ISSN 1531-0744

·I·N·F·R·A·S·T·R·U·C·T·U·R·E·
·I·N·D·U·S·T·R·I·E·S·
USA

Industry Analyses, Statistics, and Leading Companies

- A comprehensive guide to economic activity in more than 120 industries on which the rest of industrial activity rests, hence "infrastructure" industries.

- Covers five sectors, including Mining, Utilities, Construction, Transportation, and some coverage of Agriculture.

- Provides data in the new NAICS format in a pre-analyzed format, with graphics, maps, and ratios.

- Presents SIC data for bridging between the old and the new formats.

- Includes contact information on more than 7,000 companies, showing addresses, telephone numbers, and contact name, as well as providing sales and employment data.

Arsen J. Darnay, Editor

GALE GROUP

Detroit
New York
San Francisco
London
Boston
Woodbridge, CT

Arsen J. Darnay, *Editor*

Editorial Code & Data Inc. Staff

Sherae R. Carroll, *Data Entry*
Joyce Piwowarski, *Data Processing*

Gale Group Staff

Eric Hoss, *Editorial Coordinator*
Mary Beth Trimper, *Production Director*
Nekita McKee, *Buyer*
Kenn Zorn, *Product Design Manager*
Mike Logusz, *Graphic Artist*
Theresa Rocklin, *Technical Support Services Manager*
Richard Antonowicz, *Programmer*

This book is printed on acid-free paper that meets the minimum requirements of American National Standard for Information Sciences — Permanence Paper for Printed Library Materials, ANSI Z39.48-1984.

This book is printed on recycled paper that meets Environmental Protection Agency standards.

Gale Group
27500 Drake Road
Farmington Hills, MI 48331-3535

ISBN 0-7876-5057-9
ISSN 1531-0744

Printed in the United States of America

TABLE OF CONTENTS

Introduction

Infrastructure Industries USA (II-USA) presents information on five economic sectors as defined by the North American Industry Classifcation System (NAICS). Data are drawn from a variety of Federal Government statistical sources and are combined with information on leading public and private corporations from the *Ward's Business Directory of U.S. Private and Public Companies*.

This volume is named "infrastructure industries" because Agriculture, Mining, Utilities, Construction, and Transportation may be viewed as the sectors on which all else is built. They form the first layer of economic activity — providing raw materials, energy, structures, and the means of moving goods and people throughout the economy.

History

Gale's "USA" series grew out of a need to present federal statistical data, from different agencies, in a more "user friendly" format. To make these statistics even more useful, they were combined with data on corporate participation in various industries. The series features preanalyzed data, ratios, and projections — in a standard format — so that all the data are handily available to the analyst or student in one place. This approach continues with *II-USA*.

II-USA contains information heretofore presented as follows:

- Statistics on Agriculture, Mining, and Construction were presented formerly in *Agriculture, Mining, and Construction USA*.

- Data on Utilities and Transportation were published in *Transportation and Public Utilities USA*.

II-USA combines these two titles as *Infrastructure Industries USA* using, for the first time, the new NAICS coding system.

This first edition of *II-USA* is, of necessity, a transitional product. The statistical world is making a transition between the old Standard Industrial Classification (SIC) coding to the new North American Industry Classification System (NAICS). *II-USA* contains data in NAICS format. During the transition, a number of industries have remained unchanged — if renumbered. For these, it is possible to show multiple years of data under NAICS codes. They are, of course, cross-referenced to the old SIC system. In other cases, the majority, NAICS tables have been augmented with statistics that show the performance of their SIC "predecessors." For the first time, data for agriculture are presented in NAICS formats from the *1997 Census of Agriculture*.

'The Most Current Data Available'

II-USA reports the most current data available at the time of the book's preparation. The objective is to present *hard* information — data based on actual survey by authoritative bodies — for all industries within these sectors. Where at all possible, the data presented are comparable across industries. In this volume, the exception is Agriculture (Part I), which has its own census. The data are "rich," but they are not comparable to data in other sectors.

Most industries rely on the *Economic Census* to track their own performance. A few may collect more recent information through industry associations or other bodies. Similarly, estimates are published on this or that industry based on the analyses and guesses of knowledgeable individuals. These data are rarely in the same format as the Federal data and are not available for a large cross section of industry. Therefore, the data in *II-USA* are, indeed, the most current at this level of detail and spanning the entirety of the activities profiled. The book is meant to serve as the foundation on which others can base their own projections.

In addition to presenting current survey data, the editors also provide projected data for most categories from 1997 to the year 2001 where a time series is available.

Scope and Coverage

II-USA presents statistical data on 137 distinct industries, usually 6-digit NAICS-demonimated activities. Of this total only 41 are equivalent to the earlier 4-digit SIC definitions. The rest represent newly defined industries. In most cases, old SIC industries have been divided into new industries. In other cases, a NAICS industry may contain all or parts of two or more NAICS industries. To get a flavor of the manner in which SIC industries have been transformed into NAICS industries, please examine the SIC index (p. 831). More information on content is presented in *Overview of Contents and Sources*.

NAICS Presentation. For the majority of the industries, data are presented for the year 1997 — the first NAICS Economic Census year. Those industries that have remained essentially unchanged feature a full time series, from 1982 or 1987 forward, with projections to 2001. Those industries that do not have SIC equivalents feature a table entitled *SIC Industries Related to NAICS 000000*, where the 0s stand for a NAICS code. The table presents, where available, data from 1990 to 1997. These tables enable the user to see which SIC industry or industries make up the NAICS account. For some sectors (Mining, Construction), a table entitled *Distribution Among SIC-Based Industries - 1997* is also provided. It shows the SIC contributions to the NAICS industry for one year.

All presentation feature indices of change and selected, precalculated ratios (for 1997). State level information, also for 1997, is also provided for all sectors except Agriculture. State data for Agriculture, albeit not NAICS-based, is presented in Appendix I. Metro area data, in NAICS format, is presented in Appendices II and III for Utilities and Transportation respectively.

SIC and NAICS

The Bureau of the Census implemented the transition between SIC and NAICS in the 1997 Economic Census. Some kind of updating of the industrial classification system had long been overdue. The Bureau had made some minor modifications in 1987 — which were but a "tweaking" of the 1982 classification. Much had changed since then. The new NAICS coding — which is used by the U.S., Canada, and Mexico — represents a major revamping. Additional sectors have been created (e.g., Information) and the "services" categories have increased substantially.

In *II-USA*, looking to the future, the organization of data is based on the "new order," but as much help as possible is provided to die-hard SIC users as the federal data sources allow — if for no other reason than to provide longer time series. But the SIC system is definitely on the way out. Adapting to the new coding will benefit analysts in the long run. We hope that the Bureau of the Census will soon publish "retrospective" series on at least some of the new industries so that analysts everywhere can once more anchor their work in good data. Major changes in national coding inevitably mean some loss of information. Restatement of past years in NAICS terms will require some time — provided budgets for it are available. In some cases, no data for years before 1997 will ever be available. Only time will correct the deficiency.

Under the NAICS coding, 6-digit industry codes replace the familiar 4-digit SIC codes. The first two digits indicate the sector, the last four specify the industry. The code 212221 - Gold Ore Mining, can be parsed as follows: 21 is the sector code used for *Mining*; 211 is *Mining (except Oil & Gas)*, the industry group; 2221 is the actual industry designation. 212221 might be better presented as 21-2221, the dash offsetting the sector from the "industry." In current practice, all six digits are used to designate the industry. In the NAICS manual, a trailing zero is suppressed. The zero appears in published data series, however, and is also used in *II-USA*.

Organization and Content

II-USA presents data on five economic sectors. Each sector is a distinct part of the book. Parts are numbered in Roman format, as shown below. Two tables, on the next page, show the layout for each category of industry. As in the former *Agriculture, Mining, and Construction USA*, data on Agriculture are treated uniquely. All other data have a similar "look and feel" and permit comparisons across sectors. Data for some 6-digit industries in the NAICS series were not always available. Codes not shown in this volume are identified below.

Part I - Agriculture - NAICS 111000 to 115000

> Part I shows 15 industries for which the *1997 Census of Agriculture* provided data and for one industry (113310 - Logging) for which the *Economic Census* provided data. Logging is shown under Agriculture, but only national data for this industry were available, without ratios, because the entire "forestry" sector, part of Agriculture, remains to be surveyed by the Bureau of the Census. Data from the Department of Agriculture are not in the same format as from the *Economic Census* and are thus not comparable to the presentation in the rest of the book.

Part II - Mining - NAICS 211111 to 213115

Part III - Utilities - NAICS 221111 to 221330

Part IV - Construction - NAICS 233110 to 235990

Part V - Transportation and Warehousing - NAICS 481111 to 493190
> Excluded because the government does not provide data:
>> 482111 - Line-haul railroads
>> 482112 - Short line railroads
>> 491110 - Postal service

Each industry begins on a new page. The order of graphics and tables is invariable. In some instances, data may not be available in a category, e.g., company data or geographical data. The absence of data is indicated in each section. Tables presented for each industry are shown in the two layouts that follow:

Tables for Agricultural Industries

1	General Statistics	Summary statistics for the agricultural industry.
2	Land in Farms According to Use	Data on land, by use, in acres.
3	Market Value of Agricultural Products Sold	Data by commodity and animals, all farms.
4	Market Value of Agricultural Products Sold - 2	Data for farms with sales of $50,000 or more.
5	Government Payments and Other Income	Data showing supplemental income streams.
6	Commodity Credit Corporation Loans	Data showing subsidized loans for farms.
7	Selected Machinery and Equipment	Data on number of vehicles and major implements.
8	Farm Production Expenses	Expenses, in dollars, by category.
9	Net Cash Returns and Farms with Gains/Losses	Statistics in dollars and farm counts.
10	Characteristics of Farm Operators	Counts of farm operators in various categories.
11	Farms by Type of Organization	Counts of farms based on organization.
12	Livestock Inventories and Sales	Counts of livestock by type for this industry.
13	Poultry Inventories and Sales	Counts of birds by type for this industry.
14	Selected Crops Harvested	Data for crops by type and acres on which grown.
15	Leading Companies	Up to 75 companies per industry when available.

Graphics and Tables for Economic Census Industries

1	Trend Graphic	Provided when multiple years of data are available.
2	General Statistics	National statistics.
3	Distribution Among SIC-Based Industries - 1997	Mining and Construction only.
4	SIC Industries Related to NAICS	Provided when NAICS-SIC do not match exactly.
5	Indices of Change	National data in index format.
6	Selected Ratios	Precalculated ratios for the industry for 1997.
7	Leading Companies	Up to 75 companies per industry when available.
8	Cost Details	Only available for Construction sector.
9	Product Details	Only available for Mining and Construction sectors.
10	Maps	States and regions where the industry is active.
11	Industry Data by State	State-level statistics.

Three appendixes provide additional information on Agriculture, Utilities, and Transportation & Warehousing.

- **Appendix I - Agricultural Data by State**. This appendix provides detailed information on agriculture at the state level (but not in NAICS divisions), for 1987, 1992, and 1997.

- **Appendix II - Metro Data - Utilities**. This appendix presents data, in NAICS format, for 220 metropolitan areas in alphabetical order by city and then by NAICS order within the table. Only industries with data for employment and revenues are shown.

- **Appendix II - Metro Data - Transportation**. The last appendix presents data, in NAICS format, for 346 metropolitan areas, as above.

Four indexes complete the volume:

- **SIC Index**. Data are arranged, first, by SIC number and then in alphabetical order by SIC name. One or more NAICS industries in which the SIC is present are shown as dashed items beneath each SIC. Page references are provided to the start of the relevant NAICS industry or industries in which the SIC is fully or partially included.

- **NAICS Index**. The NAICS index is also in two parts — by NAICS code and by industry name arranged in alphabetical order. Page references are to the page on which the industry begins.

- **Subject Index**. Activities, services, products, and references to metro areas are show in an alphabetical arrangement. One or more page references are provided to the first page of the industry concerned with the indexed topic or the page on which the metro area appears.

- **Company Index**. The company index holds all corporations shown in *II-USA*'s *Leading Companies* table. Company names are labelled by the NAICS code where each is listed. References are to the pages where the tables that hold the organizations appear.

In other editions of this series, an occupational index has been provided in the past. This time — and we hope only temporarily — the occupational index has been omitted because occupational data are not, as yet, available in NAICS formats.

For more detailed information on *II-USA*'s industry profiles, please consult the *Overview of Contents and Sources*, which follows.

Comments and Suggestions are Welcome

Comments on this volume — or suggestions on how to improve it — are welcome. Every effort is made to maintain accuracy, but errors may occasionally occur. The editor will be grateful if these are called to his attention. Please contact the editor below with comments and suggestsion. To discuss technical matters, call the editor directly at Editorial Code & Data, Inc. at (248) 356-6990.

Editor
Infrastructure Industries USA
Gale Group
27500 Drake Road
Farmington Hills, MI 48331-3535
248-699-GALE

Overview of Content and Sources

Industry Coding Structure

Data in *II-USA* are ordered in conformity with the 1997 North American Industry Classification System (NAICS).

The NAICS coding system is new. Many industries have been reclassified so that they no longer resemble the SIC codes. However, a fair number of NAICS codes correspond directly — without change — to the older SIC codes. Of the 137 NAICS industries presented in *II-USA*, 41 have direct SIC equivalents. When the industries coincide, multiple years of data are provided. In each case, the data are presented under NAICS codes, but an asterisk is used to mark the industry, and the equivalent SIC code is supplied at the bottom of the page. New industries that have no SIC equivalent show only one year of data, for 1997 — but in most cases, data for the period 1990 to 1997 are presented for the SIC industries that make up the NAICS.

Naming Conventions

Industry and sector names are taken from *North American Industry Classification System*, Office of Management and Budget, 1997. Names of sectors and of industries have been generally left unchanged, with one exception. Industries that begin with the word "Other" or "All Other" have been modified using the old SIC designation of "nec," meaning "not elsewhere classified." NEC is well known to users of the *USA* series.

Industry Profiles - Agriculture

The 15 tables for each of the 15 agricultural industries shown in *II-USA* are unlike the usual presentation of industry data in the Gale *USA* series. This is dictated by the manner in which data for agriculture are collected and reported by the U.S. Department of Agriculture in its *1997 Census of Agriculture*, the source of all but one of these tables.

General Description

Statistics are presented in 14 tables for the year 1997. The 15th table is for *Leading Companies* and is in the same format as for the Economic Census industries. The first table, *General Statistics*, features summary data for the industry as a whole. The next

13 tables then provide additional detail on elements summarized in *General Statistics*.

All tables provide information on the entire U.S. agricultural sector in the first column followed by data for the NAICS industry under consideration. The NAICS industry is labeled "This Agriculture Sector," "This Agric. Sector," or "This Sector" in text above the table columns. The NAICS industry is shown as a "% of U.S." to provide a useful ratio in every case.

Tables are divided into three parts. The leftmost columns show totals and percentages. The middle columns are typically averages per farm, and the last two columns always show the "universe" of farms on which the averages are based (*Number of farms reporting category*). The last two columns are important because not all farms report on every item. Data on the value of machinery and equipment, for example, are provided by 1,911,601 farms nationally, out of a total universe of 1,911,859 farms. Thus the basis for reporting changes from item to item and must be taken into consideration. These data are provided for the user's convenience. Where the subject of the table is number of farms, these last two columns are not shown again.

Denomination of Data

Data are shown in numbers, acres, dollars, bushels, tons, hundredweight (cwt), bales, and pounds. Dollars may be in millions and other values in 1,000s. Negative dollar amounts are enclosed in parentheses. In most instances, the data denominations are shown in column headers or in the columns themselves. Where no denomination is explicitly shown, it is a simple count.

Sources and Comments

The source of the statistical tables is the *1997 Census of Agriculture*, U.S. Department of Agriculture, National Agricultural Statistics Service. The source of the *Leading Companies* tables is *Ward's Business Directory of U.S. Private and Public Companies* for 2000. More information about that table is presented below. Comments necessary for understanding of each table, including explanation of abbreviations, is included in the source note below each table, where necessary.

Industry Profiles - Census Industries

Each industry profile drawn from the Economic Census contains the tables and graphics listed in the second table of the *Introduction*. A detailed discussion of each graphic and table follows; the meaning of each data element is explained, and the sources from which the data were obtained are cited.

Trends Graphics

At the beginning of each industry profile, two graphs are presented showing (1) industry revenues and (2) employment plotted for the years 1982 to 2001 on logarithmic scale. The curves are provided primarily to give the user an at-a-glance assessment of important trends in the industry. The logarithmic scale ensures that the revenue and employment trends can be compared visually despite different magnitudes and denominations of the data (millions of dollars and thousands of employees); in this mode of presentation, if two curves have the same slope, the values are growing or declining at the same rate. If the values fit within a single cycle (1 to 9, 10 to 90, etc.), a single cycle is shown; if the values bridge two cycles, both are shown.

The data graphed are derived from the first table, *General Statistics*. All available years of data are plotted. If data gaps appear in the series, missing points are calculated using a least-squares curve fitting algorithm.

In the case of a few industries, data discontinuities are present in the general statistics; data for the 1982-1986 period are not strictly comparable to the data for 1987 and later. In such cases, the line of the graph is interrupted between 1986 and 1987 to show this discontinuity.

Those portions of curves based on projections by the editors are shown in a dotted-line format.

General Statistics

Mining. If the industry is equivalent to the earlier SIC definition, data are shown for 1977, 1982, and for 1987 through 2001. In other cases, only 1997 is shown. Census years are shown in bold. The table shows Companies, Establishments (total and with 20 or more employees), Employment (total), Workers, and Hours. Included under the Compensation heading are Payroll (total) and Wages per Hour. Shown under the Production heading are Cost of Materials, Value Added by Mining, Value of Shipments, and Capital Investment.

Construction. Data are shown for the same years as in Mining. The contents of the table are slightly different. Categories are Establishments, Employment, Construction Workers, Payroll (total), Worker Payroll, Total Cost, Cost of Materials, Value Added, Revenues, and Capital Investment. Under the heading of Revenues, data are provided for Revenues (all sources), Revenues from Construction (total), and Revenues from Construction (net of subcontracted work).

Utilities and **Transportation & Warehousing**. If the industry is equivalent to an earlier SIC definition, data for 1982-2001 or 1987-2001 are shown. If the NAICS industry is new, only data for 1997 are presented. Four elements of data and three ratios are displayed. Data shown are Establishments (number), Employment (number), Payroll (in millions of dollars), and Revenues (in millions of dollars). The ratios shown are Employees per Establishment (number), Revenues per Establishment (in dollars), and Payroll per Employee (in dollars). Data for the period 1998-2001 are projected by the editors. A discussion of the methods of projection is presented below. Projected data are followed by the letter "p". Some data are extrapolations to fill gaps in the data series. These figures are marked with an "e".

Data for 1982, 1987, 1992, and 1997 are from Economic Census held in each of those years. Data for other years are extrapolations or projections. New industries created in the 1987 SIC reclassification will not show data earlier than 1987. In all of these cases, the SIC data and the NAICS data are identical.

Distribution Among SIC-Based Industries - 1997

This table appears only for those Mining and Construction industries that are newly formed under the NAICS coding. It shows data for 1997 only.

For **Mining**, the categories shown are SIC code, name of the Industry, Establishments, Employment, Compensation, and Production. The Employment category is subdivided further into Total employment and Production employment. Production employment is subdivided into Workers and Hours (in millions). Compensation shows total Payroll in millions of dollars and Wages in dollars per hour. Production is divided into Cost of Materials and Value of Shipments.

For **Construction**, the categories are SIC code, name of the Industry, Establishments, Employment, Cost of Power and Materials, Revenues, and Value Added. Employment is divided into Total employment, in thousands, and Payroll, in millions of dollars. Revenues are divided into All Sources and Construction, with the construction category further divided into Total and Net — the net being construction revenue less the cost of subcontracts.

In cases where the SIC code ends in 00, the entire SIC industry is included in the NAICS industry. If the last two digits are not zero, they indicate a component of a 4-digit SIC industry.

SIC Industries Related to NAICS

This table is present only in those situations where the NAICS industry is new. The purpose of the table is to show where the NAICS industry "comes from." New industries are constructed from pieces of one or more of the old SIC industries. Where parts of an SIC have been incorporated, the SIC industry name is followed by an asterisk (*). In cases where the entire SIC industry is now embedded in the NAICS industry, only the name is shown. **Please note**: The statistics shown for each such SIC industry are the statistics for that industry *as a whole*, not just that portion which is now reported under the NAICS classification. It is possible to get some feel for how much the SIC industry contributes to the NAICS by comparing items for 1997 from this table to the data in the *General Statistics* table.

This table shows, for each "participating" SIC, the SIC code, the industry name (with or without the asterisk). Thereafter, statistics are shown for the period 1990 to 1997 for Establishments (number), Employment (in thousands), and Revenues (in millions of dollars). Where the precursor industry is a manufacturing enterprise, Value of Shipments is shown in place of Revenues.

This table is presented even in those instances where no SIC data are available. This is frequently the case in financial categories. In that sector, data in the *USA* series have usually been reported at a higher level (3-digit rather than 4-digit SIC) and are therefore not suitable for display in this context. In some instances, only partial data are available, e.g., for the year 1992.

Indices of Change

The data presented in the *General Statistics* table are partially restated as indices for all industries where multiple years of data are available. The purpose of the table is to show the user rapidly how different categories of the industry have changed since 1997. Indices are shown for the census years (1982, 1987, 1992, and 1997) and for the years 1998 through 2001.

The year 1997 is used as the base and is therefore shown as 100 in every category. Other values are expressed in relation to the 1997 value.

Values of 100 indicate no change in relation to the base year; values above 100 mean "better" and values below 100 indicate "worse" performance — all relative to the 1997 base. Note, however, that these are *indices* rather than compounded annual rates of growth or decline.

Indexes based on projections by the editors are followed by a "p".

A table of Indices of Change is also provided for industries that have only one year of data. All values shown are 100. No other data being available, no "change" can be shown. These tables are shown, nevertheless, to ensure a consistent presentation, industry to industry.

Selected Ratios

To understand an industry, analysts calculate ratios of various kinds so that the absolute numbers can be placed in a more global perspective. Twenty ratios are provided for Mining, 22 for Construction, and six each for Utilities and Transportation & Warehousing. Ratios are based on the sector averages, which are also shown.

The ratios are calculated for the most recent complete year available, 1997.

The first column of values represents the **Average of Sector**. These ratios are calculated by (1) using reported totals for each sector and (2) calculating the ratios based on the totals.

The second column of values shows the ratios for the **Analyzed Industry**, i.e., the industry currently under consideration.

The third column is an **Index** comparing the Analyzed Industry to the Average of Sector. The index is useful for determining quickly and consistently how the Analyzed Industry stands in relation to its sector, e.g., Mining or Construction. Index values of 100 mean that the Analyzed Industry, within a given ratio, is identical to the average of all industries. An index value of 500 means that the Analyzed Industry is five times the average — for instance, that it has five times as many employees per establishment or pays five times as much. An index value of 50 would indicate that the Analyzed Industry is half of the average of all industries (50%). Similarly, an index of 105 means 5% above average and 95 indicates 5% below.

Leading Companies

The table of *Leading Companies* shows up to 75 companies that participate in the industry. The listings are sorted in descending order of sales and show the company name, address, name of the Chief Executive Officer (or person with a similar title), telephone, company type, sales (in millions of dollars) and employment (in thousands of employees). The number of companies shown, their total sales, and total employment are summed at the top of the table for the user's convenience.

The data are from the *Ward's Business Directory of U.S. Private and Public Companies* for 2000. Public and private corporations, divisions, subsidiaries, joint ventures, and corporate groups are shown. Thus a listing for an industry may show the parent company as well as important divisions and subsidiaries of the same company (usually in a different location).

While this method of presentation has the disadvantage of duplication (the sales of a parent corporation include the sales of any divisions listed separately), it has the advantage of providing the user with information on major components of an enterprise at different locations. In any event, the user should *not* assume that the sum of the sales (or employment) shown in the *Leading Companies* table represents the total sales (or employment) of an industry. The Revenues column of the *General Statistics* table is a better guide to industry sales.

The company's type (private, public, division, etc.) is shown under the column headed "Co Type," thus providing the user with a means of roughly determining the total "net" sales (or employment) represented in the table; this can be accomplished by adding the values and then deducting values corresponding to divisions and subsidiaries of parent organizations also shown in the table. The code used is as follows:

P	Public corporation
R	Private corporation
S	Subsidiary
D	Division
J	Joint venture
G	Corporate group

An asterisk (*) placed behind the sales volume indicates an estimate; the absence of an asterisk indicates that the sales value has been obtained from annual reports, other formal submissions to regulatory bodies, or from the corporation. The symbol "<" appears in front of some employment values to indicate that the actual value is "less than" the value shown. Thus the value of "<0.1" means that the company employs fewer than 100 people.

Company data were sometimes unavailable for a NAICS industry. In those cases, the absence of data is noted in the company profile with the phrase: *No company data available for this industry*. As databases are updated and old SIC coding is replaced with NAICS coding, more company data will become available in future editions.

Cost Details

For the Construction sector only, data on costs are presented in one table. Costs are shown in total and then by categories. The cost for a category, in millions of dollars, is followed by cost as a percent of total cost and in dollars per $1,000 of revenue.

Product Details

In the **Mining** sector, the table is titled *Mining Product Details* and shows the output of mined product(s). The units of measurement are followed by Quantity and Value of product shipments. Quantity is subdivided into Production and Shipments categories for 1997. Value of Product Shipments is divided into millions of dollars and percent of total for 1992 and 1997.

In the **Construction** sector, the table is titled *Construction Product Details*. All data are in millions of dollars or in percent and show the value of construction work divided into four categories: Total; New Construction; Additions, alterations, reconstruction; and Mainenance and repair. Dollar values are followed by "percent of total" columns.

Map Graphics

The geographical presentation of data begins with two maps titled *Location by State* and *Regional Concentration*.

In the first map, those states are shaded on the map where the industry's activity is proportionally *greater* than would be indicated by the state's share of total U.S. population. An example will illustrate the procedure used. If a state's share of industry revenues was 4.5 percent, and its share of the U.S. population was 2.3 percent, the state is shaded on the map. But if the state share of revenues was 5.0 percent, and its population share 7.5, the state on the map is left blank.

This procedure is used for Utilities, Construction, and Transportation & Warehousing. In Mining, states are shaded if the industry is present *at all*.

In the second map, the industry's concentration is shown by Census region. The two maps, together, tell the user at a glance where the industry is most active and which regions rank first, second, and third in revenues or in number of establishments; establishment counts are used for ranking in those industries where shipment data are withheld (the (D) symbol) for the majority of states. In the case of some industries, only one or two regions are shaded because the industry is concentrated in a few states. The data for ranking are taken from the table on *Industry Data by State* which immediately follows the maps.

The regional boundaries are those of the Census Regions and are named, from left to right and top to bottom as follows:

Pacific (includes Alaska and Hawaii)	East South Central
Mountain	New England
West North Central	Middle Atlantic
West South Central	South Atlantic
East North Central	

In the case of the Pacific region, all parts of the region are shaded (including Alaska and Hawaii), even if the basis for the ranking is the industry's predominance in California (the usual case).

Although regional data are only graphed and not reported in a separate table, the table of *Industry Data by State* provides all the necessary information for constructing a regional table.

Industry Data by State

The table on *Industry Data by State* provides several data elements for each state in which the industry is active. The data come from the 1997 Economic Census, the most recently available data set on states. Even in this series, certain data elements are suppressed by the Bureau of the Census to prevent disclosure of competitive information. This may come about in instances where only a few operations are present in the state or they are operated by a small number of companies. The states are shown in descending order of revenues.

Elements provided for **Mining** and **Construction** are:

- Establishments

- Employment — total, workers, and total as a percent of the U.S.

- Compensation — payroll per employee and wages per worker in dollars.

- Production — costs, value added, revenues, and revenues as a percent of the U.S. Dollar values are in millions.

- Capital expenditures in millions of dollars.

Elements provided for **Utilities** and **Transportation & Warehousing** are:

- Establishments — total number and as a percent of all establishments in this industry.

- Employment — total number, as a percent of industry employment, and employees per establishment.

- Payroll — total, in millions of dollars, and payroll per employee, in dollars.

- Revenues — total, in millions of dollars, as a percent of total industry revenues, and revenues per establishment, in dollars.

The symbol (D) is used when data are withheld to prevent disclosure of proprietary information. Dashes are used to indicate that the corresponding data element cannot be calculated because some part of the ratio is missing or withheld.

Where revenue and payroll data are withheld, the Bureau of the Census still provides two values: number of establishments and an employment range. *II-USA* shows the midpoint of a range when an employment range is used. The ranges, and their midpoints, are shown in the following table:

Range	Midpoint
0-19	10
20-99	60
100-249	175
250-499	375
500-999	750
1000-2499	1750
2500-4999	3750
5000-9999	7500
10000-24999	17500
25000-99999	37500
100000+	100000+

Projected Data Series

As a service to the busy user of this book, *II-USA* features trend projections of data — when a sufficient number of years of data is available.

Projections are based on a curve-fitting algorithm using the least-squares method. In essence, the algorithm calculates a trend line for the data using existing data points. Extensions of the trend line are used to predict future years of data.

Projections are simply means of detecting trends. But extensions of a trend line into the future may not be legitimate — if conditions suddenly change. The projections in *II-USA*, therefore, are not as reliable as actual survey data. Most analysts trying to project the future routinely turn to trend projection. In *II-USA*, the work of doing the projections has been done for the user in advance.

Appendices

Additional data are presented in three appendices. These are briefly described in what follows.

Appendix I - Agricultural Data for States

This appendix presents state-by-state data from the *1997 Census of Agriculture*. The appendix is arranged alphabetically by state. Each state is profiled in three tables: *General Statistics*, *Livestock Statistics*, and *Crop Statistics*.

Each table holds information for 1987, 1992, and 1997. Data shown are described on the left of each table. Columns present value and percent of the U.S. total for the category. The last two columns show percent change in the values from 1987 to 1992 and from 1992 to 1997.

The data series used for this presentation lacked U.S. totals for some categories. For that reason, the "% of U.S." column is sometimes blank — as noted in the source note.

Appendices II and III - Metro Data

Data for metropolitan areas were available for **Utilities** and **Transportation & Warehousing** from the Economic Census and were included in two appendices.

Both appendices are arranged alphabetically by metro area. Each metro area has its own table, which is arranged by NAICS code. In this series, 7-digit NAICS codes are included, where appropriate.

Data for these tables were selected only if both employment and revenue data were available. The absence of an industry should not be interpreted as meaning that the industry does not exist in the metro area. The only implication is that no meaningful values were reported by the Bureau of the Census.

Categories shown in the tables are NAICS code, Industry name, Establishments, Employment, Payroll, and Sales or revenues in millions of dollars. The Payroll heading is divided into Total Payroll, in millions, and Payroll per Employee, in dollars.

MSAs, CMSAs, and PMSAs. Each metro area is followed by one of these abbreviations. MSAs are "metropolitan statistical areas" — areas with at least one city with 50,000 inhabitants and a metropolitan area of at least 100,000. MSAs of 1 million or more population qualify for the designation of CMSA — "consolidated metropolitan statistical areas." PMSAs — "primary metropolitan statistical areas" — are components of CMSAs. Thus the hierarchy is MSA, PMSA (an MSA that is part of a CMSA), and CMSA, the largest aggregation.

Part I

AGRICULTURE

NAICS 111100 - OILSEED AND GRAIN FARMING

GENERAL STATISTICS

Item	U.S. Total	This Agri-culture Sector	% of U.S.	Value shown as	Category average per farm			Number of farms reporting category	
					U.S.	This Agric. Sector	% of U.S.	U.S.	This Sector
Farms - number	1,911,859	462,877	24.2	-	-	-	-	-	-
Land in farms - mil. acres	931.795	285.180	30.6	Acres	487	616	126.5	1,911,859	462,877
Value of land, buildings - $ mil.	859,839.2	299,006.6	34.8	$	449,748	643,635	143.1	524,066	464,559
Value of machinery and equip-ment - $ mil.	110,256.8	42,984.5	39.0	$	57,678	92,544	160.4	1,911,601	464,477
Sales of Ag Products - $ mil.	196,864.6	44,404.7	22.6	$	102,970	95,932	93.2	1,911,859	462,877
Government payments - $ mil.	5,054.5	3,178.6	62.9	$	7,378	8,848	119.9	685,029	359,251
Other farm-related income - $ mil.	3,272.3	1,129.0	34.5	$	5,999	6,146	102.5	545,480	183,692
Expenses - $ mil.	150,591.0	31,691.2	21.0	$	78,771	68,219	86.6	1,911,766	464,548
Payroll - $ mil.	14,841.0	1,617.5	10.9	$	22,811	10,449	45.8	650,623	154,796
Workers - 150 days or more a year	890,467	100,567	11.3	Number	3.4	1.7	49.9	259,631	58,784
Workers - less than 150 days	2,461,561	335,725	13.6	Number	4.2	2.4	57.7	581,658	137,412
Net Cash Return - $ mil.	42,557.9	11,859.0	27.9	$	22,260	25,527	114.7	1,911,824	464,559

Source: *1997 Census of Agriculture*, U.S. Department of Agriculture, National Agricultural Statistics Service. Table shows totals for the U.S. agriculture sector and for the NAICS subdivision of it, shown as "This Agric. Sector" or as "This Sector." Not all farms report on every category. For this reason, the reporting universe is shown in the last two columns. Averages are based on these columns.

LAND IN FARMS ACCORDING TO USE

Item	U.S. Total (000 acres)	This Sector (000 acres)	% of U.S.	Average acres per farms			Number of farms reporting category	
				U.S.	This Agric. Sector	% of U.S.	U.S.	This Sector
Total cropland	431,144.9	224,863.6	52.2	260	504	-	1,661,395	446,342
Harvested cropland	309,395.5	180,062.7	58.2	219	456	-	1,410,606	394,743
Cropland:								
Pasture or grazing	64,466.5	10,468.8	16.2	85	102	-	754,170	103,012
In cover crops, legumes, grasses	13,531.2	7,511.0	55.5	88	114	-	153,177	65,619
On which all crops failed	3,449.4	1,727.6	50.1	67	90	-	51,673	19,290
In cultivated summer fallow	20,905.9	15,222.0	72.8	256	358	-	81,702	42,520
Idle	19,396.3	9,871.5	50.9	83	115	-	232,961	85,605
Total woodland	71,465.4	12,386.6	17.3	96	85	-	743,011	146,408
Woodland pastured	29,693.9	2,673.9	9.0	84	68	-	352,217	39,468
Woodland not pastured	41,771.5	9,712.7	23.3	79	78	-	531,846	124,652
Other pasture/rangeland	396,884.6	37,700.0	9.5	721	392	-	550,619	96,267
Land for house lots, ponds, roads, wasteland	32,300.4	10,230.0	31.7	28	36	-	1,142,618	280,642
Irrigated land	55,058.1	20,078.2	36.5	197	417	-	279,442	48,172
Harvested cropland	50,013.5	19,802.8	39.6	198	417	-	252,679	47,506
Pasture and other	5,044.7	275.4	5.5	87	89	-	58,258	3,101
Conservation Reserve/Wetlands Reserve Lands	29,489.1	18,232.6	61.8	131	138	-	225,410	131,687

Source: *1997 Census of Agriculture*, U.S. Department of Agriculture, National Agricultural Statistics Service. Table shows totals for the U.S. agriculture sector and for the NAICS subdivision of it, shown as "This Agric. Sector" or as "This Sector." Not all farms report on every category. For this reason, the reporting universe is shown in the last two columns. Averages are based on these columns. The Conservation Reserve and Wetlands Reserve programs provide support for land conservation/preservation. Cover crops are not harvested or pastured.

MARKET VALUE OF AGRICULTURAL PRODUCTS SOLD: ALL FARMS

Item	U.S. Total ($ mil.)	This Sector ($ mil.)	% of Sector Sales	% of U.S.	Average sales per farm - $			Number of farms reporting category	
					U.S.	This Agric. Sector	% of U.S.	U.S.	This Sector
Grains	46,617.1	38,854.5	87.50	83.3	79,095	99,882	126.3	589,379	389,004
Corn for grain	18,884.8	16,159.6	36.39	85.6	52,506	61,797	117.7	359,666	261,496
Wheat	7,173.9	5,423.7	12.21	75.6	29,726	34,240	115.2	241,334	158,404
Soybeans	15,622.4	13,260.8	29.86	84.9	44,185	49,660	112.4	353,566	267,031
Sorghum for grain	1,140.0	873.5	1.97	76.6	25,360	26,815	105.7	44,955	32,574
Barley	709.6	476.8	1.07	67.2	23,191	25,579	110.3	30,598	18,641
Oats	121.3	68.9	0.16	56.8	3,114	3,534	113.5	38,940	19,489
Other grains	2,965.1	2,591.3	5.84	87.4	67,540	79,570	117.8	43,901	32,566
Cotton and cotton seed	5,975.5	419.5	0.94	7.0	189,963	99,588	52.4	31,456	4,212
Tobacco	2,924.7	90.6	0.20	3.1	32,662	27,153	83.1	89,544	3,335
Hay, silage, and field seeds	4,670.5	749.9	1.69	16.1	13,174	10,231	77.7	354,523	73,293
Vegetables, sweet corn, and melons	8,401.7	213.1	0.48	2.5	156,628	34,997	22.3	53,641	6,089
Fruits and berries	12,660.3	26.7	0.06	0.2	147,259	20,044	13.6	85,973	1,331
Nursery and greenhouse crops	10,942.8	16.6	0.04	0.2	161,360	17,316	10.7	67,816	960
Other crops	5,863.1	334.8	0.75	5.7	153,907	73,793	47.9	38,095	4,537
Poultry and poultry products	22,262.6	18.1	0.04	0.1	352,000	6,522	1.9	63,246	2,773
Dairy products	18,997.3	193.8	0.44	1.0	191,432	68,101	35.6	99,238	2,846
Cattle and calves	40,524.8	2,435.9	5.49	6.0	40,052	20,444	51.0	1,011,809	119,149
Hogs and pigs	13,804.8	988.1	2.23	7.2	135,201	44,966	33.3	102,106	21,974
Sheep, lambs, and wool	682.9	38.1	0.09	5.6	10,913	4,345	39.8	62,579	8,768
Other livestock	2,536.5	25.2	0.06	1.0	20,506	5,017	24.5	123,695	5,017
Products sold to public directly	13,096.7	758.4	1.71	5.8	377,610	118,216	31.3	34,683	6,415

Source: 1997 Census of Agriculture, U.S. Department of Agriculture, National Agricultural Statistics Service. Table shows totals for the U.S. agriculture sector and for the NAICS subdivision of it, shown as "This Agric. Sector" or as "This Sector." Not all farms report on every category. For this reason, the reporting universe is shown in the last two columns. Averages are based on these columns. Farms classified in one sector routinely produce categories in other sectors as well. Products sold to the public are sold for direct consumption.

MARKET VALUE OF PRODUCTS SOLD: FARMS WITH SALES OF $50,000 OR MORE

Item	U.S. Total ($ mil.)	This Sector ($ mil.)	% of Sector Sales	% of U.S.	Average sales per farm - $			Number of farms reporting category	
					U.S.	This Agric. Sector	% of U.S.	U.S.	This Sector
Grains	40,973.4	35,147.1	79.15	85.8	183,623	192,367	104.8	223,138	182,709
Cotton and cotton seed	5,743.9	378.8	0.85	6.6	286,562	171,113	59.7	20,044	2,214
Tobacco	2,060.2	54.3	0.12	2.6	175,907	119,540	68.0	11,712	454
Hay, silage, and field seeds	2,781.9	288.7	0.65	10.4	188,959	117,225	62.0	14,722	2,463
Vegetables, sweet corn, and melons	7,966.8	147.3	0.33	1.8	673,443	139,932	20.8	11,830	1,053
Fruits and berries	12,072.3	19.9	0.04	0.2	478,927	151,924	31.7	25,207	131
Nursery and greenhouse crops	10,412.0	10.0	0.02	0.1	578,025	141,282	24.4	18,013	71
Other crops	5,586.6	290.3	0.65	5.2	363,758	153,617	42.2	15,358	1,890
Poultry and poultry products	22,171.7	14.4	0.03	0.1	778,637	175,012	22.5	28,475	82
Dairy products	18,344.3	159.8	0.36	0.9	250,075	118,454	47.4	73,355	1,349
Cattle and calves	32,358.6	1,157.5	2.61	3.6	386,685	105,178	27.2	83,682	11,005
Hogs and pigs	13,096.7	758.4	1.71	5.8	377,610	118,216	31.3	34,683	6,415
Sheep, lambs, and wool	478.6	7.9	0.02	1.7	278,730	99,125	35.6	1,717	80
Other livestock	2,026.6	11.2	0.03	0.6	369,685	99,723	27.0	5,482	112

Source: 1997 Census of Agriculture, U.S. Department of Agriculture, National Agricultural Statistics Service. Table shows totals for the U.S. agriculture sector and for the NAICS subdivision of it, shown as "This Agric. Sector" or as "This Sector." Not all farms report on every category. For this reason, the reporting universe is shown in the last two columns. Averages are based on these columns. Farms classified in one sector routinely produce categories in other sectors as well.

GOVERNMENT PAYMENTS AND OTHER FARM-RELATED INCOME

Item	U.S. Total ($ mil.)	This Sector ($ mil.)	% of Sector Gov/Oth. Income	% of U.S.	Average receipts per farm - $			Number of farms reporting category	
					U.S.	This Agric. Sector	% of U.S.	U.S.	This Sector
Government payments	5,054.5	3,178.6	73.79	62.9	7,378	8,848	119.9	685,029	359,251
Other farm-related income	3,272.3	1,129.0	26.21	34.5	5,999	6,146	102.5	545,480	183,692
Custom work and other agricultural services	1,235.1	474.1	11.01	38.4	8,646	8,856	102.4	142,854	53,534
Gross cash rent or share payments	1,207.9	445.7	10.35	36.9	6,867	8,868	129.1	175,901	50,257
Forest products, excluding Christmas trees and maple products	344.3	45.5	1.06	13.2	7,417	7,388	99.6	46,426	6,163
Other farm-related income sources	484.9	163.7	3.80	33.8	1,595	1,305	81.8	303,908	125,488

Source: *1997 Census of Agriculture*, U.S. Department of Agriculture, National Agricultural Statistics Service. Table shows totals for the U.S. agriculture sector and for the NAICS subdivision of it, shown as "This Agric. Sector" or as "This Sector." Not all farms report on every category. For this reason, the reporting universe is shown in the last two columns. Averages are based on these columns. Government payments are agricultural subsidies under various programs.

COMMODITY CREDIT CORPORATION LOANS

Item	U.S. Total ($ mil.)	This Sector ($ mil.)	% of Sector Loan Total	% of U.S.	Average loan value per farm - $			Number of farms reporting category	
					U.S.	This Agric. Sector	% of U.S.	U.S.	This Sector
Total loans	3,034.7	2,376.3	100.00	78.3	36,419	41,776	114.7	83,328	56,881
Corn	1,333.9	1,076.8	45.31	80.7	26,419	30,426	115.2	50,489	35,390
Wheat	415.4	332.0	13.97	79.9	18,093	20,566	113.7	22,961	16,144
Soybeans	774.0	667.6	28.10	86.3	30,370	32,146	105.8	25,487	20,769
Sorghum, barley, and oats	54.8	42.5	1.79	77.5	8,603	10,173	118.3	6,375	4,180
Cotton	191.4	20.1	0.84	10.5	43,275	33,235	76.8	4,422	604
Sunflower seed, flaxseed, safflower, canola, other rapeseed, and mustard seed	17.3	15.6	0.66	90.3	25,159	26,639	105.9	686	585
Peanuts, rice, and tobacco	247.9	221.7	9.33	89.4	60,421	79,823	132.1	4,103	2,777

Source: *1997 Census of Agriculture*, U.S. Department of Agriculture, National Agricultural Statistics Service. Table shows totals for the U.S. agriculture sector and for the NAICS subdivision of it, shown as "This Agric. Sector" or as "This Sector." Not all farms report on every category. For this reason, the reporting universe is shown in the last two columns. Averages are based on these columns. The Commodity Credit Corporation provides low interest loans to farmers.

SELECTED MACHINERY AND EQUIPMENT

Item	U.S. Total (number)	This Agric. Sector (number)	% of U.S.	Average number per farm			Number of farms reporting category	
				U.S.	This Agric. Sector	% of U.S.	U.S.	This Sector
Motortrucks, including pickups	3,497,735	1,032,509	29.5	2.07	2.44	118.0	1,688,303	422,506
Wheel tractors	3,936,014	1,253,213	31.8	2.31	2.90	125.7	1,707,384	432,609
Less than 40 horsepower (PTO)	1,262,688	293,779	23.3	1.44	1.53	106.0	877,119	192,436
40 horsepower (PTO) or more	2,673,326	959,434	35.9	2.02	2.46	121.7	1,321,084	389,539
40 to 99 horsepower (PTO)	1,808,105	500,678	27.7	1.58	1.65	104.3	1,145,466	304,061
100 horsepower (PTO)	865,221	458,756	53.0	1.68	1.79	106.2	513,773	256,596
Grain and bean combines	460,606	297,088	64.5	1.16	1.18	101.4	395,934	251,821
Cotton pickers and strippers	38,294	4,745	12.4	1.48	1.33	90.0	25,874	3,563
Mower conditioners	608,443	107,766	17.7	1.12	1.08	96.8	543,565	99,437
Pickup balers	717,245	138,425	19.3	1.24	1.20	96.7	579,440	115,635

Source: *1997 Census of Agriculture*, U.S. Department of Agriculture, National Agricultural Statistics Service. Table shows totals for the U.S. agriculture sector and for the NAICS subdivision of it, shown as "This Agric. Sector" or as "This Sector." Not all farms report on every category. For this reason, the reporting universe is shown in the last two columns. Averages are based on these columns. PTO stands for "power take off."

FARM PRODUCTION EXPENSES

Item	U.S. Total ($ mil.)	This Sector ($ mil.)	% of Sector Total Expense	% of U.S.	Average expense per farm - $			Number of farms reporting category	
					U.S.	This Agric. Sector	% of U.S.	U.S.	This Sector
Total farm production expenses	150,591.0	31,691.2	100.00	21.0	78,771	68,219	86.6	1,911,766	464,548
Livestock and poultry purchased	21,614.6	835.3	2.64	3.9	38,807	11,765	30.3	556,980	70,997
Feed for livestock and poultry	32,760.0	773.6	2.44	2.4	32,059	6,443	20.1	1,021,849	120,076
Commercially mixed formula feeds	21,236.2	329.4	1.04	1.6	34,459	4,937	14.3	616,280	66,718
Seeds, bulbs, plants, and trees	5,725.9	2,786.8	8.79	48.7	6,388	7,526	117.8	896,339	370,280
Commercial fertilizer	9,597.1	4,764.5	15.03	49.6	8,060	13,200	163.8	1,190,733	360,948
Agricultural chemicals	7,581.4	3,549.2	11.20	46.8	8,056	10,326	128.2	941,136	343,702
Petroleum products	6,371.5	2,244.6	7.08	35.2	3,619	5,335	147.4	1,760,642	420,713
Gasoline and gasohol	1,886.6	556.7	1.76	29.5	1,380	1,633	118.3	1,366,915	340,828
Diesel fuel	2,846.0	1,143.8	3.61	40.2	2,164	3,182	147.1	1,315,397	359,449
Natural gas	432.9	144.5	0.46	33.4	6,091	5,643	92.6	71,069	25,599
LP gas, fuel oil, kerosene, motor oil, grease, etc.	1,206.1	399.7	1.26	33.1	945	1,125	119.0	1,276,331	355,317
Electricity	2,751.1	520.3	1.64	18.9	2,247	1,640	73.0	1,224,374	317,184
Hired farm labor	14,841.0	1,617.5	5.10	10.9	22,811	10,449	45.8	650,623	154,796
Contract labor	2,959.0	177.4	0.56	6.0	13,040	4,464	34.2	226,909	39,753
Repair and maintenance	8,637.7	2,748.2	8.67	31.8	5,616	7,227	128.7	1,538,058	380,263
Custom work, machine hire, and rental of equipment	3,210.3	1,122.9	3.54	35.0	5,372	5,615	104.5	597,624	199,970
Interest	8,928.1	2,741.3	8.65	30.7	11,016	11,021	100.0	810,476	248,737
Secured by real estate	5,449.6	1,582.6	4.99	29.0	9,564	9,544	99.8	569,775	165,830
Not secured by real estate	3,478.5	1,158.7	3.66	33.3	7,540	7,089	94.0	461,326	163,458
Cash rent	6,915.7	3,588.8	11.32	51.9	14,244	20,404	143.2	485,512	175,889
Property taxes	3,920.1	1,198.2	3.78	30.6	2,213	2,871	129.8	1,771,787	417,367
All other farm production expenses	14,777.4	3,022.7	9.54	20.5	8,747	7,208	82.4	1,689,391	419,321

Source: 1997 Census of Agriculture, U.S. Department of Agriculture, National Agricultural Statistics Service. Table shows totals for the U.S. agriculture sector and for the NAICS subdivision of it, shown as "This Agric. Sector" or as "This Sector." Not all farms report on every category. For this reason, the reporting universe is shown in the last two columns. Averages are based on these columns. LP gas stands for "liquid petroleum gas," i.e., butane or propane.

NET CASH RETURN AND FARMS WITH GAINS AND LOSSES

Item	Number of farms and %				Average gain or loss per farm - $		
	U.S.	% of U.S.	This Agriculture Sector	% of Sector	U.S.	This Agriculture Sector	% of U.S.
All farms	1,911,824	100.0	464,559	100.0	22,260	25,527	114.7
Number of farms with net gains	985,718	51.6	279,671	60.2	51,296	48,249	94.1
Gain of -							
Less than $1,000	120,163	6.3	15,175	3.3	-	-	-
$1,000 to $9,999	370,611	19.4	77,859	16.8	-	-	-
$10,000 to $49,999	292,484	15.3	107,348	23.1	-	-	-
$50,000 or more	202,460	10.6	79,289	17.1	-	-	-
Number of farms with net losses	926,106	48.4	184,888	39.8	(8,645)	(8,843)	102.3
Loss of -							
Less than $1,000	165,390	8.7	36,070	7.8	-	-	-
$1,000 to $9,999	591,517	30.9	108,224	23.3	-	-	-
$10,000 to $49,999	152,649	8.0	35,719	7.7	-	-	-
$50,000 or more	16,550	0.9	4,875	1.0	-	-	-

Source: 1997 Census of Agriculture, U.S. Department of Agriculture, National Agricultural Statistics Service. Table shows totals for the U.S. agriculture sector and for the NAICS subdivision of it, shown as "This Agric. Sector" or as "This Sector." Not all farms report on every category. For this reason, the reporting universe is shown in the last two columns. Averages are based on these columns. Net gains are income less cost for farm operations; they exclude non-farm earnings. Values in parentheses are losses.

CHARACTERISTICS OF FARM OPERATORS

Farm Operators	U.S.	This Agric. Sector	% of U.S.	Farm Operators	U.S.	This Agric. Sector	% of U.S.
Place of residence:				By age group:			
On farm operated	1,361,766	297,637	21.9	Under 25 years	20,850	7,159	34.3
Not on farm operated	412,554	127,730	31.0	25 to 34 years	128,455	33,489	26.1
Not reported	137,539	37,510	27.3	35 to 44 years	371,442	91,949	24.8
Principal occupation:				45 to 49 years	232,845	54,047	23.2
Farming	961,560	279,994	29.1	50 to 54 years	233,884	51,707	22.1
Other	950,299	182,883	19.2	55 to 59 years	222,736	51,068	22.9
Days worked off farm:				60 to 64 years	204,618	50,074	24.5
None	755,254	207,963	27.5	65 to 69 years	179,858	43,877	24.4
Any	1,042,158	222,762	21.4	70 years and over	317,171	79,507	25.1
1 to 99 days	164,957	48,416	29.4	Average age	54	54	99.8
100 to 199 days	167,922	36,551	21.8	By sex:			
200 days or more	709,279	137,795	19.4	Male	1,746,757	435,199	24.9
Not reported	114,447	32,152	28.1	Female	165,102	27,678	16.8
Years on present farm:				Spanish, Hispanic/Latino origin	27,717	2,547	9.2
2 years or less	92,574	17,160	18.5	Tenure of operator:			
3 or 4 years	126,791	19,476	15.4	All operators	1,911,859	462,877	24.2
5 to 9 years	263,642	44,300	16.8	Full owners	1,146,891	208,661	18.2
10 years or more	1,113,839	300,906	27.0	Part owners	573,839	185,342	32.3
Ave. years on this farm	20	23	116.9	Tenants	191,129	68,874	36.0
Not reported	315,013	81,035	25.7				

Source: 1997 Census of Agriculture, U.S. Department of Agriculture, National Agricultural Statistics Service. Table shows totals for the U.S. agriculture sector and for the NAICS subdivision of it, shown as "This Agric. Sector" or as "This Sector." Not all farms report on every category. For this reason, the reporting universe is shown in the last two columns. Averages are based on these columns. All values shown are number of farm operators in each category or percent.

FARMS BY TYPE OF ORGANIZATION

Item	Number of farms and percent				Total acres and percent		
	U.S.	% of U.S.	This Agriculture Sector	% of Sector	U.S.	This Agriculture Sector	% of U.S.
Individual or family (sole proprietorship)	1,643,424	100.0	386,688	100.0	585,464,911	200,055,932	34.2
Partnership	169,462	10.3	47,941	12.4	149,321,484	45,275,642	30.3
Corporation:							
Family held	76,103	4.6	22,600	5.8	119,559,203	30,883,835	25.8
More than 10 stockholders	1,795	0.1	378	0.1	-	-	-
10 or less stockholders	74,308	4.5	22,222	5.7	-	-	-
Other than family held	7,899	0.5	1,412	0.4	11,904,053	1,287,709	10.8
More than 10 stockholders	1,029	0.1	212	0.1	-	-	-
10 or less stockholders	6,870	0.4	1,200	0.3	-	-	-
Other cooperative, estate or trust, institutional, etc.	14,971	0.9	4,236	1.1	65,545,604	7,677,074	11.7

Source: 1997 Census of Agriculture, U.S. Department of Agriculture, National Agricultural Statistics Service. Table shows totals for the U.S. agriculture sector and for the NAICS subdivision of it, shown as "This Agric. Sector" or as "This Sector." Not all farms report on every category. For this reason, the reporting universe is shown in the last two columns. Averages are based on these columns.

LIVESTOCK INVENTORIES AND SALES

Item	U.S. (number)	This Agric. Sector (number)	% of U.S.	Average number per farm			Number of farms reporting category	
				U.S.	This Agric. Sector	% of U.S.	U.S.	This Sector
Cattle and calves inventory	98,989,244	9,752,083	9.9	94.6	79.3	83.9	1,046,863	122,946
Cows and heifers that had calved	43,162,054	4,442,757	10.3	48.3	44.3	91.8	894,110	100,215
Beef cows	34,066,615	4,311,747	12.7	42.3	44.2	104.4	804,595	97,589
Milk cows	9,095,439	131,010	1.4	77.8	31.6	40.6	116,874	4,142
Heifers and heifer calves	26,988,697	2,327,831	8.6	33.6	25.9	77.2	803,985	89,778
Steers, steer calves, bulls, and bull calves	28,838,493	2,981,495	10.3	32.6	27.7	84.8	883,983	107,737
Cattle and calves sold	74,089,046	5,002,005	6.8	73.2	42.0	57.3	1,011,809	119,149
Calves	16,480,293	1,248,171	7.6	26.8	26.8	99.9	615,177	46,616
Cattle	57,608,753	3,753,834	6.5	78.0	39.8	51.0	738,696	94,337
Fattened on grain and concentrates	27,328,190	899,704	3.3	247.0	34.4	13.9	110,620	26,166
Hogs and pigs inventory	61,206,236	5,744,009	9.4	557.7	270.4	48.5	109,754	21,244
Used or to be used for breeding	6,831,564	582,744	8.5	106.7	44.7	41.9	64,029	13,027
Other	54,374,672	5,161,265	9.5	528.0	255.2	48.3	102,977	20,221
Hogs and pigs sold	142,611,882	9,070,756	6.4	1,396.7	412.8	29.6	102,106	21,974
Feeder pigs	34,988,718	1,046,616	3.0	2,037.8	422.4	20.7	17,170	2,478
Litters of pigs farrowed between Dec. 1 of preceding year and Nov. 30	11,497,523	849,916	7.4	170.3	61.3	36.0	67,514	13,857
Dec. 1 and May 31	5,697,371	431,504	7.6	91.0	33.7	37.0	62,622	12,816
June 1 and Nov. 30	5,800,152	418,412	7.2	99.7	34.4	34.5	58,204	12,164
Sheep and lambs of all ages inventory	7,821,885	527,665	6.7	118.9	59.5	50.0	65,790	8,868
Ewes 1 year old or older	4,408,683	313,729	7.1	78.1	40.1	51.4	56,414	7,815
Sheep and lambs sold	7,331,545	440,072	6.0	123.1	51.8	42.1	59,575	8,499
Sheep and lambs shorn	6,139,140	397,680	6.5	118.4	53.5	45.2	51,869	7,440
Horses and ponies inventory	2,427,277	135,132	5.6	6.5	4.5	69.9	375,218	29,881
Horses and ponies sold	325,306	8,690	2.7	4.1	2.8	68.9	79,516	3,083
Goats inventory	1,989,799	43,249	2.2	34.4	14.2	41.3	57,925	3,052
Goats sold	740,597	16,257	2.2	31.5	18.4	58.4	23,520	884

Source: *1997 Census of Agriculture*, U.S. Department of Agriculture, National Agricultural Statistics Service. Table shows totals for the U.S. agriculture sector and for the NAICS subdivision of it, shown as "This Agric. Sector" or as "This Sector." Not all farms report on every category. For this reason, the reporting universe is shown in the last two columns. Averages are based on these columns.

POULTRY INVENTORIES AND SALES

Item	U.S. (number)	This Agric. Sector (number)	% of U.S.	Average number per farm			Number of farms reporting category	
				U.S.	This Agric. Sector	% of U.S.	U.S.	This Sector
Layers and pullets 13 weeks old and older inventory	366,989,851	1,150,558	0.3	5,053.8	209.0	4.1	72,616	5,505
Layers 20 weeks old and older	313,851,480	841,992	0.3	4,499.0	157.9	3.5	69,761	5,332
Pullets 13 weeks old and older but less than 20 weeks old	53,138,371	308,566	0.6	4,031.7	396.1	9.8	13,180	779
Layers, pullets, and pullet chicks sold	331,563,736	867,141	0.3	24,636.9	2,026.0	8.2	13,458	428
Broilers and other meat type chickens sold	6,741,927,110	3,982,487	0.1	281,653.0	6,164.8	2.2	23,937	646
Turkey hens kept for breeding	5,504,808	13,539	0.2	968.1	44.8	4.6	5,686	302
Turkeys sold	307,586,680	269,205	0.1	51,000.9	1,416.9	2.8	6,031	190

Source: *1997 Census of Agriculture*, U.S. Department of Agriculture, National Agricultural Statistics Service. Table shows totals for the U.S. agriculture sector and for the NAICS subdivision of it, shown as "This Agric. Sector" or as "This Sector." Not all farms report on every category. For this reason, the reporting universe is shown in the last two columns. Averages are based on these columns.

SELECTED CROPS HARVESTED

Item	In 1,000	Crop harvested			Acres used for crop (000)			Number of farms reporting category	
		U.S.	This Agric. Sector	% of U.S.	U.S.	This Agric. Sector	% of U.S.	U.S.	This Sector
Corn for grain or seed	bushels	8,578,635	6,690,141	78.0	69,796.7	53,664.5	76.9	430,711	265,126
Irrigated		-	-	-	10,638.9	8,416.9	79.1	40,574	27,600
Corn for silage or green chop	tons, green	88,381	16,430	18.6	5,727.6	1,026.7	17.9	119,308	23,882
Irrigated		-	-	-	1,033.3	286.2	27.7	10,815	3,176
Sorghum for grain or seed	bushels	559,070	412,580	73.8	8,470.4	6,070.4	71.7	49,397	33,491
Irrigated		-	-	-	875.6	507.3	57.9	5,793	3,281
Wheat for grain	bushels	2,204,027	1,655,685	75.1	58,836.3	44,927.9	76.4	243,568	158,852
Irrigated		-	-	-	3,990.9	1,950.0	48.9	20,385	9,648
Barley for grain	bushels	336,435	218,122	64.8	5,945.0	4,118.4	69.3	41,930	19,594
Irrigated		-	-	-	1,060.7	355.7	33.5	8,847	2,511
Oats for grain	bushels	151,327	60,698	40.1	2,681.0	1,055.8	39.4	89,606	30,356
Irrigated		-	-	-	121.0	32.3	26.7	2,788	558
Rice	cwt	182,231	172,376	94.6	3,122.1	2,958.1	94.7	9,291	8,607
Irrigated		-	-	-	3,122.1	2,958.1	94.7	9,291	8,607
Cotton	bales	17,879	1,362	7.6	13,235.2	1,061.1	8.0	31,493	4,216
Irrigated		-	-	-	4,888.0	333.0	6.8	12,434	1,485
Tobacco	pounds	1,747,702	54,874	3.1	838.5	25.9	3.1	89,706	3,347
Irrigated		-	-	-	138.7	1.6	1.1	7,090	133
Soybeans for beans	bushels	2,504,307	2,111,837	84.3	66,147.7	55,197.9	83.4	354,692	267,302
Irrigated		-	-	-	4,152.1	3,568.9	86.0	20,619	16,612
Dry edible beans, excluding dry limas	cwt	27,224	20,289	74.5	1,691.9	1,294.0	76.5	10,911	7,626
Irrigated		-	-	-	577.0	376.4	65.2	4,882	2,935
Potatoes, excluding sweetpotatoes	cwt	459,886	10,978	2.4	1,355.2	48.2	3.6	10,523	645
Irrigated		-	-	-	1,070.3	27.1	2.5	4,843	255
Sugar beets for sugar	tons	29,775	6,846	23.0	1,453.8	374.8	25.8	7,102	2,386
Irrigated		-	-	-	616.4	99.5	16.1	3,492	819
Peanuts for nuts	pounds	3,377,143	97,291	2.9	1,352.2	47.3	3.5	12,221	893
Irrigated		-	-	-	412.3	11.6	2.8	3,125	122
Hay alfalfa, other tame, small grain, wild, grass silage, green chop	tons, dry	139,365	19,650	14.1	60,799.8	8,502.1	14.0	888,597	143,446
Irrigated		-	-	-	9,564.3	717.2	7.5	79,406	8,661
Alfalfa hay	tons, dry	65,863	11,921	18.1	21,309.8	4,071.5	19.1	358,365	92,635
Irrigated		-	-	-	5,980.5	540.3	9.0	57,854	7,202
Vegetables harvested for sale		-	-	-	3,773.2	378.7	10.0	53,727	6,102
Irrigated		-	-	-	2,641.8	101.6	3.8	23,203	1,350
Land in orchards		-	-	-	5,158.1	49.3	1.0	106,069	2,295
Irrigated		-	-	-	4,107.9	26.2	0.6	61,606	604

Source: *1997 Census of Agriculture*, U.S. Department of Agriculture, National Agricultural Statistics Service. Table shows totals for the U.S. agriculture sector and for the NAICS subdivision of it, shown as "This Agric. Sector" or as "This Sector." Not all farms report on every category. For this reason, the reporting universe is shown in the last two columns. Averages are based on these columns. "Green tons" are weight of product as harvested, i.e., moist. cwt stands for "hundredweight."

LEADING COMPANIES   Number shown: **15**   Total sales ($ mil): **5,673**   Total employment (000): **14.9**

Company Name	Address				CEO Name	Phone	Co. Type	Sales ($ mil)	Empl. (000)
Dow AgroSciences	9330 Zionsville Rd	Indianapolis	IN	46268	A Charles Fischer	317-337-3000	S	2,000	3.1
Pioneer Hi-Bred International Inc.	PO Box 14453	Des Moines	IA	50306	Jerry Chicoine	515-248-4800	P	1,835	5.0
DEKALB Genetics Corp.	3100 Sycamore Rd	Dekalb	IL	60115	Bruce Bicker	815-758-3461	S	502	2.1
Busch Agricultural Resources Inc.	10733 Sunset Office	St. Louis	MO	63127	Don Koth	314-909-3800	S	362*	0.6
Delta and Pine Land Co.	1 Cotton Row	Scott	MS	38772	Roger D Malkin	662-742-4500	P	260	0.6
NEW Cooperative Inc.	PO Box 818	Fort Dodge	IA	50501	Paul Pingle	515-955-2040	R	240	0.1
John I. Haas Inc.	5185 MacArthur	Washington	DC	20016	HF V Eichel	202-777-4800	R	160*	2.0
J.C. Robinson Seed Co.	100 J C Robinson	Waterloo	NE	68069	Ed Robinson	402-779-2531	R	115*	0.3
OH Kruse Grain and Milling	P O Box 51493	Ontario	CA	91761	Kevin Kruse	909-983-1771	R	53*	0.2
Central Washington Grain	Ash & Baker Sts	Waterville	WA	98858		509-745-8551	R	40	0.4
American Pop Corn Co.	PO Box 178	Sioux City	IA	51102		712-239-1232	R	36*	0.1
E. Ritter and Co.	106 Frisco St	Marked Tree	AR	72365	ER Arnold	870-358-2200	R	35	0.2
Moews Seed Company Inc.	PO Box 214	Granville	IL	61326	Tom Navin	815-339-2201	R	21*	0.1
Abt Systems	PO Box 12447	Fresno	CA	93777	Doug Elkins	559-233-8823	S	12	<0.1
Grand Forks Bean Company Inc.	P O Box 5357	Grand Forks	ND	58206	Glen Shoemacher	701-775-3984	R	1*	<0.1

Source: Ward's Business Directory of U.S. Private and Public Companies, Volumes 1 and 2, 2000. The company type code used is as follows: P - Public, R - Private, S - Subsidiary, D - Division, J - Joint Venture, A - Affiliate, G - Group, N - Company type not reported. Sales are in millions of dollars, employees are in thousands. An asterisk (*) indicates an estimated sales volume. The symbol < stands for 'less than'. Company names and addresses are truncated, in some cases, to fit into the available space.

NAICS 111200 - VEGETABLE AND MELON FARMING

GENERAL STATISTICS

Item	U.S. Total	This Agri- culture Sector	% of U.S.	Category average per farm				Number of farms reporting category	
				Value shown as	U.S.	This Agric. Sector	% of U.S.	U.S.	This Sector
Farms - number	1,911,859	31,030	1.6	-	-	-	-	-	-
Land in farms - mil. acres	931.795	10.244	1.1	Acres	487	330	67.8	1,911,859	31,030
Value of land, buildings - $ mil.	859,839.2	23,658.0	2.8	$	449,748	761,370	169.3	524,066	31,073
Value of machinery and equip- ment - $ mil.	110,256.8	3,393.2	3.1	$	57,678	109,215	189.4	1,911,601	31,069
Sales of Ag Products - $ mil.	196,864.6	10,779.2	5.5	$	102,970	347,381	337.4	1,911,859	31,030
Government payments - $ mil.	5,054.5	63.5	1.3	$	7,378	9,267	125.6	685,029	6,853
Other farm-related income - $ mil.	3,272.3	88.5	2.7	$	5,999	11,743	195.8	545,480	7,534
Expenses - $ mil.	150,591.0	7,336.4	4.9	$	78,771	236,094	299.7	1,911,766	31,074
Payroll - $ mil.	14,841.0	1,716.4	11.6	$	22,811	108,047	473.7	650,623	15,886
Workers - 150 days or more a year	890,467	89,310	10.0	Number	3.4	10.5	305.7	259,631	8,518
Workers - less than 150 days	2,461,561	219,712	8.9	Number	4.2	15.1	356.9	581,658	14,547
Net Cash Return - $ mil.	42,557.9	3,366.1	7.9	$	22,260	108,324	486.6	1,911,824	31,074

Source: *1997 Census of Agriculture*, U.S. Department of Agriculture, National Agricultural Statistics Service. Table shows totals for the U.S. agriculture sector and for the NAICS subdivision of it, shown as "This Agric. Sector" or as "This Sector." Not all farms report on every category. For this reason, the reporting universe is shown in the last two columns. Averages are based on these columns.

LAND IN FARMS ACCORDING TO USE

Item	U.S. Total (000 acres)	This Sector (000 acres)	% of U.S.	Average acres per farms			Number of farms reporting category	
				U.S.	This Agric. Sector	% of U.S.	U.S.	This Sector
Total cropland	431,144.9	7,734.5	1.8	260	249	-	1,661,395	31,021
Harvested cropland	309,395.5	6,763.4	2.2	219	218	-	1,410,606	31,012
Cropland:								
Pasture or grazing	64,466.5	272.4	0.4	85	48	-	754,170	5,640
In cover crops, legumes, grasses	13,531.2	163.1	1.2	88	44	-	153,177	3,682
On which all crops failed	3,449.4	79.3	2.3	67	29	-	51,673	2,690
In cultivated summer fallow	20,905.9	99.7	0.5	256	65	-	81,702	1,523
Idle	19,396.3	356.6	1.8	83	52	-	232,961	6,893
Total woodland	71,465.4	807.6	1.1	96	74	-	743,011	10,874
Woodland pastured	29,693.9	147.2	0.5	84	60	-	352,217	2,443
Woodland not pastured	41,771.5	660.5	1.6	79	70	-	531,846	9,497
Other pasture/rangeland	396,884.6	1,210.0	0.3	721	351	-	550,619	3,451
Land for house lots, ponds, roads, wasteland	32,300.4	492.3	1.5	28	27	-	1,142,618	18,199
Irrigated land	55,058.1	4,697.5	8.5	197	287	-	279,442	16,370
Harvested cropland	50,013.5	4,633.4	9.3	198	284	-	252,679	16,331
Pasture and other	5,044.7	64.1	1.3	87	75	-	58,258	859
Conservation Reserve/Wetlands Reserve Lands	29,489.1	142.6	0.5	131	94	-	225,410	1,520

Source: *1997 Census of Agriculture*, U.S. Department of Agriculture, National Agricultural Statistics Service. Table shows totals for the U.S. agriculture sector and for the NAICS subdivision of it, shown as "This Agric. Sector" or as "This Sector." Not all farms report on every category. For this reason, the reporting universe is shown in the last two columns. Averages are based on these columns. The Conservation Reserve and Wetlands Reserve programs provide support for land conservation/preservation. Cover crops are not harvested or pastured.

MARKET VALUE OF AGRICULTURAL PRODUCTS SOLD: ALL FARMS

Item	U.S. Total ($ mil.)	This Sector ($ mil.)	% of Sector Sales	% of U.S.	Average sales per farm - $			Number of farms reporting category	
					U.S.	This Agric. Sector	% of U.S.	U.S.	This Sector
Grains	46,617.1	624.1	5.79	1.3	79,095	82,057	103.7	589,379	7,606
Corn for grain	18,884.8	163.8	1.52	0.9	52,506	52,592	100.2	359,666	3,115
Wheat	7,173.9	244.9	2.27	3.4	29,726	70,735	238.0	241,334	3,462
Soybeans	15,622.4	60.8	0.56	0.4	44,185	28,962	65.5	353,566	2,098
Sorghum for grain	1,140.0	7.5	0.07	0.7	25,360	32,151	126.8	44,955	232
Barley	709.6	66.1	0.61	9.3	23,191	60,878	262.5	30,598	1,085
Oats	121.3	5.7	0.05	4.7	3,114	7,996	256.7	38,940	710
Other grains	2,965.1	75.5	0.70	2.5	67,540	60,174	89.1	43,901	1,254
Cotton and cotton seed	5,975.5	190.4	1.77	3.2	189,963	298,912	157.4	31,456	637
Tobacco	2,924.7	22.8	0.21	0.8	32,662	70,650	216.3	89,544	323
Hay, silage, and field seeds	4,670.5	197.3	1.83	4.2	13,174	44,556	338.2	354,523	4,428
Vegetables, sweet corn, and melons	8,401.7	7,234.3	67.11	86.1	156,628	262,979	167.9	53,641	27,509
Fruits and berries	12,660.3	181.6	1.68	1.4	147,259	45,248	30.7	85,973	4,013
Nursery and greenhouse crops	10,942.8	76.1	0.71	0.7	161,360	28,422	17.6	67,816	2,678
Other crops	5,863.1	2,168.3	20.12	37.0	153,907	311,721	202.5	38,095	6,956
Poultry and poultry products	22,262.6	2.3	0.02	0.0	352,000	1,896	0.5	63,246	1,192
Dairy products	18,997.3	11.7	0.11	0.1	191,432	92,402	48.3	99,238	127
Cattle and calves	40,524.8	58.3	0.54	0.1	40,052	15,265	38.1	1,011,809	3,820
Hogs and pigs	13,804.8	9.1	0.08	0.1	135,201	11,790	8.7	102,106	775
Sheep, lambs, and wool	682.9	1.1	0.01	0.2	10,913	1,644	15.1	62,579	661
Other livestock	2,536.5	1.8	0.02	0.1	20,506	1,622	7.9	123,695	1,082
Products sold to public directly	13,096.7	6.8	0.06	0.1	377,610	272,120	72.1	34,683	25

Source: *1997 Census of Agriculture*, U.S. Department of Agriculture, National Agricultural Statistics Service. Table shows totals for the U.S. agriculture sector and for the NAICS subdivision of it, shown as "This Agric. Sector" or as "This Sector." Not all farms report on every category. For this reason, the reporting universe is shown in the last two columns. Averages are based on these columns. Farms classified in one sector routinely produce categories in other sectors as well. Products sold to the public are sold for direct consumption.

MARKET VALUE OF PRODUCTS SOLD: FARMS WITH SALES OF $50,000 OR MORE

Item	U.S. Total ($ mil.)	This Sector ($ mil.)	% of Sector Sales	% of U.S.	Average sales per farm - $			Number of farms reporting category	
					U.S.	This Agric. Sector	% of U.S.	U.S.	This Sector
Grains	40,973.4	563.5	5.23	1.4	183,623	224,944	122.5	223,138	2,505
Cotton and cotton seed	5,743.9	186.8	1.73	3.3	286,562	412,402	143.9	20,044	453
Tobacco	2,060.2	20.2	0.19	1.0	175,907	315,359	179.3	11,712	64
Hay, silage, and field seeds	2,781.9	172.4	1.60	6.2	188,959	258,087	136.6	14,722	668
Vegetables, sweet corn, and melons	7,966.8	7,005.1	64.99	87.9	673,443	909,877	135.1	11,830	7,699
Fruits and berries	12,072.3	163.2	1.51	1.4	478,927	360,289	75.2	25,207	453
Nursery and greenhouse crops	10,412.0	59.3	0.55	0.6	578,025	237,176	41.0	18,013	250
Other crops	5,586.6	2,140.7	19.86	38.3	363,758	640,151	176.0	15,358	3,344
Poultry and poultry products	22,171.7	1.2	0.01	0.0	778,637	113,455	14.6	28,475	11
Dairy products	18,344.3	11.0	0.10	0.1	250,075	243,356	97.3	73,355	45
Cattle and calves	32,358.6	35.1	0.33	0.1	386,685	156,124	40.4	83,682	225
Hogs and pigs	13,096.7	6.8	0.06	0.1	377,610	272,120	72.1	34,683	25
Sheep, lambs, and wool	478.6	0.2	0.00	0.0	278,730	57,500	20.6	1,717	4
Other livestock	2,026.6	0.3	0.00	0.0	369,685	87,333	23.6	5,482	3

Source: *1997 Census of Agriculture*, U.S. Department of Agriculture, National Agricultural Statistics Service. Table shows totals for the U.S. agriculture sector and for the NAICS subdivision of it, shown as "This Agric. Sector" or as "This Sector." Not all farms report on every category. For this reason, the reporting universe is shown in the last two columns. Averages are based on these columns. Farms classified in one sector routinely produce categories in other sectors as well.

GOVERNMENT PAYMENTS AND OTHER FARM-RELATED INCOME

| Item | U.S. Total ($ mil.) | This Sector ($ mil.) | % of Sector Gov/Oth. Income | % of U.S. | Average receipts per farm - $ | | | Number of farms reporting category | |
					U.S.	This Agric. Sector	% of U.S.	U.S.	This Sector
Government payments	5,054.5	63.5	41.79	1.3	7,378	9,267	125.6	685,029	6,853
Other farm-related income	3,272.3	88.5	58.21	2.7	5,999	11,743	195.8	545,480	7,534
Custom work and other agricultural services	1,235.1	36.9	24.25	3.0	8,646	15,035	173.9	142,854	2,451
Gross cash rent or share payments	1,207.9	34.8	22.91	2.9	6,867	13,077	190.4	175,901	2,662
Forest products, excluding Christmas trees and maple products	344.3	5.2	3.42	1.5	7,417	5,140	69.3	46,426	1,012
Other farm-related income sources	484.9	11.6	7.64	2.4	1,595	3,592	225.1	303,908	3,232

Source: 1997 Census of Agriculture, U.S. Department of Agriculture, National Agricultural Statistics Service. Table shows totals for the U.S. agriculture sector and for the NAICS subdivision of it, shown as "This Agric. Sector" or as "This Sector." Not all farms report on every category. For this reason, the reporting universe is shown in the last two columns. Averages are based on these columns. Government payments are agricultural subsidies under various programs.

COMMODITY CREDIT CORPORATION LOANS

| Item | U.S. Total ($ mil.) | This Sector ($ mil.) | % of Sector Loan Total | % of U.S. | Average loan value per farm - $ | | | Number of farms reporting category | |
					U.S.	This Agric. Sector	% of U.S.	U.S.	This Sector
Total loans	3,034.7	21.7	100.00	0.7	36,419	40,874	112.2	83,328	530
Corn	1,333.9	6.3	29.10	0.5	26,419	33,717	127.6	50,489	187
Wheat	415.4	9.9	45.62	2.4	18,093	34,436	190.3	22,961	287
Soybeans	774.0	1.7	7.78	0.2	30,370	36,652	120.7	25,487	46
Sorghum, barley, and oats	54.8	-	-	-	8,603	-	-	6,375	68
Cotton	191.4	1.1	4.91	0.6	43,275	21,280	49.2	4,422	50
Sunflower seed, flaxseed, safflower, canola, other rapeseed, and mustard seed	17.3	-	-	-	25,159	-	-	686	1
Peanuts, rice, and tobacco	247.9	1.8	8.27	0.7	60,421	68,885	114.0	4,103	26

Source: 1997 Census of Agriculture, U.S. Department of Agriculture, National Agricultural Statistics Service. Table shows totals for the U.S. agriculture sector and for the NAICS subdivision of it, shown as "This Agric. Sector" or as "This Sector." Not all farms report on every category. For this reason, the reporting universe is shown in the last two columns. Averages are based on these columns. The Commodity Credit Corporation provides low interest loans to farmers.

SELECTED MACHINERY AND EQUIPMENT

| Item | U.S. Total (number) | This Agric. Sector (number) | % of U.S. | Average number per farm | | | Number of farms reporting category | |
				U.S.	This Agric. Sector	% of U.S.	U.S.	This Sector
Motortrucks, including pickups	3,497,735	92,433	2.6	2.07	3.33	160.8	1,688,303	27,750
Wheel tractors	3,936,014	84,778	2.2	2.31	3.05	132.3	1,707,384	27,799
Less than 40 horsepower (PTO)	1,262,688	31,321	2.5	1.44	1.79	124.2	877,119	17,523
40 horsepower (PTO) or more	2,673,326	53,457	2.0	2.02	2.76	136.6	1,321,084	19,345
40 to 99 horsepower (PTO)	1,808,105	35,438	2.0	1.58	2.06	130.3	1,145,466	17,234
100 horsepower (PTO)	865,221	18,019	2.1	1.68	2.55	151.5	513,773	7,063
Grain and bean combines	460,606	4,980	1.1	1.16	1.27	108.8	395,934	3,933
Cotton pickers and strippers	38,294	1,011	2.6	1.48	1.76	119.2	25,874	573
Mower conditioners	608,443	5,534	0.9	1.12	1.16	103.5	543,565	4,778
Pickup balers	717,245	4,934	0.7	1.24	1.21	98.0	579,440	4,066

Source: 1997 Census of Agriculture, U.S. Department of Agriculture, National Agricultural Statistics Service. Table shows totals for the U.S. agriculture sector and for the NAICS subdivision of it, shown as "This Agric. Sector" or as "This Sector." Not all farms report on every category. For this reason, the reporting universe is shown in the last two columns. Averages are based on these columns. PTO stands for "power take off."

13

FARM PRODUCTION EXPENSES

Item	U.S. Total ($ mil.)	This Sector ($ mil.)	% of Sector Total Expense	% of U.S.	Average expense per farm - $			Number of farms reporting category	
					U.S.	This Agric. Sector	% of U.S.	U.S.	This Sector
Total farm production expenses	150,591.0	7,336.4	100.00	4.9	78,771	236,094	299.7	1,911,766	31,074
Livestock and poultry purchased	21,614.6	20.0	0.27	0.1	38,807	5,789	14.9	556,980	3,453
Feed for livestock and poultry	32,760.0	22.1	0.30	0.1	32,059	3,695	11.5	1,021,849	5,990
Commercially mixed formula feeds	21,236.2	11.9	0.16	0.1	34,459	3,210	9.3	616,280	3,711
Seeds, bulbs, plants, and trees	5,725.9	517.2	7.05	9.0	6,388	18,552	290.4	896,339	27,879
Commercial fertilizer	9,597.1	687.7	9.37	7.2	8,060	23,912	296.7	1,190,733	28,761
Agricultural chemicals	7,581.4	666.6	9.09	8.8	8,056	28,683	356.1	941,136	23,241
Petroleum products	6,371.5	290.0	3.95	4.6	3,619	9,625	266.0	1,760,642	30,132
Gasoline and gasohol	1,886.6	94.3	1.29	5.0	1,380	3,783	274.1	1,366,915	24,938
Diesel fuel	2,846.0	144.6	1.97	5.1	2,164	6,848	316.5	1,315,397	21,114
Natural gas	432.9	14.5	0.20	3.4	6,091	9,696	159.2	71,069	1,496
LP gas, fuel oil, kerosene, motor oil, grease, etc.	1,206.1	36.6	0.50	3.0	945	1,662	175.9	1,276,331	22,015
Electricity	2,751.1	222.1	3.03	8.1	2,247	10,800	480.7	1,224,374	20,567
Hired farm labor	14,841.0	1,716.4	23.40	11.6	22,811	108,047	473.7	650,623	15,886
Contract labor	2,959.0	618.4	8.43	20.9	13,040	96,417	739.4	226,909	6,414
Repair and maintenance	8,637.7	441.8	6.02	5.1	5,616	16,385	291.8	1,538,058	26,962
Custom work, machine hire, and rental of equipment	3,210.3	257.0	3.50	8.0	5,372	26,626	495.7	597,624	9,651
Interest	8,928.1	378.1	5.15	4.2	11,016	28,745	260.9	810,476	13,152
Secured by real estate	5,449.6	202.3	2.76	3.7	9,564	22,987	240.3	569,775	8,802
Not secured by real estate	3,478.5	175.7	2.40	5.1	7,540	22,720	301.3	461,326	7,734
Cash rent	6,915.7	412.4	5.62	6.0	14,244	38,295	268.8	485,512	10,769
Property taxes	3,920.1	127.9	1.74	3.3	2,213	4,664	210.8	1,771,787	27,433
All other farm production expenses	14,777.4	958.6	13.07	6.5	8,747	33,752	385.9	1,689,391	28,400

Source: 1997 Census of Agriculture, U.S. Department of Agriculture, National Agricultural Statistics Service. Table shows totals for the U.S. agriculture sector and for the NAICS subdivision of it, shown as "This Agric. Sector" or as "This Sector." Not all farms report on every category. For this reason, the reporting universe is shown in the last two columns. Averages are based on these columns. LP gas stands for "liquid petroleum gas," i.e., butane or propane.

NET CASH RETURN AND FARMS WITH GAINS AND LOSSES

Item	Number of farms and %				Average gain or loss per farm - $		
	U.S.	% of U.S.	This Agriculture Sector	% of Sector	U.S.	This Agriculture Sector	% of U.S.
All farms	1,911,824	100.0	31,074	100.0	22,260	108,324	486.6
Number of farms with net gains	985,718	51.6	23,035	74.1	51,296	151,137	294.6
Gain of -							
Less than $1,000	120,163	6.3	1,887	6.1	-	-	-
$1,000 to $9,999	370,611	19.4	8,336	26.8	-	-	-
$10,000 to $49,999	292,484	15.3	6,767	21.8	-	-	-
$50,000 or more	202,460	10.6	6,045	19.5	-	-	-
Number of farms with net losses	926,106	48.4	8,039	25.9	(8,645)	(14,352)	166.0
Loss of -							
Less than $1,000	165,390	8.7	1,842	5.9	-	-	-
$1,000 to $9,999	591,517	30.9	4,670	15.0	-	-	-
$10,000 to $49,999	152,649	8.0	1,158	3.7	-	-	-
$50,000 or more	16,550	0.9	369	1.2	-	-	-

Source: 1997 Census of Agriculture, U.S. Department of Agriculture, National Agricultural Statistics Service. Table shows totals for the U.S. agriculture sector and for the NAICS subdivision of it, shown as "This Agric. Sector" or as "This Sector." Not all farms report on every category. For this reason, the reporting universe is shown in the last two columns. Averages are based on these columns. Net gains are income less cost for farm operations; they exclude non-farm earnings. Values in parentheses are losses.

CHARACTERISTICS OF FARM OPERATORS

Farm Operators	U.S.	This Agric. Sector	% of U.S.	Farm Operators	U.S.	This Agric. Sector	% of U.S.
Place of residence:				By age group:			
On farm operated	1,361,766	21,027	1.5	Under 25 years	20,850	347	1.7
Not on farm operated	412,554	7,060	1.7	25 to 34 years	128,455	2,213	1.7
Not reported	137,539	2,943	2.1	35 to 44 years	371,442	6,530	1.8
Principal occupation:				45 to 49 years	232,845	4,224	1.8
Farming	961,560	19,434	2.0	50 to 54 years	233,884	3,965	1.7
Other	950,299	11,596	1.2	55 to 59 years	222,736	3,581	1.6
Days worked off farm:				60 to 64 years	204,618	3,020	1.5
None	755,254	14,105	1.9	65 to 69 years	179,858	2,672	1.5
Any	1,042,158	14,560	1.4	70 years and over	317,171	4,478	1.4
1 to 99 days	164,957	3,284	2.0	Average age	54	53	98.0
100 to 199 days	167,922	3,049	1.8	By sex:			
200 days or more	709,279	8,227	1.2	Male	1,746,757	28,408	1.6
Not reported	114,447	2,365	2.1	Female	165,102	2,622	1.6
Years on present farm:				Spanish, Hispanic/Latino origin	27,717	1,017	3.7
2 years or less	92,574	2,133	2.3	Tenure of operator:			
3 or 4 years	126,791	2,451	1.9	All operators	1,911,859	31,030	1.6
5 to 9 years	263,642	4,478	1.7	Full owners	1,146,891	16,336	1.4
10 years or more	1,113,839	16,420	1.5	Part owners	573,839	9,690	1.7
Ave. years on this farm	20	19	92.0	Tenants	191,129	5,004	2.6
Not reported	315,013	5,548	1.8				

Source: *1997 Census of Agriculture*, U.S. Department of Agriculture, National Agricultural Statistics Service. Table shows totals for the U.S. agriculture sector and for the NAICS subdivision of it, shown as "This Agric. Sector" or as "This Sector." Not all farms report on every category. For this reason, the reporting universe is shown in the last two columns. Averages are based on these columns. All values shown are number of farm operators in each category or percent.

FARMS BY TYPE OF ORGANIZATION

Item	Number of farms and percent				Total acres and percent		
	U.S.	% of U.S.	This Agriculture Sector	% of Sector	U.S.	This Agriculture Sector	% of U.S.
Individual or family (sole proprietorship)	1,643,424	100.0	24,964	100.0	585,464,911	4,337,115	0.7
Partnership	169,462	10.3	3,070	12.3	149,321,484	2,242,104	1.5
Corporation:							
Family held	76,103	4.6	2,467	9.9	119,559,203	2,853,519	2.4
More than 10 stockholders	1,795	0.1	71	0.3	-	-	-
10 or less stockholders	74,308	4.5	2,396	9.6	-	-	-
Other than family held	7,899	0.5	289	1.2	11,904,053	395,289	3.3
More than 10 stockholders	1,029	0.1	31	0.1	-	-	-
10 or less stockholders	6,870	0.4	258	1.0	-	-	-
Other cooperative, estate or trust, institutional, etc.	14,971	0.9	240	1.0	65,545,604	416,422	0.6

Source: *1997 Census of Agriculture*, U.S. Department of Agriculture, National Agricultural Statistics Service. Table shows totals for the U.S. agriculture sector and for the NAICS subdivision of it, shown as "This Agric. Sector" or as "This Sector." Not all farms report on every category. For this reason, the reporting universe is shown in the last two columns. Averages are based on these columns.

LIVESTOCK INVENTORIES AND SALES

Item	U.S. (number)	This Agric. Sector (number)	% of U.S.	Average number per farm			Number of farms reporting category	
				U.S.	This Agric. Sector	% of U.S.	U.S.	This Sector
Cattle and calves inventory	98,989,244	288,110	0.3	94.6	61.9	65.5	1,046,863	4,652
Cows and heifers that had calved	43,162,054	151,596	0.4	48.3	41.5	86.0	894,110	3,650
Beef cows	34,066,615	144,519	0.4	42.3	42.4	100.2	804,595	3,406
Milk cows	9,095,439	7,077	0.1	77.8	17.9	23.0	116,874	396
Heifers and heifer calves	26,988,697	67,947	0.3	33.6	21.5	64.0	803,985	3,163
Steers, steer calves, bulls, and bull calves	28,838,493	68,567	0.2	32.6	18.6	57.1	883,983	3,682
Cattle and calves sold	74,089,046	136,474	0.2	73.2	35.7	48.8	1,011,809	3,820
Calves	16,480,293	52,083	0.3	26.8	23.7	88.5	615,177	2,198
Cattle	57,608,753	84,391	0.1	78.0	32.6	41.8	738,696	2,586
Fattened on grain and concentrates	27,328,190	9,480	0.0	247.0	22.0	8.9	110,620	431
Hogs and pigs inventory	61,206,236	51,970	0.1	557.7	51.6	9.2	109,754	1,008
Used or to be used for breeding	6,831,564	6,407	0.1	106.7	14.6	13.6	64,029	440
Other	54,374,672	45,563	0.1	528.0	48.6	9.2	102,977	938
Hogs and pigs sold	142,611,882	93,820	0.1	1,396.7	121.1	8.7	102,106	775
Feeder pigs	34,988,718	29,157	0.1	2,037.8	239.0	11.7	17,170	122
Litters of pigs farrowed between Dec. 1 of preceding year and Nov. 30	11,497,523	10,122	0.1	170.3	21.2	12.5	67,514	477
Dec. 1 and May 31	5,697,371	5,055	0.1	91.0	12.1	13.3	62,622	417
June 1 and Nov. 30	5,800,152	5,067	0.1	99.7	14.7	14.8	58,204	344
Sheep and lambs of all ages inventory	7,821,885	23,656	0.3	118.9	31.8	26.7	65,790	744
Ewes 1 year old or older	4,408,683	12,945	0.3	78.1	21.8	27.8	56,414	595
Sheep and lambs sold	7,331,545	14,754	0.2	123.1	26.0	21.1	59,575	568
Sheep and lambs shorn	6,139,140	13,473	0.2	118.4	25.3	21.4	51,869	532
Horses and ponies inventory	2,427,277	11,544	0.5	6.5	4.3	67.1	375,218	2,659
Horses and ponies sold	325,306	662	0.2	4.1	2.6	63.5	79,516	255
Goats inventory	1,989,799	9,016	0.5	34.4	9.4	27.5	57,925	955
Goats sold	740,597	2,874	0.4	31.5	9.4	29.9	23,520	305

Source: 1997 Census of Agriculture, U.S. Department of Agriculture, National Agricultural Statistics Service. Table shows totals for the U.S. agriculture sector and for the NAICS subdivision of it, shown as "This Agric. Sector" or as "This Sector." Not all farms report on every category. For this reason, the reporting universe is shown in the last two columns. Averages are based on these columns.

POULTRY INVENTORIES AND SALES

Item	U.S. (number)	This Agric. Sector (number)	% of U.S.	Average number per farm			Number of farms reporting category	
				U.S.	This Agric. Sector	% of U.S.	U.S.	This Sector
Layers and pullets 13 weeks old and older inventory	366,989,851	126,772	0.0	5,053.8	72.6	1.4	72,616	1,747
Layers 20 weeks old and older	313,851,480	81,305	0.0	4,499.0	48.0	1.1	69,761	1,693
Pullets 13 weeks old and older but less than 20 weeks old	53,138,371	45,467	0.1	4,031.7	146.7	3.6	13,180	310
Layers, pullets, and pullet chicks sold	331,563,736	62,867	0.0	24,636.9	275.7	1.1	13,458	228
Broilers and other meat type chickens sold	6,741,927,110	536,328	0.0	281,653.0	2,603.5	0.9	23,937	206
Turkey hens kept for breeding	5,504,808	3,567	0.1	968.1	31.3	3.2	5,686	114
Turkeys sold	307,586,680	7,380	0.0	51,000.9	57.2	0.1	6,031	129

Source: 1997 Census of Agriculture, U.S. Department of Agriculture, National Agricultural Statistics Service. Table shows totals for the U.S. agriculture sector and for the NAICS subdivision of it, shown as "This Agric. Sector" or as "This Sector." Not all farms report on every category. For this reason, the reporting universe is shown in the last two columns. Averages are based on these columns.

SELECTED CROPS HARVESTED

Item	In 1,000	Crop harvested			Acres used for crop (000)			Number of farms reporting category	
		U.S.	This Agric. Sector	% of U.S.	U.S.	This Agric. Sector	% of U.S.	U.S.	This Sector
Corn for grain or seed	bushels	8,578,635	64,544	0.8	69,796.7	483.4	0.7	430,711	3,852
Irrigated		-	-	-	10,638.9	223.6	2.1	40,574	994
Corn for silage or green chop	tons, green	88,381	848	1.0	5,727.6	41.4	0.7	119,308	724
Irrigated		-	-	-	1,033.3	28.5	2.8	10,815	266
Sorghum for grain or seed	bushels	559,070	4,446	0.8	8,470.4	51.0	0.6	49,397	261
Irrigated		-	-	-	875.6	26.7	3.0	5,793	138
Wheat for grain	bushels	2,204,027	72,422	3.3	58,836.3	953.4	1.6	243,568	3,534
Irrigated		-	-	-	3,990.9	576.6	14.4	20,385	1,779
Barley for grain	bushels	336,435	23,932	7.1	5,945.0	269.1	4.5	41,930	1,154
Irrigated		-	-	-	1,060.7	189.6	17.9	8,847	688
Oats for grain	bushels	151,327	4,278	2.8	2,681.0	61.7	2.3	89,606	985
Irrigated		-	-	-	121.0	8.1	6.7	2,788	84
Rice	cwt	182,231	1,021	0.6	3,122.1	12.8	0.4	9,291	33
Irrigated		-	-	-	3,122.1	12.8	0.4	9,291	33
Cotton	bales	17,879	495	2.8	13,235.2	238.2	1.8	31,493	639
Irrigated		-	-	-	4,888.0	184.0	3.8	12,434	478
Tobacco	pounds	1,747,702	13,655	0.8	838.5	6.3	0.8	89,706	333
Irrigated		-	-	-	138.7	2.7	1.9	7,090	80
Soybeans for beans	bushels	2,504,307	9,651	0.4	66,147.7	295.7	0.4	354,692	2,143
Irrigated		-	-	-	4,152.1	44.9	1.1	20,619	291
Dry edible beans, excluding dry limas	cwt	27,224	1,362	5.0	1,691.9	74.4	4.4	10,911	605
Irrigated		-	-	-	577.0	50.4	8.7	4,882	402
Potatoes, excluding sweetpotatoes	cwt	459,886	388,857	84.6	1,355.2	1,116.5	82.4	10,523	5,603
Irrigated		-	-	-	1,070.3	896.7	83.8	4,843	3,100
Sugar beets for sugar	tons	29,775	1,771	5.9	1,453.8	68.1	4.7	7,102	310
Irrigated		-	-	-	616.4	57.9	9.4	3,492	256
Peanuts for nuts	pounds	3,377,143	86,558	2.6	1,352.2	33.8	2.5	12,221	361
Irrigated		-	-	-	412.3	15.5	3.7	3,125	123
Hay alfalfa, other tame, small grain, wild, grass silage, green chop	tons, dry	139,365	2,120	1.5	60,799.8	504.5	0.8	888,597	6,637
Irrigated		-	-	-	9,564.3	326.7	3.4	79,406	1,768
Alfalfa hay	tons, dry	65,863	1,626	2.5	21,309.8	301.3	1.4	358,365	2,944
Irrigated		-	-	-	5,980.5	251.0	4.2	57,854	1,356
Vegetables harvested for sale		-	-	-	3,773.2	2,680.7	71.0	53,727	27,523
Irrigated		-	-	-	2,641.8	2,102.6	79.6	23,203	13,670
Land in orchards		-	-	-	5,158.1	85.2	1.7	106,069	3,301
Irrigated		-	-	-	4,107.9	64.9	1.6	61,606	1,595

Source: *1997 Census of Agriculture*, U.S. Department of Agriculture, National Agricultural Statistics Service. Table shows totals for the U.S. agriculture sector and for the NAICS subdivision of it, shown as "This Agric. Sector" or as "This Sector." Not all farms report on every category. For this reason, the reporting universe is shown in the last two columns. Averages are based on these columns. "Green tons" are weight of product as harvested, i.e., moist. cwt stands for "hundredweight."

LEADING COMPANIES   Number shown: **26**   Total sales ($ mil): **3,191**   Total employment (000): **20.5**

Company Name	Address				CEO Name	Phone	Co. Type	Sales ($ mil)	Empl. (000)
R.D. Offutt Co.	P O Box 7160	Fargo	ND	58106	Ronald D Offutt	701-237-6062	R	720*	2.0
United States Sugar Corp.	P O Drawer 1207	Clewiston	FL	33440	J Nelson Fairbanks	813-983-2721	R	430*	2.7
Tanimura and Antle Inc.	PO Box 4070	Salinas	CA	93912	Rick Antle	408-455-2950	R	378*	2.7
Dole Fresh Vegetables	PO Box 1759	Salinas	CA	93902	Lawrence Kern	408-422-8871	S	250*	3.0
United Foods Inc.	PO Box 119	Bells	TN	38006	J Haltom	901-422-7600	P	206	2.1
Harry Singh and Sons	P O Box 1850	Oceanside	CA	92054	Harry Singh	760-758-9299	R	199*	0.9
Harris Farms Inc.	Rte 1, Box 426	Coalinga	CA	93210	John C Harris	559-884-2859	R	168*	1.2
William Bolthouse Farms Inc.	7200 E Brundage Ln	Bakersfield	CA	93307	Bill Bolthouse	661-366-7205	R	167*	2.0
Furman Foods Inc.	PO Box 500	Northumberland	PA	17857	David Geise	570-473-3516	R	100*	0.5
Nash De Camp Co.	3300 S Demaree Rd	Visalia	CA	93277	Stephen C Biswell	559-622-1850	S	90*	1.0
Growers Vegetable Express	PO Box 948	Salinas	CA	93902	Ron Frudden	831-757-9951	R	83*	0.4
Petoseed Co.	PO Box 4206	Ventura	CA	93007	Alexandro Rodriquez	805-647-1188	D	62*	0.3
Deardorff-Jackson Co.	PO Box 1188	Oxnard	CA	93032	Thomas D Deardorff	805-487-7801	R	56*	0.3
Agri-Empire	PO Box 490	San Jacinto	CA	92581	Larry Minor	909-654-7311	R	46	0.2
Pecos Cantaloupe Shed Inc.	PO Box 1389	Pecos	TX	79772	Randy Taylor	915-447-2123	R	44*	0.2
John Kautz Farms	5490 E Bear Creek	Lodi	CA	95240	John Kautz	209-334-4786	R	35*	0.2
Merrill Farms Inc.	PO Box 659	Salinas	CA	93902	Thomas Merrill	831-424-7365	R	34*	0.2
Royal Packing Co.	639 South Sandborn	Salinas	CA	93901	Larry Kern	831-424-0975	D	28	0.2
Wilson Farms Inc.	10 Pleasant St	Lexington	MA	02173	AB Wilson	781-862-3900	R	25	0.1
Taylor and Fulton Inc.	PO Box 1087	Palmetto	FL	34220	R Jay Taylor	941-729-3883	R	22	0.1
Anthony Farms Inc.	PO Box 4	Scandinavia	WI	54977	Victor Anthony Jr	715-467-2212	R	14*	<0.1
Bianchi and Sons Packing Co.	PO Box 190	Merced	CA	95341	Larry Bianchi	209-722-8134	R	12*	0.1
Nunes Co.	P O Box 673	Salinas	CA	93902	Bob Nunes	831-424-7206	R	9*	<0.1
Russo Farms Inc.	1962 S East Ave	Vineland	NJ	08360		856-692-5942	R	8	0.1
Salyer American Corp.	PO Box 488	Corcoran	CA	93212	Fred Salyer	559-992-2131	R	3*	<0.1
De Bruyn Produce Company Inc.	PO Box 76	Zeeland	MI	49464	Robert D De Bruyn	616-772-2102	R	2*	<0.1

Source: Ward's Business Directory of U.S. Private and Public Companies, Volumes 1 and 2, 2000. The company type code used is as follows: P - Public, R - Private, S - Subsidiary, D - Division, J - Joint Venture, A - Affiliate, G - Group, N - Company type not reported. Sales are in millions of dollars, employees are in thousands. An asterisk (*) indicates an estimated sales volume. The symbol < stands for 'less than'. Company names and addresses are truncated, in some cases, to fit into the available space.

NAICS 111300 - FRUIT AND TREE NUT FARMING

GENERAL STATISTICS

Item	U.S. Total	This Agri-culture Sector	% of U.S.	Category average per farm				Number of farms reporting category	
				Value shown as	U.S.	This Agric. Sector	% of U.S.	U.S.	This Sector
Farms - number	1,911,859	81,956	4.3	-	-	-	-	-	-
Land in farms - mil. acres	931.795	10.377	1.1	Acres	487	127	26.1	1,911,859	81,956
Value of land, buildings - $ mil.	859,839.2	47,973.7	5.6	$	449,748	584,517	130.0	524,066	82,074
Value of machinery and equip-ment - $ mil.	110,256.8	4,182.7	3.8	$	57,678	50,984	88.4	1,911,601	82,040
Sales of Ag Products - $ mil.	196,864.6	12,405.1	6.3	$	102,970	151,363	147.0	1,911,859	81,956
Government payments - $ mil.	5,054.5	25.7	0.5	$	7,378	4,744	64.3	685,029	5,420
Other farm-related income - $ mil.	3,272.3	196.8	6.0	$	5,999	12,040	200.7	545,480	16,342
Expenses - $ mil.	150,591.0	8,656.4	5.7	$	78,771	105,475	133.9	1,911,766	82,071
Payroll - $ mil.	14,841.0	2,331.4	15.7	$	22,811	56,705	248.6	650,623	41,115
Workers - 150 days or more a year	890,467	135,837	15.3	Number	3.4	7.2	210.9	259,631	18,780
Workers - less than 150 days	2,461,561	547,405	22.2	Number	4.2	14.5	341.5	581,658	37,876
Net Cash Return - $ mil.	42,557.9	3,689.2	8.7	$	22,260	44,949	201.9	1,911,824	82,074

Source: 1997 Census of Agriculture, U.S. Department of Agriculture, National Agricultural Statistics Service. Table shows totals for the U.S. agriculture sector and for the NAICS subdivision of it, shown as "This Agric. Sector" or as "This Sector." Not all farms report on every category. For this reason, the reporting universe is shown in the last two columns. Averages are based on these columns.

LAND IN FARMS ACCORDING TO USE

Item	U.S. Total (000 acres)	This Sector (000 acres)	% of U.S.	Average acres per farms			Number of farms reporting category	
				U.S.	This Agric. Sector	% of U.S.	U.S.	This Sector
Total cropland	431,144.9	6,213.5	1.4	260	76	-	1,661,395	81,956
Harvested cropland	309,395.5	5,212.9	1.7	219	64	-	1,410,606	81,956
Cropland:								
Pasture or grazing	64,466.5	338.3	0.5	85	47	-	754,170	7,203
In cover crops, legumes, grasses	13,531.2	99.3	0.7	88	28	-	153,177	3,508
On which all crops failed	3,449.4	18.0	0.5	67	19	-	51,673	942
In cultivated summer fallow	20,905.9	40.0	0.2	256	38	-	81,702	1,063
Idle	19,396.3	505.1	2.6	83	40	-	232,961	12,726
Total woodland	71,465.4	1,398.3	2.0	96	87	-	743,011	16,028
Woodland pastured	29,693.9	236.8	0.8	84	83	-	352,217	2,843
Woodland not pastured	41,771.5	1,161.5	2.8	79	82	-	531,846	14,243
Other pasture/rangeland	396,884.6	1,703.1	0.4	721	303	-	550,619	5,618
Land for house lots, ponds, roads, wasteland	32,300.4	1,061.6	3.3	28	24	-	1,142,618	44,280
Irrigated land	55,058.1	4,238.4	7.7	197	74	-	279,442	57,131
Harvested cropland	50,013.5	4,172.7	8.3	198	73	-	252,679	56,994
Pasture and other	5,044.7	65.8	1.3	87	30	-	58,258	2,201
Conservation Reserve/Wetlands Reserve Lands	29,489.1	125.3	0.4	131	68	-	225,410	1,838

Source: 1997 Census of Agriculture, U.S. Department of Agriculture, National Agricultural Statistics Service. Table shows totals for the U.S. agriculture sector and for the NAICS subdivision of it, shown as "This Agric. Sector" or as "This Sector." Not all farms report on every category. For this reason, the reporting universe is shown in the last two columns. Averages are based on these columns. The Conservation Reserve and Wetlands Reserve programs provide support for land conservation/preservation. Cover crops are not harvested or pastured.

MARKET VALUE OF AGRICULTURAL PRODUCTS SOLD: ALL FARMS

Item	U.S. Total ($ mil.)	This Sector ($ mil.)	% of Sector Sales	% of U.S.	Average sales per farm - $			Number of farms reporting category	
					U.S.	This Agric. Sector	% of U.S.	U.S.	This Sector
Grains	46,617.1	58.8	0.47	0.1	79,095	40,241	50.9	589,379	1,460
Corn for grain	18,884.8	13.5	0.11	0.1	52,506	24,532	46.7	359,666	549
Wheat	7,173.9	14.0	0.11	0.2	29,726	24,625	82.8	241,334	570
Soybeans	15,622.4	6.3	0.05	0.0	44,185	20,041	45.4	353,566	315
Sorghum for grain	1,140.0	0.6	0.00	0.1	25,360	13,636	53.8	44,955	44
Barley	709.6	0.7	0.01	0.1	23,191	13,196	56.9	30,598	51
Oats	121.3	0.7	0.01	0.6	3,114	5,307	170.4	38,940	127
Other grains	2,965.1	23.0	0.19	0.8	67,540	80,947	119.9	43,901	284
Cotton and cotton seed	5,975.5	33.2	0.27	0.6	189,963	161,859	85.2	31,456	205
Tobacco	2,924.7	0.3	0.00	0.0	32,662	6,977	21.4	89,544	44
Hay, silage, and field seeds	4,670.5	46.0	0.37	1.0	13,174	18,718	142.1	354,523	2,455
Vegetables, sweet corn, and melons	8,401.7	121.5	0.98	1.4	156,628	45,924	29.3	53,641	2,645
Fruits and berries	12,660.3	12,010.9	96.82	94.9	147,259	177,350	120.4	85,973	67,724
Nursery and greenhouse crops	10,942.8	35.4	0.29	0.3	161,360	28,045	17.4	67,816	1,261
Other crops	5,863.1	26.9	0.22	0.5	153,907	67,525	43.9	38,095	398
Poultry and poultry products	22,262.6	4.0	0.03	0.0	352,000	6,694	1.9	63,246	602
Dairy products	18,997.3	2.0	0.02	0.0	191,432	70,607	36.9	99,238	28
Cattle and calves	40,524.8	57.6	0.46	0.1	40,052	17,659	44.1	1,011,809	3,263
Hogs and pigs	13,804.8	1.7	0.01	0.0	135,201	5,814	4.3	102,106	295
Sheep, lambs, and wool	682.9	1.8	0.01	0.3	10,913	2,490	22.8	62,579	722
Other livestock	2,536.5	5.2	0.04	0.2	20,506	3,972	19.4	123,695	1,313
Products sold to public directly	13,096.7	0.9	0.01	0.0	377,610	117,250	31.1	34,683	8

Source: *1997 Census of Agriculture*, U.S. Department of Agriculture, National Agricultural Statistics Service. Table shows totals for the U.S. agriculture sector and for the NAICS subdivision of it, shown as "This Agric. Sector" or as "This Sector." Not all farms report on every category. For this reason, the reporting universe is shown in the last two columns. Averages are based on these columns. Farms classified in one sector routinely produce categories in other sectors as well. Products sold to the public are sold for direct consumption.

MARKET VALUE OF PRODUCTS SOLD: FARMS WITH SALES OF $50,000 OR MORE

Item	U.S. Total ($ mil.)	This Sector ($ mil.)	% of Sector Sales	% of U.S.	Average sales per farm - $			Number of farms reporting category	
					U.S.	This Agric. Sector	% of U.S.	U.S.	This Sector
Grains	40,973.4	46.1	0.37	0.1	183,623	194,650	106.0	223,138	237
Cotton and cotton seed	5,743.9	31.3	0.25	0.5	286,562	250,528	87.4	20,044	125
Tobacco	2,060.2	-	-	-	175,907	-	-	11,712	-
Hay, silage, and field seeds	2,781.9	32.5	0.26	1.2	188,959	149,982	79.4	14,722	217
Vegetables, sweet corn, and melons	7,966.8	103.1	0.83	1.3	673,443	259,113	38.5	11,830	398
Fruits and berries	12,072.3	11,497.9	92.69	95.2	478,927	489,066	102.1	25,207	23,510
Nursery and greenhouse crops	10,412.0	27.7	0.22	0.3	578,025	234,975	40.7	18,013	118
Other crops	5,586.6	24.7	0.20	0.4	363,758	425,362	116.9	15,358	58
Poultry and poultry products	22,171.7	3.6	0.03	0.0	778,637	328,182	42.1	28,475	11
Dairy products	18,344.3	1.8	0.01	0.0	250,075	180,500	72.2	73,355	10
Cattle and calves	32,358.6	38.7	0.31	0.1	386,685	217,303	56.2	83,682	178
Hogs and pigs	13,096.7	0.9	0.01	0.0	377,610	117,250	31.1	34,683	8
Sheep, lambs, and wool	478.6	0.8	0.01	0.2	278,730	156,000	56.0	1,717	5
Other livestock	2,026.6	1.5	0.01	0.1	369,685	107,786	29.2	5,482	14

Source: *1997 Census of Agriculture*, U.S. Department of Agriculture, National Agricultural Statistics Service. Table shows totals for the U.S. agriculture sector and for the NAICS subdivision of it, shown as "This Agric. Sector" or as "This Sector." Not all farms report on every category. For this reason, the reporting universe is shown in the last two columns. Averages are based on these columns. Farms classified in one sector routinely produce categories in other sectors as well.

GOVERNMENT PAYMENTS AND OTHER FARM-RELATED INCOME

| Item | U.S. Total ($ mil.) | This Sector ($ mil.) | % of Sector Gov/Oth. Income | % of U.S. | Average receipts per farm - $ | | | Number of farms reporting category | |
					U.S.	This Agric. Sector	% of U.S.	U.S.	This Sector
Government payments	5,054.5	25.7	11.56	0.5	7,378	4,744	64.3	685,029	5,420
Other farm-related income	3,272.3	196.8	88.44	6.0	5,999	12,040	200.7	545,480	16,342
Custom work and other agricultural services	1,235.1	85.3	38.34	6.9	8,646	19,286	223.1	142,854	4,422
Gross cash rent or share payments	1,207.9	64.6	29.05	5.3	6,867	13,335	194.2	175,901	4,846
Forest products, excluding Christmas trees and maple products	344.3	14.8	6.63	4.3	7,417	8,158	110.0	46,426	1,808
Other farm-related income sources	484.9	32.1	14.43	6.6	1,595	4,198	263.1	303,908	7,646

Source: 1997 Census of Agriculture, U.S. Department of Agriculture, National Agricultural Statistics Service. Table shows totals for the U.S. agriculture sector and for the NAICS subdivision of it, shown as "This Agric. Sector" or as "This Sector." Not all farms report on every category. For this reason, the reporting universe is shown in the last two columns. Averages are based on these columns. Government payments are agricultural subsidies under various programs.

COMMODITY CREDIT CORPORATION LOANS

| Item | U.S. Total ($ mil.) | This Sector ($ mil.) | % of Sector Loan Total | % of U.S. | Average loan value per farm - $ | | | Number of farms reporting category | |
					U.S.	This Agric. Sector	% of U.S.	U.S.	This Sector
Total loans	3,034.7	3.2	100.00	0.1	36,419	38,916	106.9	83,328	83
Corn	1,333.9	0.1	4.30	0.0	26,419	5,792	21.9	50,489	24
Wheat	415.4	0.2	7.71	0.1	18,093	9,960	55.0	22,961	25
Soybeans	774.0	0.0	0.93	0.0	30,370	3,750	12.3	25,487	8
Sorghum, barley, and oats	54.8	-	-	-	8,603	-	-	6,375	2
Cotton	191.4	-	-	-	43,275	-	-	4,422	15
Sunflower seed, flaxseed, safflower, canola, other rapeseed, and mustard seed	17.3	-	-	-	25,159	-	-	686	-
Peanuts, rice, and tobacco	247.9	2.7	82.69	1.1	60,421	116,130	192.2	4,103	23

Source: 1997 Census of Agriculture, U.S. Department of Agriculture, National Agricultural Statistics Service. Table shows totals for the U.S. agriculture sector and for the NAICS subdivision of it, shown as "This Agric. Sector" or as "This Sector." Not all farms report on every category. For this reason, the reporting universe is shown in the last two columns. Averages are based on these columns. The Commodity Credit Corporation provides low interest loans to farmers.

SELECTED MACHINERY AND EQUIPMENT

| Item | U.S. Total (number) | This Agric. Sector (number) | % of U.S. | Average number per farm | | | Number of farms reporting category | |
				U.S.	This Agric. Sector	% of U.S.	U.S.	This Sector
Motortrucks, including pickups	3,497,735	145,881	4.2	2.07	2.18	105.0	1,688,303	67,034
Wheel tractors	3,936,014	146,719	3.7	2.31	2.13	92.2	1,707,384	69,044
Less than 40 horsepower (PTO)	1,262,688	66,648	5.3	1.44	1.53	106.2	877,119	43,614
40 horsepower (PTO) or more	2,673,326	80,071	3.0	2.02	1.93	95.4	1,321,084	41,484
40 to 99 horsepower (PTO)	1,808,105	70,471	3.9	1.58	1.82	115.3	1,145,466	38,712
100 horsepower (PTO)	865,221	9,600	1.1	1.68	1.60	95.0	513,773	6,003
Grain and bean combines	460,606	1,191	0.3	1.16	1.18	101.2	395,934	1,012
Cotton pickers and strippers	38,294	343	0.9	1.48	2.09	141.3	25,874	164
Mower conditioners	608,443	13,744	2.3	1.12	1.21	107.7	543,565	11,400
Pickup balers	717,245	2,759	0.4	1.24	1.16	93.3	579,440	2,388

Source: 1997 Census of Agriculture, U.S. Department of Agriculture, National Agricultural Statistics Service. Table shows totals for the U.S. agriculture sector and for the NAICS subdivision of it, shown as "This Agric. Sector" or as "This Sector." Not all farms report on every category. For this reason, the reporting universe is shown in the last two columns. Averages are based on these columns. PTO stands for "power take off."

FARM PRODUCTION EXPENSES

Item	U.S. Total ($ mil.)	This Sector ($ mil.)	% of Sector Total Expense	% of U.S.	Average expense per farm - $			Number of farms reporting category	
					U.S.	This Agric. Sector	% of U.S.	U.S.	This Sector
Total farm production expenses	150,591.0	8,656.4	100.00	5.7	78,771	105,475	133.9	1,911,766	82,071
Livestock and poultry purchased	21,614.6	14.4	0.17	0.1	38,807	5,554	14.3	556,980	2,589
Feed for livestock and poultry	32,760.0	17.6	0.20	0.1	32,059	2,895	9.0	1,021,849	6,097
Commercially mixed formula feeds	21,236.2	9.3	0.11	0.0	34,459	2,790	8.1	616,280	3,315
Seeds, bulbs, plants, and trees	5,725.9	152.7	1.76	2.7	6,388	7,016	109.8	896,339	21,768
Commercial fertilizer	9,597.1	478.9	5.53	5.0	8,060	7,614	94.5	1,190,733	62,894
Agricultural chemicals	7,581.4	819.7	9.47	10.8	8,056	12,519	155.4	941,136	65,479
Petroleum products	6,371.5	246.1	2.84	3.9	3,619	3,484	96.3	1,760,642	70,632
Gasoline and gasohol	1,886.6	97.1	1.12	5.1	1,380	1,740	126.1	1,366,915	55,818
Diesel fuel	2,846.0	107.2	1.24	3.8	2,164	2,247	103.9	1,315,397	47,695
Natural gas	432.9	11.5	0.13	2.6	6,091	5,555	91.2	71,069	2,064
LP gas, fuel oil, kerosene, motor oil, grease, etc.	1,206.1	30.3	0.35	2.5	945	657	69.6	1,276,331	46,136
Electricity	2,751.1	249.7	2.88	9.1	2,247	4,706	209.4	1,224,374	53,060
Hired farm labor	14,841.0	2,331.4	26.93	15.7	22,811	56,705	248.6	650,623	41,115
Contract labor	2,959.0	1,170.4	13.52	39.6	13,040	40,174	308.1	226,909	29,133
Repair and maintenance	8,637.7	440.2	5.09	5.1	5,616	7,100	126.4	1,538,058	62,005
Custom work, machine hire, and rental of equipment	3,210.3	293.8	3.39	9.2	5,372	11,255	209.5	597,624	26,102
Interest	8,928.1	690.0	7.97	7.7	11,016	24,815	225.3	810,476	27,808
Secured by real estate	5,449.6	527.3	6.09	9.7	9,564	23,741	248.2	569,775	22,211
Not secured by real estate	3,478.5	162.7	1.88	4.7	7,540	14,852	197.0	461,326	10,957
Cash rent	6,915.7	158.2	1.83	2.3	14,244	20,554	144.3	485,512	7,696
Property taxes	3,920.1	320.9	3.71	8.2	2,213	4,110	185.7	1,771,787	78,075
All other farm production expenses	14,777.4	1,272.4	14.70	8.6	8,747	17,675	202.1	1,689,391	71,989

Source: 1997 Census of Agriculture, U.S. Department of Agriculture, National Agricultural Statistics Service. Table shows totals for the U.S. agriculture sector and for the NAICS subdivision of it, shown as "This Agric. Sector" or as "This Sector." Not all farms report on every category. For this reason, the reporting universe is shown in the last two columns. Averages are based on these columns. LP gas stands for "liquid petroleum gas," i.e., butane or propane.

NET CASH RETURN AND FARMS WITH GAINS AND LOSSES

Item	Number of farms and %				Average gain or loss per farm - $		
	U.S.	% of U.S.	This Agriculture Sector	% of Sector	U.S.	This Agriculture Sector	% of U.S.
All farms	1,911,824	100.0	82,074	100.0	22,260	44,949	201.9
Number of farms with net gains	985,718	51.6	41,884	51.0	51,296	96,216	187.6
Gain of -							
Less than $1,000	120,163	6.3	3,783	4.6	-	-	-
$1,000 to $9,999	370,611	19.4	12,763	15.6	-	-	-
$10,000 to $49,999	292,484	15.3	13,969	17.0	-	-	-
$50,000 or more	202,460	10.6	11,369	13.9	-	-	-
Number of farms with net losses	926,106	48.4	40,190	49.0	(8,645)	(8,479)	98.1
Loss of -							
Less than $1,000	165,390	8.7	7,194	8.8	-	-	-
$1,000 to $9,999	591,517	30.9	25,945	31.6	-	-	-
$10,000 to $49,999	152,649	8.0	6,335	7.7	-	-	-
$50,000 or more	16,550	0.9	716	0.9	-	-	-

Source: 1997 Census of Agriculture, U.S. Department of Agriculture, National Agricultural Statistics Service. Table shows totals for the U.S. agriculture sector and for the NAICS subdivision of it, shown as "This Agric. Sector" or as "This Sector." Not all farms report on every category. For this reason, the reporting universe is shown in the last two columns. Averages are based on these columns. Net gains are income less cost for farm operations; they exclude non-farm earnings. Values in parentheses are losses.

CHARACTERISTICS OF FARM OPERATORS

Farm Operators	U.S.	This Agric. Sector	% of U.S.	Farm Operators	U.S.	This Agric. Sector	% of U.S.
Place of residence:				By age group:			
On farm operated	1,361,766	53,880	4.0	Under 25 years	20,850	225	1.1
Not on farm operated	412,554	23,498	5.7	25 to 34 years	128,455	2,642	2.1
Not reported	137,539	4,578	3.3	35 to 44 years	371,442	12,279	3.3
Principal occupation:				45 to 49 years	232,845	9,745	4.2
Farming	961,560	38,775	4.0	50 to 54 years	233,884	10,653	4.6
Other	950,299	43,181	4.5	55 to 59 years	222,736	10,299	4.6
Days worked off farm:				60 to 64 years	204,618	9,606	4.7
None	755,254	32,748	4.3	65 to 69 years	179,858	9,111	5.1
Any	1,042,158	45,151	4.3	70 years and over	317,171	17,396	5.5
1 to 99 days	164,957	7,741	4.7	Average age	54	58	105.9
100 to 199 days	167,922	7,926	4.7	By sex:			
200 days or more	709,279	29,484	4.2	Male	1,746,757	73,003	4.2
Not reported	114,447	4,057	3.5	Female	165,102	8,953	5.4
Years on present farm:				Spanish, Hispanic/Latino origin	27,717	3,859	13.9
2 years or less	92,574	3,687	4.0	Tenure of operator:			
3 or 4 years	126,791	5,575	4.4	All operators	1,911,859	81,956	4.3
5 to 9 years	263,642	13,377	5.1	Full owners	1,146,891	69,127	6.0
10 years or more	1,113,839	49,310	4.4	Part owners	573,839	8,330	1.5
Ave. years on this farm	20	18	90.0	Tenants	191,129	4,499	2.4
Not reported	315,013	10,007	3.2				

Source: 1997 Census of Agriculture, U.S. Department of Agriculture, National Agricultural Statistics Service. Table shows totals for the U.S. agriculture sector and for the NAICS subdivision of it, shown as "This Agric. Sector" or as "This Sector." Not all farms report on every category. For this reason, the reporting universe is shown in the last two columns. Averages are based on these columns. All values shown are number of farm operators in each category or percent.

FARMS BY TYPE OF ORGANIZATION

Item	Number of farms and percent				Total acres and percent		
	U.S.	% of U.S.	This Agriculture Sector	% of Sector	U.S.	This Agriculture Sector	% of U.S.
Individual or family (sole proprietorship)	1,643,424	100.0	64,354	100.0	585,464,911	4,451,792	0.8
Partnership	169,462	10.3	9,526	14.8	149,321,484	2,097,854	1.4
Corporation:							
Family held	76,103	4.6	5,909	9.2	119,559,203	2,728,750	2.3
More than 10 stockholders	1,795	0.1	227	0.4	-	-	-
10 or less stockholders	74,308	4.5	5,682	8.8	-	-	-
Other than family held	7,899	0.5	911	1.4	11,904,053	902,417	7.6
More than 10 stockholders	1,029	0.1	175	0.3	-	-	-
10 or less stockholders	6,870	0.4	736	1.1	-	-	-
Other cooperative, estate or trust, institutional, etc.	14,971	0.9	1,256	2.0	65,545,604	195,699	0.3

Source: 1997 Census of Agriculture, U.S. Department of Agriculture, National Agricultural Statistics Service. Table shows totals for the U.S. agriculture sector and for the NAICS subdivision of it, shown as "This Agric. Sector" or as "This Sector." Not all farms report on every category. For this reason, the reporting universe is shown in the last two columns. Averages are based on these columns.

LIVESTOCK INVENTORIES AND SALES

Item	U.S. (number)	This Agric. Sector (number)	% of U.S.	Average number per farm			Number of farms reporting category	
				U.S.	This Agric. Sector	% of U.S.	U.S.	This Sector
Cattle and calves inventory	98,989,244	351,908	0.4	94.6	74.9	79.2	1,046,863	4,698
Cows and heifers that had calved	43,162,054	197,501	0.5	48.3	53.8	111.5	894,110	3,670
Beef cows	34,066,615	196,158	0.6	42.3	55.3	130.6	804,595	3,548
Milk cows	9,095,439	1,343	0.0	77.8	7.1	9.1	116,874	190
Heifers and heifer calves	26,988,697	75,634	0.3	33.6	24.6	73.3	803,985	3,075
Steers, steer calves, bulls, and bull calves	28,838,493	78,773	0.3	32.6	22.4	68.8	883,983	3,510
Cattle and calves sold	74,089,046	147,620	0.2	73.2	45.2	61.8	1,011,809	3,263
Calves	16,480,293	73,987	0.4	26.8	36.6	136.6	615,177	2,022
Cattle	57,608,753	73,633	0.1	78.0	34.8	44.6	738,696	2,117
Fattened on grain and concentrates	27,328,190	2,483	0.0	247.0	11.8	4.8	110,620	211
Hogs and pigs inventory	61,206,236	9,840	0.0	557.7	19.1	3.4	109,754	516
Used or to be used for breeding	6,831,564	1,566	0.0	106.7	9.7	9.1	64,029	162
Other	54,374,672	8,274	0.0	528.0	17.8	3.4	102,977	464
Hogs and pigs sold	142,611,882	16,533	0.0	1,396.7	56.0	4.0	102,106	295
Feeder pigs	34,988,718	5,009	0.0	2,037.8	100.2	4.9	17,170	50
Litters of pigs farrowed between Dec. 1 of preceding year and Nov. 30	11,497,523	1,817	0.0	170.3	10.2	6.0	67,514	179
Dec. 1 and May 31	5,697,371	946	0.0	91.0	6.1	6.8	62,622	154
June 1 and Nov. 30	5,800,152	871	0.0	99.7	7.1	7.2	58,204	122
Sheep and lambs of all ages inventory	7,821,885	33,733	0.4	118.9	37.6	31.7	65,790	896
Ewes 1 year old or older	4,408,683	19,218	0.4	78.1	27.5	35.1	56,414	700
Sheep and lambs sold	7,331,545	20,856	0.3	123.1	32.6	26.5	59,575	640
Sheep and lambs shorn	6,139,140	22,996	0.4	118.4	40.6	34.3	51,869	566
Horses and ponies inventory	2,427,277	20,161	0.8	6.5	4.3	67.2	375,218	4,636
Horses and ponies sold	325,306	922	0.3	4.1	2.7	65.5	79,516	344
Goats inventory	1,989,799	13,724	0.7	34.4	13.7	39.8	57,925	1,005
Goats sold	740,597	4,682	0.6	31.5	18.9	60.0	23,520	248

Source: *1997 Census of Agriculture*, U.S. Department of Agriculture, National Agricultural Statistics Service. Table shows totals for the U.S. agriculture sector and for the NAICS subdivision of it, shown as "This Agric. Sector" or as "This Sector." Not all farms report on every category. For this reason, the reporting universe is shown in the last two columns. Averages are based on these columns.

POULTRY INVENTORIES AND SALES

Item	U.S. (number)	This Agric. Sector (number)	% of U.S.	Average number per farm			Number of farms reporting category	
				U.S.	This Agric. Sector	% of U.S.	U.S.	This Sector
Layers and pullets 13 weeks old and older inventory	366,989,851	-	-	5,053.8	-	-	72,616	1,514
Layers 20 weeks old and older	313,851,480	154,051	0.0	4,499.0	103.9	2.3	69,761	1,482
Pullets 13 weeks old and older but less than 20 weeks old	53,138,371	-	-	4,031.7	-	-	13,180	252
Layers, pullets, and pullet chicks sold	331,563,736	370,101	0.1	24,636.9	2,984.7	12.1	13,458	124
Broilers and other meat type chickens sold	6,741,927,110	653,895	0.0	281,653.0	8,383.3	3.0	23,937	78
Turkey hens kept for breeding	5,504,808	286	0.0	968.1	3.4	0.3	5,686	85
Turkeys sold	307,586,680	-	-	51,000.9	-	-	6,031	46

Source: *1997 Census of Agriculture*, U.S. Department of Agriculture, National Agricultural Statistics Service. Table shows totals for the U.S. agriculture sector and for the NAICS subdivision of it, shown as "This Agric. Sector" or as "This Sector." Not all farms report on every category. For this reason, the reporting universe is shown in the last two columns. Averages are based on these columns.

SELECTED CROPS HARVESTED

Item	In 1,000	Crop harvested			Acres used for crop (000)			Number of farms reporting category	
		U.S.	This Agric. Sector	% of U.S.	U.S.	This Agric. Sector	% of U.S.	U.S.	This Sector
Corn for grain or seed	bushels	8,578,635	5,625	0.1	69,796.7	45.5	0.1	430,711	700
Irrigated		-	-	-	10,638.9	14.4	0.1	40,574	159
Corn for silage or green chop	tons, green	88,381	270	0.3	5,727.6	12.5	0.2	119,308	262
Irrigated		-	-	-	1,033.3	10.8	1.0	10,815	175
Sorghum for grain or seed	bushels	559,070	255	0.0	8,470.4	4.3	0.1	49,397	52
Irrigated		-	-	-	875.6	1.9	0.2	5,793	15
Wheat for grain	bushels	2,204,027	3,946	0.2	58,836.3	63.9	0.1	243,568	584
Irrigated		-	-	-	3,990.9	32.6	0.8	20,385	239
Barley for grain	bushels	336,435	295	0.1	5,945.0	5.3	0.1	41,930	64
Irrigated		-	-	-	1,060.7	3.4	0.3	8,847	30
Oats for grain	bushels	151,327	374	0.2	2,681.0	5.5	0.2	89,606	197
Irrigated		-	-	-	121.0	2.2	1.8	2,788	24
Rice	cwt	182,231	1,259	0.7	3,122.1	16.2	0.5	9,291	56
Irrigated		-	-	-	3,122.1	16.2	0.5	9,291	56
Cotton	bales	17,879	89	0.5	13,235.2	42.2	0.3	31,493	206
Irrigated		-	-	-	4,888.0	35.7	0.7	12,434	174
Tobacco	pounds	1,747,702	229	0.0	838.5	0.1	0.0	89,706	45
Irrigated		-	-	-	138.7	-	-	7,090	2
Soybeans for beans	bushels	2,504,307	1,040	0.0	66,147.7	32.9	0.0	354,692	323
Irrigated		-	-	-	4,152.1	1.3	0.0	20,619	22
Dry edible beans, excluding dry limas	cwt	27,224	122	0.4	1,691.9	6.0	0.4	10,911	74
Irrigated		-	-	-	577.0	5.7	1.0	4,882	62
Potatoes, excluding sweetpotatoes	cwt	459,886	886	0.2	1,355.2	2.3	0.2	10,523	163
Irrigated		-	-	-	1,070.3	2.2	0.2	4,843	78
Sugar beets for sugar	tons	29,775	32	0.1	1,453.8	1.3	0.1	7,102	16
Irrigated		-	-	-	616.4	1.3	0.2	3,492	16
Peanuts for nuts	pounds	3,377,143	6,798	0.2	1,352.2	3.5	0.3	12,221	69
Irrigated		-	-	-	412.3	0.9	0.2	3,125	16
Hay alfalfa, other tame, small grain, wild, grass silage, green chop	tons, dry	139,365	564	0.4	60,799.8	181.4	0.3	888,597	4,663
Irrigated		-	-	-	9,564.3	74.3	0.8	79,406	1,258
Alfalfa hay	tons, dry	65,863	331	0.5	21,309.8	63.8	0.3	358,365	1,476
Irrigated		-	-	-	5,980.5	49.7	0.8	57,854	807
Vegetables harvested for sale		-	-	-	3,773.2	64.0	1.7	53,727	2,656
Irrigated		-	-	-	2,641.8	46.9	1.8	23,203	1,584
Land in orchards		-	-	-	5,158.1	4,544.2	88.1	106,069	75,096
Irrigated		-	-	-	4,107.9	3,782.0	92.1	61,606	51,709

Source: 1997 Census of Agriculture, U.S. Department of Agriculture, National Agricultural Statistics Service. Table shows totals for the U.S. agriculture sector and for the NAICS subdivision of it, shown as "This Agric. Sector" or as "This Sector." Not all farms report on every category. For this reason, the reporting universe is shown in the last two columns. Averages are based on these columns. "Green tons" are weight of product as harvested, i.e., moist. cwt stands for "hundredweight."

LEADING COMPANIES   Number shown: **75**   Total sales ($ mil): **14,037**   Total employment (000): **122.9**

Company Name	Address				CEO Name	Phone	Co. Type	Sales ($ mil)	Empl. (000)
Dole Food Company Inc.	PO Box 5132	Westlake Village	CA	91359	David De Lorenzo	818-879-6600	P	4,424	53.5
Chiquita Brands International Inc.	250 E 5th St	Cincinnati	OH	45202	H Carl Lindner	513-784-8000	P	2,556	37.0
Canandaigua Brands Inc.	300 Wilwbrk Of	Fairport	NY	14450	Richard Sands	716-218-2169	P	1,497	4.2
Lykes Bros. Inc.	PO Box 1690	Tampa	FL	33601		813-223-3981	R	1,100	3.0
A and B Hawaii Inc.	PO Box 3440	Honolulu	HI	96801	W Allen Doane	808-525-6611	S	588	1.2
National Grape Cooperative	2 S Portage St	Westfield	NY	14787		716-326-3131		550	1.3
Beringer Wine Estates Holdings	PO Box 4500	Napa	CA	94558	Walter T Klenz	707-259-4500	P	407*	0.8
Robert Mondavi Corp.	7801 St Helena Hwy	Oakville	CA	94562	R Michael Mondavi	707-259-9463	P	371	0.8
Dole Fresh Vegetables	PO Box 1759	Salinas	CA	93902	Lawrence Kern	408-422-8871	S	250*	3.0
Calavo Growers of California	PO Box 26081	Santa Ana	CA	92799	Lee Cole	949-223-1111	R	150	0.3
Sutter Home Winery Inc.	P O Box 248	St. Helena	CA	94574	Louis B Trinchero	707-963-3104	R	140*	0.3
John J. Kovacevich and Sons Inc.	P O Bin 488	Arvin	CA	93203		616-854-5591	R	122*	0.7
Northland Cranberries Inc.	PO Box 8020	Wisc Rapids	WI	54495	Robert E Hawk	715-424-4444	P	113	1.2
Amfac/JMB Hawaii Inc.	900 N Michigan Ave	Chicago	IL	60611	Edward G Karl	312-440-4800	S	100*	1.0
Giumarra Vineyards Corp.	PO Bin 1969	Bakersfield	CA	93303	Sal Giumarra	661-395-7000	R	100*	3.5
Limoneira Co.	1141 Cummings Rd	Santa Paula	CA	93060	Pierre Tada	805-525-5541	R	99*	0.3
Stimson Lane Ltd.	PO Box 1976	Woodinville	WA	98072	Allen C Shoup	425-488-1133	S	97*	0.6
C. Brewer and Company Ltd.	PO Box 1826	Papaikou	HI	96781	James Andrasick	808-969-1826	S	92*	1.5
Nash De Camp Co.	3300 S Demaree Rd	Visalia	CA	93277	Stephen C Biswell	559-622-1850	S	90*	1.0
Maui Pineapple Company Ltd.	PO Box 187	Kahului	HI	96733	Douglas R Schenk	808-877-3351	S	85	1.5
Delicato Vineyards	12001 S Hwy 99	Manteca	CA	95336	Eric Morham	209-842-3600	R	79*	0.3
Royal Citrus Co.	PO Box 288	Riverside	CA	92502	Lou Cardey	909-686-0987	R	72*	0.6
Clos du Bois Wines	PO Box 940	Geyserville	CA	95441	Jon Moramarco Jr	707-857-1651	S	58*	0.1
Sebastiani Vineyards Inc.	PO Box AA	Sonoma	CA	95476	Richard Cuneo	707-938-5532	R	58*	0.4
Deardorff-Jackson Co.	PO Box 1188	Oxnard	CA	93032	Thomas D Deardorff	805-487-7801	R	56*	0.3
Biltmore Co.	1 N Pack Sq	Asheville	NC	28801	William Cecil	828-255-1776	R	50	0.5
Ben Hill Griffin Inc.	PO Box 127	Frostproof	FL	33843	Ben Hill Griffin III	941-635-2251	R	47*	0.2
Chalone Wine Group Ltd.	621 Airpark Rd	Napa	CA	94558		707-254-4200	P	44	0.1
Alico Inc.	P O Box 338	LaBelle	FL	33975	Ben H Griffin III	863-675-2966	P	43	0.1
C.M. Holtzinger Fruit Inc.	PO Box 169	Yakima	WA	98907	Charles M Holtzinger	509-452-5834	R	42*	0.5
Rodney Strong Vineyards	PO Box 6010	Healdsburg	CA	95448	Al Nirenstein	707-433-6521	D	40	0.2
P-R Farms Inc.	2917 E Shepherd	Clovis	CA	93612	Pat Ricchiuti Sr	559-299-7270	R	37*	0.4
John Kautz Farms	5490 E Bear Creek	Lodi	CA	95240	John Kautz	209-334-4786	R	35*	0.2
Symms Fruit Ranch Inc.	14068 Sunnyslope	Caldwell	ID	83607	RA Symms	208-459-4821	R	35*	0.2
Haines City Citrus Growers	P O Box 337	Haines City	FL	33845	Dennis Broadawaay	941-422-1174	R	30*	0.6
Jasper Wyman and Son Inc.	PO Box 100	Milbridge	ME	04658	Edward Flanagan	207-546-2311	R	28	<0.1
Wells and Wade Fruit Co.	PO Box 259	East Wenatchee	WA	98802	David Green	509-886-0547	S	25	0.3
Buena Vista Winery Inc.	PO Box 182	Sonoma	CA	95476	Harry Parsley	707-252-7117	R	22*	<0.1
Kenwood Vineyards	PO Box 447	Kenwood	CA	95452	Gary Heck	707-833-5891	R	22*	0.2
Modern Development Co.	3333 W Coast #400	Newport Beach	CA	92663		949-646-6400	R	20*	0.2
Jordan Vineyard and Winery	PO Box 878	Healdsburg	CA	95448	Thomas N Jordan, Jr	707-431-5250	R	18	<0.1
National Raisin Co.	P O Box 219	Fowler	CA	93625	Ernest Bedrosian	559-834-5981	R	18*	0.1
Scheid Vineyards Inc.	13470 Washington	Marina del Rey	CA	90292	Alfred G Scheid	310-301-1555	P	18	<0.1
Bob Paul Inc.	P O Box 898	Winter Haven	FL	33882	John R Paul Jr	863-293-9906	R	13*	<0.1
East-Side Winery	6100 E Hwy 12	Lodi	CA	95241	Bruce Mettler	209-369-4768	R	13*	<0.1
Mirassou Sales Co.	3000 Aborn Rd	San Jose	CA	95135	Daniel Mirassou	408-274-4000	R	13	<0.1
Hess Collection Winery	PO Box 4140	Napa	CA	94558	Clement Firko	707-255-1144	R	12	0.2
Maine Wild Blueberry Co.	PO Box 128	Cherryfield	ME	04622		207-255-8364	S	12	0.1
Rice Fruit Co.	PO Box 66	Gardners	PA	17324	David Rice	717-677-8131	R	12*	0.1
Kendall Foods Corp.	PO Box 8	Goulds	FL	33170	Peter HJ Kendall	305-258-1631	R	10*	<0.1
Pine Ridge Winery	PO Box 2508	Yountville	CA	94599	R Gary Andrus	707-253-7500	R	10*	<0.1
Valley Fig Growers Inc.	PO Box 1987	Fresno	CA	93718	Michael Emigh	559-237-3893	S	10	<0.1
Wailuku Agribusiness Inc.	255 E Waiko Rd	Wailuku	HI	96793		808-244-9570	S	10*	<0.1
Weibel Inc.	P O Box 3398	Fremont	CA	94539	Fred E Weibel Jr		R	8	<0.1
D. DeFranco and Sons Inc.	1000 Lawrence St	Los Angeles	CA	90021	Jerald DeFranco	213-627-8575	R	7*	<0.1
Willamette Valley Vineyards Inc.	8800 Enchanted SE	Turner	OR	97392	James Bernau	503-588-9463	P	6	<0.1
Chateau Montelena	1429 Tubbs Ln	Calistoga	CA	94515	J Barrett	707-942-5105	R	6	<0.1
Sonoma-Cutrer Vineyards Inc.	PO Box 9	Fulton	CA	95439	Brice Cutrer Jones	707-528-1181	R	6*	<0.1
Markham Vineyards	P O Box 636	St. Helena	CA	94574	Bryan Del Bondio	707-963-5292	R	5*	<0.1
Tedeschi Vineyards Ltd.	PO Box 953	Kula	HI	96790	Pard Erdman	808-878-6058	R	5*	<0.1
Vavin Inc.	HCR 4, Box 77	Leon	VA	22725	Stephen B Lane	540-547-3707	R	5*	<0.1
Williamsburg Winery Ltd.	5800 Wessex	Williamsburg	VA	23185		757-229-0999	R	4	<0.1
Fess Parker Winery and Vineyard	PO Box 908	Los Olivos	CA	93441	Eli Parker	805-688-1545	S	4*	<0.1
Made in Nature Inc.	100 Stony Point Rd	Santa Rosa	CA	95401	Gerald E Prolman	415-499-3309	S	4*	<0.1
Navarro Vineyards and Winery	PO Box 47	Philo	CA	95466	Deborah Cahn	707-895-3686	R	4*	<0.1
Schramsberg Vineyards Co.	1400 Schramsberg	Calistoga	CA	94515	Jamie Davies	707-942-4558	R	4*	<0.1
Byron Vineyard and Winery	5230 Tepusquet Rd	Santa Maria	CA	93454		805-937-7288	S	3*	<0.1
Cain Cellars Inc.	3800 Langtry Rd	Saint Helena	CA	94574		707-963-1616	R	3*	<0.1
Fisher Vineyard	6200 St Helena Rd	Santa Rosa	CA	95404	Fred Fisher	707-539-7511	R	3	<0.1
Geyser Peak Winery	PO Box 25	Geyserville	CA	95441	Dennis Pasquini	707-857-9463	R	3*	<0.1
Silverado Vineyards	6121 Silverado Trl	Napa	CA	94558	Diane Miller	707-257-1770	R	3*	<0.1
St. Supery Vineyards and Winery	PO Box 38	Rutherford	CA	94573	Michaela Rodeno	707-963-4507	R	3	0.1
Swanson Vineyards and Winery	P O Box 459	Rutherford	CA	94573	W Clarke Swanson Jr	707-944-1642	R	3*	<0.1
Peter Michael Winery Inc.	12400 Ida Clayton	Calistoga	CA	94515	Scott Rodde	707-942-4459	R	3	<0.1
Chateau Potelle Winery	3875 Mount Veeder	Napa	CA	94558	Jean-Noel Fourmeaux	707-255-9440	R	2	<0.1

Source: Ward's Business Directory of U.S. Private and Public Companies, Volumes 1 and 2, 2000. The company type code used is as follows: P - Public, R - Private, S - Subsidiary, D - Division, J - Joint Venture, A - Affiliate, G - Group, N - Company type not reported. Sales are in millions of dollars, employees are in thousands. An asterisk (*) indicates an estimated sales volume. The symbol < stands for 'less than'. Company names and addresses are truncated, in some cases, to fit into the available space.

NAICS 111400 - GREENHOUSE, NURSERY, AND FLORICULTURE PRODUCTION

GENERAL STATISTICS

Item	U.S. Total	This Agri-culture Sector	% of U.S.	Category average per farm				Number of farms reporting category	
				Value shown as	U.S.	This Agric. Sector	% of U.S.	U.S.	This Sector
Farms - number	1,911,859	57,192	3.0	-	-	-	-	-	-
Land in farms - mil. acres	931.795	3.931	0.4	Acres	487	69	14.2	1,911,859	57,192
Value of land, buildings - $ mil.	859,839.2	19,751.3	2.3	$	449,748	346,204	77.0	524,066	57,051
Value of machinery and equipment - $ mil.	110,256.8	3,052.1	2.8	$	57,678	53,501	92.8	1,911,601	57,048
Sales of Ag Products - $ mil.	196,864.6	10,873.4	5.5	$	102,970	190,121	184.6	1,911,859	57,192
Government payments - $ mil.	5,054.5	15.0	0.3	$	7,378	3,583	48.6	685,029	4,191
Other farm-related income - $ mil.	3,272.3	58.4	1.8	$	5,999	6,921	115.4	545,480	8,433
Expenses - $ mil.	150,591.0	7,009.7	4.7	$	78,771	122,893	156.0	1,911,766	57,039
Payroll - $ mil.	14,841.0	2,835.4	19.1	$	22,811	97,588	427.8	650,623	29,055
Workers - 150 days or more a year	890,467	150,177	16.9	Number	3.4	9.2	267.8	259,631	16,351
Workers - less than 150 days	2,461,561	202,583	8.2	Number	4.2	7.9	186.7	581,658	25,634
Net Cash Return - $ mil.	42,557.9	3,744.3	8.8	$	22,260	65,631	294.8	1,911,824	57,051

Source: 1997 Census of Agriculture, U.S. Department of Agriculture, National Agricultural Statistics Service. Table shows totals for the U.S. agriculture sector and for the NAICS subdivision of it, shown as "This Agric. Sector" or as "This Sector." Not all farms report on every category. For this reason, the reporting universe is shown in the last two columns. Averages are based on these columns.

LAND IN FARMS ACCORDING TO USE

Item	U.S. Total (000 acres)	This Sector (000 acres)	% of U.S.	Average acres per farms			Number of farms reporting category	
				U.S.	This Agric. Sector	% of U.S.	U.S.	This Sector
Total cropland	431,144.9	1,989.7	0.5	260	35	-	1,661,395	57,192
Harvested cropland	309,395.5	1,419.8	0.5	219	25	-	1,410,606	57,192
Cropland:								
Pasture or grazing	64,466.5	180.8	0.3	85	31	-	754,170	5,872
In cover crops, legumes, grasses	13,531.2	86.2	0.6	88	27	-	153,177	3,229
On which all crops failed	3,449.4	10.9	0.3	67	12	-	51,673	918
In cultivated summer fallow	20,905.9	24.9	0.1	256	30	-	81,702	836
Idle	19,396.3	267.1	1.4	83	27	-	232,961	9,899
Total woodland	71,465.4	1,137.3	1.6	96	62	-	743,011	18,266
Woodland pastured	29,693.9	168.9	0.6	84	56	-	352,217	3,010
Woodland not pastured	41,771.5	968.4	2.3	79	58	-	531,846	16,612
Other pasture/rangeland	396,884.6	375.6	0.1	721	88	-	550,619	4,252
Land for house lots, ponds, roads, wasteland	32,300.4	428.3	1.3	28	12	-	1,142,618	34,561
Irrigated land	55,058.1	612.0	1.1	197	20	-	279,442	31,250
Harvested cropland	50,013.5	586.7	1.2	198	19	-	252,679	31,086
Pasture and other	5,044.7	25.3	0.5	87	21	-	58,258	1,234
Conservation Reserve/Wetlands Reserve Lands	29,489.1	49.9	0.2	131	42	-	225,410	1,202

Source: 1997 Census of Agriculture, U.S. Department of Agriculture, National Agricultural Statistics Service. Table shows totals for the U.S. agriculture sector and for the NAICS subdivision of it, shown as "This Agric. Sector" or as "This Sector." Not all farms report on every category. For this reason, the reporting universe is shown in the last two columns. Averages are based on these columns. The Conservation Reserve and Wetlands Reserve programs provide support for land conservation/preservation. Cover crops are not harvested or pastured.

MARKET VALUE OF AGRICULTURAL PRODUCTS SOLD: ALL FARMS

Item	U.S. Total ($ mil.)	This Sector ($ mil.)	% of Sector Sales	% of U.S.	Average sales per farm - $			Number of farms reporting category	
					U.S.	This Agric. Sector	% of U.S.	U.S.	This Sector
Grains	46,617.1	22.8	0.21	0.0	79,095	19,082	24.1	589,379	1,196
Corn for grain	18,884.8	6.7	0.06	0.0	52,506	12,462	23.7	359,666	535
Wheat	7,173.9	5.2	0.05	0.1	29,726	14,286	48.1	241,334	367
Soybeans	15,622.4	7.1	0.07	0.0	44,185	15,281	34.6	353,566	463
Sorghum for grain	1,140.0	0.4	0.00	0.0	25,360	18,600	73.3	44,955	20
Barley	709.6	0.7	0.01	0.1	23,191	12,863	55.5	30,598	51
Oats	121.3	0.2	0.00	0.2	3,114	2,821	90.6	38,940	84
Other grains	2,965.1	2.6	0.02	0.1	67,540	25,225	37.3	43,901	102
Cotton and cotton seed	5,975.5	2.5	0.02	0.0	189,963	113,955	60.0	31,456	22
Tobacco	2,924.7	3.7	0.03	0.1	32,662	15,729	48.2	89,544	236
Hay, silage, and field seeds	4,670.5	22.0	0.20	0.5	13,174	9,260	70.3	354,523	2,375
Vegetables, sweet corn, and melons	8,401.7	51.6	0.47	0.6	156,628	22,023	14.1	53,641	2,344
Fruits and berries	12,660.3	29.4	0.27	0.2	147,259	14,790	10.0	85,973	1,990
Nursery and greenhouse crops	10,942.8	10,701.6	98.42	97.8	161,360	187,117	116.0	67,816	57,192
Other crops	5,863.1	11.9	0.11	0.2	153,907	27,165	17.7	38,095	437
Poultry and poultry products	22,262.6	1.8	0.02	0.0	352,000	2,390	0.7	63,246	751
Dairy products	18,997.3	1.6	0.01	0.0	191,432	60,115	31.4	99,238	26
Cattle and calves	40,524.8	20.0	0.18	0.0	40,052	8,537	21.3	1,011,809	2,345
Hogs and pigs	13,804.8	1.0	0.01	0.0	135,201	3,928	2.9	102,106	251
Sheep, lambs, and wool	682.9	0.6	0.01	0.1	10,913	816	7.5	62,579	686
Other livestock	2,536.5	2.9	0.03	0.1	20,506	2,769	13.5	123,695	1,045
Products sold to public directly	13,096.7	0.6	0.01	0.0	377,610	196,333	52.0	34,683	3

Source: 1997 Census of Agriculture, U.S. Department of Agriculture, National Agricultural Statistics Service. Table shows totals for the U.S. agriculture sector and for the NAICS subdivision of it, shown as "This Agric. Sector" or as "This Sector." Not all farms report on every category. For this reason, the reporting universe is shown in the last two columns. Averages are based on these columns. Farms classified in one sector routinely produce categories in other sectors as well. Products sold to the public are sold for direct consumption.

MARKET VALUE OF PRODUCTS SOLD: FARMS WITH SALES OF $50,000 OR MORE

Item	U.S. Total ($ mil.)	This Sector ($ mil.)	% of Sector Sales	% of U.S.	Average sales per farm - $			Number of farms reporting category	
					U.S.	This Agric. Sector	% of U.S.	U.S.	This Sector
Grains	40,973.4	14.7	0.14	0.0	183,623	129,947	70.8	223,138	113
Cotton and cotton seed	5,743.9	2.4	0.02	0.0	286,562	213,818	74.6	20,044	11
Tobacco	2,060.2	1.8	0.02	0.1	175,907	132,000	75.0	11,712	14
Hay, silage, and field seeds	2,781.9	14.2	0.13	0.5	188,959	309,543	163.8	14,722	46
Vegetables, sweet corn, and melons	7,966.8	35.3	0.32	0.4	673,443	179,096	26.6	11,830	197
Fruits and berries	12,072.3	21.0	0.19	0.2	478,927	199,810	41.7	25,207	105
Nursery and greenhouse crops	10,412.0	10,232.1	94.10	98.3	578,025	597,428	103.4	18,013	17,127
Other crops	5,586.6	10.4	0.10	0.2	363,758	433,375	119.1	15,358	24
Poultry and poultry products	22,171.7	1.3	0.01	0.0	778,637	128,400	16.5	28,475	10
Dairy products	18,344.3	1.4	0.01	0.0	250,075	120,167	48.1	73,355	12
Cattle and calves	32,358.6	9.6	0.09	0.0	386,685	241,075	62.3	83,682	40
Hogs and pigs	13,096.7	0.6	0.01	0.0	377,610	196,333	52.0	34,683	3
Sheep, lambs, and wool	478.6	-	-	-	278,730	-	-	1,717	-
Other livestock	2,026.6	1.1	0.01	0.1	369,685	119,222	32.2	5,482	9

Source: 1997 Census of Agriculture, U.S. Department of Agriculture, National Agricultural Statistics Service. Table shows totals for the U.S. agriculture sector and for the NAICS subdivision of it, shown as "This Agric. Sector" or as "This Sector." Not all farms report on every category. For this reason, the reporting universe is shown in the last two columns. Averages are based on these columns. Farms classified in one sector routinely produce categories in other sectors as well.

GOVERNMENT PAYMENTS AND OTHER FARM-RELATED INCOME

Item	U.S. Total ($ mil.)	This Sector ($ mil.)	% of Sector Gov/Oth. Income	% of U.S.	Average receipts per farm - $			Number of farms reporting category	
					U.S.	This Agric. Sector	% of U.S.	U.S.	This Sector
Government payments	5,054.5	15.0	20.46	0.3	7,378	3,583	48.6	685,029	4,191
Other farm-related income	3,272.3	58.4	79.54	1.8	5,999	6,921	115.4	545,480	8,433
Custom work and other agricultural services	1,235.1	24.7	33.64	2.0	8,646	11,817	136.7	142,854	2,089
Gross cash rent or share payments	1,207.9	13.7	18.63	1.1	6,867	3,949	57.5	175,901	3,461
Forest products, excluding Christmas trees and maple products	344.3	13.4	18.24	3.9	7,417	6,292	84.8	46,426	2,127
Other farm-related income sources	484.9	6.6	9.03	1.4	1,595	3,303	207.0	303,908	2,007

Source: 1997 Census of Agriculture, U.S. Department of Agriculture, National Agricultural Statistics Service. Table shows totals for the U.S. agriculture sector and for the NAICS subdivision of it, shown as "This Agric. Sector" or as "This Sector." Not all farms report on every category. For this reason, the reporting universe is shown in the last two columns. Averages are based on these columns. Government payments are agricultural subsidies under various programs.

COMMODITY CREDIT CORPORATION LOANS

Item	U.S. Total ($ mil.)	This Sector ($ mil.)	% of Sector Loan Total	% of U.S.	Average loan value per farm - $			Number of farms reporting category	
					U.S.	This Agric. Sector	% of U.S.	U.S.	This Sector
Total loans	3,034.7	0.5	100.00	0.0	36,419	20,652	56.7	83,328	23
Corn	1,333.9	0.3	55.37	0.0	26,419	16,437	62.2	50,489	16
Wheat	415.4	0.0	2.32	0.0	18,093	2,200	12.2	22,961	5
Soybeans	774.0	0.2	36.21	0.0	30,370	57,333	188.8	25,487	3
Sorghum, barley, and oats	54.8	-	-	-	8,603	-	-	6,375	2
Cotton	191.4	-	-	-	43,275	-	-	4,422	1
Sunflower seed, flaxseed, safflower, canola, other rapeseed, and mustard seed	17.3	-	-	-	25,159	-	-	686	-
Peanuts, rice, and tobacco	247.9	-	-	-	60,421	-	-	4,103	2

Source: 1997 Census of Agriculture, U.S. Department of Agriculture, National Agricultural Statistics Service. Table shows totals for the U.S. agriculture sector and for the NAICS subdivision of it, shown as "This Agric. Sector" or as "This Sector." Not all farms report on every category. For this reason, the reporting universe is shown in the last two columns. Averages are based on these columns. The Commodity Credit Corporation provides low interest loans to farmers.

SELECTED MACHINERY AND EQUIPMENT

Item	U.S. Total (number)	This Agric. Sector (number)	% of U.S.	Average number per farm			Number of farms reporting category	
				U.S.	This Agric. Sector	% of U.S.	U.S.	This Sector
Motortrucks, including pickups	3,497,735	112,940	3.2	2.07	2.31	111.3	1,688,303	48,994
Wheel tractors	3,936,014	100,007	2.5	2.31	2.17	94.1	1,707,384	46,091
Less than 40 horsepower (PTO)	1,262,688	57,035	4.5	1.44	1.66	115.0	877,119	34,447
40 horsepower (PTO) or more	2,673,326	42,972	1.6	2.02	1.84	90.9	1,321,084	23,361
40 to 99 horsepower (PTO)	1,808,105	35,760	2.0	1.58	1.66	105.2	1,145,466	21,533
100 horsepower (PTO)	865,221	7,212	0.8	1.68	1.47	87.1	513,773	4,915
Grain and bean combines	460,606	812	0.2	1.16	1.10	94.7	395,934	737
Cotton pickers and strippers	38,294	-	-	1.48	-	-	25,874	19
Mower conditioners	608,443	6,167	1.0	1.12	1.19	106.2	543,565	5,188
Pickup balers	717,245	2,356	0.3	1.24	1.14	91.9	579,440	2,071

Source: 1997 Census of Agriculture, U.S. Department of Agriculture, National Agricultural Statistics Service. Table shows totals for the U.S. agriculture sector and for the NAICS subdivision of it, shown as "This Agric. Sector" or as "This Sector." Not all farms report on every category. For this reason, the reporting universe is shown in the last two columns. Averages are based on these columns. PTO stands for "power take off."

FARM PRODUCTION EXPENSES

Item	U.S. Total ($ mil.)	This Sector ($ mil.)	% of Sector Total Expense	% of U.S.	Average expense per farm - $			Number of farms reporting category	
					U.S.	This Agric. Sector	% of U.S.	U.S.	This Sector
Total farm production expenses	150,591.0	7,009.7	100.00	4.7	78,771	122,892	156.0	1,911,766	57,039
Livestock and poultry purchased	21,614.6	5.1	0.07	0.0	38,807	2,361	6.1	556,980	2,172
Feed for livestock and poultry	32,760.0	7.3	0.10	0.0	32,059	1,594	5.0	1,021,849	4,585
Commercially mixed formula feeds	21,236.2	4.0	0.06	0.0	34,459	1,436	4.2	616,280	2,768
Seeds, bulbs, plants, and trees	5,725.9	779.7	11.12	13.6	6,388	22,210	347.7	896,339	35,104
Commercial fertilizer	9,597.1	181.8	2.59	1.9	8,060	4,842	60.1	1,190,733	37,552
Agricultural chemicals	7,581.4	140.3	2.00	1.9	8,056	3,871	48.0	941,136	36,251
Petroleum products	6,371.5	317.8	4.53	5.0	3,619	5,964	164.8	1,760,642	53,295
Gasoline and gasohol	1,886.6	73.5	1.05	3.9	1,380	1,724	124.9	1,366,915	42,652
Diesel fuel	2,846.0	79.9	1.14	2.8	2,164	2,679	123.8	1,315,397	29,834
Natural gas	432.9	101.2	1.44	23.4	6,091	17,879	293.5	71,069	5,660
LP gas, fuel oil, kerosene, motor oil, grease, etc.	1,206.1	63.2	0.90	5.2	945	1,757	185.9	1,276,331	35,967
Electricity	2,751.1	156.9	2.24	5.7	2,247	4,107	182.8	1,224,374	38,190
Hired farm labor	14,841.0	2,835.4	40.45	19.1	22,811	97,588	427.8	650,623	29,055
Contract labor	2,959.0	231.4	3.30	7.8	13,040	22,797	174.8	226,909	10,150
Repair and maintenance	8,637.7	374.9	5.35	4.3	5,616	8,103	144.3	1,538,058	46,272
Custom work, machine hire, and rental of equipment	3,210.3	82.0	1.17	2.6	5,372	7,790	145.0	597,624	10,530
Interest	8,928.1	291.1	4.15	3.3	11,016	14,317	130.0	810,476	20,333
Secured by real estate	5,449.6	184.6	2.63	3.4	9,564	12,781	133.6	569,775	14,440
Not secured by real estate	3,478.5	106.5	1.52	3.1	7,540	10,651	141.3	461,326	10,003
Cash rent	6,915.7	106.0	1.51	1.5	14,244	13,669	96.0	485,512	7,755
Property taxes	3,920.1	137.0	1.95	3.5	2,213	2,628	118.8	1,771,787	52,107
All other farm production expenses	14,777.4	1,362.9	19.44	9.2	8,747	26,152	299.0	1,689,391	52,114

Source: *1997 Census of Agriculture*, U.S. Department of Agriculture, National Agricultural Statistics Service. Table shows totals for the U.S. agriculture sector and for the NAICS subdivision of it, shown as "This Agric. Sector" or as "This Sector." Not all farms report on every category. For this reason, the reporting universe is shown in the last two columns. Averages are based on these columns. LP gas stands for "liquid petroleum gas," i.e., butane or propane.

NET CASH RETURN AND FARMS WITH GAINS AND LOSSES

Item	Number of farms and %				Average gain or loss per farm - $		
	U.S.	% of U.S.	This Agriculture Sector	% of Sector	U.S.	This Agriculture Sector	% of U.S.
All farms	1,911,824	100.0	57,051	100.0	22,260	65,631	294.8
Number of farms with net gains	985,718	51.6	40,955	71.8	51,296	94,663	184.5
Gain of -							
Less than $1,000	120,163	6.3	4,148	7.3	-	-	-
$1,000 to $9,999	370,611	19.4	13,697	24.0	-	-	-
$10,000 to $49,999	292,484	15.3	13,451	23.6	-	-	-
$50,000 or more	202,460	10.6	9,659	16.9	-	-	-
Number of farms with net losses	926,106	48.4	16,096	28.2	(8,645)	(8,240)	95.3
Loss of -							
Less than $1,000	165,390	8.7	3,588	6.3	-	-	-
$1,000 to $9,999	591,517	30.9	10,078	17.7	-	-	-
$10,000 to $49,999	152,649	8.0	2,129	3.7	-	-	-
$50,000 or more	16,550	0.9	301	0.5	-	-	-

Source: *1997 Census of Agriculture*, U.S. Department of Agriculture, National Agricultural Statistics Service. Table shows totals for the U.S. agriculture sector and for the NAICS subdivision of it, shown as "This Agric. Sector" or as "This Sector." Not all farms report on every category. For this reason, the reporting universe is shown in the last two columns. Averages are based on these columns. Net gains are income less cost for farm operations; they exclude non-farm earnings. Values in parentheses are losses.

CHARACTERISTICS OF FARM OPERATORS

Farm Operators	U.S.	This Agric. Sector	% of U.S.	Farm Operators	U.S.	This Agric. Sector	% of U.S.
Place of residence:				By age group:			
On farm operated	1,361,766	37,251	2.7	Under 25 years	20,850	226	1.1
Not on farm operated	412,554	16,238	3.9	25 to 34 years	128,455	2,763	2.2
Not reported	137,539	3,703	2.7	35 to 44 years	371,442	12,895	3.5
Principal occupation:				45 to 49 years	232,845	8,801	3.8
Farming	961,560	25,171	2.6	50 to 54 years	233,884	8,350	3.6
Other	950,299	32,021	3.4	55 to 59 years	222,736	7,248	3.3
Days worked off farm:				60 to 64 years	204,618	5,804	2.8
None	755,254	24,158	3.2	65 to 69 years	179,858	4,694	2.6
Any	1,042,158	30,332	2.9	70 years and over	317,171	6,411	2.0
1 to 99 days	164,957	5,232	3.2	Average age	54	53	97.4
100 to 199 days	167,922	5,640	3.4	By sex:			
200 days or more	709,279	19,460	2.7	Male	1,746,757	48,936	2.8
Not reported	114,447	2,702	2.4	Female	165,102	8,256	5.0
Years on present farm:				Spanish, Hispanic/Latino origin	27,717	1,216	4.4
2 years or less	92,574	2,841	3.1	Tenure of operator:			
3 or 4 years	126,791	4,251	3.4	All operators	1,911,859	57,192	3.0
5 to 9 years	263,642	10,481	4.0	Full owners	1,146,891	45,183	3.9
10 years or more	1,113,839	32,450	2.9	Part owners	573,839	6,193	1.1
Ave. years on this farm	20	16	78.1	Tenants	191,129	5,816	3.0
Not reported	315,013	7,169	2.3				

Source: 1997 Census of Agriculture, U.S. Department of Agriculture, National Agricultural Statistics Service. Table shows totals for the U.S. agriculture sector and for the NAICS subdivision of it, shown as "This Agric. Sector" or as "This Sector." Not all farms report on every category. For this reason, the reporting universe is shown in the last two columns. Averages are based on these columns. All values shown are number of farm operators in each category or percent.

FARMS BY TYPE OF ORGANIZATION

Item	Number of farms and percent				Total acres and percent			
	U.S.	% of U.S.	This Agriculture Sector	% of Sector	U.S.	This Agriculture Sector	% of U.S.
Individual or family (sole proprietorship)	1,643,424	100.0	41,467	100.0	585,464,911	2,072,061	0.4
Partnership	169,462	10.3	4,827	11.6	149,321,484	528,722	0.4
Corporation:							
Family held	76,103	4.6	8,931	21.5	119,559,203	1,058,824	0.9
More than 10 stockholders	1,795	0.1	112	0.3	-	-	-
10 or less stockholders	74,308	4.5	8,819	21.3	-	-	-
Other than family held	7,899	0.5	1,385	3.3	11,904,053	210,016	1.8
More than 10 stockholders	1,029	0.1	98	0.2	-	-	-
10 or less stockholders	6,870	0.4	1,287	3.1	-	-	-
Other cooperative, estate or trust, institutional, etc.	14,971	0.9	582	1.4	65,545,604	61,366	0.1

Source: 1997 Census of Agriculture, U.S. Department of Agriculture, National Agricultural Statistics Service. Table shows totals for the U.S. agriculture sector and for the NAICS subdivision of it, shown as "This Agric. Sector" or as "This Sector." Not all farms report on every category. For this reason, the reporting universe is shown in the last two columns. Averages are based on these columns.

LIVESTOCK INVENTORIES AND SALES

Item	U.S. (number)	This Agric. Sector (number)	% of U.S.	Average number per farm			Number of farms reporting category	
				U.S.	This Agric. Sector	% of U.S.	U.S.	This Sector
Cattle and calves inventory	98,989,244	94,164	0.1	94.6	29.5	31.2	1,046,863	3,187
Cows and heifers that had calved	43,162,054	52,140	0.1	48.3	22.0	45.5	894,110	2,374
Beef cows	34,066,615	51,094	0.1	42.3	22.5	53.3	804,595	2,266
Milk cows	9,095,439	1,046	0.0	77.8	6.1	7.8	116,874	172
Heifers and heifer calves	26,988,697	23,028	0.1	33.6	11.7	34.7	803,985	1,976
Steers, steer calves, bulls, and bull calves	28,838,493	18,996	0.1	32.6	8.1	25.0	883,983	2,332
Cattle and calves sold	74,089,046	48,719	0.1	73.2	20.8	28.4	1,011,809	2,345
Calves	16,480,293	21,396	0.1	26.8	16.3	60.9	615,177	1,312
Cattle	57,608,753	27,323	0.0	78.0	16.8	21.6	738,695	1,625
Fattened on grain and concentrates	27,328,190	1,984	0.0	247.0	7.8	3.2	110,620	254
Hogs and pigs inventory	61,206,236	5,811	0.0	557.7	12.8	2.3	109,754	453
Used or to be used for breeding	6,831,564	464	0.0	106.7	4.1	3.8	64,029	113
Other	54,374,672	5,347	0.0	528.0	12.4	2.3	102,977	431
Hogs and pigs sold	142,611,882	9,230	0.0	1,396.7	36.8	2.6	102,106	251
Feeder pigs	34,988,718	905	0.0	2,037.8	26.6	1.3	17,170	34
Litters of pigs farrowed between Dec. 1 of preceding year and Nov. 30	11,497,523	561	0.0	170.3	4.6	2.7	67,514	123
Dec. 1 and May 31	5,697,371	323	0.0	91.0	2.9	3.1	62,622	113
June 1 and Nov. 30	5,800,152	238	0.0	99.7	3.4	3.4	58,204	71
Sheep and lambs of all ages inventory	7,821,885	11,626	0.1	118.9	14.1	11.9	65,790	824
Ewes 1 year old or older	4,408,683	7,133	0.2	78.1	11.0	14.1	56,414	647
Sheep and lambs sold	7,331,545	7,803	0.1	123.1	14.0	11.4	59,575	558
Sheep and lambs shorn	6,139,140	8,293	0.1	118.4	14.8	12.5	51,869	562
Horses and ponies inventory	2,427,277	12,876	0.5	6.5	4.1	62.7	375,218	3,175
Horses and ponies sold	325,306	580	0.2	4.1	2.0	49.6	79,516	286
Goats inventory	1,989,799	7,967	0.4	34.4	9.1	26.4	57,925	879
Goats sold	740,597	2,007	0.3	31.5	8.2	26.0	23,520	245

Source: 1997 Census of Agriculture, U.S. Department of Agriculture, National Agricultural Statistics Service. Table shows totals for the U.S. agriculture sector and for the NAICS subdivision of it, shown as "This Agric. Sector" or as "This Sector." Not all farms report on every category. For this reason, the reporting universe is shown in the last two columns. Averages are based on these columns.

POULTRY INVENTORIES AND SALES

Item	U.S. (number)	This Agric. Sector (number)	% of U.S.	Average number per farm			Number of farms reporting category	
				U.S.	This Agric. Sector	% of U.S.	U.S.	This Sector
Layers and pullets 13 weeks old and older inventory	366,989,851	-	-	5,053.8	-	-	72,616	1,337
Layers 20 weeks old and older	313,851,480	80,596	0.0	4,499.0	61.5	1.4	69,761	1,310
Pullets 13 weeks old and older but less than 20 weeks old	53,138,371	-	-	4,031.7	-	-	13,180	207
Layers, pullets, and pullet chicks sold	331,563,736	47,435	0.0	24,636.9	343.7	1.4	13,458	138
Broilers and other meat type chickens sold	6,741,927,110	542,997	0.0	281,653.0	5,838.7	2.1	23,937	93
Turkey hens kept for breeding	5,504,808	509	0.0	968.1	4.9	0.5	5,686	103
Turkeys sold	307,586,680	-	-	51,000.9	-	-	6,031	61

Source: 1997 Census of Agriculture, U.S. Department of Agriculture, National Agricultural Statistics Service. Table shows totals for the U.S. agriculture sector and for the NAICS subdivision of it, shown as "This Agric. Sector" or as "This Sector." Not all farms report on every category. For this reason, the reporting universe is shown in the last two columns. Averages are based on these columns.

SELECTED CROPS HARVESTED

Item	In 1,000	Crop harvested			Acres used for crop (000)			Number of farms reporting category	
		U.S.	This Agric. Sector	% of U.S.	U.S.	This Agric. Sector	% of U.S.	U.S.	This Sector
Corn for grain or seed	bushels	8,578,635	2,854	0.0	69,796.7	25.9	0.0	430,711	711
Irrigated		-	-	-	10,638.9	3.6	0.0	40,574	100
Corn for silage or green chop	tons, green	88,381	33	0.0	5,727.6	2.3	0.0	119,308	130
Irrigated		-	-	-	1,033.3	0.6	0.1	10,815	28
Sorghum for grain or seed	bushels	559,070	172	0.0	8,470.4	2.1	0.0	49,397	32
Irrigated		-	-	-	875.6	1.5	0.2	5,793	10
Wheat for grain	bushels	2,204,027	1,536	0.1	58,836.3	24.7	0.0	243,568	387
Irrigated		-	-	-	3,990.9	10.0	0.2	20,385	100
Barley for grain	bushels	336,435	195	0.1	5,945.0	2.9	0.0	41,930	60
Irrigated		-	-	-	1,060.7	2.1	0.2	8,847	26
Oats for grain	bushels	151,327	154	0.1	2,681.0	2.4	0.1	89,606	145
Irrigated		-	-	-	121.0	0.1	0.1	2,788	11
Rice	cwt	182,231	134	0.1	3,122.1	2.1	0.1	9,291	5
Irrigated		-	-	-	3,122.1	2.1	0.1	9,291	5
Cotton	bales	17,879	7	0.0	13,235.2	4.0	0.0	31,493	22
Irrigated		-	-	-	4,888.0	1.9	0.0	12,434	10
Tobacco	pounds	1,747,702	2,187	0.1	838.5	1.1	0.1	89,706	238
Irrigated		-	-	-	138.7	0.2	0.1	7,090	31
Soybeans for beans	bushels	2,504,307	1,159	0.0	66,147.7	34.6	0.1	354,692	494
Irrigated		-	-	-	4,152.1	2.8	0.1	20,619	37
Dry edible beans, excluding dry limas	cwt	27,224	26	0.1	1,691.9	1.5	0.1	10,911	41
Irrigated		-	-	-	577.0	1.4	0.2	4,882	25
Potatoes, excluding sweetpotatoes	cwt	459,886	910	0.2	1,355.2	2.9	0.2	10,523	203
Irrigated		-	-	-	1,070.3	2.7	0.3	4,843	82
Sugar beets for sugar	tons	29,775	21	0.1	1,453.8	0.7	0.0	7,102	11
Irrigated		-	-	-	616.4	0.7	0.1	3,492	10
Peanuts for nuts	pounds	3,377,143	-	-	1,352.2	-	-	12,221	13
Irrigated		-	-	-	412.3	0.8	0.2	3,125	8
Hay alfalfa, other tame, small grain, wild, grass silage, green chop	tons, dry	139,365	244	0.2	60,799.8	109.3	0.2	888,597	4,535
Irrigated		-	-	-	9,564.3	19.2	0.2	79,406	521
Alfalfa hay	tons, dry	65,863	98	0.1	21,309.8	26.4	0.1	358,365	1,132
Irrigated		-	-	-	5,980.5	11.8	0.2	57,854	251
Vegetables harvested for sale		-	-	-	3,773.2	29.8	0.8	53,727	2,347
Irrigated		-	-	-	2,641.8	15.9	0.6	23,203	1,246
Land in orchards		-	-	-	5,158.1	24.3	0.5	106,069	3,033
Irrigated		-	-	-	4,107.9	13.0	0.3	61,606	1,430

Source: 1997 Census of Agriculture, U.S. Department of Agriculture, National Agricultural Statistics Service. Table shows totals for the U.S. agriculture sector and for the NAICS subdivision of it, shown as "This Agric. Sector" or as "This Sector." Not all farms report on every category. For this reason, the reporting universe is shown in the last two columns. Averages are based on these columns. "Green tons" are weight of product as harvested, i.e., moist. cwt stands for "hundredweight."

LEADING COMPANIES   Number shown: 25   Total sales ($ mil): 1,703   Total employment (000): 12.0

Company Name	Address				CEO Name	Phone	Co. Type	Sales ($ mil)	Empl. (000)
AgriBioTech Inc.	120 Corporate Park	Henderson	NV	89014	Kenneth Budd	702-566-2440	P	371	1.0
Monrovia Nursery Co.	P O Box 1385	Azusa	CA	91702	Miles Rosedale	626-334-9321	R	190*	1.5
Earl May Seed and Nursery L.P.	208 N Elm St	Shenandoah	IA	51603	Betty Shaw	712-246-1020	R	181*	0.8
Yoder Brothers Inc.	115 3rd St S E	Barberton	OH	44203	Thomas D Doak	330-745-2143	R	181*	1.6
Novartis Seeds Inc. (Boise, Idaho)	P O Box 4188	Boise	ID	83704	John Sorenson	208-322-7272	S	140*	0.6
Gurney Seed and Nursery Corp.	110 Capitol St	Yankton	SD	57078	Al Lingor	605-665-4451	R	88*	0.7
Zelenka Nursery Inc.	16127 Winans St	Grand Haven	MI	49417	Richard H Brolick	616-842-1367	R	82*	0.7
Wight Nurseries Inc.	P O Box 390	Cairo	GA	31728	R VanLandingham	912-377-3033	R	76*	0.6
Mycogen Seeds	5501 Oberlin Dr	San Diego	CA	92121	Charles Fischer	619-453-8030	S	65*	1.0
Green Circle Growers Inc.	15650 State Rte 511	Oberlin	OH	44074	John Vanwingerden	440-775-1411	R	57*	0.5
Stark Brothers Nurseries	PO Box 10	Louisiana	MO	63353		573-754-5511	R	38*	0.3
DSI Industries Inc.	5211 Brownfield	Lubbock	TX	79407	S Howard Norton III	806-785-8460	P	36	0.5
Speedling Inc.	PO Box 7220	Sun City	FL	33586	Berl Thomas	813-645-3221	S	35	0.2
Conrad Fafard Inc.	PO Box 790	Agawam	MA	01001		413-786-4343	R	33	0.1
American Nursery Products Inc.	7010 S Yale, Ste 101	Tulsa	OK	74136	J Wayne Fields	918-523-9665	R	25	0.9
LG Seeds Inc.	4001 N War Mem	Peoria	IL	61614	Bruno Carette	309-681-0300	R	20	0.1
Van Wingerden International Inc.	556 Jeffress Rd	Fletcher	NC	28732	Bert Lemkes	828-891-4116	R	20*	0.3
Conard-Pyle Co.	372 Rosehill Rd	West Grove	PA	19390	Steven B Hutton	610-869-2426	R	19*	0.2
Alf Christianson Seed Co.	P O Box 98	Mount Vernon	WA	98273	K G Christianson	360-336-9727	R	15*	<0.1
Hermann Engelmann Greenhouses	P O Box 1147	Apopka	FL	32704	Hermann Engelmann	407-886-3434	R	11	0.2
Color Spot Lone Star Growers	PO Box 330	Waco	TX	76703		254-752-9711	D	10*	0.1
Margo Caribe Inc.	Road 690	Vega Alta	PR	00692	Michael J Spector	787-883-2570	P	5	0.1
Charles C. Hart Seed Co.	304 Main St	Wethersfield	CT	06109	Charles H Hart	860-529-2537	R	3*	<0.1
Genecorp Inc.	910 Duncan Rd	Glen RidLima	CA	95045		831-757-0169	R	2*	<0.1
Sonoma Flower Co.	6683 Sonoma Hwy	Santa Rosa	CA	95409	E Farmer-Bowers	707-539-2000	S	1	<0.1

Source: Ward's Business Directory of U.S. Private and Public Companies, Volumes 1 and 2, 2000. The company type code used is as follows: P - Public, R - Private, S - Subsidiary, D - Division, J - Joint Venture, A - Affiliate, G - Group, N - Company type not reported. Sales are in millions of dollars, employees are in thousands. An asterisk (*) indicates an estimated sales volume. The symbol < stands for 'less than'. Company names and addresses are truncated, in some cases, to fit into the available space.

NAICS 111900 - OTHER CROP FARMING

GENERAL STATISTICS

Item	U.S. Total	This Agri-culture Sector	% of U.S.	Category average per farm				Number of farms reporting category	
				Value shown as	U.S.	This Agric. Sector	% of U.S.	U.S.	This Sector
Farms - number	1,911,859	269,317	14.1	-	-	-	-	-	-
Land in farms - mil. acres	931.795	93.837	10.1	Acres	487	348	71.5	1,911,859	269,317
Value of land, buildings - $ mil.	859,839.2	109,093.0	12.7	$	449,748	410,511	91.3	524,066	265,749
Value of machinery and equip-ment - $ mil.	110,256.8	15,339.4	13.9	$	57,678	57,727	100.1	1,911,601	265,722
Sales of Ag Products - $ mil.	196,864.6	19,262.4	9.8	$	102,970	71,523	69.5	1,911,859	269,317
Government payments - $ mil.	5,054.5	617.1	12.2	$	7,378	7,433	100.7	685,029	83,021
Other farm-related income - $ mil.	3,272.3	496.3	15.2	$	5,999	6,572	109.6	545,480	75,510
Expenses - $ mil.	150,591.0	14,036.4	9.3	$	78,771	52,819	67.1	1,911,766	265,747
Payroll - $ mil.	14,841.0	1,855.4	12.5	$	22,811	17,678	77.5	650,623	104,956
Workers - 150 days or more a year	890,467	107,145	12.0	Number	3.4	2.9	85.8	259,631	36,412
Workers - less than 150 days	2,461,561	464,017	18.9	Number	4.2	4.8	112.4	581,658	97,549
Net Cash Return - $ mil.	42,557.9	4,712.4	11.1	$	22,260	17,733	79.7	1,911,824	265,749

Source: *1997 Census of Agriculture*, U.S. Department of Agriculture, National Agricultural Statistics Service. Table shows totals for the U.S. agriculture sector and for the NAICS subdivision of it, shown as "This Agric. Sector" or as "This Sector." Not all farms report on every category. For this reason, the reporting universe is shown in the last two columns. Averages are based on these columns.

LAND IN FARMS ACCORDING TO USE

Item	U.S. Total (000 acres)	This Sector (000 acres)	% of U.S.	Average acres per farms			Number of farms reporting category	
				U.S.	This Agric. Sector	% of U.S.	U.S.	This Sector
Total cropland	431,144.9	57,577.1	13.4	260	215	-	1,661,395	268,195
Harvested cropland	309,395.5	44,060.2	14.2	219	164	-	1,410,606	267,944
Cropland:								
Pasture or grazing	64,466.5	6,973.4	10.8	85	68	-	754,170	102,110
In cover crops, legumes, grasses	13,531.2	1,647.0	12.2	88	56	-	153,177	29,328
On which all crops failed	3,449.4	489.4	14.2	67	51	-	51,673	9,626
In cultivated summer fallow	20,905.9	1,180.6	5.6	256	99	-	81,702	11,944
Idle	19,396.3	3,226.5	16.6	83	70	-	232,961	46,272
Total woodland	71,465.4	12,178.7	17.0	96	96	-	743,011	127,448
Woodland pastured	29,693.9	3,189.9	10.7	84	66	-	352,217	48,566
Woodland not pastured	41,771.5	8,988.8	21.5	79	89	-	531,846	100,879
Other pasture/rangeland	396,884.6	19,955.8	5.0	721	376	-	550,619	53,055
Land for house lots, ponds, roads, wasteland	32,300.4	4,125.4	12.8	28	25	-	1,142,618	165,198
Irrigated land	55,058.1	13,896.2	25.2	197	280	-	279,442	49,695
Harvested cropland	50,013.5	13,348.4	26.7	198	271	-	252,679	49,211
Pasture and other	5,044.7	547.8	10.9	87	72	-	58,258	7,653
Conservation Reserve/Wetlands Reserve Lands	29,489.1	2,639.6	9.0	131	111	-	225,410	23,868

Source: *1997 Census of Agriculture*, U.S. Department of Agriculture, National Agricultural Statistics Service. Table shows totals for the U.S. agriculture sector and for the NAICS subdivision of it, shown as "This Agric. Sector" or as "This Sector." Not all farms report on every category. For this reason, the reporting universe is shown in the last two columns. Averages are based on these columns. The Conservation Reserve and Wetlands Reserve programs provide support for land conservation/preservation. Cover crops are not harvested or pastured.

MARKET VALUE OF AGRICULTURAL PRODUCTS SOLD: ALL FARMS

Item	U.S. Total ($ mil.)	This Sector ($ mil.)	% of Sector Sales	% of U.S.	Average sales per farm - $			Number of farms reporting category	
					U.S.	This Agric. Sector	% of U.S.	U.S.	This Sector
Grains	46,617.1	2,675.7	13.89	5.7	79,095	42,442	53.7	589,379	63,044
Corn for grain	18,884.8	788.5	4.09	4.2	52,506	26,037	49.6	359,666	30,284
Wheat	7,173.9	676.1	3.51	9.4	29,726	25,200	84.8	241,334	26,830
Soybeans	15,622.4	739.8	3.84	4.7	44,185	29,788	67.4	353,566	24,837
Sorghum for grain	1,140.0	153.8	0.80	13.5	25,360	27,475	108.3	44,955	5,599
Barley	709.6	107.7	0.56	15.2	23,191	23,201	100.0	30,598	4,641
Oats	121.3	18.1	0.09	15.0	3,114	2,853	91.6	38,940	6,362
Other grains	2,965.1	191.6	0.99	6.5	67,540	42,630	63.1	43,901	4,494
Cotton and cotton seed	5,975.5	5,235.3	27.18	87.6	189,963	208,510	109.8	31,456	25,108
Tobacco	2,924.7	2,555.5	13.27	87.4	32,662	35,740	109.4	89,544	71,502
Hay, silage, and field seeds	4,670.5	2,954.4	15.34	63.3	13,174	17,518	133.0	354,523	168,647
Vegetables, sweet corn, and melons	8,401.7	690.7	3.59	8.2	156,628	79,854	51.0	53,641	8,650
Fruits and berries	12,660.3	315.6	1.64	2.5	147,259	66,985	45.5	85,973	4,712
Nursery and greenhouse crops	10,942.8	96.8	0.50	0.9	161,360	29,584	18.3	67,816	3,272
Other crops	5,863.1	3,198.1	16.60	54.5	153,907	147,190	95.6	38,095	21,728
Poultry and poultry products	22,262.6	49.8	0.26	0.2	352,000	13,699	3.9	63,246	3,638
Dairy products	18,997.3	96.4	0.50	0.5	191,432	64,658	33.8	99,238	1,491
Cattle and calves	40,524.8	1,049.2	5.45	2.6	40,052	12,545	31.3	1,011,809	83,638
Hogs and pigs	13,804.8	282.5	1.47	2.0	135,201	37,456	27.7	102,106	7,542
Sheep, lambs, and wool	682.9	33.7	0.18	4.9	10,913	6,186	56.7	62,579	5,452
Other livestock	2,536.5	28.6	0.15	1.1	20,506	3,554	17.3	123,695	8,057
Products sold to public directly	13,096.7	225.2	1.17	1.7	377,610	141,549	37.5	34,683	1,591

Source: *1997 Census of Agriculture*, U.S. Department of Agriculture, National Agricultural Statistics Service. Table shows totals for the U.S. agriculture sector and for the NAICS subdivision of it, shown as "This Agric. Sector" or as "This Sector." Not all farms report on every category. For this reason, the reporting universe is shown in the last two columns. Averages are based on these columns. Farms classified in one sector routinely produce categories in other sectors as well. Products sold to the public are sold for direct consumption.

MARKET VALUE OF PRODUCTS SOLD: FARMS WITH SALES OF $50,000 OR MORE

Item	U.S. Total ($ mil.)	This Sector ($ mil.)	% of Sector Sales	% of U.S.	Average sales per farm - $			Number of farms reporting category	
					U.S.	This Agric. Sector	% of U.S.	U.S.	This Sector
Grains	40,973.4	2,121.5	11.01	5.2	183,623	154,392	84.1	223,138	13,741
Cotton and cotton seed	5,743.9	5,062.6	26.28	88.1	286,562	301,113	105.1	20,044	16,813
Tobacco	2,060.2	1,854.1	9.63	90.0	175,907	180,925	102.9	11,712	10,248
Hay, silage, and field seeds	2,781.9	2,013.2	10.45	72.4	188,959	217,813	115.3	14,722	9,243
Vegetables, sweet corn, and melons	7,966.8	627.3	3.26	7.9	673,443	297,162	44.1	11,830	2,111
Fruits and berries	12,072.3	293.2	1.52	2.4	478,927	416,447	87.0	25,207	704
Nursery and greenhouse crops	10,412.0	75.9	0.39	0.7	578,025	198,584	34.4	18,013	382
Other crops	5,586.6	3,024.9	15.70	54.1	363,758	316,912	87.1	15,358	9,545
Poultry and poultry products	22,171.7	45.4	0.24	0.2	778,637	308,585	39.6	28,475	147
Dairy products	18,344.3	80.7	0.42	0.4	250,075	136,008	54.4	73,355	593
Cattle and calves	32,358.6	475.5	2.47	1.5	386,685	123,568	32.0	83,682	3,848
Hogs and pigs	13,096.7	225.2	1.17	1.7	377,610	141,549	37.5	34,683	1,591
Sheep, lambs, and wool	478.6	18.4	0.10	3.8	278,730	156,940	56.3	1,717	117
Other livestock	2,026.6	12.0	0.06	0.6	369,685	235,549	63.7	5,482	51

Source: *1997 Census of Agriculture*, U.S. Department of Agriculture, National Agricultural Statistics Service. Table shows totals for the U.S. agriculture sector and for the NAICS subdivision of it, shown as "This Agric. Sector" or as "This Sector." Not all farms report on every category. For this reason, the reporting universe is shown in the last two columns. Averages are based on these columns. Farms classified in one sector routinely produce categories in other sectors as well.

GOVERNMENT PAYMENTS AND OTHER FARM-RELATED INCOME

Item	U.S. Total ($ mil.)	This Sector ($ mil.)	% of Sector Gov/Oth. Income	% of U.S.	Average receipts per farm - $			Number of farms reporting category	
					U.S.	This Agric. Sector	% of U.S.	U.S.	This Sector
Government payments	5,054.5	617.1	55.43	12.2	7,378	7,433	100.7	685,029	83,021
Other farm-related income	3,272.3	496.3	44.57	15.2	5,999	6,572	109.6	545,480	75,510
Custom work and other agricultural services	1,235.1	207.2	18.61	16.8	8,646	8,770	101.4	142,854	23,625
Gross cash rent or share payments	1,207.9	141.6	12.72	11.7	6,867	5,093	74.2	175,901	27,795
Forest products, excluding Christmas trees and maple products	344.3	66.5	5.98	19.3	7,417	7,597	102.4	46,426	8,758
Other farm-related income sources	484.9	81.0	7.28	16.7	1,595	2,509	157.2	303,908	32,288

Source: 1997 Census of Agriculture, U.S. Department of Agriculture, National Agricultural Statistics Service. Table shows totals for the U.S. agriculture sector and for the NAICS subdivision of it, shown as "This Agric. Sector" or as "This Sector." Not all farms report on every category. For this reason, the reporting universe is shown in the last two columns. Averages are based on these columns. Government payments are agricultural subsidies under various programs.

COMMODITY CREDIT CORPORATION LOANS

Item	U.S. Total ($ mil.)	This Sector ($ mil.)	% of Sector Loan Total	% of U.S.	Average loan value per farm - $			Number of farms reporting category	
					U.S.	This Agric. Sector	% of U.S.	U.S.	This Sector
Total loans	3,034.7	277.1	100.00	9.1	36,419	29,514	81.0	83,328	9,389
Corn	1,333.9	33.4	12.07	2.5	26,419	10,786	40.8	50,489	3,100
Wheat	415.4	31.2	11.27	7.5	18,093	12,228	67.6	22,961	2,553
Soybeans	774.0	17.8	6.43	2.3	30,370	15,910	52.4	25,487	1,120
Sorghum, barley, and oats	54.8	5.6	2.04	10.3	8,603	6,739	78.3	6,375	838
Cotton	191.4	168.6	60.86	88.1	43,275	46,394	107.2	4,422	3,635
Sunflower seed, flaxseed, safflower, canola, other rapeseed, and mustard seed	17.3	0.3	0.12	1.8	25,159	15,950	63.4	686	20
Peanuts, rice, and tobacco	247.9	20.0	7.23	8.1	60,421	18,008	29.8	4,103	1,112

Source: 1997 Census of Agriculture, U.S. Department of Agriculture, National Agricultural Statistics Service. Table shows totals for the U.S. agriculture sector and for the NAICS subdivision of it, shown as "This Agric. Sector" or as "This Sector." Not all farms report on every category. For this reason, the reporting universe is shown in the last two columns. Averages are based on these columns. The Commodity Credit Corporation provides low interest loans to farmers.

SELECTED MACHINERY AND EQUIPMENT

Item	U.S. Total (number)	This Agric. Sector (number)	% of U.S.	Average number per farm			Number of farms reporting category	
				U.S.	This Agric. Sector	% of U.S.	U.S.	This Sector
Motortrucks, including pickups	3,497,735	466,481	13.3	2.07	2.04	98.7	1,688,303	228,218
Wheel tractors	3,936,014	566,236	14.4	2.31	2.30	99.8	1,707,384	246,046
Less than 40 horsepower (PTO)	1,262,688	198,947	15.8	1.44	1.49	103.2	877,119	133,928
40 horsepower (PTO) or more	2,673,326	367,289	13.7	2.02	1.94	95.8	1,321,084	189,409
40 to 99 horsepower (PTO)	1,808,105	258,500	14.3	1.58	1.56	98.5	1,145,466	166,213
100 horsepower (PTO)	865,221	108,789	12.6	1.68	1.84	109.0	513,773	59,279
Grain and bean combines	460,606	44,078	9.6	1.16	1.18	101.5	395,934	37,318
Cotton pickers and strippers	38,294	30,987	80.9	1.48	1.49	100.8	25,874	20,772
Mower conditioners	608,443	110,910	18.2	1.12	1.13	101.3	543,565	97,841
Pickup balers	717,245	133,503	18.6	1.24	1.25	101.1	579,440	106,675

Source: 1997 Census of Agriculture, U.S. Department of Agriculture, National Agricultural Statistics Service. Table shows totals for the U.S. agriculture sector and for the NAICS subdivision of it, shown as "This Agric. Sector" or as "This Sector." Not all farms report on every category. For this reason, the reporting universe is shown in the last two columns. Averages are based on these columns. PTO stands for "power take off."

FARM PRODUCTION EXPENSES

Item	U.S. Total ($ mil.)	This Sector ($ mil.)	% of Sector Total Expense	% of U.S.	Average expense per farm - $			Number of farms reporting category	
					U.S.	This Agric. Sector	% of U.S.	U.S.	This Sector
Total farm production expenses	150,591.0	14,036.4	100.00	9.3	78,771	52,819	67.1	1,911,766	265,747
Livestock and poultry purchased	21,614.6	312.0	2.22	1.4	38,807	7,008	18.1	556,980	44,523
Feed for livestock and poultry	32,760.0	334.5	2.38	1.0	32,059	4,016	12.5	1,021,849	83,275
Commercially mixed formula feeds	21,236.2	166.3	1.18	0.8	34,459	3,577	10.4	616,280	46,481
Seeds, bulbs, plants, and trees	5,725.9	727.0	5.18	12.7	6,388	5,102	79.9	896,339	142,494
Commercial fertilizer	9,597.1	1,617.0	11.52	16.8	8,060	8,100	100.5	1,190,733	199,625
Agricultural chemicals	7,581.4	1,539.3	10.97	20.3	8,056	10,789	133.9	941,136	142,668
Petroleum products	6,371.5	964.1	6.87	15.1	3,619	3,812	105.3	1,760,642	252,907
Gasoline and gasohol	1,886.6	264.9	1.89	14.0	1,380	1,384	100.3	1,366,915	191,393
Diesel fuel	2,846.0	480.7	3.42	16.9	2,164	2,495	115.3	1,315,397	192,671
Natural gas	432.9	49.7	0.35	11.5	6,091	5,551	91.1	71,069	8,955
LP gas, fuel oil, kerosene, motor oil, grease, etc.	1,206.1	168.8	1.20	14.0	945	975	103.1	1,276,331	173,184
Electricity	2,751.1	356.7	2.54	13.0	2,247	2,291	101.9	1,224,374	155,747
Hired farm labor	14,841.0	1,855.4	13.22	12.5	22,811	17,678	77.5	650,623	104,956
Contract labor	2,959.0	361.9	2.58	12.2	13,040	9,360	71.8	226,909	38,667
Repair and maintenance	8,637.7	1,207.6	8.60	14.0	5,616	5,730	102.0	1,538,058	210,765
Custom work, machine hire, and rental of equipment	3,210.3	592.8	4.22	18.5	5,372	7,344	136.7	597,624	80,715
Interest	8,928.1	1,062.2	7.57	11.9	11,016	10,196	92.6	810,476	104,183
Secured by real estate	5,449.6	601.4	4.28	11.0	9,564	8,223	86.0	569,775	73,137
Not secured by real estate	3,478.5	460.8	3.28	13.2	7,540	8,204	108.8	461,326	56,172
Cash rent	6,915.7	1,040.2	7.41	15.0	14,244	17,619	123.7	485,512	59,037
Property taxes	3,920.1	475.2	3.39	12.1	2,213	1,921	86.8	1,771,787	247,328
All other farm production expenses	14,777.4	1,590.4	11.33	10.8	8,747	7,051	80.6	1,689,391	225,574

Source: 1997 Census of Agriculture, U.S. Department of Agriculture, National Agricultural Statistics Service. Table shows totals for the U.S. agriculture sector and for the NAICS subdivision of it, shown as "This Agric. Sector" or as "This Sector." Not all farms report on every category. For this reason, the reporting universe is shown in the last two columns. Averages are based on these columns. LP gas stands for "liquid petroleum gas," i.e., butane or propane.

NET CASH RETURN AND FARMS WITH GAINS AND LOSSES

Item	Number of farms and %				Average gain or loss per farm - $		
	U.S.	% of U.S.	This Agriculture Sector	% of Sector	U.S.	This Agriculture Sector	% of U.S.
All farms	1,911,824	100.0	265,749	100.0	22,260	17,733	79.7
Number of farms with net gains	985,718	51.6	154,651	58.2	51,296	35,632	69.5
Gain of -							
Less than $1,000	120,163	6.3	21,188	8.0	-	-	-
$1,000 to $9,999	370,611	19.4	71,439	26.9	-	-	-
$10,000 to $49,999	292,484	15.3	39,806	15.0	-	-	-
$50,000 or more	202,460	10.6	22,218	8.4	-	-	-
Number of farms with net losses	926,106	48.4	111,098	41.8	(8,645)	(7,184)	83.1
Loss of -							
Less than $1,000	165,390	8.7	22,666	8.5	-	-	-
$1,000 to $9,999	591,517	30.9	71,399	26.9	-	-	-
$10,000 to $49,999	152,649	8.0	15,302	5.8	-	-	-
$50,000 or more	16,550	0.9	1,731	0.7	-	-	-

Source: 1997 Census of Agriculture, U.S. Department of Agriculture, National Agricultural Statistics Service. Table shows totals for the U.S. agriculture sector and for the NAICS subdivision of it, shown as "This Agric. Sector" or as "This Sector." Not all farms report on every category. For this reason, the reporting universe is shown in the last two columns. Averages are based on these columns. Net gains are income less cost for farm operations; they exclude non-farm earnings. Values in parentheses are losses.

CHARACTERISTICS OF FARM OPERATORS

Farm Operators	U.S.	This Agric. Sector	% of U.S.	Farm Operators	U.S.	This Agric. Sector	% of U.S.
Place of residence:				By age group:			
On farm operated	1,361,766	191,227	14.0	Under 25 years	20,850	2,901	13.9
Not on farm operated	412,554	57,593	14.0	25 to 34 years	128,455	18,405	14.3
Not reported	137,539	20,497	14.9	35 to 44 years	371,442	51,350	13.8
Principal occupation:				45 to 49 years	232,845	32,950	14.2
Farming	961,560	124,692	13.0	50 to 54 years	233,884	33,402	14.3
Other	950,299	144,625	15.2	55 to 59 years	222,736	31,713	14.2
Days worked off farm:				60 to 64 years	204,618	28,254	13.8
None	755,254	99,332	13.2	65 to 69 years	179,858	24,956	13.9
Any	1,042,158	152,859	14.7	70 years and over	317,171	45,386	14.3
1 to 99 days	164,957	23,347	14.2	Average age	54	54	100.2
100 to 199 days	167,922	25,180	15.0	By sex:			
200 days or more	709,279	104,332	14.7	Male	1,746,757	248,983	14.3
Not reported	114,447	17,126	15.0	Female	165,102	20,334	12.3
Years on present farm:				Spanish, Hispanic/Latino origin	27,717	3,758	13.6
2 years or less	92,574	14,452	15.6	Tenure of operator:			
3 or 4 years	126,791	18,263	14.4	All operators	1,911,859	269,317	14.1
5 to 9 years	263,642	37,049	14.1	Full owners	1,146,891	167,334	14.6
10 years or more	1,113,839	151,923	13.6	Part owners	573,839	76,199	13.3
Ave. years on this farm	20	20	98.5	Tenants	191,129	25,784	13.5
Not reported	315,013	47,630	15.1				

Source: *1997 Census of Agriculture*, U.S. Department of Agriculture, National Agricultural Statistics Service. Table shows totals for the U.S. agriculture sector and for the NAICS subdivision of it, shown as "This Agric. Sector" or as "This Sector." Not all farms report on every category. For this reason, the reporting universe is shown in the last two columns. Averages are based on these columns. All values shown are number of farm operators in each category or percent.

FARMS BY TYPE OF ORGANIZATION

Item	Number of farms and percent				Total acres and percent		
	U.S.	% of U.S.	This Agriculture Sector	% of Sector	U.S.	This Agriculture Sector	% of U.S.
Individual or family (sole proprietorship)	1,643,424	100.0	234,479	100.0	585,464,911	58,826,359	10.0
Partnership	169,462	10.3	24,488	10.4	149,321,484	16,167,485	10.8
Corporation:							
Family held	76,103	4.6	7,779	3.3	119,559,203	9,772,322	8.2
More than 10 stockholders	1,795	0.1	197	0.1	-	-	-
10 or less stockholders	74,308	4.5	7,582	3.2	-	-	-
Other than family held	7,899	0.5	769	0.3	11,904,053	2,222,655	18.7
More than 10 stockholders	1,029	0.1	103	0.0	-	-	-
10 or less stockholders	6,870	0.4	666	0.3	-	-	-
Other cooperative, estate or trust, institutional, etc.	14,971	0.9	1,802	0.8	65,545,604	6,848,039	10.4

Source: *1997 Census of Agriculture*, U.S. Department of Agriculture, National Agricultural Statistics Service. Table shows totals for the U.S. agriculture sector and for the NAICS subdivision of it, shown as "This Agric. Sector" or as "This Sector." Not all farms report on every category. For this reason, the reporting universe is shown in the last two columns. Averages are based on these columns.

LIVESTOCK INVENTORIES AND SALES

Item	U.S. (number)	This Agric. Sector (number)	% of U.S.	Average number per farm			Number of farms reporting category	
				U.S.	This Agric. Sector	% of U.S.	U.S.	This Sector
Cattle and calves inventory	98,989,244	5,005,237	5.1	94.6	54.0	57.2	1,046,863	92,611
Cows and heifers that had calved	43,162,054	2,484,470	5.8	48.3	32.6	67.6	894,110	76,129
Beef cows	34,066,615	2,418,261	7.1	42.3	32.6	77.0	804,595	74,214
Milk cows	9,095,439	66,209	0.7	77.8	18.9	24.3	116,874	3,507
Heifers and heifer calves	26,988,697	1,207,708	4.5	33.6	17.8	53.1	803,985	67,707
Steers, steer calves, bulls, and bull calves	28,838,493	1,313,059	4.6	32.6	17.0	52.2	883,983	77,087
Cattle and calves sold	74,089,046	2,417,477	3.3	73.2	28.9	39.5	1,011,809	83,638
Calves	16,480,293	896,871	5.4	26.8	17.9	66.9	615,177	50,016
Cattle	57,608,753	1,520,606	2.6	78.0	26.8	34.4	738,696	56,700
Fattened on grain and concentrates	27,328,190	231,047	0.8	247.0	30.8	12.5	110,620	7,490
Hogs and pigs inventory	61,206,236	1,373,800	2.2	557.7	153.3	27.5	109,754	8,959
Used or to be used for breeding	6,831,564	151,474	2.2	106.7	31.1	29.2	64,029	4,864
Other	54,374,672	1,222,326	2.2	528.0	146.7	27.8	102,977	8,332
Hogs and pigs sold	142,611,882	2,645,247	1.9	1,396.7	350.7	25.1	102,106	7,542
Feeder pigs	34,988,718	264,885	0.8	2,037.8	243.0	11.9	17,170	1,090
Litters of pigs farrowed between Dec. 1 of preceding year and Nov. 30	11,497,523	229,487	2.0	170.3	44.5	26.1	67,514	5,154
Dec. 1 and May 31	5,697,371	117,960	2.1	91.0	24.9	27.4	62,622	4,740
June 1 and Nov. 30	5,800,152	111,527	1.9	99.7	26.3	26.4	58,204	4,246
Sheep and lambs of all ages inventory	7,821,885	471,628	6.0	118.9	79.0	66.4	65,790	5,971
Ewes 1 year old or older	4,408,683	252,360	5.7	78.1	50.6	64.8	56,414	4,987
Sheep and lambs sold	7,331,545	389,925	5.3	123.1	78.0	63.4	59,575	5,001
Sheep and lambs shorn	6,139,140	334,474	5.4	118.4	73.8	62.3	51,869	4,533
Horses and ponies inventory	2,427,277	221,101	9.1	6.5	5.0	77.6	375,218	44,061
Horses and ponies sold	325,306	11,089	3.4	4.1	2.3	57.3	79,516	4,734
Goats inventory	1,989,799	85,103	4.3	34.4	14.9	43.3	57,925	5,723
Goats sold	740,597	25,418	3.4	31.5	14.7	46.6	23,520	1,732

Source: 1997 Census of Agriculture, U.S. Department of Agriculture, National Agricultural Statistics Service. Table shows totals for the U.S. agriculture sector and for the NAICS subdivision of it, shown as "This Agric. Sector" or as "This Sector." Not all farms report on every category. For this reason, the reporting universe is shown in the last two columns. Averages are based on these columns.

POULTRY INVENTORIES AND SALES

Item	U.S. (number)	This Agric. Sector (number)	% of U.S.	Average number per farm			Number of farms reporting category	
				U.S.	This Agric. Sector	% of U.S.	U.S.	This Sector
Layers and pullets 13 weeks old and older inventory	366,989,851	1,350,529	0.4	5,053.8	177.7	3.5	72,616	7,599
Layers 20 weeks old and older	313,851,480	1,028,658	0.3	4,499.0	139.6	3.1	69,761	7,371
Pullets 13 weeks old and older but less than 20 weeks old	53,138,371	321,871	0.6	4,031.7	270.0	6.7	13,180	1,192
Layers, pullets, and pullet chicks sold	331,563,736	1,803,578	0.5	24,636.9	2,265.8	9.2	13,458	796
Broilers and other meat type chickens sold	6,741,927,110	14,406,019	0.2	281,653.0	25,633.5	9.1	23,937	562
Turkey hens kept for breeding	5,504,808	11,222	0.2	968.1	20.2	2.1	5,686	556
Turkeys sold	307,586,680	1,079,331	0.4	51,000.9	3,573.9	7.0	6,031	302

Source: 1997 Census of Agriculture, U.S. Department of Agriculture, National Agricultural Statistics Service. Table shows totals for the U.S. agriculture sector and for the NAICS subdivision of it, shown as "This Agric. Sector" or as "This Sector." Not all farms report on every category. For this reason, the reporting universe is shown in the last two columns. Averages are based on these columns.

SELECTED CROPS HARVESTED

Item	In 1,000	Crop harvested			Acres used for crop (000)			Number of farms reporting category	
		U.S.	This Agric. Sector	% of U.S.	U.S.	This Agric. Sector	% of U.S.	U.S.	This Sector
Corn for grain or seed	bushels	8,578,635	352,361	4.1	69,796.7	3,215.9	4.6	430,711	36,139
Irrigated		-	-	-	10,638.9	760.6	7.1	40,574	4,918
Corn for silage or green chop	tons, green	88,381	5,651	6.4	5,727.6	321.1	5.6	119,308	7,653
Irrigated		-	-	-	1,033.3	168.4	16.3	10,815	1,619
Sorghum for grain or seed	bushels	559,070	70,350	12.6	8,470.4	1,231.8	14.5	49,397	6,047
Irrigated		-	-	-	875.6	256.2	29.3	5,793	1,701
Wheat for grain	bushels	2,204,027	201,875	9.2	58,836.3	4,570.5	7.8	243,568	27,356
Irrigated		-	-	-	3,990.9	1,025.8	25.7	20,385	5,737
Barley for grain	bushels	336,435	44,025	13.1	5,945.0	614.8	10.3	41,930	5,355
Irrigated		-	-	-	1,060.7	322.8	30.4	8,847	2,723
Oats for grain	bushels	151,327	15,359	10.1	2,681.0	271.8	10.1	89,606	10,441
Irrigated		-	-	-	121.0	31.3	25.9	2,788	730
Rice	cwt	182,231	6,670	3.7	3,122.1	118.3	3.8	9,291	467
Irrigated		-	-	-	3,122.1	118.3	3.8	9,291	467
Cotton	bales	17,879	15,642	87.5	13,235.2	11,636.1	87.9	31,493	25,123
Irrigated		-	-	-	4,888.0	4,285.1	87.7	12,434	9,986
Tobacco	pounds	1,747,702	1,515,840	86.7	838.5	724.9	86.5	89,706	71,531
Irrigated		-	-	-	138.7	126.7	91.4	7,090	6,204
Soybeans for beans	bushels	2,504,307	119,107	4.8	66,147.7	4,025.1	6.1	354,692	25,049
Irrigated		-	-	-	4,152.1	357.0	8.6	20,619	1,827
Dry edible beans, excluding dry limas	cwt	27,224	3,981	14.6	1,691.9	232.9	13.8	10,911	1,728
Irrigated		-	-	-	577.0	98.7	17.1	4,882	1,055
Potatoes, excluding sweetpotatoes	cwt	459,886	51,905	11.3	1,355.2	165.8	12.2	10,523	2,360
Irrigated		-	-	-	1,070.3	126.2	11.8	4,843	1,079
Sugar beets for sugar	tons	29,775	20,178	67.8	1,453.8	962.6	66.2	7,102	4,029
Irrigated		-	-	-	616.4	427.9	69.4	3,492	2,149
Peanuts for nuts	pounds	3,377,143	3,049,816	90.3	1,352.2	1,199.8	88.7	12,221	9,716
Irrigated		-	-	-	412.3	367.0	89.0	3,125	2,618
Hay alfalfa, other tame, small grain, wild, grass silage, green chop	tons, dry	139,365	37,398	26.8	60,799.8	13,287.1	21.9	888,597	201,805
Irrigated		-	-	-	9,564.3	3,709.8	38.8	79,406	27,568
Alfalfa hay	tons, dry	65,863	21,685	32.9	21,309.8	5,497.9	25.8	358,365	77,871
Irrigated		-	-	-	5,980.5	2,848.0	47.6	57,854	22,074
Vegetables harvested for sale		-	-	-	3,773.2	494.9	13.1	53,727	8,673
Irrigated		-	-	-	2,641.8	343.2	13.0	23,203	3,803
Land in orchards		-	-	-	5,158.1	230.1	4.5	106,069	7,739
Irrigated		-	-	-	4,107.9	159.3	3.9	61,606	2,728

Source: 1997 Census of Agriculture, U.S. Department of Agriculture, National Agricultural Statistics Service. Table shows totals for the U.S. agriculture sector and for the NAICS subdivision of it, shown as "This Agric. Sector" or as "This Sector." Not all farms report on every category. For this reason, the reporting universe is shown in the last two columns. Averages are based on these columns. "Green tons" are weight of product as harvested, i.e., moist. cwt stands for "hundredweight."

LEADING COMPANIES   Number shown: **22**   Total sales ($ mil): **1,920**   Total employment (000): **6.3**

Company Name	Address				CEO Name	Phone	Co. Type	Sales ($ mil)	Empl. (000)
A and B Hawaii Inc.	PO Box 3440	Honolulu	HI	96801	W Allen Doane	808-525-6611	S	588	1.2
Busch Agricultural Resources Inc.	10733 Sunset Office	St. Louis	MO	63127	Don Koth	314-909-3800	S	362*	0.6
Delta and Pine Land Co.	1 Cotton Row	Scott	MS	38772	Roger D Malkin	662-742-4500	P	260	0.6
Harris Farms Inc.	Rte 1, Box 426	Coalinga	CA	93210	John C Harris	559-884-2859	R	168*	1.2
Deltic Timber Corp.	PO Box 7200	El Dorado	AR	71731	Robert Nalon	870-881-9400	R	125	0.5
Agrinorthwest	PO Box 2308	Pasco	WA	99302	Don Sleight	509-735-6461	R	80	0.3
Agripro Seeds Inc.	P O Box 2962	Shawnee Msn	KS	66201	Milton Allen	913-384-4940	S	55*	0.3
Sterling Sugars Inc.	PO Box 572	Franklin	LA	70538	Bernard Boudreaux Jr	318-828-0620	P	45	0.2
E. Ritter and Co.	106 Frisco St	Marked Tree	AR	72365	E Ritter Arnold	870-358-2200	R	35	0.2
John Kautz Farms	5490 E Bear Creek	Lodi	CA	95240	John Kautz	209-334-4786	R	35*	0.2
Speedling Inc.	PO Box 7220	Sun City	FL	33586	Berl Thomas	813-645-3221	S	35	0.2
Arends Brothers Inc.	Rte 54 N	Melvin	IL	60952	Kent Arends	217-388-7717	R	20	<0.1
Walter Lasley and Sons Inc.	PO Box 168	Stratford	TX	79084	Walter Lasley	806-753-4411	R	19	<0.1
Wolfsen Inc.	P O Box 311	Los Banos	CA	93635	Donald C Skinner	209-827-7700	R	18*	0.3
Culbro Tobacco	55 Griffin Road S	Bloomfield	CT	06002		860-243-4500	D	16*	0.2
Barenbrug U.S.A. Inc.	P O Box 239	Tangent	OR	97389	Don Herb	541-926-5801	S	15*	<0.1
Pike Creek Turf Sports Group Inc.	Rte 2, Box 376A	Adel	GA	31620	Jaimie Allen	912-896-7581	R	13*	<0.1
Abt Systems	PO Box 12447	Fresno	CA	93777	Doug Elkins	559-233-8823	S	12	<0.1
J.C. Watson Company Inc.	P O Box 300	Parma	ID	83660	Jon C Watson	208-722-5141	R	10*	0.1
Morrison Ventures	P O Box 737	Salina	KS	67402	Roger Morrison	785-827-9331	R	4*	<0.1
Salyer American Corp.	PO Box 488	Corcoran	CA	93212	Fred Salyer	559-992-2131	R	3*	<0.1
Seven J Stock Farm Inc.	99 Travis St	Houston	TX	77060	John R Parten	713-228-8900	P	1*	<0.1

Source: *Ward's Business Directory of U.S. Private and Public Companies*, Volumes 1 and 2, 2000. The company type code used is as follows: P - Public, R - Private, S - Subsidiary, D - Division, J - Joint Venture, A - Affiliate, G - Group, N - Company type not reported. Sales are in millions of dollars, employees are in thousands. An asterisk (*) indicates an estimated sales volume. The symbol < stands for 'less than'. Company names and addresses are truncated, in some cases, to fit into the available space.

NAICS 111910 - TOBACCO FARMING

GENERAL STATISTICS

Item	U.S. Total	This Agri-culture Sector	% of U.S.	Value shown as	Category average per farm			Number of farms reporting category	
					U.S.	This Agric. Sector	% of U.S.	U.S.	This Sector
Farms - number	1,911,859	65,755	3.4	-	-	-	-	-	-
Land in farms - mil. acres	931.795	9.863	1.1	Acres	487	150	30.8	1,911,859	65,755
Value of land, buildings - $ mil.	859,839.2	14,962.9	1.7	$	449,748	226,663	50.4	524,066	66,014
Value of machinery and equip-ment - $ mil.	110,256.8	2,356.0	2.1	$	57,678	35,689	61.9	1,911,601	66,013
Sales of Ag Products - $ mil.	196,864.6	2,876.9	1.5	$	102,970	43,751	42.5	1,911,859	65,755
Government payments - $ mil.	5,054.5	31.9	0.6	$	7,378	2,105	28.5	685,029	15,177
Other farm-related income - $ mil.	3,272.3	52.5	1.6	$	5,999	3,558	59.3	545,480	14,769
Expenses - $ mil.	150,591.0	1,736.2	1.2	$	78,771	26,300	33.4	1,911,766	66,013
Payroll - $ mil.	14,841.0	301.0	2.0	$	22,811	8,188	35.9	650,623	36,764
Workers - 150 days or more a year	890,467	19,535	2.2	Number	3.4	2.4	70.6	259,631	8,072
Workers - less than 150 days	2,461,561	200,230	8.1	Number	4.2	5.6	132.1	581,658	35,820
Net Cash Return - $ mil.	42,557.9	1,007.1	2.4	$	22,260	15,255	68.5	1,911,824	66,014

Source: 1997 Census of Agriculture, U.S. Department of Agriculture, National Agricultural Statistics Service. Table shows totals for the U.S. agriculture sector and for the NAICS subdivision of it, shown as "This Agric. Sector" or as "This Sector." Not all farms report on every category. For this reason, the reporting universe is shown in the last two columns. Averages are based on these columns.

LAND IN FARMS ACCORDING TO USE

Item	U.S. Total (000 acres)	This Sector (000 acres)	% of U.S.	Average acres per farms			Number of farms reporting category	
				U.S.	This Agric. Sector	% of U.S.	U.S.	This Sector
Total cropland	431,144.9	5,701.0	1.3	260	87	-	1,661,395	65,755
Harvested cropland	309,395.5	3,129.9	1.0	219	48	-	1,410,606	65,755
Cropland:								
Pasture or grazing	64,466.5	1,809.2	2.8	85	58	-	754,170	31,120
In cover crops, legumes, grasses	13,531.2	225.4	1.7	88	20	-	153,177	11,311
On which all crops failed	3,449.4	32.9	1.0	67	15	-	51,673	2,143
In cultivated summer fallow	20,905.9	54.6	0.3	256	15	-	81,702	3,529
Idle	19,396.3	448.9	2.3	83	32	-	232,961	14,164
Total woodland	71,465.4	2,973.0	4.2	96	77	-	743,011	38,786
Woodland pastured	29,693.9	710.9	2.4	84	38	-	352,217	18,505
Woodland not pastured	41,771.5	2,262.1	5.4	79	78	-	531,846	28,902
Other pasture/rangeland	396,884.6	650.0	0.2	721	61	-	550,619	10,696
Land for house lots, ponds, roads, wasteland	32,300.4	538.8	1.7	28	13	-	1,142,618	41,812
Irrigated land	55,058.1	145.5	0.3	197	24	-	279,442	6,168
Harvested cropland	50,013.5	141.2	0.3	198	23	-	252,679	6,087
Pasture and other	5,044.7	4.4	0.1	87	19	-	58,258	229
Conservation Reserve/Wetlands Reserve Lands	29,489.1	140.9	0.5	131	39	-	225,410	3,632

Source: 1997 Census of Agriculture, U.S. Department of Agriculture, National Agricultural Statistics Service. Table shows totals for the U.S. agriculture sector and for the NAICS subdivision of it, shown as "This Agric. Sector" or as "This Sector." Not all farms report on every category. For this reason, the reporting universe is shown in the last two columns. Averages are based on these columns. The Conservation Reserve and Wetlands Reserve programs provide support for land conservation/preservation. Cover crops are not harvested or pastured.

MARKET VALUE OF AGRICULTURAL PRODUCTS SOLD: ALL FARMS

Item	U.S. Total ($ mil.)	This Sector ($ mil.)	% of Sector Sales	% of U.S.	Average sales per farm - $			Number of farms reporting category	
					U.S.	This Agric. Sector	% of U.S.	U.S.	This Sector
Grains	46,617.1	224.1	7.79	0.5	79,095	21,517	27.2	589,379	10,413
Corn for grain	18,884.8	78.3	2.72	0.4	52,506	13,562	25.8	359,666	5,775
Wheat	7,173.9	41.5	1.44	0.6	29,726	9,555	32.1	241,334	4,344
Soybeans	15,622.4	102.5	3.56	0.7	44,185	16,293	36.9	353,566	6,292
Sorghum for grain	1,140.0	0.2	0.01	0.0	25,360	3,947	15.6	44,955	57
Barley	709.6	0.2	0.01	0.0	23,191	2,446	10.5	30,598	65
Oats	121.3	0.8	0.03	0.6	3,114	2,976	95.6	38,940	253
Other grains	2,965.1	0.6	0.02	0.0	67,540	3,355	5.0	43,901	172
Cotton and cotton seed	5,975.5	74.1	2.57	1.2	189,963	88,924	46.8	31,456	833
Tobacco	2,924.7	2,292.8	79.70	78.4	32,662	34,877	106.8	89,544	65,739
Hay, silage, and field seeds	4,670.5	27.8	0.97	0.6	13,174	3,016	22.9	354,523	9,207
Vegetables, sweet corn, and melons	8,401.7	17.0	0.59	0.2	156,628	15,871	10.1	53,641	1,068
Fruits and berries	12,660.3	2.2	0.08	0.0	147,259	7,288	4.9	85,973	302
Nursery and greenhouse crops	10,942.8	6.8	0.24	0.1	161,360	13,316	8.3	67,816	510
Other crops	5,863.1	30.8	1.07	0.5	153,907	30,996	20.1	38,095	993
Poultry and poultry products	22,262.6	6.7	0.23	0.0	352,000	21,310	6.1	63,246	316
Dairy products	18,997.3	9.5	0.33	0.0	191,432	37,813	19.8	99,238	251
Cattle and calves	40,524.8	171.6	5.97	0.4	40,052	6,436	16.1	1,011,809	26,669
Hogs and pigs	13,804.8	10.2	0.35	0.1	135,201	12,732	9.4	102,106	798
Sheep, lambs, and wool	682.9	0.4	0.02	0.1	10,913	1,293	11.9	62,579	341
Other livestock	2,536.5	3.0	0.10	0.1	20,506	2,706	13.2	123,695	1,109
Products sold to public directly	13,096.7	5.7	0.20	0.0	377,610	141,925	37.6	34,683	40

Source: 1997 Census of Agriculture, U.S. Department of Agriculture, National Agricultural Statistics Service. Table shows totals for the U.S. agriculture sector and for the NAICS subdivision of it, shown as "This Agric. Sector" or as "This Sector." Not all farms report on every category. For this reason, the reporting universe is shown in the last two columns. Averages are based on these columns. Farms classified in one sector routinely produce categories in other sectors as well. Products sold to the public are sold for direct consumption.

MARKET VALUE OF PRODUCTS SOLD: FARMS WITH SALES OF $50,000 OR MORE

Item	U.S. Total ($ mil.)	This Sector ($ mil.)	% of Sector Sales	% of U.S.	Average sales per farm - $			Number of farms reporting category	
					U.S.	This Agric. Sector	% of U.S.	U.S.	This Sector
Grains	40,973.4	138.8	4.83	0.3	183,623	115,977	63.2	223,138	1,197
Cotton and cotton seed	5,743.9	65.6	2.28	1.1	286,562	153,979	53.7	20,044	426
Tobacco	2,060.2	1,640.0	57.01	79.6	175,907	179,552	102.1	11,712	9,134
Hay, silage, and field seeds	2,781.9	0.9	0.03	0.0	188,959	70,462	37.3	14,722	13
Vegetables, sweet corn, and melons	7,966.8	9.6	0.33	0.1	673,443	108,202	16.1	11,830	89
Fruits and berries	12,072.3	0.9	0.03	0.0	478,927	146,000	30.5	25,207	6
Nursery and greenhouse crops	10,412.0	2.8	0.10	0.0	578,025	111,920	19.4	18,013	25
Other crops	5,586.6	21.1	0.73	0.4	363,758	130,932	36.0	15,358	161
Poultry and poultry products	22,171.7	6.0	0.21	0.0	778,637	149,300	19.2	28,475	40
Dairy products	18,344.3	5.9	0.21	0.0	250,075	107,618	43.0	73,355	55
Cattle and calves	32,358.6	22.4	0.78	0.1	386,685	85,954	22.2	83,682	261
Hogs and pigs	13,096.7	5.7	0.20	0.0	377,610	141,925	37.6	34,683	40
Sheep, lambs, and wool	478.6	-	-	-	278,730	-	-	1,717	-
Other livestock	2,026.6	0.7	0.02	0.0	369,685	119,333	32.3	5,482	6

Source: 1997 Census of Agriculture, U.S. Department of Agriculture, National Agricultural Statistics Service. Table shows totals for the U.S. agriculture sector and for the NAICS subdivision of it, shown as "This Agric. Sector" or as "This Sector." Not all farms report on every category. For this reason, the reporting universe is shown in the last two columns. Averages are based on these columns. Farms classified in one sector routinely produce categories in other sectors as well.

GOVERNMENT PAYMENTS AND OTHER FARM-RELATED INCOME

Item	U.S. Total ($ mil.)	This Sector ($ mil.)	% of Sector Gov/Oth. Income	% of U.S.	Average receipts per farm - $			Number of farms reporting category	
					U.S.	This Agric. Sector	% of U.S.	U.S.	This Sector
Government payments	5,054.5	31.9	37.81	0.6	7,378	2,105	28.5	685,029	15,177
Other farm-related income	3,272.3	52.5	62.19	1.6	5,999	3,558	59.3	545,480	14,769
Custom work and other agricultural services	1,235.1	23.9	28.30	1.9	8,646	5,621	65.0	142,854	4,254
Gross cash rent or share payments	1,207.9	14.6	17.27	1.2	6,867	2,909	42.4	175,901	5,017
Forest products, excluding Christmas trees and maple products	344.3	10.4	12.28	3.0	7,417	7,729	104.2	46,426	1,342
Other farm-related income sources	484.9	3.7	4.34	0.8	1,595	597	37.4	303,908	6,144

Source: 1997 Census of Agriculture, U.S. Department of Agriculture, National Agricultural Statistics Service. Table shows totals for the U.S. agriculture sector and for the NAICS subdivision of it, shown as "This Agric. Sector" or as "This Sector." Not all farms report on every category. For this reason, the reporting universe is shown in the last two columns. Averages are based on these columns. Government payments are agricultural subsidies under various programs.

COMMODITY CREDIT CORPORATION LOANS

Item	U.S. Total ($ mil.)	This Sector ($ mil.)	% of Sector Loan Total	% of U.S.	Average loan value per farm - $			Number of farms reporting category	
					U.S.	This Agric. Sector	% of U.S.	U.S.	This Sector
Total loans	3,034.7	12.9	100.00	0.4	36,419	6,609	18.1	83,328	1,951
Corn	1,333.9	2.6	20.19	0.2	26,419	2,969	11.2	50,489	877
Wheat	415.4	0.9	7.06	0.2	18,093	1,908	10.5	22,961	477
Soybeans	774.0	1.3	10.35	0.2	30,370	5,252	17.3	25,487	254
Sorghum, barley, and oats	54.8	0.0	0.15	0.0	8,603	1,188	13.8	6,375	16
Cotton	191.4	0.5	3.54	0.2	43,275	6,437	14.9	4,422	71
Sunflower seed, flaxseed, safflower, canola, other rapeseed, and mustard seed	17.3	-	-	-	25,159	-	-	686	-
Peanuts, rice, and tobacco	247.9	7.6	58.71	3.1	60,421	11,489	19.0	4,103	659

Source: 1997 Census of Agriculture, U.S. Department of Agriculture, National Agricultural Statistics Service. Table shows totals for the U.S. agriculture sector and for the NAICS subdivision of it, shown as "This Agric. Sector" or as "This Sector." Not all farms report on every category. For this reason, the reporting universe is shown in the last two columns. Averages are based on these columns. The Commodity Credit Corporation provides low interest loans to farmers.

SELECTED MACHINERY AND EQUIPMENT

Item	U.S. Total (number)	This Agric. Sector (number)	% of U.S.	Average number per farm			Number of farms reporting category	
				U.S.	This Agric. Sector	% of U.S.	U.S.	This Sector
Motortrucks, including pickups	3,497,735	104,885	3.0	2.07	1.82	87.6	1,688,303	57,768
Wheel tractors	3,936,014	133,951	3.4	2.31	2.18	94.8	1,707,384	61,310
Less than 40 horsepower (PTO)	1,262,688	62,549	5.0	1.44	1.52	105.6	877,119	41,130
40 horsepower (PTO) or more	2,673,326	71,402	2.7	2.02	1.60	79.1	1,321,084	44,593
40 to 99 horsepower (PTO)	1,808,105	62,008	3.4	1.58	1.46	92.7	1,145,466	42,356
100 horsepower (PTO)	865,221	9,394	1.1	1.68	1.35	80.4	513,773	6,937
Grain and bean combines	460,606	6,069	1.3	1.16	1.12	96.5	395,934	5,407
Cotton pickers and strippers	38,294	738	1.9	1.48	1.20	80.9	25,874	616
Mower conditioners	608,443	18,166	3.0	1.12	1.14	101.6	543,565	15,980
Pickup balers	717,245	24,132	3.4	1.24	1.24	100.2	579,440	19,455

Source: 1997 Census of Agriculture, U.S. Department of Agriculture, National Agricultural Statistics Service. Table shows totals for the U.S. agriculture sector and for the NAICS subdivision of it, shown as "This Agric. Sector" or as "This Sector." Not all farms report on every category. For this reason, the reporting universe is shown in the last two columns. Averages are based on these columns. PTO stands for "power take off."

FARM PRODUCTION EXPENSES

Item	U.S. Total ($ mil.)	This Sector ($ mil.)	% of Sector Total Expense	% of U.S.	Average expense per farm - $			Number of farms reporting category	
					U.S.	This Agric. Sector	% of U.S.	U.S.	This Sector
Total farm production expenses	150,591.0	1,736.2	100.00	1.2	78,771	26,300	33.4	1,911,766	66,013
Livestock and poultry purchased	21,614.6	27.5	1.59	0.1	38,807	2,920	7.5	556,980	9,429
Feed for livestock and poultry	32,760.0	39.6	2.28	0.1	32,059	1,829	5.7	1,021,849	21,668
Commercially mixed formula feeds	21,236.2	20.0	1.15	0.1	34,459	1,856	5.4	616,280	10,759
Seeds, bulbs, plants, and trees	5,725.9	81.8	4.71	1.4	6,388	1,630	25.5	896,339	50,191
Commercial fertilizer	9,597.1	201.8	11.62	2.1	8,060	3,057	37.9	1,190,733	66,005
Agricultural chemicals	7,581.4	120.3	6.93	1.6	8,056	2,497	31.0	941,136	48,193
Petroleum products	6,371.5	161.4	9.30	2.5	3,619	2,497	69.0	1,760,642	64,632
Gasoline and gasohol	1,886.6	45.7	2.63	2.4	1,380	913	66.2	1,366,915	49,992
Diesel fuel	2,846.0	49.1	2.83	1.7	2,164	975	45.1	1,315,397	50,352
Natural gas	432.9	5.7	0.33	1.3	6,091	2,775	45.6	71,069	2,044
LP gas, fuel oil, kerosene, motor oil, grease, etc.	1,206.1	60.9	3.51	5.1	945	1,394	147.5	1,276,331	43,725
Electricity	2,751.1	38.0	2.19	1.4	2,247	991	44.1	1,224,374	38,330
Hired farm labor	14,841.0	301.0	17.34	2.0	22,811	8,188	35.9	650,623	36,764
Contract labor	2,959.0	66.5	3.83	2.2	13,040	5,936	45.5	226,909	11,206
Repair and maintenance	8,637.7	153.5	8.84	1.8	5,616	2,944	52.4	1,538,058	52,160
Custom work, machine hire, and rental of equipment	3,210.3	33.1	1.91	1.0	5,372	1,975	36.8	597,624	16,775
Interest	8,928.1	138.2	7.96	1.5	11,016	5,330	48.4	810,476	25,926
Secured by real estate	5,449.6	95.3	5.49	1.7	9,564	5,063	52.9	569,775	18,831
Not secured by real estate	3,478.5	42.8	2.47	1.2	7,540	3,364	44.6	461,326	12,737
Cash rent	6,915.7	128.4	7.40	1.9	14,244	10,189	71.5	485,512	12,604
Property taxes	3,920.1	55.2	3.18	1.4	2,213	911	41.2	1,771,787	60,620
All other farm production expenses	14,777.4	189.7	10.92	1.3	8,747	3,294	37.7	1,689,391	57,577

Source: 1997 Census of Agriculture, U.S. Department of Agriculture, National Agricultural Statistics Service. Table shows totals for the U.S. agriculture sector and for the NAICS subdivision of it, shown as "This Agric. Sector" or as "This Sector." Not all farms report on every category. For this reason, the reporting universe is shown in the last two columns. Averages are based on these columns. LP gas stands for "liquid petroleum gas," i.e., butane or propane.

NET CASH RETURN AND FARMS WITH GAINS AND LOSSES

Item	Number of farms and %				Average gain or loss per farm - $		
	U.S.	% of U.S.	This Agriculture Sector	% of Sector	U.S.	This Agriculture Sector	% of U.S.
All farms	1,911,824	100.0	66,014	100.0	22,260	15,255	68.5
Number of farms with net gains	985,718	51.6	53,463	81.0	51,296	19,894	38.8
Gain of -							
Less than $1,000	120,163	6.3	4,963	7.5	-	-	-
$1,000 to $9,999	370,611	19.4	28,378	43.0	-	-	-
$10,000 to $49,999	292,484	15.3	15,663	23.7	-	-	-
$50,000 or more	202,460	10.6	4,459	6.8	-	-	-
Number of farms with net losses	926,106	48.4	12,551	19.0	(8,645)	(4,504)	52.1
Loss of -							
Less than $1,000	165,390	8.7	3,360	5.1	-	-	-
$1,000 to $9,999	591,517	30.9	8,037	12.2	-	-	-
$10,000 to $49,999	152,649	8.0	1,074	1.6	-	-	-
$50,000 or more	16,550	0.9	80	0.1	-	-	-

Source: 1997 Census of Agriculture, U.S. Department of Agriculture, National Agricultural Statistics Service. Table shows totals for the U.S. agriculture sector and for the NAICS subdivision of it, shown as "This Agric. Sector" or as "This Sector." Not all farms report on every category. For this reason, the reporting universe is shown in the last two columns. Averages are based on these columns. Net gains are income less cost for farm operations; they exclude non-farm earnings. Values in parentheses are losses.

CHARACTERISTICS OF FARM OPERATORS

Farm Operators	U.S.	This Agric. Sector	% of U.S.	Farm Operators	U.S.	This Agric. Sector	% of U.S.
Place of residence:				By age group:			
On farm operated	1,361,766	45,711	3.4	Under 25 years	20,850	1,060	5.1
Not on farm operated	412,554	14,519	3.5	25 to 34 years	128,455	5,533	4.3
Not reported	137,539	5,525	4.0	35 to 44 years	371,442	12,494	3.4
Principal occupation:				45 to 49 years	232,845	7,777	3.3
Farming	961,560	31,239	3.2	50 to 54 years	233,884	8,012	3.4
Other	950,299	34,516	3.6	55 to 59 years	222,736	7,925	3.6
Days worked off farm:				60 to 64 years	204,618	7,030	3.4
None	755,254	24,432	3.2	65 to 69 years	179,858	5,730	3.2
Any	1,042,158	36,941	3.5	70 years and over	317,171	10,194	3.2
1 to 99 days	164,957	5,565	3.4	Average age	54	53	98.5
100 to 199 days	167,922	6,117	3.6	By sex:			
200 days or more	709,279	25,259	3.6	Male	1,746,757	60,473	3.5
Not reported	114,447	4,382	3.8	Female	165,102	5,282	3.2
Years on present farm:				Spanish, Hispanic/Latino origin	27,717	405	1.5
2 years or less	92,574	3,451	3.7	Tenure of operator:			
3 or 4 years	126,791	3,447	2.7	All operators	1,911,859	65,755	3.4
5 to 9 years	263,642	8,728	3.3	Full owners	1,146,891	39,614	3.5
10 years or more	1,113,839	35,346	3.2	Part owners	573,839	18,932	3.3
Ave. years on this farm	20	20	100.0	Tenants	191,129	7,209	3.8
Not reported	315,013	14,783	4.7				

Source: *1997 Census of Agriculture*, U.S. Department of Agriculture, National Agricultural Statistics Service. Table shows totals for the U.S. agriculture sector and for the NAICS subdivision of it, shown as "This Agric. Sector" or as "This Sector." Not all farms report on every category. For this reason, the reporting universe is shown in the last two columns. Averages are based on these columns. All values shown are number of farm operators in each category or percent.

FARMS BY TYPE OF ORGANIZATION

Item	Number of farms and percent				Total acres and percent		
	U.S.	% of U.S.	This Agriculture Sector	% of Sector	U.S.	This Agriculture Sector	% of U.S.
Individual or family (sole proprietorship)	1,643,424	100.0	57,162	100.0	585,464,911	7,916,756	1.4
Partnership	169,462	10.3	7,700	13.5	149,321,484	1,531,283	1.0
Corporation:							
Family held	76,103	4.6	584	1.0	119,559,203	351,571	0.3
More than 10 stockholders	1,795	0.1	14	0.0	-	-	-
10 or less stockholders	74,308	4.5	570	1.0	-	-	-
Other than family held	7,899	0.5	85	0.1	11,904,053	25,470	0.2
More than 10 stockholders	1,029	0.1	-	-	-	-	-
10 or less stockholders	6,870	0.4	85	0.1	-	-	-
Other cooperative, estate or trust, institutional, etc.	14,971	0.9	224	0.4	65,545,604	37,707	0.1

Source: *1997 Census of Agriculture*, U.S. Department of Agriculture, National Agricultural Statistics Service. Table shows totals for the U.S. agriculture sector and for the NAICS subdivision of it, shown as "This Agric. Sector" or as "This Sector." Not all farms report on every category. For this reason, the reporting universe is shown in the last two columns. Averages are based on these columns.

LIVESTOCK INVENTORIES AND SALES

Item	U.S. (number)	This Agric. Sector (number)	% of U.S.	Average number per farm			Number of farms reporting category	
				U.S.	This Agric. Sector	% of U.S.	U.S.	This Sector
Cattle and calves inventory	98,989,244	1,141,390	1.2	94.6	39.6	41.9	1,046,863	28,793
Cows and heifers that had calved	43,162,054	639,059	1.5	48.3	24.8	51.4	894,110	25,777
Beef cows	34,066,615	629,122	1.8	42.3	24.8	58.5	804,595	25,406
Milk cows	9,095,439	9,937	0.1	77.8	12.3	15.8	116,874	807
Heifers and heifer calves	26,988,697	235,837	0.9	33.6	11.1	33.0	803,985	21,258
Steers, steer calves, bulls, and bull calves	28,838,493	266,494	0.9	32.6	10.9	33.5	883,983	24,360
Cattle and calves sold	74,089,046	489,931	0.7	73.2	18.4	25.1	1,011,809	26,669
Calves	16,480,293	269,052	1.6	26.8	13.7	51.2	615,177	19,629
Cattle	57,608,753	220,879	0.4	78.0	14.4	18.4	738,696	15,384
Fattened on grain and concentrates	27,328,190	9,841	0.0	247.0	11.7	4.7	110,620	844
Hogs and pigs inventory	61,206,236	62,402	0.1	557.7	49.8	8.9	109,754	1,252
Used or to be used for breeding	6,831,564	8,311	0.1	106.7	12.6	11.8	64,029	662
Other	54,374,672	54,091	0.1	528.0	47.2	8.9	102,977	1,146
Hogs and pigs sold	142,611,882	106,078	0.1	1,396.7	132.9	9.5	102,106	798
Feeder pigs	34,988,718	17,831	0.1	2,037.8	141.5	6.9	17,170	126
Litters of pigs farrowed between Dec. 1 of preceding year and Nov. 30	11,497,523	10,465	0.1	170.3	14.8	8.7	67,514	705
Dec. 1 and May 31	5,697,371	5,343	0.1	91.0	8.5	9.4	62,622	625
June 1 and Nov. 30	5,800,152	5,122	0.1	99.7	9.9	9.9	58,204	519
Sheep and lambs of all ages inventory	7,821,885	9,001	0.1	118.9	22.3	18.8	65,790	403
Ewes 1 year old or older	4,408,683	5,545	0.1	78.1	17.4	22.3	56,414	318
Sheep and lambs sold	7,331,545	6,551	0.1	123.1	21.5	17.5	59,575	305
Sheep and lambs shorn	6,139,140	6,978	0.1	118.4	27.8	23.5	51,869	251
Horses and ponies inventory	2,427,277	28,576	1.2	6.5	4.2	64.7	375,218	6,832
Horses and ponies sold	325,306	1,515	0.5	4.1	2.3	56.7	79,516	653
Goats inventory	1,989,799	12,357	0.6	34.4	10.9	31.8	57,925	1,131
Goats sold	740,597	3,416	0.5	31.5	11.3	35.8	23,520	303

Source: 1997 Census of Agriculture, U.S. Department of Agriculture, National Agricultural Statistics Service. Table shows totals for the U.S. agriculture sector and for the NAICS subdivision of it, shown as "This Agric. Sector" or as "This Sector." Not all farms report on every category. For this reason, the reporting universe is shown in the last two columns. Averages are based on these columns.

POULTRY INVENTORIES AND SALES

Item	U.S. (number)	This Agric. Sector (number)	% of U.S.	Average number per farm			Number of farms reporting category	
				U.S.	This Agric. Sector	% of U.S.	U.S.	This Sector
Layers and pullets 13 weeks old and older inventory	366,989,851	384,400	0.1	5,053.8	316.1	6.3	72,616	1,216
Layers 20 weeks old and older	313,851,480	217,647	0.1	4,499.0	187.5	4.2	69,761	1,161
Pullets 13 weeks old and older but less than 20 weeks old	53,138,371	166,753	0.3	4,031.7	744.4	18.5	13,180	224
Layers, pullets, and pullet chicks sold	331,563,736	-	-	24,636.9	-	-	13,458	108
Broilers and other meat type chickens sold	6,741,927,110	-	-	281,653.0	-	-	23,937	36
Turkey hens kept for breeding	5,504,808	-	-	968.1	-	-	5,686	102
Turkeys sold	307,586,680	-	-	51,000.9	-	-	6,031	18

Source: 1997 Census of Agriculture, U.S. Department of Agriculture, National Agricultural Statistics Service. Table shows totals for the U.S. agriculture sector and for the NAICS subdivision of it, shown as "This Agric. Sector" or as "This Sector." Not all farms report on every category. For this reason, the reporting universe is shown in the last two columns. Averages are based on these columns.

SELECTED CROPS HARVESTED

Item	In 1,000	Crop harvested			Acres used for crop (000)			Number of farms reporting category	
		U.S.	This Agric. Sector	% of U.S.	U.S.	This Agric. Sector	% of U.S.	U.S.	This Sector
Corn for grain or seed	bushels	8,578,635	31,184	0.4	69,796.7	383.0	0.5	430,711	8,311
Irrigated		-	-	-	10,638.9	7.6	0.1	40,574	147
Corn for silage or green chop	tons, green	88,381	312	0.4	5,727.6	24.0	0.4	119,308	1,243
Irrigated		-	-	-	1,033.3	0.5	0.0	10,815	15
Sorghum for grain or seed	bushels	559,070	132	0.0	8,470.4	2.8	0.0	49,397	103
Irrigated		-	-	-	875.6	-	-	5,793	3
Wheat for grain	bushels	2,204,027	13,950	0.6	58,836.3	309.2	0.5	243,568	4,557
Irrigated		-	-	-	3,990.9	1.3	0.0	20,385	49
Barley for grain	bushels	336,435	105	0.0	5,945.0	1.8	0.0	41,930	116
Irrigated		-	-	-	1,060.7	0.0	0.0	8,847	3
Oats for grain	bushels	151,327	605	0.4	2,681.0	10.1	0.4	89,606	514
Irrigated		-	-	-	121.0	0.2	0.2	2,788	9
Rice	cwt	182,231	-	-	3,122.1	-	-	9,291	-
Irrigated		-	-	-	3,122.1	-	-	9,291	-
Cotton	bales	17,879	235	1.3	13,235.2	179.2	1.4	31,493	836
Irrigated		-	-	-	4,888.0	2.3	0.0	12,434	28
Tobacco	pounds	1,747,702	1,353,027	77.4	838.5	648.0	77.3	89,706	65,755
Irrigated		-	-	-	138.7	114.0	82.2	7,090	5,712
Soybeans for beans	bushels	2,504,307	16,823	0.7	66,147.7	677.9	1.0	354,692	6,384
Irrigated		-	-	-	4,152.1	2.4	0.1	20,619	61
Dry edible beans, excluding dry limas	cwt	27,224	-	-	1,691.9	-	-	10,911	3
Irrigated		-	-	-	577.0	-	-	4,882	1
Potatoes, excluding sweetpotatoes	cwt	459,886	166	0.0	1,355.2	1.1	0.1	10,523	352
Irrigated		-	-	-	1,070.3	0.0	0.0	4,843	18
Sugar beets for sugar	tons	29,775	-	-	1,453.8	-	-	7,102	-
Irrigated		-	-	-	616.4	-	-	3,492	-
Peanuts for nuts	pounds	3,377,143	70,279	2.1	1,352.2	29.3	2.2	12,221	563
Irrigated		-	-	-	412.3	4.1	1.0	3,125	53
Hay alfalfa, other tame, small grain, wild, grass silage, green chop	tons, dry	139,365	2,101	1.5	60,799.8	1,070.4	1.8	888,597	30,302
Irrigated		-	-	-	9,564.3	2.8	0.0	79,406	173
Alfalfa hay	tons, dry	65,863	257	0.4	21,309.8	102.2	0.5	358,365	6,155
Irrigated		-	-	-	5,980.5	0.3	0.0	57,854	29
Vegetables harvested for sale		-	-	-	3,773.2	13.7	0.4	53,727	1,070
Irrigated		-	-	-	2,641.8	4.6	0.2	23,203	278
Land in orchards		-	-	-	5,158.1	1.9	0.0	106,069	357
Irrigated		-	-	-	4,107.9	0.4	0.0	61,606	25

Source: 1997 Census of Agriculture, U.S. Department of Agriculture, National Agricultural Statistics Service. Table shows totals for the U.S. agriculture sector and for the NAICS subdivision of it, shown as "This Agric. Sector" or as "This Sector." Not all farms report on every category. For this reason, the reporting universe is shown in the last two columns. Averages are based on these columns. "Green tons" are weight of product as harvested, i.e., moist. cwt stands for "hundredweight."

LEADING COMPANIES   Number shown: **2**   Total sales ($ mil): **51**   Total employment (000): **0.4**

Company Name	Address				CEO Name	Phone	Co. Type	Sales ($ mil)	Empl. (000)
Speedling Inc.	PO Box 7220	Sun City	FL	33586	Berl Thomas	813-645-3221	S	35	0.2
Culbro Tobacco	55 Griffin Road S	Bloomfield	CT	06002		860-243-4500	D	16*	0.2

Source: *Ward's Business Directory of U.S. Private and Public Companies*, Volumes 1 and 2, 2000. The company type code used is as follows: P - Public, R - Private, S - Subsidiary, D - Division, J - Joint Venture, A - Affiliate, G - Group, N - Company type not reported. Sales are in millions of dollars, employees are in thousands. An asterisk (*) indicates an estimated sales volume. The symbol < stands for 'less than'. Company names and addresses are truncated, in some cases, to fit into the available space.

NAICS 111920 - COTTON FARMING

GENERAL STATISTICS

Item	U.S. Total	This Agri- culture Sector	% of U.S.	Value shown as	Category average per farm			Number of farms reporting category	
					U.S.	This Agric. Sector	% of U.S.	U.S.	This Sector
Farms - number	1,911,859	18,994	1.0	-	-	-	-	-	-
Land in farms - mil. acres	931.795	20.281	2.2	Acres	487	1,068	219.3	1,911,859	18,994
Value of land, buildings - $ mil.	859,839.2	19,980.0	2.3	$	449,748	1,091,148	242.6	524,066	18,311
Value of machinery and equip- ment - $ mil.	110,256.8	3,360.4	3.0	$	57,678	183,677	318.5	1,911,601	18,295
Sales of Ag Products - $ mil.	196,864.6	5,854.6	3.0	$	102,970	308,235	299.3	1,911,859	18,994
Government payments - $ mil.	5,054.5	284.8	5.6	$	7,378	18,994	257.4	685,029	14,995
Other farm-related income - $ mil.	3,272.3	124.9	3.8	$	5,999	17,668	294.5	545,480	7,067
Expenses - $ mil.	150,591.0	4,233.1	2.8	$	78,771	231,181	293.5	1,911,766	18,311
Payroll - $ mil.	14,841.0	521.1	3.5	$	22,811	39,990	175.3	650,623	13,030
Workers - 150 days or more a year	890,467	29,486	3.3	Number	3.4	3.3	96.1	259,631	8,949
Workers - less than 150 days	2,461,561	56,750	2.3	Number	4.2	5.3	124.9	581,658	10,735
Net Cash Return - $ mil.	42,557.9	1,460.4	3.4	$	22,260	79,754	358.3	1,911,824	18,311

Source: *1997 Census of Agriculture*, U.S. Department of Agriculture, National Agricultural Statistics Service. Table shows totals for the U.S. agriculture sector and for the NAICS subdivision of it, shown as "This Agric. Sector" or as "This Sector." Not all farms report on every category. For this reason, the reporting universe is shown in the last two columns. Averages are based on these columns.

LAND IN FARMS ACCORDING TO USE

Item	U.S. Total (000 acres)	This Sector (000 acres)	% of U.S.	Average acres per farms			Number of farms reporting category	
				U.S.	This Agric. Sector	% of U.S.	U.S.	This Sector
Total cropland	431,144.9	17,083.4	4.0	260	899	-	1,661,395	18,994
Harvested cropland	309,395.5	14,789.5	4.8	219	779	-	1,410,606	18,994
Cropland:								
Pasture or grazing	64,466.5	530.1	0.8	85	153	-	754,170	3,466
In cover crops, legumes, grasses	13,531.2	387.1	2.9	88	174	-	153,177	2,231
On which all crops failed	3,449.4	157.8	4.6	67	117	-	51,673	1,343
In cultivated summer fallow	20,905.9	247.3	1.2	256	170	-	81,702	1,455
Idle	19,396.3	971.6	5.0	83	192	-	232,961	5,049
Total woodland	71,465.4	1,007.7	1.4	96	246	-	743,011	4,103
Woodland pastured	29,693.9	145.3	0.5	84	137	-	352,217	1,064
Woodland not pastured	41,771.5	862.3	2.1	79	244	-	531,846	3,528
Other pasture/rangeland	396,884.6	1,650.7	0.4	721	491	-	550,619	3,364
Land for house lots, ponds, roads, wasteland	32,300.4	539.1	1.7	28	61	-	1,142,618	8,867
Irrigated land	55,058.1	5,257.9	9.5	197	611	-	279,442	8,601
Harvested cropland	50,013.5	5,236.9	10.5	198	610	-	252,679	8,582
Pasture and other	5,044.7	20.9	0.4	87	81	-	58,258	257
Conservation Reserve/Wetlands Reserve Lands	29,489.1	539.3	1.8	131	187	-	225,410	2,886

Source: *1997 Census of Agriculture*, U.S. Department of Agriculture, National Agricultural Statistics Service. Table shows totals for the U.S. agriculture sector and for the NAICS subdivision of it, shown as "This Agric. Sector" or as "This Sector." Not all farms report on every category. For this reason, the reporting universe is shown in the last two columns. Averages are based on these columns. The Conservation Reserve and Wetlands Reserve programs provide support for land conservation/preservation. Cover crops are not harvested or pastured.

MARKET VALUE OF AGRICULTURAL PRODUCTS SOLD: ALL FARMS

Item	U.S. Total ($ mil.)	This Sector ($ mil.)	% of Sector Sales	% of U.S.	Average sales per farm - $			Number of farms reporting category	
					U.S.	This Agric. Sector	% of U.S.	U.S.	This Sector
Grains	46,617.1	825.4	14.10	1.8	79,095	78,318	99.0	589,379	10,539
Corn for grain	18,884.8	202.5	3.46	1.1	52,506	62,668	119.4	359,666	3,232
Wheat	7,173.9	130.7	2.23	1.8	29,726	30,147	101.4	241,334	4,334
Soybeans	15,622.4	305.5	5.22	2.0	44,185	62,225	140.8	353,566	4,910
Sorghum for grain	1,140.0	109.1	1.86	9.6	25,360	35,852	141.4	44,955	3,044
Barley	709.6	15.1	0.26	2.1	23,191	64,132	276.5	30,598	235
Oats	121.3	1.1	0.02	0.9	3,114	8,758	281.2	38,940	124
Other grains	2,965.1	61.4	1.05	2.1	67,540	75,309	111.5	43,901	815
Cotton and cotton seed	5,975.5	4,452.9	76.06	74.5	189,963	234,511	123.5	31,456	18,988
Tobacco	2,924.7	40.9	0.70	1.4	32,662	102,624	314.2	89,544	399
Hay, silage, and field seeds	4,670.5	131.1	2.24	2.8	13,174	72,780	552.5	354,523	1,802
Vegetables, sweet corn, and melons	8,401.7	100.1	1.71	1.2	156,628	151,396	96.7	53,641	661
Fruits and berries	12,660.3	27.9	0.48	0.2	147,259	68,115	46.3	85,973	410
Nursery and greenhouse crops	10,942.8	1.4	0.02	0.0	161,360	44,688	27.7	67,816	32
Other crops	5,863.1	193.7	3.31	3.3	153,907	75,194	48.9	38,095	2,576
Poultry and poultry products	22,262.6	1.3	0.02	0.0	352,000	49,852	14.2	63,246	27
Dairy products	18,997.3	0.8	0.01	0.0	191,432	57,786	30.2	99,238	14
Cattle and calves	40,524.8	65.5	1.12	0.2	40,052	17,515	43.7	1,011,809	3,738
Hogs and pigs	13,804.8	8.8	0.15	0.1	135,201	36,667	27.1	102,106	240
Sheep, lambs, and wool	682.9	1.9	0.03	0.3	10,913	16,786	153.8	62,579	112
Other livestock	2,536.5	2.8	0.05	0.1	20,506	15,659	76.4	123,695	179
Products sold to public directly	13,096.7	7.0	0.12	0.1	377,610	194,639	51.5	34,683	36

Source: *1997 Census of Agriculture*, U.S. Department of Agriculture, National Agricultural Statistics Service. Table shows totals for the U.S. agriculture sector and for the NAICS subdivision of it, shown as "This Agric. Sector" or as "This Sector." Not all farms report on every category. For this reason, the reporting universe is shown in the last two columns. Averages are based on these columns. Farms classified in one sector routinely produce categories in other sectors as well. Products sold to the public are sold for direct consumption.

MARKET VALUE OF PRODUCTS SOLD: FARMS WITH SALES OF $50,000 OR MORE

Item	U.S. Total ($ mil.)	This Sector ($ mil.)	% of Sector Sales	% of U.S.	Average sales per farm - $			Number of farms reporting category	
					U.S.	This Agric. Sector	% of U.S.	U.S.	This Sector
Grains	40,973.4	718.6	12.27	1.8	183,623	173,964	94.7	223,138	4,131
Cotton and cotton seed	5,743.9	4,335.0	74.04	75.5	286,562	322,687	112.6	20,044	13,434
Tobacco	2,060.2	37.3	0.64	1.8	175,907	179,990	102.3	11,712	207
Hay, silage, and field seeds	2,781.9	120.2	2.05	4.3	188,959	245,249	129.8	14,722	490
Vegetables, sweet corn, and melons	7,966.8	94.0	1.61	1.2	673,443	308,233	45.8	11,830	305
Fruits and berries	12,072.3	25.3	0.43	0.2	478,927	241,305	50.4	25,207	105
Nursery and greenhouse crops	10,412.0	1.2	0.02	0.0	578,025	231,400	40.0	18,013	5
Other crops	5,586.6	167.6	2.86	3.0	363,758	144,070	39.6	15,358	1,163
Poultry and poultry products	22,171.7	1.3	0.02	0.0	778,637	422,667	54.3	28,475	3
Dairy products	18,344.3	0.7	0.01	0.0	250,075	87,750	35.1	73,355	8
Cattle and calves	32,358.6	27.6	0.47	0.1	386,685	106,486	27.5	83,682	259
Hogs and pigs	13,096.7	7.0	0.12	0.1	377,610	194,639	51.5	34,683	36
Sheep, lambs, and wool	478.6	1.1	0.02	0.2	278,730	120,000	43.1	1,717	9
Other livestock	2,026.6	2.0	0.03	0.1	369,685	170,667	46.2	5,482	12

Source: *1997 Census of Agriculture*, U.S. Department of Agriculture, National Agricultural Statistics Service. Table shows totals for the U.S. agriculture sector and for the NAICS subdivision of it, shown as "This Agric. Sector" or as "This Sector." Not all farms report on every category. For this reason, the reporting universe is shown in the last two columns. Averages are based on these columns. Farms classified in one sector routinely produce categories in other sectors as well.

GOVERNMENT PAYMENTS AND OTHER FARM-RELATED INCOME

Item	U.S. Total ($ mil.)	This Sector ($ mil.)	% of Sector Gov/Oth. Income	% of U.S.	Average receipts per farm - $			Number of farms reporting category	
					U.S.	This Agric. Sector	% of U.S.	U.S.	This Sector
Government payments	5,054.5	284.8	69.52	5.6	7,378	18,994	257.4	685,029	14,995
Other farm-related income	3,272.3	124.9	30.48	3.8	5,999	17,668	294.5	545,480	7,067
Custom work and other agricul- tural services	1,235.1	50.1	12.23	4.1	8,646	22,124	255.9	142,854	2,265
Gross cash rent or share payments	1,207.9	24.3	5.93	2.0	6,867	14,183	206.5	175,901	1,712
Forest products, excluding Christ- mas trees and maple products	344.3	5.5	1.33	1.6	7,417	21,174	285.5	46,426	258
Other farm-related income sources	484.9	45.0	10.99	9.3	1,595	9,202	576.8	303,908	4,891

Source: 1997 Census of Agriculture, U.S. Department of Agriculture, National Agricultural Statistics Service. Table shows totals for the U.S. agriculture sector and for the NAICS subdivision of it, shown as "This Agric. Sector" or as "This Sector." Not all farms report on every category. For this reason, the reporting universe is shown in the last two columns. Averages are based on these columns. Government payments are agricultural subsidies under various programs.

COMMODITY CREDIT CORPORATION LOANS

Item	U.S. Total ($ mil.)	This Sector ($ mil.)	% of Sector Loan Total	% of U.S.	Average loan value per farm - $			Number of farms reporting category	
					U.S.	This Agric. Sector	% of U.S.	U.S.	This Sector
Total loans	3,034.7	169.9	100.00	5.6	36,419	52,165	143.2	83,328	3,257
Corn	1,333.9	3.9	2.32	0.3	26,419	13,311	50.4	50,489	296
Wheat	415.4	2.1	1.25	0.5	18,093	5,185	28.7	22,961	410
Soybeans	774.0	1.8	1.08	0.2	30,370	8,738	28.8	25,487	210
Sorghum, barley, and oats	54.8	1.9	1.12	3.5	8,603	6,622	77.0	6,375	288
Cotton	191.4	154.9	91.15	80.9	43,275	51,077	118.0	4,422	3,032
Sunflower seed, flaxseed, saf- flower, canola, other rapeseed, and mustard seed	17.3	-	-	-	25,159	-	-	686	-
Peanuts, rice, and tobacco	247.9	5.2	3.08	2.1	60,421	37,619	62.3	4,103	139

Source: 1997 Census of Agriculture, U.S. Department of Agriculture, National Agricultural Statistics Service. Table shows totals for the U.S. agriculture sector and for the NAICS subdivision of it, shown as "This Agric. Sector" or as "This Sector." Not all farms report on every category. For this reason, the reporting universe is shown in the last two columns. Averages are based on these columns. The Commodity Credit Corporation provides low interest loans to farmers.

SELECTED MACHINERY AND EQUIPMENT

Item	U.S. Total (number)	This Agric. Sector (number)	% of U.S.	Average number per farm			Number of farms reporting category	
				U.S.	This Agric. Sector	% of U.S.	U.S.	This Sector
Motortrucks, including pickups	3,497,735	52,537	1.5	2.07	3.01	145.4	1,688,303	17,443
Wheel tractors	3,936,014	53,125	1.3	2.31	3.20	138.8	1,707,384	16,604
Less than 40 horsepower (PTO)	1,262,688	6,399	0.5	1.44	1.58	109.5	877,119	4,061
40 horsepower (PTO) or more	2,673,326	46,726	1.7	2.02	3.00	148.3	1,321,084	15,567
40 to 99 horsepower (PTO)	1,808,105	16,062	0.9	1.58	1.90	120.3	1,145,466	8,459
100 horsepower (PTO)	865,221	30,664	3.5	1.68	2.59	153.5	513,773	11,861
Grain and bean combines	460,606	6,037	1.3	1.16	1.19	102.5	395,934	5,061
Cotton pickers and strippers	38,294	23,991	62.6	1.48	1.52	102.7	25,874	15,790
Mower conditioners	608,443	2,604	0.4	1.12	1.17	104.7	543,565	2,221
Pickup balers	717,245	2,002	0.3	1.24	1.31	105.7	579,440	1,530

Source: 1997 Census of Agriculture, U.S. Department of Agriculture, National Agricultural Statistics Service. Table shows totals for the U.S. agriculture sector and for the NAICS subdivision of it, shown as "This Agric. Sector" or as "This Sector." Not all farms report on every category. For this reason, the reporting universe is shown in the last two columns. Averages are based on these columns. PTO stands for "power take off."

FARM PRODUCTION EXPENSES

Item	U.S. Total ($ mil.)	This Sector ($ mil.)	% of Sector Total Expense	% of U.S.	Average expense per farm - $			Number of farms reporting category	
					U.S.	This Agric. Sector	% of U.S.	U.S.	This Sector
Total farm production expenses	150,591.0	4,233.1	100.00	2.8	78,771	231,181	293.5	1,911,766	18,311
Livestock and poultry purchased	21,614.6	14.9	0.35	0.1	38,807	8,938	23.0	556,980	1,668
Feed for livestock and poultry	32,760.0	15.1	0.36	0.0	32,059	4,739	14.8	1,021,849	3,182
Commercially mixed formula feeds	21,236.2	6.4	0.15	0.0	34,459	3,629	10.5	616,280	1,763
Seeds, bulbs, plants, and trees	5,725.9	226.7	5.35	4.0	6,388	12,432	194.6	896,339	18,234
Commercial fertilizer	9,597.1	501.5	11.85	5.2	8,060	29,818	370.0	1,190,733	16,820
Agricultural chemicals	7,581.4	748.9	17.69	9.9	8,056	43,997	546.2	941,136	17,021
Petroleum products	6,371.5	294.4	6.95	4.6	3,619	16,258	449.3	1,760,642	18,108
Gasoline and gasohol	1,886.6	62.5	1.48	3.3	1,380	4,561	330.5	1,366,915	13,702
Diesel fuel	2,846.0	173.5	4.10	6.1	2,164	10,207	471.8	1,315,397	17,000
Natural gas	432.9	22.1	0.52	5.1	6,091	9,404	154.4	71,069	2,350
LP gas, fuel oil, kerosene, motor oil, grease, etc.	1,206.1	36.3	0.86	3.0	945	2,164	229.0	1,276,331	16,773
Electricity	2,751.1	96.3	2.28	3.5	2,247	6,747	300.3	1,224,374	14,280
Hired farm labor	14,841.0	521.1	12.31	3.5	22,811	39,990	175.3	650,623	13,030
Contract labor	2,959.0	98.3	2.32	3.3	13,040	15,731	120.6	226,909	6,246
Repair and maintenance	8,637.7	334.7	7.91	3.9	5,616	20,317	361.8	1,538,058	16,475
Custom work, machine hire, and rental of equipment	3,210.3	228.9	5.41	7.1	5,372	21,909	407.9	597,624	10,448
Interest	8,928.1	269.7	6.37	3.0	11,016	20,804	188.9	810,476	12,965
Secured by real estate	5,449.6	115.9	2.74	2.1	9,564	17,264	180.5	569,775	6,711
Not secured by real estate	3,478.5	153.9	3.63	4.4	7,540	15,994	212.1	461,326	9,620
Cash rent	6,915.7	323.8	7.65	4.7	14,244	36,040	253.0	485,512	8,985
Property taxes	3,920.1	64.0	1.51	1.6	2,213	4,190	189.4	1,771,787	15,287
All other farm production expenses	14,777.4	494.8	11.69	3.3	8,747	27,605	315.6	1,689,391	17,924

Source: 1997 Census of Agriculture, U.S. Department of Agriculture, National Agricultural Statistics Service. Table shows totals for the U.S. agriculture sector and for the NAICS subdivision of it, shown as "This Agric. Sector" or as "This Sector." Not all farms report on every category. For this reason, the reporting universe is shown in the last two columns. Averages are based on these columns. LP gas stands for "liquid petroleum gas," i.e., butane or propane.

NET CASH RETURN AND FARMS WITH GAINS AND LOSSES

Item	Number of farms and %				Average gain or loss per farm - $		
	U.S.	% of U.S.	This Agriculture Sector	% of Sector	U.S.	This Agriculture Sector	% of U.S.
All farms	1,911,824	100.0	18,311	100.0	22,260	79,754	358.3
Number of farms with net gains	985,718	51.6	14,551	79.5	51,296	109,323	213.1
Gain of -							
Less than $1,000	120,163	6.3	381	2.1	-	-	-
$1,000 to $9,999	370,611	19.4	2,399	13.1	-	-	-
$10,000 to $49,999	292,484	15.3	4,667	25.5	-	-	-
$50,000 or more	202,460	10.6	7,104	38.8	-	-	-
Number of farms with net losses	926,106	48.4	3,760	20.5	(8,645)	(34,675)	401.1
Loss of -							
Less than $1,000	165,390	8.7	288	1.6	-	-	-
$1,000 to $9,999	591,517	30.9	1,406	7.7	-	-	-
$10,000 to $49,999	152,649	8.0	1,429	7.8	-	-	-
$50,000 or more	16,550	0.9	637	3.5	-	-	-

Source: 1997 Census of Agriculture, U.S. Department of Agriculture, National Agricultural Statistics Service. Table shows totals for the U.S. agriculture sector and for the NAICS subdivision of it, shown as "This Agric. Sector" or as "This Sector." Not all farms report on every category. For this reason, the reporting universe is shown in the last two columns. Averages are based on these columns. Net gains are income less cost for farm operations; they exclude non-farm earnings. Values in parentheses are losses.

CHARACTERISTICS OF FARM OPERATORS

Farm Operators	U.S.	This Agric. Sector	% of U.S.	Farm Operators	U.S.	This Agric. Sector	% of U.S.
Place of residence:				By age group:			
On farm operated	1,361,766	9,274	0.7	Under 25 years	20,850	361	1.7
Not on farm operated	412,554	7,061	1.7	25 to 34 years	128,455	1,858	1.4
Not reported	137,539	2,659	1.9	35 to 44 years	371,442	4,237	1.1
Principal occupation:				45 to 49 years	232,845	2,371	1.0
Farming	961,560	15,589	1.6	50 to 54 years	233,884	2,110	0.9
Other	950,299	3,405	0.4	55 to 59 years	222,736	2,205	1.0
Days worked off farm:				60 to 64 years	204,618	2,068	1.0
None	755,254	11,020	1.5	65 to 69 years	179,858	1,555	0.9
Any	1,042,158	5,472	0.5	70 years and over	317,171	2,229	0.7
1 to 99 days	164,957	1,621	1.0	Average age	54	52	95.0
100 to 199 days	167,922	994	0.6	By sex:			
200 days or more	709,279	2,857	0.4	Male	1,746,757	18,247	1.0
Not reported	114,447	2,502	2.2	Female	165,102	747	0.5
Years on present farm:				Spanish, Hispanic/Latino origin	27,717	524	1.9
2 years or less	92,574	962	1.0	Tenure of operator:			
3 or 4 years	126,791	913	0.7	All operators	1,911,859	18,994	1.0
5 to 9 years	263,642	2,070	0.8	Full owners	1,146,891	5,022	0.4
10 years or more	1,113,839	10,927	1.0	Part owners	573,839	8,869	1.5
Ave. years on this farm	20	21	104.5	Tenants	191,129	5,103	2.7
Not reported	315,013	4,122	1.3				

Source: *1997 Census of Agriculture*, U.S. Department of Agriculture, National Agricultural Statistics Service. Table shows totals for the U.S. agriculture sector and for the NAICS subdivision of it, shown as "This Agric. Sector" or as "This Sector." Not all farms report on every category. For this reason, the reporting universe is shown in the last two columns. Averages are based on these columns. All values shown are number of farm operators in each category or percent.

FARMS BY TYPE OF ORGANIZATION

Item	Number of farms and percent				Total acres and percent		
	U.S.	% of U.S.	This Agriculture Sector	% of Sector	U.S.	This Agriculture Sector	% of U.S.
Individual or family (sole proprietorship)	1,643,424	100.0	13,632	100.0	585,464,911	11,626,150	2.0
Partnership	169,462	10.3	3,450	25.3	149,321,484	5,910,484	4.0
Corporation:							
Family held	76,103	4.6	1,671	12.3	119,559,203	2,376,860	2.0
More than 10 stockholders	1,795	0.1	24	0.2	-	-	-
10 or less stockholders	74,308	4.5	1,647	12.1	-	-	-
Other than family held	7,899	0.5	110	0.8	11,904,053	172,432	1.4
More than 10 stockholders	1,029	0.1	11	0.1	-	-	-
10 or less stockholders	6,870	0.4	99	0.7	-	-	-
Other cooperative, estate or trust, institutional, etc.	14,971	0.9	131	1.0	65,545,604	195,045	0.3

Source: *1997 Census of Agriculture*, U.S. Department of Agriculture, National Agricultural Statistics Service. Table shows totals for the U.S. agriculture sector and for the NAICS subdivision of it, shown as "This Agric. Sector" or as "This Sector." Not all farms report on every category. For this reason, the reporting universe is shown in the last two columns. Averages are based on these columns.

LIVESTOCK INVENTORIES AND SALES

Item	U.S. (number)	This Agric. Sector (number)	% of U.S.	Average number per farm			Number of farms reporting category	
				U.S.	This Agric. Sector	% of U.S.	U.S.	This Sector
Cattle and calves inventory	98,989,244	348,092	0.4	94.6	90.8	96.0	1,046,863	3,835
Cows and heifers that had calved	43,162,054	181,936	0.4	48.3	53.3	110.5	894,110	3,411
Beef cows	34,066,615	181,346	0.5	42.3	53.4	126.2	804,595	3,393
Milk cows	9,095,439	590	0.0	77.8	11.6	14.9	116,874	51
Heifers and heifer calves	26,988,697	73,745	0.3	33.6	24.9	74.0	803,985	2,967
Steers, steer calves, bulls, and bull calves	28,838,493	92,411	0.3	32.6	27.0	82.8	883,983	3,421
Cattle and calves sold	74,089,046	166,522	0.2	73.2	44.5	60.8	1,011,809	3,738
Calves	16,480,293	73,859	0.4	26.8	31.0	115.9	615,177	2,379
Cattle	57,608,753	92,663	0.2	78.0	38.7	49.6	738,696	2,397
Fattened on grain and concentrates	27,328,190	2,086	0.0	247.0	25.8	10.4	110,620	81
Hogs and pigs inventory	61,206,236	56,418	0.1	557.7	204.4	36.7	109,754	276
Used or to be used for breeding	6,831,564	7,264	0.1	106.7	45.4	42.6	64,029	160
Other	54,374,672	49,154	0.1	528.0	186.9	35.4	102,977	263
Hogs and pigs sold	142,611,882	89,728	0.1	1,396.7	373.9	26.8	102,106	240
Feeder pigs	34,988,718	5,697	0.0	2,037.8	183.8	9.0	17,170	31
Litters of pigs farrowed between Dec. 1 of preceding year and Nov. 30	11,497,523	10,147	0.1	170.3	61.5	36.1	67,514	165
Dec. 1 and May 31	5,697,371	5,039	0.1	91.0	34.5	37.9	62,622	146
June 1 and Nov. 30	5,800,152	5,108	0.1	99.7	36.0	36.1	58,204	142
Sheep and lambs of all ages inventory	7,821,885	27,154	0.3	118.9	222.6	187.2	65,790	122
Ewes 1 year old or older	4,408,683	14,678	0.3	78.1	161.3	206.4	56,414	91
Sheep and lambs sold	7,331,545	21,501	0.3	123.1	192.0	156.0	59,575	112
Sheep and lambs shorn	6,139,140	20,325	0.3	118.4	236.3	199.7	51,869	86
Horses and ponies inventory	2,427,277	4,077	0.2	6.5	4.3	66.9	375,218	942
Horses and ponies sold	325,306	247	0.1	4.1	3.5	86.3	79,516	70
Goats inventory	1,989,799	12,706	0.6	34.4	66.2	192.6	57,925	192
Goats sold	740,597	2,050	0.3	31.5	29.7	94.4	23,520	69

Source: 1997 Census of Agriculture, U.S. Department of Agriculture, National Agricultural Statistics Service. Table shows totals for the U.S. agriculture sector and for the NAICS subdivision of it, shown as "This Agric. Sector" or as "This Sector." Not all farms report on every category. For this reason, the reporting universe is shown in the last two columns. Averages are based on these columns.

POULTRY INVENTORIES AND SALES

Item	U.S. (number)	This Agric. Sector (number)	% of U.S.	Average number per farm			Number of farms reporting category	
				U.S.	This Agric. Sector	% of U.S.	U.S.	This Sector
Layers and pullets 13 weeks old and older inventory	366,989,851	1,740	0.0	5,053.8	17.6	0.3	72,616	99
Layers 20 weeks old and older	313,851,480	1,524	0.0	4,499.0	16.4	0.4	69,761	93
Pullets 13 weeks old and older but less than 20 weeks old	53,138,371	216	0.0	4,031.7	12.7	0.3	13,180	17
Layers, pullets, and pullet chicks sold	331,563,736	-	-	24,636.9	-	-	13,458	1
Broilers and other meat type chickens sold	6,741,927,110	-	-	281,653.0	-	-	23,937	6
Turkey hens kept for breeding	5,504,808	-	-	968.1	-	-	5,686	8
Turkeys sold	307,586,680	-	-	51,000.9	-	-	6,031	2

Source: 1997 Census of Agriculture, U.S. Department of Agriculture, National Agricultural Statistics Service. Table shows totals for the U.S. agriculture sector and for the NAICS subdivision of it, shown as "This Agric. Sector" or as "This Sector." Not all farms report on every category. For this reason, the reporting universe is shown in the last two columns. Averages are based on these columns.

SELECTED CROPS HARVESTED

Item	In 1,000	Crop harvested			Acres used for crop (000)			Number of farms reporting category	
		U.S.	This Agric. Sector	% of U.S.	U.S.	This Agric. Sector	% of U.S.	U.S.	This Sector
Corn for grain or seed	bushels	8,578,635	78,062	0.9	69,796.7	663.9	1.0	430,711	3,390
Irrigated		-	-	-	10,638.9	257.2	2.4	40,574	1,333
Corn for silage or green chop	tons, green	88,381	939	1.1	5,727.6	42.3	0.7	119,308	313
Irrigated		-	-	-	1,033.3	35.7	3.5	10,815	244
Sorghum for grain or seed	bushels	559,070	48,175	8.6	8,470.4	854.4	10.1	49,397	3,108
Irrigated		-	-	-	875.6	167.9	19.2	5,793	1,094
Wheat for grain	bushels	2,204,027	37,017	1.7	58,836.3	953.5	1.6	243,568	4,360
Irrigated		-	-	-	3,990.9	235.0	5.9	20,385	1,161
Barley for grain	bushels	336,435	4,946	1.5	5,945.0	58.1	1.0	41,930	236
Irrigated		-	-	-	1,060.7	57.4	5.4	8,847	226
Oats for grain	bushels	151,327	716	0.5	2,681.0	13.6	0.5	89,606	206
Irrigated		-	-	-	121.0	2.6	2.1	2,788	32
Rice	cwt	182,231	4,714	2.6	3,122.1	85.4	2.7	9,291	372
Irrigated		-	-	-	3,122.1	85.4	2.7	9,291	372
Cotton	bales	17,879	13,305	74.4	13,235.2	9,941.1	75.1	31,493	18,994
Irrigated		-	-	-	4,888.0	3,740.5	76.5	12,434	8,098
Tobacco	pounds	1,747,702	25,693	1.5	838.5	12.3	1.5	89,706	400
Irrigated		-	-	-	138.7	2.2	1.6	7,090	72
Soybeans for beans	bushels	2,504,307	47,641	1.9	66,147.7	1,669.8	2.5	354,692	4,921
Irrigated		-	-	-	4,152.1	297.4	7.2	20,619	1,212
Dry edible beans, excluding dry limas	cwt	27,224	-	-	1,691.9	-	-	10,911	55
Irrigated		-	-	-	577.0	-	-	4,882	45
Potatoes, excluding sweetpotatoes	cwt	459,886	265	0.1	1,355.2	1.3	0.1	10,523	22
Irrigated		-	-	-	1,070.3	1.1	0.1	4,843	14
Sugar beets for sugar	tons	29,775	288	1.0	1,453.8	10.8	0.7	7,102	72
Irrigated		-	-	-	616.4	10.8	1.8	3,492	71
Peanuts for nuts	pounds	3,377,143	725,816	21.5	1,352.2	281.3	20.8	12,221	2,432
Irrigated		-	-	-	412.3	88.3	21.4	3,125	717
Hay alfalfa, other tame, small grain, wild, grass silage, green chop	tons, dry	139,365	1,256	0.9	60,799.8	309.1	0.5	888,597	3,230
Irrigated		-	-	-	9,564.3	158.4	1.7	79,406	915
Alfalfa hay	tons, dry	65,863	840	1.3	21,309.8	121.9	0.6	358,365	773
Irrigated		-	-	-	5,980.5	116.5	1.9	57,854	657
Vegetables harvested for sale		-	-	-	3,773.2	63.3	1.7	53,727	665
Irrigated		-	-	-	2,641.8	53.4	2.0	23,203	429
Land in orchards		-	-	-	5,158.1	33.7	0.7	106,069	627
Irrigated		-	-	-	4,107.9	23.8	0.6	61,606	284

Source: *1997 Census of Agriculture*, U.S. Department of Agriculture, National Agricultural Statistics Service. Table shows totals for the U.S. agriculture sector and for the NAICS subdivision of it, shown as "This Agric. Sector" or as "This Sector." Not all farms report on every category. For this reason, the reporting universe is shown in the last two columns. Averages are based on these columns. "Green tons" are weight of product as harvested, i.e., moist. cwt stands for "hundredweight."

LEADING COMPANIES   Number shown: **6**   Total sales ($ mil): **480**   Total employment (000): **2.0**

Company Name	Address				CEO Name	Phone	Co. Type	Sales ($ mil)	Empl. (000)
Delta and Pine Land Co.	1 Cotton Row	Scott	MS	38772	Roger D Malkin	662-742-4500	P	260	0.6
Harris Farms Inc.	Rte 1, Box 426	Coalinga	CA	93210	John C Harris	559-884-2859	R	168*	1.2
E. Ritter and Co.	106 Frisco St	Marked Tree	AR	72365	E Ritter Arnold	870-358-2200	R	35	0.2
Abt Systems	PO Box 12447	Fresno	CA	93777	Doug Elkins	559-233-8823	S	12	<0.1
Salyer American Corp.	PO Box 488	Corcoran	CA	93212	Fred Salyer	559-992-2131	R	3*	<0.1
Seven J Stock Farm Inc.	99 Travis St	Houston	TX	77060	John R Parten	713-228-8900	P	1*	<0.1

Source: *Ward's Business Directory of U.S. Private and Public Companies*, Volumes 1 and 2, 2000. The company type code used is as follows: P - Public, R - Private, S - Subsidiary, D - Division, J - Joint Venture, A - Affiliate, G - Group, N - Company type not reported. Sales are in millions of dollars, employees are in thousands. An asterisk (*) indicates an estimated sales volume. The symbol < stands for 'less than'. Company names and addresses are truncated, in some cases, to fit into the available space.

NAICS 11193-94-99 - SUGARCANE, HAY, AND ALL OTHER CROPS

GENERAL STATISTICS

Item	U.S. Total	This Agri-culture Sector	% of U.S.	Category average per farm				Number of farms reporting category	
				Value shown as	U.S.	This Agric. Sector	% of U.S.	U.S.	This Sector
Farms - number	1,911,859	184,568	9.7	-	-	-	-	-	-
Land in farms - mil. acres	931.795	63.693	6.8	Acres	487	345	70.8	1,911,859	184,568
Value of land, buildings - $ mil.	859,839.2	74,150.1	8.6	$	449,748	408,711	90.9	524,066	181,424
Value of machinery and equipment - $ mil.	110,256.8	9,623.0	8.7	$	57,678	53,045	92.0	1,911,601	181,414
Sales of Ag Products - $ mil.	196,864.6	10,530.9	5.3	$	102,970	57,057	55.4	1,911,859	184,568
Government payments - $ mil.	5,054.5	300.4	5.9	$	7,378	5,684	77.0	685,029	52,849
Other farm-related income - $ mil.	3,272.3	318.9	9.7	$	5,999	5,941	99.0	545,480	53,674
Expenses - $ mil.	150,591.0	8,067.1	5.4	$	78,771	44,466	56.4	1,911,766	181,423
Payroll - $ mil.	14,841.0	1,033.4	7.0	$	22,811	18,733	82.1	650,623	55,162
Workers - 150 days or more a year	890,467	58,124	6.5	Number	3.4	3.0	87.4	259,631	19,391
Workers - less than 150 days	2,461,561	207,037	8.4	Number	4.2	4.1	95.9	581,658	50,994
Net Cash Return - $ mil.	42,557.9	2,245.0	5.3	$	22,260	12,374	55.6	1,911,824	181,424

Source: *1997 Census of Agriculture*, U.S. Department of Agriculture, National Agricultural Statistics Service. Table shows totals for the U.S. agriculture sector and for the NAICS subdivision of it, shown as "This Agric. Sector" or as "This Sector." Not all farms report on every category. For this reason, the reporting universe is shown in the last two columns. Averages are based on these columns.

LAND IN FARMS ACCORDING TO USE

Item	U.S. Total (000 acres)	This Sector (000 acres)	% of U.S.	Average acres per farms			Number of farms reporting category	
				U.S.	This Agric. Sector	% of U.S.	U.S.	This Sector
Total cropland	431,144.9	34,792.6	8.1	260	190	-	1,661,395	183,446
Harvested cropland	309,395.5	26,140.8	8.4	219	143	-	1,410,606	183,195
Cropland:								
Pasture or grazing	64,466.5	4,634.1	7.2	85	69	-	754,170	67,524
In cover crops, legumes, grasses	13,531.2	1,034.4	7.6	88	66	-	153,177	15,786
On which all crops failed	3,449.4	298.7	8.7	67	49	-	51,673	6,140
In cultivated summer fallow	20,905.9	878.6	4.2	256	126	-	81,702	6,960
Idle	19,396.3	1,806.0	9.3	83	67	-	232,961	27,059
Total woodland	71,465.4	8,198.0	11.5	96	97	-	743,011	84,559
Woodland pastured	29,693.9	2,333.6	7.9	84	80	-	352,217	28,997
Woodland not pastured	41,771.5	5,864.4	14.0	79	86	-	531,846	68,449
Other pasture/rangeland	396,884.6	17,655.1	4.4	721	453	-	550,619	38,995
Land for house lots, ponds, roads, wasteland	32,300.4	3,047.4	9.4	28	27	-	1,142,618	114,519
Irrigated land	55,058.1	8,492.8	15.4	197	243	-	279,442	34,926
Harvested cropland	50,013.5	7,970.3	15.9	198	231	-	252,679	34,542
Pasture and other	5,044.7	522.5	10.4	87	73	-	58,258	7,167
Conservation Reserve/Wetlands Reserve Lands	29,489.1	1,959.3	6.6	131	113	-	225,410	17,350

Source: *1997 Census of Agriculture*, U.S. Department of Agriculture, National Agricultural Statistics Service. Table shows totals for the U.S. agriculture sector and for the NAICS subdivision of it, shown as "This Agric. Sector" or as "This Sector." Not all farms report on every category. For this reason, the reporting universe is shown in the last two columns. Averages are based on these columns. The Conservation Reserve and Wetlands Reserve programs provide support for land conservation/preservation. Cover crops are not harvested or pastured.

MARKET VALUE OF AGRICULTURAL PRODUCTS SOLD: ALL FARMS

Item	U.S. Total ($ mil.)	This Sector ($ mil.)	% of Sector Sales	% of U.S.	Average sales per farm - $			Number of farms reporting category	
					U.S.	This Agric. Sector	% of U.S.	U.S.	This Sector
Grains	46,617.1	1,626.2	15.44	3.5	79,095	38,635	48.8	589,379	42,092
Corn for grain	18,884.8	507.6	4.82	2.7	52,506	23,858	45.4	359,666	21,277
Wheat	7,173.9	504.0	4.79	7.0	29,726	27,763	93.4	241,334	18,152
Soybeans	15,622.4	331.8	3.15	2.1	44,185	24,334	55.1	353,566	13,635
Sorghum for grain	1,140.0	44.5	0.42	3.9	25,360	17,804	70.2	44,955	2,498
Barley	709.6	92.4	0.88	13.0	23,191	21,296	91.8	30,598	4,341
Oats	121.3	16.3	0.15	13.4	3,114	2,725	87.5	38,940	5,985
Other grains	2,965.1	129.6	1.23	4.4	67,540	36,962	54.7	43,901	3,507
Cotton and cotton seed	5,975.5	708.3	6.73	11.9	189,963	133,969	70.5	31,456	5,287
Tobacco	2,924.7	221.7	2.11	7.6	32,662	41,340	126.6	89,544	5,364
Hay, silage, and field seeds	4,670.5	2,795.4	26.55	59.9	13,174	17,733	134.6	354,523	157,638
Vegetables, sweet corn, and melons	8,401.7	573.7	5.45	6.8	156,628	82,894	52.9	53,641	6,921
Fruits and berries	12,660.3	285.5	2.71	2.3	147,259	71,376	48.5	85,973	4,000
Nursery and greenhouse crops	10,942.8	88.6	0.84	0.8	161,360	32,447	20.1	67,816	2,730
Other crops	5,863.1	2,973.7	28.24	50.7	153,907	163,757	106.4	38,095	18,159
Poultry and poultry products	22,262.6	41.8	0.40	0.2	352,000	12,673	3.6	63,246	3,295
Dairy products	18,997.3	86.1	0.82	0.5	191,432	70,232	36.7	99,238	1,226
Cattle and calves	40,524.8	812.1	7.71	2.0	40,052	15,257	38.1	1,011,809	53,231
Hogs and pigs	13,804.8	263.5	2.50	1.9	135,201	40,519	30.0	102,106	6,504
Sheep, lambs, and wool	682.9	31.4	0.30	4.6	10,913	6,282	57.6	62,579	4,999
Other livestock	2,536.5	22.8	0.22	0.9	20,506	3,373	16.4	123,695	6,769
Products sold to public directly	13,096.7	212.5	2.02	1.6	377,610	140,277	37.1	34,683	1,515

Source: *1997 Census of Agriculture*, U.S. Department of Agriculture, National Agricultural Statistics Service. Table shows totals for the U.S. agriculture sector and for the NAICS subdivision of it, shown as "This Agric. Sector" or as "This Sector." Not all farms report on every category. For this reason, the reporting universe is shown in the last two columns. Averages are based on these columns. Farms classified in one sector routinely produce categories in other sectors as well. Products sold to the public are sold for direct consumption.

MARKET VALUE OF PRODUCTS SOLD: FARMS WITH SALES OF $50,000 OR MORE

Item	U.S. Total ($ mil.)	This Sector ($ mil.)	% of Sector Sales	% of U.S.	Average sales per farm - $			Number of farms reporting category	
					U.S.	This Agric. Sector	% of U.S.	U.S.	This Sector
Grains	40,973.4	1,264.0	12.00	3.1	183,623	150,248	81.8	223,138	8,413
Cotton and cotton seed	5,743.9	662.0	6.29	11.5	286,562	224,195	78.2	20,044	2,953
Tobacco	2,060.2	176.8	1.68	8.6	175,907	194,972	110.8	11,712	907
Hay, silage, and field seeds	2,781.9	1,892.2	17.97	68.0	188,959	216,493	114.6	14,722	8,740
Vegetables, sweet corn, and melons	7,966.8	523.7	4.97	6.6	673,443	304,990	45.3	11,830	1,717
Fruits and berries	12,072.3	267.0	2.54	2.2	478,927	450,197	94.0	25,207	593
Nursery and greenhouse crops	10,412.0	71.9	0.68	0.7	578,025	204,276	35.3	18,013	352
Other crops	5,586.6	2,836.3	26.93	50.8	363,758	345,006	94.8	15,358	8,221
Poultry and poultry products	22,171.7	38.1	0.36	0.2	778,637	366,567	47.1	28,475	104
Dairy products	18,344.3	74.0	0.70	0.4	250,075	139,683	55.9	73,355	530
Cattle and calves	32,358.6	425.5	4.04	1.3	386,685	127,848	33.1	83,682	3,328
Hogs and pigs	13,096.7	212.5	2.02	1.6	377,610	140,277	37.1	34,683	1,515
Sheep, lambs, and wool	478.6	17.3	0.16	3.6	278,730	160,019	57.4	1,717	108
Other livestock	2,026.6	9.2	0.09	0.5	369,685	280,273	75.8	5,482	33

Source: *1997 Census of Agriculture*, U.S. Department of Agriculture, National Agricultural Statistics Service. Table shows totals for the U.S. agriculture sector and for the NAICS subdivision of it, shown as "This Agric. Sector" or as "This Sector." Not all farms report on every category. For this reason, the reporting universe is shown in the last two columns. Averages are based on these columns. Farms classified in one sector routinely produce categories in other sectors as well.

GOVERNMENT PAYMENTS AND OTHER FARM-RELATED INCOME

Item	U.S. Total ($ mil.)	This Sector ($ mil.)	% of Sector Gov/Oth. Income	% of U.S.	Average receipts per farm - $			Number of farms reporting category	
					U.S.	This Agric. Sector	% of U.S.	U.S.	This Sector
Government payments	5,054.5	300.4	48.51	5.9	7,378	5,684	77.0	685,029	52,849
Other farm-related income	3,272.3	318.9	51.49	9.7	5,999	5,941	99.0	545,480	53,674
Custom work and other agricultural services	1,235.1	133.2	21.50	10.8	8,646	7,784	90.0	142,854	17,106
Gross cash rent or share payments	1,207.9	102.7	16.58	8.5	6,867	4,875	71.0	175,901	21,066
Forest products, excluding Christmas trees and maple products	344.3	50.7	8.19	14.7	7,417	7,082	95.5	46,426	7,158
Other farm-related income sources	484.9	32.3	5.22	6.7	1,595	1,521	95.3	303,908	21,253

Source: 1997 Census of Agriculture, U.S. Department of Agriculture, National Agricultural Statistics Service. Table shows totals for the U.S. agriculture sector and for the NAICS subdivision of it, shown as "This Agric. Sector" or as "This Sector." Not all farms report on every category. For this reason, the reporting universe is shown in the last two columns. Averages are based on these columns. Government payments are agricultural subsidies under various programs.

COMMODITY CREDIT CORPORATION LOANS

Item	U.S. Total ($ mil.)	This Sector ($ mil.)	% of Sector Loan Total	% of U.S.	Average loan value per farm - $			Number of farms reporting category	
					U.S.	This Agric. Sector	% of U.S.	U.S.	This Sector
Total loans	3,034.7	94.3	100.00	3.1	36,419	22,557	61.9	83,328	4,181
Corn	1,333.9	26.9	28.52	2.0	26,419	13,956	52.8	50,489	1,927
Wheat	415.4	28.2	29.88	6.8	18,093	16,917	93.5	22,961	1,666
Soybeans	774.0	14.7	15.53	1.9	30,370	22,332	73.5	25,487	656
Sorghum, barley, and oats	54.8	3.7	3.95	6.8	8,603	6,968	81.0	6,375	534
Cotton	191.4	13.3	14.12	7.0	43,275	25,038	57.9	4,422	532
Sunflower seed, flaxseed, safflower, canola, other rapeseed, and mustard seed	17.3	0.3	0.34	1.8	25,159	15,950	63.4	686	20
Peanuts, rice, and tobacco	247.9	7.2	7.66	2.9	60,421	23,010	38.1	4,103	314

Source: 1997 Census of Agriculture, U.S. Department of Agriculture, National Agricultural Statistics Service. Table shows totals for the U.S. agriculture sector and for the NAICS subdivision of it, shown as "This Agric. Sector" or as "This Sector." Not all farms report on every category. For this reason, the reporting universe is shown in the last two columns. Averages are based on these columns. The Commodity Credit Corporation provides low interest loans to farmers.

SELECTED MACHINERY AND EQUIPMENT

Item	U.S. Total (number)	This Agric. Sector (number)	% of U.S.	Average number per farm			Number of farms reporting category	
				U.S.	This Agric. Sector	% of U.S.	U.S.	This Sector
Motortrucks, including pickups	3,497,735	309,059	8.8	2.07	2.02	97.5	1,688,303	153,007
Wheel tractors	3,936,014	379,160	9.6	2.31	2.26	97.8	1,707,384	168,132
Less than 40 horsepower (PTO)	1,262,688	129,999	10.3	1.44	1.46	101.8	877,119	88,737
40 horsepower (PTO) or more	2,673,326	249,161	9.3	2.02	1.93	95.3	1,321,084	129,249
40 to 99 horsepower (PTO)	1,808,105	180,430	10.0	1.58	1.56	99.1	1,145,466	115,398
100 horsepower (PTO)	865,221	68,731	7.9	1.68	1.70	100.8	513,773	40,481
Grain and bean combines	460,606	31,972	6.9	1.16	1.19	102.4	395,934	26,850
Cotton pickers and strippers	38,294	6,258	16.3	1.48	1.43	96.8	25,874	4,366
Mower conditioners	608,443	90,140	14.8	1.12	1.13	101.1	543,565	79,640
Pickup balers	717,245	107,369	15.0	1.24	1.25	101.2	579,440	85,690

Source: 1997 Census of Agriculture, U.S. Department of Agriculture, National Agricultural Statistics Service. Table shows totals for the U.S. agriculture sector and for the NAICS subdivision of it, shown as "This Agric. Sector" or as "This Sector." Not all farms report on every category. For this reason, the reporting universe is shown in the last two columns. Averages are based on these columns. PTO stands for "power take off."

FARM PRODUCTION EXPENSES

Item	U.S. Total ($ mil.)	This Sector ($ mil.)	% of Sector Total Expense	% of U.S.	Average expense per farm - $			Number of farms reporting category	
					U.S.	This Agric. Sector	% of U.S.	U.S.	This Sector
Total farm production expenses	150,591.0	8,067.1	100.00	5.4	78,771	44,466	56.4	1,911,766	181,423
Livestock and poultry purchased	21,614.6	269.6	3.34	1.2	38,807	8,064	20.8	556,980	33,426
Feed for livestock and poultry	32,760.0	279.8	3.47	0.9	32,059	4,788	14.9	1,021,849	58,425
Commercially mixed formula feeds	21,236.2	139.9	1.73	0.7	34,459	4,120	12.0	616,280	33,959
Seeds, bulbs, plants, and trees	5,725.9	418.5	5.19	7.3	6,388	5,650	88.4	896,339	74,069
Commercial fertilizer	9,597.1	913.7	11.33	9.5	8,060	7,823	97.1	1,190,733	116,800
Agricultural chemicals	7,581.4	670.1	8.31	8.8	8,056	8,651	107.4	941,136	77,454
Petroleum products	6,371.5	508.3	6.30	8.0	3,619	2,987	82.5	1,760,642	170,167
Gasoline and gasohol	1,886.6	156.8	1.94	8.3	1,380	1,228	88.9	1,366,915	127,969
Diesel fuel	2,846.0	258.1	3.20	9.1	2,164	2,059	95.2	1,315,397	125,319
Natural gas	432.9	21.9	0.27	5.1	6,091	4,810	79.0	71,069	4,561
LP gas, fuel oil, kerosene, motor oil, grease, etc.	1,206.1	71.5	0.89	5.9	945	635	67.2	1,276,331	112,686
Electricity	2,751.1	222.4	2.76	8.1	2,247	2,157	96.0	1,224,374	103,137
Hired farm labor	14,841.0	1,033.4	12.81	7.0	22,811	18,733	82.1	650,623	55,162
Contract labor	2,959.0	197.1	2.44	6.7	13,040	9,293	71.3	226,909	21,215
Repair and maintenance	8,637.7	719.4	8.92	8.3	5,616	5,061	90.1	1,538,058	142,130
Custom work, machine hire, and rental of equipment	3,210.3	330.8	4.10	10.3	5,372	6,183	115.1	597,624	53,492
Interest	8,928.1	654.3	8.11	7.3	11,016	10,022	91.0	810,476	65,292
Secured by real estate	5,449.6	390.2	4.84	7.2	9,564	8,199	85.7	569,775	47,595
Not secured by real estate	3,478.5	264.1	3.27	7.6	7,540	7,811	103.6	461,326	33,815
Cash rent	6,915.7	588.0	7.29	8.5	14,244	15,701	110.2	485,512	37,448
Property taxes	3,920.1	355.9	4.41	9.1	2,213	2,076	93.8	1,771,787	171,421
All other farm production expenses	14,777.4	906.0	11.23	6.1	8,747	6,037	69.0	1,689,391	150,073

Source: 1997 Census of Agriculture, U.S. Department of Agriculture, National Agricultural Statistics Service. Table shows totals for the U.S. agriculture sector and for the NAICS subdivision of it, shown as "This Agric. Sector" or as "This Sector." Not all farms report on every category. For this reason, the reporting universe is shown in the last two columns. Averages are based on these columns. LP gas stands for "liquid petroleum gas," i.e., butane or propane.

NET CASH RETURN AND FARMS WITH GAINS AND LOSSES

Item	Number of farms and %				Average gain or loss per farm - $		
	U.S.	% of U.S.	This Agriculture Sector	% of Sector	U.S.	This Agriculture Sector	% of U.S.
All farms	1,911,824	100.0	181,424	100.0	22,260	12,374	55.6
Number of farms with net gains	985,718	51.6	86,637	47.8	51,296	32,968	64.3
Gain of -							
Less than $1,000	120,163	6.3	15,844	8.7	-	-	-
$1,000 to $9,999	370,611	19.4	40,662	22.4	-	-	-
$10,000 to $49,999	292,484	15.3	19,476	10.7	-	-	-
$50,000 or more	202,460	10.6	10,655	5.9	-	-	-
Number of farms with net losses	926,106	48.4	94,787	52.2	(8,645)	(6,449)	74.6
Loss of -							
Less than $1,000	165,390	8.7	19,018	10.5	-	-	-
$1,000 to $9,999	591,517	30.9	61,956	34.1	-	-	-
$10,000 to $49,999	152,649	8.0	12,799	7.1	-	-	-
$50,000 or more	16,550	0.9	1,014	0.6	-	-	-

Source: 1997 Census of Agriculture, U.S. Department of Agriculture, National Agricultural Statistics Service. Table shows totals for the U.S. agriculture sector and for the NAICS subdivision of it, shown as "This Agric. Sector" or as "This Sector." Not all farms report on every category. For this reason, the reporting universe is shown in the last two columns. Averages are based on these columns. Net gains are income less cost for farm operations; they exclude non-farm earnings. Values in parentheses are losses.

CHARACTERISTICS OF FARM OPERATORS

Farm Operators	U.S.	This Agric. Sector	% of U.S.	Farm Operators	U.S.	This Agric. Sector	% of U.S.
Place of residence:				By age group:			
On farm operated	1,361,766	136,242	10.0	Under 25 years	20,850	1,480	7.1
Not on farm operated	412,554	36,013	8.7	25 to 34 years	128,455	11,014	8.6
Not reported	137,539	12,313	9.0	35 to 44 years	371,442	34,619	9.3
Principal occupation:				45 to 49 years	232,845	22,802	9.8
Farming	961,560	77,864	8.1	50 to 54 years	233,884	23,280	10.0
Other	950,299	106,704	11.2	55 to 59 years	222,736	21,583	9.7
Days worked off farm:				60 to 64 years	204,618	19,156	9.4
None	755,254	63,880	8.5	65 to 69 years	179,858	17,671	9.8
Any	1,042,158	110,446	10.6	70 years and over	317,171	32,963	10.4
1 to 99 days	164,957	16,161	9.8	Average age	54	55	101.3
100 to 199 days	167,922	18,069	10.8	By sex:			
200 days or more	709,279	76,216	10.7	Male	1,746,757	170,263	9.7
Not reported	114,447	10,242	8.9	Female	165,102	14,305	8.7
Years on present farm:				Spanish, Hispanic/Latino origin	27,717	2,829	10.2
2 years or less	92,574	10,039	10.8	Tenure of operator:			
3 or 4 years	126,791	13,903	11.0	All operators	1,911,859	184,568	9.7
5 to 9 years	263,642	26,251	10.0	Full owners	1,146,891	122,698	10.7
10 years or more	1,113,839	105,650	9.5	Part owners	573,839	48,398	8.4
Ave. years on this farm	20	20	97.5	Tenants	191,129	13,472	7.0
Not reported	315,013	28,725	9.1				

Source: *1997 Census of Agriculture*, U.S. Department of Agriculture, National Agricultural Statistics Service. Table shows totals for the U.S. agriculture sector and for the NAICS subdivision of it, shown as "This Agric. Sector" or as "This Sector." Not all farms report on every category. For this reason, the reporting universe is shown in the last two columns. Averages are based on these columns. All values shown are number of farm operators in each category or percent.

FARMS BY TYPE OF ORGANIZATION

Item	Number of farms and percent				Total acres and percent		
	U.S.	% of U.S.	This Agriculture Sector	% of Sector	U.S.	This Agriculture Sector	% of U.S.
Individual or family (sole proprietorship)	1,643,424	100.0	163,685	100.0	585,464,911	39,283,453	6.7
Partnership	169,462	10.3	13,338	8.1	149,321,484	8,725,718	5.8
Corporation:							
Family held	76,103	4.6	5,524	3.4	119,559,203	7,043,891	5.9
More than 10 stockholders	1,795	0.1	159	0.1	-	-	-
10 or less stockholders	74,308	4.5	5,365	3.3	-	-	-
Other than family held	7,899	0.5	574	0.4	11,904,053	2,024,753	17.0
More than 10 stockholders	1,029	0.1	92	0.1	-	-	-
10 or less stockholders	6,870	0.4	482	0.3	-	-	-
Other cooperative, estate or trust, institutional, etc.	14,971	0.9	1,447	0.9	65,545,604	6,615,287	10.1

Source: *1997 Census of Agriculture*, U.S. Department of Agriculture, National Agricultural Statistics Service. Table shows totals for the U.S. agriculture sector and for the NAICS subdivision of it, shown as "This Agric. Sector" or as "This Sector." Not all farms report on every category. For this reason, the reporting universe is shown in the last two columns. Averages are based on these columns.

LIVESTOCK INVENTORIES AND SALES

Item	U.S. (number)	This Agric. Sector (number)	% of U.S.	Average number per farm			Number of farms reporting category	
				U.S.	This Agric. Sector	% of U.S.	U.S.	This Sector
Cattle and calves inventory	98,989,244	3,515,755	3.6	94.6	58.6	62.0	1,046,863	59,983
Cows and heifers that had calved	43,162,054	1,663,475	3.9	48.3	35.4	73.4	894,110	46,941
Beef cows	34,066,615	1,607,793	4.7	42.3	35.4	83.6	804,595	45,415
Milk cows	9,095,439	55,682	0.6	77.8	21.0	27.0	116,874	2,649
Heifers and heifer calves	26,988,697	898,126	3.3	33.6	20.7	61.5	803,985	43,482
Steers, steer calves, bulls, and bull calves	28,838,493	954,154	3.3	32.6	19.4	59.3	883,983	49,306
Cattle and calves sold	74,089,046	1,761,024	2.4	73.2	33.1	45.2	1,011,809	53,231
Calves	16,480,293	553,960	3.4	26.8	19.8	73.8	615,177	28,008
Cattle	57,608,753	1,207,064	2.1	78.0	31.0	39.8	738,696	38,919
Fattened on grain and concentrates	27,328,190	219,120	0.8	247.0	33.4	13.5	110,620	6,565
Hogs and pigs inventory	61,206,236	1,254,980	2.1	557.7	168.9	30.3	109,754	7,431
Used or to be used for breeding	6,831,564	135,899	2.0	106.7	33.6	31.5	64,029	4,042
Other	54,374,672	1,119,081	2.1	528.0	161.6	30.6	102,977	6,923
Hogs and pigs sold	142,611,882	2,449,441	1.7	1,396.7	376.6	27.0	102,106	6,504
Feeder pigs	34,988,718	241,357	0.7	2,037.8	258.7	12.7	17,170	933
Litters of pigs farrowed between Dec. 1 of preceding year and Nov. 30	11,497,523	208,875	1.8	170.3	48.8	28.6	67,514	4,284
Dec. 1 and May 31	5,697,371	107,578	1.9	91.0	27.1	29.8	62,622	3,969
June 1 and Nov. 30	5,800,152	101,297	1.7	99.7	28.3	28.4	58,204	3,585
Sheep and lambs of all ages inventory	7,821,885	435,473	5.6	118.9	80.0	67.3	65,790	5,446
Ewes 1 year old or older	4,408,683	232,137	5.3	78.1	50.7	64.9	56,414	4,578
Sheep and lambs sold	7,331,545	361,873	4.9	123.1	78.9	64.1	59,575	4,584
Sheep and lambs shorn	6,139,140	307,171	5.0	118.4	73.2	61.9	51,869	4,196
Horses and ponies inventory	2,427,277	188,448	7.8	6.5	5.2	80.3	375,218	36,287
Horses and ponies sold	325,306	9,327	2.9	4.1	2.3	56.8	79,516	4,011
Goats inventory	1,989,799	60,040	3.0	34.4	13.6	39.7	57,925	4,400
Goats sold	740,597	19,952	2.7	31.5	14.7	46.6	23,520	1,360

Source: 1997 Census of Agriculture, U.S. Department of Agriculture, National Agricultural Statistics Service. Table shows totals for the U.S. agriculture sector and for the NAICS subdivision of it, shown as "This Agric. Sector" or as "This Sector." Not all farms report on every category. For this reason, the reporting universe is shown in the last two columns. Averages are based on these columns.

POULTRY INVENTORIES AND SALES

Item	U.S. (number)	This Agric. Sector (number)	% of U.S.	Average number per farm			Number of farms reporting category	
				U.S.	This Agric. Sector	% of U.S.	U.S.	This Sector
Layers and pullets 13 weeks old and older inventory	366,989,851	964,389	0.3	5,053.8	153.5	3.0	72,616	6,284
Layers 20 weeks old and older	313,851,480	809,487	0.3	4,499.0	132.3	2.9	69,761	6,117
Pullets 13 weeks old and older but less than 20 weeks old	53,138,371	154,902	0.3	4,031.7	162.9	4.0	13,180	951
Layers, pullets, and pullet chicks sold	331,563,736	1,069,434	0.3	24,636.9	1,556.7	6.3	13,458	687
Broilers and other meat type chickens sold	6,741,927,110	12,499,383	0.2	281,653.0	24,037.3	8.5	23,937	520
Turkey hens kept for breeding	5,504,808	2,143	0.0	968.1	4.8	0.5	5,686	446
Turkeys sold	307,586,680	970,470	0.3	51,000.9	3,441.4	6.7	6,031	282

Source: 1997 Census of Agriculture, U.S. Department of Agriculture, National Agricultural Statistics Service. Table shows totals for the U.S. agriculture sector and for the NAICS subdivision of it, shown as "This Agric. Sector" or as "This Sector." Not all farms report on every category. For this reason, the reporting universe is shown in the last two columns. Averages are based on these columns.

SELECTED CROPS HARVESTED

Item	In 1,000	Crop harvested			Acres used for crop (000)			Number of farms reporting category	
		U.S.	This Agric. Sector	% of U.S.	U.S.	This Agric. Sector	% of U.S.	U.S.	This Sector
Corn for grain or seed	bushels	8,578,635	243,116	2.8	69,796.7	2,168.9	3.1	430,711	24,438
Irrigated		-	-	-	10,638.9	495.8	4.7	40,574	3,438
Corn for silage or green chop	tons, green	88,381	4,400	5.0	5,727.6	254.8	4.4	119,308	6,097
Irrigated		-	-	-	1,033.3	132.2	12.8	10,815	1,360
Sorghum for grain or seed	bushels	559,070	22,043	3.9	8,470.4	374.6	4.4	49,397	2,836
Irrigated		-	-	-	875.6	-	-	5,793	604
Wheat for grain	bushels	2,204,027	150,908	6.8	58,836.3	3,307.8	5.6	243,568	18,439
Irrigated		-	-	-	3,990.9	789.5	19.8	20,385	4,527
Barley for grain	bushels	336,435	38,974	11.6	5,945.0	554.9	9.3	41,930	5,003
Irrigated		-	-	-	1,060.7	265.4	25.0	8,847	2,494
Oats for grain	bushels	151,327	14,038	9.3	2,681.0	248.2	9.3	89,606	9,721
Irrigated		-	-	-	121.0	28.6	23.6	2,788	689
Rice	cwt	182,231	1,956	1.1	3,122.1	33.0	1.1	9,291	95
Irrigated		-	-	-	3,122.1	33.0	1.1	9,291	95
Cotton	bales	17,879	2,102	11.8	13,235.2	1,515.8	11.5	31,493	5,293
Irrigated		-	-	-	4,888.0	542.2	11.1	12,434	1,860
Tobacco	pounds	1,747,702	137,120	7.8	838.5	64.6	7.7	89,706	5,376
Irrigated		-	-	-	138.7	10.5	7.6	7,090	420
Soybeans for beans	bushels	2,504,307	54,644	2.2	66,147.7	1,677.4	2.5	354,692	13,744
Irrigated		-	-	-	4,152.1	57.2	1.4	20,619	554
Dry edible beans, excluding dry limas	cwt	27,224	3,846	14.1	1,691.9	225.8	13.3	10,911	1,670
Irrigated		-	-	-	577.0	92.6	16.0	4,882	1,009
Potatoes, excluding sweetpotatoes	cwt	459,886	51,475	11.2	1,355.2	163.4	12.1	10,523	1,986
Irrigated		-	-	-	1,070.3	125.1	11.7	4,843	1,047
Sugar beets for sugar	tons	29,775	19,890	66.8	1,453.8	951.8	65.5	7,102	3,957
Irrigated		-	-	-	616.4	417.0	67.7	3,492	2,078
Peanuts for nuts	pounds	3,377,143	2,253,721	66.7	1,352.2	889.2	65.8	12,221	6,721
Irrigated		-	-	-	412.3	274.6	66.6	3,125	1,848
Hay alfalfa, other tame, small grain, wild, grass silage, green chop	tons, dry	139,365	34,041	24.4	60,799.8	11,907.5	19.6	888,597	168,273
Irrigated		-	-	-	9,564.3	3,548.6	37.1	79,406	26,480
Alfalfa hay	tons, dry	65,863	20,588	31.3	21,309.8	5,273.8	24.7	358,365	70,943
Irrigated		-	-	-	5,980.5	2,731.2	45.7	57,854	21,388
Vegetables harvested for sale		-	-	-	3,773.2	417.9	11.1	53,727	6,938
Irrigated		-	-	-	2,641.8	285.2	10.8	23,203	3,096
Land in orchards		-	-	-	5,158.1	194.5	3.8	106,069	6,755
Irrigated		-	-	-	4,107.9	135.0	3.3	61,606	2,419

Source: 1997 Census of Agriculture, U.S. Department of Agriculture, National Agricultural Statistics Service. Table shows totals for the U.S. agriculture sector and for the NAICS subdivision of it, shown as "This Agric. Sector" or as "This Sector." Not all farms report on every category. For this reason, the reporting universe is shown in the last two columns. Averages are based on these columns. "Green tons" are weight of product as harvested, i.e., moist. cwt stands for "hundredweight."

LEADING COMPANIES   Number shown: **15**   Total sales ($ mil): **1,401**   Total employment (000): **4.0**

Company Name	Address				CEO Name	Phone	Co. Type	Sales ($ mil)	Empl. (000)
A and B Hawaii Inc.	PO Box 3440	Honolulu	HI	96801	W Allen Doane	808-525-6611	S	588	1.2
Busch Agricultural Resources Inc.	10733 Sunset Office	St. Louis	MO	63127	Don Koth	314-909-3800	S	362*	0.6
Deltic Timber Corp.	PO Box 7200	El Dorado	AR	71731	Robert Nalon	870-881-9400	R	125	0.5
Agrinorthwest	PO Box 2308	Pasco	WA	99302	Don Sleight	509-735-6461	R	80	0.3
Agripro Seeds Inc.	P O Box 2962	Shawnee Msn	KS	66201	Milton Allen	913-384-4940	S	55*	0.3
Sterling Sugars Inc.	PO Box 572	Franklin	LA	70538	Bernard Boudreaux Jr	318-828-0620	P	45	0.2
John Kautz Farms	5490 E Bear Creek	Lodi	CA	95240	John Kautz	209-334-4786	R	35*	0.2
Arends Brothers Inc.	Rte 54 N	Melvin	IL	60952	Kent Arends	217-388-7717	R	20	<0.1
Walter Lasley and Sons Inc.	PO Box 168	Stratford	TX	79084	Walter Lasley	806-753-4411	R	19	<0.1
Wolfsen Inc.	P O Box 311	Los Banos	CA	93635	Donald C Skinner	209-827-7700	R	18*	0.3
Barenbrug U.S.A. Inc.	P O Box 239	Tangent	OR	97389	Don Herb	541-926-5801	S	15*	<0.1
Pike Creek Turf Sports Group Inc.	Rte 2, Box 376A	Adel	GA	31620	Jaimie Allen	912-896-7581	R	13*	<0.1
Abt Systems	PO Box 12447	Fresno	CA	93777	Doug Elkins	559-233-8823	S	12	<0.1
J.C. Watson Company Inc.	P O Box 300	Parma	ID	83660	Jon C Watson	208-722-5141	R	10*	0.1
Morrison Ventures	P O Box 737	Salina	KS	67402	Roger Morrison	785-827-9331	R	4*	<0.1

Source: *Ward's Business Directory of U.S. Private and Public Companies*, Volumes 1 and 2, 2000. The company type code used is as follows: P - Public, R - Private, S - Subsidiary, D - Division, J - Joint Venture, A - Affiliate, G - Group, N - Company type not reported. Sales are in millions of dollars, employees are in thousands. An asterisk (*) indicates an estimated sales volume. The symbol < stands for 'less than'. Company names and addresses are truncated, in some cases, to fit into the available space.

NAICS 112111 - BEEF CATTLE RANCHING AND FARMING

GENERAL STATISTICS

Item	U.S. Total	This Agriculture Sector	% of U.S.	Category average per farm				Number of farms reporting category	
				Value shown as	U.S.	This Agric. Sector	% of U.S.	U.S.	This Sector
Farms - number	1,911,859	656,181	34.3	-	-	-	-	-	-
Land in farms - mil. acres	931.795	423.921	45.5	Acres	487	646	132.6	1,911,859	656,181
Value of land, buildings - $ mil.	859,839.2	230,197.9	26.8	$	449,748	346,998	77.2	524,066	663,398
Value of machinery and equipment - $ mil.	110,256.8	20,222.1	18.3	$	57,678	30,485	52.9	1,911,601	663,343
Sales of Ag Products - $ mil.	196,864.6	18,044.2	9.2	$	102,970	27,499	26.7	1,911,859	656,181
Government payments - $ mil.	5,054.5	583.1	11.5	$	7,378	4,670	63.3	685,029	124,873
Other farm-related income - $ mil.	3,272.3	682.1	20.8	$	5,999	4,557	76.0	545,480	149,697
Expenses - $ mil.	150,591.0	16,092.5	10.7	$	78,771	24,258	30.8	1,911,766	663,393
Payroll - $ mil.	14,841.0	832.1	5.6	$	22,811	4,933	21.6	650,623	168,663
Workers - 150 days or more a year	890,467	78,455	8.8	Number	3.4	1.6	46.5	259,631	49,204
Workers - less than 150 days	2,461,561	344,986	14.0	Number	4.2	2.2	52.0	581,658	156,761
Net Cash Return - $ mil.	42,557.9	1,703.2	4.0	$	22,260	2,567	11.5	1,911,824	663,398

Source: 1997 Census of Agriculture, U.S. Department of Agriculture, National Agricultural Statistics Service. Table shows totals for the U.S. agriculture sector and for the NAICS subdivision of it, shown as "This Agric. Sector" or as "This Sector." Not all farms report on every category. For this reason, the reporting universe is shown in the last two columns. Averages are based on these columns.

LAND IN FARMS ACCORDING TO USE

Item	U.S. Total (000 acres)	This Sector (000 acres)	% of U.S.	Average acres per farms			Number of farms reporting category	
				U.S.	This Agric. Sector	% of U.S.	U.S.	This Sector
Total cropland	431,144.9	85,058.7	19.7	260	166	-	1,661,395	511,907
Harvested cropland	309,395.5	36,661.6	11.8	219	97	-	1,410,606	376,877
Cropland:								
Pasture or grazing	64,466.5	37,090.3	57.5	85	102	-	754,170	363,989
In cover crops, legumes, grasses	13,531.2	3,110.5	23.0	88	107	-	153,177	29,080
On which all crops failed	3,449.4	825.9	23.9	67	80	-	51,673	10,279
In cultivated summer fallow	20,905.9	3,612.5	17.3	256	207	-	81,702	17,414
Idle	19,396.3	3,757.9	19.4	83	89	-	232,961	42,054
Total woodland	71,465.4	32,501.6	45.5	96	117	-	743,011	276,711
Woodland pastured	29,693.9	19,159.2	64.5	84	102	-	352,217	187,424
Woodland not pastured	41,771.5	13,342.4	31.9	79	86	-	531,846	155,558
Other pasture/rangeland	396,884.6	295,390.8	74.4	721	1,077	-	550,619	274,224
Land for house lots, ponds, roads, wasteland	32,300.4	10,970.2	34.0	28	31	-	1,142,618	356,535
Irrigated land	55,058.1	8,312.6	15.1	197	170	-	279,442	48,964
Harvested cropland	50,013.5	4,839.6	9.7	198	144	-	252,679	33,637
Pasture and other	5,044.7	3,473.0	68.8	87	122	-	58,258	28,482
Conservation Reserve/Wetlands Reserve Lands	29,489.1	6,549.3	22.2	131	151	-	225,410	43,276

Source: 1997 Census of Agriculture, U.S. Department of Agriculture, National Agricultural Statistics Service. Table shows totals for the U.S. agriculture sector and for the NAICS subdivision of it, shown as "This Agric. Sector" or as "This Sector." Not all farms report on every category. For this reason, the reporting universe is shown in the last two columns. Averages are based on these columns. The Conservation Reserve and Wetlands Reserve programs provide support for land conservation/preservation. Cover crops are not harvested or pastured.

MARKET VALUE OF AGRICULTURAL PRODUCTS SOLD: ALL FARMS

Item	U.S. Total ($ mil.)	This Sector ($ mil.)	% of Sector Sales	% of U.S.	Average sales per farm - $			Number of farms reporting category	
					U.S.	This Agric. Sector	% of U.S.	U.S.	This Sector
Grains	46,617.1	1,331.8	7.38	2.9	79,095	23,947	30.3	589,379	55,613
Corn for grain	18,884.8	404.9	2.24	2.1	52,506	19,184	36.5	359,666	21,104
Wheat	7,173.9	536.9	2.98	7.5	29,726	18,861	63.5	241,334	28,464
Soybeans	15,622.4	235.0	1.30	1.5	44,185	14,855	33.6	353,566	15,822
Sorghum for grain	1,140.0	68.0	0.38	6.0	25,360	14,008	55.2	44,955	4,853
Barley	709.6	33.3	0.18	4.7	23,191	10,209	44.0	30,598	3,258
Oats	121.3	12.6	0.07	10.4	3,114	2,713	87.1	38,940	4,628
Other grains	2,965.1	41.2	0.23	1.4	67,540	15,210	22.5	43,901	2,710
Cotton and cotton seed	5,975.5	24.1	0.13	0.4	189,963	33,547	17.7	31,456	718
Tobacco	2,924.7	87.9	0.49	3.0	32,662	9,267	28.4	89,544	9,484
Hay, silage, and field seeds	4,670.5	362.7	2.01	7.8	13,174	5,344	40.6	354,523	67,870
Vegetables, sweet corn, and melons	8,401.7	23.1	0.13	0.3	156,628	10,350	6.6	53,641	2,229
Fruits and berries	12,660.3	29.3	0.16	0.2	147,259	7,461	5.1	85,973	3,933
Nursery and greenhouse crops	10,942.8	6.2	0.03	0.1	161,360	5,073	3.1	67,816	1,217
Other crops	5,863.1	35.8	0.20	0.6	153,907	21,639	14.1	38,095	1,653
Poultry and poultry products	22,262.6	17.8	0.10	0.1	352,000	2,101	0.6	63,246	8,469
Dairy products	18,997.3	379.8	2.10	2.0	191,432	58,402	30.5	99,238	6,503
Cattle and calves	40,524.8	15,464.2	85.70	38.2	40,052	24,827	62.0	1,011,809	622,883
Hogs and pigs	13,804.8	118.6	0.66	0.9	135,201	9,754	7.2	102,106	12,159
Sheep, lambs, and wool	682.9	86.1	0.48	12.6	10,913	5,672	52.0	62,579	15,185
Other livestock	2,536.5	77.0	0.43	3.0	20,506	2,712	13.2	123,695	28,380
Products sold to public directly	13,096.7	67.8	0.38	0.5	377,610	119,412	31.6	34,683	568

Source: *1997 Census of Agriculture*, U.S. Department of Agriculture, National Agricultural Statistics Service. Table shows totals for the U.S. agriculture sector and for the NAICS subdivision of it, shown as "This Agric. Sector" or as "This Sector." Not all farms report on every category. For this reason, the reporting universe is shown in the last two columns. Averages are based on these columns. Farms classified in one sector routinely produce categories in other sectors as well. Products sold to the public are sold for direct consumption.

MARKET VALUE OF PRODUCTS SOLD: FARMS WITH SALES OF $50,000 OR MORE

Item	U.S. Total ($ mil.)	This Sector ($ mil.)	% of Sector Sales	% of U.S.	Average sales per farm - $			Number of farms reporting category	
					U.S.	This Agric. Sector	% of U.S.	U.S.	This Sector
Grains	40,973.4	818.9	4.54	2.0	183,623	123,169	67.1	223,138	6,649
Cotton and cotton seed	5,743.9	16.9	0.09	0.3	286,562	115,479	40.3	20,044	146
Tobacco	2,060.2	23.0	0.13	1.1	175,907	107,252	61.0	11,712	214
Hay, silage, and field seeds	2,781.9	99.9	0.55	3.6	188,959	107,223	56.7	14,722	932
Vegetables, sweet corn, and melons	7,966.8	13.0	0.07	0.2	673,443	143,889	21.4	11,830	90
Fruits and berries	12,072.3	17.7	0.10	0.1	478,927	199,146	41.6	25,207	89
Nursery and greenhouse crops	10,412.0	2.2	0.01	0.0	578,025	117,526	20.3	18,013	19
Other crops	5,586.6	24.8	0.14	0.4	363,758	147,619	40.6	15,358	168
Poultry and poultry products	22,171.7	12.1	0.07	0.1	778,637	195,435	25.1	28,475	62
Dairy products	18,344.3	303.5	1.68	1.7	250,075	130,689	52.3	73,355	2,322
Cattle and calves	32,358.6	10,721.9	59.42	33.1	386,685	214,863	55.6	83,682	49,901
Hogs and pigs	13,096.7	67.8	0.38	0.5	377,610	119,412	31.6	34,683	568
Sheep, lambs, and wool	478.6	39.5	0.22	8.2	278,730	132,852	47.7	1,717	297
Other livestock	2,026.6	14.1	0.08	0.7	369,685	106,598	28.8	5,482	132

Source: *1997 Census of Agriculture*, U.S. Department of Agriculture, National Agricultural Statistics Service. Table shows totals for the U.S. agriculture sector and for the NAICS subdivision of it, shown as "This Agric. Sector" or as "This Sector." Not all farms report on every category. For this reason, the reporting universe is shown in the last two columns. Averages are based on these columns. Farms classified in one sector routinely produce categories in other sectors as well.

GOVERNMENT PAYMENTS AND OTHER FARM-RELATED INCOME

Item	U.S. Total ($ mil.)	This Sector ($ mil.)	% of Sector Gov/Oth. Income	% of U.S.	Average receipts per farm - $			Number of farms reporting category	
					U.S.	This Agric. Sector	% of U.S.	U.S.	This Sector
Government payments	5,054.5	583.1	46.09	11.5	7,378	4,670	63.3	685,029	124,873
Other farm-related income	3,272.3	682.1	53.91	20.8	5,999	4,557	76.0	545,480	149,697
Custom work and other agricultural services	1,235.1	184.4	14.57	14.9	8,646	5,459	63.1	142,854	33,777
Gross cash rent or share payments	1,207.9	317.3	25.08	26.3	6,867	5,287	77.0	175,901	60,024
Forest products, excluding Christmas trees and maple products	344.3	132.7	10.49	38.5	7,417	7,376	99.5	46,426	17,990
Other farm-related income sources	484.9	47.7	3.77	9.8	1,595	724	45.4	303,908	65,889

Source: 1997 Census of Agriculture, U.S. Department of Agriculture, National Agricultural Statistics Service. Table shows totals for the U.S. agriculture sector and for the NAICS subdivision of it, shown as "This Agric. Sector" or as "This Sector." Not all farms report on every category. For this reason, the reporting universe is shown in the last two columns. Averages are based on these columns. Government payments are agricultural subsidies under various programs.

COMMODITY CREDIT CORPORATION LOANS

Item	U.S. Total ($ mil.)	This Sector ($ mil.)	% of Sector Loan Total	% of U.S.	Average loan value per farm - $			Number of farms reporting category	
					U.S.	This Agric. Sector	% of U.S.	U.S.	This Sector
Total loans	3,034.7	74.9	100.00	2.5	36,419	14,171	38.9	83,328	5,287
Corn	1,333.9	29.7	39.68	2.2	26,419	13,237	50.1	50,489	2,246
Wheat	415.4	30.6	40.79	7.4	18,093	11,089	61.3	22,961	2,756
Soybeans	774.0	9.5	12.74	1.2	30,370	14,798	48.7	25,487	645
Sorghum, barley, and oats	54.8	2.9	3.81	5.2	8,603	4,571	53.1	6,375	625
Cotton	191.4	0.4	0.53	0.2	43,275	6,108	14.1	4,422	65
Sunflower seed, flaxseed, safflower, canola, other rapeseed, and mustard seed	17.3	1.1	1.47	6.4	25,159	17,508	69.6	686	63
Peanuts, rice, and tobacco	247.9	0.7	0.97	0.3	60,421	6,887	11.4	4,103	106

Source: 1997 Census of Agriculture, U.S. Department of Agriculture, National Agricultural Statistics Service. Table shows totals for the U.S. agriculture sector and for the NAICS subdivision of it, shown as "This Agric. Sector" or as "This Sector." Not all farms report on every category. For this reason, the reporting universe is shown in the last two columns. Averages are based on these columns. The Commodity Credit Corporation provides low interest loans to farmers.

SELECTED MACHINERY AND EQUIPMENT

Item	U.S. Total (number)	This Agric. Sector (number)	% of U.S.	Average number per farm			Number of farms reporting category	
				U.S.	This Agric. Sector	% of U.S.	U.S.	This Sector
Motortrucks, including pickups	3,497,735	1,020,141	29.2	2.07	1.76	84.8	1,688,303	580,398
Wheel tractors	3,936,014	1,085,337	27.6	2.31	1.85	80.1	1,707,384	588,125
Less than 40 horsepower (PTO)	1,262,688	390,706	30.9	1.44	1.33	92.1	877,119	294,564
40 horsepower (PTO) or more	2,673,326	694,631	26.0	2.02	1.59	78.5	1,321,084	437,429
40 to 99 horsepower (PTO)	1,808,105	563,633	31.2	1.58	1.42	90.2	1,145,466	396,023
100 horsepower (PTO)	865,221	130,998	15.1	1.68	1.32	78.3	513,773	99,347
Grain and bean combines	460,606	50,585	11.0	1.16	1.13	97.4	395,934	44,625
Cotton pickers and strippers	38,294	519	1.4	1.48	1.55	104.7	25,874	335
Mower conditioners	608,443	226,351	37.2	1.12	1.12	100.3	543,565	201,573
Pickup balers	717,245	279,101	38.9	1.24	1.25	100.8	579,440	223,581

Source: 1997 Census of Agriculture, U.S. Department of Agriculture, National Agricultural Statistics Service. Table shows totals for the U.S. agriculture sector and for the NAICS subdivision of it, shown as "This Agric. Sector" or as "This Sector." Not all farms report on every category. For this reason, the reporting universe is shown in the last two columns. Averages are based on these columns. PTO stands for "power take off."

FARM PRODUCTION EXPENSES

Item	U.S. Total ($ mil.)	This Sector ($ mil.)	% of Sector Total Expense	% of U.S.	Average expense per farm - $			Number of farms reporting category	
					U.S.	This Agric. Sector	% of U.S.	U.S.	This Sector
Total farm production expenses	150,591.0	16,092.5	100.00	10.7	78,771	24,258	30.8	1,911,766	663,393
Livestock and poultry purchased	21,614.6	4,089.8	25.41	18.9	38,807	16,174	41.7	556,980	252,865
Feed for livestock and poultry	32,760.0	2,631.2	16.35	8.0	32,059	5,199	16.2	1,021,849	506,106
Commercially mixed formula feeds	21,236.2	1,006.7	6.26	4.7	34,459	3,691	10.7	616,280	272,720
Seeds, bulbs, plants, and trees	5,725.9	198.4	1.23	3.5	6,388	1,255	19.7	896,339	158,063
Commercial fertilizer	9,597.1	847.6	5.27	8.8	8,060	2,528	31.4	1,190,733	335,256
Agricultural chemicals	7,581.4	263.9	1.64	3.5	8,056	1,431	17.8	941,136	184,483
Petroleum products	6,371.5	922.8	5.73	14.5	3,619	1,489	41.2	1,760,642	619,676
Gasoline and gasohol	1,886.6	416.1	2.59	22.1	1,380	910	65.9	1,366,915	457,330
Diesel fuel	2,846.0	366.2	2.28	12.9	2,164	830	38.4	1,315,397	441,290
Natural gas	432.9	18.4	0.11	4.3	6,091	1,670	27.4	71,069	11,036
LP gas, fuel oil, kerosene, motor oil, grease, etc.	1,206.1	122.1	0.76	10.1	945	301	31.8	1,276,331	405,833
Electricity	2,751.1	269.2	1.67	9.8	2,247	724	32.2	1,224,374	372,038
Hired farm labor	14,841.0	832.1	5.17	5.6	22,811	4,933	21.6	650,623	168,663
Contract labor	2,959.0	137.0	0.85	4.6	13,040	2,132	16.3	226,909	64,281
Repair and maintenance	8,637.7	1,237.1	7.69	14.3	5,616	2,384	42.4	1,538,058	519,027
Custom work, machine hire, and rental of equipment	3,210.3	318.3	1.98	9.9	5,372	2,005	37.3	597,624	158,781
Interest	8,928.1	1,278.6	7.95	14.3	11,016	5,764	52.3	810,476	221,836
Secured by real estate	5,449.6	825.8	5.13	15.2	9,564	5,381	56.3	569,775	153,447
Not secured by real estate	3,478.5	452.8	2.81	13.0	7,540	3,866	51.3	461,326	117,129
Cash rent	6,915.7	611.9	3.80	8.8	14,244	4,587	32.2	485,512	133,388
Property taxes	3,920.1	824.0	5.12	21.0	2,213	1,321	59.7	1,771,787	623,578
All other farm production expenses	14,777.4	1,630.5	10.13	11.0	8,747	2,849	32.6	1,689,391	572,245

Source: *1997 Census of Agriculture*, U.S. Department of Agriculture, National Agricultural Statistics Service. Table shows totals for the U.S. agriculture sector and for the NAICS subdivision of it, shown as "This Agric. Sector" or as "This Sector." Not all farms report on every category. For this reason, the reporting universe is shown in the last two columns. Averages are based on these columns. LP gas stands for "liquid petroleum gas," i.e., butane or propane.

NET CASH RETURN AND FARMS WITH GAINS AND LOSSES

Item	Number of farms and %				Average gain or loss per farm - $		
	U.S.	% of U.S.	This Agriculture Sector	% of Sector	U.S.	This Agriculture Sector	% of U.S.
All farms	1,911,824	100.0	663,398	100.0	22,260	2,567	11.5
Number of farms with net gains	985,718	51.6	274,502	41.4	51,296	15,286	29.8
Gain of -							
Less than $1,000	120,163	6.3	60,571	9.1	-	-	-
$1,000 to $9,999	370,611	19.4	147,409	22.2	-	-	-
$10,000 to $49,999	292,484	15.3	50,959	7.7	-	-	-
$50,000 or more	202,460	10.6	15,563	2.3	-	-	-
Number of farms with net losses	926,106	48.4	388,896	58.6	(8,645)	(6,410)	74.1
Loss of -							
Less than $1,000	165,390	8.7	71,866	10.8	-	-	-
$1,000 to $9,999	591,517	30.9	258,410	39.0	-	-	-
$10,000 to $49,999	152,649	8.0	55,311	8.3	-	-	-
$50,000 or more	16,550	0.9	3,309	0.5	-	-	-

Source: *1997 Census of Agriculture*, U.S. Department of Agriculture, National Agricultural Statistics Service. Table shows totals for the U.S. agriculture sector and for the NAICS subdivision of it, shown as "This Agric. Sector" or as "This Sector." Not all farms report on every category. For this reason, the reporting universe is shown in the last two columns. Averages are based on these columns. Net gains are income less cost for farm operations; they exclude non-farm earnings. Values in parentheses are losses.

CHARACTERISTICS OF FARM OPERATORS

Farm Operators	U.S.	This Agric. Sector	% of U.S.	Farm Operators	U.S.	This Agric. Sector	% of U.S.
Place of residence:				By age group:			
On farm operated	1,361,766	470,727	34.6	Under 25 years	20,850	5,966	28.6
Not on farm operated	412,554	141,176	34.2	25 to 34 years	128,455	38,999	30.4
Not reported	137,539	44,278	32.2	35 to 44 years	371,442	109,290	29.4
Principal occupation:				45 to 49 years	232,845	71,975	30.9
Farming	961,560	275,553	28.7	50 to 54 years	233,884	77,988	33.3
Other	950,299	380,628	40.1	55 to 59 years	222,736	77,124	34.6
Days worked off farm:				60 to 64 years	204,618	74,650	36.5
None	755,254	223,322	29.6	65 to 69 years	179,858	70,196	39.0
Any	1,042,158	396,911	38.1	70 years and over	317,171	129,993	41.0
1 to 99 days	164,957	49,108	29.8	Average age	54	56	103.1
100 to 199 days	167,922	61,455	36.6	By sex:			
200 days or more	709,279	286,348	40.4	Male	1,746,757	600,985	34.4
Not reported	114,447	35,948	31.4	Female	165,102	55,196	33.4
Years on present farm:				Spanish, Hispanic/Latino origin	27,717	11,227	40.5
2 years or less	92,574	32,939	35.6	Tenure of operator:			
3 or 4 years	126,791	48,632	38.4	All operators	1,911,859	656,181	34.3
5 to 9 years	263,642	96,529	36.6	Full owners	1,146,891	418,556	36.5
10 years or more	1,113,839	367,004	32.9	Part owners	573,839	185,728	32.4
Ave. years on this farm	20	20	98.5	Tenants	191,129	51,897	27.2
Not reported	315,013	111,077	35.3				

Source: *1997 Census of Agriculture*, U.S. Department of Agriculture, National Agricultural Statistics Service. Table shows totals for the U.S. agriculture sector and for the NAICS subdivision of it, shown as "This Agric. Sector" or as "This Sector." Not all farms report on every category. For this reason, the reporting universe is shown in the last two columns. Averages are based on these columns. All values shown are number of farm operators in each category or percent.

FARMS BY TYPE OF ORGANIZATION

Item	Number of farms and percent				Total acres and percent		
	U.S.	% of U.S.	This Agriculture Sector	% of Sector	U.S.	This Agriculture Sector	% of U.S.
Individual or family (sole proprietorship)	1,643,424	100.0	590,502	100.0	585,464,911	251,045,602	42.9
Partnership	169,462	10.3	47,614	8.1	149,321,484	64,225,432	43.0
Corporation:							
Family held	76,103	4.6	12,049	2.0	119,559,203	56,622,735	47.4
More than 10 stockholders	1,795	0.1	354	0.1	-	-	-
10 or less stockholders	74,308	4.5	11,695	2.0	-	-	-
Other than family held	7,899	0.5	1,174	0.2	11,904,053	5,620,054	47.2
More than 10 stockholders	1,029	0.1	99	0.0	-	-	-
10 or less stockholders	6,870	0.4	1,075	0.2	-	-	-
Other cooperative, estate or trust, institutional, etc.	14,971	0.9	4,842	0.8	65,545,604	46,407,441	70.8

Source: *1997 Census of Agriculture*, U.S. Department of Agriculture, National Agricultural Statistics Service. Table shows totals for the U.S. agriculture sector and for the NAICS subdivision of it, shown as "This Agric. Sector" or as "This Sector." Not all farms report on every category. For this reason, the reporting universe is shown in the last two columns. Averages are based on these columns.

LIVESTOCK INVENTORIES AND SALES

Item	U.S. (number)	This Agric. Sector (number)	% of U.S.	Average number per farm			Number of farms reporting category	
				U.S.	This Agric. Sector	% of U.S.	U.S.	This Sector
Cattle and calves inventory	98,989,244	50,085,292	50.6	94.6	79.6	84.1	1,046,863	629,498
Cows and heifers that had calved	43,162,054	24,201,550	56.1	48.3	44.0	91.1	894,110	550,379
Beef cows	34,066,615	23,946,963	70.3	42.3	44.0	104.0	804,595	543,946
Milk cows	9,095,439	254,587	2.8	77.8	14.7	18.9	116,874	17,276
Heifers and heifer calves	26,988,697	12,109,145	44.9	33.6	24.8	73.8	803,985	488,507
Steers, steer calves, bulls, and bull calves	28,838,493	13,774,597	47.8	32.6	25.2	77.2	883,983	546,816
Cattle and calves sold	74,089,046	33,709,803	45.5	73.2	54.1	73.9	1,011,809	622,883
Calves	16,480,293	10,482,837	63.6	26.8	25.7	96.1	615,177	407,233
Cattle	57,608,753	23,226,966	40.3	78.0	52.9	67.9	738,696	438,730
Fattened on grain and concentrates	27,328,190	422,838	1.5	247.0	24.3	9.8	110,620	17,407
Hogs and pigs inventory	61,206,236	767,654	1.3	557.7	44.5	8.0	109,754	17,260
Used or to be used for breeding	6,831,564	92,231	1.4	106.7	12.6	11.8	64,029	7,304
Other	54,374,672	675,423	1.2	528.0	42.8	8.1	102,977	15,770
Hogs and pigs sold	142,611,882	1,166,232	0.8	1,396.7	95.9	6.9	102,106	12,159
Feeder pigs	34,988,718	217,182	0.6	2,037.8	103.1	5.1	17,170	2,107
Litters of pigs farrowed between Dec. 1 of preceding year and Nov. 30	11,497,523	124,319	1.1	170.3	15.9	9.3	67,514	7,830
Dec. 1 and May 31	5,697,371	64,138	1.1	91.0	9.5	10.5	62,622	6,744
June 1 and Nov. 30	5,800,152	60,181	1.0	99.7	10.8	10.8	58,204	5,585
Sheep and lambs of all ages inventory	7,821,885	1,531,999	19.6	118.9	91.1	76.7	65,790	16,810
Ewes 1 year old or older	4,408,683	999,251	22.7	78.1	71.8	91.9	56,414	13,920
Sheep and lambs sold	7,331,545	1,032,673	14.1	123.1	71.8	58.3	59,575	14,390
Sheep and lambs shorn	6,139,140	1,175,166	19.1	118.4	98.5	83.2	51,869	11,934
Horses and ponies inventory	2,427,277	766,421	31.6	6.5	4.9	76.4	375,218	155,058
Horses and ponies sold	325,306	49,582	15.2	4.1	2.8	69.1	79,516	17,535
Goats inventory	1,989,799	789,934	39.7	34.4	37.3	108.5	57,925	21,196
Goats sold	740,597	238,041	32.1	31.5	30.4	96.4	23,520	7,842

Source: *1997 Census of Agriculture*, U.S. Department of Agriculture, National Agricultural Statistics Service. Table shows totals for the U.S. agriculture sector and for the NAICS subdivision of it, shown as "This Agric. Sector" or as "This Sector." Not all farms report on every category. For this reason, the reporting universe is shown in the last two columns. Averages are based on these columns.

POULTRY INVENTORIES AND SALES

Item	U.S. (number)	This Agric. Sector (number)	% of U.S.	Average number per farm			Number of farms reporting category	
				U.S.	This Agric. Sector	% of U.S.	U.S.	This Sector
Layers and pullets 13 weeks old and older inventory	366,989,851	1,398,614	0.4	5,053.8	55.7	1.1	72,616	25,116
Layers 20 weeks old and older	313,851,480	940,480	0.3	4,499.0	38.6	0.9	69,761	24,354
Pullets 13 weeks old and older but less than 20 weeks old	53,138,371	458,134	0.9	4,031.7	104.7	2.6	13,180	4,375
Layers, pullets, and pullet chicks sold	331,563,736	1,535,406	0.5	24,636.9	866.5	3.5	13,458	1,772
Broilers and other meat type chickens sold	6,741,927,110	5,331,426	0.1	281,653.0	4,608.0	1.6	23,937	1,157
Turkey hens kept for breeding	5,504,808	22,326	0.4	968.1	11.3	1.2	5,686	1,972
Turkeys sold	307,586,680	168,905	0.1	51,000.9	296.3	0.6	6,031	570

Source: *1997 Census of Agriculture*, U.S. Department of Agriculture, National Agricultural Statistics Service. Table shows totals for the U.S. agriculture sector and for the NAICS subdivision of it, shown as "This Agric. Sector" or as "This Sector." Not all farms report on every category. For this reason, the reporting universe is shown in the last two columns. Averages are based on these columns.

SELECTED CROPS HARVESTED

Item	In 1,000	Crop harvested			Acres used for crop (000)			Number of farms reporting category	
		U.S.	This Agric. Sector	% of U.S.	U.S.	This Agric. Sector	% of U.S.	U.S.	This Sector
Corn for grain or seed	bushels	8,578,635	231,455	2.7	69,796.7	2,159.1	3.1	430,711	35,106
Irrigated		-	-	-	10,638.9	425.8	4.0	40,574	2,902
Corn for silage or green chop	tons, green	88,381	9,349	10.6	5,727.6	699.0	12.2	119,308	17,845
Irrigated		-	-	-	1,033.3	138.5	13.4	10,815	1,958
Sorghum for grain or seed	bushels	559,070	40,214	7.2	8,470.4	688.5	8.1	49,397	6,358
Irrigated		-	-	-	875.6	64.7	7.4	5,793	471
Wheat for grain	bushels	2,204,027	180,121	8.2	58,836.3	6,212.8	10.6	243,568	29,023
Irrigated		-	-	-	3,990.9	271.6	6.8	20,385	2,014
Barley for grain	bushels	336,435	21,744	6.5	5,945.0	454.6	7.6	41,930	5,852
Irrigated		-	-	-	1,060.1	94.9	8.9	8,847	1,663
Oats for grain	bushels	151,327	24,970	16.5	2,681.0	515.6	19.2	89,606	15,171
Irrigated		-	-	-	121.0	31.9	26.4	2,788	954
Rice	cwt	182,231	496	0.3	3,122.1	10.4	0.3	9,291	90
Irrigated		-	-	-	3,122.1	10.4	0.3	9,291	90
Cotton	bales	17,879	79	0.4	13,235.2	99.5	0.8	31,493	728
Irrigated		-	-	-	4,888.0	20.8	0.4	12,434	156
Tobacco	pounds	1,747,702	57,113	3.3	838.5	31.3	3.7	89,706	9,572
Irrigated		-	-	-	138.7	2.0	1.5	7,090	319
Soybeans for beans	bushels	2,504,307	41,409	1.7	66,147.7	1,178.9	1.8	354,692	15,996
Irrigated		-	-	-	4,152.1	47.0	1.1	20,619	519
Dry edible beans, excluding dry limas	cwt	27,224	446	1.6	1,691.9	25.6	1.5	10,911	367
Irrigated		-	-	-	577.0	16.2	2.8	4,882	236
Potatoes, excluding sweetpotatoes	cwt	459,886	1,479	0.3	1,355.2	5.4	0.4	10,523	808
Irrigated		-	-	-	1,070.3	4.2	0.4	4,843	104
Sugar beets for sugar	tons	29,775	306	1.0	1,453.8	15.6	1.1	7,102	160
Irrigated		-	-	-	616.4	12.9	2.1	3,492	139
Peanuts for nuts	pounds	3,377,143	52,066	1.5	1,352.2	31.6	2.3	12,221	634
Irrigated		-	-	-	412.3	9.8	2.4	3,125	139
Hay alfalfa, other tame, small grain, wild, grass silage, green chop	tons, dry	139,365	46,630	33.5	60,799.8	24,764.1	40.7	888,597	354,453
Irrigated		-	-	-	9,564.3	3,685.7	38.5	79,406	28,173
Alfalfa hay	tons, dry	65,863	14,672	22.3	21,309.8	6,322.7	29.7	358,365	87,799
Irrigated		-	-	-	5,980.5	1,702.9	28.5	57,854	18,829
Vegetables harvested for sale		-	-	-	3,773.2	28.9	0.8	53,727	2,238
Irrigated		-	-	-	2,641.8	8.9	0.3	23,203	525
Land in orchards		-	-	-	5,158.1	166.3	3.2	106,069	9,912
Irrigated		-	-	-	4,107.9	31.0	0.8	61,606	1,928

Source: 1997 *Census of Agriculture*, U.S. Department of Agriculture, National Agricultural Statistics Service. Table shows totals for the U.S. agriculture sector and for the NAICS subdivision of it, shown as "This Agric. Sector" or as "This Sector." Not all farms report on every category. For this reason, the reporting universe is shown in the last two columns. Averages are based on these columns. "Green tons" are weight of product as harvested, i.e., moist. cwt stands for "hundredweight."

LEADING COMPANIES   Number shown: **11**   Total sales ($ mil): **622**   Total employment (000): **2.0**

Company Name	Address				CEO Name	Phone	Co. Type	Sales ($ mil)	Empl. (000)
King Ranch Inc.	1415 Louisiana	Houston	TX	77002	Jack Hunt	713-752-5700	R	300*	0.7
Lykes Agriculture	7 Lykes Rd	Lake Placid	FL	33852	Pat Hamilton	941-465-4127	S	143*	0.5
Tejon Ranch Co.	PO Box 1000	Lebec	CA	93243	Robert A Stine	661-248-3000	P	52	<0.1
Alico Inc.	P O Box 338	LaBelle	FL	33975	Ben H Griffin III	863-675-2966	P	43	0.1
Bay Houston Towing Co.	P O Box 3006	Houston	TX	77253	Mark E Kuebler	713-529-3755	R	38	0.4
Bridwell Oil Co.	PO Box 1830	Wichita Falls	TX	76307	GH Shores	940-723-4351	R	22	<0.1
H.C. Spinks Clay Company Inc.	PO Box 820	Paris	TN	38242	R Carothers	901-642-5414	R	15*	0.1
J.R. Resources	P O Box 188	Ringgold	PA	15770		814-365-5821	R	4	<0.1
Midland Cattle Co.	P O Box 495	Red Oak	IA	51566	Gordon Reisinger	712-623-5158	P	3*	<0.1
Seven J Stock Farm Inc.	99 Travis St	Houston	TX	77060	John R Parten	713-228-8900	P	1*	<0.1
Bar-D Ranch Div.	P O Box 3006	Houston	TX	77253	Mark E Kuebler	713-529-3755	D	1	<0.1

Source: *Ward's Business Directory of U.S. Private and Public Companies*, Volumes 1 and 2, 2000. The company type code used is as follows: P - Public, R - Private, S - Subsidiary, D - Division, J - Joint Venture, A - Affiliate, G - Group, N - Company type not reported. Sales are in millions of dollars, employees are in thousands. An asterisk (*) indicates an estimated sales volume. The symbol < stands for 'less than'. Company names and addresses are truncated, in some cases, to fit into the available space.

NAICS 112112 - CATTLE FEEDLOTS

GENERAL STATISTICS

Item	U.S. Total	This Agri-culture Sector	% of U.S.	Category average per farm				Number of farms reporting category	
				Value shown as	U.S.	This Agric. Sector	% of U.S.	U.S.	This Sector
Farms - number	1,911,859	43,469	2.3	-	-	-	-	-	-
Land in farms - mil. acres	931.795	20.453	2.2	Acres	487	471	96.7	1,911,859	43,469
Value of land, buildings - $ mil.	859,839.2	18,734.0	2.2	$	449,748	431,899	96.0	524,066	43,376
Value of machinery and equip-ment - $ mil.	110,256.8	2,652.2	2.4	$	57,678	61,154	106.0	1,911,601	43,369
Sales of Ag Products - $ mil.	196,864.6	19,998.5	10.2	$	102,970	460,064	446.8	1,911,859	43,469
Government payments - $ mil.	5,054.5	118.6	2.3	$	7,378	8,292	112.4	685,029	14,301
Other farm-related income - $ mil.	3,272.3	97.4	3.0	$	5,999	7,253	120.9	545,480	13,424
Expenses - $ mil.	150,591.0	17,374.2	11.5	$	78,771	400,550	508.5	1,911,766	43,376
Payroll - $ mil.	14,841.0	456.4	3.1	$	22,811	33,392	146.4	650,623	13,668
Workers - 150 days or more a year	890,467	23,180	2.6	Number	3.4	4.1	120.1	259,631	5,626
Workers - less than 150 days	2,461,561	40,222	1.6	Number	4.2	3.4	79.4	581,658	11,967
Net Cash Return - $ mil.	42,557.9	2,492.6	5.9	$	22,260	57,464	258.1	1,911,824	43,376

Source: *1997 Census of Agriculture*, U.S. Department of Agriculture, National Agricultural Statistics Service. Table shows totals for the U.S. agriculture sector and for the NAICS subdivision of it, shown as "This Agric. Sector" or as "This Sector." Not all farms report on every category. For this reason, the reporting universe is shown in the last two columns. Averages are based on these columns.

LAND IN FARMS ACCORDING TO USE

Item	U.S. Total (000 acres)	This Sector (000 acres)	% of U.S.	Average acres per farms			Number of farms reporting category	
				U.S.	This Agric. Sector	% of U.S.	U.S.	This Sector
Total cropland	431,144.9	8,280.0	1.9	260	234	-	1,661,395	35,338
Harvested cropland	309,395.5	5,915.6	1.9	219	207	-	1,410,606	28,550
Cropland:								
Pasture or grazing	64,466.5	1,632.0	2.5	85	73	-	754,170	22,437
In cover crops, legumes, grasses	13,531.2	184.0	1.4	88	67	-	153,177	2,743
On which all crops failed	3,449.4	46.8	1.4	67	48	-	51,673	983
In cultivated summer fallow	20,905.9	256.0	1.2	256	200	-	81,702	1,279
Idle	19,396.3	245.6	1.3	83	70	-	232,961	3,494
Total woodland	71,465.4	1,271.4	1.8	96	73	-	743,011	17,522
Woodland pastured	29,693.9	562.2	1.9	84	58	-	352,217	9,637
Woodland not pastured	41,771.5	709.2	1.7	79	59	-	531,846	12,009
Other pasture/rangeland	396,884.6	10,224.2	2.6	721	670	-	550,619	15,254
Land for house lots, ponds, roads, wasteland	32,300.4	677.2	2.1	28	24	-	1,142,618	28,141
Irrigated land	55,058.1	1,080.0	2.0	197	277	-	279,442	3,900
Harvested cropland	50,013.5	947.0	1.9	198	320	-	252,679	2,957
Pasture and other	5,044.7	133.1	2.6	87	80	-	58,258	1,666
Conservation Reserve/Wetlands Reserve Lands	29,489.1	395.4	1.3	131	103	-	225,410	3,838

Source: *1997 Census of Agriculture*, U.S. Department of Agriculture, National Agricultural Statistics Service. Table shows totals for the U.S. agriculture sector and for the NAICS subdivision of it, shown as "This Agric. Sector" or as "This Sector." Not all farms report on every category. For this reason, the reporting universe is shown in the last two columns. Averages are based on these columns. The Conservation Reserve and Wetlands Reserve programs provide support for land conservation/preservation. Cover crops are not harvested or pastured.

MARKET VALUE OF AGRICULTURAL PRODUCTS SOLD: ALL FARMS

Item	U.S. Total ($ mil.)	This Sector ($ mil.)	% of Sector Sales	% of U.S.	Average sales per farm - $			Number of farms reporting category	
					U.S.	This Agric. Sector	% of U.S.	U.S.	This Sector
Grains	46,617.1	617.4	3.09	1.3	79,095	52,307	66.1	589,379	11,803
Corn for grain	18,884.8	271.5	1.36	1.4	52,506	40,410	77.0	359,666	6,719
Wheat	7,173.9	69.8	0.35	1.0	29,726	18,297	61.6	241,334	3,816
Soybeans	15,622.4	238.2	1.19	1.5	44,185	34,316	77.7	353,566	6,941
Sorghum for grain	1,140.0	15.3	0.08	1.3	25,360	43,777	172.6	44,955	350
Barley	709.6	3.3	0.02	0.5	23,191	9,579	41.3	30,598	349
Oats	121.3	2.2	0.01	1.8	3,114	1,892	60.8	38,940	1,159
Other grains	2,965.1	17.0	0.09	0.6	67,540	32,886	48.7	43,901	517
Cotton and cotton seed	5,975.5	8.0	0.04	0.1	189,963	348,652	183.5	31,456	23
Tobacco	2,924.7	5.3	0.03	0.2	32,662	13,901	42.6	89,544	382
Hay, silage, and field seeds	4,670.5	61.4	0.31	1.3	13,174	9,966	75.6	354,523	6,160
Vegetables, sweet corn, and melons	8,401.7	5.1	0.03	0.1	156,628	11,967	7.6	53,641	426
Fruits and berries	12,660.3	2.3	0.01	0.0	147,259	11,069	7.5	85,973	204
Nursery and greenhouse crops	10,942.8	0.4	0.00	0.0	161,360	3,576	2.2	67,816	125
Other crops	5,863.1	31.1	0.16	0.5	153,907	147,919	96.1	38,095	210
Poultry and poultry products	22,262.6	4.2	0.02	0.0	352,000	3,341	0.9	63,246	1,262
Dairy products	18,997.3	15.5	0.08	0.1	191,432	71,373	37.3	99,238	217
Cattle and calves	40,524.8	19,103.7	95.53	47.1	40,052	439,478	1,097.3	1,011,809	43,469
Hogs and pigs	13,804.8	129.9	0.65	0.9	135,201	39,971	29.6	102,106	3,249
Sheep, lambs, and wool	682.9	9.4	0.05	1.4	10,913	6,265	57.4	62,579	1,501
Other livestock	2,536.5	4.9	0.02	0.2	20,506	3,116	15.2	123,695	1,565
Products sold to public directly	13,096.7	109.3	0.55	0.8	377,610	160,507	42.5	34,683	681

Source: 1997 Census of Agriculture, U.S. Department of Agriculture, National Agricultural Statistics Service. Table shows totals for the U.S. agriculture sector and for the NAICS subdivision of it, shown as "This Agric. Sector" or as "This Sector." Not all farms report on every category. For this reason, the reporting universe is shown in the last two columns. Averages are based on these columns. Farms classified in one sector routinely produce categories in other sectors as well. Products sold to the public are sold for direct consumption.

MARKET VALUE OF PRODUCTS SOLD: FARMS WITH SALES OF $50,000 OR MORE

Item	U.S. Total ($ mil.)	This Sector ($ mil.)	% of Sector Sales	% of U.S.	Average sales per farm - $			Number of farms reporting category	
					U.S.	This Agric. Sector	% of U.S.	U.S.	This Sector
Grains	40,973.4	507.9	2.54	1.2	183,623	159,963	87.1	223,138	3,175
Cotton and cotton seed	5,743.9	-	-	-	286,562	-	-	20,044	8
Tobacco	2,060.2	1.5	0.01	0.1	175,907	105,143	59.8	11,712	14
Hay, silage, and field seeds	2,781.9	35.5	0.18	1.3	188,959	153,632	81.3	14,722	231
Vegetables, sweet corn, and melons	7,966.8	2.4	0.01	0.0	673,443	134,000	19.9	11,830	18
Fruits and berries	12,072.3	1.9	0.01	0.0	478,927	266,571	55.7	25,207	7
Nursery and greenhouse crops	10,412.0	-	-	-	578,025	-	-	18,013	2
Other crops	5,586.6	29.7	0.15	0.5	363,758	494,600	136.0	15,358	60
Poultry and poultry products	22,171.7	3.2	0.02	0.0	778,637	198,875	25.5	28,475	16
Dairy products	18,344.3	13.4	0.07	0.1	250,075	212,143	84.8	73,355	63
Cattle and calves	32,358.6	18,773.1	93.87	58.0	386,685	1,933,575	500.0	83,682	9,709
Hogs and pigs	13,096.7	109.3	0.55	0.8	377,610	160,507	42.5	34,683	681
Sheep, lambs, and wool	478.6	6.5	0.03	1.4	278,730	646,500	231.9	1,717	10
Other livestock	2,026.6	2.2	0.01	0.1	369,685	180,583	48.8	5,482	12

Source: 1997 Census of Agriculture, U.S. Department of Agriculture, National Agricultural Statistics Service. Table shows totals for the U.S. agriculture sector and for the NAICS subdivision of it, shown as "This Agric. Sector" or as "This Sector." Not all farms report on every category. For this reason, the reporting universe is shown in the last two columns. Averages are based on these columns. Farms classified in one sector routinely produce categories in other sectors as well.

GOVERNMENT PAYMENTS AND OTHER FARM-RELATED INCOME

Item	U.S. Total ($ mil.)	This Sector ($ mil.)	% of Sector Gov/Oth. Income	% of U.S.	Average receipts per farm - $			Number of farms reporting category	
					U.S.	This Agric. Sector	% of U.S.	U.S.	This Sector
Government payments	5,054.5	118.6	54.91	2.3	7,378	8,292	112.4	685,029	14,301
Other farm-related income	3,272.3	97.4	45.09	3.0	5,999	7,253	120.9	545,480	13,424
Custom work and other agricultural services	1,235.1	40.5	18.75	3.3	8,646	12,385	143.2	142,854	3,270
Gross cash rent or share payments	1,207.9	42.7	19.75	3.5	6,867	9,146	133.2	175,901	4,664
Forest products, excluding Christmas trees and maple products	344.3	6.4	2.95	1.9	7,417	5,935	80.0	46,426	1,074
Other farm-related income sources	484.9	7.8	3.63	1.6	1,595	990	62.1	303,908	7,911

Source: *1997 Census of Agriculture*, U.S. Department of Agriculture, National Agricultural Statistics Service. Table shows totals for the U.S. agriculture sector and for the NAICS subdivision of it, shown as "This Agric. Sector" or as "This Sector." Not all farms report on every category. For this reason, the reporting universe is shown in the last two columns. Averages are based on these columns. Government payments are agricultural subsidies under various programs.

COMMODITY CREDIT CORPORATION LOANS

Item	U.S. Total ($ mil.)	This Sector ($ mil.)	% of Sector Loan Total	% of U.S.	Average loan value per farm - $			Number of farms reporting category	
					U.S.	This Agric. Sector	% of U.S.	U.S.	This Sector
Total loans	3,034.7	56.2	100.00	1.9	36,419	35,310	97.0	83,328	1,591
Corn	1,333.9	38.2	68.06	2.9	26,419	29,389	111.2	50,489	1,301
Wheat	415.4	3.8	6.68	0.9	18,093	15,629	86.4	22,961	240
Soybeans	774.0	13.3	23.59	1.7	30,370	31,782	104.6	25,487	417
Sorghum, barley, and oats	54.8	0.8	1.38	1.4	8,603	7,653	89.0	6,375	101
Cotton	191.4	-	-	-	43,275	-	-	4,422	2
Sunflower seed, flaxseed, safflower, canola, other rapeseed, and mustard seed	17.3	0.1	0.16	0.5	25,159	30,667	121.9	686	3
Peanuts, rice, and tobacco	247.9	-	-	-	60,421	-	-	4,103	7

Source: *1997 Census of Agriculture*, U.S. Department of Agriculture, National Agricultural Statistics Service. Table shows totals for the U.S. agriculture sector and for the NAICS subdivision of it, shown as "This Agric. Sector" or as "This Sector." Not all farms report on every category. For this reason, the reporting universe is shown in the last two columns. Averages are based on these columns. The Commodity Credit Corporation provides low interest loans to farmers.

SELECTED MACHINERY AND EQUIPMENT

Item	U.S. Total (number)	This Agric. Sector (number)	% of U.S.	Average number per farm			Number of farms reporting category	
				U.S.	This Agric. Sector	% of U.S.	U.S.	This Sector
Motortrucks, including pickups	3,497,735	76,622	2.2	2.07	1.99	96.0	1,688,303	38,522
Wheel tractors	3,936,014	97,099	2.5	2.31	2.49	107.9	1,707,384	39,041
Less than 40 horsepower (PTO)	1,262,688	29,924	2.4	1.44	1.45	100.7	877,119	20,649
40 horsepower (PTO) or more	2,673,326	67,175	2.5	2.02	2.20	108.6	1,321,084	30,559
40 to 99 horsepower (PTO)	1,808,105	46,718	2.6	1.58	1.68	106.7	1,145,466	27,740
100 horsepower (PTO)	865,221	20,457	2.4	1.68	1.81	107.5	513,773	11,298
Grain and bean combines	460,606	10,526	2.3	1.16	1.11	95.5	395,934	9,474
Cotton pickers and strippers	38,294	51	0.1	1.48	2.13	143.6	25,874	24
Mower conditioners	608,443	19,372	3.2	1.12	1.09	97.4	543,565	17,760
Pickup balers	717,245	23,236	3.2	1.24	1.24	100.0	579,440	18,778

Source: *1997 Census of Agriculture*, U.S. Department of Agriculture, National Agricultural Statistics Service. Table shows totals for the U.S. agriculture sector and for the NAICS subdivision of it, shown as "This Agric. Sector" or as "This Sector." Not all farms report on every category. For this reason, the reporting universe is shown in the last two columns. Averages are based on these columns. PTO stands for "power take off."

FARM PRODUCTION EXPENSES

Item	U.S. Total ($ mil.)	This Sector ($ mil.)	% of Sector Total Expense	% of U.S.	Average expense per farm - $			Number of farms reporting category	
					U.S.	This Agric. Sector	% of U.S.	U.S.	This Sector
Total farm production expenses	150,591.0	17,374.2	100.00	11.5	78,771	400,550	508.5	1,911,766	43,376
Livestock and poultry purchased	21,614.6	9,838.5	56.63	45.5	38,807	347,170	894.6	556,980	28,339
Feed for livestock and poultry	32,760.0	4,738.3	27.27	14.5	32,059	121,620	379.4	1,021,849	38,960
Commercially mixed formula feeds	21,236.2	997.5	5.74	4.7	34,459	42,264	122.7	616,280	23,602
Seeds, bulbs, plants, and trees	5,725.9	93.4	0.54	1.6	6,388	4,763	74.6	896,339	19,613
Commercial fertilizer	9,597.1	165.8	0.95	1.7	8,060	6,583	81.7	1,190,733	25,186
Agricultural chemicals	7,581.4	105.9	0.61	1.4	8,056	5,280	65.5	941,136	20,048
Petroleum products	6,371.5	203.3	1.17	3.2	3,619	4,913	135.7	1,760,642	41,380
Gasoline and gasohol	1,886.6	64.1	0.37	3.4	1,380	1,906	138.1	1,366,915	33,645
Diesel fuel	2,846.0	90.2	0.52	3.2	2,164	3,067	141.8	1,315,397	29,420
Natural gas	432.9	19.7	0.11	4.5	6,091	12,861	211.1	71,069	1,530
LP gas, fuel oil, kerosene, motor oil, grease, etc.	1,206.1	29.3	0.17	2.4	945	975	103.2	1,276,331	29,998
Electricity	2,751.1	84.9	0.49	3.1	2,247	2,671	118.9	1,224,374	31,797
Hired farm labor	14,841.0	456.4	2.63	3.1	22,811	33,392	146.4	650,623	13,668
Contract labor	2,959.0	25.6	0.15	0.9	13,040	7,170	55.0	226,909	3,570
Repair and maintenance	8,637.7	301.7	1.74	3.5	5,616	8,178	145.6	1,538,058	36,894
Custom work, machine hire, and rental of equipment	3,210.3	91.7	0.53	2.9	5,372	6,283	117.0	597,624	14,599
Interest	8,928.1	354.2	2.04	4.0	11,016	19,267	174.9	810,476	18,385
Secured by real estate	5,449.6	143.9	0.83	2.6	9,564	11,196	117.1	569,775	12,849
Not secured by real estate	3,478.5	210.4	1.21	6.0	7,540	19,918	264.2	461,326	10,561
Cash rent	6,915.7	151.0	0.87	2.2	14,244	14,167	99.5	485,512	10,655
Property taxes	3,920.1	112.4	0.65	2.9	2,213	2,741	123.9	1,771,787	41,000
All other farm production expenses	14,777.4	651.2	3.75	4.4	8,747	16,261	185.9	1,689,391	40,044

Source: *1997 Census of Agriculture*, U.S. Department of Agriculture, National Agricultural Statistics Service. Table shows totals for the U.S. agriculture sector and for the NAICS subdivision of it, shown as "This Agric. Sector" or as "This Sector." Not all farms report on every category. For this reason, the reporting universe is shown in the last two columns. Averages are based on these columns. LP gas stands for "liquid petroleum gas," i.e., butane or propane.

NET CASH RETURN AND FARMS WITH GAINS AND LOSSES

Item	Number of farms and %				Average gain or loss per farm - $		
	U.S.	% of U.S.	This Agriculture Sector	% of Sector	U.S.	This Agriculture Sector	% of U.S.
All farms	1,911,824	100.0	43,376	100.0	22,260	57,464	258.1
Number of farms with net gains	985,718	51.6	19,038	43.9	51,296	153,698	299.6
Gain of -							
Less than $1,000	120,163	6.3	3,020	7.0	-	-	-
$1,000 to $9,999	370,611	19.4	7,736	17.8	-	-	-
$10,000 to $49,999	292,484	15.3	4,760	11.0	-	-	-
$50,000 or more	202,460	10.6	3,522	8.1	-	-	-
Number of farms with net losses	926,106	48.4	24,338	56.1	(8,645)	(17,813)	206.0
Loss of -							
Less than $1,000	165,390	8.7	3,311	7.6	-	-	-
$1,000 to $9,999	591,517	30.9	15,536	35.8	-	-	-
$10,000 to $49,999	152,649	8.0	4,738	10.9	-	-	-
$50,000 or more	16,550	0.9	753	1.7	-	-	-

Source: *1997 Census of Agriculture*, U.S. Department of Agriculture, National Agricultural Statistics Service. Table shows totals for the U.S. agriculture sector and for the NAICS subdivision of it, shown as "This Agric. Sector" or as "This Sector." Not all farms report on every category. For this reason, the reporting universe is shown in the last two columns. Averages are based on these columns. Net gains are income less cost for farm operations; they exclude non-farm earnings. Values in parentheses are losses.

CHARACTERISTICS OF FARM OPERATORS

Farm Operators	U.S.	This Agric. Sector	% of U.S.	Farm Operators	U.S.	This Agric. Sector	% of U.S.
Place of residence:				By age group:			
On farm operated	1,361,766	34,492	2.5	Under 25 years	20,850	560	2.7
Not on farm operated	412,554	6,425	1.6	25 to 34 years	128,455	2,900	2.3
Not reported	137,539	2,552	1.9	35 to 44 years	371,442	8,785	2.4
Principal occupation:				45 to 49 years	232,845	5,184	2.2
Farming	961,560	20,993	2.2	50 to 54 years	233,884	4,921	2.1
Other	950,299	22,476	2.4	55 to 59 years	222,736	4,984	2.2
Days worked off farm:				60 to 64 years	204,618	4,649	2.3
None	755,254	16,156	2.1	65 to 69 years	179,858	4,273	2.4
Any	1,042,158	24,856	2.4	70 years and over	317,171	7,213	2.3
1 to 99 days	164,957	3,342	2.0	Average age	54	54	99.8
100 to 199 days	167,922	3,590	2.1	By sex:			
200 days or more	709,279	17,924	2.5	Male	1,746,757	40,820	2.3
Not reported	114,447	2,457	2.1	Female	165,102	2,649	1.6
Years on present farm:				Spanish, Hispanic/Latino origin	27,717	428	1.5
2 years or less	92,574	1,710	1.8	Tenure of operator:			
3 or 4 years	126,791	2,826	2.2	All operators	1,911,859	43,469	2.3
5 to 9 years	263,642	6,032	2.3	Full owners	1,146,891	27,026	2.4
10 years or more	1,113,839	26,276	2.4	Part owners	573,839	13,248	2.3
Ave. years on this farm	20	21	104.5	Tenants	191,129	3,195	1.7
Not reported	315,013	6,625	2.1				

Source: *1997 Census of Agriculture*, U.S. Department of Agriculture, National Agricultural Statistics Service. Table shows totals for the U.S. agriculture sector and for the NAICS subdivision of it, shown as "This Agric. Sector" or as "This Sector." Not all farms report on every category. For this reason, the reporting universe is shown in the last two columns. Averages are based on these columns. All values shown are number of farm operators in each category or percent.

FARMS BY TYPE OF ORGANIZATION

Item	Number of farms and percent				Total acres and percent		
	U.S.	% of U.S.	This Agriculture Sector	% of Sector	U.S.	This Agriculture Sector	% of U.S.
Individual or family (sole proprietorship)	1,643,424	100.0	37,625	100.0	585,464,911	11,304,423	1.9
Partnership	169,462	10.3	3,519	9.4	149,321,484	3,575,469	2.4
Corporation:							
Family held	76,103	4.6	1,859	4.9	119,559,203	4,731,471	4.0
More than 10 stockholders	1,795	0.1	70	0.2	-	-	-
10 or less stockholders	74,308	4.5	1,789	4.8	-	-	-
Other than family held	7,899	0.5	223	0.6	11,904,053	518,737	4.4
More than 10 stockholders	1,029	0.1	29	0.1	-	-	-
10 or less stockholders	6,870	0.4	194	0.5	-	-	-
Other cooperative, estate or trust, institutional, etc.	14,971	0.9	243	0.6	65,545,604	322,746	0.5

Source: *1997 Census of Agriculture*, U.S. Department of Agriculture, National Agricultural Statistics Service. Table shows totals for the U.S. agriculture sector and for the NAICS subdivision of it, shown as "This Agric. Sector" or as "This Sector." Not all farms report on every category. For this reason, the reporting universe is shown in the last two columns. Averages are based on these columns.

LIVESTOCK INVENTORIES AND SALES

Item	U.S. (number)	This Agric. Sector (number)	% of U.S.	Average number per farm			Number of farms reporting category	
				U.S.	This Agric. Sector	% of U.S.	U.S.	This Sector
Cattle and calves inventory	98,989,244	15,029,722	15.2	94.6	363.6	384.5	1,046,863	41,336
Cows and heifers that had calved	43,162,054	1,254,354	2.9	48.3	47.3	98.0	894,110	26,504
Beef cows	34,066,615	1,242,879	3.6	42.3	47.7	112.6	804,595	26,067
Milk cows	9,095,439	11,475	0.1	77.8	11.9	15.3	116,874	961
Heifers and heifer calves	26,988,697	5,153,846	19.1	33.6	185.9	553.8	803,985	27,724
Steers, steer calves, bulls, and bull calves	28,838,493	8,621,522	29.9	32.6	229.9	704.8	883,983	37,496
Cattle and calves sold	74,089,046	25,861,229	34.9	73.2	594.9	812.5	1,011,809	43,469
Calves	16,480,293	223,857	1.4	26.8	24.0	89.6	615,177	9,325
Cattle	57,608,753	25,637,372	44.5	78.0	589.8	756.3	738,696	43,469
Fattened on grain and concentrates	27,328,190	25,192,622	92.2	247.0	579.6	234.6	110,620	43,469
Hogs and pigs inventory	61,206,236	675,518	1.1	557.7	208.0	37.3	109,754	3,247
Used or to be used for breeding	6,831,564	55,708	0.8	106.7	43.9	41.2	64,029	1,268
Other	54,374,672	619,810	1.1	528.0	199.2	37.7	102,977	3,112
Hogs and pigs sold	142,611,882	1,127,435	0.8	1,396.7	347.0	24.8	102,106	3,249
Feeder pigs	34,988,718	87,608	0.3	2,037.8	312.9	15.4	17,170	280
Litters of pigs farrowed between Dec. 1 of preceding year and Nov. 30	11,497,523	80,771	0.7	170.3	59.3	34.8	67,514	1,363
Dec. 1 and May 31	5,697,371	40,525	0.7	91.0	32.7	35.9	62,622	1,241
June 1 and Nov. 30	5,800,152	40,246	0.7	99.7	36.4	36.5	58,204	1,107
Sheep and lambs of all ages inventory	7,821,885	74,286	0.9	118.9	49.7	41.8	65,790	1,495
Ewes 1 year old or older	4,408,683	37,119	0.8	78.1	30.7	39.3	56,414	1,210
Sheep and lambs sold	7,331,545	119,070	1.6	123.1	84.1	68.3	59,575	1,416
Sheep and lambs shorn	6,139,140	100,346	1.6	118.4	90.3	76.3	51,869	1,111
Horses and ponies inventory	2,427,277	40,563	1.7	6.5	4.7	72.3	375,218	8,667
Horses and ponies sold	325,306	2,423	0.7	4.1	2.8	68.6	79,516	863
Goats inventory	1,989,799	14,040	0.7	34.4	11.4	33.3	57,925	1,227
Goats sold	740,597	4,618	0.6	31.5	10.1	32.0	23,520	459

Source: *1997 Census of Agriculture*, U.S. Department of Agriculture, National Agricultural Statistics Service. Table shows totals for the U.S. agriculture sector and for the NAICS subdivision of it, shown as "This Agric. Sector" or as "This Sector." Not all farms report on every category. For this reason, the reporting universe is shown in the last two columns. Averages are based on these columns.

POULTRY INVENTORIES AND SALES

Item	U.S. (number)	This Agric. Sector (number)	% of U.S.	Average number per farm			Number of farms reporting category	
				U.S.	This Agric. Sector	% of U.S.	U.S.	This Sector
Layers and pullets 13 weeks old and older inventory	366,989,851	234,728	0.1	5,053.8	106.5	2.1	72,616	2,205
Layers 20 weeks old and older	313,851,480	171,732	0.1	4,499.0	81.0	1.8	69,761	2,119
Pullets 13 weeks old and older but less than 20 weeks old	53,138,371	62,996	0.1	4,031.7	149.3	3.7	13,180	422
Layers, pullets, and pullet chicks sold	331,563,736	330,725	0.1	24,636.9	1,312.4	5.3	13,458	252
Broilers and other meat type chickens sold	6,741,927,110	727,844	0.0	281,653.0	2,260.4	0.8	23,937	322
Turkey hens kept for breeding	5,504,808	-	-	968.1	-	-	5,686	152
Turkeys sold	307,586,680	-	-	51,000.9	-	-	6,031	114

Source: *1997 Census of Agriculture*, U.S. Department of Agriculture, National Agricultural Statistics Service. Table shows totals for the U.S. agriculture sector and for the NAICS subdivision of it, shown as "This Agric. Sector" or as "This Sector." Not all farms report on every category. For this reason, the reporting universe is shown in the last two columns. Averages are based on these columns.

SELECTED CROPS HARVESTED

Item	In 1,000	Crop harvested			Acres used for crop (000)			Number of farms reporting category	
		U.S.	This Agric. Sector	% of U.S.	U.S.	This Agric. Sector	% of U.S.	U.S.	This Sector
Corn for grain or seed	bushels	8,578,635	259,316	3.0	69,796.7	2,069.4	3.0	430,711	13,600
Irrigated		-	-	-	10,638.9	463.2	4.4	40,574	1,341
Corn for silage or green chop	tons, green	88,381	5,979	6.8	5,727.6	375.7	6.6	119,308	6,962
Irrigated		-	-	-	1,033.3	93.2	9.0	10,815	838
Sorghum for grain or seed	bushels	559,070	11,764	2.1	8,470.4	160.5	1.9	49,397	677
Irrigated		-	-	-	875.6	9.1	1.0	5,793	58
Wheat for grain	bushels	2,204,027	23,323	1.1	58,836.3	586.5	1.0	243,568	3,930
Irrigated		-	-	-	3,990.9	62.5	1.6	20,385	257
Barley for grain	bushels	336,435	3,266	1.0	5,945.0	53.9	0.9	41,930	1,194
Irrigated		-	-	-	1,060.7	14.2	1.3	8,847	192
Oats for grain	bushels	151,327	4,966	3.3	2,681.0	85.8	3.2	89,606	4,034
Irrigated		-	-	-	121.0	1.9	1.6	2,788	76
Rice	cwt	182,231	-	-	3,122.1	-	-	9,291	1
Irrigated		-	-	-	3,122.1	-	-	9,291	1
Cotton	bales	17,879	21	0.1	13,235.2	32.6	0.2	31,493	25
Irrigated		-	-	-	4,888.0	0.8	0.0	12,434	7
Tobacco	pounds	1,747,702	3,612	0.2	838.5	1.8	0.2	89,706	383
Irrigated		-	-	-	138.7	0.2	0.1	7,090	14
Soybeans for beans	bushels	2,504,307	40,417	1.6	66,147.7	969.1	1.5	354,692	6,992
Irrigated		-	-	-	4,152.1	45.1	1.1	20,619	388
Dry edible beans, excluding dry limas	cwt	27,224	564	2.1	1,691.9	31.0	1.8	10,911	153
Irrigated		-	-	-	577.0	21.0	3.6	4,882	90
Potatoes, excluding sweetpotatoes	cwt	459,886	2,977	0.6	1,355.2	7.9	0.6	10,523	121
Irrigated		-	-	-	1,070.3	7.8	0.7	4,843	30
Sugar beets for sugar	tons	29,775	319	1.1	1,453.8	15.6	1.1	7,102	75
Irrigated		-	-	-	616.4	9.8	1.6	3,492	58
Peanuts for nuts	pounds	3,377,143	928	0.0	1,352.2	0.4	0.0	12,221	14
Irrigated		-	-	-	412.3	-	-	3,125	1
Hay alfalfa, other tame, small grain, wild, grass silage, green chop	tons, dry	139,365	3,875	2.8	60,799.8	1,597.8	2.6	888,597	24,992
Irrigated		-	-	-	9,564.3	216.3	2.3	79,406	1,769
Alfalfa hay	tons, dry	65,863	2,250	3.4	21,309.8	714.2	3.4	358,365	14,113
Irrigated		-	-	-	5,980.5	142.5	2.4	57,854	1,323
Vegetables harvested for sale		-	-	-	3,773.2	7.7	0.2	53,727	426
Irrigated		-	-	-	2,641.8	2.1	0.1	23,203	104
Land in orchards		-	-	-	5,158.1	5.2	0.1	106,069	446
Irrigated		-	-	-	4,107.9	0.8	0.0	61,606	112

Source: 1997 Census of Agriculture, U.S. Department of Agriculture, National Agricultural Statistics Service. Table shows totals for the U.S. agriculture sector and for the NAICS subdivision of it, shown as "This Agric. Sector" or as "This Sector." Not all farms report on every category. For this reason, the reporting universe is shown in the last two columns. Averages are based on these columns. "Green tons" are weight of product as harvested, i.e., moist. cwt stands for "hundredweight."

LEADING COMPANIES Number shown: **16** Total sales ($ mil): **10,857** Total employment (000): **32.5**

Company Name	Address				CEO Name	Phone	Co. Type	Sales ($ mil)	Empl. (000)
Monfort Inc.	PO Box G	Greeley	CO	80632		970-353-2311	S	7,093*	19.0
J.R. Simplot Co.	PO Box 27	Boise	ID	83707	Stephen Beebe	208-336-2110	R	2,800	12.0
Cactus Feeders Inc.	P O Box 3050	Amarillo	TX	79116	Paul F Engler	806-373-2333	R	325	0.4
National Farms Inc.	1600 Genessee St	Kansas City	MO	64102	Bill Haw	816-221-4501	R	266*	0.5
Caprock Industries Inc.	905 S Fillmore St	Amarillo	TX	79101	Zay Gilbreath	806-371-3700	S	130*	0.2
AzTx Cattle Co.	P O Box 390	Hereford	TX	79045	John Josserand	806-364-8871	R	115*	0.2
Texas County Feedyard L.L.C.	P O Box 1029	Guymon	OK	73942		580-338-7714	S	21*	<0.1
Walter Lasley and Sons Inc.	PO Box 168	Stratford	TX	79084	Walter Lasley	806-753-4411	R	19	<0.1
Ingalls Feed Yard	10505 U S Hwy 50	Ingalls	KS	67853		316-335-5174	R	17*	<0.1
Great Bend Feeding Inc.	R R 5, Box 150	Great Bend	KS	67530	Roger Murphy	316-792-2508	R	15	<0.1
Kearny County Feeders Inc.	N Hwy 25	Lakin	KS	67860	Bradner A Tate	316-355-6630	R	15	<0.1
Reeve Cattle Co.	P O Box 1036	Garden City	KS	67846	MP Reeve	316-275-0234	R	13*	<0.1
El Toro Land and Cattle Co.	PO Box G	Heber	CA	92249	Robert Odell	760-352-6312	R	12	<0.1
Fall River Feedyard L.L.C.	PO Box 892	Hot Springs	SD	57747		605-745-4109	R	8	<0.1
Roode Packing Company Inc.	PO Box 510	Fairbury	NE	68352	Tom Roode	402-729-2253	R	5	<0.1
Schaake Packing Co.	PO Box 450	Yakima	WA	98907	John Kincaid	509-925-5346	R	3*	<0.1

Source: *Ward's Business Directory of U.S. Private and Public Companies*, Volumes 1 and 2, 2000. The company type code used is as follows: P - Public, R - Private, S - Subsidiary, D - Division, J - Joint Venture, A - Affiliate, G - Group, N - Company type not reported. Sales are in millions of dollars, employees are in thousands. An asterisk (*) indicates an estimated sales volume. The symbol < stands for 'less than'. Company names and addresses are truncated, in some cases, to fit into the available space.

NAICS 112120 - DAIRY CATTLE AND MILK PRODUCTION

GENERAL STATISTICS

Item	U.S. Total	This Agri-culture Sector	% of U.S.	Category average per farm				Number of farms reporting category	
				Value shown as	U.S.	This Agric. Sector	% of U.S.	U.S.	This Sector
Farms - number	1,911,859	86,022	4.5	-	-	-	-	-	-
Land in farms - mil. acres	931.795	30.612	3.3	Acres	487	356	73.1	1,911,859	86,022
Value of land, buildings - $ mil.	859,839.2	42,227.2	4.9	$	449,748	500,245	111.2	524,066	84,413
Value of machinery and equip-ment - $ mil.	110,256.8	8,779.0	8.0	$	57,678	104,000	180.3	1,911,601	84,413
Sales of Ag Products - $ mil.	196,864.6	20,922.0	10.6	$	102,970	243,217	236.2	1,911,859	86,022
Government payments - $ mil.	5,054.5	193.7	3.8	$	7,378	4,514	61.2	685,029	42,921
Other farm-related income - $ mil.	3,272.3	202.6	6.2	$	5,999	4,865	81.1	545,480	41,648
Expenses - $ mil.	150,591.0	15,456.5	10.3	$	78,771	183,105	232.5	1,911,766	84,413
Payroll - $ mil.	14,841.0	1,549.2	10.4	$	22,811	29,393	128.9	650,623	52,708
Workers - 150 days or more a year	890,467	101,383	11.4	Number	3.4	2.9	84.1	259,631	35,145
Workers - less than 150 days	2,461,561	114,302	4.6	Number	4.2	3.0	71.5	581,658	37,796
Net Cash Return - $ mil.	42,557.9	5,038.5	11.8	$	22,260	59,689	268.1	1,911,824	84,413

Source: *1997 Census of Agriculture*, U.S. Department of Agriculture, National Agricultural Statistics Service. Table shows totals for the U.S. agriculture sector and for the NAICS subdivision of it, shown as "This Agric. Sector" or as "This Sector." Not all farms report on every category. For this reason, the reporting universe is shown in the last two columns. Averages are based on these columns.

LAND IN FARMS ACCORDING TO USE

Item	U.S. Total (000 acres)	This Sector (000 acres)	% of U.S.	Average acres per farms			Number of farms reporting category	
				U.S.	This Agric. Sector	% of U.S.	U.S.	This Sector
Total cropland	431,144.9	21,436.8	5.0	260	262	-	1,661,395	81,711
Harvested cropland	309,395.5	17,312.9	5.6	219	220	-	1,410,606	78,609
Cropland:								
Pasture or grazing	64,466.5	3,361.6	5.2	85	65	-	754,170	51,701
In cover crops, legumes, grasses	13,531.2	187.5	1.4	88	37	-	153,177	5,126
On which all crops failed	3,449.4	104.3	3.0	67	33	-	51,673	3,166
In cultivated summer fallow	20,905.9	168.0	0.8	256	64	-	81,702	2,618
Idle	19,396.3	302.5	1.6	83	43	-	232,961	6,972
Total woodland	71,465.4	4,035.1	5.6	96	80	-	743,011	50,534
Woodland pastured	29,693.9	1,211.6	4.1	84	52	-	352,217	23,328
Woodland not pastured	41,771.5	2,823.5	6.8	79	69	-	531,846	40,782
Other pasture/rangeland	396,884.6	3,629.3	0.9	721	122	-	550,619	29,643
Land for house lots, ponds, roads, wasteland	32,300.4	1,511.1	4.7	28	25	-	1,142,618	60,216
Irrigated land	55,058.1	1,162.2	2.1	197	194	-	279,442	5,979
Harvested cropland	50,013.5	1,024.1	2.0	198	193	-	252,679	5,307
Pasture and other	5,044.7	138.1	2.7	87	72	-	58,258	1,910
Conservation Reserve/Wetlands Reserve Lands	29,489.1	306.0	1.0	131	61	-	225,410	4,998

Source: *1997 Census of Agriculture*, U.S. Department of Agriculture, National Agricultural Statistics Service. Table shows totals for the U.S. agriculture sector and for the NAICS subdivision of it, shown as "This Agric. Sector" or as "This Sector." Not all farms report on every category. For this reason, the reporting universe is shown in the last two columns. Averages are based on these columns. The Conservation Reserve and Wetlands Reserve programs provide support for land conservation/preservation. Cover crops are not harvested or pastured.

MARKET VALUE OF AGRICULTURAL PRODUCTS SOLD: ALL FARMS

Item	U.S. Total ($ mil.)	This Sector ($ mil.)	% of Sector Sales	% of U.S.	Average sales per farm - $			Number of farms reporting category	
					U.S.	This Agric. Sector	% of U.S.	U.S.	This Sector
Grains	46,617.1	807.6	3.86	1.7	79,095	26,484	33.5	589,379	30,495
Corn for grain	18,884.8	442.9	2.12	2.3	52,506	23,580	44.9	359,666	18,782
Wheat	7,173.9	88.1	0.42	1.2	29,726	8,478	28.5	241,334	10,390
Soybeans	15,622.4	241.2	1.15	1.5	44,185	16,810	38.0	353,566	14,347
Sorghum for grain	1,140.0	5.7	0.03	0.5	25,360	15,380	60.6	44,955	371
Barley	709.6	12.3	0.06	1.7	23,191	6,869	29.6	30,598	1,785
Oats	121.3	8.3	0.04	6.8	3,114	2,087	67.0	38,940	3,968
Other grains	2,965.1	9.3	0.04	0.3	67,540	7,747	11.5	43,901	1,194
Cotton and cotton seed	5,975.5	17.1	0.08	0.3	189,963	178,448	93.9	31,456	96
Tobacco	2,924.7	56.8	0.27	1.9	32,662	20,765	63.6	89,544	2,735
Hay, silage, and field seeds	4,670.5	176.6	0.84	3.8	13,174	18,117	137.5	354,523	9,750
Vegetables, sweet corn, and melons	8,401.7	31.0	0.15	0.4	156,628	17,781	11.4	53,641	1,746
Fruits and berries	12,660.3	38.1	0.18	0.3	147,259	68,427	46.5	85,973	557
Nursery and greenhouse crops	10,942.8	3.1	0.01	0.0	161,360	13,229	8.2	67,816	231
Other crops	5,863.1	24.2	0.12	0.4	153,907	20,862	13.6	38,095	1,162
Poultry and poultry products	22,262.6	19.3	0.09	0.1	352,000	9,715	2.8	63,246	1,985
Dairy products	18,997.3	18,129.5	86.65	95.4	191,432	211,177	110.3	99,238	85,850
Cattle and calves	40,524.8	1,541.4	7.37	3.8	40,052	18,001	44.9	1,011,809	85,629
Hogs and pigs	13,804.8	67.3	0.32	0.5	135,201	18,709	13.8	102,106	3,598
Sheep, lambs, and wool	682.9	3.1	0.01	0.5	10,913	2,071	19.0	62,579	1,502
Other livestock	2,536.5	6.7	0.03	0.3	20,506	2,665	13.0	123,695	2,528
Products sold to public directly	13,096.7	37.5	0.18	0.3	377,610	102,292	27.1	34,683	367

Source: 1997 Census of Agriculture, U.S. Department of Agriculture, National Agricultural Statistics Service. Table shows totals for the U.S. agriculture sector and for the NAICS subdivision of it, shown as "This Agric. Sector" or as "This Sector." Not all farms report on every category. For this reason, the reporting universe is shown in the last two columns. Averages are based on these columns. Farms classified in one sector routinely produce categories in other sectors as well. Products sold to the public are sold for direct consumption.

MARKET VALUE OF PRODUCTS SOLD: FARMS WITH SALES OF $50,000 OR MORE

Item	U.S. Total ($ mil.)	This Sector ($ mil.)	% of Sector Sales	% of U.S.	Average sales per farm - $			Number of farms reporting category	
					U.S.	This Agric. Sector	% of U.S.	U.S.	This Sector
Grains	40,973.4	433.1	2.07	1.1	183,623	99,256	54.1	223,138	4,363
Cotton and cotton seed	5,743.9	16.5	0.08	0.3	286,562	257,422	89.8	20,044	64
Tobacco	2,060.2	17.3	0.08	0.8	175,907	85,634	48.7	11,712	202
Hay, silage, and field seeds	2,781.9	102.3	0.49	3.7	188,959	137,491	72.8	14,722	744
Vegetables, sweet corn, and melons	7,966.8	14.9	0.07	0.2	673,443	127,009	18.9	11,830	117
Fruits and berries	12,072.3	35.7	0.17	0.3	478,927	315,513	65.9	25,207	113
Nursery and greenhouse crops	10,412.0	1.4	0.01	0.0	578,025	95,800	16.6	18,013	15
Other crops	5,586.6	16.1	0.08	0.3	363,758	166,495	45.8	15,358	97
Poultry and poultry products	22,171.7	15.9	0.08	0.1	778,637	186,494	24.0	28,475	85
Dairy products	18,344.3	17,624.8	84.24	96.1	250,075	259,066	103.6	73,355	68,032
Cattle and calves	32,358.6	709.9	3.39	2.2	386,685	132,080	34.2	83,682	5,375
Hogs and pigs	13,096.7	37.5	0.18	0.3	377,610	102,292	27.1	34,683	367
Sheep, lambs, and wool	478.6	0.4	0.00	0.1	278,730	96,000	34.4	1,717	4
Other livestock	2,026.6	1.3	0.01	0.1	369,685	147,333	39.9	5,482	9

Source: 1997 Census of Agriculture, U.S. Department of Agriculture, National Agricultural Statistics Service. Table shows totals for the U.S. agriculture sector and for the NAICS subdivision of it, shown as "This Agric. Sector" or as "This Sector." Not all farms report on every category. For this reason, the reporting universe is shown in the last two columns. Averages are based on these columns. Farms classified in one sector routinely produce categories in other sectors as well.

GOVERNMENT PAYMENTS AND OTHER FARM-RELATED INCOME

Item	U.S. Total ($ mil.)	This Sector ($ mil.)	% of Sector Gov/Oth. Income	% of U.S.	Average receipts per farm - $			Number of farms reporting category	
					U.S.	This Agric. Sector	% of U.S.	U.S.	This Sector
Government payments	5,054.5	193.7	48.88	3.8	7,378	4,514	61.2	685,029	42,921
Other farm-related income	3,272.3	202.6	51.12	6.2	5,999	4,865	81.1	545,480	41,648
Custom work and other agricultural services	1,235.1	60.3	15.22	4.9	8,646	7,499	86.7	142,854	8,046
Gross cash rent or share payments	1,207.9	25.0	6.30	2.1	6,867	7,713	112.3	175,901	3,235
Forest products, excluding Christmas trees and maple products	344.3	28.8	7.26	8.4	7,417	9,027	121.7	46,426	3,188
Other farm-related income sources	484.9	88.5	22.34	18.3	1,595	2,453	153.7	303,908	36,099

Source: *1997 Census of Agriculture*, U.S. Department of Agriculture, National Agricultural Statistics Service. Table shows totals for the U.S. agriculture sector and for the NAICS subdivision of it, shown as "This Agric. Sector" or as "This Sector." Not all farms report on every category. For this reason, the reporting universe is shown in the last two columns. Averages are based on these columns. Government payments are agricultural subsidies under various programs.

COMMODITY CREDIT CORPORATION LOANS

Item	U.S. Total ($ mil.)	This Sector ($ mil.)	% of Sector Loan Total	% of U.S.	Average loan value per farm - $			Number of farms reporting category	
					U.S.	This Agric. Sector	% of U.S.	U.S.	This Sector
Total loans	3,034.7	58.9	100.00	1.9	36,419	12,556	34.5	83,328	4,694
Corn	1,333.9	44.2	74.98	3.3	26,419	10,625	40.2	50,489	4,159
Wheat	415.4	3.1	5.27	0.7	18,093	6,275	34.7	22,961	495
Soybeans	774.0	10.3	17.50	1.3	30,370	15,076	49.6	25,487	684
Sorghum, barley, and oats	54.8	0.9	1.49	1.6	8,603	2,335	27.1	6,375	376
Cotton	191.4	0.1	0.16	0.1	43,275	13,714	31.7	4,422	7
Sunflower seed, flaxseed, safflower, canola, other rapeseed, and mustard seed	17.3	0.0	0.06	0.2	25,159	9,500	37.8	686	4
Peanuts, rice, and tobacco	247.9	0.3	0.53	0.1	60,421	14,318	23.7	4,103	22

Source: *1997 Census of Agriculture*, U.S. Department of Agriculture, National Agricultural Statistics Service. Table shows totals for the U.S. agriculture sector and for the NAICS subdivision of it, shown as "This Agric. Sector" or as "This Sector." Not all farms report on every category. For this reason, the reporting universe is shown in the last two columns. Averages are based on these columns. The Commodity Credit Corporation provides low interest loans to farmers.

SELECTED MACHINERY AND EQUIPMENT

Item	U.S. Total (number)	This Agric. Sector (number)	% of U.S.	Average number per farm			Number of farms reporting category	
				U.S.	This Agric. Sector	% of U.S.	U.S.	This Sector
Motortrucks, including pickups	3,497,735	172,437	4.9	2.07	2.20	106.2	1,688,303	78,404
Wheel tractors	3,936,014	260,922	6.6	2.31	3.35	145.2	1,707,384	77,953
Less than 40 horsepower (PTO)	1,262,688	58,688	4.6	1.44	1.58	109.8	877,119	37,113
40 horsepower (PTO) or more	2,673,326	202,234	7.6	2.02	2.83	140.1	1,321,084	71,350
40 to 99 horsepower (PTO)	1,808,105	140,091	7.7	1.58	2.09	132.7	1,145,466	66,883
100 horsepower (PTO)	865,221	62,143	7.2	1.68	1.69	100.5	513,773	36,720
Grain and bean combines	460,606	27,922	6.1	1.16	1.09	93.3	395,934	25,733
Cotton pickers and strippers	38,294	172	0.4	1.48	1.98	133.6	25,874	87
Mower conditioners	608,443	70,896	11.7	1.12	1.13	101.3	543,565	62,496
Pickup balers	717,245	82,042	11.4	1.24	1.30	104.6	579,440	63,335

Source: *1997 Census of Agriculture*, U.S. Department of Agriculture, National Agricultural Statistics Service. Table shows totals for the U.S. agriculture sector and for the NAICS subdivision of it, shown as "This Agric. Sector" or as "This Sector." Not all farms report on every category. For this reason, the reporting universe is shown in the last two columns. Averages are based on these columns. PTO stands for "power take off."

FARM PRODUCTION EXPENSES

Item	U.S. Total ($ mil.)	This Sector ($ mil.)	% of Sector Total Expense	% of U.S.	Average expense per farm - $			Number of farms reporting category	
					U.S.	This Agric. Sector	% of U.S.	U.S.	This Sector
Total farm production expenses	150,591.0	15,456.5	100.00	10.3	78,771	183,105	232.5	1,911,766	84,413
Livestock and poultry purchased	21,614.6	929.2	6.01	4.3	38,807	23,022	59.3	556,980	40,361
Feed for livestock and poultry	32,760.0	6,142.2	39.74	18.7	32,059	74,621	232.8	1,021,849	82,312
Commercially mixed formula feeds	21,236.2	3,148.3	20.37	14.8	34,459	40,705	118.1	616,280	77,343
Seeds, bulbs, plants, and trees	5,725.9	267.9	1.73	4.7	6,388	3,867	60.5	896,339	69,287
Commercial fertilizer	9,597.1	510.3	3.30	5.3	8,060	7,336	91.0	1,190,733	69,559
Agricultural chemicals	7,581.4	252.1	1.63	3.3	8,056	4,067	50.5	941,136	61,991
Petroleum products	6,371.5	463.9	3.00	7.3	3,619	5,568	153.9	1,760,642	83,308
Gasoline and gasohol	1,886.6	141.8	0.92	7.5	1,380	1,975	143.1	1,366,915	71,777
Diesel fuel	2,846.0	236.7	1.53	8.3	2,164	3,125	144.4	1,315,397	75,756
Natural gas	432.9	10.6	0.07	2.5	6,091	1,968	32.3	71,069	5,400
LP gas, fuel oil, kerosene, motor oil, grease, etc.	1,206.1	74.7	0.48	6.2	945	934	98.9	1,276,331	79,994
Electricity	2,751.1	431.9	2.79	15.7	2,247	5,169	230.1	1,224,374	83,562
Hired farm labor	14,841.0	1,549.2	10.02	10.4	22,811	29,393	128.9	650,623	52,708
Contract labor	2,959.0	79.8	0.52	2.7	13,040	7,963	61.1	226,909	10,015
Repair and maintenance	8,637.7	951.6	6.16	11.0	5,616	11,685	208.1	1,538,058	81,438
Custom work, machine hire, and rental of equipment	3,210.3	272.5	1.76	8.5	5,372	5,915	110.1	597,624	46,071
Interest	8,928.1	1,001.6	6.48	11.2	11,016	16,249	147.5	810,476	61,645
Secured by real estate	5,449.6	611.8	3.96	11.2	9,564	13,642	142.6	569,775	44,848
Not secured by real estate	3,478.5	389.8	2.52	11.2	7,540	9,639	127.8	461,326	40,445
Cash rent	6,915.7	401.2	2.60	5.8	14,244	8,923	62.6	485,512	44,968
Property taxes	3,920.1	320.7	2.07	8.2	2,213	4,105	185.5	1,771,787	78,122
All other farm production expenses	14,777.4	1,882.3	12.18	12.7	8,747	22,336	255.4	1,689,391	84,268

Source: 1997 Census of Agriculture, U.S. Department of Agriculture, National Agricultural Statistics Service. Table shows totals for the U.S. agriculture sector and for the NAICS subdivision of it, shown as "This Agric. Sector" or as "This Sector." Not all farms report on every category. For this reason, the reporting universe is shown in the last two columns. Averages are based on these columns. LP gas stands for "liquid petroleum gas," i.e., butane or propane.

NET CASH RETURN AND FARMS WITH GAINS AND LOSSES

Item	Number of farms and %				Average gain or loss per farm - $		
	U.S.	% of U.S.	This Agriculture Sector	% of Sector	U.S.	This Agriculture Sector	% of U.S.
All farms	1,911,824	100.0	84,413	100.0	22,260	59,689	268.1
Number of farms with net gains	985,718	51.6	73,412	87.0	51,296	71,671	139.7
Gain of -							
Less than $1,000	120,163	6.3	1,009	1.2	-	-	-
$1,000 to $9,999	370,611	19.4	9,891	11.7	-	-	-
$10,000 to $49,999	292,484	15.3	35,244	41.8	-	-	-
$50,000 or more	202,460	10.6	27,268	32.3	-	-	-
Number of farms with net losses	926,106	48.4	11,001	13.0	(8,645)	(20,271)	234.5
Loss of -							
Less than $1,000	165,390	8.7	904	1.1	-	-	-
$1,000 to $9,999	591,517	30.9	4,932	5.8	-	-	-
$10,000 to $49,999	152,649	8.0	4,409	5.2	-	-	-
$50,000 or more	16,550	0.9	756	0.9	-	-	-

Source: 1997 Census of Agriculture, U.S. Department of Agriculture, National Agricultural Statistics Service. Table shows totals for the U.S. agriculture sector and for the NAICS subdivision of it, shown as "This Agric. Sector" or as "This Sector." Not all farms report on every category. For this reason, the reporting universe is shown in the last two columns. Averages are based on these columns. Net gains are income less cost for farm operations; they exclude non-farm earnings. Values in parentheses are losses.

CHARACTERISTICS OF FARM OPERATORS

Farm Operators	U.S.	This Agric. Sector	% of U.S.	Farm Operators	U.S.	This Agric. Sector	% of U.S.
Place of residence:				By age group:	20,850	1,176	5.6
On farm operated	1,361,766	74,564	5.5	Under 25 years	20,850	1,176	5.6
Not on farm operated	412,554	5,776	1.4	25 to 34 years	128,455	8,940	7.0
Not reported	137,539	5,682	4.1	35 to 44 years	371,442	23,128	6.2
Principal occupation:				45 to 49 years	232,845	11,928	5.1
Farming	961,560	79,627	8.3	50 to 54 years	233,884	10,648	4.6
Other	950,299	6,395	0.7	55 to 59 years	222,736	9,585	4.3
Days worked off farm:				60 to 64 years	204,618	8,100	4.0
None	755,254	62,744	8.3	65 to 69 years	179,858	5,420	3.0
Any	1,042,158	16,655	1.6	70 years and over	317,171	7,097	2.2
1 to 99 days	164,957	7,051	4.3	Average age	54	50	91.5
100 to 199 days	167,922	3,119	1.9	By sex:			
200 days or more	709,279	6,485	0.9	Male	1,746,757	82,773	4.7
Not reported	114,447	6,623	5.8	Female	165,102	3,249	2.0
Years on present farm:				Spanish, Hispanic/Latino origin	27,717	637	2.3
2 years or less	92,574	3,365	3.6	Tenure of operator:			
3 or 4 years	126,791	4,103	3.2	All operators	1,911,859	86,022	4.5
5 to 9 years	263,642	9,514	3.6	Full owners	1,146,891	31,093	2.7
10 years or more	1,113,839	56,683	5.1	Part owners	573,839	45,510	7.9
Ave. years on this farm	20	22	107.5	Tenants	191,129	9,419	4.9
Not reported	315,013	12,357	3.9				

Source: 1997 Census of Agriculture, U.S. Department of Agriculture, National Agricultural Statistics Service. Table shows totals for the U.S. agriculture sector and for the NAICS subdivision of it, shown as "This Agric. Sector" or as "This Sector." Not all farms report on every category. For this reason, the reporting universe is shown in the last two columns. Averages are based on these columns. All values shown are number of farm operators in each category or percent.

FARMS BY TYPE OF ORGANIZATION

Item	Number of farms and percent				Total acres and percent		
	U.S.	% of U.S.	This Agriculture Sector	% of Sector	U.S.	This Agriculture Sector	% of U.S.
Individual or family (sole proprietorship)	1,643,424	100.0	68,336	100.0	585,464,911	21,126,579	3.6
Partnership	169,462	10.3	13,282	19.4	149,321,484	6,332,488	4.2
Corporation:							
Family held	76,103	4.6	3,854	5.6	119,559,203	2,763,612	2.3
More than 10 stockholders	1,795	0.1	60	0.1	-	-	-
10 or less stockholders	74,308	4.5	3,794	5.6	-	-	-
Other than family held	7,899	0.5	150	0.2	11,904,053	74,209	0.6
More than 10 stockholders	1,029	0.1	18	0.0	-	-	-
10 or less stockholders	6,870	0.4	132	0.2	-	-	-
Other cooperative, estate or trust, institutional, etc.	14,971	0.9	400	0.6	65,545,604	315,510	0.5

Source: 1997 Census of Agriculture, U.S. Department of Agriculture, National Agricultural Statistics Service. Table shows totals for the U.S. agriculture sector and for the NAICS subdivision of it, shown as "This Agric. Sector" or as "This Sector." Not all farms report on every category. For this reason, the reporting universe is shown in the last two columns. Averages are based on these columns.

LIVESTOCK INVENTORIES AND SALES

Item	U.S. (number)	This Agric. Sector (number)	% of U.S.	Average number per farm			Number of farms reporting category	
				U.S.	This Agric. Sector	% of U.S.	U.S.	This Sector
Cattle and calves inventory	98,989,244	15,233,787	15.4	94.6	177.6	187.8	1,046,863	85,772
Cows and heifers that had calved	43,162,054	8,918,726	20.7	48.3	104.4	216.3	894,110	85,403
Beef cows	34,066,615	394,036	1.2	42.3	35.4	83.6	804,595	11,137
Milk cows	9,095,439	8,524,690	93.7	77.8	100.1	128.7	116,874	85,137
Heifers and heifer calves	26,988,697	5,233,173	19.4	33.6	66.0	196.7	803,985	79,239
Steers, steer calves, bulls, and bull calves	28,838,493	1,081,888	3.8	32.6	19.5	59.8	883,983	55,461
Cattle and calves sold	74,089,046	5,110,734	6.9	73.2	59.7	81.5	1,011,809	85,629
Calves	16,480,293	2,936,924	17.8	26.8	42.4	158.2	615,177	69,302
Cattle	57,608,753	2,173,810	3.8	78.0	32.8	42.1	738,696	66,279
Fattened on grain and concentrates	27,328,190	199,350	0.7	247.0	26.3	10.6	110,620	7,584
Hogs and pigs inventory	61,206,236	409,316	0.7	557.7	98.5	17.7	109,754	4,157
Used or to be used for breeding	6,831,564	50,941	0.7	106.7	22.1	20.7	64,029	2,304
Other	54,374,672	358,375	0.7	528.0	92.8	17.6	102,977	3,863
Hogs and pigs sold	142,611,882	689,489	0.5	1,396.7	191.6	13.7	102,106	3,598
Feeder pigs	34,988,718	157,276	0.4	2,037.8	214.3	10.5	17,170	734
Litters of pigs farrowed between Dec. 1 of preceding year and Nov. 30	11,497,523	74,266	0.6	170.3	30.5	17.9	67,514	2,437
Dec. 1 and May 31	5,697,371	37,434	0.7	91.0	17.0	18.7	62,622	2,196
June 1 and Nov. 30	5,800,152	36,832	0.6	99.7	17.8	17.8	58,204	2,073
Sheep and lambs of all ages inventory	7,821,885	58,502	0.7	118.9	34.0	28.6	65,790	1,722
Ewes 1 year old or older	4,408,683	35,182	0.8	78.1	25.3	32.3	56,414	1,393
Sheep and lambs sold	7,331,545	41,356	0.6	123.1	30.8	25.0	59,575	1,342
Sheep and lambs shorn	6,139,140	42,695	0.7	118.4	34.8	29.4	51,869	1,228
Horses and ponies inventory	2,427,277	68,569	2.8	6.5	5.6	85.8	375,218	12,352
Horses and ponies sold	325,306	4,560	1.4	4.1	2.4	59.9	79,516	1,862
Goats inventory	1,989,799	12,566	0.6	34.4	9.9	28.9	57,925	1,265
Goats sold	740,597	3,476	0.5	31.5	12.0	38.1	23,520	290

Source: 1997 Census of Agriculture, U.S. Department of Agriculture, National Agricultural Statistics Service. Table shows totals for the U.S. agriculture sector and for the NAICS subdivision of it, shown as "This Agric. Sector" or as "This Sector." Not all farms report on every category. For this reason, the reporting universe is shown in the last two columns. Averages are based on these columns.

POULTRY INVENTORIES AND SALES

Item	U.S. (number)	This Agric. Sector (number)	% of U.S.	Average number per farm			Number of farms reporting category	
				U.S.	This Agric. Sector	% of U.S.	U.S.	This Sector
Layers and pullets 13 weeks old and older inventory	366,989,851	801,717	0.2	5,053.8	207.7	4.1	72,616	3,860
Layers 20 weeks old and older	313,851,480	679,942	0.2	4,499.0	181.5	4.0	69,761	3,747
Pullets 13 weeks old and older but less than 20 weeks old	53,138,371	121,775	0.2	4,031.7	204.7	5.1	13,180	595
Layers, pullets, and pullet chicks sold	331,563,736	1,093,552	0.3	24,636.9	2,268.8	9.2	13,458	482
Broilers and other meat type chickens sold	6,741,927,110	3,648,382	0.1	281,653.0	10,453.8	3.7	23,937	349
Turkey hens kept for breeding	5,504,808	25,627	0.5	968.1	179.2	18.5	5,686	143
Turkeys sold	307,586,680	518,689	0.2	51,000.9	3,758.6	7.4	6,031	138

Source: 1997 Census of Agriculture, U.S. Department of Agriculture, National Agricultural Statistics Service. Table shows totals for the U.S. agriculture sector and for the NAICS subdivision of it, shown as "This Agric. Sector" or as "This Sector." Not all farms report on every category. For this reason, the reporting universe is shown in the last two columns. Averages are based on these columns.

SELECTED CROPS HARVESTED

Item	In 1,000	Crop harvested U.S.	This Agric. Sector	% of U.S.	Acres used for crop (000) U.S.	This Agric. Sector	% of U.S.	Number of farms reporting category U.S.	This Sector
Corn for grain or seed	bushels	8,578,635	422,329	4.9	69,796.7	3,653.1	5.2	430,711	46,019
Irrigated		-	-	-	10,638.9	96.0	0.9	40,574	1,026
Corn for silage or green chop	tons, green	88,381	47,479	53.7	5,727.6	3,090.2	54.0	119,308	56,502
Irrigated		-	-	-	1,033.3	297.5	28.8	10,815	2,499
Sorghum for grain or seed	bushels	559,070	4,774	0.9	8,470.4	73.5	0.9	49,397	765
Irrigated		-	-	-	875.6	2.8	0.3	5,793	32
Wheat for grain	bushels	2,204,027	28,206	1.3	58,836.3	646.4	1.1	243,568	10,606
Irrigated		-	-	-	3,990.9	37.0	0.9	20,385	320
Barley for grain	bushels	336,435	16,512	4.9	5,945.0	273.0	4.6	41,930	6,695
Irrigated		-	-	-	1,060.7	61.4	5.8	8,847	733
Oats for grain	bushels	151,327	31,337	20.7	2,681.0	534.2	19.9	89,606	20,785
Irrigated		-	-	-	121.0	8.1	6.7	2,788	161
Rice	cwt	182,231	149	0.1	3,122.1	2.0	0.1	9,291	12
Irrigated		-	-	-	3,122.1	2.0	0.1	9,291	12
Cotton	bales	17,879	46	0.3	13,235.2	20.4	0.2	31,493	97
Irrigated		-	-	-	4,888.0	17.2	0.4	12,434	74
Tobacco	pounds	1,747,702	36,122	2.1	838.5	18.0	2.1	89,706	2,740
Irrigated		-	-	-	138.7	1.2	0.9	7,090	138
Soybeans for beans	bushels	2,504,307	41,743	1.7	66,147.7	1,075.3	1.6	354,692	14,546
Irrigated		-	-	-	4,152.1	10.4	0.3	20,619	187
Dry edible beans, excluding dry limas	cwt	27,224	217	0.8	1,691.9	13.8	0.8	10,911	186
Irrigated		-	-	-	577.0	2.7	0.5	4,882	35
Potatoes, excluding sweetpotatoes	cwt	459,886	1,446	0.3	1,355.2	4.3	0.3	10,523	261
Irrigated		-	-	-	1,070.3	2.9	0.3	4,843	35
Sugar beets for sugar	tons	29,775	140	0.5	1,453.8	6.5	0.4	7,102	63
Irrigated		-	-	-	616.4	3.3	0.5	3,492	26
Peanuts for nuts	pounds	3,377,143	11,895	0.4	1,352.2	5.4	0.4	12,221	65
Irrigated		-	-	-	412.3	2.2	0.5	3,125	25
Hay alfalfa, other tame, small grain, wild, grass silage, green chop	tons, dry	139,365	23,029	16.5	60,799.8	9,154.3	15.1	888,597	75,356
Irrigated		-	-	-	9,564.3	577.2	6.0	79,406	3,792
Alfalfa hay	tons, dry	65,863	11,031	16.7	21,309.8	3,496.1	16.4	358,365	53,297
Irrigated		-	-	-	5,980.5	292.3	4.9	57,854	2,330
Vegetables harvested for sale		-	-	-	3,773.2	50.0	1.3	53,727	1,753
Irrigated		-	-	-	2,641.8	6.3	0.2	23,203	261
Land in orchards		-	-	-	5,158.1	18.7	0.4	106,069	556
Irrigated		-	-	-	4,107.9	14.4	0.4	61,606	169

Source: *1997 Census of Agriculture*, U.S. Department of Agriculture, National Agricultural Statistics Service. Table shows totals for the U.S. agriculture sector and for the NAICS subdivision of it, shown as "This Agric. Sector" or as "This Sector." Not all farms report on every category. For this reason, the reporting universe is shown in the last two columns. Averages are based on these columns. "Green tons" are weight of product as harvested, i.e., moist. cwt stands for "hundredweight."

LEADING COMPANIES   Number shown: **4**   Total sales ($ mil): **104**   Total employment (000): **0.4**

Company Name	Address				CEO Name	Phone	Co. Type	Sales ($ mil)	Empl. (000)
Wilcox Farms Inc.	40400 Hrts LkVly	Roy	WA	98580	Barrie Wilcox	206-458-7774	R	90	0.3
Coach Farm Inc.	105 Mill Hill Rd	Pine Plains	NY	12567	Miles Cahn	518-398-5325	R	7*	<0.1
Prices Producers Inc.	201 E Main St	El Paso	TX	79901	JV Curlin	915-532-2296	R	4	<0.1
Maytag Dairy Farms Inc.	PO Box 806	Newton	IA	50208	James W Stevens	515-792-1133	R	3	<0.1

Source: *Ward's Business Directory of U.S. Private and Public Companies*, Volumes 1 and 2, 2000. The company type code used is as follows: P - Public, R - Private, S - Subsidiary, D - Division, J - Joint Venture, A - Affiliate, G - Group, N - Company type not reported. Sales are in millions of dollars, employees are in thousands. An asterisk (*) indicates an estimated sales volume. The symbol < stands for 'less than'. Company names and addresses are truncated, in some cases, to fit into the available space.

NAICS 112200 - HOG AND PIG FARMING

GENERAL STATISTICS

Item	U.S. Total	This Agri-culture Sector	% of U.S.	Category average per farm				Number of farms reporting category	
				Value shown as	U.S.	This Agric. Sector	% of U.S.	U.S.	This Sector
Farms - number	1,911,859	46,353	2.4	-	-	-	-	-	-
Land in farms - mil. acres	931.795	11.704	1.3	Acres	487	253	52.0	1,911,859	46,353
Value of land, buildings - $ mil.	859,839.2	20,194.4	2.3	$	449,748	441,669	98.2	524,066	45,723
Value of machinery and equip-ment - $ mil.	110,256.8	3,451.5	3.1	$	57,678	75,487	130.9	1,911,601	45,723
Sales of Ag Products - $ mil.	196,864.6	13,748.1	7.0	$	102,970	296,597	288.0	1,911,859	46,353
Government payments - $ mil.	5,054.5	154.3	3.1	$	7,378	7,590	102.9	685,029	20,331
Other farm-related income - $ mil.	3,272.3	91.7	2.8	$	5,999	5,991	99.9	545,480	15,312
Expenses - $ mil.	150,591.0	10,144.2	6.7	$	78,771	221,887	281.7	1,911,766	45,718
Payroll - $ mil.	14,841.0	639.6	4.3	$	22,811	33,904	148.6	650,623	18,866
Workers - 150 days or more a year	890,467	33,933	3.8	Number	3.4	3.6	105.7	259,631	9,359
Workers - less than 150 days	2,461,561	54,496	2.2	Number	4.2	3.4	80.1	581,658	16,071
Net Cash Return - $ mil.	42,557.9	3,180.7	7.5	$	22,260	69,565	312.5	1,911,824	45,723

Source: 1997 Census of Agriculture, U.S. Department of Agriculture, National Agricultural Statistics Service. Table shows totals for the U.S. agriculture sector and for the NAICS subdivision of it, shown as "This Agric. Sector" or as "This Sector." Not all farms report on every category. For this reason, the reporting universe is shown in the last two columns. Averages are based on these columns.

LAND IN FARMS ACCORDING TO USE

Item	U.S. Total (000 acres)	This Sector (000 acres)	% of U.S.	Average acres per farms			Number of farms reporting category	
				U.S.	This Agric. Sector	% of U.S.	U.S.	This Sector
Total cropland	431,144.9	8,950.3	2.1	260	260	-	1,661,395	34,378
Harvested cropland	309,395.5	7,693.3	2.5	219	264	-	1,410,606	29,187
Cropland:								
Pasture or grazing	64,466.5	769.7	1.2	85	53	-	754,170	14,421
In cover crops, legumes, grasses	13,531.2	143.1	1.1	88	43	-	153,177	3,347
On which all crops failed	3,449.4	37.0	1.1	67	35	-	51,673	1,059
In cultivated summer fallow	20,905.9	89.2	0.4	256	105	-	81,702	851
Idle	19,396.3	217.9	1.1	83	46	-	232,961	4,774
Total woodland	71,465.4	942.3	1.3	96	62	-	743,011	15,127
Woodland pastured	29,693.9	279.1	0.9	84	44	-	352,217	6,402
Woodland not pastured	41,771.5	663.2	1.6	79	57	-	531,846	11,547
Other pasture/rangeland	396,884.6	1,113.6	0.3	721	108	-	550,619	10,270
Land for house lots, ponds, roads, wasteland	32,300.4	698.1	2.2	28	21	-	1,142,618	33,992
Irrigated land	55,058.1	292.6	0.5	197	111	-	279,442	2,626
Harvested cropland	50,013.5	272.7	0.5	198	133	-	252,679	2,056
Pasture and other	5,044.7	19.9	0.4	87	24	-	58,258	817
Conservation Reserve/Wetlands Reserve Lands	29,489.1	264.8	0.9	131	64	-	225,410	4,128

Source: 1997 Census of Agriculture, U.S. Department of Agriculture, National Agricultural Statistics Service. Table shows totals for the U.S. agriculture sector and for the NAICS subdivision of it, shown as "This Agric. Sector" or as "This Sector." Not all farms report on every category. For this reason, the reporting universe is shown in the last two columns. Averages are based on these columns. The Conservation Reserve and Wetlands Reserve programs provide support for land conservation/preservation. Cover crops are not harvested or pastured.

MARKET VALUE OF AGRICULTURAL PRODUCTS SOLD: ALL FARMS

Item	U.S. Total ($ mil.)	This Sector ($ mil.)	% of Sector Sales	% of U.S.	Average sales per farm - $			Number of farms reporting category	
					U.S.	This Agric. Sector	% of U.S.	U.S.	This Sector
Grains	46,617.1	1,209.9	8.80	2.6	79,095	61,288	77.5	589,379	19,741
Corn for grain	18,884.8	455.8	3.32	2.4	52,506	39,652	75.5	359,666	11,494
Wheat	7,173.9	63.4	0.46	0.9	29,726	11,169	37.6	241,334	5,673
Soybeans	15,622.4	670.1	4.87	4.3	44,185	41,027	92.9	353,566	16,333
Sorghum for grain	1,140.0	8.7	0.06	0.8	25,360	18,721	73.8	44,955	466
Barley	709.6	2.1	0.02	0.3	23,191	10,010	43.2	30,598	207
Oats	121.3	2.8	0.02	2.3	3,114	1,811	58.1	38,940	1,560
Other grains	2,965.1	7.1	0.05	0.2	67,540	17,282	25.6	43,901	408
Cotton and cotton seed	5,975.5	20.1	0.15	0.3	189,963	117,637	61.9	31,456	171
Tobacco	2,924.7	55.9	0.41	1.9	32,662	88,340	270.5	89,544	633
Hay, silage, and field seeds	4,670.5	40.8	0.30	0.9	13,174	6,416	48.7	354,523	6,356
Vegetables, sweet corn, and melons	8,401.7	12.4	0.09	0.1	156,628	16,344	10.4	53,641	761
Fruits and berries	12,660.3	2.9	0.02	0.0	147,259	11,530	7.8	85,973	249
Nursery and greenhouse crops	10,942.8	2.0	0.01	0.0	161,360	12,000	7.4	67,816	167
Other crops	5,863.1	11.6	0.08	0.2	153,907	31,116	20.2	38,095	372
Poultry and poultry products	22,262.6	135.9	0.99	0.6	352,000	69,609	19.8	63,246	1,953
Dairy products	18,997.3	49.5	0.36	0.3	191,432	51,891	27.1	99,238	954
Cattle and calves	40,524.8	325.9	2.37	0.8	40,052	19,906	49.7	1,011,809	16,373
Hogs and pigs	13,804.8	11,869.9	86.34	86.0	135,201	258,378	191.1	102,106	45,940
Sheep, lambs, and wool	682.9	7.5	0.05	1.1	10,913	3,148	28.8	62,579	2,377
Other livestock	2,536.5	3.8	0.03	0.1	20,506	1,969	9.6	123,695	1,926
Products sold to public directly	13,096.7	11,594.3	84.33	88.5	377,610	493,142	130.6	34,683	23,511

Source: 1997 Census of Agriculture, U.S. Department of Agriculture, National Agricultural Statistics Service. Table shows totals for the U.S. agriculture sector and for the NAICS subdivision of it, shown as "This Agric. Sector" or as "This Sector." Not all farms report on every category. For this reason, the reporting universe is shown in the last two columns. Averages are based on these columns. Farms classified in one sector routinely produce categories in other sectors as well. Products sold to the public are sold for direct consumption.

MARKET VALUE OF PRODUCTS SOLD: FARMS WITH SALES OF $50,000 OR MORE

Item	U.S. Total ($ mil.)	This Sector ($ mil.)	% of Sector Sales	% of U.S.	Average sales per farm - $			Number of farms reporting category	
					U.S.	This Agric. Sector	% of U.S.	U.S.	This Sector
Grains	40,973.4	994.3	7.23	2.4	183,623	133,032	72.4	223,138	7,474
Cotton and cotton seed	5,743.9	18.3	0.13	0.3	286,562	215,435	75.2	20,044	85
Tobacco	2,060.2	49.9	0.36	2.4	175,907	200,277	113.9	11,712	249
Hay, silage, and field seeds	2,781.9	8.8	0.06	0.3	188,959	138,968	73.5	14,722	63
Vegetables, sweet corn, and melons	7,966.8	6.3	0.05	0.1	673,443	107,136	15.9	11,830	59
Fruits and berries	12,072.3	2.1	0.02	0.0	478,927	209,900	43.8	25,207	10
Nursery and greenhouse crops	10,412.0	1.0	0.01	0.0	578,025	100,700	17.4	18,013	10
Other crops	5,586.6	8.7	0.06	0.2	363,758	132,212	36.3	15,358	66
Poultry and poultry products	22,171.7	133.6	0.97	0.6	778,637	472,085	60.6	28,475	283
Dairy products	18,344.3	39.6	0.29	0.2	250,075	131,950	52.8	73,355	300
Cattle and calves	32,358.6	186.2	1.35	0.6	386,685	128,681	33.3	83,682	1,447
Hogs and pigs	13,096.7	11,594.3	84.33	88.5	377,610	493,142	130.6	34,683	23,511
Sheep, lambs, and wool	478.6	2.1	0.02	0.4	278,730	94,773	34.0	1,717	22
Other livestock	2,026.6	1.0	0.01	0.0	369,685	107,556	29.1	5,482	9

Source: 1997 Census of Agriculture, U.S. Department of Agriculture, National Agricultural Statistics Service. Table shows totals for the U.S. agriculture sector and for the NAICS subdivision of it, shown as "This Agric. Sector" or as "This Sector." Not all farms report on every category. For this reason, the reporting universe is shown in the last two columns. Averages are based on these columns. Farms classified in one sector routinely produce categories in other sectors as well.

GOVERNMENT PAYMENTS AND OTHER FARM-RELATED INCOME

Item	U.S. Total ($ mil.)	This Sector ($ mil.)	% of Sector Gov/Oth. Income	% of U.S.	Average receipts per farm - $			Number of farms reporting category	
					U.S.	This Agric. Sector	% of U.S.	U.S.	This Sector
Government payments	5,054.5	154.3	62.72	3.1	7,378	7,590	102.9	685,029	20,331
Other farm-related income	3,272.3	91.7	37.28	2.8	5,999	5,991	99.9	545,480	15,312
Custom work and other agricultural services	1,235.1	37.4	15.21	3.0	8,646	8,565	99.1	142,854	4,368
Gross cash rent or share payments	1,207.9	35.1	14.28	2.9	6,867	8,888	129.4	175,901	3,952
Forest products, excluding Christmas trees and maple products	344.3	4.4	1.78	1.3	7,417	6,134	82.7	46,426	714
Other farm-related income sources	484.9	14.8	6.02	3.1	1,595	1,491	93.5	303,908	9,937

Source: 1997 Census of Agriculture, U.S. Department of Agriculture, National Agricultural Statistics Service. Table shows totals for the U.S. agriculture sector and for the NAICS subdivision of it, shown as "This Agric. Sector" or as "This Sector." Not all farms report on every category. For this reason, the reporting universe is shown in the last two columns. Averages are based on these columns. Government payments are agricultural subsidies under various programs.

COMMODITY CREDIT CORPORATION LOANS

Item	U.S. Total ($ mil.)	This Sector ($ mil.)	% of Sector Loan Total	% of U.S.	Average loan value per farm - $			Number of farms reporting category	
					U.S.	This Agric. Sector	% of U.S.	U.S.	This Sector
Total loans	3,034.7	136.9	100.00	4.5	36,419	35,750	98.2	83,328	3,830
Corn	1,333.9	88.6	64.70	6.6	26,419	26,879	101.7	50,489	3,296
Wheat	415.4	2.3	1.69	0.6	18,093	8,981	49.6	22,961	257
Soybeans	774.0	44.9	32.76	5.8	30,370	30,579	100.7	25,487	1,467
Sorghum, barley, and oats	54.8	0.9	0.67	1.7	8,603	7,888	91.7	6,375	116
Cotton	191.4	0.0	0.03	0.0	43,275	3,667	8.5	4,422	12
Sunflower seed, flaxseed, safflower, canola, other rapeseed, and mustard seed	17.3	0.0	0.02	0.2	25,159	8,000	31.8	686	4
Peanuts, rice, and tobacco	247.9	0.2	0.13	0.1	60,421	13,231	21.9	4,103	13

Source: 1997 Census of Agriculture, U.S. Department of Agriculture, National Agricultural Statistics Service. Table shows totals for the U.S. agriculture sector and for the NAICS subdivision of it, shown as "This Agric. Sector" or as "This Sector." Not all farms report on every category. For this reason, the reporting universe is shown in the last two columns. Averages are based on these columns. The Commodity Credit Corporation provides low interest loans to farmers.

SELECTED MACHINERY AND EQUIPMENT

Item	U.S. Total (number)	This Agric. Sector (number)	% of U.S.	Average number per farm			Number of farms reporting category	
				U.S.	This Agric. Sector	% of U.S.	U.S.	This Sector
Motortrucks, including pickups	3,497,735	93,803	2.7	2.07	2.21	106.9	1,688,303	42,355
Wheel tractors	3,936,014	99,560	2.5	2.31	2.51	108.8	1,707,384	39,677
Less than 40 horsepower (PTO)	1,262,688	26,291	2.1	1.44	1.41	97.6	877,119	18,707
40 horsepower (PTO) or more	2,673,326	73,269	2.7	2.02	2.23	110.1	1,321,084	32,894
40 to 99 horsepower (PTO)	1,808,105	46,295	2.6	1.58	1.63	103.3	1,145,466	28,399
100 horsepower (PTO)	865,221	26,974	3.1	1.68	1.69	100.2	513,773	15,993
Grain and bean combines	460,606	16,052	3.5	1.16	1.09	93.7	395,934	14,729
Cotton pickers and strippers	38,294	161	0.4	1.48	1.25	84.3	25,874	129
Mower conditioners	608,443	11,178	1.8	1.12	1.08	96.8	543,565	10,312
Pickup balers	717,245	15,815	2.2	1.24	1.19	96.3	579,440	13,267

Source: 1997 Census of Agriculture, U.S. Department of Agriculture, National Agricultural Statistics Service. Table shows totals for the U.S. agriculture sector and for the NAICS subdivision of it, shown as "This Agric. Sector" or as "This Sector." Not all farms report on every category. For this reason, the reporting universe is shown in the last two columns. Averages are based on these columns. PTO stands for "power take off."

FARM PRODUCTION EXPENSES

Item	U.S. Total ($ mil.)	This Sector ($ mil.)	% of Sector Total Expense	% of U.S.	Average expense per farm - $			Number of farms reporting category	
					U.S.	This Agric. Sector	% of U.S.	U.S.	This Sector
Total farm production expenses	150,591.0	10,144.2	100.00	6.7	78,771	221,887	281.7	1,911,766	45,718
Livestock and poultry purchased	21,614.6	2,125.2	20.95	9.8	38,807	63,639	164.0	556,980	33,395
Feed for livestock and poultry	32,760.0	4,208.8	41.49	12.8	32,059	98,711	307.9	1,021,849	42,638
Commercially mixed formula feeds	21,236.2	2,434.4	24.00	11.5	34,459	86,061	249.8	616,280	28,287
Seeds, bulbs, plants, and trees	5,725.9	152.1	1.50	2.7	6,388	6,138	96.1	896,339	24,774
Commercial fertilizer	9,597.1	230.9	2.28	2.4	8,060	9,242	114.7	1,190,733	24,987
Agricultural chemicals	7,581.4	165.7	1.63	2.2	8,056	7,093	88.1	941,136	23,354
Petroleum products	6,371.5	278.6	2.75	4.4	3,619	6,465	178.6	1,760,642	43,097
Gasoline and gasohol	1,886.6	65.9	0.65	3.5	1,380	1,830	132.6	1,366,915	36,036
Diesel fuel	2,846.0	97.2	0.96	3.4	2,164	3,131	144.7	1,315,397	31,057
Natural gas	432.9	17.3	0.17	4.0	6,091	6,831	112.1	71,069	2,536
LP gas, fuel oil, kerosene, motor oil, grease, etc.	1,206.1	98.1	0.97	8.1	945	2,742	290.2	1,276,331	35,788
Electricity	2,751.1	160.9	1.59	5.8	2,247	4,279	190.4	1,224,374	37,608
Hired farm labor	14,841.0	639.6	6.31	4.3	22,811	33,904	148.6	650,623	18,866
Contract labor	2,959.0	46.5	0.46	1.6	13,040	11,814	90.6	226,909	3,936
Repair and maintenance	8,637.7	374.2	3.69	4.3	5,616	9,294	165.5	1,538,058	40,267
Custom work, machine hire, and rental of equipment	3,210.3	89.8	0.89	2.8	5,372	5,269	98.1	597,624	17,050
Interest	8,928.1	493.0	4.86	5.5	11,016	17,849	162.0	810,476	27,622
Secured by real estate	5,449.6	294.9	2.91	5.4	9,564	14,352	150.1	569,775	20,550
Not secured by real estate	3,478.5	198.1	1.95	5.7	7,540	11,861	157.3	461,326	16,701
Cash rent	6,915.7	297.2	2.93	4.3	14,244	20,731	145.5	485,512	14,337
Property taxes	3,920.1	122.1	1.20	3.1	2,213	2,881	130.2	1,771,787	42,383
All other farm production expenses	14,777.4	759.4	7.49	5.1	8,747	17,703	202.4	1,689,391	42,896

Source: *1997 Census of Agriculture*, U.S. Department of Agriculture, National Agricultural Statistics Service. Table shows totals for the U.S. agriculture sector and for the NAICS subdivision of it, shown as "This Agric. Sector" or as "This Sector." Not all farms report on every category. For this reason, the reporting universe is shown in the last two columns. Averages are based on these columns. LP gas stands for "liquid petroleum gas," i.e., butane or propane.

NET CASH RETURN AND FARMS WITH GAINS AND LOSSES

Item	Number of farms and %				Average gain or loss per farm - $		
	U.S.	% of U.S.	This Agriculture Sector	% of Sector	U.S.	This Agriculture Sector	% of U.S.
All farms	1,911,824	100.0	45,723	100.0	22,260	69,565	312.5
Number of farms with net gains	985,718	51.6	29,523	64.6	51,296	116,299	226.7
Gain of -							
Less than $1,000	120,163	6.3	2,014	4.4	-	-	-
$1,000 to $9,999	370,611	19.4	6,900	15.1	-	-	-
$10,000 to $49,999	292,484	15.3	8,749	19.1	-	-	-
$50,000 or more	202,460	10.6	11,860	25.9	-	-	-
Number of farms with net losses	926,106	48.4	16,200	35.4	(8,645)	(15,603)	180.5
Loss of -							
Less than $1,000	165,390	8.7	2,480	5.4	-	-	-
$1,000 to $9,999	591,517	30.9	9,904	21.7	-	-	-
$10,000 to $49,999	152,649	8.0	3,253	7.1	-	-	-
$50,000 or more	16,550	0.9	563	1.2	-	-	-

Source: *1997 Census of Agriculture*, U.S. Department of Agriculture, National Agricultural Statistics Service. Table shows totals for the U.S. agriculture sector and for the NAICS subdivision of it, shown as "This Agric. Sector" or as "This Sector." Not all farms report on every category. For this reason, the reporting universe is shown in the last two columns. Averages are based on these columns. Net gains are income less cost for farm operations; they exclude non-farm earnings. Values in parentheses are losses.

CHARACTERISTICS OF FARM OPERATORS

Farm Operators	U.S.	This Agric. Sector	% of U.S.	Farm Operators	U.S.	This Agric. Sector	% of U.S.
Place of residence:				By age group:			
On farm operated	1,361,766	36,539	2.7	Under 25 years	20,850	1,057	5.1
Not on farm operated	412,554	6,191	1.5	25 to 34 years	128,455	5,758	4.5
Not reported	137,539	3,623	2.6	35 to 44 years	371,442	13,797	3.7
Principal occupation:				45 to 49 years	232,845	6,405	2.8
Farming	961,560	27,727	2.9	50 to 54 years	233,884	5,209	2.2
Other	950,299	18,626	2.0	55 to 59 years	222,736	4,605	2.1
Days worked off farm:				60 to 64 years	204,618	3,775	1.8
None	755,254	19,541	2.6	65 to 69 years	179,858	2,512	1.4
Any	1,042,158	23,959	2.3	70 years and over	317,171	3,235	1.0
1 to 99 days	164,957	4,111	2.5	Average age	54	48	88.4
100 to 199 days	167,922	3,437	2.0	By sex:			
200 days or more	709,279	16,411	2.3	Male	1,746,757	44,287	2.5
Not reported	114,447	2,853	2.5	Female	165,102	2,066	1.3
Years on present farm:				Spanish, Hispanic/Latino origin	27,717	445	1.6
2 years or less	92,574	2,407	2.6	Tenure of operator:			
3 or 4 years	126,791	3,289	2.6	All operators	1,911,859	46,353	2.4
5 to 9 years	263,642	7,182	2.7	Full owners	1,146,891	26,187	2.3
10 years or more	1,113,839	25,828	2.3	Part owners	573,839	15,079	2.6
Ave. years on this farm	20	18	90.0	Tenants	191,129	5,087	2.7
Not reported	315,013	7,647	2.4				

Source: 1997 Census of Agriculture, U.S. Department of Agriculture, National Agricultural Statistics Service. Table shows totals for the U.S. agriculture sector and for the NAICS subdivision of it, shown as "This Agric. Sector" or as "This Sector." Not all farms report on every category. For this reason, the reporting universe is shown in the last two columns. Averages are based on these columns. All values shown are number of farm operators in each category or percent.

FARMS BY TYPE OF ORGANIZATION

Item	Number of farms and percent				Total acres and percent			
	U.S.	% of U.S.	This Agriculture Sector	% of Sector	U.S.	This Agriculture Sector	% of U.S.
Individual or family (sole proprietorship)	1,643,424	100.0	37,942	100.0	585,464,911	7,830,082	1.3
Partnership	169,462	10.3	4,599	12.1	149,321,484	1,753,545	1.2
Corporation:							
Family held	76,103	4.6	3,123	8.2	119,559,203	1,847,083	1.5
More than 10 stockholders	1,795	0.1	68	0.2	-	-	-
10 or less stockholders	74,308	4.5	3,055	8.1	-	-	-
Other than family held	7,899	0.5	454	1.2	11,904,053	195,804	1.6
More than 10 stockholders	1,029	0.1	106	0.3	-	-	-
10 or less stockholders	6,870	0.4	348	0.9	-	-	-
Other cooperative, estate or trust, institutional, etc.	14,971	0.9	235	0.6	65,545,604	77,753	0.1

Source: 1997 Census of Agriculture, U.S. Department of Agriculture, National Agricultural Statistics Service. Table shows totals for the U.S. agriculture sector and for the NAICS subdivision of it, shown as "This Agric. Sector" or as "This Sector." Not all farms report on every category. For this reason, the reporting universe is shown in the last two columns. Averages are based on these columns.

LIVESTOCK INVENTORIES AND SALES

Item	U.S. (number)	This Agric. Sector (number)	% of U.S.	Average number per farm			Number of farms reporting category	
				U.S.	This Agric. Sector	% of U.S.	U.S.	This Sector
Cattle and calves inventory	98,989,244	1,047,307	1.1	94.6	55.7	58.9	1,046,863	18,797
Cows and heifers that had calved	43,162,054	428,396	1.0	48.3	31.2	64.7	894,110	13,721
Beef cows	34,066,615	398,325	1.2	42.3	31.7	74.9	804,595	12,554
Milk cows	9,095,439	30,071	0.3	77.8	17.6	22.6	116,874	1,711
Heifers and heifer calves	26,988,697	269,856	1.0	33.6	20.6	61.4	803,985	13,103
Steers, steer calves, bulls, and bull calves	28,838,493	349,055	1.2	32.6	22.2	68.0	883,983	15,740
Cattle and calves sold	74,089,046	600,879	0.8	73.2	36.7	50.1	1,011,809	16,373
Calves	16,480,293	141,290	0.9	26.8	19.5	72.9	615,177	7,238
Cattle	57,608,753	459,589	0.8	78.0	37.2	47.7	738,696	12,354
Fattened on grain and concentrates	27,328,190	216,399	0.8	247.0	48.0	19.4	110,620	4,511
Hogs and pigs inventory	61,206,236	50,398,074	82.3	557.7	1,146.5	205.6	109,754	43,957
Used or to be used for breeding	6,831,564	5,710,464	83.6	106.7	187.1	175.4	64,029	30,513
Other	54,374,672	44,687,610	82.2	528.0	1,077.0	204.0	102,977	41,491
Hogs and pigs sold	142,611,882	124,365,477	87.2	1,396.7	2,707.1	193.8	102,106	45,940
Feeder pigs	34,988,718	32,591,890	93.1	2,037.8	3,504.9	172.0	17,170	9,299
Litters of pigs farrowed between Dec. 1 of preceding year and Nov. 30	11,497,523	9,836,360	85.6	170.3	308.8	181.3	67,514	31,850
Dec. 1 and May 31	5,697,371	4,851,785	85.2	91.0	160.0	175.9	62,622	30,321
June 1 and Nov. 30	5,800,152	4,984,575	85.9	99.7	171.4	172.0	58,204	29,079
Sheep and lambs of all ages inventory	7,821,885	118,678	1.5	118.9	46.8	39.4	65,790	2,534
Ewes 1 year old or older	4,408,683	52,864	1.2	78.1	25.9	33.2	56,414	2,040
Sheep and lambs sold	7,331,545	91,799	1.3	123.1	40.4	32.8	59,575	2,272
Sheep and lambs shorn	6,139,140	73,397	1.2	118.4	42.2	35.6	51,869	1,740
Horses and ponies inventory	2,427,277	31,558	1.3	6.5	4.8	74.2	375,218	6,571
Horses and ponies sold	325,306	2,314	0.7	4.1	2.6	62.4	79,516	907
Goats inventory	1,989,799	25,595	1.3	34.4	12.7	36.9	57,925	2,020
Goats sold	740,597	9,675	1.3	31.5	13.1	41.5	23,520	741

Source: 1997 Census of Agriculture, U.S. Department of Agriculture, National Agricultural Statistics Service. Table shows totals for the U.S. agriculture sector and for the NAICS subdivision of it, shown as "This Agric. Sector" or as "This Sector." Not all farms report on every category. For this reason, the reporting universe is shown in the last two columns. Averages are based on these columns.

POULTRY INVENTORIES AND SALES

Item	U.S. (number)	This Agric. Sector (number)	% of U.S.	Average number per farm			Number of farms reporting category	
				U.S.	This Agric. Sector	% of U.S.	U.S.	This Sector
Layers and pullets 13 weeks old and older inventory	366,989,851	1,260,539	0.3	5,053.8	392.1	7.8	72,616	3,215
Layers 20 weeks old and older	313,851,480	589,934	0.2	4,499.0	191.2	4.2	69,761	3,086
Pullets 13 weeks old and older but less than 20 weeks old	53,138,371	670,605	1.3	4,031.7	1,034.9	25.7	13,180	648
Layers, pullets, and pullet chicks sold	331,563,736	2,340,831	0.7	24,636.9	5,737.3	23.3	13,458	408
Broilers and other meat type chickens sold	6,741,927,110	25,839,353	0.4	281,653.0	52,095.5	18.5	23,937	496
Turkey hens kept for breeding	5,504,808	-		968.1	-	-	5,686	329
Turkeys sold	307,586,680	7,835,131	2.5	51,000.9	21,644.0	42.4	6,031	362

Source: 1997 Census of Agriculture, U.S. Department of Agriculture, National Agricultural Statistics Service. Table shows totals for the U.S. agriculture sector and for the NAICS subdivision of it, shown as "This Agric. Sector" or as "This Sector." Not all farms report on every category. For this reason, the reporting universe is shown in the last two columns. Averages are based on these columns.

SELECTED CROPS HARVESTED

Item	In 1,000	Crop harvested			Acres used for crop (000)			Number of farms reporting category	
		U.S.	This Agric. Sector	% of U.S.	U.S.	This Agric. Sector	% of U.S.	U.S.	This Sector
Corn for grain or seed	bushels	8,578,635	449,572	5.2	69,796.7	3,605.5	5.2	430,711	20,989
Irrigated		-	-	-	10,638.9	164.5	1.5	40,574	984
Corn for silage or green chop	tons, green	88,381	1,010	1.1	5,727.6	69.2	1.2	119,308	2,694
Irrigated		-	-	-	1,033.3	2.7	0.3	10,815	89
Sorghum for grain or seed	bushels	559,070	10,230	1.8	8,470.4	126.6	1.5	49,397	1,070
Irrigated		-	-	-	875.6	3.1	0.4	5,793	53
Wheat for grain	bushels	2,204,027	20,521	0.9	58,836.3	451.4	0.8	243,568	5,769
Irrigated		-	-	-	3,990.9	8.7	0.2	20,385	97
Barley for grain	bushels	336,435	3,292	1.0	5,945.0	67.9	1.1	41,930	948
Irrigated		-	-	-	1,060.7	3.2	0.3	8,847	51
Oats for grain	bushels	151,327	5,641	3.7	2,681.0	85.5	3.2	89,606	4,592
Irrigated		-	-	-	121.0	0.4	0.3	2,788	31
Rice	cwt	182,231	-	-	3,122.1	-	-	9,291	-
Irrigated		-	-	-	3,122.1	-	-	9,291	-
Cotton	bales	17,879	64	0.4	13,235.2	44.7	0.3	31,493	173
Irrigated		-	-	-	4,888.0	1.0	0.0	12,434	17
Tobacco	pounds	1,747,702	35,390	2.0	838.5	15.6	1.9	89,706	634
Irrigated		-	-	-	138.7	1.5	1.1	7,090	74
Soybeans for beans	bushels	2,504,307	112,233	4.5	66,147.7	2,632.8	4.0	354,692	16,396
Irrigated		-	-	-	4,152.1	47.8	1.2	20,619	479
Dry edible beans, excluding dry limas	cwt	27,224	133	0.5	1,691.9	8.1	0.5	10,911	68
Irrigated		-	-	-	577.0	1.4	0.2	4,882	13
Potatoes, excluding sweetpotatoes	cwt	459,886	128	0.0	1,355.2	0.6	0.0	10,523	97
Irrigated		-	-	-	1,070.3	0.1	0.0	4,843	14
Sugar beets for sugar	tons	29,775	95	0.3	1,453.8	5.2	0.4	7,102	30
Irrigated		-	-	-	616.4	-	-	3,492	4
Peanuts for nuts	pounds	3,377,143	23,805	0.7	1,352.2	9.7	0.7	12,221	188
Irrigated		-	-	-	412.3	0.9	0.2	3,125	24
Hay alfalfa, other tame, small grain, wild, grass silage, green chop	tons, dry	139,365	1,714	1.2	60,799.8	700.2	1.2	888,597	16,192
Irrigated		-	-	-	9,564.3	34.3	0.4	79,406	740
Alfalfa hay	tons, dry	65,863	887	1.3	21,309.8	284.1	1.3	358,365	9,102
Irrigated		-	-	-	5,980.5	13.6	0.2	57,854	338
Vegetables harvested for sale		-	-	-	3,773.2	19.6	0.5	53,727	761
Irrigated		-	-	-	2,641.8	2.0	0.1	23,203	162
Land in orchards		-	-	-	5,158.1	4.8	0.1	106,069	418
Irrigated		-	-	-	4,107.9	1.9	0.0	61,606	126

Source: *1997 Census of Agriculture*, U.S. Department of Agriculture, National Agricultural Statistics Service. Table shows totals for the U.S. agriculture sector and for the NAICS subdivision of it, shown as "This Agric. Sector" or as "This Sector." Not all farms report on every category. For this reason, the reporting universe is shown in the last two columns. Averages are based on these columns. "Green tons" are weight of product as harvested, i.e., moist. cwt stands for "hundredweight."

LEADING COMPANIES   Number shown: **6**   Total sales ($ mil): **1,273**   Total employment (000): **4.0**

Company Name	Address				CEO Name	Phone	Co. Type	Sales ($ mil)	Empl. (000)
Murphy Family Farms Inc.	PO Box 759	Rose Hill	NC	28458	Jerry Godwin	910-289-2111	R	600	1.9
National Farms Inc.	1600 Genessee St	Kansas City	MO	64102	Bill Haw	816-221-4501	R	266*	0.5
Pig Improvement Company Inc.	P O Box 348	Franklin	KY	42134	Gregg Be Vier	502-586-9226	S	179	0.7
National Hog Farms Inc.	25000 Weld Co 69	Kersey	CO	80644	Bill Haw	970-353-9960	S	93*	0.2
Midwest Farms Inc.	2700 Midwest Dr	Onalaska	WI	54650	Ron Houser	608-783-7130	D	89*	0.3
DEKALB Swine Breeders Inc.	2210 Bethany Road	Sycamore	IL	60178	Gary Kahle	815-758-9152	S	46*	0.4

Source: *Ward's Business Directory of U.S. Private and Public Companies*, Volumes 1 and 2, 2000. The company type code used is as follows: P - Public, R - Private, S - Subsidiary, D - Division, J - Joint Venture, A - Affiliate, G - Group, N - Company type not reported. Sales are in millions of dollars, employees are in thousands. An asterisk (*) indicates an estimated sales volume. The symbol < stands for 'less than'. Company names and addresses are truncated, in some cases, to fit into the available space.

NAICS 112300 - POULTRY AND EGG PRODUCTION

GENERAL STATISTICS

Item	U.S. Total	This Agri-culture Sector	% of U.S.	Value shown as	Category average per farm			Number of farms reporting category	
					U.S.	This Agric. Sector	% of U.S.	U.S.	This Sector
Farms - number	1,911,859	36,944	1.9	-	-	-	-	-	-
Land in farms - mil. acres	931.795	5.460	0.6	Acres	487	148	30.4	1,911,859	36,944
Value of land, buildings - $ mil.	859,839.2	13,223.0	1.5	$	449,748	396,838	88.2	524,066	33,321
Value of machinery and equip-ment - $ mil.	110,256.8	2,410.3	2.2	$	57,678	72,335	125.4	1,911,601	33,321
Sales of Ag Products - $ mil.	196,864.6	22,720.6	11.5	$	102,970	615,001	597.3	1,911,859	36,944
Government payments - $ mil.	5,054.5	38.0	0.8	$	7,378	6,279	85.1	685,029	6,047
Other farm-related income - $ mil.	3,272.3	80.3	2.5	$	5,999	11,499	191.7	545,480	6,981
Expenses - $ mil.	150,591.0	19,508.7	13.0	$	78,771	585,547	743.4	1,911,766	33,317
Payroll - $ mil.	14,841.0	679.4	4.6	$	22,811	42,778	187.5	650,623	15,881
Workers - 150 days or more a year	890,467	43,323	4.9	Number	3.4	5.0	145.4	259,631	8,690
Workers - less than 150 days	2,461,561	58,503	2.4	Number	4.2	4.4	103.8	581,658	13,322
Net Cash Return - $ mil.	42,557.9	2,410.5	5.7	$	22,260	72,342	325.0	1,911,824	33,321

Source: *1997 Census of Agriculture*, U.S. Department of Agriculture, National Agricultural Statistics Service. Table shows totals for the U.S. agriculture sector and for the NAICS subdivision of it, shown as "This Agric. Sector" or as "This Sector." Not all farms report on every category. For this reason, the reporting universe is shown in the last two columns. Averages are based on these columns.

LAND IN FARMS ACCORDING TO USE

Item	U.S. Total (000 acres)	This Sector (000 acres)	% of U.S.	Average acres per farms			Number of farms reporting category	
				U.S.	This Agric. Sector	% of U.S.	U.S.	This Sector
Total cropland	431,144.9	2,788.2	0.6	260	114	-	1,661,395	24,477
Harvested cropland	309,395.5	1,673.7	0.5	219	94	-	1,410,606	17,722
Cropland:								
Pasture or grazing	64,466.5	886.5	1.4	85	64	-	754,170	13,872
In cover crops, legumes, grasses	13,531.2	71.8	0.5	88	41	-	153,177	1,739
On which all crops failed	3,449.4	15.5	0.5	67	32	-	51,673	488
In cultivated summer fallow	20,905.9	11.2	0.1	256	34	-	81,702	325
Idle	19,396.3	129.6	0.7	83	38	-	232,961	3,453
Total woodland	71,465.4	1,278.0	1.8	96	71	-	743,011	17,997
Woodland pastured	29,693.9	396.1	1.3	84	48	-	352,217	8,194
Woodland not pastured	41,771.5	881.9	2.1	79	67	-	531,846	13,133
Other pasture/rangeland	396,884.6	868.6	0.2	721	98	-	550,619	8,835
Land for house lots, ponds, roads, wasteland	32,300.4	525.4	1.6	28	19	-	1,142,618	27,474
Irrigated land	55,058.1	108.0	0.2	197	66	-	279,442	1,640
Harvested cropland	50,013.5	98.0	0.2	198	76	-	252,679	1,294
Pasture and other	5,044.7	10.0	0.2	87	21	-	58,258	476
Conservation Reserve/Wetlands Reserve Lands	29,489.1	119.9	0.4	131	71	-	225,410	1,698

Source: *1997 Census of Agriculture*, U.S. Department of Agriculture, National Agricultural Statistics Service. Table shows totals for the U.S. agriculture sector and for the NAICS subdivision of it, shown as "This Agric. Sector" or as "This Sector." Not all farms report on every category. For this reason, the reporting universe is shown in the last two columns. Averages are based on these columns. The Conservation Reserve and Wetlands Reserve programs provide support for land conservation/preservation. Cover crops are not harvested or pastured.

MARKET VALUE OF AGRICULTURAL PRODUCTS SOLD: ALL FARMS

Item	U.S. Total ($ mil.)	This Sector ($ mil.)	% of Sector Sales	% of U.S.	Average sales per farm - $			Number of farms reporting category	
					U.S.	This Agric. Sector	% of U.S.	U.S.	This Sector
Grains	46,617.1	210.8	0.93	0.5	79,095	53,644	67.8	589,379	3,929
Corn for grain	18,884.8	101.9	0.45	0.5	52,506	37,150	70.8	359,666	2,743
Wheat	7,173.9	22.4	0.10	0.3	29,726	15,098	50.8	241,334	1,485
Soybeans	15,622.4	79.1	0.35	0.5	44,185	30,799	69.7	353,566	2,567
Sorghum for grain	1,140.0	2.2	0.01	0.2	25,360	12,099	47.7	44,955	181
Barley	709.6	2.1	0.01	0.3	23,191	7,897	34.1	30,598	262
Oats	121.3	0.3	0.00	0.2	3,114	2,121	68.1	38,940	140
Other grains	2,965.1	2.8	0.01	0.1	67,540	20,650	30.6	43,901	137
Cotton and cotton seed	5,975.5	20.4	0.09	0.3	189,963	95,472	50.3	31,456	214
Tobacco	2,924.7	38.0	0.17	1.3	32,662	76,941	235.6	89,544	494
Hay, silage, and field seeds	4,670.5	28.5	0.13	0.6	13,174	6,173	46.9	354,523	4,616
Vegetables, sweet corn, and melons	8,401.7	16.2	0.07	0.2	156,628	25,465	16.3	53,641	636
Fruits and berries	12,660.3	19.6	0.09	0.2	147,259	45,473	30.9	85,973	431
Nursery and greenhouse crops	10,942.8	2.7	0.01	0.0	161,360	12,132	7.5	67,816	219
Other crops	5,863.1	16.8	0.07	0.3	153,907	47,969	31.2	38,095	350
Poultry and poultry products	22,262.6	21,968.8	96.69	98.7	352,000	609,093	173.0	63,246	36,068
Dairy products	18,997.3	77.4	0.34	0.4	191,432	127,044	66.4	99,238	609
Cattle and calves	40,524.8	211.3	0.93	0.5	40,052	14,799	36.9	1,011,809	14,281
Hogs and pigs	13,804.8	104.1	0.46	0.8	135,201	87,362	64.6	102,106	1,192
Sheep, lambs, and wool	682.9	2.0	0.01	0.3	10,913	2,278	20.9	62,579	872
Other livestock	2,536.5	4.1	0.02	0.2	20,506	2,662	13.0	123,695	1,523
Products sold to public directly	13,096.7	98.1	0.43	0.7	377,610	308,585	81.7	34,683	318

Source: *1997 Census of Agriculture*, U.S. Department of Agriculture, National Agricultural Statistics Service. Table shows totals for the U.S. agriculture sector and for the NAICS subdivision of it, shown as "This Agric. Sector" or as "This Sector." Not all farms report on every category. For this reason, the reporting universe is shown in the last two columns. Averages are based on these columns. Farms classified in one sector routinely produce categories in other sectors as well. Products sold to the public are sold for direct consumption.

MARKET VALUE OF PRODUCTS SOLD: FARMS WITH SALES OF $50,000 OR MORE

Item	U.S. Total ($ mil.)	This Sector ($ mil.)	% of Sector Sales	% of U.S.	Average sales per farm - $			Number of farms reporting category	
					U.S.	This Agric. Sector	% of U.S.	U.S.	This Sector
Grains	40,973.4	171.2	0.75	0.4	183,623	159,744	87.0	223,138	1,072
Cotton and cotton seed	5,743.9	17.9	0.08	0.3	286,562	167,673	58.5	20,044	107
Tobacco	2,060.2	33.3	0.15	1.6	175,907	154,767	88.0	11,712	215
Hay, silage, and field seeds	2,781.9	7.5	0.03	0.3	188,959	149,120	78.9	14,722	50
Vegetables, sweet corn, and melons	7,966.8	11.1	0.05	0.1	673,443	135,744	20.2	11,830	82
Fruits and berries	12,072.3	17.7	0.08	0.1	478,927	248,958	52.0	25,207	71
Nursery and greenhouse crops	10,412.0	1.4	0.01	0.0	578,025	119,833	20.7	18,013	12
Other crops	5,586.6	13.5	0.06	0.2	363,758	162,084	44.6	15,358	83
Poultry and poultry products	22,171.7	21,903.1	96.40	98.8	778,637	791,297	101.6	28,475	27,680
Dairy products	18,344.3	73.0	0.32	0.4	250,075	187,697	75.1	73,355	389
Cattle and calves	32,358.6	85.7	0.38	0.3	386,685	114,293	29.6	83,682	750
Hogs and pigs	13,096.7	98.1	0.43	0.7	377,610	308,585	81.7	34,683	318
Sheep, lambs, and wool	478.6	0.5	0.00	0.1	278,730	88,833	31.9	1,717	6
Other livestock	2,026.6	1.6	0.01	0.1	369,685	198,500	53.7	5,482	8

Source: *1997 Census of Agriculture*, U.S. Department of Agriculture, National Agricultural Statistics Service. Table shows totals for the U.S. agriculture sector and for the NAICS subdivision of it, shown as "This Agric. Sector" or as "This Sector." Not all farms report on every category. For this reason, the reporting universe is shown in the last two columns. Averages are based on these columns. Farms classified in one sector routinely produce categories in other sectors as well.

GOVERNMENT PAYMENTS AND OTHER FARM-RELATED INCOME

Item	U.S. Total ($ mil.)	This Sector ($ mil.)	% of Sector Gov/Oth. Income	% of U.S.	Average receipts per farm - $			Number of farms reporting category	
					U.S.	This Agric. Sector	% of U.S.	U.S.	This Sector
Government payments	5,054.5	38.0	32.11	0.8	7,378	6,279	85.1	685,029	6,047
Other farm-related income	3,272.3	80.3	67.89	2.5	5,999	11,499	191.7	545,480	6,981
Custom work and other agricul- tural services	1,235.1	45.1	38.12	3.6	8,646	26,147	302.4	142,854	1,724
Gross cash rent or share payments	1,207.9	13.8	11.66	1.1	6,867	6,138	89.4	175,901	2,246
Forest products, excluding Christ- mas trees and maple products	344.3	11.1	9.38	3.2	7,417	13,892	187.3	46,426	798
Other farm-related income sources	484.9	10.3	8.73	2.1	1,595	2,820	176.8	303,908	3,660

Source: *1997 Census of Agriculture*, U.S. Department of Agriculture, National Agricultural Statistics Service. Table shows totals for the U.S. agriculture sector and for the NAICS subdivision of it, shown as "This Agric. Sector" or as "This Sector." Not all farms report on every category. For this reason, the reporting universe is shown in the last two columns. Averages are based on these columns. Government payments are agricultural subsidies under various programs.

COMMODITY CREDIT CORPORATION LOANS

Item	U.S. Total ($ mil.)	This Sector ($ mil.)	% of Sector Loan Total	% of U.S.	Average loan value per farm - $			Number of farms reporting category	
					U.S.	This Agric. Sector	% of U.S.	U.S.	This Sector
Total loans	3,034.7	11.6	100.00	0.4	36,419	31,632	86.9	83,328	367
Corn	1,333.9	5.9	51.11	0.4	26,419	21,653	82.0	50,489	274
Wheat	415.4	0.8	6.94	0.2	18,093	11,681	64.6	22,961	69
Soybeans	774.0	4.3	37.01	0.6	30,370	33,302	109.7	25,487	129
Sorghum, barley, and oats	54.8	0.1	1.25	0.3	8,603	9,667	112.4	6,375	15
Cotton	191.4	0.3	2.42	0.1	43,275	10,407	24.0	4,422	27
Sunflower seed, flaxseed, saf- flower, canola, other rapeseed, and mustard seed	17.3	-	-	-	25,159	-	-	686	-
Peanuts, rice, and tobacco	247.9	0.1	1.27	0.1	60,421	14,800	24.5	4,103	10

Source: *1997 Census of Agriculture*, U.S. Department of Agriculture, National Agricultural Statistics Service. Table shows totals for the U.S. agriculture sector and for the NAICS subdivision of it, shown as "This Agric. Sector" or as "This Sector." Not all farms report on every category. For this reason, the reporting universe is shown in the last two columns. Averages are based on these columns. The Commodity Credit Corporation provides low interest loans to farmers.

SELECTED MACHINERY AND EQUIPMENT

Item	U.S. Total (number)	This Agric. Sector (number)	% of U.S.	Average number per farm			Number of farms reporting category	
				U.S.	This Agric. Sector	% of U.S.	U.S.	This Sector
Motortrucks, including pickups	3,497,735	85,285	2.4	2.07	2.69	129.6	1,688,303	31,757
Wheel tractors	3,936,014	60,361	1.5	2.31	2.09	90.8	1,707,384	28,843
Less than 40 horsepower (PTO)	1,262,688	21,580	1.7	1.44	1.39	96.3	877,119	15,562
40 horsepower (PTO) or more	2,673,326	38,781	1.5	2.02	1.82	90.1	1,321,084	21,259
40 to 99 horsepower (PTO)	1,808,105	32,443	1.8	1.58	1.61	102.3	1,145,466	20,092
100 horsepower (PTO)	865,221	6,338	0.7	1.68	1.53	90.6	513,773	4,152
Grain and bean combines	460,606	2,506	0.5	1.16	1.12	96.6	395,934	2,230
Cotton pickers and strippers	38,294	244	0.6	1.48	1.32	89.1	25,874	185
Mower conditioners	608,443	7,627	1.3	1.12	1.14	101.7	543,565	6,702
Pickup balers	717,245	8,996	1.3	1.24	1.25	100.7	579,440	7,218

Source: *1997 Census of Agriculture*, U.S. Department of Agriculture, National Agricultural Statistics Service. Table shows totals for the U.S. agriculture sector and for the NAICS subdivision of it, shown as "This Agric. Sector" or as "This Sector." Not all farms report on every category. For this reason, the reporting universe is shown in the last two columns. Averages are based on these columns. PTO stands for "power take off."

FARM PRODUCTION EXPENSES

Item	U.S. Total ($ mil.)	This Sector ($ mil.)	% of Sector Total Expense	% of U.S.	Average expense per farm - $			Number of farms reporting category	
					U.S.	This Agric. Sector	% of U.S.	U.S.	This Sector
Total farm production expenses	150,591.0	19,508.7	100.00	13.0	78,771	585,547	743.4	1,911,766	33,317
Livestock and poultry purchased	21,614.6	2,865.2	14.69	13.3	38,807	94,850	244.4	556,980	30,208
Feed for livestock and poultry	32,760.0	13,134.7	67.33	40.1	32,059	428,260	1,335.8	1,021,849	30,670
Commercially mixed formula feeds	21,236.2	12,782.7	65.52	60.2	34,459	421,648	1,223.6	616,280	30,316
Seeds, bulbs, plants, and trees	5,725.9	23.7	0.12	0.4	6,388	3,330	52.1	896,339	7,116
Commercial fertilizer	9,597.1	48.3	0.25	0.5	8,060	5,077	63.0	1,190,733	9,520
Agricultural chemicals	7,581.4	38.8	0.20	0.5	8,056	3,797	47.1	941,136	10,232
Petroleum products	6,371.5	291.1	1.49	4.6	3,619	9,558	264.1	1,760,642	30,454
Gasoline and gasohol	1,886.6	41.5	0.21	2.2	1,380	1,731	125.4	1,366,915	24,006
Diesel fuel	2,846.0	46.8	0.24	1.6	2,164	2,107	97.4	1,315,397	22,191
Natural gas	432.9	42.6	0.22	9.8	6,091	9,820	161.2	71,069	4,340
LP gas, fuel oil, kerosene, motor oil, grease, etc.	1,206.1	160.1	0.82	13.3	945	6,276	664.1	1,276,331	25,519
Electricity	2,751.1	212.0	1.09	7.7	2,247	7,168	319.0	1,224,374	29,574
Hired farm labor	14,841.0	679.4	3.48	4.6	22,811	42,778	187.5	650,623	15,881
Contract labor	2,959.0	72.0	0.37	2.4	13,040	12,062	92.5	226,909	5,970
Repair and maintenance	8,637.7	289.3	1.48	3.3	5,616	9,663	172.1	1,538,058	29,934
Custom work, machine hire, and rental of equipment	3,210.3	46.9	0.24	1.5	5,372	4,845	90.2	597,624	9,678
Interest	8,928.1	393.8	2.02	4.4	11,016	17,476	158.6	810,476	22,534
Secured by real estate	5,449.6	303.1	1.55	5.6	9,564	15,357	160.6	569,775	19,737
Not secured by real estate	3,478.5	90.7	0.46	2.6	7,540	9,757	129.4	461,326	9,296
Cash rent	6,915.7	78.3	0.40	1.1	14,244	13,305	93.4	485,512	5,882
Property taxes	3,920.1	83.2	0.43	2.1	2,213	2,582	116.7	1,771,787	32,240
All other farm production expenses	14,777.4	1,251.9	6.42	8.5	8,747	39,561	452.3	1,689,391	31,645

Source: *1997 Census of Agriculture*, U.S. Department of Agriculture, National Agricultural Statistics Service. Table shows totals for the U.S. agriculture sector and for the NAICS subdivision of it, shown as "This Agric. Sector" or as "This Sector." Not all farms report on every category. For this reason, the reporting universe is shown in the last two columns. Averages are based on these columns. LP gas stands for "liquid petroleum gas," i.e., butane or propane.

NET CASH RETURN AND FARMS WITH GAINS AND LOSSES

Item	Number of farms and %				Average gain or loss per farm - $		
	U.S.	% of U.S.	This Agriculture Sector	% of Sector	U.S.	This Agriculture Sector	% of U.S.
All farms	1,911,824	100.0	33,321	100.0	22,260	72,342	325.0
Number of farms with net gains	985,718	51.6	20,611	61.9	51,296	153,030	298.3
Gain of -							
Less than $1,000	120,163	6.3	671	2.0	-	-	-
$1,000 to $9,999	370,611	19.4	2,223	6.7	-	-	-
$10,000 to $49,999	292,484	15.3	5,561	16.7	-	-	-
$50,000 or more	202,460	10.6	12,156	36.5	-	-	-
Number of farms with net losses	926,106	48.4	12,710	38.1	(8,645)	(58,505)	676.7
Loss of -							
Less than $1,000	165,390	8.7	1,458	4.4	-	-	-
$1,000 to $9,999	591,517	30.9	5,870	17.6	-	-	-
$10,000 to $49,999	152,649	8.0	3,171	9.5	-	-	-
$50,000 or more	16,550	0.9	2,211	6.6	-	-	-

Source: *1997 Census of Agriculture*, U.S. Department of Agriculture, National Agricultural Statistics Service. Table shows totals for the U.S. agriculture sector and for the NAICS subdivision of it, shown as "This Agric. Sector" or as "This Sector." Not all farms report on every category. For this reason, the reporting universe is shown in the last two columns. Averages are based on these columns. Net gains are income less cost for farm operations; they exclude non-farm earnings. Values in parentheses are losses.

CHARACTERISTICS OF FARM OPERATORS

Farm Operators	U.S.	This Agric. Sector	% of U.S.	Farm Operators	U.S.	This Agric. Sector	% of U.S.
Place of residence:				By age group:			
On farm operated	1,361,766	29,865	2.2	Under 25 years	20,850	315	1.5
Not on farm operated	412,554	3,854	0.9	25 to 34 years	128,455	3,234	2.5
Not reported	137,539	3,225	2.3	35 to 44 years	371,442	8,966	2.4
Principal occupation:				45 to 49 years	232,845	5,383	2.3
Farming	961,560	24,182	2.5	50 to 54 years	233,884	5,228	2.2
Other	950,299	12,762	1.3	55 to 59 years	222,736	4,951	2.2
Days worked off farm:				60 to 64 years	204,618	3,754	1.8
None	755,254	17,403	2.3	65 to 69 years	179,858	2,363	1.3
Any	1,042,158	16,594	1.6	70 years and over	317,171	2,750	0.9
1 to 99 days	164,957	2,914	1.8	Average age	54	51	93.0
100 to 199 days	167,922	2,882	1.7	By sex:			
200 days or more	709,279	10,798	1.5	Male	1,746,757	32,270	1.8
Not reported	114,447	2,947	2.6	Female	165,102	4,674	2.8
Years on present farm:				Spanish, Hispanic/Latino origin	27,717	411	1.5
2 years or less	92,574	2,013	2.2	Tenure of operator:			
3 or 4 years	126,791	3,430	2.7	All operators	1,911,859	36,944	1.9
5 to 9 years	263,642	6,412	2.4	Full owners	1,146,891	27,745	2.4
10 years or more	1,113,839	19,193	1.7	Part owners	573,839	7,696	1.3
Ave. years on this farm	20	16	80.6	Tenants	191,129	1,503	0.8
Not reported	315,013	5,896	1.9				

Source: 1997 Census of Agriculture, U.S. Department of Agriculture, National Agricultural Statistics Service. Table shows totals for the U.S. agriculture sector and for the NAICS subdivision of it, shown as "This Agric. Sector" or as "This Sector." Not all farms report on every category. For this reason, the reporting universe is shown in the last two columns. Averages are based on these columns. All values shown are number of farm operators in each category or percent.

FARMS BY TYPE OF ORGANIZATION

Item	Number of farms and percent				Total acres and percent		
	U.S.	% of U.S.	This Agriculture Sector	% of Sector	U.S.	This Agriculture Sector	% of U.S.
Individual or family (sole proprietorship)	1,643,424	100.0	31,307	100.0	585,464,911	3,987,238	0.7
Partnership	169,462	10.3	2,856	9.1	149,321,484	639,853	0.4
Corporation:							
Family held	76,103	4.6	2,293	7.3	119,559,203	669,214	0.6
More than 10 stockholders	1,795	0.1	158	0.5	-	-	-
10 or less stockholders	74,308	4.5	2,135	6.8	-	-	-
Other than family held	7,899	0.5	350	1.1	11,904,053	67,674	0.6
More than 10 stockholders	1,029	0.1	96	0.3	-	-	-
10 or less stockholders	6,870	0.4	254	0.8	-	-	-
Other cooperative, estate or trust, institutional, etc.	14,971	0.9	138	0.4	65,545,604	96,279	0.1

Source: 1997 Census of Agriculture, U.S. Department of Agriculture, National Agricultural Statistics Service. Table shows totals for the U.S. agriculture sector and for the NAICS subdivision of it, shown as "This Agric. Sector" or as "This Sector." Not all farms report on every category. For this reason, the reporting universe is shown in the last two columns. Averages are based on these columns.

LIVESTOCK INVENTORIES AND SALES

Item	U.S. (number)	This Agric. Sector (number)	% of U.S.	Average number per farm			Number of farms reporting category	
				U.S.	This Agric. Sector	% of U.S.	U.S.	This Sector
Cattle and calves inventory	98,989,244	1,053,475	1.1	94.6	65.5	69.3	1,046,863	16,076
Cows and heifers that had calved	43,162,054	567,088	1.3	48.3	41.1	85.1	894,110	13,800
Beef cows	34,066,615	527,394	1.5	42.3	40.1	94.8	804,595	13,146
Milk cows	9,095,439	39,694	0.4	77.8	40.8	52:4	116,874	974
Heifers and heifer calves	26,988,697	243,836	0.9	33.6	19.8	59.0	803,985	12,310
Steers, steer calves, bulls, and bull calves	28,838,493	242,551	0.8	32.6	17.6	54.1	883,983	13,751
Cattle and calves sold	74,089,046	530,019	0.7	73.2	37.1	50.7	1,011,809	14,281
Calves	16,480,293	255,348	1.5	26.8	24.3	90.6	615,177	10,523
Cattle	57,608,753	274,671	0.5	78.0	30.0	38.5	738,696	9,154
Fattened on grain and concentrates	27,328,190	30,907	0.1	247.0	41.5	16.8	110,620	745
Hogs and pigs inventory	61,206,236	522,246	0.9	557.7	321.4	57.6	109,754	1,625
Used or to be used for breeding	6,831,564	48,688	0.7	106.7	68.7	64.4	64,029	709
Other	54,374,672	473,558	0.9	528.0	317.6	60.2	102,977	1,491
Hogs and pigs sold	142,611,882	1,353,404	0.9	1,396.7	1,135.4	81.3	102,106	1,192
Feeder pigs	34,988,718	392,541	1.1	2,037.8	1,721.7	84.5	17,170	228
Litters of pigs farrowed between Dec. 1 of preceding year and Nov. 30	11,497,523	86,142	0.7	170.3	114.2	67.1	67,514	754
Dec. 1 and May 31	5,697,371	44,852	0.8	91.0	66.5	73.1	62,622	674
June 1 and Nov. 30	5,800,152	41,290	0.7	99.7	67.2	67.5	58,204	614
Sheep and lambs of all ages inventory	7,821,885	33,941	0.4	118.9	32.0	26.9	65,790	1,061
Ewes 1 year old or older	4,408,683	18,995	0.4	78.1	22.7	29.1	56,414	835
Sheep and lambs sold	7,331,545	23,893	0.3	123.1	31.1	25.3	59,575	768
Sheep and lambs shorn	6,139,140	22,266	0.4	118.4	33.4	28.2	51,869	667
Horses and ponies inventory	2,427,277	25,849	1.1	6.5	4.5	69.4	375,218	5,761
Horses and ponies sold	325,306	1,627	0.5	4.1	2.9	71.0	79,516	560
Goats inventory	1,989,799	19,117	1.0	34.4	11.0	32.1	57,925	1,733
Goats sold	740,597	7,585	1.0	31.5	13.2	41.8	23,520	576

Source: 1997 Census of Agriculture, U.S. Department of Agriculture, National Agricultural Statistics Service. Table shows totals for the U.S. agriculture sector and for the NAICS subdivision of it, shown as "This Agric. Sector" or as "This Sector." Not all farms report on every category. For this reason, the reporting universe is shown in the last two columns. Averages are based on these columns.

POULTRY INVENTORIES AND SALES

Item	U.S. (number)	This Agric. Sector (number)	% of U.S.	Average number per farm			Number of farms reporting category	
				U.S.	This Agric. Sector	% of U.S.	U.S.	This Sector
Layers and pullets 13 weeks old and older inventory	366,989,851	358,775,357	97.8	5,053.8	35,909.9	710.5	72,616	9,991
Layers 20 weeks old and older	313,851,480	307,993,337	98.1	4,499.0	34,122.9	758.5	69,761	9,026
Pullets 13 weeks old and older but less than 20 weeks old	53,138,371	50,782,020	95.6	4,031.7	22,479.9	557.6	13,180	2,259
Layers, pullets, and pullet chicks sold	331,563,736	321,165,777	96.9	24,636.9	42,269.8	171.6	13,458	7,598
Broilers and other meat type chickens sold	6,741,927,110	6,683,231,401	99.1	281,653.0	346,209.7	122.9	23,937	19,304
Turkey hens kept for breeding	5,504,808	5,344,356	97.1	968.1	6,100.9	630.2	5,686	876
Turkeys sold	307,586,680	295,738,076	96.1	51,000.9	79,778.3	156.4	6,031	3,707

Source: 1997 Census of Agriculture, U.S. Department of Agriculture, National Agricultural Statistics Service. Table shows totals for the U.S. agriculture sector and for the NAICS subdivision of it, shown as "This Agric. Sector" or as "This Sector." Not all farms report on every category. For this reason, the reporting universe is shown in the last two columns. Averages are based on these columns.

SELECTED CROPS HARVESTED

Item	In 1,000	Crop harvested			Acres used for crop (000)			Number of farms reporting category	
		U.S.	This Agric. Sector	% of U.S.	U.S.	This Agric. Sector	% of U.S.	U.S.	This Sector
Corn for grain or seed	bushels	8,578,635	44,858	0.5	69,796.7	401.3	0.6	430,711	3,466
Irrigated		-	-	-	10,638.9	31.9	0.3	40,574	244
Corn for silage or green chop	tons, green	88,381	672	0.8	5,727.6	43.9	0.8	119,308	1,019
Irrigated		-	-	-	1,033.3	2.4	0.2	10,815	48
Sorghum for grain or seed	bushels	559,070	987	0.2	8,470.4	16.0	0.2	49,397	213
Irrigated		-	-	-	875.6	0.2	0.0	5,793	9
Wheat for grain	bushels	2,204,027	7,191	0.3	58,836.3	136.4	0.2	243,568	1,530
Irrigated		-	-	-	3,990.9	5.3	0.1	20,385	71
Barley for grain	bushels	336,435	1,256	0.4	5,945.0	17.2	0.3	41,930	395
Irrigated		-	-	-	1,060.7	0.9	0.1	8,847	26
Oats for grain	bushels	151,327	429	0.3	2,681.0	7.2	0.3	89,606	401
Irrigated		-	-	-	121.0	0.1	0.1	2,788	5
Rice	cwt	182,231	28	0.0	3,122.1	0.5	0.0	9,291	6
Irrigated		-	-	-	3,122.1	0.5	0.0	9,291	6
Cotton	bales	17,879	60	0.3	13,235.2	46.5	0.4	31,493	214
Irrigated		-	-	-	4,888.0	5.9	0.1	12,434	28
Tobacco	pounds	1,747,702	23,760	1.4	838.5	11.1	1.3	89,706	494
Irrigated		-	-	-	138.7	2.1	1.5	7,090	79
Soybeans for beans	bushels	2,504,307	12,261	0.5	66,147.7	368.6	0.6	354,692	2,596
Irrigated		-	-	-	4,152.1	13.3	0.3	20,619	135
Dry edible beans, excluding dry limas	cwt	27,224	43	0.2	1,691.9	2.3	0.1	10,911	7
Irrigated		-	-	-	577.0	2.0	0.3	4,882	3
Potatoes, excluding sweetpotatoes	cwt	459,886	229	0.0	1,355.2	0.9	0.1	10,523	87
Irrigated		-	-	-	1,070.3	0.3	0.0	4,843	23
Sugar beets for sugar	tons	29,775	-	-	1,453.8	-	-	7,102	1
Irrigated		-	-	-	616.4	-	-	3,492	-
Peanuts for nuts	pounds	3,377,143	42,658	1.3	1,352.2	18.0	1.3	12,221	225
Irrigated		-	-	-	412.3	2.8	0.7	3,125	38
Hay alfalfa, other tame, small grain, wild, grass silage, green chop	tons, dry	139,365	1,621	1.2	60,799.8	658.8	1.1	888,597	14,183
Irrigated		-	-	-	9,564.3	14.6	0.2	79,406	317
Alfalfa hay	tons, dry	65,863	153	0.2	21,309.8	50.5	0.2	358,365	1,828
Irrigated		-	-	-	5,980.5	6.9	0.1	57,854	153
Vegetables harvested for sale		-	-	-	3,773.2	16.8	0.4	53,727	639
Irrigated		-	-	-	2,641.8	11.2	0.4	23,203	287
Land in orchards		-	-	-	5,158.1	13.9	0.3	106,069	856
Irrigated		-	-	-	4,107.9	8.6	0.2	61,606	316

Source: 1997 Census of Agriculture, U.S. Department of Agriculture, National Agricultural Statistics Service. Table shows totals for the U.S. agriculture sector and for the NAICS subdivision of it, shown as "This Agric. Sector" or as "This Sector." Not all farms report on every category. For this reason, the reporting universe is shown in the last two columns. Averages are based on these columns. "Green tons" are weight of product as harvested, i.e., moist. cwt stands for "hundredweight."

LEADING COMPANIES Number shown: 26   Total sales ($ mil): 7,212   Total employment (000): 56.7

Company Name	Address				CEO Name	Phone	Co. Type	Sales ($ mil)	Empl. (000)
Seaboard Corp.	9000 W 67th St	Shawnee Msn	KS	66202	HH Bresky	913-676-8800	P	1,780	15.0
Pilgrim's Pride Corp.	PO Box 93	Pittsburg	TX	75686	Lonnie Pilgrim	903-855-1000	P	1,357	13.0
Foster Poultry Farms Inc.	PO Box 457	Livingston	CA	95334	Robert Fox	209-394-7901	R	1,250	7.5
Wampler Foods	P O Box 7275	Broadway	VA	22815	James T Keeler	540-896-7000	P	888	7.2
Cal-Maine Foods Inc.	PO Box 2960	Jackson	MS	39207	Fred Adams	601-948-6813	P	288	1.6
George's Inc.	PO Drawer G	Springdale	AR	72765	Gary George	501-751-4686	R	250*	2.0
Cuddy Farms Inc.	6140 W Marshville	Marshville	NC	28103	Rick Vandestek	704-624-5055	R	238*	1.1
Turkey Store Co.	34 N 7th St	Barron	WI	54812	Jerome Jerome	715-537-3131	R	220*	2.5
Nash Johnson & Sons' Farms Inc.	PO Box 699	Rose Hill	NC	28458	EM Johnson	910-289-3113	R	200*	1.7
ConAgra Food Co. Arkansas	PO Box 2127	Batesville	AR	72503		870-793-8700	S	170	1.5
Arbor Acres Farm Inc.	439 Marlborough Rd	Glastonbury	CT	06033	Dr Colin Baxter-Jones	860-633-4681	S	164	0.8
Tyson Foods Inc. Monroe Div.	PO Box 965	Monroe	NC	28111		704-283-7571	S	94	1.1
Olson Farms Inc.	521 N Arden Dr	Beverly Hills	CA	90210	Michael Mills	310-278-3590	R	39*	0.1
Keith Smith Company Inc.	PO Box 6480	SJ Bautista	AR	71902		501-321-9990	R	38*	0.1
Allen's Hatchery Inc.	126 N Shipley St	Seaford	DE	19973		302-629-9163	R	33*	0.3
Zephyr Egg Co.	PO Box 9005	Zephyrhills	FL	33539	Lois Linville	813-782-1521	R	30	0.2
Ward Egg Ranch Corp.	2900 Harmny Gr	Escondido	CA	92029	Edward Wilgenburg	760-745-5689	R	28*	<0.1
J.S. West Milling Company Inc.	PO Box 1041	Modesto	CA	95353	Robert Benson	209-577-3221	R	25*	0.1
Wilson Farms Inc.	10 Pleasant St	Lexington	MA	02173	AB Wilson	781-862-3900	R	25	0.1
Caldwell Milling Company Inc.	PO Box 179	Rose Bud	AR	72137		501-556-5121	R	23*	<0.1
CWT International Inc.	P O Box 1396	Gainesville	GA	30501	Cees Boudewrjn	770-532-3181	D	20	0.1
Nicholas Turkey Breeding Farms	PO Box Y	Sonoma	CA	95476	Steve Clausen	707-938-1111	D	19	0.2
Feather Crest Farms Inc.	14374 E SH 21	Bryan	TX	77808	DR Barrett	409-589-2576	R	14*	<0.1
Tatum Farms, International Inc.	PO Box 3098	Dawsonville	GA	30534	WL Tatum	706-265-3211	R	9*	<0.1
Hylive	15302 N C 38	Redmond	WA	98052		425-885-1414	S	8*	0.2
Elkin Co.	W 222 Cheaney	Waukesha	WI	53186		262-548-0864	R	2*	<0.1

Source: *Ward's Business Directory of U.S. Private and Public Companies*, Volumes 1 and 2, 2000. The company type code used is as follows: P - Public, R - Private, S - Subsidiary, D - Division, J - Joint Venture, A - Affiliate, G - Group, N - Company type not reported. Sales are in millions of dollars, employees are in thousands. An asterisk (*) indicates an estimated sales volume. The symbol < stands for 'less than'. Company names and addresses are truncated, in some cases, to fit into the available space.

NAICS 112400 - SHEEP AND GOAT FARMING

GENERAL STATISTICS

Item	U.S. Total	This Agri-culture Sector	% of U.S.	Category average per farm				Number of farms reporting category	
				Value shown as	U.S.	This Agric. Sector	% of U.S.	U.S.	This Sector
Farms - number	1,911,859	29,938	1.6	-	-	-	-	-	-
Land in farms - mil. acres	931.795	20.359	2.2	Acres	487	680	139.6	1,911,859	29,938
Value of land, buildings - $ mil.	859,839.2	8,917.2	1.0	$	449,748	294,919	65.6	524,066	30,236
Value of machinery and equip-ment - $ mil.	110,256.8	694.3	0.6	$	57,678	22,962	39.8	1,911,601	30,236
Sales of Ag Products - $ mil.	196,864.6	625.4	0.3	$	102,970	20,889	20.3	1,911,859	29,938
Government payments - $ mil.	5,054.5	13.2	0.3	$	7,378	2,895	39.2	685,029	4,573
Other farm-related income - $ mil.	3,272.3	24.4	0.7	$	5,999	4,080	68.0	545,480	5,990
Expenses - $ mil.	150,591.0	576.0	0.4	$	78,771	19,051	24.2	1,911,766	30,235
Payroll - $ mil.	14,841.0	40.0	0.3	$	22,811	5,441	23.9	650,623	7,347
Workers - 150 days or more a year	890,467	4,345	0.5	Number	3.4	1.7	50.7	259,631	2,498
Workers - less than 150 days	2,461,561	16,451	0.7	Number	4.2	2.4	55.5	581,658	6,999
Net Cash Return - $ mil.	42,557.9	58.9	0.1	$	22,260	1,949	8.8	1,911,824	30,236

Source: *1997 Census of Agriculture*, U.S. Department of Agriculture, National Agricultural Statistics Service. Table shows totals for the U.S. agriculture sector and for the NAICS subdivision of it, shown as "This Agric. Sector" or as "This Sector." Not all farms report on every category. For this reason, the reporting universe is shown in the last two columns. Averages are based on these columns.

LAND IN FARMS ACCORDING TO USE

Item	U.S. Total (000 acres)	This Sector (000 acres)	% of U.S.	Average acres per farms			Number of farms reporting category	
				U.S.	This Agric. Sector	% of U.S.	U.S.	This Sector
Total cropland	431,144.9	1,519.0	0.4	260	77	-	1,661,395	19,731
Harvested cropland	309,395.5	567.3	0.2	219	49	-	1,410,606	11,572
Cropland:								
Pasture or grazing	64,466.5	656.6	1.0	85	47	-	754,170	14,007
In cover crops, legumes, grasses	13,531.2	72.5	0.5	88	61	-	153,177	1,183
On which all crops failed	3,449.4	25.4	0.7	67	55	-	51,673	461
In cultivated summer fallow	20,905.9	71.9	0.3	256	169	-	81,702	426
Idle	19,396.3	125.3	0.6	83	54	-	232,961	2,305
Total woodland	71,465.4	1,159.7	1.6	96	120	-	743,011	9,698
Woodland pastured	29,693.9	838.5	2.8	84	174	-	352,217	4,827
Woodland not pastured	41,771.5	321.2	0.8	79	48	-	531,846	6,656
Other pasture/rangeland	396,884.6	17,222.4	4.3	721	1,360	-	550,619	12,661
Land for house lots, ponds, roads, wasteland	32,300.4	458.2	1.4	28	25	-	1,142,618	18,602
Irrigated land	55,058.1	276.3	0.5	197	73	-	279,442	3,799
Harvested cropland	50,013.5	142.8	0.3	198	70	-	252,679	2,053
Pasture and other	5,044.7	133.4	2.6	87	51	-	58,258	2,613
Conservation Reserve/Wetlands Reserve Lands	29,489.1	141.9	0.5	131	90	-	225,410	1,582

Source: *1997 Census of Agriculture*, U.S. Department of Agriculture, National Agricultural Statistics Service. Table shows totals for the U.S. agriculture sector and for the NAICS subdivision of it, shown as "This Agric. Sector" or as "This Sector." Not all farms report on every category. For this reason, the reporting universe is shown in the last two columns. Averages are based on these columns. The Conservation Reserve and Wetlands Reserve programs provide support for land conservation/preservation. Cover crops are not harvested or pastured.

MARKET VALUE OF AGRICULTURAL PRODUCTS SOLD: ALL FARMS

Item	U.S. Total ($ mil.)	This Sector ($ mil.)	% of Sector Sales	% of U.S.	Average sales per farm - $			Number of farms reporting category	
					U.S.	This Agric. Sector	% of U.S.	U.S.	This Sector
Grains	46,617.1	15.2	2.43	0.0	79,095	12,995	16.4	589,379	1,171
Corn for grain	18,884.8	3.5	0.56	0.0	52,506	8,385	16.0	359,666	421
Wheat	7,173.9	6.1	0.98	0.1	29,726	13,745	46.2	241,334	444
Soybeans	15,622.4	2.6	0.42	0.0	44,185	10,027	22.7	353,566	263
Sorghum for grain	1,140.0	0.6	0.09	0.0	25,360	15,389	60.7	44,955	36
Barley	709.6	1.5	0.24	0.2	23,191	12,846	55.4	30,598	117
Oats	121.3	0.4	0.07	0.4	3,114	2,651	85.1	38,940	166
Other grains	2,965.1	0.5	0.07	0.0	67,540	9,020	13.4	43,901	50
Cotton and cotton seed	5,975.5	0.9	0.15	0.0	189,963	83,091	43.7	31,456	11
Tobacco	2,924.7	0.1	0.01	0.0	32,662	2,852	8.7	89,544	27
Hay, silage, and field seeds	4,670.5	9.3	1.48	0.2	13,174	4,233	32.1	354,523	2,185
Vegetables, sweet corn, and melons	8,401.7	0.9	0.15	0.0	156,628	4,863	3.1	53,641	190
Fruits and berries	12,660.3	0.4	0.06	0.0	147,259	1,232	0.8	85,973	297
Nursery and greenhouse crops	10,942.8	0.2	0.03	0.0	161,360	1,351	0.8	67,816	148
Other crops	5,863.1	1.7	0.27	0.0	153,907	20,202	13.1	38,095	84
Poultry and poultry products	22,262.6	0.7	0.11	0.0	352,000	353	0.1	63,246	1,948
Dairy products	18,997.3	0.5	0.08	0.0	191,432	9,500	5.0	99,238	50
Cattle and calves	40,524.8	57.2	9.15	0.1	40,052	11,491	28.7	1,011,809	4,981
Hogs and pigs	13,804.8	2.9	0.46	0.0	135,201	3,472	2.6	102,106	832
Sheep, lambs, and wool	682.9	487.7	77.98	71.4	10,913	22,006	201.6	62,579	22,161
Other livestock	2,536.5	47.8	7.64	1.9	20,506	4,859	23.7	123,695	9,834
Products sold to public directly	13,096.7	1.6	0.26	0.0	377,610	164,900	43.7	34,683	10

Source: *1997 Census of Agriculture*, U.S. Department of Agriculture, National Agricultural Statistics Service. Table shows totals for the U.S. agriculture sector and for the NAICS subdivision of it, shown as "This Agric. Sector" or as "This Sector." Not all farms report on every category. For this reason, the reporting universe is shown in the last two columns. Averages are based on these columns. Farms classified in one sector routinely produce categories in other sectors as well. Products sold to the public are sold for direct consumption.

MARKET VALUE OF PRODUCTS SOLD: FARMS WITH SALES OF $50,000 OR MORE

Item	U.S. Total ($ mil.)	This Sector ($ mil.)	% of Sector Sales	% of U.S.	Average sales per farm - $			Number of farms reporting category	
					U.S.	This Agric. Sector	% of U.S.	U.S.	This Sector
Grains	40,973.4	8.2	1.31	0.0	183,623	134,656	73.3	223,138	61
Cotton and cotton seed	5,743.9	-	-	-	286,562	-	-	20,044	4
Tobacco	2,060.2	-	-	-	175,907	-	-	11,712	-
Hay, silage, and field seeds	2,781.9	3.8	0.60	0.1	188,959	129,724	68.7	14,722	29
Vegetables, sweet corn, and melons	7,966.8	-	-	-	673,443	-	-	11,830	2
Fruits and berries	12,072.3	-	-	-	478,927	-	-	25,207	1
Nursery and greenhouse crops	10,412.0	-	-	-	578,025	-	-	18,013	-
Other crops	5,586.6	1.6	0.25	0.0	363,758	141,364	38.9	15,358	11
Poultry and poultry products	22,171.7	-	-	-	778,637	-	-	28,475	-
Dairy products	18,344.3	0.2	0.04	0.0	250,075	61,750	24.7	73,355	4
Cattle and calves	32,358.6	31.5	5.03	0.1	386,685	124,451	32.2	83,682	253
Hogs and pigs	13,096.7	1.6	0.26	0.0	377,610	164,900	43.7	34,683	10
Sheep, lambs, and wool	478.6	396.6	63.42	82.9	278,730	350,702	125.8	1,717	1,131
Other livestock	2,026.6	17.1	2.73	0.8	369,685	112,197	30.3	5,482	152

Source: *1997 Census of Agriculture*, U.S. Department of Agriculture, National Agricultural Statistics Service. Table shows totals for the U.S. agriculture sector and for the NAICS subdivision of it, shown as "This Agric. Sector" or as "This Sector." Not all farms report on every category. For this reason, the reporting universe is shown in the last two columns. Averages are based on these columns. Farms classified in one sector routinely produce categories in other sectors as well.

GOVERNMENT PAYMENTS AND OTHER FARM-RELATED INCOME

Item	U.S. Total ($ mil.)	This Sector ($ mil.)	% of Sector Gov/Oth. Income	% of U.S.	Average receipts per farm - $			Number of farms reporting category	
					U.S.	This Agric. Sector	% of U.S.	U.S.	This Sector
Government payments	5,054.5	13.2	35.14	0.3	7,378	2,895	39.2	685,029	4,573
Other farm-related income	3,272.3	24.4	64.86	0.7	5,999	4,080	68.0	545,480	5,990
Custom work and other agricultural services	1,235.1	4.0	10.50	0.3	8,646	3,777	43.7	142,854	1,047
Gross cash rent or share payments	1,207.9	14.1	37.45	1.2	6,867	5,482	79.8	175,901	2,574
Forest products, excluding Christmas trees and maple products	344.3	3.4	8.98	1.0	7,417	4,568	61.6	46,426	741
Other farm-related income sources	484.9	3.0	7.93	0.6	1,595	1,150	72.1	303,908	2,597

Source: 1997 Census of Agriculture, U.S. Department of Agriculture, National Agricultural Statistics Service. Table shows totals for the U.S. agriculture sector and for the NAICS subdivision of it, shown as "This Agric. Sector" or as "This Sector." Not all farms report on every category. For this reason, the reporting universe is shown in the last two columns. Averages are based on these columns. Government payments are agricultural subsidies under various programs.

COMMODITY CREDIT CORPORATION LOANS

Item	U.S. Total ($ mil.)	This Sector ($ mil.)	% of Sector Loan Total	% of U.S.	Average loan value per farm - $			Number of farms reporting category	
					U.S.	This Agric. Sector	% of U.S.	U.S.	This Sector
Total loans	3,034.7	0.4	100.00	0.0	36,419	7,279	20.0	83,328	61
Corn	1,333.9	0.1	31.76	0.0	26,419	4,862	18.4	50,489	29
Wheat	415.4	0.2	41.44	0.0	18,093	7,667	42.4	22,961	24
Soybeans	774.0	0.1	11.94	0.0	30,370	6,625	21.8	25,487	8
Sorghum, barley, and oats	54.8	0.1	14.86	0.1	8,603	4,714	54.8	6,375	14
Cotton	191.4	-	-	-	43,275	-	-	4,422	-
Sunflower seed, flaxseed, safflower, canola, other rapeseed, and mustard seed	17.3	-	-	-	25,159	-	-	686	-
Peanuts, rice, and tobacco	247.9	-	-	-	60,421	-	-	4,103	-

Source: 1997 Census of Agriculture, U.S. Department of Agriculture, National Agricultural Statistics Service. Table shows totals for the U.S. agriculture sector and for the NAICS subdivision of it, shown as "This Agric. Sector" or as "This Sector." Not all farms report on every category. For this reason, the reporting universe is shown in the last two columns. Averages are based on these columns. The Commodity Credit Corporation provides low interest loans to farmers.

SELECTED MACHINERY AND EQUIPMENT

Item	U.S. Total (number)	This Agric. Sector (number)	% of U.S.	Average number per farm			Number of farms reporting category	
				U.S.	This Agric. Sector	% of U.S.	U.S.	This Sector
Motortrucks, including pickups	3,497,735	43,038	1.2	2.07	1.64	79.1	1,688,303	26,278
Wheel tractors	3,936,014	39,307	1.0	2.31	1.66	71.8	1,707,384	23,750
Less than 40 horsepower (PTO)	1,262,688	19,476	1.5	1.44	1.31	91.0	877,119	14,868
40 horsepower (PTO) or more	2,673,326	19,831	0.7	2.02	1.45	71.7	1,321,084	13,677
40 to 99 horsepower (PTO)	1,808,105	16,690	0.9	1.58	1.34	84.9	1,145,466	12,456
100 horsepower (PTO)	865,221	3,141	0.4	1.68	1.27	75.4	513,773	2,473
Grain and bean combines	460,606	1,160	0.3	1.16	1.12	96.5	395,934	1,033
Cotton pickers and strippers	38,294	-	-	1.48	-	-	25,874	1
Mower conditioners	608,443	6,327	1.0	1.12	1.08	96.7	543,565	5,848
Pickup balers	717,245	7,131	1.0	1.24	1.17	94.3	579,440	6,106

Source: 1997 Census of Agriculture, U.S. Department of Agriculture, National Agricultural Statistics Service. Table shows totals for the U.S. agriculture sector and for the NAICS subdivision of it, shown as "This Agric. Sector" or as "This Sector." Not all farms report on every category. For this reason, the reporting universe is shown in the last two columns. Averages are based on these columns. PTO stands for "power take off."

FARM PRODUCTION EXPENSES

Item	U.S. Total ($ mil.)	This Sector ($ mil.)	% of Sector Total Expense	% of U.S.	Average expense per farm - $			Number of farms reporting category	
					U.S.	This Agric. Sector	% of U.S.	U.S.	This Sector
Total farm production expenses	150,591.0	576.0	100.00	0.4	78,771	19,051	24.2	1,911,766	30,235
Livestock and poultry purchased	21,614.6	129.1	22.41	0.6	38,807	9,678	24.9	556,980	13,339
Feed for livestock and poultry	32,760.0	118.6	20.58	0.4	32,059	4,779	14.9	1,021,849	24,807
Commercially mixed formula feeds	21,236.2	40.4	7.01	0.2	34,459	2,876	8.3	616,280	14,032
Seeds, bulbs, plants, and trees	5,725.9	3.7	0.64	0.1	6,388	669	10.5	896,339	5,491
Commercial fertilizer	9,597.1	9.4	1.63	0.1	8,060	1,173	14.6	1,190,733	7,992
Agricultural chemicals	7,581.4	8.8	1.53	0.1	8,056	1,364	16.9	941,136	6,472
Petroleum products	6,371.5	28.5	4.94	0.4	3,619	1,113	30.8	1,760,642	25,589
Gasoline and gasohol	1,886.6	15.9	2.76	0.8	1,380	778	56.4	1,366,915	20,439
Diesel fuel	2,846.0	8.3	1.44	0.3	2,164	643	29.7	1,315,397	12,919
Natural gas	432.9	0.3	0.05	0.1	6,091	637	10.5	71,069	454
LP gas, fuel oil, kerosene, motor oil, grease, etc.	1,206.1	4.0	0.69	0.3	945	277	29.3	1,276,331	14,365
Electricity	2,751.1	11.6	2.02	0.4	2,247	616	27.4	1,224,374	18,880
Hired farm labor	14,841.0	40.0	6.94	0.3	22,811	5,441	23.9	650,623	7,347
Contract labor	2,959.0	7.5	1.31	0.3	13,040	2,064	15.8	226,909	3,653
Repair and maintenance	8,637.7	40.5	7.03	0.5	5,616	1,794	31.9	1,538,058	22,557
Custom work, machine hire, and rental of equipment	3,210.3	12.1	2.10	0.4	5,372	2,090	38.9	597,624	5,780
Interest	8,928.1	47.1	8.17	0.5	11,016	5,224	47.4	810,476	9,011
Secured by real estate	5,449.6	32.7	5.67	0.6	9,564	4,855	50.8	569,775	6,728
Not secured by real estate	3,478.5	14.4	2.50	0.4	7,540	3,605	47.8	461,326	3,999
Cash rent	6,915.7	17.6	3.05	0.3	14,244	4,765	33.5	485,512	3,684
Property taxes	3,920.1	37.7	6.55	1.0	2,213	1,340	60.6	1,771,787	28,169
All other farm production expenses	14,777.4	63.9	11.10	0.4	8,747	2,463	28.2	1,689,391	25,955

Source: *1997 Census of Agriculture*, U.S. Department of Agriculture, National Agricultural Statistics Service. Table shows totals for the U.S. agriculture sector and for the NAICS subdivision of it, shown as "This Agric. Sector" or as "This Sector." Not all farms report on every category. For this reason, the reporting universe is shown in the last two columns. Averages are based on these columns. LP gas stands for "liquid petroleum gas," i.e., butane or propane.

NET CASH RETURN AND FARMS WITH GAINS AND LOSSES

Item	Number of farms and %				Average gain or loss per farm - $		
	U.S.	% of U.S.	This Agriculture Sector	% of Sector	U.S.	This Agriculture Sector	% of U.S.
All farms	1,911,824	100.0	30,236	100.0	22,260	1,949	8.8
Number of farms with net gains	985,718	51.6	7,468	24.7	51,296	23,334	45.5
Gain of -							
Less than $1,000	120,163	6.3	2,507	8.3	-	-	-
$1,000 to $9,999	370,611	19.4	3,251	10.8	-	-	-
$10,000 to $49,999	292,484	15.3	1,233	4.1	-	-	-
$50,000 or more	202,460	10.6	477	1.6	-	-	-
Number of farms with net losses	926,106	48.4	22,768	75.3	(8,645)	(5,065)	58.6
Loss of -							
Less than $1,000	165,390	8.7	4,062	13.4	-	-	-
$1,000 to $9,999	591,517	30.9	16,339	54.0	-	-	-
$10,000 to $49,999	152,649	8.0	2,267	7.5	-	-	-
$50,000 or more	16,550	0.9	100	0.3	-	-	-

Source: *1997 Census of Agriculture*, U.S. Department of Agriculture, National Agricultural Statistics Service. Table shows totals for the U.S. agriculture sector and for the NAICS subdivision of it, shown as "This Agric. Sector" or as "This Sector." Not all farms report on every category. For this reason, the reporting universe is shown in the last two columns. Averages are based on these columns. Net gains are income less cost for farm operations; they exclude non-farm earnings. Values in parentheses are losses.

CHARACTERISTICS OF FARM OPERATORS

Farm Operators	U.S.	This Agric. Sector	% of U.S.	Farm Operators	U.S.	This Agric. Sector	% of U.S.
Place of residence:				By age group:			
On farm operated	1,361,766	24,901	1.8	Under 25 years	20,850	310	1.5
Not on farm operated	412,554	3,441	0.8	25 to 34 years	128,455	1,757	1.4
Not reported	137,539	1,596	1.2	35 to 44 years	371,442	6,488	1.7
Principal occupation:				45 to 49 years	232,845	4,378	1.9
Farming	961,560	10,074	1.0	50 to 54 years	233,884	4,362	1.9
Other	950,299	19,864	2.1	55 to 59 years	222,736	3,594	1.6
Days worked off farm:				60 to 64 years	204,618	2,903	1.4
None	755,254	8,066	1.1	65 to 69 years	179,858	2,348	1.3
Any	1,042,158	20,685	2.0	70 years and over	317,171	3,798	1.2
1 to 99 days	164,957	2,293	1.4	Average age	54	53	97.4
100 to 199 days	167,922	3,246	1.9	By sex:			
200 days or more	709,279	15,146	2.1	Male	1,746,757	24,608	1.4
Not reported	114,447	1,187	1.0	Female	165,102	5,330	3.2
Years on present farm:				Spanish, Hispanic/Latino origin	27,717	622	2.2
2 years or less	92,574	1,677	1.8	Tenure of operator:			
3 or 4 years	126,791	2,651	2.1	All operators	1,911,859	29,938	1.6
5 to 9 years	263,642	5,739	2.2	Full owners	1,146,891	22,591	2.0
10 years or more	1,113,839	15,882	1.4	Part owners	573,839	4,969	0.9
Ave. years on this farm	20	16	81.1	Tenants	191,129	2,378	1.2
Not reported	315,013	3,989	1.3				

Source: *1997 Census of Agriculture*, U.S. Department of Agriculture, National Agricultural Statistics Service. Table shows totals for the U.S. agriculture sector and for the NAICS subdivision of it, shown as "This Agric. Sector" or as "This Sector." Not all farms report on every category. For this reason, the reporting universe is shown in the last two columns. Averages are based on these columns. All values shown are number of farm operators in each category or percent.

FARMS BY TYPE OF ORGANIZATION

Item	Number of farms and percent				Total acres and percent		
	U.S.	% of U.S.	This Agriculture Sector	% of Sector	U.S.	This Agriculture Sector	% of U.S.
Individual or family (sole proprietorship)	1,643,424	100.0	27,560	100.0	585,464,911	10,983,797	1.9
Partnership	169,462	10.3	1,630	5.9	149,321,484	4,587,930	3.1
Corporation:							
Family held	76,103	4.6	505	1.8	119,559,203	3,457,417	2.9
More than 10 stockholders	1,795	0.1	12	0.0	-	-	-
10 or less stockholders	74,308	4.5	493	1.8	-	-	-
Other than family held	7,899	0.5	56	0.2	11,904,053	51,862	0.4
More than 10 stockholders	1,029	0.1	5	0.0	-	-	-
10 or less stockholders	6,870	0.4	51	0.2	-	-	-
Other cooperative, estate or trust, institutional, etc.	14,971	0.9	187	0.7	65,545,604	1,278,270	2.0

Source: *1997 Census of Agriculture*, U.S. Department of Agriculture, National Agricultural Statistics Service. Table shows totals for the U.S. agriculture sector and for the NAICS subdivision of it, shown as "This Agric. Sector" or as "This Sector." Not all farms report on every category. For this reason, the reporting universe is shown in the last two columns. Averages are based on these columns.

LIVESTOCK INVENTORIES AND SALES

Item	U.S. (number)	This Agric. Sector (number)	% of U.S.	Average number per farm			Number of farms reporting category	
				U.S.	This Agric. Sector	% of U.S.	U.S.	This Sector
Cattle and calves inventory	98,989,244	332,076	0.3	94.6	41.2	43.6	1,046,863	8,063
Cows and heifers that had calved	43,162,054	175,500	0.4	48.3	30.4	63.0	894,110	5,770
Beef cows	34,066,615	173,938	0.5	42.3	32.5	76.7	804,595	5,358
Milk cows	9,095,439	1,562	0.0	77.8	2.3	2.9	116,874	693
Heifers and heifer calves	26,988,697	81,299	0.3	33.6	15.1	44.9	803,985	5,398
Steers, steer calves, bulls, and bull calves	28,838,493	75,277	0.3	32.6	12.3	37.7	883,983	6,116
Cattle and calves sold	74,089,046	139,738	0.2	73.2	28.1	38.3	1,011,809	4,981
Calves	16,480,293	54,120	0.3	26.8	19.6	73.3	615,177	2,755
Cattle	57,608,753	85,618	0.1	78.0	25.8	33.0	738,696	3,324
Fattened on grain and concentrates	27,328,190	4,645	0.0	247.0	11.6	4.7	110,620	400
Hogs and pigs inventory	61,206,236	18,093	0.0	557.7	12.7	2.3	109,754	1,423
Used or to be used for breeding	6,831,564	1,920	0.0	106.7	4.6	4.4	64,029	413
Other	54,374,672	16,173	0.0	528.0	12.6	2.4	102,977	1,288
Hogs and pigs sold	142,611,882	25,664	0.0	1,396.7	30.8	2.2	102,106	832
Feeder pigs	34,988,718	2,126	0.0	2,037.8	18.2	0.9	17,170	117
Litters of pigs farrowed between Dec. 1 of preceding year and Nov. 30	11,497,523	2,076	0.0	170.3	4.6	2.7	67,514	447
Dec. 1 and May 31	5,697,371	1,100	0.0	91.0	2.9	3.2	62,622	383
June 1 and Nov. 30	5,800,152	976	0.0	99.7	3.5	3.5	58,204	277
Sheep and lambs of all ages inventory	7,821,885	4,765,053	60.9	118.9	222.6	187.2	65,790	21,407
Ewes 1 year old or older	4,408,683	2,560,442	58.1	78.1	130.0	166.3	56,414	19,698
Sheep and lambs sold	7,331,545	5,016,062	68.4	123.1	232.0	188.5	59,575	21,621
Sheep and lambs shorn	6,139,140	3,826,187	62.3	118.4	195.6	165.3	51,869	19,558
Horses and ponies inventory	2,427,277	41,507	1.7	6.5	4.7	72.3	375,218	8,878
Horses and ponies sold	325,306	1,579	0.5	4.1	2.1	52.0	79,516	742
Goats inventory	1,989,799	891,636	44.8	34.4	76.6	222.9	57,925	11,643
Goats sold	740,597	394,892	53.3	31.5	48.7	154.7	23,520	8,106

Source: *1997 Census of Agriculture*, U.S. Department of Agriculture, National Agricultural Statistics Service. Table shows totals for the U.S. agriculture sector and for the NAICS subdivision of it, shown as "This Agric. Sector" or as "This Sector." Not all farms report on every category. For this reason, the reporting universe is shown in the last two columns. Averages are based on these columns.

POULTRY INVENTORIES AND SALES

Item	U.S. (number)	This Agric. Sector (number)	% of U.S.	Average number per farm			Number of farms reporting category	
				U.S.	This Agric. Sector	% of U.S.	U.S.	This Sector
Layers and pullets 13 weeks old and older inventory	366,989,851	85,208	0.0	5,053.8	21.5	0.4	72,616	3,962
Layers 20 weeks old and older	313,851,480	72,574	0.0	4,499.0	18.7	0.4	69,761	3,871
Pullets 13 weeks old and older but less than 20 weeks old	53,138,371	12,634	0.0	4,031.7	15.8	0.4	13,180	799
Layers, pullets, and pullet chicks sold	331,563,736	22,483	0.0	24,636.9	48.1	0.2	13,458	467
Broilers and other meat type chickens sold	6,741,927,110	39,381	0.0	281,653.0	122.3	0.0	23,937	322
Turkey hens kept for breeding	5,504,808	1,417	0.0	968.1	3.3	0.3	5,686	430
Turkeys sold	307,586,680	-	-	51,000.9	--	-	6,031	158

Source: *1997 Census of Agriculture*, U.S. Department of Agriculture, National Agricultural Statistics Service. Table shows totals for the U.S. agriculture sector and for the NAICS subdivision of it, shown as "This Agric. Sector" or as "This Sector." Not all farms report on every category. For this reason, the reporting universe is shown in the last two columns. Averages are based on these columns.

SELECTED CROPS HARVESTED

Item	In 1,000	Crop harvested			Acres used for crop (000)			Number of farms reporting category	
		U.S.	This Agric. Sector	% of U.S.	U.S.	This Agric. Sector	% of U.S.	U.S.	This Sector
Corn for grain or seed	bushels	8,578,635	2,624	0.0	69,796.7	24.9	0.0	430,711	889
Irrigated		-	-	-	10,638.9	5.3	0.0	40,574	70
Corn for silage or green chop	tons, green	88,381	87	0.1	5,727.6	4.8	0.1	119,308	192
Irrigated		-	-	-	1,033.3	2.6	0.2	10,815	46
Sorghum for grain or seed	bushels	559,070	346	0.1	8,470.4	7.4	0.1	49,397	72
Irrigated		-	-	-	875.6	0.9	0.1	5,793	11
Wheat for grain	bushels	2,204,027	2,084	0.1	58,836.3	75.5	0.1	243,568	481
Irrigated		-	-	-	3,990.9	5.0	0.1	20,385	67
Barley for grain	bushels	336,435	975	0.3	5,945.0	16.6	0.3	41,930	277
Irrigated		-	-	-	1,060.7	7.5	0.7	8,847	132
Oats for grain	bushels	151,327	793	0.5	2,681.0	16.7	0.6	89,606	631
Irrigated		-	-	-	121.0	3.2	2.7	2,788	87
Rice	cwt	182,231	-	-	3,122.1	-	-	9,291	1
Irrigated		-	-	-	3,122.1	-	-	9,291	1
Cotton	bales	17,879	3	0.0	13,235.2	1.9	0.0	31,493	11
Irrigated		-	-	-	4,888.0	1.3	0.0	12,434	7
Tobacco	pounds	1,747,702	52	0.0	838.5	0.0	0.0	89,706	28
Irrigated		-	-	-	138.7	-	-	7,090	1
Soybeans for beans	bushels	2,504,307	459	0.0	66,147.7	12.1	0.0	354,692	284
Irrigated		-	-	-	4,152.1	0.2	0.0	20,619	4
Dry edible beans, excluding dry limas	cwt	27,224	13	0.0	1,691.9	0.7	0.0	10,911	25
Irrigated		-	-	-	577.0	-	-	4,882	18
Potatoes, excluding sweetpotatoes	cwt	459,886	59	0.0	1,355.2	0.2	0.0	10,523	47
Irrigated		-	-	-	1,070.3	0.1	0.0	4,843	17
Sugar beets for sugar	tons	29,775	44	0.1	1,453.8	2.1	0.1	7,102	14
Irrigated		-	-	-	616.4	2.1	0.3	3,492	13
Peanuts for nuts	pounds	3,377,143	-	-	1,352.2	-	-	12,221	2
Irrigated		-	-	-	412.3	-	-	3,125	2
Hay alfalfa, other tame, small grain, wild, grass silage, green chop	tons, dry	139,365	814	0.6	60,799.8	404.8	0.7	888,597	10,092
Irrigated		-	-	-	9,564.3	113.7	1.2	79,406	1,549
Alfalfa hay	tons, dry	65,863	494	0.8	21,309.8	190.2	0.9	358,365	4,427
Irrigated		-	-	-	5,980.5	76.8	1.3	57,854	1,097
Vegetables harvested for sale		-	-	-	3,773.2	0.7	0.0	53,727	192
Irrigated		-	-	-	2,641.8	0.4	0.0	23,203	66
Land in orchards		-	-	-	5,158.1	6.1	0.1	106,069	941
Irrigated		-	-	-	4,107.9	2.2	0.1	61,606	355

Source: 1997 Census of Agriculture, U.S. Department of Agriculture, National Agricultural Statistics Service. Table shows totals for the U.S. agriculture sector and for the NAICS subdivision of it, shown as "This Agric. Sector" or as "This Sector." Not all farms report on every category. For this reason, the reporting universe is shown in the last two columns. Averages are based on these columns. "Green tons" are weight of product as harvested, i.e., moist. cwt stands for "hundredweight."

LEADING COMPANIES   Number shown: **1**   Total sales ($ mil): **6**   Total employment (000): **0.0**

Company Name	Address				CEO Name	Phone	Co. Type	Sales ($ mil)	Empl. (000)
Superior Farms Inc.	34561 E Walls Rd	Hermiston	OR	97838	Thomas Watson	541-567-2954	S	6*	<0.1

Source: Ward's Business Directory of U.S. Private and Public Companies, Volumes 1 and 2, 2000. The company type code used is as follows: P - Public, R - Private, S - Subsidiary, D - Division, J - Joint Venture, A - Affiliate, G - Group, N - Company type not reported. Sales are in millions of dollars, employees are in thousands. An asterisk (*) indicates an estimated sales volume. The symbol < stands for 'less than'. Company names and addresses are truncated, in some cases, to fit into the available space.

NAICS 112500-112900 - ANIMAL AQUACULTURE AND OTHER ANIMAL PRODUCTIONS

GENERAL STATISTICS

Item	U.S. Total	This Agri-culture Sector	% of U.S.	Category average per farm				Number of farms reporting category	
				Value shown as	U.S.	This Agric. Sector	% of U.S.	U.S.	This Sector
Farms - number	1,911,859	110,580	5.8	-	-	-	-	-	-
Land in farms - mil. acres	931.795	15.716	1.7	Acres	487	142	29.2	1,911,859	110,580
Value of land, buildings - $ mil.	859,839.2	26,862.9	3.1	$	449,748	242,336	53.9	524,066	110,850
Value of machinery and equip-ment - $ mil.	110,256.8	3,095.6	2.8	$	57,678	27,928	48.4	1,911,601	110,840
Sales of Ag Products - $ mil.	196,864.6	3,080.9	1.6	$	102,970	27,861	27.1	1,911,859	110,580
Government payments - $ mil.	5,054.5	53.6	1.1	$	7,378	4,044	54.8	685,029	13,247
Other farm-related income - $ mil.	3,272.3	124.9	3.8	$	5,999	5,970	99.5	545,480	20,917
Expenses - $ mil.	150,591.0	2,708.6	1.8	$	78,771	24,439	31.0	1,911,766	110,835
Payroll - $ mil.	14,841.0	288.1	1.9	$	22,811	10,408	45.6	650,623	27,682
Workers - 150 days or more a year	890,467	22,812	2.6	Number	3.4	2.2	64.8	259,631	10,264
Workers - less than 150 days	2,461,561	63,159	2.6	Number	4.2	2.5	58.0	581,658	25,724
Net Cash Return - $ mil.	42,557.9	302.4	0.7	$	22,260	2,728	12.3	1,911,824	110,850

Source: 1997 Census of Agriculture, U.S. Department of Agriculture, National Agricultural Statistics Service. Table shows totals for the U.S. agriculture sector and for the NAICS subdivision of it, shown as "This Agric. Sector" or as "This Sector." Not all farms report on every category. For this reason, the reporting universe is shown in the last two columns. Averages are based on these columns.

LAND IN FARMS ACCORDING TO USE

Item	U.S. Total (000 acres)	This Sector (000 acres)	% of U.S.	Average acres per farms			Number of farms reporting category	
				U.S.	This Agric. Sector	% of U.S.	U.S.	This Sector
Total cropland	431,144.9	4,733.4	1.1	260	68	-	1,661,395	69,147
Harvested cropland	309,395.5	2,052.2	0.7	219	58	-	1,410,606	35,242
Cropland:								
Pasture or grazing	64,466.5	1,836.1	2.8	85	37	-	754,170	49,906
In cover crops, legumes, grasses	13,531.2	255.1	1.9	88	56	-	153,177	4,593
On which all crops failed	3,449.4	69.3	2.0	67	39	-	51,673	1,771
In cultivated summer fallow	20,905.9	130.0	0.6	256	144	-	81,702	903
Idle	19,396.3	390.7	2.0	83	46	-	232,961	8,514
Total woodland	71,465.4	2,368.9	3.3	96	65	-	743,011	36,398
Woodland pastured	29,693.9	830.7	2.8	84	52	-	352,217	16,075
Woodland not pastured	41,771.5	1,538.2	3.7	79	59	-	531,846	26,278
Other pasture/rangeland	396,884.6	7,491.1	1.9	721	202	-	550,619	37,089
Land for house lots, ponds, roads, wasteland	32,300.4	1,122.6	3.5	28	15	-	1,142,618	74,778
Irrigated land	55,058.1	304.1	0.6	197	31	-	279,442	9,916
Harvested cropland	50,013.5	145.3	0.3	198	34	-	252,679	4,247
Pasture and other	5,044.7	158.8	3.1	87	22	-	58,258	7,246
Conservation Reserve/Wetlands Reserve Lands	29,489.1	521.8	1.8	131	90	-	225,410	5,775

Source: 1997 Census of Agriculture, U.S. Department of Agriculture, National Agricultural Statistics Service. Table shows totals for the U.S. agriculture sector and for the NAICS subdivision of it, shown as "This Agric. Sector" or as "This Sector." Not all farms report on every category. For this reason, the reporting universe is shown in the last two columns. Averages are based on these columns. The Conservation Reserve and Wetlands Reserve programs provide support for land conservation/preservation. Cover crops are not harvested or pastured.

MARKET VALUE OF AGRICULTURAL PRODUCTS SOLD: ALL FARMS

Item	U.S. Total ($ mil.)	This Sector ($ mil.)	% of Sector Sales	% of U.S.	Average sales per farm - $			Number of farms reporting category	
					U.S.	This Agric. Sector	% of U.S.	U.S.	This Sector
Grains	46,617.1	188.5	6.12	0.4	79,095	43,667	55.2	589,379	4,317
Corn for grain	18,884.8	72.3	2.35	0.4	52,506	29,826	56.8	359,666	2,424
Wheat	7,173.9	23.3	0.75	0.3	29,726	16,276	54.8	241,334	1,429
Soybeans	15,622.4	81.4	2.64	0.5	44,185	31,947	72.3	353,566	2,549
Sorghum for grain	1,140.0	3.8	0.12	0.3	25,360	16,773	66.1	44,955	229
Barley	709.6	3.2	0.10	0.5	23,191	21,272	91.7	30,598	151
Oats	121.3	1.1	0.03	0.9	3,114	1,967	63.2	38,940	547
Other grains	2,965.1	3.4	0.11	0.1	67,540	18,335	27.1	43,901	185
Cotton and cotton seed	5,975.5	4.0	0.13	0.1	189,963	101,462	53.4	31,456	39
Tobacco	2,924.7	7.8	0.25	0.3	32,662	22,479	68.8	89,544	349
Hay, silage, and field seeds	4,670.5	21.8	0.71	0.5	13,174	3,409	25.9	354,523	6,388
Vegetables, sweet corn, and melons	8,401.7	1.7	0.06	0.0	156,628	4,149	2.6	53,641	416
Fruits and berries	12,660.3	3.5	0.11	0.0	147,259	6,622	4.5	85,973	532
Nursery and greenhouse crops	10,942.8	1.8	0.06	0.0	161,360	5,090	3.2	67,816	346
Other crops	5,863.1	1.9	0.06	0.0	153,907	9,327	6.1	38,095	208
Poultry and poultry products	22,262.6	39.9	1.30	0.2	352,000	15,318	4.4	63,246	2,605
Dairy products	18,997.3	39.7	1.29	0.2	191,432	73,944	38.6	99,238	537
Cattle and calves	40,524.8	200.0	6.49	0.5	40,052	16,700	41.7	1,011,809	11,978
Hogs and pigs	13,804.8	229.7	7.46	1.7	135,201	53,435	39.5	102,106	4,299
Sheep, lambs, and wool	682.9	11.9	0.39	1.7	10,913	4,411	40.4	62,579	2,692
Other livestock	2,536.5	2,328.6	75.58	91.8	20,506	37,910	184.9	123,695	61,425
Products sold to public directly	13,096.7	196.0	6.36	1.5	377,610	165,298	43.8	34,683	1,186

Source: *1997 Census of Agriculture*, U.S. Department of Agriculture, National Agricultural Statistics Service. Table shows totals for the U.S. agriculture sector and for the NAICS subdivision of it, shown as "This Agric. Sector" or as "This Sector." Not all farms report on every category. For this reason, the reporting universe is shown in the last two columns. Averages are based on these columns. Farms classified in one sector routinely produce categories in other sectors as well. Products sold to the public are sold for direct consumption.

MARKET VALUE OF PRODUCTS SOLD: FARMS WITH SALES OF $50,000 OR MORE

Item	U.S. Total ($ mil.)	This Sector ($ mil.)	% of Sector Sales	% of U.S.	Average sales per farm - $			Number of farms reporting category	
					U.S.	This Agric. Sector	% of U.S.	U.S.	This Sector
Grains	40,973.4	146.8	4.76	0.4	183,623	141,280	76.9	223,138	1,039
Cotton and cotton seed	5,743.9	3.6	0.12	0.1	286,562	259,214	90.5	20,044	14
Tobacco	2,060.2	4.9	0.16	0.2	175,907	129,763	73.8	11,712	38
Hay, silage, and field seeds	2,781.9	3.0	0.10	0.1	188,959	83,722	44.3	14,722	36
Vegetables, sweet corn, and melons	7,966.8	-	-	-	673,443	-	-	11,830	4
Fruits and berries	12,072.3	-	-	-	478,927	-	-	25,207	13
Nursery and greenhouse crops	10,412.0	-	-	-	578,025	-	-	18,013	7
Other crops	5,586.6	1.2	0.04	0.0	363,758	103,000	28.3	15,358	12
Poultry and poultry products	22,171.7	38.0	1.23	0.2	778,637	431,568	55.4	28,475	88
Dairy products	18,344.3	35.2	1.14	0.2	250,075	148,983	59.6	73,355	236
Cattle and calves	32,358.6	133.9	4.35	0.4	386,685	140,778	36.4	83,682	951
Hogs and pigs	13,096.7	196.0	6.36	1.5	377,610	165,298	43.8	34,683	1,186
Sheep, lambs, and wool	478.6	5.7	0.19	1.2	278,730	139,268	50.0	1,717	41
Other livestock	2,026.6	1,963.4	63.73	96.9	369,685	394,974	106.8	5,482	4,971

Source: *1997 Census of Agriculture*, U.S. Department of Agriculture, National Agricultural Statistics Service. Table shows totals for the U.S. agriculture sector and for the NAICS subdivision of it, shown as "This Agric. Sector" or as "This Sector." Not all farms report on every category. For this reason, the reporting universe is shown in the last two columns. Averages are based on these columns. Farms classified in one sector routinely produce categories in other sectors as well.

GOVERNMENT PAYMENTS AND OTHER FARM-RELATED INCOME

Item	U.S. Total ($ mil.)	This Sector ($ mil.)	% of Sector Gov/Oth. Income	% of U.S.	Average receipts per farm - $			Number of farms reporting category	
					U.S.	This Agric. Sector	% of U.S.	U.S.	This Sector
Government payments	5,054.5	53.6	30.02	1.1	7,378	4,044	54.8	685,029	13,247
Other farm-related income	3,272.3	124.9	69.98	3.8	5,999	5,970	99.5	545,480	20,917
Custom work and other agricultural services	1,235.1	35.4	19.82	2.9	8,646	7,858	90.9	142,854	4,501
Gross cash rent or share payments	1,207.9	59.6	33.42	4.9	6,867	5,854	85.3	175,901	10,185
Forest products, excluding Christmas trees and maple products	344.3	12.2	6.86	3.6	7,417	5,959	80.3	46,426	2,053
Other farm-related income sources	484.9	17.6	9.89	3.6	1,595	2,467	154.6	303,908	7,154

Source: *1997 Census of Agriculture*, U.S. Department of Agriculture, National Agricultural Statistics Service. Table shows totals for the U.S. agriculture sector and for the NAICS subdivision of it, shown as "This Agric. Sector" or as "This Sector." Not all farms report on every category. For this reason, the reporting universe is shown in the last two columns. Averages are based on these columns. Government payments are agricultural subsidies under various programs.

COMMODITY CREDIT CORPORATION LOANS

Item	U.S. Total ($ mil.)	This Sector ($ mil.)	% of Sector Loan Total	% of U.S.	Average loan value per farm - $			Number of farms reporting category	
					U.S.	This Agric. Sector	% of U.S.	U.S.	This Sector
Total loans	3,034.7	16.9	100.00	0.6	36,419	28,618	78.6	83,328	592
Corn	1,333.9	10.1	59.86	0.8	26,419	21,715	82.2	50,489	467
Wheat	415.4	1.3	7.84	0.3	18,093	12,538	69.3	22,961	106
Soybeans	774.0	4.4	25.80	0.6	30,370	22,885	75.4	25,487	191
Sorghum, barley, and oats	54.8	0.1	0.68	0.2	8,603	3,053	35.5	6,375	38
Cotton	191.4	-	-	-	43,275	-	-	4,422	4
Sunflower seed, flaxseed, safflower, canola, other rapeseed, and mustard seed	17.3	-	-	-	25,159	-	-	686	6
Peanuts, rice, and tobacco	247.9	-	-	-	60,421	-	-	4,103	5

Source: *1997 Census of Agriculture*, U.S. Department of Agriculture, National Agricultural Statistics Service. Table shows totals for the U.S. agriculture sector and for the NAICS subdivision of it, shown as "This Agric. Sector" or as "This Sector." Not all farms report on every category. For this reason, the reporting universe is shown in the last two columns. Averages are based on these columns. The Commodity Credit Corporation provides low interest loans to farmers.

SELECTED MACHINERY AND EQUIPMENT

Item	U.S. Total (number)	This Agric. Sector (number)	% of U.S.	Average number per farm			Number of farms reporting category	
				U.S.	This Agric. Sector	% of U.S.	U.S.	This Sector
Motortrucks, including pickups	3,497,735	156,165	4.5	2.07	1.63	78.4	1,688,303	96,087
Wheel tractors	3,936,014	142,475	3.6	2.31	1.61	69.9	1,707,384	88,406
Less than 40 horsepower (PTO)	1,262,688	68,293	5.4	1.44	1.27	88.3	877,119	53,708
40 horsepower (PTO) or more	2,673,326	74,182	2.8	2.02	1.46	72.2	1,321,084	50,778
40 to 99 horsepower (PTO)	1,808,105	61,388	3.4	1.58	1.33	84.3	1,145,466	46,120
100 horsepower (PTO)	865,221	12,794	1.5	1.68	1.29	76.5	513,773	9,934
Grain and bean combines	460,606	3,706	0.8	1.16	1.13	96.9	395,934	3,289
Cotton pickers and strippers	38,294	32	0.1	1.48	1.45	98.3	25,874	22
Mower conditioners	608,443	22,571	3.7	1.12	1.12	99.7	543,565	20,230
Pickup balers	717,245	18,947	2.6	1.24	1.16	93.8	579,440	16,320

Source: *1997 Census of Agriculture*, U.S. Department of Agriculture, National Agricultural Statistics Service. Table shows totals for the U.S. agriculture sector and for the NAICS subdivision of it, shown as "This Agric. Sector" or as "This Sector." Not all farms report on every category. For this reason, the reporting universe is shown in the last two columns. Averages are based on these columns. PTO stands for "power take off."

FARM PRODUCTION EXPENSES

Item	U.S. Total ($ mil.)	This Sector ($ mil.)	% of Sector Total Expense	% of U.S.	Average expense per farm - $			Number of farms reporting category	
					U.S.	This Agric. Sector	% of U.S.	U.S.	This Sector
Total farm production expenses	150,591.0	2,708.6	100.00	1.8	78,771	24,439	31.0	1,911,766	110,835
Livestock and poultry purchased	21,614.6	450.7	16.64	2.1	38,807	12,974	33.4	556,980	34,739
Feed for livestock and poultry	32,760.0	631.0	23.29	1.9	32,059	8,266	25.8	1,021,849	76,333
Commercially mixed formula feeds	21,236.2	305.5	11.28	1.4	34,459	6,502	18.9	616,280	46,987
Seeds, bulbs, plants, and trees	5,725.9	23.2	0.86	0.4	6,388	1,606	25.1	896,339	14,470
Commercial fertilizer	9,597.1	54.8	2.02	0.6	8,060	1,927	23.9	1,190,733	28,453
Agricultural chemicals	7,581.4	31.1	1.15	0.4	8,056	1,339	16.6	941,136	23,215
Petroleum products	6,371.5	120.7	4.45	1.9	3,619	1,349	37.3	1,760,642	89,459
Gasoline and gasohol	1,886.6	54.7	2.02	2.9	1,380	803	58.2	1,366,915	68,053
Diesel fuel	2,846.0	44.2	1.63	1.6	2,164	851	39.3	1,315,397	52,001
Natural gas	432.9	2.6	0.10	0.6	6,091	1,302	21.4	71,069	1,999
LP gas, fuel oil, kerosene, motor oil, grease, etc.	1,206.1	19.1	0.71	1.6	945	366	38.8	1,276,331	52,215
Electricity	2,751.1	74.8	2.76	2.7	2,247	1,130	50.3	1,224,374	66,167
Hired farm labor	14,841.0	288.1	10.64	1.9	22,811	10,408	45.6	650,623	27,682
Contract labor	2,959.0	31.0	1.15	1.0	13,040	2,729	20.9	226,909	11,367
Repair and maintenance	8,637.7	230.6	8.51	2.7	5,616	2,824	50.3	1,538,058	81,674
Custom work, machine hire, and rental of equipment	3,210.3	30.5	1.13	0.9	5,372	1,631	30.4	597,624	18,697
Interest	8,928.1	196.9	7.27	2.2	11,016	5,590	50.7	810,476	35,230
Secured by real estate	5,449.6	139.2	5.14	2.6	9,564	5,119	53.5	569,775	27,196
Not secured by real estate	3,478.5	57.7	2.13	1.7	7,540	3,882	51.5	461,326	14,871
Cash rent	6,915.7	53.0	1.96	0.8	14,244	4,625	32.5	485,512	11,452
Property taxes	3,920.1	160.8	5.94	4.1	2,213	1,547	69.9	1,771,787	103,985
All other farm production expenses	14,777.4	331.3	12.23	2.2	8,747	3,490	39.9	1,689,391	94,940

Source: 1997 Census of Agriculture, U.S. Department of Agriculture, National Agricultural Statistics Service. Table shows totals for the U.S. agriculture sector and for the NAICS subdivision of it, shown as "This Agric. Sector" or as "This Sector." Not all farms report on every category. For this reason, the reporting universe is shown in the last two columns. Averages are based on these columns. LP gas stands for "liquid petroleum gas," i.e., butane or propane.

NET CASH RETURN AND FARMS WITH GAINS AND LOSSES

Item	Number of farms and %				Average gain or loss per farm - $		
	U.S.	% of U.S.	This Agriculture Sector	% of Sector	U.S.	This Agriculture Sector	% of U.S.
All farms	1,911,824	100.0	110,850	100.0	22,260	2,728	12.3
Number of farms with net gains	985,718	51.6	20,968	18.9	51,296	48,904	95.3
Gain of -							
Less than $1,000	120,163	6.3	4,190	3.8	-	-	-
$1,000 to $9,999	370,611	19.4	9,107	8.2	-	-	-
$10,000 to $49,999	292,484	15.3	4,637	4.2	-	-	-
$50,000 or more	202,460	10.6	3,034	2.7	-	-	-
Number of farms with net losses	926,106	48.4	89,882	81.1	(8,645)	(8,044)	93.0
Loss of -							
Less than $1,000	165,390	8.7	9,949	9.0	-	-	-
$1,000 to $9,999	591,517	30.9	60,210	54.3	-	-	-
$10,000 to $49,999	152,649	8.0	18,857	17.0	-	-	-
$50,000 or more	16,550	0.9	866	0.8	-	-	-

Source: 1997 Census of Agriculture, U.S. Department of Agriculture, National Agricultural Statistics Service. Table shows totals for the U.S. agriculture sector and for the NAICS subdivision of it, shown as "This Agric. Sector" or as "This Sector." Not all farms report on every category. For this reason, the reporting universe is shown in the last two columns. Averages are based on these columns. Net gains are income less cost for farm operations; they exclude non-farm earnings. Values in parentheses are losses.

CHARACTERISTICS OF FARM OPERATORS

Farm Operators	U.S.	This Agric. Sector	% of U.S.	Farm Operators	U.S.	This Agric. Sector	% of U.S.
Place of residence:				By age group:			
On farm operated	1,361,766	89,656	6.6	Under 25 years	20,850	608	2.9
Not on farm operated	412,554	13,572	3.3	25 to 34 years	128,455	7,355	5.7
Not reported	137,539	7,352	5.3	35 to 44 years	371,442	25,985	7.0
Principal occupation:				45 to 49 years	232,845	17,825	7.7
Farming	961,560	35,338	3.7	50 to 54 years	233,884	17,451	7.5
Other	950,299	75,242	7.9	55 to 59 years	222,736	13,984	6.3
Days worked off farm:				60 to 64 years	204,618	10,029	4.9
None	755,254	29,716	3.9	65 to 69 years	179,858	7,436	4.1
Any	1,042,158	76,834	7.4	70 years and over	317,171	9,907	3.1
1 to 99 days	164,957	8,118	4.9	Average age	54	51	94.7
100 to 199 days	167,922	11,847	7.1	By sex:			
200 days or more	709,279	56,869	8.0	Male	1,746,757	86,485	5.0
Not reported	114,447	4,030	3.5	Female	165,102	24,095	14.6
Years on present farm:				Spanish, Hispanic/Latino origin	27,717	1,550	5.6
2 years or less	92,574	8,190	8.8	Tenure of operator:			
3 or 4 years	126,791	11,844	9.3	All operators	1,911,859	110,580	5.8
5 to 9 years	263,642	22,549	8.6	Full owners	1,146,891	87,052	7.6
10 years or more	1,113,839	51,964	4.7	Part owners	573,839	15,855	2.8
Ave. years on this farm	20	14	69.2	Tenants	191,129	7,673	4.0
Not reported	315,013	16,033	5.1				

Source: *1997 Census of Agriculture*, U.S. Department of Agriculture, National Agricultural Statistics Service. Table shows totals for the U.S. agriculture sector and for the NAICS subdivision of it, shown as "This Agric. Sector" or as "This Sector." Not all farms report on every category. For this reason, the reporting universe is shown in the last two columns. Averages are based on these columns. All values shown are number of farm operators in each category or percent.

FARMS BY TYPE OF ORGANIZATION

Item	Number of farms and percent				Total acres and percent		
	U.S.	% of U.S.	This Agriculture Sector	% of Sector	U.S.	This Agriculture Sector	% of U.S.
Individual or family (sole proprietorship)	1,643,424	100.0	98,200	100.0	585,464,911	9,443,931	1.6
Partnership	169,462	10.3	6,110	6.2	149,321,484	1,894,960	1.3
Corporation:							
Family held	76,103	4.6	4,734	4.8	119,559,203	2,170,421	1.8
More than 10 stockholders	1,795	0.1	88	0.1	-	-	-
10 or less stockholders	74,308	4.5	4,646	4.7	-	-	-
Other than family held	7,899	0.5	726	0.7	11,904,053	357,627	3.0
More than 10 stockholders	1,029	0.1	57	0.1	-	-	-
10 or less stockholders	6,870	0.4	669	0.7	-	-	-
Other cooperative, estate or trust, institutional, etc.	14,971	0.9	810	0.8	65,545,604	1,849,005	2.8

Source: *1997 Census of Agriculture*, U.S. Department of Agriculture, National Agricultural Statistics Service. Table shows totals for the U.S. agriculture sector and for the NAICS subdivision of it, shown as "This Agric. Sector" or as "This Sector." Not all farms report on every category. For this reason, the reporting universe is shown in the last two columns. Averages are based on these columns.

LIVESTOCK INVENTORIES AND SALES

Item	U.S. (number)	This Agric. Sector (number)	% of U.S.	Average number per farm			Number of farms reporting category	
				U.S.	This Agric. Sector	% of U.S.	U.S.	This Sector
Cattle and calves inventory	98,989,244	716,083	0.7	94.6	37.2	39.4	1,046,863	19,227
Cows and heifers that had calved	43,162,054	287,976	0.7	48.3	23.0	47.7	894,110	12,495
Beef cows	34,066,615	261,301	0.8	42.3	23.0	54.3	804,595	11,364
Milk cows	9,095,439	26,675	0.3	77.8	15.6	20.0	116,874	1,715
Heifers and heifer calves	26,988,697	195,394	0.7	33.6	16.3	48.5	803,985	12,005
Steers, steer calves, bulls, and bull calves	28,838,493	232,713	0.8	32.6	16.3	50.0	883,983	14,255
Cattle and calves sold	74,089,046	384,349	0.5	73.2	32.1	43.8	1,011,809	11,978
Calves	16,480,293	93,409	0.6	26.8	14.1	52.5	615,177	6,637
Cattle	57,608,753	290,940	0.5	78.0	36.3	46.5	738,696	8,021
Fattened on grain and concentrates	27,328,190	116,731	0.4	247.0	59.8	24.2	110,620	1,952
Hogs and pigs inventory	61,206,236	1,229,905	2.0	557.7	208.3	37.3	109,754	5,905
Used or to be used for breeding	6,831,564	128,957	1.9	106.7	44.3	41.5	64,029	2,912
Other	54,374,672	1,100,948	2.0	528.0	197.4	37.4	102,977	5,576
Hogs and pigs sold	142,611,882	2,048,595	1.4	1,396.7	476.5	34.1	102,106	4,299
Feeder pigs	34,988,718	193,523	0.6	2,037.8	306.7	15.1	17,170	631
Litters of pigs farrowed between Dec. 1 of preceding year and Nov. 30	11,497,523	201,686	1.8	170.3	66.3	38.9	67,514	3,043
Dec. 1 and May 31	5,697,371	101,749	1.8	91.0	36.0	39.6	62,622	2,823
June 1 and Nov. 30	5,800,152	99,937	1.7	99.7	39.6	39.8	58,204	2,522
Sheep and lambs of all ages inventory	7,821,885	171,118	2.2	118.9	49.5	41.6	65,790	3,458
Ewes 1 year old or older	4,408,683	99,445	2.3	78.1	38.6	49.4	56,414	2,574
Sheep and lambs sold	7,331,545	133,282	1.8	123.1	53.3	43.3	59,575	2,500
Sheep and lambs shorn	6,139,140	122,167	2.0	118.4	61.1	51.7	51,869	1,998
Horses and ponies inventory	2,427,277	1,051,996	43.3	6.5	11.2	173.9	375,218	93,519
Horses and ponies sold	325,306	241,278	74.2	4.1	5.0	122.0	79,516	48,345
Goats inventory	1,989,799	77,852	3.9	34.4	10.8	31.4	57,925	7,227
Goats sold	740,597	31,072	4.2	31.5	14.9	47.2	23,520	2,092

Source: 1997 Census of Agriculture, U.S. Department of Agriculture, National Agricultural Statistics Service. Table shows totals for the U.S. agriculture sector and for the NAICS subdivision of it, shown as "This Agric. Sector" or as "This Sector." Not all farms report on every category. For this reason, the reporting universe is shown in the last two columns. Averages are based on these columns.

POULTRY INVENTORIES AND SALES

Item	U.S. (number)	This Agric. Sector (number)	% of U.S.	Average number per farm			Number of farms reporting category	
				U.S.	This Agric. Sector	% of U.S.	U.S.	This Sector
Layers and pullets 13 weeks old and older inventory	366,989,851	1,453,112	0.4	5,053.8	221.3	4.4	72,616	6,565
Layers 20 weeks old and older	313,851,480	1,216,879	0.4	4,499.0	191.0	4.2	69,761	6,370
Pullets 13 weeks old and older but less than 20 weeks old	53,138,371	236,233	0.4	4,031.7	176.0	4.4	13,180	1,342
Layers, pullets, and pullet chicks sold	331,563,736	1,923,840	0.6	24,636.9	2,514.8	10.2	13,458	765
Broilers and other meat type chickens sold	6,741,927,110	2,987,597	0.0	281,653.0	7,431.8	2.6	23,937	402
Turkey hens kept for breeding	5,504,808	2,392	0.0	968.1	3.8	0.4	5,686	624
Turkeys sold	307,586,680	1,661,398	0.5	51,000.9	6,540.9	12.8	6,031	254

Source: 1997 Census of Agriculture, U.S. Department of Agriculture, National Agricultural Statistics Service. Table shows totals for the U.S. agriculture sector and for the NAICS subdivision of it, shown as "This Agric. Sector" or as "This Sector." Not all farms report on every category. For this reason, the reporting universe is shown in the last two columns. Averages are based on these columns.

SELECTED CROPS HARVESTED

Item	In 1,000	Crop harvested			Acres used for crop (000)			Number of farms reporting category	
		U.S.	This Agric. Sector	% of U.S.	U.S.	This Agric. Sector	% of U.S.	U.S.	This Sector
Corn for grain or seed	bushels	8,578,635	52,956	0.6	69,796.7	448.2	0.6	430,711	4,114
Irrigated		-	-	-	10,638.9	33.0	0.3	40,574	236
Corn for silage or green chop	tons, green	88,381	573	0.6	5,727.6	40.9	0.7	119,308	1,443
Irrigated		-	-	-	1,033.3	2.0	0.2	10,815	73
Sorghum for grain or seed	bushels	559,070	2,951	0.5	8,470.4	38.3	0.5	49,397	359
Irrigated		-	-	-	875.6	1.1	0.1	5,793	14
Wheat for grain	bushels	2,204,027	7,117	0.3	58,836.3	187.0	0.3	243,568	1,516
Irrigated		-	-	-	3,990.9	5.8	0.1	20,385	56
Barley for grain	bushels	336,435	2,818	0.8	5,945.0	51.3	0.9	41,930	342
Irrigated		-	-	-	1,060.7	4.9	0.5	8,847	72
Oats for grain	bushels	151,327	2,328	1.5	2,681.0	38.9	1.5	89,606	1,868
Irrigated		-	-	-	121.0	1.4	1.1	2,788	67
Rice	cwt	182,231	90	0.0	3,122.1	1.5	0.0	9,291	13
Irrigated		-	-	-	3,122.1	1.5	0.0	9,291	13
Cotton	bales	17,879	12	0.1	13,235.2	7.9	0.1	31,493	39
Irrigated		-	-	-	4,888.0	1.5	0.0	12,434	12
Tobacco	pounds	1,747,702	4,868	0.3	838.5	2.3	0.3	89,706	361
Irrigated		-	-	-	138.7	0.4	0.3	7,090	15
Soybeans for beans	bushels	2,504,307	12,991	0.5	66,147.7	324.9	0.5	354,692	2,571
Irrigated		-	-	-	4,152.1	13.4	0.3	20,619	118
Dry edible beans, excluding dry limas	cwt	27,224	28	0.1	1,691.9	1.7	0.1	10,911	31
Irrigated		-	-	-	577.0	-	-	4,882	8
Potatoes, excluding sweetpotatoes	cwt	459,886	31	0.0	1,355.2	0.2	0.0	10,523	128
Irrigated		-	-	-	1,070.3	0.0	0.0	4,843	26
Sugar beets for sugar	tons	29,775	-	-	1,453.8	-	-	7,102	7
Irrigated		-	-	-	616.4	-	-	3,492	2
Peanuts for nuts	pounds	3,377,143	3,466	0.1	1,352.2	1.6	0.1	12,221	41
Irrigated		-	-	-	412.3	0.6	0.2	3,125	9
Hay alfalfa, other tame, small grain, wild, grass silage, green chop	tons, dry	139,365	1,705	1.2	60,799.8	935.4	1.5	888,597	32,243
Irrigated		-	-	-	9,564.3	75.3	0.8	79,406	3,290
Alfalfa hay	tons, dry	65,863	715	1.1	21,309.8	291.1	1.4	358,365	11,741
Irrigated		-	-	-	5,980.5	44.6	0.7	57,854	2,094
Vegetables harvested for sale		-	-	-	3,773.2	1.5	0.0	53,727	417
Irrigated		-	-	-	2,641.8	0.6	0.0	23,203	145
Land in orchards		-	-	-	5,158.1	9.8	0.2	106,069	1,476
Irrigated		-	-	-	4,107.9	3.7	0.1	61,606	534

Source: *1997 Census of Agriculture*, U.S. Department of Agriculture, National Agricultural Statistics Service. Table shows totals for the U.S. agriculture sector and for the NAICS subdivision of it, shown as "This Agric. Sector" or as "This Sector." Not all farms report on every category. For this reason, the reporting universe is shown in the last two columns. Averages are based on these columns. "Green tons" are weight of product as harvested, i.e., moist. cwt stands for "hundredweight."

LEADING COMPANIES   Number shown: **10**   Total sales ($ mil): **3,673**   Total employment (000): **9.2**

Company Name	Address				CEO Name	Phone	Co. Type	Sales ($ mil)	Empl. (000)
Stolt-Nielsen Inc.	P O Box 2300	Greenwich	CT	06836	Jacob Stolt-Nielsen Jr	203-625-9400	S	3,215*	6.0
Charles River Laboratories	251 Ballardvale St	Wilmington	MA	01887	James C Foster	978-658-6000	S	221*	1.5
Delta Pride Catfish Inc.	PO Box 850	Indianola	MS	38751		601-887-5401	R	114	0.9
Farm Fresh Catfish Co.	PO Box 85	Hollandale	MS	38748	Jim Hoffman	601-827-2204	S	30*	0.3
Nevada Nile Ranch Inc.	PO Box 1150	Lovelock	NV	89419	RA McDougal	775-273-2646	R	30*	<0.1
Covance Research Products Inc.	PO Box 7200	Denver	PA	17517		717-336-4921	S	25	0.2
Larson Products Inc.	PO Box 5	Sargeant	MN	55973	Vance Larson	507-584-2269	R	16	<0.1
Farrar Oil Co.	PO Box 747	Mount Vernon	IL	62864		618-242-1717	R	14*	0.1
Calumet Farm Inc.	3301 Versailles Rd	Lexington	KY	40510	H De Kwiatkowski	606-231-8272	R	4*	<0.1
Farm Fish Inc.	P O Box 23109	Jackson	MS	39225	Thomas R Slough Jr	601-354-3801	P	4	<0.1

Source: *Ward's Business Directory of U.S. Private and Public Companies*, Volumes 1 and 2, 2000. The company type code used is as follows: P - Public, R - Private, S - Subsidiary, D - Division, J - Joint Venture, A - Affiliate, G - Group, N - Company type not reported. Sales are in millions of dollars, employees are in thousands. An asterisk (*) indicates an estimated sales volume. The symbol < stands for 'less than'. Company names and addresses are truncated, in some cases, to fit into the available space.

NAICS 113310 - LOGGING*

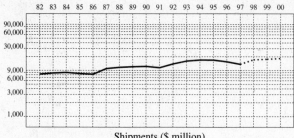

Shipments ($ million)

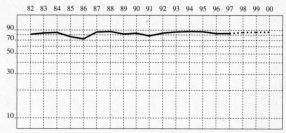

Employment (000)

GENERAL STATISTICS

| Year | Com-panies | Establishments | | Employment | | | Compensation | | Production ($ million) | | | |
		Total	with 20 or more employees	Total (000)	Production Workers (000)	Hours (Mil)	Payroll ($ mil)	Wages ($/hr)	Cost of Materials	Value Added by Manufacture	Value of Shipments	Capital Invest.
1982	11,541	11,658	657	80.8	69.1	121.3	1,207.9	8.27	5,630.2	2,501.9	8,274.0	249.0
1983				83.5	73.0	129.2	1,310.8	8.54	5,916.6	2,780.9	8,731.0	237.0
1984				84.7	72.1	131.5	1,362.5	8.47	5,993.2	2,939.3	8,987.9	328.2
1985				76.3	65.2	116.1	1,259.5	8.90	5,524.9	2,944.0	8,518.0	356.0
1986				72.3	60.6	112.2	1,250.0	9.11	5,306.5	2,892.3	8,235.7	341.3
1987	11,852	11,936	803	85.8	72.2	131.3	1,515.5	9.14	6,801.5	4,075.2	10,938.2	349.3
1988				86.9	73.0	136.5	1,591.4	9.09	7,350.6	4,324.0	11,663.8	221.5
1989		11,915	814	81.7	68.0	132.4	1,595.6	9.50	7,576.3	4,512.6	12,017.4	353.9
1990				83.4	68.9	134.4	1,647.3	9.55	7,930.4	4,313.2	12,229.0	405.9
1991				78.1	65.4	126.0	1,560.6	9.80	7,280.2	4,097.4	11,434.3	292.9
1992	12,916	13,010	727	83.6	69.4	131.2	1,693.1	9.96	8,763.3	5,119.3	13,844.5	375.5
1993				86.2	71.6	138.9	1,774.9	9.86	10,121.3	5,904.4	15,976.4	366.0
1994				87.2	71.7	142.4	1,820.2	9.96	10,856.7	5,947.6	16,817.7	469.0
1995				86.8	71.0	140.7	1,890.8	10.41	10,707.4	6,133.2	16,775.5	592.4
1996				83.0	68.3	134.1	1,856.0	10.76	9,660.5	5,775.3	15,411.1	539.4
1997	13,461	13,533	727	83.2	72.6	113.5	2,011.9	13.86	7,427.0	6,166.0	13,613.3	789.6
1998				85.4p	70.5p	135.0p	2,015.8p	11.64p	10,416.9p	6,670.2p	17,035.9p	598.3p
1999				85.7p	70.6p	135.6p	2,066.6p	11.87p	10,739.2p	6,937.0p	17,617.5p	622.7p
2000				86.0p	70.7p	136.3p	2,117.4p	12.09p	11,061.4p	7,203.9p	18,199.2p	647.0p

Sources: *Economic Census of the United States*, 1977, 1982, 1987, 1992, and 1997. Data for those years are from the 5-year censuses of the economy. Other values are extrapolations. Data after 1997 are projections by the editor and marked with a *p*. Logging data are the only data for the agricultural sector published in the Economic Census. They are included with Manufacturing. No totals for Agriculture are published, hence no ratios can be presented.

INDICES OF CHANGE

| Year | Com-panies | Establishments | | Employment | | | Compensation | | Production ($ million) | | | |
		Total	with 20 or more employees	Total (000)	Production Workers (000)	Hours (Mil)	Payroll ($ mil)	Wages ($/hr)	Cost of Materials	Value Added by Manufacture	Value of Shipments	Capital Invest.
1982	86	86	90	97	95	107	60	60	76	41	61	32
1983				100	101	114	65	62	80	45	64	30
1984				102	99	116	68	61	81	48	66	42
1985				92	90	102	63	64	74	48	63	45
1986				87	83	99	62	66	71	47	60	43
1987	88	88	110	103	99	116	75	66	92	66	80	44
1988				104	101	120	79	66	99	70	86	28
1989		88	112	98	94	117	79	69	102	73	88	45
1990				100	95	118	82	69	107	70	90	51
1991				94	90	111	78	71	98	66	84	37
1992	96	96	100	100	96	116	84	72	118	83	102	48
1993				104	99	122	88	71	136	96	117	46
1994				105	99	125	90	72	146	96	124	59
1995				104	98	124	94	75	144	99	123	75
1996				100	94	118	92	78	130	94	113	68
1997	100	100	100	100	100	100	100	100	100	100	100	100
1998				103p	97p	119p	100p	84p	140p	108p	125p	76p
1999				103p	97p	120p	103p	86p	145p	113p	129p	79p
2000				103p	97p	120p	105p	87p	149p	117p	134p	82p

Sources: Same as General Statistics. The values shown reflect change from the base year, 1997. Values above 100 mean greater than 1997, values below 100 mean less than 1997, and a value of 100 in years other than 1997 means same as 1997.

*Equivalent to SIC 2411.

123

Part II

MINING

NAICS 211111 - CRUDE PETROLEUM AND NATURAL GAS EXTRACTION*

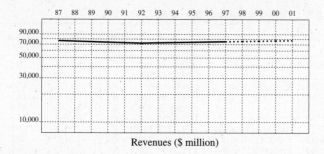

Revenues ($ million)

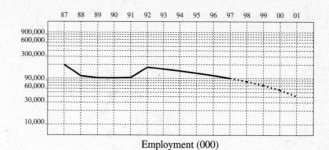

Employment (000)

GENERAL STATISTICS

| Year | Com-panies | Establishments | | Employment | | | Compensation | | Production ($ million) | | | |
		Total	with 20 or more employees	Total (No.)	Production Workers (No.)	Hours (Mil)	Payroll ($ mil)	Wages ($/hr)	Cost of Materials	Value Added by Mining	Value of Shipments	Capital Invest.
1977	6,217	8,573	981	139,700	59,900	118.0	2,738.2	8.69	13,418.7	38,327.1	40,829.8	10,916.0
1982	8,676	12,087	-	264,200	102,300	213.6	8,084.3	12.76	43,214.9	126,035.2	134,969.4	34,280.8
1987	8,120	10,203	1,171	198,800	69,400	142.3	7,510.0	15.14	19,112.2	67,954.9	76,518.1	10,549.0
1988	8,032	8,580[1]	843[1]	112,265[1]	68,349	139.9	3,981.6[1]	15.98	18,601.5	67,663.2	75,643.8	-
1989	7,944	7,659[1]	783[1]	101,933[1]	67,313	137.6	3,680.2[1]	16.87	18,104.4	67,372.7	74,779.5	-
1990	7,858	7,443[1]	776[1]	101,800[1]	66,293	135.3	3,927.6[1]	17.81	17,620.6	67,083.4	73,925.1	-
1991	7,773	7,281[1]	771[1]	103,376[1]	65,289	133.1	4,062.2[1]	18.81	17,149.7	66,795.5	73,080.4	-
1992	7,688	9,391	1,015	174,300	64,300	130.9	8,404.3	19.86	16,691.4	66,508.7	72,245.4	10,954.7
1993	7,511	9,069	954	159,502	63,098	128.1	7,717.2	20.55	17,734.8	68,081.4	72,828.8	-
1994	7,334	8,747	893	144,703	61,896	125.2	7,030.1	21.23	18,778.1	69,654.1	73,412.3	-
1995	7,156	8,425	832	129,905	60,693	122.4	6,342.9	21.92	19,821.5	71,226.8	73,995.7	-
1996	6,979	8,103	771	115,106	59,491	119.5	5,655.8	22.60	20,864.8	72,799.5	74,579.2	-
1997	6,802	7,781	710	100,308	58,289	116.7	4,968.7	23.29	21,908.2	74,372.2	75,162.6	21,117.9
1998	6,625p	7,459p	649p	85,510p	57,087p	113.9p	4,281.6p	23.98p	22,951.6p	75,944.9p	75,746.0p	-
1999	6,448p	7,137p	588p	70,711p	55,885p	111.0p	3,594.5p	24.66p	23,994.9p	77,517.6p	76,329.5p	-
2000	6,270p	6,815p	527p	55,913p	54,682p	108.2p	2,907.3p	25.35p	25,038.3p	79,090.3p	76,912.9p	-
2001	6,093p	6,493p	466p	41,114p	53,480p	105.3p	2,220.2p	26.03p	26,081.6p	80,663.0p	77,496.4p	-

Sources: *Economic Census of the United States*, 1977, 1982, 1987, 1992, and 1997. Data for those years (years are in **bold** type) are from the 5-year censuses of the economy. Other values, unless otherwise noted, are extrapolations. Values footnoted 1 are from the *County Business Patterns* for the years indicated. Values marked with *p* are projections. Data are the most recent available at this level of detail.

INDICES OF CHANGE

| Year | Com-panies | Establishments | | Employment | | | Compensation | | Production ($ million) | | | |
		Total	with 20 or more employees	Total (No.)	Production Workers (No.)	Hours (Mil)	Payroll ($ mil)	Wages ($/hr)	Cost of Materials	Value Added by Mining	Value of Shipments	Capital Invest.
1977	91.4	110.2	138.2	139.3	102.8	101.1	55.1	37.3	61.2	51.5	54.3	51.7
1982	127.6	155.3	-	263.4	175.5	183.0	162.7	54.8	197.3	169.5	179.6	162.3
1987	119.4	131.1	164.9	198.2	119.1	121.9	151.1	65.0	87.2	91.4	101.8	50.0
1992	113.0	120.7	143.0	173.8	110.3	112.2	169.1	85.3	76.2	89.4	96.1	51.9
1997	100.0	100.0	100.0	100.0	100.0	100.0	100.0	100.0	100.0	100.0	100.0	100.0

Sources: Same as General Statistics. The values shown reflect change from the base year, 1997. Values above 100 mean greater than 1997, values below 100 mean less than 1997, and a value of 100 in years other than 1997 means same as 1997. Indices are calculated only for Census years. Data are the most recent available at this level of detail.

SELECTED RATIOS

For 1992	Avg. of Sector	Analyzed Industry	Index	For 1992	Avg. of Sector	Analyzed Industry	Index
Employees per Establishment	20.4	12.9	63	Value Added per Production Worker	335,283	1,275,922	381
Payroll per Establishment	831,719	638,568	77	Cost per Establishment	2,854,087	2,815,602	99
Payroll per Employee	40,815	49,534	121	Cost per Employee	140,057	218,409	156
Production Workers per Establishment	15.6	7.5	48	Cost per Production Worker	183,057	375,855	205
Wages per Establishment	613,139	349,305	57	Shipments per Establishment	6,840,788	9,659,761	141
Wages per Production Worker	39,326	46,629	119	Shipments per Employee	335,695	749,318	223
Hours per Production Worker	2,075	2,002	96	Shipments per Production Worker	438,757	1,289,482	294
Wages per Hour	18.96	23.29	123	Investment per Establishment	1,242,441	2,714,034	218
Value Added per Establishment	5,227,487	9,558,180	183	Investment per Employee	60,970	210,531	345
Value Added per Employee	256,526	741,438	289	Investment per Production Worker	79,688	362,296	455

Sources: Same as General Statistics. The 'Average of Sector' column represents the average for all industries in this sector. The Index shows the relationship between the Average and the Analyzed Industry. For example, 100 means that they are equal; 500 that the Analyzed Industry is five times the average; 50 means that the Analyzed Industry is half the national average. 'na' is used to show that data are 'not available'.

*Equivalent to SIC 1311.

LEADING COMPANIES   Number shown: 75   Total sales ($ mil): **717,078**   Total employment (000): **658.5**

Company Name	Address				CEO Name	Phone	Co. Type	Sales ($ mil)	Empl. (000)
Exxon Mobil Corp.	5959 Las Colinas	Irving	TX	75039	Lee Raymond	972-444-1000	P	186,906	79.0
Mobil Oil Corp.	3225 Gallows Rd	Fairfax	VA	22037	Eugene A Renna	703-849-3000	S	41,990	39.1
Enron Corp.	P O Box 1188	Houston	TX	77251	Kenneth L Lay	713-853-6161	P	40,112	17.8
BP Amoco Chemicals	200 E Randolph St	Chicago	IL	60601		312-856-3200	S	36,287*	43.5
Koch Industries Inc.	PO Box 2256	Wichita	KS	67201		316-828-5500	R	36,200	15.6
Texaco Inc.	2000 Westchester	White Plains	NY	10650	Peter I Bijur	914-253-4000	P	35,698	24.6
Conoco Inc.	PO Box 2197	Houston	TX	77252	Archie W Dunham	281-293-1000	P	27,309	16.6
Chevron Corp.	PO Box 7753	San Francisco	CA	94120	David J O'Reilly	415-894-7700	P	26,187	39.2
Amoco Co.	200 E Randolph St	Chicago	IL	60601	Frederick S Addy	312-856-3200	S	25,042*	39.0
Marathon Oil Co.	PO Box 3128	Houston	TX	77253	Thomas J Usher	713-629-6600	P	24,212	24.3
USX Corp.	600 Grant St	Pittsburgh	PA	15219		412-433-1121	P	22,375	32.9
Exxon Mobil U.S.A.	PO Box 2180	Houston	TX	77252		713-656-3636	S	16,410	17.0
Shell Oil Co.	P O Box 2463	Houston	TX	77252	Philip J Carroll	713-241-6161	S	15,451	19.8
Phillips Petroleum Co.	411 S Keeler Ave	Bartlesville	OK	74003	JJ Mulva	918-661-6600	P	13,852	17.3
Atlantic Richfield Co.	515 S Flower St	Los Angeles	CA	90071	Michael Bowlin	213-486-3511	P	13,055	18.4
PacifiCorp	700 N E Multnomah	Portland	OR	97232	Alan Richardson	503-731-2000	S	12,989	9.1
Sunoco Inc.	1801 Market St	Philadelphia	PA	19103	Robert Campbell	215-977-3000	P	10,068	0.0
Coastal Corp.	9 E Greenway Plz	Houston	TX	77046		713-877-1400	P	7,368	13.2
Columbia Energy Group	13880 Dulles Corner	Herndon	VA	20171	Oliver G Richard III	703-561-6000	P	6,969*	8.6
Occidental Petroleum Corp.	10889 Wilshire Blvd	Los Angeles	CA	90024	Ray Irani	310-208-8800	P	6,596	9.2
Amerada Hess Corp.	1185 Av Americas	New York	NY	10036	WSH Laidlaw	212-997-8500	P	6,590	9.8
Consolidated Natural Gas Co.	625 Liberty Ave	Pittsburgh	PA	15222	GA Davidson Jr.	412-690-1000	P	6,362	6.2
CMS Energy Corp.	330 Town Center Dr	Dearborn	MI	48126	Victor Fryling	313-436-9200	P	6,103	9.7
BP Exploration Inc.	200 Westlake Park	Houston	TX	77079	Andrew G Inglis	281-560-8500	S	5,600*	1.0
Unocal Corp.	2141 Rosecrans Ave	El Segundo	CA	90245	Roger C Beach	310-726-7600	P	5,003*	7.9
Texaco North America Production	P O Box 1404	Houston	TX	77251	Peter I Bijur	713-752-6000	S	4,600	4.6
FINA Inc.	P O Box 2159	Dallas	TX	75221	Paul D Meek	214-750-2400	P	4,463	2.9
MCN Energy Group Inc.	500 Griswold St	Detroit	MI	48226	Stephen E Ewing	313-256-5500	P	4,393	3.0
Adair International Oil & Gas Inc.	P O Box 22658	Houston	TX	77227	John W Adair	713-621-8241	P	3,380	<0.1
Statoil Energy Inc.	2800 Eisenhower	Alexandria	VA	22314	David A Dresner	703-317-2300	S	3,000	0.7
MarketSpan Corp.	175 E Old Country	Hicksville	NY	11801	Robert B Catell	718-403-2000	P	2,955	7.9
ENSERCH Corp.	Energy Plz	Dallas	TX	75201	David W Biegler	214-651-8700	S	2,790*	3.0
Sedco Forex	P O Box 1569	Channelview	TX	77530	Jean-Marie Brodin	281-457-7400	S	2,735*	5.0
Kerr-McGee Corp.	PO Box 25861	Oklahoma City	OK	73125	Luke R Corbett	405-270-1313	P	2,696	3.4
Brooklyn Union Gas Co.	1 MetroTech Cntr	Brooklyn	NY	11201	Robert B Catell	718-403-2000	P	2,290*	3.3
Murphy Oil USA Inc.	PO Box 7000	El Dorado	AR	71731		870-862-6411	S	2,100	1.3
Burlington Resources Inc.	PO Box 4239	Houston	TX	77210	Bobby S Shackouls	713-624-9500	P	2,065	1.7
Marathon Ashland Petroleum	539 S Main St	Findlay	OH	45840		419-422-2121	R	2,000	30.0
Occidental Oil and Gas Corp.	PO Box 12021	Bakersfield	CA	93389	Dale R Laurence	661-321-6000	P	2,000*	2.6
Adams Resources and Energy Inc.	P O Box 844	Houston	TX	77001	KS Adams Jr	713-881-3600	P	1,974	0.6
TransMontaigne Oil Co.	370 17th St	Denver	CO	80202	Richard E Gathright	303-626-8200	P	1,968	0.4
BP Amoco Business Corp.	550 Westlake Park	Houston	TX	77079	John Brown	281-366-5953	D	1,919*	2.7
Western Gas Resources Inc.	12200 Pecos St	Denver	CO	80234		303-452-5603	P	1,911	0.9
Equitable Resources Inc.	1 Oxford Ctr	Pittsburgh	PA	15219	Murry S Gerber	412-553-5700	P	1,854	1.6
Union Pacific Resources Group	PO Box 7	Fort Worth	TX	76101	George Lindahl III	817-321-6000	P	1,728	2.9
Murphy Oil Corp.	PO Box 7000	El Dorado	AR	71731	Claiborne P Deming	870-862-6411	P	1,699	1.6
Cabot Corp.	75 State St	Boston	MA	02109	Samuel Bodman	617-345-0100	P	1,648	4.8
American Trading & Production	P O Box 238	Baltimore	MD	21203	Sanford Schmidt	410-347-7000	R	1,644*	3.0
Tesoro Petroleum Corp.	8700 Tesoro Dr	San Antonio	TX	78217	Tom Moody	210-828-8484	P	1,487	2.1
Montana Power Co.	40 E Broadway	Butte	MT	59701	Robert P Gannon	406-723-5421	P	1,342	2.9
TOTAL America Inc.	P O Box 4826	Houston	TX	77210		713-739-3400	S	1,300	4.0
Plains Resources Inc.	500 Dallas St	Houston	TX	77002	Greg L Armstrong	713-654-1414	P	1,293	0.4
Western Atlas International Inc.	PO Box 1407	Houston	TX	77251	John R Russell	713-972-4000	S	1,180*	10.0
Burlington Resources (Subsidiary)	PO Box 4239	Houston	TX	77210	Bobby Shackouls	713-624-9000	S	1,117*	1.6
Samedan Oil Corp.	P O Box 909	Ardmore	OK	73402	Robert Kelley	580-223-4110	S	1,044*	0.6
Vastar Resources Inc.	15375 Mem Dr	Houston	TX	77079	Chester D Davidson	281-584-6000	P	941	1.1
Questar Corp.	PO Box 45433	Salt Lake City	UT	84145	R Cash	801-324-5000	P	924	2.3
Noble Affiliates Inc.	PO Box 1967	Ardmore	OK	73402	Robert Kelley	580-223-4110	P	910	0.6
New Jersey Resources Corp.	PO Box 1468	Wall	NJ	07719	Laurence M Downes	732-938-1480	P	904	0.8
Baker Hughes INTEQ	PO Box 670968	Houston	TX	77267		713-625-4200	S	901*	5.0
Arctic Slope Regional Corp.	PO Box 129	Barrow	AK	99723	Jacob Adams	907-852-8633	R	880	0.0
Apache Corp.	2000 Post Oak Blvd	Houston	TX	77056	G Steven Farris	713-296-6000	P	876	1.3
Barrett Resources Corp.	1515 Arapahoe St	Denver	CO	80202	William Barrett	303-572-3900	P	839	0.2
Global Marine Inc.	777 N Eldridge	Houston	TX	77079	Robert E Rose	281-596-5100	P	791	2.7
Mitchell Energy Corp.	2002 Timberloch Pl	The Woodlands	TX	77380	George P Mitchell	713-377-5500	S	790	1.1
EOG Resources Inc.	P O Box 4362	Houston	TX	77210	Mark G Papa	713-853-6161	P	769	1.2
Devon Energy Corp.	20 N Broadway Ave	Oklahoma City	OK	73102	J Larry Nichols	405-235-3611	P	734	0.8
Pennzoil Exploration	PO Box 2967	Houston	TX	77252	Donald A Pesident	713-546-4000	S	732	1.3
Pioneer Natural Resources Co.	5205 N O Connor	Irving	TX	75039	Scott D Sheffield	972-444-9001	P	710	1.0
Hunt Consolidated Inc.	1445 Ross at Field	Dallas	TX	75202	Ray L Hunt	214-978-8000	R	705	2.6
Mitchell Energy & Development	2001 Timberloch Pl	The Woodlands	TX	77380	George P Mitchell	713-377-5500	P	701	0.9
Anadarko Petroleum Corp.	PO Box 1330	Houston	TX	77251	Robert J Allison Jr	281-875-1101	P	701	1.5
Tredegar Industries Inc.	1100 Boulders Pkwy	Chesterfield	VA	23832	John D Gottwald	804-330-1000	P	700	3.4
Southwestern Energy Co.	PO Box 1408	Fayetteville	AR	72702	Harold M Korell	501-521-1141	P	648	0.7
Maxus Energy Corp.	717 N Harwood St	Dallas	TX	75201	Mario Rosso	214-953-2000	S	614*	1.8

Source: *Ward's Business Directory of U.S. Private and Public Companies*, Volumes 1 and 2, 2000. The company type code used is as follows: P - Public, R - Private, S - Subsidiary, D - Division, J - Joint Venture, A - Affiliate, G - Group, N - Company type not reported. Sales are in millions of dollars, employees are in thousands. An asterisk (*) indicates an estimated sales volume. The symbol < stands for 'less than'. Company names and addresses are truncated, in some cases, to fit into the available space.

MINING PRODUCT DETAILS

Products	Units	Quantity of (000s)		Value of product shipments			
		Produc-tion 1997	Ship-ments 1997	1992		1997	
				($ mil)	% of total	($ mil)	% of total
Crude petroleum and natural gas		NA	NA	71,607.7	100.0	74,458.8	100.0
Crude petroleum, including lease condensate (volumes corrected to 60 degrees F) shipped	mil bbl	NA	1,804	36,628.1	51.2	32,187.6	43.2
Crude petroleum shipped from stripper well leases	mil bbl	NA	123	NA	-	NA	-
Lease condensate produced (volumes corrected to 60 degrees F)	mil bbl	NA	128	NA	-	NA	-
Natural gas (volumes adjusted to pressure base of 14.73 lb absolute at 60 degrees F) shipped to consumers	bil cu ft	NA	14,576	27,775.1	38.8	34,467.2	46.3
Crude petroleum and natural gas, nsk[1]		NA	NA	7,204.5	10.1	7,804.0	10.5

Source: Economic Census of the U.S., 1997. Notes: 1. Includes value for establishments that did not report detailed data and estimates for small companies (estimates were made from administrative-record data rather than collected from respondents). NA stands for not applicable. (D) means data are withheld to avoid disclosure of competitive information. (S) indicates that data did not meet publication standards. - means not available or zero.

LOCATION BY STATE AND REGIONAL CONCENTRATION

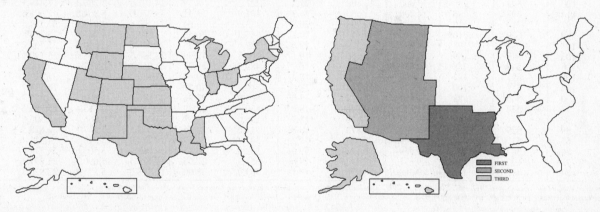

FIRST
SECOND
THIRD

INDUSTRY DATA BY STATE

State	Estab-lish-ments	Employment			Compensation		Production				Capital Exp. ($ mil)
		Total	Workers	Total as % of US	Payroll per Employee	Wages per Worker	Costs ($ mil)	Value Added ($ mil)	Reve-nues ($ mil)	% of US	
Texas	3,064	39,679	22,409	39.56	50,517	45,249	7,046.6	23,920.6	23,030.9	30.97	7,936.3
Louisiana	473	15,324	9,190	15.28	55,964	54,388	5,103.3	16,954.6	16,594.5	22.31	5,463.4
California	215	4,866	2,938	4.85	58,675	55,207	2,646.9	5,276.4	7,084.0	9.53	839.2
Oklahoma	1,070	10,704	5,031	10.67	44,855	41,867	1,114.2	4,037.7	4,143.4	5.57	1,008.5
New Mexico	199	2,239	1,645	2.23	45,052	44,507	616.2	3,461.2	3,354.7	4.51	722.7
Wyoming	20	1,643	1,208	1.64	52,915	53,410	1,365.8	3,931.9	3,292.5	4.43	2,005.2
Wyoming	173	1,863	1,405	1.86	48,493	49,434	475.8	2,703.8	2,810.3	3.78	369.2
Colorado	317	4,531	1,876	4.52	46,103	48,132	480.3	1,862.6	1,958.0	2.63	384.8
Kansas	470	3,396	2,424	3.39	33,389	31,122	277.5	1,744.7	1,826.9	2.46	195.4
North Dakota	55	950	826	0.95	51,949	52,430	155.8	651.2	690.0	0.93	116.9
Utah	64	1,035	612	1.03	44,913	38,948	175.6	680.1	683.8	0.92	171.9
Alabama	45	484	299	0.48	39,236	37,589	(D)	525.4	543.8	0.73	(D)
Michigan	110	910	530	0.91	39,069	35,425	77.4	553.5	512.9	0.73	87.9
Ohio	242	2,132	1,271	2.13	34,383	31,245	103.1	558.9	525.0	0.71	137.0
Mississippi	128	704	434	0.70	40,531	37,668	110.0	302.0	337.3	0.45	74.8
Montana	89	900	343	0.90	41,744	35,609	75.0	247.3	253.3	0.34	68.9
Illinois	200	906	598	0.90	23,857	21,933	(D)	133.1	162.7	0.22	(D)
New York	55	311	199	0.31	33,277	31,879	17.4	49.1	57.7	0.08	8.8
Indiana	60	265	148	0.26	31,649	17,804	13.0	41.2	49.4	0.07	4.8
Nebraska	30	147	98	0.15	31,027	27,347	8.0	27.3	30.0	0.04	5.3
Tennessee	15	103	63	0.10	29,495	25,587	(D)	16.0	19.2	0.03	(D)
West Virginia	223	1,750*	(D)	1.74	-	(D)	(D)	(D)	(D)	-	(D)
Pennsylvania	133	1,750*	(D)	1.74	-	(D)	(D)	(D)	(D)	-	(D)
Arkansas	120	750*	(D)	0.75	-	(D)	(D)	(D)	(D)	-	(D)
Kentucky	95	750*	(D)	0.75	-	(D)	(D)	(D)	(D)	-	(D)
Virginia	21	175*	(D)	0.17	-	(D)	(D)	(D)	(D)	-	(D)
Alaska	19	1,750*	(D)	1.74	-	(D)	(D)	(D)	(D)	-	(D)

Source: Economic Census of the U.S., 1997. Data are sorted by 1997 revenues or establishments. (D) means data suppression to prevent disclosure of company data. A dash (-) is used when data are unavailable or cannot be calculated. Data followed by an * indicate the midpoint of a range. The ranges are: for 10, 0-19; for 60, 20-99, for 175, 100-249, for 375, 250-499, for 750, 500-999. Higher values are multiples of those shown, e.g., 3,750 is the midpoint of the range 2,500-4,999. Shaded *states* indicate states in which the industry was active in 1997. Shaded *regions* indicate where the industry is regionally most concentrated.

NAICS 211112 - NATURAL GAS LIQUID EXTRACTION*

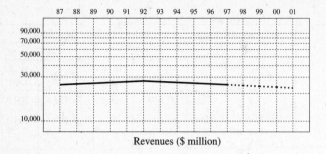

Revenues ($ million)

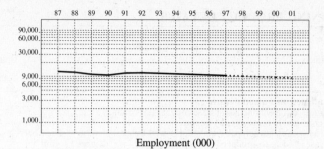

Employment (000)

GENERAL STATISTICS

| Year | Com-panies | Establishments | | Employment | | | Compensation | | Production ($ million) | | | |
		Total	with 20 or more employees	Total (No.)	Production Workers (No.)	Hours (Mil)	Payroll ($ mil)	Wages ($/hr)	Cost of Materials	Value Added by Mining	Value of Shipments	Capital Invest.
1977	100	692	209	13,000	10,600	21.2	227.3	8.39	14,491.8	3,286.3	17,449.1	328.9
1982	114	793	236	14,200	11,600	24.3	401.9	13.31	33,276.0	8,864.8	41,009.6	1,131.1
1987	97	714	210	12,700	9,700	20.2	433.0	15.84	21,107.4	4,024.9	24,749.5	382.7
1988	99	629[1]	210[1]	12,240[1]	9,513	19.8	445.2[1]	16.53	21,581.4	4,067.5	25,223.8	-
1989	101	583[1]	193[1]	11,053[1]	9,329	19.5	389.9[1]	17.25	22,066.0	4,110.5	25,707.2	-
1990	103	549[1]	189[1]	10,677[1]	9,150	19.1	405.8[1]	17.99	22,561.5	4,153.9	26,199.9	-
1991	106	548[1]	188[1]	11,836[1]	8,973	18.7	489.2[1]	18.77	23,068.1	4,197.8	26,702.1	-
1992	108	591	197	12,000	8,800	18.4	513.7	19.59	23,586.1	4,242.2	27,213.8	614.6
1993	104	579	190	11,710	8,814	18.5	519.3	20.52	22,940.8	4,423.3	26,736.7	-
1994	100	566	183	11,420	8,828	18.6	524.9	21.46	22,295.5	4,604.3	26,259.7	-
1995	97	554	177	11,129	8,842	18.6	530.4	22.39	21,650.1	4,785.4	25,782.6	-
1996	93	541	170	10,839	8,856	18.7	536.0	23.33	21,004.8	4,966.4	25,305.6	-
1997	89	529	163	10,549	8,870	18.8	541.6	24.26	20,359.5	5,147.5	24,828.5	678.5
1998	85p	517p	156p	10,259p	8,884p	18.9p	547.2p	25.19p	19,714.2p	5,328.6p	24,351.4p	-
1999	81p	504p	149p	9,969p	8,898p	19.0p	552.8p	26.13p	19,068.9p	5,509.6p	23,874.4p	-
2000	78p	492p	143p	9,678p	8,912p	19.0p	558.3p	27.06p	18,423.5p	5,690.7p	23,397.3p	-
2001	74p	479p	136p	9,388p	8,926p	19.1p	563.9p	28.00p	17,778.2p	5,871.7p	22,920.3p	-

Sources: *Economic Census of the United States*, 1977, 1982, 1987, 1992, and 1997. Data for those years (years are in **bold** type) are from the 5-year censuses of the economy. Other values, unless otherwise noted, are extrapolations. Values footnoted 1 are from the *County Business Patterns* for the years indicated. Values marked with *p* are projections. Data are the most recent available at this level of detail.

INDICES OF CHANGE

| Year | Com-panies | Establishments | | Employment | | | Compensation | | Production ($ million) | | | |
		Total	with 20 or more employees	Total (No.)	Production Workers (No.)	Hours (Mil)	Payroll ($ mil)	Wages ($/hr)	Cost of Materials	Value Added by Mining	Value of Shipments	Capital Invest.
1977	112.4	130.8	128.2	123.2	119.5	112.8	42.0	34.6	71.2	63.8	70.3	48.5
1982	128.1	149.9	144.8	134.6	130.8	129.3	74.2	54.9	163.4	172.2	165.2	166.7
1987	109.0	135.0	128.8	120.4	109.4	107.4	79.9	65.3	103.7	78.2	99.7	56.4
1992	121.3	111.7	120.9	113.8	99.2	97.9	94.8	80.8	115.8	82.4	109.6	90.6
1997	100.0	100.0	100.0	100.0	100.0	100.0	100.0	100.0	100.0	100.0	100.0	100.0

Sources: Same as General Statistics. The values shown reflect change from the base year, 1997. Values above 100 mean greater than 1997, values below 100 mean less than 1997, and a value of 100 in years other than 1997 means same as 1997. Indices are calculated only for Census years. Data are the most recent available at this level of detail.

SELECTED RATIOS

For 1992	Avg. of Sector	Analyzed Industry	Index	For 1992	Avg. of Sector	Analyzed Industry	Index
Employees per Establishment	20.4	19.9	98	Value Added per Production Worker	335,283	580,327	173
Payroll per Establishment	831,719	1,023,819	123	Cost per Establishment	2,854,087	38,486,767	1,348
Payroll per Employee	40,815	51,341	126	Cost per Employee	140,057	1,929,993	1,378
Production Workers per Establishment	15.6	16.8	107	Cost per Production Worker	183,057	2,295,321	1,254
Wages per Establishment	613,139	862,170	141	Shipments per Establishment	6,840,788	46,934,783	686
Wages per Production Worker	39,326	51,419	131	Shipments per Employee	335,695	2,353,635	701
Hours per Production Worker	2,075	2,120	102	Shipments per Production Worker	438,757	2,799,154	638
Wages per Hour	18.96	24.26	128	Investment per Establishment	1,242,441	1,282,609	103
Value Added per Establishment	5,227,487	9,730,624	186	Investment per Employee	60,970	64,319	105
Value Added per Employee	256,526	487,961	190	Investment per Production Worker	79,688	76,494	96

Sources: Same as General Statistics. The 'Average of Sector' column represents the average for all industries in this sector. The Index shows the relationship between the Average and the Analyzed Industry. For example, 100 means that they are equal; 500 that the Analyzed Industry is five times the average; 50 means that the Analyzed Industry is half the national average. 'na' is used to show that data are 'not available'.

*Equivalent to SIC 1321.

LEADING COMPANIES Number shown: 16   Total sales ($ mil): 22,935   Total employment (000): 15.1

Company Name	Address				CEO Name	Phone	Co. Type	Sales ($ mil)	Empl. (000)
Dynegy Inc.	PO Box 4777	Houston	TX	77210	Stephen W Bergstrom	713-507-6400	P	15,430	2.4
Union Pacific Resources Group	PO Box 7	Fort Worth	TX	76101	George Lindahl III	817-321-6000	P	1,728	2.9
Cabot Corp.	75 State St	Boston	MA	02109	Samuel Bodman	617-345-0100	P	1,648	4.8
Phillips Gas Co.	1300 Post Oak Blvd	Houston	TX	77056		713-297-6066	S	1,306	1.1-
Enterprise Products Partners L.P.	P O Box 4324	Houston	TX	77210	OS Andras	713-880-6500	R	739	0.5
Mitchell Energy & Development	2001 Timberloch Pl	The Woodlands	TX	77380	George P Mitchell	713-377-5500	P	701	0.9
Sonat Exploration Co.	P O Box 1513	Houston	TX	77251	Donald G Russell	713-940-4000	S	533	0.7
Energy Corporation of America	4643 S Ulster St	Denver	CO	80237	John Mork	303-694-2667	R	270*	0.7
Midgard Energy Corp.	P O Box 400	Amarillo	TX	79188		806-371-4555	D	241*	0.3
Sid Richardson Carbon	201 Main St	Fort Worth	TX	76102	John M Hogg	817-390-8600	R	144*	0.5
Aeropres Corp.	PO Box 78588	Shreveport	LA	71137		318-221-6282	R	63	0.2
Imperial Petroleum Inc.	100 Northwest 2nd	Evansville	IN	47708	Jeffrey T Wilson	812-424-7948	P	60	<0.1
Huffco Group Inc.	P O Box 4337	Houston	TX	77210	David A Trice	713-753-1000	R	27*	<0.1
Ecogas Corp.	3321 Beecaves Rd	Austin	TX	78746	Jerrel D Branson	512-347-1441	R	20	<0.1
Kentucky Hydrocarbon Co.	72 Maple Dr	Langley	KY	41645		606-285-3949	S	20*	<0.1
Yukon-Pacific Corp.	1049 W 5th Ave	Anchorage	AK	99501	Jeff B Lowenfels	907-265-3100	S	5*	<0.1

Source: Ward's Business Directory of U.S. Private and Public Companies, Volumes 1 and 2, 2000. The company type code used is as follows: P - Public, R - Private, S - Subsidiary, D - Division, J - Joint Venture, A - Affiliate, G - Group, N - Company type not reported. Sales are in millions of dollars, employees are in thousands. An asterisk (*) indicates an estimated sales volume. The symbol < stands for 'less than'. Company names and addresses are truncated, in some cases, to fit into the available space.

MINING PRODUCT DETAILS

Products	Units	Quantity of (000s)		Value of product shipments			
		Produc-tion 1997	Ship-ments 1997	1992		1997	
				($ mil)	% of total	($ mil)	% of total
Natural gas liquids		NA	NA	27,401.0	100.0	25,147.2	100.0
Isopentane and natural gasoline	mil bbl	69	69	1,580.3	5.8	1,244.2	4.9
Propane	mil bbl	167	166	2,470.2	9.0	2,458.4	9.8
Butane	mil bbl	101	101	2,157.3	7.9	1,893.2	7.5
Plant condensate from natural gas liquids plants	mil bbl	14	15	177.4	0.6	259.7	1.0
Ethane	mil bbl	199	199	1,662.6	6.1	1,738.9	6.9
Gas mixtures from natural gas liquids plants	mil bbl	27	27	225.8	0.8	423.5	1.7
Other natural gas liquids	mil bbl	87	87	1,137.4	4.2	1,166.3	4.6
Residue gas shipped from natural gas liquids plants	bil cu ft	NA	6,595	17,804.0	65.0	15,810.8	62.9
Natural gas liquids, nsk[1]		NA	NA	186.0	0.7	152.2	0.6

Source: Economic Census of the U.S., 1997. *Notes:* 1. Includes value for establishments that did not report detailed data and estimates for small companies (estimates were made from administrative-record data rather than collected from respondents). NA stands for not applicable. (D) means data are withheld to avoid disclosure of competitive information. (S) indicates that data did not meet publication standards. - means not available or zero.

LOCATION BY STATE AND REGIONAL CONCENTRATION

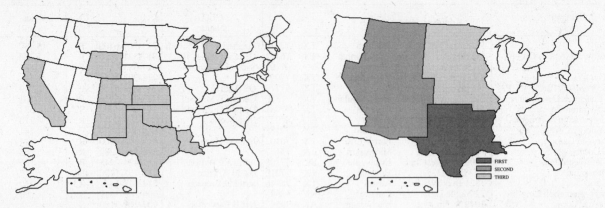

INDUSTRY DATA BY STATE

State	Estab lish- ments	Employment			Compensation		Production				Capital Exp. ($ mil)
		Total	Workers	Total as % of US	Payroll per Employee	Wages per Worker	Costs ($ mil)	Value Added ($ mil)	Reve- nues ($ mil)	% of US	
Texas	211	3,993	3,273	37.85	50,857	50,767	8,877.5	2,838.6	11,411.4	221.69	304.7
Louisiana	98	1,838	1,636	17.42	57,082	56,745	4,784.7	938.7	5,615.2	109.09	108.2
New Mexico	35	1,031	933	9.77	50,905	51,135	1,605.8	318.2	1,831.0	35.57	93.1
Oklahoma	56	961	750	9.11	46,698	48,796	1,325.0	320.8	1,615.8	31.39	30.0
Wyoming	37	791	735	7.50	47,527	47,461	1,138.2	129.8	1,210.6	23.52	57.4
Kansas	13	185	128	1.75	53,897	56,164	872.7	125.6	990.6	19.24	7.7
California	25	812	656	7.70	49,196	48,125	630.3	120.5	728.2	14.15	22.6
Colorado	15	287	236	2.72	56,955	56,725	374.6	90.3	451.7	8.78	13.3
Alabama	4	122	122	1.16	47,369	47,369	(D)	47.7	187.9	3.65	(D)
Michigan	5	138	96	1.31	60,080	57,250	85.1	52.2	134.5	2.61	2.8

Source: Economic Census of the U.S., 1997. Data are sorted by 1997 revenues or establishments. (D) means data suppression to prevent disclosure of company data. A dash (-) is used when data are unavailable or cannot be calculated. Data followed by an * indicate the midpoint of a range. The ranges are: for 10, 0-19; for 60, 20-99, for 175, 100-249, for 375, 250-499, for 750, 500-999. Higher values are multiples of those shown, e.g., 3,750 is the midpoint of the range 2,500-4,999. Shaded *states* indicate states in which the industry was active in 1997. Shaded *regions* indicate where the industry is regionally most concentrated.

NAICS 212111 - BITUMINOUS COAL AND LIGNITE SURFACE MINING*

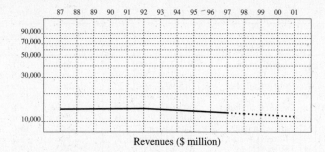

Revenues ($ million)

Employment (000)

GENERAL STATISTICS

Year	Companies	Establishments		Employment			Compensation		Production ($ million)			
		Total	with 20 or more employees	Total (No.)	Production Workers (No.)	Hours (Mil)	Payroll ($ mil)	Wages ($/hr)	Cost of Materials	Value Added by Mining	Value of Shipments	Capital Invest.
1977	-	-	-	-	-	-	-	-	-	-	-	-
1982	-	-	-	-	-	-	-	-	-	-	-	-
1987	1,367	1,804	612	63,800	48,000	99.5	2,204.0	15.88	6,460.3	7,893.7	13,617.5	736.4
1988	1,307	1,581[1]	574[1]	59,474[1]	46,735	97.7	2,043.2[1]	16.24	6,507.5	7,920.0	13,658.6	-
1989	1,250	1,305[1]	510[1]	53,673[1]	45,503	96.0	1,940.1[1]	16.62	6,555.0	7,946.3	13,699.9	-
1990	1,195	1,226[1]	509[1]	55,123[1]	44,304	94.2	2,105.1[1]	17.00	6,602.9	7,972.8	13,741.3	-
1991	1,142	1,169[1]	466[1]	51,468[1]	43,137	92.6	1,990.8[1]	17.39	6,651.1	7,999.3	13,782.8	-
1992	1,092	1,503	555	55,500	42,000	90.9	2,272.1	17.78	6,699.7	8,025.9	13,824.4	901.2
1993	996	1,369	518	51,700	39,668	85.7	2,147.2	18.31	6,547.0	7,869.9	13,542.7	-
1994	900	1,235	482	47,901	37,336	80.4	2,022.2	18.85	6,394.4	7,713.9	13,261.0	-
1995	803	1,102	445	44,101	35,003	75.2	1,897.3	19.38	6,241.7	7,557.9	12,979.4	-
1996	707	968	409	40,302	32,671	69.9	1,772.5	19.92	6,089.1	7,401.9	12,697.7	-
1997	611	834	372	36,502	30,339	64.7	1,647.4	20.45	5,936.4	7,245.9	12,416.0	766.3
1998	515p	700p	335p	32,702p	28,007p	59.5p	1,522.5p	20.98p	5,783.7p	7,089.9p	12,134.3p	-
1999	419p	566p	299p	28,903p	25,675p	54.2p	1,397.5p	21.52p	5,631.1p	6,933.9p	11,852.6p	-
2000	322p	433p	262p	25,103p	23,342p	49.0p	1,272.6p	22.05p	5,478.4p	6,777.9p	11,571.0p	-
2001	226p	299p	226p	21,304p	21,010p	43.7p	1,147.6p	22.59p	5,325.8p	6,621.9p	11,289.3p	-

Sources: Economic Census of the United States, 1977, 1982, 1987, 1992, and 1997. Data for those years (years are in **bold** type) are from the 5-year censuses of the economy. Other values, unless otherwise noted, are extrapolations. Values footnoted 1 are from the *County Business Patterns* for the years indicated. Values marked with *p* are projections. Data are the most recent available at this level of detail.

INDICES OF CHANGE

Year	Companies	Establishments		Employment			Compensation		Production ($ million)			
		Total	with 20 or more employees	Total (No.)	Production Workers (No.)	Hours (Mil)	Payroll ($ mil)	Wages ($/hr)	Cost of Materials	Value Added by Mining	Value of Shipments	Capital Invest.
1977	-	-	-	-	-	-	-	-	-	-	-	-
1982	-	-	-	-	-	-	-	-	-	-	-	-
1987	223.7	216.3	164.5	174.8	158.2	153.8	133.8	77.7	108.8	108.9	109.7	96.1
1992	178.7	180.2	149.2	152.0	138.4	140.5	137.9	86.9	112.9	110.8	111.3	117.6
1997	100.0	100.0	100.0	100.0	100.0	100.0	100.0	100.0	100.0	100.0	100.0	100.0

Sources: Same as General Statistics. The values shown reflect change from the base year, 1997. Values above 100 mean greater than 1997, values below 100 mean less than 1997, and a value of 100 in years other than 1997 means same as 1997. Indices are calculated only for Census years. Data are the most recent available at this level of detail.

SELECTED RATIOS

For 1992	Avg. of Sector	Analyzed Industry	Index	For 1992	Avg. of Sector	Analyzed Industry	Index
Employees per Establishment	20.4	43.8	215	Value Added per Production Worker	335,283	238,831	71
Payroll per Establishment	831,719	1,975,300	237	Cost per Establishment	2,854,087	7,117,986	249
Payroll per Employee	40,815	45,132	111	Cost per Employee	140,057	162,632	116
Production Workers per Establishment	15.6	36.4	233	Cost per Production Worker	183,057	195,669	107
Wages per Establishment	613,139	1,586,469	259	Shipments per Establishment	6,840,788	14,887,290	218
Wages per Production Worker	39,326	43,611	111	Shipments per Employee	335,695	340,146	101
Hours per Production Worker	2,075	2,133	103	Shipments per Production Worker	438,757	409,242	93
Wages per Hour	18.96	20.45	108	Investment per Establishment	1,242,441	918,825	74
Value Added per Establishment	5,227,487	8,688,129	166	Investment per Employee	60,970	20,993	34
Value Added per Employee	256,526	198,507	77	Investment per Production Worker	79,688	25,258	32

Sources: Same as General Statistics. The 'Average of Sector' column represents the average for all industries in this sector. The Index shows the relationship between the Average and the Analyzed Industry. For example, 100 means that they are equal; 500 that the Analyzed Industry is five times the average; 50 means that the Analyzed Industry is half the national average. 'na' is used to show that data are 'not available'.

*Equivalent to SIC 1221.

LEADING COMPANIES   Number shown: **43**   Total sales ($ mil): **73,925**   Total employment (000): **180.3**

Company Name	Address				CEO Name	Phone	Co. Type	Sales ($ mil)	Empl. (000)
PacifiCorp	700 N E Multnomah	Portland	OR	97232	Alan Richardson	503-731-2000	S	12,989	9.1
Fluor Corp.	1 Enterprise Dr	Aliso Viejo	CA	92656	Philip J Carroll Jr	949-349-2000	P	12,417	53.6
Sunoco Inc.	1801 Market St	Philadelphia	PA	19103	Robert Campbell	215-977-3000	P	10,068	0.0
Coastal Corp.	9 E Greenway Plz	Houston	TX	77046		713-877-1400	P	7,368	13.2
Cyprus Amax Coal Co.	9100 E Mineral Cir	Englewood	CO	80112	Gerald R Spindler	303-643-5100	S	3,199*	4.8
Kerr-McGee Corp.	PO Box 25861	Oklahoma City	OK	73125	Luke R Corbett	405-270-1313	P	2,696	3.4
NACCO Industries Inc.	5875 Landerbrook	Cleveland	OH	44124	Alfred Rankin	440-449-9600	P	2,603	13.6
Cyprus Amax Minerals Co.	P O Box 3299	Englewood	CO	80112	Milton H Ward	303-643-5000	P	2,566	7.2
CONSOL Inc.	1800 Washington Rd	Pittsburgh	PA	15241	J Brett Harvey	412-831-4000	S	2,327*	7.8
Peabody Group	701 Market St	St. Louis	MO	63101	Irl F Engelhardt	314-342-3400	S	2,224	6.9
TECO Energy Inc.	PO Box 111	Tampa	FL	33601	Robert D Fagan	813-228-4111	P	1,983	5.5
Arch Coal Inc.	CityPlace 1, #300	St. Louis	MO	63141	Steven F Leer	314-994-2700	P	1,600	4.4
Montana Power Co.	40 E Broadway	Butte	MT	59701	Robert P Gannon	406-723-5421	P	1,342	2.9
Berwind Corp.	3000 Center Sq W	Philadelphia	PA	19102	Edward Kosmik	215-563-2800	R	1,156	4.8
CONSOL Energy Inc.	1800 Washington	Pittsburgh	PA	15201	J Brett Harvey	412-831-4000	P	1,111	8.6
A.T. Massey Coal Company Inc.	P O Box 26765	Richmond	VA	23261	Don L Blankenship	804-788-1800	S	1,100	3.1
Mueller Industries Inc.	PO Box 382100	Germantown	TN	38183	Harvey Karp	901-753-3200	P	929	2.3
ANR Coal Company L.L.C.	PO Box 1871	Roanoke	VA	24008		540-983-0222	S	854*	0.8
Drummond Company Inc.	PO Box 10246	Birmingham	AL	35202	Gary Drummond	205-945-6500	R	739*	2.8
Tredegar Industries Inc.	1100 Boulders Pkwy	Chesterfield	VA	23832	John D Gottwald	804-330-1000	P	700	3.4
Black Hills Corp.	PO Box 1400	Rapid City	SD	57709	Daniel P Landguth	605-348-1700	P	559*	0.5
Pittston Minerals Group	PO Box 4229	Glen Allen	VA	23058	Karl K Kindig	540-889-6000	P	519	1.8
MAPCO Coal Inc.	PO Box 22027	Tulsa	OK	74121	Joseph Craft	918-586-4380	R	472*	1.4
Pittsburg & Midway Coal Mining	PO Box 6518	Englewood	CO	80155		303-930-4115	S	400*	1.5
Kerr-McGee Chemicl Corp.	PO Box 25861	Oklahoma City	OK	73125	Luke R Corbet	405-270-1313	S	317	1.0
Oglebay Norton Co.	1100 Superior Ave E	Cleveland	OH	44114	John N Lauer	216-861-3300	P	294	1.8
Coal Properties Corp.	P O Box 1233	Charleston	WV	25324	HDouglas Dahl	304-340-1700	S	266*	1.0
North American Coal Corp.	14785 Preston Rd	Dallas	TX	75240	Cliff Miercort	972-239-2625	S	259*	1.0
Exxon Coal and Minerals Co.	2401 S Gessner Rd	Houston	TX	77063	Lee R Raymond	713-978-5333	S	177	7.4
Amvest Corp.	PO Box 5347	Charlottesville	VA	22905		804-977-3350	R	133*	0.8
Bridger Coal Co.	PO Box 2068	Rock Springs	WY	82902		307-382-9741	S	97*	0.4
Gatliff Coal Co.	PO Box 39	Nevisdale	KY	40754		606-549-5452	S	85*	0.3
Solar Sources Inc.	PO Box 47068	Indianapolis	IN	46247		317-788-0084	R	85	0.3
Peabody Coal Co.	P O Box 1990	Henderson	KY	42420	H Douglas Dahl	502-827-0800	S	79*	2.1
Falkirk Mining Co.	P O Box 1087	Underwood	ND	58576	Dan W Swetich	701-442-5751	S	60	0.2
Phoenix Cement Co.	PO Box 43740	Phoenix	AZ	85080		602-264-0511	R	50*	0.2
Usibelli Coal Mine Inc.	P O Box 1000	Healy	AK	99743	Joseph E Usibelli Jr	907-683-2226	R	35	0.1
Wyodak Resources Development	13126 State Hwy 51	Gillette	WY	82718		307-682-3410	S	31*	<0.1
Cravat Coal Company Inc.	40580 Cadiz Pied	Cadiz	OH	43907	Michael Puskarich	740-942-4656	R	13*	<0.1
Red River Mining	PO Box 741	Coushatta	LA	71019		318-932-6721	R	11	<0.1
Reitz Coal Co.	509 15th St	Windber	PA	15963	Anthony Sossong	814-467-4519	S	7*	<0.1
GeoResources Inc.	PO Box 1505	Williston	ND	58802	Jeffrey P Vickers	701-572-2020	P	2	<0.1
Phillips Coal Co.	2929 N Central	Richardson	TX	75080	Paul M Thompson	972-669-1200	S	2	<0.1

Source: *Ward's Business Directory of U.S. Private and Public Companies*, Volumes 1 and 2, 2000. The company type code used is as follows: P - Public, R - Private, S - Subsidiary, D - Division, J - Joint Venture, A - Affiliate, G - Group, N - Company type not reported. Sales are in millions of dollars, employees are in thousands. An asterisk (*) indicates an estimated sales volume. The symbol < stands for 'less than'. Company names and addresses are truncated, in some cases, to fit into the available space.

MINING PRODUCT DETAILS

Products	Units	Quantity of (000s)		Value of product shipments			
		Produc-tion 1997	Ship-ments 1997	1992		1997	
				($ mil)	% of total	($ mil)	% of total
Bituminous coal and lignite from surface operations[1]		NA	NA	13,689.5	100.0	12,303.3	100.0
Run-of-mine (raw) bituminous coal and lignite shipped from surface mining operations, for use without processing	mil s tons	NA	23	644.5	4.7	502.3	4.1
Run-of-mine (raw) bituminous coal and lignite shipped from surface mining operations, for processing at other establishments	mil s tons	NA	68	1,172.0	8.6	1,106.9	9.0
Processed bituminous coal and lignite shipped from surface operations, washed by wet-washing, pneumatic, or other methods	mil s tons	NA	182	5,350.2	39.1	4,811.2	39.1
Processed bituminous coal shipped from surface operations (mechanically crushed, screened, or sized only)	mil s tons	NA	114	2,601.3	19.0	2,671.5	21.7
Processed subbituminous coal shipped from surface operations (mechanically crushed, screened, or sized only)	mil s tons	NA	308	2,083.2	15.2	1,888.2	15.3
Processed lignite coal shipped from surface operations (mechanically crushed, screened, or sized only)	mil s tons	NA	81	797.0	5.8	847.0	6.9
Bituminous coal and lignite surface mining, nsk[2]		NA	NA	1,041.2	7.6	476.3	3.9

Source: Economic Census of the U.S., 1997. *Notes*: 1. Value of net shipments for 1997 is 9,258,892 thousand dollars. In 1992 it was 9,848,180 thousand dollars. Net shipments represent gross shipments excluding coal not specified by kind and less coal recieved for preparation. 2. Represents value for establishments that did not report detailed data. NA stands for not applicable. (D) means data are withheld to avoid disclosure of competitive information. (S) indicates that data did not meet publication standards. - means not available or zero.

LOCATION BY STATE AND REGIONAL CONCENTRATION

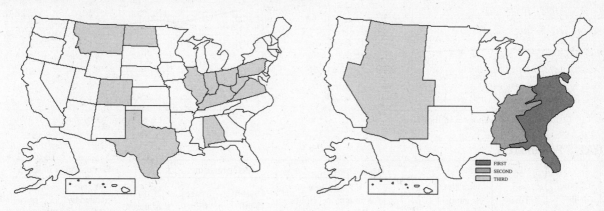

INDUSTRY DATA BY STATE

State	Estab lish- ments	Employment			Compensation		Production				Capital Exp. ($ mil)
		Total	Workers	Total as % of US	Payroll per Employee	Wages per Worker	Costs ($ mil)	Value Added ($ mil)	Reve- nues ($ mil)	% of US	
West Virginia	151	5,771	5,005	15.81	45,855	45,136	1,411.8	1,223.7	2,489.0	34.35	146.5
Kentucky	170	6,365	5,551	17.44	37,058	36,729	1,364.5	1,083.1	2,321.3	32.04	126.3
Pennsylvania	178	3,392	2,843	9.29	31,634	31,574	595.4	415.2	949.1	13.10	61.6
Virginia	61	1,830	1,619	5.01	39,133	39,503	482.6	278.1	724.3	10.00	36.4
New Mexico	5	1,633	1,178	4.47	56,604	52,345	(D)	549.7	672.4	9.28	(D)
Texas	10	2,600	1,713	7.12	53,735	50,079	253.3	378.9	621.3	8.57	11.0
Montana	8	860	670	2.36	47,516	45,307	112.4	361.5	460.9	6.36	13.0
Indiana	31	1,873	1,678	5.13	52,043	51,318	192.3	319.1	460.7	6.36	50.6
Ohio	65	1,711	1,356	4.69	39,295	38,466	157.4	269.6	390.7	5.39	36.3
Illinois	18	963	772	2.64	50,374	47,030	255.2	125.9	368.3	5.08	12.9
Alabama	46	1,573	1,329	4.31	38,879	38,995	132.4	235.6	348.7	4.81	19.3
North Dakota	9	992	795	2.72	56,339	55,019	61.3	193.9	235.9	3.26	19.3
Colorado	7	658	551	1.80	52,974	50,630	57.2	100.0	145.5	2.01	11.7
Tennessee	15	429	351	1.18	30,688	26,795	(D)	49.3	90.1	1.24	(D)
Wyoming	25	3,750*	(D)	10.27	-	(D)	(D)	(D)	(D)	-	(D)
Maryland	12	175*	(D)	0.48	-	(D)	(D)	(D)	(D)	-	(D)
Oklahoma	8	375*	(D)	1.03	-	(D)	(D)	(D)	(D)	-	(D)
Arizona	2	750*	(D)	2.05	-	(D)	(D)	(D)	(D)	-	(D)
Louisiana	2	175*	(D)	0.48	-	(D)	(D)	(D)	(D)	-	(D)
Washington	2	750*	(D)	2.05	-	(D)	(D)	(D)	(D)	-	(D)
Alaska	1	175*	(D)	0.48	-	(D)	(D)	(D)	(D)	-	(D)

Source: *Economic Census of the U.S., 1997*. Data are sorted by 1997 revenues or establishments. (D) means data suppression to prevent disclosure of company data. A dash (-) is used when data are unavailable or cannot be calculated. Data followed by an * indicate the midpoint of a range. The ranges are: for 10, 0-19; for 60, 20-99, for 175, 100-249, for 375, 250-499, for 750, 500-999. Higher values are multiples of those shown, e.g., 3,750 is the midpoint of the range 2,500-4,999. Shaded *states* indicate states in which the industry was active in 1997. Shaded *regions* indicate where the industry is regionally most concentrated.

NAICS 212112 - BITUMINOUS COAL UNDERGROUND MINING*

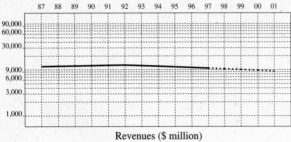

Revenues ($ million)

Employment (000)

GENERAL STATISTICS

Year	Com-panies	Establishments		Employment			Compensation		Production ($ million)			
		Total	with 20 or more employees	Total (No.)	Production Workers (No.)	Hours (Mil)	Payroll ($ mil)	Wages ($/hr)	Cost of Materials	Value Added by Mining	Value of Shipments	Capital Invest.
1977	-	-	-	-	-	-	-	-	-	-	-	-
1982	-	-	-	-	-	-	-	-	-	-	-	-
1987	1,302	1,703	723	93,700	75,800	149.9	3,206.1	16.98	3,821.8	8,785.2	11,729.3	877.7
1988	1,179	1,489[1]	661[1]	86,831[1]	72,672	144.8	3,063.3[1]	17.44	4,011.9	8,777.9	11,900.2	-
1989	1,067	1,132[1]	571[1]	78,768[1]	69,674	139.8	2,882.2[1]	17.91	4,211.4	8,770.7	12,073.6	-
1990	966	1,016[1]	517[1]	73,190[1]	66,799	135.1	2,902.4[1]	18.40	4,420.8	8,763.4	12,249.5	-
1991	875	920[1]	476[1]	68,585[1]	64,043	130.5	2,684.7[1]	18.90	4,640.7	8,756.1	12,428.0	-
1992	792	1,133	600	73,000	61,400	126.0	3,011.5	19.41	4,871.5	8,748.9	12,609.1	1,011.2
1993	726	1,029	555	68,439	57,946	119.1	2,868.2	19.80	4,661.9	8,635.8	12,244.0	-
1994	660	925	510	63,879	54,492	112.2	2,724.9	20.19	4,452.4	8,522.7	11,878.8	-
1995	594	822	465	59,318	51,038	105.4	2,581.7	20.57	4,242.8	8,409.5	11,513.7	-
1996	528	718	420	54,758	47,584	98.5	2,438.4	20.96	4,033.3	8,296.4	11,148.5	-
1997	462	614	375	50,197	44,130	91.6	2,295.1	21.35	3,823.7	8,183.3	10,783.4	1,223.6
1998	396p	510p	330p	45,636p	40,676p	84.7p	2,151.8p	21.74p	3,614.1p	8,070.2p	10,418.3p	-
1999	330p	406p	285p	41,076p	37,222p	77.8p	2,008.5p	22.13p	3,404.6p	7,957.1p	10,053.1p	-
2000	264p	303p	240p	36,515p	33,768p	71.0p	1,865.3p	22.51p	3,195.0p	7,843.9p	9,688.0p	-
2001	198p	199p	195p	31,955p	30,314p	64.1p	1,722.0p	22.90p	2,985.5p	7,730.8p	9,322.8p	-

Sources: Economic Census of the United States, 1977, 1982, 1987, 1992, and 1997. Data for those years (years are in bold type) are from the 5-year censuses of the economy. Other values, unless otherwise noted, are extrapolations. Values footnoted 1 are from the County Business Patterns for the years indicated. Values marked with p are projections. Data are the most recent available at this level of detail.

INDICES OF CHANGE

Year	Com-panies	Establishments		Employment			Compensation		Production ($ million)			
		Total	with 20 or more employees	Total (No.)	Production Workers (No.)	Hours (Mil)	Payroll ($ mil)	Wages ($/hr)	Cost of Materials	Value Added by Mining	Value of Shipments	Capital Invest.
1977	-	-	-	-	-	-	-	-	-	-	-	-
1982	-	-	-	-	-	-	-	-	-	-	-	-
1987	281.8	277.4	192.8	186.7	171.8	163.6	139.7	79.5	100.0	107.4	108.8	71.7
1992	171.4	184.5	160.0	145.4	139.1	137.6	131.2	90.9	127.4	106.9	116.9	82.6
1997	100.0	100.0	100.0	100.0	100.0	100.0	100.0	100.0	100.0	100.0	100.0	100.0

Sources: Same as General Statistics. The values shown reflect change from the base year, 1997. Values above 100 mean greater than 1997, values below 100 mean less than 1997, and a value of 100 in years other than 1997 means same as 1997. Indices are calculated only for Census years. Data are the most recent available at this level of detail.

SELECTED RATIOS

For 1992	Avg. of Sector	Analyzed Industry	Index	For 1992	Avg. of Sector	Analyzed Industry	Index
Employees per Establishment	20.4	81.8	401	Value Added per Production Worker	335,283	185,436	55
Payroll per Establishment	831,719	3,737,948	449	Cost per Establishment	2,854,087	6,227,524	218
Payroll per Employee	40,815	45,722	112	Cost per Employee	140,057	76,174	54
Production Workers per Establishment	15.6	71.9	461	Cost per Production Worker	183,057	86,646	47
Wages per Establishment	613,139	3,185,114	519	Shipments per Establishment	6,840,788	17,562,541	257
Wages per Production Worker	39,326	44,316	113	Shipments per Employee	335,695	214,822	64
Hours per Production Worker	2,075	2,076	100	Shipments per Production Worker	438,757	244,355	56
Wages per Hour	18.96	21.35	113	Investment per Establishment	1,242,441	1,992,834	160
Value Added per Establishment	5,227,487	13,327,850	255	Investment per Employee	60,970	24,376	40
Value Added per Employee	256,526	163,024	64	Investment per Production Worker	79,688	27,727	35

Sources: Same as General Statistics. The 'Average of Sector' column represents the average for all industries in this sector. The Index shows the relationship between the Average and the Analyzed Industry. For example, 100 means that they are equal; 500 that the Analyzed Industry is five times the average; 50 means that the Analyzed Industry is half the national average. 'na' is used to show that data are 'not available'.

*Equivalent to SIC 1222.

LEADING COMPANIES   Number shown: **23**   Total sales ($ mil): **18,389**   Total employment (000): **95.0**

Company Name	Address				CEO Name	Phone	Co. Type	Sales ($ mil)	Empl. (000)
Pittston Co.	PO Box 4229	Glen Allen	VA	23058	Michael T Dan	804-553-3600	R	3,747	41.0
Cyprus Amax Minerals Co.	P O Box 3299	Englewood	CO	80112	Milton H Ward	303-643-5000	P	2,566	7.2
CONSOL Inc.	1800 Washington Rd	Pittsburgh	PA	15241	J Brett Harvey	412-831-4000	S	2,327*	7.8
Peabody Group	701 Market St	St. Louis	MO	63101	Irl F Engelhardt	314-342-3400	S	2,224	6.9
Walter Industries Inc.	PO Box 31601	Tampa	FL	33631	Kenneth Hyatt	813-871-4811	P	1,618	7.7
CONSOL Energy Inc.	1800 Washington	Pittsburgh	PA	15201	J Brett Harvey	412-831-4000	P	1,111	8.6
ANR Coal Company L.L.C.	PO Box 1871	Roanoke	VA	24008		540-983-0222	S	854*	0.8
Zeigler Coal Holding Co.	50 Jerome Ln	Fairview H.	IL	62208	Chand B Vyas	618-394-2400	P	801	2.2
Drummond Company Inc.	PO Box 10246	Birmingham	AL	35202	Gary Drummond	205-945-6500	R	739*	2.8
Pittston Minerals Group	PO Box 4229	Glen Allen	VA	23058	Karl K Kindig	540-889-6000	P	519	1.8
MAPCO Coal Inc.	PO Box 22027	Tulsa	OK	74121	Joseph Craft	918-586-4380	R	472*	1.4
Pittsburg & Midway Coal Mining	PO Box 6518	Englewood	CO	80155		303-930-4115	S	400*	1.5
U.S. Steel Mining Company Inc.	600 Grant St	Pittsburgh	PA	15219	Paul J Wilhelm	412-433-1121	S	324*	1.2
Kerr-McGee Chemicl Corp.	PO Box 25861	Oklahoma City	OK	73125	Luke R Corbet	405-270-1313	S	317	1.0
Westmoreland Coal Co.	2 N Cascade Ave	Co Springs	CO	80903	Christopher K Seglem	719-442-2600	P	109	<0.1
Solar Sources Inc.	PO Box 47068	Indianapolis	IN	46247		317-788-0084	R	85	0.3
Peabody Coal Co.	P O Box 1990	Henderson	KY	42420	H Douglas Dahl	502-827-0800	S	79*	2.1
Progress Capital Holdings Inc.	1 Progress Plz	St. Petersburg	FL	33701	Darryl A LeClair	813-824-6400	S	44	0.2
McCoy Elkhorn Coal Corp.	1148 Long Fork Rd	Kimper	KY	41539		606-835-2233	S	39	0.2
Washington Corporations	P O Box 16630	Missoula	MT	59808	Mike Haizht	406-523-1300	R	12*	0.1
Cyprus Shoshone Coal Corp.	PO Box 830	Hanna	WY	82327		307-325-9471	S	2	<0.1
Double Eagle Petroleum	PO Box 766	Casper	WY	82601	Stephen H Hollis	307-237-9330	P	1	<0.1
Wesco Resources Inc.	PO Box 1181	Billings	MT	59103	Mike Gustafson	406-252-5695	R	1	<0.1

Source: *Ward's Business Directory of U.S. Private and Public Companies*, Volumes 1 and 2, 2000. The company type code used is as follows: P - Public, R - Private, S - Subsidiary, D - Division, J - Joint Venture, A - Affiliate, G - Group, N - Company type not reported. Sales are in millions of dollars, employees are in thousands. An asterisk (*) indicates an estimated sales volume. The symbol < stands for 'less than'. Company names and addresses are truncated, in some cases, to fit into the available space.

MINING PRODUCT DETAILS

Products	Units	Quantity of (000s)		Value of product shipments				
		Produc-tion 1997	Ship-ments 1997	1992			1997	
				($ mil)	% of total		($ mil)	% of total
Bituminous coal from underground operations[1]		NA	NA	12,451.8	100.0		10,703.8	100.0
Run-of-mine (raw) bituminous coal shipped from underground mining operations, for use without processing	mil s tons	NA	8	318.5	2.6		159.9	1.5
Run-of-mine (raw) bituminous coal shipped from underground mining operations, for processing at other establishments	mil s tons	NA	138	2,730.7	21.9		2,036.8	19.0
Processed bituminous coal shipped from underground mining operations, washed by wet-washing, pneumatic, or other methods	mil s tons	NA	261	7,892.7	63.4		7,296.4	68.2
Processed bituminous coal shipped from underground mining operations (mechanically crushed, screened, or sized only)	mil s tons	NA	46	998.1	8.0		872.2	8.1
Bituminous coal underground mining, nsk[2]		NA	NA	511.7	4.1		338.5	3.2

Source: Economic Census of the U.S., 1997. *Notes*: 1. Value of net shipments for 1997 is 10,088,405 thousand dollars. In 1992 it was 11,434,443 thousand dollars. Net shipments represent gross shipments excluding coal not specified by kind and less coal recieved for preparation. 2. Represents value for establishments that did not report detailed data. NA stands for not applicable. (D) means data are withheld to avoid disclosure of competitive information. (S) indicates that data did not meet publication standards. - means not available or zero.

LOCATION BY STATE AND REGIONAL CONCENTRATION

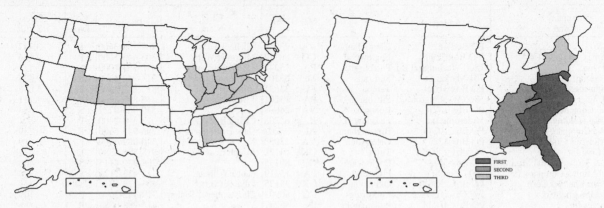

INDUSTRY DATA BY STATE

State	Estab lish- ments	Employment			Compensation		Production				Capital Exp. ($ mil)
		Total	Workers	Total as % of US	Payroll per Employee	Wages per Worker	Costs ($ mil)	Value Added ($ mil)	Reve- nues ($ mil)	% of US	
West Virginia	152	12,581	11,248	25.06	47,708	46,485	1,187.4	2,256.9	3,066.3	37.47	378.1
Kentucky	183	11,148	10,087	22.21	40,334	39,822	845.4	1,671.8	2,308.2	28.21	209.0
Pennsylvania	45	5,526	4,839	11.01	51,390	50,126	429.5	1,035.7	1,311.5	16.03	153.7
Virginia	146	5,866	5,104	11.69	38,432	36,954	408.8	677.2	1,018.4	12.44	67.6
Alabama	12	3,790	3,150	7.55	50,934	48,778	148.8	634.3	728.4	8.90	54.6
Illinois	18	3,950	3,459	7.87	47,072	45,244	230.9	544.6	723.5	8.84	51.9
Utah	19	2,611	2,244	5.20	47,997	46,415	208.7	596.7	610.3	7.46	195.1
Ohio	7	1,889	1,472	3.76	54,680	50,414	175.7	306.6	434.6	5.31	47.7
Colorado	9	844	670	1.68	60,325	59,804	79.6	201.3	235.5	2.88	45.4
Indiana	7	1,106	989	2.20	37,119	38,333	69.4	130.2	188.7	2.31	10.8
Tennessee	10	375*	(D)	0.75	-	(D)	(D)	(D)	(D)	-	(D)
Oklahoma	3	175*	(D)	0.35	-	(D)	(D)	(D)	(D)	-	(D)
Maryland	1	375*	(D)	0.75	-	(D)	(D)	(D)	(D)	-	(D)
Wyoming	1	175*	(D)	0.35	-	(D)	(D)	(D)	(D)	-	(D)

Source: *Economic Census of the U.S., 1997*. Data are sorted by 1997 revenues or establishments. (D) means data suppression to prevent disclosure of company data. A dash (-) is used when data are unavailable or cannot be calculated. Data followed by an * indicate the midpoint of a range. The ranges are: for 10, 0-19; for 60, 20-99, for 175, 100-249, for 375, 250-499, for 750, 500-999. Higher values are multiples of those shown, e.g., 3,750 is the midpoint of the range 2,500-4,999. Shaded *states* indicate states in which the industry was active in 1997. Shaded *regions* indicate where the industry is regionally most concentrated.

NAICS 212113 - ANTHRACITE MINING*

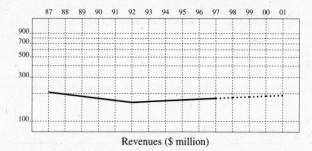

Revenues ($ million)

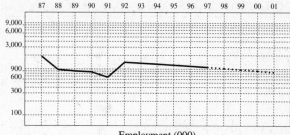

Employment (000)

GENERAL STATISTICS

Year	Companies	Establishments		Employment			Compensation		Production ($ million)			
		Total	with 20 or more employees	Total (No.)	Production Workers (No.)	Hours (Mil)	Payroll ($ mil)	Wages ($/hr)	Cost of Materials	Value Added by Mining	Value of Shipments	Capital Invest.
1977	127	156	38	3,300	2,700	5.4	47.5	7.04	109.8	116.0	217.0	8.8
1982	128	152	40	3,400	2,900	5.5	66.9	10.13	137.7	171.7	286.6	22.9
1987	88	107	26	1,900	1,600	2.9	41.2	11.17	109.0	109.4	206.3	12.1
1988	83	25[1]	10[1]	973[1]	1,484	2.7	22.8[1]	11.61	99.0	106.8	196.2	-
1989	77	23[1]	10[1]	901[1]	1,377	2.6	19.3[1]	12.07	89.9	104.3	186.5	-
1990	73	27[1]	11[1]	867[1]	1,278	2.5	23.7[1]	12.54	81.6	101.9	177.4	-
1991	68	29[1]	9[1]	664[1]	1,186	2.3	16.8[1]	13.03	74.1	99.5	168.7	-
1992	64	76	18	1,400	1,100	2.2	38.6	13.55	67.3	97.2	160.4	4.1
1993	63	74	17	1,339	1,057	2.1	37.8	13.90	77.2	97.1	163.9	-
1994	61	73	16	1,278	1,014	2.0	37.0	14.25	87.1	97.0	167.4	-
1995	60	71	16	1,216	972	1.9	36.3	14.61	97.0	96.8	170.8	-
1996	58	70	15	1,155	929	1.8	35.5	14.96	106.9	96.7	174.3	-
1997	57	68	14	1,094	886	1.7	34.7	15.31	116.8	96.6	177.8	35.7
1998	56p	66p	13p	1,033p	843p	1.6p	33.9p	15.66p	126.7p	96.5p	181.3p	-
1999	54p	65p	12p	972p	800p	1.5p	33.1p	16.01p	136.6p	96.4p	184.8p	-
2000	53p	63p	12p	910p	758p	1.4p	32.4p	16.37p	146.5p	96.2p	188.2p	-
2001	51p	62p	11p	849p	715p	1.3p	31.6p	16.72p	156.4p	96.1p	191.7p	-

Sources: *Economic Census of the United States*, 1977, 1982, 1987, 1992, and 1997. Data for those years (years are in **bold** type) are from the 5-year censuses of the economy. Other values, unless otherwise noted, are extrapolations. Values footnoted 1 are from the *County Business Patterns* for the years indicated. Values marked with *p* are projections. Data are the most recent available at this level of detail.

INDICES OF CHANGE

Year	Companies	Establishments		Employment			Compensation		Production ($ million)			
		Total	with 20 or more employees	Total (No.)	Production Workers (No.)	Hours (Mil)	Payroll ($ mil)	Wages ($/hr)	Cost of Materials	Value Added by Mining	Value of Shipments	Capital Invest.
1977	222.8	229.4	271.4	301.6	304.7	317.6	136.9	46.0	94.0	120.1	122.0	24.6
1982	224.6	223.5	285.7	310.8	327.3	323.5	192.8	66.2	117.9	177.7	161.2	64.1
1987	154.4	157.4	185.7	173.7	180.6	170.6	118.7	73.0	93.3	113.3	116.0	33.9
1992	112.3	111.8	128.6	128.0	124.2	129.4	111.2	88.5	57.6	100.6	90.2	11.5
1997	100.0	100.0	100.0	100.0	100.0	100.0	100.0	100.0	100.0	100.0	100.0	100.0

Sources: Same as General Statistics. The values shown reflect change from the base year, 1997. Values above 100 mean greater than 1997, values below 100 mean less than 1997, and a value of 100 in years other than 1997 means same as 1997. Indices are calculated only for Census years. Data are the most recent available at this level of detail.

SELECTED RATIOS

For 1992	Avg. of Sector	Analyzed Industry	Index	For 1992	Avg. of Sector	Analyzed Industry	Index
Employees per Establishment	20.4	16.1	79	Value Added per Production Worker	335,283	109,029	33
Payroll per Establishment	831,719	510,294	61	Cost per Establishment	2,854,087	1,717,647	60
Payroll per Employee	40,815	31,718	78	Cost per Employee	140,057	106,764	76
Production Workers per Establishment	15.6	13.0	84	Cost per Production Worker	183,057	131,828	72
Wages per Establishment	613,139	382,750	62	Shipments per Establishment	6,840,788	2,614,706	38
Wages per Production Worker	39,326	29,376	75	Shipments per Employee	335,695	162,523	48
Hours per Production Worker	2,075	1,919	92	Shipments per Production Worker	438,757	200,677	46
Wages per Hour	18.96	15.31	81	Investment per Establishment	1,242,441	525,000	42
Value Added per Establishment	5,227,487	1,420,588	27	Investment per Employee	60,970	32,633	54
Value Added per Employee	256,526	88,300	34	Investment per Production Worker	79,688	40,293	51

Sources: Same as General Statistics. The 'Average of Sector' column represents the average for all industries in this sector. The Index shows the relationship between the Average and the Analyzed Industry. For example, 100 means that they are equal; 500 that the Analyzed Industry is five times the average; 50 means that the Analyzed Industry is half the national average. 'na' is used to show that data are 'not available'.

*Equivalent to SIC 1231.

LEADING COMPANIES   Number shown: **1**   Total sales ($ mil): **30**   Total employment (000): **0.3**

Company Name	Address				CEO Name	Phone	Co. Type	Sales ($ mil)	Empl. (000)
Reading Anthracite Co.	PO Box 1200	Pottsville	PA	17901		717-622-5150	R	30	0.3

Source: Ward's Business Directory of U.S. Private and Public Companies, Volumes 1 and 2, 2000. The company type code used is as follows: P - Public, R - Private, S - Subsidiary, D - Division, J - Joint Venture, A - Affiliate, G - Group, N - Company type not reported. Sales are in millions of dollars, employees are in thousands. An asterisk (*) indicates an estimated sales volume. The symbol < stands for 'less than'. Company names and addresses are truncated, in some cases, to fit into the available space.

MINING PRODUCT DETAILS

Products	Units	Quantity of (000s)		Value of product shipments			
		Production 1997	Ship-ments 1997	1992 ($ mil)	1992 % of total	1997 ($ mil)	1997 % of total
Anthracite[1]		NA	NA	150.9	100.0	169.6	100.0
Run-of-mine (raw) anthracite shipped for use without processing	1,000 s tons	NA	442	-	-	7.4	4.4
Run-of-mine (raw) anthracite shipped for processing at other establishments[2]	1,000 s tons	NA	2,243	20.3	13.5	43.5	25.6
Processed anthracite, washed by wet-washing, pneumatic, or other methods	1,000 s tons	NA	1,345	111.0	73.5	89.8	53.0
Processed anthracite (mechanically crushed, screened, or sized only)	1,000 s tons	NA	508	6.1	4.1	16.7	9.8
Anthracite mining, nsk[3]		NA	NA	13.5	8.9	12.2	7.2

Source: Economic Census of the U.S., 1997. *Notes:* 1. Quantity and value of net shipments in 1997 are 2,294.5 thousand short tons and 113.9 million dollars. In 1992 they were 1,890.4 thousand short tons and 117.1 million dollars. Net shipments represent raw coal for use without preparation plus prepared coal. 2. Includes estimates for small companies (estimates were made from administrative-record data rather than collected from respondents). 3. Represents value for establishments that did not report detailed data. NA stands for not applicable. (D) means data are withheld to avoid disclosure of competitive information. (S) indicates that data did not meet publication standards. - means not available or zero.

LOCATION BY STATE AND REGIONAL CONCENTRATION

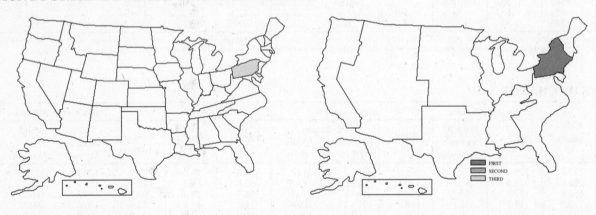

FIRST
SECOND
THIRD

INDUSTRY DATA BY STATE

State	Estab-lish-ments	Employment			Compensation		Production				Capital Exp. ($ mil)
		Total	Workers	Total as % of US	Payroll per Employee	Wages per Worker	Costs ($ mil)	Value Added ($ mil)	Reve-nues ($ mil)	% of US	
Pennsylvania	68	1,141	925	104.30	31,837	29,562	118.6	99.9	182.5	188.87	36.0

Source: Economic Census of the U.S., 1997. Data are sorted by 1997 revenues or establishments. (D) means data suppression to prevent disclosure of company data. A dash (-) is used when data are unavailable or cannot be calculated. Data followed by an * indicate the midpoint of a range. The ranges are: for 10, 0-19; for 60, 20-99; for 175, 100-249; for 375, 250-499; for 750, 500-999. Higher values are multiples of those shown, e.g., 3,750 is the midpoint of the range 2,500-4,999. Shaded *states* indicate states in which the industry was active in 1997. Shaded *regions* indicate where the industry is regionally most concentrated.

NAICS 212210 - IRON ORE MINING*

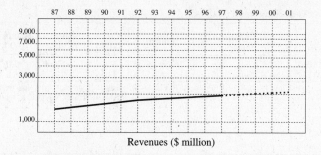

Revenues ($ million)

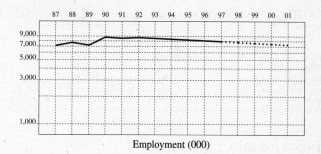

Employment (000)

GENERAL STATISTICS

Year	Com-panies	Establishments		Employment			Compensation		Production ($ million)			
		Total	with 20 or more employees	Total (No.)	Production Workers (No.)	Hours (Mil)	Payroll ($ mil)	Wages ($/hr)	Cost of Materials	Value Added by Mining	Value of Shipments	Capital Invest.
1977	70	97	61	19,300	13,900	28.5	372.3	8.89	1,026.6	1,046.4	1,614.4	458.5
1982	50	78	40	11,700	7,000	12.6	339.8	15.97	706.7	770.3	1,414.3	62.7
1987	39	51	16	7,100	5,600	11.2	224.2	14.80	618.5	767.9	1,362.4	24.0
1988	36	51[1]	15[1]	7,686[1]	5,889	11.9	257.2[1]	15.46	648.3	807.2	1,426.5	-
1989	33	44[1]	15[1]	7,192[1]	6,192	12.6	254.0[1]	16.15	679.4	848.5	1,493.7	-
1990	31	52[1]	17[1]	8,774[1]	6,511	13.3	301.1[1]	16.87	712.1	891.8	1,564.0	-
1991	28	41[1]	13[1]	8,549[1]	6,847	14.1	324.4[1]	17.62	746.4	937.5	1,637.7	-
1992	26	40	18	8,700	7,200	14.9	348.2	18.40	782.3	985.4	1,714.8	53.0
1993	26	38	17	8,544	7,117	15.0	357.3	19.04	834.8	985.1	1,759.4	-
1994	26	37	16	8,388	7,035	15.1	366.5	19.68	887.3	984.8	1,804.0	-
1995	26	35	14	8,232	6,952	15.1	375.6	20.32	939.7	984.5	1,848.5	-
1996	26	34	13	8,076	6,870	15.2	384.8	20.96	992.2	984.2	1,893.1	-
1997	26	32	12	7,920	6,787	15.3	393.9	21.60	1,044.7	983.9	1,937.7	90.9
1998	26p	30p	11p	7,764p	6,704p	15.4p	403.0p	22.24p	1,097.2p	983.6p	1,982.3p	-
1999	26p	29p	10p	7,608p	6,622p	15.5p	412.2p	22.88p	1,149.7p	983.3p	2,026.9p	-
2000	26p	27p	8p	7,452p	6,539p	15.5p	421.3p	23.52p	1,202.1p	983.0p	2,071.4p	-
2001	26p	26p	7p	7,296p	6,457p	15.6p	430.5p	24.16p	1,254.6p	982.7p	2,116.0p	-

Sources: *Economic Census of the United States*, 1977, 1982, 1987, 1992, and 1997. Data for those years (years are in **bold** type) are from the 5-year censuses of the economy. Other values, unless otherwise noted, are extrapolations. Values footnoted 1 are from the *County Business Patterns* for the years indicated. Values marked with *p* are projections. Data are the most recent available at this level of detail.

INDICES OF CHANGE

Year	Com-panies	Establishments		Employment			Compensation		Production ($ million)			
		Total	with 20 or more employees	Total (No.)	Production Workers (No.)	Hours (Mil)	Payroll ($ mil)	Wages ($/hr)	Cost of Materials	Value Added by Mining	Value of Shipments	Capital Invest.
1977	269.2	303.1	508.3	243.7	204.8	186.3	94.5	41.2	98.3	106.4	83.3	504.4
1982	192.3	243.8	333.3	147.7	103.1	82.4	86.3	73.9	67.6	78.3	73.0	69.0
1987	150.0	159.4	133.3	89.6	82.5	73.2	56.9	68.5	59.2	78.0	70.3	26.4
1992	100.0	125.0	150.0	109.8	106.1	97.4	88.4	85.2	74.9	100.2	88.5	58.3
1997	100.0	100.0	100.0	100.0	100.0	100.0	100.0	100.0	100.0	100.0	100.0	100.0

Sources: Same as General Statistics. The values shown reflect change from the base year, 1997. Values above 100 mean greater than 1997, values below 100 mean less than 1997, and a value of 100 in years other than 1997 means same as 1997. Indices are calculated only for Census years. Data are the most recent available at this level of detail.

SELECTED RATIOS

For 1992	Avg. of Sector	Analyzed Industry	Index	For 1992	Avg. of Sector	Analyzed Industry	Index
Employees per Establishment	20.4	247.5	1,213	Value Added per Production Worker	335,283	144,968	43
Payroll per Establishment	831,719	12,309,375	1,480	Cost per Establishment	2,854,087	32,646,875	1,144
Payroll per Employee	40,815	49,735	122	Cost per Employee	140,057	131,907	94
Production Workers per Establishment	15.6	212.1	1,360	Cost per Production Worker	183,057	153,927	84
Wages per Establishment	613,139	10,327,500	1,684	Shipments per Establishment	6,840,788	60,553,125	885
Wages per Production Worker	39,326	48,693	124	Shipments per Employee	335,695	244,659	73
Hours per Production Worker	2,075	2,254	109	Shipments per Production Worker	438,757	285,502	65
Wages per Hour	18.96	21.60	114	Investment per Establishment	1,242,441	2,840,625	229
Value Added per Establishment	5,227,487	30,746,875	588	Investment per Employee	60,970	11,477	19
Value Added per Employee	256,526	124,230	48	Investment per Production Worker	79,688	13,393	17

Sources: Same as General Statistics. The 'Average of Sector' column represents the average for all industries in this sector. The Index shows the relationship between the Average and the Analyzed Industry. For example, 100 means that they are equal; 500 that the Analyzed Industry is five times the average; 50 means that the Analyzed Industry is half the national average. 'na' is used to show that data are 'not available'.

*Equivalent to SIC 1011.

LEADING COMPANIES　Number shown: **2**　　Total sales ($ mil): **973**　　Total employment (000): **6.8**

Company Name	Address				CEO Name	Phone	Co. Type	Sales ($ mil)	Empl. (000)
Cleveland-Cliffs Inc.	1100 Superior Ave E	Cleveland	OH	44114	John S Brinzo	216-694-5700	P	679	5.0
Oglebay Norton Co.	1100 Superior Ave E	Cleveland	OH	44114	John N Lauer	216-861-3300	P	294	1.8

Source: Ward's Business Directory of U.S. Private and Public Companies, Volumes 1 and 2, 2000. The company type code used is as follows: P - Public, R - Private, S - Subsidiary, D - Division, J - Joint Venture, A - Affiliate, G - Group, N - Company type not reported. Sales are in millions of dollars, employees are in thousands. An asterisk (*) indicates an estimated sales volume. The symbol < stands for 'less than'. Company names and addresses are truncated, in some cases, to fit into the available space.

MINING PRODUCT DETAILS

Products	Units	Quantity of (000s)		Value of product shipments			
		Produc-tion 1997	Ship-ments 1997	1992		1997	
				($ mil)	% of total	($ mil)	% of total
Iron ore[1]		NA	NA	1,715.2	100.0	1,915.9	100.0
Direct-shipping crude iron ore[2]	mil metric tons	3	2	4.7	0.3	20.3	1.1
Crude iron ore for treatment, concentration, etc.	mil metric tons	209	(D)	(D)	-	(D)	-
Iron ore concentrates (including washed material) for consumption	mil metric tons	0	0	28.5	1.7	17.8	0.9
Iron ore concentrates (including washed material) for agglomeration plants not at blast furnaces	mil metric tons	62	-	-	-	-	-
Iron agglomerates (pellets, sinter, briquets, and other)	mil metric tons	61	60	1,657.9	96.7	1,820.8	95.0
Iron ores, nsk[3]		NA	NA	(D)	-	(D)	-

Source: Economic Census of the U.S., 1997. *Notes:* 1. Net shipments represented by the sum of direct-shipping ore, iron ore concentrates for consumption, and iron agglomerates were 63.2 million metric tons and 1,858.8 million dollars for 1997. 2. Includes estimates for small companies (estimates were made from administrative-record data rather than collected from respondents). 3. Represents value for establishments that did not report detailed data. NA stands for not applicable. (D) means data are withheld to avoid disclosure of competitive information. (S) indicates that data did not meet publication standards. - means not available or zero.

LOCATION BY STATE AND REGIONAL CONCENTRATION

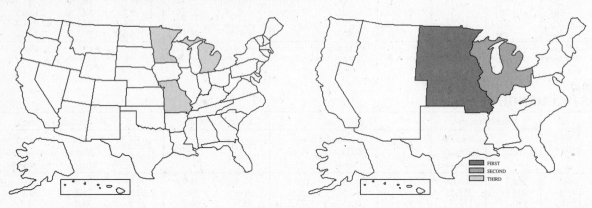

INDUSTRY DATA BY STATE

State	Estab-lish-ments	Employment			Compensation		Production				Capital Exp. ($ mil)
		Total	Workers	Total as % of US	Payroll per Employee	Wages per Worker	Costs ($ mil)	Value Added ($ mil)	Reve-nues ($ mil)	% of US	
Minnesota	16	7,500*	(D)	94.70	-	(D)	(D)	(D)	(D)	-	(D)
Michigan	6	1,750*	(D)	22.10	-	(D)	(D)	(D)	(D)	-	(D)
Missouri	1	175*	(D)	2.21	-	(D)	(D)	(D)	(D)	-	(D)

Source: Economic Census of the U.S., 1997. Data are sorted by 1997 revenues or establishments. (D) means data suppression to prevent disclosure of company data. A dash (-) is used when data are unavailable or cannot be calculated. Data followed by an * indicate the midpoint of a range. The ranges are: for 10, 0-19; for 60, 20-99; for 175, 100-249; for 375, 250-499; for 750, 500-999. Higher values are multiples of those shown, e.g., 3,750 is the midpoint of the range 2,500-4,999. Shaded *states* indicate states in which the industry was active in 1997. Shaded *regions* indicate where the industry is regionally most concentrated.

NAICS 212221 - GOLD ORE MINING*

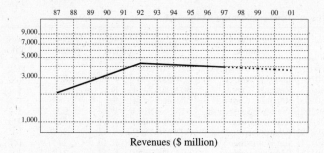

Revenues ($ million)

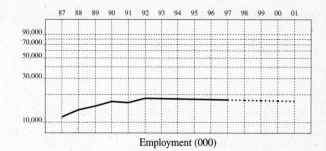

Employment (000)

GENERAL STATISTICS

Year	Companies	Establishments		Employment			Compensation		Production ($ million)			
		Total	with 20 or more employees	Total (No.)	Production Workers (No.)	Hours (Mil)	Payroll ($ mil)	Wages ($/hr)	Cost of Materials	Value Added by Mining	Value of Shipments	Capital Invest.
1977	119	126	8	2,600	2,000	3.8	39.5	7.39	42.5	78.2	99.0	21.7
1982	260	286	59	7,700	5,200	10.2	187.9	11.73	246.4	479.2	521.1	204.5
1987	260	319	91	11,400	8,900	18.2	371.5	14.49	920.6	1,689.1	2,067.1	542.6
1988	263	267[1]	83[1]	13,634[1]	9,840	20.3	481.6[1]	15.17	1,033.5	1,963.8	2,397.7	-
1989	266	272[1]	98[1]	14,980[1]	10,878	22.6	537.4[1]	15.87	1,160.2	2,283.3	2,781.1	-
1990	269	280[1]	97[1]	16,768[1]	12,027	25.2	631.4[1]	16.60	1,302.5	2,654.6	3,225.8	-
1991	273	271[1]	94[1]	16,331[1]	13,296	28.2	646.1[1]	17.37	1,462.2	3,086.4	3,741.7	-
1992	276	403	110	18,200	14,700	31.4	784.0	18.18	1,641.5	3,588.4	4,340.0	889.9
1993	271	383	104	18,062	14,858	31.5	782.7	18.76	1,774.2	3,428.0	4,262.4	-
1994	265	362	98	17,924	15,017	31.6	781.5	19.34	1,906.9	3,267.5	4,184.8	-
1995	260	342	91	17,785	15,175	31.8	780.2	19.93	2,039.5	3,107.1	4,107.3	-
1996	254	321	85	17,647	15,334	31.9	779.0	20.51	2,172.2	2,946.6	4,029.7	-
1997	249	301	79	17,509	15,492	32.0	777.7	21.09	2,304.9	2,786.2	3,952.1	1,139.0
1998	244p	281p	73p	17,371p	15,650p	32.1p	776.4p	21.67p	2,437.6p	2,625.8p	3,874.5p	-
1999	238p	260p	67p	17,233p	15,809p	32.2p	775.2p	22.25p	2,570.3p	2,465.3p	3,796.9p	-
2000	233p	240p	60p	17,094p	15,967p	32.4p	773.9p	22.84p	2,702.9p	2,304.9p	3,719.4p	-
2001	227p	219p	54p	16,956p	16,126p	32.5p	772.7p	23.42p	2,835.6p	2,144.4p	3,641.8p	-

Sources: *Economic Census of the United States*, 1977, 1982, 1987, 1992, and 1997. Data for those years (years are in **bold** type) are from the 5-year censuses of the economy. Other values, unless otherwise noted, are extrapolations. Values footnoted 1 are from the *County Business Patterns* for the years indicated. Values marked with *p* are projections. Data are the most recent available at this level of detail.

INDICES OF CHANGE

Year	Companies	Establishments		Employment			Compensation		Production ($ million)			
		Total	with 20 or more employees	Total (No.)	Production Workers (No.)	Hours (Mil)	Payroll ($ mil)	Wages ($/hr)	Cost of Materials	Value Added by Mining	Value of Shipments	Capital Invest.
1977	47.8	41.9	10.1	14.8	12.9	11.9	5.1	35.0	1.8	2.8	2.5	1.9
1982	104.4	95.0	74.7	44.0	33.6	31.9	24.2	55.6	10.7	17.2	13.2	18.0
1987	104.4	106.0	115.2	65.1	57.4	56.9	47.8	68.7	39.9	60.6	52.3	47.6
1992	110.8	133.9	139.2	103.9	94.9	98.1	100.8	86.2	71.2	128.8	109.8	78.1
1997	100.0	100.0	100.0	100.0	100.0	100.0	100.0	100.0	100.0	100.0	100.0	100.0

Sources: Same as General Statistics. The values shown reflect change from the base year, 1997. Values above 100 mean greater than 1997, values below 100 mean less than 1997, and a value of 100 in years other than 1997 means same as 1997. Indices are calculated only for Census years. Data are the most recent available at this level of detail.

SELECTED RATIOS

For 1992	Avg. of Sector	Analyzed Industry	Index	For 1992	Avg. of Sector	Analyzed Industry	Index
Employees per Establishment	20.4	58.2	285	Value Added per Production Worker	335,283	179,848	54
Payroll per Establishment	831,719	2,583,721	311	Cost per Establishment	2,854,087	7,657,475	268
Payroll per Employee	40,815	44,417	109	Cost per Employee	140,057	131,641	94
Production Workers per Establishment	15.6	51.5	330	Cost per Production Worker	183,057	148,780	81
Wages per Establishment	613,139	2,242,126	366	Shipments per Establishment	6,840,788	13,129,900	192
Wages per Production Worker	39,326	43,563	111	Shipments per Employee	335,695	225,718	67
Hours per Production Worker	2,075	2,066	100	Shipments per Production Worker	438,757	255,106	58
Wages per Hour	18.96	21.09	111	Investment per Establishment	1,242,441	3,784,053	305
Value Added per Establishment	5,227,487	9,256,478	177	Investment per Employee	60,970	65,052	107
Value Added per Employee	256,526	159,130	62	Investment per Production Worker	79,688	73,522	92

Sources: Same as General Statistics. The 'Average of Sector' column represents the average for all industries in this sector. The Index shows the relationship between the Average and the Analyzed Industry. For example, 100 means that they are equal; 500 that the Analyzed Industry is five times the average; 50 means that the Analyzed Industry is half the national average. 'na' is used to show that data are 'not available'.

*Equivalent to SIC 1041.

143

LEADING COMPANIES   Number shown: **49**   Total sales ($ mil): **11,105**   Total employment (000): **40.1**

Company Name	Address				CEO Name	Phone	Co. Type	Sales ($ mil)	Empl. (000)
Asarco Inc.	180 Maiden Ln	New York	NY	10038	Francis R McAllister	212-510-2000	P	2,233	11.1
Freeport-McMoRan Copper	PO Box 61119	New Orleans	LA	70161	James R Moffett	504-582-4000	P	1,887	6.3
Newmont Mining Corp.	1700 Lincoln St	Denver	CO	80203	Ronald Cambre	303-863-7414	P	1,432	5.7
Newmont Gold Co.	1700 Lincoln St	Denver	CO	80203	Ronald C Cambre	303-863-7414	S	1,380*	0.3
Homestake Mining Co.	650 California St	San Francisco	CA	94108	Walter T Segsworth	415-981-8150	P	803	1.4
Pittston Minerals Group	PO Box 4229	Glen Allen	VA	23058	Karl K Kindig	540-889-6000	P	519	1.8
Trelleborg Corp.	PO Box 8985	Wilmington	DE	19899	Fredrik Arp	302-656-7909	S	364*	0.7
AngloGold North America Inc.	5251 DTC Pkwy	Englewood	CO	80111	Jim Komadina	303-889-0700	R	344*	0.7
ChemFirst Inc.	PO Box 1249	Jackson	MS	39215	RM Summerford	601-948-7550	P	312	1.1
Battle Mountain Gold Company	333 Clay St	Houston	TX	77002	Ian D Bayer	713-650-6400	P	277	1.5
Echo Bay Mines Inc.	6400 Fiddlers Grn	Englewood	CO	80111	Robert Leclerc	303-714-8600	P	232	1.3
Battle Mountain Gold Co.	333 Clay St	Houston	TX	77002	Karl E Elers	713-650-6400	P	228	1.5
Pegasus Gold Inc.	601 W 1st Ave	Spokane	WA	99204	Werner Nennecker	509-624-4653	P	226	0.6
Hecla Mining Co.	P O Box C8000	Coeur D Alene	ID	83814	Arthur Brown	208-769-4100	P	159	1.2
N.A. Degerstrom Inc.	3303 N Sullivan Rd	Spokane	WA	99216	Neal Degerstrom	509-928-3333	R	143*	0.3
Anglogold Colorado Corp.	P O Box 191	Victor	CO	80860		719-689-2977	R	132*	0.3
Coeur d'Alene Mines Corp.	PO Box I	Coeur D Alene	ID	83816	Dennis E Wheeler	208-667-3511	P	102	0.8
Getchell Gold Corp.	5460 S Quebec St	Englewood	CO	80111	GW Thompson	303-771-9000	P	53	0.6
D.H. Blattner and Sons Inc.	400 Cty Road 50	Avon	MN	56310	WH Blattner Jr	320-356-7351	R	41*	0.5
Canyon Resources Corp.	14142 Denver W	Golden	CO	80401	Richard H De Voto	303-278-8464	P	35	0.2
Glamis Gold Ltd.	5190 Neil Rd	Reno	NV	89502	C Kevin McArthur	702-827-4600	P	33*	0.1
Western States Minerals Corp.	4975 Van Gordon St	Wheat Ridge	CO	80033	Arden B Morrow	303-425-7042	R	28*	<0.1
Arabian Shield Development Co.	10830 N Central	Dallas	TX	75231	Hatem El-Khalidi	214-692-7872	P	25	<0.1
MK Gold Co.	60 E South Temple	Salt Lake City	UT	84111	G Frank Joklik	801-237-1700	P	20	0.1
Alta Gold Co.	601 Whitney Ranch	Henderson	NV	89014		702-433-8525	P	17	0.2
Stratford American Corp.	2400 E AZ Biltmr	Phoenix	AZ	85016	David H Eaton	602-956-7809	P	11	<0.1
U.S. Energy Corp.	877 N 8th St W	Riverton	WY	82501	John Larsen	307-856-9271	P	11	<0.1
Global Outdoors Inc.	P O Box 3040	Fallbrook	CA	92028	Perry Massie	760-728-6620	P	7	<0.1
Royal Crescent Valley Inc.	1660 Wynkoop St	Denver	CO	80202	Stanley Dempsey	303-573-1660	S	6*	<0.1
J.A.B. International Inc.	1013 Fairway Drive	Winter Park	FL	32792	Jefferson Bootes	407-629-7373	P	5	<0.1
Atlas Corp.	370 7th St	Denver	CO	80202	Gregg B Shafter	303-629-2440	P	5*	0.2
Daugherty Resources Inc.	131 Prosperous Pl	Lexington	KY	40509	William Daugherty	606-263-3948	P	5	<0.1
Earth Sciences Inc.	910 12th St	Golden	CO	80401	Ramon Bisque	303-279-7641	P	5	<0.1
Crested Corp.	877 N 8th St W	Riverton	WY	82501	Max Evans	307-856-9271	P	4	<0.1
Mallon Resources Corp.	999 18th St	Denver	CO	80202	George O Mallon, Jr	303-293-2333	P	4	<0.1
Casmyn Corp.	380 Chickadee Dr	Reno	NV	89506	Amyn S Dahya	702-331-5524	R	3	0.6
Piedmont Mining Company Inc.	PO Box 240722	Charlotte	NC	28224	Earl M Jones	704-523-6866	P	3	<0.1
Golden Cycle Gold Corp.	2340 Robinson St	Co Springs	CO	80904	Birl W Worley Jr	719-471-9013	J	2	0.3
Original Sixteen to One Mine Inc.	P O Box 1621	Alleghany	CA	95910	Michael M Miller	530-287-3223	P	2	<0.1
Americomm Resources Corp.	15 E 5th St	Tulsa	OK	74103	Thomas R Bradley	918-587-8093	P	1	<0.1
Aspen Exploration Corp.	2050 S Oneida St	Denver	CO	80224	RV Bailey	303-639-9860	P	1	<0.1
Kinross Gold U.S.A. Inc.	185 S State St	Salt Lake City	UT	84111	Robert M Buchan	801-363-9152	S	1*	<0.1
U.S. Gold Corp.	2201 Kipling St	Lakewood	CO	80215	William W Reid	303-238-1438	P	1	<0.1
Gold Standard Inc.	712 Kearns Bldg	Salt Lake City	UT	84101	Scott L Smith	801-328-4452	P	1	<0.1
Solitario Resources Corp.	1675 Broadway	Denver	CO	80202	Christopher E Herald	303-534-1030	R	0	<0.1
Golden Star Resources Ltd.	One Norwest Center	Denver	CO	80264	James Askew	303-830-9000	P	0	0.2
Gold Reserve Corp.	926 W Sprague Ave	Spokane	WA	99201	Rockne J Timm	509-623-1500	P	0	<0.1
Crown Resources Corp.	1675 Broadway	Denver	CO	80202	Christopher E Herald	303-534-1030	P	0	<0.1
Chief Consolidated Mining Co.	500 5th Ave	New York	NY	10110	Leonard Weitz	212-354-4044	P	0	<0.1

Source: Ward's Business Directory of U.S. Private and Public Companies, Volumes 1 and 2, 2000. The company type code used is as follows: P - Public, R - Private, S - Subsidiary, D - Division, J - Joint Venture, A - Affiliate, G - Group, N - Company type not reported. Sales are in millions of dollars, employees are in thousands. An asterisk (*) indicates an estimated sales volume. The symbol < stands for 'less than'. Company names and addresses are truncated, in some cases, to fit into the available space.

MINING PRODUCT DETAILS

Products	Units	Quantity of (000s)		Value of product shipments			
		Production 1997	Shipments 1997	1992		1997	
				($ mil)	% of total	($ mil)	% of total
Gold ore		NA	NA	3,418.0	100.0	3,933.2	100.0
Crude lode gold ores mined	1,000 metric tons	275,507	NA	NA	-	NA	-
Crude lode gold ores and residues shipped to smelters	1,000 metric tons	NA	-	(D)	-	-	-
Crude lode gold ores and residues shipped to mills	1,000 metric tons	NA	(D)	(D)	-	(D)	-
Gold concentrates	1,000 metric tons	190	204	79.0	2.3	164.5	4.2
Gold mill bullion, dore, and precipitates		NA	NA	3,222.4	94.3	3,607.8	91.7
Placer gold	kilograms	2,333	2,323	54.9	1.6	23.9	0.6
Gold ores, nsk[1]		NA	NA	(D)	-	(D)	-

Source: Economic Census of the U.S., 1997. Notes: 1. Includes value for establishments that did not report detailed data and estimates for small companies (estimates were made from administrative-record data rather than collected from respondents). NA stands for not applicable. (D) means data are withheld to avoid disclosure of competitive information. (S) indicates that data did not meet publication standards. - means not available or zero.

LOCATION BY STATE AND REGIONAL CONCENTRATION

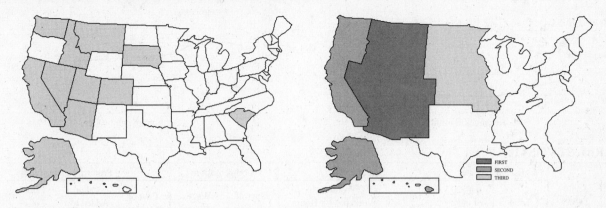

INDUSTRY DATA BY STATE

State	Estab lish- ments	Employment			Compensation		Production				Capital Exp. ($ mil)
		Total	Workers	Total as % of US	Payroll per Employee	Wages per Worker	Costs ($ mil)	Value Added ($ mil)	Reve- nues ($ mil)	% of US	
Nevada	100	10,816	9,788	61.77	46,143	45,644	(D)	1,628.7	2,719.2	97.60	(D)
South Dakota	8	1,295	1,170	7.40	39,269	38,732	(D)	115.7	185.8	6.67	(D)
Colorado	30	587	506	3.35	44,920	40,458	(D)	75.6	95.3	3.42	(D)
Arizona	17	226	162	1.29	33,429	37,926	5.2	16.9	15.7	0.56	6.4
California	47	1,750*	(D)	9.99	-	(D)	(D)	(D)	(D)	-	(D)
Alaska	34	750*	(D)	4.28	-	(D)	(D)	(D)	(D)	-	(D)
Idaho	18	750*	(D)	4.28	-	(D)	(D)	(D)	(D)	-	(D)
Montana	12	750*	(D)	4.28	-	(D)	(D)	(D)	(D)	-	(D)
Utah	12	375*	(D)	2.14	-	(D)	(D)	(D)	(D)	-	(D)
Washington	7	375*	(D)	2.14	-	(D)	(D)	(D)	(D)	-	(D)
South Carolina	3	175*	(D)	1.00	-	(D)	(D)	(D)	(D)	-	(D)

Source: *Economic Census of the U.S., 1997*. Data are sorted by 1997 revenues or establishments. (D) means data suppression to prevent disclosure of company data. A dash (-) is used when data are unavailable or can- not be calculated. Data followed by an * indicate the midpoint of a range. The ranges are: for 10, 0-19; for 60, 20-99, for 175, 100-249, for 375, 250-499, for 750, 500-999. Higher values are multiples of those shown, e.g., 3,750 is the midpoint of the range 2,500-4,999. Shaded *states* indicate states in which the industry was active in 1997. Shaded *regions* indicate where the industry is regionally most concentrated.

NAICS 212222 - SILVER ORE MINING*

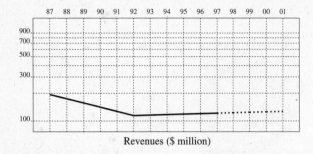

Revenues ($ million)

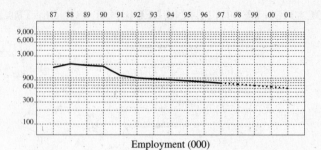

Employment (000)

GENERAL STATISTICS

| Year | Com-panies | Establishments | | Employment | | | Compensation | | Production ($ million) | | | |
		Total	with 20 or more employees	Total (No.)	Production Workers (No.)	Hours (Mil)	Payroll ($ mil)	Wages ($/hr)	Cost of Materials	Value Added by Mining	Value of Shipments	Capital Invest.
1977	45	49	12	2,000	1,700	3.2	31.6	7.94	35.7	82.9	99.6	19.0
1982	73	85	21	2,600	2,200	4.5	74.8	13.60	82.7	170.6	220.3	33.0
1987	45	53	10	1,700	1,500	3.1	51.5	13.29	80.8	125.1	193.8	12.2
1988	38	42[1]	13[1]	2,040[1]	1,323	2.7	58.5[1]	14.04	-	107.1	174.5	-
1989	33	36[1]	13[1]	1,896[1]	1,167	2.4	56.7[1]	14.83	-	91.7	157.1	-
1990	28	31[1]	12[1]	1,813[1]	1,029	2.2	55.9[1]	15.66	-	78.6	141.4	-
1991	24	27[1]	10[1]	1,139[1]	907	1.9	32.8[1]	16.54	-	67.3	127.3	-
1992	20	24	6	1,000	800	1.7	41.3	17.47	-	57.6	114.6	-
1993	19	22	6	956	781	1.7	39.6	17.63	-	63.0	116.0	-
1994	18	21	6	912	762	1.7	37.9	17.79	-	68.5	117.4	-
1995	17	19	5	868	742	1.6	36.2	17.96	-	73.9	118.7	-
1996	16	18	5	824	723	1.6	34.5	18.12	-	79.4	120.1	-
1997	15	16	5	780	704	1.6	32.8	18.28	43.1	84.8	121.5	6.4
1998	14p	14p	5p	736p	685p	1.6p	31.1p	18.44p	-	90.2p	122.9p	-
1999	13p	13p	5p	692p	666p	1.6p	29.4p	18.60p	-	95.7p	124.3p	-
2000	12p	11p	4p	648p	646p	1.5p	27.7p	18.77p	-	101.1p	125.6p	-
2001	11p	10p	4p	604p	627p	1.5p	26.0p	18.93p	-	106.6p	127.0p	-

Sources: Economic Census of the United States, 1977, 1982, 1987, 1992, and 1997. Data for those years (years are in **bold** type) are from the 5-year censuses of the economy. Other values, unless otherwise noted, are extrapolations. Values footnoted 1 are from the *County Business Patterns* for the years indicated. Values marked with *p* are projections. Data are the most recent available at this level of detail.

INDICES OF CHANGE

| Year | Com-panies | Establishments | | Employment | | | Compensation | | Production ($ million) | | | |
		Total	with 20 or more employees	Total (No.)	Production Workers (No.)	Hours (Mil)	Payroll ($ mil)	Wages ($/hr)	Cost of Materials	Value Added by Mining	Value of Shipments	Capital Invest.
1977	300.0	306.3	240.0	256.4	241.5	200.0	96.3	43.4	82.8	97.8	82.0	296.9
1982	486.7	531.3	420.0	333.3	312.5	281.3	228.0	74.4	191.9	201.2	181.3	515.6
1987	300.0	331.3	200.0	217.9	213.1	193.7	157.0	72.7	187.5	147.5	159.5	190.6
1992	133.3	150.0	120.0	128.2	113.6	106.3	125.9	95.6	-	67.9	94.3	-
1997	100.0	100.0	100.0	100.0	100.0	100.0	100.0	100.0	100.0	100.0	100.0	100.0

Sources: Same as General Statistics. The values shown reflect change from the base year, 1997. Values above 100 mean greater than 1997, values below 100 mean less than 1997, and a value of 100 in years other than 1997 means same as 1997. Indices are calculated only for Census years. Data are the most recent available at this level of detail.

SELECTED RATIOS

For 1992	Avg. of Sector	Analyzed Industry	Index	For 1992	Avg. of Sector	Analyzed Industry	Index
Employees per Establishment	20.4	48.8	239	Value Added per Production Worker	335,283	120,455	36
Payroll per Establishment	831,719	2,050,000	246	Cost per Establishment	2,854,087	2,693,750	94
Payroll per Employee	40,815	42,051	103	Cost per Employee	140,057	55,256	39
Production Workers per Establishment	15.6	44.0	282	Cost per Production Worker	183,057	61,222	33
Wages per Establishment	613,139	1,828,000	298	Shipments per Establishment	6,840,788	7,593,750	111
Wages per Production Worker	39,326	41,545	106	Shipments per Employee	335,695	155,769	46
Hours per Production Worker	2,075	2,273	110	Shipments per Production Worker	438,757	172,585	39
Wages per Hour	18.96	18.28	96	Investment per Establishment	1,242,441	400,000	32
Value Added per Establishment	5,227,487	5,300,000	101	Investment per Employee	60,970	8,205	13
Value Added per Employee	256,526	108,718	42	Investment per Production Worker	79,688	9,091	11

Sources: Same as General Statistics. The 'Average of Sector' column represents the average for all industries in this sector. The Index shows the relationship between the Average and the Analyzed Industry. For example, 100 means that they are equal; 500 that the Analyzed Industry is five times the average; 50 means that the Analyzed Industry is half the national average. 'na' is used to show that data are 'not available'.

*Equivalent to SIC 1044.

LEADING COMPANIES

Number shown: **14**   Total sales ($ mil): **3,521**   Total employment (000): **12.6**

Company Name	Address				CEO Name	Phone	Co. Type	Sales ($ mil)	Empl. (000)
Freeport-McMoRan Copper	PO Box 61119	New Orleans	LA	70161	James R Moffett	504-582-4000	P	1,887	6.3
Homestake Mining Co.	650 California St	San Francisco	CA	94108	Walter T Segsworth	415-981-8150	P	803	1.4
Echo Bay Mines Inc.	6400 Fiddlers Grn	Englewood	CO	80111	Robert Leclerc	303-714-8600	P	232	1.3
Pegasus Gold Inc.	601 W 1st Ave	Spokane	WA	99204	Werner Nennecker	509-624-4653	P	226	0.6
Hecla Mining Co.	P O Box C8000	Coeur D Alene	ID	83814	Arthur Brown	208-769-4100	P	159	1.2
Coeur d'Alene Mines Corp.	PO Box I	Coeur D Alene	ID	83816	Dennis E Wheeler	208-667-3511	P	102	0.8
Canyon Resources Corp.	14142 Denver W	Golden	CO	80401	Richard H De Voto	303-278-8464	P	35	0.2
Sunshine Mining and Refining Co.	877 W Main St	Boise	ID	83702	John S Simko	208-345-0660	P	32	0.3
Alta Gold Co.	601 Whitney Ranch	Henderson	NV	89014		702-433-8525	P	17	0.2
Goldfield Corp.	100 Rialto Place	Melbourne	FL	32901	John H Sottile	407-724-1700	P	16	0.1
Daugherty Resources Inc.	131 Prosperous Pl	Lexington	KY	40509	William Daugherty	606-263-3948	P	5	<0.1
Mallon Resources Corp.	999 18th St	Denver	CO	80202	George O Mallon, Jr	303-293-2333	P	4	<0.1
U.S. Gold Corp.	2201 Kipling St	Lakewood	CO	80215	William W Reid	303-238-1438	P	1	<0.1
Chief Consolidated Mining Co.	500 5th Ave	New York	NY	10110	Leonard Weitz	212-354-4044	P	0	<0.1

Source: *Ward's Business Directory of U.S. Private and Public Companies*, Volumes 1 and 2, 2000. The company type code used is as follows: P - Public, R - Private, S - Subsidiary, D - Division, J - Joint Venture, A - Affiliate, G - Group, N - Company type not reported. Sales are in millions of dollars, employees are in thousands. An asterisk (*) indicates an estimated sales volume. The symbol < stands for 'less than'. Company names and addresses are truncated, in some cases, to fit into the available space.

MINING PRODUCT DETAILS

Products	Units	Quantity of (000s)		Value of product shipments			
		Production 1997	Shipments 1997	1992 ($ mil)	1992 % of total	1997 ($ mil)	1997 % of total
Silver ore		NA	NA	110.4	100.0	130.3	100.0
Crude silver ores mined	1,000 metric tons	(D)	NA	NA	-	NA	-
Crude silver ores and residues shipped to smelters	1,000 metric tons	NA	-	(D)	-	-	-
Crude silver ores and residues shipped to mills	1,000 metric tons	NA	-	(D)	-	-	-
Silver concentrates	1,000 metric tons	(D)	(D)	(D)	-	(D)	-
Silver mill bullion, dore, and precipitates		NA	NA	(D)	-	(D)	-
Placer silver	kilograms	(D)	(D)	(D)	-	(D)	-
Silver ores, nsk[1]		NA	NA	2.9	2.6	2.7	2.0

Source: Economic Census of the U.S., 1997. Notes: 1. Includes a value for establishments that did not report detailed data and estimates for small companies (estimates were made from administrative-record data rather than collected from respondents). NA stands for not applicable. (D) means data are withheld to avoid disclosure of competitive information. (S) indicates that data did not meet publication standards. - means not available or zero.

LOCATION BY STATE AND REGIONAL CONCENTRATION

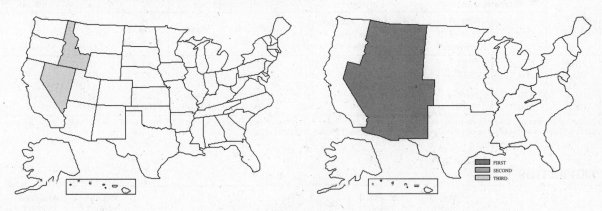

FIRST
SECOND
THIRD

INDUSTRY DATA BY STATE

State	Establishments	Employment Total	Employment Workers	Employment Total as % of US	Compensation Payroll per Employee	Compensation Wages per Worker	Production Costs ($ mil)	Production Value Added ($ mil)	Production Revenues ($ mil)	Production % of US	Capital Exp. ($ mil)
Idaho	8	375* (D)		48.08	-	(D)	(D)	(D)	(D)	-	(D)
Nevada	3	375* (D)		48.08	-	(D)	(D)	(D)	(D)	-	(D)

Source: Economic Census of the U.S., 1997. Data are sorted by 1997 revenues or establishments. (D) means data suppression to prevent disclosure of company data. A dash (-) is used when data are unavailable or cannot be calculated. Data followed by an * indicate the midpoint of a range. The ranges are: for 10, 0-19; for 60, 20-99, for 175, 100-249, for 375, 250-499, for 750, 500-999. Higher values are multiples of those shown, e.g., 3,750 is the midpoint of the range 2,500-4,999. Shaded *states* indicate states in which the industry was active in 1997. Shaded *regions* indicate where the industry is regionally most concentrated.

NAICS 212231 - LEAD ORE AND ZINC ORE MINING*

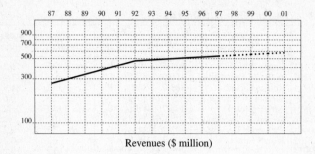

Revenues ($ million)

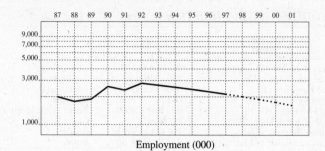

Employment (000)

GENERAL STATISTICS

| Year | Com-panies | Establishments | | Employment | | | Compensation | | Production ($ million) | | | |
		Total	with 20 or more employees	Total (No.)	Production Workers (No.)	Hours (Mil)	Payroll ($ mil)	Wages ($/hr)	Cost of Materials	Value Added by Mining	Value of Shipments	Capital Invest.
1977	54	88	41	7,100	5,400	10.7	105.1	7.01	131.5	329.1	418.4	42.1
1982	39	71	28	4,300	2,900	5.8	111.8	12.26	174.5	200.6	318.3	56.8
1987	21	39	19	2,000	1,400	3.0	58.3	13.33	104.1	176.2	268.3	11.9
1988	21	30[1]	16[1]	1,777[1]	1,532	3.3	58.6[1]	14.27	119.5	194.3	300.4	-
1989	21	32[1]	16[1]	1,884[1]	1,677	3.6	72.7[1]	15.28	137.1	214.2	336.3	-
1990	22	36[1]	19[1]	2,582[1]	1,836	3.9	92.0[1]	16.35	157.4	236.2	376.5	-
1991	22	35[1]	19[1]	2,362[1]	2,010	4.2	86.8[1]	17.51	180.6	260.4	421.5	-
1992	22	44	24	2,800	2,200	4.6	113.3	18.74	207.3	287.1	471.9	22.4
1993	22	42	22	2,668	2,115	4.4	108.4	18.75	211.0	313.1	484.1	-
1994	21	40	20	2,536	2,030	4.2	103.6	18.76	214.6	339.0	496.3	-
1995	21	38	19	2,404	1,946	4.0	98.7	18.76	218.3	365.0	508.5	-
1996	20	36	17	2,272	1,861	3.8	93.9	18.77	221.9	390.9	520.7	-
1997	20	34	15	2,140	1,776	3.6	89.0	18.78	225.6	416.9	532.9	109.6
1998	20p	32p	13p	2,008p	1,691p	3.4p	84.1p	18.79p	229.3p	442.9p	545.1p	-
1999	19p	30p	11p	1,876p	1,606p	3.2p	79.3p	18.80p	232.9p	468.8p	557.3p	-
2000	19p	28p	10p	1,744p	1,522p	3.0p	74.4p	18.80p	236.6p	494.8p	569.5p	-
2001	18p	26p	8p	1,612p	1,437p	2.8p	69.6p	18.81p	240.2p	520.7p	581.7p	-

Sources: Economic Census of the United States, 1977, 1982, 1987, 1992, and 1997. Data for those years (years are in **bold** type) are from the 5-year censuses of the economy. Other values, unless otherwise noted, are extrapolations. Values footnoted 1 are from the *County Business Patterns* for the years indicated. Values marked with *p* are projections. Data are the most recent available at this level of detail.

INDICES OF CHANGE

| Year | Com-panies | Establishments | | Employment | | | Compensation | | Production ($ million) | | | |
		Total	with 20 or more employees	Total (No.)	Production Workers (No.)	Hours (Mil)	Payroll ($ mil)	Wages ($/hr)	Cost of Materials	Value Added by Mining	Value of Shipments	Capital Invest.
1977	270.0	258.8	273.3	331.8	304.1	297.2	118.1	37.3	58.3	78.9	78.5	38.4
1982	195.0	208.8	186.7	200.9	163.3	161.1	125.6	65.3	77.3	48.1	59.7	51.8
1987	105.0	114.7	126.7	93.5	78.8	83.3	65.5	71.0	46.1	42.3	50.3	10.9
1992	110.0	129.4	160.0	130.8	123.9	127.8	127.3	99.8	91.9	68.9	88.6	20.4
1997	100.0	100.0	100.0	100.0	100.0	100.0	100.0	100.0	100.0	100.0	100.0	100.0

Sources: Same as General Statistics. The values shown reflect change from the base year, 1997. Values above 100 mean greater than 1997, values below 100 mean less than 1997, and a value of 100 in years other than 1997 means same as 1997. Indices are calculated only for Census years. Data are the most recent available at this level of detail.

SELECTED RATIOS

For 1992	Avg. of Sector	Analyzed Industry	Index	For 1992	Avg. of Sector	Analyzed Industry	Index
Employees per Establishment	20.4	62.9	309	Value Added per Production Worker	335,283	234,741	70
Payroll per Establishment	831,719	2,617,647	315	Cost per Establishment	2,854,087	6,635,294	232
Payroll per Employee	40,815	41,589	102	Cost per Employee	140,057	105,421	75
Production Workers per Establishment	15.6	52.2	335	Cost per Production Worker	183,057	127,027	69
Wages per Establishment	613,139	1,988,471	324	Shipments per Establishment	6,840,788	15,673,529	229
Wages per Production Worker	39,326	38,068	97	Shipments per Employee	335,695	249,019	74
Hours per Production Worker	2,075	2,027	98	Shipments per Production Worker	438,757	300,056	68
Wages per Hour	18.96	18.78	99	Investment per Establishment	1,242,441	3,223,529	259
Value Added per Establishment	5,227,487	12,261,765	235	Investment per Employee	60,970	51,215	84
Value Added per Employee	256,526	194,813	76	Investment per Production Worker	79,688	61,712	77

Sources: Same as General Statistics. The 'Average of Sector' column represents the average for all industries in this sector. The Index shows the relationship between the Average and the Analyzed Industry. For example, 100 means that they are equal; 500 that the Analyzed Industry is five times the average; 50 means that the Analyzed Industry is half the national average. 'na' is used to show that data are 'not available'.

*Equivalent to SIC 1031.

LEADING COMPANIES   Number shown: **7**   Total sales ($ mil): **3,280**   Total employment (000): **17.8**

Company Name	Address				CEO Name	Phone	Co. Type	Sales ($ mil)	Empl. (000)
Asarco Inc.	180 Maiden Ln	New York	NY	10038	Francis R McAllister	212-510-2000	P	2,233	11.1
Doe Run Co.	1801 Park 270 Dr	St. Louis	MO	63146	Jeffrey Zelms	314-453-7177	S	800	5.0
Hecla Mining Co.	P O Box C8000	Coeur D Alene	ID	83814	Arthur Brown	208-769-4100	P	159	1.2
Savage Zinc Inc.	PO Box 1104	Clarksville	TN	37041		931-552-4200	R	45*	0.2
Arabian Shield Development Co.	10830 N Central	Dallas	TX	75231	Hatem El-Khalidi	214-692-7872	P	25	<0.1
Goldfield Corp.	100 Rialto Place	Melbourne	FL	32901	John H Sottile	407-724-1700	P	16	0.1
Resurrection Mining Co.	1700 Lincoln St	Denver	CO	80203	David Baker	303-863-7414	S	2*	<0.1

Source: Ward's Business Directory of U.S. Private and Public Companies, Volumes 1 and 2, 2000. The company type code used is as follows: P - Public, R - Private, S - Subsidiary, D - Division, J - Joint Venture, A - Affiliate, G - Group, N - Company type not reported. Sales are in millions of dollars, employees are in thousands. An asterisk (*) indicates an estimated sales volume. The symbol < stands for 'less than'. Company names and addresses are truncated, in some cases, to fit into the available space.

MINING PRODUCT DETAILS

Products	Units	Quantity of (000s)		Value of product shipments			
		Produc-tion 1997	Ship-ments 1997	1992		1997	
				($ mil)	% of total	($ mil)	% of total
Lead and zinc ores		NA	NA	496.6	100.0	529.7	100.0
Crude lead and zinc ores mined	mil metric tons	13	NA	NA	-	NA	-
Crude lead and zinc ores and residues shipped to smelters	mil metric tons	NA	(D)	-	-	(D)	-
Crude lead and zinc ores and residues shipped to mills	mil metric tons	NA	(D)	(D)	-	(D)	-
Lead concentrates	mil metric tons	1	1	(D)	-	144.7	27.3
Zinc concentrates	mil metric tons	1	1	360.9	72.7	333.5	63.0
Lead and zinc ores, nsk[1]		NA	NA	1.4	0.3	3.9	0.7

Source: Economic Census of the U.S., 1997. Notes: 1. Includes value for establishments that did not report detailed data and estimates for small companies (estimates were made from administrative-record data rather than collected from respondents). NA stands for not applicable. (D) means data are withheld to avoid disclosure of competitive information. (S) indicates that data did not meet publication standards. - means not available or zero.

LOCATION BY STATE AND REGIONAL CONCENTRATION

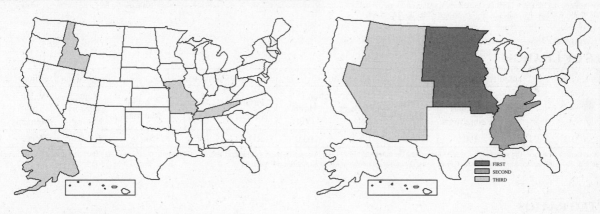

INDUSTRY DATA BY STATE

State	Estab-lish-ments	Employment			Compensation		Production				Capital Exp. ($ mil)
		Total	Workers	Total as % of US	Payroll per Employee	Wages per Worker	Costs ($ mil)	Value Added ($ mil)	Reve-nues ($ mil)	% of US	
Missouri	8	750*	(D)	35.05	-	(D)	(D)	(D)	(D)	-	(D)
Tennessee	8	750*	(D)	35.05	-	(D)	(D)	(D)	(D)	-	(D)
Idaho	4	175*	(D)	8.18	-	(D)	(D)	(D)	(D)	-	(D)
Alaska	1	375*	(D)	17.52	-	(D)	(D)	(D)	(D)	-	(D)

Source: Economic Census of the U.S., 1997. Data are sorted by 1997 revenues or establishments. (D) means data suppression to prevent disclosure of company data. A dash (-) is used when data are unavailable or cannot be calculated. Data followed by an * indicate the midpoint of a range. The ranges are: for 10, 0-19; for 60, 20-99, for 175, 100-249, for 375, 250-499, for 750, 500-999. Higher values are multiples of those shown, e.g., 3,750 is the midpoint of the range 2,500-4,999. Shaded states indicate states in which the industry was active in 1997. Shaded regions indicate where the industry is regionally most concentrated.

NAICS 212234 - COPPER ORE AND NICKEL ORE MINING

GENERAL STATISTICS

| Year | Com-panies | Establishments | | Employment | | | Compensation | | Production ($ million) | | | |
		Total	with 20 or more employees	Total (No.)	Production Workers (No.)	Hours (Mil)	Payroll ($ mil)	Wages ($/hr)	Cost of Materials	Value Added by Mining	Value of Shipments	Capital Invest.
1997	22	48	25	13,744	11,680	25.2	550.9	17.72	1,912.5	2,634.4	4,017.8	529.0

Source: Economic Census of the United States, 1997. This is a newly defined industry. Data for prior years were unavailable at the time of publication but may become available over time.

DISTRIBUTION AMONG SIC-BASED INDUSTRIES - 1997

| SIC | Industry | Estab-lish-ments | Employment | | | Compensation | | Production ($ mil) | |
			Total	Production Workers	Hours (Mil)	Payroll ($ mil)	Wages ($/hr)	Cost of Materials	Value of Shipments
102100	Copper ores	48	13,744	11,680	25.2	550.9	17.69	1,912.5	4,017.8
109910	Miscellaneous metal ores, nec, & ferroalloy ores, exc vanadium (pt)	-	-	-	-	-	-	-	-

Source: 1997 Economic Census. U.S. Census Bureau, U.S. Department of Commerce, August 1997. SIC codes ending in two zeroes represent complete 4-digit SICs. All others are parts of 4-digit SIC industries. Items showing a dash (-) indicate that data are not available because of disclosure problems.

SIC INDUSTRIES RELATED TO NAICS 212234

SIC	Industry	1990	1991	1992	1993	1994	1995	1996	1997
1021	**Copper Ores**								
	Establishments (number)	47	50	62	50	46	45	63p	63p
	Employment (thousands)	12.9	13.7	14.9	15.2	14.7	13.7	15.8e	16.0e
	Revenues ($ million)	2,817.8e	3,083.8e	3,374.9	3,693.5e	4,042.2e	4,423.8e	4,841.4e	5,298.4e
1061	**Ferroalloy Ores, Except Vanadium***	-	-	-	-	-	-	-	-

*Source: Economic Census of the United States, 1992, annual surveys of economic sectors conducted by the Bureau of the Census, and estimates or projections based on the 1982-1992 period; not all data are shown. 'e' marks estimates made by the editors; 'p' indicates projections based on time series. A dash (-) indicates that data for this SIC or year were not available. * Indicates that only a portion of this industry is present within the NAICS data. If no * is shown, the entire industry is contained within the NAICS data.*

INDICES OF CHANGE

| Year | Com-panies | Establishments | | Employment | | | Compensation | | Production ($ million) | | | |
		Total	with 20 or more employees	Total (No.)	Production Workers (No.)	Hours (Mil)	Payroll ($ mil)	Wages ($/hr)	Cost of Materials	Value Added by Mining	Value of Shipments	Capital Invest.
1997	100.0	100.0	100.0	100.0	100.0	100.0	100.0	100.0	100.0	100.0	100.0	100.0

Sources: Same as General Statistics. The values shown reflect change from the base year, 1997. Values above 100 mean greater than 1997, values below 100 mean less than 1997, and a value of 100 in years other than 1997 means same as 1997. Indices are calculated only for Census years. Data are the most recent available at this level of detail.

SELECTED RATIOS

For 1992	Avg. of Sector	Analyzed Industry	Index	For 1992	Avg. of Sector	Analyzed Industry	Index
Employees per Establishment	20.4	286.3	1,404	Value Added per Production Worker	335,283	225,548	67
Payroll per Establishment	831,719	11,477,083	1,380	Cost per Establishment	2,854,087	39,843,750	1,396
Payroll per Employee	40,815	40,083	98	Cost per Employee	140,057	139,152	99
Production Workers per Establishment	15.6	243.3	1,560	Cost per Production Worker	183,057	163,741	89
Wages per Establishment	613,139	9,303,000	1,517	Shipments per Establishment	6,840,788	83,704,167	1,224
Wages per Production Worker	39,326	38,232	97	Shipments per Employee	335,695	292,331	87
Hours per Production Worker	2,075	2,158	104	Shipments per Production Worker	438,757	343,990	78
Wages per Hour	18.96	17.72	93	Investment per Establishment	1,242,441	11,020,833	887
Value Added per Establishment	5,227,487	54,883,333	1,050	Investment per Employee	60,970	38,490	63
Value Added per Employee	256,526	191,676	75	Investment per Production Worker	79,688	45,291	57

Sources: Same as General Statistics. The 'Average of Sector' column represents the average for all industries in this sector. The Index shows the relationship between the Average and the Analyzed Industry. For example, 100 means that they are equal; 500 that the Analyzed Industry is five times the average; 50 means that the Analyzed Industry is half the national average. 'na' is used to show that data are 'not available'.

LEADING COMPANIES   Number shown: **13**   Total sales ($ mil): **13,310**   Total employment (000): **62.9**

Company Name	Address				CEO Name	Phone	Co. Type	Sales ($ mil)	Empl. (000)
Phelps Dodge Corp.	2600 N Central Ave	Phoenix	AZ	85004		602-234-8100	P	3,114	13.9
Cyprus Amax Minerals Co.	P O Box 3299	Englewood	CO	80112	Milton H Ward	303-643-5000	P	2,566	7.2
Asarco Inc.	180 Maiden Ln	New York	NY	10038	Francis R McAllister	212-510-2000	P	2,233	11.1
Freeport-McMoRan Copper	PO Box 61119	New Orleans	LA	70161	James R Moffett	504-582-4000	P	1,887	6.3
Kennecott Utah Copper Corp.	PO Box 6001	Magna	UT	84044	Robert R Dimock	801-252-3000	S	900*	2.0
BHP Copper North American	7400 N Oracle Rd	Tucson	AZ	85704	J Winter	520-575-5600	S	821*	4.4
Doe Run Co.	1801 Park 270 Dr	St. Louis	MO	63146	Jeffrey Zelms	314-453-7177	S	800	5.0
Southern Peru Copper Corp.	180 Maiden Ln	New York	NY	10038	Richard de J Osborne	212-510-2000	S	412	4.6
Trelleborg Corp.	PO Box 8985	Wilmington	DE	19899	Fredrik Arp	302-656-7909	S	364*	0.7
Exxon Coal and Minerals Co.	2401 S Gessner Rd	Houston	TX	77063	Lee R Raymond	713-978-5333	S	177	7.4
Alta Gold Co.	601 Whitney Ranch	Henderson	NV	89014		702-433-8525	P	17	0.2
Goldfield Corp.	100 Rialto Place	Melbourne	FL	32901	John H Sottile	407-724-1700	P	16	0.1
Azco Mining Inc.	PO Box 1895	Ferndale	WA	98248	Alan P Lindsay	360-380-4467	P	1	<0.1

Source: Ward's Business Directory of U.S. Private and Public Companies, Volumes 1 and 2, 2000. The company type code used is as follows: P - Public, R - Private, S - Subsidiary, D - Division, J - Joint Venture, A - Affiliate, G - Group, N - Company type not reported. Sales are in millions of dollars, employees are in thousands. An asterisk (*) indicates an estimated sales volume. The symbol < stands for 'less than'. Company names and addresses are truncated, in some cases, to fit into the available space.

MINING PRODUCT DETAILS

Products	Units	Quantity of (000s)		Value of product shipments			
		Produc-tion 1997	Ship-ments 1997	1992 ($ mil)	1992 % of total	1997 ($ mil)	1997 % of total
Copper and nickel ores		NA	NA	-	-	3,860.6	100.0
Crude copper ores mined[1]	mil metric tons	745	NA	NA	-	NA	-
Crude copper ores and residues shipped to smelters	mil metric tons	NA	(D)	-	-	(D)	-
Crude copper ores and residues shipped to mills	mil metric tons	NA	(D)	204.0	-	(D)	-
Copper concentrates	mil metric tons	4	4	1,982.2	-	2,340.8	60.6
Copper precipitates	1,000 metric tons	24	22	40.7	-	25.2	0.7
Electrowon copper recovered from leaching operations	1,000 metric tons	582	580	1,052.3	-	1,237.6	32.1
Copper ores, nsk, and nickel ores and concentrates[2]		NA	NA	-	-	8.0	0.2

Source: Economic Census of the U.S., 1997. Notes: 1. Includes material for leaching 2. Includes a value for establishments that did not report detailed data and estimates for small companies (estimates were made from administrative-record data rather than collected from respondents). NA stands for not applicable. (D) means data are withheld to avoid disclosure of competitive information. (S) indicates that data did not meet publication standards. - means not available or zero.

LOCATION BY STATE AND REGIONAL CONCENTRATION

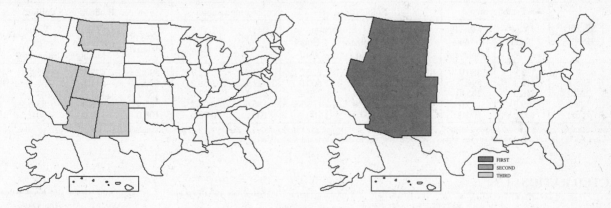

FIRST
SECOND
THIRD

INDUSTRY DATA BY STATE

State	Estab-lish-ments	Employment			Compensation		Production				Capital Exp. ($ mil)
		Total	Workers	Total as % of US	Payroll per Employee	Wages per Worker	Costs ($ mil)	Value Added ($ mil)	Reve-nues ($ mil)	% of US	
Arizona	25	9,911	8,330	72.11	40,117	38,189	1,080.9	1,833.4	2,615.2	99.27	299.1
Nevada	7	375*	(D)	2.73	-	(D)	(D)	(D)	(D)	-	(D)
New Mexico	6	1,750*	(D)	12.73	-	(D)	(D)	(D)	(D)	-	(D)
Utah	4	1,750*	(D)	12.73	-	(D)	(D)	(D)	(D)	-	(D)
Montana	3	375*	(D)	2.73	-	(D)	(D)	(D)	(D)	-	(D)

Source: Economic Census of the U.S., 1997. Data are sorted by 1997 revenues or establishments. (D) means data suppression to prevent disclosure of company data. A dash (-) is used when data are unavailable or cannot be calculated. Data followed by an * indicate the midpoint of a range. The ranges are: for 10, 0-19; for 60, 20-99, for 175, 100-249, for 375, 250-499, for 750, 500-999. Higher values are multiples of those shown, e.g., 3,750 is the midpoint of the range 2,500-4,999. Shaded *states* indicate states in which the industry was active in 1997. Shaded *regions* indicate where the industry is regionally most concentrated.

NAICS 212291 - URANIUM-RADIUM-VANADIUM ORE MINING*

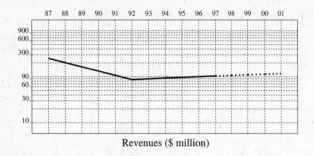

Revenues ($ million)

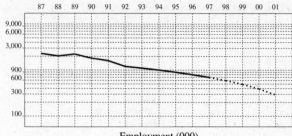

Employment (000)

GENERAL STATISTICS

Year	Com-panies	Establishments		Employment			Compensation		Production ($ million)			
		Total	with 20 or more employees	Total (No.)	Production Workers (No.)	Hours (Mil)	Payroll ($ mil)	Wages ($/hr)	Cost of Materials	Value Added by Mining	Value of Shipments	Capital Invest.
1977	-	225	66	12,000	9,600	20.0	203.2	7.76	435.0	431.6	614.5	252.1
1982	123	215	71	10,500	7,100	14.4	285.4	12.41	420.2	578.8	775.1	223.9
1987	59	101	27	2,300	1,500	2.9	72.1	15.03	115.8	174.7	251.5	39.0
1988	57	73[1]	26[1]	2,032[1]	1,249	2.4	66.4[1]	15.50	96.1	145.2	203.1	-
1989	54	82[1]	25[1]	2,232[1]	1,040	2.0	75.6[1]	15.98	79.8	120.8	164.0	-
1990	52	79[1]	24[1]	1,814[1]	866	1.7	63.9[1]	16.47	66.2	100.4	132.4	-
1991	50	73[1]	21[1]	1,593[1]	721	1.4	56.7[1]	16.98	54.9	83.5	106.9	-
1992	48	78	21	1,200	600	1.2	49.6	17.50	45.6	69.4	86.3	28.7
1993	43	68	19	1,099	583	1.1	45.0	17.64	51.2	73.6	89.7	-
1994	37	58	17	998	565	1.1	40.4	17.78	56.8	77.7	93.1	-
1995	32	49	16	897	548	1.0	35.8	17.91	62.5	81.9	96.4	-
1996	26	39	14	796	530	1.0	31.2	18.05	68.1	86.0	99.8	-
1997	21	29	12	695	513	0.9	26.6	18.19	73.7	90.2	103.2	60.7
1998	16p	19p	10p	594p	496p	0.8p	22.0p	18.33p	79.3p	94.4p	106.6p	-
1999	10p	9p	8p	493p	478p	0.8p	17.4p	18.47p	84.9p	98.5p	110.0p	-
2000	5p	-	7p	392p	461p	0.7p	12.8p	18.60p	90.6p	102.7p	113.3p	-
2001	-1	-10	5p	291p	443p	0.7p	8.2p	18.74p	96.2p	106.8p	116.7p	-

Sources: *Economic Census of the United States*, 1977, 1982, 1987, 1992, and 1997. Data for those years (years are in **bold** type) are from the 5-year censuses of the economy. Other values, unless otherwise noted, are extrapolations. Values footnoted 1 are from the *County Business Patterns* for the years indicated. Values marked with *p* are projections. Data are the most recent available at this level of detail.

INDICES OF CHANGE

Year	Com-panies	Establishments		Employment			Compensation		Production ($ million)			
		Total	with 20 or more employees	Total (No.)	Production Workers (No.)	Hours (Mil)	Payroll ($ mil)	Wages ($/hr)	Cost of Materials	Value Added by Mining	Value of Shipments	Capital Invest.
1977	-	775.9	550.0	1,726.6	1,871.3	2,222.2	763.9	42.7	590.2	478.5	595.4	415.3
1982	585.7	741.4	591.7	1,510.8	1,384.0	1,600.0	1,072.9	68.2	570.1	641.7	751.1	368.9
1987	281.0	348.3	225.0	330.9	292.4	322.2	271.1	82.6	157.1	193.7	243.7	64.3
1992	228.6	269.0	175.0	172.7	117.0	133.3	186.5	96.2	61.9	76.9	83.6	47.3
1997	100.0	100.0	100.0	100.0	100.0	100.0	100.0	100.0	100.0	100.0	100.0	100.0

Sources: Same as General Statistics. The values shown reflect change from the base year, 1997. Values above 100 mean greater than 1997, values below 100 mean less than 1997, and a value of 100 in years other than 1997 means same as 1997. Indices are calculated only for Census years. Data are the most recent available at this level of detail.

SELECTED RATIOS

For 1992	Avg. of Sector	Analyzed Industry	Index	For 1992	Avg. of Sector	Analyzed Industry	Index
Employees per Establishment	20.4	24.0	117	Value Added per Production Worker	335,283	175,828	52
Payroll per Establishment	831,719	917,241	110	Cost per Establishment	2,854,087	2,541,379	89
Payroll per Employee	40,815	38,273	94	Cost per Employee	140,057	106,043	76
Production Workers per Establishment	15.6	17.7	113	Cost per Production Worker	183,057	143,665	78
Wages per Establishment	613,139	564,517	92	Shipments per Establishment	6,840,788	3,558,621	52
Wages per Production Worker	39,326	31,912	81	Shipments per Employee	335,695	148,489	44
Hours per Production Worker	2,075	1,754	85	Shipments per Production Worker	438,757	201,170	46
Wages per Hour	18.96	18.19	96	Investment per Establishment	1,242,441	2,093,103	168
Value Added per Establishment	5,227,487	3,110,345	59	Investment per Employee	60,970	87,338	143
Value Added per Employee	256,526	129,784	51	Investment per Production Worker	79,688	118,324	148

Sources: Same as General Statistics. The 'Average of Sector' column represents the average for all industries in this sector. The Index shows the relationship between the Average and the Analyzed Industry. For example, 100 means that they are equal; 500 that the Analyzed Industry is five times the average; 50 means that the Analyzed Industry is half the national average. 'na' is used to show that data are 'not available'.

*Equivalent to SIC 1094.

LEADING COMPANIES   Number shown: **10**   Total sales ($ mil): **187,123**   Total employment (000): **79.7**

Company Name	Address				CEO Name	Phone	Co. Type	Sales ($ mil)	Empl. (000)
Exxon Mobil Corp.	5959 Las Colinas	Irving	TX	75039	Lee Raymond	972-444-1000	P	186,906	79.0
Cogema Inc.	7401 Wisconsin Ave	Bethesda	MD	20814	Michael McMurphy	301-986-8585	R	92*	0.3
Shirley Basin Mine	Shirley Basin Mine	Shirley Basin	WY	82615	George J Simchuk	307-356-4312	D	57*	0.2
Uranium Resources Inc.	12750 Merit Dr	Dallas	TX	75251	Paul Willmott	972-387-7777	P	23	<0.1
Cotter Corp.	12596 W Bayaud	Lakewood	CO	80228	Richard Cherry	303-980-1292	S	20*	0.1
U.S. Energy Corp.	877 N 8th St W	Riverton	WY	82501	John Larsen	307-856-9271	P	11	<0.1
Earth Sciences Inc.	910 12th St	Golden	CO	80401	Ramon Bisque	303-279-7641	P	5	<0.1
Crested Corp.	877 N 8th St W	Riverton	WY	82501	Max Evans	307-856-9271	P	4	<0.1
Reserve Industries Corp.	20 1st Plz	Albuquerque	NM	87102	Frank C Melfi	505-247-2384	P	4	<0.1
Double Eagle Petroleum	PO Box 766	Casper	WY	82601	Stephen H Hollis	307-237-9330	P	1	<0.1

Source: *Ward's Business Directory of U.S. Private and Public Companies*, Volumes 1 and 2, 2000. The company type code used is as follows: P - Public, R - Private, S - Subsidiary, D - Division, J - Joint Venture, A - Affiliate, G - Group, N - Company type not reported. Sales are in millions of dollars, employees are in thousands. An asterisk (*) indicates an estimated sales volume. The symbol < stands for 'less than'. Company names and addresses are truncated, in some cases, to fit into the available space.

MINING PRODUCT DETAILS

Products	Units	Quantity of (000s)		Value of product shipments			
		Produc- tion 1997	Ship- ments 1997	1992		1997	
				($ mil)	% of total	($ mil)	% of total
Uranium-radium-vanadium ores		NA	NA	86.2	100.0	85.6	100.0
Crude uranium-vanadium ores	1,000 metric tons	(D)	(D)	-	-	(D)	-
Uranium concentrates[1]	1,000 metric tons	(D)	(D)	-	-	(D)	-
Vanadium concentrates	1,000 metric tons	(D)	(D)	(D)	-	(D)	-
Uranium-radium-vanadium ores, nsk[2]		NA	NA	40.8	47.4	(D)	-

Source: Economic Census of the U.S., 1997. *Notes:* 1. Byproduct uranium oxide not associated with the mining and milling of ores is included in Product Code 3251317331, Other Organic Chemicals, nec. 2. Includes value for establishments that did not report detailed data and estimates for small companies (estimates were made from administrative-record data rather than collected from respondents). NA stands for not applicable. (D) means data are withheld to avoid disclosure of competitive information. (S) indicates that data did not meet publication standards. - means not available or zero.

LOCATION BY STATE AND REGIONAL CONCENTRATION

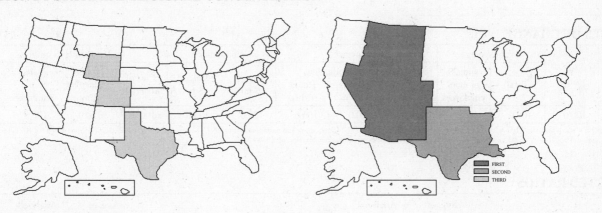

INDUSTRY DATA BY STATE

State	Estab- lish- ments	Employment			Compensation		Production				Capital Exp. ($ mil)
		Total	Workers	Total as % of US	Payroll per Employee	Wages per Worker	Costs ($ mil)	Value Added ($ mil)	Reve- nues ($ mil)	% of US	
Wyoming	8	172	125	24.75	54,145	43,536	(D)	47.5	32.2	35.77	(D)
Colorado	6	175*	(D)	25.18	-	(D)	(D)	(D)	(D)	-	(D)
Texas	6	175*	(D)	25.18	-	(D)	(D)	(D)	(D)	-	(D)

Source: Economic Census of the U.S., 1997. Data are sorted by 1997 revenues or establishments. (D) means data suppression to prevent disclosure of company data. A dash (-) is used when data are unavailable or cannot be calculated. Data followed by an * indicate the midpoint of a range. The ranges are: for 10, 0-19; for 60, 20-99, for 175, 100-249, for 375, 250-499, for 750, 500-999. Higher values are multiples of those shown, e.g., 3,750 is the midpoint of the range 2,500-4,999. Shaded *states* indicate states in which the industry was active in 1997. Shaded *regions* indicate where the industry is regionally most concentrated.

NAICS 212299 - METAL ORE MINING NEC

GENERAL STATISTICS

Year	Com-panies	Establishments		Employment			Compensation		Production ($ million)			
		Total	with 20 or more employees	Total (No.)	Production Workers (No.)	Hours (Mil)	Payroll ($ mil)	Wages ($/hr)	Cost of Materials	Value Added by Mining	Value of Shipments	Capital Invest.
1997	41	42	10	2,711	2,174	5.0	122.5	17.89	238.9	377.6	541.8	74.7

Source: *Economic Census of the United States*, 1997. This is a newly defined industry. Data for prior years were unavailable at the time of publication but may become available over time.

DISTRIBUTION AMONG SIC-BASED INDUSTRIES - 1997

SIC	Industry	Estab-lish-ments	Employment			Compensation		Production ($ mil)	
			Total	Production Workers	Hours (Mil)	Payroll ($ mil)	Wages ($/hr)	Cost of Materials	Value of Shipments
109920	Miscellaneous metal ores, nec, & ferroalloy ores, exc vanadium (pt)	42	2,711	2,174	5.0	122.5	18.03	238.9	541.8

Source: 1997 *Economic Census*. U.S. Census Bureau, U.S. Department of Commerce, August 1997. SIC codes ending in two zeroes represent complete 4-digit SICs. All others are parts of 4-digit SIC industries. Items showing a dash (-) indicate that data are not available because of disclosure problems.

SIC INDUSTRIES RELATED TO NAICS 212299

SIC	Industry	1990	1991	1992	1993	1994	1995	1996	1997
1099	**Metal Ores, n.e.c.**								
	Establishments (number)	80	70	108	88	83	71	90p	86p
	Employment (thousands)	2.0	1.5	2.8	2.3	1.9	2.0	2.7e	2.7e
	Revenues ($ million)	310.3e	311.2e	312.2	313.2e	314.1e	315.1e	316.1e	317.1e
1061	**Ferroalloy Ores, Except Vanadium***	-	-	-	-	-	-	-	-

Source: *Economic Census of the United States*, 1992, annual surveys of economic sectors conducted by the Bureau of the Census, and estimates or projections based on the 1982-1992 period; not all data are shown. 'e' marks estimates made by the editors; 'p' indicates projections based on time series. A dash (-) indicates that data for this SIC or year were not available. * Indicates that only a portion of this industry is present within the NAICS data. If no * is shown, the entire industry is contained within the NAICS data.

INDICES OF CHANGE

Year	Com-panies	Establishments		Employment			Compensation		Production ($ million)			
		Total	with 20 or more employees	Total (No.)	Production Workers (No.)	Hours (Mil)	Payroll ($ mil)	Wages ($/hr)	Cost of Materials	Value Added by Mining	Value of Shipments	Capital Invest.
1997	100.0	100.0	100.0	100.0	100.0	100.0	100.0	100.0	100.0	100.0	100.0	100.0

Sources: Same as General Statistics. The values shown reflect change from the base year, 1997. Values above 100 mean greater than 1997, values below 100 mean less than 1997, and a value of 100 in years other than 1997 means same as 1997. Indices are calculated only for Census years. Data are the most recent available at this level of detail.

SELECTED RATIOS

For 1992	Avg. of Sector	Analyzed Industry	Index	For 1992	Avg. of Sector	Analyzed Industry	Index
Employees per Establishment	20.4	64.5	316	Value Added per Production Worker	335,283	173,689	52
Payroll per Establishment	831,719	2,916,667	351	Cost per Establishment	2,854,087	5,688,095	199
Payroll per Employee	40,815	45,186	111	Cost per Employee	140,057	88,122	63
Production Workers per Establishment	15.6	51.8	332	Cost per Production Worker	183,057	109,890	60
Wages per Establishment	613,139	2,129,762	347	Shipments per Establishment	6,840,788	12,900,000	189
Wages per Production Worker	39,326	41,145	105	Shipments per Employee	335,695	199,852	60
Hours per Production Worker	2,075	2,300	111	Shipments per Production Worker	438,757	249,218	57
Wages per Hour	18.96	17.89	94	Investment per Establishment	1,242,441	1,778,571	143
Value Added per Establishment	5,227,487	8,990,476	172	Investment per Employee	60,970	27,554	45
Value Added per Employee	256,526	139,284	54	Investment per Production Worker	79,688	34,361	43

Sources: Same as General Statistics. The 'Average of Sector' column represents the average for all industries in this sector. The Index shows the relationship between the Average and the Analyzed Industry. For example, 100 means that they are equal; 500 that the Analyzed Industry is five times the average; 50 means that the Analyzed Industry is half the national average. 'na' is used to show that data are 'not available'.

LEADING COMPANIES   Number shown: **17**   Total sales ($ mil): **9,099**   Total employment (000): **31.6**

Company Name	Address				CEO Name	Phone	Co. Type	Sales ($ mil)	Empl. (000)
U.S. Steel Group	600 Grant St	Pittsburgh	PA	15219	Thomas J Usher	412-433-1121	S	5,314	19.3
Cyprus Amax Minerals Co.	P O Box 3299	Englewood	CO	80112	Milton H Ward	303-643-5000	P	2,566	7.2
Pittston Minerals Group	PO Box 4229	Glen Allen	VA	23058	Karl K Kindig	540-889-6000	P	519	1.8
Morrison Knudsen Corp. Mining	P O Box 73	Boise	ID	83729	Dennis Washington	208-386-5000	D	219*	0.7
Stillwater Mining Co.	1200 17th St Ste 900	Denver	CO	80202	John E Andrews	303-978-2525	P	153	0.9
Magnesium Corporation	238 N 2200 W	Salt Lake City	UT	84116	Michael Legge	801-532-2043	S	90	0.6
GCO Minerals Co.	1600 Smith	Houston	TX	77002	James R Montague	713-651-9261	S	85*	0.1
Cominco American Inc.	PO Box 3087	Spokane	WA	99216		509-459-4428	S	50*	0.3
Sunshine Mining and Refining Co.	877 W Main St	Boise	ID	83702	John S Simko	208-345-0660	P	32	0.3
RGC (USA) Mineral Sands Inc.	1223 Warner Rd	Wisc Rapids	FL	32043		904-284-9832	R	30	0.1
Alta Gold Co.	601 Whitney Ranch	Henderson	NV	89014		702-433-8525	P	17	0.2
U.S. Energy Corp.	877 N 8th St W	Riverton	WY	82501	John Larsen	307-856-9271	P	11	<0.1
Avocet Tungsten Inc.	Rte 2, Pine Creek Rd	Bishop	CA	93514		760-387-2501	R	7*	<0.1
Crested Corp.	877 N 8th St W	Riverton	WY	82501	Max Evans	307-856-9271	P	4	<0.1
Double Eagle Petroleum	PO Box 766	Casper	WY	82601	Stephen H Hollis	307-237-9330	P	1	<0.1
Tri-Valley Corp.	230 S Montclair St	Bakersfield	CA	93309	F Lynn Blystone	661-837-9300	P	1	<0.1
Nord Resources Corp.	201 3rd St	Albuquerque	NM	87102	W Pierce Carson	505-766-9955	P	0	<0.1

Source: Ward's Business Directory of U.S. Private and Public Companies, Volumes 1 and 2, 2000. The company type code used is as follows: P - Public, R - Private, S - Subsidiary, D - Division, J - Joint Venture, A - Affiliate, G - Group, N - Company type not reported. Sales are in millions of dollars, employees are in thousands. An asterisk (*) indicates an estimated sales volume. The symbol < stands for 'less than'. Company names and addresses are truncated, in some cases, to fit into the available space.

MINING PRODUCT DETAILS

Products	Units	Quantity of (000s)		Value of product shipments			
		Produc-tion 1997	Ship-ments 1997	1992		1997	
				($ mil)	% of total	($ mil)	% of total
All other metal ores		NA	NA	-	-	718.5	100.0
Bauxite	mil metric tons (dry)	(D)	(D)	-	-	(D)	-
Crude ferroalloy ores, such as manganese and manganiferous ores, chromium, molybdenum, tungsten, etc. (except vanadium and nickel)	1,000 metric tons	18,554	(D)	-	-	(D)	-
Molybdenum concentrates	1,000 mt cont. moly	50	48	208.8	-	421.3	58.6
Miscellaneous metal ores and concentrates, such as antimony, beryllium, mercury, rare-earth metals, tin, and titanium[1]	1,000 metric tons	(S)	(S)	-	-	267.6	37.2
Other metal ores, nsk[2]		NA	NA	-	-	10.8	1.5

Source: Economic Census of the U.S., 1997. Notes: 1. Includes value for platinum-group metals. 2. Includes value for establishments that did not report detailed data and estimates for small companies (estimates were made from administrative-record data rather than collected from respondents). NA stands for not applicable. (D) means data are withheld to avoid disclosure of competitive information. (S) indicates that data did not meet publication standards. - means not available or zero.

LOCATION BY STATE AND REGIONAL CONCENTRATION

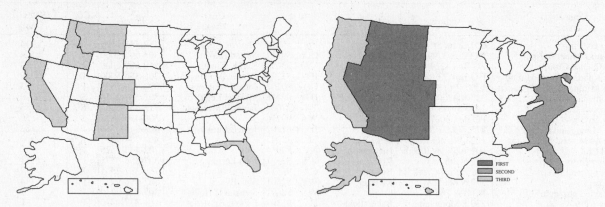

FIRST
SECOND
THIRD

INDUSTRY DATA BY STATE

State	Estab lish- ments	Employment			Compensation		Production				Capital Exp. ($ mil)
		Total	Workers	Total as % of US	Payroll per Employee	Wages per Worker	Costs ($ mil)	Value Added ($ mil)	Reve- nues ($ mil)	% of US	
Colorado	9	750*	(D)	27.67	-	(D)	(D)	(D)	(D)	-	(D)
New Mexico	4	375*	(D)	13.83	-	(D)	(D)	(D)	(D)	-	(D)
Florida	3	375*	(D)	13.83	-	(D)	(D)	(D)	(D)	-	(D)
Montana	3	750*	(D)	27.67	-	(D)	(D)	(D)	(D)	-	(D)
California	2	375*	(D)	13.83	-	(D)	(D)	(D)	(D)	-	(D)
Idaho	2	175*	(D)	6.46	-	(D)	(D)	(D)	(D)	-	(D)

Source: Economic Census of the U.S., 1997. Data are sorted by 1997 revenues or establishments. (D) means data suppression to prevent disclosure of company data. A dash (-) is used when data are unavailable or can-not be calculated. Data followed by an * indicate the midpoint of a range. The ranges are: for 10, 0-19; for 60, 20-99, for 175, 100-249, for 375, 250-499, for 750, 500-999. Higher values are multiples of those shown, e.g., 3,750 is the midpoint of the range 2,500-4,999. Shaded *states* indicate states in which the industry was active in 1997. Shaded *regions* indicate where the industry is regionally most concentrated.

NAICS 212311 - DIMENSION STONE MINING AND QUARRYING*

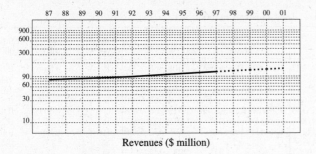

Revenues ($ million)

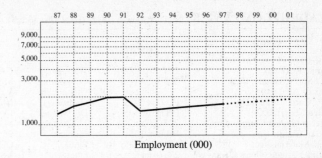

Employment (000)

GENERAL STATISTICS

Year	Com-panies	Establishments		Employment			Compensation		Production ($ million)			
		Total	with 20 or more employees	Total (No.)	Production Workers (No.)	Hours (Mil)	Payroll ($ mil)	Wages ($/hr)	Cost of Materials	Value Added by Mining	Value of Shipments	Capital Invest.
1977	185	209	23	1,900	1,600	2.7	18.6	5.19	13.2	38.5	49.0	2.7
1982	137	154	22	1,500	1,200	2.1	21.2	7.62	16.8	50.2	63.8	3.3
1987	130	149	19	1,300	1,100	2.0	24.5	8.85	25.2	64.7	85.8	4.0
1988	132	170[1]	25[1]	1,585[1]	1,100	2.0	32.3[1]	9.10	25.5	66.9	88.3	-
1989	134	176[1]	25[1]	1,753[1]	1,100	2.0	36.4[1]	9.36	25.8	69.3	90.8	-
1990	136	190[1]	33[1]	1,963[1]	1,100	2.1	42.0[1]	9.63	26.0	71.7	93.4	-
1991	139	198[1]	30[1]	1,983[1]	1,100	2.1	41.7[1]	9.91	26.3	74.1	96.1	-
1992	141	166	17	1,400	1,100	2.1	30.5	10.19	26.6	76.7	98.9	4.5
1993	145	169	18	1,453	1,163	2.2	32.1	10.62	28.6	81.2	104.3	-
1994	148	172	19	1,506	1,226	2.3	33.6	11.05	30.5	85.7	109.7	-
1995	152	174	19	1,558	1,289	2.3	35.2	11.47	32.5	90.1	115.1	-
1996	155	177	20	1,611	1,352	2.4	36.7	11.90	34.4	94.6	120.5	-
1997	159	180	21	1,664	1,415	2.5	38.3	12.33	36.4	99.1	125.9	9.6
1998	163p	183p	22p	1,717p	1,478p	2.6p	39.9p	12.76p	38.4p	103.6p	131.3p	-
1999	166p	186p	23p	1,770p	1,541p	2.7p	41.4p	13.19p	40.3p	108.1p	136.7p	-
2000	170p	188p	23p	1,822p	1,604p	2.7p	43.0p	13.61p	42.3p	112.5p	142.1p	-
2001	173p	191p	24p	1,875p	1,667p	2.8p	44.5p	14.04p	44.2p	117.0p	147.5p	-

*Sources: Economic Census of the United States, 1977, 1982, 1987, 1992, and 1997. Data for those years (years are in **bold** type) are from the 5-year censuses of the economy. Other values, unless otherwise noted, are extrapolations. Values footnoted 1 are from the County Business Patterns for the years indicated. Values marked with p are projections. Data are the most recent available at this level of detail.*

INDICES OF CHANGE

Year	Com-panies	Establishments		Employment			Compensation		Production ($ million)			
		Total	with 20 or more employees	Total (No.)	Production Workers (No.)	Hours (Mil)	Payroll ($ mil)	Wages ($/hr)	Cost of Materials	Value Added by Mining	Value of Shipments	Capital Invest.
1977	116.4	116.1	109.5	114.2	113.1	108.0	48.6	42.1	36.3	38.8	38.9	28.1
1982	86.2	85.6	104.8	90.1	84.8	84.0	55.4	61.8	46.2	50.7	50.7	34.4
1987	81.8	82.8	90.5	78.1	77.7	80.0	64.0	71.8	69.2	65.3	68.1	41.7
1992	88.7	92.2	81.0	84.1	77.7	84.0	79.6	82.6	73.1	77.4	78.6	46.9
1997	100.0	100.0	100.0	100.0	100.0	100.0	100.0	100.0	100.0	100.0	100.0	100.0

Sources: Same as General Statistics. The values shown reflect change from the base year, 1997. Values above 100 mean greater than 1997, values below 100 mean less than 1997, and a value of 100 in years other than 1997 means same as 1997. Indices are calculated only for Census years. Data are the most recent available at this level of detail.

SELECTED RATIOS

For 1992	Avg. of Sector	Analyzed Industry	Index	For 1992	Avg. of Sector	Analyzed Industry	Index
Employees per Establishment	20.4	9.2	45	Value Added per Production Worker	335,283	70,035	21
Payroll per Establishment	831,719	212,778	26	Cost per Establishment	2,854,087	202,222	7
Payroll per Employee	40,815	23,017	56	Cost per Employee	140,057	21,875	16
Production Workers per Establishment	15.6	7.9	50	Cost per Production Worker	183,057	25,724	14
Wages per Establishment	613,139	171,250	28	Shipments per Establishment	6,840,788	699,444	10
Wages per Production Worker	39,326	21,784	55	Shipments per Employee	335,695	75,661	23
Hours per Production Worker	2,075	1,767	85	Shipments per Production Worker	438,757	88,975	20
Wages per Hour	18.96	12.33	65	Investment per Establishment	1,242,441	53,333	4
Value Added per Establishment	5,227,487	550,556	11	Investment per Employee	60,970	5,769	9
Value Added per Employee	256,526	59,555	23	Investment per Production Worker	79,688	6,784	9

Sources: Same as General Statistics. The 'Average of Sector' column represents the average for all industries in this sector. The Index shows the relationship between the Average and the Analyzed Industry. For example, 100 means that they are equal; 500 that the Analyzed Industry is five times the average; 50 means that the Analyzed Industry is half the national average. 'na' is used to show that data are 'not available'.

*Equivalent to SIC 1411.

LEADING COMPANIES   Number shown: **10**   Total sales ($ mil): **540**   Total employment (000): **4.1**

Company Name	Address				CEO Name	Phone	Co. Type	Sales ($ mil)	Empl. (000)
Granite Rock Co.	P O Box 50001	Watsonville	CA	95077	Bruce W Woolpert	408-768-2000	R	155*	0.6
Cold Spring Granite Co.	202 3rd Ave S	Cold Spring	MN	56320		320-685-3621	R	120	1.4
Rock of Ages Corp.	772 Granitevillve Rd	Graniteville	VT	05654	Kurt M Swenson	802-476-3121	P	83	1.0
FMC Corp. Lithium Div.	PO Box 3925	Gastonia	NC	28054		704-868-5300	S	82*	0.5
Hallett Materials Co.	PO Box 3365	Des Moines	IA	50316	James E Rasmussen	515-266-9928	S	60*	0.4
Fletcher Granite Company Inc.	275 Groton Rd	N. Chelmsford	MA	01863	Duke Pointer	978-251-4031	R	15	0.2
Dakota Granite Co.	PO Box 1351	Milbank	SD	57252	Charles Monson	605-432-5580	R	13	0.0
Piqua Materials Inc.	1750 W Statler Rd	Piqua	OH	45356		937-773-4824	S	7*	<0.1
Martin Marietta (Ottawa, Kansas)	2807 San Creek Rd	Ottawa	KS	66067		785-242-3232	D	4*	<0.1
Jacob's Creek Stone Inc.	PO Box 608	Denton	NC	27239	RJ McKinney	336-857-2602	R	2	<0.1

Source: *Ward's Business Directory of U.S. Private and Public Companies*, Volumes 1 and 2, 2000. The company type code used is as follows: P - Public, R - Private, S - Subsidiary, D - Division, J - Joint Venture, A - Affiliate, G - Group, N - Company type not reported. Sales are in millions of dollars, employees are in thousands. An asterisk (*) indicates an estimated sales volume. The symbol < stands for 'less than'. Company names and addresses are truncated, in some cases, to fit into the available space.

MINING PRODUCT DETAILS

Products	Units	Quantity of (000s)		Value of product shipments			
		Produc- tion 1997	Ship- ments 1997	1992		1997	
				($ mil)	% of total	($ mil)	% of total
Dimension stone		NA	NA	107.4	100.0	137.7	100.0
Rough dimension limestone	1,000 s tons	391	384	20.2	18.8	32.3	23.4
Rough dimension granite	1,000 s tons	342	331	51.9	48.4	56.6	41.1
Other rough dimension stone (slate, marble, trap rock, sandstone, and miscellaneous stone)	1,000 s tons	320	317	13.2	12.3	30.8	22.4
Dimension stone, nsk[1]		NA	NA	22.0	20.5	18.0	13.1

Source: *Economic Census of the U.S.*, 1997. Notes: 1. Includes value for establishments that did not report detailed data and estimates for small companies (estimates were made from administrative-record data rather than collected from respondents. NA stands for not applicable. (D) means data are withheld to avoid disclosure of competitive information. (S) indicates that data did not meet publication standards. - means not available or zero.

LOCATION BY STATE AND REGIONAL CONCENTRATION

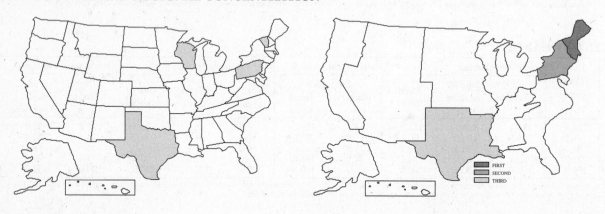

FIRST
SECOND
THIRD

INDUSTRY DATA BY STATE

State	Estab- lish- ments	Employment			Compensation		Production				Capital Exp. ($ mil)
		Total	Workers	Total as % of US	Payroll per Employee	Wages per Worker	Costs ($ mil)	Value Added ($ mil)	Reve- nues ($ mil)	% of US	
Vermont	8	165	152	9.92	22,248	21,197	3.8	17.6	20.5	20.68	0.8
Pennsylvania	21	129	103	7.75	28,496	25,126	3.1	12.9	15.2	15.39	0.7
Texas	18	249	226	14.96	21,843	20,973	5.0	11.0	14.9	15.02	1.1
Wisconsin	8	120	93	7.21	31,750	29,946	5.9	8.7	13.2	13.33	1.3
Georgia	32	375*	(D)	22.54	-	(D)	(D)	(D)	(D)	-	(D)

Source: *Economic Census of the U.S.*, 1997. Data are sorted by 1997 revenues or establishments. (D) means data suppression to prevent disclosure of company data. A dash (-) is used when data are unavailable or cannot be calculated. Data followed by an * indicate the midpoint of a range. The ranges are: for 10, 0-19; for 60, 20-99; for 175, 100-249; for 375, 250-499; for 750, 500-999. Higher values are multiples of those shown, e.g., 3,750 is the midpoint of the range 2,500-4,999. Shaded *states* indicate states in which the industry was active in 1997. Shaded *regions* indicate where the industry is regionally most concentrated.

NAICS 212312 - CRUSHED AND BROKEN LIMESTONE MINING AND QUARRYING*

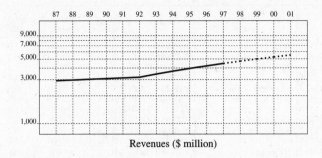

Revenues ($ million)

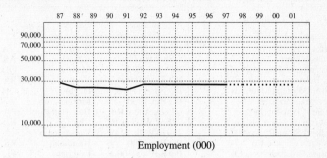

Employment (000)

GENERAL STATISTICS

Year	Com-panies	Establishments		Employment			Compensation		Production ($ million)			
		Total	with 20 or more employees	Total (No.)	Production Workers (No.)	Hours (Mil)	Payroll ($ mil)	Wages ($/hr)	Cost of Materials	Value Added by Mining	Value of Shipments	Capital Invest.
1977	837	1,457	452	29,100	23,200	47.4	392.1	5.92	553.6	1,002.9	1,378.5	178.1
1982	787	1,314	378	25,800	19,800	40.0	497.9	8.76	712.1	1,228.7	1,756.1	184.7
1987	714	1,335	456	28,900	21,600	47.0	702.3	10.27	1,161.8	2,091.4	2,914.4	338.7
1988	714	1,218[1]	394[1]	25,582[1]	21,354	46.5	715.0[1]	10.60	1,162.3	2,126.0	2,965.4	-
1989	715	1,175[1]	374[1]	25,579[1]	21,112	45.9	736.3[1]	10.93	1,162.8	2,161.1	3,017.2	-
1990	715	1,180[1]	387[1]	25,232[1]	20,872	45.4	742.8[1]	11.27	1,163.2	2,196.8	3,070.0	-
1991	716	1,179[1]	381[1]	24,233[1]	20,635	44.9	707.9[1]	11.62	1,163.7	2,233.1	3,123.7	-
1992	716	1,432	422	27,700	20,400	44.4	784.8	11.99	1,164.2	2,270.0	3,178.3	255.9
1993	714	1,433	424	27,673	20,779	45.2	819.5	12.64	1,263.1	2,480.3	3,437.7	-
1994	712	1,434	426	27,646	21,158	46.0	854.3	13.28	1,362.0	2,690.7	3,697.2	-
1995	710	1,434	428	27,619	21,538	46.9	889.0	13.93	1,460.9	2,901.0	3,956.6	-
1996	708	1,435	430	27,592	21,917	47.7	923.8	14.57	1,559.8	3,111.4	4,216.1	-
1997	706	1,436	432	27,565	22,296	48.5	958.5	15.22	1,658.7	3,321.7	4,475.5	504.8
1998	704p	1,437p	434p	27,538p	22,675p	49.3p	993.2p	15.87p	1,757.6p	3,532.0p	4,734.9p	-
1999	702p	1,438p	436p	27,511p	23,054p	50.1p	1,028.0p	16.51p	1,856.5p	3,742.4p	4,994.4p	-
2000	700p	1,438p	438p	27,484p	23,434p	51.0p	1,062.7p	17.16p	1,955.4p	3,952.7p	5,253.8p	-
2001	698p	1,439p	440p	27,457p	23,813p	51.8p	1,097.5p	17.80p	2,054.3p	4,163.1p	5,513.3p	-

*Sources: Economic Census of the United States, 1977, 1982, 1987, 1992, and 1997. Data for those years (years are in **bold** type) are from the 5-year censuses of the economy. Other values, unless otherwise noted, are extrapolations. Values footnoted 1 are from the County Business Patterns for the years indicated. Values marked with p are projections. Data are the most recent available at this level of detail.*

INDICES OF CHANGE

Year	Com-panies	Establishments		Employment			Compensation		Production ($ million)			
		Total	with 20 or more employees	Total (No.)	Production Workers (No.)	Hours (Mil)	Payroll ($ mil)	Wages ($/hr)	Cost of Materials	Value Added by Mining	Value of Shipments	Capital Invest.
1977	118.6	101.5	104.6	105.6	104.1	97.7	40.9	38.9	33.4	30.2	30.8	35.3
1982	111.5	91.5	87.5	93.6	88.8	82.5	51.9	57.6	42.9	37.0	39.2	36.6
1987	101.1	93.0	105.6	104.8	96.9	96.9	73.3	67.5	70.0	63.0	65.1	67.1
1992	101.4	99.7	97.7	100.5	91.5	91.5	81.9	78.8	70.2	68.3	71.0	50.7
1997	100.0	100.0	100.0	100.0	100.0	100.0	100.0	100.0	100.0	100.0	100.0	100.0

Sources: Same as General Statistics. The values shown reflect change from the base year, 1997. Values above 100 mean greater than 1997, values below 100 mean less than 1997, and a value of 100 in years other than 1997 means same as 1997. Indices are calculated only for Census years. Data are the most recent available at this level of detail.

SELECTED RATIOS

For 1992	Avg. of Sector	Analyzed Industry	Index	For 1992	Avg. of Sector	Analyzed Industry	Index
Employees per Establishment	20.4	19.2	94	Value Added per Production Worker	335,283	148,982	44
Payroll per Establishment	831,719	667,479	80	Cost per Establishment	2,854,087	1,155,084	40
Payroll per Employee	40,815	34,772	85	Cost per Employee	140,057	60,174	43
Production Workers per Establishment	15.6	15.5	100	Cost per Production Worker	183,057	74,395	41
Wages per Establishment	613,139	514,046	84	Shipments per Establishment	6,840,788	3,116,643	46
Wages per Production Worker	39,326	33,108	84	Shipments per Employee	335,695	162,362	48
Hours per Production Worker	2,075	2,175	105	Shipments per Production Worker	438,757	200,731	46
Wages per Hour	18.96	15.22	80	Investment per Establishment	1,242,441	351,532	28
Value Added per Establishment	5,227,487	2,313,162	44	Investment per Employee	60,970	18,313	30
Value Added per Employee	256,526	120,504	47	Investment per Production Worker	79,688	22,641	28

Sources: Same as General Statistics. The 'Average of Sector' column represents the average for all industries in this sector. The Index shows the relationship between the Average and the Analyzed Industry. For example, 100 means that they are equal; 500 that the Analyzed Industry is five times the average; 50 means that the Analyzed Industry is half the national average. 'na' is used to show that data are 'not available'.

*Equivalent to SIC 1422.

LEADING COMPANIES   Number shown: **28**   Total sales ($ mil): **2,366**   Total employment (000): **12.9**

Company Name	Address				CEO Name	Phone	Co. Type	Sales ($ mil)	Empl. (000)
Tarmac America Inc.	PO Box 2016	Norfolk	VA	23501	John D Carr	757-858-6500	R	400*	2.3
Sealaska Corp.	1 Sealaska Plz	Juneau	AK	99801	Robert Loesher	907-586-1512	R	237*	0.5
S.E. Johnson Companies Inc.	P O Box 29-A	Maumee	OH	43537	JT Bearss	419-893-8731	R	225*	1.4
J.E. Baker Co.	PO Box 1189	York	PA	17405		717-848-1501	R	185	0.7
Martin Marietta Materials	PO Box 137515	Dayton	OH	45413	Geoffrey C Harris	937-454-1128	S	185	0.8
Greer Industries Inc.	PO Box 1900	Morgantown	WV	26507	John R Raese	304-594-1768	R	150*	0.7
Stabler Company Inc.	635 Lucknow Rd	Harrisburg	PA	17110		717-236-9307	R	115	1.5
Continental Materials Corp.	225 W Wacker Dr	Chicago	IL	60606	James Gidwitz	312-541-7200	P	109	0.7
Redland Stone Products Co.	17910 W Ih 10	San Antonio	TX	78257	Bruce Vaio	210-696-8500	S	100*	0.4
Monarch Cement Co.	PO Box 1000	Humboldt	KS	66748		316-473-2225	P	100	0.6
Florida Crushed Stone Co.	PO Box 490300	Leesburg	FL	34749	F Gregg	352-787-0608	R	92	0.5
Capitol Aggregates Ltd.	PO Box 33240	San Antonio	TX	78265	Robert Engberg	210-655-3010	S	91*	0.6
National Lime and Stone Co.	PO Box 120	Findlay	OH	45839	Carl Palmer	419-422-4341	R	75	0.4
Harper Bros. Inc.	14860 6 Mile Cyp	Fort Myers	FL	33912		941-481-2350	R	67*	0.4
W.W. Boxley Co.	PO Box 13527	Roanoke	VA	24035	Abney S Boxley III	540-344-6601	R	40	0.3
Michigan Foundation Co.	1 W Jefferson Ave	Trenton	MI	48183		734-282-9100	R	30	0.1
Presque Isle Corp.	203 N Broadway	Lorain	OH	44052	RJ Hipple	440-246-3555	S	27*	0.2
Santa Fe International	2 Lincoln Ctr	Dallas	TX	75240	Sted Gasher	972-701-7300	R	23*	0.1
N.R. Hamm Quarry Inc.	Hwy 24	Perry	KS	66073	N Rodney Hamm	785-597-5111	R	18*	0.1
E. Dillon and Co.	P O Box 160	Swords Creek	VA	24649	David Skidmore	540-873-6816	R	18*	0.1
Stuart M. Perry Inc.	117 Limestone Ln	Winchester	VA	22602	DW Perry	540-662-3431	R	18*	0.1
Elmhurst-Chicago Stone	400 W 1st St	Elmhurst	IL	60126	Peter M Greco	630-832-4000	R	13	0.2
Columbia River Carbonates	PO Box 2350	Woodland	WA	98674		360-225-6505	R	13*	<0.1
Countyline Quarry Inc.	PO Box 99	Wrightsville	PA	17368		717-252-1584	R	12*	0.1
Meckley's Limestone Products	P O Box 950	Herndon	PA	17830	Fred J Meckley	717-758-3011	R	10	<0.1
Piqua Materials Inc.	1750 W Statler Rd	Piqua	OH	45356		937-773-4824	S	7*	<0.1
Greenville Quarries Inc.	P O Box 388	Greenville	KY	42345	John A Stovall	270-338-2300	R	5*	<0.1
Trans-Tex Fabricating Inc.	105 Humble Ave	San Antonio	TX	78225	John Schuepbach	210-924-4431	R	2	<0.1

Source: Ward's Business Directory of U.S. Private and Public Companies, Volumes 1 and 2, 2000. The company type code used is as follows: P - Public, R - Private, S - Subsidiary, D - Division, J - Joint Venture, A - Affiliate, G - Group, N - Company type not reported. Sales are in millions of dollars, employees are in thousands. An asterisk (*) indicates an estimated sales volume. The symbol < stands for 'less than'. Company names and addresses are truncated, in some cases, to fit into the available space.

MINING PRODUCT DETAILS

Products	Units	Quantity of (000s)		Value of product shipments			
		Production 1997	Shipments 1997	1992		1997	
				($ mil)	% of total	($ mil)	% of total
Limestone		NA	NA	3,099.1	100.0	4,469.5	100.0
Crushed and broken limestone	mil s tons	957	934	3,099.1	100.0	4,469.5	100.0

Source: Economic Census of the U.S., 1997. *Notes*: 1. NA stands for not applicable. (D) means data are withheld to avoid disclosure of competitive information. (S) indicates that data did not meet publication standards. - means not available or zero.

LOCATION BY STATE AND REGIONAL CONCENTRATION

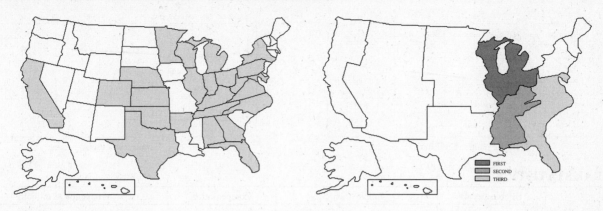

FIRST
SECOND
THIRD

INDUSTRY DATA BY STATE

State	Estab lish- ments	Employment			Compensation		Production				Capital Exp. ($ mil)
		Total	Workers	Total as % of US	Payroll per Employee	Wages per Worker	Costs ($ mil)	Value Added ($ mil)	Reve- nues ($ mil)	% of US	
Pennsylvania	112	2,501	1,957	9.07	37,186	34,033	127.6	300.2	391.6	11.79	36.2
Illinois	105	1,944	1,544	7.05	39,555	39,380	124.9	277.7	356.5	10.73	46.1
Ohio	90	1,926	1,509	6.99	35,346	33,380	130.7	220.9	314.1	9.46	37.5
Missouri	167	2,337	1,826	8.48	31,784	31,299	(D)	230.3	308.3	9.28	(D)
Tennessee	85	1,473	1,195	5.34	31,710	28,675	98.9	218.5	292.5	8.81	24.8
Kentucky	70	1,586	1,348	5.75	31,408	29,073	84.3	192.1	253.1	7.62	23.3
Alabama	37	1,303	1,091	4.73	34,665	31,111	84.2	181.1	234.2	7.05	31.1
Indiana	76	1,375	1,149	4.99	36,314	34,848	74.1	178.0	225.0	6.77	27.0
Florida	47	1,450	1,250	5.26	31,952	30,788	92.9	147.7	223.2	6.72	17.3
Texas	50	1,131	969	4.10	33,730	32,669	71.9	140.5	192.3	5.79	20.1
New York	58	943	763	3.42	41,692	39,181	65.8	116.7	163.6	4.92	18.9
Wisconsin	43	917	624	3.33	44,170	41,713	73.6	113.1	157.4	4.74	29.3
Michigan	17	698	565	2.53	43,842	42,110	55.8	87.3	131.1	3.95	11.9
Virginia	38	1,120	868	4.06	28,848	27,040	41.7	95.2	124.1	3.74	12.8
Georgia	23	534	487	1.94	31,277	30,390	28.1	68.8	90.4	2.72	6.5
Maryland	11	365	327	1.32	36,781	35,098	28.8	63.8	87.7	2.64	4.9
Oklahoma	34	810	715	2.94	26,458	25,483	36.4	64.9	85.8	2.58	15.6
Kansas	65	616	508	2.23	26,844	25,780	31.1	60.5	80.9	2.44	10.6
West Virginia	24	617	448	2.24	25,428	26,250	34.6	49.0	68.2	2.05	15.4
California	18	386	290	1.40	44,205	42,014	24.3	48.8	66.0	1.99	7.1
North Carolina	16	215	174	0.78	40,940	42,190	16.5	37.0	50.0	1.51	3.5
Minnesota	20	243	176	0.88	46,239	48,506	14.6	37.2	48.0	1.44	3.9
South Carolina	10	151	134	0.55	35,623	35,373	(D)	26.8	35.9	1.08	(D)
Washington	13	178	134	0.65	34,399	32,731	(D)	20.2	28.0	0.84	(D)
Colorado	15	132	104	0.48	34,523	33,442	4.5	12.6	15.7	0.47	1.4
Iowa	108	1,750*	(D)	6.35	-	(D)	(D)	(D)	(D)	-	(D)
Arkansas	13	175*	(D)	0.63	-	(D)	(D)	(D)	(D)	-	10.5
Nebraska	11	175*	(D)	0.63	-	(D)	(D)	(D)	(D)	-	5.1
South Dakota	4	175*	(D)	0.63	-	(D)	(D)	(D)	(D)	-	(D)
Vermont	3	175*	(D)	0.63	-	(D)	(D)	(D)	(D)	-	(D)

Source: Economic Census of the U.S., 1997. Data are sorted by 1997 revenues or establishments. (D) means data suppression to prevent disclosure of company data. A dash (-) is used when data are unavailable or can- not be calculated. Data followed by an * indicate the midpoint of a range. The ranges are: for 10, 0-19; for 60, 20-99; for 175, 100-249; for 375, 250-499; for 750, 500-999. Higher values are multiples of those shown, e.g., 3,750 is the midpoint of the range 2,500-4,999. Shaded *states* indicate states in which the industry was active in 1997. Shaded *regions* indicate where the industry is regionally most concentrated.

NAICS 212313 - CRUSHED AND BROKEN GRANITE MINING AND QUARRYING*

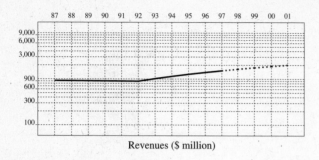

Revenues ($ million)

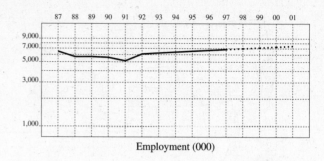

Employment (000)

GENERAL STATISTICS

Year	Companies	Establishments		Employment			Compensation		Production ($ million)			
		Total	with 20 or more employees	Total (No.)	Production Workers (No.)	Hours (Mil)	Payroll ($ mil)	Wages ($/hr)	Cost of Materials	Value Added by Mining	Value of Shipments	Capital Invest.
1977	69	162	93	4,400	3,900	8.7	51.2	4.83	112.7	192.0	272.5	32.2
1982	85	189	90	4,500	3,700	7.6	76.7	7.46	164.2	259.0	384.2	39.1
1987	104	238	129	6,500	5,000	11.7	168.6	10.29	339.2	696.2	922.7	112.7
1988	105	211[1]	121[1]	5,677[1]	4,980	11.5	157.3[1]	10.74	332.1	688.7	917.2	-
1989	105	211[1]	124[1]	5,688[1]	4,960	11.3	158.8[1]	11.20	325.2	681.3	911.6	-
1990	106	206[1]	120[1]	5,589[1]	4,940	11.2	160.8[1]	11.69	318.4	674.0	906.2	-
1991	106	213[1]	108[1]	5,130[1]	4,920	11.0	145.0[1]	12.19	311.8	666.8	900.7	-
1992	107	264	126	6,100	4,900	10.8	184.6	12.72	305.3	659.6	895.3	69.6
1993	110	269	128	6,248	5,037	11.3	202.2	13.45	358.9	755.9	1,019.1	-
1994	113	275	130	6,397	5,174	11.7	219.8	14.17	412.5	852.2	1,142.9	-
1995	117	280	131	6,545	5,312	12.2	237.3	14.90	466.0	948.6	1,266.7	-
1996	120	286	133	6,694	5,449	12.6	254.9	15.62	519.6	1,044.9	1,390.5	-
1997	123	291	135	6,842	5,586	13.1	272.5	16.35	573.2	1,141.2	1,514.3	200.1
1998	126p	296p	137p	6,990p	5,723p	13.6p	290.1p	17.08p	626.8p	1,237.5p	1,638.1p	-
1999	129p	302p	139p	7,139p	5,860p	14.0p	307.7p	17.80p	680.4p	1,333.8p	1,761.9p	-
2000	133p	307p	140p	7,287p	5,998p	14.5p	325.2p	18.53p	733.9p	1,430.2p	1,885.7p	-
2001	136p	313p	142p	7,436p	6,135p	14.9p	342.8p	19.25p	787.5p	1,526.5p	2,009.5p	-

Sources: Economic Census of the United States, 1977, 1982, 1987, 1992, and 1997. Data for those years (years are in **bold** type) are from the 5-year censuses of the economy. Other values, unless otherwise noted, are extrapolations. Values footnoted 1 are from the *County Business Patterns* for the years indicated. Values marked with *p* are projections. Data are the most recent available at this level of detail.

INDICES OF CHANGE

Year	Companies	Establishments		Employment			Compensation		Production ($ million)			
		Total	with 20 or more employees	Total (No.)	Production Workers (No.)	Hours (Mil)	Payroll ($ mil)	Wages ($/hr)	Cost of Materials	Value Added by Mining	Value of Shipments	Capital Invest.
1977	56.1	55.7	68.9	64.3	69.8	66.4	18.8	29.5	19.7	16.8	18.0	16.1
1982	69.1	64.9	66.7	65.8	66.2	58.0	28.1	45.6	28.6	22.7	25.4	19.5
1987	84.6	81.8	95.6	95.0	89.5	89.3	61.9	62.9	59.2	61.0	60.9	56.3
1992	87.0	90.7	93.3	89.2	87.7	82.4	67.7	77.8	53.3	57.8	59.1	34.8
1997	100.0	100.0	100.0	100.0	100.0	100.0	100.0	100.0	100.0	100.0	100.0	100.0

Sources: Same as General Statistics. The values shown reflect change from the base year, 1997. Values above 100 mean greater than 1997, values below 100 mean less than 1997, and a value of 100 in years other than 1997 means same as 1997. Indices are calculated only for Census years. Data are the most recent available at this level of detail.

SELECTED RATIOS

For 1992	Avg. of Sector	Analyzed Industry	Index	For 1992	Avg. of Sector	Analyzed Industry	Index
Employees per Establishment	20.4	23.5	115	Value Added per Production Worker	335,283	204,296	61
Payroll per Establishment	831,719	936,426	113	Cost per Establishment	2,854,087	1,969,759	69
Payroll per Employee	40,815	39,828	98	Cost per Employee	140,057	83,777	60
Production Workers per Establishment	15.6	19.2	123	Cost per Production Worker	183,057	102,614	56
Wages per Establishment	613,139	736,031	120	Shipments per Establishment	6,840,788	5,203,780	76
Wages per Production Worker	39,326	38,343	98	Shipments per Employee	335,695	221,324	66
Hours per Production Worker	2,075	2,345	113	Shipments per Production Worker	438,757	271,088	62
Wages per Hour	18.96	16.35	86	Investment per Establishment	1,242,441	687,629	55
Value Added per Establishment	5,227,487	3,921,649	75	Investment per Employee	60,970	29,246	48
Value Added per Employee	256,526	166,793	65	Investment per Production Worker	79,688	35,822	45

Sources: Same as General Statistics. The 'Average of Sector' column represents the average for all industries in this sector. The Index shows the relationship between the Average and the Analyzed Industry. For example, 100 means that they are equal; 500 that the Analyzed Industry is five times the average; 50 means that the Analyzed Industry is half the national average. 'na' is used to show that data are 'not available'.

*Equivalent to SIC 1423.

LEADING COMPANIES   Number shown: **5**   Total sales ($ mil): **182**   Total employment (000): **1.2**

Company Name	Address				CEO Name	Phone	Co. Type	Sales ($ mil)	Empl. (000)
Luck Stone Corp.	PO Box 29682	Richmond	VA	23242		804-784-6300	R	95	0.5
W.W. Boxley Co.	PO Box 13527	Roanoke	VA	24035	Abney S Boxley III	540-344-6601	R	40	0.3
North Carolina Granite Corp.	PO Box 151	Mount Airy	NC	27030		336-786-5141	R	24*	0.2
Barretto Granite Corp.	Groton Rd	N. Chelmsford	MA	01863	Duke Pointer	978-251-4031	R	17*	0.2
Vulcan Materials Co. Mideast Div.	PO Box 99	Skippers	VA	23879	Donald M James	804-634-4158	S	6*	<0.1

Source: Ward's Business Directory of U.S. Private and Public Companies, Volumes 1 and 2, 2000. The company type code used is as follows: P - Public, R - Private, S - Subsidiary, D - Division, J - Joint Venture, A - Affiliate, G - Group, N - Company type not reported. Sales are in millions of dollars, employees are in thousands. An asterisk (*) indicates an estimated sales volume. The symbol < stands for 'less than'. Company names and addresses are truncated, in some cases, to fit into the available space.

MINING PRODUCT DETAILS

Products	Units	Quantity of (000s)		Value of product shipments			
		Produc-tion 1997	Ship-ments 1997	1992		1997	
				($ mil)	% of total	($ mil)	% of total
Granite		NA	NA	900.9	100.0	1,523.9	100.0
Crushed and broken granite	mil s tons	256	247	900.9	100.0	1,523.9	100.0

Source: Economic Census of the U.S., 1997. *Notes:* 1. NA stands for not applicable. (D) means data are withheld to avoid disclosure of competitive information. (S) indicates that data did not meet publication standards. - means not available or zero.

LOCATION BY STATE AND REGIONAL CONCENTRATION

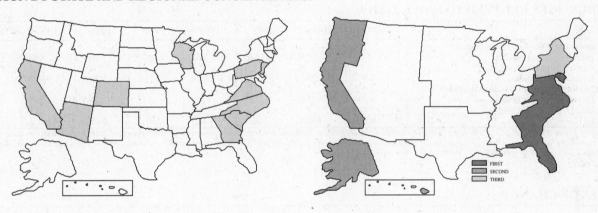

FIRST
SECOND
THIRD

INDUSTRY DATA BY STATE

State	Estab-lish-ments	Employment			Compensation		Production				Capital Exp. ($ mil)
		Total	Workers	Total as % of US	Payroll per Employee	Wages per Worker	Costs ($ mil)	Value Added ($ mil)	Reve-nues ($ mil)	% of US	
North Carolina	71	1,483	1,251	21.67	39,662	37,779	142.5	297.3	381.0	33.38	58.9
Georgia	55	1,339	1,151	19.57	37,032	36,138	130.6	237.3	335.7	29.42	32.2
Virginia	35	824	673	12.04	37,746	35,985	58.2	124.7	163.1	14.29	19.8
California	20	499	399	7.29	47,745	46,398	41.7	94.4	128.6	11.27	7.5
South Carolina	17	381	303	5.57	35,163	35,076	34.9	75.8	96.4	8.45	14.3
New Jersey	7	427	358	6.24	59,190	54,383	23.8	43.5	56.9	4.99	10.4
Maryland	3	107	91	1.56	41,318	27,824	(D)	20.8	26.7	2.34	(D)
Colorado	7	177	105	2.59	35,277	40,267	8.2	15.1	21.5	1.88	1.8
Pennsylvania	7	141	94	2.06	30,645	27,043	8.5	10.5	18.0	1.57	1.1
Oklahoma	6	108	94	1.58	31,065	32,702	(D)	14.2	17.8	1.56	(D)
Wisconsin	7	170	126	2.48	41,494	41,452	7.7	10.2	15.1	1.33	2.8
Arizona	10	113	69	1.65	35,699	33,290	3.3	10.9	12.2	1.06	2.1
Arkansas	2	375*	(D)	5.48	-	(D)	(D)	(D)	(D)	-	(D)
Missouri	1	175*	(D)	2.56	-	(D)	(D)	(D)	(D)	-	(D)

Source: Economic Census of the U.S., 1997. Data are sorted by 1997 revenues or establishments. (D) means data suppression to prevent disclosure of company data. A dash (-) is used when data are unavailable or cannot be calculated. Data followed by an * indicate the midpoint of a range. The ranges are: for 10, 0-19; for 60, 20-99, for 175, 100-249, for 375, 250-499, for 750, 500-999. Higher values are multiples of those shown, e.g., 3,750 is the midpoint of the range 2,500-4,999. Shaded *states* indicate states in which the industry was active in 1997. Shaded *regions* indicate where the industry is regionally most concentrated.

NAICS 212319 - CRUSHED AND BROKEN STONE MINING AND QUARRYING NEC

GENERAL STATISTICS

| Year | Com-panies | Establishments | | Employment | | | Compensation | | Production ($ million) | | | |
		Total	with 20 or more employees	Total (No.)	Production Workers (No.)	Hours (Mil)	Payroll ($ mil)	Wages ($/hr)	Cost of Materials	Value Added by Mining	Value of Shipments	Capital Invest.
1997	395	462	122	8,036	6,014	12.2	283.7	17.11	426.4	986.6	1,279.2	134.4

Source: *Economic Census of the United States*, 1997. This is a newly defined industry. Data for prior years were unavailable at the time of publication but may become available over time.

DISTRIBUTION AMONG SIC-BASED INDUSTRIES - 1997

| SIC | Industry | Estab-lish-ments | Employment | | | Compensation | | Production ($ mil) | |
			Total	Production Workers	Hours (Mil)	Payroll ($ mil)	Wages ($/hr)	Cost of Materials	Value of Shipments
142900	Crushed & broken stone, nec	457	7,942	5,933	12.0	281.0	17.13	422.0	1,261.0
149910	Miscellaneous nonmetallic minerals, except fuels (pt)	5	94	81	0.1	2.7	16.39	4.3	18.2

Source: 1997 *Economic Census*. U.S. Census Bureau, U.S. Department of Commerce, August 1997. SIC codes ending in two zeroes represent complete 4-digit SICs. All others are parts of 4-digit SIC industries. Items showing a dash (-) indicate that data are not available because of disclosure problems.

SIC INDUSTRIES RELATED TO NAICS 212319

SIC	Industry	1990	1991	1992	1993	1994	1995	1996	1997
1429	**Crushed and Broken Stone, n.e.c.**								
	Establishments (number)	360	359	446	444	444	440	460p	464p
	Employment (thousands)	7.1	6.6	7.8	7.6	8.1	8.6	7.4e	7.3e
	Revenues ($ million)	929.4e	928.8e	928.3	927.8e	927.2e	926.7e	926.1e	925.6e
1499	**Miscellaneous Nonmetallic Minerals***								
	Establishments (number)	304	296	281	268	272	285	235p	224p
	Employment (thousands)	6.8	6.4	5.5	5.2	5.1	5.1	4.5e	4.3e
	Revenues ($ million)	604.0e	600.1e	596.3	592.5e	588.7e	585.0e	581.2e	577.5e

Source: *Economic Census of the United States*, 1992, annual surveys of economic sectors conducted by the Bureau of the Census, and estimates or projections based on the 1982-1992 period; not all data are shown. 'e' marks estimates made by the editors; 'p' indicates projections based on time series. A dash (-) indicates that data for this SIC or year were not available. * Indicates that only a portion of this industry is present within the NAICS data. If no * is shown, the entire industry is contained within the NAICS data.

INDICES OF CHANGE

| Year | Com-panies | Establishments | | Employment | | | Compensation | | Production ($ million) | | | |
		Total	with 20 or more employees	Total (No.)	Production Workers (No.)	Hours (Mil)	Payroll ($ mil)	Wages ($/hr)	Cost of Materials	Value Added by Mining	Value of Shipments	Capital Invest.
1997	100.0	100.0	100.0	100.0	100.0	100.0	100.0	100.0	100.0	100.0	100.0	100.0

Sources: Same as General Statistics. The values shown reflect change from the base year, 1997. Values above 100 mean greater than 1997, values below 100 mean less than 1997, and a value of 100 in years other than 1997 means same as 1997. Indices are calculated only for Census years. Data are the most recent available at this level of detail.

SELECTED RATIOS

For 1992	Avg. of Sector	Analyzed Industry	Index	For 1992	Avg. of Sector	Analyzed Industry	Index
Employees per Establishment	20.4	17.4	85	Value Added per Production Worker	335,283	164,051	49
Payroll per Establishment	831,719	614,069	74	Cost per Establishment	2,854,087	922,944	32
Payroll per Employee	40,815	35,304	86	Cost per Employee	140,057	53,061	38
Production Workers per Establishment	15.6	13.0	83	Cost per Production Worker	183,057	70,901	39
Wages per Establishment	613,139	451,823	74	Shipments per Establishment	6,840,788	2,768,831	40
Wages per Production Worker	39,326	34,709	88	Shipments per Employee	335,695	159,184	47
Hours per Production Worker	2,075	2,029	98	Shipments per Production Worker	438,757	212,704	48
Wages per Hour	18.96	17.11	90	Investment per Establishment	1,242,441	290,909	23
Value Added per Establishment	5,227,487	2,135,498	41	Investment per Employee	60,970	16,725	27
Value Added per Employee	256,526	122,773	48	Investment per Production Worker	79,688	22,348	28

Sources: Same as General Statistics. The 'Average of Sector' column represents the average for all industries in this sector. The Index shows the relationship between the Average and the Analyzed Industry. For example, 100 means that they are equal; 500 that the Analyzed Industry is five times the average; 50 means that the Analyzed Industry is half the national average. 'na' is used to show that data are 'not available'.

LEADING COMPANIES   Number shown: **17**   Total sales ($ mil): **4,263**   Total employment (000): **16.3**

Company Name	Address				CEO Name	Phone	Co. Type	Sales ($ mil)	Empl. (000)
Vulcan Materials Co.	PO Box 285014	Birmingham	AL	35238	Donald M James	205-298-3000	P	2,356	7.0
Martin Marietta Materials Inc.	P O Box 30013	Raleigh	NC	27622	Stephen P Zelnak Jr	919-781-4550	P	1,259	5.7
Pike Industries Inc.	3 Eastgate Park Dr	Belmont	NH	03220	Randolph Pike	603-527-5100	S	160	1.0
Trap Rock Industries Inc.	PO Box 419	Kingston	NJ	08528	Joseph Stavola	609-924-0300	R	100	0.4
Mt. Hope Rock Products Inc.	625 Mt Hope Rd	Wharton	NJ	07885	Robert E Carballal	973-366-7741	R	74*	0.5
Hallett Materials Co.	PO Box 3365	Des Moines	IA	50316	James E Rasmussen	515-266-9928	S	60*	0.4
Southern Ready Mix Inc.	4200 Colonnade	Birmingham	AL	35243	C Reed	205-970-2400	R	45*	0.3
Alico Inc.	P O Box 338	LaBelle	FL	33975	Ben H Griffin III	863-675-2966	P	43	0.1
Lynn Sand and Stone Co.	30 Danvers Rd	Swampscott	MA	01907		781-595-0820	S	43*	0.1
Dutra Group	1000 Pt S Pedro	San Rafael	CA	94901	Bill Dutra	415-258-6876	R	38*	0.3
Seubert Excavators Inc.	PO Box 57	Cottonwood	ID	83522	John Seubert	208-962-3314	R	20	0.2
Amis Materials Co.	P O Box 1871	Oklahoma City	OK	73101	WD Amis Jr	405-235-3555	R	17*	0.1
S.M. Lorusso and Sons Inc.	PO Box 230	Walpole	MA	02081	Tony Lorusso	508-668-2600	R	15	0.1
Wingra Stone Company Inc.	PO Box 44284	Madison	WI	53719	RF Shea	608-271-5555	R	13*	0.2
York Hill Trap Rock Quarry	PO Box 748	Meriden	CT	06450		203-237-8421	R	12	0.1
San Rafael Rock Quarry Inc.	1000 Pt S Pedro	San Rafael	CA	94901	Bill Dutra	415-459-7740	S	5	<0.1
Cayuga Crushed Stone Inc.	PO Box 41	Lansing	NY	14882	Tom Besemer	607-533-4273	R	3*	<0.1

Source: Ward's Business Directory of U.S. Private and Public Companies, Volumes 1 and 2, 2000. The company type code used is as follows: P - Public, R - Private, S - Subsidiary, D - Division, J - Joint Venture, A - Affiliate, G - Group, N - Company type not reported. Sales are in millions of dollars, employees are in thousands. An asterisk (*) indicates an estimated sales volume. The symbol < stands for 'less than'. Company names and addresses are truncated, in some cases, to fit into the available space.

MINING PRODUCT DETAILS

Products	Units	Quantity of (000s)		Value of product shipments			
		Production 1997	Shipments 1997	1992 ($ mil)	% of total	1997 ($ mil)	% of total
Other stone		NA	NA	-	-	1,303.0	100.0
Bituminous limestone and bituminous sandstone	1,000 metric tons	2,954	2,904	-	-	18.1	1.4
Other crushed and broken stone	mil s tons	228	214	950.8	-	1,286.8	98.8
Bituminous limestone, bituminous sandstone, and other crushed and broken stone, nsk[1]		NA	NA	-	-	-1,899.0	-

Source: Economic Census of the U.S., 1997. *Notes:* 1. Includes value for establishments that did not report detailed data and estimates for small companies (estimates were made from administrative-record data rather than collected from respondents). NA stands for not applicable. (D) means data are withheld to avoid disclosure of competitive information. (S) indicates that data did not meet publication standards. - means not available or zero.

LOCATION BY STATE AND REGIONAL CONCENTRATION

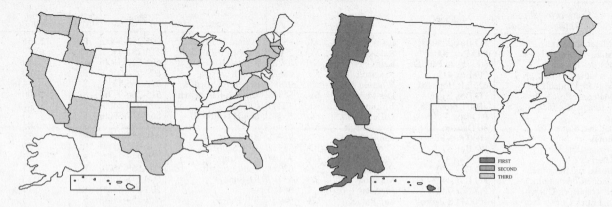

INDUSTRY DATA BY STATE

State	Estab lish- ments	Employment			Compensation		Production				Capital Exp. ($ mil)
		Total	Workers	Total as % of US	Payroll per Employee	Wages per Worker	Costs ($ mil)	Value Added ($ mil)	Reve- nues ($ mil)	% of US	
Washington	25	761	548	9.47	34,317	34,675	36.4	95.3	114.6	11.62	17.1
California	36	623	500	7.75	39,064	39,502	27.7	80.1	101.0	10.24	6.8
New Jersey	10	419	301	5.21	47,026	43,027	29.7	76.8	99.0	10.03	7.6
Pennsylvania	36	576	427	7.17	33,366	33,260	30.5	74.6	92.5	9.38	12.6
Connecticut	14	250	193	3.11	55,940	52,150	18.2	67.1	82.3	8.34	3.0
Wisconsin	10	227	170	2.82	47,599	46,088	13.8	66.4	78.0	7.91	2.1
Massachusetts	17	433	306	5.39	40,732	41,026	28.6	58.5	76.1	7.71	11.0
Virginia	14	398	322	4.95	34,995	33,342	28.8	56.9	73.2	7.42	12.5
Oregon	46	620	398	7.72	32,647	33,211	(D)	50.5	68.7	6.96	(D)
Texas	17	454	367	5.65	23,463	22,926	18.0	38.2	50.9	5.16	5.3
New York	21	335	236	4.17	35,675	39,525	14.4	39.0	50.7	5.14	2.7
Maryland	12	217	182	2.70	38,502	39,407	(D)	35.7	50.4	5.11	(D)
Florida	7	185	163	2.30	33,800	31,773	18.0	21.4	35.1	3.55	4.3
Arkansas	9	217	199	2.70	34,415	32,402	(D)	29.8	34.9	3.53	(D)
Idaho	13	288	173	3.58	43,038	32,503	13.3	19.7	30.9	3.14	2.0
Arizona	18	253	187	3.15	22,036	20,888	9.1	13.4	20.6	2.09	2.0
Oklahoma	10	140	95	1.74	26,100	27,558	(D)	11.4	17.3	1.75	(D)
Vermont	14	175*	(D)	2.18	-	(D)	(D)	(D)	(D)	-	(D)
Tennessee	10	175*	(D)	2.18	-	(D)	(D)	(D)	(D)	-	(D)
Missouri	7	175*	(D)	2.18	-	(D)	(D)	(D)	(D)	-	(D)
Georgia	5	175*	(D)	2.18	-	(D)	(D)	(D)	(D)	-	(D)

Source: *Economic Census of the U.S., 1997.* Data are sorted by 1997 revenues or establishments. (D) means data suppression to prevent disclosure of company data. A dash (-) is used when data are unavailable or can-not be calculated. Data followed by an * indicate the midpoint of a range. The ranges are: for 10, 0-19; for 60, 20-99, for 175, 100-249, for 375, 250-499, for 750, 500-999. Higher values are multiples of those shown, e.g., 3,750 is the midpoint of the range 2,500-4,999. Shaded *states* indicate states in which the industry was active in 1997. Shaded *regions* indicate where the industry is regionally most concentrated.

NAICS 212321 - CONSTRUCTION SAND AND GRAVEL MINING*

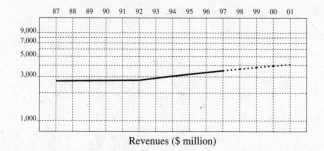

Revenues ($ million)

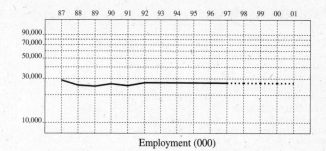

Employment (000)

GENERAL STATISTICS

Year	Com-panies	Establishments		Employment			Compensation		Production ($ million)			
		Total	with 20 or more employees	Total (No.)	Production Workers (No.)	Hours (Mil)	Payroll ($ mil)	Wages ($/hr)	Cost of Materials	Value Added by Mining	Value of Shipments	Capital Invest.
1977	2,111	2,619	362	25,900	19,600	40.7	354.4	6.36	456.8	861.4	1,177.9	140.3
1982	2,059	2,552	275	23,400	17,400	34.9	437.2	9.30	593.6	1,112.1	1,535.3	170.4
1987	2,087	2,559	371	28,900	21,100	45.4	673.0	10.78	899.3	2,011.6	2,696.8	214.1
1988	2,066	2,299[1]	332[1]	25,450[1]	20,706	44.8	715.2[1]	11.12	907.8	2,017.3	2,707.3	-
1989	2,044	2,197[1]	325[1]	24,770[1]	20,318	44.3	723.1[1]	11.47	916.3	2,023.0	2,717.8	-
1990	2,023	2,146[1]	365[1]	26,360[1]	19,939	43.8	775.3[1]	11.83	925.0	2,028.7	2,728.4	-
1991	2,003	2,132[1]	343[1]	25,178[1]	19,566	43.2	734.2[1]	12.20	933.7	2,034.4	2,739.0	-
1992	1,982	2,516	379	27,100	19,200	42.7	790.3	12.59	942.5	2,040.2	2,749.7	233.1
1993	1,961	2,486	376	27,063	19,362	42.2	813.9	13.44	995.6	2,163.9	2,899.3	-
1994	1,940	2,457	373	27,025	19,524	41.8	837.5	14.28	1,048.7	2,287.6	3,048.9	-
1995	1,918	2,427	369	26,988	19,686	41.3	861.2	15.13	1,101.9	2,411.3	3,198.5	-
1996	1,897	2,398	366	26,950	19,848	40.9	884.8	15.97	1,155.0	2,535.0	3,348.1	-
1997	1,876	2,368	363	26,913	20,010	40.4	908.4	16.82	1,208.1	2,658.7	3,497.7	370.5
1998	1,855p	2,338p	360p	26,876p	20,172p	39.9p	932.0p	17.67p	1,261.2p	2,782.4p	3,647.3p	-
1999	1,834p	2,309p	357p	26,838p	20,334p	39.5p	955.6p	18.51p	1,314.3p	2,906.1p	3,796.9p	-
2000	1,812p	2,279p	353p	26,801p	20,496p	39.0p	979.3p	19.36p	1,367.5p	3,029.8p	3,946.5p	-
2001	1,791p	2,250p	350p	26,763p	20,658p	38.6p	1,002.9p	20.20p	1,420.6p	3,153.5p	4,096.1p	-

Sources: *Economic Census of the United States*, 1977, 1982, 1987, 1992, and 1997. Data for those years (years are in **bold** type) are from the 5-year censuses of the economy. Other values, unless otherwise noted, are extrapolations. Values footnoted 1 are from the *County Business Patterns* for the years indicated. Values marked with *p* are projections. Data are the most recent available at this level of detail.

INDICES OF CHANGE

Year	Com-panies	Establishments		Employment			Compensation		Production ($ million)			
		Total	with 20 or more employees	Total (No.)	Production Workers (No.)	Hours (Mil)	Payroll ($ mil)	Wages ($/hr)	Cost of Materials	Value Added by Mining	Value of Shipments	Capital Invest.
1977	112.5	110.6	99.7	96.2	98.0	100.7	39.0	37.8	37.8	32.4	33.7	37.9
1982	109.8	107.8	75.8	86.9	87.0	86.4	48.1	55.3	49.1	41.8	43.9	46.0
1987	111.2	108.1	102.2	107.4	105.4	112.4	74.1	64.1	74.4	75.7	77.1	57.8
1992	105.7	106.3	104.4	100.7	96.0	105.7	87.0	74.9	78.0	76.7	78.6	62.9
1997	100.0	100.0	100.0	100.0	100.0	100.0	100.0	100.0	100.0	100.0	100.0	100.0

Sources: Same as General Statistics. The values shown reflect change from the base year, 1997. Values above 100 mean greater than 1997, values below 100 mean less than 1997, and a value of 100 in years other than 1997 means same as 1997. Indices are calculated only for Census years. Data are the most recent available at this level of detail.

SELECTED RATIOS

For 1992	Avg. of Sector	Analyzed Industry	Index	For 1992	Avg. of Sector	Analyzed Industry	Index
Employees per Establishment	20.4	11.4	56	Value Added per Production Worker	335,283	132,869	40
Payroll per Establishment	831,719	383,615	46	Cost per Establishment	2,854,087	510,177	18
Payroll per Employee	40,815	33,753	83	Cost per Employee	140,057	44,889	32
Production Workers per Establishment	15.6	8.5	54	Cost per Production Worker	183,057	60,375	33
Wages per Establishment	613,139	286,963	47	Shipments per Establishment	6,840,788	1,477,069	22
Wages per Production Worker	39,326	33,959	86	Shipments per Employee	335,695	129,963	39
Hours per Production Worker	2,075	2,019	97	Shipments per Production Worker	438,757	174,798	40
Wages per Hour	18.96	16.82	89	Investment per Establishment	1,242,441	156,461	13
Value Added per Establishment	5,227,487	1,122,762	21	Investment per Employee	60,970	13,767	23
Value Added per Employee	256,526	98,789	39	Investment per Production Worker	79,688	18,516	23

Sources: Same as General Statistics. The 'Average of Sector' column represents the average for all industries in this sector. The Index shows the relationship between the Average and the Analyzed Industry. For example, 100 means that they are equal; 500 that the Analyzed Industry is five times the average; 50 means that the Analyzed Industry is half the national average. 'na' is used to show that data are 'not available'.

*Equivalent to SIC 1442.

167

LEADING COMPANIES   Number shown: **21**   Total sales ($ mil): **5,538**   Total employment (000): **24.0**

Company Name	Address				CEO Name	Phone	Co. Type	Sales ($ mil)	Empl. (000)
Vulcan Materials Co.	PO Box 285014	Birmingham	AL	35238	Donald M James	205-298-3000	P	2,356	7.0
Hanson Building Materials	1350 Campus Pkwy	Neptune	NJ	07753	Alan J Murray	732-919-9777	S	1,500	7.5
Florida Rock Industries Inc.	PO Box 4667	Jacksonville	FL	32201	John D Baker II	904-355-1781	P	579	2.8
Rogers Group Inc.	PO Box 25250	Nashville	TN	37202	Don Williamson	615-242-0585	R	269*	1.6
Martin Marietta Materials	PO Box 137515	Dayton	OH	45413	Geoffrey C Harris	937-454-1128	S	185	0.8
Pike Industries Inc.	3 Eastgate Park Dr	Belmont	NH	03220	Randolph Pike	603-527-5100	S	160	1.0
Vulcan Materials Co. Midwest	747 E 22nd St	Lombard	IL	60148	Will Glusac	630-261-8600	S	119*	0.8
Monroc Inc.	PO Box 537	Salt Lake City	UT	84110		801-359-3701	P	61	0.5
Superior Ready Mix Concrete L.P.	1508 Mission Rd	Escondido	CA	92029	Jack Browwer	760-745-0556	R	58*	0.4
Harper Investments Inc.	P O Box 18400	Kearns	UT	84118	RJ Harper	801-250-0132	R	46	0.4
Fisher Sand and Gravel Co.	PO Box 1034	Dickinson	ND	58602	Gene Fisher	701-225-9184	R	40	0.3
Florida Rock and Sand Inc.	PO Box 3004	Florida City	FL	33034		305-247-3011	R	32*	0.2
Wyoming Sand and Stone Co.	6 Wyoming Sand Rd	Tunkhannock	PA	18657	William Eyar-Price Jr	570-836-2117	R	26	0.2
Hanson Permanente Cement	PO Box 580	Pleasanton	CA	94566		925-846-8800	S	24*	0.1
Grand Rapids Gravel Co.	PO Box 9160	Grand Rapids	MI	49509	Andrew Dykema	616-538-9000	R	22*	0.1
Hilltop Basic Resources Inc.	1 W 4th St Ste 1100	Cincinnati	OH	45202		513-651-5000	R	20*	0.2
Valco Inc.	PO Box 550	Rocky Ford	CO	81067	Tom Brubaker	719-254-7464	R	17*	0.1
J.C. Compton Company Inc.	P O Box 768	McMinnville	OR	97128	Mike Flanagan	503-472-4155	R	10*	<0.1
Mount Carmel Sand & Gravel Inc.	PO Box 458	Mount Carmel	IL	62863		618-262-5118	R	8*	<0.1
Madison Sand and Gravel Inc.	5349 Norway Grv	De Forest	WI	53532	Calvin Ziegler	608-244-6726	R	4*	<0.1
Lucky Sand and Gravel Co	12018 Frost Rd	Mantua	OH	44255	Bernard Udelson	330-562-6196	R	2*	<0.1

Source: *Ward's Business Directory of U.S. Private and Public Companies*, Volumes 1 and 2, 2000. The company type code used is as follows: P - Public, R - Private, S - Subsidiary, D - Division, J - Joint Venture, A - Affiliate, G - Group, N - Company type not reported. Sales are in millions of dollars, employees are in thousands. An asterisk (*) indicates an estimated sales volume. The symbol < stands for 'less than'. Company names and addresses are truncated, in some cases, to fit into the available space.

MINING PRODUCT DETAILS

Products	Units	Quantity of (000s)		Value of product shipments				
		Produc-tion 1997	Ship-ments 1997	1992		1997		
				($ mil)	% of total	($ mil)	% of total	
Construction sand and gravel		NA	NA	2,998.3	100.0	3,789.0	100.0	
Construction sand (run of pit or bank)	mil s tons	51	48	115.3	3.8	170.4	4.5	
Construction gravel (run of pit or bank)	mil s tons	53	48	114.4	3.8	180.1	4.8	
Construction sand (washed, screened, or otherwise treated)	mil s tons	226	216	755.2	25.2	937.2	24.7	
Construction gravel (washed, screened, or otherwise treated)	mil s tons	203	196	895.4	29.9	1,020.6	26.9	
Construction sand and gravel, nsk[1]		NA	NA	1,118.0	37.3	1,480.8	39.1	

Source: *Economic Census of the U.S.*, 1997. Notes: 1. Includes value for establishments that did not report detailed data and estimates for small companies (estimates were made from administrative-record data rather than collected from respondents). NA stands for not applicable. (D) means data are withheld to avoid disclosure of competitive information. (S) indicates that data did not meet publication standards. - means not available or zero.

LOCATION BY STATE AND REGIONAL CONCENTRATION

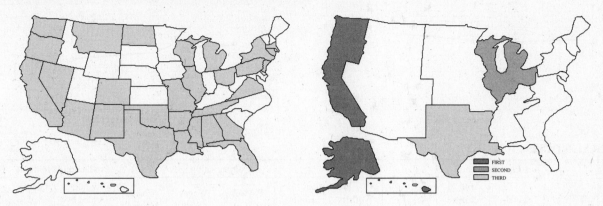

INDUSTRY DATA BY STATE

State	Estab lish- ments	Employment			Compensation		Production				Capital Exp. ($ mil)
		Total	Workers	Total as % of US	Payroll per Employee	Wages per Worker	Costs ($ mil)	Value Added ($ mil)	Reve- nues ($ mil)	% of US	
California	151	2,602	2,069	9.67	43,891	44,871	142.1	417.1	520.7	19.58	38.5
Texas	154	2,426	1,943	9.01	27,925	28,207	95.4	196.7	263.6	9.91	28.5
Ohio	153	1,693	1,295	6.29	33,060	32,399	73.0	159.9	208.4	7.84	24.5
Illinois	90	1,097	693	4.08	41,624	38,603	47.5	126.8	156.3	5.88	18.1
Michigan	125	967	705	3.59	38,010	40,594	58.9	114.4	152.6	5.74	20.7
New York	145	1,155	828	4.29	36,996	37,225	46.6	115.6	146.7	5.52	15.5
Florida	53	767	556	2.85	29,356	32,412	38.4	76.9	102.3	3.85	13.1
Arizona	45	914	672	3.40	35,791	35,634	36.9	74.0	101.7	3.82	9.2
Pennsylvania	86	883	674	3.28	32,318	33,099	33.6	74.0	100.1	3.77	7.5
Washington	55	636	441	2.36	36,585	35,966	40.6	59.8	96.1	3.62	4.3
New Jersey	38	494	321	1.84	42,178	41,312	22.7	72.6	84.3	3.17	11.1
North Dakota	16	471	361	1.75	44,820	46,515	24.4	51.6	69.4	2.61	6.7
Tennessee	29	587	450	2.18	28,114	25,769	28.1	50.5	68.2	2.57	10.3
Wisconsin	63	572	372	2.13	34,879	38,618	24.0	53.8	64.2	2.41	13.5
New Hampshire	28	370	271	1.37	45,481	45,314	(D)	38.9	63.0	2.37	(D)
Massachusetts	46	509	320	1.89	37,116	35,525	23.5	40.7	57.6	2.17	6.6
Colorado	56	546	340	2.03	29,342	32,303	22.1	40.3	56.2	2.11	6.2
Louisiana	53	528	422	1.96	23,498	23,555	19.3	41.7	54.3	2.04	6.7
Virginia	33	376	286	1.40	31,912	33,049	16.9	37.9	47.6	1.79	7.2
Mississippi	46	563	435	2.09	22,053	21,343	17.8	32.0	47.4	1.78	2.3
Iowa	63	362	316	1.35	30,224	30,731	(D)	37.3	46.2	1.74	(D)
Kansas	33	366	241	1.36	34,355	34,871	(D)	30.4	44.3	1.67	(D)
Alabama	38	438	344	1.63	24,308	24,794	16.1	32.1	43.9	1.65	4.3
North Carolina	42	523	414	1.94	25,451	26,138	(D)	33.5	43.0	1.62	(D)
Kentucky	16	247	201	0.92	33,895	32,851	(D)	32.0	42.5	1.60	(D)
Arkansas	36	402	325	1.49	26,286	26,637	16.4	30.6	41.6	1.57	5.3
Nevada	28	322	211	1.20	28,429	29,986	12.2	29.3	37.2	1.40	4.3
Missouri	47	402	303	1.49	28,891	27,106	13.3	27.4	35.7	1.34	5.0
Oklahoma	41	415	327	1.54	22,125	23,336	12.1	29.9	35.6	1.34	6.4
South Carolina	21	263	195	0.98	27,878	28,621	(D)	20.0	26.6	1.00	(D)
New Mexico	16	284	223	1.06	27,081	27,283	8.5	17.3	23.7	0.89	2.2
Georgia	21	190	152	0.71	28,742	27,921	6.6	15.2	20.1	0.75	1.7
Utah	14	151	102	0.56	35,477	37,206	(D)	12.2	15.3	0.58	(D)
Montana	19	107	78	0.40	29,224	31,885	3.1	7.2	9.1	0.34	1.2
Indiana	98	750*	(D)	2.79	-	(D)	(D)	(D)	(D)	-	(D)
Minnesota	74	750*	(D)	2.79	-	(D)	(D)	(D)	(D)	-	(D)
Nebraska	54	375*	(D)	1.39	-	(D)	(D)	(D)	(D)	-	(D)
Oregon	49	750*	(D)	2.79	-	(D)	(D)	(D)	(D)	-	11.9
Connecticut	36	375*	(D)	1.39	-	(D)	(D)	(D)	(D)	-	2.5
Maryland	34	375*	(D)	1.39	-	(D)	(D)	(D)	(D)	-	(D)
Idaho	25	175*	(D)	0.65	-	(D)	(D)	(D)	(D)	-	(D)

Source: Economic Census of the U.S., 1997. Data are sorted by 1997 revenues or establishments. (D) means data suppression to prevent disclosure of company data. A dash (-) is used when data are unavailable or can-not be calculated. Data followed by an * indicate the midpoint of a range. The ranges are: for 10, 0-19; for 60, 20-99, for 175, 100-249, for 375, 250-499, for 750, 500-999. Higher values are multiples of those shown, e.g., 3,750 is the midpoint of the range 2,500-4,999. Shaded *states* indicate states in which the industry was active in 1997. Shaded *regions* indicate where the industry is regionally most concentrated.

NAICS 212322 - INDUSTRIAL SAND MINING*

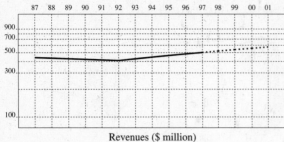

Revenues ($ million)

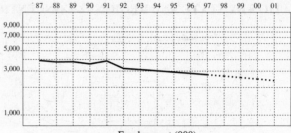

Employment (000)

GENERAL STATISTICS

| Year | Com-panies | Establishments | | Employment | | | Compensation | | Production ($ million) | | | |
		Total	with 20 or more employees	Total (No.)	Production Workers (No.)	Hours (Mil)	Payroll ($ mil)	Wages ($/hr)	Cost of Materials	Value Added by Mining	Value of Shipments	Capital Invest.
1977	115	188	68	4,700	3,500	7.6	63.1	5.72	128.4	155.2	249.7	33.9
1982	132	206	68	4,300	3,200	6.6	83.2	8.35	159.3	223.5	341.9	40.9
1987	121	191	65	3,900	2,800	5.7	98.9	10.79	157.4	308.3	442.1	23.5
1988	116	176[1]	64[1]	3,764[1]	2,668	5.5	100.6[1]	11.05	157.7	301.9	435.7	-
1989	112	176[1]	64[1]	3,780[1]	2,543	5.2	106.2[1]	11.32	157.9	295.7	429.3	-
1990	108	173[1]	64[1]	3,582[1]	2,423	5.0	97.2[1]	11.59	158.2	289.6	423.0	-
1991	104	171[1]	65[1]	3,855[1]	2,309	4.8	102.0[1]	11.87	158.4	283.6	416.9	-
1992	100	161	60	3,200	2,200	4.6	97.6	12.15	158.7	277.8	410.8	25.6
1993	97	157	58	3,108	2,173	4.5	95.9	12.52	161.5	294.7	429.1	-
1994	94	153	56	3,016	2,147	4.5	94.1	12.90	164.2	311.6	447.4	-
1995	90	148	55	2,923	2,120	4.4	92.4	13.27	167.0	328.4	465.6	-
1996	87	144	53	2,831	2,094	4.4	90.6	13.65	169.7	345.3	483.9	-
1997	84	140	51	2,739	2,067	4.3	88.9	14.02	172.5	362.2	502.2	32.5
1998	81p	136p	49p	2,647p	2,040p	4.2p	87.2p	14.39p	175.3p	379.1p	520.5p	-
1999	78p	132p	47p	2,555p	2,014p	4.2p	85.4p	14.77p	178.0p	396.0p	538.8p	-
2000	74p	127p	46p	2,462p	1,987p	4.1p	83.7p	15.14p	180.8p	412.8p	557.0p	-
2001	71p	123p	44p	2,370p	1,961p	4.1p	81.9p	15.52p	183.5p	429.7p	575.3p	-

Sources: *Economic Census of the United States*, 1977, 1982, 1987, 1992, and 1997. Data for those years (years are in **bold** type) are from the 5-year censuses of the economy. Other values, unless otherwise noted, are extrapolations. Values footnoted 1 are from the *County Business Patterns* for the years indicated. Values marked with *p* are projections. Data are the most recent available at this level of detail.

INDICES OF CHANGE

| Year | Com-panies | Establishments | | Employment | | | Compensation | | Production ($ million) | | | |
		Total	with 20 or more employees	Total (No.)	Production Workers (No.)	Hours (Mil)	Payroll ($ mil)	Wages ($/hr)	Cost of Materials	Value Added by Mining	Value of Shipments	Capital Invest.
1977	136.9	134.3	133.3	171.6	169.3	176.7	71.0	40.8	74.4	42.8	49.7	104.3
1982	157.1	147.1	133.3	157.0	154.8	153.5	93.6	59.6	92.3	61.7	68.1	125.8
1987	144.0	136.4	127.5	142.4	135.5	132.6	111.2	77.0	91.2	85.1	88.0	72.3
1992	119.0	115.0	117.6	116.8	106.4	107.0	109.8	86.7	92.0	76.7	81.8	78.8
1997	100.0	100.0	100.0	100.0	100.0	100.0	100.0	100.0	100.0	100.0	100.0	100.0

Sources: Same as General Statistics. The values shown reflect change from the base year, 1997. Values above 100 mean greater than 1997, values below 100 mean less than 1997, and a value of 100 in years other than 1997 means same as 1997. Indices are calculated only for Census years. Data are the most recent available at this level of detail.

SELECTED RATIOS

For 1992	Avg. of Sector	Analyzed Industry	Index	For 1992	Avg. of Sector	Analyzed Industry	Index
Employees per Establishment	20.4	19.6	96	Value Added per Production Worker	335,283	175,230	52
Payroll per Establishment	831,719	635,000	76	Cost per Establishment	2,854,087	1,232,143	43
Payroll per Employee	40,815	32,457	80	Cost per Employee	140,057	62,979	45
Production Workers per Establishment	15.6	14.8	95	Cost per Production Worker	183,057	83,454	46
Wages per Establishment	613,139	430,614	70	Shipments per Establishment	6,840,788	3,587,143	52
Wages per Production Worker	39,326	29,166	74	Shipments per Employee	335,695	183,352	55
Hours per Production Worker	2,075	2,080	100	Shipments per Production Worker	438,757	242,961	55
Wages per Hour	18.96	14.02	74	Investment per Establishment	1,242,441	232,143	19
Value Added per Establishment	5,227,487	2,587,143	49	Investment per Employee	60,970	11,866	19
Value Added per Employee	256,526	132,238	52	Investment per Production Worker	79,688	15,723	20

Sources: Same as General Statistics. The 'Average of Sector' column represents the average for all industries in this sector. The Index shows the relationship between the Average and the Analyzed Industry. For example, 100 means that they are equal; 500 that the Analyzed Industry is five times the average; 50 means that the Analyzed Industry is half the national average. 'na' is used to show that data are 'not available'.

*Equivalent to SIC 1446.

LEADING COMPANIES   Number shown: **8**   Total sales ($ mil): **2,433**   Total employment (000): **8.6**

Company Name	Address				CEO Name	Phone	Co. Type	Sales ($ mil)	Empl. (000)
J.M. Huber Corp.	333 Thornall St	Edison	NJ	08837		732-549-8600	R	1,500	5.0
South Jersey Industries Inc.	1 S Jersey Plaza	Folsom	NJ	08037	Charles Biscieglia	609-561-9000	P	392	0.7
U.S. Borax Inc.	26877 Tourney Rd	Valencia	CA	91355		661-287-5400	S	310*	1.0
U.S. Silica Co.	PO Box 187	Berkeley Sprgs	WV	25411	Richard Goodell	304-258-2500	S	120*	0.8
Zemex Industrial Minerals Inc.	1040 Crown Pointe	Atlanta	GA	30338	Peter J Goodwin Jr	770-392-8660	S	58*	0.3
South Jersey Industry	1 S Jersey Plz	Folsom	NJ	08037	Charles Biscieglia	609-561-9000	S	27	0.7
Short Mountain Silica Co.	170 Silica Rd	Mooresburg	TN	37811	J D Nicewonder	423-272-5700	S	22*	0.1
Reserve Industries Corp.	20 1st Plz	Albuquerque	NM	87102	Frank C Melfi	505-247-2384	P	4	<0.1

Source: Ward's Business Directory of U.S. Private and Public Companies, Volumes 1 and 2, 2000. The company type code used is as follows: P - Public, R - Private, S - Subsidiary, D - Division, J - Joint Venture, A - Affiliate, G - Group, N - Company type not reported. Sales are in millions of dollars, employees are in thousands. An asterisk (*) indicates an estimated sales volume. The symbol < stands for 'less than'. Company names and addresses are truncated, in some cases, to fit into the available space.

MINING PRODUCT DETAILS

Products	Units	Quantity of (000s)		Value of product shipments				
		Production 1997	Shipments 1997	1992		1997		
				($ mil)	% of total	($ mil)	% of total	
Industrial sand		NA	NA	413.9	100.0	495.0	100.0	
Industrial glass sand	mil s tons	13	13	177.9	43.0	211.9	42.8	
Industrial molding sand	mil s tons	6	6	69.0	16.7	83.1	16.8	
Other industrial sand	mil s tons	7	7	138.9	33.5	175.3	35.4	
Industrial sand, nsk[1]		NA	NA	28.1	6.8	24.7	5.0	

Source: Economic Census of the U.S., 1997. Notes: 1. Includes value for establishments that did not report detailed data and estimates for small companies (estimates were made from administrative-record data rather than collected from respondents). NA stands for not applicable. (D) means data are withheld to avoid disclosure of competitive information. (S) indicates that data did not meet publication standards. - means not available or zero.

LOCATION BY STATE AND REGIONAL CONCENTRATION

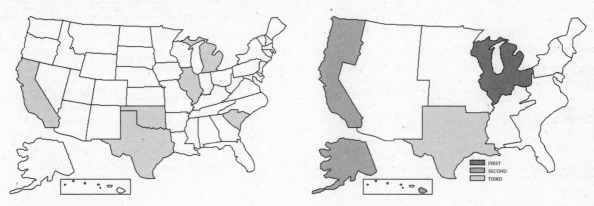

INDUSTRY DATA BY STATE

State	Estab- lish- ments	Employment			Compensation		Production				Capital Exp. ($ mil)
		Total	Workers	Total as % of US	Payroll per Employee	Wages per Worker	Costs ($ mil)	Value Added ($ mil)	Reve- nues ($ mil)	% of US	
Illinois	10	383	280	13.98	37,094	33,904	26.4	66.6	89.1	24.60	3.8
California	10	180	143	6.57	35,133	34,930	12.9	21.5	33.2	9.16	1.3
New Jersey	8	180	130	6.57	38,556	34,862	(D)	19.1	32.2	8.88	(D)
Michigan	11	124	91	4.53	35,218	32,176	9.8	18.1	27.0	7.47	0.9
Oklahoma	3	105	94	3.83	32,133	31,468	6.8	20.4	26.4	7.30	0.8
Texas	15	375*	(D)	13.69	-	(D)	(D)	(D)	(D)	-	2.8
Ohio	7	175*	(D)	6.39	-	(D)	(D)	(D)	(D)	-	(D)
South Carolina	7	175*	(D)	6.39	-	(D)	(D)	(D)	(D)	-	3.5
Tennessee	4	175*	(D)	6.39	-	(D)	(D)	(D)	(D)	-	(D)
Wisconsin	4	175*	(D)	6.39	-	(D)	(D)	(D)	(D)	-	(D)

Source: Economic Census of the U.S., 1997. Data are sorted by 1997 revenues or establishments. (D) means data suppression to prevent disclosure of company data. A dash (-) is used when data are unavailable or cannot be calculated. Data followed by an * indicate the midpoint of a range. The ranges are: for 10, 0-19; for 60, 20-99; for 175, 100-249; for 375, 250-499; for 750, 500-999. Higher values are multiples of those shown, e.g., 3,750 is the midpoint of the range 2,500-4,999. Shaded *states* indicate states in which the industry was active in 1997. Shaded *regions* indicate where the industry is regionally most concentrated.

NAICS 212324 - KAOLIN AND BALL CLAY MINING

GENERAL STATISTICS

| Year | Com-panies | Establishments | | Employment | | | Compensation | | Production ($ million) | | | |
		Total	with 20 or more employees	Total (No.)	Production Workers (No.)	Hours (Mil)	Payroll ($ mil)	Wages ($/hr)	Cost of Materials	Value Added by Mining	Value of Shipments	Capital Invest.
1997	20	33	29	3,530	2,546	5.6	141.3	16.09	363.5	630.2	917.3	76.4

Source: Economic Census of the United States, 1997. This is a newly defined industry. Data for prior years were unavailable at the time of publication but may become available over time.

DISTRIBUTION AMONG SIC-BASED INDUSTRIES - 1997

| SIC | Industry | Estab-lish-ments | Employment | | | Compensation | | Production ($ mil) | |
			Total	Production Workers	Hours (Mil)	Payroll ($ mil)	Wages ($/hr)	Cost of Materials	Value of Shipments
145500	Kaolin & ball clay	33	3,530	2,546	5.6	141.3	15.96	363.5	917.3

Source: 1997 Economic Census. U.S. Census Bureau, U.S. Department of Commerce, August 1997. SIC codes ending in two zeroes represent complete 4-digit SICs. All others are parts of 4-digit SIC industries. Items showing a dash (-) indicate that data are not available because of disclosure problems.

SIC INDUSTRIES RELATED TO NAICS 212324

SIC	Industry	1990	1991	1992	1993	1994	1995	1996	1997
1455	**Kaolin and Ball Clay**								
	Establishments (number)	36	34	45	41	40	40	45*p*	45*p*
	Employment (thousands)	3.7	3.9	5.0	3.9	3.9	4.0	4.8*e*	4.7*e*
	Revenues ($ million)	768.3*e*	774.3*e*	780.4	786.5*e*	792.7*e*	798.9*e*	805.2*e*	811.5*e*
3295	**Minerals & Earths Ground Etc.***								
	Establishments (number)	347	354	368	357	349	355	328*p*	320*p*
	Employment (thousands)	10.7	8.7	9.5	9.4	9.4	10.2	10.5	9.9*p*
	Value of Shipments ($ million)	1,499.8	1,523.3	1,774.4	1,847.6	1,830.1	1,993.0	1,990.8	1,997.5*p*

Source: Economic Census of the United States, 1992, annual surveys of economic sectors conducted by the Bureau of the Census, and estimates or projections based on the 1982-1992 period; not all data are shown. 'e' marks estimates made by the editors; 'p' indicates projections based on time series. A dash (-) indicates that data for this SIC or year were not available. * Indicates that only a portion of this industry is present within the NAICS data. If no * is shown, the entire industry is contained within the NAICS data.

INDICES OF CHANGE

| Year | Com-panies | Establishments | | Employment | | | Compensation | | Production ($ million) | | | |
		Total	with 20 or more employees	Total (No.)	Production Workers (No.)	Hours (Mil)	Payroll ($ mil)	Wages ($/hr)	Cost of Materials	Value Added by Mining	Value of Shipments	Capital Invest.
1997	100.0	100.0	100.0	100.0	100.0	100.0	100.0	100.0	100.0	100.0	100.0	100.0

Sources: Same as General Statistics. The values shown reflect change from the base year, 1997. Values above 100 mean greater than 1997, values below 100 mean less than 1997, and a value of 100 in years other than 1997 means same as 1997. Indices are calculated only for Census years. Data are the most recent available at this level of detail.

SELECTED RATIOS

For 1992	Avg. of Sector	Analyzed Industry	Index	For 1992	Avg. of Sector	Analyzed Industry	Index
Employees per Establishment	20.4	107.0	524	Value Added per Production Worker	335,283	247,526	74
Payroll per Establishment	831,719	4,281,818	515	Cost per Establishment	2,854,087	11,015,152	386
Payroll per Employee	40,815	40,028	98	Cost per Employee	140,057	102,975	74
Production Workers per Establishment	15.6	77.2	495	Cost per Production Worker	183,057	142,773	78
Wages per Establishment	613,139	2,730,424	445	Shipments per Establishment	6,840,788	27,796,970	406
Wages per Production Worker	39,326	35,390	90	Shipments per Employee	335,695	259,858	77
Hours per Production Worker	2,075	2,200	106	Shipments per Production Worker	438,757	360,291	82
Wages per Hour	18.96	16.09	85	Investment per Establishment	1,242,441	2,315,152	186
Value Added per Establishment	5,227,487	19,096,970	365	Investment per Employee	60,970	21,643	35
Value Added per Employee	256,526	178,527	70	Investment per Production Worker	79,688	30,008	38

Sources: Same as General Statistics. The 'Average of Sector' column represents the average for all industries in this sector. The Index shows the relationship between the Average and the Analyzed Industry. For example, 100 means that they are equal; 500 that the Analyzed Industry is five times the average; 50 means that the Analyzed Industry is half the national average. 'na' is used to show that data are 'not available'.

LEADING COMPANIES   Number shown: **5**   Total sales ($ mil): **262**   Total employment (000): **1.8**

Company Name	Address				CEO Name	Phone	Co. Type	Sales ($ mil)	Empl. (000)
Hecla Mining Co.	P O Box C8000	Coeur D Alene	ID	83814	Arthur Brown	208-769-4100	P	159	1.2
Zemex Industrial Minerals Inc.	1040 Crown Pointe	Atlanta	GA	30338	Peter J Goodwin Jr	770-392-8660	S	58*	0.3
Kentucky-Tennessee Clay Co.	PO Box 6002	Mayfield	KY	42066	Robert M Carland	502-247-3061	S	30*	0.2
H.C. Spinks Clay Company Inc.	PO Box 820	Paris	TN	38242	R Carothers	901-642-5414	R	15*	0.1
Nord Resources Corp.	201 3rd St	Albuquerque	NM	87102	W Pierce Carson	505-766-9955	P	0	<0.1

Source: *Ward's Business Directory of U.S. Private and Public Companies*, Volumes 1 and 2, 2000. The company type code used is as follows: P - Public, R - Private, S - Subsidiary, D - Division, J - Joint Venture, A - Affiliate, G - Group, N - Company type not reported. Sales are in millions of dollars, employees are in thousands. An asterisk (*) indicates an estimated sales volume. The symbol < stands for 'less than'. Company names and addresses are truncated, in some cases, to fit into the available space.

MINING PRODUCT DETAILS

Products	Units	Quantity of (000s)		Value of product shipments				
		Production 1997	Shipments 1997	1992		1997		
				($ mil)	% of total	($ mil)	% of total	
Kaolin and ball clay		NA	NA	749.9	100.0	871.9	100.0	
Kaolin	1,000 metric tons	NA	9,375	-	-	820.2	94.1	
Ball clay	1,000 metric tons	NA	1,093	-	-	51.7	5.9	
Kaolin and ball clay, nsk[1]		NA	NA	-	-	-	-	

Source: *Economic Census of the U.S., 1997. Notes:* 1. Incudes value for establishments that did not report detailed data and estimates for small companies (estimates were made from administrative-record data rather than collected from respondents). NA stands for not applicable. (D) means data are withheld to avoid disclosure of competitive information. (S) indicates that data did not meet publication standards. - means not available or zero.

LOCATION BY STATE AND REGIONAL CONCENTRATION

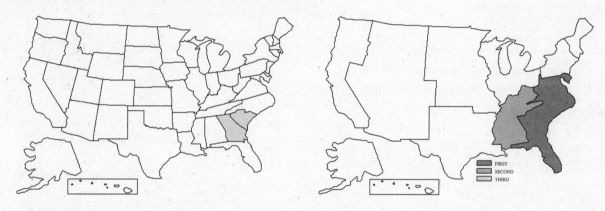

INDUSTRY DATA BY STATE

State	Establishments	Employment			Compensation		Production				Capital Exp. ($ mil)
		Total	Workers	Total as % of US	Payroll per Employee	Wages per Worker	Costs ($ mil)	Value Added ($ mil)	Revenues ($ mil)	% of US	
Georgia	17	2,857	2,059	80.93	41,532	37,095	330.2	574.1	834.3	132.39	70.0
Tennessee	3	235	165	6.66	35,340	28,721	(D)	23.6	28.5	4.52	(D)
South Carolina	5	200	156	5.67	35,510	30,333	13.9	14.7	26.5	4.20	2.1
Kentucky	2	175*	(D)	4.96	-	(D)	(D)	(D)	(D)	-	(D)

Source: *Economic Census of the U.S., 1997.* Data are sorted by 1997 revenues or establishments. (D) means data suppression to prevent disclosure of company data. A dash (-) is used when data are unavailable or cannot be calculated. Data followed by an * indicate the midpoint of a range. The ranges are: for 10, 0-19; for 60, 20-99, for 175, 100-249, for 375, 250-499, for 750, 500-999. Higher values are multiples of those shown, e.g., 3,750 is the midpoint of the range 2,500-4,999. Shaded *states* indicate states in which the industry was active in 1997. Shaded *regions* indicate where the industry is regionally most concentrated.

NAICS 212325 - CLAY AND CERAMIC AND REFRACTORY MINERALS MINING

GENERAL STATISTICS

Year	Companies	Establishments		Employment			Compensation		Production ($ million)			
		Total	with 20 or more employees	Total (No.)	Production Workers (No.)	Hours (Mil)	Payroll ($ mil)	Wages ($/hr)	Cost of Materials	Value Added by Mining	Value of Shipments	Capital Invest.
1997	99	131	55	3,778	2,953	6.0	118.3	14.52	256.4	434.0	618.3	72.2

Source: Economic Census of the United States, 1997. This is a newly defined industry. Data for prior years were unavailable at the time of publication but may become available over time.

DISTRIBUTION AMONG SIC-BASED INDUSTRIES - 1997

SIC	Industry	Establishments	Employment			Compensation		Production ($ mil)	
			Total	Production Workers	Hours (Mil)	Payroll ($ mil)	Wages ($/hr)	Cost of Materials	Value of Shipments
145900	Clay, ceramic, & refractory minerals, nec	131	3,778	2,953	6.0	118.3	14.55	256.5	618.3

Source: 1997 Economic Census. U.S. Census Bureau, U.S. Department of Commerce, August 1997. SIC codes ending in two zeroes represent complete 4-digit SICs. All others are parts of 4-digit SIC industries. Items showing a dash (-) indicate that data are not available because of disclosure problems.

SIC INDUSTRIES RELATED TO NAICS 212325

SIC	Industry	1990	1991	1992	1993	1994	1995	1996	1997
1459	**Clay and Related Minerals, n.e.c.**								
	Establishments (number) . . . , . . .	128	125	155	145	139	136	157p	158p
	Employment (thousands)	4.9	4.8	5.0	4.7	5.2e	4.8	5.3e	5.4e
	Revenues ($ million)	567.9e	593.3e	619.8	647.5e	676.4e	706.7e	738.2e	771.2e
3295	**Minerals & Earths Ground Etc.***								
	Establishments (number)	347	354	368	357	349	355	328p	320p
	Employment (thousands)	10.7	8.7	9.5	9.4	9.4	10.2	10.5	9.9p
	Value of Shipments ($ million) . .	1,499.8	1,523.3	1,774.4	1,847.6	1,830.1	1,993.0	1,990.8	1,997.5p

*Source: Economic Census of the United States, 1992, annual surveys of economic sectors conducted by the Bureau of the Census, and estimates or projections based on the 1982-1992 period; not all data are shown. 'e' marks estimates made by the editors; 'p' indicates projections based on time series. A dash (-) indicates that data for this SIC or year were not available. * Indicates that only a portion of this industry is present within the NAICS data. If no * is shown, the entire industry is contained within the NAICS data.*

INDICES OF CHANGE

Year	Companies	Establishments		Employment			Compensation		Production ($ million)			
		Total	with 20 or more employees	Total (No.)	Production Workers (No.)	Hours (Mil)	Payroll ($ mil)	Wages ($/hr)	Cost of Materials	Value Added by Mining	Value of Shipments	Capital Invest.
1997	100.0	100.0	100.0	100.0	100.0	100.0	100.0	100.0	100.0	100.0	100.0	100.0

Sources: Same as General Statistics. The values shown reflect change from the base year, 1997. Values above 100 mean greater than 1997, values below 100 mean less than 1997, and a value of 100 in years other than 1997 means same as 1997. Indices are calculated only for Census years. Data are the most recent available at this level of detail.

SELECTED RATIOS

For 1992	Avg. of Sector	Analyzed Industry	Index	For 1992	Avg. of Sector	Analyzed Industry	Index
Employees per Establishment	20.4	28.8	141	Value Added per Production Worker	335,283	146,969	44
Payroll per Establishment	831,719	903,053	109	Cost per Establishment	2,854,087	1,957,252	69
Payroll per Employee	40,815	31,313	77	Cost per Employee	140,057	67,867	48
Production Workers per Establishment	15.6	22.5	144	Cost per Production Worker	183,057	86,827	47
Wages per Establishment	613,139	665,038	108	Shipments per Establishment	6,840,788	4,719,847	69
Wages per Production Worker	39,326	29,502	75	Shipments per Employee	335,695	163,658	49
Hours per Production Worker	2,075	2,032	98	Shipments per Production Worker	438,757	209,380	48
Wages per Hour	18.96	14.52	77	Investment per Establishment	1,242,441	551,145	44
Value Added per Establishment	5,227,487	3,312,977	63	Investment per Employee	60,970	19,111	31
Value Added per Employee	256,526	114,876	45	Investment per Production Worker	79,688	24,450	31

Sources: Same as General Statistics. The 'Average of Sector' column represents the average for all industries in this sector. The Index shows the relationship between the Average and the Analyzed Industry. For example, 100 means that they are equal; 500 that the Analyzed Industry is five times the average; 50 means that the Analyzed Industry is half the national average. 'na' is used to show that data are 'not available'.

LEADING COMPANIES   Number shown: **5**   Total sales ($ mil): **675**   Total employment (000): **2.3**

Company Name	Address				CEO Name	Phone	Co. Type	Sales ($ mil)	Empl. (000)
AMCOL International Corp.	1500 W Shure Dr	Arlington H.	IL	60004	John Hughes	847-394-8730	P	552	1.6
Zemex Industrial Minerals Inc.	1040 Crown Pointe	Atlanta	GA	30338	Peter J Goodwin Jr	770-392-8660	S	58*	0.3
Kentucky-Tennessee Clay Co.	PO Box 6002	Mayfield	KY	42066	Robert M Carland	502-247-3061	S	30*	0.2
Black Hills Bentonite L.L.C.	PO Box 9	Mills	WY	82644	Tom Thorson	307-265-3740	R	29*	0.2
Vanderbilt Mineral Corp.	PO Box 5150	Norwalk	CT	06856		203-853-1400	S	6	<0.1

Source: Ward's Business Directory of U.S. Private and Public Companies, Volumes 1 and 2, 2000. The company type code used is as follows: P - Public, R - Private, S - Subsidiary, D - Division, J - Joint Venture, A - Affiliate, G - Group, N - Company type not reported. Sales are in millions of dollars, employees are in thousands. An asterisk (*) indicates an estimated sales volume. The symbol < stands for 'less than'. Company names and addresses are truncated, in some cases, to fit into the available space.

MINING PRODUCT DETAILS

Products	Units	Quantity of (000s)		Value of product shipments			
		Production 1997	Shipments 1997	1992		1997	
				($ mil)	% of total	($ mil)	% of total
Clay, ceramic and refractory minerals		NA	NA	611.1	100.0	611.0	100.0
Bentonite	1,000 metric tons	NA	4,107	142.5	23.3	180.5	29.5
Fire clay[1]	1,000 metric tons	NA	319	-	-	2.8	0.5
Fuller's earth	1,000 metric tons	NA	1,553	180.5	29.5	225.7	36.9
Feldspar (crude, crushed, or ground)	1,000 metric tons	NA	644	96.7	15.8	37.3	6.1
Crude common (miscellaneous) clay and shale	1,000 metric tons	NA	725	7.5	1.2	5.1	0.8
Prepared common (miscellaneous) clay and shale	1,000 metric tons	NA	3,750	79.8	13.1	86.9	14.2
Other clay, ceramic, and refractory minerals including magnesite and brucite	1,000 metric tons	NA	1,085	84.4	13.8	61.4	10.0
Other clay, ceramic, and refractory minerals, nsk[2]		NA	NA	13.8	2.3	11.4	1.9

Source: Economic Census of the U.S., 1997. Notes: 1. Excludes quantity of crude clay mined and used at establishments classified in manufacturing industries. 2. Includes value for establishments that did not report detailed data and estimates for small companies (estimates were made from administrative-record data rather than collected from respondents). NA stands for not applicable. (D) means data are withheld to avoid disclosure of competitive information. (S) indicates that data did not meet publication standards. - means not available or zero.

LOCATION BY STATE AND REGIONAL CONCENTRATION

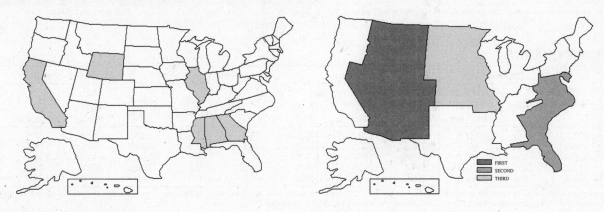

FIRST
SECOND
THIRD

INDUSTRY DATA BY STATE

State	Establishments	Employment			Compensation		Production				Capital Exp. ($ mil)
		Total	Workers	Total as % of US	Payroll per Employee	Wages per Worker	Costs ($ mil)	Value Added ($ mil)	Revenues ($ mil)	% of US	
Wyoming	13	519	441	13.74	34,368	33,440	68.4	85.5	145.9	33.62	8.0
Missouri	12	224	186	5.93	30,277	29,532	(D)	50.3	64.5	14.86	(D)
Georgia	7	469	385	12.41	31,341	28,914	21.3	46.2	62.4	14.39	5.1
Texas	9	288	181	7.62	35,295	29,768	(D)	40.5	62.0	14.29	(D)
Mississippi	9	400	340	10.59	25,950	23,838	22.1	33.5	49.6	11.44	6.0
Illinois	3	172	125	4.55	29,145	33,104	14.7	20.9	35.0	8.07	0.6
California	10	149	99	3.94	37,074	28,303	6.7	25.2	30.7	7.08	1.1
North Carolina	4	168	138	4.45	39,810	36,261	(D)	19.6	27.9	6.42	(D)
Alabama	9	206	164	5.45	25,699	23,604	8.2	11.2	18.1	4.17	1.3
Florida	9	288	216	7.62	26,361	24,023	(D)	5.7	13.5	3.10	(D)
Virginia	5	375*	(D)	9.93	-	(D)	(D)	(D)	(D)	-	(D)

*Source: Economic Census of the U.S., 1997. Data are sorted by 1997 revenues or establishments. (D) means data suppression to prevent disclosure of company data. A dash (-) is used when data are unavailable or cannot be calculated. Data followed by an * indicate the midpoint of a range. The ranges are: for 10, 0-19; for 60, 20-99, for 175, 100-249, for 375, 250-499, for 750, 500-999. Higher values are multiples of those shown, e.g., 3,750 is the midpoint of the range 2,500-4,999. Shaded states indicate states in which the industry was active in 1997. Shaded regions indicate where the industry was regionally most concentrated.*

NAICS 212391 - POTASH, SODA, AND BORATE MINERAL MINING*

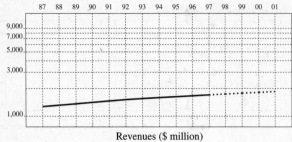

Revenues ($ million)

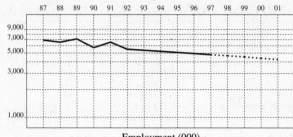

Employment (000)

GENERAL STATISTICS

Year	Com- panies	Establishments		Employment			Compensation		Production ($ million)			
		Total	with 20 or more employees	Total (No.)	Production Workers (No.)	Hours (Mil)	Payroll ($ mil)	Wages ($/hr)	Cost of Materials	Value Added by Mining	Value of Shipments	Capital Invest.
1977	23	31	25	9,400	6,900	14.3	151.8	7.29	426.6	562.8	816.5	172.9
1982	25	37	28	10,500	7,200	15.1	310.5	12.73	569.4	954.3	1,290.8	232.9
1987	25	30	19	6,900	5,300	11.4	234.5	15.53	439.1	915.0	1,271.8	82.3
1988	24	30¹	19¹	6,553¹	5,083	10.8	225.3¹	15.94	436.2	958.6	1,317.2	-
1989	23	28¹	21¹	7,101¹	4,875	10.3	275.5¹	16.37	433.4	1,004.3	1,364.3	-
1990	22	24¹	18¹	5,718¹	4,675	9.8	240.3¹	16.81	430.5	1,052.1	1,413.0	-
1991	21	28¹	18¹	6,554¹	4,484	9.4	273.8¹	17.27	427.7	1,102.3	1,463.4	-
1992	20	33	24	5,500	4,300	8.9	225.4	17.73	424.9	1,154.8	1,515.7	64.0
1993	20	32	23	5,361	4,210	8.7	227.8	18.63	451.4	1,183.0	1,553.2	-
1994	19	31	22	5,222	4,120	8.5	230.2	19.53	478.0	1,211.2	1,590.6	-
1995	19	29	21	5,083	4,029	8.4	232.6	20.42	504.5	1,239.5	1,628.1	-
1996	18	28	20	4,944	3,939	8.2	235.0	21.32	531.1	1,267.7	1,665.5	-
1997	18	27	19	4,805	3,849	8.0	237.4	22.22	557.6	1,295.9	1,703.0	150.5
1998	18p	26p	18p	4,666p	3,759p	7.8p	239.8p	23.12p	584.1p	1,324.1p	1,740.5p	-
1999	17p	25p	17p	4,527p	3,669p	7.6p	242.2p	24.02p	610.7p	1,352.3p	1,777.9p	-
2000	17p	23p	16p	4,388p	3,578p	7.5p	244.6p	24.91p	637.2p	1,380.6p	1,815.4p	-
2001	16p	22p	15p	4,249p	3,488p	7.3p	247.0p	25.81p	663.8p	1,408.8p	1,852.8p	-

Sources: *Economic Census of the United States*, 1977, 1982, 1987, 1992, and 1997. Data for those years (years are in **bold** type) are from the 5-year censuses of the economy. Other values, unless otherwise noted, are extrapolations. Values footnoted 1 are from the *County Business Patterns* for the years indicated. Values marked with *p* are projections. Data are the most recent available at this level of detail.

INDICES OF CHANGE

Year	Com- panies	Establishments		Employment			Compensation		Production ($ million)			
		Total	with 20 or more employees	Total (No.)	Production Workers (No.)	Hours (Mil)	Payroll ($ mil)	Wages ($/hr)	Cost of Materials	Value Added by Mining	Value of Shipments	Capital Invest.
1977	127.8	114.8	131.6	195.6	179.3	178.8	63.9	32.8	76.5	43.4	47.9	114.9
1982	138.9	137.0	147.4	218.5	187.1	188.8	130.8	57.3	102.1	73.6	75.8	154.8
1987	138.9	111.1	100.0	143.6	137.7	142.5	98.8	69.9	78.7	70.6	74.7	54.7
1992	111.1	122.2	126.3	114.5	111.7	111.2	94.9	79.8	76.2	89.1	89.0	42.5
1997	100.0	100.0	100.0	100.0	100.0	100.0	100.0	100.0	100.0	100.0	100.0	100.0

Sources: Same as General Statistics. The values shown reflect change from the base year, 1997. Values above 100 mean greater than 1997, values below 100 mean less than 1997, and a value of 100 in years other than 1997 means same as 1997. Indices are calculated only for Census years. Data are the most recent available at this level of detail.

SELECTED RATIOS

For 1992	Avg. of Sector	Analyzed Industry	Index	For 1992	Avg. of Sector	Analyzed Industry	Index
Employees per Establishment	20.4	178.0	872	Value Added per Production Worker	335,283	336,685	100
Payroll per Establishment	831,719	8,792,593	1,057	Cost per Establishment	2,854,087	20,651,852	724
Payroll per Employee	40,815	49,407	121	Cost per Employee	140,057	116,046	83
Production Workers per Establishment	15.6	142.6	914	Cost per Production Worker	183,057	144,869	79
Wages per Establishment	613,139	6,583,704	1,074	Shipments per Establishment	6,840,788	63,074,074	922
Wages per Production Worker	39,326	46,183	117	Shipments per Employee	335,695	354,422	106
Hours per Production Worker	2,075	2,078	100	Shipments per Production Worker	438,757	442,453	101
Wages per Hour	18.96	22.22	117	Investment per Establishment	1,242,441	5,574,074	449
Value Added per Establishment	5,227,487	47,996,296	918	Investment per Employee	60,970	31,322	51
Value Added per Employee	256,526	269,698	105	Investment per Production Worker	79,688	39,101	49

Sources: Same as General Statistics. The 'Average of Sector' column represents the average for all industries in this sector. The Index shows the relationship between the Average and the Analyzed Industry. For example, 100 means that they are equal; 500 that the Analyzed Industry is five times the average; 50 means that the Analyzed Industry is half the national average. 'na' is used to show that data are 'not available'.

*Equivalent to SIC 1474.

LEADING COMPANIES   Number shown: **6**   Total sales ($ mil): **2,374**   Total employment (000): **8.5**

Company Name	Address				CEO Name	Phone	Co. Type	Sales ($ mil)	Empl. (000)
IMC Chemicals Inc.	8300 College Blvd	Overland Park	KS	66210	Jon Tancredi	913-344-9200	S	840*	3.2
IMC Kalium	2345 Waukegan Rd	Bannockburn	IL	60015	John H Huber	847-607-3000	S	600*	2.5
Trans-Resources Inc.	9 W 57th St	New York	NY	10019	Arie Genger	212-888-3044	R	376	0.9
U.S. Borax Inc.	26877 Tourney Rd	Valencia	CA	91355		661-287-5400	S	310*	1.0
Mississippi Potash Inc.	PO Box 101	Carlsbad	NM	88221		505-887-5591	S	141*	0.5
TG Soda Ash Inc.	PO Box 100	Granger	WY	82934		307-875-2700	S	107*	0.4

Source: *Ward's Business Directory of U.S. Private and Public Companies*, Volumes 1 and 2, 2000. The company type code used is as follows: P - Public, R - Private, S - Subsidiary, D - Division, J - Joint Venture, A - Affiliate, G - Group, N - Company type not reported. Sales are in millions of dollars, employees are in thousands. An asterisk (*) indicates an estimated sales volume. The symbol < stands for 'less than'. Company names and addresses are truncated, in some cases, to fit into the available space.

MINING PRODUCT DETAILS

Products	Units	Quantity of (000s)		Value of product shipments				
		Produc- tion 1997	Ship- ments 1997	1992		1997		
				($ mil)	% of total	($ mil)	% of total	
Potash, soda, and borate		NA	NA	1,505.5	100.0	1,689.6	100.0	
Potassium salts and boron compounds	1,000 metric tons	4,425	4,320	-	-	725.0	42.9	
Sodium carbonate (natural)	1,000 metric tons	NA	(D)	832.9	55.3	(D)	-	
Sodium sulfate (natural)	1,000 metric tons	NA	(D)	27.6	1.8	(D)	-	
Potash, soda, and borate minerals, nsk[1]		NA	NA	4.3	0.3	-	-	

Source: *Economic Census of the U.S., 1997. Notes:* 1. Includes value for establishments that did not report detailed data and estimates for small companies (estimates were made from administrative record data rather than collected from respondents). NA stands for not applicable. (D) means data are withheld to avoid disclosure of competitive information. (S) indicates that data did not meet publication standards. - means not available or zero.

LOCATION BY STATE AND REGIONAL CONCENTRATION

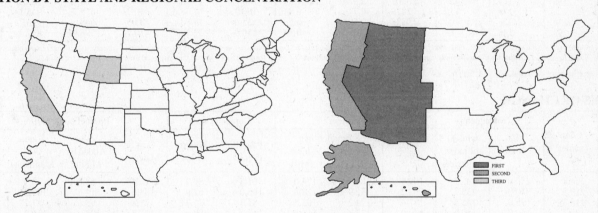

FIRST
SECOND
THIRD

INDUSTRY DATA BY STATE

State	Estab- lish- ments	Employment			Compensation		Production				Capital Exp. ($ mil)
		Total	Workers	Total as % of US	Payroll per Employee	Wages per Worker	Costs ($ mil)	Value Added ($ mil)	Reve- nues ($ mil)	% of US	
Wyoming	6	2,750	2,171	57.23	56,687	54,910	375.6	565.3	838.6	64.71	102.3
California	8	472	385	9.82	48,568	42,935	82.0	474.3	544.1	41.99	12.2
Utah	3	122	105	2.54	36,098	31,171	(D)	63.6	71.4	5.51	(D)
New Mexico	6	1,750*	(D)	36.42	-	(D)	(D)	(D)	(D)	-	(D)

Source: *Economic Census of the U.S., 1997.* Data are sorted by 1997 revenues or establishments. (D) means data suppression to prevent disclosure of company data. A dash (-) is used when data are unavailable or cannot be calculated. Data followed by an * indicate the midpoint of a range. The ranges are: for 10, 0-19; for 60, 20-99; for 175, 100-249; for 375, 250-499; for 750, 500-999. Higher values are multiples of those shown, e.g., 3,750 is the midpoint of the range 2,500-4,999. Shaded *states* indicate states in which the industry was active in 1997. Shaded *regions* indicate where the industry is regionally most concentrated.

NAICS 212392 - PHOSPHATE ROCK MINING*

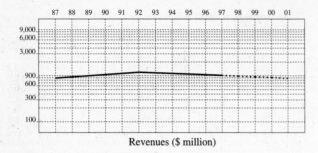

Revenues ($ million)

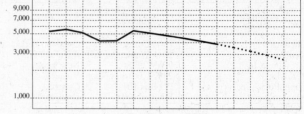

Employment (000)

GENERAL STATISTICS

| Year | Com-panies | Establishments | | Employment | | | Compensation | | Production ($ million) | | | |
		Total	with 20 or more employees	Total (No.)	Production Workers (No.)	Hours (Mil)	Payroll ($ mil)	Wages ($/hr)	Cost of Materials	Value Added by Mining	Value of Shipments	Capital Invest.
1977	31	50	33	7,700	5,900	12.7	104.7	6.23	384.6	439.7	751.2	73.1
1982	32	48	33	7,800	4,800	9.4	179.6	10.54	538.3	732.5	1,047.7	223.0
1987	32	39	26	5,300	3,900	7.7	139.5	12.01	365.9	595.1	886.7	74.3
1988	30	35[1]	20[1]	5,573[1]	3,958	7.9	141.7[1]	12.55	408.4	613.0	940.3	-
1989	28	30[1]	22[1]	5,127[1]	4,017	8.0	140.3[1]	13.12	455.9	631.4	997.1	-
1990	26	28[1]	18[1]	4,168[1]	4,077	8.2	133.1[1]	13.71	508.8	650.3	1,057.3	-
1991	24	25[1]	18[1]	4,191[1]	4,138	8.4	134.4[1]	14.32	567.9	669.9	1,121.2	-
1992	22	28	21	5,400	4,200	8.6	192.7	14.97	633.9	690.0	1,188.9	134.9
1993	21	26	20	5,092	3,988	8.3	188.1	15.33	609.1	679.8	1,154.5	-
1994	19	25	18	4,783	3,776	8.1	183.4	15.69	584.3	669.6	1,120.1	-
1995	18	23	17	4,475	3,564	7.8	178.8	16.04	559.5	659.5	1,085.7	-
1996	16	22	15	4,166	3,352	7.6	174.1	16.40	534.7	649.3	1,051.3	-
1997	15	20	14	3,858	3,140	7.3	169.5	16.76	509.9	639.1	1,016.9	132.0
1998	14p	18p	13p	3,550p	2,928p	7.0p	164.9p	17.12p	485.1p	628.9p	982.5p	-
1999	12p	17p	11p	3,241p	2,716p	6.8p	160.2p	17.48p	460.3p	618.7p	948.1p	-
2000	11p	15p	10p	2,933p	2,504p	6.5p	155.6p	17.83p	435.5p	608.6p	913.7p	-
2001	9p	14p	8p	2,624p	2,292p	6.3p	150.9p	18.19p	410.7p	598.4p	879.3p	-

Sources: Economic Census of the United States, 1977, 1982, 1987, 1992, and 1997. Data for those years (years are in **bold** type) are from the 5-year censuses of the economy. Other values, unless otherwise noted, are extrapolations. Values footnoted 1 are from the *County Business Patterns* for the years indicated. Values marked with *p* are projections. Data are the most recent available at this level of detail.

INDICES OF CHANGE

| Year | Com-panies | Establishments | | Employment | | | Compensation | | Production ($ million) | | | |
		Total	with 20 or more employees	Total (No.)	Production Workers (No.)	Hours (Mil)	Payroll ($ mil)	Wages ($/hr)	Cost of Materials	Value Added by Mining	Value of Shipments	Capital Invest.
1977	206.7	250.0	235.7	199.6	187.9	174.0	61.8	37.2	75.4	68.8	73.9	55.4
1982	213.3	240.0	235.7	202.2	152.9	128.8	106.0	62.9	105.6	114.6	103.0	168.9
1987	213.3	195.0	185.7	137.4	124.2	105.5	82.3	71.7	71.8	93.1	87.2	56.3
1992	146.7	140.0	150.0	140.0	133.8	117.8	113.7	89.3	124.3	108.0	116.9	102.2
1997	100.0	100.0	100.0	100.0	100.0	100.0	100.0	100.0	100.0	100.0	100.0	100.0

Sources: Same as General Statistics. The values shown reflect change from the base year, 1997. Values above 100 mean greater than 1997, values below 100 mean less than 1997, and a value of 100 in years other than 1997 means same as 1997. Indices are calculated only for Census years. Data are the most recent available at this level of detail.

SELECTED RATIOS

For 1992	Avg. of Sector	Analyzed Industry	Index	For 1992	Avg. of Sector	Analyzed Industry	Index
Employees per Establishment	20.4	192.9	946	Value Added per Production Worker	335,283	203,535	61
Payroll per Establishment	831,719	8,475,000	1,019	Cost per Establishment	2,854,087	25,495,000	893
Payroll per Employee	40,815	43,935	108	Cost per Employee	140,057	132,167	94
Production Workers per Establishment	15.6	157.0	1,006	Cost per Production Worker	183,057	162,389	89
Wages per Establishment	613,139	6,117,400	998	Shipments per Establishment	6,840,788	50,845,000	743
Wages per Production Worker	39,326	38,964	99	Shipments per Employee	335,695	263,582	79
Hours per Production Worker	2,075	2,325	112	Shipments per Production Worker	438,757	323,854	74
Wages per Hour	18.96	16.76	88	Investment per Establishment	1,242,441	6,600,000	531
Value Added per Establishment	5,227,487	31,955,000	611	Investment per Employee	60,970	34,215	56
Value Added per Employee	256,526	165,656	65	Investment per Production Worker	79,688	42,038	53

Sources: Same as General Statistics. The 'Average of Sector' column represents the average for all industries in this sector. The Index shows the relationship between the Average and the Analyzed Industry. For example, 100 means that they are equal; 500 that the Analyzed Industry is five times the average; 50 means that the Analyzed Industry is half the national average. 'na' is used to show that data are 'not available'.

*Equivalent to SIC 1475.

LEADING COMPANIES   Number shown: **1**   Total sales ($ mil): **184**   Total employment (000): **0.4**

Company Name	Address			CEO Name	Phone	Co. Type	Sales ($ mil)	Empl. (000)
IMC-Agrico Co.	7250 Hwy 44	Uncle Sam	LA 70792		225-562-3501	S	184*	0.4

Source: Ward's Business Directory of U.S. Private and Public Companies, Volumes 1 and 2, 2000. The company type code used is as follows: P - Public, R - Private, S - Subsidiary, D - Division, J - Joint Venture, A - Affiliate, G - Group, N - Company type not reported. Sales are in millions of dollars, employees are in thousands. An asterisk (*) indicates an estimated sales volume. The symbol < stands for 'less than'. Company names and addresses are truncated, in some cases, to fit into the available space.

MINING PRODUCT DETAILS

Products	Units	Quantity of (000s)		Value of product shipments			
		Produc-tion 1997	Ship-ments 1997	1992		1997	
				($ mil)	% of total	($ mil)	% of total
Phosphate rock[1]		NA	NA	1,193.9	100.0	1,006.4	100.0
Crude phosphate rock (ore or matrix)	mil metric tons (dry)	162	4	-	-	55.9	5.6
Washed and concentrated phosphate rock shipments	mil metric tons (dry)	(D)	(D)	-	-	(D)	-
Dried, calcined, sintered, or nodulized phosphate rock	mil metric tons (dry)	(D)	(D)	383.8	32.2	(D)	-
Phosphate rock, nsk[2]		NA	NA	0.7	0.1	-	-

Source: Economic Census of the U.S., 1997. Notes: 1. In 1997 the quantity and value of net shipments represented by gross shipments less minerals received for preparation were 42.3 million metric tons and 1,006.4 million dollars. 2. Includes value for establishments that did not report report detailed data and estimates for small companies (estimates were made from administrative-record data rather than collected from respondents. NA stands for not applicable. (D) means data are withheld to avoid disclosure of competitive information. (S) indicates that data did not meet publication standards. - means not available or zero.

LOCATION BY STATE AND REGIONAL CONCENTRATION

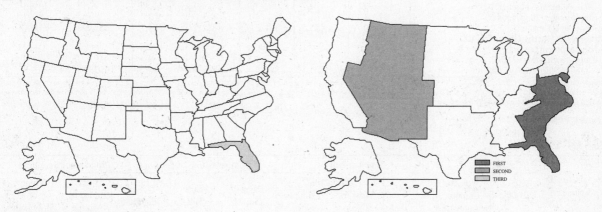

FIRST
SECOND
THIRD

INDUSTRY DATA BY STATE

State	Estab-lish-ments	Employment			Compensation		Production				Capital Exp. ($ mil)
		Total	Workers	Total as % of US	Payroll per Employee	Wages per Worker	Costs ($ mil)	Value Added ($ mil)	Reve-nues ($ mil)	% of US	
Florida	11	2,961	2,478	76.75	43,183	37,393	370.9	505.8	764.0	119.55	112.7
Idaho	5	561	402	14.54	48,911	47,575	(D)	74.5	111.5	17.44	(D)
North Carolina	1	175*	(D)	4.54	-	(D)	(D)	(D)	(D)	-	(D)
Utah	1	175*	(D)	4.54	-	(D)	(D)	(D)	(D)	-	(D)

Source: Economic Census of the U.S., 1997. Data are sorted by 1997 revenues or establishments. (D) means data suppression to prevent disclosure of company data. A dash (-) is used when data are unavailable or cannot be calculated. Data followed by an * indicate the midpoint of a range. The ranges are: for 10, 0-19; for 60, 20-99, for 175, 100-249, for 375, 250-499, for 750, 500-999. Higher values are multiples of those shown, e.g., 3,750 is the midpoint of the range 2,500-4,999. Shaded states indicate states in which the industry was active in 1997. Shaded regions indicate where the industry is regionally most concentrated.

NAICS 212393 - CHEMICAL AND FERTILIZER MINERAL MINING NEC

GENERAL STATISTICS

Year	Com-panies	Establishments		Employment			Compensation		Production ($ million)			
		Total	with 20 or more employees	Total (No.)	Production Workers (No.)	Hours (Mil)	Payroll ($ mil)	Wages ($/hr)	Cost of Materials	Value Added by Mining	Value of Shipments	Capital Invest.
1997	41	50	18	2,177	1,585	3.3	88.6	18.55	147.2	240.3	363.0	24.5

Source: Economic Census of the United States, 1997. This is a newly defined industry. Data for prior years were unavailable at the time of publication but may become available over time.

DISTRIBUTION AMONG SIC-BASED INDUSTRIES - 1997

SIC	Industry	Estab-lish-ments	Employment			Compensation		Production ($ mil)	
			Total	Production Workers	Hours (Mil)	Payroll ($ mil)	Wages ($/hr)	Cost of Materials	Value of Shipments
147900	Chemical & fertilizer mineral mining, nec	50	2,177	1,585	3.3	88.6	18.54	147.2	363.0

Source: 1997 Economic Census. U.S. Census Bureau, U.S. Department of Commerce, August 1997. SIC codes ending in two zeroes represent complete 4-digit SICs. All others are parts of 4-digit SIC industries. Items showing a dash (-) indicate that data are not available because of disclosure problems.

SIC INDUSTRIES RELATED TO NAICS 212393

SIC	Industry	1990	1991	1992	1993	1994	1995	1996	1997
1479	**Chemical and Fertilizer Mining, n.e.c.**								
	Establishments (number)	61	67	99	69	70	67	119p	124p
	Employment (thousands)	3.4	3.1	4.1	3.2	3.2	2.8	4.0e	4.0e
	Revenues ($ million)	490.7e	455.5e	422.8	392.5e	364.3e	338.2e	313.9e	291.4e
3295	**Minerals & Earths Ground Etc.***								
	Establishments (number)	347	354	368	357	349	355	328p	320p
	Employment (thousands)	10.7	8.7	9.5	9.4	9.4	10.2	10.5	9.9p
	Value of Shipments ($ million) . .	1,499.8	1,523.3	1,774.4	1,847.6	1,830.1	1,993.0	1,990.8	1,997.5p

*Source: Economic Census of the United States, 1992, annual surveys of economic sectors conducted by the Bureau of the Census, and estimates or projections based on the 1982-1992 period; not all data are shown. 'e' marks estimates made by the editors; 'p' indicates projections based on time series. A dash (-) indicates that data for this SIC or year were not available. * Indicates that only a portion of this industry is present within the NAICS data. If no * is shown, the entire industry is contained within the NAICS data.*

INDICES OF CHANGE

Year	Com-panies	Establishments		Employment			Compensation		Production ($ million)			
		Total	with 20 or more employees	Total (No.)	Production Workers (No.)	Hours (Mil)	Payroll ($ mil)	Wages ($/hr)	Cost of Materials	Value Added by Mining	Value of Shipments	Capital Invest.
1997	100.0	100.0	100.0	100.0	100.0	100.0	100.0	100.0	100.0	100.0	100.0	100.0

Sources: Same as General Statistics. The values shown reflect change from the base year, 1997. Values above 100 mean greater than 1997, values below 100 mean less than 1997, and a value of 100 in years other than 1997 means same as 1997. Indices are calculated only for Census years. Data are the most recent available at this level of detail.

SELECTED RATIOS

For 1992	Avg. of Sector	Analyzed Industry	Index	For 1992	Avg. of Sector	Analyzed Industry	Index
Employees per Establishment	20.4	43.5	213	Value Added per Production Worker	335,283	151,609	45
Payroll per Establishment	831,719	1,772,000	213	Cost per Establishment	2,854,087	2,944,000	103
Payroll per Employee	40,815	40,698	100	Cost per Employee	140,057	67,616	48
Production Workers per Establishment	15.6	31.7	203	Cost per Production Worker	183,057	92,871	51
Wages per Establishment	613,139	1,224,300	200	Shipments per Establishment	6,840,788	7,260,000	106
Wages per Production Worker	39,326	38,621	98	Shipments per Employee	335,695	166,743	50
Hours per Production Worker	2,075	2,082	100	Shipments per Production Worker	438,757	229,022	52
Wages per Hour	18.96	18.55	98	Investment per Establishment	1,242,441	490,000	39
Value Added per Establishment	5,227,487	4,806,000	92	Investment per Employee	60,970	11,254	18
Value Added per Employee	256,526	110,381	43	Investment per Production Worker	79,688	15,457	19

Sources: Same as General Statistics. The 'Average of Sector' column represents the average for all industries in this sector. The Index shows the relationship between the Average and the Analyzed Industry. For example, 100 means that they are equal; 500 that the Analyzed Industry is five times the average; 50 means that the Analyzed Industry is half the national average. 'na' is used to show that data are 'not available'.

LEADING COMPANIES   Number shown: **5**   Total sales ($ mil): **943**   Total employment (000): **2.3**

Company Name	Address				CEO Name	Phone	Co. Type	Sales ($ mil)	Empl. (000)
PennzEnergy Co.	PO Box 2967	Houston	TX	77252		713-546-6000	S	551	1.1
Freeport Sulphur Co.	1615 Poydras St	New Orleans	LA	70112	James Moffett	504-582-4000	S	212*	0.4
Chemetall Foote Corp.	348 Holiday Inn Rd	Kings Mountain	NC	28086	Juergen Deberitz	704-739-2501	S	125*	0.4
United Salt Corp.	4800 San Felipe St	Houston	TX	77056	Dan Sutton	713-877-2600	S	34	0.2
Randall and Blake Inc.	821 E Southlake	Southlake	TX	76092	Richard Randall	303-795-2582	R	21*	0.2

Source: *Ward's Business Directory of U.S. Private and Public Companies*, Volumes 1 and 2, 2000. The company type code used is as follows: P - Public, R - Private, S - Subsidiary, D - Division, J - Joint Venture, A - Affiliate, G - Group, N - Company type not reported. Sales are in millions of dollars, employees are in thousands. An asterisk (*) indicates an estimated sales volume. The symbol < stands for 'less than'. Company names and addresses are truncated, in some cases, to fit into the available space.

MINING PRODUCT DETAILS

Products	Units	Quantity of (000s)		Value of product shipments			
		Production 1997	Shipments 1997	1992 ($ mil)	1992 % of total	1997 ($ mil)	1997 % of total
Other chemical and fertilizer minerals		NA	NA	410.9	100.0	355.2	100.0
Barite	1,000 metric tons	(D)	(D)	13.0	3.2	(D)	-
Rock salt[1]	1,000 s tons	NA	12,585	198.5	48.3	220.8	62.2
Native sulfur	1,000 metric tons	(D)	(D)	147.0	35.8	(D)	-
Other chemical and fertilizer minerals[2]		NA	NA	39.1	9.5	(D)	-
Chemical and fertilizer mining, nsk[3]		NA	NA	13.4	3.3	(D)	-

Source: *Economic Census of the U.S.*, 1997. Notes: 1. Includes some rock salt shipped as brine. 2. Represents pyrites and such other miscellaneous chemical and fertilizer minerals as fluorspar, spodumene, lithium carbonate, wollastonite, natural wollastonite, and natural iron oxide pigments. 3. Includes value for establishments that did not report detailed data and estimates for small companies (estimates were made from administrative-record data rather than collected from respondents). NA stands for not applicable. (D) means data are withheld to avoid disclosure of competitive information. (S) indicates that data did not meet publication standards. - means not available or zero.

LOCATION BY STATE AND REGIONAL CONCENTRATION

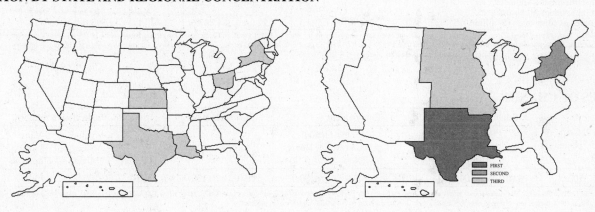

FIRST
SECOND
THIRD

INDUSTRY DATA BY STATE

State	Establishments	Employment Total	Employment Workers	Employment Total as % of US	Compensation Payroll per Employee	Compensation Wages per Worker	Production Costs ($ mil)	Production Value Added ($ mil)	Production Revenues ($ mil)	Production % of US	Capital Exp. ($ mil)
Louisiana	8	750*	(D)	34.45	-	(D)	(D)	(D)	(D)	-	(D)
New York	5	375*	(D)	17.23	-	(D)	(D)	(D)	(D)	-	(D)
Texas	5	375*	(D)	17.23	-	(D)	(D)	(D)	(D)	-	(D)
Kansas	3	175*	(D)	8.04	-	(D)	(D)	(D)	(D)	-	(D)
Ohio	3	375*	(D)	17.23	-	(D)	(D)	(D)	(D)	-	(D)

Source: *Economic Census of the U.S.*, 1997. Data are sorted by 1997 revenues or establishments. (D) means data suppression to prevent disclosure of company data. A dash (-) is used when data are unavailable or cannot be calculated. Data followed by an * indicate the midpoint of a range. The ranges are: for 10, 0-19; for 60, 20-99; for 175, 100-249; for 375, 250-499; for 750, 500-999. Higher values are multiples of those shown, e.g., 3,750 is the midpoint of the range 2,500-4,999. Shaded *states* indicate states in which the industry was active in 1997. Shaded *regions* indicate where the industry is regionally most concentrated.

NAICS 212399 - NONMETALLIC MINERAL MINING NEC

GENERAL STATISTICS

Year	Com-panies	Establishments		Employment			Compensation		Production ($ million)			
		Total	with 20 or more employees	Total (No.)	Production Workers (No.)	Hours (Mil)	Payroll ($ mil)	Wages ($/hr)	Cost of Materials	Value Added by Mining	Value of Shipments	Capital Invest.
1997	178	209	56	3,953	3,014	6.2	136.9	15.65	267.8	447.2	612.6	102.4

Source: *Economic Census of the United States*, 1997. This is a newly defined industry. Data for prior years were unavailable at the time of publication but may become available over time.

DISTRIBUTION AMONG SIC-BASED INDUSTRIES - 1997

SIC	Industry	Estab-lish-ments	Employment			Compensation		Production ($ mil)	
			Total	Production Workers	Hours (Mil)	Payroll ($ mil)	Wages ($/hr)	Cost of Materials	Value of Shipments
149920	Miscellaneous nonmetallic minerals, except fuels (pt)	209	3,953	3,014	6.2	136.9	15.71	267.8	612.6

Source: 1997 *Economic Census*. U.S. Census Bureau, U.S. Department of Commerce, August 1997. SIC codes ending in two zeroes represent complete 4-digit SICs. All others are parts of 4-digit SIC industries. Items showing a dash (-) indicate that data are not available because of disclosure problems.

SIC INDUSTRIES RELATED TO NAICS 212399

SIC	Industry	1990	1991	1992	1993	1994	1995	1996	1997
1499	**Miscellaneous Nonmetallic Minerals***								
	Establishments (number)	304	296	281	268	272	285	235*p*	224*p*
	Employment (thousands)	6.8	6.4	5.5	5.2	5.1	5.1	4.5*e*	4.3*e*
	Revenues ($ million)	604.0*e*	600.1*e*	596.3	592.5*e*	588.7*e*	585.0*e*	581.2*e*	577.5*e*
3295	**Minerals & Earths Ground Etc.***								
	Establishments (number)	347	354	368	357	349	355	328*p*	320*p*
	Employment (thousands)	10.7	8.7	9.5	9.4	9.4	10.2	10.5	9.9*p*
	Value of Shipments ($ million)	1,499.8	1,523.3	1,774.4	1,847.6	1,830.1	1,993.0	1,990.8	1,997.5*p*

Source: *Economic Census of the United States*, 1992, annual surveys of economic sectors conducted by the Bureau of the Census, and estimates or projections based on the 1982-1992 period; not all data are shown. 'e' marks estimates made by the editors; 'p' indicates projections based on time series. A dash (-) indicates that data for this SIC or year were not available. * Indicates that only a portion of this industry is present within the NAICS data. If no * is shown, the entire industry is contained within the NAICS data.

INDICES OF CHANGE

Year	Com-panies	Establishments		Employment			Compensation		Production ($ million)			
		Total	with 20 or more employees	Total (No.)	Production Workers (No.)	Hours (Mil)	Payroll ($ mil)	Wages ($/hr)	Cost of Materials	Value Added by Mining	Value of Shipments	Capital Invest.
1997	100.0	100.0	100.0	100.0	100.0	100.0	100.0	100.0	100.0	100.0	100.0	100.0

Sources: Same as General Statistics. The values shown reflect change from the base year, 1997. Values above 100 mean greater than 1997, values below 100 mean less than 1997, and a value of 100 in years other than 1997 means same as 1997. Indices are calculated only for Census years. Data are the most recent available at this level of detail.

SELECTED RATIOS

For 1992	Avg. of Sector	Analyzed Industry	Index	For 1992	Avg. of Sector	Analyzed Industry	Index
Employees per Establishment	20.4	18.9	93	Value Added per Production Worker	335,283	148,374	44
Payroll per Establishment	831,719	655,024	79	Cost per Establishment	2,854,087	1,281,340	45
Payroll per Employee	40,815	34,632	85	Cost per Employee	140,057	67,746	48
Production Workers per Establishment	15.6	14.4	92	Cost per Production Worker	183,057	88,852	49
Wages per Establishment	613,139	464,258	76	Shipments per Establishment	6,840,788	2,931,100	43
Wages per Production Worker	39,326	32,193	82	Shipments per Employee	335,695	154,971	46
Hours per Production Worker	2,075	2,057	99	Shipments per Production Worker	438,757	203,251	46
Wages per Hour	18.96	15.65	83	Investment per Establishment	1,242,441	489,952	39
Value Added per Establishment	5,227,487	2,139,713	41	Investment per Employee	60,970	25,904	42
Value Added per Employee	256,526	113,129	44	Investment per Production Worker	79,688	33,975	43

Sources: Same as General Statistics. The 'Average of Sector' column represents the average for all industries in this sector. The Index shows the relationship between the Average and the Analyzed Industry. For example, 100 means that they are equal; 500 that the Analyzed Industry is five times the average; 50 means that the Analyzed Industry is half the national average. 'na' is used to show that data are 'not available'.

LEADING COMPANIES   Number shown: **16**   Total sales ($ mil): **3,072**   Total employment (000): **16.0**

Company Name	Address				CEO Name	Phone	Co. Type	Sales ($ mil)	Empl. (000)
Hanson Building Materials	1350 Campus Pkwy	Neptune	NJ	07753	Alan J Murray	732-919-9777	S	1,500	7.5
Alleghany Corp.	375 Park Ave	New York	NY	10152	John J Burns Jr	212-752-1356	P	919	2.9
World Minerals Inc.	137 W Central Ave	Lompoc	CA	93436	William J Woods Jr	805-735-7791	S	200	1.9
Celite Corp.	PO Box 519	Lompoc	CA	93438		805-735-7791	S	124*	1.1
Rio Tinto Services Inc.	100 Roosevelt	Garden City	NY	11530	Arthur Glass	516-794-4949	S	66*	0.4
Luzenac America Inc.	9000 E Nichols Ave	Englewood	CO	80112		303-643-0400	S	60*	0.4
Zemex Industrial Minerals Inc.	1040 Crown Pointe	Atlanta	GA	30338	Peter J Goodwin Jr	770-392-8660	S	58*	0.3
NYCO Minerals Inc.	PO Box 368	Willsboro	NY	12996	Tom Krowl	403-260-9894	S	38	0.1
Canyon Resources Corp.	14142 Denver W	Golden	CO	80401	Richard H De Voto	303-278-8464	P	35	0.2
Harborlite Corp.	137 W Central Ave	Lompoc	CA	93436	William J Woods Jr	805-735-7791	S	35*	0.2
Grefco Minerals Inc.	23705 Crenshaw	Torrance	CA	90509	Glenn P Jones	310-517-0700	S	16*	0.1
United Oil and Minerals Inc.	1001 Westbank Dr	Austin	TX	78746	Michael T Peays	512-328-8184	S	12*	<0.1
Atlas Corp.	370 7th St	Denver	CO	80202	Gregg B Shafter	303-629-2440	P	5*	0.2
Casmyn Corp.	380 Chickadee Dr	Reno	NV	89506	Amyn S Dahya	702-331-5524	R	3	0.6
Digital Gem Corp.	PO Box 4729	Helena	MT	59604	Vic Alboini	406-458-3200	P	1	<0.1
American Absorbents Natural	3800 Hudson Bend	Austin	TX	78734	Robert Bitterli	512-266-2481	P	0	<0.1

Source: *Ward's Business Directory of U.S. Private and Public Companies*, Volumes 1 and 2, 2000. The company type code used is as follows: P - Public, R - Private, S - Subsidiary, D - Division, J - Joint Venture, A - Affiliate, G - Group, N - Company type not reported. Sales are in millions of dollars, employees are in thousands. An asterisk (*) indicates an estimated sales volume. The symbol < stands for 'less than'. Company names and addresses are truncated, in some cases, to fit into the available space.

MINING PRODUCT DETAILS

Products	Units	Quantity of (000s)		Value of product shipments			
		Production 1997	Shipments 1997	1992		1997	
				($ mil)	% of total	($ mil)	% of total
All other nonmetallic minerals		NA	NA	-	-	636.4	100.0
Diatomite, crude and prepared	1,000 metric tons	768	687	139.3	-	128.9	20.3
Gypsum[1]	mil s tons	18	7	-	-	66.1	10.4
Talc, soapstone, and pyrophyllite[2]	1,000 metric tons	1,169	1,084	-	-	95.6	15.0
Mica	1,000 metric tons	112	108	21.3	-	9.4	1.5
Native asphalt and bitumens (except bituminous limestone and bituminous sandstone)[3]	1,000 metric tons	448	449	-	-	19.0	3.0
Pumice and pumicite[4]	1,000 metric tons	662	687	26.0	-	20.3	3.2
Natural abrasives, except sand	1,000 metric tons	55	56	18.7	-	22.0	3.5
Peat	1,000 s tons	459	403	15.8	-	12.8	2.0
Perlite	1,000 s tons	840	812	22.2	-	34.8	5.5
Shell, crushed or broken[5]	1,000 s tons	1,943	1,870	29.9	-	10.8	1.7
All other nonmetallic minerals[6]		NA	NA	-	-	172.7	27.1
Miscellaneous nonmetallic minerals, nsk[7]		NA	NA	-	-	43.7	6.9

Source: *Economic Census of the U.S.*, 1997. *Notes:* 1. Quantity of production for all purposes includes gypsum mined and used in the same establishment manufacturing gypsum products. 2. Excludes data for prepared talc, soapstone, and pyrophyllite produced at establishments classified in manufacturing industries. 3. Includes gilsonite. 4. Includes volcanic ash and scoria. 5. Excludes production and shipments of shell produced and used by establishments primarily classified in construction or manufacturing industries, such as those producing cement or concrete products. 6. Represents other miscellaneous nonmetallic minerals, such as vermiculite, gem stones, wollastonite, etc. 7. Includes value for establishments that did not report detailed data and estimates for small companies (estimates were made from administrative-record data rather than collected from respondents). NA stands for not applicable. (D) means data are withheld to avoid disclosure of competitive information. (S) indicates that data did not meet publication standards. - means not available or zero.

LOCATION BY STATE AND REGIONAL CONCENTRATION

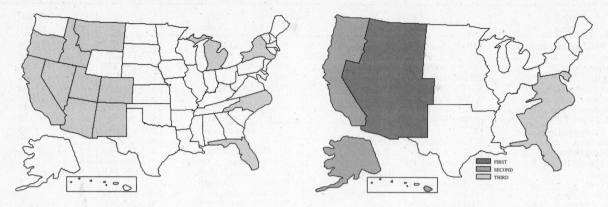

FIRST
SECOND
THIRD

INDUSTRY DATA BY STATE

State	Estab lish- ments	Employment			Compensation		Production				Capital Exp. ($ mil)
		Total	Workers	Total as % of US	Payroll per Employee	Wages per Worker	Costs ($ mil)	Value Added ($ mil)	Reve- nues ($ mil)	% of US	
New York	8	382	253	9.66	37,694	36,557	(D)	61.7	79.3	17.73	(D)
Nevada	9	334	212	8.45	33,311	30,231	21.2	37.9	57.9	12.95	1.2
Florida	15	192	104	4.86	31,542	27,856	7.0	16.3	21.3	4.76	2.0
Oregon	8	120	91	3.04	27,775	28,473	(D)	12.4	18.2	4.07	(D)
Idaho	7	115	100	2.91	31,870	30,600	(D)	12.9	14.2	3.18	(D)
Colorado	7	105	84	2.66	29,048	26,012	(D)	7.2	10.1	2.25	(D)
California	19	750*	(D)	18.97	-	(D)	(D)	(D)	(D)	-	(D)
Arizona	15	175*	(D)	4.43	-	(D)	(D)	(D)	(D)	-	(D)
Montana	10	375*	(D)	9.49	-	(D)	(D)	(D)	(D)	-	(D)
Michigan	8	175*	(D)	4.43	-	(D)	(D)	(D)	(D)	-	(D)
New Mexico	8	175*	(D)	4.43	-	(D)	(D)	(D)	(D)	-	(D)
North Carolina	8	375*	(D)	9.49	-	(D)	(D)	(D)	(D)	-	(D)
Utah	7	175*	(D)	4.43	-	(D)	(D)	(D)	(D)	-	0.9

Source: *Economic Census of the U.S., 1997.* Data are sorted by 1997 revenues or establishments. (D) means data suppression to prevent disclosure of company data. A dash (-) is used when data are unavailable or cannot be calculated. Data followed by an * indicate the midpoint of a range. The ranges are: for 10, 0-19; for 60, 20-99, for 175, 100-249, for 375, 250-499, for 750, 500-999. Higher values are multiples of those shown, e.g., 3,750 is the midpoint of the range 2,500-4,999. Shaded *states* indicate states in which the industry was active in 1997. Shaded *regions* indicate where the industry is regionally most concentrated.

NAICS 213111 - DRILLING OIL AND GAS WELLS*

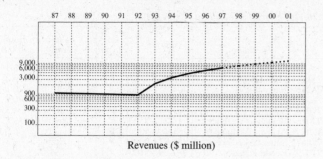

Revenues ($ million)

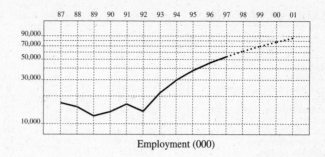

Employment (000)

GENERAL STATISTICS

Year	Com-panies	Establishments		Employment			Compensation		Production ($ million)			
		Total	with 20 or more employees	Total (No.)	Production Workers (No.)	Hours (Mil)	Payroll ($ mil)	Wages ($/hr)	Cost of Materials	Value Added by Mining	Value of Shipments	Capital Invest.
1977	-	1,252	116	17,800	13,700	32.4	220.2	5.27	189.5	545.2	665.0	69.7
1982	2,402	2,934	-	41,800	33,300	73.1	809.5	8.50	1,044.8	2,306.4	2,960.4	390.8
1987	1,591	1,917	143	16,900	12,800	27.1	452.1	11.46	394.1	771.3	1,096.2	69.3
1988	1,535	1,584[1]	122[1]	15,298[1]	11,766	25.2	398.5[1]	11.67	397.4	761.8	1,068.5	-
1989	1,481	1,421[1]	122[1]	12,174[1]	10,815	23.5	386.1[1]	11.88	400.8	752.4	1,041.5	-
1990	1,429	1,401[1]	123[1]	13,554[1]	9,941	21.9	465.2[1]	12.09	404.2	743.2	1,015.2	-
1991	1,379	1,541[1]	152[1]	16,391[1]	9,138	20.4	543.4[1]	12.30	407.6	734.0	989.6	-
1992	1,331	1,490	84	13,700	8,400	19.0	460.3	12.52	411.1	725.0	964.6	171.5
1993	1,339	1,520	147	21,733	15,764	33.6	751.9	13.36	1,088.3	1,725.8	2,235.3	-
1994	1,347	1,549	211	29,766	23,128	48.2	1,043.4	14.20	1,765.6	2,726.7	3,506.0	-
1995	1,355	1,579	274	37,799	30,491	62.9	1,335.0	15.03	2,442.8	3,727.5	4,776.6	-
1996	1,363	1,608	338	45,832	37,855	77.5	1,626.5	15.87	3,120.1	4,728.4	6,047.3	-
1997	1,371	1,638	401	53,865	45,219	92.1	1,918.1	16.71	3,797.3	5,729.2	7,318.0	2,209.3
1998	1,379p	1,668p	464p	61,898p	52,583p	106.7p	2,209.7p	17.55p	4,474.5p	6,730.0p	8,588.7p	-
1999	1,387p	1,697p	528p	69,931p	59,947p	121.3p	2,501.2p	18.39p	5,151.8p	7,730.9p	9,859.4p	-
2000	1,395p	1,727p	591p	77,964p	67,310p	136.0p	2,792.8p	19.22p	5,829.0p	8,731.7p	11,130.0p	-
2001	1,403p	1,756p	655p	85,997p	74,674p	150.6p	3,084.3p	20.06p	6,506.3p	9,732.6p	12,400.7p	-

Sources: *Economic Census of the United States*, 1977, 1982, 1987, 1992, and 1997. Data for those years (years are in **bold** type) are from the 5-year censuses of the economy. Other values, unless otherwise noted, are extrapolations. Values footnoted 1 are from the *County Business Patterns* for the years indicated. Values marked with *p* are projections. Data are the most recent available at this level of detail.

INDICES OF CHANGE

Year	Com-panies	Establishments		Employment			Compensation		Production ($ million)			
		Total	with 20 or more employees	Total (No.)	Production Workers (No.)	Hours (Mil)	Payroll ($ mil)	Wages ($/hr)	Cost of Materials	Value Added by Mining	Value of Shipments	Capital Invest.
1977	-	76.4	28.9	33.0	30.3	35.2	11.5	31.5	5.0	9.5	9.1	3.2
1982	175.2	179.1	-	77.6	73.6	79.4	42.2	50.9	27.5	40.3	40.5	17.7
1987	116.0	117.0	35.7	31.4	28.3	29.4	23.6	68.6	10.4	13.5	15.0	3.1
1992	97.1	91.0	20.9	25.4	18.6	20.6	24.0	74.9	10.8	12.7	13.2	7.8
1997	100.0	100.0	100.0	100.0	100.0	100.0	100.0	100.0	100.0	100.0	100.0	100.0

Sources: Same as General Statistics. The values shown reflect change from the base year, 1997. Values above 100 mean greater than 1997, values below 100 mean less than 1997, and a value of 100 in years other than 1997 means same as 1997. Indices are calculated only for Census years. Data are the most recent available at this level of detail.

SELECTED RATIOS

For 1992	Avg. of Sector	Analyzed Industry	Index	For 1992	Avg. of Sector	Analyzed Industry	Index
Employees per Establishment	20.4	32.9	161	Value Added per Production Worker	335,283	126,699	38
Payroll per Establishment	831,719	1,171,001	141	Cost per Establishment	2,854,087	2,318,254	81
Payroll per Employee	40,815	35,609	87	Cost per Employee	140,057	70,497	50
Production Workers per Establishment	15.6	27.6	177	Cost per Production Worker	183,057	83,976	46
Wages per Establishment	613,139	939,555	153	Shipments per Establishment	6,840,788	4,467,643	65
Wages per Production Worker	39,326	34,034	87	Shipments per Employee	335,695	135,858	40
Hours per Production Worker	2,075	2,037	98	Shipments per Production Worker	438,757	161,835	37
Wages per Hour	18.96	16.71	88	Investment per Establishment	1,242,441	1,348,779	109
Value Added per Establishment	5,227,487	3,497,680	67	Investment per Employee	60,970	41,016	67
Value Added per Employee	256,526	106,362	41	Investment per Production Worker	79,688	48,858	61

Sources: Same as General Statistics. The 'Average of Sector' column represents the average for all industries in this sector. The Index shows the relationship between the Average and the Analyzed Industry. For example, 100 means that they are equal; 500 that the Analyzed Industry is five times the average; 50 means that the Analyzed Industry is half the national average. 'na' is used to show that data are 'not available'.

*Equivalent to SIC 1382.

LEADING COMPANIES   Number shown: **75**   Total sales ($ mil): **63,726,179**   Total employment (000): **118.2**

Company Name	Address				CEO Name	Phone	Co. Type	Sales ($ mil)	Empl. (000)
Helmerich & Payne Intern.	1579 E 21st St	Tulsa	OK	74114	George S Dotson	918-742-5531	S	63,664,000*	3.3
DLB Oil and Gas Inc.	1601 NW Exprwy	Oklahoma City	OK	73118	Mike Liddell	405-424-4327	P	41,692*	0.2
Boggs Natural Gas Co.	882 Charleston Rd	Spencer	WV	25276	Harry Boggs	304-927-1236	R	2,991*	<0.1
South Texas Drilling	9310 Broadway	San Antonio	TX	78217	William Locke	210-828-7689	P	1,806*	<0.1
Diamond Offshore Drilling Inc.	15415 Katy Fwy	Houston	TX	77094	Laurence R Dickerson	281-492-5300	P	1,209	4.3
Transocean Offshore Inc.	PO Box 2765	Houston	TX	77046	W Dennis Heagney	713-871-7500	P	1,090*	3.8
R and B Falcon Corp.	901 Threadneedle	Houston	TX	77079	Andrew Bakonyi	281-496-5000	P	1,033*	6.2
Nabors Industries Inc.	515 W Greens Rd	Houston	TX	77067	Eugene M Isenberg	281-874-0035	P	969*	6.8
Global Marine Inc.	777 N Eldridge	Houston	TX	77079	Robert E Rose	281-596-5100	P	791	2.7
Mitchell Energy Corp.	2002 Timberloch Pl	The Woodlands	TX	77380	George P Mitchell	713-377-5500	S	790	1.1
Noble Drilling Corp.	10370 Richmond	Houston	TX	77042	Robert D Campbell	713-974-3131	P	788	3.3
Santa Fe International Corp.	2 Lincoln Centre	Dallas	TX	75240	Gordon M Anderson	972-701-7300	P	614	5.8
Anadrill Schlumberger	900 Threadneedle	Houston	TX	77079	Mohamed Awad	281-275-8000	S	600	3.7
Global Marine Drilling Co.	P O Box 4379	Houston	TX	77210	Jon A Marshall	281-496-8000	S	579	2.5
Helmerich and Payne Inc.	Utica at 21st St	Tulsa	OK	74114	Hans Helmerich	918-742-5531	P	564	3.4
Noble Drilling International Inc.	10370 Richmond	Houston	TX	77042	James C Day	713-974-3131	S	533*	1.5
Key Energy Group Inc.	2 Tower Ctr	East Brunswick	NJ	08816	Francis D John	732-247-4822	P	489	5.6
Rowan Companies Inc.	2800 Post Oak Blvd	Houston	TX	77056	C R Palmer	713-621-7800	P	461	4.9
Nabors Drilling USA Inc.	515 W Greens Rd	Houston	TX	77067	Richard Stratton	281-874-0035	S	439*	5.6
ENSCO International Inc.	2700 Fountain Pl	Dallas	TX	75202	Carl F Thorne	214-922-1500	P	364	31.0
Chesapeake Energy Corp.	P O Box 18496	Oklahoma City	OK	73154	Aubrey K McClendon	405-848-8000	P	355	0.5
KLT Inc.	P O Box 410233	Kansas City	MO	64141	Ronald G Wasson	816-654-1900	S	347	<0.1
Cliffs Drilling Co.	1200 Smith St	Houston	TX	77002	Douglas E Swanson	713-651-9426	P	336	1.6
Parker Drilling Co.	8 E 3rd St	Tulsa	OK	74103	Robert Parker Jr	918-585-8221	P	325	4.5
Layne Christensen Co.	1900 Shawn Msn	Mission Woods	KS	66205	Andrew B Schmitt	913-362-0510	P	284	3.0
Abarta Inc.	1000 R I D C Plz	Pittsburgh	PA	15238	John F Bitzer III	412-963-6226	R	280*	1.2
Grey Wolf Inc.	10370 Richmond	Houston	TX	77042	Thomas P Richards	713-435-6100	P	241	1.3
UTI Energy Corp.	16800 Greenspoint	Houston	TX	77060	Vaughn E Drum	281-873-4111	P	186	1.1
Cabot Oil and Gas Corp.	15375 Mem Dr	Houston	TX	77079		281-589-4600	P	182	0.4
Noble Offshore Corp.	10370 Richmond	Houston	TX	77042	James Day	713-974-3131	S	179*	0.5
Key Energy Drilling Inc.	812 9th St #B	Levelland	TX	79336	Joe Dee Brooks	806-894-7386	S	163*	0.5
Atwood Oceanics Inc.	PO Box 218350	Houston	TX	77218	John R Irwin	281-492-2929	P	150	0.7
Ramos Oil Company Inc.	1515 S River Rd	W. Sacramento	CA	95691	Kent Ramos	916-371-2570	R	130	0.2
Marine Drilling Companies Inc.	1 Sugar Creek Ctr	Sugar Land	TX	77478	Jan Rask	281-243-3000	P	115	0.9
Union Drilling Div.	PO Drawer 40	Buckhannon	WV	26201		304-472-4610	D	107*	0.3
BP Exploration (Alaska) Inc.	P O Box 196612	Anchorage	AK	99519	Richard Campbell	907-561-5111	S	100	1.2
Torch Operating Co.	1221 LaMar St	Houston	TX	77010	Ken White	713-650-1246	S	98*	0.3
Justiss Oil Company Inc.	1810 E Oak St	Jena	LA	71342	JF Justiss Jr	318-992-4111	R	72*	0.2
True Drilling Co.	PO Box 2360	Casper	WY	82602		307-237-9301	R	71	0.7
Chesapeake Operating Inc.	P O Box 18496	Oklahoma City	OK	73154	Aubrey McClendon	405-840-3000	S	63*	0.4
Gary Drilling Company Inc.	7001 Charity Ave	Bakersfield	CA	93308	Edward C Green	661-589-0111	R	62*	0.2
Nabors Drilling International Ltd.	515 W Greens Rd	Houston	TX	77067	Siegfried Meissner	281-874-0035	S	49*	0.5
Unit Drilling Co.	P O Box 702500	Tulsa	OK	74170		918-493-7700	S	46	<0.1
Kriti Holdings Inc.	1010 Lamar St	Houston	TX	77002	James Riner	713-655-7070	R	45	<0.1
DSI Industries Inc.	5211 Brownfield	Lubbock	TX	79407	S Howard Norton III	806-785-8460	P	36	0.5
Brammer Engineering Inc.	333 Texas Ste	Shreveport	LA	71101	Keith Evans	318-429-2345	R	34*	<0.1
Cyclone Drilling Inc.	P O Box 908	Gillette	WY	82717	James J Hladky	307-682-4161	R	32*	<0.1
Martex Drilling Co.	P O Box 2069	Marshall	TX	75671	Richard Roark		R	30	0.2
Norton Drilling Services Inc.	5211 Brownfield	Lubbock	TX	79407	S Howard Norton III	806-785-8400	P	29	0.2
McVay Drilling Co.	P O Box 924	Hobbs	NM	88240	Ted McVay	505-397-3311	R	27*	<0.1
Leonard Hudson Drilling Inc.	PO Box 1876	Pampa	TX	79066	LR Hudson	806-665-1816	R	20	0.1
Calpine Natural Gas Co.	1000 Louisiana	Houston	TX	77002	Peter Cartwright	713-651-7899	P	20	<0.1
Maynard Oil Co.	8080 N Central	Dallas	TX	75206	James G Maynard	214-891-8880	P	16	<0.1
Barnwell Industries Inc.	1100 Alakea St	Honolulu	HI	96813	Morton H Kinzler	808-531-8400	P	15	<0.1
TMBR-Sharp Drilling Inc.	4607 W Ind Blvd	Midland	TX	79703	Thomas C Brown	915-699-5050	P	14	0.1
Reunion Energy Co.	2801 Post Oak Blvd	Houston	TX	77056	Richard Bowman	713-627-9277	S	14*	<0.1
Hickman Drilling Co.	P O Box 38	Woodward	OK	73802		580-256-8688	D	12	0.2
Harken Energy Corp.	16285 Park 10 Plc	Houston	TX	77084	Mikel D Faulkner	781-717-1300	P	11	0.1
Dynamic Inc.	2801 Glenda Ave	Fort Worth	TX	76117	John H Harvison	817-838-1800	R	9	<0.1
Fairman Drilling Co.	P O Box 288	Du Bois	PA	15801		814-371-8410	R	8*	<0.1
Dynamic Production Inc.	2801 Glenda Ave	Fort Worth	TX	76117	John H Harvison	817-838-1800	R	8*	<0.1
ONEOK Resources Co.	PO Box 871	Tulsa	OK	74102	JD Holbird	918-588-7700	S	7*	<0.1
Elenburg Exploration Inc.	P O Box 2440	Casper	WY	82602	Nicolas Wendland	307-235-8609	R	5	<0.1
Central Industries Inc.	329 Westgate Rd	Lafayette	LA	70506	W F Stevenson Jr	318-233-3171	R	5*	<0.1
Zenith Drilling Corp.	1861 N Rock Rd	Wichita	KS	67206	C Robert Buford	316-684-9777	R	5*	<0.1
Penwell Energy Inc.	600 N Marienfeld	Midland	TX	79701	William M Ford	915-683-2534	R	5*	<0.1
OGE Drilling Inc.	6430 Hillcroft St	Houston	TX	77081	TB O'Brien	713-270-1190	D	4*	<0.1
Wasatch Pharmaceutical Inc.	714 E 7200 S	Midvale	UT	84047	Gary V Heesch	801-424-2424	P	4*	<0.1
Berenergy Corp.	1801 California St	Denver	CO	80202	Robert M Goodyear Jr	303-295-2323	R	4*	<0.1
E and H Drilling Company Inc.	P O Box 1058	Graham	TX	76450	Ray Herring	940-549-0370	R	3	<0.1
Les Wilson Inc.	204 Industrial Dr	Carmi	IL	62821	LW Wilson	618-382-4666	R	3*	<0.1
W.O. Operating Co.	P O Box 960	Pampa	TX	79066	Miles O'Loughlin	806-665-8298	R	3	<0.1
Hall-Houston Oil Co.	700 Louisiana St	Houston	TX	77002	Gary L Hall	713-228-0711	R	3*	<0.1
Chandler and Associates Inc.	475 17th St	Denver	CO	80202	Mitchell Solich	303-295-0400	R	3	<0.1
Delta Petroleum Corp.	555 17th St	Denver	CO	80202	Aleron H Larson Jr	303-293-9133	P	2	<0.1

Source: *Ward's Business Directory of U.S. Private and Public Companies*, Volumes 1 and 2, 2000. The company type code used is as follows: P - Public, R - Private, S - Subsidiary, D - Division, J - Joint Venture, A - Affiliate, G - Group, N - Company type not reported. Sales are in millions of dollars, employees are in thousands. An asterisk (*) indicates an estimated sales volume. The symbol < stands for 'less than'. Company names and addresses are truncated, in some cases, to fit into the available space.

MINING PRODUCT DETAILS

Products	Units	Quantity of (000s)		Value of product shipments			
		Produc-tion 1997	Ship-ments 1997	1992		1997	
				($ mil)	% of total	($ mil)	% of total
Drilling oil and gas wells		NA	NA	3,669.3	100.0	7,350.1	100.0
Drilling oil, gas, dry, or service wells	mil ft	NA	(S)	2,229.1	60.8	5,700.1	77.6
Drilling in, spudding in, or tailing in oil and gas wells	mil ft	NA	5	79.2	2.2	57.0	0.8
Reworking oil and gas wells		NA	NA	670.5	18.3	742.0	10.1
Oil and gas well directional drilling control		NA	NA	128.7	3.5	373.2	5.1
Drilling oil and gas wells, nsk[1]		NA	NA	561.8	15.3	477.8	6.5

Source: Economic Census of the U.S., 1997. Notes: 1. Includes value for establishments that did not report detailed data and estimates for small companies (estimates were made from administrative-record data rather than collected from respondents). NA stands for not applicable. (D) means data are withheld to avoid disclosure of competitive information. (S) indicates that data did not meet publication standards. - means not available or zero.

LOCATION BY STATE AND REGIONAL CONCENTRATION

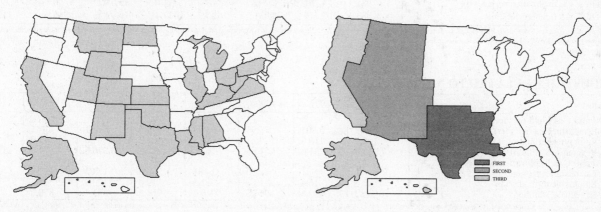

INDUSTRY DATA BY STATE

State	Estab lish-ments	Employment			Compensation		Production				Capital Exp. ($ mil)
		Total	Workers	Total as % of US	Payroll per Employee	Wages per Worker	Costs ($ mil)	Value Added ($ mil)	Reve-nues ($ mil)	% of US	
Louisiana	165	11,940	9,331	22.17	45,165	42,757	1,351.7	1,659.0	2,239.1	39.08	771.6
Wyoming	9	8,348	7,405	15.50	35,998	34,389	761.9	1,465.1	1,686.9	29.44	540.1
Texas	448	14,322	12,347	26.59	33,562	31,461	740.6	1,206.9	1,577.6	27.54	369.9
Oklahoma	164	3,680	3,109	6.83	28,508	28,613	175.9	273.7	358.3	6.25	91.4
California	61	2,312	1,901	4.29	34,913	32,281	144.1	160.0	208.3	3.64	95.7
Wyoming	49	1,607	1,394	2.98	37,373	38,996	79.0	158.2	201.5	3.52	35.7
New Mexico	54	1,961	1,656	3.64	32,442	30,657	84.4	126.5	176.4	3.08	34.6
Alaska	11	1,023	791	1.90	53,570	58,614	172.0	111.6	131.9	2.30	151.7
Colorado	57	744	608	1.38	34,081	34,783	31.8	58.8	80.4	1.40	10.1
Mississippi	39	730	602	1.36	24,299	22,051	33.5	53.0	72.9	1.27	13.6
Kansas	66	784	666	1.46	28,417	26,985	24.3	48.5	67.7	1.18	5.1
North Dakota	17	468	441	0.87	33,064	32,680	26.9	41.7	52.2	0.91	16.5
Montana	16	388	343	0.72	35,601	35,662	21.5	40.0	50.8	0.89	10.7
Alabama	20	171	143	0.32	25,064	23,965	29.6	39.7	50.7	0.88	18.6
Ohio	71	549	444	1.02	27,087	27,507	14.1	33.4	44.4	0.78	3.0
Pennsylvania	43	451	365	0.84	27,007	27,537	14.1	31.9	42.8	0.75	3.2
Michigan	33	549	419	1.02	28,066	30,165	13.6	32.1	42.0	0.73	3.7
Utah	31	444	397	0.82	34,113	32,476	16.0	33.3	41.7	0.73	7.7
West Virginia	30	506	437	0.94	23,490	22,778	11.6	32.8	39.0	0.68	5.3
Virginia	4	132	121	0.25	39,227	36,620	6.0	11.9	16.7	0.29	1.2
Kentucky	30	211	149	0.39	22,583	25,094	4.0	9.6	12.5	0.22	1.1
Illinois	42	238	198	0.44	18,244	18,869	2.7	10.2	11.5	0.20	1.4
Nebraska	13	111	96	0.21	24,396	24,240	(D)	3.4	7.0	0.12	(D)
Arkansas	31	750*	(D)	1.39	-	(D)	(D)	(D)	(D)	-	(D)

Source: Economic Census of the U.S., 1997. Data are sorted by 1997 revenues or establishments. (D) means data suppression to prevent disclosure of company data. A dash (-) is used when data are unavailable or cannot be calculated. Data followed by an * indicate the midpoint of a range. The ranges are: for 10, 0-19; for 60, 20-99, for 175, 100-249, for 375, 250-499, for 750, 500-999. Higher values are multiples of those shown, e.g., 3,750 is the midpoint of the range 2,500-4,999. Shaded *states* indicate states in which the industry was active in 1997. Shaded *regions* indicate where the industry is regionally most concentrated.

NAICS 213112 - SUPPORT ACTIVITIES FOR OIL AND GAS OPERATIONS

GENERAL STATISTICS

Year	Companies	Establishments		Employment			Compensation		Production ($ million)			
		Total	with 20 or more employees	Total (No.)	Production Workers (No.)	Hours (Mil)	Payroll ($ mil)	Wages ($/hr)	Cost of Materials	Value Added by Mining	Value of Shipments	Capital Invest.
1997	6,385	7,068	968	106,339	80,734	166.6	3,628.4	16.94	3,076.0	9,597.9	11,547.6	1,165.0

Source: Economic Census of the United States, 1997. This is a newly defined industry. Data for prior years were unavailable at the time of publication but may become available over time.

DISTRIBUTION AMONG SIC-BASED INDUSTRIES - 1997

SIC	Industry	Establishments	Employment			Compensation		Production ($ mil)	
			Total	Production Workers	Hours (Mil)	Payroll ($ mil)	Wages ($/hr)	Cost of Materials	Value of Shipments
138210	Oil & gas exploration services (pt)	985	4,161	2,703	4.9	111.0	15.07	90.1	299.0
138900	Oil & gas field services, nec	6,083	102,178	78,031	161.7	3,517.4	16.99	2,985.9	11,248.6

Source: 1997 *Economic Census.* U.S. Census Bureau, U.S. Department of Commerce, August 1997. SIC codes ending in two zeroes represent complete 4-digit SICs. All others are parts of 4-digit SIC industries. Items showing a dash (-) indicate that data are not available because of disclosure problems.

SIC INDUSTRIES RELATED TO NAICS 213112

SIC	Industry	1990	1991	1992	1993	1994	1995	1996	1997
1389	**Oil and Gas Field Services, n.e.c.**								
	Establishments (number)	5,643	5,805	7,294	6,090	5,959	5,661	7,145*p*	7,108*p*
	Employment (thousands)	105.1	116.5	96.4	88.5	102.2	93.0	97.9*e*	98.2*e*
	Revenues ($ million)	7,035.8*e*	7,271.6*e*	7,515.3	7,767.2*e*	8,027.5*e*	8,296.6*e*	8,574.7*e*	8,862.1*e*
1382	**Oil and Gas Exploration Services***								
	Establishments (number)	1,401	1,541	1,490	1,487	1,420	1,004	1,218*p*	1,158*p*
	Employment (thousands)	13.6	16.4	13.7	12.3	12.0	10.9	11.6*e*	11.1*e*
	Revenues ($ million)	1,015.2*e*	989.6*e*	964.6	940.2*e*	916.5*e*	893.4*e*	870.8*e*	848.8*e*

Source: Economic Census of the United States, 1992, annual surveys of economic sectors conducted by the Bureau of the Census, and estimates or projections based on the 1982-1992 period; not all data are shown. 'e' marks estimates made by the editors; 'p' indicates projections based on time series. A dash (-) indicates that data for this SIC or year were not available. * Indicates that only a portion of this industry is present within the NAICS data. If no * is shown, the entire industry is contained within the NAICS data.

INDICES OF CHANGE

Year	Companies	Establishments		Employment			Compensation		Production ($ million)			
		Total	with 20 or more employees	Total (No.)	Production Workers (No.)	Hours (Mil)	Payroll ($ mil)	Wages ($/hr)	Cost of Materials	Value Added by Mining	Value of Shipments	Capital Invest.
1997	100.0	100.0	100.0	100.0	100.0	100.0	100.0	100.0	100.0	100.0	100.0	100.0

Sources: Same as General Statistics. The values shown reflect change from the base year, 1997. Values above 100 mean greater than 1997, values below 100 mean less than 1997, and a value of 100 in years other than 1997 means same as 1997. Indices are calculated only for Census years. Data are the most recent available at this level of detail.

SELECTED RATIOS

For 1992	Avg. of Sector	Analyzed Industry	Index	For 1992	Avg. of Sector	Analyzed Industry	Index
Employees per Establishment	20.4	15.0	74	Value Added per Production Worker	335,283	118,883	35
Payroll per Establishment	831,719	513,356	62	Cost per Establishment	2,854,087	435,201	15
Payroll per Employee	40,815	34,121	84	Cost per Employee	140,057	28,926	21
Production Workers per Establishment	15.6	11.4	73	Cost per Production Worker	183,057	38,100	21
Wages per Establishment	613,139	399,293	65	Shipments per Establishment	6,840,788	1,633,786	24
Wages per Production Worker	39,326	34,957	89	Shipments per Employee	335,695	108,592	32
Hours per Production Worker	2,075	2,064	99	Shipments per Production Worker	438,757	143,033	33
Wages per Hour	18.96	16.94	89	Investment per Establishment	1,242,441	164,827	13
Value Added per Establishment	5,227,487	1,357,937	26	Investment per Employee	60,970	10,956	18
Value Added per Employee	256,526	90,258	35	Investment per Production Worker	79,688	14,430	18

Sources: Same as General Statistics. The 'Average of Sector' column represents the average for all industries in this sector. The Index shows the relationship between the Average and the Analyzed Industry. For example, 100 means that they are equal; 500 that the Analyzed Industry is five times the average; 50 means that the Analyzed Industry is half the national average. 'na' is used to show that data are 'not available'.

LEADING COMPANIES   Number shown: **75**   Total sales ($ mil): **158,016**   Total employment (000): **514.8**

Company Name	Address				CEO Name	Phone	Co. Type	Sales ($ mil)	Empl. (000)
USX-Marathon Group	PO Box 3128	Houston	TX	77253	Victor G Beghini	713-629-6600	P	22,075	32.9
Exxon Mobil U.S.A.	PO Box 2180	Houston	TX	77252		713-656-3636	S	16,410	17.0
Halliburton Co.	3600 Lincoln Plaza	Dallas	TX	75201	Williams Bradford	214-978-2600	P	14,898	107.8
Phillips Petroleum Co.	411 S Keeler Ave	Bartlesville	OK	74003	JJ Mulva	918-661-6600	P	13,852	17.3
Atlantic Richfield Co.	515 S Flower St	Los Angeles	CA	90071	Michael Bowlin	213-486-3511	P	13,055	18.4
Union Pacific Corp.	1416 Dodge St	Omaha	NE	68179	Richard K Davidson	401-271-5000	P	11,273	65.0
Schlumberger Ltd.	277 Park Ave	New York	NY	10172	D Evan Baird	212-350-9400	P	8,752	64.0
Union Oil Company of California	2141 Rosecrans Ave	El Segundo	CA	90245	Roger Beach	310-726-7600	S	6,064*	8.4
Litton Industries Inc.	21240 Burbank Blvd	Woodland Hills	CA	91367	Michael R Brown	818-598-5000	P	4,827	34.8
FINA Inc.	P O Box 2159	Dallas	TX	75221	Paul D Meek	214-750-2400	P	4,463	2.9
Petrofina Delaware Inc.	P O Box 2159	Dallas	TX	75201	Ron W Haddock	214-750-2400	S	4,081	2.7
Fina Oil and Chemical Co.	PO Box 2159	Dallas	TX	75221	Ron W Haddock	972-801-2000	S	4,081*	2.7
Chevron Overseas Petroleum Inc.	P O Box 5046	San Ramon	CA	94583	Richard H Matzke	925-842-3518	S	3,180	5.7
Lefrak Organization Inc.	97-77 Queens Blvd	Rego Park	NY	11374	Samuel J LeFrak	718-459-9021	R	2,750	16.0
Halliburton Energy Services Div.	5151 San Felipe St	Houston	TX	77056	Edgar Ortiz	713-624-2000	S	2,623	20.0
Oklahoma Energy Corp.	321 N Harvey	Oklahoma City	OK	73101	Steven E Moore	405-553-3000	P	2,172	2.8
South Texas Drilling	9310 Broadway	San Antonio	TX	78217	William Locke	210-828-7689	P	1,806*	<0.1
NICOR Inc.	PO Box 3014	Naperville	IL	60566	Thomas L Fisher	630-305-9500	P	1,615	3.3
National Fuel Gas Co.	10 Lafayette Sq	Buffalo	NY	14203	Philip C Ackerman	716-857-6980	P	1,263	3.8
Western Atlas International Inc.	PO Box 1407	Houston	TX	77251	John R Russell	713-972-4000	S	1,180*	10.0
BJ Services Co.	PO Box 4442	Houston	TX	77210	J Stewart	713-462-4239	P	1,131	7.6
Coastal Oil and Gas Corp.	9 E Greenway Plz	Houston	TX	77046		713-877-1400	S	994*	1.7
Nabors Industries Inc.	515 W Greens Rd	Houston	TX	77067	Eugene M Isenberg	281-874-0035	P	969*	6.8
Apache Corp.	2000 Post Oak Blvd	Houston	TX	77056	G Steven Farris	713-296-6000	P	876	1.3
Pride International Inc.	5847 San Felipe	Houston	TX	77057	Paul A Bragg	713-789-1400	P	837	7.5
Mitchell Energy Corp.	2002 Timberloch Pl	The Woodlands	TX	77380	George P Mitchell	713-377-5500	S	790	1.1
EOG Resources Inc.	P O Box 4362	Houston	TX	77210	Mark G Papa	713-853-6161	P	769	1.2
Amoco Tulsa Technology Center	4502 41st St	Tulsa	OK	74135		918-660-3000	R	750*	1.0
TransTexas Exploration Corp.	1300 N S Houston E	Houston	TX	77032		281-987-8600	S	723	2.5
Tuboscope Inc.	PO Box 808	Houston	TX	77001	John Lauletta	713-799-5100	P	568	4.4
Helmerich and Payne Inc.	Utica at 21st St	Tulsa	OK	74114	Hans Helmerich	918-742-5531	P	564	3.4
Key Energy Group Inc.	2 Tower Ctr	East Brunswick	NJ	08816	Francis D John	732-247-4822	P	489	5.6
Oceaneering International Inc.	PO Box 40494	Houston	TX	77240		713-329-4500	P	400	2.6
Western Atlas Logging Services	PO Box 1407	Houston	TX	77251	Gary Jones	713-972-4000	S	400*	3.8
Veritas DGC Inc.	3701 Kirby Dr	Houston	TX	77098	Stephen J Ludlow	713-512-8300	P	389	2.8
Global Industries Ltd.	8000 Global Dr	Sulphur	LA	70665	William J Dore	318-583-5000	P	388	2.2
New Jersey Natural Gas Co.	P O Box 1468	Wall	NJ	07719	Larry Downes	732-938-1074	S	365*	0.8
KLT Inc.	P O Box 410233	Kansas City	MO	64141	Ronald G Wasson	816-654-1900	S	347	<0.1
Cliffs Drilling Co.	1200 Smith St	Houston	TX	77002	Douglas E Swanson	713-651-9426	P	336	1.6
Frontier Oil Corp.	10000 Mem Dr	Houston	TX	77024	James R Gibbs	713-688-9600	P	299	0.3
Public Service of North Carolina	PO Box 1398	Gastonia	NC	28053	Charles E Zeigler Jr	704-864-6731	P	299	0.9
Forcenergy Inc.	2730 Southwest 3rd	Miami	FL	33129	Stig Wennerstrom	305-856-8500	P	274	0.3
Newpark Resources Inc.	3850 N Causeway	Metairie	LA	70002	James D Cole	504-838-8222	P	266	1.2
ICO Inc.	11490 Westheimer	Houston	TX	77077	Sylvia Pacholder	281-721-4200	P	262	2.0
Nuevo Energy Co.	1331 Lamar St	Houston	TX	77010	Douglas Foshee	713-652-0706	P	245*	0.9
McMoRan Exploration Co.	1615 Poydras Street	New Orleans	LA	70112	Richard C Adkerson	504-582-4000	P	244	0.3
RPC Inc.	PO Box 647	Atlanta	GA	30301	Richard A Hubbell	404-321-2140	P	231	1.6
Chevron Industries	PO Box 7753	San Francisco	CA	94120		415-894-7700	S	227*	0.3
Schlumberger Technologies Inc.	277 Park Ave	New York	NY	10172	Euan Baird	212-350-9400	P	220*	1.6
Patterson Energy Inc.	P O Drawer 1416	Snyder	TX	79550	A Glenn Patterson	915-573-1104	P	187	1.2
UTI Energy Corp.	16800 Greenspoint	Houston	TX	77060	Vaughn E Drum	281-873-4111	P	186	1.1
Cabot Oil and Gas Corp.	15375 Mem Dr	Houston	TX	77079		281-589-4600	P	182	0.4
Howell Corp. (Houston, Texas)	1111 Fannin St	Houston	TX	77002		713-658-4000	P	166	0.1
Trinity Industries Leasing Co.	PO Box 39	Quincy	IL	62306		217-228-6150	S	155	0.0
Atwood Oceanics Inc.	PO Box 218350	Houston	TX	77218	John R Irwin	281-492-2929	P	150	0.7
Quintana Petroleum Corp.	P O Box 3331	Houston	TX	77253		713-651-8600	R	150*	0.2
Pride Offshore Inc.	410 S Van Ave	Houma	LA	70363		504-872-4700	S	144*	1.7
Ceanic Corp.	900 Twn & Cntry	Houston	TX	77024	Rod Stanley	713-430-1100	R	133	1.1
Eagle Geophysical Inc.	2603 Augusta	Houston	TX	77057	William Lurie	713-243-6100	P	122	0.7
Unichem (The Woodlands, Texas)	14505 Torrey Ch	Houston	TX	77014	William Mooo	281 631 8450	D	115*	0.2
Coho Resources Inc.	14785 Preston Rd	Dallas	TX	75240	Jeffrey Clarke	972-991-9493	S	105*	0.1
Peak Oilfield Services Co.	2525 C St	Anchorage	AK	99503	Michael R O'Connor	907-263-7000	R	97*	0.6
Elf Exploration Inc.	1000 Louisiana St	Houston	TX	77002	Guy Feneyrou	713-658-9811	R	94*	<0.1
Total Minatome Corp.	PO Box 4326	Houston	TX	77210	J Guillermou	713-739-3000	S	90	0.2
AMBAR Inc.	16825 N Chase	Houston	TX	77060	Jerry Blumberg	281-873-7600	S	90*	0.4
GulfMark Offshore Inc.	5 Post Oak Park	Houston	TX	77027	David J Butters	713-963-9522	P	86	0.8
Anschutz Corp.	555 17th St	Denver	CO	80202	Philip F Anschutz	303-298-1000	R	84*	0.2
Petroleum Development Corp.	PO Box 26	Bridgeport	WV	26330	James N Ryan	304-842-3597	P	83	<0.1
Fairfield Maxwell Corp.	277 Park Ave	New York	NY	10172	KG Sugahara	212-421-2850	R	80*	0.6
Boots and Coots Group	777 Post Oak Blvd	Houston	TX	77056	Larry H Ramming	713-621-7911	R	76	0.6
Maple Resources Corp.	2626 Cole Ave	Dallas	TX	75204	John Hanks	214-880-0400	R	75*	0.1
Alexander Energy Corp.	701 Cedar Lake	Oklahoma City	OK	73114	Bob G Alexander	405-478-8686	P	75	<0.1
Nana Regional Corporation Inc.	Shore Ave	Kotzebue	AK	99752	Charlie A Curtis	907-442-3301	R	73*	0.5
KCI Inc.	6105 W 68th St	Tulsa	OK	74131	Neal Cartwright	918-446-1801	R	72	0.2
Justiss Oil Company Inc.	1810 E Oak St	Jena	LA	71342	JF Justiss Jr	318-992-4111	R	72*	0.2

Source: *Ward's Business Directory of U.S. Private and Public Companies*, Volumes 1 and 2, 2000. The company type code used is as follows: P - Public, R - Private, S - Subsidiary, D - Division, J - Joint Venture, A - Affiliate, G - Group, N - Company type not reported. Sales are in millions of dollars, employees are in thousands. An asterisk (*) indicates an estimated sales volume. The symbol < stands for 'less than'. Company names and addresses are truncated, in some cases, to fit into the available space.

MINING PRODUCT DETAILS

Products	Units	Quantity of (000s)		Value of product shipments				
		Produc-tion 1997	Ship-ments 1997	1992		1997	
				($ mil)	% of total	($ mil)	% of total
Support activities for oil and gas field operations		NA	NA	-	-	10,969.8	100.0
Oil and gas field geophysical exploration work, except mapping and surveying services		NA	NA	-	-	386.3	3.5
Other oil and gas field exploration services		NA	NA	57.7	-	4.0	0.0
Cementing oil and gas wells		NA	NA	472.3	-	834.2	7.6
Oil and gas well surveying and well logging		NA	NA	545.2	-	1,224.0	11.2
Hydraulic fracturing of oil and gas wells	1,000 wells	NA	(S)	1,027.2	-	1,121.0	10.2
Running, cutting, and pulling casings, tubes, or rods for oil and gas wells		NA	NA	333.8	-	222.0	2.0
Acidizing and other chemical treatment of oil and gas wells, excluding hydraulic fracturing	1,000 wells	NA	78	246.5	-	272.8	2.5
Perforating oil and gas well casings		NA	NA	99.4	-	120.1	1.1
Installing oil and gas field production equipment, such as wellhead fittings, pumps, and engines		NA	NA	165.2	-	110.3	1.0
Cleaning out, bailing out, or swabbing oil and gas wells		NA	NA	131.2	-	211.4	1.9
Pumping oil and gas wells but not operating leases		NA	NA	105.7	-	132.5	1.2
All other oil and gas field services		NA	NA	2,129.6	-	3,633.7	33.1
Oil and gas field operations, nsk[1]		NA	NA	-	-	2,697.5	24.6

Source: Economic Census of the U.S., 1997. *Notes:* 1. Includes value for establishments that did not report detailed data and estimates for small companies (estimates were made from adminstrative-record data rather than collected from respondents). NA stands for not applicable. (D) means data are withheld to avoid disclosure of competitive information. (S) indicates that data did not meet publication standards. - means not available or zero.

LOCATION BY STATE AND REGIONAL CONCENTRATION

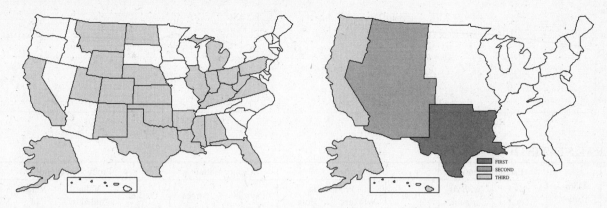

FIRST
SECOND
THIRD

INDUSTRY DATA BY STATE

State	Estab lish- ments	Employment			Compensation		Production				Capital Exp. ($ mil)
		Total	Workers	Total as % of US	Payroll per Employee	Wages per Worker	Costs ($ mil)	Value Added ($ mil)	Reve- nues ($ mil)	% of US	
Texas	2,367	39,033	29,234	36.71	34,113	35,604	1,248.2	3,574.4	4,287.0	44.67	535.6
Louisiana	795	22,029	16,844	20.72	33,663	33,528	667.9	2,140.4	2,560.9	26.68	247.4
Oklahoma	856	8,476	6,223	7.97	33,086	32,108	288.2	696.6	911.2	9.49	73.5
Alaska	46	5,071	3,782	4.77	56,027	61,189	104.3	518.8	584.1	6.09	39.0
California	256	6,542	5,329	6.15	33,515	32,361	136.0	448.1	550.5	5.74	33.5
Wyoming	12	1,144	1,104	1.08	58,987	56,914	58.2	384.8	432.3	4.50	10.8
New Mexico	248	3,776	2,825	3.55	30,721	31,311	109.5	315.2	369.8	3.85	54.9
Wyoming	313	3,246	2,462	3.05	32,569	33,389	85.3	281.3	332.0	3.46	34.6
Colorado	294	2,193	1,626	2.06	33,880	35,680	66.1	214.0	257.1	2.68	22.9
Kansas	361	2,320	1,749	2.18	25,969	25,990	50.6	142.7	181.1	1.89	12.3
Mississippi	141	1,598	1,211	1.50	26,615	26,310	33.8	98.0	120.1	1.25	11.7
Michigan	111	1,100	791	1.03	33,467	33,918	30.5	87.1	109.2	1.14	8.5
Utah	115	1,105	843	1.04	29,016	28,668	30.0	80.3	99.3	1.03	10.9
North Dakota	123	1,076	845	1.01	26,826	27,857	24.8	65.6	83.9	0.87	6.5
West Virginia	99	985	729	0.93	27,379	28,335	21.1	65.3	76.1	0.79	10.3
Pennsylvania	82	746	541	0.70	27,326	27,564	27.8	53.8	74.3	0.77	7.3
Ohio	146	872	625	0.82	25,843	27,226	17.2	51.0	62.2	0.65	6.0
Kentucky	54	592	484	0.56	29,829	33,267	14.9	50.5	61.3	0.64	4.0
Alabama	53	708	566	0.67	26,794	25,687	13.6	49.1	58.2	0.61	4.4
Montana	110	687	506	0.65	25,856	27,289	12.3	44.9	52.1	0.54	5.0
Illinois	135	673	508	0.63	23,449	24,872	11.8	42.1	51.0	0.53	3.0
Arkansas	77	606	492	0.57	28,467	28,130	13.7	44.2	49.8	0.52	8.1
Missouri	13	161	132	0.15	18,870	17,492	(D)	13.1	16.4	0.17	(D)
Indiana	32	200	156	0.19	25,605	26,231	2.7	12.1	13.9	0.15	0.8
Florida	27	147	101	0.14	30,898	31,574	2.9	9.6	11.2	0.12	1.3
New York	25	143	104	0.13	24,657	24,837	(D)	8.3	9.8	0.10	(D)
Nebraska	34	143	116	0.13	18,888	18,974	2.0	7.7	9.2	0.10	0.5
Virginia	22	175*	(D)	0.16		(D)	(D)	(D)	(D)	-	1.6

Source: *Economic Census of the U.S., 1997.* Data are sorted by 1997 revenues or establishments. (D) means data suppression to prevent disclosure of company data. A dash (-) is used when data are unavailable or can- not be calculated. Data followed by an * indicate the midpoint of a range. The ranges are: for 10, 0-19; for 60, 20-99, for 175, 100-249, for 375, 250-499, for 750, 500-999. Higher values are multiples of those shown, e.g., 3,750 is the midpoint of the range 2,500-4,999. Shaded *states* indicate states in which the industry was active in 1997. Shaded *regions* indicate where the industry is regionally most concentrated.

NAICS 213113 - SUPPORT ACTIVITIES FOR COAL MINING*

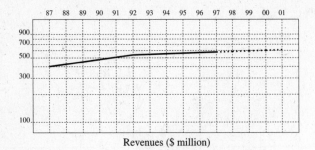

Revenues ($ million)

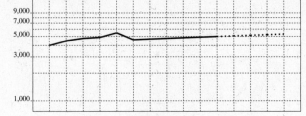

Employment (000)

GENERAL STATISTICS

Year	Com-panies	Establishments		Employment			Compensation		Production ($ million)			
		Total	with 20 or more employees	Total (No.)	Production Workers (No.)	Hours (Mil)	Payroll ($ mil)	Wages ($/hr)	Cost of Materials	Value Added by Mining	Value of Shipments	Capital Invest.
1977	-	351	85	6,800	6,000	11.6	118.9	8.85	154.6	313.3	417.6	50.3
1982	368	422	-	6,900	5,700	11.0	168.2	12.15	212.2	418.1	572.0	58.4
1987	254	291	57	4,000	3,300	6.8	115.7	13.78	161.4	279.6	402.0	39.0
1988	266	254[1]	67[1]	4,479[1]	3,394	7.0	128.0[1]	13.82	166.1	297.0	426.2	-
1989	279	232[1]	74[1]	4,755[1]	3,492	7.3	168.4[1]	13.85	170.9	315.5	451.8	-
1990	292	243[1]	74[1]	4,882[1]	3,591	7.6	168.5[1]	13.89	175.9	335.2	479.0	-
1991	306	251[1]	84[1]	5,484[1]	3,694	7.8	178.2[1]	13.93	181.0	356.1	507.8	-
1992	320	358	65	4,600	3,800	8.1	140.5	13.96	186.2	378.3	538.4	26.2
1993	312	348	65	4,678	3,883	8.2	147.1	14.58	185.4	387.9	546.3	-
1994	304	337	66	4,756	3,965	8.3	153.7	15.21	184.7	397.5	554.3	-
1995	296	327	66	4,834	4,048	8.3	160.2	15.83	183.9	407.0	562.2	-
1996	288	316	67	4,912	4,130	8.4	166.8	16.46	183.2	416.6	570.2	-
1997	280	306	67	4,990	4,213	8.5	173.4	17.08	182.4	426.2	578.1	30.5
1998	272p	296p	67p	5,068p	4,296p	8.6p	180.0p	17.70p	181.6p	435.8p	586.0p	-
1999	264p	285p	68p	5,146p	4,378p	8.7p	186.6p	18.33p	180.9p	445.4p	594.0p	-
2000	256p	275p	68p	5,224p	4,461p	8.7p	193.1p	18.95p	180.1p	454.9p	601.9p	-
2001	248p	264p	69p	5,302p	4,543p	8.8p	199.7p	19.58p	179.4p	464.5p	609.9p	-

Sources: Economic Census of the United States, 1977, 1982, 1987, 1992, and 1997. Data for those years (years are in bold type) are from the 5-year censuses of the economy. Other values, unless otherwise noted, are extrapolations. Values footnoted 1 are from the County Business Patterns for the years indicated. Values marked with p are projections. Data are the most recent available at this level of detail.

INDICES OF CHANGE

Year	Com-panies	Establishments		Employment			Compensation		Production ($ million)			
		Total	with 20 or more employees	Total (No.)	Production Workers (No.)	Hours (Mil)	Payroll ($ mil)	Wages ($/hr)	Cost of Materials	Value Added by Mining	Value of Shipments	Capital Invest.
1977	-	114.7	126.9	136.3	142.4	136.5	68.6	51.8	84.8	73.5	72.2	164.9
1982	131.4	137.9	-	138.3	135.3	129.4	97.0	71.1	116.3	98.1	98.9	191.5
1987	90.7	95.1	85.1	80.2	78.3	80.0	66.7	80.7	88.5	65.6	69.5	127.9
1992	114.3	117.0	97.0	92.2	90.2	95.3	81.0	81.7	102.1	88.8	93.1	85.9
1997	100.0	100.0	100.0	100.0	100.0	100.0	100.0	100.0	100.0	100.0	100.0	100.0

Sources: Same as General Statistics. The values shown reflect change from the base year, 1997. Values above 100 mean greater than 1997, values below 100 mean less than 1997, and a value of 100 in years other than 1997 means same as 1997. Indices are calculated only for Census years. Data are the most recent available at this level of detail.

SELECTED RATIOS

For 1992	Avg. of Sector	Analyzed Industry	Index	For 1992	Avg. of Sector	Analyzed Industry	Index
Employees per Establishment	20.4	16.3	80	Value Added per Production Worker	335,283	101,163	30
Payroll per Establishment	831,719	566,667	68	Cost per Establishment	2,854,087	596,078	21
Payroll per Employee	40,815	34,749	85	Cost per Employee	140,057	36,553	26
Production Workers per Establishment	15.6	13.8	88	Cost per Production Worker	183,057	43,295	24
Wages per Establishment	613,139	474,444	77	Shipments per Establishment	6,840,788	1,889,216	28
Wages per Production Worker	39,326	34,460	88	Shipments per Employee	335,695	115,852	35
Hours per Production Worker	2,075	2,018	97	Shipments per Production Worker	438,757	137,218	31
Wages per Hour	18.96	17.08	90	Investment per Establishment	1,242,441	99,673	8
Value Added per Establishment	5,227,487	1,392,810	27	Investment per Employee	60,970	6,112	10
Value Added per Employee	256,526	85,411	33	Investment per Production Worker	79,688	7,239	9

Sources: Same as General Statistics. The 'Average of Sector' column represents the average for all industries in this sector. The Index shows the relationship between the Average and the Analyzed Industry. For example, 100 means that they are equal; 500 that the Analyzed Industry is five times the average; 50 means that the Analyzed Industry is half the national average. 'na' is used to show that data are 'not available'.

*Equivalent to SIC 1241.

LEADING COMPANIES   Number shown: **3**   Total sales ($ mil): **181**   Total employment (000): **7.4**

Company Name	Address				CEO Name	Phone	Co. Type	Sales ($ mil)	Empl. (000)
Exxon Coal and Minerals Co.	2401 S Gessner Rd	Houston	TX	77063	Lee R Raymond	713-978-5333	S	177	7.4
CQ Inc.	160 Quality Ctr	Homer City	PA	15748	Clark D Harrison	724-479-3503	R	2	<0.1
TECO Coalbed Methane Inc.	P O Box 111	Tampa	FL	33601	Rober Fagan	813-228-4111	S	2*	<0.1

Source: Ward's Business Directory of U.S. Private and Public Companies, Volumes 1 and 2, 2000. The company type code used is as follows: P - Public, R - Private, S - Subsidiary, D - Division, J - Joint Venture, A - Affiliate, G - Group, N - Company type not reported. Sales are in millions of dollars, employees are in thousands. An asterisk (*) indicates an estimated sales volume. The symbol < stands for 'less than'. Company names and addresses are truncated, in some cases, to fit into the available space.

MINING PRODUCT DETAILS

Products	Units	Quantity of (000s)		Value of product shipments			
		Produc-tion 1997	Ship-ments 1997	1992		1997	
				($ mil)	% of total	($ mil)	% of total
Support activities for coal mining		NA	NA	536.5	100.0	585.3	100.0
Strip mining coal not for own account	1,000 s tons	NA	12,432	95.8	17.9	67.4	11.5
Coal mining overburden stripping services		NA	NA	52.9	9.9	81.3	13.9
Coal mining prospect and test drilling services		NA	NA	17.0	3.2	16.8	2.9
Coal mine drilling services, other than prospect and test drilling, including blasting		NA	NA	25.2	4.7	36.3	6.2
Recovering culm bank material and auger mining coal not for own account	1,000 s tons	NA	1,043	6.7	1.2	8.7	1.5
Sinking coal mine shafts and driving coal mine tunnels services		NA	NA	38.5	7.2	34.6	5.9
Other coal mining services, nec		NA	NA	101.5	18.9	199.2	34.0
Coal mining services, nsk[1]		NA	NA	198.9	37.1	141.0	24.1

Source: Economic Census of the U.S., 1997. *Notes:* 1. Includes value for establishments that did not report detailed data and estimates for small companies (estimates were made from administrative-record data rather than collected from respondents). NA stands for not applicable. (D) means data are withheld to avoid disclosure of competitive information. (S) indicates that data did not meet publication standards. - means not available or zero.

LOCATION BY STATE AND REGIONAL CONCENTRATION

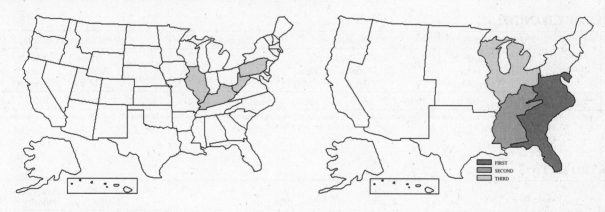

INDUSTRY DATA BY STATE

State	Estab-lish-ments	Employment			Compensation		Production				Capital Exp. ($ mil)
		Total	Workers	Total as % of US	Payroll per Employee	Wages per Worker	Costs ($ mil)	Value Added ($ mil)	Reve-nues ($ mil)	% of US	
West Virginia	63	1,453	1,210	29.12	40,551	41,412	52.2	155.9	197.1	46.25	11.0
Kentucky	57	1,064	961	21.32	30,783	30,287	49.5	74.6	117.8	27.63	6.4
Pennsylvania	77	664	526	13.31	28,747	27,249	19.0	45.0	61.2	14.35	2.8
Ohio	22	462	385	9.26	33,052	32,623	(D)	47.7	58.4	13.70	(D)
Virginia	28	395	330	7.92	27,848	27,985	(D)	21.4	28.5	6.70	(D)
Illinois	8	300	263	6.01	47,470	45,745	8.0	18.3	24.5	5.75	1.8
Texas	4	175*	(D)	3.51	-	(D)	(D)	(D)	(D)	-	(D)
Montana	1	175*	(D)	3.51	-	(D)	(D)	(D)	(D)	-	(D)

Source: Economic Census of the U.S., 1997. Data are sorted by 1997 revenues or establishments. (D) means data suppression to prevent disclosure of company data. A dash (-) is used when data are unavailable or cannot be calculated. Data followed by an * indicate the midpoint of a range. The ranges are: for 10, 0-19; for 60, 20-99; for 175, 100-249; for 375, 250-499; for 750, 500-999. Higher values are multiples of those shown, e.g., 3,750 is the midpoint of the range 2,500-4,999. Shaded *states* indicate states in which the industry was active in 1997. Shaded *regions* indicate where the industry is regionally most concentrated.

NAICS 213114 - SUPPORT ACTIVITIES FOR METAL MINING

GENERAL STATISTICS

| Year | Companies | Establishments | | Employment | | | Compensation | | Production ($ million) | | | |
		Total	with 20 or more employees	Total (No.)	Production Workers (No.)	Hours (Mil)	Payroll ($ mil)	Wages ($/hr)	Cost of Materials	Value Added by Mining	Value of Shipments	Capital Invest.
1997	141	189	39	3,031	2,565	5.0	109.2	18.32	125.7	237.6	339.8	23.5

Source: *Economic Census of the United States*, 1997. This is a newly defined industry. Data for prior years were unavailable at the time of publication but may become available over time.

DISTRIBUTION AMONG SIC-BASED INDUSTRIES - 1997

| SIC | Industry | Establishments | Employment | | | Compensation | | Production ($ mil) | |
			Total	Production Workers	Hours (Mil)	Payroll ($ mil)	Wages ($/hr)	Cost of Materials	Value of Shipments
108110	Metal mining services (pt)	189	3,031	2,565	5.0	109.2	18.29	125.7	339.7

Source: 1997 *Economic Census*. U.S. Census Bureau, U.S. Department of Commerce, August 1997. SIC codes ending in two zeroes represent complete 4-digit SICs. All others are parts of 4-digit SIC industries. Items showing a dash (-) indicate that data are not available because of disclosure problems.

SIC INDUSTRIES RELATED TO NAICS 213114

SIC	Industry	1990	1991	1992	1993	1994	1995	1996	1997
1081	**Metal Mining Services***								
	Establishments (number)	218	224	266	210	193	193	264p	264p
	Employment (thousands)	3.4	3.6	3.3	2.3	2.7	2.7	3.8e	3.9e
	Revenues ($ million)	306.8e	327.9e	350.4	374.5e	400.2e	427.7e	457.2e	488.6e

Source: *Economic Census of the United States*, 1992, annual surveys of economic sectors conducted by the Bureau of the Census, and estimates or projections based on the 1982-1992 period; not all data are shown. 'e' marks estimates made by the editors; 'p' indicates projections based on time series. A dash (-) indicates that data for this SIC or year were not available. * Indicates that only a portion of this industry is present within the NAICS data. If no * is shown, the entire industry is contained within the NAICS data.

INDICES OF CHANGE

| Year | Companies | Establishments | | Employment | | | Compensation | | Production ($ million) | | | |
		Total	with 20 or more employees	Total (No.)	Production Workers (No.)	Hours (Mil)	Payroll ($ mil)	Wages ($/hr)	Cost of Materials	Value Added by Mining	Value of Shipments	Capital Invest.
1997	100.0	100.0	100.0	100.0	100.0	100.0	100.0	100.0	100.0	100.0	100.0	100.0

Sources: Same as General Statistics. The values shown reflect change from the base year, 1997. Values above 100 mean greater than 1997, values below 100 mean less than 1997, and a value of 100 in years other than 1997 means same as 1997. Indices are calculated only for Census years. Data are the most recent available at this level of detail.

SELECTED RATIOS

For 1992	Avg. of Sector	Analyzed Industry	Index	For 1992	Avg. of Sector	Analyzed Industry	Index
Employees per Establishment	20.4	16.0	79	Value Added per Production Worker	335,283	92,632	28
Payroll per Establishment	831,719	577,778	69	Cost per Establishment	2,854,087	665,079	23
Payroll per Employee	40,815	36,028	88	Cost per Employee	140,057	41,471	30
Production Workers per Establishment	15.6	13.6	87	Cost per Production Worker	183,057	49,006	27
Wages per Establishment	613,139	484,656	79	Shipments per Establishment	6,840,788	1,797,884	26
Wages per Production Worker	39,326	35,712	91	Shipments per Employee	335,695	112,108	33
Hours per Production Worker	2,075	1,949	94	Shipments per Production Worker	438,757	132,476	30
Wages per Hour	18.96	18.32	97	Investment per Establishment	1,242,441	124,339	10
Value Added per Establishment	5,227,487	1,257,143	24	Investment per Employee	60,970	7,753	13
Value Added per Employee	256,526	78,390	31	Investment per Production Worker	79,688	9,162	11

Sources: Same as General Statistics. The 'Average of Sector' column represents the average for all industries in this sector. The Index shows the relationship between the Average and the Analyzed Industry. For example, 100 means that they are equal; 500 that the Analyzed Industry is five times the average; 50 means that the Analyzed Industry is half the national average. 'na' is used to show that data are 'not available'.

LEADING COMPANIES   Number shown: **6**   Total sales ($ mil): **168**   Total employment (000): **0.6**

Company Name	Address				CEO Name	Phone	Co. Type	Sales ($ mil)	Empl. (000)
N.A. Degerstrom Inc.	3303 N Sullivan Rd	Spokane	WA	99216	Neal Degerstrom	509-928-3333	R	143*	0.3
American Mine Services Inc.	11808 Hwy 93	Boulder	CO	80303	Brian Micke	303-371-4000	R	15	0.1
Century Geophysical Corp.	7517 E Pine St	Tulsa	OK	74115	John McCormick	918-838-9811	R	6	<0.1
Environmental & Foundation	217 Raemisch Rd	Waunakee	WI	53597	Gregory Anderson	608-849-9896	R	3	<0.1
Royal Gold Inc.	1660 Wynkoop St	Denver	CO	80202	Stanley Dempsey	303-573-1660	P	1	<0.1
Metallica Resources Inc.	3979 E Arapahoe Rd	Littleton	CO	80122	Louis A Lepry Jr	303-796-0229	P	0	0.1

Source: *Ward's Business Directory of U.S. Private and Public Companies*, Volumes 1 and 2, 2000. The company type code used is as follows: P - Public, R - Private, S - Subsidiary, D - Division, J - Joint Venture, A - Affiliate, G - Group, N - Company type not reported. Sales are in millions of dollars, employees are in thousands. An asterisk (*) indicates an estimated sales volume. The symbol < stands for 'less than'. Company names and addresses are truncated, in some cases, to fit into the available space.

MINING PRODUCT DETAILS

Products	Units	Quantity of (000s)		Value of product shipments			
		Produc-tion 1997	Ship-ments 1997	1992		1997	
				($ mil)	% of total	($ mil)	% of total
Support activities for metal mining		NA	NA	-	-	334.4	100.0
Metal mining exploration work, except prospect and test drilling and geophysical surveying services		NA	NA	-	-	32.0	9.6
Open-pit metal mining ores not for own account		NA	NA	114.5	-	54.4	16.3
Metal mining prospect services and test drilling services		NA	NA	60.4	-	148.5	44.4
Sinking metal mine shafts and driving metal mine tunnels services		NA	NA	10.8	-	36.0	10.8
Other metal mining services, nec		NA	NA	8.9	-	8.1	2.4
Metal mining services, nsk[1]		NA	NA	-	-	55.5	16.6

Source: *Economic Census of the U.S.*, 1997. Notes: 1. Includes value for establishments that did not report detailed data and estimates for small companies (estimates were made from administrative-record data rather than collected from respondents). NA stands for not applicable. (D) means data are withheld to avoid disclosure of competitive information. (S) indicates that data did not meet publication standards. - means not available or zero.

LOCATION BY STATE AND REGIONAL CONCENTRATION

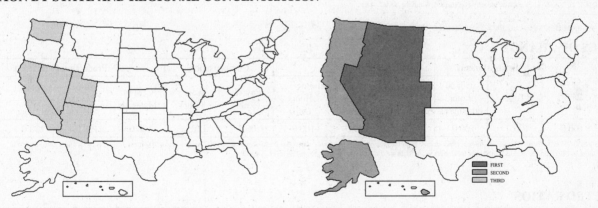

INDUSTRY DATA BY STATE

State	Estab-lish-ments	Employment			Compensation		Production				Capital Exp. ($ mil)
		Total	Workers	Total as % of US	Payroll per Employee	Wages per Worker	Costs ($ mil)	Value Added ($ mil)	Reve-nues ($ mil)	% of US	
Nevada	35	1,169	1,025	38.57	42,932	42,565	58.1	91.7	142.0	59.79	7.8
Arizona	20	329	263	10.85	34,195	32,483	16.5	36.5	51.2	21.53	1.9
Alaska	10	133	118	4.39	45,782	45,856	(D)	18.4	24.2	10.18	(D)
California	17	181	154	5.97	29,757	30,351	5.9	13.2	17.7	7.43	1.4
Utah	8	230	192	7.59	23,991	22,396	5.8	11.9	17.0	7.15	0.7
Montana	12	175*	(D)	5.77	-	(D)	(D)	(D)	(D)	-	(D)
Washington	5	175*	(D)	5.77	-	(D)	(D)	(D)	(D)	-	0.9
Minnesota	2	175*	(D)	5.77	-	(D)	(D)	(D)	(D)	-	(D)

Source: *Economic Census of the U.S.*, 1997. Data are sorted by 1997 revenues or establishments. (D) means data suppression to prevent disclosure of company data. A dash (-) is used when data are unavailable or cannot be calculated. Data followed by an * indicate the midpoint of a range. The ranges are: for 10, 0-19; for 60, 20-99, for 175, 100-249, for 375, 250-499, for 750, 500-999. Higher values are multiples of those shown, e.g., 3,750 is the midpoint of the range 2,500-4,999. Shaded *states* indicate states in which the industry was active in 1997. Shaded *regions* indicate where the industry is regionally most concentrated.

NAICS 213115 - SUPPORT ACTIVITIES FOR NONMETALLIC MINERALS (EXCEPT FUELS)

GENERAL STATISTICS

| Year | Companies | Establishments | | Employment | | | Compensation | | Production ($ million) | | | |
		Total	with 20 or more employees	Total (No.)	Production Workers (No.)	Hours (Mil)	Payroll ($ mil)	Wages ($/hr)	Cost of Materials	Value Added by Mining	Value of Shipments	Capital Invest.
1997	137	144	20	1,623	1,248	2.6	57.1	16.33	62.1	125.4	172.0	15.5

Source: *Economic Census of the United States*, 1997. This is a newly defined industry. Data for prior years were unavailable at the time of publication but may become available over time.

DISTRIBUTION AMONG SIC-BASED INDUSTRIES - 1997

| SIC | Industry | Establish-ments | Employment | | | Compensation | | Production ($ mil) | |
			Total	Production Workers	Hours (Mil)	Payroll ($ mil)	Wages ($/hr)	Cost of Materials	Value of Shipments
148110	Nonmetallic minerals services, except fuels (pt)	144	1,623	1,248	2.6	57.1	16.33	62.1	172.0

Source: 1997 *Economic Census*. U.S. Census Bureau, U.S. Department of Commerce, August 1997. SIC codes ending in two zeroes represent complete 4-digit SICs. All others are parts of 4-digit SIC industries. Items showing a dash (-) indicate that data are not available because of disclosure problems.

SIC INDUSTRIES RELATED TO NAICS 213115

SIC	Industry	1990	1991	1992	1993	1994	1995	1996	1997
1481	**Nonmetallic Minerals Services***								
	Establishments (number)	161	160	178	138	143	106	179*p*	179*p*
	Employment (thousands)	1.8	1.9	2.0	1.5	1.6	1.3	2.2*e*	2.2*e*
	Revenues ($ million)	179.1*e*	183.9*e*	188.9	194.0*e*	199.2*e*	204.6*e*	210.1*e*	215.7*e*

Source: *Economic Census of the United States*, 1992, annual surveys of economic sectors conducted by the Bureau of the Census, and estimates or projections based on the 1982-1992 period; not all data are shown. 'e' marks estimates made by the editors; 'p' indicates projections based on time series. A dash (-) indicates that data for this SIC or year were not available. * Indicates that only a portion of this industry is present within the NAICS data. If no * is shown, the entire industry is contained within the NAICS data.

INDICES OF CHANGE

| Year | Companies | Establishments | | Employment | | | Compensation | | Production ($ million) | | | |
		Total	with 20 or more employees	Total (No.)	Production Workers (No.)	Hours (Mil)	Payroll ($ mil)	Wages ($/hr)	Cost of Materials	Value Added by Mining	Value of Shipments	Capital Invest.
1997	100.0	100.0	100.0	100.0	100.0	100.0	100.0	100.0	100.0	100.0	100.0	100.0

Sources: Same as General Statistics. The values shown reflect change from the base year, 1997. Values above 100 mean greater than 1997, values below 100 mean less than 1997, and a value of 100 in years other than 1997 means same as 1997. Indices are calculated only for Census years. Data are the most recent available at this level of detail.

SELECTED RATIOS

For 1992	Avg. of Sector	Analyzed Industry	Index	For 1992	Avg. of Sector	Analyzed Industry	Index
Employees per Establishment	20.4	11.3	55	Value Added per Production Worker	335,283	100,481	30
Payroll per Establishment	831,719	396,528	48	Cost per Establishment	2,854,087	431,250	15
Payroll per Employee	40,815	35,182	86	Cost per Employee	140,057	38,262	27
Production Workers per Establishment	15.6	8.7	56	Cost per Production Worker	183,057	49,760	27
Wages per Establishment	613,139	294,847	48	Shipments per Establishment	6,840,788	1,194,444	17
Wages per Production Worker	39,326	34,021	87	Shipments per Employee	335,695	105,977	32
Hours per Production Worker	2,075	2,083	100	Shipments per Production Worker	438,757	137,821	31
Wages per Hour	18.96	16.33	86	Investment per Establishment	1,242,441	107,639	9
Value Added per Establishment	5,227,487	870,833	17	Investment per Employee	60,970	9,550	16
Value Added per Employee	256,526	77,264	30	Investment per Production Worker	79,688	12,420	16

Sources: Same as General Statistics. The 'Average of Sector' column represents the average for all industries in this sector. The Index shows the relationship between the Average and the Analyzed Industry. For example, 100 means that they are equal; 500 that the Analyzed Industry is five times the average; 50 means that the Analyzed Industry is half the national average. 'na' is used to show that data are 'not available'.

LEADING COMPANIES   Number shown: **1**   Total sales ($ mil): **50**   Total employment (000): **0.3**

Company Name	Address			CEO Name	Phone	Co. Type	Sales ($ mil)	Empl. (000)
Cominco American Inc.	PO Box 3087	Spokane	WA 99216		509-459-4428	S	50*	0.3

Source: Ward's Business Directory of U.S. Private and Public Companies, Volumes 1 and 2, 2000. The company type code used is as follows: P - Public, R - Private, S - Subsidiary, D - Division, J - Joint Venture, A - Affiliate, G - Group, N - Company type not reported. Sales are in millions of dollars, employees are in thousands. An asterisk (*) indicates an estimated sales volume. The symbol < stands for 'less than'. Company names and addresses are truncated, in some cases, to fit into the available space.

MINING PRODUCT DETAILS

Products	Units	Quantity of (000s)		Value of product shipments			
		Produc-tion 1997	Ship-ments 1997	1992		1997	
				($ mil)	% of total	($ mil)	% of total
Support activities for nonmetallic minerals (except fuels)		NA	NA	-	-	223.9	100.0
Open-pit or quarry mining nonmetallic minerals not for own account		NA	NA	46.7	-	50.4	22.5
Nonmetallic mineral overburden stripping services		NA	NA	19.4	-	17.9	8.0
Nonmetallic mineral prospect and test drilling services		NA	NA	7.7	-	20.3	9.1
Nonmetallic mineral drilling services, other than prospect and test drilling, including blasting		NA	NA	17.9	-	43.5	19.4
Other nonmetallic minerals services (except fuels), nec		NA	NA	-	-	12.4	5.6
Nonmetallic minerals services (except fuels), nsk[1]		NA	NA	-	-	79.5	35.5

Source: Economic Census of the U.S., 1997. Notes: 1. Includes value for establishments that did not report detailed data and estimates for small companies (estimates were made from administrative-record data rather than collected from respondents). NA stands for not applicable. (D) means data are withheld to avoid disclosure of competitive information. (S) indicates that data did not meet publication standards. - means not available or zero.

LOCATION BY STATE AND REGIONAL CONCENTRATION

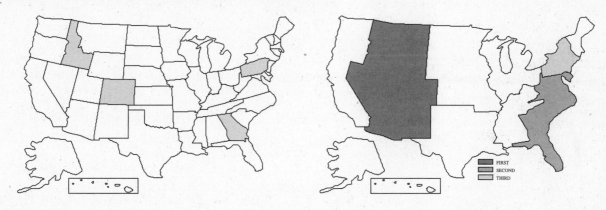

FIRST
SECOND
THIRD

INDUSTRY DATA BY STATE

State	Estab-lish-ments	Employment			Compensation		Production				Capital Exp. ($ mil)
		Total	Workers	Total as % of US	Payroll per Employee	Wages per Worker	Costs ($ mil)	Value Added ($ mil)	Reve-nues ($ mil)	% of US	
Idaho	4	161	142	9.92	41,118	41,049	6.3	19.4	24.9	19.87	0.8
Colorado	10	261	236	16.08	28,054	25,504	5.1	19.2	23.3	18.60	1.0
Georgia	12	205	140	12.63	28,776	26,457	6.4	15.4	17.7	14.11	4.1
Pennsylvania	11	145	110	8.93	36,683	37,036	4.7	9.5	13.2	10.51	1.0
Utah	3	175*	(D)	10.78	-	(D)	(D)	(D)	(D)	-	(D)

Source: Economic Census of the U.S., 1997. Data are sorted by 1997 revenues or establishments. (D) means data suppression to prevent disclosure of company data. A dash (-) is used when data are unavailable or cannot be calculated. Data followed by an * indicate the midpoint of a range. The ranges are: for 10, 0-19; for 60, 20-99, for 175, 100-249, for 375, 250-499, for 750, 500-999. Higher values are multiples of those shown, e.g., 3,750 is the midpoint of the range 2,500-4,999. Shaded *states* indicate states in which the industry was active in 1997. Shaded *regions* indicate where the industry is regionally most concentrated.

Part III

UTILITIES

NAICS 221111 - HYDROELECTRIC POWER GENERATION

GENERAL STATISTICS

Year	Establishments (number)	Employment (number)	Payroll ($ million)	Revenues ($ million)	Employees per Establishment (number)	Revenues per Establishment ($)	Payroll per Employee ($)
1997	353	7,380	394.1	3,073.9	20.9	8,707,955	53,406

Source: Economic Census of the United States, 1997. This is a newly defined industry. Data for prior years were unavailable at the time of publication but may become available over time.

SIC INDUSTRIES RELATED TO NAICS 221111

SIC	Industry	1990	1991	1992	1993	1994	1995	1996	1997
4911	**Electric Services***	-	-	-	-	-	-	-	-
4931	**Electric and Other Services Combined***								
	Establishments (number)	738	891	1,589	1,507	1,597	1,610	1,564	1,882*p*
	Employment (thousands)	105.1	117.3	216.0	207.5	198.4	188.2	191.0	226.5*p*
	Revenues ($ million)			68,726.0					
4939	**Combination Utilities, nec***								
	Establishments (number)	145	247	101	103	141	145	161	150*p*
	Employment (thousands)	4.5	6.0	1.7	1.2	3.6	4.6	4.5	3.5*p*
	Revenues ($ million)		-	502.9					

Source: Economic Census of the United States, 1992, annual surveys of economic sectors conducted by the Bureau of the Census, and estimates or projections based on the 1982-1992 period; not all data are shown. 'e' marks estimates made by the editors; 'p' indicates projections based on time series. A dash (-) indicates that data for this SIC or year were not available. * Indicates that only a portion of this industry is present within the NAICS data. If no * is shown, the entire industry is contained within the NAICS data.

INDICES OF CHANGE

Year	Establishments (number)	Employment (number)	Payroll ($ million)	Revenues ($ million)	Employees per Establishment (number)	Revenues per Establishment ($)	Payroll per Employee ($)
1997	100.0	100.0	100.0	100.0	100.0	100.0	100.0

Sources: Same as General Statistics. The values shown reflect change from the base year, 1997. Values above 100 mean greater than 1997, values below 100 mean less than 1997, and a value of 100 in years other than 1997 means same as 1997. Indices are calculated only for Census years. Data are the most recent available at this level of detail.

SELECTED RATIOS

For 1997	Avg. of Sector	Analyzed Industry	Index	For 1997	Avg. of Sector	Analyzed Industry	Index
Employees per establishment	45	21	46	Payroll per establishment	2,358,969	1,116,431	47
Revenue per establishment	26,539,891	8,707,932	33	Payroll as % of revenue	9	13	144
Revenue per employee	585,899	416,518	71	Payroll per employee	52,077	53,401	103

Sources: Same as General Statistics. The 'Average of Sector' column represents the average for all industries in this sector. The Index shows the relationship between the Average and the Analyzed Industry. For example, 100 means that they are equal; 500 that the Analyzed Industry is five times the average; 50 means that the Analyzed Industry is half the national average. 'na' is used to show that data are 'not available'.

LEADING COMPANIES
No company data available for this industry.

LOCATION BY STATE AND REGIONAL CONCENTRATION

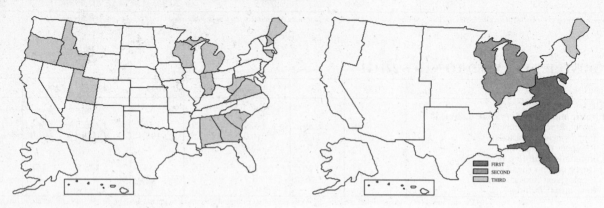

INDUSTRY DATA BY STATE

State	Establishments Total (number)	Establishments % of U.S.	Employment Total (number)	Employment % of U.S.	Employment Per Estab.	Payroll Total ($ mil.)	Payroll Per Empl. ($)	Revenues Total ($ mil.)	Revenues % of U.S.	Revenues Per Estab. ($)
Massachusetts	7	2.0	271	3.7	39	13.7	50,572	135.0	4.4	19,290,000
Pennsylvania	13	3.7	207	2.8	16	10.8	52,280	99.5	3.2	7,655,846
Michigan	16	4.5	324	4.4	20	26.3	81,142	84.1	2.7	5,257,500
Wisconsin	24	6.8	194	2.6	8	9.0	46,397	69.2	2.3	2,882,458
Idaho	16	4.5	126	1.7	8	6.8	54,111	42.5	1.4	2,659,125
California	25	7.1	375*	-	-	(D)	-	(D)	-	-
West Virginia	23	6.5	750*	-	-	(D)	-	(D)	-	-
Maine	20	5.7	60*	-	-	(D)	-	(D)	-	-
Virginia	20	5.7	375*	-	-	(D)	-	(D)	-	-
Indiana	18	5.1	750*	-	-	(D)	-	(D)	-	-
New York	17	4.8	60*	-	-	(D)	-	(D)	-	-
Alabama	14	4.0	175*	-	-	(D)	-	(D)	-	-
New Hampshire	14	4.0	175*	-	-	(D)	-	(D)	-	-
Oregon	14	4.0	1,750*	-	-	(D)	-	(D)	-	-
Connecticut	12	3.4	175*	-	-	(D)	-	(D)	-	-
Utah	12	3.4	60*	-	-	(D)	-	(D)	-	-
Georgia	10	2.8	175*	-	-	(D)	-	(D)	-	-
North Carolina	7	2.0	175*	-	-	(D)	-	(D)	-	-
South Carolina	6	1.7	60*	-	-	(D)	-	(D)	-	-
Washington	6	1.7	60*	-	-	(D)	-	(D)	-	-

Source: 1997 *Economic Census*. The states are in descending order of revenues or establishments (if revenue data are missing for the majority). The symbol (D) appears when data are withheld to prevent disclosure of competitive information. States marked with (D) are sorted by number of establishments. A dash (-) indicates that the data element cannot be calculated. * indicates the midpoint of a range; 175, for example is the range 100-249. Shaded *states* on the state map indicate those states which have proportionately greater representation in the industry than would be indicated by the state's population; the ratio is based on total revenues or number of establishments. Shaded *regions* indicate where the industry is regionally most concentrated.

NAICS 221112 - FOSSIL FUEL ELECTRIC POWER GENERATION

GENERAL STATISTICS

Year	Establishments (number)	Employment (number)	Payroll ($ million)	Revenues ($ million)	Employees per Establishment (number)	Revenues per Establishment ($)	Payroll per Employee ($)
1997	1,009	93,765	5,048.6	48,324.0	92.9	47,892,971	53,843

Source: *Economic Census of the United States*, 1997. This is a newly defined industry. Data for prior years were unavailable at the time of publication but may become available over time.

SIC INDUSTRIES RELATED TO NAICS 221112

SIC	Industry	1990	1991	1992	1993	1994	1995	1996	1997
4911	**Electric Services***	-	-	-	-	-	-	-	-
4931	**Electric and Other Services Combined***								
	Establishments (number)	738	891	1,589	1,507	1,597	1,610	1,564	1,882p
	Employment (thousands)	105.1	117.3	216.0	207.5	198.4	188.2	191.0	226.5p
	Revenues ($ million)	-	-	68,726.0	-	-	-	-	-
4939	**Combination Utilities, nec***								
	Establishments (number)	145	247	101	103	141	145	161	150p
	Employment (thousands)	4.5	6.0	1.7	1.2	3.6	4.6	4.5	3.5p
	Revenues ($ million)	-	-	502.9	-	-	-	-	-

Source: *Economic Census of the United States*, 1992, annual surveys of economic sectors conducted by the Bureau of the Census, and estimates or projections based on the 1982-1992 period; not all data are shown. 'e' marks estimates made by the editors; 'p' indicates projections based on time series. A dash (-) indicates that data for this SIC or year were not available. * Indicates that only a portion of this industry is present within the NAICS data. If no * is shown, the entire industry is contained within the NAICS data.

INDICES OF CHANGE

Year	Establishments (number)	Employment (number)	Payroll ($ million)	Revenues ($ million)	Employees per Establishment (number)	Revenues per Establishment ($)	Payroll per Employee ($)
1997	100.0	100.0	100.0	100.0	100.0	100.0	100.0

Sources: Same as General Statistics. The values shown reflect change from the base year, 1997. Values above 100 mean greater than 1997, values below 100 mean less than 1997, and a value of 100 in years other than 1997 means same as 1997. Indices are calculated only for Census years. Data are the most recent available at this level of detail.

SELECTED RATIOS

For 1997	Avg. of Sector	Analyzed Industry	Index	For 1997	Avg. of Sector	Analyzed Industry	Index
Employees per establishment	45	93	205	Payroll per establishment	2,358,969	5,003,568	212
Revenue per establishment	26,539,891	47,892,963	180	Payroll as % of revenue	9	10	118
Revenue per employee	585,899	515,374	88	Payroll per employee	52,077	53,843	103

Sources: Same as General Statistics. The 'Average of Sector' column represents the average for all industries in this sector. The Index shows the relationship between the Average and the Analyzed Industry. For example, 100 means that they are equal; 500 that the Analyzed Industry is five times the average; 50 means that the Analyzed Industry is half the national average. 'na' is used to show that data are 'not available'.

LEADING COMPANIES
No company data available for this industry.

LOCATION BY STATE AND REGIONAL CONCENTRATION

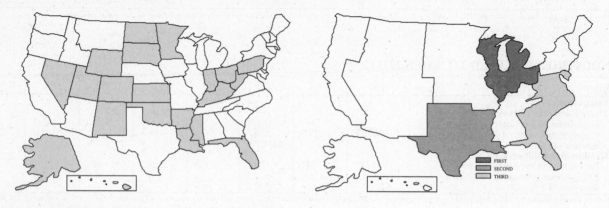

FIRST
SECOND
THIRD

INDUSTRY DATA BY STATE

State	Establishments Total (number)	% of U.S.	Employment Total (number)	% of U.S.	Per Estab.	Payroll Total ($ mil.)	Per Empl. ($)	Revenues Total ($ mil.)	% of U.S.	Per Estab. ($)
Pennsylvania	61	6.0	5,902	6.3	97	341.8	57,912	3,263.3	6.8	53,497,279
Florida	105	10.4	5,992	6.4	57	327.0	54,580	3,123.2	6.5	29,744,429
Texas	59	5.8	4,975	5.3	84	189.3	38,048	2,660.7	5.5	45,096,966
New York	19	1.9	3,701	3.9	195	209.8	56,687	2,642.9	5.5	139,100,684
Oklahoma	62	6.1	3,497	3.7	56	169.7	48,524	1,428.4	3.0	23,039,339
Michigan	16	1.6	1,660	1.8	104	93.9	56,587	1,254.0	2.6	78,374,438
California	45	4.5	1,458	1.6	32	76.2	52,289	1,175.4	2.4	26,119,000
Connecticut	12	1.2	1,306	1.4	109	80.2	61,435	1,063.9	2.2	88,655,833
Massachusetts	12	1.2	1,251	1.3	104	80.9	64,681	837.2	1.7	69,768,667
Arkansas	16	1.6	734	0.8	46	37.6	51,198	829.3	1.7	51,830,063
Minnesota	19	1.9	2,405	2.6	127	137.2	57,044	828.0	1.7	43,577,842
Virginia	25	2.5	1,701	1.8	68	80.1	47,113	749.0	1.5	29,958,600
Missouri	11	1.1	1,208	1.3	110	61.5	50,872	690.7	1.4	62,786,545
Wisconsin	14	1.4	1,490	1.6	106	82.4	55,277	542.6	1.1	38,755,429
Mississippi	14	1.4	736	0.8	53	37.5	50,924	537.8	1.1	38,416,929
Utah	9	0.9	1,218	1.3	135	67.1	55,093	387.2	0.8	43,021,778
Alaska	30	3.0	856	0.9	29	54.1	63,216	279.0	0.6	9,299,533
Iowa	6	0.6	224	0.2	37	10.0	44,482	90.2	0.2	15,038,167
Ohio	119	11.8	7,500*	-	-	(D)	-	(D)	-	-
Louisiana	58	5.7	1,750*	-	-	(D)	-	(D)	-	-
New Mexico	40	4.0	3,750*	-	-	(D)	-	(D)	-	-
Indiana	32	3.2	7,500*	-	-	(D)	-	(D)	-	-
Illinois	25	2.5	7,500*	-	-	(D)	-	(D)	-	-
Kentucky	20	2.0	3,750*	-	-	(D)	-	(D)	-	-
New Jersey	20	2.0	1,750*	-	-	(D)	-	(D)	-	-
Colorado	15	1.5	750*	-	-	(D)	-	(D)	-	-
South Dakota	15	1.5	375*	-	-	(D)	-	(D)	-	-
West Virginia	14	1.4	1,750*	-	-	(D)	-	(D)	-	-
Kansas	11	1.1	1,750*	-	-	(D)	-	(D)	-	-
Maryland	10	1.0	1,750*	-	-	(D)	-	(D)	-	-
South Carolina	10	1.0	1,750*	-	-	(D)	-	(D)	-	-
Wyoming	10	1.0	1,750*	-	-	(D)	-	(D)	-	-
Georgia	9	0.9	1,750*	-	-	(D)	-	(D)	-	-
North Carolina	9	0.9	175*	-	-	(D)	-	(D)	-	-
Hawaii	8	0.8	1,750*	-	-	(D)	-	(D)	-	-
North Dakota	7	0.7	1,750*	-	-	(D)	-	(D)	-	-
Arizona	6	0.6	7,500*	-	-	(D)	-	(D)	-	-
Nevada	6	0.6	1,750*	-	-	(D)	-	(D)	-	-

Source: 1997 *Economic Census*. The states are in descending order of revenues or establishments (if revenue data are missing for the majority). The symbol (D) appears when data are withheld to prevent disclosure of competitive information. States marked with (D) are sorted by number of establishments. A dash (-) indicates that the data element cannot be calculated. * indicates the midpoint of a range; 175, for example is the range 100-249. Shaded *states* on the state map indicate those states which have proportionately greater representation in the industry than would be indicated by the state's population; the ratio is based on total revenues or number of establishments. Shaded *regions* indicate where the industry is regionally most concentrated.

NAICS 221113 - NUCLEAR ELECTRIC POWER GENERATION

GENERAL STATISTICS

Year	Establishments (number)	Employment (number)	Payroll ($ million)	Revenues ($ million)	Employees per Establishment (number)	Revenues per Establishment ($)	Payroll per Employee ($)
1997	67	34,381	2,201.9	13,966.6	513.1	208,456,955	64,045

Source: Economic Census of the United States, 1997. This is a newly defined industry. Data for prior years were unavailable at the time of publication but may become available over time.

SIC INDUSTRIES RELATED TO NAICS 221113

SIC	Industry	1990	1991	1992	1993	1994	1995	1996	1997
4911	**Electric Services***	-	-	-	-	-	-	-	-
4931	**Electric and Other Services Combined***								
	Establishments (number)	738	891	1,589	1,507	1,597	1,610	1,564	1,882p
	Employment (thousands)	105.1	117.3	216.0	207.5	198.4	188.2	191.0	226.5p
	Revenues ($ million)	-	-	68,726.0	-	-	-	-	-
4939	**Combination Utilities, nec***								
	Establishments (number)	145	247	101	103	141	145	161	150p
	Employment (thousands)	4.5	6.0	1.7	1.2	3.6	4.6	4.5	3.5p
	Revenues ($ million)	-	-	502.9	-	-	-	-	-

Source: Economic Census of the United States, 1992, annual surveys of economic sectors conducted by the Bureau of the Census, and estimates or projections based on the 1982-1992 period; not all data are shown. 'e' marks estimates made by the editors; 'p' indicates projections based on time series. A dash (-) indicates that data for this SIC or year were not available. * Indicates that only a portion of this industry is present within the NAICS data. If no * is shown, the entire industry is contained within the NAICS data.

INDICES OF CHANGE

Year	Establishments (number)	Employment (number)	Payroll ($ million)	Revenues ($ million)	Employees per Establishment (number)	Revenues per Establishment ($)	Payroll per Employee ($)
1997	100.0	100.0	100.0	100.0	100.0	100.0	100.0

Sources: Same as General Statistics. The values shown reflect change from the base year, 1997. Values above 100 mean greater than 1997, values below 100 mean less than 1997, and a value of 100 in years other than 1997 means same as 1997. Indices are calculated only for Census years. Data are the most recent available at this level of detail.

SELECTED RATIOS

For 1997	Avg. of Sector	Analyzed Industry	Index	For 1997	Avg. of Sector	Analyzed Industry	Index
Employees per establishment	45	513	1,133	Payroll per establishment	2,358,969	32,864,179	1,393
Revenue per establishment	26,539,891	208,456,716	785	Payroll as % of revenue	9	16	177
Revenue per employee	585,899	406,230	69	Payroll per employee	52,077	64,044	123

Sources: Same as General Statistics. The 'Average of Sector' column represents the average for all industries in this sector. The Index shows the relationship between the Average and the Analyzed Industry. For example, 100 means that they are equal; 500 that the Analyzed Industry is five times the average; 50 means that the Analyzed Industry is half the national average. 'na' is used to show that data are 'not available'.

LEADING COMPANIES

No company data available for this industry.

LOCATION BY STATE AND REGIONAL CONCENTRATION

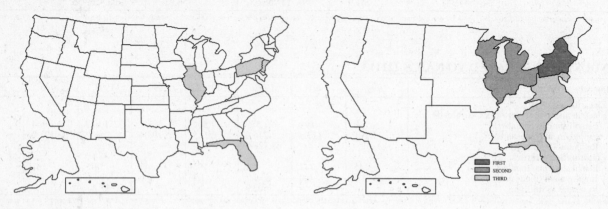

FIRST
SECOND
THIRD

INDUSTRY DATA BY STATE

State	Establishments		Employment			Payroll		Revenues		
	Total (number)	% of U.S.	Total (number)	% of U.S.	Per Estab.	Total ($ mil.)	Per Empl. ($)	Total ($ mil.)	% of U.S.	Per Estab. ($)
Pennsylvania	7	10.4	3,610	10.5	516	225.2	62,396	2,334.4	16.7	333,492,143
Illinois	8	11.9	7,500*	-	-	(D)	-	(D)	-	-
Florida	6	9.0	3,750*	-	-	(D)	-	(D)	-	-
New Jersey	6	9.0	3,750*	-	-	(D)	-	(D)	-	-

Source: 1997 *Economic Census*. The states are in descending order of revenues or establishments (if revenue data are missing for the majority). The symbol (D) appears when data are withheld to prevent disclosure of competitive information. States marked with (D) are sorted by number of establishments. A dash (-) indicates that the data element cannot be calculated. * indicates the midpoint of a range; 175, for example is the range 100-249. Shaded *states* on the state map indicate those states which have proportionately greater representation in the industry than would be indicated by the state's population; the ratio is based on total revenues or number of establishments. Shaded *regions* indicate where the industry is regionally most concentrated.

NAICS 221119 - ELECTRIC POWER GENERATION NEC

GENERAL STATISTICS

Year	Establishments (number)	Employment (number)	Payroll ($ million)	Revenues ($ million)	Employees per Establishment (number)	Revenues per Establishment ($)	Payroll per Employee ($)
1997	316	13,160	724.7	8,010.8	41.6	25,350,604	55,069

Source: Economic Census of the United States, 1997. This is a newly defined industry. Data for prior years were unavailable at the time of publication but may become available over time.

SIC INDUSTRIES RELATED TO NAICS 221119

SIC	Industry	1990	1991	1992	1993	1994	1995	1996	1997
4911	**Electric Services***	-	-	-	-	-	-	-	-
4931	**Electric and Other Services Combined***								
	Establishments (number)	738	891	1,589	1,507	1,597	1,610	1,564	1,882p
	Employment (thousands)	105.1	117.3	216.0	207.5	198.4	188.2	191.0	226.5p
	Revenues ($ million)	-	-	68,726.0	-	-	-	-	-
4939	**Combination Utilities, nec***								
	Establishments (number)	145	247	101	103	141	145	161	150p
	Employment (thousands)	4.5	6.0	1.7	1.2	3.6	4.6	4.5	3.5p
	Revenues ($ million)	-	-	502.9	-	-	-	-	-

Source: Economic Census of the United States, 1992, annual surveys of economic sectors conducted by the Bureau of the Census, and estimates or projections based on the 1982-1992 period; not all data are shown. 'e' marks estimates made by the editors; 'p' indicates projections based on time series. A dash (-) indicates that data for this SIC or year were not available. * Indicates that only a portion of this industry is present within the NAICS data. If no * is shown, the entire industry is contained within the NAICS data.

INDICES OF CHANGE

Year	Establishments (number)	Employment (number)	Payroll ($ million)	Revenues ($ million)	Employees per Establishment (number)	Revenues per Establishment ($)	Payroll per Employee ($)
1997	100.0	100.0	100.0	100.0	100.0	100.0	100.0

Sources: Same as General Statistics. The values shown reflect change from the base year, 1997. Values above 100 mean greater than 1997, values below 100 mean less than 1997, and a value of 100 in years other than 1997 means same as 1997. Indices are calculated only for Census years. Data are the most recent available at this level of detail.

SELECTED RATIOS

For 1997	Avg. of Sector	Analyzed Industry	Index	For 1997	Avg. of Sector	Analyzed Industry	Index
Employees per establishment	45	42	92	Payroll per establishment	2,358,969	2,293,354	97
Revenue per establishment	26,539,891	25,350,633	96	Payroll as % of revenue	9	9	102
Revenue per employee	585,899	608,723	104	Payroll per employee	52,077	55,068	106

Sources: Same as General Statistics. The 'Average of Sector' column represents the average for all industries in this sector. The Index shows the relationship between the Average and the Analyzed Industry. For example, 100 means that they are equal; 500 that the Analyzed Industry is five times the average; 50 means that the Analyzed Industry is half the national average. 'na' is used to show that data are 'not available'.

LEADING COMPANIES
No company data available for this industry.

LOCATION BY STATE AND REGIONAL CONCENTRATION

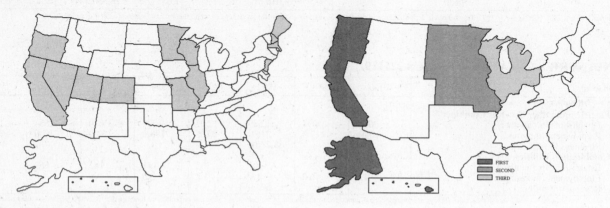

FIRST
SECOND
THIRD

INDUSTRY DATA BY STATE

State	Establishments		Employment			Payroll		Revenues		
	Total (number)	% of U.S.	Total (number)	% of U.S.	Per Estab.	Total ($ mil.)	Per Empl. ($)	Total ($ mil.)	% of U.S.	Per Estab. ($)
Massachusetts	10	3.2	714	5.4	71	50.3	70,494	1,155.1	14.4	115,510,000
New Hampshire	6	1.9	113	0.9	19	6.1	53,690	76.8	1.0	12,792,333
Michigan	11	3.5	138	1.0	13	5.6	40,710	62.7	0.8	5,695,909
Pennsylvania	7	2.2	116	0.9	17	6.0	52,069	40.5	0.5	5,783,714
California	66	20.9	1,750*	-	-	(D)	-	(D)	-	-
Minnesota	20	6.3	375*	-	-	(D)	-	(D)	-	-
Missouri	16	5.1	750*	-	-	(D)	-	(D)	-	-
Illinois	15	4.7	3,750*	-	-	(D)	-	(D)	-	-
Florida	13	4.1	750*	-	-	(D)	-	(D)	-	-
Texas	12	3.8	375*	-	-	(D)	-	(D)	-	-
Maine	11	3.5	175*	-	-	(D)	-	(D)	-	-
New Jersey	10	3.2	175*	-	-	(D)	-	(D)	-	-
Colorado	9	2.8	175*	-	-	(D)	-	(D)	-	-
New York	8	2.5	175*	-	-	(D)	-	(D)	-	-
Utah	8	2.5	175*	-	-	(D)	-	(D)	-	-
Wisconsin	8	2.5	750*	-	-	(D)	-	(D)	-	-
Nevada	7	2.2	60*	-	-	(D)	-	(D)	-	-
Oregon	6	1.9	175*	-	-	(D)	-	(D)	-	-

Source: 1997 *Economic Census*. The states are in descending order of revenues or establishments (if revenue data are missing for the majority). The symbol (D) appears when data are withheld to prevent disclosure of competitive information. States marked with (D) are sorted by number of establishments. A dash (-) indicates that the data element cannot be calculated. * indicates the midpoint of a range; 175, for example is the range 100-249. Shaded *states* on the state map indicate those states which have proportionately greater representation in the industry than would be indicated by the state's population; the ratio is based on total revenues or number of establishments. Shaded *regions* indicate where the industry is regionally most concentrated.

NAICS 221121 - ELECTRIC BULK POWER TRANSMISSION AND CONTROL

GENERAL STATISTICS

Year	Establishments (number)	Employment (number)	Payroll ($ million)	Revenues ($ million)	Employees per Establishment (number)	Revenues per Establishment ($)	Payroll per Employee ($)
1997	120	2,418	115.7	956.0	20.1	7,966,533	47,852

Source: *Economic Census of the United States*, 1997. This is a newly defined industry. Data for prior years were unavailable at the time of publication but may become available over time.

SIC INDUSTRIES RELATED TO NAICS 221121

SIC	Industry	1990	1991	1992	1993	1994	1995	1996	1997
4911	**Electric Services***	-	-	-	-	-	-	-	-
4931	**Electric and Other Services Combined***								
	Establishments (number)	738	891	1,589	1,507	1,597	1,610	1,564	1,882p
	Employment (thousands)	105.1	117.3	216.0	207.5	198.4	188.2	191.0	226.5p
	Revenues ($ million)	-	-	68,726.0	-	-	-	-	-
4939	**Combination Utilities, nec***								
	Establishments (number)	145	247	101	103	141	145	161	150p
	Employment (thousands)	4.5	6.0	1.7	1.2	3.6	4.6	4.5	3.5p
	Revenues ($ million)	-	-	502.9	-	-	-	-	-

Source: *Economic Census of the United States*, 1992, annual surveys of economic sectors conducted by the Bureau of the Census, and estimates or projections based on the 1982-1992 period; not all data are shown. 'e' marks estimates made by the editors; 'p' indicates projections based on time series. A dash (-) indicates that data for this SIC or year were not available. * Indicates that only a portion of this industry is present within the NAICS data. If no * is shown, the entire industry is contained within the NAICS data.

INDICES OF CHANGE

Year	Establishments (number)	Employment (number)	Payroll ($ million)	Revenues ($ million)	Employees per Establishment (number)	Revenues per Establishment ($)	Payroll per Employee ($)
1997	100.0	100.0	100.0	100.0	100.0	100.0	100.0

Sources: Same as General Statistics. The values shown reflect change from the base year, 1997. Values above 100 mean greater than 1997, values below 100 mean less than 1997, and a value of 100 in years other than 1997 means same as 1997. Indices are calculated only for Census years. Data are the most recent available at this level of detail.

SELECTED RATIOS

For 1997	Avg. of Sector	Analyzed Industry	Index	For 1997	Avg. of Sector	Analyzed Industry	Index
Employees per establishment	45	20	44	Payroll per establishment	2,358,969	964,167	41
Revenue per establishment	26,539,891	7,966,667	30	Payroll as % of revenue	9	12	136
Revenue per employee	585,899	395,368	67	Payroll per employee	52,077	47,849	92

Sources: Same as General Statistics. The 'Average of Sector' column represents the average for all industries in this sector. The Index shows the relationship between the Average and the Analyzed Industry. For example, 100 means that they are equal; 500 that the Analyzed Industry is five times the average; 50 means that the Analyzed Industry is half the national average. 'na' is used to show that data are 'not available'.

LEADING COMPANIES

No company data available for this industry.

LOCATION BY STATE AND REGIONAL CONCENTRATION

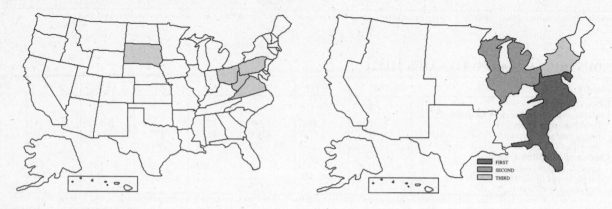

FIRST
SECOND
THIRD

INDUSTRY DATA BY STATE

State	Establishments		Employment			Payroll		Revenues		
	Total (number)	% of U.S.	Total (number)	% of U.S.	Per Estab.	Total ($ mil.)	Per Empl. ($)	Total ($ mil.)	% of U.S.	Per Estab. ($)
Texas	7	5.8	33	1.4	5	1.0	31,697	11.8	1.2	1,679,571
Ohio	16	13.3	60*	-	-	(D)	-	(D)	-	-
Pennsylvania	12	10.0	375*	-	-	(D)	-	(D)	-	-
Virginia	12	10.0	175*	-	-	(D)	-	(D)	-	-
West Virginia	7	5.8	10*	-	-	(D)	-	(D)	-	-
South Dakota	6	5.0	60*	-	-	(D)	-	(D)	-	-

Source: 1997 *Economic Census*. The states are in descending order of revenues or establishments (if revenue data are missing for the majority). The symbol (D) appears when data are withheld to prevent disclosure of competitive information. States marked with (D) are sorted by number of establishments. A dash (-) indicates that the data element cannot be calculated. * indicates the midpoint of a range; 175, for example is the range 100-249. Shaded *states* on the state map indicate those states which have proportionately greater representation in the industry than would be indicated by the state's population; the ratio is based on total revenues or number of establishments. Shaded *regions* indicate where the industry is regionally most concentrated.

NAICS 221122 - ELECTRIC POWER DISTRIBUTION

GENERAL STATISTICS

Year	Establishments (number)	Employment (number)	Payroll ($ million)	Revenues ($ million)	Employees per Establishment (number)	Revenues per Establishment ($)	Payroll per Employee ($)
1997	6,070	413,421	21,954.7	194,763.9	68.1	32,086,315	53,105

Source: Economic Census of the United States, 1997. This is a newly defined industry. Data for prior years were unavailable at the time of publication but may become available over time.

SIC INDUSTRIES RELATED TO NAICS 221122

SIC	Industry	1990	1991	1992	1993	1994	1995	1996	1997
4911	**Electric Services***	-	-	-	-	-	-	-	-
4931	**Electric and Other Services Combined***								
	Establishments (number)	738	891	1,589	1,507	1,597	1,610	1,564	1,882p
	Employment (thousands)	105.1	117.3	216.0	207.5	198.4	188.2	191.0	226.5p
	Revenues ($ million)	-	-	68,726.0	-	-	-	-	-
4939	**Combination Utilities, nec***								
	Establishments (number)	145	247	101	103	141	145	161	150p
	Employment (thousands)	4.5	6.0	1.7	1.2	3.6	4.6	4.5	3.5p
	Revenues ($ million)	-	-	502.9	-	-	-	-	-

*Source: Economic Census of the United States, 1992, annual surveys of economic sectors conducted by the Bureau of the Census, and estimates or projections based on the 1982-1992 period; not all data are shown. 'e' marks estimates made by the editors; 'p' indicates projections based on time series. A dash (-) indicates that data for this SIC or year were not available. * Indicates that only a portion of this industry is present within the NAICS data. If no * is shown, the entire industry is contained within the NAICS data.*

INDICES OF CHANGE

Year	Establishments (number)	Employment (number)	Payroll ($ million)	Revenues ($ million)	Employees per Establishment (number)	Revenues per Establishment ($)	Payroll per Employee ($)
1997	100.0	100.0	100.0	100.0	100.0	100.0	100.0

Sources: Same as General Statistics. The values shown reflect change from the base year, 1997. Values above 100 mean greater than 1997, values below 100 mean less than 1997, and a value of 100 in years other than 1997 means same as 1997. Indices are calculated only for Census years. Data are the most recent available at this level of detail.

SELECTED RATIOS

For 1997	Avg. of Sector	Analyzed Industry	Index	For 1997	Avg. of Sector	Analyzed Industry	Index
Employees per establishment	45	68	150	Payroll per establishment	2,358,969	3,616,919	153
Revenue per establishment	26,539,891	32,086,310	121	Payroll as % of revenue	9	11	127
Revenue per employee	585,899	471,103	80	Payroll per employee	52,077	53,105	102

Sources: Same as General Statistics. The 'Average of Sector' column represents the average for all industries in this sector. The Index shows the relationship between the Average and the Analyzed Industry. For example, 100 means that they are equal; 500 that the Analyzed Industry is five times the average; 50 means that the Analyzed Industry is half the national average. 'na' is used to show that data are 'not available'.

LEADING COMPANIES   Number shown: **75**   Total sales ($ mil): **4,751,457**   Total employment (000): **572.3**

Company Name	Address				CEO Name	Phone	Co. Type	Sales ($ mil)	Empl. (000)
Niagara Mohawk Power Corp.	300 Erie Blvd W	Syracuse	NY	13202	William E Davis	315-474-1511	S	3,827,340	7.3
Wisconsin Energy Corp.	PO Box 2949	Milwaukee	WI	53201	Richard A Abdoo	414-221-2345	P	208,989	5.3
TXU	1601 Bryan St	Dallas	TX	75201		214-812-4600	P	39,514	22.1
Pacific Gas and Electric Co.	P O Box 770000	San Francisco	CA	94177	Robert Glynn	415-973-7000	P	33,234	23.0
Commonwealth Edison Co.	P O Box 767	Chicago	IL	60690	John Rowe	312-394-4321	S	25,707	16.0
Southern California Edison Co.	PO Box 800	Rosemead	CA	91770	John E Bryson	626-302-1212	P	24,698	13.2
Entergy Corp.	PO Box 61000	New Orleans	LA	70161	Donald C Hintz	504-529-5262	P	22,848	12.8
Reliant Energy Inc.	PO Box 4567	Houston	TX	77210	Steve Letbetter	713-207-3000	P	22,000	12.9
Duke Energy Corp.	PO Box 1005	Charlotte	NC	28242	PM Anderson	704-594-6200	P	21,742	22.0
Hawaiian Electric Company Inc.	PO Box 730	Honolulu	HI	96808	T Michael May	808-543-7771	S	20,600	2.2
Texas Utilities Electric Co.	1601 Bryan St	Dallas	TX	75201		214-812-4600	S	18,405	8.4
Public Service Enterprise Group	P O Box 1171	Newark	NJ	07101	Lawrence R Codey	973-430-7000	P	18,100	10.6
Dominion Resources Inc.	PO Box 26532	Richmond	VA	23261	Thomas E Capps	804-819-2000	P	17,517	11.0
American Electric Power Inc.	PO Box 16631	Columbus	OH	43216	E Linn Draper	614-223-1000	P	16,916	17.9
Vermont Electric Cooperative Inc.	182 School St	Johnson	VT	05656		802-635-2331	R	15,781	<0.1
Public Service Electric & Gas Co.	P O Box 570	Newark	NJ	07101	Robert J Dougherty Jr	973-430-7000	S	14,920	10.1
Consolidated Edison Inc.	4 Irving Pl	New York	NY	10003	J Michael Evans	212-460-4600	P	14,381	15.0
Central and South West Corp.	PO Box 660614	Dallas	TX	75266	ER Brooks	214-777-1000	P	13,744	11.0
Cloverland Electric Coop.	2916 W M-28	Dafter	MI	49724		906-635-6800	R	13,000	<0.1
PacifiCorp	700 N E Multnomah	Portland	OR	97232	Alan Richardson	503-731-2000	S	12,989	9.1
Florida Power and Light Co.	P O Box 14000	Juno Beach	FL	33408	James L Broadhead	561-694-4644	S	12,029	9.8
Long Island Lighting Co.	333 Earle Ovington	Uniondale	NY	11553	Richard M Kessel	516-222-7700	P	11,901	5.2
Southern Co.	270 Peachtree St	Atlanta	GA	30303	AW Dahlberg	404-506-5000	P	11,585	31.8
Detroit Edison Co.	2000 2nd Ave	Detroit	MI	48226	John E Lobbia	313-237-8000	S	11,223	8.5
Southern Energy Inc.	900 Ashwood Pkwy	Atlanta	GA	30338	Thomas G Boren	770-379-7000	S	10,000	15.0
Georgia Power Co.	333 Piedmont Ave	Atlanta	GA	30308	H Allen Franklin	404-526-6526	S	9,927*	8.4
Consumers Energy Co.	212 W Michigan	Jackson	MI	49201	Michael G Morris	517-788-0550	S	9,793	8.6
Pennsylvania Power and Light Co.	2 N 9th St	Allentown	PA	18101	William F Hecht	610-774-5151	S	9,472	6.4
Florida Public Utilities Co.	PO Box 3395	W. Palm Beach	FL	33402	John T English	561-832-2461	P	9,240	0.3
Ohio Edison Co.	76 S Main St	Akron	OH	44308	H Peter Burg	330-384-5100	S	8,977	6.2
Ameren Corp.	PO Box 66149	St. Louis	MO	63166	Charles w Mueller	314-621-3222	P	8,847	7.4
Houston Lighting and Power Co.	P O Box 1700	Houston	TX	77251	David M McClanahan	713-207-1111	S	8,669*	8.0
Alabama Power Co.	600 N 18th St	Birmingham	AL	35291	Elmer B Harris	205-257-1000	S	8,309*	6.5
Avista Corp.	P O Box 3727	Spokane	WA	99220	Thomas M Matthews	509-489-0500	P	7,900	3.7
Unicom Corp.	P O Box A-3005	Chicago	IL	60690	John W Rowe	312-394-7399	P	7,151	16.0
Public Service of Colorado	P O Box 840	Denver	CO	80201	Wayne H Brunetti	303-571-7511	S	6,973*	6.0
Illinova Corp.	500 S 27th St	Decatur	IL	62521	Charles E Bayless	217-424-6600	P	6,801	4.0
Cleveland Electric Illuminating	55 Public Sq	Cleveland	OH	44101	H Peter Burg	216-622-9800	S	6,440*	3.2
FPL Group Inc.	PO Box 14000	Juno Beach	FL	33408	James L Broadhead	561-694-4000	P	6,438	9.8
Arizona Public Service Co.	P O Box 53999	Phoenix	AZ	85072	William J Post	602-250-1000	S	6,392	6.1
Mississippi Power	2992 W Beach Blvd	Gulfport	MS	39501	Dwight H Evans	228-864-1211	S	6,330	1.3
FirstEnergy Corp.	76 S Main St	Akron	OH	44308	H P Burg	330-384-5100	P	6,320	1.9
Entergy Gulf States Inc.	350 Pine St	Beaumont	TX	77701	Edwin Lupberger	409-838-6631	S	6,317	1.5
CMS Energy Corp.	330 Town Center Dr	Dearborn	MI	48126	Victor Fryling	313-436-9200	P	6,103	9.7
Connecticut Light and Power Co.	107 Selden St	Berlin	CT	06037	Hugh C MacKenzie	203-665-5000	S	6,050	2.3
UtiliCorp United Inc.	PO Box 13287	Kansas City	MO	64199	Robert K Green	816-421-6600	P	5,991	4.6
CINergy Corp.	139 East 4th St	Cincinnati	OH	45202	Jackson Randolph	513-421-9500	P	5,938	8.8
Salt River Project Agricultural	PO Box 52025	Phoenix	AZ	85072	William P Schrader	602-236-8888	R	5,938	4.0
Illinova Generating Co.	500 S 27th St	Decatur	IL	62525	Alec G Dreyer	217-424-6600	S	5,733*	4.0
SCANA Corp.	1426 Main St	Columbia	SC	29201	W B Timmerman	803-217-9000	P	5,685	4.7
Illinois Power Co.	500 S 27th St	Decatur	IL	62525	Larry D Haab	217-424-6600	S	5,583	3.7
Sempra Energy	101 Ash St	San Diego	CA	92101	Stephen L Baum	619-696-2034	P	5,481	11.1
PECO Energy Co.	PO Box 8699	Philadelphia	PA	19101	Corbin A McNeill, Jr	215-841-4000	P	5,434	6.8
Edison Mission Energy	18101 Von Karman	Irvine	CA	92602	Edward R Muller	949-752-5588	S	4,985*	1.1
Northern Indiana Public Service	5265 Hohman Ave	Hammond	IN	46320	Gary L Neale	219-853-5200	S	4,937	6.0
South Carolina Electric & Gas Co.	1426 Main St	Columbia	SC	29201	JL Skolds	803-748-3000	S	4,900	4.3
Central Power and Light Co.	P O Box 2121	Corpus Christi	TX	78403	Gonzalo Sandoval	512-881-5300	S	4,813	1.6
Florida Power Corp.	100 Central St	St. Petersburg	FL	33701	Joseph H Richardson	727-866-5151	S	4,757*	4.7
DTE Energy Co.	2000 2nd Ave	Detroit	MI	48226	Anthony F Earley Jr	313-235-4000	P	4,728	8.5
San Diego Gas and Electric Co.	101 Ash St	San Diego	CA	92101	Edwin A Guiles	619-696-2000	S	4,654	3.6
Virginia Power	PO Box 26666	Richmond	VA	23261	Edgar M Roach Jr	804-771-3000	S	4,600	8.9
PP and L Resources Inc.	2 N 9th St	Allentown	PA	18101	William F Hecht	610-774-5151	P	4,590	7.6
Oglethorpe Power Corp.	P O Box 1349	Tucker	GA	30085	Jack L King	770-270-7600	R	4,506	0.1
Northeast Utilities	174 Brush Hill Ave	West Springfield	MA	01090	Michael G Morris	413-785-5871	P	4,471	9.1
GPU Energy	300 Madison Ave	Morristown	NJ	07962	D Baldassari	973-455-8200	S	4,465*	3.1
MidAmerican Energy Holdings	P O Box 657	Des Moines	IA	50303	Gregory E Able	515-252-6400	P	4,399	9.7
Entergy Louisiana Inc.	639 Loyola Ave	New Orleans	LA	70113	Edwin Lupberger	504-529-5262	S	4,279*	0.8
Duquesne Light Co.	411 7th Ave	Pittsburgh	PA	15219	David D Marshall	412-393-6000	S	4,181*	3.6
Appalachian Power Co.	40 Franklin Rd S W	Roanoke	VA	24022	E Linn Draper Jr	540-985-2300	S	3,883	4.1
Florida Progress Corp.	PO Box 33042	St. Petersburg	FL	33733	Richard Korpan	727-824-6400	P	3,845	4.7
North Carolina Eastern Municipal	P O Box 29513	Raleigh	NC	27626	Jesse C Tilton III	919-760-6000	R	3,600*	<0.1
System Energy Resources Inc.	PO Box 31995	Jackson	MS	39286	Donald C Hintz	601-984-9000	S	3,432	0.0
New Century Energies Inc.	P O Box 840	Denver	CO	80202	Wayne H Brunetti	303-571-7511	P	3,375	6.3
Carolina Power and Light Co.	PO Box 1551	Raleigh	NC	27602	W Cavanaugh III	919-546-6111	P	3,358	7.2
AES Corp.	1001 N 19th St	Arlington	VA	22209	Dennis W Bakke	703-522-1315	P	3,300	11.7

Source: *Ward's Business Directory of U.S. Private and Public Companies*, Volumes 1 and 2, 2000. The company type code used is as follows: P - Public, R - Private, S - Subsidiary, D - Division, J - Joint Venture, A - Affiliate, G - Group, N - Company type not reported. Sales are in millions of dollars, employees are in thousands. An asterisk (*) indicates an estimated sales volume. The symbol < stands for 'less than'. Company names and addresses are truncated, in some cases, to fit into the available space.

LOCATION BY STATE AND REGIONAL CONCENTRATION

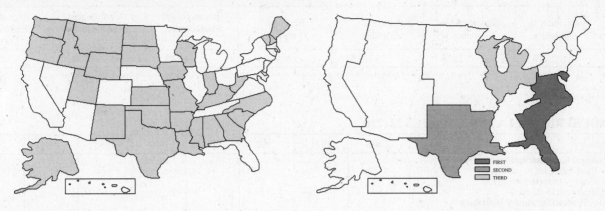

FIRST
SECOND
THIRD

INDUSTRY DATA BY STATE

State	Establishments Total (number)	Establishments % of U.S.	Employment Total (number)	Employment % of U.S.	Employment Per Estab.	Payroll Total ($ mil.)	Payroll Per Empl. ($)	Revenues Total ($ mil.)	Revenues % of U.S.	Revenues Per Estab. ($)
California	255	4.2	42,551	10.3	167	2,603.0	61,174	21,377.7	11.0	83,834,239
Texas	621	10.2	29,441	7.1	47	1,449.3	49,226	19,419.0	10.0	31,270,523
Massachusetts	92	1.5	8,880	2.1	97	534.5	60,191	7,730.1	4.0	84,022,435
Georgia	351	5.8	14,793	3.6	42	796.0	53,810	6,839.6	3.5	19,486,046
Kentucky	167	2.8	6,915	1.7	41	305.2	44,133	4,415.2	2.3	26,438,198
Maryland	61	1.0	9,142	2.2	150	540.2	59,091	3,936.5	2.0	64,533,492
Wisconsin	141	2.3	9,055	2.2	64	470.5	51,957	3,350.4	1.7	23,761,894
Indiana	137	2.3	7,068	1.7	52	326.3	46,164	3,229.7	1.7	23,574,693
Iowa	212	3.5	7,438	1.8	35	325.8	43,796	2,891.1	1.5	13,637,401
Arizona	36	0.6	1,414	0.3	39	66.0	46,665	2,886.2	1.5	80,172,528
Connecticut	44	0.7	4,761	1.2	108	301.8	63,383	2,582.6	1.3	58,696,023
Washington	126	2.1	4,280	1.0	34	209.5	48,943	2,464.6	1.3	19,560,698
Kansas	121	2.0	5,620	1.4	46	275.6	49,036	2,408.7	1.2	19,906,240
Mississippi	182	3.0	4,529	1.1	25	199.2	43,974	2,078.7	1.1	11,421,659
Arkansas	125	2.1	3,257	0.8	26	155.4	47,721	1,743.6	0.9	13,948,536
Utah	63	1.0	2,490	0.6	40	144.5	58,029	1,619.4	0.8	25,705,032
Tennessee	86	1.4	2,017	0.5	23	77.3	38,315	1,060.7	0.5	12,333,733
Idaho	66	1.1	2,314	0.6	35	122.4	52,878	905.8	0.5	13,723,758
New Hampshire	52	0.9	1,406	0.3	27	70.0	49,778	879.1	0.5	16,905,404
New Mexico	49	0.8	1,851	0.4	38	79.6	42,982	788.9	0.4	16,099,694
Vermont	31	0.5	1,217	0.3	39	60.3	49,588	585.3	0.3	18,879,516
North Dakota	40	0.7	1,349	0.3	34	61.0	45,241	467.3	0.2	11,682,900
South Dakota	62	1.0	1,393	0.3	22	54.7	39,266	373.1	0.2	6,017,694
Wyoming	51	0.8	858	0.2	17	40.9	47,666	333.3	0.2	6,535,451
Nebraska	8	0.1	249	0.1	31	19.0	76,301	223.6	0.1	27,945,250
Alabama	267	4.4	17,500*	-	-	(D)	-	(D)	-	-
Michigan	226	3.7	17,500*	-	-	(D)	-	(D)	-	-
New York	191	3.1	37,500*	-	-	(D)	-	(D)	-	-
North Carolina	181	3.0	17,500*	-	-	(D)	-	(D)	-	-
Ohio	175	2.9	17,500*	-	-	(D)	-	(D)	-	-
Missouri	166	2.7	17,500*	-	-	(D)	-	(D)	-	-
South Carolina	165	2.7	17,500*	-	-	(D)	-	(D)	-	-
Pennsylvania	158	2.6	17,500*	-	-	(D)	-	(D)	-	-
Louisiana	152	2.5	7,500*	-	-	(D)	-	(D)	-	-
Illinois	138	2.3	17,500*	-	-	(D)	-	(D)	-	-
New Jersey	132	2.2	17,500*	-	-	(D)	-	(D)	-	-
Montana	128	2.1	1,750*	-	-	(D)	-	(D)	-	-
Virginia	124	2.0	17,500*	-	-	(D)	-	(D)	-	-
Florida	123	2.0	17,500*	-	-	(D)	-	(D)	-	-
Minnesota	104	1.7	7,500*	-	-	(D)	-	(D)	-	-
Oregon	96	1.6	3,750*	-	-	(D)	-	(D)	-	-
Oklahoma	95	1.6	3,750*	-	-	(D)	-	(D)	-	-
West Virginia	70	1.2	1,750*	-	-	(D)	-	(D)	-	-
Colorado	65	1.1	7,500*	-	-	(D)	-	(D)	-	-
Maine	37	0.6	1,750*	-	-	(D)	-	(D)	-	-
Alaska	29	0.5	750*	-	-	(D)	-	(D)	-	-
Nevada	27	0.4	1,750*	-	-	(D)	-	(D)	-	-
D.C.	22	0.4	3,750*	-	-	(D)	-	(D)	-	-
Hawaii	7	0.1	750*	-	-	(D)	-	(D)	-	-
Rhode Island	7	0.1	1,750*	-	-	(D)	-	(D)	-	-
Delaware	6	0.1	1,750*	-	-	(D)	-	(D)	-	-

Source: 1997 *Economic Census*. The states are in descending order of revenues or establishments (if revenue data are missing for the majority). The symbol (D) appears when data are withheld to prevent disclosure of competitive information. States marked with (D) are sorted by number of establishments. A dash (-) indicates that the data element cannot be calculated. * indicates the midpoint of a range; 175, for example is the range 100-249. Shaded *states* on the state map indicate those states which have proportionately greater representation in the industry than would be indicated by the state's population; the ratio is based on total revenues or number of establishments. Shaded *regions* indicate where the industry is regionally most concentrated.

NAICS 221210 - NATURAL GAS DISTRIBUTION

GENERAL STATISTICS

Year	Establishments (number)	Employment (number)	Payroll ($ million)	Revenues ($ million)	Employees per Establishment (number)	Revenues per Establishment ($)	Payroll per Employee ($)
1997	2,747	102,878	5,109.5	136,995.4	37.5	49,870,898	49,666

Source: Economic Census of the United States, 1997. This is a newly defined industry. Data for prior years were unavailable at the time of publication but may become available over time.

SIC INDUSTRIES RELATED TO NAICS 221210

SIC	Industry	1990	1991	1992	1993	1994	1995	1996	1997
4924	**Natural Gas Distribution**								
	Establishments (number)	-	-	1,734	-	-	-	-	-
	Employment (thousands)	-	-	65.2	-	-	-	-	-
	Revenues ($ million)	-	-	37,152.4	-	-	-	-	-
4925	**Gas Production and/or Distribution**								
	Establishments (number)	-	-	71	-	-	-	-	-
	Employment (thousands)	-	-	0.4	-	-	-	-	-
	Revenues ($ million)	-	-	536.7	-	-	-	-	-
4932	**Gas and Other Services Combined**								
	Establishments (number)	161	216	124	88	120	123	135	111p
	Employment (thousands)	44.4	44.3	4.5	1.7	4.7	4.7	4.1	-
	Revenues ($ million)	-	-	1,474.0	-	-	-	-	-
4923	**Natural Gas Transmission and Distribution***								
	Establishments (number)	-	-	1,648	-	-	-	-	-
	Employment (thousands)	-	-	69.3	-	-	-	-	-
	Revenues ($ million)	-	-	29,313.7	-	-	-	-	-
4931	**Electric and Other Services Combined***								
	Establishments (number)	738	891	1,589	1,507	1,597	1,610	1,564	1,882p
	Employment (thousands)	105.1	117.3	216.0	207.5	198.4	188.2	191.0	226.5p
	Revenues ($ million)	-	-	68,726.0	-	-	-	-	-
4939	**Combination Utilities, nec***								
	Establishments (number)	145	247	101	103	141	145	161	150p
	Employment (thousands)	4.5	6.0	1.7	1.2	3.6	4.6	4.5	3.5p
	Revenues ($ million)	-	-	502.9	-	-	-	-	-

Source: Economic Census of the United States, 1992, annual surveys of economic sectors conducted by the Bureau of the Census, and estimates or projections based on the 1982-1992 period; not all data are shown. 'e' marks estimates made by the editors; 'p' indicates projections based on time series. A dash (-) indicates that data for this SIC or year were not available. * Indicates that only a portion of this industry is present within the NAICS data. If no * is shown, the entire industry is contained within the NAICS data.

INDICES OF CHANGE

Year	Establishments (number)	Employment (number)	Payroll ($ million)	Revenues ($ million)	Employees per Establishment (number)	Revenues per Establishment ($)	Payroll per Employee ($)
1997	100.0	100.0	100.0	100.0	100.0	100.0	100.0

Sources: Same as General Statistics. The values shown reflect change from the base year, 1997. Values above 100 mean greater than 1997, values below 100 mean less than 1997, and a value of 100 in years other than 1997 means same as 1997. Indices are calculated only for Census years. Data are the most recent available at this level of detail.

SELECTED RATIOS

For 1997	Avg. of Sector	Analyzed Industry	Index	For 1997	Avg. of Sector	Analyzed Industry	Index
Employees per establishment	45	37	83	Payroll per establishment	2,358,969	1,860,029	79
Revenue per establishment	26,539,891	49,870,914	188	Payroll as % of revenue	9	4	42
Revenue per employee	585,899	1,331,630	227	Payroll per employee	52,077	49,666	95

Sources: Same as General Statistics. The 'Average of Sector' column represents the average for all industries in this sector. The Index shows the relationship between the Average and the Analyzed Industry. For example, 100 means that they are equal; 500 that the Analyzed Industry is five times the average; 50 means that the Analyzed Industry is half the national average. 'na' is used to show that data are 'not available'.

LEADING COMPANIES   Number shown: **75**   Total sales ($ mil): **867,291**   Total employment (000): **229.9**

Company Name	Address				CEO Name	Phone	Co. Type	Sales ($ mil)	Empl. (000)
NW Natural	220 Northwest 2nd	Portland	OR	97209	Richard G Reiten	503-226-4211	P	455,834	1.3
Wisconsin Energy Corp.	PO Box 2949	Milwaukee	WI	53201	Richard A Abdoo	414-221-2345	P	208,989	5.3
Enron Corp.	P O Box 1188	Houston	TX	77251	Kenneth L Lay	713-853-6161	P	40,112	17.8
Conoco Inc.	PO Box 2197	Houston	TX	77252	Archie W Dunham	281-293-1000	P	27,309	16.6
Northern Illinois Gas Co.	1844 Ferry Rd	Naperville	IL	60563	Thomas L Fisher	708-983-8676	S	17,000	2.2
Colorado Interstate Gas Co.	PO Box 1087	Co Springs	CO	80944	David A Arledge	713-877-6754	S	8,250*	11.0
Columbia Energy Group	13880 Dulles Corner	Herndon	VA	20171	Oliver G Richard III	703-561-6000	P	6,969*	8.6
Consolidated Natural Gas Co.	625 Liberty Ave	Pittsburgh	PA	15222	GA Davidson Jr.	412-690-1000	P	6,362	6.2
Sempra Energy	101 Ash St	San Diego	CA	92101	Stephen L Baum	619-696-2034	P	5,481	11.1
Citizens Utilities Co.	PO Box 3801	Stamford	CT	06905	Rudy J Graf	203-614-5600	P	5,293	6.7
San Diego Gas and Electric Co.	101 Ash St	San Diego	CA	92101	Edwin A Guiles	619-696-2000	S	4,654	3.6
Southern California Gas Co.	P O Box 3249	Los Angeles	CA	90051	Warren I Mitchell	213-244-1200	S	4,462	7.2
MCN Energy Group Inc.	500 Griswold St	Detroit	MI	48226	Stephen E Ewing	313-256-5500	P	4,393	3.0
KeySpan Corp.	175 E Old Country	Hicksville	NY	11801	Robert B Catell		P	2,955	7.9
Northern States Power Co.	414 Nicollet Mall	Minneapolis	MN	55401	James J Howard	612-330-5500	P	2,869	7.9
ENSERCH Corp.	Energy Plz	Dallas	TX	75201	David W Biegler	214-651-8700	S	2,790*	3.0
Coral Energy L.P.	1301 McKinney	Houston	TX	77010	Charles R Crisp	713-230-3000	P	2,600*	1.2
Brooklyn Union Gas Co.	1 MetroTech Cntr	Brooklyn	NY	11201	Robert B Catell	718-403-2000	S	2,290*	3.3
Energy East Corp.	Ithaca-Dryden Rd	Ithaca	NY	14852	W W von Schack	607-347-4131	P	2,279	4.0
Alliant Energy	222 W Washington	Madison	WI	53703	Erroll B Davis Jr	608-252-3311	P	2,198	6.4
MCN Energy Group	500 Griswold St	Detroit	MI	48226		313-965-2430	P	2,136	3.0
Sierra Pacific Resources	P O Box 30150	Reno	NV	89520	Michael Niggli	775-834-4011	P	2,041	1.5
TEPPCO Partners L.P.	PO Box 2521	Houston	TX	77252		713-759-3636	P	1,935	0.7
Equitable Resources Inc.	1 Oxford Ctr	Pittsburgh	PA	15219	Murry S Gerber	412-553-5700	P	1,854	1.6
ONEOK Inc.	PO Box 871	Tulsa	OK	74102		918-588-7000	P	1,835	3.2
Southwest Gas Corp.	PO Box 98510	Las Vegas	NV	89193	Thomas Y Hartley	702-876-7237	P	1,772	2.4
NICOR Inc.	PO Box 3014	Naperville	IL	60566	Thomas L Fisher	630-305-9500	P	1,615	3.3
Peoples Gas Light and Coke Co.	130 E Randolph Dr	Chicago	IL	60603	J Bruce Hasch	312-240-4000	S	1,558	2.6
Duke Energy Field Services	PO Box 5493	Denver	CO	80217	JW Mogg	303-595-3331	S	1,500*	1.8
Sierra Pacific Power Co.	P O Box 10100	Reno	NV	89520	Malyn Malquist	702-689-4011	S	1,418*	1.5
UGI Corp.	PO Box 858	Valley Forge	PA	19482	Lon R Greenberg	610-337-1000	P	1,384	5.0
SEMCO Energy Services Inc.	P O Box 5026	Port Huron	MI	48061	William L Johnson	810-987-2200	S	1,338*	1.6
CH Energy Group Inc.	284 South Ave	Poughkeepsie	NY	12601	Paul J Ganci	914-452-2000	P	1,316	1.1
CILCORP Inc.	300 Hamilton Blvd	Peoria	IL	61602	Robert O Viets	309-675-8810	P	1,313	1.3
Orange and Rockland Utilities Inc.	1 Blue Hill Plz	Pearl River	NY	10965	D Louis Peoples	914-352-6000	P	1,308	1.4
Phillips Gas Co.	1300 Post Oak Blvd	Houston	TX	77056		713-297-6066	S	1,306	1.1
Columbia Gas Of Ohio Inc.	200 Civic Center Dr	Columbus	OH	43215	Robert C Skaggs Jr	614-460-6000	S	1,300	3.0
Atlanta Gas Light Co.	P O Box 4569	Atlanta	GA	30302	Walter Higgins	404-584-4000	P	1,298	3.0
National Fuel Gas Co.	10 Lafayette Sq	Buffalo	NY	14203	Philip C Ackerman	716-857-6980	P	1,263	3.8
AmeriGas Inc.	P O Box 965	Valley Forge	PA	19482	Lon R Greenberg	610-337-1000	P	1,217	5.1
Peoples Energy Corp.	130 E Randolph Dr	Chicago	IL	60601	Thomas M Patrick	312-240-4299	P	1,194	2.8
Minnesota Power and Light Co.	30 W Superior St	Duluth	MN	55802	Edwin L Russell	218-722-2641	P	1,132	0.0
Washington Gas Light Co.	1100 H St N W	Washington	DC	20080	JH DeGraffenreidt	202-750-4440	P	1,112	2.1
AGL Resources Inc.	PO Box 4569	Atlanta	GA	30302	Walter M Higgins	404-584-9470	P	1,069	2.9
Wicor Inc.	626 E Wisconsin	Milwaukee	WI	53201	Thomas Schrader	414-291-7026	P	1,010	3.5
Wisconsin Electric Power Co.	P O Box 2046	Milwaukee	WI	53201	Richard A Abdoo	414-221-2345	S	1,001	4.5
Southwest Gas Corp. Central Div.	P O Box 52075	Phoenix	AZ	85072		602-861-1555	D	980*	0.6
Eastern Enterprises	9 Riverside Rd	Weston	MA	02493	J Atwood Ives	781-647-2300	P	979	1.4
Questar Corp.	PO Box 45433	Salt Lake City	UT	84145	R Cash	801-324-5000	P	924	2.3
New Jersey Resources Corp.	PO Box 1468	Wall	NJ	07719	Laurence M Downes	732-938-1480	P	904	0.8
Boston Gas Co.	1 Beacon St	Boston	MA	02108	Chester R Messer	617-742-8400	S	878	1.4
ATMOS Energy Corp.	PO Box 650205	Dallas	TX	75265	Robert W Best	972-934-9227	P	848	2.2
NUI Corp.	PO Box 760	Bedminster	NJ	07921	John Kean Jr	908-781-0500	P	828	1.0
South Jersey Gas Co.	1 S Jersey Plz	Folsom	NJ	08037	William F Ryan	609-561-9000	S	796*	0.7
Piedmont Natural Gas Inc.	PO Box 33068	Charlotte	NC	28233	John H Maxheim	704-364-3120	P	686	1.8
Columbia Gas of Pennsylvania	650 Washington Rd	Pittsburgh	PA	15228	Gary J Robinson	412-344-9800	S	666*	0.9
Southwestern Energy Co.	PO Box 1408	Fayetteville	AR	72702	Harold M Korell	501-521-1141	P	648	0.7
Aquila Gas Pipeline Corp.	100 NE Lp 410	San Antonio	TX	78216	F Joseph Becraft	210-342-0685	P	646	0.3
Southern Union Co.	504 Lavaca St	Austin	TX	78701	Peter H Kelley	512-477-5852	P	605	1.6
Yankee Energy System Inc.	599 Research Pkwy	Meriden	CT	06450	Charles E Gooley	203-639-4000	P	540	0.8
Enogex Inc.	PO Box 24300	Oklahoma City	OK	73124	Roger A Farrell	405-525-7788	S	509	0.6
Energen Corp.	605 21st St N	Birmingham	AL	35203		205-326-2742	P	503	1.4
Laclede Gas Co.	720 Olive St	St. Louis	MO	63101	Douglas H Yaeger	314-342-0500	P	492	2.0
Connecticut Natural Gas Corp.	PO Box 1500	Hartford	CT	06144	Arthur C Marquardt	860-727-3000	S	480	0.5
UGI Utilities Inc.	PO Box 858	Valley Forge	PA	19482	Richard L Bunn	610-796-3400	S	422	1.2
Indiana Energy Inc.	1630 N Meridian St	Indianapolis	IN	46202	Niel C Ellerbrook	317-926-3351	P	421	0.9
United Cities Gas Co.	810 Crescent Centre	Franklin	TN	37067	Thomas R Blose	615-771-8300	S	407*	1.0
Commonwealth Gas Co.	157 Cordaville Rd	Southborough	MA	01772	Debra McLaughlin	508-481-7900	S	396	0.6
South Jersey Industries Inc.	1 S Jersey Plaza	Folsom	NJ	08037	Charles Biscieglia	609-561-9000	P	392	0.7
Colorado Springs Utilities	P O Box 1103	Co Springs	CO	80947		719-448-8000	R	390	1.9
SEMCO Energy Inc.	P O Box 5026	Port Huron	MI	48061	William L Johnson	810-987-2200	P	385	0.9
Yankee Gas Services Co.	599 Research Pkwy	Meriden	CT	06450	Charles E Gooley	203-639-4000	P	325	0.6
Columbia Gas of Virginia Inc.	P O Box 35674	Richmond	VA	23235	Anthony Trubisz Jr	804-323-5300	S	324*	0.4
Peoples Natural Gas Co.	625 Liberty Ave	Pittsburgh	PA	15222		412-471-5100	S	303	0.9
Martin Resource Management	PO Box Drawer 191	Kilgore	TX	75662	Rubin Martin Jr	903-983-6200	R	300*	1.3

Source: Ward's Business Directory of U.S. Private and Public Companies, Volumes 1 and 2, 2000. The company type code used is as follows: P - Public, R - Private, S - Subsidiary, D - Division, J - Joint Venture, A - Affiliate, G - Group, N - Company type not reported. Sales are in millions of dollars, employees are in thousands. An asterisk (*) indicates an estimated sales volume. The symbol < stands for 'less than'. Company names and addresses are truncated, in some cases, to fit into the available space.

LOCATION BY STATE AND REGIONAL CONCENTRATION

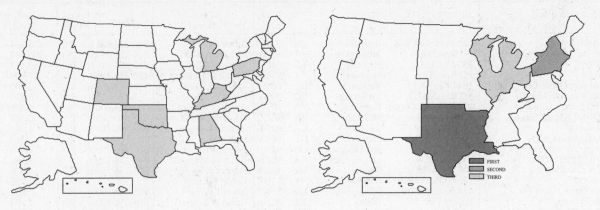

FIRST
SECOND
THIRD

INDUSTRY DATA BY STATE

State	Establishments Total (number)	Establishments % of U.S.	Employment Total (number)	Employment % of U.S.	Employment Per Estab.	Payroll Total ($ mil.)	Payroll Per Empl. ($)	Revenues Total ($ mil.)	Revenues % of U.S.	Revenues Per Estab. ($)
Texas	451	16.4	18,386	17.9	41	1,003.6	54,583	50,459.4	36.8	111,883,348
Pennsylvania	152	5.5	6,820	6.6	45	333.1	48,849	24,904.1	18.2	163,842,855
Michigan	89	3.2	4,090	4.0	46	240.7	58,847	5,723.0	4.2	64,302,933
Ohio	125	4.6	5,742	5.6	46	271.5	47,286	4,141.9	3.0	33,135,320
Illinois	86	3.1	5,590	5.4	65	289.3	51,751	3,775.6	2.8	43,901,942
Virginia	39	1.4	2,844	2.8	73	141.4	49,733	3,339.8	2.4	85,636,615
New York	57	2.1	5,255	5.1	92	310.8	59,143	2,815.0	2.1	49,385,947
Kentucky	77	2.8	1,183	1.1	15	54.6	46,150	2,664.0	1.9	34,597,442
Oklahoma	76	2.8	1,287	1.3	17	69.4	53,925	2,527.2	1.8	33,252,539
Alabama	54	2.0	2,034	2.0	38	96.0	47,209	2,357.5	1.7	43,657,333
Colorado	95	3.5	2,027	2.0	21	104.4	51,494	2,353.0	1.7	24,768,811
Indiana	76	2.8	1,820	1.8	24	76.3	41,908	2,033.8	1.5	26,760,355
California	39	1.4	2,075	2.0	53	109.7	52,879	1,871.8	1.4	47,994,410
New Jersey	40	1.5	2,505	2.4	63	116.2	46,371	1,720.9	1.3	43,021,875
Louisiana	88	3.2	2,289	2.2	26	99.5	43,486	1,510.1	1.1	17,159,716
Georgia	65	2.4	2,496	2.4	38	98.4	39,438	1,378.3	1.0	21,205,046
Missouri	66	2.4	3,313	3.2	50	149.1	45,013	1,066.1	0.8	16,153,394
North Carolina	79	2.9	2,898	2.8	37	117.9	40,669	1,046.4	0.8	13,245,430
Wisconsin	46	1.7	1,752	1.7	38	79.9	45,615	1,003.6	0.7	21,817,739
Minnesota	60	2.2	1,877	1.8	31	82.5	43,934	844.4	0.6	14,073,917
West Virginia	61	2.2	1,234	1.2	20	52.3	42,397	837.0	0.6	13,720,869
Tennessee	26	0.9	1,149	1.1	44	56.7	49,377	667.5	0.5	25,674,731
Kansas	72	2.6	770	0.7	11	31.6	40,979	549.2	0.4	7,627,722
Florida	40	1.5	1,905	1.9	48	60.9	31,963	470.2	0.3	11,754,250
Mississippi	67	2.4	1,167	1.1	17	37.4	32,019	393.5	0.3	5,872,672
Washington	19	0.7	443	0.4	23	21.5	48,465	276.4	0.2	14,547,474
Wyoming	47	1.7	512	0.5	11	19.9	38,859	172.2	0.1	3,664,851
South Carolina	12	0.4	326	0.3	27	12.5	38,212	165.7	0.1	13,805,333
New Mexico	18	0.7	380	0.4	21	17.1	44,982	120.6	0.1	6,699,833
Montana	27	1.0	299	0.3	11	11.4	38,000	78.3	0.1	2,901,333
Nebraska	108	3.9	1,750*	-	-	(D)	-	(D)	-	-
Arkansas	56	2.0	1,750*	-	-	(D)	-	(D)	-	-
North Dakota	56	2.0	750*	-	-	(D)	-	(D)	-	-
Massachusetts	54	2.0	3,750*	-	-	(D)	-	(D)	-	-
Arizona	41	1.5	1,750*	-	-	(D)	-	(D)	-	-
Connecticut	28	1.0	1,750*	-	-	(D)	-	(D)	-	-
Iowa	21	0.8	375*	-	-	(D)	-	(D)	-	-
Oregon	21	0.8	1,750*	-	-	(D)	-	(D)	-	-
South Dakota	20	0.7	175*	-	-	(D)	-	(D)	-	-
Nevada	17	0.6	1,750*	-	-	(D)	-	(D)	-	-
Maryland	13	0.5	750*	-	-	(D)	-	(D)	-	-
Utah	13	0.5	1,750*	-	-	(D)	-	(D)	-	-
New Hampshire	11	0.4	175*	-	-	(D)	-	(D)	-	-
Rhode Island	10	0.4	750*	-	-	(D)	-	(D)	-	-
Idaho	9	0.3	375*	-	-	(D)	-	(D)	-	-
Alaska	7	0.3	175*	-	-	(D)	-	(D)	-	-

Source: 1997 *Economic Census*. The states are in descending order of revenues or establishments (if revenue data are missing for the majority). The symbol (D) appears when data are withheld to prevent disclosure of competitive information. States marked with (D) are sorted by number of establishments. A dash (-) indicates that the data element cannot be calculated. * indicates the midpoint of a range; 175, for example is the range 100-249. Shaded *states* on the state map indicate those states which have proportionately greater representation in the industry than would be indicated by the state's population; the ratio is based on total revenues or number of establishments. Shaded *regions* indicate where the industry is regionally most concentrated.

NAICS 221310 - WATER SUPPLY AND IRRIGATION SYSTEMS

GENERAL STATISTICS

Year	Establishments (number)	Employment (number)	Payroll ($ million)	Revenues ($ million)	Employees per Establishment (number)	Revenues per Establishment ($)	Payroll per Employee ($)
1997	4,052	27,933	825.4	4,453.8	6.9	1,099,170	29,550

Source: Economic Census of the United States, 1997. This is a newly defined industry. Data for prior years were unavailable at the time of publication but may become available over time.

SIC INDUSTRIES RELATED TO NAICS 221310

SIC	Industry	1990	1991	1992	1993	1994	1995	1996	1997
4941	**Water Supply**	-	-	-	-	-	-	-	-
4971	**Irrigation Systems**	-	-	-	-	-	-	-	-

Source: Economic Census of the United States, 1992, annual surveys of economic sectors conducted by the Bureau of the Census, and estimates or projections based on the 1982-1992 period; not all data are shown. 'e' marks estimates made by the editors; 'p' indicates projections based on time series. A dash (-) indicates that data for this SIC or year were not available. * Indicates that only a portion of this industry is present within the NAICS data. If no * is shown, the entire industry is contained within the NAICS data.

INDICES OF CHANGE

Year	Establishments (number)	Employment (number)	Payroll ($ million)	Revenues ($ million)	Employees per Establishment (number)	Revenues per Establishment ($)	Payroll per Employee ($)
1997	100.0	100.0	100.0	100.0	100.0	100.0	100.0

Sources: Same as General Statistics. The values shown reflect change from the base year, 1997. Values above 100 mean greater than 1997, values below 100 mean less than 1997, and a value of 100 in years other than 1997 means same as 1997. Indices are calculated only for Census years. Data are the most recent available at this level of detail.

SELECTED RATIOS

For 1997	Avg. of Sector	Analyzed Industry	Index	For 1997	Avg. of Sector	Analyzed Industry	Index
Employees per establishment	45	7	15	Payroll per establishment	2,358,969	203,702	9
Revenue per establishment	26,539,891	1,099,161	4	Payroll as % of revenue	9	19	208
Revenue per employee	585,899	159,446	27	Payroll per employee	52,077	29,549	57

Sources: Same as General Statistics. The 'Average of Sector' column represents the average for all industries in this sector. The Index shows the relationship between the Average and the Analyzed Industry. For example, 100 means that they are equal; 500 that the Analyzed Industry is five times the average; 50 means that the Analyzed Industry is half the national average. 'na' is used to show that data are 'not available'.

LEADING COMPANIES   Number shown: **63**   Total sales ($ mil): **398,517**   Total employment (000): **60.2**

Company Name	Address				CEO Name	Phone	Co. Type	Sales ($ mil)	Empl. (000)
United Water Resources	200 Old Hook Rd	Harrington Park	NJ	07640	Donald Correll	201-784-9434	S	356,210	1.4
Florida Public Utilities Co.	PO Box 3395	W. Palm Beach	FL	33402	John T English	561-832-2461	P	9,240	0.3
Salt River Project Agricultural	PO Box 52025	Phoenix	AZ	85072	William P Schrader	602-236-8888	R	5,938	4.0
Citizens Utilities Co.	PO Box 3801	Stamford	CT	06905	Rudy J Graf	203-614-5600	P	5,293	6.7
United States Filter Corp.	40-004 Cook St	Palm Desert	CA	92211	Richard J Heckmann	760-340-0098	S	3,235	18.5
JEA	21 W Church St	Jacksonville	FL	32202	Walter P Bussells	904-632-7410	R	2,009*	2.6
United Water Resources Inc.	200 Old Hook Rd	Harrington Park	NJ	07640	Donald L Correll	201-784-9434	P	1,769	1.4
Sierra Pacific Power Co.	P O Box 10100	Reno	NV	89520	Malyn Malquist	702-689-4011	S	1,418*	1.5
Snohomish County Public Utility	P O Box 1107	Everett	WA	98206		425-783-1000	R	1,220	1.0
Public Service of New Mexico	Alvarado Sq	Albuquerque	NM	87158	JT Ackerman	505-241-2700	P	1,157	2.7
Minnesota Power and Light Co.	30 W Superior St	Duluth	MN	55802	Edwin L Russell	218-722-2641	P	1,132	0.0
E'town Corp.	P O Box 788	Westfield	NJ	07091	Robert W Kean Jr	908-654-1234	P	779	0.5
Tacoma Public Utilities	P O Box 11007	Tacoma	WA	98411		253-383-2471	R	750	1.1
Philadelphia Suburban Corp.	762 W Lancaster	Bryn Mawr	PA	19010	N DeBenedictis	610-527-8000	P	701	0.5
Philadelphia Suburban Water Co.	762 Lancaster Ave	Bryn Mawr	PA	19010	N DeBenedictis	610-527-8000	S	665*	0.6
Empire District Electric Co.	PO Box 127	Joplin	MO	64802	Myron W McKinney	417-625-5100	P	653	0.6
California Water Service Group	1720 N 1st St	San Jose	CA	95112	Peter C Nelson	408-367-8200	P	548*	0.7
Las Vegas Valley Water District	1001 S Valley View	Las Vegas	NV	89107		702-870-2011	R	529*	1.0
Southern California Water Co.	630 E Foothill Blvd	San Dimas	CA	91773	Floyd E Wicks	909-394-3600	P	457*	0.5
Colorado Springs Utilities	P O Box 1103	Co Springs	CO	80947		719-448-8000	R	390	1.9
San Jose Water Co.	374 W Santa Clara	San Jose	CA	95196	W R Roth	408-279-7962	S	323	0.3
Newhall Land and Farming Co.	23823 Valencia Blvd	Valencia	CA	91355	Gary M Cusumano	661-255-4000	P	322	0.2
Professional Services Group Inc.	14950 Heathrow	Houston	TX	77032	Patrick L McMahon	281-985-5427	S	233*	1.5
Dalton Utilities	P O Box 869	Dalton	GA	30722	Don Cope	706-278-1313	R	226*	0.3
BHC Co.	835 Main St	Bridgeport	CT	06604	James S McInerney	203-367-6621	S	217	0.3
San Gabriel Valley Water Co.	P O Box 6010	El Monte	CA	91734	Michael Whitehead	626-448-6183	P	214*	0.2
Baton Rouge Water Works Co.	8755 Goodwood	Baton Rouge	LA	70806	Gene Owen	225-928-1000	R	212*	0.2
Middlesex Water Co.	PO Box 1500	Iselin	NJ	08830	J Richard Tompkins	732-634-1500	P	203	0.1
Connecticut Water Co.	93 W Main St	Clinton	CT	06413	Michael T Chiaraluce	860-669-8636	S	195	0.2
Laurel Holdings Inc.	PO Box 1287	Johnstown	PA	15907	Kim Kunkle	814-533-5777	P	191*	0.3
American Water Works Inc.	PO Box 1770	Voorhees	NJ	08043	J James Barr	856-346-8200	P	148	4.1
Artesian Resources Corp.	664 Churchmans Rd	Newark	DE	19702	Dian C Taylor	302-453-6900	P	137*	0.2
Suburban Water Systems	PO Box 6105	Covina	CA	91722		626-966-2090	S	123*	0.1
Connecticut American Water Co.	75 Holly Hill Ln	Greenwich	CT	06830	James bARR	856-346-8360	S	122*	0.1
SJW Corp.	374 W Santa Clara	San Jose	CA	95196	W Richard Roth	408-279-7900	P	117	0.3
United Water Idaho Inc.	PO Box 7488	Boise	ID	83707		208-362-1300	S	116*	<0.1
Mesa Consolidated Water District	PO Box 5008	Costa Mesa	CA	92628		949-631-1200	R	114*	<0.1
Park Water Co.	9750 E Washburn	Downey	CA	90241	Henry H Wheeler	562-923-0711	R	108*	0.1
York Water Co.	130 E Market St	York	PA	17405	William T Morris	717-845-3601	P	102	<0.1
Southwest Water Co.	225 N Barranca Ave	West Covina	CA	91791	Anton C Garnier	626-915-1551	P	81	0.5
Indianapolis Water Co.	P O Box 1220	Indianapolis	IN	46206	Joseph R Broyles	317-639-1501	S	80	0.4
Louisville Water Co.	550 S 3rd St	Louisville	KY	40202	John L Huber	502-569-3600	R	78*	0.4
Northern Illinois Water Co.	PO Box 9018	Champaign	IL	61826		217-352-7001	S	74*	0.1
Pennichuck Corp.	PO Box 448	Nashua	NH	03061	Maurice L Arel	603-882-5191	P	71	<0.1
Valley Center Municipal Water	PO Box 67	Valley Center	CA	92082		760-749-1600	R	67*	<0.1
East Valley Water District	PO Box 3427	San Bernardino	CA	92413		909-889-9501	R	62*	<0.1
Dominguez Water Co.	21718 S Alameda St	Long Beach	CA	90810	Brian J Brady	310-834-2625	S	52	<0.1
Kaiser Ventures Inc.	3633 E Inland	Ontario	CA	91764	Richard E Stoddard	909-483-8500	P	52	<0.1
Consolidated Mutual Water Co.	12700 W 27th Ave	Lakewood	CO	80215	Walter S Welton	303-238-0451	R	46	<0.1
Ohio-American Water Co.	365 E Center St	Marion	OH	43302	Robert J Gallo	740-387-2293	S	46*	0.1
Pennsylvania-American Water Co.	800 W Hersheypark	Hershey	PA	17033	Robert M Ross	717-533-5000	S	44	1.1
Columbia Power & Water System	P O Box 379	Columbia	TN	38402		931-388-4833	R	40	<0.1
Goleta Water District	4699 Hollister Ave	Santa Barbara	CA	93110		805-964-6761	R	32*	<0.1
Municipal Authority	PO Box 730	Greensburg	PA	15601	Donald Ruscitti	724-834-6500	R	31*	0.3
Cedar Falls Utilities	P O Box 769	Cedar Falls	IA	50613		319-266-1761	R	30	0.1
Elmira Water Board	P O Box 267	Elmira	NY	14902		607-733-9179	R	29	<0.1
Shepaug Corp.	54 E 64th St	New York	NY	10021	Arthur Carter	212-751-6633	R	28*	0.3
New Mexico Utilities Inc.	4700 Irving N W	Albuquerque	NM	87114	Robert L Swartwout	505-898-2661	S	21*	<0.1
Sun Belt Water Inc.	PO Box 92229	Santa Barbara	CA	93190	Jack B Lindsey	805-966-5928	R	18*	<0.1
Virginia American Water Co.	P O Box 25405	Alexandria	VA	22313		703-549-7080	R	7*	<0.1
Birmingham Utilites Inc.	P O Box 426	Ansonia	CT	06401	Betsy Henley-Cohn	203-735-1888	P	4	<0.1
Beckley Water Co.	PO Drawer U	Beckley	WV	25802	Jack R Vickers	304-255-5121	R	4	<0.1
Monroeville Water Authority	4185 Old Wm Penn	Monroeville	PA	15146		412-372-2677	R	3*	<0.1

Source: Ward's Business Directory of U.S. Private and Public Companies, Volumes 1 and 2, 2000. The company type code used is as follows: P - Public, R - Private, S - Subsidiary, D - Division, J - Joint Venture, A - Affiliate, G - Group, N - Company type not reported. Sales are in millions of dollars, employees are in thousands. An asterisk (*) indicates an estimated sales volume. The symbol < stands for 'less than'. Company names and addresses are truncated, in some cases, to fit into the available space.

LOCATION BY STATE AND REGIONAL CONCENTRATION

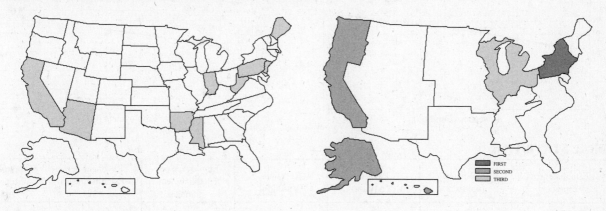

INDUSTRY DATA BY STATE

State	Establishments Total (number)	Establishments % of U.S.	Employment Total (number)	Employment % of U.S.	Employment Per Estab.	Payroll Total ($ mil.)	Payroll Per Empl. ($)	Revenues Total ($ mil.)	Revenues % of U.S.	Revenues Per Estab. ($)
California	421	10.4	3,014	10.8	7	108.7	36,076	755.1	17.0	1,793,572
New Jersey	52	1.3	1,692	6.1	33	85.2	50,366	557.2	12.5	10,714,519
Pennsylvania	129	3.2	2,573	9.2	20	101.6	39,487	499.7	11.2	3,873,845
Texas	618	15.3	2,586	9.3	4	51.0	19,710	249.5	5.6	403,704
Indiana	115	2.8	1,274	4.6	11	41.8	32,805	217.1	4.9	1,887,626
Florida	146	3.6	1,478	5.3	10	36.1	24,445	201.3	4.5	1,378,884
New York	42	1.0	657	2.4	16	25.7	39,055	153.1	3.4	3,644,286
Illinois	84	2.1	879	3.1	10	27.3	31,007	151.5	3.4	1,803,048
Arizona	141	3.5	1,263	4.5	9	40.7	32,261	140.5	3.2	996,504
Ohio	64	1.6	692	2.5	11	19.3	27,821	119.3	2.7	1,864,391
West Virginia	43	1.1	541	1.9	13	19.1	35,342	82.9	1.9	1,927,814
Mississippi	335	8.3	1,006	3.6	3	12.7	12,603	64.9	1.5	193,827
Kentucky	44	1.1	374	1.3	9	10.2	27,307	58.1	1.3	1,319,795
North Carolina	84	2.1	585	2.1	7	14.0	23,968	56.5	1.3	672,940
Arkansas	141	3.5	572	2.0	4	10.5	18,435	55.5	1.2	393,433
Colorado	113	2.8	534	1.9	5	10.9	20,326	43.4	1.0	383,637
Tennessee	31	0.8	276	1.0	9	8.7	31,620	41.7	0.9	1,344,129
Virginia	50	1.2	291	1.0	6	7.0	24,172	40.9	0.9	818,280
Oklahoma	107	2.6	360	1.3	3	5.2	14,361	25.6	0.6	239,168
Maine	24	0.6	192	0.7	8	4.9	25,286	24.5	0.6	1,021,750
Georgia	40	1.0	149	0.5	4	2.8	18,913	14.5	0.3	362,625
Montana	46	1.1	147	0.5	3	3.1	21,034	13.4	0.3	290,500
Utah	45	1.1	140	0.5	3	2.4	17,307	12.2	0.3	270,733
Hawaii	12	0.3	52	0.2	4	1.5	28,538	7.2	0.2	598,000
Michigan	12	0.3	66	0.2	6	0.8	12,788	4.1	0.1	344,750
Wisconsin	6	0.1	21	0.1	4	0.3	15,714	2.0	0.0	325,167
Louisiana	193	4.8	750*	-	-	(D)	-	(D)	-	-
Washington	173	4.3	750*	-	-	(D)	-	(D)	-	-
Alabama	98	2.4	375*	-	-	(D)	-	(D)	-	-
New Mexico	96	2.4	375*	-	-	(D)	-	(D)	-	-
Oregon	77	1.9	375*	-	-	(D)	-	(D)	-	-
Idaho	68	1.7	375*	-	-	(D)	-	(D)	-	-
Missouri	59	1.5	750*	-	-	(D)	-	(D)	-	-
South Carolina	54	1.3	375*	-	-	(D)	-	(D)	-	-
Kansas	39	1.0	175*	-	-	(D)	-	(D)	-	-
Connecticut	33	0.8	1,750*	-	-	(D)	-	(D)	-	-
South Dakota	30	0.7	175*	-	-	(D)	-	(D)	-	-
Iowa	27	0.7	175*	-	-	(D)	-	(D)	-	-
Nevada	25	0.6	60*	-	-	(D)	-	(D)	-	-
North Dakota	24	0.6	60*	-	-	(D)	-	(D)	-	-
Massachusetts	23	0.6	175*	-	-	(D)	-	(D)	-	-
Wyoming	20	0.5	60*	-	-	(D)	-	(D)	-	-
Nebraska	17	0.4	60*	-	-	(D)	-	(D)	-	-
New Hampshire	11	0.3	175*	-	-	(D)	-	(D)	-	-
Delaware	9	0.2	375*	-	-	(D)	-	(D)	-	-
Maryland	8	0.2	60*	-	-	(D)	-	(D)	-	-
Minnesota	7	0.2	60*	-	-	(D)	-	(D)	-	-
Vermont	7	0.2	60*	-	-	(D)	-	(D)	-	-
Alaska	6	0.1	10*	-	-	(D)	-	(D)	-	-

Source: 1997 *Economic Census*. The states are in descending order of revenues or establishments (if revenue data are missing for the majority). The symbol (D) appears when data are withheld to prevent disclosure of competitive information. States marked with (D) are sorted by number of establishments. A dash (-) indicates that the data element cannot be calculated. * indicates the midpoint of a range; 175, for example is the range 100-249. Shaded *states* on the state map indicate those states which have proportionately greater representation in the industry than would be indicated by the state's population; the ratio is based on total revenues or number of establishments. Shaded *regions* indicate where the industry is regionally most concentrated.

NAICS 221320 - SEWAGE TREATMENT FACILITIES*

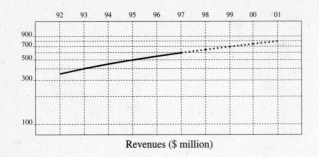

Revenues ($ million)

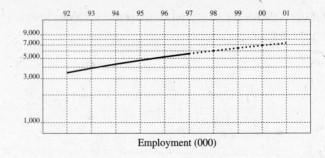

Employment (000)

GENERAL STATISTICS

Year	Establishments (number)	Employment (number)	Payroll ($ million)	Revenues ($ million)	Employees per Establishment (number)	Revenues per Establishment ($)	Payroll per Employee ($)
1987	-	-	-	-	-	-	-
1988	-	-	-	-	-	-	-
1989	-	-	-	-	-	-	-
1990	-	-	-	-	-	-	-
1991	-	-	-	-	-	-	-
1992	470	3,470	82.5	351.9	7.4	748,823	23,781
1993	515	3,896	93.8	400.7	7.5	770,275	23,988
1994	560	4,322	105.1	449.5	7.6	791,727	24,195
1995	606	4,748	116.4	498.2	7.8	813,179	24,402
1996	651	5,174	127.7	547.0	7.9	834,631	24,609
1997	696	5,600	139.0	595.8	8.0	856,083	24,816
1998	741 p	6,026 p	150.3 p	644.6 p	8.1 p	877,535 p	25,023 p
1999	786 p	6,452 p	161.6 p	693.4 p	8.2 p	898,987 p	25,230 p
2000	832 p	6,878 p	172.9 p	742.1 p	8.4 p	920,439 p	25,437 p
2001	877 p	7,304 p	184.2 p	790.9 p	8.5 p	941,891 p	25,644 p

Sources: Economic Census of the United States, 1987, 1992 and 1997. Data for those years (years are in **bold** type) are from the 5-year censuses of the economy. Other values, unless otherwise noted, are extrapolations. Values marked with *p* are projections. Data are the most recent available at this level of detail.

INDICES OF CHANGE

Year	Establishments (number)	Employment (number)	Payroll ($ million)	Revenues ($ million)	Employees per Establishment (number)	Revenues per Establishment ($)	Payroll per Employee ($)
1987	-	-	-	-	-	-	-
1992	67.5	62.0	59.4	59.1	92.5	87.5	95.8
1993	74.0	69.6	67.5	67.3	93.8	90.0	96.7
1994	80.5	77.2	75.6	75.4	95.0	92.5	97.5
1995	87.1	84.8	83.7	83.6	97.5	95.0	98.3
1996	93.5	92.4	91.9	91.8	98.8	97.5	99.2
1997	100.0	100.0	100.0	100.0	100.0	100.0	100.0
1998	106.5 p	107.6 p	108.1 p	108.2 p	101.3 p	102.5 p	100.8 p
1999	112.9 p	115.2 p	116.3 p	116.4 p	102.5 p	105.0 p	101.7 p
2000	119.5 p	122.8 p	124.4 p	124.6 p	105.0 p	107.5 p	102.5 p
2001	126.0 p	130.4 p	132.5 p	132.7 p	106.3 p	110.0 p	103.3 p

Sources: Same as General Statistics. The values shown reflect change from the base year, 1997. Values above 100 mean greater than 1997, values below 100 mean less than 1997, and a value of 100 in years other than 1997 means same as 1997. Indices are calculated only for Census years. Data are the most recent available at this level of detail.

SELECTED RATIOS

For 1997	Avg. of Sector	Analyzed Industry	Index	For 1997	Avg. of Sector	Analyzed Industry	Index
Employees per establishment	45	8	18	Payroll per establishment	2,358,969	199,713	8
Revenue per establishment	26,539,891	856,034	3	Payroll as % of revenue	9	23	262
Revenue per employee	585,899	106,393	18	Payroll per employee	52,077	24,821	48

Sources: Same as General Statistics. The 'Average of Sector' column represents the average for all industries in this sector. The Index shows the relationship between the Average and the Analyzed Industry. For example, 100 means that they are equal; 500 that the Analyzed Industry is five times the average; 50 means that the Analyzed Industry is half the national average. 'na' is used to show that data are 'not available'.

*Equivalent to SIC 4952.

LEADING COMPANIES   Number shown: **14**   Total sales ($ mil): **8,651**   Total employment (000): **27.8**

Company Name	Address				CEO Name	Phone	Co. Type	Sales ($ mil)	Empl. (000)
United States Filter Corp.	40-004 Cook St	Palm Desert	CA	92211	Richard J Heckmann	760-340-0098	S	3,235	18.5
JEA	21 W Church St	Jacksonville	FL	32202	Walter P Bussells	904-632-7410	R	2,009*	2.6
United Water Resources Inc.	200 Old Hook Rd	Harrington Park	NJ	07640	Donald L Correll	201-784-9434	P	1,769	1.4
Carylon Corp.	2500 W Arthington	Chicago	IL	60612	Julius Hemmelstein	312-666-7700	R	530*	1.1
Colorado Springs Utilities	P O Box 1103	Co Springs	CO	80947		719-448-8000	R	390	1.9
Professional Services Group Inc.	14950 Heathrow	Houston	TX	77032	Patrick L McMahon	281-985-5427	S	233*	1.5
Dalton Utilities	P O Box 869	Dalton	GA	30722	Don Cope	706-278-1313	R	226*	0.3
Lyles Diversified Inc.	P O Box 4376	Fresno	CA	93744	William Lyles	559-441-1190	R	62*	0.3
East Valley Water District	PO Box 3427	San Bernardino	CA	92413		909-889-9501	R	62*	<0.1
IT Corp.	23456 Hawthorne	Torrance	CA	90505	E Brian Smith	310-378-9933	S	61*	<0.1
W.M. Lyles Co.	P O Box 4376	Fresno	CA	93744	Michael A Burson	559-441-1900	S	50*	0.2
New Mexico Utilities Inc.	4700 Irving N W	Albuquerque	NM	87114	Robert L Swartwout	505-898-2661	S	21*	<0.1
Intrepid Capital Corp.	50 N Laura	Jacksonville	FL	32202	William J Long	904-350-9999	P	3	<0.1
Facilities Management Inc.	PO Box 10	Taylor	MI	48180	Dave Vago	734-947-9700	S	0	<0.1

Source: Ward's Business Directory of U.S. Private and Public Companies, Volumes 1 and 2, 2000. The company type code used is as follows: P - Public, R - Private, S - Subsidiary, D - Division, J - Joint Venture, A - Affiliate, G - Group, N - Company type not reported. Sales are in millions of dollars, employees are in thousands. An asterisk (*) indicates an estimated sales volume. The symbol < stands for 'less than'. Company names and addresses are truncated, in some cases, to fit into the available space.

LOCATION BY STATE AND REGIONAL CONCENTRATION

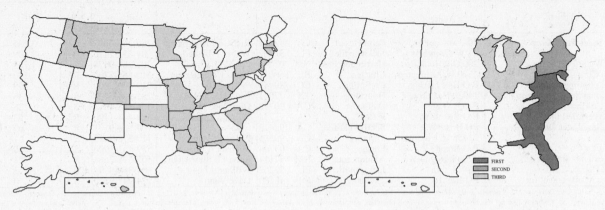

INDUSTRY DATA BY STATE

State	Establishments Total (number)	Establishments % of U.S.	Employment Total (number)	Employment % of U.S.	Employment Per Estab.	Payroll Total ($ mil.)	Payroll Per Empl. ($)	Revenues Total ($ mil.)	Revenues % of U.S.	Revenues Per Estab. ($)
Maryland	9	1.3	107	1.9	12	2.7	25,664	15.4	2.6	1,713,667
California	27	3.9	116	2.1	4	2.1	18,060	12.3	2.1	455,519
West Virginia	20	2.9	94	1.7	5	1.6	16,830	7.8	1.3	391,850
Arizona	8	1.1	40	0.7	5	0.9	22,800	7.6	1.3	945,375
Colorado	14	2.0	51	0.9	4	1.5	29,000	5.8	1.0	412,214
Kentucky	13	1.9	116	2.1	9	1.9	16,405	5.2	0.9	403,692
Wisconsin	13	1.9	47	0.8	4	0.4	8,000	1.7	0.3	129,231
Michigan	10	1.4	24	0.4	2	0.6	25,667	1.7	0.3	165,800
Idaho	6	0.9	20	0.4	3	0.3	14,800	0.9	0.2	156,500
Florida	88	12.6	750*	-	-	(D)	-	(D)	-	-
Pennsylvania	59	8.5	375*	-	-	(D)	-	(D)	-	-
Texas	38	5.5	750*	-	-	(D)	-	(D)	-	-
Indiana	30	4.3	175*	-	-	(D)	-	(D)	-	-
New York	28	4.0	175*	-	-	(D)	-	(D)	-	-
Illinois	27	3.9	175*	-	-	(D)	-	(D)	-	-
New Jersey	24	3.4	750*	-	-	(D)	-	(D)	-	-
Louisiana	21	3.0	175*	-	-	(D)	-	(D)	-	-
Massachusetts	21	3.0	375*	-	-	(D)	-	(D)	-	-
Ohio	19	2.7	175*	-	-	(D)	-	(D)	-	-
North Carolina	18	2.6	60*	-	-	(D)	-	(D)	-	-
Missouri	15	2.2	60*	-	-	(D)	-	(D)	-	-
Mississippi	14	2.0	60*	-	-	(D)	-	(D)	-	-
Alabama	13	1.9	175*	-	-	(D)	-	(D)	-	-
Hawaii	13	1.9	175*	-	-	(D)	-	(D)	-	-
Minnesota	13	1.9	60*	-	-	(D)	-	(D)	-	-
South Carolina	12	1.7	60*	-	-	(D)	-	(D)	-	-
Virginia	12	1.7	60*	-	-	(D)	-	(D)	-	-
Tennessee	11	1.6	175*	-	-	(D)	-	(D)	-	-
Georgia	10	1.4	60*	-	-	(D)	-	(D)	-	-
Arkansas	9	1.3	60*	-	-	(D)	-	(D)	-	-
Connecticut	9	1.3	60*	-	-	(D)	-	(D)	-	-
Oklahoma	9	1.3	175*	-	-	(D)	-	(D)	-	-
Washington	8	1.1	60*	-	-	(D)	-	(D)	-	-
Iowa	7	1.0	60*	-	-	(D)	-	(D)	-	-
Oregon	7	1.0	60*	-	-	(D)	-	(D)	-	-
Montana	6	0.9	10*	-	-	(D)	-	(D)	-	-

Source: 1997 *Economic Census*. The states are in descending order of revenues or establishments (if revenue data are missing for the majority). The symbol (D) appears when data are withheld to prevent disclosure of competitive information. States marked with (D) are sorted by number of establishments. A dash (-) indicates that the data element cannot be calculated. * indicates the midpoint of a range; 175, for example is the range 100-249. Shaded *states* on the state map indicate those states which have proportionately greater representation in the industry than would be indicated by the state's population; the ratio is based on total revenues or number of establishments. Shaded *regions* indicate where the industry is regionally most concentrated.

NAICS 221330 - STEAM AND AIR-CONDITIONING SUPPLY

GENERAL STATISTICS

Year	Establishments (number)	Employment (number)	Payroll ($ million)	Revenues ($ million)	Employees per Establishment (number)	Revenues per Establishment ($)	Payroll per Employee ($)
1997	83	1,767	81.0	573.1	21.3	6,904,373	45,838

Source: Economic Census of the United States, 1997. This is a newly defined industry. Data for prior years were unavailable at the time of publication but may become available over time.

SIC INDUSTRIES RELATED TO NAICS 221330

SIC	Industry	1990	1991	1992	1993	1994	1995	1996	1997
4961	**Steam and Air-Conditioning Supply**	-	-	-	-	-	-	-	-

Source: Economic Census of the United States, 1992, annual surveys of economic sectors conducted by the Bureau of the Census, and estimates or projections based on the 1982-1992 period; not all data are shown. 'e' marks estimates made by the editors; 'p' indicates projections based on time series. A dash (-) indicates that data for this SIC or year were not available. * Indicates that only a portion of this industry is present within the NAICS data. If no * is shown, the entire industry is contained within the NAICS data.

INDICES OF CHANGE

Year	Establishments (number)	Employment (number)	Payroll ($ million)	Revenues ($ million)	Employees per Establishment (number)	Revenues per Establishment ($)	Payroll per Employee ($)
1997	100.0	100.0	100.0	100.0	100.0	100.0	100.0

Sources: Same as General Statistics. The values shown reflect change from the base year, 1997. Values above 100 mean greater than 1997, values below 100 mean less than 1997, and a value of 100 in years other than 1997 means same as 1997. Indices are calculated only for Census years. Data are the most recent available at this level of detail.

SELECTED RATIOS

For 1997	Avg. of Sector	Analyzed Industry	Index	For 1997	Avg. of Sector	Analyzed Industry	Index
Employees per establishment	45	21	47	Payroll per establishment	2,358,969	975,904	41
Revenue per establishment	26,539,891	6,904,819	26	Payroll as % of revenue	9	14	159
Revenue per employee	585,899	324,335	55	Payroll per employee	52,077	45,840	88

Sources: Same as General Statistics. The 'Average of Sector' column represents the average for all industries in this sector. The Index shows the relationship between the Average and the Analyzed Industry. For example, 100 means that they are equal; 500 that the Analyzed Industry is five times the average; 50 means that the Analyzed Industry is half the national average. 'na' is used to show that data are 'not available'.

LEADING COMPANIES   Number shown: **8**   Total sales ($ mil): **15,159**   Total employment (000): **16.1**

Company Name	Address				CEO Name	Phone	Co. Type	Sales ($ mil)	Empl. (000)
Consolidated Edison Inc.	4 Irving Pl	New York	NY	10003	J Michael Evans	212-460-4600	P	14,381	15.0
Trigen Energy Corp.	1 Water St	White Plains	NY	10601	Thomas R Casten	914-286-6600	P	618	0.7
Trigen-Boston Energy Corp.	210 South St	Boston	MA	02111	Richard S Strong	617-482-8080	S	82*	<0.1
Thermal Ventures Inc.	29 E Front St	Youngstown	OH	44503	Carl Avers	330-747-4604	R	30	0.1
Imperial Power Services Inc.	PO Box 1538	Heber	CA	92249	Mark Elliot	760-353-9630	R	27*	<0.1
AES Warrior Run Inc.	11600 Mexico Fms	Cumberland	MD	21502		301-777-0055	R	17*	<0.1
Youngstown Thermal L.P.	205 North Ave	Youngstown	OH	44502	Jim Mullen		R	3	<0.1
Natural Power Inc.	3000 Gresham Lake	Raleigh	NC	27615	Bill I Rowland	919-876-6722	R	1	<0.1

Source: Ward's Business Directory of U.S. Private and Public Companies, Volumes 1 and 2, 2000. The company type code used is as follows: P - Public, R - Private, S - Subsidiary, D - Division, J - Joint Venture, A - Affiliate, G - Group, N - Company type not reported. Sales are in millions of dollars, employees are in thousands. An asterisk (*) indicates an estimated sales volume. The symbol < stands for 'less than'. Company names and addresses are truncated, in some cases, to fit into the available space.

LOCATION BY STATE AND REGIONAL CONCENTRATION

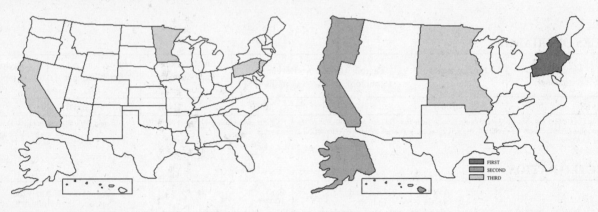

FIRST
SECOND
THIRD

INDUSTRY DATA BY STATE

State	Establishments Total (number)	% of U.S.	Employment Total (number)	% of U.S.	Per Estab.	Payroll Total ($ mil.)	Per Empl. ($)	Revenues Total ($ mil.)	% of U.S.	Per Estab. ($)
California	11	13.3	269	15.2	24	8.5	31,491	69.2	12.1	6,288,273
Pennsylvania	8	9.6	175*	-	-	(D)	-	(D)	-	-
Minnesota	7	8.4	175*	-	-	(D)	-	(D)	-	-
New Jersey	6	7.2	175*	-	-	(D)	-	(D)	-	-

Source: 1997 Economic Census. The states are in descending order of revenues or establishments (if revenue data are missing for the majority). The symbol (D) appears when data are withheld to prevent disclosure of competitive information. States marked with (D) are sorted by number of establishments. A dash (-) indicates that the data element cannot be calculated. * indicates the midpoint of a range; 175, for example is the range 100-249. Shaded *states* on the state map indicate those states which have proportionately greater representation in the industry than would be indicated by the state's population; the ratio is based on total revenues or number of establishments. Shaded *regions* indicate where the industry is regionally most concentrated.

Part IV

CONSTRUCTION

NAICS 233110 - LAND SUBDIVISION AND LAND DEVELOPMENT*

GENERAL STATISTICS

Years	Estab-lish-ments	Employment		Payroll ($ mil)		Costs ($ mil)		Value Added ($ mil)	Revenues ($ mil)			Capital expend. ($ mil)
		Total	Constr. workers	Total	Worker payroll	Total	Cost of materials		All sources	Construction		
										Total	Net	
1997	8,186	41,827	10,977	1,509.8	254.2	1,867.4	1,778.2	9,154.6	14,409.8	13,635.5	10,247.8	276.8

Source: Economic Census of the United States, 1997. This is a newly defined industry. Data for prior years were unavailable at the time of publication but may become available over time. "Net" under "Construction" is construction revenue net of the costs of subcontracts.

DISTRIBUTION AMONG SIC-BASED INDUSTRIES - 1997

SIC	Industry	Estab-lish-ments	Employment		Cost of Power & Materials ($ mil)	Revenues ($ mil)			Value Added ($ mil)
			Total (000)	Payroll ($ mil)		All Sources	Construction		
							Total	Net	
655200	Land subdividers & developers, except cemeteries	8,186.0	41,827	1,509.8	1,867.4	14,409.7	13,635.5	10,247.8	9,154.63

Source: 1997 Economic Census. U.S. Census Bureau, U.S. Department of Commerce, August 1997. SIC codes ending in two zeroes represent complete 4-digit SICs. All others are parts of 4-digit SIC industries. Items showing a dash (-) indicate that data are not available because of disclosure problems.

SIC INDUSTRIES RELATED TO NAICS 233110

SIC	Industry	1990	1991	1992	1993	1994	1995	1996	1997
6552	**Subdividers and Developers, nec**	-	-	-	-	-	-	-	-

*Source: Economic Census of the United States, 1992, annual surveys of economic sectors conducted by the Bureau of the Census, and estimates or projections based on the 1982-1992 period; not all data are shown. 'e' marks estimates made by the editors; 'p' indicates projections based on time series. A dash (-) indicates that data for this SIC or year were not available. * Indicates that only a portion of this industry is present within the NAICS data. If no * is shown, the entire industry is contained within the NAICS data.*

INDICES OF CHANGE

Years	Estab-lish-ments	Employment		Payroll ($ mil)		Costs ($ mil)		Value Added ($ mil)	Revenues ($ mil)			Capital expend. ($ mil)
		Total	Constr. workers	Total	Worker payroll	Total	Cost of materials		All sources	Construction		
										Total	Net	
1997	100.0	100.0	100.0	100.0	100.0	100.0	100.0	100.0	100.0	100.0	100.0	100.0

Sources: Same as General Statistics. The values shown reflect change from the base year, 1997. Values above 100 mean greater than 1997, values below 100 mean less than 1997, and a value of 100 in years other than 1997 means same as 1997. Indices are calculated only for Census years. Data are the most recent available at this level of detail.

SELECTED RATIOS

For 1997	Avg. of Sector	Analyzed Industry	Index	For 1997	Avg. of Sector	Analyzed Industry	Index
Employees per establishment	8.6	5.1	59	Value added per establishment	584,730	1,118,324	191
Construction workers per establishment	6.6	1.3	20	Value added per employee	67,759	218,868	323
Payroll per establishment	265,343	184,437	70	Value added per construction worker	88,592	833,980	941
Payroll per employee	30,748	36,096	117	Revenues per establishment	1,307,915	1,760,298	135
Payroll per construction worker	27,622	23,158	84	Revenues per employee	151,563	344,510	227
Costs per establishment	367,737	228,121	62	Revenues per construction worker	198,161	1,312,727	662
Costs per employee	42,614	44,646	105	CR as % of total revenues	98.48	94.63	96
Costs per construction worker	55,716	170,119	305	Net CR as % of CR	72.40	75.16	104
Materials as % of costs	95.75	95.22	99	Investment per establishment	22,948	33,814	147
Costs as % of revenues	28.12	12.96	46	Investment per employee	2,659	6,618	249
Costs as % of construction revenues	28.55	13.70	48	Investment per construction worker	3,477	25,216	725

Sources: Same as General Statistics. The 'Average of Sector' column represents the average for all industries in this sector. The Index shows the relationship between the Average and the Analyzed Industry. For example, 100 means that they are equal; 500 that the Analyzed Industry is five times the average; 50 means that the Analyzed Industry is half the national average. 'na' is used to show that data are 'not available'. CR stands for "construction revenues" and "Net CR" is construction revenues net of subcontract expenses.

*Equivalent to SIC 6552.

LEADING COMPANIES   Number shown: **65**   Total sales ($ mil): **44,504**   Total employment (000): **93.8**

Company Name	Address				CEO Name	Phone	Co. Type	Sales ($ mil)	Empl. (000)
Dominion Resources Inc.	PO Box 26532	Richmond	VA	23261	Thomas E Capps	804-819-2000	P	17,517	11.0
Centex Corp.	PO Box 19000	Dallas	TX	75219	Laurence E Hirsch	214-981-5000	P	5,155	13.2
Lefrak Organization Inc.	97-77 Queens Blvd	Rego Park	NY	11374	Samuel J LeFrak	718-459-9021	R	2,750	16.0
Pinnacle West Capital Corp.	P O Box 52132	Phoenix	AZ	85072	Bill Post	602-379-2500	P	2,423	7.3
Hawaiian Electric Industries Inc.	PO Box 730	Honolulu	HI	96808	Robert F Clarke	808-543-5662	P	1,523	3.7
Lincoln Property Co.	P O Box 1920	Dallas	TX	75201	Mack Pogue	214-740-3300	R	1,398	4.5
Opus Corp.	10350 Bren Rd W	Minnetonka	MN	55343	Mark Ravenhorst	952-656-4444	R	1,200	0.0
A.G. Spanos Construction Inc.	P O Box 7126	Stockton	CA	95267	Dean Spanos	209-478-7954	R	1,175	0.6
Perini Corp.	Box 9160	Framingham	MA	01701	Robert Band	508-628-2000	P	1,036	2.7
Alexander and Baldwin Inc.	PO Box 3440	Honolulu	HI	96813	Alexander Baldwin	808-525-6611	P	959	2.3
New Jersey Resources Corp.	PO Box 1468	Wall	NJ	07719	Laurence M Downes	732-938-1480	P	904	0.8
Watkins Associated Industries Inc.	P O Box 1738	Atlanta	GA	30371	William Freeman	404-872-3841	R	800	8.5
Southern Union Co.	504 Lavaca St	Austin	TX	78701	Peter H Kelley	512-477-5852	P	605	1.6
A and B Hawaii Inc.	PO Box 3440	Honolulu	HI	96801	W Allen Doane	808-525-6611	S	588	1.2
Helmerich and Payne Inc.	Utica at 21st St	Tulsa	OK	74114	Hans Helmerich	918-742-5531	P	564	3.4
Shapell Industries Inc.	8383 Wilshire Blvd	Beverly Hills	CA	90211	Nathan Shapell	323-655-7330	R	554	0.4
Kraus-Anderson Inc.	523 S 8th St	Minneapolis	MN	55404	Burton F Dahlberg	612-332-7281	R	540	1.0
St. Joe Paper Co.	1650 Prudential Dr	Jacksonville	FL	32207	Peter S Rummell	904-396-6600	P	392*	2.1
John Wieland Homes Inc.	1950 Sullivan Rd	Atlanta	GA	30337	Russell Terry	770-996-1400	R	389	0.8
Newhall Land and Farming Co.	23823 Valencia Blvd	Valencia	CA	91355	Gary M Cusumano	661-255-4000	P	322	0.2
Devcon Construction Inc.	555 Los Coches St	Milpitas	CA	95035	Gary Filizetti	408-942-8200	R	300*	0.3
Florida East Coast Industries Inc.	1 Malaga St	St. Augustine	FL	32084	Robert W Anestis	904-829-3421	P	248	1.0
Donohoe Companies Inc.	2101 Wisconsin NW	Washington	DC	20007	James A Donohoe III	202-333-0880	R	240*	0.4
Casden Co.	9090 Wilshire Blvd	Beverly Hills	CA	90211	Henry Casden	310-274-5553	R	202*	0.3
JPI Investments Inc.	600 E Colinas	Irving	TX	75039	Robert D Page	972-556-1700	R	200	1.0
AMREP Corp.	641 Lexington Ave	New York	NY	10022	Edward B Cloues II	212-541-7300	P	184	1.2
Buzz Oates Cos.	8615 Eldercreek Rd	Sacramento	CA	95828		916-381-3600	R	135*	0.2
Cooper Communities Inc.	1801 Forest Hills	Bella Vista	AR	72715	John Cooper Jr	501-855-6151	R	130*	0.5
William E. Buchan Inc.	11555 Northop Way	Bellevue	WA	98004	William E Buchan	425-828-6424	R	126*	0.1
Salient 3 Communications Inc.	PO Box 1498	Reading	PA	19603	Timothy S Cobb	610-856-5500	P	123	0.8
Avatar Holdings Inc.	201 Alhambra Cir	Coral Gables	FL	33134	Gerald D Kelfer	305-442-7000	P	114*	0.9
Capital Development Co.	691 Sleater-Kinney	Olympia	WA	98503	Robert L Blume	360-459-8744	R	103*	0.2
Amfac/JMB Hawaii Inc.	900 N Michigan Ave	Chicago	IL	60611	Edward G Karl	312-440-4800	S	100*	1.0
Grupe Co.	3255 W March Ln	Stockton	CA	95219	Greenlaw Grupe Jr	209-473-6000	R	100*	0.4
Corporex Companies Inc.	655 Eden Park Dr	Cincinnati	OH	45206	William P Butler	513-292-5500	R	100*	0.1
Saxton Inc.	5440 W Sahara Ave	Las Vegas	NV	89146	James C Saxton	702-221-1111	P	92	0.9
Ryan Companies US Inc.	900 2nd Ave S	Minneapolis	MN	55402	James R Ryan	612-336-1200	R	85*	0.1
Richmond American Homes	17310 Red Hill Ave	Irvine	CA	92614	Robert Shiota	949-756-7373	S	83*	<0.1
FRP Properties Inc.	155 E 21st St	Jacksonville	FL	32206	John E Anderson	904-355-1781	P	82	0.9
Elliott Homes Inc.	2390 E Bidwell St	Folsom	CA	95630	Harry C Elliott III	916-984-1300	R	75*	0.1
Standard Pacific	3825 Hopyard Rd	Pleasanton	CA	94588	MC Cortney	925-847-8700	S	72*	<0.1
Pennichuck Corp.	PO Box 448	Nashua	NH	03061	Maurice L Arel	603-882-5191	P	71	<0.1
Al Neyer Inc.	3800 Red Bank Rd	Cincinnati	OH	45227	David F Neter	513-271-6400	R	70	0.2
M.J. Peterson Real Estate Inc.	501 Audubon	Amherst	NY	14228	Victor L Peterson Jr	716-688-1234	R	68*	0.1
Skinner-Broadbent Company Inc.	201 N Illinois St	Indianapolis	IN	46204	George P Broadbent	317-237-2900	R	62*	<0.1
Kaiser Ventures Inc.	3633 E Inland	Ontario	CA	91764	Richard E Stoddard	909-483-8500	P	52	<0.1
Allen and O'Hara Inc.	530 Oak Court Dr	Memphis	TN	38117	Paul O'Bower	901-345-7620	R	48*	<0.1
Mayer Homes Inc.	755 S New Ballas	St. Louis	MO	63141	J Randall Mayer	314-997-2300	R	48*	<0.1
Kriti Holdings Inc.	1010 Lamar St	Houston	TX	77002	James Riner	713-655-7070	R	45	<0.1
Progress Capital Holdings Inc.	1 Progress Plz	St. Petersburg	FL	33701	Darryl A LeClair	813-824-6400	S	44	0.2
Westwood Swinerton	3030 S W Moody	Portland	OR	97201	Carl Grossman	503-222-2000	D	43*	0.1
Reliable Contracting Inc.	1 Churchview Rd	Millersville	MD	21108	Thomas I Baldwin	410-987-0313	R	40	0.4
Maracay Homes Arizona I L.L.C.	15160 N Hayden Rd	Scottsdale	AZ	85260	Dave Bessey	480-970-6000	R	40	<0.1
Interstate General Company L.P.	5160 Parkstone Dr	Chantilly	VA	20151	Mark Augenblick	703-263-1191	P	33	<0.1
Giordano Construction Inc.	P O Box 802	Branford	CT	06405		203-488-7264	R	32*	<0.1
Forbes Homes Inc.	2635 Millersport	Getzville	NY	14068	Elliot Lasky	716-688-5597	R	24	<0.1
Russell Lands Inc.	1 Willow Point Rd	Alexander City	AL	35010	Benjamin Russell	256-329-8424	R	19	0.2
Kickerillo Building Co.	1306 S Fry Blvd	Katy	TX	77450	Mary Kickerillo	713-951-0666	D	17*	<0.1
ERC Properties Inc.	P O Box 3945	Fort Smith	AR	72913	ER Coleman	501-452-9950	R	16	<0.1
Focus Group Inc.	3565 Piedmont Rd	Atlanta	GA	30305	Michael Blonder	404-816-6300	R	12*	<0.1
Marina L.P.	1691 Fall Creek Rd	Indianapolis	IN	46256	Allen E Rosenberg	317-845-0270	P	11	<0.1
Consolidated-Tomoka Land Co.	149 S Ridgewood	Daytona Beach	FL	32114	Bob D Allen	904-255-7558	P	6	0.1
Gierczyk Inc.	17475 Jovanna Dr	Homewood	IL	60430	James P Gierczyk	708-647-4747	R	6*	<0.1
Foster Brothers Inc.	3975 University Dr	Fairfax	VA	22030	Arthur E Foster	703-385-8900	R	4*	<0.1
Hope Communities Inc.	2444 Washington St	Denver	CO	80205		303-860-7747	R	2	<0.1

Source: Ward's Business Directory of U.S. Private and Public Companies, Volumes 1 and 2, 2000. The company type code used is as follows: P - Public, R - Private, S - Subsidiary, D - Division, J - Joint Venture, A - Affiliate, G - Group, N - Company type not reported. Sales are in millions of dollars, employees are in thousands. An asterisk (*) indicates an estimated sales volume. The symbol < stands for 'less than'. Company names and addresses are truncated, in some cases, to fit into the available space.

COST DETAILS

Item	Cost ($ mil)	% of total	Per $1,000 of Revenue	Item	Cost ($ mil)	% of total	Per $1,000 of Revenue
All costs	5,255.1	100.000	364.7	Total Rentals	80.8	1.538	5.6
Cost of supplies	1,778.2	33.837	123.4	Equipment	(S)	-	-
Subcontracts	3,387.7	64.465	235.1	Buildings	36.3	0.690	2.5
Power, fuel, lubricants	89.3	1.698	6.2	Services purchased	103.4	1.967	7.2
Electricity	31.2	0.594	2.2	Communications	54.0	1.028	3.7
Natural gas	9.1	0.173	0.6	Building repairs	10.1	0.191	0.7
Gasoline and diesel	46.6	0.887	3.2	Machinery repairs	39.3	0.748	2.7
Highway	37.8	0.720	2.6				
Offroad	8.8	0.167	0.6				
Other power	(S)	-	-				

Source: Economic Census of the United States, 1997. Revenues referred to are total industry revenues for the current NAICS industry.

CONSTRUCTION PRODUCT DETAILS

Construction type	Value of construction work ($ mil and %)							
	Total		New construction		Additions, alterations, reconstruction		Maintenance and repair	
	Value	%	Value	%	Value	%	Value	%
Total	**13,635.5**	**100.0**	**12,784.3**	**100.0**	**94.1**	**100.0**	**(S)**	**-**
Building construction, total	**12,005.9**	**88.0**	**11,913.3**	**93.2**	**71.1**	**75.5**	**(S)**	**-**
Single-family houses, detached	7,220.3	53.0	7,188.1	56.2	20.7	22.0	11.5	-
Single-family houses, attached	472.9	3.5	472.1	3.7	(S)	-	(S)	-
Apartment buildings, condos and cooperatives	1,746.8	12.8	1,714.9	13.4	29.1	30.9	(S)	-
Manufacturing and light industrial buildings	117.0	0.9	114.6	0.9	(S)	-	-	-
Office buildings	268.5	2.0	260.0	2.0	7.2	7.6	1.3	-
All other commercial buildings, nec	1,205.4	8.8	1,195.8	9.4	8.3	8.8	1.4	-
Other building construction	975.0	7.2	967.7	7.6	3.2	3.4	(S)	-
Nonbuilding construction, total	**900.8**	**6.6**	**871.0**	**6.8**	**(S)**	**-**	**(S)**	**-**
Other nonbuilding construction, nec	900.8	6.6	871.0	6.8	(S)	-	(S)	-
Construction work, nsk	**728.8**	**5.3**	**NA**	**-**	**NA**	**-**	**NA**	**-**

Source: Economic Census of the United States, 1997. Bold items are headers. (D) stands for data withheld to protect competitive information. (S) indicates instances where data do not meet publications standards.

LOCATION BY STATE AND REGIONAL CONCENTRATION

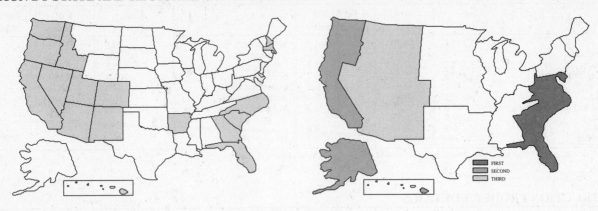

FIRST
SECOND
THIRD

INDUSTRY DATA BY STATE

| State | Estab- lish- ments | Employment | | | Compensation | | Production | | | | Capital Exp. ($ mil) |
		Total	Workers	Total as % of US	Payroll per Employee	Wages per Worker	Costs ($ mil)	Value Added ($ mil)	Reve- nues ($ mil)	% of US	
California	796	4,764	(S)	11.39	44,865	-	229.1	1,277.4	1,985.7	13.78	28.6
Florida	698	4,733	1,086	11.32	33,099	-	196.2	1,011.9	1,534.3	10.65	(S)
Georgia	340	1,613	380	3.86	35,821	24,424	107.2	698.4	1,031.5	7.16	12.4
Texas	643	2,683	725	6.41	39,471	19,894	126.0	635.5	901.6	6.26	(S)
Arizona	228	1,540	323	3.68	34,362	20,746	40.6	352.6	645.4	4.48	12.8
Illinois	286	1,454	430	3.48	43,054	26,521	63.6	423.5	644.8	4.47	7.3
South Carolina	164	1,832	317	4.38	30,187	18,744	57.0	339.2	527.7	3.66	8.3
Nevada	116	976	213	2.33	47,633	35,052	61.1	228.5	507.1	3.52	11.5
Ohio	271	1,565	313	3.74	32,773	21,010	62.7	337.7	483.7	3.36	10.1
North Carolina	366	1,851	388	4.43	26,499	18,575	74.7	290.0	450.4	3.13	(S)
New Jersey	228	1,082	299	2.59	35,977	30,846	61.7	287.8	430.4	2.99	(S)
Washington	267	1,089	375	2.60	40,713	26,696	52.8	275.0	426.2	2.96	(S)
Massachusetts	220	1,055	288	2.52	40,156	28,163	68.2	241.9	390.0	2.71	(S)
New York	260	1,354	311	3.24	40,702	27,415	73.5	239.6	381.9	2.65	(S)
Colorado	219	1,063	287	2.54	34,815	21,686	33.3	184.7	342.9	2.38	3.8
Virginia	199	1,228	243	2.94	32,900	24,992	41.7	225.4	336.3	2.33	6.9
Pennsylvania	240	1,070	281	2.56	31,217	23,100	49.0	180.3	300.2	2.08	10.3
Indiana	212	808	289	1.93	34,303	21,343	29.5	143.3	242.0	1.68	7.9
Tennessee	174	601	137	1.44	32,514	29,584	36.9	131.3	200.7	1.39	(S)
Oregon	127	489	174	1.17	44,828	37,534	18.7	105.3	195.4	1.36	7.6
Minnesota	120	436	95	1.04	41,885	27,147	(S)	119.2	170.6	1.18	(S)
Maryland	139	582	281	1.39	41,478	26,039	17.2	94.2	159.5	1.11	(S)
Hawaii	54	637	170	1.52	36,016	26,359	27.6	82.6	147.2	1.02	(S)
Arkansas	85	546	47	1.31	27,592	11,106	20.4	112.6	140.8	0.98	3.1
Missouri	175	712	312	1.70	27,444	14,705	27.9	78.5	133.7	0.93	2.0
Utah	128	539	197	1.29	38,434	21,406	15.9	64.3	116.1	0.81	2.7
New Mexico	76	424	65	1.01	37,649	14,231	12.5	73.4	115.5	0.80	1.4
Alabama	99	254	74	0.61	37,055	19,838	15.3	71.6	110.6	0.77	2.1
Wisconsin	103	401	112	0.96	31,666	21,429	(S)	68.5	93.6	0.65	(S)
Connecticut	91	640	246	1.53	27,822	18,455	15.9	53.7	93.6	0.65	3.5
Oklahoma	104	289	141	0.69	25,325	17,716	15.1	69.2	90.9	0.63	(S)
Kentucky	80	272	(D)	0.65	27,912	-	14.2	50.3	85.7	0.59	3.7
Louisiana	61	307	63	0.73	26,932	10,111	12.5	54.1	78.2	0.54	2.7
New Hampshire	38	142	38	0.34	37,817	20,421	13.7	43.2	73.3	0.51	0.5
Rhode Island	77	160	(S)	0.38	50,656	-	(S)	56.3	69.4	0.48	(S)
Kansas	56	221	129	0.53	33,276	20,977	14.8	31.0	67.2	0.47	0.8
Idaho	67	214	71	0.51	29,603	19,113	9.5	29.8	63.6	0.44	0.7
Mississippi	44	219	128	0.52	21,694	11,711	6.5	22.7	35.8	0.25	0.7
West Virginia	35	108	(S)	0.26	27,444	-	5.4	22.7	32.4	0.23	1.4
Nebraska	25	75	26	0.18	47,773	25,192	3.6	13.9	22.2	0.15	0.3
Alaska	27	145	27	0.35	22,910	22,815	3.2	13.4	18.3	0.13	0.3
Iowa	39	66	28	0.16	25,985	10,464	2.5	10.0	17.1	0.12	0.1
Montana	31	62	4	0.15	24,145	11,750	2.4	11.0	15.6	0.11	0.1
Wyoming	12	54	43	0.13	20,130	20,093	(S)	7.8	9.7	0.07	(S)
Delaware	17	59	47	0.14	21,000	17,979	1.7	4.6	9.5	0.07	0.2
Vermont	17	92	70	0.22	20,620	14,886	1.3	6.3	9.3	0.06	0.5
Maine	19	64	17	0.15	47,156	33,176	1.2	5.8	8.5	0.06	0.2
South Dakota	17	54	24	0.13	32,426	15,542	1.5	4.5	7.9	0.05	(S)
Michigan	278	1,039	369	2.48	33,958	21,182	70.6	(S)	(S)	-	7.6
D.C.	15	157	(S)	0.38	-	-	(S)	(S)	(S)	-	(S)
North Dakota	5	7	(D)	0.02	-	-	(S)	(S)	(S)	-	(S)

Source: Economic Census of the U.S., 1997. Data are sorted by 1997 revenues or establishments. (D) means data suppression to prevent disclosure of company data. (S) means that data did not meet statistical standards for publication. A dash (-) is used when data are unavailable or cannot be calculated. Data followed by an * indicate the midpoint of a range. The ranges are: for 10, 0-19; for 60, 20-99, for 175, 100-249, for 375, 250-499, for 750, 500-999. Higher values are multiples of those shown, e.g., 3,750 is the midpoint of the range 2,500-4,999. Shaded *states* on the state map indicate those states which have proportionately greater representation in the industry than would be indicated by the state's population; the ratio is based on total revenues or number of establishments. Shaded *regions* indicate where the industry is regionally most concentrated.

NAICS 233210 - SINGLE-FAMILY HOUSING CONSTRUCTION

GENERAL STATISTICS

Years	Estab-lish-ments	Employment		Payroll ($ mil)		Costs ($ mil)		Value Added ($ mil)	Revenues ($ mil)			Capital expend. ($ mil)
		Total	Constr. workers	Total	Worker payroll	Total	Cost of materials		All sources	Construction		
										Total	Net	
1997	138,850	570,990	367,719	14,964.6	7,739.9	41,947.7	41,052.5	52,585.9	148,530.3	146,798.8	92,802.2	1,211.1

Source: *Economic Census of the United States*, 1997. This is a newly defined industry. Data for prior years were unavailable at the time of publication but may become available over time. "Net" under "Construction" is construction revenue net of the costs of subcontracts.

DISTRIBUTION AMONG SIC-BASED INDUSTRIES - 1997

SIC	Industry	Estab-lish-ments	Employment		Cost of Power & Materials ($ mil)	Revenues ($ mil)			Value Added ($ mil)
			Total (000)	Payroll ($ mil)		All Sources	Construction		
							Total	Net	
152100	General contractors--single-family houses	116,537.0	438,033	10,314.5	24,427.0	79,380.9	78,546.1	52,802.4	29,210.23
153110	Operative builders (pt)	19,781.0	125,106	4,402.2	17,285.8	67,838.2	66,965.1	39,024.2	22,611.46
874121	Management services (pt)	2,531.0	7,852	247.9	235.0	1,311.2	1,287.5	975.5	764.24

Source: 1997 *Economic Census*. U.S. Census Bureau, U.S. Department of Commerce, August 1997. SIC codes ending in two zeroes represent complete 4-digit SICs. All others are parts of 4-digit SIC industries. Items showing a dash (-) indicate that data are not available because of disclosure problems.

SIC INDUSTRIES RELATED TO NAICS 233210

SIC	Industry	1990	1991	1992	1993	1994	1995	1996	1997
1521	**Single-Family Housing Construction**								
	Establishments (number)	100,290e	103,830e	107,495	111,289p	115,218p	119,284p	123,495p	127,854p
	Employment (thousands)	400.8e	402.3e	403.8	405.3e	406.8e	408.3e	409.8e	411.4e
	Revenues ($ million)	45,486.2e	47,435.7e	49,468.8	51,589.1e	53,800.2e	56,106.1e	58,510.8e	61,018.6e
1531	**Operative Builders***								
	Establishments (number)	10,396	9,279	16,989	11,225	15,678p	15,061p	14,468p	13,899p
	Employment (thousands)	120.5	88.7	114.2	96.7	97.6e	90.3e	83.5e	77.2e
	Revenues ($ million)	50,369.3e	48,201.9e	46,127.7	44,142.8e	42,243.3e	40,425.6e	38,686.0e	37,021.3e
8741	**Management Services***								
	Establishments (number)	15,267	16,556	20,186	21,920	23,803	21,674	23,348p	24,255p
	Employment (thousands)	285.2	306.6	285.1	357.7	386.3	312.7	368.9p	381.9p
	Revenues ($ million)	20,627.0	21,788.0	23,774.0	23,373.0	24,328.0	27,611.0	27,569.0	28,870.9p

Source: *Economic Census of the United States*, 1992, annual surveys of economic sectors conducted by the Bureau of the Census, and estimates or projections based on the 1982-1992 period; not all data are shown. 'e' marks estimates made by the editors; 'p' indicates projections based on time series. A dash (-) indicates that data for this SIC or year were not available. * Indicates that only a portion of this industry is present within the NAICS data. If no * is shown, the entire industry is contained within the NAICS data.

INDICES OF CHANGE

Years	Estab-lish-ments	Employment		Payroll ($ mil)		Costs ($ mil)		Value Added ($ mil)	Revenues ($ mil)			Capital expend. ($ mil)
		Total	Constr. workers	Total	Worker payroll	Total	Cost of materials		All sources	Construction		
										Total	Net	
1997	100.0	100.0	100.0	100.0	100.0	100.0	100.0	100.0	100.0	100.0	100.0	100.0

Sources: Same as General Statistics. The values shown reflect change from the base year, 1997. Values above 100 mean greater than 1997, values below 100 mean less than 1997, and a value of 100 in years other than 1997 means same as 1997. Indices are calculated only for Census years. Data are the most recent available at this level of detail.

SELECTED RATIOS

For 1997	Avg. of Sector	Analyzed Industry	Index	For 1997	Avg. of Sector	Analyzed Industry	Index
Employees per establishment	8.6	4.1	48	Value added per establishment	584,730	378,725	65
Construction workers per establishment	6.6	2.6	40	Value added per employee	67,759	92,096	136
Payroll per establishment	265,343	107,775	41	Value added per construction worker	88,592	143,006	161
Payroll per employee	30,748	26,208	85	Revenues per establishment	1,307,915	1,069,718	82
Payroll per construction worker	27,622	21,048	76	Revenues per employee	151,563	260,128	172
Costs per establishment	367,737	302,108	82	Revenues per construction worker	198,161	403,923	204
Costs per employee	42,614	73,465	172	CR as % of total revenues	98.48	98.83	100
Costs per construction worker	55,716	114,075	205	Net CR as % of CR	72.40	63.22	87
Materials as % of costs	95.75	97.87	102	Investment per establishment	22,948	8,722	38
Costs as % of revenues	28.12	28.24	100	Investment per employee	2,659	2,121	80
Costs as % of construction revenues	28.55	28.57	100	Investment per construction worker	3,477	3,294	95

Sources: Same as General Statistics. The 'Average of Sector' column represents the average for all industries in this sector. The Index shows the relationship between the Average and the Analyzed Industry. For example, 100 means that they are equal; 500 that the Analyzed Industry is five times the average; 50 means that the Analyzed Industry is half the national average. 'na' is used to show that data are 'not available'. CR stands for "construction revenues" and "Net CR" is construction revenues net of subcontract expenses.

LEADING COMPANIES   Number shown: **75**   Total sales ($ mil): **59,445**   Total employment (000): **111.4**

Company Name	Address				CEO Name	Phone	Co. Type	Sales ($ mil)	Empl. (000)
Centex Corp.	PO Box 19000	Dallas	TX	75219	Laurence E Hirsch	214-981-5000	P	5,155	13.2
Hechinger Investment Co.	1801 McCormick Dr	Largo	MD	20774	Mark Schwartz Jr	301-341-1000	R	4,100	26.0
Kaufman and Broad Home Corp.	10990 Wilshire Blvd	Los Angeles	CA	90024	Bruce Karatz	310-231-4000	P	3,836	3.5
Pulte Corp.	33 Bloomfield Hills	Bloomfield Hills	MI	48304	Robert K Burgess	248-647-2750	P	3,830	4.3
D.R. Horton Inc.	1901 Ascension	Arlington	TX	76006	Ricard Beckwilt	817-856-8200	P	3,156	3.4
Lennar Corp.	700 NW 107th Ave	Miami	FL	33172	Leonard Miller	305-559-4000	P	3,119	4.1
Ryland Group Inc.	11000 Broken Land	Columbia	MD	21044	R Chad Dreier	410-715-7000	P	2,009	2.1
NVR Inc.	7601 Lewinsville Rd	McLean	VA	22102	Dwight C Schar	703-761-2000	P	1,943	3.1
Pulte Diversified Companies Inc.	33 Bloomfield Hill	Bloomfield Hills	MI	48304	Robert K Burgess	248-644-7300	S	1,851*	3.0
Walter Industries Inc.	PO Box 31601	Tampa	FL	33631	Kenneth Hyatt	813-871-4811	P	1,618	7.7
Turner Steiner International	375 Hudson St	New York	NY	10014	Thomas Leppert	212-229-6157	R	1,578*	3.2
U.S. Home Corp.	PO Box 2863	Houston	TX	77252	Isaac Heimbinder	713-877-2311	P	1,498	2.0
Toll Brothers Inc.	3103 Philmont Ave	Hopewell Jctn	PA	19006	Robert I Toll	215-938-8000	P	1,456	1.6
Beazer Homes USA Inc.	5775 Peachtree	Atlanta	GA	30342	Brian Beazer	404-250-3420	P	1,394	1.5
Richmond American Homes Inc.	3600 S Yosemite St	Denver	CO	80237	Larry A Mizel	307-773-1100	S	1,260	1.4
Shea Homes (Walnut, California)	655 Brea Canyon Rd	Walnut	CA	91789	Roy Humphreys	909-598-1841	D	1,245	0.6
Standard Pacific Corp.	1565 W MacArthur	Costa Mesa	CA	92626	S J Scarborough	714-668-4300	P	1,199	0.6
A.G. Spanos Construction Inc.	P O Box 7126	Stockton	CA	95267	Dean Spanos	209-478-7954	R	1,175	0.6
Continental Homes Holding Corp.	7001 N Scottsdale	Scottsdale	AZ	85253	W Thomas Hickcox	602-483-0006	P	1,124	1.0
Rouse Co.	10275 L Patuxent	Columbia	MD	21044	Anothy W Deering	410-992-6000	P	977	4.1
Hovnanian Enterprises Inc.	PO Box 500	Red Bank	NJ	07701	Ara K Hovnanian	732-747-7800	P	948	1.2
M/I Schottenstein Homes Inc.	3 Eastern Oval, #500	Columbus	OH	43219	Irving E Schottenstein	614-418-8000	P	852	0.8
Engle Homes Inc.	123 NW 13th St	Boca Raton	FL	33432	Alec Engelstein	561-391-4012	P	742	0.9
Lewis Homes	P O Box 670	Upland	CA	91785	John Goodman	909-985-0971	R	700*	0.9
Weekley Homes Inc.	1300 Post Oak Blvd	Houston	TX	77056	David Weekley	713-963-0500	R	607	0.8
Shapell Industries Inc.	8383 Wilshire Blvd	Beverly Hills	CA	90211	Nathan Shapell	323-655-7330	R	554	0.4
Greystone Homes Inc.	6767 Forest Lawn	Los Angeles	CA	90068	Jack R Harter	213-436-6300	S	525*	0.5
Jim Walter Homes Inc.	P O Box 31601	Tampa	FL	33631	Robert W Michael	813-871-4611	S	459*	1.1
Crossmann Communities Inc.	9210 N Meridian St	Indianapolis	IN	46260	Richard H Crosser	317-843-9514	P	422	0.6
John Wieland Homes Inc.	1950 Sullivan Rd	Atlanta	GA	30337	Russell Terry	770-996-1400	R	389	0.8
Drees Co.	211 Grandview Dr	Fort Mitchell	KY	41017	Ralph A Drees	606-578-4200	R	366	0.7
Washington Homes Inc.	1802 Brightseat Rd	Landover	MD	20785	G A DeCesaris Jr	301-772-8900	P	359	0.4
Arvida/JMB Partners	900 N Michigan Ave	Chicago	IL	60611	Judd D Malkin	312-915-1987	R	356*	0.7
Fralin and Waldron Inc.	PO Box 20069	Roanoke	VA	24018	Karen Waldron	540-774-4415	R	354*	0.3
Schult Homes Corp.	PO Box 151	Middlebury	IN	46540	Walter Wells	219-825-5881	R	348	0.2
Henry Fischer Builder Inc.	2670 Chancellor Dr	Crestview Hills	KY	41017	Henry Fischer	606-341-4709	R	311*	0.3
Midwest Drywall Company Inc.	PO Box 771170	Wichita	KS	67277	Steve Nienke	316-722-9559	R	300*	1.2
Devcon Construction Inc.	555 Los Coches St	Milpitas	CA	95035	Gary Filizetti	408-942-8200	R	300*	0.3
Taylor-Morley Inc.	1224 Fernridge	St. Louis	MO	63141	Harry Morley	314-434-9000	R	293*	0.3
Dominion Homes Inc.	P O Box 7166	Dublin	OH	43017	Douglas G Borror	614-761-6000	P	278	0.4
Lexington Homes Inc.	800 S Milwaukee	Arlington H.	IL	60004	Douglas Brown	847-362-9100	S	271*	0.3
John Mourier Construction Inc.	1830 Vernon St	Roseville	CA	95678	John Mourier	916-786-3040	R	269*	0.2
Zaring National Corp.	11300 Cornell	Cincinnati	OH	45242	Daniel W Jones	513-489-8849	P	268	0.5
Meritage Corp.	6613 N Scottsdale	Scottsdale	AZ	85250	Steven J Hilton	480-998-7000	P	262	0.2
Town and Country Homes Inc.	1603 16th St	Oak Brook	IL	60521	Micheal Ryan	708-617-5577	R	261*	0.3
Diamond Home Services Inc.	222 Church St	Woodstock	IL	60098	Geoffrey H Foreman	815-334-1414	P	245	1.2
Colony Homes L.P.	5134 Hwy 92 E	Woodstock	GA	30188	Thomas Bradbury	404-928-0092	R	241*	0.2
Levitt Corp.	7777 Glades Rd	Boca Raton	FL	33434	Elliott Wiener	561-482-5100	S	241*	0.2
Ryan Homes	7601 Lewinsville Rd	Mc Lean	VA	22102	Dwight Schar	703-761-3000	S	222*	1.0
Paul W. Davis Systems Inc.	1 Independent Dr	Jacksonville	FL	32202	Scott Baker	904-737-2779	R	220*	<0.1
CHI Construction Co.	7001 N Scottsdale	Scottsdale	AZ	85253	Tom Davis	480-483-0006	R	199*	0.2
Capital Pacific Holdings Inc.	4100 MacArthur	Newport Beach	CA	92660	Hadi Makarechain	949-622-8400	P	192	0.3
New Fortis Corp.	PO Box 485	King	NC	27021	Marvin Gentry	336-983-4321	R	191*	0.2
Estridge Group	1041 W Main St	Carmel	IN	46032	Paul Estridge Jr	317-846-7311	R	190*	0.2
AMREP Corp.	641 Lexington Ave	New York	NY	10022	Edward B Cloues II	212-541-7300	P	184	1.2
H.J. Russell and Co.	504 Fair St S W	Atlanta	GA	30313	Herman J Russell	404-330-0800	R	184	0.7
Croom Construction Co.	4733 N A-1-A	Vero Beach	FL	32963	David Croom	561-231-1703	R	179*	0.2
Kopf Construction Corp.	420 Avon Beldin Rd	Avon Lake	OH	44012	HR Kopf	440-933-6908	R	178*	0.2
G. L. Homes of Florida	1401 Univ Drv	Coral Springs	FL	33071		954-753-1730	R	175	0.2
Melody Homes Inc.	11031 Sheridan Blvd	Westminster	CO	80030	Dave L Oyler	303-466-1831	S	172	0.2
Starrett Corp.	One Park Ave	New York	NY	10022	Bruce Reshen	212-751-3100	P	167	1.6
Dura Companies	5740 Decateur Blvd	Indianapolis	IN	46241	Paul Shoopman	317-821-8100	R	158*	0.1
J.R. Roberts Enterprises Inc.	7745 Greenback Ln	Citrus Heights	CA	95610	Robert C Hall Jr	916-729-5600	R	153*	0.2
Pasquinelli Construction Co.	905 W 175th St	Homewood	IL	60430	Bruno Pasquinelli	708-957-9020	R	152*	0.1
A.P. Orleans Co.	1 Greenwood Sq	Bensalem	PA	19020	Jeffrey P Orleans	215-245-7500	P	151	0.2
Warmington Homes	3090 Pullman St	Costa Mesa	CA	92626	Timothy P Hogan	714-557-5511	R	150*	0.1
Wohlsen Construction Co.	PO Box 7066	Lancaster	PA	17604	J Gary Langmuir	717-299-2500	R	149*	0.4
All American Homes Inc.	PO Box 451	Decatur	IN	46733		219-724-9171	S	146*	0.5
Bradbury & Stamm Construction	P O Box 10850	Albuquerque	NM	87184	James N King	505-765-1200	R	145	0.3
H.J. Stabile and Son Inc.	21 Manchester St	Merrimack	NH	03054	John P Stabile	603-889-0318	R	131*	0.1
Cooper Communities Inc.	1801 Forest Hills	Bella Vista	AR	72715	John Cooper Jr	501-855-6151	R	130*	0.5
William E. Buchan Inc.	11555 Northop Way	Bellevue	WA	98004	William E Buchan	425-828-6424	R	126*	0.1
Royce Homes Inc.	14614 Falling Creek	Houston	TX	77068	Michael Manners	281-440-5091	R	120	0.1
Miller Construction Co.	614 S Federal Hwy	Fort Lauderdale	FL	33301	Tom Miller	954-764-6550	R	119*	0.1
BOR-SON Cos.	2001 Killebrew	Minneapolis	MN	55440	W Arthur Young	612-854-8444	R	117	0.4

Source: *Ward's Business Directory of U.S. Private and Public Companies, Volumes 1 and 2, 2000.* The company type code used is as follows: P - Public, R - Private, S - Subsidiary, D - Division, J - Joint Venture, A - Affiliate, G - Group, N - Company type not reported. Sales are in millions of dollars, employees are in thousands. An asterisk (*) indicates an estimated sales volume. The symbol < stands for 'less than'. Company names and addresses are truncated, in some cases, to fit into the available space.

COST DETAILS

Item	Cost ($ mil)	% of total	Per $1,000 of Revenue	Item	Cost ($ mil)	% of total	Per $1,000 of Revenue
All costs	95,944.3	100.000	646.0	Total Rentals	668.0	0.696	4.5
Cost of supplies	41,052.5	42.788	276.4	Equipment	304.9	0.318	2.1
Subcontracts	53,996.6	56.279	363.5	Buildings	363.1	0.378	2.4
Power, fuel, lubricants	895.2	0.933	6.0	Services purchased	1,130.9	1.179	7.6
Electricity	279.1	0.291	1.9	Communications	610.2	0.636	4.1
Natural gas	65.8	0.069	0.4	Building repairs	92.1	0.096	0.6
Gasoline and diesel	523.6	0.546	3.5	Machinery repairs	428.6	0.447	2.9
Highway	448.2	0.467	3.0				
Offroad	75.3	0.079	0.5				
Other power	26.7	0.028	0.2				

Source: Economic Census of the United States, 1997. Revenues referred to are total industry revenues for the current NAICS industry.

CONSTRUCTION PRODUCT DETAILS

Construction type	Value of construction work ($ mil and %)							
	Total		New construction		Additions, alterations, reconstruction		Maintenance and repair	
	Value	%	Value	%	Value	%	Value	%
Total	**146,798.8**	**100.0**	**117,641.7**	**100.0**	**22,881.9**	**100.0**	**5,143.5**	**100.0**
Building construction, total	**145,310.5**	**99.0**	**117,338.8**	**99.7**	**22,839.9**	**99.8**	**5,131.9**	**99.8**
Single-family houses, detached	123,563.6	84.2	101,825.0	86.6	17,990.1	78.6	3,748.5	72.9
Single-family houses, attached	15,460.7	10.5	12,276.4	10.4	2,513.7	11.0	670.6	13.0
Apartment buildings, condos and cooperatives	1,971.8	1.3	1,144.2	1.0	552.0	2.4	(S)	-
Office buildings	1,186.0	0.8	559.2	0.5	507.5	2.2	(S)	-
All other commercial buildings, nec	1,152.4	0.8	533.9	0.5	497.7	2.2	120.8	2.3
Other building construction	1,976.1	1.3	1,000.1	0.9	778.9	3.4	197.1	3.8
Nonbuilding construction, total	**356.6**	**0.2**	**303.0**	**0.3**	**42.1**	**0.2**	**11.6**	**0.2**
Other nonbuilding construction, nec	356.6	0.2	303.0	0.3	42.1	0.2	11.6	0.2
Construction work, nsk	**1,131.6**	**0.8**	NA	-	NA	-	NA	-

Source: Economic Census of the United States, 1997. Bold items are headers. (D) stands for data withheld to protect competitive information. (S) indicates instances where data do not meet publications standards.

LOCATION BY STATE AND REGIONAL CONCENTRATION

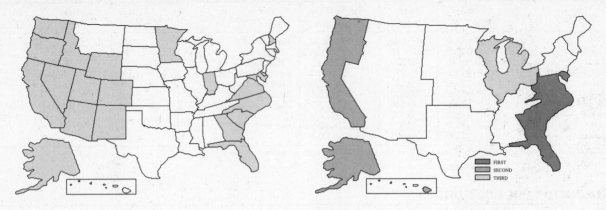

FIRST
SECOND
THIRD

INDUSTRY DATA BY STATE

State	Estab lish- ments	Employment			Compensation		Production				Capital Exp. ($ mil)
		Total	Workers	Total as % of US	Payroll per Employee	Wages per Worker	Costs ($ mil)	Value Added ($ mil)	Reve- nues ($ mil)	% of US	
California	12,998	61,091	40,283	10.70	29,998	23,836	3,358.1	7,407.7	18,382.6	12.38	124.9
Florida	6,739	35,519	17,231	6.22	28,350	21,179	3,520.1	3,836.0	12,217.3	8.23	87.6
Texas	5,142	25,564	11,512	4.48	33,054	21,505	2,948.6	3,198.6	10,138.2	6.83	57.7
Illinois	5,705	24,050	14,750	4.21	28,410	22,321	1,504.7	2,330.7	6,165.4	4.15	53.9
North Carolina	5,455	23,313	15,078	4.08	24,416	19,434	1,984.4	2,136.3	6,068.2	4.09	43.6
Ohio	5,386	22,061	13,926	3.86	25,517	20,930	1,675.7	1,977.2	5,445.1	3.67	42.1
Pennsylvania	6,317	25,506	17,211	4.47	24,388	20,949	1,719.5	1,930.9	5,242.1	3.53	47.3
Virginia	4,881	20,967	13,176	3.67	24,732	19,606	1,566.0	1,741.5	5,209.7	3.51	33.2
Michigan	6,083	24,791	16,766	4.34	24,501	20,557	1,432.4	1,924.7	5,179.5	3.49	44.1
Arizona	2,305	14,612	8,721	2.56	29,030	21,360	903.7	1,497.2	4,950.8	3.33	35.4
Georgia	3,595	12,844	7,396	2.25	26,663	20,316	1,602.7	1,619.9	4,771.7	3.21	27.9
New York	6,842	22,738	15,571	3.98	25,786	23,634	1,501.1	1,728.9	4,614.1	3.11	41.5
New Jersey	4,615	16,331	10,678	2.86	29,224	22,751	1,186.9	1,708.1	4,434.2	2.99	28.3
Washington	5,660	18,805	13,406	3.29	24,897	21,688	1,197.0	1,602.5	4,219.2	2.84	101.6
Maryland	3,675	15,773	9,711	2.76	28,497	22,849	1,246.7	1,356.3	4,092.9	2.76	26.5
Colorado	3,026	12,842	7,547	2.25	29,908	22,624	937.0	1,327.1	4,091.0	2.75	30.1
Indiana	3,769	16,532	11,229	2.90	24,120	20,037	1,186.1	1,298.7	3,567.8	2.40	33.3
Minnesota	2,640	9,927	6,180	1.74	27,671	22,585	919.2	968.4	2,988.0	2.01	27.6
Nevada	976	7,344	4,435	1.29	32,131	24,378	481.6	1,035.3	2,873.2	1.93	28.3
Tennessee	2,588	10,454	7,170	1.83	22,872	17,748	957.4	887.7	2,710.9	1.83	23.9
Missouri	3,204	14,220	10,030	2.49	22,448	20,013	856.5	968.5	2,590.0	1.74	24.8
Oregon	3,150	9,715	6,801	1.70	23,782	19,761	756.5	886.2	2,516.3	1.69	17.7
Wisconsin	2,959	11,185	7,723	1.96	24,249	21,278	690.5	841.2	2,502.1	1.68	22.8
Massachusetts	2,840	10,513	7,024	1.84	28,559	24,006	768.7	950.2	2,499.9	1.68	22.4
South Carolina	2,436	8,616	5,772	1.51	21,883	17,394	828.5	728.2	2,314.9	1.56	16.1
Kentucky	1,733	7,292	4,677	1.28	22,197	17,292	632.4	620.3	1,785.5	1.20	12.3
Alabama	1,977	7,735	5,065	1.35	19,720	16,057	563.8	560.9	1,608.5	1.08	11.5
Connecticut	1,800	5,845	3,750	1.02	30,161	25,699	436.7	522.4	1,439.0	0.97	12.4
Kansas	1,373	5,888	4,270	1.03	21,685	18,576	423.5	463.7	1,409.3	0.95	12.7
Utah	1,662	5,920	4,269	1.04	23,833	19,658	357.9	524.3	1,380.8	0.93	11.5
New Mexico	1,343	5,914	4,659	1.04	22,679	19,771	359.3	337.8	1,075.7	0.72	10.8
Louisiana	1,287	4,560	2,857	0.80	21,387	16,375	320.4	290.7	908.3	0.61	7.3
Iowa	1,531	6,211	4,854	1.09	20,100	18,343	304.4	342.5	883.4	0.59	10.8
Nebraska	919	3,290	2,481	0.58	22,211	18,911	243.2	309.2	791.0	0.53	7.3
Oklahoma	878	3,012	1,633	0.53	22,984	20,124	257.2	265.5	766.0	0.52	5.9
Idaho	1,123	3,697	2,869	0.65	20,848	17,318	239.4	249.1	699.1	0.47	(S)
New Hampshire	831	2,998	2,072	0.53	26,028	22,624	228.7	250.6	658.1	0.44	6.4
Mississippi	896	3,162	2,348	0.55	18,749	16,109	247.5	194.9	604.5	0.41	4.1
Arkansas	1,028	3,110	2,158	0.54	19,876	17,564	198.0	203.1	551.1	0.37	5.5
Delaware	556	2,248	1,548	0.39	25,784	20,244	180.4	153.7	515.8	0.35	4.3
Maine	956	3,298	2,493	0.58	21,110	18,957	150.2	173.7	456.8	0.31	5.6
West Virginia	1,504	4,908	3,965	0.86	16,729	15,125	187.5	175.3	445.0	0.30	6.7
Montana	959	2,534	1,966	0.44	17,880	16,467	138.0	136.0	381.4	0.26	4.3
Alaska	429	1,808	1,353	0.32	23,392	21,090	137.4	144.6	363.4	0.24	4.4
Wyoming	541	2,216	1,857	0.39	21,806	20,160	104.9	127.8	342.9	0.23	3.8
Rhode Island	610	1,881	1,364	0.33	23,404	20,594	81.3	167.4	335.1	0.23	3.1
Vermont	641	2,220	1,636	0.39	22,218	19,756	106.8	123.0	333.0	0.22	2.9
South Dakota	438	1,530	1,250	0.27	20,412	19,002	89.4	87.5	252.6	0.17	2.0
North Dakota	285	979	768	0.17	17,473	15,754	47.4	42.7	114.1	0.08	1.5
D.C.	54	393	252	0.07	25,173	20,905	13.6	14.1	46.3	0.03	0.3
Hawaii	510	3,028	1,979	0.53	31,126	25,444	169.0	(S)	(S)	-	(S)

Source: Economic Census of the U.S., 1997. Data are sorted by 1997 revenues or establishments. (D) means data suppression to prevent disclosure of company data. (S) means that data did not meet statistical standards for publication. A dash (-) is used when data are unavailable or cannot be calculated. Data followed by an * indicate the midpoint of a range. The ranges are: for 10, 0-19; for 60, 20-99, for 175, 100-249, for 375, 250-499, for 750, 500-999. Higher values are multiples of those shown, e.g., 3,750 is the midpoint of the range 2,500-4,999. Shaded *states* on the state map indicate those states which have proportionately greater representation in the industry than would be indicated by the state's population; the ratio is based on total revenues or number of establishments. Shaded *regions* indicate where the industry is regionally most concentrated.

NAICS 233220 - MULTIFAMILY HOUSING CONSTRUCTION

GENERAL STATISTICS

Years	Estab-lish-ments	Employment		Payroll ($ mil)		Costs ($ mil)		Value Added ($ mil)	Revenues ($ mil)			Capital expend. ($ mil)
		Total	Constr. workers	Total	Worker payroll	Total	Cost of materials		All sources	Construction Total	Net	
1997	7,544	58,896	40,082	1,766.6	1,022.3	3,762.6	3,678.1	3,788.8	14,716.7	14,487.3	7,322.0	95.8

Source: *Economic Census of the United States*, 1997. This is a newly defined industry. Data for prior years were unavailable at the time of publication but may become available over time. "Net" under "Construction" is construction revenue net of the costs of subcontracts.

DISTRIBUTION AMONG SIC-BASED INDUSTRIES - 1997

SIC	Industry	Estab-lish-ments	Employment		Cost of Power & Materials ($ mil)	Revenues ($ mil)			Value Added ($ mil)
			Total (000)	Payroll ($ mil)		All Sources	Construction Total	Net	
152220	General contractors--residential buildings, other than single-family (pt)	6,341.0	47,742	1,396.4	2,816.6	11,059.4	10,929.3	5,527.4	2,840.84
153120	Operative builders (pt)	693.0	8,541	274.4	775.0	2,902.0	2,816.4	1,459.6	770.26
874122	Management services (pt)	510.0	2,613	95.8	171.0	755.3	741.6	335.0	177.68

Source: 1997 *Economic Census*. U.S. Census Bureau, U.S. Department of Commerce, August 1997. SIC codes ending in two zeroes represent complete 4-digit SICs. All others are parts of 4-digit SIC industries. Items showing a dash (-) indicate that data are not available because of disclosure problems.

SIC INDUSTRIES RELATED TO NAICS 233220

SIC	Industry	1990	1991	1992	1993	1994	1995	1996	1997
1522	**Residential Construction, n.e.c.***								
	Establishments (number)	7,107e	6,791e	6,490	6,202p	5,927p	5,664p	5,413p	5,173p
	Employment (thousands)	60.0e	54.1e	48.8	44.0e	39.7e	35.8e	32.3e	29.1e
	Revenues ($ million)	9,855.5e	8,853.8e	7,954.0	7,145.6e	6,419.4e	5,767.0e	5,180.9e	4,654.3e
1531	**Operative Builders***								
	Establishments (number)	10,396	9,279	16,989	11,225	15,678p	15,061p	14,468p	13,899p
	Employment (thousands)	120.5	88.7	114.2	96.7	97.6e	90.3e	83.5e	77.2e
	Revenues ($ million)	50,369.3e	48,201.9e	46,127.7	44,142.8e	42,243.3e	40,425.6e	38,686.0e	37,021.3e
8741	**Management Services***								
	Establishments (number)	15,267	16,556	20,186	21,920	23,803	21,674	23,348p	24,255p
	Employment (thousands)	285.2	306.6	285.1	357.7	386.3	312.7	368.9p	381.9p
	Revenues ($ million)	20,627.0	21,788.0	23,774.0	23,373.0	24,328.0	27,611.0	27,569.0	28,870.9p

Source: *Economic Census of the United States*, 1992, annual surveys of economic sectors conducted by the Bureau of the Census, and estimates or projections based on the 1982-1992 period; not all data are shown. 'e' marks estimates made by the editors; 'p' indicates projections based on time series. A dash (-) indicates that data for this SIC or year were not available. * Indicates that only a portion of this industry is present within the NAICS data. If no * is shown, the entire industry is contained within the NAICS data.

INDICES OF CHANGE

Years	Estab-lish-ments	Employment		Payroll ($ mil)		Costs ($ mil)		Value Added ($ mil)	Revenues ($ mil)			Capital expend. ($ mil)
		Total	Constr. workers	Total	Worker payroll	Total	Cost of materials		All sources	Construction Total	Net	
1997	100.0	100.0	100.0	100.0	100.0	100.0	100.0	100.0	100.0	100.0	100.0	100.0

Sources: Same as General Statistics. The values shown reflect change from the base year, 1997. Values above 100 mean greater than 1997, values below 100 mean less than 1997, and a value of 100 in years other than 1997 means same as 1997. Indices are calculated only for Census years. Data are the most recent available at this level of detail.

SELECTED RATIOS

For 1997	Avg. of Sector	Analyzed Industry	Index	For 1997	Avg. of Sector	Analyzed Industry	Index
Employees per establishment	8.6	7.8	90	Value added per establishment	584,730	502,227	86
Construction workers per establishment	6.6	5.3	81	Value added per employee	67,759	64,330	95
Payroll per establishment	265,343	234,173	88	Value added per construction worker	88,592	94,526	107
Payroll per employee	30,748	29,995	98	Revenues per establishment	1,307,915	1,950,782	149
Payroll per construction worker	27,622	25,505	92	Revenues per employee	151,563	249,876	165
Costs per establishment	367,737	498,754	136	Revenues per construction worker	198,161	367,165	185
Costs per employee	42,614	63,885	150	CR as % of total revenues	98.48	98.44	100
Costs per construction worker	55,716	93,873	168	Net CR as % of CR	72.40	50.54	70
Materials as % of costs	95.75	97.75	102	Investment per establishment	22,948	12,699	55
Costs as % of revenues	28.12	25.57	91	Investment per employee	2,659	1,627	61
Costs as % of construction revenues	28.55	25.97	91	Investment per construction worker	3,477	2,390	69

Sources: Same as General Statistics. The 'Average of Sector' column represents the average for all industries in this sector. The Index shows the relationship between the Average and the Analyzed Industry. For example, 100 means that they are equal; 500 that the Analyzed Industry is five times the average; 50 means that the Analyzed Industry is half the national average. 'na' is used to show that data are 'not available'. CR stands for "construction revenues" and "Net CR" is construction revenues net of subcontract expenses.

LEADING COMPANIES   Number shown: **75**   Total sales ($ mil): **26,996**   Total employment (000): **91.7**

Company Name	Address				CEO Name	Phone	Co. Type	Sales ($ mil)	Empl. (000)
Bechtel Corp.	50 Beale St	San Francisco	CA	94105	RP Bechtel	415-768-1234	R	8,250*	30.0
Turner Corp.	901 Main St	Dallas	TX	75202	Robert E Fee	214-752-4323	P	3,699	32.0
Turner Construction Co.	375 Hudson St	New York	NY	10014	Robert Fee	212-229-6000	R	1,407*	3.4
Shea Homes (Walnut, California)	655 Brea Canyon Rd	Walnut	CA	91789	Roy Humphreys	909-598-1841	D	1,245	0.6
Perini Corp.	Box 9160	Framingham	MA	01701	Robert Band	508-628-2000	P	1,036	2.7
Hovnanian Enterprises Inc.	PO Box 500	Red Bank	NJ	07701	Ara K Hovnanian	732-747-7800	P	948	1.2
Lewis Homes	P O Box 670	Upland	CA	91785	John Goodman	909-985-0971	R	700*	0.9
Fortress Group Inc.	1650 Tysons Blvd	McLean	VA	22102	George C Yeonas	703-442-4545	P	693	1.2
Suffolk Construction Inc.	65 Allerton St	Boston	MA	02119	John F Fish	617-445-3500	R	540	0.5
Hardaway Group Inc.	615 Main St	Nashville	TN	37206	LH Hardaway Jr	615-254-5461	R	388*	0.9
Drees Co.	211 Grandview Dr	Fort Mitchell	KY	41017	Ralph A Drees	606-578-4200	R	366	0.7
Arvida/JMB Partners	900 N Michigan Ave	Chicago	IL	60611	Judd D Malkin	312-915-1987	R	356*	0.7
Fralin and Waldron Inc.	PO Box 20069	Roanoke	VA	24018	Karen Waldron	540-774-4415	R	354*	0.3
Pardee Construction Co.	10880 Wilshire	Los Angeles	CA	90024	David Landon	310-475-3525	S	339*	0.4
Henry Fischer Builder Inc.	2670 Chancellor Dr	Crestview Hills	KY	41017	Henry Fischer	606-341-4709	R	311*	0.3
Midwest Drywall Company Inc.	PO Box 771170	Wichita	KS	67277	Steve Nienke	316-722-9559	R	300*	1.2
Devcon Construction Inc.	555 Los Coches St	Milpitas	CA	95035	Gary Filizetti	408-942-8200	R	300*	0.3
Kitchell Corp.	1707 E Highland	Phoenix	AZ	85016	William C Schubert	602-264-4411	R	289	0.7
Lexington Homes Inc.	800 S Milwaukee	Arlington H.	IL	60004	Douglas Brown	847-362-9100	S	271*	0.3
Lease Crutcher Lewis	107 Spring St	Seattle	WA	98104	Bill Lewis	206-622-0500	R	251	0.5
Fletcher Pacific Construction Ltd.	707 Richards St	Honolulu	HI	96813	Dennis N Watts	808-533-5000	R	250	0.8
McBride & Son Management Co.	1 McBride	Chesterfield	MO	63005	Michael Arri	314-537-2000	R	225*	0.5
JPI Investments Inc.	600 E Colinas	Irving	TX	75039	Robert D Page	972-556-1700	R	200	1.0
Capital Pacific Holdings Inc.	4100 MacArthur	Newport Beach	CA	92660	Hadi Makarechain	949-622-8400	P	192	0.3
Croom Construction Co.	4733 N A-1-A	Vero Beach	FL	32963	David Croom	561-231-1703	R	179*	0.2
Kopf Construction Corp.	420 Avon Beldin Rd	Avon Lake	OH	44012	HR Kopf	440-933-6908	R	178*	0.2
Hunt Building Corp.	PO Box 12220	El Paso	TX	79913	Woddy L Hunt	915-533-1122	R	171	0.2
Bradbury & Stamm Construction	P O Box 10850	Albuquerque	NM	87184	James N King	505-765-1200	R	145	0.3
H.J. Stabile and Son Inc.	21 Manchester St	Merrimack	NH	03054	John P Stabile	603-889-0318	R	131*	0.1
Cooper Communities Inc.	1801 Forest Hills	Bella Vista	AR	72715	John Cooper Jr	501-855-6151	R	130*	0.5
A.J. Etkin Construction Co.	30445 Northwestern	Farmington Hills	MI	48333	Thomas H Landry	248-737-5800	S	128*	0.2
Centex-Rooney Construction Inc.	6300 N W 5th Way	Fort Lauderdale	FL	33309	Bob L Moss	954-771-7122	S	120*	0.2
Miller Construction Co.	614 S Federal Hwy	Fort Lauderdale	FL	33301	Tom Miller	954-764-6550	R	119*	0.1
Wesseln Construction Inc.	292 N Wilshire	Anaheim	CA	92801	Henry B Wesseln	714-772-0888	R	114*	0.3
Palace Construction Company Inc.	90 Galapago St	Denver	CO	80223	Lou Jahde	303-777-7999	R	108*	<0.1
Harkins Builders Inc.	12301 Old Columbia	Silver Spring	MD	20904	J P Blase Cooke	301-622-9000	R	106	0.2
Grupe Co.	3255 W March Ln	Stockton	CA	95219	Greenlaw Grupe Jr	209-473-6000	R	100*	0.4
Boyd and Co.	PO Box 23589	Columbia	SC	29224	Darnall W Boyd	803-788-3800	R	100*	0.2
Engelberth Construction Inc.	463 Mountain View	Colchester	VT	05446	Otto Engelberth	802-655-0100	R	95	0.2
Oriole Homes Corp.	1690 S Congress	Delray Beach	FL	33445	Mark A Levy	561-274-2000	P	87	0.1
Tompkins Builders	1333 H St NW	Washington	DC	20005	Edward Smalls	202-789-0770	R	85*	0.2
United Interior Resources Inc.	8200 Lovett Ave	Dallas	TX	75227	William H Holden	214-381-0101	R	85*	0.2
William Lyon Homes Inc.	P O Box 7520	Newport Beach	CA	92658	Doug Bauer	949-833-3600	R	84	0.2
Paul Risk Associates Inc.	11 W State St	Quarryville	PA	17566	Paul D Risk	717-786-7308	R	83*	<0.1
Shaw Construction L.L.C.	111 Kalamath St	Denver	CO	80223	Steve Meyer	303-825-4740	R	83	0.1
All Pool and Spa Inc.	905 Kalanianaole	Kailua	HI	96734	John King	808-261-8991	R	82*	<0.1
George Sollitt Construction Co.	790 N Central Ave	Wood Dale	IL	60191	Donald Maziarka	630-860-7333	R	80	0.2
Horst Construction Company Inc.	PO Box 3310	Lancaster	PA	17604	Randall L Horst	717-581-9900	S	78	0.2
Amerihost Properties Inc.	2400 E Devon Ave	Des Plaines	IL	60018	Michael P Holtz	847-298-4500	P	69	1.8
R.E. Purcell Construction Co.	PO Box 837	Odessa	FL	33556	Raymond Purcell	727-785-6567	R	67*	0.2
Tocci Building Corp.	130 New Boston St	Woburn	MA	01801	John L Tocci	781-935-5500	R	65	<0.1
Ukpeagvik Inupiat Corp.	PO Box 890	Barrow	AK	99723	Van D Edwardsen	907-852-4460	R	60*	0.2
Albert D. Seeno Construction Co.	4021 Port Chicago	Concord	CA	94520	Albert D Seeno JR	925-671-7711	R	60*	0.2
Segal and Morel Inc.	991 Route 22 W	Bridgewater	NJ	08807	Kenneth Segal	908-722-0505	R	59*	<0.1
DeLuca Enterprises Inc.	842 Durham Rd	Newtown	PA	18940	Alfonso DeLuca	215-598-3451	R	57*	<0.1
Masters Inc.	7891 Beachcraft Ave	Gaithersburg	MD	20879	Ron Bryant	301-948-8950	P	56	0.5
NorAm Construction Co.	1530 S W Taylor St	Portland	OR	97205	John Bradley	503-228-7177	R	54*	0.1
Greater Construction Corp.	1105 Kensington	Altamonte Sprgs	FL	32714	Robert A Mandell	407-869-0300	R	54	<0.1
Greenbriar Corp.	4265 Kellway Cir	Dallas	TX	75244	James R Gilley	972-407-8400	P	53	1.2
Abco Builders Inc.	2680 Abco Ct	Lithonia	GA	30058	CP Richards Jr	770-981-0350	R	53*	0.1
State Wide Investors Inc.	4401 Atlantic Ave	Long Beach	CA	90807	RE Hearrean	562-984-3500	R	53*	0.1
Glen Construction Company Inc.	9055 Comprint Ct	Gaithersburg	MD	20877	Michael Hubert	301-258-2700	R	51*	0.1
Bush Construction Corp.	4029 Ironbound Rd	Williamsburg	VA	23188	John J Digges	757-220-2874	R	50*	0.1
Calhoun Builders Inc.	PO Box 799	Mansfield	LA	71052	R Calhoun Jr	318-872-0286	R	50*	0.1
Dan Vos Construction Co.	6160 E Fulton	Ada	MI	49301	GL Vos	616-676-9169	R	50	<0.1
E.W. Corrigan Construction Co.	1900 Spring Rd	Oak Brook	IL	60521	William Nagy	630-571-4755	R	50*	<0.1
Allen and O'Hara Inc.	530 Oak Court Dr	Memphis	TN	38117	Paul O'Bower	901-345-7620	R	48*	<0.1
Andrew Roby General Contractor	P O Box 221416	Charlotte	NC	28222	Glen Haston	704-334-5477	R	47*	<0.1
Pangere Corp.	4050 W 4th Ave	Gary	IN	46406	Steve Pangere	219-949-1368	R	46*	0.3
Green Valley Corp.	701 N 1st St	San Jose	CA	95112	Barry Swenson	408-287-0246	R	46*	0.1
McStain Enterprises Inc.	75 Manhattan Dr	Boulder	CO	80303	TR Hoyt	303-494-5900	R	45	0.1
James K. Schuler & Associates	828 Fort Street Mall	Honolulu	HI	96813	James K Schuler	808-521-5661	R	45*	<0.1
Gethmann Construction Inc.	PO Box 160	Marshalltown	IA	50158	JB Gethmann	515-753-3555	R	43*	0.1
Stevens Construction Corp.	4001 W Mill Rd	Milwaukee	WI	53209	Gerald Henrich	414-358-3505	R	43*	0.1
McBride Construction Resources	224 Nickerson St	Seattle	WA	98109	Ken McBride	206-283-7121	R	42*	0.1

Source: Ward's Business Directory of U.S. Private and Public Companies, Volumes 1 and 2, 2000. The company type code used is as follows: P - Public, R - Private, S - Subsidiary, D - Division, J - Joint Venture, A - Affiliate, G - Group, N - Company type not reported. Sales are in millions of dollars, employees are in thousands. An asterisk (*) indicates an estimated sales volume. The symbol < stands for 'less than'. Company names and addresses are truncated, in some cases, to fit into the available space.

COST DETAILS

Item	Cost ($ mil)	% of total	Per $1,000 of Revenue	Item	Cost ($ mil)	% of total	Per $1,000 of Revenue
All costs	10,927.9	100.000	742.6	Total Rentals	90.2	0.825	6.1
Cost of supplies	3,678.1	33.658	249.9	Equipment	52.3	0.478	3.6
Subcontracts	7,165.3	65.569	486.9	Buildings	37.9	0.347	2.6
Power, fuel, lubricants	84.5	0.773	5.7	Services purchased	94.1	0.861	6.4
Electricity	33.6	0.307	2.3	Communications	57.9	0.530	3.9
Natural gas	5.8	0.053	0.4	Building repairs	7.0	0.064	0.5
Gasoline and diesel	42.7	0.390	2.9	Machinery repairs	29.2	0.268	2.0
Highway	37.0	0.338	2.5				
Offroad	5.7	0.052	0.4				
Other power	2.4	0.022	0.2				

Source: Economic Census of the United States, 1997. Revenues referred to are total industry revenues for the current NAICS industry.

CONSTRUCTION PRODUCT DETAILS

Construction type	Value of construction work ($ mil and %)							
	Total		New construction		Additions, alterations, reconstruction		Maintenance and repair	
	Value	%	Value	%	Value	%	Value	%
Total	**14,487.3**	**100.0**	**10,179.0**	**100.0**	**3,328.6**	**100.0**	**893.7**	**100.0**
Building construction, total	**14,283.3**	**98.6**	**10,081.2**	**99.0**	**3,312.8**	**99.5**	**889.3**	**99.5**
Single-family houses, detached	610.5	4.2	461.0	4.5	118.2	3.6	(S)	-
Single-family houses, attached	184.7	1.3	122.7	1.2	51.5	1.5	10.6	1.2
Apartment buildings, condos and cooperatives	11,543.8	79.7	8,289.5	81.4	2,514.9	75.6	739.4	82.7
All other residential buildings	338.1	2.3	203.1	2.0	(S)	-	(S)	-
Manufacturing and light industrial buildings	118.2	0.8	58.2	0.6	56.0	1.7	4.1	0.5
Manufacturing and light industrial warehouses	44.0	0.3	27.2	0.3	9.1	0.3	7.7	0.9
Hotels and motels	216.3	1.5	165.4	1.6	49.5	1.5	1.4	0.2
Office buildings	290.4	2.0	134.2	1.3	136.5	4.1	19.6	2.2
All other commercial buildings, nec	305.4	2.1	204.1	2.0	84.4	2.5	16.8	1.9
Educational buildings	177.1	1.2	77.8	0.8	89.7	2.7	9.6	1.1
Health care and institutional buildings	180.7	1.2	143.0	1.4	36.7	1.1	1.0	0.1
Public safety buildings	40.4	0.3	33.7	0.3	4.3	0.1	2.4	0.3
Amusement, social, and recreational buildings	78.4	0.5	54.6	0.5	22.6	0.7	1.2	0.1
Other building construction	155.4	1.1	106.9	1.0	42.4	1.3	(S)	-
Nonbuilding construction, total	**118.0**	**0.8**	**97.8**	**1.0**	**15.8**	**0.5**	**4.4**	**0.5**
Other nonbuilding construction, nec	118.0	0.8	97.8	1.0	15.8	0.5	4.4	0.5
Construction work, nsk	**86.0**	**0.6**	**NA**	**-**	**NA**	**-**	**NA**	**-**

Source: Economic Census of the United States, 1997. Bold items are headers. (D) stands for data withheld to protect competitive information. (S) indicates instances where data do not meet publications standards.

LOCATION BY STATE AND REGIONAL CONCENTRATION

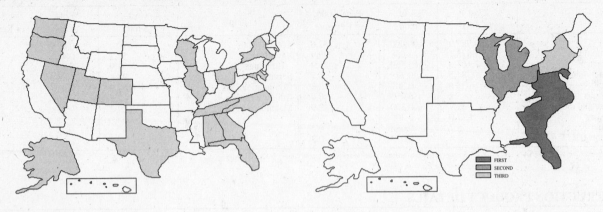

FIRST
SECOND
THIRD

INDUSTRY DATA BY STATE

State	Estab lish- ments	Employment			Compensation		Production				Capital Exp. ($ mil)
		Total	Workers	Total as % of US	Payroll per Employee	Wages per Worker	Costs ($ mil)	Value Added ($ mil)	Reve- nues ($ mil)	% of US	
Florida	485	7,490	4,728	12.72	33,052	26,626	648.9	578.4	2,385.5	16.21	22.5
New York	1,017	6,268	4,654	10.64	31,143	27,702	287.6	344.7	1,243.4	8.45	5.7
California	736	5,848	3,915	9.93	30,281	25,805	166.0	323.6	1,129.1	7.67	4.2
Texas	325	3,685	2,258	6.26	30,476	23,061	250.3	244.9	1,032.2	7.01	6.6
Ohio	267	2,731	1,479	4.64	26,372	23,446	220.6	132.0	745.7	5.07	5.2
Illinois	400	2,621	1,723	4.45	32,614	27,272	204.6	195.7	715.6	4.86	3.2
Georgia	156	1,263	779	2.14	31,013	23,275	160.8	100.3	506.3	3.44	2.6
North Carolina	234	1,693	1,133	2.87	29,173	23,120	131.9	118.6	496.9	3.38	4.6
Washington	292	1,780	1,173	3.02	32,561	30,494	103.1	110.2	424.8	2.89	1.7
Pennsylvania	291	1,604	1,199	2.72	27,640	26,003	116.2	98.6	394.5	2.68	1.9
New Jersey	263	1,393	1,066	2.37	30,263	26,459	107.7	83.8	363.3	2.47	2.3
Tennessee	123	1,374	1,054	2.33	27,376	24,360	101.0	88.8	351.8	2.39	1.8
Maryland	133	1,078	653	1.83	36,844	26,625	70.0	84.9	345.5	2.35	1.4
Michigan	146	1,135	763	1.93	31,535	25,498	77.4	89.8	334.8	2.27	9.7
Virginia	198	2,096	1,430	3.56	24,757	18,169	86.2	107.3	308.8	2.10	1.2
Colorado	209	1,004	591	1.70	28,833	26,080	64.9	89.7	306.9	2.09	1.2
Wisconsin	239	1,351	918	2.29	27,920	25,060	87.4	81.6	302.5	2.06	1.4
Massachusetts	163	1,458	1,077	2.48	32,451	28,950	53.8	99.3	276.3	1.88	1.4
Alabama	68	1,090	884	1.85	30,509	29,321	109.5	79.6	271.0	1.84	1.5
Oregon	179	1,024	676	1.74	30,909	28,675	91.7	52.2	260.9	1.77	1.7
Minnesota	98	491	354	0.83	34,159	31,065	46.3	40.8	228.7	1.55	0.4
Indiana	156	935	641	1.59	24,202	21,270	73.7	51.4	222.6	1.51	0.6
Utah	95	735	521	1.25	25,117	18,566	33.0	50.9	184.1	1.25	0.8
Missouri	235	975	724	1.66	22,897	20,228	46.2	57.9	183.0	1.24	1.0
Arizona	87	642	429	1.09	26,298	22,345	24.0	41.9	175.9	1.20	1.0
South Carolina	55	334	227	0.57	32,132	21,855	32.1	20.1	137.7	0.94	0.4
Iowa	94	534	354	0.91	28,483	21,299	30.7	48.6	137.5	0.93	1.0
Kentucky	66	737	573	1.25	25,406	22,550	34.9	40.0	132.9	0.90	0.5
Louisiana	48	699	566	1.19	28,960	24,456	33.6	45.5	116.1	0.79	0.8
Kansas	44	568	421	0.96	33,484	28,919	26.6	31.8	116.1	0.79	1.5
Nevada	43	456	396	0.77	24,412	21,242	27.4	27.2	104.6	0.71	0.2
Alaska	30	342	252	0.58	40,529	37,869	20.9	19.3	78.8	0.54	0.3
Nebraska	12	185	114	0.31	27,876	23,447	16.8	8.9	58.5	0.40	0.5
Connecticut	78	277	209	0.47	29,617	26,311	13.0	20.7	52.3	0.36	0.3
Arkansas	24	286	213	0.49	25,406	23,700	13.1	18.7	48.9	0.33	0.5
Mississippi	5	102	75	0.17	22,333	18,213	14.8	4.8	32.4	0.22	(D)
Maine	15	177	84	0.30	26,395	18,762	10.5	11.6	31.5	0.21	0.3
Oklahoma	55	154	108	0.26	24,786	20,500	2.4	9.2	28.3	0.19	0.6
New Hampshire	16	87	61	0.15	30,839	18,508	7.2	6.5	28.2	0.19	0.4
Montana	31	118	75	0.20	28,576	24,653	7.1	9.1	25.6	0.17	0.1
Rhode Island	58	225	175	0.38	18,973	17,069	7.2	8.9	22.6	0.15	0.2
Vermont	32	75	57	0.13	18,933	20,211	4.9	3.7	15.3	0.10	0.2
Delaware	14	118	64	0.20	20,898	28,906	2.9	4.0	15.2	0.10	-
Wyoming	8	50	(D)	0.08	27,160	-	(D)	(D)	14.6	0.10	0.1
West Virginia	76	241	188	0.41	16,207	14,303	(S)	8.3	(D)	-	0.1
Idaho	47	325	240	0.55	34,188	34,792	(D)	26.2	(D)	-	0.6
North Dakota	41	218	181	0.37	25,225	19,221	(D)	10.0	(D)	-	0.2
Hawaii	33	196	123	0.33	36,954	28,431	(D)	14.1	(D)	-	0.2
D.C.	12	240	162	0.41	32,325	38,772	(D)	14.5	(D)	-	(D)
New Mexico	10	383	296	0.65	-	-	24.7	25.8	(D)	-	(D)
South Dakota	3	8	(D)	0.01	-	-	(D)	(D)	(D)	-	(D)

Source: Economic Census of the U.S., 1997. Data are sorted by 1997 revenues or establishments. (D) means data suppression to prevent disclosure of company data. (S) means that data did not meet statistical standards for publication. A dash (-) is used when data are unavailable or cannot be calculated. Data followed by an * indicate the midpoint of a range. The ranges are: for 10, 0-19; for 60, 20-99, for 175, 100-249, for 375, 250-499, for 750, 500-999. Higher values are multiples of those shown, e.g., 3,750 is the midpoint of the range 2,500-4,999. Shaded *states* on the state map indicate those states which have proportionately greater representation in the industry than would be indicated by the state's population; the ratio is based on total revenues or number of establishments. Shaded *regions* indicate where the industry is regionally most concentrated.

NAICS 233310 - MANUFACTURING AND INDUSTRIAL BUILDING CONSTRUCTION

GENERAL STATISTICS

Years	Estab-lish-ments	Employment		Payroll ($ mil)		Costs ($ mil)		Value Added ($ mil)	Revenues ($ mil)			Capital expend. ($ mil)
		Total	Constr. workers	Total	Worker payroll	Total	Cost of materials		All sources	Construction Total	Net	
1997	7,280	143,066	107,180	5,129.0	3,322.3	7,296.3	7,118.4	10,429.8	34,038.4	33,514.3	17,202.1	309.9

Source: Economic Census of the United States, 1997. This is a newly defined industry. Data for prior years were unavailable at the time of publication but may become available over time. "Net" under "Construction" is construction revenue net of the costs of subcontracts.

DISTRIBUTION AMONG SIC-BASED INDUSTRIES - 1997

SIC	Industry	Estab-lish-ments	Employment		Cost of Power & Materials ($ mil)	Revenues ($ mil)			Value Added ($ mil)
			Total (000)	Payroll ($ mil)		All Sources	Construction Total	Net	
153130	Operative builders (pt)	85.0	1,555	61.5	51.0	493.6	461.0	257.2	238.79
154120	General contractors--industrial buildings & warehouses (pt)	6,800.0	138,294	4,926.7	7,139.7	32,661.3	32,185.0	16,581.4	9,917.94
874123	Management services (pt)	395.0	3,216	140.8	105.6	883.4	868.3	363.5	273.12

Source: 1997 Economic Census. U.S. Census Bureau, U.S. Department of Commerce, August 1997. SIC codes ending in two zeroes represent complete 4-digit SICs. All others are parts of 4-digit SIC industries. Items showing a dash (-) indicate that data are not available because of disclosure problems.

SIC INDUSTRIES RELATED TO NAICS 233310

SIC	Industry	1990	1991	1992	1993	1994	1995	1996	1997
1531	**Operative Builders***								
	Establishments (number)	10,396	9,279	16,989	11,225	15,678p	15,061p	14,468p	13,899p
	Employment (thousands)	120.5	88.7	114.2	96.7	97.6e	90.3e	83.5e	77.2e
	Revenues ($ million)	50,369.3e	48,201.9e	46,127.7	44,142.8e	42,243.3e	40,425.6e	38,686.0e	37,021.3e
1541	**Industrial Buildings and Warehouses***								
	Establishments (number)	7,414e	7,552e	7,693	7,836p	7,983p	8,132p	8,283p	8,438p
	Employment (thousands)	130.6e	126.7e	123.0	119.3e	115.8e	112.3e	109.0e	105.7e
	Revenues ($ million)	21,511.9e	21,250.1e	20,991.4	20,735.9e	20,483.6e	20,234.3e	19,988.0e	19,744.7e
8741	**Management Services***								
	Establishments (number)	15,267	16,556	20,186	21,920	23,803	21,674	23,348p	24,255p
	Employment (thousands)	285.2	306.6	285.1	357.7	386.3	312.7	368.9p	381.9p
	Revenues ($ million)	20,627.0	21,788.0	23,774.0	23,373.0	24,328.0	27,611.0	27,569.0	28,870.9p

*Source: Economic Census of the United States, 1992, annual surveys of economic sectors conducted by the Bureau of the Census, and estimates or projections based on the 1982-1992 period; not all data are shown. 'e' marks estimates made by the editors; 'p' indicates projections based on time series. A dash (-) indicates that data for this SIC or year were not available. * Indicates that only a portion of this industry is present within the NAICS data. If no * is shown, the entire industry is contained within the NAICS data.*

INDICES OF CHANGE

Years	Estab-lish-ments	Employment		Payroll ($ mil)		Costs ($ mil)		Value Added ($ mil)	Revenues ($ mil)			Capital expend. ($ mil)
		Total	Constr. workers	Total	Worker payroll	Total	Cost of materials		All sources	Construction Total	Net	
1997	100.0	100.0	100.0	100.0	100.0	100.0	100.0	100.0	100.0	100.0	100.0	100.0

Sources: Same as General Statistics. The values shown reflect change from the base year, 1997. Values above 100 mean greater than 1997, values below 100 mean less than 1997, and a value of 100 in years other than 1997 means same as 1997. Indices are calculated only for Census years. Data are the most recent available at this level of detail.

SELECTED RATIOS

For 1997	Avg. of Sector	Analyzed Industry	Index	For 1997	Avg. of Sector	Analyzed Industry	Index
Employees per establishment	8.6	19.7	228	Value added per establishment	584,730	1,432,665	245
Construction workers per establishment	6.6	14.7	223	Value added per employee	67,759	72,902	108
Payroll per establishment	265,343	704,533	266	Value added per construction worker	88,592	97,311	110
Payroll per employee	30,748	35,851	117	Revenues per establishment	1,307,915	4,675,604	357
Payroll per construction worker	27,622	30,997	112	Revenues per employee	151,563	237,921	157
Costs per establishment	367,737	1,002,239	273	Revenues per construction worker	198,161	317,582	160
Costs per employee	42,614	51,000	120	CR as % of total revenues	98.48	98.46	100
Costs per construction worker	55,716	68,075	122	Net CR as % of CR	72.40	51.33	71
Materials as % of costs	95.75	97.56	102	Investment per establishment	22,948	42,569	186
Costs as % of revenues	28.12	21.44	76	Investment per employee	2,659	2,166	81
Costs as % of construction revenues	28.55	21.77	76	Investment per construction worker	3,477	2,891	83

Sources: Same as General Statistics. The 'Average of Sector' column represents the average for all industries in this sector. The Index shows the relationship between the Average and the Analyzed Industry. For example, 100 means that they are equal; 500 that the Analyzed Industry is five times the average; 50 means that the Analyzed Industry is half the national average. 'na' is used to show that data are 'not available'. CR stands for "construction revenues" and "Net CR" is construction revenues net of subcontract expenses.

LEADING COMPANIES   Number shown: 75   Total sales ($ mil): 82,516   Total employment (000): 307.1

Company Name	Address				CEO Name	Phone	Co. Type	Sales ($ mil)	Empl. (000)
Fluor Corp.	1 Enterprise Dr	Aliso Viejo	CA	92656	Philip J Carroll Jr	949-349-2000	P	12,417	53.6
Bechtel Corp.	50 Beale St	San Francisco	CA	94105	RP Bechtel	415-768-1234	R	8,250*	30.0
Brown and Root Inc.	PO Box 3	Houston	TX	77001		713-676-3011	S	3,062	30.0
Raytheon Engineers	1 Broadway	Cambridge	MA	02142	Shay Assad	617-494-7000	S	2,700	16.0
Foster Wheeler International Corp.	Perryville Corp Park	Clinton	NJ	08809	John C Blythe	908-730-4030	S	2,381*	7.2
Raytheon Engineers	1 Broadway	Cambridge	MA	02142	Shay Assad	617-494-7000	S	2,100	8.6
Gilbane Building Co.	7 Jackson Walkway	Providence	RI	02903	Paul J Choquette Jr	401-456-5800	R	2,100	1.2
HBE Corp.	P O Box 419039	St. Louis	MO	63141	Fred S Kummer	314-567-9000	R	2,000*	8.0
Parsons Corp.	100 W Walnut St	Pasadena	CA	91124	James F McNulty	626-440-2000	R	1,710*	11.4
Turner Steiner International	375 Hudson St	New York	NY	10014	Thomas Leppert	212-229-6157	R	1,578*	3.2
Parsons Overseas Co.	100 W Walnut St	Pasadena	CA	91124	William Hall	626-440-2000	S	1,500*	10.0
Clark Construction Group Inc.	7500 Old Gtown	Bethesda	MD	20814	Peter C Forster	301-272-8100	S	1,475	3.0
Turner Construction Co.	375 Hudson St	New York	NY	10014	Robert Fee	212-229-6000	R	1,407*	3.4
Weitz Company Inc. Denver Div.	899 Logan St	Denver	CO	80203	Glenn De Stigter	303-860-6600	D	1,385*	0.9
Kaiser Engineers	9300 Lee Hwy	Fairfax	VA	22031	James O Maiwurm	703-934-3600	P	1,210	4.8
J.A. Jones Construction Co.	J A Jones Dr	Charlotte	NC	28287	Bob Hambright	704-553-3000	S	1,200*	10.0
Opus Corp.	10350 Bren Rd W	Minnetonka	MN	55343	Mark Ravenhorst	952-656-4444	R	1,200	0.0
Dillingham Construction Corp.	5960 Inglewood Dr	Pleasanton	CA	94588	DE Sundgren	925-463-3300	S	1,175	8.0
Whiting-Turner Contracting Co.	300 E Joppa Rd	Baltimore	MD	21286	Willard Hackerman	410-821-1100	R	1,050*	1.8
Huber, Hunt and Nichols Inc.	2450 S Tibbs Ave	Indianapolis	IN	46241	Robert G Hunt	317-227-7800	S	1,032	0.6
Beers Construction Co.	70 Ellis St	Atlanta	GA	30303	Joe Riedel	404-659-1970	S	1,000	3.0
Hunt Corp. (Indianapolis, Indiana)	250 E 96th St	Indianapolis	IN	46240	Robert G Hunt	317-575-6301	R	1,000	0.5
McCarthy Building Cos.	1341 N Rock Hill	St. Louis	MO	63124	Michael Hurst	314-968-3300	R	980	1.5
Swinerton Inc.	580 California St	San Francisco	CA	94104	James R Gillette	415-421-2980	R	902	1.0
McCarthy Building	1341 N Rock Hill	St. Louis	MO	63124	Michael M McCarthy	314-968-3300	R	900	1.5
Morse-Diesel International Inc.	18 Broad St	New York	NY	10005	Donald H Piser	212-514-8880	R	900*	0.6
Dunn Industries Inc.	929 Holmes	Kansas City	MO	64106	Terrence Dunn	816-474-8600	R	871	1.6
Barton Malow Enterprises Inc.	27777 Franklin Rd	Southfield	MI	48034	Ben C Maibach III	248-351-4500	R	850	1.5
Perini Building Company Inc.	73 Mount Wayte	Framingham	MA	01701	Richard J Rizzo	508-628-2000	S	811*	1.0
Austin Industries Inc.	P O Box 1590	Dallas	TX	75221	William T Solomon	214-443-5500	R	808	6.3
M.A. Mortenson Co.	700 Meadow Ln	Minneapolis	MN	55422	MA Mortenson Jr	612-522-2100	R	804	1.7
Rooney Brothers Co.	111 W 5th St	Tulsa	OK	74103	Timothy P Rooney	918-583-6900	R	770	2.0
TIC Holdings, Inc.	P O Box 774848	Steamboat Sprgs	CO	80477	Ronald W McKenzie	970-879-2561	R	745	5.0
Barton Malow Co.	P O Box 35200	Detroit	MI	48235	Ben C Maibach III	248-351-4500	R	727	1.3
Austin Co.	3650 Mayfield Rd	Cleveland	OH	44121	J William Melsop	864-291-6625	R	700*	1.2
Lewis Homes	P O Box 670	Upland	CA	91785	John Goodman	909-985-0971	R	700*	0.9
Caddell Construction Inc.	PO Box 210099	Montgomery	AL	36121	John A Caddell	334-272-7723	R	680*	1.8
TIC Holdings Inc.	P O Box 774848	Steamboat Sprgs	CO	80477	RW McKenzie	303-879-2561	R	625*	5.0
Pepper Companies Inc.	643 N Orleans St	Chicago	IL	60610	J David Pepper	312-266-4703	R	623	1.3
Dunn Investment Co.	PO Box 247	Birmingham	AL	35201	JSM French	205-592-8908	R	622*	1.5
Turner Industries Ltd.	8687 United Plaza	Baton Rouge	LA	70809	Bert S Turner	225-922-5050	R	600*	9.8
Rudolph and Sletten Inc.	989 E Hillsdale Blvd	Foster City	CA	94404	John Rudolph	650-572-1919	R	600*	0.9
Pitt-Des Moines Inc.	1450 Lake Robbins	The Woodlands	TX	77380	William W McKee	281-765-4600	P	567	2.5
Weitz Co.	400 Locust, #300	Des Moines	IA	50309	Glenn H DeStigter	515-698-4260	R	556*	0.9
Alberici Corp.	2150 Kienlen Ave	St. Louis	MO	63121	Robert F McCoole	314-261-2611	R	554	1.7
Kraus-Anderson Inc.	523 S 8th St	Minneapolis	MN	55404	Burton F Dahlberg	612-332-7281	R	540	1.0
Suffolk Construction Inc.	65 Allerton St	Boston	MA	02119	John F Fish	617-445-3500	R	540	0.5
Dick Corp.	PO Box 10896	Pittsburgh	PA	15236	Douglas P Dick	412-384-1000	R	530	3.0
Michael Baker Corp.	PO Box 12259	Pittsburgh	PA	15231	Richard L Shaw	412-269-6300	P	521	3.7
Hoffman Corp.	PO Box 1300	Portland	OR	97207	Wayne A Drinkward	503-221-8811	R	516	0.7
Ralph M. Parsons Co.	100 W Walnut St	Pasadena	CA	91124	James S McNulty	626-440-2000	S	514*	4.0
J.E. Dunn Construction Co.	929 Holmes	Kansas City	MO	64106	Terrence Dunn	816-474-8600	S	500*	1.0
Kokosing Construction Inc.	P O Box 226	Fredericktown	OH	43019	William B Burgett	740-694-6315	R	497*	1.2
Brasfield & Gorrie General	P O Box 10383	Birmingham	AL	35202	Miller Gorrie	205-328-4000	R	477*	1.5
Okland Construction Inc.	1978 SW Temple	Salt Lake City	UT	84115	J Randy Okland	801-486-0144	R	455	0.4
Danis Cos.	2 River Pl	Dayton	OH	45405	Thomas J Danis	937-228-1225	R	454*	1.1
Baugh Enterprises Inc.	PO Box 14135	Seattle	WA	98114	Louis E Kapcsandy	206-726-8000	R	450	1.1
Austin Commercial Inc.	P O Box 2879	Dallas	TX	75221	David B Wallls	214-443-5700	S	450	0.9
Perini Building Inc. Western U.S.	360 E Coronado Rd	Phoenix	AZ	85004	Craig Shaw	602-256-6777	D	449	0.4
Fru-Con Construction Corp.	PO Box 100	Ballwin	MO	63022	Bruce A Frust	314-391-6700	R	442	2.8
Manhattan Construction Co.	3890 W Northwest	Dallas	TX	75220	Timothy P Rooney	214-357-7400	S	425	0.9
O and G Industries Inc.	112 Wall St	Torrington	CT	06790	David Oneglia	860-489-9261	R	421*	1.0
Sundt Corp.	P O Box 26685	Tucson	AZ	85726	J D Pruitt	520-748-7555	R	417	1.5
Oscar J. Boldt Construction Co.	PO Box 419	Appleton	WI	54912	Warren Parsons	920-739-6321	S	402*	2.0
Hathaway Dinwiddie Construction	275 Battery St	San Francisco	CA	94111	Donald Warmby	415-986-2718	R	400	0.5
Weitz Company Inc. Phoenix Div.	2255 N 44th St	Phoenix	AZ	85008	Larry Mohr	602-225-0225	D	400	0.1
Haskell Co.	P O Box 44100	Jacksonville	FL	32202	Preston H Haskell	904-791-4500	R	390	0.6
Drees Co.	211 Grandview Dr	Fort Mitchell	KY	41017	Ralph A Drees	606-578-4200	R	366	0.7
Watkins Engineers & Constructors	P O Box 2194	Tallahassee	FL	32316	Eddie Aaron	850-576-7181	S	330	4.0
Stellar Group Inc.	2900 Hartley Rd	Jacksonville	FL	32257	H Bobby Cothren	904-260-2900	R	318*	0.8
Flint Industries Inc.	P O Box 490	Tulsa	OK	74101	John Bates	918-587-8451	R	300*	1.5
Alex J. Etkin Inc.	30445 Northwestern	Farmington Hills	MI	48333	Thomas H Landry	248-737-5800	R	300	0.3
Centex-Rodgers Inc.	2620 Elm Hill Pike	Nashville	TN	37214	Douglas H Jones	615-889-4400	S	300	0.2
Suitt Construction Company Inc.	PO Box 8858	Greenville	SC	29604	TH Suitt	864-250-5000	S	294*	1.3
Tellepsen Builders L.P.	777 Benmar, #400	Houston	TX	77060	Howard Fellepsen	281-447-8100	R	290*	0.7

Source: Ward's Business Directory of U.S. Private and Public Companies, Volumes 1 and 2, 2000. The company type code used is as follows: P - Public, R - Private, S - Subsidiary, D - Division, J - Joint Venture, A - Affiliate, G - Group, N - Company type not reported. Sales are in millions of dollars, employees are in thousands. An asterisk (*) indicates an estimated sales volume. The symbol < stands for 'less than'. Company names and addresses are truncated, in some cases, to fit into the available space.

COST DETAILS

Item	Cost ($ mil)	% of total	Per $1,000 of Revenue	Item	Cost ($ mil)	% of total	Per $1,000 of Revenue
All costs	23,608.5	100.000	693.6	Total Rentals	347.7	1.473	10.2
Cost of supplies	7,118.4	30.152	209.1	Equipment	260.0	1.101	7.6
Subcontracts	16,312.3	69.095	479.2	Buildings	87.7	0.372	2.6
Power, fuel, lubricants	177.9	0.753	5.2	Services purchased	237.9	1.008	7.0
Electricity	39.3	0.166	1.2	Communications	90.1	0.382	2.6
Natural gas	11.6	0.049	0.3	Building repairs	19.3	0.082	0.6
Gasoline and diesel	119.1	0.504	3.5	Machinery repairs	128.5	0.544	3.8
Highway	94.9	0.402	2.8				
Offroad	24.2	0.103	0.7				
Other power	7.9	0.034	0.2				

Source: Economic Census of the United States, 1997. Revenues referred to are total industry revenues for the current NAICS industry.

CONSTRUCTION PRODUCT DETAILS

Construction type	Value of construction work ($ mil and %)							
	Total		New construction		Additions, alterations, reconstruction		Maintenance and repair	
	Value	%	Value	%	Value	%	Value	%
Total	**33,514.3**	**100.0**	**22,359.1**	**100.0**	**8,099.1**	**100.0**	**3,053.8**	**100.0**
Building construction, total	**33,008.1**	**98.5**	**22,042.4**	**98.6**	**7,975.3**	**98.5**	**2,990.4**	**97.9**
Manufacturing and light industrial buildings	17,590.1	52.5	10,914.5	48.8	4,280.1	52.8	2,395.5	78.4
Manufacturing and light industrial warehouses	7,058.1	21.1	5,421.8	24.2	1,358.9	16.8	277.5	9.1
Hotels and motels	432.8	1.3	-	-	49.6	0.6	9.9	0.3
Office buildings	2,478.6	7.4	1,570.3	7.0	810.8	10.0	97.5	3.2
All other commercial buildings, nec	1,141.6	3.4	799.5	3.6	298.2	3.7	43.9	1.4
Commercial warehouses	1,040.7	3.1	883.4	4.0	131.0	1.6	26.3	0.9
Educational buildings	823.0	2.5	541.1	2.4	255.5	3.2	26.4	0.9
Health care and institutional buildings	862.9	2.6	464.8	2.1	355.1	4.4	43.0	1.4
Other building construction	1,580.2	4.7	1,073.8	4.8	436.0	5.4	70.5	2.3
Nonbuilding construction, total	**504.0**	**1.5**	**316.7**	**1.4**	**123.8**	**1.5**	**63.4**	**2.1**
Other nonbuilding construction, nec	504.0	1.5	316.7	1.4	123.8	1.5	63.4	2.1
Construction work, nsk	**2.3**	**-**	**NA**	**-**	**NA**	**-**	**NA**	**-**

Source: Economic Census of the United States, 1997. Bold items are headers. (D) stands for data withheld to protect competitive information. (S) indicates instances where data do not meet publications standards.

LOCATION BY STATE AND REGIONAL CONCENTRATION

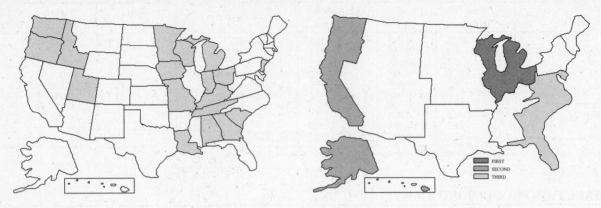

INDUSTRY DATA BY STATE

State	Estab lish- ments	Employment			Compensation		Production				Capital Exp. ($ mil)
		Total	Workers	Total as % of US	Payroll per Employee	Wages per Worker	Costs ($ mil)	Value Added ($ mil)	Reve- nues ($ mil)	% of US	
California	792	9,606	6,219	6.71	42,406	33,971	626.4	678.4	3,836.0	11.27	22.4
Michigan	339	6,095	3,994	4.26	41,101	35,152	382.8	487.5	2,621.9	7.70	22.6
Ohio	338	6,899	4,940	4.82	37,481	32,605	404.3	534.3	1,881.2	5.53	18.0
Texas	412	11,963	9,735	8.36	35,955	33,786	398.2	702.8	1,706.2	5.01	21.3
Illinois	389	5,402	4,171	3.78	38,328	35,752	334.6	505.1	1,385.1	4.07	10.4
Alabama	104	9,024	7,103	6.31	36,985	31,874	365.5	425.8	1,225.8	3.60	10.4
Missouri	136	4,031	2,826	2.82	43,508	38,209	240.9	339.1	1,223.6	3.59	21.8
Georgia	266	4,532	3,467	3.17	31,417	25,963	254.2	279.4	1,158.5	3.40	8.4
New Jersey	196	2,048	1,048	1.43	51,601	42,001	158.9	508.5	1,150.3	3.38	5.6
Washington	213	3,541	2,525	2.48	45,108	37,421	123.8	281.9	1,140.9	3.35	5.4
Florida	234	3,724	2,407	2.60	35,759	23,984	466.1	262.7	1,124.4	3.30	5.3
Tennessee	174	5,678	4,499	3.97	30,414	26,053	229.5	329.1	1,045.5	3.07	12.2
Pennsylvania	311	4,998	3,833	3.49	33,603	29,112	212.4	340.9	1,017.3	2.99	14.3
Indiana	201	5,588	4,508	3.91	36,680	34,716	236.7	469.1	1,011.0	2.97	11.8
New York	308	3,574	2,505	2.50	34,615	31,774	191.1	246.6	918.1	2.70	7.3
Idaho	66	4,434	3,486	3.10	37,054	33,321	198.1	439.3	807.5	2.37	(D)
Minnesota	209	2,728	2,052	1.91	36,971	30,909	180.7	215.3	795.5	2.34	5.4
South Carolina	165	5,723	4,756	4.00	28,336	26,327	177.9	215.0	762.4	2.24	4.7
North Carolina	220	4,654	3,687	3.25	29,708	25,100	186.8	215.1	744.4	2.19	10.4
Wisconsin	138	3,387	2,621	2.37	36,139	31,308	147.7	258.0	725.2	2.13	7.3
Oregon	203	2,692	2,079	1.88	44,853	38,550	126.6	263.2	721.2	2.12	3.8
Kentucky	133	2,901	2,076	2.03	32,318	26,848	144.1	195.7	688.6	2.02	6.3
Louisiana	77	4,145	3,490	2.90	32,087	28,857	143.1	228.4	615.5	1.81	6.4
Iowa	82	2,308	1,844	1.61	28,515	25,259	136.2	160.1	491.3	1.44	5.1
Arizona	104	1,568	1,151	1.10	34,997	27,228	51.9	114.6	380.9	1.12	2.4
Arkansas	114	1,376	1,168	0.96	20,102	18,260	59.0	120.8	298.0	0.88	2.9
Utah	121	1,468	1,013	1.03	35,864	30,785	114.2	73.0	287.0	0.84	2.5
Mississippi	76	1,767	1,499	1.24	26,228	23,907	86.9	93.4	257.0	0.75	2.3
Connecticut	110	771	482	0.54	43,956	36,079	36.5	66.5	230.3	0.68	1.6
Colorado	107	949	589	0.66	32,673	28,007	37.8	96.7	229.7	0.67	2.1
Maryland	41	1,204	929	0.84	39,049	34,790	46.6	107.5	228.3	0.67	2.5
Virginia	133	1,557	1,161	1.09	28,588	24,515	61.3	76.7	205.5	0.60	2.1
Maine	50	897	683	0.63	29,651	25,646	24.3	51.3	158.9	0.47	1.3
West Virginia	35	857	668	0.60	32,608	30,916	54.9	54.0	143.9	0.42	1.8
Nevada	23	169	108	0.12	35,314	30,954	5.0	19.9	35.5	0.10	(D)
Montana	5	82	62	0.06	21,049	19,758	1.8	6.8	18.6	0.05	-
Massachusetts	125	1,139	714	0.80	44,414	37,894	(D)	93.7	(D)	-	2.3
Oklahoma	117	1,368	966	0.96	28,947	24,587	(D)	76.3	(D)	-	1.6
Kansas	88	1,557	1,188	1.09	27,595	26,263	(D)	84.3	(D)	-	1.7
New Mexico	56	2,519	2,139	1.76	35,389	31,107	(D)	151.8	(D)	-	1.6
Nebraska	54	876	715	0.61	33,918	29,319	(D)	52.4	(D)	-	2.4
New Hampshire	50	480	309	0.34	24,431	17,359	(D)	20.2	(D)	-	0.6
Rhode Island	46	896	409	0.63	28,161	25,729	(D)	343.4	(D)	-	7.6
Wyoming	28	534	419	0.37	35,414	32,993	(D)	54.4	(D)	-	0.7
South Dakota	25	247	187	0.17	26,162	23,818	13.4	9.6	(D)	-	0.5
Delaware	20	491	(S)	0.34	37,914	-	(D)	40.4	(D)	-	(S)
North Dakota	18	389	306	0.27	29,576	24,993	(D)	18.7	(D)	-	0.8
Alaska	13	121	81	0.08	46,587	45,025	(D)	16.2	(D)	-	0.1
Vermont	9	53	35	0.04	20,717	20,914	(D)	2.0	(D)	-	-
Hawaii	6	(D)	(D)	-	-	-	(S)	(D)	(D)	-	(D)
D.C.	1	(D)	(D)	-	-	-	(D)	(D)	(D)	-	(D)

Source: Economic Census of the U.S., 1997. Data are sorted by 1997 revenues or establishments. (D) means data suppression to prevent disclosure of company data. (S) means that data did not meet statistical standards for publication. A dash (-) is used when data are unavailable or cannot be calculated. Data followed by an * indicate the midpoint of a range. The ranges are: for 10, 0-19; for 60, 20-99; for 175, 100-249; for 375, 250-499; for 750, 500-999. Higher values are multiples of those shown, e.g., 3,750 is the midpoint of the range 2,500-4,999. Shaded *states* on the state map indicate those states which have proportionately greater representation in the industry than would be indicated by the state's population; the ratio is based on total revenues or number of establishments. Shaded *regions* indicate where the industry is regionally most concentrated.

NAICS 233320 - COMMERCIAL AND INSTITUTIONAL BUILDING CONSTRUCTION

GENERAL STATISTICS

Years	Estab-lish-ments	Employment		Payroll ($ mil)		Costs ($ mil)		Value Added ($ mil)	Revenues ($ mil)			Capital expend. ($ mil)
		Total	Constr. workers	Total	Worker payroll	Total	Cost of materials		All sources	Construction Total	Net	
1997	37,430	528,173	359,981	19,176.2	10,797.1	28,914.4	28,087.3	44,363.5	175,230.8	173,205.7	71,252.8	1,144.4

Source: *Economic Census of the United States*, 1997. This is a newly defined industry. Data for prior years were unavailable at the time of publication but may become available over time. "Net" under "Construction" is construction revenue net of the costs of subcontracts.

DISTRIBUTION AMONG SIC-BASED INDUSTRIES - 1997

SIC	Industry	Estab-lish-ments	Employment		Cost of Power & Materials ($ mil)	Revenues ($ mil)			Value Added ($ mil)
			Total (000)	Payroll ($ mil)		All Sources	Construction Total	Net	
152210	General contractors--residential buildings, other than single-family (pt)	1,112.0	13,807	500.3	853.5	4,928.2	4,882.7	2,422.4	1,614.31
153140	Operative builders (pt)	441.0	3,743	132.4	337.7	1,967.0	1,727.9	1,233.2	1,134.45
154110	General contractors--industrial buildings & warehouses (pt)	1,910.0	19,856	638.6	1,054.9	5,524.9	5,468.5	2,678.4	1,679.88
154200	General contractors--nonresidential buildings	30,817.0	472,611	17,205.1	26,002.2	158,795.8	157,182.7	62,498.7	38,109.60
874124	Management services (pt)	3,150.0	18,156	699.8	666.0	4,015.0	3,943.8	2,420.1	1,825.29

Source: 1997 *Economic Census*. U.S. Census Bureau, U.S. Department of Commerce, August 1997. SIC codes ending in two zeroes represent complete 4-digit SICs. All others are parts of 4-digit SIC industries. Items showing a dash (-) indicate that data are not available because of disclosure problems.

SIC INDUSTRIES RELATED TO NAICS 233320

SIC	Industry	1990	1991	1992	1993	1994	1995	1996	1997
1542	**Nonresidential Construction, n.e.c.**								
	Establishments (number)	30,368e	30,052e	29,739	29,429p	29,123p	28,820p	28,519p	28,222p
	Employment (thousands)	437.9e	422.2e	407.1	392.6e	378.5e	365.0e	351.9e	339.3e
	Revenues ($ million)	94,072.7e	94,877.5e	95,689.2	96,507.9e	97,333.5e	98,166.2e	99,006.1e	99,853.1e
1522	**Residential Construction, n.e.c.***								
	Establishments (number)	7,107e	6,791e	6,490	6,202p	5,927p	5,664p	5,413p	5,173p
	Employment (thousands)	60.0e	54.1e	48.8	44.0e	39.7e	35.8e	32.3e	29.1e
	Revenues ($ million)	9,855.5e	8,853.8e	7,954.0	7,145.6e	6,419.4e	5,767.0e	5,180.9e	4,654.3e
1531	**Operative Builders***								
	Establishments (number)	10,396	9,279	16,989	11,225	15,678p	15,061p	14,468p	13,899p
	Employment (thousands)	120.5	88.7	114.2	96.7	97.6e	90.3e	83.5e	77.2e
	Revenues ($ million)	50,369.3e	48,201.9e	46,127.7	44,142.8e	42,243.3e	40,425.6e	38,686.0e	37,021.3e
1541	**Industrial Buildings and Warehouses***								
	Establishments (number)	7,414e	7,552e	7,693	7,836p	7,983p	8,132p	8,283p	8,438p
	Employment (thousands)	130.6e	126.7e	123.0	119.3e	115.8e	112.3e	109.0e	105.7e
	Revenues ($ million)	21,511.9e	21,250.1e	20,991.4	20,735.9e	20,483.6e	20,234.3e	19,988.0e	19,744.7e
8741	**Management Services***								
	Establishments (number)	15,267	16,556	20,186	21,920	23,803	21,674	23,348p	24,255p
	Employment (thousands)	285.2	306.6	285.1	357.7	386.3	312.7	368.9p	381.9p
	Revenues ($ million)	20,627.0	21,788.0	23,774.0	23,373.0	24,328.0	27,611.0	27,569.0	28,870.9p

Source: *Economic Census of the United States*, 1992, annual surveys of economic sectors conducted by the Bureau of the Census, and estimates or projections based on the 1982-1992 period; not all data are shown. 'e' marks estimates made by the editors; 'p' indicates projections based on time series. A dash (-) indicates that data for this SIC or year were not available. * Indicates that only a portion of this industry is present within the NAICS data. If no * is shown, the entire industry is contained within the NAICS data.

SELECTED RATIOS

For 1997	Avg. of Sector	Analyzed Industry	Index	For 1997	Avg. of Sector	Analyzed Industry	Index
Employees per establishment	8.6	14.1	164	Value added per establishment	584,730	1,185,239	203
Construction workers per establishment	6.6	9.6	146	Value added per employee	67,759	83,994	124
Payroll per establishment	265,343	512,322	193	Value added per construction worker	88,592	123,238	139
Payroll per employee	30,748	36,307	118	Revenues per establishment	1,307,915	4,681,560	358
Payroll per construction worker	27,622	29,994	109	Revenues per employee	151,563	331,768	219
Costs per establishment	367,737	772,493	210	Revenues per construction worker	198,161	486,778	246
Costs per employee	42,614	54,744	128	CR as % of total revenues	98.48	98.84	100
Costs per construction worker	55,716	80,322	144	Net CR as % of CR	72.40	41.14	57
Materials as % of costs	95.75	97.14	101	Investment per establishment	22,948	30,574	133
Costs as % of revenues	28.12	16.50	59	Investment per employee	2,659	2,167	81
Costs as % of construction revenues	28.55	16.69	58	Investment per construction worker	3,477	3,179	91

Sources: Same as General Statistics. The 'Average of Sector' column represents the average for all industries in this sector. The Index shows the relationship between the Average and the Analyzed Industry. For example, 100 means that they are equal; 500 that the Analyzed Industry is five times the average; 50 means that the Analyzed Industry is half the national average. 'na' is used to show that data are 'not available'. CR stands for "construction revenues" and "Net CR" is construction revenues net of subcontract expenses.

LEADING COMPANIES   Number shown: **75**   Total sales ($ mil): **63,540**   Total employment (000): **203.3**

Company Name	Address				CEO Name	Phone	Co. Type	Sales ($ mil)	Empl. (000)
Turner Corp.	901 Main St	Dallas	TX	75202	Robert E Fee	214-752-4323	P	3,699	32.0
United Dominion Industries Inc.	301 S College St	Charlotte	NC	28202	William Holland	704-347-6800	P	2,148	12.0
Gilbane Building Co.	7 Jackson Walkway	Providence	RI	02903	Paul J Choquette Jr	401-456-5800	R	2,100	1.2
Kiewit Construction Group Inc.	1000 Kiewit Plz	Omaha	NE	68131	Kenneth E Stinson	402-342-2052	S	2,000*	11.0
HBE Corp.	P O Box 419039	St. Louis	MO	63141	Fred S Kummer	314-567-9000	R	2,000*	8.0
Kiewit Construction Co.	1000 Kiewit Plz	Omaha	NE	68131	Ken Stinson	402-342-2052	S	1,900*	2.9
Turner Steiner International	375 Hudson St	New York	NY	10014	Thomas Leppert	212-229-6157	R	1,578*	3.2
Clark Construction Group Inc.	7500 Old Gtown	Bethesda	MD	20814	Peter C Forster	301-272-8100	S	1,475	3.0
Turner Construction Co.	375 Hudson St	New York	NY	10014	Robert Fee	212-229-6000	R	1,407*	3.4
Clark Enterprises Inc.	7500 Old Gtown	Bethesda	MD	20814	A James Clark	301-657-7100	R	1,400	2.5
Lincoln Property Co.	P O Box 1920	Dallas	TX	75201	Mack Pogue	214-740-3300	R	1,398	4.5
Weitz Company Inc. Denver Div.	899 Logan St	Denver	CO	80203	Glenn De Stigter	303-860-6600	D	1,385*	0.9
DPR Construction Inc.	555 Twin Dolphin	Redwood City	CA	94065	Peter Nosler	650-592-4800	R	1,300	2.5
Skanska USA Inc.	60 Arch St	Greenwich	CT	06830	Stuart Graham	203-629-8840	R	1,261*	3.0
J.A. Jones Construction Co.	J A Jones Dr	Charlotte	NC	28287	Bob Hambright	704-553-3000	S	1,200*	10.0
Opus Corp.	10350 Bren Rd W	Minnetonka	MN	55343	Mark Ravenhorst	952-656-4444	R	1,200	0.0
Dillingham Construction Corp.	5960 Inglewood Dr	Pleasanton	CA	94588	DE Sundgren	925-463-3300	S	1,175	8.0
Whiting-Turner Contracting Co.	300 E Joppa Rd	Baltimore	MD	21286	Willard Hackerman	410-821-1100	R	1,050*	1.8
Perini Corp.	Box 9160	Framingham	MA	01701	Robert Band	508-628-2000	P	1,036	2.7
Huber, Hunt and Nichols Inc.	2450 S Tibbs Ave	Indianapolis	IN	46241	Robert G Hunt	317-227-7800	S	1,032	0.6
Dillingham Construction Holdings	5960 Inglewood Dr	Pleasanton	CA	94588	Donald Sumden	925-463-3300	R	1,023*	8.0
Beers Construction Co.	70 Ellis St	Atlanta	GA	30303	Joe Riedel	404-659-1970	S	1,000	3.0
McCarthy Building Cos.	1341 N Rock Hill	St. Louis	MO	63124	Michael Hurst	314-968-3300	R	980	1.5
Butler Manufacturing Co.	PO Box 419917	Kansas City	MO	64141	john Holland	816-968-3000	P	973	5.2
Hensel Phelps Construction Co.	PO Box 0	Greeley	CO	80632	Jerry Morgensen	970-352-6565	R	934	1.9
Swinerton Inc.	580 California St	San Francisco	CA	94104	James R Gillette	415-421-2980	R	902	1.0
McCarthy Building	1341 N Rock Hill	St. Louis	MO	63124	Michael M McCarthy	314-968-3300	R	900	1.5
Morse-Diesel International Inc.	18 Broad St	New York	NY	10005	Donald H Piser	212-514-8880	R	900*	0.6
Dunn Industries Inc.	929 Holmes	Kansas City	MO	64106	Terrence Dunn	816-474-8600	R	871	1.6
Perini Building Company Inc.	73 Mount Wayte	Framingham	MA	01701	Richard J Rizzo	508-628-2000	S	811*	1.0
Austin Industries Inc.	P O Box 1590	Dallas	TX	75221	William T Solomon	214-443-5500	R	808	6.3
M.A. Mortenson Co.	700 Meadow Ln	Minneapolis	MN	55422	MA Mortenson Jr	612-522-2100	R	804	1.7
Rooney Brothers Co.	111 W 5th St	Tulsa	OK	74103	Timothy P Rooney	918-583-6900	R	770	2.0
TIC Holdings, Inc.	P O Box 774848	Steamboat Sprgs	CO	80477	Ronald W McKenzie	970-879-2561	R	745	5.0
Centex Construction Group Inc.	PO Box 199000	Dallas	TX	75219	Brice E Hill	214-981-5000	S	725*	1.5
Austin Co.	3650 Mayfield Rd	Cleveland	OH	44121	J William Melsop	864-291-6625	R	700*	1.2
Lewis Homes	P O Box 670	Upland	CA	91785	John Goodman	909-985-0971	R	700*	0.9
Colson & Colson Construction	2250 McGilchrist	Salem	OR	97302	William Colson	503-370-7070	R	674	6.4
McDevitt Street Bovis Inc.	P O Box 32755	Charlotte	NC	28232	Luther Cochrane	704-357-1919	S	642*	0.9
Pepper Companies Inc.	643 N Orleans St	Chicago	IL	60610	J David Pepper	312-266-4703	R	623	1.3
Dunn Investment Co.	PO Box 247	Birmingham	AL	35201	JSM French	205-592-8908	R	622*	1.5
Rudolph and Sletten Inc.	989 E Hillsdale Blvd	Foster City	CA	94404	John Rudolph	650-572-1919	R	600*	0.9
HCB Contractors	1700 Pacific Ave	Dallas	TX	75201	Lawrence A Wilson	214-965-1100	R	560	0.5
Weitz Co.	400 Locust, #300	Des Moines	IA	50309	Glenn H DeStigter	515-698-4260	R	556*	0.9
Beck Group	1700 Pacific Ave	Dallas	TX	75201	Lawrence Wilson	214-965-1100	R	555	0.5
Alberici Corp.	2150 Kienlen Ave	St. Louis	MO	63121	Robert F McCoole	314-261-2611	R	554	1.7
Suffolk Construction Inc.	65 Allerton St	Boston	MA	02119	John F Fish	617-445-3500	R	540	0.5
Michael Baker Corp.	PO Box 12259	Pittsburgh	PA	15231	Richard L Shaw	412-269-6300	P	521	3.7
Hoffman Corp.	PO Box 1300	Portland	OR	97207	Wayne A Drinkward	503-221-8811	R	516	0.7
J.E. Dunn Construction Co.	929 Holmes	Kansas City	MO	64106	Terrence Dunn	816-474-8600	S	500*	1.0
Kokosing Construction Inc.	P O Box 226	Fredericktown	OH	43019	William B Burgett	740-694-6315	R	497*	1.2
Okland Construction Inc.	1978 SW Temple	Salt Lake City	UT	84115	J Randy Okland	801-486-0144	R	455	0.4
Danis Cos.	2 River Pl	Dayton	OH	45405	Thomas J Danis	937-228-1225	R	454*	1.1
Boldt Group Inc.	P O Box 373	Appleton	WI	54912	Oscar C Boldt	920-739-7800	R	450*	2.3
Baugh Enterprises Inc.	PO Box 14135	Seattle	WA	98114	Louis E Kapcsandy	206-726-8000	R	450	1.1
Perini Building Inc. Western U.S.	360 E Coronado Rd	Phoenix	AZ	85004	Craig Shaw	602-256-6777	D	449	0.4
Carlson Group Inc.	959 Concord St	Framingham	MA	01701		508-370-0100	R	444*	0.5
Fru-Con Construction Corp.	PO Box 100	Ballwin	MO	63022	Bruce A Frust	314-391-6700	R	442	2.8
Manhattan Construction Co.	3890 W Northwest	Dallas	TX	75220	Timothy P Rooney	214-357-7400	S	425	0.9
O and G Industries Inc.	112 Wall St	Torrington	CT	06790	David Oneglia	860-489-9261	R	421*	1.0
Sundt Corp.	P O Box 26685	Tucson	AZ	85726	J D Pruitt	520-748-7555	R	417	1.5
Hathaway Dinwiddie Construction	275 Battery St	San Francisco	CA	94111	Donald Warmby	415-986-2718	R	400	0.5
Centex Construction Inc.	P O Box 299009	Dallas	TX	75229	Robert Van Cleave	214-357-1891	P	400	0.2
Weitz Company Inc. Phoenix Div.	2255 N 44th St	Phoenix	AZ	85008	Larry Mohr	602-225-0225	D	400	0.1
Haskell Co.	P O Box 44100	Jacksonville	FL	32202	Preston H Haskell	904-791-4500	R	390	0.6
Presley Cos.	19 Corporate Plz	Newport Beach	CA	92660	General W Lyon	949-640-6400	R	367	0.4
Drees Co.	211 Grandview Dr	Fort Mitchell	KY	41017	Ralph A Drees	606-578-4200	R	366	0.7
Hardin Construction Group Inc.	1380 W Paces Ferry	Atlanta	GA	30327	Earl L Shell Jr	404-264-0404	R	340	0.3
Pardee Construction Co.	10880 Wilshire	Los Angeles	CA	90024	David Landon	310-475-3525	S	339*	0.4
Edward Rose Building Enterprises	30057 Orchard Lake	Farmington Hills	MI	48333	Sheldon Rose	248-539-2255	R	331	1.5
Watkins Engineers & Constructors	P O Box 2194	Tallahassee	FL	32316	Eddie Aaron	850-576-7181	S	330	4.0
Stellar Group Inc.	2900 Hartley Rd	Jacksonville	FL	32257	H Bobby Cothren	904-260-2900	R	318*	0.8
Flint Industries Inc.	P O Box 490	Tulsa	OK	74101	John Bates	918-587-8451	R	300*	1.5
Midwest Drywall Company Inc.	PO Box 771170	Wichita	KS	67277	Steve Nienke	316-722-9559	R	300*	1.2
Alex J. Etkin Inc.	30445 Northwestern	Farmington Hills	MI	48333	Thomas H Landry	248-737-5800	R	300	0.3

Source: Ward's Business Directory of U.S. Private and Public Companies, Volumes 1 and 2, 2000. The company type code used is as follows: P - Public, R - Private, S - Subsidiary, D - Division, J - Joint Venture, A - Affiliate, G - Group, N - Company type not reported. Sales are in millions of dollars, employees are in thousands. An asterisk (*) indicates an estimated sales volume. The symbol < stands for 'less than'. Company names and addresses are truncated, in some cases, to fit into the available space.

COST DETAILS

Item	Cost ($ mil)	% of total	Per $1,000 of Revenue	Item	Cost ($ mil)	% of total	Per $1,000 of Revenue
All costs	130,867.3	100.000	746.8	Total Rentals	1,154.6	0.882	6.6
Cost of supplies	28,087.3	21.462	160.3	Equipment	742.2	0.567	4.2
Subcontracts	101,952.9	77.906	581.8	Buildings	412.4	0.315	2.4
Power, fuel, lubricants	827.2	0.632	4.7	Services purchased	1,061.6	0.811	6.1
Electricity	247.1	0.189	1.4	Communications	502.6	0.384	2.9
Natural gas	51.3	0.039	0.3	Building repairs	84.8	0.065	0.5
Gasoline and diesel	494.6	0.378	2.8	Machinery repairs	474.2	0.362	2.7
Highway	415.9	0.318	2.4				
Offroad	78.7	0.060	0.4				
Other power	34.2	0.026	0.2				

Source: Economic Census of the United States, 1997. Revenues referred to are total industry revenues for the current NAICS industry.

CONSTRUCTION PRODUCT DETAILS

Construction type	Value of construction work ($ mil and %)							
	Total		New construction		Additions, alterations, reconstruction		Maintenance and repair	
	Value	%	Value	%	Value	%	Value	%
Total	**173,205.7**	**100.0**	**113,315.5**	**100.0**	**51,530.5**	**100.0**	**6,063.7**	**100.0**
Building construction, total	**166,818.2**	**96.3**	**110,618.2**	**97.6**	**50,325.0**	**97.7**	**5,875.1**	**96.9**
Single-family houses, detached	2,178.5	1.3	1,194.7	1.1	820.0	1.6	163.8	2.7
Single-family houses, attached	512.4	0.3	278.4	0.2	180.1	0.3	53.8	0.9
Apartment buildings, condos and cooperatives	4,081.5	2.4	2,905.2	2.6	1,016.1	2.0	160.2	2.6
Manufacturing and light industrial buildings	8,083.7	4.7	5,201.9	4.6	2,425.4	4.7	456.4	7.5
Manufacturing and light industrial warehouses	3,325.8	1.9	2,428.7	2.1	776.3	1.5	120.8	2.0
Hotels and motels	8,313.6	4.8	6,433.1	5.7	1,679.9	3.3	200.6	3.3
Office buildings	36,148.0	20.9	21,235.7	18.7	13,524.4	26.2	1,387.9	22.9
All other commercial buildings, nec	32,715.0	18.9	21,866.9	19.3	9,631.1	18.7	1,217.0	20.1
Commercial warehouses	6,929.5	4.0	5,465.6	4.8	1,215.7	2.4	248.2	4.1
Religious buildings	4,324.0	2.5	2,870.7	2.5	1,342.6	2.6	110.7	1.8
Educational buildings	23,974.8	13.8	15,587.1	13.8	7,893.5	15.3	494.2	8.2
Health care and institutional buildings	17,466.7	10.1	11,187.6	9.9	5,917.4	11.5	361.7	6.0
Public safety buildings	5,345.6	3.1	4,183.2	3.7	1,064.7	2.1	97.7	1.6
Farm buildings, nonresidential	1,904.1	1.1	1,508.4	1.3	272.8	0.5	122.9	2.0
Amusement, social, and recreational buildings	6,529.9	3.8	5,141.5	4.5	1,275.0	2.5	113.4	1.9
Other building construction	3,429.7	2.0	1,984.7	1.8	895.5	1.7	549.4	9.1
Nonbuilding construction, total	**4,091.5**	**2.4**	**2,697.4**	**2.4**	**1,205.5**	**2.3**	**188.7**	**3.1**
Highways, streets, and related work	812.6	0.5	521.3	0.5	236.6	0.5	54.7	0.9
Bridges, tunnels, and elevated highways	506.0	0.3	251.2	0.2	-	-	26.1	0.4
Other nonbuilding construction, nec	2,772.9	1.6	1,924.9	1.7	740.2	1.4	107.9	1.8
Construction work, nsk	**2,295.9**	**1.3**	NA	-	NA	-	NA	-

Source: Economic Census of the United States, 1997. Bold items are headers. (D) stands for data withheld to protect competitive information. (S) indicates instances where data do not meet publications standards.

245

LOCATION BY STATE AND REGIONAL CONCENTRATION

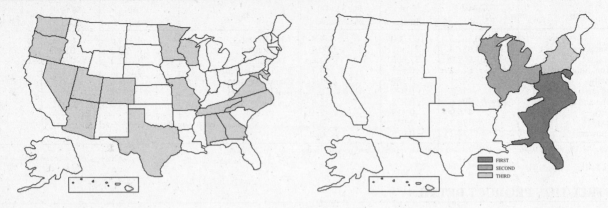

INDUSTRY DATA BY STATE

State	Estab lish- ments	Employment Total	Employment Workers	Total as % of US	Payroll per Employee	Wages per Worker	Costs ($ mil)	Value Added ($ mil)	Reve- nues ($ mil)	% of US	Capital Exp. ($ mil)
California	3,722	48,044	31,204	9.10	42,543	35,428	2,377.0	4,315.2	18,120.5	10.34	106.0
Texas	2,857	35,917	24,052	6.80	32,817	25,221	2,015.5	3,077.2	12,624.8	7.20	65.6
New York	2,743	31,168	18,714	5.90	42,551	34,557	1,459.7	3,006.6	11,703.0	6.68	60.1
Florida	1,975	25,772	16,274	4.88	32,794	25,998	1,272.2	2,028.7	8,285.1	4.73	39.2
Georgia	1,195	18,670	12,527	3.53	35,554	27,609	1,427.1	1,922.1	7,931.9	4.53	41.3
Illinois	1,439	19,797	13,430	3.75	41,317	37,187	961.7	1,917.0	7,708.8	4.40	44.1
Pennsylvania	1,317	21,534	14,719	4.08	38,069	32,954	1,138.9	1,893.2	7,091.2	4.05	52.2
Ohio	1,582	19,713	13,151	3.73	35,790	31,056	940.1	1,658.7	5,785.6	3.30	42.5
North Carolina	919	17,929	12,213	3.39	33,906	26,318	1,092.4	1,220.8	5,382.6	3.07	53.0
Maryland	910	15,299	10,100	2.90	36,515	29,374	825.7	1,386.3	5,118.8	2.92	26.2
Michigan	1,261	12,496	8,638	2.37	37,951	30,641	734.6	1,136.2	4,720.4	2.69	27.3
New Jersey	918	12,320	7,872	2.33	43,881	37,305	726.7	1,691.8	4,615.4	2.63	23.2
Virginia	1,018	16,163	10,654	3.06	33,637	25,295	799.8	1,080.4	4,612.9	2.63	31.7
Missouri	746	16,486	12,534	3.12	32,018	25,693	967.6	859.3	4,558.5	2.60	31.3
Minnesota	702	10,428	7,319	1.97	41,677	38,964	683.7	1,004.9	4,275.7	2.44	20.8
Washington	1,084	14,733	10,315	2.79	36,871	33,116	834.1	966.5	4,250.3	2.43	20.4
Colorado	722	10,949	6,553	2.07	38,267	29,378	624.0	871.5	4,196.6	2.39	25.5
Tennessee	603	12,450	8,909	2.36	34,782	26,454	720.2	816.3	3,877.6	2.21	29.0
Alabama	620	12,365	8,965	2.34	28,593	24,921	891.3	858.8	3,688.8	2.11	32.5
Wisconsin	663	13,451	9,963	2.55	38,610	34,112	711.2	1,104.5	3,524.9	2.01	41.1
Indiana	842	12,906	9,368	2.44	34,311	29,804	588.7	996.2	3,265.6	1.86	26.8
Arizona	684	8,571	4,878	1.62	35,185	27,107	461.1	646.5	3,222.7	1.84	15.4
Oregon	635	6,456	4,473	1.22	40,766	36,525	463.6	577.4	2,714.2	1.55	29.2
Nevada	254	5,996	4,436	1.14	47,944	45,797	218.4	1,144.3	2,380.9	1.36	(D)
Utah	330	5,421	3,857	1.03	34,102	29,382	340.2	464.3	2,133.1	1.22	10.1
Connecticut	421	4,589	2,726	0.87	47,051	37,333	270.2	477.6	2,074.8	1.18	8.7
Mississippi	318	7,049	5,581	1.33	31,460	25,865	471.6	460.2	1,771.8	1.01	(D)
South Carolina	355	6,699	4,797	1.27	29,067	22,625	356.5	525.8	1,662.3	0.95	10.8
Arkansas	296	5,503	4,230	1.04	26,002	20,998	346.7	428.1	1,588.5	0.91	13.5
Kentucky	532	6,918	(D)	1.31	27,551	-	283.7	435.2	1,553.1	0.89	11.1
Louisiana	526	7,489	5,789	1.42	26,031	20,907	313.3	420.9	1,532.2	0.87	12.0
Iowa	579	7,442	5,814	1.41	30,619	28,264	400.5	444.4	1,524.5	0.87	22.7
Montana	166	1,585	1,264	0.30	-	-	80.6	103.1	355.2	0.20	3.5
Maine	239	1,477	1,029	0.28	26,378	23,376	73.1	93.0	309.5	0.18	4.8
Massachusetts	767	10,398	6,275	1.97	44,193	36,481	(D)	1,256.8	(D)	-	(S)
Oklahoma	468	6,363	4,878	1.20	27,016	21,350	(D)	457.6	(D)	-	9.8
Kansas	385	6,045	4,474	1.14	30,027	25,036	(D)	356.8	(D)	-	15.4
Idaho	368	(D)	(D)	-	-	-	(D)	185.0	(D)	-	(D)
New Mexico	331	3,072	2,218	0.58	-	-	(D)	199.1	(D)	-	(D)
Nebraska	318	3,788	2,948	0.72	30,048	25,194	(D)	274.3	(D)	-	8.7
West Virginia	247	(D)	(D)	-	-	-	80.2	146.0	(D)	-	6.2
Hawaii	210	(D)	2,400	-	-	-	(D)	(D)	(D)	-	(D)
South Dakota	208	2,345	(D)	0.44	-	-	(D)	(D)	(D)	-	(D)
North Dakota	171	1,902		0.36	-	-	(D)	83.9	(D)	-	5.7
Alaska	169	1,755	1,223	0.33	45,937	44,357	(D)	143.1	(D)	-	7.4
New Hampshire	131	2,131	1,410	0.40	35,917	25,079	(D)	169.8	(D)	-	4.5
Vermont	121	1,098	761	0.21	32,270	27,138	(D)	55.8	(D)	-	2.6
Wyoming	115	953	(D)	0.18	23,717	-	(D)	(D)	(D)	-	1.9
Delaware	98	1,412	972	0.27	34,219	30,731	(D)	138.4	(D)	-	3.7
Rhode Island	91	1,371	678	0.26	46,981	29,124	(D)	256.3	(D)	-	2.6
D.C.	57	(D)	(D)	-	-	-	(D)	(D)	(D)	-	(D)

Source: Economic Census of the U.S., 1997. Data are sorted by 1997 revenues or establishments. (D) means data suppression to prevent disclosure of company data. (S) means that data did not meet statistical standards for publication. A dash (-) is used when data are unavailable or cannot be calculated. Data followed by an * indicate the midpoint of a range. The ranges are: for 10, 0-19; for 60, 20-99; for 175, 100-249, for 375, 250-499, for 750, 500-999. Higher values are multiples of those shown, e.g., 3,750 is the midpoint of the range 2,500-4,999. Shaded *states* on the state map indicate those states which have proportionately greater representation in the industry than would be indicated by the state's population; the ratio is based on total revenues or number of establishments. Shaded *regions* indicate where the industry is regionally most concentrated.

NAICS 234110 - HIGHWAY AND STREET CONSTRUCTION

GENERAL STATISTICS

Years	Establishments	Employment		Payroll ($ mil)		Costs ($ mil)		Value Added ($ mil)	Revenues ($ mil)			Capital expend. ($ mil)
		Total	Constr. workers	Total	Worker payroll	Total	Cost of materials		All sources	Construction		
										Total	Net	
1997	11,270	277,979	227,066	9,527.6	7,095.1	17,699.6	16,283.2	22,983.9	50,053.8	48,472.3	39,102.1	2,189.1

Source: Economic Census of the United States, 1997. This is a newly defined industry. Data for prior years were unavailable at the time of publication but may become available over time. "Net" under "Construction" is construction revenue net of the costs of subcontracts.

DISTRIBUTION AMONG SIC-BASED INDUSTRIES - 1997

SIC	Industry	Establishments	Employment		Cost of Power & Materials ($ mil)	Revenues ($ mil)			Value Added ($ mil)
			Total (000)	Payroll ($ mil)		All Sources	Construction		
							Total	Net	
161100	Highway & street construction contractors	11,162.0	277,073	9,472.3	17,676.6	49,920.8	48,347.2	39,026.2	22,923.20
874131	Management services (pt)	108.0	906	55.4	23.1	133.0	125.1	75.9	60.71

Source: 1997 Economic Census. U.S. Census Bureau, U.S. Department of Commerce, August 1997. SIC codes ending in two zeroes represent complete 4-digit SICs. All others are parts of 4-digit SIC industries. Items showing a dash (-) indicate that data are not available because of disclosure problems.

SIC INDUSTRIES RELATED TO NAICS 234110

SIC	Industry	1990	1991	1992	1993	1994	1995	1996	1997
1611	**Highway and Street Construction**								
	Establishments (number)	8,476	8,563	10,090	9,833	9,752p	9,588p	9,426p	9,267p
	Employment (thousands)	215.2	194.6	257.4	194.5	247.3e	242.4e	237.6e	232.9e
	Revenues ($ million)	36,194.6e	36,419.5e	36,645.8	36,873.6e	37,102.7e	37,333.3e	37,565.3e	37,798.8e
8741	**Management Services***								
	Establishments (number)	15,267	16,556	20,186	21,920	23,803	21,674	23,348p	24,255p
	Employment (thousands)	285.2	306.6	285.1	357.7	386.3	312.7	368.9p	381.9p
	Revenues ($ million)	20,627.0	21,788.0	23,774.0	23,373.0	24,328.0	27,611.0	27,569.0	28,870.9p

Source: Economic Census of the United States, 1992, annual surveys of economic sectors conducted by the Bureau of the Census, and estimates or projections based on the 1982-1992 period; not all data are shown. 'e' marks estimates made by the editors; 'p' indicates projections based on time series. A dash (-) indicates that data for this SIC or year were not available. * Indicates that only a portion of this industry is present within the NAICS data. If no * is shown, the entire industry is contained within the NAICS data.

INDICES OF CHANGE

Years	Establishments	Employment		Payroll ($ mil)		Costs ($ mil)		Value Added ($ mil)	Revenues ($ mil)			Capital expend. ($ mil)
		Total	Constr. workers	Total	Worker payroll	Total	Cost of materials		All sources	Construction		
										Total	Net	
1997	100.0	100.0	100.0	100.0	100.0	100.0	100.0	100.0	100.0	100.0	100.0	100.0

Sources: Same as General Statistics. The values shown reflect change from the base year, 1997. Values above 100 mean greater than 1997, values below 100 mean less than 1997, and a value of 100 in years other than 1997 means same as 1997. Indices are calculated only for Census years. Data are the most recent available at this level of detail.

SELECTED RATIOS

For 1997	Avg. of Sector	Analyzed Industry	Index	For 1997	Avg. of Sector	Analyzed Industry	Index
Employees per establishment	8.6	24.7	286	Value added per establishment	584,730	2,039,388	349
Construction workers per establishment	6.6	20.1	305	Value added per employee	67,759	82,682	122
Payroll per establishment	265,343	845,395	319	Value added per construction worker	88,592	101,221	114
Payroll per employee	30,748	34,275	111	Revenues per establishment	1,307,915	4,441,331	340
Payroll per construction worker	27,622	31,247	113	Revenues per employee	151,563	180,063	119
Costs per establishment	367,737	1,570,506	427	Revenues per construction worker	198,161	220,437	111
Costs per employee	42,614	63,672	149	CR as % of total revenues	98.48	96.84	98
Costs per construction worker	55,716	77,949	140	Net CR as % of CR	72.40	80.67	111
Materials as % of costs	95.75	92.00	96	Investment per establishment	22,948	194,241	846
Costs as % of revenues	28.12	35.36	126	Investment per employee	2,659	7,875	296
Costs as % of construction revenues	28.55	36.51	128	Investment per construction worker	3,477	9,641	277

Sources: Same as General Statistics. The 'Average of Sector' column represents the average for all industries in this sector. The Index shows the relationship between the Average and the Analyzed Industry. For example, 100 means that they are equal; 500 that the Analyzed Industry is five times the average; 50 means that the Analyzed Industry is half the national average. 'na' is used to show that data are 'not available'. CR stands for "construction revenues" and "Net CR" is construction revenues net of subcontract expenses.

LEADING COMPANIES Number shown: 75 Total sales ($ mil): 35,066 Total employment (000): 146.2

Company Name	Address				CEO Name	Phone	Co. Type	Sales ($ mil)	Empl. (000)
Bechtel Group Inc.	50 Beale St	San Francisco	CA	94105	Riley Bechtel	415-768-1234	R	11,329	30.0
Peter Kiewit Sons' Inc.	1000 Kiewit Plz	Omaha	NE	68131		402-342-2052	R	3,403	16.2
Kiewit Construction Group Inc.	1000 Kiewit Plz	Omaha	NE	68131	Kenneth E Stinson	402-342-2052	S	2,000*	11.0
Granite Construction Inc.	PO Box 50085	Watsonville	CA	95077	David H Watts	831-724-1011	P	1,329	3.9
APAC Inc.	900 Ashwood Pkwy	Atlanta	GA	30338	C Potts	770-392-5300	S	1,300	7.5
J.A. Jones Construction Co.	J A Jones Dr	Charlotte	NC	28287	Bob Hambright	704-553-3000	S	1,200*	10.0
Huber, Hunt and Nichols Inc.	2450 S Tibbs Ave	Indianapolis	IN	46241	Robert G Hunt	317-227-7800	S	1,032	0.6
McCarthy Building Cos.	1341 N Rock Hill	St. Louis	MO	63124	Michael Hurst	314-968-3300	R	980	1.5
Hensel Phelps Construction Co.	PO Box 0	Greeley	CO	80632	Jerry Morgensen	970-352-6565	R	934	1.9
Austin Industries Inc.	P O Box 1590	Dallas	TX	75221	William T Solomon	214-443-5500	R	808	6.3
Halliburton/Brown and Root Inc.	400 Clinton Dr	Houston	TX	77020		713-676-3011	S	675*	1.5
Michael Baker Corp.	PO Box 12259	Pittsburgh	PA	15231	Richard L Shaw	412-269-6300	P	521	3.7
Michael Baker Jr. Inc.	PO Box 12259	Pittsburgh	PA	15231	Charles I Homan	412-269-6300	S	521	3.8
Kokosung Construction Inc.	PO Box 226	Fredricktown	ID	43019	Brian Burgett	740-694-6315	R	435	1.5
Sundt Corp.	P O Box 26685	Tucson	AZ	85726	J D Pruitt	520-748-7555	R	417	1.5
Lane Industries Inc.	965 E Main St	Meriden	CT	06450	Byron F Wetmore	203-235-3351	R	346	1.6
Lafarge Inc.	1400 West 64th Ave	Denver	CO	80221	Patrick Walker	303-426-1166	S	334*	2.0
Tidewater Skanska Group Inc.	PO Box 57	Norfolk	VA	23501	DJ Eastwood	757-578-4100	S	320	2.5
Lane Construction Corp.	965 E Main St	Meriden	CT	06450	BF Wetmue	203-235-3351	S	314	1.6
Slattery Skanska Inc.	16-16 Whitestone	Whitestone	NY	11357	Stuart E Graham	718-767-2600	S	300	1.0
Rogers Group Inc.	PO Box 25250	Nashville	TN	37202	Don Williamson	615-242-0585	R	269*	1.6
T.L. James and Company Inc.	PO Box 1260	Ruston	LA	71273	William J Deasy	318-255-7912	R	264*	2.0
Fletcher Pacific Construction Ltd.	707 Richards St	Honolulu	HI	96813	Dennis N Watts	808-533-5000	S	250	0.8
S.E. Johnson Companies Inc.	P O Box 29-A	Maumee	OH	43537	JT Bearss	419-893-8731	R	225*	1.4
Flatiron Structures L.L.C.	PO Box 2239	Longmont	CO	80502	Scott Lynn	303-444-1760	R	206*	0.5
Boh Bros. Construction L.L.C.	PO Box 53266	New Orleans	LA	70153		504-821-2400	R	200	2.0
Hubbard Construction Co.	P O Box 547217	Orlando	FL	32854	Jean-Marc Allard	407-645-5500	S	200*	1.3
Vecellio Contracting Corp.	P O Box 15065	W. Palm Beach	FL	33416	Leo Vecellio Jr	561-793-2102	S	200	1.3
Meadow Valley Corp.	P O Box 60726	Phoenix	AZ	85082	Bradley E Larson	602-437-5400	P	187	0.6
Dick Enterprises Inc.	PO Box 10896	Pittsburgh	PA	15236	David Dick	412-384-1100	S	184*	0.5
Barnhill Contracting Co.	P O Box 31765	Raleigh	NC	27622	Robert E Barnhill Jr	919-781-7210	R	163	1.0
James McHugh Construction Co.	2222 S Indiana Ave	Chicago	IL	60616	Bruce E Lake	312-842-8400	S	157*	0.4
Cianbro Corp.	PO Box 1000	Pittsfield	ME	04967	Alton Cianchette	207-487-3311	R	150*	1.5
Driggs Corp.	8700 Ashwood Dr	Capitol Heights	MD	20743	John Driggs	301-499-1950	R	150*	1.1
United Metro Materials Inc.	PO Box 52140	Phoenix	AZ	85072	John Fowler	602-220-5000	S	150*	0.9
N.A. Degerstrom Inc.	3303 N Sullivan Rd	Spokane	WA	99216	Neal Degerstrom	509-928-3333	R	143*	0.3
Ritchie Corp.	PO Box 4048	Wichita	KS	67204	H Ritchie	316-838-9301	R	137*	1.0
Hawaiian Bitumuls & Paving	PO Box 2240	Honolulu	HI	96804	Bill Paik	808-845-3991	S	134*	0.5
Herzog Contracting Corp.	P O Box 1089	St. Joseph	MO	64502	William E Herzog	816-233-9001	R	130	0.9
C.C. Myers Inc.	3286 Fitzgerald Rd	Rancho Cordova	CA	95742	CC Myers	916-635-9370	R	125	0.4
Sim J. Harris Co.	P O Box 639069	San Diego	CA	92163	Dave Hummel	858-277-5481	S	124*	0.8
James Cape and Sons Co.	6422 N Hwy 31	Racine	WI	53402	WR Cape	414-639-2552	R	120*	0.7
Gohmann Asphalt & Construction	PO Box 2428	Clarksville	IN	47131	J Gohmann	812-282-1349	R	110	0.7
McHugh Enterprises Inc.	2222 S Indiana Ave	Chicago	IL	60616	James R McHugh	312-842-8400	R	110	0.5
K-Five Construction Corp.	13769 Main St	Lemont	IL	60439	George Krug, Jr	630-257-5600	R	108	0.5
Western Mobile Denver Paving	P O Box 21588	Denver	CO	80221	Patrick Walker	303-657-4200	D	105*	0.3
Matsco Inc.	1600 Kenview Dr	Marietta	GA	30061	Bob Mathews	770-422-7520	R	103*	0.6
Hardaway Co.	P O Box 1360	Columbus	GA	31902	Mason H Lampton	706-322-3274	R	100*	0.5
Trap Rock Industries Inc.	PO Box 419	Kingston	NJ	08528	Joseph Stavola	609-924-0300	R	100	0.4
Interstate Highway Construction	PO Box 4356	Englewood	CO	80155	J Kenyon Schaeffer	303-790-9100	R	90	0.4
C.W. Matthews Contracting	1600 Kenview Dr	Marietta	GA	30060	Robert E Matthews	770-422-7520	S	85*	0.5
Johnson Brothers Corp.	23577 Minnesota 22	Litchfield	MN	55355		612-693-2871	R	83	0.6
Koester Equipment Inc.	14649 Hwy	Evansville	IN	47711	Homer Fruit	812-867-6635	R	83	0.3
Plote Inc.	1100 Brandt Dr	Elgin	IL	60120		847-695-9300	R	82*	0.6
Manatts Inc.	PO Box 535	Brooklyn	IA	52211	Brad Manatt	515-522-9206	R	81*	0.5
Harper Industries Inc.	616 Northview St	Paducah	KY	42001	Billy Harper	502-442-2753	R	80	1.0
Lakeside Industries	PO Box 7016	Issaquah	WA	98027	Timothy Lee	425-313-2600	R	80	0.6
Staker Paving & Construction Inc.	P O Box 27598	Salt Lake City	UT	84127	S Val Staker	801-298-7500	P	80	0.6
Freesen Inc.	PO Box 350	Bluffs	IL	62621	Thomas Oetgen	217-754-3304	R	80	0.5
Bankhead Enterprises Inc.	P O Box 93006	Atlanta	GA	30318	Glenn E Taylor	404-894-7900	R	80*	0.5
Phillips and Jordan Inc.	PO Box 52050	Knoxville	TN	37950	William T Phillips Sr	423-688-8342	R	80*	0.4
Summers-Taylor Inc.	P O Box 1628	Elizabethton	TN	37644	Robert T Summers	423-543-3181	R	77*	0.5
H.E. Sargent Inc.	101 Bennoch Rd	Stillwater	ME	04489	John Simpson	207-827-4435	R	76	0.5
Northern Improvement Co.	PO Box 2846	Fargo	ND	58108	Thomas McCormick	701-277-1225	S	75*	0.6
Glasgow Inc.	PO Box 1089	Glenside	PA	19038	Bruce Rambo	215-884-8800	R	75	0.5
Hardrives of Delray Inc.	2350 S Congress	Delray Beach	FL	33445	George T Elmore	561-278-0456	R	75*	0.4
Mt. Hope Rock Products Inc.	625 Mt Hope Rd	Wharton	NJ	07885	Robert E Carballal	973-366-7741	R	74*	0.5
Hinkle Corp.	PO Box 200	Paris	KY	40362		606-987-3670	R	72*	0.4
Kasler Corp.	P O Box 600	Highland	CA	92346	Tony Ferreccio	909-425-4200	S	71*	0.4
Bellezza Company Inc.	2 Fish House Rd	South Kearny	NJ	07032	Alan Bellezza	201-997-4445	R	68*	0.4
Condotte America Inc.	9200 S Dadeland	Miami	FL	33156	Chiassredo Bellero	305-670-7585	R	68*	0.2
Harper Bros. Inc.	14860 6 Mile Cyp	Fort Myers	FL	33912		941-481-2350	R	67*	0.4
Kiewit Western Co.	7926 S Platte	Littleton	CO	80128	Walter Scott	303-979-9330	S	62*	0.4
Ruhlin Co.	P O Box 190	Sharon Center	OH	44274	James L Ruhlin	330-239-2800	R	60	0.4
Lionmark Inc.	1620 Woodson Rd	St. Louis	MO	63114	Edward Gomes Jr	314-991-2180	R	60*	0.4

Source: Ward's Business Directory of U.S. Private and Public Companies, Volumes 1 and 2, 2000. The company type code used is as follows: P - Public, R - Private, S - Subsidiary, D - Division, J - Joint Venture, A - Affiliate, G - Group, N - Company type not reported. Sales are in millions of dollars, employees are in thousands. An asterisk (*) indicates an estimated sales volume. The symbol < stands for 'less than'. Company names and addresses are truncated, in some cases, to fit into the available space.

COST DETAILS

Item	Cost ($ mil)	% of total	Per $1,000 of Revenue	Item	Cost ($ mil)	% of total	Per $1,000 of Revenue
All costs	27,069.8	100.000	540.8	Total Rentals	1,547.0	5.715	30.9
Cost of supplies	16,283.2	60.153	325.3	Equipment	1,418.4	5.240	28.3
Subcontracts	9,370.2	34.615	187.2	Buildings	128.6	0.475	2.6
Power, fuel, lubricants	1,416.4	5.233	28.3	Services purchased	1,698.3	6.274	33.9
Electricity	139.4	0.515	2.8	Communications	204.7	0.756	4.1
Natural gas	122.1	0.451	2.4	Building repairs	82.3	0.304	1.6
Gasoline and diesel	1,036.5	3.829	20.7	Machinery repairs	1,411.3	5.213	28.2
Highway	515.1	1.903	10.3				
Offroad	521.4	1.926	10.4				
Other power	118.4	0.437	2.4				

Source: *Economic Census of the United States*, 1997. Revenues referred to are total industry revenues for the current NAICS industry.

CONSTRUCTION PRODUCT DETAILS

Construction type	Value of construction work ($ mil and %)							
	Total		New construction		Additions, alterations, reconstruction		Maintenance and repair	
	Value	%	Value	%	Value	%	Value	%
Total	**48,472.3**	**100.0**	**24,670.8**	**100.0**	**16,107.2**	**100.0**	**7,694.2**	**100.0**
Building construction, total	**893.6**	**1.8**	**696.0**	**2.8**	**143.5**	**0.9**	**54.1**	**0.7**
Nonbuilding construction, total	**47,578.5**	**98.2**	**23,974.7**	**97.2**	**15,963.7**	**99.1**	**7,640.0**	**99.3**
Highways, streets, and related work	38,171.1	78.7	18,421.3	74.7	13,133.1	81.5	6,616.7	86.0
Airport runways and related work	1,434.2	3.0	676.3	2.7	577.3	3.6	180.6	2.3
Private driveways and parking areas	2,651.7	5.5	1,475.8	6.0	682.7	4.2	493.3	6.4
Bridges, tunnels, and elevated highways	1,872.8	3.9	1,020.1	4.1	710.9	4.4	141.7	1.8
Sewers, water mains, and related facilities	1,958.7	4.0	1,428.2	5.8	432.2	2.7	98.3	1.3
Water mains and related facilities	748.6	1.5	535.0	2.2	169.7	1.1	43.9	0.6
Sewage and water treatment plants	227.5	0.5	125.4	0.5	88.5	0.5	13.6	0.2
Conservation and development construction	245.3	0.5	176.5	0.7	40.4	0.3	28.4	0.4
Recreational facilities	159.9	0.3	129.4	0.5	25.6	0.2	4.9	0.1
Other nonbuilding construction, nec	857.3	1.8	521.7	2.1	273.0	1.7	62.5	0.8

Source: *Economic Census of the United States*, 1997. Bold items are headers. (D) stands for data withheld to protect competitive information. (S) indicates instances where data do not meet publications standards.

LOCATION BY STATE AND REGIONAL CONCENTRATION

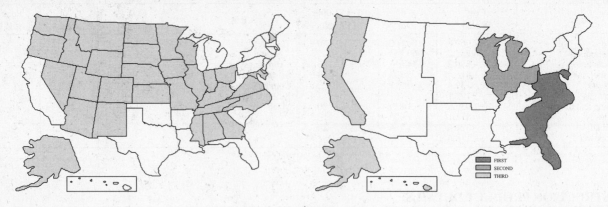

INDUSTRY DATA BY STATE

State	Estab lish- ments	Employment			Compensation		Production				Capital Exp. ($ mil)
		Total	Workers	Total as % of US	Payroll per Employee	Wages per Worker	Costs ($ mil)	Value Added ($ mil)	Reve- nues ($ mil)	% of US	
California	827	19,540	15,153	7.03	44,171	41,494	1,339.6	2,184.1	4,363.6	8.72	135.6
Texas	556	20,748	17,627	7.46	24,958	21,735	1,155.7	1,141.4	2,766.0	5.53	131.9
Florida	380	15,288	12,254	5.50	29,795	26,422	825.5	1,143.4	2,512.0	5.02	115.5
Illinois	475	11,999	9,744	4.32	41,607	39,347	790.1	1,121.1	2,386.1	4.77	90.2
Ohio	397	10,433	8,316	3.75	40,616	39,686	817.5	997.5	2,241.6	4.48	60.6
New York	622	11,037	8,872	3.97	40,838	38,787	708.8	1,025.1	2,165.8	4.33	64.8
Pennsylvania	507	11,590	9,298	4.17	35,931	32,715	674.5	1,000.1	1,985.2	3.97	89.3
North Carolina	381	11,964	9,746	4.30	27,987	25,375	615.7	753.5	1,741.0	3.48	85.1
Virginia	420	11,309	9,591	4.07	26,773	23,496	609.1	653.0	1,547.8	3.09	63.5
Michigan	352	5,789	4,771	2.08	44,557	40,786	481.2	673.0	1,466.8	2.93	64.0
Washington	364	6,975	5,561	2.51	42,420	39,015	410.8	753.8	1,415.5	2.83	80.0
Georgia	316	7,103	5,888	2.56	31,186	25,887	590.5	524.8	1,380.0	2.76	79.2
Tennessee	216	7,680	6,713	2.76	28,068	24,163	439.5	655.4	1,312.0	2.62	67.3
Minnesota	262	5,839	4,929	2.10	42,813	39,497	382.6	605.6	1,271.2	2.54	58.1
Missouri	221	5,952	4,872	2.14	36,939	34,157	494.6	514.6	1,189.7	2.38	51.3
Indiana	173	5,041	3,652	1.81	41,357	43,495	543.4	393.5	1,155.2	2.31	47.1
New Jersey	406	5,677	4,403	2.04	40,980	36,863	369.2	568.2	1,124.5	2.25	37.5
Maryland	204	7,716	6,385	2.78	30,595	26,790	360.2	527.0	1,095.0	2.19	51.0
Wisconsin	182	4,739	4,049	1.70	47,403	46,250	404.1	468.9	1,071.7	2.14	56.9
Kansas	134	5,505	4,533	1.98	32,506	27,346	339.2	468.9	1,063.5	2.12	57.5
Colorado	228	5,476	4,365	1.97	32,771	29,281	363.9	466.7	1,047.5	2.09	43.8
Iowa	165	5,197	4,541	1.87	34,368	30,355	492.7	342.1	994.0	1.99	60.2
Massachusetts	245	4,016	3,073	1.44	42,755	38,809	348.3	398.4	950.6	1.90	26.3
Arizona	184	5,345	4,461	1.92	30,731	28,565	355.0	395.8	945.6	1.89	36.1
Alabama	308	6,577	5,503	2.37	23,738	21,749	338.3	423.0	931.0	1.86	49.5
Louisiana	144	5,467	4,376	1.97	26,045	22,062	352.3	340.4	802.1	1.60	33.4
Kentucky	155	3,969	3,227	1.43	32,833	30,537	267.6	337.6	742.0	1.48	37.0
Mississippi	141	4,140	3,572	1.49	25,368	21,596	265.5	311.6	695.0	1.39	24.5
South Carolina	211	4,290	3,619	1.54	25,314	21,931	286.0	286.7	680.7	1.36	30.4
Oregon	300	3,641	2,927	1.31	36,034	33,915	226.1	296.5	617.0	1.23	30.0
Utah	97	2,796	2,253	1.01	33,461	30,461	169.3	299.7	588.4	1.18	25.0
Connecticut	232	2,753	2,171	0.99	39,997	37,752	165.7	261.1	531.2	1.06	22.1
Nevada	46	2,523	2,194	0.91	41,171	40,328	149.5	303.2	511.9	1.02	20.7
Oklahoma	114	3,099	2,568	1.11	27,412	23,550	199.2	231.2	498.1	1.00	19.3
Nebraska	116	2,954	2,512	1.06	29,168	26,854	189.1	193.9	493.6	0.99	23.6
Idaho	140	2,368	2,025	0.85	29,616	26,888	109.1	237.4	456.2	0.91	(S)
New Mexico	75	3,512	2,740	1.26	28,513	26,924	149.9	225.8	448.4	0.90	19.4
Alaska	124	1,785	1,515	0.64	55,186	55,454	93.3	249.4	408.4	0.82	19.6
Montana	109	2,168	1,874	0.78	27,559	24,419	106.1	145.8	305.1	0.61	25.2
West Virginia	77	1,816	1,375	0.65	31,635	25,732	63.4	193.0	290.1	0.58	22.6
North Dakota	109	1,732	1,526	0.62	33,096	30,484	80.7	143.4	279.0	0.56	13.8
New Hampshire	96	1,208	938	0.43	35,469	31,614	85.9	86.0	225.4	0.45	29.2
Wyoming	33	1,338	1,194	0.48	31,071	30,126	63.3	104.4	196.4	0.39	17.5
South Dakota	110	1,415	1,120	0.51	26,322	25,656	67.0	100.6	186.8	0.37	11.1
Delaware	44	1,028	826	0.37	29,655	27,374	67.6	61.7	154.8	0.31	6.9
Maine	47	954	772	0.34	29,482	26,278	42.7	57.6	116.7	0.23	5.8
Arkansas	97	1,751	1,415	0.63	23,995	21,249	(D)	97.6	(D)	-	9.3
Hawaii	50	996	682	0.36	46,409	43,425	(D)	99.5	(D)	-	5.4
Rhode Island	42	619	467	0.22	41,326	39,330	(D)	44.6	(D)	-	(S)
Vermont	30	360	301	0.13	27,781	25,412	(D)	24.9	(D)	-	2.3
D.C.	8	764	580	0.27	36,880	37,324	(D)	51.5	(D)	-	5.2

Source: Economic Census of the U.S., 1997. Data are sorted by 1997 revenues or establishments. (D) means data suppression to prevent disclosure of company data. (S) means that data did not meet statistical standards for publication. A dash (-) is used when data are unavailable or cannot be calculated. Data followed by an * indicate the midpoint of a range. The ranges are: for 10, 0-19; for 60, 20-99, for 175, 100-249, for 375, 250-499, for 750, 500-999. Higher values are multiples of those shown, e.g., 3,750 is the midpoint of the range 2,500-4,999. Shaded *states* on the state map indicate those states which have proportionately greater representation in the industry than would be indicated by the state's population; the ratio is based on total revenues or number of establishments. Shaded *regions* indicate where the industry is regionally most concentrated.

NAICS 234120 - BRIDGE AND TUNNEL CONSTRUCTION

GENERAL STATISTICS

| Years | Estab-lish-ments | Employment | | Payroll ($ mil) | | Costs ($ mil) | | Value Added ($ mil) | Revenues ($ mil) | | | Capital expend. ($ mil) |
| | | Total | Constr. workers | Total | Worker payroll | Total | Cost of materials | | All sources | Construction | | |
										Total	Net	
1997	1,177	47,764	38,201	1,847.2	1,378.8	2,695.9	2,575.4	4,493.6	9,556.4	9,539.0	7,172.0	242.3

Source: *Economic Census of the United States*, 1997. This is a newly defined industry. Data for prior years were unavailable at the time of publication but may become available over time. "Net" under "Construction" is construction revenue net of the costs of subcontracts.

DISTRIBUTION AMONG SIC-BASED INDUSTRIES - 1997

| SIC | Industry | Estab-lish-ments | Employment | | Cost of Power & Materials ($ mil) | Revenues ($ mil) | | | Value Added ($ mil) |
| | | | Total (000) | Payroll ($ mil) | | All Sources | Construction | | |
							Total	Net	
162200	Bridge, tunnel, & elevated highway construction contractors	1,171.0	47,681	1,843.7	2,694.1	9,547.8	9,530.8	7,165.6	4,488.51
874132	Management services (pt)	6.0	84	3.5	1.8	8.6	8.2	6.4	5.04

Source: 1997 *Economic Census*. U.S. Census Bureau, U.S. Department of Commerce, August 1997. SIC codes ending in two zeroes represent complete 4-digit SICs. All others are parts of 4-digit SIC industries. Items showing a dash (-) indicate that data are not available because of disclosure problems.

SIC INDUSTRIES RELATED TO NAICS 234120

SIC	Industry	1990	1991	1992	1993	1994	1995	1996	1997
1622	**Bridge, Tunnel, and Elevated Highway**								
	Establishments (number)	1,087e	1,064e	1,041	1,019p	997p	976p	955p	935p
	Employment (thousands)	45.2e	44.4e	43.7	43.0e	42.3e	41.6e	40.9e	40.2e
	Revenues ($ million)	6,548.8e	6,908.0e	7,286.9	7,686.6e	8,108.3e	8,553.0e	9,022.2e	9,517.0e
8741	**Management Services***								
	Establishments (number)	15,267	16,556	20,186	21,920	23,803	21,674	23,348p	24,255p
	Employment (thousands)	285.2	306.6	285.1	357.7	386.3	312.7	368.9p	381.9p
	Revenues ($ million)	20,627.0	21,788.0	23,774.0	23,373.0	24,328.0	27,611.0	27,569.0	28,870.9p

Source: *Economic Census of the United States*, 1992, annual surveys of economic sectors conducted by the Bureau of the Census, and estimates or projections based on the 1982-1992 period; not all data are shown. 'e' marks estimates made by the editors; 'p' indicates projections based on time series. A dash (-) indicates that data for this SIC or year were not available. * Indicates that only a portion of this industry is present within the NAICS data. If no * is shown, the entire industry is contained within the NAICS data.

INDICES OF CHANGE

| Years | Estab-lish-ments | Employment | | Payroll ($ mil) | | Costs ($ mil) | | Value Added ($ mil) | Revenues ($ mil) | | | Capital expend. ($ mil) |
| | | Total | Constr. workers | Total | Worker payroll | Total | Cost of materials | | All sources | Construction | | |
										Total	Net	
1997	100.0	100.0	100.0	100.0	100.0	100.0	100.0	100.0	100.0	100.0	100.0	100.0

Sources: Same as General Statistics. The values shown reflect change from the base year, 1997. Values above 100 mean greater than 1997, values below 100 mean less than 1997, and a value of 100 in years other than 1997 means same as 1997. Indices are calculated only for Census years. Data are the most recent available at this level of detail.

SELECTED RATIOS

For 1997	Avg. of Sector	Analyzed Industry	Index	For 1997	Avg. of Sector	Analyzed Industry	Index
Employees per establishment	8.6	40.6	470	Value added per establishment	584,730	3,817,842	653
Construction workers per establishment	6.6	32.5	492	Value added per employee	67,759	94,079	139
Payroll per establishment	265,343	1,569,414	591	Value added per construction worker	88,592	117,630	133
Payroll per employee	30,748	38,673	126	Revenues per establishment	1,307,915	8,119,286	621
Payroll per construction worker	27,622	36,093	131	Revenues per employee	151,563	200,075	132
Costs per establishment	367,737	2,290,484	623	Revenues per construction worker	198,161	250,161	126
Costs per employee	42,614	56,442	132	CR as % of total revenues	98.48	99.82	101
Costs per construction worker	55,716	70,571	127	Net CR as % of CR	72.40	75.19	104
Materials as % of costs	95.75	95.53	100	Investment per establishment	22,948	205,862	897
Costs as % of revenues	28.12	28.21	100	Investment per employee	2,659	5,073	191
Costs as % of construction revenues	28.55	28.26	99	Investment per construction worker	3,477	6,343	182

Sources: Same as General Statistics. The 'Average of Sector' column represents the average for all industries in this sector. The Index shows the relationship between the Average and the Analyzed Industry. For example, 100 means that they are equal; 500 that the Analyzed Industry is five times the average; 50 means that the Analyzed Industry is half the national average. 'na' is used to show that data are 'not available'. CR stands for "construction revenues" and "Net CR" is construction revenues net of subcontract expenses.

LEADING COMPANIES   Number shown: **75**   Total sales ($ mil): **16,188**   Total employment (000): **87.3**

Company Name	Address				CEO Name	Phone	Co. Type	Sales ($ mil)	Empl. (000)
Brown and Root Inc.	PO Box 3	Houston	TX	77001		713-676-3011	S	3,062	30.0
J.F. Shea Co.	PO Box 489	Walnut	CA	91788	John Shea	909-594-9500	R	1,621	2.0
Granite Construction Inc.	PO Box 50085	Watsonville	CA	95077	David H Watts	831-724-1011	P	1,329	3.9
McCarthy Building	1341 N Rock Hill	St. Louis	MO	63124	Michael M McCarthy	314-968-3300	R	900	1.5
Austin Industries Inc.	P O Box 1590	Dallas	TX	75221	William T Solomon	214-443-5500	R	808	6.3
Chicago Bridge and Iron Co.	1501 N Division St	Plainfield	IL	60544		815-439-6000	P	776	6.5
Michael Baker Jr. Inc.	PO Box 12259	Pittsburgh	PA	15231	Charles I Homan	412-269-6300	S	521	3.8
Kokosung Construction Inc.	PO Box 226	Fredricktown	ID	43019	Brian Burgett	740-694-6315	R	435	1.5
Lane Construction Corp.	965 E Main St	Meriden	CT	06450	BF Wetmue	203-235-3351	S	314	1.6
Slattery Skanska Inc.	16-16 Whitestone	Whitestone	NY	11357	Stuart E Graham	718-767-2600	S	300	1.0
Mosser Construction Inc.	122 S Wilson Ave	Fremont	OH	43420	Art Carter	419-334-3801	S	299*	0.7
Rogers Group Inc.	PO Box 25250	Nashville	TN	37202	Don Williamson	615-242-0585	R	269*	1.6
T.L. James and Company Inc.	PO Box 1260	Ruston	LA	71273	William J Deasy	318-255-7912	R	264*	2.0
WMOG Inc.	122 S Wilson Ave	Fremont	OH	43420	Robert Moyer	419-334-3801	R	256*	0.6
S.E. Johnson Companies Inc.	P O Box 29-A	Maumee	OH	43537	JT Bearss	419-893-8731	R	225*	1.4
Flatiron Structures L.L.C.	PO Box 2239	Longmont	CO	80502	Scott Lynn	303-444-1760	R	206*	0.5
Meadow Valley Corp.	P O Box 60726	Phoenix	AZ	85082	Bradley E Larson	602-437-5400	P	187	0.6
Traylor Brothers Inc.	P O Box 5165	Evansville	IN	47716	Thomas W Traylor	812-477-1542	R	186	1.0
Rieth-Riley Company Inc.	PO Box 477	Goshen	IN	46527	R McCormick	219-875-5183	R	170*	0.8
Gilbert Southern Corp.	510 Plaza Dr	College Park	GA	30349	Scott Cassels	404-768-4145	S	170	0.3
James McHugh Construction Co.	2222 S Indiana Ave	Chicago	IL	60616	Bruce E Lake	312-842-8400	S	157*	0.4
Cianbro Corp.	PO Box 1000	Pittsfield	ME	04967	Alton Cianchette	207-487-3311	R	150*	1.5
National Engineering	12608 Alameda Dr	Cleveland	OH	44136	Marty Cohen	440-238-3331	R	150*	0.6
I and OA Slutzky Inc.	Rte 296	Hunter	NY	12442		518-263-4268	R	149*	0.4
Bradbury & Stamm Construction	P O Box 10850	Albuquerque	NM	87184	James N King	505-765-1200	R	145	0.3
N.A. Degerstrom Inc.	3303 N Sullivan Rd	Spokane	WA	99216	Neal Degerstrom	509-928-3333	R	143*	0.3
Herzog Contracting Corp.	P O Box 1089	St. Joseph	MO	64502	William E Herzog	816-233-9001	R	130	0.9
Crowder Construction Co.	P O Box 30007	Charlotte	NC	28230	Otis A Crowder	704-372-3541	R	130	0.7
C.C. Myers Inc.	3286 Fitzgerald Rd	Rancho Cordova	CA	95742	CC Myers	916-635-9370	R	125	0.4
MCM Construction Inc.	6413 32nd St	North Highlands	CA	95660	James Carter	916-334-1221	R	115	0.4
McHugh Enterprises Inc.	2222 S Indiana Ave	Chicago	IL	60616	James R McHugh	312-842-8400	R	110	0.5
Western Mobile Denver Paving	P O Box 21588	Denver	CO	80221	Patrick Walker	303-657-4200	D	105*	0.3
Hardaway Co.	P O Box 1360	Columbus	GA	31902	Mason H Lampton	706-322-3274	R	100*	0.5
CRSS-Constructors Inc.	4848 Loop Central	Houston	TX	77081	WM Dean	314-436-7600	S	97*	0.9
Jensen Construction Co.	5550 N E 22nd St	Des Moines	IA	50313		515-266-5173	R	91*	0.5
Glenn O. Hawbaker Inc.	PO Box 135	State College	PA	16804	Daniel Hawbaker	814-237-1444	R	88	0.7
Johnson Brothers Corp.	23577 Minnesota 22	Litchfield	MN	55355		612-693-2871	R	83	0.6
Freesen Inc.	PO Box 350	Bluffs	IL	62621	Thomas Oetgen	217-754-3304	R	80	0.5
Neosho Construction Co.	P O Box 4526	Topeka	KS	66604	Steve Hutchinson	785-273-0200	R	80	0.4
Northern Improvement Co.	PO Box 2846	Fargo	ND	58108	Thomas McCormick	701-277-1225	S	75*	0.6
Manson Construction Co.	P O Box 24067	Seattle	WA	98124	Glenn A Edwards	206-762-0850	R	75*	0.3
Kasler Corp.	P O Box 600	Highland	CA	92346	Tony Ferreccio	909-425-4200	S	71*	0.4
Bellezza Company Inc.	2 Fish House Rd	South Kearny	NJ	07032	Alan Bellezza	201-997-4445	R	68*	0.4
Karl Koch Erecting Co.	400 Roosevelt Ave	Carteret	NJ	07008	John Daly	732-969-1700	S	68*	0.4
Zenith Tech Inc.	PO Box 1028	Waukesha	WI	53187	Ned W Bechthold	414-524-1800	R	60	0.5
Steve P. Rados Inc.	2002	Santa Ana	CA	92735	Alex S Rados	714-835-4612	S	60*	0.2
Hickory Construction Co.	1728 9th Ave N W	Hickory	NC	28601		828-322-9234	R	60	0.2
Flippo Construction Company Inc.	3820 Penn Belt Pl	Forestville	MD	20747	Michael Haluka	301-967-6800	R	59*	0.4
James D. Morrissey Inc.	9119 Frankford Ave	Philadelphia	PA	19114	James D Morrissey Jr	215-333-8000	R	58*	0.3
J.F. White Contracting Co.	P O Box 9020	Framingham	MA	01701	Peter T White	617-964-0100	R	53*	0.4
Peterson Contractors Inc.	P O Box A	Reinbeck	IA	50669	Cordell Q Peterson	319-345-2713	R	51*	0.3
Ranger Construction	1801 S Nova Rd	Daytona Beach	FL	32119	Mike Slade	904-761-8383	R	51*	0.3
Massman Construction Co.	2401 State Line Rd	Kansas City	MO	64114	HJ Massman IV	816-523-1000	R	50*	0.2
Sletten Construction Co.	PO Box 2467	Great Falls	MT	59403	J Robert Sletten	406-761-7920	S	50	0.2
VSL Corp.	1671 Dell Ave	Campbell	CA	95008		408-866-6777	R	49*	0.3
APAC Construction Group	PO Box 19855	Atlanta	GA	30325	Frank Nichols	404-603-2654	S	44*	0.2
C.A. Hull Company Inc.	8177 Goldie	Walled Lake	MI	48390	Joseph R Malloure	248-363-3813	R	42	0.3
D.H. Blattner and Sons Inc.	400 Cty Road 50	Avon	MN	56310	WH Blattner Jr	320-356-7351	R	41*	0.5
W.L. Hailey and Company Inc.	PO Box 40646	Nashville	TN	37204	G David Waller	615-255-3161	R	41*	0.3
L.C. Whitford Company Inc.	164 N Main St	Wellsville	NY	14895		716-593-3601	R	40	0.3
George and Lynch Inc.	113 W 6th St	New Castle	DE	19720	Will Robinson	302-328-6275	R	40*	0.2
Max J. Kuney Co.	PO Box 4008	Spokane	WA	99202	Max J Kuney III	509-535-0651	R	40	0.2
D.A. Collins Construction Co.	PO Box 191	Mechanicville	NY	12118	Thomas F Longe	518-664-9855	R	40	0.1
Brutoco Engineering	P O Box 429	Fontana	CA	92334	Michael H King	909-350-3535	R	38*	0.2
GAL Construction Company Inc.	PO Box 127	Belle Vernon	PA	15012	Luis Ruscitto	724-929-3000	R	36*	0.2
Affholder Inc.	17988 Edison Ave	Chesterfield	MO	63005	Robert W Affholder	636-530-2833	S	35	0.2
C.S. McCrossan Inc.	7865 Jefferson Hwy	Maple Grove	MN	55369	Charles McCrossan	612-425-4167	R	34*	0.2
Otto Baum and Sons Inc.	866 N Main St	Morton	IL	61550	Kenneth D Baum	309-266-7114	R	34	0.2
Greggo and Ferrara Inc.	4048 New Castle	New Castle	DE	19720	Nicholas Ferrara Jr	302-658-5241	R	30*	0.3
South Coast Inc.	4049 Tongass Hwy	Ketchikan	AK	99901	Gerry Renich	907-225-6125	R	30	0.3
DeFoe Corp.	800 S Columbus	Mount Vernon	NY	10550		914-699-7440	R	30*	0.2
J.M. Foster Inc.	PO Box M-750	Gary	IN	46401	Martha B Lee	219-949-4020	R	30	0.2
Howell Asphalt Company Inc.	PO Box 1009	Mattoon	IL	61938	Kenneth Ozier	217-234-8877	R	27*	0.3
Buckley and Co.	3401 Moore St	Philadelphia	PA	19145	Robert R Buckley	215-334-7500	R	26*	0.2
General Construction Co.	19472 Powder Hill	Poulsbo	WA	98370	William Urban	360-779-3200	R	26*	0.2

Source: Ward's *Business Directory of U.S. Private and Public Companies*, Volumes 1 and 2, 2000. The company type code used is as follows: P - Public, R - Private, S - Subsidiary, D - Division, J - Joint Venture, A - Affiliate, G - Group, N - Company type not reported. Sales are in millions of dollars, employees are in thousands. An asterisk (*) indicates an estimated sales volume. The symbol < stands for 'less than'. Company names and addresses are truncated, in some cases, to fit into the available space.

COST DETAILS

Item	Cost ($ mil)	% of total	Per $1,000 of Revenue	Item	Cost ($ mil)	% of total	Per $1,000 of Revenue
All costs	5,062.9	100.000	529.8	Total Rentals	256.4	5.064	26.8
Cost of supplies	2,575.4	50.868	269.5	Equipment	225.0	4.445	23.5
Subcontracts	2,367.0	46.753	247.7	Buildings	31.3	0.619	3.3
Power, fuel, lubricants	120.5	2.379	12.6	Services purchased	166.8	3.295	17.5
Electricity	23.2	0.458	2.4	Communications	27.6	0.546	2.9
Natural gas	4.3	0.084	0.4	Building repairs	7.3	0.143	0.8
Gasoline and diesel	84.1	1.662	8.8	Machinery repairs	131.9	2.605	13.8
Highway	49.9	0.985	5.2				
Offroad	34.3	0.677	3.6				
Other power	8.9	0.175	0.9				

Source: *Economic Census of the United States*, 1997. Revenues referred to are total industry revenues for the current NAICS industry.

CONSTRUCTION PRODUCT DETAILS

Construction type	Value of construction work ($ mil and %)							
	Total		New construction		Additions, alterations, reconstruction		Maintenance and repair	
	Value	%	Value	%	Value	%	Value	%
Total	**9,539.0**	**100.0**	**6,417.8**	**100.0**	**2,512.1**	**100.0**	**609.1**	**100.0**
Building construction, total	**227.9**	**2.4**	**170.9**	**2.7**	**51.8**	**2.1**	**5.1**	**0.8**
Manufacturing and light industrial buildings	84.6	0.9	72.4	1.1	10.5	0.4	1.7	0.3
Other building construction	-	-	-	-	-	-	3.3	0.5
Nonbuilding construction, total	**9,311.2**	**97.6**	**6,246.9**	**97.3**	**2,460.3**	**97.9**	**604.0**	**99.2**
Highways, streets, and related work	807.6	8.5	486.3	7.6	247.4	9.8	73.9	12.1
Bridges, tunnels, and elevated highways	7,526.1	78.9	5,062.9	78.9	1,965.1	78.2	498.1	81.8
Bridges and elevated highways	6,039.5	63.3	3,773.7	58.8	1,817.5	72.3	448.3	73.6
Tunnels	1,486.6	15.6	1,289.2	20.1	147.6	5.9	49.8	8.2
Sewers, water mains, and related facilities	211.6	2.2	170.8	2.7	33.3	1.3	7.5	1.2
Sewage treatment plants	-	-	-	-	(D)	-	(D)	-
Water treatment plants	-	-	-	-	(D)	-	(D)	-
Mass transit construction	-	-	-	-	58.3	2.3	-	-
Urban mass transit construction	-	-	-	-	(D)	-	(D)	-
Railroad construction	111.6	1.2	-	-	(D)	-	(D)	-
Marine construction	-	-	-	-	10.5	0.4	-	-
Other nonbuilding construction, nec	388.8	4.1	243.9	3.8	127.4	5.1	17.4	2.9

Source: *Economic Census of the United States*, 1997. Bold items are headers. (D) stands for data withheld to protect competitive information. (S) indicates instances where data do not meet publications standards.

LOCATION BY STATE AND REGIONAL CONCENTRATION

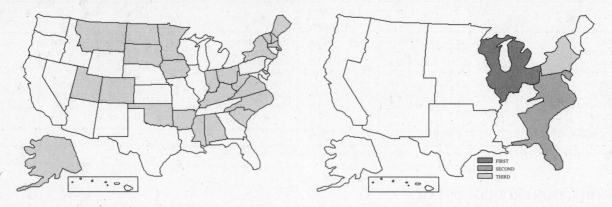

FIRST
SECOND
THIRD

INDUSTRY DATA BY STATE

State	Establishments	Employment			Compensation		Production				Capital Exp. ($ mil)
		Total	Workers	Total as % of US	Payroll per Employee	Wages per Worker	Costs ($ mil)	Value Added ($ mil)	Revenues ($ mil)	% of US	
Massachusetts	38	3,862	2,811	8.09	46,357	42,788	214.9	931.5	1,333.1	13.95	12.3
California	85	3,796	3,026	7.95	43,261	40,729	203.6	405.3	885.3	9.26	15.2
New York	105	3,247	2,602	6.80	50,665	50,192	173.0	424.5	742.9	7.77	19.6
Illinois	46	2,512	1,960	5.26	38,397	37,791	147.2	220.8	617.8	6.47	17.9
Indiana	46	1,867	1,594	3.91	37,829	34,163	101.9	125.3	301.7	3.16	8.4
Wisconsin	15	920	808	1.93	44,157	42,670	64.8	92.7	247.3	2.59	6.5
Oklahoma	22	997	923	2.09	24,925	21,567	61.2	76.2	173.8	1.82	5.7
Maryland	18	910	728	1.91	32,179	30,647	44.8	50.0	138.2	1.45	3.9
North Carolina	33	844	609	1.77	31,185	31,507	33.3	82.5	132.6	1.39	4.1
Colorado	17	590	457	1.24	38,620	36,341	50.6	43.2	130.5	1.37	2.7
Kentucky	40	728	630	1.52	31,526	28,222	46.9	45.1	120.6	1.26	4.1
Utah	13	428	351	0.90	34,362	32,835	24.3	37.7	113.0	1.18	3.1
Georgia	23	906	612	1.90	28,406	25,005	27.3	60.7	110.5	1.16	5.0
Oregon	13	438	347	0.92	45,854	43,052	36.7	41.6	107.7	1.13	2.5
South Carolina	28	763	675	1.60	30,239	28,360	33.9	33.6	95.1	0.99	1.1
Connecticut	13	504	380	1.06	43,532	38,084	27.4	44.1	91.2	0.95	2.5
Arizona	14	732	590	1.53	25,877	25,900	34.0	33.8	86.2	0.90	(D)
West Virginia	18	361	307	0.76	44,839	42,352	28.6	20.2	66.0	0.69	1.5
North Dakota	6	446	394	0.93	37,437	34,429	23.0	32.0	64.8	0.68	3.8
Arkansas	19	267	228	0.56	27,371	24,044	12.4	13.5	33.4	0.35	0.7
South Dakota	9	206	144	0.43	47,233	42,090	3.6	21.9	32.4	0.34	2.5
Delaware	4	234	202	0.49	39,838	35,084	9.8	13.9	30.9	0.32	(D)
Louisiana	8	250	217	0.52	31,116	26,857	9.2	16.6	29.4	0.31	0.9
New Mexico	4	62	41	0.13	-	-	3.3	(S)	(S)	-	(S)
Ohio	72	1,926	1,464	4.03	42,147	40,126	(D)	148.7	(D)	-	8.6
Texas	71	1,998	1,607	4.18	30,243	29,121	(D)	128.7	(D)	-	6.7
Pennsylvania	44	2,333	1,804	4.88	44,715	44,563	(D)	181.9	(D)	-	14.3
Iowa	42	1,161	970	2.43	36,220	33,155	(D)	82.5	(D)	-	4.8
Michigan	40	886	745	1.85	47,675	45,427	(D)	92.3	(D)	-	5.8
Virginia	37	2,950	2,437	6.18	32,646	27,557	(D)	177.0	(D)	-	15.3
Florida	26	1,879	1,554	3.93	30,243	-	(D)	117.6	(D)	-	(S)
New Jersey	26	641	493	1.34	48,583	46,783	(D)	59.1	(D)	-	6.7
Tennessee	22	1,117	908	2.34	35,650	32,431	(D)	104.5	(D)	-	7.0
Alabama	21	563	441	1.18	28,234	24,132	(D)	30.3	(D)	-	3.4
Minnesota	21	835	678	1.75	40,357	36,709	(D)	99.5	(D)	-	2.2
Washington	21	859	620	1.80	50,884	49,456	(D)	109.4	(D)	-	3.6
Missouri	18	989	838	2.07	35,223	33,197	(D)	60.7	(D)	-	6.0
Mississippi	14	583	500	1.22	24,381	23,816	(D)	17.6	(D)	-	2.6
Kansas	11	558	483	1.17	41,181	37,609	(D)	50.3	(D)	-	6.2
Maine	11	574	486	1.20	27,249	23,986	(D)	31.0	(D)	-	1.3
New Hampshire	7	168	137	0.35	38,964	28,555	(D)	10.4	(D)	-	0.9
Vermont	7	94	76	0.20	27,702	-	(D)	3.5	(D)	-	0.6
Nebraska	6	(D)	(D)	-	-	-	(D)	18.6	(D)	-	(D)
Rhode Island	5	(S)	(S)	-	-	-	(S)	(D)	(D)	-	(D)
Montana	4	248	(D)	0.52	-	-	15.2	14.2	(D)	-	(D)
Alaska	3	37	26	0.08	60,459	61,000	(D)	5.8	(D)	-	0.4
Hawaii	3	45	(D)	0.09	-	-	(D)	(D)	(D)	-	0.1
D.C.	2	(D)	(D)	-	-	-	(D)	(D)	(D)	-	(D)
Idaho	2	(D)	(D)	-	-	-	(D)	(D)	(D)	-	(D)
Nevada	2	(D)	(D)	-	-	-	(D)	(D)	(D)	-	(D)
Wyoming	2	(D)	(D)	-	-	-	(D)	(D)	(D)	-	(D)

Source: Economic Census of the U.S., 1997. Data are sorted by 1997 revenues or establishments. (D) means data suppression to prevent disclosure of company data. (S) means that data did not meet statistical standards for publication. A dash (-) is used when data are unavailable or cannot be calculated. Data followed by an * indicate the midpoint of a range. The ranges are: for 10, 0-19; for 60, 20-99; for 175, 100-249, for 375, 250-499, for 750, 500-999. Higher values are multiples of those shown, e.g., 3,750 is the midpoint of the range 2,500-4,999. Shaded *states* on the state map indicate those states which have proportionately greater representation in the industry than would be indicated by the state's population; the ratio is based on total revenues or number of establishments. Shaded *regions* indicate where the industry is regionally most concentrated.

NAICS 234910 - WATER, SEWER, AND PIPELINE CONSTRUCTION

GENERAL STATISTICS

| Years | Estab-lish-ments | Employment | | Payroll ($ mil) | | Costs ($ mil) | | Value Added ($ mil) | Revenues ($ mil) | | | Capital expend. ($ mil) |
| | | Total | Constr. workers | Total | Worker payroll | Total | Cost of materials | | All sources | Construction | | |
										Total	Net	
1997	8,042	162,566	134,023	5,522.3	4,087.0	7,062.3	6,557.7	12,280.1	22,419.8	22,204.1	19,126.7	945.0

Source: *Economic Census of the United States*, 1997. This is a newly defined industry. Data for prior years were unavailable at the time of publication but may become available over time. "Net" under "Construction" is construction revenue net of the costs of subcontracts.

DISTRIBUTION AMONG SIC-BASED INDUSTRIES - 1997

| SIC | Industry | Estab-lish-ments | Employment | | Cost of Power & Materials ($ mil) | Revenues ($ mil) | | | Value Added ($ mil) |
| | | | Total (000) | Payroll ($ mil) | | All Sources | Construction | | |
							Total	Net	
162310	Water, sewer, pipeline, & communications & power line construction (pt)	8,013.0	162,401	5,514.4	7,057.6	22,388.4	22,173.1	19,107.9	12,265.61
874133	Management services (pt)	29.0	165	7.9	4.7	31.3	31.0	18.8	14.48

Source: 1997 *Economic Census*. U.S. Census Bureau, U.S. Department of Commerce, August 1997. SIC codes ending in two zeroes represent complete 4-digit SICs. All others are parts of 4-digit SIC industries. Items showing a dash (-) indicate that data are not available because of disclosure problems.

SIC INDUSTRIES RELATED TO NAICS 234910

SIC	Industry	1990	1991	1992	1993	1994	1995	1996	1997
1623	**Water, Sewer, and Utility Lines***								
	Establishments (number)	10,106e	10,169e	10,233	10,297p	10,361p	10,426p	10,491p	10,557p
	Employment (thousands)	195.6e	194.9e	194.3	193.6e	192.9e	192.3e	191.6e	190.9e
	Revenues ($ million)	19,095.2e	19,751.2e	20,429.8	21,131.6e	21,857.6e	22,608.5e	23,385.3e	24,188.7e
8741	**Management Services***								
	Establishments (number)	15,267	16,556	20,186	21,920	23,803	21,674	23,348p	24,255p
	Employment (thousands)	285.2	306.6	285.1	357.7	386.3	312.7	368.9p	381.9p
	Revenues ($ million)	20,627.0	21,788.0	23,774.0	23,373.0	24,328.0	27,611.0	27,569.0	28,870.9p

Source: *Economic Census of the United States*, 1992, annual surveys of economic sectors conducted by the Bureau of the Census, and estimates or projections based on the 1982-1992 period; not all data are shown. 'e' marks estimates made by the editors; 'p' indicates projections based on time series. A dash (-) indicates that data for this SIC or year were not available. * Indicates that only a portion of this industry is present within the NAICS data. If no * is shown, the entire industry is contained within the NAICS data.

INDICES OF CHANGE

| Years | Estab-lish-ments | Employment | | Payroll ($ mil) | | Costs ($ mil) | | Value Added ($ mil) | Revenues ($ mil) | | | Capital expend. ($ mil) |
| | | Total | Constr. workers | Total | Worker payroll | Total | Cost of materials | | All sources | Construction | | |
										Total	Net	
1997	100.0	100.0	100.0	100.0	100.0	100.0	100.0	100.0	100.0	100.0	100.0	100.0

Sources: Same as General Statistics. The values shown reflect change from the base year, 1997. Values above 100 mean greater than 1997, values below 100 mean less than 1997, and a value of 100 in years other than 1997 means same as 1997. Indices are calculated only for Census years. Data are the most recent available at this level of detail.

SELECTED RATIOS

For 1997	Avg. of Sector	Analyzed Industry	Index	For 1997	Avg. of Sector	Analyzed Industry	Index
Employees per establishment	8.6	20.2	234	Value added per establishment	584,730	1,526,996	261
Construction workers per establishment	6.6	16.7	253	Value added per employee	67,759	75,539	111
Payroll per establishment	265,343	686,682	259	Value added per construction worker	88,592	91,627	103
Payroll per employee	30,748	33,970	110	Revenues per establishment	1,307,915	2,787,839	213
Payroll per construction worker	27,622	30,495	110	Revenues per employee	151,563	137,912	91
Costs per establishment	367,737	878,177	239	Revenues per construction worker	198,161	167,283	84
Costs per employee	42,614	43,443	102	CR as % of total revenues	98.48	99.04	101
Costs per construction worker	55,716	52,695	95	Net CR as % of CR	72.40	86.14	119
Materials as % of costs	95.75	92.86	97	Investment per establishment	22,948	117,508	512
Costs as % of revenues	28.12	31.50	112	Investment per employee	2,659	5,813	219
Costs as % of construction revenues	28.55	31.81	111	Investment per construction worker	3,477	7,051	203

Sources: Same as General Statistics. The 'Average of Sector' column represents the average for all industries in this sector. The Index shows the relationship between the Average and the Analyzed Industry. For example, 100 means that they are equal; 500 that the Analyzed Industry is five times the average; 50 means that the Analyzed Industry is half the national average. 'na' is used to show that data are 'not available'. CR stands for "construction revenues" and "Net CR" is construction revenues net of subcontract expenses.

LEADING COMPANIES

No company data available for this industry.

COST DETAILS

Item	Cost ($ mil)	% of total	Per $1,000 of Revenue	Item	Cost ($ mil)	% of total	Per $1,000 of Revenue
All costs	10,139.7	100.000	452.3	Total Rentals	880.4	8.683	39.3
Cost of supplies	6,557.7	64.673	292.5	Equipment	782.3	7.716	34.9
Subcontracts	3,077.3	30.349	137.3	Buildings	98.1	0.967	4.4
Power, fuel, lubricants	504.7	4.977	22.5	Services purchased	785.0	7.741	35.0
Electricity	44.3	0.437	2.0	Communications	113.8	1.122	5.1
Natural gas	8.0	0.079	0.4	Building repairs	40.3	0.398	1.8
Gasoline and diesel	410.8	4.051	18.3	Machinery repairs	630.9	6.222	28.1
Highway	205.9	2.031	9.2				
Offroad	204.9	2.020	9.1				
Other power	41.7	0.411	1.9				

Source: *Economic Census of the United States*, 1997. Revenues referred to are total industry revenues for the current NAICS industry.

CONSTRUCTION PRODUCT DETAILS

Construction type	Value of construction work ($ mil and %)							
	Total		New construction		Additions, alterations, reconstruction		Maintenance and repair	
	Value	%	Value	%	Value	%	Value	%
Total	**22,204.1**	**100.0**	**15,921.1**	**100.0**	**3,627.2**	**100.0**	**2,591.0**	**100.0**
Building construction, total	**610.5**	**2.7**	**479.2**	**3.0**	**80.7**	**2.2**	**50.6**	**2.0**
Nonbuilding construction, total	**21,528.8**	**97.0**	**15,441.9**	**97.0**	**3,546.5**	**97.8**	**2,540.3**	**98.0**
Highways, streets, and related work	1,219.5	5.5	863.8	5.4	243.8	6.7	112.0	4.3
Private driveways and parking areas	199.9	0.9	125.3	0.8	33.5	0.9	41.1	1.6
Bridges, tunnels, and elevated highways	281.7	1.3	186.0	1.2	66.7	1.8	29.0	1.1
Sewers, water mains, and related facilities	13,742.1	61.9	10,299.6	64.7	2,097.9	57.8	1,344.6	51.9
Pipeline construction ex sewer or water	4,643.8	20.9	2,969.9	18.7	804.9	22.2	869.0	33.5
Power and communication lines, cables, towers, etc.	314.9	1.4	231.2	1.5	39.3	1.1	44.5	1.7
Sewage and water treatment plants	412.3	1.9	239.4	1.5	154.4	4.3	18.5	0.7
Sewage treatment plants	205.6	0.9	128.5	0.8	66.8	1.8	10.4	0.4
Water treatment plants	206.7	0.9	110.9	0.7	87.7	2.4	8.1	0.3
Conservation and development construction	220.4	1.0	168.4	1.1	12.1	0.3	39.9	1.5
Other nonbuilding construction, nec	494.2	2.2	358.4	2.3	93.9	2.6	41.9	1.6
Construction work, nsk	**64.8**	**0.3**	NA	-	NA	-	NA	-

Source; *Economic Census of the United States*, 1997. Bold items are headers. (D) stands for data withheld to protect competitive information. (S) indicates instances where data do not meet publications standards.

LOCATION BY STATE AND REGIONAL CONCENTRATION

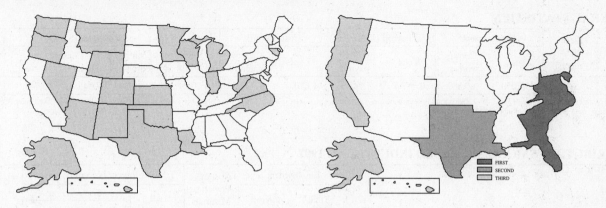

FIRST
SECOND
THIRD

INDUSTRY DATA BY STATE

State	Estab lish- ments	Employment			Compensation		Production				Capital Exp. ($ mil)
		Total	Workers	Total as % of US	Payroll per Employee	Wages per Worker	Costs ($ mil)	Value Added ($ mil)	Reve- nues ($ mil)	% of US	
California	651	13,220	10,645	8.13	42,412	38,327	686.1	1,249.1	2,322.3	10.36	62.0
Texas	511	18,134	15,590	11.15	31,857	28,089	684.3	1,288.6	2,277.9	10.16	79.2
Florida	295	7,685	6,334	4.73	30,444	26,980	389.0	596.6	1,169.8	5.22	44.8
Michigan	281	5,323	4,301	3.27	42,454	36,740	339.7	479.1	950.9	4.24	48.6
Virginia	240	7,768	6,449	4.78	29,890	25,207	288.7	475.6	888.5	3.96	55.1
Louisiana	168	6,838	5,994	4.21	31,481	27,928	300.5	445.2	822.1	3.67	29.2
Washington	288	4,407	3,319	2.71	42,451	38,823	234.2	405.1	783.1	3.49	27.0
Illinois	342	5,691	4,841	3.50	33,856	31,160	263.2	391.7	769.5	3.43	35.8
Ohio	270	5,062	4,121	3.11	35,703	31,658	211.9	394.9	710.4	3.17	33.8
North Carolina	347	6,278	5,154	3.86	26,870	23,178	200.7	400.1	676.9	3.02	31.8
Pennsylvania	272	4,842	3,791	2.98	34,997	31,630	175.3	380.3	643.7	2.87	35.1
Minnesota	216	3,641	2,947	2.24	38,027	36,271	196.1	336.7	642.0	2.86	28.3
New York	276	4,492	3,526	2.76	44,864	41,981	170.2	392.0	620.8	2.77	18.7
Indiana	203	3,968	3,244	2.44	34,837	33,119	174.3	348.1	582.2	2.60	31.2
Georgia	321	4,442	3,537	2.73	28,565	24,882	190.5	281.4	570.3	2.54	28.0
Colorado	207	3,968	3,364	2.44	31,772	28,598	222.6	254.1	548.2	2.45	21.1
New Jersey	194	3,821	3,111	2.35	44,461	42,050	120.9	348.9	539.2	2.40	13.8
Arizona	128	4,276	3,614	2.63	31,193	27,727	156.3	264.5	502.4	2.24	16.4
Wisconsin	107	2,644	2,256	1.63	41,847	38,246	161.2	223.7	445.9	1.99	25.2
Massachusetts	229	2,542	1,958	1.56	38,057	34,141	122.9	207.9	413.8	1.85	31.7
Oregon	223	2,796	2,312	1.72	36,269	34,791	135.8	212.6	408.7	1.82	17.1
Missouri	238	2,570	2,103	1.58	32,937	31,462	136.7	192.7	377.5	1.68	13.0
Nevada	51	2,402	2,088	1.48	36,072	33,120	131.3	200.3	376.5	1.68	17.6
Maryland	122	2,826	2,245	1.74	35,413	29,009	148.2	176.3	375.1	1.67	11.1
Alabama	142	2,768	2,267	1.70	28,702	21,866	116.0	201.3	358.1	1.60	20.1
Oklahoma	243	3,410	2,877	2.10	28,955	26,831	86.3	222.5	343.2	1.53	21.8
Kansas	53	2,536	2,149	1.56	27,239	26,344	115.1	195.1	337.3	1.50	15.7
Tennessee	167	2,842	2,482	1.75	26,394	24,712	122.4	172.2	329.2	1.47	19.1
Connecticut	93	1,234	951	0.76	39,729	36,074	76.2	190.8	297.1	1.33	10.0
New Mexico	59	3,078	2,676	1.89	28,860	26,500	94.0	156.1	273.4	1.22	10.8
Iowa	166	1,397	1,147	0.86	34,506	32,735	55.1	144.3	231.6	1.03	6.2
South Carolina	135	2,159	1,770	1.33	24,603	20,012	85.0	100.6	217.8	0.97	10.3
Mississippi	66	1,972	1,472	1.21	24,576	21,955	52.3	111.5	191.1	0.85	10.7
Kentucky	151	1,730	1,370	1.06	28,491	26,593	60.1	102.5	190.9	0.85	9.0
West Virginia	82	1,684	1,439	1.04	31,736	28,942	46.6	125.7	178.5	0.80	9.3
Montana	82	904	722	0.56	27,157	25,449	56.7	51.6	115.7	0.52	8.3
Utah	62	902	659	0.55	24,931	26,082	37.2	71.0	115.6	0.52	4.6
Hawaii	12	645	505	0.40	44,174	42,331	22.3	71.0	111.5	0.50	1.7
Delaware	22	871	741	0.54	34,458	29,314	24.4	61.0	93.5	0.42	4.7
Nebraska	52	624	488	0.38	30,465	28,928	32.4	55.8	93.2	0.42	1.3
Arkansas	65	922	785	0.57	22,014	19,776	19.2	47.1	76.8	0.34	4.6
Wyoming	27	568	490	0.35	31,234	31,063	17.3	35.9	72.3	0.32	3.0
Idaho	26	512	439	0.31	27,998	25,212	(D)	34.1	65.6	0.29	2.2
Alaska	29	342	267	0.21	48,649	45,453	17.5	40.9	64.2	0.29	4.8
Maine	18	364	305	0.22	38,918	34,711	13.3	33.0	55.9	0.25	3.1
South Dakota	38	404	319	0.25	23,371	19,608	13.8	24.1	42.0	0.19	1.6
Rhode Island	20	277	213	0.17	34,090	25,263	9.7	25.1	38.7	0.17	2.3
North Dakota	29	235	190	0.14	36,847	31,211	15.0	19.4	38.5	0.17	1.5
New Hampshire	9	305	274	0.19	25,190	24,303	9.9	20.7	38.4	0.17	1.2
Vermont	18	(D)	(D)	-	-	-	(D)	(D)	(D)	-	(D)
D.C.	2	(D)	(D)	-	-	-	(D)	(D)	(D)	-	(D)

Source: Economic Census of the U.S., 1997. Data are sorted by 1997 revenues or establishments. (D) means data suppression to prevent disclosure of company data. (S) means that data did not meet statistical standards for publication. A dash (-) is used when data are unavailable or cannot be calculated. Data followed by an * indicate the midpoint of a range. The ranges are: for 10, 0-19; for 60, 20-99; for 175, 100-249; for 375, 250-499, for 750, 500-999. Higher values are multiples of those shown, e.g., 3,750 is the midpoint of the range 2,500-4,999. Shaded *states* on the state map indicate those states which have proportionately greater representation in the industry than would be indicated by the state's population; the ratio is based on total revenues or number of establishments. Shaded *regions* indicate where the industry is regionally most concentrated.

NAICS 234920 - POWER AND COMMUNICATION TRANSMISSION LINE CONSTRUCTION

GENERAL STATISTICS

Years	Estab-lish-ments	Employment		Payroll ($ mil)		Costs ($ mil)		Value Added ($ mil)	Revenues ($ mil)			Capital expend. ($ mil)
		Total	Constr. workers	Total	Worker payroll	Total	Cost of materials		All sources	Construction Total	Net	
1997	3,300	74,050	60,880	2,387.4	1,748.7	1,610.6	1,412.5	5,201.4	7,919.5	7,849.4	6,741.9	428.3

Source: *Economic Census of the United States*, 1997. This is a newly defined industry. Data for prior years were unavailable at the time of publication but may become available over time. "Net" under "Construction" is construction revenue net of the costs of subcontracts.

DISTRIBUTION AMONG SIC-BASED INDUSTRIES - 1997

SIC	Industry	Estab-lish-ments	Employment		Cost of Power & Materials ($ mil)	Revenues ($ mil)			Value Added ($ mil)
			Total (000)	Payroll ($ mil)		All Sources	Construction Total	Net	
162320	Water, sewer, pipeline, & communications & power line construction (pt)	3,236.0	73,584	2,366.1	1,592.3	7,799.9	7,730.2	6,677.8	5,155.24
874134	Management services (pt)	64.0	466	21.3	18.3	119.6	119.3	64.2	46.19

Source: 1997 *Economic Census*. U.S. Census Bureau, U.S. Department of Commerce, August 1997. SIC codes ending in two zeroes represent complete 4-digit SICs. All others are parts of 4-digit SIC industries. Items showing a dash (-) indicate that data are not available because of disclosure problems.

SIC INDUSTRIES RELATED TO NAICS 234920

SIC	Industry	1990	1991	1992	1993	1994	1995	1996	1997
1623	**Water, Sewer, and Utility Lines***								
	Establishments (number)	10,106e	10,169e	10,233	10,297p	10,361p	10,426p	10,491p	10,557p
	Employment (thousands)	195.6e	194.9e	194.3	193.6e	192.9e	192.3e	191.6e	190.9e
	Revenues ($ million)	19,095.2e	19,751.2e	20,429.8	21,131.6e	21,857.6e	22,608.5e	23,385.3e	24,188.7e
8741	**Management Services***								
	Establishments (number)	15,267	16,556	20,186	21,920	23,803	21,674	23,348p	24,255p
	Employment (thousands)	285.2	306.6	285.1	357.7	386.3	312.7	368.9p	381.9p
	Revenues ($ million)	20,627.0	21,788.0	23,774.0	23,373.0	24,328.0	27,611.0	27,569.0	28,870.9p

Source: *Economic Census of the United States*, 1992, annual surveys of economic sectors conducted by the Bureau of the Census, and estimates or projections based on the 1982-1992 period; not all data are shown. 'e' marks estimates made by the editors; 'p' indicates projections based on time series. A dash (-) indicates that data for this SIC or year were not available. * Indicates that only a portion of this industry is present within the NAICS data. If no * is shown, the entire industry is contained within the NAICS data.

INDICES OF CHANGE

Years	Estab-lish-ments	Employment		Payroll ($ mil)		Costs ($ mil)		Value Added ($ mil)	Revenues ($ mil)			Capital expend. ($ mil)
		Total	Constr. workers	Total	Worker payroll	Total	Cost of materials		All sources	Construction Total	Net	
1997	100.0	100.0	100.0	100.0	100.0	100.0	100.0	100.0	100.0	100.0	100.0	100.0

Sources: Same as General Statistics. The values shown reflect change from the base year, 1997. Values above 100 mean greater than 1997, values below 100 mean less than 1997, and a value of 100 in years other than 1997 means same as 1997. Indices are calculated only for Census years. Data are the most recent available at this level of detail.

SELECTED RATIOS

For 1997	Avg. of Sector	Analyzed Industry	Index	For 1997	Avg. of Sector	Analyzed Industry	Index
Employees per establishment	8.6	22.4	260	Value added per establishment	584,730	1,576,182	270
Construction workers per establishment	6.6	18.4	280	Value added per employee	67,759	70,242	104
Payroll per establishment	265,343	723,455	273	Value added per construction worker	88,592	85,437	96
Payroll per employee	30,748	32,240	105	Revenues per establishment	1,307,915	2,399,848	183
Payroll per construction worker	27,622	28,724	104	Revenues per employee	151,563	106,948	71
Costs per establishment	367,737	488,061	133	Revenues per construction worker	198,161	130,084	66
Costs per employee	42,614	21,750	51	CR as % of total revenues	98.48	99.11	101
Costs per construction worker	55,716	26,455	47	Net CR as % of CR	72.40	85.89	119
Materials as % of costs	95.75	87.70	92	Investment per establishment	22,948	129,788	566
Costs as % of revenues	28.12	20.34	72	Investment per employee	2,659	5,784	218
Costs as % of construction revenues	28.55	20.52	72	Investment per construction worker	3,477	7,035	202

Sources: Same as General Statistics. The 'Average of Sector' column represents the average for all industries in this sector. The Index shows the relationship between the Average and the Analyzed Industry. For example, 100 means that they are equal; 500 that the Analyzed Industry is five times the average; 50 means that the Analyzed Industry is half the national average. 'na' is used to show that data are 'not available'. CR stands for "construction revenues" and "Net CR" is construction revenues net of subcontract expenses.

LEADING COMPANIES

Number shown: **67**   Total sales ($ mil): **8,029**   Total employment (000): **63.3**

Company Name	Address				CEO Name	Phone	Co. Type	Sales ($ mil)	Empl. (000)
EMCOR Group Inc.	101 Merritt	Norwalk	CT	06851	Jeffrey Levy	203-849-7848	P	2,210	15.0
MasTec Inc.	3155 NW 77th Ave	Miami	FL	33122	Joel-Tomas Citron	305-599-1800	P	1,059	9.9
H.B. Zachry Co.	527 Logwood	San Antonio	TX	78221	Henry B Zachary Jr	210-475-8000	R	661	7.5
MYR Group Inc.	1701 W Golf Rd	Rolling Mdws	IL	60008	C M Brennan III	847-290-1891	P	459	3.7
Henkels and McCoy Inc.	985 Jolly Rd	Blue Bell	PA	19422	Kenneth L Rose	215-283-7600	P	450*	5.0
Kaneb Services Inc.	2435 N Cen Expwy	Richardson	TX	75080	John R Barnes	972-699-4023	P	376	1.8
Parsons Energy & Chemicals	100 W Walnut St	Pasadena	CA	91124	William E Hall	626-440-2000	S	340*	2.5
Able Telcom Holding Corp.	1601 Forum Pl	W. Palm Beach	FL	33401	Frazier Gaines	561-688-0400	P	217	2.2
Murphy Brothers Inc.	3150 5th Ave	East Moline	IL	61244	William Murphy	309-752-1227	R	123*	0.8
Flint Engineering & Construction	P O Box 3044	Tulsa	OK	74101	Gary Whipple	918-584-0033	S	120	1.2
Irby Construction Co.	P O Box 1819	Jackson	MS	39215	Charles L Irby	601-969-1811	R	114*	0.7
Reynolds Inc.	PO Box 186	Orleans	IN	47452	Jack Reynolds	812-865-3232	R	102*	0.7
Irish Construction	2641 River Ave	Rosemead	CA	91770	Bill Willbanks	626-288-8530	R	90*	0.6
Associated Pipe Line Contractors	3535 Briarpark	Houston	TX	77042	Ralph Pendarvis	713-789-4311	R	81*	0.5
UTILX Corp.	P O Box 97009	Kent	WA	98064	William M Weisfield	253-395-0200	P	79	0.8
Henkels & McCoy Inc. Northeast	985 Jolly Rd	Blue Bell	PA	19422		215-283-7600	D	75*	0.1
B. Frank Joy Company Inc.	5355 Kilmer Pl	Bladensburg	MD	20710	T Kenneth Joy	301-779-9400	R	73*	0.5
Rowe Corp.	5200-77 Center Dr	Charlotte	NC	28217	Robert Dunn	704-527-3336	R	72*	0.5
Hood Corp.	P O Box 4368	Whittier	CA	90607	Bruce Svatos	562-698-8402	R	71*	0.5
Underground Construction Inc.	PO Box 2000	Benicia	CA	94510	Lynn Barr	707-746-8800	R	70	0.4
Asplundh Construction Corp.	93 Sills Rd	Yaphank	NY	11980	Scott Asplundh	516-205-9340	R	67*	0.5
AmeriLink Corp.	1900 E D-Granville	Columbus	OH	43229	Larry R Linhart	614-895-1313	S	65	0.5
Garney Holding Company Inc.	1331 NW Vivion Rd	Kansas City	MO	64118	James I Dorman	816-741-4600	R	65*	0.3
Flippo Construction Company Inc.	3820 Penn Belt Pl	Forestville	MD	20747	Michael Haluka	301-967-6800	R	59*	0.4
Penn Line Service Inc.	300 Scottdale Ave	Scottdale	PA	15683	Paul Mongell	724-887-9110	R	51	0.7
R.H. White Construction Inc.	PO Box 404	Auburn	MA	01501		508-832-3295	S	50	0.3
Sheehan Pipe Line Construction	1924 S Utica Ave	Tulsa	OK	74104	R David Sheehan, Jr	918-747-3471	R	50	<0.1
Hall Contracting Corp.	PO Box 37270	Louisville	KY	40233		502-367-6151	R	41	0.4
W.L. Hailey and Company Inc.	PO Box 40646	Nashville	TN	37204	G David Waller	615-255-3161	R	41*	0.3
Nelson Pipeline Constructors Inc.	6215 Colorado Blvd	Commerce City	CO	80022	Jon Andrews	303-289-5971	R	37	0.2
Argonaut Constructors Inc.	P O Box 639	Santa Rosa	CA	95402	Michael D Smith	707-542-4862	R	36	0.3
Mueller Pipeliners Inc.	PO Box 510650	New Berlin	WI	53151	Robert C Osborn	262-782-6160	R	34	0.5
Utilities Construction Inc.	P O Box 20485	Charleston	SC	29413	James C Murray	843-722-0161	R	34*	0.5
Atrex Inc.	175 Ind Loop S	Orange Park	FL	32073	David Bradford	904-264-9086	R	33*	0.2
C.J. Hughes Construction Co.	P O Box 7305	Huntington	WV	25776	James D Hughes	304-522-3868	R	33*	0.2
W.G. Lockhart Construction Co.	800 W Waterloo Rd	Akron	OH	44314	Alexander Lockhart	330-745-6520	R	33*	0.2
E. Sambol Corp.	PO Box 5110	Toms River	NJ	08754	Eric Sambol	732-349-2900	R	28	0.2
Woodruff and Sons Inc.	PO Box 10127	Bradenton	FL	34282	Roy Woodruff	941-756-1871	R	27*	0.2
Yantis Corp.	P O Box 17045	San Antonio	TX	78217	Thomas G Yantis	210-655-3780	R	26	0.2
Suburban Grading and Utilities	1190 Harmony Rd	Norfolk	VA	23502		757-461-1800	R	26*	0.2
Napp-Grecco Co.	1500 McCarter Hwy	Newark	NJ	07104	Joseph M Napp	973-482-3500	R	25*	0.2
Barbarossa and Sons Inc.	P O Box 367	Osseo	MN	55369	Robert R Barbarosa	612-425-4146	R	25	0.1
Kay and Kay Contracting Inc.	1355 Keavy Rd	London	KY	40741	William Robinson	606-864-7384	R	24*	0.2
Max Foote Construction Inc.	PO Box 1208	Mandeville	LA	70470	Max E Foote	504-624-8569	R	24*	0.2
Insituform East Inc.	3421 Pennsy Dr	Landover	MD	20785	Robert Erickson	301-386-4100	P	23	0.2
Utility Contractors Inc.	P O Box 2079	Wichita	KS	67201	Charles F Grier	316-265-9506	R	22	0.2
Rhode Construction Co.	PO Box 53370	Lubbock	TX	79453	Robert Rhode	806-792-0185	R	21*	0.1
Insituform Plains Inc.	P O Box 12664	Wichita	KS	67277	James Tadtman	316-942-5996	S	20	<0.1
R. Roese Contracting Inc.	PO Box 158	Kawkawlin	MI	48631	RF Roese	517-684-5121	R	17*	0.2
P. Gioioso and Sons Inc.	50 Sprague St	Boston	MA	02136	L Gioioso	617-364-5800	R	16*	0.1
Super Excavators Inc.	N59 Boblink	Menomonee Fls	WI	53051	Robert Schraufnagel	414-252-3200	R	16*	0.1
R.L. Coolsaet Construction Co.	PO Box 279	Taylor	MI	48180	JA Coolsaet	734-946-9300	R	15*	0.3
H.N. Donahoo Contracting Inc.	P O Box 2345	Birmingham	AL	35201	Robert Steakman	205-252-9246	R	15*	<0.1
T.A. Chapman Inc.	P O Box 125	Milton	WV	25541	DA Chapman	304-743-6885	R	13	0.1
M.A. Bongiovanni Inc.	1400 Jamesville Ave	Syracuse	NY	13205	J J Bongiovanni Sr	315-475-9937	R	12	<0.1
Highlines Construction Inc.	PO Box 408	Westwego	LA	70096	HD Hughes	504-436-3961	S	10	0.2
Crain Brothers Inc.	2715 Grand Chenier	Grand Chenier	LA	70643	Malcolm L Crain	318-538-2411	R	9*	0.1
Custom Electrical Contractors Inc.	11366 Amalgam	Rancho Cordova	CA	95670		916-638-4110	R	8*	<0.1
Insituform Technologies USA Inc.	P O Box 250	Owosso	MI	48867	Robert Affholder	517-725-9525	S	8*	<0.1
Richard A. Heaps Electrical	8909 Florin Rd	Sacramento	CA	95829	Diane Meehan	916-386-8857	R	8*	<0.1
Davis Electric	5921 Landis Ave	Carmichael	CA	95608	Mary A Stolecki	916-489-1643	R	4*	<0.1
Perfection Electric Co.	5710 Auburn Blvd	Sacramento	CA	95841	Steve Leibovitz	916-348-7788	R	4*	<0.1
G and S Electric	1604 Basler St	Sacramento	CA	95814	Gary Krezman	916-442-7714	R	3*	<0.1
Blacksher and Son Inc.	Rte 5, Box 1460-A	Orange	TX	77630	Robert Blacksher	409-735-6515	R	2*	<0.1
CRC-Evans Rehabilitation	6911 Breen Rd	Houston	TX	77086		281-999-2181	D	2*	<0.1
Dorfman Construction Inc.	5525 Oakdale Ave	Woodland Hills	CA	91364	Gerald E Dorfman	818-702-9731	R	2	<0.1
All City Electric	6201 Enterprise Dr	Diamond Sprgs	CA	95619	Mike Meschi	530-626-5802	R	1*	<0.1

Source: Ward's Business Directory of U.S. Private and Public Companies, Volumes 1 and 2, 2000. The company type code used is as follows: P - Public, R - Private, S - Subsidiary, D - Division, J - Joint Venture, A - Affiliate, G - Group, N - Company type not reported. Sales are in millions of dollars, employees are in thousands. An asterisk (*) indicates an estimated sales volume. The symbol < stands for 'less than'. Company names and addresses are truncated, in some cases, to fit into the available space.

COST DETAILS

Item	Cost ($ mil)	% of total	Per $1,000 of Revenue	Item	Cost ($ mil)	% of total	Per $1,000 of Revenue
All costs	2,718.1	100.000	343.2	Total Rentals	267.4	9.836	33.8
Cost of supplies	1,412.5	51.967	178.4	Equipment	225.4	8.292	28.5
Subcontracts	1,107.5	40.745	139.8	Buildings	42.0	1.544	5.3
Power, fuel, lubricants	198.1	7.287	25.0	Services purchased	305.2	11.227	38.5
Electricity	19.7	0.724	2.5	Communications	62.8	2.310	7.9
Natural gas	2.4	0.090	0.3	Building repairs	16.0	0.590	2.0
Gasoline and diesel	163.9	6.030	20.7	Machinery repairs	226.4	8.328	28.6
Highway	110.7	4.073	14.0				
Offroad	53.2	1.957	6.7				
Other power	12.1	0.444	1.5				

Source: *Economic Census of the United States*, 1997. Revenues referred to are total industry revenues for the current NAICS industry.

CONSTRUCTION PRODUCT DETAILS

Construction type	Value of construction work ($ mil and %)							
	Total		New construction		Additions, alterations, reconstruction		Maintenance and repair	
	Value	%	Value	%	Value	%	Value	%
Total	**7,849.4**	**100.0**	**5,029.0**	**100.0**	**1,351.2**	**100.0**	**1,402.9**	**100.0**
Building construction, total	**115.5**	**1.5**	**87.8**	**1.7**	**22.6**	**1.7**	**5.0**	**0.4**
Nonbuilding construction, total	**7,667.6**	**97.7**	**4,941.1**	**98.3**	**1,328.6**	**98.3**	**1,397.8**	**99.6**
Sewers, water mains, and related facilities	127.1	1.6	102.4	2.0	11.2	0.8	13.5	1.0
Pipeline construction ex sewer and water	92.5	1.2	59.1	1.2	15.2	1.1	18.2	1.3
Power and communication lines, cables, towers, etc.	7,251.8	92.4	4,644.7	92.4	1,278.7	94.6	1,328.3	94.7
Other nonbuilding construction, nec	196.2	2.5	134.9	2.7	23.5	1.7	37.8	2.7
Construction work, nsk	-	-	NA	-	NA	-	NA	-

Source: *Economic Census of the United States*, 1997. Bold items are headers. (D) stands for data withheld to protect competitive information. (S) indicates instances where data do not meet publications standards.

LOCATION BY STATE AND REGIONAL CONCENTRATION

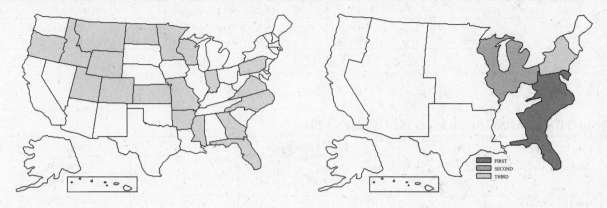

FIRST
SECOND
THIRD

INDUSTRY DATA BY STATE

State	Estab lish- ments	Employment			Compensation		Production				Capital Exp. ($ mil)
		Total	Workers	Total as % of US	Payroll per Employee	Wages per Worker	Costs ($ mil)	Value Added ($ mil)	Reve- nues ($ mil)	% of US	
Pennsylvania	89	6,681	5,585	9.02	32,065	29,177	155.8	466.6	740.1	9.35	36.1
California	176	5,198	4,291	7.02	34,250	32,064	113.2	370.6	564.0	7.12	24.0
Florida	237	5,550	4,515	7.49	25,343	23,473	87.8	312.2	468.9	5.92	27.8
Colorado	74	3,537	2,912	4.78	41,218	36,577	92.5	294.1	440.8	5.57	16.0
North Carolina	151	4,653	3,903	6.28	26,727	25,170	49.1	247.7	354.8	4.48	15.5
Virginia	69	3,246	2,837	4.38	27,891	25,967	53.5	191.5	260.1	3.28	12.5
Georgia	98	2,119	1,696	2.86	31,268	29,604	47.6	137.8	256.0	3.23	9.0
Missouri	99	2,144	1,819	2.90	26,711	16,732	40.7	151.9	246.4	3.11	13.4
Wisconsin	74	1,595	1,331	2.15	45,507	40,783	26.1	163.1	216.1	2.73	13.9
Michigan	59	1,686	1,415	2.28	40,273	35,204	39.7	158.0	209.8	2.65	8.0
Oregon	31	1,465	1,212	1.98	47,783	43,315	39.1	138.6	206.7	2.61	10.0
Indiana	170	2,159	1,868	2.92	27,380	26,270	21.3	138.8	181.7	2.29	17.2
Minnesota	64	(D)	(D)	-	-	-	24.2	116.3	171.8	2.17	(D)
Ohio	109	1,842	1,507	2.49	29,150	27,952	31.3	117.0	163.9	2.07	9.4
Kansas	126	1,408	1,109	1.90	29,305	25,653	16.9	103.8	137.9	1.74	7.8
Mississippi	30	1,411	1,140	1.91	30,140	29,203	19.3	99.0	132.7	1.68	19.4
Tennessee	102	1,427	1,220	1.93	26,589	25,289	22.7	90.4	132.5	1.67	9.9
Arkansas	135	1,636	1,337	2.21	21,942	19,396	23.7	88.5	122.2	1.54	3.9
Maryland	71	1,559	1,281	2.11	27,918	24,011	18.0	83.7	120.3	1.52	3.4
New Jersey	47	948	787	1.28	34,895	33,779	24.7	79.8	112.8	1.42	6.7
South Carolina	54	1,181	1,005	1.59	30,051	26,965	13.5	65.8	87.7	1.11	3.9
Utah	21	752	611	1.02	32,826	29,408	14.7	56.3	81.5	1.03	2.5
Idaho	36	535	462	0.72	37,697	36,013	10.9	53.3	70.2	0.89	3.2
Kentucky	40	620	500	0.84	25,540	21,462	18.6	30.6	59.6	0.75	2.1
Montana	7	343	315	0.46	38,840	38,467	(D)	30.8	49.2	0.62	1.1
Wyoming	30	308	207	0.42	30,903	29,116	7.2	25.8	46.5	0.59	3.4
Massachusetts	36	307	268	0.41	39,788	38,429	(S)	26.6	43.6	0.55	3.4
Nevada	20	514	437	0.69	30,821	26,359	8.9	30.1	40.7	0.51	3.7
West Virginia	27	580	485	0.78	22,710	23,825	5.0	26.2	32.5	0.41	1.2
North Dakota	7	155	126	0.21	29,277	28,032	4.5	16.3	31.8	0.40	1.1
Rhode Island	7	141	(S)	0.19	54,504	-	3.9	18.7	28.1	0.35	0.6
Oklahoma	31	214	185	0.29	17,299	14,476	5.7	11.3	24.3	0.31	2.5
Iowa	30	140	117	0.19	44,414	41,197	(D)	10.6	17.8	0.22	2.8
South Dakota	17	101	65	0.14	31,109	31,523	5.0	9.6	17.3	0.22	0.6
Connecticut	16	62	45	0.08	32,774	27,089	1.5	6.2	11.3	0.14	0.8
Alaska	10	(S)	47	-	-	29,702	(S)	6.4	8.9	0.11	0.3
Delaware	14	104	82	0.14	21,423	17,988	1.6	5.5	7.7	0.10	0.5
Hawaii	6	62	49	0.08	29,500	28,224	(D)	3.1	6.3	0.08	0.1
Vermont	12	74	70	0.10	25,405	25,571	(S)	4.1	5.8	0.07	(S)
Texas	366	5,706	4,821	7.71	29,204	25,504	(D)	340.4	(D)	-	29.7
Illinois	107	1,421	1,155	1.92	46,059	42,248	35.5	147.7	(D)	-	4.2
Washington	91	1,786	1,470	2.41	35,613	33,118	(D)	80.0	(D)	-	9.4
New York	75	995	849	1.34	39,675	35,700	(D)	78.3	(D)	-	5.6
Alabama	63	1,524	1,296	2.06	26,301	22,107	(D)	89.0	(D)	-	4.2
Louisiana	49	840	641	1.13	28,263	23,048	27.6	62.0	(D)	-	4.4
Arizona	32	1,932	1,600	2.61	27,618	26,241	(D)	117.0	(D)	-	8.5
Nebraska	28	1,226	407	1.66	67,420	-	(D)	204.5	(D)	-	49.1
New Hampshire	26	651	543	0.88	40,280	39,192	(D)	64.2	(D)	-	6.0
Maine	25	179	138	0.24	35,737	31,188	(D)	19.6	(D)	-	0.8
D.C.	2	(D)	(D)	-	-	-	(D)	(D)	(D)	-	(D)

Source: Economic Census of the U.S., 1997. Data are sorted by 1997 revenues or establishments. (D) means data suppression to prevent disclosure of company data. (S) means that data did not meet statistical standards for publication. A dash (-) is used when data are unavailable or cannot be calculated. Data followed by an * indicate the midpoint of a range. The ranges are: for 10, 0-19; for 60, 20-99, for 175, 100-249, for 375, 250-499, for 750, 500-999. Higher values are multiples of those shown, e.g., 3,750 is the midpoint of the range 2,500-4,999. Shaded *states* on the state map indicate those states which have proportionately greater representation in the industry than would be indicated by the state's population; the ratio is based on total revenues or number of establishments. Shaded *regions* indicate where the industry is regionally most concentrated.

NAICS 234930 - INDUSTRIAL NONBUILDING STRUCTURE CONSTRUCTION

GENERAL STATISTICS

Years	Estab-lish-ments	Employment		Payroll ($ mil)		Costs ($ mil)		Value Added ($ mil)	Revenues ($ mil)			Capital expend. ($ mil)
		Total	Constr. workers	Total	Worker payroll	Total	Cost of materials		All sources	Construction Total	Net	
1997	531	98,555	79,473	3,722.4	2,734.0	1,894.7	1,822.8	6,288.7	9,309.0	9,255.2	8,129.7	135.4

Source: *Economic Census of the United States*, 1997. This is a newly defined industry. Data for prior years were unavailable at the time of publication but may become available over time. "Net" under "Construction" is construction revenue net of the costs of subcontracts.

DISTRIBUTION AMONG SIC-BASED INDUSTRIES - 1997

SIC	Industry	Estab-lish-ments	Employment		Cost of Power & Materials ($ mil)	Revenues ($ mil)			Value Added ($ mil)
			Total (000)	Payroll ($ mil)		All Sources	Construction Total	Net	
162910	Heavy construction, nec (pt)	484.0	97,883	3,687.8	1,863.5	9,111.1	9,058.9	7,974.7	6,163.49
874135	Management services (pt)	47.0	672	34.6	31.2	197.8	196.3	154.9	125.21

Source: 1997 *Economic Census*. U.S. Census Bureau, U.S. Department of Commerce, August 1997. SIC codes ending in two zeroes represent complete 4-digit SICs. All others are parts of 4-digit SIC industries. Items showing a dash (-) indicate that data are not available because of disclosure problems.

SIC INDUSTRIES RELATED TO NAICS 234930

SIC	Industry	1990	1991	1992	1993	1994	1995	1996	1997
1629	**Heavy Construction, n.e.c.***								
	Establishments (number)	15,289e	15,550e	15,816	16,086p	16,361p	16,640p	16,924p	17,213p
	Employment (thousands)	301.5e	302.8e	304.1	305.4e	306.8e	308.1e	309.4e	310.7e
	Revenues ($ million)	31,238.0e	32,669.1e	34,165.7	35,730.8e	37,367.7e	39,079.5e	40,869.8e	42,742.1e
8741	**Management Services***								
	Establishments (number)	15,267	16,556	20,186	21,920	23,803	21,674	23,348p	24,255p
	Employment (thousands)	285.2	306.6	285.1	357.7	386.3	312.7	368.9p	381.9p
	Revenues ($ million)	20,627.0	21,788.0	23,774.0	23,373.0	24,328.0	27,611.0	27,569.0	28,870.9p

Source: *Economic Census of the United States*, 1992, annual surveys of economic sectors conducted by the Bureau of the Census, and estimates or projections based on the 1982-1992 period; not all data are shown. 'e' marks estimates made by the editors; 'p' indicates projections based on time series. A dash (-) indicates that data for this SIC or year were not available. * Indicates that only a portion of this industry is present within the NAICS data. If no * is shown, the entire industry is contained within the NAICS data.

INDICES OF CHANGE

Years	Estab-lish-ments	Employment		Payroll ($ mil)		Costs ($ mil)		Value Added ($ mil)	Revenues ($ mil)			Capital expend. ($ mil)
		Total	Constr. workers	Total	Worker payroll	Total	Cost of materials		All sources	Construction Total	Net	
1997	100.0	100.0	100.0	100.0	100.0	100.0	100.0	100.0	100.0	100.0	100.0	100.0

Sources: Same as General Statistics. The values shown reflect change from the base year, 1997. Values above 100 mean greater than 1997, values below 100 mean less than 1997, and a value of 100 in years other than 1997 means same as 1997. Indices are calculated only for Census years. Data are the most recent available at this level of detail.

SELECTED RATIOS

For 1997	Avg. of Sector	Analyzed Industry	Index	For 1997	Avg. of Sector	Analyzed Industry	Index
Employees per establishment	8.6	185.6	2,151	Value added per establishment	584,730	11,843,126	2,025
Construction workers per establishment	6.6	149.7	2,268	Value added per employee	67,759	63,809	94
Payroll per establishment	265,343	7,010,169	2,642	Value added per construction worker	88,592	79,130	89
Payroll per employee	30,748	37,770	123	Revenues per establishment	1,307,915	17,531,073	1,340
Payroll per construction worker	27,622	34,402	125	Revenues per employee	151,563	94,455	62
Costs per establishment	367,737	3,568,173	970	Revenues per construction worker	198,161	117,134	59
Costs per employee	42,614	19,225	45	CR as % of total revenues	98.48	99.42	101
Costs per construction worker	55,716	23,841	43	Net CR as % of CR	72.40	87.84	121
Materials as % of costs	95.75	96.21	100	Investment per establishment	22,948	254,991	1,111
Costs as % of revenues	28.12	20.35	72	Investment per employee	2,659	1,374	52
Costs as % of construction revenues	28.55	20.47	72	Investment per construction worker	3,477	1,704	49

Sources: Same as General Statistics. The 'Average of Sector' column represents the average for all industries in this sector. The Index shows the relationship between the Average and the Analyzed Industry. For example, 100 means that they are equal; 500 that the Analyzed Industry is five times the average; 50 means that the Analyzed Industry is half the national average. 'na' is used to show that data are 'not available'. CR stands for "construction revenues" and "Net CR" is construction revenues net of subcontract expenses.

LEADING COMPANIES   Number shown: **4**   Total sales ($ mil): **604**   Total employment (000): **1.6**

Company Name	Address				CEO Name	Phone	Co. Type	Sales ($ mil)	Empl. (000)
Bradco Supply Corp.	13 Production Way	Avenel	NJ	07001	Barry Segal	732-382-3400	R	475*	1.1
Horizon Offshore	2500 City West Blvd	Houston	TX	77042	Bill J Lam	713-361-2600	P	120	0.4
Blue Ridge Construction Inc.	1622 Rainier Dr	Co Springs	CO	80901		719-578-5225	R	9	<0.1
ETS Pacific Inc.	222 SW Harrison	Portland	OR	97201		503-222-5840	N	0	<0.1

Source: Ward's Business Directory of U.S. Private and Public Companies, Volumes 1 and 2, 2000. The company type code used is as follows: P - Public, R - Private, S - Subsidiary, D - Division, J - Joint Venture, A - Affiliate, G - Group, N - Company type not reported. Sales are in millions of dollars, employees are in thousands. An asterisk (*) indicates an estimated sales volume. The symbol < stands for 'less than'. Company names and addresses are truncated, in some cases, to fit into the available space.

COST DETAILS

Item	Cost ($ mil)	% of total	Per $1,000 of Revenue	Item	Cost ($ mil)	% of total	Per $1,000 of Revenue
All costs	3,020.3	100.000	324.4	Total Rentals	234.2	7.755	25.2
Cost of supplies	1,822.8	60.352	195.8	Equipment	204.9	6.784	22.0
Subcontracts	1,125.6	37.267	120.9	Buildings	29.3	0.970	3.1
Power, fuel, lubricants	71.9	2.381	7.7	Services purchased	100.6	3.332	10.8
Electricity	10.9	0.362	1.2	Communications	39.0	1.292	4.2
Natural gas	4.3	0.144	0.5	Building repairs	6.0	0.198	0.6
Gasoline and diesel	51.5	1.706	5.5	Machinery repairs	55.6	1.842	6.0
Highway	25.4	0.842	2.7				
Offroad	26.1	0.863	2.8				
Other power	5.1	0.170	0.6				

Source: Economic Census of the United States, 1997. Revenues referred to are total industry revenues for the current NAICS industry.

CONSTRUCTION PRODUCT DETAILS

Construction type	Value of construction work ($ mil and %)							
	Total		New construction		Additions, alterations, reconstruction		Maintenance and repair	
	Value	%	Value	%	Value	%	Value	%
Total	**9,255.2**	**100.0**	**4,348.7**	**100.0**	**1,474.1**	**100.0**	**3,407.9**	**100.0**
Building construction, total	**240.6**	**2.6**	**120.9**	**2.8**	**30.0**	**2.0**	**-**	**-**
Manufacturing and light industrial buildings	87.4	0.9	52.3	1.2	16.4	1.1	-	-
Other building construction	153.2	1.7	68.6	1.6	13.5	0.9	-	-
Nonbuilding construction, total	**8,990.2**	**97.1**	**4,227.8**	**97.2**	**1,444.1**	**98.0**	**3,318.2**	**97.4**
Highways, streets, and related work	-	-	(D)	-	(D)	-	0.5	-
Bridges, tunnels, and elevated highways	99.9	1.1	(D)	-	(D)	-	10.1	0.3
Power plants	-	-	-	-	-	-	779.5	22.9
Blast furnaces, refineries, chemical complexes, etc	6,177.8	66.7	2,688.4	61.8	992.9	67.4	2,496.5	73.3
Sewage and water treatment plants	109.5	1.2	60.4	1.4	41.5	2.8	(S)	-
Other nonbuilding construction, nec	427.6	4.6	371.8	8.6	31.9	2.2	23.9	0.7
Construction work, nsk	**-**	**-**	**NA**	**-**	**NA**	**-**	**NA**	**-**

Source: Economic Census of the United States, 1997. Bold items are headers. (D) stands for data withheld to protect competitive information. (S) indicates instances where data do not meet publications standards.

LOCATION BY STATE AND REGIONAL CONCENTRATION

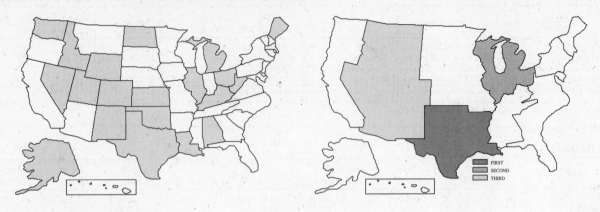

FIRST
SECOND
THIRD

INDUSTRY DATA BY STATE

State	Establishments	Employment			Compensation		Production				Capital Exp. ($ mil)
		Total	Workers	Total as % of US	Payroll per Employee	Wages per Worker	Costs ($ mil)	Value Added ($ mil)	Revenues ($ mil)	% of US	
California	30	3,796	3,023	3.85	37,480	34,088	89.0	271.4	445.4	4.78	4.5
New Jersey	12	2,439	1,936	2.47	48,457	41,001	(D)	310.2	394.6	4.24	3.0
Kentucky	9	1,126	1,029	1.14	47,719	48,868	13.1	190.3	208.2	2.24	0.4
West Virginia	11	(D)	940	-	-	30,878	33.5	80.3	141.3	1.52	2.1
Arkansas	4	1,016	815	1.03	33,602	28,985	10.5	83.8	111.4	1.20	(D)
Maryland	6	61	18	0.06	53,197	24,000	(D)	5.4	13.1	0.14	0.3
Massachusetts	5	49	32	0.05	41,490	-	1.3	4.1	6.8	0.07	0.7
Texas	110	44,312	36,584	44.96	37,891	33,510	(D)	2,688.7	(D)	-	48.8
Illinois	31	665	578	0.67	47,620	47,633	(D)	60.3	(D)	-	1.3
Michigan	27	404	365	0.41	46,255	43,937	(D)	29.2	(D)	-	0.6
Ohio	26	2,811	2,413	2.85	48,435	46,986	(D)	218.7	(D)	-	3.5
Colorado	25	770	582	0.78	37,175	35,423	(D)	59.6	(D)	-	6.7
Florida	25	1,234	943	1.25	46,408	45,287	(D)	119.8	(D)	-	6.7
Pennsylvania	25	2,230	1,963	2.26	37,974	34,974	(D)	130.9	(D)	-	2.6
Louisiana	23	15,518	13,726	15.75	35,037	34,375	(D)	782.9	(D)	-	13.3
Washington	20	1,210	906	1.23	42,719	36,031	(D)	70.5	(D)	-	5.4
Oklahoma	19	930	822	0.94	25,228	21,824	(D)	44.0	(D)	-	1.1
Utah	11	586	530	0.59	35,722	33,925	(D)	38.6	(D)	-	1.7
Alabama	10	800	746	0.81	30,029	28,241	(D)	39.7	(D)	-	1.5
Indiana	9	2,572	2,335	2.61	39,550	38,196	(D)	175.6	(D)	-	1.8
New York	9	116	70	0.12	55,569	45,943	(D)	12.3	(D)	-	0.3
Idaho	8	(D)	(D)	-	-	-	(D)	(D)	(D)	-	(D)
Kansas	7	392	352	0.40	37,689	35,804	(D)	16.4	(D)	-	0.6
New Mexico	7	(D)	(D)	-	-	-	(D)	(D)	(D)	-	(S)
Alaska	6	261	216	0.26	41,874	36,644	(D)	26.0	(D)	-	1.6
Virginia	6	203	129	0.21	-	22,031	(D)	(S)	(D)	-	(S)
Georgia	5	795	511	0.81	36,351	27,337	(D)	82.0	(D)	-	2.0
Minnesota	5	(D)	(D)	-	-	-	(D)	55.6	(D)	-	(D)
Nevada	5	(D)	(D)	-	-	-	(D)	(D)	(D)	-	(D)
Tennessee	4	272	212	0.28	39,176	35,467	(D)	18.8	(D)	-	4.8
Arizona	3	(D)	(D)	-	-	-	(D)	(D)	(D)	-	(D)
Connecticut	3	(D)	(D)	-	-	-	(D)	(D)	(D)	-	(D)
Maine	3	(D)	(D)	-	-	-	(D)	(D)	(D)	-	(D)
South Carolina	3	612	454	0.62	58,441	-	(D)	(D)	(D)	-	3.0
Wyoming	3	(D)	(D)	-	-	-	(D)	(D)	(D)	-	(D)
Hawaii	2	(D)	(D)	-	-	-	(D)	(D)	(D)	-	(D)
Missouri	2	(D)	(D)	-	-	-	(D)	(D)	(D)	-	(D)
New Hampshire	2	(D)	(D)	-	-	-	-	(D)	(D)	-	-
North Dakota	2	(D)	(D)	-	-	-	(D)	(D)	(D)	-	(D)
Oregon	2	(D)	(D)	-	-	-	(D)	(D)	(D)	-	(D)
Delaware	1	(D)	(D)	-	-	-	(D)	(D)	(D)	-	(D)
Mississippi	1	(D)	(D)	-	-	-	(D)	(D)	(D)	-	-
Nebraska	1	(D)	(D)	-	-	-	(D)	(D)	(D)	-	(D)
North Carolina	1	(D)	(D)	-	-	-	(D)	(D)	(D)	-	(D)
South Dakota	1	(D)	(D)	-	-	-	(D)	(D)	(D)	-	-
Wisconsin	1	(D)	(D)	-	-	-	(D)	(D)	(D)	-	-

Source: Economic Census of the U.S., 1997. Data are sorted by 1997 revenues or establishments. (D) means data suppression to prevent disclosure of company data. (S) means that data did not meet statistical standards for publication. A dash (-) is used when data are unavailable or cannot be calculated. Data followed by an * indicate the midpoint of a range. The ranges are: for 10, 0-19; for 60, 20-99; for 175, 100-249; for 375, 250-499, for 750, 500-999. Higher values are multiples of those shown, e.g., 3,750 is the midpoint of the range 2,500-4,999. Shaded *states* on the state map indicate those states which have proportionately greater representation in the industry than would be indicated by the state's population; the ratio is based on total revenues or number of establishments. Shaded *regions* indicate where the industry is regionally most concentrated.

NAICS 234990 - HEAVY CONSTRUCTION NEC

GENERAL STATISTICS

Years	Estab-lish-ments	Employment		Payroll ($ mil)		Costs ($ mil)		Value Added ($ mil)	Revenues ($ mil)			Capital expend. ($ mil)
		Total	Constr. workers	Total	Worker payroll	Total	Cost of materials		All sources	Construction		
										Total	Net	
1997	18,236	219,486	171,254	7,285.0	5,174.9	8,853.2	8,004.2	17,528.3	31,536.1	30,521.6	25,366.9	1,373.2

Source: Economic Census of the United States, 1997. This is a newly defined industry. Data for prior years were unavailable at the time of publication but may become available over time. "Net" under "Construction" is construction revenue net of the costs of subcontracts.

DISTRIBUTION AMONG SIC-BASED INDUSTRIES - 1997

SIC	Industry	Estab-lish-ments	Employment		Cost of Power & Materials ($ mil)	Revenues ($ mil)			Value Added ($ mil)
			Total (000)	Payroll ($ mil)		All Sources	Construction		
							Total	Net	
162920	Heavy construction, nec (pt)	15,475.0	192,974	6,334.0	8,122.9	28,096.1	27,318.2	22,631.1	15,286.02
735320	Heavy construction equipment rental (pt)	2,295.0	23,586	834.1	597.2	2,734.7	2,524.5	2,349.9	1,962.93
874136	Management services (pt)	465.0	2,926	116.9	133.0	705.3	678.8	386.0	279.34

Source: 1997 Economic Census. U.S. Census Bureau, U.S. Department of Commerce, August 1997. SIC codes ending in two zeroes represent complete 4-digit SICs. All others are parts of 4-digit SIC industries. Items showing a dash (-) indicate that data are not available because of disclosure problems.

SIC INDUSTRIES RELATED TO NAICS 234990

SIC	Industry	1990	1991	1992	1993	1994	1995	1996	1997
1629	**Heavy Construction, n.e.c.***								
	Establishments (number)	15,289e	15,550e	15,816	16,086p	16,361p	16,640p	16,924p	17,213p
	Employment (thousands)	301.5e	302.8e	304.1	305.4e	306.8e	308.1e	309.4e	310.7e
	Revenues ($ million)	31,238.0e	32,669.1e	34,165.7	35,730.8e	37,367.7e	39,079.5e	40,869.8e	42,742.1e
7353	**Heavy Construction Equipment Rental***								
	Establishments (number)	3,764	3,634	3,853	3,796	3,661	3,624	3,394p	3,290p
	Employment (thousands)	39.6	36.1	34.7	36.8	37.3	39.7	37.0p	36.8p
	Revenues ($ million)	5,091.0	4,537.0	4,090.0	4,393.0	4,836.0	5,740.0	6,076.0	5,838.6p
8741	**Management Services***								
	Establishments (number)	15,267	16,556	20,186	21,920	23,803	21,674	23,348p	24,255p
	Employment (thousands)	285.2	306.6	285.1	357.7	386.3	312.7	368.9p	381.9p
	Revenues ($ million)	20,627.0	21,788.0	23,774.0	23,373.0	24,328.0	27,611.0	27,569.0	28,870.9p

Source: Economic Census of the United States, 1992, annual surveys of economic sectors conducted by the Bureau of the Census, and estimates or projections based on the 1982-1992 period; not all data are shown. 'e' marks estimates made by the editors; 'p' indicates projections based on time series. A dash (-) indicates that data for this SIC or year were not available. * Indicates that only a portion of this industry is present within the NAICS data. If no * is shown, the entire industry is contained within the NAICS data.

INDICES OF CHANGE

Years	Estab-lish-ments	Employment		Payroll ($ mil)		Costs ($ mil)		Value Added ($ mil)	Revenues ($ mil)			Capital expend. ($ mil)
		Total	Constr. workers	Total	Worker payroll	Total	Cost of materials		All sources	Construction		
										Total	Net	
1997	100.0	100.0	100.0	100.0	100.0	100.0	100.0	100.0	100.0	100.0	100.0	100.0

Sources: Same as General Statistics. The values shown reflect change from the base year, 1997. Values above 100 mean greater than 1997, values below 100 mean less than 1997, and a value of 100 in years other than 1997 means same as 1997. Indices are calculated only for Census years. Data are the most recent available at this level of detail.

SELECTED RATIOS

For 1997	Avg. of Sector	Analyzed Industry	Index	For 1997	Avg. of Sector	Analyzed Industry	Index
Employees per establishment	8.6	12.0	139	Value added per establishment	584,730	961,192	164
Construction workers per establishment	6.6	9.4	142	Value added per employee	67,759	79,861	118
Payroll per establishment	265,343	399,485	151	Value added per construction worker	88,592	102,353	116
Payroll per employee	30,748	33,191	108	Revenues per establishment	1,307,915	1,729,332	132
Payroll per construction worker	27,622	30,218	109	Revenues per employee	151,563	143,682	95
Costs per establishment	367,737	485,479	132	Revenues per construction worker	198,161	184,148	93
Costs per employee	42,614	40,336	95	CR as % of total revenues	98.48	96.78	98
Costs per construction worker	55,716	51,696	93	Net CR as % of CR	72.40	83.11	115
Materials as % of costs	95.75	90.41	94	Investment per establishment	22,948	75,302	328
Costs as % of revenues	28.12	28.07	100	Investment per employee	2,659	6,256	235
Costs as % of construction revenues	28.55	29.01	102	Investment per construction worker	3,477	8,018	231

Sources: Same as General Statistics. The 'Average of Sector' column represents the average for all industries in this sector. The Index shows the relationship between the Average and the Analyzed Industry. For example, 100 means that they are equal; 500 that the Analyzed Industry is five times the average; 50 means that the Analyzed Industry is half the national average. 'na' is used to show that data are 'not available'. CR stands for "construction revenues" and "Net CR" is construction revenues net of subcontract expenses.

LEADING COMPANIES   Number shown: **75**   Total sales ($ mil): **67,896**   Total employment (000): **376.4**

Company Name	Address				CEO Name	Phone	Co. Type	Sales ($ mil)	Empl. (000)
Halliburton Co.	3600 Lincoln Plaza	Dallas	TX	75201	Williams Bradford	214-978-2600	P	14,898	107.8
Fluor Corp.	1 Enterprise Dr	Aliso Viejo	CA	92656	Philip J Carroll Jr	949-349-2000	P	12,417	53.6
Foster Wheeler Corp.	Perryville Corporate	Clinton	NJ	08809	Richard J Swift	908-730-4000	P	3,944	11.1
Peter Kiewit Sons' Inc.	1000 Kiewit Plz	Omaha	NE	68131		402-342-2052	R	3,403	16.2
McDermott International Inc.	PO Box 60035	New Orleans	LA	70160	Robert Rawle	504-587-5400	P	3,150	20.3
BOC Process Plants	575 Mountain Ave	Murray Hill	NJ	07974		908-464-8100	D	3,000	0.7
McDermott International nc.	PO Box 60035	New Orleans	LA	70160	Roger E Terrault	504-587-4411	S	1,891	17.5
Morrison Knudsen Corp.	PO Box 73	Boise	ID	83729	Dennis R Washington	208-386-5000	P	1,862	9.0
Black and Veatch L.L.P.	P O Box 8405	Kansas City	MO	64114	PJ Adam	913-458-2000	R	1,800	8.0
Skanska USA Inc.	60 Arch St	Greenwich	CT	06830	Stuart Graham	203-629-8840	R	1,261*	3.0
M.W. Kellogg Co.	P O Box 4557	Houston	TX	77210	A Jack Stanley	713-753-2000	S	1,234*	3.0
J.A. Jones Construction Co.	J A Jones Dr	Charlotte	NC	28287	Bob Hambright	704-553-3000	S	1,200*	10.0
Dillingham Construction Corp.	5960 Inglewood Dr	Pleasanton	CA	94588	DE Sundgren	925-463-3300	S	1,175	8.0
GE Nuclear Energy	175 Curtner Ave	San Jose	CA	95125		408-925-1000	S	1,000	2.5
Foster Wheeler Power Systems	Perryville Corp Park	Clinton	NJ	08809	Claudio Ferrari	908-713-2701	S	875*	0.5
Tutor-Saliba Corp.	15901 Olden St	Sylmar	CA	91342	Ronald Tutor	818-362-8391	R	791	2.5
Chicago Bridge and Iron Co.	1501 N Division St	Plainfield	IL	60544		815-439-6000	P	776	6.5
Rocky Flats Environmental	PO Box 464	Golden	CO	80403	RG Card	303-966-7000	S	629	5.0
Bechtel National Inc.	P O Box 193965	San Francisco	CA	94119	Riley P Bechtel	415-768-1234	S	568*	3.0
Alberici Corp.	2150 Kienlen Ave	St. Louis	MO	63121	Robert F McCoole	314-261-2611	R	554	1.7
Progress Rail Services Corp.	PO Box 1037	Albertville	AL	35950	Bill Ainsworth	256-593-1260	S	475	2.3
Fru-Con Construction Corp.	PO Box 100	Ballwin	MO	63022	Bruce A Frust	314-391-6700	R	442	2.8
Bechtel Group Inc.	So Beale Street	San Francisco	CA	94105	Riley P Bechtel	415-768-1234	R	413	30.0
Oscar J. Boldt Construction Co.	PO Box 419	Appleton	WI	54912	Warren Parsons	920-739-6321	S	402*	2.0
Oceaneering International Inc.	PO Box 40494	Houston	TX	77240		713-329-4500	P	400	2.6
Centex Construction Inc.	P O Box 299009	Dallas	TX	75229	Robert Van Cleave	214-357-1891	P	400	0.2
Parsons Energy & Chemicals	100 W Walnut St	Pasadena	CA	91124	William E Hall	626-440-2000	S	340*	2.5
Enron Power Corp.	1200 Smith St	Houston	TX	77002	Lincoln Jones III	713-646-6000	S	340*	0.4
Irwin Industries Inc.	2679 Redondo Ave	Long Beach	CA	90806	Robert J Gierat	562-427-0946	S	338*	1.4
Lane Construction Corp.	965 E Main St	Meriden	CT	06450	BF Wetmue	203-235-3351	R	314	1.6
Flint Industries Inc.	P O Box 490	Tulsa	OK	74101	John Bates	918-587-8451	R	300*	1.5
Slattery Skanska Inc.	16-16 Whitestone	Whitestone	NY	11357	Stuart E Graham	718-767-2600	S	300	1.0
Weeks Marine Inc.	216 N Ave E	Cranford	NJ	07016	Richard S Weeks	908-272-4010	R	300	1.0
American Eco Corp.	11011 Jones Rd	Houston	TX	77070	Michael E McGinnis	281-774-7000	P	300	2.2
Dillingham Construction Pacific	614 Kapahulu Ave	Honolulu	HI	96815	William J Wilson	808-735-3211	S	275	0.7
T.L. James and Company Inc.	PO Box 1260	Ruston	LA	71273	William J Deasy	318-255-7912	R	264*	2.0
Auchter Co.	PO Box 1193	Jacksonville	FL	32201	WH Glass	904-355-3536	R	260*	0.1
Landscapes Unlimited Inc.	1601 Cheney Rd	Lincoln	NE	68516	William Kubly	402-423-6653	R	254*	1.0
W.A. Klinger Inc.	P O Box 8800	Sioux City	IA	51102	John W Gleeson	712-277-3900	S	248*	0.6
Pizzagalli Construction Co.	PO Box 2009	S. Burlington	VT	05407	Peter Bernhardt	802-658-4100	R	230	1.0
Eby Corp.	P O Box 1679	Wichita	KS	67201	James R Grier III	316-268-3500	R	221	1.2
National Energy Production Corp.	18578 NE 67th Ct	Redmond	WA	98052	John H Gillis	425-869-3000	S	215	0.9
Matrix Service Inc.	10701 E Ute St	Tulsa	OK	74116	Martin L Rinehart	918-838-8822	P	215	2.5
Martin K. Eby Construction Inc.	PO Box 1679	Wichita	KS	67201	James R Grier III	316-268-3500	D	212	1.0
Burns and Roe Enterprises Inc.	800 Kinderkamack	Oradell	NJ	07649	K Keith Roe	201-265-2000	R	204*	0.8
Hubbard Construction Co.	P O Box 547217	Orlando	FL	32854	Jean-Marc Allard	407-645-5500	S	200*	1.3
Gulf Island Fabrication Inc.	PO Box 310	Houma	LA	70361	Kerry Chauvin	504-872-2100	P	192	1.3
Traylor Brothers Inc.	P O Box 5165	Evansville	IN	47716	Thomas W Traylor	812-477-1542	R	186	1.0
KTI Fish Inc.	1990 Post Oak, #200	Houston	TX	77056	Gerald L Turner	281-548-4000	S	180*	1.8
Rieth-Riley Company Inc.	PO Box 477	Goshen	IN	46527	R McCormick	219-875-5183	R	170*	0.8
S & B Engineers & Constructors	7825 Park Pl	Houston	TX	77087	William A Brookshire	713-645-4141	R	160*	1.0
Eichleay Corp.	6585 Penn Ave	Pittsburgh	PA	15206	Theodore W Nelson	412-363-9000	S	150*	2.0
Cianbro Corp.	PO Box 1000	Pittsfield	ME	04967	Alton Cianchette	207-487-3311	R	150*	1.5
National Engineering	12608 Alameda Dr	Cleveland	OH	44136	Marty Cohen	440-238-3331	R	150*	0.6
Walsh Construction Co.	P O Box 0400	Trumbull	CT	06611			D	149*	0.1
Foster Wheeler USA Corp.	Perryville Corporate	Clinton	NJ	08809	Richard Swift	908-730-4000	S	132*	1.1
Herzog Contracting Corp.	P O Box 1089	St. Joseph	MO	64502	William E Herzog	816-233-9001	R	130	0.9
Williard Inc.	PO Box 9002	Jenkintown	PA	19046	Joseph Doody	215-885-5000	S	130*	0.8
Crowder Construction Co.	P O Box 30007	Charlotte	NC	28230	Otis A Crowder	704-372-3541	R	130	0.7
CCC Group Inc.	PO Box 200242	San Antonio	TX	78220	Orvis Maxey	210-661-4251	R	120	1.1
Hardaway Construction	615 Main St	Nashville	TN	37206	LH Hardaway Jr	615-254-5461	S	115	0.4
Loram Maintenance of Way Inc.	PO Box 188	Hamel	MN	55340		612-478-6014	R	112*	0.5
Foster Wheeler Constructors Inc.	Perryville Corporate	Clinton	NJ	08809	Robert J Burcin	908-730-5500	D	110	0.5
Ref-Chem Corp.	1128 S Grandview	Odessa	TX	79761	Bob Cranshaw	915-332-8531	R	107	0.7
Reynolds Inc.	PO Box 186	Orleans	IN	47452	Jack Reynolds	812-865-3232	R	102*	0.7
C.F. Bean Corp.	P O Box 237	Belle Chasse	LA	70037	JW Bean	504-391-7000	R	101*	0.4
Hardaway Co.	P O Box 1360	Columbus	GA	31902	Mason H Lampton	706-322-3274	R	100*	0.5
Grupe Inc.	3255 W March Ln	Stockton	CA	95219	Greenlaw Grupe Jr	209-473-6000	R	100*	0.4
Frontier-Kemper Constructors Inc.	PO Box 6548	Evansville	IN	47719	Galyn G Rippentrop	812-426-2741	R	99	0.3
Sevenson Environmental Services	P O Box 396	Niagara Falls	NY	14302	Michael A Elia	716-284-0431	P	95	0.2
Arctic Slope World Services Inc.	3033 Gold Canal Dr	Rancho Cordova	CA	95670	Mike Taylor	916-363-2224	S	90	0.9
Valley Crest Landscape Inc.	24121 Ventura Blvd	Calabasas	CA	91302	Richard Sperber	818-223-8500	S	88	1.1
Advanco Constructors Inc.	PO Box 1210	Upland	CA	91785	Pete Seley	909-982-8803	S	88*	0.4
Sherwood Construction Inc.	P O Box 9163	Wichita	KS	67277	John Curtis	316-943-0211	R	88*	0.4
Koester Equipment Inc.	14649 Hwy	Evansville	IN	47711	Homer Fruit	812-867-6635	R	83	0.3

Source: Ward's Business Directory of U.S. Private and Public Companies, Volumes 1 and 2, 2000. The company type code used is as follows: P - Public, R - Private, S - Subsidiary, D - Division, J - Joint Venture, A - Affiliate, G - Group, N - Company type not reported. Sales are in millions of dollars, employees are in thousands. An asterisk (*) indicates an estimated sales volume. The symbol < stands for 'less than'. Company names and addresses are truncated, in some cases, to fit into the available space.

COST DETAILS

Item	Cost ($ mil)	% of total	Per $1,000 of Revenue	Item	Cost ($ mil)	% of total	Per $1,000 of Revenue
All costs	14,007.8	100.000	444.2	Total Rentals	1,112.4	7.941	35.3
Cost of supplies	8,004.2	57.141	253.8	Equipment	997.0	7.117	31.6
Subcontracts	5,154.6	36.798	163.5	Buildings	115.4	0.824	3.7
Power, fuel, lubricants	848.9	6.060	26.9	Services purchased	1,130.5	8.070	35.8
Electricity	102.6	0.733	3.3	Communications	199.9	1.427	6.3
Natural gas	19.1	0.137	0.6	Building repairs	37.0	0.264	1.2
Gasoline and diesel	662.9	4.732	21.0	Machinery repairs	893.5	6.379	28.3
Highway	293.1	2.093	9.3				
Offroad	369.8	2.640	11.7				
Other power	64.2	0.459	2.0				

Source: *Economic Census of the United States*, 1997. Revenues referred to are total industry revenues for the current NAICS industry.

CONSTRUCTION PRODUCT DETAILS

Construction type	Value of construction work ($ mil and %)							
	Total		New construction		Additions, alterations, reconstruction		Maintenance and repair	
	Value	%	Value	%	Value	%	Value	%
Total	**30,521.6**	**100.0**	**20,444.2**	**100.0**	**5,380.0**	**100.0**	**3,993.8**	**100.0**
Building construction, total	**3,130.7**	**10.3**	**2,163.3**	**10.6**	**579.8**	**10.8**	**387.7**	**9.7**
Single-family houses, detached and attached	496.8	1.6	412.3	2.0	51.6	1.0	32.9	0.8
Manufacturing and light industrial buildings	782.2	2.6	394.0	1.9	221.4	4.1	166.9	4.2
Office buildings	451.7	1.5	342.3	1.7	78.4	1.5	31.0	0.8
All other commercial buildings, nec	549.3	1.8	430.1	2.1	66.2	1.2	53.1	1.3
Other building construction	850.7	2.8	584.5	2.9	162.2	3.0	103.9	2.6
Nonbuilding construction, total	**26,687.3**	**87.4**	**18,280.9**	**89.4**	**4,800.3**	**89.2**	**3,606.1**	**90.3**
Highways, streets, and related work	1,929.0	6.3	1,038.5	5.1	529.1	9.8	361.5	9.1
Private driveways and parking areas	817.6	2.7	587.8	2.9	112.3	2.1	117.5	2.9
Bridges, tunnels, and elevated highways	907.3	3.0	656.3	3.2	175.3	3.3	75.7	1.9
Sewers, water mains, and related facilities	3,400.1	11.1	2,563.6	12.5	502.3	9.3	334.3	8.4
Pipeline construction ex sewer and water	568.6	1.9	358.8	1.8	99.4	1.8	110.3	2.8
Power and communication lines, cables, towers, etc.	640.4	2.1	454.6	2.2	94.2	1.8	91.7	2.3
Power plants	713.7	2.3	562.2	2.8	66.1	1.2	85.4	2.1
Blast furnaces, refineries, chemical complexes, etc	294.4	1.0	139.2	0.7	32.9	0.6	122.3	3.1
Sewage treatment plants	2,634.9	8.6	1,637.3	8.0	898.3	16.7	99.2	2.5
Water treatment plants	1,913.3	6.3	1,326.3	6.5	527.8	9.8	59.3	1.5
Mass transit construction	1,796.7	5.9	1,020.2	5.0	355.6	6.6	420.8	10.5
Railroad construction	1,190.8	3.9	565.6	2.8	277.0	5.1	348.3	8.7
Conservation and development construction	2,441.9	8.0	1,766.7	8.6	324.2	6.0	351.1	8.8
Dam and reservoir construction	654.4	2.1	548.9	2.7	32.4	0.6	73.1	1.8
Dry/solid waste disposal	899.8	2.9	614.4	3.0	157.3	2.9	128.0	3.2
Harbor and port facilities	581.7	1.9	439.5	2.1	97.2	1.8	44.9	1.1
Marine construction	1,836.8	6.0	804.7	3.9	301.3	5.6	730.8	18.3
Recreational facilities	1,809.0	5.9	1,417.9	6.9	271.7	5.0	119.5	3.0
Other nonbuilding construction, nec	2,847.5	9.3	2,343.9	11.5	222.7	4.1	280.8	7.0
Construction work, nsk	**703.6**	**2.3**	NA	-	NA	-	NA	-

Source: *Economic Census of the United States*, 1997. Bold items are headers. (D) stands for data withheld to protect competitive information. (S) indicates instances where data do not meet publications standards.

LOCATION BY STATE AND REGIONAL CONCENTRATION

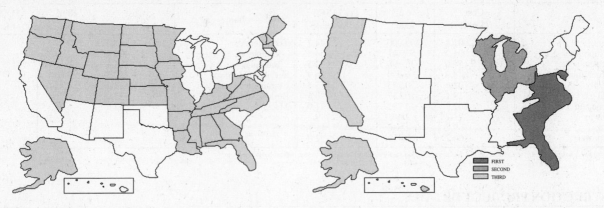

FIRST
SECOND
THIRD

INDUSTRY DATA BY STATE

State	Estab lish- ments	Employment			Compensation		Production				Capital Exp. ($ mil)
		Total	Workers	Total as % of US	Payroll per Employee	Wages per Worker	Costs ($ mil)	Value Added ($ mil)	Reve- nues ($ mil)	% of US	
California	1,427	20,045	15,774	9.13	43,677	40,896	1,074.3	1,893.3	3,606.8	11.44	124.4
Texas	1,223	17,947	14,452	8.18	28,136	24,175	626.9	1,206.0	2,096.8	6.65	88.8
Ohio	649	6,427	5,006	2.93	34,677	32,129	283.8	522.8	1,011.2	3.21	38.8
Washington	573	5,753	4,493	2.62	40,828	38,598	268.2	573.6	976.0	3.09	42.0
Massachusetts	431	5,343	4,145	2.43	39,832	37,452	283.4	446.5	973.5	3.09	37.6
Maryland	224	3,511	2,608	1.60	30,719	28,304	(D)	244.4	465.7	1.48	20.5
Nevada	170	2,596	2,067	1.18	35,741	34,811	(D)	189.9	427.7	1.36	26.2
Kentucky	342	3,102	(D)	1.41	27,072	-	135.0	199.3	391.8	1.24	16.2
West Virginia	242	3,655	3,246	1.67	20,329	16,277	78.1	201.9	319.0	1.01	(S)
Wyoming	111	1,350	(D)	0.62	24,196	-	(D)	77.1	114.7	0.36	9.4
Florida	1,064	13,448	10,632	6.13	27,902	24,777	(D)	960.9	(D)	-	77.1
New York	805	9,464	7,202	4.31	39,684	36,350	(D)	931.7	(D)	-	57.0
North Carolina	706	(D)	(D)	-	-	-	(D)	(D)	(D)	-	(D)
Michigan	664	5,279	4,204	2.41	38,668	36,094	(D)	481.1	(D)	-	44.5
Pennsylvania	592	7,979	5,837	3.64	33,017	30,830	(D)	707.9	(D)	-	45.0
Missouri	571	(D)	(D)	-	-	-	(D)	(D)	(D)	-	(D)
Illinois	529	6,800	5,578	3.10	39,914	37,622	(D)	801.8	(D)	-	61.9
Georgia	503	8,330	6,866	3.80	29,732	25,123	(D)	548.7	(D)	-	56.9
Virginia	482	4,826	4,059	2.20	30,325	27,450	(D)	341.4	(D)	-	34.4
Minnesota	452	(D)	(D)	-	-	-	(D)	503.2	(D)	-	52.6
New Jersey	443	4,610	3,458	2.10	40,092	33,883	(D)	463.1	(D)	-	37.4
Indiana	402	4,596	3,402	2.09	34,342	31,184	(D)	380.8	(D)	-	33.8
Tennessee	383	6,294	5,226	2.87	30,809	25,626	(D)	355.6	(D)	-	29.5
Louisiana	368	6,683	5,085	3.04	31,770	29,722	(D)	473.5	(D)	-	35.6
Alabama	354	3,229	2,613	1.47	24,100	20,084	(D)	238.4	(D)	-	14.6
Wisconsin	350	(D)	(D)	-	-	-	(D)	(D)	(D)	-	23.7
Mississippi	345	(D)	(D)	-	-	-	(D)	(D)	(D)	-	21.5
Oregon	293	(D)	(D)	-	-	-	(D)	(D)	(D)	-	(D)
Iowa	287	1,610	1,294	0.73	24,986	25,264	(D)	94.0	(D)	-	17.4
Arkansas	261	2,876	2,547	1.31	21,686	19,196	(D)	129.9	(D)	-	(D)
Colorado	261	4,222	3,276	1.92	32,876	29,481	(D)	346.0	(D)	-	16.5
Kansas	251	2,912	2,222	1.33	29,201	28,735	118.9	224.8	(D)	-	28.1
Nebraska	231	(D)	(D)	-	-	-	(D)	(D)	(D)	-	22.2
Oklahoma	229	2,028	1,624	0.92	22,530	21,369	(D)	87.8	(D)	-	8.2
Arizona	227	(D)	(D)	-	-	-	(D)	(D)	(D)	-	(D)
Idaho	214	(D)	2,694	-	-	41,681	(D)	747.2	(D)	-	9.5
South Carolina	172	2,509	1,984	1.14	28,950	-	(D)	(D)	(D)	-	14.8
Montana	171	1,012	(D)	0.46	-	-	(D)	73.5	(D)	-	(D)
Connecticut	168	(D)	(D)	-	-	-	(D)	(D)	(D)	-	(D)
Utah	156	1,444	1,230	0.66	31,675	28,168	(D)	84.8	(D)	-	9.6
Maine	148	(D)	(D)	-	-	-	(D)	(D)	(D)	-	(D)
New Hampshire	135	(D)	(D)	-	-	-	(D)	(D)	(D)	-	3.6
Vermont	101	(D)	(D)	-	-	-	(D)	(D)	(D)	-	(D)
Alaska	100	(S)	448	-	-	42,078	(D)	85.9	(D)	-	(S)
New Mexico	92	533	393	0.24	23,546	-	(D)	34.3	(D)	-	2.2
Rhode Island	91	613	407	0.28	32,669	31,720	(D)	(D)	(D)	-	(D)
South Dakota	82	(D)	(D)	-	-	-	(D)	(D)	(D)	-	3.3
Hawaii	71	(D)	(D)	-	-	-	26.4	(D)	(D)	-	(D)
North Dakota	55	(D)	(D)	-	-	-	(D)	(D)	(D)	-	(D)
Delaware	30	(D)	(D)	-	-	-	(D)	(D)	(D)	-	4.5
D.C.	6	(D)	(D)	-	-	-	(D)	(D)	(D)	-	1.7

Source: Economic Census of the U.S., 1997. Data are sorted by 1997 revenues or establishments. (D) means data suppression to prevent disclosure of company data. (S) means that data did not meet statistical standards for publication. A dash (-) is used when data are unavailable or cannot be calculated. Data followed by an * indicate the midpoint of a range. The ranges are: for 10, 0-19; for 60, 20-99, for 175, 100-249, for 375, 250-499, for 750, 500-999. Higher values are multiples of those shown, e.g., 3,750 is the midpoint of the range 2,500-4,999. Shaded *states* on the state map indicate those states which have proportionately greater representation in the industry than would be indicated by the state's population; the ratio is based on total revenues or number of establishments. Shaded *regions* indicate where the industry is regionally most concentrated.

NAICS 235110 - PLUMBING, HEATING, AND AIR-CONDITIONING CONTRACTORS

GENERAL STATISTICS

Years	Estab-lish-ments	Employment		Payroll ($ mil)		Costs ($ mil)		Value Added ($ mil)	Revenues ($ mil)			Capital expend. ($ mil)
		Total	Constr. workers	Total	Worker payroll	Total	Cost of materials		All sources	Construction Total	Net	
1997	84,876	788,930	599,940	25,720.2	18,279.7	33,016.8	31,879.5	46,576.8	88,427.4	87,330.2	78,496.4	1,361.6

Source: *Economic Census of the United States*, 1997. This is a newly defined industry. Data for prior years were unavailable at the time of publication but may become available over time. "Net" under "Construction" is construction revenue net of the costs of subcontracts.

DISTRIBUTION AMONG SIC-BASED INDUSTRIES - 1997

SIC	Industry	Estab-lish-ments	Employment		Cost of Power & Materials ($ mil)	Revenues ($ mil)			Value Added ($ mil)
			Total (000)	Payroll ($ mil)		All Sources	Construction Total	Net	
171100	Plumbing, heating, & air-conditioning contractors	84,876.0	788,930	25,720.2	33,016.8	88,427.4	87,330.2	78,496.4	46,576.81

Source: 1997 *Economic Census*. U.S. Census Bureau, U.S. Department of Commerce, August 1997. SIC codes ending in two zeroes represent complete 4-digit SICs. All others are parts of 4-digit SIC industries. Items showing a dash (-) indicate that data are not available because of disclosure problems.

SIC INDUSTRIES RELATED TO NAICS 235110

SIC	Industry	1990	1991	1992	1993	1994	1995	1996	1997
1711	**Plumbing, Heating, and Air Conditioning**								
	Establishments (number)	71,791	72,047	75,395	77,162	77,861p	79,124p	80,408p	81,712p
	Employment (thousands)	645.2	592.7	612.5	608.7	610.6e	609.6e	608.7e	607.7e
	Revenues ($ million)	54,564.5e	56,094.8e	57,668.0	59,285.3e	60,948.0e	62,657.3e	64,414.5e	66,221.0e
7699	**Repair Services, nec***								
	Establishments (number)	27,822	29,303	34,103	34,618	34,136	34,391	35,001p	35,792p
	Employment (thousands)	181.0	181.4	191.0	201.5	207.4	220.2	219.6p	226.2p
	Revenues ($ million)	-	-	15,059.4	15,563.6p	16,427.9p	17,292.2p	18,156.5p	19,020.8p

Source: *Economic Census of the United States*, 1992, annual surveys of economic sectors conducted by the Bureau of the Census, and estimates or projections based on the 1982-1992 period; not all data are shown. 'e' marks estimates made by the editors; 'p' indicates projections based on time series. A dash (-) indicates that data for this SIC or year were not available. * Indicates that only a portion of this industry is present within the NAICS data. If no * is shown, the entire industry is contained within the NAICS data.

INDICES OF CHANGE

Years	Estab-lish-ments	Employment		Payroll ($ mil)		Costs ($ mil)		Value Added ($ mil)	Revenues ($ mil)			Capital expend. ($ mil)
		Total	Constr. workers	Total	Worker payroll	Total	Cost of materials		All sources	Construction Total	Net	
1997	100.0	100.0	100.0	100.0	100.0	100.0	100.0	100.0	100.0	100.0	100.0	100.0

Sources: Same as General Statistics. The values shown reflect change from the base year, 1997. Values above 100 mean greater than 1997, values below 100 mean less than 1997, and a value of 100 in years other than 1997 means same as 1997. Indices are calculated only for Census years. Data are the most recent available at this level of detail.

SELECTED RATIOS

For 1997	Avg. of Sector	Analyzed Industry	Index	For 1997	Avg. of Sector	Analyzed Industry	Index
Employees per establishment	8.6	9.3	108	Value added per establishment	584,730	548,763	94
Construction workers per establishment	6.6	7.1	107	Value added per employee	67,759	59,038	87
Payroll per establishment	265,343	303,033	114	Value added per construction worker	88,592	77,636	88
Payroll per employee	30,748	32,601	106	Revenues per establishment	1,307,915	1,041,842	80
Payroll per construction worker	27,622	30,469	110	Revenues per employee	151,563	112,085	74
Costs per establishment	367,737	389,000	106	Revenues per construction worker	198,161	147,394	74
Costs per employee	42,614	41,850	98	CR as % of total revenues	98.48	98.76	100
Costs per construction worker	55,716	55,034	99	Net CR as % of CR	72.40	89.88	124
Materials as % of costs	95.75	96.56	101	Investment per establishment	22,948	16,042	70
Costs as % of revenues	28.12	37.34	133	Investment per employee	2,659	1,726	65
Costs as % of construction revenues	28.55	37.81	132	Investment per construction worker	3,477	2,270	65

Sources: Same as General Statistics. The 'Average of Sector' column represents the average for all industries in this sector. The Index shows the relationship between the Average and the Analyzed Industry. For example, 100 means that they are equal; 500 that the Analyzed Industry is five times the average; 50 means that the Analyzed Industry is half the national average. 'na' is used to show that data are 'not available'. CR stands for "construction revenues" and "Net CR" is construction revenues net of subcontract expenses.

LEADING COMPANIES   Number shown: **75**   Total sales ($ mil): **14,423**   Total employment (000): **145.1**

Company Name	Address				CEO Name	Phone	Co. Type	Sales ($ mil)	Empl. (000)
EMCOR Group Inc.	101 Merritt	Norwalk	CT	06851	Jeffrey Levy	203-849-7848	P	2,210	15.0
McDermott International nc.	PO Box 60035	New Orleans	LA	70160	Roger E Terrault	504-587-4411	S	1,891	17.5
ABM Industries Inc.	160 Pacific Ave	San Francisco	CA	94111	William W Steele	415-597-4500	P	1,502	55.0
Comfort Systems USA Inc.	777 Post Oak Blvd	Houston	TX	77056	Fred M Ferreira	713-830-9600	P	854	8.9
American Residential Services	5051 Westheimer Rd	Houston	TX	77056	Thomas N Amonett	713-599-0100	P	506	5.0
MYR Group Inc.	1701 W Golf Rd	Rolling Mdws	IL	60008	C M Brennan III	847-290-1891	P	459	3.7
Anjou Intern. Management	800 3rd Ave	New York	NY	10022		212-753-2000	R	440*	4.0
Service Experts Inc.	6 Cadillac Dr	Brentwood	TN	37027	Alan R Sielbeck	615-371-9990	R	408	4.5
Burns Brothers Contractors	400 Leavenworth	Syracuse	NY	13204	DS Burns	315-422-0261	R	350*	0.3
Poole and Kent Co.	4530 Hollins Ferry	Baltimore	MD	21227	William W Thomas	410-247-2200	S	320*	1.0
Montour Oil Service Co.	112 Broad St	Montoursville	PA	17754	Steven M Sleboda	570-368-8611	D	246*	0.3
Scott Company of California Inc.	1717 Doolittle Dr	San Leandro	CA	94577	Joseph A Guglielmo	510-895-2333	R	225*	1.2
Rudolph/Libbe Companies Inc.	6494 Latcha Rd	Walbridge	OH	43465	Frederick Rudolph	419-241-5000	R	220	0.8
Ivey Mechanical Company Inc.	514 N Wells St	Kosciusko	MS	39090		662-289-3646	R	200*	1.2
W.W. Gay Mechanical	524 Stockton St	Jacksonville	FL	32204	David Boree	904-388-2696	R	141*	0.9
Harder Mechanical Contractors	2148 NE ML King	Portland	OR	97212	Steve Harder	503-281-1112	R	140	0.7
TDIndustries Inc.	13850 Diplomat Dr	Dallas	TX	75234	Jack Lowe Jr	972-888-9500	R	135	1.0
Buzz Oates Cos.	8615 Eldercreek Rd	Sacramento	CA	95828		916-381-3600	R	135*	0.2
Williard Inc.	PO Box 9002	Jenkintown	PA	19046	Joseph Doody	215-885-5000	S	130*	0.8
Grucon Corp.	1100 W Anderson Ct	Oak Creek	WI	53154	Paul Grunau	414-216-6900	R	125	0.5
BGE Home Products and Services	7161 Columbia Gate	Columbia	MD	21045	William H Munn	410-720-6619	S	118*	0.7
Airtron Inc.	7813 N Dixie Ave	Dayton	OH	45414	Eric Salzer	937-898-0826	R	117*	0.7
Apex Industries Inc.	PO Box 88030-A	Indianapolis	IN	46208		317-257-7141	R	115*	0.7
Reedy Industries Inc.	1701 E Lake Ave	Glenview	IL	60025	Thomas W Reedy	847-729-9450	R	114*	0.7
Corrigan Brothers Inc.	3545 Gratiot St	St. Louis	MO	63103	Tom Corrigan	314-771-6200	R	113*	0.7
U.S. Engineering Co.	3433 Roanoke Rd	Kansas City	MO	64111		816-753-6969	R	109	0.6
General Heating Engineering Inc.	9070 Euclid Ave	Manassas	VA	20110	Frank Menditch	703-631-2690	P	100*	0.6
AC Corp.	PO Box 16367	Greensboro	NC	27416	D Nickell	336-273-4472	R	100*	0.6
Egan Co.	7100 Medicine Lake	Minneapolis	MN	55427	Gerald L Egan	612-544-4131	R	98*	0.6
Carson Oil Company Inc.	P O Box 10948	Portland	OR	97296	JA Carson	503-224-8500	R	96*	0.3
O'Connor Constructors Inc.	45 Industrial Dr	Canton	MA	02021		617-364-9000	R	94*	0.5
DualStar Technologies Corp.	11-30 47th Ave	Long Island City	NY	11101	Gregory Cuneo	718-340-6655	P	93	0.4
Kirk & Blum Mfg Inc.	3120 Forrer St	Cincinnati	OH	45209	Richard Blum	513-458-2600	D	92*	0.6
Morrison Construction Co.	P O Box 747	Hammond	IN	46320	JM Morrison	219-932-5036	R	92*	0.6
MCC Group L.L.C.	P O Box 7460	Metairie	LA	70010	Joseph A Jaeger Jr	504-833-8291	R	90*	0.6
Roth Bros. Inc.	PO Box 4209	Youngstown	OH	44515	Richard Thomas	330-793-5571	S	82*	0.5
Jupiter Industries Inc.	2215 Sanders Rd	Northbrook	IL	60062	George E Murphy	847-753-8200	R	78*	0.5
Henkels & McCoy Inc. Northeast	985 Jolly Rd	Blue Bell	PA	19422		215-283-7600	D	75*	0.1
McClure Co.	PO Box 1579	Harrisburg	PA	17105	W E McClure, Jr	717-237-2801	D	70*	<0.1
Stanley Jones Corp.	119 Morris St	South Fulton	TN	38257	Stanley G Jones II	901-479-2311	R	69	0.6
Fluidics Inc.	4140 Whitaker Ave	Philadelphia	PA	19124	Edward A Quinn	215-425-4800	P	67*	0.4
Harry Grodsky and Company Inc.	33 Shaws Ln	Springfield	MA	01104	Ronald D Grodsky	413-785-1947	R	67	0.2
Cleveland Consolidated	1281 Fulton Ind NW	Atlanta	GA	30336	James R Cleveland Jr	404-696-4550	S	66*	0.5
Frank A. McBride Co.	P O Box 22	Hawthorne	NJ	07507	Joseph A McBride	973-423-1123	R	66*	0.4
Kirk and Blum Manufacturing Inc.	3120 Forrer St	Cincinnati	OH	45209	Richard J Blum	513-458-2600	R	65*	0.6
Hooper Construction Corp.	PO Box 7455	Madison	WI	53707	Don Gardner	608-249-0451	R	63*	0.5
Southern Air Inc.	2655 Lakeside Dr	Lynchburg	VA	24502	Ronald Kidd Jr	804-385-6200	R	62*	0.6
Gruno Company Inc.	PO Box 479	Milwaukee	WI	53201		414-216-6900	S	62	0.4
Herman Goldner Company Inc.	7777 Brewster Ave	Philadelphia	PA	19153	HE Goldner	215-365-5400	R	62*	0.2
Colonial Mechanical Corp.	3017 Vernon Rd	Richmond	VA	23228	Robert Norton	804-264-5522	S	60*	0.7
Chapman Corp.	331 S Main St	Washington	PA	15301	Arthur Hathaway	724-228-1900	R	60	0.5
Elliott-Lewis Corp.	2701 Grant Ave	Philadelphia	PA	19114	William Sautter	215-698-4400	R	58*	0.4
Letsos Co.	P O Box 36927	Houston	TX	77236	James Letsos III	713-783-3200	R	57	0.3
Masters Inc.	7891 Beachcraft Ave	Gaithersburg	MD	20879	Ron Bryant	301-948-8950	P	56	0.5
McCarl's Inc.	PO Box 191	Beaver Falls	PA	15010	F McCarl	724-843-5660	P	55	0.4
Joseph Davis Inc.	120 W Tupper St	Buffalo	NY	14201	Jeffrey Davis	716-842-1500	R	55	0.3
Daw Technologies Inc.	2700 S 900 W	Salt Lake City	UT	84119	Ronald Daw	801-977-3100	P	53	0.4
Pacer International Inc.	551 S E 8th St	Delray Beach	FL	33483		561-272-2702	R	53	0.1
Great Lakes Plumbing & Heating	4521 W Diverse Ave	Chicago	IL	60639	Geaorge Treutelaar	773-489-0400	R	51*	0.3
Peyronnin Construction Inc.	P O Box 3317	Evansville	IN	47732	Edward Peyronnin	812-423-6241	R	51*	0.1
MewMech Companies Inc.	1633 Eustis St	St. Paul	MN	55108	Ron Pearson	651-645-0451	R	50	0.6
Lomanco Inc.	PO Box 519	Jacksonville	AR	72078	Lynn Cooper	501-982-6511	R	50	0.3
Shumate Air Conditioning	2805 Premiere Pkwy	Duluth	GA	30097	Harold Shumate	678-584-0880	R	50	0.3
Meccon Industries Inc.	P O Box 206	Lansing	IL	60438	John D Curran	708-474-8300	R	50	0.3
Todd-Ford Management Co.	1914 Breeden	San Antonio	TX	78212	John G Ford	210-732-9791	R	49	0.2
Egan Mechanical Contractors Inc.	7100 Medicine Lake	Minneapolis	MN	55427	Craig Sulentic	612-544-4131	S	48*	0.2
Morrison Inc.	PO Box 747	Hammond	IN	46320	JM Morrison	219-932-5036	S	47*	0.3
Gruno Project Development Inc.	101 W Pleasnt St	Oak Creek	WI	53154	Robert Schmitt	920-233-6901	S	47*	<0.1
Azco Group Ltd.	PO Box 567	Appleton	WI	54912	Mark W Loper	920-734-5791	R	44	0.5
Cosco Fire Protection Inc.	321 E Gardena Blvd	Gardena	CA	90247	Daniel Pool	213-321-5155	S	42*	0.4
H and H Group Inc.	P O Box 44267	Madison	WI	53744	Frank J Hoffman	608-273-3434	R	42	0.4
Way Co.	P O Box 36530	Houston	TX	77236	Peter M Way	713-666-3541	R	42*	0.3
Nashville Machine Company Inc.	P O Box 101603	Nashville	TN	37224	Donald C Orr	615-244-2030	R	41	0.4
CommAir Mechanical Services	1266 14th St	Oakland	CA	94607	Jack Lofy	510-839-1500	D	41*	0.3
John W. Danforth Co.	1940 Fillmore Ave	Buffalo	NY	14214	Emmett Reilly	716-832-1940	R	40	0.3

Source: Ward's Business Directory of U.S. Private and Public Companies, Volumes 1 and 2, 2000. The company type code used is as follows: P - Public, R - Private, S - Subsidiary, D - Division, J - Joint Venture, A - Affiliate, G - Group, N - Company type not reported. Sales are in millions of dollars, employees are in thousands. An asterisk (*) indicates an estimated sales volume. The symbol < stands for 'less than'. Company names and addresses are truncated, in some cases, to fit into the available space.

COST DETAILS

Item	Cost ($ mil)	% of total	Per $1,000 of Revenue	Item	Cost ($ mil)	% of total	Per $1,000 of Revenue
All costs	41,850.6	100.000	473.3	Total Rentals	1,315.3	3.143	14.9
Cost of supplies	31,879.5	76.174	360.5	Equipment	647.7	1.548	7.3
Subcontracts	8,833.8	21.108	99.9	Buildings	667.7	1.595	7.6
Power, fuel, lubricants	1,137.3	2.718	12.9	Services purchased	1,401.1	3.348	15.8
Electricity	193.4	0.462	2.2	Communications	678.1	1.620	7.7
Natural gas	55.0	0.131	0.6	Building repairs	120.1	0.287	1.4
Gasoline and diesel	850.7	2.033	9.6	Machinery repairs	602.9	1.441	6.8
Highway	762.4	1.822	8.6				
Offroad	88.3	0.211	1.0				
Other power	38.3	0.091	0.4				

Source: *Economic Census of the United States*, 1997. Revenues referred to are total industry revenues for the current NAICS industry.

CONSTRUCTION PRODUCT DETAILS

Construction type	Value of construction work ($ mil and %)							
	Total		New construction		Additions, alterations, reconstruction		Maintenance and repair	
	Value	%	Value	%	Value	%	Value	%
Total	**87,330.2**	**100.0**	**44,209.6**	**100.0**	**22,527.4**	**100.0**	**20,282.2**	**100.0**
Building construction, total	**82,150.1**	**94.1**	**42,071.1**	**95.2**	**21,241.1**	**94.3**	**18,838.0**	**92.9**
Single-family houses, detached	19,889.4	22.8	10,064.3	22.8	3,933.3	17.5	5,891.8	29.0
Single-family houses, attached	3,314.2	3.8	1,759.1	4.0	536.1	2.4	1,019.0	5.0
Apartment buildings, condos and cooperatives	4,514.5	5.2	2,504.2	5.7	708.8	3.1	1,301.5	6.4
Manufacturing and light industrial buildings	12,568.2	14.4	5,666.3	12.8	4,140.1	18.4	2,761.8	13.6
Manufacturing and light industrial warehouses	2,392.5	2.7	1,302.0	2.9	635.0	2.8	455.5	2.2
Hotels and motels	2,190.2	2.5	1,483.0	3.4	384.6	1.7	322.6	1.6
Office buildings	9,473.3	10.8	4,457.4	10.1	2,878.8	12.8	2,137.2	10.5
All other commercial buildings, nec	7,488.2	8.6	3,605.6	8.2	1,759.9	7.8	2,122.7	10.5
Commercial warehouses	1,722.4	2.0	1,021.6	2.3	417.3	1.9	283.6	1.4
Religious buildings	1,248.7	1.4	557.1	1.3	344.2	1.5	347.4	1.7
Educational buildings	7,135.4	8.2	3,834.1	8.7	2,472.9	11.0	828.4	4.1
Health care and institutional buildings	5,529.0	6.3	2,682.8	6.1	2,114.6	9.4	731.6	3.6
Public safety buildings	1,420.4	1.6	906.1	2.0	370.1	1.6	144.2	0.7
Other building construction	3,263.6	3.7	2,227.6	5.0	545.3	2.4	490.7	2.4
Nonbuilding construction, total	**4,869.1**	**5.6**	**2,138.5**	**4.8**	**1,286.3**	**5.7**	**1,444.3**	**7.1**
Sewers, sewer lines, septic systems, and related facilities	705.6	0.8	342.2	0.8	147.2	0.7	216.2	1.1
Water mains and related facilities	509.8	0.6	246.5	0.6	94.0	0.4	169.2	0.8
Blast furnaces, refineries, chemical complexes, etc	997.1	1.1	-	-	362.0	1.6	351.0	1.7
Sewage and water treatment plants	866.6	1.0	527.8	1.2	261.5	1.2	77.2	0.4
Other nonbuilding construction, nec	1,790.0	2.0	737.8	1.7	421.6	1.9	630.6	3.1
Construction work, nsk	**310.9**	**0.4**	**NA**	**-**	**NA**	**-**	**NA**	**-**

Source: *Economic Census of the United States*, 1997. Bold items are headers. (D) stands for data withheld to protect competitive information. (S) indicates instances where data do not meet publications standards.

LOCATION BY STATE AND REGIONAL CONCENTRATION

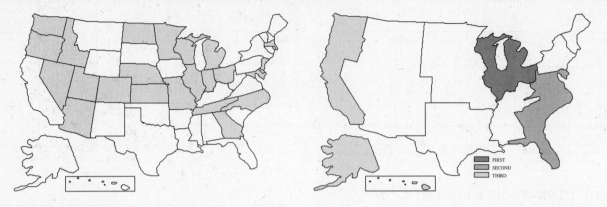

FIRST
SECOND
THIRD

INDUSTRY DATA BY STATE

State	Estab lish- ments	Employment			Compensation		Production				Capital Exp. ($ mil)
		Total	Workers	Total as % of US	Payroll per Employee	Wages per Worker	Costs ($ mil)	Value Added ($ mil)	Reve- nues ($ mil)	% of US	
California	6,776	64,396	48,875	8.16	38,828	37,435	3,074.4	4,450.0	8,277.1	9.36	118.1
Texas	5,516	56,618	43,479	7.18	29,045	26,382	2,482.1	2,995.4	6,048.9	6.84	83.6
New York	5,234	42,540	30,533	5.39	35,865	33,160	1,887.1	2,818.9	5,371.4	6.07	62.0
Illinois	3,756	36,423	27,791	4.62	41,048	39,978	1,612.3	2,681.7	4,715.2	5.33	70.6
Florida	4,803	44,510	33,003	5.64	27,189	24,503	1,743.2	2,181.7	4,312.2	4.88	77.1
Pennsylvania	3,546	33,498	25,353	4.25	34,850	32,770	1,485.2	2,151.9	4,068.1	4.60	54.9
Ohio	3,329	34,872	26,575	4.42	33,208	31,675	1,349.2	2,052.2	3,885.4	4.39	58.0
Michigan	3,187	27,022	20,554	3.43	36,220	34,289	1,168.7	1,820.9	3,376.5	3.82	54.2
North Carolina	3,057	31,326	24,450	3.97	27,928	24,873	1,184.3	1,598.4	3,020.8	3.42	55.4
New Jersey	3,320	21,391	15,758	2.71	38,380	36,707	995.7	1,481.6	2,825.8	3.20	37.1
Georgia	2,589	26,088	19,813	3.31	28,581	25,729	1,068.1	1,451.0	2,745.2	3.10	44.2
Maryland	2,037	23,109	17,207	2.93	32,979	30,137	996.3	1,311.4	2,739.3	3.10	32.3
Indiana	1,973	21,461	16,402	2.72	35,159	33,636	880.5	1,329.4	2,458.3	2.78	39.8
Massachusetts	2,172	15,548	11,677	1.97	37,316	34,677	788.9	1,072.6	2,215.7	2.51	26.8
Wisconsin	1,981	19,290	14,478	2.45	36,153	35,421	740.1	1,241.2	2,149.7	2.43	38.7
Virginia	2,391	24,055	18,959	3.05	27,958	25,067	864.0	1,138.7	2,145.7	2.43	38.6
Tennessee	1,612	18,810	14,504	2.38	30,249	26,221	815.8	984.4	1,987.4	2.25	36.1
Washington	1,746	16,774	12,145	2.13	35,452	34,373	693.6	1,114.9	1,942.6	2.20	31.1
Missouri	1,824	16,587	12,594	2.10	34,337	32,658	630.7	1,006.4	1,860.4	2.10	32.4
Minnesota	1,416	13,656	10,211	1.73	38,284	36,855	645.0	932.7	1,763.2	1.99	28.8
Colorado	1,654	16,541	12,884	2.10	30,167	27,963	681.1	872.7	1,717.0	1.94	31.0
Arizona	1,344	15,358	11,784	1.95	28,937	26,708	670.6	793.4	1,569.4	1.77	25.5
Oregon	1,079	10,884	8,332	1.38	40,419	39,901	498.3	719.4	1,366.5	1.55	13.5
Alabama	1,413	14,066	11,172	1.78	26,697	23,418	469.6	699.2	1,240.7	1.40	22.4
South Carolina	1,351	14,067	11,260	1.78	25,505	23,279	484.6	605.8	1,200.0	1.36	20.1
Kentucky	1,178	12,006	9,422	1.52	26,413	24,750	420.4	582.8	1,074.9	1.22	16.9
Louisiana	1,200	10,148	7,674	1.29	27,392	24,657	390.0	526.6	1,040.3	1.18	11.5
Connecticut	1,254	8,868	6,479	1.12	34,329	32,636	363.9	553.9	1,010.2	1.14	15.7
Kansas	1,065	9,054	6,886	1.15	30,495	28,971	413.2	495.3	997.5	1.13	12.9
Iowa	938	9,125	6,819	1.16	30,192	29,562	333.3	542.4	965.8	1.09	20.0
Utah	835	7,899	6,254	1.00	29,695	27,753	313.8	481.9	910.3	1.03	22.8
Nevada	515	7,491	6,175	0.95	34,132	31,567	355.9	462.7	888.7	1.01	10.4
Oklahoma	1,156	7,288	5,644	0.92	25,623	23,796	292.0	397.9	749.6	0.85	10.8
Arkansas	980	7,214	5,611	0.91	23,448	21,994	233.5	330.4	602.8	0.68	11.6
Nebraska	662	5,598	4,369	0.71	31,257	28,896	228.1	306.5	589.3	0.67	10.1
Mississippi	746	6,793	5,279	0.86	21,416	19,703	246.5	302.7	586.8	0.66	10.4
Idaho	546	4,961	3,863	0.63	27,179	25,795	203.0	268.8	543.8	0.62	12.2
Delaware	288	3,942	3,029	0.50	35,364	32,158	137.5	239.6	410.1	0.46	7.2
New Mexico	600	4,824	3,893	0.61	25,734	24,119	155.5	208.1	399.1	0.45	6.6
New Hampshire	462	3,097	2,304	0.39	30,966	29,808	140.3	179.2	362.5	0.41	9.6
West Virginia	496	3,488	2,809	0.44	24,051	23,510	138.7	155.7	310.2	0.35	8.2
Maine	552	2,930	2,181	0.37	26,871	25,137	109.3	145.7	277.4	0.31	4.0
Hawaii	243	1,976	1,337	0.25	39,913	40,185	84.4	154.9	270.4	0.31	2.4
Montana	412	2,350	1,799	0.30	29,077	28,463	110.9	122.7	253.8	0.29	3.8
Rhode Island	356	1,893	1,417	0.24	33,099	30,933	91.2	113.4	241.2	0.27	3.8
North Dakota	248	2,359	1,947	0.30	28,630	26,829	84.5	122.2	226.9	0.26	6.1
Alaska	187	1,333	961	0.17	41,632	40,648	62.1	108.1	197.3	0.22	2.3
South Dakota	311	1,760	1,327	0.22	28,372	25,777	71.7	89.2	176.5	0.20	3.1
Vermont	245	1,657	1,286	0.21	27,273	26,267	55.0	84.2	151.1	0.17	3.1
Wyoming	264	1,527	1,039	0.19	25,607	25,048	52.7	69.4	134.8	0.15	3.2
D.C.	31	461	342	0.06	35,967	33,132	19.8	26.8	53.5	0.06	0.6

Source: Economic Census of the U.S., 1997. Data are sorted by 1997 revenues or establishments. (D) means data suppression to prevent disclosure of company data. (S) means that data did not meet statistical standards for publication. A dash (-) is used when data are unavailable or cannot be calculated. Data followed by an * indicate the midpoint of a range. The ranges are: for 10, 0-19; for 60, 20-99, for 175, 100-249, for 375, 250-499, for 750, 500-999. Higher values are multiples of those shown, e.g., 3,750 is the midpoint of the range 2,500-4,999. Shaded *states* on the state map indicate those states which have proportionately greater representation in the industry than would be indicated by the state's population; the ratio is based on total revenues or number of establishments. Shaded *regions* indicate where the industry is regionally most concentrated.

NAICS 235210 - PAINTING AND WALL COVERING CONTRACTORS

GENERAL STATISTICS

Years	Estab-lish-ments	Employment		Payroll ($ mil)		Costs ($ mil)		Value Added ($ mil)	Revenues ($ mil)			Capital expend. ($ mil)
		Total	Constr. workers	Total	Worker payroll	Total	Cost of materials		All sources	Construction		
										Total	Net	
1997	37,480	195,331	160,740	4,543.5	3,430.5	3,313.8	3,095.9	8,787.4	13,067.3	13,015.7	12,049.6	306.4

Source: Economic Census of the United States, 1997. This is a newly defined industry. Data for prior years were unavailable at the time of publication but may become available over time. "Net" under "Construction" is construction revenue net of the costs of subcontracts.

DISTRIBUTION AMONG SIC-BASED INDUSTRIES - 1997

SIC	Industry	Estab-lish-ments	Employment		Cost of Power & Materials ($ mil)	Revenues ($ mil)			Value Added ($ mil)
			Total (000)	Payroll ($ mil)		All Sources	Construction		
							Total	Net	
172100	Painting & paper hanging contractors	36,339.0	191,073	4,472.3	3,247.4	12,793.2	12,742.0	11,810.0	8,613.78
179910	Special trade contractors, nec (pt)	1,141.0	4,258	71.2	66.4	274.1	273.6	239.6	173.65

Source: 1997 Economic Census. U.S. Census Bureau, U.S. Department of Commerce, August 1997. SIC codes ending in two zeroes represent complete 4-digit SICs. All others are parts of 4-digit SIC industries. Items showing a dash (-) indicate that data are not available because of disclosure problems.

SIC INDUSTRIES RELATED TO NAICS 235210

SIC	Industry	1990	1991	1992	1993	1994	1995	1996	1997
1721	**Painting and Paper Hanging**								
	Establishments (number)	29,393	29,715	31,920	33,542	32,780p	33,219p	33,664p	34,114p
	Employment (thousands)	164.9	146.4	162.6	155.8	159.7e	158.3e	156.9e	155.5e
	Revenues ($ million)	8,447.8e	8,592.5e	8,739.8	8,889.5e	9,041.9e	9,196.8e	9,354.4e	9,514.7e
1799	**Special Trade Contractors, n.e.c.***								
	Establishments (number)	22,471	22,634	25,270	27,296	26,150p	26,601p	27,060p	27,527p
	Employment (thousands)	197.0	186.3	204.3	207.1	216.9e	223.4e	230.2e	237.1e
	Revenues ($ million)	12,936.7e	13,535.6e	14,162.3	14,818.0e	15,504.1e	16,221.9e	16,973.0e	17,758.8e

Source: Economic Census of the United States, 1992, annual surveys of economic sectors conducted by the Bureau of the Census, and estimates or projections based on the 1982-1992 period; not all data are shown. 'e' marks estimates made by the editors; 'p' indicates projections based on time series. A dash (-) indicates that data for this SIC or year were not available. * Indicates that only a portion of this industry is present within the NAICS data. If no * is shown, the entire industry is contained within the NAICS data.

INDICES OF CHANGE

Years	Estab-lish-ments	Employment		Payroll ($ mil)		Costs ($ mil)		Value Added ($ mil)	Revenues ($ mil)			Capital expend. ($ mil)
		Total	Constr. workers	Total	Worker payroll	Total	Cost of materials		All sources	Construction		
										Total	Net	
1997	100.0	100.0	100.0	100.0	100.0	100.0	100.0	100.0	100.0	100.0	100.0	100.0

Sources: Same as General Statistics. The values shown reflect change from the base year, 1997. Values above 100 mean greater than 1997, values below 100 mean less than 1997, and a value of 100 in years other than 1997 means same as 1997. Indices are calculated only for Census years. Data are the most recent available at this level of detail.

SELECTED RATIOS

For 1997	Avg. of Sector	Analyzed Industry	Index	For 1997	Avg. of Sector	Analyzed Industry	Index
Employees per establishment	8.6	5.2	60	Value added per establishment	584,730	234,456	40
Construction workers per establishment	6.6	4.3	65	Value added per employee	67,759	44,987	66
Payroll per establishment	265,343	121,225	46	Value added per construction worker	88,592	54,668	62
Payroll per employee	30,748	23,261	76	Revenues per establishment	1,307,915	348,647	27
Payroll per construction worker	27,622	21,342	77	Revenues per employee	151,563	66,898	44
Costs per establishment	367,737	88,415	24	Revenues per construction worker	198,161	81,295	41
Costs per employee	42,614	16,965	40	CR as % of total revenues	98.48	99.61	101
Costs per construction worker	55,716	20,616	37	Net CR as % of CR	72.40	92.58	128
Materials as % of costs	95.75	93.42	98	Investment per establishment	22,948	8,175	36
Costs as % of revenues	28.12	25.36	90	Investment per employee	2,659	1,569	59
Costs as % of construction revenues	28.55	25.46	89	Investment per construction worker	3,477	1,906	55

Sources: Same as General Statistics. The 'Average of Sector' column represents the average for all industries in this sector. The Index shows the relationship between the Average and the Analyzed Industry. For example, 100 means that they are equal; 500 that the Analyzed Industry is five times the average; 50 means that the Analyzed Industry is half the national average. 'na' is used to show that data are 'not available'. CR stands for "construction revenues" and "Net CR" is construction revenues net of subcontract expenses.

LEADING COMPANIES   Number shown: **17**   Total sales ($ mil): **957**   Total employment (000): **7.9**

Company Name	Address				CEO Name	Phone	Co. Type	Sales ($ mil)	Empl. (000)
Williams Group International	2076 W Park Place	Stone Mountain	GA	30087	Virgil Williams	770-498-2020	R	260*	1.4
Brock Enterprises Inc.	P O Box 306	Beaumont	TX	77704	Jerry Brock	409-833-6226	R	203*	2.5
White Cap Industries Inc.	3120 Airway	Costa Mesa	CA	92626	Gregory E Grosch	714-850-0900	R	187	0.8
Cannon Sline Inc.	5600 Woodland Ave	Philadelphia	PA	19143	Roger Gossett	215-729-4600	S	50	0.7
Pangere Corp.	4050 W 4th Ave	Gary	IN	46406	Steve Pangere	219-949-1368	R	46*	0.3
Cannon Sline Inc.	6900 N Loop E	Houston	TX	77028	Ralph A Trallo	713-675-3141	D	40*	0.1
Long Painting Co.	PO Box 81435	Seattle	WA	98108	Mike Cassidy	206-763-8433	R	39	0.3
WesTower Corp.	7001 N E 40th Ave	Vancouver	WA	98661	Calvin J Payne	360-750-9355	P	23*	0.7
M.L. McDonald Sales Inc.	50 Oakland St	Watertown	MA	02472	Peter Patch	617-923-0900	R	23*	0.2
Swanson and Youngdale Inc.	6565 W 23rd St	Minneapolis	MN	55426	Robert E Swanson	612-545-2541	R	22*	0.2
M. Ecker and Company Inc.	5374 N Elston Ave	Chicago	IL	60630	Frank Vuvricki	773-685-5500	R	15*	0.3
W.G. Thompson Inc.	PO Box 4028	Richmond	CA	94804	Cary Gaidano	510-233-5883	R	14*	0.1
Hartman-Walsh Painting Co.	7144 N Market St	St. Louis	MO	63133	Edward C Smith	314-863-1800	R	12	0.2
Irvin H. Whitehouse and Sons Co.	4600 Jennings Ln	Louisville	KY	40218	Alfred Carpenter	502-966-4176	R	10	0.2
Craddock Finishing Corp.	PO Box 269	Evansville	IN	47702	Marc C Craddock	812-425-2691	R	8	0.1
HPC Inc.	2809 Mokumoa St	Honolulu	HI	96819	Grace H Wong	808-839-2777	R	3	<0.1
Honolulu Painting Company Ltd.	2809 Mokumoa St	Honolulu	HI	96819	Ronald Yanagi	808-839-2777	S	2*	<0.1

Source: *Ward's Business Directory of U.S. Private and Public Companies*, Volumes 1 and 2, 2000. The company type code used is as follows: P - Public, R - Private, S - Subsidiary, D - Division, J - Joint Venture, A - Affiliate, G - Group, N - Company type not reported. Sales are in millions of dollars, employees are in thousands. An asterisk (*) indicates an estimated sales volume. The symbol < stands for 'less than'. Company names and addresses are truncated, in some cases, to fit into the available space.

COST DETAILS

Item	Cost ($ mil)	% of total	Per $1,000 of Revenue	Item	Cost ($ mil)	% of total	Per $1,000 of Revenue
All costs	4,279.9	100.000	327.5	Total Rentals	241.7	5.648	18.5
Cost of supplies	3,095.9	72.337	236.9	Equipment	147.0	3.435	11.3
Subcontracts	966.1	22.573	73.9	Buildings	94.7	2.213	7.2
Power, fuel, lubricants	217.8	5.089	16.7	Services purchased	287.9	6.726	22.0
Electricity	44.7	1.044	3.4	Communications	119.3	2.787	9.1
Natural gas	9.7	0.227	0.7	Building repairs	19.7	0.461	1.5
Gasoline and diesel	156.6	3.660	12.0	Machinery repairs	148.9	3.478	11.4
Highway	130.6	3.051	10.0				
Offroad	26.0	0.609	2.0				
Other power	6.8	0.158	0.5				

Source: *Economic Census of the United States*, 1997. Revenues referred to are total industry revenues for the current NAICS industry.

CONSTRUCTION PRODUCT DETAILS

Construction type	Value of construction work ($ mil and %)							
	Total		New construction		Additions, alterations, reconstruction		Maintenance and repair	
	Value	%	Value	%	Value	%	Value	%
Total	**13,015.7**	**100.0**	**5,039.8**	**100.0**	**2,615.9**	**100.0**	**5,184.7**	**100.0**
Building construction, total	**11,062.2**	**85.0**	**4,558.7**	**90.5**	**2,330.5**	**89.1**	**4,173.1**	**80.5**
Single-family houses, detached	3,657.1	28.1	1,813.1	36.0	562.8	21.5	1,281.1	24.7
Single-family houses, attached	652.4	5.0	301.5	6.0	104.7	4.0	246.2	4.7
Apartment buildings, condos and cooperatives	1,202.6	9.2	330.3	6.6	207.7	7.9	664.6	12.8
Manufacturing and light industrial buildings	924.3	7.1	277.2	5.5	185.3	7.1	461.8	8.9
Manufacturing and light industrial warehouses	272.9	2.1	117.9	2.3	51.7	2.0	103.3	2.0
Hotels and motels	325.3	2.5	139.3	2.8	81.7	3.1	104.2	2.0
Office buildings	1,509.7	11.6	504.6	10.0	489.8	18.7	515.3	9.9
All other commercial buildings, nec	852.8	6.6	392.7	7.8	188.4	7.2	271.7	5.2
Commercial warehouses	221.2	1.7	109.9	2.2	45.5	1.7	65.8	1.3
Religious buildings	167.5	1.3	43.5	0.9	51.9	2.0	72.1	1.4
Educational buildings	446.9	3.4	176.1	3.5	136.7	5.2	134.1	2.6
Health care and institutional buildings	450.7	3.5	192.9	3.8	154.3	5.9	103.4	2.0
Other building construction	379.0	2.9	159.8	3.2	69.7	2.7	149.5	2.9
Nonbuilding construction, total	**1,778.2**	**13.7**	**481.1**	**9.5**	**285.5**	**10.9**	**1,011.6**	**19.5**
Highways, streets, and related work	562.8	4.3	213.9	4.2	139.8	5.3	209.2	4.0
Bridges, tunnels, and elevated highways	247.2	1.9	41.9	0.8	38.0	1.5	167.3	3.2
Blast furnaces, refineries, chemical complexes, etc	320.8	2.5	54.8	1.1	30.4	1.2	235.6	4.5
Sewage and water treatment plants	147.1	1.1	57.9	1.1	37.8	1.4	51.4	1.0
Water storage facilities	183.2	1.4	34.9	0.7	14.4	0.5	134.0	2.6
Ships	100.9	0.8	36.6	0.7	(S)	-	60.4	1.2
Other nonbuilding construction, nec	216.1	1.7	41.1	0.8	21.4	0.8	153.6	3.0
Construction work, nsk	**175.2**	**1.3**	**NA**	**-**	**NA**	**-**	**NA**	**-**

Source: *Economic Census of the United States*, 1997. Bold items are headers. (D) stands for data withheld to protect competitive information. (S) indicates instances where data do not meet publications standards.

LOCATION BY STATE AND REGIONAL CONCENTRATION

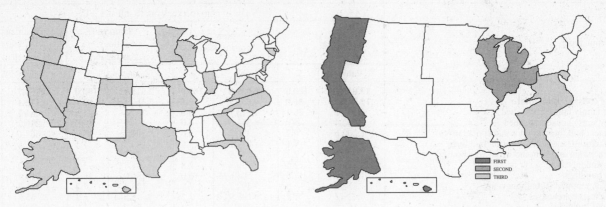

INDUSTRY DATA BY STATE

| State | Estab-lish-ments | Employment | | | Compensation | | Production | | | | Capital Exp. ($ mil) |
		Total	Workers	Total as % of US	Payroll per Employee	Wages per Worker	Costs ($ mil)	Value Added ($ mil)	Reve-nues ($ mil)	% of US	
California	4,402	25,146	21,153	12.87	24,003	22,249	433.6	1,213.3	1,724.9	13.20	39.5
Texas	1,871	14,567	12,195	7.46	22,316	19,736	284.8	596.3	959.3	7.34	22.4
Florida	2,283	11,697	9,090	5.99	20,015	17,467	203.3	503.4	832.8	6.37	15.1
New York	2,215	10,218	8,291	5.23	26,806	24,477	175.4	560.3	772.2	5.91	12.3
Illinois	1,597	8,007	6,394	4.10	30,228	29,206	138.2	410.1	576.6	4.41	12.4
Pennsylvania	1,415	7,533	6,241	3.86	25,768	24,370	126.5	387.8	550.3	4.21	13.7
Ohio	1,467	7,483	6,083	3.83	23,888	22,222	126.1	333.2	484.1	3.70	15.1
Michigan	1,320	6,256	5,188	3.20	24,772	22,336	103.0	343.4	473.2	3.62	10.8
New Jersey	1,278	4,785	3,885	2.45	27,275	24,560	99.6	284.0	420.2	3.22	5.3
Georgia	855	5,471	4,512	2.80	22,151	18,686	122.2	233.8	417.1	3.19	9.7
North Carolina	1,310	6,788	5,560	3.48	19,852	17,682	102.0	241.3	413.5	3.16	7.7
Virginia	1,349	7,309	6,107	3.74	20,078	18,312	113.0	260.2	407.3	3.12	10.5
Washington	1,182	5,443	4,555	2.79	24,889	23,057	91.4	269.2	381.8	2.92	8.0
Missouri	892	5,114	4,413	2.62	26,056	23,968	92.6	226.7	341.2	2.61	12.2
Indiana	900	4,877	4,141	2.50	24,871	22,848	73.1	206.4	293.0	2.24	8.5
Wisconsin	953	4,106	3,302	2.10	24,641	23,294	79.9	190.1	287.9	2.20	8.2
Minnesota	624	3,365	2,779	1.72	27,563	26,420	61.9	187.4	265.1	2.03	7.8
Massachusetts	870	3,517	2,720	1.80	27,235	25,551	61.8	182.8	260.5	1.99	4.5
Arizona	648	4,610	3,811	2.36	19,654	18,686	78.7	152.5	242.3	1.85	3.8
Colorado	915	4,166	3,605	2.13	20,870	18,588	60.2	164.3	239.3	1.83	4.3
Oregon	658	3,069	2,299	1.57	21,144	21,929	52.7	125.9	199.4	1.53	4.5
Louisiana	349	3,575	2,795	1.83	21,202	19,793	56.6	130.4	195.8	1.50	3.7
Connecticut	586	2,262	1,685	1.16	25,719	23,431	44.1	124.4	182.1	1.39	4.2
Alabama	460	2,966	2,399	1.52	21,298	18,594	39.7	111.8	158.6	1.21	6.6
Kentucky	438	2,102	1,703	1.08	19,978	18,867	36.7	73.7	118.2	0.90	(S)
Hawaii	166	1,262	986	0.65	37,872	33,916	19.8	87.4	112.8	0.86	2.2
Kansas	441	1,617	1,336	0.83	20,727	19,763	25.5	62.2	93.6	0.72	(S)
Oklahoma	339	1,572	1,334	0.80	17,443	16,144	23.7	53.6	91.9	0.70	2.1
Iowa	353	1,762	1,413	0.90	18,328	17,916	23.2	60.5	85.8	0.66	4.6
Nevada	186	1,294	1,148	0.66	23,280	21,999	21.5	54.7	78.0	0.60	1.7
Arkansas	204	1,073	867	0.55	21,084	20,099	10.7	52.6	70.6	0.54	2.4
Nebraska	272	1,231	1,074	0.63	19,359	18,588	21.0	41.3	65.3	0.50	2.2
Mississippi	219	1,001	801	0.51	18,382	17,080	(S)	41.8	63.7	0.49	1.6
Idaho	353	1,015	899	0.52	14,921	14,676	16.2	36.0	53.6	0.41	1.3
Rhode Island	263	774	565	0.40	18,258	19,044	8.5	33.8	44.4	0.34	0.8
Maine	186	799	715	0.41	16,543	16,175	12.8	28.8	43.4	0.33	(S)
Alaska	113	449	336	0.23	23,846	22,062	7.7	26.8	37.2	0.28	0.6
New Hampshire	185	718	638	0.37	19,039	17,332	9.0	25.4	36.2	0.28	0.9
New Mexico	225	625	540	0.32	18,510	15,235	10.7	23.0	34.8	0.27	0.8
Delaware	100	501	414	0.26	23,719	21,304	10.3	18.7	33.1	0.25	0.3
Montana	125	399	312	0.20	18,880	16,654	8.6	21.1	31.1	0.24	1.0
North Dakota	95	402	310	0.21	19,244	18,387	10.6	16.1	29.9	0.23	1.6
Vermont	149	597	522	0.31	15,399	13,929	5.9	18.7	25.7	0.20	(S)
South Dakota	115	441	401	0.23	16,005	15,105	(S)	15.4	24.0	0.18	0.4
Wyoming	114	313	275	0.16	16,693	14,709	6.1	13.9	23.8	0.18	0.4
D.C.	16	225	186	0.12	24,493	22,973	2.2	9.1	13.3	0.10	(S)
Maryland	875	5,052	4,109	2.59	23,708	21,518	(D)	239.9	(D)	-	7.4
South Carolina	603	2,878	2,420	1.47	17,800	15,571	(D)	99.6	(D)	-	2.8
Tennessee	513	2,813	2,422	1.44	22,278	18,646	(D)	114.7	(D)	-	5.0
Utah	339	1,673	1,509	0.86	18,679	18,089	(D)	64.4	(D)	-	6.0
West Virginia	92	413	303	0.21	21,625	23,703	(D)	15.5	(D)	-	0.5

Source: Economic Census of the U.S., 1997. Data are sorted by 1997 revenues or establishments. (D) means data suppression to prevent disclosure of company data. (S) means that data did not meet statistical standards for publication. A dash (-) is used when data are unavailable or cannot be calculated. Data followed by an * indicate the midpoint of a range. The ranges are: for 10, 0-19; for 60, 20-99; for 175, 100-249, for 375, 250-499, for 750, 500-999. Higher values are multiples of those shown, e.g., 3,750 is the midpoint of the range 2,500-4,999. Shaded *states* on the state map indicate those states which have proportionately greater representation in the industry than would be indicated by the state's population; the ratio is based on total revenues or number of establishments. Shaded *regions* indicate where the industry is regionally most concentrated.

NAICS 235310 - ELECTRICAL CONTRACTORS*

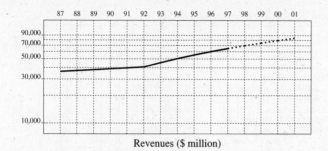

Revenues ($ million)

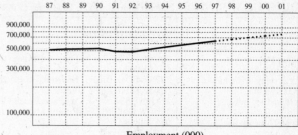

Employment (000)

GENERAL STATISTICS

Years	Estab-lish-ments	Employment		Payroll ($ mil)		Costs ($ mil)		Value Added ($ mil)	Revenues ($ mil)			Capital expend. ($ mil)
		Total	Constr. workers	Total	Worker payroll	Total	Cost of materials		All sources	Construction Total	Net	
1977	36,764	356,591	296,946	5,482.5	4,496.7	5,733.4	5,240.0	8,748.5	14,481.8	14,221.3	13,919.1	-
1982	39,563	434,764	351,894	9,106.6	7,346.5	11,318.5	10,234.6	15,122.6	26,441.1	25,948.5	25,252.4	-
1987	49,436	509,309	405,982	12,663.5	9,622.0	14,458.7	12,788.5	21,816.6	36,275.3	35,838.2	34,657.8	495.6
1988	49,144	518,989	400,447	13,931.4	9,704.0	14,965.8	13,184.1	22,152.4	37,124.9	36,681.8	35,401.8	-
1989	52,127	522,019	394,988	14,165.2	9,786.6	15,490.8	13,592.0	22,493.4	37,994.4	37,545.2	36,161.8	-
1990	52,201	528,603	389,603	14,628.9	9,870.0	16,034.2	14,012.4	22,839.7	38,884.3	38,429.0	36,938.1	-
1991	52,928	490,747	384,291	13,919.6	9,954.1	16,596.6	14,445.9	23,191.3	39,795.0	39,333.6	37,731.0	-
1992	54,022	487,072	379,052	13,623.8	10,038.9	17,178.7	14,892.8	23,548.3	40,727.0	40,259.4	38,541.0	508.2
1993	55,500	518,055	405,426	15,235.0	11,283.4	18,382.0	16,416.6	26,554.7	45,564.6	45,059.6	43,057.0	-
1994	56,979	549,037	431,800	16,846.3	12,527.8	19,585.4	17,940.4	29,561.2	50,402.2	49,859.8	47,573.0	-
1995	58,457	580,020	458,173	18,457.5	13,772.3	20,788.7	19,464.2	32,567.6	55,239.9	54,659.9	52,089.1	-
1996	59,936	611,002	484,547	20,068.8	15,016.7	21,992.1	20,988.0	35,574.1	60,077.5	59,460.1	56,605.1	-
1997	61,414	641,985	510,921	21,680.0	16,261.2	23,195.4	22,511.8	38,580.5	64,915.1	64,260.3	61,121.1	1,015.9
1998	62,892p	672,968p	537,295p	23,291.2p	17,505.7p	24,398.7p	24,035.6p	41,586.9p	69,752.7p	69,060.5p	65,637.1p	-
1999	64,371p	703,950p	563,669p	24,902.5p	18,750.1p	25,602.1p	25,559.4p	44,593.4p	74,590.3p	73,860.7p	70,153.1p	-
2000	65,849p	734,933p	590,042p	26,513.7p	19,994.6p	26,805.4p	27,083.2p	47,599.8p	79,428.0p	78,660.8p	74,669.2p	-
2001	67,328p	765,915p	616,416p	28,125.0p	21,239.0p	28,008.8p	28,607.0p	50,606.3p	84,265.6p	83,461.0p	79,185.2p	-

*Sources: Economic Census of the United States, 1977, 1982, 1987, 1992, and 1997. Data for those years (years are in **bold** type) are from the 5-year censuses of the economy. Other values, unless otherwise noted, are extrapolations. Values footnoted 1 are from the* County Business Patterns *for the years indicated. Values marked with p are projections. Data are the most recent available at this level of detail. "Net" under "Construction" is construction revenues net of the costs of subcontracts.*

INDICES OF CHANGE

Years	Estab-lish-ments	Employment		Payroll ($ mil)		Costs ($ mil)		Value Added ($ mil)	Revenues ($ mil)			Capital expend. ($ mil)
		Total	Constr. workers	Total	Worker payroll	Total	Cost of materials		All sources	Construction Total	Net	
1977	59.9	55.5	58.1	25.3	27.7	24.7	23.3	22.7	22.3	22.1	22.8	-
1982	64.4	67.7	68.9	42.0	45.2	48.8	45.5	39.2	40.7	40.4	41.3	-
1987	80.5	79.3	79.5	58.4	59.2	62.3	56.8	56.5	55.9	55.8	56.7	48.8
1992	88.0	75.9	74.2	62.8	61.7	74.1	66.2	61.0	62.7	62.7	63.1	50.0
1997	100.0	100.0	100.0	100.0	100.0	100.0	100.0	100.0	100.0	100.0	100.0	100.0

Sources: Same as General Statistics. The values shown reflect change from the base year, 1997. Values above 100 mean greater than 1997, values below 100 mean less than 1997, and a value of 100 in years other than 1997 means same as 1997. Indices are calculated only for Census years. Data are the most recent available at this level of detail.

SELECTED RATIOS

For 1997	Avg. of Sector	Analyzed Industry	Index	For 1997	Avg. of Sector	Analyzed Industry	Index
Employees per establishment	8.6	10.5	121	Value added per establishment	584,730	628,204	107
Construction workers per establishment	6.6	8.3	126	Value added per employee	67,759	60,096	89
Payroll per establishment	265,343	353,014	133	Value added per construction worker	88,592	75,512	85
Payroll per employee	30,748	33,770	110	Revenues per establishment	1,307,915	1,057,008	81
Payroll per construction worker	27,622	31,827	115	Revenues per employee	151,563	101,116	67
Costs per establishment	367,737	377,689	103	Revenues per construction worker	198,161	127,055	64
Costs per employee	42,614	36,131	85	CR as % of total revenues	98.48	98.99	101
Costs per construction worker	55,716	45,399	81	Net CR as % of CR	72.40	95.11	131
Materials as % of costs	95.75	97.05	101	Investment per establishment	22,948	16,542	72
Costs as % of revenues	28.12	35.73	127	Investment per employee	2,659	1,582	60
Costs as % of construction revenues	28.55	36.10	126	Investment per construction worker	3,477	1,988	57

Sources: Same as General Statistics. The 'Average of Sector' column represents the average for all industries in this sector. The Index shows the relationship between the Average and the Analyzed Industry. For example, 100 means that they are equal; 500 that the Analyzed Industry is five times the average; 50 means that the Analyzed Industry is half the national average. 'na' is used to show that data are 'not available'. CR stands for "construction revenues" and "Net CR" is construction revenues net of subcontract expenses.

*Equivalent to SIC 1731.

LEADING COMPANIES   Number shown: **75**   Total sales ($ mil): **32,215**   Total employment (000): **143.6**

Company Name	Address				CEO Name	Phone	Co. Type	Sales ($ mil)	Empl. (000)
AutoNation Inc.	110 SE 6th St	Fort Lauderdale	FL	33301	John Costello	954-769-6000	P	20,112	42.0
EMCOR Group Inc.	101 Merritt	Norwalk	CT	06851	Jeffrey Levy	203-849-7848	P	2,210	15.0
Comfort Systems USA Inc.	777 Post Oak Blvd	Houston	TX	77056	Fred M Ferreira	713-830-9600	P	854	8.9
MATCO Group Inc.	320 N Jensen Rd	Vestal	NY	13850	Jim Matthews	607-729-8973	R	500*	5.6
Dycom Industries Inc.	PO Box 3524	W. Palm Beach	FL	33402	Steven E Nielsen	561-627-7171	P	470	5.8
MYR Group Inc.	1701 W Golf Rd	Rolling Mdws	IL	60008	C M Brennan III	847-290-1891	P	459	3.7
Henkels and McCoy Inc.	985 Jolly Rd	Blue Bell	PA	19422	Kenneth L Rose	215-283-7600	R	450*	5.0
Tetra Tech Inc.	670 N Rosemead	Pasadena	CA	91107	Li-San Hwang	626-351-4664	P	432	5.4
Arguss Communications Group	P O Box 459	Epsom	NH	03234		603-736-4766	S	412*	1.6
Dynalectric Co.	1420 Spring Hill Rd	McLean	VA	22102	Jeffrey M Levy	703-556-8000	S	325*	2.0
Newtron Group Inc.	8183 W El Cajon Dr	Baton Rouge	LA	70815	NB Thomas	225-927-8921	R	275*	1.8
Mass. Electric Construction Co.	180 Guest St	Boston	MA	02135	Francis C Angino	617-254-1015	S	275*	1.4
Volt Telecommunications Group	6801 Lakeworth Rd	Lake Worth	FL	33461		561-357-9779	S	273*	1.8
Rudolph/Libbe Companies Inc.	6494 Latcha Rd	Walbridge	OH	43465	Frederick Rudolph	419-241-5000	R	220	0.8
Able Telcom Holding Corp.	1601 Forum Pl	W. Palm Beach	FL	33401	Frazier Gaines	561-688-0400	P	217	2.2
Tri-City Electrical Contractors Inc.	430 West Dr	Altamonte Sprgs	FL	32714	HL Eidel	407-788-3500	R	214*	1.4
TIE Systems Inc.	10975 Grandview Dr	Overland Park	KS	66210	Charlie McNane	913-344-0400	S	210	0.6
Concorp Inc.	P O Box 429	Nitro	WV	25143	RS McDavid	304-755-8178	R	160*	8.8
L.K. Comstock and Company Inc.	1 N Lexington Ave	White Plains	NY	10601	Michael Azarela	914-323-3000	R	160*	1.0
Midstates Development Inc.	P O Box 338	Fergus Falls	MN	56538	Lauras N Molbert	218-736-4712	S	160*	0.8
Helix Electric Inc.	8260 Cam S Fe	San Diego	CA	92121	Michael Stone	858-535-0505	R	151*	1.0
Arguss Holdings Inc.	1 Church St	Rockville	MD	20850	Ranier Busselmann	301-315-0027	P	145	1.3
Williard Inc.	PO Box 9002	Jenkintown	PA	19046	Joseph Doody	215-885-5000	S	130*	0.8
SecurityLink	111 Windsor Dr	Oak Brook	IL	60523		630-572-1200	R	129*	0.8
Synergism Inc.	722 E Evelyn Ave	Sunnyvale	CA	94086	Eugene A Ravizza	408-739-5000	R	120*	0.6
BGE Home Products and Services	7161 Columbia Gate	Columbia	MD	21045	William H Munn	410-720-6619	S	118*	0.7
Sachs Electric Co.	16300 Justus Post	Chesterfield	MO	63017	LN Plunkett	636-532-2000	R	109*	0.7
Electro Management Inc.	111 S W Jackson	Des Moines	IA	50315	Britt Baker	515-288-6774	R	100*	0.1
Cochran Inc.	PO Box 33524	Seattle	WA	98133	Robert Cochran	206-367-1900	R	97	0.7
Morrow-Meadows Corp.	610 Reyes Dr	Walnut	CA	91789	Jesse R Meadows	909-598-7700	R	96*	0.6
Watson Electrical Construction	P O Box 3105	Wilson	NC	27895	WE Boyette	252-237-7511	S	94*	1.2
DualStar Technologies Corp.	11-30 47th Ave	Long Island City	NY	11101	Gregory Cuneo	718-340-6655	P	93	0.4
PhoneTel Technologies Inc.	1001 Lakeside	Cleveland	OH	44114	John D Chichester	216-241-2555	P	91	0.4
MCC Group L.L.C.	P O Box 7460	Metairie	LA	70010	Joseph A Jaeger Jr	504-833-8291	R	90*	0.6
Electric Machinery Enterprises	2515 E Hanna Ave	Tampa	FL	33610	Jaime Jurado	813-238-5010	R	80	0.5
Bryant Electric Company Inc.	215 Balfour Dr	Archdale	NC	27263	John Wall	336-861-1800	R	76*	0.5
Miller Electric Co.	P O Box 1799	Jacksonville	FL	32201	Henry Autrey	904-388-8000	R	76*	0.5
Truland Systems Corp.	3330 Washington	Arlington	VA	22201	Robert Truland	703-516-2600	R	76*	0.5
Sargent Electric Co.	PO Box 30	Pittsburgh	PA	15230	Frederic B Sargent	412-391-0588	R	75	0.6
Hood Corp.	P O Box 4368	Whittier	CA	90607	Bruce Svatos	562-698-8402	R	71*	0.5
Kirkwood Dynalectric Co.	P O Box 3012	Los Alamitos	CA	90720	Chris Pesavento	714-828-7000	S	70*	0.3
North Pittsburgh Systems Inc.	4008 Gibsonia Rd	Gibsonia	PA	15044	Harry R Brown	724-443-9600	P	67	0.3
Cleveland Consolidated	1281 Fulton Ind NW	Atlanta	GA	30351	James R Cleveland Jr	404-696-4550	S	66*	0.5
Guarantee Electrical Co.	3405 Bent Ave	St. Louis	MO	63116	Charles W Oertli	314-772-5400	R	65*	0.6
Rex Moore Electrical Contractors	P O Box 980010	W. Sacramento	CA	95691	Steven R Moore	916-372-1300	R	65*	0.6
Hooper Construction Corp.	PO Box 7455	Madison	WI	53707	Don Gardner	608-249-0451	R	63*	0.5
Baker Support Services Inc.	4801 Spring Valley	Dallas	TX	75244	Daniel W McDonald	972-991-0800	S	62	1.9
Southern Air Inc.	2655 Lakeside Dr	Lynchburg	VA	24502	Ronald Kidd Jr	804-385-6200	R	62*	0.6
Meade Electric Company Inc.	9550 W 55th St	La Grange	IL	60525	A Hirsth	630-850-3500	R	61*	0.4
RTK Corp.	120 Floral Ave	New Providence	NJ	07974	Roy D Tartaglia	908-665-0133	S	60*	0.6
Chapman Corp.	331 S Main St	Washington	PA	15301	Arthur Hathaway	724-228-1900	R	60	0.5
O'Connell Electric Company Inc.	830 Phillips Rd	Victor	NY	14564	WT Parkes	716-924-2176	R	58	0.5
John E. Green Co.	220 Victor Ave	Highland Park	MI	48203	Peter J Green	313-868-2400	R	56*	0.4
SECO Industries Inc.	3838 N Causeway	Metairie	LA	70002	Brian Landry	504-834-8100	S	55	0.8
Joseph Davis Inc.	120 W Tupper St	Buffalo	NY	14201	Jeffrey Davis	716-842-1500	R	55	0.3
Ermco Inc.	1631 W Thompson	Indianapolis	IN	46217	Darrell Gossett	317-780-2923	R	53	0.5
Koontz-Wagner Electric Inc.	3801 Voorde Dr	South Bend	IN	46628	Richard Pfeil	219-232-2051	R	52	0.5
Miller-Eads Company Inc.	4125 N Keystone	Indianapolis	IN	46205	Tom Chastain	317-545-7101	R	51*	0.2
Electrical Construction Co.	P O Box 10286	Portland	OR	97296	WK Deshler	503-224-3511	R	50	0.4
Zwicker Electric Company Inc.	200 Park Ave S	New York	NY	10003	DP Pinter	212-477-8400	R	50	0.3
Commercial Light Co.	245 Fencl Ln	Hillside	IL	60162	TC Halperin	708-449-6900	R	46*	0.3
Delta Diversified Enterprises Inc.	425 W Gemini Dr	Tempe	AZ	85283	LR Donaldson	602-831-0532	R	46*	0.3
Long Electric Company Inc.	1310 S Franklin Rd	Indianapolis	IN	46239	Yvonne Shaheen	317-356-2455	R	46*	0.3
Pritchard Electric Company Inc.	P O Box 2503	Huntington	WV	25703		304-529-2566	R	46*	0.3
Starr Electric Company Inc.	6 Battleground Ct	Greensboro	NC	27408	John D Starr	336-275-0241	R	46*	0.3
Henderson Electric Company Inc.	4502 Poplar Level	Louisville	KY	40213	Rodney Henderson	502-452-6327	P	44	0.4
H and H Group Inc.	P O Box 44267	Madison	WI	53744	Frank J Hoffman	608-273-3434	R	42	0.4
Vista Network Integration	2195 Foxmail	Herndon	VA	20171	Bruce Jacobs	703-561-4000	S	41*	0.3
RFI Communications & Security	360 Turtle Creek Ct	San Jose	CA	95125	Larry Reece	408-298-5400	R	41*	0.3
Cannon and Wendt Electric Inc.	4020 N 16th St	Phoenix	AZ	85016	Albert G Wendt	602-279-1681	R	39*	0.3
Staff Electric Company Inc.	PO Box 917	Butler	WI	53007	Mike Lochmann	414-781-8230	R	39*	0.3
Total Engineering Services Team	PO Box 10	Harvey	LA	70059	David Volz	504-371-3000	R	38*	0.3
Commonwealth Electric	P O Box 80638	Lincoln	NE	68501	Thomas M Price	402-474-1341	R	38*	0.3
Harry F. Ortlip Co.	780 Lancaster Ave	Bryn Mawr	PA	19010	Alfred B Pentony	610-527-7000	R	38*	0.3
Intermountain Electric Inc.	602 S Lipan St	Denver	CO	80223	Elliot Robbins	303-733-7248	R	38*	0.3

Source: Ward's Business Directory of U.S. Private and Public Companies, Volumes 1 and 2, 2000. The company type code used is as follows: P - Public, R - Private, S - Subsidiary, D - Division, J - Joint Venture, A - Affiliate, G - Group, N - Company type not reported. Sales are in millions of dollars, employees are in thousands. An asterisk (*) indicates an estimated sales volume. The symbol < stands for 'less than'. Company names and addresses are truncated, in some cases, to fit into the available space.

COST DETAILS

Item	Cost ($ mil)	% of total	Per $1,000 of Revenue	Item	Cost ($ mil)	% of total	Per $1,000 of Revenue
All costs	26,334.5	100.000	405.7	Total Rentals	818.6	3.109	12.6
Cost of supplies	22,511.9	85.484	346.8	Equipment	424.7	1.613	6.5
Subcontracts	3,139.2	11.920	48.4	Buildings	393.9	1.496	6.1
Power, fuel, lubricants	683.5	2.595	10.5	Services purchased	929.9	3.531	14.3
Electricity	114.1	0.433	1.8	Communications	441.3	1.676	6.8
Natural gas	22.3	0.085	0.3	Building repairs	82.7	0.314	1.3
Gasoline and diesel	524.5	1.992	8.1	Machinery repairs	405.9	1.541	6.3
Highway	459.9	1.746	7.1				
Offroad	64.6	0.245	1.0				
Other power	22.6	0.086	0.3				

Source: *Economic Census of the United States*, 1997. Revenues referred to are total industry revenues for the current NAICS industry.

CONSTRUCTION PRODUCT DETAILS

Construction type	Value of construction work ($ mil and %)							
	Total		New construction		Additions, alterations, reconstruction		Maintenance and repair	
	Value	%	Value	%	Value	%	Value	%
Total	**64,260.3**	**100.0**	**33,538.4**	**100.0**	**19,830.7**	**100.0**	**10,447.5**	**100.0**
Building construction, total	**54,044.5**	**84.1**	**28,002.1**	**83.5**	**17,241.7**	**86.9**	**8,800.6**	**84.2**
Single-family houses, detached	6,645.6	10.3	4,246.2	12.7	1,253.9	6.3	1,145.4	11.0
Single-family houses, attached	1,034.3	1.6	628.8	1.9	198.5	1.0	207.0	2.0
Apartment buildings, condos and cooperatives	1,897.4	3.0	1,127.1	3.4	431.4	2.2	338.8	3.2
All other residential buildings	136.5	0.2	80.3	0.2	25.9	0.1	30.2	0.3
Manufacturing and light industrial buildings	9,787.6	15.2	4,232.3	12.6	3,579.5	18.1	1,975.8	18.9
Manufacturing and light industrial warehouses	2,280.0	3.5	1,134.6	3.4	735.1	3.7	410.2	3.9
Hotels and motels	1,353.8	2.1	927.2	2.8	275.8	1.4	150.9	1.4
Office buildings	10,899.4	17.0	4,805.9	14.3	4,271.6	21.5	1,821.8	17.4
All other commercial buildings, nec	7,109.3	11.1	3,840.3	11.5	2,106.4	10.6	1,162.6	11.1
Commercial warehouses	1,625.4	2.5	937.6	2.8	420.1	2.1	267.7	2.6
Religious buildings	739.4	1.2	363.7	1.1	245.6	1.2	130.1	1.2
Educational buildings	4,470.4	7.0	2,333.7	7.0	1,715.4	8.7	421.3	4.0
Health care and institutional buildings	3,697.5	5.8	1,786.2	5.3	1,427.3	7.2	483.9	4.6
Public safety buildings	967.6	1.5	647.6	1.9	230.0	1.2	89.9	0.9
Farm buildings, nonresidential	243.3	0.4	118.2	0.4	60.0	0.3	65.2	0.6
Amusement, social, and recreational buildings	680.5	1.1	468.5	1.4	152.2	0.8	59.8	0.6
Other building construction	476.6	0.7	323.9	1.0	112.8	0.6	39.8	0.4
Nonbuilding construction, total	**9,772.1**	**15.2**	**5,536.2**	**16.5**	**2,588.9**	**13.1**	**1,646.9**	**15.8**
Highways, streets, and related work	1,745.8	2.7	1,165.4	3.5	374.3	1.9	206.1	2.0
Power and communication lines, cables, towers, etc.	4,504.2	7.0	2,645.0	7.9	1,100.1	5.5	759.1	7.3
Power and cogeneration plants, except hydroelectric	361.7	0.6	165.3	0.5	137.6	0.7	58.8	0.6
Power plants, hydroelectric	74.2	0.1	45.1	0.1	15.6	0.1	13.6	0.1
Blast furnaces, refineries, chemical complexes, etc	716.1	1.1	242.0	0.7	221.9	1.1	252.2	2.4
Sewage treatment plants	509.7	0.8	263.3	0.8	179.7	0.9	66.6	0.6
Water treatment plants	397.3	0.6	183.8	0.5	163.9	0.8	49.6	0.5
Mass transit construction	454.3	0.7	249.2	0.7	177.7	0.9	27.4	0.3
Railroad construction	78.1	0.1	56.5	0.2	16.1	0.1	5.4	0.1
Other nonbuilding construction, nec	1,008.8	1.6	577.3	1.7	218.0	1.1	213.5	2.0
Construction work, nsk	**443.7**	**0.7**	NA	-	NA	-	NA	-

Source: *Economic Census of the United States*, 1997. Bold items are headers. (D) stands for data withheld to protect competitive information. (S) indicates instances where data do not meet publications standards.

LOCATION BY STATE AND REGIONAL CONCENTRATION

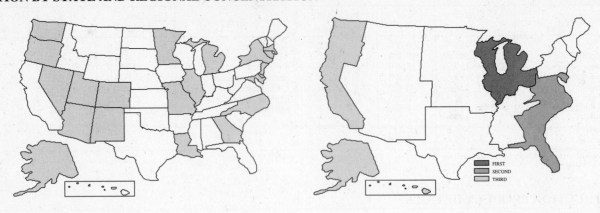

FIRST
SECOND
THIRD

INDUSTRY DATA BY STATE

State	Estab lish- ments	Employment			Compensation		Production				Capital Exp. ($ mil)
		Total	Workers	Total as % of US	Payroll per Employee	Wages per Worker	Costs ($ mil)	Value Added ($ mil)	Reve- nues ($ mil)	% of US	
California	6,011	61,932	47,837	9.65	38,265	36,306	2,623.1	4,297.0	7,392.2	11.39	100.8
New York	3,869	41,413	33,069	6.45	39,038	37,503	1,645.2	2,977.6	4,848.6	7.47	52.7
Texas	3,547	47,054	37,416	7.33	29,413	26,376	1,526.3	2,409.2	4,092.7	6.30	67.7
Florida	3,775	40,728	32,285	6.34	26,329	24,125	1,300.6	1,858.2	3,401.3	5.24	53.4
Illinois	2,561	26,818	21,240	4.18	44,394	42,224	1,072.0	1,973.3	3,265.0	5.03	42.6
Michigan	2,157	24,523	20,121	3.82	38,364	36,877	874.9	1,864.9	2,838.3	4.37	48.2
Pennsylvania	2,523	24,337	19,159	3.79	35,611	34,157	935.6	1,629.4	2,631.4	4.05	40.9
Ohio	2,123	24,576	19,113	3.83	35,040	33,206	882.4	1,485.0	2,475.7	3.81	41.1
New Jersey	2,661	18,540	14,341	2.89	39,829	38,504	836.7	1,215.1	2,170.6	3.34	28.8
Georgia	1,879	22,416	17,951	3.49	29,633	26,979	821.3	1,071.8	2,012.9	3.10	31.8
North Carolina	2,295	23,631	19,806	3.68	27,073	24,789	610.0	1,298.4	2,002.1	3.08	37.3
Massachusetts	1,779	14,693	11,663	2.29	37,923	36,075	610.6	1,018.2	1,751.6	2.70	22.1
Virginia	1,578	19,218	15,166	2.99	29,496	26,422	598.2	946.1	1,625.7	2.50	23.3
Washington	1,317	14,355	11,381	2.24	36,045	34,182	580.2	906.5	1,578.9	2.43	21.6
Colorado	1,355	15,097	12,138	2.35	33,676	33,217	538.0	897.7	1,524.4	2.35	25.2
Maryland	1,334	14,449	11,413	2.25	34,146	31,810	546.2	835.4	1,405.4	2.16	22.5
Missouri	990	12,425	10,043	1.94	36,905	34,125	465.5	882.0	1,403.1	2.16	23.4
Indiana	1,178	13,683	10,745	2.13	35,764	34,648	504.3	837.3	1,392.5	2.15	22.4
Minnesota	1,299	11,918	9,415	1.86	36,922	36,331	464.4	772.7	1,282.0	1.97	24.3
Louisiana	966	15,048	12,309	2.34	28,523	27,721	407.3	803.4	1,260.9	1.94	13.8
Wisconsin	1,235	12,394	9,433	1.93	36,245	35,429	436.3	782.6	1,250.2	1.93	19.5
Tennessee	885	14,082	11,713	2.19	29,391	26,179	457.6	655.8	1,204.8	1.86	20.2
Oregon	774	8,888	6,936	1.38	39,440	38,557	350.7	639.7	1,042.2	1.61	20.1
Arizona	1,051	11,633	9,132	1.81	29,389	27,595	385.2	572.4	998.1	1.54	19.4
Connecticut	1,102	7,264	5,646	1.13	37,962	35,117	311.2	467.6	862.3	1.33	14.1
Kentucky	797	9,092	7,420	1.42	29,292	27,450	286.2	468.3	781.0	1.20	19.8
South Carolina	907	10,838	8,941	1.69	24,374	22,952	262.7	450.2	751.7	1.16	13.2
Nevada	398	6,614	5,398	1.03	34,743	32,406	246.8	422.1	685.5	1.06	7.0
Alabama	897	8,531	6,922	1.33	25,956	24,022	261.9	364.4	643.2	0.99	10.0
Utah	543	6,066	5,157	0.94	32,888	31,912	238.1	341.2	603.8	0.93	10.5
Iowa	651	5,927	4,770	0.92	32,815	32,348	240.2	329.7	589.4	0.91	15.1
Oklahoma	833	5,689	4,033	0.89	28,527	25,978	205.6	352.7	584.9	0.90	8.9
Kansas	543	5,012	4,004	0.78	36,097	34,422	210.8	319.7	544.1	0.84	11.4
Nebraska	489	4,499	3,582	0.70	29,644	27,207	147.0	250.3	407.0	0.63	8.5
New Mexico	501	4,488	3,690	0.70	30,541	28,956	133.7	246.8	406.2	0.63	10.6
Arkansas	450	3,485	2,921	0.54	29,931	27,518	115.2	191.4	313.0	0.48	7.6
Mississippi	452	3,941	3,310	0.61	23,851	22,311	85.9	199.6	289.7	0.45	8.0
Hawaii	269	2,172	1,663	0.34	40,490	40,031	101.8	169.1	283.7	0.44	3.5
Idaho	405	2,992	2,412	0.47	31,224	31,219	99.2	152.8	260.4	0.40	4.1
Alaska	222	2,130	1,750	0.33	42,892	41,889	78.0	172.2	256.8	0.40	5.9
Delaware	235	2,602	2,101	0.41	32,978	31,543	80.6	153.7	240.4	0.37	3.0
Rhode Island	304	2,132	1,551	0.33	33,826	30,303	90.5	137.7	238.0	0.37	4.1
New Hampshire	407	2,465	1,980	0.38	28,888	26,313	97.0	123.7	227.3	0.35	3.3
Maine	391	2,203	1,815	0.34	31,055	29,719	106.4	110.4	223.1	0.34	3.8
West Virginia	292	2,611	2,122	0.41	31,610	31,930	66.3	122.4	192.7	0.30	2.7
Montana	271	1,776	1,529	0.28	27,417	27,377	61.4	93.5	157.2	0.24	3.8
North Dakota	222	1,257	1,011	0.20	31,508	30,598	54.2	85.8	143.8	0.22	3.6
South Dakota	224	1,579	1,226	0.25	24,099	23,366	58.1	75.3	137.9	0.21	4.2
Wyoming	195	1,242	965	0.19	27,676	26,672	41.9	67.3	113.8	0.18	3.2
Vermont	231	1,162	908	0.18	26,031	23,887	33.3	61.1	96.0	0.15	1.9
D.C.	40	367	270	0.06	33,997	30,689	8.7	22.0	31.3	0.05	0.8

Source: Economic Census of the U.S., 1997. Data are sorted by 1997 revenues or establishments. (D) means data suppression to prevent disclosure of company data. (S) means that data did not meet statistical standards for publication. A dash (-) is used when data are unavailable or cannot be calculated. Data followed by an * indicate the midpoint of a range. The ranges are: for 10, 0-19; for 60, 20-99, for 175, 100-249, for 375, 250-499, for 750, 500-999. Higher values are multiples of those shown, e.g., 3,750 is the midpoint of the range 2,500-4,999. Shaded *states* on the state map indicate those states which have proportionately greater representation in the industry than would be indicated by the state's population; the ratio is based on total revenues or number of establishments. Shaded *regions* indicate where the industry is regionally most concentrated.

NAICS 235410 - MASONRY AND STONE CONTRACTORS*

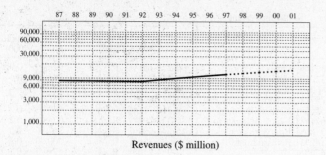

Revenues ($ million)

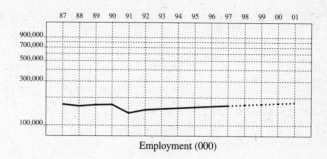

Employment (000)

GENERAL STATISTICS

| Years | Estab-lish-ments | Employment | | Payroll ($ mil) | | Costs ($ mil) | | Value Added ($ mil) | Revenues ($ mil) | | | Capital expend. ($ mil) |
		Total	Constr. workers	Total	Worker payroll	Total	Cost of materials		All sources	Construction Total	Net	
1977	24,815	152,167	142,797	1,493.2	1,350.3	1,388.4	1,219.6	2,416.7	3,805.1	3,775.4	3,677.6	-
1982	20,188	120,600	109,576	1,550.8	1,344.2	1,665.4	1,353.2	2,667.2	4,332.6	4,269.4	4,046.4	-
1987	23,284	168,978	150,308	2,947.0	2,461.6	3,302.8	2,715.4	5,475.8	8,778.6	8,714.2	8,269.2	157.1
1988	21,590	161,459	145,954	3,116.3	2,442.3	3,312.8	2,711.8	5,408.2	8,722.0	8,662.3	8,205.6	-
1989	21,974	166,667	141,726	3,163.7	2,423.1	3,322.9	2,708.2	5,341.4	8,665.8	8,610.7	8,142.4	-
1990	21,572	168,297	137,620	3,119.5	2,404.0	3,332.9	2,704.6	5,275.5	8,609.9	8,559.5	8,079.8	-
1991	20,923	136,446	133,633	2,685.8	2,385.1	3,343.0	2,701.1	5,210.4	8,554.4	8,508.5	8,017.6	-
1992	22,637	147,892	129,762	2,882.5	2,366.4	3,353.1	2,697.5	5,146.1	8,499.3	8,457.9	7,955.9	135.4
1993	22,632	151,161	132,993	3,119.7	2,562.9	3,464.6	2,908.0	5,635.6	9,259.0	9,212.7	8,652.4	-
1994	22,628	154,430	136,225	3,356.9	2,759.3	3,576.1	3,118.5	6,125.1	10,018.7	9,967.5	9,348.9	-
1995	22,623	157,698	139,456	3,594.1	2,955.8	3,687.6	3,329.1	6,614.7	10,778.3	10,722.3	10,045.5	-
1996	22,619	160,967	142,688	3,831.3	3,152.2	3,799.1	3,539.6	7,104.2	11,538.0	11,477.1	10,742.0	-
1997	22,614	164,236	145,919	4,068.5	3,348.7	3,910.6	3,750.1	7,593.7	12,297.7	12,231.9	11,438.5	231.5
1998	22,609p	167,505p	149,150p	4,305.7p	3,545.2p	4,022.1p	3,960.6p	8,083.2p	13,057.4p	12,986.7p	12,135.0p	-
1999	22,605p	170,774p	152,382p	4,542.9p	3,741.6p	4,133.6p	4,171.1p	8,572.7p	13,817.1p	13,741.5p	12,831.5p	-
2000	22,600p	174,042p	155,613p	4,780.1p	3,938.1p	4,245.1p	4,381.7p	9,062.3p	14,576.7p	14,496.3p	13,528.1p	-
2001	22,596p	177,311p	158,845p	5,017.3p	4,134.5p	4,356.6p	4,592.2p	9,551.8p	15,336.4p	15,251.1p	14,224.6p	-

Sources: *Economic Census of the United States*, 1977, 1982, 1987, 1992, and 1997. Data for those years (years are in **bold** type) are from the 5-year censuses of the economy. Other values, unless otherwise noted, are extrapolations. Values footnoted 1 are from the *County Business Patterns* for the years indicated. Values marked with p are projections. Data are the most recent available at this level of detail. "Net" under "Construction" is construction revenues net of the costs of subcontracts.

INDICES OF CHANGE

| Years | Estab-lish-ments | Employment | | Payroll ($ mil) | | Costs ($ mil) | | Value Added ($ mil) | Revenues ($ mil) | | | Capital expend. ($ mil) |
		Total	Constr. workers	Total	Worker payroll	Total	Cost of materials		All sources	Construction Total	Net	
1977	109.7	92.7	97.9	36.7	40.3	35.5	32.5	31.8	30.9	30.9	32.2	-
1982	89.3	73.4	75.1	38.1	40.1	42.6	36.1	35.1	35.2	34.9	35.4	-
1987	103.0	102.9	103.0	72.4	73.5	84.5	72.4	72.1	71.4	71.2	72.3	67.9
1992	100.1	90.0	88.9	70.8	70.7	85.7	71.9	67.8	69.1	69.1	69.6	58.5
1997	100.0	100.0	100.0	100.0	100.0	100.0	100.0	100.0	100.0	100.0	100.0	100.0

Sources: Same as General Statistics. The values shown reflect change from the base year, 1997. Values above 100 mean greater than 1997, values below 100 mean less than 1997, and a value of 100 in years other than 1997 means same as 1997. Indices are calculated only for Census years. Data are the most recent available at this level of detail.

SELECTED RATIOS

For 1997	Avg. of Sector	Analyzed Industry	Index	For 1997	Avg. of Sector	Analyzed Industry	Index
Employees per establishment	8.6	7.3	84	Value added per establishment	584,730	335,796	57
Construction workers per establishment	6.6	6.5	98	Value added per employee	67,759	46,237	68
Payroll per establishment	265,343	179,911	68	Value added per construction worker	88,592	52,041	59
Payroll per employee	30,748	24,772	81	Revenues per establishment	1,307,915	543,809	42
Payroll per construction worker	27,622	22,949	83	Revenues per employee	151,563	74,878	49
Costs per establishment	367,737	172,928	47	Revenues per construction worker	198,161	84,278	43
Costs per employee	42,614	23,811	56	CR as % of total revenues	98.48	99.46	101
Costs per construction worker	55,716	26,800	48	Net CR as % of CR	72.40	93.51	129
Materials as % of costs	95.75	95.90	100	Investment per establishment	22,948	10,237	45
Costs as % of revenues	28.12	31.80	113	Investment per employee	2,659	1,410	53
Costs as % of construction revenues	28.55	31.97	112	Investment per construction worker	3,477	1,586	46

Sources: Same as General Statistics. The 'Average of Sector' column represents the average for all industries in this sector. The Index shows the relationship between the Average and the Analyzed Industry. For example, 100 means that they are equal; 500 that the Analyzed Industry is five times the average; 50 means that the Analyzed Industry is half the national average. 'na' is used to show that data are 'not available'. CR stands for "construction revenues" and "Net CR" is construction revenues net of subcontract expenses.

*Equivalent to SIC 1741.

LEADING COMPANIES   Number shown: **11**   Total sales ($ mil): **380**   Total employment (000): **3.3**

Company Name	Address				CEO Name	Phone	Co. Type	Sales ($ mil)	Empl. (000)
Saxton Inc.	5440 W Sahara Ave	Las Vegas	NV	89146	James C Saxton	702-221-1111	P	92	0.9
Seedorff Masonry Inc.	PO Box 38	Strawberry Point	IA	52076	Mark H Guetzko	319-933-2296	R	58*	0.4
Sun Valley Masonry Inc.	10828 N Cave Creek	Phoenix	AZ	85020	Robert L Baum	602-943-6106	R	47	0.4
Dee Brown Inc.	P O Box 28335	Dallas	TX	75228	Robert V Barnes Jr	214-321-6443	R	35	0.5
Otto Baum and Sons Inc.	866 N Main St	Morton	IL	61550	Kenneth D Baum	309-266-7114	R	34	0.2
Manganaro Industries Inc.	P O Box 363	Malden	MA	02148	John B Manganaro Jr	781-322-7929	R	33*	0.2
Wasco Inc.	1138 2nd Ave N	Nashville	TN	37208	Brad S Proctor	615-244-9090	R	30	0.5
International Chimney Corp.	PO Box 260	Buffalo	NY	14231	Richard Lohr	716-634-3967	R	20	0.2
Bruns-Gutzwiller Inc.	305 S John St	Batesville	IN	47006		812-934-2105	R	17*	<0.1
Brencal Contractors Inc.	6686 E McNichols	Detroit	MI	48212	Brian Brickel	313-365-4300	S	14	<0.1
ICOS Corporation of America	PO Box 749	Englewood	NJ	07631	A Ressi	201-568-4411	R	0	<0.1

Source: Ward's Business Directory of U.S. Private and Public Companies, Volumes 1 and 2, 2000. The company type code used is as follows: P - Public, R - Private, S - Subsidiary, D - Division, J - Joint Venture, A - Affiliate, G - Group, N - Company type not reported. Sales are in millions of dollars, employees are in thousands. An asterisk (*) indicates an estimated sales volume. The symbol < stands for 'less than'. Company names and addresses are truncated, in some cases, to fit into the available space.

COST DETAILS

Item	Cost ($ mil)	% of total	Per $1,000 of Revenue	Item	Cost ($ mil)	% of total	Per $1,000 of Revenue
All costs	4,704.0	100.000	382.5	Total Rentals	195.5	4.156	15.9
Cost of supplies	3,750.1	79.721	304.9	Equipment	142.1	3.021	11.6
Subcontracts	793.4	16.866	64.5	Buildings	53.4	1.135	4.3
Power, fuel, lubricants	160.5	3.412	13.1	Services purchased	227.0	4.825	18.5
Electricity	18.2	0.387	1.5	Communications	78.5	1.668	6.4
Natural gas	6.1	0.130	0.5	Building repairs	11.8	0.250	1.0
Gasoline and diesel	128.6	2.733	10.5	Machinery repairs	136.7	2.907	11.1
Highway	106.8	2.270	8.7				
Offroad	21.8	0.463	1.8				
Other power	7.7	0.163	0.6				

Source: Economic Census of the United States, 1997. Revenues referred to are total industry revenues for the current NAICS industry.

CONSTRUCTION PRODUCT DETAILS

Construction type	Value of construction work ($ mil and %)							
	Total		New construction		Additions, alterations, reconstruction		Maintenance and repair	
	Value	%	Value	%	Value	%	Value	%
Total	**12,231.9**	**100.0**	**8,712.1**	**100.0**	**1,899.8**	**100.0**	**1,501.1**	**100.0**
Building construction, total	**11,223.6**	**91.8**	**8,359.6**	**96.0**	**1,774.0**	**93.4**	**1,090.0**	**72.6**
Single-family houses, detached	3,221.7	26.3	2,597.0	29.8	395.2	20.8	229.5	15.3
Single-family houses, attached	678.2	5.5	556.3	6.4	79.6	4.2	42.3	2.8
Apartment buildings, condos and cooperatives	565.8	4.6	363.8	4.2	77.3	4.1	124.8	8.3
Manufacturing and light industrial buildings	658.8	5.4	390.8	4.5	108.1	5.7	159.8	10.6
Manufacturing and light industrial warehouses	238.2	1.9	176.9	2.0	35.9	1.9	25.4	1.7
Hotels and motels	238.6	2.0	193.7	2.2	22.6	1.2	22.2	1.5
Office buildings	1,047.0	8.6	722.8	8.3	169.8	8.9	154.4	10.3
All other commercial buildings, nec	1,254.3	10.3	1,023.9	11.8	153.4	8.1	77.0	5.1
Commercial warehouses	348.7	2.9	294.2	3.4	37.0	1.9	17.4	1.2
Religious buildings	351.2	2.9	199.3	2.3	93.2	4.9	58.7	3.9
Educational buildings	1,559.0	12.7	1,058.7	12.2	399.4	21.0	100.9	6.7
Health care and institutional buildings	443.2	3.6	303.9	3.5	96.9	5.1	42.3	2.8
Public safety buildings	319.4	2.6	257.0	2.9	46.3	2.4	16.1	1.1
Amusement, social, and recreational buildings	188.8	1.5	142.2	1.6	37.4	2.0	9.2	0.6
Other building construction	110.8	0.9	79.0	0.9	21.8	1.1	10.0	0.7
Nonbuilding construction, total	**889.5**	**7.3**	**352.4**	**4.0**	**125.9**	**6.6**	**411.2**	**27.4**
Blast furnaces, refineries, chemical complexes, etc	437.0	3.6	77.6	0.9	65.2	3.4	294.3	19.6
Other nonbuilding construction, nec	452.5	3.7	274.9	3.2	60.7	3.2	116.9	7.8
Construction work, nsk	**118.8**	**1.0**	**NA**	**-**	**NA**	**-**	**NA**	**-**

Source: Economic Census of the United States, 1997. Bold items are headers. (D) stands for data withheld to protect competitive information. (S) indicates instances where data do not meet publications standards.

LOCATION BY STATE AND REGIONAL CONCENTRATION

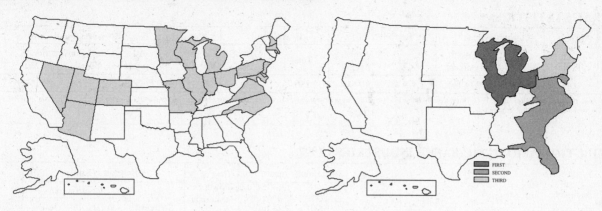

INDUSTRY DATA BY STATE

State	Estab lish- ments	Employment			Compensation		Production				Capital Exp. ($ mil)
		Total	Workers	Total as % of US	Payroll per Employee	Wages per Worker	Costs ($ mil)	Value Added ($ mil)	Reve- nues ($ mil)	% of US	
California	1,291	9,967	8,789	6.07	26,636	24,777	312.3	516.3	855.2	6.95	12.3
Pennsylvania	1,439	10,349	9,097	6.30	26,082	23,831	256.5	526.5	839.5	6.83	17.2
New York	1,281	7,960	6,530	4.85	28,333	25,604	227.3	474.4	812.8	6.61	10.8
Illinois	1,115	8,223	7,314	5.01	33,390	31,477	207.9	506.0	753.7	6.13	12.9
Ohio	1,212	8,475	7,485	5.16	26,299	25,042	199.3	421.4	666.8	5.42	12.2
Texas	969	9,335	8,398	5.68	21,125	19,341	203.5	367.3	629.7	5.12	12.3
Michigan	996	6,245	5,551	3.80	30,162	28,577	188.6	332.8	552.3	4.49	11.9
Florida	833	7,713	6,905	4.70	21,068	19,162	147.8	317.3	514.2	4.18	9.0
North Carolina	1,415	8,737	7,977	5.32	19,005	17,803	133.7	330.5	498.9	4.06	11.3
New Jersey	865	4,427	3,771	2.70	28,110	26,555	137.9	272.4	453.6	3.69	8.8
Virginia	949	7,718	6,951	4.70	20,107	18,549	115.8	254.0	386.5	3.14	8.7
Maryland	547	5,850	5,191	3.56	23,517	21,325	124.2	219.2	364.6	2.96	5.6
Wisconsin	580	3,831	3,314	2.33	30,439	29,223	104.7	213.2	340.0	2.76	6.7
Minnesota	498	3,118	2,649	1.90	34,415	31,475	105.3	207.0	324.6	2.64	6.4
Massachusetts	487	3,244	2,750	1.98	31,926	30,006	96.3	193.4	321.6	2.62	4.4
Indiana	652	4,670	4,172	2.84	24,190	23,108	84.8	201.3	310.7	2.53	9.0
Missouri	515	3,867	3,473	2.35	27,629	25,868	83.2	199.8	292.9	2.38	5.1
Arizona	336	4,106	3,793	2.50	23,251	21,608	131.9	149.7	291.6	2.37	5.0
Georgia	510	3,908	3,456	2.38	19,646	17,896	97.3	145.3	271.9	2.21	3.9
Colorado	392	3,292	2,994	2.00	26,394	23,798	87.1	139.9	235.9	1.92	5.0
Tennessee	427	3,947	3,644	2.40	22,503	20,061	69.5	144.2	221.3	1.80	5.3
Washington	391	2,123	1,837	1.29	33,098	31,706	71.1	135.0	218.4	1.78	2.8
Nevada	132	2,458	2,274	1.50	22,769	21,507	75.2	103.8	180.4	1.47	2.0
Kentucky	383	3,313	3,060	2.02	19,510	18,379	39.7	129.1	177.1	1.44	4.6
Alabama	385	3,239	2,893	1.97	19,236	17,458	67.5	98.0	172.8	1.41	3.2
Louisiana	180	2,014	1,729	1.23	24,468	21,016	74.6	84.7	161.7	1.32	3.8
Connecticut	294	1,512	1,348	0.92	27,960	25,224	39.9	87.4	137.8	1.12	2.0
South Carolina	573	3,109	2,813	1.89	15,633	14,843	24.8	96.8	134.3	1.09	2.1
Iowa	229	1,623	1,448	0.99	25,559	23,999	37.2	79.9	119.8	0.97	4.9
Utah	277	1,382	1,269	0.84	23,664	22,810	42.1	58.3	103.8	0.84	1.8
Oklahoma	223	1,676	1,546	1.02	20,036	18,417	18.0	71.1	97.1	0.79	1.5
Oregon	212	990	897	0.60	28,257	26,627	40.2	49.8	92.2	0.75	2.1
Kansas	198	1,413	1,315	0.86	23,006	21,592	25.7	57.6	86.2	0.70	1.9
Rhode Island	109	604	511	0.37	35,255	34,166	31.4	37.9	70.7	0.57	1.1
Nebraska	206	1,167	1,089	0.71	21,259	20,298	17.8	49.4	69.4	0.56	2.7
Arkansas	201	1,127	1,014	0.69	17,831	16,514	24.6	39.8	66.2	0.54	0.8
New Hampshire	116	662	585	0.40	27,080	27,181	23.8	34.2	64.3	0.52	2.1
Delaware	137	793	652	0.48	22,898	21,385	17.2	36.2	55.3	0.45	1.0
New Mexico	97	917	810	0.56	17,744	16,106	19.4	28.6	51.9	0.42	1.3
West Virginia	192	851	773	0.52	16,051	15,618	13.5	24.5	42.3	0.34	0.8
Idaho	63	517	477	0.31	28,017	25,985	23.5	17.8	42.1	0.34	0.7
Mississippi	171	977	900	0.59	14,911	12,913	(S)	27.5	37.9	0.31	0.5
South Dakota	50	505	485	0.31	21,485	20,940	10.4	19.6	31.2	0.25	0.8
Maine	140	546	466	0.33	19,747	18,685	12.7	16.6	30.3	0.25	1.0
Hawaii	74	343	289	0.21	28,452	27,657	5.4	23.5	29.1	0.24	0.3
Vermont	95	(S)	282	-		21,504	8.8	13.6	23.3	0.19	0.8
Montana	67	350	333	0.21	19,237	18,060	7.0	13.8	20.9	0.17	0.3
North Dakota	37	295	270	0.18	20,919	18,359	5.9	10.4	16.5	0.13	(S)
Wyoming	45	225	204	0.14	20,627	19,824	4.8	8.7	(D)	-	0.2
Alaska	22	128	112	0.08	24,500	22,973	3.1	6.4	(D)	-	0.2
D.C.	7	(S)	(S)	-	-	-	(S)	(S)	(D)	-	(S)

Source: Economic Census of the U.S., 1997. Data are sorted by 1997 revenues or establishments. (D) means data suppression to prevent disclosure of company data. (S) means that data did not meet statistical standards for publication. A dash (-) is used when data are unavailable or cannot be calculated. Data followed by an * indicate the midpoint of a range. The ranges are: for 10, 0-19; for 60, 20-99; for 175, 100-249; for 375, 250-499, for 750, 500-999. Higher values are multiples of those shown, e.g., 3,750 is the midpoint of the range 2,500-4,999. Shaded *states* on the state map indicate those states which have proportionately greater representation in the industry than would be indicated by the state's population; the ratio is based on total revenues or number of establishments. Shaded *regions* indicate where the industry is regionally most concentrated.

283

NAICS 235420 - DRYWALL, PLASTERING, ACOUSTICAL, AND INSULATION CONTRACTORS

GENERAL STATISTICS

Years	Estab-lish-ments	Employment		Payroll ($ mil)		Costs ($ mil)		Value Added ($ mil)	Revenues ($ mil)			Capital expend. ($ mil)
		Total	Constr. workers	Total	Worker payroll	Total	Cost of materials		All sources	Construction		
										Total	Net	
1997	20,457	266,710	229,934	7,479.4	5,940.4	7,290.7	7,070.5	13,082.5	22,628.7	22,369.4	20,113.9	269.0

Source: *Economic Census of the United States*, 1997. This is a newly defined industry. Data for prior years were unavailable at the time of publication but may become available over time. "Net" under "Construction" is construction revenue net of the costs of subcontracts.

DISTRIBUTION AMONG SIC-BASED INDUSTRIES - 1997

SIC	Industry	Estab-lish-ments	Employment		Cost of Power & Materials ($ mil)	Revenues ($ mil)			Value Added ($ mil)
			Total (000)	Payroll ($ mil)		All Sources	Construction		
							Total	Net	
174200	Plastering, drywall, acoustical contractors	19,333.0	256,538	7,258.3	7,054.9	21,906.2	21,652.6	19,475.7	12,674.45
174310	Terrazzo, tile, marble, & mosaic work (pt)	-	-	-	-	-	-	-	-
177110	Concrete work contractors (pt)	1,124.0	10,172	221.2	235.8	722.4	716.8	638.3	408.09

Source: 1997 *Economic Census*. U.S. Census Bureau, U.S. Department of Commerce, August 1997. SIC codes ending in two zeroes represent complete 4-digit SICs. All others are parts of 4-digit SIC industries. Items showing a dash (-) indicate that data are not available because of disclosure problems.

SIC INDUSTRIES RELATED TO NAICS 235420

SIC	Industry	1990	1991	1992	1993	1994	1995	1996	1997
1742	**Plastering, Dry Wall, and Insulation**								
	Establishments (number)	16,005	16,233	18,648	18,903	18,995p	19,170p	19,348p	19,527p
	Employment (thousands)	255.0	208.1	206.7	203.4	190.4e	182.8e	175.5e	168.4e
	Revenues ($ million)	15,187.6e	14,699.6e	14,227.3	13,770.2e	13,327.8e	12,899.6e	12,485.1e	12,084.0e
1743	**Terrazzo, Tile, Marble, and Mosaic Work***								
	Establishments (number)	4,541	4,491	6,499	5,849	7,167p	7,526p	7,903p	8,300p
	Employment (thousands)	33.1	28.6	34.0	30.3	33.9e	33.8e	33.7e	33.6e
	Revenues ($ million)	2,414.0e	2,447.7e	2,481.8	2,516.5e	2,551.6e	2,587.2e	2,623.3e	2,659.9e
1771	**Concrete Work***								
	Establishments (number)	21,496	21,212	26,123	25,835	27,289p	27,891p	28,506p	29,135p
	Employment (thousands)	198.2	164.9	192.5	182.0	183.1e	178.6e	174.2e	169.9e
	Revenues ($ million)	14,839.4e	14,717.2e	14,596.0	14,475.9e	14,356.7e	14,238.5e	14,121.2e	14,005.0e

Source: *Economic Census of the United States*, 1992, annual surveys of economic sectors conducted by the Bureau of the Census, and estimates or projections based on the 1982-1992 period; not all data are shown. 'e' marks estimates made by the editors; 'p' indicates projections based on time series. A dash (-) indicates that data for this SIC or year were not available. * Indicates that only a portion of this industry is present within the NAICS data. If no * is shown, the entire industry is contained within the NAICS data.

INDICES OF CHANGE

Years	Estab-lish-ments	Employment		Payroll ($ mil)		Costs ($ mil)		Value Added ($ mil)	Revenues ($ mil)			Capital expend. ($ mil)
		Total	Constr. workers	Total	Worker payroll	Total	Cost of materials		All sources	Construction		
										Total	Net	
1997	100.0	100.0	100.0	100.0	100.0	100.0	100.0	100.0	100.0	100.0	100.0	100.0

Sources: Same as General Statistics. The values shown reflect change from the base year, 1997. Values above 100 mean greater than 1997, values below 100 mean less than 1997, and a value of 100 in years other than 1997 means same as 1997. Indices are calculated only for Census years. Data are the most recent available at this level of detail.

SELECTED RATIOS

For 1997	Avg. of Sector	Analyzed Industry	Index	For 1997	Avg. of Sector	Analyzed Industry	Index
Employees per establishment	8.6	13.0	151	Value added per establishment	584,730	639,512	109
Construction workers per establishment	6.6	11.2	170	Value added per employee	67,759	49,051	72
Payroll per establishment	265,343	365,616	138	Value added per construction worker	88,592	56,897	64
Payroll per employee	30,748	28,043	91	Revenues per establishment	1,307,915	1,106,159	85
Payroll per construction worker	27,622	25,835	94	Revenues per employee	151,563	84,844	56
Costs per establishment	367,737	356,391	97	Revenues per construction worker	198,161	98,414	50
Costs per employee	42,614	27,336	64	CR as % of total revenues	98.48	98.85	100
Costs per construction worker	55,716	31,708	57	Net CR as % of CR	72.40	89.92	124
Materials as % of costs	95.75	96.98	101	Investment per establishment	22,948	13,150	57
Costs as % of revenues	28.12	32.22	115	Investment per employee	2,659	1,009	38
Costs as % of construction revenues	28.55	32.59	114	Investment per construction worker	3,477	1,170	34

Sources: Same as General Statistics. The 'Average of Sector' column represents the average for all industries in this sector. The Index shows the relationship between the Average and the Analyzed Industry. For example, 100 means that they are equal; 500 that the Analyzed Industry is five times the average; 50 means that the Analyzed Industry is half the national average. 'na' is used to show that data are 'not available'. CR stands for "construction revenues" and "Net CR" is construction revenues net of subcontract expenses.

LEADING COMPANIES　Number shown: **28**　　Total sales ($ mil): **2,743**　　Total employment (000): **20.0**

Company Name	Address				CEO Name	Phone	Co. Type	Sales ($ mil)	Empl. (000)
APi Group Inc.	2366 Rose Pl	St. Paul	MN	55113	Lee R Anderson	612-636-4320	R	535	3.5
Performance Contracting Inc.	P O Box 2198	Shawnee Msn	KS	66201	Craig Sallon	913-888-8600	S	481*	3.2
Pacific Coast Building Products	PO Box 160488	Sacramento	CA	95816	David Luccetti	916-444-9304	R	360*	2.5
Irex Corp.	PO Box 1268	Lancaster	PA	17608	W kirk Lidell	717-397-3633	P	315	0.4
C.H. Heist Corp.	810 N Belcher Rd	Clearwater	FL	33758	W David Foster	727-461-5656	P	136	4.0
Young Sales Corp.	1054 Central Ind	St. Louis	MO	63110	W Todd McCane	314-771-3080	R	129*	0.7
AC and S Inc.	P O Box 1548	Lancaster	PA	17608	Dave Andrew	717-397-3631	S	110	0.2
Saxton Inc.	5440 W Sahara Ave	Las Vegas	NV	89146	James C Saxton	702-221-1111	P	92	0.9
Building Service Inc.	11925 W Carmen	Milwaukee	WI	53225	Ralph T Kuehn	414-353-3600	R	85*	0.2
King and Company Inc.	P O Box 50263	New Orleans	LA	70150	Cyril P Geary Jr	504-486-9195	R	82*	0.6
Anning-Johnson Co.	1959 Anson Dr	Melrose Park	IL	60160		708-681-1300	S	75*	0.8
Allied Construction Services Inc.	PO Box 937	Des Moines	IA	50304	Robert L Maddox Jr	515-288-4855	R	58*	0.4
Davis Acoustical Corp.	PO Box 1150	Troy	NY	12181	Burton Fisher	518-271-7400	R	45*	0.3
Manganaro Industries Inc.	P O Box 363	Malden	MA	02148	John B Manganaro Jr	781-322-7929	R	33*	0.2
Acmat Corp.	P O Box 2350	New Britain	CT	06050	Henry W Nozko Sr	860-229-9000	P	29	<0.1
Precision Walls Inc.	PO Box 33309	Raleigh	NC	27636	Loy Allen	919-832-0380	R	25	0.5
M.L. McDonald Sales Inc.	50 Oakland St	Watertown	MA	02472	Peter Patch	617-923-0900	R	23*	0.2
B.J. McGlone and Company Inc.	40 Brunswick Ave	Edison	NJ	08817	BJ McGlone	732-287-8600	R	21*	0.2
Sullivan Brothers Inc.	2515 S Stoughton	Madison	WI	53716	RJ Sullivan	608-222-1277	R	18	0.2
F. Richard Wilton Jr. Inc.	PO Box 949	Glen Allen	VA	23060	W Scott Brannan	804-798-1637	R	17*	0.1
M. Ecker and Company Inc.	5374 N Elston Ave	Chicago	IL	60630	Frank Vuvricki	773-685-5500	R	15*	0.3
Jacobson and Company Inc.	1079 E Grand St	Elizabeth	NJ	07207	J Jacobson	908-355-5200	R	14*	0.1
Eckel Industries Inc.	155 Fawcett St	Cambridge	MA	02138	Alan Eckel	617-491-3221	R	13	0.1
Marek Brothers Co.	2201 Judi Way	Houston	TX	77018		713-681-9213	R	12	0.2
Transco Products Inc.	55 E Jackson Blvd	Chicago	IL	60604		312-427-2818	S	12	<0.1
Field and Associates Inc.	2187 W 1st St	Springfield	OH	45504	Stephen C Field	937-323-5518	S	4	<0.1
Armor Deck Inc.	6315 S Kyrene Rd	Tempe	AZ	85280	Tim Maas	602-456-0555	R	2	<0.1
K. Reinke Jr. and Co.	P O Box 68	Dundee	IL	60118	Karl Reinke Jr	847-428-5555	R	2*	<0.1

Source: Ward's Business Directory of U.S. Private and Public Companies, Volumes 1 and 2, 2000. The company type code used is as follows: P - Public, R - Private, S - Subsidiary, D - Division, J - Joint Venture, A - Affiliate, G - Group, N - Company type not reported. Sales are in millions of dollars, employees are in thousands. An asterisk (*) indicates an estimated sales volume. The symbol < stands for 'less than'. Company names and addresses are truncated, in some cases, to fit into the available space.

COST DETAILS

Item	Cost ($ mil)	% of total	Per $1,000 of Revenue	Item	Cost ($ mil)	% of total	Per $1,000 of Revenue
All costs	9,546.1	100.000	421.9	Total Rentals	265.5	2.781	11.7
Cost of supplies	7,070.5	74.066	312.5	Equipment	137.3	1.438	6.1
Subcontracts	2,255.4	23.627	99.7	Buildings	128.2	1.343	5.7
Power, fuel, lubricants	220.2	2.307	9.7	Services purchased	266.8	2.795	11.8
Electricity	32.3	0.338	1.4	Communications	120.5	1.262	5.3
Natural gas	7.5	0.079	0.3	Building repairs	18.1	0.189	0.8
Gasoline and diesel	173.4	1.817	7.7	Machinery repairs	128.3	1.344	5.7
Highway	157.5	1.649	7.0				
Offroad	16.0	0.167	0.7				
Other power	7.0	0.074	0.3				

Source: Economic Census of the United States, 1997. Revenues referred to are total industry revenues for the current NAICS industry.

CONSTRUCTION PRODUCT DETAILS

Construction type	Value of construction work ($ mil and %)							
	Total		New construction		Additions, alterations, reconstruction		Maintenance and repair	
	Value	%	Value	%	Value	%	Value	%
Total	**22,369.4**	**100.0**	**16,218.8**	**100.0**	**4,796.5**	**100.0**	**1,247.7**	**100.0**
Building construction, total	**21,841.2**	**97.6**	**16,135.4**	**99.5**	**4,683.0**	**97.6**	**1,022.8**	**82.0**
Single-family houses, detached	6,046.4	27.0	5,232.3	32.3	569.9	11.9	244.2	19.6
Single-family houses, attached	1,010.0	4.5	869.2	5.4	87.4	1.8	53.4	4.3
Apartment buildings, condos and cooperatives	1,371.3	6.1	1,185.2	7.3	135.4	2.8	50.6	4.1
Manufacturing and light industrial buildings	930.8	4.2	545.3	3.4	262.6	5.5	122.9	9.9
Manufacturing and light industrial warehouses	459.4	2.1	333.1	2.1	93.4	1.9	32.8	2.6
Hotels and motels	926.8	4.1	768.3	4.7	136.8	2.9	21.7	1.7
Office buildings	4,077.6	18.2	2,386.4	14.7	1,494.1	31.2	197.1	15.8
All other commercial buildings, nec	2,322.6	10.4	1,562.8	9.6	672.3	14.0	87.5	7.0
Commercial warehouses	407.8	1.8	313.2	1.9	78.8	1.6	15.8	1.3
Religious buildings	433.5	1.9	292.9	1.8	112.8	2.4	27.9	2.2
Educational buildings	1,540.6	6.9	1,034.6	6.4	445.4	9.3	60.6	4.9
Health care and institutional buildings	1,430.7	6.4	944.2	5.8	424.6	8.9	61.9	5.0
Public safety buildings	360.5	1.6	274.7	1.7	70.5	1.5	15.2	1.2
Amusement, social, and recreational buildings	353.6	1.6	259.8	1.6	70.9	1.5	22.9	1.8
Other building construction	169.6	0.8	133.2	0.8	28.0	0.6	8.4	0.7
Nonbuilding construction, total	**421.8**	**1.9**	**83.4**	**0.5**	**113.5**	**2.4**	**224.9**	**18.0**
Blast furnaces, refineries, chemical complexes, etc	238.5	1.1	32.8	0.2	76.1	1.6	129.6	10.4
Other nonbuilding construction, nec	183.3	0.8	50.6	0.3	37.4	0.8	95.3	7.6
Construction work, nsk	**106.3**	**0.5**	**NA**	**-**	**NA**	**-**	**NA**	**-**

Source: *Economic Census of the United States*, 1997. Bold items are headers. (D) stands for data withheld to protect competitive information. (S) indicates instances where data do not meet publications standards.

LOCATION BY STATE AND REGIONAL CONCENTRATION

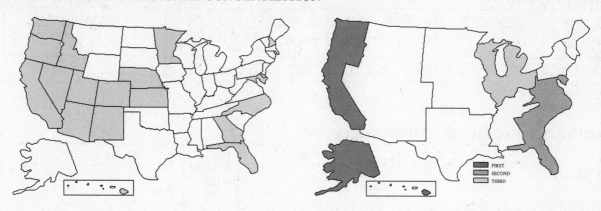

INDUSTRY DATA BY STATE

State	Estab lish- ments	Employment			Compensation		Production				Capital Exp. ($ mil)
		Total	Workers	Total as % of US	Payroll per Employee	Wages per Worker	Costs ($ mil)	Value Added ($ mil)	Reve- nues ($ mil)	% of US	
California	2,590	39,210	34,795	14.70	28,113	26,175	905.1	1,851.3	2,951.1	13.04	32.4
Florida	1,760	17,959	15,009	6.73	25,130	22,666	591.0	834.9	1,732.6	7.66	19.7
Texas	983	16,479	14,402	6.18	22,481	20,324	427.5	669.2	1,236.8	5.47	15.6
New York	839	11,284	9,421	4.23	38,576	36,088	313.0	779.4	1,225.2	5.41	11.7
Illinois	692	10,268	8,741	3.85	34,822	33,102	301.7	622.7	1,021.6	4.51	13.1
Arizona	494	13,866	12,532	5.20	22,241	20,114	295.1	475.5	797.5	3.52	10.1
Pennsylvania	601	8,087	7,076	3.03	33,821	32,149	245.9	475.3	780.6	3.45	7.8
Michigan	643	7,069	6,181	2.65	30,896	28,028	226.2	368.0	694.5	3.07	8.7
North Carolina	643	7,151	5,907	2.68	25,228	22,401	241.1	332.9	676.6	2.99	10.9
Ohio	638	7,610	6,480	2.85	28,480	26,211	222.2	369.5	665.8	2.94	5.3
Washington	810	8,927	7,811	3.35	27,490	26,025	196.0	425.5	664.5	2.94	7.8
Maryland	441	7,367	6,230	2.76	29,418	27,298	207.1	357.3	636.9	2.81	6.5
Georgia	592	6,223	5,063	2.33	24,581	22,013	229.1	292.1	616.7	2.73	7.5
New Jersey	504	5,178	4,189	1.94	35,952	34,672	165.7	342.8	569.4	2.52	4.0
Virginia	477	7,623	6,314	2.86	24,426	21,537	183.5	303.6	541.9	2.39	6.4
Colorado	558	6,921	6,079	2.59	27,750	24,714	168.3	316.5	528.3	2.33	7.6
Minnesota	416	4,496	3,767	1.69	34,293	31,892	151.3	282.0	476.2	2.10	5.9
Indiana	507	5,005	4,338	1.88	28,253	26,285	128.1	255.4	436.7	1.93	5.5
Massachusetts	426	3,849	3,145	1.44	32,365	30,286	130.1	248.7	429.4	1.90	5.3
Nevada	167	6,729	6,036	2.52	26,116	24,401	138.1	271.0	421.5	1.86	3.8
Wisconsin	513	4,917	4,265	1.84	29,077	27,220	134.9	252.4	419.8	1.86	6.7
Missouri	457	4,916	4,242	1.84	31,576	29,293	133.3	261.5	419.5	1.85	6.0
Tennessee	284	4,614	4,023	1.73	25,686	21,974	123.2	198.0	355.2	1.57	4.0
Louisiana	136	4,653	4,230	1.74	29,177	27,813	111.0	207.7	337.8	1.49	3.3
Utah	369	4,239	3,866	1.59	26,972	25,322	105.2	206.0	327.8	1.45	3.9
Oregon	400	3,841	3,328	1.44	29,370	27,761	114.8	191.7	326.8	1.44	4.6
South Carolina	307	3,480	2,941	1.30	22,171	19,566	111.3	160.0	302.6	1.34	3.5
Alabama	281	4,023	3,494	1.51	22,977	20,344	103.8	161.0	296.9	1.31	5.8
Kansas	153	2,422	2,010	0.91	31,768	28,504	86.1	133.3	270.8	1.20	2.0
Nebraska	183	2,166	1,744	0.81	27,326	24,350	90.6	131.1	261.2	1.15	2.8
Kentucky	255	3,689	3,046	1.38	22,368	19,944	82.7	151.3	254.3	1.12	3.4
Connecticut	154	2,025	1,671	0.76	38,068	35,151	64.6	134.8	233.0	1.03	2.0
Iowa	261	2,491	2,142	0.93	27,888	24,938	78.1	136.3	228.4	1.01	5.2
Mississippi	142	2,531	2,157	0.95	26,479	24,796	62.0	127.6	205.1	0.91	3.6
New Mexico	201	2,525	2,217	0.95	19,704	18,739	49.2	95.5	152.4	0.67	2.4
Rhode Island	134	1,006	847	0.38	44,846	42,289	42.1	74.4	137.7	0.61	1.1
Idaho	266	1,890	1,760	0.71	21,282	20,202	40.1	73.3	122.7	0.54	(D)
Arkansas	157	1,488	1,245	0.56	21,239	20,476	39.7	61.1	121.5	0.54	1.4
Oklahoma	185	1,501	1,301	0.56	22,919	19,995	43.9	69.6	119.9	0.53	1.8
Hawaii	90	1,110	914	0.42	38,459	38,854	37.2	80.6	119.8	0.53	0.9
New Hampshire	79	1,120	936	0.42	33,981	31,165	39.2	60.5	107.3	0.47	1.2
Delaware	60	687	532	0.26	35,863	34,278	28.3	42.5	81.7	0.36	1.0
Maine	108	1,010	872	0.38	19,705	18,377	21.9	38.3	67.1	0.30	0.8
North Dakota	69	614	529	0.23	22,674	19,711	16.8	28.5	46.2	0.20	0.8
Alaska	79	360	293	0.13	39,906	36,901	14.3	27.2	45.7	0.20	0.2
South Dakota	82	383	346	0.14	25,339	24,457	10.1	21.5	32.8	0.15	0.2
Wyoming	59	495	433	0.19	23,798	20,986	10.8	20.6	31.7	0.14	0.7
West Virginia	58	403	328	0.15	27,452	26,835	7.9	21.7	31.0	0.14	0.3
Montana	126	309	268	0.12	-	-	10.2	16.4	29.1	0.13	0.4
Vermont	24	(D)	(D)	-	-	-	(D)	(D)	(D)	-	0.5
D.C.	3	(D)	(D)	-	-	-	(D)	(D)	(D)	-	(D)

Source: Economic Census of the U.S., 1997. Data are sorted by 1997 revenues or establishments. (D) means data suppression to prevent disclosure of company data. (S) means that data did not meet statistical standards for publication. A dash (-) is used when data are unavailable or cannot be calculated. Data followed by an * indicate the midpoint of a range. The ranges are: for 10, 0-19; for 60, 20-99; for 175, 100-249; for 375, 250-499, for 750, 500-999. Higher values are multiples of those shown, e.g., 3,750 is the midpoint of the range 2,500-4,999. Shaded *states* on the state map indicate those states which have proportionately greater representation in the industry than would be indicated by the state's population; the ratio is based on total revenues or number of establishments. Shaded *regions* indicate where the industry is regionally most concentrated.

NAICS 235430 - TILE, MARBLE, TERRAZZO, AND MOSAIC CONTRACTORS

GENERAL STATISTICS

Years	Estab-lish-ments	Employment		Payroll ($ mil)		Costs ($ mil)		Value Added ($ mil)	Revenues ($ mil)			Capital expend. ($ mil)
		Total	Constr. workers	Total	Worker payroll	Total	Cost of materials		All sources	Construction Total	Net	
1997	6,847	39,755	31,847	1,064.2	783.8	1,339.6	1,293.4	1,992.7	3,533.0	3,491.7	3,291.0	47.9

Source: Economic Census of the United States, 1997. This is a newly defined industry. Data for prior years were unavailable at the time of publication but may become available over time. "Net" under "Construction" is construction revenue net of the costs of subcontracts.

DISTRIBUTION AMONG SIC-BASED INDUSTRIES - 1997

SIC	Industry	Estab-lish-ments	Employment		Cost of Power & Materials ($ mil)	Revenues ($ mil)			Value Added ($ mil)
			Total (000)	Payroll ($ mil)		All Sources	Construction Total	Net	
174320	Terrazzo, tile, marble, & mosaic work (pt)	6,847.0	39,755	1,064.2	1,339.6	3,533.0	3,491.6	3,291.0	1,992.73

Source: 1997 Economic Census. U.S. Census Bureau, U.S. Department of Commerce, August 1997. SIC codes ending in two zeroes represent complete 4-digit SICs. All others are parts of 4-digit SIC industries. Items showing a dash (-) indicate that data are not available because of disclosure problems.

SIC INDUSTRIES RELATED TO NAICS 235430

SIC	Industry	1990	1991	1992	1993	1994	1995	1996	1997
1743	**Terrazzo, Tile, Marble, and Mosaic Work***								
	Establishments (number)	4,541	4,491	6,499	5,849	7,167p	7,526p	7,903p	8,300p
	Employment (thousands)	33.1	28.6	34.0	30.3	33.9e	33.8e	33.7e	33.6e
	Revenues ($ million)	2,414.0e	2,447.7e	2,481.8	2,516.5e	2,551.6e	2,587.2e	2,623.3e	2,659.9e

Source: Economic Census of the United States, 1992, annual surveys of economic sectors conducted by the Bureau of the Census, and estimates or projections based on the 1982-1992 period; not all data are shown. 'e' marks estimates made by the editors; 'p' indicates projections based on time series. A dash (-) indicates that data for this SIC or year were not available. * Indicates that only a portion of this industry is present within the NAICS data. If no * is shown, the entire industry is contained within the NAICS data.

INDICES OF CHANGE

Years	Estab-lish-ments	Employment		Payroll ($ mil)		Costs ($ mil)		Value Added ($ mil)	Revenues ($ mil)			Capital expend. ($ mil)
		Total	Constr. workers	Total	Worker payroll	Total	Cost of materials		All sources	Construction Total	Net	
1997	100.0	100.0	100.0	100.0	100.0	100.0	100.0	100.0	100.0	100.0	100.0	100.0

Sources: Same as General Statistics. The values shown reflect change from the base year, 1997. Values above 100 mean greater than 1997, values below 100 mean less than 1997, and a value of 100 in years other than 1997 means same as 1997. Indices are calculated only for Census years. Data are the most recent available at this level of detail.

SELECTED RATIOS

For 1997	Avg. of Sector	Analyzed Industry	Index	For 1997	Avg. of Sector	Analyzed Industry	Index
Employees per establishment	8.6	5.8	67	Value added per establishment	584,730	291,033	50
Construction workers per establishment	6.6	4.7	70	Value added per employee	67,759	50,125	74
Payroll per establishment	265,343	155,426	59	Value added per construction worker	88,592	62,571	71
Payroll per employee	30,748	26,769	87	Revenues per establishment	1,307,915	515,992	39
Payroll per construction worker	27,622	24,611	89	Revenues per employee	151,563	88,869	59
Costs per establishment	367,737	195,648	53	Revenues per construction worker	198,161	110,937	56
Costs per employee	42,614	33,696	79	CR as % of total revenues	98.48	98.83	100
Costs per construction worker	55,716	42,064	75	Net CR as % of CR	72.40	94.25	130
Materials as % of costs	95.75	96.55	101	Investment per establishment	22,948	6,996	30
Costs as % of revenues	28.12	37.92	135	Investment per employee	2,659	1,205	45
Costs as % of construction revenues	28.55	38.37	134	Investment per construction worker	3,477	1,504	43

Sources: Same as General Statistics. The 'Average of Sector' column represents the average for all industries in this sector. The Index shows the relationship between the Average and the Analyzed Industry. For example, 100 means that they are equal; 500 that the Analyzed Industry is five times the average; 50 means that the Analyzed Industry is half the national average. 'na' is used to show that data are 'not available'. CR stands for "construction revenues" and "Net CR" is construction revenues net of subcontract expenses.

LEADING COMPANIES
No company data available for this industry.

COST DETAILS

Item	Cost ($ mil)	% of total	Per $1,000 of Revenue	Item	Cost ($ mil)	% of total	Per $1,000 of Revenue
All costs	1,540.3	100.000	436.0	Total Rentals	37.3	2.424	10.6
Cost of supplies	1,293.4	83.975	366.1	Equipment	10.1	0.657	2.9
Subcontracts	200.7	13.028	56.8	Buildings	27.2	1.767	7.7
Power, fuel, lubricants	46.2	2.998	13.1	Services purchased	50.5	3.281	14.3
Electricity	7.7	0.498	2.2	Communications	26.7	1.734	7.6
Natural gas	2.0	0.132	0.6	Building repairs	2.4	0.156	0.7
Gasoline and diesel	34.8	2.263	9.9	Machinery repairs	21.4	1.390	6.1
Highway	32.5	2.110	9.2				
Offroad	2.3	0.153	0.7				
Other power	1.6	0.104	0.5				

Source: *Economic Census of the United States*, 1997. Revenues referred to are total industry revenues for the current NAICS industry.

CONSTRUCTION PRODUCT DETAILS

Construction type	Value of construction work ($ mil and %)							
	Total		New construction		Additions, alterations, reconstruction		Maintenance and repair	
	Value	%	Value	%	Value	%	Value	%
Total	**3,491.7**	**100.0**	**2,364.6**	**100.0**	**900.3**	**100.0**	**205.3**	**100.0**
Building construction, total	**3,433.9**	**98.3**	**2,341.8**	**99.0**	**889.8**	**98.8**	**202.3**	**98.5**
Single-family houses, detached	1,440.0	41.2	1,022.9	43.3	352.7	39.2	64.4	31.4
Single-family houses, attached	198.0	5.7	128.2	5.4	56.8	6.3	13.0	6.3
Apartment buildings, condos and cooperatives	160.2	4.6	99.2	4.2	43.6	4.8	17.4	8.5
Manufacturing and light industrial buildings	91.7	2.6	58.9	2.5	21.3	2.4	11.5	5.6
Hotels and motels	150.0	4.3	95.7	4.0	42.1	4.7	12.1	5.9
Office buildings	333.9	9.6	217.6	9.2	98.3	10.9	18.0	8.8
All other commercial buildings, nec	447.5	12.8	308.4	13.0	109.4	12.1	29.7	14.5
Religious buildings	51.3	1.5	26.8	1.1	19.6	2.2	5.0	2.4
Educational buildings	236.4	6.8	162.7	6.9	62.3	6.9	11.3	5.5
Health care and institutional buildings	118.3	3.4	63.9	2.7	47.1	5.2	7.3	3.6
Public safety buildings	49.8	1.4	36.7	1.6	10.5	1.2	2.6	1.3
Amusement, social, and recreational buildings	42.3	1.2	31.3	1.3	8.4	0.9	2.5	1.2
Other building construction	114.6	3.3	89.5	3.8	17.7	2.0	7.4	3.6
Nonbuilding construction, total	**36.2**	**1.0**	**22.8**	**1.0**	**10.4**	**1.2**	**3.0**	**1.5**
Other nonbuilding construction, nec	36.2	1.0	22.8	1.0	10.4	1.2	3.0	1.5
Construction work, nsk	**21.5**	**0.6**	NA	-	NA	-	NA	-

Source: *Economic Census of the United States*, 1997. Bold items are headers. (D) stands for data withheld to protect competitive information. (S) indicates instances where data do not meet publications standards.

LOCATION BY STATE AND REGIONAL CONCENTRATION

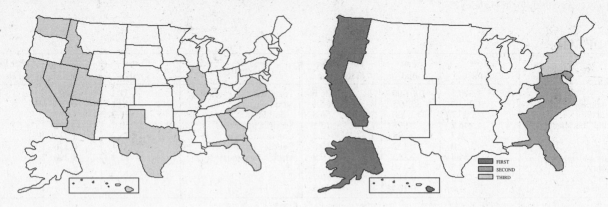

FIRST
SECOND
THIRD

INDUSTRY DATA BY STATE

| State | Estab lish- ments | Employment | | | Compensation | | Production | | | | Capital Exp. ($ mil) |
		Total	Workers	Total as % of US	Payroll per Employee	Wages per Worker	Costs ($ mil)	Value Added ($ mil)	Reve- nues ($ mil)	% of US	
California	1,187	7,575	6,396	19.05	27,324	25,364	249.4	376.0	652.5	18.47	7.4
Florida	795	3,658	2,887	9.20	21,837	19,865	137.3	169.5	342.2	9.69	5.2
Texas	428	2,961	2,376	7.45	25,397	21,770	97.4	132.4	257.5	7.29	3.7
New York	365	2,055	1,597	5.17	33,612	31,076	87.2	132.6	235.6	6.67	2.5
Illinois	189	1,420	1,085	3.57	36,172	34,294	62.5	104.3	172.5	4.88	3.0
Pennsylvania	150	1,158	930	2.91	32,519	29,617	50.1	68.9	125.2	3.54	1.4
North Carolina	244	1,421	1,089	3.57	22,677	20,309	48.1	62.3	120.0	3.40	2.2
New Jersey	253	1,072	786	2.70	31,837	29,274	39.1	61.4	106.8	3.02	1.3
Nevada	114	1,261	1,059	3.17	25,914	23,081	39.3	59.7	103.3	2.92	0.9
Arizona	253	1,588	1,275	3.99	22,037	20,355	34.6	61.0	98.8	2.80	1.6
Georgia	139	1,005	753	2.53	24,728	24,270	39.6	51.2	96.7	2.74	1.4
Virginia	158	1,322	1,065	3.33	24,315	20,878	38.0	53.6	95.0	2.69	1.4
Ohio	152	967	770	2.43	28,512	27,821	31.7	46.7	83.1	2.35	1.0
Washington	135	784	585	1.97	33,180	33,285	28.6	47.9	79.1	2.24	1.3
Michigan	160	707	587	1.78	32,320	29,889	24.5	40.8	67.5	1.91	0.9
Tennessee	125	785	642	1.97	26,531	20,662	25.9	36.4	67.1	1.90	1.3
Utah	149	1,047	871	2.63	21,147	19,509	22.9	39.9	65.3	1.85	0.8
Indiana	89	713	579	1.79	27,321	25,356	21.0	33.0	55.9	1.58	0.7
Missouri	81	604	467	1.52	29,336	26,889	18.3	34.9	55.4	1.57	1.6
Minnesota	106	520	394	1.31	35,369	33,485	21.6	31.5	55.1	1.56	0.5
Maryland	137	819	664	2.06	22,411	21,642	19.4	31.4	53.4	1.51	0.7
Wisconsin	99	424	318	1.07	29,696	29,075	14.5	28.1	43.9	1.24	0.5
Alabama	78	595	495	1.50	25,803	22,616	17.2	25.0	43.9	1.24	0.6
Massachusetts	95	393	294	0.99	32,206	32,949	14.4	25.4	41.6	1.18	0.3
Colorado	130	364	258	0.92	28,657	29,256	14.9	22.6	41.1	1.16	0.3
Oklahoma	82	359	257	0.90	22,582	20,619	17.9	20.3	40.7	1.15	0.4
Louisiana	77	535	436	1.35	21,548	18,835	10.1	21.7	32.0	0.91	0.9
Hawaii	47	315	250	0.79	32,790	28,428	9.5	20.2	31.8	0.90	0.3
Iowa	50	305	244	0.77	23,056	23,520	14.3	15.6	31.6	0.90	0.5
Kentucky	65	332	289	0.84	28,904	26,031	11.9	16.6	28.9	0.82	0.2
South Carolina	113	414	321	1.04	19,577	19,143	10.1	15.8	27.8	0.79	0.4
Connecticut	71	218	166	0.55	32,427	32,301	8.8	12.8	23.8	0.67	0.2
Oregon	90	287	222	0.72	24,756	25,617	8.6	12.7	22.7	0.64	0.4
Idaho	63	256	206	0.64	17,133	17,845	6.5	11.5	18.1	0.51	0.2
Kansas	40	225	192	0.57	25,600	21,188	6.3	10.6	17.8	0.51	0.3
Arkansas	75	319	275	0.80	15,389	15,182	6.2	10.8	17.0	0.48	0.4
New Mexico	72	182	158	0.46	22,291	21,722	5.2	9.0	14.5	0.41	0.1
Nebraska	23	149	115	0.37	27,597	25,478	4.9	6.7	11.7	0.33	0.2
Rhode Island	54	111	91	0.28	23,595	20,319	2.5	5.7	8.7	0.25	0.1
South Dakota	6	69	49	0.17	26,536	26,224	4.9	3.7	8.6	0.24	0.1
Montana	23	118	100	0.30	22,627	20,280	2.9	5.0	8.0	0.23	0.1
Mississippi	16	113	85	0.28	23,027	18,424	2.9	4.1	7.3	0.21	0.1
Alaska	14	30	22	0.08	38,033	42,727	1.9	2.3	4.3	0.12	0.1
Delaware	12	44	34	0.11	34,773	29,882	1.6	2.4	4.3	0.12	0.1
New Hampshire	12	35	26	0.09	33,057	32,462	0.9	2.2	3.4	0.10	-
Wyoming	9	43	29	0.11	19,558	16,897	1.0	1.6	2.7	0.08	-
Maine	6	19	13	0.05	25,316	24,692	0.9	1.2	2.3	0.06	0.2
North Dakota	4	20	15	0.05	11,100	9,733	0.5	0.9	1.4	0.04	-
Vermont	6	16	14	0.04	22,125	23,429	0.4	0.6	1.0	0.03	-
West Virginia	8	26	19	0.07	-	-	(S)	(S)	(S)	-	(S)

Source: Economic Census of the U.S., 1997. Data are sorted by 1997 revenues or establishments. (D) means data suppression to prevent disclosure of company data. (S) means that data did not meet statistical standards for publication. A dash (-) is used when data are unavailable or cannot be calculated. Data followed by an * indicate the midpoint of a range. The ranges are: for 10, 0-19; for 60, 20-99; for 175, 100-249; for 375, 250-499, for 750, 500-999. Higher values are multiples of those shown, e.g., 3,750 is the midpoint of the range 2,500-4,999. Shaded *states* on the state map indicate those states which have proportionately greater representation in the industry than would be indicated by the state's population; the ratio is based on total revenues or number of establishments. Shaded *regions* indicate where the industry is regionally most concentrated.

NAICS 235510 - CARPENTRY CONTRACTORS*

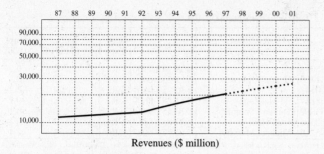

Revenues ($ million)

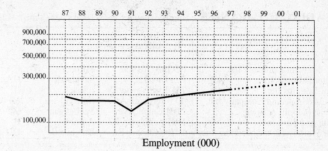

Employment (000)

GENERAL STATISTICS

Years	Estab-lish-ments	Employment		Payroll ($ mil)		Costs ($ mil)		Value Added ($ mil)	Revenues ($ mil)			Capital expend. ($ mil)
		Total	Constr. workers	Total	Worker payroll	Total	Cost of materials		All sources	Construction Total	Net	
1977	24,388	124,646	114,673	1,202.2	1,060.7	1,563.9	1,231.1	2,083.1	3,647.0	3,597.2	3,328.4	-
1982	30,765	132,543	116,973	1,612.0	1,352.2	2,583.5	1,771.6	2,928.7	5,512.2	5,451.2	4,758.5	-
1987	36,009	190,431	164,191	3,272.2	2,609.9	5,374.6	3,997.5	6,077.6	11,452.2	11,243.9	10,038.9	147.9
1988	29,840	171,895	160,247	3,186.9	2,624.4	5,542.9	4,102.3	6,208.3	11,751.7	11,548.6	10,285.6	-
1989	28,175	172,021	156,397	3,301.7	2,639.0	5,716.5	4,209.7	6,341.8	12,059.1	11,861.5	10,538.4	-
1990	29,267	171,123	152,640	3,156.5	2,653.6	5,895.6	4,320.0	6,478.1	12,374.6	12,183.0	10,797.3	-
1991	27,946	133,059	148,973	2,710.4	2,668.3	6,080.3	4,433.2	6,617.4	12,698.3	12,513.2	11,062.6	-
1992	38,210	177,601	145,394	3,488.8	2,683.1	6,270.7	4,549.4	6,759.7	13,030.5	12,852.3	11,334.5	155.1
1993	39,540	188,163	153,437	3,889.1	2,963.7	6,477.9	5,044.8	7,614.0	14,553.0	14,344.0	12,668.8	-
1994	40,869	198,724	161,480	4,289.5	3,244.3	6,685.1	5,540.2	8,468.4	16,075.5	15,835.8	14,003.1	-
1995	42,199	209,286	169,524	4,689.8	3,525.0	6,892.2	6,035.5	9,322.7	17,597.9	17,327.5	15,337.5	-
1996	43,528	219,847	177,567	5,090.2	3,805.6	7,099.4	6,530.9	10,177.1	19,120.4	18,819.3	16,671.8	-
1997	44,858	230,409	185,610	5,490.5	4,086.2	7,306.6	7,026.3	11,031.4	20,642.9	20,311.0	18,006.1	251.2
1998	46,188p	240,971p	193,653p	5,890.8p	4,366.8p	7,513.8p	7,521.7p	11,885.7p	22,165.4p	21,802.7p	19,340.4p	-
1999	47,517p	251,532p	201,696p	6,291.2p	4,647.4p	7,721.0p	8,017.1p	12,740.1p	23,687.9p	23,294.5p	20,674.7p	-
2000	48,847p	262,094p	209,740p	6,691.5p	4,928.1p	7,928.1p	8,512.4p	13,594.4p	25,210.3p	24,786.2p	22,009.1p	-
2001	50,176p	272,655p	217,783p	7,091.9p	5,208.7p	8,135.3p	9,007.8p	14,448.8p	26,732.8p	26,278.0p	23,343.4p	-

Sources: Economic Census of the United States, 1977, 1982, 1987, 1992, and 1997. Data for those years (years are in **bold** type) are from the 5-year censuses of the economy. Other values, unless otherwise noted, are extrapolations. Values footnoted 1 are from the *County Business Patterns* for the years indicated. Values marked with *p* are projections. Data are the most recent available at this level of detail. "Net" under "Construction" is construction revenues net of the costs of subcontracts.

INDICES OF CHANGE

Years	Estab-lish-ments	Employment		Payroll ($ mil)		Costs ($ mil)		Value Added ($ mil)	Revenues ($ mil)			Capital expend. ($ mil)
		Total	Constr. workers	Total	Worker payroll	Total	Cost of materials		All sources	Construction Total	Net	
1977	54.4	54.1	61.8	21.9	26.0	21.4	17.5	18.9	17.7	17.7	18.5	-
1982	68.6	57.5	63.0	29.4	33.1	35.4	25.2	26.5	26.7	26.8	26.4	-
1987	80.3	82.6	88.5	59.6	63.9	73.6	56.9	55.1	55.5	55.4	55.8	58.9
1992	85.2	77.1	78.3	63.5	65.7	85.8	64.7	61.3	63.1	63.3	62.9	61.7
1997	100.0	100.0	100.0	100.0	100.0	100.0	100.0	100.0	100.0	100.0	100.0	100.0

Sources: Same as General Statistics. The values shown reflect change from the base year, 1997. Values above 100 mean greater than 1997, values below 100 mean less than 1997, and a value of 100 in years other than 1997 means same as 1997. Indices are calculated only for Census years. Data are the most recent available at this level of detail.

SELECTED RATIOS

For 1997	Avg. of Sector	Analyzed Industry	Index	For 1997	Avg. of Sector	Analyzed Industry	Index
Employees per establishment	8.6	5.1	60	Value added per establishment	584,730	245,918	42
Construction workers per establishment	6.6	4.1	63	Value added per employee	67,759	47,877	71
Payroll per establishment	265,343	122,397	46	Value added per construction worker	88,592	59,433	67
Payroll per employee	30,748	23,829	77	Revenues per establishment	1,307,915	460,183	35
Payroll per construction worker	27,622	22,015	80	Revenues per employee	151,563	89,592	59
Costs per establishment	367,737	162,883	44	Revenues per construction worker	198,161	111,217	56
Costs per employee	42,614	31,711	74	CR as % of total revenues	98.48	98.39	100
Costs per construction worker	55,716	39,365	71	Net CR as % of CR	72.40	88.65	122
Materials as % of costs	95.75	96.16	100	Investment per establishment	22,948	5,600	24
Costs as % of revenues	28.12	35.40	126	Investment per employee	2,659	1,090	41
Costs as % of construction revenues	28.55	35.97	126	Investment per construction worker	3,477	1,353	39

Sources: Same as General Statistics. The 'Average of Sector' column represents the average for all industries in this sector. The Index shows the relationship between the Average and the Analyzed Industry. For example, 100 means that they are equal; 500 that the Analyzed Industry is five times the average; 50 means that the Analyzed Industry is half the national average. 'na' is used to show that data are 'not available'. CR stands for "construction revenues" and "Net CR" is construction revenues net of subcontract expenses.

*Equivalent to SIC 1751.

LEADING COMPANIES   Number shown: **7**   Total sales ($ mil): **125**   Total employment (000): **0.9**

Company Name	Address				CEO Name	Phone	Co. Type	Sales ($ mil)	Empl. (000)
B.T. Mancini Company Inc.	PO Box 361930	Milpitas	CA	95036		408-942-7900	R	42*	0.2
Center Brothers Inc.	P O Box 22278	Savannah	GA	31403	Henry Tuton	912-232-6491	R	23*	0.3
Door Systems Inc.	751 Expressway Dr	Itasca	IL	60143		630-250-0101	R	21*	0.2
B.J. McGlone and Company Inc.	40 Brunswick Ave	Edison	NJ	08817	BJ McGlone	732-287-8600	R	21*	0.2
Joseph Schmitt & Sons	2104 Union Ave	Sheboygan	WI	53082	Steven J Schmitt	920-457-9474	R	14*	0.1
J Mar and Sons Inc.	1941 Selmarten Rd	Aurora	IL	60505	Joe Peters	630-851-0814	R	3	<0.1
Don Murphy Door Specialties Inc.	10390 Chester Rd	Cincinnati	OH	45215	Michael Murphy	513-771-6087	R	1*	<0.1

Source: Ward's Business Directory of U.S. Private and Public Companies, Volumes 1 and 2, 2000. The company type code used is as follows: P - Public, R - Private, S - Subsidiary, D - Division, J - Joint Venture, A - Affiliate, G - Group, N - Company type not reported. Sales are in millions of dollars, employees are in thousands. An asterisk (*) indicates an estimated sales volume. The symbol < stands for 'less than'. Company names and addresses are truncated, in some cases, to fit into the available space.

COST DETAILS

Item	Cost ($ mil)	% of total	Per $1,000 of Revenue	Item	Cost ($ mil)	% of total	Per $1,000 of Revenue
All costs	9,611.5	100.000	465.6	Total Rentals	265.9	2.766	12.9
Cost of supplies	7,026.3	73.103	340.4	Equipment	135.1	1.405	6.5
Subcontracts	2,304.9	23.981	111.7	Buildings	130.8	1.361	6.3
Power, fuel, lubricants	280.3	2.916	13.6	Services purchased	325.7	3.388	15.8
Electricity	65.3	0.680	3.2	Communications	152.6	1.587	7.4
Natural gas	9.9	0.102	0.5	Building repairs	18.5	0.192	0.9
Gasoline and diesel	196.3	2.042	9.5	Machinery repairs	154.6	1.608	7.5
Highway	167.5	1.743	8.1				
Offroad	28.8	0.299	1.4				
Other power	8.8	0.092	0.4				

Source: Economic Census of the United States, 1997. Revenues referred to are total industry revenues for the current NAICS industry.

CONSTRUCTION PRODUCT DETAILS

Construction type	Total		New construction		Additions, alterations, reconstruction		Maintenance and repair	
	Value	%	Value	%	Value	%	Value	%
Total	**20,311.0**	**100.0**	**12,638.9**	**100.0**	**5,397.7**	**100.0**	**1,912.0**	**100.0**
Building construction, total	**19,781.4**	**97.4**	**12,530.1**	**99.1**	**5,360.1**	**99.3**	**1,891.1**	**98.9**
Single-family houses, detached	10,599.8	52.2	7,120.7	56.3	2,547.7	47.2	931.4	48.7
Single-family houses, attached	1,800.9	8.9	1,221.5	9.7	402.9	7.5	176.5	9.2
Apartment buildings, condos and cooperatives	1,638.1	8.1	1,215.2	9.6	296.8	5.5	126.1	6.6
Manufacturing and light industrial buildings	520.1	2.6	246.6	2.0	144.2	2.7	129.3	6.8
Manufacturing and light industrial warehouses	290.8	1.4	144.5	1.1	90.1	1.7	56.2	2.9
Hotels and motels	274.9	1.4	188.2	1.5	65.2	1.2	21.5	1.1
Office buildings	1,288.4	6.3	550.7	4.4	631.9	11.7	105.8	5.5
All other commercial buildings, nec	1,328.5	6.5	741.2	5.9	463.8	8.6	123.5	6.5
Commercial warehouses	400.0	2.0	244.3	1.9	88.5	1.6	67.3	3.5
Educational buildings	574.5	2.8	260.1	2.1	289.7	5.4	24.7	1.3
Health care and institutional buildings	387.8	1.9	204.4	1.6	166.7	3.1	16.7	0.9
Farm buildings, nonresidential	130.2	0.6	99.5	0.8	16.7	0.3	13.9	0.7
Other building construction	547.4	2.7	293.3	2.3	156.0	2.9	98.1	5.1
Nonbuilding construction, total	**167.2**	**0.8**	**108.8**	**0.9**	**37.5**	**0.7**	**20.9**	**1.1**
Other nonbuilding construction, nec	167.2	0.8	108.8	0.9	37.5	0.7	20.9	1.1
Construction work, nsk	**362.5**	**1.8**	NA	-	NA	-	NA	-

Source: Economic Census of the United States, 1997. Bold items are headers. (D) stands for data withheld to protect competitive information. (S) indicates instances where data do not meet publications standards.

LOCATION BY STATE AND REGIONAL CONCENTRATION

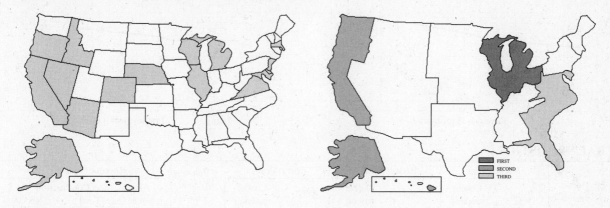

FIRST
SECOND
THIRD

INDUSTRY DATA BY STATE

State	Estab lish- ments	Employment			Compensation		Production				Capital Exp. ($ mil)
		Total	Workers	Total as % of US	Payroll per Employee	Wages per Worker	Costs ($ mil)	Value Added ($ mil)	Reve- nues ($ mil)	% of US	
California	2,733	33,707	28,925	14.63	25,880	23,490	1,276.2	1,490.4	2,944.9	14.27	30.2
Illinois	2,335	14,976	12,169	6.50	31,617	30,195	523.7	847.6	1,544.3	7.48	17.4
New York	3,161	13,166	10,043	5.71	27,147	24,724	434.1	747.9	1,367.9	6.63	15.1
Texas	1,761	9,791	7,907	4.25	20,655	17,641	278.0	595.0	1,024.3	4.96	12.1
Florida	2,287	10,656	8,198	4.62	21,367	18,741	353.2	503.7	999.7	4.84	10.4
Arizona	609	10,880	9,618	4.72	23,779	21,506	545.8	429.6	997.5	4.83	10.0
Michigan	2,024	10,448	8,371	4.53	25,289	24,155	270.3	497.3	861.0	4.17	10.0
Pennsylvania	1,870	7,886	5,958	3.42	22,306	20,999	280.9	396.2	797.6	3.86	9.9
Ohio	1,878	9,250	7,148	4.01	22,224	21,252	256.2	428.7	797.2	3.86	9.3
New Jersey	1,728	6,598	5,019	2.86	26,391	23,689	275.8	358.5	737.7	3.57	7.3
Nevada	259	5,982	5,247	2.60	27,636	24,573	276.2	295.4	591.7	2.87	4.5
Virginia	1,265	6,263	4,823	2.72	23,796	21,982	191.5	304.0	569.5	2.76	10.5
Colorado	1,426	5,278	3,902	2.29	21,242	20,119	178.8	248.5	513.3	2.49	7.3
Massachusetts	1,061	4,244	3,309	1.84	26,486	25,095	159.8	254.2	497.5	2.41	7.9
North Carolina	1,699	7,067	5,339	3.07	20,135	18,727	144.0	279.5	485.0	2.35	7.0
Maryland	971	5,239	4,235	2.27	25,016	21,983	133.8	248.2	459.3	2.23	6.7
Wisconsin	1,360	5,157	3,997	2.24	23,345	22,916	148.3	253.5	451.8	2.19	7.4
Washington	1,374	4,865	3,951	2.11	23,029	21,124	120.2	242.5	406.1	1.97	5.0
Indiana	1,239	5,343	3,862	2.32	21,404	20,125	153.7	208.2	399.8	1.94	5.8
Missouri	1,148	5,455	4,569	2.37	22,595	21,496	89.3	239.1	360.0	1.74	4.9
Minnesota	1,080	3,867	3,104	1.68	26,473	25,556	104.9	200.7	336.0	1.63	7.2
Georgia	924	3,927	3,073	1.70	19,815	17,393	(S)	164.1	314.0	1.52	3.4
Oregon	775	3,467	2,930	1.50	21,528	19,975	62.9	157.8	251.8	1.22	3.4
Tennessee	639	3,134	2,434	1.36	16,929	15,383	80.3	117.7	234.4	1.14	2.4
Connecticut	635	2,103	1,556	0.91	28,562	27,868	72.5	115.3	220.7	1.07	2.3
Iowa	726	2,681	2,241	1.16	18,609	18,350	71.7	108.9	196.7	0.95	4.0
South Carolina	744	2,799	2,283	1.21	19,987	19,457	51.4	111.3	182.6	0.88	3.7
Louisiana	536	1,947	1,673	0.85	16,414	14,527	68.4	73.2	169.9	0.82	2.2
Kentucky	636	2,254	1,750	0.98	20,673	18,424	50.1	95.8	162.2	0.79	1.6
Kansas	685	2,448	2,127	1.06	19,659	17,795	48.7	98.9	161.7	0.78	1.3
Nebraska	479	2,067	1,504	0.90	19,093	17,615	40.9	91.3	155.7	0.75	2.2
Alabama	493	1,719	1,361	0.75	18,269	17,536	53.4	78.5	141.8	0.69	1.3
Utah	465	1,471	1,203	0.64	20,537	19,803	39.9	57.4	105.1	0.51	2.0
Idaho	428	1,733	1,364	0.75	17,696	17,732	(S)	64.0	104.9	0.51	2.0
Maine	438	988	779	0.43	20,635	21,146	31.1	58.3	98.9	0.48	1.4
Rhode Island	266	886	686	0.38	22,085	20,031	37.4	43.0	90.3	0.44	1.4
New Mexico	192	1,161	966	0.50	16,441	14,913	38.5	32.6	81.5	0.39	0.9
Mississippi	234	708	633	0.31	20,753	18,130	(D)	46.7	72.7	0.35	1.0
Delaware	189	1,017	863	0.44	23,220	22,019	21.6	38.2	70.2	0.34	0.7
Arkansas	250	831	652	0.36	17,970	16,492	22.4	31.2	57.0	0.28	1.1
Alaska	107	582	485	0.25	26,017	23,118	12.5	34.7	56.5	0.27	0.1
West Virginia	214	757	678	0.33	16,629	15,286	15.9	31.4	50.8	0.25	0.6
North Dakota	182	555	499	0.24	18,258	16,303	14.1	31.5	49.7	0.24	0.2
South Dakota	197	506	404	0.22	21,180	18,874	18.6	26.3	48.2	0.23	0.6
Vermont	182	430	395	0.19	16,402	15,142	7.5	15.4	26.5	0.13	0.5
Oklahoma	326	1,593	1,322	0.69	21,279	18,466	(D)	68.9	(D)	-	0.9
New Hampshire	294	926	762	0.40	26,620	24,853	(D)	68.4	(D)	-	1.1
Montana	182	700	600	0.30	16,356	16,432	(D)	26.1	(D)	-	1.5
Wyoming	103	277	240	0.12	13,495	-	(D)	8.7	(D)	-	(S)
Hawaii	59	548	394	0.24	37,770	38,741	(D)	58.4	(D)	-	(D)
D.C.	9	75	57	0.03	26,133	-	(D)	8.8	(D)	-	(D)

Source: Economic Census of the U.S., 1997. Data are sorted by 1997 revenues or establishments. (D) means data suppression to prevent disclosure of company data. (S) means that data did not meet statistical standards for publication. A dash (-) is used when data are unavailable or cannot be calculated. Data followed by an * indicate the midpoint of a range. The ranges are: for 10, 0-19; for 60, 20-99, for 175, 100-249, for 375, 250-499, for 750, 500-999. Higher values are multiples of those shown, e.g., 3,750 is the midpoint of the range 2,500-4,999. Shaded *states* on the state map indicate those states which have proportionately greater representation in the industry than would be indicated by the state's population; the ratio is based on total revenues or number of establishments. Shaded *regions* indicate where the industry is regionally most concentrated.

NAICS 235520 - FLOOR LAYING AND OTHER FLOOR CONTRACTORS*

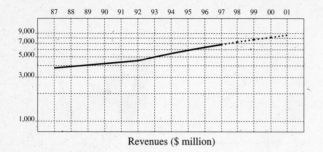

Revenues ($ million)

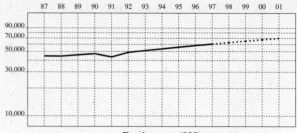

Employment (000)

GENERAL STATISTICS

Years	Estab-lish-ments	Employment		Payroll ($ mil)		Costs ($ mil)		Value Added ($ mil)	Revenues ($ mil)			Capital expend. ($ mil)
		Total	Constr. workers	Total	Worker payroll	Total	Cost of materials		All sources	Construction Total	Net	
1977	8,969	40,990	33,724	453.1	352.2	850.2	749.8	823.7	1,673.9	1,616.9	1,547.9	-
1982	6,673	32,349	25,410	496.8	364.2	940.8	806.9	913.3	1,854.1	1,793.8	1,697.6	-
1987	8,174	44,579	34,666	906.2	645.5	1,891.7	1,548.3	1,880.3	3,772.0	3,651.4	3,371.2	41.4
1988	7,440	44,465	35,013	956.6	660.4	1,979.8	1,614.7	1,934.2	3,914.6	3,794.9	3,494.1	-
1989	7,439	45,882	35,363	1,003.6	675.6	2,072.0	1,683.8	1,989.7	4,062.6	3,944.0	3,621.6	-
1990	8,172	47,256	35,716	1,035.8	691.3	2,168.5	1,755.9	2,046.7	4,216.2	4,099.0	3,753.7	-
1991	8,286	43,581	36,073	961.0	707.2	2,269.6	1,831.2	2,105.4	4,375.6	4,260.1	3,890.6	-
1992	10,196	48,948	36,434	1,065.2	723.6	2,375.3	1,909.6	2,165.8	4,541.1	4,427.5	4,032.5	46.2
1993	10,572	51,265	37,680	1,186.6	784.9	2,445.7	2,053.5	2,423.7	4,996.0	4,877.1	4,434.5	-
1994	10,949	53,582	38,926	1,308.0	846.1	2,516.1	2,197.5	2,681.6	5,450.9	5,326.8	4,836.5	-
1995	11,325	55,899	40,171	1,429.5	907.4	2,586.4	2,341.4	2,939.4	5,905.7	5,776.4	5,238.6	-
1996	11,702	58,216	41,417	1,550.9	968.6	2,656.8	2,485.4	3,197.3	6,360.6	6,226.1	5,640.6	-
1997	12,078	60,533	42,663	1,672.3	1,029.9	2,727.2	2,629.3	3,455.2	6,815.5	6,675.7	6,042.6	75.9
1998	12,454p	62,850p	43,909p	1,793.7p	1,091.2p	2,797.6p	2,773.2p	3,713.1p	7,270.4p	7,125.3p	6,444.6p	-
1999	12,831p	65,167p	45,155p	1,915.1p	1,152.4p	2,868.0p	2,917.2p	3,971.0p	7,725.3p	7,575.0p	6,846.6p	-
2000	13,207p	67,484p	46,400p	2,036.6p	1,213.7p	2,938.3p	3,061.1p	4,228.8p	8,180.1p	8,024.6p	7,248.7p	-
2001	13,584p	69,801p	47,646p	2,158.0p	1,274.9p	3,008.7p	3,205.1p	4,486.7p	8,635.0p	8,474.3p	7,650.7p	-

Sources: Economic Census of the United States, 1977, 1982, 1987, 1992, and 1997. Data for those years (years are in **bold** type) are from the 5-year censuses of the economy. Other values, unless otherwise noted, are extrapolations. Values footnoted 1 are from the *County Business Patterns* for the years indicated. Values marked with *p* are projections. Data are the most recent available at this level of detail. "Net" under "Construction" is construction revenues net of the costs of subcontracts.

INDICES OF CHANGE

Years	Estab-lish-ments	Employment		Payroll ($ mil)		Costs ($ mil)		Value Added ($ mil)	Revenues ($ mil)			Capital expend. ($ mil)
		Total	Constr. workers	Total	Worker payroll	Total	Cost of materials		All sources	Construction Total	Net	
1977	74.3	67.7	79.0	27.1	34.2	31.2	28.5	23.8	24.6	24.2	25.6	-
1982	55.2	53.4	59.6	29.7	35.4	34.5	30.7	26.4	27.2	26.9	28.1	54.5
1987	67.7	73.6	81.3	54.2	62.7	69.4	58.9	54.4	55.3	54.7	55.8	54.5
1992	84.4	80.9	85.4	63.7	70.3	87.1	72.6	62.7	66.6	66.3	66.7	60.9
1997	100.0	100.0	100.0	100.0	100.0	100.0	100.0	100.0	100.0	100.0	100.0	100.0

Sources: Same as General Statistics. The values shown reflect change from the base year, 1997. Values above 100 mean greater than 1997, values below 100 mean less than 1997, and a value of 100 in years other than 1997 means same as 1997. Indices are calculated only for Census years. Data are the most recent available at this level of detail.

SELECTED RATIOS

For 1997	Avg. of Sector	Analyzed Industry	Index	For 1997	Avg. of Sector	Analyzed Industry	Index
Employees per establishment	8.6	5.0	58	Value added per establishment	584,730	286,074	49
Construction workers per establishment	6.6	3.5	54	Value added per employee	67,759	57,080	84
Payroll per establishment	265,343	138,458	52	Value added per construction worker	88,592	80,988	91
Payroll per employee	30,748	27,626	90	Revenues per establishment	1,307,915	564,290	43
Payroll per construction worker	27,622	24,140	87	Revenues per employee	151,563	112,591	74
Costs per establishment	367,737	225,799	61	Revenues per construction worker	198,161	159,752	81
Costs per employee	42,614	45,053	106	CR as % of total revenues	98.48	97.95	99
Costs per construction worker	55,716	63,924	115	Net CR as % of CR	72.40	90.52	125
Materials as % of costs	95.75	96.41	101	Investment per establishment	22,948	6,284	27
Costs as % of revenues	28.12	40.01	142	Investment per employee	2,659	1,254	47
Costs as % of construction revenues	28.55	40.85	143	Investment per construction worker	3,477	1,779	51

Sources: Same as General Statistics. The 'Average of Sector' column represents the average for all industries in this sector. The Index shows the relationship between the Average and the Analyzed Industry. For example, 100 means that they are equal; 500 that the Analyzed Industry is five times the average; 50 means that the Analyzed Industry is half the national average. 'na' is used to show that data are 'not available'. CR stands for "construction revenues" and "Net CR" is construction revenues net of subcontract expenses.

*Equivalent to SIC 1752.

LEADING COMPANIES   Number shown: **10**   Total sales ($ mil): **351**   Total employment (000): **1.6**

Company Name	Address				CEO Name	Phone	Co. Type	Sales ($ mil)	Empl. (000)
Stonhard Inc.	PO Box 308	Maple Shade	NJ	08052	Jeffrey Stork	609-779-7500	S	180	0.8
B.T. Mancini Company Inc.	PO Box 361930	Milpitas	CA	95036		408-942-7900	R	42*	0.2
Acmat Corp.	P O Box 2350	New Britain	CT	06050	Henry W Nozko Sr	860-229-9000	P	29	<0.1
Center Brothers Inc.	P O Box 22278	Savannah	GA	31403	Henry Tuton	912-232-6491	R	23*	0.3
Continental Flooring Co.	5111 N Scottsdale	Scottsdale	AZ	85250	James GF Coleman	602-949-8509	R	22	<0.1
Donald E. McNabb Co.	PO Box 448	Milford	MI	48381	Doug McNabb	248-437-8146	R	17*	0.1
Kalman Floor Co.	1202 Bergen	Evergreen	CO	80439	Carl N Ytterberg	303-674-2290	R	16*	<0.1
Hagopian Fire & Flood Services	1400 W 8 Mile Rd	Oak Park	MI	48237	Edmond Hagopian	248-399-2323	D	10*	0.1
Pioneer Randustrial Corp.	4529 Ind Pkwy	Cleveland	OH	44135	James Schattinger	216-671-5500	S	9*	0.1
Kaswell and Company Inc.	PO Box 549	Framingham	MA	01701	Norman Kaswell	508-879-1120	R	3	<0.1

Source: Ward's Business Directory of U.S. Private and Public Companies, Volumes 1 and 2, 2000. The company type code used is as follows: P - Public, R - Private, S - Subsidiary, D - Division, J - Joint Venture, A - Affiliate, G - Group, N - Company type not reported. Sales are in millions of dollars, employees are in thousands. An asterisk (*) indicates an estimated sales volume. The symbol < stands for 'less than'. Company names and addresses are truncated, in some cases, to fit into the available space.

COST DETAILS

Item	Cost ($ mil)	% of total	Per $1,000 of Revenue	Item	Cost ($ mil)	% of total	Per $1,000 of Revenue
All costs	3,360.4	100.000	493.0	Total Rentals	95.0	2.828	13.9
Cost of supplies	2,629.3	78.245	385.8	Equipment	24.0	0.714	3.5
Subcontracts	633.1	18.841	92.9	Buildings	71.0	2.113	10.4
Power, fuel, lubricants	97.9	2.915	14.4	Services purchased	97.7	2.907	14.3
Electricity	33.0	0.983	4.8	Communications	51.6	1.534	7.6
Natural gas	5.2	0.154	0.8	Building repairs	6.9	0.206	1.0
Gasoline and diesel	57.7	1.718	8.5	Machinery repairs	39.2	1.166	5.8
Highway	53.0	1.577	7.8				
Offroad	4.7	0.141	0.7				
Other power	2.0	0.060	0.3				

Source: Economic Census of the United States, 1997. Revenues referred to are total industry revenues for the current NAICS industry.

CONSTRUCTION PRODUCT DETAILS

Construction type	Value of construction work ($ mil and %)							
	Total		New construction		Additions, alterations, reconstruction		Maintenance and repair	
	Value	%	Value	%	Value	%	Value	%
Total	**6,675.7**	**100.0**	**3,290.9**	**100.0**	**2,208.2**	**100.0**	**965.5**	**100.0**
Building construction, total	**6,393.1**	**95.8**	**3,249.5**	**98.7**	**2,190.3**	**99.2**	**953.2**	**98.7**
Single-family houses, detached	2,424.0	36.3	1,497.5	45.5	599.8	27.2	326.7	33.8
Single-family houses, attached	390.7	5.9	228.4	6.9	111.3	5.0	51.1	5.3
Apartment buildings, condos and cooperatives	448.9	6.7	175.1	5.3	146.2	6.6	127.6	13.2
Manufacturing and light industrial buildings	225.0	3.4	76.6	2.3	81.3	3.7	67.0	6.9
Manufacturing and light industrial warehouses	67.4	1.0	32.9	1.0	24.1	1.1	10.4	1.1
Hotels and motels	149.8	2.2	67.5	2.1	60.8	2.8	21.5	2.2
Office buildings	1,059.9	15.9	410.1	12.5	532.1	24.1	117.7	12.2
All other commercial buildings, nec	549.8	8.2	297.7	9.0	185.0	8.4	67.2	7.0
Commercial warehouses	50.0	0.7	24.8	0.8	13.8	0.6	11.4	1.2
Religious buildings	96.3	1.4	34.0	1.0	47.9	2.2	14.3	1.5
Educational buildings	438.9	6.6	181.2	5.5	188.0	8.5	69.8	7.2
Health care and institutional buildings	313.5	4.7	112.6	3.4	153.5	7.0	47.4	4.9
Amusement, social, and recreational buildings	89.7	1.3	57.4	1.7	18.8	0.8	13.6	1.4
Other building construction	89.1	1.3	53.6	1.6	27.9	1.3	7.6	0.8
Nonbuilding construction, total	**71.5**	**1.1**	**41.3**	**1.3**	**17.9**	**0.8**	**12.3**	**1.3**
Other nonbuilding construction, nec	71.5	1.1	41.3	1.3	17.9	0.8	12.3	1.3
Construction work, nsk	**211.2**	**3.2**	**NA**	**-**	**NA**	**-**	**NA**	**-**

Source: Economic Census of the United States, 1997. Bold items are headers. (D) stands for data withheld to protect competitive information. (S) indicates instances where data do not meet publications standards.

LOCATION BY STATE AND REGIONAL CONCENTRATION

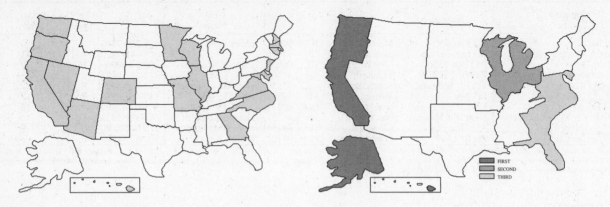

FIRST
SECOND
THIRD

INDUSTRY DATA BY STATE

State	Estab lish- ments	Employment			Compensation		Production				Capital Exp. ($ mil)
		Total	Workers	Total as % of US	Payroll per Employee	Wages per Worker	Costs ($ mil)	Value Added ($ mil)	Reve- nues ($ mil)	% of US	
California	1,519	9,466	6,929	15.64	28,741	24,875	441.0	540.2	1,090.0	15.99	12.6
New York	720	3,465	2,300	5.72	28,049	22,208	202.1	195.4	432.4	6.34	4.1
Illinois	576	3,430	2,460	5.67	31,732	30,525	143.0	233.3	398.3	5.84	6.0
Texas	442	2,764	1,719	4.57	27,301	22,064	143.9	178.2	354.6	5.20	2.6
Maryland	301	2,081	1,344	3.44	27,994	21,818	118.6	127.9	288.0	4.23	4.2
Pennsylvania	491	2,025	1,358	3.35	29,007	27,455	105.4	128.2	255.3	3.75	3.0
Ohio	372	2,440	1,785	4.03	28,360	24,658	106.6	122.8	254.0	3.73	2.8
New Jersey	424	2,009	1,283	3.32	32,586	28,903	95.7	138.2	253.2	3.71	2.0
Florida	509	1,969	1,150	3.25	26,547	24,307	101.6	108.6	243.0	3.57	1.8
Virginia	390	2,057	1,358	3.40	26,910	21,493	95.3	117.1	239.6	3.52	2.8
Colorado	281	2,060	1,417	3.40	29,944	28,465	99.0	108.7	225.3	3.31	2.1
Michigan	413	1,669	1,107	2.76	29,316	25,334	83.5	104.0	204.0	2.99	2.2
North Carolina	444	1,943	1,552	3.21	24,335	21,890	82.4	89.0	190.7	2.80	2.3
Georgia	284	1,258	818	2.08	27,727	22,079	80.8	81.0	189.0	2.77	2.0
Massachusetts	251	1,250	800	2.06	32,253	26,595	57.5	106.4	186.4	2.73	2.2
Washington	486	1,698	1,222	2.81	25,576	24,020	63.0	101.6	182.5	2.68	1.8
Missouri	242	1,881	1,405	3.11	28,028	23,293	66.8	104.4	178.3	2.62	1.9
Arizona	236	1,542	1,115	2.55	27,110	21,752	67.1	66.4	159.4	2.34	(S)
Wisconsin	371	1,446	1,145	2.39	27,982	24,786	50.6	85.9	142.3	2.09	2.3
Indiana	248	1,086	663	1.79	29,470	24,548	55.9	67.7	137.4	2.02	1.4
Minnesota	263	1,355	1,016	2.24	28,723	26,466	44.3	78.0	126.5	1.86	2.8
Connecticut	166	910	668	1.50	29,138	28,105	48.1	58.2	119.5	1.75	(S)
Oregon	344	1,169	890	1.93	23,065	21,473	31.9	54.0	90.3	1.33	0.9
Alabama	160	687	485	1.13	26,460	21,868	33.6	49.1	86.7	1.27	0.2
Nevada	82	1,147	978	1.89	23,605	20,688	27.1	54.7	85.5	1.25	0.7
Louisiana	128	731	502	1.21	21,595	18,809	26.6	32.2	64.4	0.95	0.7
Kansas	149	723	501	1.19	24,959	23,413	26.9	30.8	64.2	0.94	0.7
Tennessee	165	680	501	1.12	23,903	22,018	20.3	36.1	62.3	0.91	0.7
Kentucky	157	647	493	1.07	21,600	20,552	21.3	28.2	54.4	0.80	0.6
South Carolina	227	579	459	0.96	17,933	18,183	18.6	26.4	52.4	0.77	0.8
Iowa	133	505	382	0.83	23,485	18,785	19.5	20.9	42.6	0.62	0.6
Nebraska	116	360	232	0.59	21,561	21,457	21.6	14.3	40.1	0.59	0.4
New Hampshire	36	187	127	0.31	29,791	24,071	10.8	16.3	32.1	0.47	0.1
Hawaii	62	349	246	0.58	31,782	29,423	11.5	18.1	31.8	0.47	0.8
Oklahoma	83	336	246	0.56	20,679	18,610	11.1	10.8	24.5	0.36	0.1
New Mexico	50	143	117	0.24	25,420	21,265	9.0	8.9	20.7	0.30	(S)
Arkansas	57	220	155	0.36	23,409	20,052	6.7	12.3	19.8	0.29	0.7
Alaska	30	73	41	0.12	32,356	20,244	4.4	7.0	12.2	0.18	0.1
Vermont	33	74	60	0.12	16,095	17,900	4.3	3.1	7.7	0.11	0.2
North Dakota	34	71	56	0.12	19,042	-	1.8	3.6	5.6	0.08	-
Montana	42	55	40	0.09	13,527	12,625	2.0	2.6	4.6	0.07	-
Wyoming	33	43	39	0.07	19,279	-	0.8	1.8	2.7	0.04	(D)
Utah	99	311	228	0.51	23,264	23,689	(D)	13.0	(D)	-	0.5
Idaho	88	319	237	0.53	20,103	16,481	(D)	13.2	(D)	-	0.1
Mississippi	81	243	190	0.40	31,313	35,142	(D)	7.3	(D)	-	0.1
Maine	74	309	232	0.51	25,476	21,647	(D)	15.3	(D)	-	0.2
West Virginia	67	210	180	0.35	15,667	14,539	(D)	6.0	(D)	-	0.1
Delaware	55	275	225	0.45	22,004	20,431	(D)	13.4	(D)	-	(S)
Rhode Island	48	128	98	0.21	22,578	22,816	(D)	8.1	(D)	-	0.1
D.C.	8	97	71	0.16	29,845	22,549	(D)	4.7	(D)	-	(D)
South Dakota	8	56	41	0.09	19,946	22,610	(D)	2.0	(D)	-	(S)

Source: Economic Census of the U.S., 1997. Data are sorted by 1997 revenues or establishments. (D) means data suppression to prevent disclosure of company data. (S) means that data did not meet statistical standards for publication. A dash (-) is used when data are unavailable or cannot be calculated. Data followed by an * indicate the midpoint of a range. The ranges are: for 10, 0-19; for 60, 20-99, for 175, 100-249, for 375, 250-499, for 750, 500-999. Higher values are multiples of those shown, e.g., 3,750 is the midpoint of the range 2,500-4,999. Shaded *states* on the state map indicate those states which have proportionately greater representation in the industry than would be indicated by the state's population; the ratio is based on total revenues or number of establishments. Shaded *regions* indicate where the industry is regionally most concentrated.

NAICS 235610 - ROOFING, SIDING, AND SHEET METAL CONTRACTORS*

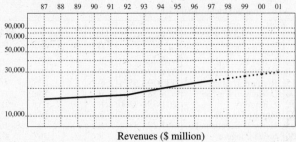

Revenues ($ million)

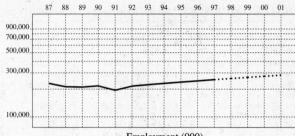

Employment (000)

GENERAL STATISTICS

| Years | Estab- lish- ments | Employment | | Payroll ($ mil) | | Costs ($ mil) | | Value Added ($ mil) | Revenues ($ mil) | | | Capital expend. ($ mil) |
		Total	Constr. workers	Total	Worker payroll	Total	Cost of materials		All sources	Construction Total	Net	
1977	20,577	171,931	146,307	1,967.8	1,555.3	2,900.3	2,535.6	3,420.4	6,320.7	6,200.4	5,938.8	-
1982	21,152	191,489	158,901	3,034.8	2,320.7	4,573.7	3,848.6	5,459.9	10,033.5	9,836.5	9,315.2	-
1987	25,673	231,137	186,916	4,313.7	3,111.0	6,734.5	5,637.2	8,524.4	15,258.9	15,027.8	14,182.8	249.2
1988	22,598	212,204	183,136	4,410.5	3,134.4	6,982.4	5,812.7	8,599.4	15,587.6	15,364.4	14,453.7	-
1989	22,978	210,564	179,432	4,496.6	3,158.0	7,239.4	5,993.7	8,675.0	15,923.3	15,708.6	14,729.7	-
1990	23,200	216,752	175,803	4,631.7	3,181.8	7,505.9	6,180.3	8,751.3	16,266.3	16,060.4	15,011.0	-
1991	23,564	194,514	172,248	4,315.7	3,205.8	7,782.2	6,372.8	8,828.3	16,616.7	16,420.2	15,297.7	-
1992	27,569	215,545	168,764	4,622.5	3,230.0	8,068.6	6,571.2	8,906.0	16,974.6	16,788.0	15,589.8	232.7
1993	28,167	223,099	174,470	4,997.0	3,458.0	8,243.2	6,974.8	9,769.0	18,410.3	18,223.8	16,867.0	-
1994	28,764	230,653	180,176	5,371.5	3,685.9	8,417.8	7,378.4	10,631.9	19,846.1	19,659.6	18,144.3	-
1995	29,362	238,207	185,882	5,745.9	3,913.9	8,592.3	7,781.9	11,494.9	21,281.8	21,095.5	19,421.5	-
1996	29,959	245,761	191,588	6,120.4	4,141.8	8,766.9	8,185.5	12,357.8	22,717.6	22,531.3	20,698.8	-
1997	30,557	253,315	197,294	6,494.9	4,369.8	8,941.5	8,589.1	13,220.8	24,153.3	23,967.1	21,976.0	417.1
1998	31,155p	260,869p	203,000p	6,869.4p	4,597.8p	9,116.1p	8,992.7p	14,083.8p	25,589.0p	25,402.9p	23,253.2p	-
1999	31,752p	268,423p	208,706p	7,243.9p	4,825.7p	9,290.7p	9,396.3p	14,946.7p	27,024.8p	26,838.7p	24,530.5p	-
2000	32,350p	275,977p	214,412p	7,618.3p	5,053.7p	9,465.2p	9,799.8p	15,809.7p	28,460.5p	28,274.6p	25,807.7p	-
2001	32,947p	283,531p	220,118p	7,992.8p	5,281.6p	9,639.8p	10,203.4p	16,672.6p	29,896.3p	29,710.4p	27,085.0p	-

Sources: Economic Census of the United States, 1977, 1982, 1987, 1992, and 1997. Data for those years (years are in **bold** type) are from the 5-year censuses of the economy. Other values, unless otherwise noted, are extrapolations. Values footnoted 1 are from the *County Business Patterns* for the years indicated. Values marked with *p* are projections. Data are the most recent available at this level of detail. "Net" under "Construction" is construction revenues net of the costs of subcontracts.

INDICES OF CHANGE

| Years | Estab- lish- ments | Employment | | Payroll ($ mil) | | Costs ($ mil) | | Value Added ($ mil) | Revenues ($ mil) | | | Capital expend. ($ mil) |
		Total	Constr. workers	Total	Worker payroll	Total	Cost of materials		All sources	Construction Total	Net	
1977	67.3	67.9	74.2	30.3	35.6	32.4	29.5	25.9	26.2	25.9	27.0	-
1982	69.2	75.6	80.5	46.7	53.1	51.2	44.8	41.3	41.5	41.0	42.4	59.7
1987	84.0	91.2	94.7	66.4	71.2	75.3	65.6	64.5	63.2	62.7	64.5	59.7
1992	90.2	85.1	85.5	71.2	73.9	90.2	76.5	67.4	70.3	70.0	70.9	55.8
1997	100.0	100.0	100.0	100.0	100.0	100.0	100.0	100.0	100.0	100.0	100.0	100.0

Sources: Same as General Statistics. The values shown reflect change from the base year, 1997. Values above 100 mean greater than 1997, values below 100 mean less than 1997, and a value of 100 in years other than 1997 means same as 1997. Indices are calculated only for Census years. Data are the most recent available at this level of detail.

SELECTED RATIOS

For 1997	Avg. of Sector	Analyzed Industry	Index	For 1997	Avg. of Sector	Analyzed Industry	Index
Employees per establishment	8.6	8.3	96	Value added per establishment	584,730	432,660	74
Construction workers per establishment	6.6	6.5	98	Value added per employee	67,759	52,191	77
Payroll per establishment	265,343	212,550	80	Value added per construction worker	88,592	67,011	76
Payroll per employee	30,748	25,640	83	Revenues per establishment	1,307,915	790,434	60
Payroll per construction worker	27,622	22,149	80	Revenues per employee	151,563	95,349	63
Costs per establishment	367,737	292,617	80	Revenues per construction worker	198,161	122,423	62
Costs per employee	42,614	35,298	83	CR as % of total revenues	98.48	99.23	101
Costs per construction worker	55,716	45,321	81	Net CR as % of CR	72.40	91.69	127
Materials as % of costs	95.75	96.06	100	Investment per establishment	22,948	13,650	59
Costs as % of revenues	28.12	37.02	132	Investment per employee	2,659	1,647	62
Costs as % of construction revenues	28.55	37.31	131	Investment per construction worker	3,477	2,114	61

Sources: Same as General Statistics. The 'Average of Sector' column represents the average for all industries in this sector. The Index shows the relationship between the Average and the Analyzed Industry. For example, 100 means that they are equal; 500 that the Analyzed Industry is five times the average; 50 means that the Analyzed Industry is half the national average. 'na' is used to show that data are 'not available'. CR stands for "construction revenues" and "Net CR" is construction revenues net of subcontract expenses.

LEADING COMPANIES   Number shown: **23**   Total sales ($ mil): **1,167**   Total employment (000): **7.5**

Company Name	Address				CEO Name	Phone	Co. Type	Sales ($ mil)	Empl. (000)
Pacific Coast Building Products	PO Box 160488	Sacramento	CA	95816	David Luccetti	916-444-9304	R	360*	2.5
Young Sales Corp.	1054 Central Ind	St. Louis	MO	63110	W Todd McCane	314-771-3080	R	129*	0.7
Roth Bros. Inc.	PO Box 4209	Youngstown	OH	44515	Richard Thomas	330-793-5571	S	82*	0.5
North American Roofing Systems	3 Winners Cir	Arden	NC	28704	C Michael Verble	828-687-7767	R	74*	0.4
Industrial Roofing Co.	38 Ridgewood Ave	Ridgewood	NJ	07450	E Komito	201-791-7300	R	65*	0.1
Sheriff-Goslin Company Inc.	10 Avenue C	Battle Creek	MI	49015	Robert Sherriff	616-962-4036	R	56*	0.3
Mountain Co.	P O Box 5310	Vienna	WV	26105	Harry H Esbenshade	304-295-3311	R	50	0.6
Pangere Corp.	4050 W 4th Ave	Gary	IN	46406	Steve Pangere	219-949-1368	R	46*	0.3
B.T. Mancini Company Inc.	PO Box 361930	Milpitas	CA	95036		408-942-7900	R	42*	0.2
Snyder Roofing & Sheet Metal	PO Box 23819	Tigard	OR	97281	Harold Johnston	503-620-5252	R	35	0.2
Crown Corr Inc.	PO Box 1750	Highland	IN	46322	Richard J Peller	219-949-8080	R	33*	0.2
Johnson Contracting Inc.	2750 Morton Dr	East Moline	IL	61244	C Johnson	309-755-0601	R	29*	0.2
Standard Taylor Industries Inc.	516 N McDonough	Montgomery	AL	36102	Pete Taylor	334-834-3000	R	20	0.2
Straus Systems Inc.	P O Box 1189	Stafford	TX	77497	Steve Kemble	281-498-1689	S	20	0.2
Midland Engineering Inc.	52369 U S 33 N	South Bend	IN	46637	Chas W Frazier	219-272-0200	R	19	0.2
CEI West Roofing Co.	1881 W 13th Ave	Denver	CO	80204	Frederick Holland	303-573-5953	R	18	0.2
Luckinbill Inc.	304 E Broadway	Enid	OK	73701	Dennis Luckinbill	580-233-2026	R	17*	0.1
Honolulu Shipyard Inc.	PO Box 30989	Honolulu	HI	96820	Steven Loui	808-848-6211	S	17	0.2
A. Zahner Co.	1400 E 9th St	Kansas City	MO	64106		816-474-8882	R	16*	0.1
CSM Mechanical Inc.	2055 N 25th Ave	Melrose Park	IL	60160	Louise A Cripe	847-451-7700	R	15*	<0.1
Charles F. Evans Company Inc.	800 Canal St	Elmira	NY	14901	Garey Stout	607-734-8151	S	12	0.1
Pioneer Randustrial Corp.	4529 Ind Pkwy	Cleveland	OH	44135	James Schattinger	216-671-5500	S	9*	0.1
Field and Associates Inc.	2187 W 1st St	Springfield	OH	45504	Stephen C Field	937-323-5518	S	4	<0.1

Source: Ward's Business Directory of U.S. Private and Public Companies, Volumes 1 and 2, 2000. The company type code used is as follows: P - Public, R - Private, S - Subsidiary, D - Division, J - Joint Venture, A - Affiliate, G - Group, N - Company type not reported. Sales are in millions of dollars, employees are in thousands. An asterisk (*) indicates an estimated sales volume. The symbol < stands for 'less than'. Company names and addresses are truncated, in some cases, to fit into the available space.

COST DETAILS

Item	Cost ($ mil)	% of total	Per $1,000 of Revenue	Item	Cost ($ mil)	% of total	Per $1,000 of Revenue
All costs	10,932.6	100.000	452.6	Total Rentals	335.3	3.067	13.9
Cost of supplies	8,589.2	78.565	355.6	Equipment	163.5	1.495	6.8
Subcontracts	1,991.1	18.212	82.4	Buildings	171.8	1.571	7.1
Power, fuel, lubricants	352.4	3.223	14.6	Services purchased	449.7	4.114	18.6
Electricity	54.0	0.494	2.2	Communications	193.5	1.770	8.0
Natural gas	30.5	0.279	1.3	Building repairs	34.3	0.314	1.4
Gasoline and diesel	253.7	2.321	10.5	Machinery repairs	221.9	2.030	9.2
Highway	230.6	2.110	9.5				
Offroad	23.1	0.211	1.0				
Other power	14.1	0.129	0.6				

Source: Economic Census of the United States, 1997. Revenues referred to are total industry revenues for the current NAICS industry.

CONSTRUCTION PRODUCT DETAILS

Construction type	Value of construction work ($ mil and %)							
	Total		New construction		Additions, alterations, reconstruction		Maintenance and repair	
	Value	%	Value	%	Value	%	Value	%
Total	**23,967.1**	**100.0**	**8,652.9**	**100.0**	**9,244.5**	**100.0**	**5,704.8**	**100.0**
Building construction, total	**23,383.3**	**97.6**	**8,589.8**	**99.3**	**9,149.9**	**99.0**	**5,643.6**	**98.9**
Single-family houses, detached	6,956.1	29.0	2,555.9	29.5	2,714.3	29.4	1,685.9	29.6
Single-family houses, attached	1,415.7	5.9	534.7	6.2	528.8	5.7	352.2	6.2
Apartment buildings, condos and cooperatives	1,348.2	5.6	359.2	4.2	603.5	6.5	385.4	6.8
Manufacturing and light industrial buildings	2,991.7	12.5	945.1	10.9	1,247.3	13.5	799.3	14.0
Manufacturing and light industrial warehouses	1,029.8	4.3	388.1	4.5	380.8	4.1	260.8	4.6
Hotels and motels	411.8	1.7	203.3	2.3	118.6	1.3	89.9	1.6
Office buildings	1,898.5	7.9	797.1	9.2	673.8	7.3	427.6	7.5
All other commercial buildings, nec	2,264.5	9.4	978.6	11.3	717.5	7.8	568.5	10.0
Commercial warehouses	1,024.6	4.3	363.7	4.2	439.8	4.8	221.0	3.9
Religious buildings	485.3	2.0	126.8	1.5	207.8	2.2	150.6	2.6
Educational buildings	2,078.0	8.7	723.2	8.4	942.7	10.2	412.0	7.2
Health care and institutional buildings	710.8	3.0	280.0	3.2	299.5	3.2	131.4	2.3
Public safety buildings	335.8	1.4	146.0	1.7	125.5	1.4	64.4	1.1
Other building construction	432.7	1.8	188.2	2.2	149.9	1.6	94.6	1.7
Nonbuilding construction, total	**218.8**	**0.9**	**63.1**	**0.7**	**94.6**	**1.0**	**61.2**	**1.1**
Other nonbuilding construction, nec	218.8	0.9	63.1	0.7	94.6	1.0	61.2	1.1
Construction work, nsk	**364.9**	**1.5**	**NA**	**-**	**NA**	**-**	**NA**	**-**

Source: *Economic Census of the United States*, 1997. Bold items are headers. (D) stands for data withheld to protect competitive information. (S) indicates instances where data do not meet publications standards.

LOCATION BY STATE AND REGIONAL CONCENTRATION

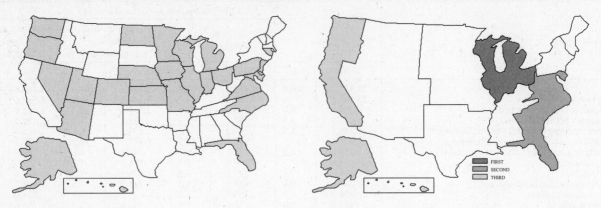

INDUSTRY DATA BY STATE

State	Establishments	Employment			Compensation		Production				Capital Exp. ($ mil)
		Total	Workers	Total as % of US	Payroll per Employee	Wages per Worker	Costs ($ mil)	Value Added ($ mil)	Revenues ($ mil)	% of US	
California	3,033	27,560	22,279	10.88	25,925	22,609	1,109.1	1,503.4	2,759.5	11.43	39.9
Florida	1,944	16,766	12,464	6.62	23,404	19,599	526.7	856.3	1,475.3	6.11	22.2
Illinois	1,388	12,816	9,273	5.06	31,192	28,471	460.9	800.1	1,436.1	5.95	21.1
Texas	1,593	13,697	10,066	5.41	23,509	18,530	489.0	677.0	1,343.8	5.56	24.5
Pennsylvania	1,497	12,245	9,561	4.83	29,001	25,998	453.6	746.1	1,278.9	5.29	28.3
Ohio	1,614	12,827	10,314	5.06	24,767	21,475	437.6	642.9	1,174.9	4.86	18.2
New York	1,509	10,888	8,304	4.30	25,792	23,249	385.6	588.9	1,068.2	4.42	16.2
Michigan	1,019	8,078	6,432	3.19	30,471	26,537	318.0	513.5	929.1	3.85	15.5
New Jersey	970	6,323	4,535	2.50	33,532	30,338	284.4	399.1	802.8	3.32	9.4
Virginia	922	9,225	7,562	3.64	23,541	20,032	260.9	410.1	735.2	3.04	9.8
North Carolina	1,130	8,389	6,666	3.31	22,247	18,647	292.9	357.7	723.2	2.99	9.8
Indiana	786	7,367	5,676	2.91	24,558	21,577	240.5	372.5	653.0	2.70	12.1
Washington	957	6,381	4,970	2.52	26,323	22,064	241.2	336.8	609.2	2.52	12.5
Minnesota	566	5,193	3,870	2.05	26,949	22,761	243.8	286.4	587.7	2.43	14.4
Colorado	596	5,591	4,085	2.21	25,879	22,272	221.8	303.4	571.5	2.37	7.3
Maryland	501	5,631	4,520	2.22	29,122	24,806	215.8	277.2	551.9	2.28	10.5
Georgia	734	5,938	4,779	2.34	27,227	22,099	193.0	299.3	549.2	2.27	10.9
Missouri	887	5,886	4,686	2.32	26,956	22,692	172.7	310.4	521.7	2.16	8.7
Wisconsin	776	5,330	4,285	2.10	27,108	24,217	178.5	288.0	484.3	2.01	9.8
Massachusetts	566	3,817	2,825	1.51	30,640	25,663	172.5	258.8	469.7	1.94	4.7
Tennessee	564	4,996	4,044	1.97	22,462	18,774	148.1	231.2	412.4	1.71	9.0
Oregon	640	4,728	3,763	1.87	24,614	21,374	148.7	226.1	401.9	1.66	7.0
Arizona	406	4,836	3,963	1.91	23,349	20,588	163.8	199.9	372.6	1.54	6.8
Connecticut	421	2,688	1,851	1.06	36,428	30,751	106.0	194.3	355.0	1.47	4.9
Kentucky	440	4,155	3,400	1.64	21,584	18,895	125.5	183.3	333.6	1.38	5.8
Alabama	426	3,737	3,004	1.48	20,821	18,763	111.5	163.5	311.1	1.29	9.0
Louisiana	450	3,460	2,594	1.37	21,915	19,265	123.8	134.8	286.8	1.19	4.5
Iowa	408	3,132	2,440	1.24	27,060	23,903	107.8	160.1	285.5	1.18	4.6
South Carolina	472	3,686	2,878	1.46	19,567	16,788	99.7	152.2	284.4	1.18	3.8
Kansas	382	2,931	2,331	1.16	23,418	20,764	91.4	143.0	245.6	1.02	6.1
Utah	337	2,770	2,353	1.09	22,647	20,431	104.6	115.7	229.7	0.95	3.2
Oklahoma	284	2,397	1,833	0.95	18,817	17,338	77.4	102.6	195.9	0.81	2.9
Nevada	110	2,373	2,010	0.94	22,700	20,770	66.0	112.1	181.9	0.75	2.8
Nebraska	189	1,585	1,144	0.63	26,167	20,783	62.3	91.5	175.1	0.73	6.7
Mississippi	245	2,446	1,940	0.97	16,809	13,755	68.0	77.4	154.0	0.64	5.9
Hawaii	128	1,119	806	0.44	29,145	25,207	36.0	94.4	140.4	0.58	1.5
West Virginia	193	1,314	1,108	0.52	23,058	20,879	37.5	83.9	127.3	0.53	2.1
Arkansas	204	1,661	1,403	0.66	18,856	16,497	42.3	65.8	114.0	0.47	2.3
Maine	67	1,072	821	0.42	25,038	22,180	36.9	54.0	94.3	0.39	2.6
New Hampshire	107	807	540	0.32	29,415	23,933	30.1	48.1	81.8	0.34	1.4
Delaware	81	716	521	0.28	30,536	24,355	26.7	46.7	79.0	0.33	1.0
North Dakota	101	1,063	805	0.42	20,377	18,078	29.9	43.7	78.1	0.32	3.5
Rhode Island	129	769	616	0.30	26,740	24,010	22.9	44.4	70.2	0.29	1.3
New Mexico	150	961	791	0.38	19,413	16,750	25.0	38.2	64.3	0.27	0.9
Alaska	67	387	316	0.15	40,765	39,782	24.0	36.5	62.0	0.26	2.4
South Dakota	71	747	611	0.29	18,070	15,624	20.8	28.7	52.2	0.22	2.6
Montana	126	672	498	0.27	19,644	17,380	15.1	33.9	51.1	0.21	1.4
Vermont	110	594	459	0.23	23,114	22,636	20.9	23.7	45.7	0.19	1.7
Idaho	171	1,048	859	0.41	22,976	20,508	(D)	39.7	(D)	-	2.5
Wyoming	76	475	401	0.19	20,981	18,763	(D)	22.3	(D)	-	1.1
D.C.	16	44	36	0.02	23,023	19,056	(D)	1.4	(D)	-	0.1

Source: Economic Census of the U.S., 1997. Data are sorted by 1997 revenues or establishments. (D) means data suppression to prevent disclosure of company data. (S) means that data did not meet statistical standards for publication. A dash (-) is used when data are unavailable or cannot be calculated. Data followed by an * indicate the midpoint of a range. The ranges are: for 10, 0-19; for 60, 20-99; for 175, 100-249, for 375, 250-499, for 750, 500-999. Higher values are multiples of those shown, e.g., 3,750 is the midpoint of the range 2,500-4,999. Shaded *states* on the state map indicate those states which have proportionately greater representation in the industry than would be indicated by the state's population; the ratio is based on total revenues or number of establishments. Shaded *regions* indicate where the industry is regionally most concentrated.

NAICS 235710 - CONCRETE CONTRACTORS

GENERAL STATISTICS

Years	Estab-lish-ments	Employment		Payroll ($ mil)		Costs ($ mil)		Value Added ($ mil)	Revenues ($ mil)			Capital expend. ($ mil)
		Total	Constr. workers	Total	Worker payroll	Total	Cost of materials		All sources	Construction Total	Net	
1997	30,417	262,256	222,121	6,858.1	5,298.5	9,762.1	9,250.7	14,159.4	26,166.6	25,848.8	23,603.7	701.5

Source: *Economic Census of the United States*, 1997. This is a newly defined industry. Data for prior years were unavailable at the time of publication but may become available over time. "Net" under "Construction" is construction revenue net of the costs of subcontracts.

DISTRIBUTION AMONG SIC-BASED INDUSTRIES - 1997

SIC	Industry	Estab-lish-ments	Employment		Cost of Power & Materials ($ mil)	Revenues ($ mil)			Value Added ($ mil)
			Total (000)	Payroll ($ mil)		All Sources	Construction Total	Net	
177120	Concrete work contractors (pt)	30,417.0	262,256	6,858.1	9,762.1	26,166.6	25,848.9	23,603.7	14,159.43

Source: 1997 *Economic Census*. U.S. Census Bureau, U.S. Department of Commerce, August 1997. SIC codes ending in two zeroes represent complete 4-digit SICs. All others are parts of 4-digit SIC industries. Items showing a dash (-) indicate that data are not available because of disclosure problems.

SIC INDUSTRIES RELATED TO NAICS 235710

SIC	Industry	1990	1991	1992	1993	1994	1995	1996	1997
1771	**Concrete Work***								
	Establishments (number)	21,496	21,212	26,123	25,835	27,289p	27,891p	28,506p	29,135p
	Employment (thousands) . . . . / . .	198.2	164.9	192.5	182.0	183.1e	178.6e	174.2e	169.9e
	Revenues ($ million)	14,839.4e	14,717.2e	14,596.0	14,475.9e	14,356.7e	14,238.5e	14,121.2e	14,005.0e

Source: *Economic Census of the United States*, 1992, annual surveys of economic sectors conducted by the Bureau of the Census, and estimates or projections based on the 1982-1992 period; not all data are shown. 'e' marks estimates made by the editors; 'p' indicates projections based on time series. A dash (-) indicates that data for this SIC or year were not available. * Indicates that only a portion of this industry is present within the NAICS data. If no * is shown, the entire industry is contained within the NAICS data.

INDICES OF CHANGE

Years	Estab-lish-ments	Employment		Payroll ($ mil)		Costs ($ mil)		Value Added ($ mil)	Revenues ($ mil)			Capital expend. ($ mil)
		Total	Constr. workers	Total	Worker payroll	Total	Cost of materials		All sources	Construction Total	Net	
1997	100.0	100.0	100.0	100.0	100.0	100.0	100.0	100.0	100.0	100.0	100.0	100.0

Sources: Same as General Statistics. The values shown reflect change from the base year, 1997. Values above 100 mean greater than 1997, values below 100 mean less than 1997, and a value of 100 in years other than 1997 means same as 1997. Indices are calculated only for Census years. Data are the most recent available at this level of detail.

SELECTED RATIOS

For 1997	Avg. of Sector	Analyzed Industry	Index	For 1997	Avg. of Sector	Analyzed Industry	Index
Employees per establishment	8.6	8.6	100	Value added per establishment	584,730	465,509	80
Construction workers per establishment	6.6	7.3	111	Value added per employee	67,759	53,991	80
Payroll per establishment	265,343	225,469	85	Value added per construction worker	88,592	63,746	72
Payroll per employee	30,748	26,150	85	Revenues per establishment	1,307,915	860,262	66
Payroll per construction worker	27,622	23,854	86	Revenues per employee	151,563	99,775	66
Costs per establishment	367,737	320,942	87	Revenues per construction worker	198,161	117,803	59
Costs per employee	42,614	37,224	87	CR as % of total revenues	98.48	98.79	100
Costs per construction worker	55,716	43,949	79	Net CR as % of CR	72.40	91.31	126
Materials as % of costs	95.75	94.76	99	Investment per establishment	22,948	23,063	101
Costs as % of revenues	28.12	37.31	133	Investment per employee	2,659	2,675	101
Costs as % of construction revenues	28.55	37.77	132	Investment per construction worker	3,477	3,158	91

Sources: Same as General Statistics. The 'Average of Sector' column represents the average for all industries in this sector. The Index shows the relationship between the Average and the Analyzed Industry. For example, 100 means that they are equal; 500 that the Analyzed Industry is five times the average; 50 means that the Analyzed Industry is half the national average. 'na' is used to show that data are 'not available'. CR stands for "construction revenues" and "Net CR" is construction revenues net of subcontract expenses.

LEADING COMPANIES   Number shown: 29   Total sales ($ mil): 3,085   Total employment (000): 16.3

Company Name	Address				CEO Name	Phone	Co. Type	Sales ($ mil)	Empl. (000)
Walsh Group Ltd.	929 W Adams	Chicago	IL	60607	Matthew Walsh	312-563-5400	R	1,170	3.5
A. Teichert and Son Inc.	P O Box 15002	Sacramento	CA	95851	Louis Riggs	916-484-3011	R	280*	2.1
Ray Wilson Co.	199 S Los Robles	Pasadena	CA	91101	Nobu Kawasaki	626-795-7900	S	200*	0.4
Baker Concrete Construction Inc.	900 N Garver Rd	Monroe	OH	45050	Daniel L Baker	513-539-4000	R	180*	1.5
Fuller Co.	2040 Avenue C	Bethlehem	PA	18017		610-264-6011	S	168*	0.8
Driggs Corp.	8700 Ashwood Dr	Capitol Heights	MD	20743	John Driggs	301-499-1950	R	150*	1.1
James Cape and Sons Co.	6422 N Hwy 31	Racine	WI	53402	WR Cape	414-639-2552	R	120*	0.7
Jack B. Parson Cos.	PO Box 3429	Ogden	UT	84409	John Parson	801-731-1111	S	100	0.9
Saxton Inc.	5440 W Sahara Ave	Las Vegas	NV	89146	James C Saxton	702-221-1111	P	92	0.9
Penhall Co.	P O Box 4609	Anaheim	CA	92803	John Sawyer	714-772-6450	S	86*	0.8
Kasler Corp.	P O Box 600	Highland	CA	92346	Tony Ferreccio	909-425-4200	S	71*	0.4
Penhall International Inc.	PO Box 4609	Anaheim	CA	92803	John Sawyer	714-772-6450	R	70	0.7
Case Foundation Co.	P O Box 40	Roselle	IL	60172	John E O'Malley	630-529-2911	S	58	0.5
Stevens Painton Corp.	7850 Freeway Cir	Middleburg H.	OH	44130	Robert Navarro	440-237-1300	R	45	0.3
P. Flanigan and Sons Inc.	2444 Loch Raven Rd	Baltimore	MD	21218	Pierce Flanigan	410-467-5900	R	45	0.2
Border States Paving Inc.	PO Box 2586	Fargo	ND	58108	Dan L Thompson	701-237-4860	R	33*	0.2
Nicholson Construction Co.	12 McClane St	Cuddy	PA	15031	Peter J Nicholson	412-221-4500	R	30*	0.1
Dance Brothers Inc.	825-C Ham Ferr	Linthicum H.	MD	21090	Anderson Dance	410-789-8200	R	25*	0.2
Superior Gunite	12306 Van Nuys	Grn Cv Sprgs	CA	91342	Anthony L Federico	818-896-9199	R	20*	0.1
Central Allied Enterprises Inc.	PO Box 80489	Canton	OH	44708	John Bartley	330-477-6751	R	19	0.3
Conduit & Foundation	33 Rock Hill Rd	Bala Cynwyd	PA	19004	Richard Halloran	610-668-8400	R	18*	<0.1
J.W. Conner and Sons Inc.	P O Box 2522	Tampa	FL	33601	Donald L Conner	813-247-4441	R	16*	<0.1
Kalman Floor Co.	1202 Bergen	Evergreen	CO	80439	Carl N Ytterberg	303-674-2290	R	16*	<0.1
L.R. Hubbard Construction Inc.	7485 Ronson Rd	San Diego	CA	92111	George Byrom	619-277-9300	R	15	0.1
Stein Construction Company Inc.	PO Box 5246	Chattanooga	TN	37406	Frank D Stein	423-698-0271	R	15*	<0.1
Wingra Stone Company Inc.	PO Box 44284	Madison	WI	53719	RF Shea	608-271-5555	R	13*	0.2
Carson Concrete Corp.	PO Box 550	Conshohocken	PA	19428	Anthony Samango	610-825-8600	R	12*	0.2
Merco Inc.	1117 Rte 31, S	Lebanon	NJ	08833	CE Mergentime	908-730-9172	R	10*	<0.1
Conco Cement Co.	5151 Port Chicago	Concord	CA	94520	Steve Gonsalves	925-685-6799	R	8*	<0.1

Source: *Ward's Business Directory of U.S. Private and Public Companies*, Volumes 1 and 2, 2000. The company type code used is as follows: P - Public, R - Private, S - Subsidiary, D - Division, J - Joint Venture, A - Affiliate, G - Group, N - Company type not reported. Sales are in millions of dollars, employees are in thousands. An asterisk (*) indicates an estimated sales volume. The symbol < stands for 'less than'. Company names and addresses are truncated, in some cases, to fit into the available space.

COST DETAILS

Item	Cost ($ mil)	% of total	Per $1,000 of Revenue	Item	Cost ($ mil)	% of total	Per $1,000 of Revenue
All costs	12,007.2	100.000	458.9	Total Rentals	511.5	4.260	19.5
Cost of supplies	9,250.7	77.043	353.5	Equipment	384.2	3.200	14.7
Subcontracts	2,245.1	18.698	85.8	Buildings	127.3	1.060	4.9
Power, fuel, lubricants	511.4	4.259	19.5	Services purchased	635.1	5.289	24.3
Electricity	50.0	0.416	1.9	Communications	187.5	1.561	7.2
Natural gas	20.4	0.170	0.8	Building repairs	29.4	0.245	1.1
Gasoline and diesel	411.5	3.427	15.7	Machinery repairs	418.2	3.483	16.0
Highway	330.6	2.753	12.6				
Offroad	81.0	0.674	3.1				
Other power	29.5	0.246	1.1				

Source: *Economic Census of the United States*, 1997. Revenues referred to are total industry revenues for the current NAICS industry.

CONSTRUCTION PRODUCT DETAILS

Construction type	Value of construction work ($ mil and %)							
	Total		New construction		Additions, alterations, reconstruction		Maintenance and repair	
	Value	%	Value	%	Value	%	Value	%
Total	**25,848.8**	**100.0**	**18,737.9**	**100.0**	**3,558.6**	**100.0**	**3,217.9**	**100.0**
Building construction, total	**17,221.9**	**66.6**	**14,031.9**	**74.9**	**1,871.6**	**52.6**	**1,318.4**	**41.0**
Single-family houses, detached	5,632.1	21.8	4,882.9	26.1	456.3	12.8	292.9	9.1
Single-family houses, attached	1,186.8	4.6	1,032.8	5.5	95.2	2.7	58.9	1.8
Apartment buildings, condos and cooperatives	1,103.7	4.3	895.1	4.8	85.0	2.4	123.6	3.8
Manufacturing and light industrial buildings	1,436.5	5.6	1,001.0	5.3	233.8	6.6	201.7	6.3
Manufacturing and light industrial warehouses	835.2	3.2	686.4	3.7	85.1	2.4	63.7	2.0
Hotels and motels	341.0	1.3	286.2	1.5	24.6	0.7	30.3	0.9
Office buildings	1,495.3	5.8	1,196.4	6.4	170.7	4.8	128.2	4.0
All other commercial buildings, nec	1,888.6	7.3	1,434.5	7.7	234.4	6.6	219.7	6.8
Commercial warehouses	1,093.3	4.2	934.3	5.0	101.6	2.9	57.4	1.8
Religious buildings	225.4	0.9	151.9	0.8	50.6	1.4	22.9	0.7
Educational buildings	742.9	2.9	545.5	2.9	154.5	4.3	42.9	1.3
Health care and institutional buildings	429.5	1.7	325.8	1.7	73.9	2.1	29.7	0.9
Other building construction	811.6	3.1	659.1	3.5	105.8	3.0	46.7	1.4
Nonbuilding construction, total	**8,292.6**	**32.1**	**4,706.0**	**25.1**	**1,687.0**	**47.4**	**1,899.6**	**59.0**
Highways, streets, and related work	1,516.7	5.9	909.6	4.9	316.1	8.9	290.9	9.0
Private driveways and parking areas	5,278.3	20.4	2,822.7	15.1	1,131.7	31.8	1,323.9	41.1
Bridges, tunnels, and elevated highways	200.9	0.8	112.1	0.6	31.1	0.9	57.7	1.8
Sewers, water mains, and related facilities	260.5	1.0	154.4	0.8	38.5	1.1	67.6	2.1
Other nonbuilding construction, nec	1,036.2	4.0	707.2	3.8	169.6	4.8	159.4	5.0
Construction work, nsk	**334.4**	**1.3**	**NA**	**-**	**NA**	**-**	**NA**	**-**

Source: Economic Census of the United States, 1997. Bold items are headers. (D) stands for data withheld to protect competitive information. (S) indicates instances where data do not meet publications standards.

LOCATION BY STATE AND REGIONAL CONCENTRATION

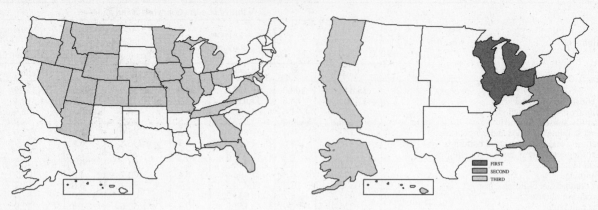

FIRST
SECOND
THIRD

INDUSTRY DATA BY STATE

State	Estab lish- ments	Employment			Compensation		Production				Capital Exp. ($ mil)
		Total	Workers	Total as % of US	Payroll per Employee	Wages per Worker	Costs ($ mil)	Value Added ($ mil)	Reve- nues ($ mil)	% of US	
California	2,471	28,919	24,828	11.03	28,828	25,998	1,109.3	1,665.7	3,108.0	11.88	60.7
Texas	1,873	21,697	18,578	8.27	21,329	19,171	668.9	910.9	1,756.8	6.71	38.5
Illinois	1,472	12,951	10,808	4.94	33,081	31,271	591.7	871.3	1,596.5	6.10	42.7
Ohio	1,527	13,236	11,057	5.05	30,457	28,268	645.0	840.4	1,594.7	6.09	41.0
Florida	1,773	15,250	12,853	5.81	23,266	20,516	495.3	736.2	1,394.0	5.33	33.1
Michigan	1,439	10,411	8,694	3.97	31,396	28,659	563.9	699.2	1,391.8	5.32	40.1
New York	1,173	10,010	8,153	3.82	29,192	27,257	379.9	595.2	1,060.4	4.05	28.5
Pennsylvania	1,366	9,801	8,234	3.74	25,742	23,716	415.0	548.7	1,035.8	3.96	30.6
Colorado	842	9,047	8,006	3.45	26,070	24,013	295.5	489.3	827.4	3.16	23.6
Arizona	471	8,771	7,615	3.34	25,491	22,290	296.0	422.8	772.2	2.95	16.9
Georgia	619	7,520	6,345	2.87	24,437	21,997	284.9	378.4	744.0	2.84	21.4
Missouri	1,007	7,593	6,487	2.90	24,722	22,335	284.2	399.0	729.8	2.79	21.6
Maryland	592	7,560	6,188	2.88	26,478	23,921	262.5	400.7	714.1	2.73	19.5
Virginia	805	8,429	7,099	3.21	23,267	20,645	272.4	376.2	698.1	2.67	21.6
Wisconsin	939	5,878	4,944	2.24	29,461	27,960	278.7	348.2	682.2	2.61	25.3
Indiana	812	6,361	5,338	2.43	25,682	23,434	240.4	356.3	645.4	2.47	18.7
Minnesota	708	5,341	4,463	2.04	31,863	30,117	242.2	328.0	611.2	2.34	18.7
New Jersey	705	4,974	4,226	1.90	27,706	25,360	219.6	301.8	572.5	2.19	13.5
Tennessee	486	4,248	3,568	1.62	27,111	23,750	190.7	246.5	519.8	1.99	15.7
North Carolina	768	5,730	4,805	2.18	21,861	18,688	153.5	264.4	467.1	1.79	15.2
Nevada	176	4,095	3,617	1.56	31,968	29,328	164.4	251.9	443.8	1.70	12.1
Kansas	444	3,893	3,371	1.48	23,670	21,557	145.3	196.9	412.3	1.58	12.0
Washington	905	4,955	4,217	1.89	24,793	22,892	133.9	259.5	412.2	1.58	11.3
Massachusetts	570	3,918	3,203	1.49	29,752	28,002	131.0	244.0	399.7	1.53	9.0
Iowa	520	3,629	3,164	1.38	23,494	21,517	141.0	196.8	365.4	1.40	13.6
Oregon	568	3,892	3,328	1.48	27,174	26,438	113.5	205.9	334.0	1.28	10.0
Kentucky	509	3,941	3,361	1.50	20,487	18,527	111.8	178.9	322.4	1.23	9.8
South Carolina	392	2,520	2,068	0.96	22,301	19,184	79.3	134.1	233.3	0.89	5.8
Connecticut	349	2,127	1,677	0.81	28,020	27,028	84.6	129.1	225.3	0.86	5.8
Utah	482	2,758	2,424	1.05	22,029	21,133	72.8	131.1	214.2	0.82	2.8
Alabama	393	2,648	2,186	1.01	21,763	19,865	60.5	118.0	187.8	0.72	6.9
Oklahoma	291	1,966	1,685	0.75	20,601	18,053	73.7	86.4	172.7	0.66	4.8
Nebraska	326	2,138	1,812	0.82	20,167	18,805	62.0	99.2	170.4	0.65	6.1
Idaho	368	2,054	1,815	0.78	17,817	17,017	56.2	89.6	153.5	0.59	4.6
Louisiana	227	2,043	1,769	0.78	19,139	17,620	49.9	78.8	136.3	0.52	3.3
Delaware	91	959	780	0.37	26,301	24,641	35.9	56.7	112.0	0.43	3.2
Mississippi	153	1,370	1,221	0.52	19,452	17,925	38.2	54.0	111.8	0.43	3.8
Arkansas	186	1,385	1,190	0.53	21,399	18,573	40.7	58.8	106.6	0.41	4.1
New Mexico	141	1,166	990	0.44	22,057	19,497	38.8	53.7	101.1	0.39	2.9
Montana	187	1,027	898	0.39	18,131	17,454	31.9	46.6	86.9	0.33	2.5
South Dakota	213	650	604	0.25	21,918	20,929	28.7	38.4	70.1	0.27	1.9
Maine	188	793	686	0.30	21,528	20,813	30.6	37.9	69.2	0.26	2.6
New Hampshire	149	706	606	0.27	27,901	24,649	25.8	37.8	67.3	0.26	3.6
West Virginia	134	821	663	0.31	19,269	18,658	24.6	34.3	60.6	0.23	2.8
Rhode Island	130	601	484	0.23	23,789	22,174	15.6	39.9	57.1	0.22	1.1
North Dakota	135	739	601	0.28	16,991	16,203	24.7	25.5	55.2	0.21	2.6
Wyoming	147	646	557	0.25	18,260	16,469	14.5	30.9	49.4	0.19	1.8
Vermont	101	448	350	0.17	25,612	24,700	22.4	22.5	47.0	0.18	2.7
Hawaii	44	450	345	0.17	34,244	30,719	11.1	32.5	46.1	0.18	0.6
Alaska	47	159	130	0.06	28,170	27,892	8.2	8.4	17.3	0.07	0.4
D.C.	4	34	26	0.01	40,559	40,692	1.0	2.3	3.6	0.01	0.1

Source: Economic Census of the U.S., 1997. Data are sorted by 1997 revenues or establishments. (D) means data suppression to prevent disclosure of company data. (S) means that data did not meet statistical standards for publication. A dash (-) is used when data are unavailable or cannot be calculated. Data followed by an * indicate the midpoint of a range. The ranges are: for 10, 0-19; for 60, 20-99; for 175, 100-249, for 375, 250-499, for 750, 500-999. Higher values are multiples of those shown, e.g., 3,750 is the midpoint of the range 2,500-4,999. Shaded *states* on the state map indicate those states which have proportionately greater representation in the industry than would be indicated by the state's population; the ratio is based on total revenues or number of establishments. Shaded *regions* indicate where the industry is regionally most concentrated.

NAICS 235810 - WATER WELL DRILLING CONTRACTORS*

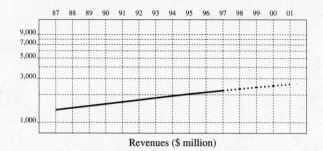

Revenues ($ million)

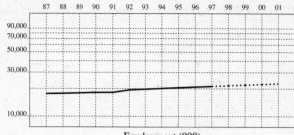

Employment (000)

GENERAL STATISTICS

| Years | Estab-lish-ments | Employment | | Payroll ($ mil) | | Costs ($ mil) | | Value Added ($ mil) | Revenues ($ mil) | | | Capital expend. ($ mil) |
		Total	Constr. workers	Total	Worker payroll	Total	Cost of materials		All sources	Construction Total	Net	
1977	4,305	22,352	18,720	237.0	188.3	489.5	435.4	628.8	1,118.3	1,090.4	1,077.8	-
1982	3,551	17,153	13,703	249.0	190.2	454.2	374.0	577.5	1,031.7	1,013.9	984.9	-
1987	3,414	17,598	13,628	335.2	248.5	588.7	495.7	779.6	1,368.3	1,330.1	1,299.3	61.7
1988	3,194	17,717	13,833	378.9	261.8	619.0	520.2	818.6	1,437.6	1,401.4	1,367.2	-
1989	3,069	17,910	14,041	399.1	275.8	650.8	545.8	859.5	1,510.3	1,476.6	1,438.6	-
1990	3,261	18,128	14,252	425.5	290.6	684.3	572.7	902.4	1,586.7	1,555.9	1,513.7	-
1991	3,359	18,170	14,466	433.9	306.2	719.5	600.9	947.5	1,667.0	1,639.4	1,592.8	-
1992	3,638	19,346	14,683	443.6	322.6	756.5	630.5	994.8	1,751.3	1,727.4	1,676.0	69.5
1993	3,683	19,720	14,818	470.1	337.9	771.6	653.0	1,062.0	1,845.5	1,820.2	1,767.2	-
1994	3,728	20,093	14,954	496.6	353.2	786.6	675.6	1,129.3	1,939.7	1,913.0	1,858.4	-
1995	3,772	20,467	15,089	523.2	368.5	801.7	698.1	1,196.5	2,033.8	2,005.7	1,949.5	-
1996	3,817	20,840	15,225	549.7	383.8	816.7	720.7	1,263.8	2,128.0	2,098.5	2,040.7	-
1997	3,862	21,214	15,360	576.2	399.1	831.8	743.2	1,331.0	2,222.2	2,191.3	2,131.9	129.0
1998	3,907p	21,588p	15,495p	602.7p	414.4p	846.9p	765.7p	1,398.2p	2,316.4p	2,284.1p	2,223.1p	
1999	3,952p	21,961p	15,631p	629.2p	429.7p	861.9p	788.3p	1,465.5p	2,410.6p	2,376.9p	2,314.3p	
2000	3,996p	22,335p	15,766p	655.8p	445.0p	877.0p	810.8p	1,532.7p	2,504.7p	2,469.6p	2,405.4p	
2001	4,041p	22,708p	15,902p	682.3p	460.3p	892.0p	833.4p	1,600.0p	2,598.9p	2,562.4p	2,496.6p	

Sources: Economic Census of the United States, 1977, 1982, 1987, 1992, and 1997. Data for those years (years are in **bold** type) are from the 5-year censuses of the economy. Other values, unless otherwise noted, are extrapolations. Values footnoted 1 are from the *County Business Patterns* for the years indicated. Values marked with *p* are projections. Data are the most recent available at this level of detail. "Net" under "Construction" is construction revenues net of the costs of subcontracts.

INDICES OF CHANGE

| Years | Estab-lish-ments | Employment | | Payroll ($ mil) | | Costs ($ mil) | | Value Added ($ mil) | Revenues ($ mil) | | | Capital expend. ($ mil) |
		Total	Constr. workers	Total	Worker payroll	Total	Cost of materials		All sources	Construction Total	Net	
1977	111.5	105.4	121.9	41.1	47.2	58.8	58.6	47.2	50.3	49.8	50.6	-
1982	91.9	80.9	89.2	43.2	47.7	54.6	50.3	43.4	46.4	46.3	46.2	-
1987	88.4	83.0	88.7	58.2	62.3	70.8	66.7	58.6	61.6	60.7	60.9	47.8
1992	94.2	91.2	95.6	77.0	80.8	90.9	84.8	74.7	78.8	78.8	78.6	53.9
1997	100.0	100.0	100.0	100.0	100.0	100.0	100.0	100.0	100.0	100.0	100.0	100.0

Sources: Same as General Statistics. The values shown reflect change from the base year, 1997. Values above 100 mean greater than 1997, values below 100 mean less than 1997, and a value of 100 in years other than 1997 means same as 1997. Indices are calculated only for Census years. Data are the most recent available at this level of detail.

SELECTED RATIOS

For 1997	Avg. of Sector	Analyzed Industry	Index	For 1997	Avg. of Sector	Analyzed Industry	Index
Employees per establishment	8.6	5.5	64	Value added per establishment	584,730	344,640	59
Construction workers per establishment	6.6	4.0	60	Value added per employee	67,759	62,742	93
Payroll per establishment	265,343	149,197	56	Value added per construction worker	88,592	86,654	98
Payroll per employee	30,748	27,161	88	Revenues per establishment	1,307,915	575,401	44
Payroll per construction worker	27,622	25,983	94	Revenues per employee	151,563	104,752	69
Costs per establishment	367,737	215,381	59	Revenues per construction worker	198,161	144,674	73
Costs per employee	42,614	39,210	92	CR as % of total revenues	98.48	98.61	100
Costs per construction worker	55,716	54,154	97	Net CR as % of CR	72.40	97.29	134
Materials as % of costs	95.75	89.35	93	Investment per establishment	22,948	33,402	146
Costs as % of revenues	28.12	37.43	133	Investment per employee	2,659	6,081	229
Costs as % of construction revenues	28.55	37.96	133	Investment per construction worker	3,477	8,398	242

Sources: Same as General Statistics. The 'Average of Sector' column represents the average for all industries in this sector. The Index shows the relationship between the Average and the Analyzed Industry. For example, 100 means that they are equal; 500 that the Analyzed Industry is five times the average; 50 means that the Analyzed Industry is half the national average. 'na' is used to show that data are 'not available'. CR stands for "construction revenues" and "Net CR" is construction revenues net of subcontract expenses.

LEADING COMPANIES   Number shown: **4**   Total sales ($ mil): **86**   Total employment (000): **0.6**

Company Name	Address				CEO Name	Phone	Co. Type	Sales ($ mil)	Empl. (000)
Beylik Drilling Inc.	555 S Harbor Blvd	La Habra	CA	90631	Robert Beylik	714-870-5360	R	53*	0.3
Barnwell Industries Inc.	1100 Alakea St	Honolulu	HI	96813	Morton H Kinzler	808-531-8400	P	15	<0.1
Water Resources International Inc.	P O Box 44301	Kamuela	HI	96743	Morton H Kinzler	808-882-7207	S	11*	<0.1
Raba-Kistner Consultants Inc.	12821 W Golden Ln	San Antonio	TX	78249	Bunny Jean Raba	210-699-9090	R	7*	0.2

Source: *Ward's Business Directory of U.S. Private and Public Companies*, Volumes 1 and 2, 2000. The company type code used is as follows: P - Public, R - Private, S - Subsidiary, D - Division, J - Joint Venture, A - Affiliate, G - Group, N - Company type not reported. Sales are in millions of dollars, employees are in thousands. An asterisk (*) indicates an estimated sales volume. The symbol < stands for 'less than'. Company names and addresses are truncated, in some cases, to fit into the available space.

COST DETAILS

Item	Cost ($ mil)	% of total	Per $1,000 of Revenue	Item	Cost ($ mil)	% of total	Per $1,000 of Revenue
All costs	891.2	100.000	401.0	Total Rentals	47.5	5.334	21.4
Cost of supplies	743.2	83.395	334.4	Equipment	25.8	2.895	11.6
Subcontracts	59.4	6.663	26.7	Buildings	21.7	2.441	9.8
Power, fuel, lubricants	88.6	9.942	39.9	Services purchased	113.9	12.781	51.3
Electricity	11.0	1.240	5.0	Communications	29.0	3.254	13.1
Natural gas	2.5	0.286	1.1	Building repairs	5.0	0.561	2.3
Gasoline and diesel	67.9	7.622	30.6	Machinery repairs	79.9	8.965	36.0
Highway	41.6	4.668	18.7				
Offroad	26.3	2.953	11.8				
Other power	7.1	0.793	3.2				

Source: *Economic Census of the United States*, 1997. Revenues referred to are total industry revenues for the current NAICS industry.

CONSTRUCTION PRODUCT DETAILS

Construction type	Value of construction work ($ mil and %)							
	Total		New construction		Additions, alterations, reconstruction		Maintenance and repair	
	Value	%	Value	%	Value	%	Value	%
Total	**2,191.3**	**100.0**	**1,604.4**	**100.0**	**170.4**	**100.0**	**376.2**	**100.0**
Building construction, total	**662.3**	**30.2**	**470.0**	**29.3**	**76.9**	**45.1**	**115.4**	**30.7**
Single-family houses, detached	505.6	23.1	361.5	22.5	53.6	31.5	90.5	24.0
Single-family houses, attached	44.9	2.0	33.2	2.1	6.0	3.5	5.6	1.5
Office buildings	14.8	0.7	9.9	0.6	3.5	2.0	1.4	0.4
All other commercial buildings, nec	25.8	1.2	20.2	1.3	1.7	1.0	3.8	1.0
Farm buildings, nonresidential	21.6	1.0	12.5	0.8	2.7	1.6	6.5	1.7
Other building construction	49.6	2.3	32.6	2.0	(S)	-	7.7	2.0
Nonbuilding construction, total	**1,488.8**	**67.9**	**1,134.4**	**70.7**	**93.5**	**54.9**	**260.8**	**69.3**
Water mains and related facilities	1,312.9	59.9	1,005.1	62.6	78.1	45.8	229.7	61.1
Sewage treatment plants	23.6	1.1	19.7	1.2	(D)	-	(D)	-
Water treatment plants	29.4	1.3	9.5	0.6	(D)	-	(D)	-
Water storage facilities	21.9	1.0	15.7	1.0	(S)	-	3.0	0.8
Other nonbuilding construction, nec	92.8	4.2	78.2	4.9	4.5	2.7	10.0	2.7
Construction work, nsk	**40.2**	**1.8**	**NA**	**-**	**NA**	**-**	**NA**	**-**

Source: *Economic Census of the United States*, 1997. Bold items are headers. (D) stands for data withheld to protect competitive information. (S) indicates instances where data do not meet publications standards.

LOCATION BY STATE AND REGIONAL CONCENTRATION

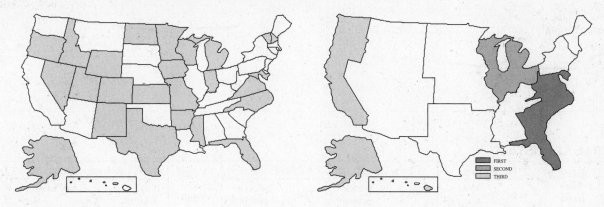

FIRST
SECOND
THIRD

INDUSTRY DATA BY STATE

State	Estab lish- ments	Employment			Compensation		Production				Capital Exp. ($ mil)
		Total	Workers	Total as % of US	Payroll per Employee	Wages per Worker	Costs ($ mil)	Value Added ($ mil)	Reve- nues ($ mil)	% of US	
California	229	1,675	1,242	7.90	34,849	30,936	76.5	141.2	224.1	10.09	15.1
Florida	251	1,820	1,285	8.58	28,797	25,559	63.1	98.1	172.3	7.76	13.1
Texas	311	1,609	1,236	7.58	23,874	21,184	63.1	87.1	154.9	6.97	8.1
Michigan	268	1,183	877	5.58	24,839	24,599	40.6	75.8	120.5	5.42	7.3
North Carolina	167	890	608	4.20	23,583	21,319	29.8	53.8	85.0	3.83	6.2
Colorado	88	554	374	2.61	30,477	31,508	27.7	46.8	75.2	3.38	2.8
Pennsylvania	139	709	522	3.34	25,622	24,550	27.5	44.4	72.6	3.27	5.3
Wisconsin	152	605	417	2.85	30,564	32,607	28.4	41.1	71.6	3.22	4.8
Minnesota	104	687	489	3.24	25,071	25,384	22.9	44.0	68.4	3.08	5.0
Virginia	90	587	394	2.77	23,596	23,322	21.0	37.1	58.8	2.64	5.8
Illinois	96	572	395	2.70	33,815	33,924	23.3	34.6	58.6	2.64	1.9
New York	130	560	376	2.64	26,430	27,274	18.7	35.8	55.4	2.49	2.1
New Jersey	60	442	314	2.08	34,792	34,401	18.2	33.9	54.3	2.44	1.9
Maryland	78	542	420	2.55	27,876	27,374	19.2	31.5	50.7	2.28	3.1
Indiana	97	472	375	2.22	25,074	24,024	19.2	30.0	50.0	2.25	2.7
Georgia	120	542	386	2.55	19,358	18,710	17.8	29.4	48.1	2.16	2.6
Missouri	85	399	288	1.88	25,093	24,219	19.9	25.4	46.4	2.09	2.9
Ohio	85	438	305	2.06	28,484	28,134	15.3	28.7	44.5	2.00	1.9
Washington	105	443	341	2.09	28,190	26,079	16.2	27.5	44.4	2.00	3.0
Massachusetts	41	288	179	1.36	41,292	39,492	10.3	28.1	41.4	1.86	1.3
Mississippi	34	353	270	1.66	23,875	22,644	19.5	15.5	37.5	1.69	1.3
Arkansas	42	381	247	1.80	22,583	22,320	14.4	19.4	34.5	1.55	1.4
Arizona	39	405	288	1.91	34,467	35,122	12.4	20.1	33.3	1.50	1.1
Oregon	100	362	261	1.71	23,854	18,598	10.3	21.3	31.8	1.43	0.9
Idaho	73	295	182	1.39	20,322	22,929	12.0	19.1	31.5	1.42	1.5
Tennessee	49	290	212	1.37	24,093	23,057	9.6	19.6	29.5	1.33	2.7
New Hampshire	38	310	235	1.46	32,213	26,813	12.7	16.4	29.4	1.32	1.8
Iowa	60	270	199	1.27	21,693	22,382	10.9	14.5	25.8	1.16	1.5
Nevada	37	201	141	0.95	30,368	28,418	11.3	14.0	25.5	1.15	1.1
Kansas	30	239	167	1.13	28,197	26,695	10.1	14.1	25.4	1.14	0.9
New Mexico	41	260	195	1.23	26,858	25,979	8.2	16.1	24.4	1.10	1.4
Connecticut	37	192	130	0.91	36,063	37,646	9.8	13.3	23.8	1.07	1.4
South Carolina	80	235	174	1.11	21,945	21,695	9.9	12.5	23.5	1.06	1.3
Utah	16	137	113	0.65	35,693	33,434	9.0	13.5	23.1	1.04	0.5
Louisiana	37	199	145	0.94	18,397	15,283	(D)	12.0	18.3	0.82	0.7
Oklahoma	46	229	178	1.08	19,594	21,298	8.2	8.5	16.7	.0.75	0.9
Wyoming	26	140	123	0.66	33,436	34,976	7.2	7.6	15.3	0.69	0.7
Alabama	25	120	95	0.57	24,267	20,147	(D)	6.8	11.5	0.52	0.5
Vermont	19	120	102	0.57	25,475	26,294	3.1	7.9	11.4	0.51	0.5
North Dakota	23	99	80	0.47	20,596	19,737	3.9	4.3	8.3	0.37	0.9
Alaska	19	61	46	0.29	31,705	31,891	2.4	5.1	7.4	0.33	0.4
Kentucky	21	64	41	0.30	23,187	28,732	2.6	3.6	6.2	0.28	0.1
Rhode Island	11	50	21	0.24	29,380	45,429	1.1	4.3	5.4	0.24	(S)
West Virginia	28	50	31	0.24	17,020	23,742	2.4	2.4	5.0	0.23	0.1
South Dakota	21	59	47	0.28	17,746	16,574	(S)	2.2	4.3	0.19	0.2
Delaware	13	51	38	0.24	23,294	24,947	1.8	2.4	4.3	0.19	0.2
Hawaii	10	36	21	0.17	33,667	33,762	2.0	2.1	4.2	0.19	0.6
Nebraska	86	646	508	3.05	24,997	24,935	(D)	36.1	(D)	-	5.5
Montana	61	202	152	0.95	20,807	21,309	(D)	15.5	(D)	-	0.9
Maine	48	138	95	0.65	18,529	21,589	(D)	6.6	(D)	-	1.2

Source: *Economic Census of the U.S., 1997*. Data are sorted by 1997 revenues or establishments. (D) means data suppression to prevent disclosure of company data. (S) means that data did not meet statistical standards for publication. A dash (-) is used when data are unavailable or cannot be calculated. Data followed by an * indicate the midpoint of a range. The ranges are: for 10, 0-19; for 60, 20-99, for 175, 100-249, for 375, 250-499, for 750, 500-999. Higher values are multiples of those shown, e.g., 3,750 is the midpoint of the range 2,500-4,999. Shaded *states* on the state map indicate those states which have proportionately greater representation in the industry than would be indicated by the state's population; the ratio is based on total revenues or number of establishments. Shaded *regions* indicate where the industry is regionally most concentrated.

NAICS 235910 - STRUCTURAL STEEL ERECTION CONTRACTORS*

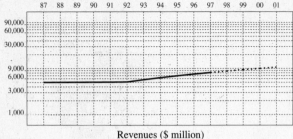

Revenues ($ million)

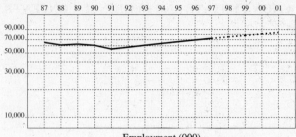

Employment (000)

GENERAL STATISTICS

Years	Estab-lish-ments	Employment		Payroll ($ mil)		Costs ($ mil)		Value Added ($ mil)	Revenues ($ mil)			Capital expend. ($ mil)
		Total	Constr. workers	Total	Worker payroll	Total	Cost of materials		All sources	Construction Total	Net	
1977	2,592	47,166	40,911	673.8	556.5	698.0	574.8	1,184.4	1,882.4	1,803.3	1,709.5	-
1982	3,705	61,588	52,645	1,291.2	1,056.1	1,273.6	903.5	2,376.2	3,649.8	3,540.7	3,233.1	-
1987	4,017	65,348	54,729	1,594.0	1,231.6	1,750.5	1,318.1	3,253.3	5,003.9	4,862.7	4,510.2	71.3
1988	3,415	61,208	53,119	1,628.6	1,230.7	1,810.9	1,358.5	3,205.5	5,021.9	4,880.4	4,505.5	-
1989	3,209	62,571	51,556	1,737.1	1,229.7	1,873.3	1,400.2	3,158.3	5,040.0	4,898.2	4,500.8	-
1990	3,356	60,697	50,039	1,736.6	1,228.8	1,937.8	1,443.1	3,111.9	5,058.2	4,916.1	4,496.1	-
1991	3,308	55,351	48,567	1,540.7	1,227.8	2,004.6	1,487.3	3,066.1	5,076.4	4,934.0	4,491.4	-
1992	3,792	57,986	47,138	1,628.9	1,226.9	2,073.7	1,532.9	3,021.0	5,094.7	4,952.0	4,486.7	77.3
1993	3,881	60,849	49,695	1,780.5	1,346.1	2,158.3	1,704.6	3,389.5	5,706.3	5,563.4	5,032.8	-
1994	3,970	63,712	52,252	1,932.2	1,465.2	2,242.9	1,876.2	3,758.0	6,317.9	6,174.9	5,578.8	-
1995	4,060	66,575	54,809	2,083.8	1,584.4	2,327.6	2,047.9	4,126.6	6,929.5	6,786.3	6,124.9	-
1996	4,149	69,438	57,366	2,235.5	1,703.5	2,412.2	2,219.5	4,495.1	7,541.1	7,397.8	6,670.9	-
1997	4,238	72,301	59,923	2,387.1	1,822.7	2,496.8	2,391.2	4,863.6	8,152.7	8,009.2	7,217.0	120.9
1998	4,327p	75,164p	62,480p	2,538.7p	1,941.9p	2,581.4p	2,562.9p	5,232.1p	8,764.3p	8,620.6p	7,763.1p	-
1999	4,416p	78,027p	65,037p	2,690.4p	2,061.0p	2,666.0p	2,734.5p	5,600.6p	9,375.9p	9,232.1p	8,309.1p	-
2000	4,506p	80,890p	67,594p	2,842.0p	2,180.2p	2,750.7p	2,906.2p	5,969.2p	9,987.5p	9,843.5p	8,855.2p	-
2001	4,595p	83,753p	70,151p	2,993.7p	2,299.3p	2,835.3p	3,077.8p	6,337.7p	10,599.1p	10,455.0p	9,401.2p	-

Sources: *Economic Census of the United States*, 1977, 1982, 1987, 1992, and 1997. Data for those years (years are in **bold** type) are from the 5-year censuses of the economy. Other values, unless otherwise noted, are extrapolations. Values footnoted 1 are from the *County Business Patterns* for the years indicated. Values marked with *p* are projections. Data are the most recent available at this level of detail. "Net" under "Construction" is construction revenues net of the costs of subcontracts.

INDICES OF CHANGE

Years	Estab-lish-ments	Employment		Payroll ($ mil)		Costs ($ mil)		Value Added ($ mil)	Revenues ($ mil)			Capital expend. ($ mil)
		Total	Constr. workers	Total	Worker payroll	Total	Cost of materials		All sources	Construction Total	Net	
1977	61.2	65.2	68.3	28.2	30.5	28.0	24.0	24.4	23.1	22.5	23.7	-
1982	87.4	85.2	87.9	54.1	57.9	51.0	37.8	48.9	44.8	44.2	44.8	-
1987	94.8	90.4	91.3	66.8	67.6	70.1	55.1	66.9	61.4	60.7	62.5	59.0
1992	89.5	80.2	78.7	68.2	67.3	83.1	64.1	62.1	62.5	61.8	62.2	63.9
1997	100.0	100.0	100.0	100.0	100.0	100.0	100.0	100.0	100.0	100.0	100.0	100.0

Sources: Same as General Statistics. The values shown reflect change from the base year, 1997. Values above 100 mean greater than 1997, values below 100 mean less than 1997, and a value of 100 in years other than 1997 means same as 1997. Indices are calculated only for Census years. Data are the most recent available at this level of detail.

SELECTED RATIOS

For 1997	Avg. of Sector	Analyzed Industry	Index	For 1997	Avg. of Sector	Analyzed Industry	Index
Employees per establishment	8.6	17.1	198	Value added per establishment	584,730	1,147,617	196
Construction workers per establishment	6.6	14.1	214	Value added per employee	67,759	67,269	99
Payroll per establishment	265,343	563,261	212	Value added per construction worker	88,592	81,164	92
Payroll per employee	30,748	33,016	107	Revenues per establishment	1,307,915	1,923,714	147
Payroll per construction worker	27,622	30,417	110	Revenues per employee	151,563	112,761	74
Costs per establishment	367,737	589,146	160	Revenues per construction worker	198,161	136,053	69
Costs per employee	42,614	34,533	81	CR as % of total revenues	98.48	98.24	100
Costs per construction worker	55,716	41,667	75	Net CR as % of CR	72.40	90.11	124
Materials as % of costs	95.75	95.77	100	Investment per establishment	22,948	28,528	124
Costs as % of revenues	28.12	30.63	109	Investment per employee	2,659	1,672	63
Costs as % of construction revenues	28.55	31.17	109	Investment per construction worker	3,477	2,018	58

Sources: Same as General Statistics. The 'Average of Sector' column represents the average for all industries in this sector. The Index shows the relationship between the Average and the Analyzed Industry. For example, 100 means that they are equal; 500 that the Analyzed Industry is five times the average; 50 means that the Analyzed Industry is half the national average. 'na' is used to show that data are 'not available'. CR stands for "construction revenues" and "Net CR" is construction revenues net of subcontract expenses.

*Equivalent to SIC 1791.

LEADING COMPANIES　Number shown: **17**　Total sales ($ mil): **699**　Total employment (000): **4.8**

Company Name	Address				CEO Name	Phone	Co. Type	Sales ($ mil)	Empl. (000)
Schuff Steel Co.	PO Box 39670	Phoenix	AZ	85069	David Schuff	602-252-7787	P	190	1.4
Harmon Contract	2001 Killebrew Dr	Bloomington	MN	55425	Peter Koukos	612-851-9949	S	85	0.3
Havens Steel Co.	7219 E 17th St	Kansas City	MO	64126		816-231-5724	R	65*	0.5
Pangere Corp.	4050 W 4th Ave	Gary	IN	46406	Steve Pangere	219-949-1368	R	46*	0.3
Azco Group Ltd.	PO Box 567	Appleton	WI	54912	Mark W Loper	920-734-5791	R	44	0.5
Derr Construction Co.	P O Box 637	Euless	TX	76039	Bob Derr	817-267-4433	R	44*	0.2
Eagle Precast Co.	PO Box 537	Salt Lake City	UT	84110	Ronald Davis	801-322-4400	S	33*	0.2
Globe Iron Construction Inc.	PO Box 2354	Norfolk	VA	23501	Arthur Peregoff	757-625-2542	R	32	0.2
Williams Industries Inc.	PO Box 506	Merrifield	VA	22116	Frank Williams	703-560-5196	P	29	0.3
Goodhart Sons Inc.	PO Box 10308	Lancaster	PA	17605	Gary Goodhart	717-656-2404	R	23*	0.2
Fisher Tank Co.	3131 W 4th St	Chester	PA	19013	Leo Pasini	610-494-7200	R	22	0.2
PSF Industries Inc.	PO Box 3747	Seattle	WA	98124	Stanley Miller	206-622-1252	R	20	0.2
Universal Steel Buildings Inc.	PO Box 818	Grenada	MS	38901	Robert Kennington	601-226-4512	R	18	<0.1
Snodgrass Construction Inc.	2700 G Washington	Wichita	KS	67210	James L Snodgrass	316-687-3110	R	16*	<0.1
DBM Contractors Inc.	PO Box 6139	Federal Way	WA	98063	Donald B Murphy	253-927-8510	R	15	0.4
Higgins Erectors and Haulers Inc.	PO Box 1008	Buffalo	NY	14240	Jeffrey Higgins	716-821-8000	R	15*	0.1
Busch Industries Inc.	900 E Paris Ave SE	Grand Rapids	MI	49546	John Busch	616-957-3737	R	2	<0.1

Source: *Ward's Business Directory of U.S. Private and Public Companies*, Volumes 1 and 2, 2000. The company type code used is as follows: P - Public, R - Private, S - Subsidiary, D - Division, J - Joint Venture, A - Affiliate, G - Group, N - Company type not reported. Sales are in millions of dollars, employees are in thousands. An asterisk (*) indicates an estimated sales volume. The symbol < stands for 'less than'. Company names and addresses are truncated, in some cases, to fit into the available space.

COST DETAILS

Item	Cost ($ mil)	% of total	Per $1,000 of Revenue	Item	Cost ($ mil)	% of total	Per $1,000 of Revenue
All costs	3,289.0	100.000	403.4	Total Rentals	229.4	6.974	28.1
Cost of supplies	2,391.3	72.703	293.3	Equipment	175.6	5.338	21.5
Subcontracts	792.3	24.088	97.2	Buildings	53.8	1.636	6.6
Power, fuel, lubricants	105.6	3.209	12.9	Services purchased	131.1	3.985	16.1
Electricity	22.2	0.674	2.7	Communications	47.0	1.430	5.8
Natural gas	5.6	0.171	0.7	Building repairs	10.8	0.329	1.3
Gasoline and diesel	72.8	2.214	8.9	Machinery repairs	73.2	2.226	9.0
Highway	56.7	1.725	7.0				
Offroad	16.1	0.489	2.0				
Other power	5.0	0.151	0.6				

Source: *Economic Census of the United States*, 1997. Revenues referred to are total industry revenues for the current NAICS industry.

CONSTRUCTION PRODUCT DETAILS

Construction type	Value of construction work ($ mil and %)							
	Total		New construction		Additions, alterations, reconstruction		Maintenance and repair	
	Value	%	Value	%	Value	%	Value	%
Total	**8,009.2**	**100.0**	**6,037.1**	**100.0**	**1,267.5**	**100.0**	**627.9**	**100.0**
Building construction, total	**5,751.9**	**71.8**	**4,640.2**	**76.9**	**860.7**	**67.9**	**251.1**	**40.0**
Single-family houses, detached and attached	172.5	2.2	136.2	2.3	27.5	2.2	8.7	1.4
Apartment buildings, condos and cooperatives	91.6	1.1	66.8	1.1	9.8	0.8	(S)	-
Manufacturing and light industrial buildings	1,016.5	12.7	722.1	12.0	195.7	15.4	98.6	15.7
Manufacturing and light industrial warehouses	523.2	6.5	432.1	7.2	72.5	5.7	18.6	3.0
Hotels and motels	220.1	2.7	185.1	3.1	28.8	2.3	6.3	1.0
Office buildings	1,089.8	13.6	928.6	15.4	128.9	10.2	32.3	5.2
All other commercial buildings, nec	680.4	8.5	567.6	9.4	92.1	7.3	20.8	3.3
Commercial warehouses	558.2	7.0	497.1	8.2	46.1	3.6	15.1	2.4
Religious buildings	100.0	1.2	77.8	1.3	20.3	1.6	1.8	0.3
Educational buildings	571.8	7.1	450.0	7.5	110.8	8.7	11.0	1.8
Health care and institutional buildings	341.7	4.3	256.9	4.3	72.2	5.7	(S)	-
Public safety buildings	149.2	1.9	115.1	1.9	31.9	2.5	2.1	0.3
Amusement, social, and recreational buildings	78.4	1.0	58.5	1.0	17.0	1.3	2.9	0.5
Other building construction	158.6	2.0	146.1	2.4	7.2	0.6	5.3	0.8
Nonbuilding construction, total	**2,180.5**	**27.2**	**1,396.9**	**23.1**	**406.8**	**32.1**	**376.8**	**60.0**
Highways, streets, and related work	219.8	2.7	155.6	2.6	42.5	3.4	21.7	3.5
Bridges, tunnels, and elevated highways	400.4	5.0	206.6	3.4	158.7	12.5	35.1	5.6
Sewers, water mains, and related facilities	80.5	1.0	63.3	1.0	11.7	0.9	5.5	0.9
Power plants	119.7	1.5	71.8	1.2	24.9	2.0	23.0	3.7
Blast furnaces, refineries, chemical complexes, etc	-	-	56.9	0.9	-	-	-	-
Sewage and water treatment plants	133.3	1.7	103.2	1.7	25.9	2.0	4.3	0.7
Water storage facilities	365.8	4.6	297.3	4.9	12.1	1.0	56.4	9.0
Tank storage facilities other than water	459.0	5.7	295.9	4.9	57.7	4.5	105.5	16.8
Other nonbuilding construction, nec	183.4	2.3	146.2	2.4	17.8	1.4	19.3	3.1
Construction work, nsk	**76.8**	**1.0**	**NA**	**-**	**NA**	**-**	**NA**	**-**

Source: *Economic Census of the United States*, 1997. Bold items are headers. (D) stands for data withheld to protect competitive information. (S) indicates instances where data do not meet publications standards.

LOCATION BY STATE AND REGIONAL CONCENTRATION

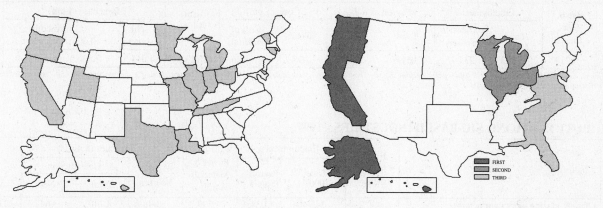

INDUSTRY DATA BY STATE

State	Estab lish- ments	Employment			Compensation		Production				Capital Exp. ($ mil)
		Total	Workers	Total as % of US	Payroll per Employee	Wages per Worker	Costs ($ mil)	Value Added ($ mil)	Reve- nues ($ mil)	% of US	
California	482	9,784	7,962	13.53	35,424	32,478	415.3	717.0	1,216.8	14.93	13.8
Texas	300	6,552	5,583	9.06	28,706	26,549	174.6	343.3	571.5	7.01	11.2
New York	297	3,400	2,670	4.70	36,080	34,874	118.9	246.4	419.6	5.15	4.9
Ohio	166	3,227	2,643	4.46	34,460	31,439	122.2	241.0	417.2	5.12	5.6
Illinois	205	2,833	2,301	3.92	37,544	35,992	146.6	215.9	401.5	4.93	6.1
Michigan	127	2,118	1,748	2.93	37,491	35,387	108.5	174.9	339.9	4.17	4.6
Florida	180	3,204	2,598	4.43	29,104	26,721	105.7	180.5	332.5	4.08	3.8
Missouri	95	2,082	1,772	2.88	34,625	31,566	59.1	150.6	228.9	2.81	4.2
Indiana	93	2,339	1,968	3.24	33,945	31,109	55.2	155.6	226.4	2.78	3.3
Tennessee	100	1,848	1,520	2.56	26,996	24,084	88.3	110.5	217.2	2.66	4.3
Oregon	80	1,608	1,403	2.22	34,630	32,560	44.3	149.8	205.7	2.52	2.9
Connecticut	59	1,244	1,029	1.72	44,605	38,507	59.4	104.2	203.0	2.49	2.9
Pennsylvania	121	1,813	1,503	2.51	33,544	31,076	49.8	119.1	192.2	2.36	2.6
Washington	170	1,598	1,385	2.21	32,265	30,225	45.8	105.1	164.2	2.01	2.1
Virginia	92	1,716	1,433	2.37	27,131	24,395	38.0	107.5	155.6	1.91	2.4
Louisiana	85	1,358	1,133	1.88	28,728	26,225	45.6	97.1	153.7	1.89	(S)
Minnesota	57	1,392	1,134	1.93	39,149	37,526	37.5	100.9	152.4	1.87	2.9
Utah	56	985	823	1.36	34,340	32,091	51.7	62.7	123.9	1.52	2.2
North Carolina	99	1,292	1,024	1.79	27,755	25,551	47.0	68.5	121.7	1.49	1.7
Maryland	49	1,185	997	1.64	33,504	30,932	31.8	68.1	111.0	1.36	1.7
Arizona	87	1,074	930	1.49	32,423	30,267	35.6	64.0	108.2	1.33	(S)
Wisconsin	64	930	750	1.29	38,759	35,959	21.9	70.1	103.2	1.27	2.2
South Carolina	68	1,185	1,032	1.64	26,084	24,376	22.9	52.7	81.2	1.00	1.3
Iowa	62	789	663	1.09	25,721	21,566	21.2	45.6	79.1	0.97	1.1
Kansas	63	931	852	1.29	24,958	24,284	22.2	42.5	67.1	0.82	1.5
Kentucky	34	736	639	1.02	29,299	29,066	17.2	47.5	66.3	0.81	0.7
Delaware	11	315	249	0.44	41,340	35,538	18.9	25.9	53.8	0.66	0.8
Mississippi	54	732	563	1.01	24,374	22,604	11.0	39.9	53.6	0.66	1.0
Hawaii	19	352	288	0.49	42,665	43,288	(D)	28.8	50.7	0.62	0.8
Nebraska	71	481	419	0.67	27,010	25,764	6.7	37.2	44.5	0.55	0.2
Rhode Island	12	309	254	0.43	39,113	34,358	9.9	26.9	40.4	0.50	0.2
New Mexico	14	234	205	0.32	30,966	30,249	6.3	18.2	25.2	0.31	(D)
Arkansas	55	287	228	0.40	20,181	17,018	5.6	15.5	22.2	0.27	0.3
Vermont	9	133	107	0.18	37,060	33,206	7.5	11.5	19.9	0.24	0.2
South Dakota	26	184	147	0.25	23,929	22,136	6.7	9.1	18.4	0.23	0.5
Alaska	13	119	97	0.16	45,336	42,454	(D)	11.1	16.6	0.20	0.4
West Virginia	19	107	81	0.15	35,215	37,728	5.0	8.5	14.7	0.18	(D)
Montana	17	146	135	0.20	19,158	19,259	2.3	6.3	9.6	0.12	(S)
Maine	8	77	66	0.11	23,455	21,212	2.4	5.3	8.0	0.10	0.1
New Hampshire	6	29	23	0.04	35,241	33,391	0.5	1.5	2.1	0.03	-
New Jersey	155	2,638	2,165	3.65	40,025	35,225	(D)	188.7	(D)	-	4.8
Georgia	134	1,832	1,503	2.53	31,275	27,724	(D)	115.1	(D)	-	4.0
Colorado	87	1,814	1,533	2.51	29,598	26,470	(D)	109.9	(D)	-	2.5
Massachusetts	69	(S)	(S)	-	-	-	(D)	(S)	(D)	-	(S)
Alabama	55	1,441	1,202	1.99	31,291	29,071	(D)	83.9	(D)	-	3.0
Oklahoma	36	878	699	1.21	30,804	28,930	(D)	52.6	(D)	-	1.2
Idaho	34	467	402	0.65	23,480	22,473	(D)	24.6	(D)	-	0.8
Nevada	27	1,151	923	1.59	38,935	36,044	(D)	91.8	(D)	-	2.4
North Dakota	11	147	113	0.20	32,211	29,717	7.8	14.8	(D)	-	0.3
Wyoming	4	40	30	0.06	26,550	20,800	(D)	2.9	(D)	-	-

Source: Economic Census of the U.S., 1997. Data are sorted by 1997 revenues or establishments. (D) means data suppression to prevent disclosure of company data. (S) means that data did not meet statistical standards for publication. A dash (-) is used when data are unavailable or cannot be calculated. Data followed by an * indicate the midpoint of a range. The ranges are: for 10, 0-19; for 60, 20-99, for 175, 100-249, for 375, 250-499, for 750, 500-999. Higher values are multiples of those shown, e.g., 3,750 is the midpoint of the range 2,500-4,999. Shaded *states* on the state map indicate those states which have proportionately greater representation in the industry than would be indicated by the state's population; the ratio is based on total revenues or number of establishments. Shaded *regions* indicate where the industry is regionally most concentrated.

NAICS 235920 - GLASS AND GLAZING CONTRACTORS

GENERAL STATISTICS

Years	Estab-lish-ments	Employment		Payroll ($ mil)		Costs ($ mil)		Value Added ($ mil)	Revenues ($ mil)			Capital expend. ($ mil)
		Total	Constr. workers	Total	Worker payroll	Total	Cost of materials		All sources	Construction		
										Total	Net	
1997	4,714	35,823	23,207	1,051.6	623.7	1,826.1	1,775.6	2,123.5	4,045.5	3,830.9	3,735.0	47.4

Source: Economic Census of the United States, 1997. This is a newly defined industry. Data for prior years were unavailable at the time of publication but may become available over time. "Net" under "Construction" is construction revenue net of the costs of subcontracts.

DISTRIBUTION AMONG SIC-BASED INDUSTRIES - 1997

SIC	Industry	Estab-lish-ments	Employment		Cost of Power & Materials ($ mil)	Revenues ($ mil)			Value Added ($ mil)
			Total (000)	Payroll ($ mil)		All Sources	Construction		
							Total	Net	
179300	Glass & glazing work contractors	4,472.0	34,740	1,024.4	1,797.2	3,948.8	3,740.1	3,647.3	2,058.78
179920	Special trade contractors, nec (pt)	242.0	1,084	27.1	29.0	-	-	-	-

Source: 1997 Economic Census. U.S. Census Bureau, U.S. Department of Commerce, August 1997. SIC codes ending in two zeroes represent complete 4-digit SICs. All others are parts of 4-digit SIC industries. Items showing a dash (-) indicate that data are not available because of disclosure problems.

SIC INDUSTRIES RELATED TO NAICS 235920

SIC	Industry	1990	1991	1992	1993	1994	1995	1996	1997
1793	**Glass and Glazing Work**								
	Establishments (number)	4,013	4,012	4,590	4,583	4,572p	4,563p	4,554p	4,544p
	Employment (thousands)	39.1	35.0	32.1	32.7	29.2e	27.9e	26.6e	25.4e
	Revenues ($ million)	3,111.5e	3,011.1e	2,913.9	2,819.8e	2,728.8e	2,640.8e	2,555.6e	2,473.1e
1799	**Special Trade Contractors, n.e.c.***								
	Establishments (number)	22,471	22,634	25,270	27,296	26,150p	26,601p	27,060p	27,527p
	Employment (thousands)	197.0	186.3	204.3	207.1	216.9e	223.4e	230.2e	237.1e
	Revenues ($ million)	12,936.7e	13,535.6e	14,162.3	14,818.0e	15,504.1e	16,221.9e	16,973.0e	17,758.8e

Source: Economic Census of the United States, 1992, annual surveys of economic sectors conducted by the Bureau of the Census, and estimates or projections based on the 1982-1992 period; not all data are shown. 'e' marks estimates made by the editors; 'p' indicates projections based on time series. A dash (-) indicates that data for this SIC or year were not available. * Indicates that only a portion of this industry is present within the NAICS data. If no * is shown, the entire industry is contained within the NAICS data.

INDICES OF CHANGE

Years	Estab-lish-ments	Employment		Payroll ($ mil)		Costs ($ mil)		Value Added ($ mil)	Revenues ($ mil)			Capital expend. ($ mil)
		Total	Constr. workers	Total	Worker payroll	Total	Cost of materials		All sources	Construction		
										Total	Net	
1997	100.0	100.0	100.0	100.0	100.0	100.0	100.0	100.0	100.0	100.0	100.0	100.0

Sources: Same as General Statistics. The values shown reflect change from the base year, 1997. Values above 100 mean greater than 1997, values below 100 mean less than 1997, and a value of 100 in years other than 1997 means same as 1997. Indices are calculated only for Census years. Data are the most recent available at this level of detail.

SELECTED RATIOS

For 1997	Avg. of Sector	Analyzed Industry	Index	For 1997	Avg. of Sector	Analyzed Industry	Index
Employees per establishment	8.6	7.6	88	Value added per establishment	584,730	450,467	77
Construction workers per establishment	6.6	4.9	75	Value added per employee	67,759	59,278	87
Payroll per establishment	265,343	223,080	84	Value added per construction worker	88,592	91,503	103
Payroll per employee	30,748	29,355	95	Revenues per establishment	1,307,915	858,188	66
Payroll per construction worker	27,622	26,876	97	Revenues per employee	151,563	112,930	75
Costs per establishment	367,737	387,378	105	Revenues per construction worker	198,161	174,322	88
Costs per employee	42,614	50,976	120	CR as % of total revenues	98.48	94.70	96
Costs per construction worker	55,716	78,687	141	Net CR as % of CR	72.40	97.50	135
Materials as % of costs	95.75	97.23	102	Investment per establishment	22,948	10,055	44
Costs as % of revenues	28.12	45.14	161	Investment per employee	2,659	1,323	50
Costs as % of construction revenues	28.55	47.67	167	Investment per construction worker	3,477	2,042	59

Sources: Same as General Statistics. The 'Average of Sector' column represents the average for all industries in this sector. The Index shows the relationship between the Average and the Analyzed Industry. For example, 100 means that they are equal; 500 that the Analyzed Industry is five times the average; 50 means that the Analyzed Industry is half the national average. 'na' is used to show that data are 'not available'. CR stands for "construction revenues" and "Net CR" is construction revenues net of subcontract expenses.

LEADING COMPANIES   Number shown: **5**   Total sales ($ mil): **291**   Total employment (000): **1.0**

Company Name	Address				CEO Name	Phone	Co. Type	Sales ($ mil)	Empl. (000)
Benson Industries Inc.	1650 NW Naito	Portland	OR	97209	Lou Niles	503-226-7611	R	106*	0.3
Harmon Contract	2001 Killebrew Dr	Bloomington	MN	55425	Peter Koukos	612-851-9949	S	85	0.3
Norment Industries Inc.	PO Drawer 6129	Montgomery	AL	36106	Dennis A Flynn	334-281-8440	S	70*	0.4
Gump Glass	1265 S Broadway	Denver	CO	80210		303-778-1155	D	18*	<0.1
Model Glass Co.	4907 E Landon Dr	Anaheim	CA	92807	Tom Metz	714-777-7714	R	12*	<0.1

Source: Ward's Business Directory of U.S. Private and Public Companies, Volumes 1 and 2, 2000. The company type code used is as follows: P - Public, R - Private, S - Subsidiary, D - Division, J - Joint Venture, A - Affiliate, G - Group, N - Company type not reported. Sales are in millions of dollars, employees are in thousands. An asterisk (*) indicates an estimated sales volume. The symbol < stands for 'less than'. Company names and addresses are truncated, in some cases, to fit into the available space.

COST DETAILS

Item	Cost ($ mil)	% of total	Per $1,000 of Revenue	Item	Cost ($ mil)	% of total	Per $1,000 of Revenue
All costs	1,922.0	100.000	475.1	Total Rentals	75.5	3.927	18.7
Cost of supplies	1,775.6	92.383	438.9	Equipment	22.0	1.147	5.4
Subcontracts	95.9	4.987	23.7	Buildings	53.4	2.780	13.2
Power, fuel, lubricants	50.5	2.630	12.5	Services purchased	50.0	2.602	12.4
Electricity	13.1	0.682	3.2	Communications	26.9	1.399	6.6
Natural gas	3.6	0.189	0.9	Building repairs	4.5	0.232	1.1
Gasoline and diesel	32.1	1.668	7.9	Machinery repairs	18.7	0.971	4.6
Highway	29.0	1.509	7.2				
Offroad	3.1	0.159	0.8				
Other power	1.7	0.091	0.4				

Source: Economic Census of the United States, 1997. Revenues referred to are total industry revenues for the current NAICS industry.

CONSTRUCTION PRODUCT DETAILS

Construction type	Value of construction work ($ mil and %)							
	Total		New construction		Additions, alterations, reconstruction		Maintenance and repair	
	Value	%	Value	%	Value	%	Value	%
Total	**3,830.9**	**100.0**	**2,262.6**	**100.0**	**780.2**	**100.0**	**651.0**	**100.0**
Building construction, total	**3,688.5**	**96.3**	**2,259.6**	**99.9**	**778.7**	**99.8**	**650.2**	**99.9**
Single-family houses, detached	565.7	14.8	322.7	14.3	117.8	15.1	125.3	19.2
Single-family houses, attached	113.2	3.0	54.2	2.4	22.3	2.9	36.7	5.6
Apartment buildings, condos and cooperatives	138.7	3.6	55.9	2.5	26.9	3.4	55.9	8.6
Manufacturing and light industrial buildings	190.5	5.0	130.4	5.8	32.5	4.2	27.6	4.2
Manufacturing and light industrial warehouses	114.5	3.0	79.1	3.5	18.2	2.3	17.2	2.6
Hotels and motels	182.4	4.8	119.0	5.3	34.1	4.4	29.3	4.5
Office buildings	899.0	23.5	607.3	26.8	180.4	23.1	111.3	17.1
All other commercial buildings, nec	638.6	16.7	377.0	16.7	123.6	15.8	138.1	21.2
Commercial warehouses	79.6	2.1	56.0	2.5	13.4	1.7	10.2	1.6
Religious buildings	94.6	2.5	50.9	2.2	26.4	3.4	17.3	2.7
Educational buildings	347.2	9.1	203.7	9.0	107.5	13.8	36.0	5.5
Health care and institutional buildings	191.5	5.0	118.1	5.2	50.7	6.5	22.6	3.5
Public safety buildings	93.2	2.4	64.3	2.8	16.1	2.1	12.8	2.0
Other building construction	39.8	1.0	21.1	0.9	8.8	1.1	9.8	1.5
Nonbuilding construction, total	**5.3**	**0.1**	**3.0**	**0.1**	**1.4**	**0.2**	**0.8**	**0.1**
Other nonbuilding construction, nec	5.3	0.1	3.0	0.1	1.4	0.2	0.8	0.1
Construction work, nsk	**137.2**	**3.6**	NA	-	NA	-	NA	-

Source: Economic Census of the United States, 1997. Bold items are headers. (D) stands for data withheld to protect competitive information. (S) indicates instances where data do not meet publications standards

LOCATION BY STATE AND REGIONAL CONCENTRATION

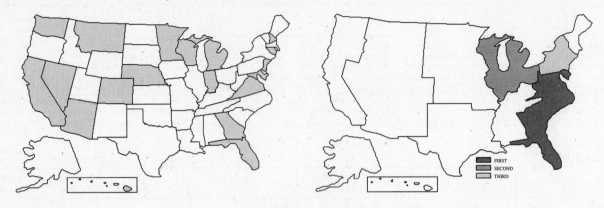

FIRST
SECOND
THIRD

INDUSTRY DATA BY STATE

State	Estab lish- ments	Employment			Compensation		Production				Capital Exp. ($ mil)
		Total	Workers	Total as % of US	Payroll per Employee	Wages per Worker	Costs ($ mil)	Value Added ($ mil)	Reve- nues ($ mil)	% of US	
California	700	4,370	2,709	12.20	29,308	29,050	224.0	286.9	521.5	12.89	4.0
Florida	387	2,612	1,804	7.29	24,589	21,766	111.8	148.4	267.3	6.61	3.0
New York	326	1,966	1,231	5.49	30,442	27,045	107.6	135.1	251.3	6.21	3.2
Texas	281	2,144	1,540	5.98	26,961	22,036	90.5	106.5	198.9	4.92	1.7
Michigan	191	1,337	876	3.73	33,883	30,486	81.8	101.1	188.7	4.66	2.5
Illinois	219	1,710	1,068	4.77	31,942	29,288	82.0	98.7	183.4	4.53	2.1
Pennsylvania	145	1,403	854	3.92	31,800	31,854	78.0	81.6	163.5	4.04	1.5
Maryland	99	1,151	758	3.21	30,283	27,323	70.8	61.0	138.0	3.41	1.4
New Jersey	149	912	594	2.55	37,723	35,736	57.4	67.5	129.7	3.21	2.0
Wisconsin	65	1,156	598	3.23	34,689	31,962	53.8	70.4	126.9	3.14	3.5
Georgia	148	1,193	833	3.33	25,608	22,893	62.4	60.2	126.0	3.11	1.3
Washington	136	996	593	2.78	32,749	31,546	62.2	57.8	121.9	3.01	1.4
Ohio	152	1,069	667	2.98	27,829	26,018	49.9	62.4	116.2	2.87	1.7
Virginia	90	897	607	2.50	32,777	29,532	47.0	59.9	111.8	2.76	1.3
Nevada	58	755	571	2.11	36,099	33,545	44.2	62.0	107.5	2.66	0.6
North Carolina	126	1,076	626	3.00	26,661	23,214	49.2	49.5	106.0	2.62	2.4
Indiana	91	885	599	2.47	29,285	28,067	54.4	41.0	96.8	2.39	0.5
Massachusetts	97	771	479	2.15	32,123	30,065	37.9	45.1	85.3	2.11	1.4
Arizona	96	701	449	1.96	26,244	21,561	43.2	39.0	82.8	2.05	1.0
Minnesota	73	643	417	1.79	35,017	34,499	37.3	43.9	82.0	2.03	1.6
Missouri	77	601	395	1.68	34,775	33,425	31.3	45.9	80.9	2.00	0.8
Colorado	84	808	613	2.26	26,749	25,772	39.5	40.8	80.7	2.00	1.4
Tennessee	74	635	416	1.77	26,687	21,108	27.3	31.2	58.9	1.46	0.5
Connecticut	69	486	302	1.36	36,755	32,026	21.7	34.8	57.7	1.43	0.4
South Carolina	60	524	346	1.46	23,565	21,046	19.5	27.7	47.9	1.18	0.6
Alabama	59	554	353	1.55	22,128	15,802	19.6	25.4	46.3	1.15	0.4
Oregon	64	326	206	0.91	31,914	31,053	16.2	22.2	38.5	0.95	0.5
Louisiana	58	396	292	1.11	22,891	21,031	14.7	17.6	32.6	0.81	0.3
Oklahoma	40	284	182	0.79	20,599	18,390	18.0	13.6	31.7	0.78	0.9
Nebraska	43	223	155	0.62	30,247	24,581	(D)	10.2	25.8	0.64	0.3
Kansas	32	269	176	0.75	30,093	25,756	9.5	15.8	25.6	0.63	0.3
Hawaii	29	184	117	0.51	33,125	34,658	11.5	12.2	24.7	0.61	(D)
Iowa	21	233	162	0.65	23,592	17,944	9.4	11.8	21.6	0.53	0.3
Arkansas	42	269	164	0.75	25,851	24,335	8.5	12.7	21.3	0.53	0.4
New Hampshire	29	176	89	0.49	29,398	29,921	10.2	9.8	20.3	0.50	0.3
Montana	24	156	85	0.44	19,481	14,529	9.1	9.4	18.7	0.46	0.2
Utah	33	172	127	0.48	22,994	19,929	10.3	7.9	18.5	0.46	0.3
Mississippi	29	164	87	0.46	23,537	26,092	(D)	7.1	15.5	0.38	0.1
Maine	17	119	80	0.33	27,782	24,900	8.0	6.3	14.3	0.35	0.1
West Virginia	22	136	87	0.38	21,838	18,816	4.4	9.2	13.6	0.34	0.1
Delaware	11	73	47	0.20	29,507	26,191	5.6	4.3	9.9	0.25	(D)
North Dakota	10	80	58	0.22	22,837	19,897	5.9	3.7	9.9	0.24	0.2
South Dakota	18	144	100	0.40	18,444	17,960	3.9	5.4	9.3	0.23	0.1
Vermont	21	85	56	0.24	27,141	28,893	4.3	4.1	8.5	0.21	0.1
D.C.	4	49	32	0.14	28,510	24,437	1.8	2.2	4.0	0.10	0.1
Alaska	6	(S)	(S)	-	-	-	(S)	(S)	(S)	-	(D)
Kentucky	46	455	346	1.27	24,980	23,642	(D)	24.9	(D)	-	0.2
Idaho	22	140	90	0.39	21,743	20,200	(D)	6.1	(D)	-	0.1
New Mexico	18	112	62	0.31	22,625	16,935	(D)	4.6	(D)	-	0.1
Rhode Island	17	167	(S)	0.47	33,347	-	11.6	14.8	(D)	-	0.2
Wyoming	7	(S)	(S)	-	-	-	(D)	(S)	(D)	-	(D)

Source: Economic Census of the U.S., 1997. Data are sorted by 1997 revenues or establishments. (D) means data suppression to prevent disclosure of company data. (S) means that data did not meet statistical standards for publication. A dash (-) is used when data are unavailable or cannot be calculated. Data followed by an * indicate the midpoint of a range. The ranges are: for 10, 0-19; for 60, 20-99, for 175, 100-249, for 375, 250-499, for 750, 500-999. Higher values are multiples of those shown, e.g., 3,750 is the midpoint of the range 2,500-4,999. Shaded *states* on the state map indicate those states which have proportionately greater representation in the industry than would be indicated by the state's population; the ratio is based on total revenues or number of establishments. Shaded *regions* indicate where the industry is regionally most concentrated.

NAICS 235930 - EXCAVATION CONTRACTORS*

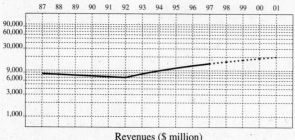

Revenues ($ million)

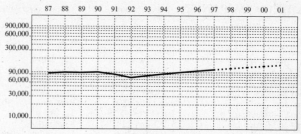

Employment (000)

GENERAL STATISTICS

Years	Estab-lish-ments	Employment		Payroll ($ mil)		Costs ($ mil)		Value Added ($ mil)	Revenues ($ mil)			Capital expend. ($ mil)
		Total	Constr. workers	Total	Worker payroll	Total	Cost of materials		All sources	Construction		
										Total	Net	
1977	16,521	104,092	91,522	1,207.7	1,020.9	1,376.6	883.8	2,993.6	4,370.2	4,215.7	3,929.7	-
1982	19,646	135,968	115,059	2,151.9	1,756.7	2,965.4	1,575.4	5,507.2	8,472.6	8,181.3	7,337.0	-
1987	13,422	95,329	79,198	2,059.8	1,597.5	2,744.7	1,582.8	5,707.7	8,452.4	8,244.4	7,491.0	465.5
1988	14,800	99,404	75,520	2,515.8	1,556.0	2,738.6	1,589.6	5,403.3	8,152.1	7,949.0	7,196.3	-
1989	15,065	98,589	72,012	2,577.1	1,515.6	2,732.5	1,596.4	5,115.1	7,862.5	7,664.3	6,913.3	-
1990	15,376	101,144	68,667	2,580.0	1,476.3	2,726.5	1,603.2	4,842.3	7,583.2	7,389.7	6,641.4	-
1991	15,513	90,727	65,478	2,302.5	1,438.0	2,720.4	1,610.1	4,584.1	7,313.8	7,124.9	6,380.1	-
1992	13,898	77,126	62,437	1,816.8	1,400.6	2,714.4	1,617.0	4,339.6	7,054.0	6,869.7	6,129.2	331.4
1993	14,764	84,948	68,516	2,124.2	1,625.7	2,886.9	1,892.4	5,288.9	8,481.9	8,245.1	7,346.6	-
1994	15,630	92,770	74,594	2,431.6	1,850.7	3,059.4	2,167.8	6,238.2	9,909.8	9,620.5	8,564.0	-
1995	16,497	100,593	80,673	2,739.1	2,075.8	3,231.9	2,443.3	7,187.6	11,337.8	10,995.8	9,781.3	-
1996	17,363	108,415	86,751	3,046.5	2,300.8	3,404.4	2,718.7	8,136.9	12,765.7	12,371.2	10,998.7	-
1997	18,229	116,237	92,830	3,353.9	2,525.9	3,576.9	2,994.1	9,086.2	14,193.6	13,746.6	12,216.1	994.7
1998	19,095p	124,059p	98,909p	3,661.3p	2,751.0p	3,749.4p	3,269.5p	10,035.5p	15,621.5p	15,122.0p	13,433.5p	-
1999	19,961p	131,881p	104,987p	3,968.7p	2,976.0p	3,921.9p	3,544.9p	10,984.8p	17,049.4p	16,497.4p	14,650.9p	-
2000	20,828p	139,704p	111,066p	4,276.2p	3,201.1p	4,094.4p	3,820.4p	11,934.2p	18,477.4p	17,872.7p	15,868.2p	-
2001	21,694p	147,526p	117,144p	4,583.6p	3,426.1p	4,266.9p	4,095.8p	12,883.5p	19,905.3p	19,248.1p	17,085.6p	-

Sources: Economic Census of the United States, 1977, 1982, 1987, 1992, and 1997. Data for those years (years are in **bold** type) are from the 5-year censuses of the economy. Other values, unless otherwise noted, are extrapolations. Values footnoted 1 are from the *County Business Patterns* for the years indicated. Values marked with *p* are projections. Data are the most recent available at this level of detail. "Net" under "Construction" is construction revenues net of the costs of subcontracts.

INDICES OF CHANGE

Years	Estab-lish-ments	Employment		Payroll ($ mil)		Costs ($ mil)		Value Added ($ mil)	Revenues ($ mil)			Capital expend. ($ mil)
		Total	Constr. workers	Total	Worker payroll	Total	Cost of materials		All sources	Construction		
										Total	Net	
1977	90.6	89.6	98.6	36.0	40.4	38.5	29.5	32.9	30.8	30.7	32.2	-
1982	107.8	117.0	123.9	64.2	69.5	82.9	52.6	60.6	59.7	59.5	60.1	-
1987	73.6	82.0	85.3	61.4	63.2	76.7	52.9	62.8	59.6	60.0	61.3	46.8
1992	76.2	66.4	67.3	54.2	55.4	75.9	54.0	47.8	49.7	50.0	50.2	33.3
1997	100.0	100.0	100.0	100.0	100.0	100.0	100.0	100.0	100.0	100.0	100.0	100.0

Sources: Same as General Statistics. The values shown reflect change from the base year, 1997. Values above 100 mean greater than 1997, values below 100 mean less than 1997, and a value of 100 in years other than 1997 means same as 1997. Indices are calculated only for Census years. Data are the most recent available at this level of detail.

SELECTED RATIOS

For 1997	Avg. of Sector	Analyzed Industry	Index	For 1997	Avg. of Sector	Analyzed Industry	Index
Employees per establishment	8.6	6.4	74	Value added per establishment	584,730	498,448	85
Construction workers per establishment	6.6	5.1	77	Value added per employee	67,759	78,170	115
Payroll per establishment	265,343	183,987	69	Value added per construction worker	88,592	97,880	110
Payroll per employee	30,748	28,854	94	Revenues per establishment	1,307,915	778,627	60
Payroll per construction worker	27,622	27,210	99	Revenues per employee	151,563	122,109	81
Costs per establishment	367,737	196,220	53	Revenues per construction worker	198,161	152,899	77
Costs per employee	42,614	30,772	72	CR as % of total revenues	98.48	96.85	98
Costs per construction worker	55,716	38,532	69	Net CR as % of CR	72.40	88.87	123
Materials as % of costs	95.75	83.71	87	Investment per establishment	22,948	54,567	238
Costs as % of revenues	28.12	25.20	90	Investment per employee	2,659	8,558	322
Costs as % of construction revenues	28.55	26.02	91	Investment per construction worker	3,477	10,715	308

Sources: Same as General Statistics. The 'Average of Sector' column represents the average for all industries in this sector. The Index shows the relationship between the Average and the Analyzed Industry. For example, 100 means that they are equal; 500 that the Analyzed Industry is five times the average; 50 means that the Analyzed Industry is half the national average. 'na' is used to show that data are 'not available'. CR stands for "construction revenues" and "Net CR" is construction revenues net of subcontract expenses.

*Equivalent to SIC 1794.

LEADING COMPANIES   Number shown: **41**   Total sales ($ mil): **2,877**   Total employment (000): **13.9**

Company Name	Address				CEO Name	Phone	Co. Type	Sales ($ mil)	Empl. (000)
Walsh Group Ltd.	929 W Adams	Chicago	IL	60607	Matthew Walsh	312-563-5400	R	1,170	3.5
Driggs Corp.	8700 Ashwood Dr	Capitol Heights	MD	20743	John Driggs	301-499-1950	R	150*	1.1
National Engineering	12608 Alameda Dr	Cleveland	OH	44136	Marty Cohen	440-238-3331	R	150*	0.6
Koester Equipment Inc.	14649 Hwy	Evansville	IN	47711	Homer Fruit	812-867-6635	R	83	0.3
Freesen Inc.	PO Box 350	Bluffs	IL	62621	Thomas Oetgen	217-754-3304	R	80	0.5
Neosho Construction Co.	P O Box 4526	Topeka	KS	66604	Steve Hutchinson	785-273-0200	R	80	0.4
Phillips and Jordan Inc.	PO Box 52050	Knoxville	TN	37950	William T Phillips Sr	423-688-8342	R	80*	0.4
Ryan Incorporated Central	P O Box 206	Janesville	WI	53547	Patrick Ryan	608-754-2291	R	78	0.5
Glasgow Inc.	PO Box 1089	Glenside	PA	19038	Bruce Rambo	215-884-8800	R	75	0.5
Devcon International Corp.	1350 E Newport	Deerfield Beach	FL	33442	Donald L Smith Jr	954-429-1500	P	66	0.4
Case Foundation Co.	P O Box 40	Roselle	IL	60172	John E O'Malley	630-529-2911	S	58	0.5
George J. Igel and Company Inc.	2040 Alum Creek Dr	Columbus	OH	43207	John B Igel	614-445-8421	R	50	0.3
Dykema Excavators Inc.	1730 3 Mile Rd NE	Grand Rapids	MI	49505	A Dykema	616-363-6895	R	50	0.1
Harper Investments Inc.	P O Box 18400	Kearns	UT	84118	RJ Harper	801-250-0132	R	46	0.4
Stevens Painton Corp.	7850 Freeway Cir	Middleburg H.	OH	44130	Robert Navarro	440-237-1300	R	45	0.3
Kamminga and Roodvoets Inc.	3435 Broadmoor SE	Grand Rapids	MI	49512	Richard Steigenga	616-949-0800	R	43*	0.3
Harper Contracting	P O Box 18400	Kearns	UT	84118	RJ Harper	801-250-0132	S	41	0.2
Beaver Excavating Co.	4650 Southway	Canton	OH	44706	W Sterling	330-478-2151	R	40	0.4
Carl Bolander and Sons Co.	PO Box 7216	St. Paul	MN	55107	Bruce Bolander	651-224-6299	R	38*	0.2
Geo-Con Inc.	4075 Monroeville	Monroeville	PA	15146	Brian H Jasperse	412-856-7700	S	37	0.1
Brubacher Excavating Inc.	PO Box 528	Bowmansville	PA	17507	B S Brubacher	717-445-4571	R	36	0.3
Ebensteiner Co.	5311 Deery Ave	Agoura Hills	CA	91301	Paul Ebensteiner	818-706-0608	R	32*	0.2
Independence Excavating Inc.	5720 Schaaf Rd	Cleveland	OH	44131	Victor DiGeronimo	216-524-1700	R	32*	0.2
Pleasant Excavating Co.	24024 Frederick Rd	Clarksburg	MD	20871	WD Pleasants Jr	301-428-0800	R	32*	0.2
Tschiggfrie Excavating	P O Box 3280	Dubuque	IA	52001	Ed Tschiggfrie	319-557-7450	R	32*	0.2
R.A. Bright Construction Inc.	9001 Hanslik Ct	Naperville	IL	60564	Robert Bright	630-851-3750	R	29*	0.2
Kanawha Stone Co.	PO Box 503	Nitro	WV	25143	Arthur L King	304-755-8271	R	25	0.2
P.T. Ferro Construction Co.	PO Box 156	Joliet	IL	60434	John T Ferro	815-726-6284	R	24*	0.2
Perry Engineering Company Inc.	1945 Millwood Pike	Winchester	VA	22602	RW Werner	540-667-4310	R	20*	0.3
Sukut Construction Inc.	4010 W Chandler	Santa Ana	CA	92704	Michael Crawford	714-540-5351	R	20*	0.2
Conduit & Foundation	33 Rock Hill Rd	Bala Cynwyd	PA	19004	Richard Halloran	610-668-8400	R	18*	<0.1
Millgard Corp.	12822 Stark Rd	Livonia	MI	48150	D Millgard	734-425-8550	R	17	0.2
Gallagher and Burk Inc.	PO Box 7227	Oakland	CA	94601	David DeSilva	510-261-0466	R	17*	0.1
J.D. Contractors	38881 Schoolcraft St	Livonia	MI	48150	Thomas S Di Ponio	734-591-3400	R	16*	0.1
DBM Contractors Inc.	PO Box 6139	Federal Way	WA	98063	Donald B Murphy	253-927-8510	R	15	0.4
Redgwick Construction Co.	25599 Huntwood	Hayward	CA	94544	DA Redgwick	510-782-0400	R	12	<0.1
N.E. Finch Co.	PO Box 5187	Peoria	IL	61601	Thomas E Finch	309-671-1433	R	12	<0.1
Henderson Excavating Co.	2524 Birmingham	Birmingham	AL	35224		205-787-3314	R	10*	<0.1
Merco Inc.	1117 Rte 31, S	Lebanon	NJ	08833	CE Mergentime	908-730-9172	R	10*	<0.1
Rose Construction Co.	PO Box 309	Northport	AL	35476	Wayne Rose	502-348-9241	R	8*	<0.1
Altair International	1725 Sheridan Ave	Cody	WY	82414	William P Long	307-587-8245	P	0	<0.1

Source: *Ward's Business Directory of U.S. Private and Public Companies*, Volumes 1 and 2, 2000. The company type code used is as follows: P - Public, R - Private, S - Subsidiary, D - Division, J - Joint Venture, A - Affiliate, G - Group, N - Company type not reported. Sales are in millions of dollars, employees are in thousands. An asterisk (*) indicates an estimated sales volume. The symbol < stands for 'less than'. Company names and addresses are truncated, in some cases, to fit into the available space.

COST DETAILS

Item	Cost ($ mil)	% of total	Per $1,000 of Revenue	Item	Cost ($ mil)	% of total	Per $1,000 of Revenue
All costs	5,107.4	100.000	359.8	Total Rentals	601.3	11.773	42.4
Cost of supplies	2,994.1	58.623	210.9	Equipment	525.4	10.287	37.0
Subcontracts	1,530.5	29.966	107.8	Buildings	75.9	1.485	5.3
Power, fuel, lubricants	582.8	11.412	41.1	Services purchased	777.8	15.229	54.8
Electricity	34.3	0.671	2.4	Communications	110.2	2.157	7.8
Natural gas	10.7	0.210	0.8	Building repairs	24.1	0.472	1.7
Gasoline and diesel	490.6	9.606	34.6	Machinery repairs	643.5	12.599	45.3
Highway	240.3	4.705	16.9				
Offroad	250.3	4.901	17.6				
Other power	47.2	0.925	3.3				

Source: *Economic Census of the United States*, 1997. Revenues referred to are total industry revenues for the current NAICS industry.

CONSTRUCTION PRODUCT DETAILS

Construction type	Value of construction work ($ mil and %)							
	Total		New construction		Additions, alterations, reconstruction		Maintenance and repair	
	Value	%	Value	%	Value	%	Value	%
Total	**13,746.6**	**100.0**	**11,073.2**	**100.0**	**1,587.2**	**100.0**	**809.7**	**100.0**
Building construction, total	**10,909.9**	**79.4**	**9,159.2**	**82.7**	**1,178.6**	**74.3**	**572.1**	**70.6**
Single-family houses, detached	3,947.5	28.7	3,455.2	31.2	275.9	17.4	216.5	26.7
Single-family houses, attached	698.7	5.1	595.8	5.4	63.3	4.0	39.6	4.9
Apartment buildings, condos and cooperatives	547.0	4.0	465.2	4.2	45.1	2.8	36.7	4.5
Manufacturing and light industrial buildings	916.1	6.7	689.9	6.2	159.0	10.0	67.3	8.3
Manufacturing and light industrial warehouses	316.7	2.3	254.3	2.3	46.9	3.0	15.5	1.9
Hotels and motels	154.9	1.1	137.4	1.2	12.2	0.8	5.3	0.6
Office buildings	948.6	6.9	808.9	7.3	108.9	6.9	30.7	3.8
All other commercial buildings, nec	1,889.8	13.7	1,623.6	14.7	187.3	11.8	78.9	9.7
Commercial warehouses	334.9	2.4	290.5	2.6	33.5	2.1	10.9	1.3
Religious buildings	131.9	1.0	94.2	0.9	29.0	1.8	8.7	1.1
Educational buildings	394.4	2.9	272.1	2.5	109.1	6.9	13.2	1.6
Health care and institutional buildings	223.1	1.6	160.6	1.5	56.0	3.5	6.5	0.8
Other building construction	406.4	3.0	311.5	2.8	52.5	3.3	(S)	-
Nonbuilding construction, total	**2,560.3**	**18.6**	**1,914.0**	**17.3**	**408.7**	**25.7**	**237.7**	**29.4**
Highways, streets, and related work	581.7	4.2	368.6	3.3	143.0	9.0	70.2	8.7
Private driveways and parking areas	437.0	3.2	351.8	3.2	51.2	3.2	34.0	4.2
Sewers, water mains, and related facilities	968.2	7.0	805.6	7.3	95.3	6.0	67.3	8.3
Other nonbuilding construction, nec	573.3	4.2	387.9	3.5	119.3	7.5	66.2	8.2
Construction work, nsk	**276.5**	**2.0**	NA	-	NA	-	NA	-

Source: *Economic Census of the United States*, 1997. Bold items are headers. (D) stands for data withheld to protect competitive information. (S) indicates instances where data do not meet publications standards.

LOCATION BY STATE AND REGIONAL CONCENTRATION

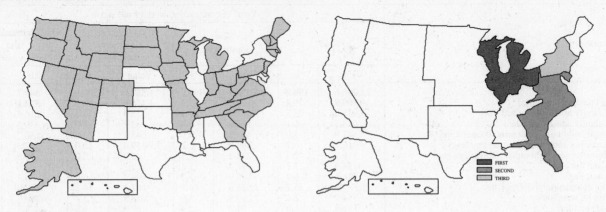

FIRST
SECOND
THIRD

INDUSTRY DATA BY STATE

State	Estab lish- ments	Employment			Compensation		Production				Capital Exp. ($ mil)
		Total	Workers	Total as % of US	Payroll per Employee	Wages per Worker	Costs ($ mil)	Value Added ($ mil)	Reve- nues ($ mil)	% of US	
California	1,000	8,168	6,585	7.03	35,895	34,992	282.2	851.4	1,271.9	8.96	63.8
Pennsylvania	970	6,946	5,477	5.98	27,923	26,608	185.8	542.5	812.6	5.73	59.8
Ohio	840	5,636	4,413	4.85	30,101	29,310	219.8	432.1	754.9	5.32	51.6
Texas	688	6,876	5,423	5.92	26,829	23,652	221.1	430.0	748.4	5.27	55.2
Michigan	927	5,042	4,098	4.34	32,171	31,330	147.8	437.1	632.8	4.46	57.2
Illinois	744	4,540	3,538	3.91	38,047	36,080	130.5	416.1	624.7	4.40	38.7
Georgia	545	4,397	3,736	3.78	26,214	22,513	109.0	416.4	594.7	4.19	38.0
New York	756	3,883	3,027	3.34	32,001	30,214	139.4	313.9	519.8	3.66	36.1
Massachusetts	615	3,907	2,955	3.36	32,152	28,751	136.2	303.0	487.4	3.43	30.6
Indiana	542	3,414	2,786	2.94	27,835	27,917	99.7	264.0	404.1	2.85	28.5
Colorado	542	3,653	3,002	3.14	29,526	27,001	89.2	284.2	403.7	2.84	28.9
Wisconsin	541	3,165	2,394	2.72	32,782	33,439	90.2	257.2	376.3	2.65	34.2
Virginia	470	3,471	2,794	2.99	23,709	22,224	88.7	229.2	363.9	2.56	28.0
Utah	283	2,001	1,755	1.72	25,475	24,631	77.2	163.9	254.5	1.79	15.0
Oregon	362	2,121	1,729	1.82	27,214	26,072	76.2	144.9	248.2	1.75	18.5
Connecticut	389	1,867	1,430	1.61	30,342	29,590	46.1	148.2	213.7	1.51	15.7
Kentucky	272	1,401	1,098	1.21	23,591	21,981	57.4	106.9	181.5	1.28	(S)
Iowa	244	1,363	1,085	1.17	26,377	23,594	37.5	112.7	163.8	1.15	8.9
Maine	324	1,420	1,182	1.22	22,618	22,009	32.4	95.0	139.6	0.98	13.0
New Hampshire	271	1,168	932	1.00	24,878	25,377	29.0	84.8	124.1	0.87	9.3
Alaska	98	474	399	0.41	39,876	39,078	24.5	43.3	75.0	0.53	5.9
North Carolina	704	(D)	(D)	-	-	-	(D)	224.2	(D)	-	36.5
Florida	591	4,324	3,351	3.72	23,680	22,266	(D)	346.6	(D)	-	36.4
New Jersey	591	3,809	2,937	3.28	31,824	31,639	(D)	307.3	(D)	-	30.3
Minnesota	517	2,765	2,191	2.38	30,662	29,524	(D)	246.4	(D)	-	30.0
Washington	454	2,277	1,798	1.96	31,514	31,182	(D)	195.5	(D)	-	17.6
Missouri	413	2,532	1,946	2.18	28,338	26,422	(D)	165.0	(D)	-	19.9
Tennessee	401	2,105	1,648	1.81	25,542	23,712	(D)	176.5	(D)	-	20.4
Maryland	317	2,762	2,330	2.38	29,122	27,281	(D)	146.3	(D)	-	17.5
Arizona	296	1,824	1,400	1.57	28,751	25,290	(D)	131.4	(D)	-	13.7
South Carolina	289	1,872	1,581	1.61	24,307	21,287	(D)	114.6	(D)	-	14.6
Alabama	242	1,343	1,049	1.16	22,123	20,733	(D)	83.4	(D)	-	13.4
Arkansas	200	1,281	(D)	1.10	20,719	-	(D)	73.0	(D)	-	9.6
Idaho	175	(D)	370	-	-	25,400	(D)	40.1	(D)	-	4.0
Vermont	175	737	(D)	0.63	21,833	-	(D)	49.2	(D)	-	6.3
Nevada	165	1,736	1,443	1.49	35,432	33,931	(D)	150.6	(D)	-	14.7
West Virginia	165	843	692	0.73	22,076	21,514	(D)	69.1	(D)	-	8.9
Louisiana	156	1,108	886	0.95	21,947	21,131	(D)	72.6	(D)	-	13.9
Oklahoma	137	704	583	0.61	21,210	18,130	(D)	48.3	(D)	-	5.3
Kansas	126	709	565	0.61	33,285	27,241	(D)	57.4	(D)	-	5.8
Montana	107	266	238	0.23	-	-	(D)	22.1	(D)	-	0.9
Mississippi	95	(D)	(D)	-	-	-	28.4	(D)	(D)	-	5.5
Nebraska	93	622	519	0.54	-	-	(D)	(D)	(D)	-	5.4
New Mexico	69	676	545	0.58	21,598	17,683	(D)	47.2	(D)	-	4.1
North Dakota	67	(D)	(D)	-	-	-	(D)	(D)	(D)	-	1.6
Wyoming	66	339	(D)	0.29	19,021	-	(D)	20.9	(D)	-	2.2
Rhode Island	61	381	310	0.33	30,480	30,742	(D)	(D)	(D)	-	(S)
South Dakota	60	(D)	(D)	-	-	-	(D)	17.3	(D)	-	1.5
Delaware	49	255	(D)	0.22	-	-	(D)	(D)	(D)	-	3.8
Hawaii	24	127	86	0.11	39,299	40,302	(D)	8.1	(D)	-	(D)
D.C.	3	(D)	(D)	-	-	-	(D)	(D)	(D)	-	(D)

Source: Economic Census of the U.S., 1997. Data are sorted by 1997 revenues or establishments. (D) means data suppression to prevent disclosure of company data. (S) means that data did not meet statistical standards for publication. A dash (-) is used when data are unavailable or cannot be calculated. Data followed by an * indicate the midpoint of a range. The ranges are: for 10, 0-19; for 60, 20-99, for 175, 100-249, for 375, 250-499, for 750, 500-999. Higher values are multiples of those shown, e.g., 3,750 is the midpoint of the range 2,500-4,999. Shaded *states* on the state map indicate those states which have proportionately greater representation in the industry than would be indicated by the state's population; the ratio is based on total revenues or number of establishments. Shaded *regions* indicate where the industry is regionally most concentrated.

NAICS 235940 - WRECKING AND DEMOLITION CONTRACTORS*

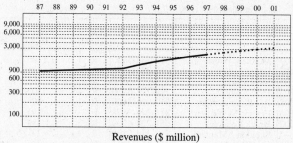

Revenues ($ million)

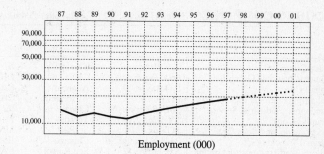

Employment (000)

GENERAL STATISTICS

Years	Estab-lish-ments	Employment		Payroll ($ mil)		Costs ($ mil)		Value Added ($ mil)	Revenues ($ mil)			Capital expend. ($ mil)
		Total	Constr. workers	Total	Worker payroll	Total	Cost of materials		All sources	Construction Total	Net	
1977	978	8,295	6,998	89.0	70.2	47.6	25.9	210.6	258.2	240.6	229.2	-
1982	890	8,402	7,201	130.1	107.2	89.2	32.9	313.8	403.0	376.9	340.7	-
1987	1,240	14,109	11,686	261.5	195.4	177.0	79.2	781.9	958.8	912.5	844.7	40.9
1988	765	12,043	11,419	291.2	199.1	201.5	93.2	780.5	988.0	940.1	860.7	-
1989	747	13,056	11,157	303.3	202.9	229.4	109.5	779.1	1,018.0	968.5	877.1	-
1990	832	11,961	10,902	299.6	206.7	261.2	128.8	777.8	1,048.9	997.8	893.7	-
1991	857	11,379	10,653	298.1	210.6	297.3	151.5	776.4	1,080.7	1,028.0	910.7	-
1992	966	13,112	10,409	296.0	214.6	338.5	178.2	775.0	1,113.5	1,059.1	928.0	23.1
1993	1,081	14,254	11,224	355.2	254.6	335.1	194.6	966.5	1,351.6	1,280.1	1,125.2	-
1994	1,196	15,395	12,040	414.5	294.6	331.7	211.0	1,158.0	1,589.7	1,501.1	1,322.4	-
1995	1,312	16,537	12,855	473.7	334.6	328.2	227.5	1,349.4	1,827.8	1,722.2	1,519.5	-
1996	1,427	17,678	13,671	533.0	374.6	324.8	243.9	1,540.9	2,065.9	1,943.2	1,716.7	-
1997	1,542	18,820	14,486	592.2	414.6	321.4	260.3	1,732.4	2,304.0	2,164.2	1,913.9	109.9
1998	1,657p	19,962p	15,301p	651.4p	454.6p	318.0p	276.7p	1,923.9p	2,542.1p	2,385.2p	2,111.1p	-
1999	1,772p	21,103p	16,117p	710.7p	494.6p	314.6p	293.1p	2,115.4p	2,780.2p	2,606.2p	2,308.3p	-
2000	1,888p	22,245p	16,932p	769.9p	534.6p	311.1p	309.6p	2,306.8p	3,018.3p	2,827.3p	2,505.4p	-
2001	2,003p	23,386p	17,748p	829.2p	574.6p	307.7p	326.0p	2,498.3p	3,256.4p	3,048.3p	2,702.6p	-

Sources: Economic Census of the United States, 1977, 1982, 1987, 1992, and 1997. Data for those years (years are in **bold** type) are from the 5-year censuses of the economy. Other values, unless otherwise noted, are extrapolations. Values footnoted 1 are from the *County Business Patterns* for the years indicated. Values marked with *p* are projections. Data are the most recent available at this level of detail. "Net" under "Construction" is construction revenues net of the costs of subcontracts.

INDICES OF CHANGE

Years	Estab-lish-ments	Employment		Payroll ($ mil)		Costs ($ mil)		Value Added ($ mil)	Revenues ($ mil)			Capital expend. ($ mil)
		Total	Constr. workers	Total	Worker payroll	Total	Cost of materials		All sources	Construction Total	Net	
1977	63.4	44.1	48.3	15.0	16.9	14.8	10.0	12.2	11.2	11.1	12.0	-
1982	57.7	44.6	49.7	22.0	25.9	27.8	12.6	18.1	17.5	17.4	17.8	-
1987	80.4	75.0	80.7	44.2	47.1	55.1	30.4	45.1	41.6	42.2	44.1	37.2
1992	62.6	69.7	71.9	50.0	51.8	105.3	68.5	44.7	48.3	48.9	48.5	21.0
1997	100.0	100.0	100.0	100.0	100.0	100.0	100.0	100.0	100.0	100.0	100.0	100.0

Sources: Same as General Statistics. The values shown reflect change from the base year, 1997. Values above 100 mean greater than 1997, values below 100 mean less than 1997, and a value of 100 in years other than 1997 means same as 1997. Indices are calculated only for Census years. Data are the most recent available at this level of detail.

SELECTED RATIOS

For 1997	Avg. of Sector	Analyzed Industry	Index	For 1997	Avg. of Sector	Analyzed Industry	Index
Employees per establishment	8.6	12.2	141	Value added per establishment	584,730	1,123,476	192
Construction workers per establishment	6.6	9.4	142	Value added per employee	67,759	92,051	136
Payroll per establishment	265,343	384,047	145	Value added per construction worker	88,592	119,591	135
Payroll per employee	30,748	31,467	102	Revenues per establishment	1,307,915	1,494,163	114
Payroll per construction worker	27,622	28,621	104	Revenues per employee	151,563	122,423	81
Costs per establishment	367,737	208,431	57	Revenues per construction worker	198,161	159,050	80
Costs per employee	42,614	17,078	40	CR as % of total revenues	98.48	93.93	95
Costs per construction worker	55,716	22,187	40	Net CR as % of CR	72.40	88.43	122
Materials as % of costs	95.75	80.99	85	Investment per establishment	22,948	71,271	311
Costs as % of revenues	28.12	13.95	50	Investment per employee	2,659	5,840	220
Costs as % of construction revenues	28.55	14.85	52	Investment per construction worker	3,477	7,587	218

Sources: Same as General Statistics. The 'Average of Sector' column represents the average for all industries in this sector. The Index shows the relationship between the Average and the Analyzed Industry. For example, 100 means that they are equal; 500 that the Analyzed Industry is five times the average; 50 means that the Analyzed Industry is half the national average. 'na' is used to show that data are 'not available'. CR stands for "construction revenues" and "Net CR" is construction revenues net of subcontract expenses.

*Equivalent to SIC 1795.

LEADING COMPANIES　Number shown: **12**　Total sales ($ mil): **1,750**　Total employment (000): **7.3**

Company Name	Address				CEO Name	Phone	Co. Type	Sales ($ mil)	Empl. (000)
Walsh Group Ltd.	929 W Adams	Chicago	IL	60607	Matthew Walsh	312-563-5400	R	1,170	3.5
Columbia National Group Inc.	6600 Grant Ave	Cleveland	OH	44105	David Miller	216-883-4972	R	180*	0.5
Penhall Co.	P O Box 4609	Anaheim	CA	92803	John Sawyer	714-772-6450	S	86*	0.8
Penhall International Inc.	PO Box 4609	Anaheim	CA	92803	John Sawyer	714-772-6450	R	70	0.7
Brandenburg Industrial Service	2625 S Loomis St	Chicago	IL	60608	Bill Sommerville	312-326-5800	R	60*	0.5
Kimmins Corp.	1501 2nd Ave E	Tampa	FL	33605	Francis M Williams	813-248-3878	P	59	0.7
Carl Bolander and Sons Co.	PO Box 7216	St. Paul	MN	55107	Bruce Bolander	651-224-6299	R	38*	0.2
National Wrecking Co.	2441 N Leavitt St	Chicago	IL	60647	Sheldon J Mandell	773-384-2800	R	27*	0.2
Ghilotti Brothers Construction Inc.	525 Jacoby St	San Rafael	CA	94901	Eva Ghilotti	415-454-7011	R	21*	0.1
Mainline Contracting Corp.	PO Box 933	Buffalo	NY	14205	David Franjoine	716-842-0860	R	21*	0.1
U.S. Dismantlement L.L.C.	2600 S Throop St	Chicago	IL	60608	T Harry Gieschen	312-328-1400	R	10	0.1
Plant Reclamation	912 Harbour Way S	Richmond	CA	94804	Fred Glueck	510-233-6552	R	8*	<0.1

Source: *Ward's Business Directory of U.S. Private and Public Companies*, Volumes 1 and 2, 2000. The company type code used is as follows: P - Public, R - Private, S - Subsidiary, D - Division, J - Joint Venture, A - Affiliate, G - Group, N - Company type not reported. Sales are in millions of dollars, employees are in thousands. An asterisk (*) indicates an estimated sales volume. The symbol < stands for 'less than'. Company names and addresses are truncated, in some cases, to fit into the available space.

COST DETAILS

Item	Cost ($ mil)	% of total	Per $1,000 of Revenue	Item	Cost ($ mil)	% of total	Per $1,000 of Revenue
All costs	571.6	100.000	248.1	Total Rentals	105.8	18.508	45.9
Cost of supplies	260.3	45.532	113.0	Equipment	90.0	15.746	39.1
Subcontracts	250.3	43.781	108.6	Buildings	15.8	2.762	6.9
Power, fuel, lubricants	61.1	10.687	26.5	Services purchased	113.6	19.874	49.3
Electricity	4.7	0.815	2.0	Communications	23.2	4.065	10.1
Natural gas	2.3	0.397	1.0	Building repairs	4.4	0.763	1.9
Gasoline and diesel	49.6	8.677	21.5	Machinery repairs	86.0	15.046	37.3
Highway	31.2	5.451	13.5				
Offroad	18.4	3.226	8.0				
Other power	4.6	0.798	2.0				

Source: *Economic Census of the United States*, 1997. Revenues referred to are total industry revenues for the current NAICS industry.

CONSTRUCTION PRODUCT DETAILS

Construction type	Value of construction work ($ mil and %)							
	Total		New construction		Additions, alterations, reconstruction		Maintenance and repair	
	Value	%	Value	%	Value	%	Value	%
Total	**2,164.2**	**100.0**	(S)	-	(S)	-	(S)	-
Building construction, total	**1,640.7**	**75.8**	(S)	-	(S)	-	(S)	-
Single-family houses, detached	200.0	9.2	(S)	-	(S)	-	(S)	-
Single-family houses, attached	16.9	0.8	(S)	-	(S)	-	(S)	-
Apartment buildings, condos and cooperatives	64.2	3.0	(S)	-	(S)	-	(S)	-
Manufacturing and light industrial buildings	299.4	13.8	(S)	-	(S)	-	(S)	-
Hotels and motels	21.8	1.0	(S)	-	(S)	-	(S)	-
Office buildings	259.3	12.0	(S)	-	(S)	-	(S)	-
All other commercial buildings, nec	393.7	18.2	(S)	-	(S)	-	(S)	-
Commercial warehouses	98.2	4.5	(S)	-	(S)	-	(S)	-
Educational buildings	51.2	2.4	(S)	-	(S)	-	(S)	-
Health care and institutional buildings	53.5	2.5	(S)	-	(S)	-	(S)	-
Other building construction	69.3	3.2	(S)	-	(S)	-	(S)	-
Nonbuilding construction, total	**476.0**	**22.0**	(S)	-	(S)	-	(S)	-
Highways, streets, and related work	93.5	4.3	(S)	-	(S)	-	(S)	-
Bridges, tunnels, and elevated highways	56.6	2.6	(S)	-	(S)	-	(S)	-
Sewers, water mains, and related facilities	20.2	0.9	(S)	-	(S)	-	(S)	-
Tank storage facilities other than water	84.0	3.9	(S)	-	(S)	-	(S)	-
Other nonbuilding construction, nec	221.8	10.2	(S)	-	(S)	-	(S)	-
Construction work, nsk	**47.5**	**2.2**	NA	-	NA	-	NA	-

Source: *Economic Census of the United States*, 1997. Bold items are headers. (D) stands for data withheld to protect competitive information. (S) indicates instances where data do not meet publications standards.

LOCATION BY STATE AND REGIONAL CONCENTRATION

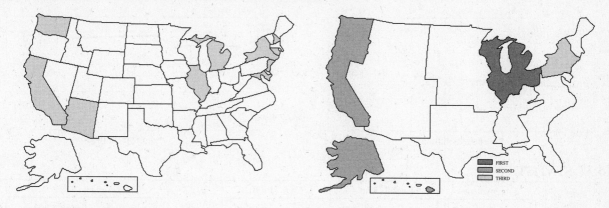

FIRST
SECOND
THIRD

INDUSTRY DATA BY STATE

State	Estab lish- ments	Employment			Compensation		Production				Capital Exp. ($ mil)
		Total	Workers	Total as % of US	Payroll per Employee	Wages per Worker	Costs ($ mil)	Value Added ($ mil)	Reve- nues ($ mil)	% of US	
California	197	3,306	2,528	17.57	31,108	27,394	34.3	314.3	397.8	17.27	13.6
New York	128	1,647	1,276	8.75	31,649	29,608	26.7	165.7	221.4	9.61	(S)
Illinois	91	1,389	1,126	7.38	46,857	43,041	33.1	157.5	205.0	8.90	8.9
Michigan	76	1,245	976	6.62	35,789	33,179	20.5	123.8	166.0	7.20	10.6
Texas	89	1,204	881	6.40	24,120	23,059	20.3	87.5	128.8	5.59	2.8
New Jersey	63	965	773	5.13	34,352	32,796	16.8	93.9	123.4	5.36	6.7
Ohio	66	764	572	4.06	30,737	28,049	13.9	66.1	88.3	3.83	2.8
Maryland	37	625	506	3.32	30,173	28,123	14.1	47.7	69.5	3.02	1.5
Pennsylvania	70	598	469	3.18	25,298	20,959	7.9	53.7	67.0	2.91	(S)
Washington	37	459	324	2.44	42,638	40,722	5.0	51.0	60.9	2.64	3.6
Connecticut	58	364	275	1.93	45,668	46,225	11.9	36.7	55.3	2.40	1.6
Virginia	31	534	427	2.84	25,648	20,354	12.8	31.6	48.9	2.12	3.2
Missouri	34	280	191	1.49	26,500	21,550	2.9	38.7	45.1	1.96	0.4
Arizona	19	297	196	1.58	25,215	23,224	2.5	39.1	43.4	1.88	1.4
Tennessee	31	384	305	2.04	25,305	21,505	4.6	28.8	37.4	1.62	1.5
Wisconsin	26	188	124	1.00	30,777	29,823	5.0	30.0	37.4	1.62	3.4
Indiana	52	336	223	1.79	28,310	28,135	4.4	27.8	34.1	1.48	4.8
Georgia	28	298	234	1.58	22,624	19,397	5.8	15.4	25.7	1.12	2.2
Oklahoma	18	194	139	1.03	26,948	21,655	2.6	16.8	20.9	0.91	1.9
Oregon	19	143	98	0.76	33,741	30,316	3.5	12.1	17.5	0.76	(S)
New Hampshire	10	115	93	0.61	37,391	30,215	3.4	11.2	16.1	0.70	1.1
Kentucky	14	125	92	0.66	28,200	26,859	1.9	10.9	13.4	0.58	0.8
Alabama	24	97	75	0.52	21,557	21,987	3.7	6.7	13.3	0.58	0.4
Iowa	8	55	41	0.29	26,036	19,732	1.0	4.4	5.9	0.26	0.3
West Virginia	25	69	42	0.37	14,101	13,952	0.5	5.1	5.7	0.25	0.2
Montana	3	66	64	0.35	19,258	19,516	0.9	2.1	3.2	0.14	0.1
Colorado	19	248	203	1.32	25,577	19,379	(D)	(S)	(S)	-	0.9
Nevada	7	76	58	0.40	30,474	24,759	1.0	(S)	(S)	-	0.2
South Carolina	7	(S)	(S)	-	-	-	(S)	(S)	(S)	-	(S)
Massachusetts	61	667	540	3.54	31,681	27,531	(D)	72.1	(D)	-	5.8
Florida	38	315	214	1.67	24,143	21,136	(D)	20.9	(D)	-	1.4
Utah	26	(S)	(S)	-	-	-	(D)	(S)	(D)	-	1.1
Minnesota	19	183	145	0.97	35,634	32,228	(D)	18.0	(D)	-	1.8
Louisiana	16	125	91	0.66	23,184	18,549	(D)	10.7	(D)	-	0.2
Kansas	12	80	69	0.43	25,238	22,348	(D)	4.8	(D)	-	0.5
Rhode Island	10	96	74	0.51	32,552	32,486	(D)	8.4	(D)	-	0.5
North Carolina	9	(D)	(D)	-	-	-	(D)	17.6	(D)	-	(D)
Maine	8	(S)	(S)	-	-	-	0.9	1.5	(D)	-	(S)
Alaska	6	61	43	0.32	42,639	43,558	(D)	6.7	(D)	-	(S)
Nebraska	5	101	77	0.54	-	-	(D)	(D)	(D)	-	(D)
New Mexico	5	56	44	0.30	25,375	23,205	(D)	2.6	(D)	-	0.5
Arkansas	4	40	(D)	0.21	28,075	-	(D)	3.8	(D)	-	(S)
Mississippi	4	(D)	(D)	-	-	-	(D)	(D)	(D)	-	(D)
Delaware	3	(S)	(D)	-	-	-	(S)	(D)	(D)	-	(D)
Hawaii	3	97	81	0.52	25,216	23,481	0.8	7.0	(D)	-	(D)
Vermont	3	(S)	(S)	-	-	-	(D)	(S)	(D)	-	(S)
North Dakota	2	(D)	(D)	-	-	-	(D)	(D)	(D)	-	(S)
D.C.	1	(D)	(D)	-	-	-	(D)	(D)	(D)	-	(D)
Idaho	(S)	(D)	(S)	-	-	-	(D)	(S)	(D)	-	(D)

Source: Economic Census of the U.S., 1997. Data are sorted by 1997 revenues or establishments. (D) means data suppression to prevent disclosure of company data. (S) means that data did not meet statistical standards for publication. A dash (-) is used when data are unavailable or cannot be calculated. Data followed by an * indicate the midpoint of a range. The ranges are: for 10, 0-19; for 60, 20-99; for 175, 100-249; for 375, 250-499; for 750, 500-999. Higher values are multiples of those shown, e.g., 3,750 is the midpoint of the range 2,500-4,999. Shaded *states* on the state map indicate those states which have proportionately greater representation in the industry than would be indicated by the state's population; the ratio is based on total revenues or number of establishments. Shaded *regions* indicate where the industry is regionally most concentrated.

NAICS 235950 - BUILDING EQUIPMENT AND OTHER MACHINERY INSTALLATION CONTRACTORS*

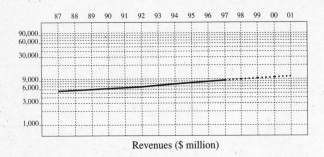

Revenues ($ million)

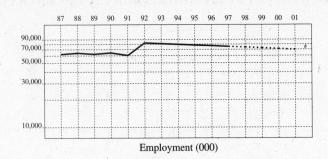

Employment (000)

GENERAL STATISTICS

Years	Estab-lish-ments	Employment		Payroll ($ mil)		Costs ($ mil)		Value Added ($ mil)	Revenues ($ mil)			Capital expend. ($ mil)
		Total	Constr. workers	Total	Worker payroll	Total	Cost of materials		All sources	Construction Total	Net	
1977	2,442	40,474	32,630	752.4	601.6	562.0	469.2	1,385.0	1,947.0	1,899.0	1,829.2	-
1982	3,754	60,169	49,101	1,449.3	1,144.8	1,303.8	1,038.7	2,952.0	4,255.8	4,189.3	3,970.6	-
1987	3,777	62,151	50,244	1,857.7	1,447.5	1,779.9	1,363.6	3,723.1	5,502.9	5,359.8	5,009.8	49.1
1988	2,976	64,029	52,798	2,157.3	1,502.1	1,866.2	1,425.0	3,865.9	5,732.4	5,589.5	5,216.5	-
1989	2,852	62,360	55,482	2,067.4	1,558.8	1,956.8	1,489.2	4,014.3	5,971.5	5,829.1	5,431.7	-
1990	3,040	64,454	58,302	2,216.1	1,617.7	2,051.8	1,556.2	4,168.3	6,220.5	6,078.9	5,655.8	-
1991	3,108	60,445	61,266	2,137.9	1,678.7	2,151.3	1,626.3	4,328.3	6,479.9	6,339.4	5,889.1	-
1992	3,889	82,648	64,380	2,324.1	1,742.1	2,255.8	1,699.6	4,494.4	6,750.1	6,611.0	6,132.1	71.5
1993	4,009	81,219	62,746	2,488.9	1,845.7	2,228.1	1,763.9	4,918.8	7,268.7	7,131.8	6,626.9	-
1994	4,129	79,789	61,112	2,653.7	1,949.3	2,200.4	1,828.3	5,343.2	7,787.2	7,652.7	7,121.7	-
1995	4,249	78,360	59,479	2,818.4	2,052.9	2,172.8	1,892.6	5,767.5	8,305.8	8,173.5	7,616.4	-
1996	4,369	76,930	57,845	2,983.2	2,156.5	2,145.1	1,957.0	6,191.9	8,824.3	8,694.4	8,111.2	-
1997	4,489	75,501	56,211	3,148.0	2,260.1	2,117.4	2,021.3	6,616.3	9,342.9	9,215.2	8,606.0	181.0
1998	4,609p	74,072p	54,577p	3,312.8p	2,363.7p	2,089.7p	2,085.6p	7,040.7p	9,861.5p	9,736.0p	9,100.8p	-
1999	4,729p	72,642p	52,943p	3,477.6p	2,467.3p	2,062.0p	2,150.0p	7,465.1p	10,380.0p	10,256.9p	9,595.6p	-
2000	4,849p	71,213p	51,310p	3,642.3p	2,570.9p	2,034.4p	2,214.3p	7,889.4p	10,898.6p	10,777.7p	10,090.3p	-
2001	4,969p	69,783p	49,676p	3,807.1p	2,674.5p	2,006.7p	2,278.7p	8,313.8p	11,417.1p	11,298.6p	10,585.1p	-

*Sources: Economic Census of the United States, 1977, 1982, 1987, 1992, and 1997. Data for those years (years are in **bold** type) are from the 5-year censuses of the economy. Other values, unless otherwise noted, are extrapolations. Values footnoted 1 are from the County Business Patterns for the years indicated. Values marked with p are projections. Data are the most recent available at this level of detail. "Net" under "Construction" is construction revenues net of the costs of subcontracts.*

INDICES OF CHANGE

Years	Estab-lish-ments	Employment		Payroll ($ mil)		Costs ($ mil)		Value Added ($ mil)	Revenues ($ mil)			Capital expend. ($ mil)
		Total	Constr. workers	Total	Worker payroll	Total	Cost of materials		All sources	Construction Total	Net	
1977	54.4	53.6	58.0	23.9	26.6	26.5	23.2	20.9	20.8	20.6	21.3	-
1982	83.6	79.7	87.4	46.0	50.7	61.6	51.4	44.6	45.6	45.5	46.1	-
1987	84.1	82.3	89.4	59.0	64.0	84.1	67.5	56.3	58.9	58.2	58.2	27.1
1992	86.6	109.5	114.5	73.8	77.1	106.5	84.1	67.9	72.2	71.7	71.3	39.5
1997	100.0	100.0	100.0	100.0	100.0	100.0	100.0	100.0	100.0	100.0	100.0	100.0

Sources: Same as General Statistics. The values shown reflect change from the base year, 1997. Values above 100 mean greater than 1997, values below 100 mean less than 1997, and a value of 100 in years other than 1997 means same as 1997. Indices are calculated only for Census years. Data are the most recent available at this level of detail.

SELECTED RATIOS

For 1997	Avg. of Sector	Analyzed Industry	Index	For 1997	Avg. of Sector	Analyzed Industry	Index
Employees per establishment	8.6	16.8	195	Value added per establishment	584,730	1,473,892	252
Construction workers per establishment	6.6	12.5	190	Value added per employee	67,759	87,632	129
Payroll per establishment	265,343	701,270	264	Value added per construction worker	88,592	117,705	133
Payroll per employee	30,748	41,695	136	Revenues per establishment	1,307,915	2,081,288	159
Payroll per construction worker	27,622	40,207	146	Revenues per employee	151,563	123,745	82
Costs per establishment	367,737	471,686	128	Revenues per construction worker	198,161	166,211	84
Costs per employee	42,614	28,045	66	CR as % of total revenues	98.48	98.63	100
Costs per construction worker	55,716	37,669	68	Net CR as % of CR	72.40	93.39	129
Materials as % of costs	95.75	95.46	100	Investment per establishment	22,948	40,321	176
Costs as % of revenues	28.12	22.66	81	Investment per employee	2,659	2,397	90
Costs as % of construction revenues	28.55	22.98	80	Investment per construction worker	3,477	3,220	93

Sources: Same as General Statistics. The 'Average of Sector' column represents the average for all industries in this sector. The Index shows the relationship between the Average and the Analyzed Industry. For example, 100 means that they are equal; 500 that the Analyzed Industry is five times the average; 50 means that the Analyzed Industry is half the national average. 'na' is used to show that data are 'not available'. CR stands for "construction revenues" and "Net CR" is construction revenues net of subcontract expenses.

*Equivalent to SIC 1796.

LEADING COMPANIES   Number shown: **22**   Total sales ($ mil): **1,261**   Total employment (000): **8.7**

Company Name	Address				CEO Name	Phone	Co. Type	Sales ($ mil)	Empl. (000)
Oscar J. Boldt Construction Co.	PO Box 419	Appleton	WI	54912	Warren Parsons	920-739-6321	S	402*	2.0
Millar Elevator Service Co.	PO Box 960	Holland	OH	43528	Tim Shea	419-867-5100	D	187*	2.5
Harco Technologies Div.	1055 W Smith Rd	Medina	OH	44256	Joseph W Rog	330-725-6681	D	150*	0.8
Thyssen Elevator Co.	PO Box 1702	Baltimore	MD	21203	William R Herbst	410-789-0200	S	93*	0.5
Henkels & McCoy Inc. Northeast	985 Jolly Rd	Blue Bell	PA	19422		215-283-7600	D	75*	0.1
M-E-C Co.	PO Box 330	Neodesha	KS	66757	David Parker	316-325-2673	R	45	0.3
Nashville Machine Company Inc.	P O Box 101603	Nashville	TN	37224	Donald C Orr	615-244-2030	R	41	0.4
T.E. Ibberson Co.	828 5th St S	Hopkins	MN	55343	Walter Hanson	612-938-7007	S	37*	<0.1
D.W. Nicholson Corp.	PO Box 4197	Hayward	CA	94540	JL Nicholson	510-887-0900	R	33	0.2
M and S Systems Inc.	PO Box 541777	Dallas	TX	75354	Brad Farris	214-358-3196	S	25	0.3
Proven Alternatives Inc.	1740 Army St	San Francisco	CA	94124	Charles T Condy	415-285-0800	R	25	<0.1
Don R. Fruchey Inc.	5608 Old Maumee	Fort Wayne	IN	46803	Robert L Fruchey	219-749-8502	R	22	0.1
PSF Industries Inc.	PO Box 3747	Seattle	WA	98124	Stanley Miller	206-622-1252	R	20	0.2
Hy-Tek Material Handling Inc.	2222 Post Rd	Columbus	OH	43217	William J Miller	614-497-2500	R	20	0.1
Raygal Inc.	2719 White Rd	Irvine	CA	92614	Ygal Sonenshine	949-474-1000	R	20*	<0.1
PS Marcato Elevator Inc.	44-11 11th St	Long Island City	NY	11101	David N Marcato	718-392-6400	R	18	0.2
Staley Elevator Company Inc.	4724 27th St	Long Island City	NY	11101	Kevin Leo	718-786-4300	R	14*	0.1
Coast Machinery Movers	2431 Chico Ave	South El Monte	CA	91733	Larry Beard	626-579-4510	R	9	<0.1
All Chemical Disposal Inc.	21 Great Oaks Blvd	San Jose	CA	95119	Fred Murabito	408-363-1660	R	9*	<0.1
Reliance Elevator Co.	1101 W Adams St	Chicago	IL	60607	Thomson Grunnah	312-666-4022	R	8*	<0.1
Tele-Tech, Company Inc.	2628 Wilhite Ct	Lexington	KY	40503		606-277-8000	N	7	0.5
Colt Temperature Control & Tube	2332 Rockview Dr	Sandy	UT	84092	Rual Coray	801-943-4195	R	1*	<0.1

Source: *Ward's Business Directory of U.S. Private and Public Companies*, Volumes 1 and 2, 2000. The company type code used is as follows: P - Public, R - Private, S - Subsidiary, D - Division, J - Joint Venture, A - Affiliate, G - Group, N - Company type not reported. Sales are in millions of dollars, employees are in thousands. An asterisk (*) indicates an estimated sales volume. The symbol < stands for 'less than'. Company names and addresses are truncated, in some cases, to fit into the available space.

COST DETAILS

Item	Cost ($ mil)	% of total	Per $1,000 of Revenue	Item	Cost ($ mil)	% of total	Per $1,000 of Revenue
All costs	2,726.6	100.000	291.8	Total Rentals	172.1	6.313	18.4
Cost of supplies	2,021.3	74.134	216.3	Equipment	103.2	3.785	11.0
Subcontracts	609.2	22.342	65.2	Buildings	68.9	2.528	7.4
Power, fuel, lubricants	96.1	3.523	10.3	Services purchased	143.4	5.260	15.3
Electricity	15.3	0.563	1.6	Communications	69.4	2.545	7.4
Natural gas	6.1	0.224	0.7	Building repairs	9.4	0.346	1.0
Gasoline and diesel	68.8	2.524	7.4	Machinery repairs	64.6	2.369	6.9
Highway	59.2	2.172	6.3				
Offroad	9.6	0.352	1.0				
Other power	5.8	0.212	0.6				

Source: *Economic Census of the United States*, 1997. Revenues referred to are total industry revenues for the current NAICS industry.

CONSTRUCTION PRODUCT DETAILS

Construction type	Value of construction work ($ mil and %)							
	Total		New construction		Additions, alterations, reconstruction		Maintenance and repair	
	Value	%	Value	%	Value	%	Value	%
Total	**9,215.2**	**100.0**	**3,358.4**	**100.0**	**1,990.9**	**100.0**	**3,596.0**	**100.0**
Building construction, total	**8,196.7**	**88.9**	**3,096.3**	**92.2**	**1,780.2**	**89.4**	**3,320.3**	**92.3**
Single-family houses, detached	155.1	1.7	94.2	2.8	25.2	1.3	35.7	1.0
Single-family houses, attached	44.7	0.5	22.2	0.7	11.0	0.6	11.5	0.3
Apartment buildings, condos and cooperatives	732.3	7.9	215.1	6.4	117.7	5.9	399.5	11.1
Manufacturing and light industrial buildings	2,761.7	30.0	910.5	27.1	901.1	45.3	950.1	26.4
Manufacturing and light industrial warehouses	286.4	3.1	93.1	2.8	92.4	4.6	100.9	2.8
Hotels and motels	580.1	6.3	290.9	8.7	57.6	2.9	231.6	6.4
Office buildings	-	-	-	-	203.4	10.2	689.6	19.2
All other commercial buildings, nec	702.7	7.6	227.8	6.8	161.3	8.1	313.6	8.7
Commercial warehouses	100.5	1.1	53.6	1.6	23.8	1.2	23.2	0.6
Educational buildings	361.3	3.9	149.9	4.5	49.5	2.5	161.9	4.5
Health care and institutional buildings	490.4	5.3	161.8	4.8	74.3	3.7	254.3	7.1
Public safety buildings	103.7	1.1	30.4	0.9	17.2	0.9	-	-
Farm buildings, nonresidential	93.1	1.0	32.1	1.0	17.7	0.9	43.2	1.2
Other building construction	277.7	3.0	200.6	6.0	28.0	1.4	49.1	1.4
Nonbuilding construction, total	**748.5**	**8.1**	**262.1**	**7.8**	**210.7**	**10.6**	**275.7**	**7.7**
Power plants	114.0	1.2	-	-	13.2	0.7	76.9	2.1
Blast furnaces, refineries, chemical complexes, etc	445.9	4.8	-	-	158.5	8.0	141.7	3.9
Other nonbuilding construction, nec	188.6	2.0	92.5	2.8	39.0	2.0	57.2	1.6
Construction work, nsk	**269.9**	**2.9**	**NA**	**-**	**NA**	**-**	**NA**	**-**

Source: *Economic Census of the United States*, 1997. Bold items are headers. (D) stands for data withheld to protect competitive information. (S) indicates instances where data do not meet publications standards.

LOCATION BY STATE AND REGIONAL CONCENTRATION

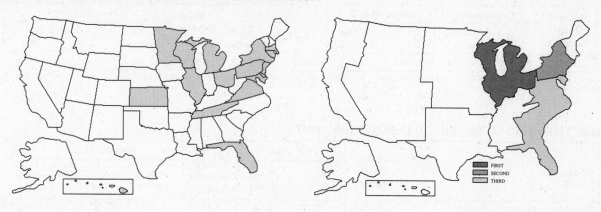

INDUSTRY DATA BY STATE

State	Estab lish- ments	Employment			Compensation		Production				Capital Exp. ($ mil)
		Total	Workers	Total as % of US	Payroll per Employee	Wages per Worker	Costs ($ mil)	Value Added ($ mil)	Reve- nues ($ mil)	% of US	
California	338	6,427	4,741	8.51	51,382	51,314	214.1	671.6	944.8	10.11	19.5
New York	305	6,361	4,601	8.43	46,945	45,894	166.2	607.3	792.7	8.48	8.3
Florida	183	5,327	4,117	7.06	37,108	33,818	204.5	337.8	581.9	6.23	4.9
Illinois	286	4,323	3,232	5.73	46,938	46,347	114.4	414.3	551.9	5.91	8.0
Texas	261	4,103	3,171	5.43	36,854	34,178	135.7	392.0	537.5	5.75	6.5
Michigan	174	2,836	2,228	3.76	48,945	47,905	71.4	316.9	530.5	5.68	14.8
Pennsylvania	231	3,964	2,767	5.25	41,642	38,595	82.7	370.3	485.2	5.19	7.4
Ohio	186	3,250	2,426	4.30	44,007	42,731	76.4	298.1	412.6	4.42	11.7
New Jersey	184	2,575	1,873	3.41	47,130	44,396	85.2	245.5	342.6	3.67	5.4
Tennessee	143	3,129	2,066	4.14	34,066	34,506	89.7	209.7	332.2	3.56	13.9
Massachusetts	127	1,855	1,361	2.46	50,666	51,179	58.1	202.7	266.1	2.85	3.9
Virginia	93	2,123	1,457	2.81	38,838	38,744	51.3	189.8	256.3	2.74	8.4
Maryland	81	1,958	1,442	2.59	44,784	43,498	61.0	185.2	255.2	2.73	2.6
Indiana	103	1,826	1,400	2.42	38,545	37,744	36.0	142.3	207.4	2.22	7.1
North Carolina	174	2,076	1,585	2.75	32,069	31,283	57.6	133.5	201.1	2.15	5.3
Wisconsin	131	1,963	1,437	2.60	38,548	32,981	33.4	153.8	197.2	2.11	6.3
Georgia	135	1,986	1,564	2.63	34,068	32,595	41.6	141.2	192.2	2.06	4.9
Minnesota	104	1,322	943	1.75	43,182	42,665	42.7	123.8	173.3	1.86	3.3
Missouri	80	1,110	845	1.47	43,109	41,199	31.4	98.1	138.4	1.48	2.0
Louisiana	54	1,412	1,167	1.87	37,287	36,391	32.6	105.2	138.4	1.48	4.0
Kansas	56	1,135	850	1.50	35,258	30,715	29.9	89.8	136.8	1.46	4.5
Connecticut	57	926	676	1.23	47,887	48,553	24.7	104.0	132.1	1.41	2.4
Iowa	84	974	780	1.29	33,958	31,426	26.3	68.7	99.0	1.06	3.2
Oregon	74	790	608	1.05	35,305	35,439	15.4	59.7	79.1	0.85	1.4
Hawaii	16	367	272	0.49	57,139	58,471	11.4	47.5	59.4	0.64	0.4
Utah	31	350	277	0.46	37,903	35,917	11.0	31.5	43.1	0.46	2.0
Delaware	28	327	259	0.43	28,661	24,973	11.5	26.3	39.1	0.42	0.3
Oklahoma	58	364	286	0.48	33,096	32,210	8.9	26.5	35.5	0.38	0.5
New Mexico	11	367	336	0.49	23,286	20,607	2.2	19.8	22.7	0.24	0.2
D.C.	4	222	174	0.29	37,495	35,718	(D)	15.7	20.5	0.22	0.1
Rhode Island	12	120	82	0.16	51,008	52,866	(D)	11.7	15.5	0.17	0.1
Idaho	17	(S)	(S)	-	-	-	(D)	7.8	10.0	0.11	(D)
Alaska	9	55	34	0.07	57,200	57,147	(D)	5.1	7.2	0.08	-
Washington	79	1,142	881	1.51	44,390	42,701	(D)	108.2	(D)		1.8
Kentucky	74	1,364	925	1.81	36,523	37,935	(D)	90.4	(D)	-	4.0
Alabama	67	1,060	857	1.40	35,922	33,862	(D)	75.8	(D)	-	2.6
Colorado	67	1,049	711	1.39	36,048	39,117	(D)	88.6	(D)	-	1.2
Arizona	52	543	399	0.72	35,505	33,546	(D)	46.6	(D)	-	0.8
Arkansas	51	524	380	0.69	36,141	33,884	(D)	40.1	(D)	-	0.6
South Carolina	51	843	682	1.12	31,868	29,720	(D)	56.8	(D)	-	1.2
Mississippi	42	396	333	0.52	27,412	21,348	(D)	26.5	(D)	-	0.8
Nevada	40	739	533	0.98	48,553	51,698	(D)	96.9	(D)	-	2.0
North Dakota	26	153	115	0.20	22,542	16,365	(D)	8.0	(D)	-	0.4
Maine	25	738	614	0.98	41,982	37,233	4.5	48.0	(D)	-	0.3
West Virginia	23	172	133	0.23	40,017	38,940	(D)	14.6	(D)	-	0.2
Nebraska	22	303	229	0.40	41,360	37,843	(D)	22.8	(D)	-	0.5
New Hampshire	14	209	148	0.28	50,359	49,628	(D)	18.1	(D)	-	0.4
Montana	10	91	65	0.12	36,484	36,015	(D)	6.8	(D)	-	0.1
South Dakota	6	43	26	0.06	40,233	41,269	0.6	3.7	(D)	-	
Wyoming	6	27	23	0.04	22,074	23,652	(D)	0.9	(D)	-	(S)
Vermont	5	91	35	0.12	28,945	32,143	(D)	10.4	(D)	-	(D)

*Source: Economic Census of the U.S., 1997. Data are sorted by 1997 revenues or establishments. (D) means data suppression to prevent disclosure of company data. (S) means that data did not meet statistical standards for publication. A dash (-) is used when data are unavailable or cannot be calculated. Data followed by an * indicate the midpoint of a range. The ranges are: for 10, 0-19; for 60, 20-99; for 175, 100-249, for 375, 250-499, for 750, 500-999. Higher values are multiples of those shown, e.g., 3,750 is the midpoint of the range 2,500-4,999. Shaded states on the state map indicate those states which have proportionately greater representation in the industry than would be indicated by the state's population; the ratio is based on total revenues or number of establishments. Shaded regions indicate where the industry is regionally most concentrated.*

NAICS 235990 - SPECIAL TRADE CONTRACTORS NEC

GENERAL STATISTICS

| Years | Estab-lish-ments | Employment | | Payroll ($ mil) | | Costs ($ mil) | | Value Added ($ mil) | Revenues ($ mil) | | | Capital expend. ($ mil) |
| | | Total | Constr. workers | Total | Worker payroll | Total | Cost of materials | | All sources | Construction | | |
										Total	Net	
1997	25,932	198,141	146,894	5,166.2	3,447.6	5,821.2	5,491.3	10,513.5	17,952.1	17,401.3	15,783.9	452.0

Source: *Economic Census of the United States*, 1997. This is a newly defined industry. Data for prior years were unavailable at the time of publication but may become available over time. "Net" under "Construction" is construction revenue net of the costs of subcontracts.

DISTRIBUTION AMONG SIC-BASED INDUSTRIES - 1997

| SIC | Industry | Estab-lish-ments | Employment | | Cost of Power & Materials ($ mil) | Revenues ($ mil) | | | Value Added ($ mil) |
| | | | Total (000) | Payroll ($ mil) | | All Sources | Construction | | |
							Total	Net	
179940	Special trade contractors, nec (pt)	25,932.0	198,141	5,166.1	5,821.2	17,952.1	17,401.3	15,783.8	10,513.53

Source: 1997 *Economic Census*. U.S. Census Bureau, U.S. Department of Commerce, August 1997. SIC codes ending in two zeroes represent complete 4-digit SICs. All others are parts of 4-digit SIC industries. Items showing a dash (-) indicate that data are not available because of disclosure problems.

SIC INDUSTRIES RELATED TO NAICS 235990

SIC	Industry	1990	1991	1992	1993	1994	1995	1996	1997
1799	**Special Trade Contractors, n.e.c.***								
	Establishments (number)	22,471	22,634	25,270	27,296	26,150*p*	26,601*p*	27,060*p*	27,527*p*
	Employment (thousands)	197.0	186.3	204.3	207.1	216.9*e*	223.4*e*	230.2*e*	237.1*e*
	Revenues ($ million)	12,936.7*e*	13,535.6*e*	14,162.3	14,818.0*e*	15,504.1*e*	16,221.9*e*	16,973.0*e*	17,758.8*e*

Source: *Economic Census of the United States*, 1992, annual surveys of economic sectors conducted by the Bureau of the Census, and estimates or projections based on the 1982-1992 period; not all data are shown. 'e' marks estimates made by the editors; 'p' indicates projections based on time series. A dash (-) indicates that data for this SIC or year were not available. * Indicates that only a portion of this industry is present within the NAICS data. If no * is shown, the entire industry is contained within the NAICS data.

INDICES OF CHANGE

| Years | Estab-lish-ments | Employment | | Payroll ($ mil) | | Costs ($ mil) | | Value Added ($ mil) | Revenues ($ mil) | | | Capital expend. ($ mil) |
| | | Total | Constr. workers | Total | Worker payroll | Total | Cost of materials | | All sources | Construction | | |
										Total	Net	
1997	100.0	100.0	100.0	100.0	100.0	100.0	100.0	100.0	100.0	100.0	100.0	100.0

Sources: Same as General Statistics. The values shown reflect change from the base year, 1997. Values above 100 mean greater than 1997, values below 100 mean less than 1997, and a value of 100 in years other than 1997 means same as 1997. Indices are calculated only for Census years. Data are the most recent available at this level of detail.

SELECTED RATIOS

For 1997	Avg. of Sector	Analyzed Industry	Index	For 1997	Avg. of Sector	Analyzed Industry	Index
Employees per establishment	8.6	7.6	89	Value added per establishment	584,730	405,426	69
Construction workers per establishment	6.6	5.7	86	Value added per employee	67,759	53,061	78
Payroll per establishment	265,343	199,221	75	Value added per construction worker	88,592	71,572	81
Payroll per employee	30,748	26,073	85	Revenues per establishment	1,307,915	692,276	53
Payroll per construction worker	27,622	23,470	85	Revenues per employee	151,563	90,603	60
Costs per establishment	367,737	224,479	61	Revenues per construction worker	198,161	122,211	62
Costs per employee	42,614	29,379	69	CR as % of total revenues	98.48	96.93	98
Costs per construction worker	55,716	39,629	71	Net CR as % of CR	72.40	90.71	125
Materials as % of costs	95.75	94.33	99	Investment per establishment	22,948	17,430	76
Costs as % of revenues	28.12	32.43	115	Investment per employee	2,659	2,281	86
Costs as % of construction revenues	28.55	33.45	117	Investment per construction worker	3,477	3,077	88

Sources: Same as General Statistics. The 'Average of Sector' column represents the average for all industries in this sector. The Index shows the relationship between the Average and the Analyzed Industry. For example, 100 means that they are equal; 500 that the Analyzed Industry is five times the average; 50 means that the Analyzed Industry is half the national average. 'na' is used to show that data are 'not available'. CR stands for "construction revenues" and "Net CR" is construction revenues net of subcontract expenses.

LEADING COMPANIES   Number shown: **75**   Total sales ($ mil): **3,784**   Total employment (000): **28.0**

Company Name	Address				CEO Name	Phone	Co. Type	Sales ($ mil)	Empl. (000)
Tetra Tech Inc.	670 N Rosemead	Pasadena	CA	91107	Li-San Hwang	626-351-4664	P	432	5.4
American Eco Corp.	11011 Jones Rd	Houston	TX	77070	Michael E McGinnis	281-774-7000	P	300	2.2
Ray Wilson Co.	199 S Los Robles	Pasadena	CA	91101	Nobu Kawasaki	626-795-7900	S	200*	0.4
Western Waterproofing Inc.	1637 N Warson Rd	St. Louis	MO	63132	William L Bishop	314-427-6733	S	120	1.3
LVI Services Inc.	470 Park Ave S	New York	NY	10016	Burton T Fried	212-951-3660	R	111	1.5
NSC Corp.	49 Danton Dr	Methuen	MA	01844	Darryl G Schimeck	978-557-7300	P	100	1.0
Arctic Slope World Services Inc.	3033 Gold Canal Dr	Rancho Cordova	CA	95670	Mike Taylor	916-363-2224	S	90	0.9
CST Environmental Inc.	404 N Berry	Brea	CA	92821	Subhas Khara	714-991-8300	R	88*	0.4
King and Company Inc.	P O Box 50263	New Orleans	LA	70150	Cyril P Geary Jr	504-486-9195	R	82*	0.6
All Pool and Spa Inc.	905 Kalanianaole	Kailua	HI	96734	John King	808-261-8991	R	82*	<0.1
Shasta Industries Inc.	2950 N 7th St	Phoenix	AZ	85014	Edward Ast	602-258-8981	R	80	0.6
Bankhead Enterprises Inc.	P O Box 93006	Atlanta	GA	30318	Glenn E Taylor	404-894-7900	R	80*	0.5
Serrot Corp.	PO Box 1519	Huntington Bch	CA	92647		714-895-3010	R	80*	0.3
Bigge Crane and Rigging Co.	10700 Bigge St	San Leandro	CA	94577	Brock Settlemier	510-638-8100	R	76*	0.4
Henkels & McCoy Inc. Northeast	985 Jolly Rd	Blue Bell	PA	19422		215-283-7600	D	75*	0.1
Norment Industries Inc.	PO Drawer 6129	Montgomery	AL	36106	Dennis A Flynn	334-281-8440	S	70*	0.4
Minnotte Contracting Corp.	Minnotte Sq	Pittsburgh	PA	15220	David W Minnotte	412-922-1633	R	70	<0.1
Lloyd's Refrigeration Inc.	3550 W Tompkins	Las Vegas	NV	89103	Gary Lloyds	702-798-1010	R	64*	0.2
KDI Corp.	3975 McMann Rd	Cincinnati	OH	45245	Jim Gitzinger	513-943-2000	R	58*	0.4
John E. Green Co.	220 Victor Ave	Highland Park	MI	48203	Peter J Green	313-868-2400	R	56*	0.4
Stebbins Engineering and Mfg Co.	363 Eastern Blvd	Watertown	NY	13601	Alfred Calligaris	315-782-3000	R	55*	0.4
MARCOR Remediation Inc.	P O Box 1043	Hunt Valley	MD	21030	Richard Ehrlich	410-785-0001	R	53	0.6
Sylvan Pools Executive Offices	Rte 611 Box 1449	Doylestown	PA	18901	Rick Kelso	215-348-9011	R	51*	0.3
Cannon Sline Inc.	5600 Woodland Ave	Philadelphia	PA	19143	Roger Gossett	215-729-4600	S	50	0.7
MewMech Companies Inc.	1633 Eustis St	St. Paul	MN	55108	Ron Pearson	651-645-0451	R	50	0.6
Davis Acoustical Corp.	PO Box 1150	Troy	NY	12181	Burton Fisher	518-271-7400	R	45*	0.3
PCI Energy Services	PO Box 3000	Lake Bluff	IL	60044	Michael McGough	847-680-8100	S	44*	0.3
Hodges Truck Company Inc.	P O Box 270660	Oklahoma City	OK	73137	HL Hodges	405-947-7764	R	44*	0.3
McDaniel Fire Systems Inc.	P O Box 70	Valparaiso	IN	46383	Gene A Grieger	219-462-0571	R	42	0.3
Way Co.	P O Box 36530	Houston	TX	77236	Peter M Way	713-666-3541	R	42*	0.3
Texas Aluminum Industries Inc.	2900 Patio Dr	Houston	TX	77017		713-946-9000	S	41*	0.3
Cannon Sline Inc.	6900 N Loop E	Houston	TX	77028	Ralph A Trallo	713-675-3141	D	40*	0.1
Long Painting Co.	PO Box 81435	Seattle	WA	98108	Mike Cassidy	206-763-8433	R	39	0.3
GeoTrans Wireless	46050 Manekin Plz	Sterling	VA	20166		703-444-7000	D	39*	0.2
G.S.I. of California Inc.	1503 Loveridge Rd	Pittsburg	CA	94565	Jim Heath	925-439-3195	S	38	0.4
PDG Environmental Inc.	300 Oxford Dr	Monroeville	PA	15146	John C Regan	412-856-2200	P	37	0.3
Bloom Engineering Company Inc.	5460 Horning Rd	Pittsburgh	PA	15236	James Johns	412-653-3500	R	36*	0.3
Eastern Maintenance & Services	PO Box 669	Benson	NC	27504	John M Aldridge Jr	919-894-7101	R	35*	0.2
Dunbar Mechanical Inc.	PO Box 352350	Toledo	OH	43635	Harley G Dunbar	419-537-1900	S	32	0.3
CRC-Evans Automatic Welding	11601 N H-Rosslyn	Houston	TX	77086	R L Jones	281-999-8920	D	30*	0.2
Nicholson Construction Co.	12 McClane St	Cuddy	PA	15031	Peter J Nicholson	412-221-4500	R	30*	0.1
Advanced Office Interiors Inc.	8801 S 137th Cir	Omaha	NE	68138	Martin McCormick	402-896-5520	R	30	0.1
Hayward Baker Inc.	1875 Mayfield Rd	Odenton	MD	21113	Tom Dobson	410-621-9400	P	29	0.4
Larson Company Inc.	6701 S Midvale Park	Tucson	AZ	85746	G Douglas Young	520-294-3900	R	29*	0.2
P.W. Stephens Residential Inc.	15201 Pipeline Ln	Huntington Bch	CA	92649	Scott Johnson	626-330-7221	S	28*	0.3
PetroChem Insulation Inc.	110 Corporate Pl	Vallejo	CA	94590	Arthur Lewis	707-644-7455	R	28	0.3
Cable Services Company Inc.	2113 Marydale Ave	Williamsport	PA	17701	John M Roskowski	570-323-8518	R	27*	0.2
Transaction Technology Corp.	22 S Main St	Greenville	SC	29601	Ed Harrison	843-271-6522	R	26*	0.2
Mechanical Construction Corp.	P O Box 752	Poughkeepsie	NY	12602	Don McKAY	518-465-3426	R	25*	0.2
Proven Alternatives Inc.	1740 Army St	San Francisco	CA	94124	Charles T Condy	415-285-0800	R	25	<0.1
NEO Corp.	PO Box 646	Waynesville	NC	28786	George Escaravage	828-456-4332	R	24*	0.1
HSI GeoTrans Inc.	46050 Manekin	Sterling	VA	20166	Charles R Faust		S	22*	0.1
Taft Contracting Company Inc.	5525 W Roosevelt	Chicago	IL	60804	Richard J Walsh	708-656-7500	R	22*	0.2
Continental Flooring Co.	5111 N Scottsdale	Scottsdale	AZ	85250	James GF Coleman	602-949-8509	R	22	<0.1
Gary Pools Inc.	438 Sandau Rd	San Antonio	TX	78216	Hugh Lynch Jr	210-341-5153	R	21*	0.1
Brisk Waterproofing Co.	720 Grand Ave	Ridgefield	NJ	07657	Steve Brisk	201-945-0210	D	20	0.3
C-Tec Inc.	PO Box 8828	Kentwood	MI	49518		616-977-8600	S	20*	0.1
Rock-Tred Corp.	3415 W Howard St	Skokie	IL	60076	Mark G Moran	847-673-8200	R	20*	<0.1
Alcorn Fence Co.	P O Box 1249	Sun Valley	CA	91353	Greg Erikson	818-983-0650	R	16*	0.2
P. Gioioso and Sons Inc.	50 Sprague St	Boston	MA	02136	L Gioioso	617-364-5800	R	16*	0.1
Clark Grave Vault Co.	PO Box 8250	Columbus	OH	43201	Mark A Beck	614-294-3761	R	15	0.1
Sauer Industries Inc.	30 51st St	Pittsburgh	PA	15201	William Steitz	412-687-4100	R	14*	0.3
Hartman-Walsh Painting Co.	7144 N Market St	St. Louis	MO	63133	Edward C Smith	314-863-1800	R	12	0.2
Marek Brothers Co.	2201 Judi Way	Houston	TX	77018		713-681-9213	R	12	0.2
Concise Industries Inc.	1101 Estes Ave	Elk Grove Vill.	IL	60007	Fred J Rieble	847-439-4550	R	12*	<0.1
Transco Products Inc.	55 E Jackson Blvd	Chicago	IL	60604		312-427-2818	S	12	<0.1
Metalclad Insulation Corp.	2198 S Dupont Dr	Anaheim	CA	92806	Dave Duclett	714-634-9050	S	11	0.2
Marine Steel Painting Corp.	2064 Zoeller Rd	Amherst	NY	14226	Leon Hatzitetros	716-937-3765	R	11*	<0.1
Metalclad Corp.	2 Corporate Plz	Newport Beach	CA	92660	Grant S Kesler	949-719-1234	P	10	0.1
Anthony Pools	1500 Brittmoore Rd	Houston	TX	77043		713-467-6458	R	8	<0.1
Raba-Kistner Consultants Inc.	12821 W Golden Ln	San Antonio	TX	78249	Bunny Jean Raba	210-699-9090	R	7*	0.2
Ramcon Engineering	P O Box 1026	W. Sacramento	CA	95691	Michael S Ramos	916-372-7535	R	6	<0.1
D.J. Plastics Inc.	PO Box 337	Folsom	CA	95763	Daniel Spence	916-351-0161	R	6	<0.1
D.P.C. General Contractors Inc.	250 Arizona Ave	Atlanta	GA	30307	David Sever	404-373-0561	D	6*	<0.1
Cardinal Fence and Security Inc.	4617 Illinois Ave	Louisville	KY	40213	David Shedd	502-459-1505	R	6*	<0.1

Source: Ward's Business Directory of U.S. Private and Public Companies, Volumes 1 and 2, 2000. The company type code used is as follows: P - Public, R - Private, S - Subsidiary, D - Division, J - Joint Venture, A - Affiliate, G - Group, N - Company type not reported. Sales are in millions of dollars, employees are in thousands. An asterisk (*) indicates an estimated sales volume. The symbol < stands for 'less than'. Company names and addresses are truncated, in some cases, to fit into the available space.

COST DETAILS

Item	Cost ($ mil)	% of total	Per $1,000 of Revenue	Item	Cost ($ mil)	% of total	Per $1,000 of Revenue
All costs	7,438.6	100.000	414.4	Total Rentals	396.1	5.325	22.1
Cost of supplies	5,491.3	73.821	305.9	Equipment	222.7	2.994	12.4
Subcontracts	1,617.4	21.744	90.1	Buildings	173.4	2.331	9.7
Power, fuel, lubricants	329.9	4.435	18.4	Services purchased	407.8	5.483	22.7
Electricity	57.1	0.767	3.2	Communications	185.1	2.488	10.3
Natural gas	11.5	0.155	0.6	Building repairs	26.0	0.350	1.5
Gasoline and diesel	246.7	3.317	13.7	Machinery repairs	196.7	2.644	11.0
Highway	212.4	2.855	11.8				
Offroad	34.4	0.462	1.9				
Other power	14.5	0.196	0.8				

Source: Economic Census of the United States, 1997. Revenues referred to are total industry revenues for the current NAICS industry.

CONSTRUCTION PRODUCT DETAILS

Construction type	Value of construction work ($ mil and %)							
	Total		New construction		Additions, alterations, reconstruction		Maintenance and repair	
	Value	%	Value	%	Value	%	Value	%
Total	**17,401.3**	**100.0**	**10,035.2**	**100.0**	**3,522.4**	**100.0**	**3,590.2**	**100.0**
Building construction, total	**9,862.4**	**56.7**	**5,080.2**	**50.6**	**2,591.7**	**73.6**	**2,190.5**	**61.0**
Single-family houses, detached	2,041.5	11.7	974.0	9.7	576.7	16.4	490.8	13.7
Single-family houses, attached	229.1	1.3	122.8	1.2	55.3	1.6	51.0	1.4
Apartment buildings, condos and cooperatives	388.0	2.2	188.5	1.9	104.6	3.0	94.8	2.6
Manufacturing and light industrial buildings	1,167.2	6.7	526.8	5.2	262.6	7.5	377.9	10.5
Manufacturing and light industrial warehouses	241.6	1.4	138.1	1.4	48.6	1.4	54.8	1.5
Hotels and motels	230.2	1.3	169.8	1.7	30.0	0.9	30.4	0.8
Office buildings	1,685.3	9.7	988.5	9.8	416.4	11.8	280.4	7.8
All other commercial buildings, nec	2,236.6	12.9	988.8	9.9	697.5	19.8	550.2	15.3
Commercial warehouses	174.6	1.0	114.5	1.1	31.7	0.9	28.4	0.8
Religious buildings	100.6	0.6	50.2	0.5	25.6	0.7	24.9	0.7
Educational buildings	415.6	2.4	209.5	2.1	138.4	3.9	67.7	1.9
Health care and institutional buildings	250.8	1.4	141.3	1.4	67.5	1.9	41.9	1.2
Public safety buildings	145.5	0.8	104.0	1.0	28.9	0.8	12.6	0.3
Other building construction	555.8	3.2	363.3	3.6	107.8	3.1	84.7	2.4
Nonbuilding construction, total	**7,285.4**	**41.9**	**4,954.9**	**49.4**	**930.8**	**26.4**	**1,399.7**	**39.0**
Highways, streets, and related work	230.5	1.3	139.4	1.4	45.3	1.3	45.7	1.3
Sewers, water mains, and related facilities	161.9	0.9	102.2	1.0	26.2	0.7	33.6	0.9
Power plants	160.9	0.9	31.9	0.3	16.0	0.5	113.0	3.1
Blast furnaces, refineries, chemical complexes, etc	520.6	3.0	86.4	0.9	74.9	2.1	359.4	10.0
Outdoor swimming pools	2,962.7	17.0	2,305.9	23.0	289.7	8.2	367.1	10.2
Fencing	2,428.9	14.0	1,791.7	17.9	358.2	10.2	279.0	7.8
Other nonbuilding construction, nec	819.8	4.7	497.4	5.0	120.5	3.4	201.9	5.6
Construction work, nsk	**253.5**	**1.5**	**NA**	**-**	**NA**	**-**	**NA**	**-**

Source: Economic Census of the United States, 1997. Bold items are headers. (D) stands for data withheld to protect competitive information. (S) indicates instances where data do not meet publications standards.

LOCATION BY STATE AND REGIONAL CONCENTRATION

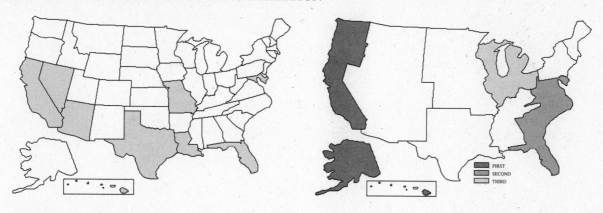

INDUSTRY DATA BY STATE

State	Estab lish- ments	Employment			Compensation		Production				Capital Exp. ($ mil)
		Total	Workers	Total as % of US	Payroll per Employee	Wages per Worker	Costs ($ mil)	Value Added ($ mil)	Reve- nues ($ mil)	% of US	
California	2,962	24,783	18,668	12.51	27,792	24,745	751.0	1,392.3	2,380.0	13.26	56.8
Texas	2,187	20,653	16,060	10.42	24,781	22,445	581.7	1,037.0	1,816.3	10.12	44.3
Florida	2,057	14,014	9,685	7.07	24,158	21,108	495.2	757.3	1,488.8	8.29	29.8
New York	1,437	10,232	7,183	5.16	29,223	26,076	356.5	617.6	1,082.8	6.03	28.2
Illinois	882	6,981	4,973	3.52	32,814	30,763	200.5	424.3	679.5	3.78	15.3
Pennsylvania	984	7,309	5,510	3.69	25,540	22,761	218.6	384.3	642.5	3.58	17.9
Arizona	626	6,253	4,525	3.16	25,948	22,770	192.1	313.3	597.7	3.33	14.5
Michigan	747	6,023	4,286	3.04	28,307	26,463	161.1	341.0	547.1	3.05	13.3
Ohio	873	6,708	4,559	3.39	25,147	22,335	180.3	334.6	546.7	3.05	13.3
New Jersey	848	5,679	4,162	2.87	28,194	25,737	155.1	321.3	511.6	2.85	12.3
Maryland	584	5,571	3,993	2.81	27,011	24,266	158.9	286.1	497.5	2.77	14.3
Louisiana	397	6,228	5,168	3.14	25,716	23,692	128.4	276.6	438.3	2.44	8.8
Missouri	547	5,465	4,152	2.76	26,139	23,816	127.0	277.8	426.1	2.37	10.2
Virginia	703	5,048	3,702	2.55	23,373	21,320	128.0	230.2	385.5	2.15	8.9
Washington	710	4,037	3,034	2.04	25,765	23,416	115.6	204.9	335.7	1.87	10.1
Indiana	457	3,709	2,781	1.87	24,279	22,613	101.2	192.7	308.9	1.72	5.6
Nevada	257	2,676	1,994	1.35	29,226	24,462	99.6	155.8	293.3	1.63	8.1
Tennessee	363	2,766	1,916	1.40	25,693	22,108	80.5	142.2	241.0	1.34	6.4
Wisconsin	357	1,942	1,337	0.98	27,893	25,739	78.0	114.2	213.5	1.19	5.9
Connecticut	333	2,168	1,537	1.09	30,697	27,100	69.1	118.9	200.9	1.12	5.3
Oregon	346	1,974	1,539	1.00	28,249	24,779	60.1	115.7	189.7	1.06	4.1
Alabama	363	2,463	1,874	1.24	22,116	20,387	60.1	115.1	185.0	1.03	5.1
South Carolina	408	2,388	1,700	1.21	20,159	18,871	67.2	100.3	181.1	1.01	4.5
Kentucky	280	1,805	1,307	0.91	21,080	17,650	44.7	84.1	136.0	0.76	3.4
Oklahoma	334	1,660	1,232	0.84	20,842	19,747	39.0	76.1	121.6	0.68	5.7
Iowa	179	1,218	885	0.61	23,984	20,642	36.3	64.0	105.1	0.59	2.6
Kansas	168	1,226	905	0.62	23,322	21,310	34.7	56.5	96.0	0.53	2.6
Nebraska	172	1,267	954	0.64	22,301	19,292	(D)	53.1	95.2	0.53	(D)
Hawaii	98	848	595	0.43	30,409	27,992	30.9	54.6	89.8	0.50	(D)
West Virginia	124	831	(D)	0.42	24,905	-	19.6	45.9	69.0	0.38	(D)
Idaho	171	837	666	0.42	18,970	18,101	(D)	35.0	57.4	0.32	(D)
Montana	105	359	291	0.18	-	-	16.1	24.8	44.4	0.25	1.1
Wyoming	110	394	(D)	0.20	22,419	-	(D)	21.8	31.9	0.18	(D)
South Dakota	63	298	(D)	0.15	21,470	-	6.4	17.0	24.2	0.14	1.0
North Carolina	895	5,796	4,517	2.93	-	-	(D)	262.5	(D)	-	(D)
Georgia	843	7,361	5,835	3.72	26,249	23,776	(D)	371.7	(D)	-	14.8
Massachusetts	571	4,004	2,857	2.02	29,147	27,106	(D)	246.2	(D)	-	10.5
Colorado	550	3,374	2,575	1.70	24,929	20,879	(D)	189.7	(D)	-	7.8
Minnesota	355	2,742	2,131	1.38	25,891	24,002	(D)	145.4	(D)	-	6.9
Utah	251	1,285	874	0.65	22,595	21,542	(D)	68.1	(D)	-	3.0
New Mexico	226	1,221	823	0.62	22,128	20,501	(D)	64.0	(D)	-	(D)
Arkansas	173	1,158	863	0.58	20,894	19,025	(D)	64.0	(D)	-	3.0
Mississippi	170	1,064	(D)	0.54	23,637	-	(D)	64.9	(D)	-	(D)
Maine	142	856	655	0.43	21,242	18,760	(D)	50.2	(D)	-	3.8
New Hampshire	131	935	717	0.47	23,767	20,768	(D)	46.5	(D)	-	1.9
Delaware	112	606	491	0.31	28,465	26,305	(D)	(D)	(D)	-	(D)
Rhode Island	99	787	575	0.40	32,475	34,501	(D)	54.2	(D)	-	2.3
Vermont	77	(D)	(D)	-	-	-	(D)	(D)	(D)	-	(D)
Alaska	57	298	221	0.15	33,426	32,543	(D)	18.8	(D)	-	(D)
North Dakota	41	423	337	0.21	27,350	25,442	(D)	28.6	(D)	-	(D)
D.C.	6	(D)	(D)	-	-	-	1.0	(D)	(D)	-	(D)

Source: Economic Census of the U.S., 1997. Data are sorted by 1997 revenues or establishments. (D) means data suppression to prevent disclosure of company data. (S) means that data did not meet statistical standards for publication. A dash (-) is used when data are unavailable or cannot be calculated. Data followed by an * indicate the midpoint of a range. The ranges are: for 10, 0-19; for 60, 20-99; for 175, 100-249; for 375, 250-499; for 750, 500-999. Higher values are multiples of those shown, e.g., 3,750 is the midpoint of the range 2,500-4,999. Shaded *states* on the state map indicate those states which have proportionately greater representation in the industry than would be indicated by the state's population; the ratio is based on total revenues or number of establishments. Shaded *regions* indicate where the industry is regionally most concentrated.

Part V

TRANSPORTATION & WAREHOUSING

NAICS 481111 - SCHEDULED PASSENGER AIR TRANSPORTATION*

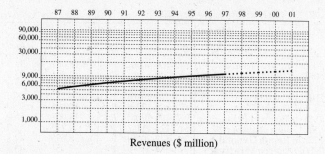

Revenues ($ million)

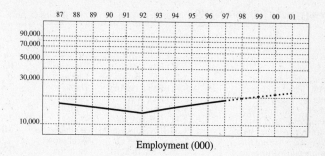

Employment (000)

GENERAL STATISTICS

Year	Establishments (number)	Employment (number)	Payroll ($ million)	Revenues ($ million)	Employees per Establishment (number)	Revenues per Establishment ($)	Payroll per Employee ($)
1987	273	16,787	577.7	5,220.8	61.5	19,123,810	34,414
1988	285	16,096	588.0	5,874.8	56.5	20,613,333	36,531
1989	297	15,406	598.3	6,528.7	51.9	21,982,155	38,836
1990	310	14,715	608.6	7,182.6	47.5	23,169,677	41,359
1991	322	14,025	618.9	7,836.5	43.6	24,336,957	44,128
1992	334	13,334	629.2	8,490.5	39.9	25,420,659	47,188
1993	365	14,376	671.7	9,106.5	39.4	24,976,796	46,724
1994	395	15,417	714.2	9,722.6	39.0	24,601,670	46,322
1995	426	16,459	756.6	10,338.6	38.7	24,280,460	45,972
1996	456	17,500	799.1	10,954.7	38.3	24,002,323	45,663
1997	487	18,542	841.6	11,570.7	38.1	23,759,138	45,389
1998	518 *p*	19,584 *p*	884.1 *p*	12,186.7 *p*	37.8 *p*	23,544,706 *p*	45,144 *p*
1999	548 *p*	20,625 *p*	926.6 *p*	12,802.8 *p*	37.6 *p*	23,354,214 *p*	44,924 *p*
2000	579 *p*	21,667 *p*	969.0 *p*	13,418.8 *p*	37.4 *p*	23,183,863 *p*	44,725 *p*
2001	609 *p*	22,708 *p*	1,011.5 *p*	14,034.9 *p*	37.3 *p*	23,030,620 *p*	44,544 *p*

Sources: Economic Census of the United States, 1987, 1992 and 1997. Data for those years (years are in **bold** type) are from the 5-year censuses of the economy. Other values, unless otherwise noted, are extrapolations. Values marked with *p* are projections. Data are the most recent available at this level of detail.

INDICES OF CHANGE

Year	Establishments (number)	Employment (number)	Payroll ($ million)	Revenues ($ million)	Employees per Establishment (number)	Revenues per Establishment ($)	Payroll per Employee ($)
1987	56.1	90.5	68.6	45.1	161.4	80.5	75.8
1992	68.6	71.9	74.8	73.4	104.7	107.0	104.0
1993	74.9	77.5	79.8	78.7	103.4	105.1	102.9
1994	81.1	83.1	84.9	84.0	102.4	103.5	102.1
1995	87.5	88.8	89.9	89.4	101.6	102.2	101.3
1996	93.6	94.4	95.0	94.7	100.5	101.0	100.6
1997	100.0	100.0	100.0	100.0	100.0	100.0	100.0
1998	106.4 *p*	105.6 *p*	105.0 *p*	105.3 *p*	99.2 *p*	99.1 *p*	99.5 *p*
1999	112.5 *p*	111.2 *p*	110.1 *p*	110.6 *p*	98.7 *p*	98.3 *p*	99.0 *p*
2000	118.9 *p*	116.9 *p*	115.1 *p*	116.0 *p*	98.2 *p*	97.6 *p*	98.5 *p*
2001	125.1 *p*	122.5 *p*	120.2 *p*	121.3 *p*	97.9 *p*	96.9 *p*	98.1 *p*

Sources: Same as General Statistics. The values shown reflect change from the base year, 1997. Values above 100 mean greater than 1997, values below 100 mean less than 1997, and a value of 100 in years other than 1997 means same as 1997. Indices are calculated only for Census years. Data are the most recent available at this level of detail.

SELECTED RATIOS

For 1997	Avg. of Sector	Analyzed Industry	Index	For 1997	Avg. of Sector	Analyzed Industry	Index
Employees per establishment	16	38	232	Payroll per establishment	462,554	1,728,131	374
Revenue per establishment	1,787,642	23,759,138	1,329	Payroll as % of revenue	26	7	28
Revenue per employee	108,959	624,027	573	Payroll per employee	28,193	45,389	161

Sources: Same as General Statistics. The 'Average of Sector' column represents the average for all industries in this sector. The Index shows the relationship between the Average and the Analyzed Industry. For example, 100 means that they are equal; 500 that the Analyzed Industry is five times the average; 50 means that the Analyzed Industry is half the national average. 'na' is used to show that data are 'not available'.

*Equivalent to SIC 4412.

LEADING COMPANIES Number shown: **75** Total sales ($ mil): **156,027** Total employment (000): **922.1**

Company Name	Address				CEO Name	Phone	Co. Type	Sales ($ mil)	Empl. (000)
UAL Corp.	PO Box 66919	Chicago	IL	60666	Rono J Dutta	847-700-4000	P	18,027	95.0
United Air Lines Inc.	PO Box 66100	Chicago	IL	60666	Gerald Greenwald	847-700-6796	S	17,561	93.0
AMR Corp.	PO Box 619616	Dallas	TX	75261	Donald J Carty	817-963-1234	P	15,192*	92.0
Delta Air Lines Inc.	PO Box 20706	Atlanta	GA	30320	Leo F Mullin	404-715-2600	P	14,711	74.0
American Airlines Inc.	P O Box 619616	Dallas	TX	75261	Donald J Carty	817-963-1234	S	14,695	92.0
Kimberly-Clark Corp.	PO Box 619100	Dallas	TX	75261	Thomas J Folk	972-281-1200	P	13,007	55.0
Northwest Airlines Inc.	5101 Northwest Dr	St. Paul	MN	55121	John Dasburg	612-726-2111	P	9,715	49.0
US Airways Group Inc.	2345 Crystal Dr	Arlington	VA	22227	Rakesh Gangwal	703-872-7000	P	8,595	42.7
Continental Airlines Inc.	1600 Smith St	Houston	TX	77002	Gordon M Bethune	713-324-5000	P	7,951	43.9
Southwest Airlines Co.	P O Box 36611	Dallas	TX	75235	Herbert D Kelleher	214-792-4000	P	4,736	29.0
Pittston Co.	PO Box 4229	Glen Allen	VA	23058	Michael T Dan	804-553-3600	R	3,747	41.0
Trans World Airlines Inc.	515 N 6th St	St. Louis	MO	63101	William F Compton	314-589-3000	P	3,309	21.3
America West Holdings Corp.	111 W Rio Salado	Tempe	AZ	85281	William A Franke	480-693-0800	P	2,211	13.5
Alaska Air Group Inc.	PO Box 68947	Seattle	WA	98188	William S Ayer	206-431-7040	P	2,082	9.2
America West Airlines Inc.	51 W 3rd St	Tempe	AZ	85281	William A Franke	602-693-0800	P	2,023	12.2
Pittston BAX Group	P O Box 19571	Irvine	CA	92623	C Robert Campbell	949-752-4000	P	1,800	7.6
BAX Global Inc.	16808 Armstrong	Irvine	CA	92606	C Robert Campbel	949-752-4000	S	1,700*	6.3
Alaska Airlines Inc.	P O Box 68900	Seattle	WA	98168	John F Kelly	206-433-3200	S	1,448	8.6
Amtran Inc.	P O Box 51609	Indianapolis	IN	46251	John P Tague	317-247-4000	P	1,122	7.0
NWA Inc.	5101 Northwest Dr	St. Paul	MN	55111	John H Dasburg	612-726-2111	S	1,100	52.0
American Trans Air Inc.	P O Box 51609	Indianapolis	IN	46251	John Tague	317-247-4000	S	773*	5.6
Comair Holdings Inc.	P O Box 75021	Cincinnati	OH	45275	David R Mueller	606-767-2550	P	763	4.4
Atlas Air Inc.	538 Commons Dr	Golden	CO	80401	Michael A Chowdry	303-526-5050	P	637	0.9
Continental Express Inc.	1600 Smith St	Houston	TX	77002	Dave Siegel	713-324-2639	S	534	3.4
AirTran Holdings Inc.	9955 AirTran Blvd	Orlando	FL	32827	Joseph Pl Leonard	407-251-5600	P	524	3.5
AirTran Airlines Inc.	9955 AirTran Blvd	Orlando	FL	32827	Joseph B Leonard	407-251-5600	S	500	3.7
Tower Air Inc.	Hanger 17	Jamaica	NY	11430	Morris K Nachtomi	718-553-4300	P	484	1.9
Midwest Express Airlines Inc.	6744 S Howell Ave	Oak Creek	WI	53154	Timothy E Hoeksema	414-570-4000	P	444*	2.8
Hawaiian Airlines Inc.	P O Box 30008	Honolulu	HI	96820	Paul J Casey	808-835-3700	P	412	2.6
Mesa Air Group Inc.	410 N 44th St	Phoenix	AZ	85008	Jonathon Ornstein	602-685-4000	P	405	3.4
Skywest Inc.	444 S River Rd	St. George	UT	84790	Jerry C Atkin	435-634-3000	P	389	3.2
Horizon Air Industries Inc.	P O Box 48309	Seattle	WA	98148	George Bagley	206-241-6757	S	380	3.2
Atlantic Coast Airlines Inc.	515-A Shaw Rd	Dulles	VA	20166	Kerry B Skeen	703-925-6000	P	347	2.5
Mesaba Holdings Inc.	7501 26th Ave S	Minneapolis	MN	55450	Paul F Foley	651-726-5151	P	332	3.0
Coca-Cola Swire Pacific Holdings	12634 263 W	Draper	UT	84020	Jack Pelo	801-816-5300	S	306*	1.5
Skywest Airlines Inc.	444 S River Rd	St. George	UT	84790	Jerry C Atkin	435-634-3000	S	304*	3.0
Evergreen Intern. Aviation Inc.	3850 3 Mile Ln	McMinnville	OR	97128	Delford M Smith	503-472-9361	R	300*	2.3
Atlantic Coast Airlines Holdings	515 Ashaw Rd	Dulles	VA	20166	C Edward Acker	703-925-6000	S	289	2.2
Comair Inc.	P O Box 75021	Cincinnati	OH	45275	DR Mueller	513-767-2550	S	280*	2.6
World Airways Inc.	13873 Park Center	Herndon	VA	20171	Russell L Ray Jr	703-834-9200	P	271	0.8
Trans States Airlines Inc.	9275 Genaire Dr	St. Louis	MO	63134	Hulas Kanodia	314-895-8700	R	264*	2.0
Aloha Airgroup Inc.	PO Box 30028	Honolulu	HI	96820	Glenn Zanzar	808-836-4200	R	260	2.3
Arrow Air Inc.	P O Box 026062	Miami	FL	33102	Guillermo Cabezq	305-526-0900	R	176*	0.5
Wings West Airlines Inc.	835 Arpt Dr	San Luis Obispo	CA	93401	Robert Cordes	805-541-1010	S	175	1.4
PSA Airlines Inc.	3400 Terminal Dr	Vandalia	OH	45377	Richard Psennig	937-454-1116	S	159*	1.0
Challenge Air Cargo Inc.	PO Box 523979	Miami	FL	33152	Bill Spohrer	305-869-8333	R	131*	0.8
Air Wisconsin Airline Corp.	W6390 Challenger	Appleton	WI	54915	Geoffrey Crowley	920-739-5123	R	130*	0.8
Great Lakes Aviation Ltd.	1965 330th St	Spencer	IA	51301	Douglas G Voss	712-262-1000	P	114	1.4
Vanguard Airlines Inc.	533 MexCit	Kansas City	MO	64153	Robert Spane	913-789-1388	P	104	0.9
Era Aviation Inc.	6160 Carl Brady Dr	Anchorage	AK	99502	Charles Johnson	907-248-4422	S	100	0.6
Corporate Jets Inc.	57 Allegh Cty Apt	West Mifflin	PA	15122	Fred S Shavlis	412-466-2500	R	90*	0.5
Commutair Inc.	518 Rugar St	Plattsburgh	NY	12901		518-562-2700	R	72*	0.5
CCAIR Inc.	4700 Yorkmont Rd	Charlotte	NC	28208	Kenneth W Gann	704-359-8990	S	71	0.7
Ameriflight Inc.	4700 Empire Ave	Burbank	CA	91505	Gary Richards	818-980-5005	R	71	0.6
Express One International Inc.	3890 W Northwest	Dallas	TX	75220	Charles Hamm	214-902-2501	R	70*	0.5
Spirit Airlines Inc.	18121 Eight Mile Rd	Eastpointe	MI	48021	Ned Homfield	810-779-2700	R	66*	0.8
USA Jet Airlines Inc.	2064 D St	Belleville	MI	48111	Martin R Goldman	734-483-7833	R	60	0.4
Peninsula Airways Inc.	6100 Boeing Av	Anchorage	AK	99502	Orin Sybert	907-243-2485	R	56*	0.4
IslandAir	99 Kapalulu Pl	Honolulu	HI	96819	Neil Takekawa	808-836-7693	S	45*	0.3
Astral Airlines Inc.	1190 W Rawson	Oak Creek	WI	53154	David C Reeve	414-570-2300	R	42	0.4
Capital Cargo Airlines	6200 Hazeltime	Orlando	FL	32822		407-855-2004	R	40*	0.3
Island Air	99 Kapalulu Pl	Honolulu	HI	96819	Neil Takekawa	808-836-7693	S	36	0.3
Reeve Aleutian Airways Inc.	4700 W Int Apt	Anchorage	AK	99502	Richard D Reeve	907-243-1112	R	36*	0.3
Priester Aviation Inc.	1126 S Milwaukee	Wheeling	IL	60090	Charles Priester	847-537-1200	R	30*	0.1
Piedmont Airlines Inc.	5443 Arpt Terminal	Salisbury	MD	21804	John Leonard	410-742-2996	S	29*	0.2
Empire Airlines Inc.	2115 Government	Coeur D Alene	ID	83814	Mel Spelde	208-667-5400	R	27*	0.2
Aloha Airlines Inc.	P O Box 30028	Honolulu	HI	96820	Glenn Zander	808-836-4113	S	26*	2.0
Aero California Inc.	1960 E Grand 1200	El Segundo	CA	90245	Raul A Arechiga	310-647-6100	R	24*	0.2
KOA Holdings Inc.	550 N 31st St	Billings	MT	59101	Art Peterson	406-248-7444	R	23*	0.4
Gulfstream Intern. Airlines Inc.	P O Box 777	Miami Springs	FL	33266	Thomas Cooper	954-266-3000	R	23*	0.1
Taquan Air	1007 Water St	Ketchikan	AK	99901	Gail Mathers	907-828-8800	R	23*	0.1
Air Vegas Airlines	P O Box 11008	Las Vegas	NV	89111	James Petty	702-736-3599	R	14	0.1
Kitty Hawk Cargo	110 Keehi Pl	Honolulu	HI	96819		808-836-0656	D	13*	<0.1
Ross Aviation Inc.	PO Box 9124	Albuquerque	NM	87119		505-845-4091	R	12*	<0.1
Air Transport Association	1301 Penn NW	Washington	DC	20004	Carol Hallett	202-626-4000	R	11	0.1

Source: Ward's Business Directory of U.S. Private and Public Companies, Volumes 1 and 2, 2000. The company type code used is as follows: P - Public, R - Private, S - Subsidiary, D - Division, J - Joint Venture, A - Affiliate, G - Group, N - Company type not reported. Sales are in millions of dollars, employees are in thousands. An asterisk (*) indicates an estimated sales volume. The symbol < stands for 'less than'. Company names and addresses are truncated, in some cases, to fit into the available space.

LOCATION BY STATE AND REGIONAL CONCENTRATION

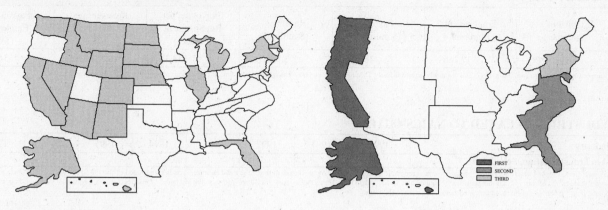

FIRST
SECOND
THIRD

INDUSTRY DATA BY STATE

State	Establishments Total (number)	% of U.S.	Employment Total (number)	% of U.S.	Per Estab.	Payroll Total ($ mil.)	Per Empl. ($)	Revenues Total ($ mil.)	% of U.S.	Per Estab. ($)
New York	150	10.5	7,520	17.6	50	295.5	39,292	2,779.8	22.8	18,532,133
California	177	12.3	5,418	12.7	31	181.2	33,436	2,553.8	20.9	14,427,983
Florida	147	10.3	4,186	9.8	28	116.6	27,862	941.9	7.7	6,407,340
Illinois	71	5.0	1,119	2.6	16	39.5	35,309	649.4	5.3	9,145,803
Texas	91	6.3	1,989	4.7	22	64.1	32,233	644.4	5.3	7,080,846
Pennsylvania	46	3.2	1,701	4.0	37	42.6	25,021	394.4	3.2	8,574,239
Virginia	30	2.1	1,751	4.1	58	51.7	29,543	322.1	2.6	10,738,233
Michigan	57	4.0	1,345	3.1	24	34.6	25,752	213.9	1.8	3,752,789
Maryland	12	0.8	769	1.8	64	21.5	27,902	197.9	1.6	16,488,167
Alaska	57	4.0	1,796	4.2	32	56.1	31,229	178.0	1.5	3,122,807
Georgia	30	2.1	662	1.5	22	20.5	30,974	160.2	1.3	5,338,933
Minnesota	19	1.3	760	1.8	40	26.1	34,301	122.1	1.0	6,428,000
Wisconsin	16	1.1	161	0.4	10	3.9	24,273	98.4	0.8	6,150,500
Nevada	11	0.8	508	1.2	46	12.9	25,372	67.3	0.6	6,118,091
Ohio	30	2.1	562	1.3	19	15.6	27,804	54.7	0.4	1,824,000
Oregon	12	0.8	103	0.2	9	3.8	36,553	37.3	0.3	3,112,333
Tennessee	12	0.8	198	0.5	16	4.6	23,131	25.5	0.2	2,127,417
Missouri	8	0.6	152	0.4	19	4.1	26,875	17.2	0.1	2,153,500
West Virginia	9	0.6	100	0.2	11	1.8	17,780	15.4	0.1	1,705,889
Kansas	13	0.9	146	0.3	11	3.5	23,678	14.4	0.1	1,110,000
Connecticut	11	0.8	373	0.9	34	9.8	26,201	13.0	0.1	1,181,273
Massachusetts	47	3.3	750*	-	-	(D)	-	(D)	-	-
Washington	34	2.4	375*	-	-	(D)	-	(D)	-	-
Arizona	32	2.2	375*	-	-	(D)	-	(D)	-	-
Colorado	31	2.2	1,750*	-	-	(D)	-	(D)	-	-
D.C.	31	2.2	375*	-	-	(D)	-	(D)	-	-
New Jersey	27	1.9	375*	-	-	(D)	-	(D)	-	-
North Carolina	22	1.5	750*	-	-	(D)	-	(D)	-	-
New Mexico	17	1.2	375*	-	-	(D)	-	(D)	-	-
Nebraska	15	1.0	375*	-	-	(D)	-	(D)	-	-
Iowa	14	1.0	375*	-	-	(D)	-	(D)	-	-
Hawaii	13	0.9	750*	-	-	(D)	-	(D)	-	-
Louisiana	13	0.9	375*	-	-	(D)	-	(D)	-	-
South Dakota	13	0.9	175*	-	-	(D)	-	(D)	-	-
Wyoming	13	0.9	175*	-	-	(D)	-	(D)	-	-
Indiana	12	0.8	175*	-	-	(D)	-	(D)	-	-
Montana	12	0.8	60*	-	-	(D)	-	(D)	-	-
South Carolina	12	0.8	60*	-	-	(D)	-	(D)	-	-
North Dakota	9	0.6	60*	-	-	(D)	-	(D)	-	-
Utah	9	0.6	750*	-	-	(D)	-	(D)	-	-
Arkansas	8	0.6	60*	-	-	(D)	-	(D)	-	-
Idaho	7	0.5	175*	-	-	(D)	-	(D)	-	-
Kentucky	7	0.5	3,750*	-	-	(D)	-	(D)	-	-

Source: 1997 *Economic Census*. The states are in descending order of revenues or establishments (if revenue data are missing for the majority). The symbol (D) appears when data are withheld to prevent disclosure of competitive information. States marked with (D) are sorted by number of establishments. A dash (-) indicates that the data element cannot be calculated. * indicates the midpoint of a range; 175, for example is the range 100-249. Shaded *states* on the state map indicate those states which have proportionately greater representation in the industry than would be indicated by the state's population; the ratio is based on total revenues or number of establishments. Shaded *regions* indicate where the industry is regionally most concentrated.

NAICS 481112 - SCHEDULED FREIGHT AIR TRANSPORTATION

GENERAL STATISTICS

Year	Establishments (number)	Employment (number)	Payroll ($ million)	Revenues ($ million)	Employees per Establishment (number)	Revenues per Establishment ($)	Payroll per Employee ($)
1997	80	12,266	380.3	3,908.1	153.3	48,851,250	31,004

Source: *Economic Census of the United States*, 1997. This is a newly defined industry. Data for prior years were unavailable at the time of publication but may become available over time.

SIC INDUSTRIES RELATED TO NAICS 481112

SIC	Industry	1990	1991	1992	1993	1994	1995	1996	1997
4512	**Air Transportation, Scheduled***	-	-	-	-	-	-	-	-

Source: *Economic Census of the United States*, 1992, annual surveys of economic sectors conducted by the Bureau of the Census, and estimates or projections based on the 1982-1992 period; not all data are shown. 'e' marks estimates made by the editors; 'p' indicates projections based on time series. A dash (-) indicates that data for this SIC or year were not available. * Indicates that only a portion of this industry is present within the NAICS data. If no * is shown, the entire industry is contained within the NAICS data.

INDICES OF CHANGE

Year	Establishments (number)	Employment (number)	Payroll ($ million)	Revenues ($ million)	Employees per Establishment (number)	Revenues per Establishment ($)	Payroll per Employee ($)
1997	100.0	100.0	100.0	100.0	100.0	100.0	100.0

Sources: Same as General Statistics. The values shown reflect change from the base year, 1997. Values above 100 mean greater than 1997, values below 100 mean less than 1997, and a value of 100 in years other than 1997 means same as 1997. Indices are calculated only for Census years. Data are the most recent available at this level of detail.

SELECTED RATIOS

For 1997	Avg. of Sector	Analyzed Industry	Index	For 1997	Avg. of Sector	Analyzed Industry	Index
Employees per establishment	16	153	935	Payroll per establishment	462,554	4,753,750	1,028
Revenue per establishment	1,787,642	48,851,250	2,733	Payroll as % of revenue	26	10	38
Revenue per employee	108,959	318,612	292	Payroll per employee	28,193	31,004	110

Sources: Same as General Statistics. The 'Average of Sector' column represents the average for all industries in this sector. The Index shows the relationship between the Average and the Analyzed Industry. For example, 100 means that they are equal; 500 that the Analyzed Industry is five times the average; 50 means that the Analyzed Industry is half the national average. 'na' is used to show that data are 'not available'.

LEADING COMPANIES　　Number shown: **75**　　Total sales ($ mil): **156,027**　　Total employment (000): **922.1**

Company Name	Address				CEO Name	Phone	Co. Type	Sales ($ mil)	Empl. (000)
UAL Corp.	PO Box 66919	Chicago	IL	60666	Rono J Dutta	847-700-4000	P	18,027	95.0
United Air Lines Inc.	PO Box 66100	Chicago	IL	60666	Gerald Greenwald	847-700-6796	S	17,561	93.0
AMR Corp.	PO Box 619616	Dallas	TX	75261	Donald J Carty	817-963-1234	P	15,192*	92.0
Delta Air Lines Inc.	PO Box 20706	Atlanta	GA	30320	Leo F Mullin	404-715-2600	P	14,711	74.0
American Airlines Inc.	P O Box 619616	Dallas	TX	75261	Donald J Carty	817-963-1234	S	14,695	92.0
Kimberly-Clark Corp.	PO Box 619100	Dallas	TX	75261	Thomas J Folk	972-281-1200	P	13,007	55.0
Northwest Airlines Inc.	5101 Northwest Dr	St. Paul	MN	55121	John Dasburg	612-726-2111	P	9,715	49.0
US Airways Group Inc.	2345 Crystal Dr	Arlington	VA	22227	Rakesh Gangwal	703-872-7000	P	8,595	42.7
Continental Airlines Inc.	1600 Smith St	Houston	TX	77002	Gordon M Bethune	713-324-5000	P	7,951	43.9
Southwest Airlines Co.	P O Box 36611	Dallas	TX	75235	Herbert D Kelleher	214-792-4000	P	4,736	29.0
Pittston Co.	PO Box 4229	Glen Allen	VA	23058	Michael T Dan	804-553-3600	R	3,747	41.0
Trans World Airlines Inc.	515 N 6th St	St. Louis	MO	63101	William F Compton	314-589-3000	P	3,309	21.3
America West Holdings Corp.	111 W Rio Salado	Tempe	AZ	85281	William A Franke	480-693-0800	P	2,211	13.5
Alaska Air Group Inc.	PO Box 68947	Seattle	WA	98188	William S Ayer	206-431-7040	P	2,082	9.2
America West Airlines Inc.	51 W 3rd St	Tempe	AZ	85281	William A Franke	602-693-0800	P	2,023	12.2
Pittston BAX Group	P O Box 19571	Irvine	CA	92623	C Robert Campbell	949-752-4000	P	1,800	7.6
BAX Global Inc.	16808 Armstrong	Irvine	CA	92606	C Robert Campbel	949-752-4000	S	1,700*	6.3
Alaska Airlines Inc.	P O Box 68900	Seattle	WA	98168	John F Kelly	206-433-3200	S	1,448	8.6
Amtran Inc.	P O Box 51609	Indianapolis	IN	46251	John P Tague	317-247-4000	P	1,122	7.0
NWA Inc.	5101 Northwest Dr	St. Paul	MN	55111	John H Dasburg	612-726-2111	S	1,100	52.0
American Trans Air Inc.	P O Box 51609	Indianapolis	IN	46251	John Tague	317-247-4000	S	773*	5.6
Comair Holdings Inc.	P O Box 75021	Cincinnati	OH	45275	David R Mueller	606-767-2550	P	763	4.4
Atlas Air Inc.	538 Commons Dr	Golden	CO	80401	Michael A Chowdry	303-526-5050	P	637	0.9
Continental Express Inc.	1600 Smith St	Houston	TX	77002	Dave Siegel	713-324-2639	S	534	3.4
AirTran Holdings Inc.	9955 AirTran Blvd	Orlando	FL	32827	Joseph Pl Leonard	407-251-5600	P	524	3.5
AirTran Airlines Inc.	9955 AirTran Blvd	Orlando	FL	32827	Joseph B Leonard	407-251-5600	S	500	3.7
Tower Air Inc.	Hanger 17	Jamaica	NY	11430	Morris K Nachtomi	718-553-4300	P	484	1.9
Midwest Express Airlines Inc.	6744 S Howell Ave	Oak Creek	WI	53154	Timothy E Hoeksema	414-570-4000	P	444*	2.8
Hawaiian Airlines Inc.	P O Box 30008	Honolulu	HI	96820	Paul J Casey	808-835-3700	P	412	2.6
Mesa Air Group Inc.	410 N 44th St	Phoenix	AZ	85008	Jonathon Ornstein	602-685-4000	P	405	3.4
Skywest Inc.	444 S River Rd	St. George	UT	84790	Jerry C Atkin	435-634-3000	P	389	3.2
Horizon Air Industries Inc.	P O Box 48309	Seattle	WA	98148	George Bagley	206-241-6757	S	380	3.2
Atlantic Coast Airlines Inc.	515-A Shaw Rd	Dulles	VA	20166	Kerry B Skeen	703-925-6000	P	347	2.5
Mesaba Holdings Inc.	7501 26th Ave S	Minneapolis	MN	55450	Paul F Foley	651-726-5151	P	332	3.0
Coca-Cola Swire Pacific Holdings	12634 263 W	Draper	UT	84020	Jack Pelo	801-816-5300	S	306*	1.5
Skywest Airlines Inc.	444 S River Rd	St. George	UT	84790	Jerry C Atkin	435-634-3000	S	304*	3.0
Evergreen Intern. Aviation Inc.	3850 3 Mile Ln	McMinnville	OR	97128	Delford M Smith	503-472-9361	R	300*	2.3
Atlantic Coast Airlines Holdings	515 Ashaw Rd	Dulles	VA	20166	C Edward Acker	703-925-6000	S	289	2.2
Comair Inc.	P O Box 75021	Cincinnati	OH	45275	DR Mueller	513-767-2550	S	280*	2.6
World Airways Inc.	13873 Park Center	Herndon	VA	20171	Russell L Ray Jr	703-834-9200	P	271	0.8
Trans States Airlines Inc.	9275 Genaire Dr	St. Louis	MO	63134	Hulas Kanodia	314-895-8700	R	264*	2.0
Aloha Airgroup Inc.	PO Box 30028	Honolulu	HI	96820	Glenn Zanzar	808-836-4200	R	260	2.3
Arrow Air Inc.	P O Box 026062	Miami	FL	33102	Guillermo Cabezq	305-526-0900	R	176*	0.5
Wings West Airlines Inc.	835 Arpt Dr	San Luis Obispo	CA	93401	Robert Cordes	805-541-1010	S	175	1.4
PSA Airlines Inc.	3400 Terminal Dr	Vandalia	OH	45377	Richard Psennig	937-454-1116	S	159*	1.0
Challenge Air Cargo Inc.	PO Box 523979	Miami	FL	33152	Bill Spohrer	305-869-8333	R	131*	0.8
Air Wisconsin Airline Corp.	W6390 Challenger	Appleton	WI	54915	Geoffrey Crowley	920-739-5123	R	130*	0.8
Great Lakes Aviation Ltd.	1965 330th St	Spencer	IA	51301	Douglas G Voss	712-262-1000	P	114	1.4
Vanguard Airlines Inc.	533 MexCit	Kansas City	MO	64153	Robert Spane	913-789-1388	P	104	0.9
Era Aviation Inc.	6160 Carl Brady Dr	Anchorage	AK	99502	Charles Johnson	907-248-4422	S	100	0.6
Corporate Jets Inc.	57 Allegh Cty Apt	West Mifflin	PA	15122	Fred S Shavlis	412-466-2500	R	90*	0.5
Commutair Inc.	518 Rugar St	Plattsburgh	NY	12901		518-562-2700	R	72*	0.5
CCAIR Inc.	4700 Yorkmont Rd	Charlotte	NC	28208	Kenneth W Gann	704-359-8990	S	71	0.7
Ameriflight Inc.	4700 Empire Ave	Burbank	CA	91505	Gary Richards	818-980-5005	R	71	0.6
Express One International Inc.	3890 W Northwest	Dallas	TX	75220	Charles Hamm	214-902-2501	R	70*	0.5
Spirit Airlines Inc.	18121 Eight Mile Rd	Eastpointe	MI	48021	Ned Homfield	810-779-2700	R	66*	0.8
USA Jet Airlines Inc.	2064 D St	Belleville	MI	48111	Martin R Goldman	734-483-7833	R	60	0.4
Peninsula Airways Inc.	6100 Boeing Av	Anchorage	AK	99502	Orin Sybert	907-243-2485	R	56*	0.4
IslandAir	99 Kapalulu Pl	Honolulu	HI	96819	Neil Takekawa	808-836-7693	S	45*	0.3
Astral Airlines Inc.	1190 W Rawson	Oak Creek	WI	53154	David C Reeve	414-570-2300	S	42	0.4
Capital Cargo Airlines	6200 Hazeltime	Orlando	FL	32822		407-855-2004	R	40*	0.3
Island Air	99 Kapalulu Pl	Honolulu	HI	96819	Neil Takekawa	808-836-7693	S	36	0.3
Reeve Aleutian Airways Inc.	4700 W Int Apt	Anchorage	AK	99502	Richard D Reeve	907-243-1112	R	36*	0.3
Priester Aviation Inc.	1126 S Milwaukee	Wheeling	IL	60090	Charles Priester	847-537-1200	R	30*	0.1
Piedmont Airlines Inc.	5443 Arpt Terminal	Salisbury	MD	21804	John Leonard	410-742-2996	S	29*	0.2
Empire Airlines Inc.	2115 Government	Coeur D Alene	ID	83814	Mel Spelde	208-667-5400	R	27*	0.2
Aloha Airlines Inc.	P O Box 30028	Honolulu	HI	96820	Glenn Zander	808-836-4113	S	26*	2.0
Aero California Inc.	1960 E Grand 1200	El Segundo	CA	90245	Raul A Arechiga	310-647-6100	R	24*	0.2
KOA Holdings Inc.	550 N 31st St	Billings	MT	59101	Art Peterson	406-248-7444	R	23*	0.4
Gulfstream Intern. Airlines Inc.	P O Box 777	Miami Springs	FL	33266	Thomas Cooper	954-266-3000	R	23*	0.1
Taquan Air	1007 Water St	Ketchikan	AK	99901	Gail Mathers	907-828-8800	R	23*	0.1
Air Vegas Airlines	P O Box 11008	Las Vegas	NV	89111	James Petty	702-736-3599	R	14	0.1
Kitty Hawk Cargo	110 Keehi Pl	Honolulu	HI	96819		808-836-0656	D	13*	<0.1
Ross Aviation Inc.	PO Box 9124	Albuquerque	NM	87119		505-845-4091	R	12*	<0.1
Air Transport Association	1301 Penn NW	Washington	DC	20004	Carol Hallett	202-626-4000	R	11	0.1

Source: Ward's Business Directory of U.S. Private and Public Companies, Volumes 1 and 2, 2000. The company type code used is as follows: P - Public, R - Private, S - Subsidiary, D - Division, J - Joint Venture, A - Affiliate, G - Group, N - Company type not reported. Sales are in millions of dollars, employees are in thousands. An asterisk (*) indicates an estimated sales volume. The symbol < stands for 'less than'. Company names and addresses are truncated, in some cases, to fit into the available space.

LOCATION BY STATE AND REGIONAL CONCENTRATION

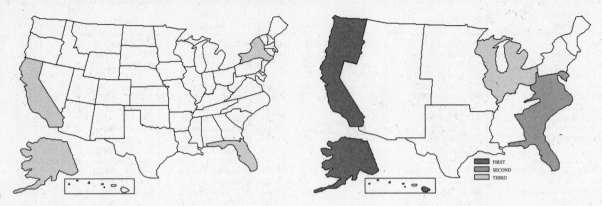

INDUSTRY DATA BY STATE

State	Establishments		Employment			Payroll		Revenues		
	Total (number)	% of U.S.	Total (number)	% of U.S.	Per Estab.	Total ($ mil.)	Per Empl. ($)	Total ($ mil.)	% of U.S.	Per Estab. ($)
California	51	14.0	4,857	20.9	95	145.2	29,895	1,430.2	35.0	28,042,353
Florida	39	10.7	2,992	12.9	77	86.2	28,807	591.9	14.5	15,177,385
New York	33	9.1	973	4.2	29	40.3	41,377	393.3	9.6	11,918,212
Illinois	21	5.8	377	1.6	18	13.0	34,483	170.0	4.2	8,093,381
Michigan	10	2.7	838	3.6	84	27.3	32,556	127.7	3.1	12,772,000
Ohio	8	2.2	1,187	5.1	148	42.5	35,812	112.5	2.8	14,065,500
Alaska	25	6.9	547	2.4	22	21.8	39,872	95.8	2.3	3,832,720
Texas	19	5.2	240	1.0	13	9.1	38,017	68.6	1.7	3,608,053
Georgia	9	2.5	92	0.4	10	3.7	40,652	34.5	0.8	3,833,111
Virginia	9	2.5	98	0.4	11	6.9	70,122	27.4	0.7	3,049,333
Wisconsin	8	2.2	177	0.8	22	4.4	24,610	22.7	0.6	2,839,625
Pennsylvania	6	1.6	138	0.6	23	3.2	23,058	17.4	0.4	2,895,833
Maryland	8	2.2	45	0.2	6	1.3	29,778	8.1	0.2	1,011,250
Missouri	8	2.2	47	0.2	6	0.7	15,170	6.5	0.2	814,000
New Jersey	12	3.3	175*	-	-	(D)	-	(D)	-	-
Massachusetts	8	2.2	60*	-	-	(D)	-	(D)	-	-
North Carolina	8	2.2	375*	-	-	(D)	-	(D)	-	-
Washington	8	2.2	60*	-	-	(D)	-	(D)	-	-
Idaho	7	1.9	60*	-	-	(D)	-	(D)	-	-
Indiana	7	1.9	750*	-	-	(D)	-	(D)	-	-
Utah	6	1.6	60*	-	-	(D)	-	(D)	-	-

Source: 1997 *Economic Census*. The states are in descending order of revenues or establishments (if revenue data are missing for the majority). The symbol (D) appears when data are withheld to prevent disclosure of competitive information. States marked with (D) are sorted by number of establishments. A dash (-) indicates that the data element cannot be calculated. * indicates the midpoint of a range; 175, for example is the range 100-249. Shaded *states* on the state map indicate those states which have proportionately greater representation in the industry than would be indicated by the state's population; the ratio is based on total revenues or number of establishments. Shaded *regions* indicate where the industry is regionally most concentrated.

NAICS 481211 - NONSCHEDULED CHARTERED PASSENGER AIR TRANSPORTATION

GENERAL STATISTICS

Year	Establishments (number)	Employment (number)	Payroll ($ million)	Revenues ($ million)	Employees per Establishment (number)	Revenues per Establishment ($)	Payroll per Employee ($)
1997	616	21,690	925.5	4,677.9	35.2	7,593,994	42,669

Source: Economic Census of the United States, 1997. This is a newly defined industry. Data for prior years were unavailable at the time of publication but may become available over time.

SIC INDUSTRIES RELATED TO NAICS 481211

SIC	Industry	1990	1991	1992	1993	1994	1995	1996	1997
4522	**Air Transportation, Nonscheduled***								
	Establishments (number)	928	1,441	1,791	1,714	1,692	1,621	1,831	2,052p
	Employment (thousands)	15.3	20.5	23.1	24.4	29.1	27.7	28.8	33.2p
	Revenues ($ million)	-	-	3,432.7	-	-	-	-	-

*Source: Economic Census of the United States, 1992, annual surveys of economic sectors conducted by the Bureau of the Census, and estimates or projections based on the 1982-1992 period; not all data are shown. 'e' marks estimates made by the editors; 'p' indicates projections based on time series. A dash (-) indicates that data for this SIC or year were not available. * Indicates that only a portion of this industry is present within the NAICS data. If no * is shown, the entire industry is contained within the NAICS data.*

INDICES OF CHANGE

Year	Establishments (number)	Employment (number)	Payroll ($ million)	Revenues ($ million)	Employees per Establishment (number)	Revenues per Establishment ($)	Payroll per Employee ($)
1997	100.0	100.0	100.0	100.0	100.0	100.0	100.0

Sources: Same as General Statistics. The values shown reflect change from the base year, 1997. Values above 100 mean greater than 1997, values below 100 mean less than 1997, and a value of 100 in years other than 1997 means same as 1997. Indices are calculated only for Census years. Data are the most recent available at this level of detail.

SELECTED RATIOS

For 1997	Avg. of Sector	Analyzed Industry	Index	For 1997	Avg. of Sector	Analyzed Industry	Index
Employees per establishment	16	35	215	Payroll per establishment	462,554	1,502,435	325
Revenue per establishment	1,787,642	7,593,994	425	Payroll as % of revenue	26	20	76
Revenue per employee	108,959	215,671	198	Payroll per employee	28,193	42,669	151

Sources: Same as General Statistics. The 'Average of Sector' column represents the average for all industries in this sector. The Index shows the relationship between the Average and the Analyzed Industry. For example, 100 means that they are equal; 500 that the Analyzed Industry is five times the average; 50 means that the Analyzed Industry is half the national average. 'na' is used to show that data are 'not available'.

LEADING COMPANIES   Number shown: **29**   Total sales ($ mil): **5,572**   Total employment (000): **29.6**

Company Name	Address				CEO Name	Phone	Co. Type	Sales ($ mil)	Empl. (000)
Amtran Inc.	P O Box 51609	Indianapolis	IN	46251	John P Tague	317-247-4000	P	1,122	7.0
Kitty Hawk Aircargo Inc.	P O Box 612787	Dallas	TX	75261	M Tom Christopher	972-456-2200	S	1,070*	2.1
American Trans Air Inc.	P O Box 51609	Indianapolis	IN	46251	John Tague	317-247-4000	S	773*	5.6
Kitty Hawk Inc.	PO Box 612787	Dallas	TX	75261	M Tom Christopher	972-456-2200	P	715	3.8
Offshore Logistics Inc.	PO Box 5-C	Lafayette	LA	70505	George M Small	318-233-1221	P	468	3.2
Evergreen Intern. Airlines Inc.	3850 3 Mile Ln	McMinnville	OR	97128	Delford M Smith	503-472-0011	S	260*	0.5
Petroleum Helicopters Inc.	PO Box 578	Metairie	LA	70004	Carroll W Suggs	504-828-3323	P	247	2.1
Jet Charter	7930 Arpt Blvd	Houston	TX	77061	Marcel White	713-643-5387	S	220*	1.0
Southern Air Transport Inc.	PO Box 328988	Columbus	OH	43232	William G Langton	614-751-1100	R	200	0.7
Columbia Helicopters Inc.	PO Box 3500	Portland	OR	97208		503-678-1222	R	100	0.9
Lynden Air Freight Inc.	PO Box 84167	Seattle	WA	98124	Dennis Patrick	206-777-5300	S	52*	0.3
Air Methods Corp.	7301 S Peoria St	Englewood	CO	80112	George Belsey	303-792-7400	P	49	0.4
Richmor Aviation Inc.	PO Box 423	Hudson	NY	12534	Mahlom W Richards	518-828-9461	R	43*	0.2
Executive Jet Inc.	625 N Hamilton Rd	Columbus	OH	43219	Richard Santulli	614-239-5580	S	32*	0.2
Epps Aviation Inc.	DeKalb Airport	Atlanta	GA	30341	E Patrick Epps	770-458-9851	R	30*	0.1
Flight Services Group Inc.	611 Access Rd	Stratford	CT	06615	David C Hurley	203-337-4600	S	29	0.1
Eagle Airlines Inc.	275 E Tropicana	Las Vegas	NV	89109	Clifford Evarts	702-736-3333	S	25	0.2
Scenic Airlines Inc.	275 E Tropicana	Las Vegas	NV	89109	Grant Murray	702-736-3333	D	22*	0.4
Flight International Inc.	Williamsbrg Apt	Newport News	VA	23602	David E Sandlin	757-886-5500	S	22	0.2
Phoenix Air Group Inc.	100 Phoenix Air Dr	Cartersville	GA	30120	Mark Thompson	770-387-2000	R	17	0.1
Tex-Air Helicopters Inc.	8919 Paul B Koonce	Houston	TX	77061	Ed Behne	713-649-6300	R	17*	<0.1
JetCorp	18152 Edison Ave	Chesterfield	MO	63005	Douglas R McCollum	363-530-7000	R	13*	0.2
St. Louis Helicopter Airways Inc.	P O Box 809	Chesterfield	MO	63006	Jack R Russell	314-532-1177	R	11	<0.1
Eagle Aviation Resources Ltd.	275 E Tropicana	Las Vegas	NV	89109	Norm Freeman	702-736-1830	R	10	<0.1
Mercy Air Service Inc.	P O Box 2532	Fontana	CA	92334	David Dolstein	909-357-9006	R	10*	<0.1
Emery Air Charter Inc.	P O Box 6067	Rockford	IL	61125	John C Emery	815-968-8287	R	8*	<0.1
P-K Air Charter	8402 Nelms	Houston	TX	77061	Floyd Bigelow	713-649-2800	R	3*	<0.1
Zantop International Airlines Inc.	840 Willow Run	Ypsilanti	MI	48198	James M Zantop	734-485-8900	R	2*	0.2
Helicopters Services Inc.	19931 Stuebner	Spring	TX	77379	Robin Simpson	281-370-4354	R	2	<0.1

Source: *Ward's Business Directory of U.S. Private and Public Companies*, Volumes 1 and 2, 2000. The company type code used is as follows: P - Public, R - Private, S - Subsidiary, D - Division, J - Joint Venture, A - Affiliate, G - Group, N - Company type not reported. Sales are in millions of dollars, employees are in thousands. An asterisk (*) indicates an estimated sales volume. The symbol < stands for 'less than'. Company names and addresses are truncated, in some cases, to fit into the available space.

LOCATION BY STATE AND REGIONAL CONCENTRATION

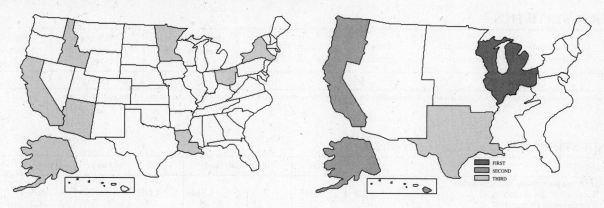

INDUSTRY DATA BY STATE

State	Establishments Total (number)	% of U.S.	Employment Total (number)	% of U.S.	Per Estab.	Payroll Total ($ mil.)	Per Empl. ($)	Revenues Total ($ mil.)	% of U.S.	Per Estab. ($)
California	143	10.5	1,605	10.6	11	63.9	39,809	349.4	12.9	2,443,224
Louisiana	34	2.5	2,153	14.2	63	87.7	40,742	270.2	10.0	7,947,294
Ohio	45	3.3	738	4.9	16	24.3	32,936	256.2	9.5	5,692,733
New York	56	4.1	826	5.4	15	33.1	40,091	193.5	7.2	3,456,089
Texas	95	7.0	718	4.7	8	31.6	43,992	185.6	6.9	1,953,453
Florida	108	7.9	567	3.7	5	16.6	29,240	114.0	4.2	1,055,824
Michigan	42	3.1	551	3.6	13	22.3	40,459	96.7	3.6	2,301,690
Alaska	82	6.0	731	4.8	9	25.2	34,536	79.8	3.0	972,573
Illinois	32	2.3	464	3.1	15	16.0	34,522	79.7	2.9	2,490,594
Minnesota	27	2.0	348	2.3	13	12.0	34,621	64.3	2.4	2,379,815
Pennsylvania	44	3.2	350	2.3	8	10.2	29,209	54.4	2.0	1,236,136
Arizona	22	1.6	249	1.6	11	8.6	34,438	44.0	1.6	1,999,500
Georgia	23	1.7	257	1.7	11	9.1	35,377	43.9	1.6	1,908,609
Wisconsin	23	1.7	324	2.1	14	7.4	22,784	36.9	1.4	1,602,304
Missouri	22	1.6	259	1.7	12	9.2	35,398	36.7	1.4	1,667,682
Washington	31	2.3	272	1.8	9	7.2	26,640	30.3	1.1	976,742
North Carolina	40	2.9	183	1.2	5	5.6	30,727	30.0	1.1	751,100
Colorado	21	1.5	313	2.1	15	7.0	22,473	29.5	1.1	1,405,095
Tennessee	29	2.1	174	1.1	6	5.2	29,684	27.1	1.0	934,759
Indiana	24	1.8	138	0.9	6	3.9	28,536	21.4	0.8	890,375
Oregon	14	1.0	167	1.1	12	3.7	21,898	16.4	0.6	1,171,214
Oklahoma	14	1.0	81	0.5	6	1.7	20,691	14.8	0.5	1,059,571
Idaho	15	1.1	80	0.5	5	2.6	32,450	12.7	0.5	847,667
Hawaii	13	1.0	130	0.9	10	2.9	22,438	12.1	0.4	934,308
New Mexico	18	1.3	128	0.8	7	4.3	33,766	11.2	0.4	624,667
Iowa	18	1.3	108	0.7	6	1.8	17,111	10.5	0.4	581,111
Maine	16	1.2	101	0.7	6	1.7	16,802	10.0	0.4	622,813
Kansas	14	1.0	73	0.5	5	1.2	16,945	6.2	0.2	444,429
West Virginia	9	0.7	63	0.4	7	1.3	20,429	6.1	0.2	679,667
New Jersey	34	2.5	375*	-	-	(D)	-	(D)	-	-
Virginia	29	2.1	175*	-	-	(D)	-	(D)	-	-
Nevada	25	1.8	750*	-	-	(D)	-	(D)	-	-
Kentucky	23	1.7	175*	-	-	(D)	-	(D)	-	-
Connecticut	22	1.6	375*	-	-	(D)	-	(D)	-	-
Massachusetts	21	1.5	60*	-	-	(D)	-	(D)	-	-
Maryland	17	1.2	175*	-	-	(D)	-	(D)	-	-
Alabama	15	1.1	60*	-	-	(D)	-	(D)	-	-
Nebraska	12	0.9	60*	-	-	(D)	-	(D)	-	-
New Hampshire	12	0.9	60*	-	-	(D)	-	(D)	-	-
South Carolina	12	0.9	60*	-	-	(D)	-	(D)	-	-
Montana	10	0.7	175*	-	-	(D)	-	(D)	-	-
Mississippi	9	0.7	60*	-	-	(D)	-	(D)	-	-
Utah	8	0.6	750*	-	-	(D)	-	(D)	-	-
Wyoming	8	0.6	60*	-	-	(D)	-	(D)	-	-
Arkansas	7	0.5	60*	-	-	(D)	-	(D)	-	-
Delaware	7	0.5	10*	-	-	(D)	-	(D)	-	-
South Dakota	7	0.5	60*	-	-	(D)	-	(D)	-	-

Source: 1997 Economic Census. The states are in descending order of revenues or establishments (if revenue data are missing for the majority). The symbol (D) appears when data are withheld to prevent disclosure of competitive information. States marked with (D) are sorted by number of establishments. A dash (-) indicates that the data element cannot be calculated. * indicates the midpoint of a range; 175, for example is the range 100-249. Shaded states on the state map indicate those states which have proportionately greater representation in the industry than would be indicated by the state's population; the ratio is based on total revenues or number of establishments. Shaded regions indicate where the industry is regionally most concentrated.

NAICS 481212 - NONSCHEDULED CHARTERED FREIGHT AIR TRANSPORTATION

GENERAL STATISTICS

Year	Establishments (number)	Employment (number)	Payroll ($ million)	Revenues ($ million)	Employees per Establishment (number)	Revenues per Establishment ($)	Payroll per Employee ($)
1997	125	1,802	50.2	182.1	14.4	1,456,800	27,858

Source: *Economic Census of the United States*, 1997. This is a newly defined industry. Data for prior years were unavailable at the time of publication but may become available over time.

SIC INDUSTRIES RELATED TO NAICS 481212

SIC	Industry	1990	1991	1992	1993	1994	1995	1996	1997
4522	**Air Transportation, Nonscheduled***								
	Establishments (number)	928	1,441	1,791	1,714	1,692	1,621	1,831	2,052*p*
	Employment (thousands)	15.3	20.5	23.1	24.4	29.1	27.7	28.8	33.2*p*
	Revenues ($ million)	-	-	3,432.7	-	-	-	-	-

Source: *Economic Census of the United States*, 1992, annual surveys of economic sectors conducted by the Bureau of the Census, and estimates or projections based on the 1982-1992 period; not all data are shown. 'e' marks estimates made by the editors; 'p' indicates projections based on time series. A dash (-) indicates that data for this SIC or year were not available. * Indicates that only a portion of this industry is present within the NAICS data. If no * is shown, the entire industry is contained within the NAICS data.

INDICES OF CHANGE

Year	Establishments (number)	Employment (number)	Payroll ($ million)	Revenues ($ million)	Employees per Establishment (number)	Revenues per Establishment ($)	Payroll per Employee ($)
1997	100.0	100.0	100.0	100.0	100.0	100.0	100.0

Sources: Same as General Statistics. The values shown reflect change from the base year, 1997. Values above 100 mean greater than 1997, values below 100 mean less than 1997, and a value of 100 in years other than 1997 means same as 1997. Indices are calculated only for Census years. Data are the most recent available at this level of detail.

SELECTED RATIOS

For 1997	Avg. of Sector	Analyzed Industry	Index	For 1997	Avg. of Sector	Analyzed Industry	Index
Employees per establishment	16	14	88	Payroll per establishment	462,554	401,600	87
Revenue per establishment	1,787,642	1,456,800	81	Payroll as % of revenue	26	28	107
Revenue per employee	108,959	101,054	93	Payroll per employee	28,193	27,858	99

Sources: Same as General Statistics. The 'Average of Sector' column represents the average for all industries in this sector. The Index shows the relationship between the Average and the Analyzed Industry. For example, 100 means that they are equal; 500 that the Analyzed Industry is five times the average; 50 means that the Analyzed Industry is half the national average. 'na' is used to show that data are 'not available'.

LEADING COMPANIES
No company data available for this industry.

LOCATION BY STATE AND REGIONAL CONCENTRATION

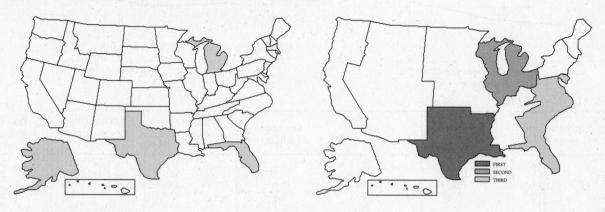

FIRST
SECOND
THIRD

INDUSTRY DATA BY STATE

State	Establishments		Employment			Payroll		Revenues		
	Total (number)	% of U.S.	Total (number)	% of U.S.	Per Estab.	Total ($ mil.)	Per Empl. ($)	Total ($ mil.)	% of U.S.	Per Estab. ($)
Texas	24	14.5	1,264	31.5	53	47.1	37,259	317.6	41.2	13,235,167
Michigan	7	4.2	585	14.6	84	21.0	35,834	117.3	15.2	16,754,571
Florida	23	13.9	413	10.3	18	14.9	36,002	111.8	14.5	4,859,000
Alaska	9	5.5	117	2.9	13	4.3	36,667	25.4	3.3	2,822,111
California	14	8.5	202	5.0	14	12.7	62,921	21.4	2.8	1,530,143
Indiana	6	3.6	44	1.1	7	1.3	30,386	9.7	1.3	1,614,167
Ohio	7	4.2	60*	-	-	(D)	-	(D)	-	-

Source: 1997 *Economic Census*. The states are in descending order of revenues or establishments (if revenue data are missing for the majority). The symbol (D) appears when data are withheld to prevent disclosure of competitive information. States marked with (D) are sorted by number of establishments. A dash (-) indicates that the data element cannot be calculated. * indicates the midpoint of a range; 175, for example is the range 100-249. Shaded *states* on the state map indicate those states which have proportionately greater representation in the industry than would be indicated by the state's population; the ratio is based on total revenues or number of establishments. Shaded *regions* indicate where the industry is regionally most concentrated.

NAICS 481219 - NONSCHEDULED AIR TRANSPORTATION NEC*

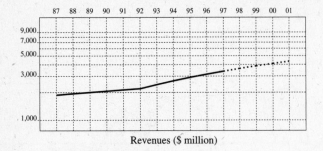

Revenues ($ million)

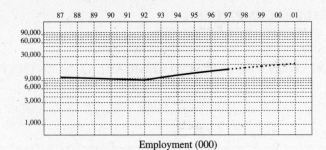

Employment (000)

GENERAL STATISTICS

Year	Establishments (number)	Employment (number)	Payroll ($ million)	Revenues ($ million)	Employees per Establishment (number)	Revenues per Establishment ($)	Payroll per Employee ($)
1987	282	10,606	285.3	1,875.2	37.6	6,649,645	26,900
1988	265	10,320	286.9	1,939.6	38.9	7,319,245	27,800
1989	247	10,034	288.5	2,003.9	40.6	8,112,955	28,752
1990	230	9,748	290.1	2,068.2	42.4	8,992,174	29,760
1991	212	9,462	291.8	2,132.6	44.6	10,059,434	30,839
1992	195	9,176	293.4	2,196.9	47.1	11,266,154	31,975
1993	233	10,473	345.2	2,434.9	45.0	10,468,358	32,960
1994	270	11,771	397.0	2,673.0	43.6	9,892,598	33,728
1995	308	13,068	448.8	2,911.0	42.5	9,457,505	34,343
1996	345	14,366	500.6	3,149.1	41.6	9,117,140	34,847
1997	383	15,663	552.4	3,387.1	40.9	8,843,603	35,268
1998	421 *p*	16,960 *p*	604.2 *p*	3,625.1 *p*	40.3 *p*	8,618,973 *p*	35,624 *p*
1999	458 *p*	18,258 *p*	656.0 *p*	3,863.2 *p*	39.8 *p*	8,431,209 *p*	35,930 *p*
2000	496 *p*	19,555 *p*	707.8 *p*	4,101.2 *p*	39.4 *p*	8,271,924 *p*	36,195 *p*
2001	533 *p*	20,853 *p*	759.6 *p*	4,339.3 *p*	39.1 *p*	8,135,096 *p*	36,427 *p*

Sources: Economic Census of the United States, 1987, 1992 and 1997. Data for those years (years are in bold type) are from the 5-year censuses of the economy. Other values, unless otherwise noted, are extrapolations. Values marked with p are projections. Data are the most recent available at this level of detail.

INDICES OF CHANGE

Year	Establishments (number)	Employment (number)	Payroll ($ million)	Revenues ($ million)	Employees per Establishment (number)	Revenues per Establishment ($)	Payroll per Employee ($)
1987	73.6	67.7	51.6	55.4	91.9	75.2	76.3
1992	50.9	58.6	53.1	64.9	115.2	127.4	90.7
1993	60.8	66.9	62.5	71.9	110.0	118.4	93.5
1994	70.5	75.2	71.9	78.9	106.6	111.9	95.6
1995	80.4	83.4	81.2	85.9	103.9	106.9	97.4
1996	90.1	91.7	90.6	93.0	101.7	103.1	98.8
1997	100.0	100.0	100.0	100.0	100.0	100.0	100.0
1998	109.9 *p*	108.3 *p*	109.4 *p*	107.0 *p*	98.5 *p*	97.5 *p*	101.0 *p*
1999	119.6 *p*	116.6 *p*	118.8 *p*	114.1 *p*	97.3 *p*	95.3 *p*	101.9 *p*
2000	129.5 *p*	124.8 *p*	128.1 *p*	121.1 *p*	96.3 *p*	93.5 *p*	102.6 *p*
2001	139.2 *p*	133.1 *p*	137.5 *p*	128.1 *p*	95.6 *p*	92.0 *p*	103.3 *p*

Sources: Same as General Statistics. The values shown reflect change from the base year, 1997. Values above 100 mean greater than 1997, values below 100 mean less than 1997, and a value of 100 in years other than 1997 means same as 1997. Indices are calculated only for Census years. Data are the most recent available at this level of detail.

SELECTED RATIOS

For 1997	Avg. of Sector	Analyzed Industry	Index	For 1997	Avg. of Sector	Analyzed Industry	Index
Employees per establishment	16	41	249	Payroll per establishment	462,554	1,442,298	312
Revenue per establishment	1,787,642	8,843,603	495	Payroll as % of revenue	26	16	63
Revenue per employee	108,959	216,248	198	Payroll per employee	28,193	35,268	125

Sources: Same as General Statistics. The 'Average of Sector' column represents the average for all industries in this sector. The Index shows the relationship between the Average and the Analyzed Industry. For example, 100 means that they are equal; 500 that the Analyzed Industry is five times the average; 50 means that the Analyzed Industry is half the national average. 'na' is used to show that data are 'not available'.

*Equivalent to SIC 4449.

LEADING COMPANIES

No company data available for this industry.

LOCATION BY STATE AND REGIONAL CONCENTRATION

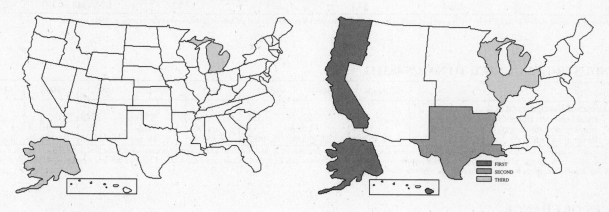

FIRST
SECOND
THIRD

INDUSTRY DATA BY STATE

State	Establishments Total (number)	Establishments % of U.S.	Employment Total (number)	Employment % of U.S.	Employment Per Estab.	Payroll Total ($ mil.)	Payroll Per Empl. ($)	Revenues Total ($ mil.)	Revenues % of U.S.	Revenues Per Estab. ($)
California	28	10.4	261	6.6	9	9.6	36,843	48.9	10.0	1,747,321
Alaska	10	3.7	100	2.5	10	4.4	43,750	24.1	4.9	2,414,800
Texas	21	7.8	185	4.7	9	5.7	30,984	21.2	4.3	1,007,476
Michigan	6	2.2	678	17.2	113	16.7	24,693	20.0	4.1	3,331,167
Florida	17	6.3	70	1.8	4	2.1	29,557	10.7	2.2	629,059
Washington	13	4.8	66	1.7	5	2.0	30,636	7.6	1.5	585,000
Illinois	9	3.3	43	1.1	5	1.0	24,256	4.3	0.9	472,667
Louisiana	8	3.0	47	1.2	6	1.1	23,043	4.0	0.8	503,125
Oregon	19	7.0	1,750*	-	-	(D)	-	(D)	-	-
Colorado	10	3.7	60*	-	-	(D)	-	(D)	-	-
Montana	10	3.7	60*	-	-	(D)	-	(D)	-	-
Idaho	8	3.0	60*	-	-	(D)	-	(D)	-	-
North Carolina	7	2.6	60*	-	-	(D)	-	(D)	-	-
Wisconsin	7	2.6	60*	-	-	(D)	-	(D)	-	-
Arkansas	6	2.2	10*	-	-	(D)	-	(D)	-	-
New York	6	2.2	60*	-	-	(D)	-	(D)	-	-

Source: 1997 *Economic Census*. The states are in descending order of revenues or establishments (if revenue data are missing for the majority). The symbol (D) appears when data are withheld to prevent disclosure of competitive information. States marked with (D) are sorted by number of establishments. A dash (-) indicates that the data element cannot be calculated. * indicates the midpoint of a range; 175, for example is the range 100-249. Shaded *states* on the state map indicate those states which have proportionately greater representation in the industry than would be indicated by the state's population; the ratio is based on total revenues or number of establishments. Shaded *regions* indicate where the industry is regionally most concentrated.

NAICS 483111 - DEEP SEA FREIGHT TRANSPORTATION

GENERAL STATISTICS

Year	Establishments (number)	Employment (number)	Payroll ($ million)	Revenues ($ million)	Employees per Establishment (number)	Revenues per Establishment ($)	Payroll per Employee ($)
1997	230	2,894	84.1	293.1	12.6	1,274,348	29,060

Source: Economic Census of the United States, 1997. This is a newly defined industry. Data for prior years were unavailable at the time of publication but may become available over time.

SIC INDUSTRIES RELATED TO NAICS 483111

SIC	Industry	1990	1991	1992	1993	1994	1995	1996	1997
4412	**Deep Sea Foreign Freight**								
	Establishments (number)	310e	322e	334	346p	358p	371p	383p	395p
	Employment (thousands)	14.7e	14.0e	13.3	12.6p	12.0p	11.3p	10.6p	9.9p
	Revenues ($ million)	7,182.6e	7,836.5e	8,490.5	9,144.4p	9,798.3p	10,452.2p	11,106.2p	11,760.1p

Source: Economic Census of the United States, 1992, annual surveys of economic sectors conducted by the Bureau of the Census, and estimates or projections based on the 1982-1992 period; not all data are shown. 'e' marks estimates made by the editors; 'p' indicates projections based on time series. A dash (-) indicates that data for this SIC or year were not available. * Indicates that only a portion of this industry is present within the NAICS data. If no * is shown, the entire industry is contained within the NAICS data.

INDICES OF CHANGE

Year	Establishments (number)	Employment (number)	Payroll ($ million)	Revenues ($ million)	Employees per Establishment (number)	Revenues per Establishment ($)	Payroll per Employee ($)
1997	100.0	100.0	100.0	100.0	100.0	100.0	100.0

Sources: Same as General Statistics. The values shown reflect change from the base year, 1997. Values above 100 mean greater than 1997, values below 100 mean less than 1997, and a value of 100 in years other than 1997 means same as 1997. Indices are calculated only for Census years. Data are the most recent available at this level of detail.

SELECTED RATIOS

For 1997	Avg. of Sector	Analyzed Industry	Index	For 1997	Avg. of Sector	Analyzed Industry	Index
Employees per establishment	16	13	77	Payroll per establishment	462,554	365,652	79
Revenue per establishment	1,787,642	1,274,348	71	Payroll as % of revenue	26	29	111
Revenue per employee	108,959	101,279	93	Payroll per employee	28,193	29,060	103

Sources: Same as General Statistics. The 'Average of Sector' column represents the average for all industries in this sector. The Index shows the relationship between the Average and the Analyzed Industry. For example, 100 means that they are equal; 500 that the Analyzed Industry is five times the average; 50 means that the Analyzed Industry is half the national average. 'na' is used to show that data are 'not available'.

LEADING COMPANIES   Number shown: **33**   Total sales ($ mil): **47,021**   Total employment (000): **315.2**

Company Name	Address				CEO Name	Phone	Co. Type	Sales ($ mil)	Empl. (000)
Federal Express Corp.	U S Mail Box 727	Memphis	TN	38194	Frederick W Smith	901-369-3600	D	16,774	141.0
FedEx Corp.	6075 Poplar Ave	Memphis	TN	38119	Fredrick W Smith	901-369-3600	P	16,774	141.0
Stolt-Nielsen Inc.	P O Box 2300	Greenwich	CT	06836	Jacob Stolt-Nielsen Jr	203-625-9400	S	3,215*	6.0
Sea-Land Service Inc.	6000 Carnegie Blvd	Charlotte	NC	28209	John P Clancey	704-571-2000	S	2,623*	6.0
American President Lines Ltd.	1111 Broadway	Oakland	CA	94607	TJ Rhein	510-272-8000	S	1,910*	4.0
Mark VII Inc.	965 Ridge Lake	Memphis	TN	38120	RC Matney	901-767-4455	P	725	0.4
SeaRiver Maritime Inc.	PO Box 1512	Houston	TX	77251	Gus Elmer	713-758-5000	S	455*	0.9
Overseas Shipholding Group Inc.	511 Fifth Ave	New York	NY	10017	Morton P Hyman	212-869-1222	P	442	2.2
Hvide Marine Inc.	P O Box 13038	Fort Lauderdale	FL	33316	J Erik Hvide	954-523-2200	R	402	3.1
Con-Way Truckload Services Inc.	2322 Gravel Dr	Fort Worth	TX	76118	J Ronald Linkous	817-284-7800	S	400*	0.8
SEACOR SMIT Inc.	11200 Westheimer	Houston	TX	77042	Charles Fabrikant	713-782-5990	P	386	1.8
International Shipholding Corp.	650 Poydras St	New Orleans	LA	70130	Erik F Johnsen	504-529-5461	P	373	1.0
ATC Leasing Co.	4316 39th Ave	Kenosha	WI	53144	Dennis Troha	414-658-4831	S	286*	0.9
Stolt Parcel Tankers Inc.	PO Box 2300	Greenwich	CT	06836	Samuel Cooperman	203-625-9400	R	271*	0.5
Atlantic Container Line	50 Cragwood Rd	South Plainfield	NJ	07080		908-668-5400	P	260	0.5
Lykes Lines Limited L.L.C.	401 E Jackson St	Tampa	FL	33602	Frank Halliwell	813-276-4600	S	246*	0.5
Waterman Steamship Corp.	P O Box 53306	New Orleans	LA	70153	Eric S Johnson	504-529-5461	S	180	0.2
Central Gulf Lines Inc.	P O Box 53366	New Orleans	LA	70130	Erik F Johnsen	504-529-5461	S	162*	0.3
Westwood Shipping Lines	PO Box 9777	Federal Way	WA	98063	Arnfinn Giske	253-924-4399	S	150*	0.1
OMI Corp.	1 Station Pl	Stamford	CT	06902	Craig H Stevenson Jr	203-602-6700	P	143	0.7
Columbus Line USA Inc.	465 South St	Morristown	NJ	07960	Klaus Meves	973-775-5300	R	133*	0.3
Marine Transport Lines Inc.	1200 Harbor Blvd	Weehawken	NJ	07087	Richard Du Moulin	201-330-0200	R	120	1.8
Tecmarine Lines Co.	2051 SE 35th	Port Everglades	FL	33316	Jeremy Chester	954-331-2000	R	107*	0.2
Farrell Lines Inc.	1 Whitehall St	New York	NY	10004	Richard F Gronda	212-440-4200	R	90*	<0.1
Alcoa Steamship Company Inc.	1501	Pittsburgh	PA	15219	Merv R Thede	412-553-2545	S	86*	<0.1
Chevron Shipping Co.	555 Market St	San Francisco	CA	94105	Thomas R Moore	415-894-5515	S	82*	0.2
Fairfield Maxwell Corp.	277 Park Ave	New York	NY	10172	KG Sugahara	212-421-2850	R	80*	0.6
LASH Intermodal Terminal Co.	2725 Riverport Rd	Memphis	TN	38109		901-774-5049	J	50*	<0.1
OOCL (USA) Inc.	4141 Hacienda Dr	Pleasanton	CA	94588	Philip Chow	925-460-4800	R	42*	0.2
Cosco Agencies Los Angeles Inc.	606 S Olive St	Los Angeles	CA	90014	Zhou Hu	213-689-6700	S	28*	<0.1
Liberty Maritime Corp.	1979 Marcus Ave	Lake Success	NY	11042	Philip Shapiro	516-488-8800	R	11*	<0.1
SEACOR Marine Inc.	5005 Railroad Ave	Morgan City	LA	70380	Milton Rose	713-782-5990	S	11*	<0.1
Forest Lines Inc.	650 Poydras St	New Orleans	LA	70130	Erik L Johnsen	504-529-5461	P	5*	<0.1

Source: *Ward's Business Directory of U.S. Private and Public Companies*, Volumes 1 and 2, 2000. The company type code used is as follows: P - Public, R - Private, S - Subsidiary, D - Division, J - Joint Venture, A - Affiliate, G - Group, N - Company type not reported. Sales are in millions of dollars, employees are in thousands. An asterisk (*) indicates an estimated sales volume. The symbol < stands for 'less than'. Company names and addresses are truncated, in some cases, to fit into the available space.

LOCATION BY STATE AND REGIONAL CONCENTRATION

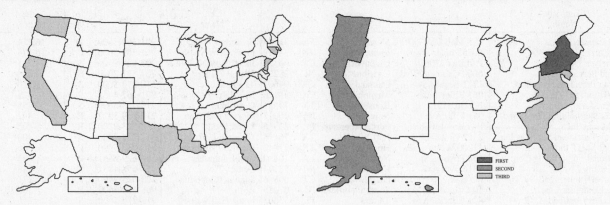

INDUSTRY DATA BY STATE

State	Establishments Total (number)	Establishments % of U.S.	Employment Total (number)	Employment % of U.S.	Employment Per Estab.	Payroll Total ($ mil.)	Payroll Per Empl. ($)	Revenues Total ($ mil.)	Revenues % of U.S.	Revenues Per Estab. ($)
New Jersey	35	7.2	3,088	16.7	88	123.0	39,825	2,151.8	18.6	61,480,486
Florida	56	11.5	2,929	15.8	52	122.2	41,725	1,859.3	16.1	33,201,893
California	39	8.0	2,683	14.5	69	157.6	58,735	1,673.3	14.5	42,903,949
Texas	54	11.1	2,356	12.7	44	95.6	40,587	1,093.1	9.4	20,242,944
Washington	21	4.3	984	5.3	47	55.2	56,089	940.8	8.1	44,800,524
New York	57	11.7	1,628	8.8	29	84.3	51,776	674.1	5.8	11,826,877
Connecticut	18	3.7	345	1.9	19	23.1	67,049	461.4	4.0	25,632,444
Louisiana	35	7.2	1,696	9.1	48	35.1	20,722	327.1	2.8	9,346,171
Illinois	18	3.7	406	2.2	23	17.9	44,200	229.1	2.0	12,725,333
Massachusetts	10	2.1	383	2.1	38	23.0	59,940	208.9	1.8	20,889,300
Georgia	17	3.5	348	1.9	20	15.4	44,161	193.5	1.7	11,380,235
South Carolina	9	1.8	167	0.9	19	6.8	40,653	106.1	0.9	11,790,111
North Carolina	6	1.2	16	0.1	3	0.7	46,250	47.5	0.4	7,919,333
Virginia	21	4.3	750*	-	-	(D)	-	(D)	-	-
Pennsylvania	15	3.1	60*	-	-	(D)	-	(D)	-	-
Maryland	12	2.5	175*	-	-	(D)	-	(D)	-	-
Ohio	11	2.3	60*	-	-	(D)	-	(D)	-	-
Missouri	7	1.4	10*	-	-	(D)	-	(D)	-	-
Alaska	6	1.2	175*	-	-	(D)	-	(D)	-	-
Oregon	6	1.2	60*	-	-	(D)	-	(D)	-	-

Source: 1997 Economic Census. The states are in descending order of revenues or establishments (if revenue data are missing for the majority). The symbol (D) appears when data are withheld to prevent disclosure of competitive information. States marked with (D) are sorted by number of establishments. A dash (-) indicates that the data element cannot be calculated. * indicates the midpoint of a range; 175, for example is the range 100-249. Shaded *states* on the state map indicate those states which have proportionately greater representation in the industry than would be indicated by the state's population; the ratio is based on total revenues or number of establishments. Shaded *regions* indicate where the industry is regionally most concentrated.

NAICS 483112 - DEEP SEA PASSENGER TRANSPORTATION

GENERAL STATISTICS

Year	Establishments (number)	Employment (number)	Payroll ($ million)	Revenues ($ million)	Employees per Establishment (number)	Revenues per Establishment ($)	Payroll per Employee ($)
1997	15,460	134,777	3,522.1	12,273.3	8.7	793,875	26,133

Source: *Economic Census of the United States*, 1997. This is a newly defined industry. Data for prior years were unavailable at the time of publication but may become available over time.

SIC INDUSTRIES RELATED TO NAICS 483112

SIC	Industry	1990	1991	1992	1993	1994	1995	1996	1997
4481	**Deep Sea Transportation Except by Ferry***								
	Establishments (number)	86	101	72	83	72	80	105	80*p*
	Employment (thousands)	8.8	13.4	12.5	11.4	11.3	12.5	11.3	12.3*p*
	Revenues ($ million)	2,734.6*e*	3,001.5*e*	3,268.5	3,535.4*p*	3,802.3*p*	4,069.2*p*	4,336.1*p*	4,603.0*p*

Source: *Economic Census of the United States*, 1992, annual surveys of economic sectors conducted by the Bureau of the Census, and estimates or projections based on the 1982-1992 period; not all data are shown. 'e' marks estimates made by the editors; 'p' indicates projections based on time series. A dash (-) indicates that data for this SIC or year were not available. * Indicates that only a portion of this industry is present within the NAICS data. If no * is shown, the entire industry is contained within the NAICS data.

INDICES OF CHANGE

Year	Establishments (number)	Employment (number)	Payroll ($ million)	Revenues ($ million)	Employees per Establishment (number)	Revenues per Establishment ($)	Payroll per Employee ($)
1997	100.0	100.0	100.0	100.0	100.0	100.0	100.0

Sources: Same as General Statistics. The values shown reflect change from the base year, 1997. Values above 100 mean greater than 1997, values below 100 mean less than 1997, and a value of 100 in years other than 1997 means same as 1997. Indices are calculated only for Census years. Data are the most recent available at this level of detail.

SELECTED RATIOS

For 1997	Avg. of Sector	Analyzed Industry	Index	For 1997	Avg. of Sector	Analyzed Industry	Index
Employees per establishment	16	9	53	Payroll per establishment	462,554	227,820	49
Revenue per establishment	1,787,642	793,875	44	Payroll as % of revenue	26	29	111
Revenue per employee	108,959	91,064	84	Payroll per employee	28,193	26,133	93

Sources: Same as General Statistics. The 'Average of Sector' column represents the average for all industries in this sector. The Index shows the relationship between the Average and the Analyzed Industry. For example, 100 means that they are equal; 500 that the Analyzed Industry is five times the average; 50 means that the Analyzed Industry is half the national average. 'na' is used to show that data are 'not available'.

LEADING COMPANIES   Number shown: **15**   Total sales ($ mil): **11,196**   Total employment (000): **63.2**

Company Name	Address				CEO Name	Phone	Co. Type	Sales ($ mil)	Empl. (000)
Carnival Corp.	PO Box 1347	Miami	FL	33178	Micky Arison	305-599-2600	P	3,498	22.0
Seabourn Cruise Line	6100 Blue Lagoon	Miami	FL	33126	LB Pimentel	305-463-3000	S	2,922*	2.7
Royal Caribbean Cruises Ltd.	1050 Caribbean Way	Miami	FL	33132	Richard D Fain	305-539-6000	P	2,546	21.0
Norwegian Cruise Line Ltd.	7665 Corp. Center	Miami	FL	33126	Hans Golteus	305-436-4000	S	1,020*	7.0
Holland America Line Westours	300 Elliott Ave W	Seattle	WA	98119	A Kirk Lanterman	206-281-3535	S	594	6.0
Cunard Line	6100 Blue Lagoon	Miami	FL	33126	Larry Pimentel	305-463-3000	S	306*	2.7
Renaissance Cruises Inc.	P O Box 350307	Fort Lauderdale	FL	33335	Edward B Rudner	954-463-0982	S	151*	0.7
European Cruises Inc.	241 E Commercial	Fort Lauderdale	FL	33334	Eric Heindl	954-491-0333	R	65*	0.3
Europa Cruise Line Ltd.	150 153rd Ave	Madeira Beach	FL	33708	Debbrah Vitlie	727-393-2885	S	22*	0.1
Costa Cruise Lines N.V.	P O Box 01964	Miami	FL	33101	Dino Schibuola	305-358-7325	S	19*	0.2
Europa Cruises Corp.	150 153rd Ave	Madeira Beach	FL	33708	Deborah A Vitale	727-393-2885	P	17	0.4
Orient Lines	1510 S E 17th St	Fort Lauderdale	FL	33316	Deborah Natansohn	954-527-6660	S	14*	<0.1
Classical Cruises	132 E 70th St	New York	NY	10021	George Papagapitos	212-794-3200	R	11*	<0.1
Star Clippers Ltd.	4101 Salzedo Ave	Miami	FL	33146	Mikael Krafft	305-442-0550	S	8*	<0.1
Unique World Travel Inc.	154 Village Rd	Manhasset	NY	11030	Misha Radulovic	516-627-2636	R	4	<0.1

Source: *Ward's Business Directory of U.S. Private and Public Companies*, Volumes 1 and 2, 2000. The company type code used is as follows: P - Public, R - Private, S - Subsidiary, D - Division, J - Joint Venture, A - Affiliate, G - Group, N - Company type not reported. Sales are in millions of dollars, employees are in thousands. An asterisk (*) indicates an estimated sales volume. The symbol < stands for 'less than'. Company names and addresses are truncated, in some cases, to fit into the available space.

LOCATION BY STATE AND REGIONAL CONCENTRATION

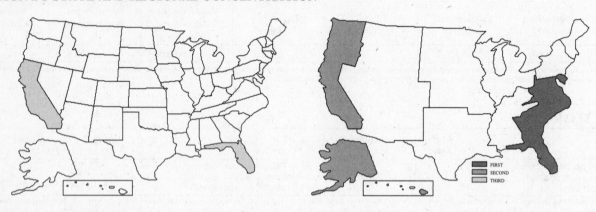

FIRST
SECOND
THIRD

INDUSTRY DATA BY STATE

State	Establishments		Employment			Payroll		Revenues		
	Total (number)	% of U.S.	Total (number)	% of U.S.	Per Estab.	Total ($ mil.)	Per Empl. ($)	Total ($ mil.)	% of U.S.	Per Estab. ($)
Florida	32	40.0	7,736	63.1	242	271.7	35,128	2,924.9	74.8	91,402,188
California	9	11.3	2,658	21.7	295	72.0	27,083	609.9	15.6	67,768,333

Source: 1997 *Economic Census*. The states are in descending order of revenues or establishments (if revenue data are missing for the majority). The symbol (D) appears when data are withheld to prevent disclosure of competitive information. States marked with (D) are sorted by number of establishments. A dash (-) indicates that the data element cannot be calculated. * indicates the midpoint of a range; 175, for example is the range 100-249. Shaded *states* on the state map indicate those states which have proportionately greater representation in the industry than would be indicated by the state's population; the ratio is based on total revenues or number of establishments. Shaded *regions* indicate where the industry is regionally most concentrated.

NAICS 483113 - COASTAL AND GREAT LAKES FREIGHT TRANSPORTATION

GENERAL STATISTICS

Year	Establishments (number)	Employment (number)	Payroll ($ million)	Revenues ($ million)	Employees per Establishment (number)	Revenues per Establishment ($)	Payroll per Employee ($)
1997	23,111	425,758	12,690.1	51,142.1	18.4	2,212,890	29,806

Source: *Economic Census of the United States*, 1997. This is a newly defined industry. Data for prior years were unavailable at the time of publication but may become available over time.

SIC INDUSTRIES RELATED TO NAICS 483113

SIC	Industry	1990	1991	1992	1993	1994	1995	1996	1997
4424	**Deep Sea Domestic Freight**								
	Establishments (number)	247e	264e	281	298p	315p	331p	348p	365p
	Employment (thousands)	12.8e	13.1e	13.5	13.8p	14.2p	14.5p	14.9p	15.2p
	Revenues ($ million)	3,120.0e	3,288.8e	3,457.7	3,626.5p	3,795.3p	3,964.2p	4,133.0p	4,301.9p
4432	**Freight Transportation on The Great Lakes**								
	Establishments (number)	25e	26e	26	26p	27p	27p	28p	28p
	Employment (thousands)	1.2e	1.2e	1.3	1.3p	1.3p	1.4p	1.5p	1.5p
	Revenues ($ million)	427.1e	493.1e	559.2	625.3p	691.3p	757.4p	823.5p	889.5p

Source: *Economic Census of the United States*, 1992, annual surveys of economic sectors conducted by the Bureau of the Census, and estimates or projections based on the 1982-1992 period; not all data are shown. 'e' marks estimates made by the editors; 'p' indicates projections based on time series. A dash (-) indicates that data for this SIC or year were not available. * Indicates that only a portion of this industry is present within the NAICS data. If no * is shown, the entire industry is contained within the NAICS data.

INDICES OF CHANGE

Year	Establishments (number)	Employment (number)	Payroll ($ million)	Revenues ($ million)	Employees per Establishment (number)	Revenues per Establishment ($)	Payroll per Employee ($)
1997	100.0	100.0	100.0	100.0	100.0	100.0	100.0

Sources: Same as General Statistics. The values shown reflect change from the base year, 1997. Values above 100 mean greater than 1997, values below 100 mean less than 1997, and a value of 100 in years other than 1997 means same as 1997. Indices are calculated only for Census years. Data are the most recent available at this level of detail.

SELECTED RATIOS

For 1997	Avg. of Sector	Analyzed Industry	Index	For 1997	Avg. of Sector	Analyzed Industry	Index
Employees per establishment	16	18	112	Payroll per establishment	462,554	549,094	119
Revenue per establishment	1,787,642	2,212,890	124	Payroll as % of revenue	26	25	96
Revenue per employee	108,959	120,120	110	Payroll per employee	28,193	29,806	106

Sources: Same as General Statistics. The 'Average of Sector' column represents the average for all industries in this sector. The Index shows the relationship between the Average and the Analyzed Industry. For example, 100 means that they are equal; 500 that the Analyzed Industry is five times the average; 50 means that the Analyzed Industry is half the national average. 'na' is used to show that data are 'not available'.

LEADING COMPANIES   Number shown: **26**   Total sales ($ mil): **6,843**   Total employment (000): **23.2**

Company Name	Address				CEO Name	Phone	Co. Type	Sales ($ mil)	Empl. (000)
Crowley American Transport Inc.	9487 Regency Squ	Jacksonville	FL	32225	P Elliott Burnside	904-727-2200	S	1,111*	3.5
Alexander and Baldwin Inc.	PO Box 3440	Honolulu	HI	96813	Alexander Baldwin	808-525-6611	P	959	2.3
Matson Navigation Company Inc.	PO Box 7452	San Francisco	CA	94120	C Bradley Mulholland	415-957-4000	S	700*	0.7
Overseas Shipholding Group Inc.	511 Fifth Ave	New York	NY	10017	Morton P Hyman	212-869-1222	P	442	2.2
Hvide Marine Inc.	P O Box 13038	Fort Lauderdale	FL	33316	J Erik Hvide	954-523-2200	R	402	3.1
Con-Way Truckload Services Inc.	2322 Gravel Dr	Fort Worth	TX	76118	J Ronald Linkous	817-284-7800	S	400*	0.8
Oglebay Norton Co.	1100 Superior Ave E	Cleveland	OH	44114	John N Lauer	216-861-3300	P	294	1.8
P & O Containers Ltd.	1 Meadowlands Plz	East Rutherford	NJ	07073	Michael Seymour	201-896-6200	D	291*	0.9
ATC Leasing Co.	4316 39th Ave	Kenosha	WI	53144	Dennis Troha	414-658-4831	S	286*	0.9
Birdsall Inc.	PO Box 10683	Riviera Beach	FL	33419	Rick Murrell	561-881-3900	S	285*	0.9
Midland Enterprises Inc.	300 Pike St	Cincinnati	OH	45202	Fred C Raskin	513-721-2111	S	269	1.4
Lykes Lines Limited L.L.C.	401 E Jackson St	Tampa	FL	33602	Frank Halliwell	813-276-4600	S	246*	0.5
Salt Chuk Resources	1111 Fairview N	Duvall	WA	98019		206-652-1111	R	220*	1.1
Maritrans Inc. Eastern Div.	Fort Mifflin Rd	Philadelphia	PA	19153	Steve VanDyck	215-492-8100	D	190*	0.6
Central Gulf Lines Inc.	P O Box 53366	New Orleans	LA	70130	Erik F Johnsen	504-529-5461	S	162*	0.3
Maritrans Inc.	1 Logan Sq	Philadelphia	PA	19103	Stephen A Van Dyck	215-864-1200	P	152*	0.6
Western Pioneer Inc.	P O Box 70438	Seattle	WA	98107		206-789-1930	R	100*	0.3
American Steamship Co.	500 Essjay Rd	Buffalo	NY	14221	Ned A Smith	716-635-0222	S	90	0.4
Electro-Coal Transfer	14537 Hwy 15	Braithwaite	LA	70040		504-333-7200	S	66*	0.2
Lynden Transport Inc.	P O Box 3725	Seattle	WA	98124	David B Neely	253-872-3020	S	65*	0.2
Coastal Transportation Inc.	4025 13th Ave W	Seattle	WA	98119	Peter Strong	206-282-9979	R	35*	0.1
Mormac Marine Group Inc.	3 Landmark Sq	Stamford	CT	06901	Paul R Tregurtha	203-977-8900	R	29	0.2
Express Marine Inc.	P O Box 329	Pennsauken	NJ	08110	Richard Walling	609-541-4600	R	21*	<0.1
Washington Corporations	P O Box 16630	Missoula	MT	59808	Mike Haizht	406-523-1300	R	12*	0.1
KCBX Terminals Co.	3259 E 100th St	Chicago	IL	60617		773-375-3700	S	11*	<0.1
Forest Lines Inc.	650 Poydras St	New Orleans	LA	70130	Erik L Johnsen	504-529-5461	P	5*	<0.1

Source: *Ward's Business Directory of U.S. Private and Public Companies*, Volumes 1 and 2, 2000. The company type code used is as follows: P - Public, R - Private, S - Subsidiary, D - Division, J - Joint Venture, A - Affiliate, G - Group, N - Company type not reported. Sales are in millions of dollars, employees are in thousands. An asterisk (*) indicates an estimated sales volume. The symbol < stands for 'less than'. Company names and addresses are truncated, in some cases, to fit into the available space.

LOCATION BY STATE AND REGIONAL CONCENTRATION

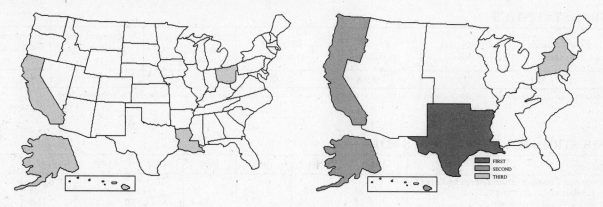

INDUSTRY DATA BY STATE

State	Establishments		Employment			Payroll		Revenues		
	Total (number)	% of U.S.	Total (number)	% of U.S.	Per Estab.	Total ($ mil.)	Per Empl. ($)	Total ($ mil.)	% of U.S.	Per Estab. ($)
Louisiana	184	29.9	6,957	32.1	38	230.0	33,060	963.3	20.6	5,235,239
California	25	4.1	1,485	6.8	59	87.4	58,842	696.7	14.9	27,869,320
Ohio	15	2.4	752	3.5	50	45.8	60,951	216.1	4.6	14,406,467
Pennsylvania	18	2.9	903	4.2	50	49.3	54,632	185.1	4.0	10,281,500
Florida	51	8.3	693	3.2	14	35.2	50,864	159.8	3.4	3,134,255
Alaska	30	4.9	444	2.0	15	25.2	56,705	115.2	2.5	3,838,533
New Jersey	15	2.4	208	1.0	14	11.4	54,625	114.5	2.4	7,633,133
Hawaii	10	1.6	399	1.8	40	20.4	51,195	69.8	1.5	6,977,800
Michigan	8	1.3	225	1.0	28	13.8	61,187	44.7	1.0	5,592,375
Massachusetts	9	1.5	183	0.8	20	5.0	27,230	17.0	0.4	1,892,667
New York	71	11.5	1,750*	-	-	(D)	-	(D)	-	-
Texas	34	5.5	1,750*	-	-	(D)	-	(D)	-	-
Washington	34	5.5	3,750*	-	-	(D)	-	(D)	-	-
Virginia	18	2.9	750*	-	-	(D)	-	(D)	-	-
Connecticut	12	1.9	750*	-	-	(D)	-	(D)	-	-
Alabama	11	1.8	375*	-	-	(D)	-	(D)	-	-
Illinois	8	1.3	175*	-	-	(D)	-	(D)	-	-
Maryland	7	1.1	175*	-	-	(D)	-	(D)	-	-
Mississippi	6	1.0	375*	-	-	(D)	-	(D)	-	-

Source: 1997 *Economic Census*. The states are in descending order of revenues or establishments (if revenue data are missing for the majority). The symbol (D) appears when data are withheld to prevent disclosure of competitive information. States marked with (D) are sorted by number of establishments. A dash (-) indicates that the data element cannot be calculated. * indicates the midpoint of a range; 175, for example is the range 100-249. Shaded *states* on the state map indicate those states which have proportionately greater representation in the industry than would be indicated by the state's population; the ratio is based on total revenues or number of establishments. Shaded *regions* indicate where the industry is regionally most concentrated.

NAICS 483114 - COASTAL AND GREAT LAKES PASSENGER TRANSPORTATION

GENERAL STATISTICS

Year	Establishments (number)	Employment (number)	Payroll ($ million)	Revenues ($ million)	Employees per Establishment (number)	Revenues per Establishment ($)	Payroll per Employee ($)
1997	6,210	258,972	9,509.9	25,010.1	41.7	4,027,391	36,722

Source: Economic Census of the United States, 1997. This is a newly defined industry. Data for prior years were unavailable at the time of publication but may become available over time.

SIC INDUSTRIES RELATED TO NAICS 483114

SIC	Industry	1990	1991	1992	1993	1994	1995	1996	1997
4481	**Deep Sea Transportation Except by Ferry***								
	Establishments (number)	86	101	72	83	72	80	105	80p
	Employment (thousands)	8.8	13.4	12.5	11.4	11.3	12.5	11.3	12.3p
	Revenues ($ million)	2,734.6e	3,001.5e	3,268.5	3,535.4p	3,802.3p	4,069.2p	4,336.1p	4,603.0p
4482	**Ferries***								
	Establishments (number)	96	104	118	125	117	115	130	128p
	Employment (thousands)	1.7	1.7	1.8	1.7	1.6	1.8	1.8	1.8p
	Revenues ($ million)	131.0e	142.9e	154.7	166.5p	178.3p	190.1p	201.9p	213.7p

*Source: Economic Census of the United States, 1992, annual surveys of economic sectors conducted by the Bureau of the Census, and estimates or projections based on the 1982-1992 period; not all data are shown. 'e' marks estimates made by the editors; 'p' indicates projections based on time series. A dash (-) indicates that data for this SIC or year were not available. * Indicates that only a portion of this industry is present within the NAICS data. If no * is shown, the entire industry is contained within the NAICS data.*

INDICES OF CHANGE

Year	Establishments (number)	Employment (number)	Payroll ($ million)	Revenues ($ million)	Employees per Establishment (number)	Revenues per Establishment ($)	Payroll per Employee ($)
1997	100.0	100.0	100.0	100.0	100.0	100.0	100.0

Sources: Same as General Statistics. The values shown reflect change from the base year, 1997. Values above 100 mean greater than 1997, values below 100 mean less than 1997, and a value of 100 in years other than 1997 means same as 1997. Indices are calculated only for Census years. Data are the most recent available at this level of detail.

SELECTED RATIOS

For 1997	Avg. of Sector	Analyzed Industry	Index	For 1997	Avg. of Sector	Analyzed Industry	Index
Employees per establishment	16	42	254	Payroll per establishment	462,554	1,531,385	331
Revenue per establishment	1,787,642	4,027,391	225	Payroll as % of revenue	26	38	147
Revenue per employee	108,959	96,575	89	Payroll per employee	28,193	36,722	130

Sources: Same as General Statistics. The 'Average of Sector' column represents the average for all industries in this sector. The Index shows the relationship between the Average and the Analyzed Industry. For example, 100 means that they are equal; 500 that the Analyzed Industry is five times the average; 50 means that the Analyzed Industry is half the national average. 'na' is used to show that data are 'not available'.

LEADING COMPANIES   Number shown: **15**   Total sales ($ mil): **11,196**   Total employment (000): **63.2**

Company Name	Address				CEO Name	Phone	Co. Type	Sales ($ mil)	Empl. (000)
Carnival Corp.	PO Box 1347	Miami	FL	33178	Micky Arison	305-599-2600	P	3,498	22.0
Seabourn Cruise Line	6100 Blue Lagoon	Miami	FL	33126	LB Pimentel	305-463-3000	S	2,922*	2.7
Royal Caribbean Cruises Ltd.	1050 Caribbean Way	Miami	FL	33132	Richard D Fain	305-539-6000	P	2,546	21.0
Norwegian Cruise Line Ltd.	7665 Corp. Center	Miami	FL	33126	Hans Golteus	305-436-4000	S	1,020*	7.0
Holland America Line Westours	300 Elliott Ave W	Seattle	WA	98119	A Kirk Lanterman	206-281-3535	S	594	6.0
Cunard Line	6100 Blue Lagoon	Miami	FL	33126	Larry Pimentel	305-463-3000	S	306*	2.7
Renaissance Cruises Inc.	P O Box 350307	Fort Lauderdale	FL	33335	Edward B Rudner	954-463-0982	S	151*	0.7
European Cruises Inc.	241 E Commercial	Fort Lauderdale	FL	33334	Eric Heindl	954-491-0333	R	65*	0.3
Europa Cruise Line Ltd.	150 153rd Ave	Madeira Beach	FL	33708	Debbrah Vitlie	727-393-2885	S	22*	0.1
Costa Cruise Lines N.V.	P O Box 01964	Miami	FL	33101	Dino Schibuola	305-358-7325	S	19*	0.2
Europa Cruises Corp.	150 153rd Ave	Madeira Beach	FL	33708	Deborah A Vitale	727-393-2885	P	17	0.4
Orient Lines	1510 S E 17th St	Fort Lauderdale	FL	33316	Deborah Natansohn	954-527-6660	S	14*	<0.1
Classical Cruises	132 E 70th St	New York	NY	10021	George Papagapitos	212-794-3200	R	11*	<0.1
Star Clippers Ltd.	4101 Salzedo Ave	Miami	FL	33146	Mikael Krafft	305-442-0550	S	8*	<0.1
Unique World Travel Inc.	154 Village Rd	Manhasset	NY	11030	Misha Radulovic	516-627-2636	R	4	<0.1

Source: Ward's Business Directory of U.S. Private and Public Companies, Volumes 1 and 2, 2000. The company type code used is as follows: P - Public, R - Private, S - Subsidiary, D - Division, J - Joint Venture, A - Affiliate, G - Group, N - Company type not reported. Sales are in millions of dollars, employees are in thousands. An asterisk (*) indicates an estimated sales volume. The symbol < stands for 'less than'. Company names and addresses are truncated, in some cases, to fit into the available space.

LOCATION BY STATE AND REGIONAL CONCENTRATION

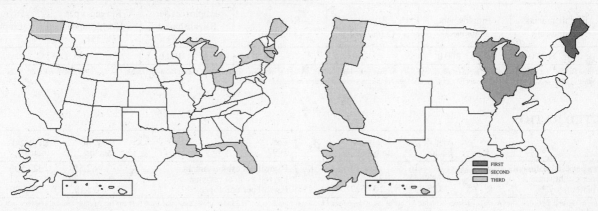

FIRST
SECOND
THIRD

INDUSTRY DATA BY STATE

State	Establishments		Employment			Payroll		Revenues		
	Total (number)	% of U.S.	Total (number)	% of U.S.	Per Estab.	Total ($ mil.)	Per Empl. ($)	Total ($ mil.)	% of U.S.	Per Estab. ($)
California	7	5.6	263	14.6	38	6.5	24,719	21.3	11.7	3,046,857
Florida	15	12.0	250	13.9	17	3.7	14,676	16.3	9.0	1,089,067
Maine	13	10.4	36	2.0	3	1.0	29,056	3.4	1.9	263,923
Michigan	15	12.0	175*	-	-	(D)	-	(D)	-	-
New York	11	8.8	60*	-	-	(D)	-	(D)	-	-
Washington	8	6.4	175*	-	-	(D)	-	(D)	-	-
Louisiana	7	5.6	60*	-	-	(D)	-	(D)	-	-
Massachusetts	7	5.6	60*	-	-	(D)	-	(D)	-	-
Connecticut	6	4.8	175*	-	-	(D)	-	(D)	-	-
Ohio	6	4.8	60*	-	-	(D)	-	(D)	-	-

Source: 1997 Economic Census. The states are in descending order of revenues or establishments (if revenue data are missing for the majority). The symbol (D) appears when data are withheld to prevent disclosure of competitive information. States marked with (D) are sorted by number of establishments. A dash (-) indicates that the data element cannot be calculated. * indicates the midpoint of a range; 175, for example is the range 100-249. Shaded *states* on the state map indicate those states which have proportionately greater representation in the industry than would be indicated by the state's population; the ratio is based on total revenues or number of establishments. Shaded *regions* indicate where the industry is regionally most concentrated.

NAICS 483211 - INLAND WATER FREIGHT TRANSPORTATION

GENERAL STATISTICS

Year	Establishments (number)	Employment (number)	Payroll ($ million)	Revenues ($ million)	Employees per Establishment (number)	Revenues per Establishment ($)	Payroll per Employee ($)
1997	9,100	121,550	2,943.9	12,583.7	13.4	1,382,824	24,220

Source: *Economic Census of the United States*, 1997. This is a newly defined industry. Data for prior years were unavailable at the time of publication but may become available over time.

SIC INDUSTRIES RELATED TO NAICS 483211

SIC	Industry	1990	1991	1992	1993	1994	1995	1996	1997
4449	**Water Transportation of Freight, nec**								
	Establishments (number)	230e	212e	195	178p	160p	143p	125p	108p
	Employment (thousands)	9.7e	9.5e	9.2	8.9p	8.6p	8.3p	8.0p	7.7p
	Revenues ($ million)	2,068.2e	2,132.6e	2,196.9	2,261.2p	2,325.5p	2,389.9p	2,454.2p	2,518.5p

Source: *Economic Census of the United States*, 1992, annual surveys of economic sectors conducted by the Bureau of the Census, and estimates or projections based on the 1982-1992 period; not all data are shown. 'e' marks estimates made by the editors; 'p' indicates projections based on time series. A dash (-) indicates that data for this SIC or year were not available. * Indicates that only a portion of this industry is present within the NAICS data. If no * is shown, the entire industry is contained within the NAICS data.

INDICES OF CHANGE

Year	Establishments (number)	Employment (number)	Payroll ($ million)	Revenues ($ million)	Employees per Establishment (number)	Revenues per Establishment ($)	Payroll per Employee ($)
1997	100.0	100.0	100.0	100.0	100.0	100.0	100.0

Sources: Same as General Statistics. The values shown reflect change from the base year, 1997. Values above 100 mean greater than 1997, values below 100 mean less than 1997, and a value of 100 in years other than 1997 means same as 1997. Indices are calculated only for Census years. Data are the most recent available at this level of detail.

SELECTED RATIOS

For 1997	Avg. of Sector	Analyzed Industry	Index	For 1997	Avg. of Sector	Analyzed Industry	Index
Employees per establishment	16	13	81	Payroll per establishment	462,554	323,505	70
Revenue per establishment	1,787,642	1,382,824	77	Payroll as % of revenue	26	23	90
Revenue per employee	108,959	103,527	95	Payroll per employee	28,193	24,220	86

Sources: Same as General Statistics. The 'Average of Sector' column represents the average for all industries in this sector. The Index shows the relationship between the Average and the Analyzed Industry. For example, 100 means that they are equal; 500 that the Analyzed Industry is five times the average; 50 means that the Analyzed Industry is half the national average. 'na' is used to show that data are 'not available'.

LEADING COMPANIES   Number shown: **20**   Total sales ($ mil): **23,543**   Total employment (000): **68.3**

Company Name	Address				CEO Name	Phone	Co. Type	Sales ($ mil)	Empl. (000)
CSX Corp.	PO Box 85629	Richmond	VA	23219	John Snow	804-782-1400	P	10,811	46.1
Ingram Industries Inc.	P O Box 23049	Nashville	TN	37202	Martha Ingram	615-298-8200	R	6,930*	6.3
TECO Energy Inc.	PO Box 111	Tampa	FL	33601	Robert D Fagan	813-228-4111	P	1,983	5.5
Eastern Enterprises	9 Riverside Rd	Weston	MA	02493	J Atwood Ives	781-647-2300	P	979	1.4
American Commercial Lines Inc.	1701 E Market St	Jeffersonville	IN	47130	Mike Hagan	812-288-0100	S	639	4.3
ADM-Growmark Inc.	PO Box 1470	Decatur	IL	62525	Burnell Kraft	217-424-5900	S	584*	0.7
Kirby Corp.	P O Box 1745	Houston	TX	77251	JH Pyne	713-435-1000	P	366	1.3
NACO Inc. (Lisle, Illinois)	2001 Butterfiel Rd	Downers Grove	IL	60515		630-852-1300	R	268*	<0.1
Trico Marine Services Inc.	PO Box 2468	Houma	LA	70361	Thomas E Fairley	504-851-3833	P	186	1.2
Trinity Industries Leasing Co.	PO Box 39	Quincy	IL	62306		217-228-6150	S	155	0.0
American River Transportation	P O Box 1470	Decatur	IL	62525	Royce Wilken	217-424-5555	S	140*	0.1
Western Pioneer Inc.	P O Box 70438	Seattle	WA	98107		206-789-1930	R	100*	0.3
Crounse Corp.	2626 Broadway	Paducah	KY	42001	William R Dibert	502-444-9611	R	100*	0.2
Port Amherst Ltd.	2 Port Amherst Dr	Charleston	WV	25306	Charles T Jones	304-926-1100	R	85*	0.2
Marine Terminals of Arkansas Inc.	P O Box 160	Armorel	AR	72310	Rick Ellis	870-763-5923	R	63*	0.2
Alter Barge Co.	2117 State St	Bettendorf	IA	52722	Jeff Goldstein	319-344-5100	R	59*	0.1
Progress Capital Holdings Inc.	1 Progress Plz	St. Petersburg	FL	33701	Darryl A LeClair	813-824-6400	S	44	0.2
Parker Towing Co.	P O Box 20908	Tuscaloosa	AL	35402	Tim Parker Jr	205-349-1677	R	40*	0.2
Alter Barge Line Inc.	2117 State St	Bettendorf	IA	52722		319-344-5100	R	7*	<0.1
Superior Barge Lines Inc.	100 N Broadway	St. Louis	MO	63102	Stephen Sheridan	314-992-0100	S	5*	<0.1

Source: *Ward's Business Directory of U.S. Private and Public Companies*, Volumes 1 and 2, 2000. The company type code used is as follows: P - Public, R - Private, S - Subsidiary, D - Division, J - Joint Venture, A - Affiliate, G - Group, N - Company type not reported. Sales are in millions of dollars, employees are in thousands. An asterisk (*) indicates an estimated sales volume. The symbol < stands for 'less than'. Company names and addresses are truncated, in some cases, to fit into the available space.

LOCATION BY STATE AND REGIONAL CONCENTRATION

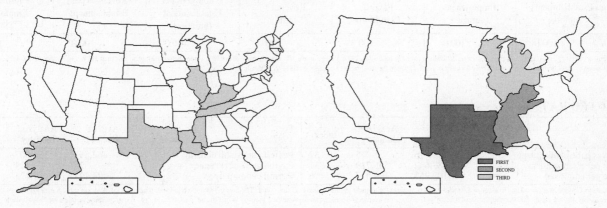

INDUSTRY DATA BY STATE

State	Establishments Total (number)	% of U.S.	Employment Total (number)	% of U.S.	Per Estab.	Payroll Total ($ mil.)	Per Empl. ($)	Revenues Total ($ mil.)	% of U.S.	Per Estab. ($)
Louisiana	115	30.0	2,656	17.0	23	86.1	32,406	512.7	15.1	4,458,539
Illinois	20	5.2	1,168	7.5	58	41.5	35,520	496.5	14.7	24,823,650
Kentucky	21	5.5	2,442	15.6	116	83.4	34,148	356.1	10.5	16,957,905
Texas	35	9.1	1,914	12.2	55	60.2	31,429	302.9	8.9	8,653,514
Mississippi	17	4.4	791	5.1	47	27.4	34,627	118.7	3.5	6,983,176
Tennessee	14	3.7	659	4.2	47	24.1	36,587	97.2	2.9	6,939,429
Washington	16	4.2	251	1.6	16	11.9	47,311	65.6	1.9	4,102,000
Florida	12	3.1	411	2.6	34	11.7	28,399	36.6	1.1	3,049,667
Alaska	6	1.6	26	0.2	4	2.5	94,923	10.1	0.3	1,685,833
Missouri	18	4.7	750*	-	-	(D)	-	(D)	-	-
New York	15	3.9	175*	-	-	(D)	-	(D)	-	-
Pennsylvania	13	3.4	375*	-	-	(D)	-	(D)	-	-
New Jersey	9	2.3	60*	-	-	(D)	-	(D)	-	-
Ohio	9	2.3	750*	-	-	(D)	-	(D)	-	-
Alabama	8	2.1	375*	-	-	(D)	-	(D)	-	-
Maryland	8	2.1	60*	-	-	(D)	-	(D)	-	-
Indiana	6	1.6	1,750*	-	-	(D)	-	(D)	-	-
Oregon	6	1.6	175*	-	-	(D)	-	(D)	-	-

Source: 1997 *Economic Census*. The states are in descending order of revenues or establishments (if revenue data are missing for the majority). The symbol (D) appears when data are withheld to prevent disclosure of competitive information. States marked with (D) are sorted by number of establishments. A dash (-) indicates that the data element cannot be calculated. * indicates the midpoint of a range; 175, for example is the range 100-249. Shaded *states* on the state map indicate those states which have proportionately greater representation in the industry than would be indicated by the state's population; the ratio is based on total revenues or number of establishments. Shaded *regions* indicate where the industry is regionally most concentrated.

NAICS 483212 - INLAND WATER PASSENGER TRANSPORTATION

GENERAL STATISTICS

Year	Establishments (number)	Employment (number)	Payroll ($ million)	Revenues ($ million)	Employees per Establishment (number)	Revenues per Establishment ($)	Payroll per Employee ($)
1997	35,478	188,106	4,754.3	19,715.8	5.3	555,719	25,275

Source: *Economic Census of the United States*, 1997. This is a newly defined industry. Data for prior years were unavailable at the time of publication but may become available over time.

SIC INDUSTRIES RELATED TO NAICS 483212

SIC	Industry	1990	1991	1992	1993	1994	1995	1996	1997
4482	**Ferries***								
	Establishments (number)	96	104	118	125	117	115	130	128p
	Employment (thousands)	1.7	1.7	1.8	1.7	1.6	1.8	1.8	1.8p
	Revenues ($ million)	131.0e	142.9e	154.7	166.5p	178.3p	190.1p	201.9p	213.7p
4489	**Water Passenger Transportation, nec***								
	Establishments (number)	321	374	843	773	751	733	809	916p
	Employment (thousands)	4.7	5.2	9.0	8.6	8.7	9.6	10.1	11.0p
	Revenues ($ million)	551.0e	630.4e	709.8	789.2p	868.6p	948.0p	1,027.4p	1,106.8p

Source: *Economic Census of the United States*, 1992, annual surveys of economic sectors conducted by the Bureau of the Census, and estimates or projections based on the 1982-1992 period; not all data are shown. 'e' marks estimates made by the editors; 'p' indicates projections based on time series. A dash (-) indicates that data for this SIC or year were not available. * Indicates that only a portion of this industry is present within the NAICS data. If no * is shown, the entire industry is contained within the NAICS data.

INDICES OF CHANGE

Year	Establishments (number)	Employment (number)	Payroll ($ million)	Revenues ($ million)	Employees per Establishment (number)	Revenues per Establishment ($)	Payroll per Employee ($)
1997	100.0	100.0	100.0	100.0	100.0	100.0	100.0

Sources: Same as General Statistics. The values shown reflect change from the base year, 1997. Values above 100 mean greater than 1997, values below 100 mean less than 1997, and a value of 100 in years other than 1997 means same as 1997. Indices are calculated only for Census years. Data are the most recent available at this level of detail.

SELECTED RATIOS

For 1997	Avg. of Sector	Analyzed Industry	Index	For 1997	Avg. of Sector	Analyzed Industry	Index
Employees per establishment	16	5	32	Payroll per establishment	462,554	134,007	29
Revenue per establishment	1,787,642	555,719	31	Payroll as % of revenue	26	24	93
Revenue per employee	108,959	104,812	96	Payroll per employee	28,193	25,275	90

Sources: Same as General Statistics. The 'Average of Sector' column represents the average for all industries in this sector. The Index shows the relationship between the Average and the Analyzed Industry. For example, 100 means that they are equal; 500 that the Analyzed Industry is five times the average; 50 means that the Analyzed Industry is half the national average. 'na' is used to show that data are 'not available'.

LEADING COMPANIES   Number shown: 1   Total sales ($ mil): 15   Total employment (000): 0.3

Company Name	Address				CEO Name	Phone	Co. Type	Sales ($ mil)	Empl. (000)
Catalina Channel Express Inc.	Berth 95	San Pedro	CA	90731	Greg Bombard	310-519-1212	R	15*	0.3

Source: Ward's Business Directory of U.S. Private and Public Companies, Volumes 1 and 2, 2000. The company type code used is as follows: P - Public, R - Private, S - Subsidiary, D - Division, J - Joint Venture, A - Affiliate, G - Group, N - Company type not reported. Sales are in millions of dollars, employees are in thousands. An asterisk (*) indicates an estimated sales volume. The symbol < stands for 'less than'. Company names and addresses are truncated, in some cases, to fit into the available space.

LOCATION BY STATE AND REGIONAL CONCENTRATION

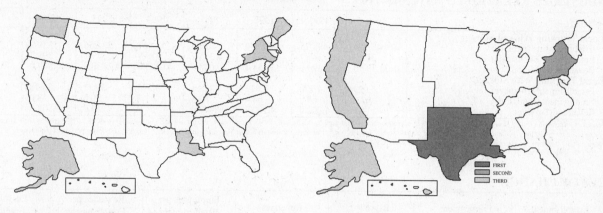

INDUSTRY DATA BY STATE

State	Establishments		Employment			Payroll		Revenues		
	Total (number)	% of U.S.	Total (number)	% of U.S.	Per Estab.	Total ($ mil.)	Per Empl. ($)	Total ($ mil.)	% of U.S.	Per Estab. ($)
Louisiana	41	17.8	1,091	37.7	27	27.1	24,837	120.1	41.0	2,930,415
New York	11	4.8	351	12.1	32	14.2	40,353	49.3	16.8	4,483,909
California	13	5.7	103	3.6	8	7.8	75,456	22.0	7.5	1,689,538
Washington	11	4.8	167	5.8	15	4.8	28,677	12.9	4.4	1,175,455
Florida	32	13.9	196	6.8	6	3.6	18,199	11.6	4.0	361,969
Texas	7	3.0	62	2.1	9	1.4	21,952	5.4	1.8	769,000
Alaska	6	2.6	13	0.4	2	0.5	41,385	2.6	0.9	426,667
Maine	8	3.5	17	0.6	2	0.7	38,588	2.0	0.7	247,750
New Jersey	12	5.2	375*	-	-	(D)	-	(D)	-	-
Massachusetts	11	4.8	175*	-	-	(D)	-	(D)	-	-
Maryland	8	3.5	60*	-	-	(D)	-	(D)	-	-
Michigan	6	2.6	10*	-	-	(D)	-	(D)	-	-

Source: 1997 *Economic Census*. The states are in descending order of revenues or establishments (if revenue data are missing for the majority). The symbol (D) appears when data are withheld to prevent disclosure of competitive information. States marked with (D) are sorted by number of establishments. A dash (-) indicates that the data element cannot be calculated. * indicates the midpoint of a range; 175, for example is the range 100-249. Shaded *states* on the state map indicate those states which have proportionately greater representation in the industry than would be indicated by the state's population; the ratio is based on total revenues or number of establishments. Shaded *regions* indicate where the industry is regionally most concentrated.

NAICS 484110 - GENERAL FREIGHT TRUCKING, LOCAL

GENERAL STATISTICS

Year	Establishments (number)	Employment (number)	Payroll ($ million)	Revenues ($ million)	Employees per Establishment (number)	Revenues per Establishment ($)	Payroll per Employee ($)
1997	14,439	164,627	5,050.9	20,500.4	11.4	1,419,794	30,681

Source: Economic Census of the United States, 1997. This is a newly defined industry. Data for prior years were unavailable at the time of publication but may become available over time.

SIC INDUSTRIES RELATED TO NAICS 484110

SIC	Industry	1990	1991	1992	1993	1994	1995	1996	1997
4212	**Local Trucking Without Storage***								
	Establishments (number)	48,279e	49,075e	49,870	50,665p	51,461p	52,256p	53,052p	53,847p
	Employment (thousands)	332.7e	343.7e	354.7	365.7p	376.7p	387.7p	398.7p	409.7p
	Revenues ($ million)	31,397.0	30,890.0	33,554.4	36,648.0	40,903.0	43,830.0	46,589.0	49,972.0
4214	**Local Trucking With Storage***								
	Establishments (number)	5,029e	4,770e	4,512	4,254p	3,995p	3,737p	3,478p	3,220p
	Employment (thousands)	67.6e	66.0e	64.4	62.8p	61.2p	59.6p	58.0p	56.4p
	Revenues ($ million)	4,115.0	4,022.0	4,190.7	4,487.0	4,757.0	5,154.0	5,502.0	5,860.0

*Source: Economic Census of the United States, 1992, annual surveys of economic sectors conducted by the Bureau of the Census, and estimates or projections based on the 1982-1992 period; not all data are shown. 'e' marks estimates made by the editors; 'p' indicates projections based on time series. A dash (-) indicates that data for this SIC or year were not available. * Indicates that only a portion of this industry is present within the NAICS data. If no * is shown, the entire industry is contained within the NAICS data.*

INDICES OF CHANGE

Year	Establishments (number)	Employment (number)	Payroll ($ million)	Revenues ($ million)	Employees per Establishment (number)	Revenues per Establishment ($)	Payroll per Employee ($)
1997	100.0	100.0	100.0	100.0	100.0	100.0	100.0

Sources: Same as General Statistics. The values shown reflect change from the base year, 1997. Values above 100 mean greater than 1997, values below 100 mean less than 1997, and a value of 100 in years other than 1997 means same as 1997. Indices are calculated only for Census years. Data are the most recent available at this level of detail.

SELECTED RATIOS

For 1997	Avg. of Sector	Analyzed Industry	Index	For 1997	Avg. of Sector	Analyzed Industry	Index
Employees per establishment	16	11	69	Payroll per establishment	462,554	349,810	76
Revenue per establishment	1,787,642	1,419,794	79	Payroll as % of revenue	26	25	95
Revenue per employee	108,959	124,526	114	Payroll per employee	28,193	30,681	109

Sources: Same as General Statistics. The 'Average of Sector' column represents the average for all industries in this sector. The Index shows the relationship between the Average and the Analyzed Industry. For example, 100 means that they are equal; 500 that the Analyzed Industry is five times the average; 50 means that the Analyzed Industry is half the national average. 'na' is used to show that data are 'not available'.

LEADING COMPANIES Number shown: 75   Total sales ($ mil): 57,020   Total employment (000): 432.2

Company Name	Address				CEO Name	Phone	Co. Type	Sales ($ mil)	Empl. (000)
Federal Express Corp.	U S Mail Box 727	Memphis	TN	38194	Frederick W Smith	901-369-3600	D	16,774	141.0
FedEx Corp.	6075 Poplar Ave	Memphis	TN	38119	Fredrick W Smith	901-369-3600	P	16,774	141.0
Schneider National Inc.	P O Box 2545	Green Bay	WI	54306	Donald J Schneider	920-592-5100	R	2,510	16.5
J.B. Hunt Transport Services Inc.	PO Box 130	Lowell	AR	72745	Kirk Thompson	501-820-0000	P	2,045	14.2
Adams Resources and Energy Inc.	P O Box 844	Houston	TX	77001	KS Adams Jr	713-881-3600	P	1,974	0.6
Con-Way Transportation Services	110 Parkland Plz	Ann Arbor	MI	48103	Gerald L Detter	734-769-0203	S	1,700	16.6
Landstar System Inc.	4160 Woodcock Dr	Jacksonville	FL	32207	Jeffrey C Crowe	904-390-1234	P	1,284	1.3
Leprino Foods Co.	PO Box 173400	Denver	CO	80217	Wes Allen	303-480-2605	R	1,250	2.5
American Freightways Corp.	2200 Forward Dr	Harrison	AR	72601	F Sheridan Garrison	870-741-9000	P	1,167	13.2
Allied Holdings Inc.	160 Clairmont Ave	Decatur	GA	30030	Robert J Rutland	404-373-4285	P	1,027	8.5
Atlas World Group Inc.	1212 St George Rd	Evansville	IN	47711	Wally E Saubert	812-424-4326	R	689*	0.8
Con-Way Central Express	4880 Venture Dr	Ann Arbor	MI	48108	Richard V Palazzo	734-994-6600	D	678*	7.5
General Electric Capital Fleet	3 Capital Dr	Eden Prairie	MN	55344	Rick Smith	612-828-1000	S	627*	2.2
U.S. Xpress Inc.	1535 New Hope	Tunnel Hill	GA	30755	William K Farris	706-673-6592	P	513	5.6
Atlas Van Lines Inc.	1212 St George Rd	Evansville	IN	47711	Dick Arneson	812-424-4326	S	490*	0.6
Acme Truck Line Inc.	P O Box 183	Harvey	LA	70059	Doyle Coatney	504-368-2510	R	466*	1.6
Old Dominion Freight Line Inc.	PO Box 2006	High Point	NC	27262	David S Congdon	336-889-5000	R	426	5.3
Customized Transportation Inc.	PO Box 40083	Jacksonville	FL	32203	David Kulik	904-928-1400	S	409	3.8
Southeastern Freight Lines Inc.	PO Box 2104	West Columbia	SC	29171		803-794-7300	R	377*	4.7
Saia Motor Freight Line Inc.	P O Box A, Sta 1	Houma	LA	70363	Jimmy D Crisp	504-868-1030	R	305*	4.5
Transport Corporation of America	1769 Yankee Doodle	Eagan	MN	55121	Robert J Meyers	651-686-2500	P	286	1.2
Burlington Motor Carriers Inc.	14611 W Commerce	Daleville	IN	47334	Ralph Arthur	765-378-0261	R	240	3.0
Global Transportation Services	PO Box 24504	Seattle	WA	98124	Eddie Kelly	206-624-4354	R	232	0.1
RPC Inc.	PO Box 647	Atlanta	GA	30301	Richard A Hubbell	404-321-2140	P	231	1.6
Exel Logistics Inc.	501 W Schrock Rd	Westerville	OH	43081	Bruce Edwards	614-890-1730	S	225	6.0
Bekins Van Lines Corp.	330 S Mannheim Rd	Hillside	IL	60162	Laurence Marzullo	708-547-2000	S	225	0.4
Salem National Corp.	PO Box 24788	Winston-Salem	NC	27114	Thomas L Teague	336-768-6800	R	195*	0.6
The Suddath Companies	815 S Main St	Jacksonville	FL	32207	AQ Bell	904-390-7100	R	180	1.2
Merchants Home Delivery Service	2400 Latigo St	Oxnard	CA	93030	James Allyn	805-485-7979	S	175*	0.6
Bekins Co.	330 S Mannheim Rd	Hillside	IL	60162	Larry Marzullo	708-547-2000	R	167*	1.2
Savage Industries Inc.	5250 S Commerce	Salt Lake City	UT	84107	Allan Alexander	801-263-9400	R	161*	1.0
A-P-A Transport Corp.	2100 88th St	North Bergen	NJ	07047	Armand Pohan	201-869-6600	R	160	1.9
Ward Trucking Corp.	P O Box 1553	Altoona	PA	16603	David K Ward	814-944-0803	R	154*	0.9
Morgan Group Inc.	P O Box 1168	Elkhart	IN	46515	Charles C Baum	219-295-2200	P	150	0.4
Paul Arpin Van Lines	P O Box 1302	East Greenwich	RI	02818	David A Arpin	401-828-8111	R	147	0.4
Solid Waste Services Inc.	320 Godshall Dr	Harleysville	PA	19438	Pat Mascaro	215-256-1900	R	139*	0.8
Forward Air Corp.	P O Box 1058	Greeneville	TN	37744	Scott M Niswonger	423-636-7100	P	130	1.3
Etranco Inc.	6169 W 300 N	Greenfield	IN	46140	Lanny Wilhelm	317-894-2900	R	120*	0.7
Artic Express Inc.	PO Box 129	Hilliard	OH	43026	Richard E Durst	614-876-4008	R	107*	0.6
Schilli Corp.	2275 Cassens Dr	Fenton	MO	63026	RB Schilli	636-343-1877	R	107*	0.6
Arnold Transportation Service	9523 Florida Mining	Jacksonville	FL	32257	Mike Walters	904-262-4285	S	103*	0.7
Total Logistic Control	8300 Logistic Dr	Zeeland	MI	49464	Gary Sarner	616-772-9009	S	100	0.8
Market Transport Ltd.	110 N Marine Dr	Portland	OR	97217	Brian Fitzgerald	503-283-2405	R	98*	0.5
Schneider National Bulk Carriers	PO Box 2700	Green Bay	WI	54306	John Lanigan	920-592-5025	S	93*	1.0
Manfredi Motor Transit Co.	14841 Sperry Rd	Newbury	OH	44065	Richard Manfredi	440-338-1010	R	87*	0.5
Rail Van Inc.	400 W Wilson Br	Worthington	OH	43085	Jeff Brashares	614-436-6262	R	85*	0.5
A. Duie Pyle Inc.	P O Box 564	West Chester	PA	19381	Peter Latta	610-696-5800	R	80	1.0
Safety-Kleen Corp. Oklahoma	2 NE 9th St	Oklahoma City	OK	73104	Kenneth Winger	803-934-4200	D	80*	0.4
Hallamore Corp.	795 Plymouth St	Holbrook	MA	02343	Joseph L Barry Jr	781-767-2000	R	78*	0.4
Ploof Truck Lines Inc.	1414 Lindrose St	Jacksonville	FL	32206	Dan Copeland	904-353-8641	R	70*	0.4
Alvan Motor Freight Inc.	3600 Alvan Rd	Kalamazoo	MI	49001	Charles A Van Zoeren	616-382-1500	R	65	0.7
K and R Express Systems Inc.	15 W 460 Frontage	Hinsdale	IL	60521		630-323-3230	R	65*	0.4
Lewis Truck Lines Inc.	4001 12th Ave N W	Fargo	ND	58102	Bob Lewis Sr	701-282-5330	R	60*	0.4
Johnson Storage and Moving Inc.	221 Broadway	Denver	CO	80203		303-778-6683	R	58*	0.3
Standard Corp.	1400 Main St	Columbia	SC	29201	Claude Walker	803-771-6785	R	55*	1.7
Transwood Inc.	2565 St Marys Ave	Omaha	NE	68105	Brian Wood	402-346-8092	R	55	0.0
Two Men & A Truck/Intern. Inc.	2152 Commons Pky	Okemos	MI	48864	Mary Ellen Sheets		R	52	1.1
D.D. Jones Transfer & Warehouse	2626 Indian River	Chesapeake	VA	23325	Robert Jones Jr	757-494-0200	R	52*	0.3
Elston-Richards Inc.	4880 Corp Ex	Grand Rapids	MI	49512	John E Holmes	616-698-2698	R	51*	0.3
Electronic Data Carriers Inc.	PO Box 920680	Houston	TX	77292	George Gilbert	713-680-9600	R	44*	0.3
Hodges Truck Company Inc.	P O Box 270660	Oklahoma City	OK	73137	HL Hodges	405-947-7764	R	44*	0.3
Howard's Express Inc.	83 Senneca St	Geneva	NY	14456	SG Boncaro	315-789-1900	R	44*	0.3
Perkins Specialized Transportation	PO Box 78130	Indianapolis	IN	46278	James H Card	317-297-3550	R	44*	0.3
Mayfield Transfer Company Inc.	3200 W Lake St	Melrose Park	IL	60160	Ray Emerick	708-681-4440	R	43*	0.3
MGM Transport Corp.	P O Box 536	Totowa	NJ	07512	George Massood	973-256-6500	R	42	0.5
Di Salvo Trucking Co.	PO Box 193765	San Francisco	CA	94119	Bob J Lawlor	415-495-1800	S	40*	0.3
Romar Transportation Systems	3500 S Kedzie Ave	Chicago	IL	60632	Michael Marden	773-376-8800	R	39*	0.2
MME Inc.	P O Box 1058	Bismarck	ND	58502	John T Roswick	701-223-1880	R	36	0.4
Triad Transport Inc.	P O Box 818	McAlester	OK	74502	John Titswor	918-426-4751	R	36*	0.2
Federal Warehouse Co.	200 National Rd	East Peoria	IL	61611	Donald L Ullman	309-694-4500	R	35	0.6
Kinard Trucking Inc.	310 N Zarfoss Dr	York	PA	17404	Ronald Workman	717-792-3632	R	35*	0.2
Parker Motor Freight Inc.	1025 Ken-O-Sha Ind	Grand Rapids	MI	49508	John H Parker	616-241-3641	R	34	0.3
Hahn Transportation Inc.	90 W Main St	New Market	MD	21774	Rebecca Windsor	301-865-5467	R	34*	0.2
Terminal Trucking Co.	PO Box 1623	Concord	NC	28026	Gene Isenhour	704-786-0189	R	34*	0.2
Paxton Van Lines Inc.	5300 Port Royal Rd	Springfield	VA	22151	Frederick D Paxton	703-321-7600	R	33*	0.2

Source: *Ward's Business Directory of U.S. Private and Public Companies*, Volumes 1 and 2, 2000. The company type code used is as follows: P - Public, R - Private, S - Subsidiary, D - Division, J - Joint Venture, A - Affiliate, G - Group, N - Company type not reported. Sales are in millions of dollars, employees are in thousands. An asterisk (*) indicates an estimated sales volume. The symbol < stands for 'less than'. Company names and addresses are truncated, in some cases, to fit into the available space.

LOCATION BY STATE AND REGIONAL CONCENTRATION

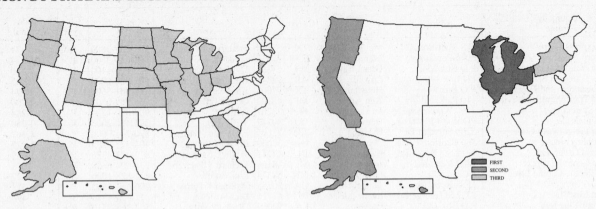

FIRST
SECOND
THIRD

INDUSTRY DATA BY STATE

State	Establishments Total (number)	% of U.S.	Employment Total (number)	% of U.S.	Per Estab.	Payroll Total ($ mil.)	Per Empl. ($)	Revenues Total ($ mil.)	% of U.S.	Per Estab. ($)
California	1,648	10.7	20,384	15.1	12	558.1	27,378	2,015.0	16.4	1,222,690
Illinois	1,111	7.2	10,011	7.4	9	302.0	30,166	988.3	8.1	889,526
Texas	1,085	7.0	9,683	7.2	9	219.5	22,667	769.8	6.3	709,482
New Jersey	854	5.5	7,306	5.4	9	223.8	30,635	747.1	6.1	874,794
Ohio	769	5.0	7,648	5.7	10	206.3	26,976	701.9	5.7	912,785
Michigan	499	3.2	5,170	3.8	10	167.5	32,391	643.1	5.2	1,288,830
New York	825	5.3	6,767	5.0	8	173.0	25,563	529.0	4.3	641,222
Florida	617	4.0	3,559	2.6	6	89.4	25,117	356.1	2.9	577,081
Georgia	397	2.6	4,044	3.0	10	100.6	24,865	349.9	2.9	881,373
Wisconsin	430	2.8	3,925	2.9	9	107.2	27,313	344.4	2.8	800,842
Pennsylvania	468	3.0	3,865	2.9	8	87.6	22,677	320.2	2.6	684,239
Missouri	499	3.2	3,425	2.5	7	83.8	24,470	306.7	2.5	614,643
Indiana	394	2.5	3,542	2.6	9	93.1	26,282	300.8	2.5	763,401
Minnesota	377	2.4	2,706	2.0	7	72.5	26,807	276.2	2.3	732,613
North Carolina	431	2.8	3,416	2.5	8	72.2	21,146	266.7	2.2	618,803
Washington	276	1.8	3,017	2.2	11	86.2	28,580	261.1	2.1	945,928
Tennessee	309	2.0	2,419	1.8	8	60.0	24,793	235.3	1.9	761,625
Virginia	351	2.3	2,552	1.9	7	66.0	25,854	204.8	1.7	583,390
Massachusetts	264	1.7	2,056	1.5	8	60.3	29,330	175.5	1.4	664,848
Oregon	177	1.1	2,173	1.6	12	59.7	27,468	174.1	1.4	983,480
Iowa	262	1.7	1,775	1.3	7	41.0	23,094	172.4	1.4	658,084
Alabama	264	1.7	1,820	1.4	7	40.3	22,170	168.7	1.4	638,883
Arizona	200	1.3	2,113	1.6	11	48.1	22,770	156.3	1.3	781,680
Kansas	175	1.1	1,604	1.2	9	39.3	24,478	146.2	1.2	835,389
Maryland	197	1.3	1,865	1.4	9	44.8	24,044	138.5	1.1	703,178
Colorado	184	1.2	1,563	1.2	8	37.7	24,115	133.3	1.1	724,212
Kentucky	227	1.5	1,709	1.3	8	39.7	23,232	128.7	1.0	567,004
Mississippi	213	1.4	1,262	0.9	6	27.9	22,082	114.9	0.9	539,380
Louisiana	199	1.3	1,394	1.0	7	27.4	19,664	110.2	0.9	553,583
Utah	111	0.7	1,091	0.8	10	26.7	24,464	99.3	0.8	894,631
Connecticut	97	0.6	751	0.6	8	21.5	28,636	91.5	0.7	943,144
South Carolina	159	1.0	1,012	0.8	6	21.8	21,512	88.3	0.7	555,553
Nebraska	170	1.1	944	0.7	6	23.1	24,417	86.4	0.7	508,218
Oklahoma	159	1.0	997	0.7	6	20.4	20,412	78.7	0.6	495,245
Hawaii	54	0.3	947	0.7	18	26.1	27,534	69.5	0.6	1,287,519
Arkansas	170	1.1	723	0.5	4	15.2	20,997	58.8	0.5	345,659
Idaho	82	0.5	660	0.5	8	12.9	19,605	50.4	0.4	614,488
West Virginia	114	0.7	630	0.5	6	14.9	23,671	48.0	0.4	421,070
North Dakota	62	0.4	700	0.5	11	14.5	20,646	46.9	0.4	756,081
South Dakota	91	0.6	454	0.3	5	10.3	22,670	45.2	0.4	496,231
Nevada	57	0.4	648	0.5	11	16.9	26,111	44.1	0.4	773,544
Alaska	42	0.3	332	0.2	8	13.2	39,614	43.7	0.4	1,040,000
Maine	83	0.5	536	0.4	6	12.1	22,638	42.2	0.3	508,723
New Mexico	51	0.3	309	0.2	6	8.3	26,812	31.3	0.3	614,098
New Hampshire	59	0.4	337	0.3	6	9.1	26,864	28.7	0.2	486,831
Rhode Island	38	0.2	173	0.1	5	5.9	33,884	27.9	0.2	733,132
Montana	64	0.4	318	0.2	5	6.3	19,814	26.2	0.2	410,109
Delaware	31	0.2	215	0.2	7	4.8	22,153	20.3	0.2	653,968
Vermont	23	0.1	88	0.1	4	1.6	18,091	4.3	0.0	188,087
Wyoming	40	0.3	175*	-	-	(D)	-	(D)	-	-

Source: 1997 *Economic Census*. The states are in descending order of revenues or establishments (if revenue data are missing for the majority). The symbol (D) appears when data are withheld to prevent disclosure of competitive information. States marked with (D) are sorted by number of establishments. A dash (-) indicates that the data element cannot be calculated. * indicates the midpoint of a range; 175, for example is the range 100-249. Shaded *states* on the state map indicate those states which have proportionately greater representation in the industry than would be indicated by the state's population; the ratio is based on total revenues or number of establishments. Shaded *regions* indicate where the industry is regionally most concentrated.

NAICS 484121 - GENERAL FREIGHT TRUCKING, LONG-DISTANCE, TRUCKLOAD (TL)

GENERAL STATISTICS

Year	Establishments (number)	Employment (number)	Payroll ($ million)	Revenues ($ million)	Employees per Establishment (number)	Revenues per Establishment ($)	Payroll per Employee ($)
1997	28	759	24.1	51.6	27.1	1,842,857	31,752

Source: Economic Census of the United States, 1997. This is a newly defined industry. Data for prior years were unavailable at the time of publication but may become available over time.

SIC INDUSTRIES RELATED TO NAICS 484121

SIC	Industry	1990	1991	1992	1993	1994	1995	1996	1997
4213	**Trucking, Except Local***								
	Establishments (number)	39,589e	40,205e	40,821	41,437p	42,053p	42,668p	43,284p	43,900p
	Employment (thousands)	748.5e	753.5e	758.4	763.4p	768.4p	773.4p	778.3p	783.3p
	Revenues ($ million)	74,465.0	73,982.0	78,357.5	81,317.0	89,369.0	91,675.0	97,586.0	103,847.0

Source: Economic Census of the United States, 1992, annual surveys of economic sectors conducted by the Bureau of the Census, and estimates or projections based on the 1982-1992 period; not all data are shown. 'e' marks estimates made by the editors; 'p' indicates projections based on time series. A dash (-) indicates that data for this SIC or year were not available. * Indicates that only a portion of this industry is present within the NAICS data. If no * is shown, the entire industry is contained within the NAICS data.

INDICES OF CHANGE

Year	Establishments (number)	Employment (number)	Payroll ($ million)	Revenues ($ million)	Employees per Establishment (number)	Revenues per Establishment ($)	Payroll per Employee ($)
1997	100.0	100.0	100.0	100.0	100.0	100.0	100.0

Sources: Same as General Statistics. The values shown reflect change from the base year, 1997. Values above 100 mean greater than 1997, values below 100 mean less than 1997, and a value of 100 in years other than 1997 means same as 1997. Indices are calculated only for Census years. Data are the most recent available at this level of detail.

SELECTED RATIOS

For 1997	Avg. of Sector	Analyzed Industry	Index	For 1997	Avg. of Sector	Analyzed Industry	Index
Employees per establishment	16	27	165	Payroll per establishment	462,554	860,714	186
Revenue per establishment	1,787,642	1,842,857	103	Payroll as % of revenue	26	47	181
Revenue per employee	108,959	67,984	62	Payroll per employee	28,193	31,752	113

Sources: Same as General Statistics. The 'Average of Sector' column represents the average for all industries in this sector. The Index shows the relationship between the Average and the Analyzed Industry. For example, 100 means that they are equal; 500 that the Analyzed Industry is five times the average; 50 means that the Analyzed Industry is half the national average. 'na' is used to show that data are 'not available'.

LEADING COMPANIES　　Number shown: **75**　　　Total sales ($ mil): **119,857**　　　Total employment (000): **748.6**

Company Name	Address				CEO Name	Phone	Co. Type	Sales ($ mil)	Empl. (000)
FedEx Corp.	6075 Poplar Ave	Memphis	TN	38119	Fredrick W Smith	901-369-3600	P	16,774	141.0
Union Pacific Corp.	1416 Dodge St	Omaha	NE	68179	Richard K Davidson	401-271-5000	P	11,273	65.0
CSX Corp.	PO Box 85629	Richmond	VA	23219	John Snow	804-782-1400	P	10,811	46.1
Coastal Corp.	9 E Greenway Plz	Houston	TX	77046		713-877-1400	P	7,368	13.2
CNF Transportation Inc.	3240 Hillview Ave	Palo Alto	CA	94304	Gregory L Quesnel	650-494-2900	P	5,593	33.7
Norfolk Southern Corp.	3 Commercial Pl	Norfolk	VA	23510	David R Goode	757-629-2600	P	5,195	24.3
Yellow Corp.	PO Box 7563	Overland Park	KS	66207	William Zollars	913-696-6100	P	3,227	29.7
Roadway Express Inc.	PO Box 471	Akron	OH	44309	James D Staley	330-384-1717	P	2,813	28.0
United Van Lines Inc.	1 United Dr	Fenton	MO	63026	Robert J Baer	314-326-3100	S	2,742*	1.8
Schneider National Inc.	P O Box 2545	Green Bay	WI	54306	Donald J Schneider	920-592-5100	R	2,510	16.5
Consolidated Freightways Corp.	175 Linfield Dr	Menlo Park	CA	94025	Patrick H Blake	650-326-1700	P	2,379	21.0
Yellow Freight System Inc.	P O Box 7563	Overland Park	KS	66207	William D Zollars	913-344-3000	S	2,330*	24.0
Consolidated Freightways	175 Linfield Dr	Menlo Park	CA	94025	W Roger Curry	650-326-1700	S	2,238	21.0
USFreightways Corp.	9700 Higgins Rd	Rosemont	IL	60018	J Campbell Carruth	847-696-0200	P	2,222	19.2
J.B. Hunt Transport Services Inc.	PO Box 130	Lowell	AR	72745	Kirk Thompson	501-820-0000	P	2,045	14.2
UniGroup Inc.	1 United Dr	Fenton	MO	63026	Robert J Baer	636-305-5000	R	1,800	1.6
CGB Enterprises Inc.	P O Box 249	Mandeville	LA	70470	Richard Wilcox	504-867-3500	R	1,800	0.9
Arkansas Best Corp.	PO Box 10048	Fort Smith	AR	72917	Robert A Young III	501-785-6000	P	1,722	14.8
Landstar System Holdings Inc.	4160 Woockock Dr	Jacksonville	FL	32207	Jeffrey C Crowe	904-390-1234	S	1,313	2.0
ABF Freight System Inc.	PO Box 10048	Fort Smith	AR	72917	Robert Young III	501-785-8700	S	1,311*	14.0
Plains Resources Inc.	500 Dallas St	Houston	TX	77002	Greg L Armstrong	713-654-1414	P	1,293	0.4
Landstar System Inc.	4160 Woodcock Dr	Jacksonville	FL	32207	Jeffrey C Crowe	904-390-1234	P	1,284	1.3
Leprino Foods Co.	PO Box 173400	Denver	CO	80217	Wes Allen	303-480-2605	R	1,250	2.5
Arkansas Best Holdings Corp.	PO Box 10048	Fort Smith	AR	72917	Robert A Young III	501-785-6000	R	1,225*	13.1
Navajo L.T.L. Inc.	PO Box 5002	Commerce City	CO	80037	David Congdon		S	1,170*	6.0
American Freightways Corp.	2200 Forward Dr	Harrison	AR	72601	F Sheridan Garrison	870-741-9000	P	1,167	13.2
Lykes Bros. Inc.	PO Box 1690	Tampa	FL	33601		813-223-3981	R	1,100	3.0
Werner Enterprises Inc.	P O Box 45308	Omaha	NE	68145	Clarence L Werner	402-895-6640	P	1,052	8.9
Allied Holdings Inc.	160 Clairmont Ave	Decatur	GA	30030	Robert J Rutland	404-373-4285	P	1,027	8.5
EOTT Energy Corp.	P O Box 4666	Houston	TX	77210	Michael Burke	713-993-5000	S	912*	1.4
Swift Transportation Inc.	PO Box 29243	Phoenix	AZ	85038	Jerry C Moyes	602-269-9700	S	873	9.6
Sparks Finance Co.	1455 Hulda Way	Sparks	NV	89431	Jerry C Moyes	702-359-9031	P	873*	9.6
Overnite Transportation Co.	P O Box 1216	Richmond	VA	23218	Leo Suggs	804-231-8000	S	836*	13.0
Watkins Associated Industries Inc.	P O Box 1738	Atlanta	GA	30371	William Freeman	404-872-3841	R	800	8.5
Mark VII Inc.	965 Ridge Lake	Memphis	TN	38120	RC Matney	901-767-4455	P	725	0.4
Atlas World Group Inc.	1212 St George Rd	Evansville	IN	47711	Wally E Saubert	812-424-4326	S	689*	0.8
USF Holland Inc.	750 E 40th St	Holland	MI	49423	Peter B Neydon	616-392-3101	S	654*	7.5
Watkins Motor Lines Inc.	P O Box 95002	Lakeland	FL	33804	John F Watkins	941-687-4545	R	650*	10.0
North American Van Lines Inc.	PO Box 988	Fort Wayne	IN	46801	Barry Uber	219-429-2511	R	634*	2.4
General Electric Capital Fleet	3 Capital Dr	Eden Prairie	MN	55344	Rick Smith	612-828-1000	S	627*	2.2
M.S. Carriers Inc.	P O Box 30788	Memphis	TN	38130	Michael S Starnes	901-332-2500	P	620	3.3
U.S. Express	4080 Jenkins Rd	Chattanooga	TN	37421	Max Fuller	423-510-3000	P	581	8.0
AMCOL International Corp.	1500 W Shure Dr	Arlington H.	IL	60004	John Hughes	847-394-8730	P	552	1.6
Giant Industries Inc.	PO Box 12999	Scottsdale	AZ	85267	James E Acridge	602-585-8888	P	526	2.7
U.S. Xpress Inc.	1535 New Hope	Tunnel Hill	GA	30755	William K Farris	706-673-6592	P	513	5.6
Atlas Van Lines Inc.	1212 St George Rd	Evansville	IN	47711	Dick Arneson	812-424-4326	S	490*	0.6
Lynch Corp.	401 Theodore Fremd	Rye	NY	10580	Mario J Gabelli	914-921-7601	P	468	1.9
Acme Truck Line Inc.	P O Box 183	Harvey	LA	70059	Doyle Coatney	504-368-2510	R	466*	1.6
Estes Express Lines Inc.	P O Box 25612	Richmond	VA	23260		804-232-6793	R	442*	6.5
Landstar Inway Inc.	PO Box 7013	Rockford	IL	61125	Jeff Pundt	815-972-6902	S	430	0.4
Old Dominion Freight Line Inc.	PO Box 2006	High Point	NC	27262	David S Congdon	336-889-5000	P	426	5.3
Triple Crown Services Co.	2720 Dupont	Fort Wayne	IN	46825	Dan Cushman	219-434-3600	S	410*	0.3
Customized Transportation Inc.	PO Box 40083	Jacksonville	FL	32203	David Kulik	904-928-1400	S	409	3.8
Arnold Industries Inc.	P O Box 11963	Lebanon	PA	17042	EH Arnold	717-273-9058	P	404*	1.5
Quality Distribution Inc.	3802 Corporex Dr	Tampa	FL	33619	Jack Elrod	813-630-5826	R	398	2.5
Comet Transport Inc.	3880 Salem Lake Dr	Long Grove	IL	60047	Douglas Christanson	847-726-4500	R	394*	2.0
Centra Inc.	12225 Stephen Rd	Warren	MI	48089	Matty J Moroun	810-939-7000	R	389*	2.0
Dart Transit Company Inc.	P O Box 64110	St. Paul	MN	55164	Donald Oren	612-688-2000	R	386*	0.6
Southeastern Freight Lines Inc.	PO Box 2104	West Columbia	SC	29171		803-794-7300	R	377*	4.7
AAA Cooper Transportation	PO Box 6827	Dothan	AL	36302	G Mack Dove	334-793-2284	R	367	4.3
Celadon Trucking Services Inc.	9503 East 33rd St	Indianapolis	IN	46235	Stephen Russell	317-972-7000	S	352*	1.8
Frozen Food Express Industries	PO Box 655888	Dallas	TX	75265	Stoney M Stubbs Jr	214-630-8090	P	350	2.6
Cassens Corp.	PO Box 468	Edwardsville	IL	62025	Albert Cassens	618-656-3006	R	331*	1.7
CRST International Inc.	PO Box 68	Cedar Rapids	IA	52406	John M Smith	319-396-4400	R	330	3.7
Trism Specialized Carriers	P O Box 9000	Kennesaw	GA	30144	Ed McCormick	770-795-4700	S	330	2.0
C.R. England Inc.	4701 W 2100 South	Salt Lake City	UT	84120	Dan England		R	320	4.1
Mayflower Transit Inc.	PO Box 26150	Fenton	MO	63026	John J Temporiti	314-305-4000	S	311*	0.5
Saia Motor Freight Line Inc.	P O Box A, Sta 1	Houma	LA	70363	Jimmy D Crisp	504-868-1030	S	305*	4.5
TRISM Inc.	P O Box 9000	Kennesaw	GA	30144	Edward L McCormick	770-795-4600	P	292	2.5
Transport Corporation of America	1769 Yankee Doodle	Eagan	MN	55121	Robert J Meyers	651-686-2500	P	286	1.2
Celadon Group Inc.	9503 E 33rd St	Indianapolis	IN	46235	Stepen Russell	317-972-7000	P	282	2.1
Intrenet Inc.	400 TechneCenter	Milford	OH	45150	John P Delavan	513-576-6666	P	263	1.9
Heartland Express Inc.	2777 Heartland Dr	Coralville	IA	52241	Russell A Gerdin	319-645-2728	P	261	1.2
Contract Freighters Inc.	P O Box 2547	Joplin	MO	64803	Glenn Brown	417-623-5229	R	250	2.5
Burlington Motor Carriers Inc.	14611 W Commerce	Daleville	IN	47334	Ralph Arthur	765-378-0261	R	240	3.0

Source: Ward's Business Directory of U.S. Private and Public Companies, Volumes 1 and 2, 2000. The company type code used is as follows: P - Public, R - Private, S - Subsidiary, D - Division, J - Joint Venture, A - Affiliate, G - Group, N - Company type not reported. Sales are in millions of dollars, employees are in thousands. An asterisk (*) indicates an estimated sales volume. The symbol < stands for 'less than'. Company names and addresses are truncated, in some cases, to fit into the available space.

LOCATION BY STATE AND REGIONAL CONCENTRATION

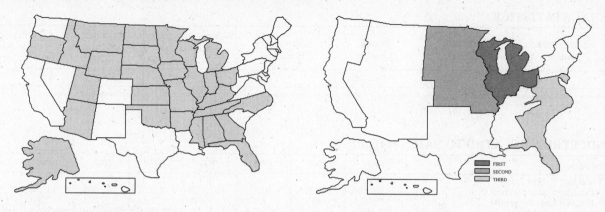

INDUSTRY DATA BY STATE

State	Establishments Total (number)	% of U.S.	Employment Total (number)	% of U.S.	Per Estab.	Payroll Total ($ mil.)	Per Empl. ($)	Revenues Total ($ mil.)	% of U.S.	Per Estab. ($)
Florida	733	3.2	19,556	4.6	27	770.0	39,375	2,902.0	5.7	3,959,112
Texas	1,794	7.8	24,631	5.8	14	681.3	27,661	2,645.5	5.2	1,474,632
Wisconsin	946	4.1	20,734	4.9	22	693.4	33,440	2,609.4	5.1	2,758,336
Illinois	1,026	4.4	18,907	4.4	18	603.9	31,940	2,396.4	4.7	2,335,668
Ohio	1,068	4.6	17,349	4.1	16	532.4	30,688	2,378.3	4.7	2,226,895
Tennessee	859	3.7	21,173	5.0	25	617.2	29,150	2,261.1	4.4	2,632,289
Indiana	973	4.2	19,744	4.6	20	567.9	28,765	2,172.6	4.2	2,232,889
Michigan	675	2.9	14,059	3.3	21	399.9	28,443	2,124.9	4.2	3,147,961
Pennsylvania	805	3.5	17,374	4.1	22	526.9	30,327	2,085.4	4.1	2,590,609
California	1,025	4.4	18,206	4.3	18	552.9	30,367	2,072.4	4.1	2,021,874
Iowa	755	3.3	13,450	3.2	18	386.7	28,754	1,821.3	3.6	2,412,258
Nebraska	418	1.8	9,282	2.2	22	295.6	31,852	1,789.0	3.5	4,280,005
Missouri	1,029	4.5	14,760	3.5	14	406.9	27,568	1,635.2	3.2	1,589,137
Alabama	648	2.8	15,178	3.6	23	386.4	25,460	1,624.5	3.2	2,506,873
Minnesota	594	2.6	10,087	2.4	17	308.9	30,625	1,607.2	3.1	2,705,670
Arkansas	570	2.5	15,885	3.7	28	456.2	28,718	1,604.1	3.1	2,814,163
North Carolina	771	3.3	14,830	3.5	19	434.1	29,269	1,494.2	2.9	1,937,951
Georgia	724	3.1	12,605	3.0	17	383.1	30,395	1,407.6	2.8	1,944,225
New Jersey	449	1.9	8,506	2.0	19	303.7	35,708	1,218.4	2.4	2,713,577
Arizona	283	1.2	12,380	2.9	44	298.9	24,146	1,073.3	2.1	3,792,548
Utah	249	1.1	10,507	2.5	42	290.7	27,667	1,004.2	2.0	4,032,775
Washington	436	1.9	7,951	1.9	18	252.8	31,790	942.7	1.8	2,162,236
Kentucky	396	1.7	5,750	1.4	15	160.9	27,975	864.7	1.7	2,183,616
Oklahoma	371	1.6	7,402	1.7	20	209.3	28,279	794.1	1.6	2,140,491
Virginia	562	2.4	7,896	1.9	14	216.4	27,401	786.6	1.5	1,399,680
New York	516	2.2	6,321	1.5	12	187.7	29,697	682.5	1.3	1,322,686
Mississippi	422	1.8	6,242	1.5	15	169.5	27,147	634.6	1.2	1,503,694
Kansas	359	1.6	5,743	1.3	16	172.5	30,036	632.6	1.2	1,762,058
Louisiana	403	1.7	6,979	1.6	17	189.6	27,161	625.8	1.2	1,552,806
Oregon	324	1.4	4,831	1.1	15	140.0	28,986	592.2	1.2	1,827,821
Colorado	310	1.3	4,326	1.0	14	126.0	29,129	556.8	1.1	1,795,987
South Carolina	348	1.5	5,331	1.3	15	140.3	26,324	514.1	1.0	1,477,207
Maryland	234	1.0	3,913	0.9	17	123.1	31,455	493.6	1.0	2,109,248
South Dakota	237	1.0	2,415	0.6	10	58.4	24,196	402.5	0.8	1,698,215
North Dakota	224	1.0	2,863	0.7	13	76.9	26,847	347.5	0.7	1,551,147
Massachusetts	190	0.8	2,509	0.6	13	84.1	33,534	299.8	0.6	1,577,805
Alaska	41	0.2	941	0.2	23	41.7	44,351	297.1	0.6	7,245,780
Montana	137	0.6	1,693	0.4	12	41.7	24,631	268.0	0.5	1,955,861
Idaho	226	1.0	2,153	0.5	10	60.5	28,094	237.2	0.5	1,049,496
New Mexico	117	0.5	1,969	0.5	17	64.6	32,802	226.0	0.4	1,931,359
Maine	176	0.8	1,785	0.4	10	51.6	28,934	211.6	0.4	1,202,472
West Virginia	147	0.6	1,640	0.4	11	45.3	27,637	165.4	0.3	1,125,510
Connecticut	97	0.4	1,068	0.3	11	35.0	32,750	131.5	0.3	1,356,021
Wyoming	92	0.4	963	0.2	10	30.5	31,620	103.1	0.2	1,120,283
Nevada	83	0.4	833	0.2	10	25.9	31,128	92.4	0.2	1,113,048
New Hampshire	71	0.3	844	0.2	12	24.6	29,116	81.1	0.2	1,141,817
Delaware	65	0.3	742	0.2	11	20.8	28,051	76.0	0.1	1,169,431
Rhode Island	46	0.2	565	0.1	12	19.2	34,044	67.1	0.1	1,458,978
Vermont	70	0.3	659	0.2	9	17.3	26,320	62.5	0.1	892,657
Hawaii	16	0.1	175 *	-	-	(D)	-	(D)	-	-

Source: 1997 *Economic Census*. The states are in descending order of revenues or establishments (if revenue data are missing for the majority). The symbol (D) appears when data are withheld to prevent disclosure of competitive information. States marked with (D) are sorted by number of establishments. A dash (-) indicates that the data element cannot be calculated. * indicates the midpoint of a range; 175, for example is the range 100-249. Shaded *states* on the state map indicate those states which have proportionately greater representation in the industry than would be indicated by the state's population; the ratio is based on total revenues or number of establishments. Shaded *regions* indicate where the industry is regionally most concentrated.

NAICS 484122 - GENERAL FREIGHT TRUCKING, LONG-DISTANCE, LESS THAN TRUCKLOAD (LTL)

GENERAL STATISTICS

Year	Establishments (number)	Employment (number)	Payroll ($ million)	Revenues ($ million)	Employees per Establishment (number)	Revenues per Establishment ($)	Payroll per Employee ($)
1997	16	3,750*	(D)	(D)	-	-	-

Source: Economic Census of the United States, 1997. This is a newly defined industry. Data for prior years were unavailable at the time of publication but may become available over time.

SIC INDUSTRIES RELATED TO NAICS 484122

SIC	Industry	1990	1991	1992	1993	1994	1995	1996	1997
4213	**Trucking, Except Local***								
	Establishments (number)	39,589e	40,205e	40,821	41,437p	42,053p	42,668p	43,284p	43,900p
	Employment (thousands)	748.5e	753.5e	758.4	763.4p	768.4p	773.4p	778.3p	783.3p
	Revenues ($ million)	74,465.0	73,982.0	78,357.5	81,317.0	89,369.0	91,675.0	97,586.0	103,847.0

Source: Economic Census of the United States, 1992, annual surveys of economic sectors conducted by the Bureau of the Census, and estimates or projections based on the 1982-1992 period; not all data are shown. 'e' marks estimates made by the editors; 'p' indicates projections based on time series. A dash (-) indicates that data for this SIC or year were not available. * Indicates that only a portion of this industry is present within the NAICS data. If no * is shown, the entire industry is contained within the NAICS data.

INDICES OF CHANGE

Year	Establishments (number)	Employment (number)	Payroll ($ million)	Revenues ($ million)	Employees per Establishment (number)	Revenues per Establishment ($)	Payroll per Employee ($)
1997	100.0	100.0	-	-	-	-	-

Sources: Same as General Statistics. The values shown reflect change from the base year, 1997. Values above 100 mean greater than 1997, values below 100 mean less than 1997, and a value of 100 in years other than 1997 means same as 1997. Indices are calculated only for Census years. Data are the most recent available at this level of detail.

SELECTED RATIOS

For 1997	Avg. of Sector	Analyzed Industry	Index	For 1997	Avg. of Sector	Analyzed Industry	Index
Employees per establishment	16	234	1,429	Payroll per establishment	462,554	na	na
Revenue per establishment	1,787,642	na	na	Payroll as % of revenue	26	na	na
Revenue per employee	108,959	na	na	Payroll per employee	28,193	na	na

Sources: Same as General Statistics. The 'Average of Sector' column represents the average for all industries in this sector. The Index shows the relationship between the Average and the Analyzed Industry. For example, 100 means that they are equal; 500 that the Analyzed Industry is five times the average; 50 means that the Analyzed Industry is half the national average. 'na' is used to show that data are 'not available'.

LEADING COMPANIES Number shown: **75**   Total sales ($ mil): **119,857**   Total employment (000): **748.6**

Company Name	Address				CEO Name	Phone	Co. Type	Sales ($ mil)	Empl. (000)
FedEx Corp.	6075 Poplar Ave	Memphis	TN	38119	Fredrick W Smith	901-369-3600	P	16,774	141.0
Union Pacific Corp.	1416 Dodge St	Omaha	NE	68179	Richard K Davidson	401-271-5000	P	11,273	65.0
CSX Corp.	PO Box 85629	Richmond	VA	23219	John Snow	804-782-1400	P	10,811	46.1
Coastal Corp.	9 E Greenway Plz	Houston	TX	77046		713-877-1400	P	7,368	13.2
CNF Transportation Inc.	3240 Hillview Ave	Palo Alto	CA	94304	Gregory L Quesnel	650-494-2900	P	5,593	33.7
Norfolk Southern Corp.	3 Commercial Pl	Norfolk	VA	23510	David R Goode	757-629-2600	P	5,195	24.3
Yellow Corp.	PO Box 7563	Overland Park	KS	66207	William Zollars	913-696-6100	P	3,227	29.7
Roadway Express Inc.	PO Box 471	Akron	OH	44309	James D Staley	330-384-1717	P	2,813	28.0
United Van Lines Inc.	1 United Dr	Fenton	MO	63026	Robert J Baer	314-326-3100	S	2,742*	1.8
Schneider National Inc.	P O Box 2545	Green Bay	WI	54306	Donald J Schneider	920-592-5100	R	2,510	16.5
Consolidated Freightways Corp.	175 Linfield Dr	Menlo Park	CA	94025	Patrick H Blake	650-326-1700	P	2,379	21.0
Yellow Freight System Inc.	P O Box 7563	Overland Park	KS	66207	William D Zollars	913-344-3000	S	2,330*	24.0
Consolidated Freightways	175 Linfield Dr	Menlo Park	CA	94025	W Roger Curry	650-326-1700	S	2,238	21.0
USFreightways Corp.	9700 Higgins Rd	Rosemont	IL	60018	J Campbell Carruth	847-696-0200	P	2,222	19.2
J.B. Hunt Transport Services Inc.	PO Box 130	Lowell	AR	72745	Kirk Thompson	501-820-0000	P	2,045	14.2
UniGroup Inc.	1 United Dr	Fenton	MO	63026	Robert J Baer	636-305-5000	R	1,800	1.6
CGB Enterprises Inc.	P O Box 249	Mandeville	LA	70470	Richard Wilcox	504-867-3500	R	1,800	0.9
Arkansas Best Corp.	PO Box 10048	Fort Smith	AR	72917	Robert A Young III	501-785-6000	P	1,722	14.8
Landstar System Holdings Inc.	4160 Woockock Dr	Jacksonville	FL	32207	Jeffrey C Crowe	904-390-1234	S	1,313	2.0
ABF Freight System Inc.	PO Box 10048	Fort Smith	AR	72917	Robert Young III	501-785-8700	S	1,311*	14.0
Plains Resources Inc.	500 Dallas St	Houston	TX	77002	Greg L Armstrong	713-654-1414	P	1,293	0.4
Landstar System Inc.	4160 Woodcock Dr	Jacksonville	FL	32207	Jeffrey C Crowe	904-390-1234	P	1,284	1.3
Leprino Foods Co.	PO Box 173400	Denver	CO	80217	Wes Allen	303-480-2605	R	1,250	2.5
Arkansas Best Holdings Corp.	PO Box 10048	Fort Smith	AR	72917	Robert A Young III	501-785-6000	S	1,225*	13.1
Navajo L.T.L. Inc.	PO Box 5002	Commerce City	CO	80037	David Congdon		S	1,170*	6.0
American Freightways Corp.	2200 Forward Dr	Harrison	AR	72601	F Sheridan Garrison	870-741-9000	P	1,167	13.2
Lykes Bros. Inc.	PO Box 1690	Tampa	FL	33601		813-223-3981	R	1,100	3.0
Werner Enterprises Inc.	P O Box 45308	Omaha	NE	68145	Clarence L Werner	402-895-6640	P	1,052	8.9
Allied Holdings Inc.	160 Clairmont Ave	Decatur	GA	30030	Robert J Rutland	404-373-4285	P	1,027	8.5
EOTT Energy Corp.	P O Box 4666	Houston	TX	77210	Michael Burke	713-993-5000	S	912*	1.4
Swift Transportation Inc.	PO Box 29243	Phoenix	AZ	85038	Jerry C Moyes	602-269-9700	S	873	9.6
Sparks Finance Co.	1455 Hulda Way	Sparks	NV	89431	Jerry C Moyes	702-359-9031	P	873*	9.6
Overnite Transportation Co.	P O Box 1216	Richmond	VA	23218	Leo Suggs	804-231-8000	S	836*	13.0
Watkins Associated Industries Inc.	P O Box 1738	Atlanta	GA	30371	William Freeman	404-872-3841	R	800	8.5
Mark VII Inc.	965 Ridge Lake	Memphis	TN	38120	RC Matney	901-767-4455	P	725	0.4
Atlas World Group Inc.	1212 St George Rd	Evansville	IN	47711	Wally E Saubert	812-424-4326	R	689*	0.8
USF Holland Inc.	750 E 40th St	Holland	MI	49423	Peter B Neydon	616-392-3101	S	654*	7.5
Watkins Motor Lines Inc.	P O Box 95002	Lakeland	FL	33804	John F Watkins	941-687-4545	R	650*	10.0
North American Van Lines Inc.	PO Box 988	Fort Wayne	IN	46801	Barry Uber	219-429-2511	R	634*	2.4
General Electric Capital Fleet	3 Capital Dr	Eden Prairie	MN	55344	Rick Smith	612-828-1000	S	627*	2.2
M.S. Carriers Inc.	P O Box 30788	Memphis	TN	38130	Michael S Starnes	901-332-2500	P	620	3.3
U.S. Express	4080 Jenkins Rd	Chattanooga	TN	37421	Max Fuller	423-510-3000	P	581	8.0
AMCOL International Corp.	1500 W Shure Dr	Arlington H.	IL	60004	John Hughes	847-394-8730	P	552	1.6
Giant Industries Inc.	PO Box 12999	Scottsdale	AZ	85267	James E Acridge	602-585-8888	P	526	2.7
U.S. Xpress Inc.	1535 New Hope	Tunnel Hill	GA	30755	William K Farris	706-673-6592	P	513	5.6
Atlas Van Lines Inc.	1212 St George Rd	Evansville	IN	47711	Dick Arneson	812-424-4326	S	490*	0.6
Lynch Corp.	401 Theodore Fremd	Rye	NY	10580	Mario J Gabelli	914-921-7601	P	468	1.9
Acme Truck Line Inc.	P O Box 183	Harvey	LA	70059	Doyle Coatney	504-368-2510	R	466*	1.6
Estes Express Lines Inc.	P O Box 25612	Richmond	VA	23260		804-232-6793	R	442*	6.5
Landstar Inway Inc.	PO Box 7013	Rockford	IL	61125	Jeff Pundt	815-972-6902	S	430	0.4
Old Dominion Freight Line Inc.	PO Box 2006	High Point	NC	27262	David S Congdon	336-889-5000	P	426	5.3
Triple Crown Services Co.	2720 Dupont	Fort Wayne	IN	46825	Dan Cushman	219-434-3600	S	410*	0.3
Customized Transportation Inc.	PO Box 40083	Jacksonville	FL	32203	David Kulik	904-928-1400	S	409	3.8
Arnold Industries Inc.	P O Box 11963	Lebanon	PA	17042	EH Arnold	717-273-9058	P	404*	1.5
Quality Distribution Inc.	3802 Corporex Dr	Tampa	FL	33619	Jack Elrod	813-630-5826	R	398	2.5
Comet Transport Inc.	3880 Salem Lake Dr	Long Grove	IL	60047	Douglas Christanson	847-726-4500	R	394*	2.0
Centra Inc.	12225 Stephen Rd	Warren	MI	48089	Matty J Moroun	810-939-7000	R	389*	2.0
Dart Transit Company Inc.	P O Box 64110	St. Paul	MN	55164	Donald Oren	612-688-2000	R	386*	0.6
Southeastern Freight Lines Inc.	PO Box 2104	West Columbia	SC	29171		803-794-7300	R	377*	4.7
A A A Cooper Transportation	PO Box 6827	Dothan	AL	36302	G Mack Dove	334-793-2284	R	367	4.3
Celadon Trucking Services Inc.	9503 East 33rd St	Indianapolis	IN	46235	Stephen Russell	317-972-7000	S	352*	1.8
Frozen Food Express Industries	PO Box 655888	Dallas	TX	75265	Stoney M Stubbs Jr	214-630-8090	P	350	2.6
Cassens Corp.	PO Box 468	Edwardsville	IL	62025	Albert Cassens	618-656-3006	R	331*	1.7
CRST International Inc.	PO Box 68	Cedar Rapids	IA	52406	John M Smith	319-396-4400	R	330	3.7
Trism Specialized Carriers	P O Box 9000	Kennesaw	GA	30144	Ed McCormick	770-795-4700	S	330	2.0
C.R. England Inc.	4701 W 2100 South	Salt Lake City	UT	84120	Dan England		R	320	4.1
Mayflower Transit Inc.	PO Box 26150	Fenton	MO	63026	John J Temporiti	314-305-4000	S	311*	0.5
Saia Motor Freight Line Inc.	P O Box A, Sta 1	Houma	LA	70363	Jimmy D Crisp	504-868-1030	S	305*	4.5
TRISM Inc.	P O Box 9000	Kennesaw	GA	30144	Edward L McCormick	770-795-4600	P	292	2.5
Transport Corporation of America	1769 Yankee Doodle	Eagan	MN	55121	Robert J Meyers	651-686-2500	P	286	1.2
Celadon Group Inc.	9503 E 33rd St	Indianapolis	IN	46235	Stepen Russell	317-972-7000	P	282	2.1
Intrenet Inc.	400 TechneCenter	Milford	OH	45150	John P Delavan	513-576-6666	P	263	1.9
Heartland Express Inc.	2777 Heartland Dr	Coralville	IA	52241	Russell A Gerdin	319-645-2728	P	261	1.2
Contract Freighters Inc.	P O Box 2547	Joplin	MO	64803	Glenn Brown	417-623-5229	R	250	2.5
Burlington Motor Carriers Inc.	14611 W Commerce	Daleville	IN	47334	Ralph Arthur	765-378-0261	R	240	3.0

Source: Ward's Business Directory of U.S. Private and Public Companies, Volumes 1 and 2, 2000. The company type code used is as follows: P - Public, R - Private, S - Subsidiary, D - Division, J - Joint Venture, A - Affiliate, G - Group, N - Company type not reported. Sales are in millions of dollars, employees are in thousands. An asterisk (*) indicates an estimated sales volume. The symbol < stands for 'less than'. Company names and addresses are truncated, in some cases, to fit into the available space.

LOCATION BY STATE AND REGIONAL CONCENTRATION

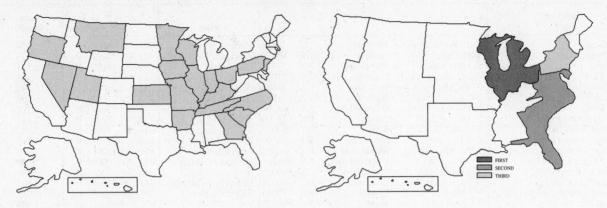

FIRST
SECOND
THIRD

INDUSTRY DATA BY STATE

State	Establishments Total (number)	% of U.S.	Employment Total (number)	% of U.S.	Per Estab.	Payroll Total ($ mil.)	Per Empl. ($)	Revenues Total ($ mil.)	% of U.S.	Per Estab. ($)
California	456	7.3	19,125	7.4	42	702.0	36,707	2,307.4	9.2	5,060,145
Illinois	313	5.0	16,590	6.4	53	670.8	40,436	1,643.6	6.6	5,251,249
Texas	426	6.9	18,004	7.0	42	614.3	34,119	1,639.2	6.6	3,847,969
Ohio	275	4.4	14,764	5.7	54	612.5	41,489	1,376.2	5.5	5,004,218
New Jersey	184	3.0	11,566	4.5	63	463.1	40,041	1,228.4	4.9	6,676,082
Pennsylvania	242	3.9	15,264	5.9	63	591.9	38,781	1,223.7	4.9	5,056,479
North Carolina	264	4.3	15,150	5.9	57	512.5	33,828	1,152.0	4.6	4,363,572
Tennessee	211	3.4	13,738	5.3	65	532.7	38,777	1,111.7	4.4	5,268,630
Georgia	210	3.4	13,369	5.2	64	479.6	35,871	1,089.3	4.4	5,187,276
Indiana	201	3.2	8,055	3.1	40	299.5	37,187	978.9	3.9	4,869,920
Florida	218	3.5	8,507	3.3	39	279.8	32,895	863.6	3.5	3,961,514
Michigan	200	3.2	6,918	2.7	35	277.0	40,047	854.5	3.4	4,272,355
New York	206	3.3	7,588	2.9	37	306.0	40,322	817.9	3.3	3,970,248
Wisconsin	217	3.5	5,137	2.0	24	180.7	35,181	668.1	2.7	3,078,700
Missouri	198	3.2	7,333	2.8	37	276.7	37,740	614.2	2.5	3,101,899
Massachusetts	104	1.7	3,852	1.5	37	149.8	38,887	483.7	1.9	4,651,010
Arkansas	101	1.6	6,068	2.3	60	197.1	32,489	478.3	1.9	4,735,950
Virginia	139	2.2	4,761	1.8	34	169.3	35,556	465.4	1.9	3,348,043
Minnesota	128	2.1	3,708	1.4	29	144.5	38,972	458.5	1.8	3,582,047
Kentucky	95	1.5	3,678	1.4	39	131.5	35,759	421.1	1.7	4,433,084
Washington	127	2.0	3,129	1.2	25	113.7	36,328	414.6	1.7	3,264,654
Oregon	101	1.6	4,740	1.8	47	175.1	36,932	387.1	1.5	3,832,347
South Carolina	112	1.8	4,877	1.9	44	166.8	34,192	371.4	1.5	3,316,438
Alabama	127	2.0	3,947	1.5	31	124.4	31,518	365.9	1.5	2,881,189
Maryland	67	1.1	2,995	1.2	45	118.8	39,663	341.2	1.4	5,092,418
Colorado	106	1.7	3,797	1.5	36	142.9	37,629	325.1	1.3	3,066,830
Iowa	133	2.1	3,624	1.4	27	116.1	32,048	288.9	1.2	2,172,180
Arizona	85	1.4	2,712	1.0	32	90.9	33,511	255.1	1.0	3,001,235
Louisiana	108	1.7	3,101	1.2	29	88.7	28,596	240.1	1.0	2,222,991
Kansas	80	1.3	2,870	1.1	36	102.7	35,790	239.6	1.0	2,994,563
Oklahoma	89	1.4	2,676	1.0	30	84.1	31,410	236.5	0.9	2,657,663
Utah	46	0.7	2,772	1.1	60	93.9	33,875	228.6	0.9	4,968,978
Mississippi	98	1.6	3,085	1.2	31	106.4	34,501	223.4	0.9	2,279,735
Connecticut	49	0.8	1,773	0.7	36	72.4	40,842	198.7	0.8	4,056,041
Nevada	48	0.8	1,395	0.5	29	47.3	33,938	182.7	0.7	3,806,479
Nebraska	59	1.0	1,296	0.5	22	44.9	34,633	133.9	0.5	2,270,017
Montana	39	0.6	990	0.4	25	27.4	27,725	101.1	0.4	2,591,949
New Hampshire	26	0.4	544	0.2	21	19.2	35,296	62.9	0.3	2,417,385
Idaho	40	0.6	618	0.2	15	17.8	28,822	60.8	0.2	1,519,350
Maine	38	0.6	490	0.2	13	18.0	36,712	57.8	0.2	1,521,500
Rhode Island	20	0.3	494	0.2	25	17.6	35,565	55.9	0.2	2,794,950
Vermont	29	0.5	589	0.2	20	18.2	30,956	55.4	0.2	1,910,655
Alaska	11	0.2	388	0.1	35	12.7	32,856	52.2	0.2	4,744,818
New Mexico	40	0.6	778	0.3	19	31.9	40,981	50.9	0.2	1,273,475
North Dakota	43	0.7	673	0.3	16	17.0	25,212	49.7	0.2	1,156,209
West Virginia	28	0.5	571	0.2	20	18.7	32,681	49.1	0.2	1,752,464
Delaware	14	0.2	284	0.1	20	11.6	40,835	41.7	0.2	2,981,643
South Dakota	36	0.6	433	0.2	12	15.2	34,998	38.6	0.2	1,073,306
Wyoming	12	0.2	60*	-	-	(D)	-	(D)	-	-
Hawaii	10	0.2	60*	-	-	(D)	-	(D)	-	-

Source: 1997 *Economic Census*. The states are in descending order of revenues or establishments (if revenue data are missing for the majority). The symbol (D) appears when data are withheld to prevent disclosure of competitive information. States marked with (D) are sorted by number of establishments. A dash (-) indicates that the data element cannot be calculated. * indicates the midpoint of a range; 175, for example is the range 100-249. Shaded *states* on the state map indicate those states which have proportionately greater representation in the industry than would be indicated by the state's population; the ratio is based on total revenues or number of establishments. Shaded *regions* indicate where the industry is regionally most concentrated.

NAICS 484210 - USED HOUSEHOLD AND OFFICE GOODS MOVING

GENERAL STATISTICS

Year	Establishments (number)	Employment (number)	Payroll ($ million)	Revenues ($ million)	Employees per Establishment (number)	Revenues per Establishment ($)	Payroll per Employee ($)
1997	542	27,448	744.4	1,152.5	50.6	2,126,384	27,120

Source: *Economic Census of the United States*, 1997. This is a newly defined industry. Data for prior years were unavailable at the time of publication but may become available over time.

SIC INDUSTRIES RELATED TO NAICS 484210

SIC	Industry	1990	1991	1992	1993	1994	1995	1996	1997
4212	**Local Trucking Without Storage***								
	Establishments (number)	48,279e	49,075e	49,870	50,665p	51,461p	52,256p	53,052p	53,847p
	Employment (thousands)	332.7e	343.7e	354.7	365.7p	376.7p	387.7p	398.7p	409.7p
	Revenues ($ million)	31,397.0	30,890.0	33,554.4	36,648.0	40,903.0	43,830.0	46,589.0	49,972.0
4213	**Trucking, Except Local***								
	Establishments (number)	39,589e	40,205e	40,821	41,437p	42,053p	42,668p	43,284p	43,900p
	Employment (thousands)	748.5e	753.5e	758.4	763.4p	768.4p	773.4p	778.3p	783.3p
	Revenues ($ million)	74,465.0	73,982.0	78,357.5	81,317.0	89,369.0	91,675.0	97,586.0	103,847.0
4214	**Local Trucking With Storage***								
	Establishments (number)	5,029e	4,770e	4,512	4,254p	3,995p	3,737p	3,478p	3,220p
	Employment (thousands)	67.6e	66.0e	64.4	62.8p	61.2p	59.6p	58.0p	56.4p
	Revenues ($ million)	4,115.0	4,022.0	4,190.7	4,487.0	4,757.0	5,154.0	5,502.0	5,860.0

Source: *Economic Census of the United States*, 1992, annual surveys of economic sectors conducted by the Bureau of the Census, and estimates or projections based on the 1982-1992 period; not all data are shown. 'e' marks estimates made by the editors; 'p' indicates projections based on time series. A dash (-) indicates that data for this SIC or year were not available. * Indicates that only a portion of this industry is present within the NAICS data. If no * is shown, the entire industry is contained within the NAICS data.

INDICES OF CHANGE

Year	Establishments (number)	Employment (number)	Payroll ($ million)	Revenues ($ million)	Employees per Establishment (number)	Revenues per Establishment ($)	Payroll per Employee ($)
1997	100.0	100.0	100.0	100.0	100.0	100.0	100.0

Sources: Same as General Statistics. The values shown reflect change from the base year, 1997. Values above 100 mean greater than 1997, values below 100 mean less than 1997, and a value of 100 in years other than 1997 means same as 1997. Indices are calculated only for Census years. Data are the most recent available at this level of detail.

SELECTED RATIOS

For 1997	Avg. of Sector	Analyzed Industry	Index	For 1997	Avg. of Sector	Analyzed Industry	Index
Employees per establishment	16	51	309	Payroll per establishment	462,554	1,373,432	297
Revenue per establishment	1,787,642	2,126,384	119	Payroll as % of revenue	26	65	250
Revenue per employee	108,959	41,988	39	Payroll per employee	28,193	27,120	96

Sources: Same as General Statistics. The 'Average of Sector' column represents the average for all industries in this sector. The Index shows the relationship between the Average and the Analyzed Industry. For example, 100 means that they are equal; 500 that the Analyzed Industry is five times the average; 50 means that the Analyzed Industry is half the national average. 'na' is used to show that data are 'not available'.

LEADING COMPANIES
No company data available for this industry.

LOCATION BY STATE AND REGIONAL CONCENTRATION

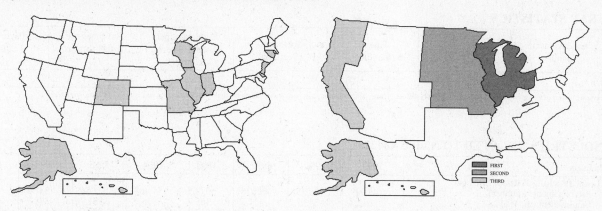

FIRST
SECOND
THIRD

INDUSTRY DATA BY STATE

State	Establishments Total (number)	Establishments % of U.S.	Employment Total (number)	Employment % of U.S.	Employment Per Estab.	Payroll Total ($ mil.)	Payroll Per Empl. ($)	Revenues Total ($ mil.)	Revenues % of U.S.	Revenues Per Estab. ($)
Missouri	245	2.7	4,166	3.4	17	92.2	22,131	1,718.2	13.7	7,012,980
Indiana	178	2.0	6,307	5.2	35	190.8	30,248	1,507.0	12.0	8,466,354
California	1,206	13.3	14,348	11.8	12	348.9	24,314	1,228.9	9.8	1,018,989
Illinois	396	4.4	5,671	4.7	14	163.5	28,829	1,162.3	9.2	2,935,020
Texas	618	6.8	8,429	6.9	14	183.0	21,715	638.8	5.1	1,033,623
New York	620	6.8	7,536	6.2	12	163.5	21,694	503.8	4.0	812,518
New Jersey	390	4.3	4,709	3.9	12	132.6	28,151	413.2	3.3	1,059,569
Florida	599	6.6	5,032	4.1	8	103.4	20,543	380.6	3.0	635,331
Wisconsin	189	2.1	2,216	1.8	12	61.2	27,625	355.7	2.8	1,882,106
Virginia	267	2.9	4,659	3.8	17	110.4	23,688	308.8	2.5	1,156,367
Ohio	275	3.0	4,019	3.3	15	97.6	24,280	305.1	2.4	1,109,484
Pennsylvania	301	3.3	4,017	3.3	13	101.8	25,346	300.0	2.4	996,701
Georgia	223	2.5	3,521	2.9	16	87.6	24,870	278.3	2.2	1,247,991
North Carolina	289	3.2	3,907	3.2	14	90.0	23,028	251.0	2.0	868,637
Washington	227	2.5	3,064	2.5	13	76.6	25,012	248.4	2.0	1,094,427
Massachusetts	262	2.9	3,228	2.7	12	86.4	26,758	242.9	1.9	927,229
Michigan	225	2.5	2,843	2.3	13	82.2	28,911	242.0	1.9	1,075,422
Maryland	204	2.2	3,677	3.0	18	75.0	20,410	227.2	1.8	1,113,505
Connecticut	143	1.6	1,910	1.6	13	58.9	30,815	205.5	1.6	1,436,965
Colorado	165	1.8	2,467	2.0	15	64.4	26,103	172.2	1.4	1,043,448
Minnesota	144	1.6	1,622	1.3	11	43.5	26,834	168.5	1.3	1,170,208
Tennessee	152	1.7	1,831	1.5	12	43.2	23,573	141.2	1.1	929,270
Rhode Island	46	0.5	526	0.4	11	14.3	27,135	124.4	1.0	2,704,109
Arizona	141	1.5	2,110	1.7	15	42.7	20,218	120.1	1.0	851,723
Iowa	108	1.2	1,445	1.2	13	31.9	22,107	111.8	0.9	1,035,157
Kentucky	95	1.0	1,230	1.0	13	24.8	20,163	98.6	0.8	1,038,189
Kansas	86	0.9	1,549	1.3	18	30.9	19,928	98.0	0.8	1,139,302
Oregon	83	0.9	1,215	1.0	15	31.7	26,059	82.8	0.7	997,747
Oklahoma	90	1.0	1,082	0.9	12	23.9	22,065	77.1	0.6	856,322
South Carolina	102	1.1	1,402	1.2	14	29.9	21,325	76.9	0.6	753,657
Alabama	134	1.5	1,423	1.2	11	27.4	19,250	74.3	0.6	554,679
Louisiana	91	1.0	1,185	1.0	13	21.1	17,842	69.5	0.6	763,538
Hawaii	25	0.3	888	0.7	36	27.7	31,238	65.9	0.5	2,637,200
Nebraska	79	0.9	735	0.6	9	15.3	20,782	61.5	0.5	778,620
Alaska	45	0.5	600	0.5	13	17.0	28,250	49.8	0.4	1,107,667
Utah	45	0.5	743	0.6	17	15.7	21,194	49.2	0.4	1,092,578
Mississippi	65	0.7	663	0.5	10	14.9	22,424	47.4	0.4	728,815
Nevada	37	0.4	593	0.5	16	15.2	25,567	44.9	0.4	1,213,054
Maine	40	0.4	497	0.4	12	11.8	23,730	40.5	0.3	1,012,150
New Hampshire	48	0.5	493	0.4	10	10.8	21,856	38.2	0.3	796,479
Delaware	31	0.3	597	0.5	19	13.1	22,007	36.5	0.3	1,176,742
Montana	39	0.4	352	0.3	9	6.8	19,312	34.2	0.3	877,103
New Mexico	55	0.6	528	0.4	10	10.4	19,614	32.3	0.3	587,545
Idaho	47	0.5	409	0.3	9	9.1	22,318	30.2	0.2	641,702
Arkansas	75	0.8	560	0.5	7	8.7	15,620	30.1	0.2	400,787
West Virginia	52	0.6	383	0.3	7	7.1	18,601	21.3	0.2	409,385
North Dakota	35	0.4	291	0.2	8	5.5	18,777	17.3	0.1	494,486
South Dakota	30	0.3	244	0.2	8	5.4	22,189	14.7	0.1	489,700
Wyoming	24	0.3	224	0.2	9	4.3	19,098	14.3	0.1	596,292
Vermont	25	0.3	175*	-	-	(D)	-	(D)	-	-
D.C.	9	0.1	175*	-	-	(D)	-	(D)	-	-

Source: 1997 *Economic Census*. The states are in descending order of revenues or establishments (if revenue data are missing for the majority). The symbol (D) appears when data are withheld to prevent disclosure of competitive information. States marked with (D) are sorted by number of establishments. A dash (-) indicates that the data element cannot be calculated. * indicates the midpoint of a range; 175, for example is the range 100-249. Shaded *states* on the state map indicate those states which have proportionately greater representation in the industry than would be indicated by the state's population; the ratio is based on total revenues or number of establishments. Shaded *regions* indicate where the industry is regionally most concentrated.

371

NAICS 484220 - SPECIALIZED FREIGHT (EXCEPT USED GOODS) TRUCKING, LOCAL

GENERAL STATISTICS

Year	Establishments (number)	Employment (number)	Payroll ($ million)	Revenues ($ million)	Employees per Establishment (number)	Revenues per Establishment ($)	Payroll per Employee ($)
1997	32	750*	(D)	(D)	-	-	-

Source: Economic Census of the United States, 1997. This is a newly defined industry. Data for prior years were unavailable at the time of publication but may become available over time.

SIC INDUSTRIES RELATED TO NAICS 484220

SIC	Industry	1990	1991	1992	1993	1994	1995	1996	1997
4212	**Local Trucking Without Storage***								
	Establishments (number)	48,279e	49,075e	49,870	50,665p	51,461p	52,256p	53,052p	53,847p
	Employment (thousands)	332.7e	343.7e	354.7	365.7p	376.7p	387.7p	398.7p	409.7p
	Revenues ($ million)	31,397.0	30,890.0	33,554.4	36,648.0	40,903.0	43,830.0	46,589.0	49,972.0
4214	**Local Trucking With Storage***								
	Establishments (number)	5,029e	4,770e	4,512	4,254p	3,995p	3,737p	3,478p	3,220p
	Employment (thousands)	67.6e	66.0e	64.4	62.8p	61.2p	59.6p	58.0p	56.4p
	Revenues ($ million)	4,115.0	4,022.0	4,190.7	4,487.0	4,757.0	5,154.0	5,502.0	5,860.0

Source: Economic Census of the United States, 1992, annual surveys of economic sectors conducted by the Bureau of the Census, and estimates or projections based on the 1982-1992 period; not all data are shown. 'e' marks estimates made by the editors; 'p' indicates projections based on time series. A dash (-) indicates that data for this SIC or year were not available. * Indicates that only a portion of this industry is present within the NAICS data. If no * is shown, the entire industry is contained within the NAICS data.

INDICES OF CHANGE

Year	Establishments (number)	Employment (number)	Payroll ($ million)	Revenues ($ million)	Employees per Establishment (number)	Revenues per Establishment ($)	Payroll per Employee ($)
1997	100.0	100.0	-	-	-	-	-

Sources: Same as General Statistics. The values shown reflect change from the base year, 1997. Values above 100 mean greater than 1997, values below 100 mean less than 1997, and a value of 100 in years other than 1997 means same as 1997. Indices are calculated only for Census years. Data are the most recent available at this level of detail.

SELECTED RATIOS

For 1997	Avg. of Sector	Analyzed Industry	Index	For 1997	Avg. of Sector	Analyzed Industry	Index
Employees per establishment	16	23	143	Payroll per establishment	462,554	na	na
Revenue per establishment	1,787,642	na	na	Payroll as % of revenue	26	na	na
Revenue per employee	108,959	na	na	Payroll per employee	28,193	na	na

Sources: Same as General Statistics. The 'Average of Sector' column represents the average for all industries in this sector. The Index shows the relationship between the Average and the Analyzed Industry. For example, 100 means that they are equal; 500 that the Analyzed Industry is five times the average; 50 means that the Analyzed Industry is half the national average. 'na' is used to show that data are 'not available'.

LEADING COMPANIES

No company data available for this industry.

LOCATION BY STATE AND REGIONAL CONCENTRATION

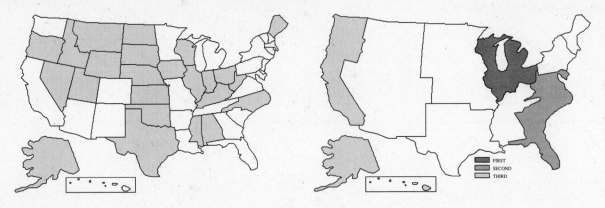

INDUSTRY DATA BY STATE

State	Establishments Total (number)	Establishments % of U.S.	Employment Total (number)	Employment % of U.S.	Employment Per Estab.	Payroll Total ($ mil.)	Payroll Per Empl. ($)	Revenues Total ($ mil.)	Revenues % of U.S.	Revenues Per Estab. ($)
California	2,805	7.9	20,472	10.9	7	544.1	26,578	2,354.2	11.9	839,291
Texas	2,158	6.1	14,790	7.9	7	362.8	24,533	1,523.7	7.7	706,077
Illinois	1,781	5.0	8,451	4.5	5	251.3	29,735	1,040.2	5.3	584,081
Ohio	1,613	4.5	7,786	4.1	5	209.6	26,918	1,030.9	5.2	639,099
New York	1,380	3.9	8,515	4.5	6	228.9	26,885	831.6	4.2	602,632
Pennsylvania	1,371	3.9	7,673	4.1	6	193.8	25,263	796.9	4.0	581,233
Michigan	992	2.8	5,655	3.0	6	201.3	35,592	729.5	3.7	735,369
Florida	1,161	3.3	6,306	3.4	5	145.4	23,051	718.2	3.6	618,581
Indiana	926	2.6	6,323	3.4	7	176.1	27,852	689.1	3.5	744,217
New Jersey	934	2.6	5,432	2.9	6	166.9	30,716	600.6	3.0	643,073
Wisconsin	1,415	4.0	5,386	2.9	4	146.6	27,220	562.5	2.9	397,551
North Carolina	1,206	3.4	6,497	3.5	5	156.0	24,009	560.3	2.8	464,601
Kentucky	1,095	3.1	5,665	3.0	5	122.8	21,670	515.7	2.6	471,005
Georgia	944	2.7	5,299	2.8	6	120.9	22,815	480.6	2.4	509,147
Virginia	1,268	3.6	5,743	3.1	5	126.3	21,984	477.9	2.4	376,882
West Virginia	621	1.8	4,307	2.3	7	102.5	23,795	404.3	2.1	651,011
Missouri	924	2.6	3,937	2.1	4	88.5	22,484	401.8	2.0	434,834
Washington	750	2.1	3,278	1.7	4	89.8	27,387	356.6	1.8	475,517
Alabama	744	2.1	3,604	1.9	5	70.2	19,466	351.4	1.8	472,257
Massachusetts	522	1.5	2,544	1.4	5	66.9	26,278	335.8	1.7	643,333
Minnesota	817	2.3	2,781	1.5	3	65.2	23,462	330.9	1.7	405,031
Tennessee	661	1.9	3,598	1.9	5	75.1	20,864	320.8	1.6	485,356
Maryland	624	1.8	3,482	1.9	6	78.8	22,639	312.2	1.6	500,316
Louisiana	713	2.0	3,464	1.8	5	69.3	20,010	291.7	1.5	409,184
Oregon	723	2.0	2,866	1.5	4	70.8	24,696	289.7	1.5	400,651
Oklahoma	431	1.2	2,664	1.4	6	60.3	22,652	248.3	1.3	576,035
Iowa	717	2.0	2,365	1.3	3	48.3	20,442	236.0	1.2	329,216
Colorado	455	1.3	2,277	1.2	5	60.4	26,545	229.9	1.2	505,310
Mississippi	637	1.8	2,570	1.4	4	49.2	19,125	225.9	1.1	354,615
South Carolina	348	1.0	2,429	1.3	7	56.3	23,199	224.0	1.1	643,807
Kansas	551	1.6	2,258	1.2	4	49.9	22,096	221.3	1.1	401,666
Arizona	376	1.1	2,402	1.3	6	56.7	23,604	215.0	1.1	571,691
Arkansas	580	1.6	1,902	1.0	3	36.2	19,023	179.0	0.9	308,671
Utah	214	0.6	1,418	0.8	7	44.0	31,024	162.8	0.8	760,949
Alaska	68	0.2	853	0.5	13	51.2	60,019	157.0	0.8	2,309,235
Nebraska	411	1.2	1,423	0.8	3	28.6	20,128	139.2	0.7	338,640
Maine	361	1.0	1,247	0.7	3	28.7	23,010	136.4	0.7	377,776
Idaho	338	1.0	1,453	0.8	4	32.7	22,538	136.2	0.7	403,006
Connecticut	232	0.7	1,019	0.5	4	33.6	32,965	124.2	0.6	535,198
Nevada	125	0.4	1,104	0.6	9	30.1	27,227	110.5	0.6	884,208
New Mexico	191	0.5	1,110	0.6	6	27.5	24,747	107.7	0.5	564,099
Montana	222	0.6	1,148	0.6	5	24.8	21,596	103.4	0.5	465,716
North Dakota	219	0.6	929	0.5	4	17.0	18,309	83.4	0.4	380,895
New Hampshire	155	0.4	631	0.3	4	16.1	25,479	79.6	0.4	513,568
South Dakota	186	0.5	609	0.3	3	13.9	22,854	65.9	0.3	354,559
Wyoming	128	0.4	537	0.3	4	13.5	25,101	56.6	0.3	442,086
Delaware	80	0.2	480	0.3	6	12.6	26,321	45.8	0.2	571,912
Vermont	125	0.4	375 *	-	-	(D)	-	(D)	-	-
Rhode Island	89	0.3	375 *	-	-	(D)	-	(D)	-	-
Hawaii	83	0.2	750 *	-	-	(D)	-	(D)	-	-
D.C.	8	-	60 *	-	-	(D)	-	(D)	-	-

Source: 1997 *Economic Census.* The states are in descending order of revenues or establishments (if revenue data are missing for the majority). The symbol (D) appears when data are withheld to prevent disclosure of competitive information. States marked with (D) are sorted by number of establishments. A dash (-) indicates that the data element cannot be calculated. * indicates the midpoint of a range; 175, for example is the range 100-249. Shaded *states* on the state map indicate those states which have proportionately greater representation in the industry than would be indicated by the state's population; the ratio is based on total revenues or number of establishments. Shaded *regions* indicate where the industry is regionally most concentrated.

NAICS 484230 - SPECIALIZED FREIGHT (EXCEPT USED GOODS) TRUCKING, LONG-DISTANCE

GENERAL STATISTICS

Year	Establishments (number)	Employment (number)	Payroll ($ million)	Revenues ($ million)	Employees per Establishment (number)	Revenues per Establishment ($)	Payroll per Employee ($)
1997	407	19,900	549.7	1,147.4	48.9	2,819,165	27,623

Source: Economic Census of the United States, 1997. This is a newly defined industry. Data for prior years were unavailable at the time of publication but may become available over time.

SIC INDUSTRIES RELATED TO NAICS 484230

SIC	Industry	1990	1991	1992	1993	1994	1995	1996	1997
4213	**Trucking, Except Local***								
	Establishments (number)	39,589e	40,205e	40,821	41,437p	42,053p	42,668p	43,284p	43,900p
	Employment (thousands)	748.5e	753.5e	758.4	763.4p	768.4p	773.4p	778.3p	783.3p
	Revenues ($ million)	74,465.0	73,982.0	78,357.5	81,317.0	89,369.0	91,675.0	97,586.0	103,847.0

Source: Economic Census of the United States, 1992, annual surveys of economic sectors conducted by the Bureau of the Census, and estimates or projections based on the 1982-1992 period; not all data are shown. 'e' marks estimates made by the editors; 'p' indicates projections based on time series. A dash (-) indicates that data for this SIC or year were not available. * Indicates that only a portion of this industry is present within the NAICS data. If no * is shown, the entire industry is contained within the NAICS data.

INDICES OF CHANGE

Year	Establishments (number)	Employment (number)	Payroll ($ million)	Revenues ($ million)	Employees per Establishment (number)	Revenues per Establishment ($)	Payroll per Employee ($)
1997	100.0	100.0	100.0	100.0	100.0	100.0	100.0

Sources: Same as General Statistics. The values shown reflect change from the base year, 1997. Values above 100 mean greater than 1997, values below 100 mean less than 1997, and a value of 100 in years other than 1997 means same as 1997. Indices are calculated only for Census years. Data are the most recent available at this level of detail.

SELECTED RATIOS

For 1997	Avg. of Sector	Analyzed Industry	Index	For 1997	Avg. of Sector	Analyzed Industry	Index
Employees per establishment	16	49	298	Payroll per establishment	462,554	1,350,614	292
Revenue per establishment	1,787,642	2,819,165	158	Payroll as % of revenue	26	48	185
Revenue per employee	108,959	57,658	53	Payroll per employee	28,193	27,623	98

Sources: Same as General Statistics. The 'Average of Sector' column represents the average for all industries in this sector. The Index shows the relationship between the Average and the Analyzed Industry. For example, 100 means that they are equal; 500 that the Analyzed Industry is five times the average; 50 means that the Analyzed Industry is half the national average. 'na' is used to show that data are 'not available'.

LEADING COMPANIES

No company data available for this industry.

LOCATION BY STATE AND REGIONAL CONCENTRATION

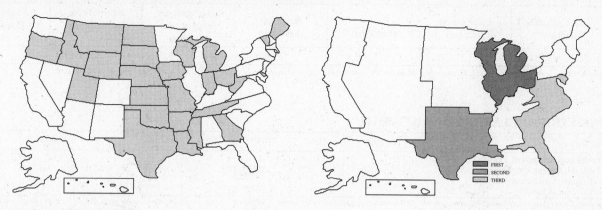

INDUSTRY DATA BY STATE

State	Establishments Total (number)	% of U.S.	Employment Total (number)	% of U.S.	Per Estab.	Payroll Total ($ mil.)	Per Empl. ($)	Revenues Total ($ mil.)	% of U.S.	Per Estab. ($)
Texas	1,127	7.8	17,609	10.7	16	510.2	28,973	2,409.8	11.8	2,138,282
California	894	6.2	11,140	6.8	12	355.1	31,880	1,394.5	6.8	1,559,849
Ohio	513	3.6	8,434	5.1	16	276.9	32,837	1,256.9	6.1	2,450,148
Florida	594	4.1	9,164	5.6	15	264.1	28,819	928.8	4.5	1,563,636
Pennsylvania	474	3.3	6,303	3.8	13	212.9	33,785	907.3	4.4	1,914,084
Georgia	382	2.6	8,998	5.5	24	251.4	27,937	856.0	4.2	2,240,846
Missouri	453	3.1	5,103	3.1	11	158.7	31,103	820.0	4.0	1,810,055
Michigan	405	2.8	5,411	3.3	13	243.9	45,078	807.9	3.9	1,994,844
Indiana	528	3.7	5,567	3.4	11	163.7	29,408	779.7	3.8	1,476,650
Illinois	590	4.1	5,239	3.2	9	182.8	34,892	694.4	3.4	1,176,905
Tennessee	312	2.2	4,375	2.7	14	156.6	35,789	598.9	2.9	1,919,436
New Jersey	328	2.3	4,404	2.7	13	159.0	36,103	572.9	2.8	1,746,616
Wisconsin	462	3.2	3,959	2.4	9	122.1	30,832	517.8	2.5	1,120,710
North Carolina	458	3.2	4,648	2.8	10	133.2	28,660	480.9	2.3	1,049,930
New York	382	2.6	3,947	2.4	10	118.4	29,988	424.8	2.1	1,112,092
Washington	393	2.7	3,846	2.3	10	117.1	30,454	402.0	2.0	1,022,896
Louisiana	313	2.2	3,178	1.9	10	96.8	30,466	386.5	1.9	1,234,885
Arkansas	286	2.0	3,369	2.0	12	88.6	26,291	380.9	1.9	1,331,657
Kansas	371	2.6	2,539	1.5	7	72.0	28,376	373.0	1.8	1,005,458
Minnesota	348	2.4	2,356	1.4	7	71.8	30,455	354.6	1.7	1,018,845
Oregon	267	1.8	3,654	2.2	14	112.3	30,723	340.7	1.7	1,275,981
Nebraska	308	2.1	2,077	1.3	7	52.3	25,180	319.3	1.6	1,036,649
Mississippi	262	1.8	2,877	1.7	11	78.2	27,176	312.4	1.5	1,192,313
Iowa	440	3.0	2,409	1.5	5	58.9	24,451	287.4	1.4	653,275
Oklahoma	276	1.9	2,883	1.8	10	75.3	26,129	286.6	1.4	1,038,333
Virginia	297	2.1	3,214	2.0	11	101.7	31,648	286.2	1.4	963,519
Alabama	312	2.2	2,494	1.5	8	69.8	27,990	279.4	1.4	895,381
South Carolina	207	1.4	2,135	1.3	10	66.3	31,037	258.0	1.3	1,246,324
Kentucky	241	1.7	2,190	1.3	9	70.6	32,243	255.2	1.2	1,058,780
Colorado	217	1.5	1,305	0.8	6	35.8	27,405	249.9	1.2	1,151,521
Massachusetts	143	1.0	2,357	1.4	16	77.3	32,803	248.7	1.2	1,738,944
Utah	122	0.8	1,951	1.2	16	56.4	28,932	236.8	1.2	1,941,066
Arizona	151	1.0	1,750	1.1	12	49.4	28,231	197.5	1.0	1,307,815
Maryland	143	1.0	1,646	1.0	12	57.0	34,659	196.6	1.0	1,374,874
West Virginia	138	1.0	1,364	0.8	10	39.3	28,820	182.2	0.9	1,320,239
Maine	153	1.1	1,234	0.7	8	31.4	25,479	151.0	0.7	987,163
Idaho	154	1.1	1,513	0.9	10	35.6	23,517	139.3	0.7	904,396
South Dakota	160	1.1	862	0.5	5	21.1	24,490	136.6	0.7	853,869
Montana	136	0.9	1,050	0.6	8	32.0	30,518	133.7	0.7	983,397
New Mexico	113	0.8	1,331	0.8	12	36.1	27,131	115.8	0.6	1,024,540
North Dakota	143	1.0	839	0.5	6	20.4	24,278	114.4	0.6	800,112
Wyoming	107	0.7	943	0.6	9	25.3	26,780	94.8	0.5	885,561
Vermont	62	0.4	712	0.4	11	20.5	28,772	79.3	0.4	1,278,532
Nevada	52	0.4	510	0.3	10	18.1	35,531	58.2	0.3	1,119,365
Connecticut	56	0.4	529	0.3	9	18.8	35,463	57.0	0.3	1,018,232
Delaware	58	0.4	603	0.4	10	17.0	28,126	54.9	0.3	945,862
New Hampshire	56	0.4	284	0.2	5	7.8	27,514	32.7	0.2	583,446
Alaska	24	0.2	131	0.1	5	3.4	26,244	16.0	0.1	668,208
Rhode Island	26	0.2	175 *	-	-	(D)	-	(D)	-	-

Source: 1997 *Economic Census*. The states are in descending order of revenues or establishments (if revenue data are missing for the majority). The symbol (D) appears when data are withheld to prevent disclosure of competitive information. States marked with (D) are sorted by number of establishments. A dash (-) indicates that the data element cannot be calculated. * indicates the midpoint of a range; 175, for example is the range 100-249. Shaded *states* on the state map indicate those states which have proportionately greater representation in the industry than would be indicated by the state's population; the ratio is based on total revenues or number of establishments. Shaded *regions* indicate where the industry is regionally most concentrated.

NAICS 485111 - MIXED MODE TRANSIT SYSTEMS

GENERAL STATISTICS

Year	Establishments (number)	Employment (number)	Payroll ($ million)	Revenues ($ million)	Employees per Establishment (number)	Revenues per Establishment ($)	Payroll per Employee ($)
1997	3,184	27,850	392.8	1,280.6	8.7	402,198	14,104

Source: Economic Census of the United States, 1997. This is a newly defined industry. Data for prior years were unavailable at the time of publication but may become available over time.

SIC INDUSTRIES RELATED TO NAICS 485111

SIC	Industry	1990	1991	1992	1993	1994	1995	1996	1997
4111	**Local and Suburban Transit***								
	Establishments (number)	678	927	1,135	1,114	1,059	1,107	1,221	1,302p
	Employment (thousands)	41.0	52.4	37.7	40.3	43.7	44.1	45.7	45.9p
	Revenues ($ million)	-	-	1,364.0					

Source: Economic Census of the United States, 1992, annual surveys of economic sectors conducted by the Bureau of the Census, and estimates or projections based on the 1982-1992 period; not all data are shown. 'e' marks estimates made by the editors; 'p' indicates projections based on time series. A dash (-) indicates that data for this SIC or year were not available. * Indicates that only a portion of this industry is present within the NAICS data. If no * is shown, the entire industry is contained within the NAICS data.

INDICES OF CHANGE

Year	Establishments (number)	Employment (number)	Payroll ($ million)	Revenues ($ million)	Employees per Establishment (number)	Revenues per Establishment ($)	Payroll per Employee ($)
1997	100.0	100.0	100.0	100.0	100.0	100.0	100.0

Sources: Same as General Statistics. The values shown reflect change from the base year, 1997. Values above 100 mean greater than 1997, values below 100 mean less than 1997, and a value of 100 in years other than 1997 means same as 1997. Indices are calculated only for Census years. Data are the most recent available at this level of detail.

SELECTED RATIOS

For 1997	Avg. of Sector	Analyzed Industry	Index	For 1997	Avg. of Sector	Analyzed Industry	Index
Employees per establishment	16	9	53	Payroll per establishment	462,554	123,367	27
Revenue per establishment	1,787,642	402,198	22	Payroll as % of revenue	26	31	119
Revenue per employee	108,959	45,982	42	Payroll per employee	28,193	14,104	50

Sources: Same as General Statistics. The 'Average of Sector' column represents the average for all industries in this sector. The Index shows the relationship between the Average and the Analyzed Industry. For example, 100 means that they are equal; 500 that the Analyzed Industry is five times the average; 50 means that the Analyzed Industry is half the national average. 'na' is used to show that data are 'not available'.

LEADING COMPANIES   Number shown: **1**   Total sales ($ mil): **804**   Total employment (000): **12.4**

Company Name	Address	CEO Name	Phone	Co. Type	Sales ($ mil)	Empl. (000)
Coach USA Inc.	1 Riverway, Ste 500 Houston TX 77056	Lawrence K King	713-888-0104	P	804	12.4

Source: *Ward's Business Directory of U.S. Private and Public Companies*, Volumes 1 and 2, 2000. The company type code used is as follows: P - Public, R - Private, S - Subsidiary, D - Division, J - Joint Venture, A - Affiliate, G - Group, N - Company type not reported. Sales are in millions of dollars, employees are in thousands. An asterisk (*) indicates an estimated sales volume. The symbol < stands for 'less than'. Company names and addresses are truncated, in some cases, to fit into the available space.

INDUSTRY DATA BY STATE

State-level data are not available.

NAICS 485112 - COMMUTER RAIL SYSTEMS

GENERAL STATISTICS

Year	Establishments (number)	Employment (number)	Payroll ($ million)	Revenues ($ million)	Employees per Establishment (number)	Revenues per Establishment ($)	Payroll per Employee ($)
1997	3,234	29,432	487.9	1,873.9	9.1	579,437	16,577

Source: Economic Census of the United States, 1997. This is a newly defined industry. Data for prior years were unavailable at the time of publication but may become available over time.

SIC INDUSTRIES RELATED TO NAICS 485112

SIC	Industry	1990	1991	1992	1993	1994	1995	1996	1997
4111	**Local and Suburban Transit***								
	Establishments (number)	678	927	1,135	1,114	1,059	1,107	1,221	1,302p
	Employment (thousands)	41.0	52.4	37.7	40.3	43.7	44.1	45.7	45.9p
	Revenues ($ million)	-	-	1,364.0	-	-	-	-	-

Source: Economic Census of the United States, 1992, annual surveys of economic sectors conducted by the Bureau of the Census, and estimates or projections based on the 1982-1992 period; not all data are shown. 'e' marks estimates made by the editors; 'p' indicates projections based on time series. A dash (-) indicates that data for this SIC or year were not available. * Indicates that only a portion of this industry is present within the NAICS data. If no * is shown, the entire industry is contained within the NAICS data.

INDICES OF CHANGE

Year	Establishments (number)	Employment (number)	Payroll ($ million)	Revenues ($ million)	Employees per Establishment (number)	Revenues per Establishment ($)	Payroll per Employee ($)
1997	100.0	100.0	100.0	100.0	100.0	100.0	100.0

Sources: Same as General Statistics. The values shown reflect change from the base year, 1997. Values above 100 mean greater than 1997, values below 100 mean less than 1997, and a value of 100 in years other than 1997 means same as 1997. Indices are calculated only for Census years. Data are the most recent available at this level of detail.

SELECTED RATIOS

For 1997	Avg. of Sector	Analyzed Industry	Index	For 1997	Avg. of Sector	Analyzed Industry	Index
Employees per establishment	16	9	55	Payroll per establishment	462,554	150,866	33
Revenue per establishment	1,787,642	579,437	32	Payroll as % of revenue	26	26	101
Revenue per employee	108,959	63,669	58	Payroll per employee	28,193	16,577	59

Sources: Same as General Statistics. The 'Average of Sector' column represents the average for all industries in this sector. The Index shows the relationship between the Average and the Analyzed Industry. For example, 100 means that they are equal; 500 that the Analyzed Industry is five times the average; 50 means that the Analyzed Industry is half the national average. 'na' is used to show that data are 'not available'.

LEADING COMPANIES   Number shown: **17**   Total sales ($ mil): **1,577**   Total employment (000): **41.2**

Company Name	Address				CEO Name	Phone	Co. Type	Sales ($ mil)	Empl. (000)
New Jersey Transit Corp.	1 Penn Plz	Newark	NJ	07105		973-491-7000	R	513*	9.2
AHL Services Inc.	3353 Peachtree N E	Atlanta	GA	30326	Frank Argenbright Jr	404-267-2222	P	476	13.0
Argenbright Inc.	3465 N Desert Dr	Atlanta	GA	30326	Thomas J Marano	404-766-1212	S	193	12.0
Oahu Transit Services Inc.	811 Middle St	Honolulu	HI	96819		808-848-4500	R	100	1.4
Mears Transportation Group	324 W Gore St	Orlando	FL	32806	P Mears Jr	407-422-4561	R	97*	2.0
Blue Bird Coach Lines Inc.	1 Blue Bird Sq	Olean	NY	14760	Louis A Magnano	716-372-5500	R	32*	0.3
Bell Trans Inc.	1900 Industrial Rd	Las Vegas	NV	89102	Jim A Bell	702-739-7990	R	24*	0.5
Central New York Regional	PO Box 820	Syracuse	NY	13205		315-442-3333	R	24*	0.5
Triboro Coach Corp.	8501 24th Ave	East Elmhurst	NY	11370	S Eagar	718-335-1000	R	21*	0.5
Grayline of Seattle	4500 W Marginal	Seattle	WA	98106		206-624-5077	S	21	0.3
Connecticut Limousine Service	230 Old Gate Ln	Milford	CT	06460		203-878-6867	S	19*	0.4
Connecticut Limousine L.L.C.	230 Old Gate Ln	Milford	CT	06460	Andy Anastasio Jr	203-878-6867	R	18*	0.4
Continental Air Transport Co.	730 W Lake St	Chicago	IL	60661	Lynda Hawkins	312-454-7800	R	14*	0.3
Jamaica Buses Inc.	114-15 Brewer	Jamaica	NY	11434	Jerome Cooper	718-526-0800	R	11*	0.2
Commuter Transportation Co.	E Service Dr	Detroit	MI	48242	Timothy J McCarthy	313-292-2000	R	9	0.2
Kahului Trucking and Storage Inc.	140 Hobron Ave	Kahului	HI	96732		808-877-5001	S	3*	<0.1
Trolley Tours of Cleveland Inc.	1831 Columbus Rd	Cleveland	OH	44113	Sherry Paul	216-771-4484	R	2*	<0.1

Source: Ward's Business Directory of U.S. Private and Public Companies, Volumes 1 and 2, 2000. The company type code used is as follows: P - Public, R - Private, S - Subsidiary, D - Division, J - Joint Venture, A - Affiliate, G - Group, N - Company type not reported. Sales are in millions of dollars, employees are in thousands. An asterisk (*) indicates an estimated sales volume. The symbol < stands for 'less than'. Company names and addresses are truncated, in some cases, to fit into the available space.

INDUSTRY DATA BY STATE

State-level data are not available.

NAICS 485113 - BUS AND MOTOR VEHICLE TRANSIT SYSTEMS

GENERAL STATISTICS

Year	Establishments (number)	Employment (number)	Payroll ($ million)	Revenues ($ million)	Employees per Establishment (number)	Revenues per Establishment ($)	Payroll per Employee ($)
1997	4,484	151,664	1,878.0	4,392.8	33.8	979,661	12,383

Source: Economic Census of the United States, 1997. This is a newly defined industry. Data for prior years were unavailable at the time of publication but may become available over time.

SIC INDUSTRIES RELATED TO NAICS 485113

SIC	Industry	1990	1991	1992	1993	1994	1995	1996	1997
4111	**Local and Suburban Transit***								
	Establishments (number)	678	927	1,135	1,114	1,059	1,107	1,221	1,302p
	Employment (thousands)	41.0	52.4	37.7	40.3	43.7	44.1	45.7	45.9p
	Revenues ($ million)	-	-	1,364.0	-	-	-	-	-

Source: Economic Census of the United States, 1992, annual surveys of economic sectors conducted by the Bureau of the Census, and estimates or projections based on the 1982-1992 period; not all data are shown. 'e' marks estimates made by the editors; 'p' indicates projections based on time series. A dash (-) indicates that data for this SIC or year were not available. * Indicates that only a portion of this industry is present within the NAICS data. If no * is shown, the entire industry is contained within the NAICS data.

INDICES OF CHANGE

Year	Establishments (number)	Employment (number)	Payroll ($ million)	Revenues ($ million)	Employees per Establishment (number)	Revenues per Establishment ($)	Payroll per Employee ($)
1997	100.0	100.0	100.0	100.0	100.0	100.0	100.0

Sources: Same as General Statistics. The values shown reflect change from the base year, 1997. Values above 100 mean greater than 1997, values below 100 mean less than 1997, and a value of 100 in years other than 1997 means same as 1997. Indices are calculated only for Census years. Data are the most recent available at this level of detail.

SELECTED RATIOS

For 1997	Avg. of Sector	Analyzed Industry	Index	For 1997	Avg. of Sector	Analyzed Industry	Index
Employees per establishment	16	34	206	Payroll per establishment	462,554	418,822	91
Revenue per establishment	1,787,642	979,661	55	Payroll as % of revenue	26	43	165
Revenue per employee	108,959	28,964	27	Payroll per employee	28,193	12,383	44

Sources: Same as General Statistics. The 'Average of Sector' column represents the average for all industries in this sector. The Index shows the relationship between the Average and the Analyzed Industry. For example, 100 means that they are equal; 500 that the Analyzed Industry is five times the average; 50 means that the Analyzed Industry is half the national average. 'na' is used to show that data are 'not available'.

LEADING COMPANIES   Number shown: **17**   Total sales ($ mil): **1,577**   Total employment (000): **41.2**

Company Name	Address				CEO Name	Phone	Co. Type	Sales ($ mil)	Empl. (000)
New Jersey Transit Corp.	1 Penn Plz	Newark	NJ	07105		973-491-7000	R	513*	9.2
AHL Services Inc.	3353 Peachtree N E	Atlanta	GA	30326	Frank Argenbright Jr	404-267-2222	P	476	13.0
Argenbright Inc.	3465 N Desert Dr	Atlanta	GA	30326	Thomas J Marano	404-766-1212	S	193	12.0
Oahu Transit Services Inc.	811 Middle St	Honolulu	HI	96819		808-848-4500	R	100	1.4
Mears Transportation Group	324 W Gore St	Orlando	FL	32806	P Mears Jr	407-422-4561	R	97*	2.0
Blue Bird Coach Lines Inc.	1 Blue Bird Sq	Olean	NY	14760	Louis A Magnano	716-372-5500	R	32*	0.3
Bell Trans Inc.	1900 Industrial Rd	Las Vegas	NV	89102	Jim A Bell	702-739-7990	R	24*	0.5
Central New York Regional	PO Box 820	Syracuse	NY	13205		315-442-3333	R	24*	0.5
Triboro Coach Corp.	8501 24th Ave	East Elmhurst	NY	11370	S Eagar	718-335-1000	R	21*	0.5
Grayline of Seattle	4500 W Marginal	Seattle	WA	98106		206-624-5077	S	21	0.3
Connecticut Limousine Service	230 Old Gate Ln	Milford	CT	06460		203-878-6867	S	19*	0.4
Connecticut Limousine L.L.C.	230 Old Gate Ln	Milford	CT	06460	Andy Anastasio Jr	203-878-6867	R	18*	0.4
Continental Air Transport Co.	730 W Lake St	Chicago	IL	60661	Lynda Hawkins	312-454-7800	R	14*	0.3
Jamaica Buses Inc.	114-15 Brewer	Jamaica	NY	11434	Jerome Cooper	718-526-0800	R	11*	0.2
Commuter Transportation Co.	E Service Dr	Detroit	MI	48242	Timothy J McCarthy	313-292-2000	R	9	0.2
Kahului Trucking and Storage Inc.	140 Hobron Ave	Kahului	HI	96732		808-877-5001	S	3*	<0.1
Trolley Tours of Cleveland Inc.	1831 Columbus Rd	Cleveland	OH	44113	Sherry Paul	216-771-4484	R	2*	<0.1

Source: *Ward's Business Directory of U.S. Private and Public Companies*, Volumes 1 and 2, 2000. The company type code used is as follows: P - Public, R - Private, S - Subsidiary, D - Division, J - Joint Venture, A - Affiliate, G - Group, N - Company type not reported. Sales are in millions of dollars, employees are in thousands. An asterisk (*) indicates an estimated sales volume. The symbol < stands for 'less than'. Company names and addresses are truncated, in some cases, to fit into the available space.

LOCATION BY STATE AND REGIONAL CONCENTRATION

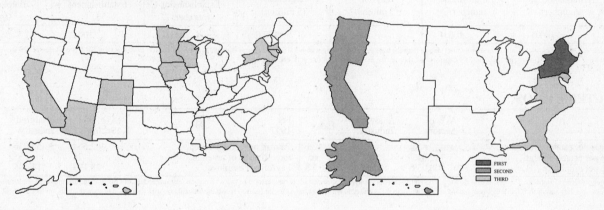

FIRST
SECOND
THIRD

INDUSTRY DATA BY STATE

State	Establishments Total (number)	% of U.S.	Employment Total (number)	% of U.S.	Per Estab.	Payroll Total ($ mil.)	Per Empl. ($)	Revenues Total ($ mil.)	% of U.S.	Per Estab. ($)
California	72	13.3	4,584	16.7	64	109.8	23,952	196.2	17.0	2,725,653
Louisiana	7	1.3	1,544	5.6	221	66.7	43,168	106.8	9.3	15,250,571
Arizona	9	1.7	1,243	4.5	138	33.6	27,025	38.8	3.4	4,314,778
Massachusetts	26	4.8	949	3.5	37	20.0	21,066	36.0	3.1	1,386,000
Illinois	20	3.7	686	2.5	34	16.3	23,746	30.1	2.6	1,504,800
Connecticut	8	1.5	234	0.9	29	5.2	22,090	9.9	0.9	1,240,250
Missouri	11	2.0	113	0.4	10	2.2	19,540	5.8	0.5	524,182
Michigan	9	1.7	145	0.5	16	3.4	23,421	5.6	0.5	621,667
New Jersey	71	13.1	1,750*	-	-	(D)	-	(D)	-	-
New York	58	10.7	3,750*	-	-	(D)	-	(D)	-	-
Florida	34	6.3	750*	-	-	(D)	-	(D)	-	-
Texas	23	4.2	3,750*	-	-	(D)	-	(D)	-	-
Pennsylvania	21	3.9	375*	-	-	(D)	-	(D)	-	-
Virginia	13	2.4	1,750*	-	-	(D)	-	(D)	-	-
Wisconsin	12	2.2	375*	-	-	(D)	-	(D)	-	-
Colorado	11	2.0	750*	-	-	(D)	-	(D)	-	-
Iowa	11	2.0	60*	-	-	(D)	-	(D)	-	-
Minnesota	11	2.0	375*	-	-	(D)	-	(D)	-	-
North Carolina	11	2.0	375*	-	-	(D)	-	(D)	-	-
Maryland	10	1.8	175*	-	-	(D)	-	(D)	-	-
Hawaii	6	1.1	1,750*	-	-	(D)	-	(D)	-	-
Ohio	6	1.1	175*	-	-	(D)	-	(D)	-	-
Oregon	6	1.1	60*	-	-	(D)	-	(D)	-	-
South Carolina	6	1.1	175*	-	-	(D)	-	(D)	-	-
Tennessee	6	1.1	375*	-	-	(D)	-	(D)	-	-

Source: 1997 *Economic Census*. The states are in descending order of revenues or establishments (if revenue data are missing for the majority). The symbol (D) appears when data are withheld to prevent disclosure of competitive information. States marked with (D) are sorted by number of establishments. A dash (-) indicates that the data element cannot be calculated. * indicates the midpoint of a range; 175, for example is the range 100-249. Shaded *states* on the state map indicate those states which have proportionately greater representation in the industry than would be indicated by the state's population; the ratio is based on total revenues or number of establishments. Shaded *regions* indicate where the industry is regionally most concentrated.

NAICS 485119 - URBAN TRANSIT SYSTEMS NEC

GENERAL STATISTICS

Year	Establishments (number)	Employment (number)	Payroll ($ million)	Revenues ($ million)	Employees per Establishment (number)	Revenues per Establishment ($)	Payroll per Employee ($)
1997	1,531	31,483	548.0	1,768.2	20.6	1,154,931	17,406

Source: Economic Census of the United States, 1997. This is a newly defined industry. Data for prior years were unavailable at the time of publication but may become available over time.

SIC INDUSTRIES RELATED TO NAICS 485119

SIC	Industry	1990	1991	1992	1993	1994	1995	1996	1997
4111	**Local and Suburban Transit***								
	Establishments (number)	678	927	1,135	1,114	1,059	1,107	1,221	1,302p
	Employment (thousands)	41.0	52.4	37.7	40.3	43.7	44.1	45.7	45.9p
	Revenues ($ million)	-	-	1,364.0	-	-	-	-	-

Source: Economic Census of the United States, 1992, annual surveys of economic sectors conducted by the Bureau of the Census, and estimates or projections based on the 1982-1992 period; not all data are shown. 'e' marks estimates made by the editors; 'p' indicates projections based on time series. A dash (-) indicates that data for this SIC or year were not available. * Indicates that only a portion of this industry is present within the NAICS data. If no * is shown, the entire industry is contained within the NAICS data.

INDICES OF CHANGE

Year	Establishments (number)	Employment (number)	Payroll ($ million)	Revenues ($ million)	Employees per Establishment (number)	Revenues per Establishment ($)	Payroll per Employee ($)
1997	100.0	100.0	100.0	100.0	100.0	100.0	100.0

Sources: Same as General Statistics. The values shown reflect change from the base year, 1997. Values above 100 mean greater than 1997, values below 100 mean less than 1997, and a value of 100 in years other than 1997 means same as 1997. Indices are calculated only for Census years. Data are the most recent available at this level of detail.

SELECTED RATIOS

For 1997	Avg. of Sector	Analyzed Industry	Index	For 1997	Avg. of Sector	Analyzed Industry	Index
Employees per establishment	16	21	125	Payroll per establishment	462,554	357,936	77
Revenue per establishment	1,787,642	1,154,931	65	Payroll as % of revenue	26	31	120
Revenue per employee	108,959	56,164	52	Payroll per employee	28,193	17,406	62

Sources: Same as General Statistics. The 'Average of Sector' column represents the average for all industries in this sector. The Index shows the relationship between the Average and the Analyzed Industry. For example, 100 means that they are equal; 500 that the Analyzed Industry is five times the average; 50 means that the Analyzed Industry is half the national average. 'na' is used to show that data are 'not available'.

LEADING COMPANIES   Number shown: **17**   Total sales ($ mil): **1,577**   Total employment (000): **41.2**

Company Name	Address				CEO Name	Phone	Co. Type	Sales ($ mil)	Empl. (000)
New Jersey Transit Corp.	1 Penn Plz	Newark	NJ	07105		973-491-7000	R	513*	9.2
AHL Services Inc.	3353 Peachtree N E	Atlanta	GA	30326	Frank Argenbright Jr	404-267-2222	P	476	13.0
Argenbright Inc.	3465 N Desert Dr	Atlanta	GA	30326	Thomas J Marano	404-766-1212	S	193	12.0
Oahu Transit Services Inc.	811 Middle St	Honolulu	HI	96819		808-848-4500	R	100	1.4
Mears Transportation Group	324 W Gore St	Orlando	FL	32806	P Mears Jr	407-422-4561	R	97*	2.0
Blue Bird Coach Lines Inc.	1 Blue Bird Sq	Olean	NY	14760	Louis A Magnano	716-372-5500	R	32*	0.3
Bell Trans Inc.	1900 Industrial Rd	Las Vegas	NV	89102	Jim A Bell	702-739-7990	R	24*	0.5
Central New York Regional	PO Box 820	Syracuse	NY	13205		315-442-3333	R	24*	0.5
Triboro Coach Corp.	8501 24th Ave	East Elmhurst	NY	11370	S Eagar	718-335-1000	R	21*	0.5
Grayline of Seattle	4500 W Marginal	Seattle	WA	98106		206-624-5077	S	21	0.3
Connecticut Limousine Service	230 Old Gate Ln	Milford	CT	06460		203-878-6867	S	19*	0.4
Connecticut Limousine L.L.C.	230 Old Gate Ln	Milford	CT	06460	Andy Anastasio Jr	203-878-6867	R	18*	0.4
Continental Air Transport Co.	730 W Lake St	Chicago	IL	60661	Lynda Hawkins	312-454-7800	R	14*	0.3
Jamaica Buses Inc.	114-15 Brewer	Jamaica	NY	11434	Jerome Cooper	718-526-0800	R	11*	0.2
Commuter Transportation Co.	E Service Dr	Detroit	MI	48242	Timothy J McCarthy	313-292-2000	R	9	0.2
Kahului Trucking and Storage Inc.	140 Hobron Ave	Kahului	HI	96732		808-877-5001	S	3*	<0.1
Trolley Tours of Cleveland Inc.	1831 Columbus Rd	Cleveland	OH	44113	Sherry Paul	216-771-4484	R	2*	<0.1

Source: Ward's Business Directory of U.S. Private and Public Companies, Volumes 1 and 2, 2000. The company type code used is as follows: P - Public, R - Private, S - Subsidiary, D - Division, J - Joint Venture, A - Affiliate, G - Group, N - Company type not reported. Sales are in millions of dollars, employees are in thousands. An asterisk (*) indicates an estimated sales volume. The symbol < stands for 'less than'. Company names and addresses are truncated, in some cases, to fit into the available space.

INDUSTRY DATA BY STATE

State-level data are not available.

NAICS 485210 - INTERURBAN AND RURAL BUS TRANSPORTATION

GENERAL STATISTICS

Year	Establishments (number)	Employment (number)	Payroll ($ million)	Revenues ($ million)	Employees per Establishment (number)	Revenues per Establishment ($)	Payroll per Employee ($)
1997	1,789	31,791	486.7	1,141.4	17.8	638,010	15,309

Source: *Economic Census of the United States*, 1997. This is a newly defined industry. Data for prior years were unavailable at the time of publication but may become available over time.

SIC INDUSTRIES RELATED TO NAICS 485210

SIC	Industry	1990	1991	1992	1993	1994	1995	1996	1997
4131	**Intercity & Rural Bus Transportation**	-	-	-	-	-	-	-	-

Source: *Economic Census of the United States*, 1992, annual surveys of economic sectors conducted by the Bureau of the Census, and estimates or projections based on the 1982-1992 period; not all data are shown. 'e' marks estimates made by the editors; 'p' indicates projections based on time series. A dash (-) indicates that data for this SIC or year were not available. * Indicates that only a portion of this industry is present within the NAICS data. If no * is shown, the entire industry is contained within the NAICS data.

INDICES OF CHANGE

Year	Establishments (number)	Employment (number)	Payroll ($ million)	Revenues ($ million)	Employees per Establishment (number)	Revenues per Establishment ($)	Payroll per Employee ($)
1997	100.0	100.0	100.0	100.0	100.0	100.0	100.0

Sources: Same as General Statistics. The values shown reflect change from the base year, 1997. Values above 100 mean greater than 1997, values below 100 mean less than 1997, and a value of 100 in years other than 1997 means same as 1997. Indices are calculated only for Census years. Data are the most recent available at this level of detail.

SELECTED RATIOS

For 1997	Avg. of Sector	Analyzed Industry	Index	For 1997	Avg. of Sector	Analyzed Industry	Index
Employees per establishment	16	18	108	Payroll per establishment	462,554	272,051	59
Revenue per establishment	1,787,642	638,010	36	Payroll as % of revenue	26	43	165
Revenue per employee	108,959	35,903	33	Payroll per employee	28,193	15,309	54

Sources: Same as General Statistics. The 'Average of Sector' column represents the average for all industries in this sector. The Index shows the relationship between the Average and the Analyzed Industry. For example, 100 means that they are equal; 500 that the Analyzed Industry is five times the average; 50 means that the Analyzed Industry is half the national average. 'na' is used to show that data are 'not available'.

LEADING COMPANIES   Number shown: **10**   Total sales ($ mil): **1,581**   Total employment (000): **25.9**

Company Name	Address				CEO Name	Phone	Co. Type	Sales ($ mil)	Empl. (000)
Greyhound Lines Inc.	P O Box 660362	Dallas	TX	75266	Thomas G Plaskett	972-789-7000	P	846	13.4
New Jersey Transit Corp.	1 Penn Plz	Newark	NJ	07105		973-491-7000	R	513*	9.2
Peter Pan Bus Lines Inc.	PO Box 1776	Springfield	MA	01102	Peter A Picknelly Jr	413-781-2900	R	64*	0.8
San Diego Transit Corp.	PO Box 12251	San Diego	CA	92112		619-238-0100	R	60	1.0
Blue Bird Coach Lines Inc.	1 Blue Bird Sq	Olean	NY	14760	Louis A Magnano	716-372-5500	R	32*	0.3
Jefferson Partners L.P.	2100 E 26th St	Minneapolis	MN	55404	Charles A Zelle	612-332-8745	R	17	0.2
Carolina Coach Company Inc.	P O Box 28088	Raleigh	NC	27611	William C Steele	919-833-3601	S	17	0.2
Texas, New Mexico & Oklahoma	P O Box 1800	Lubbock	TX	79408	Robert D Greenhill	806-763-5389	S	12*	0.2
Greater Richmond Transit Co.	PO Box 27323	Richmond	VA	23261		804-358-4782	R	11*	0.4
Bonanza Bus Lines Inc.	1 Bonanza Way	Providence	RI	02940		401-331-7500	R	9*	0.2

Source: *Ward's Business Directory of U.S. Private and Public Companies*, Volumes 1 and 2, 2000. The company type code used is as follows: P - Public, R - Private, S - Subsidiary, D - Division, J - Joint Venture, A - Affiliate, G - Group, N - Company type not reported. Sales are in millions of dollars, employees are in thousands. An asterisk (*) indicates an estimated sales volume. The symbol < stands for 'less than'. Company names and addresses are truncated, in some cases, to fit into the available space.

LOCATION BY STATE AND REGIONAL CONCENTRATION

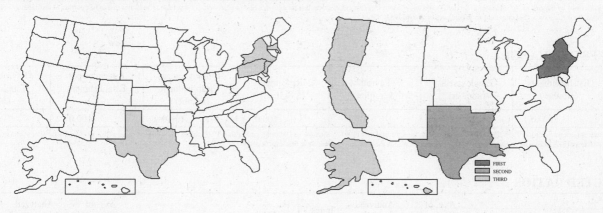

INDUSTRY DATA BY STATE

State	Establishments Total (number)	% of U.S.	Employment Total (number)	% of U.S.	Per Estab.	Payroll Total ($ mil.)	Per Empl. ($)	Revenues Total ($ mil.)	% of U.S.	Per Estab. ($)
New Jersey	40	9.8	6,935	34.8	173	252.5	36,412	320.6	27.9	8,014,650
Texas	45	11.1	1,843	9.3	41	34.6	18,772	111.6	9.7	2,480,200
New York	30	7.4	1,651	8.3	55	53.7	32,498	107.7	9.4	3,589,300
California	42	10.3	1,834	9.2	44	35.4	19,278	89.5	7.8	2,130,190
Massachusetts	10	2.5	894	4.5	89	23.7	26,474	67.5	5.9	6,751,000
Pennsylvania	20	4.9	848	4.3	42	21.9	25,874	57.8	5.0	2,888,850
Florida	21	5.2	583	2.9	28	11.1	19,029	43.4	3.8	2,064,381
North Carolina	11	2.7	231	1.2	21	6.5	28,312	22.4	1.9	2,032,455
Louisiana	10	2.5	246	1.2	25	4.6	18,732	15.1	1.3	1,509,900
Alabama	6	1.5	401	2.0	67	8.0	19,950	14.3	1.2	2,375,667
Colorado	6	1.5	265	1.3	44	5.0	18,830	13.8	1.2	2,296,000
Virginia	10	2.5	156	0.8	16	5.0	31,929	13.6	1.2	1,363,100
Oregon	8	2.0	212	1.1	27	5.2	24,533	12.7	1.1	1,585,875
Minnesota	12	2.9	274	1.4	23	3.7	13,562	12.5	1.1	1,043,833
Mississippi	6	1.5	115	0.6	19	1.7	14,504	5.6	0.5	925,167
Maryland	6	1.5	17	0.1	3	0.5	26,647	2.7	0.2	450,000
Idaho	6	1.5	86	0.4	14	0.8	9,407	2.2	0.2	374,667
Georgia	9	2.2	175*	-	-	(D)	-	(D)	-	-
Ohio	8	2.0	375*	-	-	(D)	-	(D)	-	-
South Carolina	8	2.0	175*	-	-	(D)	-	(D)	-	-
Missouri	7	1.7	175*	-	-	(D)	-	(D)	-	-
Arizona	6	1.5	60*	-	-	(D)	-	(D)	-	-
Tennessee	6	1.5	175*	-	-	(D)	-	(D)	-	-

Source: 1997 *Economic Census*. The states are in descending order of revenues or establishments (if revenue data are missing for the majority). The symbol (D) appears when data are withheld to prevent disclosure of competitive information. States marked with (D) are sorted by number of establishments. A dash (-) indicates that the data element cannot be calculated. * indicates the midpoint of a range; 175, for example is the range 100-249. Shaded *states* on the state map indicate those states which have proportionately greater representation in the industry than would be indicated by the state's population; the ratio is based on total revenues or number of establishments. Shaded *regions* indicate where the industry is regionally most concentrated.

NAICS 485310 - TAXI SERVICE

GENERAL STATISTICS

Year	Establishments (number)	Employment (number)	Payroll ($ million)	Revenues ($ million)	Employees per Establishment (number)	Revenues per Establishment ($)	Payroll per Employee ($)
1997	766	14,513	233.2	669.4	18.9	873,890	16,068

Source: Economic Census of the United States, 1997. This is a newly defined industry. Data for prior years were unavailable at the time of publication but may become available over time.

SIC INDUSTRIES RELATED TO NAICS 485310

SIC	Industry	1990	1991	1992	1993	1994	1995	1996	1997
4121	**Taxicabs**	-	-	-	-	-	-	-	-
4899	**Communications Services, nec***								
	Establishments (number)	1,201	1,320	1,008	1,105	1,034	1,305	1,488	468*p*
	Employment (thousands)	34.6	25.0	9.7	15.3	13.1	20.0	22.4	-
	Revenues ($ million)	-	-	2,357.9	-	-	-	-	-

*Source: Economic Census of the United States, 1992, annual surveys of economic sectors conducted by the Bureau of the Census, and estimates or projections based on the 1982-1992 period; not all data are shown. 'e' marks estimates made by the editors; 'p' indicates projections based on time series. A dash (-) indicates that data for this SIC or year were not available. * Indicates that only a portion of this industry is present within the NAICS data. If no * is shown, the entire industry is contained within the NAICS data.*

INDICES OF CHANGE

Year	Establishments (number)	Employment (number)	Payroll ($ million)	Revenues ($ million)	Employees per Establishment (number)	Revenues per Establishment ($)	Payroll per Employee ($)
1997	100.0	100.0	100.0	100.0	100.0	100.0	100.0

Sources: Same as General Statistics. The values shown reflect change from the base year, 1997. Values above 100 mean greater than 1997, values below 100 mean less than 1997, and a value of 100 in years other than 1997 means same as 1997. Indices are calculated only for Census years. Data are the most recent available at this level of detail.

SELECTED RATIOS

For 1997	Avg. of Sector	Analyzed Industry	Index	For 1997	Avg. of Sector	Analyzed Industry	Index
Employees per establishment	16	19	115	Payroll per establishment	462,554	304,439	66
Revenue per establishment	1,787,642	873,890	49	Payroll as % of revenue	26	35	135
Revenue per employee	108,959	46,124	42	Payroll per employee	28,193	16,068	57

Sources: Same as General Statistics. The 'Average of Sector' column represents the average for all industries in this sector. The Index shows the relationship between the Average and the Analyzed Industry. For example, 100 means that they are equal; 500 that the Analyzed Industry is five times the average; 50 means that the Analyzed Industry is half the national average. 'na' is used to show that data are 'not available'.

LEADING COMPANIES   Number shown: **3**   Total sales ($ mil): **83**   Total employment (000): **0.1**

Company Name	Address				CEO Name	Phone	Co. Type	Sales ($ mil)	Empl. (000)
Yellow Cab Company Inc.	1730 S Indiana Ave	Chicago	IL	60616	Jeffrey Feldman	312-225-7440	S	42*	0.1
Yellow Cab-Delaware Inc.	1227 E 15th St	Wilmington	DE	19802	Joseph Longo	302-658-7321	R	25*	<0.1
SCSM Holdings Inc.	1266 E Main St	Stamford	CT	06902		203-425-2070	S	16*	<0.1

Source: *Ward's Business Directory of U.S. Private and Public Companies*, Volumes 1 and 2, 2000. The company type code used is as follows: P - Public, R - Private, S - Subsidiary, D - Division, J - Joint Venture, A - Affiliate, G - Group, N - Company type not reported. Sales are in millions of dollars, employees are in thousands. An asterisk (*) indicates an estimated sales volume. The symbol < stands for 'less than'. Company names and addresses are truncated, in some cases, to fit into the available space.

LOCATION BY STATE AND REGIONAL CONCENTRATION

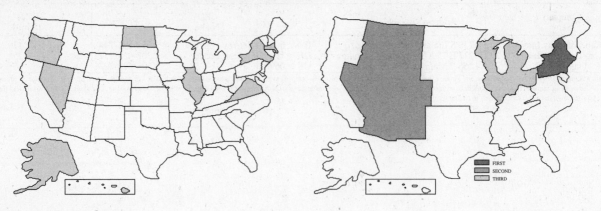

INDUSTRY DATA BY STATE

State	Establishments Total (number)	% of U.S.	Employment Total (number)	% of U.S.	Per Estab.	Payroll Total ($ mil.)	Per Empl. ($)	Revenues Total ($ mil.)	% of U.S.	Per Estab. ($)
New York	923	29.0	3,735	13.4	4	52.9	14,174	266.4	20.8	288,670
Nevada	20	0.6	4,123	14.8	206	67.0	16,257	150.6	11.8	7,531,650
California	132	4.1	1,838	6.6	14	31.5	17,131	114.4	8.9	866,333
Illinois	154	4.8	828	3.0	5	13.4	16,187	67.2	5.2	436,442
Texas	93	2.9	1,280	4.6	14	18.1	14,137	64.7	5.0	695,333
Massachusetts	170	5.3	1,330	4.8	8	21.3	15,978	57.7	4.5	339,224
Florida	125	3.9	933	3.4	7	15.3	16,353	55.2	4.3	441,464
Virginia	88	2.8	799	2.9	9	11.0	13,760	45.6	3.6	518,443
Ohio	70	2.2	713	2.6	10	10.1	14,227	35.4	2.8	505,700
New Jersey	161	5.1	1,000	3.6	6	11.1	11,106	32.5	2.5	202,161
Pennsylvania	119	3.7	780	2.8	7	9.5	12,160	30.4	2.4	255,487
Wisconsin	67	2.1	917	3.3	14	9.9	10,850	21.5	1.7	320,463
Michigan	61	1.9	486	1.7	8	6.5	13,274	17.7	1.4	290,344
Missouri	41	1.3	366	1.3	9	5.3	14,566	16.9	1.3	412,829
Minnesota	47	1.5	441	1.6	9	6.3	14,388	16.5	1.3	351,723
Kentucky	45	1.4	611	2.2	14	8.1	13,254	16.2	1.3	359,133
Colorado	17	0.5	306	1.1	18	4.9	15,931	16.1	1.3	944,412
Indiana	38	1.2	351	1.3	9	4.6	13,191	15.8	1.2	414,921
North Carolina	108	3.4	551	2.0	5	5.0	9,034	15.6	1.2	144,222
Oregon	35	1.1	473	1.7	14	5.1	10,786	15.0	1.2	427,571
Georgia	61	1.9	312	1.1	5	3.7	11,955	13.0	1.0	213,410
Connecticut	29	0.9	243	0.9	8	4.5	18,354	12.9	1.0	443,966
Washington	30	0.9	211	0.8	7	3.0	14,455	11.8	0.9	392,067
South Carolina	45	1.4	292	1.0	6	3.8	12,959	10.1	0.8	223,889
Arizona	17	0.5	288	1.0	17	3.6	12,361	9.1	0.7	532,588
Hawaii	18	0.6	186	0.7	10	2.9	15,844	8.7	0.7	484,222
New Mexico	11	0.3	264	0.9	24	3.6	13,458	7.8	0.6	707,545
Tennessee	34	1.1	197	0.7	6	2.4	12,234	7.5	0.6	221,559
Louisiana	35	1.1	187	0.7	5	2.2	11,620	6.7	0.5	191,114
D.C.	10	0.3	150	0.5	15	2.3	15,327	6.2	0.5	620,400
Alaska	31	1.0	171	0.6	6	1.7	9,988	5.3	0.4	170,194
West Virginia	16	0.5	143	0.5	9	1.7	11,951	5.0	0.4	309,500
Nebraska	9	0.3	209	0.8	23	2.3	10,770	4.9	0.4	546,000
Iowa	22	0.7	220	0.8	10	2.0	9,159	4.8	0.4	218,182
Maine	30	0.9	227	0.8	8	1.7	7,626	4.7	0.4	157,867
Rhode Island	28	0.9	72	0.3	3	1.1	14,681	4.6	0.4	165,750
Alabama	21	0.7	123	0.4	6	1.2	9,976	4.3	0.3	204,667
North Dakota	9	0.3	208	0.7	23	2.4	11,769	4.3	0.3	474,222
Kansas	22	0.7	199	0.7	9	1.5	7,744	4.1	0.3	186,773
Utah	7	0.2	92	0.3	13	1.3	14,043	3.6	0.3	517,000
Oklahoma	14	0.4	119	0.4	9	1.4	11,538	3.5	0.3	247,143
Montana	13	0.4	128	0.5	10	1.3	10,117	3.2	0.2	244,154
New Hampshire	17	0.5	137	0.5	8	1.1	7,759	3.1	0.2	180,000
Vermont	14	0.4	125	0.4	9	1.1	8,616	2.8	0.2	199,929
Arkansas	11	0.3	81	0.3	7	0.9	10,753	2.8	0.2	259,091
South Dakota	9	0.3	186	0.7	21	1.5	8,183	2.7	0.2	296,333
Mississippi	15	0.5	98	0.4	7	1.0	9,878	2.5	0.2	168,267
Wyoming	10	0.3	83	0.3	8	0.7	8,482	1.5	0.1	147,200
Maryland	70	2.2	750*	-	-	(D)	-	(D)	-	-
Idaho	9	0.3	60*	-	-	(D)	-	(D)	-	-

Source: 1997 *Economic Census*. The states are in descending order of revenues or establishments (if revenue data are missing for the majority). The symbol (D) appears when data are withheld to prevent disclosure of competitive information. States marked with (D) are sorted by number of establishments. A dash (-) indicates that the data element cannot be calculated. * indicates the midpoint of a range; 175, for example is the range 100-249. Shaded *states* on the state map indicate those states which have proportionately greater representation in the industry than would be indicated by the state's population; the ratio is based on total revenues or number of establishments. Shaded *regions* indicate where the industry is regionally most concentrated.

NAICS 485320 - LIMOUSINE SERVICE

GENERAL STATISTICS

Year	Establishments (number)	Employment (number)	Payroll ($ million)	Revenues ($ million)	Employees per Establishment (number)	Revenues per Establishment ($)	Payroll per Employee ($)
1997	382	7,960	479.5	4,364.6	20.8	11,425,654	60,239

Source: Economic Census of the United States, 1997. This is a newly defined industry. Data for prior years were unavailable at the time of publication but may become available over time.

SIC INDUSTRIES RELATED TO NAICS 485320

SIC	Industry	1990	1991	1992	1993	1994	1995	1996	1997
4119	**Local Passenger Transportation, nec***								
	Establishments (number)	5,187	5,991	7,140	7,652	7,915	7,800	8,305	8,988p
	Employment (thousands)	94.0	94.6	115.6	124.4	130.7	139.0	149.0	156.0p
	Revenues ($ million)	-	-	4,604.0	-	-	-	-	-

Source: Economic Census of the United States, 1992, annual surveys of economic sectors conducted by the Bureau of the Census, and estimates or projections based on the 1982-1992 period; not all data are shown. 'e' marks estimates made by the editors; 'p' indicates projections based on time series. A dash (-) indicates that data for this SIC or year were not available. * Indicates that only a portion of this industry is present within the NAICS data. If no * is shown, the entire industry is contained within the NAICS data.

INDICES OF CHANGE

Year	Establishments (number)	Employment (number)	Payroll ($ million)	Revenues ($ million)	Employees per Establishment (number)	Revenues per Establishment ($)	Payroll per Employee ($)
1997	100.0	100.0	100.0	100.0	100.0	100.0	100.0

Sources: Same as General Statistics. The values shown reflect change from the base year, 1997. Values above 100 mean greater than 1997, values below 100 mean less than 1997, and a value of 100 in years other than 1997 means same as 1997. Indices are calculated only for Census years. Data are the most recent available at this level of detail.

SELECTED RATIOS

For 1997	Avg. of Sector	Analyzed Industry	Index	For 1997	Avg. of Sector	Analyzed Industry	Index
Employees per establishment	16	21	127	Payroll per establishment	462,554	1,255,236	271
Revenue per establishment	1,787,642	11,425,654	639	Payroll as % of revenue	26	11	42
Revenue per employee	108,959	548,317	503	Payroll per employee	28,193	60,239	214

Sources: Same as General Statistics. The 'Average of Sector' column represents the average for all industries in this sector. The Index shows the relationship between the Average and the Analyzed Industry. For example, 100 means that they are equal; 500 that the Analyzed Industry is five times the average; 50 means that the Analyzed Industry is half the national average. 'na' is used to show that data are 'not available'.

LEADING COMPANIES

No company data available for this industry.

LOCATION BY STATE AND REGIONAL CONCENTRATION

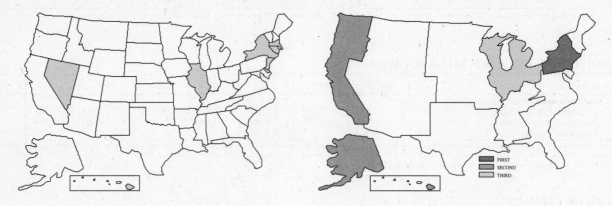

FIRST
SECOND
THIRD

INDUSTRY DATA BY STATE

State	Establishments		Employment			Payroll		Revenues		
	Total (number)	% of U.S.	Total (number)	% of U.S.	Per Estab.	Total ($ mil.)	Per Empl. ($)	Total ($ mil.)	% of U.S.	Per Estab. ($)
New York	681	21.1	5,613	19.1	8	108.8	19,387	651.8	34.8	957,094
New Jersey	413	12.8	4,057	13.8	10	72.7	17,913	219.7	11.7	531,869
California	326	10.1	3,847	13.1	12	58.1	15,098	201.4	10.7	617,856
Illinois	243	7.5	1,883	6.4	8	40.3	21,389	133.7	7.1	550,181
Connecticut	115	3.6	1,589	5.4	14	35.6	22,398	87.1	4.6	757,183
Massachusetts	121	3.7	1,712	5.8	14	30.5	17,800	66.9	3.6	553,223
D.C.	15	0.5	268	0.9	18	9.3	34,616	63.3	3.4	4,219,000
Florida	178	5.5	878	3.0	5	12.7	14,432	60.1	3.2	337,663
Pennsylvania	94	2.9	1,116	3.8	12	16.1	14,405	47.0	2.5	500,436
Texas	113	3.5	992	3.4	9	14.9	14,985	44.0	2.4	389,796
Nevada	9	0.3	618	2.1	69	9.3	15,008	24.9	1.3	2,767,000
Georgia	50	1.5	217	0.7	4	3.2	14,714	22.2	1.2	444,100
Ohio	75	2.3	554	1.9	7	5.7	10,273	19.8	1.1	263,800
Minnesota	41	1.3	387	1.3	9	5.2	13,419	17.8	1.0	434,463
Michigan	48	1.5	345	1.2	7	3.9	11,183	15.5	0.8	323,708
Arizona	33	1.0	302	1.0	9	4.3	14,278	14.7	0.8	446,545
Louisiana	38	1.2	377	1.3	10	4.0	10,623	13.4	0.7	351,921
Colorado	37	1.1	292	1.0	8	3.3	11,240	11.5	0.6	310,757
Missouri	36	1.1	328	1.1	9	3.7	11,375	10.5	0.6	293,028
Hawaii	25	0.8	225	0.8	9	3.8	16,778	10.4	0.6	416,600
Wisconsin	53	1.6	360	1.2	7	3.5	9,689	10.3	0.6	195,113
Oregon	29	0.9	253	0.9	9	3.0	11,897	8.3	0.4	287,483
North Carolina	31	1.0	255	0.9	8	2.6	10,184	8.2	0.4	264,677
New Hampshire	24	0.7	227	0.8	9	2.9	12,634	7.2	0.4	299,833
Indiana	32	1.0	161	0.5	5	1.7	10,839	6.1	0.3	189,313
Tennessee	19	0.6	180	0.6	9	2.2	12,417	6.1	0.3	321,053
Delaware	14	0.4	129	0.4	9	1.7	13,481	5.4	0.3	383,643
Maine	10	0.3	98	0.3	10	1.4	14,469	3.9	0.2	386,500
Kansas	18	0.6	62	0.2	3	0.6	9,516	3.0	0.2	169,000
Alabama	11	0.3	42	0.1	4	0.4	10,048	1.6	0.1	144,727
Oklahoma	8	0.2	63	0.2	8	0.5	7,698	1.4	0.1	176,875
Utah	7	0.2	36	0.1	5	0.4	11,722	1.4	0.1	196,714
West Virginia	6	0.2	34	0.1	6	0.5	13,882	1.4	0.1	235,667
Iowa	16	0.5	74	0.3	5	0.4	4,757	1.3	0.1	79,375
Nebraska	10	0.3	59	0.2	6	0.4	6,542	1.3	0.1	131,900
Arkansas	8	0.2	33	0.1	4	0.3	10,303	1.2	0.1	146,625
South Dakota	9	0.3	42	0.1	5	0.2	4,976	0.9	0.0	95,222
Vermont	8	0.2	40	0.1	5	0.2	4,825	0.9	0.0	110,000
Virginia	68	2.1	375*	-	-	(D)	-	(D)	-	-
Maryland	50	1.5	375*	-	-	(D)	-	(D)	-	-
Washington	37	1.1	375*	-	-	(D)	-	(D)	-	-
Kentucky	21	0.6	175*	-	-	(D)	-	(D)	-	-
South Carolina	14	0.4	175*	-	-	(D)	-	(D)	-	-
Rhode Island	11	0.3	60*	-	-	(D)	-	(D)	-	-
North Dakota	9	0.3	60*	-	-	(D)	-	(D)	-	-

Source: 1997 *Economic Census*. The states are in descending order of revenues or establishments (if revenue data are missing for the majority). The symbol (D) appears when data are withheld to prevent disclosure of competitive information. States marked with (D) are sorted by number of establishments. A dash (-) indicates that the data element cannot be calculated. * indicates the midpoint of a range; 175, for example is the range 100-249. Shaded *states* on the state map indicate those states which have proportionately greater representation in the industry than would be indicated by the state's population; the ratio is based on total revenues or number of establishments. Shaded *regions* indicate where the industry is regionally most concentrated.

NAICS 485410 - SCHOOL AND EMPLOYEE BUS TRANSPORTATION

GENERAL STATISTICS

Year	Establishments (number)	Employment (number)	Payroll ($ million)	Revenues ($ million)	Employees per Establishment (number)	Revenues per Establishment ($)	Payroll per Employee ($)
1997	1,434	42,754	1,308.1	12,196.1	29.8	8,504,951	30,596

Source: *Economic Census of the United States*, 1997. This is a newly defined industry. Data for prior years were unavailable at the time of publication but may become available over time.

SIC INDUSTRIES RELATED TO NAICS 485410

SIC	Industry	1990	1991	1992	1993	1994	1995	1996	1997
4154	**School Buses**	-	-	-	-	-	-	-	-
4119	**Local Passenger Transportation, nec***								
	Establishments (number)	5,187	5,991	7,140	7,652	7,915	7,800	8,305	8,988p
	Employment (thousands)	94.0	94.6	115.6	124.4	130.7	139.0	149.0	156.0p
	Revenues ($ million)	-	-	4,604.0	-	-	-	-	-

Source: *Economic Census of the United States*, 1992, annual surveys of economic sectors conducted by the Bureau of the Census, and estimates or projections based on the 1982-1992 period; not all data are shown. 'e' marks estimates made by the editors; 'p' indicates projections based on time series. A dash (-) indicates that data for this SIC or year were not available. * Indicates that only a portion of this industry is present within the NAICS data. If no * is shown, the entire industry is contained within the NAICS data.

INDICES OF CHANGE

Year	Establishments (number)	Employment (number)	Payroll ($ million)	Revenues ($ million)	Employees per Establishment (number)	Revenues per Establishment ($)	Payroll per Employee ($)
1997	100.0	100.0	100.0	100.0	100.0	100.0	100.0

Sources: Same as General Statistics. The values shown reflect change from the base year, 1997. Values above 100 mean greater than 1997, values below 100 mean less than 1997, and a value of 100 in years other than 1997 means same as 1997. Indices are calculated only for Census years. Data are the most recent available at this level of detail.

SELECTED RATIOS

For 1997	Avg. of Sector	Analyzed Industry	Index	For 1997	Avg. of Sector	Analyzed Industry	Index
Employees per establishment	16	30	182	Payroll per establishment	462,554	912,204	197
Revenue per establishment	1,787,642	8,504,951	476	Payroll as % of revenue	26	11	41
Revenue per employee	108,959	285,262	262	Payroll per employee	28,193	30,596	109

Sources: Same as General Statistics. The 'Average of Sector' column represents the average for all industries in this sector. The Index shows the relationship between the Average and the Analyzed Industry. For example, 100 means that they are equal; 500 that the Analyzed Industry is five times the average; 50 means that the Analyzed Industry is half the national average. 'na' is used to show that data are 'not available'.

LEADING COMPANIES   Number shown: **4**   Total sales ($ mil): **838**   Total employment (000): **24.8**

Company Name	Address				CEO Name	Phone	Co. Type	Sales ($ mil)	Empl. (000)
Atlantic Express Transportation	7 North St	Staten Island	NY	10302	Domenic Gatto	718-442-7000	R	262	5.8
Laidlaw Transit Services Inc.	PO Box 7941	Shawnee Msn	KS	66207		913-345-1986	S	236	10.0
Ryder Student Transportation	3600 N W 82nd Ave	Miami	FL	33166	John Dorr	305-593-4112	D	189*	5.0
Durham Transportation Inc.	9011 Mtn Ridge	Austin	TX	78759	Larry K Durham	512-343-6292	R	151	4.0

Source: Ward's Business Directory of U.S. Private and Public Companies, Volumes 1 and 2, 2000. The company type code used is as follows: P - Public, R - Private, S - Subsidiary, D - Division, J - Joint Venture, A - Affiliate, G - Group, N - Company type not reported. Sales are in millions of dollars, employees are in thousands. An asterisk (*) indicates an estimated sales volume. The symbol < stands for 'less than'. Company names and addresses are truncated, in some cases, to fit into the available space.

LOCATION BY STATE AND REGIONAL CONCENTRATION

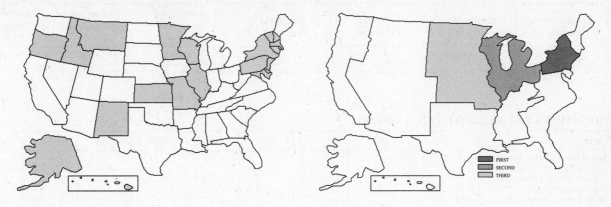

FIRST
SECOND
THIRD

INDUSTRY DATA BY STATE

State	Establishments Total (number)	% of U.S.	Employment Total (number)	% of U.S.	Per Estab.	Payroll Total ($ mil.)	Per Empl. ($)	Revenues Total ($ mil.)	% of U.S.	Per Estab. ($)
New York	422	9.4	27,218	17.9	64	454.9	16,713	940.1	21.4	2,227,749
Pennsylvania	647	14.4	16,195	10.7	25	167.9	10,369	437.5	10.0	676,230
Illinois	239	5.3	12,779	8.4	53	149.4	11,693	380.4	8.7	1,591,498
New Jersey	224	5.0	12,641	8.3	56	153.6	12,154	338.6	7.7	1,511,527
California	104	2.3	8,734	5.8	84	136.3	15,601	319.5	7.3	3,071,750
Wisconsin	268	6.0	8,827	5.8	33	92.1	10,434	227.3	5.2	848,011
Minnesota	245	5.5	8,128	5.4	33	90.3	11,104	215.1	4.9	878,016
Massachusetts	170	3.8	7,536	5.0	44	87.8	11,647	201.4	4.6	1,184,518
Connecticut	115	2.6	5,080	3.3	44	71.1	13,997	175.2	4.0	1,523,461
Missouri	188	4.2	6,809	4.5	36	67.7	9,944	165.0	3.8	877,564
Maryland	443	9.9	3,704	2.4	8	41.6	11,243	109.7	2.5	247,707
Kansas	62	1.4	2,703	1.8	44	40.7	15,043	93.5	2.1	1,507,919
Ohio	56	1.2	2,920	1.9	52	34.1	11,690	77.3	1.8	1,380,179
Texas	40	0.9	2,827	1.9	71	23.0	8,125	55.5	1.3	1,387,450
Oregon	50	1.1	2,019	1.3	40	20.4	10,101	53.3	1.2	1,065,760
New Mexico	86	1.9	1,942	1.3	23	18.5	9,544	46.1	1.0	535,674
New Hampshire	51	1.1	1,730	1.1	34	18.2	10,540	45.2	1.0	887,137
Washington	18	0.4	1,451	1.0	81	19.5	13,429	44.6	1.0	2,475,222
Florida	127	2.8	1,467	1.0	12	15.2	10,358	41.8	1.0	329,165
Tennessee	173	3.9	1,485	1.0	9	15.0	10,094	40.7	0.9	235,121
Rhode Island	31	0.7	1,580	1.0	51	16.6	10,513	38.9	0.9	1,254,613
Indiana	83	1.9	1,360	0.9	16	14.1	10,369	33.7	0.8	406,048
Alaska	27	0.6	1,103	0.7	41	13.9	12,638	30.0	0.7	1,111,370
Delaware	117	2.6	1,116	0.7	10	10.8	9,667	29.9	0.7	255,598
Michigan	31	0.7	958	0.6	31	12.8	13,361	28.7	0.7	926,581
Hawaii	21	0.5	1,104	0.7	53	10.7	9,659	23.9	0.5	1,137,381
Idaho	27	0.6	958	0.6	35	8.4	8,788	21.2	0.5	784,963
Montana	78	1.7	916	0.6	12	7.1	7,799	19.1	0.4	244,859
Colorado	11	0.2	563	0.4	51	7.9	14,034	14.1	0.3	1,277,727
Nebraska	22	0.5	565	0.4	26	5.5	9,690	13.5	0.3	615,682
Maine	18	0.4	450	0.3	25	4.7	10,511	12.8	0.3	708,833
Vermont	24	0.5	462	0.3	19	5.9	12,703	12.4	0.3	517,292
Georgia	26	0.6	448	0.3	17	4.6	10,174	11.9	0.3	457,231
Iowa	21	0.5	497	0.3	24	4.8	9,740	10.8	0.2	513,762
Alabama	14	0.3	428	0.3	31	3.5	8,199	8.6	0.2	615,214
South Dakota	23	0.5	443	0.3	19	3.2	7,246	8.5	0.2	369,957
North Dakota	26	0.6	324	0.2	12	2.4	7,293	7.0	0.2	267,615
North Carolina	27	0.6	157	0.1	6	1.2	7,841	3.8	0.1	141,741
Mississippi	17	0.4	165	0.1	10	1.1	6,745	2.7	0.1	157,588
Louisiana	23	0.5	61	0.0	3	0.6	10,639	1.7	0.0	72,913
Arizona	14	0.3	375*	-	-	(D)	-	(D)	-	-
Kentucky	14	0.3	375*	-	-	(D)	-	(D)	-	-
Virginia	14	0.3	175*	-	-	(D)	-	(D)	-	-
Oklahoma	11	0.2	60*	-	-	(D)	-	(D)	-	-
Arkansas	8	0.2	60*	-	-	(D)	-	(D)	-	-
Utah	8	0.2	375*	-	-	(D)	-	(D)	-	-
South Carolina	7	0.2	375*	-	-	(D)	-	(D)	-	-

Source: 1997 *Economic Census*. The states are in descending order of revenues or establishments (if revenue data are missing for the majority). The symbol (D) appears when data are withheld to prevent disclosure of competitive information. States marked with (D) are sorted by number of establishments. A dash (-) indicates that the data element cannot be calculated. * indicates the midpoint of a range; 175, for example is the range 100-249. Shaded *states* on the state map indicate those states which have proportionately greater representation in the industry than would be indicated by the state's population; the ratio is based on total revenues or number of establishments. Shaded *regions* indicate where the industry is regionally most concentrated.

NAICS 485510 - CHARTER BUS INDUSTRY

GENERAL STATISTICS

Year	Establishments (number)	Employment (number)	Payroll ($ million)	Revenues ($ million)	Employees per Establishment (number)	Revenues per Establishment ($)	Payroll per Employee ($)
1997	364	23,234	612.8	4,088.8	63.8	11,232,967	26,375

Source: *Economic Census of the United States*, 1997. This is a newly defined industry. Data for prior years were unavailable at the time of publication but may become available over time.

SIC INDUSTRIES RELATED TO NAICS 485510

SIC	Industry	1990	1991	1992	1993	1994	1995	1996	1997
4141	**Local Bus Charter Service**								
	Establishments (number)	244	352	429	424	406	405	424	490p
	Employment (thousands)	7.3	9.4	7.7	8.4	8.4	8.7	9.5	9.7p
	Revenues ($ million)	-	-	375.2	-	-	-	-	-
4142	**Bus Charter Service, Except Local**								
	Establishments (number)	357	413	878	870	885	854	919	1,073p
	Employment (thousands)	8.3	10.9	16.9	17.5	18.1	18.7	19.2	21.8p
	Revenues ($ million)	-	-	893.9	-	-	-	-	-

Source: *Economic Census of the United States*, 1992, annual surveys of economic sectors conducted by the Bureau of the Census, and estimates or projections based on the 1982-1992 period; not all data are shown. 'e' marks estimates made by the editors; 'p' indicates projections based on time series. A dash (-) indicates that data for this SIC or year were not available. * Indicates that only a portion of this industry is present within the NAICS data. If no * is shown, the entire industry is contained within the NAICS data.

INDICES OF CHANGE

Year	Establishments (number)	Employment (number)	Payroll ($ million)	Revenues ($ million)	Employees per Establishment (number)	Revenues per Establishment ($)	Payroll per Employee ($)
1997	100.0	100.0	100.0	100.0	100.0	100.0	100.0

Sources: Same as General Statistics. The values shown reflect change from the base year, 1997. Values above 100 mean greater than 1997, values below 100 mean less than 1997, and a value of 100 in years other than 1997 means same as 1997. Indices are calculated only for Census years. Data are the most recent available at this level of detail.

SELECTED RATIOS

For 1997	Avg. of Sector	Analyzed Industry	Index	For 1997	Avg. of Sector	Analyzed Industry	Index
Employees per establishment	16	64	389	Payroll per establishment	462,554	1,683,516	364
Revenue per establishment	1,787,642	11,232,967	628	Payroll as % of revenue	26	15	58
Revenue per employee	108,959	175,983	162	Payroll per employee	28,193	26,375	94

Sources: Same as General Statistics. The 'Average of Sector' column represents the average for all industries in this sector. The Index shows the relationship between the Average and the Analyzed Industry. For example, 100 means that they are equal; 500 that the Analyzed Industry is five times the average; 50 means that the Analyzed Industry is half the national average. 'na' is used to show that data are 'not available'.

LEADING COMPANIES   Number shown: **7**   Total sales ($ mil): **400**   Total employment (000): **11.8**

Company Name	Address				CEO Name	Phone	Co. Type	Sales ($ mil)	Empl. (000)
Laidlaw Transit Services Inc.	PO Box 7941	Shawnee Msn	KS	66207		913-345-1986	S	236	10.0
Peter Pan Bus Lines Inc.	PO Box 1776	Springfield	MA	01102	Peter A Picknelly Jr	413-781-2900	R	64*	0.8
Blue Bird Coach Lines Inc.	1 Blue Bird Sq	Olean	NY	14760	Louis A Magnano	716-372-5500	R	32*	0.3
Park Holdings Inc.	2060 Mount Paran	Atlanta	GA	30327	Frederick D Clemente	404-264-1000	R	27*	<0.1
Connecticut Limousine L.L.C.	230 Old Gate Ln	Milford	CT	06460	Andy Anastasio Jr	203-878-6867	R	18*	0.4
Jefferson Partners L.P.	2100 E 26th St	Minneapolis	MN	55404	Charles A Zelle	612-332-8745	R	17	0.2
Classic Transportation Group	1600 Locust Ave	Bohemia	NY	11716	William Schoolman	516-567-5100	R	6*	<0.1

Source: *Ward's Business Directory of U.S. Private and Public Companies*, Volumes 1 and 2, 2000. The company type code used is as follows: P - Public, R - Private, S - Subsidiary, D - Division, J - Joint Venture, A - Affiliate, G - Group, N - Company type not reported. Sales are in millions of dollars, employees are in thousands. An asterisk (*) indicates an estimated sales volume. The symbol < stands for 'less than'. Company names and addresses are truncated, in some cases, to fit into the available space.

LOCATION BY STATE AND REGIONAL CONCENTRATION

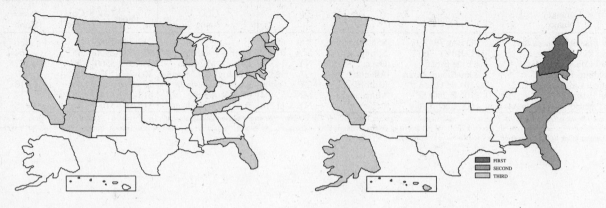

FIRST
SECOND
THIRD

INDUSTRY DATA BY STATE

State	Establishments Total (number)	Establishments % of U.S.	Employment Total (number)	Employment % of U.S.	Employment Per Estab.	Payroll Total ($ mil.)	Payroll Per Empl. ($)	Revenues Total ($ mil.)	Revenues % of U.S.	Revenues Per Estab. ($)
California	195	12.7	3,674	11.7	19	70.7	19,248	229.7	13.0	1,178,123
New York	114	7.4	2,700	8.6	24	52.1	19,294	157.7	8.9	1,383,289
Pennsylvania	79	5.2	2,710	8.6	34	46.3	17,086	147.2	8.3	1,863,899
Florida	83	5.4	1,903	6.0	23	29.2	15,357	93.9	5.3	1,131,687
Massachusetts	35	2.3	1,283	4.1	37	26.3	20,535	75.8	4.3	2,165,629
New Jersey	77	5.0	1,167	3.7	15	26.5	22,743	74.8	4.2	971,273
Illinois	63	4.1	1,197	3.8	19	20.2	16,881	64.8	3.7	1,029,302
Texas	72	4.7	1,119	3.6	16	16.5	14,718	63.6	3.6	883,083
Ohio	51	3.3	991	3.1	19	16.8	16,980	54.2	3.1	1,061,765
Maryland	50	3.3	852	2.7	17	15.7	18,473	53.5	3.0	1,070,460
Tennessee	31	2.0	713	2.3	23	14.9	20,955	50.1	2.8	1,616,742
Michigan	41	2.7	950	3.0	23	17.2	18,134	49.9	2.8	1,218,220
Virginia	44	2.9	951	3.0	22	15.4	16,174	45.5	2.6	1,034,159
North Carolina	55	3.6	707	2.2	13	10.3	14,515	45.0	2.5	817,618
Connecticut	14	0.9	515	1.6	37	16.2	31,396	44.9	2.5	3,209,286
Wisconsin	28	1.8	800	2.5	29	12.9	16,172	44.6	2.5	1,594,286
Indiana	32	2.1	763	2.4	24	11.9	15,532	40.9	2.3	1,277,500
Minnesota	47	3.1	833	2.6	18	10.9	13,096	35.1	2.0	747,638
Arizona	30	2.0	528	1.7	18	8.2	15,568	30.0	1.7	998,933
Washington	28	1.8	561	1.8	20	9.4	16,693	29.2	1.7	1,042,393
Louisiana	23	1.5	572	1.8	25	9.2	16,089	29.0	1.6	1,262,348
Georgia	32	2.1	481	1.5	15	8.0	16,538	27.9	1.6	871,469
Colorado	19	1.2	414	1.3	22	8.4	20,220	27.2	1.5	1,431,684
Alabama	31	2.0	577	1.8	19	6.8	11,735	24.0	1.4	772,968
Missouri	25	1.6	334	1.1	13	5.2	15,431	19.6	1.1	785,880
Iowa	18	1.2	329	1.0	18	4.6	14,064	17.1	1.0	951,000
Utah	7	0.5	358	1.1	51	5.7	16,036	15.8	0.9	2,260,143
Kansas	17	1.1	243	0.8	14	3.3	13,737	12.3	0.7	724,294
South Carolina	24	1.6	313	1.0	13	3.1	9,939	11.0	0.6	460,375
Kentucky	14	0.9	255	0.8	18	4.1	15,886	10.6	0.6	758,500
Oklahoma	10	0.7	165	0.5	16	2.4	14,309	9.6	0.5	964,500
Nebraska	13	0.8	221	0.7	17	3.6	16,127	9.1	0.5	700,615
Mississippi	17	1.1	241	0.8	14	3.0	12,618	9.0	0.5	529,118
Idaho	10	0.7	173	0.5	17	1.9	11,064	6.4	0.4	641,800
Montana	10	0.7	183	0.6	18	1.8	9,852	6.4	0.4	641,500
Arkansas	12	0.8	103	0.3	9	1.7	16,592	5.7	0.3	478,333
Vermont	7	0.5	56	0.2	8	1.6	27,696	5.3	0.3	758,286
South Dakota	6	0.4	99	0.3	16	1.2	12,121	5.0	0.3	833,167
West Virginia	9	0.6	110	0.3	12	1.5	13,218	4.2	0.2	464,000
Alaska	6	0.4	26	0.1	4	0.3	10,385	1.3	0.1	211,500
Nevada	10	0.7	750*	-	-	(D)	-	(D)	-	-
Rhode Island	7	0.5	175*	-	-	(D)	-	(D)	-	-
North Dakota	6	0.4	60*	-	-	(D)	-	(D)	-	-

Source: 1997 *Economic Census*. The states are in descending order of revenues or establishments (if revenue data are missing for the majority). The symbol (D) appears when data are withheld to prevent disclosure of competitive information. States marked with (D) are sorted by number of establishments. A dash (-) indicates that the data element cannot be calculated. * indicates the midpoint of a range; 175, for example is the range 100-249. Shaded *states* on the state map indicate those states which have proportionately greater representation in the industry than would be indicated by the state's population; the ratio is based on total revenues or number of establishments. Shaded *regions* indicate where the industry is regionally most concentrated.

NAICS 485991 - SPECIAL NEEDS TRANSPORTATION

GENERAL STATISTICS

Year	Establishments (number)	Employment (number)	Payroll ($ million)	Revenues ($ million)	Employees per Establishment (number)	Revenues per Establishment ($)	Payroll per Employee ($)
1997	1,365	15,175	535.6	2,702.8	11.1	1,980,073	35,295

Source: *Economic Census of the United States*, 1997. This is a newly defined industry. Data for prior years were unavailable at the time of publication but may become available over time.

SIC INDUSTRIES RELATED TO NAICS 485991

SIC	Industry	1990	1991	1992	1993	1994	1995	1996	1997
4119	**Local Passenger Transportation, nec***								
	Establishments (number)	5,187	5,991	7,140	7,652	7,915	7,800	8,305	8,988*p*
	Employment (thousands)	94.0	94.6	115.6	124.4	130.7	139.0	149.0	156.0*p*
	Revenues ($ million)	-	-	4,604.0	-	-	-	-	-

Source: *Economic Census of the United States*, 1992, annual surveys of economic sectors conducted by the Bureau of the Census, and estimates or projections based on the 1982-1992 period; not all data are shown. 'e' marks estimates made by the editors; 'p' indicates projections based on time series. A dash (-) indicates that data for this SIC or year were not available. * Indicates that only a portion of this industry is present within the NAICS data. If no * is shown, the entire industry is contained within the NAICS data.

INDICES OF CHANGE

Year	Establishments (number)	Employment (number)	Payroll ($ million)	Revenues ($ million)	Employees per Establishment (number)	Revenues per Establishment ($)	Payroll per Employee ($)
1997	100.0	100.0	100.0	100.0	100.0	100.0	100.0

Sources: Same as General Statistics. The values shown reflect change from the base year, 1997. Values above 100 mean greater than 1997, values below 100 mean less than 1997, and a value of 100 in years other than 1997 means same as 1997. Indices are calculated only for Census years. Data are the most recent available at this level of detail.

SELECTED RATIOS

For 1997	Avg. of Sector	Analyzed Industry	Index	For 1997	Avg. of Sector	Analyzed Industry	Index
Employees per establishment	16	11	68	Payroll per establishment	462,554	392,381	85
Revenue per establishment	1,787,642	1,980,073	111	Payroll as % of revenue	26	20	77
Revenue per employee	108,959	178,109	163	Payroll per employee	28,193	35,295	125

Sources: Same as General Statistics. The 'Average of Sector' column represents the average for all industries in this sector. The Index shows the relationship between the Average and the Analyzed Industry. For example, 100 means that they are equal; 500 that the Analyzed Industry is five times the average; 50 means that the Analyzed Industry is half the national average. 'na' is used to show that data are 'not available'.

LEADING COMPANIES

No company data available for this industry.

LOCATION BY STATE AND REGIONAL CONCENTRATION

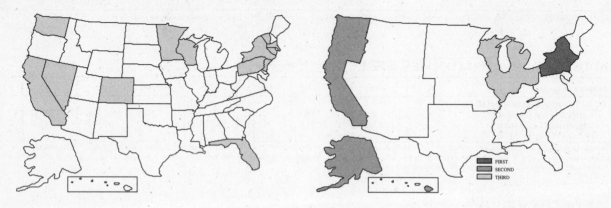

FIRST
SECOND
THIRD

INDUSTRY DATA BY STATE

State	Establishments		Employment			Payroll		Revenues		
	Total (number)	% of U.S.	Total (number)	% of U.S.	Per Estab.	Total ($ mil.)	Per Empl. ($)	Total ($ mil.)	% of U.S.	Per Estab. ($)
California	182	10.2	4,436	14.0	24	69.7	15,719	182.7	16.0	1,003,830
New York	258	14.4	4,892	15.4	19	84.4	17,245	180.0	15.8	697,853
Pennsylvania	59	3.3	2,422	7.6	41	37.6	15,507	110.7	9.7	1,875,915
Massachusetts	92	5.1	2,146	6.8	23	31.8	14,802	69.1	6.1	750,761
Florida	142	7.9	1,679	5.3	12	26.6	15,843	65.9	5.8	464,042
New Jersey	100	5.6	1,476	4.6	15	25.1	16,985	54.2	4.7	542,000
Washington	36	2.0	1,118	3.5	31	18.2	16,305	46.3	4.1	1,286,361
Minnesota	63	3.5	1,354	4.3	21	22.2	16,412	45.6	4.0	724,079
Illinois	62	3.5	1,117	3.5	18	20.4	18,224	39.5	3.5	636,306
Wisconsin	128	7.2	1,241	3.9	10	15.6	12,551	36.2	3.2	283,117
Texas	32	1.8	686	2.2	21	10.1	14,717	23.8	2.1	743,562
Tennessee	31	1.7	739	2.3	24	8.7	11,789	21.8	1.9	702,806
Ohio	51	2.9	874	2.7	17	9.9	11,287	21.2	1.9	415,176
Connecticut	27	1.5	536	1.7	20	10.4	19,491	20.6	1.8	763,704
Georgia	48	2.7	557	1.8	12	6.8	12,162	19.8	1.7	412,729
Michigan	33	1.8	405	1.3	12	6.4	15,805	18.1	1.6	549,455
Indiana	32	1.8	659	2.1	21	8.5	12,885	18.0	1.6	562,875
Missouri	29	1.6	721	2.3	25	8.9	12,390	17.1	1.5	588,000
Colorado	18	1.0	481	1.5	27	7.5	15,545	15.9	1.4	885,611
Arizona	21	1.2	457	1.4	22	6.9	15,059	15.4	1.3	731,238
Nevada	7	0.4	327	1.0	47	5.0	15,327	10.7	0.9	1,522,714
North Carolina	34	1.9	239	0.8	7	3.2	13,280	7.1	0.6	209,706
Oregon	25	1.4	231	0.7	9	2.8	12,121	6.2	0.5	248,560
D.C.	12	0.7	147	0.5	12	1.9	13,170	4.3	0.4	358,333
Arkansas	8	0.4	87	0.3	11	1.1	12,575	4.2	0.4	521,500
Vermont	7	0.4	79	0.2	11	1.2	14,861	3.3	0.3	471,857
New Hampshire	6	0.3	22	0.1	4	0.8	38,318	2.2	0.2	366,667
Kansas	12	0.7	66	0.2	6	0.7	10,985	1.7	0.2	145,250
South Dakota	13	0.7	79	0.2	6	0.7	9,342	1.5	0.1	119,000
New Mexico	6	0.3	24	0.1	4	0.5	20,583	1.3	0.1	212,833
Louisiana	39	2.2	175*	-	-	(D)	-	(D)	-	-
Virginia	36	2.0	375*	-	-	(D)	-	(D)	-	-
Maryland	34	1.9	375*	-	-	(D)	-	(D)	-	-
Kentucky	21	1.2	375*	-	-	(D)	-	(D)	-	-
Iowa	18	1.0	175*	-	-	(D)	-	(D)	-	-
Alabama	10	0.6	175*	-	-	(D)	-	(D)	-	-
South Carolina	9	0.5	175*	-	-	(D)	-	(D)	-	-

Source: 1997 *Economic Census*. The states are in descending order of revenues or establishments (if revenue data are missing for the majority). The symbol (D) appears when data are withheld to prevent disclosure of competitive information. States marked with (D) are sorted by number of establishments. A dash (-) indicates that the data element cannot be calculated. * indicates the midpoint of a range; 175, for example is the range 100-249. Shaded *states* on the state map indicate those states which have proportionately greater representation in the industry than would be indicated by the state's population; the ratio is based on total revenues or number of establishments. Shaded *regions* indicate where the industry is regionally most concentrated.

NAICS 485999 - TRANSIT AND GROUND PASSENGER TRANSPORTATION NEC

GENERAL STATISTICS

Year	Establishments (number)	Employment (number)	Payroll ($ million)	Revenues ($ million)	Employees per Establishment (number)	Revenues per Establishment ($)	Payroll per Employee ($)
1997	165	4,009	148.9	770.2	24.3	4,667,879	37,141

Source: Economic Census of the United States, 1997. This is a newly defined industry. Data for prior years were unavailable at the time of publication but may become available over time.

SIC INDUSTRIES RELATED TO NAICS 485999

SIC	Industry	1990	1991	1992	1993	1994	1995	1996	1997
4111	**Local and Suburban Transit***								
	Establishments (number)	678	927	1,135	1,114	1,059	1,107	1,221	1,302p
	Employment (thousands)	41.0	52.4	37.7	40.3	43.7	44.1	45.7	45.9p
	Revenues ($ million)	-	-	1,364.0	-	-	-	-	-
4119	**Local Passenger Transportation, nec***								
	Establishments (number)	5,187	5,991	7,140	7,652	7,915	7,800	8,305	8,988p
	Employment (thousands)	94.0	94.6	115.6	124.4	130.7	139.0	149.0	156.0p
	Revenues ($ million)	-	-	4,604.0	-	-	-	-	-

Source: Economic Census of the United States, 1992, annual surveys of economic sectors conducted by the Bureau of the Census, and estimates or projections based on the 1982-1992 period; not all data are shown. 'e' marks estimates made by the editors; 'p' indicates projections based on time series. A dash (-) indicates that data for this SIC or year were not available. * Indicates that only a portion of this industry is present within the NAICS data. If no * is shown, the entire industry is contained within the NAICS data.

INDICES OF CHANGE

Year	Establishments (number)	Employment (number)	Payroll ($ million)	Revenues ($ million)	Employees per Establishment (number)	Revenues per Establishment ($)	Payroll per Employee ($)
1997	100.0	100.0	100.0	100.0	100.0	100.0	100.0

Sources: Same as General Statistics. The values shown reflect change from the base year, 1997. Values above 100 mean greater than 1997, values below 100 mean less than 1997, and a value of 100 in years other than 1997 means same as 1997. Indices are calculated only for Census years. Data are the most recent available at this level of detail.

SELECTED RATIOS

For 1997	Avg. of Sector	Analyzed Industry	Index	For 1997	Avg. of Sector	Analyzed Industry	Index
Employees per establishment	16	24	148	Payroll per establishment	462,554	902,424	195
Revenue per establishment	1,787,642	4,667,879	261	Payroll as % of revenue	26	19	75
Revenue per employee	108,959	192,118	176	Payroll per employee	28,193	37,141	132

Sources: Same as General Statistics. The 'Average of Sector' column represents the average for all industries in this sector. The Index shows the relationship between the Average and the Analyzed Industry. For example, 100 means that they are equal; 500 that the Analyzed Industry is five times the average; 50 means that the Analyzed Industry is half the national average. 'na' is used to show that data are 'not available'.

LEADING COMPANIES   Number shown: 16   Total sales ($ mil): 2,515   Total employment (000): 44.2

Company Name	Address				CEO Name	Phone	Co. Type	Sales ($ mil)	Empl. (000)
American Medical Response Inc.	2821 S Parker Rd	Aurora	CO	80014	George DeHuff III	303-614-8500	S	1,012	24.0
Rural/Metro Corp.	8401 E Ind Schl	Scottsdale	AZ	85251	Warren S Rustand	480-994-3886	P	561	12.0
Emergency Medical Service	55-30 58th St	Maspeth	NY	11378	David Diggs	718-416-7000	R	464*	3.5
Carey International Inc.	4530 Wisconsin Ave	Washington	DC	20016	Vincent Wolfington	202-895-1200	P	191	1.8
Tauck Tours Inc.	276 Post Rd W	Westport	CT	06880	Peter Tauck	203-226-6911	R	50*	0.4
Buck Medical Services Inc.	P O Box 15339	Portland	OR	97215	Trace Skeen	503-231-6300	R	42*	0.3
Metro Ambulance Service Inc.	4349 Monticello	South Euclid	OH	44121	John Furman	216-381-6001	S	40*	0.3
Rural Metro Inc.	3969 Meadows Dr	Indianapolis	IN	46205	John Karozack	317-546-1581	S	39*	0.3
Hunter Ambulette-Ambulance Inc.	28 Sheridan Blvd	Inwood	NY	11696	Roberta LaBowitz	516-371-2622	R	33*	0.3
TransCare Pennsylvania	706-B Long Run Rd	Mc Keesport	PA	15132	Jayme Bursman	412-829-8086	D	24*	0.2
Community Medical Transport	4 Gannett Dr	White Plains	NY	10604	Dean Sloane	914-697-9233	P	18	0.5
Network Ambulance	4730 Market St	Philadelphia	PA	19139	Dean Bolendorph	215-476-3800	S	18	0.4
Custom Transportation Service	20 Rex Dr	Braintree	MA	02184	John M Greene		S	6*	0.2
Thompson and Ward Leasing Co.	1131 W 5th Ave	Columbus	OH	43212	Jim Ward	614-297-8880	R	6*	<0.1
Classic Transportation Group	1600 Locust Ave	Bohemia	NY	11716	William Schoolman	516-567-5100	R	6*	<0.1
Carey Limousine of San Fancisco	137 S Linden Ave	S. San Francisco	CA	94080		650-761-3000	R	4*	<0.1

Source: Ward's Business Directory of U.S. Private and Public Companies, Volumes 1 and 2, 2000. The company type code used is as follows: P - Public, R - Private, S - Subsidiary, D - Division, J - Joint Venture, A - Affiliate, G - Group, N - Company type not reported. Sales are in millions of dollars, employees are in thousands. An asterisk (*) indicates an estimated sales volume. The symbol < stands for 'less than'. Company names and addresses are truncated, in some cases, to fit into the available space.

LOCATION BY STATE AND REGIONAL CONCENTRATION

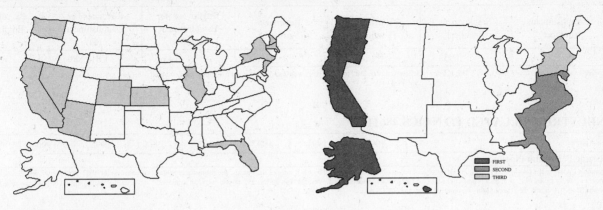

FIRST
SECOND
THIRD

INDUSTRY DATA BY STATE

State	Establishments		Employment			Payroll		Revenues		
	Total (number)	% of U.S.	Total (number)	% of U.S.	Per Estab.	Total ($ mil.)	Per Empl. ($)	Total ($ mil.)	% of U.S.	Per Estab. ($)
California	118	15.4	3,179	21.9	27	51.2	16,110	141.4	21.1	1,198,492
Florida	71	9.3	1,483	10.2	21	27.0	18,194	93.7	14.0	1,320,408
New York	60	7.8	888	6.1	15	21.6	24,339	56.5	8.4	942,333
New Jersey	46	6.0	539	3.7	12	12.1	22,488	42.6	6.4	926,935
Illinois	29	3.8	775	5.3	27	12.4	16,035	41.7	6.2	1,436,793
Colorado	24	3.1	846	5.8	35	11.5	13,643	30.6	4.6	1,273,583
Massachusetts	30	3.9	453	3.1	15	9.2	20,325	26.2	3.9	873,200
Arizona	25	3.3	577	4.0	23	8.4	14,558	17.8	2.7	712,520
Washington	16	2.1	483	3.3	30	7.6	15,669	16.8	2.5	1,049,063
Texas	21	2.7	483	3.3	23	5.6	11,582	15.9	2.4	757,190
Michigan	14	1.8	317	2.2	23	5.2	16,312	15.2	2.3	1,088,786
Indiana	10	1.3	239	1.6	24	4.4	18,397	14.1	2.1	1,408,900
Pennsylvania	19	2.5	355	2.4	19	4.7	13,270	13.4	2.0	704,316
Virginia	16	2.1	273	1.9	17	3.5	12,821	11.5	1.7	716,125
Nevada	7	0.9	270	1.9	39	4.4	16,330	9.6	1.4	1,367,000
Georgia	25	3.3	311	2.1	12	4.0	12,717	8.0	1.2	319,440
Minnesota	15	2.0	237	1.6	16	2.6	11,055	7.2	1.1	483,067
Kansas	11	1.4	242	1.7	22	2.9	12,186	6.4	1.0	578,727
New Hampshire	9	1.2	205	1.4	23	2.4	11,922	5.4	0.8	604,889
Missouri	12	1.6	175	1.2	15	1.7	9,520	4.3	0.6	359,250
North Carolina	15	2.0	150	1.0	10	1.4	9,467	3.5	0.5	235,733
Utah	6	0.8	75	0.5	13	0.8	10,400	2.8	0.4	472,667
Connecticut	7	0.9	38	0.3	5	0.5	12,211	2.7	0.4	380,143
Tennessee	11	1.4	93	0.6	8	1.0	10,452	2.2	0.3	198,000
New Mexico	10	1.3	63	0.4	6	0.8	12,905	1.9	0.3	194,800
Oregon	9	1.2	48	0.3	5	0.5	9,396	1.1	0.2	122,222
Wisconsin	10	1.3	47	0.3	5	0.4	7,532	1.0	0.1	97,000
Maryland	24	3.1	375*	-	-	(D)	-	(D)	-	-
Ohio	19	2.5	375*	-	-	(D)	-	(D)	-	-
Hawaii	11	1.4	175*	-	-	(D)	-	(D)	-	-
Iowa	7	0.9	60*	-	-	(D)	-	(D)	-	-
South Carolina	7	0.9	60*	-	-	(D)	-	(D)	-	-
Delaware	6	0.8	175*	-	-	(D)	-	(D)	-	-
Kentucky	6	0.8	60*	-	-	(D)	-	(D)	-	-

Source: 1997 *Economic Census*. The states are in descending order of revenues or establishments (if revenue data are missing for the majority). The symbol (D) appears when data are withheld to prevent disclosure of competitive information. States marked with (D) are sorted by number of establishments. A dash (-) indicates that the data element cannot be calculated. * indicates the midpoint of a range; 175, for example is the range 100-249. Shaded *states* on the state map indicate those states which have proportionately greater representation in the industry than would be indicated by the state's population; the ratio is based on total revenues or number of establishments. Shaded *regions* indicate where the industry is regionally most concentrated.

NAICS 486110 - PIPELINE TRANSPORTATION OF CRUDE OIL

GENERAL STATISTICS

Year	Establishments (number)	Employment (number)	Payroll ($ million)	Revenues ($ million)	Employees per Establishment (number)	Revenues per Establishment ($)	Payroll per Employee ($)
1997	270	3,953	142.6	491.1	14.6	1,818,889	36,074

Source: *Economic Census of the United States*, 1997. This is a newly defined industry. Data for prior years were unavailable at the time of publication but may become available over time.

SIC INDUSTRIES RELATED TO NAICS 486110

SIC	Industry	1990	1991	1992	1993	1994	1995	1996	1997
4612	**Crude Petroleum Pipelines**	-	-	-	-	-	-	-	-

Source: *Economic Census of the United States*, 1992, annual surveys of economic sectors conducted by the Bureau of the Census, and estimates or projections based on the 1982-1992 period; not all data are shown. 'e' marks estimates made by the editors; 'p' indicates projections based on time series. A dash (-) indicates that data for this SIC or year were not available. * Indicates that only a portion of this industry is present within the NAICS data. If no * is shown, the entire industry is contained within the NAICS data.

INDICES OF CHANGE

Year	Establishments (number)	Employment (number)	Payroll ($ million)	Revenues ($ million)	Employees per Establishment (number)	Revenues per Establishment ($)	Payroll per Employee ($)
1997	100.0	100.0	100.0	100.0	100.0	100.0	100.0

Sources: Same as General Statistics. The values shown reflect change from the base year, 1997. Values above 100 mean greater than 1997, values below 100 mean less than 1997, and a value of 100 in years other than 1997 means same as 1997. Indices are calculated only for Census years. Data are the most recent available at this level of detail.

SELECTED RATIOS

For 1997	Avg. of Sector	Analyzed Industry	Index	For 1997	Avg. of Sector	Analyzed Industry	Index
Employees per establishment	16	15	89	Payroll per establishment	462,554	528,148	114
Revenue per establishment	1,787,642	1,818,889	102	Payroll as % of revenue	26	29	112
Revenue per employee	108,959	124,235	114	Payroll per employee	28,193	36,074	128

Sources: Same as General Statistics. The 'Average of Sector' column represents the average for all industries in this sector. The Index shows the relationship between the Average and the Analyzed Industry. For example, 100 means that they are equal; 500 that the Analyzed Industry is five times the average; 50 means that the Analyzed Industry is half the national average. 'na' is used to show that data are 'not available'.

LEADING COMPANIES   Number shown: **25**   Total sales ($ mil): **50,302**   Total employment (000): **58.5**

Company Name	Address				CEO Name	Phone	Co. Type	Sales ($ mil)	Empl. (000)
Koch Industries Inc.	PO Box 2256	Wichita	KS	67201		316-828-5500	R	36,200	15.6
Mobil Pipe Line Co.	P O Box 900	Dallas	TX	75221			S	3,000*	3.0
Marathon Ashland Petroleum	539 S Main St	Findlay	OH	45840		419-422-2121	R	2,000	30.0
TransMontaigne Oil Co.	370 17th St	Denver	CO	80202	Richard E Gathright	303-626-8200	P	1,968	0.4
Shell Services International	PO Box 2648	Houston	TX	77252	Steven Miller	713-241-6161	D	1,940	2.0
Plains All American Pipeline L.P.	500 Dallas St	Houston	TX	77002	Greg L Armstrong	713-654-1414	J	1,120	0.2
Sun Pipe Line Co.	907 S Detroit Ave	Tulsa	OK	74120	Deborah M Fretz	918-586-6700	S	725*	0.6
Coscol Petroleum Corp.	9 Greenway Plz	Houston	TX	77046	David A Arledge	713-877-1400	S	575*	0.5
TEPPCO	PO Box 2521	Houston	TX	77252	William Thacker	713-759-3636	J	429	0.7
Enbrery Inc	21 W Superior St	Duluth	MN	55802	Larry Brian	218-725-0100	S	395*	0.5
Pride Companies L.P.	PO Box 3237	Abilene	TX	79604	Brad Stephens	915-674-8000	P	380	0.2
Kaneb Services Inc.	2435 N Cen Expwy	Richardson	TX	75080	John R Barnes	972-699-4023	P	376	1.8
Lakehead Pipe Line Partners L.P.	21 W Superior St	Duluth	MN	55802	EC Hambrook	218-725-0100	P	313	0.4
Phillips Pipeline Co.	411 S Keeler Ave	Bartlesville	OK	74003	JT Webster	918-661-4550	S	189*	0.6
Marathon Ashland Pipe Line	539 S Main St	Findlay	OH	45840	DL Porter	419-422-2121	S	157	0.5
Unocal Pipeline Co.	376 S Valencia Ave	Brea	CA	92821	Brian C Conners	714-577-3153	S	150	0.2
BP Exploration (Alaska) Inc.	P O Box 196612	Anchorage	AK	99519	Richard Campbell	907-561-5111	S	100	1.2
El Paso Energy Partners L.P.	El Paso Energy Bldg	Houston	TX	77002	James H Lytal	713-420-2131	P	97	<0.1
Jayhawk Pipeline Corp.	P O Box 1404	McPherson	KS	67460	JF Loving	316-755-0241	J	76*	<0.1
All American Pipeline Co.	P O Box 40160	Bakersfield	CA	93384	Greg Armstrong	661-664-5300	S	63*	<0.1
Platte Pipe Line Company Inc.	539 S Main St	Findlay	OH	45840		419-422-2121	R	21	<0.1
Portal Pipe Line Co.	2625 5th Ave N E	Minot	ND	58703	mark Kinblom	701-857-0800	J	15*	<0.1
KLT Gas Inc.	P O Box 412612	Kansas City	MO	64141	David M McCoy	816-556-2881	S	6	<0.1
Longhorn Partners Pipeline L.P.	3633 Allen Pkwy	Houston	TX	77019	Carter R Montgomery	713-529-1555	R	5	<0.1
Blue Dolphin Energy Co.	801 Travis	Houston	TX	77002	Michael J Jacobson	713-227-7600	P	4	<0.1

Source: *Ward's Business Directory of U.S. Private and Public Companies*, Volumes 1 and 2, 2000. The company type code used is as follows: P - Public, R - Private, S - Subsidiary, D - Division, J - Joint Venture, A - Affiliate, G - Group, N - Company type not reported. Sales are in millions of dollars, employees are in thousands. An asterisk (*) indicates an estimated sales volume. The symbol < stands for 'less than'. Company names and addresses are truncated, in some cases, to fit into the available space.

LOCATION BY STATE AND REGIONAL CONCENTRATION

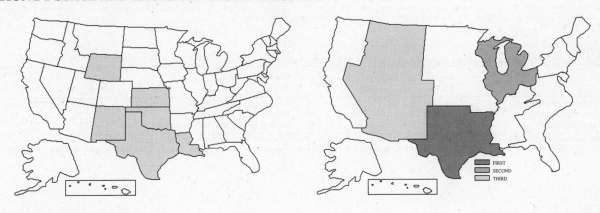

INDUSTRY DATA BY STATE

State	Establishments Total (number)	% of U.S.	Employment Total (number)	% of U.S.	Per Estab.	Payroll Total ($ mil.)	Per Empl. ($)	Revenues Total ($ mil.)	% of U.S.	Per Estab. ($)
Texas	123	32.2	2,383	29.9	19	130.0	54,563	1,099.3	25.2	8,937,447
Louisiana	35	9.2	487	6.1	14	25.9	53,164	287.0	6.6	8,199,000
Illinois	21	5.5	495	6.2	24	30.9	62,414	177.2	4.1	8,438,619
Oklahoma	20	5.2	429	5.4	21	19.8	46,098	156.9	3.6	7,844,150
Wyoming	19	5.0	330	4.1	17	15.2	45,921	109.2	2.5	5,745,000
Kansas	14	3.7	360	4.5	26	15.8	43,781	55.9	1.3	3,995,000
Colorado	8	2.1	108	1.4	14	6.1	56,528	51.6	1.2	6,449,125
New Mexico	15	3.9	150	1.9	10	6.4	42,693	48.6	1.1	3,241,133
Ohio	10	2.6	235	3.0	23	11.3	48,149	41.0	0.9	4,098,900
Mississippi	8	2.1	63	0.8	8	3.0	47,952	18.4	0.4	2,305,000
California	26	6.8	750*	-	-	(D)	-	(D)	-	-
Michigan	7	1.8	175*	-	-	(D)	-	(D)	-	-
Missouri	7	1.8	60*	-	-	(D)	-	(D)	-	-
Kentucky	6	1.6	60*	-	-	(D)	-	(D)	-	-

Source: 1997 *Economic Census*. The states are in descending order of revenues or establishments (if revenue data are missing for the majority). The symbol (D) appears when data are withheld to prevent disclosure of competitive information. States marked with (D) are sorted by number of establishments. A dash (-) indicates that the data element cannot be calculated. * indicates the midpoint of a range; 175, for example is the range 100-249. Shaded *states* on the state map indicate those states which have proportionately greater representation in the industry than would be indicated by the state's population; the ratio is based on total revenues or number of establishments. Shaded *regions* indicate where the industry is regionally most concentrated.

NAICS 486210 - PIPELINE TRANSPORTATION OF NATURAL GAS

GENERAL STATISTICS

Year	Establishments (number)	Employment (number)	Payroll ($ million)	Revenues ($ million)	Employees per Establishment (number)	Revenues per Establishment ($)	Payroll per Employee ($)
1997	1,450	35,789	1,870.9	19,626.8	24.7	13,535,724	52,276

Source: *Economic Census of the United States*, 1997. This is a newly defined industry. Data for prior years were unavailable at the time of publication but may become available over time.

SIC INDUSTRIES RELATED TO NAICS 486210

SIC	Industry	1990	1991	1992	1993	1994	1995	1996	1997
4922	**Natural Gas Transmission**								
	Establishments (number)	-	-	515	-	-	-	-	-
	Employment (thousands)	-	-	12.9	-	-	-	-	-
	Revenues ($ million)	-	-	8,739.6	-	-	-	-	-
4923	**Natural Gas Transmission and Distribution***								
	Establishments (number)	-	-	1,648	-	-	-	-	-
	Employment (thousands)	-	-	69.3	-	-	-	-	-
	Revenues ($ million)	-	-	29,313.7	-	-	-	-	-

Source: *Economic Census of the United States*, 1992, annual surveys of economic sectors conducted by the Bureau of the Census, and estimates or projections based on the 1982-1992 period; not all data are shown. 'e' marks estimates made by the editors; 'p' indicates projections based on time series. A dash (-) indicates that data for this SIC or year were not available. * Indicates that only a portion of this industry is present within the NAICS data. If no * is shown, the entire industry is contained within the NAICS data.

INDICES OF CHANGE

Year	Establishments (number)	Employment (number)	Payroll ($ million)	Revenues ($ million)	Employees per Establishment (number)	Revenues per Establishment ($)	Payroll per Employee ($)
1997	100.0	100.0	100.0	100.0	100.0	100.0	100.0

Sources: Same as General Statistics. The values shown reflect change from the base year, 1997. Values above 100 mean greater than 1997, values below 100 mean less than 1997, and a value of 100 in years other than 1997 means same as 1997. Indices are calculated only for Census years. Data are the most recent available at this level of detail.

SELECTED RATIOS

For 1997	Avg. of Sector	Analyzed Industry	Index	For 1997	Avg. of Sector	Analyzed Industry	Index
Employees per establishment	16	25	150	Payroll per establishment	462,554	1,290,276	279
Revenue per establishment	1,787,642	13,535,724	757	Payroll as % of revenue	26	10	37
Revenue per employee	108,959	548,403	503	Payroll per employee	28,193	52,276	185

Sources: Same as General Statistics. The 'Average of Sector' column represents the average for all industries in this sector. The Index shows the relationship between the Average and the Analyzed Industry. For example, 100 means that they are equal; 500 that the Analyzed Industry is five times the average; 50 means that the Analyzed Industry is half the national average. 'na' is used to show that data are 'not available'.

LEADING COMPANIES   Number shown: **55**   Total sales ($ mil): **294,515**   Total employment (000): **184.6**

Company Name	Address				CEO Name	Phone	Co. Type	Sales ($ mil)	Empl. (000)
Exxon Mobil Corp.	5959 Las Colinas	Irving	TX	75039	Lee Raymond	972-444-1000	P	186,906	79.0
Citrus Corp.	P O Box 1188	Houston	TX	77251	Ken Lay	713-853-6161	J	11,390*	4.0
PanEnergy Corp.	P O Box 1642	Houston	TX	77251	Paul M Anderson	713-627-5400	S	10,385	8.3
Southern Energy Inc.	900 Ashwood Pkwy	Atlanta	GA	30338	Thomas G Boren	770-379-7000	S	10,000	15.0
Valero Energy Corp.	PO Box 500	San Antonio	TX	78292	William Greehey	210-370-2000	P	7,961	2.5
Texas Eastern Corp.	P O Box 1642	Houston	TX	77251	Richard Priory	713-627-5400	S	7,727*	2.0
Williams Companies Inc.	1 Williams Ctr	Tulsa	OK	74172	Keith Bailey	918-573-2000	P	7,658	21.0
El Paso Energy Corp.	1001 Louisiana St	Houston	TX	77002	Ronald Kuehn Jr	713-420-2131	P	5,782	3.6
El Paso Energy	1001 Louisane St	Houston	TX	77002	William Wise	713-420-2131	R	5,696*	2.0
Algonquin Gas Transmission Co.	1284 Soldiers Field	Boston	MA	02135		617-254-4050	S	4,760*	2.0
MCN Energy Group Inc.	500 Griswold St	Detroit	MI	48226	Stephen E Ewing	313-256-5500	P	4,393	3.0
Texas Eastern Transmission Corp.	P O Box 1642	Houston	TX	77251	Robert B Evans	713-627-4094	S	4,250	1.1
Northwestern Corp.	PO Box 1318	Huron	SD	57350	Richard R Hylland	605-978-2908	P	3,004	6.1
El Paso Natural Gas Co.	1001 Louisiana St	Houston	TX	77002		713-757-2131	P	2,786	0.8
LG and E Energy Corp.	PO Box 32030	Louisville	KY	40232	Roger W Hale	502-627-2000	P	2,707	5.4
CNG Transmission Corp.	445 W Main St	Clarksburg	WV	26302	George A Davidson Jr	412-690-1200	S	2,245*	6.5
TransMontaigne Oil Co.	370 17th St	Denver	CO	80202	Richard E Gathright	303-626-8200	P	1,968	0.4
Panhandle Eastern Pipeline Co.	P O Box 1642	Houston	TX	77251	Steven M Roverud	713-627-5400	S	1,906	1.0
Union Pacific Resources Group	PO Box 7	Fort Worth	TX	76101	George Lindahl III	817-321-6000	P	1,728	2.9
Mountaineer Gas Co.	414 Summer St	Charleston	WV	25301	Michael S Fletcher	304-347-0595	S	1,384*	0.5
Pakhoed Corp.	2000 W Loop S	Houston	TX	77027	Darwin H Simpson	713-623-0000	R	1,372*	0.5
MDU Resources Group Inc.	PO Box 5650	Bismarck	ND	58506	John Schuchart	701-222-7900	P	1,280	3.8
Great Lakes Gas Transmission	1 Woodward Ave	Detroit	MI	48226	Mike Durnin	313-596-4400	J	854*	0.3
Columbia Gas Transmission Corp.	12801 Fair Lakes	Fairfax	VA	22033	Catherine Abbott	703-227-3292	S	850*	2.5
ANR Pipeline Co.	500 Renaissance Ctr	Detroit	MI	48243	Jeffrey A Connelly	313-496-0200	S	662	1.9
Northern Natural Gas Co.	1111 S 103rd St	Omaha	NE	68124	William C Cordes	402-398-7200	S	600*	0.2
Enogex Inc.	PO Box 24300	Oklahoma City	OK	73124	Roger A Farrell	405-525-7788	S	509	0.6
Trunkline Gas Co.	P O Box 1642	Houston	TX	77251	Steven M Roverud	713-627-5400	S	470	0.3
Kinder Morgan Energy Partners	1301 McKinney St	Houston	TX	77010	William V Allison	713-844-9500	P	429	1.2
Southern Natural Gas Co.	AmSouth Tower	Birmingham	AL	35203	James C Yardley	205-325-7410	S	394	1.0
PG & E Gas Transmission	2100 S W River	Portland	OR	97201	Tom King	503-833-4000	S	340*	0.2
Northern Border Partners L.P.	1400 Smith St	Houston	TX	77002	Larry L DeRoin	713-853-6161	P	319	0.3
Columbia Gulf Transmission Co.	P O Box 683	Houston	TX	77001	Terrence L McGill	713-267-4100	S	294	0.5
Nuevo Energy Co.	1331 Lamar St	Houston	TX	77010	Douglas Foshee	713-652-0706	P	245*	0.9
Dominion Energy Inc.	PO Box 26532	Richmond	VA	23261	Thomas Farrell II	804-775-5700	S	215*	0.2
Questar Pipeline Co.	PO Box 45360	Salt Lake City	UT	84101	David N Rose	801-324-2684	S	211*	0.3
Cook Inlet Energy Supply	10100 Santa Monica	Los Angeles	CA	90067	Greg Craig	310-556-8956	R	150*	<0.1
El Paso Energy Partners L.P.	El Paso Energy Bldg	Houston	TX	77002	James H Lytal	713-420-2131	P	97	<0.1
Unit Corp.	1000 Kens Twr	Tulsa	OK	74136	King P Kirchner	918-493-7700	P	93	0.5
Williston Basin Interstate Pipeline	1250 W Century	Bismarck	ND	58501	John K Castleberry	701-530-1600	S	76	0.2
Fitchburg Gas & Electric Light	560 John Fitch Hwy	Fitchburg	MA	01420		978-343-6931	S	67*	0.1
Castle Energy Corp.	1 Radnor Corporate	Radnor	PA	19087	Joseph L Castle II	610-995-9400	P	57	<0.1
Oasis Pipe Line Texas L.P.	1000 Louisiana	Houston	TX	77002	MR Roper	713-758-9800	R	57*	<0.1
Encina Gas Marketing Inc.	1734 N Padre Island	Corpus Christi	TX	78403	Doug Williams	512-289-5875	S	57*	<0.1
Delta Natural Gas Company Inc.	3617 Lexington Rd	Winchester	KY	40391	Glenn R Jennings	606-744-6171	P	39	0.2
High Island Offshore System	500 Renaissance Ctr	Detroit	MI	48243		313-496-0200	R	29*	<0.1
Equitrans L.P.	3500 Park Ln	Pittsburgh	PA	15275	Murry Gerber	412-788-6066	S	28*	<0.1
Tenaska Inc.	1044 N 115th St	Omaha	NE	68154	Howard L Hawks	402-691-9500	R	21*	0.2
Cedar Falls Municipal Gas	P O Box 769	Cedar Falls	IA	50613		319-268-5222	R	19*	<0.1
Falcon Seaboard Resources Inc.	5 Post Oak Park	Houston	TX	77027	David H Dewhurst	713-622-0055	R	15*	<0.1
Wolverine Gas and Oil Co.	One Riverfront Plaza	Grand Rapids	MI	49503	Sid Jansma Jr	616-458-1150	S	11*	<0.1
Tennessee Gas Pipeline Co.	750 Old Hickory	Brentwood	TN	37027	J W Somerhalder II	615-661-5551	S	7	1.7
Bluefield Gas Co.	P O Box 589	Bluefield	WV	24701	John Williamson	304-327-7161	S	6	<0.1
Mountain Front Pipeline Co.	P O Box 702500	Tulsa	OK	74170	John Nikkel	918-493-7700	S	6*	<0.1
Basin Pipeline Corp.	2101 6th Ave N	Birmingham	AL	35203	Mike Warren	205-326-2700	S	1	0.0

Source: Ward's Business Directory of U.S. Private and Public Companies, Volumes 1 and 2, 2000. The company type code used is as follows: P - Public, R - Private, S - Subsidiary, D - Division, J - Joint Venture, A - Affiliate, G - Group, N - Company type not reported. Sales are in millions of dollars, employees are in thousands. An asterisk (*) indicates an estimated sales volume. The symbol < stands for 'less than'. Company names and addresses are truncated, in some cases, to fit into the available space.

407

LOCATION BY STATE AND REGIONAL CONCENTRATION

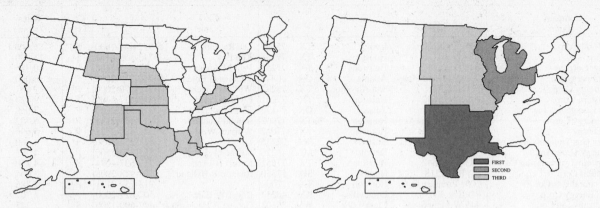

INDUSTRY DATA BY STATE

State	Establishments Total (number)	Establishments % of U.S.	Employment Total (number)	Employment % of U.S.	Employment Per Estab.	Payroll Total ($ mil.)	Payroll Per Empl. ($)	Revenues Total ($ mil.)	Revenues % of U.S.	Revenues Per Estab. ($)
Texas	285	19.7	6,289	17.6	22	400.9	63,750	5,519.4	28.1	19,366,147
Oklahoma	109	7.5	3,093	8.6	28	139.9	45,215	1,839.0	9.4	16,871,734
Louisiana	100	6.9	2,256	6.3	23	113.8	50,422	1,047.8	5.3	10,478,260
Pennsylvania	86	5.9	1,244	3.5	14	59.8	48,088	607.3	3.1	7,061,047
Michigan	41	2.8	1,494	4.2	36	80.9	54,157	595.1	3.0	14,515,463
New Mexico	33	2.3	350	1.0	11	20.7	59,109	455.1	2.3	13,789,667
Illinois	39	2.7	1,003	2.8	26	57.6	57,379	440.8	2.2	11,301,949
Kansas	70	4.8	920	2.6	13	46.0	49,974	406.7	2.1	5,809,743
Ohio	53	3.7	889	2.5	17	44.6	50,130	347.9	1.8	6,565,057
Kentucky	28	1.9	1,131	3.2	40	53.9	47,698	304.8	1.6	10,884,000
Mississippi	27	1.9	469	1.3	17	25.5	54,311	248.3	1.3	9,195,926
Nebraska	8	0.6	289	0.8	36	18.2	63,135	224.4	1.1	28,052,750
Iowa	26	1.8	363	1.0	14	21.4	59,000	211.6	1.1	8,137,038
Virginia	33	2.3	513	1.4	16	37.6	73,386	203.8	1.0	6,174,303
Alabama	20	1.4	283	0.8	14	18.3	64,583	203.8	1.0	10,187,850
Indiana	31	2.1	343	1.0	11	17.5	50,956	154.0	0.8	4,968,194
Wisconsin	16	1.1	142	0.4	9	6.9	48,852	131.9	0.7	8,243,312
Tennessee	20	1.4	233	0.7	12	13.0	55,661	110.6	0.6	5,532,300
Minnesota	26	1.8	234	0.7	9	12.1	51,551	89.8	0.5	3,453,115
Arkansas	10	0.7	139	0.4	14	7.0	50,626	86.7	0.4	8,670,400
Wyoming	9	0.6	205	0.6	23	10.2	49,615	78.3	0.4	8,699,556
Missouri	15	1.0	166	0.5	11	7.7	46,530	73.6	0.4	4,905,267
New York	26	1.8	190	0.5	7	9.4	49,495	69.7	0.4	2,680,385
Colorado	7	0.5	78	0.2	11	5.0	64,205	25.3	0.1	3,611,143
California	131	9.0	7,500*	-	-	(D)	-	(D)	-	-
West Virginia	75	5.2	1,750*	-	-	(D)	-	(D)	-	-
Arizona	20	1.4	175*	-	-	(D)	-	(D)	-	-
Florida	18	1.2	175*	-	-	(D)	-	(D)	-	-
New Jersey	12	0.8	175*	-	-	(D)	-	(D)	-	-
Georgia	9	0.6	175*	-	-	(D)	-	(D)	-	-
Maryland	8	0.6	60*	-	-	(D)	-	(D)	-	-
D.C.	6	0.4	60*	-	-	(D)	-	(D)	-	-
Utah	6	0.4	750*	-	-	(D)	-	(D)	-	-
Washington	6	0.4	375*	-	-	(D)	-	(D)	-	-

Source: 1997 *Economic Census*. The states are in descending order of revenues or establishments (if revenue data are missing for the majority). The symbol (D) appears when data are withheld to prevent disclosure of competitive information. States marked with (D) are sorted by number of establishments. A dash (-) indicates that the data element cannot be calculated. * indicates the midpoint of a range; 175, for example is the range 100-249. Shaded *states* on the state map indicate those states which have proportionately greater representation in the industry than would be indicated by the state's population; the ratio is based on total revenues or number of establishments. Shaded *regions* indicate where the industry is regionally most concentrated.

NAICS 486910 - PIPELINE TRANSPORTATION OF REFINED PETROLEUM PRODUCTS*

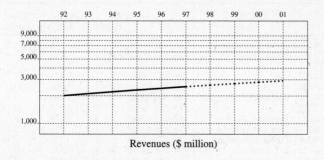

Revenues ($ million)

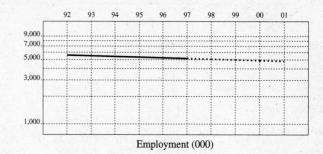

Employment (000)

GENERAL STATISTICS

Year	Establishments (number)	Employment (number)	Payroll ($ million)	Revenues ($ million)	Employees per Establishment (number)	Revenues per Establishment ($)	Payroll per Employee ($)
1992	358	5,578	251.9	2,010.0	15.6	5,614,525	45,160
1993	376	5,494	259.5	2,111.2	14.6	5,614,947	47,244
1994	394	5,409	267.2	2,212.4	13.7	5,615,330	49,394
1995	412	5,325	274.8	2,313.7	12.9	5,615,680	51,611
1996	430	5,240	282.5	2,414.9	12.2	5,616,000	53,900
1997	448	5,156	290.1	2,516.1	11.5	5,616,295	56,265
1998	466 *p*	5,072 *p*	297.7 *p*	2,617.3 *p*	10.9 *p*	5,616,567 *p*	58,707 *p*
1999	484 *p*	4,987 *p*	305.4 *p*	2,718.5 *p*	10.3 *p*	5,616,818 *p*	61,233 *p*
2000	502 *p*	4,903 *p*	313.0 *p*	2,819.8 *p*	9.8 *p*	5,617,052 *p*	63,845 *p*
2001	520 *p*	4,818 *p*	320.7 *p*	2,921.0 *p*	9.3 *p*	5,617,269 *p*	66,549 *p*

Sources: *Economic Census of the United States*, 1987, 1992 and 1997. Data for those years (years are in **bold** type) are from the 5-year censuses of the economy. Other values, unless otherwise noted, are extrapolations. Values marked with *p* are projections. Data are the most recent available at this level of detail.

INDICES OF CHANGE

Year	Establishments (number)	Employment (number)	Payroll ($ million)	Revenues ($ million)	Employees per Establishment (number)	Revenues per Establishment ($)	Payroll per Employee ($)
1992	79.9	108.2	86.8	79.9	135.7	100.0	80.3
1993	83.9	106.6	89.5	83.9	127.0	100.0	84.0
1994	87.9	104.9	92.1	87.9	119.1	100.0	87.8
1995	92.0	103.3	94.7	92.0	112.2	100.0	91.7
1996	96.0	101.6	97.4	96.0	106.1	100.0	95.8
1997	100.0	100.0	100.0	100.0	100.0	100.0	100.0
1998	104.0 *p*	98.4 *p*	102.6 *p*	104.0 *p*	94.8 *p*	100.0 *p*	104.3 *p*
1999	108.0 *p*	96.7 *p*	105.3 *p*	108.0 *p*	89.6 *p*	100.0 *p*	108.8 *p*
2000	112.1 *p*	95.1 *p*	107.9 *p*	112.1 *p*	85.2 *p*	100.0 *p*	113.5 *p*
2001	116.1 *p*	93.4 *p*	110.5 *p*	116.1 *p*	80.9 *p*	100.0 *p*	118.3 *p*

Sources: Same as General Statistics. The values shown reflect change from the base year, 1997. Values above 100 mean greater than 1997, values below 100 mean less than 1997, and a value of 100 in years other than 1997 means same as 1997. Indices are calculated only for Census years. Data are the most recent available at this level of detail.

SELECTED RATIOS

For 1997	Avg. of Sector	Analyzed Industry	Index	For 1997	Avg. of Sector	Analyzed Industry	Index
Employees per establishment	16	12	70	Payroll per establishment	462,554	647,545	140
Revenue per establishment	1,787,642	5,616,295	314	Payroll as % of revenue	26	12	45
Revenue per employee	108,959	487,995	448	Payroll per employee	28,193	56,265	200

Sources: Same as General Statistics. The 'Average of Sector' column represents the average for all industries in this sector. The Index shows the relationship between the Average and the Analyzed Industry. For example, 100 means that they are equal; 500 that the Analyzed Industry is five times the average; 50 means that the Analyzed Industry is half the national average. 'na' is used to show that data are 'not available'.

*Equivalent to SIC 4613.

LEADING COMPANIES   Number shown: **19**   Total sales ($ mil): **35,538**   Total employment (000): **74.7**

Company Name	Address				CEO Name	Phone	Co. Type	Sales ($ mil)	Empl. (000)
CITGO Petroleum Corp.	PO Box 3758	Tulsa	OK	74102	David Tippeconnic	918-495-4000	S	10,912	4.5
Williams Companies Inc.	1 Williams Ctr	Tulsa	OK	74172	Keith Bailey	918-573-2000	P	7,658	21.0
Mobil Pipe Line Co.	P O Box 900	Dallas	TX	75221			S	3,000*	3.0
National Fuel Gas Supply Corp.	10 Lafayette Sq	Buffalo	NY	14203		716-857-7000	R	2,575*	3.2
Marathon Ashland Petroleum	539 S Main St	Findlay	OH	45840		419-422-2121	R	2,000	30.0
TransMontaigne Oil Co.	370 17th St	Denver	CO	80202	Richard E Gathright	303-626-8200	P	1,968	0.4
TEPPCO Partners L.P.	PO Box 2521	Houston	TX	77252		713-759-3636	P	1,935	0.7
GATX Corp.	500 W Monroe St	Chicago	IL	60661	Ronald H Zech	312-621-6200	P	1,859	6.0
Sun Pipe Line Co.	907 S Detroit Ave	Tulsa	OK	74120	Deborah M Fretz	918-586-6700	S	725*	0.6
Coscol Petroleum Corp.	9 Greenway Plz	Houston	TX	77046	David A Arledge	713-877-1400	S	575*	0.5
Colonial Pipeline Co.	PO Box 18855	Atlanta	GA	31126	D L Lemmon	404-261-1470	R	528*	0.7
TEPPCO	PO Box 2521	Houston	TX	77252	William Thacker	713-759-3636	J	429	0.7
Kinder Morgan Energy Partners	1301 McKinney St	Houston	TX	77010	William V Allison	713-844-9500	P	429	1.2
Buckeye Partners L.P.	5 Radnor Corporate	Radnor	PA	19087	Alfred W Martinelli	610-770-4000	P	306	0.5
Phillips Pipeline Co.	411 S Keeler Ave	Bartlesville	OK	74003	JT Webster	918-661-4550	S	189*	0.6
Buckeye Partners L.P.	PO Box 368	Emmaus	PA	18049	Alfred W Martinelli	610-770-4000	P	184	0.5
Marathon Ashland Pipe Line	539 S Main St	Findlay	OH	45840	DL Porter	419-422-2121	S	157	0.5
Kaneb Pipe Line Operating	2435 N Cen Expwy	Richardson	TX	75080	Edward D Doherty	972-699-4055	S	61	0.0
Calnev Pipe Line Co.	PO Box 6346	San Bernardino	CA	92412		909-888-7771	S	48*	<0.1

Source: *Ward's Business Directory of U.S. Private and Public Companies*, Volumes 1 and 2, 2000. The company type code used is as follows: P - Public, R - Private, S - Subsidiary, D - Division, J - Joint Venture, A - Affiliate, G - Group, N - Company type not reported. Sales are in millions of dollars, employees are in thousands. An asterisk (*) indicates an estimated sales volume. The symbol < stands for 'less than'. Company names and addresses are truncated, in some cases, to fit into the available space.

LOCATION BY STATE AND REGIONAL CONCENTRATION

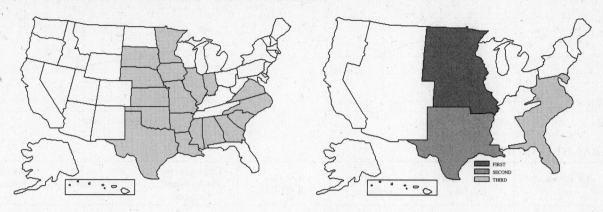

INDUSTRY DATA BY STATE

State	Establishments Total (number)	Establishments % of U.S.	Employment Total (number)	Employment % of U.S.	Employment Per Estab.	Payroll Total ($ mil.)	Payroll Per Empl. ($)	Revenues Total ($ mil.)	Revenues % of U.S.	Revenues Per Estab. ($)
Texas	43	9.6	723	14.0	17	43.6	60,369	357.2	14.2	8,306,721
Georgia	28	6.3	461	8.9	16	26.7	57,959	325.8	12.9	11,636,893
California	21	4.7	443	8.6	21	30.1	67,959	221.8	8.8	10,563,762
Pennsylvania	20	4.5	561	10.9	28	29.9	53,258	208.8	8.3	10,437,500
Kansas	29	6.5	279	5.4	10	14.6	52,283	84.9	3.4	2,926,276
Mississippi	11	2.5	59	1.1	5	3.1	52,797	50.8	2.0	4,618,091
Ohio	13	2.9	210	4.1	16	9.9	47,195	50.3	2.0	3,872,000
Nebraska	14	3.1	71	1.4	5	4.3	60,592	36.5	1.5	2,606,857
Missouri	14	3.1	77	1.5	6	3.9	51,234	33.5	1.3	2,392,929
South Carolina	12	2.7	49	1.0	4	2.6	52,531	32.6	1.3	2,716,750
Illinois	21	4.7	175*	-	-	(D)	-	(D)	-	-
Oklahoma	19	4.2	750*	-	-	(D)	-	(D)	-	-
Iowa	17	3.8	175*	-	-	(D)	-	(D)	-	-
North Carolina	17	3.8	175*	-	-	(D)	-	(D)	-	-
Indiana	16	3.6	175*	-	-	(D)	-	(D)	-	-
Louisiana	16	3.6	175*	-	-	(D)	-	(D)	-	-
Virginia	14	3.1	60*	-	-	(D)	-	(D)	-	-
Alabama	13	2.9	60*	-	-	(D)	-	(D)	-	-
Michigan	11	2.5	60*	-	-	(D)	-	(D)	-	-
Minnesota	9	2.0	60*	-	-	(D)	-	(D)	-	-
Florida	8	1.8	60*	-	-	(D)	-	(D)	-	-
New York	8	1.8	175*	-	-	(D)	-	(D)	-	-
South Dakota	7	1.6	60*	-	-	(D)	-	(D)	-	-
Tennessee	7	1.6	60*	-	-	(D)	-	(D)	-	-
Arkansas	6	1.3	60*	-	-	(D)	-	(D)	-	-
Colorado	6	1.3	60*	-	-	(D)	-	(D)	-	-

Source: 1997 *Economic Census*. The states are in descending order of revenues or establishments (if revenue data are missing for the majority). The symbol (D) appears when data are withheld to prevent disclosure of competitive information. States marked with (D) are sorted by number of establishments. A dash (-) indicates that the data element cannot be calculated. * indicates the midpoint of a range; 175, for example is the range 100-249. Shaded *states* on the state map indicate those states which have proportionately greater representation in the industry than would be indicated by the state's population; the ratio is based on total revenues or number of establishments. Shaded *regions* indicate where the industry is regionally most concentrated.

NAICS 486990 - PIPELINE TRANSPORTATION NEC*

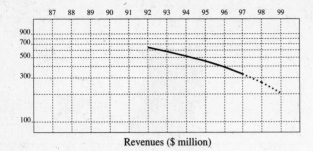

Revenues ($ million)

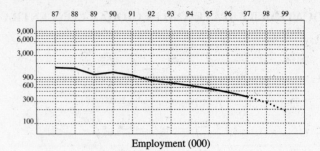

Employment (000)

GENERAL STATISTICS

Year	Establishments (number)	Employment (number)	Payroll ($ million)	Revenues ($ million)	Employees per Establishment (number)	Revenues per Establishment ($)	Payroll per Employee ($)
1987	47	1,616	55.7	-	34.4	-	34,468
1988	73	1,561	52.3	-	21.4	-	33,504
1989	47	1,149	43.3	-	24.4	-	37,685
1990	54	1,280	47.5	-	23.7	-	37,109
1991	46	1,100	44.9	-	23.9	-	40,818
1992	81	846	38.0	643.8	10.4	7,948,148	44,917
1993	71	752	34.4	580.9	10.6	8,182,254	45,757
1994	61	658	30.8	518.1	10.8	8,493,115	46,837
1995	51	563	27.2	455.2	11.0	8,925,882	48,278
1996	41	469	23.6	392.4	11.4	9,569,756	50,298
1997	31	375	20.0	329.5	12.1	10,629,032	53,333
1998	21 p	281 p	16.4 p	266.6 p	13.4 p	12,697,143 p	58,405 p
1999	11 p	187 p	12.8 p	203.8 p	17.0 p	18,525,455 p	68,596 p

*Sources: Economic Census of the United States, 1987, 1992 and 1997. Data for those years (years are in **bold** type) are from the 5-year censuses of the economy. Other values, unless otherwise noted, are extrapolations. Values marked with p are projections. Data are the most recent available at this level of detail.*

INDICES OF CHANGE

Year	Establishments (number)	Employment (number)	Payroll ($ million)	Revenues ($ million)	Employees per Establishment (number)	Revenues per Establishment ($)	Payroll per Employee ($)
1987	151.6	430.9	278.5	-	284.3	-	64.6
1992	261.3	225.6	190.0	195.4	86.0	74.8	84.2
1993	229.0	200.5	172.0	176.3	87.6	77.0	85.8
1994	196.8	175.5	154.0	157.2	89.3	79.9	87.8
1995	164.5	150.1	136.0	138.1	90.9	84.0	90.5
1996	132.3	125.1	118.0	119.1	94.2	90.0	94.3
1997	100.0	100.0	100.0	100.0	100.0	100.0	100.0
1998	67.7 p	74.9 p	82.0 p	80.9 p	110.7 p	119.5 p	109.5 p
1999	35.5 p	49.9 p	64.0 p	61.9 p	140.5 p	174.3 p	128.6 p

Sources: Same as General Statistics. The values shown reflect change from the base year, 1997. Values above 100 mean greater than 1997, values below 100 mean less than 1997, and a value of 100 in years other than 1997 means same as 1997. Indices are calculated only for Census years. Data are the most recent available at this level of detail.

SELECTED RATIOS

For 1997	Avg. of Sector	Analyzed Industry	Index	For 1997	Avg. of Sector	Analyzed Industry	Index
Employees per establishment	16	12	74	Payroll per establishment	462,554	645,161	139
Revenue per establishment	1,787,642	10,629,032	595	Payroll as % of revenue	26	6	23
Revenue per employee	108,959	878,667	806	Payroll per employee	28,193	53,333	189

Sources: Same as General Statistics. The 'Average of Sector' column represents the average for all industries in this sector. The Index shows the relationship between the Average and the Analyzed Industry. For example, 100 means that they are equal; 500 that the Analyzed Industry is five times the average; 50 means that the Analyzed Industry is half the national average. 'na' is used to show that data are 'not available'.

*Equivalent to SIC 4619.

LEADING COMPANIES　　Number shown: **3**　　Total sales ($ mil): **464**　　Total employment (000): **1.3**

Company Name	Address				CEO Name	Phone	Co. Type	Sales ($ mil)	Empl. (000)
Kinder Morgan Energy Partners	1301 McKinney St	Houston	TX	77010	William V Allison	713-844-9500	P	429	1.2
Black Mesa Pipeline Inc.	1509 E Butler Ave	Flagstaff	AZ	86001	HJ Brolick	602-774-5076	S	21	<0.1
Sabine Pipe Line Co.	1111 Bagby St	Houston	TX	77002	Deborah Plattsmier	713-752-4046	S	14	<0.1

Source: Ward's Business Directory of U.S. Private and Public Companies, Volumes 1 and 2, 2000. The company type code used is as follows: P - Public, R - Private, S - Subsidiary, D - Division, J - Joint Venture, A - Affiliate, G - Group, N - Company type not reported. Sales are in millions of dollars, employees are in thousands. An asterisk (*) indicates an estimated sales volume. The symbol < stands for 'less than'. Company names and addresses are truncated, in some cases, to fit into the available space.

LOCATION BY STATE AND REGIONAL CONCENTRATION

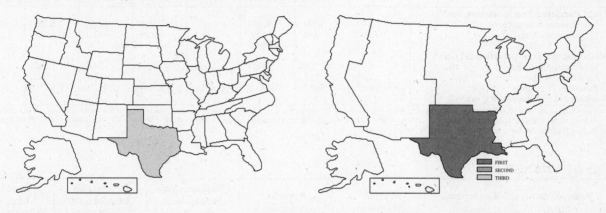

FIRST
SECOND
THIRD

INDUSTRY DATA BY STATE

State	Establishments		Employment			Payroll		Revenues		
	Total (number)	% of U.S.	Total (number)	% of U.S.	Per Estab.	Total ($ mil.)	Per Empl. ($)	Total ($ mil.)	% of U.S.	Per Estab. ($)
Texas	9	29.0	210	56.0	23	11.9	56,471	235.5	71.5	26,163,333

Source: 1997 *Economic Census*. The states are in descending order of revenues or establishments (if revenue data are missing for the majority). The symbol (D) appears when data are withheld to prevent disclosure of competitive information. States marked with (D) are sorted by number of establishments. A dash (-) indicates that the data element cannot be calculated. * indicates the midpoint of a range; 175, for example is the range 100-249. Shaded *states* on the state map indicate those states which have proportionately greater representation in the industry than would be indicated by the state's population; the ratio is based on total revenues or number of establishments. Shaded *regions* indicate where the industry is regionally most concentrated.

NAICS 487110 - SCENIC AND SIGHTSEEING TRANSPORTATION, LAND

GENERAL STATISTICS

Year	Establishments (number)	Employment (number)	Payroll ($ million)	Revenues ($ million)	Employees per Establishment (number)	Revenues per Establishment ($)	Payroll per Employee ($)
1997	454	8,227	169.6	557.6	18.1	1,228,194	20,615

Source: *Economic Census of the United States*, 1997. This is a newly defined industry. Data for prior years were unavailable at the time of publication but may become available over time.

SIC INDUSTRIES RELATED TO NAICS 487110

SIC	Industry	1990	1991	1992	1993	1994	1995	1996	1997
4119	**Local Passenger Transportation, nec***								
	Establishments (number)	5,187	5,991	7,140	7,652	7,915	7,800	8,305	8,988*p*
	Employment (thousands)	94.0	94.6	115.6	124.4	130.7	139.0	149.0	156.0*p*
	Revenues ($ million)	-	-	4,604.0	-	-	-	-	-
4789	**Miscellaneous Transportation Services***								
	Establishments (number)	995*e*	1,009*e*	1,024	1,039*p*	1,053*p*	1,068*p*	1,082*p*	1,097*p*
	Employment (thousands)	17.3*e*	16.8*e*	16.4	15.9*p*	15.5*p*	15.1*p*	14.6*p*	14.2*p*
	Revenues ($ million)	1,231.2*e*	1,382.5*e*	1,533.8	1,685.1*p*	1,836.4*p*	1,987.7*p*	2,139.0*p*	2,290.3*p*
7999	**Amusement and Recreation, nec***	-	-	-	-	-	-	-	-

Source: *Economic Census of the United States*, 1992, annual surveys of economic sectors conducted by the Bureau of the Census, and estimates or projections based on the 1982-1992 period; not all data are shown. 'e' marks estimates made by the editors; 'p' indicates projections based on time series. A dash (-) indicates that data for this SIC or year were not available. * Indicates that only a portion of this industry is present within the NAICS data. If no * is shown, the entire industry is contained within the NAICS data.

INDICES OF CHANGE

Year	Establishments (number)	Employment (number)	Payroll ($ million)	Revenues ($ million)	Employees per Establishment (number)	Revenues per Establishment ($)	Payroll per Employee ($)
1997	100.0	100.0	100.0	100.0	100.0	100.0	100.0

Sources: Same as General Statistics. The values shown reflect change from the base year, 1997. Values above 100 mean greater than 1997, values below 100 mean less than 1997, and a value of 100 in years other than 1997 means same as 1997. Indices are calculated only for Census years. Data are the most recent available at this level of detail.

SELECTED RATIOS

For 1997	Avg. of Sector	Analyzed Industry	Index	For 1997	Avg. of Sector	Analyzed Industry	Index
Employees per establishment	16	18	110	Payroll per establishment	462,554	373,568	81
Revenue per establishment	1,787,642	1,228,194	69	Payroll as % of revenue	26	30	118
Revenue per employee	108,959	67,777	62	Payroll per employee	28,193	20,615	73

Sources: Same as General Statistics. The 'Average of Sector' column represents the average for all industries in this sector. The Index shows the relationship between the Average and the Analyzed Industry. For example, 100 means that they are equal; 500 that the Analyzed Industry is five times the average; 50 means that the Analyzed Industry is half the national average. 'na' is used to show that data are 'not available'.

LEADING COMPANIES

No company data available for this industry.

LOCATION BY STATE AND REGIONAL CONCENTRATION

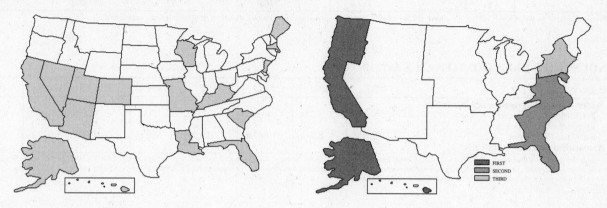

FIRST
SECOND
THIRD

INDUSTRY DATA BY STATE

State	Establishments Total (number)	% of U.S.	Employment Total (number)	% of U.S.	Per Estab.	Payroll Total ($ mil.)	Per Empl. ($)	Revenues Total ($ mil.)	% of U.S.	Per Estab. ($)
Hawaii	32	7.0	2,293	27.9	72	42.5	18,539	107.5	19.3	3,358,656
New Jersey	14	3.1	526	6.4	38	15.3	29,025	55.8	10.0	3,985,000
Alaska	15	3.3	132	1.6	9	5.8	44,227	38.4	6.9	2,558,467
Florida	33	7.3	330	4.0	10	6.6	19,858	29.8	5.3	903,818
Texas	13	2.9	393	4.8	30	6.6	16,763	21.0	3.8	1,613,615
Arizona	12	2.6	279	3.4	23	3.7	13,373	15.0	2.7	1,246,667
Pennsylvania	20	4.4	172	2.1	9	3.5	20,483	11.2	2.0	560,300
Colorado	18	4.0	57	0.7	3	2.2	39,439	8.6	1.5	476,167
South Carolina	14	3.1	147	1.8	10	1.9	12,755	7.4	1.3	526,500
Tennessee	8	1.8	112	1.4	14	1.1	9,795	6.5	1.2	813,375
Maine	7	1.5	96	1.2	14	2.1	22,052	6.5	1.2	934,286
Missouri	12	2.6	81	1.0	7	1.2	14,432	4.6	0.8	385,083
Wisconsin	10	2.2	33	0.4	3	0.5	15,394	1.9	0.3	185,500
Utah	6	1.3	64	0.8	11	0.5	8,578	1.2	0.2	199,000
California	57	12.6	1,750*	-	-	(D)	-	(D)	-	-
New York	24	5.3	175*	-	-	(D)	-	(D)	-	-
Massachusetts	14	3.1	60*	-	-	(D)	-	(D)	-	-
Ohio	11	2.4	60*	-	-	(D)	-	(D)	-	-
Michigan	10	2.2	60*	-	-	(D)	-	(D)	-	-
North Carolina	10	2.2	60*	-	-	(D)	-	(D)	-	-
Illinois	9	2.0	175*	-	-	(D)	-	(D)	-	-
Kentucky	9	2.0	60*	-	-	(D)	-	(D)	-	-
Georgia	8	1.8	175*	-	-	(D)	-	(D)	-	-
Louisiana	8	1.8	175*	-	-	(D)	-	(D)	-	-
Indiana	7	1.5	60*	-	-	(D)	-	(D)	-	-
Maryland	7	1.5	60*	-	-	(D)	-	(D)	-	-
Nevada	7	1.5	375*	-	-	(D)	-	(D)	-	-
Minnesota	6	1.3	10*	-	-	(D)	-	(D)	-	-
Washington	6	1.3	175*	-	-	(D)	-	(D)	-	-

Source: 1997 Economic Census. The states are in descending order of revenues or establishments (if revenue data are missing for the majority). The symbol (D) appears when data are withheld to prevent disclosure of competitive information. States marked with (D) are sorted by number of establishments. A dash (-) indicates that the data element cannot be calculated. * indicates the midpoint of a range; 175, for example is the range 100-249. Shaded states on the state map indicate those states which have proportionately greater representation in the industry than would be indicated by the state's population; the ratio is based on total revenues or number of establishments. Shaded regions indicate where the industry is regionally most concentrated.

NAICS 487210 - SCENIC AND SIGHTSEEING TRANSPORTATION, WATER

GENERAL STATISTICS

Year	Establishments (number)	Employment (number)	Payroll ($ million)	Revenues ($ million)	Employees per Establishment (number)	Revenues per Establishment ($)	Payroll per Employee ($)
1997	1,692	14,185	282.8	1,128.6	8.4	667,021	19,937

Source: *Economic Census of the United States*, 1997. This is a newly defined industry. Data for prior years were unavailable at the time of publication but may become available over time.

SIC INDUSTRIES RELATED TO NAICS 487210

SIC	Industry	1990	1991	1992	1993	1994	1995	1996	1997
4489	**Water Passenger Transportation, nec***								
	Establishments (number)	321	374	843	773	751	733	809	916*p*
	Employment (thousands)	4.7	5.2	9.0	8.6	8.7	9.6	10.1	11.0*p*
	Revenues ($ million)	551.0*e*	630.4*e*	709.8	789.2*p*	868.6*p*	948.0*p*	1,027.4*p*	1,106.8*p*
7999	**Amusement and Recreation, nec***	-	-	-	-	-	-	-	-

Source: *Economic Census of the United States*, 1992, annual surveys of economic sectors conducted by the Bureau of the Census, and estimates or projections based on the 1982-1992 period; not all data are shown. 'e' marks estimates made by the editors; 'p' indicates projections based on time series. A dash (-) indicates that data for this SIC or year were not available. * Indicates that only a portion of this industry is present within the NAICS data. If no * is shown, the entire industry is contained within the NAICS data.

INDICES OF CHANGE

Year	Establishments (number)	Employment (number)	Payroll ($ million)	Revenues ($ million)	Employees per Establishment (number)	Revenues per Establishment ($)	Payroll per Employee ($)
1997	100.0	100.0	100.0	100.0	100.0	100.0	100.0

Sources: Same as General Statistics. The values shown reflect change from the base year, 1997. Values above 100 mean greater than 1997, values below 100 mean less than 1997, and a value of 100 in years other than 1997 means same as 1997. Indices are calculated only for Census years. Data are the most recent available at this level of detail.

SELECTED RATIOS

For 1997	Avg. of Sector	Analyzed Industry	Index	For 1997	Avg. of Sector	Analyzed Industry	Index
Employees per establishment	16	8	51	Payroll per establishment	462,554	167,139	36
Revenue per establishment	1,787,642	667,021	37	Payroll as % of revenue	26	25	97
Revenue per employee	108,959	79,563	73	Payroll per employee	28,193	19,937	71

Sources: Same as General Statistics. The 'Average of Sector' column represents the average for all industries in this sector. The Index shows the relationship between the Average and the Analyzed Industry. For example, 100 means that they are equal; 500 that the Analyzed Industry is five times the average; 50 means that the Analyzed Industry is half the national average. 'na' is used to show that data are 'not available'.

LEADING COMPANIES   Number shown: **7**   Total sales ($ mil): **462**   Total employment (000): **2.7**

Company Name	Address				CEO Name	Phone	Co. Type	Sales ($ mil)	Empl. (000)
American Classic Voyages Co.	2 N Riverside Plz	Chicago	IL	60606	Philip C Calian	312-258-1890	P	192	1.4
World Yacht Inc.	W 41st St	New York	NY	10011	August J Ceradini	212-630-8100	R	67*	0.2
New Commodore Cruise Line Ltd.	4000 Hollywood	Hollywood	FL	33021	Fred Mayer	954-967-2100	P	61	0.1
Clipper Navigation Inc.	2701 Alaskan Way	Seattle	WA	98121	Merideth Tall	206-443-2560	R	55*	0.2
Spirit Cruises Inc.	501 Front St	Norfolk	VA	23510	Francois Vincent	757-627-2900	S	50*	0.4
Bay Houston Towing Co. Harbor	P O Box 3006	Houston	TX	77253	Mark E Kuebler	713-529-3755	D	18	0.3
Windsor Inc.	7711 Bonhomme	Clayton	MO	63105	Paul H Duynhouwer	314-727-2929	S	18*	<0.1

Source: Ward's Business Directory of U.S. Private and Public Companies, Volumes 1 and 2, 2000. The company type code used is as follows: P - Public, R - Private, S - Subsidiary, D - Division, J - Joint Venture, A - Affiliate, G - Group, N - Company type not reported. Sales are in millions of dollars, employees are in thousands. An asterisk (*) indicates an estimated sales volume. The symbol < stands for 'less than'. Company names and addresses are truncated, in some cases, to fit into the available space.

LOCATION BY STATE AND REGIONAL CONCENTRATION

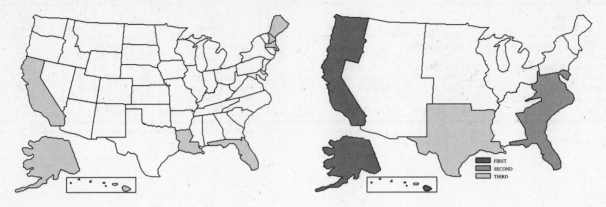

FIRST
SECOND
THIRD

INDUSTRY DATA BY STATE

State	Establishments Total (number)	% of U.S.	Employment Total (number)	% of U.S.	Per Estab.	Payroll Total ($ mil.)	Per Empl. ($)	Revenues Total ($ mil.)	% of U.S.	Per Estab. ($)
Florida	360	21.3	2,966	20.9	8	46.4	15,647	195.5	17.3	542,994
Louisiana	39	2.3	1,352	9.5	35	37.3	27,589	177.1	15.7	4,541,667
California	204	12.1	1,999	14.1	10	37.7	18,861	144.6	12.8	708,593
Hawaii	97	5.7	1,642	11.6	17	27.1	16,524	103.0	9.1	1,062,216
New York	109	6.4	732	5.2	7	18.2	24,810	69.2	6.1	635,147
Alaska	105	6.2	245	1.7	2	9.5	38,873	46.2	4.1	440,333
Massachusetts	50	3.0	293	2.1	6	10.5	35,809	40.1	3.5	801,220
Illinois	19	1.1	553	3.9	29	13.9	25,128	37.8	3.3	1,986,842
Texas	51	3.0	321	2.3	6	5.0	15,436	20.3	1.8	397,196
Pennsylvania	13	0.8	326	2.3	25	5.6	17,117	17.2	1.5	1,326,077
South Carolina	31	1.8	224	1.6	7	3.6	16,183	12.9	1.1	415,677
Minnesota	15	0.9	160	1.1	11	3.0	18,494	10.7	0.9	712,533
North Carolina	58	3.4	169	1.2	3	3.1	18,337	10.2	0.9	175,534
Wisconsin	21	1.2	42	0.3	2	2.2	52,333	8.3	0.7	395,714
Maine	31	1.8	33	0.2	1	1.6	47,758	7.9	0.7	253,323
Ohio	36	2.1	53	0.4	1	2.2	40,849	7.4	0.7	204,389
Michigan	30	1.8	107	0.8	4	1.8	16,402	7.3	0.7	244,833
New Hampshire	12	0.7	29	0.2	2	1.6	54,414	5.6	0.5	470,500
Arkansas	6	0.4	68	0.5	11	0.7	10,338	4.0	0.4	673,333
Alabama	27	1.6	53	0.4	2	0.7	12,925	2.5	0.2	93,407
Montana	8	0.5	20	0.1	3	0.4	18,150	1.4	0.1	175,500
Mississippi	9	0.5	14	0.1	2	0.5	34,429	1.1	0.1	125,333
New Jersey	85	5.0	175*	-	-	(D)	-	(D)	-	-
Washington	52	3.1	375*	-	-	(D)	-	(D)	-	-
Maryland	35	2.1	175*	-	-	(D)	-	(D)	-	-
Oregon	33	2.0	175*	-	-	(D)	-	(D)	-	-
Virginia	24	1.4	175*	-	-	(D)	-	(D)	-	-
Georgia	16	0.9	60*	-	-	(D)	-	(D)	-	-
Connecticut	13	0.8	60*	-	-	(D)	-	(D)	-	-
Rhode Island	12	0.7	60*	-	-	(D)	-	(D)	-	-
Missouri	9	0.5	60*	-	-	(D)	-	(D)	-	-
Nevada	9	0.5	175*	-	-	(D)	-	(D)	-	-
Arizona	8	0.5	60*	-	-	(D)	-	(D)	-	-
Vermont	8	0.5	10*	-	-	(D)	-	(D)	-	-
Kentucky	7	0.4	375*	-	-	(D)	-	(D)	-	-
Colorado	6	0.4	10*	-	-	(D)	-	(D)	-	-
Idaho	6	0.4	10*	-	-	(D)	-	(D)	-	-
Utah	6	0.4	60*	-	-	(D)	-	(D)	-	-

Source: 1997 *Economic Census*. The states are in descending order of revenues or establishments (if revenue data are missing for the majority). The symbol (D) appears when data are withheld to prevent disclosure of competitive information. States marked with (D) are sorted by number of establishments. A dash (-) indicates that the data element cannot be calculated. * indicates the midpoint of a range; 175, for example is the range 100-249. Shaded *states* on the state map indicate those states which have proportionately greater representation in the industry than would be indicated by the state's population; the ratio is based on total revenues or number of establishments. Shaded *regions* indicate where the industry is regionally most concentrated.

NAICS 487990 - SCENIC AND SIGHTSEEING TRANSPORTATION NEC

GENERAL STATISTICS

Year	Establishments (number)	Employment (number)	Payroll ($ million)	Revenues ($ million)	Employees per Establishment (number)	Revenues per Establishment ($)	Payroll per Employee ($)
1997	179	1,495	40.0	207.2	8.4	1,157,542	26,756

Source: Economic Census of the United States, 1997. This is a newly defined industry. Data for prior years were unavailable at the time of publication but may become available over time.

SIC INDUSTRIES RELATED TO NAICS 487990

SIC	Industry	1990	1991	1992	1993	1994	1995	1996	1997
4522	**Air Transportation, Nonscheduled***								
	Establishments (number)	928	1,441	1,791	1,714	1,692	1,621	1,831	2,052p
	Employment (thousands)	15.3	20.5	23.1	24.4	29.1	27.7	28.8	33.2p
	Revenues ($ million)	-	-	3,432.7	-	-	-	-	-
7999	**Amusement and Recreation, nec***	-	-	-	-	-	-	-	-

Source: Economic Census of the United States, 1992, annual surveys of economic sectors conducted by the Bureau of the Census, and estimates or projections based on the 1982-1992 period; not all data are shown. 'e' marks estimates made by the editors; 'p' indicates projections based on time series. A dash (-) indicates that data for this SIC or year were not available. * Indicates that only a portion of this industry is present within the NAICS data. If no * is shown, the entire industry is contained within the NAICS data.

INDICES OF CHANGE

Year	Establishments (number)	Employment (number)	Payroll ($ million)	Revenues ($ million)	Employees per Establishment (number)	Revenues per Establishment ($)	Payroll per Employee ($)
1997	100.0	100.0	100.0	100.0	100.0	100.0	100.0

Sources: Same as General Statistics. The values shown reflect change from the base year, 1997. Values above 100 mean greater than 1997, values below 100 mean less than 1997, and a value of 100 in years other than 1997 means same as 1997. Indices are calculated only for Census years. Data are the most recent available at this level of detail.

SELECTED RATIOS

For 1997	Avg. of Sector	Analyzed Industry	Index	For 1997	Avg. of Sector	Analyzed Industry	Index
Employees per establishment	16	8	51	Payroll per establishment	462,554	223,464	48
Revenue per establishment	1,787,642	1,157,542	65	Payroll as % of revenue	26	19	75
Revenue per employee	108,959	138,595	127	Payroll per employee	28,193	26,756	95

Sources: Same as General Statistics. The 'Average of Sector' column represents the average for all industries in this sector. The Index shows the relationship between the Average and the Analyzed Industry. For example, 100 means that they are equal; 500 that the Analyzed Industry is five times the average; 50 means that the Analyzed Industry is half the national average. 'na' is used to show that data are 'not available'.

LEADING COMPANIES
No company data available for this industry.

LOCATION BY STATE AND REGIONAL CONCENTRATION

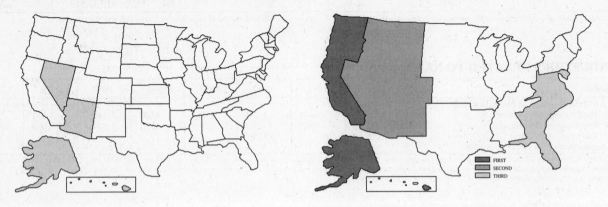

FIRST
SECOND
THIRD

INDUSTRY DATA BY STATE

State	Establishments		Employment			Payroll		Revenues		
	Total (number)	% of U.S.	Total (number)	% of U.S.	Per Estab.	Total ($ mil.)	Per Empl. ($)	Total ($ mil.)	% of U.S.	Per Estab. ($)
Hawaii	21	11.7	411	27.5	20	11.9	28,888	56.8	27.4	2,706,000
Nevada	10	5.6	225	15.1	23	6.0	26,782	45.1	21.8	4,508,100
Alaska	14	7.8	100	6.7	7	5.8	58,330	20.2	9.7	1,441,714
Arizona	13	7.3	182	12.2	14	4.1	22,769	16.3	7.9	1,256,462
Florida	13	7.3	63	4.2	5	1.1	17,984	6.8	3.3	520,692
Texas	12	6.7	35	2.3	3	1.1	32,771	6.5	3.1	541,917
California	10	5.6	60*	-	-	(D)	-	(D)	-	-
Michigan	8	4.5	10*	-	-	(D)	-	(D)	-	-
New York	7	3.9	60*	-	-	(D)	-	(D)	-	-
Pennsylvania	6	3.4	60*	-	-	(D)	-	(D)	-	-
Washington	6	3.4	60*	-	-	(D)	-	(D)	-	-

Source: 1997 *Economic Census*. The states are in descending order of revenues or establishments (if revenue data are missing for the majority). The symbol (D) appears when data are withheld to prevent disclosure of competitive information. States marked with (D) are sorted by number of establishments. A dash (-) indicates that the data element cannot be calculated. * indicates the midpoint of a range; 175, for example is the range 100-249. Shaded *states* on the state map indicate those states which have proportionately greater representation in the industry than would be indicated by the state's population; the ratio is based on total revenues or number of establishments. Shaded *regions* indicate where the industry is regionally most concentrated.

NAICS 488111 - AIR TRAFFIC CONTROL

GENERAL STATISTICS

Year	Establishments (number)	Employment (number)	Payroll ($ million)	Revenues ($ million)	Employees per Establishment (number)	Revenues per Establishment ($)	Payroll per Employee ($)
1997	114	502	21.2	43.5	4.4	381,579	42,231

Source: *Economic Census of the United States*, 1997. This is a newly defined industry. Data for prior years were unavailable at the time of publication but may become available over time.

SIC INDUSTRIES RELATED TO NAICS 488111

SIC	Industry	1990	1991	1992	1993	1994	1995	1996	1997
4581	**Airports, Flying Fields and Services***								
	Establishments (number)	2,777	2,968	3,252	3,382	3,503	3,629	4,014	3,958p
	Employment (thousands)	84.3	83.9	80.0	90.8	90.2	96.6	104.6	103.5p
	Revenues ($ million)	-	-	6,167.6	-	-	-	-	-

Source: *Economic Census of the United States*, 1992, annual surveys of economic sectors conducted by the Bureau of the Census, and estimates or projections based on the 1982-1992 period; not all data are shown. 'e' marks estimates made by the editors; 'p' indicates projections based on time series. A dash (-) indicates that data for this SIC or year were not available. * Indicates that only a portion of this industry is present within the NAICS data. If no * is shown, the entire industry is contained within the NAICS data.

INDICES OF CHANGE

Year	Establishments (number)	Employment (number)	Payroll ($ million)	Revenues ($ million)	Employees per Establishment (number)	Revenues per Establishment ($)	Payroll per Employee ($)
1997	100.0	100.0	100.0	100.0	100.0	100.0	100.0

Sources: Same as General Statistics. The values shown reflect change from the base year, 1997. Values above 100 mean greater than 1997, values below 100 mean less than 1997, and a value of 100 in years other than 1997 means same as 1997. Indices are calculated only for Census years. Data are the most recent available at this level of detail.

SELECTED RATIOS

For 1997	Avg. of Sector	Analyzed Industry	Index	For 1997	Avg. of Sector	Analyzed Industry	Index
Employees per establishment	16	4	27	Payroll per establishment	462,554	185,965	40
Revenue per establishment	1,787,642	381,579	21	Payroll as % of revenue	26	49	188
Revenue per employee	108,959	86,653	80	Payroll per employee	28,193	42,231	150

Sources: Same as General Statistics. The 'Average of Sector' column represents the average for all industries in this sector. The Index shows the relationship between the Average and the Analyzed Industry. For example, 100 means that they are equal; 500 that the Analyzed Industry is five times the average; 50 means that the Analyzed Industry is half the national average. 'na' is used to show that data are 'not available'.

LEADING COMPANIES

No company data available for this industry.

LOCATION BY STATE AND REGIONAL CONCENTRATION

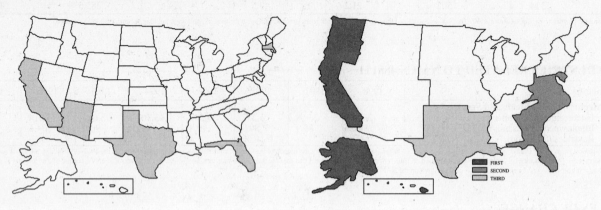

FIRST
SECOND
THIRD

INDUSTRY DATA BY STATE

State	Establishments		Employment			Payroll		Revenues		
	Total (number)	% of U.S.	Total (number)	% of U.S.	Per Estab.	Total ($ mil.)	Per Empl. ($)	Total ($ mil.)	% of U.S.	Per Estab. ($)
California	18	15.8	175*	-	-	(D)	-	(D)	-	-
Florida	14	12.3	60*	-	-	(D)	-	(D)	-	-
Texas	8	7.0	60*	-	-	(D)	-	(D)	-	-
Massachusetts	7	6.1	10*	-	-	(D)	-	(D)	-	-
Arizona	6	5.3	60*	-	-	(D)	-	(D)	-	-

Source: 1997 *Economic Census*. The states are in descending order of revenues or establishments (if revenue data are missing for the majority). The symbol (D) appears when data are withheld to prevent disclosure of competitive information. States marked with (D) are sorted by number of establishments. A dash (-) indicates that the data element cannot be calculated. * indicates the midpoint of a range; 175, for example is the range 100-249. Shaded *states* on the state map indicate those states which have proportionately greater representation in the industry than would be indicated by the state's population; the ratio is based on total revenues or number of establishments. Shaded *regions* indicate where the industry is regionally most concentrated.

NAICS 488119 - AIRPORT OPERATIONS NEC

GENERAL STATISTICS

Year	Establishments (number)	Employment (number)	Payroll ($ million)	Revenues ($ million)	Employees per Establishment (number)	Revenues per Establishment ($)	Payroll per Employee ($)
1997	1,717	61,636	1,085.0	3,250.2	35.9	1,892,953	17,603

Source: Economic Census of the United States, 1997. This is a newly defined industry. Data for prior years were unavailable at the time of publication but may become available over time.

SIC INDUSTRIES RELATED TO NAICS 488119

SIC	Industry	1990	1991	1992	1993	1994	1995	1996	1997
4581	**Airports, Flying Fields and Services***								
	Establishments (number)	2,777	2,968	3,252	3,382	3,503	3,629	4,014	3,958p
	Employment (thousands)	84.3	83.9	80.0	90.8	90.2	96.6	104.6	103.5p
	Revenues ($ million)	-	-	6,167.6	-	-	-	-	-
4959	**Sanitary Services, nec***								
	Establishments (number)	-	-	1,277	-	-	-	-	-
	Employment (thousands)	-	-	8.1	-	-	-	-	-
	Revenues ($ million)	-	-	702.4	-	-	-	-	-

*Source: Economic Census of the United States, 1992, annual surveys of economic sectors conducted by the Bureau of the Census, and estimates or projections based on the 1982-1992 period; not all data are shown. 'e' marks estimates made by the editors; 'p' indicates projections based on time series. A dash (-) indicates that data for this SIC or year were not available. * Indicates that only a portion of this industry is present within the NAICS data. If no * is shown, the entire industry is contained within the NAICS data.*

INDICES OF CHANGE

Year	Establishments (number)	Employment (number)	Payroll ($ million)	Revenues ($ million)	Employees per Establishment (number)	Revenues per Establishment ($)	Payroll per Employee ($)
1997	100.0	100.0	100.0	100.0	100.0	100.0	100.0

Sources: Same as General Statistics. The values shown reflect change from the base year, 1997. Values above 100 mean greater than 1997, values below 100 mean less than 1997, and a value of 100 in years other than 1997 means same as 1997. Indices are calculated only for Census years. Data are the most recent available at this level of detail.

SELECTED RATIOS

For 1997	Avg. of Sector	Analyzed Industry	Index	For 1997	Avg. of Sector	Analyzed Industry	Index
Employees per establishment	16	36	219	Payroll per establishment	462,554	631,916	137
Revenue per establishment	1,787,642	1,892,953	106	Payroll as % of revenue	26	33	129
Revenue per employee	108,959	52,732	48	Payroll per employee	28,193	17,603	62

Sources: Same as General Statistics. The 'Average of Sector' column represents the average for all industries in this sector. The Index shows the relationship between the Average and the Analyzed Industry. For example, 100 means that they are equal; 500 that the Analyzed Industry is five times the average; 50 means that the Analyzed Industry is half the national average. 'na' is used to show that data are 'not available'.

LEADING COMPANIES   Number shown: **45**   Total sales ($ mil): **8,189**   Total employment (000): **116.7**

Company Name	Address				CEO Name	Phone	Co. Type	Sales ($ mil)	Empl. (000)
Ogden Services Corp.	2 Penn Plz	New York	NY	10121	R Richard Ablon	212-868-6000	S	1,750*	39.0
DynCorp.	2000 Edmund Halley	Reston	VA	20191	Dan Bannister	703-264-0330	R	1,527	16.0
Signature Flight Support	401 Industrial Ave	Teterboro	NJ	07608	David A Van Dyke	201-288-1880	R	753*	5.0
Lockheed Martin Space	6801 Rockledge Dr	Bethesda	MD	20817	Paul Smith	301-897-6000	S	500	5.3
B.F. Goodrich Aerospace	3100 112th St	Everett	WA	98204		425-347-3030	S	491*	2.3
Signature Flight Support Corp.	201 S Orange Ave	Orlando	FL	32801	Bruce Van Allen	407-648-7200	R	325*	5.2
Lear Siegler Services Inc.	175 Adm Cochrane	Annapolis	MD	21401	John Moellering	410-266-1380	R	300*	4.0
Airport Group International Inc.	330 N Brand Blvd	Glendale	CA	91214	George Casey	818-409-7500	S	250*	2.5
International Total Services Inc.	1200 Crown Center	Cleveland	OH	44131	Steven Johnson	216-642-4522	P	230	15.0
Mercury Air Group Inc.	5456 McConnell	Los Angeles	CA	90066	Joseph A Czyzyk	310-827-2737	P	225	1.7
Aircraft Service International Inc.	1815 Griffin Rd	Dania	FL	33004	Steve Townes	954-926-2000	S	220	3.2
McDonnell Douglas Services Inc.	P O Box 516	St. Louis	MO	63166		314-233-5005	S	189*	1.0
Hudson General Corp.	PO Box 355	Great Neck	NY	11022	Jay B Langner	516-487-8610	P	169	4.3
Duncan Aviation Inc.	PO Box 81887	Lincoln	NE	68501	Aaron Hilkemann	402-475-2611	R	160*	1.4
Kay and Associates Inc.	3820 N Ventura Dr	Arlington H.	IL	60004	Gregory Kay	847-255-8444	R	125*	0.9
Triad Intern. Maintenance Corp.	623 Radar Rd	Greensboro	NC	27410	Charles H Bell	336-668-4410	S	104*	1.3
Aero Corp.	PO Box 1909	Lake City	FL	32056	John Affeltranger	904-758-3000	S	100	0.8
DynCorp. Fort Rucker Div.	P O Box 620039	Fort Rucker	AL	36362		334-598-0433	D	92*	0.6
AAR Oklahoma	6611 S Meridian	Oklahoma City	OK	73159	David Storch	405-681-3000	D	77	3.0
Hawthorne Corp.	PO Box 61000	Charleston	SC	29419	Dean Harton	843-797-8484	R	76*	0.5
Dalfort Corp.	PO Box 7556	Dallas	TX	75209	Steve Lim	214-358-6019	R	63*	0.8
Miller Aviation Corp.	Binghamton Reg	Johnson City	NY	13790	James P Miller	607-770-1093	R	50	0.2
Raytheon Aerospace Co.	555 Industrial Dr S	Madison	MS	39110	Dan Grafton	601-856-2274	S	42*	0.3
Hartsfield Atlanta Intern. Airport	PO Box 20509	Atlanta	GA	30320		404-209-1700	R	38*	0.3
Keystone Helicopter Corp.	1420 Phoenixville	West Chester	PA	19380	Peter Wright Jr	610-644-4430	R	35	0.2
Curtiss-Wright Accessory Services	3950 N W 28th St	Miami	FL	33142		305-871-3383	D	32*	0.2
Carrier Aircraft Interiors	6201 W Imperial	Los Angeles	CA	90045	Jim Zentgras	310-568-3870	R	30*	0.2
Piedmont Airlines Inc.	5443 Arpt Terminal	Salisbury	MD	21804	John Leonard	410-742-2996	S	29*	0.2
Flight International Group Inc.	Williamsbrg Apt	Newport News	VA	23602	David E Sandlin	757-886-5500	P	25	0.2
Banyan Air Service Inc.	1575 W Commercial	Fort Lauderdale	FL	33309	Donald Campion	954-491-3170	R	23	0.1
Aviation Group Inc.	700 N Pearl St	Dallas	TX	75201	Lee Sanders	214-922-8100	P	23	0.4
Jet Centers Inc.	7625 S Peoria St	Englewood	CO	80112	Charles Haas	303-790-4321	R	20*	0.1
Western Aircraft Inc.	4444 Aeronca St	Boise	ID	83705	John Penn	208-338-1800	S	20*	<0.1
Avjet Airport Services	923 E Layton Ave	Milwaukee	WI	53207		407-648-7000	D	19*	0.1
Galvin Flying Service Inc.	7149 Perimeter Rd	Seattle	WA	98108	Peter G Anderson	206-763-0350	R	15*	0.1
Muncie Aviation Co.	PO Box 1169	Muncie	IN	47308	Otto Arrington	765-289-7141	R	15	<0.1
Aero Precision Repair & Overhaul	580 S Military Trail	Deerfield Beach	FL	33442	Alex Tearle	954-428-9500	R	13*	<0.1
Northern Air Inc.	P O Box 888380	Grand Rapids	MI	49588		616-336-4773	R	13*	<0.1
Aero Services International Inc.	660 N-Yardley	Newtown	PA	18940	R Ted Brant	215-860-5600	S	5*	<0.1
Lockheed Martin Logistics	105 Edinburgh Ct	Greenville	SC	29607		817-261-0295	S	5	<0.1
AirFlite Inc.	3250 AirFlite Way	Long Beach	CA	90807	Yoshimi Inaba	562-490-6200	S	4*	<0.1
William Penn Aviation Inc.	3441 N Aviation Dr	Burlington	NC	27215	Allan Ostroff	336-227-1278	R	3*	<0.1
Hudson General L.L.C.	P O Box 355	Great Neck	NY	11022	Barry Regnstien	516-487-8610	S	2*	<0.1
Texas Skyways Inc.	308 Boerne Stage	Boerne	TX	78006	Jack Johnson	830-755-8989	R	1*	<0.1
D.Z. Inc.	P O Box 8069	Red Bluff	CA	96080	Jim Thompson	530-529-2560	R	1*	<0.1

Source: Ward's Business Directory of U.S. Private and Public Companies, Volumes 1 and 2, 2000. The company type code used is as follows: P - Public, R - Private, S - Subsidiary, D - Division, J - Joint Venture, A - Affiliate, G - Group, N - Company type not reported. Sales are in millions of dollars, employees are in thousands. An asterisk (*) indicates an estimated sales volume. The symbol < stands for 'less than'. Company names and addresses are truncated, in some cases, to fit into the available space.

LOCATION BY STATE AND REGIONAL CONCENTRATION

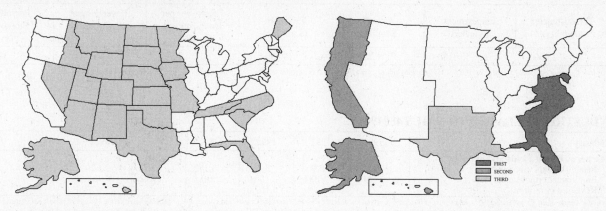

INDUSTRY DATA BY STATE

State	Establishments Total (number)	Establishments % of U.S.	Employment Total (number)	Employment % of U.S.	Employment Per Estab.	Payroll Total ($ mil.)	Payroll Per Empl. ($)	Revenues Total ($ mil.)	Revenues % of U.S.	Revenues Per Estab. ($)
New Jersey	33	1.9	1,743	2.8	53	37.1	21,264	146.8	4.5	4,449,697
Minnesota	36	2.1	838	1.4	23	16.9	20,144	110.8	3.4	3,076,944
Virginia	43	2.5	2,047	3.3	48	35.0	17,082	105.2	3.2	2,446,535
Illinois	48	2.8	1,305	2.1	27	24.3	18,619	81.1	2.5	1,689,229
Michigan	50	2.9	1,244	2.0	25	19.7	15,875	69.2	2.1	1,383,140
Missouri	39	2.3	3,836	6.2	98	40.4	10,533	67.7	2.1	1,735,385
Indiana	38	2.2	1,176	1.9	31	22.1	18,812	58.5	1.8	1,539,842
Colorado	42	2.4	1,542	2.5	37	20.4	13,251	41.6	1.3	990,214
Hawaii	14	0.8	1,095	1.8	78	19.5	17,806	41.4	1.3	2,953,857
Maryland	18	1.0	860	1.4	48	13.6	15,797	37.1	1.1	2,061,056
Mississippi	18	1.0	754	1.2	42	21.1	28,050	37.0	1.1	2,053,500
Utah	20	1.2	918	1.5	46	12.4	13,532	33.9	1.0	1,695,050
Kansas	19	1.1	481	0.8	25	13.3	27,672	31.9	1.0	1,676,421
Wisconsin	30	1.7	316	0.5	11	6.1	19,370	26.2	0.8	872,533
Kentucky	22	1.3	353	0.6	16	6.9	19,561	20.2	0.6	919,409
Iowa	24	1.4	266	0.4	11	3.6	13,410	16.6	0.5	691,875
Nebraska	17	1.0	174	0.3	10	3.4	19,713	15.9	0.5	932,765
Maine	10	0.6	137	0.2	14	3.4	24,737	15.5	0.5	1,550,100
Montana	20	1.2	223	0.4	11	3.3	15,004	12.3	0.4	616,200
North Dakota	10	0.6	151	0.2	15	2.8	18,517	11.6	0.4	1,164,900
Delaware	7	0.4	65	0.1	9	2.8	43,062	9.8	0.3	1,405,286
South Dakota	7	0.4	70	0.1	10	1.7	24,571	9.0	0.3	1,286,571
Wyoming	15	0.9	120	0.2	8	1.9	15,650	8.2	0.3	548,400
California	166	9.7	7,500*	-	-	(D)	-	(D)	-	-
Florida	166	9.7	7,500*	-	-	(D)	-	(D)	-	-
Texas	150	8.7	3,750*	-	-	(D)	-	(D)	-	-
New York	75	4.4	7,500*	-	-	(D)	-	(D)	-	-
Pennsylvania	52	3.0	1,750*	-	-	(D)	-	(D)	-	-
Ohio	50	2.9	1,750*	-	-	(D)	-	(D)	-	-
North Carolina	46	2.7	1,750*	-	-	(D)	-	(D)	-	-
Georgia	45	2.6	1,750*	-	-	(D)	-	(D)	-	-
Oklahoma	37	2.2	750*	-	-	(D)	-	(D)	-	-
Arizona	35	2.0	1,750*	-	-	(D)	-	(D)	-	-
Tennessee	35	2.0	375*	-	-	(D)	-	(D)	-	-
Washington	35	2.0	1,750*	-	-	(D)	-	(D)	-	-
Alabama	28	1.6	750*	-	-	(D)	-	(D)	-	-
South Carolina	26	1.5	375*	-	-	(D)	-	(D)	-	-
Connecticut	21	1.2	750*	-	-	(D)	-	(D)	-	-
Nevada	21	1.2	750*	-	-	(D)	-	(D)	-	-
Louisiana	19	1.1	750*	-	-	(D)	-	(D)	-	-
Oregon	19	1.1	375*	-	-	(D)	-	(D)	-	-
Alaska	18	1.0	750*	-	-	(D)	-	(D)	-	-
Arkansas	16	0.9	375*	-	-	(D)	-	(D)	-	-
Idaho	16	0.9	175*	-	-	(D)	-	(D)	-	-
Massachusetts	16	0.9	750*	-	-	(D)	-	(D)	-	-
New Mexico	16	0.9	375*	-	-	(D)	-	(D)	-	-
New Hampshire	7	0.4	60*	-	-	(D)	-	(D)	-	-
Rhode Island	7	0.4	375*	-	-	(D)	-	(D)	-	-
West Virginia	7	0.4	60*	-	-	(D)	-	(D)	-	-

Source: 1997 *Economic Census*. The states are in descending order of revenues or establishments (if revenue data are missing for the majority). The symbol (D) appears when data are withheld to prevent disclosure of competitive information. States marked with (D) are sorted by number of establishments. A dash (-) indicates that the data element cannot be calculated. * indicates the midpoint of a range; 175, for example is the range 100-249. Shaded *states* on the state map indicate those states which have proportionately greater representation in the industry than would be indicated by the state's population; the ratio is based on total revenues or number of establishments. Shaded *regions* indicate where the industry is regionally most concentrated.

NAICS 488190 - SUPPORT ACTIVITIES FOR AIR TRANSPORTATION NEC

GENERAL STATISTICS

Year	Establishments (number)	Employment (number)	Payroll ($ million)	Revenues ($ million)	Employees per Establishment (number)	Revenues per Establishment ($)	Payroll per Employee ($)
1997	2,400	53,318	1,713.9	5,859.6	22.2	2,441,500	32,145

Source: Economic Census of the United States, 1997. This is a newly defined industry. Data for prior years were unavailable at the time of publication but may become available over time.

SIC INDUSTRIES RELATED TO NAICS 488190

SIC	Industry	1990	1991	1992	1993	1994	1995	1996	1997
4581	**Airports, Flying Fields and Services***								
	Establishments (number)	2,777	2,968	3,252	3,382	3,503	3,629	4,014	3,958p
	Employment (thousands)	84.3	83.9	80.0	90.8	90.2	96.6	104.6	103.5p
	Revenues ($ million)	-	-	6,167.6	-	-	-	-	-

Source: Economic Census of the United States, 1992, annual surveys of economic sectors conducted by the Bureau of the Census, and estimates or projections based on the 1982-1992 period; not all data are shown. 'e' marks estimates made by the editors; 'p' indicates projections based on time series. A dash (-) indicates that data for this SIC or year were not available. * Indicates that only a portion of this industry is present within the NAICS data. If no * is shown, the entire industry is contained within the NAICS data.

INDICES OF CHANGE

Year	Establishments (number)	Employment (number)	Payroll ($ million)	Revenues ($ million)	Employees per Establishment (number)	Revenues per Establishment ($)	Payroll per Employee ($)
1997	100.0	100.0	100.0	100.0	100.0	100.0	100.0

Sources: Same as General Statistics. The values shown reflect change from the base year, 1997. Values above 100 mean greater than 1997, values below 100 mean less than 1997, and a value of 100 in years other than 1997 means same as 1997. Indices are calculated only for Census years. Data are the most recent available at this level of detail.

SELECTED RATIOS

For 1997	Avg. of Sector	Analyzed Industry	Index	For 1997	Avg. of Sector	Analyzed Industry	Index
Employees per establishment	16	22	135	Payroll per establishment	462,554	714,125	154
Revenue per establishment	1,787,642	2,441,500	137	Payroll as % of revenue	26	29	113
Revenue per employee	108,959	109,899	101	Payroll per employee	28,193	32,145	114

Sources: Same as General Statistics. The 'Average of Sector' column represents the average for all industries in this sector. The Index shows the relationship between the Average and the Analyzed Industry. For example, 100 means that they are equal; 500 that the Analyzed Industry is five times the average; 50 means that the Analyzed Industry is half the national average. 'na' is used to show that data are 'not available'.

LEADING COMPANIES

No company data available for this industry.

LOCATION BY STATE AND REGIONAL CONCENTRATION

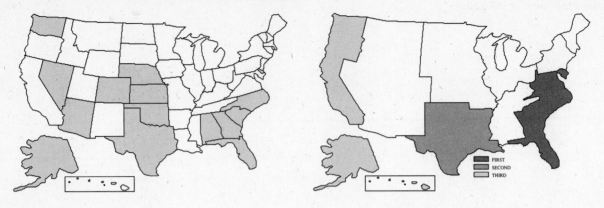

FIRST
SECOND
THIRD

INDUSTRY DATA BY STATE

State	Establishments Total (number)	% of U.S.	Employment Total (number)	% of U.S.	Per Estab.	Payroll Total ($ mil.)	Per Empl. ($)	Revenues Total ($ mil.)	% of U.S.	Per Estab. ($)
Texas	272	11.3	6,748	12.7	25	248.8	36,866	1,146.9	19.6	4,216,702
Florida	296	12.3	7,047	13.2	24	235.7	33,442	723.3	12.3	2,443,530
California	294	12.3	5,614	10.5	19	152.8	27,220	481.6	8.2	1,637,929
New York	78	3.3	2,206	4.1	28	77.4	35,097	282.5	4.8	3,621,821
South Carolina	23	1.0	2,654	5.0	115	103.7	39,088	258.0	4.4	11,215,261
Washington	62	2.6	2,984	5.6	48	104.2	34,925	250.3	4.3	4,037,419
Illinois	57	2.4	1,845	3.5	32	60.9	33,015	241.5	4.1	4,236,316
Georgia	61	2.5	1,192	2.2	20	31.5	26,398	172.4	2.9	2,826,213
North Carolina	52	2.2	1,868	3.5	36	64.6	34,592	170.2	2.9	3,273,154
Alabama	26	1.1	2,239	4.2	86	77.9	34,814	145.5	2.5	5,595,846
Nebraska	22	0.9	809	1.5	37	30.6	37,763	135.5	2.3	6,160,227
Oklahoma	81	3.4	1,462	2.7	18	41.3	28,279	124.0	2.1	1,531,272
Colorado	60	2.5	1,162	2.2	19	26.9	23,180	123.8	2.1	2,062,817
Arizona	61	2.5	1,008	1.9	17	33.4	33,150	118.3	2.0	1,939,902
Kansas	39	1.6	851	1.6	22	28.2	33,134	113.6	1.9	2,913,564
Tennessee	35	1.5	843	1.6	24	24.2	28,683	97.7	1.7	2,790,171
Michigan	53	2.2	1,039	1.9	20	28.8	27,758	92.7	1.6	1,749,264
Ohio	71	3.0	680	1.3	10	19.5	28,625	71.6	1.2	1,008,380
Wisconsin	29	1.2	459	0.9	16	18.8	40,885	71.1	1.2	2,452,034
Alaska	44	1.8	374	0.7	9	10.9	29,233	70.9	1.2	1,611,409
Maryland	26	1.1	1,225	2.3	47	41.9	34,198	70.8	1.2	2,724,731
New Jersey	36	1.5	437	0.8	12	15.9	36,444	65.3	1.1	1,814,472
Connecticut	30	1.3	516	1.0	17	18.5	35,903	62.8	1.1	2,094,567
Pennsylvania	39	1.6	586	1.1	15	17.4	29,654	60.8	1.0	1,559,795
Indiana	29	1.2	620	1.2	21	16.9	27,234	59.8	1.0	2,062,552
Missouri	42	1.8	707	1.3	17	14.9	21,027	57.6	1.0	1,371,262
Virginia	42	1.8	785	1.5	19	21.4	27,214	56.1	1.0	1,336,643
Arkansas	46	1.9	498	0.9	11	12.4	24,847	47.4	0.8	1,029,348
Delaware	15	0.6	310	0.6	21	10.4	33,468	43.6	0.7	2,906,533
Louisiana	30	1.3	495	0.9	16	10.7	21,580	38.2	0.7	1,271,933
Oregon	42	1.8	429	0.8	10	10.2	23,737	37.4	0.6	890,286
Minnesota	39	1.6	246	0.5	6	8.2	33,366	34.3	0.6	879,923
Massachusetts	35	1.5	345	0.6	10	9.5	27,461	33.6	0.6	958,829
Nevada	22	0.9	346	0.6	16	8.0	23,197	32.9	0.6	1,496,545
New Mexico	22	0.9	323	0.6	15	7.4	22,932	19.6	0.3	891,182
Kentucky	14	0.6	86	0.2	6	2.2	25,267	16.6	0.3	1,187,571
Idaho	21	0.9	123	0.2	6	2.3	18,520	9.5	0.2	454,095
North Dakota	9	0.4	42	0.1	5	1.3	32,000	4.8	0.1	531,556
Montana	12	0.5	39	0.1	3	0.8	20,359	4.4	0.1	362,917
Iowa	19	0.8	73	0.1	4	1.1	14,822	3.8	0.1	197,895
Maine	12	0.5	73	0.1	6	1.5	19,959	3.5	0.1	291,583
South Dakota	8	0.3	18	0.0	2	0.4	21,389	2.0	0.0	256,125
Wyoming	6	0.3	13	0.0	2	0.2	18,231	1.1	0.0	177,000
Mississippi	24	1.0	1,750*	-	-	(D)	-	(D)	-	-
Utah	17	0.7	60*	-	-	(D)	-	(D)	-	-
New Hampshire	13	0.5	60*	-	-	(D)	-	(D)	-	-
Hawaii	10	0.4	60*	-	-	(D)	-	(D)	-	-
West Virginia	10	0.4	375*	-	-	(D)	-	(D)	-	-
Rhode Island	7	0.3	60*	-	-	(D)	-	(D)	-	-
Vermont	7	0.3	60*	-	-	(D)	-	(D)	-	-

Source: 1997 *Economic Census*. The states are in descending order of revenues or establishments (if revenue data are missing for the majority). The symbol (D) appears when data are withheld to prevent disclosure of competitive information. States marked with (D) are sorted by number of establishments. A dash (-) indicates that the data element cannot be calculated. * indicates the midpoint of a range; 175, for example is the range 100-249. Shaded *states* on the state map indicate those states which have proportionately greater representation in the industry than would be indicated by the state's population; the ratio is based on total revenues or number of establishments. Shaded *regions* indicate where the industry is regionally most concentrated.

NAICS 488210 - SUPPORT ACTIVITIES FOR RAIL TRANSPORTATION

GENERAL STATISTICS

Year	Establishments (number)	Employment (number)	Payroll ($ million)	Revenues ($ million)	Employees per Establishment (number)	Revenues per Establishment ($)	Payroll per Employee ($)
1997	816	18,865	514.6	2,066.7	23.1	2,532,721	27,278

Source: Economic Census of the United States, 1997. This is a newly defined industry. Data for prior years were unavailable at the time of publication but may become available over time.

SIC INDUSTRIES RELATED TO NAICS 488210

SIC	Industry	1990	1991	1992	1993	1994	1995	1996	1997
4013	**Switching and Terminal Services***	-	-	-	-	-	-	-	-
4741	**Rental of Railroad Cars***								
	Establishments (number)	148	147	125	123	113	111	116	111p
	Employment (thousands)	2.6	2.3	1.9	2.0	1.9	2.1	2.3	2.0p
	Revenues ($ million)	1,829.5e	1,855.3e	1,881.1	1,906.9p	1,932.7p	1,958.5p	1,984.3p	2,010.1p
4789	**Miscellaneous Transportation Services***								
	Establishments (number)	995e	1,009e	1,024	1,039p	1,053p	1,068p	1,082p	1,097p
	Employment (thousands)	17.3e	16.8e	16.4	15.9p	15.5p	15.1p	15.1p	14.2p
	Revenues ($ million)	1,231.2e	1,382.5e	1,533.8	1,685.1p	1,836.4p	1,987.7p	2,139.0p	2,290.3p

Source: Economic Census of the United States, 1992, annual surveys of economic sectors conducted by the Bureau of the Census, and estimates or projections based on the 1982-1992 period; not all data are shown. 'e' marks estimates made by the editors; 'p' indicates projections based on time series. A dash (-) indicates that data for this SIC or year were not available. * Indicates that only a portion of this industry is present within the NAICS data. If no * is shown, the entire industry is contained within the NAICS data.

INDICES OF CHANGE

Year	Establishments (number)	Employment (number)	Payroll ($ million)	Revenues ($ million)	Employees per Establishment (number)	Revenues per Establishment ($)	Payroll per Employee ($)
1997	100.0	100.0	100.0	100.0	100.0	100.0	100.0

Sources: Same as General Statistics. The values shown reflect change from the base year, 1997. Values above 100 mean greater than 1997, values below 100 mean less than 1997, and a value of 100 in years other than 1997 means same as 1997. Indices are calculated only for Census years. Data are the most recent available at this level of detail.

SELECTED RATIOS

For 1997	Avg. of Sector	Analyzed Industry	Index	For 1997	Avg. of Sector	Analyzed Industry	Index
Employees per establishment	16	23	141	Payroll per establishment	462,554	630,637	136
Revenue per establishment	1,787,642	2,532,721	142	Payroll as % of revenue	26	25	96
Revenue per employee	108,959	109,552	101	Payroll per employee	28,193	27,278	97

Sources: Same as General Statistics. The 'Average of Sector' column represents the average for all industries in this sector. The Index shows the relationship between the Average and the Analyzed Industry. For example, 100 means that they are equal; 500 that the Analyzed Industry is five times the average; 50 means that the Analyzed Industry is half the national average. 'na' is used to show that data are 'not available'.

LEADING COMPANIES Number shown: **8**   Total sales ($ mil): **960**   Total employment (000): **5.8**

Company Name	Address				CEO Name	Phone	Co. Type	Sales ($ mil)	Empl. (000)
Illinois Central Corp.	455 N Ctyfrnt	Chicago	IL	60611	E Hunter Harrison	312-755-7500	S	700*	3.6
Indiana Harbor Belt Railroad Co.	2721 161st St	Hammond	IN	46323		219-989-4703	S	88	0.8
Belt Railway of Chicago	6900 S Central Ave	Bedford Park	IL	60638	T Shurstad	708-496-4000	R	78*	0.6
Terminal Railroad Association	700 N 2nd St	St. Louis	MO	63102	WD Spencer	314-231-5196	P	36*	0.3
Emons Transportation Group Inc.	96 S George St	York	PA	17401	Robert Grossman	717-771-1700	P	23	0.2
Cuyahoga Valley Railway	3060 Eggers Ave	Cleveland	OH	44105	DP Hennessy	216-429-7256	S	19	0.2
Peoria & Pekin Union Railway	101 Wesley Rd	Creve Coeur	IL	61610	PD Feltenstein	309-694-8600	P	13*	0.1
Brandywine Valley Railroad Co.	50 S 1st Ave	Coatesville	PA	19320	Brian McComski	610-383-2780	S	3*	<0.1

Source: Ward's Business Directory of U.S. Private and Public Companies, Volumes 1 and 2, 2000. The company type code used is as follows: P - Public, R - Private, S - Subsidiary, D - Division, J - Joint Venture, A - Affiliate, G - Group, N - Company type not reported. Sales are in millions of dollars, employees are in thousands. An asterisk (*) indicates an estimated sales volume. The symbol < stands for 'less than'. Company names and addresses are truncated, in some cases, to fit into the available space.

LOCATION BY STATE AND REGIONAL CONCENTRATION

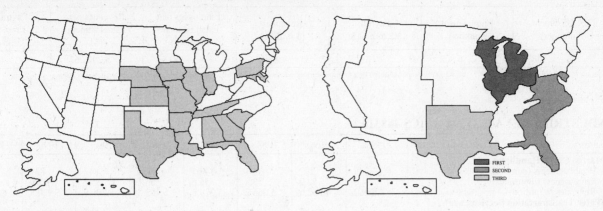

INDUSTRY DATA BY STATE

State	Establishments		Employment			Payroll		Revenues		
	Total (number)	% of U.S.	Total (number)	% of U.S.	Per Estab.	Total ($ mil.)	Per Empl. ($)	Total ($ mil.)	% of U.S.	Per Estab. ($)
Illinois	79	9.7	2,931	15.5	37	88.8	30,290	402.4	19.5	5,093,658
Texas	75	9.2	2,440	12.9	33	73.6	30,159	236.6	11.4	3,154,267
California	56	6.9	1,644	8.7	29	44.2	26,893	158.0	7.6	2,821,107
Florida	44	5.4	1,139	6.0	26	25.3	22,233	136.9	6.6	3,110,568
Pennsylvania	32	3.9	859	4.6	27	24.4	28,390	103.5	5.0	3,234,156
Georgia	27	3.3	653	3.5	24	16.7	25,556	93.0	4.5	3,445,222
Ohio	35	4.3	657	3.5	19	17.3	26,315	81.3	3.9	2,321,514
Alabama	18	2.2	408	2.2	23	10.8	26,407	66.9	3.2	3,718,611
Louisiana	23	2.8	306	1.6	13	7.9	25,882	65.7	3.2	2,858,087
Indiana	21	2.6	621	3.3	30	18.0	28,992	65.4	3.2	3,115,238
Kansas	15	1.8	463	2.5	31	12.0	25,890	65.1	3.1	4,339,800
Maryland	12	1.5	555	2.9	46	11.8	21,247	57.3	2.8	4,778,750
New Jersey	22	2.7	307	1.6	14	10.3	33,537	46.7	2.3	2,121,318
Michigan	34	4.2	704	3.7	21	21.7	30,875	46.0	2.2	1,354,206
Missouri	29	3.6	587	3.1	20	19.6	33,310	43.9	2.1	1,512,621
Tennessee	22	2.7	304	1.6	14	6.1	20,076	40.7	2.0	1,847,818
Iowa	11	1.3	342	1.8	31	9.3	27,316	33.5	1.6	3,042,182
South Carolina	17	2.1	191	1.0	11	4.3	22,644	31.9	1.5	1,876,118
Nebraska	11	1.3	263	1.4	24	6.7	25,422	29.8	1.4	2,712,091
Kentucky	20	2.5	556	2.9	28	13.2	23,707	29.7	1.4	1,487,250
Washington	23	2.8	320	1.7	14	9.0	28,247	24.4	1.2	1,062,348
North Carolina	18	2.2	247	1.3	14	6.0	24,433	20.3	1.0	1,126,833
Arkansas	9	1.1	224	1.2	25	6.3	28,286	19.9	1.0	2,205,556
Colorado	14	1.7	205	1.1	15	5.9	28,717	15.5	0.7	1,106,071
Oregon	6	0.7	192	1.0	32	5.3	27,703	15.3	0.7	2,552,167
Massachusetts	8	1.0	114	0.6	14	3.7	32,789	13.7	0.7	1,711,250
New York	18	2.2	228	1.2	13	5.1	22,522	13.3	0.6	739,722
Wisconsin	13	1.6	85	0.5	7	2.7	31,365	12.0	0.6	921,692
Virginia	8	1.0	102	0.5	13	3.0	29,539	11.2	0.5	1,403,750
Utah	13	1.6	185	1.0	14	2.6	14,146	8.2	0.4	632,538
Oklahoma	10	1.2	122	0.6	12	3.1	25,451	7.0	0.3	704,900
West Virginia	11	1.3	99	0.5	9	2.2	21,960	6.8	0.3	620,727
Minnesota	13	1.6	108	0.6	8	2.9	27,065	6.1	0.3	468,538
Mississippi	7	0.9	63	0.3	9	1.2	18,857	4.7	0.2	667,143
Delaware	6	0.7	175 *	-	-	(D)	-	(D)	-	-

Source: 1997 *Economic Census*. The states are in descending order of revenues or establishments (if revenue data are missing for the majority). The symbol (D) appears when data are withheld to prevent disclosure of competitive information. States marked with (D) are sorted by number of establishments. A dash (-) indicates that the data element cannot be calculated. * indicates the midpoint of a range; 175, for example is the range 100-249. Shaded *states* on the state map indicate those states which have proportionately greater representation in the industry than would be indicated by the state's population; the ratio is based on total revenues or number of establishments. Shaded *regions* indicate where the industry is regionally most concentrated.

NAICS 488310 - PORT AND HARBOR OPERATIONS

GENERAL STATISTICS

Year	Establishments (number)	Employment (number)	Payroll ($ million)	Revenues ($ million)	Employees per Establishment (number)	Revenues per Establishment ($)	Payroll per Employee ($)
1997	168	6,802	237.7	889.1	40.5	5,292,262	34,946

Source: *Economic Census of the United States*, 1997. This is a newly defined industry. Data for prior years were unavailable at the time of publication but may become available over time.

SIC INDUSTRIES RELATED TO NAICS 488310

SIC	Industry	1990	1991	1992	1993	1994	1995	1996	1997
4491	**Marine Cargo Handling***								
	Establishments (number)	746	797	871	865	854	842	831	851*p*
	Employment (thousands)	54.6	52.9	58.8	56.6	55.1	55.7	52.9	53.4*p*
	Revenues ($ million)	4,639.0*e*	4,852.6*e*	5,066.2	5,279.8*p*	5,493.3*p*	5,706.9*p*	5,920.5*p*	6,134.0*p*
4499	**Water Transportation Services, nec***								
	Establishments (number)	1,111	1,187	1,118	1,180	1,209	1,244	1,394	1,261*p*
	Employment (thousands)	10.6	13.1	9.4	8.7	8.6	9.4	9.7	9.1*p*
	Revenues ($ million)	1,151.3*e*	1,060.9*e*	970.6	880.3*p*	789.9*p*	699.6*p*	609.3*p*	519.0*p*

Source: *Economic Census of the United States*, 1992, annual surveys of economic sectors conducted by the Bureau of the Census, and estimates or projections based on the 1982-1992 period; not all data are shown. 'e' marks estimates made by the editors; 'p' indicates projections based on time series. A dash (-) indicates that data for this SIC or year were not available. * Indicates that only a portion of this industry is present within the NAICS data. If no * is shown, the entire industry is contained within the NAICS data.

INDICES OF CHANGE

Year	Establishments (number)	Employment (number)	Payroll ($ million)	Revenues ($ million)	Employees per Establishment (number)	Revenues per Establishment ($)	Payroll per Employee ($)
1997	100.0	100.0	100.0	100.0	100.0	100.0	100.0

Sources: Same as General Statistics. The values shown reflect change from the base year, 1997. Values above 100 mean greater than 1997, values below 100 mean less than 1997, and a value of 100 in years other than 1997 means same as 1997. Indices are calculated only for Census years. Data are the most recent available at this level of detail.

SELECTED RATIOS

For 1997	Avg. of Sector	Analyzed Industry	Index	For 1997	Avg. of Sector	Analyzed Industry	Index
Employees per establishment	16	40	247	Payroll per establishment	462,554	1,414,881	306
Revenue per establishment	1,787,642	5,292,262	296	Payroll as % of revenue	26	27	103
Revenue per employee	108,959	130,712	120	Payroll per employee	28,193	34,946	124

Sources: Same as General Statistics. The 'Average of Sector' column represents the average for all industries in this sector. The Index shows the relationship between the Average and the Analyzed Industry. For example, 100 means that they are equal; 500 that the Analyzed Industry is five times the average; 50 means that the Analyzed Industry is half the national average. 'na' is used to show that data are 'not available'.

LEADING COMPANIES

No company data available for this industry.

LOCATION BY STATE AND REGIONAL CONCENTRATION

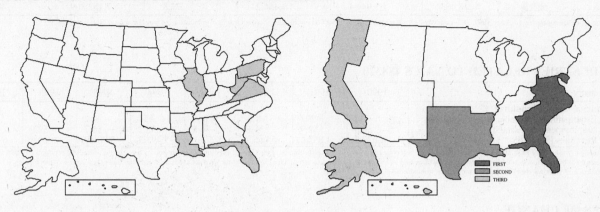

FIRST
SECOND
THIRD

INDUSTRY DATA BY STATE

State	Establishments		Employment			Payroll		Revenues		
	Total (number)	% of U.S.	Total (number)	% of U.S.	Per Estab.	Total ($ mil.)	Per Empl. ($)	Total ($ mil.)	% of U.S.	Per Estab. ($)
Louisiana	15	8.9	940	13.8	63	30.7	32,662	183.6	20.7	12,241,200
Virginia	7	4.2	1,388	20.4	198	64.5	46,451	145.8	16.4	20,824,857
California	11	6.5	110	1.6	10	8.4	76,436	89.6	10.1	8,147,545
Florida	21	12.5	1,404	20.6	67	21.4	15,233	67.7	7.6	3,222,667
Illinois	14	8.3	217	3.2	15	7.8	35,816	60.2	6.8	4,301,571
Pennsylvania	10	6.0	815	12.0	81	39.7	48,698	57.8	6.5	5,776,700
Ohio	7	4.2	172	2.5	25	6.7	38,913	21.2	2.4	3,033,571
West Virginia	7	4.2	134	2.0	19	4.1	30,858	18.7	2.1	2,670,857
Tennessee	6	3.6	65	1.0	11	2.6	39,846	11.4	1.3	1,899,333
Texas	7	4.2	175*	-	-	(D)	-	(D)	-	-

Source: 1997 *Economic Census*. The states are in descending order of revenues or establishments (if revenue data are missing for the majority). The symbol (D) appears when data are withheld to prevent disclosure of competitive information. States marked with (D) are sorted by number of establishments. A dash (-) indicates that the data element cannot be calculated. * indicates the midpoint of a range; 175, for example is the range 100-249. Shaded *states* on the state map indicate those states which have proportionately greater representation in the industry than would be indicated by the state's population; the ratio is based on total revenues or number of establishments. Shaded *regions* indicate where the industry is regionally most concentrated.

NAICS 488320 - MARINE CARGO HANDLING

GENERAL STATISTICS

Year	Establishments (number)	Employment (number)	Payroll ($ million)	Revenues ($ million)	Employees per Establishment (number)	Revenues per Establishment ($)	Payroll per Employee ($)
1997	623	48,463	1,941.4	4,456.2	77.8	7,152,809	40,059

Source: Economic Census of the United States, 1997. This is a newly defined industry. Data for prior years were unavailable at the time of publication but may become available over time.

SIC INDUSTRIES RELATED TO NAICS 488320

SIC	Industry	1990	1991	1992	1993	1994	1995	1996	1997
4491	**Marine Cargo Handling***								
	Establishments (number)	746	797	871	865	854	842	831	851*p*
	Employment (thousands)	54.6	52.9	58.8	56.6	55.1	55.7	52.9	53.4*p*
	Revenues ($ million)	4,639.0*e*	4,852.6*e*	5,066.2	5,279.8*p*	5,493.3*p*	5,706.9*p*	5,920.5*p*	6,134.0*p*

Source: Economic Census of the United States, 1992, annual surveys of economic sectors conducted by the Bureau of the Census, and estimates or projections based on the 1982-1992 period; not all data are shown. 'e' marks estimates made by the editors; 'p' indicates projections based on time series. A dash (-) indicates that data for this SIC or year were not available. * Indicates that only a portion of this industry is present within the NAICS data. If no * is shown, the entire industry is contained within the NAICS data.

INDICES OF CHANGE

Year	Establishments (number)	Employment (number)	Payroll ($ million)	Revenues ($ million)	Employees per Establishment (number)	Revenues per Establishment ($)	Payroll per Employee ($)
1997	100.0	100.0	100.0	100.0	100.0	100.0	100.0

Sources: Same as General Statistics. The values shown reflect change from the base year, 1997. Values above 100 mean greater than 1997, values below 100 mean less than 1997, and a value of 100 in years other than 1997 means same as 1997. Indices are calculated only for Census years. Data are the most recent available at this level of detail.

SELECTED RATIOS

For 1997	Avg. of Sector	Analyzed Industry	Index	For 1997	Avg. of Sector	Analyzed Industry	Index
Employees per establishment	16	78	474	Payroll per establishment	462,554	3,116,212	674
Revenue per establishment	1,787,642	7,152,809	400	Payroll as % of revenue	26	44	168
Revenue per employee	108,959	91,951	84	Payroll per employee	28,193	40,059	142

Sources: Same as General Statistics. The 'Average of Sector' column represents the average for all industries in this sector. The Index shows the relationship between the Average and the Analyzed Industry. For example, 100 means that they are equal; 500 that the Analyzed Industry is five times the average; 50 means that the Analyzed Industry is half the national average. 'na' is used to show that data are 'not available'.

LEADING COMPANIES   Number shown: **26**   Total sales ($ mil): **3,996**   Total employment (000): **48.0**

Company Name	Address				CEO Name	Phone	Co. Type	Sales ($ mil)	Empl. (000)
Crowley Maritime Corp.	155 Grand Ave	Oakland	CA	94612	Thomas Crowley	510-251-7500	R	1,153	4.5
Stevedoring Services of America	1131 SW Klickitat	Seattle	WA	98134	Frederick D Smith	206-623-0304	R	850	7.5
International Shipholding Corp.	650 Poydras St	New Orleans	LA	70130	Erik F Johnsen	504-529-5461	P	373	1.0
ENSCO International Inc.	2700 Fountain Pl	Dallas	TX	75202	Carl F Thorne	214-922-1500	P	364	31.0
Weeks Marine Inc.	216 N Ave E	Cranford	NJ	07016	Richard S Weeks	908-272-4010	R	300	1.0
L and L Oil and Services Inc.	PO Box 6984	Metairie	LA	70009	FL Levy	504-832-8600	R	200	0.2
Matson Navigation	PO Box 7452	San Francisco	CA	94120	Bradly Mulholland	415-957-4000	S	113*	0.4
Direct Container Line Inc.	857 E 230th St	Carson	CA	90745	Owen Glenn	310-835-8900	R	103*	0.4
Trailer Bridge Inc.	10405 New Berlin E	Jacksonville	FL	32226	Ralph W Heim	904-751-7100	P	77	0.3
Electro-Coal Transfer	14537 Hwy 15	Braithwaite	LA	70040		504-333-7200	S	66*	0.2
Marine Terminals of Arkansas Inc.	P O Box 160	Armorel	AR	72310	Rick Ellis	870-763-5923	R	63*	0.2
New Haven Terminal Inc.	100 Waterfront St	New Haven	CT	06512	Joseph D Crowley	203-468-0805	R	46*	0.2
Universal Maritime Service Corp.	10710 Midlothian	Richmond	VA	23235	Phil Conners	804-897-3888	S	43*	0.2
Intern. Terminal Operating Inc.	1 Evertrust Plz	Jersey City	NJ	07302	James Field	201-915-3100	R	42*	0.2
Parker Towing Co.	P O Box 20908	Tuscaloosa	AL	35402	Tim Parker Jr	205-349-1677	R	40*	0.2
Hub Group	751 Walnut Knoll	Cordova	TN	38018	David Yeager	901-758-0020	S	29*	0.1
APC Warehouse Co.	P O Box C	Madison	IL	62060	Richard Kerns	618-451-4222	R	28*	0.1
Penn Warehousing & Distribution	2147 S Delaware	Philadelphia	PA	19148	John Brown	215-468-5232	R	23*	<0.1
Dix Industries Inc.	PO Box 3466	Brownsville	TX	78523	Robert Ostos	956-831-4228	R	17*	<0.1
James J. Flanagan Stevedores	1111 E Navigation	Houston	TX	77012	James Flanagan	713-928-5683	D	17*	<0.1
Lake Charles Stevedores Inc.	150 Marine St	Lake Charles	LA	70602	Daryl Didier	318-439-9473	R	17*	<0.1
Pinney Dock and Transport Co.	1149 E 5th St	Ashtabula	OH	44004	Maynard Walker	440-964-7186	R	13*	<0.1
Levin Enterprises Inc.	550 Hamilton Ave	Palo Alto	CA	94301	Gary Levin	650-324-3025	R	6*	<0.1
Golden Stevedoring Company Inc.	PO Box 8697	Rowland H.	CA	91748	Edgard H Gonzalez	334-433-3726	R	5	0.1
Shipyard River Coal Terminal Co.	1801 Milford	Charleston	SC	29405		843-722-2878	S	5*	<0.1
Lambert's Point Docks Inc.	PO Box 89	Norfolk	VA	23501	R L Taylor	757-446-1200	S	3*	<0.1

Source: *Ward's Business Directory of U.S. Private and Public Companies*, Volumes 1 and 2, 2000. The company type code used is as follows: P - Public, R - Private, S - Subsidiary, D - Division, J - Joint Venture, A - Affiliate, G - Group, N - Company type not reported. Sales are in millions of dollars, employees are in thousands. An asterisk (*) indicates an estimated sales volume. The symbol < stands for 'less than'. Company names and addresses are truncated, in some cases, to fit into the available space.

LOCATION BY STATE AND REGIONAL CONCENTRATION

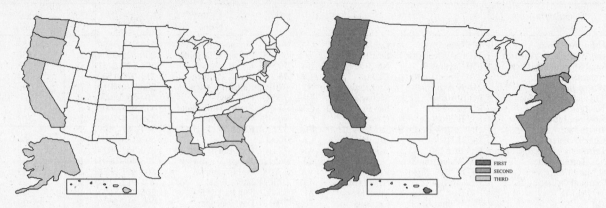

INDUSTRY DATA BY STATE

State	Establishments		Employment			Payroll		Revenues		
	Total (number)	% of U.S.	Total (number)	% of U.S.	Per Estab.	Total ($ mil.)	Per Empl. ($)	Total ($ mil.)	% of U.S.	Per Estab. ($)
California	58	9.3	10,350	21.4	178	743.8	71,861	1,663.3	37.3	28,677,172
New Jersey	23	3.7	3,552	7.3	154	160.4	45,161	411.4	9.2	17,886,696
Washington	35	5.6	2,234	4.6	64	176.6	79,066	311.6	7.0	8,901,657
Louisiana	69	11.1	3,167	6.5	46	100.9	31,857	299.8	6.7	4,345,304
Florida	68	10.9	5,843	12.1	86	107.0	18,308	238.6	5.4	3,508,235
Texas	60	9.6	4,281	8.8	71	82.8	19,333	211.5	4.7	3,525,433
Oregon	11	1.8	1,171	2.4	106	92.2	78,738	151.3	3.4	13,758,273
Georgia	17	2.7	2,708	5.6	159	53.9	19,898	131.4	2.9	7,732,059
South Carolina	15	2.4	2,711	5.6	181	46.6	17,190	103.3	2.3	6,884,133
Virginia	15	2.4	1,654	3.4	110	46.3	27,995	100.0	2.2	6,663,600
Pennsylvania	19	3.0	853	1.8	45	31.2	36,596	79.7	1.8	4,192,368
New York	17	2.7	962	2.0	57	29.5	30,701	76.1	1.7	4,473,765
Hawaii	7	1.1	651	1.3	93	35.0	53,822	65.4	1.5	9,341,143
Illinois	21	3.4	445	0.9	21	18.8	42,249	62.9	1.4	2,993,714
Alaska	12	1.9	645	1.3	54	27.4	42,451	56.4	1.3	4,700,917
Ohio	17	2.7	566	1.2	33	16.0	28,228	44.6	1.0	2,620,941
Alabama	23	3.7	990	2.0	43	25.3	25,543	42.3	1.0	1,841,000
Mississippi	13	2.1	563	1.2	43	12.8	22,824	35.1	0.8	2,698,769
Arkansas	10	1.6	213	0.4	21	7.2	33,770	33.5	0.8	3,349,700
North Carolina	9	1.4	918	1.9	102	13.4	14,584	32.2	0.7	3,575,556
Tennessee	10	1.6	123	0.3	12	2.7	22,171	17.9	0.4	1,793,400
Kentucky	12	1.9	118	0.2	10	3.4	29,169	13.8	0.3	1,146,667
Maine	9	1.4	128	0.3	14	2.8	21,992	10.9	0.2	1,209,667
Maryland	16	2.6	1,750*	-	-	(D)	-	(D)	-	-
Minnesota	9	1.4	60*	-	-	(D)	-	(D)	-	-
Iowa	6	1.0	60*	-	-	(D)	-	(D)	-	-

Source: 1997 *Economic Census*. The states are in descending order of revenues or establishments (if revenue data are missing for the majority). The symbol (D) appears when data are withheld to prevent disclosure of competitive information. States marked with (D) are sorted by number of establishments. A dash (-) indicates that the data element cannot be calculated. * indicates the midpoint of a range; 175, for example is the range 100-249. Shaded *states* on the state map indicate those states which have proportionately greater representation in the industry than would be indicated by the state's population; the ratio is based on total revenues or number of establishments. Shaded *regions* indicate where the industry is regionally most concentrated.

NAICS 488330 - NAVIGATIONAL SERVICES TO SHIPPING

GENERAL STATISTICS

Year	Establishments (number)	Employment (number)	Payroll ($ million)	Revenues ($ million)	Employees per Establishment (number)	Revenues per Establishment ($)	Payroll per Employee ($)
1997	865	10,800	376.7	1,513.2	12.5	1,749,364	34,880

Source: *Economic Census of the United States*, 1997. This is a newly defined industry. Data for prior years were unavailable at the time of publication but may become available over time.

SIC INDUSTRIES RELATED TO NAICS 488330

SIC	Industry	1990	1991	1992	1993	1994	1995	1996	1997
4492	**Towing and Tugboat Service***								
	Establishments (number)	713	732	941	914	884	867	890	906p
	Employment (thousands)	19.7	19.2	24.6	22.2	21.8	21.5	22.5	23.1p
	Revenues ($ million)	2,202.0e	2,441.9e	2,681.9	2,921.9p	3,161.8p	3,401.8p	3,641.8p	3,881.8p
4499	**Water Transportation Services, nec***								
	Establishments (number)	1,111	1,187	1,118	1,180	1,209	1,244	1,394	1,261p
	Employment (thousands)	10.6	13.1	9.4	8.7	8.6	9.4	9.7	9.1p
	Revenues ($ million)	1,151.3e	1,060.9e	970.6	880.3p	789.9p	699.6p	609.3p	519.0p

Source: *Economic Census of the United States*, 1992, annual surveys of economic sectors conducted by the Bureau of the Census, and estimates or projections based on the 1982-1992 period; not all data are shown. 'e' marks estimates made by the editors; 'p' indicates projections based on time series. A dash (-) indicates that data for this SIC or year were not available. * Indicates that only a portion of this industry is present within the NAICS data. If no * is shown, the entire industry is contained within the NAICS data.

INDICES OF CHANGE

Year	Establishments (number)	Employment (number)	Payroll ($ million)	Revenues ($ million)	Employees per Establishment (number)	Revenues per Establishment ($)	Payroll per Employee ($)
1997	100.0	100.0	100.0	100.0	100.0	100.0	100.0

Sources: Same as General Statistics. The values shown reflect change from the base year, 1997. Values above 100 mean greater than 1997, values below 100 mean less than 1997, and a value of 100 in years other than 1997 means same as 1997. Indices are calculated only for Census years. Data are the most recent available at this level of detail.

SELECTED RATIOS

For 1997	Avg. of Sector	Analyzed Industry	Index	For 1997	Avg. of Sector	Analyzed Industry	Index
Employees per establishment	16	12	76	Payroll per establishment	462,554	435,491	94
Revenue per establishment	1,787,642	1,749,364	98	Payroll as % of revenue	26	25	96
Revenue per employee	108,959	140,111	129	Payroll per employee	28,193	34,880	124

Sources: Same as General Statistics. The 'Average of Sector' column represents the average for all industries in this sector. The Index shows the relationship between the Average and the Analyzed Industry. For example, 100 means that they are equal; 500 that the Analyzed Industry is five times the average; 50 means that the Analyzed Industry is half the national average. 'na' is used to show that data are 'not available'.

LEADING COMPANIES   Number shown: **12**   Total sales ($ mil): **3,004**   Total employment (000): **19.4**

Company Name	Address				CEO Name	Phone	Co. Type	Sales ($ mil)	Empl. (000)
Crowley Maritime Corp.	155 Grand Ave	Oakland	CA	94612	Thomas Crowley	510-251-7500	R	1,153	4.5
Tidewater Inc.	PO Box 61117	New Orleans	LA	70161	William O'Malley	504-568-1010	P	969	8.1
Hvide Marine Inc.	P O Box 13038	Fort Lauderdale	FL	33316	J Erik Hvide	954-523-2200	R	402	3.1
Foss Maritime Co.	660 W Ewing St	Seattle	WA	98119	Thomas Van Dawark	206-281-3800	S	139*	1.0
Moran Towing Corp.	2 Greenwich Plz	Greenwich	CT	06830	Malcolm W MacLeod	203-625-7800	R	89*	0.9
Coastal Towing Inc.	8401 W Monroe Rd	Houston	TX	77061	Edgar Griffin	713-943-5000	R	70*	0.5
Allied Marine Industries Inc.	P O Box 717	Norfolk	VA	23501	William Law	757-545-7301	R	44*	0.3
Bay Houston Towing Co.	P O Box 3006	Houston	TX	77253	Mark E Kuebler	713-529-3755	R	38	0.4
Jantran Inc.	P O Box 397	Rosedale	MS	38769	Joseph W Janoush	662-759-6841	R	35*	0.2
Le Beouf Brothers Towing Inc.	PO Box 9036	Houma	LA	70361	Richard Gonsoulin	504-594-6691	R	31*	0.2
McAllister Towing	17 Battery Pl	New York	NY	10004	Brian A McAllister	212-269-3200	R	17*	0.1
Shaver Transportation Co.	P O Box 10324	Portland	OR	97210	Harry L Shaver	503-228-8850	R	17*	<0.1

Source: Ward's Business Directory of U.S. Private and Public Companies, Volumes 1 and 2, 2000. The company type code used is as follows: P - Public, R - Private, S - Subsidiary, D - Division, J - Joint Venture, A - Affiliate, G - Group, N - Company type not reported. Sales are in millions of dollars, employees are in thousands. An asterisk (*) indicates an estimated sales volume. The symbol < stands for 'less than'. Company names and addresses are truncated, in some cases, to fit into the available space.

LOCATION BY STATE AND REGIONAL CONCENTRATION

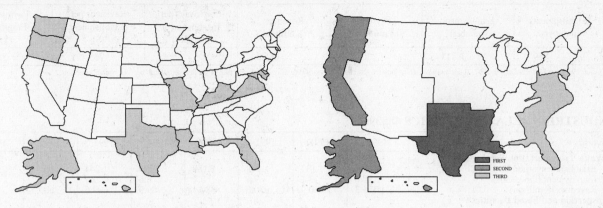

INDUSTRY DATA BY STATE

State	Establishments Total (number)	Establishments % of U.S.	Employment Total (number)	Employment % of U.S.	Employment Per Estab.	Payroll Total ($ mil.)	Payroll Per Empl. ($)	Revenues Total ($ mil.)	Revenues % of U.S.	Revenues Per Estab. ($)
Louisiana	160	18.5	3,072	28.4	19	91.8	29,891	393.5	26.0	2,459,656
Texas	103	11.9	805	7.5	8	37.1	46,103	140.6	9.3	1,364,864
California	40	4.6	697	6.5	17	29.9	42,859	105.8	7.0	2,645,500
Florida	122	14.1	725	6.7	6	27.2	37,550	90.8	6.0	744,172
Kentucky	8	0.9	193	1.8	24	4.7	24,233	89.8	5.9	11,224,750
New York	36	4.2	591	5.5	16	21.5	36,299	66.4	4.4	1,845,639
Illinois	29	3.4	742	6.9	26	22.8	30,763	60.7	4.0	2,092,828
Maryland	11	1.3	348	3.2	32	19.0	54,529	58.8	3.9	5,349,545
Missouri	16	1.8	320	3.0	20	8.8	27,481	55.2	3.6	3,450,437
Virginia	15	1.7	376	3.5	25	8.9	23,782	49.9	3.3	3,327,733
Washington	56	6.5	250	2.3	4	13.4	53,732	47.2	3.1	843,518
Oregon	26	3.0	329	3.0	13	14.4	43,909	45.6	3.0	1,752,269
Alaska	33	3.8	104	1.0	3	6.4	61,356	44.3	2.9	1,342,485
New Jersey	13	1.5	105	1.0	8	7.1	67,590	30.6	2.0	2,354,385
Hawaii	8	0.9	173	1.6	22	7.1	40,827	22.8	1.5	2,851,000
Alabama	15	1.7	267	2.5	18	6.0	22,554	20.9	1.4	1,393,467
Ohio	13	1.5	181	1.7	14	4.9	27,177	17.7	1.2	1,363,692
Georgia	10	1.2	181	1.7	18	5.3	29,215	17.1	1.1	1,710,200
Delaware	10	1.2	74	0.7	7	2.7	36,595	15.2	1.0	1,524,000
South Carolina	12	1.4	148	1.4	12	3.1	21,142	12.6	0.8	1,048,167
Iowa	7	0.8	161	1.5	23	4.7	28,950	12.6	0.8	1,806,000
Wisconsin	9	1.0	80	0.7	9	2.6	32,050	11.6	0.8	1,287,889
Tennessee	6	0.7	108	1.0	18	3.2	29,343	9.7	0.6	1,623,333
Massachusetts	8	0.9	55	0.5	7	1.2	21,345	8.8	0.6	1,099,250
Michigan	8	0.9	46	0.4	6	2.9	63,326	7.3	0.5	910,125
Maine	18	2.1	56	0.5	3	2.7	48,446	6.6	0.4	368,167
Rhode Island	8	0.9	31	0.3	4	1.2	38,903	6.3	0.4	791,750
North Carolina	7	0.8	57	0.5	8	1.8	30,789	5.5	0.4	781,143
Minnesota	9	1.0	24	0.2	3	1.1	47,375	3.4	0.2	381,889
Pennsylvania	13	1.5	175*	-	-	(D)	-	(D)	-	-
Mississippi	11	1.3	60*	-	-	(D)	-	(D)	-	-
Indiana	7	0.8	175*	-	-	(D)	-	(D)	-	-

Source: 1997 Economic Census. The states are in descending order of revenues or establishments (if revenue data are missing for the majority). The symbol (D) appears when data are withheld to prevent disclosure of competitive information. States marked with (D) are sorted by number of establishments. A dash (-) indicates that the data element cannot be calculated. * indicates the midpoint of a range; 175, for example is the range 100-249. Shaded *states* on the state map indicate those states which have proportionately greater representation in the industry than would be indicated by the state's population; the ratio is based on total revenues or number of establishments. Shaded *regions* indicate where the industry is regionally most concentrated.

NAICS 488390 - SUPPORT ACTIVITIES FOR WATER TRANSPORTATION NEC

GENERAL STATISTICS

Year	Establishments (number)	Employment (number)	Payroll ($ million)	Revenues ($ million)	Employees per Establishment (number)	Revenues per Establishment ($)	Payroll per Employee ($)
1997	869	6,415	207.5	656.2	7.4	755,121	32,346

Source: *Economic Census of the United States*, 1997. This is a newly defined industry. Data for prior years were unavailable at the time of publication but may become available over time.

SIC INDUSTRIES RELATED TO NAICS 488390

SIC	Industry	1990	1991	1992	1993	1994	1995	1996	1997
4499	**Water Transportation Services, nec***								
	Establishments (number)	1,111	1,187	1,118	1,180	1,209	1,244	1,394	1,261p
	Employment (thousands)	10.6	13.1	9.4	8.7	8.6	9.4	9.7	9.1p
	Revenues ($ million)	1,151.3e	1,060.9e	970.6	880.3p	789.9p	699.6p	609.3p	519.0p
4785	**Inspection and Fixed Facilities***								
	Establishments (number)	222e	242e	263	284p	304p	325p	345p	366p
	Employment (thousands)	2.3e	2.5e	2.8	3.1p	3.4p	3.6p	3.9p	4.2p
	Revenues ($ million)	181.0e	201.0e	221.0	241.0p	261.0p	281.0p	301.0p	321.0p
7699	**Repair Services, nec***								
	Establishments (number)	27,822	29,303	34,103	34,618	34,136	34,391	35,001p	35,792p
	Employment (thousands)	181.0	181.4	191.0	201.5	207.4	220.2	219.6p	226.2p
	Revenues ($ million)	-	-	15,059.4	15,563.6p	16,427.9p	17,292.2p	18,156.5p	19,020.8p

Source: *Economic Census of the United States*, 1992, annual surveys of economic sectors conducted by the Bureau of the Census, and estimates or projections based on the 1982-1992 period; not all data are shown. 'e' marks estimates made by the editors; 'p' indicates projections based on time series. A dash (-) indicates that data for this SIC or year were not available. * Indicates that only a portion of this industry is present within the NAICS data. If no * is shown, the entire industry is contained within the NAICS data.

INDICES OF CHANGE

Year	Establishments (number)	Employment (number)	Payroll ($ million)	Revenues ($ million)	Employees per Establishment (number)	Revenues per Establishment ($)	Payroll per Employee ($)
1997	100.0	100.0	100.0	100.0	100.0	100.0	100.0

Sources: Same as General Statistics. The values shown reflect change from the base year, 1997. Values above 100 mean greater than 1997, values below 100 mean less than 1997, and a value of 100 in years other than 1997 means same as 1997. Indices are calculated only for Census years. Data are the most recent available at this level of detail.

SELECTED RATIOS

For 1997	Avg. of Sector	Analyzed Industry	Index	For 1997	Avg. of Sector	Analyzed Industry	Index
Employees per establishment	16	7	45	Payroll per establishment	462,554	238,780	52
Revenue per establishment	1,787,642	755,121	42	Payroll as % of revenue	26	32	122
Revenue per employee	108,959	102,292	94	Payroll per employee	28,193	32,346	115

Sources: Same as General Statistics. The 'Average of Sector' column represents the average for all industries in this sector. The Index shows the relationship between the Average and the Analyzed Industry. For example, 100 means that they are equal; 500 that the Analyzed Industry is five times the average; 50 means that the Analyzed Industry is half the national average. 'na' is used to show that data are 'not available'.

LEADING COMPANIES   Number shown: **5**   Total sales ($ mil): **308**   Total employment (000): **1.6**

Company Name	Address				CEO Name	Phone	Co. Type	Sales ($ mil)	Empl. (000)
Edison Chouest Offshore Inc.	P O Box 310	Galliano	LA	70354	Gary J Chouest	504-632-7144	R	196*	1.0
Biehl International Corp.	5200 Hollister St	Houston	TX	77040	John Springer	713-690-7200	R	98*	0.5
Fleet Yacht Charters	164 Norhtern Ave	Boston	MA	02210	Charles G Moretto	617-439-5678	R	10*	<0.1
MTL Petrolink Corp.	4606 FM 1960 W	Houston	TX	77069	Bob Carson	281-580-2888	S	2*	<0.1
Lady Cyana Divers Inc.	P O Box 1157	Islamorada	FL	33036	Gloria J Teague	305-664-8717	R	2*	<0.1

Source: Ward's Business Directory of U.S. Private and Public Companies, Volumes 1 and 2, 2000. The company type code used is as follows: P - Public, R - Private, S - Subsidiary, D - Division, J - Joint Venture, A - Affiliate, G - Group, N - Company type not reported. Sales are in millions of dollars, employees are in thousands. An asterisk (*) indicates an estimated sales volume. The symbol < stands for 'less than'. Company names and addresses are truncated, in some cases, to fit into the available space.

LOCATION BY STATE AND REGIONAL CONCENTRATION

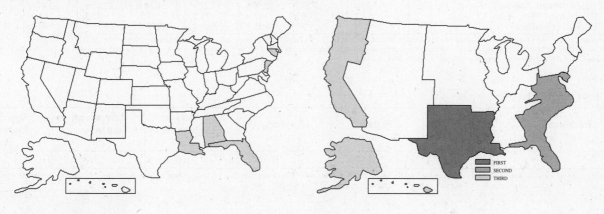

INDUSTRY DATA BY STATE

State	Establishments Total (number)	% of U.S.	Employment Total (number)	% of U.S.	Per Estab.	Payroll Total ($ mil.)	Per Empl. ($)	Revenues Total ($ mil.)	% of U.S.	Per Estab. ($)
Louisiana	109	12.5	1,840	28.7	17	48.8	26,507	145.0	22.1	1,329,899
Florida	162	18.6	536	8.4	3	20.4	38,019	85.0	13.0	524,870
California	70	8.1	556	8.7	8	16.3	29,333	59.8	9.1	854,000
New Jersey	51	5.9	460	7.2	9	19.6	42,715	49.2	7.5	963,922
Alabama	18	2.1	98	1.5	5	3.3	33,765	31.6	4.8	1,757,833
Illinois	23	2.6	140	2.2	6	4.2	30,229	19.7	3.0	854,522
Connecticut	19	2.2	204	3.2	11	8.3	40,843	18.0	2.7	949,737
Ohio	14	1.6	207	3.2	15	5.9	28,454	13.2	2.0	944,929
Virginia	19	2.2	149	2.3	8	3.2	21,550	8.7	1.3	456,842
Tennessee	7	0.8	79	1.2	11	2.0	25,038	5.1	0.8	729,143
Kentucky	7	0.8	46	0.7	7	1.2	26,391	4.1	0.6	579,571
South Carolina	9	1.0	50	0.8	6	1.5	29,800	3.5	0.5	383,889
Oregon	12	1.4	37	0.6	3	1.1	28,432	3.2	0.5	262,917
Michigan	21	2.4	46	0.7	2	1.0	21,696	3.0	0.5	143,333
Wisconsin	7	0.8	48	0.7	7	1.1	22,521	2.7	0.4	382,000
North Carolina	12	1.4	50	0.8	4	1.1	21,800	2.5	0.4	208,000
Massachusetts	9	1.0	22	0.3	2	0.7	31,773	2.3	0.3	251,667
Texas	96	11.0	750*	-	-	(D)	-	(D)	-	-
Washington	52	6.0	175*	-	-	(D)	-	(D)	-	-
New York	37	4.3	375*	-	-	(D)	-	(D)	-	-
Maryland	21	2.4	60*	-	-	(D)	-	(D)	-	-
Alaska	14	1.6	60*	-	-	(D)	-	(D)	-	-
Pennsylvania	11	1.3	175*	-	-	(D)	-	(D)	-	-
Maine	9	1.0	10*	-	-	(D)	-	(D)	-	-
Minnesota	9	1.0	10*	-	-	(D)	-	(D)	-	-
Georgia	8	0.9	60*	-	-	(D)	-	(D)	-	-
Rhode Island	7	0.8	60*	-	-	(D)	-	(D)	-	-
Hawaii	6	0.7	60*	-	-	(D)	-	(D)	-	-

Source: 1997 Economic Census. The states are in descending order of revenues or establishments (if revenue data are missing for the majority). The symbol (D) appears when data are withheld to prevent disclosure of competitive information. States marked with (D) are sorted by number of establishments. A dash (-) indicates that the data element cannot be calculated. * indicates the midpoint of a range; 175, for example is the range 100-249. Shaded states on the state map indicate those states which have proportionately greater representation in the industry than would be indicated by the state's population; the ratio is based on total revenues or number of establishments. Shaded regions indicate where the industry is regionally most concentrated.

NAICS 488410 - MOTOR VEHICLE TOWING

GENERAL STATISTICS

Year	Establishments (number)	Employment (number)	Payroll ($ million)	Revenues ($ million)	Employees per Establishment (number)	Revenues per Establishment ($)	Payroll per Employee ($)
1997	5,893	36,845	747.4	2,295.2	6.3	389,479	20,285

Source: Economic Census of the United States, 1997. This is a newly defined industry. Data for prior years were unavailable at the time of publication but may become available over time.

SIC INDUSTRIES RELATED TO NAICS 488410

SIC	Industry	1990	1991	1992	1993	1994	1995	1996	1997
7549	**Automotive Services, nec***								
	Establishments (number)	7,856	8,721	10,906	11,269	11,704	12,058	12,470p	13,093p
	Employment (thousands)	54.2	55.9	67.4	71.2	77.1	85.5	85.8p	90.6p
	Revenues ($ million)	-	-	3,402.8	3,589.4p	3,858.4p	4,127.4p	4,396.4p	4,665.4p

*Source: Economic Census of the United States, 1992, annual surveys of economic sectors conducted by the Bureau of the Census, and estimates or projections based on the 1982-1992 period; not all data are shown. 'e' marks estimates made by the editors; 'p' indicates projections based on time series. A dash (-) indicates that data for this SIC or year were not available. * Indicates that only a portion of this industry is present within the NAICS data. If no * is shown, the entire industry is contained within the NAICS data.*

INDICES OF CHANGE

Year	Establishments (number)	Employment (number)	Payroll ($ million)	Revenues ($ million)	Employees per Establishment (number)	Revenues per Establishment ($)	Payroll per Employee ($)
1997	100.0	100.0	100.0	100.0	100.0	100.0	100.0

Sources: Same as General Statistics. The values shown reflect change from the base year, 1997. Values above 100 mean greater than 1997, values below 100 mean less than 1997, and a value of 100 in years other than 1997 means same as 1997. Indices are calculated only for Census years. Data are the most recent available at this level of detail.

SELECTED RATIOS

For 1997	Avg. of Sector	Analyzed Industry	Index	For 1997	Avg. of Sector	Analyzed Industry	Index
Employees per establishment	16	6	38	Payroll per establishment	462,554	126,828	27
Revenue per establishment	1,787,642	389,479	22	Payroll as % of revenue	26	33	126
Revenue per employee	108,959	62,293	57	Payroll per employee	28,193	20,285	72

Sources: Same as General Statistics. The 'Average of Sector' column represents the average for all industries in this sector. The Index shows the relationship between the Average and the Analyzed Industry. For example, 100 means that they are equal; 500 that the Analyzed Industry is five times the average; 50 means that the Analyzed Industry is half the national average. 'na' is used to show that data are 'not available'.

LEADING COMPANIES

No company data available for this industry.

LOCATION BY STATE AND REGIONAL CONCENTRATION

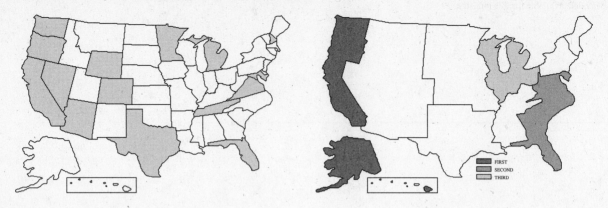

FIRST
SECOND
THIRD

INDUSTRY DATA BY STATE

State	Establishments Total (number)	Establishments % of U.S.	Employment Total (number)	Employment % of U.S.	Employment Per Estab.	Payroll Total ($ mil.)	Payroll Per Empl. ($)	Revenues Total ($ mil.)	Revenues % of U.S.	Revenues Per Estab. ($)
California	917	15.6	8,084	21.9	9	188.0	23,262	529.4	23.1	577,303
Texas	385	6.5	2,420	6.6	6	51.2	21,141	160.5	7.0	416,961
Florida	373	6.3	2,379	6.5	6	43.1	18,135	136.0	5.9	364,702
Illinois	253	4.3	1,418	3.8	6	31.6	22,288	94.6	4.1	373,731
Michigan	244	4.1	1,467	4.0	6	28.4	19,380	87.9	3.8	360,410
New York	258	4.4	1,171	3.2	5	22.9	19,534	82.7	3.6	320,473
Ohio	246	4.2	1,584	4.3	6	28.3	17,896	80.0	3.5	325,191
New Jersey	205	3.5	907	2.5	4	20.7	22,770	67.6	2.9	329,829
Tennessee	121	2.1	840	2.3	7	19.5	23,248	66.6	2.9	550,785
Virginia	187	3.2	1,089	3.0	6	22.1	20,318	65.8	2.9	351,765
Washington	166	2.8	1,142	3.1	7	22.3	19,502	65.4	2.8	393,946
Georgia	178	3.0	961	2.6	5	18.8	19,570	60.0	2.6	336,837
Oregon	104	1.8	813	2.2	8	15.8	19,405	50.2	2.2	482,654
Maryland	134	2.3	768	2.1	6	16.4	21,323	47.9	2.1	357,604
Indiana	134	2.3	844	2.3	6	16.1	19,026	47.8	2.1	356,597
North Carolina	153	2.6	706	1.9	5	14.5	20,606	47.7	2.1	311,490
Massachusetts	126	2.1	714	1.9	6	13.6	19,000	46.5	2.0	368,937
Arizona	131	2.2	808	2.2	6	16.6	20,587	46.1	2.0	352,053
Minnesota	110	1.9	771	2.1	7	14.3	18,486	43.4	1.9	394,255
Pennsylvania	174	3.0	735	2.0	4	12.3	16,672	43.1	1.9	247,920
Colorado	109	1.8	693	1.9	6	13.6	19,610	41.1	1.8	377,211
Missouri	104	1.8	734	2.0	7	13.6	18,561	38.3	1.7	368,365
Louisiana	93	1.6	505	1.4	5	9.3	18,354	34.5	1.5	370,677
Alabama	75	1.3	397	1.1	5	7.8	19,746	28.1	1.2	374,733
Nevada	40	0.7	493	1.3	12	10.1	20,430	25.7	1.1	641,375
Wisconsin	79	1.3	409	1.1	5	7.0	17,174	22.4	1.0	283,975
Kentucky	55	0.9	363	1.0	7	6.1	16,744	21.5	0.9	391,255
Kansas	42	0.7	320	0.9	8	6.2	19,328	20.5	0.9	489,262
South Carolina	80	1.4	299	0.8	4	4.7	15,682	18.2	0.8	228,100
Oklahoma	63	1.1	322	0.9	5	5.8	17,950	17.0	0.7	269,762
Iowa	57	1.0	301	0.8	5	5.3	17,445	16.8	0.7	294,754
Arkansas	48	0.8	257	0.7	5	4.0	15,669	14.6	0.6	304,167
Mississippi	49	0.8	187	0.5	4	3.6	19,369	12.3	0.5	250,510
West Virginia	40	0.7	217	0.6	5	3.3	15,018	11.1	0.5	278,625
New Hampshire	27	0.5	151	0.4	6	3.1	20,384	11.0	0.5	407,296
Utah	32	0.5	161	0.4	5	3.0	18,776	10.6	0.5	330,969
New Mexico	42	0.7	186	0.5	4	3.0	15,957	8.8	0.4	208,786
Nebraska	28	0.5	158	0.4	6	2.8	17,430	8.1	0.4	287,750
Maine	32	0.5	133	0.4	4	1.7	12,970	7.3	0.3	228,156
Idaho	30	0.5	120	0.3	4	1.7	14,525	6.4	0.3	213,500
Hawaii	18	0.3	122	0.3	7	1.5	12,090	5.0	0.2	278,611
Delaware	11	0.2	69	0.2	6	1.6	22,739	4.5	0.2	410,636
Montana	18	0.3	62	0.2	3	1.0	16,532	4.4	0.2	244,889
Wyoming	16	0.3	90	0.2	6	1.2	13,422	3.9	0.2	241,125
Alaska	12	0.2	37	0.1	3	0.7	18,432	2.5	0.1	209,500
Connecticut	36	0.6	375*	-	-	(D)	-	(D)	-	-
Rhode Island	27	0.5	60*	-	-	(D)	-	(D)	-	-
South Dakota	9	0.2	60*	-	-	(D)	-	(D)	-	-
North Dakota	8	0.1	60*	-	-	(D)	-	(D)	-	-
D.C.	7	0.1	60*	-	-	(D)	-	(D)	-	-
Vermont	7	0.1	10*	-	-	(D)	-	(D)	-	-

Source: 1997 *Economic Census*. The states are in descending order of revenues or establishments (if revenue data are missing for the majority). The symbol (D) appears when data are withheld to prevent disclosure of competitive information. States marked with (D) are sorted by number of establishments. A dash (-) indicates that the data element cannot be calculated. * indicates the midpoint of a range; 175, for example is the range 100-249. Shaded *states* on the state map indicate those states which have proportionately greater representation in the industry than would be indicated by the state's population; the ratio is based on total revenues or number of establishments. Shaded *regions* indicate where the towing industry is regionally most concentrated.

NAICS 488490 - SUPPORT ACTIVITIES FOR ROAD TRANSPORTATION NEC

GENERAL STATISTICS

Year	Establishments (number)	Employment (number)	Payroll ($ million)	Revenues ($ million)	Employees per Establishment (number)	Revenues per Establishment ($)	Payroll per Employee ($)
1997	531	7,480	153.6	388.0	14.1	730,697	20,535

Source: Economic Census of the United States, 1997. This is a newly defined industry. Data for prior years were unavailable at the time of publication but may become available over time.

SIC INDUSTRIES RELATED TO NAICS 488490

SIC	Industry	1990	1991	1992	1993	1994	1995	1996	1997
4173	**Bus Terminal and Service Facilities**	-	-	-	-	-	-	-	-
4231	**Trucking Terminal Facilities**	-	-	-	-	-	-	-	-
4785	**Inspection and Fixed Facilities***								
	Establishments (number)	222e	242e	263	284p	304p	325p	345p	366p
	Employment (thousands)	2.3e	2.5e	2.8	3.1p	3.4p	3.6p	3.9p	4.2p
	Revenues ($ million)	181.0e	201.0e	221.0	241.0p	261.0p	281.0p	301.0p	321.0p

*Source: Economic Census of the United States, 1992, annual surveys of economic sectors conducted by the Bureau of the Census, and estimates or projections based on the 1982-1992 period; not all data are shown. 'e' marks estimates made by the editors; 'p' indicates projections based on time series. A dash (-) indicates that data for this SIC or year were not available. * Indicates that only a portion of this industry is present within the NAICS data. If no * is shown, the entire industry is contained within the NAICS data.*

INDICES OF CHANGE

Year	Establishments (number)	Employment (number)	Payroll ($ million)	Revenues ($ million)	Employees per Establishment (number)	Revenues per Establishment ($)	Payroll per Employee ($)
1997	100.0	100.0	100.0	100.0	100.0	100.0	100.0

Sources: Same as General Statistics. The values shown reflect change from the base year, 1997. Values above 100 mean greater than 1997, values below 100 mean less than 1997, and a value of 100 in years other than 1997 means same as 1997. Indices are calculated only for Census years. Data are the most recent available at this level of detail.

SELECTED RATIOS

For 1997	Avg. of Sector	Analyzed Industry	Index	For 1997	Avg. of Sector	Analyzed Industry	Index
Employees per establishment	16	14	86	Payroll per establishment	462,554	289,266	63
Revenue per establishment	1,787,642	730,697	41	Payroll as % of revenue	26	40	153
Revenue per employee	108,959	51,872	48	Payroll per employee	28,193	20,535	73

Sources: Same as General Statistics. The 'Average of Sector' column represents the average for all industries in this sector. The Index shows the relationship between the Average and the Analyzed Industry. For example, 100 means that they are equal; 500 that the Analyzed Industry is five times the average; 50 means that the Analyzed Industry is half the national average. 'na' is used to show that data are 'not available'.

LEADING COMPANIES   Number shown: **2**   Total sales ($ mil): **1,834**   Total employment (000): **1.1**

Company Name	Address				CEO Name	Phone	Co. Type	Sales ($ mil)	Empl. (000)
CGB Enterprises Inc.	P O Box 249	Mandeville	LA	70470	Richard Wilcox	504-867-3500	R	1,800	0.9
U.S. Water L.L.C.	480 Quadrangle Dr	Bolingbrook	IL	60440	Michael Belsante	630-699-7100	J	34*	0.2

Source: Ward's Business Directory of U.S. Private and Public Companies, Volumes 1 and 2, 2000. The company type code used is as follows: P - Public, R - Private, S - Subsidiary, D - Division, J - Joint Venture, A - Affiliate, G - Group, N - Company type not reported. Sales are in millions of dollars, employees are in thousands. An asterisk (*) indicates an estimated sales volume. The symbol < stands for 'less than'. Company names and addresses are truncated, in some cases, to fit into the available space.

LOCATION BY STATE AND REGIONAL CONCENTRATION

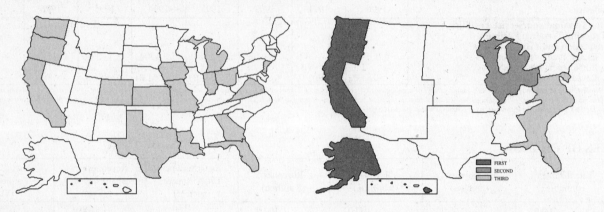

INDUSTRY DATA BY STATE

State	Establishments Total (number)	% of U.S.	Employment Total (number)	% of U.S.	Per Estab.	Payroll Total ($ mil.)	Per Empl. ($)	Revenues Total ($ mil.)	% of U.S.	Per Estab. ($)
California	59	11.1	849	11.4	14	18.8	22,184	55.9	14.4	947,729
Texas	48	9.0	908	12.1	19	15.2	16,735	34.4	8.9	716,333
Florida	36	6.8	803	10.7	22	13.1	16,301	28.8	7.4	800,000
Michigan	15	2.8	345	4.6	23	9.6	27,832	22.6	5.8	1,504,333
New York	14	2.6	351	4.7	25	9.8	28,003	22.2	5.7	1,584,429
Colorado	13	2.4	199	2.7	15	5.0	25,256	20.2	5.2	1,552,923
Ohio	24	4.5	294	3.9	12	6.7	22,796	20.1	5.2	838,542
Virginia	14	2.6	145	1.9	10	3.7	25,303	17.0	4.4	1,214,143
New Jersey	12	2.3	166	2.2	14	6.9	41,277	16.2	4.2	1,349,000
Illinois	21	4.0	115	1.5	5	4.0	34,930	13.0	3.3	616,714
Georgia	22	4.1	153	2.0	7	4.2	27,529	10.8	2.8	489,545
Washington	22	4.1	272	3.6	12	4.6	16,989	9.7	2.5	438,864
Louisiana	16	3.0	143	1.9	9	4.2	29,566	9.6	2.5	598,500
Missouri	15	2.8	211	2.8	14	4.3	20,275	9.5	2.4	632,333
Pennsylvania	15	2.8	203	2.7	14	3.4	16,700	9.5	2.4	633,333
Indiana	11	2.1	85	1.1	8	1.6	18,424	9.2	2.4	833,455
Oregon	7	1.3	242	3.2	35	4.2	17,339	7.7	2.0	1,099,571
North Carolina	19	3.6	229	3.1	12	4.2	18,480	7.3	1.9	381,842
Tennessee	13	2.4	201	2.7	15	3.9	19,303	5.8	1.5	444,615
Arizona	10	1.9	171	2.3	17	2.7	15,737	5.2	1.3	518,500
Iowa	9	1.7	84	1.1	9	1.9	22,714	4.9	1.3	548,000
Kansas	7	1.3	107	1.4	15	1.9	18,150	4.1	1.1	584,714
Oklahoma	9	1.7	127	1.7	14	1.7	13,535	3.8	1.0	424,778
Minnesota	7	1.3	72	1.0	10	1.3	18,319	3.3	0.8	466,714
Utah	6	1.1	94	1.3	16	1.1	11,989	1.9	0.5	310,833
Wisconsin	6	1.1	57	0.8	10	0.8	13,579	1.2	0.3	192,000
Nebraska	8	1.5	45	0.6	6	0.4	8,178	1.0	0.3	130,875
Maryland	15	2.8	175*	-	-	(D)	-	(D)	-	-
Kentucky	8	1.5	60*	-	-	(D)	-	(D)	-	-

Source: 1997 *Economic Census*. The states are in descending order of revenues or establishments (if revenue data are missing for the majority). The symbol (D) appears when data are withheld to prevent disclosure of competitive information. States marked with (D) are sorted by number of establishments. A dash (-) indicates that the data element cannot be calculated. * indicates the midpoint of a range; 175, for example is the range 100-249. Shaded *states* on the state map indicate those states which have proportionately greater representation in the industry than would be indicated by the state's population; the ratio is based on total revenues or number of establishments. Shaded *regions* indicate where the industry is regionally most concentrated.

NAICS 488510 - FREIGHT TRANSPORTATION ARRANGEMENT

GENERAL STATISTICS

Year	Establishments (number)	Employment (number)	Payroll ($ million)	Revenues ($ million)	Employees per Establishment (number)	Revenues per Establishment ($)	Payroll per Employee ($)
1997	15,782	141,488	5,014.6	16,250.8	9.0	1,029,705	35,442

Source: Economic Census of the United States, 1997. This is a newly defined industry. Data for prior years were unavailable at the time of publication but may become available over time.

SIC INDUSTRIES RELATED TO NAICS 488510

SIC	Industry	1990	1991	1992	1993	1994	1995	1996	1997
4731	**Freight Transportation Arrangement***								
	Establishments (number)	8,905	9,584	12,553	12,995	13,388	13,778	14,771	15,292p
	Employment (thousands)	116.0	112.7	107.0	111.5	117.8	130.1	137.5	132.8p
	Revenues ($ million)	8,125.9e	8,642.3e	9,158.6	9,675.0p	10,191.3p	10,707.6p	11,224.0p	11,740.3p

*Source: Economic Census of the United States, 1992, annual surveys of economic sectors conducted by the Bureau of the Census, and estimates or projections based on the 1982-1992 period; not all data are shown. 'e' marks estimates made by the editors; 'p' indicates projections based on time series. A dash (-) indicates that data for this SIC or year were not available. * Indicates that only a portion of this industry is present within the NAICS data. If no * is shown, the entire industry is contained within the NAICS data.*

INDICES OF CHANGE

Year	Establishments (number)	Employment (number)	Payroll ($ million)	Revenues ($ million)	Employees per Establishment (number)	Revenues per Establishment ($)	Payroll per Employee ($)
1997	100.0	100.0	100.0	100.0	100.0	100.0	100.0

Sources: Same as General Statistics. The values shown reflect change from the base year, 1997. Values above 100 mean greater than 1997, values below 100 mean less than 1997, and a value of 100 in years other than 1997 means same as 1997. Indices are calculated only for Census years. Data are the most recent available at this level of detail.

SELECTED RATIOS

For 1997	Avg. of Sector	Analyzed Industry	Index	For 1997	Avg. of Sector	Analyzed Industry	Index
Employees per establishment	16	9	55	Payroll per establishment	462,554	317,742	69
Revenue per establishment	1,787,642	1,029,705	58	Payroll as % of revenue	26	31	119
Revenue per employee	108,959	114,856	105	Payroll per employee	28,193	35,442	126

Sources: Same as General Statistics. The 'Average of Sector' column represents the average for all industries in this sector. The Index shows the relationship between the Average and the Analyzed Industry. For example, 100 means that they are equal; 500 that the Analyzed Industry is five times the average; 50 means that the Analyzed Industry is half the national average. 'na' is used to show that data are 'not available'.

LEADING COMPANIES   Number shown: **75**   Total sales ($ mil): **45,163**   Total employment (000): **160.7**

Company Name	Address				CEO Name	Phone	Co. Type	Sales ($ mil)	Empl. (000)
CSX Intermodal Inc.	301 W Bay St	Jacksonville	FL	32202	Lester M Passa	904-633-1070	S	6,453*	10.0
CNF Transportation Inc.	3240 Hillview Ave	Palo Alto	CA	94304	Gregory L Quesnel	650-494-2900	P	5,593	33.7
Yellow Corp.	PO Box 7563	Overland Park	KS	66207	William Zollars	913-696-6100	P	3,227	29.7
Airborne Freight Corp.	P O Box 662	Seattle	WA	98111	Robert G Brazier	206-285-4600	P	3,140	2.3
C.H. Robinson Company Inc.	8100 Mitchell Rd	Eden Prairie	MN	55344	Daryl R Verdoorn	612-937-8500	P	2,038*	2.2
UniGroup Inc.	1 United Dr	Fenton	MO	63026	Robert J Baer	636-305-5000	R	1,800	1.6
Hawaiian Electric Industries Inc.	PO Box 730	Honolulu	HI	96808	Robert F Clarke	808-543-5662	P	1,523	3.7
Air Express International Corp.	120 Tokeneke Rd	Darien	CT	06820	Guenter Rohrmann	203-655-7900	P	1,513	7.4
Union-Transport	19443 Laurel	R. Dominguez	CA	90220	Roger MacFarlane	310-604-9516	R	1,487*	3.0
Landstar Logistics Inc.	13410 Sutton park S	Jacksonville	FL	32224	James R Hertwig	904-399-8909	S	1,400	<0.1
Fritz Companies Inc.	706 Mission St	San Francisco	CA	94103	Lynn C Fritz	415-904-8360	P	1,388	10.0
Hub Group Inc.	377 E Butterfield Rd	Lombard	IL	60148	Thomas L Hardin	630-271-3600	P	1,145	1.3
Expeditors Intern. of Washington	1015 3rd Ave	Seattle	WA	98104	Peter J Rose	206-674-3400	P	1,064	5.3
EOTT Energy Operating L.P.	P O Box 4666	Houston	TX	77210		713-993-5200	S	1,000*	0.7
Midland Co.	PO Box 1256	Cincinnati	OH	45201	John W Hayden	513-943-7100	P	837	0.9
Circle International Group Inc.	260 Townsend St	San Francisco	CA	94107	David I Beatson	415-978-0600	P	790	4.6
Mark VII Inc.	965 Ridge Lake	Memphis	TN	38120	RC Matney	901-767-4455	P	725	0.4
Kitty Hawk Inc.	PO Box 612787	Dallas	TX	75261	M Tom Christopher	972-456-2200	P	715	3.8
Atlas World Group Inc.	1212 St George Rd	Evansville	IN	47711	Wally E Saubert	812-424-4326	R	689*	0.8
Eagle USA Airfreight Inc.	15350 Vickery Dr	Houston	TX	77032	James R Crane	281-618-3100	P	595	2.6
F.X. Coughlin Co.	27050 Wick Rd	Taylor	MI	48180	Joseph Coughlin	734-946-9510	R	496*	1.0
Atlas Van Lines Inc.	1212 St George Rd	Evansville	IN	47711	Dick Arneson	812-424-4326	S	490*	0.6
Alliance Shippers Inc.	15515 S 70th Ct	Orland Park	IL	60462	Ronald Lefcourt	708-802-7000	R	460	0.5
Averitt Express Inc.	P O Box 3166	Cookeville	TN	38502	Gary D Sasser	931-526-3306	R	429	5.5
Brambles USA Inc.	400 N Michigan Ave	Chicago	IL	60611	Robert J Anderson	312-836-0200	S	380*	2.0
Pacer International	5800 E Sheila St	Los Angeles	CA	90040		323-720-1771	R	355*	0.7
J.B. Hunt Logistics Inc.	P O Box 130	Lowell	AR	72745	Jun-Sheng Li	501-820-0000	S	292	0.2
Comdata Corp.	5301 Maryland Way	Brentwood	TN	37027	Tony Holcombe	615-370-7000	S	286*	1.9
USF Logistics	3880 Salem Lake Dr	Long Grove	IL	60047	Doug Christensen	847-726-4500	S	279*	3.0
Transoceanic Shipping Inc.	32 E Airline Hwy	Kenner	LA	70062	Gregory Rusovich	504-465-1000	R	270*	0.6
Tower Group International Inc.	128 Dearborn St	Buffalo	NY	14207	Mike Hehir	716-874-1227	S	258*	1.6
Landstar Express America Inc.	P O Box 19136	Jacksonville	FL	32245	Ronald G Stanley	904-390-4848	S	255	<0.1
Gateway Cargo Service Center	11099 S LaCienega	Los Angeles	CA	90045	Jack Keery	310-646-1982	R	251*	0.5
Global Transportation Services	PO Box 24504	Seattle	WA	98124	Eddie Kelly	206-624-4354	R	232	0.1
Exel Logistics Inc.	501 W Schrock Rd	Westerville	OH	43081	Bruce Edwards	614-890-1730	S	225	6.0
Tricor America	12441 Eucalyptus	Hawthorne	CA	90250		310-215-5600	S	223*	0.5
Nissin International Transport Inc.	1580 W Carson St	Long Beach	CA	90810	K Yamaguchi	310-816-5741	R	222*	0.5
Pittsburgh Logistics Systems Inc.	2060 Pennsylvania	Monaca	PA	15061	Gregg A Troian	724-709-9000	R	208*	0.2
Pilot Air Freight Corp.	P O Box 97	Mex Cty-KCI	PA	19037	Richard G Phillips	610-891-8100	R	167	1.5
A.N. Deringer Inc.	PO Box 1309	St. Albans	VT	05478	Wayne Burl	802-524-8110	R	165*	0.6
Danzas Corp.	3650 131st Ave S E	Bellevue	WA	98015	Hans Toggweiler	425-649-9339	S	130*	0.8
Matson Intermodal System Inc.	PO Box 7452	San Francisco	CA	94120	James S Sells	415-957-4911	S	130	<0.1
AEI (Cranford, New Jersey)	25 Commerce Dr	Cranford	NJ	07016	Guenter Rohrmann	908-709-1500	D	100*	0.2
Adcom Express Inc.	PO Box 390048	Edina	MN	55439	Robert F Friedman	612-829-7990	R	100*	<0.1
Central Transport Intern. Inc.	12225 Stephen Rd	Warren	MI	48089	Joe Goril	810-939-7000	S	98*	2.0
Clipper Exxpress Co.	15700 W 103rd St	Lemont	IL	60439	Andy H Fan Sze	708-739-0700	S	94	0.2
Hale Transport, Inc.	1801 S Clinton St	Baltimore	MD	21224	Steven Jones	410-342-1500	R	89*	0.2
ABX Logistics (USA) Inc.	8010 Roswell Rd	Atlanta	GA	30350	Frank Guenzerodt	404-353-4200	S	80	0.3
Target Logistics Inc.	112 E 25th St	Baltimore	MD	21218	Stuart Hettleman	410-338-0127	P	77	0.2
Tricor International	12441 Eucalyptus	Hawthorne	CA	90250		310-215-5600	R	76*	0.2
Saga Transport (U.S.A.) Inc.	5306 Clinton Dr	Houston	TX	77020	Wolfgan Anderson	281-443-1904	R	71*	0.2
Daniel F. Young Inc.	17 Battery Pl	New York	NY	10004	Joseph G Kearns	212-248-1700	R	69*	0.4
Alexander International	PO Box 30209	Memphis	TN	38130	W L Wadsworth Jr	901-345-5420	S	68*	0.1
Air Cargo Inc.	1819 Bay Ridge Ave	Annapolis	MD	21403	CB Wilder	410-280-5578	R	67	0.2
Allen Lund Company Inc.	P O Box 1369	La Canada	CA	91012	D Allen Lund	818-790-8412	R	67*	0.2
International Cargo Group Inc.	301 Edgewater Pl	Wakefield	MA	01880	Fred Glantz	781-246-5870	R	60	0.2
James J. Flanagan Shipping Corp.	490 Park St	Beaumont	TX	77701	Thomas M Flanagan	409-833-5053	R	59*	0.1
TLR-Total Logistics Resource Inc.	5362 N E 112th Ave	Portland	OR	97220	Steve Buffam	503-257-0513	R	52*	<0.1
Seino America Inc.	8728 Aviation Blvd	Inglewood	CA	90301	Norizumi Fuma	310-215-0500	R	51*	0.1
Hale Trans Inc.	1801 S Clinton St	Baltimore	MD	21224	Melody Blades	410-342-5900	P	50	0.4
AIT Freight Systems inc.	P O Box 66730	Chicago	IL	60666	Steven L Leturno	708-766-8300	R	50*	0.5
Network Courier Service Inc.	9010 Bellanca Ave	Los Angeles	CA	90045	Rudy B Markmiller	310-410-7777	R	49*	0.5
A.W. Fenton Company Inc.	P O Box 81179	Cleveland	OH	44181	Kenneth Lashutka	440-243-5900	R	46*	<0.1
WestEx Inc.	2920 N 44th St	Phoenix	AZ	85018	Frank E Myers	602-952-2929	S	45*	1.0
Air-Sea Forwarders Inc.	9009 LaCienega	Inglewood	CA	90301	Erwin Rautenberg	310-216-1616	R	45	0.2
James J. Boyle and Co.	160 Sansome St	San Francisco	CA	94104	TM Hatada	415-288-9780	R	45*	0.1
Rock-it Cargo USA Inc.	5438 W 104th St	Los Angeles	CA	90045	Doug Masterson	310-410-0935	R	45*	0.1
BDP International Inc.	510 Walnut St	Philadelphia	PA	19106	Richard J Bolte	215-629-8900	R	30*	0.6
CASAS Intern. Brokerage Inc.	10030 Marconi Dr	San Diego	CA	92173	Sylvia Casas-Jolliffe	619-661-6162	R	25	0.1
Service By Air Inc.	55 E Ames Ct	Plainview	NY	11803	Karl Zirbes	516-576-0500	R	25*	<0.1
Union Transport Corp.	2701 ElSegundo	Hawthorne	CA	90250	Roger MacFarlane	323-756-9988	S	25*	<0.1
Miami International Forwarders	1801 NW 82nd Ave	Miami	FL	33126	Leonard C Roberts	305-594-0038	R	24	0.3
Inter-Maritime Forwarding Inc.	39 Broadway	New York	NY	10006	Howard Mann	212-791-1234	R	22*	0.1
Wice Freight Service Inc.	701 W Manchester	Inglewood	CA	90301	Paul Dunn	310-674-3300	R	19	<0.1
John S. Connor Inc.	401 E Platt	Baltimore	MD	21202	Lee Connor	410-332-4800	R	16*	<0.1

Source: Ward's Business Directory of U.S. Private and Public Companies, Volumes 1 and 2, 2000. The company type code used is as follows: P - Public, R - Private, S - Subsidiary, D - Division, J - Joint Venture, A - Affiliate, G - Group, N - Company type not reported. Sales are in millions of dollars, employees are in thousands. An asterisk (*) indicates an estimated sales volume. The symbol < stands for 'less than'. Company names and addresses are truncated, in some cases, to fit into the available space.

LOCATION BY STATE AND REGIONAL CONCENTRATION

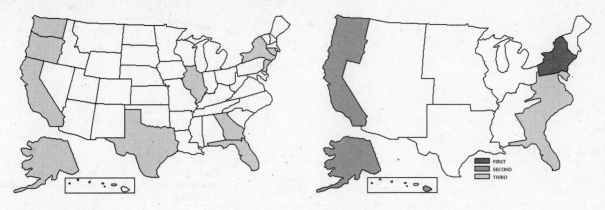

INDUSTRY DATA BY STATE

State	Establishments Total (number)	% of U.S.	Employment Total (number)	% of U.S.	Per Estab.	Payroll Total ($ mil.)	Per Empl. ($)	Revenues Total ($ mil.)	% of U.S.	Per Estab. ($)
California	2,104	13.3	22,698	16.0	11	842.4	37,113	2,731.3	16.8	1,298,155
New York	1,565	9.9	13,597	9.6	9	569.4	41,878	1,791.1	11.0	1,144,493
Texas	1,650	10.5	17,289	12.2	10	516.0	29,844	1,515.0	9.3	918,165
New Jersey	830	5.3	10,102	7.1	12	435.1	43,073	1,281.8	7.9	1,544,327
Illinois	873	5.5	10,006	7.1	11	388.4	38,814	1,205.7	7.4	1,381,149
Florida	1,595	10.1	9,893	7.0	6	304.4	30,771	1,080.6	6.6	677,521
Pennsylvania	383	2.4	4,036	2.9	11	136.1	33,709	513.2	3.2	1,339,984
Georgia	519	3.3	4,427	3.1	9	153.0	34,562	494.7	3.0	953,227
Ohio	495	3.1	4,293	3.0	9	146.1	34,039	480.7	3.0	971,020
Washington	459	2.9	4,326	3.1	9	151.6	35,039	472.7	2.9	1,029,745
Michigan	312	2.0	3,770	2.7	12	116.5	30,915	390.6	2.4	1,251,952
Massachusetts	316	2.0	2,737	1.9	9	101.8	37,186	325.6	2.0	1,030,399
Connecticut	183	1.2	1,437	1.0	8	94.9	66,052	294.2	1.8	1,607,481
Virginia	282	1.8	2,449	1.7	9	87.4	35,682	286.6	1.8	1,016,465
Minnesota	253	1.6	2,157	1.5	9	80.7	37,431	269.6	1.7	1,065,802
North Carolina	345	2.2	2,376	1.7	7	76.8	32,314	252.5	1.6	731,913
Tennessee	249	1.6	2,629	1.9	11	88.2	33,539	244.0	1.5	980,040
Wisconsin	166	1.1	1,357	1.0	8	45.1	33,219	230.9	1.4	1,390,747
Maryland	256	1.6	2,282	1.6	9	78.7	34,500	230.2	1.4	899,227
Arizona	209	1.3	1,380	1.0	7	40.0	28,957	195.5	1.2	935,172
Oregon	215	1.4	1,633	1.2	8	57.0	34,910	194.1	1.2	903,005
Louisiana	264	1.7	2,173	1.5	8	68.2	31,380	189.2	1.2	716,716
Missouri	318	2.0	1,815	1.3	6	58.4	32,154	185.3	1.1	582,783
Indiana	208	1.3	1,382	1.0	7	41.7	30,175	146.5	0.9	704,313
South Carolina	171	1.1	1,306	0.9	8	40.8	31,234	141.2	0.9	825,491
Colorado	166	1.1	940	0.7	6	30.7	32,693	137.1	0.8	826,205
Kentucky	131	0.8	1,328	0.9	10	35.8	26,977	123.1	0.8	939,351
Alabama	143	0.9	1,010	0.7	7	30.2	29,935	97.4	0.6	680,804
Arkansas	101	0.6	686	0.5	7	22.4	32,615	78.2	0.5	774,059
Kansas	105	0.7	664	0.5	6	19.9	29,976	75.6	0.5	720,305
Utah	85	0.5	536	0.4	6	17.4	32,489	71.4	0.4	839,482
Nevada	66	0.4	360	0.3	5	8.8	24,567	57.6	0.4	872,288
Iowa	92	0.6	458	0.3	5	13.7	29,886	54.3	0.3	590,554
Alaska	49	0.3	503	0.4	10	15.9	31,660	52.1	0.3	1,062,694
Hawaii	63	0.4	318	0.2	5	10.7	33,607	43.8	0.3	695,413
Oklahoma	84	0.5	452	0.3	5	12.2	26,996	41.9	0.3	498,226
Mississippi	69	0.4	296	0.2	4	8.0	27,000	37.5	0.2	543,304
Maine	52	0.3	306	0.2	6	6.8	22,307	33.9	0.2	652,692
Idaho	37	0.2	232	0.2	6	6.9	29,866	32.9	0.2	888,541
Nebraska	58	0.4	366	0.3	6	11.3	30,913	30.9	0.2	533,466
Rhode Island	34	0.2	264	0.2	8	8.8	33,265	24.8	0.2	728,971
Montana	38	0.2	262	0.2	7	5.3	20,305	23.9	0.1	630,211
North Dakota	22	0.1	228	0.2	10	6.0	26,132	18.6	0.1	843,409
D.C.	25	0.2	97	0.1	4	7.1	73,165	17.3	0.1	691,800
New Hampshire	23	0.1	91	0.1	4	4.5	49,736	11.0	0.1	477,522
Vermont	29	0.2	173	0.1	6	4.1	23,584	10.8	0.1	371,034
Delaware	21	0.1	105	0.1	5	4.1	38,781	10.4	0.1	497,048
New Mexico	30	0.2	91	0.1	3	1.6	17,286	9.3	0.1	311,200
West Virginia	16	0.1	92	0.1	6	2.0	21,500	6.9	0.0	432,188
South Dakota	16	0.1	62	0.0	4	1.5	24,758	6.5	0.0	406,438
Wyoming	7	-	18	0.0	3	0.3	13,944	0.7	0.0	101,429

Source: 1997 *Economic Census*. The states are in descending order of revenues or establishments (if revenue data are missing for the majority). The symbol (D) appears when data are withheld to prevent disclosure of competitive information. States marked with (D) are sorted by number of establishments. A dash (-) indicates that the data element cannot be calculated. * indicates the midpoint of a range; 175, for example is the range 100-249. Shaded *states* on the state map indicate those states which have proportionately greater representation in the industry than would be indicated by the state's population; the ratio is based on total revenues or number of establishments. Shaded *regions* indicate where the industry is regionally most concentrated.

NAICS 488991 - PACKING AND CRATING*

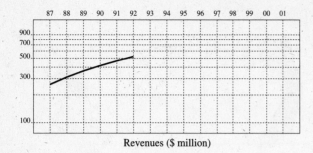

Revenues ($ million)

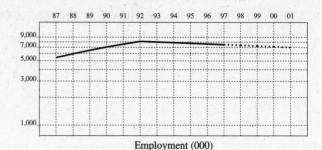

Employment (000)

GENERAL STATISTICS

Year	Establishments (number)	Employment (number)	Payroll ($ million)	Revenues ($ million)	Employees per Establishment (number)	Revenues per Establishment ($)	Payroll per Employee ($)
1987	481	5,405	82.2	259.9	11.2	540,333	15,208
1988	552	5,949	96.6	312.4	10.8	565,942	16,238
1989	623	6,492	111.1	365.0	10.4	585,875	17,113
1990	693	7,036	125.6	417.5	10.2	602,453	17,851
1991	764	7,579	140.0	470.0	9.9	615,183	18,472
1992	835	8,123	154.5	522.5	9.7	625,749	19,020
1993	827	7,998	-	-	9.7	-	-
1994	819	7,874	-	-	9.6	-	-
1995	811	7,749	-	-	9.6	-	-
1996	803	7,625	-	-	9.5	-	-
1997	795	7,500 *	(D)	(D)	-	-	-
1998	787 p	7,375 p	-	-	9.4 p	-	-
1999	779 p	7,251 p	-	-	9.3 p	-	-
2000	771 p	7,126 p	-	-	9.2 p	-	-
2001	763 p	7,002 p	-	-	9.2 p	-	-

Sources: Economic Census of the United States, 1987, 1992 and 1997. Data for those years (years are in **bold** type) are from the 5-year censuses of the economy. Other values, unless otherwise noted, are extrapolations. Values marked with *p* are projections. Data are the most recent available at this level of detail.

INDICES OF CHANGE

Year	Establishments (number)	Employment (number)	Payroll ($ million)	Revenues ($ million)	Employees per Establishment (number)	Revenues per Establishment ($)	Payroll per Employee ($)
1987	60.5	72.1	-	-	-	-	-
1992	105.0	108.3	-	-	-	-	-
1993	104.0	106.6	-	-	-	-	-
1994	103.0	105.0	-	-	-	-	-
1995	102.0	103.3	-	-	-	-	-
1996	101.0	101.7	-	-	-	-	-
1997	100.0	100.0	-	-	-	-	-
1998	99.0 p	98.3 p	-	-	-	-	-
1999	98.0 p	96.7 p	- p	- p	-	-	-
2000	97.0 p	95.0 p	- p	- p	-	-	-
2001	96.0 p	93.4 p	- p	- p	-	-	-

Sources: Same as General Statistics. The values shown reflect change from the base year, 1997. Values above 100 mean greater than 1997, values below 100 mean less than 1997, and a value of 100 in years other than 1997 means same as 1997. Indices are calculated only for Census years. Data are the most recent available at this level of detail.

SELECTED RATIOS

For 1997	Avg. of Sector	Analyzed Industry	Index	For 1997	Avg. of Sector	Analyzed Industry	Index
Employees per establishment	16	9	57	Payroll per establishment	462,554	na	na
Revenue per establishment	1,787,642	na	na	Payroll as % of revenue	26	na	na
Revenue per employee	108,959	na	na	Payroll per employee	28,193	na	na

Sources: Same as General Statistics. The 'Average of Sector' column represents the average for all industries in this sector. The Index shows the relationship between the Average and the Analyzed Industry. For example, 100 means that they are equal; 500 that the Analyzed Industry is five times the average; 50 means that the Analyzed Industry is half the national average. 'na' is used to show that data are 'not available'.

*Equivalent to SIC 4783.

LEADING COMPANIES   Number shown: 3   Total sales ($ mil): 189   Total employment (000): 0.7

Company Name	Address				CEO Name	Phone	Co. Type	Sales ($ mil)	Empl. (000)
Venchurs Packaging	800 S Center St	Adrian	MI	49221		517-263-8937	R	111	<0.1
SOPAKCO Packaging	PO Box 1047	Mullins	SC	29574		843-464-7851	S	50	0.5
Newstar Fresh Food L.L.C.	P O Box 5999	Salinas	CA	93915	Robert Jenkins	831-758-7800	R	28*	0.1

Source: Ward's Business Directory of U.S. Private and Public Companies, Volumes 1 and 2, 2000. The company type code used is as follows: P - Public, R - Private, S - Subsidiary, D - Division, J - Joint Venture, A - Affiliate, G - Group, N - Company type not reported. Sales are in millions of dollars, employees are in thousands. An asterisk (*) indicates an estimated sales volume. The symbol < stands for 'less than'. Company names and addresses are truncated, in some cases, to fit into the available space.

LOCATION BY STATE AND REGIONAL CONCENTRATION

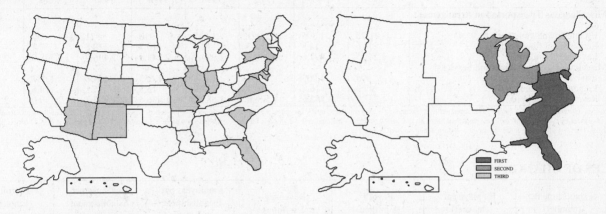

FIRST
SECOND
THIRD

INDUSTRY DATA BY STATE

State	Establishments Total (number)	% of U.S.	Employment Total (number)	% of U.S.	Per Estab.	Payroll Total ($ mil.)	Per Empl. ($)	Revenues Total ($ mil.)	% of U.S.	Per Estab. ($)
California	87	10.9	649	0.0	7	16.2	24,941	60.3	0.0	692,747
New York	61	7.7	813	0.0	13	14.9	18,349	47.1	0.0	772,230
South Carolina	13	1.6	115	0.0	9	2.9	24,861	22.8	0.0	1,757,308
Tennessee	15	1.9	388	0.0	26	4.8	12,299	13.8	0.0	917,267
Georgia	21	2.6	102	0.0	5	2.5	24,549	9.1	0.0	435,429
Louisiana	11	1.4	83	0.0	8	1.6	19,410	5.7	0.0	520,545
Arkansas	7	0.9	114	0.0	16	1.9	16,956	5.2	0.0	743,143
Arizona	19	2.4	90	0.0	5	1.1	12,356	5.0	0.0	261,000
New Mexico	8	1.0	26	0.0	3	0.7	25,654	2.4	0.0	294,625
Florida	75	9.4	375*	-	-	(D)	-	(D)	-	-
Texas	53	6.7	750*	-	-	(D)	-	(D)	-	-
Illinois	47	5.9	1,750*	-	-	(D)	-	(D)	-	-
New Jersey	41	5.2	375*	-	-	(D)	-	(D)	-	-
Pennsylvania	34	4.3	375*	-	-	(D)	-	(D)	-	-
Ohio	32	4.0	750*	-	-	(D)	-	(D)	-	-
Michigan	26	3.3	750*	-	-	(D)	-	(D)	-	-
Indiana	23	2.9	375*	-	-	(D)	-	(D)	-	-
Virginia	23	2.9	175*	-	-	(D)	-	(D)	-	-
Colorado	17	2.1	60*	-	-	(D)	-	(D)	-	-
Massachusetts	17	2.1	175*	-	-	(D)	-	(D)	-	-
Missouri	17	2.1	60*	-	-	(D)	-	(D)	-	-
Maryland	16	2.0	175*	-	-	(D)	-	(D)	-	-
Wisconsin	15	1.9	375*	-	-	(D)	-	(D)	-	-
Minnesota	13	1.6	60*	-	-	(D)	-	(D)	-	-
North Carolina	11	1.4	60*	-	-	(D)	-	(D)	-	-
Washington	11	1.4	175*	-	-	(D)	-	(D)	-	-
Connecticut	9	1.1	175*	-	-	(D)	-	(D)	-	-
Kentucky	8	1.0	175*	-	-	(D)	-	(D)	-	-

Source: 1997 Economic Census. The states are in descending order of revenues or establishments (if revenue data are missing for the majority). The symbol (D) appears when data are withheld to prevent disclosure of competitive information. States marked with (D) are sorted by number of establishments. A dash (-) indicates that the data element cannot be calculated. * indicates the midpoint of a range; 175, for example is the range 100-249. Shaded states on the state map indicate those states which have proportionately greater representation in the industry than would be indicated by the state's population; the ratio is based on total revenues or number of establishments. Shaded regions indicate where the industry is regionally most concentrated.

NAICS 488999 - SUPPORT ACTIVITIES FOR TRANSPORTATION NEC

GENERAL STATISTICS

Year	Establishments (number)	Employment (number)	Payroll ($ million)	Revenues ($ million)	Employees per Establishment (number)	Revenues per Establishment ($)	Payroll per Employee ($)
1997	102	7,500*	(D)	(D)	-	-	-

Source: Economic Census of the United States, 1997. This is a newly defined industry. Data for prior years were unavailable at the time of publication but may become available over time.

SIC INDUSTRIES RELATED TO NAICS 488999

SIC	Industry	1990	1991	1992	1993	1994	1995	1996	1997
4729	**Miscellaneous Transportation Arrangement, nec***								
	Establishments (number)	1,320	1,306	1,097	1,022	910	871	852	658p
	Employment (thousands)	14.6	14.8	13.3	12.1	10.7	10.8	9.7	11.1p
	Revenues ($ million)	1,241.5e	1,492.6e	1,743.7	1,994.7p	2,245.8p	2,496.9p	2,748.0p	2,999.1p
4789	**Miscellaneous Transportation Services***								
	Establishments (number)	995e	1,009e	1,024	1,039p	1,053p	1,068p	1,082p	1,097p
	Employment (thousands)	17.3e	16.8e	16.4	15.9p	15.5p	15.1p	14.6p	14.2p
	Revenues ($ million)	1,231.2e	1,382.5e	1,533.8	1,685.1p	1,836.4p	1,987.7p	2,139.0p	2,290.3p

*Source: Economic Census of the United States, 1992, annual surveys of economic sectors conducted by the Bureau of the Census, and estimates or projections based on the 1982-1992 period; not all data are shown. 'e' marks estimates made by the editors; 'p' indicates projections based on time series. A dash (-) indicates that data for this SIC or year were not available. * Indicates that only a portion of this industry is present within the NAICS data. If no * is shown, the entire industry is contained within the NAICS data.*

INDICES OF CHANGE

Year	Establishments (number)	Employment (number)	Payroll ($ million)	Revenues ($ million)	Employees per Establishment (number)	Revenues per Establishment ($)	Payroll per Employee ($)
1997	100.0	100.0	-	-	-	-	-

Sources: Same as General Statistics. The values shown reflect change from the base year, 1997. Values above 100 mean greater than 1997, values below 100 mean less than 1997, and a value of 100 in years other than 1997 means same as 1997. Indices are calculated only for Census years. Data are the most recent available at this level of detail.

SELECTED RATIOS

For 1997	Avg. of Sector	Analyzed Industry	Index	For 1997	Avg. of Sector	Analyzed Industry	Index
Employees per establishment	16	74	448	Payroll per establishment	462,554	na	na
Revenue per establishment	1,787,642	na	na	Payroll as % of revenue	26	na	na
Revenue per employee	108,959	na	na	Payroll per employee	28,193	na	na

Sources: Same as General Statistics. The 'Average of Sector' column represents the average for all industries in this sector. The Index shows the relationship between the Average and the Analyzed Industry. For example, 100 means that they are equal; 500 that the Analyzed Industry is five times the average; 50 means that the Analyzed Industry is half the national average. 'na' is used to show that data are 'not available'.

LEADING COMPANIES   Number shown: 15   Total sales ($ mil): **4,967**   Total employment (000): **27.7**

Company Name	Address				CEO Name	Phone	Co. Type	Sales ($ mil)	Empl. (000)
Dome Railway Services	2850 S Broadway	St. Louis	MO	63118	August Busch III	314-577-7518	S	4,440*	24.0
Rescar Inc.	1101 31st St	Downers Grove	IL	60515	Joe Schieszler	630-963-1114	R	190*	1.0
Hulcher Services Inc.	P O Box 271	Denton	TX	76202	Byron Hart	940-387-0099	R	108*	0.6
Arctic Slope World Services Inc.	3033 Gold Canal Dr	Rancho Cordova	CA	95670	Mike Taylor	916-363-2224	S	90	0.9
Romar Transportation Systems	3500 S Kedzie Ave	Chicago	IL	60632	Michael Marden	773-376-8800	R	39*	0.2
Federal Warehouse Co.	200 National Rd	East Peoria	IL	61611	Donald L Ullman	309-694-4500	R	35	0.6
Freight Traffic Services	58 Chambers Brook	Somerville	NJ	08876		908-526-8700	N	20	0.2
Allied Realty Co.	P O Box 1700	Huntington	WV	25717	L Polan III	304-525-9125	R	18	0.2
Indiana Freight Traffic Analysts	1111 E 54	Indianapolis	IN	46220		317-253-5111	N	14	<0.1
TransNuclear West Inc.	39300 Civic Center	Fremont	CA	94538	Allen Hanson	510-795-9800	R	9*	<0.1
Traffic Service Bureau Inc.	PO Box 460	Middletown	PA	17057		717-944-4618	N	3	<0.1
LunaCorp.	4350 N Fairfax Dr	Arlington	VA	22203	David Gump	703-841-9500	R	1*	<0.1
Trans-Continental Traffic Service	1771 N Powerline 4	Pompano Beach	FL	33069		954-977-6888	N	1	<0.1
Interstate Registration Service Inc.	PO Box 200005	Arlington	TX	76006		817-633-7887	N	1	<0.1
Freight Management Resources	PO Box 14466	Spokane	WA	99214		509-891-0625	N	0	<0.1

Source: *Ward's Business Directory of U.S. Private and Public Companies*, Volumes 1 and 2, 2000. The company type code used is as follows: P - Public, R - Private, S - Subsidiary, D - Division, J - Joint Venture, A - Affiliate, G - Group, N - Company type not reported. Sales are in millions of dollars, employees are in thousands. An asterisk (*) indicates an estimated sales volume. The symbol < stands for 'less than'. Company names and addresses are truncated, in some cases, to fit into the available space.

LOCATION BY STATE AND REGIONAL CONCENTRATION

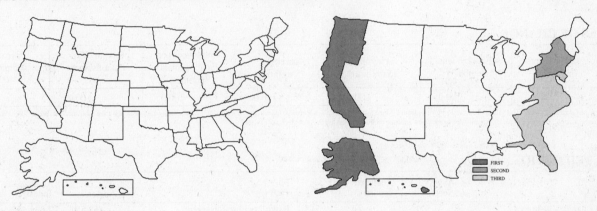

INDUSTRY DATA BY STATE

State	Establishments		Employment			Payroll		Revenues		
	Total (number)	% of U.S.	Total (number)	% of U.S.	Per Estab.	Total ($ mil.)	Per Empl. ($)	Total ($ mil.)	% of U.S.	Per Estab. ($)
California	7	6.9	185	0.0	26	5.3	28,578	15.2	0.0	2,172,714
New York	12	11.8	70	0.0	6	1.8	25,471	7.1	0.0	593,250
South Carolina	6	5.9	84	0.0	14	1.1	13,274	1.7	0.0	285,500
Florida	14	13.7	3,750*	-	-	(D)	-	(D)	-	-
Texas	13	12.7	3,750*	-	-	(D)	-	(D)	-	-
Pennsylvania	7	6.9	60*	-	-	(D)	-	(D)	-	-

Source: 1997 *Economic Census*. The states are in descending order of revenues or establishments (if revenue data are missing for the majority). The symbol (D) appears when data are withheld to prevent disclosure of competitive information. States marked with (D) are sorted by number of establishments. A dash (-) indicates that the data element cannot be calculated. * indicates the midpoint of a range; 175, for example is the range 100-249. Shaded *states* on the state map indicate those states which have proportionately greater representation in the industry than would be indicated by the state's population; the ratio is based on total revenues or number of establishments. Shaded *regions* indicate where the industry is regionally most concentrated.

NAICS 492110 - COURIERS

GENERAL STATISTICS

Year	Establishments (number)	Employment (number)	Payroll ($ million)	Revenues ($ million)	Employees per Establishment (number)	Revenues per Establishment ($)	Payroll per Employee ($)
1997	5,503	463,426	12,829.9	36,293.3	84.2	6,595,184	27,685

Source: *Economic Census of the United States*, 1997. This is a newly defined industry. Data for prior years were unavailable at the time of publication but may become available over time.

SIC INDUSTRIES RELATED TO NAICS 492110

SIC	Industry	1990	1991	1992	1993	1994	1995	1996	1997
4215	**Courier Services, Except by Air***								
	Establishments (number)	5,961e	5,964e	5,966	5,968p	5,971p	5,973p	5,976p	5,978p
	Employment (thousands)	290.5e	298.8e	307.1	315.4p	323.7p	331.9p	340.2p	348.5p
	Revenues ($ million)	17,337.0	17,878.0	19,334.3	20,095.0	20,684.0	21,147.0	23,066.0	23,474.0
4513	**Air Courier Services**								
	Establishments (number)	-	-	2,639	-	-	-	-	-
	Employment (thousands)	-	-	99.0	-	-	-	-	-
	Revenues ($ million)	-	-	11,012.7	-	-	-	-	-

Source: *Economic Census of the United States*, 1992, annual surveys of economic sectors conducted by the Bureau of the Census, and estimates or projections based on the 1982-1992 period; not all data are shown. 'e' marks estimates made by the editors; 'p' indicates projections based on time series. A dash (-) indicates that data for this SIC or year were not available. * Indicates that only a portion of this industry is present within the NAICS data. If no * is shown, the entire industry is contained within the NAICS data.

INDICES OF CHANGE

Year	Establishments (number)	Employment (number)	Payroll ($ million)	Revenues ($ million)	Employees per Establishment (number)	Revenues per Establishment ($)	Payroll per Employee ($)
1997	100.0	100.0	100.0	100.0	100.0	100.0	100.0

Sources: Same as General Statistics. The values shown reflect change from the base year, 1997. Values above 100 mean greater than 1997, values below 100 mean less than 1997, and a value of 100 in years other than 1997 means same as 1997. Indices are calculated only for Census years. Data are the most recent available at this level of detail.

SELECTED RATIOS

For 1997	Avg. of Sector	Analyzed Industry	Index	For 1997	Avg. of Sector	Analyzed Industry	Index
Employees per establishment	16	84	513	Payroll per establishment	462,554	2,331,437	504
Revenue per establishment	1,787,642	6,595,184	369	Payroll as % of revenue	26	35	137
Revenue per employee	108,959	78,315	72	Payroll per employee	28,193	27,685	98

Sources: Same as General Statistics. The 'Average of Sector' column represents the average for all industries in this sector. The Index shows the relationship between the Average and the Analyzed Industry. For example, 100 means that they are equal; 500 that the Analyzed Industry is five times the average; 50 means that the Analyzed Industry is half the national average. 'na' is used to show that data are 'not available'.

LEADING COMPANIES   Number shown: **49**   Total sales ($ mil): **107,190**   Total employment (000): **963.3**

Company Name	Address				CEO Name	Phone	Co. Type	Sales ($ mil)	Empl. (000)
United Parcel Service of America	55 Glenlake Pkwy	Atlanta	GA	30328	James P Kelly	404-828-6000	P	27,052	
Federal Express Corp.	U S Mail Box 727	Memphis	TN	38194	Frederick W Smith	901-369-3600	D	16,774	
FedEx Corp.	6075 Poplar Ave	Memphis	TN	38119	Fredrick W Smith	901-369-3600	P	16,774	
AMR Corp.	PO Box 619616	Dallas	TX	75261	Donald J Carty	817-963-1234	P	15,192*	
Continental Airlines Inc.	1600 Smith St	Houston	TX	77002	Gordon M Bethune	713-324-5000	P	7,951	
CNF Transportation Inc.	3240 Hillview Ave	Palo Alto	CA	94304	Gregory L Quesnel	650-494-2900	P	5,593	
Airborne Freight Corp.	P O Box 662	Seattle	WA	98111	Robert G Brazier	206-285-4600	P	3,140	
DHL Airways Inc.	333 Twin Dolphin	Redwood City	CA	94065	Patrick Foley	650-593-7474	R	3,100*	
Corporate Express Delivery	11 Greenway Plz	Houston	TX	77046	Clarence Gabriel	713-867-5070	S	2,875*	
Emery Worldwide	1 Lagoon Dr	Redwood City	CA	94065	Roger Piazza	650-596-9600	P	2,100	
BAX Global Inc.	16808 Armstrong	Irvine	CA	92606	C Robert Campbel	949-752-4000	S	1,700*	1
Burns International Services Corp.	200 S Michigan Ave	Chicago	IL	60604	John A Edwardson	312-322-8500	P	1,323	73
ABX Air Inc.	145 Hunter Dr	Wilmington	OH	45177	Carl D Donaway	937-382-5591	S	869*	7.
Hawaiian Airlines Inc.	P O Box 30008	Honolulu	HI	96820	Paul J Casey	808-835-3700	P	412	2.
Dynamex Inc.	1431 Greenway Dr	Irving	TX	75038	R K McClelland	972-756-8180	P	240	2.8
Consolidated Delivery & Logistics	380 Allwood Rd	Clifton	NJ	07012	William T Brannan	973-471-1005	P	186	3.5
Skyway Freight Systems Inc.	P O Box 1810	Santa Cruz	CA	95061	Kip Hawley	831-722-3133	S	175*	1.6
Transit Group Inc.	2859 Paces Ferry Rd	Atlanta	GA	30339	Philip A Belyew	770-444-0240	P	174	2.0
United Couriers Inc.	3220 Winona Ave	Burbank	CA	91504	Richard Irvin	818-845-8883	S	158*	1.0
Pony Express Delivery Services	6165 Barfield Rd	Atlanta	GA	30328	Dick Williams	404-847-3120	S	140	2.5
Sky Courier	21240 Ridge Top	Sterling	VA	20166		703-433-2800	S	140*	0.5
AirNet Systems	3939 Int Gtway	Columbus	OH	43219	J G Mercer	614-237-9777	P	114	1.2
Amerijet International Inc.	498 S W 34th St	Fort Lauderdale	FL	33315	David Basset	954-359-0077	R	110*	0.7
Guaranteed Overnight Delivery	P O Box 100	Kearny	NJ	07032	Walter A Riley	973-344-3013	R	105*	0.6
Adcom Express Inc.	PO Box 390048	Edina	MN	55439	Robert F Friedman	612-829-7990	R	100*	<0.1
Lanter Co.	PO Box 68	Madison	IL	62060	Steve Lanter	618-452-9500	R	75*	0.9
Hartco Inc.	11235 Mastin St	Overland Park	KS	66210	John E Hartman	913-661-9777	R	62*	0.4
USA Jet Airlines Inc.	2064 D St	Belleville	MI	48111	Martin R Goldman	734-483-7833	R	60	0.4
Air T Inc.	3524 Arpt Rd	Maiden	NC	28650	J Hugh Bingham	828-465-1336	P	52	0.4
Courier Express Inc.	1250 W Sunset Blvd	Los Angeles	CA	90026	Richard L Williams	213-250-4013	R	48*	0.9
Global Mail Ltd.	22560 Glen Dr #105	Sterling	VA	20164	Harry Geller	703-405-5777	R	47*	0.3
IslandAir	99 Kapalulu Pl	Honolulu	HI	96819	Neil Takekawa	808-836-7693	S	45*	0.3
Packaging Store Inc.	5675 DTC Blvd	Englewood	CO	80111	Mark A Challis	303-741-6626	R	45	<0.1
Mailfast	200 Garden Cty	Garden City	NY	11530	John Costanzo	516-535-1000	S	33*	0.4
Matheson Postal Service	PO Box 970	Elk Grove	CA	95759	Robert B Matheson	916-687-4800	D	32*	0.2
Trans-Box Systems Inc.	P O Box 6278	Oakland	CA	94603	Ron Boehm	510-568-8890	R	30*	0.5
SonicAir Inc.	15150 N Hayden Rd	Scottsdale	AZ	85260	R Thurston	480-991-1891	S	30	0.3
Empire Airlines Inc.	2115 Government	Coeur D Alene	ID	83814	Mel Spelde	208-667-5400	R	27*	0.2
Bellair Expediting Service Inc.	3745 25th Ave	Schiller Park	IL	60176	Ed Becht	847-928-1500	R	20	<0.1
Dahlsten Truck Line Inc.	PO Box 95	Clay Center	NE	68933	Vayle Hayes	402-762-3511	R	18	0.2
Mid-Georgia Courier Inc.	1564 Norman Dr	College Park	GA	30349	Larry Friday	770-991-1084	R	17*	0.1
Aero Special Delivery Service Inc.	1900 3rd St	San Francisco	CA	94107	Kurt Sparks	415-495-8333	J	12	0.3
Single Source Transportation Inc.	26986 Trolly Ind Dr	Taylor	MI	48180	Gary A Maccagnone	313-295-3390	R	12	<0.1
Corporate Express Delivery	733 Lambert Dr	Atlanta	GA	30324	Shawn Friden	404-873-5052	R	9*	<0.1
United States Cargo Service Corp.	900 Williams Ave	Columbus	OH	43212	Ralph E Richter Jr	614-358-1356	R	8*	0.3
ABC Messenger Service Inc.	16900 Valleyview	La Mirada	CA	90638	Scott Leveridge	714-994-1615	R	5*	<0.1
City Sprint	1851 Cobb Pkwy	Marietta	GA	30062		770-955-3278	R	4*	<0.1
Zantop International Airlines Inc.	840 Willow Run	Ypsilanti	MI	48198	James M Zantop	734-485-8900	R	2*	<0.1
Choice Parcel Service Inc.	9532 Deereco Rd	Timonium	MD	21093	Debra Dudderar	410-560-0607	R	1*	0.2

Source: *Ward's Business Directory of U.S. Private and Public Companies*, Volumes 1 and 2, 2000. The company type code used is as follows: P - Public, R - Private, S - Subsidiary, D - Division, J - Joint Venture, A - Affiliate, G - Group, N - Company type not reported. Sales are in millions of dollars, employees are in thousands. An asterisk (*) indicates an estimated sales volume. The symbol < stands for 'less than'. Company names and addresses are truncated, in some cases, to fit into the available space.

OCATION BY STATE AND REGIONAL CONCENTRATION

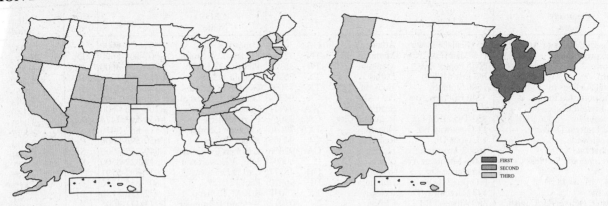

FIRST
SECOND
THIRD

INDUSTRY DATA BY STATE

State	Establishments Total (number)	% of U.S.	Employment Total (number)	% of U.S.	Per Estab.	Payroll Total ($ mil.)	Per Empl. ($)	Revenues Total ($ mil.)	% of U.S.	Per Estab. ($)
California	694	12.6	62,901	13.6	91	1,639.7	26,068	4,735.1	13.0	6,822,924
New York	407	7.4	30,650	6.6	75	883.9	28,838	2,653.3	7.3	6,519,170
Illinois	207	3.8	32,913	7.1	159	730.7	22,201	2,223.7	6.1	10,742,618
Texas	377	6.9	25,848	5.6	69	670.9	25,954	2,187.6	6.0	5,802,682
Kentucky	57	1.0	6,637	1.4	116	398.2	59,999	2,033.3	5.6	35,671,281
Florida	418	7.6	21,565	4.7	52	617.6	28,638	1,840.9	5.1	4,404,048
New Jersey	184	3.3	19,914	4.3	108	540.1	27,122	1,783.4	4.9	9,692,435
Pennsylvania	173	3.1	22,951	5.0	133	637.3	27,770	1,677.7	4.6	9,697,838
Ohio	144	2.6	27,905	6.0	194	824.9	29,562	1,430.0	3.9	9,930,451
Michigan	143	2.6	14,650	3.2	102	469.7	32,058	1,187.9	3.3	8,306,993
Tennessee	208	3.8	11,297	2.4	54	379.6	33,605	1,039.8	2.9	4,998,841
Georgia	144	2.6	12,895	2.8	90	317.0	24,583	980.5	2.7	6,808,694
North Carolina	143	2.6	12,612	2.7	88	319.8	25,360	849.9	2.3	5,943,315
Massachusetts	141	2.6	9,673	2.1	69	280.4	28,986	764.9	2.1	5,425,014
Indiana	85	1.5	11,413	2.5	134	282.7	24,766	740.1	2.0	8,707,047
Virginia	137	2.5	8,332	1.8	61	234.5	28,142	686.2	1.9	5,008,883
Colorado	107	1.9	9,083	2.0	85	246.2	27,102	681.5	1.9	6,369,318
Maryland	86	1.6	8,667	1.9	101	292.3	33,731	659.5	1.8	7,668,663
Arizona	94	1.7	9,554	2.1	102	224.0	23,446	656.2	1.8	6,980,766
Washington	123	2.2	8,730	1.9	71	233.3	26,728	607.2	1.7	4,936,902
Minnesota	84	1.5	8,463	1.8	101	218.5	25,821	605.5	1.7	7,207,810
Missouri	118	2.1	7,382	1.6	63	208.7	28,273	576.4	1.6	4,884,992
Wisconsin	100	1.8	7,640	1.6	76	210.5	27,555	535.2	1.5	5,351,640
Connecticut	63	1.1	6,652	1.4	106	205.8	30,942	510.6	1.4	8,105,063
New Hampshire	37	0.7	6,860	1.5	185	176.2	25,682	426.2	1.2	11,517,919
Oregon	67	1.2	5,775	1.2	86	162.6	28,157	420.4	1.2	6,275,045
Louisiana	85	1.5	6,337	1.4	75	164.2	25,916	415.7	1.1	4,890,435
Kansas	60	1.1	5,683	1.2	95	154.3	27,147	367.1	1.0	6,118,667
Arkansas	48	0.9	5,392	1.2	112	142.1	26,352	356.3	1.0	7,422,521
South Carolina	54	1.0	4,804	1.0	89	117.1	24,367	339.0	0.9	6,276,870
Utah	44	0.8	4,918	1.1	112	134.4	27,321	336.5	0.9	7,647,364
Alabama	62	1.1	4,699	1.0	76	141.7	30,151	334.0	0.9	5,387,355
Iowa	68	1.2	4,301	0.9	63	112.2	26,097	280.6	0.8	4,126,206
Nebraska	50	0.9	4,212	0.9	84	112.1	26,607	267.6	0.7	5,351,060
Oklahoma	54	1.0	3,410	0.7	63	94.6	27,730	265.9	0.7	4,924,667
Alaska	42	0.8	1,069	0.2	25	63.0	58,979	154.7	0.4	3,682,786
Nevada	44	0.8	955	0.2	22	23.9	25,023	94.3	0.3	2,142,568
Hawaii	26	0.5	1,009	0.2	39	28.3	28,051	72.9	0.2	2,803,423
New Mexico	33	0.6	724	0.2	22	16.6	22,941	56.7	0.2	1,717,242
Maine	26	0.5	600	0.1	23	15.2	25,258	54.7	0.2	2,103,385
Mississippi	43	0.8	695	0.1	16	14.9	21,406	53.8	0.1	1,251,442
Vermont	16	0.3	615	0.1	38	9.4	15,281	40.8	0.1	2,550,625
Idaho	39	0.7	471	0.1	12	10.8	22,947	36.2	0.1	929,410
West Virginia	27	0.5	421	0.1	16	10.9	25,952	35.1	0.1	1,298,222
South Dakota	25	0.5	273	0.1	11	6.8	24,890	25.0	0.1	999,560
Montana	30	0.5	375*	-	-	(D)	-	(D)	-	-
D.C.	27	0.5	750*	-	-	(D)	-	(D)	-	-
North Dakota	18	0.3	175*	-	-	(D)	-	(D)	-	-
Wyoming	16	0.3	175*	-	-	(D)	-	(D)	-	-
Rhode Island	14	0.3	375*	-	-	(D)	-	(D)	-	-
Delaware	11	0.2	375*	-	-	(D)	-	(D)	-	-

Source: 1997 *Economic Census*. The states are in descending order of revenues or establishments (if revenue data are missing for the majority). The symbol (D) appears when data are withheld to prevent disclosure of competitive information. States marked with (D) are sorted by number of establishments. A dash (-) indicates that the data element cannot be calculated. * indicates the midpoint of a range; 175, for example is the range 100-249. Shaded *states* on the state map indicate those states which have proportionately greater representation in the industry than would be indicated by the state's population; the ratio is based on total revenues or number of establishments. Shaded *regions* indicate where the industry is regionally most concentrated.

NAICS 492210 - LOCAL MESSENGERS AND LOCAL DELIVERY

GENERAL STATISTICS

Year	Establishments (number)	Employment (number)	Payroll ($ million)	Revenues ($ million)	Employees per Establishment (number)	Revenues per Establishment ($)	Payroll per Employee ($)
1997	5,384	67,413	1,241.7	3,519.1	12.5	653,622	18,419

Source: Economic Census of the United States, 1997. This is a newly defined industry. Data for prior years were unavailable at the time of publication but may become available over time.

SIC INDUSTRIES RELATED TO NAICS 492210

SIC	Industry	1990	1991	1992	1993	1994	1995	1996	1997
4215	**Courier Services, Except by Air***								
	Establishments (number)	5,961e	5,964e	5,966	5,968p	5,971p	5,973p	5,976p	5,978p
	Employment (thousands)	290.5e	298.8e	307.1	315.4p	323.7p	331.9p	340.2p	348.5p
	Revenues ($ million)	17,337.0	17,878.0	19,334.3	20,095.0	20,684.0	21,147.0	23,066.0	23,474.0

Source: Economic Census of the United States, 1992, annual surveys of economic sectors conducted by the Bureau of the Census, and estimates or projections based on the 1982-1992 period; not all data are shown. 'e' marks estimates made by the editors; 'p' indicates projections based on time series. A dash (-) indicates that data for this SIC or year were not available. * Indicates that only a portion of this industry is present within the NAICS data. If no * is shown, the entire industry is contained within the NAICS data.

INDICES OF CHANGE

Year	Establishments (number)	Employment (number)	Payroll ($ million)	Revenues ($ million)	Employees per Establishment (number)	Revenues per Establishment ($)	Payroll per Employee ($)
1997	100.0	100.0	100.0	100.0	100.0	100.0	100.0

Sources: Same as General Statistics. The values shown reflect change from the base year, 1997. Values above 100 mean greater than 1997, values below 100 mean less than 1997, and a value of 100 in years other than 1997 means same as 1997. Indices are calculated only for Census years. Data are the most recent available at this level of detail.

SELECTED RATIOS

For 1997	Avg. of Sector	Analyzed Industry	Index	For 1997	Avg. of Sector	Analyzed Industry	Index
Employees per establishment	16	13	76	Payroll per establishment	462,554	230,628	50
Revenue per establishment	1,787,642	653,622	37	Payroll as % of revenue	26	35	136
Revenue per employee	108,959	52,202	48	Payroll per employee	28,193	18,419	65

Sources: Same as General Statistics. The 'Average of Sector' column represents the average for all industries in this sector. The Index shows the relationship between the Average and the Analyzed Industry. For example, 100 means that they are equal; 500 that the Analyzed Industry is five times the average; 50 means that the Analyzed Industry is half the national average. 'na' is used to show that data are 'not available'.

LEADING COMPANIES

No company data available for this industry.

LOCATION BY STATE AND REGIONAL CONCENTRATION

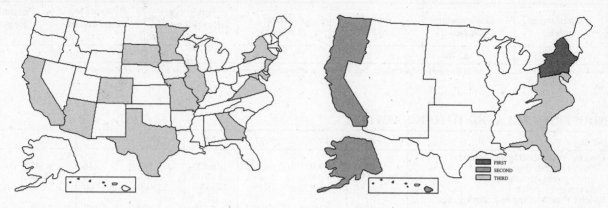

INDUSTRY DATA BY STATE

State	Establishments Total (number)	% of U.S.	Employment Total (number)	% of U.S.	Per Estab.	Payroll Total ($ mil.)	Per Empl. ($)	Revenues Total ($ mil.)	% of U.S.	Per Estab. ($)
California	612	11.4	14,044	20.8	23	228.1	16,244	542.8	15.4	887,008
New York	509	9.5	10,377	15.4	20	181.3	17,474	496.5	14.1	975,356
Texas	412	7.7	3,862	5.7	9	95.7	24,768	298.5	8.5	724,607
Illinois	237	4.4	3,435	5.1	14	70.2	20,448	185.2	5.3	781,574
Florida	372	6.9	2,131	3.2	6	41.6	19,504	168.0	4.8	451,632
New Jersey	243	4.5	1,966	2.9	8	45.9	23,369	165.3	4.7	680,193
Minnesota	127	2.4	2,516	3.7	20	48.1	19,128	141.6	4.0	1,115,228
Ohio	171	3.2	1,712	2.5	10	38.2	22,326	139.5	4.0	815,608
Maryland	146	2.7	1,621	2.4	11	30.0	18,476	116.6	3.3	798,390
Georgia	119	2.2	2,010	3.0	17	39.2	19,480	113.7	3.2	955,866
Missouri	179	3.3	1,619	2.4	9	34.3	21,206	103.3	2.9	576,994
Virginia	155	2.9	2,021	3.0	13	33.3	16,489	99.8	2.8	644,032
Pennsylvania	151	2.8	1,241	1.8	8	24.7	19,910	83.4	2.4	552,603
Massachusetts	105	2.0	1,131	1.7	11	21.4	18,900	63.2	1.8	601,695
Michigan	139	2.6	1,381	2.0	10	31.7	22,966	57.8	1.6	415,993
Arizona	87	1.6	1,243	1.8	14	24.8	19,977	56.3	1.6	646,586
Colorado	93	1.7	1,434	2.1	15	24.6	17,181	54.8	1.6	589,075
Tennessee	96	1.8	936	1.4	10	17.8	18,994	51.1	1.5	532,594
Washington	104	1.9	1,174	1.7	11	21.4	18,215	48.0	1.4	461,125
North Carolina	118	2.2	1,136	1.7	10	15.4	13,534	42.1	1.2	356,780
Connecticut	48	0.9	478	0.7	10	10.3	21,653	40.8	1.2	850,333
Wisconsin	116	2.2	951	1.4	8	17.0	17,903	39.4	1.1	339,466
Indiana	102	1.9	529	0.8	5	9.8	18,618	36.3	1.0	355,716
Kentucky	71	1.3	881	1.3	12	12.6	14,296	31.6	0.9	445,112
Louisiana	49	0.9	537	0.8	11	8.9	16,484	27.4	0.8	559,857
Kansas	60	1.1	561	0.8	9	9.2	16,342	26.4	0.7	439,267
Oklahoma	60	1.1	451	0.7	8	7.6	16,829	25.9	0.7	431,217
Iowa	68	1.3	633	0.9	9	8.3	13,092	22.0	0.6	323,456
Alabama	49	0.9	541	0.8	11	8.7	16,161	20.2	0.6	412,490
Arkansas	34	0.6	371	0.6	11	7.2	19,456	20.2	0.6	593,853
Oregon	61	1.1	492	0.7	8	8.8	17,831	19.8	0.6	324,148
Nebraska	47	0.9	354	0.5	8	7.2	20,398	17.3	0.5	368,447
South Carolina	53	1.0	470	0.7	9	6.1	12,962	15.7	0.4	296,208
Nevada	41	0.8	213	0.3	5	4.2	19,756	11.4	0.3	278,659
South Dakota	22	0.4	250	0.4	11	3.4	13,496	11.3	0.3	514,591
West Virginia	25	0.5	285	0.4	11	3.8	13,382	11.2	0.3	446,280
Utah	29	0.5	259	0.4	9	4.4	17,058	11.0	0.3	380,207
Mississippi	18	0.3	288	0.4	16	4.7	16,153	10.8	0.3	601,778
Hawaii	28	0.5	220	0.3	8	3.8	17,145	10.3	0.3	366,321
Idaho	29	0.5	259	0.4	9	2.7	10,398	7.3	0.2	250,931
Maine	16	0.3	106	0.2	7	1.9	17,821	4.5	0.1	283,437
New Mexico	18	0.3	120	0.2	7	1.8	14,750	4.4	0.1	246,778
Alaska	18	0.3	87	0.1	5	1.9	21,494	4.3	0.1	241,444
Vermont	8	0.1	18	0.0	2	0.2	13,389	0.8	0.0	99,000
Rhode Island	36	0.7	175*	-	-	(D)	-	(D)	-	-
Montana	23	0.4	175*	-	-	(D)	-	(D)	-	-
D.C.	22	0.4	175*	-	-	(D)	-	(D)	-	-
New Hampshire	22	0.4	175*	-	-	(D)	-	(D)	-	-
North Dakota	15	0.3	175*	-	-	(D)	-	(D)	-	-
Wyoming	15	0.3	60*	-	-	(D)	-	(D)	-	-
Delaware	6	0.1	175*	-	-	(D)	-	(D)	-	-

Source: 1997 *Economic Census*. The states are in descending order of revenues or establishments (if revenue data are missing for the majority). The symbol (D) appears when data are withheld to prevent disclosure of competitive information. States marked with (D) are sorted by number of establishments. A dash (-) indicates that the data element cannot be calculated. * indicates the midpoint of a range; 175, for example is the range 100-249. Shaded *states* on the state map indicate those states which have proportionally greater representation in the industry than would be indicated by the state's population; the ratio is based on total revenues or number of establishments. Shaded *regions* indicate where the industry is regionally most concentrated.

NAICS 493110 - GENERAL WAREHOUSING AND STORAGE

GENERAL STATISTICS

Year	Establishments (number)	Employment (number)	Payroll ($ million)	Revenues ($ million)	Employees per Establishment (number)	Revenues per Establishment ($)	Payroll per Employee ($)
1997	3,921	62,784	1,623.0	5,321.4	16.0	1,357,154	25,851

Source: Economic Census of the United States, 1997. This is a newly defined industry. Data for prior years were unavailable at the time of publication but may become available over time.

SIC INDUSTRIES RELATED TO NAICS 493110

SIC	Industry	1990	1991	1992	1993	1994	1995	1996	1997
4225	**General Warehousing and Storage***								
	Establishments (number)	4,495	5,921	6,753	6,825	7,171	7,338	8,588	8,754p
	Employment (thousands)	45.1	47.6	49.1	51.7	57.2	61.3	66.8	66.8p
	Revenues ($ million)	3,257.0	3,568.0	3,919.2	4,633.0	5,294.0	6,143.0	6,522.0	7,457.0
4226	**Special Warehousing and Storage, nec***								
	Establishments (number)	1,126	1,158	1,452	1,490	1,479	1,547	1,648	1,670p
	Employment (thousands)	16.3	16.5	20.6	24.0	22.0	24.0	25.8	26.6p
	Revenues ($ million)	1,796.0	1,752.0	2,009.5	1,882.0	1,911.0	1,875.0	2,050.0	2,262.0

Source: Economic Census of the United States, 1992, annual surveys of economic sectors conducted by the Bureau of the Census, and estimates or projections based on the 1982-1992 period; not all data are shown. 'e' marks estimates made by the editors; 'p' indicates projections based on time series. A dash (-) indicates that data for this SIC or year were not available. * Indicates that only a portion of this industry is present within the NAICS data. If no * is shown, the entire industry is contained within the NAICS data.

INDICES OF CHANGE

Year	Establishments (number)	Employment (number)	Payroll ($ million)	Revenues ($ million)	Employees per Establishment (number)	Revenues per Establishment ($)	Payroll per Employee ($)
1997	100.0	100.0	100.0	100.0	100.0	100.0	100.0

Sources: Same as General Statistics. The values shown reflect change from the base year, 1997. Values above 100 mean greater than 1997, values below 100 mean less than 1997, and a value of 100 in years other than 1997 means same as 1997. Indices are calculated only for Census years. Data are the most recent available at this level of detail.

SELECTED RATIOS

For 1997	Avg. of Sector	Analyzed Industry	Index	For 1997	Avg. of Sector	Analyzed Industry	Index
Employees per establishment	16	16	98	Payroll per establishment	462,554	413,925	89
Revenue per establishment	1,787,642	1,357,154	76	Payroll as % of revenue	26	30	118
Revenue per employee	108,959	84,757	78	Payroll per employee	28,193	25,851	92

Sources: Same as General Statistics. The 'Average of Sector' column represents the average for all industries in this sector. The Index shows the relationship between the Average and the Analyzed Industry. For example, 100 means that they are equal; 500 that the Analyzed Industry is five times the average; 50 means that the Analyzed Industry is half the national average. 'na' is used to show that data are not available.

LEADING COMPANIES   Number shown: **50**   Total sales ($ mil): **3,796**   Total employment (000): **41.9**

Company Name	Address				CEO Name	Phone	Co. Type	Sales ($ mil)	Empl. (000)
Overnite Transportation Co.	P O Box 1216	Richmond	VA	23218	Leo Suggs	804-231-8000	S	836*	13.0
Arnold Industries Inc.	P O Box 11963	Lebanon	PA	17042	EH Arnold	717-273-9058	P	404*	1.5
GATX Logistics Inc.	1301 Riverplace	Jacksonville	FL	32207	Joseph A Nicosia	904-396-2517	P	294	3.2
Iron Mountain Inc.	745 Atlantic Ave	Boston	MA	02111	JPeter Pierce	617-535-4766	P	270	3.3
Global Transportation Services	PO Box 24504	Seattle	WA	98124	Eddie Kelly	206-624-4354	R	232	0.1
Exel Logistics Inc.	501 W Schrock Rd	Westerville	OH	43081	Bruce Edwards	614-890-1730	S	225	6.0
A.N. Deringer Inc.	PO Box 1309	St. Albans	VT	05478	Wayne Burl	802-524-8110	R	165*	0.6
Kenco Group	P O Box 1607	Chattanooga	TN	37401	Jim Kennedy III	423-756-5552	R	110	2.5
Tecma Maquila Services Inc.	2000 Wyoming A	El Paso	TX	79903	Alan Russell	915-534-4252	R	69*	0.5
Capital City Companies Inc.	1295 Johnson St N E	Salem	OR	97303	WB Loch	503-362-5558	R	61*	0.3
Nelson Westerberg Inc.	1500 Arthur Ave	Elk Grove Vill.	IL	60007	Allen S Mileski	847-437-2080	R	60	0.4
Jacobson Warehouse Inc.	P O Box 224	Des Moines	IA	50301		515-265-6171	R	58	0.6
Kenco Group Inc.	520 W 31st St	Chattanooga	TN	37401	James D Kennedy III	423-622-1113	R	57*	0.4
Standard Corp.	1400 Main St	Columbia	SC	29201	Claude Walker	803-771-6785	R	55*	1.7
Kane is Able Inc.	P O Box 931	Scranton	PA	18501	Eugene J Kane Sr	717-343-5263	R	52	0.5
D.D. Jones Transfer & Warehouse	2626 Indian River	Chesapeake	VA	23325	Robert Jones Jr	757-494-0200	R	52*	0.3
C.C.W. Group	PO Box 20107	Greensboro	NC	27420	Jay Bitner	336-273-3465	R	50	1.8
LASH Intermodal Terminal Co.	2725 Riverport Rd	Memphis	TN	38109		901-774-5049	J	50*	<0.1
Saddle Creek Corp.	3010 Saddle Creek	Lakeland	FL	33801	David P Lyons	941-665-0966	R	49*	0.6
Gra-Bell Truck Line Inc.	P O Box 1019	Holland	MI	49422	Tom Van Wyk		R	49*	0.3
Dry Ridge Distribution Inc.	10000 Business Blvd	Dry Ridge	KY	41035	William Verst	606-824-3400	R	47*	0.3
Hub Group Distribution Services	3250 N Arl Hght	Arlington H.	IL	60004	Thomas Juedes	847-253-6800	S	43	<0.1
Distribution Technology Inc.	6100 Wheaton Dr	Atlanta	GA	30336	Rock J Miralia	404-349-9578	R	40*	0.3
Romar Transportation Systems	3500 S Kedzie Ave	Chicago	IL	60632	Michael Marden	773-376-8800	R	39*	0.2
Federal Warehouse Co.	200 National Rd	East Peoria	IL	61611	Donald L Ullman	309-694-4500	R	35	0.6
Curtice-Burns Foods Inc. Sodus	4125 S Pipestone Rd	Sodus	MI	49126	Dennis Mullen	616-926-8233	D	31*	0.2
Columbian Logistics Network	900 Hall St S W	Grand Rapids	MI	49503	John Zevalkink	616-452-3231	R	30*	0.2
Distribution Services of America	208 North St	Foxboro	MA	02035	David Petic	508-543-3313	R	29*	0.2
Terminal Corp.	1922 Greenspring Dr	Timonium	MD	21093	John T Menzies	410-560-4590	R	28*	0.2
APC Warehouse Co.	P O Box C	Madison	IL	62060	Richard Kerns	618-451-4222	R	28*	0.1
Belt's Corp.	608 Folcroft St	Baltimore	MD	21224	Skip Brown	410-633-7060	R	25*	0.2
Distribution & Marking Services	PO Box 7112	Charlotte	NC	28241	Michael Faucett	704-587-3674	R	22*	0.3
ACME Distribution Centers Inc.	18101 E Colfax Ave	Aurora	CO	80011	Jack L Grunwald	303-340-2100	R	21*	0.3
Leicht Transfer and Storage Co.	P O Box 2447	Green Bay	WI	54306	Russell G Leicht	920-432-8632	R	20	0.2
Oregon Transfer Co.	9304 SE Main St	Milwaukie	OR	97222	Gary Iichman	503-653-2660	R	19*	0.1
Gay Johnson's Inc.	P O Box 1829	Grand Junction	CO	81502	Bert Johnson	970-245-7992	R	19	<0.1
Allied Realty Co.	P O Box 1700	Huntington	WV	25717	L Polan III	304-525-9125	R	18	0.2
TGC Industries Inc.	1304 Summit Ave	Plano	TX	75074	Wayne Whitener	972-881-1099	P	17	0.1
Floyd and Beasley Transfer	PO Box 8	Sycamore	AL	35149	Jeff McGrady	256-245-4385	R	17	0.3
California Cartage Co.	PO Box 92829	Long Beach	CA	90809	Robert A Curry Sr	562-427-1143	R	13*	0.2
Pinney Dock and Transport Co.	1149 E 5th St	Ashtabula	OH	44004	Maynard Walker	440-964-7186	R	13*	<0.1
Single Source Transportation Inc.	26986 Trolly Ind Dr	Taylor	MI	48180	Gary A Maccagnone	313-295-3390	R	12	<0.1
Holman United	1599 Rockmountain	Stone Mountain	GA	30083	Joe Wansley	770-496-8188	S	8	<0.1
Patterson Warehouses Inc.	PO Box 30817	Memphis	TN	38130	Samuel B Bell	901-344-2600	R	7*	0.1
New Orleans Cold Storage	PO Box 26308	New Orleans	LA	70186	Gary Escoffier	504-944-4400	R	5*	0.1
Service Parts Supply Co.	11345 Century	Cincinnati	OH	45246		513-671-2800	R	4	<0.1
Empire State Coca-Cola Co.	Creighton Rd	Malone	NY	12953	Marvin Herb	802-655-9660	D	4*	<0.1
Exhibit Systems Inc.	1367 S 700 W	Salt Lake City	UT	84104	Randy Pridgen	801-978-9000	R	2	<0.1
Anderson Transfer	231 Burton Ave	Washington	PA	15301	Barbara Moore	412-341-0820	S	2*	<0.1
Rite Stuff Foods Inc.	10890 Paramount	Downey	CA	90241	Tom Madden	562-622-5500	R	0*	<0.1

Source: *Ward's Business Directory of U.S. Private and Public Companies*, Volumes 1 and 2, 2000. The company type code used is as follows: P - Public, R - Private, S - Subsidiary, D - Division, J - Joint Venture, A - Affiliate, G - Group, N - Company type not reported. Sales are in millions of dollars, employees are in thousands. An asterisk (*) indicates an estimated sales volume. The symbol < stands for 'less than'. Company names and addresses are truncated, in some cases, to fit into the available space.

LOCATION BY STATE AND REGIONAL CONCENTRATION

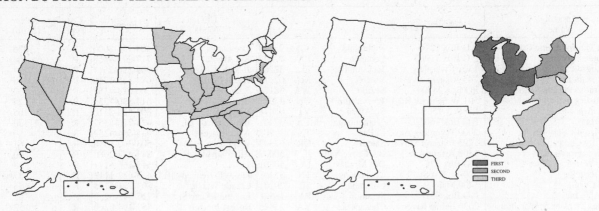

FIRST
SECOND
THIRD

INDUSTRY DATA BY STATE

State	Establishments Total (number)	Establishments % of U.S.	Employment Total (number)	Employment % of U.S.	Employment Per Estab.	Payroll Total ($ mil.)	Payroll Per Empl. ($)	Revenues Total ($ mil.)	Revenues % of U.S.	Revenues Per Estab. ($)
California	401	10.2	8,636	13.8	22	226.5	26,225	675.0	12.7	1,683,322
New Jersey	276	7.0	6,758	10.8	24	177.6	26,274	554.8	10.4	2,010,054
Illinois	209	5.3	3,975	6.3	19	121.3	30,512	385.8	7.3	1,845,967
Ohio	194	4.9	3,767	6.0	19	93.9	24,922	343.2	6.4	1,769,108
Texas	299	7.6	3,538	5.6	12	85.4	24,137	315.7	5.9	1,055,779
Pennsylvania	156	4.0	2,877	4.6	18	77.1	26,814	230.9	4.3	1,480,212
Georgia	143	3.6	2,226	3.5	16	57.6	25,889	210.4	4.0	1,471,510
New York	195	5.0	2,734	4.4	14	66.8	24,432	199.9	3.8	1,025,118
Florida	202	5.2	2,654	4.2	13	60.7	22,870	175.0	3.3	866,243
Tennessee	127	3.2	1,971	3.1	16	55.4	28,116	160.4	3.0	1,262,732
Indiana	106	2.7	2,233	3.6	21	55.2	24,704	150.7	2.8	1,421,726
Michigan	104	2.7	1,351	2.2	13	35.8	26,491	148.9	2.8	1,431,875
Massachusetts	107	2.7	1,395	2.2	13	42.6	30,509	147.5	2.8	1,378,841
North Carolina	131	3.3	1,990	3.2	15	48.4	24,331	142.0	2.7	1,084,244
Wisconsin	93	2.4	1,236	2.0	13	31.8	25,752	119.4	2.2	1,283,978
South Carolina	89	2.3	1,723	2.7	19	36.0	20,901	118.4	2.2	1,330,438
Missouri	103	2.6	1,377	2.2	13	30.3	22,031	114.7	2.2	1,113,718
Kentucky	66	1.7	1,088	1.7	16	30.2	27,800	108.4	2.0	1,641,758
Maryland	64	1.6	1,022	1.6	16	28.2	27,598	106.5	2.0	1,663,813
Washington	77	2.0	1,018	1.6	13	30.1	29,541	105.8	2.0	1,373,883
Minnesota	40	1.0	495	0.8	12	13.0	26,291	101.1	1.9	2,527,325
Virginia	90	2.3	1,169	1.9	13	28.6	24,482	93.9	1.8	1,043,567
Alabama	66	1.7	1,042	1.7	16	24.9	23,910	76.6	1.4	1,161,348
Louisiana	58	1.5	792	1.3	14	19.4	24,439	61.5	1.2	1,060,397
Iowa	49	1.2	924	1.5	19	22.7	24,553	60.8	1.1	1,240,429
Colorado	52	1.3	469	0.7	9	17.4	37,030	53.2	1.0	1,023,654
Connecticut	35	0.9	543	0.9	16	13.4	24,757	48.7	0.9	1,391,743
Nevada	28	0.7	498	0.8	18	11.8	23,612	33.8	0.6	1,208,821
Mississippi	22	0.6	296	0.5	13	7.8	26,348	29.7	0.6	1,348,591
Arizona	50	1.3	394	0.6	8	9.2	23,358	29.0	0.5	579,800
Arkansas	34	0.9	345	0.5	10	7.7	22,223	28.0	0.5	823,206
Oregon	37	0.9	225	0.4	6	6.7	29,742	25.0	0.5	674,946
Kansas	28	0.7	296	0.5	11	7.1	23,946	23.7	0.4	845,429
Maine	9	0.2	235	0.4	26	5.8	24,643	22.8	0.4	2,534,111
West Virginia	18	0.5	150	0.2	8	3.5	23,293	16.2	0.3	899,667
Hawaii	9	0.2	140	0.2	16	3.2	23,114	11.9	0.2	1,319,778
Nebraska	16	0.4	165	0.3	10	4.1	24,818	10.7	0.2	671,812
New Hampshire	8	0.2	97	0.2	12	2.6	26,557	10.4	0.2	1,294,500
Utah	15	0.4	96	0.2	6	2.5	26,240	9.3	0.2	618,733
Oklahoma	24	0.6	124	0.2	5	2.5	20,129	8.3	0.2	347,500
New Mexico	15	0.4	67	0.1	4	1.5	22,104	5.4	0.1	362,400
Idaho	12	0.3	65	0.1	5	1.7	25,600	2.7	0.1	228,333
Vermont	8	0.2	50	0.1	6	0.4	8,020	1.6	0.0	203,000
North Dakota	6	0.2	20	0.0	3	0.3	13,550	0.8	0.0	136,833
Delaware	15	0.4	175*	-	-	(D)	-	(D)	-	-
Rhode Island	11	0.3	60*	-	-	(D)	-	(D)	-	-
Montana	9	0.2	60*	-	-	(D)	-	(D)	-	-

Source: 1997 *Economic Census*. The states are in descending order of revenues or establishments (if revenue data are missing for the majority). The symbol (D) appears when data are withheld to prevent disclosure of competitive information. States marked with (D) are sorted by number of establishments. A dash (-) indicates that the data element cannot be calculated. * indicates the midpoint of a range; 175, for example is the range 100-249. Shaded *states* on the state map indicate those states which have proportionately greater representation in the industry than would be indicated by the state's population; the ratio is based on total revenues or number of establishments. Shaded *regions* indicate where the industry is regionally most concentrated.

NAICS 493120 - REFRIGERATED WAREHOUSING AND STORAGE

GENERAL STATISTICS

Year	Establishments (number)	Employment (number)	Payroll ($ million)	Revenues ($ million)	Employees per Establishment (number)	Revenues per Establishment ($)	Payroll per Employee ($)
1997	877	22,121	609.6	2,270.3	25.2	2,588,712	27,558

Source: Economic Census of the United States, 1997. This is a newly defined industry. Data for prior years were unavailable at the time of publication but may become available over time.

SIC INDUSTRIES RELATED TO NAICS 493120

SIC	Industry	1990	1991	1992	1993	1994	1995	1996	1997
4222	**Refrigerated Warehousing and Storage**								
	Establishments (number)	934	963	929	958	966	971	944	955p
	Employment (thousands)	19.6	19.9	19.0	19.9	20.3	22.4	22.3	22.9p
	Revenues ($ million)	1,469.0	1,554.0	1,744.8	1,756.0	1,869.0	2,107.0	2,203.0	2,321.0
4226	**Special Warehousing and Storage, nec***								
	Establishments (number)	1,126	1,158	1,452	1,490	1,479	1,547	1,648	1,670p
	Employment (thousands)	16.3	16.5	20.6	24.0	22.0	24.0	25.8	26.6p
	Revenues ($ million)	1,796.0	1,752.0	2,009.5	1,882.0	1,911.0	1,875.0	2,050.0	2,262.0

Source: Economic Census of the United States, 1992, annual surveys of economic sectors conducted by the Bureau of the Census, and estimates or projections based on the 1982-1992 period; not all data are shown. 'e' marks estimates made by the editors; 'p' indicates projections based on time series. A dash (-) indicates that data for this SIC or year were not available. * Indicates that only a portion of this industry is present within the NAICS data. If no * is shown, the entire industry is contained within the NAICS data.

INDICES OF CHANGE

Year	Establishments (number)	Employment (number)	Payroll ($ million)	Revenues ($ million)	Employees per Establishment (number)	Revenues per Establishment ($)	Payroll per Employee ($)
1997	100.0	100.0	100.0	100.0	100.0	100.0	100.0

Sources: Same as General Statistics. The values shown reflect change from the base year, 1997. Values above 100 mean greater than 1997, values below 100 mean less than 1997, and a value of 100 in years other than 1997 means same as 1997. Indices are calculated only for Census years. Data are the most recent available at this level of detail.

SELECTED RATIOS

For 1997	Avg. of Sector	Analyzed Industry	Index	For 1997	Avg. of Sector	Analyzed Industry	Index
Employees per establishment	16	25	154	Payroll per establishment	462,554	695,097	150
Revenue per establishment	1,787,642	2,588,712	145	Payroll as % of revenue	26	27	104
Revenue per employee	108,959	102,631	94	Payroll per employee	28,193	27,558	98

Sources: Same as General Statistics. The 'Average of Sector' column represents the average for all industries in this sector. The Index shows the relationship between the Average and the Analyzed Industry. For example, 100 means that they are equal; 500 that the Analyzed Industry is five times the average; 50 means that the Analyzed Industry is half the national average. 'na' is used to show that data are 'not available'.

LEADING COMPANIES   Number shown: **25**   Total sales ($ mil): **2,906**   Total employment (000): **17.7**

Company Name	Address				CEO Name	Phone	Co. Type	Sales ($ mil)	Empl. (000)
Stone and Webster Inc.	245 Summer St	Boston	MA	02210		617-589-5111	P	1,249	5.5
WLR Foods Inc.	PO Box 7000	Broadway	VA	22815	James Keeler	540-896-7001	P	888	7.1
Burris Refrigerated Services	P O Box 219	Milford	DE	19963	Robert Burris	302-422-4531	R	186*	1.0
United States Cold Storage Inc.	100 Dobbs Ln	Cherry Hill	NJ	08034	Timothy Bridgeman	856-354-8181	S	144*	0.8
Total Logistic Control	8300 Logistic Dr	Zeeland	MI	49464	Gary Sarner	616-772-9009	S	100	0.8
Kane is Able Inc.	P O Box 931	Scranton	PA	18501	Eugene J Kane Sr	717-343-5263	R	52	0.5
Chief Wenatchee	P O Box 1091	Wenatchee	WA	98807	Brian Birdsall	509-662-5197	R	27*	0.3
Hall's Warehouse Corp.	P O Box 378	South Plainfield	NJ	07080	William E Jayne	908-756-5037	R	25*	0.2
Bellingham Cold Storage Co.	2825 Roeder Ave	Bellingham	WA	98225	Doug Thomas	360-733-1640	R	24*	0.1
Nordic Refrigerated Services	4300 Pleasdl NE	Atlanta	GA	30340		770-448-7400	S	23*	0.1
Select Foods Inc.	PO Box 3097	Hayward	CA	94540	Edmond R Rasnick	510-785-1000	R	22*	<0.1
ACME Distribution Centers Inc.	18101 E Colfax Ave	Aurora	CO	80011	Jack L Grunwald	303-340-2100	R	21*	0.3
Central Cold Storage Inc.	P O Box 610	Castroville	CA	95012	John Thornton	831-633-4011	R	19*	0.1
Merchants Terminal Corp.	501 N Kresson St	Baltimore	MD	21224	Roy Johnson	410-342-9300	R	19*	0.1
Associated Freezers Inc.	318 Cadiz St	Dallas	TX	75207		214-426-5151	R	17	0.2
Union Ice Co.	6100 E Sheila St	Los Angeles	CA	90040	Richard L Burke	323-890-3803	R	13	<0.1
Riechmann Distribution Inc.	1110 98th Ave	Oakland	CA	94603	Mr Whitman	510-632-5064	R	13*	<0.1
Americold Logistics	10 Glennlake Pkwy	Atlanta	GA	30328	Ronald H Dykehouse	678-441-1400	R	12*	<0.1
Konoike-Pacific California Inc.	1420 Coil Ave	Wilmington	CA	90744	K Kita	310-518-1000	S	12*	<0.1
Main Street Produce Inc.	2165 W Main St	Santa Maria	CA	93454	Paul Allen	805-349-7170	R	12	<0.1
Los Angeles Cold Storage Co.	400 S Central Ave	Los Angeles	CA	90013	Larry Rauch	213-624-1831	S	10*	0.1
Barber's Poultry Inc.	PO Box 363	Broomfield	CO	80038	David R Barber	303-466-7338	R	6*	<0.1
New Orleans Cold Storage	PO Box 26308	New Orleans	LA	70186	Gary Escoffier	504-944-4400	R	5*	0.1
Rainier Cold Storage Inc.	6004 Arpt Way S	Seattle	WA	98108	Robert King	206-762-8800	R	5*	0.1
VC Glass Carpet Co.	801 Logan St	Louisville	KY	40204	Ray Glass	502-584-5324	R	2*	<0.1

Source: Ward's Business Directory of U.S. Private and Public Companies, Volumes 1 and 2, 2000. The company type code used is as follows: P - Public, R - Private, S - Subsidiary, D - Division, J - Joint Venture, A - Affiliate, G - Group, N - Company type not reported. Sales are in millions of dollars, employees are in thousands. An asterisk (*) indicates an estimated sales volume. The symbol < stands for 'less than'. Company names and addresses are truncated, in some cases, to fit into the available space.

LOCATION BY STATE AND REGIONAL CONCENTRATION

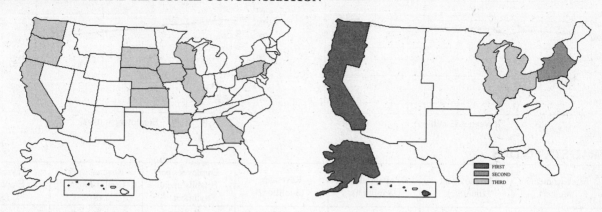

FIRST
SECOND
THIRD

INDUSTRY DATA BY STATE

State	Establishments Total (number)	% of U.S.	Employment Total (number)	% of U.S.	Per Estab.	Payroll Total ($ mil.)	Per Empl. ($)	Revenues Total ($ mil.)	% of U.S.	Per Estab. ($)
California	123	14.0	3,104	14.0	25	93.1	29,999	363.3	16.0	2,954,033
Washington	54	6.2	1,686	7.6	31	44.2	26,202	152.3	6.7	2,819,833
Pennsylvania	31	3.5	1,459	6.6	47	45.5	31,158	145.5	6.4	4,694,484
Texas	45	5.1	1,189	5.4	26	29.6	24,865	116.3	5.1	2,583,578
Illinois	23	2.6	1,264	5.7	55	34.3	27,103	115.0	5.1	4,998,783
Georgia	39	4.4	1,077	4.9	28	36.9	34,224	108.2	4.8	2,773,795
Florida	51	5.8	979	4.4	19	23.1	23,547	95.2	4.2	1,866,863
New York	43	4.9	652	2.9	15	19.0	29,124	89.3	3.9	2,076,930
New Jersey	27	3.1	883	4.0	33	28.7	32,451	88.6	3.9	3,281,333
Oregon	20	2.3	520	2.4	26	15.3	29,465	85.4	3.8	4,271,000
Wisconsin	30	3.4	727	3.3	24	18.4	25,254	84.8	3.7	2,827,600
Iowa	36	4.1	798	3.6	22	20.0	25,073	71.3	3.1	1,981,694
Arkansas	17	1.9	667	3.0	39	16.3	24,505	63.1	2.8	3,710,824
Kansas	12	1.4	414	1.9	35	13.2	31,829	58.0	2.6	4,835,750
Nebraska	19	2.2	454	2.1	24	13.1	28,797	49.7	2.2	2,616,211
Ohio	25	2.9	543	2.5	22	13.8	25,383	46.1	2.0	1,844,400
Michigan	28	3.2	363	1.6	13	9.4	25,871	39.5	1.7	1,411,214
Virginia	16	1.8	729	3.3	46	13.4	18,340	38.3	1.7	2,394,125
Missouri	12	1.4	467	2.1	39	12.1	25,859	38.3	1.7	3,191,917
Tennessee	13	1.5	367	1.7	28	13.1	35,793	35.7	1.6	2,746,769
North Carolina	19	2.2	350	1.6	18	8.0	22,823	34.9	1.5	1,837,579
Indiana	17	1.9	391	1.8	23	10.5	26,747	34.4	1.5	2,025,529
Alabama	17	1.9	356	1.6	21	7.3	20,371	28.5	1.3	1,678,529
Minnesota	23	2.6	247	1.1	11	6.8	27,510	25.6	1.1	1,110,913
Mississippi	10	1.1	306	1.4	31	5.7	18,565	20.1	0.9	2,009,500
Louisiana	10	1.1	228	1.0	23	5.9	25,899	18.6	0.8	1,857,900
Colorado	9	1.0	151	0.7	17	4.1	27,146	18.5	0.8	2,052,444
South Carolina	13	1.5	171	0.8	13	4.5	26,035	16.8	0.7	1,292,769
Utah	9	1.0	125	0.6	14	2.9	23,480	15.3	0.7	1,704,333
Arizona	8	0.9	173	0.8	22	4.5	26,029	13.0	0.6	1,621,750
South Dakota	9	1.0	101	0.5	11	1.7	17,307	8.0	0.4	892,000
Kentucky	6	0.7	77	0.3	13	3.2	42,052	7.6	0.3	1,266,833
Oklahoma	6	0.7	60	0.3	10	1.5	25,267	6.1	0.3	1,010,333
Massachusetts	20	2.3	375 *	-	-	(D)	-	(D)	-	-
Maryland	8	0.9	175 *	-	-	(D)	-	(D)	-	-

Source. 1997 Economic Census. The states are in descending order of revenues or establishments (if revenue data are missing for the majority). The symbol (D) appears when data are withheld to prevent disclosure of competitive information. States marked with (D) are sorted by number of establishments. A dash (-) indicates that the data element cannot be calculated. * indicates the midpoint of a range; 175, for example is the range 100-249. Shaded *states* on the state map indicate those states which have proportionately greater representation in the industry than would be indicated by the state's population; the ratio is based on total revenues or number of establishments. Shaded *regions* indicate where the industry is regionally most concentrated.

NAICS 493130 - FARM PRODUCT WAREHOUSING AND STORAGE*

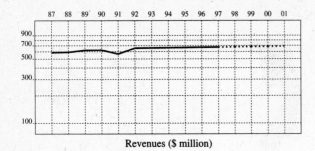

Revenues ($ million)

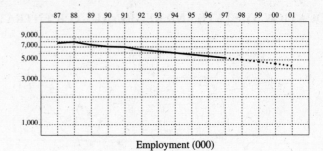

Employment (000)

GENERAL STATISTICS

Year	Establishments (number)	Employment (number)	Payroll ($ million)	Revenues ($ million)	Employees per Establishment (number)	Revenues per Establishment ($)	Payroll per Employee ($)
1987	751	7,729	131.0	586.2	10.3	780,559	16,949
1988	775	7,922	109.0	591.0	10.2	762,581	13,759
1989	721	7,372	115.0	621.0	10.2	861,304	15,600
1990	723	7,044	125.0	625.0	9.7	864,454	17,746
1991	693	6,979	116.0	566.0	10.1	816,739	16,621
1992	584	6,497	129.6	656.5	11.1	1,124,144	19,948
1993	564	6,254	127.4	659.8	11.1	1,169,100	20,369
1994	545	6,010	125.2	663.2	11.0	1,217,291	20,825
1995	525	5,767	122.9	666.5	11.0	1,269,078	21,319
1996	506	5,523	120.7	669.9	10.9	1,324,881	21,856
1997	486	5,280	118.5	673.2	10.9	1,385,185	22,443
1998	466 *p*	5,037 *p*	116.3 *p*	676.5 *p*	10.8 *p*	1,450,557 *p*	23,087 *p*
1999	447 *p*	4,793 *p*	114.1 *p*	679.9 *p*	10.7 *p*	1,521,665 *p*	23,796 *p*
2000	427 *p*	4,550 *p*	111.8 *p*	683.2 *p*	10.7 *p*	1,599,298 *p*	24,581 *p*
2001	408 *p*	4,306 *p*	109.6 *p*	686.6 *p*	10.6 *p*	1,684,396 *p*	25,455 *p*

*Sources: Economic Census of the United States, 1987, 1992 and 1997. Data for those years (years are in **bold** type) are from the 5-year censuses of the economy. Other values, unless otherwise noted, are extrapolations. Values marked with p are projections. Data are the most recent available at this level of detail.*

INDICES OF CHANGE

Year	Establishments (number)	Employment (number)	Payroll ($ million)	Revenues ($ million)	Employees per Establishment (number)	Revenues per Establishment ($)	Payroll per Employee ($)
1987	154.5	146.4	110.5	87.1	94.5	56.4	75.5
1992	120.2	123.0	109.4	97.5	101.8	81.2	88.9
1993	116.0	118.4	107.5	98.0	101.8	84.4	90.8
1994	112.1	113.8	105.7	98.5	100.9	87.9	92.8
1995	108.0	109.2	103.7	99.0	100.9	91.6	95.0
1996	104.1	104.6	101.9	99.5	100.0	95.6	97.4
1997	100.0	100.0	100.0	100.0	100.0	100.0	100.0
1998	95.9 *p*	95.4 *p*	98.1 *p*	100.5 *p*	99.1 *p*	104.7 *p*	102.9 *p*
1999	92.0 *p*	90.8 *p*	96.3 *p*	101.0 *p*	98.2 *p*	109.9 *p*	106.0 *p*
2000	87.9 *p*	86.2 *p*	94.3 *p*	101.5 *p*	98.2 *p*	115.5 *p*	109.5 *p*
2001	84.0 *p*	81.6 *p*	92.5 *p*	102.0 *p*	97.2 *p*	121.6 *p*	113.4 *p*

Sources: Same as General Statistics. The values shown reflect change from the base year, 1997. Values above 100 mean greater than 1997, values below 100 mean less than 1997, and a value of 100 in years other than 1997 means same as 1997. Indices are calculated only for Census years. Data are the most recent available at this level of detail.

SELECTED RATIOS

For 1997	Avg. of Sector	Analyzed Industry	Index	For 1997	Avg. of Sector	Analyzed Industry	Index
Employees per establishment	16	11	66	Payroll per establishment	462,554	243,827	53
Revenue per establishment	1,787,642	1,385,185	77	Payroll as % of revenue	26	18	68
Revenue per employee	108,959	127,500	117	Payroll per employee	28,193	22,443	80

Sources: Same as General Statistics. The 'Average of Sector' column represents the average for all industries in this sector. The Index shows the relationship between the Average and the Analyzed Industry. For example, 100 means that they are equal; 500 that the Analyzed Industry is five times the average; 50 means that the Analyzed Industry is half the national average. 'na' is used to show that data are 'not available'.

*Equivalent to SIC 4221.

LEADING COMPANIES Number shown: 52   Total sales ($ mil): 7,875   Total employment (000): 6.6

Company Name	Address				CEO Name	Phone	Co. Type	Sales ($ mil)	Empl. (000)
Scoular Co.	2027 Dodge St	Omaha	NE	68102	Duane A Fischer	402-342-3500	R	2,458*	0.3
Federal Compress & Warehouse	PO Box 77	Memphis	TN	38101	Larry Lively	901-524-4000	R	1,305*	1.6
Farmland Grain	10100 N Exec Hls	Kansas City	MO	64153		816-459-3300	S	1,060*	0.4
Bartlett and Co.	4800 Main St	Kansas City	MO	64112		816-753-6300	R	750	0.6
Collingwood Grain Inc.	PO Box 2150	Hutchinson	KS	67504	Lowell Downey	316-663-7121	S	586*	0.7
Farmers Cooperative Compress	P O Box 2877	Lubbock	TX	79408		806-763-9431	R	132*	0.2
Meadowland Farmers Co-op	PO Box 338	Lamberton	MN	56152		507-752-7352	R	120	<0.1
Inland-Joseph Fruit Co.	300 N Frontage Rd	Wapato	WA	98951	Susan Putnam	509-877-2126	R	111*	0.5
Prairie Land Coop.	PO Box 99	Windom	MN	56101	Randy Kruger	507-831-2527	R	100	<0.1
Sunray Coop.	P O Box 430	Sunray	TX	79086		806-948-4121	R	92*	0.1
Farmers Cooperative	PO Box 47	Dayton	IA	50530		515-547-2813	D	90*	0.1
Prairie Central Cooperative Inc.	Rte 1, Box 230	Chenoa	IL	61726		815-945-7866	R	88*	<0.1
G.F. Vaughan Tobacco Co.	PO Box 160	Lexington	KY	40588	Derek Vaughan	606-252-1733	R	77*	0.1
Attebury Grain Inc.	PO Box 2707	Amarillo	TX	79105	Sam L Attebury	806-335-1639	R	76*	0.1
Ray-Carroll County Grain	PO Box 158	Richmond	MO	64085	V Tracy	816-776-2291	R	55	0.1
Farmers Coop.	PO Box 100	Carmen	OK	73726		580-987-2234	R	50*	<0.1
Elkhart Cooperative Equity	P O Box G	Elkhart	KS	67950		316-697-2135	R	50	<0.1
Iuka Cooperative Inc.	PO Box 175	Iuka	KS	67066	Bruce Krettbiel	316-546-2231	R	46*	<0.1
Adams County Co-operative	109 E Andrews St	Monroe	IN	46772			R	41*	<0.1
Central Washington Grain	Ash & Baker Sts	Waterville	WA	98858		509-745-8551	R	40	0.4
Farmers Cooperative Association	428 Barnes Ave	Alva	OK	73717	Randy Schwerdtfeger	580-327-3854	R	37*	<0.1
Wolcott and Lincoln Inc.	4800 Main St	Kansas City	MO	64112		816-753-6750	R	37*	<0.1
Trout Inc.	P O Box 669	Chelan	WA	98816		509-682-2591	R	33*	0.2
Wallace County Cooperative	P O Box 280	Sharon Springs	KS	67758	Dean Schemm	785-852-4241	R	32*	<0.1
Minn-Kota Ag Products Inc.	P O Box 175	Breckenridge	MN	56520	George M Schuler III	218-643-8464	R	32*	<0.1
Walla Walla Grain Growers Inc.	P O Box 310	Walla Walla	WA	99362	Scott Erwin	509-525-6510	R	31*	<0.1
North Central Grain Coop.	PO Box 8	Bisbee	ND	58317	Dwayne Kaleva	701-656-3263	R	30	<0.1
Farmers Cooperative Mill Elevator	106 S Broadway	Carnegie	OK	73015		580-654-1016	R	29*	<0.1
Ottawa Cooperative Association	302 N Main St	Ottawa	KS	66067		785-242-5170	R	28*	<0.1
Carwell Elevator Company Inc.	PO Box 184	Cherry Valley	AR	72324		870-588-3381	R	24	<0.1
Farmers Co-op Elevator	P O Box 909	Dighton	KS	67839	Jay Cook	316-397-5343	R	24*	<0.1
Fasco Mills Co.	PO Box 170	Mendota	IL	61342	Curt Zimmerman	815-539-7491	R	21*	<0.1
Nehawka Farmers Coop.	PO Box 159	Nehawka	NE	68413		402-227-2715	R	20	<0.1
Alderman-Cave Feeds	PO Box 217	Winters	TX	79567	Murray Edwards	915-754-4546	R	17	<0.1
Poag Grain Inc.	PO Box 2037	Chickasha	OK	73023	Steve Poag	405-224-6350	R	15	<0.1
Blair Milling and Elevator Inc.	PO Box 437	Atchison	KS	66002	W Blair	913-367-2310	R	13*	<0.1
Emma Cooperative Elevator Co.	125 Lexington Ave	Sweet Springs	MO	65351	Rick Alexander	660-335-6355	R	12	<0.1
Haverhill Coop.	PO Box 50	Haverhill	IA	50120		515-475-3221	S	12	<0.1
Lyford Gin Association	PO Box 70	Lyford	TX	78569	Russell Klostermann	956-347-3541	R	11*	<0.1
Edmonson Wheat Growers Inc.	P O Box 32	Edmonson	TX	79032	Jack Witten	806-864-3327	R	10	<0.1
Associated Potato Growers Inc.	2001 M 6th St	Grand Forks	ND	58203		701-775-4614	R	10*	0.1
Morrisonville Farmers	PO Box 17	Morrisonville	IL	62546	Glenn Fesser	217-526-3123	R	9*	<0.1
Frontier Equity Exchange	PO Box 998	Goodland	KS	67735	Kenny Davis	785-899-3681	R	7*	<0.1
Rugby Farmers Union Elevator	105 E Dewey St	Rugby	ND	58368	Steve Fritle	701-776-5214	R	7	<0.1
ABJ Enterprises Inc.	P O Box 428	Dunn	NC	28335	Alsey B Johnson	910-892-1357	R	7*	<0.1
Farmers Association Talmage	PO Box 68	Abilene	KS	67410		785-263-1660	R	7*	<0.1
Topflight Grain Co.	P O Box 69	Cisco	IL	61830	Richard Thomas	217-669-2141	R	7*	<0.1
Bond Food Products Inc.	PO Box 18	Oconto	WI	54153	John Kelly	920-834-4433	R	6*	<0.1
Bethany Grain Company Inc.	P O Box 350	Bethany	IL	61914	Harry L Bennett	217-665-3392	R	6	<0.1
Grower Shipper Potato Co.	P O Box 432	Monte Vista	CO	81144	Kris Miner	719-852-3569	R	5*	<0.1
Hale Center Wheat Growers Inc.	PO Drawer F	Hale Center	TX	79041	JA Nivens	806-839-2426	R	5	<0.1
Hamilton Elevator Company Inc.	PO Box 177	Campus	IL	60920	Rodney W Carlson	815-567-3311	R	5*	<0.1

Source: *Ward's Business Directory of U.S. Private and Public Companies*, Volumes 1 and 2, 2000. The company type code used is as follows: P - Public, R - Private, S - Subsidiary, D - Division, J - Joint Venture, A - Affiliate, G - Group, N - Company type not reported. Sales are in millions of dollars, employees are in thousands. An asterisk (*) indicates an estimated sales volume. The symbol < stands for 'less than'. Company names and addresses are truncated, in some cases, to fit into the available space.

LOCATION BY STATE AND REGIONAL CONCENTRATION

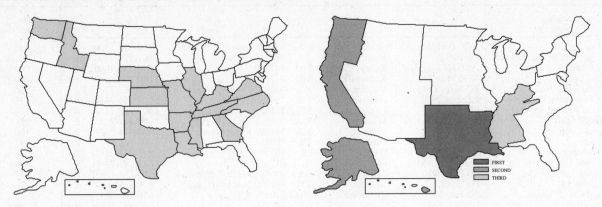

INDUSTRY DATA BY STATE

State	Establishments		Employment			Payroll		Revenues		
	Total (number)	% of U.S.	Total (number)	% of U.S.	Per Estab.	Total ($ mil.)	Per Empl. ($)	Total ($ mil.)	% of U.S.	Per Estab. ($)
Texas	72	14.8	959	18.2	13	21.6	22,533	121.1	18.0	1,682,194
California	40	8.2	514	9.7	13	13.2	25,626	73.2	10.9	1,829,350
Arkansas	37	7.6	368	7.0	10	8.6	23,348	57.5	8.5	1,553,000
Louisiana	18	3.7	421	8.0	23	8.5	20,290	54.4	8.1	3,021,944
Washington	18	3.7	299	5.7	17	8.4	28,107	45.4	6.7	2,523,944
Illinois	20	4.1	114	2.2	6	2.8	25,000	35.4	5.3	1,771,600
Mississippi	25	5.1	321	6.1	13	6.4	19,794	32.8	4.9	1,314,000
Georgia	24	4.9	281	5.3	12	5.7	20,374	29.7	4.4	1,235,917
Missouri	15	3.1	146	2.8	10	2.5	17,432	28.1	4.2	1,874,267
Tennessee	23	4.7	190	3.6	8	4.3	22,432	23.5	3.5	1,020,348
North Carolina	39	8.0	152	2.9	4	5.2	34,020	20.1	3.0	514,949
Virginia	13	2.7	165	3.1	13	5.3	31,939	19.7	2.9	1,512,769
Kentucky	13	2.7	222	4.2	17	3.0	13,387	14.9	2.2	1,147,692
Nebraska	9	1.9	54	1.0	6	1.1	20,370	13.6	2.0	1,516,000
New Jersey	6	1.2	192	3.6	32	4.3	22,573	12.9	1.9	2,142,667
Minnesota	7	1.4	35	0.7	5	1.0	28,743	10.6	1.6	1,517,857
Kansas	18	3.7	91	1.7	5	2.3	25,473	9.2	1.4	510,389
Alabama	10	2.1	169	3.2	17	2.0	11,994	7.4	1.1	743,300
Idaho	9	1.9	67	1.3	7	1.1	16,045	6.3	0.9	704,778
South Carolina	17	3.5	60	1.1	4	1.1	18,200	6.0	0.9	351,824

Source: 1997 *Economic Census*. The states are in descending order of revenues or establishments (if revenue data are missing for the majority). The symbol (D) appears when data are withheld to prevent disclosure of competitive information. States marked with (D) are sorted by number of establishments. A dash (-) indicates that the data element cannot be calculated. * indicates the midpoint of a range; 175, for example is the range 100-249. Shaded *states* on the state map indicate those states which have proportionately greater representation in the industry than would be indicated by the state's population; the ratio is based on total revenues or number of establishments. Shaded *regions* indicate where the industry is regionally most concentrated.

NAICS 493190 - WAREHOUSING AND STORAGE NEC

GENERAL STATISTICS

Year	Establishments (number)	Employment (number)	Payroll ($ million)	Revenues ($ million)	Employees per Establishment (number)	Revenues per Establishment ($)	Payroll per Employee ($)
1997	1,213	19,575	575.0	2,393.0	16.1	1,972,795	29,374

Source: Economic Census of the United States, 1997. This is a newly defined industry. Data for prior years were unavailable at the time of publication but may become available over time.

SIC INDUSTRIES RELATED TO NAICS 493190

SIC	Industry	1990	1991	1992	1993	1994	1995	1996	1997
4226	**Special Warehousing and Storage, nec***								
	Establishments (number)	1,126	1,158	1,452	1,490	1,479	1,547	1,648	1,670p
	Employment (thousands)	16.3	16.5	20.6	24.0	22.0	24.0	25.8	26.6p
	Revenues ($ million)	1,796.0	1,752.0	2,009.5	1,882.0	1,911.0	1,875.0	2,050.0	2,262.0

*Source: Economic Census of the United States, 1992, annual surveys of economic sectors conducted by the Bureau of the Census, and estimates or projections based on the 1982-1992 period; not all data are shown. 'e' marks estimates made by the editors; 'p' indicates projections based on time series. A dash (-) indicates that data for this SIC or year were not available. * Indicates that only a portion of this industry is present within the NAICS data. If no * is shown, the entire industry is contained within the NAICS data.*

INDICES OF CHANGE

Year	Establishments (number)	Employment (number)	Payroll ($ million)	Revenues ($ million)	Employees per Establishment (number)	Revenues per Establishment ($)	Payroll per Employee ($)
1997	100.0	100.0	100.0	100.0	100.0	100.0	100.0

Sources: Same as General Statistics. The values shown reflect change from the base year, 1997. Values above 100 mean greater than 1997, values below 100 mean less than 1997, and a value of 100 in years other than 1997 means same as 1997. Indices are calculated only for Census years. Data are the most recent available at this level of detail.

SELECTED RATIOS

For 1997	Avg. of Sector	Analyzed Industry	Index	For 1997	Avg. of Sector	Analyzed Industry	Index
Employees per establishment	16	16	98	Payroll per establishment	462,554	474,031	102
Revenue per establishment	1,787,642	1,972,795	110	Payroll as % of revenue	26	24	93
Revenue per employee	108,959	122,248	112	Payroll per employee	28,193	29,374	104

Sources: Same as General Statistics. The 'Average of Sector' column represents the average for all industries in this sector. The Index shows the relationship between the Average and the Analyzed Industry. For example, 100 means that they are equal; 500 that the Analyzed Industry is five times the average; 50 means that the Analyzed Industry is half the national average. 'na' is used to show that data are 'not available'.

LEADING COMPANIES
No company data available for this industry.

LOCATION BY STATE AND REGIONAL CONCENTRATION

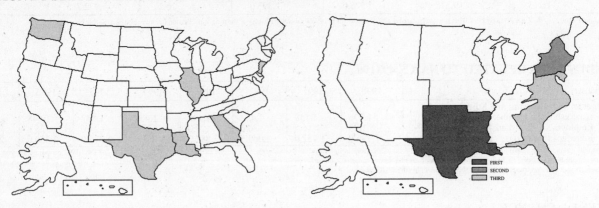

FIRST
SECOND
THIRD

INDUSTRY DATA BY STATE

State	Establishments		Employment			Payroll		Revenues		
	Total (number)	% of U.S.	Total (number)	% of U.S.	Per Estab.	Total ($ mil.)	Per Empl. ($)	Total ($ mil.)	% of U.S.	Per Estab. ($)
Texas	103	8.5	2,528	12.9	25	90.5	35,782	474.6	19.8	4,608,058
New Jersey	67	5.5	1,483	7.6	22	54.4	36,715	246.3	10.3	3,675,403
California	126	10.4	1,823	9.3	14	53.6	29,425	219.4	9.2	1,741,198
Illinois	57	4.7	1,293	6.6	23	39.3	30,405	126.0	5.3	2,209,719
New York	82	6.8	731	3.7	9	21.0	28,710	123.6	5.2	1,507,549
Louisiana	34	2.8	775	4.0	23	28.9	37,240	120.8	5.0	3,553,559
Florida	61	5.0	621	3.2	10	16.7	26,862	108.3	4.5	1,774,902
Georgia	57	4.7	931	4.8	16	24.7	26,579	93.1	3.9	1,633,088
Ohio	46	3.8	1,038	5.3	23	26.4	25,407	82.5	3.4	1,792,870
Washington	32	2.6	485	2.5	15	15.9	32,748	56.3	2.4	1,759,156
Indiana	25	2.1	369	1.9	15	9.9	26,748	36.1	1.5	1,443,880
North Carolina	46	3.8	382	2.0	8	10.3	26,861	36.0	1.5	781,978
Tennessee	26	2.1	405	2.1	16	9.6	23,681	35.4	1.5	1,362,923
Virginia	35	2.9	391	2.0	11	9.4	24,128	30.0	1.3	856,200
Kentucky	17	1.4	319	1.6	19	6.6	20,806	24.1	1.0	1,418,412
South Carolina	17	1.4	272	1.4	16	6.9	25,235	23.7	1.0	1,393,000
Minnesota	8	0.7	202	1.0	25	6.0	29,743	18.5	0.8	2,317,000
Arkansas	14	1.2	55	0.3	4	2.0	35,582	13.0	0.5	928,500
Missouri	21	1.7	110	0.6	5	3.0	27,364	10.6	0.4	504,810
Alabama	18	1.5	99	0.5	6	2.5	25,152	9.6	0.4	530,722
Oklahoma	16	1.3	64	0.3	4	1.7	26,047	8.2	0.3	509,438
Arizona	17	1.4	108	0.6	6	2.1	19,435	6.2	0.3	362,824
Iowa	7	0.6	47	0.2	7	0.9	18,468	5.7	0.2	817,857
Mississippi	11	0.9	48	0.2	4	0.8	15,625	4.3	0.2	394,545
New Mexico	6	0.5	20	0.1	3	0.4	17,850	1.9	0.1	317,833
Idaho	6	0.5	20	0.1	3	0.3	14,450	1.2	0.0	196,000
Nebraska	6	0.5	14	0.1	2	0.2	17,643	0.7	0.0	123,667
Pennsylvania	55	4.5	1,750*	-	-	(D)	-	(D)	-	-
Michigan	35	2.9	375*	-	-	(D)	-	(D)	-	-
Colorado	21	1.7	175*	-	-	(D)	-	(D)	-	-
Massachusetts	20	1.6	375*	-	-	(D)	-	(D)	-	-
Wisconsin	16	1.3	175*	-	-	(D)	-	(D)	-	-
Maryland	15	1.2	175*	-	-	(D)	-	(D)	-	-
Oregon	11	0.9	175*	-	-	(D)	-	(D)	-	-
Utah	11	0.9	60*	-	-	(D)	-	(D)	-	-
Connecticut	10	0.8	60*	-	-	(D)	-	(D)	-	-
Nevada	10	0.8	750*	-	-	(D)	-	(D)	-	-
Delaware	6	0.5	175*	-	-	(D)	-	(D)	-	-
New Hampshire	6	0.5	60*	-	-	(D)	-	(D)	-	-

Source: 1997 *Economic Census.* The states are in descending order of revenues or establishments (if revenue data are missing for the majority). The symbol (D) appears when data are withheld to prevent disclosure of competitive information. States marked with (D) are sorted by number of establishments. A dash (-) indicates that the data element cannot be calculated. * indicates the midpoint of a range; 175, for example is the range 100-249. Shaded *states* on the state map indicate those states which have proportionately greater representation in the industry than would be indicated by the state's population; the ratio is based on total revenues or number of establishments. Shaded *regions* indicate where the industry is regionally most concentrated.

Appendix I

AGRICULTURAL DATA FOR STATES

ALABAMA

GENERAL STATISTICS FOR ALABAMA

Item	1987 Value	1987 % of U.S.	1992 Value	1992 % of U.S.	1997 Value	1997 % of U.S.	Percent change 1987-1992	Percent change 1992-1997
Farms (number)	43,318	2.1	37,905	2.0	41,384	2.2	-12.5	9.2
Land in farms (acres)	9,145,753	0.9	8,450,823	0.9	8,704,385	0.9	-7.6	3.0
Average size of farm (acres)	211	45.7	223	45.4	210	43.1	5.7	-5.8
Median size of farm (acres)	NA	-	NA	-	81	67.5	-	-
Market value of land and buildings:								
Average per farm (dollars)	168,161	58.1	220,265	61.7	298,244	66.3	31.0	35.4
Average per acre (dollars)	800	127.6	1,000	137.6	1,442	154.6	25.0	44.2
Market value of machinery/equipment -								
average per farm (dollars)	25,831	62.7	30,354	62.5	35,914	62.3	17.5	18.3
Farms by size:								
1 to 9 acres	2,602	1.4	1,902	1.1	2,141	1.4	-26.9	12.6
10 to 49 acres	12,356	3.0	10,165	2.6	11,854	2.9	-17.7	16.6
50 to 179 acres	16,514	2.6	14,929	2.6	16,015	2.7	-9.6	7.3
180 to 499 acres	7,776	1.6	7,162	1.7	7,561	1.9	-7.9	5.6
500 to 999 acres	2,469	1.2	2,244	1.2	2,277	1.3	-9.1	1.5
1,000 acres or more	1,601	0.9	1,503	0.9	1,536	0.9	-6.1	2.2
Total cropland								
Farms	37,148	2.0	32,327	1.9	34,407	2.1	-13.0	6.4
Acres	4,496,607	1.0	4,237,057	1.0	4,197,670	1.0	-5.8	-0.9
Harvested cropland (farms)	28,509	1.7	24,780	1.7	24,819	1.8	-13.1	0.2
Harvested cropland (acres)	2,231,623	0.8	2,104,064	0.7	2,077,139	0.7	-5.7	-1.3
Irrigated land (farms)	1,344	0.5	1,380	0.5	1,301	0.5	2.7	-5.7
Irrigated land (acres)	84,054	0.2	82,015	0.2	76,871	0.1	-2.4	-6.3
Market value of agricultural products sold:								
Total sales ($1,000)	1,908,303	1.4	2,369,179	1.5	3,098,989	1.6	24.2	30.8
Average per farm (dollars)	44,053	67.6	62,503	74.0	74,884	72.7	41.9	19.8
Agricultural products only ($1,000)	497,992	0.8	649,110	0.9	632,978	0.6	30.3	-2.5
Livestock, poultry, and products ($1,000)	1,410,311	1.8	1,720,070	2.0	2,466,010	2.5	22.0	43.4
Farms by value of sales:								
Less than $2,500	15,082	3.1	11,663	2.8	15,286	3.1	-22.7	31.1
$2,500 to $4,999	7,726	2.9	6,506	2.8	6,940	3.0	-15.8	6.7
$5,000 to $9,999	6,534	2.4	5,936	2.4	6,279	2.6	-9.2	5.8
$10,000 to $24,999	5,210	1.6	5,076	1.7	4,985	1.8	-2.6	-1.8
$25,000 to $49,999	2,324	1.1	2,178	1.1	1,842	1.1	-6.3	-15.4
$50,000 to $99,999	1,956	0.9	1,661	0.9	1,358	0.9	-15.1	-18.2
$100,000 or more	4,486	1.5	4,885	1.5	4,694	1.4	8.9	-3.9
Total farm production expenses ($1,000)	1,610,833	1.5	1,930,063	1.5	2,509,917	1.7	19.8	30.0
Average expenses per farm (dollars)	37,190	71.8	50,912	74.9	60,661	77.0	36.9	19.1
Net cash return for the farm unit:								
Number of farms	43,316	2.1	37,910	2.0	41,377	2.2	-12.5	9.1
Value ($1000)	223,741	0.8	381,882	1.3	490,081	1.2	70.7	28.3
Average per farm (dollars)	5,165	40.8	10,073	63.7	11,844	53.2	95.0	17.6
Operators by principal occupation:								
Farming	16,398	1.4	15,712	1.5	15,568	1.6	-4.2	-0.9
Other	26,920	2.8	22,193	2.5	25,816	2.7	-17.6	16.3
Operators by days worked off farm:								
Any	26,899	2.4	21,921	2.2	25,259	2.4	-18.5	15.2
200 days or more	20,154	2.7	16,343	2.5	18,677	2.6	-18.9	14.3

Source: 1997 Census of Agriculture, U.S. Department of Agriculture, National Agricultural Statistics Service. NA stands for "not available." (D) is shown when data are withheld to prevent disclosure of competitive information. A dash (-) is shown where no data were reported. The market value of land and buildings, and of machinery and equipment, is an estimated amount. Net cash return for the farm unit includes only returns from agricultural activities.

LIVESTOCK STATISTICS FOR ALABAMA

Item	1987 Value	1987 % of U.S.	1992 Value	1992 % of U.S.	1997 Value	1997 % of U.S.	Percent change 1987-1992	Percent change 1992-1997
Cattle and calves								
Number of farms	29,844	2.5	26,360	2.5	28,450	2.7	-11.7	7.9
Number of animals	1,450,416	1.5	1,453,137	1.5	1,530,566	1.5	0.2	5.3
Beef cows (farms)	25,879	3.1	23,925	3.0	25,384	3.2	-7.6	6.1
Beef cows (number)	748,002	2.4	771,151	2.4	832,298	2.4	3.1	7.9
Milk cows (farms)	1,336	0.7	995	0.6	608	0.5	-25.5	-38.9
Milk cows (number)	45,994	0.5	45,454	0.5	27,848	0.3	-1.2	-38.7
Cattle and calves sold (farms)	29,320	2.5	25,532	2.5	27,705	2.7	-12.9	8.5
Cattle and calves sold (number)	831,908	1.1	676,215	1.0	767,806	1.0	-18.7	13.5
Hogs and pigs								
Number of farms	3,585	1.5	1,880	1.0	932	0.8	-47.6	-50.4
Number of animals	353,062	0.7	307,672	0.5	183,811	0.3	-12.9	-40.3
Hogs and pigs sold (farms)	3,220	1.3	1,715	0.9	750	0.7	-46.7	-56.3
Hogs and pigs sold (number)	648,262	0.7	571,680	0.5	380,853	0.3	-11.8	-33.4
Sheep and lambs								
Number of farms	214	0.2	320	0.4	294	0.4	49.5	-8.1
Number of animals	5,334	0.0	11,016	0.1	8,173	0.1	106.5	-25.8
Layers and pullets 13 weeks old and older								
Number of farms	2,785	1.9	1,643	1.9	1,250	1.7	-41.0	-23.9
Number of birds	15,107,005	4.0	14,493,030	4.1	13,432,845	3.7	-4.1	-7.3
Broilers and other meat-type chickens sold								
Number of farms	2,557	9.2	2,460	10.3	2,477	10.3	-3.8	0.7
Number of birds sold	564,583,477	8.4	737,608,903	13.6	871,123,702	12.9	30.6	18.1

Source: *1997 Census of Agriculture*, U.S. Department of Agriculture, National Agricultural Statistics Service. NA stands for "not available." (D) is shown when data are withheld to prevent disclosure of competitive information. A dash (-) is shown where no data were reported.

CROP STATISTICS FOR ALABAMA

Item	1987 Value	1987 % of U.S.	1992 Value	1992 % of U.S.	1997 Value	1997 % of U.S.	Percent change 1987-1992	Percent change 1992-1997
Corn for grain or seed								
Number of farms	7,413	1.2	5,305	1.1	3,687	0.9	-28.4	-30.5
Number of acres	234,669	0.4	281,053	0.4	230,484	0.3	19.8	-18.0
Number of bushels	15,623,257	-	24,941,228	0.3	19,735,218	0.2	59.6	-20.9
Corn for silage or green chop								
Number of farms	-	-	-	-	-	-	-	-
Number of acres	-	-	-	-	-	-	-	-
Weight in tons, green	-	-	-	-	-	-	-	-
Sorghum for grain or seed								
Number of farms	-	-	-	-	-	-	-	-
Number of acres	-	-	-	-	-	-	-	-
Number of bushels	-	-	-	-	-	-	-	-
Wheat for grain								
Number of farms	1,914	0.5	870	0.3	732	0.3	-54.5	-15.9
Number of acres	156,466	0.3	86,071	0.1	82,440	0.1	-45.0	-4.2
Number of bushels	4,903,608	0.3	3,461,454	0.2	3,326,421	0.2	-29.4	-3.9
Barley for grain								
Number of farms	-	-	-	-	-	-	-	-
Number of acres	-	-	-	-	-	-	-	-
Number of bushels	-	-	-	-	-	-	-	-
Oats for grain								
Number of farms	-	-	-	-	-	-	-	-
Number of acres	-	-	-	-	-	-	-	-
Number of bushels	-	-	-	-	-	-	-	-
Rice								
Number of farms	-	-	-	-	-	-	-	-
Number of acres	-	-	-	-	-	-	-	-
Weight in hundredweight	-	-	-	-	-	-	-	-
Sunflower seed								
Number of farms	-	-	-	-	-	-	-	-
Number of acres	-	-	-	-	-	-	-	-
Weight in pounds	-	-	-	-	-	-	-	-
Cotton								
Number of farms	1,820	4.2	1,469	4.2	1,470	4.7	-19.3	0.1
Number of acres	346,013	3.5	431,665	3.9	433,160	3.3	24.8	0.3
Number of bales	380,936	2.9	601,506	3.9	523,864	2.9	57.9	-12.9

Continued.

CROP STATISTICS FOR ALABAMA - Continued

Item	1987 Value	1987 % of U.S.	1992 Value	1992 % of U.S.	1997 Value	1997 % of U.S.	Percent change 1987-1992	Percent change 1992-1997
Tobacco								
Number of farms	-	-	-	-	-	-	-	-
Number of acres	-	-	-	-	-	-	-	-
Weight in pounds	-	-	-	-	-	-	-	-
Soybeans for beans								
Number of farms	4,124	0.9	2,065	0.5	1,889	0.5	-49.9	-8.5
Number of acres	575,370	1.0	305,713	0.5	316,019	0.5	-46.9	3.4
Number of bushels	11,633,904	0.6	8,871,365	0.4	7,867,880	0.3	-23.7	-11.3
Dry edible beans, excluding dry limas								
Number of farms	-	-	-	-	-	-	-	-
Number of acres	-	-	-	-	-	-	-	-
Weight in hundredweight	-	-	-	-	-	-	-	-
Potatoes, excluding sweetpotatoes								
Number of farms	-	-	-	-	-	-	-	-
Number of acres	-	-	-	-	-	-	-	-
Weight in hundredweight	-	-	-	-	-	-	-	-
Sugar beets for sugar								
Number of farms	-	-	-	-	-	-	-	-
Number of acres	-	-	-	-	-	-	-	-
Weight in tons	-	-	-	-	-	-	-	-
Sugarcane for sugar								
Number of farms	-	-	-	-	-	-	-	-
Number of acres	-	-	-	-	-	-	-	-
Weight in tons	-	-	-	-	-	-	-	-
Pineapples harvested								
Number of farms	-	-	-	-	-	-	-	-
Number of acres	-	-	-	-	-	-	-	-
Weight in tons	-	-	-	-	-	-	-	-
Peanuts for nuts								
Number of farms	2,655	-	2,254	-	1,510	-	-15.1	-33.0
Number of acres	207,963	-	237,516	-	181,393	-	14.2	-23.6
Weight in pounds	429,000,017	-	586,013,571	-	356,492,286	-	36.6	-39.2
Hay - all types, including alfalfa								
Number of farms	19,061	1.9	17,480	1.9	19,085	2.1	-8.3	9.2
Number of acres	647,843	1.1	678,726	1.2	778,602	1.3	4.8	14.7
Weight in tons, dry	1,186,655	0.9	1,409,044	1.1	1,750,870	1.3	18.7	24.3
Vegetables harvested for sale								
Number of farms	-	-	-	-	-	-	-	-
Number of acres	-	-	-	-	-	-	-	-
Land in orchards								
Number of farms	-	-	-	-	-	-	-	-
Number of acres	-	-	-	-	-	-	-	-

Source: *1997 Census of Agriculture*, U.S. Department of Agriculture, National Agricultural Statistics Service. NA stands for "not available." (D) is shown when data are withheld to prevent disclosure of competitive information. A dash (-) is shown where no data were reported. Not all states report growing all crops, but all crop categories in the census are shown for every state. The data series used for this presentation did not report U.S. totals for a number of categories; for that reason, the "% of U.S." column is sometimes blank.

ALASKA

GENERAL STATISTICS FOR ALASKA

Item	1987 Value	1987 % of U.S.	1992 Value	1992 % of U.S.	1997 Value	1997 % of U.S.	Percent change 1987-1992	Percent change 1992-1997
Farms (number)	574	0.0	512	0.0	548	0.0	-10.8	7.0
Land in farms (acres)	1,026,732	0.1	923,037	0.1	881,045	0.1	-10.1	-4.5
Average size of farm (acres)	1,789	387.2	1,803	367.2	1,608	330.2	0.8	-10.8
Median size of farm (acres)	NA	-	NA	-	107	89.2	-	-
Market value of land and buildings:								
Average per farm (dollars)	553,000	191.1	486,550	136.3	486,827	108.2	-12.0	0.1
Average per acre (dollars)	309	49.3	270	37.1	303	32.5	-12.6	12.2
Market value of machinery/equipment - average per farm (dollars)	38,901	94.4	43,795	90.1	53,003	91.9	12.6	21.0
Farms by size:								
1 to 9 acres	96	0.1	76	0.0	96	0.1	-20.8	26.3
10 to 49 acres	113	0.0	93	0.0	98	0.0	-17.7	5.4
50 to 179 acres	172	0.0	160	0.0	171	0.0	-7.0	6.9
180 to 499 acres	97	0.0	85	0.0	93	0.0	-12.4	9.4
500 to 999 acres	24	0.0	41	0.0	33	0.0	70.8	-19.5
1,000 acres or more	72	0.0	57	0.0	57	0.0	-20.8	-
Total cropland								
Farms	454	0.0	419	0.0	434	0.0	-7.7	3.6
Acres	66,305	0.0	84,061	0.0	94,810	0.0	26.8	12.8
Harvested cropland (farms)	397	0.0	352	0.0	381	0.0	-11.3	8.2
Harvested cropland (acres)	28,949	0.0	22,699	0.0	34,227	0.0	-21.6	50.8
Irrigated land (farms)	74	0.0	93	0.0	114	0.0	25.7	22.6
Irrigated land (acres)	1,826	0.0	1,566	0.0	2,667	0.0	-14.2	70.3
Market value of agricultural products sold:								
Total sales ($1,000)	17,972	0.0	15,351	0.0	24,650	0.0	-14.6	60.6
Average per farm (dollars)	31,309	48.0	29,982	35.5	44,982	43.7	-4.2	50.0
Agricultural products only ($1,000)	10,768	0.0	11,228	0.0	15,968	0.0	4.3	42.2
Livestock, poultry, and products ($1,000)	7,204	0.0	4,123	0.0	8,682	0.0	-42.8	110.6
Farms by value of sales:								
Less than $2,500	242	0.0	211	0.0	187	0.0	-12.8	-11.4
$2,500 to $4,999	92	0.0	75	0.0	75	0.0	-18.5	-
$5,000 to $9,999	73	0.0	67	0.0	66	0.0	-8.2	-1.5
$10,000 to $24,999	65	0.0	70	0.0	99	0.0	7.7	41.4
$25,000 to $49,999	38	0.0	30	0.0	44	0.0	-21.1	46.7
$50,000 to $99,999	25	0.0	25	0.0	30	0.0	-	20.0
$100,000 or more	39	0.0	34	0.0	47	0.0	-12.8	38.2
Total farm production expenses ($1,000)	15,774	0.0	16,308	0.0	21,821	0.0	3.4	33.8
Average expenses per farm (dollars)	27,480	53.1	31,851	46.9	39,820	50.6	15.9	25.0
Net cash return for the farm unit:								
Number of farms	574	0.0	512	0.0	548	0.0	-10.8	7.0
Value ($1000)	2,198	0.0	-	-	2,829	0.0	-	-
Average per farm (dollars)	3,829	30.2	-	-	5,162	23.2	-	-
Operators by principal occupation:								
Farming	248	0.0	273	0.0	306	0.0	10.1	12.1
Other	326	0.0	239	0.0	242	0.0	-26.7	1.3
Operators by days worked off farm:								
Any	369	0.0	308	0.0	314	0.0	-16.5	1.9
200 days or more	182	0.0	145	0.0	145	0.0	-20.3	-

Source: *1997 Census of Agriculture*, U.S. Department of Agriculture, National Agricultural Statistics Service. NA stands for "not available." (D) is shown when data are withheld to prevent disclosure of competitive information. A dash (-) is shown where no data were reported. The market value of land and buildings, and of machinery and equipment, is an estimated amount. Net cash return for the farm unit includes only returns from agricultural activities.

LIVESTOCK STATISTICS FOR ALASKA

Item	1987 Value	1987 % of U.S.	1992 Value	1992 % of U.S.	1997 Value	1997 % of U.S.	Percent change 1987-1992	Percent change 1992-1997
Cattle and calves								
Number of farms	170	0.0	132	0.0	120	0.0	-22.4	-9.1
Number of animals	9,433	0.0	8,002	0.0	11,111	0.0	-15.2	38.9
Beef cows (farms)	112	0.0	97	0.0	84	0.0	-13.4	-13.4
Beef cows (number)	3,199	0.0	3,224	0.0	3,694	0.0	0.8	14.6
Milk cows (farms)	50	0.0	34	0.0	30	0.0	-32.0	-11.8
Milk cows (number)	1,713	0.0	715	0.0	1,101	0.0	-58.3	54.0
Cattle and calves sold (farms)	134	0.0	115	0.0	92	0.0	-14.2	-20.0
Cattle and calves sold (number)	2,538	0.0	1,672	0.0	2,847	0.0	-34.1	70.3
Hogs and pigs								
Number of farms	45	0.0	45	0.0	53	0.0	-	17.8
Number of animals	573	0.0	2,135	0.0	2,112	0.0	272.6	-1.1
Hogs and pigs sold (farms)	37	0.0	40	0.0	33	0.0	8.1	-17.5
Hogs and pigs sold (number)	1,100	0.0	2,800	0.0	2,532	0.0	154.5	-9.6
Sheep and lambs								
Number of farms	27	0.0	27	0.0	40	0.1	-	48.1
Number of animals	2,394	0.0	2,233	0.0	1,605	0.0	-6.7	-28.1
Layers and pullets 13 weeks old and older								
Number of farms	82	0.1	51	0.1	63	0.1	-37.8	23.5
Number of birds	2,385	0.0	1,974	0.0	2,138	0.0	-17.2	8.3
Broilers and other meat-type chickens sold								
Number of farms	12	0.0	7	0.0	9	0.0	-41.7	28.6
Number of birds sold	4,141	0.0	(D)	-	1,860	0.0	-	-

Source: *1997 Census of Agriculture*, U.S. Department of Agriculture, National Agricultural Statistics Service. NA stands for "not available." (D) is shown when data are withheld to prevent disclosure of competitive information. A dash (-) is shown where no data were reported.

CROP STATISTICS FOR ALASKA

Item	1987 Value	1987 % of U.S.	1992 Value	1992 % of U.S.	1997 Value	1997 % of U.S.	Percent change 1987-1992	Percent change 1992-1997
Corn for grain or seed								
Number of farms	-	-	-	-	-	-	-	-
Number of acres	-	-	-	-	-	-	-	-
Number of bushels	-	-	-	-	-	-	-	-
Corn for silage or green chop								
Number of farms	-	-	-	-	-	-	-	-
Number of acres	-	-	-	-	-	-	-	-
Weight in tons, green	-	-	-	-	-	-	-	-
Sorghum for grain or seed								
Number of farms	-	-	-	-	-	-	-	-
Number of acres	-	-	-	-	-	-	-	-
Number of bushels	-	-	-	-	-	-	-	-
Wheat for grain								
Number of farms	-	-	-	-	-	-	-	-
Number of acres	-	-	-	-	-	-	-	-
Number of bushels	-	-	-	-	-	-	-	-
Barley for grain								
Number of farms	35	-	22	-	31	-	-37.1	40.9
Number of acres	5,666	-	2,676	-	7,106	-	-52.8	165.5
Number of bushels	235,417	-	136,228	-	164,015	-	-42.1	20.4
Oats for grain								
Number of farms	21	-	12	-	22	-	-42.9	83.3
Number of acres	749	-	547	-	1,463	-	-27.0	167.5
Number of bushels	44,463	-	25,944	-	64,140	-	-41.7	147.2
Rice								
Number of farms	-	-	-	-	-	-	-	-
Number of acres	-	-	-	-	-	-	-	-
Weight in hundredweight	-	-	-	-	-	-	-	-
Sunflower seed								
Number of farms	-	-	-	-	-	-	-	-
Number of acres	-	-	-	-	-	-	-	-
Weight in pounds	-	-	-	-	-	-	-	-
Cotton								
Number of farms	-	-	-	-	-	-	-	-
Number of acres	-	-	-	-	-	-	-	-
Number of bales	-	-	-	-	-	-	-	-

Continued.

CROP STATISTICS FOR ALASKA - Continued

Item	1987		1992		1997		Percent change	
	Value	% of U.S.	Value	% of U.S.	Value	% of U.S.	1987-1992	1992-1997
Tobacco								
Number of farms	-	-	-	-	-	-	-	-
Number of acres	-	-	-	-	-	-	-	-
Weight in pounds	-	-	-	-	-	-	-	-
Soybeans for beans								
Number of farms	-	-	-	-	-	-	-	-
Number of acres	-	-	-	-	-	-	-	-
Number of bushels	-	-	-	-	-	-	-	-
Dry edible beans, excluding dry limas								
Number of farms	-	-	-	-	-	-	-	-
Number of acres	-	-	-	-	-	-	-	-
Weight in hundredweight	-	-	-	-	-	-	-	-
Potatoes, excluding sweetpotatoes								
Number of farms	54	-	56	-	63	-	3.7	12.5
Number of acres	743	-	629	-	814	-	-15.3	29.4
Weight in hundredweight	145,635	-	127,559	-	159,056	-	-12.4	24.7
Sugar beets for sugar								
Number of farms	-	-	-	-	-	-	-	-
Number of acres	-	-	-	-	-	-	-	-
Weight in tons	-	-	-	-	-	-	-	-
Sugarcane for sugar								
Number of farms	-	-	-	-	-	-	-	-
Number of acres	-	-	-	-	-	-	-	-
Weight in tons	-	-	-	-	-	-	-	-
Pineapples harvested								
Number of farms	-	-	-	-	-	-	-	-
Number of acres	-	-	-	-	-	-	-	-
Weight in tons	-	-	-	-	-	-	-	-
Peanuts for nuts								
Number of farms	-	-	-	-	-	-	-	-
Number of acres	-	-	-	-	-	-	-	-
Weight in pounds	-	-	-	-	-	-	-	-
Hay - all types, including alfalfa								
Number of farms	290	0.0	230	0.0	267	0.0	-20.7	16.1
Number of acres	21,254	0.0	(D)	-	24,023	0.0	-	-
Weight in tons, dry	28,615	0.0	23,510	0.0	28,664	0.0	-17.8	21.9
Vegetables harvested for sale								
Number of farms	46	0.1	54	0.1	48	0.1	17.4	-11.1
Number of acres	347	0.0	262	0.0	315	0.0	-24.5	20.2
Land in orchards								
Number of farms	-	-	-	-	-	-	-	-
Number of acres	-	-	-	-	-	-	-	-

Source: 1997 Census of Agriculture, U.S. Department of Agriculture, National Agricultural Statistics Service. NA stands for "not available." (D) is shown when data are withheld to prevent disclosure of competitive information. A dash (-) is shown where no data were reported. Not all states report growing all crops, but all crop categories in the census are shown for every state. The data series used for this presentation did not report U.S. totals for a number of categories; for that reason, the "% of U.S." column is sometimes blank.

ARIZONA

GENERAL STATISTICS FOR ARIZONA

Item	1987 Value	1987 % of U.S.	1992 Value	1992 % of U.S.	1997 Value	1997 % of U.S.	Percent change 1987-1992	Percent change 1992-1997
Farms (number)	7,669	0.4	6,773	0.4	6,135	0.3	-11.7	-9.4
Land in farms (acres)	36,287,794	3.8	35,037,618	3.7	26,866,722	2.9	-3.4	-23.3
Average size of farm (acres)	4,732	1,024.2	5,173	1,053.6	4,379	899.2	9.3	-15.3
Median size of farm (acres)	NA	-	NA	-	80	66.7	-	-
Market value of land and buildings:								
Average per farm (dollars)	1,317,765	455.4	1,621,530	454.1	1,689,258	375.6	23.1	4.2
Average per acre (dollars)	279	44.5	316	43.5	388	41.6	13.3	22.8
Market value of machinery/equipment -								
average per farm (dollars)	55,702	135.1	59,607	122.6	70,817	122.8	7.0	18.8
Farms by size:								
1 to 9 acres	2,158	1.2	1,678	1.0	1,444	0.9	-22.2	-13.9
10 to 49 acres	1,510	0.4	1,418	0.4	1,303	0.3	-6.1	-8.1
50 to 179 acres	1,133	0.2	1,048	0.2	1,008	0.2	-7.5	-3.8
180 to 499 acres	910	0.2	741	0.2	717	0.2	-18.6	-3.2
500 to 999 acres	678	0.3	613	0.3	581	0.3	-9.6	-5.2
1,000 acres or more	1,280	0.8	1,275	0.7	1,082	0.6	-0.4	-15.1
Total cropland								
Farms	4,840	0.3	4,356	0.3	3,711	0.2	-10.0	-14.8
Acres	1,453,852	0.3	1,344,091	0.3	1,277,169	0.3	-7.5	-5.0
Harvested cropland (farms)	3,646	0.2	3,323	0.2	2,765	0.2	-8.9	-16.8
Harvested cropland (acres)	865,817	0.3	911,355	0.3	969,602	0.3	5.3	6.4
Irrigated land (farms)	4,241	1.5	3,965	1.4	3,426	1.2	-6.5	-13.6
Irrigated land (acres)	913,841	2.0	956,454	1.9	1,013,902	1.8	4.7	6.0
Market value of agricultural products sold:								
Total sales ($1,000)	1,628,544	1.2	1,515,384	0.9	1,903,408	1.0	-6.9	25.6
Average per farm (dollars)	212,354	325.9	223,739	264.9	310,254	301.3	5.4	38.7
Agricultural products only ($1,000)	896,681	1.5	899,242	1.2	1,222,891	1.2	0.3	36.0
Livestock, poultry, and products ($1,000)	731,863	0.9	616,141	0.7	680,517	0.7	-15.8	10.4
Farms by value of sales:								
Less than $2,500	2,494	0.5	2,241	0.5	1,918	0.4	-10.1	-14.4
$2,500 to $4,999	820	0.3	695	0.3	655	0.3	-15.2	-5.8
$5,000 to $9,999	775	0.3	648	0.3	620	0.3	-16.4	-4.3
$10,000 to $24,999	757	0.2	779	0.3	765	0.3	2.9	-1.8
$25,000 to $49,999	583	0.3	485	0.2	496	0.3	-16.8	2.3
$50,000 to $99,999	533	0.2	462	0.2	333	0.2	-13.3	-27.9
$100,000 or more	1,707	0.6	1,463	0.4	1,348	0.4	-14.3	-7.9
Total farm production expenses ($1,000)	1,301,666	1.2	1,239,020	0.9	1,479,713	1.0	-4.8	19.4
Average expenses per farm (dollars)	169,642	327.5	182,908	269.3	241,271	306.3	7.8	31.9
Net cash return for the farm unit:								
Number of farms	7,673	0.4	6,774	0.4	6,133	0.3	-11.7	-9.5
Value ($1000)	306,975	1.2	247,273	0.8	417,135	1.0	-19.4	68.7
Average per farm (dollars)	40,007	316.0	36,503	231.0	68,015	305.5	-8.8	86.3
Operators by principal occupation:								
Farming	3,782	0.3	3,613	0.3	3,250	0.3	-4.5	-10.0
Other	3,887	0.4	3,160	0.4	2,885	0.3	-18.7	-8.7
Operators by days worked off farm:								
Any	4,423	0.4	3,583	0.4	3,223	0.3	-19.0	-10.0
200 days or more	2,997	0.4	2,382	0.4	2,068	0.3	-20.5	-13.2

Source: 1997 Census of Agriculture, U.S. Department of Agriculture, National Agricultural Statistics Service. NA stands for "not available." (D) is shown when data are withheld to prevent disclosure of competitive information. A dash (-) is shown where no data were reported. The market value of land and buildings, and of machinery and equipment, is an estimated amount. Net cash return for the farm unit includes only returns from agricultural activities.

LIVESTOCK STATISTICS FOR ARIZONA

Item	1987 Value	1987 % of U.S.	1992 Value	1992 % of U.S.	1997 Value	1997 % of U.S.	Percent change 1987-1992	Percent change 1992-1997
Cattle and calves								
Number of farms	3,521	0.3	3,064	0.3	2,881	0.3	-13.0	-6.0
Number of animals	1,110,912	1.2	928,783	1.0	822,273	0.8	-16.4	-11.5
Beef cows (farms)	2,497	0.3	2,288	0.3	2,164	0.3	-8.4	-5.4
Beef cows (number)	334,851	1.1	292,848	0.9	263,878	0.8	-12.5	-9.9
Milk cows (farms)	476	0.2	305	0.2	247	0.2	-35.9	-19.0
Milk cows (number)	86,280	0.9	88,582	0.9	123,371	1.4	2.7	39.3
Cattle and calves sold (farms)	3,302	0.3	2,777	0.3	2,639	0.3	-15.9	-5.0
Cattle and calves sold (number)	1,009,492	1.4	744,147	1.1	688,560	0.9	-26.3	-7.5
Hogs and pigs								
Number of farms	331	0.1	281	0.1	206	0.2	-15.1	-26.7
Number of animals	135,414	0.3	83,262	0.1	141,112	0.2	-38.5	69.5
Hogs and pigs sold (farms)	242	0.1	181	0.1	125	0.1	-25.2	-30.9
Hogs and pigs sold (number)	237,623	0.2	150,140	0.1	200,790	0.1	-36.8	33.7
Sheep and lambs								
Number of farms	456	0.5	427	0.5	270	0.4	-6.4	-36.8
Number of animals	301,279	2.7	247,068	2.3	140,602	1.8	-18.0	-43.1
Layers and pullets 13 weeks old and older								
Number of farms	741	0.5	513	0.6	383	0.5	-30.8	-25.3
Number of birds	331,462	0.1	391,979	0.1	(D)	-	18.3	-
Broilers and other meat-type chickens sold								
Number of farms	23	0.1	15	0.1	20	0.1	-34.8	33.3
Number of birds sold	(D)	-	(D)	-	(D)	-	-	-

Source: 1997 Census of Agriculture, U.S. Department of Agriculture, National Agricultural Statistics Service. NA stands for "not available." (D) is shown when data are withheld to prevent disclosure of competitive information. A dash (-) is shown where no data were reported.

CROP STATISTICS FOR ARIZONA

Item	1987 Value	1987 % of U.S.	1992 Value	1992 % of U.S.	1997 Value	1997 % of U.S.	Percent change 1987-1992	Percent change 1992-1997
Corn for grain or seed								
Number of farms	166	0.0	108	0.0	140	0.0	-34.9	29.6
Number of acres	12,794	0.0	15,547	0.0	40,091	0.1	21.5	157.9
Number of bushels	1,530,568	-	2,104,384	0.0	6,498,484	0.1	37.5	208.8
Corn for silage or green chop								
Number of farms	-	-	-	-	-	-	-	-
Number of acres	-	-	-	-	-	-	-	-
Weight in tons, green	-	-	-	-	-	-	-	-
Sorghum for grain or seed								
Number of farms	-	-	-	-	-	-	-	-
Number of acres	-	-	-	-	-	-	-	-
Number of bushels	-	-	-	-	-	-	-	-
Wheat for grain								
Number of farms	443	0.1	310	0.1	304	0.1	-30.0	-1.9
Number of acres	97,407	0.2	80,533	0.1	103,121	0.2	-17.3	28.0
Number of bushels	7,991,708	0.4	6,823,397	0.3	9,114,709	0.4	-14.6	33.6
Barley for grain								
Number of farms	168	-	165	-	315	-	-1.8	90.9
Number of acres	14,654	-	19,984	-	66,215	-	36.4	231.3
Number of bushels	1,365,067	-	1,952,678	-	6,660,644	-	43.0	241.1
Oats for grain								
Number of farms	-	-	-	-	-	-	-	-
Number of acres	-	-	-	-	-	-	-	-
Number of bushels	-	-	-	-	-	-	-	-
Rice								
Number of farms	-	-	-	-	-	-	-	-
Number of acres	-	-	-	-	-	-	-	-
Weight in hundredweight	-	-	-	-	-	-	-	-
Sunflower seed								
Number of farms	-	-	-	-	-	-	-	-
Number of acres	-	-	-	-	-	-	-	-
Weight in pounds	-	-	-	-	-	-	-	-
Cotton								
Number of farms	1,199	2.8	887	2.5	643	2.0	-26.0	-27.5
Number of acres	381,733	3.9	428,637	3.9	331,699	2.5	12.3	-22.6
Number of bales	1,005,493	7.6	895,992	5.8	837,643	4.7	-10.9	-6.5

Continued.

CROP STATISTICS FOR ARIZONA - Continued

Item	1987		1992		1997		Percent change	
	Value	% of U.S.	Value	% of U.S.	Value	% of U.S.	1987-1992	1992-1997
Tobacco								
Number of farms	-	-	-	-	-	-	-	-
Number of acres	-	-	-	-	-	-	-	-
Weight in pounds	-	-	-	-	-	-	-	-
Soybeans for beans								
Number of farms	-	-	-	-	-	-	-	-
Number of acres	-	-	-	-	-	-	-	-
Number of bushels	-	-	-	-	-	-	-	-
Dry edible beans, excluding dry limas								
Number of farms	-	-	-	-	-	-	-	-
Number of acres	-	-	-	-	-	-	-	-
Weight in hundredweight	-	-	-	-	-	-	-	-
Potatoes, excluding sweetpotatoes								
Number of farms	-	-	-	-	-	-	-	-
Number of acres	-	-	-	-	-	-	-	-
Weight in hundredweight	-	-	-	-	-	-	-	-
Sugar beets for sugar								
Number of farms	-	-	-	-	-	-	-	-
Number of acres	-	-	-	-	-	-	-	-
Weight in tons	-	-	-	-	-	-	-	-
Sugarcane for sugar								
Number of farms	-	-	-	-	-	-	-	-
Number of acres	-	-	-	-	-	-	-	-
Weight in tons	-	-	-	-	-	-	-	-
Pineapples harvested								
Number of farms	-	-	-	-	-	-	-	-
Number of acres	-	-	-	-	-	-	-	-
Weight in tons	-	-	-	-	-	-	-	-
Peanuts for nuts								
Number of farms	-	-	-	-	-	-	-	-
Number of acres	-	-	-	-	-	-	-	-
Weight in pounds	-	-	-	-	-	-	-	-
Hay - all types, including alfalfa								
Number of farms	1,402	0.1	1,242	0.1	1,170	0.1	-11.4	-5.8
Number of acres	181,319	0.3	191,277	0.3	243,946	0.4	5.5	27.5
Weight in tons, dry	1,040,321	0.8	1,037,443	0.8	1,667,752	1.2	-0.3	60.8
Vegetables harvested for sale								
Number of farms	328	0.5	360	0.6	302	0.6	9.8	-16.1
Number of acres	98,138	2.8	118,125	3.1	131,204	3.5	20.4	11.1
Land in orchards								
Number of farms	1,141	0.9	1,162	1.0	843	0.8	1.8	-27.5
Number of acres	74,921	1.6	68,465	1.4	67,459	1.3	-8.6	-1.5

Source: 1997 Census of Agriculture, U.S. Department of Agriculture, National Agricultural Statistics Service. NA stands for "not available." (D) is shown when data are withheld to prevent disclosure of competitive information. A dash (-) is shown where no data were reported. Not all states report growing all crops, but all crop categories in the census are shown for every state. The data series used for this presentation did not report U.S. totals for a number of categories; for that reason, the "% of U.S." column is sometimes blank.

ARKANSAS

GENERAL STATISTICS FOR ARKANSAS

Item	1987 Value	1987 % of U.S.	1992 Value	1992 % of U.S.	1997 Value	1997 % of U.S.	Percent change 1987-1992	Percent change 1992-1997
Farms (number)	48,242	2.3	43,937	2.3	45,142	2.4	-8.9	2.7
Land in farms (acres)	14,355,611	1.5	14,127,711	1.5	14,364,955	1.5	-1.6	1.7
Average size of farm (acres)	298	64.5	322	65.6	318	65.3	8.1	-1.2
Median size of farm (acres)	NA	-	NA	-	123	102.5	-	-
Market value of land and buildings:								
Average per farm (dollars)	225,604	78.0	282,389	79.1	360,114	80.1	25.2	27.5
Average per acre (dollars)	761	121.4	880	121.0	1,151	123.4	15.6	30.8
Market value of machinery/equipment -								
average per farm (dollars)	34,505	83.7	44,601	91.8	55,619	96.4	29.3	24.7
Farms by size:								
1 to 9 acres	2,249	1.2	1,727	1.0	1,686	1.1	-23.2	-2.4
10 to 49 acres	9,723	2.4	8,295	2.1	9,186	2.2	-14.7	10.7
50 to 179 acres	17,551	2.7	15,771	2.7	16,450	2.8	-10.1	4.3
180 to 499 acres	11,173	2.3	10,719	2.5	10,437	2.6	-4.1	-2.6
500 to 999 acres	4,371	2.2	4,188	2.2	4,049	2.3	-4.2	-3.3
1,000 acres or more	3,175	1.9	3,237	1.9	3,334	1.9	2.0	3.0
Total cropland								
Farms	40,536	2.2	37,408	2.2	37,205	2.2	-7.7	-0.5
Acres	9,950,401	2.2	10,064,948	2.3	10,062,289	2.3	1.2	-0.0
Harvested cropland (farms)	32,248	2.0	30,441	2.0	30,125	2.1	-5.6	-1.0
Harvested cropland (acres)	6,477,365	2.3	7,295,095	2.5	7,665,490	2.5	12.6	5.1
Irrigated land (farms)	7,269	2.5	6,682	2.4	6,593	2.4	-8.1	-1.3
Irrigated land (acres)	2,406,338	5.2	2,701,651	5.5	3,717,217	6.8	12.3	37.6
Market value of agricultural products sold:								
Total sales ($1,000)	3,320,258	2.4	4,159,505	2.6	5,479,692	2.8	25.3	31.7
Average per farm (dollars)	68,825	105.6	94,670	112.1	121,388	117.9	37.6	28.2
Agricultural products only ($1,000)	1,246,686	2.1	1,714,842	2.3	2,188,026	2.2	37.6	27.6
Livestock, poultry, and products ($1,000)	2,073,572	2.7	2,444,663	2.8	3,291,665	3.3	17.9	34.6
Farms by value of sales:								
Less than $2,500	12,130	2.5	9,566	2.3	11,029	2.2	-21.1	15.3
$2,500 to $4,999	7,609	2.9	6,405	2.8	6,901	3.0	-15.8	7.7
$5,000 to $9,999	7,101	2.6	6,844	2.7	6,723	2.8	-3.6	-1.8
$10,000 to $24,999	6,088	1.9	6,071	2.0	6,071	2.2	-0.3	-
$25,000 to $49,999	2,885	1.3	2,717	1.4	2,408	1.4	-5.8	-11.4
$50,000 to $99,999	3,329	1.5	2,614	1.4	1,978	1.3	-21.5	-24.3
$100,000 or more	9,100	3.1	9,720	2.9	10,032	2.9	6.8	3.2
Total farm production expenses ($1,000)	2,454,097	2.3	3,245,341	2.5	4,161,029	2.8	32.2	28.2
Average expenses per farm (dollars)	50,869	98.2	73,865	108.7	92,183	117.0	45.2	24.8
Net cash return for the farm unit:								
Number of farms	48,243	2.3	43,936	2.3	45,139	2.4	-8.9	2.7
Value ($1000)	643,726	2.4	778,566	2.6	1,007,988	2.4	20.9	29.5
Average per farm (dollars)	13,343	105.4	17,720	112.1	22,331	100.3	32.8	26.0
Operators by principal occupation:								
Farming	24,210	2.1	23,273	2.2	22,300	2.3	-3.9	-4.2
Other	24,032	2.5	20,664	2.4	22,842	2.4	-14.0	10.5
Operators by days worked off farm:								
Any	26,208	2.3	22,755	2.3	24,906	2.4	-13.2	9.5
200 days or more	18,417	2.5	16,181	2.4	17,855	2.5	-12.1	10.3

Source: *1997 Census of Agriculture*, U.S. Department of Agriculture, National Agricultural Statistics Service. NA stands for "not available." (D) is shown when data are withheld to prevent disclosure of competitive information. A dash (-) is shown where no data were reported. The market value of land and buildings, and of machinery and equipment, is an estimated amount. Net cash return for the farm unit includes only returns from agricultural activities.

LIVESTOCK STATISTICS FOR ARKANSAS

Item	1987 Value	% of U.S.	1992 Value	% of U.S.	1997 Value	% of U.S.	Percent change 1987-1992	1992-1997
Cattle and calves								
Number of farms	31,606	2.7	29,162	2.7	30,369	2.9	-7.7	4.1
Number of animals	1,562,243	1.6	1,632,666	1.7	1,770,248	1.8	4.5	8.4
Beef cows (farms)	27,297	3.2	26,011	3.2	26,981	3.4	-4.7	3.7
Beef cows (number)	786,183	2.5	826,306	2.5	927,357	2.7	5.1	12.2
Milk cows (farms)	2,252	1.1	1,688	1.1	1,193	1.0	-25.0	-29.3
Milk cows (number)	70,926	0.7	64,427	0.7	49,012	0.5	-9.2	-23.9
Cattle and calves sold (farms)	31,315	2.7	28,545	2.8	29,903	3.0	-8.8	4.8
Cattle and calves sold (number)	888,755	1.2	817,838	1.2	978,007	1.3	-8.0	19.6
Hogs and pigs								
Number of farms	2,467	1.0	1,883	1.0	1,247	1.1	-23.7	-33.8
Number of animals	452,930	0.9	725,497	1.3	858,741	1.4	60.2	18.4
Hogs and pigs sold (farms)	2,168	0.9	1,666	0.9	1,019	1.0	-23.2	-38.8
Hogs and pigs sold (number)	1,211,130	1.3	2,016,536	1.8	2,762,914	1.9	66.5	37.0
Sheep and lambs								
Number of farms	351	0.4	420	0.5	400	0.6	19.7	-4.8
Number of animals	10,943	0.1	12,006	0.1	8,284	0.1	9.7	-31.0
Layers and pullets 13 weeks old and older								
Number of farms	3,263	2.3	2,123	2.4	1,835	2.5	-34.9	-13.6
Number of birds	24,085,427	6.4	22,115,272	6.3	20,213,603	5.5	-8.2	-8.6
Broilers and other meat-type chickens sold								
Number of farms	4,132	14.9	3,666	15.3	3,650	15.2	-11.3	-0.4
Number of birds sold	719,764,548	10.7	862,403,824	15.9	1,003,161,769	14.9	19.8	16.3

Source: 1997 Census of Agriculture, U.S. Department of Agriculture, National Agricultural Statistics Service. NA stands for "not available." (D) is shown when data are withheld to prevent disclosure of competitive information. A dash (-) is shown where no data were reported.

CROP STATISTICS FOR ARKANSAS

Item	1987 Value	% of U.S.	1992 Value	% of U.S.	1997 Value	% of U.S.	Percent change 1987-1992	1992-1997
Corn for grain or seed								
Number of farms	-	-	-	-	-	-		-
Number of acres	-	-	-	-	-	-		-
Number of bushels	-	-	-	-	-	-		-
Corn for silage or green chop								
Number of farms	-	-	-	-	-	-		-
Number of acres	-	-	-	-	-	-		-
Weight in tons, green	-	-	-	-	-	-		-
Sorghum for grain or seed								
Number of farms	3,631	-	2,343	-	875	-	-35.5	-62.7
Number of acres	334,569	-	344,936	-	130,948	-	3.1	-62.0
Number of bushels	22,351,651	-	23,339,497	-	8,988,578	-	4.4	-61.5
Wheat for grain								
Number of farms	5,329	1.5	4,134	1.4	3,361	1.4	-22.4	-18.7
Number of acres	859,405	1.6	815,096	1.4	763,388	1.3	-5.2	-6.3
Number of bushels	33,241,332	1.8	35,234,257	1.6	35,361,702	1.6	6.0	0.4
Barley for grain								
Number of farms	-	-	-	-	-	-		-
Number of acres	-	-	-	-	-	-		-
Number of bushels	-	-	-	-	-	-		-
Oats for grain								
Number of farms	-	-	-	-	-	-		-
Number of acres	-	-	-	-	-	-		-
Number of bushels	-	-	-	-	-	-		-
Rice								
Number of farms	5,613	-	4,924	-	4,207	-	-12.3	-14.6
Number of acres	1,041,433	-	1,363,237	-	1,384,969	-	30.9	1.6
Weight in hundredweight	54,663,266	-	75,410,027	-	78,882,488	-	38.0	4.6
Sunflower seed								
Number of farms	-	-	-	-	-	-	-	-
Number of acres	-	-	-	-	-	-	-	-
Weight in pounds	-	-	-	-	-	-	-	-
Cotton								
Number of farms	2,479	5.8	2,279	6.5	1,730	5.5	-8.1	-24.1
Number of acres	529,636	5.4	947,973	8.6	962,272	7.3	79.0	1.5
Number of bales	816,723	6.1	1,574,664	10.2	1,621,344	9.1	92.8	3.0

Continued.

CROP STATISTICS FOR ARKANSAS - Continued

Item	1987 Value	1987 % of U.S.	1992 Value	1992 % of U.S.	1997 Value	1997 % of U.S.	Percent change 1987-1992	Percent change 1992-1997
Tobacco								
Number of farms	-	-	-	-	-	-	-	-
Number of acres	-	-	-	-	-	-	-	-
Weight in pounds	-	-	-	-	-	-	-	-
Soybeans for beans								
Number of farms	8,983	2.0	7,604	2.0	6,889	1.9	-15.4	-9.4
Number of acres	3,160,746	5.7	3,164,168	5.6	3,571,342	5.4	0.1	12.9
Number of bushels	73,279,691	4.0	99,219,546	4.8	103,074,994	4.1	35.4	3.9
Dry edible beans, excluding dry limas								
Number of farms	-	-	-	-	-	-	-	-
Number of acres	-	-	-	-	-	-	-	-
Weight in hundredweight	-	-	-	-	-	-	-	-
Potatoes, excluding sweetpotatoes								
Number of farms	-	-	-	-	-	-	-	-
Number of acres	-	-	-	-	-	-	-	-
Weight in hundredweight	-	-	-	-	-	-	-	-
Sugar beets for sugar								
Number of farms	-	-	-	-	-	-	-	-
Number of acres	-	-	-	-	-	-	-	-
Weight in tons	-	-	-	-	-	-	-	-
Sugarcane for sugar								
Number of farms	-	-	-	-	-	-	-	-
Number of acres	-	-	-	-	-	-	-	-
Weight in tons	-	-	-	-	-	-	-	-
Pineapples harvested								
Number of farms	-	-	-	-	-	-	-	-
Number of acres	-	-	-	-	-	-	-	-
Weight in tons	-	-	-	-	-	-	-	-
Peanuts for nuts								
Number of farms	-	-	-	-	-	-	-	-
Number of acres	-	-	-	-	-	-	-	-
Weight in pounds	-	-	-	-	-	-	-	-
Hay - all types, including alfalfa								
Number of farms	21,832	2.2	21,542	2.4	22,201	2.5	-1.3	3.1
Number of acres	944,470	1.6	1,111,909	2.0	1,232,771	2.0	17.7	10.9
Weight in tons, dry	1,511,459	1.2	2,106,936	1.7	2,396,515	1.7	39.4	13.7
Vegetables harvested for sale								
Number of farms	-	-	-	-	-	-	-	-
Number of acres	-	-	-	-	-	-	-	-
Land in orchards								
Number of farms	-	-	-	-	-	-	-	-
Number of acres	-	-	-	-	-	-	-	-

Source: 1997 Census of Agriculture, U.S. Department of Agriculture, National Agricultural Statistics Service. NA stands for "not available." (D) is shown when data are withheld to prevent disclosure of competitive information. A dash (-) is shown where no data were reported. Not all states report growing all crops, but all crop categories in the census are shown for every state. The data series used for this presentation did not report U.S. totals for a number of categories; for that reason, the "% of U.S." column is sometimes blank.

CALIFORNIA

GENERAL STATISTICS FOR CALIFORNIA

Item	1987 Value	1987 % of U.S.	1992 Value	1992 % of U.S.	1997 Value	1997 % of U.S.	Percent change 1987-1992	Percent change 1992-1997
Farms (number)	83,217	4.0	77,669	4.0	74,126	3.9	-6.7	-4.6
Land in farms (acres)	30,598,178	3.2	28,978,997	3.1	27,698,779	3.0	-5.3	-4.4
Average size of farm (acres)	368	79.7	373	76.0	374	76.8	1.4	0.3
Median size of farm (acres)	NA	-	NA	-	28	23.3	-	-
Market value of land and buildings:								
Average per farm (dollars)	583,668	201.7	820,063	229.7	941,170	209.3	40.5	14.8
Average per acre (dollars)	1,575	251.2	2,213	304.4	2,605	279.2	40.5	17.7
Market value of machinery/equipment -								
average per farm (dollars)	49,223	119.4	56,485	116.2	69,590	120.7	14.8	23.2
Farms by size:								
1 to 9 acres	22,697	12.4	21,485	12.9	20,662	13.5	-5.3	-3.8
10 to 49 acres	28,498	6.9	26,089	6.7	24,250	5.9	-8.5	-7.0
50 to 179 acres	15,017	2.3	13,883	2.4	13,288	2.2	-7.6	-4.3
180 to 499 acres	8,028	1.7	7,512	1.8	7,270	1.8	-6.4	-3.2
500 to 999 acres	3,804	1.9	3,702	2.0	3,572	2.0	-2.7	-3.5
1,000 acres or more	5,173	3.1	4,998	2.9	5,084	2.9	-3.4	1.7
Total cropland								
Farms	68,266	3.7	64,417	3.8	62,269	3.7	-5.6	-3.3
Acres	10,894,503	2.5	10,479,268	2.4	10,803,804	2.5	-3.8	3.1
Harvested cropland (farms)	59,259	3.6	56,785	3.8	55,590	3.9	-4.2	-2.1
Harvested cropland (acres)	7,676,287	2.7	7,760,773	2.6	8,543,159	2.8	1.1	10.1
Irrigated land (farms)	58,868	20.2	56,546	20.2	55,920	20.0	-3.9	-1.1
Irrigated land (acres)	7,596,091	16.4	7,571,313	15.3	8,712,893	15.8	-0.3	15.1
Market value of agricultural products sold:								
Total sales ($1,000)	13,922,234	10.2	17,051,912	10.5	23,032,259	11.7	22.5	35.1
Average per farm (dollars)	167,300	256.7	219,546	259.9	310,718	301.8	31.2	41.5
Agricultural products only ($1,000)	9,269,389	15.7	11,747,474	15.6	17,033,714	17.4	26.7	45.0
Livestock, poultry, and products ($1,000)	4,652,845	6.0	5,304,438	6.1	5,998,545	6.1	14.0	13.1
Farms by value of sales:								
Less than $2,500	23,187	4.7	22,692	5.4	19,473	3.9	-2.1	-14.2
$2,500 to $4,999	8,661	3.3	7,160	3.1	6,516	2.9	-17.3	-9.0
$5,000 to $9,999	8,512	3.1	7,417	2.9	6,498	2.7	-12.9	-12.4
$10,000 to $24,999	11,028	3.4	9,324	3.1	8,621	3.1	-15.5	-7.5
$25,000 to $49,999	7,863	3.6	6,899	3.5	6,747	4.0	-12.3	-2.2
$50,000 to $99,999	6,895	3.2	6,360	3.4	6,544	4.1	-7.8	2.9
$100,000 or more	17,071	5.8	17,817	5.3	19,727	5.7	4.4	10.7
Total farm production expenses ($1,000)	10,917,593	10.1	13,804,983	10.6	16,817,253	11.2	26.4	21.8
Average expenses per farm (dollars)	131,205	253.3	177,755	261.7	226,868	288.0	35.5	27.6
Net cash return for the farm unit:								
Number of farms	83,210	4.0	77,663	4.0	74,129	3.9	-6.7	-4.6
Value ($1000)	2,927,279	11.1	3,179,111	10.5	6,118,086	14.4	8.6	92.4
Average per farm (dollars)	35,179	277.9	40,935	259.1	82,533	370.8	16.4	101.6
Operators by principal occupation:								
Farming	41,906	3.7	40,215	3.8	39,267	4.1	-4.0	-2.4
Other	41,311	4.4	37,454	4.3	34,859	3.7	-9.3	-6.9
Operators by days worked off farm:								
Any	47,085	4.2	41,278	4.2	37,919	3.6	-12.3	-8.1
200 days or more	30,948	4.2	26,681	4.0	24,012	3.4	-13.8	-10.0

Source: 1997 Census of Agriculture, U.S. Department of Agriculture, National Agricultural Statistics Service. NA stands for "not available." (D) is shown when data are withheld to prevent disclosure of competitive information. A dash (-) is shown where no data were reported. The market value of land and buildings, and of machinery and equipment, is an estimated amount. Net cash return for the farm unit includes only returns from agricultural activities.

LIVESTOCK STATISTICS FOR CALIFORNIA

Item	1987 Value	1987 % of U.S.	1992 Value	1992 % of U.S.	1997 Value	1997 % of U.S.	Percent change 1987-1992	Percent change 1992-1997
Cattle and calves								
Number of farms	22,119	1.9	19,097	1.8	17,335	1.7	-13.7	-9.2
Number of animals	4,570,667	4.8	4,702,114	4.9	4,968,679	5.0	2.9	5.7
Beef cows (farms)	14,966	1.8	13,105	1.6	12,158	1.5	-12.4	-7.2
Beef cows (number)	906,006	2.9	862,971	2.7	890,805	2.6	-4.7	3.2
Milk cows (farms)	3,631	1.8	3,124	2.0	2,650	2.3	-14.0	-15.2
Milk cows (number)	1,070,366	10.6	1,249,038	13.2	1,403,217	15.4	16.7	12.3
Cattle and calves sold (farms)	20,486	1.8	17,205	1.7	16,007	1.6	-16.0	-7.0
Cattle and calves sold (number)	3,097,084	4.3	2,993,538	4.2	3,107,562	4.2	-3.3	3.8
Hogs and pigs								
Number of farms	2,699	1.1	2,221	1.2	1,593	1.5	-17.7	-28.3
Number of animals	150,931	0.3	258,130	0.4	212,088	0.3	71.0	-17.8
Hogs and pigs sold (farms)	2,297	1.0	1,761	0.9	1,193	1.2	-23.3	-32.3
Hogs and pigs sold (number)	303,406	0.3	481,270	0.4	373,352	0.3	58.6	-22.4
Sheep and lambs								
Number of farms	4,602	5.0	3,692	4.6	3,014	4.6	-19.8	-18.4
Number of animals	979,506	8.9	859,835	8.0	784,041	10.0	-12.2	-8.8
Layers and pullets 13 weeks old and older								
Number of farms	5,354	3.7	3,592	4.1	2,731	3.8	-32.9	-24.0
Number of birds	45,377,564	12.1	33,253,782	9.5	34,149,987	9.3	-26.7	2.7
Broilers and other meat-type chickens sold								
Number of farms	298	1.1	298	1.2	240	1.0	-	-19.5
Number of birds sold	209,376,014	3.1	225,074,862	4.1	237,723,294	3.5	7.5	5.6

Source: 1997 Census of Agriculture, U.S. Department of Agriculture, National Agricultural Statistics Service. NA stands for "not available." (D) is shown when data are withheld to prevent disclosure of competitive information. A dash (-) is shown where no data were reported.

CROP STATISTICS FOR CALIFORNIA

Item	1987 Value	1987 % of U.S.	1992 Value	1992 % of U.S.	1997 Value	1997 % of U.S.	Percent change 1987-1992	Percent change 1992-1997
Corn for grain or seed								
Number of farms	-	-	-	-	-	-	-	-
Number of acres	-	-	-	-	-	-	-	-
Number of bushels	-	-	-	-	-	-	-	-
Corn for silage or green chop								
Number of farms	-	-	-	-	-	-	-	-
Number of acres	-	-	-	-	-	-	-	-
Weight in tons, green	-	-	-	-	-	-	-	-
Sorghum for grain or seed								
Number of farms	-	-	-	-	-	-	-	-
Number of acres	-	-	-	-	-	-	-	-
Number of bushels	-	-	-	-	-	-	-	-
Wheat for grain								
Number of farms	2,841	0.8	2,236	0.8	2,065	0.8	-21.3	-7.6
Number of acres	562,302	1.1	569,044	1.0	581,071	1.0	1.2	2.1
Number of bushels	40,004,786	2.1	39,456,581	1.8	42,372,177	1.9	-1.4	7.4
Barley for grain								
Number of farms	1,431	-	933	-	574	-	-34.8	-38.5
Number of acres	269,845	-	204,119	-	129,549	-	-24.4	-36.5
Number of bushels	14,560,411	-	12,183,472	-	7,475,447	-	-16.3	-38.6
Oats for grain								
Number of farms	-	-	-	-	-	-	-	-
Number of acres	-	-	-	-	-	-	-	-
Number of bushels	-	-	-	-	-	-	-	-
Rice								
Number of farms	1,654	-	1,575	-	1,544	-	-4.8	-2.0
Number of acres	399,193	-	401,194	-	514,081	-	0.5	28.1
Weight in hundredweight	28,566,209	-	31,865,036	-	41,457,650	-	11.5	30.1
Sunflower seed								
Number of farms	-	-	-	-	-	-	-	-
Number of acres	-	-	-	-	-	-	-	-
Weight in pounds	-	-	-	-	-	-	-	-
Cotton								
Number of farms	3,037	7.1	2,351	6.8	1,833	5.8	-22.6	-22.0
Number of acres	1,083,811	11.0	1,066,060	9.7	1,036,316	7.8	-1.6	-2.8
Number of bales	2,619,934	19.7	2,792,443	18.2	2,543,194	14.2	6.6	-8.9

Continued.

CROP STATISTICS FOR CALIFORNIA - Continued

Item	1987 Value	1987 % of U.S.	1992 Value	1992 % of U.S.	1997 Value	1997 % of U.S.	Percent change 1987-1992	Percent change 1992-1997
Tobacco								
Number of farms	-	-	-	-	-	-	-	-
Number of acres	-	-	-	-	-	-	-	-
Weight in pounds	-	-	-	-	-	-	-	-
Soybeans for beans								
Number of farms	-	-	-	-	-	-	-	-
Number of acres	-	-	-	-	-	-	-	-
Number of bushels	-	-	-	-	-	-	-	-
Dry edible beans, excluding dry limas								
Number of farms	-	-	-	-	-	-	-	-
Number of acres	-	-	-	-	-	-	-	-
Weight in hundredweight	-	-	-	-	-	-	-	-
Potatoes, excluding sweetpotatoes								
Number of farms	-	-	-	-	-	-	-	-
Number of acres	-	-	-	-	-	-	-	-
Weight in hundredweight	-	-	-	-	-	-	-	-
Sugar beets for sugar								
Number of farms	-	-	-	-	-	-	-	-
Number of acres	-	-	-	-	-	-	-	-
Weight in tons	-	-	-	-	-	-	-	-
Sugarcane for sugar								
Number of farms	-	-	-	-	-	-	-	-
Number of acres	-	-	-	-	-	-	-	-
Weight in tons	-	-	-	-	-	-	-	-
Pineapples harvested								
Number of farms	-	-	-	-	-	-	-	-
Number of acres	-	-	-	-	-	-	-	-
Weight in tons	-	-	-	-	-	-	-	-
Peanuts for nuts								
Number of farms	-	-	-	-	-	-	-	-
Number of acres	-	-	-	-	-	-	-	-
Weight in pounds	-	-	-	-	-	-	-	-
Hay - all types, including alfalfa								
Number of farms	10,638	1.1	9,286	1.0	8,636	1.0	-12.7	-7.0
Number of acres	1,532,777	2.6	1,531,230	2.7	1,698,773	2.8	-0.1	10.9
Weight in tons, dry	7,304,837	5.7	7,567,342	6.0	8,344,564	6.0	3.6	10.3
Vegetables harvested for sale								
Number of farms	3,787	6.2	3,713	6.0	4,490	8.4	-2.0	20.9
Number of acres	882,741	25.5	1,016,744	26.9	1,209,259	32.0	15.2	18.9
Land in orchards								
Number of farms	41,021	34.1	40,298	34.7	38,747	36.5	-1.8	-3.8
Number of acres	2,152,664	47.2	2,245,781	47.1	2,582,084	50.1	4.3	15.0

Source: *1997 Census of Agriculture*, U.S. Department of Agriculture, National Agricultural Statistics Service. NA stands for "not available." (D) is shown when data are withheld to prevent disclosure of competitive information. A dash (-) is shown where no data were reported. Not all states report growing all crops, but all crop categories in the census are shown for every state. The data series used for this presentation did not report U.S. totals for a number of categories; for that reason, the "% of U.S." column is sometimes blank.

COLORADO

GENERAL STATISTICS FOR COLORADO

Item	1987 Value	1987 % of U.S.	1992 Value	1992 % of U.S.	1997 Value	1997 % of U.S.	Percent change 1987-1992	Percent change 1992-1997
Farms (number)	27,284	1.3	27,152	1.4	28,268	1.5	-0.5	4.1
Land in farms (acres)	34,048,433	3.5	33,983,029	3.6	32,634,221	3.5	-0.2	-4.0
Average size of farm (acres)	1,248	270.1	1,252	255.0	1,154	237.0	0.3	-7.8
Median size of farm (acres)	NA	-	NA	-	200	166.7	-	-
Market value of land and buildings:								
Average per farm (dollars)	458,906	158.6	536,510	150.3	707,165	157.2	16.9	31.8
Average per acre (dollars)	369	58.9	426	58.6	618	66.2	15.4	45.1
Market value of machinery/equipment -								
average per farm (dollars)	49,534	120.1	54,868	112.9	71,417	123.8	10.8	30.2
Farms by size:								
1 to 9 acres	2,725	1.5	2,424	1.5	2,502	1.6	-11.0	3.2
10 to 49 acres	4,352	1.1	4,867	1.3	5,516	1.3	11.8	13.3
50 to 179 acres	5,111	0.8	5,371	0.9	5,748	1.0	5.1	7.0
180 to 499 acres	4,862	1.0	4,594	1.1	4,833	1.2	-5.5	5.2
500 to 999 acres	3,355	1.7	3,188	1.7	3,030	1.7	-5.0	-5.0
1,000 acres or more	6,879	4.1	6,708	3.9	6,639	3.8	-2.5	-1.0
Total cropland								
Farms	22,334	1.2	21,882	1.3	22,357	1.3	-2.0	2.2
Acres	10,988,853	2.5	10,933,484	2.5	10,509,384	2.4	-0.5	-3.9
Harvested cropland (farms)	19,446	1.2	18,573	1.2	18,406	1.3	-4.5	-0.9
Harvested cropland (acres)	5,522,216	2.0	5,532,964	1.9	5,896,984	1.9	0.2	6.6
Irrigated land (farms)	14,913	5.1	15,193	5.4	15,470	5.5	1.9	1.8
Irrigated land (acres)	3,013,773	6.5	3,169,839	6.4	3,430,129	6.2	5.2	8.2
Market value of agricultural products sold:								
Total sales ($1,000)	3,143,131	2.3	4,115,552	2.5	4,534,213	2.3	30.9	10.2
Average per farm (dollars)	115,201	176.8	151,575	179.5	160,401	155.8	31.6	5.8
Agricultural products only ($1,000)	781,934	1.3	1,036,174	1.4	1,326,944	1.4	32.5	28.1
Livestock, poultry, and products ($1,000)	2,361,197	3.1	3,079,378	3.5	3,207,269	3.2	30.4	4.2
Farms by value of sales:								
Less than $2,500	6,607	1.3	6,365	1.5	7,328	1.5	-3.7	15.1
$2,500 to $4,999	2,582	1.0	2,637	1.1	2,849	1.2	2.1	8.0
$5,000 to $9,999	3,008	1.1	3,005	1.2	3,220	1.4	-0.1	7.2
$10,000 to $24,999	4,245	1.3	4,249	1.4	4,427	1.6	0.1	4.2
$25,000 to $49,999	3,316	1.5	3,135	1.6	3,060	1.8	-5.5	-2.4
$50,000 to $99,999	3,117	1.4	2,866	1.5	2,620	1.7	-8.1	-8.6
$100,000 or more	4,409	1.5	4,895	1.5	4,764	1.4	11.0	-2.7
Total farm production expenses ($1,000)	2,700,407	2.5	3,569,175	2.7	3,725,343	2.5	32.2	4.4
Average expenses per farm (dollars)	98,989	191.1	131,442	193.5	131,768	167.3	32.8	0.2
Net cash return for the farm unit:								
Number of farms	27,281	1.3	27,154	1.4	28,272	1.5	-0.5	4.1
Value ($1000)	422,200	1.6	515,763	1.7	803,321	1.9	22.2	55.8
Average per farm (dollars)	15,476	122.2	18,994	120.2	28,414	127.6	22.7	49.6
Operators by principal occupation:								
Farming	16,504	1.5	16,181	1.5	15,399	1.6	-2.0	-4.8
Other	10,780	1.1	10,971	1.3	12,869	1.4	1.8	17.3
Operators by days worked off farm:								
Any	14,202	1.3	13,914	1.4	15,459	1.5	-2.0	11.1
200 days or more	8,311	1.1	8,353	1.3	9,615	1.4	0.5	15.1

Source: 1997 Census of Agriculture, U.S. Department of Agriculture, National Agricultural Statistics Service. NA stands for "not available." (D) is shown when data are withheld to prevent disclosure of competitive information. A dash (-) is shown where no data were reported. The market value of land and buildings, and of machinery and equipment, is an estimated amount. Net cash return for the farm unit includes only returns from agricultural activities.

LIVESTOCK STATISTICS FOR COLORADO

Item	1987		1992		1997		Percent change	
	Value	% of U.S.	Value	% of U.S.	Value	% of U.S.	1987-1992	1992-1997
Cattle and calves								
Number of farms	14,637	1.2	14,797	1.4	15,592	1.5	1.1	5.4
Number of animals	2,946,334	3.1	3,086,717	3.2	3,307,301	3.3	4.8	7.1
Beef cows (farms)	11,132	1.3	11,596	1.4	12,243	1.5	4.2	5.6
Beef cows (number)	830,216	2.6	900,347	2.8	918,891	2.7	8.4	2.1
Milk cows (farms)	1,714	0.8	1,162	0.7	814	0.7	-32.2	-29.9
Milk cows (number)	76,285	0.8	81,825	0.9	79,617	0.9	7.3	-2.7
Cattle and calves sold (farms)	14,569	1.3	14,439	1.4	15,124	1.5	-0.9	4.7
Cattle and calves sold (number)	3,476,740	4.8	3,569,739	5.1	3,751,788	5.1	2.7	5.1
Hogs and pigs								
Number of farms	1,685	0.7	1,643	0.9	1,225	1.1	-2.5	-25.4
Number of animals	258,725	0.5	464,479	0.8	787,440	1.3	79.5	69.5
Hogs and pigs sold (farms)	1,620	0.7	1,558	0.8	1,035	1.0	-3.8	-33.6
Hogs and pigs sold (number)	460,359	0.5	878,515	0.8	1,452,164	1.0	90.8	65.3
Sheep and lambs								
Number of farms	1,981	2.1	1,911	2.4	1,628	2.5	-3.5	-14.8
Number of animals	708,070	6.4	730,272	6.8	593,755	7.6	3.1	-18.7
Layers and pullets 13 weeks old and older								
Number of farms	2,709	1.9	1,767	2.0	1,628	2.2	-34.8	-7.9
Number of birds	3,118,767	0.8	4,257,327	1.2	3,793,457	1.0	36.5	-10.9
Broilers and other meat-type chickens sold								
Number of farms	112	0.4	74	0.3	74	0.3	-33.9	-
Number of birds sold	43,706	0.0	(D)	-	11,933	0.0	-	-

Source: *1997 Census of Agriculture*, U.S. Department of Agriculture, National Agricultural Statistics Service. NA stands for "not available." (D) is shown when data are withheld to prevent disclosure of competitive information. A dash (-) is shown where no data were reported.

CROP STATISTICS FOR COLORADO

Item	1987		1992		1997		Percent change	
	Value	% of U.S.	Value	% of U.S.	Value	% of U.S.	1987-1992	1992-1997
Corn for grain or seed								
Number of farms	4,295	0.7	4,066	0.8	3,579	0.8	-5.3	-12.0
Number of acres	685,568	1.2	891,720	1.3	919,784	1.3	30.1	3.1
Number of bushels	98,919,585	-	126,076,043	1.4	130,170,731	1.5	27.5	3.2
Corn for silage or green chop								
Number of farms	1,525	-	1,341	-	1,160	-	-12.1	-13.5
Number of acres	100,798	-	98,838	-	96,344	-	-1.9	-2.5
Weight in tons, green	2,101,438	-	2,102,940	-	2,021,799	-	0.1	-3.9
Sorghum for grain or seed								
Number of farms	1,039	-	709	-	504	-	-31.8	-28.9
Number of acres	190,554	-	163,850	-	148,004	-	-14.0	-9.7
Number of bushels	7,327,665	-	6,280,126	-	5,272,619	-	-14.3	-16.0
Wheat for grain								
Number of farms	6,992	2.0	5,597	1.9	5,407	2.2	-20.0	-3.4
Number of acres	2,421,603	4.5	2,384,979	4.0	2,515,100	4.3	-1.5	5.5
Number of bushels	81,581,401	4.3	71,825,463	3.3	76,656,526	3.5	-12.0	6.7
Barley for grain								
Number of farms	2,404	-	1,053	-	657	-	-56.2	-37.6
Number of acres	203,226	-	115,321	-	84,564	-	-43.3	-26.7
Number of bushels	12,386,192	-	8,934,199	-	8,639,798	-	-27.9	-3.3
Oats for grain								
Number of farms	-	-	-	-	-	-	-	-
Number of acres	-	-	-	-	-	-	-	-
Number of bushels	-	-	-	-	-	-	-	-
Rice								
Number of farms	-	-	-	-	-	-	-	-
Number of acres	-	-	-	-	-	-	-	-
Weight in hundredweight	-	-	-	-	-	-	-	-
Sunflower seed								
Number of farms	-	-	-	-	-	-	-	-
Number of acres	-	-	-	-	-	-	-	-
Weight in pounds	-	-	-	-	-	-	-	-
Cotton								
Number of farms	-	-	-	-	-	-	-	-
Number of acres	-	-	-	-	-	-	-	-
Number of bales	-	-	-	-	-	-	-	-

Continued.

CROP STATISTICS FOR COLORADO - Continued

Item	1987 Value	% of U.S.	1992 Value	% of U.S.	1997 Value	% of U.S.	Percent change 1987-1992	Percent change 1992-1997
Tobacco								
Number of farms	-	-	-	-	-	-	-	-
Number of acres	-	-	-	-	-	-	-	-
Weight in pounds	-	-	-	-	-	-	-	-
Soybeans for beans								
Number of farms	-	-	-	-	-	-	-	-
Number of acres	-	-	-	-	-	-	-	-
Number of bushels	-	-	-	-	-	-	-	-
Dry edible beans, excluding dry limas								
Number of farms	1,689	-	1,533	-	1,095	-	-9.2	-28.6
Number of acres	169,506	-	150,824	-	116,544	-	-11.0	-22.7
Weight in hundredweight	2,521,626	-	2,509,515	-	2,028,685	-	-0.5	-19.2
Potatoes, excluding sweetpotatoes								
Number of farms	-	-			-	-	-	-
Number of acres	-	-			-	-	-	-
Weight in hundredweight	-	-			-	-	-	-
Sugar beets for sugar								
Number of farms	-	-	-	-	-	-	-	-
Number of acres	-	-	-	-	-	-	-	-
Weight in tons	-	-	-	-	-	-	-	-
Sugarcane for sugar								
Number of farms	-	-	-	-	-	-	-	-
Number of acres	-	-	-	-	-	-	-	-
Weight in tons	-	-	-	-	-	-	-	-
Pineapples harvested								
Number of farms	-	-		-	-	-	-	-
Number of acres	-	-		-	-	-	-	-
Weight in tons	-	-		-	-	-	-	-
Peanuts for nuts								
Number of farms	-	-	-	-	-	-	-	-
Number of acres	-	-	-	-	-	-	-	-
Weight in pounds	-	-	-	-	-	-	-	-
Hay - all types, including alfalfa								
Number of farms	13,535	1.4	13,160	1.5	13,446	1.5	-2.8	2.2
Number of acres	1,423,807	2.5	1,449,177	2.6	1,607,991	2.6	1.8	11.0
Weight in tons, dry	3,088,681	2.4	3,464,389	2.7	3,989,176	2.9	12.2	15.1
Vegetables harvested for sale								
Number of farms	-	-	-	-	-	-	-	-
Number of acres	-	-	-	-	-	-	-	-
Land in orchards								
Number of farms	-	-	-	-	-	-	-	-
Number of acres	-	-	-	-	-	-	-	-

Source: 1997 Census of Agriculture, U.S. Department of Agriculture, National Agricultural Statistics Service. NA stands for "not available." (D) is shown when data are withheld to prevent disclosure of competitive information. A dash (-) is shown where no data were reported. Not all states report growing all crops, but all crop categories in the census are shown for every state. The data series used for this presentation did not report U.S. totals for a number of categories; for that reason, the "% of U.S." column is sometimes blank.

CONNECTICUT

GENERAL STATISTICS FOR CONNECTICUT

Item	1987 Value	1987 % of U.S.	1992 Value	1992 % of U.S.	1997 Value	1997 % of U.S.	Percent change 1987-1992	Percent change 1992-1997
Farms (number)	3,580	0.2	3,427	0.2	3,687	0.2	-4.3	7.6
Land in farms (acres)	398,400	0.0	358,743	0.0	359,313	0.0	-10.0	0.2
Average size of farm (acres)	111	24.0	105	21.4	97	19.9	-5.4	-7.6
Median size of farm (acres)	NA	-	NA	-	40	33.3	-	-
Market value of land and buildings:								
Average per farm (dollars)	467,677	161.6	624,135	174.8	571,074	127.0	33.5	-8.5
Average per acre (dollars)	4,171	665.2	5,959	819.7	5,949	637.6	42.9	-0.2
Market value of machinery/equipment -								
average per farm (dollars)	36,996	89.7	36,557	75.2	41,194	71.4	-1.2	12.7
Farms by size:								
1 to 9 acres	560	0.3	606	0.4	744	0.5	8.2	22.8
10 to 49 acres	1,176	0.3	1,172	0.3	1,273	0.3	-0.3	8.6
50 to 179 acres	1,176	0.2	1,082	0.2	1,129	0.2	-8.0	4.3
180 to 499 acres	546	0.1	455	0.1	436	0.1	-16.7	-4.2
500 to 999 acres	95	0.0	86	0.0	75	0.0	-9.5	-12.8
1,000 acres or more	27	0.0	26	0.0	30	0.0	-3.7	15.4
Total cropland								
Farms	3,163	0.2	3,058	0.2	3,289	0.2	-3.3	7.6
Acres	210,012	0.0	192,756	0.0	181,043	0.0	-8.2	-6.1
Harvested cropland (farms)	2,876	0.2	2,789	0.2	3,032	0.2	-3.0	8.7
Harvested cropland (acres)	153,715	0.1	143,782	0.0	140,513	0.0	-6.5	-2.3
Irrigated land (farms)	430	0.1	524	0.2	674	0.2	21.9	28.6
Irrigated land (acres)	7,245	0.0	5,893	0.0	7,366	0.0	-18.7	25.0
Market value of agricultural products sold:								
Total sales ($1,000)	357,702	0.3	336,983	0.2	421,648	0.2	-5.8	25.1
Average per farm (dollars)	99,917	153.3	98,332	116.4	114,361	111.1	-1.6	16.3
Agricultural products only ($1,000)	164,664	0.3	183,300	0.2	263,799	0.3	11.3	43.9
Livestock, poultry, and products ($1,000)	193,039	0.3	153,683	0.2	157,850	0.2	-20.4	2.7
Farms by value of sales:								
Less than $2,500	1,166	0.2	1,120	0.3	1,165	0.2	-3.9	4.0
$2,500 to $4,999	482	0.2	442	0.2	555	0.2	-8.3	25.6
$5,000 to $9,999	445	0.2	476	0.2	500	0.2	7.0	5.0
$10,000 to $24,999	436	0.1	480	0.2	511	0.2	10.1	6.5
$25,000 to $49,999	275	0.1	249	0.1	271	0.2	-9.5	8.8
$50,000 to $99,999	247	0.1	214	0.1	221	0.1	-13.4	3.3
$100,000 or more	529	0.2	446	0.1	464	0.1	-15.7	4.0
Total farm production expenses ($1,000)	255,212	0.2	282,694	0.2	330,902	0.2	10.8	17.1
Average expenses per farm (dollars)	71,288	137.6	82,514	121.5	89,846	114.1	15.7	8.9
Net cash return for the farm unit:								
Number of farms	3,580	0.2	3,426	0.2	3,684	0.2	-4.3	7.5
Value ($1000)	97,787	0.4	53,863	0.2	87,211	0.2	-44.9	61.9
Average per farm (dollars)	27,315	215.8	15,722	99.5	23,673	106.3	-42.4	50.6
Operators by principal occupation:								
Farming	1,842	0.2	1,828	0.2	1,824	0.2	-0.8	-0.2
Other	1,738	0.2	1,599	0.2	1,863	0.2	-8.0	16.5
Operators by days worked off farm:								
Any	1,940	0.2	1,751	0.2	1,953	0.2	-9.7	11.5
200 days or more	1,304	0.2	1,098	0.2	1,310	0.2	-15.8	19.3

Source: 1997 Census of Agriculture, U.S. Department of Agriculture, National Agricultural Statistics Service. NA stands for "not available." (D) is shown when data are withheld to prevent disclosure of competitive information. A dash (-) is shown where no data were reported. The market value of land and buildings, and of machinery and equipment, is an estimated amount. Net cash return for the farm unit includes only returns from agricultural activities.

LIVESTOCK STATISTICS FOR CONNECTICUT

Item	1987		1992		1997		Percent change	
	Value	% of U.S.	Value	% of U.S.	Value	% of U.S.	1987-1992	1992-1997
Cattle and calves								
Number of farms	1,596	0.1	1,345	0.1	1,227	0.1	-15.7	-8.8
Number of animals	89,306	0.1	78,044	0.1	65,645	0.1	-12.6	-15.9
Beef cows (farms)	887	0.1	770	0.1	721	0.1	-13.2	-6.4
Beef cows (number)	7,146	0.0	6,878	0.0	6,887	0.0	-3.8	0.1
Milk cows (farms)	630	0.3	486	0.3	370	0.3	-22.9	-23.9
Milk cows (number)	41,691	0.4	34,552	0.4	28,017	0.3	-17.1	-18.9
Cattle and calves sold (farms)	1,335	0.1	1,103	0.1	983	0.1	-17.4	-10.9
Cattle and calves sold (number)	41,093	0.1	31,200	0.0	25,237	0.0	-24.1	-19.1
Hogs and pigs								
Number of farms	254	0.1	293	0.2	210	0.2	15.4	-28.3
Number of animals	5,429	0.0	5,588	0.0	4,521	0.0	2.9	-19.1
Hogs and pigs sold (farms)	195	0.1	201	0.1	160	0.2	3.1	-20.4
Hogs and pigs sold (number)	8,776	0.0	8,232	0.0	9,408	0.0	-6.2	14.3
Sheep and lambs								
Number of farms	326	0.4	312	0.4	254	0.4	-4.3	-18.6
Number of animals	7,347	0.1	7,501	0.1	5,010	0.1	2.1	-33.2
Layers and pullets 13 weeks old and older								
Number of farms	443	0.3	391	0.4	387	0.5	-11.7	-1.0
Number of birds	4,913,031	1.3	4,494,659	1.3	3,992,919	1.1	-8.5	-11.2
Broilers and other meat-type chickens sold								
Number of farms	40	0.1	42	0.2	30	0.1	5.0	-28.6
Number of birds sold	850,969	0.0	943,569	0.0	342,656	0.0	10.9	-63.7

Source: 1997 Census of Agriculture, U.S. Department of Agriculture, National Agricultural Statistics Service. NA stands for "not available." (D) is shown when data are withheld to prevent disclosure of competitive information. A dash (-) is shown where no data were reported.

CROP STATISTICS FOR CONNECTICUT

Item	1987		1992		1997		Percent change	
	Value	% of U.S.	Value	% of U.S.	Value	% of U.S.	1987-1992	1992-1997
Corn for grain or seed								
Number of farms	115	0.0	81	0.0	75	0.0	-29.6	-7.4
Number of acres	3,953	0.0	5,357	0.0	5,460	0.0	35.5	1.9
Number of bushels	335,317	-	630,547	0.0	605,666	0.0	88.0	-3.9
Corn for silage or green chop								
Number of farms	624	-	500	-	403	-	-19.9	-19.4
Number of acres	42,865	-	37,825	-	32,219	-	-11.8	-14.8
Weight in tons, green	783,403	-	689,551	-	610,198	-	-12.0	-11.5
Sorghum for grain or seed								
Number of farms	-	-	-	-	-	-	-	-
Number of acres	-	-	-	-	-	-	-	-
Number of bushels	-	-	-	-	-	-	-	-
Wheat for grain								
Number of farms	-	-	-	-	-	-	-	-
Number of acres	-	-	-	-	-	-	-	-
Number of bushels	-	-	-	-	-	-	-	-
Barley for grain								
Number of farms	-	-	-	-	-	-	-	-
Number of acres	-	-	-	-	-	-	-	-
Number of bushels	-	-	-	-	-	-	-	-
Oats for grain								
Number of farms	-	-	-	-	-	-	-	-
Number of acres	-	-	-	-	-	-	-	-
Number of bushels	-	-	-	-	-	-	-	-
Rice								
Number of farms	-	-	-	-	-	-	-	-
Number of acres	-	-	-	-	-	-	-	-
Weight in hundredweight	-	-	-	-	-	-	-	-
Sunflower seed								
Number of farms	-	-	-	-	-	-	-	-
Number of acres	-	-	-	-	-	-	-	-
Weight in pounds	-	-	-	-	-	-	-	-
Cotton								
Number of farms	-	-	-	-	-	-	-	-
Number of acres	-	-	-	-	-	-	-	-
Number of bales	-	-	-	-	-	-	-	-

Continued.

CROP STATISTICS FOR CONNECTICUT - Continued

Item	1987		1992		1997		Percent change	
	Value	% of U.S.	Value	% of U.S.	Value	% of U.S.	1987-1992	1992-1997
Tobacco								
Number of farms	-	-	-	-	-	-	-	-
Number of acres	-	-	-	-	-	-	-	-
Weight in pounds	-	-	-	-	-	-	-	-
Soybeans for beans								
Number of farms	-	-	-	-	-	-	-	-
Number of acres	-	-	-	-	-	-	-	-
Number of bushels	-	-	-	-	-	-	-	-
Dry edible beans, excluding dry limas								
Number of farms	-	-	-	-	-	-	-	-
Number of acres	-	-	-	-	-	-	-	-
Weight in hundredweight	-	-	-	-	-	-	-	-
Potatoes, excluding sweetpotatoes								
Number of farms	37	-	47	-	58	-	27.0	23.4
Number of acres	544	-	279	-	151	-	-48.7	-45.9
Weight in hundredweight	114,633	-	57,401	-	37,907	-	-49.9	-34.0
Sugar beets for sugar								
Number of farms	-	-	-	-	-	-	-	-
Number of acres	-	-	-	-	-	-	-	-
Weight in tons	-	-	-	-	-	-	-	-
Sugarcane for sugar								
Number of farms	-	-	-	-	-	-	-	-
Number of acres	-	-	-	-	-	-	-	-
Weight in tons	-	-	-	-	-	-	-	-
Pineapples harvested								
Number of farms	-	-	-	-	-	-	-	-
Number of acres	-	-	-	-	-	-	-	-
Weight in tons	-	-	-	-	-	-	-	-
Peanuts for nuts								
Number of farms	-	-	-	-	-	-	-	-
Number of acres	-	-	-	-	-	-	-	-
Weight in pounds	-	-	-	-	-	-	-	-
Hay - all types, including alfalfa								
Number of farms	1,984	0.2	1,752	0.2	1,670	0.2	-11.7	-4.7
Number of acres	86,038	0.1	81,281	0.1	81,752	0.1	-5.5	0.6
Weight in tons, dry	184,080	0.1	176,190	0.1	158,978	0.1	-4.3	-9.8
Vegetables harvested for sale								
Number of farms	451	0.7	579	0.9	620	1.2	28.4	7.1
Number of acres	8,608	0.2	9,994	0.3	10,008	0.3	16.1	0.1
Land in orchards								
Number of farms	308	0.3	332	0.3	253	0.2	7.8	-23.8
Number of acres	5,122	0.1	4,481	0.1	3,546	0.1	-12.5	-20.9

Source: *1997 Census of Agriculture*, U.S. Department of Agriculture, National Agricultural Statistics Service. NA stands for "not available." (D) is shown when data are withheld to prevent disclosure of competitive information. A dash (-) is shown where no data were reported. Not all states report growing all crops, but all crop categories in the census are shown for every state. The data series used for this presentation did not report U.S. totals for a number of categories; for that reason, the "% of U.S." column is sometimes blank.

DELAWARE

GENERAL STATISTICS FOR DELAWARE

Item	1987 Value	1987 % of U.S.	1992 Value	1992 % of U.S.	1997 Value	1997 % of U.S.	Percent change 1987-1992	Percent change 1992-1997
Farms (number)	2,966	0.1	2,633	0.1	2,460	0.1	-11.2	-6.6
Land in farms (acres)	608,245	0.1	589,189	0.1	579,545	0.1	-3.1	-1.6
Average size of farm (acres)	205	44.4	224	45.6	236	48.5	9.3	5.4
Median size of farm (acres)	NA	-	NA	-	56	46.7	-	-
Market value of land and buildings:								
Average per farm (dollars)	369,751	127.8	514,156	144.0	609,974	135.6	39.1	18.6
Average per acre (dollars)	1,765	281.5	2,246	308.9	2,660	285.1	27.3	18.4
Market value of machinery/equipment - average per farm (dollars)	53,447	129.6	67,843	139.6	76,183	132.1	26.9	12.3
Farms by size:								
1 to 9 acres	514	0.3	421	0.3	399	0.3	-18.1	-5.2
10 to 49 acres	867	0.2	797	0.2	772	0.2	-8.1	-3.1
50 to 179 acres	788	0.1	725	0.1	638	0.1	-8.0	-12.0
180 to 499 acres	481	0.1	398	0.1	359	0.1	-17.3	-9.8
500 to 999 acres	188	0.1	161	0.1	155	0.1	-14.4	-3.7
1,000 acres or more	128	0.1	131	0.1	137	0.1	2.3	4.6
Total cropland								
Farms	2,397	0.1	2,162	0.1	1,981	0.1	-9.8	-8.4
Acres	501,290	0.1	495,156	0.1	486,981	0.1	-1.2	-1.7
Harvested cropland (farms)	2,172	0.1	1,956	0.1	1,810	0.1	-9.9	-7.5
Harvested cropland (acres)	441,502	0.2	470,348	0.2	466,555	0.2	6.5	-0.8
Irrigated land (farms)	384	0.1	352	0.1	415	0.1	-8.3	17.9
Irrigated land (acres)	60,812	0.1	61,774	0.1	72,635	0.1	1.6	17.6
Market value of agricultural products sold:								
Total sales ($1,000)	443,575	0.3	559,766	0.3	690,794	0.4	26.2	23.4
Average per farm (dollars)	149,553	229.5	212,596	251.7	280,811	272.7	42.2	32.1
Agricultural products only ($1,000)	96,118	0.2	142,963	0.2	174,845	0.2	48.7	22.3
Livestock, poultry, and products ($1,000)	347,456	0.5	416,802	0.5	515,949	0.5	20.0	23.8
Farms by value of sales:								
Less than $2,500	540	0.1	392	0.1	375	0.1	-27.4	-4.3
$2,500 to $4,999	270	0.1	213	0.1	173	0.1	-21.1	-18.8
$5,000 to $9,999	297	0.1	252	0.1	195	0.1	-15.2	-22.6
$10,000 to $24,999	280	0.1	301	0.1	262	0.1	7.5	-13.0
$25,000 to $49,999	214	0.1	202	0.1	200	0.1	-5.6	-1.0
$50,000 to $99,999	257	0.1	182	0.1	177	0.1	-29.2	-2.7
$100,000 or more	1,108	0.4	1,091	0.3	1,078	0.3	-1.5	-1.2
Total farm production expenses ($1,000)	377,102	0.3	448,199	0.3	620,297	0.4	18.9	38.4
Average expenses per farm (dollars)	127,184	245.5	170,613	251.2	252,358	320.4	34.1	47.9
Net cash return for the farm unit:								
Number of farms	2,965	0.1	2,627	0.1	2,458	0.1	-11.4	-6.4
Value ($1000)	65,300	0.2	108,998	0.4	68,563	0.2	66.9	-37.1
Average per farm (dollars)	22,023	174.0	41,491	262.6	27,894	125.3	88.4	-32.8
Operators by principal occupation:								
Farming	1,774	0.2	1,578	0.1	1,497	0.2	-11.0	-5.1
Other	1,192	0.1	1,055	0.1	963	0.1	-11.5	-8.7
Operators by days worked off farm:								
Any	1,426	0.1	1,287	0.1	1,097	0.1	-9.7	-14.8
200 days or more	955	0.1	849	0.1	744	0.1	-11.1	-12.4

Source: 1997 Census of Agriculture, U.S. Department of Agriculture, National Agricultural Statistics Service. NA stands for "not available." (D) is shown when data are withheld to prevent disclosure of competitive information. A dash (-) is shown where no data were reported. The market value of land and buildings, and of machinery and equipment, is an estimated amount. Net cash return for the farm unit includes only returns from agricultural activities.

LIVESTOCK STATISTICS FOR DELAWARE

Item	1987		1992		1997		Percent change	
	Value	% of U.S.	Value	% of U.S.	Value	% of U.S.	1987-1992	1992-1997
Cattle and calves								
Number of farms	461	0.0	411	0.0	434	0.0	-10.8	5.6
Number of animals	31,191	0.0	28,838	0.0	27,968	0.0	-7.5	-3.0
Beef cows (farms)	216	0.0	204	0.0	224	0.0	-5.6	9.8
Beef cows (number)	2,187	0.0	2,856	0.0	3,685	0.0	30.6	29.0
Milk cows (farms)	169	0.1	137	0.1	132	0.1	-18.9	-3.6
Milk cows (number)	9,354	0.1	8,659	0.1	9,241	0.1	-7.4	6.7
Cattle and calves sold (farms)	376	0.0	337	0.0	370	0.0	-10.4	9.8
Cattle and calves sold (number)	26,934	0.0	22,655	0.0	18,179	0.0	-15.9	-19.8
Hogs and pigs								
Number of farms	301	0.1	205	0.1	132	0.1	-31.9	-35.6
Number of animals	49,714	0.1	58,913	0.1	33,355	0.1	18.5	-43.4
Hogs and pigs sold (farms)	310	0.1	195	0.1	115	0.1	-37.1	-41.0
Hogs and pigs sold (number)	109,600	0.1	118,100	0.1	60,245	0.0	7.8	-49.0
Sheep and lambs								
Number of farms	50	0.1	72	0.1	50	0.1	44.0	-30.6
Number of animals	1,667	0.0	1,856	0.0	1,167	0.0	11.3	-37.1
Layers and pullets 13 weeks old and older								
Number of farms	175	0.1	117	0.1	87	0.1	-33.1	-25.6
Number of birds	834,287	0.2	739,248	0.2	(D)	-	-11.4	-
Broilers and other meat-type chickens sold								
Number of farms	1,001	3.6	870	3.6	805	3.4	-13.1	-7.5
Number of birds sold	210,492,139	3.1	223,328,864	4.1	223,298,115	3.3	6.1	-0.0

Source: 1997 Census of Agriculture, U.S. Department of Agriculture, National Agricultural Statistics Service. NA stands for "not available." (D) is shown when data are withheld to prevent disclosure of competitive information. A dash (-) is shown where no data were reported.

CROP STATISTICS FOR DELAWARE

Item	1987		1992		1997		Percent change	
	Value	% of U.S.	Value	% of U.S.	Value	% of U.S.	1987-1992	1992-1997
Corn for grain or seed								
Number of farms	1,076	0.2	1,029	0.2	985	0.2	-4.4	-4.3
Number of acres	130,234	0.2	154,240	0.2	157,011	0.2	18.4	1.8
Number of bushels	9,876,539	-	18,142,044	0.2	15,670,883	0.2	83.7	-13.6
Corn for silage or green chop								
Number of farms	-	-	-	-	-	-	-	-
Number of acres	-	-	-	-	-	-	-	-
Weight in tons, green	-	-	-	-	-	-	-	-
Sorghum for grain or seed								
Number of farms	-	-	-	-	-	-	-	-
Number of acres	-	-	-	-	-	-	-	-
Number of bushels	-	-	-	-	-	-	-	-
Wheat for grain								
Number of farms	630	0.2	599	0.2	652	0.3	-4.9	8.8
Number of acres	43,573	0.1	61,754	0.1	75,265	0.1	41.7	21.9
Number of bushels	1,827,869	0.1	3,324,145	0.2	4,987,739	0.2	81.9	50.0
Barley for grain								
Number of farms	360	-	323	-	242	-	-10.3	-25.1
Number of acres	32,642	-	37,520	-	32,311	-	14.9	-13.9
Number of bushels	1,897,161	-	2,605,621	-	2,700,574	-	37.3	3.6
Oats for grain								
Number of farms	-	-	-	-	-	-	-	-
Number of acres	-	-	-	-	-	-	-	-
Number of bushels	-	-	-	-	-	-	-	-
Rice								
Number of farms	-	-	-	-	-	-	-	-
Number of acres	-	-	-	-	-	-	-	-
Weight in hundredweight	-	-	-	-	-	-	-	-
Sunflower seed								
Number of farms	-	-	-	-	-	-	-	-
Number of acres	-	-	-	-	-	-	-	-
Weight in pounds	-	-	-	-	-	-	-	-
Cotton								
Number of farms	-	-	-	-	-	-	-	-
Number of acres	-	-	-	-	-	-	-	-
Number of bales	-	-	-	-	-	-	-	-

Continued.

CROP STATISTICS FOR DELAWARE - Continued

Item	1987		1992		1997		Percent change	
	Value	% of U.S.	Value	% of U.S.	Value	% of U.S.	1987-1992	1992-1997
Tobacco								
Number of farms	-	-	-	-	-	-	-	-
Number of acres	-	-	-	-	-	-	-	-
Weight in pounds	-	-	-	-	-	-	-	-
Soybeans for beans								
Number of farms	1,515	0.3	1,324	0.3	1,125	0.3	-12.6	-15.0
Number of acres	219,941	0.4	231,872	0.4	222,785	0.3	5.4	-3.9
Number of bushels	4,143,975	0.2	6,948,357	0.3	6,560,094	0.3	67.7	-5.6
Dry edible beans, excluding dry limas								
Number of farms	-	-	-	-	-	-	-	-
Number of acres	-	-	-	-	-	-	-	-
Weight in hundredweight	-	-	-	-	-	-	-	-
Potatoes, excluding sweetpotatoes								
Number of farms	-	-	-	-	-	-	-	-
Number of acres	-	-	-	-	-	-	-	-
Weight in hundredweight	-	-	-	-	-	-	-	-
Sugar beets for sugar								
Number of farms	-	-	-	-	-	-	-	-
Number of acres	-	-	-	-	-	-	-	-
Weight in tons	-	-	-	-	-	-	-	-
Sugarcane for sugar								
Number of farms	-	-	-	-	-	-	-	-
Number of acres	-	-	-	-	-	-	-	-
Weight in tons	-	-	-	-	-	-	-	-
Pineapples harvested								
Number of farms	-	-	-	-	-	-	-	-
Number of acres	-	-	-	-	-	-	-	-
Weight in tons	-	-	-	-	-	-	-	-
Peanuts for nuts								
Number of farms	-	-	-	-	-	-	-	-
Number of acres	-	-	-	-	-	-	-	-
Weight in pounds	-	-	-	-	-	-	-	-
Hay - all types, including alfalfa								
Number of farms	539	0.1	428	0.0	467	0.1	-20.6	9.1
Number of acres	18,341	0.0	11,947	0.0	15,918	0.0	-34.9	33.2
Weight in tons, dry	43,254	0.0	30,451	0.0	37,696	0.0	-29.6	23.8
Vegetables harvested for sale								
Number of farms	317	0.5	271	0.4	270	0.5	-14.5	-0.4
Number of acres	43,036	1.2	42,380	1.1	45,491	1.2	-1.5	7.3
Land in orchards								
Number of farms	-	-	-	-	-	-	-	-
Number of acres	-	-	-	-	-	-	-	-

Source: 1997 Census of Agriculture, U.S. Department of Agriculture, National Agricultural Statistics Service. NA stands for "not available." (D) is shown when data are withheld to prevent disclosure of competitive information. A dash (-) is shown where no data were reported. Not all states report growing all crops, but all crop categories in the census are shown for every state. The data series used for this presentation did not report U.S. totals for a number of categories; for that reason, the "% of U.S." column is sometimes blank.

FLORIDA

GENERAL STATISTICS FOR FLORIDA

Item	1987 Value	1987 % of U.S.	1992 Value	1992 % of U.S.	1997 Value	1997 % of U.S.	Percent change 1987-1992	Percent change 1992-1997
Farms (number)	36,556	1.8	35,204	1.8	34,799	1.8	-3.7	-1.2
Land in farms (acres)	11,194,090	1.2	10,766,077	1.1	10,454,217	1.1	-3.8	-2.9
Average size of farm (acres)	306	66.2	306	62.3	300	61.6	-	-2.0
Median size of farm (acres)	NA	-	NA	-	35	29.2	-	-
Market value of land and buildings:								
Average per farm (dollars)	543,830	187.9	619,265	173.4	662,538	147.3	13.9	7.0
Average per acre (dollars)	1,790	285.5	2,037	280.2	2,241	240.2	13.8	10.0
Market value of machinery/equipment - average per farm (dollars)	34,799	84.4	40,898	84.1	40,869	70.9	17.5	-0.1
Farms by size:								
1 to 9 acres	7,300	4.0	7,664	4.6	7,394	4.8	5.0	-3.5
10 to 49 acres	13,346	3.2	12,692	3.3	12,750	3.1	-4.9	0.5
50 to 179 acres	8,379	1.3	7,738	1.3	7,932	1.3	-7.7	2.5
180 to 499 acres	4,255	0.9	4,011	0.9	3,687	0.9	-5.7	-8.1
500 to 999 acres	1,598	0.8	1,451	0.8	1,390	0.8	-9.2	-4.2
1,000 acres or more	1,678	1.0	1,648	1.0	1,646	0.9	-1.8	-0.1
Total cropland								
Farms	29,386	1.6	28,702	1.7	27,141	1.6	-2.3	-5.4
Acres	3,790,599	0.9	3,841,505	0.9	3,639,850	0.8	1.3	-5.2
Harvested cropland (farms)	22,677	1.4	22,556	1.5	21,017	1.5	-0.5	-6.8
Harvested cropland (acres)	2,240,831	0.8	2,400,704	0.8	2,435,702	0.8	7.1	1.5
Irrigated land (farms)	11,981	4.1	13,500	4.8	12,673	4.5	12.7	-6.1
Irrigated land (acres)	1,622,750	3.5	1,782,680	3.6	1,862,404	3.4	9.9	4.5
Market value of agricultural products sold:								
Total sales ($1,000)	4,351,383	3.2	5,266,033	3.2	6,004,554	3.1	21.0	14.0
Average per farm (dollars)	119,033	182.7	149,586	177.1	172,550	167.6	25.7	15.4
Agricultural products only ($1,000)	3,317,823	5.6	4,197,420	5.6	4,817,261	4.9	26.5	14.8
Livestock, poultry, and products ($1,000)	1,033,560	1.3	1,068,613	1.2	1,187,292	1.2	3.4	11.1
Farms by value of sales:								
Less than $2,500	12,551	2.6	11,790	2.8	11,530	2.3	-6.1	-2.2
$2,500 to $4,999	4,868	1.9	4,318	1.9	4,405	1.9	-11.3	2.0
$5,000 to $9,999	4,470	1.6	4,151	1.6	4,122	1.7	-7.1	-0.7
$10,000 to $24,999	4,765	1.5	4,674	1.5	4,572	1.7	-1.9	-2.2
$25,000 to $49,999	2,833	1.3	2,901	1.5	2,805	1.6	2.4	-3.3
$50,000 to $99,999	2,273	1.0	2,262	1.2	2,188	1.4	-0.5	-3.3
$100,000 or more	4,796	1.6	5,108	1.5	5,177	1.5	6.5	1.4
Total farm production expenses ($1,000)	3,200,405	3.0	4,082,659	3.1	4,384,423	2.9	27.6	7.4
Average expenses per farm (dollars)	87,534	169.0	115,971	170.7	126,043	160.0	32.5	8.7
Net cash return for the farm unit:								
Number of farms	36,562	1.8	35,204	1.8	34,787	1.8	-3.7	-1.2
Value ($1000)	1,087,317	4.1	1,139,072	3.7	1,573,154	3.7	4.8	38.1
Average per farm (dollars)	29,739	234.9	32,356	204.8	45,222	203.2	8.8	39.8
Operators by principal occupation:								
Farming	15,821	1.4	16,557	1.6	15,782	1.6	4.7	-4.7
Other	20,735	2.2	18,647	2.1	19,017	2.0	-10.1	2.0
Operators by days worked off farm:								
Any	21,196	1.9	18,791	1.9	18,337	1.8	-11.3	-2.4
200 days or more	15,349	2.1	13,330	2.0	13,152	1.9	-13.2	-1.3

Source: 1997 Census of Agriculture, U.S. Department of Agriculture, National Agricultural Statistics Service. NA stands for "not available." (D) is shown when data are withheld to prevent disclosure of competitive information. A dash (-) is shown where no data were reported. The market value of land and buildings, and of machinery and equipment, is an estimated amount. Net cash return for the farm unit includes only returns from agricultural activities.

LIVESTOCK STATISTICS FOR FLORIDA

Item	1987 Value	1987 % of U.S.	1992 Value	1992 % of U.S.	1997 Value	1997 % of U.S.	Percent change 1987-1992	Percent change 1992-1997
Cattle and calves								
Number of farms	17,321	1.5	15,522	1.4	15,849	1.5	-10.4	2.1
Number of animals	1,879,124	2.0	1,783,968	1.9	1,808,900	1.8	-5.1	1.4
Beef cows (farms)	14,672	1.7	13,423	1.7	13,600	1.7	-8.5	1.3
Beef cows (number)	995,250	3.1	962,527	3.0	1,003,072	2.9	-3.3	4.2
Milk cows (farms)	1,073	0.5	877	0.6	666	0.6	-18.3	-24.1
Milk cows (number)	176,993	1.8	171,675	1.8	159,614	1.8	-3.0	-7.0
Cattle and calves sold (farms)	16,071	1.4	14,127	1.4	14,600	1.4	-12.1	3.3
Cattle and calves sold (number)	1,025,178	1.4	897,455	1.3	869,219	1.2	-12.5	-3.1
Hogs and pigs								
Number of farms	2,487	1.0	1,926	1.0	1,431	1.3	-22.6	-25.7
Number of animals	156,137	0.3	114,899	0.2	50,309	0.1	-26.4	-56.2
Hogs and pigs sold (farms)	2,103	0.9	1,551	0.8	971	1.0	-26.2	-37.4
Hogs and pigs sold (number)	266,652	0.3	200,375	0.2	96,512	0.1	-24.9	-51.8
Sheep and lambs								
Number of farms	304	0.3	305	0.4	336	0.5	0.3	10.2
Number of animals	8,867	0.1	7,465	0.1	5,722	0.1	-15.8	-23.3
Layers and pullets 13 weeks old and older								
Number of farms	2,275	1.6	1,454	1.6	1,203	1.7	-36.1	-17.3
Number of birds	12,964,760	3.5	10,802,573	3.1	12,605,047	3.4	-16.7	16.7
Broilers and other meat-type chickens sold								
Number of farms	402	1.5	363	1.5	321	1.3	-9.7	-11.6
Number of birds sold	93,224,832	1.4	97,854,566	1.8	105,967,210	1.6	5.0	8.3

Source: 1997 Census of Agriculture, U.S. Department of Agriculture, National Agricultural Statistics Service. NA stands for "not available." (D) is shown when data are withheld to prevent disclosure of competitive information. A dash (-) is shown where no data were reported.

CROP STATISTICS FOR FLORIDA

Item	1987 Value	1987 % of U.S.	1992 Value	1992 % of U.S.	1997 Value	1997 % of U.S.	Percent change 1987-1992	Percent change 1992-1997
Corn for grain or seed								
Number of farms	2,088	0.3	1,548	0.3	1,268	0.3	-25.9	-18.1
Number of acres	95,874	0.2	86,407	0.1	69,623	0.1	-9.9	-19.4
Number of bushels	6,628,740	-	6,377,801	0.1	5,440,956	0.1	-3.8	-14.7
Corn for silage or green chop								
Number of farms	-	-	-	-	-	-		-
Number of acres	-	-	-	-	-	-		-
Weight in tons, green	-	-	-	-	-	-		-
Sorghum for grain or seed								
Number of farms	-	-	-	-	-	-		-
Number of acres	-	-	-	-	-	-		-
Number of bushels	-	-	-	-	-	-		-
Wheat for grain								
Number of farms	-	-	-	-	-	-		-
Number of acres	-	-	-	-	-	-		-
Number of bushels	-	-	-	-	-	-		-
Barley for grain								
Number of farms	-	-	-	-	-	-		-
Number of acres	-	-	-	-	-	-		-
Number of bushels	-	-	-	-	-	-		-
Oats for grain								
Number of farms	-	-	-	-	-	-		-
Number of acres	-	-	-	-	-	-		-
Number of bushels	-	-	-	-	-	-		-
Rice								
Number of farms	-	-	-	-	-	-		-
Number of acres	-	-	-	-	-	-		-
Weight in hundredweight	-	-	-	-	-	-		-
Sunflower seed								
Number of farms	-	-	-	-	-	-		-
Number of acres	-	-	-	-	-	-		-
Weight in pounds	-	-	-	-	-	-		-
Cotton								
Number of farms	-	-	-	-	-	-		-
Number of acres	-	-	-	-	-	-		-
Number of bales	-	-	-	-	-	-		-

Continued.

CROP STATISTICS FOR FLORIDA - Continued

Item	1987 Value	1987 % of U.S.	1992 Value	1992 % of U.S.	1997 Value	1997 % of U.S.	Percent change 1987-1992	Percent change 1992-1997
Tobacco								
Number of farms	-	-	-	-	-	-	-	-
Number of acres	-	-	-	-	-	-	-	-
Weight in pounds	-	-	-	-	-	-	-	-
Soybeans for beans								
Number of farms	708	0.2	415	0.1	404	0.1	-41.4	-2.7
Number of acres	89,938	0.2	49,072	0.1	41,021	0.1	-45.4	-16.4
Number of bushels	2,257,392	0.1	1,523,227	0.1	1,025,521	0.0	-32.5	-32.7
Dry edible beans, excluding dry limas								
Number of farms	-	-	-	-	-	-	-	-
Number of acres	-	-	-	-	-	-	-	-
Weight in hundredweight	-	-	-	-	-	-	-	-
Potatoes, excluding sweetpotatoes								
Number of farms	-	-	-	-	-	-	-	-
Number of acres	-	-	-	-	-	-	-	-
Weight in hundredweight	-	-	-	-	-	-	-	-
Sugar beets for sugar								
Number of farms	-	-	-	-	-	-	-	-
Number of acres	-	-	-	-	-	-	-	-
Weight in tons	-	-	-	-	-	-	-	-
Sugarcane for sugar								
Number of farms	138	-	139	-	152	-	0.7	9.4
Number of acres	403,014	-	431,677	-	421,421	-	7.1	-2.4
Weight in tons	13,586,040	-	16,151,380	-	15,718,897	-	18.9	-2.7
Pineapples harvested								
Number of farms	-	-	-	-	-	-	-	-
Number of acres	-	-	-	-	-	-	-	-
Weight in tons	-	-	-	-	-	-	-	-
Peanuts for nuts								
Number of farms	-	-	-	-	-	-	-	-
Number of acres	-	-	-	-	-	-	-	-
Weight in pounds	-	-	-	-	-	-	-	-
Hay - all types, including alfalfa								
Number of farms	5,643	0.6	4,892	0.5	4,798	0.5	-13.3	-1.9
Number of acres	280,639	0.5	270,404	0.5	265,985	0.4	-3.6	-1.6
Weight in tons, dry	687,019	0.5	664,029	0.5	697,410	0.5	-3.3	5.0
Vegetables harvested for sale								
Number of farms	2,053	3.4	1,988	3.2	1,500	2.8	-3.2	-24.5
Number of acres	311,659	9.0	299,867	7.9	250,562	6.6	-3.8	-16.4
Land in orchards								
Number of farms	9,965	8.3	10,258	8.8	9,379	8.8	2.9	-8.6
Number of acres	762,068	16.7	914,642	19.2	981,910	19.0	20.0	7.4

Source: 1997 Census of Agriculture, U.S. Department of Agriculture, National Agricultural Statistics Service. NA stands for "not available." (D) is shown when data are withheld to prevent disclosure of competitive information. A dash (-) is shown where no data were reported. Not all states report growing all crops, but all crop categories in the census are shown for every state. The data series used for this presentation did not report U.S. totals for a number of categories; for that reason, the "% of U.S." column is sometimes blank.

GEORGIA

GENERAL STATISTICS FOR GEORGIA

Item	1987 Value	1987 % of U.S.	1992 Value	1992 % of U.S.	1997 Value	1997 % of U.S.	Percent change 1987-1992	Percent change 1992-1997
Farms (number)	43,552	2.1	40,759	2.1	40,334	2.1	-6.4	-1.0
Land in farms (acres)	10,744,718	1.1	10,025,581	1.1	10,671,246	1.1	-6.7	6.4
Average size of farm (acres)	247	53.5	246	50.1	265	54.4	-0.4	7.7
Median size of farm (acres)	NA	-	NA	-	96	80.0	-	-
Market value of land and buildings:								
Average per farm (dollars)	226,217	78.2	280,562	78.6	392,577	87.3	24.0	39.9
Average per acre (dollars)	920	146.7	1,131	155.6	1,505	161.3	22.9	33.1
Market value of machinery/equipment - average per farm (dollars)	32,477	78.8	34,904	71.8	44,392	77.0	7.5	27.2
Farms by size:								
1 to 9 acres	2,875	1.6	2,859	1.7	2,399	1.6	-0.6	-16.1
10 to 49 acres	10,953	2.7	10,443	2.7	10,255	2.5	-4.7	-1.8
50 to 179 acres	15,602	2.4	14,470	2.5	14,677	2.5	-7.3	1.4
180 to 499 acres	8,868	1.9	7,987	1.9	7,910	2.0	-9.9	-1.0
500 to 999 acres	3,197	1.6	2,972	1.6	2,795	1.6	-7.0	-6.0
1,000 acres or more	2,057	1.2	2,028	1.2	2,298	1.3	-1.4	13.3
Total cropland								
Farms	37,689	2.0	34,600	2.0	32,816	2.0	-8.2	-5.2
Acres	5,780,330	1.3	5,475,712	1.3	5,370,844	1.2	-5.3	-1.9
Harvested cropland (farms)	30,301	1.8	27,177	1.8	25,082	1.8	-10.3	-7.7
Harvested cropland (acres)	3,298,268	1.2	3,332,666	1.1	3,762,559	1.2	1.0	12.9
Irrigated land (farms)	4,985	1.7	4,701	1.7	4,372	1.6	-5.7	-7.0
Irrigated land (acres)	640,256	1.4	724,792	1.5	748,520	1.4	13.2	3.3
Market value of agricultural products sold:								
Total sales ($1,000)	2,814,592	2.1	3,521,217	2.2	4,992,918	2.5	25.1	41.8
Average per farm (dollars)	64,626	99.2	86,391	102.3	123,789	120.2	33.7	43.3
Agricultural products only ($1,000)	1,005,664	1.7	1,428,964	1.9	1,920,598	2.0	42.1	34.4
Livestock, poultry, and products ($1,000)	1,808,928	2.3	2,092,253	2.4	3,072,320	3.1	15.7	46.8
Farms by value of sales:								
Less than $2,500	13,176	2.7	12,070	2.9	13,731	2.8	-8.4	13.8
$2,500 to $4,999	6,460	2.5	5,983	2.6	5,503	2.4	-7.4	-8.0
$5,000 to $9,999	5,805	2.1	5,402	2.1	5,154	2.2	-6.9	-4.6
$10,000 to $24,999	5,320	1.6	5,200	1.7	4,694	1.7	-2.3	-9.7
$25,000 to $49,999	3,012	1.4	2,659	1.4	2,174	1.3	-11.7	-18.2
$50,000 to $99,999	2,883	1.3	2,397	1.3	1,908	1.2	-16.9	-20.4
$100,000 or more	6,896	2.3	7,048	2.1	7,170	2.1	2.2	1.7
Total farm production expenses ($1,000)	2,338,551	2.2	2,867,358	2.2	3,840,117	2.6	22.6	33.9
Average expenses per farm (dollars)	53,698	103.7	70,342	103.6	95,168	120.8	31.0	35.3
Net cash return for the farm unit:								
Number of farms	43,550	2.1	40,763	2.1	40,353	2.1	-6.4	-1.0
Value ($1000)	390,427	1.5	561,686	1.8	976,666	2.3	43.9	73.9
Average per farm (dollars)	8,965	70.8	13,779	87.2	24,203	108.7	53.7	75.7
Operators by principal occupation:								
Farming	19,449	1.7	18,817	1.8	17,523	1.8	-3.2	-6.9
Other	24,103	2.5	21,942	2.5	22,811	2.4	-9.0	4.0
Operators by days worked off farm:								
Any	25,029	2.2	21,843	2.2	21,902	2.1	-12.7	0.3
200 days or more	18,426	2.5	16,051	2.4	16,295	2.3	-12.9	1.5

Source: *1997 Census of Agriculture*, U.S. Department of Agriculture, National Agricultural Statistics Service. NA stands for "not available." (D) is shown when data are withheld to prevent disclosure of competitive information. A dash (-) is shown where no data were reported. The market value of land and buildings, and of machinery and equipment, is an estimated amount. Net cash return for the farm unit includes only returns from agricultural activities.

LIVESTOCK STATISTICS FOR GEORGIA

Item	1987 Value	1987 % of U.S.	1992 Value	1992 % of U.S.	1997 Value	1997 % of U.S.	Percent change 1987-1992	Percent change 1992-1997
Cattle and calves								
Number of farms	25,349	2.2	23,339	2.2	21,874	2.1	-7.9	-6.3
Number of animals	1,266,679	1.3	1,258,062	1.3	1,244,489	1.3	-0.7	-1.1
Beef cows (farms)	21,952	2.6	20,549	2.6	19,180	2.4	-6.4	-6.7
Beef cows (number)	606,750	1.9	599,899	1.8	613,731	1.8	-1.1	2.3
Milk cows (farms)	1,475	0.7	1,168	0.8	984	0.8	-20.8	-15.8
Milk cows (number)	97,763	1.0	102,001	1.1	98,931	1.1	4.3	-3.0
Cattle and calves sold (farms)	24,604	2.1	22,162	2.1	21,015	2.1	-9.9	-5.2
Cattle and calves sold (number)	681,238	0.9	612,588	0.9	613,950	0.8	-10.1	0.2
Hogs and pigs								
Number of farms	5,805	2.4	3,844	2.0	1,764	1.6	-33.8	-54.1
Number of animals	1,060,377	2.0	1,000,813	1.7	514,029	0.8	-5.6	-48.6
Hogs and pigs sold (farms)	5,634	2.4	3,745	2.0	1,561	1.5	-33.5	-58.3
Hogs and pigs sold (number)	1,869,236	1.9	1,865,702	1.7	1,030,187	0.7	-0.2	-44.8
Sheep and lambs								
Number of farms	348	0.4	374	0.5	335	0.5	7.5	-10.4
Number of animals	8,726	0.1	8,237	0.1	7,318	0.1	-5.6	-11.2
Layers and pullets 13 weeks old and older								
Number of farms	2,629	1.8	1,800	2.0	1,295	1.8	-31.5	-28.1
Number of birds	26,274,511	7.0	24,144,218	6.9	21,525,495	5.9	-8.1	-10.8
Broilers and other meat-type chickens sold								
Number of farms	2,815	10.2	2,407	10.1	2,245	9.4	-14.5	-6.7
Number of birds sold	609,503,009	9.1	749,018,187	13.8	1,017,501,305	15.1	22.9	35.8

Source: *1997 Census of Agriculture*, U.S. Department of Agriculture, National Agricultural Statistics Service. NA stands for "not available." (D) is shown when data are withheld to prevent disclosure of competitive information. A dash (-) is shown where no data were reported.

CROP STATISTICS FOR GEORGIA

Item	1987 Value	1987 % of U.S.	1992 Value	1992 % of U.S.	1997 Value	1997 % of U.S.	Percent change 1987-1992	Percent change 1992-1997
Corn for grain or seed								
Number of farms	10,561	1.7	7,896	1.6	5,196	1.2	-25.2	-34.2
Number of acres	548,498	0.9	647,833	0.9	404,268	0.6	18.1	-37.6
Number of bushels	43,332,343	-	60,513,790	0.7	40,568,303	0.5	39.7	-33.0
Corn for silage or green chop								
Number of farms	-	-	-	-	-	-	-	-
Number of acres	-	-	-	-	-	-	-	-
Weight in tons, green	-	-	-	-	-	-	-	-
Sorghum for grain or seed								
Number of farms	-	-	-	-	-	-	-	-
Number of acres	-	-	-	-	-	-	-	-
Number of bushels	-	-	-	-	-	-	-	-
Wheat for grain								
Number of farms	4,704	1.3	2,332	0.8	2,115	0.9	-50.4	-9.3
Number of acres	416,997	0.8	292,362	0.5	299,188	0.5	-29.9	2.3
Number of bushels	13,269,742	0.7	12,371,069	0.6	12,691,834	0.6	-6.8	2.6
Barley for grain								
Number of farms	-	-	-	-	-	-	-	-
Number of acres	-	-	-	-	-	-	-	-
Number of bushels	-	-	-	-	-	-	-	-
Oats for grain								
Number of farms	-	-	-	-	-	-	-	-
Number of acres	-	-	-	-	-	-	-	-
Number of bushels	-	-	-	-	-	-	-	-
Rice								
Number of farms	-	-	-	-	-	-	-	-
Number of acres	-	-	-	-	-	-	-	-
Weight in hundredweight	-	-	-	-	-	-	-	-
Sunflower seed								
Number of farms	-	-	-	-	-	-	-	-
Number of acres	-	-	-	-	-	-	-	-
Weight in pounds	-	-	-	-	-	-	-	-
Cotton								
Number of farms	1,733	4.0	2,015	5.8	4,188	13.3	16.3	107.8
Number of acres	231,635	2.4	431,625	3.9	1,367,620	10.3	86.3	216.9
Number of bales	286,188	2.2	668,950	4.4	1,764,127	9.9	133.7	163.7

Continued.

501

CROP STATISTICS FOR GEORGIA - Continued

Item	1987 Value	1987 % of U.S.	1992 Value	1992 % of U.S.	1997 Value	1997 % of U.S.	Percent change 1987-1992	Percent change 1992-1997
Tobacco								
Number of farms	2,061	-	1,658	-	1,180	-	-19.6	-28.8
Number of acres	30,853	-	40,403	-	41,083	-	31.0	1.7
Weight in pounds	65,722,067	-	88,150,533	-	85,789,611	-	34.1	-2.7
Soybeans for beans								
Number of farms	6,036	1.4	4,193	1.1	2,864	0.8	-30.5	-31.7
Number of acres	759,582	1.4	513,781	0.9	351,359	0.5	-32.4	-31.6
Number of bushels	16,725,741	0.9	14,391,870	0.7	7,078,444	0.3	-14.0	-50.8
Dry edible beans, excluding dry limas								
Number of farms	-	-	-	-	-	-	-	-
Number of acres	-	-	-	-	-	-	-	-
Weight in hundredweight	-	-	-	-	-	-	-	-
Potatoes, excluding sweetpotatoes								
Number of farms	-	-	-	-	-	-	-	-
Number of acres	-	-	-	-	-	-	-	-
Weight in hundredweight	-	-	-	-	-	-	-	-
Sugar beets for sugar								
Number of farms	-	-	-	-	-	-	-	-
Number of acres	-	-	-	-	-	-	-	-
Weight in tons	-	-	-	-	-	-	-	-
Sugarcane for sugar								
Number of farms	-	-	-	-	-	-	-	-
Number of acres	-	-	-	-	-	-	-	-
Weight in tons	-	-	-	-	-	-	-	-
Pineapples harvested								
Number of farms	-	-	-	-	-	-	-	-
Number of acres	-	-	-	-	-	-	-	-
Weight in tons	-	-	-	-	-	-	-	-
Peanuts for nuts								
Number of farms	7,067	-	6,095	-	4,695	-	-13.8	-23.0
Number of acres	562,034	-	630,305	-	511,954	-	12.1	-18.8
Weight in pounds	1,449,659,693	-	1,717,836,338	-	1,284,532,488	-	18.5	-25.2
Hay - all types, including alfalfa								
Number of farms	16,221	1.6	14,241	1.6	14,066	1.6	-12.2	-1.2
Number of acres	536,670	0.9	508,575	0.9	553,243	0.9	-5.2	8.8
Weight in tons, dry	1,076,223	0.8	1,221,143	1.0	1,340,678	1.0	13.5	9.8
Vegetables harvested for sale								
Number of farms	-	-	-	-	-	-	-	-
Number of acres	-	-	-	-	-	-	-	-
Land in orchards								
Number of farms	-	-	-	-	-	-	-	-
Number of acres	-	-	-	-	-	-	-	-

Source: 1997 Census of Agriculture, U.S. Department of Agriculture, National Agricultural Statistics Service. NA stands for "not available." (D) is shown when data are withheld to prevent disclosure of competitive information. A dash (-) is shown where no data were reported. Not all states report growing all crops, but all crop categories in the census are shown for every state. The data series used for this presentation did not report U.S. totals for a number of categories; for that reason, the "% of U.S." column is sometimes blank.

HAWAII

GENERAL STATISTICS FOR HAWAII

Item	1987 Value	1987 % of U.S.	1992 Value	1992 % of U.S.	1997 Value	1997 % of U.S.	Percent change 1987-1992	Percent change 1992-1997
Farms (number)	4,870	0.2	5,336	0.3	5,473	0.3	9.6	2.6
Land in farms (acres)	1,721,521	0.2	1,588,843	0.2	1,439,071	0.2	-7.7	-9.4
Average size of farm (acres)	353	76.4	298	60.7	263	54.0	-15.6	-11.7
Median size of farm (acres)	NA	-	NA	-	5	4.2	-	-
Market value of land and buildings:								
Average per farm (dollars)	603,435	208.5	722,189	202.3	632,281	140.6	19.7	-12.4
Average per acre (dollars)	1,707	272.2	2,425	333.6	2,405	257.8	42.1	-0.8
Market value of machinery/equipment - average per farm (dollars)	41,208	100.0	53,207	109.5	38,709	67.1	29.1	-27.2
Farms by size:								
1 to 9 acres	2,855	1.6	3,410	2.0	3,456	2.3	19.4	1.3
10 to 49 acres	1,401	0.3	1,342	0.3	1,417	0.3	-4.2	5.6
50 to 179 acres	341	0.1	313	0.1	318	0.1	-8.2	1.6
180 to 499 acres	128	0.0	133	0.0	139	0.0	3.9	4.5
500 to 999 acres	31	0.0	34	0.0	43	0.0	9.7	26.5
1,000 acres or more	114	0.1	104	0.1	100	0.1	-8.8	-3.8
Total cropland								
Farms	4,170	0.2	4,735	0.3	4,882	0.3	13.5	3.1
Acres	327,396	0.1	293,371	0.1	292,107	0.1	-10.4	-0.4
Harvested cropland (farms)	3,837	0.2	4,472	0.3	4,594	0.3	16.5	2.7
Harvested cropland (acres)	152,719	0.1	136,431	0.0	100,094	0.0	-10.7	-26.6
Irrigated land (farms)	1,827	0.6	2,220	0.8	2,241	0.8	21.5	0.9
Irrigated land (acres)	148,884	0.3	134,338	0.3	76,971	0.1	-9.8	-42.7
Market value of agricultural products sold:								
Total sales ($1,000)	609,741	0.4	552,054	0.3	496,935	0.3	-9.5	-10.0
Average per farm (dollars)	125,203	192.1	103,458	122.5	90,798	88.2	-17.4	-12.2
Agricultural products only ($1,000)	498,317	0.8	453,410	0.6	401,411	0.4	-9.0	-11.5
Livestock, poultry, and products ($1,000)	111,424	0.1	98,644	0.1	95,524	0.1	-11.5	-3.2
Farms by value of sales:								
Less than $2,500	1,402	0.3	1,790	0.4	1,638	0.3	27.7	-8.5
$2,500 to $4,999	674	0.3	754	0.3	743	0.3	11.9	-1.5
$5,000 to $9,999	745	0.3	715	0.3	797	0.3	-4.0	11.5
$10,000 to $24,999	911	0.3	863	0.3	989	0.4	-5.3	14.6
$25,000 to $49,999	476	0.2	484	0.2	535	0.3	1.7	10.5
$50,000 to $99,999	287	0.1	291	0.2	323	0.2	1.4	11.0
$100,000 or more	375	0.1	439	0.1	448	0.1	17.1	2.1
Total farm production expenses ($1,000)	495,759	0.5	466,826	0.4	398,567	0.3	-5.8	-14.6
Average expenses per farm (dollars)	101,840	196.6	87,486	128.8	72,851	92.5	-14.1	-16.7
Net cash return for the farm unit:								
Number of farms	4,869	0.2	5,336	0.3	5,473	0.3	9.6	2.6
Value ($1000)	113,904	0.4	85,228	0.3	98,368	0.2	-25.2	15.4
Average per farm (dollars)	23,394	184.8	15,972	101.1	17,973	80.7	-31.7	12.5
Operators by principal occupation:								
Farming	2,816	0.2	2,926	0.3	3,052	0.3	3.9	4.3
Other	2,054	0.2	2,410	0.3	2,421	0.3	17.3	0.5
Operators by days worked off farm:								
Any	2,728	0.2	2,864	0.3	2,827	0.3	5.0	-1.3
200 days or more	1,476	0.2	1,487	0.2	1,566	0.2	0.7	5.3

Source: *1997 Census of Agriculture*, U.S. Department of Agriculture, National Agricultural Statistics Service. NA stands for "not available." (D) is shown when data are withheld to prevent disclosure of competitive information. A dash (-) is shown where no data were reported. The market value of land and buildings, and of machinery and equipment, is an estimated amount. Net cash return for the farm unit includes only returns from agricultural activities.

LIVESTOCK STATISTICS FOR HAWAII

Item	1987 Value	1987 % of U.S.	1992 Value	1992 % of U.S.	1997 Value	1997 % of U.S.	Percent change 1987-1992	Percent change 1992-1997
Cattle and calves								
Number of farms	1,003	0.1	874	0.1	829	0.1	-12.9	-5.1
Number of animals	211,045	0.2	191,230	0.2	181,732	0.2	-9.4	-5.0
Beef cows (farms)	724	0.1	655	0.1	625	0.1	-9.5	-4.6
Beef cows (number)	83,427	0.3	87,620	0.3	93,711	0.3	5.0	7.0
Milk cows (farms)	73	0.0	57	0.0	44	0.0	-21.9	-22.8
Milk cows (number)	11,836	0.1	10,816	0.1	8,389	0.1	-8.6	-22.4
Cattle and calves sold (farms)	807	0.1	699	0.1	660	0.1	-13.4	-5.6
Cattle and calves sold (number)	101,315	0.1	82,788	0.1	66,726	0.1	-18.3	-19.4
Hogs and pigs								
Number of farms	372	0.2	253	0.1	248	0.2	-32.0	-2.0
Number of animals	47,564	0.1	28,570	0.0	29,440	0.0	-39.9	3.0
Hogs and pigs sold (farms)	307	0.1	200	0.1	190	0.2	-34.9	-5.0
Hogs and pigs sold (number)	69,019	0.1	47,831	0.0	38,066	0.0	-30.7	-20.4
Sheep and lambs								
Number of farms	42	0.0	62	0.1	104	0.2	47.6	67.7
Number of animals	21,908	0.2	22,938	0.2	22,541	0.3	4.7	-1.7
Layers and pullets 13 weeks old and older								
Number of farms	181	0.1	177	0.2	140	0.2	-2.2	-20.9
Number of birds	(D)	-	935,278	0.3	726,534	0.2	-	-22.3
Broilers and other meat-type chickens sold								
Number of farms	12	0.0	14	0.1	9	0.0	16.7	-35.7
Number of birds sold	2,069,316	0.0	1,201,331	0.0	478,672	0.0	-41.9	-60.2

Source: *1997 Census of Agriculture*, U.S. Department of Agriculture, National Agricultural Statistics Service. NA stands for "not available." (D) is shown when data are withheld to prevent disclosure of competitive information. A dash (-) is shown where no data were reported.

CROP STATISTICS FOR HAWAII

Item	1987 Value	1987 % of U.S.	1992 Value	1992 % of U.S.	1997 Value	1997 % of U.S.	Percent change 1987-1992	Percent change 1992-1997
Corn for grain or seed								
Number of farms	-	-	-	-	-	-	-	-
Number of acres	-	-	-	-	-	-	-	-
Number of bushels	-	-	-	-	-	-	-	-
Corn for silage or green chop								
Number of farms	-	-	-	-	-	-	-	-
Number of acres	-	-	-	-	-	-	-	-
Weight in tons, green	-	-	-	-	-	-	-	-
Sorghum for grain or seed								
Number of farms	-	-	-	-	-	-	-	-
Number of acres	-	-	-	-	-	-	-	-
Number of bushels	-	-	-	-	-	-	-	-
Wheat for grain								
Number of farms	-	-	-	-	-	-	-	-
Number of acres	-	-	-	-	-	-	-	-
Number of bushels	-	-	-	-	-	-	-	-
Barley for grain								
Number of farms	-	-	-	-	-	-	-	-
Number of acres	-	-	-	-	-	-	-	-
Number of bushels	-	-	-	-	-	-	-	-
Oats for grain								
Number of farms	-	-	-	-	-	-	-	-
Number of acres	-	-	-	-	-	-	-	-
Number of bushels	-	-	-	-	-	-	-	-
Rice								
Number of farms	-	-	-	-	-	-	-	-
Number of acres	-	-	-	-	-	-	-	-
Weight in hundredweight	-	-	-	-	-	-	-	-
Sunflower seed								
Number of farms	-	-	-	-	-	-	-	-
Number of acres	-	-	-	-	-	-	-	-
Weight in pounds	-	-	-	-	-	-	-	-
Cotton								
Number of farms	-	-	-	-	-	-	-	-
Number of acres	-	-	-	-	-	-	-	-
Number of bales	-	-	-	-	-	-	-	-

Continued.

CROP STATISTICS FOR HAWAII - Continued

Item	1987 Value	1987 % of U.S.	1992 Value	1992 % of U.S.	1997 Value	1997 % of U.S.	Percent change 1987-1992	Percent change 1992-1997
Tobacco								
Number of farms	-	-	-	-	-	-	-	-
Number of acres	-	-	-	-	-	-	-	-
Weight in pounds	-	-	-	-	-	-	-	-
Soybeans for beans								
Number of farms	-	-	-	-	-	-	-	-
Number of acres	-	-	-	-	-	-	-	-
Number of bushels	-	-	-	-	-	-	-	-
Dry edible beans, excluding dry limas								
Number of farms	-	-	-	-	-	-	-	-
Number of acres	-	-	-	-	-	-	-	-
Weight in hundredweight	-	-	-	-	-	-	-	-
Potatoes, excluding sweetpotatoes								
Number of farms	-	-	-	-	-	-	-	-
Number of acres	-	-	-	-	-	-	-	-
Weight in hundredweight	-	-	-	-	-	-	-	-
Sugar beets for sugar								
Number of farms	-	-	-	-	-	-	-	-
Number of acres	-	-	-	-	-	-	-	-
Weight in tons	-	-	-	-	-	-	-	-
Sugarcane for sugar								
Number of farms	79	-	31	-	13	-	-60.8	-58.1
Number of acres	79,234	-	62,915	-	31,483	-	-20.6	-50.0
Weight in tons	7,934,181	-	5,488,214	-	2,873,712	-	-30.8	-47.6
Pineapples harvested								
Number of farms	18	-	21	-	27	-	16.7	28.6
Number of acres	22,262	-	15,500	-	12,992	-	-30.4	-16.2
Weight in tons	683,182	-	556,748	-	348,428	-	-18.5	-37.4
Peanuts for nuts								
Number of farms	-	-	-	-	-	-	-	-
Number of acres	-	-	-	-	-	-	-	-
Weight in pounds	-	-	-	-	-	-	-	-
Hay - all types, including alfalfa								
Number of farms	-	-	-	-	-	-	-	-
Number of acres	-	-	-	-	-	-	-	-
Weight in tons, dry	-	-	-	-	-	-	-	-
Vegetables harvested for sale								
Number of farms	710	1.2	602	1.0	657	1.2	-15.2	9.1
Number of acres	5,587	0.2	5,129	0.1	6,549	0.2	-8.2	27.7
Land in orchards								
Number of farms	2,128	1.8	2,537	2.2	2,786	2.6	19.2	9.8
Number of acres	33,564	0.7	38,590	0.8	37,906	0.7	15.0	-1.8

Source: *1997 Census of Agriculture*, U.S. Department of Agriculture, National Agricultural Statistics Service. NA stands for "not available." (D) is shown when data are withheld to prevent disclosure of competitive information. A dash (-) is shown where no data were reported. Not all states report growing all crops, but all crop categories in the census are shown for every state. The data series used for this presentation did not report U.S. totals for a number of categories; for that reason, the "% of U.S." column is sometimes blank.

IDAHO

GENERAL STATISTICS FOR IDAHO

Item	1987 Value	1987 % of U.S.	1992 Value	1992 % of U.S.	1997 Value	1997 % of U.S.	Percent change 1987-1992	Percent change 1992-1997
Farms (number)	24,142	1.2	22,124	1.1	22,314	1.2	-8.4	0.9
Land in farms (acres)	13,931,875	1.4	13,468,992	1.4	11,830,167	1.3	-3.3	-12.2
Average size of farm (acres)	577	124.9	609	124.0	530	108.8	5.5	-13.0
Median size of farm (acres)	NA	-	NA	-	100	83.3	-	-
Market value of land and buildings:								
Average per farm (dollars)	336,615	116.3	410,206	114.9	536,521	119.3	21.9	30.8
Average per acre (dollars)	572	91.2	682	93.8	1,017	109.0	19.2	49.1
Market value of machinery/equipment - average per farm (dollars)	55,327	134.2	67,841	139.6	77,916	135.1	22.6	14.9
Farms by size:								
1 to 9 acres	3,021	1.6	2,785	1.7	3,092	2.0	-7.8	11.0
10 to 49 acres	5,268	1.3	5,017	1.3	5,621	1.4	-4.8	12.0
50 to 179 acres	5,685	0.9	5,070	0.9	4,757	0.8	-10.8	-6.2
180 to 499 acres	4,716	1.0	4,182	1.0	3,812	0.9	-11.3	-8.8
500 to 999 acres	2,446	1.2	2,270	1.2	2,199	1.3	-7.2	-3.1
1,000 acres or more	3,006	1.8	2,800	1.6	2,833	1.6	-6.9	1.2
Total cropland								
Farms	21,085	1.1	19,204	1.1	18,994	1.1	-8.9	-1.1
Acres	6,742,285	1.5	6,301,862	1.4	6,308,877	1.5	-6.5	0.1
Harvested cropland (farms)	18,270	1.1	16,023	1.1	15,494	1.1	-12.3	-3.3
Harvested cropland (acres)	4,349,122	1.5	4,225,273	1.4	4,478,862	1.4	-2.8	6.0
Irrigated land (farms)	16,620	5.7	15,487	5.5	15,191	5.4	-6.8	-1.9
Irrigated land (acres)	3,219,192	6.9	3,260,006	6.6	3,493,542	6.3	1.3	7.2
Market value of agricultural products sold:								
Total sales ($1,000)	2,269,404	1.7	2,964,216	1.8	3,345,864	1.7	30.6	12.9
Average per farm (dollars)	94,002	144.3	133,982	158.6	149,945	145.6	42.5	11.9
Agricultural products only ($1,000)	1,097,255	1.9	1,492,103	2.0	1,773,699	1.8	36.0	18.9
Livestock, poultry, and products ($1,000)	1,172,149	1.5	1,472,113	1.7	1,572,166	1.6	25.6	6.8
Farms by value of sales:								
Less than $2,500	5,329	1.1	4,726	1.1	5,663	1.1	-11.3	19.8
$2,500 to $4,999	2,519	1.0	2,186	0.9	2,350	1.0	-13.2	7.5
$5,000 to $9,999	2,627	1.0	2,433	1.0	2,362	1.0	-7.4	-2.9
$10,000 to $24,999	3,646	1.1	3,266	1.1	3,182	1.2	-10.4	-2.6
$25,000 to $49,999	2,781	1.3	2,370	1.2	2,068	1.2	-14.8	-12.7
$50,000 to $99,999	2,787	1.3	2,253	1.2	1,898	1.2	-19.2	-15.8
$100,000 or more	4,453	1.5	4,890	1.5	4,791	1.4	9.8	-2.0
Total farm production expenses ($1,000)	1,862,264	1.7	2,445,017	1.9	2,705,028	1.8	31.3	10.6
Average expenses per farm (dollars)	77,148	148.9	110,489	162.7	121,117	153.8	43.2	9.6
Net cash return for the farm unit:								
Number of farms	24,140	1.2	22,129	1.1	22,334	1.2	-8.3	0.9
Value ($1000)	387,910	1.5	493,797	1.6	590,283	1.4	27.3	19.5
Average per farm (dollars)	16,069	126.9	22,314	141.2	26,430	118.7	38.9	18.4
Operators by principal occupation:								
Farming	14,550	1.3	13,082	1.2	12,049	1.3	-10.1	-7.9
Other	9,592	1.0	9,042	1.0	10,265	1.1	-5.7	13.5
Operators by days worked off farm:								
Any	12,614	1.1	11,342	1.1	12,230	1.2	-10.1	7.8
200 days or more	7,555	1.0	7,214	1.1	7,885	1.1	-4.5	9.3

Source: *1997 Census of Agriculture*, U.S. Department of Agriculture, National Agricultural Statistics Service. NA stands for "not available." (D) is shown when data are withheld to prevent disclosure of competitive information. A dash (-) is shown where no data were reported. The market value of land and buildings, and of machinery and equipment, is an estimated amount. Net cash return for the farm unit includes only returns from agricultural activities.

LIVESTOCK STATISTICS FOR IDAHO

Item	1987 Value	% of U.S.	1992 Value	% of U.S.	1997 Value	% of U.S.	Percent change 1987-1992	1992-1997
Cattle and calves								
Number of farms	13,481	1.1	12,527	1.2	12,063	1.2	-7.1	-3.7
Number of animals	1,772,756	1.8	1,812,720	1.9	1,908,097	1.9	2.3	5.3
Beef cows (farms)	8,604	1.0	8,393	1.0	8,405	1.0	-2.5	0.1
Beef cows (number)	558,229	1.8	565,016	1.7	555,676	1.6	1.2	-1.7
Milk cows (farms)	2,769	1.4	1,990	1.3	1,404	1.2	-28.1	-29.4
Milk cows (number)	157,665	1.6	181,785	1.9	265,854	2.9	15.3	46.2
Cattle and calves sold (farms)	13,321	1.2	12,230	1.2	11,684	1.2	-8.2	-4.5
Cattle and calves sold (number)	1,502,218	2.1	1,646,112	2.3	1,578,375	2.1	9.6	-4.1
Hogs and pigs								
Number of farms	1,258	0.5	1,141	0.6	714	0.7	-9.3	-37.4
Number of animals	76,882	0.1	67,343	0.1	29,026	0.0	-12.4	-56.9
Hogs and pigs sold (farms)	1,113	0.5	940	0.5	573	0.6	-15.5	-39.0
Hogs and pigs sold (number)	119,188	0.1	104,723	0.1	44,626	0.0	-12.1	-57.4
Sheep and lambs								
Number of farms	1,464	1.6	1,316	1.6	1,097	1.7	-10.1	-16.6
Number of animals	316,112	2.9	347,678	3.2	273,804	3.5	10.0	-21.2
Layers and pullets 13 weeks old and older								
Number of farms	1,839	1.3	1,119	1.3	886	1.2	-39.2	-20.8
Number of birds	1,425,572	0.4	1,488,472	0.4	(D)	-	4.4	-
Broilers and other meat-type chickens sold								
Number of farms	85	0.3	59	0.2	55	0.2	-30.6	-6.8
Number of birds sold	8,733	0.0	27,206	0.0	6,043	0.0	211.5	-77.8

Source: *1997 Census of Agriculture*, U.S. Department of Agriculture, National Agricultural Statistics Service. NA stands for "not available." (D) is shown when data are withheld to prevent disclosure of competitive information. A dash (-) is shown where no data were reported.

CROP STATISTICS FOR IDAHO

Item	1987 Value	% of U.S.	1992 Value	% of U.S.	1997 Value	% of U.S.	Percent change 1987-1992	1992-1997
Corn for grain or seed								
Number of farms	-	-	-	-	-	-	-	-
Number of acres	-	-	-	-	-	-	-	-
Number of bushels	-	-	-	-	-	-	-	-
Corn for silage or green chop								
Number of farms	-	-	-	-	-	-	-	-
Number of acres	-	-	-	-	-	-	-	-
Weight in tons, green	-	-	-	-	-	-	-	-
Sorghum for grain or seed								
Number of farms	-	-	-	-	-	-	-	-
Number of acres	-	-	-	-	-	-	-	-
Number of bushels	-	-	-	-	-	-	-	-
Wheat for grain								
Number of farms	7,706	2.2	6,106	2.1	5,199	2.1	-20.8	-14.9
Number of acres	1,239,480	2.3	1,384,893	2.3	1,410,978	2.4	11.7	1.9
Number of bushels	83,250,152	4.4	94,094,326	4.3	108,941,849	4.9	13.0	15.8
Barley for grain								
Number of farms	7,852	-	5,149	-	4,178	-	-34.4	-18.9
Number of acres	833,225	-	691,273	-	711,504	-	-17.0	2.9
Number of bushels	59,437,911	-	48,647,384	-	54,317,070	-	-18.2	11.7
Oats for grain								
Number of farms	-	-	-	-	-	-	-	-
Number of acres	-	-	-	-	-	-	-	-
Number of bushels	-	-	-	-	-	-	-	-
Rice								
Number of farms	-	-	-	-	-	-	-	-
Number of acres	-	-	-	-	-	-	-	-
Weight in hundredweight	-	-	-	-	-	-	-	-
Sunflower seed								
Number of farms	-	-	-	-	-	-	-	-
Number of acres	-	-	-	-	-	-	-	-
Weight in pounds	-	-	-	-	-	-	-	-
Cotton								
Number of farms	-	-	-	-	-	-	-	-
Number of acres	-	-	-	-	-	-	-	-
Number of bales	-	-	-	-	-	-	-	-

Continued.

CROP STATISTICS FOR IDAHO - Continued

Item	1987		1992		1997		Percent change	
	Value	% of U.S.	Value	% of U.S.	Value	% of U.S.	1987-1992	1992-1997
Tobacco								
Number of farms	-	-	-	-	-	-	-	-
Number of acres	-	-	-	-	-	-	-	-
Weight in pounds	-	-	-	-	-	-	-	-
Soybeans for beans								
Number of farms	-	-	-	-	-	-	-	-
Number of acres	-	-	-	-	-	-	-	-
Number of bushels	-	-	-	-	-	-	-	-
Dry edible beans, excluding dry limas								
Number of farms	2,043	-	1,494	-	1,138	-	-26.9	-23.8
Number of acres	160,078	-	114,896	-	92,743	-	-28.2	-19.3
Weight in hundredweight	3,097,637	-	2,064,725	-	2,036,315	-	-33.3	-1.4
Potatoes, excluding sweetpotatoes								
Number of farms	1,792	-	1,616	-	1,402	-	-9.8	-13.2
Number of acres	352,670	-	372,028	-	394,977	-	5.5	6.2
Weight in hundredweight	99,392,607	-	119,060,333	-	135,578,736	-	19.8	13.9
Sugar beets for sugar								
Number of farms	1,397	-	1,406	-	921	-	0.6	-34.5
Number of acres	168,352	-	202,115	-	195,651	-	20.1	-3.2
Weight in tons	4,319,597	-	4,828,489	-	5,078,013	-	11.8	5.2
Sugarcane for sugar								
Number of farms	-	-	-	-	-	-	-	-
Number of acres	-	-	-	-	-	-	-	-
Weight in tons	-	-	-	-	-	-	-	-
Pineapples harvested								
Number of farms	-	-	-	-	-	-	-	-
Number of acres	-	-	-	-	-	-	-	-
Weight in tons	-	-	-	-	-	-	-	-
Peanuts for nuts								
Number of farms	-	-	-	-	-	-	-	-
Number of acres	-	-	-	-	-	-	-	-
Weight in pounds	-	-	-	-	-	-	-	-
Hay - all types, including alfalfa								
Number of farms	13,717	1.4	11,940	1.3	11,960	1.3	-13.0	0.2
Number of acres	1,173,475	2.0	1,063,292	1.9	1,260,010	2.1	-9.4	18.5
Weight in tons, dry	3,563,558	2.8	3,389,557	2.7	4,395,396	3.2	-4.9	29.7
Vegetables harvested for sale								
Number of farms	-	-	-	-	-	-	-	-
Number of acres	-	-	-	-	-	-	-	-
Land in orchards								
Number of farms	-	-	-	-	-	-	-	-
Number of acres	-	-	-	-	-	-	-	-

Source: *1997 Census of Agriculture*, U.S. Department of Agriculture, National Agricultural Statistics Service. NA stands for "not available." (D) is shown when data are withheld to prevent disclosure of competitive information. A dash (-) is shown where no data were reported. Not all states report growing all crops, but all crop categories in the census are shown for every state. The data series used for this presentation did not report U.S. totals for a number of categories; for that reason, the "% of U.S." column is sometimes blank.

ILLINOIS

GENERAL STATISTICS FOR ILLINOIS

Item	1987 Value	1987 % of U.S.	1992 Value	1992 % of U.S.	1997 Value	1997 % of U.S.	Percent change 1987-1992	Percent change 1992-1997
Farms (number)	88,786	4.3	77,610	4.0	73,051	3.8	-12.6	-5.9
Land in farms (acres)	28,526,664	3.0	27,250,340	2.9	27,204,780	2.9	-4.5	-0.2
Average size of farm (acres)	321	69.5	351	71.5	372	76.4	9.3	6.0
Median size of farm (acres)	NA	-	NA	-	180	150.0	-	-
Market value of land and buildings:								
Average per farm (dollars)	402,970	139.2	539,181	151.0	773,141	171.9	33.8	43.4
Average per acre (dollars)	1,262	201.3	1,548	212.9	2,126	227.9	22.7	37.3
Market value of machinery/equipment - average per farm (dollars)	60,935	147.8	71,219	146.5	90,447	156.8	16.9	27.0
Farms by size:								
1 to 9 acres	5,931	3.2	5,026	3.0	4,254	2.8	-15.3	-15.4
10 to 49 acres	12,971	3.1	12,191	3.1	12,604	3.1	-6.0	3.4
50 to 179 acres	23,824	3.7	20,239	3.5	19,606	3.3	-15.0	-3.1
180 to 499 acres	26,720	5.6	21,327	5.0	18,231	4.5	-20.2	-14.5
500 to 999 acres	14,320	7.2	12,833	6.9	11,619	6.6	-10.4	-9.5
1,000 acres or more	5,020	3.0	5,994	3.5	6,737	3.8	19.4	12.4
Total cropland								
Farms	83,056	4.5	72,626	4.3	68,082	4.1	-12.6	-6.3
Acres	25,102,092	5.7	24,164,457	5.6	23,920,923	5.5	-3.7	-1.0
Harvested cropland (farms)	79,986	4.9	69,425	4.7	62,712	4.4	-13.2	-9.7
Harvested cropland (acres)	20,102,388	7.1	21,868,287	7.4	22,274,230	7.2	8.8	1.9
Irrigated land (farms)	1,635	0.6	2,061	0.7	2,021	0.7	26.1	-1.9
Irrigated land (acres)	208,105	0.4	328,316	0.7	349,799	0.6	57.8	6.5
Market value of agricultural products sold:								
Total sales ($1,000)	6,376,801	4.7	7,336,864	4.5	8,556,486	4.3	15.1	16.6
Average per farm (dollars)	71,822	110.2	94,535	111.9	117,130	113.8	31.6	23.9
Agricultural products only ($1,000)	4,158,936	7.1	5,251,328	7.0	6,567,164	6.7	26.3	25.1
Livestock, poultry, and products ($1,000)	2,217,865	2.9	2,085,535	2.4	1,989,323	2.0	-6.0	-4.6
Farms by value of sales:								
Less than $2,500	10,630	2.2	9,178	2.2	12,210	2.5	-13.7	33.0
$2,500 to $4,999	6,741	2.6	5,613	2.4	5,107	2.2	-16.7	-9.0
$5,000 to $9,999	8,728	3.2	6,898	2.7	5,949	2.5	-21.0	-13.8
$10,000 to $24,999	14,962	4.6	11,800	3.9	9,082	3.3	-21.1	-23.0
$25,000 to $49,999	13,313	6.1	10,363	5.3	8,243	4.8	-22.2	-20.5
$50,000 to $99,999	14,765	6.8	11,572	6.2	9,290	5.9	-21.6	-19.7
$100,000 or more	19,647	6.6	22,186	6.6	23,170	6.7	12.9	4.4
Total farm production expenses ($1,000)	4,557,450	4.2	5,088,894	3.9	5,542,904	3.7	11.7	8.9
Average expenses per farm (dollars)	51,330	99.1	65,573	96.5	75,882	96.3	27.7	15.7
Net cash return for the farm unit:								
Number of farms	88,788	4.3	77,606	4.0	73,046	3.8	-12.6	-5.9
Value ($1000)	1,730,879	6.5	2,169,423	7.1	2,729,334	6.4	25.3	25.8
Average per farm (dollars)	19,495	154.0	27,954	176.9	37,365	167.9	43.4	33.7
Operators by principal occupation:								
Farming	57,122	5.0	47,875	4.5	41,645	4.3	-16.2	-13.0
Other	31,664	3.3	29,735	3.4	31,406	3.3	-6.1	5.6
Operators by days worked off farm:								
Any	43,651	3.9	38,703	3.9	37,953	3.6	-11.3	-1.9
200 days or more	26,001	3.5	24,056	3.6	24,220	3.4	-7.5	0.7

Source: 1997 Census of Agriculture, U.S. Department of Agriculture, National Agricultural Statistics Service. NA stands for "not available." (D) is shown when data are withheld to prevent disclosure of competitive information. A dash (-) is shown where no data were reported. The market value of land and buildings, and of machinery and equipment, is an estimated amount. Net cash return for the farm unit includes only returns from agricultural activities.

LIVESTOCK STATISTICS FOR ILLINOIS

Item	1987 Value	1987 % of U.S.	1992 Value	1992 % of U.S.	1997 Value	1997 % of U.S.	Percent change 1987-1992	Percent change 1992-1997
Cattle and calves								
Number of farms	33,305	2.8	27,405	2.6	24,452	2.3	-17.7	-10.8
Number of animals	1,885,444	2.0	1,601,261	1.7	1,437,697	1.5	-15.1	-10.2
Beef cows (farms)	23,087	2.7	19,392	2.4	17,682	2.2	-16.0	-8.8
Beef cows (number)	511,188	1.6	447,201	1.4	453,127	1.3	-12.5	1.3
Milk cows (farms)	4,304	2.1	3,050	2.0	2,238	1.9	-29.1	-26.6
Milk cows (number)	186,371	1.8	151,503	1.6	127,702	1.4	-18.7	-15.7
Cattle and calves sold (farms)	32,798	2.9	26,419	2.6	23,622	2.3	-19.4	-10.6
Cattle and calves sold (number)	1,407,670	1.9	1,130,433	1.6	949,478	1.3	-19.7	-16.0
Hogs and pigs								
Number of farms	17,084	7.0	13,433	7.0	7,168	6.5	-21.4	-46.6
Number of animals	5,642,991	10.8	5,641,115	9.8	4,679,166	7.6	-0.0	-17.1
Hogs and pigs sold (farms)	17,837	7.5	14,142	7.5	7,447	7.3	-20.7	-47.3
Hogs and pigs sold (number)	9,879,960	10.2	10,330,124	9.3	9,374,726	6.6	4.6	-9.2
Sheep and lambs								
Number of farms	3,950	4.3	3,204	4.0	2,263	3.4	-18.9	-29.4
Number of animals	137,913	1.2	110,302	1.0	72,544	0.9	-20.0	-34.2
Layers and pullets 13 weeks old and older								
Number of farms	4,013	2.8	2,248	2.5	1,747	2.4	-44.0	-22.3
Number of birds	4,396,092	1.2	4,170,867	1.2	3,722,915	1.0	-5.1	-10.7
Broilers and other meat-type chickens sold								
Number of farms	296	1.1	123	0.5	115	0.5	-58.4	-6.5
Number of birds sold	435,555	0.0	60,004	0.0	363,353	0.0	-86.2	505.5

Source: 1997 Census of Agriculture, U.S. Department of Agriculture, National Agricultural Statistics Service. NA stands for "not available." (D) is shown when data are withheld to prevent disclosure of competitive information. A dash (-) is shown where no data were reported.

CROP STATISTICS FOR ILLINOIS

Item	1987 Value	1987 % of U.S.	1992 Value	1992 % of U.S.	1997 Value	1997 % of U.S.	Percent change 1987-1992	Percent change 1992-1997
Corn for grain or seed								
Number of farms	66,600	10.6	55,685	11.1	48,443	11.2	-16.4	-13.0
Number of acres	9,162,711	15.6	10,770,985	15.5	10,710,072	15.3	17.6	-0.6
Number of bushels	1,168,644,485	-	1,532,681,088	17.6	1,363,015,453	15.9	31.2	-11.1
Corn for silage or green chop								
Number of farms	5,451	-	5,005	-	3,774	-	-8.2	-24.6
Number of acres	149,419	-	164,698	-	119,116	-	10.2	-27.7
Weight in tons, green	2,480,171	-	2,659,536	-	1,892,873	-	7.2	-28.8
Sorghum for grain or seed								
Number of farms	-	-	-	-	-	-	-	-
Number of acres	-	-	-	-	-	-	-	-
Number of bushels	-	-	-	-	-	-	-	-
Wheat for grain								
Number of farms	21,356	6.1	17,061	5.8	14,822	6.1	-20.1	-13.1
Number of acres	954,990	1.8	1,075,805	1.8	983,556	1.7	12.7	-8.6
Number of bushels	48,850,664	2.6	54,096,203	2.5	53,954,013	2.4	10.7	-0.3
Barley for grain								
Number of farms	-	-	-	-	-	-	-	-
Number of acres	-	-	-	-	-	-	-	-
Number of bushels	-	-	-	-	-	-	-	-
Oats for grain								
Number of farms	-	-	-	-	-	-	-	-
Number of acres	-	-	-	-	-	-	-	-
Number of bushels	-	-	-	-	-	-	-	-
Rice								
Number of farms	-	-	-	-	-	-	-	-
Number of acres	-	-	-	-	-	-	-	-
Weight in hundredweight	-	-	-	-	-	-	-	-
Sunflower seed								
Number of farms	-	-	-	-	-	-	-	-
Number of acres	-	-	-	-	-	-	-	-
Weight in pounds	-	-	-	-	-	-	-	-
Cotton								
Number of farms	-	-	-	-	-	-	-	-
Number of acres	-	-	-	-	-	-	-	-
Number of bales	-	-	-	-	-	-	-	-

Continued.

CROP STATISTICS FOR ILLINOIS - Continued

Item	1987 Value	1987 % of U.S.	1992 Value	1992 % of U.S.	1997 Value	1997 % of U.S.	Percent change 1987-1992	Percent change 1992-1997
Tobacco								
Number of farms	-	-	-	-	-	-	-	-
Number of acres	-	-	-	-	-	-	-	-
Weight in pounds	-	-	-	-	-	-	-	-
Soybeans for beans								
Number of farms	61,547	13.9	52,339	13.7	47,008	13.3	-15.0	-10.2
Number of acres	8,768,833	15.9	8,932,399	15.9	9,825,475	14.9	1.9	10.0
Number of bushels	329,323,117	17.9	373,563,650	18.2	415,716,620	16.6	13.4	11.3
Dry edible beans, excluding dry limas								
Number of farms	-	-	-	-	-	-	-	-
Number of acres	-	-	-	-	-	-	-	-
Weight in hundredweight	-	-	-	-	-	-	-	-
Potatoes, excluding sweetpotatoes								
Number of farms	-	-	-	-	-	-	-	-
Number of acres	-	-	-	-	-	-	-	-
Weight in hundredweight	-	-	-	-	-	-	-	-
Sugar beets for sugar								
Number of farms	-	-	-	-	-	-	-	-
Number of acres	-	-	-	-	-	-	-	-
Weight in tons	-	-	-	-	-	-	-	-
Sugarcane for sugar								
Number of farms	-	-	-	-	-	-	-	-
Number of acres	-	-	-	-	-	-	-	-
Weight in tons	-	-	-	-	-	-	-	-
Pineapples harvested								
Number of farms	-	-	-	-	-	-	-	-
Number of acres	-	-	-	-	-	-	-	-
Weight in tons	-	-	-	-	-	-	-	-
Peanuts for nuts								
Number of farms	-	-	-	-	-	-	-	-
Number of acres	-	-	-	-	-	-	-	-
Weight in pounds	-	-	-	-	-	-	-	-
Hay - all types, including alfalfa								
Number of farms	30,589	3.1	27,481	3.0	24,156	2.7	-10.2	-12.1
Number of acres	986,808	1.7	902,899	1.6	822,508	1.4	-8.5	-8.9
Weight in tons, dry	2,720,838	2.1	2,463,316	1.9	2,248,811	1.6	-9.5	-8.7
Vegetables harvested for sale								
Number of farms	1,466	2.4	1,714	2.8	1,262	2.3	16.9	-26.4
Number of acres	79,492	2.3	99,422	2.6	66,780	1.8	25.1	-32.8
Land in orchards								
Number of farms	-	-	-	-	-	-	-	-
Number of acres	-	-	-	-	-	-	-	-

Source: *1997 Census of Agriculture*, U.S. Department of Agriculture, National Agricultural Statistics Service. NA stands for "not available." (D) is shown when data are withheld to prevent disclosure of competitive information. A dash (-) is shown where no data were reported. Not all states report growing all crops, but all crop categories in the census are shown for every state. The data series used for this presentation did not report U.S. totals for a number of categories; for that reason, the "% of U.S." column is sometimes blank.

INDIANA

GENERAL STATISTICS FOR INDIANA

Item	1987 Value	1987 % of U.S.	1992 Value	1992 % of U.S.	1997 Value	1997 % of U.S.	Percent change 1987-1992	Percent change 1992-1997
Farms (number)	70,506	3.4	62,778	3.3	57,916	3.0	-11.0	-7.7
Land in farms (acres)	16,170,895	1.7	15,618,831	1.7	15,111,022	1.6	-3.4	-3.3
Average size of farm (acres)	229	49.6	249	50.7	261	53.6	8.7	4.8
Median size of farm (acres)	NA	-	NA	-	100	83.3	-	-
Market value of land and buildings:								
Average per farm (dollars)	265,446	91.7	346,199	97.0	532,663	118.4	30.4	53.9
Average per acre (dollars)	1,158	184.7	1,395	191.9	2,064	221.2	20.5	48.0
Market value of machinery/equipment - average per farm (dollars)	44,502	107.9	55,440	114.1	64,050	111.0	24.6	15.5
Farms by size:								
1 to 9 acres	5,444	3.0	5,141	3.1	4,183	2.7	-5.6	-18.6
10 to 49 acres	15,010	3.6	14,234	3.7	13,987	3.4	-5.2	-1.7
50 to 179 acres	24,892	3.9	21,268	3.6	19,913	3.4	-14.6	-6.4
180 to 499 acres	15,902	3.3	12,928	3.0	11,099	2.8	-18.7	-14.1
500 to 999 acres	6,670	3.3	6,000	3.2	5,268	3.0	-10.0	-12.2
1,000 acres or more	2,588	1.5	3,207	1.9	3,466	2.0	23.9	8.1
Total cropland								
Farms	65,529	3.5	58,117	3.4	53,256	3.2	-11.3	-8.4
Acres	13,592,873	3.1	13,366,034	3.1	12,848,950	3.0	-1.7	-3.9
Harvested cropland (farms)	61,689	3.8	54,252	3.6	47,613	3.4	-12.1	-12.2
Harvested cropland (acres)	10,706,298	3.8	11,834,675	4.0	11,716,704	3.8	10.5	-1.0
Irrigated land (farms)	1,481	0.5	1,742	0.6	1,753	0.6	17.6	0.6
Irrigated land (acres)	169,703	0.4	240,898	0.5	250,050	0.5	42.0	3.8
Market value of agricultural products sold:								
Total sales ($1,000)	4,067,684	3.0	4,633,090	2.8	5,229,977	2.7	13.9	12.9
Average per farm (dollars)	57,693	88.5	73,801	87.4	90,303	87.7	27.9	22.4
Agricultural products only ($1,000)	2,127,135	3.6	2,698,335	3.6	3,246,617	3.3	26.9	20.3
Livestock, poultry, and products ($1,000)	1,940,549	2.5	1,934,755	2.2	1,983,359	2.0	-0.3	2.5
Farms by value of sales:								
Less than $2,500	12,433	2.5	11,189	2.6	13,022	2.6	-10.0	16.4
$2,500 to $4,999	8,072	3.1	6,848	3.0	5,710	2.5	-15.2	-16.6
$5,000 to $9,999	9,515	3.5	8,053	3.2	6,579	2.8	-15.4	-18.3
$10,000 to $24,999	12,820	3.9	10,642	3.5	8,757	3.2	-17.0	-17.7
$25,000 to $49,999	8,682	4.0	7,296	3.7	6,057	3.5	-16.0	-17.0
$50,000 to $99,999	8,031	3.7	6,694	3.6	5,728	3.6	-16.6	-14.4
$100,000 or more	10,953	3.7	12,056	3.6	12,063	3.5	10.1	0.1
Total farm production expenses ($1,000)	3,178,679	2.9	3,645,379	2.8	4,011,772	2.7	14.7	10.1
Average expenses per farm (dollars)	45,084	87.0	58,073	85.5	69,262	87.9	28.8	19.3
Net cash return for the farm unit:								
Number of farms	70,506	3.4	62,772	3.3	57,922	3.0	-11.0	-7.7
Value ($1000)	883,642	3.3	961,902	3.2	1,163,605	2.7	8.9	21.0
Average per farm (dollars)	12,533	99.0	15,324	97.0	20,089	90.2	22.3	31.1
Operators by principal occupation:								
Farming	36,654	3.2	31,547	3.0	26,993	2.8	-13.9	-14.4
Other	33,852	3.6	31,231	3.6	30,923	3.3	-7.7	-1.0
Operators by days worked off farm:								
Any	40,682	3.6	35,397	3.6	33,959	3.3	-13.0	-4.1
200 days or more	28,153	3.8	25,237	3.8	24,216	3.4	-10.4	-4.0

Source: 1997 Census of Agriculture, U.S. Department of Agriculture, National Agricultural Statistics Service. NA stands for "not available." (D) is shown when data are withheld to prevent disclosure of competitive information. A dash (-) is shown where no data were reported. The market value of land and buildings, and of machinery and equipment, is an estimated amount. Net cash return for the farm unit includes only returns from agricultural activities.

LIVESTOCK STATISTICS FOR INDIANA

Item	1987 Value	1987 % of U.S.	1992 Value	1992 % of U.S.	1997 Value	1997 % of U.S.	Percent change 1987-1992	Percent change 1992-1997
Cattle and calves								
Number of farms	30,340	2.6	25,974	2.4	23,025	2.2	-14.4	-11.4
Number of animals	1,236,480	1.3	1,113,473	1.2	976,701	1.0	-9.9	-12.3
Beef cows (farms)	19,150	2.3	16,783	2.1	15,164	1.9	-12.4	-9.6
Beef cows (number)	315,784	1.0	293,836	0.9	277,797	0.8	-7.0	-5.5
Milk cows (farms)	5,204	2.6	3,958	2.5	3,216	2.8	-23.9	-18.7
Milk cows (number)	163,867	1.6	144,532	1.5	131,630	1.4	-11.8	-8.9
Cattle and calves sold (farms)	28,905	2.5	24,215	2.3	21,585	2.1	-16.2	-10.9
Cattle and calves sold (number)	881,663	1.2	763,919	1.1	667,846	0.9	-13.4	-12.6
Hogs and pigs								
Number of farms	14,834	6.1	11,987	6.3	6,442	5.9	-19.2	-46.3
Number of animals	4,372,294	8.4	4,618,663	8.0	3,972,060	6.5	5.6	-14.0
Hogs and pigs sold (farms)	15,458	6.5	12,559	6.7	6,623	6.5	-18.8	-47.3
Hogs and pigs sold (number)	8,024,713	8.3	8,760,626	7.9	7,584,642	5.3	9.2	-13.4
Sheep and lambs								
Number of farms	3,008	3.3	2,553	3.2	1,927	2.9	-15.1	-24.5
Number of animals	82,757	0.7	72,386	0.7	54,227	0.7	-12.5	-25.1
Layers and pullets 13 weeks old and older								
Number of farms	3,713	2.6	2,348	2.7	1,846	2.5	-36.8	-21.4
Number of birds	26,787,315	7.2	22,256,785	6.3	22,731,425	6.2	-16.9	2.1
Broilers and other meat-type chickens sold								
Number of farms	311	1.1	188	0.8	204	0.9	-39.5	8.5
Number of birds sold	22,306,685	0.3	21,081,124	0.4	10,391,178	0.2	-5.5	-50.7

Source: 1997 Census of Agriculture, U.S. Department of Agriculture, National Agricultural Statistics Service. NA stands for "not available." (D) is shown when data are withheld to prevent disclosure of competitive information. A dash (-) is shown where no data were reported.

CROP STATISTICS FOR INDIANA

Item	1987 Value	1987 % of U.S.	1992 Value	1992 % of U.S.	1997 Value	1997 % of U.S.	Percent change 1987-1992	Percent change 1992-1997
Corn for grain or seed								
Number of farms	45,383	7.2	37,005	7.3	30,642	7.1	-18.5	-17.2
Number of acres	4,884,114	8.3	5,828,308	8.4	5,473,792	7.8	19.3	-6.1
Number of bushels	619,045,978	-	805,637,216	9.3	652,547,322	7.6	30.1	-19.0
Corn for silage or green chop								
Number of farms	4,710	-	4,039	-	3,365	-	-14.2	-16.7
Number of acres	112,812	-	110,919	-	102,464	-	-1.7	-7.6
Weight in tons, green	1,961,381	-	1,944,771	-	1,639,160	-	-0.8	-15.7
Sorghum for grain or seed								
Number of farms	-	-	-	-	-	-	-	-
Number of acres	-	-	-	-	-	-	-	-
Number of bushels	-	-	-	-	-	-	-	-
Wheat for grain								
Number of farms	18,294	5.2	12,936	4.4	10,658	4.4	-29.3	-17.6
Number of acres	590,920	1.1	542,058	0.9	545,027	0.9	-8.3	0.5
Number of bushels	30,789,151	1.6	25,048,728	1.1	29,209,090	1.3	-18.6	16.6
Barley for grain								
Number of farms	-	-	-	-	-	-	-	-
Number of acres	-	-	-	-	-	-	-	-
Number of bushels	-	-	-	-	-	-	-	-
Oats for grain								
Number of farms	4,982	-	2,905	-	1,739	-	-41.7	-40.1
Number of acres	69,063	-	41,538	-	23,551	-	-39.9	-43.3
Number of bushels	4,317,321	-	2,603,270	-	1,445,213	-	-39.7	-44.5
Rice								
Number of farms	-	-	-	-	-	-	-	-
Number of acres	-	-	-	-	-	-	-	-
Weight in hundredweight	-	-	-	-	-	-	-	-
Sunflower seed								
Number of farms	-	-	-	-	-	-	-	-
Number of acres	-	-	-	-	-	-	-	-
Weight in pounds	-	-	-	-	-	-	-	-
Cotton								
Number of farms	-	-	-	-	-	-	-	-
Number of acres	-	-	-	-	-	-	-	-
Number of bales	-	-	-	-	-	-	-	-

Continued.

CROP STATISTICS FOR INDIANA - Continued

Item	1987 Value	1987 % of U.S.	1992 Value	1992 % of U.S.	1997 Value	1997 % of U.S.	Percent change 1987-1992	Percent change 1992-1997
Tobacco								
Number of farms	-	-	-	-	-	-	-	-
Number of acres	-	-	-	-	-	-	-	-
Weight in pounds	-	-	-	-	-	-	-	-
Soybeans for beans								
Number of farms	40,068	9.1	33,568	8.8	28,056	7.9	-16.2	-16.4
Number of acres	4,397,253	8.0	4,729,880	8.4	5,003,186	7.6	7.6	5.8
Number of bushels	169,749,051	9.2	195,049,717	9.5	210,645,005	8.4	14.9	8.0
Dry edible beans, excluding dry limas								
Number of farms	-	-	-	-	-	-	-	-
Number of acres	-	-	-	-	-	-	-	-
Weight in hundredweight	-	-	-	-	-	-	-	-
Potatoes, excluding sweetpotatoes								
Number of farms	-	-	-	-	-	-	-	-
Number of acres	-	-	-	-	-	-	-	-
Weight in hundredweight	-	-	-	-	-	-	-	-
Sugar beets for sugar								
Number of farms	-	-	-	-	-	-	-	-
Number of acres	-	-	-	-	-	-	-	-
Weight in tons	-	-	-	-	-	-	-	-
Sugarcane for sugar								
Number of farms	-	-	-	-	-	-	-	-
Number of acres	-	-	-	-	-	-	-	-
Weight in tons	-	-	-	-	-	-	-	-
Pineapples harvested								
Number of farms	-	-	-	-	-	-	-	-
Number of acres	-	-	-	-	-	-	-	-
Weight in tons	-	-	-	-	-	-	-	-
Peanuts for nuts								
Number of farms	-	-	-	-	-	-	-	-
Number of acres	-	-	-	-	-	-	-	-
Weight in pounds	-	-	-	-	-	-	-	-
Hay - all types, including alfalfa								
Number of farms	27,050	2.7	24,321	2.7	22,923	2.6	-10.1	-5.7
Number of acres	720,914	1.2	686,707	1.2	674,789	1.1	-4.7	-1.7
Weight in tons, dry	1,892,446	1.5	1,712,613	1.3	1,756,825	1.3	-9.5	2.6
Vegetables harvested for sale								
Number of farms	1,203	2.0	1,302	2.1	1,125	2.1	8.2	-13.6
Number of acres	32,934	0.9	33,860	0.9	30,139	0.8	2.8	-11.0
Land in orchards								
Number of farms	-	-	-	-	-	-	-	-
Number of acres	-	-	-	-	-	-	-	-

Source: 1997 Census of Agriculture, U.S. Department of Agriculture, National Agricultural Statistics Service. NA stands for "not available." (D) is shown when data are withheld to prevent disclosure of competitive information. A dash (-) is shown where no data were reported. Not all states report growing all crops, but all crop categories in the census are shown for every state. The data series used for this presentation did not report U.S. totals for a number of categories; for that reason, the "% of U.S." column is sometimes blank.

IOWA

GENERAL STATISTICS FOR IOWA

Item	1987 Value	1987 % of U.S.	1992 Value	1992 % of U.S.	1997 Value	1997 % of U.S.	Percent change 1987-1992	Percent change 1992-1997
Farms (number)	105,180	5.0	96,543	5.0	90,792	4.7	-8.2	-6.0
Land in farms (acres)	31,638,130	3.3	31,346,565	3.3	31,166,699	3.3	-0.9	-0.6
Average size of farm (acres)	301	65.2	325	66.2	343	70.4	8.0	5.5
Median size of farm (acres)	NA	-	NA	-	206	171.7	-	-
Market value of land and buildings:								
Average per farm (dollars)	283,597	98.0	394,267	110.4	566,587	126.0	39.0	43.7
Average per acre (dollars)	947	151.0	1,212	166.7	1,697	181.9	28.0	40.0
Market value of machinery/equipment -								
average per farm (dollars)	52,844	128.2	68,967	141.9	80,651	139.8	30.5	16.9
Farms by size:								
1 to 9 acres	7,974	4.4	7,129	4.3	5,049	3.3	-10.6	-29.2
10 to 49 acres	10,981	2.7	10,345	2.7	11,580	2.8	-5.8	11.9
50 to 179 acres	27,556	4.3	24,518	4.2	24,525	4.1	-11.0	0.0
180 to 499 acres	39,071	8.2	33,988	7.9	28,918	7.2	-13.0	-14.9
500 to 999 acres	15,874	7.9	15,830	8.5	14,833	8.4	-0.3	-6.3
1,000 acres or more	3,724	2.2	4,733	2.7	5,887	3.3	27.1	24.4
Total cropland								
Farms	96,749	5.2	88,224	5.2	83,375	5.0	-8.8	-5.5
Acres	27,290,868	6.2	27,195,676	6.2	26,821,844	6.2	-0.3	-1.4
Harvested cropland (farms)	92,878	5.7	84,009	5.6	74,951	5.3	-9.5	-10.8
Harvested cropland (acres)	20,484,178	7.3	22,826,308	7.7	23,323,249	7.5	11.4	2.2
Irrigated land (farms)	851	0.3	1,063	0.4	957	0.3	24.9	-10.0
Irrigated land (acres)	92,247	0.2	115,724	0.2	124,983	0.2	25.5	8.0
Market value of agricultural products sold:								
Total sales ($1,000)	8,926,799	6.6	10,099,786	6.2	11,947,894	6.1	13.1	18.3
Average per farm (dollars)	84,872	130.2	104,614	123.9	131,596	127.8	23.3	25.8
Agricultural products only ($1,000)	3,660,117	6.2	4,641,155	6.2	6,187,269	6.3	26.8	33.3
Livestock, poultry, and products ($1,000)	5,266,682	6.8	5,458,631	6.2	5,760,625	5.8	3.6	5.5
Farms by value of sales:								
Less than $2,500	8,799	1.8	7,636	1.8	13,191	2.7	-13.2	72.7
$2,500 to $4,999	5,498	2.1	4,753	2.0	4,577	2.0	-13.6	-3.7
$5,000 to $9,999	8,252	3.0	7,030	2.8	5,878	2.5	-14.8	-16.4
$10,000 to $24,999	17,436	5.3	13,820	4.6	10,507	3.8	-20.7	-24.0
$25,000 to $49,999	17,752	8.1	14,852	7.6	11,448	6.7	-16.3	-22.9
$50,000 to $99,999	20,656	9.5	17,570	9.4	13,735	8.7	-14.9	-21.8
$100,000 or more	26,787	9.1	30,882	9.2	31,456	9.1	15.3	1.9
Total farm production expenses ($1,000)	6,647,645	6.1	7,744,947	5.9	8,405,838	5.6	16.5	8.5
Average expenses per farm (dollars)	63,200	122.0	80,232	118.1	92,590	117.5	26.9	15.4
Net cash return for the farm unit:								
Number of farms	105,184	5.0	96,541	5.0	90,786	4.7	-8.2	-6.0
Value ($1000)	2,146,997	8.1	2,193,209	7.2	2,969,179	7.0	2.2	35.4
Average per farm (dollars)	20,412	161.2	22,718	143.8	32,705	146.9	11.3	44.0
Operators by principal occupation:								
Farming	75,279	6.6	66,885	6.4	56,256	5.9	-11.2	-15.9
Other	29,901	3.1	29,658	3.4	34,536	3.6	-0.8	16.4
Operators by days worked off farm:								
Any	46,229	4.1	42,672	4.3	45,408	4.4	-7.7	6.4
200 days or more	25,928	3.5	25,568	3.8	28,673	4.0	-1.4	12.1

Source: 1997 Census of Agriculture, U.S. Department of Agriculture, National Agricultural Statistics Service. NA stands for "not available." (D) is shown when data are withheld to prevent disclosure of competitive information. A dash (-) is shown where no data were reported. The market value of land and buildings, and of machinery and equipment, is an estimated amount. Net cash return for the farm unit includes only returns from agricultural activities.

LIVESTOCK STATISTICS FOR IOWA

Item	1987		1992		1997		Percent change	
	Value	% of U.S.	Value	% of U.S.	Value	% of U.S.	1987-1992	1992-1997
Cattle and calves								
Number of farms	49,469	4.2	43,610	4.1	38,435	3.7	-11.8	-11.9
Number of animals	4,303,682	4.5	3,963,602	4.1	3,647,129	3.7	-7.9	-8.0
Beef cows (farms)	32,279	3.8	29,987	3.7	27,452	3.4	-7.1	-8.5
Beef cows (number)	1,123,745	3.6	1,065,744	3.3	1,029,172	3.0	-5.2	-3.4
Milk cows (farms)	7,748	3.8	5,878	3.8	4,208	3.6	-24.1	-28.4
Milk cows (number)	294,888	2.9	258,925	2.7	222,142	2.4	-12.2	-14.2
Cattle and calves sold (farms)	50,509	4.4	43,780	4.2	38,548	3.8	-13.3	-12.0
Cattle and calves sold (number)	3,539,020	4.9	3,223,645	4.6	2,881,122	3.9	-8.9	-10.6
Hogs and pigs								
Number of farms	36,670	15.1	31,790	16.6	17,243	15.7	-13.3	-45.8
Number of animals	12,983,074	24.8	14,153,158	24.6	14,651,919	23.9	9.0	3.5
Hogs and pigs sold (farms)	38,638	16.2	34,058	18.1	18,370	18.0	-11.9	-46.1
Hogs and pigs sold (number)	23,483,812	24.3	26,812,736	24.1	27,495,818	19.3	14.2	2.5
Sheep and lambs								
Number of farms	8,636	9.3	6,760	8.4	4,431	6.7	-21.7	-34.5
Number of animals	451,617	4.1	405,354	3.8	265,305	3.4	-10.2	-34.5
Layers and pullets 13 weeks old and older								
Number of farms	4,897	3.4	2,633	3.0	1,892	2.6	-46.2	-28.1
Number of birds	9,580,666	2.6	12,560,235	3.6	24,876,834	6.8	31.1	98.1
Broilers and other meat-type chickens sold								
Number of farms	1,060	3.8	652	2.7	519	2.2	-38.5	-20.4
Number of birds sold	666,016	0.0	9,199,943	0.2	6,852,810	0.1	1,281.3	-25.5

Source: 1997 Census of Agriculture, U.S. Department of Agriculture, National Agricultural Statistics Service. NA stands for "not available." (D) is shown when data are withheld to prevent disclosure of competitive information. A dash (-) is shown where no data were reported.

CROP STATISTICS FOR IOWA

Item	1987		1992		1997		Percent change	
	Value	% of U.S.	Value	% of U.S.	Value	% of U.S.	1987-1992	1992-1997
Corn for grain or seed								
Number of farms	83,301	13.3	72,756	14.4	61,860	14.4	-12.7	-15.0
Number of acres	10,147,051	17.3	12,512,815	18.0	11,595,308	16.6	23.3	-7.3
Number of bushels	1,274,388,346	-	1,754,149,889	20.2	1,537,482,128	17.9	37.6	-12.4
Corn for silage or green chop								
Number of farms	7,934	-	9,575	-	8,405	-	20.7	-12.2
Number of acres	205,176	-	260,770	-	241,549	-	27.1	-7.4
Weight in tons, green	3,251,394	-	4,096,921	-	3,993,158	-	26.0	-2.5
Sorghum for grain or seed								
Number of farms	-	-	-	-	-	-	-	-
Number of acres	-	-	-	-	-	-	-	-
Number of bushels	-	-	-	-	-	-	-	-
Wheat for grain								
Number of farms	1,345	0.4	970	0.3	719	0.3	-27.9	-25.9
Number of acres	31,047	0.1	30,072	0.1	22,123	0.0	-3.1	-26.4
Number of bushels	1,180,360	0.1	1,183,472	0.1	905,333	0.0	0.3	-23.5
Barley for grain								
Number of farms	-	-	-	-	-	-	-	-
Number of acres	-	-	-	-	-	-	-	-
Number of bushels	-	-	-	-	-	-	-	-
Oats for grain								
Number of farms	25,398	-	17,854	-	10,823	-	-29.7	-39.4
Number of acres	544,907	-	368,086	-	211,985	-	-32.4	-42.4
Number of bushels	30,918,660	-	23,246,559	-	14,293,977	-	-24.8	-38.5
Rice								
Number of farms	-	-	-	-	-	-	-	-
Number of acres	-	-	-	-	-	-	-	-
Weight in hundredweight	-	-	-	-	-	-	-	-
Sunflower seed								
Number of farms	-	-	-	-	-	-	-	-
Number of acres	-	-	-	-	-	-	-	-
Weight in pounds	-	-	-	-	-	-	-	-
Cotton								
Number of farms	-	-	-	-	-	-	-	-
Number of acres	-	-	-	-	-	-	-	-
Number of bales	-	-	-	-	-	-	-	-

Continued.

CROP STATISTICS FOR IOWA - Continued

Item	1987		1992		1997		Percent change	
	Value	% of U.S.	Value	% of U.S.	Value	% of U.S.	1987-1992	1992-1997
Tobacco								
Number of farms	-	-	-	-	-	-	-	-
Number of acres	-	-	-	-	-	-	-	-
Weight in pounds	-	-	-	-	-	-	-	-
Soybeans for beans								
Number of farms	68,278	15.5	59,945	15.7	56,436	15.9	-12.2	-5.9
Number of acres	7,903,395	14.3	8,243,067	14.6	9,944,865	15.0	4.3	20.6
Number of bushels	326,081,351	17.7	352,590,997	17.2	445,574,589	17.8	8.1	26.4
Dry edible beans, excluding dry limas								
Number of farms	-	-	-	-	-	-	-	-
Number of acres	-	-	-	-	-	-	-	-
Weight in hundredweight	-	-	-	-	-	-	-	-
Potatoes, excluding sweetpotatoes								
Number of farms	-	-	-	-	-	-	-	-
Number of acres	-	-	-	-	-	-	-	-
Weight in hundredweight	-	-	-	-	-	-	-	-
Sugar beets for sugar								
Number of farms	-	-	-	-	-	-	-	-
Number of acres	-	-	-	-	-	-	-	-
Weight in tons	-	-	-	-	-	-	-	-
Sugarcane for sugar								
Number of farms	-	-	-	-	-	-	-	-
Number of acres	-	-	-	-	-	-	-	-
Weight in tons	-	-	-	-	-	-	-	-
Pineapples harvested								
Number of farms	-	-	-	-	-	-	-	-
Number of acres	-	-	-	-	-	-	-	-
Weight in tons	-	-	-	-	-	-	-	-
Peanuts for nuts								
Number of farms	-	-	-	-	-	-	-	-
Number of acres	-	-	-	-	-	-	-	-
Weight in pounds	-	-	-	-	-	-	-	-
Hay - all types, including alfalfa								
Number of farms	48,271	4.9	44,768	4.9	37,711	4.2	-7.3	-15.8
Number of acres	1,968,207	3.4	1,762,425	3.1	1,575,777	2.6	-10.5	-10.6
Weight in tons, dry	5,612,944	4.4	5,107,237	4.0	4,365,999	3.1	-9.0	-14.5
Vegetables harvested for sale								
Number of farms	-	-	-	-	-	-	-	-
Number of acres	-	-	-	-	-	-	-	-
Land in orchards								
Number of farms	-	-	-	-	-	-	-	-
Number of acres	-	-	-	-	-	-	-	-

Source: 1997 Census of Agriculture, U.S. Department of Agriculture, National Agricultural Statistics Service. NA stands for "not available." (D) is shown when data are withheld to prevent disclosure of competitive information. A dash (-) is shown where no data were reported. Not all states report growing all crops, but all crop categories in the census are shown for every state. The data series used for this presentation did not report U.S. totals for a number of categories; for that reason, the "% of U.S." column is sometimes blank.

KANSAS

GENERAL STATISTICS FOR KANSAS

Item	1987 Value	1987 % of U.S.	1992 Value	1992 % of U.S.	1997 Value	1997 % of U.S.	Percent change 1987-1992	Percent change 1992-1997
Farms (number)	68,579	3.3	63,278	3.3	61,593	3.2	-7.7	-2.7
Land in farms (acres)	46,628,519	4.8	46,672,188	4.9	46,089,268	4.9	0.1	-1.2
Average size of farm (acres)	680	147.2	738	150.3	748	153.6	8.5	1.4
Median size of farm (acres)	NA	-	NA	-	309	257.5	-	-
Market value of land and buildings:								
Average per farm (dollars)	278,047	96.1	343,312	96.2	430,533	95.7	23.5	25.4
Average per acre (dollars)	413	65.9	463	63.7	577	61.8	12.1	24.6
Market value of machinery/equipment -								
average per farm (dollars)	50,411	122.3	58,812	121.0	74,047	128.4	16.7	25.9
Farms by size:								
1 to 9 acres	3,689	2.0	2,632	1.6	2,223	1.4	-28.7	-15.5
10 to 49 acres	6,222	1.5	6,023	1.6	6,970	1.7	-3.2	15.7
50 to 179 acres	15,510	2.4	14,221	2.4	15,118	2.5	-8.3	6.3
180 to 499 acres	16,705	3.5	15,218	3.6	13,928	3.5	-8.9	-8.5
500 to 999 acres	12,093	6.0	10,817	5.8	9,687	5.5	-10.6	-10.4
1,000 acres or more	14,360	8.5	14,367	8.3	13,667	7.8	0.0	-4.9
Total cropland								
Farms	61,615	3.3	56,389	3.3	54,145	3.3	-8.5	-4.0
Acres	31,385,090	7.1	31,119,250	7.1	30,020,580	7.0	-0.8	-3.5
Harvested cropland (farms)	57,822	3.5	52,348	3.5	48,280	3.4	-9.5	-7.8
Harvested cropland (acres)	17,729,394	6.3	18,794,787	6.4	19,839,087	6.4	6.0	5.6
Irrigated land (farms)	7,352	2.5	6,543	2.3	6,135	2.2	-11.0	-6.2
Irrigated land (acres)	2,463,073	5.3	2,680,343	5.4	2,707,489	4.9	8.8	1.0
Market value of agricultural products sold:								
Total sales ($1,000)	6,476,669	4.8	8,315,965	5.1	9,207,130	4.7	28.4	10.7
Average per farm (dollars)	94,441	144.9	131,420	155.6	149,483	145.2	39.2	13.7
Agricultural products only ($1,000)	1,693,609	2.9	2,270,577	3.0	3,221,766	3.3	34.1	41.9
Livestock, poultry, and products ($1,000)	4,783,060	6.2	6,045,388	6.9	5,985,364	6.1	26.4	-1.0
Farms by value of sales:								
Less than $2,500	9,502	1.9	8,387	2.0	10,968	2.2	-11.7	30.8
$2,500 to $4,999	6,919	2.6	5,618	2.4	5,068	2.2	-18.8	-9.8
$5,000 to $9,999	9,430	3.4	7,808	3.1	6,767	2.8	-17.2	-13.3
$10,000 to $24,999	14,070	4.3	12,132	4.0	10,293	3.8	-13.8	-15.2
$25,000 to $49,999	10,282	4.7	9,387	4.8	7,757	4.5	-8.7	-17.4
$50,000 to $99,999	8,997	4.1	8,277	4.4	7,304	4.6	-8.0	-11.8
$100,000 or more	9,379	3.2	11,669	3.5	13,436	3.9	24.4	15.1
Total farm production expenses ($1,000)	5,516,518	5.1	6,920,528	5.3	7,290,703	4.8	25.5	5.3
Average expenses per farm (dollars)	80,439	155.3	109,364	161.0	118,373	150.3	36.0	8.2
Net cash return for the farm unit:								
Number of farms	68,580	3.3	63,280	3.3	61,591	3.2	-7.7	-2.7
Value ($1000)	922,225	3.5	1,393,417	4.6	1,877,913	4.4	51.1	34.8
Average per farm (dollars)	13,447	106.2	22,020	139.4	30,490	137.0	63.8	38.5
Operators by principal occupation:								
Farming	42,607	3.7	39,324	3.7	34,979	3.6	-7.7	-11.0
Other	25,972	2.7	23,954	2.7	26,614	2.8	-7.8	11.1
Operators by days worked off farm:								
Any	34,654	3.1	30,776	3.1	31,891	3.1	-11.2	3.6
200 days or more	21,677	2.9	19,757	3.0	21,507	3.0	-8.9	8.9

Source: *1997 Census of Agriculture*, U.S. Department of Agriculture, National Agricultural Statistics Service. NA stands for "not available." (D) is shown when data are withheld to prevent disclosure of competitive information. A dash (-) is shown where no data were reported. The market value of land and buildings, and of machinery and equipment, is an estimated amount. Net cash return for the farm unit includes only returns from agricultural activities.

LIVESTOCK STATISTICS FOR KANSAS

Item	1987 Value	% of U.S.	1992 Value	% of U.S.	1997 Value	% of U.S.	Percent change 1987-1992	Percent change 1992-1997
Cattle and calves								
Number of farms	40,785	3.5	37,889	3.5	36,244	3.5	-7.1	-4.3
Number of animals	5,539,292	5.8	6,066,493	6.3	6,506,089	6.6	9.5	7.2
Beef cows (farms)	31,475	3.7	30,308	3.8	29,446	3.7	-3.7	-2.8
Beef cows (number)	1,354,649	4.3	1,434,017	4.4	1,466,429	4.3	5.9	2.3
Milk cows (farms)	3,093	1.5	2,165	1.4	1,466	1.3	-30.0	-32.3
Milk cows (number)	96,675	1.0	85,132	0.9	82,080	0.9	-11.9	-3.6
Cattle and calves sold (farms)	41,498	3.6	37,893	3.7	36,207	3.6	-8.7	-4.4
Cattle and calves sold (number)	7,310,338	10.1	7,699,746	10.9	8,271,113	11.2	5.3	7.4
Hogs and pigs								
Number of farms	6,768	2.8	5,684	3.0	2,831	2.6	-16.0	-50.2
Number of animals	1,516,878	2.9	1,584,048	2.8	1,585,224	2.6	4.4	0.1
Hogs and pigs sold (farms)	7,090	3.0	6,089	3.2	2,873	2.8	-14.1	-52.8
Hogs and pigs sold (number)	2,759,676	2.9	2,992,913	2.7	3,184,437	2.2	8.5	6.4
Sheep and lambs								
Number of farms	2,400	2.6	2,120	2.6	1,478	2.2	-11.7	-30.3
Number of animals	249,303	2.3	206,566	1.9	119,099	1.5	-17.1	-42.3
Layers and pullets 13 weeks old and older								
Number of farms	4,206	2.9	2,407	2.7	2,019	2.8	-42.8	-16.1
Number of birds	2,094,610	0.6	1,926,383	0.5	1,805,127	0.5	-8.0	-6.3
Broilers and other meat-type chickens sold								
Number of farms	132	0.5	80	0.3	93	0.4	-39.4	16.3
Number of birds sold	176,061	0.0	88,483	0.0	35,018	0.0	-49.7	-60.4

Source: 1997 Census of Agriculture, U.S. Department of Agriculture, National Agricultural Statistics Service. NA stands for "not available." (D) is shown when data are withheld to prevent disclosure of competitive information. A dash (-) is shown where no data were reported.

CROP STATISTICS FOR KANSAS

Item	1987 Value	% of U.S.	1992 Value	% of U.S.	1997 Value	% of U.S.	Percent change 1987-1992	Percent change 1992-1997
Corn for grain or seed								
Number of farms	8,944	1.4	9,604	1.9	10,833	2.5	7.4	12.8
Number of acres	1,243,969	2.1	1,748,802	2.5	2,497,516	3.6	40.6	42.8
Number of bushels	144,133,581	-	258,720,259	3.0	356,413,100	4.2	79.5	37.8
Corn for silage or green chop								
Number of farms	2,009	-	1,797	-	1,765	-	-10.6	-1.8
Number of acres	109,230	-	105,469	-	117,472	-	-3.4	11.4
Weight in tons, green	1,669,413	-	1,810,537	-	2,042,941	-	8.5	12.8
Sorghum for grain or seed								
Number of farms	32,492	-	23,820	-	20,398	-	-26.7	-14.4
Number of acres	3,399,564	-	2,957,276	-	3,077,984	-	-13.0	4.1
Number of bushels	228,045,100	-	222,145,624	-	231,561,211	-	-2.6	4.2
Wheat for grain								
Number of farms	38,638	11.0	36,623	12.5	30,392	12.5	-5.2	-17.0
Number of acres	8,679,588	16.3	9,942,149	16.8	9,560,615	16.2	14.5	-3.8
Number of bushels	292,999,442	15.5	329,082,833	14.9	407,515,802	18.5	12.3	23.8
Barley for grain								
Number of farms	-	-	-	-	-	-	-	-
Number of acres	-	-	-	-	-	-	-	-
Number of bushels	-	-	-	-	-	-	-	-
Oats for grain								
Number of farms	5,313	-	4,659	-	2,603	-	-12.3	-44.1
Number of acres	128,091	-	118,788	-	79,163	-	-7.3	-33.4
Number of bushels	4,775,729	-	6,024,886	-	4,530,823	-	26.2	-24.8
Rice								
Number of farms	-	-	-	-	-	-	-	-
Number of acres	-	-	-	-	-	-	-	-
Weight in hundredweight	-	-	-	-	-	-	-	-
Sunflower seed								
Number of farms	-	-	-	-	-	-	-	-
Number of acres	-	-	-	-	-	-	-	-
Weight in pounds	-	-	-	-	-	-	-	-
Cotton								
Number of farms	-	-	-	-	-	-	-	-
Number of acres	-	-	-	-	-	-	-	-
Number of bales	-	-	-	-	-	-	-	-

Continued.

CROP STATISTICS FOR KANSAS - Continued

Item	1987 Value	1987 % of U.S.	1992 Value	1992 % of U.S.	1997 Value	1997 % of U.S.	Percent change 1987-1992	Percent change 1992-1997
Tobacco								
Number of farms	-	-	-	-	-	-	-	-
Number of acres	-	-	-	-	-	-	-	-
Weight in pounds	-	-	-	-	-	-	-	-
Soybeans for beans								
Number of farms	18,864	4.3	14,743	3.9	14,733	4.2	-21.8	-0.1
Number of acres	1,878,978	3.4	1,669,958	3.0	2,208,642	3.3	-11.1	32.3
Number of bushels	55,789,994	3.0	56,854,327	2.8	78,563,054	3.1	1.9	38.2
Dry edible beans, excluding dry limas								
Number of farms	-	-	-	-	-	-	-	-
Number of acres	-	-	-	-	-	-	-	-
Weight in hundredweight	-	-	-	-	-	-	-	-
Potatoes, excluding sweetpotatoes								
Number of farms	-	-	-	-	-	-	-	-
Number of acres	-	-	-	-	-	-	-	-
Weight in hundredweight	-	-	-	-	-	-	-	-
Sugar beets for sugar								
Number of farms	-	-	-	-	-	-	-	-
Number of acres	-	-	-	-	-	-	-	-
Weight in tons	-	-	-	-	-	-	-	-
Sugarcane for sugar								
Number of farms	-	-	-	-	-	-	-	-
Number of acres	-	-	-	-	-	-	-	-
Weight in tons	-	-	-	-	-	-	-	-
Pineapples harvested								
Number of farms	-	-	-	-	-	-	-	-
Number of acres	-	-	-	-	-	-	-	-
Weight in tons	-	-	-	-	-	-	-	-
Peanuts for nuts								
Number of farms	-	-	-	-	-	-	-	-
Number of acres	-	-	-	-	-	-	-	-
Weight in pounds	-	-	-	-	-	-	-	-
Hay - all types, including alfalfa								
Number of farms	33,964	3.4	32,926	3.6	30,573	3.4	-3.1	-7.1
Number of acres	2,254,082	3.9	2,509,904	4.4	2,565,482	4.2	11.3	2.2
Weight in tons, dry	5,080,847	3.9	5,938,634	4.7	6,147,197	4.4	16.9	3.5
Vegetables harvested for sale								
Number of farms	-	-	-	-	-	-	-	-
Number of acres	-	-	-	-	-	-	-	-
Land in orchards								
Number of farms	-	-	-	-	-	-	-	-
Number of acres	-	-	-	-	-	-	-	-

Source: 1997 Census of Agriculture, U.S. Department of Agriculture, National Agricultural Statistics Service. NA stands for "not available." (D) is shown when data are withheld to prevent disclosure of competitive information. A dash (-) is shown where no data were reported. Not all states report growing all crops, but all crop categories in the census are shown for every state. The data series used for this presentation did not report U.S. totals for a number of categories; for that reason, the "% of U.S." column is sometimes blank.

KENTUCKY

GENERAL STATISTICS FOR KENTUCKY

Item	1987 Value	1987 % of U.S.	1992 Value	1992 % of U.S.	1997 Value	1997 % of U.S.	Percent change 1987-1992	Percent change 1992-1997
Farms (number)	92,453	4.4	90,281	4.7	82,273	4.3	-2.3	-8.9
Land in farms (acres)	14,012,700	1.5	13,665,798	1.4	13,334,234	1.4	-2.5	-2.4
Average size of farm (acres)	152	32.9	151	30.8	162	33.3	-0.7	7.3
Median size of farm (acres)	NA	-	NA	-	84	70.0	-	-
Market value of land and buildings:								
Average per farm (dollars)	135,696	46.9	163,660	45.8	230,274	51.2	20.6	40.7
Average per acre (dollars)	896	142.9	1,077	148.1	1,450	155.4	20.2	34.6
Market value of machinery/equipment -								
average per farm (dollars)	22,670	55.0	24,918	51.3	33,327	57.8	9.9	33.7
Farms by size:								
1 to 9 acres	10,648	5.8	10,402	6.2	7,114	4.6	-2.3	-31.6
10 to 49 acres	20,707	5.0	21,911	5.7	20,754	5.1	5.8	-5.3
50 to 179 acres	38,261	5.9	36,515	6.3	33,992	5.7	-4.6	-6.9
180 to 499 acres	17,920	3.7	16,586	3.9	15,522	3.9	-7.4	-6.4
500 to 999 acres	3,618	1.8	3,468	1.9	3,399	1.9	-4.1	-2.0
1,000 acres or more	1,299	0.8	1,399	0.8	1,492	0.8	7.7	6.6
Total cropland								
Farms	88,664	4.8	86,345	5.1	77,784	4.7	-2.6	-9.9
Acres	8,900,086	2.0	8,880,989	2.0	8,549,027	2.0	-0.2	-3.7
Harvested cropland (farms)	83,097	5.1	79,590	5.3	68,953	4.9	-4.2	-13.4
Harvested cropland (acres)	4,250,284	1.5	4,417,651	1.5	4,678,622	1.5	3.9	5.9
Irrigated land (farms)	3,733	1.3	2,120	0.8	4,104	1.5	-43.2	93.6
Irrigated land (acres)	37,693	0.1	27,647	0.1	58,490	0.1	-26.7	111.6
Market value of agricultural products sold:								
Total sales ($1,000)	2,075,571	1.5	2,663,702	1.6	3,064,460	1.6	28.3	15.0
Average per farm (dollars)	22,450	34.5	29,505	34.9	37,247	36.2	31.4	26.2
Agricultural products only ($1,000)	889,882	1.5	1,449,823	1.9	1,578,861	1.6	62.9	8.9
Livestock, poultry, and products ($1,000)	1,185,689	1.5	1,213,879	1.4	1,485,599	1.5	2.4	22.4
Farms by value of sales:								
Less than $2,500	24,380	5.0	17,881	4.2	19,143	3.9	-26.7	7.1
$2,500 to $4,999	16,421	6.2	14,745	6.4	12,566	5.5	-10.2	-14.8
$5,000 to $9,999	17,620	6.4	17,129	6.8	14,393	6.0	-2.8	-16.0
$10,000 to $24,999	18,078	5.5	20,354	6.7	17,388	6.3	12.6	-14.6
$25,000 to $49,999	7,880	3.6	9,623	4.9	8,339	4.9	22.1	-13.3
$50,000 to $99,999	4,527	2.1	5,519	2.9	4,843	3.1	21.9	-12.2
$100,000 or more	3,547	1.2	5,030	1.5	5,601	1.6	41.8	11.4
Total farm production expenses ($1,000)	1,485,994	1.4	1,828,743	1.4	2,033,070	1.4	23.1	11.2
Average expenses per farm (dollars)	16,073	31.0	20,256	29.8	24,714	31.4	26.0	22.0
Net cash return for the farm unit:								
Number of farms	92,453	4.4	90,280	4.7	82,264	4.3	-2.4	-8.9
Value ($1000)	579,635	2.2	817,456	2.7	979,715	2.3	41.0	19.8
Average per farm (dollars)	6,270	49.5	9,055	57.3	11,909	53.5	44.4	31.5
Operators by principal occupation:								
Farming	41,451	3.6	40,175	3.8	33,841	3.5	-3.1	-15.8
Other	51,002	5.4	50,106	5.7	48,432	5.1	-1.8	-3.3
Operators by days worked off farm:								
Any	54,464	4.9	51,075	5.1	48,491	4.7	-6.2	-5.1
200 days or more	37,893	5.1	36,497	5.5	35,100	4.9	-3.7	-3.8

Source: 1997 Census of Agriculture, U.S. Department of Agriculture, National Agricultural Statistics Service. NA stands for "not available." (D) is shown when data are withheld to prevent disclosure of competitive information. A dash (-) is shown where no data were reported. The market value of land and buildings, and of machinery and equipment, is an estimated amount. Net cash return for the farm unit includes only returns from agricultural activities.

LIVESTOCK STATISTICS FOR KENTUCKY

Item	1987		1992		1997		Percent change	
	Value	% of U.S.	Value	% of U.S.	Value	% of U.S.	1987-1992	1992-1997
Cattle and calves								
Number of farms	53,626	4.6	52,572	4.9	48,898	4.7	-2.0	-7.0
Number of animals	2,343,541	2.4	2,503,680	2.6	2,428,891	2.5	6.8	-3.0
Beef cows (farms)	41,396	4.9	42,898	5.3	41,171	5.1	3.6	-4.0
Beef cows (number)	967,856	3.1	1,088,532	3.3	1,126,748	3.3	12.5	3.5
Milk cows (farms)	7,002	3.5	4,984	3.2	3,393	2.9	-28.8	-31.9
Milk cows (number)	224,267	2.2	186,089	2.0	145,557	1.6	-17.0	-21.8
Cattle and calves sold (farms)	52,210	4.5	50,174	4.9	47,355	4.7	-3.9	-5.6
Cattle and calves sold (number)	1,305,423	1.8	1,277,661	1.8	1,388,647	1.9	-2.1	8.7
Hogs and pigs								
Number of farms	8,242	3.4	4,879	2.5	1,881	1.7	-40.8	-61.4
Number of animals	838,452	1.6	782,408	1.4	563,797	0.9	-6.7	-27.9
Hogs and pigs sold (farms)	7,602	3.2	4,345	2.3	1,523	1.5	-42.8	-64.9
Hogs and pigs sold (number)	1,497,306	1.6	1,464,686	1.3	1,100,523	0.8	-2.2	-24.9
Sheep and lambs								
Number of farms	985	1.1	1,032	1.3	795	1.2	4.8	-23.0
Number of animals	36,522	0.3	37,729	0.4	21,664	0.3	3.3	-42.6
Layers and pullets 13 weeks old and older								
Number of farms	5,989	4.1	3,126	3.5	1,991	2.7	-47.8	-36.3
Number of birds	2,103,650	0.6	2,637,061	0.8	3,500,904	1.0	25.4	32.8
Broilers and other meat-type chickens sold								
Number of farms	73	0.3	110	0.5	243	1.0	50.7	120.9
Number of birds sold	2,201,169	0.0	27,623,677	0.5	91,548,829	1.4	1,155.0	231.4

Source: 1997 Census of Agriculture, U.S. Department of Agriculture, National Agricultural Statistics Service. NA stands for "not available." (D) is shown when data are withheld to prevent disclosure of competitive information. A dash (-) is shown where no data were reported.

CROP STATISTICS FOR KENTUCKY

Item	1987		1992		1997		Percent change	
	Value	% of U.S.	Value	% of U.S.	Value	% of U.S.	1987-1992	1992-1997
Corn for grain or seed								
Number of farms	25,067	4.0	16,945	3.4	11,021	2.6	-32.4	-35.0
Number of acres	1,048,809	1.8	1,166,234	1.7	1,086,381	1.6	11.2	-6.8
Number of bushels	104,364,883	-	145,213,536	1.7	110,787,023	1.3	39.1	-23.7
Corn for silage or green chop								
Number of farms	5,344	-	3,855	-	3,062	-	-27.9	-20.6
Number of acres	134,669	-	105,077	-	104,920	-	-22.0	-0.1
Weight in tons, green	1,962,245	-	1,733,554	-	1,438,492	-	-11.7	-17.0
Sorghum for grain or seed								
Number of farms	-	-	-	-	-	-	-	-
Number of acres	-	-	-	-	-	-	-	-
Number of bushels	-	-	-	-	-	-	-	-
Wheat for grain								
Number of farms	5,361	1.5	3,881	1.3	3,180	1.3	-27.6	-18.1
Number of acres	283,742	0.5	326,268	0.6	408,771	0.7	15.0	25.3
Number of bushels	12,752,191	0.7	16,252,236	0.7	21,658,648	1.0	27.4	33.3
Barley for grain								
Number of farms	-	-	-	-	-	-	-	-
Number of acres	-	-	-	-	-	-	-	-
Number of bushels	-	-	-	-	-	-	-	-
Oats for grain								
Number of farms	-	-	-	-	-	-	-	-
Number of acres	-	-	-	-	-	-	-	-
Number of bushels	-	-	-	-	-	-	-	-
Rice								
Number of farms	-	-	-	-	-	-	-	-
Number of acres	-	-	-	-	-	-	-	-
Weight in hundredweight	-	-	-	-	-	-	-	-
Sunflower seed								
Number of farms	-	-	-	-	-	-	-	-
Number of acres	-	-	-	-	-	-	-	-
Weight in pounds	-	-	-	-	-	-	-	-
Cotton								
Number of farms	-	-	-	-	-	-	-	-
Number of acres	-	-	-	-	-	-	-	-
Number of bales	-	-	-	-	-	-	-	-

Continued.

CROP STATISTICS FOR KENTUCKY - Continued

Item	1987 Value	1987 % of U.S.	1992 Value	1992 % of U.S.	1997 Value	1997 % of U.S.	Percent change 1987-1992	Percent change 1992-1997
Tobacco								
Number of farms	61,962	-	59,373	-	44,967	-	-4.2	-24.3
Number of acres	175,957	-	268,140	-	255,053	-	52.4	-4.9
Weight in pounds	336,364,307	-	542,000,404	-	505,257,589	-	61.1	-6.8
Soybeans for beans								
Number of farms	8,765	2.0	7,185	1.9	6,644	1.9	-18.0	-7.5
Number of acres	1,021,903	1.8	1,030,180	1.8	1,214,938	1.8	0.8	17.9
Number of bushels	27,138,451	1.5	37,796,827	1.8	41,294,246	1.6	39.3	9.3
Dry edible beans, excluding dry limas								
Number of farms	-	-	-	-	-	-	-	-
Number of acres	-	-	-	-	-	-	-	-
Weight in hundredweight	-	-	-	-	-	-	-	-
Potatoes, excluding sweetpotatoes								
Number of farms	-	-	-	-	-	-	-	-
Number of acres	-	-	-	-	-	-	-	-
Weight in hundredweight	-	-	-	-	-	-	-	-
Sugar beets for sugar								
Number of farms	-	-	-	-	-	-	-	-
Number of acres	-	-	-	-	-	-	-	-
Weight in tons	-	-	-	-	-	-	-	-
Sugarcane for sugar								
Number of farms	-	-	-	-	-	-	-	-
Number of acres	-	-	-	-	-	-	-	-
Weight in tons	-	-	-	-	-	-	-	-
Pineapples harvested								
Number of farms	-	-	-	-	-	-	-	-
Number of acres	-	-	-	-	-	-	-	-
Weight in tons	-	-	-	-	-	-	-	-
Peanuts for nuts								
Number of farms	-	-	-	-	-	-	-	-
Number of acres	-	-	-	-	-	-	-	-
Weight in pounds	-	-	-	-	-	-	-	-
Hay - all types, including alfalfa								
Number of farms	51,362	5.2	47,478	5.2	46,388	5.2	-7.6	-2.3
Number of acres	1,796,635	3.1	1,837,802	3.2	2,009,061	3.3	2.3	9.3
Weight in tons, dry	3,291,951	2.6	3,757,782	3.0	4,138,965	3.0	14.2	10.1
Vegetables harvested for sale								
Number of farms	-	-	-	-	-	-	-	-
Number of acres	-	-	-	-	-	-	-	-
Land in orchards								
Number of farms	-	-	-	-	-	-	-	-
Number of acres	-	-	-	-	-	-	-	-

Source: 1997 Census of Agriculture, U.S. Department of Agriculture, National Agricultural Statistics Service. NA stands for "not available." (D) is shown when data are withheld to prevent disclosure of competitive information. A dash (-) is shown where no data were reported. Not all states report growing all crops, but all crop categories in the census are shown for every state. The data series used for this presentation did not report U.S. totals for a number of categories; for that reason, the "% of U.S." column is sometimes blank.

LOUISIANA

GENERAL STATISTICS FOR LOUISIANA

Item	1987 Value	1987 % of U.S.	1992 Value	1992 % of U.S.	1997 Value	1997 % of U.S.	Percent change 1987-1992	Percent change 1992-1997
Farms (number)	27,350	1.3	25,652	1.3	23,823	1.2	-6.2	-7.1
Land in farms (acres)	8,007,173	0.8	7,837,545	0.8	7,876,528	0.8	-2.1	0.5
Average size of farm (acres)	293	63.4	306	62.3	331	68.0	4.4	8.2
Median size of farm (acres)	NA	-	NA	-	92	76.7	-	-
Market value of land and buildings:								
Average per farm (dollars)	268,630	92.8	291,332	81.6	380,871	84.7	8.5	30.7
Average per acre (dollars)	940	149.9	972	133.7	1,206	129.3	3.4	24.1
Market value of machinery/equipment -								
average per farm (dollars)	38,323	93.0	46,299	95.3	59,330	102.9	20.8	28.1
Farms by size:								
1 to 9 acres	2,066	1.1	1,934	1.2	1,650	1.1	-6.4	-14.7
10 to 49 acres	7,799	1.9	6,895	1.8	6,485	1.6	-11.6	-5.9
50 to 179 acres	8,248	1.3	7,891	1.4	7,429	1.3	-4.3	-5.9
180 to 499 acres	4,811	1.0	4,553	1.1	4,128	1.0	-5.4	-9.3
500 to 999 acres	2,602	1.3	2,471	1.3	2,029	1.2	-5.0	-17.9
1,000 acres or more	1,824	1.1	1,908	1.1	2,102	1.2	4.6	10.2
Total cropland								
Farms	23,273	1.3	21,777	1.3	19,333	1.2	-6.4	-11.2
Acres	5,562,736	1.3	5,552,733	1.3	5,331,411	1.2	-0.2	-4.0
Harvested cropland (farms)	18,644	1.1	17,171	1.2	15,115	1.1	-7.9	-12.0
Harvested cropland (acres)	3,599,678	1.3	3,810,690	1.3	3,882,648	1.3	5.9	1.9
Irrigated land (farms)	3,929	1.3	4,064	1.5	3,400	1.2	3.4	-16.3
Irrigated land (acres)	646,677	1.4	897,641	1.8	942,528	1.7	38.8	5.0
Market value of agricultural products sold:								
Total sales ($1,000)	1,340,162	1.0	1,607,511	1.0	2,031,277	1.0	19.9	26.4
Average per farm (dollars)	49,000	75.2	62,666	74.2	85,265	82.8	27.9	36.1
Agricultural products only ($1,000)	929,858	1.6	1,111,346	1.5	1,411,472	1.4	19.5	27.0
Livestock, poultry, and products ($1,000)	410,304	0.5	496,165	0.6	619,805	0.6	20.9	24.9
Farms by value of sales:								
Less than $2,500	9,283	1.9	8,008	1.9	7,755	1.6	-13.7	-3.2
$2,500 to $4,999	4,021	1.5	3,664	1.6	3,389	1.5	-8.9	-7.5
$5,000 to $9,999	3,448	1.3	3,407	1.4	3,097	1.3	-1.2	-9.1
$10,000 to $24,999	3,050	0.9	3,149	1.0	2,825	1.0	3.2	-10.3
$25,000 to $49,999	1,776	0.8	1,593	0.8	1,358	0.8	-10.3	-14.8
$50,000 to $99,999	2,063	0.9	1,670	0.9	1,207	0.8	-19.0	-27.7
$100,000 or more	3,709	1.3	4,161	1.2	4,192	1.2	12.2	0.7
Total farm production expenses ($1,000)	1,022,931	0.9	1,309,012	1.0	1,466,483	1.0	28.0	12.0
Average expenses per farm (dollars)	37,400	72.2	51,026	75.1	61,532	78.1	36.4	20.6
Net cash return for the farm unit:								
Number of farms	27,353	1.3	25,654	1.3	23,833	1.2	-6.2	-7.1
Value ($1000)	288,943	1.1	268,077	0.9	477,426	1.1	-7.2	78.1
Average per farm (dollars)	10,563	83.4	10,450	66.1	20,032	90.0	-1.1	91.7
Operators by principal occupation:								
Farming	13,496	1.2	12,931	1.2	11,281	1.2	-4.2	-12.8
Other	13,854	1.5	12,721	1.5	12,542	1.3	-8.2	-1.4
Operators by days worked off farm:								
Any	14,388	1.3	13,024	1.3	13,128	1.3	-9.5	0.8
200 days or more	9,202	1.2	8,594	1.3	8,550	1.2	-6.6	-0.5

Source: 1997 Census of Agriculture, U.S. Department of Agriculture, National Agricultural Statistics Service. NA stands for "not available." (D) is shown when data are withheld to prevent disclosure of competitive information. A dash (-) is shown where no data were reported. The market value of land and buildings, and of machinery and equipment, is an estimated amount. Net cash return for the farm unit includes only returns from agricultural activities.

LIVESTOCK STATISTICS FOR LOUISIANA

Item	1987 Value	% of U.S.	1992 Value	% of U.S.	1997 Value	% of U.S.	Percent change 1987-1992	1992-1997
Cattle and calves								
Number of farms	16,033	1.4	15,036	1.4	14,589	1.4	-6.2	-3.0
Number of animals	813,295	0.8	844,260	0.9	877,124	0.9	3.8	3.9
Beef cows (farms)	13,551	1.6	13,112	1.6	12,669	1.6	-3.2	-3.4
Beef cows (number)	422,604	1.3	441,725	1.4	490,437	1.4	4.5	11.0
Milk cows (farms)	1,581	0.8	1,279	0.8	982	0.8	-19.1	-23.2
Milk cows (number)	83,381	0.8	78,976	0.8	64,888	0.7	-5.3	-17.8
Cattle and calves sold (farms)	15,248	1.3	14,131	1.4	13,953	1.4	-7.3	-1.3
Cattle and calves sold (number)	402,235	0.6	375,903	0.5	418,642	0.6	-6.5	11.4
Hogs and pigs								
Number of farms	1,262	0.5	844	0.4	633	0.6	-33.1	-25.0
Number of animals	51,857	0.1	37,519	0.1	20,338	0.0	-27.6	-45.8
Hogs and pigs sold (farms)	807	0.3	534	0.3	373	0.4	-33.8	-30.1
Hogs and pigs sold (number)	72,940	0.1	57,244	0.1	28,527	0.0	-21.5	-50.2
Sheep and lambs								
Number of farms	631	0.7	468	0.6	346	0.5	-25.8	-26.1
Number of animals	11,520	0.1	9,244	0.1	5,233	0.1	-19.8	-43.4
Layers and pullets 13 weeks old and older								
Number of farms	2,382	1.6	1,344	1.5	860	1.2	-43.6	-36.0
Number of birds	1,504,057	0.4	2,111,789	0.6	2,354,044	0.6	40.4	11.5
Broilers and other meat-type chickens sold								
Number of farms	312	1.1	313	1.3	319	1.3	0.3	1.9
Number of birds sold	96,147,369	1.4	115,258,369	2.1	123,132,021	1.8	19.9	6.8

Source: 1997 Census of Agriculture, U.S. Department of Agriculture, National Agricultural Statistics Service. NA stands for "not available." (D) is shown when data are withheld to prevent disclosure of competitive information. A dash (-) is shown where no data were reported.

CROP STATISTICS FOR LOUISIANA

Item	1987 Value	% of U.S.	1992 Value	% of U.S.	1997 Value	% of U.S.	Percent change 1987-1992	1992-1997
Corn for grain or seed								
Number of farms	-	-	-	-	-	-	-	-
Number of acres	-	-	-	-	-	-	-	-
Number of bushels	-	-	-	-	-	-	-	-
Corn for silage or green chop								
Number of farms	-	-	-	-	-	-	-	-
Number of acres	-	-	-	-	-	-	-	-
Weight in tons, green	-	-	-	-	-	-	-	-
Sorghum for grain or seed								
Number of farms	800	-	875	-	370	-	9.4	-57.7
Number of acres	122,030	-	179,376	-	78,445	-	47.0	-56.3
Number of bushels	7,226,766	-	11,723,104	-	5,557,996	-	62.2	-52.6
Wheat for grain								
Number of farms	1,067	0.3	682	0.2	528	0.2	-36.1	-22.6
Number of acres	151,251	0.3	119,304	0.2	98,911	0.2	-21.1	-17.1
Number of bushels	4,654,627	0.2	4,432,764	0.2	3,755,759	0.2	-4.8	-15.3
Barley for grain								
Number of farms	-	-	-	-	-	-	-	-
Number of acres	-	-	-	-	-	-	-	-
Number of bushels	-	-	-	-	-	-	-	-
Oats for grain								
Number of farms	-	-	-	-	-	-	-	-
Number of acres	-	-	-	-	-	-	-	-
Number of bushels	-	-	-	-	-	-	-	-
Rice								
Number of farms	2,273	-	2,197	-	1,736	-	-3.3	-21.0
Number of acres	417,411	-	589,752	-	579,299	-	41.3	-1.8
Weight in hundredweight	17,970,394	-	26,906,404	-	26,474,660	-	49.7	-1.6
Sunflower seed								
Number of farms	-	-	-	-	-	-	-	-
Number of acres	-	-	-	-	-	-	-	-
Weight in pounds	-	-	-	-	-	-	-	-
Cotton								
Number of farms	2,675	6.2	2,599	7.5	1,586	5.0	-2.8	-39.0
Number of acres	590,257	6.0	827,792	7.6	647,257	4.9	40.2	-21.8
Number of bales	921,867	6.9	1,219,599	7.9	970,097	5.4	32.3	-20.5

Continued.

CROP STATISTICS FOR LOUISIANA - Continued

Item	1987		1992		1997		Percent change	
	Value	% of U.S.	Value	% of U.S.	Value	% of U.S.	1987-1992	1992-1997
Tobacco								
Number of farms	-	-	-	-	-	-	-	-
Number of acres	-	-	-	-	-	-	-	-
Weight in pounds	-	-	-	-	-	-	-	-
Soybeans for beans								
Number of farms	5,017	1.1	3,903	1.0	3,511	1.0	-22.2	-10.0
Number of acres	1,540,372	2.8	1,112,815	2.0	1,260,523	1.9	-27.8	13.3
Number of bushels	40,524,474	2.2	33,360,521	1.6	36,152,458	1.4	-17.7	8.4
Dry edible beans, excluding dry limas								
Number of farms	-	-	-	-	-	-	-	-
Number of acres	-	-	-	-	-	-	-	-
Weight in hundredweight	-	-	-	-	-	-	-	-
Potatoes, excluding sweetpotatoes								
Number of farms	-	-	-	-	-	-	-	-
Number of acres	-	-	-	-	-	-	-	-
Weight in hundredweight	-	-	-	-	-	-	-	-
Sugar beets for sugar								
Number of farms	-	-	-	-	-	-	-	-
Number of acres	-	-	-	-	-	-	-	-
Weight in tons	-	-	-	-	-	-	-	-
Sugarcane for sugar								
Number of farms	687	-	755	-	705	-	9.9	-6.6
Number of acres	264,466	-	356,349	-	395,588	-	34.7	11.0
Weight in tons	6,877,798	-	9,131,174	-	12,187,651	-	32.8	33.5
Pineapples harvested								
Number of farms	-	-	-	-	-	-	-	-
Number of acres	-	-	-	-	-	-	-	-
Weight in tons	-	-	-	-	-	-	-	-
Peanuts for nuts								
Number of farms	-	-	-	-	-	-	-	-
Number of acres	-	-	-	-	-	-	-	-
Weight in pounds	-	-	-	-	-	-	-	-
Hay - all types, including alfalfa								
Number of farms	9,531	1.0	8,956	1.0	8,607	1.0	-6.0	-3.9
Number of acres	343,054	0.6	383,292	0.7	404,508	0.7	11.7	5.5
Weight in tons, dry	717,887	0.6	851,288	0.7	948,545	0.7	18.6	11.4
Vegetables harvested for sale								
Number of farms	-	-	-	-	-	-	-	-
Number of acres	-	-	-	-	-	-	-	-
Land in orchards								
Number of farms	-	-	-	-	-	-	-	-
Number of acres	-	-	-	-	-	-	-	-

Source: *1997 Census of Agriculture*, U.S. Department of Agriculture, National Agricultural Statistics Service. NA stands for "not available." (D) is shown when data are withheld to prevent disclosure of competitive information. A dash (-) is shown where no data were reported. Not all states report growing all crops, but all crop categories in the census are shown for every state. The data series used for this presentation did not report U.S. totals for a number of categories; for that reason, the "% of U.S." column is sometimes blank.

MAINE

GENERAL STATISTICS FOR MAINE

Item	1987 Value	1987 % of U.S.	1992 Value	1992 % of U.S.	1997 Value	1997 % of U.S.	Percent change 1987-1992	Percent change 1992-1997
Farms (number)	6,269	0.3	5,776	0.3	5,810	0.3	-7.9	0.6
Land in farms (acres)	1,342,588	0.1	1,258,297	0.1	1,211,648	0.1	-6.3	-3.7
Average size of farm (acres)	214	46.3	218	44.4	209	42.9	1.9	-4.1
Median size of farm (acres)	NA	-	NA	-	102	85.0	-	-
Market value of land and buildings:								
Average per farm (dollars)	210,777	72.8	241,816	67.7	251,074	55.8	14.7	3.8
Average per acre (dollars)	962	153.4	1,130	155.4	1,190	127.5	17.5	5.3
Market value of machinery/equipment - average per farm (dollars)	38,325	93.0	45,757	94.1	48,697	84.4	19.4	6.4
Farms by size:								
1 to 9 acres	419	0.2	465	0.3	533	0.3	11.0	14.6
10 to 49 acres	1,029	0.2	1,024	0.3	1,184	0.3	-0.5	15.6
50 to 179 acres	2,453	0.4	2,174	0.4	2,110	0.4	-11.4	-2.9
180 to 499 acres	1,758	0.4	1,513	0.4	1,441	0.4	-13.9	-4.8
500 to 999 acres	474	0.2	448	0.2	398	0.2	-5.5	-11.2
1,000 acres or more	136	0.1	152	0.1	144	0.1	11.8	-5.3
Total cropland								
Farms	5,919	0.3	5,495	0.3	5,372	0.3	-7.2	-2.2
Acres	592,309	0.1	559,424	0.1	539,966	0.1	-5.6	-3.5
Harvested cropland (farms)	5,486	0.3	5,141	0.3	4,875	0.3	-6.3	-5.2
Harvested cropland (acres)	410,891	0.1	399,755	0.1	403,014	0.1	-2.7	0.8
Irrigated land (farms)	359	0.1	523	0.2	671	0.2	45.7	28.3
Irrigated land (acres)	6,065	0.0	10,241	0.0	21,791	0.0	68.9	112.8
Market value of agricultural products sold:								
Total sales ($1,000)	405,484	0.3	430,324	0.3	438,673	0.2	6.1	1.9
Average per farm (dollars)	64,681	99.3	74,502	88.2	75,503	73.3	15.2	1.3
Agricultural products only ($1,000)	157,828	0.3	215,995	0.3	212,229	0.2	36.9	-1.7
Livestock, poultry, and products ($1,000)	247,656	0.3	214,329	0.2	226,444	0.2	-13.5	5.7
Farms by value of sales:								
Less than $2,500	2,059	0.4	1,690	0.4	1,923	0.4	-17.9	13.8
$2,500 to $4,999	870	0.3	775	0.3	743	0.3	-10.9	-4.1
$5,000 to $9,999	719	0.3	786	0.3	751	0.3	9.3	-4.5
$10,000 to $24,999	700	0.2	732	0.2	798	0.3	4.6	9.0
$25,000 to $49,999	466	0.2	441	0.2	438	0.3	-5.4	-0.7
$50,000 to $99,999	553	0.3	449	0.2	390	0.2	-18.8	-13.1
$100,000 or more	902	0.3	903	0.3	767	0.2	0.1	-15.1
Total farm production expenses ($1,000)	324,276	0.3	351,076	0.3	347,611	0.2	8.3	-1.0
Average expenses per farm (dollars)	51,752	99.9	60,824	89.5	59,923	76.1	17.5	-1.5
Net cash return for the farm unit:								
Number of farms	6,266	0.3	5,772	0.3	5,801	0.3	-7.9	0.5
Value ($1000)	74,252	0.3	72,781	0.2	78,187	0.2	-2.0	7.4
Average per farm (dollars)	11,850	93.6	12,609	79.8	13,478	60.5	6.4	6.9
Operators by principal occupation:								
Farming	3,220	0.3	2,981	0.3	2,872	0.3	-7.4	-3.7
Other	3,049	0.3	2,795	0.3	2,938	0.3	-8.3	5.1
Operators by days worked off farm:								
Any	3,653	0.3	3,144	0.3	3,263	0.3	-13.9	3.8
200 days or more	2,253	0.3	1,857	0.3	1,958	0.3	-17.6	5.4

Source: 1997 Census of Agriculture, U.S. Department of Agriculture, National Agricultural Statistics Service. NA stands for "not available." (D) is shown when data are withheld to prevent disclosure of competitive information. A dash (-) is shown where no data were reported. The market value of land and buildings, and of machinery and equipment, is an estimated amount. Net cash return for the farm unit includes only returns from agricultural activities.

LIVESTOCK STATISTICS FOR MAINE

Item	1987 Value	% of U.S.	1992 Value	% of U.S.	1997 Value	% of U.S.	Percent change 1987-1992	Percent change 1992-1997
Cattle and calves								
Number of farms	2,637	0.2	2,110	0.2	1,921	0.2	-20.0	-9.0
Number of animals	119,475	0.1	104,511	0.1	101,695	0.1	-12.5	-2.7
Beef cows (farms)	1,331	0.2	1,098	0.1	1,035	0.1	-17.5	-5.7
Beef cows (number)	11,782	0.0	11,412	0.0	11,782	0.0	-3.1	3.2
Milk cows (farms)	1,183	0.6	836	0.5	685	0.6	-29.3	-18.1
Milk cows (number)	49,815	0.5	42,737	0.5	40,749	0.4	-14.2	-4.7
Cattle and calves sold (farms)	2,366	0.2	1,831	0.2	1,631	0.2	-22.6	-10.9
Cattle and calves sold (number)	50,357	0.1	40,873	0.1	37,889	0.1	-18.8	-7.3
Hogs and pigs								
Number of farms	421	0.2	377	0.2	341	0.3	-10.5	-9.5
Number of animals	8,999	0.0	4,768	0.0	5,977	0.0	-47.0	25.4
Hogs and pigs sold (farms)	295	0.1	258	0.1	261	0.3	-12.5	1.2
Hogs and pigs sold (number)	13,905	0.0	9,308	0.0	9,226	0.0	-33.1	-0.9
Sheep and lambs								
Number of farms	559	0.6	457	0.6	426	0.6	-18.2	-6.8
Number of animals	15,606	0.1	12,541	0.1	10,603	0.1	-19.6	-15.5
Layers and pullets 13 weeks old and older								
Number of farms	719	0.5	562	0.6	554	0.8	-21.8	-1.4
Number of birds	6,999,685	1.9	5,200,911	1.5	6,134,383	1.7	-25.7	17.9
Broilers and other meat-type chickens sold								
Number of farms	95	0.3	74	0.3	73	0.3	-22.1	-1.4
Number of birds sold	13,679,943	0.2	638,163	0.0	199,416	0.0	-95.3	-68.8

Source: *1997 Census of Agriculture*, U.S. Department of Agriculture, National Agricultural Statistics Service. NA stands for "not available." (D) is shown when data are withheld to prevent disclosure of competitive information. A dash (-) is shown where no data were reported.

CROP STATISTICS FOR MAINE

Item	1987 Value	% of U.S.	1992 Value	% of U.S.	1997 Value	% of U.S.	Percent change 1987-1992	Percent change 1992-1997
Corn for grain or seed								
Number of farms	-	-	-	-	-	-	-	-
Number of acres	-	-	-	-	-	-	-	-
Number of bushels	-	-	-	-	-	-	-	-
Corn for silage or green chop								
Number of farms	544	-	438	-	332	-	-19.5	-24.2
Number of acres	28,711	-	28,254	-	27,537	-	-1.6	-2.5
Weight in tons, green	442,833	-	454,228	-	447,405	-	2.6	-1.5
Sorghum for grain or seed								
Number of farms	-	-	-	-	-	-	-	-
Number of acres	-	-	-	-	-	-	-	-
Number of bushels	-	-	-	-	-	-	-	-
Wheat for grain								
Number of farms	-	-	-	-	-	-	-	-
Number of acres	-	-	-	-	-	-	-	-
Number of bushels	-	-	-	-	-	-	-	-
Barley for grain								
Number of farms	-	-	-	-	-	-	-	-
Number of acres	-	-	-	-	-	-	-	-
Number of bushels	-	-	-	-	-	-	-	-
Oats for grain								
Number of farms	535	-	320	-	272	-	-40.2	-15.0
Number of acres	35,548	-	24,277	-	22,364	-	-31.7	-7.9
Number of bushels	2,728,024	-	2,014,920	-	1,643,127	-	-26.1	-18.5
Rice								
Number of farms	-	-	-	-	-	-	-	-
Number of acres	-	-	-	-	-	-	-	-
Weight in hundredweight	-	-	-	-	-	-	-	-
Sunflower seed								
Number of farms	-	-	-	-	-	-	-	-
Number of acres	-	-	-	-	-	-	-	-
Weight in pounds	-	-	-	-	-	-	-	-
Cotton								
Number of farms	-	-	-	-	-	-	-	-
Number of acres	-	-	-	-	-	-	-	-
Number of bales	-	-	-	-	-	-	-	-

Continued.

CROP STATISTICS FOR MAINE - Continued

Item	1987		1992		1997		Percent change	
	Value	% of U.S.	Value	% of U.S.	Value	% of U.S.	1987-1992	1992-1997
Tobacco								
Number of farms	-	-	-	-	-	-	-	-
Number of acres	-	-	-	-	-	-	-	-
Weight in pounds	-	-	-	-	-	-	-	-
Soybeans for beans								
Number of farms	-	-	-	-	-	-	-	-
Number of acres	-	-	-	-	-	-	-	-
Number of bushels	-	-	-	-	-	-	-	-
Dry edible beans, excluding dry limas								
Number of farms	-	-	-	-	-	-	-	-
Number of acres	-	-	-	-	-	-	-	-
Weight in hundredweight	-	-	-	-	-	-	-	-
Potatoes, excluding sweetpotatoes								
Number of farms	839	-	770	-	586	-	-8.2	-23.9
Number of acres	83,261	-	87,650	-	73,085	-	5.3	-16.6
Weight in hundredweight	22,412,030	-	25,008,230	-	19,490,474	-	11.6	-22.1
Sugar beets for sugar								
Number of farms	-	-	-	-	-	-	-	-
Number of acres	-	-	-	-	-	-	-	-
Weight in tons	-	-	-	-	-	-	-	-
Sugarcane for sugar								
Number of farms	-	-	-	-	-	-	-	-
Number of acres	-	-	-	-	-	-	-	-
Weight in tons	-	-	-	-	-	-	-	-
Pineapples harvested								
Number of farms	-	-	-	-	-	-	-	-
Number of acres	-	-	-	-	-	-	-	-
Weight in tons	-	-	-	-	-	-	-	-
Peanuts for nuts								
Number of farms	-	-	-	-	-	-	-	-
Number of acres	-	-	-	-	-	-	-	-
Weight in pounds	-	-	-	-	-	-	-	-
Hay - all types, including alfalfa								
Number of farms	3,672	0.4	3,119	0.3	2,810	0.3	-15.1	-9.9
Number of acres	221,675	0.4	214,129	0.4	214,005	0.4	-3.4	-0.1
Weight in tons, dry	393,393	0.3	332,197	0.3	332,039	0.2	-15.6	-0.0
Vegetables harvested for sale								
Number of farms	509	0.8	582	0.9	611	1.1	14.3	5.0
Number of acres	9,727	0.3	10,251	0.3	11,745	0.3	5.4	14.6
Land in orchards								
Number of farms	394	0.3	396	0.3	334	0.3	0.5	-15.7
Number of acres	7,405	0.2	6,463	0.1	5,170	0.1	-12.7	-20.0

Source: 1997 Census of Agriculture, U.S. Department of Agriculture, National Agricultural Statistics Service. NA stands for "not available." (D) is shown when data are withheld to prevent disclosure of competitive information. A dash (-) is shown where no data were reported. Not all states report growing all crops, but all crop categories in the census are shown for every state. The data series used for this presentation did not report U.S. totals for a number of categories; for that reason, the "% of U.S." column is sometimes blank.

MARYLAND

GENERAL STATISTICS FOR MARYLAND

Item	1987 Value	1987 % of U.S.	1992 Value	1992 % of U.S.	1997 Value	1997 % of U.S.	Percent change 1987-1992	Percent change 1992-1997
Farms (number)	14,776	0.7	13,037	0.7	12,084	0.6	-11.8	-7.3
Land in farms (acres)	2,396,629	0.2	2,223,476	0.2	2,154,875	0.2	-7.2	-3.1
Average size of farm (acres)	162	35.1	171	34.8	178	36.6	5.6	4.1
Median size of farm (acres)	NA	-	NA	-	64	53.3	-	-
Market value of land and buildings:								
Average per farm (dollars)	366,788	126.7	503,828	141.1	563,605	125.3	37.4	11.9
Average per acre (dollars)	2,261	360.6	2,911	400.4	3,176	340.4	28.7	9.1
Market value of machinery/equipment -								
average per farm (dollars)	44,656	108.3	50,564	104.0	60,176	104.3	13.2	19.0
Farms by size:								
1 to 9 acres	1,838	1.0	1,560	0.9	1,407	0.9	-15.1	-9.8
10 to 49 acres	4,400	1.1	3,979	1.0	3,828	0.9	-9.6	-3.8
50 to 179 acres	4,885	0.8	4,254	0.7	3,825	0.6	-12.9	-10.1
180 to 499 acres	2,591	0.5	2,252	0.5	2,038	0.5	-13.1	-9.5
500 to 999 acres	712	0.4	641	0.3	617	0.4	-10.0	-3.7
1,000 acres or more	350	0.2	351	0.2	369	0.2	0.3	5.1
Total cropland								
Farms	13,200	0.7	11,605	0.7	10,702	0.6	-12.1	-7.8
Acres	1,744,891	0.4	1,663,907	0.4	1,613,497	0.4	-4.6	-3.0
Harvested cropland (farms)	11,960	0.7	10,447	0.7	9,474	0.7	-12.7	-9.3
Harvested cropland (acres)	1,346,913	0.5	1,397,069	0.5	1,382,035	0.4	3.7	-1.1
Irrigated land (farms)	1,074	0.4	1,063	0.4	1,154	0.4	-1.0	8.6
Irrigated land (acres)	50,762	0.1	56,913	0.1	68,588	0.1	12.1	20.5
Market value of agricultural products sold:								
Total sales ($1,000)	989,061	0.7	1,169,331	0.7	1,312,086	0.7	18.2	12.2
Average per farm (dollars)	66,937	102.7	89,693	106.2	108,580	105.4	34.0	21.1
Agricultural products only ($1,000)	253,056	0.4	388,143	0.5	458,719	0.5	53.4	18.2
Livestock, poultry, and products ($1,000)	736,006	1.0	781,188	0.9	853,367	0.9	6.1	9.2
Farms by value of sales:								
Less than $2,500	4,165	0.8	3,165	0.7	3,097	0.6	-24.0	-2.1
$2,500 to $4,999	1,948	0.7	1,642	0.7	1,365	0.6	-15.7	-16.9
$5,000 to $9,999	1,881	0.7	1,698	0.7	1,551	0.7	-9.7	-8.7
$10,000 to $24,999	2,012	0.6	1,822	0.6	1,668	0.6	-9.4	-8.5
$25,000 to $49,999	1,100	0.5	1,096	0.6	952	0.6	-0.4	-13.1
$50,000 to $99,999	1,084	0.5	904	0.5	854	0.5	-16.6	-5.5
$100,000 or more	2,586	0.9	2,710	0.8	2,597	0.8	4.8	-4.2
Total farm production expenses ($1,000)	851,440	0.8	974,511	0.7	1,123,200	0.7	14.5	15.3
Average expenses per farm (dollars)	57,631	111.3	74,732	110.0	92,757	117.8	29.7	24.1
Net cash return for the farm unit:								
Number of farms	14,774	0.7	13,040	0.7	12,109	0.6	-11.7	-7.1
Value ($1000)	135,200	0.5	186,174	0.6	172,948	0.4	37.7	-7.1
Average per farm (dollars)	9,151	72.3	14,277	90.4	14,283	64.2	56.0	0.0
Operators by principal occupation:								
Farming	7,882	0.7	6,980	0.7	6,235	0.6	-11.4	-10.7
Other	6,894	0.7	6,057	0.7	5,849	0.6	-12.1	-3.4
Operators by days worked off farm:								
Any	7,985	0.7	6,745	0.7	6,362	0.6	-15.5	-5.7
200 days or more	5,504	0.7	4,563	0.7	4,317	0.6	-17.1	-5.4

Source: *1997 Census of Agriculture*, U.S. Department of Agriculture, National Agricultural Statistics Service. NA stands for "not available." (D) is shown when data are withheld to prevent disclosure of competitive information. A dash (-) is shown where no data were reported. The market value of land and buildings, and of machinery and equipment, is an estimated amount. Net cash return for the farm unit includes only returns from agricultural activities.

LIVESTOCK STATISTICS FOR MARYLAND

Item	1987		1992		1997		Percent change	
	Value	% of U.S.	Value	% of U.S.	Value	% of U.S.	1987-1992	1992-1997
Cattle and calves								
Number of farms	5,780	0.5	4,978	0.5	4,444	0.4	-13.9	-10.7
Number of animals	308,052	0.3	283,167	0.3	261,324	0.3	-8.1	-7.7
Beef cows (farms)	3,185	0.4	2,921	0.4	2,726	0.3	-8.3	-6.7
Beef cows (number)	48,454	0.2	51,676	0.2	50,619	0.1	6.6	-2.0
Milk cows (farms)	1,694	0.8	1,329	0.9	1,091	0.9	-21.5	-17.9
Milk cows (number)	110,463	1.1	94,751	1.0	84,953	0.9	-14.2	-10.3
Cattle and calves sold (farms)	5,368	0.5	4,545	0.4	4,111	0.4	-15.3	-9.5
Cattle and calves sold (number)	154,540	0.2	133,633	0.2	136,747	0.2	-13.5	2.3
Hogs and pigs								
Number of farms	1,322	0.5	910	0.5	584	0.5	-31.2	-35.8
Number of animals	197,214	0.4	145,519	0.3	80,850	0.1	-26.2	-44.4
Hogs and pigs sold (farms)	1,265	0.5	843	0.4	495	0.5	-33.4	-41.3
Hogs and pigs sold (number)	372,470	0.4	289,149	0.3	149,472	0.1	-22.4	-48.3
Sheep and lambs								
Number of farms	660	0.7	611	0.8	616	0.9	-7.4	0.8
Number of animals	24,599	0.2	25,291	0.2	21,985	0.3	2.8	-13.1
Layers and pullets 13 weeks old and older								
Number of farms	1,337	0.9	839	1.0	637	0.9	-37.2	-24.1
Number of birds	4,060,760	1.1	4,268,626	1.2	4,639,682	1.3	5.1	8.7
Broilers and other meat-type chickens sold								
Number of farms	1,381	5.0	1,109	4.6	997	4.2	-19.7	-10.1
Number of birds sold	257,070,110	3.8	257,209,663	4.7	256,926,521	3.8	0.1	-0.1

Source: 1997 Census of Agriculture, U.S. Department of Agriculture, National Agricultural Statistics Service. NA stands for "not available." (D) is shown when data are withheld to prevent disclosure of competitive information. A dash (-) is shown where no data were reported.

CROP STATISTICS FOR MARYLAND

Item	1987		1992		1997		Percent change	
	Value	% of U.S.	Value	% of U.S.	Value	% of U.S.	1987-1992	1992-1997
Corn for grain or seed								
Number of farms	5,608	0.9	4,631	0.9	3,554	0.8	-17.4	-23.3
Number of acres	432,409	0.7	454,083	0.7	405,451	0.6	5.0	-10.7
Number of bushels	31,941,714	-	52,596,358	0.6	36,823,284	0.4	64.7	-30.0
Corn for silage or green chop								
Number of farms	-	-	-	-	-	-	-	-
Number of acres	-	-	-	-	-	-	-	-
Weight in tons, green	-	-	-	-	-	-	-	-
Sorghum for grain or seed								
Number of farms	-	-	-	-	-	-	-	-
Number of acres	-	-	-	-	-	-	-	-
Number of bushels	-	-	-	-	-	-	-	-
Wheat for grain								
Number of farms	3,112	0.9	2,774	0.9	2,339	1.0	-10.9	-15.7
Number of acres	146,081	0.3	188,122	0.3	199,351	0.3	28.8	6.0
Number of bushels	6,766,273	0.4	10,233,795	0.5	12,711,370	0.6	51.2	24.2
Barley for grain								
Number of farms	1,541	-	1,291	-	972	-	-16.2	-24.7
Number of acres	59,268	-	63,024	-	47,405	-	6.3	-24.8
Number of bushels	3,707,134	-	4,240,170	-	3,489,722	-	14.4	-17.7
Oats for grain								
Number of farms	-	-	-	-	-	-	-	-
Number of acres	-	-	-	-	-	-	-	-
Number of bushels	-	-	-	-	-	-	-	-
Rice								
Number of farms	-	-	-	-	-	-	-	-
Number of acres	-	-	-	-	-	-	-	-
Weight in hundredweight	-	-	-	-	-	-	-	-
Sunflower seed								
Number of farms	-	-	-	-	-	-	-	-
Number of acres	-	-	-	-	-	-	-	-
Weight in pounds	-	-	-	-	-	-	-	-
Cotton								
Number of farms	-	-	-	-	-	-	-	-
Number of acres	-	-	-	-	-	-	-	-
Number of bales	-	-	-	-	-	-	-	-

Continued.

CROP STATISTICS FOR MARYLAND - Continued

Item	1987		1992		1997		Percent change	
	Value	% of U.S.	Value	% of U.S.	Value	% of U.S.	1987-1992	1992-1997
Tobacco								
Number of farms	1,357	-	951	-	711	-	-29.9	-25.2
Number of acres	10,780	-	8,470	-	7,939	-	-21.4	-6.3
Weight in pounds	13,751,729	-	11,794,382	-	11,987,083	-	-14.2	1.6
Soybeans for beans								
Number of farms	3,697	0.8	3,663	1.0	3,226	0.9	-0.9	-11.9
Number of acres	405,170	0.7	503,181	0.9	509,683	0.8	24.2	1.3
Number of bushels	9,352,369	0.5	16,226,822	0.8	15,171,466	0.6	73.5	-6.5
Dry edible beans, excluding dry limas								
Number of farms	-	-	-	-	-	-	-	-
Number of acres	-	-	-	-	-	-	-	-
Weight in hundredweight	-	-	-	-	-	-	-	-
Potatoes, excluding sweetpotatoes								
Number of farms	-	-	-	-	-	-	-	-
Number of acres	-	-	-	-	-	-	-	-
Weight in hundredweight	-	-	-	-	-	-	-	-
Sugar beets for sugar								
Number of farms	-	-	-	-	-	-	-	-
Number of acres	-	-	-	-	-	-	-	-
Weight in tons	-	-	-	-	-	-	-	-
Sugarcane for sugar								
Number of farms	-	-	-	-	-	-	-	-
Number of acres	-	-	-	-	-	-	-	-
Weight in tons	-	-	-	-	-	-	-	-
Pineapples harvested								
Number of farms	-	-	-	-	-	-	-	-
Number of acres	-	-	-	-	-	-	-	-
Weight in tons	-	-	-	-	-	-	-	-
Peanuts for nuts								
Number of farms	-	-	-	-	-	-	-	-
Number of acres	-	-	-	-	-	-	-	-
Weight in pounds	-	-	-	-	-	-	-	-
Hay - all types, including alfalfa								
Number of farms	6,619	0.7	5,532	0.6	5,223	0.6	-16.4	-5.6
Number of acres	255,676	0.4	222,184	0.4	223,014	0.4	-13.1	0.4
Weight in tons, dry	593,854	0.5	545,526	0.4	450,781	0.3	-8.1	-17.4
Vegetables harvested for sale								
Number of farms	1,184	1.9	1,167	1.9	951	1.8	-1.4	-18.5
Number of acres	38,238	1.1	36,313	1.0	35,958	1.0	-5.0	-1.0
Land in orchards								
Number of farms	-	-	-	-	-	-	-	-
Number of acres	-	-	-	-	-	-	-	-

Source: 1997 Census of Agriculture, U.S. Department of Agriculture, National Agricultural Statistics Service. NA stands for "not available." (D) is shown when data are withheld to prevent disclosure of competitive information. A dash (-) is shown where no data were reported. Not all states report growing all crops, but all crop categories in the census are shown for every state. The data series used for this presentation did not report U.S. totals for a number of categories; for that reason, the "% of U.S." column is sometimes blank.

MASSACHUSETTS

GENERAL STATISTICS FOR MASSACHUSETTS

Item	1987 Value	1987 % of U.S.	1992 Value	1992 % of U.S.	1997 Value	1997 % of U.S.	Percent change 1987-1992	Percent change 1992-1997
Farms (number)	6,216	0.3	5,258	0.3	5,574	0.3	-15.4	6.0
Land in farms (acres)	615,185	0.1	526,440	0.1	518,299	0.1	-14.4	-1.5
Average size of farm (acres)	99	21.4	100	20.4	93	19.1	1.0	-7.0
Median size of farm (acres)	NA	-	NA	-	37	30.8	-	-
Market value of land and buildings:								
Average per farm (dollars)	346,530	119.7	460,410	128.9	455,014	101.2	32.9	-1.2
Average per acre (dollars)	3,553	566.7	4,898	673.7	5,207	558.1	37.9	6.3
Market value of machinery/equipment - average per farm (dollars)	32,039	77.7	36,359	74.8	40,395	70.0	13.5	11.1
Farms by size:								
1 to 9 acres	1,105	0.6	1,044	0.6	1,254	0.8	-5.5	20.1
10 to 49 acres	2,125	0.5	1,738	0.4	1,865	0.5	-18.2	7.3
50 to 179 acres	2,016	0.3	1,667	0.3	1,690	0.3	-17.3	1.4
180 to 499 acres	813	0.2	654	0.2	614	0.2	-19.6	-6.1
500 to 999 acres	126	0.1	121	0.1	121	0.1	-4.0	-
1,000 acres or more	31	0.0	34	0.0	30	0.0	9.7	-11.8
Total cropland								
Farms	5,654	0.3	4,853	0.3	4,990	0.3	-14.2	2.8
Acres	272,588	0.1	235,284	0.1	223,573	0.1	-13.7	-5.0
Harvested cropland (farms)	5,084	0.3	4,417	0.3	4,587	0.3	-13.1	3.8
Harvested cropland (acres)	194,874	0.1	173,255	0.1	168,765	0.1	-11.1	-2.6
Irrigated land (farms)	1,316	0.5	1,336	0.5	1,630	0.6	1.5	22.0
Irrigated land (acres)	20,158	0.0	19,909	0.0	24,564	0.0	-1.2	23.4
Market value of agricultural products sold:								
Total sales ($1,000)	340,464	0.3	350,639	0.2	454,404	0.2	3.0	29.6
Average per farm (dollars)	54,772	84.1	66,687	79.0	81,522	79.2	21.8	22.2
Agricultural products only ($1,000)	215,855	0.4	255,138	0.3	357,377	0.4	18.2	40.1
Livestock, poultry, and products ($1,000)	124,609	0.2	95,500	0.1	97,027	0.1	-23.4	1.6
Farms by value of sales:								
Less than $2,500	2,167	0.4	1,572	0.4	1,616	0.3	-27.5	2.8
$2,500 to $4,999	830	0.3	656	0.3	664	0.3	-21.0	1.2
$5,000 to $9,999	720	0.3	655	0.3	707	0.3	-9.0	7.9
$10,000 to $24,999	770	0.2	696	0.2	753	0.3	-9.6	8.2
$25,000 to $49,999	494	0.2	476	0.2	507	0.3	-3.6	6.5
$50,000 to $99,999	515	0.2	462	0.2	468	0.3	-10.3	1.3
$100,000 or more	720	0.2	741	0.2	859	0.2	2.9	15.9
Total farm production expenses ($1,000)	251,496	0.2	266,163	0.2	311,068	0.2	5.8	16.9
Average expenses per farm (dollars)	40,460	78.1	50,621	74.5	55,897	71.0	25.1	10.4
Net cash return for the farm unit:								
Number of farms	6,216	0.3	5,258	0.3	5,571	0.3	-15.4	6.0
Value ($1000)	84,172	0.3	77,725	0.3	135,155	0.3	-7.7	73.9
Average per farm (dollars)	13,541	107.0	14,782	93.6	24,260	109.0	9.2	64.1
Operators by principal occupation:								
Farming	3,174	0.3	2,926	0.3	2,927	0.3	-7.8	0.0
Other	3,042	0.3	2,332	0.3	2,647	0.3	-23.3	13.5
Operators by days worked off farm:								
Any	3,516	0.3	2,695	0.3	2,980	0.3	-23.4	10.6
200 days or more	2,283	0.3	1,666	0.3	1,864	0.3	-27.0	11.9

Source: *1997 Census of Agriculture*, U.S. Department of Agriculture, National Agricultural Statistics Service. NA stands for "not available." (D) is shown when data are withheld to prevent disclosure of competitive information. A dash (-) is shown where no data were reported. The market value of land and buildings, and of machinery and equipment, is an estimated amount. Net cash return for the farm unit includes only returns from agricultural activities.

LIVESTOCK STATISTICS FOR MASSACHUSETTS

Item	1987		1992		1997		Percent change	
	Value	% of U.S.	Value	% of U.S.	Value	% of U.S.	1987-1992	1992-1997
Cattle and calves								
Number of farms	2,112	0.2	1,565	0.1	1,420	0.1	-25.9	-9.3
Number of animals	83,065	0.1	68,331	0.1	61,719	0.1	-17.7	-9.7
Beef cows (farms)	1,124	0.1	850	0.1	799	0.1	-24.4	-6.0
Beef cows (number)	9,692	0.0	7,347	0.0	6,858	0.0	-24.2	-6.7
Milk cows (farms)	838	0.4	606	0.4	483	0.4	-27.7	-20.3
Milk cows (number)	36,913	0.4	30,906	0.3	26,846	0.3	-16.3	-13.1
Cattle and calves sold (farms)	1,725	0.1	1,271	0.1	1,158	0.1	-26.3	-8.9
Cattle and calves sold (number)	39,668	0.1	29,839	0.0	24,849	0.0	-24.8	-16.7
Hogs and pigs								
Number of farms	498	0.2	404	0.2	383	0.3	-18.9	-5.2
Number of animals	25,816	0.0	16,439	0.0	18,297	0.0	-36.3	11.3
Hogs and pigs sold (farms)	387	0.2	296	0.2	269	0.3	-23.5	-9.1
Hogs and pigs sold (number)	40,048	0.0	25,564	0.0	23,636	0.0	-36.2	-7.5
Sheep and lambs								
Number of farms	604	0.7	520	0.6	431	0.7	-13.9	-17.1
Number of animals	14,761	0.1	11,341	0.1	8,348	0.1	-23.2	-26.4
Layers and pullets 13 weeks old and older								
Number of farms	738	0.5	535	0.6	510	0.7	-27.5	-4.7
Number of birds	1,502,202	0.4	544,401	0.2	682,853	0.2	-63.8	25.4
Broilers and other meat-type chickens sold								
Number of farms	37	0.1	45	0.2	41	0.2	21.6	-8.9
Number of birds sold	(D)	-	125,283	0.0	(D)	-	-	-

Source: 1997 Census of Agriculture, U.S. Department of Agriculture, National Agricultural Statistics Service. NA stands for "not available." (D) is shown when data are withheld to prevent disclosure of competitive information. A dash (-) is shown where no data were reported.

CROP STATISTICS FOR MASSACHUSETTS

Item	1987		1992		1997		Percent change	
	Value	% of U.S.	Value	% of U.S.	Value	% of U.S.	1987-1992	1992-1997
Corn for grain or seed								
Number of farms	152	0.0	111	0.0	99	0.0	-27.0	-10.8
Number of acres	5,681	0.0	4,893	0.0	4,951	0.0	-13.9	1.2
Number of bushels	626,829	-	488,921	0.0	590,748	0.0	-22.0	20.8
Corn for silage or green chop								
Number of farms	604	-	531	-	403	-	-12.1	-24.1
Number of acres	28,643	-	25,861	-	22,813	-	-9.7	-11.8
Weight in tons, green	524,819	-	470,201	-	445,811	-	-10.4	-5.2
Sorghum for grain or seed								
Number of farms	-	-	-	-	-	-	-	-
Number of acres	-	-	-	-	-	-	-	-
Number of bushels	-	-	-	-	-	-	-	-
Wheat for grain								
Number of farms	-	-	-	-	-	-	-	-
Number of acres	-	-	-	-	-	-	-	-
Number of bushels	-	-	-	-	-	-	-	-
Barley for grain								
Number of farms	-	-	-	-	-	-	-	-
Number of acres	-	-	-	-	-	-	-	-
Number of bushels	-	-	-	-	-	-	-	-
Oats for grain								
Number of farms	-	-	-	-	-	-	-	-
Number of acres	-	-	-	-	-	-	-	-
Number of bushels	-	-	-	-	-	-	-	-
Rice								
Number of farms	-	-	-	-	-	-	-	-
Number of acres	-	-	-	-	-	-	-	-
Weight in hundredweight	-	-	-	-	-	-	-	-
Sunflower seed								
Number of farms	-	-	-	-	-	-	-	-
Number of acres	-	-	-	-	-	-	-	-
Weight in pounds	-	-	-	-	-	-	-	-
Cotton								
Number of farms	-	-	-	-	-	-	-	-
Number of acres	-	-	-	-	-	-	-	-
Number of bales	-	-	-	-	-	-	-	-

Continued.

CROP STATISTICS FOR MASSACHUSETTS - Continued

Item	1987 Value	1987 % of U.S.	1992 Value	1992 % of U.S.	1997 Value	1997 % of U.S.	Percent change 1987-1992	Percent change 1992-1997
Tobacco								
Number of farms	-	-	-	-	-	-	-	-
Number of acres	-	-	-	-	-	-	-	-
Weight in pounds	-	-	-	-	-	-	-	-
Soybeans for beans								
Number of farms	-	-	-	-	-	-	-	-
Number of acres	-	-	-	-	-	-	-	-
Number of bushels	-	-	-	-	-	-	-	-
Dry edible beans, excluding dry limas								
Number of farms	-	-	-	-	-	-	-	-
Number of acres	-	-	-	-	-	-	-	-
Weight in hundredweight	-	-	-	-	-	-	-	-
Potatoes, excluding sweetpotatoes								
Number of farms	93	-	102	-	93	-	9.7	-8.8
Number of acres	2,628	-	3,520	-	2,964	-	33.9	-15.8
Weight in hundredweight	615,427	-	812,469	-	789,847	-	32.0	-2.8
Sugar beets for sugar								
Number of farms	-	-	-	-	-	-	-	-
Number of acres	-	-	-	-	-	-	-	-
Weight in tons	-	-	-	-	-	-	-	-
Sugarcane for sugar								
Number of farms	-	-	-	-	-	-	-	-
Number of acres	-	-	-	-	-	-	-	-
Weight in tons	-	-	-	-	-	-	-	-
Pineapples harvested								
Number of farms	-	-	-	-	-	-	-	-
Number of acres	-	-	-	-	-	-	-	-
Weight in tons	-	-	-	-	-	-	-	-
Peanuts for nuts								
Number of farms	-	-	-	-	-	-	-	-
Number of acres	-	-	-	-	-	-	-	-
Weight in pounds	-	-	-	-	-	-	-	-
Hay - all types, including alfalfa								
Number of farms	2,874	0.3	2,269	0.3	2,168	0.2	-21.1	-4.5
Number of acres	121,498	0.2	103,596	0.2	100,218	0.2	-14.7	-3.3
Weight in tons, dry	250,559	0.2	213,589	0.2	181,885	0.1	-14.8	-14.8
Vegetables harvested for sale								
Number of farms	1,008	1.7	995	1.6	935	1.7	-1.3	-6.0
Number of acres	16,325	0.5	16,577	0.4	16,039	0.4	1.5	-3.2
Land in orchards								
Number of farms	572	0.5	525	0.5	431	0.4	-8.2	-17.9
Number of acres	9,379	0.2	7,848	0.2	6,546	0.1	-16.3	-16.6

Source: *1997 Census of Agriculture*, U.S. Department of Agriculture, National Agricultural Statistics Service. NA stands for "not available." (D) is shown when data are withheld to prevent disclosure of competitive information. A dash (-) is shown where no data were reported. Not all states report growing all crops, but all crop categories in the census are shown for every state. The data series used for this presentation did not report U.S. totals for a number of categories; for that reason, the "% of U.S." column is sometimes blank.

MICHIGAN

GENERAL STATISTICS FOR MICHIGAN

Item	1987 Value	1987 % of U.S.	1992 Value	1992 % of U.S.	1997 Value	1997 % of U.S.	Percent change 1987-1992	Percent change 1992-1997
Farms (number)	51,172	2.5	46,562	2.4	46,027	2.4	-9.0	-1.1
Land in farms (acres)	10,316,861	1.1	10,088,170	1.1	9,872,812	1.1	-2.2	-2.1
Average size of farm (acres)	202	43.7	217	44.2	215	44.1	7.4	-0.9
Median size of farm (acres)	NA	-	NA	-	90	75.0	-	-
Market value of land and buildings:								
Average per farm (dollars)	196,065	67.8	247,370	69.3	358,166	79.6	26.2	44.8
Average per acre (dollars)	971	154.9	1,131	155.6	1,671	179.1	16.5	47.7
Market value of machinery/equipment -								
average per farm (dollars)	45,954	111.5	55,028	113.2	66,361	115.1	19.7	20.6
Farms by size:								
1 to 9 acres	2,866	1.6	2,562	1.5	2,611	1.7	-10.6	1.9
10 to 49 acres	12,174	3.0	11,148	2.9	12,075	2.9	-8.4	8.3
50 to 179 acres	19,779	3.1	17,449	3.0	17,439	2.9	-11.8	-0.1
180 to 499 acres	11,329	2.4	10,289	2.4	8,989	2.2	-9.2	-12.6
500 to 999 acres	3,667	1.8	3,576	1.9	3,201	1.8	-2.5	-10.5
1,000 acres or more	1,357	0.8	1,538	0.9	1,712	1.0	13.3	11.3
Total cropland								
Farms	48,653	2.6	44,320	2.6	43,017	2.6	-8.9	-2.9
Acres	8,181,320	1.8	8,156,388	1.9	7,891,802	1.8	-0.3	-3.2
Harvested cropland (farms)	46,017	2.8	41,334	2.8	37,941	2.7	-10.2	-8.2
Harvested cropland (acres)	6,172,468	2.2	6,584,251	2.2	6,724,480	2.2	6.7	2.1
Irrigated land (farms)	3,755	1.3	3,823	1.4	3,752	1.3	1.8	-1.9
Irrigated land (acres)	314,953	0.7	366,465	0.7	393,485	0.7	16.4	7.4
Market value of agricultural products sold:								
Total sales ($1,000)	2,545,078	1.9	3,028,547	1.9	3,567,825	1.8	19.0	17.8
Average per farm (dollars)	49,736	76.3	65,043	77.0	77,516	75.3	30.8	19.2
Agricultural products only ($1,000)	1,272,802	2.2	1,671,563	2.2	2,199,721	2.2	31.3	31.6
Livestock, poultry, and products ($1,000)	1,272,276	1.6	1,356,984	1.6	1,368,104	1.4	6.7	0.8
Farms by value of sales:								
Less than $2,500	12,670	2.6	10,923	2.6	12,557	2.5	-13.8	15.0
$2,500 to $4,999	6,774	2.6	5,579	2.4	5,049	2.2	-17.6	-9.5
$5,000 to $9,999	7,548	2.7	6,387	2.5	5,800	2.4	-15.4	-9.2
$10,000 to $24,999	8,460	2.6	7,752	2.6	7,213	2.6	-8.4	-7.0
$25,000 to $49,999	5,002	2.3	4,683	2.4	4,472	2.6	-6.4	-4.5
$50,000 to $99,999	4,322	2.0	4,163	2.2	3,663	2.3	-3.7	-12.0
$100,000 or more	6,396	2.2	7,075	2.1	7,273	2.1	10.6	2.8
Total farm production expenses ($1,000)	2,211,823	2.0	2,583,189	2.0	2,835,658	1.9	16.8	9.8
Average expenses per farm (dollars)	43,221	83.4	55,483	81.7	61,591	78.2	28.4	11.0
Net cash return for the farm unit:								
Number of farms	51,175	2.5	46,558	2.4	46,040	2.4	-9.0	-1.1
Value ($1000)	319,953	1.2	431,005	1.4	686,891	1.6	34.7	59.4
Average per farm (dollars)	6,252	49.4	9,257	58.6	14,919	67.0	48.1	61.2
Operators by principal occupation:								
Farming	26,112	2.3	24,396	2.3	22,043	2.3	-6.6	-9.6
Other	25,060	2.6	22,166	2.5	23,984	2.5	-11.5	8.2
Operators by days worked off farm:								
Any	29,155	2.6	25,462	2.6	25,906	2.5	-12.7	1.7
200 days or more	20,818	2.8	17,984	2.7	18,568	2.6	-13.6	3.2

Source: 1997 Census of Agriculture, U.S. Department of Agriculture, National Agricultural Statistics Service. NA stands for "not available." (D) is shown when data are withheld to prevent disclosure of competitive information. A dash (-) is shown where no data were reported. The market value of land and buildings, and of machinery and equipment, is an estimated amount. Net cash return for the farm unit includes only returns from agricultural activities.

LIVESTOCK STATISTICS FOR MICHIGAN

Item	1987		1992		1997		Percent change	
	Value	% of U.S.	Value	% of U.S.	Value	% of U.S.	1987-1992	1992-1997
Cattle and calves								
Number of farms	19,436	1.7	17,031	1.6	15,468	1.5	-12.4	-9.2
Number of animals	1,163,352	1.2	1,113,604	1.2	1,025,702	1.0	-4.3	-7.9
Beef cows (farms)	8,163	1.0	7,548	0.9	7,566	0.9	-7.5	0.2
Beef cows (number)	110,156	0.3	116,106	0.4	116,399	0.3	5.4	0.3
Milk cows (farms)	6,499	3.2	5,198	3.3	3,990	3.4	-20.0	-23.2
Milk cows (number)	344,550	3.4	316,954	3.3	300,641	3.3	-8.0	-5.1
Cattle and calves sold (farms)	18,164	1.6	15,780	1.5	14,293	1.4	-13.1	-9.4
Cattle and calves sold (number)	653,806	0.9	594,685	0.8	537,681	0.7	-9.0	-9.6
Hogs and pigs								
Number of farms	5,577	2.3	4,774	2.5	2,853	2.6	-14.4	-40.2
Number of animals	1,227,069	2.3	1,231,641	2.1	1,032,014	1.7	0.4	-16.2
Hogs and pigs sold (farms)	5,603	2.3	4,770	2.5	2,690	2.6	-14.9	-43.6
Hogs and pigs sold (number)	2,215,872	2.3	2,300,151	2.1	2,206,940	1.5	3.8	-4.1
Sheep and lambs								
Number of farms	2,057	2.2	1,831	2.3	1,628	2.5	-11.0	-11.1
Number of animals	101,330	0.9	97,433	0.9	72,107	0.9	-3.8	-26.0
Layers and pullets 13 weeks old and older								
Number of farms	3,550	2.5	2,454	2.8	2,276	3.1	-30.9	-7.3
Number of birds	8,428,623	2.3	5,388,894	1.5	6,043,468	1.6	-36.1	12.1
Broilers and other meat-type chickens sold								
Number of farms	495	1.8	386	1.6	336	1.4	-22.0	-13.0
Number of birds sold	702,431	0.0	400,262	0.0	393,028	0.0	-43.0	-1.8

Source: 1997 Census of Agriculture, U.S. Department of Agriculture, National Agricultural Statistics Service. NA stands for "not available." (D) is shown when data are withheld to prevent disclosure of competitive information. A dash (-) is shown where no data were reported.

CROP STATISTICS FOR MICHIGAN

Item	1987		1992		1997		Percent change	
	Value	% of U.S.	Value	% of U.S.	Value	% of U.S.	1987-1992	1992-1997
Corn for grain or seed								
Number of farms	25,140	4.0	18,962	3.8	16,712	3.9	-24.6	-11.9
Number of acres	1,982,401	3.4	2,221,271	3.2	2,122,283	3.0	12.0	-4.5
Number of bushels	189,779,819	-	226,824,263	2.6	238,319,129	2.8	19.5	5.1
Corn for silage or green chop								
Number of farms	-	-	-	-	-	-	-	-
Number of acres	-	-	-	-	-	-	-	-
Weight in tons, green	-	-	-	-	-	-	-	-
Sorghum for grain or seed								
Number of farms	-	-	-	-	-	-	-	-
Number of acres	-	-	-	-	-	-	-	-
Number of bushels	-	-	-	-	-	-	-	-
Wheat for grain								
Number of farms	10,327	2.9	12,433	4.3	8,976	3.7	20.4	-27.8
Number of acres	356,073	0.7	583,245	1.0	499,742	0.8	63.8	-14.3
Number of bushels	16,465,394	0.9	29,350,586	1.3	28,432,159	1.3	78.3	-3.1
Barley for grain								
Number of farms	-	-	-	-	-	-	-	-
Number of acres	-	-	-	-	-	-	-	-
Number of bushels	-	-	-	-	-	-	-	-
Oats for grain								
Number of farms	-	-	-	-	-	-	-	-
Number of acres	-	-	-	-	-	-	-	-
Number of bushels	-	-	-	-	-	-	-	-
Rice								
Number of farms	-	-	-	-	-	-	-	-
Number of acres	-	-	-	-	-	-	-	-
Weight in hundredweight	-	-	-	-	-	-	-	-
Sunflower seed								
Number of farms	-	-	-	-	-	-	-	-
Number of acres	-	-	-	-	-	-	-	-
Weight in pounds	-	-	-	-	-	-	-	-
Cotton								
Number of farms	-	-	-	-	-	-	-	-
Number of acres	-	-	-	-	-	-	-	-
Number of bales	-	-	-	-	-	-	-	-

Continued.

CROP STATISTICS FOR MICHIGAN - Continued

Item	1987		1992		1997		Percent change	
	Value	% of U.S.	Value	% of U.S.	Value	% of U.S.	1987-1992	1992-1997
Tobacco								
Number of farms	-	-	-	-	-	-	-	-
Number of acres	-	-	-	-	-	-	-	-
Weight in pounds	-	-	-	-	-	-	-	-
Soybeans for beans								
Number of farms	12,734	2.9	13,175	3.5	12,561	3.5	3.5	-4.7
Number of acres	1,023,599	1.9	1,332,114	2.4	1,694,872	2.6	30.1	27.2
Number of bushels	36,267,622	2.0	41,633,625	2.0	62,242,411	2.5	14.8	49.5
Dry edible beans, excluding dry limas								
Number of farms	4,098	-	3,176	-	2,172	-	-22.5	-31.6
Number of acres	383,687	-	322,334	-	302,767	-	-16.0	-6.1
Weight in hundredweight	4,931,689	-	4,229,224	-	4,878,076	-	-14.2	15.3
Potatoes, excluding sweetpotatoes								
Number of farms	-	-	-	-	-	-	-	-
Number of acres	-	-	-	-	-	-	-	-
Weight in hundredweight	-	-	-	-	-	-	-	-
Sugar beets for sugar								
Number of farms	-	-	-	-	-	-	-	-
Number of acres	-	-	-	-	-	-	-	-
Weight in tons	-	-	-	-	-	-	-	-
Sugarcane for sugar								
Number of farms	-	-	-	-	-	-	-	-
Number of acres	-	-	-	-	-	-	-	-
Weight in tons	-	-	-	-	-	-	-	-
Pineapples harvested								
Number of farms	-	-	-	-	-	-	-	-
Number of acres	-	-	-	-	-	-	-	-
Weight in tons	-	-	-	-	-	-	-	-
Peanuts for nuts								
Number of farms	-	-	-	-	-	-	-	-
Number of acres	-	-	-	-	-	-	-	-
Weight in pounds	-	-	-	-	-	-	-	-
Hay - all types, including alfalfa								
Number of farms	25,983	2.6	22,285	2.5	20,858	2.3	-14.2	-6.4
Number of acres	1,436,630	2.5	1,283,598	2.3	1,264,350	2.1	-10.7	-1.5
Weight in tons, dry	3,323,175	2.6	2,821,347	2.2	2,830,915	2.0	-15.1	0.3
Vegetables harvested for sale								
Number of farms	3,267	5.4	3,007	4.9	2,498	4.6	-8.0	-16.9
Number of acres	139,145	4.0	138,851	3.7	128,349	3.4	-0.2	-7.6
Land in orchards								
Number of farms	3,791	3.1	3,531	3.0	2,863	2.7	-6.9	-18.9
Number of acres	161,567	3.5	162,183	3.4	139,607	2.7	0.4	-13.9

Source: *1997 Census of Agriculture*, U.S. Department of Agriculture, National Agricultural Statistics Service. NA stands for "not available." (D) is shown when data are withheld to prevent disclosure of competitive information. A dash (-) is shown where no data were reported. Not all states report growing all crops, but all crop categories in the census are shown for every state. The data series used for this presentation did not report U.S. totals for a number of categories; for that reason, the "% of U.S." column is sometimes blank.

MINNESOTA

GENERAL STATISTICS FOR MINNESOTA

Item	1987 Value	1987 % of U.S.	1992 Value	1992 % of U.S.	1997 Value	1997 % of U.S.	Percent change 1987-1992	Percent change 1992-1997
Farms (number)	85,079	4.1	75,079	3.9	73,367	3.8	-11.8	-2.3
Land in farms (acres)	26,573,819	2.8	25,666,944	2.7	25,994,621	2.8	-3.4	1.3
Average size of farm (acres)	312	67.5	342	69.7	354	72.7	9.6	3.5
Median size of farm (acres)	NA	-	NA	-	200	166.7	-	-
Market value of land and buildings:								
Average per farm (dollars)	218,808	75.6	310,612	87.0	407,863	90.7	42.0	31.3
Average per acre (dollars)	700	111.6	910	125.2	1,164	124.8	30.0	27.9
Market value of machinery/equipment - average per farm (dollars)	55,741	135.2	69,859	143.7	84,613	146.7	25.3	21.1
Farms by size:								
1 to 9 acres	4,613	2.5	3,517	2.1	3,090	2.0	-23.8	-12.1
10 to 49 acres	9,481	2.3	8,927	2.3	10,104	2.5	-5.8	13.2
50 to 179 acres	24,947	3.9	20,967	3.6	21,535	3.6	-16.0	2.7
180 to 499 acres	30,963	6.5	26,395	6.2	23,365	5.8	-14.8	-11.5
500 to 999 acres	10,814	5.4	10,497	5.6	9,781	5.6	-2.9	-6.8
1,000 acres or more	4,261	2.5	4,776	2.8	5,492	3.1	12.1	15.0
Total cropland								
Farms	79,461	4.3	69,866	4.1	67,545	4.1	-12.1	-3.3
Acres	21,876,066	4.9	21,387,063	4.9	21,491,743	5.0	-2.2	0.5
Harvested cropland (farms)	76,537	4.7	66,549	4.5	60,726	4.3	-13.0	-8.7
Harvested cropland (acres)	16,635,264	5.9	18,201,061	6.2	18,968,607	6.1	9.4	4.2
Irrigated land (farms)	2,425	0.8	2,368	0.8	2,193	0.8	-2.4	-7.4
Irrigated land (acres)	353,504	0.8	370,404	0.7	380,394	0.7	4.8	2.7
Market value of agricultural products sold:								
Total sales ($1,000)	5,676,376	4.2	6,477,004	4.0	8,290,264	4.2	14.1	28.0
Average per farm (dollars)	66,719	102.4	86,269	102.1	112,997	109.7	29.3	31.0
Agricultural products only ($1,000)	2,500,827	4.2	3,054,747	4.1	4,200,970	4.3	22.1	37.5
Livestock, poultry, and products ($1,000)	3,175,549	4.1	3,422,257	3.9	4,089,293	4.1	7.8	19.5
Farms by value of sales:								
Less than $2,500	11,915	2.4	9,725	2.3	14,647	2.9	-18.4	50.6
$2,500 to $4,999	6,509	2.5	5,387	2.3	5,260	2.3	-17.2	-2.4
$5,000 to $9,999	8,293	3.0	7,028	2.8	6,179	2.6	-15.3	-12.1
$10,000 to $24,999	13,588	4.2	11,187	3.7	9,207	3.4	-17.7	-17.7
$25,000 to $49,999	12,983	5.9	10,168	5.2	8,033	4.7	-21.7	-21.0
$50,000 to $99,999	15,385	7.1	12,482	6.6	9,402	5.9	-18.9	-24.7
$100,000 or more	16,406	5.5	19,102	5.7	20,639	6.0	16.4	8.0
Total farm production expenses ($1,000)	4,427,445	4.1	5,244,708	4.0	6,362,110	4.2	18.5	21.3
Average expenses per farm (dollars)	52,040	100.5	69,860	102.8	86,707	110.1	34.2	24.1
Net cash return for the farm unit:								
Number of farms	85,078	4.1	75,075	3.9	73,375	3.8	-11.8	-2.3
Value ($1000)	1,233,896	4.7	1,216,890	4.0	1,835,509	4.3	-1.4	50.8
Average per farm (dollars)	14,503	114.6	16,209	102.6	25,015	112.4	11.8	54.3
Operators by principal occupation:								
Farming	58,519	5.1	51,021	4.8	44,047	4.6	-12.8	-13.7
Other	26,560	2.8	24,058	2.8	29,320	3.1	-9.4	21.9
Operators by days worked off farm:								
Any	39,567	3.5	33,932	3.4	37,550	3.6	-14.2	10.7
200 days or more	22,006	3.0	19,826	3.0	23,115	3.3	-9.9	16.6

Source: *1997 Census of Agriculture*, U.S. Department of Agriculture, National Agricultural Statistics Service. NA stands for "not available." (D) is shown when data are withheld to prevent disclosure of competitive information. A dash (-) is shown where no data were reported. The market value of land and buildings, and of machinery and equipment, is an estimated amount. Net cash return for the farm unit includes only returns from agricultural activities.

LIVESTOCK STATISTICS FOR MINNESOTA

Item	1987		1992		1997		Percent change	
	Value	% of U.S.	Value	% of U.S.	Value	% of U.S.	1987-1992	1992-1997
Cattle and calves								
Number of farms	40,222	3.4	34,501	3.2	30,913	3.0	-14.2	-10.4
Number of animals	2,700,095	2.8	2,543,373	2.6	2,395,456	2.4	-5.8	-5.8
Beef cows (farms)	15,528	1.8	15,101	1.9	15,745	2.0	-2.7	4.3
Beef cows (number)	360,153	1.1	381,869	1.2	409,184	1.2	6.0	7.2
Milk cows (farms)	17,454	8.6	13,380	8.6	9,603	8.2	-23.3	-28.2
Milk cows (number)	709,832	7.0	609,034	6.4	541,650	6.0	-14.2	-11.1
Cattle and calves sold (farms)	39,972	3.5	33,852	3.3	30,320	3.0	-15.3	-10.4
Cattle and calves sold (number)	1,474,577	2.0	1,388,581	2.0	1,339,902	1.8	-5.8	-3.5
Hogs and pigs								
Number of farms	16,042	6.6	13,125	6.9	7,512	6.8	-18.2	-42.8
Number of animals	4,236,500	8.1	4,668,590	8.1	5,722,460	9.3	10.2	22.6
Hogs and pigs sold (farms)	16,652	7.0	13,749	7.3	7,717	7.6	-17.4	-43.9
Hogs and pigs sold (number)	8,073,029	8.4	9,141,699	8.2	12,943,053	9.1	13.2	41.6
Sheep and lambs								
Number of farms	4,250	4.6	3,451	4.3	2,627	4.0	-18.8	-23.9
Number of animals	241,603	2.2	221,777	2.1	161,212	2.1	-8.2	-27.3
Layers and pullets 13 weeks old and older								
Number of farms	4,003	2.8	2,310	2.6	1,964	2.7	-42.3	-15.0
Number of birds	12,124,965	3.2	14,324,989	4.1	13,047,875	3.6	18.1	-8.9
Broilers and other meat-type chickens sold								
Number of farms	1,000	3.6	679	2.8	621	2.6	-32.1	-8.5
Number of birds sold	27,356,247	0.4	36,828,542	0.7	28,456,532	0.4	34.6	-22.7

Source: *1997 Census of Agriculture*, U.S. Department of Agriculture, National Agricultural Statistics Service. NA stands for "not available." (D) is shown when data are withheld to prevent disclosure of competitive information. A dash (-) is shown where no data were reported.

CROP STATISTICS FOR MINNESOTA

Item	1987		1992		1997		Percent change	
	Value	% of U.S.	Value	% of U.S.	Value	% of U.S.	1987-1992	1992-1997
Corn for grain or seed								
Number of farms	51,355	8.2	42,961	8.5	37,630	8.7	-16.3	-12.4
Number of acres	4,756,348	8.1	6,123,731	8.8	6,227,640	8.9	28.7	1.7
Number of bushels	567,384,166	-	669,550,546	7.7	783,739,207	9.1	18.0	17.1
Corn for silage or green chop								
Number of farms	-	-	-	-	-	-	-	-
Number of acres	-	-	-	-	-	-	-	-
Weight in tons, green	-	-	-	-	-	-	-	-
Sorghum for grain or seed								
Number of farms	-	-	-	-	-	-	-	-
Number of acres	-	-	-	-	-	-	-	-
Number of bushels	-	-	-	-	-	-	-	-
Wheat for grain								
Number of farms	20,238	5.7	12,753	4.4	9,518	3.9	-37.0	-25.4
Number of acres	2,444,294	4.6	2,609,161	4.4	2,391,598	4.1	6.7	-8.3
Number of bushels	97,967,169	5.2	126,255,763	5.7	74,531,074	3.4	28.9	-41.0
Barley for grain								
Number of farms	8,412	-	5,216	-	3,910	-	-38.0	-25.0
Number of acres	807,374	-	592,914	-	433,610	-	-26.6	-26.9
Number of bushels	44,734,800	-	42,514,551	-	21,915,338	-	-5.0	-48.5
Oats for grain								
Number of farms	25,984	-	16,658	-	10,122	-	-35.9	-39.2
Number of acres	730,864	-	465,846	-	296,188	-	-36.3	-36.4
Number of bushels	39,554,088	-	29,142,473	-	16,179,495	-	-26.3	-44.5
Rice								
Number of farms	-	-	-	-	-	-	-	-
Number of acres	-	-	-	-	-	-	-	-
Weight in hundredweight	-	-	-	-	-	-	-	-
Sunflower seed								
Number of farms	683	-	1,131	-	588	-	65.6	-48.0
Number of acres	82,278	-	202,025	-	99,245	-	145.5	-50.9
Weight in pounds	117,623,254	-	278,550,934	-	106,405,806	-	136.8	-61.8
Cotton								
Number of farms	-	-	-	-	-	-	-	-
Number of acres	-	-	-	-	-	-	-	-
Number of bales	-	-	-	-	-	-	-	-

Continued.

CROP STATISTICS FOR MINNESOTA - Continued

Item	1987		1992		1997		Percent change	
	Value	% of U.S.	Value	% of U.S.	Value	% of U.S.	1987-1992	1992-1997
Tobacco								
Number of farms	-	-	-	-	-	-	-	-
Number of acres	-	-	-	-	-	-	-	-
Weight in pounds	-	-	-	-	-	-	-	-
Soybeans for beans								
Number of farms	36,348	8.2	33,581	8.8	31,292	8.8	-7.6	-6.8
Number of acres	4,384,981	7.9	5,078,066	9.0	6,174,563	9.3	15.8	21.6
Number of bushels	166,025,760	9.0	162,137,215	7.9	233,714,926	9.3	-2.3	44.1
Dry edible beans, excluding dry limas								
Number of farms	-	-	-	-	-	-	-	-
Number of acres	-	-	-	-	-	-	-	-
Weight in hundredweight	-	-	-	-	-	-	-	-
Potatoes, excluding sweetpotatoes								
Number of farms	-	-	-	-	-	-	-	-
Number of acres	-	-	-	-	-	-	-	-
Weight in hundredweight	-	-	-	-	-	-	-	-
Sugar beets for sugar								
Number of farms	-	-	-	-	-	-	-	-
Number of acres	-	-	-	-	-	-	-	-
Weight in tons	-	-	-	-	-	-	-	-
Sugarcane for sugar								
Number of farms	-	-	-	-	-	-	-	-
Number of acres	-	-	-	-	-	-	-	-
Weight in tons	-	-	-	-	-	-	-	-
Pineapples harvested								
Number of farms	-	-	-	-	-	-	-	-
Number of acres	-	-	-	-	-	-	-	-
Weight in tons	-	-	-	-	-	-	-	-
Peanuts for nuts								
Number of farms	-	-	-	-	-	-	-	-
Number of acres	-	-	-	-	-	-	-	-
Weight in pounds	-	-	-	-	-	-	-	-
Hay - all types, including alfalfa								
Number of farms	46,531	4.7	38,336	4.2	35,500	4.0	-17.6	-7.4
Number of acres	2,418,800	4.2	2,098,145	3.7	2,168,932	3.6	-13.3	3.4
Weight in tons, dry	5,920,884	4.6	5,082,391	4.0	5,033,905	3.6	-14.2	-1.0
Vegetables harvested for sale								
Number of farms	-	-	-	-	-	-	-	-
Number of acres	-	-	-	-	-	-	-	-
Land in orchards								
Number of farms	-	-	-	-	-	-	-	-
Number of acres	-	-	-	-	-	-	-	-

Source: 1997 Census of Agriculture, U.S. Department of Agriculture, National Agricultural Statistics Service. NA stands for "not available." (D) is shown when data are withheld to prevent disclosure of competitive information. A dash (-) is shown where no data were reported. Not all states report growing all crops, but all crop categories in the census are shown for every state. The data series used for this presentation did not report U.S. totals for a number of categories; for that reason, the "% of U.S." column is sometimes blank.

MISSISSIPPI

GENERAL STATISTICS FOR MISSISSIPPI

Item	1987 Value	1987 % of U.S.	1992 Value	1992 % of U.S.	1997 Value	1997 % of U.S.	Percent change 1987-1992	Percent change 1992-1997
Farms (number)	34,074	1.6	31,998	1.7	31,318	1.6	-6.1	-2.1
Land in farms (acres)	10,746,190	1.1	10,188,362	1.1	10,124,822	1.1	-5.2	-0.6
Average size of farm (acres)	315	68.2	318	64.8	323	66.3	1.0	1.6
Median size of farm (acres)	NA	-	NA	-	124	103.3	-	-
Market value of land and buildings:								
Average per farm (dollars)	215,209	74.4	248,479	69.6	337,081	74.9	15.5	35.7
Average per acre (dollars)	697	111.2	777	106.9	1,052	112.8	11.5	35.4
Market value of machinery/equipment - average per farm (dollars)	34,900	84.7	40,616	83.6	51,801	89.8	16.4	27.5
Farms by size:								
1 to 9 acres	1,387	0.8	1,122	0.7	1,108	0.7	-19.1	-1.2
10 to 49 acres	6,240	1.5	5,796	1.5	5,863	1.4	-7.1	1.2
50 to 179 acres	13,506	2.1	12,797	2.2	12,443	2.1	-5.2	-2.8
180 to 499 acres	7,789	1.6	7,606	1.8	7,356	1.8	-2.3	-3.3
500 to 999 acres	2,884	1.4	2,524	1.4	2,415	1.4	-12.5	-4.3
1,000 acres or more	2,268	1.3	2,153	1.2	2,133	1.2	-5.1	-0.9
Total cropland								
Farms	29,785	1.6	27,625	1.6	25,289	1.5	-7.3	-8.5
Acres	6,747,639	1.5	6,518,288	1.5	5,947,311	1.4	-3.4	-8.8
Harvested cropland (farms)	24,305	1.5	22,245	1.5	19,198	1.4	-8.5	-13.7
Harvested cropland (acres)	4,272,651	1.5	4,404,612	1.5	4,338,710	1.4	3.1	-1.5
Irrigated land (farms)	2,012	0.7	2,127	0.8	1,769	0.6	5.7	-16.8
Irrigated land (acres)	636,842	1.4	882,976	1.8	1,076,231	2.0	38.6	21.9
Market value of agricultural products sold:								
Total sales ($1,000)	1,862,903	1.4	2,336,737	1.4	3,127,383	1.6	25.4	33.8
Average per farm (dollars)	54,672	83.9	73,028	86.5	99,859	97.0	33.6	36.7
Agricultural products only ($1,000)	913,913	1.6	1,146,450	1.5	1,291,365	1.3	25.4	12.6
Livestock, poultry, and products ($1,000)	948,989	1.2	1,190,287	1.4	1,836,018	1.9	25.4	54.3
Farms by value of sales:								
Less than $2,500	11,109	2.3	9,860	2.3	11,511	2.3	-11.2	16.7
$2,500 to $4,999	5,985	2.3	5,417	2.3	4,954	2.2	-9.5	-8.5
$5,000 to $9,999	5,012	1.8	5,049	2.0	4,387	1.8	0.7	-13.1
$10,000 to $24,999	4,070	1.2	4,119	1.4	3,666	1.3	1.2	-11.0
$25,000 to $49,999	1,771	0.8	1,681	0.9	1,265	0.7	-5.1	-24.7
$50,000 to $99,999	1,710	0.8	1,248	0.7	1,014	0.6	-27.0	-18.8
$100,000 or more	4,417	1.5	4,624	1.4	4,521	1.3	4.7	-2.2
Total farm production expenses ($1,000)	1,465,201	1.4	1,954,337	1.5	2,458,575	1.6	33.4	25.8
Average expenses per farm (dollars)	42,999	83.0	61,067	89.9	78,534	99.7	42.0	28.6
Net cash return for the farm unit:								
Number of farms	34,075	1.6	32,003	1.7	31,312	1.6	-6.1	-2.2
Value ($1000)	332,280	1.3	319,662	1.1	558,443	1.3	-3.8	74.7
Average per farm (dollars)	9,751	77.0	9,989	63.2	17,835	80.1	2.4	78.5
Operators by principal occupation:								
Farming	15,111	1.3	14,463	1.4	12,753	1.3	-4.3	-11.8
Other	18,963	2.0	17,535	2.0	18,565	2.0	-7.5	5.9
Operators by days worked off farm:								
Any	19,421	1.7	17,241	1.7	17,989	1.7	-11.2	4.3
200 days or more	13,518	1.8	12,119	1.8	13,004	1.8	-10.3	7.3

Source: 1997 Census of Agriculture, U.S. Department of Agriculture, National Agricultural Statistics Service. NA stands for "not available." (D) is shown when data are withheld to prevent disclosure of competitive information. A dash (-) is shown where no data were reported. The market value of land and buildings, and of machinery and equipment, is an estimated amount. Net cash return for the farm unit includes only returns from agricultural activities.

LIVESTOCK STATISTICS FOR MISSISSIPPI

Item	1987 Value	1987 % of U.S.	1992 Value	1992 % of U.S.	1997 Value	1997 % of U.S.	Percent change 1987-1992	Percent change 1992-1997
Cattle and calves								
Number of farms	22,482	1.9	21,070	2.0	19,319	1.8	-6.3	-8.3
Number of animals	1,147,219	1.2	1,152,331	1.2	1,127,442	1.1	0.4	-2.2
Beef cows (farms)	19,008	2.3	18,855	2.3	17,151	2.1	-0.8	-9.0
Beef cows (number)	579,312	1.8	588,920	1.8	590,402	1.7	1.7	0.3
Milk cows (farms)	1,643	0.8	1,216	0.8	688	0.6	-26.0	-43.4
Milk cows (number)	71,834	0.7	64,510	0.7	45,540	0.5	-10.2	-29.4
Cattle and calves sold (farms)	22,087	1.9	20,282	2.0	18,912	1.9	-8.2	-6.8
Cattle and calves sold (number)	638,685	0.9	580,526	0.8	590,771	0.8	-9.1	1.8
Hogs and pigs								
Number of farms	2,237	0.9	1,270	0.7	662	0.6	-43.2	-47.9
Number of animals	179,063	0.3	160,917	0.3	215,936	0.4	-10.1	34.2
Hogs and pigs sold (farms)	1,622	0.7	934	0.5	425	0.4	-42.4	-54.5
Hogs and pigs sold (number)	284,630	0.3	278,764	0.3	756,595	0.5	-2.1	171.4
Sheep and lambs								
Number of farms	218	0.2	237	0.3	231	0.4	8.7	-2.5
Number of animals	5,395	0.0	6,447	0.1	4,797	0.1	19.5	-25.6
Layers and pullets 13 weeks old and older								
Number of farms	2,550	1.8	1,453	1.6	941	1.3	-43.0	-35.2
Number of birds	7,027,574	1.9	6,841,469	1.9	6,537,982	1.8	-2.6	-4.4
Broilers and other meat-type chickens sold								
Number of farms	1,129	4.1	1,211	5.1	1,393	5.8	7.3	15.0
Number of birds sold	276,652,292	4.1	388,128,497	7.1	554,915,961	8.2	40.3	43.0

Source: 1997 Census of Agriculture, U.S. Department of Agriculture, National Agricultural Statistics Service. NA stands for "not available." (D) is shown when data are withheld to prevent disclosure of competitive information. A dash (-) is shown where no data were reported.

CROP STATISTICS FOR MISSISSIPPI

Item	1987 Value	1987 % of U.S.	1992 Value	1992 % of U.S.	1997 Value	1997 % of U.S.	Percent change 1987-1992	Percent change 1992-1997
Corn for grain or seed								
Number of farms	4,020	0.6	3,377	0.7	2,497	0.6	-16.0	-26.1
Number of acres	120,361	0.2	269,080	0.4	405,393	0.6	123.6	50.7
Number of bushels	9,369,093	-	23,869,788	0.3	43,851,007	0.5	154.8	83.7
Corn for silage or green chop								
Number of farms	-	-	-	-	-	-	-	-
Number of acres	-	-	-	-	-	-	-	-
Weight in tons, green	-	-	-	-	-	-	-	-
Sorghum for grain or seed								
Number of farms	1,414	-	662	-	154	-	-53.2	-76.7
Number of acres	111,250	-	105,151	-	25,499	-	-5.5	-75.8
Number of bushels	6,758,881	-	7,172,060	-	1,648,269	-	6.1	-77.0
Wheat for grain								
Number of farms	1,991	0.6	1,064	0.4	697	0.3	-46.6	-34.5
Number of acres	283,477	0.5	180,840	0.3	155,049	0.3	-36.2	-14.3
Number of bushels	9,674,702	0.5	6,749,633	0.3	6,547,211	0.3	-30.2	-3.0
Barley for grain								
Number of farms	-	-	-	-	-	-	-	-
Number of acres	-	-	-	-	-	-	-	-
Number of bushels	-	-	-	-	-	-	-	-
Oats for grain								
Number of farms	-	-	-	-	-	-	-	-
Number of acres	-	-	-	-	-	-	-	-
Number of bushels	-	-	-	-	-	-	-	-
Rice								
Number of farms	803	-	748	-	530	-	-6.8	-29.1
Number of acres	195,505	-	270,497	-	234,244	-	38.4	-13.4
Weight in hundredweight	10,466,632	-	15,630,876	-	13,330,366	-	49.3	-14.7
Sunflower seed								
Number of farms	-	-	-	-	-	-	-	-
Number of acres	-	-	-	-	-	-	-	-
Weight in pounds	-	-	-	-	-	-	-	-
Cotton								
Number of farms	4,225	9.8	3,344	9.6	1,701	5.4	-20.9	-49.1
Number of acres	1,028,249	10.5	1,332,855	12.2	966,443	7.3	29.6	-27.5
Number of bales	1,654,648	12.5	2,075,048	13.5	1,714,762	9.6	25.4	-17.4

Continued.

CROP STATISTICS FOR MISSISSIPPI - Continued

Item	1987		1992		1997		Percent change	
	Value	% of U.S.	Value	% of U.S.	Value	% of U.S.	1987-1992	1992-1997
Tobacco								
Number of farms	-	-	-	-	-	-	-	-
Number of acres	-	-	-	-	-	-	-	-
Weight in pounds	-	-	-	-	-	-	-	-
Soybeans for beans								
Number of farms	6,475	1.5	4,644	1.2	3,851	1.1	-28.3	-17.1
Number of acres	2,006,263	3.6	1,652,840	2.9	1,964,202	3.0	-17.6	18.8
Number of bushels	41,329,519	2.2	53,569,740	2.6	59,370,926	2.4	29.6	10.8
Dry edible beans, excluding dry limas								
Number of farms	-	-	-	-	-	-	-	-
Number of acres	-	-	-	-	-	-	-	-
Weight in hundredweight	-	-	-	-	-	-	-	-
Potatoes, excluding sweetpotatoes								
Number of farms	-	-	-	-	-	-	-	-
Number of acres	-	-	-	-	-	-	-	-
Weight in hundredweight	-	-	-	-	-	-	-	-
Sugar beets for sugar								
Number of farms	-	-	-	-	-	-	-	-
Number of acres	-	-	-	-	-	-	-	-
Weight in tons	-	-	-	-	-	-	-	-
Sugarcane for sugar								
Number of farms	-	-	-	-	-	-	-	-
Number of acres	-	-	-	-	-	-	-	-
Weight in tons	-	-	-	-	-	-	-	-
Pineapples harvested								
Number of farms	-	-	-	-	-	-	-	-
Number of acres	-	-	-	-	-	-	-	-
Weight in tons	-	-	-	-	-	-	-	-
Peanuts for nuts								
Number of farms	-	-	-	-	-	-	-	-
Number of acres	-	-	-	-	-	-	-	-
Weight in pounds	-	-	-	-	-	-	-	-
Hay - all types, including alfalfa								
Number of farms	15,501	1.6	15,121	1.7	13,999	1.6	-2.5	-7.4
Number of acres	585,346	1.0	639,152	1.1	648,809	1.1	9.2	1.5
Weight in tons, dry	1,092,059	0.8	1,317,502	1.0	1,486,117	1.1	20.6	12.8
Vegetables harvested for sale								
Number of farms	-	-	-	-	-	-	-	-
Number of acres	-	-	-	-	-	-	-	-
Land in orchards								
Number of farms	-	-	-	-	-	-	-	-
Number of acres	-	-	-	-	-	-	-	-

Source: *1997 Census of Agriculture*, U.S. Department of Agriculture, National Agricultural Statistics Service. NA stands for "not available." (D) is shown when data are withheld to prevent disclosure of competitive information. A dash (-) is shown where no data were reported. Not all states report growing all crops, but all crop categories in the census are shown for every state. The data series used for this presentation did not report U.S. totals for a number of categories; for that reason, the "% of U.S." column is sometimes blank.

MISSOURI

GENERAL STATISTICS FOR MISSOURI

Item	1987 Value	1987 % of U.S.	1992 Value	1992 % of U.S.	1997 Value	1997 % of U.S.	Percent change 1987-1992	Percent change 1992-1997
Farms (number)	106,105	5.1	98,082	5.1	98,860	5.2	-7.6	0.8
Land in farms (acres)	29,209,187	3.0	28,546,875	3.0	28,826,188	3.1	-2.3	1.0
Average size of farm (acres)	275	59.5	291	59.3	292	60.0	5.8	0.3
Median size of farm (acres)	NA	-	NA	-	148	123.3	-	-
Market value of land and buildings:								
Average per farm (dollars)	175,612	60.7	225,015	63.0	309,430	68.8	28.1	37.5
Average per acre (dollars)	640	102.1	774	106.5	1,069	114.6	20.9	38.1
Market value of machinery/equipment - average per farm (dollars)	28,432	69.0	36,155	74.4	41,051	71.2	27.2	13.5
Farms by size:								
1 to 9 acres	4,960	2.7	3,926	2.4	3,148	2.1	-20.8	-19.8
10 to 49 acres	17,028	4.1	16,211	4.2	16,714	4.1	-4.8	3.1
50 to 179 acres	37,413	5.8	34,654	5.9	36,346	6.1	-7.4	4.9
180 to 499 acres	30,423	6.4	27,573	6.4	27,298	6.8	-9.4	-1.0
500 to 999 acres	11,413	5.7	10,292	5.5	9,854	5.6	-9.8	-4.3
1,000 acres or more	4,868	2.9	5,426	3.1	5,500	3.1	11.5	1.4
Total cropland								
Farms	93,434	5.1	86,617	5.1	87,092	5.2	-7.3	0.5
Acres	19,378,031	4.4	19,228,832	4.4	19,229,468	4.5	-0.8	0.0
Harvested cropland (farms)	80,396	4.9	74,240	5.0	72,316	5.1	-7.7	-2.6
Harvested cropland (acres)	11,655,304	4.1	12,158,832	4.1	12,449,272	4.0	4.3	2.4
Irrigated land (farms)	2,823	1.0	2,914	1.0	2,891	1.0	3.2	-0.8
Irrigated land (acres)	534,795	1.2	708,864	1.4	881,924	1.6	32.5	24.4
Market value of agricultural products sold:								
Total sales ($1,000)	3,644,988	2.7	4,303,148	2.6	5,367,813	2.7	18.1	24.7
Average per farm (dollars)	34,353	52.7	43,873	51.9	54,297	52.7	27.7	23.8
Agricultural products only ($1,000)	1,460,850	2.5	1,861,613	2.5	2,307,009	2.4	27.4	23.9
Livestock, poultry, and products ($1,000)	2,184,138	2.8	2,441,535	2.8	3,060,803	3.1	11.8	25.4
Farms by value of sales:								
Less than $2,500	23,075	4.7	20,638	4.9	25,039	5.0	-10.6	21.3
$2,500 to $4,999	15,353	5.8	13,881	6.0	13,981	6.1	-9.6	0.7
$5,000 to $9,999	17,881	6.5	16,350	6.5	15,962	6.7	-8.6	-2.4
$10,000 to $24,999	20,749	6.4	18,998	6.3	17,863	6.5	-8.4	-6.0
$25,000 to $49,999	11,212	5.1	10,090	5.2	8,801	5.2	-10.0	-12.8
$50,000 to $99,999	8,943	4.1	7,525	4.0	6,529	4.1	-15.9	-13.2
$100,000 or more	8,892	3.0	10,600	3.2	10,685	3.1	19.2	0.8
Total farm production expenses ($1,000)	2,804,630	2.6	3,395,093	2.6	4,214,996	2.8	21.1	24.1
Average expenses per farm (dollars)	26,432	51.0	34,615	51.0	42,639	54.1	31.0	23.2
Net cash return for the farm unit:								
Number of farms	106,109	5.1	98,082	5.1	98,856	5.2	-7.6	0.8
Value ($1000)	829,853	3.1	889,365	2.9	1,097,695	2.6	7.2	23.4
Average per farm (dollars)	7,821	61.8	9,068	57.4	11,104	49.9	15.9	22.5
Operators by principal occupation:								
Farming	53,694	4.7	49,248	4.7	44,751	4.7	-8.3	-9.1
Other	52,411	5.5	48,834	5.6	54,109	5.7	-6.8	10.8
Operators by days worked off farm:								
Any	58,409	5.2	53,243	5.4	57,118	5.5	-8.8	7.3
200 days or more	40,925	5.6	37,799	5.7	41,378	5.8	-7.6	9.5

Source: *1997 Census of Agriculture*, U.S. Department of Agriculture, National Agricultural Statistics Service. NA stands for "not available." (D) is shown when data are withheld to prevent disclosure of competitive information. A dash (-) is shown where no data were reported. The market value of land and buildings, and of machinery and equipment, is an estimated amount. Net cash return for the farm unit includes only returns from agricultural activities.

LIVESTOCK STATISTICS FOR MISSOURI

Item	1987		1992		1997		Percent change	
	Value	% of U.S.	Value	% of U.S.	Value	% of U.S.	1987-1992	1992-1997
Cattle and calves								
Number of farms	73,738	6.3	68,413	6.4	67,198	6.4	-7.2	-1.8
Number of animals	4,158,226	4.3	4,165,357	4.3	4,312,716	4.4	0.2	3.5
Beef cows (farms)	61,049	7.3	58,024	7.2	57,935	7.2	-5.0	-0.2
Beef cows (number)	1,818,969	5.7	1,876,845	5.8	2,023,187	5.9	3.2	7.8
Milk cows (farms)	7,712	3.8	5,626	3.6	4,175	3.6	-27.0	-25.8
Milk cows (number)	242,039	2.4	215,920	2.3	174,669	1.9	-10.8	-19.1
Cattle and calves sold (farms)	73,947	6.4	67,044	6.5	66,350	6.6	-9.3	-1.0
Cattle and calves sold (number)	2,514,867	3.5	2,349,975	3.3	2,494,869	3.4	-6.6	6.2
Hogs and pigs								
Number of farms	14,985	6.2	11,894	6.2	5,419	4.9	-20.6	-54.4
Number of animals	2,581,954	4.9	2,908,509	5.1	3,546,972	5.8	12.6	22.0
Hogs and pigs sold (farms)	15,306	6.4	12,133	6.4	5,183	5.1	-20.7	-57.3
Hogs and pigs sold (number)	4,804,123	5.0	5,547,530	5.0	8,540,647	6.0	15.5	54.0
Sheep and lambs								
Number of farms	2,606	2.8	2,505	3.1	1,984	3.0	-3.9	-20.8
Number of animals	101,780	0.9	111,362	1.0	76,956	1.0	9.4	-30.9
Layers and pullets 13 weeks old and older								
Number of farms	7,485	5.2	4,544	5.1	3,707	5.1	-39.3	-18.4
Number of birds	8,235,467	2.2	8,343,409	2.4	8,846,447	2.4	1.3	6.0
Broilers and other meat-type chickens sold								
Number of farms	316	1.1	341	1.4	451	1.9	7.9	32.3
Number of birds sold	40,991,224	0.6	82,990,149	1.5	202,970,912	3.0	102.5	144.6

Source: 1997 Census of Agriculture, U.S. Department of Agriculture, National Agricultural Statistics Service. NA stands for "not available." (D) is shown when data are withheld to prevent disclosure of competitive information. A dash (-) is shown where no data were reported.

CROP STATISTICS FOR MISSOURI

Item	1987		1992		1997		Percent change	
	Value	% of U.S.	Value	% of U.S.	Value	% of U.S.	1987-1992	1992-1997
Corn for grain or seed								
Number of farms	25,921	4.1	21,382	4.2	18,417	4.3	-17.5	-13.9
Number of acres	2,069,238	3.5	2,445,489	3.5	2,477,027	3.5	18.2	1.3
Number of bushels	218,093,408	-	308,784,225	3.6	274,381,159	3.2	41.6	-11.1
Corn for silage or green chop								
Number of farms	2,831	-	2,387	-	2,021	-	-15.7	-15.3
Number of acres	82,412	-	81,543	-	76,404	-	-1.1	-6.3
Weight in tons, green	1,104,087	-	1,114,626	-	1,048,825	-	1.0	-5.9
Sorghum for grain or seed								
Number of farms	9,258	-	6,998	-	3,566	-	-24.4	-49.0
Number of acres	625,047	-	586,559	-	311,511	-	-6.2	-46.9
Number of bushels	50,759,064	-	53,046,665	-	26,886,487	-	4.5	-49.3
Wheat for grain								
Number of farms	12,683	3.6	16,970	5.8	12,394	5.1	33.8	-27.0
Number of acres	750,208	1.4	1,319,575	2.2	1,055,664	1.8	75.9	-20.0
Number of bushels	31,939,663	1.7	58,143,633	2.6	52,178,347	2.4	82.0	-10.3
Barley for grain								
Number of farms	-	-	-	-	-	-	-	-
Number of acres	-	-	-	-	-	-	-	-
Number of bushels	-	-	-	-	-	-	-	-
Oats for grain								
Number of farms	-	-	-	-	-	-	-	-
Number of acres	-	-	-	-	-	-	-	-
Number of bushels	-	-	-	-	-	-	-	-
Rice								
Number of farms	-	-	-	-	-	-	-	-
Number of acres	-	-	-	-	-	-	-	-
Weight in hundredweight	-	-	-	-	-	-	-	-
Sunflower seed								
Number of farms	-	-	-	-	-	-	-	-
Number of acres	-	-	-	-	-	-	-	-
Weight in pounds	-	-	-	-	-	-	-	-
Cotton								
Number of farms	1,214	2.8	1,045	3.0	863	2.7	-13.9	-17.4
Number of acres	197,598	2.0	313,226	2.9	388,725	2.9	58.5	24.1
Number of bales	305,767	2.3	500,430	3.3	554,360	3.1	63.7	10.8

Continued.

CROP STATISTICS FOR MISSOURI - Continued

Item	1987 Value	1987 % of U.S.	1992 Value	1992 % of U.S.	1997 Value	1997 % of U.S.	Percent change 1987-1992	Percent change 1992-1997
Tobacco								
Number of farms	-	-	-	-	-	-	-	-
Number of acres	-	-	-	-	-	-	-	-
Weight in pounds	-	-	-	-	-	-	-	-
Soybeans for beans								
Number of farms	33,489	7.6	26,600	7.0	24,201	6.8	-20.6	-9.0
Number of acres	4,827,272	8.7	4,208,729	7.5	4,671,797	7.1	-12.8	11.0
Number of bushels	148,272,506	8.1	150,385,224	7.3	164,562,845	6.6	1.4	9.4
Dry edible beans, excluding dry limas								
Number of farms	-	-	-	-	-	-	-	-
Number of acres	-	-	-	-	-	-	-	-
Weight in hundredweight	-	-	-	-	-	-	-	-
Potatoes, excluding sweetpotatoes								
Number of farms	-	-	-	-	-	-	-	-
Number of acres	-	-	-	-	-	-	-	-
Weight in hundredweight	-	-	-	-	-	-	-	-
Sugar beets for sugar								
Number of farms	-	-	-	-	-	-	-	-
Number of acres	-	-	-	-	-	-	-	-
Weight in tons	-	-	-	-	-	-	-	-
Sugarcane for sugar								
Number of farms	-	-	-	-	-	-	-	-
Number of acres	-	-	-	-	-	-	-	-
Weight in tons	-	-	-	-	-	-	-	-
Pineapples harvested								
Number of farms	-	-	-	-	-	-	-	-
Number of acres	-	-	-	-	-	-	-	-
Weight in tons	-	-	-	-	-	-	-	-
Peanuts for nuts								
Number of farms	-	-	-	-	-	-	-	-
Number of acres	-	-	-	-	-	-	-	-
Weight in pounds	-	-	-	-	-	-	-	-
Hay - all types, including alfalfa								
Number of farms	60,138	6.0	57,749	6.4	57,483	6.5	-4.0	-0.5
Number of acres	3,138,012	5.4	3,470,298	6.1	3,661,772	6.0	10.6	5.5
Weight in tons, dry	5,409,063	4.2	6,109,410	4.8	6,847,820	4.9	12.9	12.1
Vegetables harvested for sale								
Number of farms	-	-	-	-	-	-	-	-
Number of acres	-	-	-	-	-	-	-	-
Land in orchards								
Number of farms	-	-	-	-	-	-	-	-
Number of acres	-	-	-	-	-	-	-	-

Source: 1997 Census of Agriculture, U.S. Department of Agriculture, National Agricultural Statistics Service. NA stands for "not available." (D) is shown when data are withheld to prevent disclosure of competitive information. A dash (-) is shown where no data were reported. Not all states report growing all crops, but all crop categories in the census are shown for every state. The data series used for this presentation did not report U.S. totals for a number of categories; for that reason, the "% of U.S." column is sometimes blank.

MONTANA

GENERAL STATISTICS FOR MONTANA

Item	1987 Value	1987 % of U.S.	1992 Value	1992 % of U.S.	1997 Value	1997 % of U.S.	Percent change 1987-1992	Percent change 1992-1997
Farms (number)	24,568	1.2	22,821	1.2	24,279	1.3	-7.1	6.4
Land in farms (acres)	60,203,993	6.2	59,642,536	6.3	58,607,778	6.3	-0.9	-1.7
Average size of farm (acres)	2,451	530.5	2,613	532.2	2,414	495.7	6.6	-7.6
Median size of farm (acres)	NA	-	NA	-	609	507.5	-	-
Market value of land and buildings:								
Average per farm (dollars)	505,526	174.7	594,881	166.6	699,069	155.4	17.7	17.5
Average per acre (dollars)	205	32.7	227	31.2	294	31.5	10.7	29.5
Market value of machinery/equipment -								
average per farm (dollars)	60,754	147.4	66,472	136.8	78,157	135.5	9.4	17.6
Farms by size:								
1 to 9 acres	1,940	1.1	1,209	0.7	898	0.6	-37.7	-25.7
10 to 49 acres	2,745	0.7	2,804	0.7	3,570	0.9	2.1	27.3
50 to 179 acres	3,019	0.5	3,061	0.5	3,575	0.6	1.4	16.8
180 to 499 acres	3,315	0.7	2,964	0.7	3,372	0.8	-10.6	13.8
500 to 999 acres	2,737	1.4	2,521	1.4	2,675	1.5	-7.9	6.1
1,000 acres or more	10,812	6.4	10,262	5.9	10,189	5.8	-5.1	-0.7
Total cropland								
Farms	21,064	1.1	19,442	1.1	20,669	1.2	-7.7	6.3
Acres	17,829,766	4.0	17,494,553	4.0	17,629,001	4.1	-1.9	0.8
Harvested cropland (farms)	19,267	1.2	17,100	1.1	17,854	1.3	-11.2	4.4
Harvested cropland (acres)	9,128,013	3.2	8,199,296	2.8	9,399,718	3.0	-10.2	14.6
Irrigated land (farms)	9,520	3.3	8,883	3.2	9,059	3.2	-6.7	2.0
Irrigated land (acres)	1,996,882	4.3	1,978,167	4.0	1,994,484	3.6	-0.9	0.8
Market value of agricultural products sold:								
Total sales ($1,000)	1,547,286	1.1	1,730,237	1.1	1,870,732	1.0	11.8	8.1
Average per farm (dollars)	62,980	96.6	75,818	89.8	77,051	74.8	20.4	1.6
Agricultural products only ($1,000)	639,202	1.1	691,860	0.9	903,822	0.9	8.2	30.6
Livestock, poultry, and products ($1,000)	908,084	1.2	1,038,377	1.2	966,910	1.0	14.3	-6.9
Farms by value of sales:								
Less than $2,500	4,320	0.9	4,073	1.0	4,996	1.0	-5.7	22.7
$2,500 to $4,999	2,006	0.8	1,764	0.8	2,024	0.9	-12.1	14.7
$5,000 to $9,999	2,374	0.9	2,131	0.8	2,308	1.0	-10.2	8.3
$10,000 to $24,999	3,912	1.2	3,413	1.1	3,415	1.2	-12.8	0.1
$25,000 to $49,999	3,695	1.7	3,051	1.6	2,839	1.7	-17.4	-6.9
$50,000 to $99,999	4,064	1.9	3,528	1.9	3,340	2.1	-13.2	-5.3
$100,000 or more	4,197	1.4	4,861	1.5	5,357	1.5	15.8	10.2
Total farm production expenses ($1,000)	1,288,299	1.2	1,399,200	1.1	1,512,749	1.0	8.6	8.1
Average expenses per farm (dollars)	52,449	101.3	61,304	90.2	62,320	79.1	16.9	1.7
Net cash return for the farm unit:								
Number of farms	24,565	1.2	22,824	1.2	24,275	1.3	-7.1	6.4
Value ($1000)	260,131	1.0	333,711	1.1	334,834	0.8	28.3	0.3
Average per farm (dollars)	10,590	83.6	14,621	92.5	13,793	62.0	38.1	-5.7
Operators by principal occupation:								
Farming	17,405	1.5	16,006	1.5	15,703	1.6	-8.0	-1.9
Other	7,163	0.8	6,815	0.8	8,576	0.9	-4.9	25.8
Operators by days worked off farm:								
Any	10,764	1.0	9,838	1.0	11,280	1.1	-8.6	14.7
200 days or more	5,607	0.8	5,261	0.8	6,322	0.9	-6.2	20.2

Source: 1997 Census of Agriculture, U.S. Department of Agriculture, National Agricultural Statistics Service. NA stands for "not available." (D) is shown when data are withheld to prevent disclosure of competitive information. A dash (-) is shown where no data were reported. The market value of land and buildings, and of machinery and equipment, is an estimated amount. Net cash return for the farm unit includes only returns from agricultural activities.

LIVESTOCK STATISTICS FOR MONTANA

Item	1987 Value	% of U.S.	1992 Value	% of U.S.	1997 Value	% of U.S.	Percent change 1987-1992	1992-1997
Cattle and calves								
Number of farms	14,866	1.3	13,813	1.3	14,216	1.4	-7.1	2.9
Number of animals	2,591,391	2.7	2,645,916	2.8	2,618,319	2.6	2.1	-1.0
Beef cows (farms)	13,073	1.6	12,366	1.5	12,902	1.6	-5.4	4.3
Beef cows (number)	1,399,949	4.4	1,506,445	4.6	1,558,921	4.6	7.6	3.5
Milk cows (farms)	1,732	0.9	1,092	0.7	721	0.6	-37.0	-34.0
Milk cows (number)	26,879	0.3	22,409	0.2	18,052	0.2	-16.6	-19.4
Cattle and calves sold (farms)	14,718	1.3	13,628	1.3	14,055	1.4	-7.4	3.1
Cattle and calves sold (number)	1,644,768	2.3	1,677,932	2.4	1,654,014	2.2	2.0	-1.4
Hogs and pigs								
Number of farms	1,406	0.6	1,056	0.6	627	0.6	-24.9	-40.6
Number of animals	200,663	0.4	222,966	0.4	177,740	0.3	11.1	-20.3
Hogs and pigs sold (farms)	1,343	0.6	1,030	0.5	595	0.6	-23.3	-42.2
Hogs and pigs sold (number)	327,855	0.3	363,440	0.3	293,161	0.2	10.9	-19.3
Sheep and lambs								
Number of farms	2,625	2.8	2,507	3.1	1,981	3.0	-4.5	-21.0
Number of animals	588,150	5.3	634,361	5.9	416,012	5.3	7.9	-34.4
Layers and pullets 13 weeks old and older								
Number of farms	2,102	1.5	1,138	1.3	1,017	1.4	-45.9	-10.6
Number of birds	978,754	0.3	634,955	0.2	378,562	0.1	-35.1	-40.4
Broilers and other meat-type chickens sold								
Number of farms	100	0.4	47	0.2	61	0.3	-53.0	29.8
Number of birds sold	84,676	0.0	47,505	0.0	112,821	0.0	-43.9	137.5

Source: 1997 Census of Agriculture, U.S. Department of Agriculture, National Agricultural Statistics Service. NA stands for "not available." (D) is shown when data are withheld to prevent disclosure of competitive information. A dash (-) is shown where no data were reported.

CROP STATISTICS FOR MONTANA

Item	1987 Value	% of U.S.	1992 Value	% of U.S.	1997 Value	% of U.S.	Percent change 1987-1992	1992-1997
Corn for grain or seed								
Number of farms	-	-	-	-	-	-	-	-
Number of acres	-	-	-	-	-	-	-	-
Number of bushels	-	-	-	-	-	-	-	-
Corn for silage or green chop								
Number of farms	641	-	489	-	422	-	-23.7	-13.7
Number of acres	46,581	-	42,337	-	36,644	-	-9.1	-13.4
Weight in tons, green	793,716	-	761,758	-	736,202	-	-4.0	-3.4
Sorghum for grain or seed								
Number of farms	-	-	-	-	-	-	-	-
Number of acres	-	-	-	-	-	-	-	-
Number of bushels	-	-	-	-	-	-	-	-
Wheat for grain								
Number of farms	10,375	2.9	8,395	2.9	7,932	3.3	-19.1	-5.5
Number of acres	4,703,455	8.8	4,885,520	8.3	5,602,336	9.5	3.9	14.7
Number of bushels	143,802,744	7.6	142,893,032	6.5	172,214,482	7.8	-0.6	20.5
Barley for grain								
Number of farms	9,621	-	5,971	-	4,423	-	-37.9	-25.9
Number of acres	1,900,275	-	1,168,663	-	1,093,414	-	-38.5	-6.4
Number of bushels	79,606,320	-	47,381,536	-	55,236,960	-	-40.5	16.6
Oats for grain								
Number of farms	2,345	-	1,590	-	1,251	-	-32.2	-21.3
Number of acres	132,308	-	82,492	-	66,331	-	-37.7	-19.6
Number of bushels	6,356,871	-	4,485,707	-	3,501,669	-	-29.4	-21.9
Rice								
Number of farms	-	-	-	-	-	-	-	-
Number of acres	-	-	-	-	-	-	-	-
Weight in hundredweight	-	-	-	-	-	-	-	-
Sunflower seed								
Number of farms	-	-	-	-	-	-	-	-
Number of acres	-	-	-	-	-	-	-	-
Weight in pounds	-	-	-	-	-	-	-	-
Cotton								
Number of farms	-	-	-	-	-	-	-	-
Number of acres	-	-	-	-	-	-	-	-
Number of bales	-	-	-	-	-	-	-	-

Continued.

CROP STATISTICS FOR MONTANA - Continued

Item	1987 Value	1987 % of U.S.	1992 Value	1992 % of U.S.	1997 Value	1997 % of U.S.	Percent change 1987-1992	Percent change 1992-1997
Tobacco								
Number of farms	-	-	-	-	-	-	-	-
Number of acres	-	-	-	-	-	-	-	-
Weight in pounds	-	-	-	-	-	-	-	-
Soybeans for beans								
Number of farms	-	-	-	-	-	-	-	-
Number of acres	-	-	-	-	-	-	-	-
Number of bushels	-	-	-	-	-	-	-	-
Dry edible beans, excluding dry limas								
Number of farms	-	-	-	-	-	-	-	-
Number of acres	-	-	-	-	-	-	-	-
Weight in hundredweight	-	-	-	-	-	-	-	-
Potatoes, excluding sweetpotatoes								
Number of farms	-	-	-	-	-	-	-	-
Number of acres	-	-	-	-	-	-	-	-
Weight in hundredweight	-	-	-	-	-	-	-	-
Sugar beets for sugar								
Number of farms	429	-	476	-	415	-	11.0	-12.8
Number of acres	48,403	-	56,994	-	59,345	-	17.7	4.1
Weight in tons	1,051,273	-	1,274,952	-	1,243,622	-	21.3	-2.5
Sugarcane for sugar								
Number of farms	-	-	-	-	-	-	-	-
Number of acres	-	-	-	-	-	-	-	-
Weight in tons	-	-	-	-	-	-	-	-
Pineapples harvested								
Number of farms	-	-	-	-	-	-	-	-
Number of acres	-	-	-	-	-	-	-	-
Weight in tons	-	-	-	-	-	-	-	-
Peanuts for nuts								
Number of farms	-	-	-	-	-	-	-	-
Number of acres	-	-	-	-	-	-	-	-
Weight in pounds	-	-	-	-	-	-	-	-
Hay - all types, including alfalfa								
Number of farms	13,701	1.4	12,058	1.3	13,536	1.5	-12.0	12.3
Number of acres	2,135,438	3.7	1,983,629	3.5	2,528,517	4.2	-7.1	27.5
Weight in tons, dry	3,858,349	3.0	3,670,309	2.9	4,745,596	3.4	-4.9	29.3
Vegetables harvested for sale								
Number of farms	-	-	-	-	-	-	-	-
Number of acres	-	-	-	-	-	-	-	-
Land in orchards								
Number of farms	-	-	-	-	-	-	-	-
Number of acres	-	-	-	-	-	-	-	-

Source: 1997 Census of Agriculture, U.S. Department of Agriculture, National Agricultural Statistics Service. NA stands for "not available." (D) is shown when data are withheld to prevent disclosure of competitive information. A dash (-) is shown where no data were reported. Not all states report growing all crops, but all crop categories in the census are shown for every state. The data series used for this presentation did not report U.S. totals for a number of categories; for that reason, the "% of U.S." column is sometimes blank.

NEBRASKA

GENERAL STATISTICS FOR NEBRASKA

Item	1987 Value	1987 % of U.S.	1992 Value	1992 % of U.S.	1997 Value	1997 % of U.S.	Percent change 1987-1992	Percent change 1992-1997
Farms (number)	60,502	2.9	52,923	2.7	51,454	2.7	-12.5	-2.8
Land in farms (acres)	45,305,441	4.7	44,393,129	4.7	45,525,414	4.9	-2.0	2.6
Average size of farm (acres)	749	162.1	839	170.9	885	181.7	12.0	5.5
Median size of farm (acres)	NA	-	NA	-	378	315.0	-	-
Market value of land and buildings:								
Average per farm (dollars)	344,253	119.0	429,188	120.2	567,468	126.2	24.7	32.2
Average per acre (dollars)	457	72.9	514	70.7	645	69.1	12.5	25.5
Market value of machinery/equipment - average per farm (dollars)	58,799	142.6	69,120	142.2	84,535	146.6	17.6	22.3
Farms by size:								
1 to 9 acres	5,090	2.8	3,698	2.2	2,591	1.7	-27.3	-29.9
10 to 49 acres	4,296	1.0	4,302	1.1	4,733	1.2	0.1	10.0
50 to 179 acres	11,166	1.7	9,408	1.6	9,764	1.6	-15.7	3.8
180 to 499 acres	17,320	3.6	14,003	3.3	12,648	3.1	-19.2	-9.7
500 to 999 acres	12,153	6.1	10,966	5.9	10,338	5.9	-9.8	-5.7
1,000 acres or more	10,477	6.2	10,546	6.1	11,380	6.5	0.7	7.9
Total cropland								
Farms	53,500	2.9	46,348	2.7	45,191	2.7	-13.4	-2.5
Acres	23,320,162	5.3	22,402,132	5.1	22,092,954	5.1	-3.9	-1.4
Harvested cropland (farms)	51,175	3.1	43,879	2.9	41,652	3.0	-14.3	-5.1
Harvested cropland (acres)	15,276,151	5.4	16,146,818	5.5	17,551,212	5.7	5.7	8.7
Irrigated land (farms)	22,596	7.7	19,328	6.9	18,804	6.7	-14.5	-2.7
Irrigated land (acres)	5,681,835	12.2	6,311,633	12.8	6,939,036	12.6	11.1	9.9
Market value of agricultural products sold:								
Total sales ($1,000)	6,667,132	4.9	8,209,691	5.0	9,831,519	5.0	23.1	19.8
Average per farm (dollars)	110,197	169.1	155,125	183.7	191,074	185.6	40.8	23.2
Agricultural products only ($1,000)	2,139,116	3.6	2,651,484	3.5	3,798,462	3.9	24.0	43.3
Livestock, poultry, and products ($1,000)	4,528,016	5.9	5,558,208	6.4	6,033,057	6.1	22.8	8.5
Farms by value of sales:								
Less than $2,500	4,694	1.0	3,966	0.9	5,658	1.1	-15.5	42.7
$2,500 to $4,999	3,405	1.3	2,664	1.1	2,394	1.0	-21.8	-10.1
$5,000 to $9,999	5,515	2.0	4,021	1.6	3,497	1.5	-27.1	-13.0
$10,000 to $24,999	10,923	3.3	8,445	2.8	6,733	2.5	-22.7	-20.3
$25,000 to $49,999	10,681	4.9	8,362	4.3	6,962	4.1	-21.7	-16.7
$50,000 to $99,999	11,305	5.2	9,274	4.9	8,005	5.1	-18.0	-13.7
$100,000 or more	13,979	4.7	16,191	4.8	18,205	5.3	15.8	12.4
Total farm production expenses ($1,000)	5,409,171	5.0	6,711,544	5.1	7,596,196	5.0	24.1	13.2
Average expenses per farm (dollars)	89,403	172.6	126,824	186.7	147,628	187.4	41.9	16.4
Net cash return for the farm unit:								
Number of farms	60,503	2.9	52,920	2.7	51,456	2.7	-12.5	-2.8
Value ($1000)	1,229,040	4.7	1,462,607	4.8	2,095,114	4.9	19.0	43.2
Average per farm (dollars)	20,314	160.5	27,638	174.9	40,717	182.9	36.1	47.3
Operators by principal occupation:								
Farming	45,387	4.0	39,123	3.7	35,742	3.7	-13.8	-8.6
Other	15,115	1.6	13,800	1.6	15,712	1.7	-8.7	13.9
Operators by days worked off farm:								
Any	24,403	2.2	20,920	2.1	22,073	2.1	-14.3	5.5
200 days or more	13,099	1.8	11,927	1.8	13,129	1.9	-8.9	10.1

Source: *1997 Census of Agriculture*, U.S. Department of Agriculture, National Agricultural Statistics Service. NA stands for "not available." (D) is shown when data are withheld to prevent disclosure of competitive information. A dash (-) is shown where no data were reported. The market value of land and buildings, and of machinery and equipment, is an estimated amount. Net cash return for the farm unit includes only returns from agricultural activities.

LIVESTOCK STATISTICS FOR NEBRASKA

Item	1987 Value	1987 % of U.S.	1992 Value	1992 % of U.S.	1997 Value	1997 % of U.S.	Percent change 1987-1992	Percent change 1992-1997
Cattle and calves								
Number of farms	34,701	2.9	30,421	2.8	29,298	2.8	-12.3	-3.7
Number of animals	5,838,806	6.1	5,952,880	6.2	6,732,637	6.8	2.0	13.1
Beef cows (farms)	26,452	3.1	24,270	3.0	23,881	3.0	-8.2	-1.6
Beef cows (number)	1,823,591	5.8	1,857,347	5.7	1,966,105	5.8	1.9	5.9
Milk cows (farms)	3,339	1.7	2,122	1.4	1,352	1.2	-36.4	-36.3
Milk cows (number)	105,168	1.0	83,295	0.9	68,216	0.8	-20.8	-18.1
Cattle and calves sold (farms)	35,491	3.1	30,696	3.0	29,505	2.9	-13.5	-3.9
Cattle and calves sold (number)	5,888,192	8.1	6,238,779	8.8	7,143,061	9.6	6.0	14.5
Hogs and pigs								
Number of farms	13,363	5.5	10,826	5.7	6,017	5.5	-19.0	-44.4
Number of animals	3,944,227	7.5	4,187,389	7.3	3,452,386	5.6	6.2	-17.6
Hogs and pigs sold (farms)	14,162	5.9	11,559	6.1	6,296	6.2	-18.4	-45.5
Hogs and pigs sold (number)	7,442,810	7.7	8,405,466	7.6	7,602,587	5.3	12.9	-9.6
Sheep and lambs								
Number of farms	2,846	3.1	2,185	2.7	1,615	2.5	-23.2	-26.1
Number of animals	195,531	1.8	151,777	1.4	98,773	1.3	-22.4	-34.9
Layers and pullets 13 weeks old and older								
Number of farms	4,225	2.9	1,993	2.3	1,506	2.1	-52.8	-24.4
Number of birds	3,621,152	1.0	(D)	-	10,469,041	2.9	-	-
Broilers and other meat-type chickens sold								
Number of farms	524	1.9	289	1.2	225	0.9	-44.8	-22.1
Number of birds sold	910,980	0.0	1,887,881	0.0	725,964	0.0	107.2	-61.5

Source: *1997 Census of Agriculture*, U.S. Department of Agriculture, National Agricultural Statistics Service. NA stands for "not available." (D) is shown when data are withheld to prevent disclosure of competitive information. A dash (-) is shown where no data were reported.

CROP STATISTICS FOR NEBRASKA

Item	1987 Value	1987 % of U.S.	1992 Value	1992 % of U.S.	1997 Value	1997 % of U.S.	Percent change 1987-1992	Percent change 1992-1997
Corn for grain or seed								
Number of farms	34,717	5.5	29,679	5.9	29,149	6.8	-14.5	-1.8
Number of acres	6,090,669	10.4	7,235,528	10.4	8,279,499	11.9	18.8	14.4
Number of bushels	749,231,198	-	930,758,282	10.7	1,055,193,186	12.3	24.2	13.4
Corn for silage or green chop								
Number of farms	4,208	-	3,950	-	4,058	-	-6.1	2.7
Number of acres	181,060	-	195,029	-	209,587	-	7.7	7.5
Weight in tons, green	2,772,092	-	2,960,555	-	3,282,555	-	6.8	10.9
Sorghum for grain or seed								
Number of farms	12,576	-	10,513	-	5,965	-	-16.4	-43.3
Number of acres	1,300,713	-	1,412,747	-	720,276	-	8.6	-49.0
Number of bushels	101,004,096	-	122,513,083	-	56,264,473	-	21.3	-54.1
Wheat for grain								
Number of farms	18,124	5.1	12,671	4.3	9,826	4.0	-30.1	-22.5
Number of acres	1,962,051	3.7	1,800,432	3.0	1,772,069	3.0	-8.2	-1.6
Number of bushels	76,826,252	4.1	53,512,448	2.4	61,578,806	2.8	-30.3	15.1
Barley for grain								
Number of farms	-	-	-	-	-	-	-	-
Number of acres	-	-	-	-	-	-	-	-
Number of bushels	-	-	-	-	-	-	-	-
Oats for grain								
Number of farms	8,165	-	5,234	-	2,612	-	-35.9	-50.1
Number of acres	280,502	-	176,148	-	86,955	-	-37.2	-50.6
Number of bushels	13,643,509	-	11,341,781	-	5,113,274	-	-16.9	-54.9
Rice								
Number of farms	-	-	-	-	-	-	-	-
Number of acres	-	-	-	-	-	-	-	-
Weight in hundredweight	-	-	-	-	-	-	-	-
Sunflower seed								
Number of farms	-	-	-	-	-	-	-	-
Number of acres	-	-	-	-	-	-	-	-
Weight in pounds	-	-	-	-	-	-	-	-
Cotton								
Number of farms	-	-	-	-	-	-	-	-
Number of acres	-	-	-	-	-	-	-	-
Number of bales	-	-	-	-	-	-	-	-

Continued.

CROP STATISTICS FOR NEBRASKA - Continued

Item	1987 Value	1987 % of U.S.	1992 Value	1992 % of U.S.	1997 Value	1997 % of U.S.	Percent change 1987-1992	Percent change 1992-1997
Tobacco								
Number of farms	-	-	-	-	-	-	-	-
Number of acres	-	-	-	-	-	-	-	-
Weight in pounds	-	-	-	-	-	-		
Soybeans for beans								
Number of farms	25,598	5.8	20,687	5.4	21,072	5.9	-19.2	1.9
Number of acres	2,291,803	4.1	2,274,494	4.0	3,346,701	5.1	-0.8	47.1
Number of bushels	78,147,991	4.3	88,842,343	4.3	131,017,170	5.2	13.7	47.5
Dry edible beans, excluding dry limas								
Number of farms	-	-	-	-	-	-	-	-
Number of acres	-	-	-	-	-	-	-	-
Weight in hundredweight	-	-	-	-	-	-	-	-
Potatoes, excluding sweetpotatoes								
Number of farms	-	-	-	-	-	-	-	-
Number of acres	-	-	-	-	-	-	-	-
Weight in hundredweight	-	-	-	-	-	-	-	-
Sugar beets for sugar								
Number of farms	-	-	-	-	-	-	-	-
Number of acres	-	-	-	-	-	-	-	-
Weight in tons	-	-	-	-	-	-		-
Sugarcane for sugar								
Number of farms	-	-	-	-	-	-	-	-
Number of acres	-	-	-	-	-	-	-	-
Weight in tons	-	-	-	-	-	-		-
Pineapples harvested								
Number of farms	-	-	-	-	-	-		-
Number of acres	-	-	-	-	-	-	-	-
Weight in tons	-	-	-	-	-	-	-	-
Peanuts for nuts								
Number of farms	-	-	-	-	-	-	-	-
Number of acres	-	-	-	-	-	-	-	-
Weight in pounds	-	-	-	-	-	-	-	-
Hay - all types, including alfalfa								
Number of farms	30,224	3.0	27,433	3.0	25,215	2.8	-9.2	-8.1
Number of acres	2,868,789	4.9	2,895,217	5.1	2,932,880	4.8	0.9	1.3
Weight in tons, dry	5,951,228	4.6	6,068,201	4.8	6,118,280	4.4	2.0	0.8
Vegetables harvested for sale								
Number of farms	-	-	-	-	-	-		-
Number of acres	-	-	-	-	-	-	-	-
Land in orchards								
Number of farms	-	-	-	-	-	-	-	-
Number of acres	-	-	-	-	-	-	-	-

Source: 1997 Census of Agriculture, U.S. Department of Agriculture, National Agricultural Statistics Service. NA stands for "not available." (D) is shown when data are withheld to prevent disclosure of competitive information. A dash (-) is shown where no data were reported. Not all states report growing all crops, but all crop categories in the census are shown for every state. The data series used for this presentation did not report U.S. totals for a number of categories; for that reason, the "% of U.S." column is sometimes blank.

NEVADA

GENERAL STATISTICS FOR NEVADA

Item	1987 Value	1987 % of U.S.	1992 Value	1992 % of U.S.	1997 Value	1997 % of U.S.	Percent change 1987-1992	Percent change 1992-1997
Farms (number)	3,027	0.1	2,890	0.2	2,829	0.1	-4.5	-2.1
Land in farms (acres)	9,988,520	1.0	9,263,684	1.0	6,409,288	0.7	-7.3	-30.8
Average size of farm (acres)	3,300	714.3	3,205	652.7	2,266	465.3	-2.9	-29.3
Median size of farm (acres)	NA	-	NA	-	100	83.3	-	-
Market value of land and buildings:								
Average per farm (dollars)	749,936	259.1	811,941	227.4	876,417	194.9	8.3	7.9
Average per acre (dollars)	227	36.2	252	34.7	388	41.6	11.0	54.0
Market value of machinery/equipment -								
average per farm (dollars)	52,474	127.3	60,260	124.0	69,532	120.6	14.8	15.4
Farms by size:								
1 to 9 acres	574	0.3	445	0.3	425	0.3	-22.5	-4.5
10 to 49 acres	671	0.2	680	0.2	694	0.2	1.3	2.1
50 to 179 acres	574	0.1	599	0.1	543	0.1	4.4	-9.3
180 to 499 acres	453	0.1	431	0.1	430	0.1	-4.9	-0.2
500 to 999 acres	267	0.1	238	0.1	242	0.1	-10.9	1.7
1,000 acres or more	488	0.3	497	0.3	495	0.3	1.8	-0.4
Total cropland								
Farms	2,317	0.1	2,255	0.1	2,188	0.1	-2.7	-3.0
Acres	802,604	0.2	840,364	0.2	846,752	0.2	4.7	0.8
Harvested cropland (farms)	1,884	0.1	1,753	0.1	1,765	0.1	-7.0	0.7
Harvested cropland (acres)	526,067	0.2	408,568	0.1	526,338	0.2	-22.3	28.8
Irrigated land (farms)	2,221	0.8	2,151	0.8	2,159	0.8	-3.2	0.4
Irrigated land (acres)	778,977	1.7	556,172	1.1	764,738	1.4	-28.6	37.5
Market value of agricultural products sold:								
Total sales ($1,000)	250,458	0.2	288,139	0.2	356,565	0.2	15.0	23.7
Average per farm (dollars)	82,741	127.0	99,702	118.0	126,039	122.4	20.5	26.4
Agricultural products only ($1,000)	75,685	0.1	79,957	0.1	151,717	0.2	5.6	89.7
Livestock, poultry, and products ($1,000)	174,773	0.2	208,182	0.2	204,848	0.2	19.1	-1.6
Farms by value of sales:								
Less than $2,500	861	0.2	862	0.2	695	0.1	0.1	-19.4
$2,500 to $4,999	353	0.1	305	0.1	310	0.1	-13.6	1.6
$5,000 to $9,999	336	0.1	352	0.1	358	0.2	4.8	1.7
$10,000 to $24,999	437	0.1	375	0.1	444	0.2	-14.2	18.4
$25,000 to $49,999	278	0.1	250	0.1	259	0.2	-10.1	3.6
$50,000 to $99,999	258	0.1	264	0.1	253	0.2	2.3	-4.2
$100,000 or more	504	0.2	482	0.1	510	0.1	-4.4	5.8
Total farm production expenses ($1,000)	208,924	0.2	247,113	0.2	276,040	0.2	18.3	11.7
Average expenses per farm (dollars)	68,975	133.2	85,506	125.9	97,782	124.1	24.0	14.4
Net cash return for the farm unit:								
Number of farms	3,029	0.1	2,891	0.2	2,823	0.1	-4.6	-2.4
Value ($1000)	42,975	0.2	40,728	0.1	77,433	0.2	-5.2	90.1
Average per farm (dollars)	14,188	112.1	14,088	89.2	27,429	123.2	-0.7	94.7
Operators by principal occupation:								
Farming	1,675	0.1	1,656	0.2	1,558	0.2	-1.1	-5.9
Other	1,352	0.1	1,234	0.1	1,271	0.1	-8.7	3.0
Operators by days worked off farm:								
Any	1,654	0.1	1,518	0.2	1,515	0.1	-8.2	-0.2
200 days or more	1,042	0.1	910	0.1	939	0.1	-12.7	3.2

Source: *1997 Census of Agriculture*, U.S. Department of Agriculture, National Agricultural Statistics Service. NA stands for "not available." (D) is shown when data are withheld to prevent disclosure of competitive information. A dash (-) is shown where no data were reported. The market value of land and buildings, and of machinery and equipment, is an estimated amount. Net cash return for the farm unit includes only returns from agricultural activities.

LIVESTOCK STATISTICS FOR NEVADA

Item	1987 Value	1987 % of U.S.	1992 Value	1992 % of U.S.	1997 Value	1997 % of U.S.	Percent change 1987-1992	Percent change 1992-1997
Cattle and calves								
Number of farms	1,819	0.2	1,652	0.2	1,694	0.2	-9.2	2.5
Number of animals	575,608	0.6	523,305	0.5	518,115	0.5	-9.1	-1.0
Beef cows (farms)	1,438	0.2	1,330	0.2	1,371	0.2	-7.5	3.1
Beef cows (number)	305,018	1.0	265,690	0.8	275,801	0.8	-12.9	3.8
Milk cows (farms)	274	0.1	208	0.1	138	0.1	-24.1	-33.7
Milk cows (number)	17,646	0.2	21,769	0.2	24,902	0.3	23.4	14.4
Cattle and calves sold (farms)	1,733	0.2	1,538	0.1	1,587	0.2	-11.3	3.2
Cattle and calves sold (number)	303,567	0.4	317,233	0.4	295,007	0.4	4.5	-7.0
Hogs and pigs								
Number of farms	149	0.1	154	0.1	113	0.1	3.4	-26.6
Number of animals	16,505	0.0	7,636	0.0	7,419	0.0	-53.7	-2.8
Hogs and pigs sold (farms)	128	0.1	102	0.1	74	0.1	-20.3	-27.5
Hogs and pigs sold (number)	26,413	0.0	23,746	0.0	7,414	0.0	-10.1	-68.8
Sheep and lambs								
Number of farms	393	0.4	360	0.4	272	0.4	-8.4	-24.4
Number of animals	99,768	0.9	122,188	1.1	96,409	1.2	22.5	-21.1
Layers and pullets 13 weeks old and older								
Number of farms	397	0.3	250	0.3	203	0.3	-37.0	-18.8
Number of birds	18,245	0.0	14,826	0.0	4,503	0.0	-18.7	-69.6
Broilers and other meat-type chickens sold								
Number of farms	10	0.0	7	0.0	6	0.0	-30.0	-14.3
Number of birds sold	525	0.0	200	0.0	(D)	-	-61.9	-

Source: *1997 Census of Agriculture*, U.S. Department of Agriculture, National Agricultural Statistics Service. NA stands for "not available." (D) is shown when data are withheld to prevent disclosure of competitive information. A dash (-) is shown where no data were reported.

CROP STATISTICS FOR NEVADA

Item	1987 Value	1987 % of U.S.	1992 Value	1992 % of U.S.	1997 Value	1997 % of U.S.	Percent change 1987-1992	Percent change 1992-1997
Corn for grain or seed								
Number of farms	-	-	-	-	-	-		-
Number of acres	-	-	-	-	-	-		-
Number of bushels	-	-	-	-	-	-		-
Corn for silage or green chop								
Number of farms	-	-	-	-	-	-		-
Number of acres	-	-	-	-	-	-		-
Weight in tons, green	-	-	-	-	-	-		-
Sorghum for grain or seed								
Number of farms	-	-	-	-	-	-		-
Number of acres	-	-	-	-	-	-		-
Number of bushels	-	-	-	-	-	-		-
Wheat for grain								
Number of farms	114	0.0	57	0.0	73	0.0	-50.0	28.1
Number of acres	15,052	0.0	9,968	0.0	19,034	0.0	-33.8	91.0
Number of bushels	1,096,511	0.1	719,200	0.0	1,903,995	0.1	-34.4	164.7
Barley for grain								
Number of farms	115	-	36	-	49	-	-68.7	36.1
Number of acres	9,150	-	4,613	-	4,642	-	-49.6	0.6
Number of bushels	725,196	-	423,411	-	422,623	-	-41.6	0.2
Oats for grain								
Number of farms	-	-	-	-	-	-	-	-
Number of acres	-	-	-	-	-	-	-	-
Number of bushels	-	-	-	-	-	-	-	-
Rice								
Number of farms	-	-	-	-	-	-	-	-
Number of acres	-	-	-	-	-	-	-	-
Weight in hundredweight	-	-	-	-	-	-	-	-
Sunflower seed								
Number of farms	-	-	-	-	-	-	-	-
Number of acres	-	-	-	-	-	-	-	-
Weight in pounds	-	-	-	-	-	-	-	-
Cotton								
Number of farms	-	-	-	-	-	-	-	-
Number of acres	-	-	-	-	-	-	-	-
Number of bales	-	-	-	-	-	-	-	-

Continued.

CROP STATISTICS FOR NEVADA - Continued

Item	1987 Value	1987 % of U.S.	1992 Value	1992 % of U.S.	1997 Value	1997 % of U.S.	Percent change 1987-1992	Percent change 1992-1997
Tobacco								
Number of farms	-	-	-	-	-	-	-	-
Number of acres	-	-	-	-	-	-	-	-
Weight in pounds	-	-	-	-	-	-	-	-
Soybeans for beans								
Number of farms	-	-	-	-	-	-	-	-
Number of acres	-	-	-	-	-	-	-	-
Number of bushels	-	-	-	-	-	-	-	-
Dry edible beans, excluding dry limas								
Number of farms	-	-	-	-	-	-	-	-
Number of acres	-	-	-	-	-	-	-	-
Weight in hundredweight	-	-	-	-	-	-	-	-
Potatoes, excluding sweetpotatoes								
Number of farms	10	-	12	-	10	-	20.0	-16.7
Number of acres	7,501	-	8,111	-	6,999	-	8.1	-13.7
Weight in hundredweight	2,561,680	-	3,035,277	-	2,962,254	-	18.5	-2.4
Sugar beets for sugar								
Number of farms	-	-	-	-	-	-		
Number of acres	-	-	-	-	-	-		
Weight in tons	-	-	-	-	-	-		
Sugarcane for sugar								
Number of farms	-	-	-	-	-	-		
Number of acres	-	-	-	-	-	-		
Weight in tons	-	-	-	-	-	-		
Pineapples harvested								
Number of farms	-	-	-	-	-	-	-	-
Number of acres	-	-	-	-	-	-	-	-
Weight in tons	-	-	-	-	-	-	-	-
Peanuts for nuts								
Number of farms	-	-	-	-	-	-	-	
Number of acres	-	-	-	-	-	-	-	
Weight in pounds	-	-	-	-	-	-	-	
Hay - all types, including alfalfa								
Number of farms	1,762	0.2	1,638	0.2	1,640	0.2	-7.0	0.1
Number of acres	479,346	0.8	380,959	0.7	478,358	0.8	-20.5	25.6
Weight in tons, dry	1,223,895	1.0	1,082,233	0.9	1,458,687	1.0	-11.6	34.8
Vegetables harvested for sale								
Number of farms	-	-	-	-	-	-		-
Number of acres	-	-	-	-	-	-		-
Land in orchards								
Number of farms	-	-	-	-	-	-		-
Number of acres	-	-	-	-	-	-		-

Source: *1997 Census of Agriculture*, U.S. Department of Agriculture, National Agricultural Statistics Service. NA stands for "not available." (D) is shown when data are withheld to prevent disclosure of competitive information. A dash (-) is shown where no data were reported. Not all states report growing all crops, but all crop categories in the census are shown for every state. The data series used for this presentation did not report U.S. totals for a number of categories; for that reason, the "% of U.S." column is sometimes blank.

NEW HAMPSHIRE

GENERAL STATISTICS FOR NEW HAMPSHIRE

Item	1987 Value	1987 % of U.S.	1992 Value	1992 % of U.S.	1997 Value	1997 % of U.S.	Percent change 1987-1992	Percent change 1992-1997
Farms (number)	2,515	0.1	2,445	0.1	2,937	0.2	-2.8	20.1
Land in farms (acres)	426,237	0.0	385,832	0.0	415,031	0.0	-9.5	7.6
Average size of farm (acres)	169	36.6	158	32.2	141	29.0	-6.5	-10.8
Median size of farm (acres)	NA	-	NA	-	65	54.2	-	-
Market value of land and buildings:								
Average per farm (dollars)	358,279	123.8	342,607	96.0	323,523	71.9	-4.4	-5.6
Average per acre (dollars)	2,112	336.8	2,256	310.3	2,250	241.2	6.8	-0.3
Market value of machinery/equipment - average per farm (dollars)	33,905	82.2	34,566	71.1	37,957	65.8	1.9	9.8
Farms by size:								
1 to 9 acres	255	0.1	308	0.2	425	0.3	20.8	38.0
10 to 49 acres	567	0.1	619	0.2	784	0.2	9.2	26.7
50 to 179 acres	919	0.1	844	0.1	1,005	0.2	-8.2	19.1
180 to 499 acres	583	0.1	511	0.1	571	0.1	-12.3	11.7
500 to 999 acres	160	0.1	133	0.1	120	0.1	-16.9	-9.8
1,000 acres or more	31	0.0	30	0.0	32	0.0	-3.2	6.7
Total cropland								
Farms	2,255	0.1	2,242	0.1	2,489	0.1	-0.6	11.0
Acres	147,719	0.0	135,437	0.0	132,619	0.0	-8.3	-2.1
Harvested cropland (farms)	2,044	0.1	2,039	0.1	2,256	0.2	-0.2	10.6
Harvested cropland (acres)	106,629	0.0	100,746	0.0	101,753	0.0	-5.5	1.0
Irrigated land (farms)	253	0.1	308	0.1	429	0.2	21.7	39.3
Irrigated land (acres)	2,948	0.0	1,746	0.0	2,691	0.0	-40.8	54.1
Market value of agricultural products sold:								
Total sales ($1,000)	107,102	0.1	114,070	0.1	149,467	0.1	6.5	31.0
Average per farm (dollars)	42,585	65.3	46,654	55.2	50,891	49.4	9.6	9.1
Agricultural products only ($1,000)	35,327	0.1	45,724	0.1	73,728	0.1	29.4	61.2
Livestock, poultry, and products ($1,000)	71,775	0.1	68,346	0.1	75,739	0.1	-4.8	10.8
Farms by value of sales:								
Less than $2,500	1,020	0.2	928	0.2	1,121	0.2	-9.0	20.8
$2,500 to $4,999	371	0.1	343	0.1	460	0.2	-7.5	34.1
$5,000 to $9,999	320	0.1	325	0.1	388	0.2	1.6	19.4
$10,000 to $24,999	234	0.1	288	0.1	363	0.1	23.1	26.0
$25,000 to $49,999	131	0.1	152	0.1	187	0.1	16.0	23.0
$50,000 to $99,999	175	0.1	143	0.1	143	0.1	-18.3	-
$100,000 or more	264	0.1	266	0.1	275	0.1	0.8	3.4
Total farm production expenses ($1,000)	91,948	0.1	95,755	0.1	126,098	0.1	4.1	31.7
Average expenses per farm (dollars)	36,604	70.7	39,244	57.8	43,169	54.8	7.2	10.0
Net cash return for the farm unit:								
Number of farms	2,512	0.1	2,440	0.1	2,921	0.2	-2.9	19.7
Value ($1000)	13,954	0.1	15,953	0.1	23,567	0.1	14.3	47.7
Average per farm (dollars)	5,555	43.9	6,538	41.4	8,068	36.2	17.7	23.4
Operators by principal occupation:								
Farming	1,153	0.1	1,204	0.1	1,260	0.1	4.4	4.7
Other	1,362	0.1	1,241	0.1	1,677	0.2	-8.9	35.1
Operators by days worked off farm:								
Any	1,539	0.1	1,420	0.1	1,807	0.2	-7.7	27.3
200 days or more	959	0.1	848	0.1	1,152	0.2	-11.6	35.8

Source: *1997 Census of Agriculture*, U.S. Department of Agriculture, National Agricultural Statistics Service. NA stands for "not available." (D) is shown when data are withheld to prevent disclosure of competitive information. A dash (-) is shown where no data were reported. The market value of land and buildings, and of machinery and equipment, is an estimated amount. Net cash return for the farm unit includes only returns from agricultural activities.

LIVESTOCK STATISTICS FOR NEW HAMPSHIRE

Item	1987 Value	1987 % of U.S.	1992 Value	1992 % of U.S.	1997 Value	1997 % of U.S.	Percent change 1987-1992	Percent change 1992-1997
Cattle and calves								
Number of farms	1,148	0.1	956	0.1	953	0.1	-16.7	-0.3
Number of animals	54,012	0.1	48,419	0.1	45,115	0.0	-10.4	-6.8
Beef cows (farms)	587	0.1	494	0.1	540	0.1	-15.8	9.3
Beef cows (number)	4,229	0.0	3,727	0.0	4,206	0.0	-11.9	12.9
Milk cows (farms)	518	0.3	389	0.3	329	0.3	-24.9	-15.4
Milk cows (number)	25,110	0.2	21,659	0.2	19,563	0.2	-13.7	-9.7
Cattle and calves sold (farms)	969	0.1	766	0.1	760	0.1	-20.9	-0.8
Cattle and calves sold (number)	24,611	0.0	20,138	0.0	16,053	0.0	-18.2	-20.3
Hogs and pigs								
Number of farms	264	0.1	289	0.2	249	0.2	9.5	-13.8
Number of animals	5,040	0.0	4,458	0.0	4,373	0.0	-11.5	-1.9
Hogs and pigs sold (farms)	180	0.1	173	0.1	137	0.1	-3.9	-20.8
Hogs and pigs sold (number)	6,610	0.0	9,063	0.0	13,454	0.0	37.1	48.4
Sheep and lambs								
Number of farms	365	0.4	311	0.4	344	0.5	-14.8	10.6
Number of animals	9,180	0.1	8,052	0.1	6,925	0.1	-12.3	-14.0
Layers and pullets 13 weeks old and older								
Number of farms	404	0.3	337	0.4	405	0.6	-16.6	20.2
Number of birds	459,446	0.1	212,748	0.1	213,782	0.1	-53.7	0.5
Broilers and other meat-type chickens sold								
Number of farms	22	0.1	25	0.1	35	0.1	13.6	40.0
Number of birds sold	(D)	-	(D)	-	472,718	0.0	-	-

Source: *1997 Census of Agriculture*, U.S. Department of Agriculture, National Agricultural Statistics Service. NA stands for "not available." (D) is shown when data are withheld to prevent disclosure of competitive information. A dash (-) is shown where no data were reported.

CROP STATISTICS FOR NEW HAMPSHIRE

Item	1987 Value	1987 % of U.S.	1992 Value	1992 % of U.S.	1997 Value	1997 % of U.S.	Percent change 1987-1992	Percent change 1992-1997
Corn for grain or seed								
Number of farms	32	0.0	34	0.0	35	0.0	6.3	2.9
Number of acres	1,042	0.0	1,620	0.0	1,211	0.0	55.5	-25.2
Number of bushels	102,358	-	184,250	0.0	127,024	0.0	80.0	-31.1
Corn for silage or green chop								
Number of farms	308	-	258	-	231	-	-16.2	-10.5
Number of acres	16,979	-	16,577	-	15,957	-	-2.4	-3.7
Weight in tons, green	309,821	-	311,941	-	307,296	-	0.7	-1.5
Sorghum for grain or seed								
Number of farms	-	-	-	-	-	-	-	-
Number of acres	-	-	-	-	-	-	-	-
Number of bushels	-	-	-	-	-	-	-	-
Wheat for grain								
Number of farms	-	-	-	-	-	-	-	-
Number of acres	-	-	-	-	-	-	-	-
Number of bushels	-	-	-	-	-	-	-	-
Barley for grain								
Number of farms	-	-	-	-	-	-	-	-
Number of acres	-	-	-	-	-	-	-	-
Number of bushels	-	-	-	-	-	-	-	-
Oats for grain								
Number of farms	-	-	-	-	-	-	-	-
Number of acres	-	-	-	-	-	-	-	-
Number of bushels	-	-	-	-	-	-	-	-
Rice								
Number of farms	-	-	-	-	-	-	-	-
Number of acres	-	-	-	-	-	-	-	-
Weight in hundredweight	-	-	-	-	-	-	-	-
Sunflower seed								
Number of farms	-	-	-	-	-	-	-	-
Number of acres	-	-	-	-	-	-	-	-
Weight in pounds	-	-	-	-	-	-	-	-
Cotton								
Number of farms	-	-	-	-	-	-	-	-
Number of acres	-	-	-	-	-	-	-	-
Number of bales	-	-	-	-	-	-	-	-

Continued.

CROP STATISTICS FOR NEW HAMPSHIRE - Continued

Item	1987		1992		1997		Percent change	
	Value	% of U.S.	Value	% of U.S.	Value	% of U.S.	1987-1992	1992-1997
Tobacco								
Number of farms	-	-	-	-	-	-	-	-
Number of acres	-	-	-	-	-	-	-	-
Weight in pounds	-	-	-	-	-	-	-	-
Soybeans for beans								
Number of farms	-	-	-	-	-	-	-	-
Number of acres	-	-	-	-	-	-	-	-
Number of bushels	-	-	-	-	-	-	-	-
Dry edible beans, excluding dry limas								
Number of farms	-	-	-	-	-	-	-	-
Number of acres	-	-	-	-	-	-	-	-
Weight in hundredweight	-	-	-	-	-	-	-	-
Potatoes, excluding sweetpotatoes								
Number of farms	-	-	-	-	-	-	-	-
Number of acres	-	-	-	-	-	-	-	-
Weight in hundredweight	-	-	-	-	-	-	-	-
Sugar beets for sugar								
Number of farms	-	-	-	-	-	-	-	-
Number of acres	-	-	-	-	-	-	-	-
Weight in tons	-	-	-	-	-	-	-	-
Sugarcane for sugar								
Number of farms	-	-	-	-	-	-	-	-
Number of acres	-	-	-	-	-	-	-	-
Weight in tons	-	-	-	-	-	-	-	-
Pineapples harvested								
Number of farms	-	-	-	-	-	-	-	-
Number of acres	-	-	-	-	-	-	-	-
Weight in tons	-	-	-	-	-	-	-	-
Peanuts for nuts								
Number of farms	-	-	-	-	-	-	-	-
Number of acres	-	-	-	-	-	-	-	-
Weight in pounds	-	-	-	-	-	-	-	-
Hay - all types, including alfalfa								
Number of farms	1,586	0.2	1,492	0.2	1,462	0.2	-5.9	-2.0
Number of acres	84,617	0.1	77,605	0.1	78,832	0.1	-8.3	1.6
Weight in tons, dry	164,829	0.1	136,963	0.1	140,513	0.1	-16.9	2.6
Vegetables harvested for sale								
Number of farms	283	0.5	327	0.5	339	0.6	15.5	3.7
Number of acres	3,047	0.1	3,324	0.1	3,490	0.1	9.1	5.0
Land in orchards								
Number of farms	219	0.2	242	0.2	219	0.2	10.5	-9.5
Number of acres	3,863	0.1	3,877	0.1	3,414	0.1	0.4	-11.9

Source: 1997 Census of Agriculture, U.S. Department of Agriculture, National Agricultural Statistics Service. NA stands for "not available." (D) is shown when data are withheld to prevent disclosure of competitive information. A dash (-) is shown where no data were reported. Not all states report growing all crops, but all crop categories in the census are shown for every state. The data series used for this presentation did not report U.S. totals for a number of categories; for that reason, the "% of U.S." column is sometimes blank.

NEW JERSEY

GENERAL STATISTICS FOR NEW JERSEY

Item	1987 Value	1987 % of U.S.	1992 Value	1992 % of U.S.	1997 Value	1997 % of U.S.	Percent change 1987-1992	Percent change 1992-1997
Farms (number)	9,032	0.4	9,079	0.5	9,101	0.5	0.5	0.2
Land in farms (acres)	894,426	0.1	847,595	0.1	832,600	0.1	-5.2	-1.8
Average size of farm (acres)	99	21.4	93	18.9	91	18.7	-6.1	-2.2
Median size of farm (acres)	NA	-	NA	-	23	19.2	-	-
Market value of land and buildings:								
Average per farm (dollars)	396,198	136.9	615,430	172.4	594,206	132.1	55.3	-3.4
Average per acre (dollars)	3,969	633.0	6,942	954.9	6,642	711.9	74.9	-4.3
Market value of machinery/equipment - average per farm (dollars)	37,768	91.6	39,620	81.5	48,011	83.2	4.9	21.2
Farms by size:								
1 to 9 acres	1,862	1.0	2,099	1.3	2,249	1.5	12.7	7.1
10 to 49 acres	3,549	0.9	3,726	1.0	3,807	0.9	5.0	2.2
50 to 179 acres	2,316	0.4	2,079	0.4	1,927	0.3	-10.2	-7.3
180 to 499 acres	939	0.2	836	0.2	768	0.2	-11.0	-8.1
500 to 999 acres	292	0.1	250	0.1	238	0.1	-14.4	-4.8
1,000 acres or more	74	0.0	89	0.1	112	0.1	20.3	25.8
Total cropland								
Farms	8,268	0.4	8,221	0.5	8,322	0.5	-0.6	1.2
Acres	642,534	0.1	623,466	0.1	594,928	0.1	-3.0	-4.6
Harvested cropland (farms)	7,288	0.4	7,149	0.5	7,396	0.5	-1.9	3.5
Harvested cropland (acres)	484,805	0.2	491,518	0.2	485,187	0.2	1.4	-1.3
Irrigated land (farms)	1,846	0.6	1,911	0.7	2,089	0.7	3.5	9.3
Irrigated land (acres)	91,208	0.2	80,409	0.2	92,965	0.2	-11.8	15.6
Market value of agricultural products sold:								
Total sales ($1,000)	496,003	0.4	532,988	0.3	697,380	0.4	7.5	30.8
Average per farm (dollars)	54,916	84.3	58,706	69.5	76,627	74.4	6.9	30.5
Agricultural products only ($1,000)	370,580	0.6	431,178	0.6	592,713	0.6	16.4	37.5
Livestock, poultry, and products ($1,000)	125,423	0.2	101,810	0.1	104,666	0.1	-18.8	2.8
Farms by value of sales:								
Less than $2,500	3,089	0.6	3,136	0.7	3,352	0.7	1.5	6.9
$2,500 to $4,999	1,281	0.5	1,175	0.5	1,105	0.5	-8.3	-6.0
$5,000 to $9,999	1,163	0.4	1,144	0.5	1,097	0.5	-1.6	-4.1
$10,000 to $24,999	1,201	0.4	1,358	0.4	1,195	0.4	13.1	-12.0
$25,000 to $49,999	632	0.3	676	0.3	689	0.4	7.0	1.9
$50,000 to $99,999	578	0.3	530	0.3	502	0.3	-8.3	-5.3
$100,000 or more	1,088	0.4	1,060	0.3	1,161	0.3	-2.6	9.5
Total farm production expenses ($1,000)	387,693	0.4	430,843	0.3	513,326	0.3	11.1	19.1
Average expenses per farm (dollars)	42,920	82.9	47,434	69.8	56,447	71.7	10.5	19.0
Net cash return for the farm unit:								
Number of farms	9,034	0.4	9,083	0.5	9,094	0.5	0.5	0.1
Value ($1000)	102,318	0.4	95,771	0.3	175,896	0.4	-6.4	83.7
Average per farm (dollars)	11,326	89.5	10,544	66.7	19,342	86.9	-6.9	83.4
Operators by principal occupation:								
Farming	4,180	0.4	4,218	0.4	3,920	0.4	0.9	-7.1
Other	4,852	0.5	4,861	0.6	5,181	0.5	0.2	6.6
Operators by days worked off farm:								
Any	5,375	0.5	5,094	0.5	5,188	0.5	-5.2	1.8
200 days or more	3,666	0.5	3,396	0.5	3,478	0.5	-7.4	2.4

Source: *1997 Census of Agriculture*, U.S. Department of Agriculture, National Agricultural Statistics Service. NA stands for "not available." (D) is shown when data are withheld to prevent disclosure of competitive information. A dash (-) is shown where no data were reported. The market value of land and buildings, and of machinery and equipment, is an estimated amount. Net cash return for the farm unit includes only returns from agricultural activities.

LIVESTOCK STATISTICS FOR NEW JERSEY

Item	1987		1992		1997		Percent change	
	Value	% of U.S.	Value	% of U.S.	Value	% of U.S.	1987-1992	1992-1997
Cattle and calves								
Number of farms	2,231	0.2	1,934	0.2	1,703	0.2	-13.3	-11.9
Number of animals	77,581	0.1	69,134	0.1	56,643	0.1	-10.9	-18.1
Beef cows (farms)	1,176	0.1	1,152	0.1	1,039	0.1	-2.0	-9.8
Beef cows (number)	11,359	0.0	12,280	0.0	12,192	0.0	8.1	-0.7
Milk cows (farms)	584	0.3	450	0.3	296	0.3	-22.9	-34.2
Milk cows (number)	32,067	0.3	23,926	0.3	18,041	0.2	-25.4	-24.6
Cattle and calves sold (farms)	2,049	0.2	1,668	0.2	1,506	0.1	-18.6	-9.7
Cattle and calves sold (number)	43,257	0.1	28,989	0.0	23,362	0.0	-33.0	-19.4
Hogs and pigs								
Number of farms	680	0.3	640	0.3	431	0.4	-5.9	-32.7
Number of animals	31,968	0.1	29,645	0.1	23,189	0.0	-7.3	-21.8
Hogs and pigs sold (farms)	661	0.3	530	0.3	350	0.3	-19.8	-34.0
Hogs and pigs sold (number)	52,320	0.1	44,325	0.0	40,396	0.0	-15.3	-8.9
Sheep and lambs								
Number of farms	685	0.7	691	0.9	690	1.0	0.9	-0.1
Number of animals	12,624	0.1	12,902	0.1	13,149	0.2	2.2	1.9
Layers and pullets 13 weeks old and older								
Number of farms	950	0.7	917	1.0	827	1.1	-3.5	-9.8
Number of birds	2,130,533	0.6	1,801,049	0.5	(D)	-	-15.5	-
Broilers and other meat-type chickens sold								
Number of farms	90	0.3	93	0.4	79	0.3	3.3	-15.1
Number of birds sold	453,843	0.0	95,794	0.0	40,712	0.0	-78.9	-57.5

Source: 1997 Census of Agriculture, U.S. Department of Agriculture, National Agricultural Statistics Service. NA stands for "not available." (D) is shown when data are withheld to prevent disclosure of competitive information. A dash (-) is shown where no data were reported.

CROP STATISTICS FOR NEW JERSEY

Item	1987		1992		1997		Percent change	
	Value	% of U.S.	Value	% of U.S.	Value	% of U.S.	1987-1992	1992-1997
Corn for grain or seed								
Number of farms	1,405	0.2	1,158	0.2	1,110	0.3	-17.6	-4.1
Number of acres	74,938	0.1	83,805	0.1	89,252	0.1	11.8	6.5
Number of bushels	7,570,456	-	9,508,526	0.1	9,572,100	0.1	25.6	0.7
Corn for silage or green chop								
Number of farms	568	-	465	-	367	-	-18.1	-21.1
Number of acres	23,099	-	19,682	-	20,564	-	-14.8	4.5
Weight in tons, green	362,347	-	305,639	-	300,696	-	-15.7	-1.6
Sorghum for grain or seed								
Number of farms	-	-	-	-	-	-	-	-
Number of acres	-	-	-	-	-	-	-	-
Number of bushels	-	-	-	-	-	-	-	-
Wheat for grain								
Number of farms	-	-	-	-	-	-	-	-
Number of acres	-	-	-	-	-	-	-	-
Number of bushels	-	-	-	-	-	-	-	-
Barley for grain								
Number of farms	-	-	-	-	-	-	-	-
Number of acres	-	-	-	-	-	-	-	-
Number of bushels	-	-	-	-	-	-	-	-
Oats for grain								
Number of farms	-	-	-	-	-	-	-	-
Number of acres	-	-	-	-	-	-	-	-
Number of bushels	-	-	-	-	-	-	-	-
Rice								
Number of farms	-	-	-	-	-	-	-	-
Number of acres	-	-	-	-	-	-	-	-
Weight in hundredweight	-	-	-	-	-	-	-	-
Sunflower seed								
Number of farms	-	-	-	-	-	-	-	-
Number of acres	-	-	-	-	-	-	-	-
Weight in pounds	-	-	-	-	-	-	-	-
Cotton								
Number of farms	-	-	-	-	-	-	-	-
Number of acres	-	-	-	-	-	-	-	-
Number of bales	-	-	-	-	-	-	-	-

Continued.

CROP STATISTICS FOR NEW JERSEY - Continued

Item	1987 Value	% of U.S.	1992 Value	% of U.S.	1997 Value	% of U.S.	Percent change 1987-1992	1992-1997
Tobacco								
Number of farms	-	-	-	-	-	-	-	-
Number of acres	-	-	-	-	-	-	-	-
Weight in pounds	-	-	-	-	-	-	-	-
Soybeans for beans								
Number of farms	1,091	0.2	1,128	0.3	914	0.3	3.4	-19.0
Number of acres	106,296	0.2	131,768	0.2	116,557	0.2	24.0	-11.5
Number of bushels	3,153,039	0.2	4,378,643	0.2	3,599,073	0.1	38.9	-17.8
Dry edible beans, excluding dry limas								
Number of farms	-	-	-	-	-	-	-	-
Number of acres	-	-	-	-	-	-	-	-
Weight in hundredweight	-	-	-	-	-	-	-	-
Potatoes, excluding sweetpotatoes								
Number of farms	-	-	-	-	-	-	-	-
Number of acres	-	-	-	-	-	-	-	-
Weight in hundredweight	-	-	-	-	-	-	-	-
Sugar beets for sugar								
Number of farms	-	-	-	-	-	-	-	-
Number of acres	-	-	-	-	-	-	-	-
Weight in tons	-	-	-	-	-	-	-	-
Sugarcane for sugar								
Number of farms	-	-	-	-	-	-	-	-
Number of acres	-	-	-	-	-	-	-	-
Weight in tons	-	-	-	-	-	-	-	-
Pineapples harvested								
Number of farms	-	-	-	-	-	-	-	-
Number of acres	-	-	-	-	-	-	-	-
Weight in tons	-	-	-	-	-	-	-	-
Peanuts for nuts								
Number of farms	-	-	-	-	-	-	-	-
Number of acres	-	-	-	-	-	-	-	-
Weight in pounds	-	-	-	-	-	-	-	-
Hay - all types, including alfalfa								
Number of farms	3,226	0.3	3,060	0.3	3,022	0.3	-5.1	-1.2
Number of acres	122,451	0.2	118,536	0.2	114,523	0.2	-3.2	-3.4
Weight in tons, dry	262,323	0.2	238,792	0.2	224,259	0.2	-9.0	-6.1
Vegetables harvested for sale								
Number of farms	1,908	3.1	1,861	3.0	1,577	2.9	-2.5	-15.3
Number of acres	72,521	2.1	64,647	1.7	63,414	1.7	-10.9	-1.9
Land in orchards								
Number of farms	746	0.6	701	0.6	577	0.5	-6.0	-17.7
Number of acres	20,924	0.5	16,871	0.4	13,459	0.3	-19.4	-20.2

Source: *1997 Census of Agriculture*, U.S. Department of Agriculture, National Agricultural Statistics Service. NA stands for "not available." (D) is shown when data are withheld to prevent disclosure of competitive information. A dash (-) is shown where no data were reported. Not all states report growing all crops, but all crop categories in the census are shown for every state. The data series used for this presentation did not report U.S. totals for a number of categories; for that reason, the "% of U.S." column is sometimes blank.

NEW MEXICO

GENERAL STATISTICS FOR NEW MEXICO

Item	1987 Value	1987 % of U.S.	1992 Value	1992 % of U.S.	1997 Value	1997 % of U.S.	Percent change 1987-1992	Percent change 1992-1997
Farms (number)	14,249	0.7	14,279	0.7	14,094	0.7	0.2	-1.3
Land in farms (acres)	46,018,005	4.8	46,849,244	5.0	45,787,108	4.9	1.8	-2.3
Average size of farm (acres)	3,230	699.1	3,281	668.2	3,249	667.1	1.6	-1.0
Median size of farm (acres)	NA	-	NA	-	160	133.3	-	-
Market value of land and buildings:								
Average per farm (dollars)	582,012	201.1	645,677	180.8	625,307	139.0	10.9	-3.2
Average per acre (dollars)	180	28.7	194	26.7	195	20.9	7.8	0.5
Market value of machinery/equipment -								
average per farm (dollars)	33,093	80.3	36,992	76.1	44,047	76.4	11.8	19.1
Farms by size:								
1 to 9 acres	2,421	1.3	2,600	1.6	2,594	1.7	7.4	-0.2
10 to 49 acres	2,710	0.7	2,611	0.7	2,618	0.6	-3.7	0.3
50 to 179 acres	2,164	0.3	2,142	0.4	2,163	0.4	-1.0	1.0
180 to 499 acres	1,846	0.4	1,748	0.4	1,721	0.4	-5.3	-1.5
500 to 999 acres	1,341	0.7	1,260	0.7	1,232	0.7	-6.0	-2.2
1,000 acres or more	3,767	2.2	3,918	2.3	3,766	2.1	4.0	-3.9
Total cropland								
Farms	9,429	0.5	9,447	0.6	9,435	0.6	0.2	-0.1
Acres	2,279,119	0.5	2,252,970	0.5	2,179,428	0.5	-1.1	-3.3
Harvested cropland (farms)	7,269	0.4	7,213	0.5	7,008	0.5	-0.8	-2.8
Harvested cropland (acres)	989,214	0.4	1,060,345	0.4	1,079,953	0.3	7.2	1.8
Irrigated land (farms)	7,022	2.4	7,331	2.6	7,444	2.7	4.4	1.5
Irrigated land (acres)	718,449	1.5	738,272	1.5	804,616	1.5	2.8	9.0
Market value of agricultural products sold:								
Total sales ($1,000)	1,060,112	0.8	1,258,883	0.8	1,617,708	0.8	18.8	28.5
Average per farm (dollars)	74,399	114.2	88,163	104.4	114,780	111.5	18.5	30.2
Agricultural products only ($1,000)	261,488	0.4	375,571	0.5	462,178	0.5	43.6	23.1
Livestock, poultry, and products ($1,000)	798,624	1.0	883,312	1.0	1,155,530	1.2	10.6	30.8
Farms by value of sales:								
Less than $2,500	5,104	1.0	4,868	1.2	5,097	1.0	-4.6	4.7
$2,500 to $4,999	1,802	0.7	1,840	0.8	1,811	0.8	2.1	-1.6
$5,000 to $9,999	1,700	0.6	1,738	0.7	1,710	0.7	2.2	-1.6
$10,000 to $24,999	1,828	0.6	1,852	0.6	1,755	0.6	1.3	-5.2
$25,000 to $49,999	1,234	0.6	1,208	0.6	1,099	0.6	-2.1	-9.0
$50,000 to $99,999	966	0.4	969	0.5	896	0.6	0.3	-7.5
$100,000 or more	1,615	0.5	1,804	0.5	1,726	0.5	11.7	-4.3
Total farm production expenses ($1,000)	892,641	0.8	1,049,010	0.8	1,204,227	0.8	17.5	14.8
Average expenses per farm (dollars)	62,659	121.0	73,465	108.2	85,558	108.6	17.2	16.5
Net cash return for the farm unit:								
Number of farms	14,246	0.7	14,279	0.7	14,075	0.7	0.2	-1.4
Value ($1000)	165,007	0.6	196,574	0.6	410,261	1.0	19.1	108.7
Average per farm (dollars)	11,583	91.5	13,767	87.1	29,148	130.9	18.9	111.7
Operators by principal occupation:								
Farming	7,243	0.6	7,540	0.7	7,197	0.7	4.1	-4.5
Other	7,006	0.7	6,739	0.8	6,897	0.7	-3.8	2.3
Operators by days worked off farm:								
Any	8,137	0.7	7,590	0.8	7,506	0.7	-6.7	-1.1
200 days or more	4,937	0.7	4,673	0.7	4,592	0.6	-5.3	-1.7

Source: *1997 Census of Agriculture*, U.S. Department of Agriculture, National Agricultural Statistics Service. NA stands for "not available." (D) is shown when data are withheld to prevent disclosure of competitive information. A dash (-) is shown where no data were reported. The market value of land and buildings, and of machinery and equipment, is an estimated amount. Net cash return for the farm unit includes only returns from agricultural activities.

LIVESTOCK STATISTICS FOR NEW MEXICO

Item	1987 Value	1987 % of U.S.	1992 Value	1992 % of U.S.	1997 Value	1997 % of U.S.	Percent change 1987-1992	Percent change 1992-1997
Cattle and calves								
Number of farms	8,926	0.8	8,964	0.8	8,677	0.8	0.4	-3.2
Number of animals	1,445,062	1.5	1,589,978	1.7	1,676,171	1.7	10.0	5.4
Beef cows (farms)	6,939	0.8	7,248	0.9	6,894	0.9	4.5	-4.9
Beef cows (number)	572,828	1.8	631,738	1.9	581,812	1.7	10.3	-7.9
Milk cows (farms)	848	0.4	650	0.4	523	0.4	-23.3	-19.5
Milk cows (number)	58,606	0.6	110,422	1.2	215,844	2.4	88.4	95.5
Cattle and calves sold (farms)	8,517	0.7	8,426	0.8	8,094	0.8	-1.1	-3.9
Cattle and calves sold (number)	1,298,570	1.8	1,181,980	1.7	1,308,236	1.8	-9.0	10.7
Hogs and pigs								
Number of farms	592	0.2	496	0.3	346	0.3	-16.2	-30.2
Number of animals	44,248	0.1	20,233	0.0	6,114	0.0	-54.3	-69.8
Hogs and pigs sold (farms)	373	0.2	326	0.2	246	0.2	-12.6	-24.5
Hogs and pigs sold (number)	89,200	0.1	43,633	0.0	7,997	0.0	-51.1	-81.7
Sheep and lambs								
Number of farms	1,363	1.5	1,156	1.4	917	1.4	-15.2	-20.7
Number of animals	468,264	4.2	460,700	4.3	291,808	3.7	-1.6	-36.7
Layers and pullets 13 weeks old and older								
Number of farms	1,363	0.9	899	1.0	669	0.9	-34.0	-25.6
Number of birds	(D)	-	1,363,949	0.4	(D)	-	-	-
Broilers and other meat-type chickens sold								
Number of farms	19	0.1	20	0.1	11	0.0	5.3	-45.0
Number of birds sold	(D)	-	2,026	0.0	(D)	-	-	-

Source: 1997 Census of Agriculture, U.S. Department of Agriculture, National Agricultural Statistics Service. NA stands for "not available." (D) is shown when data are withheld to prevent disclosure of competitive information. A dash (-) is shown where no data were reported.

CROP STATISTICS FOR NEW MEXICO

Item	1987 Value	1987 % of U.S.	1992 Value	1992 % of U.S.	1997 Value	1997 % of U.S.	Percent change 1987-1992	Percent change 1992-1997
Corn for grain or seed								
Number of farms	434	0.1	398	0.1	316	0.1	-8.3	-20.6
Number of acres	37,540	0.1	72,348	0.1	80,122	0.1	92.7	10.7
Number of bushels	5,300,378	-	11,773,777	0.1	13,795,021	0.2	122.1	17.2
Corn for silage or green chop								
Number of farms	-	-	-	-	-	-	-	-
Number of acres	-	-	-	-	-	-	-	-
Weight in tons, green	-	-	-	-	-	-	-	-
Sorghum for grain or seed								
Number of farms	776	-	568	-	496	-	-26.8	-12.7
Number of acres	156,979	-	180,421	-	188,615	-	14.9	4.5
Number of bushels	8,680,130	-	8,144,520	-	7,059,484	-	-6.2	-13.3
Wheat for grain								
Number of farms	1,229	0.3	892	0.3	711	0.3	-27.4	-20.3
Number of acres	309,184	0.6	341,016	0.6	264,190	0.4	10.3	-22.5
Number of bushels	8,820,030	0.5	10,433,609	0.5	8,605,057	0.4	18.3	-17.5
Barley for grain								
Number of farms	-	-	-	-	-	-	-	-
Number of acres	-	-	-	-	-	-	-	-
Number of bushels	-	-	-	-	-	-	-	-
Oats for grain								
Number of farms	-	-	-	-	-	-	-	-
Number of acres	-	-	-	-	-	-	-	-
Number of bushels	-	-	-	-	-	-	-	-
Rice								
Number of farms	-	-	-	-	-	-	-	-
Number of acres	-	-	-	-	-	-	-	-
Weight in hundredweight	-	-	-	-	-	-	-	-
Sunflower seed								
Number of farms	-	-	-	-	-	-	-	-
Number of acres	-	-	-	-	-	-	-	-
Weight in pounds	-	-	-	-	-	-	-	-
Cotton								
Number of farms	697	1.6	459	1.3	459	1.5	-34.1	-
Number of acres	79,135	0.8	53,393	0.5	67,996	0.5	-32.5	27.4
Number of bales	113,013	0.9	74,954	0.5	113,281	0.6	-33.7	51.1

Continued.

CROP STATISTICS FOR NEW MEXICO - Continued

Item	1987 Value	1987 % of U.S.	1992 Value	1992 % of U.S.	1997 Value	1997 % of U.S.	Percent change 1987-1992	Percent change 1992-1997
Tobacco								
Number of farms	-	-	-	-	-	-	-	-
Number of acres	-	-	-	-	-	-	-	-
Weight in pounds	-	-	-	-	-	-	-	-
Soybeans for beans								
Number of farms	-	-	-	-	-	-	-	-
Number of acres	-	-	-	-	-	-	-	-
Number of bushels	-	-	-	-	-	-	-	-
Dry edible beans, excluding dry limas								
Number of farms	-	-	-	-	-	-	-	-
Number of acres	-	-	-	-	-	-	-	-
Weight in hundredweight	-	-	-	-	-	-	-	-
Potatoes, excluding sweetpotatoes								
Number of farms	-	-	-	-	-	-	-	-
Number of acres	-	-	-	-	-	-	-	-
Weight in hundredweight	-	-	-	-	-	-	-	-
Sugar beets for sugar								
Number of farms	-	-	-	-	-	-	-	-
Number of acres	-	-	-	-	-	-	-	-
Weight in tons	-	-	-	-	-	-	-	-
Sugarcane for sugar								
Number of farms	-	-	-	-	-	-	-	-
Number of acres	-	-	-	-	-	-	-	-
Weight in tons	-	-	-	-	-	-	-	-
Pineapples harvested								
Number of farms	-	-	-	-	-	-	-	-
Number of acres	-	-	-	-	-	-	-	-
Weight in tons	-	-	-	-	-	-	-	-
Peanuts for nuts								
Number of farms	-	-	-	-	-	-	-	-
Number of acres	-	-	-	-	-	-	-	-
Weight in pounds	-	-	-	-	-	-	-	-
Hay - all types, including alfalfa								
Number of farms	4,830	0.5	4,502	0.5	4,616	0.5	-6.8	2.5
Number of acres	276,861	0.5	267,507	0.5	318,213	0.5	-3.4	19.0
Weight in tons, dry	960,735	0.7	934,026	0.7	1,207,842	0.9	-2.8	29.3
Vegetables harvested for sale								
Number of farms	-	-	-	-	-	-	-	-
Number of acres	-	-	-	-	-	-	-	-
Land in orchards								
Number of farms	1,526	1.3	1,885	1.6	1,744	1.6	23.5	-7.5
Number of acres	28,529	0.6	31,648	0.7	33,600	0.7	10.9	6.2

Source: 1997 Census of Agriculture, U.S. Department of Agriculture, National Agricultural Statistics Service. NA stands for "not available." (D) is shown when data are withheld to prevent disclosure of competitive information. A dash (-) is shown where no data were reported. Not all states report growing all crops, but all crop categories in the census are shown for every state. The data series used for this presentation did not report U.S. totals for a number of categories; for that reason, the "% of U.S." column is sometimes blank.

NEW YORK

GENERAL STATISTICS FOR NEW YORK

Item	1987 Value	1987 % of U.S.	1992 Value	1992 % of U.S.	1997 Value	1997 % of U.S.	Percent change 1987-1992	Percent change 1992-1997
Farms (number)	37,743	1.8	32,306	1.7	31,757	1.7	-14.4	-1.7
Land in farms (acres)	8,416,228	0.9	7,458,015	0.8	7,254,470	0.8	-11.4	-2.7
Average size of farm (acres)	223	48.3	231	47.0	228	46.8	3.6	-1.3
Median size of farm (acres)	NA	-	NA	-	131	109.2	-	-
Market value of land and buildings:								
Average per farm (dollars)	218,934	75.7	282,546	79.1	286,620	63.7	29.1	1.4
Average per acre (dollars)	993	158.4	1,237	170.2	1,284	137.6	24.6	3.8
Market value of machinery/equipment - average per farm (dollars)	49,087	119.1	57,738	118.8	59,923	103.9	17.6	3.8
Farms by size:								
1 to 9 acres	2,517	1.4	2,129	1.3	2,226	1.5	-15.4	4.6
10 to 49 acres	6,114	1.5	5,201	1.3	5,499	1.3	-14.9	5.7
50 to 179 acres	12,991	2.0	11,147	1.9	11,319	1.9	-14.2	1.5
180 to 499 acres	12,244	2.6	10,305	2.4	9,327	2.3	-15.8	-9.5
500 to 999 acres	3,112	1.6	2,713	1.5	2,530	1.4	-12.8	-6.7
1,000 acres or more	765	0.5	811	0.5	856	0.5	6.0	5.5
Total cropland								
Farms	35,680	1.9	30,651	1.8	29,747	1.8	-14.1	-2.9
Acres	5,382,175	1.2	4,876,169	1.1	4,722,143	1.1	-9.4	-3.2
Harvested cropland (farms)	33,664	2.0	28,715	1.9	27,569	2.0	-14.7	-4.0
Harvested cropland (acres)	3,899,819	1.4	3,534,898	1.2	3,716,942	1.2	-9.4	5.1
Irrigated land (farms)	1,992	0.7	2,020	0.7	2,501	0.9	1.4	23.8
Irrigated land (acres)	50,920	0.1	46,600	0.1	69,197	0.1	-8.5	48.5
Market value of agricultural products sold:								
Total sales ($1,000)	2,441,860	1.8	2,622,001	1.6	2,834,512	1.4	7.4	8.1
Average per farm (dollars)	64,697	99.3	81,161	96.1	89,256	86.7	25.4	10.0
Agricultural products only ($1,000)	701,352	1.2	809,291	1.1	1,000,417	1.0	15.4	23.6
Livestock, poultry, and products ($1,000)	1,740,508	2.3	1,812,710	2.1	1,834,095	1.9	4.1	1.2
Farms by value of sales:								
Less than $2,500	9,168	1.9	7,324	1.7	7,707	1.6	-20.1	5.2
$2,500 to $4,999	4,061	1.5	3,389	1.5	3,424	1.5	-16.5	1.0
$5,000 to $9,999	3,892	1.4	3,536	1.4	3,484	1.5	-9.1	-1.5
$10,000 to $24,999	4,426	1.4	4,156	1.4	4,269	1.6	-6.1	2.7
$25,000 to $49,999	3,337	1.5	2,601	1.3	2,673	1.6	-22.1	2.8
$50,000 to $99,999	5,560	2.5	3,973	2.1	3,335	2.1	-28.5	-16.1
$100,000 or more	7,299	2.5	7,327	2.2	6,865	2.0	0.4	-6.3
Total farm production expenses ($1,000)	1,897,458	1.8	2,142,169	1.6	2,191,903	1.5	12.9	2.3
Average expenses per farm (dollars)	50,277	97.1	66,294	97.6	68,906	87.5	31.9	3.9
Net cash return for the farm unit:								
Number of farms	37,740	1.8	32,313	1.7	31,810	1.7	-14.4	-1.6
Value ($1000)	516,679	2.0	456,371	1.5	514,724	1.2	-11.7	12.8
Average per farm (dollars)	13,690	108.1	14,123	89.4	16,181	72.7	3.2	14.6
Operators by principal occupation:								
Farming	22,977	2.0	19,934	1.9	18,426	1.9	-13.2	-7.6
Other	14,766	1.6	12,372	1.4	13,331	1.4	-16.2	7.8
Operators by days worked off farm:								
Any	17,596	1.6	14,472	1.5	15,286	1.5	-17.8	5.6
200 days or more	11,506	1.6	9,355	1.4	9,886	1.4	-18.7	5.7

Source: 1997 Census of Agriculture, U.S. Department of Agriculture, National Agricultural Statistics Service. NA stands for "not available." (D) is shown when data are withheld to prevent disclosure of competitive information. A dash (-) is shown where no data were reported. The market value of land and buildings, and of machinery and equipment, is an estimated amount. Net cash return for the farm unit includes only returns from agricultural activities.

LIVESTOCK STATISTICS FOR NEW YORK

Item	1987 Value	1987 % of U.S.	1992 Value	1992 % of U.S.	1997 Value	1997 % of U.S.	Percent change 1987-1992	Percent change 1992-1997
Cattle and calves								
Number of farms	22,250	1.9	18,134	1.7	16,444	1.6	-18.5	-9.3
Number of animals	1,603,390	1.7	1,470,610	1.5	1,450,090	1.5	-8.3	-1.4
Beef cows (farms)	6,798	0.8	5,880	0.7	6,160	0.8	-13.5	4.8
Beef cows (number)	71,627	0.2	72,971	0.2	86,078	0.3	1.9	18.0
Milk cows (farms)	13,840	6.8	10,696	6.9	8,732	7.5	-22.7	-18.4
Milk cows (number)	814,461	8.1	721,286	7.6	700,480	7.7	-11.4	-2.9
Cattle and calves sold (farms)	21,153	1.8	17,167	1.7	15,494	1.5	-18.8	-9.7
Cattle and calves sold (number)	754,488	1.0	639,193	0.9	618,039	0.8	-15.3	-3.3
Hogs and pigs								
Number of farms	2,644	1.1	2,094	1.1	1,508	1.4	-20.8	-28.0
Number of animals	99,560	0.2	90,282	0.2	79,000	0.1	-9.3	-12.5
Hogs and pigs sold (farms)	1,957	0.8	1,498	0.8	1,001	1.0	-23.5	-33.2
Hogs and pigs sold (number)	172,072	0.2	168,196	0.2	167,201	0.1	-2.3	-0.6
Sheep and lambs								
Number of farms	1,943	2.1	1,705	2.1	1,515	2.3	-12.2	-11.1
Number of animals	76,447	0.7	76,682	0.7	61,440	0.8	0.3	-19.9
Layers and pullets 13 weeks old and older								
Number of farms	3,236	2.2	2,088	2.4	1,909	2.6	-35.5	-8.6
Number of birds	5,455,879	1.5	4,538,622	1.3	4,393,064	1.2	-16.8	-3.2
Broilers and other meat-type chickens sold								
Number of farms	206	0.7	142	0.6	172	0.7	-31.1	21.1
Number of birds sold	1,713,646	0.0	1,042,100	0.0	1,310,733	0.0	-39.2	25.8

Source: 1997 Census of Agriculture, U.S. Department of Agriculture, National Agricultural Statistics Service. NA stands for "not available." (D) is shown when data are withheld to prevent disclosure of competitive information. A dash (-) is shown where no data were reported.

CROP STATISTICS FOR NEW YORK

Item	1987 Value	1987 % of U.S.	1992 Value	1992 % of U.S.	1997 Value	1997 % of U.S.	Percent change 1987-1992	Percent change 1992-1997
Corn for grain or seed								
Number of farms	9,301	1.5	5,724	1.1	5,493	1.3	-38.5	-4.0
Number of acres	598,815	1.0	518,839	0.7	578,715	0.8	-13.4	11.5
Number of bushels	65,911,889	-	47,702,382	0.5	62,242,783	0.7	-27.6	30.5
Corn for silage or green chop								
Number of farms	11,920	-	9,862	-	8,250	-	-17.3	-16.3
Number of acres	525,458	-	544,045	-	551,365	-	3.5	1.3
Weight in tons, green	7,625,970	-	7,299,613	-	8,235,781	-	-4.3	12.8
Sorghum for grain or seed								
Number of farms	-	-	-	-	-	-	-	-
Number of acres	-	-	-	-	-	-	-	-
Number of bushels	-	-	-	-	-	-	-	-
Wheat for grain								
Number of farms	-	-	-	-	-	-	-	-
Number of acres	-	-	-	-	-	-	-	-
Number of bushels	-	-	-	-	-	-	-	-
Barley for grain								
Number of farms	-	-	-	-	-	-	-	-
Number of acres	-	-	-	-	-	-	-	-
Number of bushels	-	-	-	-	-	-	-	-
Oats for grain								
Number of farms	6,364	-	4,059	-	2,808	-	-36.2	-30.8
Number of acres	162,733	-	109,686	-	77,240	-	-32.6	-29.6
Number of bushels	9,562,189	-	6,889,878	-	4,841,802	-	-27.9	-29.7
Rice								
Number of farms	-	-	-	-	-	-	-	-
Number of acres	-	-	-	-	-	-	-	-
Weight in hundredweight	-	-	-	-	-	-	-	-
Sunflower seed								
Number of farms	-	-	-	-	-	-	-	-
Number of acres	-	-	-	-	-	-	-	-
Weight in pounds	-	-	-	-	-	-	-	-
Cotton								
Number of farms	-	-	-	-	-	-	-	-
Number of acres	-	-	-	-	-	-	-	-
Number of bales	-	-	-	-	-	-	-	-

Continued.

CROP STATISTICS FOR NEW YORK - Continued

Item	1987		1992		1997		Percent change	
	Value	% of U.S.	Value	% of U.S.	Value	% of U.S.	1987-1992	1992-1997
Tobacco								
Number of farms	-	-	-	-	-	-	-	-
Number of acres	-	-	-	-	-	-	-	-
Weight in pounds	-	-	-	-	-	-	-	-
Soybeans for beans								
Number of farms	-	-	-	-	-	-	-	-
Number of acres	-	-	-	-	-	-	-	-
Number of bushels	-	-	-	-	-	-	-	-
Dry edible beans, excluding dry limas								
Number of farms	-	-	-	-	-	-	-	-
Number of acres	-	-	-	-	-	-	-	-
Weight in hundredweight	-	-	-	-	-	-	-	-
Potatoes, excluding sweetpotatoes								
Number of farms	602	-	587	-	544	-	-2.5	-7.3
Number of acres	35,682	-	28,861	-	23,920	-	-19.1	-17.1
Weight in hundredweight	9,004,962	-	7,023,100	-	6,611,891	-	-22.0	-5.9
Sugar beets for sugar								
Number of farms	-	-	-	-	-	-	-	-
Number of acres	-	-	-	-	-	-	-	-
Weight in tons	-	-	-	-	-	-	-	-
Sugarcane for sugar								
Number of farms	-	-	-	-	-	-	-	-
Number of acres	-	-	-	-	-	-	-	-
Weight in tons	-	-	-	-	-	-	-	-
Pineapples harvested								
Number of farms	-	-	-	-	-	-	-	-
Number of acres	-	-	-	-	-	-	-	-
Weight in tons	-	-	-	-	-	-	-	-
Peanuts for nuts								
Number of farms	-	-	-	-	-	-	-	-
Number of acres	-	-	-	-	-	-	-	-
Weight in pounds	-	-	-	-	-	-	-	-
Hay - all types, including alfalfa								
Number of farms	26,877	2.7	22,376	2.5	20,805	2.3	-16.7	-7.0
Number of acres	2,259,119	3.9	2,013,646	3.6	2,073,486	3.4	-10.9	3.0
Weight in tons, dry	4,861,661	3.8	4,268,674	3.4	4,035,722	2.9	-12.2	-5.5
Vegetables harvested for sale								
Number of farms	2,822	4.6	2,758	4.5	2,720	5.1	-2.3	-1.4
Number of acres	150,054	4.3	139,841	3.7	169,331	4.5	-6.8	21.1
Land in orchards								
Number of farms	3,290	2.7	2,938	2.5	2,436	2.3	-10.7	-17.1
Number of acres	124,432	2.7	112,905	2.4	101,628	2.0	-9.3	-10.0

Source: *1997 Census of Agriculture*, U.S. Department of Agriculture, National Agricultural Statistics Service. NA stands for "not available." (D) is shown when data are withheld to prevent disclosure of competitive information. A dash (-) is shown where no data were reported. Not all states report growing all crops, but all crop categories in the census are shown for every state. The data series used for this presentation did not report U.S. totals for a number of categories; for that reason, the "% of U.S." column is sometimes blank.

NORTH CAROLINA

GENERAL STATISTICS FOR NORTH CAROLINA

Item	1987 Value	1987 % of U.S.	1992 Value	1992 % of U.S.	1997 Value	1997 % of U.S.	Percent change 1987-1992	Percent change 1992-1997
Farms (number)	59,284	2.8	51,854	2.7	49,406	2.6	-12.5	-4.7
Land in farms (acres)	9,447,705	1.0	8,936,015	0.9	9,122,379	1.0	-5.4	2.1
Average size of farm (acres)	159	34.4	172	35.0	185	38.0	8.2	7.6
Median size of farm (acres)	NA	-	NA	-	69	57.5	-	-
Market value of land and buildings:								
Average per farm (dollars)	199,781	69.0	269,000	75.3	375,895	83.6	34.6	39.7
Average per acre (dollars)	1,263	201.4	1,573	216.4	2,081	223.0	24.5	32.3
Market value of machinery/equipment - average per farm (dollars)	30,403	73.7	38,452	79.1	49,106	85.1	26.5	27.7
Farms by size:								
1 to 9 acres	5,253	2.9	4,651	2.8	3,968	2.6	-11.5	-14.7
10 to 49 acres	18,088	4.4	15,852	4.1	15,601	3.8	-12.4	-1.6
50 to 179 acres	22,680	3.5	19,366	3.3	18,259	3.1	-14.6	-5.7
180 to 499 acres	9,337	2.0	8,007	1.9	7,506	1.9	-14.2	-6.3
500 to 999 acres	2,676	1.3	2,564	1.4	2,461	1.4	-4.2	-4.0
1,000 acres or more	1,250	0.7	1,414	0.8	1,611	0.9	13.1	13.9
Total cropland								
Farms	54,972	3.0	47,497	2.8	44,502	2.7	-13.6	-6.3
Acres	5,716,256	1.3	5,578,191	1.3	5,608,388	1.3	-2.4	0.5
Harvested cropland (farms)	50,108	3.0	42,135	2.8	38,241	2.7	-15.9	-9.2
Harvested cropland (acres)	3,779,164	1.3	3,998,685	1.4	4,233,693	1.4	5.8	5.9
Irrigated land (farms)	6,445	2.2	4,337	1.6	4,695	1.7	-32.7	8.3
Irrigated land (acres)	137,858	0.3	112,630	0.2	156,250	0.3	-18.3	38.7
Market value of agricultural products sold:								
Total sales ($1,000)	3,541,419	2.6	4,834,218	3.0	7,676,523	3.9	36.5	58.8
Average per farm (dollars)	59,737	91.7	93,227	110.4	155,376	150.9	56.1	66.7
Agricultural products only ($1,000)	1,436,988	2.4	1,996,452	2.7	2,595,213	2.6	38.9	30.0
Livestock, poultry, and products ($1,000)	2,104,430	2.7	2,837,765	3.2	5,081,310	5.1	34.8	79.1
Farms by value of sales:								
Less than $2,500	16,758	3.4	12,616	3.0	13,653	2.7	-24.7	8.2
$2,500 to $4,999	8,461	3.2	7,250	3.1	6,642	2.9	-14.3	-8.4
$5,000 to $9,999	8,344	3.0	6,968	2.8	6,261	2.6	-16.5	-10.1
$10,000 to $24,999	8,515	2.6	7,641	2.5	6,470	2.4	-10.3	-15.3
$25,000 to $49,999	4,817	2.2	4,397	2.3	3,470	2.0	-8.7	-21.1
$50,000 to $99,999	4,271	2.0	3,640	1.9	2,764	1.7	-14.8	-24.1
$100,000 or more	8,118	2.7	9,342	2.8	10,146	2.9	15.1	8.6
Total farm production expenses ($1,000)	2,779,353	2.6	3,817,833	2.9	5,673,379	3.8	37.4	48.6
Average expenses per farm (dollars)	46,879	90.5	73,621	108.4	114,885	145.8	57.0	56.0
Net cash return for the farm unit:								
Number of farms	59,288	2.8	51,858	2.7	49,391	2.6	-12.5	-4.8
Value ($1000)	688,217	2.6	912,136	3.0	1,601,413	3.8	32.5	75.6
Average per farm (dollars)	11,608	91.7	17,589	111.3	32,423	145.7	51.5	84.3
Operators by principal occupation:								
Farming	30,687	2.7	27,376	2.6	24,355	2.5	-10.8	-11.0
Other	28,597	3.0	24,478	2.8	25,051	2.6	-14.4	2.3
Operators by days worked off farm:								
Any	31,914	2.9	25,958	2.6	25,856	2.5	-18.7	-0.4
200 days or more	21,702	2.9	17,989	2.7	18,028	2.5	-17.1	0.2

Source: 1997 Census of Agriculture, U.S. Department of Agriculture, National Agricultural Statistics Service. NA stands for "not available." (D) is shown when data are withheld to prevent disclosure of competitive information. A dash (-) is shown where no data were reported. The market value of land and buildings, and of machinery and equipment, is an estimated amount. Net cash return for the farm unit includes only returns from agricultural activities.

LIVESTOCK STATISTICS FOR NORTH CAROLINA

Item	1987		1992		1997		Percent change	
	Value	% of U.S.	Value	% of U.S.	Value	% of U.S.	1987-1992	1992-1997
Cattle and calves								
Number of farms	24,985	2.1	22,718	2.1	22,632	2.2	-9.1	-0.4
Number of animals	784,136	0.8	901,980	0.9	941,311	1.0	15.0	4.4
Beef cows (farms)	20,630	2.5	19,531	2.4	19,616	2.4	-5.3	0.4
Beef cows (number)	320,641	1.0	385,428	1.2	435,672	1.3	20.2	13.0
Milk cows (farms)	2,336	1.2	1,552	1.0	1,092	0.9	-33.6	-29.6
Milk cows (number)	110,127	1.1	99,291	1.0	78,400	0.9	-9.8	-21.0
Cattle and calves sold (farms)	22,682	2.0	20,771	2.0	21,286	2.1	-8.4	2.5
Cattle and calves sold (number)	395,732	0.5	399,035	0.6	443,147	0.6	0.8	11.1
Hogs and pigs								
Number of farms	6,921	2.8	4,311	2.3	2,986	2.7	-37.7	-30.7
Number of animals	2,547,127	4.9	5,100,979	8.9	9,624,860	15.7	100.3	88.7
Hogs and pigs sold (farms)	6,290	2.6	4,012	2.1	2,666	2.6	-36.2	-33.5
Hogs and pigs sold (number)	5,180,960	5.4	10,776,400	9.7	36,431,039	25.5	108.0	238.1
Sheep and lambs								
Number of farms	542	0.6	574	0.7	613	0.9	5.9	6.8
Number of animals	15,820	0.1	19,546	0.2	13,827	0.2	23.6	-29.3
Layers and pullets 13 weeks old and older								
Number of farms	3,330	2.3	2,064	2.3	1,726	2.4	-38.0	-16.4
Number of birds	20,070,337	5.4	18,133,946	5.2	16,162,563	4.4	-9.6	-10.9
Broilers and other meat-type chickens sold								
Number of farms	2,153	7.8	2,116	8.8	2,086	8.7	-1.7	-1.4
Number of birds sold	408,721,082	6.1	499,071,743	9.2	591,248,423	8.8	22.1	18.5

Source: 1997 Census of Agriculture, U.S. Department of Agriculture, National Agricultural Statistics Service. NA stands for "not available." (D) is shown when data are withheld to prevent disclosure of competitive information. A dash (-) is shown where no data were reported.

CROP STATISTICS FOR NORTH CAROLINA

Item	1987		1992		1997		Percent change	
	Value	% of U.S.	Value	% of U.S.	Value	% of U.S.	1987-1992	1992-1997
Corn for grain or seed								
Number of farms	21,000	3.3	13,052	2.6	8,862	2.1	-37.8	-32.1
Number of acres	1,056,000	1.8	1,019,871	1.5	821,039	1.2	-3.4	-19.5
Number of bushels	71,795,021	-	96,617,840	1.1	74,423,999	0.9	34.6	-23.0
Corn for silage or green chop								
Number of farms	-	-	-	-	-	-	-	-
Number of acres	-	-	-	-	-	-	-	-
Weight in tons, green	-	-	-	-	-	-	-	-
Sorghum for grain or seed								
Number of farms	-	-	-	-	-	-	-	-
Number of acres	-	-	-	-	-	-	-	-
Number of bushels	-	-	-	-	-	-	-	-
Wheat for grain								
Number of farms	7,747	2.2	6,883	2.4	5,949	2.4	-11.2	-13.6
Number of acres	378,744	0.7	490,214	0.8	616,397	1.0	29.4	25.7
Number of bushels	15,091,015	0.8	23,164,935	1.0	30,357,728	1.4	53.5	31.1
Barley for grain								
Number of farms	-	-	-	-	-	-	-	-
Number of acres	-	-	-	-	-	-	-	-
Number of bushels	-	-	-	-	-	-	-	-
Oats for grain								
Number of farms	-	-	-	-	-	-	-	-
Number of acres	-	-	-	-	-	-	-	-
Number of bushels	-	-	-	-	-	-	-	-
Rice								
Number of farms	-	-	-	-	-	-	-	-
Number of acres	-	-	-	-	-	-	-	-
Weight in hundredweight	-	-	-	-	-	-	-	-
Sunflower seed								
Number of farms	-	-	-	-	-	-	-	-
Number of acres	-	-	-	-	-	-	-	-
Weight in pounds	-	-	-	-	-	-	-	-
Cotton								
Number of farms	981	2.3	2,035	5.8	2,320	7.4	107.4	14.0
Number of acres	94,186	1.0	357,766	3.3	677,541	5.1	279.9	89.4
Number of bales	93,720	0.7	445,466	2.9	916,278	5.1	375.3	105.7

Continued.

CROP STATISTICS FOR NORTH CAROLINA - Continued

Item	1987		1992		1997		Percent change	
	Value	% of U.S.	Value	% of U.S.	Value	% of U.S.	1987-1992	1992-1997
Tobacco								
Number of farms	22,260	-	17,625	-	12,095	-	-20.8	-31.4
Number of acres	239,343	-	283,900	-	320,599	-	18.6	12.9
Weight in pounds	478,051,423	-	604,014,807	-	703,559,462	-	26.3	16.5
Soybeans for beans								
Number of farms	17,409	3.9	13,080	3.4	9,933	2.8	-24.9	-24.1
Number of acres	1,273,278	2.3	1,287,573	2.3	1,280,412	1.9	1.1	-0.6
Number of bushels	31,368,069	1.7	34,176,793	1.7	35,785,336	1.4	9.0	4.7
Dry edible beans, excluding dry limas								
Number of farms	-	-	-	-	-	-	-	-
Number of acres	-	-	-	-	-	-	-	-
Weight in hundredweight	-	-	-	-	-	-	-	-
Potatoes, excluding sweetpotatoes								
Number of farms	-	-	-	-	-	-	-	-
Number of acres	-	-	-	-	-	-	-	-
Weight in hundredweight	-	-	-	-	-	-	-	-
Sugar beets for sugar								
Number of farms	-	-	-	-	-	-	-	-
Number of acres	-	-	-	-	-	-	-	-
Weight in tons	-	-	-	-	-	-	-	-
Sugarcane for sugar								
Number of farms	-	-	-	-	-	-	-	-
Number of acres	-	-	-	-	-	-	-	-
Weight in tons	-	-	-	-	-	-	-	-
Pineapples harvested								
Number of farms	-	-	-	-	-	-	-	-
Number of acres	-	-	-	-	-	-	-	-
Weight in tons	-	-	-	-	-	-	-	-
Peanuts for nuts								
Number of farms	3,038	-	2,371	-	1,765	-	-22.0	-25.6
Number of acres	144,682	-	149,210	-	122,784	-	3.1	-17.7
Weight in pounds	379,952,977	-	398,611,000	-	325,662,397	-	4.9	-18.3
Hay - all types, including alfalfa								
Number of farms	20,733	2.1	18,268	2.0	19,761	2.2	-11.9	8.2
Number of acres	456,360	0.8	466,944	0.8	602,755	1.0	2.3	29.1
Weight in tons, dry	795,954	0.6	922,347	0.7	1,218,338	0.9	15.9	32.1
Vegetables harvested for sale								
Number of farms	-	-	-	-	-	-	-	-
Number of acres	-	-	-	-	-	-	-	-
Land in orchards								
Number of farms	-	-	-	-	-	-	-	-
Number of acres	-	-	-	-	-	-	-	-

Source: 1997 Census of Agriculture, U.S. Department of Agriculture, National Agricultural Statistics Service. NA stands for "not available." (D) is shown when data are withheld to prevent disclosure of competitive information. A dash (-) is shown where no data were reported. Not all states report growing all crops, but all crop categories in the census are shown for every state. The data series used for this presentation did not report U.S. totals for a number of categories; for that reason, the "% of U.S." column is sometimes blank.

NORTH DAKOTA

GENERAL STATISTICS FOR NORTH DAKOTA

Item	1987 Value	1987 % of U.S.	1992 Value	1992 % of U.S.	1997 Value	1997 % of U.S.	Percent change 1987-1992	Percent change 1992-1997
Farms (number)	35,289	1.7	31,123	1.6	30,504	1.6	-11.8	-2.0
Land in farms (acres)	40,336,869	4.2	39,438,144	4.2	39,359,346	4.2	-2.2	-0.2
Average size of farm (acres)	1,143	247.4	1,267	258.0	1,290	264.9	10.8	1.8
Median size of farm (acres)	NA	-	NA	-	844	703.3	-	-
Market value of land and buildings:								
Average per farm (dollars)	366,475	126.6	422,936	118.5	512,734	114.0	15.4	21.2
Average per acre (dollars)	319	50.9	335	46.1	401	43.0	5.0	19.7
Market value of machinery/equipment - average per farm (dollars)	77,505	188.0	87,290	179.6	112,015	194.2	12.6	28.3
Farms by size:								
1 to 9 acres	876	0.5	785	0.5	545	0.4	-10.4	-30.6
10 to 49 acres	1,596	0.4	1,264	0.3	1,420	0.3	-20.8	12.3
50 to 179 acres	3,025	0.5	2,945	0.5	3,573	0.6	-2.6	21.3
180 to 499 acres	6,148	1.3	4,985	1.2	5,459	1.4	-18.9	9.5
500 to 999 acres	8,637	4.3	6,714	3.6	5,867	3.3	-22.3	-12.6
1,000 acres or more	15,007	8.9	14,430	8.3	13,640	7.7	-3.8	-5.5
Total cropland								
Farms	33,179	1.8	28,967	1.7	27,994	1.7	-12.7	-3.4
Acres	28,208,099	6.4	27,469,875	6.3	27,024,895	6.3	-2.6	-1.6
Harvested cropland (farms)	32,360	2.0	27,804	1.9	25,153	1.8	-14.1	-9.5
Harvested cropland (acres)	18,363,910	6.5	19,216,531	6.5	20,438,149	6.6	4.6	6.4
Irrigated land (farms)	809	0.3	816	0.3	710	0.3	0.9	-13.0
Irrigated land (acres)	168,013	0.4	187,212	0.4	180,362	0.3	11.4	-3.7
Market value of agricultural products sold:								
Total sales ($1,000)	2,188,158	1.6	2,745,752	1.7	2,869,322	1.5	25.5	4.5
Average per farm (dollars)	62,007	95.2	88,223	104.5	94,064	91.4	42.3	6.6
Agricultural products only ($1,000)	1,497,212	2.5	2,030,900	2.7	2,193,672	2.2	35.6	8.0
Livestock, poultry, and products ($1,000)	690,946	0.9	714,852	0.8	675,649	0.7	3.5	-5.5
Farms by value of sales:								
Less than $2,500	2,260	0.5	2,139	0.5	4,164	0.8	-5.4	94.7
$2,500 to $4,999	1,750	0.7	1,363	0.6	1,313	0.6	-22.1	-3.7
$5,000 to $9,999	2,982	1.1	2,191	0.9	2,104	0.9	-26.5	-4.0
$10,000 to $24,999	6,817	2.1	4,851	1.6	4,365	1.6	-28.8	-10.0
$25,000 to $49,999	7,725	3.5	5,399	2.8	4,558	2.7	-30.1	-15.6
$50,000 to $99,999	7,808	3.6	6,502	3.5	5,341	3.4	-16.7	-17.9
$100,000 or more	5,947	2.0	8,678	2.6	8,659	2.5	45.9	-0.2
Total farm production expenses ($1,000)	1,846,305	1.7	2,090,938	1.6	2,453,342	1.6	13.2	17.3
Average expenses per farm (dollars)	52,312	101.0	67,181	98.9	80,453	102.1	28.4	19.8
Net cash return for the farm unit:								
Number of farms	35,294	1.7	31,124	1.6	30,494	1.6	-11.8	-2.0
Value ($1000)	332,673	1.3	652,308	2.1	399,832	0.9	96.1	-38.7
Average per farm (dollars)	9,426	74.5	20,958	132.6	13,112	58.9	122.3	-37.4
Operators by principal occupation:								
Farming	29,031	2.6	25,189	2.4	22,677	2.4	-13.2	-10.0
Other	6,258	0.7	5,934	0.7	7,827	0.8	-5.2	31.9
Operators by days worked off farm:								
Any	13,137	1.2	11,827	1.2	12,837	1.2	-10.0	8.5
200 days or more	5,295	0.7	4,916	0.7	6,135	0.9	-7.2	24.8

Source: *1997 Census of Agriculture*, U.S. Department of Agriculture, National Agricultural Statistics Service. NA stands for "not available." (D) is shown when data are withheld to prevent disclosure of competitive information. A dash (-) is shown where no data were reported. The market value of land and buildings, and of machinery and equipment, is an estimated amount. Net cash return for the farm unit includes only returns from agricultural activities.

LIVESTOCK STATISTICS FOR NORTH DAKOTA

Item	1987		1992		1997		Percent change	
	Value	% of U.S.	Value	% of U.S.	Value	% of U.S.	1987-1992	1992-1997
Cattle and calves								
Number of farms	17,154	1.5	15,183	1.4	14,232	1.4	-11.5	-6.3
Number of animals	1,873,839	2.0	1,723,920	1.8	1,810,409	1.8	-8.0	5.0
Beef cows (farms)	14,414	1.7	13,216	1.6	12,744	1.6	-8.3	-3.6
Beef cows (number)	886,585	2.8	837,716	2.6	920,559	2.7	-5.5	9.9
Milk cows (farms)	2,839	1.4	1,925	1.2	1,170	1.0	-32.2	-39.2
Milk cows (number)	96,366	1.0	74,885	0.8	54,024	0.6	-22.3	-27.9
Cattle and calves sold (farms)	17,428	1.5	15,249	1.5	14,426	1.4	-12.5	-5.4
Cattle and calves sold (number)	1,106,924	1.5	978,947	1.4	1,055,343	1.4	-11.6	7.8
Hogs and pigs								
Number of farms	2,365	1.0	1,932	1.0	797	0.7	-18.3	-58.7
Number of animals	294,427	0.6	346,082	0.6	197,372	0.3	17.5	-43.0
Hogs and pigs sold (farms)	2,412	1.0	2,033	1.1	814	0.8	-15.7	-60.0
Hogs and pigs sold (number)	500,107	0.5	603,910	0.5	374,733	0.3	20.8	-37.9
Sheep and lambs								
Number of farms	1,623	1.8	1,623	2.0	1,101	1.7	-	-32.2
Number of animals	182,038	1.6	217,240	2.0	130,892	1.7	19.3	-39.7
Layers and pullets 13 weeks old and older								
Number of farms	1,670	1.2	838	0.9	549	0.8	-49.8	-34.5
Number of birds	277,614	0.1	278,090	0.1	201,684	0.1	0.2	-27.5
Broilers and other meat-type chickens sold								
Number of farms	305	1.1	160	0.7	83	0.3	-47.5	-48.1
Number of birds sold	52,677	0.0	38,573	0.0	193,401	0.0	-26.8	401.4

Source: *1997 Census of Agriculture*, U.S. Department of Agriculture, National Agricultural Statistics Service. NA stands for "not available." (D) is shown when data are withheld to prevent disclosure of competitive information. A dash (-) is shown where no data were reported.

CROP STATISTICS FOR NORTH DAKOTA

Item	1987		1992		1997		Percent change	
	Value	% of U.S.	Value	% of U.S.	Value	% of U.S.	1987-1992	1992-1997
Corn for grain or seed								
Number of farms	5,313	0.8	3,353	0.7	2,812	0.7	-36.9	-16.1
Number of acres	533,379	0.9	595,347	0.9	578,953	0.8	11.6	-2.8
Number of bushels	46,983,098	-	37,487,419	0.4	54,996,430	0.6	-20.2	46.7
Corn for silage or green chop								
Number of farms	4,284	-	3,443	-	2,024	-	-19.6	-41.2
Number of acres	240,373	-	278,181	-	164,276	-	15.7	-40.9
Weight in tons, green	1,839,022	-	1,714,645	-	1,162,005	-	-6.8	-32.2
Sorghum for grain or seed								
Number of farms	-	-	-	-	-	-	-	-
Number of acres	-	-	-	-	-	-	-	-
Number of bushels	-	-	-	-	-	-	-	-
Wheat for grain								
Number of farms	28,245	8.0	22,918	7.8	19,488	8.0	-18.9	-15.0
Number of acres	8,778,869	16.5	10,627,608	18.0	10,874,126	18.5	21.1	2.3
Number of bushels	248,678,425	13.2	409,882,271	18.6	260,522,260	11.8	64.8	-36.4
Barley for grain								
Number of farms	20,825	-	13,979	-	9,565	-	-32.9	-31.6
Number of acres	2,690,972	-	2,388,696	-	2,178,700	-	-11.2	-8.8
Number of bushels	120,600,254	-	142,747,145	-	98,641,946	-	18.4	-30.9
Oats for grain								
Number of farms	9,748	-	7,843	-	4,937	-	-19.5	-37.1
Number of acres	657,196	-	557,388	-	423,877	-	-15.2	-24.0
Number of bushels	31,162,857	-	33,414,633	-	18,616,546	-	7.2	-44.3
Rice								
Number of farms	-	-	-	-	-	-	-	-
Number of acres	-	-	-	-	-	-	-	-
Weight in hundredweight	-	-	-	-	-	-	-	-
Sunflower seed								
Number of farms	7,043	-	5,287	-	5,069	-	-24.9	-4.1
Number of acres	1,407,115	-	1,130,593	-	1,347,376	-	-19.7	19.2
Weight in pounds	1,916,363,928	-	1,260,442,267	-	1,678,505,673	-	-34.2	33.2
Cotton								
Number of farms	-	-	-	-	-	-	-	-
Number of acres	-	-	-	-	-	-	-	-
Number of bales	-	-	-	-	-	-	-	-

Continued.

CROP STATISTICS FOR NORTH DAKOTA - Continued

Item	1987		1992		1997		Percent change	
	Value	% of U.S.	Value	% of U.S.	Value	% of U.S.	1987-1992	1992-1997
Tobacco								
Number of farms	-	-	-	-	-	-	-	-
Number of acres	-	-	-	-	-	-	-	-
Weight in pounds	-	-	-	-	-	-	-	-
Soybeans for beans								
Number of farms	-	-	-	-	-	-	-	-
Number of acres	-	-	-	-	-	-	-	-
Number of bushels	-	-	-	-	-	-	-	-
Dry edible beans, excluding dry limas								
Number of farms	-	-	-	-	-	-	-	-
Number of acres	-	-	-	-	-	-	-	-
Weight in hundredweight	-	-	-	-	-	-	-	-
Potatoes, excluding sweetpotatoes								
Number of farms	-	-	-	-	-	-	-	-
Number of acres	-	-	-	-	-	-	-	-
Weight in hundredweight	-	-	-	-	-	-	-	-
Sugar beets for sugar								
Number of farms	-	-	-	-	-	-	-	-
Number of acres	-	-	-	-	-	-	-	-
Weight in tons	-	-	-	-	-	-	-	-
Sugarcane for sugar								
Number of farms	-	-	-	-	-	-	-	-
Number of acres	-	-	-	-	-	-	-	-
Weight in tons	-	-	-	-	-	-	-	-
Pineapples harvested								
Number of farms	-	-	-	-	-	-	-	-
Number of acres	-	-	-	-	-	-	-	-
Weight in tons	-	-	-	-	-	-	-	-
Peanuts for nuts								
Number of farms	-	-	-	-	-	-	-	-
Number of acres	-	-	-	-	-	-	-	-
Weight in pounds	-	-	-	-	-	-	-	-
Hay - all types, including alfalfa								
Number of farms	17,956	1.8	15,695	1.7	14,707	1.7	-12.6	-6.3
Number of acres	2,635,435	4.5	2,467,853	4.4	2,702,807	4.4	-6.4	9.5
Weight in tons, dry	4,030,165	3.1	3,267,324	2.6	3,765,662	2.7	-18.9	15.3
Vegetables harvested for sale								
Number of farms	-	-	-	-	-	-	-	-
Number of acres	-	-	-	-	-	-	-	-
Land in orchards								
Number of farms	-	-	-	-	-	-	-	-
Number of acres	-	-	-	-	-	-	-	-

Source: 1997 Census of Agriculture, U.S. Department of Agriculture, National Agricultural Statistics Service. NA stands for "not available." (D) is shown when data are withheld to prevent disclosure of competitive information. A dash (-) is shown where no data were reported. Not all states report growing all crops, but all crop categories in the census are shown for every state. The data series used for this presentation did not report U.S. totals for a number of categories; for that reason, the "% of U.S." column is sometimes blank.

OHIO

GENERAL STATISTICS FOR OHIO

Item	1987 Value	1987 % of U.S.	1992 Value	1992 % of U.S.	1997 Value	1997 % of U.S.	Percent change 1987-1992	Percent change 1992-1997
Farms (number)	79,277	3.8	70,711	3.7	68,591	3.6	-10.8	-3.0
Land in farms (acres)	14,997,381	1.6	14,247,969	1.5	14,103,085	1.5	-5.0	-1.0
Average size of farm (acres)	189	40.9	201	40.9	206	42.3	6.3	2.5
Median size of farm (acres)	NA	-	NA	-	97	80.8	-	-
Market value of land and buildings:								
Average per farm (dollars)	227,341	78.6	291,766	81.7	414,773	92.2	28.3	42.2
Average per acre (dollars)	1,199	191.2	1,456	200.3	2,039	218.5	21.4	40.0
Market value of machinery/equipment - average per farm (dollars)	39,979	97.0	48,982	100.8	57,624	99.9	22.5	17.6
Farms by size:								
1 to 9 acres	6,007	3.3	5,417	3.3	5,271	3.4	-9.8	-2.7
10 to 49 acres	16,688	4.0	15,295	3.9	15,811	3.8	-8.3	3.4
50 to 179 acres	32,074	5.0	27,868	4.8	26,658	4.5	-13.1	-4.3
180 to 499 acres	17,718	3.7	15,283	3.6	14,018	3.5	-13.7	-8.3
500 to 999 acres	5,072	2.5	4,793	2.6	4,587	2.6	-5.5	-4.3
1,000 acres or more	1,718	1.0	2,055	1.2	2,246	1.3	19.6	9.3
Total cropland								
Farms	74,376	4.0	66,353	3.9	63,669	3.8	-10.8	-4.0
Acres	11,920,433	2.7	11,528,727	2.6	11,340,967	2.6	-3.3	-1.6
Harvested cropland (farms)	70,577	4.3	62,535	4.2	58,048	4.1	-11.4	-7.2
Harvested cropland (acres)	9,297,596	3.3	9,790,327	3.3	9,900,570	3.2	5.3	1.1
Irrigated land (farms)	1,562	0.5	1,755	0.6	1,778	0.6	12.4	1.3
Irrigated land (acres)	32,472	0.1	29,479	0.1	33,997	0.1	-9.2	15.3
Market value of agricultural products sold:								
Total sales ($1,000)	3,434,064	2.5	3,914,040	2.4	4,684,277	2.4	14.0	19.7
Average per farm (dollars)	43,317	66.5	55,353	65.5	68,293	66.3	27.8	23.4
Agricultural products only ($1,000)	1,750,783	3.0	2,195,985	2.9	2,827,924	2.9	25.4	28.8
Livestock, poultry, and products ($1,000)	1,683,281	2.2	1,718,055	2.0	1,856,353	1.9	2.1	8.0
Farms by value of sales:								
Less than $2,500	17,263	3.5	13,930	3.3	15,967	3.2	-19.3	14.6
$2,500 to $4,999	10,489	4.0	8,997	3.9	8,105	3.5	-14.2	-9.9
$5,000 to $9,999	11,664	4.2	9,827	3.9	8,645	3.6	-15.7	-12.0
$10,000 to $24,999	14,689	4.5	13,193	4.4	11,444	4.2	-10.2	-13.3
$25,000 to $49,999	8,953	4.1	8,311	4.3	7,538	4.4	-7.2	-9.3
$50,000 to $99,999	7,678	3.5	6,779	3.6	6,150	3.9	-11.7	-9.3
$100,000 or more	8,541	2.9	9,674	2.9	10,742	3.1	13.3	11.0
Total farm production expenses ($1,000)	2,730,026	2.5	3,119,014	2.4	3,608,839	2.4	14.2	15.7
Average expenses per farm (dollars)	34,437	66.5	44,119	64.9	52,614	66.8	28.1	19.3
Net cash return for the farm unit:								
Number of farms	79,276	3.8	70,695	3.7	68,591	3.6	-10.8	-3.0
Value ($1000)	685,358	2.6	787,050	2.6	1,039,324	2.4	14.8	32.1
Average per farm (dollars)	8,645	68.3	11,133	70.5	15,152	68.1	28.8	36.1
Operators by principal occupation:								
Farming	39,569	3.5	34,604	3.3	31,022	3.2	-12.5	-10.4
Other	39,708	4.2	36,107	4.1	37,569	4.0	-9.1	4.0
Operators by days worked off farm:								
Any	46,025	4.1	40,575	4.1	40,955	3.9	-11.8	0.9
200 days or more	32,749	4.4	29,330	4.4	29,742	4.2	-10.4	1.4

Source: 1997 Census of Agriculture, U.S. Department of Agriculture, National Agricultural Statistics Service. NA stands for "not available." (D) is shown when data are withheld to prevent disclosure of competitive information. A dash (-) is shown where no data were reported. The market value of land and buildings, and of machinery and equipment, is an estimated amount. Net cash return for the farm unit includes only returns from agricultural activities.

LIVESTOCK STATISTICS FOR OHIO

Item	1987		1992		1997		Percent change	
	Value	% of U.S.	Value	% of U.S.	Value	% of U.S.	1987-1992	1992-1997
Cattle and calves								
Number of farms	35,123	3.0	29,874	2.8	28,244	2.7	-14.9	-5.5
Number of animals	1,469,662	1.5	1,362,489	1.4	1,282,546	1.3	-7.3	-5.9
Beef cows (farms)	19,417	2.3	16,885	2.1	17,060	2.1	-13.0	1.0
Beef cows (number)	284,646	0.9	272,920	0.8	293,570	0.9	-4.1	7.6
Milk cows (farms)	9,144	4.5	6,980	4.5	5,425	4.6	-23.7	-22.3
Milk cows (number)	347,305	3.4	295,677	3.1	262,834	2.9	-14.9	-11.1
Cattle and calves sold (farms)	33,250	2.9	27,852	2.7	26,278	2.6	-16.2	-5.7
Cattle and calves sold (number)	899,517	1.2	772,063	1.1	711,149	1.0	-14.2	-7.9
Hogs and pigs								
Number of farms	11,421	4.7	9,392	4.9	5,952	5.4	-17.8	-36.6
Number of animals	2,059,174	3.9	1,957,945	3.4	1,700,491	2.8	-4.9	-13.1
Hogs and pigs sold (farms)	11,752	4.9	9,640	5.1	5,938	5.8	-18.0	-38.4
Hogs and pigs sold (number)	3,810,492	3.9	3,936,095	3.5	3,531,228	2.5	3.3	-10.3
Sheep and lambs								
Number of farms	5,491	5.9	4,329	5.4	3,549	5.4	-21.2	-18.0
Number of animals	239,519	2.2	186,444	1.7	134,906	1.7	-22.2	-27.6
Layers and pullets 13 weeks old and older								
Number of farms	5,980	4.1	3,904	4.4	3,190	4.4	-34.7	-18.3
Number of birds	21,244,883	5.7	23,226,113	6.6	29,023,796	7.9	9.3	25.0
Broilers and other meat-type chickens sold								
Number of farms	525	1.9	532	2.2	496	2.1	1.3	-6.8
Number of birds sold	8,967,735	0.1	25,257,739	0.5	41,135,469	0.6	181.7	62.9

Source: *1997 Census of Agriculture*, U.S. Department of Agriculture, National Agricultural Statistics Service. NA stands for "not available." (D) is shown when data are withheld to prevent disclosure of competitive information. A dash (-) is shown where no data were reported.

CROP STATISTICS FOR OHIO

Item	1987		1992		1997		Percent change	
	Value	% of U.S.	Value	% of U.S.	Value	% of U.S.	1987-1992	1992-1997
Corn for grain or seed								
Number of farms	45,702	7.3	37,341	7.4	31,517	7.3	-18.3	-15.6
Number of acres	3,107,822	5.3	3,486,744	5.0	3,378,205	4.8	12.2	-3.1
Number of bushels	355,339,490	-	467,163,760	5.4	429,619,833	5.0	31.5	-8.0
Corn for silage or green chop								
Number of farms	7,263	-	6,725	-	5,526	-	-7.4	-17.8
Number of acres	163,614	-	176,367	-	177,045	-	7.8	0.4
Weight in tons, green	2,691,928	-	2,969,730	-	2,710,560	-	10.3	-8.7
Sorghum for grain or seed								
Number of farms	-	-	-	-	-	-	-	-
Number of acres	-	-	-	-	-	-	-	-
Number of bushels	-	-	-	-	-	-	-	-
Wheat for grain								
Number of farms	26,086	7.4	24,054	8.2	18,747	7.7	-7.8	-22.1
Number of acres	838,496	1.6	1,089,529	1.8	994,276	1.7	29.9	-8.7
Number of bushels	42,452,489	2.2	54,020,364	2.4	55,105,157	2.5	27.2	2.0
Barley for grain								
Number of farms	-	-	-	-	-	-	-	-
Number of acres	-	-	-	-	-	-	-	-
Number of bushels	-	-	-	-	-	-	-	-
Oats for grain								
Number of farms	13,494	-	8,048	-	5,728	-	-40.4	-28.8
Number of acres	206,970	-	115,727	-	81,168	-	-44.1	-29.9
Number of bushels	13,781,107	-	7,901,758	-	5,393,500	-	-42.7	-31.7
Rice								
Number of farms	-	-	-	-	-	-	-	-
Number of acres	-	-	-	-	-	-	-	-
Weight in hundredweight	-	-	-	-	-	-	-	-
Sunflower seed								
Number of farms	-	-	-	-	-	-	-	-
Number of acres	-	-	-	-	-	-	-	-
Weight in pounds	-	-	-	-	-	-	-	-
Cotton								
Number of farms	-	-	-	-	-	-	-	-
Number of acres	-	-	-	-	-	-	-	-
Number of bales	-	-	-	-	-	-	-	-

Continued.

CROP STATISTICS FOR OHIO - Continued

Item	1987 Value	1987 % of U.S.	1992 Value	1992 % of U.S.	1997 Value	1997 % of U.S.	Percent change 1987-1992	Percent change 1992-1997
Tobacco								
Number of farms	-	-	-	-	-	-	-	-
Number of acres	-	-	-	-	-	-	-	-
Weight in pounds	-	-	-	-	-	-	-	-
Soybeans for beans								
Number of farms	36,570	8.3	31,635	8.3	28,554	8.1	-13.5	-9.7
Number of acres	3,713,340	6.7	3,776,952	6.7	4,115,575	6.2	1.7	9.0
Number of bushels	132,974,160	7.2	145,432,936	7.1	172,972,596	6.9	9.4	18.9
Dry edible beans, excluding dry limas								
Number of farms	-	-	-	-	-	-	-	-
Number of acres	-	-	-	-	-	-	-	-
Weight in hundredweight	-	-	-	-	-	-	-	-
Potatoes, excluding sweetpotatoes								
Number of farms	-	-	-	-	-	-	-	-
Number of acres	-	-	-	-	-	-	-	-
Weight in hundredweight	-	-	-	-	-	-	-	-
Sugar beets for sugar								
Number of farms	-	-	-	-	-	-	-	-
Number of acres	-	-	-	-	-	-	-	-
Weight in tons	-	-	-	-	-	-	-	-
Sugarcane for sugar								
Number of farms	-	-	-	-	-	-	-	-
Number of acres	-	-	-	-	-	-	-	-
Weight in tons	-	-	-	-	-	-	-	-
Pineapples harvested								
Number of farms	-	-	-	-	-	-	-	-
Number of acres	-	-	-	-	-	-	-	-
Weight in tons	-	-	-	-	-	-	-	-
Peanuts for nuts								
Number of farms	-	-	-	-	-	-	-	-
Number of acres	-	-	-	-	-	-	-	-
Weight in pounds	-	-	-	-	-	-	-	-
Hay - all types, including alfalfa								
Number of farms	37,730	3.8	33,080	3.7	31,475	3.5	-12.3	-4.9
Number of acres	1,271,206	2.2	1,200,789	2.1	1,196,243	2.0	-5.5	-0.4
Weight in tons, dry	3,236,378	2.5	2,949,243	2.3	2,813,975	2.0	-8.9	-4.6
Vegetables harvested for sale								
Number of farms	2,105	3.5	2,349	3.8	2,177	4.1	11.6	-7.3
Number of acres	59,093	1.7	55,024	1.5	45,591	1.2	-6.9	-17.1
Land in orchards								
Number of farms	-	-	-	-	-	-	-	-
Number of acres	-	-	-	-	-	-	-	-

Source: 1997 Census of Agriculture, U.S. Department of Agriculture, National Agricultural Statistics Service. NA stands for "not available." (D) is shown when data are withheld to prevent disclosure of competitive information. A dash (-) is shown where no data were reported. Not all states report growing all crops, but all crop categories in the census are shown for every state. The data series used for this presentation did not report U.S. totals for a number of categories; for that reason, the "% of U.S." column is sometimes blank.

OKLAHOMA

GENERAL STATISTICS FOR OKLAHOMA

Item	1987 Value	1987 % of U.S.	1992 Value	1992 % of U.S.	1997 Value	1997 % of U.S.	Percent change 1987-1992	Percent change 1992-1997
Farms (number)	70,228	3.4	66,937	3.5	74,214	3.9	-4.7	10.9
Land in farms (acres)	31,541,977	3.3	32,143,030	3.4	33,218,677	3.6	1.9	3.3
Average size of farm (acres)	449	97.2	480	97.8	448	92.0	6.9	-6.7
Median size of farm (acres)	NA	-	NA	-	160	133.3	-	-
Market value of land and buildings:								
Average per farm (dollars)	215,024	74.3	235,359	65.9	271,996	60.5	9.5	15.6
Average per acre (dollars)	480	76.6	496	68.2	610	65.4	3.3	23.0
Market value of machinery/equipment - average per farm (dollars)	29,465	71.5	31,943	65.7	36,936	64.0	8.4	15.6
Farms by size:								
1 to 9 acres	3,666	2.0	2,832	1.7	2,505	1.6	-22.7	-11.5
10 to 49 acres	10,134	2.5	9,614	2.5	12,673	3.1	-5.1	31.8
50 to 179 acres	22,331	3.5	21,099	3.6	24,681	4.2	-5.5	17.0
180 to 499 acres	18,006	3.8	17,234	4.0	18,288	4.5	-4.3	6.1
500 to 999 acres	8,405	4.2	8,202	4.4	8,155	4.6	-2.4	-0.6
1,000 acres or more	7,686	4.6	7,956	4.6	7,912	4.5	3.5	-0.6
Total cropland								
Farms	55,783	3.0	53,197	3.1	58,741	3.5	-4.6	10.4
Acres	14,443,459	3.3	14,520,063	3.3	14,843,823	3.4	0.5	2.2
Harvested cropland (farms)	43,522	2.6	42,015	2.8	44,786	3.2	-3.5	6.6
Harvested cropland (acres)	7,319,193	2.6	8,272,889	2.8	8,462,079	2.7	13.0	2.3
Irrigated land (farms)	3,029	1.0	2,581	0.9	2,710	1.0	-14.8	5.0
Irrigated land (acres)	478,437	1.0	512,487	1.0	506,459	0.9	7.1	-1.2
Market value of agricultural products sold:								
Total sales ($1,000)	2,714,892	2.0	3,562,646	2.2	4,146,351	2.1	31.2	16.4
Average per farm (dollars)	38,658	59.3	53,224	63.0	55,870	54.3	37.7	5.0
Agricultural products only ($1,000)	610,050	1.0	778,813	1.0	907,865	0.9	27.7	16.6
Livestock, poultry, and products ($1,000)	2,104,842	2.7	2,783,832	3.2	3,238,485	3.3	32.3	16.3
Farms by value of sales:								
Less than $2,500	18,501	3.8	15,902	3.8	20,476	4.1	-14.0	28.8
$2,500 to $4,999	11,073	4.2	10,189	4.4	11,713	5.1	-8.0	15.0
$5,000 to $9,999	11,999	4.4	11,208	4.4	12,341	5.2	-6.6	10.1
$10,000 to $24,999	12,805	3.9	12,543	4.2	12,869	4.7	-2.0	2.6
$25,000 to $49,999	6,300	2.9	6,493	3.3	6,234	3.7	3.1	-4.0
$50,000 to $99,999	4,479	2.1	4,609	2.5	4,285	2.7	2.9	-7.0
$100,000 or more	5,071	1.7	5,993	1.8	6,296	1.8	18.2	5.1
Total farm production expenses ($1,000)	2,359,468	2.2	3,117,869	2.4	3,576,456	2.4	32.1	14.7
Average expenses per farm (dollars)	33,594	64.9	46,580	68.6	48,186	61.2	38.7	3.4
Net cash return for the farm unit:								
Number of farms	70,235	3.4	66,936	3.5	74,222	3.9	-4.7	10.9
Value ($1000)	295,955	1.1	395,182	1.3	456,080	1.1	33.5	15.4
Average per farm (dollars)	4,214	33.3	5,904	37.4	6,145	27.6	40.1	4.1
Operators by principal occupation:								
Farming	33,052	2.9	33,279	3.2	33,060	3.4	0.7	-0.7
Other	37,176	3.9	33,658	3.9	41,154	4.3	-9.5	22.3
Operators by days worked off farm:								
Any	40,839	3.7	36,697	3.7	43,859	4.2	-10.1	19.5
200 days or more	28,495	3.9	25,827	3.9	31,803	4.5	-9.4	23.1

Source: *1997 Census of Agriculture*, U.S. Department of Agriculture, National Agricultural Statistics Service. NA stands for "not available." (D) is shown when data are withheld to prevent disclosure of competitive information. A dash (-) is shown where no data were reported. The market value of land and buildings, and of machinery and equipment, is an estimated amount. Net cash return for the farm unit includes only returns from agricultural activities.

LIVESTOCK STATISTICS FOR OKLAHOMA

Item	1987 Value	1987 % of U.S.	1992 Value	1992 % of U.S.	1997 Value	1997 % of U.S.	Percent change 1987-1992	Percent change 1992-1997
Cattle and calves								
Number of farms	53,544	4.6	52,241	4.9	58,023	5.5	-2.4	11.1
Number of animals	4,537,774	4.7	4,736,594	4.9	5,321,161	5.4	4.4	12.3
Beef cows (farms)	44,130	5.2	44,115	5.5	49,284	6.1	-0.0	11.7
Beef cows (number)	1,630,425	5.2	1,728,273	5.3	1,931,805	5.7	6.0	11.8
Milk cows (farms)	2,828	1.4	2,297	1.5	1,921	1.6	-18.8	-16.4
Milk cows (number)	90,499	0.9	90,312	1.0	87,647	1.0	-0.2	-3.0
Cattle and calves sold (farms)	53,577	4.7	51,240	5.0	56,600	5.6	-4.4	10.5
Cattle and calves sold (number)	3,630,285	5.0	3,953,960	5.6	4,346,420	5.9	8.9	9.9
Hogs and pigs								
Number of farms	3,710	1.5	3,415	1.8	3,002	2.7	-8.0	-12.1
Number of animals	187,351	0.4	260,682	0.5	1,689,700	2.8	39.1	548.2
Hogs and pigs sold (farms)	3,090	1.3	2,776	1.5	2,082	2.0	-10.2	-25.0
Hogs and pigs sold (number)	346,686	0.4	500,299	0.4	3,943,563	2.8	44.3	688.2
Sheep and lambs								
Number of farms	1,799	1.9	1,577	2.0	1,529	2.3	-12.3	-3.0
Number of animals	120,479	1.1	103,732	1.0	67,171	0.9	-13.9	-35.2
Layers and pullets 13 weeks old and older								
Number of farms	5,703	3.9	3,224	3.7	3,293	4.5	-43.5	2.1
Number of birds	5,826,714	1.6	5,051,662	1.4	5,059,373	1.4	-13.3	0.2
Broilers and other meat-type chickens sold								
Number of farms	556	2.0	529	2.2	632	2.6	-4.9	19.5
Number of birds sold	89,704,380	1.3	138,607,293	2.6	169,292,948	2.5	54.5	22.1

Source: 1997 Census of Agriculture, U.S. Department of Agriculture, National Agricultural Statistics Service. NA stands for "not available." (D) is shown when data are withheld to prevent disclosure of competitive information. A dash (-) is shown where no data were reported.

CROP STATISTICS FOR OKLAHOMA

Item	1987 Value	1987 % of U.S.	1992 Value	1992 % of U.S.	1997 Value	1997 % of U.S.	Percent change 1987-1992	Percent change 1992-1997
Corn for grain or seed								
Number of farms	-	-	-	-	-	-	-	-
Number of acres	-	-	-	-	-	-	-	-
Number of bushels	-	-	-	-	-	-	-	-
Corn for silage or green chop								
Number of farms	-	-	-	-	-	-	-	-
Number of acres	-	-	-	-	-	-	-	-
Weight in tons, green	-	-	-	-	-	-	-	-
Sorghum for grain or seed								
Number of farms	2,961	-	2,076	-	2,557	-	-29.9	23.2
Number of acres	339,368	-	281,244	-	417,872	-	-17.1	48.6
Number of bushels	15,114,650	-	13,933,273	-	18,863,920	-	-7.8	35.4
Wheat for grain								
Number of farms	18,644	5.3	16,716	5.7	13,935	5.7	-10.3	-16.6
Number of acres	4,276,344	8.0	5,197,545	8.8	4,825,074	8.2	21.5	-7.2
Number of bushels	113,464,955	6.0	138,121,986	6.3	141,302,977	6.4	21.7	2.3
Barley for grain								
Number of farms	-	-	-	-	-	-	-	-
Number of acres	-	-	-	-	-	-	-	-
Number of bushels	-	-	-	-	-	-	-	-
Oats for grain								
Number of farms	-	-	-	-	-	-	-	-
Number of acres	-	-	-	-	-	-	-	-
Number of bushels	-	-	-	-	-	-	-	-
Rice								
Number of farms	-	-	-	-	-	-	-	-
Number of acres	-	-	-	-	-	-	-	-
Weight in hundredweight	-	-	-	-	-	-	-	-
Sunflower seed								
Number of farms	-	-	-	-	-	-	-	-
Number of acres	-	-	-	-	-	-	-	-
Weight in pounds	-	-	-	-	-	-	-	-
Cotton								
Number of farms	2,913	6.8	1,726	5.0	849	2.7	-40.7	-50.8
Number of acres	360,299	3.7	296,484	2.7	176,962	1.3	-17.7	-40.3
Number of bales	306,388	2.3	212,041	1.4	190,186	1.1	-30.8	-10.3

Continued.

CROP STATISTICS FOR OKLAHOMA - Continued

Item	1987		1992		1997		Percent change	
	Value	% of U.S.	Value	% of U.S.	Value	% of U.S.	1987-1992	1992-1997
Tobacco								
Number of farms	-	-	-	-	-	-	-	-
Number of acres	-	-	-	-	-	-	-	-
Weight in pounds	-	-	-	-	-	-	-	-
Soybeans for beans								
Number of farms	1,566	0.4	1,196	0.3	1,921	0.5	-23.6	60.6
Number of acres	229,887	0.4	193,302	0.3	323,082	0.5	-15.9	67.1
Number of bushels	5,622,675	0.3	4,975,025	0.2	9,498,068	0.4	-11.5	90.9
Dry edible beans, excluding dry limas								
Number of farms	-	-	-	-	-	-	-	-
Number of acres	-	-	-	-	-	-	-	-
Weight in hundredweight	-	-	-	-	-	-	-	-
Potatoes, excluding sweetpotatoes								
Number of farms	-	-	-	-	-	-	-	-
Number of acres	-	-	-	-	-	-	-	-
Weight in hundredweight	-	-	-	-	-	-	-	-
Sugar beets for sugar								
Number of farms	-	-	-	-	-	-	-	-
Number of acres	-	-	-	-	-	-	-	-
Weight in tons	-	-	-	-	-	-	-	-
Sugarcane for sugar								
Number of farms	-	-	-	-	-	-	-	-
Number of acres	-	-	-	-	-	-	-	-
Weight in tons	-	-	-	-	-	-	-	-
Pineapples harvested								
Number of farms	-	-	-	-	-	-	-	-
Number of acres	-	-	-	-	-	-	-	-
Weight in tons	-	-	-	-	-	-	-	-
Peanuts for nuts								
Number of farms	1,088	-	908	-	662	-	-16.5	-27.1
Number of acres	86,469	-	88,449	-	68,340	-	2.3	-22.7
Weight in pounds	190,592,633	-	203,107,412	-	163,572,035	-	6.6	-19.5
Hay - all types, including alfalfa								
Number of farms	32,196	3.2	32,299	3.6	35,751	4.0	0.3	10.7
Number of acres	1,920,000	3.3	2,112,710	3.7	2,478,944	4.1	10.0	17.3
Weight in tons, dry	3,430,874	2.7	3,992,843	3.1	4,651,859	3.3	16.4	16.5
Vegetables harvested for sale								
Number of farms	-	-	-	-	-	-	-	-
Number of acres	-	-	-	-	-	-	-	-
Land in orchards								
Number of farms	-	-	-	-	-	-	-	-
Number of acres	-	-	-	-	-	-	-	-

Source: 1997 Census of Agriculture, U.S. Department of Agriculture, National Agricultural Statistics Service. NA stands for "not available." (D) is shown when data are withheld to prevent disclosure of competitive information. A dash (-) is shown where no data were reported. Not all states report growing all crops, but all crop categories in the census are shown for every state. The data series used for this presentation did not report U.S. totals for a number of categories; for that reason, the "% of U.S." column is sometimes blank.

OREGON

GENERAL STATISTICS FOR OREGON

Item	1987 Value	1987 % of U.S.	1992 Value	1992 % of U.S.	1997 Value	1997 % of U.S.	Percent change 1987-1992	Percent change 1992-1997
Farms (number)	32,014	1.5	31,892	1.7	34,030	1.8	-0.4	6.7
Land in farms (acres)	17,809,165	1.8	17,609,497	1.9	17,449,293	1.9	-1.1	-0.9
Average size of farm (acres)	556	120.3	552	112.4	513	105.3	-0.7	-7.1
Median size of farm (acres)	NA	-	NA	-	38	31.7	-	-
Market value of land and buildings:								
Average per farm (dollars)	299,755	103.6	370,938	103.9	479,385	106.6	23.7	29.2
Average per acre (dollars)	542	86.4	663	91.2	960	102.9	22.3	44.8
Market value of machinery/equipment - average per farm (dollars)	37,982	92.1	48,223	99.2	55,401	96.1	27.0	14.9
Farms by size:								
1 to 9 acres	5,476	3.0	6,319	3.8	7,202	4.7	15.4	14.0
10 to 49 acres	11,448	2.8	11,235	2.9	11,954	2.9	-1.9	6.4
50 to 179 acres	7,219	1.1	6,748	1.2	7,120	1.2	-6.5	5.5
180 to 499 acres	3,617	0.8	3,390	0.8	3,369	0.8	-6.3	-0.6
500 to 999 acres	1,560	0.8	1,508	0.8	1,601	0.9	-3.3	6.2
1,000 acres or more	2,694	1.6	2,692	1.6	2,784	1.6	-0.1	3.4
Total cropland								
Farms	27,318	1.5	26,508	1.6	28,101	1.7	-3.0	6.0
Acres	5,236,393	1.2	5,037,764	1.2	5,285,659	1.2	-3.8	4.9
Harvested cropland (farms)	21,712	1.3	20,743	1.4	22,312	1.6	-4.5	7.6
Harvested cropland (acres)	2,832,663	1.0	2,823,972	1.0	3,154,523	1.0	-0.3	11.7
Irrigated land (farms)	14,411	4.9	15,002	5.4	15,348	5.5	4.1	2.3
Irrigated land (acres)	1,648,205	3.6	1,622,235	3.3	1,948,739	3.5	-1.6	20.1
Market value of agricultural products sold:								
Total sales ($1,000)	1,846,067	1.4	2,292,973	1.4	2,969,194	1.5	24.2	29.5
Average per farm (dollars)	57,664	88.5	71,898	85.1	87,252	84.7	24.7	21.4
Agricultural products only ($1,000)	1,048,616	1.8	1,452,213	1.9	2,114,196	2.2	38.5	45.6
Livestock, poultry, and products ($1,000)	797,451	1.0	840,760	1.0	854,998	0.9	5.4	1.7
Farms by value of sales:								
Less than $2,500	11,751	2.4	11,490	2.7	12,021	2.4	-2.2	4.6
$2,500 to $4,999	4,785	1.8	4,569	2.0	5,027	2.2	-4.5	10.0
$5,000 to $9,999	3,770	1.4	3,734	1.5	3,971	1.7	-1.0	6.3
$10,000 to $24,999	3,697	1.1	3,801	1.3	4,121	1.5	2.8	8.4
$25,000 to $49,999	2,194	1.0	2,183	1.1	2,418	1.4	-0.5	10.8
$50,000 to $99,999	1,972	0.9	1,940	1.0	1,904	1.2	-1.6	-1.9
$100,000 or more	3,845	1.3	4,175	1.3	4,568	1.3	8.6	9.4
Total farm production expenses ($1,000)	1,535,162	1.4	1,881,731	1.4	2,210,747	1.5	22.6	17.5
Average expenses per farm (dollars)	47,948	92.6	59,035	86.9	64,955	82.5	23.1	10.0
Net cash return for the farm unit:								
Number of farms	32,017	1.5	31,875	1.7	34,036	1.8	-0.4	6.8
Value ($1000)	300,742	1.1	398,979	1.3	727,810	1.7	32.7	82.4
Average per farm (dollars)	9,393	74.2	12,517	79.2	21,384	96.1	33.3	70.8
Operators by principal occupation:								
Farming	15,359	1.3	15,306	1.5	15,648	1.6	-0.3	2.2
Other	16,655	1.8	16,586	1.9	18,382	1.9	-0.4	10.8
Operators by days worked off farm:								
Any	18,897	1.7	18,419	1.9	19,934	1.9	-2.5	8.2
200 days or more	12,646	1.7	12,089	1.8	13,110	1.8	-4.4	8.4

Source: *1997 Census of Agriculture*, U.S. Department of Agriculture, National Agricultural Statistics Service. NA stands for "not available." (D) is shown when data are withheld to prevent disclosure of competitive information. A dash (-) is shown where no data were reported. The market value of land and buildings, and of machinery and equipment, is an estimated amount. Net cash return for the farm unit includes only returns from agricultural activities.

LIVESTOCK STATISTICS FOR OREGON

Item	1987		1992		1997		Percent change	
	Value	% of U.S.	Value	% of U.S.	Value	% of U.S.	1987-1992	1992-1997
Cattle and calves								
Number of farms	17,515	1.5	17,088	1.6	17,122	1.6	-2.4	0.2
Number of animals	1,503,625	1.6	1,465,444	1.5	1,559,162	1.6	-2.5	6.4
Beef cows (farms)	13,369	1.6	13,105	1.6	13,393	1.7	-2.0	2.2
Beef cows (number)	618,857	2.0	629,625	1.9	695,635	2.0	1.7	10.5
Milk cows (farms)	1,937	1.0	1,541	1.0	1,052	0.9	-20.4	-31.7
Milk cows (number)	95,325	0.9	99,035	1.0	86,747	1.0	3.9	-12.4
Cattle and calves sold (farms)	16,812	1.5	15,608	1.5	15,980	1.6	-7.2	2.4
Cattle and calves sold (number)	955,484	1.3	899,088	1.3	979,199	1.3	-5.9	8.9
Hogs and pigs								
Number of farms	1,482	0.6	1,669	0.9	1,383	1.3	12.6	-17.1
Number of animals	86,293	0.2	58,276	0.1	33,152	0.1	-32.5	-43.1
Hogs and pigs sold (farms)	1,400	0.6	1,463	0.8	1,182	1.2	4.5	-19.2
Hogs and pigs sold (number)	143,661	0.1	97,427	0.1	54,864	0.0	-32.2	-43.7
Sheep and lambs								
Number of farms	4,138	4.5	3,639	4.5	3,070	4.7	-12.1	-15.6
Number of animals	470,291	4.3	392,957	3.6	282,872	3.6	-16.4	-28.0
Layers and pullets 13 weeks old and older								
Number of farms	3,178	2.2	2,480	2.8	2,241	3.1	-22.0	-9.6
Number of birds	3,049,585	0.8	2,954,237	0.8	3,272,027	0.9	-3.1	10.8
Broilers and other meat-type chickens sold								
Number of farms	225	0.8	208	0.9	156	0.7	-7.6	-25.0
Number of birds sold	14,244,387	0.2	18,921,442	0.3	18,966,576	0.3	32.8	0.2

Source: 1997 Census of Agriculture, U.S. Department of Agriculture, National Agricultural Statistics Service. NA stands for "not available." (D) is shown when data are withheld to prevent disclosure of competitive information. A dash (-) is shown where no data were reported.

CROP STATISTICS FOR OREGON

Item	1987		1992		1997		Percent change	
	Value	% of U.S.	Value	% of U.S.	Value	% of U.S.	1987-1992	1992-1997
Corn for grain or seed								
Number of farms	-	-	-	-	-	-	-	-
Number of acres	-	-	-	-	-	-	-	-
Number of bushels	-	-	-	-	-	-	-	-
Corn for silage or green chop								
Number of farms	-	-	-	-	-	-	-	-
Number of acres	-	-	-	-	-	-	-	-
Weight in tons, green	-	-	-	-	-	-	-	-
Sorghum for grain or seed								
Number of farms	-	-	-	-	-	-	-	-
Number of acres	-	-	-	-	-	-	-	-
Number of bushels	-	-	-	-	-	-	-	-
Wheat for grain								
Number of farms	3,890	1.1	3,025	1.0	2,531	1.0	-22.2	-16.3
Number of acres	838,849	1.6	924,855	1.6	882,862	1.5	10.3	-4.5
Number of bushels	51,875,186	2.7	46,527,762	2.1	54,694,903	2.5	-10.3	17.6
Barley for grain								
Number of farms	1,805	-	1,096	-	750	-	-39.3	-31.6
Number of acres	186,504	-	127,185	-	109,108	-	-31.8	-14.2
Number of bushels	12,272,482	-	7,787,057	-	7,568,675	-	-36.5	-2.8
Oats for grain								
Number of farms	1,134	-	810	-	570	-	-28.6	-29.6
Number of acres	41,551	-	38,241	-	30,173	-	-8.0	-21.1
Number of bushels	2,777,234	-	2,950,737	-	2,742,017	-	6.2	-7.1
Rice								
Number of farms	-	-	-	-	-	-	-	-
Number of acres	-	-	-	-	-	-	-	-
Weight in hundredweight	-	-	-	-	-	-	-	-
Sunflower seed								
Number of farms	-	-	-	-	-	-	-	-
Number of acres	-	-	-	-	-	-	-	-
Weight in pounds	-	-	-	-	-	-	-	-
Cotton								
Number of farms	-	-	-	-	-	-	-	-
Number of acres	-	-	-	-	-	-	-	-
Number of bales	-	-	-	-	-	-	-	-

Continued.

CROP STATISTICS FOR OREGON - Continued

Item	1987		1992		1997		Percent change	
	Value	% of U.S.	Value	% of U.S.	Value	% of U.S.	1987-1992	1992-1997
Tobacco								
Number of farms	-	-	-	-	-	-	-	-
Number of acres	-	-	-	-	-	-	-	-
Weight in pounds	-	-	-	-	-	-	-	-
Soybeans for beans								
Number of farms	-	-	-	-	-	-	-	-
Number of acres	-	-	-	-	-	-	-	-
Number of bushels	-	-	-	-	-	-	-	-
Dry edible beans, excluding dry limas								
Number of farms	-	-	-	-	-	-	-	-
Number of acres	-	-	-	-	-	-	-	-
Weight in hundredweight	-	-	-	-	-	-	-	-
Potatoes, excluding sweetpotatoes								
Number of farms	-	-	-	-	-	-	-	-
Number of acres	-	-	-	-	-	-	-	-
Weight in hundredweight	-	-	-	-	-	-	-	-
Sugar beets for sugar								
Number of farms	-	-	-	-	-	-	-	-
Number of acres	-	-	-	-	-	-	-	-
Weight in tons	-	-	-	-	-	-	-	-
Sugarcane for sugar								
Number of farms	-	-	-	-	-	-	-	-
Number of acres	-	-	-	-	-	-	-	-
Weight in tons	-	-	-	-	-	-	-	-
Pineapples harvested								
Number of farms	-	-	-	-	-	-	-	-
Number of acres	-	-	-	-	-	-	-	-
Weight in tons	-	-	-	-	-	-	-	-
Peanuts for nuts								
Number of farms	-	-	-	-	-	-	-	-
Number of acres	-	-	-	-	-	-	-	-
Weight in pounds	-	-	-	-	-	-	-	-
Hay - all types, including alfalfa								
Number of farms	13,913	1.4	12,066	1.3	12,933	1.5	-13.3	7.2
Number of acres	943,905	1.6	872,535	1.5	1,066,643	1.8	-7.6	22.2
Weight in tons, dry	2,340,999	1.8	2,276,437	1.8	3,009,247	2.2	-2.8	32.2
Vegetables harvested for sale								
Number of farms	1,529	2.5	1,509	2.4	1,432	2.7	-1.3	-5.1
Number of acres	142,236	4.1	147,616	3.9	155,242	4.1	3.8	5.2
Land in orchards								
Number of farms	4,410	3.7	4,200	3.6	3,869	3.6	-4.8	-7.9
Number of acres	91,101	2.0	96,166	2.0	96,270	1.9	5.6	0.1

Source: 1997 Census of Agriculture, U.S. Department of Agriculture, National Agricultural Statistics Service. NA stands for "not available." (D) is shown when data are withheld to prevent disclosure of competitive information. A dash (-) is shown where no data were reported. Not all states report growing all crops, but all crop categories in the census are shown for every state. The data series used for this presentation did not report U.S. totals for a number of categories; for that reason, the "% of U.S." column is sometimes blank.

PENNSYLVANIA

GENERAL STATISTICS FOR PENNSYLVANIA

Item	1987 Value	1987 % of U.S.	1992 Value	1992 % of U.S.	1997 Value	1997 % of U.S.	Percent change 1987-1992	Percent change 1992-1997
Farms (number)	51,549	2.5	44,870	2.3	45,457	2.4	-13.0	1.3
Land in farms (acres)	7,866,289	0.8	7,189,541	0.8	7,167,906	0.8	-8.6	-0.3
Average size of farm (acres)	153	33.1	160	32.6	158	32.4	4.6	-1.2
Median size of farm (acres)	NA	-	NA	-	96	80.0	-	-
Market value of land and buildings:								
Average per farm (dollars)	239,333	82.7	328,795	92.1	371,740	82.7	37.4	13.1
Average per acre (dollars)	1,579	251.8	2,056	282.8	2,390	256.2	30.2	16.2
Market value of machinery/equipment - average per farm (dollars)	41,641	101.0	49,383	101.6	53,219	92.3	18.6	7.8
Farms by size:								
1 to 9 acres	3,759	2.1	3,005	1.8	3,431	2.2	-20.1	14.2
10 to 49 acres	10,264	2.5	9,095	2.3	9,833	2.4	-11.4	8.1
50 to 179 acres	23,696	3.7	20,136	3.4	19,941	3.4	-15.0	-1.0
180 to 499 acres	11,453	2.4	10,286	2.4	9,815	2.4	-10.2	-4.6
500 to 999 acres	1,961	1.0	1,880	1.0	1,925	1.1	-4.1	2.4
1,000 acres or more	416	0.2	468	0.3	512	0.3	12.5	9.4
Total cropland								
Farms	48,546	2.6	42,390	2.5	42,573	2.6	-12.7	0.4
Acres	5,398,072	1.2	5,021,773	1.2	5,032,151	1.2	-7.0	0.2
Harvested cropland (farms)	46,157	2.8	40,090	2.7	39,689	2.8	-13.1	-1.0
Harvested cropland (acres)	4,080,153	1.4	3,861,435	1.3	4,014,564	1.3	-5.4	4.0
Irrigated land (farms)	2,208	0.8	2,121	0.8	2,814	1.0	-3.9	32.7
Irrigated land (acres)	29,505	0.1	23,096	0.0	36,150	0.1	-21.7	56.5
Market value of agricultural products sold:								
Total sales ($1,000)	3,077,523	2.3	3,570,191	2.2	3,997,565	2.0	16.0	12.0
Average per farm (dollars)	59,701	91.6	79,567	94.2	87,942	85.4	33.3	10.5
Agricultural products only ($1,000)	826,666	1.4	1,042,050	1.4	1,282,526	1.3	26.1	23.1
Livestock, poultry, and products ($1,000)	2,250,857	2.9	2,528,141	2.9	2,715,039	2.7	12.3	7.4
Farms by value of sales:								
Less than $2,500	12,747	2.6	9,634	2.3	10,299	2.1	-24.4	6.9
$2,500 to $4,999	6,517	2.5	5,314	2.3	5,036	2.2	-18.5	-5.2
$5,000 to $9,999	6,378	2.3	5,555	2.2	5,546	2.3	-12.9	-0.2
$10,000 to $24,999	6,720	2.1	6,199	2.1	6,384	2.3	-7.8	3.0
$25,000 to $49,999	4,680	2.1	3,915	2.0	3,964	2.3	-16.3	1.3
$50,000 to $99,999	6,893	3.2	5,241	2.8	4,630	2.9	-24.0	-11.7
$100,000 or more	7,614	2.6	9,012	2.7	9,598	2.8	18.4	6.5
Total farm production expenses ($1,000)	2,386,060	2.2	2,775,313	2.1	3,091,953	2.1	16.3	11.4
Average expenses per farm (dollars)	46,287	89.4	61,859	91.1	68,061	86.4	33.6	10.0
Net cash return for the farm unit:								
Number of farms	51,549	2.5	44,866	2.3	45,437	2.4	-13.0	1.3
Value ($1000)	661,804	2.5	758,341	2.5	747,503	1.8	14.6	-1.4
Average per farm (dollars)	12,838	101.4	16,902	107.0	16,451	73.9	31.7	-2.7
Operators by principal occupation:								
Farming	29,797	2.6	26,959	2.6	25,635	2.7	-9.5	-4.9
Other	21,752	2.3	17,911	2.1	19,822	2.1	-17.7	10.7
Operators by days worked off farm:								
Any	26,610	2.4	21,243	2.1	22,778	2.2	-20.2	7.2
200 days or more	17,104	2.3	13,501	2.0	14,611	2.1	-21.1	8.2

Source: *1997 Census of Agriculture*, U.S. Department of Agriculture, National Agricultural Statistics Service. NA stands for "not available." (D) is shown when data are withheld to prevent disclosure of competitive information. A dash (-) is shown where no data were reported. The market value of land and buildings, and of machinery and equipment, is an estimated amount. Net cash return for the farm unit includes only returns from agricultural activities.

LIVESTOCK STATISTICS FOR PENNSYLVANIA

Item	1987 Value	1987 % of U.S.	1992 Value	1992 % of U.S.	1997 Value	1997 % of U.S.	Percent change 1987-1992	Percent change 1992-1997
Cattle and calves								
Number of farms	33,381	2.8	27,984	2.6	26,525	2.5	-16.2	-5.2
Number of animals	1,745,617	1.8	1,699,820	1.8	1,672,295	1.7	-2.6	-1.6
Beef cows (farms)	13,429	1.6	11,461	1.4	11,237	1.4	-14.7	-2.0
Beef cows (number)	160,694	0.5	157,773	0.5	169,134	0.5	-1.8	7.2
Milk cows (farms)	15,096	7.5	12,448	8.0	10,920	9.3	-17.5	-12.3
Milk cows (number)	673,054	6.7	625,165	6.6	621,530	6.8	-7.1	-0.6
Cattle and calves sold (farms)	31,243	2.7	26,008	2.5	24,783	2.4	-16.8	-4.7
Cattle and calves sold (number)	975,472	1.3	954,013	1.4	857,149	1.2	-2.2	-10.2
Hogs and pigs								
Number of farms	6,983	2.9	5,097	2.7	3,456	3.1	-27.0	-32.2
Number of animals	919,755	1.8	1,074,574	1.9	1,100,754	1.8	16.8	2.4
Hogs and pigs sold (farms)	6,495	2.7	4,577	2.4	2,971	2.9	-29.5	-35.1
Hogs and pigs sold (number)	1,997,713	2.1	2,263,427	2.0	2,469,824	1.7	13.3	9.1
Sheep and lambs								
Number of farms	3,314	3.6	2,922	3.6	2,541	3.9	-11.8	-13.0
Number of animals	113,223	1.0	108,040	1.0	85,925	1.1	-4.6	-20.5
Layers and pullets 13 weeks old and older								
Number of farms	5,963	4.1	3,784	4.3	3,259	4.5	-36.5	-13.9
Number of birds	25,548,494	6.8	29,682,108	8.4	27,856,467	7.6	16.2	-6.2
Broilers and other meat-type chickens sold								
Number of farms	1,052	3.8	839	3.5	845	3.5	-20.2	0.7
Number of birds sold	106,382,310	1.6	108,113,026	2.0	118,545,429	1.8	1.6	9.6

Source: 1997 Census of Agriculture, U.S. Department of Agriculture, National Agricultural Statistics Service. NA stands for "not available." (D) is shown when data are withheld to prevent disclosure of competitive information. A dash (-) is shown where no data were reported.

CROP STATISTICS FOR PENNSYLVANIA

Item	1987 Value	1987 % of U.S.	1992 Value	1992 % of U.S.	1997 Value	1997 % of U.S.	Percent change 1987-1992	Percent change 1992-1997
Corn for grain or seed								
Number of farms	26,968	4.3	21,610	4.3	18,732	4.3	-19.9	-13.3
Number of acres	1,070,293	1.8	1,012,263	1.5	970,895	1.4	-5.4	-4.1
Number of bushels	99,282,796	-	112,034,518	1.3	93,320,717	1.1	12.8	-16.7
Corn for silage or green chop								
Number of farms	15,127	-	13,267	-	12,598	-	-12.3	-5.0
Number of acres	438,212	-	389,977	-	484,951	-	-11.0	24.4
Weight in tons, green	6,219,500	-	6,136,435	-	6,363,560	-	-1.3	3.7
Sorghum for grain or seed								
Number of farms	-	-	-	-	-	-	-	-
Number of acres	-	-	-	-	-	-	-	-
Number of bushels	-	-	-	-	-	-	-	-
Wheat for grain								
Number of farms	9,719	2.8	7,734	2.6	6,381	2.6	-20.4	-17.5
Number of acres	186,100	0.3	182,021	0.3	167,488	0.3	-2.2	-8.0
Number of bushels	7,663,537	0.4	8,670,089	0.4	8,526,375	0.4	13.1	-1.7
Barley for grain								
Number of farms	-	-	-	-	-	-	-	-
Number of acres	-	-	-	-	-	-	-	-
Number of bushels	-	-	-	-	-	-	-	-
Oats for grain								
Number of farms	14,900	-	11,205	-	9,041	-	-24.8	-19.3
Number of acres	243,257	-	184,186	-	144,456	-	-24.3	-21.6
Number of bushels	13,881,340	-	11,064,027	-	8,122,302	-	-20.3	-26.6
Rice								
Number of farms	-	-	-	-	-	-	-	-
Number of acres	-	-	-	-	-	-	-	-
Weight in hundredweight	-	-	-	-	-	-	-	-
Sunflower seed								
Number of farms	-	-	-	-	-	-	-	-
Number of acres	-	-	-	-	-	-	-	-
Weight in pounds	-	-	-	-	-	-	-	-
Cotton								
Number of farms	-	-	-	-	-	-	-	-
Number of acres	-	-	-	-	-	-	-	-
Number of bales	-	-	-	-	-	-	-	-

Continued.

CROP STATISTICS FOR PENNSYLVANIA - Continued

Item	1987		1992		1997		Percent change	
	Value	% of U.S.	Value	% of U.S.	Value	% of U.S.	1987-1992	1992-1997
Tobacco								
Number of farms	-	-	-	-	-	-	-	-
Number of acres	-	-	-	-	-	-	-	-
Weight in pounds	-	-	-	-	-	-	-	-
Soybeans for beans								
Number of farms	-	-	-	-	-	-	-	-
Number of acres	-	-	-	-	-	-	-	-
Number of bushels	-	-	-	-	-	-	-	-
Dry edible beans, excluding dry limas								
Number of farms	-	-	-	-	-	-	-	-
Number of acres	-	-	-	-	-	-	-	-
Weight in hundredweight	-	-	-	-	-	-	-	-
Potatoes, excluding sweetpotatoes								
Number of farms	1,113	-	956	-	740	-	-14.1	-22.6
Number of acres	21,707	-	17,393	-	12,597	-	-19.9	-27.6
Weight in hundredweight	4,428,958	-	4,030,015	-	3,082,481	-	-9.0	-23.5
Sugar beets for sugar								
Number of farms	-	-	-	-	-	-	-	-
Number of acres	-	-	-	-	-	-	-	-
Weight in tons	-	-	-	-	-	-	-	-
Sugarcane for sugar								
Number of farms	-	-	-	-	-	-	-	-
Number of acres	-	-	-	-	-	-	-	-
Weight in tons	-	-	-	-	-	-	-	-
Pineapples harvested								
Number of farms	-	-	-	-	-	-	-	-
Number of acres	-	-	-	-	-	-	-	-
Weight in tons	-	-	-	-	-	-	-	-
Peanuts for nuts								
Number of farms	-	-	-	-	-	-	-	-
Number of acres	-	-	-	-	-	-	-	-
Weight in pounds	-	-	-	-	-	-	-	-
Hay - all types, including alfalfa								
Number of farms	38,129	3.8	32,640	3.6	31,387	3.5	-14.4	-3.8
Number of acres	1,915,370	3.3	1,787,980	3.2	1,890,462	3.1	-6.7	5.7
Weight in tons, dry	4,477,463	3.5	4,091,919	3.2	3,931,973	2.8	-8.6	-3.9
Vegetables harvested for sale								
Number of farms	-	-	-	-	-	-	-	-
Number of acres	-	-	-	-	-	-	-	-
Land in orchards								
Number of farms	2,805	2.3	2,317	2.0	2,069	2.0	-17.4	-10.7
Number of acres	66,537	1.5	57,656	1.2	56,029	1.1	-13.3	-2.8

Source: 1997 Census of Agriculture, U.S. Department of Agriculture, National Agricultural Statistics Service. NA stands for "not available." (D) is shown when data are withheld to prevent disclosure of competitive information. A dash (-) is shown where no data were reported. Not all states report growing all crops, but all crop categories in the census are shown for every state. The data series used for this presentation did not report U.S. totals for a number of categories; for that reason, the "% of U.S." column is sometimes blank.

RHODE ISLAND

GENERAL STATISTICS FOR RHODE ISLAND

Item	1987 Value	1987 % of U.S.	1992 Value	1992 % of U.S.	1997 Value	1997 % of U.S.	Percent change 1987-1992	Percent change 1992-1997
Farms (number)	701	0.0	649	0.0	735	0.0	-7.4	13.3
Land in farms (acres)	58,685	0.0	49,601	0.0	55,256	0.0	-15.5	11.4
Average size of farm (acres)	84	18.2	76	15.5	75	15.4	-9.5	-1.3
Median size of farm (acres)	NA	-	NA	-	32	26.7	-	-
Market value of land and buildings:								
Average per farm (dollars)	420,279	145.2	481,783	134.9	442,402	98.4	14.6	-8.2
Average per acre (dollars)	4,748	757.3	6,304	867.1	5,885	630.8	32.8	-6.6
Market value of machinery/equipment -								
average per farm (dollars)	35,918	87.1	37,718	77.6	38,799	67.3	5.0	2.9
Farms by size:								
1 to 9 acres	131	0.1	128	0.1	181	0.1	-2.3	41.4
10 to 49 acres	250	0.1	237	0.1	257	0.1	-5.2	8.4
50 to 179 acres	241	0.0	215	0.0	221	0.0	-10.8	2.8
180 to 499 acres	66	0.0	57	0.0	61	0.0	-13.6	7.0
500 to 999 acres	11	0.0	10	0.0	13	0.0	-9.1	30.0
1,000 acres or more	2	0.0	2	0.0	2	0.0	-	-
Total cropland								
Farms	597	0.0	591	0.0	661	0.0	-1.0	11.8
Acres	26,121	0.0	24,411	0.0	25,611	0.0	-6.5	4.9
Harvested cropland (farms)	523	0.0	517	0.0	606	0.0	-1.1	17.2
Harvested cropland (acres)	18,498	0.0	18,136	0.0	19,019	0.0	-2.0	4.9
Irrigated land (farms)	105	0.0	132	0.0	180	0.1	25.7	36.4
Irrigated land (acres)	3,494	0.0	2,979	0.0	3,265	0.0	-14.7	9.6
Market value of agricultural products sold:								
Total sales ($1,000)	37,786	0.0	39,512	0.0	48,200	0.0	4.6	22.0
Average per farm (dollars)	53,903	82.7	60,882	72.1	65,578	63.7	12.9	7.7
Agricultural products only ($1,000)	26,685	0.0	27,431	0.0	39,423	0.0	2.8	43.7
Livestock, poultry, and products ($1,000)	11,100	0.0	12,082	0.0	8,777	0.0	8.8	-27.4
Farms by value of sales:								
Less than $2,500	290	0.1	175	0.0	210	0.0	-39.7	20.0
$2,500 to $4,999	79	0.0	115	0.0	91	0.0	45.6	-20.9
$5,000 to $9,999	82	0.0	85	0.0	91	0.0	3.7	7.1
$10,000 to $24,999	79	0.0	99	0.0	109	0.0	25.3	10.1
$25,000 to $49,999	41	0.0	49	0.0	73	0.0	19.5	49.0
$50,000 to $99,999	55	0.0	49	0.0	64	0.0	-10.9	30.6
$100,000 or more	75	0.0	77	0.0	97	0.0	2.7	26.0
Total farm production expenses ($1,000)	29,736	0.0	32,436	0.0	35,350	0.0	9.1	9.0
Average expenses per farm (dollars)	42,359	81.8	49,978	73.6	48,096	61.1	18.0	-3.8
Net cash return for the farm unit:								
Number of farms	702	0.0	649	0.0	735	0.0	-7.5	13.3
Value ($1000)	7,443	0.0	7,077	0.0	12,850	0.0	-4.9	81.6
Average per farm (dollars)	10,603	83.8	10,904	69.0	17,483	78.5	2.8	60.3
Operators by principal occupation:								
Farming	345	0.0	333	0.0	370	0.0	-3.5	11.1
Other	356	0.0	316	0.0	365	0.0	-11.2	15.5
Operators by days worked off farm:								
Any	395	0.0	323	0.0	381	0.0	-18.2	18.0
200 days or more	262	0.0	202	0.0	260	0.0	-22.9	28.7

Source: 1997 Census of Agriculture, U.S. Department of Agriculture, National Agricultural Statistics Service. NA stands for "not available." (D) is shown when data are withheld to prevent disclosure of competitive information. A dash (-) is shown where no data were reported. The market value of land and buildings, and of machinery and equipment, is an estimated amount. Net cash return for the farm unit includes only returns from agricultural activities.

LIVESTOCK STATISTICS FOR RHODE ISLAND

Item	1987 Value	1987 % of U.S.	1992 Value	1992 % of U.S.	1997 Value	1997 % of U.S.	Percent change 1987-1992	Percent change 1992-1997
Cattle and calves								
Number of farms	253	0.0	208	0.0	200	0.0	-17.8	-3.8
Number of animals	6,930	0.0	6,057	0.0	5,749	0.0	-12.6	-5.1
Beef cows (farms)	156	0.0	133	0.0	129	0.0	-14.7	-3.0
Beef cows (number)	1,133	0.0	967	0.0	1,062	0.0	-14.7	9.8
Milk cows (farms)	70	0.0	55	0.0	45	0.0	-21.4	-18.2
Milk cows (number)	2,975	0.0	2,565	0.0	2,239	0.0	-13.8	-12.7
Cattle and calves sold (farms)	206	0.0	162	0.0	158	0.0	-21.4	-2.5
Cattle and calves sold (number)	3,259	0.0	2,509	0.0	2,315	0.0	-23.0	-7.7
Hogs and pigs								
Number of farms	59	0.0	48	0.0	60	0.1	-18.6	25.0
Number of animals	4,719	0.0	5,488	0.0	2,764	0.0	16.3	-49.6
Hogs and pigs sold (farms)	49	0.0	41	0.0	45	0.0	-16.3	9.8
Hogs and pigs sold (number)	4,990	0.0	6,011	0.0	4,951	0.0	20.5	-17.6
Sheep and lambs								
Number of farms	76	0.1	62	0.1	69	0.1	-18.4	11.3
Number of animals	1,661	0.0	1,355	0.0	1,064	0.0	-18.4	-21.5
Layers and pullets 13 weeks old and older								
Number of farms	96	0.1	83	0.1	93	0.1	-13.5	12.0
Number of birds	205,794	0.1	242,307	0.1	58,042	0.0	17.7	-76.0
Broilers and other meat-type chickens sold								
Number of farms	6	0.0	5	0.0	5	0.0	-16.7	-
Number of birds sold	58,714	0.0	(D)	-	(D)	-	-	-

Source: *1997 Census of Agriculture*, U.S. Department of Agriculture, National Agricultural Statistics Service. NA stands for "not available." (D) is shown when data are withheld to prevent disclosure of competitive information. A dash (-) is shown where no data were reported.

CROP STATISTICS FOR RHODE ISLAND

Item	1987 Value	1987 % of U.S.	1992 Value	1992 % of U.S.	1997 Value	1997 % of U.S.	Percent change 1987-1992	Percent change 1992-1997
Corn for grain or seed								
Number of farms	9	0.0	16	0.0	9	0.0	77.8	-43.8
Number of acres	99	0.0	172	0.0	45	0.0	73.7	-73.8
Number of bushels	7,585	-	11,280	0.0	(D)	-	48.7	-
Corn for silage or green chop								
Number of farms	77	-	72	-	53	-	-6.5	-26.4
Number of acres	2,008	-	2,949	-	(D)	-	46.9	-
Weight in tons, green	33,778	-	49,638	-	(D)	-	47.0	-
Sorghum for grain or seed								
Number of farms	-	-	-	-	-	-	-	-
Number of acres	-	-	-	-	-	-	-	-
Number of bushels	-	-	-	-	-	-	-	-
Wheat for grain								
Number of farms	-	-	-	-	-	-	-	-
Number of acres	-	-	-	-	-	-	-	-
Number of bushels	-	-	-	-	-	-	-	-
Barley for grain								
Number of farms	-	-	-	-	-	-	-	-
Number of acres	-	-	-	-	-	-	-	-
Number of bushels	-	-	-	-	-	-	-	-
Oats for grain								
Number of farms	-	-	-	-	-	-	-	-
Number of acres	-	-	-	-	-	-	-	-
Number of bushels	-	-	-	-	-	-	-	-
Rice								
Number of farms	-	-	-	-	-	-	-	-
Number of acres	-	-	-	-	-	-	-	-
Weight in hundredweight	-	-	-	-	-	-	-	-
Sunflower seed								
Number of farms	-	-	-	-	-	-	-	-
Number of acres	-	-	-	-	-	-	-	-
Weight in pounds	-	-	-	-	-	-	-	-
Cotton								
Number of farms	-	-	-	-	-	-	-	-
Number of acres	-	-	-	-	-	-	-	-
Number of bales	-	-	-	-	-	-	-	-

Continued.

CROP STATISTICS FOR RHODE ISLAND - Continued

Item	1987 Value	1987 % of U.S.	1992 Value	1992 % of U.S.	1997 Value	1997 % of U.S.	Percent change 1987-1992	Percent change 1992-1997
Tobacco								
Number of farms	-	-	-	-	-	-	-	-
Number of acres	-	-	-	-	-	-	-	-
Weight in pounds	-	-	-	-	-	-	-	-
Soybeans for beans								
Number of farms	-	-	-	-	-	-	-	-
Number of acres	-	-	-	-	-	-	-	-
Number of bushels	-	-	-	-	-	-	-	-
Dry edible beans, excluding dry limas								
Number of farms	-	-	-	-	-	-	-	-
Number of acres	-	-	-	-	-	-	-	-
Weight in hundredweight	-	-	-	-	-	-	-	-
Potatoes, excluding sweetpotatoes								
Number of farms	22	-	19	-	16	-	-13.6	-15.8
Number of acres	1,410	-	1,310	-	788	-	-7.1	-39.8
Weight in hundredweight	259,958	-	374,808	-	(D)	-	44.2	-
Sugar beets for sugar								
Number of farms	-	-	-	-	-	-	-	-
Number of acres	-	-	-	-	-	-	-	-
Weight in tons	-	-	-	-	-	-	-	-
Sugarcane for sugar								
Number of farms	-	-	-	-	-	-	-	-
Number of acres	-	-	-	-	-	-	-	-
Weight in tons	-	-	-	-	-	-	-	-
Pineapples harvested								
Number of farms	-	-	-	-	-	-	-	-
Number of acres	-	-	-	-	-	-	-	-
Weight in tons	-	-	-	-	-	-	-	-
Peanuts for nuts								
Number of farms	-	-	-	-	-	-	-	-
Number of acres	-	-	-	-	-	-	-	-
Weight in pounds	-	-	-	-	-	-	-	-
Hay - all types, including alfalfa								
Number of farms	291	0.0	245	0.0	255	0.0	-15.8	4.1
Number of acres	8,126	0.0	7,614	0.0	8,189	0.0	-6.3	7.6
Weight in tons, dry	14,125	0.0	15,864	0.0	16,680	0.0	12.3	5.1
Vegetables harvested for sale								
Number of farms	99	0.2	126	0.2	126	0.2	27.3	-
Number of acres	1,947	0.1	1,868	0.0	1,907	0.1	-4.1	2.1
Land in orchards								
Number of farms	83	0.1	72	0.1	54	0.1	-13.3	-25.0
Number of acres	856	0.0	664	0.0	389	0.0	-22.4	-41.4

Source: 1997 Census of Agriculture, U.S. Department of Agriculture, National Agricultural Statistics Service. NA stands for "not available." (D) is shown when data are withheld to prevent disclosure of competitive information. A dash (-) is shown where no data were reported. Not all states report growing all crops, but all crop categories in the census are shown for every state. The data series used for this presentation did not report U.S. totals for a number of categories; for that reason, the "% of U.S." column is sometimes blank.

SOUTH CAROLINA

GENERAL STATISTICS FOR SOUTH CAROLINA

Item	1987 Value	1987 % of U.S.	1992 Value	1992 % of U.S.	1997 Value	1997 % of U.S.	Percent change 1987-1992	Percent change 1992-1997
Farms (number)	20,517	1.0	20,242	1.1	20,189	1.1	-1.3	-0.3
Land in farms (acres)	4,758,631	0.5	4,472,569	0.5	4,593,452	0.5	-6.0	2.7
Average size of farm (acres)	232	50.2	221	45.0	228	46.8	-4.7	3.2
Median size of farm (acres)	NA	-	NA	-	84	70.0	-	-
Market value of land and buildings:								
Average per farm (dollars)	201,169	69.5	251,583	70.5	324,834	72.2	25.1	29.1
Average per acre (dollars)	871	138.9	1,137	156.4	1,482	158.8	30.5	30.3
Market value of machinery/equipment - average per farm (dollars)	31,252	75.8	33,077	68.1	44,687	77.5	5.8	35.1
Farms by size:								
1 to 9 acres	1,337	0.7	1,302	0.8	1,224	0.8	-2.6	-6.0
10 to 49 acres	5,437	1.3	5,495	1.4	5,712	1.4	1.1	3.9
50 to 179 acres	7,742	1.2	7,591	1.3	7,502	1.3	-2.0	-1.2
180 to 499 acres	3,762	0.8	3,699	0.9	3,611	0.9	-1.7	-2.4
500 to 999 acres	1,303	0.7	1,263	0.7	1,225	0.7	-3.1	-3.0
1,000 acres or more	936	0.6	892	0.5	915	0.5	-4.7	2.6
Total cropland								
Farms	18,578	1.0	18,037	1.1	17,514	1.1	-2.9	-2.9
Acres	2,686,117	0.6	2,588,525	0.6	2,462,818	0.6	-3.6	-4.9
Harvested cropland (farms)	15,556	0.9	14,587	1.0	13,426	1.0	-6.2	-8.0
Harvested cropland (acres)	1,589,636	0.6	1,590,794	0.5	1,654,535	0.5	0.1	4.0
Irrigated land (farms)	1,216	0.4	1,219	0.4	1,248	0.4	0.2	2.4
Irrigated land (acres)	80,689	0.2	75,681	0.2	86,477	0.2	-6.2	14.3
Market value of agricultural products sold:								
Total sales ($1,000)	878,683	0.6	1,066,079	0.7	1,588,173	0.8	21.3	49.0
Average per farm (dollars)	42,827	65.7	52,667	62.4	78,665	76.4	23.0	49.4
Agricultural products only ($1,000)	451,285	0.8	562,036	0.7	791,104	0.8	24.5	40.8
Livestock, poultry, and products ($1,000)	427,398	0.6	504,043	0.6	797,069	0.8	17.9	58.1
Farms by value of sales:								
Less than $2,500	7,419	1.5	7,341	1.7	8,155	1.6	-1.1	11.1
$2,500 to $4,999	3,516	1.3	3,317	1.4	3,060	1.3	-5.7	-7.7
$5,000 to $9,999	2,900	1.1	2,897	1.2	2,714	1.1	-0.1	-6.3
$10,000 to $24,999	2,547	0.8	2,428	0.8	2,274	0.8	-4.7	-6.3
$25,000 to $49,999	1,276	0.6	1,301	0.7	1,003	0.6	2.0	-22.9
$50,000 to $99,999	954	0.4	937	0.5	703	0.4	-1.8	-25.0
$100,000 or more	1,905	0.6	2,021	0.6	2,280	0.7	6.1	12.8
Total farm production expenses ($1,000)	736,918	0.7	897,923	0.7	1,233,736	0.8	21.8	37.4
Average expenses per farm (dollars)	35,917	69.3	44,359	65.3	61,112	77.6	23.5	37.8
Net cash return for the farm unit:								
Number of farms	20,517	1.0	20,242	1.1	20,189	1.1	-1.3	-0.3
Value ($1000)	123,915	0.5	157,727	0.5	328,569	0.8	27.3	108.3
Average per farm (dollars)	6,040	47.7	7,792	49.3	16,275	73.1	29.0	108.9
Operators by principal occupation:								
Farming	8,983	0.8	8,866	0.8	7,959	0.8	-1.3	-10.2
Other	11,534	1.2	11,376	1.3	12,230	1.3	-1.4	7.5
Operators by days worked off farm:								
Any	11,791	1.1	11,271	1.1	11,615	1.1	-4.4	3.1
200 days or more	8,549	1.2	8,326	1.3	8,472	1.2	-2.6	1.8

Source: 1997 Census of Agriculture, U.S. Department of Agriculture, National Agricultural Statistics Service. NA stands for "not available." (D) is shown when data are withheld to prevent disclosure of competitive information. A dash (-) is shown where no data were reported. The market value of land and buildings, and of machinery and equipment, is an estimated amount. Net cash return for the farm unit includes only returns from agricultural activities.

LIVESTOCK STATISTICS FOR SOUTH CAROLINA

Item	1987 Value	% of U.S.	1992 Value	% of U.S.	1997 Value	% of U.S.	Percent change 1987-1992	Percent change 1992-1997
Cattle and calves								
Number of farms	10,227	0.9	10,026	0.9	9,902	0.9	-2.0	-1.2
Number of animals	428,491	0.4	451,719	0.5	453,631	0.5	5.4	0.4
Beef cows (farms)	8,903	1.1	8,998	1.1	8,671	1.1	1.1	-3.6
Beef cows (number)	205,344	0.6	222,566	0.7	229,048	0.7	8.4	2.9
Milk cows (farms)	697	0.3	540	0.3	394	0.3	-22.5	-27.0
Milk cows (number)	40,113	0.4	31,923	0.3	24,766	0.3	-20.4	-22.4
Cattle and calves sold (farms)	9,635	0.8	9,337	0.9	9,287	0.9	-3.1	-0.5
Cattle and calves sold (number)	218,766	0.3	200,396	0.3	216,812	0.3	-8.4	8.2
Hogs and pigs								
Number of farms	3,249	1.3	2,237	1.2	1,226	1.1	-31.1	-45.2
Number of animals	352,413	0.7	327,572	0.6	304,793	0.5	-7.0	-7.0
Hogs and pigs sold (farms)	3,031	1.3	2,048	1.1	1,031	1.0	-32.4	-49.7
Hogs and pigs sold (number)	619,986	0.6	637,592	0.6	711,109	0.5	2.8	11.5
Sheep and lambs								
Number of farms	80	0.1	169	0.2	168	0.3	111.2	-0.6
Number of animals	1,580	0.0	3,144	0.0	3,316	0.0	99.0	5.5
Layers and pullets 13 weeks old and older								
Number of farms	1,477	1.0	920	1.0	730	1.0	-37.7	-20.7
Number of birds	7,539,759	2.0	5,739,400	1.6	5,711,843	1.6	-23.9	-0.5
Broilers and other meat-type chickens sold								
Number of farms	227	0.8	292	1.2	366	1.5	28.6	25.3
Number of birds sold	60,295,197	0.9	106,171,059	2.0	158,678,646	2.4	76.1	49.5

Source: 1997 Census of Agriculture, U.S. Department of Agriculture, National Agricultural Statistics Service. NA stands for "not available." (D) is shown when data are withheld to prevent disclosure of competitive information. A dash (-) is shown where no data were reported.

CROP STATISTICS FOR SOUTH CAROLINA

Item	1987 Value	% of U.S.	1992 Value	% of U.S.	1997 Value	% of U.S.	Percent change 1987-1992	Percent change 1992-1997
Corn for grain or seed								
Number of farms	6,292	1.0	4,346	0.9	3,531	0.8	-30.9	-18.8
Number of acres	309,791	0.5	311,947	0.4	300,934	0.4	0.7	-3.5
Number of bushels	22,143,190	-	27,192,657	0.3	28,107,576	0.3	22.8	3.4
Corn for silage or green chop								
Number of farms	-	-	-	-	-	-	-	-
Number of acres	-	-	-	-	-	-	-	-
Weight in tons, green	-	-	-	-	-	-	-	-
Sorghum for grain or seed								
Number of farms	-	-	-	-	-	-	-	-
Number of acres	-	-	-	-	-	-	-	-
Number of bushels	-	-	-	-	-	-	-	-
Wheat for grain								
Number of farms	3,097	0.9	2,237	0.8	2,138	0.9	-27.8	-4.4
Number of acres	213,374	0.4	240,634	0.4	306,935	0.5	12.8	27.6
Number of bushels	7,558,179	0.4	10,470,395	0.5	14,500,101	0.7	38.5	38.5
Barley for grain								
Number of farms	-	-	-	-	-	-	-	-
Number of acres	-	-	-	-	-	-	-	-
Number of bushels	-	-	-	-	-	-	-	-
Oats for grain								
Number of farms	-	-	-	-	-	-	-	-
Number of acres	-	-	-	-	-	-	-	-
Number of bushels	-	-	-	-	-	-	-	-
Rice								
Number of farms	-	-	-	-	-	-	-	-
Number of acres	-	-	-	-	-	-	-	-
Weight in hundredweight	-	-	-	-	-	-	-	-
Sunflower seed								
Number of farms	-	-	-	-	-	-	-	-
Number of acres	-	-	-	-	-	-	-	-
Weight in pounds	-	-	-	-	-	-	-	-
Cotton								
Number of farms	744	1.7	861	2.5	894	2.8	15.7	3.8
Number of acres	116,424	1.2	191,690	1.7	285,858	2.2	64.6	49.1
Number of bales	102,078	0.8	223,658	1.5	397,545	2.2	119.1	77.7

Continued.

CROP STATISTICS FOR SOUTH CAROLINA - Continued

Item	1987		1992		1997		Percent change	
	Value	% of U.S.	Value	% of U.S.	Value	% of U.S.	1987-1992	1992-1997
Tobacco								
Number of farms	2,519	-	1,965	-	1,275	-	-22.0	-35.1
Number of acres	42,666	-	50,194	-	54,660	-	17.6	8.9
Weight in pounds	87,431,422	-	104,627,617	-	125,220,334	-	19.7	19.7
Soybeans for beans								
Number of farms	5,220	1.2	4,015	1.1	3,044	0.9	-23.1	-24.2
Number of acres	597,258	1.1	532,909	0.9	507,687	0.8	-10.8	-4.7
Number of bushels	12,872,219	0.7	11,521,171	0.6	11,554,522	0.5	-10.5	0.3
Dry edible beans, excluding dry limas								
Number of farms	-	-	-	-	-	-	-	-
Number of acres	-	-	-	-	-	-	-	-
Weight in hundredweight	-	-	-	-	-	-	-	-
Potatoes, excluding sweetpotatoes								
Number of farms	-	-	-	-	-	-	-	-
Number of acres	-	-	-	-	-	-	-	-
Weight in hundredweight	-	-	-	-	-	-	-	-
Sugar beets for sugar								
Number of farms	-	-	-	-	-	-	-	-
Number of acres	-	-	-	-	-	-	-	-
Weight in tons	-	-	-	-	-	-	-	-
Sugarcane for sugar								
Number of farms	-	-	-	-	-	-	-	-
Number of acres	-	-	-	-	-	-	-	-
Weight in tons	-	-	-	-	-	-	-	-
Pineapples harvested								
Number of farms	-	-	-	-	-	-	-	-
Number of acres	-	-	-	-	-	-	-	-
Weight in tons	-	-	-	-	-	-	-	-
Peanuts for nuts								
Number of farms	-	-	-	-	-	-	-	-
Number of acres	-	-	-	-	-	-	-	-
Weight in pounds	-	-	-	-	-	-	-	-
Hay - all types, including alfalfa								
Number of farms	7,272	0.7	7,056	0.8	7,618	0.9	-3.0	8.0
Number of acres	230,800	0.4	244,228	0.4	287,002	0.5	5.8	17.5
Weight in tons, dry	432,109	0.3	481,619	0.4	592,327	0.4	11.5	23.0
Vegetables harvested for sale								
Number of farms	-	-	-	-	-	-	-	-
Number of acres	-	-	-	-	-	-	-	-
Land in orchards								
Number of farms	1,134	0.9	1,157	1.0	885	0.8	2.0	-23.5
Number of acres	49,565	1.1	42,075	0.9	24,775	0.5	-15.1	-41.1

Source: *1997 Census of Agriculture*, U.S. Department of Agriculture, National Agricultural Statistics Service. NA stands for "not available." (D) is shown when data are withheld to prevent disclosure of competitive information. A dash (-) is shown where no data were reported. Not all states report growing all crops, but all crop categories in the census are shown for every state. The data series used for this presentation did not report U.S. totals for a number of categories; for that reason, the "% of U.S." column is sometimes blank.

SOUTH DAKOTA

GENERAL STATISTICS FOR SOUTH DAKOTA

Item	1987 Value	1987 % of U.S.	1992 Value	1992 % of U.S.	1997 Value	1997 % of U.S.	Percent change 1987-1992	Percent change 1992-1997
Farms (number)	36,376	1.7	34,057	1.8	31,284	1.6	-6.4	-8.1
Land in farms (acres)	44,157,503	4.6	44,828,124	4.7	44,354,880	4.8	1.5	-1.1
Average size of farm (acres)	1,214	262.8	1,316	268.0	1,418	291.2	8.4	7.8
Median size of farm (acres)	NA	-	NA	-	542	451.7	-	-
Market value of land and buildings:								
Average per farm (dollars)	326,333	112.8	360,111	100.9	487,039	108.3	10.4	35.2
Average per acre (dollars)	269	42.9	273	37.6	348	37.3	1.5	27.5
Market value of machinery/equipment -								
average per farm (dollars)	55,005	133.4	70,495	145.0	91,182	158.1	28.2	29.3
Farms by size:								
1 to 9 acres	1,881	1.0	1,504	0.9	1,015	0.7	-20.0	-32.5
10 to 49 acres	2,638	0.6	2,622	0.7	2,596	0.6	-0.6	-1.0
50 to 179 acres	5,083	0.8	4,977	0.9	4,844	0.8	-2.1	-2.7
180 to 499 acres	8,625	1.8	7,286	1.7	6,500	1.6	-15.5	-10.8
500 to 999 acres	7,618	3.8	6,917	3.7	5,866	3.3	-9.2	-15.2
1,000 acres or more	10,531	6.2	10,751	6.2	10,463	5.9	2.1	-2.7
Total cropland								
Farms	32,451	1.8	30,142	1.8	27,712	1.7	-7.1	-8.1
Acres	19,641,972	4.4	19,582,565	4.5	19,355,256	4.5	-0.3	-1.2
Harvested cropland (farms)	31,110	1.9	28,430	1.9	25,654	1.8	-8.6	-9.8
Harvested cropland (acres)	12,982,611	4.6	13,624,006	4.6	14,284,741	4.6	4.9	4.8
Irrigated land (farms)	1,869	0.6	1,674	0.6	1,439	0.5	-10.4	-14.0
Irrigated land (acres)	361,796	0.8	371,263	0.8	343,742	0.6	2.6	-7.4
Market value of agricultural products sold:								
Total sales ($1,000)	2,719,498	2.0	3,243,554	2.0	3,569,951	1.8	19.3	10.1
Average per farm (dollars)	74,761	114.7	95,239	112.8	114,114	110.8	27.4	19.8
Agricultural products only ($1,000)	857,373	1.5	1,072,895	1.4	1,654,044	1.7	25.1	54.2
Livestock, poultry, and products ($1,000)	1,862,125	2.4	2,170,659	2.5	1,915,907	1.9	16.6	-11.7
Farms by value of sales:								
Less than $2,500	2,888	0.6	2,792	0.7	3,338	0.7	-3.3	19.6
$2,500 to $4,999	2,020	0.8	1,658	0.7	1,605	0.7	-17.9	-3.2
$5,000 to $9,999	3,190	1.2	2,779	1.1	2,273	1.0	-12.9	-18.2
$10,000 to $24,999	6,764	2.1	5,493	1.8	4,516	1.6	-18.8	-17.8
$25,000 to $49,999	7,026	3.2	5,792	3.0	4,690	2.7	-17.6	-19.0
$50,000 to $99,999	7,706	3.5	6,829	3.6	5,415	3.4	-11.4	-20.7
$100,000 or more	6,782	2.3	8,714	2.6	9,447	2.7	28.5	8.4
Total farm production expenses ($1,000)	2,138,164	2.0	2,563,564	2.0	2,733,387	1.8	19.9	6.6
Average expenses per farm (dollars)	58,783	113.5	75,275	110.8	87,373	110.9	28.1	16.1
Net cash return for the farm unit:								
Number of farms	36,377	1.7	34,056	1.8	31,284	1.6	-6.4	-8.1
Value ($1000)	573,997	2.2	662,184	2.2	801,485	1.9	15.4	21.0
Average per farm (dollars)	15,779	124.6	19,444	123.1	25,620	115.1	23.2	31.8
Operators by principal occupation:								
Farming	28,407	2.5	26,141	2.5	22,704	2.4	-8.0	-13.1
Other	7,969	0.8	7,916	0.9	8,580	0.9	-0.7	8.4
Operators by days worked off farm:								
Any	13,553	1.2	12,540	1.3	13,049	1.3	-7.5	4.1
200 days or more	6,641	0.9	6,614	1.0	7,289	1.0	-0.4	10.2

Source: *1997 Census of Agriculture*, U.S. Department of Agriculture, National Agricultural Statistics Service. NA stands for "not available." (D) is shown when data are withheld to prevent disclosure of competitive information. A dash (-) is shown where no data were reported. The market value of land and buildings, and of machinery and equipment, is an estimated amount. Net cash return for the farm unit includes only returns from agricultural activities.

LIVESTOCK STATISTICS FOR SOUTH DAKOTA

Item	1987		1992		1997		Percent change	
	Value	% of U.S.	Value	% of U.S.	Value	% of U.S.	1987-1992	1992-1997
Cattle and calves								
Number of farms	23,998	2.0	22,576	2.1	20,502	2.0	-5.9	-9.2
Number of animals	3,630,200	3.8	3,777,822	3.9	3,723,271	3.8	4.1	-1.4
Beef cows (farms)	19,034	2.3	18,597	2.3	17,428	2.2	-2.3	-6.3
Beef cows (number)	1,502,927	4.7	1,604,838	4.9	1,675,000	4.9	6.8	4.4
Milk cows (farms)	3,940	1.9	2,873	1.8	1,802	1.5	-27.1	-37.3
Milk cows (number)	137,020	1.4	117,454	1.2	95,882	1.1	-14.3	-18.4
Cattle and calves sold (farms)	24,464	2.1	22,802	2.2	20,782	2.1	-6.8	-8.9
Cattle and calves sold (number)	2,398,208	3.3	2,500,254	3.5	2,448,551	3.3	4.3	-2.1
Hogs and pigs								
Number of farms	7,906	3.2	6,710	3.5	2,899	2.6	-15.1	-56.8
Number of animals	1,750,236	3.3	1,978,195	3.4	1,396,326	2.3	13.0	-29.4
Hogs and pigs sold (farms)	8,265	3.5	7,125	3.8	3,067	3.0	-13.8	-57.0
Hogs and pigs sold (number)	3,181,008	3.3	3,654,082	3.3	2,596,164	1.8	14.9	-29.0
Sheep and lambs								
Number of farms	3,960	4.3	3,386	4.2	2,354	3.6	-14.5	-30.5
Number of animals	603,824	5.5	661,872	6.1	416,570	5.3	9.6	-37.1
Layers and pullets 13 weeks old and older								
Number of farms	2,173	1.5	1,110	1.3	754	1.0	-48.9	-32.1
Number of birds	1,752,361	0.5	2,136,682	0.6	2,347,423	0.6	21.9	9.9
Broilers and other meat-type chickens sold								
Number of farms	269	1.0	130	0.5	92	0.4	-51.7	-29.2
Number of birds sold	237,779	0.0	121,283	0.0	285,735	0.0	-49.0	135.6

Source: 1997 Census of Agriculture, U.S. Department of Agriculture, National Agricultural Statistics Service. NA stands for "not available." (D) is shown when data are withheld to prevent disclosure of competitive information. A dash (-) is shown where no data were reported.

CROP STATISTICS FOR SOUTH DAKOTA

Item	1987		1992		1997		Percent change	
	Value	% of U.S.	Value	% of U.S.	Value	% of U.S.	1987-1992	1992-1997
Corn for grain or seed								
Number of farms	19,448	3.1	16,427	3.3	14,342	3.3	-15.5	-12.7
Number of acres	2,573,567	4.4	3,097,251	4.5	3,175,113	4.5	20.3	2.5
Number of bushels	199,208,883	-	245,398,567	2.8	295,056,391	3.4	23.2	20.2
Corn for silage or green chop								
Number of farms	6,960	-	6,235	-	4,785	-	-10.4	-23.3
Number of acres	374,158	-	394,087	-	308,116	-	5.3	-21.8
Weight in tons, green	3,077,579	-	3,335,427	-	3,061,677	-	8.4	-8.2
Sorghum for grain or seed								
Number of farms	-	-	-	-	-	-	-	-
Number of acres	-	-	-	-	-	-	-	-
Number of bushels	-	-	-	-	-	-	-	-
Wheat for grain								
Number of farms	15,273	4.3	12,014	4.1	9,561	3.9	-21.3	-20.4
Number of acres	3,229,384	6.1	3,340,644	5.7	3,177,527	5.4	3.4	-4.9
Number of bushels	91,141,128	4.8	101,053,975	4.6	89,470,811	4.1	10.9	-11.5
Barley for grain								
Number of farms	7,911	-	3,285	-	966	-	-58.5	-70.6
Number of acres	766,698	-	361,718	-	104,892	-	-52.8	-71.0
Number of bushels	29,647,024	-	17,423,745	-	4,233,108	-	-41.2	-75.7
Oats for grain								
Number of farms	13,558	-	9,055	-	3,729	-	-33.2	-58.8
Number of acres	919,997	-	627,557	-	253,972	-	-31.8	-59.5
Number of bushels	41,997,525	-	37,228,291	-	13,726,509	-	-11.4	-63.1
Rice								
Number of farms	-	-	-	-	-	-	-	-
Number of acres	-	-	-	-	-	-	-	-
Weight in hundredweight	-	-	-	-	-	-	-	-
Sunflower seed								
Number of farms	1,659	-	1,571	-	2,858	-	-5.3	81.9
Number of acres	262,847	-	349,668	-	740,707	-	33.0	111.8
Weight in pounds	315,806,323	-	427,963,785	-	1,041,102,232	-	35.5	143.3
Cotton								
Number of farms	-	-	-	-	-	-	-	-
Number of acres	-	-	-	-	-	-	-	-
Number of bales	-	-	-	-	-	-	-	-

Continued.

CROP STATISTICS FOR SOUTH DAKOTA - Continued

Item	1987		1992		1997		Percent change	
	Value	% of U.S.	Value	% of U.S.	Value	% of U.S.	1987-1992	1992-1997
Tobacco								
Number of farms	-	-	-	-	-	-	-	-
Number of acres	-	-	-	-	-	-	-	-
Weight in pounds	-	-	-	-	-	-	-	-
Soybeans for beans								
Number of farms	-	-	-	-	-	-	-	-
Number of acres	-	-	-	-	-	-	-	-
Number of bushels	-	-	-	-	-	-	-	-
Dry edible beans, excluding dry limas								
Number of farms	-	-	-	-	-	-	-	-
Number of acres	-	-	-	-	-	-	-	-
Weight in hundredweight	-	-	-	-	-	-	-	-
Potatoes, excluding sweetpotatoes								
Number of farms	-	-	-	-	-	-	-	-
Number of acres	-	-	-	-	-	-	-	-
Weight in hundredweight	-	-	-	-	-	-	-	-
Sugar beets for sugar								
Number of farms	-	-	-	-	-	-	-	-
Number of acres	-	-	-	-	-	-	-	-
Weight in tons	-	-	-	-	-	-	-	-
Sugarcane for sugar								
Number of farms	-	-	-	-	-	-	-	-
Number of acres	-	-	-	-	-	-	-	-
Weight in tons	-	-	-	-	-	-	-	-
Pineapples harvested								
Number of farms	-	-	-	-	-	-	-	-
Number of acres	-	-	-	-	-	-	-	-
Weight in tons	-	-	-	-	-	-	-	-
Peanuts for nuts								
Number of farms	-	-	-	-	-	-	-	-
Number of acres	-	-	-	-	-	-	-	-
Weight in pounds	-	-	-	-	-	-	-	-
Hay - all types, including alfalfa								
Number of farms	23,131	2.3	21,402	2.4	19,298	2.2	-7.5	-9.8
Number of acres	3,355,299	5.8	3,356,484	5.9	3,584,798	5.9	0.0	6.8
Weight in tons, dry	5,682,824	4.4	5,734,128	4.5	6,590,651	4.7	0.9	14.9
Vegetables harvested for sale								
Number of farms	-	-	-	-	-	-	-	-
Number of acres	-	-	-	-	-	-	-	-
Land in orchards								
Number of farms	-	-	-	-	-	-	-	-
Number of acres	-	-	-	-	-	-	-	-

Source: *1997 Census of Agriculture*, U.S. Department of Agriculture, National Agricultural Statistics Service. NA stands for "not available." (D) is shown when data are withheld to prevent disclosure of competitive information. A dash (-) is shown where no data were reported. Not all states report growing all crops, but all crop categories in the census are shown for every state. The data series used for this presentation did not report U.S. totals for a number of categories; for that reason, the "% of U.S." column is sometimes blank.

TENNESSEE

GENERAL STATISTICS FOR TENNESSEE

Item	1987 Value	1987 % of U.S.	1992 Value	1992 % of U.S.	1997 Value	1997 % of U.S.	Percent change 1987-1992	Percent change 1992-1997
Farms (number)	79,711	3.8	75,076	3.9	76,818	4.0	-5.8	2.3
Land in farms (acres)	11,731,386	1.2	11,169,086	1.2	11,122,363	1.2	-4.8	-0.4
Average size of farm (acres)	147	31.8	149	30.3	145	29.8	1.4	-2.7
Median size of farm (acres)	NA	-	NA	-	68	56.7	-	-
Market value of land and buildings:								
Average per farm (dollars)	146,126	50.5	186,171	52.1	261,209	58.1	27.4	40.3
Average per acre (dollars)	1,001	159.6	1,245	171.3	1,808	193.8	24.4	45.2
Market value of machinery/equipment - average per farm (dollars)	22,700	55.1	25,520	52.5	33,158	57.5	12.4	29.9
Farms by size:								
1 to 9 acres	7,306	4.0	7,336	4.4	5,919	3.9	0.4	-19.3
10 to 49 acres	23,209	5.6	22,173	5.7	24,401	5.9	-4.5	10.0
50 to 179 acres	32,266	5.0	29,572	5.1	30,719	5.2	-8.3	3.9
180 to 499 acres	12,697	2.7	11,873	2.8	11,924	3.0	-6.5	0.4
500 to 999 acres	2,906	1.5	2,707	1.5	2,544	1.4	-6.8	-6.0
1,000 acres or more	1,327	0.8	1,415	0.8	1,311	0.7	6.6	-7.3
Total cropland								
Farms	73,703	4.0	69,297	4.1	69,393	4.2	-6.0	0.1
Acres	7,185,903	1.6	7,086,879	1.6	7,069,470	1.6	-1.4	-0.2
Harvested cropland (farms)	63,754	3.9	58,527	3.9	56,016	4.0	-8.2	-4.3
Harvested cropland (acres)	3,854,302	1.4	3,817,720	1.3	4,064,058	1.3	-0.9	6.5
Irrigated land (farms)	1,899	0.7	1,544	0.6	1,768	0.6	-18.7	14.5
Irrigated land (acres)	37,776	0.1	36,974	0.1	45,581	0.1	-2.1	23.3
Market value of agricultural products sold:								
Total sales ($1,000)	1,617,636	1.2	1,933,506	1.2	2,178,389	1.1	19.5	12.7
Average per farm (dollars)	20,294	31.1	25,754	30.5	28,358	27.5	26.9	10.1
Agricultural products only ($1,000)	701,828	1.2	969,439	1.3	1,143,674	1.2	38.1	18.0
Livestock, poultry, and products ($1,000)	915,807	1.2	964,067	1.1	1,034,714	1.0	5.3	7.3
Farms by value of sales:								
Less than $2,500	27,451	5.6	21,446	5.1	27,201	5.5	-21.9	26.8
$2,500 to $4,999	16,106	6.1	14,365	6.2	14,578	6.4	-10.8	1.5
$5,000 to $9,999	14,398	5.2	14,918	5.9	13,751	5.8	3.6	-7.8
$10,000 to $24,999	11,446	3.5	13,088	4.3	11,217	4.1	14.3	-14.3
$25,000 to $49,999	4,127	1.9	4,641	2.4	3,987	2.3	12.5	-14.1
$50,000 to $99,999	2,719	1.2	2,681	1.4	2,176	1.4	-1.4	-18.8
$100,000 or more	3,464	1.2	3,937	1.2	3,908	1.1	13.7	-0.7
Total farm production expenses ($1,000)	1,282,885	1.2	1,492,457	1.1	1,641,727	1.1	16.3	10.0
Average expenses per farm (dollars)	16,094	31.1	19,879	29.3	21,371	27.1	23.5	7.5
Net cash return for the farm unit:								
Number of farms	79,712	3.8	75,078	3.9	76,821	4.0	-5.8	2.3
Value ($1000)	324,684	1.2	422,072	1.4	508,404	1.2	30.0	20.5
Average per farm (dollars)	4,073	32.2	5,622	35.6	6,618	29.7	38.0	17.7
Operators by principal occupation:								
Farming	30,745	2.7	29,878	2.8	27,680	2.9	-2.8	-7.4
Other	48,966	5.2	45,198	5.2	49,138	5.2	-7.7	8.7
Operators by days worked off farm:								
Any	48,882	4.4	44,536	4.5	47,484	4.6	-8.9	6.6
200 days or more	36,187	4.9	33,366	5.0	35,678	5.0	-7.8	6.9

Source: 1997 Census of Agriculture, U.S. Department of Agriculture, National Agricultural Statistics Service. NA stands for "not available." (D) is shown when data are withheld to prevent disclosure of competitive information. A dash (-) is shown where no data were reported. The market value of land and buildings, and of machinery and equipment, is an estimated amount. Net cash return for the farm unit includes only returns from agricultural activities.

LIVESTOCK STATISTICS FOR TENNESSEE

Item	1987 Value	1987 % of U.S.	1992 Value	1992 % of U.S.	1997 Value	1997 % of U.S.	Percent change 1987-1992	Percent change 1992-1997
Cattle and calves								
Number of farms	52,965	4.5	50,592	4.7	51,089	4.9	-4.5	1.0
Number of animals	2,008,570	2.1	2,162,660	2.2	2,145,405	2.2	7.7	-0.8
Beef cows (farms)	43,616	5.2	43,333	5.4	44,235	5.5	-0.6	2.1
Beef cows (number)	894,348	2.8	988,550	3.0	1,039,583	3.1	10.5	5.2
Milk cows (farms)	4,781	2.4	3,295	2.1	2,096	1.8	-31.1	-36.4
Milk cows (number)	180,390	1.8	152,067	1.6	111,985	1.2	-15.7	-26.4
Cattle and calves sold (farms)	51,558	4.5	47,955	4.6	49,234	4.9	-7.0	2.7
Cattle and calves sold (number)	1,077,665	1.5	1,043,627	1.5	1,126,232	1.5	-3.2	7.9
Hogs and pigs								
Number of farms	8,465	3.5	4,912	2.6	2,043	1.9	-42.0	-58.4
Number of animals	774,530	1.5	604,613	1.1	321,806	0.5	-21.9	-46.8
Hogs and pigs sold (farms)	7,874	3.3	4,522	2.4	1,579	1.5	-42.6	-65.1
Hogs and pigs sold (number)	1,484,049	1.5	1,293,654	1.2	714,999	0.5	-12.8	-44.7
Sheep and lambs								
Number of farms	623	0.7	749	0.9	773	1.2	20.2	3.2
Number of animals	15,303	0.1	18,379	0.2	13,773	0.2	20.1	-25.1
Layers and pullets 13 weeks old and older								
Number of farms	5,810	4.0	3,328	3.8	2,657	3.7	-42.7	-20.2
Number of birds	3,266,829	0.9	1,906,094	0.5	2,221,215	0.6	-41.7	16.5
Broilers and other meat-type chickens sold								
Number of farms	509	1.8	489	2.0	548	2.3	-3.9	12.1
Number of birds sold	75,974,462	1.1	98,516,358	1.8	120,830,210	1.8	29.7	22.6

Source: 1997 Census of Agriculture, U.S. Department of Agriculture, National Agricultural Statistics Service. NA stands for "not available." (D) is shown when data are withheld to prevent disclosure of competitive information. A dash (-) is shown where no data were reported.

CROP STATISTICS FOR TENNESSEE

Item	1987 Value	1987 % of U.S.	1992 Value	1992 % of U.S.	1997 Value	1997 % of U.S.	Percent change 1987-1992	Percent change 1992-1997
Corn for grain or seed								
Number of farms	13,715	2.2	9,143	1.8	5,854	1.4	-33.3	-36.0
Number of acres	553,943	0.9	605,287	0.9	575,878	0.8	9.3	-4.9
Number of bushels	47,899,079	-	67,755,811	0.8	58,459,483	0.7	41.5	-13.7
Corn for silage or green chop								
Number of farms	-	-	-	-	-	-	-	-
Number of acres	-	-	-	-	-	-	-	-
Weight in tons, green	-	-	-	-	-	-	-	-
Sorghum for grain or seed								
Number of farms	-	-	-	-	-	-	-	-
Number of acres	-	-	-	-	-	-	-	-
Number of bushels	-	-	-	-	-	-	-	-
Wheat for grain								
Number of farms	4,579	1.3	3,011	1.0	2,360	1.0	-34.2	-21.6
Number of acres	324,984	0.6	276,243	0.5	305,175	0.5	-15.0	10.5
Number of bushels	12,749,682	0.7	12,175,250	0.6	13,482,402	0.6	-4.5	10.7
Barley for grain								
Number of farms	-	-	-	-	-	-	-	-
Number of acres	-	-	-	-	-	-	-	-
Number of bushels	-	-	-	-	-	-	-	-
Oats for grain								
Number of farms	-	-	-	-	-	-	-	-
Number of acres	-	-	-	-	-	-	-	-
Number of bushels	-	-	-	-	-	-	-	-
Rice								
Number of farms	-	-	-	-	-	-	-	-
Number of acres	-	-	-	-	-	-	-	-
Weight in hundredweight	-	-	-	-	-	-	-	-
Sunflower seed								
Number of farms	-	-	-	-	-	-	-	-
Number of acres	-	-	-	-	-	-	-	-
Weight in pounds	-	-	-	-	-	-	-	-
Cotton								
Number of farms	2,545	5.9	2,137	6.1	1,156	3.7	-16.0	-45.9
Number of acres	411,100	4.2	598,838	5.5	472,165	3.6	45.7	-21.2
Number of bales	566,890	4.3	793,302	5.2	629,487	3.5	39.9	-20.6

Continued.

CROP STATISTICS FOR TENNESSEE - Continued

Item	1987 Value	1987 % of U.S.	1992 Value	1992 % of U.S.	1997 Value	1997 % of U.S.	Percent change 1987-1992	Percent change 1992-1997
Tobacco								
Number of farms	25,052	-	22,953	-	14,995	-	-8.4	-34.7
Number of acres	51,578	-	75,621	-	59,427	-	46.6	-21.4
Weight in pounds	85,715,814	-	139,367,463	-	106,785,282	-	62.6	-23.4
Soybeans for beans								
Number of farms	7,797	1.8	5,232	1.4	4,926	1.4	-32.9	-5.8
Number of acres	1,184,778	2.1	915,223	1.6	1,156,282	1.7	-22.8	26.3
Number of bushels	27,367,017	1.5	30,313,156	1.5	37,976,452	1.5	10.8	25.3
Dry edible beans, excluding dry limas								
Number of farms	-	-	-	-	-	-	-	-
Number of acres	-	-	-	-	-	-	-	-
Weight in hundredweight	-	-	-	-	-	-	-	-
Potatoes, excluding sweetpotatoes								
Number of farms	-	-	-	-	-	-	-	-
Number of acres	-	-	-	-	-	-	-	-
Weight in hundredweight	-	-	-	-	-	-	-	-
Sugar beets for sugar								
Number of farms	-	-	-	-	-	-	-	-
Number of acres	-	-	-	-	-	-	-	-
Weight in tons	-	-	-	-	-	-	-	-
Sugarcane for sugar								
Number of farms	-	-	-	-	-	-	-	-
Number of acres	-	-	-	-	-	-	-	-
Weight in tons	-	-	-	-	-	-	-	-
Pineapples harvested								
Number of farms	-	-	-	-	-	-	-	-
Number of acres	-	-	-	-	-	-	-	-
Weight in tons	-	-	-	-	-	-	-	-
Peanuts for nuts								
Number of farms	-	-	-	-	-	-	-	-
Number of acres	-	-	-	-	-	-	-	-
Weight in pounds	-	-	-	-	-	-	-	-
Hay - all types, including alfalfa								
Number of farms	44,314	4.5	40,529	4.5	44,161	5.0	-8.5	9.0
Number of acres	1,372,674	2.4	1,410,204	2.5	1,646,290	2.7	2.7	16.7
Weight in tons, dry	2,161,679	1.7	2,616,430	2.1	3,326,031	2.4	21.0	27.1
Vegetables harvested for sale								
Number of farms	-	-	-	-	-	-	-	-
Number of acres	-	-	-	-	-	-	-	-
Land in orchards								
Number of farms	-	-	-	-	-	-	-	-
Number of acres	-	-	-	-	-	-	-	-

Source: *1997 Census of Agriculture*, U.S. Department of Agriculture, National Agricultural Statistics Service. NA stands for "not available." (D) is shown when data are withheld to prevent disclosure of competitive information. A dash (-) is shown where no data were reported. Not all states report growing all crops, but all crop categories in the census are shown for every state. The data series used for this presentation did not report U.S. totals for a number of categories; for that reason, the "% of U.S." column is sometimes blank.

TEXAS

GENERAL STATISTICS FOR TEXAS

Item	1987 Value	1987 % of U.S.	1992 Value	1992 % of U.S.	1997 Value	1997 % of U.S.	Percent change 1987-1992	Percent change 1992-1997
Farms (number)	188,788	9.0	180,644	9.4	194,301	10.2	-4.3	7.6
Land in farms (acres)	130,502,792	13.5	130,886,608	13.8	131,308,286	14.1	0.3	0.3
Average size of farm (acres)	691	149.6	725	147.7	676	138.8	4.9	-6.8
Median size of farm (acres)	NA	-	NA	-	130	108.3	-	-
Market value of land and buildings:								
Average per farm (dollars)	374,742	129.5	360,153	100.9	398,126	88.5	-3.9	10.5
Average per acre (dollars)	544	86.8	499	68.6	593	63.6	-8.3	18.8
Market value of machinery/equipment -								
average per farm (dollars)	30,351	73.6	33,206	68.3	40,062	69.5	9.4	20.6
Farms by size:								
1 to 9 acres	12,770	7.0	11,122	6.7	11,930	7.8	-12.9	7.3
10 to 49 acres	37,063	9.0	34,514	8.9	41,615	10.1	-6.9	20.6
50 to 179 acres	57,666	8.9	54,214	9.3	59,420	10.0	-6.0	9.6
180 to 499 acres	39,143	8.2	38,602	9.0	39,674	9.9	-1.4	2.8
500 to 999 acres	19,327	9.7	18,800	10.1	18,495	10.5	-2.7	-1.6
1,000 acres or more	22,819	13.5	23,392	13.5	23,167	13.2	2.5	-1.0
Total cropland								
Farms	147,174	8.0	140,222	8.3	149,104	9.0	-4.7	6.3
Acres	35,610,951	8.0	36,381,847	8.4	37,662,040	8.7	2.2	3.5
Harvested cropland (farms)	110,358	6.7	104,318	7.0	108,169	7.7	-5.5	3.7
Harvested cropland (acres)	16,521,315	5.9	18,136,653	6.1	19,607,847	6.3	9.8	8.1
Irrigated land (farms)	19,806	6.8	18,784	6.7	18,756	6.7	-5.2	-0.1
Irrigated land (acres)	4,271,043	9.2	4,912,308	9.9	5,484,663	10.0	15.0	11.7
Market value of agricultural products sold:								
Total sales ($1,000)	10,548,907	7.8	12,004,385	7.4	13,766,527	7.0	13.8	14.7
Average per farm (dollars)	55,877	85.7	66,453	78.7	70,852	68.8	18.9	6.6
Agricultural products only ($1,000)	2,962,663	5.0	3,334,065	4.4	4,293,474	4.4	12.5	28.8
Livestock, poultry, and products ($1,000)	7,586,244	9.8	8,670,320	9.9	9,473,054	9.6	14.3	9.3
Farms by value of sales:								
Less than $2,500	58,693	12.0	52,446	12.4	67,440	13.6	-10.6	28.6
$2,500 to $4,999	31,227	11.9	28,770	12.4	31,746	13.9	-7.9	10.3
$5,000 to $9,999	30,076	10.9	29,303	11.6	30,136	12.7	-2.6	2.8
$10,000 to $24,999	28,350	8.7	29,226	9.7	27,410	10.0	3.1	-6.2
$25,000 to $49,999	13,467	6.1	13,701	7.0	12,317	7.2	1.7	-10.1
$50,000 to $99,999	10,598	4.9	10,147	5.4	8,252	5.2	-4.3	-18.7
$100,000 or more	16,377	5.5	17,051	5.1	17,000	4.9	4.1	-0.3
Total farm production expenses ($1,000)	8,911,631	8.2	10,431,343	8.0	11,636,594	7.7	17.1	11.6
Average expenses per farm (dollars)	47,205	91.1	57,745	85.0	59,894	76.0	22.3	3.7
Net cash return for the farm unit:								
Number of farms	188,785	9.0	180,646	9.4	194,288	10.2	-4.3	7.6
Value ($1000)	1,552,158	5.9	1,485,658	4.9	1,988,349	4.7	-4.3	33.8
Average per farm (dollars)	8,222	64.9	8,224	52.0	10,234	46.0	0.0	24.4
Operators by principal occupation:								
Farming	83,684	7.4	85,937	8.2	83,284	8.7	2.7	-3.1
Other	105,104	11.1	94,707	10.9	111,017	11.7	-9.9	17.2
Operators by days worked off farm:								
Any	113,615	10.2	101,160	10.2	114,962	11.0	-11.0	13.6
200 days or more	77,778	10.6	69,482	10.4	79,338	11.2	-10.7	14.2

Source: *1997 Census of Agriculture*, U.S. Department of Agriculture, National Agricultural Statistics Service. NA stands for "not available." (D) is shown when data are withheld to prevent disclosure of competitive information. A dash (-) is shown where no data were reported. The market value of land and buildings, and of machinery and equipment, is an estimated amount. Net cash return for the farm unit includes only returns from agricultural activities.

LIVESTOCK STATISTICS FOR TEXAS

Item	1987 Value	1987 % of U.S.	1992 Value	1992 % of U.S.	1997 Value	1997 % of U.S.	Percent change 1987-1992	Percent change 1992-1997
Cattle and calves								
Number of farms	142,244	12.1	134,669	12.5	144,354	13.8	-5.3	7.2
Number of animals	13,020,910	13.6	13,242,832	13.8	14,532,814	14.7	1.7	9.7
Beef cows (farms)	123,291	14.6	118,728	14.8	124,980	15.5	-3.7	5.3
Beef cows (number)	5,138,558	16.2	5,186,359	15.9	5,347,457	15.7	0.9	3.1
Milk cows (farms)	5,899	2.9	5,381	3.5	4,113	3.5	-8.8	-23.6
Milk cows (number)	356,538	3.5	394,587	4.2	374,816	4.1	10.7	-5.0
Cattle and calves sold (farms)	139,727	12.1	130,386	12.6	138,701	13.7	-6.7	6.4
Cattle and calves sold (number)	12,120,310	16.7	11,468,849	16.3	13,028,674	17.6	-5.4	13.6
Hogs and pigs								
Number of farms	7,717	3.2	6,537	3.4	5,428	4.9	-15.3	-17.0
Number of animals	527,942	1.0	460,175	0.8	578,664	0.9	-12.8	25.7
Hogs and pigs sold (farms)	6,190	2.6	4,995	2.7	3,659	3.6	-19.3	-26.7
Hogs and pigs sold (number)	923,228	1.0	810,047	0.7	903,226	0.6	-12.3	11.5
Sheep and lambs								
Number of farms	7,821	8.5	7,516	9.3	6,959	10.6	-3.9	-7.4
Number of animals	2,054,963	18.6	2,223,774	20.6	1,531,614	19.6	8.2	-31.1
Layers and pullets 13 weeks old and older								
Number of farms	13,201	9.1	7,595	8.6	6,473	8.9	-42.5	-14.8
Number of birds	19,601,318	5.2	19,728,363	5.6	20,184,249	5.5	0.6	2.3
Broilers and other meat-type chickens sold								
Number of farms	1,023	3.7	916	3.8	1,000	4.2	-10.5	9.2
Number of birds sold	226,038,116	3.4	292,758,887	5.4	388,114,496	5.8	29.5	32.6

Source: *1997 Census of Agriculture*, U.S. Department of Agriculture, National Agricultural Statistics Service. NA stands for "not available." (D) is shown when data are withheld to prevent disclosure of competitive information. A dash (-) is shown where no data were reported.

CROP STATISTICS FOR TEXAS

Item	1987 Value	1987 % of U.S.	1992 Value	1992 % of U.S.	1997 Value	1997 % of U.S.	Percent change 1987-1992	Percent change 1992-1997
Corn for grain or seed								
Number of farms	9,131	1.5	7,393	1.5	5,855	1.4	-19.0	-20.8
Number of acres	1,227,335	2.1	1,549,680	2.2	1,656,229	2.4	26.3	6.9
Number of bushels	123,806,676	-	180,025,937	2.1	219,361,590	2.6	45.4	21.8
Corn for silage or green chop								
Number of farms	-	-	-	-	-	-	-	-
Number of acres	-	-	-	-	-	-	-	-
Weight in tons, green	-	-	-	-	-	-	-	-
Sorghum for grain or seed								
Number of farms	15,935	-	13,942	-	10,438	-	-12.5	-25.1
Number of acres	2,665,237	-	3,984,934	-	3,041,937	-	49.5	-23.7
Number of bushels	155,573,425	-	222,512,221	-	175,279,096	-	43.0	-21.2
Wheat for grain								
Number of farms	19,386	5.5	14,877	5.1	13,669	5.6	-23.3	-8.1
Number of acres	3,649,104	6.9	3,726,217	6.3	3,860,325	6.6	2.1	3.6
Number of bushels	98,226,965	5.2	111,202,412	5.0	108,242,787	4.9	13.2	-2.7
Barley for grain								
Number of farms	-	-	-	-	-	-	-	-
Number of acres	-	-	-	-	-	-	-	-
Number of bushels	-	-	-	-	-	-	-	-
Oats for grain								
Number of farms	-	-	-	-	-	-	-	-
Number of acres	-	-	-	-	-	-	-	-
Number of bushels	-	-	-	-	-	-	-	-
Rice								
Number of farms	1,212	-	1,276	-	843	-	5.3	-33.9
Number of acres	299,388	-	369,539	-	280,676	-	23.4	-24.0
Weight in hundredweight	16,345,153	-	20,026,016	-	15,348,483	-	22.5	-23.4
Sunflower seed								
Number of farms	-	-	-	-	-	-	-	-
Number of acres	-	-	-	-	-	-	-	-
Weight in pounds	-	-	-	-	-	-	-	-
Cotton								
Number of farms	16,557	38.5	11,237	32.3	10,971	34.8	-32.1	-2.4
Number of acres	4,349,755	44.3	3,620,070	33.0	5,221,561	39.5	-16.8	44.2
Number of bales	4,071,552	30.7	3,212,770	20.9	4,828,062	27.0	-21.1	50.3

Continued.

CROP STATISTICS FOR TEXAS - Continued

Item	1987 Value	% of U.S.	1992 Value	% of U.S.	1997 Value	% of U.S.	Percent change 1987-1992	1992-1997
Tobacco								
Number of farms	-	-	-	-	-	-	-	-
Number of acres	-	-	-	-	-	-	-	-
Weight in pounds	-	-	-	-	-	-	-	-
Soybeans for beans								
Number of farms	1,118	0.3	1,985	0.5	1,705	0.5	77.5	-14.1
Number of acres	172,361	0.3	383,837	0.7	381,187	0.6	122.7	-0.7
Number of bushels	4,235,367	0.2	12,008,961	0.6	10,114,310	0.4	183.5	-15.8
Dry edible beans, excluding dry limas								
Number of farms	-	-	-	-	-	-	-	-
Number of acres	-	-	-	-	-	-	-	-
Weight in hundredweight	-	-	-	-	-	-	-	-
Potatoes, excluding sweetpotatoes								
Number of farms	-	-	-	-	-	-	-	-
Number of acres	-	-	-	-	-	-	-	-
Weight in hundredweight	-	-	-	-	-	-	-	-
Sugar beets for sugar								
Number of farms	-	-	-	-	-	-	-	-
Number of acres	-	-	-	-	-	-	-	-
Weight in tons	-	-	-	-	-	-	-	-
Sugarcane for sugar								
Number of farms	-	-	-	-	-	-	-	-
Number of acres	-	-	-	-	-	-	-	-
Weight in tons	-	-	-	-	-	-	-	-
Pineapples harvested								
Number of farms	-	-	-	-	-	-	-	-
Number of acres	-	-	-	-	-	-	-	-
Weight in tons	-	-	-	-	-	-	-	-
Peanuts for nuts								
Number of farms	-	-	-	-	-	-	-	-
Number of acres	-	-	-	-	-	-	-	-
Weight in pounds	-	-	-	-	-	-	-	-
Hay - all types, including alfalfa								
Number of farms	76,357	7.7	74,836	8.3	83,219	9.4	-2.0	11.2
Number of acres	3,252,216	5.6	3,607,387	6.4	4,277,199	7.0	10.9	18.6
Weight in tons, dry	6,684,785	5.2	8,055,561	6.3	9,605,686	6.9	20.5	19.2
Vegetables harvested for sale								
Number of farms	-	-	-	-	-	-	-	-
Number of acres	-	-	-	-	-	-	-	-
Land in orchards								
Number of farms	-	-	-	-	-	-	-	-
Number of acres	-	-	-	-	-	-	-	-

Source: 1997 Census of Agriculture, U.S. Department of Agriculture, National Agricultural Statistics Service. NA stands for "not available." (D) is shown when data are withheld to prevent disclosure of competitive information. A dash (-) is shown where no data were reported. Not all states report growing all crops, but all crop categories in the census are shown for every state. The data series used for this presentation did not report U.S. totals for a number of categories; for that reason, the "% of U.S." column is sometimes blank.

UTAH

GENERAL STATISTICS FOR UTAH

Item	1987 Value	1987 % of U.S.	1992 Value	1992 % of U.S.	1997 Value	1997 % of U.S.	Percent change 1987-1992	Percent change 1992-1997
Farms (number)	14,066	0.7	13,520	0.7	14,181	0.7	-3.9	4.9
Land in farms (acres)	9,989,073	1.0	9,624,463	1.0	12,024,661	1.3	-3.7	24.9
Average size of farm (acres)	710	153.7	712	145.0	848	174.1	0.3	19.1
Median size of farm (acres)	NA	-	NA	-	60	50.0	-	-
Market value of land and buildings:								
Average per farm (dollars)	302,838	104.6	347,982	97.5	486,235	108.1	14.9	39.7
Average per acre (dollars)	425	67.8	491	67.5	575	61.6	15.5	17.1
Market value of machinery/equipment -								
average per farm (dollars)	35,685	86.6	39,126	80.5	51,148	88.7	9.6	30.7
Farms by size:								
1 to 9 acres	2,365	1.3	2,262	1.4	2,590	1.7	-4.4	14.5
10 to 49 acres	3,835	0.9	3,735	1.0	3,978	1.0	-2.6	6.5
50 to 179 acres	3,437	0.5	3,176	0.5	3,245	0.5	-7.6	2.2
180 to 499 acres	2,137	0.4	2,057	0.5	2,042	0.5	-3.7	-0.7
500 to 999 acres	941	0.5	927	0.5	945	0.5	-1.5	1.9
1,000 acres or more	1,351	0.8	1,363	0.8	1,381	0.8	0.9	1.3
Total cropland								
Farms	12,233	0.7	11,700	0.7	12,227	0.7	-4.4	4.5
Acres	2,028,537	0.5	2,093,779	0.5	2,069,751	0.5	3.2	-1.1
Harvested cropland (farms)	10,752	0.7	10,173	0.7	10,393	0.7	-5.4	2.2
Harvested cropland (acres)	1,076,886	0.4	1,043,347	0.4	1,107,928	0.4	-3.1	6.2
Irrigated land (farms)	11,143	3.8	10,901	3.9	11,291	4.0	-2.2	3.6
Irrigated land (acres)	1,161,207	2.5	1,142,514	2.3	1,212,201	2.2	-1.6	6.1
Market value of agricultural products sold:								
Total sales ($1,000)	617,882	0.5	725,159	0.4	877,295	0.4	17.4	21.0
Average per farm (dollars)	43,927	67.4	53,636	63.5	61,864	60.1	22.1	15.3
Agricultural products only ($1,000)	130,441	0.2	181,380	0.2	247,443	0.3	39.1	36.4
Livestock, poultry, and products ($1,000)	487,442	0.6	543,779	0.6	629,852	0.6	11.6	15.8
Farms by value of sales:								
Less than $2,500	4,380	0.9	3,979	0.9	4,226	0.9	-9.2	6.2
$2,500 to $4,999	1,894	0.7	1,751	0.8	1,867	0.8	-7.6	6.6
$5,000 to $9,999	1,854	0.7	1,845	0.7	1,904	0.8	-0.5	3.2
$10,000 to $24,999	2,272	0.7	2,217	0.7	2,270	0.8	-2.4	2.4
$25,000 to $49,999	1,272	0.6	1,241	0.6	1,328	0.8	-2.4	7.0
$50,000 to $99,999	1,005	0.5	987	0.5	949	0.6	-1.8	-3.9
$100,000 or more	1,389	0.5	1,500	0.4	1,637	0.5	8.0	9.1
Total farm production expenses ($1,000)	494,641	0.5	602,812	0.5	699,532	0.5	21.9	16.0
Average expenses per farm (dollars)	35,171	67.9	44,593	65.6	49,343	62.6	26.8	10.7
Net cash return for the farm unit:								
Number of farms	14,064	0.7	13,518	0.7	14,178	0.7	-3.9	4.9
Value ($1000)	118,167	0.4	123,215	0.4	160,519	0.4	4.3	30.3
Average per farm (dollars)	8,402	66.4	9,115	57.7	11,322	50.9	8.5	24.2
Operators by principal occupation:								
Farming	6,350	0.6	6,269	0.6	5,987	0.6	-1.3	-4.5
Other	7,716	0.8	7,251	0.8	8,194	0.9	-6.0	13.0
Operators by days worked off farm:								
Any	8,688	0.8	8,142	0.8	8,726	0.8	-6.3	7.2
200 days or more	5,834	0.8	5,614	0.8	6,066	0.9	-3.8	8.1

Source: 1997 Census of Agriculture, U.S. Department of Agriculture, National Agricultural Statistics Service. NA stands for "not available." (D) is shown when data are withheld to prevent disclosure of competitive information. A dash (-) is shown where no data were reported. The market value of land and buildings, and of machinery and equipment, is an estimated amount. Net cash return for the farm unit includes only returns from agricultural activities.

LIVESTOCK STATISTICS FOR UTAH

Item	1987		1992		1997		Percent change	
	Value	% of U.S.	Value	% of U.S.	Value	% of U.S.	1987-1992	1992-1997
Cattle and calves								
Number of farms	7,854	0.7	7,530	0.7	7,986	0.8	-4.1	6.1
Number of animals	855,338	0.9	860,830	0.9	916,090	0.9	0.6	6.4
Beef cows (farms)	5,430	0.6	5,306	0.7	5,749	0.7	-2.3	8.3
Beef cows (number)	346,462	1.1	356,971	1.1	383,790	1.1	3.0	7.5
Milk cows (farms)	1,447	0.7	1,082	0.7	891	0.8	-25.2	-17.7
Milk cows (number)	76,610	0.8	80,369	0.8	92,953	1.0	4.9	15.7
Cattle and calves sold (farms)	7,520	0.7	7,212	0.7	7,598	0.8	-4.1	5.4
Cattle and calves sold (number)	499,464	0.7	506,739	0.7	524,128	0.7	1.5	3.4
Hogs and pigs								
Number of farms	748	0.3	727	0.4	511	0.5	-2.8	-29.7
Number of animals	33,643	0.1	43,017	0.1	292,472	0.5	27.9	579.9
Hogs and pigs sold (farms)	575	0.2	575	0.3	379	0.4	-	-34.1
Hogs and pigs sold (number)	48,290	0.1	61,407	0.1	330,515	0.2	27.2	438.2
Sheep and lambs								
Number of farms	1,943	2.1	1,721	2.1	1,438	2.2	-11.4	-16.4
Number of animals	595,626	5.4	519,745	4.8	438,678	5.6	-12.7	-15.6
Layers and pullets 13 weeks old and older								
Number of farms	1,008	0.7	622	0.7	535	0.7	-38.3	-14.0
Number of birds	2,089,320	0.6	1,778,605	0.5	1,921,163	0.5	-14.9	8.0
Broilers and other meat-type chickens sold								
Number of farms	23	0.1	21	0.1	19	0.1	-8.7	-9.5
Number of birds sold	7,793	0.0	5,091	0.0	(D)	-	-34.7	-

Source: *1997 Census of Agriculture*, U.S. Department of Agriculture, National Agricultural Statistics Service. NA stands for "not available." (D) is shown when data are withheld to prevent disclosure of competitive information. A dash (-) is shown where no data were reported.

CROP STATISTICS FOR UTAH

Item	1987		1992		1997		Percent change	
	Value	% of U.S.	Value	% of U.S.	Value	% of U.S.	1987-1992	1992-1997
Corn for grain or seed								
Number of farms	-	-	-	-	-	-	-	-
Number of acres	-	-	-	-	-	-	-	-
Number of bushels	-	-	-	-	-	-	-	-
Corn for silage or green chop								
Number of farms	1,352	-	1,037	-	855	-	-23.3	-17.6
Number of acres	45,437	-	41,446	-	38,495	-	-8.8	-7.1
Weight in tons, green	864,471	-	793,122	-	840,576	-	-8.3	6.0
Sorghum for grain or seed								
Number of farms	-	-	-	-	-	-	-	-
Number of acres	-	-	-	-	-	-	-	-
Number of bushels	-	-	-	-	-	-	-	-
Wheat for grain								
Number of farms	1,711	0.5	1,274	0.4	1,148	0.5	-25.5	-9.9
Number of acres	191,384	0.4	177,360	0.3	182,372	0.3	-7.3	2.8
Number of bushels	7,149,004	0.4	6,295,501	0.3	7,832,313	0.4	-11.9	24.4
Barley for grain								
Number of farms	3,139	-	2,345	-	1,929	-	-25.3	-17.7
Number of acres	126,345	-	104,213	-	94,072	-	-17.5	-9.7
Number of bushels	9,506,857	-	7,879,596	-	7,422,580	-	17.1	-5.8
Oats for grain								
Number of farms	789	-	681	-	481	-	-13.7	-29.4
Number of acres	11,107	-	11,923	-	9,208	-	7.3	-22.8
Number of bushels	699,305	-	669,910	-	643,121	-	-4.2	-4.0
Rice								
Number of farms	-	-	-	-	-	-	-	-
Number of acres	-	-	-	-	-	-	-	-
Weight in hundredweight	-	-	-	-	-	-	-	-
Sunflower seed								
Number of farms	-	-	-	-	-	-	-	-
Number of acres	-	-	-	-	-	-	-	-
Weight in pounds	-	-	-	-	-	-	-	-
Cotton								
Number of farms	-	-	-	-	-	-	-	-
Number of acres	-	-	-	-	-	-	-	-
Number of bales	-	-	-	-	-	-	-	-

Continued.

CROP STATISTICS FOR UTAH - Continued

Item	1987 Value	1987 % of U.S.	1992 Value	1992 % of U.S.	1997 Value	1997 % of U.S.	Percent change 1987-1992	Percent change 1992-1997
Tobacco								
Number of farms	-	-	-	-	-	-	-	-
Number of acres	-	-	-	-	-	-	-	-
Weight in pounds	-	-	-	-	-	-	-	-
Soybeans for beans								
Number of farms	-	-	-	-	-	-	-	-
Number of acres	-	-	-	-	-	-	-	-
Number of bushels	-	-	-	-	-	-	-	-
Dry edible beans, excluding dry limas								
Number of farms	-	-	-	-	-	-	-	-
Number of acres	-	-	-	-	-	-	-	-
Weight in hundredweight	-	-	-	-	-	-	-	-
Potatoes, excluding sweetpotatoes								
Number of farms	-	-	-	-	-	-	-	-
Number of acres	-	-	-	-	-	-	-	-
Weight in hundredweight	-	-	-	-	-	-	-	-
Sugar beets for sugar								
Number of farms	-	-	-	-	-	-	-	-
Number of acres	-	-	-	-	-	-	-	-
Weight in tons	-	-	-	-	-	-	-	-
Sugarcane for sugar								
Number of farms	-	-	-	-	-	-	-	-
Number of acres	-	-	-	-	-	-	-	-
Weight in tons	-	-	-	-	-	-	-	-
Pineapples harvested								
Number of farms	-	-	-	-	-	-	-	-
Number of acres	-	-	-	-	-	-	-	-
Weight in tons	-	-	-	-	-	-	-	-
Peanuts for nuts								
Number of farms	-	-	-	-	-	-	-	-
Number of acres	-	-	-	-	-	-	-	-
Weight in pounds	-	-	-	-	-	-	-	-
Hay - all types, including alfalfa								
Number of farms	9,114	0.9	8,660	1.0	9,033	1.0	-5.0	4.3
Number of acres	649,688	1.1	660,762	1.2	740,740	1.2	1.7	12.1
Weight in tons, dry	1,962,334	1.5	2,073,029	1.6	2,533,360	1.8	5.6	22.2
Vegetables harvested for sale								
Number of farms	-	-	-	-	-	-	-	-
Number of acres	-	-	-	-	-	-	-	-
Land in orchards								
Number of farms	865	0.7	790	0.7	631	0.6	-8.7	-20.1
Number of acres	15,113	0.3	12,833	0.3	10,162	0.2	-15.1	-20.8

Source: 1997 Census of Agriculture, U.S. Department of Agriculture, National Agricultural Statistics Service. NA stands for "not available." (D) is shown when data are withheld to prevent disclosure of competitive information. A dash (-) is shown where no data were reported. Not all states report growing all crops, but all crop categories in the census are shown for every state. The data series used for this presentation did not report U.S. totals for a number of categories; for that reason, the "% of U.S." column is sometimes blank.

VERMONT

GENERAL STATISTICS FOR VERMONT

Item	1987 Value	1987 % of U.S.	1992 Value	1992 % of U.S.	1997 Value	1997 % of U.S.	Percent change 1987-1992	Percent change 1992-1997
Farms (number)	5,877	0.3	5,436	0.3	5,828	0.3	-7.5	7.2
Land in farms (acres)	1,407,868	0.1	1,278,525	0.1	1,262,155	0.1	-9.2	-1.3
Average size of farm (acres)	240	51.9	235	47.9	217	44.6	-2.1	-7.7
Median size of farm (acres)	NA	-	NA	-	140	116.7	-	-
Market value of land and buildings:								
Average per farm (dollars)	258,713	89.4	318,131	89.1	323,107	71.8	23.0	1.6
Average per acre (dollars)	1,124	179.3	1,342	184.6	1,520	162.9	19.4	13.3
Market value of machinery/equipment - average per farm (dollars)	46,090	111.8	50,911	104.7	49,046	85.0	10.5	-3.7
Farms by size:								
1 to 9 acres	281	0.2	292	0.2	354	0.2	3.9	21.2
10 to 49 acres	834	0.2	807	0.2	1,103	0.3	-3.2	36.7
50 to 179 acres	1,800	0.3	1,692	0.3	1,925	0.3	-6.0	13.8
180 to 499 acres	2,320	0.5	2,039	0.5	1,862	0.5	-12.1	-8.7
500 to 999 acres	559	0.3	520	0.3	469	0.3	-7.0	-9.8
1,000 acres or more	83	0.0	86	0.0	115	0.1	3.6	33.7
Total cropland								
Farms	5,506	0.3	5,081	0.3	5,065	0.3	-7.7	-0.3
Acres	707,970	0.2	658,765	0.2	617,263	0.1	-7.0	-6.3
Harvested cropland (farms)	5,069	0.3	4,741	0.3	4,609	0.3	-6.5	-2.8
Harvested cropland (acres)	488,253	0.2	477,020	0.2	465,489	0.2	-2.3	-2.4
Irrigated land (farms)	178	0.1	255	0.1	333	0.1	43.3	30.6
Irrigated land (acres)	1,823	0.0	2,123	0.0	2,570	0.0	16.5	21.1
Market value of agricultural products sold:								
Total sales ($1,000)	375,537	0.3	415,253	0.3	476,343	0.2	10.6	14.7
Average per farm (dollars)	63,899	98.1	76,389	90.4	81,734	79.4	19.5	7.0
Agricultural products only ($1,000)	25,186	0.0	35,483	0.0	59,592	0.1	40.9	67.9
Livestock, poultry, and products ($1,000)	350,351	0.5	379,770	0.4	416,752	0.4	8.4	9.7
Farms by value of sales:								
Less than $2,500	1,523	0.3	1,326	0.3	1,504	0.3	-12.9	13.4
$2,500 to $4,999	589	0.2	551	0.2	655	0.3	-6.5	18.9
$5,000 to $9,999	480	0.2	567	0.2	704	0.3	18.1	24.2
$10,000 to $24,999	453	0.1	467	0.2	719	0.3	3.1	54.0
$25,000 to $49,999	446	0.2	350	0.2	344	0.2	-21.5	-1.7
$50,000 to $99,999	992	0.5	710	0.4	569	0.4	-28.4	-19.9
$100,000 or more	1,394	0.5	1,465	0.4	1,333	0.4	5.1	-9.0
Total farm production expenses ($1,000)	289,945	0.3	340,482	0.3	371,207	0.2	17.4	9.0
Average expenses per farm (dollars)	49,302	95.2	62,612	92.2	63,935	81.2	27.0	2.1
Net cash return for the farm unit:								
Number of farms	5,881	0.3	5,438	0.3	5,806	0.3	-7.5	6.8
Value ($1000)	83,417	0.3	71,810	0.2	87,572	0.2	-13.9	21.9
Average per farm (dollars)	14,184	112.0	13,205	83.6	15,083	67.8	-6.9	14.2
Operators by principal occupation:								
Farming	3,762	0.3	3,502	0.3	3,300	0.3	-6.9	-5.8
Other	2,115	0.2	1,934	0.2	2,528	0.3	-8.6	30.7
Operators by days worked off farm:								
Any	2,695	0.2	2,402	0.2	2,835	0.3	-10.9	18.0
200 days or more	1,598	0.2	1,344	0.2	1,685	0.2	-15.9	25.4

Source: 1997 Census of Agriculture, U.S. Department of Agriculture, National Agricultural Statistics Service. NA stands for "not available." (D) is shown when data are withheld to prevent disclosure of competitive information. A dash (-) is shown where no data were reported. The market value of land and buildings, and of machinery and equipment, is an estimated amount. Net cash return for the farm unit includes only returns from agricultural activities.

LIVESTOCK STATISTICS FOR VERMONT

Item	1987		1992		1997		Percent change	
	Value	% of U.S.	Value	% of U.S.	Value	% of U.S.	1987-1992	1992-1997
Cattle and calves								
Number of farms	4,128	0.4	3,558	0.3	3,203	0.3	-13.8	-10.0
Number of animals	320,189	0.3	310,518	0.3	308,267	0.3	-3.0	-0.7
Beef cows (farms)	1,180	0.1	1,048	0.1	1,057	0.1	-11.2	0.9
Beef cows (number)	9,805	0.0	11,812	0.0	12,340	0.0	20.5	4.5
Milk cows (farms)	2,846	1.4	2,373	1.5	1,940	1.7	-16.6	-18.2
Milk cows (number)	178,967	1.8	168,473	1.8	162,868	1.8	-5.9	-3.3
Cattle and calves sold (farms)	3,919	0.3	3,378	0.3	2,958	0.3	-13.8	-12.4
Cattle and calves sold (number)	170,741	0.2	145,715	0.2	142,041	0.2	-14.7	-2.5
Hogs and pigs								
Number of farms	370	0.2	347	0.2	238	0.2	-6.2	-31.4
Number of animals	5,133	0.0	3,738	0.0	2,900	0.0	-27.2	-22.4
Hogs and pigs sold (farms)	239	0.1	228	0.1	140	0.1	-4.6	-38.6
Hogs and pigs sold (number)	7,595	0.0	7,427	0.0	4,992	0.0	-2.2	-32.8
Sheep and lambs								
Number of farms	605	0.7	485	0.6	451	0.7	-19.8	-7.0
Number of animals	20,456	0.2	17,145	0.2	14,511	0.2	-16.2	-15.4
Layers and pullets 13 weeks old and older								
Number of farms	649	0.4	508	0.6	513	0.7	-21.7	1.0
Number of birds	405,869	0.1	(D)	-	256,074	0.1	-	-
Broilers and other meat-type chickens sold								
Number of farms	53	0.2	51	0.2	57	0.2	-3.8	11.8
Number of birds sold	5,231	0.0	7,266	0.0	49,535	0.0	38.9	581.7

Source: 1997 Census of Agriculture, U.S. Department of Agriculture, National Agricultural Statistics Service. NA stands for "not available." (D) is shown when data are withheld to prevent disclosure of competitive information. A dash (-) is shown where no data were reported.

CROP STATISTICS FOR VERMONT

Item	1987		1992		1997		Percent change	
	Value	% of U.S.	Value	% of U.S.	Value	% of U.S.	1987-1992	1992-1997
Corn for grain or seed								
Number of farms	210	0.0	143	0.0	131	0.0	-31.9	-8.4
Number of acres	11,191	0.0	7,567	0.0	8,233	0.0	-32.4	8.8
Number of bushels	1,031,941	-	727,744	0.0	938,996	0.0	-29.5	29.0
Corn for silage or green chop								
Number of farms	1,481	-	1,419	-	1,168	-	-4.2	-17.7
Number of acres	70,258	-	86,024	-	95,713	-	22.4	11.3
Weight in tons, green	1,154,813	-	1,362,157	-	1,702,672	-	18.0	25.0
Sorghum for grain or seed								
Number of farms	-	-	-	-	-	-	-	-
Number of acres	-	-	-	-	-	-	-	-
Number of bushels	-	-	-	-	-	-	-	-
Wheat for grain								
Number of farms	-	-	-	-	-	-	-	-
Number of acres	-	-	-	-	-	-	-	-
Number of bushels	-	-	-	-	-	-	-	-
Barley for grain								
Number of farms	-	-	-	-	-	-	-	-
Number of acres	-	-	-	-	-	-	-	-
Number of bushels	-	-	-	-	-	-	-	-
Oats for grain								
Number of farms	42	-	28	-	26	-	-33.3	-7.1
Number of acres	646	-	489	-	351	-	-24.3	-28.2
Number of bushels	28,475	-	28,885	-	13,659	-	1.4	-52.7
Rice								
Number of farms	-	-	-	-	-	-	-	-
Number of acres	-	-	-	-	-	-	-	-
Weight in hundredweight	-	-	-	-	-	-	-	-
Sunflower seed								
Number of farms	-	-	-	-	-	-	-	-
Number of acres	-	-	-	-	-	-	-	-
Weight in pounds	-	-	-	-	-	-	-	-
Cotton								
Number of farms	-	-	-	-	-	-	-	-
Number of acres	-	-	-	-	-	-	-	-
Number of bales	-	-	-	-	-	-	-	-

Continued.

CROP STATISTICS FOR VERMONT - Continued

Item	1987 Value	1987 % of U.S.	1992 Value	1992 % of U.S.	1997 Value	1997 % of U.S.	Percent change 1987-1992	Percent change 1992-1997
Tobacco								
Number of farms	-	-	-	-	-	-	-	-
Number of acres	-	-	-	-	-	-	-	-
Weight in pounds	-	-	-	-	-	-	-	-
Soybeans for beans								
Number of farms	-	-	-	-	-	-	-	-
Number of acres	-	-	-	-	-	-	-	-
Number of bushels	-	-	-	-	-	-	-	-
Dry edible beans, excluding dry limas								
Number of farms	-	-	-	-	-	-	-	-
Number of acres	-	-	-	-	-	-	-	-
Weight in hundredweight	-	-	-	-	-	-	-	-
Potatoes, excluding sweetpotatoes								
Number of farms	-	-	-	-	-	-	-	-
Number of acres	-	-	-	-	-	-	-	-
Weight in hundredweight	-	-	-	-	-	-	-	-
Sugar beets for sugar								
Number of farms	-	-	-	-	-	-	-	-
Number of acres	-	-	-	-	-	-	-	-
Weight in tons	-	-	-	-	-	-	-	-
Sugarcane for sugar								
Number of farms	-	-	-	-	-	-	-	-
Number of acres	-	-	-	-	-	-	-	-
Weight in tons	-	-	-	-	-	-	-	-
Pineapples harvested								
Number of farms	-	-	-	-	-	-	-	-
Number of acres	-	-	-	-	-	-	-	-
Weight in tons	-	-	-	-	-	-	-	-
Peanuts for nuts								
Number of farms	-	-	-	-	-	-	-	-
Number of acres	-	-	-	-	-	-	-	-
Weight in pounds	-	-	-	-	-	-	-	-
Hay - all types, including alfalfa								
Number of farms	4,640	0.5	4,200	0.5	3,782	0.4	-9.5	-10.0
Number of acres	432,881	0.7	408,552	0.7	385,562	0.6	-5.6	-5.6
Weight in tons, dry	869,548	0.7	776,231	0.6	703,077	0.5	-10.7	-9.4
Vegetables harvested for sale								
Number of farms	230	0.4	330	0.5	333	0.6	43.5	0.9
Number of acres	2,038	0.1	2,534	0.1	2,893	0.1	24.3	14.2
Land in orchards								
Number of farms	221	0.2	258	0.2	228	0.2	16.7	-11.6
Number of acres	4,797	0.1	4,894	0.1	4,311	0.1	2.0	-11.9

Source: *1997 Census of Agriculture*, U.S. Department of Agriculture, National Agricultural Statistics Service. NA stands for "not available." (D) is shown when data are withheld to prevent disclosure of competitive information. A dash (-) is shown where no data were reported. Not all states report growing all crops, but all crop categories in the census are shown for every state. The data series used for this presentation did not report U.S. totals for a number of categories; for that reason, the "% of U.S." column is sometimes blank.

VIRGINIA

GENERAL STATISTICS FOR VIRGINIA

Item	1987 Value	1987 % of U.S.	1992 Value	1992 % of U.S.	1997 Value	1997 % of U.S.	Percent change 1987-1992	Percent change 1992-1997
Farms (number)	44,799	2.1	42,222	2.2	41,095	2.1	-5.8	-2.7
Land in farms (acres)	8,676,336	0.9	8,297,011	0.9	8,228,226	0.9	-4.4	-0.8
Average size of farm (acres)	194	42.0	197	40.1	200	41.1	1.5	1.5
Median size of farm (acres)	NA	-	NA	-	92	76.7	-	-
Market value of land and buildings:								
Average per farm (dollars)	232,374	80.3	320,488	89.8	384,979	85.6	37.9	20.1
Average per acre (dollars)	1,198	191.1	1,636	225.0	1,920	205.8	36.6	17.4
Market value of machinery/equipment - average per farm (dollars)	30,249	73.4	33,090	68.1	41,835	72.5	9.4	26.4
Farms by size:								
1 to 9 acres	3,408	1.9	3,357	2.0	2,864	1.9	-1.5	-14.7
10 to 49 acres	10,753	2.6	10,361	2.7	10,283	2.5	-3.6	-0.8
50 to 179 acres	17,530	2.7	16,293	2.8	15,938	2.7	-7.1	-2.2
180 to 499 acres	9,252	1.9	8,422	2.0	8,293	2.1	-9.0	-1.5
500 to 999 acres	2,624	1.3	2,517	1.4	2,469	1.4	-4.1	-1.9
1,000 acres or more	1,232	0.7	1,272	0.7	1,248	0.7	3.2	-1.9
Total cropland								
Farms	41,491	2.2	38,779	2.3	37,177	2.2	-6.5	-4.1
Acres	4,363,106	1.0	4,311,840	1.0	4,322,425	1.0	-1.2	0.2
Harvested cropland (farms)	37,332	2.3	34,255	2.3	32,124	2.3	-8.2	-6.2
Harvested cropland (acres)	2,406,976	0.9	2,449,013	0.8	2,520,961	0.8	1.7	2.9
Irrigated land (farms)	3,054	1.0	2,312	0.8	2,337	0.8	-24.3	1.1
Irrigated land (acres)	78,681	0.2	61,759	0.1	84,926	0.2	-21.5	37.5
Market value of agricultural products sold:								
Total sales ($1,000)	1,588,770	1.2	2,055,958	1.3	2,343,518	1.2	29.4	14.0
Average per farm (dollars)	35,464	54.4	48,694	57.7	57,027	55.4	37.3	17.1
Agricultural products only ($1,000)	465,379	0.8	696,489	0.9	780,099	0.8	49.7	12.0
Livestock, poultry, and products ($1,000)	1,123,391	1.5	1,359,469	1.6	1,563,418	1.6	21.0	15.0
Farms by value of sales:								
Less than $2,500	13,622	2.8	10,546	2.5	10,999	2.2	-22.6	4.3
$2,500 to $4,999	7,995	3.0	7,161	3.1	6,754	3.0	-10.4	-5.7
$5,000 to $9,999	7,580	2.8	7,687	3.1	7,203	3.0	1.4	-6.3
$10,000 to $24,999	6,895	2.1	7,402	2.5	7,011	2.6	7.4	-5.3
$25,000 to $49,999	3,028	1.4	3,266	1.7	3,042	1.8	7.9	-6.9
$50,000 to $99,999	2,102	1.0	1,946	1.0	1,965	1.2	-7.4	1.0
$100,000 or more	3,577	1.2	4,214	1.3	4,121	1.2	17.8	-2.2
Total farm production expenses ($1,000)	1,334,393	1.2	1,699,051	1.3	1,924,690	1.3	27.3	13.3
Average expenses per farm (dollars)	29,789	57.5	40,233	59.2	46,858	59.5	35.1	16.5
Net cash return for the farm unit:								
Number of farms	44,795	2.1	42,230	2.2	41,075	2.1	-5.7	-2.7
Value ($1000)	214,860	0.8	334,280	1.1	364,331	0.9	55.6	9.0
Average per farm (dollars)	4,797	37.9	7,916	50.1	8,870	39.8	65.0	12.1
Operators by principal occupation:								
Farming	20,617	1.8	19,571	1.9	18,410	1.9	-5.1	-5.9
Other	24,182	2.5	22,651	2.6	22,685	2.4	-6.3	0.2
Operators by days worked off farm:								
Any	25,826	2.3	23,465	2.4	23,215	2.2	-9.1	-1.1
200 days or more	18,291	2.5	16,795	2.5	16,433	2.3	-8.2	-2.2

Source: 1997 Census of Agriculture, U.S. Department of Agriculture, National Agricultural Statistics Service. NA stands for "not available." (D) is shown when data are withheld to prevent disclosure of competitive information. A dash (-) is shown where no data were reported. The market value of land and buildings, and of machinery and equipment, is an estimated amount. Net cash return for the farm unit includes only returns from agricultural activities.

LIVESTOCK STATISTICS FOR VIRGINIA

Item	1987 Value	1987 % of U.S.	1992 Value	1992 % of U.S.	1997 Value	1997 % of U.S.	Percent change 1987-1992	Percent change 1992-1997
Cattle and calves								
Number of farms	28,325	2.4	27,638	2.6	26,547	2.5	-2.4	-3.9
Number of animals	1,510,920	1.6	1,653,191	1.7	1,639,058	1.7	9.4	-0.9
Beef cows (farms)	22,228	2.6	22,519	2.8	21,753	2.7	1.3	-3.4
Beef cows (number)	581,298	1.8	674,068	2.1	688,541	2.0	16.0	2.1
Milk cows (farms)	3,372	1.7	2,369	1.5	1,671	1.4	-29.7	-29.5
Milk cows (number)	157,128	1.6	140,033	1.5	121,823	1.3	-10.9	-13.0
Cattle and calves sold (farms)	28,222	2.5	26,917	2.6	26,350	2.6	-4.6	-2.1
Cattle and calves sold (number)	859,708	1.2	855,634	1.2	906,897	1.2	-0.5	6.0
Hogs and pigs								
Number of farms	3,711	1.5	2,085	1.1	1,170	1.1	-43.8	-43.9
Number of animals	345,058	0.7	412,736	0.7	385,755	0.6	19.6	-6.5
Hogs and pigs sold (farms)	3,016	1.3	1,596	0.8	823	0.8	-47.1	-48.4
Hogs and pigs sold (number)	642,863	0.7	715,452	0.6	710,320	0.5	11.3	-0.7
Sheep and lambs								
Number of farms	2,127	2.3	1,727	2.1	1,456	2.2	-18.8	-15.7
Number of animals	161,076	1.5	117,714	1.1	73,932	0.9	-26.9	-37.2
Layers and pullets 13 weeks old and older								
Number of farms	3,194	2.2	2,069	2.3	1,588	2.2	-35.2	-23.2
Number of birds	6,605,717	1.8	6,191,513	1.8	4,834,867	1.3	-6.3	-21.9
Broilers and other meat-type chickens sold								
Number of farms	567	2.1	640	2.7	671	2.8	12.9	4.8
Number of birds sold	142,971,809	2.1	201,697,436	3.7	258,684,455	3.8	41.1	28.3

Source: 1997 Census of Agriculture, U.S. Department of Agriculture, National Agricultural Statistics Service. NA stands for "not available." (D) is shown when data are withheld to prevent disclosure of competitive information. A dash (-) is shown where no data were reported.

CROP STATISTICS FOR VIRGINIA

Item	1987 Value	1987 % of U.S.	1992 Value	1992 % of U.S.	1997 Value	1997 % of U.S.	Percent change 1987-1992	Percent change 1992-1997
Corn for grain or seed								
Number of farms	8,162	1.3	6,169	1.2	4,395	1.0	-24.4	-28.8
Number of acres	341,412	0.6	361,326	0.5	318,208	0.5	5.8	-11.9
Number of bushels	20,941,850	-	40,633,506	0.5	29,480,704	0.3	94.0	-27.4
Corn for silage or green chop								
Number of farms	-	-	-	-	-	-	-	-
Number of acres	-	-	-	-	-	-	-	-
Weight in tons, green	-	-	-	-	-	-	-	-
Sorghum for grain or seed								
Number of farms	-	-	-	-	-	-	-	-
Number of acres	-	-	-	-	-	-	-	-
Number of bushels	-	-	-	-	-	-	-	-
Wheat for grain								
Number of farms	4,339	1.2	3,670	1.3	2,888	1.2	-15.4	-21.3
Number of acres	188,428	0.4	241,042	0.4	257,063	0.4	27.9	6.6
Number of bushels	8,065,684	0.4	12,598,036	0.6	15,504,394	0.7	56.2	23.1
Barley for grain								
Number of farms	-	-	-	-	-	-	-	-
Number of acres	-	-	-	-	-	-	-	-
Number of bushels	-	-	-	-	-	-	-	-
Oats for grain								
Number of farms	-	-	-	-	-	-	-	-
Number of acres	-	-	-	-	-	-	-	-
Number of bushels	-	-	-	-	-	-	-	-
Rice								
Number of farms	-	-	-	-	-	-	-	-
Number of acres	-	-	-	-	-	-	-	-
Weight in hundredweight	-	-	-	-	-	-	-	-
Sunflower seed								
Number of farms	-	-	-	-	-	-	-	-
Number of acres	-	-	-	-	-	-	-	-
Weight in pounds	-	-	-	-	-	-	-	-
Cotton								
Number of farms	-	-	-	-	-	-	-	-
Number of acres	-	-	-	-	-	-	-	-
Number of bales	-	-	-	-	-	-	-	-

Continued.

CROP STATISTICS FOR VIRGINIA - Continued

Item	1987 Value	1987 % of U.S.	1992 Value	1992 % of U.S.	1997 Value	1997 % of U.S.	Percent change 1987-1992	Percent change 1992-1997
Tobacco								
Number of farms	9,750	-	8,444	-	5,870	-	-13.4	-30.5
Number of acres	45,121	-	55,419	-	54,035	-	22.8	-2.5
Weight in pounds	80,582,854	-	113,240,049	-	115,735,107	-	40.5	2.2
Soybeans for beans								
Number of farms	4,586	1.0	3,709	1.0	3,135	0.9	-19.1	-15.5
Number of acres	459,924	0.8	507,878	0.9	487,001	0.7	10.4	-4.1
Number of bushels	10,421,715	0.6	15,742,573	0.8	11,406,611	0.5	51.1	-27.5
Dry edible beans, excluding dry limas								
Number of farms	-	-	-	-	-	-	-	-
Number of acres	-	-	-	-	-	-	-	-
Weight in hundredweight	-	-	-	-	-	-	-	-
Potatoes, excluding sweetpotatoes								
Number of farms	-	-	-	-	-	-	-	-
Number of acres	-	-	-	-	-	-	-	-
Weight in hundredweight	-	-	-	-	-	-	-	-
Sugar beets for sugar								
Number of farms	-	-	-	-	-	-	-	-
Number of acres	-	-	-	-	-	-	-	-
Weight in tons	-	-	-	-	-	-	-	-
Sugarcane for sugar								
Number of farms	-	-	-	-	-	-	-	-
Number of acres	-	-	-	-	-	-	-	-
Weight in tons	-	-	-	-	-	-	-	-
Pineapples harvested								
Number of farms	-	-	-	-	-	-	-	-
Number of acres	-	-	-	-	-	-	-	-
Weight in tons	-	-	-	-	-	-	-	-
Peanuts for nuts								
Number of farms	1,150	-	935	-	702	-	-18.7	-24.9
Number of acres	92,733	-	93,720	-	74,867	-	1.1	-20.1
Weight in pounds	243,176,261	-	258,551,252	-	190,590,588	-	6.3	-26.3
Hay - all types, including alfalfa								
Number of farms	27,244	2.7	25,282	2.8	25,028	2.8	-7.2	-1.0
Number of acres	1,075,203	1.9	1,101,530	1.9	1,189,425	2.0	2.4	8.0
Weight in tons, dry	1,832,905	1.4	2,180,604	1.7	2,291,672	1.6	19.0	5.1
Vegetables harvested for sale								
Number of farms	-	-	-	-	-	-	-	-
Number of acres	-	-	-	-	-	-	-	-
Land in orchards								
Number of farms	1,463	1.2	1,387	1.2	1,080	1.0	-5.2	-22.1
Number of acres	34,027	0.7	32,963	0.7	27,650	0.5	-3.1	-16.1

Source: *1997 Census of Agriculture*, U.S. Department of Agriculture, National Agricultural Statistics Service. NA stands for "not available." (D) is shown when data are withheld to prevent disclosure of competitive information. A dash (-) is shown where no data were reported. Not all states report growing all crops, but all crop categories in the census are shown for every state. The data series used for this presentation did not report U.S. totals for a number of categories; for that reason, the "% of U.S." column is sometimes blank.

WASHINGTON

GENERAL STATISTICS FOR WASHINGTON

Item	1987 Value	1987 % of U.S.	1992 Value	1992 % of U.S.	1997 Value	1997 % of U.S.	Percent change 1987-1992	Percent change 1992-1997
Farms (number)	33,559	1.6	30,264	1.6	29,011	1.5	-9.8	-4.1
Land in farms (acres)	16,115,568	1.7	15,726,007	1.7	15,179,710	1.6	-2.4	-3.5
Average size of farm (acres)	480	103.9	520	105.9	523	107.4	8.3	0.6
Median size of farm (acres)	NA	-	NA	-	45	37.5	-	-
Market value of land and buildings:								
Average per farm (dollars)	355,976	123.0	468,482	131.2	634,619	141.1	31.6	35.5
Average per acre (dollars)	739	117.9	892	122.7	1,192	127.8	20.7	33.6
Market value of machinery/equipment - average per farm (dollars)	45,905	111.3	61,053	125.6	69,693	120.8	33.0	14.2
Farms by size:								
1 to 9 acres	6,040	3.3	5,408	3.2	5,195	3.4	-10.5	-3.9
10 to 49 acres	11,362	2.8	10,115	2.6	9,727	2.4	-11.0	-3.8
50 to 179 acres	7,216	1.1	6,536	1.1	6,250	1.1	-9.4	-4.4
180 to 499 acres	3,796	0.8	3,336	0.8	3,138	0.8	-12.1	-5.9
500 to 999 acres	1,855	0.9	1,699	0.9	1,618	0.9	-8.4	-4.8
1,000 acres or more	3,290	1.9	3,170	1.8	3,083	1.8	-3.6	-2.7
Total cropland								
Farms	28,891	1.6	25,765	1.5	24,656	1.5	-10.8	-4.3
Acres	8,168,454	1.8	7,999,419	1.8	7,913,709	1.8	-2.1	-1.1
Harvested cropland (farms)	24,027	1.5	21,282	1.4	20,445	1.4	-11.4	-3.9
Harvested cropland (acres)	4,597,476	1.6	4,734,673	1.6	4,895,633	1.6	3.0	3.4
Irrigated land (farms)	15,437	5.3	14,068	5.0	13,131	4.7	-8.9	-6.7
Irrigated land (acres)	1,518,684	3.3	1,641,437	3.3	1,705,025	3.1	8.1	3.9
Market value of agricultural products sold:								
Total sales ($1,000)	2,919,634	2.1	3,821,222	2.3	4,767,727	2.4	30.9	24.8
Average per farm (dollars)	87,000	133.5	126,263	149.5	164,342	159.6	45.1	30.2
Agricultural products only ($1,000)	1,688,656	2.9	2,451,605	3.3	3,251,291	3.3	45.2	32.6
Livestock, poultry, and products ($1,000)	1,230,978	1.6	1,369,617	1.6	1,516,436	1.5	11.3	10.7
Farms by value of sales:								
Less than $2,500	10,599	2.2	8,980	2.1	8,698	1.8	-15.3	-3.1
$2,500 to $4,999	4,166	1.6	3,489	1.5	3,299	1.4	-16.3	-5.4
$5,000 to $9,999	3,507	1.3	3,078	1.2	2,954	1.2	-12.2	-4.0
$10,000 to $24,999	3,684	1.1	3,327	1.1	3,242	1.2	-9.7	-2.6
$25,000 to $49,999	2,668	1.2	2,305	1.2	1,972	1.2	-13.6	-14.4
$50,000 to $99,999	2,995	1.4	2,426	1.3	2,093	1.3	-19.0	-13.7
$100,000 or more	5,940	2.0	6,659	2.0	6,753	2.0	12.1	1.4
Total farm production expenses ($1,000)	2,425,028	2.2	3,122,970	2.4	3,607,282	2.4	28.8	15.5
Average expenses per farm (dollars)	72,255	139.5	103,194	151.9	124,380	157.9	42.8	20.5
Net cash return for the farm unit:								
Number of farms	33,563	1.6	30,263	1.6	29,009	1.5	-9.8	-4.1
Value ($1000)	478,484	1.8	689,113	2.3	1,132,634	2.7	44.0	64.4
Average per farm (dollars)	14,256	112.6	22,771	144.1	39,044	175.4	59.7	71.5
Operators by principal occupation:								
Farming	17,654	1.6	16,491	1.6	15,465	1.6	-6.6	-6.2
Other	15,905	1.7	13,773	1.6	13,546	1.4	-13.4	-1.6
Operators by days worked off farm:								
Any	18,561	1.7	15,691	1.6	15,079	1.4	-15.5	-3.9
200 days or more	12,330	1.7	10,441	1.6	9,924	1.4	-15.3	-5.0

Source: 1997 Census of Agriculture, U.S. Department of Agriculture, National Agricultural Statistics Service. NA stands for "not available." (D) is shown when data are withheld to prevent disclosure of competitive information. A dash (-) is shown where no data were reported. The market value of land and buildings, and of machinery and equipment, is an estimated amount. Net cash return for the farm unit includes only returns from agricultural activities.

LIVESTOCK STATISTICS FOR WASHINGTON

Item	1987 Value	1987 % of U.S.	1992 Value	1992 % of U.S.	1997 Value	1997 % of U.S.	Percent change 1987-1992	Percent change 1992-1997
Cattle and calves								
Number of farms	15,434	1.3	13,484	1.3	11,721	1.1	-12.6	-13.1
Number of animals	1,304,673	1.4	1,270,275	1.3	1,204,265	1.2	-2.6	-5.2
Beef cows (farms)	10,799	1.3	9,555	1.2	8,627	1.1	-11.5	-9.7
Beef cows (number)	334,966	1.1	310,554	1.0	304,473	0.9	-7.3	-2.0
Milk cows (farms)	2,410	1.2	1,842	1.2	1,302	1.1	-23.6	-29.3
Milk cows (number)	220,849	2.2	242,787	2.6	247,191	2.7	9.9	1.8
Cattle and calves sold (farms)	14,371	1.2	12,259	1.2	10,857	1.1	-14.7	-11.4
Cattle and calves sold (number)	1,089,642	1.5	1,014,365	1.4	1,086,270	1.5	-6.9	7.1
Hogs and pigs								
Number of farms	1,525	0.6	1,407	0.7	978	0.9	-7.7	-30.5
Number of animals	59,195	0.1	56,171	0.1	38,030	0.1	-5.1	-32.3
Hogs and pigs sold (farms)	1,355	0.6	1,150	0.6	818	0.8	-15.1	-28.9
Hogs and pigs sold (number)	104,934	0.1	93,660	0.1	72,045	0.1	-10.7	-23.1
Sheep and lambs								
Number of farms	1,609	1.7	1,364	1.7	1,189	1.8	-15.2	-12.8
Number of animals	80,177	0.7	63,584	0.6	52,298	0.7	-20.7	-17.7
Layers and pullets 13 weeks old and older								
Number of farms	2,654	1.8	1,886	2.1	1,543	2.1	-28.9	-18.2
Number of birds	5,928,036	1.6	5,499,448	1.6	5,797,721	1.6	-7.2	5.4
Broilers and other meat-type chickens sold								
Number of farms	245	0.9	164	0.7	162	0.7	-33.1	-1.2
Number of birds sold	36,068,869	0.5	33,720,007	0.6	30,183,641	0.4	-6.5	-10.5

Source: *1997 Census of Agriculture*, U.S. Department of Agriculture, National Agricultural Statistics Service. NA stands for "not available." (D) is shown when data are withheld to prevent disclosure of competitive information. A dash (-) is shown where no data were reported.

CROP STATISTICS FOR WASHINGTON

Item	1987 Value	1987 % of U.S.	1992 Value	1992 % of U.S.	1997 Value	1997 % of U.S.	Percent change 1987-1992	Percent change 1992-1997
Corn for grain or seed								
Number of farms	735	0.1	571	0.1	514	0.1	-22.3	-10.0
Number of acres	91,470	0.2	94,619	0.1	84,300	0.1	3.4	-10.9
Number of bushels	15,956,710	-	16,854,783	0.2	16,163,861	0.2	5.6	-4.1
Corn for silage or green chop								
Number of farms	-	-	-	-	-	-	-	-
Number of acres	-	-	-	-	-	-	-	-
Weight in tons, green	-	-	-	-	-	-	-	-
Sorghum for grain or seed								
Number of farms	-	-	-	-	-	-	-	-
Number of acres	-	-	-	-	-	-	-	-
Number of bushels	-	-	-	-	-	-	-	-
Wheat for grain								
Number of farms	5,562	1.6	5,032	1.7	4,097	1.7	-9.5	-18.6
Number of acres	2,160,641	4.1	2,495,940	4.2	2,422,506	4.1	15.5	-2.9
Number of bushels	114,781,997	6.1	120,833,207	5.5	151,124,143	6.9	5.3	25.1
Barley for grain								
Number of farms	3,722	-	2,428	-	1,787	-	-34.8	-26.4
Number of acres	609,133	-	422,447	-	436,299	-	-30.6	3.3
Number of bushels	31,889,132	-	19,565,135	-	30,939,269	-	-38.6	58.1
Oats for grain								
Number of farms	-	-	-	-	-	-	-	-
Number of acres	-	-	-	-	-	-	-	-
Number of bushels	-	-	-	-	-	-	-	-
Rice								
Number of farms	-	-	-	-	-	-	-	-
Number of acres	-	-	-	-	-	-	-	-
Weight in hundredweight	-	-	-	-	-	-	-	-
Sunflower seed								
Number of farms	-	-	-	-	-	-	-	-
Number of acres	-	-	-	-	-	-	-	-
Weight in pounds	-	-	-	-	-	-	-	-
Cotton								
Number of farms	-	-	-	-	-	-	-	-
Number of acres	-	-	-	-	-	-	-	-
Number of bales	-	-	-	-	-	-	-	-

Continued.

CROP STATISTICS FOR WASHINGTON - Continued

Item	1987 Value	1987 % of U.S.	1992 Value	1992 % of U.S.	1997 Value	1997 % of U.S.	Percent change 1987-1992	Percent change 1992-1997
Tobacco								
Number of farms	-	-	-	-	-	-	-	-
Number of acres	-	-	-	-	-	-	-	-
Weight in pounds	-	-	-	-	-	-	-	-
Soybeans for beans								
Number of farms	-	-	-	-	-	-	-	-
Number of acres	-	-	-	-	-	-	-	-
Number of bushels	-	-	-	-	-	-	-	-
Dry edible beans, excluding dry limas								
Number of farms	-	-	-	-	-	-	-	-
Number of acres	-	-	-	-	-	-	-	-
Weight in hundredweight	-	-	-	-	-	-	-	-
Potatoes, excluding sweetpotatoes								
Number of farms	486	-	431	-	415	-	-11.3	-3.7
Number of acres	110,157	-	129,110	-	155,074	-	17.2	20.1
Weight in hundredweight	54,358,456	-	62,345,425	-	87,208,607	-	14.7	39.9
Sugar beets for sugar								
Number of farms	-	-	-	-	-	-	-	-
Number of acres	-	-	-	-	-	-	-	-
Weight in tons	-	-	-	-	-	-	-	-
Sugarcane for sugar								
Number of farms	-	-	-	-	-	-	-	-
Number of acres	-	-	-	-	-	-	-	-
Weight in tons	-	-	-	-	-	-	-	-
Pineapples harvested								
Number of farms	-	-	-	-	-	-	-	-
Number of acres	-	-	-	-	-	-	-	-
Weight in tons	-	-	-	-	-	-	-	-
Peanuts for nuts								
Number of farms	-	-	-	-	-	-	-	-
Number of acres	-	-	-	-	-	-	-	-
Weight in pounds	-	-	-	-	-	-	-	-
Hay - all types, including alfalfa								
Number of farms	12,435	1.3	10,396	1.1	10,108	1.1	-16.4	-2.8
Number of acres	772,618	1.3	740,586	1.3	800,677	1.3	-4.1	8.1
Weight in tons, dry	2,574,944	2.0	2,669,837	2.1	3,013,551	2.2	3.7	12.9
Vegetables harvested for sale								
Number of farms	1,724	2.8	1,605	2.6	1,506	2.8	-6.9	-6.2
Number of acres	144,097	4.2	172,057	4.5	209,456	5.6	19.4	21.7
Land in orchards								
Number of farms	6,839	5.7	6,220	5.4	5,700	5.4	-9.1	-8.4
Number of acres	241,423	5.3	256,282	5.4	301,376	5.8	6.2	17.6

Source: 1997 Census of Agriculture, U.S. Department of Agriculture, National Agricultural Statistics Service. NA stands for "not available." (D) is shown when data are withheld to prevent disclosure of competitive information. A dash (-) is shown where no data were reported. Not all states report growing all crops, but all crop categories in the census are shown for every state. The data series used for this presentation did not report U.S. totals for a number of categories; for that reason, the "% of U.S." column is sometimes blank.

WEST VIRGINIA

GENERAL STATISTICS FOR WEST VIRGINIA

Item	1987 Value	1987 % of U.S.	1992 Value	1992 % of U.S.	1997 Value	1997 % of U.S.	Percent change 1987-1992	Percent change 1992-1997
Farms (number)	17,237	0.8	17,020	0.9	17,772	0.9	-1.3	4.4
Land in farms (acres)	3,372,955	0.3	3,267,188	0.3	3,455,532	0.4	-3.1	5.8
Average size of farm (acres)	196	42.4	192	39.1	194	39.8	-2.0	1.0
Median size of farm (acres)	NA	-	NA	-	115	95.8	-	-
Market value of land and buildings:								
Average per farm (dollars)	130,802	45.2	165,088	46.2	212,832	47.3	26.2	28.9
Average per acre (dollars)	682	108.8	849	116.8	1,090	116.8	24.5	28.4
Market value of machinery/equipment - average per farm (dollars)	17,482	42.4	19,257	39.6	24,315	42.2	10.2	26.3
Farms by size:								
1 to 9 acres	643	0.4	737	0.4	727	0.5	14.6	-1.4
10 to 49 acres	2,689	0.7	2,893	0.7	3,026	0.7	7.6	4.6
50 to 179 acres	8,081	1.3	7,787	1.3	8,164	1.4	-3.6	4.8
180 to 499 acres	4,518	0.9	4,350	1.0	4,522	1.1	-3.7	4.0
500 to 999 acres	1,004	0.5	948	0.5	1,012	0.6	-5.6	6.8
1,000 acres or more	302	0.2	305	0.2	321	0.2	1.0	5.2
Total cropland								
Farms	16,246	0.9	15,891	0.9	16,509	1.0	-2.2	3.9
Acres	1,285,786	0.3	1,294,134	0.3	1,336,723	0.3	0.6	3.3
Harvested cropland (farms)	15,056	0.9	14,531	1.0	15,086	1.1	-3.5	3.8
Harvested cropland (acres)	553,517	0.2	555,818	0.2	621,632	0.2	0.4	11.8
Irrigated land (farms)	255	0.1	312	0.1	268	0.1	22.4	-14.1
Irrigated land (acres)	3,132	0.0	2,769	0.0	3,285	0.0	-11.6	18.6
Market value of agricultural products sold:								
Total sales ($1,000)	270,639	0.2	364,203	0.2	447,428	0.2	34.6	22.9
Average per farm (dollars)	15,701	24.1	21,399	25.3	25,176	24.4	36.3	17.7
Agricultural products only ($1,000)	49,249	0.1	63,081	0.1	64,907	0.1	28.1	2.9
Livestock, poultry, and products ($1,000)	221,390	0.3	301,122	0.3	382,521	0.4	36.0	27.0
Farms by value of sales:								
Less than $2,500	7,977	1.6	6,927	1.6	7,819	1.6	-13.2	12.9
$2,500 to $4,999	3,463	1.3	3,499	1.5	3,415	1.5	1.0	-2.4
$5,000 to $9,999	2,547	0.9	2,848	1.1	2,863	1.2	11.8	0.5
$10,000 to $24,999	1,781	0.5	2,006	0.7	1,936	0.7	12.6	-3.5
$25,000 to $49,999	583	0.3	688	0.4	675	0.4	18.0	-1.9
$50,000 to $99,999	400	0.2	433	0.2	431	0.3	8.3	-0.5
$100,000 or more	486	0.2	619	0.2	633	0.2	27.4	2.3
Total farm production expenses ($1,000)	231,077	0.2	308,703	0.2	380,631	0.3	33.6	23.3
Average expenses per farm (dollars)	13,406	25.9	18,136	26.7	21,375	27.1	35.3	17.9
Net cash return for the farm unit:								
Number of farms	17,237	0.8	17,022	0.9	17,807	0.9	-1.2	4.6
Value ($1000)	38,395	0.1	49,571	0.2	57,522	0.1	29.1	16.0
Average per farm (dollars)	2,227	17.6	2,912	18.4	3,230	14.5	30.8	10.9
Operators by principal occupation:								
Farming	7,201	0.6	7,169	0.7	7,145	0.7	-0.4	-0.3
Other	10,036	1.1	9,851	1.1	10,627	1.1	-1.8	7.9
Operators by days worked off farm:								
Any	10,083	0.9	9,594	1.0	10,489	1.0	-4.8	9.3
200 days or more	7,278	1.0	6,985	1.0	7,554	1.1	-4.0	8.1

Source: *1997 Census of Agriculture*, U.S. Department of Agriculture, National Agricultural Statistics Service. NA stands for "not available." (D) is shown when data are withheld to prevent disclosure of competitive information. A dash (-) is shown where no data were reported. The market value of land and buildings, and of machinery and equipment, is an estimated amount. Net cash return for the farm unit includes only returns from agricultural activities.

LIVESTOCK STATISTICS FOR WEST VIRGINIA

Item	1987 Value	1987 % of U.S.	1992 Value	1992 % of U.S.	1997 Value	1997 % of U.S.	Percent change 1987-1992	Percent change 1992-1997
Cattle and calves								
Number of farms	12,897	1.1	12,431	1.2	12,284	1.2	-3.6	-1.2
Number of animals	408,129	0.4	430,708	0.4	439,462	0.4	5.5	2.0
Beef cows (farms)	10,588	1.3	10,570	1.3	10,367	1.3	-0.2	-1.9
Beef cows (number)	182,071	0.6	197,886	0.6	202,844	0.6	8.7	2.5
Milk cows (farms)	1,575	0.8	972	0.6	676	0.6	-38.3	-30.5
Milk cows (number)	27,019	0.3	23,366	0.2	18,497	0.2	-13.5	-20.8
Cattle and calves sold (farms)	12,061	1.0	11,583	1.1	11,576	1.1	-4.0	-0.1
Cattle and calves sold (number)	249,163	0.3	254,233	0.4	270,361	0.4	2.0	6.3
Hogs and pigs								
Number of farms	1,226	0.5	841	0.4	645	0.6	-31.4	-23.3
Number of animals	30,759	0.1	26,760	0.0	15,708	0.0	-13.0	-41.3
Hogs and pigs sold (farms)	868	0.4	587	0.3	402	0.4	-32.4	-31.5
Hogs and pigs sold (number)	59,181	0.1	50,642	0.0	24,884	0.0	-14.4	-50.9
Sheep and lambs								
Number of farms	1,537	1.7	1,188	1.5	979	1.5	-22.7	-17.6
Number of animals	74,987	0.7	57,091	0.5	40,709	0.5	-23.9	-28.7
Layers and pullets 13 weeks old and older								
Number of farms	2,030	1.4	1,272	1.4	1,122	1.5	-37.3	-11.8
Number of birds	691,077	0.2	1,510,412	0.4	1,806,870	0.5	118.6	19.6
Broilers and other meat-type chickens sold								
Number of farms	99	0.4	136	0.6	186	0.8	37.4	36.8
Number of birds sold	29,226,871	0.4	50,669,811	0.9	79,193,428	1.2	73.4	56.3

Source: 1997 Census of Agriculture, U.S. Department of Agriculture, National Agricultural Statistics Service. NA stands for "not available." (D) is shown when data are withheld to prevent disclosure of competitive information. A dash (-) is shown where no data were reported.

CROP STATISTICS FOR WEST VIRGINIA

Item	1987 Value	1987 % of U.S.	1992 Value	1992 % of U.S.	1997 Value	1997 % of U.S.	Percent change 1987-1992	Percent change 1992-1997
Corn for grain or seed								
Number of farms	2,097	0.3	1,517	0.3	1,150	0.3	-27.7	-24.2
Number of acres	48,953	0.1	44,564	0.1	35,499	0.1	-9.0	-20.3
Number of bushels	3,257,345	-	4,668,501	0.1	3,270,197	0.0	43.3	-30.0
Corn for silage or green chop								
Number of farms	1,477	-	1,027	-	929	-	-30.5	-9.5
Number of acres	36,870	-	27,674	-	27,642	-	-24.9	-0.1
Weight in tons, green	435,575	-	433,877	-	380,942	-	-0.4	-12.2
Sorghum for grain or seed								
Number of farms	-	-	-	-	-	-	-	-
Number of acres	-	-	-	-	-	-	-	-
Number of bushels	-	-	-	-	-	-	-	-
Wheat for grain								
Number of farms	376	0.1	307	0.1	191	0.1	-18.4	-37.8
Number of acres	7,339	0.0	9,058	0.0	7,620	0.0	23.4	-15.9
Number of bushels	316,337	0.0	438,877	0.0	421,453	0.0	38.7	-4.0
Barley for grain								
Number of farms	-	-	-	-	-	-	-	-
Number of acres	-	-	-	-	-	-	-	-
Number of bushels	-	-	-	-	-	-	-	-
Oats for grain								
Number of farms	516	-	406	-	321	-	-21.3	-20.9
Number of acres	4,605	-	3,677	-	2,720	-	-20.2	-26.0
Number of bushels	227,284	-	201,339	-	132,249	-	-11.4	-34.3
Rice								
Number of farms	-	-	-	-	-	-	-	-
Number of acres	-	-	-	-	-	-	-	-
Weight in hundredweight	-	-	-	-	-	-	-	-
Sunflower seed								
Number of farms	-	-	-	-	-	-	-	-
Number of acres	-	-	-	-	-	-	-	-
Weight in pounds	-	-	-	-	-	-	-	-
Cotton								
Number of farms	-	-	-	-	-	-	-	-
Number of acres	-	-	-	-	-	-	-	-
Number of bales	-	-	-	-	-	-	-	-

Continued.

CROP STATISTICS FOR WEST VIRGINIA - Continued

Item	1987 Value	1987 % of U.S.	1992 Value	1992 % of U.S.	1997 Value	1997 % of U.S.	Percent change 1987-1992	Percent change 1992-1997
Tobacco								
Number of farms	1,095	-	1,003	-	744	-	-8.4	-25.8
Number of acres	1,716	-	2,072	-	1,630	-	20.7	-21.3
Weight in pounds	2,158,501	-	3,101,002	-	2,737,090	-	43.7	-11.7
Soybeans for beans								
Number of farms	-	-	-	-	-	-	-	-
Number of acres	-	-	-	-	-	-	-	-
Number of bushels	-	-	-	-	-	-	-	-
Dry edible beans, excluding dry limas								
Number of farms	-	-	-	-	-	-	-	-
Number of acres	-	-	-	-	-	-	-	-
Weight in hundredweight	-	-	-	-	-	-	-	-
Potatoes, excluding sweetpotatoes								
Number of farms	-	-	-	-	-	-	-	-
Number of acres	-	-	-	-	-	-	-	-
Weight in hundredweight	-	-	-	-	-	-	-	-
Sugar beets for sugar								
Number of farms	-	-	-	-	-	-	-	-
Number of acres	-	-	-	-	-	-	-	-
Weight in tons	-	-	-	-	-	-	-	-
Sugarcane for sugar								
Number of farms	-	-	-	-	-	-	-	-
Number of acres	-	-	-	-	-	-	-	-
Weight in tons	-	-	-	-	-	-	-	-
Pineapples harvested								
Number of farms	-	-	-	-	-	-	-	-
Number of acres	-	-	-	-	-	-	-	-
Weight in tons	-	-	-	-	-	-	-	-
Peanuts for nuts								
Number of farms	-	-	-	-	-	-	-	-
Number of acres	-	-	-	-	-	-	-	-
Weight in pounds	-	-	-	-	-	-	-	-
Hay - all types, including alfalfa								
Number of farms	13,849	1.4	13,270	1.5	13,895	1.6	-4.2	4.7
Number of acres	435,446	0.8	452,480	0.8	525,257	0.9	3.9	16.1
Weight in tons, dry	673,598	0.5	753,877	0.6	886,054	0.6	11.9	17.5
Vegetables harvested for sale								
Number of farms	-	-	-	-	-	-	-	-
Number of acres	-	-	-	-	-	-	-	-
Land in orchards								
Number of farms	646	0.5	558	0.5	530	0.5	-13.6	-5.0
Number of acres	19,513	0.4	15,014	0.3	12,446	0.2	-23.1	-17.1

Source: *1997 Census of Agriculture*, U.S. Department of Agriculture, National Agricultural Statistics Service. NA stands for "not available." (D) is shown when data are withheld to prevent disclosure of competitive information. A dash (-) is shown where no data were reported. Not all states report growing all crops, but all crop categories in the census are shown for every state. The data series used for this presentation did not report U.S. totals for a number of categories; for that reason, the "% of U.S." column is sometimes blank.

WISCONSIN

GENERAL STATISTICS FOR WISCONSIN

Item	1987 Value	1987 % of U.S.	1992 Value	1992 % of U.S.	1997 Value	1997 % of U.S.	Percent change 1987-1992	Percent change 1992-1997
Farms (number)	75,131	3.6	67,959	3.5	65,602	3.4	-9.5	-3.5
Land in farms (acres)	16,606,567	1.7	15,463,551	1.6	14,900,205	1.6	-6.9	-3.6
Average size of farm (acres)	221	47.8	228	46.4	227	46.6	3.2	-0.4
Median size of farm (acres)	NA	-	NA	-	154	128.3	-	-
Market value of land and buildings:								
Average per farm (dollars)	182,950	63.2	210,179	58.9	282,135	62.7	14.9	34.2
Average per acre (dollars)	826	131.7	925	127.2	1,244	133.3	12.0	34.5
Market value of machinery/equipment - average per farm (dollars)	54,037	131.1	66,001	135.8	66,731	115.7	22.1	1.1
Farms by size:								
1 to 9 acres	4,012	2.2	3,605	2.2	3,142	2.0	-10.1	-12.8
10 to 49 acres	8,778	2.1	8,655	2.2	9,673	2.4	-1.4	11.8
50 to 179 acres	27,498	4.3	24,121	4.1	24,546	4.1	-12.3	1.8
180 to 499 acres	28,828	6.0	25,570	6.0	22,228	5.5	-11.3	-13.1
500 to 999 acres	4,923	2.5	4,790	2.6	4,573	2.6	-2.7	-4.5
1,000 acres or more	1,092	0.6	1,218	0.7	1,440	0.8	11.5	18.2
Total cropland								
Farms	71,320	3.9	64,229	3.8	61,166	3.7	-9.9	-4.8
Acres	11,618,876	2.6	10,948,614	2.5	10,353,300	2.4	-5.8	-5.4
Harvested cropland (farms)	69,141	4.2	61,125	4.1	54,369	3.9	-11.6	-11.1
Harvested cropland (acres)	9,335,007	3.3	8,843,649	3.0	8,625,011	2.8	-5.3	-2.5
Irrigated land (farms)	1,850	0.6	2,146	0.8	2,025	0.7	16.0	-5.6
Irrigated land (acres)	284,637	0.6	330,838	0.7	341,813	0.6	16.2	3.3
Market value of agricultural products sold:								
Total sales ($1,000)	4,909,869	3.6	5,259,670	3.2	5,579,861	2.8	7.1	6.1
Average per farm (dollars)	65,351	100.3	77,395	91.6	85,056	82.6	18.4	9.9
Agricultural products only ($1,000)	936,624	1.6	1,126,566	1.5	1,640,283	1.7	20.3	45.6
Livestock, poultry, and products ($1,000)	3,973,245	5.2	4,133,103	4.7	3,939,578	4.0	4.0	-4.7
Farms by value of sales:								
Less than $2,500	9,838	2.0	9,932	2.3	14,007	2.8	1.0	41.0
$2,500 to $4,999	6,039	2.3	5,355	2.3	5,161	2.3	-11.3	-3.6
$5,000 to $9,999	7,505	2.7	6,576	2.6	6,177	2.6	-12.4	-6.1
$10,000 to $24,999	10,678	3.3	8,995	3.0	8,841	3.2	-15.8	-1.7
$25,000 to $49,999	10,491	4.8	7,872	4.0	6,826	4.0	-25.0	-13.3
$50,000 to $99,999	15,223	7.0	11,916	6.3	8,818	5.6	-21.7	-26.0
$100,000 or more	15,357	5.2	17,313	5.2	15,772	4.6	12.7	-8.9
Total farm production expenses ($1,000)	3,638,957	3.4	4,029,737	3.1	4,202,802	2.8	10.7	4.3
Average expenses per farm (dollars)	48,453	93.5	59,292	87.3	64,083	81.4	22.4	8.1
Net cash return for the farm unit:								
Number of farms	75,103	3.6	67,964	3.5	65,585	3.4	-9.5	-3.5
Value ($1000)	1,253,108	4.7	1,230,986	4.0	1,318,913	3.1	-1.8	7.1
Average per farm (dollars)	16,685	131.8	18,112	114.6	20,110	90.3	8.6	11.0
Operators by principal occupation:								
Farming	53,342	4.7	46,180	4.4	39,030	4.1	-13.4	-15.5
Other	21,789	2.3	21,779	2.5	26,572	2.8	-0.0	22.0
Operators by days worked off farm:								
Any	30,014	2.7	28,081	2.8	31,303	3.0	-6.4	11.5
200 days or more	18,776	2.5	18,307	2.8	21,088	3.0	-2.5	15.2

Source: *1997 Census of Agriculture*, U.S. Department of Agriculture, National Agricultural Statistics Service. NA stands for "not available." (D) is shown when data are withheld to prevent disclosure of competitive information. A dash (-) is shown where no data were reported. The market value of land and buildings, and of machinery and equipment, is an estimated amount. Net cash return for the farm unit includes only returns from agricultural activities.

LIVESTOCK STATISTICS FOR WISCONSIN

Item	1987		1992		1997		Percent change	
	Value	% of U.S.	Value	% of U.S.	Value	% of U.S.	1987-1992	1992-1997
Cattle and calves								
Number of farms	53,315	4.5	46,052	4.3	39,593	3.8	-13.6	-14.0
Number of animals	4,138,221	4.3	3,866,998	4.0	3,440,300	3.5	-6.6	-11.0
Beef cows (farms)	10,355	1.2	10,394	1.3	11,642	1.4	0.4	12.0
Beef cows (number)	180,276	0.6	195,810	0.6	222,522	0.7	8.6	13.6
Milk cows (farms)	37,325	18.5	30,156	19.4	22,576	19.3	-19.2	-25.1
Milk cows (number)	1,743,427	17.3	1,521,969	16.0	1,336,626	14.7	-12.7	-12.2
Cattle and calves sold (farms)	52,816	4.6	45,227	4.4	38,832	3.8	-14.4	-14.1
Cattle and calves sold (number)	1,982,183	2.7	1,808,889	2.6	1,547,935	2.1	-8.7	-14.4
Hogs and pigs								
Number of farms	8,737	3.6	6,760	3.5	3,686	3.4	-22.6	-45.5
Number of animals	1,312,818	2.5	1,173,783	2.0	738,339	1.2	-10.6	-37.1
Hogs and pigs sold (farms)	8,899	3.7	6,776	3.6	3,591	3.5	-23.9	-47.0
Hogs and pigs sold (number)	2,515,246	2.6	2,244,673	2.0	1,523,490	1.1	-10.8	-32.1
Sheep and lambs								
Number of farms	2,684	2.9	2,444	3.0	2,100	3.2	-8.9	-14.1
Number of animals	94,429	0.9	84,956	0.8	76,113	1.0	-10.0	-10.4
Layers and pullets 13 weeks old and older								
Number of farms	4,658	3.2	2,860	3.2	2,534	3.5	-38.6	-11.4
Number of birds	5,156,407	1.4	3,734,208	1.1	4,117,078	1.1	-27.6	10.3
Broilers and other meat-type chickens sold								
Number of farms	674	2.4	504	2.1	587	2.5	-25.2	16.5
Number of birds sold	10,761,742	0.2	13,686,548	0.3	27,607,761	0.4	27.2	101.7

Source: 1997 Census of Agriculture, U.S. Department of Agriculture, National Agricultural Statistics Service. NA stands for "not available." (D) is shown when data are withheld to prevent disclosure of competitive information. A dash (-) is shown where no data were reported.

CROP STATISTICS FOR WISCONSIN

Item	1987		1992		1997		Percent change	
	Value	% of U.S.	Value	% of U.S.	Value	% of U.S.	1987-1992	1992-1997
Corn for grain or seed								
Number of farms	48,665	7.8	36,674	7.3	34,315	8.0	-24.6	-6.4
Number of acres	2,787,734	4.7	2,830,496	4.1	2,877,971	4.1	1.5	1.7
Number of bushels	311,689,830	-	283,709,848	3.3	362,498,739	4.2	-9.0	27.8
Corn for silage or green chop								
Number of farms	29,080	-	28,701	-	22,498	-	-1.3	-21.6
Number of acres	666,719	-	937,346	-	717,549	-	40.6	-23.4
Weight in tons, green	8,531,126	-	10,189,877	-	10,444,465	-	19.4	2.5
Sorghum for grain or seed								
Number of farms	-	-	-	-	-	-	-	-
Number of acres	-	-	-	-	-	-	-	-
Number of bushels	-	-	-	-	-	-	-	-
Wheat for grain								
Number of farms	-	-	-	-	-	-	-	-
Number of acres	-	-	-	-	-	-	-	-
Number of bushels	-	-	-	-	-	-	-	-
Barley for grain								
Number of farms	-	-	-	-	-	-	-	-
Number of acres	-	-	-	-	-	-	-	-
Number of bushels	-	-	-	-	-	-	-	-
Oats for grain								
Number of farms	31,065	-	22,195	-	14,925	-	-28.6	-32.8
Number of acres	679,203	-	488,332	-	314,722	-	-28.1	-35.6
Number of bushels	37,458,060	-	27,900,172	-	18,623,580	-	-25.5	-33.2
Rice								
Number of farms	-	-	-	-	-	-	-	-
Number of acres	-	-	-	-	-	-	-	-
Weight in hundredweight	-	-	-	-	-	-	-	-
Sunflower seed								
Number of farms	-	-	-	-	-	-	-	-
Number of acres	-	-	-	-	-	-	-	-
Weight in pounds	-	-	-	-	-	-	-	-
Cotton								
Number of farms	-	-	-	-	-	-	-	-
Number of acres	-	-	-	-	-	-	-	-
Number of bales	-	-	-	-	-	-	-	-

Continued.

CROP STATISTICS FOR WISCONSIN - Continued

Item	1987 Value	1987 % of U.S.	1992 Value	1992 % of U.S.	1997 Value	1997 % of U.S.	Percent change 1987-1992	Percent change 1992-1997
Tobacco								
Number of farms	-	-	-	-	-	-	-	-
Number of acres	-	-	-	-	-	-	-	-
Weight in pounds	-	-	-	-	-	-	-	-
Soybeans for beans								
Number of farms	5,628	1.3	8,957	2.4	12,028	3.4	59.2	34.3
Number of acres	297,226	0.5	575,087	1.0	990,531	1.5	93.5	72.2
Number of bushels	11,491,031	0.6	17,659,688	0.9	42,681,842	1.7	53.7	141.7
Dry edible beans, excluding dry limas								
Number of farms	-	-	-	-	-	-	-	-
Number of acres	-	-	-	-	-	-	-	-
Weight in hundredweight	-	-	-	-	-	-	-	-
Potatoes, excluding sweetpotatoes								
Number of farms	470	-	447	-	418	-	-4.9	-6.5
Number of acres	72,149	-	78,231	-	85,304	-	8.4	9.0
Weight in hundredweight	22,003,470	-	26,639,799	-	30,242,152	-	21.1	13.5
Sugar beets for sugar								
Number of farms	-	-	-	-	-	-	-	-
Number of acres	-	-	-	-	-	-	-	-
Weight in tons	-	-	-	-	-	-	-	-
Sugarcane for sugar								
Number of farms	-	-	-	-	-	-	-	-
Number of acres	-	-	-	-	-	-	-	-
Weight in tons	-	-	-	-	-	-	-	-
Pineapples harvested								
Number of farms	-	-	-	-	-	-	-	-
Number of acres	-	-	-	-	-	-	-	-
Weight in tons	-	-	-	-	-	-	-	-
Peanuts for nuts								
Number of farms	-	-	-	-	-	-	-	-
Number of acres	-	-	-	-	-	-	-	-
Weight in pounds	-	-	-	-	-	-	-	-
Hay - all types, including alfalfa								
Number of farms	60,404	6.1	51,238	5.7	44,115	5.0	-15.2	-13.9
Number of acres	4,784,417	8.3	3,911,258	6.9	3,554,932	5.8	-18.3	-9.1
Weight in tons, dry	12,407,639	9.6	8,621,168	6.8	8,606,243	6.2	-30.5	-0.2
Vegetables harvested for sale								
Number of farms	4,177	6.9	4,269	6.9	3,288	6.1	2.2	-23.0
Number of acres	328,902	9.5	347,581	9.2	270,130	7.2	5.7	-22.3
Land in orchards								
Number of farms	-	-	-	-	-	-	-	-
Number of acres	-	-	-	-	-	-	-	-

Source: 1997 Census of Agriculture, U.S. Department of Agriculture, National Agricultural Statistics Service. NA stands for "not available." (D) is shown when data are withheld to prevent disclosure of competitive information. A dash (-) is shown where no data were reported. Not all states report growing all crops, but all crop categories in the census are shown for every state. The data series used for this presentation did not report U.S. totals for a number of categories; for that reason, the "% of U.S." column is sometimes blank.

WYOMING

GENERAL STATISTICS FOR WYOMING

Item	1987 Value	1987 % of U.S.	1992 Value	1992 % of U.S.	1997 Value	1997 % of U.S.	Percent change 1987-1992	Percent change 1992-1997
Farms (number)	9,205	0.4	8,716	0.5	9,232	0.5	-5.3	5.9
Land in farms (acres)	33,595,135	3.5	32,876,071	3.5	34,088,692	3.7	-2.1	3.7
Average size of farm (acres)	3,650	790.0	3,772	768.2	3,692	758.1	3.3	-2.1
Median size of farm (acres)	NA	-	NA	-	500	416.7	-	-
Market value of land and buildings:								
Average per farm (dollars)	533,284	184.3	601,437	168.4	808,346	179.7	12.8	34.4
Average per acre (dollars)	147	23.4	159	21.9	222	23.8	8.2	39.6
Market value of machinery/equipment -								
average per farm (dollars)	45,709	110.9	53,862	110.8	61,161	106.0	17.8	13.6
Farms by size:								
1 to 9 acres	795	0.4	449	0.3	405	0.3	-43.5	-9.8
10 to 49 acres	989	0.2	994	0.3	1,157	0.3	0.5	16.4
50 to 179 acres	1,356	0.2	1,356	0.2	1,568	0.3	-	15.6
180 to 499 acres	1,536	0.3	1,513	0.4	1,441	0.4	-1.5	-4.8
500 to 999 acres	1,091	0.5	1,079	0.6	1,069	0.6	-1.1	-0.9
1,000 acres or more	3,438	2.0	3,325	1.9	3,592	2.0	-3.3	8.0
Total cropland								
Farms	7,237	0.4	6,756	0.4	7,122	0.4	-6.6	5.4
Acres	2,838,627	0.6	2,842,020	0.7	2,967,899	0.7	0.1	4.4
Harvested cropland (farms)	6,389	0.4	5,735	0.4	6,124	0.4	-10.2	6.8
Harvested cropland (acres)	1,717,027	0.6	1,532,732	0.5	1,743,631	0.6	-10.7	13.8
Irrigated land (farms)	5,221	1.8	5,076	1.8	5,306	1.9	-2.8	4.5
Irrigated land (acres)	1,517,891	3.3	1,464,585	3.0	1,719,463	3.1	-3.5	17.4
Market value of agricultural products sold:								
Total sales ($1,000)	676,721	0.5	824,205	0.5	898,527	0.5	21.8	9.0
Average per farm (dollars)	73,517	112.8	94,562	112.0	97,327	94.5	28.6	2.9
Agricultural products only ($1,000)	124,693	0.2	153,862	0.2	173,216	0.2	23.4	12.6
Livestock, poultry, and products ($1,000)	552,028	0.7	670,343	0.8	725,311	0.7	21.4	8.2
Farms by value of sales:								
Less than $2,500	1,987	0.4	1,531	0.4	1,709	0.3	-22.9	11.6
$2,500 to $4,999	766	0.3	722	0.3	784	0.3	-5.7	8.6
$5,000 to $9,999	977	0.4	946	0.4	959	0.4	-3.2	1.4
$10,000 to $24,999	1,497	0.5	1,385	0.5	1,470	0.5	-7.5	6.1
$25,000 to $49,999	1,241	0.6	1,092	0.6	1,238	0.7	-12.0	13.4
$50,000 to $99,999	1,154	0.5	1,185	0.6	1,172	0.7	2.7	-1.1
$100,000 or more	1,583	0.5	1,855	0.6	1,900	0.5	17.2	2.4
Total farm production expenses ($1,000)	536,980	0.5	675,225	0.5	690,403	0.5	25.7	2.2
Average expenses per farm (dollars)	58,329	112.6	77,479	114.1	74,808	95.0	32.8	-3.4
Net cash return for the farm unit:								
Number of farms	9,206	0.4	8,715	0.5	9,229	0.5	-5.3	5.9
Value ($1000)	136,366	0.5	140,895	0.5	197,249	0.5	3.3	40.0
Average per farm (dollars)	14,813	117.0	16,167	102.3	21,373	96.0	9.1	32.2
Operators by principal occupation:								
Farming	5,953	0.5	5,612	0.5	5,583	0.6	-5.7	-0.5
Other	3,252	0.3	3,104	0.4	3,649	0.4	-4.6	17.6
Operators by days worked off farm:								
Any	4,674	0.4	4,251	0.4	4,722	0.5	-9.1	11.1
200 days or more	2,640	0.4	2,435	0.4	2,771	0.4	-7.8	13.8

Source: 1997 Census of Agriculture, U.S. Department of Agriculture, National Agricultural Statistics Service. NA stands for "not available." (D) is shown when data are withheld to prevent disclosure of competitive information. A dash (-) is shown where no data were reported. The market value of land and buildings, and of machinery and equipment, is an estimated amount. Net cash return for the farm unit includes only returns from agricultural activities.

LIVESTOCK STATISTICS FOR WYOMING

Item	1987 Value	1987 % of U.S.	1992 Value	1992 % of U.S.	1997 Value	1997 % of U.S.	Percent change 1987-1992	Percent change 1992-1997
Cattle and calves								
Number of farms	5,990	0.5	5,839	0.5	6,370	0.6	-2.5	9.1
Number of animals	1,412,901	1.5	1,424,002	1.5	1,690,264	1.7	0.8	18.7
Beef cows (farms)	5,082	0.6	5,114	0.6	5,526	0.7	0.6	8.1
Beef cows (number)	689,166	2.2	746,789	2.3	862,639	2.5	8.4	15.5
Milk cows (farms)	788	0.4	523	0.3	337	0.3	-33.6	-35.6
Milk cows (number)	9,287	0.1	7,596	0.1	6,254	0.1	-18.2	-17.7
Cattle and calves sold (farms)	5,965	0.5	5,866	0.6	6,295	0.6	-1.7	7.3
Cattle and calves sold (number)	956,523	1.3	1,014,982	1.4	1,130,839	1.5	6.1	11.4
Hogs and pigs								
Number of farms	474	0.2	379	0.2	296	0.3	-20.0	-21.9
Number of animals	28,437	0.1	39,128	0.1	91,135	0.1	37.6	132.9
Hogs and pigs sold (farms)	407	0.2	342	0.2	246	0.2	-16.0	-28.1
Hogs and pigs sold (number)	54,255	0.1	60,335	0.1	227,835	0.2	11.2	277.6
Sheep and lambs								
Number of farms	1,568	1.7	1,462	1.8	1,112	1.7	-6.8	-23.9
Number of animals	917,122	8.3	921,133	8.6	713,096	9.1	0.4	-22.6
Layers and pullets 13 weeks old and older								
Number of farms	929	0.6	516	0.6	448	0.6	-44.5	-13.2
Number of birds	29,235	0.0	26,315	0.0	13,689	0.0	-10.0	-48.0
Broilers and other meat-type chickens sold								
Number of farms	37	0.1	8	0.0	17	0.1	-78.4	112.5
Number of birds sold	9,491	0.0	382	0.0	914	0.0	-96.0	139.3

Source: 1997 Census of Agriculture, U.S. Department of Agriculture, National Agricultural Statistics Service. NA stands for "not available." (D) is shown when data are withheld to prevent disclosure of competitive information. A dash (-) is shown where no data were reported.

CROP STATISTICS FOR WYOMING

Item	1987 Value	1987 % of U.S.	1992 Value	1992 % of U.S.	1997 Value	1997 % of U.S.	Percent change 1987-1992	Percent change 1992-1997
Corn for grain or seed								
Number of farms	-	-	-	-	-	-	-	-
Number of acres	-	-	-	-	-	-	-	-
Number of bushels	-	-	-	-	-	-	-	-
Corn for silage or green chop								
Number of farms	433	-	390	-	326	-	-9.9	-16.4
Number of acres	29,900	-	29,077	-	28,747	-	-2.8	-1.1
Weight in tons, green	508,205	-	482,859	-	554,416	-	-5.0	14.8
Sorghum for grain or seed								
Number of farms	-	-	-	-	-	-	-	-
Number of acres	-	-	-	-	-	-	-	-
Number of bushels	-	-	-	-	-	-	-	-
Wheat for grain								
Number of farms	924	0.3	670	0.2	656	0.3	-27.5	-2.1
Number of acres	252,784	0.5	211,312	0.4	221,041	0.4	-16.4	4.6
Number of bushels	7,207,742	0.4	5,264,505	0.2	6,520,663	0.3	-27.0	23.9
Barley for grain								
Number of farms	1,190	-	857	-	721	-	-28.0	-15.9
Number of acres	127,366	-	104,167	-	93,095	-	-18.2	-10.6
Number of bushels	8,654,469	-	8,178,366	-	7,251,158		5.5	11.3
Oats for grain								
Number of farms	-	-	-	-	-	-	-	-
Number of acres	-	-	-	-	-	-	-	-
Number of bushels	-	-	-	-	-	-	-	-
Rice								
Number of farms	-	-	-	-	-	-	-	-
Number of acres	-	-	-	-	-	-	-	-
Weight in hundredweight	-	-	-	-	-	-	-	-
Sunflower seed								
Number of farms	-	-	-	-	-	-	-	-
Number of acres	-	-	-	-	-	-	-	-
Weight in pounds	-	-	-	-	-	-	-	-
Cotton								
Number of farms	-	-	-	-	-	-	-	-
Number of acres	-	-	-	-	-	-	-	-
Number of bales	-	-	-	-	-	-	-	-

Continued.

CROP STATISTICS FOR WYOMING - Continued

Item	1987		1992		1997		Percent change	
	Value	% of U.S.	Value	% of U.S.	Value	% of U.S.	1987-1992	1992-1997
Tobacco								
Number of farms	-	-	-	-	-	-	-	-
Number of acres	-	-	-	-	-	-	-	-
Weight in pounds	-	-	-	-	-	-	-	-
Soybeans for beans								
Number of farms	-	-	-	-	-	-	-	-
Number of acres	-	-	-	-	-	-	-	-
Number of bushels	-	-	-	-	-	-	-	-
Dry edible beans, excluding dry limas								
Number of farms	394	-	346	-	317	-	-12.2	-8.4
Number of acres	33,866	-	29,709	-	29,326	-	-12.3	-1.3
Weight in hundredweight	618,740	-	517,834	-	630,995	-	-16.3	21.9
Potatoes, excluding sweetpotatoes								
Number of farms	-	-	-	-	-	-	-	-
Number of acres	-	-	-	-	-	-	-	-
Weight in hundredweight	-	-	-	-	-	-	-	-
Sugar beets for sugar								
Number of farms	400	-	497	-	356	-	24.3	-28.4
Number of acres	56,932	-	72,550	-	63,732	-	27.4	-12.2
Weight in tons	1,177,191	-	1,451,023	-	1,285,165	-	23.3	-11.4
Sugarcane for sugar								
Number of farms	-	-	-	-	-	-	-	-
Number of acres	-	-	-	-	-	-	-	-
Weight in tons	-	-	-	-	-	-	-	-
Pineapples harvested								
Number of farms	-	-	-	-	-	-	-	-
Number of acres	-	-	-	-	-	-	-	-
Weight in tons	-	-	-	-	-	-	-	-
Peanuts for nuts								
Number of farms	-	-	-	-	-	-	-	-
Number of acres	-	-	-	-	-	-	-	-
Weight in pounds	-	-	-	-	-	-	-	-
Hay - all types, including alfalfa								
Number of farms	5,682	0.6	5,032	0.6	5,601	0.6	-11.4	11.3
Number of acres	1,132,842	2.0	1,017,562	1.8	1,239,340	2.0	-10.2	21.8
Weight in tons, dry	1,904,291	1.5	1,756,092	1.4	2,295,272	1.6	-7.8	30.7
Vegetables harvested for sale								
Number of farms	-	-	-	-	-	-	-	-
Number of acres	-	-	-	-	-	-	-	-
Land in orchards								
Number of farms	-	-	-	-	-	-	-	-
Number of acres	-	-	-	-	-	-	-	-

Source: *1997 Census of Agriculture*, U.S. Department of Agriculture, National Agricultural Statistics Service. NA stands for "not available." (D) is shown when data are withheld to prevent disclosure of competitive information. A dash (-) is shown where no data were reported. Not all states report growing all crops, but all crop categories in the census are shown for every state. The data series used for this presentation did not report U.S. totals for a number of categories; for that reason, the "% of U.S." column is sometimes blank.

Appendix II

METRO DATA - UTILITIES

ABILENE, TX MSA

NAICS	Industry	Estab-lish-ments	Em-ploy-ment	Payroll		Sales, revenues ($ mil.)
				Total ($ mil.)	Per Empl. ($)	
221	Utilities	16	466	17.3	37,133	133.6

Sources: *Economic Census of the United States,* 1997. Only those industries are shown for which both employment and sales/revenue data were available. For the definition of MSAs, CMSAs, and PMSAs, please see the Introduction.

ALBANY—SCHENECTADY—TROY, NY MSA

NAICS	Industry	Estab-lish-ments	Em-ploy-ment	Payroll		Sales, revenues ($ mil.)
				Total ($ mil.)	Per Empl. ($)	
221	Utilities	20	1,652	96.2	58,214	790.3
2211	Electric power generation, transmission, and distribution	13	1,552	92.7	59,743	598.4

Sources: *Economic Census of the United States,* 1997. Only those industries are shown for which both employment and sales/revenue data were available. For the definition of MSAs, CMSAs, and PMSAs, please see the Introduction.

ALBUQUERQUE, NM MSA

NAICS	Industry	Estab-lish-ments	Em-ploy-ment	Payroll		Sales, revenues ($ mil.)
				Total ($ mil.)	Per Empl. ($)	
2213101	Water supply	12	55	1.6	29,255	8.7

Sources: *Economic Census of the United States,* 1997. Only those industries are shown for which both employment and sales/revenue data were available. For the definition of MSAs, CMSAs, and PMSAs, please see the Introduction.

ALLENTOWN—BETHLEHEM—EASTON, PA MSA

NAICS	Industry	Estab-lish-ments	Em-ploy-ment	Payroll		Sales, revenues ($ mil.)
				Total ($ mil.)	Per Empl. ($)	
221	Utilities	23	5,066	296.3	58,494	2,257.9

Sources: *Economic Census of the United States,* 1997. Only those industries are shown for which both employment and sales/revenue data were available. For the definition of MSAs, CMSAs, and PMSAs, please see the Introduction.

ALTOONA, PA MSA

NAICS	Industry	Estab-lish-ments	Em-ploy-ment	Payroll		Sales, revenues ($ mil.)
				Total ($ mil.)	Per Empl. ($)	
221	Utilities	4	189	8.6	45,307	78.1

Sources: *Economic Census of the United States,* 1997. Only those industries are shown for which both employment and sales/revenue data were available. For the definition of MSAs, CMSAs, and PMSAs, please see the Introduction.

AMARILLO, TX MSA

NAICS	Industry	Estab-lish-ments	Em-ploy-ment	Payroll		Sales, revenues ($ mil.)
				Total ($ mil.)	Per Empl. ($)	
221	Utilities	16	1,223	54.2	44,326	628.5

Sources: *Economic Census of the United States,* 1997. Only those industries are shown for which both employment and sales/revenue data were available. For the definition of MSAs, CMSAs, and PMSAs, please see the Introduction.

ANCHORAGE, AK MSA

NAICS	Industry	Estab-lish-ments	Em-ploy-ment	Payroll		Sales, revenues ($ mil.)
				Total ($ mil.)	Per Empl. ($)	
221	Utilities	15	621	41.1	66,169	309.2

Sources: Economic Census of the United States, 1997. Only those industries are shown for which both employment and sales/revenue data were available. For the definition of MSAs, CMSAs, and PMSAs, please see the Introduction.

ANN ARBOR, MI PMSA

NAICS	Industry	Estab-lish-ments	Em-ploy-ment	Payroll		Sales, revenues ($ mil.)
				Total ($ mil.)	Per Empl. ($)	
221122	Electric power distribution	13	448	29.8	66,475	212.5

Sources: Economic Census of the United States, 1997. Only those industries are shown for which both employment and sales/revenue data were available. For the definition of MSAs, CMSAs, and PMSAs, please see the Introduction.

ASHEVILLE, NC MSA

NAICS	Industry	Estab-lish-ments	Em-ploy-ment	Payroll		Sales, revenues ($ mil.)
				Total ($ mil.)	Per Empl. ($)	
221	Utilities	8	444	20.4	45,912	157.3

Sources: Economic Census of the United States, 1997. Only those industries are shown for which both employment and sales/revenue data were available. For the definition of MSAs, CMSAs, and PMSAs, please see the Introduction.

ATLANTA, GA MSA

NAICS	Industry	Estab-lish-ments	Em-ploy-ment	Payroll		Sales, revenues ($ mil.)
				Total ($ mil.)	Per Empl. ($)	
221	Utilities	177	11,340	632.1	55,740	6,712.1
2213	Water, sewage, and other systems	16	58	1.9	32,121	7.6
221310	Water supply and irrigation systems	11	32	0.9	28,844	4.0

Sources: Economic Census of the United States, 1997. Only those industries are shown for which both employment and sales/revenue data were available. For the definition of MSAs, CMSAs, and PMSAs, please see the Introduction.

AUGUSTA—AIKEN, GA—SC MSA

NAICS	Industry	Estab-lish-ments	Em-ploy-ment	Payroll		Sales, revenues ($ mil.)
				Total ($ mil.)	Per Empl. ($)	
221	Utilities	24	767	33.7	43,875	285.0
22112	Electric power transmission, control, and distribution	17	589	26.3	44,683	214.4

Sources: Economic Census of the United States, 1997. Only those industries are shown for which both employment and sales/revenue data were available. For the definition of MSAs, CMSAs, and PMSAs, please see the Introduction.

AUSTIN—SAN MARCOS, TX MSA

NAICS	Industry	Estab-lish-ments	Em-ploy-ment	Payroll		Sales, revenues ($ mil.)
				Total ($ mil.)	Per Empl. ($)	
221	Utilities	74	1,254	42.7	34,071	449.8
2211	Electric power generation, transmission, and distribution	24	399	17.6	44,008	176.5

Sources: *Economic Census of the United States*, 1997. Only those industries are shown for which both employment and sales/revenue data were available. For the definition of MSAs, CMSAs, and PMSAs, please see the Introduction.

BAKERSFIELD, CA MSA

NAICS	Industry	Estab-lish-ments	Em-ploy-ment	Payroll		Sales, revenues ($ mil.)
				Total ($ mil.)	Per Empl. ($)	
221	Utilities	53	1,313	71.5	54,470	645.9
2211	Electric power generation, transmission, and distribution	30	1,136	65.3	57,478	610.4
22111	Electric power generation	17	391	18.8	48,133	262.6
22112	Electric power transmission, control, and distribution	13	745	46.5	62,383	347.9
2213101	Water supply	20	146	5.6	38,089	32.7

Sources: *Economic Census of the United States*, 1997. Only those industries are shown for which both employment and sales/revenue data were available. For the definition of MSAs, CMSAs, and PMSAs, please see the Introduction.

BATON ROUGE, LA MSA

NAICS	Industry	Estab-lish-ments	Em-ploy-ment	Payroll		Sales, revenues ($ mil.)
				Total ($ mil.)	Per Empl. ($)	
221	Utilities	49	1,158	53.1	45,822	779.5
2211221	Electric services (electric power distribution)	27	768	38.5	50,081	618.6

Sources: *Economic Census of the United States*, 1997. Only those industries are shown for which both employment and sales/revenue data were available. For the definition of MSAs, CMSAs, and PMSAs, please see the Introduction.

BELLINGHAM, WA MSA

NAICS	Industry	Estab-lish-ments	Em-ploy-ment	Payroll		Sales, revenues ($ mil.)
				Total ($ mil.)	Per Empl. ($)	
221	Utilities	16	178	8.6	48,371	74.0

Sources: *Economic Census of the United States*, 1997. Only those industries are shown for which both employment and sales/revenue data were available. For the definition of MSAs, CMSAs, and PMSAs, please see the Introduction.

BERGEN—PASSAIC, NJ PMSA

NAICS	Industry	Estab-lish-ments	Em-ploy-ment	Payroll		Sales, revenues ($ mil.)
				Total ($ mil.)	Per Empl. ($)	
221	Utilities	31	1,725	103.7	60,090	1,025.2

Sources: *Economic Census of the United States*, 1997. Only those industries are shown for which both employment and sales/revenue data were available. For the definition of MSAs, CMSAs, and PMSAs, please see the Introduction.

BILLINGS, MT MSA

NAICS	Industry	Estab-lish-ments	Em-ploy-ment	Payroll		Sales, revenues ($ mil.)
				Total ($ mil.)	Per Empl. ($)	
221	Utilities	16	289	13.7	47,498	101.5

Sources: Economic Census of the United States, 1997. Only those industries are shown for which both employment and sales/revenue data were available. For the definition of MSAs, CMSAs, and PMSAs, please see the Introduction.

BILOXI—GULFPORT—PASCAGOULA, MS MSA

NAICS	Industry	Estab-lish-ments	Em-ploy-ment	Payroll		Sales, revenues ($ mil.)
				Total ($ mil.)	Per Empl. ($)	
221	Utilities	43	1,462	75.1	51,389	500.1
2211221	Electric services (electric power distribution)	29	947	50.7	53,589	312.1

Sources: Economic Census of the United States, 1997. Only those industries are shown for which both employment and sales/revenue data were available. For the definition of MSAs, CMSAs, and PMSAs, please see the Introduction.

BISMARCK, ND MSA

NAICS	Industry	Estab-lish-ments	Em-ploy-ment	Payroll		Sales, revenues ($ mil.)
				Total ($ mil.)	Per Empl. ($)	
221	Utilities	20	902	43.9	48,663	306.7

Sources: Economic Census of the United States, 1997. Only those industries are shown for which both employment and sales/revenue data were available. For the definition of MSAs, CMSAs, and PMSAs, please see the Introduction.

BLOOMINGTON, IN MSA

NAICS	Industry	Estab-lish-ments	Em-ploy-ment	Payroll		Sales, revenues ($ mil.)
				Total ($ mil.)	Per Empl. ($)	
221	Utilities	8	295	13.1	44,349	155.9

Sources: Economic Census of the United States, 1997. Only those industries are shown for which both employment and sales/revenue data were available. For the definition of MSAs, CMSAs, and PMSAs, please see the Introduction.

BLOOMINGTON—NORMAL, IL MSA

NAICS	Industry	Estab-lish-ments	Em-ploy-ment	Payroll		Sales, revenues ($ mil.)
				Total ($ mil.)	Per Empl. ($)	
221	Utilities	4	225	8.8	39,147	88.0

Sources: Economic Census of the United States, 1997. Only those industries are shown for which both employment and sales/revenue data were available. For the definition of MSAs, CMSAs, and PMSAs, please see the Introduction.

BOISE CITY, ID MSA

NAICS	Industry	Estab-lish-ments	Em-ploy-ment	Payroll		Sales, revenues ($ mil.)
				Total ($ mil.)	Per Empl. ($)	
221	Utilities	32	1,601	84.7	52,874	715.1

Sources: Economic Census of the United States, 1997. Only those industries are shown for which both employment and sales/revenue data were available. For the definition of MSAs, CMSAs, and PMSAs, please see the Introduction.

BOSTON, MA—NH PMSA

NAICS	Industry	Estab-lish-ments	Em-ploy-ment	Payroll		Sales, revenues ($ mil.)
				Total ($ mil.)	Per Empl. ($)	
221	Utilities	101	8,837	566.7	64,133	8,041.4
2211	Electric power generation, transmission, and distribution	50	6,223	417.8	67,138	6,594.1
22111	Electric power generation	11	1,533	116.7	76,107	850.5
221122	Electric power distribution	39	4,690	301.1	64,207	5,743.6

Sources: Economic Census of the United States, 1997. Only those industries are shown for which both employment and sales/revenue data were available. For the definition of MSAs, CMSAs, and PMSAs, please see the Introduction.

BOSTON—WORCESTER—LAWRENCE, MA—NH—ME—CT CMSA

NAICS	Industry	Estab-lish-ments	Em-ploy-ment	Payroll		Sales, revenues ($ mil.)
				Total ($ mil.)	Per Empl. ($)	
2211	Electric power generation, transmission, and distribution	105	11,012	674.0	61,204	8,658.1
221310	Water supply and irrigation systems	19	236	7.9	33,352	41.9

Sources: Economic Census of the United States, 1997. Only those industries are shown for which both employment and sales/revenue data were available. For the definition of MSAs, CMSAs, and PMSAs, please see the Introduction.

BOULDER—LONGMONT, CO PMSA

NAICS	Industry	Estab-lish-ments	Em-ploy-ment	Payroll		Sales, revenues ($ mil.)
				Total ($ mil.)	Per Empl. ($)	
221	Utilities	9	301	14.4	47,714	96.4

Sources: Economic Census of the United States, 1997. Only those industries are shown for which both employment and sales/revenue data were available. For the definition of MSAs, CMSAs, and PMSAs, please see the Introduction.

BRAZORIA, TX PMSA

NAICS	Industry	Estab-lish-ments	Em-ploy-ment	Payroll		Sales, revenues ($ mil.)
				Total ($ mil.)	Per Empl. ($)	
221	Utilities	25	325	12.9	39,738	95.8

Sources: Economic Census of the United States, 1997. Only those industries are shown for which both employment and sales/revenue data were available. For the definition of MSAs, CMSAs, and PMSAs, please see the Introduction.

BRIDGEPORT, CT PMSA

NAICS	Industry	Estab-lish-ments	Em-ploy-ment	Payroll		Sales, revenues ($ mil.)
				Total ($ mil.)	Per Empl. ($)	
221	Utilities	18	1,017	61.5	60,500	539.1

Sources: Economic Census of the United States, 1997. Only those industries are shown for which both employment and sales/revenue data were available. For the definition of MSAs, CMSAs, and PMSAs, please see the Introduction.

BROWNSVILLE—HARLINGEN—SAN BENITO, TX MSA

NAICS	Industry	Estab-lish-ments	Em-ploy-ment	Payroll		Sales, revenues ($ mil.)
				Total ($ mil.)	Per Empl. ($)	
221	Utilities	18	269	11.1	41,383	190.3

Sources: Economic Census of the United States, 1997. Only those industries are shown for which both employment and sales/revenue data were available. For the definition of MSAs, CMSAs, and PMSAs, please see the Introduction.

BUFFALO—NIAGARA FALLS, NY MSA

NAICS	Industry	Estab-lish-ments	Em-ploy-ment	Payroll		Sales, revenues ($ mil.)
				Total ($ mil.)	Per Empl. ($)	
221	Utilities	25	3,352	186.2	55,563	1,666.1

Sources: Economic Census of the United States, 1997. Only those industries are shown for which both employment and sales/revenue data were available. For the definition of MSAs, CMSAs, and PMSAs, please see the Introduction.

CANTON—MASSILLON, OH MSA

NAICS	Industry	Estab-lish-ments	Em-ploy-ment	Payroll		Sales, revenues ($ mil.)
				Total ($ mil.)	Per Empl. ($)	
221	Utilities	21	906	41.6	45,900	406.4

Sources: Economic Census of the United States, 1997. Only those industries are shown for which both employment and sales/revenue data were available. For the definition of MSAs, CMSAs, and PMSAs, please see the Introduction.

CEDAR RAPIDS, IA MSA

NAICS	Industry	Estab-lish-ments	Em-ploy-ment	Payroll		Sales, revenues ($ mil.)
				Total ($ mil.)	Per Empl. ($)	
221122	Electric power distribution	11	1,377	69.6	50,511	561.3

Sources: Economic Census of the United States, 1997. Only those industries are shown for which both employment and sales/revenue data were available. For the definition of MSAs, CMSAs, and PMSAs, please see the Introduction.

CHAMPAIGN—URBANA, IL MSA

NAICS	Industry	Estab-lish-ments	Em-ploy-ment	Payroll		Sales, revenues ($ mil.)
				Total ($ mil.)	Per Empl. ($)	
221	Utilities	5	251	10.8	43,199	78.3

Sources: Economic Census of the United States, 1997. Only those industries are shown for which both employment and sales/revenue data were available. For the definition of MSAs, CMSAs, and PMSAs, please see the Introduction.

CHARLESTON, WV MSA

NAICS	Industry	Estab-lish-ments	Em-ploy-ment	Payroll		Sales, revenues ($ mil.)
				Total ($ mil.)	Per Empl. ($)	
221	Utilities	38	1,920	90.3	47,049	1,054.6

Sources: Economic Census of the United States, 1997. Only those industries are shown for which both employment and sales/revenue data were available. For the definition of MSAs, CMSAs, and PMSAs, please see the Introduction.

CHARLOTTE—GASTONIA—ROCK HILL, NC—SC MSA

NAICS	Industry	Estab-lish-ments	Em-ploy-ment	Payroll		Sales, revenues ($ mil.)
				Total ($ mil.)	Per Empl. ($)	
221	Utilities	53	11,979	693.3	57,873	3,684.7

Sources: *Economic Census of the United States*, 1997. Only those industries are shown for which both employment and sales/revenue data were available. For the definition of MSAs, CMSAs, and PMSAs, please see the Introduction.

CHATTANOOGA, TN—GA MSA

NAICS	Industry	Estab-lish-ments	Em-ploy-ment	Payroll		Sales, revenues ($ mil.)
				Total ($ mil.)	Per Empl. ($)	
221	Utilities	11	355	15.3	43,099	152.8

Sources: *Economic Census of the United States*, 1997. Only those industries are shown for which both employment and sales/revenue data were available. For the definition of MSAs, CMSAs, and PMSAs, please see the Introduction.

CHEYENNE, WY MSA

NAICS	Industry	Estab-lish-ments	Em-ploy-ment	Payroll		Sales, revenues ($ mil.)
				Total ($ mil.)	Per Empl. ($)	
221	Utilities	6	140	6.1	43,471	68.4

Sources: *Economic Census of the United States*, 1997. Only those industries are shown for which both employment and sales/revenue data were available. For the definition of MSAs, CMSAs, and PMSAs, please see the Introduction.

CHICAGO—GARY—KENOSHA, IL—IN—WI CMSA

NAICS	Industry	Estab-lish-ments	Em-ploy-ment	Payroll		Sales, revenues ($ mil.)
				Total ($ mil.)	Per Empl. ($)	
221210	Natural gas distribution	65	5,325	276.1	51,853	4,412.5
2212102	Natural gas distribution	33	2,252	116.2	51,592	2,400.7

Sources: *Economic Census of the United States*, 1997. Only those industries are shown for which both employment and sales/revenue data were available. For the definition of MSAs, CMSAs, and PMSAs, please see the Introduction.

CHICO—PARADISE, CA MSA

NAICS	Industry	Estab-lish-ments	Em-ploy-ment	Payroll		Sales, revenues ($ mil.)
				Total ($ mil.)	Per Empl. ($)	
221	Utilities	7	79	2.9	36,228	15.7

Sources: *Economic Census of the United States*, 1997. Only those industries are shown for which both employment and sales/revenue data were available. For the definition of MSAs, CMSAs, and PMSAs, please see the Introduction.

CINCINNATI, OH—KY—IN PMSA

NAICS	Industry	Estab-lish-ments	Em-ploy-ment	Payroll		Sales, revenues ($ mil.)
				Total ($ mil.)	Per Empl. ($)	
221	Utilities	57	5,172	279.6	54,068	2,792.8

Sources: *Economic Census of the United States*, 1997. Only those industries are shown for which both employment and sales/revenue data were available. For the definition of MSAs, CMSAs, and PMSAs, please see the Introduction.

CINCINNATI—HAMILTON, OH—KY—IN CMSA

NAICS	Industry	Estab-lish-ments	Em-ploy-ment	Payroll		Sales, revenues ($ mil.)
				Total ($ mil.)	Per Empl. ($)	
221	Utilities	69	5,520	295.8	53,590	2,994.4

Sources: *Economic Census of the United States*, 1997. Only those industries are shown for which both employment and sales/revenue data were available. For the definition of MSAs, CMSAs, and PMSAs, please see the Introduction.

CLARKSVILLE—HOPKINSVILLE, TN—KY MSA

NAICS	Industry	Estab-lish-ments	Em-ploy-ment	Payroll		Sales, revenues ($ mil.)
				Total ($ mil.)	Per Empl. ($)	
221	Utilities	4	191	6.9	35,979	84.7

Sources: *Economic Census of the United States*, 1997. Only those industries are shown for which both employment and sales/revenue data were available. For the definition of MSAs, CMSAs, and PMSAs, please see the Introduction.

CLEVELAND—AKRON, OH CMSA

NAICS	Industry	Estab-lish-ments	Em-ploy-ment	Payroll		Sales, revenues ($ mil.)
				Total ($ mil.)	Per Empl. ($)	
2212102	Natural gas distribution	13	428	20.2	47,164	228.5

Sources: *Economic Census of the United States*, 1997. Only those industries are shown for which both employment and sales/revenue data were available. For the definition of MSAs, CMSAs, and PMSAs, please see the Introduction.

CLEVELAND—LORAIN—ELYRIA, OH PMSA

NAICS	Industry	Estab-lish-ments	Em-ploy-ment	Payroll		Sales, revenues ($ mil.)
				Total ($ mil.)	Per Empl. ($)	
221	Utilities	81	6,519	308.9	47,383	3,027.1
2212102	Natural gas distribution	12	427	20.1	47,187	228.5

Sources: *Economic Census of the United States*, 1997. Only those industries are shown for which both employment and sales/revenue data were available. For the definition of MSAs, CMSAs, and PMSAs, please see the Introduction.

COLORADO SPRINGS, CO MSA

NAICS	Industry	Estab-lish-ments	Em-ploy-ment	Payroll		Sales, revenues ($ mil.)
				Total ($ mil.)	Per Empl. ($)	
221	Utilities	18	630	29.4	46,625	296.0

Sources: *Economic Census of the United States*, 1997. Only those industries are shown for which both employment and sales/revenue data were available. For the definition of MSAs, CMSAs, and PMSAs, please see the Introduction.

COLUMBIA, SC MSA

NAICS	Industry	Estab-lish-ments	Em-ploy-ment	Payroll		Sales, revenues ($ mil.)
				Total ($ mil.)	Per Empl. ($)	
221	Utilities	49	2,004	97.0	48,426	1,004.2

Sources: *Economic Census of the United States*, 1997. Only those industries are shown for which both employment and sales/revenue data were available. For the definition of MSAs, CMSAs, and PMSAs, please see the Introduction.

COLUMBUS, OH MSA

NAICS	Industry	Estab-lish-ments	Em-ploy-ment	Payroll Total ($ mil.)	Payroll Per Empl. ($)	Sales, revenues ($ mil.)
221	Utilities	87	5,827	312.6	53,644	3,065.4
2211	Electric power generation, transmission, and distribution	52	3,987	223.6	56,082	1,292.4
221210	Natural gas distribution	27	1,722	85.0	49,367	1,747.1

Sources: Economic Census of the United States, 1997. Only those industries are shown for which both employment and sales/revenue data were available. For the definition of MSAs, CMSAs, and PMSAs, please see the Introduction.

CORPUS CHRISTI, TX MSA

NAICS	Industry	Estab-lish-ments	Em-ploy-ment	Payroll Total ($ mil.)	Payroll Per Empl. ($)	Sales, revenues ($ mil.)
221	Utilities	33	950	40.5	42,581	735.4

Sources: Economic Census of the United States, 1997. Only those industries are shown for which both employment and sales/revenue data were available. For the definition of MSAs, CMSAs, and PMSAs, please see the Introduction.

DALLAS, TX PMSA

NAICS	Industry	Estab-lish-ments	Em-ploy-ment	Payroll Total ($ mil.)	Payroll Per Empl. ($)	Sales, revenues ($ mil.)
221	Utilities	166	8,689	486.0	55,934	5,507.9
2211	Electric power generation, transmission, and distribution	55	5,686	325.9	57,309	2,471.0
22111	Electric power generation	11	317	19.5	61,514	227.1
22112	Electric power transmission, control, and distribution	44	5,369	306.4	57,061	2,244.0
2211221	Electric services (electric power distribution)	41	5,347	305.2	57,072	2,242.5
221210	Natural gas distribution	38	2,756	155.3	56,346	3,003.9
2213	Water, sewage, and other systems	73	247	4.9	19,680	33.0
221310	Water supply and irrigation systems	68	218	4.2	19,335	28.1

Sources: Economic Census of the United States, 1997. Only those industries are shown for which both employment and sales/revenue data were available. For the definition of MSAs, CMSAs, and PMSAs, please see the Introduction.

DALLAS—FORT WORTH, TX CMSA

NAICS	Industry	Estab-lish-ments	Em-ploy-ment	Payroll Total ($ mil.)	Payroll Per Empl. ($)	Sales, revenues ($ mil.)
221	Utilities	232	10,971	584.4	53,265	7,049.7
2211221	Electric services (electric power distribution)	57	6,852	372.5	54,365	3,140.8
221210	Natural gas distribution	54	3,227	174.8	54,182	3,505.2
2212102	Natural gas distribution	47	2,954	149.1	50,464	2,665.9
221310	Water supply and irrigation systems	90	298	5.7	19,248	37.2

Sources: Economic Census of the United States, 1997. Only those industries are shown for which both employment and sales/revenue data were available. For the definition of MSAs, CMSAs, and PMSAs, please see the Introduction.

DANVILLE, VA MSA

NAICS	Industry	Estab-lish-ments	Em-ploy-ment	Payroll Total ($ mil.)	Payroll Per Empl. ($)	Sales, revenues ($ mil.)
221	Utilities	7	71	2.9	40,901	83.2

Sources: Economic Census of the United States, 1997. Only those industries are shown for which both employment and sales/revenue data were available. For the definition of MSAs, CMSAs, and PMSAs, please see the Introduction.

DAVENPORT—MOLINE—ROCK ISLAND, IA—IL MSA

NAICS	Industry	Estab-lish-ments	Em-ploy-ment	Payroll		Sales, revenues ($ mil.)
				Total ($ mil.)	Per Empl. ($)	
221	Utilities	19	2,043	106.0	51,894	831.3

Sources: Economic Census of the United States, 1997. Only those industries are shown for which both employment and sales/revenue data were available. For the definition of MSAs, CMSAs, and PMSAs, please see the Introduction.

DAYTON—SPRINGFIELD, OH MSA

NAICS	Industry	Estab-lish-ments	Em-ploy-ment	Payroll		Sales, revenues ($ mil.)
				Total ($ mil.)	Per Empl. ($)	
221	Utilities	22	1,744	58.2	33,345	939.0

Sources: Economic Census of the United States, 1997. Only those industries are shown for which both employment and sales/revenue data were available. For the definition of MSAs, CMSAs, and PMSAs, please see the Introduction.

DAYTONA BEACH, FL MSA

NAICS	Industry	Estab-lish-ments	Em-ploy-ment	Payroll		Sales, revenues ($ mil.)
				Total ($ mil.)	Per Empl. ($)	
221	Utilities	17	640	30.0	46,908	301.1

Sources: Economic Census of the United States, 1997. Only those industries are shown for which both employment and sales/revenue data were available. For the definition of MSAs, CMSAs, and PMSAs, please see the Introduction.

DENVER, CO PMSA

NAICS	Industry	Estab-lish-ments	Em-ploy-ment	Payroll		Sales, revenues ($ mil.)
				Total ($ mil.)	Per Empl. ($)	
221	Utilities	67	4,936	252.9	51,236	3,426.6
221210	Natural gas distribution	28	895	53.1	59,276	1,862.2
2212102	Natural gas distribution	16	262	13.5	51,645	1,383.6

Sources: Economic Census of the United States, 1997. Only those industries are shown for which both employment and sales/revenue data were available. For the definition of MSAs, CMSAs, and PMSAs, please see the Introduction.

DENVER—BOULDER—GREELEY, CO CMSA

NAICS	Industry	Estab-lish-ments	Em-ploy-ment	Payroll		Sales, revenues ($ mil.)
				Total ($ mil.)	Per Empl. ($)	
221	Utilities	91	5,514	280.0	50,781	3,619.1
2211	Electric power generation, transmission, and distribution	24	4,227	214.2	50,664	1,693.3
22112	Electric power transmission, control, and distribution	16	3,713	185.7	50,006	1,450.3

Sources: Economic Census of the United States, 1997. Only those industries are shown for which both employment and sales/revenue data were available. For the definition of MSAs, CMSAs, and PMSAs, please see the Introduction.

DETROIT, MI PMSA

| NAICS | Industry | Estab-lish-ments | Em-ploy-ment | Payroll | | Sales, revenues ($ mil.) |
				Total ($ mil.)	Per Empl. ($)	
221	Utilities	131	12,328	765.9	62,125	6,677.0

Sources: *Economic Census of the United States*, 1997. Only those industries are shown for which both employment and sales/revenue data were available. For the definition of MSAs, CMSAs, and PMSAs, please see the Introduction.

DETROIT—ANN ARBOR—FLINT, MI CMSA

| NAICS | Industry | Estab-lish-ments | Em-ploy-ment | Payroll | | Sales, revenues ($ mil.) |
				Total ($ mil.)	Per Empl. ($)	
221	Utilities	157	13,466	832.2	61,802	7,154.9

Sources: *Economic Census of the United States*, 1997. Only those industries are shown for which both employment and sales/revenue data were available. For the definition of MSAs, CMSAs, and PMSAs, please see the Introduction.

EL PASO, TX MSA

| NAICS | Industry | Estab-lish-ments | Em-ploy-ment | Payroll | | Sales, revenues ($ mil.) |
				Total ($ mil.)	Per Empl. ($)	
221	Utilities	20	1,256	53.2	42,380	643.1

Sources: *Economic Census of the United States*, 1997. Only those industries are shown for which both employment and sales/revenue data were available. For the definition of MSAs, CMSAs, and PMSAs, please see the Introduction.

ERIE, PA MSA

| NAICS | Industry | Estab-lish-ments | Em-ploy-ment | Payroll | | Sales, revenues ($ mil.) |
				Total ($ mil.)	Per Empl. ($)	
221	Utilities	11	512	21.7	42,414	258.1

Sources: *Economic Census of the United States*, 1997. Only those industries are shown for which both employment and sales/revenue data were available. For the definition of MSAs, CMSAs, and PMSAs, please see the Introduction.

EUGENE—SPRINGFIELD, OR MSA

| NAICS | Industry | Estab-lish-ments | Em-ploy-ment | Payroll | | Sales, revenues ($ mil.) |
				Total ($ mil.)	Per Empl. ($)	
221	Utilities	10	158	6.9	43,715	39.5

Sources: *Economic Census of the United States*, 1997. Only those industries are shown for which both employment and sales/revenue data were available. For the definition of MSAs, CMSAs, and PMSAs, please see the Introduction.

EVANSVILLE—HENDERSON, IN—KY MSA

| NAICS | Industry | Estab-lish-ments | Em-ploy-ment | Payroll | | Sales, revenues ($ mil.) |
				Total ($ mil.)	Per Empl. ($)	
221	Utilities	21	1,230	53.2	43,220	571.9

Sources: *Economic Census of the United States*, 1997. Only those industries are shown for which both employment and sales/revenue data were available. For the definition of MSAs, CMSAs, and PMSAs, please see the Introduction.

FARGO—MOORHEAD, ND—MN MSA

NAICS	Industry	Estab-lish-ments	Em-ploy-ment	Payroll		Sales, revenues ($ mil.)
				Total ($ mil.)	Per Empl. ($)	
221	Utilities	6	209	10.0	47,928	59.7

Sources: *Economic Census of the United States*, 1997. Only those industries are shown for which both employment and sales/revenue data were available. For the definition of MSAs, CMSAs, and PMSAs, please see the Introduction.

FAYETTEVILLE, NC MSA

NAICS	Industry	Estab-lish-ments	Em-ploy-ment	Payroll		Sales, revenues ($ mil.)
				Total ($ mil.)	Per Empl. ($)	
221	Utilities	8	278	10.2	36,655	103.1

Sources: *Economic Census of the United States*, 1997. Only those industries are shown for which both employment and sales/revenue data were available. For the definition of MSAs, CMSAs, and PMSAs, please see the Introduction.

FAYETTEVILLE—SPRINGDALE—ROGERS, AR MSA

NAICS	Industry	Estab-lish-ments	Em-ploy-ment	Payroll		Sales, revenues ($ mil.)
				Total ($ mil.)	Per Empl. ($)	
221	Utilities	18	684	25.5	37,232	251.2

Sources: *Economic Census of the United States*, 1997. Only those industries are shown for which both employment and sales/revenue data were available. For the definition of MSAs, CMSAs, and PMSAs, please see the Introduction.

FITCHBURG—LEOMINSTER, MA PMSA

NAICS	Industry	Estab-lish-ments	Em-ploy-ment	Payroll		Sales, revenues ($ mil.)
				Total ($ mil.)	Per Empl. ($)	
221	Utilities	5	202	9.7	48,084	136.3

Sources: *Economic Census of the United States*, 1997. Only those industries are shown for which both employment and sales/revenue data were available. For the definition of MSAs, CMSAs, and PMSAs, please see the Introduction.

FLAGSTAFF, AZ—UT MSA

NAICS	Industry	Estab-lish-ments	Em-ploy-ment	Payroll		Sales, revenues ($ mil.)
				Total ($ mil.)	Per Empl. ($)	
221	Utilities	11	198	9.3	46,788	54.6

Sources: *Economic Census of the United States*, 1997. Only those industries are shown for which both employment and sales/revenue data were available. For the definition of MSAs, CMSAs, and PMSAs, please see the Introduction.

FORT COLLINS—LOVELAND, CO MSA

NAICS	Industry	Estab-lish-ments	Em-ploy-ment	Payroll		Sales, revenues ($ mil.)
				Total ($ mil.)	Per Empl. ($)	
221	Utilities	13	214	9.6	45,009	81.9

Sources: *Economic Census of the United States*, 1997. Only those industries are shown for which both employment and sales/revenue data were available. For the definition of MSAs, CMSAs, and PMSAs, please see the Introduction.

FORT MYERS—CAPE CORAL, FL MSA

NAICS	Industry	Estab-lish-ments	Em-ploy-ment	Payroll Total ($ mil.)	Per Empl. ($)	Sales, revenues ($ mil.)
221	Utilities	19	631	27.2	43,059	321.4

Sources: Economic Census of the United States, 1997. Only those industries are shown for which both employment and sales/revenue data were available. For the definition of MSAs, CMSAs, and PMSAs, please see the Introduction.

FORT SMITH, AR—OK MSA

NAICS	Industry	Estab-lish-ments	Em-ploy-ment	Payroll Total ($ mil.)	Per Empl. ($)	Sales, revenues ($ mil.)
221	Utilities	21	458	16.5	36,013	174.1
2213101	Water supply	13	54	1.0	17,852	5.4

Sources: Economic Census of the United States, 1997. Only those industries are shown for which both employment and sales/revenue data were available. For the definition of MSAs, CMSAs, and PMSAs, please see the Introduction.

FORT WAYNE, IN MSA

NAICS	Industry	Estab-lish-ments	Em-ploy-ment	Payroll Total ($ mil.)	Per Empl. ($)	Sales, revenues ($ mil.)
221	Utilities	20	1,828	81.0	44,314	609.1
2211	Electric power generation, transmission, and distribution	12	1,629	73.1	44,845	516.3

Sources: Economic Census of the United States, 1997. Only those industries are shown for which both employment and sales/revenue data were available. For the definition of MSAs, CMSAs, and PMSAs, please see the Introduction.

FORT WORTH—ARLINGTON, TX PMSA

NAICS	Industry	Estab-lish-ments	Em-ploy-ment	Payroll Total ($ mil.)	Per Empl. ($)	Sales, revenues ($ mil.)
221	Utilities	66	2,282	98.4	43,103	1,541.8
2211221	Electric services (electric power distribution)	16	1,505	67.3	44,746	898.3
221210	Natural gas distribution	16	471	19.6	41,522	501.3
2213101	Water supply	22	80	1.5	19,013	9.1

Sources: Economic Census of the United States, 1997. Only those industries are shown for which both employment and sales/revenue data were available. For the definition of MSAs, CMSAs, and PMSAs, please see the Introduction.

FRESNO, CA MSA

NAICS	Industry	Estab-lish-ments	Em-ploy-ment	Payroll Total ($ mil.)	Per Empl. ($)	Sales, revenues ($ mil.)
221310	Water supply and irrigation systems	18	62	1.6	25,242	7.8
2213101	Water supply	14	49	1.2	24,653	5.6

Sources: Economic Census of the United States, 1997. Only those industries are shown for which both employment and sales/revenue data were available. For the definition of MSAs, CMSAs, and PMSAs, please see the Introduction.

637

GAINESVILLE, FL MSA

NAICS	Industry	Establishments	Employment	Payroll		Sales, revenues ($ mil.)
				Total ($ mil.)	Per Empl. ($)	
221	Utilities	6	64	3.0	47,438	68.6

Sources: *Economic Census of the United States*, 1997. Only those industries are shown for which both employment and sales/revenue data were available. For the definition of MSAs, CMSAs, and PMSAs, please see the Introduction.

GALVESTON—TEXAS CITY, TX PMSA

NAICS	Industry	Establishments	Employment	Payroll		Sales, revenues ($ mil.)
				Total ($ mil.)	Per Empl. ($)	
221	Utilities	21	516	24.2	46,922	1,698.2

Sources: *Economic Census of the United States*, 1997. Only those industries are shown for which both employment and sales/revenue data were available. For the definition of MSAs, CMSAs, and PMSAs, please see the Introduction.

GARY, IN PMSA

NAICS	Industry	Establishments	Employment	Payroll		Sales, revenues ($ mil.)
				Total ($ mil.)	Per Empl. ($)	
221	Utilities	29	2,678	132.3	49,385	2,343.5

Sources: *Economic Census of the United States*, 1997. Only those industries are shown for which both employment and sales/revenue data were available. For the definition of MSAs, CMSAs, and PMSAs, please see the Introduction.

GOLDSBORO, NC MSA

NAICS	Industry	Establishments	Employment	Payroll		Sales, revenues ($ mil.)
				Total ($ mil.)	Per Empl. ($)	
221	Utilities	8	254	10.3	40,622	110.6

Sources: *Economic Census of the United States*, 1997. Only those industries are shown for which both employment and sales/revenue data were available. For the definition of MSAs, CMSAs, and PMSAs, please see the Introduction.

GRAND FORKS, ND—MN MSA

NAICS	Industry	Establishments	Employment	Payroll		Sales, revenues ($ mil.)
				Total ($ mil.)	Per Empl. ($)	
221	Utilities	9	368	18.7	50,908	126.8

Sources: *Economic Census of the United States*, 1997. Only those industries are shown for which both employment and sales/revenue data were available. For the definition of MSAs, CMSAs, and PMSAs, please see the Introduction.

GRAND JUNCTION, CO MSA

NAICS	Industry	Establishments	Employment	Payroll		Sales, revenues ($ mil.)
				Total ($ mil.)	Per Empl. ($)	
221	Utilities	8	190	9.0	47,368	63.3

Sources: *Economic Census of the United States*, 1997. Only those industries are shown for which both employment and sales/revenue data were available. For the definition of MSAs, CMSAs, and PMSAs, please see the Introduction.

GRAND RAPIDS—MUSKEGON—HOLLAND, MI MSA

NAICS	Industry	Estab-lish-ments	Em-ploy-ment	Payroll Total ($ mil.)	Payroll Per Empl. ($)	Sales, revenues ($ mil.)
221	Utilities	25	1,838	94.1	51,207	818.5

Sources: Economic Census of the United States, 1997. Only those industries are shown for which both employment and sales/revenue data were available. For the definition of MSAs, CMSAs, and PMSAs, please see the Introduction.

GREELEY, CO PMSA

NAICS	Industry	Estab-lish-ments	Em-ploy-ment	Payroll Total ($ mil.)	Payroll Per Empl. ($)	Sales, revenues ($ mil.)
221	Utilities	15	277	12.7	46,000	96.1

Sources: Economic Census of the United States, 1997. Only those industries are shown for which both employment and sales/revenue data were available. For the definition of MSAs, CMSAs, and PMSAs, please see the Introduction.

GREENSBORO—WINSTON-SALEM—HIGH POINT, NC MSA

NAICS	Industry	Estab-lish-ments	Em-ploy-ment	Payroll Total ($ mil.)	Payroll Per Empl. ($)	Sales, revenues ($ mil.)
221	Utilities	27	1,695	71.6	42,258	549.6
2211221	Electric services (electric power distribution)	12	1,227	55.8	45,486	386.1

Sources: Economic Census of the United States, 1997. Only those industries are shown for which both employment and sales/revenue data were available. For the definition of MSAs, CMSAs, and PMSAs, please see the Introduction.

GREENVILLE, NC MSA

NAICS	Industry	Estab-lish-ments	Em-ploy-ment	Payroll Total ($ mil.)	Payroll Per Empl. ($)	Sales, revenues ($ mil.)
221	Utilities	6	62	1.0	16,226	13.7

Sources: Economic Census of the United States, 1997. Only those industries are shown for which both employment and sales/revenue data were available. For the definition of MSAs, CMSAs, and PMSAs, please see the Introduction.

GREENVILLE—SPARTANBURG—ANDERSON, SC MSA

NAICS	Industry	Estab-lish-ments	Em-ploy-ment	Payroll Total ($ mil.)	Payroll Per Empl. ($)	Sales, revenues ($ mil.)
221	Utilities	40	1,767	73.9	41,847	564.1
221122	Electric power distribution	16	1,373	60.9	44,376	402.8

Sources: Economic Census of the United States, 1997. Only those industries are shown for which both employment and sales/revenue data were available. For the definition of MSAs, CMSAs, and PMSAs, please see the Introduction.

HAMILTON—MIDDLETOWN, OH PMSA

NAICS	Industry	Estab-lish-ments	Em-ploy-ment	Payroll Total ($ mil.)	Payroll Per Empl. ($)	Sales, revenues ($ mil.)
221	Utilities	12	348	16.2	46,483	201.5

Sources: Economic Census of the United States, 1997. Only those industries are shown for which both employment and sales/revenue data were available. For the definition of MSAs, CMSAs, and PMSAs, please see the Introduction.

HARRISBURG—LEBANON—CARLISLE, PA MSA

NAICS	Industry	Estab-lish-ments	Em-ploy-ment	Payroll		Sales, revenues ($ mil.)
				Total ($ mil.)	Per Empl. ($)	
221	Utilities	22	1,768	81.9	46,341	668.6

Sources: *Economic Census of the United States*, 1997. Only those industries are shown for which both employment and sales/revenue data were available. For the definition of MSAs, CMSAs, and PMSAs, please see the Introduction.

HATTIESBURG, MS MSA

NAICS	Industry	Estab-lish-ments	Em-ploy-ment	Payroll		Sales, revenues ($ mil.)
				Total ($ mil.)	Per Empl. ($)	
221	Utilities	33	515	20.4	39,550	380.6
2211221	Electric services (electric power distribution)	14	282	12.7	45,078	206.2
2213101	Water supply	12	45	0.7	15,556	3.4

Sources: *Economic Census of the United States*, 1997. Only those industries are shown for which both employment and sales/revenue data were available. For the definition of MSAs, CMSAs, and PMSAs, please see the Introduction.

HICKORY—MORGANTON—LENOIR, NC MSA

NAICS	Industry	Estab-lish-ments	Em-ploy-ment	Payroll		Sales, revenues ($ mil.)
				Total ($ mil.)	Per Empl. ($)	
221	Utilities	32	678	29.1	42,895	185.7
2211221	Electric services (electric power distribution)	13	503	23.9	47,575	141.2

Sources: *Economic Census of the United States*, 1997. Only those industries are shown for which both employment and sales/revenue data were available. For the definition of MSAs, CMSAs, and PMSAs, please see the Introduction.

HOUMA, LA MSA

NAICS	Industry	Estab-lish-ments	Em-ploy-ment	Payroll		Sales, revenues ($ mil.)
				Total ($ mil.)	Per Empl. ($)	
221	Utilities	8	176	6.9	38,943	148.8

Sources: *Economic Census of the United States*, 1997. Only those industries are shown for which both employment and sales/revenue data were available. For the definition of MSAs, CMSAs, and PMSAs, please see the Introduction.

HOUSTON, TX PMSA

NAICS	Industry	Estab-lish-ments	Em-ploy-ment	Payroll		Sales, revenues ($ mil.)
				Total ($ mil.)	Per Empl. ($)	
221	Utilities	265	18,811	1,106.3	58,813	49,252.0
2211	Electric power generation, transmission, and distribution	77	7,775	436.6	56,153	8,199.7
22111	Electric power generation	15	327	27.0	82,486	352.0
22112	Electric power transmission, control, and distribution	62	7,448	409.6	54,997	7,847.6
221210	Natural gas distribution	122	10,171	642.5	63,168	40,937.8
2212101	Natural gas transmission and distribution (distribution)	23	2,216	196.4	88,618	3,522.9
2212102	Natural gas distribution	81	4,192	216.8	51,729	22,112.3
2213	Water, sewage, and other systems	66	865	27.3	31,521	114.5
2213101	Water supply	42	222	6.8	30,685	31.8
221320	Sewage treatment facilities	15	545	16.6	30,439	55.3

Sources: *Economic Census of the United States*, 1997. Only those industries are shown for which both employment and sales/revenue data were available. For the definition of MSAs, CMSAs, and PMSAs, please see the Introduction.

HOUSTON—GALVESTON—BRAZORIA, TX CMSA

| NAICS | Industry | Estab-lish-ments | Em-ploy-ment | Payroll | | Sales, revenues ($ mil.) |
				Total ($ mil.)	Per Empl. ($)	
221	Utilities	311	19,652	1,143.5	58,186	51,046.0

Sources: *Economic Census of the United States*, 1997. Only those industries are shown for which both employment and sales/revenue data were available. For the definition of MSAs, CMSAs, and PMSAs, please see the Introduction.

HUNTINGTON—ASHLAND, WV—KY—OH MSA

| NAICS | Industry | Estab-lish-ments | Em-ploy-ment | Payroll | | Sales, revenues ($ mil.) |
				Total ($ mil.)	Per Empl. ($)	
221	Utilities	34	874	36.1	41,262	333.7

Sources: *Economic Census of the United States*, 1997. Only those industries are shown for which both employment and sales/revenue data were available. For the definition of MSAs, CMSAs, and PMSAs, please see the Introduction.

INDIANAPOLIS, IN MSA

| NAICS | Industry | Estab-lish-ments | Em-ploy-ment | Payroll | | Sales, revenues ($ mil.) |
				Total ($ mil.)	Per Empl. ($)	
221	Utilities	65	4,614	241.4	52,326	2,197.9
2211221	Electric services (electric power distribution)	17	1,604	82.2	51,277	846.3
221310	Water supply and irrigation systems	15	426	20.1	47,106	94.1

Sources: *Economic Census of the United States*, 1997. Only those industries are shown for which both employment and sales/revenue data were available. For the definition of MSAs, CMSAs, and PMSAs, please see the Introduction.

JACKSON, MS MSA

| NAICS | Industry | Estab-lish-ments | Em-ploy-ment | Payroll | | Sales, revenues ($ mil.) |
				Total ($ mil.)	Per Empl. ($)	
221	Utilities	67	1,430	65.4	45,710	704.6

Sources: *Economic Census of the United States*, 1997. Only those industries are shown for which both employment and sales/revenue data were available. For the definition of MSAs, CMSAs, and PMSAs, please see the Introduction.

JACKSONVILLE, FL MSA

| NAICS | Industry | Estab-lish-ments | Em-ploy-ment | Payroll | | Sales, revenues ($ mil.) |
				Total ($ mil.)	Per Empl. ($)	
221	Utilities	34	709	28.6	40,307	394.0
221122	Electric power distribution	11	410	18.6	45,380	341.3
221320	Sewage treatment facilities	12	148	5.6	38,135	33.4

Sources: *Economic Census of the United States*, 1997. Only those industries are shown for which both employment and sales/revenue data were available. For the definition of MSAs, CMSAs, and PMSAs, please see the Introduction.

JOHNSON CITY—KINGSPORT—BRISTOL, TN—VA MSA

NAICS	Industry	Estab-lish-ments	Em-ploy-ment	Payroll		Sales, revenues ($ mil.)
				Total ($ mil.)	Per Empl. ($)	
221	Utilities	23	464	18.1	38,931	232.6

Sources: *Economic Census of the United States*, 1997. Only those industries are shown for which both employment and sales/revenue data were available. For the definition of MSAs, CMSAs, and PMSAs, please see the Introduction.

JOHNSTOWN, PA MSA

NAICS	Industry	Estab-lish-ments	Em-ploy-ment	Payroll		Sales, revenues ($ mil.)
				Total ($ mil.)	Per Empl. ($)	
221	Utilities	28	990	46.6	47,115	387.2

Sources: *Economic Census of the United States*, 1997. Only those industries are shown for which both employment and sales/revenue data were available. For the definition of MSAs, CMSAs, and PMSAs, please see the Introduction.

JOPLIN, MO MSA

NAICS	Industry	Estab-lish-ments	Em-ploy-ment	Payroll		Sales, revenues ($ mil.)
				Total ($ mil.)	Per Empl. ($)	
221	Utilities	12	570	25.1	44,058	196.7

Sources: *Economic Census of the United States*, 1997. Only those industries are shown for which both employment and sales/revenue data were available. For the definition of MSAs, CMSAs, and PMSAs, please see the Introduction.

KANSAS CITY, MO—KS MSA

NAICS	Industry	Estab-lish-ments	Em-ploy-ment	Payroll		Sales, revenues ($ mil.)
				Total ($ mil.)	Per Empl. ($)	
221	Utilities	64	3,771	198.9	52,745	1,578.5
221122	Electric power distribution	32	2,533	138.0	54,492	1,075.7

Sources: *Economic Census of the United States*, 1997. Only those industries are shown for which both employment and sales/revenue data were available. For the definition of MSAs, CMSAs, and PMSAs, please see the Introduction.

KILLEEN—TEMPLE, TX MSA

NAICS	Industry	Estab-lish-ments	Em-ploy-ment	Payroll		Sales, revenues ($ mil.)
				Total ($ mil.)	Per Empl. ($)	
221	Utilities	22	212	8.9	41,882	119.3

Sources: *Economic Census of the United States*, 1997. Only those industries are shown for which both employment and sales/revenue data were available. For the definition of MSAs, CMSAs, and PMSAs, please see the Introduction.

KNOXVILLE, TN MSA

NAICS	Industry	Estab-lish-ments	Em-ploy-ment	Payroll		Sales, revenues ($ mil.)
				Total ($ mil.)	Per Empl. ($)	
221	Utilities	13	299	13.0	43,565	213.5

Sources: *Economic Census of the United States*, 1997. Only those industries are shown for which both employment and sales/revenue data were available. For the definition of MSAs, CMSAs, and PMSAs, please see the Introduction.

KOKOMO, IN MSA

NAICS	Industry	Estab-lish-ments	Em-ploy-ment	Payroll Total ($ mil.)	Payroll Per Empl. ($)	Sales, revenues ($ mil.)
221	Utilities	4	141	6.0	42,355	77.9

Sources: Economic Census of the United States, 1997. Only those industries are shown for which both employment and sales/revenue data were available. For the definition of MSAs, CMSAs, and PMSAs, please see the Introduction.

LAFAYETTE, IN MSA

NAICS	Industry	Estab-lish-ments	Em-ploy-ment	Payroll Total ($ mil.)	Payroll Per Empl. ($)	Sales, revenues ($ mil.)
221	Utilities	9	177	7.4	42,034	84.0

Sources: Economic Census of the United States, 1997. Only those industries are shown for which both employment and sales/revenue data were available. For the definition of MSAs, CMSAs, and PMSAs, please see the Introduction.

LAFAYETTE, LA MSA

NAICS	Industry	Estab-lish-ments	Em-ploy-ment	Payroll Total ($ mil.)	Payroll Per Empl. ($)	Sales, revenues ($ mil.)
221	Utilities	38	537	19.0	35,307	203.0
2211	Electric power generation, transmission, and distribution	14	333	13.2	39,742	161.7

Sources: Economic Census of the United States, 1997. Only those industries are shown for which both employment and sales/revenue data were available. For the definition of MSAs, CMSAs, and PMSAs, please see the Introduction.

LAKE CHARLES, LA MSA

NAICS	Industry	Estab-lish-ments	Em-ploy-ment	Payroll Total ($ mil.)	Payroll Per Empl. ($)	Sales, revenues ($ mil.)
221	Utilities	18	503	24.6	48,859	531.7

Sources: Economic Census of the United States, 1997. Only those industries are shown for which both employment and sales/revenue data were available. For the definition of MSAs, CMSAs, and PMSAs, please see the Introduction.

LAKELAND—WINTER HAVEN, FL MSA

NAICS	Industry	Estab-lish-ments	Em-ploy-ment	Payroll Total ($ mil.)	Payroll Per Empl. ($)	Sales, revenues ($ mil.)
221	Utilities	22	460	19.5	42,411	151.9
2211	Electric power generation, transmission, and distribution	12	338	15.8	46,654	124.9

Sources: Economic Census of the United States, 1997. Only those industries are shown for which both employment and sales/revenue data were available. For the definition of MSAs, CMSAs, and PMSAs, please see the Introduction.

LANCASTER, PA MSA

NAICS	Industry	Estab-lish-ments	Em-ploy-ment	Payroll Total ($ mil.)	Payroll Per Empl. ($)	Sales, revenues ($ mil.)
221	Utilities	10	432	19.7	45,567	189.8

Sources: Economic Census of the United States, 1997. Only those industries are shown for which both employment and sales/revenue data were available. For the definition of MSAs, CMSAs, and PMSAs, please see the Introduction.

LAREDO, TX MSA

NAICS	Industry	Estab-lish-ments	Em-ploy-ment	Payroll Total ($ mil.)	Payroll Per Empl. ($)	Sales, revenues ($ mil.)
221	Utilities	13	289	14.6	50,640	177.4

Sources: Economic Census of the United States, 1997. Only those industries are shown for which both employment and sales/revenue data were available. For the definition of MSAs, CMSAs, and PMSAs, please see the Introduction.

LAS CRUCES, NM MSA

NAICS	Industry	Estab-lish-ments	Em-ploy-ment	Payroll Total ($ mil.)	Payroll Per Empl. ($)	Sales, revenues ($ mil.)
221	Utilities	21	261	9.4	35,885	109.0

Sources: Economic Census of the United States, 1997. Only those industries are shown for which both employment and sales/revenue data were available. For the definition of MSAs, CMSAs, and PMSAs, please see the Introduction.

LAS VEGAS, NV—AZ MSA

NAICS	Industry	Estab-lish-ments	Em-ploy-ment	Payroll Total ($ mil.)	Payroll Per Empl. ($)	Sales, revenues ($ mil.)
221	Utilities	59	3,718	195.1	52,463	1,540.7
221122	Electric power distribution	24	1,965	104.4	53,139	888.9

Sources: Economic Census of the United States, 1997. Only those industries are shown for which both employment and sales/revenue data were available. For the definition of MSAs, CMSAs, and PMSAs, please see the Introduction.

LAWRENCE, MA—NH PMSA

NAICS	Industry	Estab-lish-ments	Em-ploy-ment	Payroll Total ($ mil.)	Payroll Per Empl. ($)	Sales, revenues ($ mil.)
221	Utilities	13	678	33.1	48,847	402.3

Sources: Economic Census of the United States, 1997. Only those industries are shown for which both employment and sales/revenue data were available. For the definition of MSAs, CMSAs, and PMSAs, please see the Introduction.

LEXINGTON, KY MSA

NAICS	Industry	Estab-lish-ments	Em-ploy-ment	Payroll Total ($ mil.)	Payroll Per Empl. ($)	Sales, revenues ($ mil.)
221	Utilities	32	1,917	84.7	44,179	775.6
2211221	Electric services (electric power distribution)	12	1,295	58.7	45,304	506.8

Sources: Economic Census of the United States, 1997. Only those industries are shown for which both employment and sales/revenue data were available. For the definition of MSAs, CMSAs, and PMSAs, please see the Introduction.

LIMA, OH MSA

NAICS	Industry	Estab-lish-ments	Em-ploy-ment	Payroll Total ($ mil.)	Payroll Per Empl. ($)	Sales, revenues ($ mil.)
221	Utilities	10	219	9.9	44,986	141.2

Sources: Economic Census of the United States, 1997. Only those industries are shown for which both employment and sales/revenue data were available. For the definition of MSAs, CMSAs, and PMSAs, please see the Introduction.

LITTLE ROCK—NORTH LITTLE ROCK, AR MSA

NAICS	Industry	Estab-lish-ments	Em-ploy-ment	Payroll		Sales, revenues ($ mil.)
				Total ($ mil.)	Per Empl. ($)	
221	Utilities	52	1,856	99.7	53,732	1,049.1

Sources: *Economic Census of the United States*, 1997. Only those industries are shown for which both employment and sales/revenue data were available. For the definition of MSAs, CMSAs, and PMSAs, please see the Introduction.

LONGVIEW—MARSHALL, TX MSA

NAICS	Industry	Estab-lish-ments	Em-ploy-ment	Payroll		Sales, revenues ($ mil.)
				Total ($ mil.)	Per Empl. ($)	
221	Utilities	36	715	30.5	42,677	451.0
2211221	Electric services (electric power distribution)	13	355	14.5	40,792	162.1

Sources: *Economic Census of the United States*, 1997. Only those industries are shown for which both employment and sales/revenue data were available. For the definition of MSAs, CMSAs, and PMSAs, please see the Introduction.

LOS ANGELES—LONG BEACH, CA PMSA

NAICS	Industry	Estab-lish-ments	Em-ploy-ment	Payroll		Sales, revenues ($ mil.)
				Total ($ mil.)	Per Empl. ($)	
221	Utilities	177	9,771	486.9	49,833	5,752.5
2211	Electric power generation, transmission, and distribution	86	7,946	411.7	51,807	4,379.4
221310	Water supply and irrigation systems	66	1,063	43.5	40,921	351.8

Sources: *Economic Census of the United States*, 1997. Only those industries are shown for which both employment and sales/revenue data were available. For the definition of MSAs, CMSAs, and PMSAs, please see the Introduction.

LOS ANGELES—RIVERSIDE—ORANGE COUNTY, CA CMSA

NAICS	Industry	Estab-lish-ments	Em-ploy-ment	Payroll		Sales, revenues ($ mil.)
				Total ($ mil.)	Per Empl. ($)	
221310	Water supply and irrigation systems	158	1,533	57.4	37,412	462.9
2213101	Water supply	138	1,474	55.9	37,948	456.6
2213102	Irrigation systems	20	59	1.4	24,017	6.3

Sources: *Economic Census of the United States*, 1997. Only those industries are shown for which both employment and sales/revenue data were available. For the definition of MSAs, CMSAs, and PMSAs, please see the Introduction.

LOUISVILLE, KY—IN MSA

NAICS	Industry	Estab-lish-ments	Em-ploy-ment	Payroll		Sales, revenues ($ mil.)
				Total ($ mil.)	Per Empl. ($)	
221	Utilities	55	3,416	165.1	48,330	4,715.9

Sources: *Economic Census of the United States*, 1997. Only those industries are shown for which both employment and sales/revenue data were available. For the definition of MSAs, CMSAs, and PMSAs, please see the Introduction.

LUBBOCK, TX MSA

NAICS	Industry	Estab-lish-ments	Em-ploy-ment	Payroll		Sales, revenues ($ mil.)
				Total ($ mil.)	Per Empl. ($)	
221	Utilities	13	504	19.5	38,738	186.6

Sources: *Economic Census of the United States*, 1997. Only those industries are shown for which both employment and sales/revenue data were available. For the definition of MSAs, CMSAs, and PMSAs, please see the Introduction.

LYNCHBURG, VA MSA

NAICS	Industry	Estab-lish-ments	Em-ploy-ment	Payroll		Sales, revenues ($ mil.)
				Total ($ mil.)	Per Empl. ($)	
221	Utilities	9	217	8.8	40,687	95.4

Sources: *Economic Census of the United States*, 1997. Only those industries are shown for which both employment and sales/revenue data were available. For the definition of MSAs, CMSAs, and PMSAs, please see the Introduction.

MACON, GA MSA

NAICS	Industry	Estab-lish-ments	Em-ploy-ment	Payroll		Sales, revenues ($ mil.)
				Total ($ mil.)	Per Empl. ($)	
2211221	Electric services (electric power distribution)	13	487	21.6	44,384	189.7

Sources: *Economic Census of the United States*, 1997. Only those industries are shown for which both employment and sales/revenue data were available. For the definition of MSAs, CMSAs, and PMSAs, please see the Introduction.

MANSFIELD, OH MSA

NAICS	Industry	Estab-lish-ments	Em-ploy-ment	Payroll		Sales, revenues ($ mil.)
				Total ($ mil.)	Per Empl. ($)	
221	Utilities	5	221	11.4	51,615	153.2

Sources: *Economic Census of the United States*, 1997. Only those industries are shown for which both employment and sales/revenue data were available. For the definition of MSAs, CMSAs, and PMSAs, please see the Introduction.

MCALLEN—EDINBURG—MISSION, TX MSA

NAICS	Industry	Estab-lish-ments	Em-ploy-ment	Payroll		Sales, revenues ($ mil.)
				Total ($ mil.)	Per Empl. ($)	
221	Utilities	17	593	18.9	31,909	264.3

Sources: *Economic Census of the United States*, 1997. Only those industries are shown for which both employment and sales/revenue data were available. For the definition of MSAs, CMSAs, and PMSAs, please see the Introduction.

MEDFORD—ASHLAND, OR MSA

NAICS	Industry	Estab-lish-ments	Em-ploy-ment	Payroll		Sales, revenues ($ mil.)
				Total ($ mil.)	Per Empl. ($)	
221	Utilities	10	293	14.0	47,792	123.1

Sources: *Economic Census of the United States*, 1997. Only those industries are shown for which both employment and sales/revenue data were available. For the definition of MSAs, CMSAs, and PMSAs, please see the Introduction.

MEMPHIS, TN—AR—MS MSA

| NAICS | Industry | Estab-lish-ments | Em-ploy-ment | Payroll | | Sales, revenues ($ mil.) |
				Total ($ mil.)	Per Empl. ($)	
221	Utilities	18	196	6.6	33,617	113.0

Sources: Economic Census of the United States, 1997. Only those industries are shown for which both employment and sales/revenue data were available. For the definition of MSAs, CMSAs, and PMSAs, please see the Introduction.

MIDDLESEX—SOMERSET—HUNTERDON, NJ PMSA

| NAICS | Industry | Estab-lish-ments | Em-ploy-ment | Payroll | | Sales, revenues ($ mil.) |
				Total ($ mil.)	Per Empl. ($)	
221	Utilities	44	2,402	133.1	55,420	1,400.6
221122	Electric power distribution	20	1,445	93.0	64,368	852.0

Sources: Economic Census of the United States, 1997. Only those industries are shown for which both employment and sales/revenue data were available. For the definition of MSAs, CMSAs, and PMSAs, please see the Introduction.

MILWAUKEE—RACINE, WI CMSA

| NAICS | Industry | Estab-lish-ments | Em-ploy-ment | Payroll | | Sales, revenues ($ mil.) |
				Total ($ mil.)	Per Empl. ($)	
221210	Natural gas distribution	12	997	49.0	49,123	576.7

Sources: Economic Census of the United States, 1997. Only those industries are shown for which both employment and sales/revenue data were available. For the definition of MSAs, CMSAs, and PMSAs, please see the Introduction.

MILWAUKEE—WAUKESHA, WI PMSA

| NAICS | Industry | Estab-lish-ments | Em-ploy-ment | Payroll | | Sales, revenues ($ mil.) |
				Total ($ mil.)	Per Empl. ($)	
221210	Natural gas distribution	12	997	49.0	49,123	576.7

Sources: Economic Census of the United States, 1997. Only those industries are shown for which both employment and sales/revenue data were available. For the definition of MSAs, CMSAs, and PMSAs, please see the Introduction.

MINNEAPOLIS—ST. PAUL, MN—WI MSA

| NAICS | Industry | Estab-lish-ments | Em-ploy-ment | Payroll | | Sales, revenues ($ mil.) |
				Total ($ mil.)	Per Empl. ($)	
221	Utilities	83	8,158	428.2	52,483	2,823.9
2211	Electric power generation, transmission, and distribution	47	6,532	355.7	54,460	2,148.3
22111	Electric power generation	18	2,442	151.2	61,926	863.8
22112	Electric power transmission, control, and distribution	29	4,090	204.5	50,002	1,284.5
221210	Natural gas distribution	21	1,443	65.1	45,141	623.8
2213	Water, sewage, and other systems	15	183	7.3	39,814	51.8

Sources: Economic Census of the United States, 1997. Only those industries are shown for which both employment and sales/revenue data were available. For the definition of MSAs, CMSAs, and PMSAs, please see the Introduction.

MOBILE, AL MSA

| NAICS | Industry | Estab- lish- ments | Em- ploy- ment | Payroll | | Sales, revenues ($ mil.) |
				Total ($ mil.)	Per Empl. ($)	
221	Utilities	45	1,302	63.9	49,062	629.8

Sources: *Economic Census of the United States*, 1997. Only those industries are shown for which both employment and sales/revenue data were available. For the definition of MSAs, CMSAs, and PMSAs, please see the Introduction.

MONMOUTH—OCEAN, NJ PMSA

| NAICS | Industry | Estab- lish- ments | Em- ploy- ment | Payroll | | Sales, revenues ($ mil.) |
				Total ($ mil.)	Per Empl. ($)	
221	Utilities	45	2,923	137.2	46,923	1,660.7

Sources: *Economic Census of the United States*, 1997. Only those industries are shown for which both employment and sales/revenue data were available. For the definition of MSAs, CMSAs, and PMSAs, please see the Introduction.

MONTGOMERY, AL MSA

| NAICS | Industry | Estab- lish- ments | Em- ploy- ment | Payroll | | Sales, revenues ($ mil.) |
				Total ($ mil.)	Per Empl. ($)	
221	Utilities	39	792	40.4	50,963	296.9

Sources: *Economic Census of the United States*, 1997. Only those industries are shown for which both employment and sales/revenue data were available. For the definition of MSAs, CMSAs, and PMSAs, please see the Introduction.

MUNCIE, IN MSA

| NAICS | Industry | Estab- lish- ments | Em- ploy- ment | Payroll | | Sales, revenues ($ mil.) |
				Total ($ mil.)	Per Empl. ($)	
221	Utilities	6	289	11.2	38,875	77.5

Sources: *Economic Census of the United States*, 1997. Only those industries are shown for which both employment and sales/revenue data were available. For the definition of MSAs, CMSAs, and PMSAs, please see the Introduction.

MYRTLE BEACH, SC MSA

| NAICS | Industry | Estab- lish- ments | Em- ploy- ment | Payroll | | Sales, revenues ($ mil.) |
				Total ($ mil.)	Per Empl. ($)	
221	Utilities	6	134	4.3	32,448	47.8

Sources: *Economic Census of the United States*, 1997. Only those industries are shown for which both employment and sales/revenue data were available. For the definition of MSAs, CMSAs, and PMSAs, please see the Introduction.

NASHUA, NH PMSA

| NAICS | Industry | Estab- lish- ments | Em- ploy- ment | Payroll | | Sales, revenues ($ mil.) |
				Total ($ mil.)	Per Empl. ($)	
221	Utilities	7	166	8.5	51,042	84.3

Sources: *Economic Census of the United States*, 1997. Only those industries are shown for which both employment and sales/revenue data were available. For the definition of MSAs, CMSAs, and PMSAs, please see the Introduction.

NASHVILLE, TN MSA

NAICS	Industry	Estab-lish-ments	Em-ploy-ment	Payroll		Sales, revenues ($ mil.)
				Total ($ mil.)	Per Empl. ($)	
221	Utilities	25	1,066	51.8	48,563	560.1
2211	Electric power generation, transmission, and distribution	13	348	14.5	41,549	225.5

Sources: *Economic Census of the United States*, 1997. Only those industries are shown for which both employment and sales/revenue data were available. For the definition of MSAs, CMSAs, and PMSAs, please see the Introduction.

NEW HAVEN—MERIDEN, CT PMSA

NAICS	Industry	Estab-lish-ments	Em-ploy-ment	Payroll		Sales, revenues ($ mil.)
				Total ($ mil.)	Per Empl. ($)	
221	Utilities	18	2,086	117.6	56,399	1,182.9

Sources: *Economic Census of the United States*, 1997. Only those industries are shown for which both employment and sales/revenue data were available. For the definition of MSAs, CMSAs, and PMSAs, please see the Introduction.

NEW LONDON—NORWICH, CT—RI MSA

NAICS	Industry	Estab-lish-ments	Em-ploy-ment	Payroll		Sales, revenues ($ mil.)
				Total ($ mil.)	Per Empl. ($)	
221	Utilities	18	2,380	155.6	65,378	526.1

Sources: *Economic Census of the United States*, 1997. Only those industries are shown for which both employment and sales/revenue data were available. For the definition of MSAs, CMSAs, and PMSAs, please see the Introduction.

NEW ORLEANS, LA MSA

NAICS	Industry	Estab-lish-ments	Em-ploy-ment	Payroll		Sales, revenues ($ mil.)
				Total ($ mil.)	Per Empl. ($)	
221	Utilities	93	4,104	227.7	55,475	1,773.9
22111	Electric power generation	12	1,156	66.6	57,615	474.1
221112	Fossil fuel electric power generation	11	381	16.2	42,593	474.1

Sources: *Economic Census of the United States*, 1997. Only those industries are shown for which both employment and sales/revenue data were available. For the definition of MSAs, CMSAs, and PMSAs, please see the Introduction.

NEW YORK, NY PMSA

NAICS	Industry	Estab-lish-ments	Em-ploy-ment	Payroll		Sales, revenues ($ mil.)
				Total ($ mil.)	Per Empl. ($)	
221	Utilities	105	34,209	1,522.8	44,514	9,823.5
22112	Electric power transmission, control, and distribution	72	30,586	1,304.4	42,647	8,296.1
221122	Electric power distribution	71	30,585	1,304.4	42,647	8,296.1

Sources: *Economic Census of the United States*, 1997. Only those industries are shown for which both employment and sales/revenue data were available. For the definition of MSAs, CMSAs, and PMSAs, please see the Introduction.

NEW YORK—NORTHERN NEW JERSEY—LONG ISLAND, NY—NJ—CT—PA CMSA

NAICS	Industry	Estab-lish-ments	Em-ploy-ment	Payroll		Sales, revenues ($ mil.)
				Total ($ mil.)	Per Empl. ($)	
221	Utilities	477	61,029	3,098.7	50,774	24,924.4
221210	Natural gas distribution	66	6,107	340.6	55,773	3,409.7
2212102	Natural gas distribution	51	5,219	297.3	56,967	2,990.7

Sources: *Economic Census of the United States*, 1997. Only those industries are shown for which both employment and sales/revenue data were available. For the definition of MSAs, CMSAs, and PMSAs, please see the Introduction.

NEWARK, NJ PMSA

NAICS	Industry	Estab-lish-ments	Em-ploy-ment	Payroll		Sales, revenues ($ mil.)
				Total ($ mil.)	Per Empl. ($)	
221	Utilities	81	6,269	384.3	61,297	3,283.1
221210	Natural gas distribution	11	770	36.9	47,948	382.7

Sources: *Economic Census of the United States*, 1997. Only those industries are shown for which both employment and sales/revenue data were available. For the definition of MSAs, CMSAs, and PMSAs, please see the Introduction.

NORFOLK—VIRGINIA BEACH—NEWPORT NEWS, VA—NC MSA

NAICS	Industry	Estab-lish-ments	Em-ploy-ment	Payroll		Sales, revenues ($ mil.)
				Total ($ mil.)	Per Empl. ($)	
221	Utilities	33	2,350	106.7	45,417	1,158.3

Sources: *Economic Census of the United States*, 1997. Only those industries are shown for which both employment and sales/revenue data were available. For the definition of MSAs, CMSAs, and PMSAs, please see the Introduction.

OCALA, FL MSA

NAICS	Industry	Estab-lish-ments	Em-ploy-ment	Payroll		Sales, revenues ($ mil.)
				Total ($ mil.)	Per Empl. ($)	
221	Utilities	26	324	13.5	41,534	119.2
221310	Water supply and irrigation systems	12	52	1.5	28,269	4.5

Sources: *Economic Census of the United States*, 1997. Only those industries are shown for which both employment and sales/revenue data were available. For the definition of MSAs, CMSAs, and PMSAs, please see the Introduction.

ODESSA—MIDLAND, TX MSA

NAICS	Industry	Estab-lish-ments	Em-ploy-ment	Payroll		Sales, revenues ($ mil.)
				Total ($ mil.)	Per Empl. ($)	
221	Utilities	23	807	30.2	37,465	985.9
221210	Natural gas distribution	16	518	14.3	27,625	797.5

Sources: *Economic Census of the United States*, 1997. Only those industries are shown for which both employment and sales/revenue data were available. For the definition of MSAs, CMSAs, and PMSAs, please see the Introduction.

OKLAHOMA CITY, OK MSA

| NAICS | Industry | Estab-lish-ments | Em-ploy-ment | Payroll | | Sales, revenues ($ mil.) |
				Total ($ mil.)	Per Empl. ($)	
221	Utilities	52	2,029	93.2	45,956	1,167.9
2212102	Natural gas distribution	16	149	8.0	53,537	335.4

Sources: *Economic Census of the United States*, 1997. Only those industries are shown for which both employment and sales/revenue data were available. For the definition of MSAs, CMSAs, and PMSAs, please see the Introduction.

ORANGE COUNTY, CA PMSA

| NAICS | Industry | Estab-lish-ments | Em-ploy-ment | Payroll | | Sales, revenues ($ mil.) |
				Total ($ mil.)	Per Empl. ($)	
2213	Water, sewage, and other systems	12	117	3.8	32,530	40.1

Sources: *Economic Census of the United States*, 1997. Only those industries are shown for which both employment and sales/revenue data were available. For the definition of MSAs, CMSAs, and PMSAs, please see the Introduction.

ORLANDO, FL MSA

| NAICS | Industry | Estab-lish-ments | Em-ploy-ment | Payroll | | Sales, revenues ($ mil.) |
				Total ($ mil.)	Per Empl. ($)	
221	Utilities	56	1,993	82.7	41,506	681.8
2211	Electric power generation, transmission, and distribution	21	1,206	62.5	51,789	579.0
221320	Sewage treatment facilities	15	107	3.3	30,495	13.6

Sources: *Economic Census of the United States*, 1997. Only those industries are shown for which both employment and sales/revenue data were available. For the definition of MSAs, CMSAs, and PMSAs, please see the Introduction.

OWENSBORO, KY MSA

| NAICS | Industry | Estab-lish-ments | Em-ploy-ment | Payroll | | Sales, revenues ($ mil.) |
				Total ($ mil.)	Per Empl. ($)	
221	Utilities	11	283	12.5	44,004	424.4

Sources: *Economic Census of the United States*, 1997. Only those industries are shown for which both employment and sales/revenue data were available. For the definition of MSAs, CMSAs, and PMSAs, please see the Introduction.

PANAMA CITY, FL MSA

| NAICS | Industry | Estab-lish-ments | Em-ploy-ment | Payroll | | Sales, revenues ($ mil.) |
				Total ($ mil.)	Per Empl. ($)	
221	Utilities	12	331	15.3	46,335	122.0

Sources: *Economic Census of the United States*, 1997. Only those industries are shown for which both employment and sales/revenue data were available. For the definition of MSAs, CMSAs, and PMSAs, please see the Introduction.

PARKERSBURG—MARIETTA, WV—OH MSA

NAICS	Industry	Estab-lish-ments	Em-ploy-ment	Payroll		Sales, revenues ($ mil.)
				Total ($ mil.)	Per Empl. ($)	
221	Utilities	18	753	35.3	46,907	354.0

Sources: *Economic Census of the United States*, 1997. Only those industries are shown for which both employment and sales/revenue data were available. For the definition of MSAs, CMSAs, and PMSAs, please see the Introduction.

PENSACOLA, FL MSA

NAICS	Industry	Estab-lish-ments	Em-ploy-ment	Payroll		Sales, revenues ($ mil.)
				Total ($ mil.)	Per Empl. ($)	
2213101	Water supply	17	138	2.8	20,130	12.6

Sources: *Economic Census of the United States*, 1997. Only those industries are shown for which both employment and sales/revenue data were available. For the definition of MSAs, CMSAs, and PMSAs, please see the Introduction.

PHILADELPHIA, PA—NJ PMSA

NAICS	Industry	Estab-lish-ments	Em-ploy-ment	Payroll		Sales, revenues ($ mil.)
				Total ($ mil.)	Per Empl. ($)	
221	Utilities	133	11,826	739.8	62,558	6,421.5
22112	Electric power transmission, control, and distribution	46	3,746	230.3	61,470	1,870.0
221320	Sewage treatment facilities	11	46	1.0	22,283	3.7

Sources: *Economic Census of the United States*, 1997. Only those industries are shown for which both employment and sales/revenue data were available. For the definition of MSAs, CMSAs, and PMSAs, please see the Introduction.

PHILADELPHIA—WILMINGTON—ATLANTIC CITY, PA—NJ—DE—MD CMSA

NAICS	Industry	Estab-lish-ments	Em-ploy-ment	Payroll		Sales, revenues ($ mil.)
				Total ($ mil.)	Per Empl. ($)	
2211	Electric power generation, transmission, and distribution	109	13,558	871.1	64,254	7,799.0

Sources: *Economic Census of the United States*, 1997. Only those industries are shown for which both employment and sales/revenue data were available. For the definition of MSAs, CMSAs, and PMSAs, please see the Introduction.

PHOENIX—MESA, AZ MSA

NAICS	Industry	Estab-lish-ments	Em-ploy-ment	Payroll		Sales, revenues ($ mil.)
				Total ($ mil.)	Per Empl. ($)	
221	Utilities	80	6,228	393.9	63,248	4,123.4
221310	Water supply and irrigation systems	46	788	30.0	38,090	91.2

Sources: *Economic Census of the United States*, 1997. Only those industries are shown for which both employment and sales/revenue data were available. For the definition of MSAs, CMSAs, and PMSAs, please see the Introduction.

PITTSBURGH, PA MSA

NAICS	Industry	Estab-lish-ments	Em-ploy-ment	Payroll		Sales, revenues ($ mil.)
				Total ($ mil.)	Per Empl. ($)	
221	Utilities	127	11,085	587.5	52,998	26,658.4
22112	Electric power transmission, control, and distribution	35	5,995	319.1	53,222	2,570.8

Sources: *Economic Census of the United States*, 1997. Only those industries are shown for which both employment and sales/revenue data were available. For the definition of MSAs, CMSAs, and PMSAs, please see the Introduction.

PITTSFIELD, MA MSA

NAICS	Industry	Estab-lish-ments	Em-ploy-ment	Payroll		Sales, revenues ($ mil.)
				Total ($ mil.)	Per Empl. ($)	
221	Utilities	5	226	11.6	51,425	123.4

Sources: *Economic Census of the United States*, 1997. Only those industries are shown for which both employment and sales/revenue data were available. For the definition of MSAs, CMSAs, and PMSAs, please see the Introduction.

POCATELLO, ID MSA

NAICS	Industry	Estab-lish-ments	Em-ploy-ment	Payroll		Sales, revenues ($ mil.)
				Total ($ mil.)	Per Empl. ($)	
221	Utilities	7	147	7.4	50,211	51.1

Sources: *Economic Census of the United States*, 1997. Only those industries are shown for which both employment and sales/revenue data were available. For the definition of MSAs, CMSAs, and PMSAs, please see the Introduction.

PORTLAND—SALEM, OR—WA CMSA

NAICS	Industry	Estab-lish-ments	Em-ploy-ment	Payroll		Sales, revenues ($ mil.)
				Total ($ mil.)	Per Empl. ($)	
2211221	Electric services (electric power distribution)	27	2,363	146.8	62,127	2,612.2

Sources: *Economic Census of the United States*, 1997. Only those industries are shown for which both employment and sales/revenue data were available. For the definition of MSAs, CMSAs, and PMSAs, please see the Introduction.

PORTLAND—VANCOUVER, OR—WA PMSA

NAICS	Industry	Estab-lish-ments	Em-ploy-ment	Payroll		Sales, revenues ($ mil.)
				Total ($ mil.)	Per Empl. ($)	
221	Utilities	53	4,715	297.1	63,004	3,740.7
2211221	Electric services (electric power distribution)	21	2,079	130.7	62,860	2,476.2
2213101	Water supply	15	67	1.9	28,164	9.3

Sources: *Economic Census of the United States*, 1997. Only those industries are shown for which both employment and sales/revenue data were available. For the definition of MSAs, CMSAs, and PMSAs, please see the Introduction.

PORTSMOUTH—ROCHESTER, NH—ME PMSA

NAICS	Industry	Estab-lish-ments	Em-ploy-ment	Payroll		Sales, revenues ($ mil.)
				Total ($ mil.)	Per Empl. ($)	
221	Utilities	13	418	20.3	48,490	336.1

Sources: *Economic Census of the United States*, 1997. Only those industries are shown for which both employment and sales/revenue data were available. For the definition of MSAs, CMSAs, and PMSAs, please see the Introduction.

PROVIDENCE—FALL RIVER—WARWICK, RI—MA MSA

NAICS	Industry	Estab-lish-ments	Em-ploy-ment	Payroll		Sales, revenues ($ mil.)
				Total ($ mil.)	Per Empl. ($)	
221	Utilities	36	2,650	135.8	51,234	1,553.6

Sources: *Economic Census of the United States*, 1997. Only those industries are shown for which both employment and sales/revenue data were available. For the definition of MSAs, CMSAs, and PMSAs, please see the Introduction.

PUEBLO, CO MSA

NAICS	Industry	Estab-lish-ments	Em-ploy-ment	Payroll		Sales, revenues ($ mil.)
				Total ($ mil.)	Per Empl. ($)	
221	Utilities	9	425	19.9	46,814	165.2

Sources: *Economic Census of the United States*, 1997. Only those industries are shown for which both employment and sales/revenue data were available. For the definition of MSAs, CMSAs, and PMSAs, please see the Introduction.

RALEIGH—DURHAM—CHAPEL HILL, NC MSA

NAICS	Industry	Estab-lish-ments	Em-ploy-ment	Payroll		Sales, revenues ($ mil.)
				Total ($ mil.)	Per Empl. ($)	
221	Utilities	44	4,369	228.5	52,310	2,557.4
2211	Electric power generation, transmission, and distribution	21	3,875	209.9	54,161	2,430.4

Sources: *Economic Census of the United States*, 1997. Only those industries are shown for which both employment and sales/revenue data were available. For the definition of MSAs, CMSAs, and PMSAs, please see the Introduction.

RAPID CITY, SD MSA

NAICS	Industry	Estab-lish-ments	Em-ploy-ment	Payroll		Sales, revenues ($ mil.)
				Total ($ mil.)	Per Empl. ($)	
221	Utilities	14	350	14.5	41,500	133.1

Sources: *Economic Census of the United States*, 1997. Only those industries are shown for which both employment and sales/revenue data were available. For the definition of MSAs, CMSAs, and PMSAs, please see the Introduction.

REDDING, CA MSA

NAICS	Industry	Estab-lish-ments	Em-ploy-ment	Payroll		Sales, revenues ($ mil.)
				Total ($ mil.)	Per Empl. ($)	
221	Utilities	19	360	21.0	58,233	229.0
2211	Electric power generation, transmission, and distribution	12	348	20.9	60,092	228.8

Sources: *Economic Census of the United States*, 1997. Only those industries are shown for which both employment and sales/revenue data were available. For the definition of MSAs, CMSAs, and PMSAs, please see the Introduction.

RICHLAND—KENNEWICK—PASCO, WA MSA

NAICS	Industry	Estab-lish-ments	Em-ploy-ment	Payroll		Sales, revenues ($ mil.)
				Total ($ mil.)	Per Empl. ($)	
221	Utilities	9	95	4.6	48,516	33.8

Sources: *Economic Census of the United States*, 1997. Only those industries are shown for which both employment and sales/revenue data were available. For the definition of MSAs, CMSAs, and PMSAs, please see the Introduction.

RICHMOND—PETERSBURG, VA MSA

NAICS	Industry	Estab-lish-ments	Em-ploy-ment	Payroll		Sales, revenues ($ mil.)
				Total ($ mil.)	Per Empl. ($)	
221	Utilities	34	4,284	256.1	59,790	2,390.0

Sources: *Economic Census of the United States*, 1997. Only those industries are shown for which both employment and sales/revenue data were available. For the definition of MSAs, CMSAs, and PMSAs, please see the Introduction.

RIVERSIDE—SAN BERNARDINO, CA PMSA

NAICS	Industry	Estab-lish-ments	Em-ploy-ment	Payroll		Sales, revenues ($ mil.)
				Total ($ mil.)	Per Empl. ($)	
221	Utilities	107	3,030	131.3	43,344	1,392.0

Sources: *Economic Census of the United States*, 1997. Only those industries are shown for which both employment and sales/revenue data were available. For the definition of MSAs, CMSAs, and PMSAs, please see the Introduction.

ROCHESTER, MN MSA

NAICS	Industry	Estab-lish-ments	Em-ploy-ment	Payroll		Sales, revenues ($ mil.)
				Total ($ mil.)	Per Empl. ($)	
221	Utilities	5	138	6.1	43,920	64.0

Sources: *Economic Census of the United States*, 1997. Only those industries are shown for which both employment and sales/revenue data were available. For the definition of MSAs, CMSAs, and PMSAs, please see the Introduction.

ROCHESTER, NY MSA

NAICS	Industry	Estab-lish-ments	Em-ploy-ment	Payroll		Sales, revenues ($ mil.)
				Total ($ mil.)	Per Empl. ($)	
221	Utilities	22	2,490	153.4	61,626	1,264.0
2211222	Electric and other services combined (electric power distribution)	14	1,775	102.7	57,857	880.7

Sources: *Economic Census of the United States*, 1997. Only those industries are shown for which both employment and sales/revenue data were available. For the definition of MSAs, CMSAs, and PMSAs, please see the Introduction.

ROCKY MOUNT, NC MSA

NAICS	Industry	Estab-lish-ments	Em-ploy-ment	Payroll		Sales, revenues ($ mil.)
				Total ($ mil.)	Per Empl. ($)	
221	Utilities	9	160	5.5	34,087	45.2

Sources: *Economic Census of the United States*, 1997. Only those industries are shown for which both employment and sales/revenue data were available. For the definition of MSAs, CMSAs, and PMSAs, please see the Introduction.

SACRAMENTO, CA PMSA

NAICS	Industry	Estab-lish-ments	Em-ploy-ment	Payroll		Sales, revenues ($ mil.)
				Total ($ mil.)	Per Empl. ($)	
221	Utilities	34	1,754	90.3	51,507	744.7

Sources: Economic Census of the United States, 1997. Only those industries are shown for which both employment and sales/revenue data were available. For the definition of MSAs, CMSAs, and PMSAs, please see the Introduction.

SALINAS, CA MSA

NAICS	Industry	Estab-lish-ments	Em-ploy-ment	Payroll		Sales, revenues ($ mil.)
				Total ($ mil.)	Per Empl. ($)	
221	Utilities	19	760	45.1	59,370	329.1

Sources: Economic Census of the United States, 1997. Only those industries are shown for which both employment and sales/revenue data were available. For the definition of MSAs, CMSAs, and PMSAs, please see the Introduction.

SALT LAKE CITY—OGDEN, UT MSA

NAICS	Industry	Estab-lish-ments	Em-ploy-ment	Payroll		Sales, revenues ($ mil.)
				Total ($ mil.)	Per Empl. ($)	
221	Utilities	52	3,568	190.2	53,297	3,283.6
2211221	Electric services (electric power distribution)	20	1,917	113.7	59,329	1,422.1
221310	Water supply and irrigation systems	15	63	1.1	17,190	5.9

Sources: Economic Census of the United States, 1997. Only those industries are shown for which both employment and sales/revenue data were available. For the definition of MSAs, CMSAs, and PMSAs, please see the Introduction.

SAN ANGELO, TX MSA

NAICS	Industry	Estab-lish-ments	Em-ploy-ment	Payroll		Sales, revenues ($ mil.)
				Total ($ mil.)	Per Empl. ($)	
221	Utilities	7	212	7.0	33,175	76.7

Sources: Economic Census of the United States, 1997. Only those industries are shown for which both employment and sales/revenue data were available. For the definition of MSAs, CMSAs, and PMSAs, please see the Introduction.

SAN ANTONIO, TX MSA

NAICS	Industry	Estab-lish-ments	Em-ploy-ment	Payroll		Sales, revenues ($ mil.)
				Total ($ mil.)	Per Empl. ($)	
221	Utilities	29	480	22.2	46,225	744.2

Sources: Economic Census of the United States, 1997. Only those industries are shown for which both employment and sales/revenue data were available. For the definition of MSAs, CMSAs, and PMSAs, please see the Introduction.

SAN DIEGO, CA MSA

NAICS	Industry	Estab-lish-ments	Em-ploy-ment	Payroll		Sales, revenues ($ mil.)
				Total ($ mil.)	Per Empl. ($)	
221	Utilities	27	4,053	249.4	61,537	2,356.0

Sources: Economic Census of the United States, 1997. Only those industries are shown for which both employment and sales/revenue data were available. For the definition of MSAs, CMSAs, and PMSAs, please see the Introduction.

SAN FRANCISCO—OAKLAND—SAN JOSE, CA CMSA

NAICS	Industry	Estab-lish-ments	Em-ploy-ment	Payroll		Sales, revenues ($ mil.)
				Total ($ mil.)	Per Empl. ($)	
2211191	Electric services (other electric power generation)	13	161	10.6	66,106	159.5

Sources: *Economic Census of the United States*, 1997. Only those industries are shown for which both employment and sales/revenue data were available. For the definition of MSAs, CMSAs, and PMSAs, please see the Introduction.

SANTA BARBARA—SANTA MARIA—LOMPOC, CA MSA

NAICS	Industry	Estab-lish-ments	Em-ploy-ment	Payroll		Sales, revenues ($ mil.)
				Total ($ mil.)	Per Empl. ($)	
221	Utilities	14	242	13.2	54,401	113.0

Sources: *Economic Census of the United States*, 1997. Only those industries are shown for which both employment and sales/revenue data were available. For the definition of MSAs, CMSAs, and PMSAs, please see the Introduction.

SANTA ROSA, CA PMSA

NAICS	Industry	Estab-lish-ments	Em-ploy-ment	Payroll		Sales, revenues ($ mil.)
				Total ($ mil.)	Per Empl. ($)	
2213101	Water supply	12	26	0.4	15,346	2.3

Sources: *Economic Census of the United States*, 1997. Only those industries are shown for which both employment and sales/revenue data were available. For the definition of MSAs, CMSAs, and PMSAs, please see the Introduction.

SARASOTA—BRADENTON, FL MSA

NAICS	Industry	Estab-lish-ments	Em-ploy-ment	Payroll		Sales, revenues ($ mil.)
				Total ($ mil.)	Per Empl. ($)	
221	Utilities	18	761	33.1	43,464	346.4

Sources: *Economic Census of the United States*, 1997. Only those industries are shown for which both employment and sales/revenue data were available. For the definition of MSAs, CMSAs, and PMSAs, please see the Introduction.

SAVANNAH, GA MSA

NAICS	Industry	Estab-lish-ments	Em-ploy-ment	Payroll		Sales, revenues ($ mil.)
				Total ($ mil.)	Per Empl. ($)	
221	Utilities	20	769	39.8	51,757	382.0

Sources: *Economic Census of the United States*, 1997. Only those industries are shown for which both employment and sales/revenue data were available. For the definition of MSAs, CMSAs, and PMSAs, please see the Introduction.

SCRANTON—WILKES-BARRE—HAZLETON, PA MSA

NAICS	Industry	Estab-lish-ments	Em-ploy-ment	Payroll		Sales, revenues ($ mil.)
				Total ($ mil.)	Per Empl. ($)	
221	Utilities	34	2,535	119.5	47,153	986.0

Sources: *Economic Census of the United States*, 1997. Only those industries are shown for which both employment and sales/revenue data were available. For the definition of MSAs, CMSAs, and PMSAs, please see the Introduction.

SEATTLE—BELLEVUE—EVERETT, WA PMSA

NAICS	Industry	Estab-lish-ments	Em-ploy-ment	Payroll		Sales, revenues ($ mil.)
				Total ($ mil.)	Per Empl. ($)	
221	Utilities	81	2,465	118.1	47,897	1,200.5

Sources: *Economic Census of the United States*, 1997. Only those industries are shown for which both employment and sales/revenue data were available. For the definition of MSAs, CMSAs, and PMSAs, please see the Introduction.

SHARON, PA MSA

NAICS	Industry	Estab-lish-ments	Em-ploy-ment	Payroll		Sales, revenues ($ mil.)
				Total ($ mil.)	Per Empl. ($)	
221	Utilities	9	193	7.7	39,819	92.6

Sources: *Economic Census of the United States*, 1997. Only those industries are shown for which both employment and sales/revenue data were available. For the definition of MSAs, CMSAs, and PMSAs, please see the Introduction.

SHERMAN—DENISON, TX MSA

NAICS	Industry	Estab-lish-ments	Em-ploy-ment	Payroll		Sales, revenues ($ mil.)
				Total ($ mil.)	Per Empl. ($)	
221	Utilities	17	211	7.5	35,469	109.8

Sources: *Economic Census of the United States*, 1997. Only those industries are shown for which both employment and sales/revenue data were available. For the definition of MSAs, CMSAs, and PMSAs, please see the Introduction.

SHREVEPORT—BOSSIER CITY, LA MSA

NAICS	Industry	Estab-lish-ments	Em-ploy-ment	Payroll		Sales, revenues ($ mil.)
				Total ($ mil.)	Per Empl. ($)	
2213101	Water supply	22	64	0.5	7,781	3.4

Sources: *Economic Census of the United States*, 1997. Only those industries are shown for which both employment and sales/revenue data were available. For the definition of MSAs, CMSAs, and PMSAs, please see the Introduction.

SIOUX FALLS, SD MSA

NAICS	Industry	Estab-lish-ments	Em-ploy-ment	Payroll		Sales, revenues ($ mil.)
				Total ($ mil.)	Per Empl. ($)	
221	Utilities	11	219	9.9	45,329	79.8

Sources: *Economic Census of the United States*, 1997. Only those industries are shown for which both employment and sales/revenue data were available. For the definition of MSAs, CMSAs, and PMSAs, please see the Introduction.

SPRINGFIELD, MA MSA

NAICS	Industry	Estab-lish-ments	Em-ploy-ment	Payroll		Sales, revenues ($ mil.)
				Total ($ mil.)	Per Empl. ($)	
221	Utilities	25	1,096	63.8	58,226	942.7
2211	Electric power generation, transmission, and distribution	18	755	46.4	61,483	772.7

Sources: *Economic Census of the United States*, 1997. Only those industries are shown for which both employment and sales/revenue data were available. For the definition of MSAs, CMSAs, and PMSAs, please see the Introduction.

SPRINGFIELD, MO MSA

| NAICS | Industry | Estab-lish-ments | Em-ploy-ment | Payroll | | Sales, revenues ($ mil.) |
				Total ($ mil.)	Per Empl. ($)	
221	Utilities	15	385	17.5	45,353	275.1

Sources: *Economic Census of the United States*, 1997. Only those industries are shown for which both employment and sales/revenue data were available. For the definition of MSAs, CMSAs, and PMSAs, please see the Introduction.

ST. LOUIS, MO—IL MSA

| NAICS | Industry | Estab-lish-ments | Em-ploy-ment | Payroll | | Sales, revenues ($ mil.) |
				Total ($ mil.)	Per Empl. ($)	
221	Utilities	96	8,152	431.5	52,935	2,944.7
221320	Sewage treatment facilities	11	70	2.1	30,586	6.7

Sources: *Economic Census of the United States*, 1997. Only those industries are shown for which both employment and sales/revenue data were available. For the definition of MSAs, CMSAs, and PMSAs, please see the Introduction.

STAMFORD—NORWALK, CT PMSA

| NAICS | Industry | Estab-lish-ments | Em-ploy-ment | Payroll | | Sales, revenues ($ mil.) |
				Total ($ mil.)	Per Empl. ($)	
221	Utilities	19	803	50.5	62,839	867.4

Sources: *Economic Census of the United States*, 1997. Only those industries are shown for which both employment and sales/revenue data were available. For the definition of MSAs, CMSAs, and PMSAs, please see the Introduction.

STATE COLLEGE, PA MSA

| NAICS | Industry | Estab-lish-ments | Em-ploy-ment | Payroll | | Sales, revenues ($ mil.) |
				Total ($ mil.)	Per Empl. ($)	
221	Utilities	10	127	5.6	44,079	48.3

Sources: *Economic Census of the United States*, 1997. Only those industries are shown for which both employment and sales/revenue data were available. For the definition of MSAs, CMSAs, and PMSAs, please see the Introduction.

STEUBENVILLE—WEIRTON, OH—WV MSA

| NAICS | Industry | Estab-lish-ments | Em-ploy-ment | Payroll | | Sales, revenues ($ mil.) |
				Total ($ mil.)	Per Empl. ($)	
221	Utilities	8	1,017	52.1	51,192	629.4

Sources: *Economic Census of the United States*, 1997. Only those industries are shown for which both employment and sales/revenue data were available. For the definition of MSAs, CMSAs, and PMSAs, please see the Introduction.

STOCKTON—LODI, CA MSA

| NAICS | Industry | Estab-lish-ments | Em-ploy-ment | Payroll | | Sales, revenues ($ mil.) |
				Total ($ mil.)	Per Empl. ($)	
221	Utilities	14	215	11.4	53,088	129.7

Sources: *Economic Census of the United States*, 1997. Only those industries are shown for which both employment and sales/revenue data were available. For the definition of MSAs, CMSAs, and PMSAs, please see the Introduction.

SUMTER, SC MSA

NAICS	Industry	Estab-lish-ments	Em-ploy-ment	Payroll Total ($ mil.)	Payroll Per Empl. ($)	Sales, revenues ($ mil.)
221	Utilities	6	128	5.5	43,266	43.1

Sources: *Economic Census of the United States*, 1997. Only those industries are shown for which both employment and sales/revenue data were available. For the definition of MSAs, CMSAs, and PMSAs, please see the Introduction.

SYRACUSE, NY MSA

NAICS	Industry	Estab-lish-ments	Em-ploy-ment	Payroll Total ($ mil.)	Payroll Per Empl. ($)	Sales, revenues ($ mil.)
221	Utilities	17	4,701	283.3	60,271	2,907.3
2211	Electric power generation, transmission, and distribution	14	4,693	283.2	60,348	2,906.0

Sources: *Economic Census of the United States*, 1997. Only those industries are shown for which both employment and sales/revenue data were available. For the definition of MSAs, CMSAs, and PMSAs, please see the Introduction.

TACOMA, WA PMSA

NAICS	Industry	Estab-lish-ments	Em-ploy-ment	Payroll Total ($ mil.)	Payroll Per Empl. ($)	Sales, revenues ($ mil.)
221	Utilities	42	641	27.5	42,835	252.5
221122	Electric power distribution	12	467	22.7	48,627	236.7

Sources: *Economic Census of the United States*, 1997. Only those industries are shown for which both employment and sales/revenue data were available. For the definition of MSAs, CMSAs, and PMSAs, please see the Introduction.

TAMPA—ST. PETERSBURG—CLEARWATER, FL MSA

NAICS	Industry	Estab-lish-ments	Em-ploy-ment	Payroll Total ($ mil.)	Payroll Per Empl. ($)	Sales, revenues ($ mil.)
221	Utilities	65	6,226	300.9	48,331	2,545.1
2211	Electric power generation, transmission, and distribution	40	5,498	281.1	51,128	2,385.3

Sources: *Economic Census of the United States*, 1997. Only those industries are shown for which both employment and sales/revenue data were available. For the definition of MSAs, CMSAs, and PMSAs, please see the Introduction.

TERRE HAUTE, IN MSA

NAICS	Industry	Estab-lish-ments	Em-ploy-ment	Payroll Total ($ mil.)	Payroll Per Empl. ($)	Sales, revenues ($ mil.)
221	Utilities	17	740	35.8	48,339	369.1

Sources: *Economic Census of the United States*, 1997. Only those industries are shown for which both employment and sales/revenue data were available. For the definition of MSAs, CMSAs, and PMSAs, please see the Introduction.

TOLEDO, OH MSA

NAICS	Industry	Estab-lish-ments	Em-ploy-ment	Payroll		Sales, revenues ($ mil.)
				Total ($ mil.)	Per Empl. ($)	
221	Utilities	24	1,173	54.6	46,580	651.1

Sources: *Economic Census of the United States*, 1997. Only those industries are shown for which both employment and sales/revenue data were available. For the definition of MSAs, CMSAs, and PMSAs, please see the Introduction.

TOPEKA, KS MSA

NAICS	Industry	Estab-lish-ments	Em-ploy-ment	Payroll		Sales, revenues ($ mil.)
				Total ($ mil.)	Per Empl. ($)	
221	Utilities	8	1,432	79.0	55,179	932.6

Sources: *Economic Census of the United States*, 1997. Only those industries are shown for which both employment and sales/revenue data were available. For the definition of MSAs, CMSAs, and PMSAs, please see the Introduction.

TUCSON, AZ MSA

NAICS	Industry	Estab-lish-ments	Em-ploy-ment	Payroll		Sales, revenues ($ mil.)
				Total ($ mil.)	Per Empl. ($)	
221	Utilities	29	1,862	90.2	48,459	888.2
221310	Water supply and irrigation systems	22	89	1.7	19,494	8.5

Sources: *Economic Census of the United States*, 1997. Only those industries are shown for which both employment and sales/revenue data were available. For the definition of MSAs, CMSAs, and PMSAs, please see the Introduction.

TULSA, OK MSA

NAICS	Industry	Estab-lish-ments	Em-ploy-ment	Payroll		Sales, revenues ($ mil.)
				Total ($ mil.)	Per Empl. ($)	
221	Utilities	76	2,785	142.5	51,184	2,244.8
221210	Natural gas distribution	28	628	43.8	69,798	1,797.1
2212102	Natural gas distribution	21	208	13.2	63,692	1,431.1

Sources: *Economic Census of the United States*, 1997. Only those industries are shown for which both employment and sales/revenue data were available. For the definition of MSAs, CMSAs, and PMSAs, please see the Introduction.

TYLER, TX MSA

NAICS	Industry	Estab-lish-ments	Em-ploy-ment	Payroll		Sales, revenues ($ mil.)
				Total ($ mil.)	Per Empl. ($)	
221	Utilities	18	300	11.7	38,887	141.9

Sources: *Economic Census of the United States*, 1997. Only those industries are shown for which both employment and sales/revenue data were available. For the definition of MSAs, CMSAs, and PMSAs, please see the Introduction.

UTICA—ROME, NY MSA

NAICS	Industry	Estab-lish-ments	Em-ploy-ment	Payroll		Sales, revenues ($ mil.)
				Total ($ mil.)	Per Empl. ($)	
221	Utilities	8	598	30.9	51,600	273.9

Sources: *Economic Census of the United States*, 1997. Only those industries are shown for which both employment and sales/revenue data were available. For the definition of MSAs, CMSAs, and PMSAs, please see the Introduction.

VENTURA, CA PMSA

NAICS	Industry	Estab-lish-ments	Em-ploy-ment	Payroll		Sales, revenues ($ mil.)
				Total ($ mil.)	Per Empl. ($)	
221	Utilities	46	715	33.5	46,902	354.8

Sources: *Economic Census of the United States*, 1997. Only those industries are shown for which both employment and sales/revenue data were available. For the definition of MSAs, CMSAs, and PMSAs, please see the Introduction.

VICTORIA, TX MSA

NAICS	Industry	Estab-lish-ments	Em-ploy-ment	Payroll		Sales, revenues ($ mil.)
				Total ($ mil.)	Per Empl. ($)	
221	Utilities	10	296	12.0	40,409	199.7

Sources: *Economic Census of the United States*, 1997. Only those industries are shown for which both employment and sales/revenue data were available. For the definition of MSAs, CMSAs, and PMSAs, please see the Introduction.

WACO, TX MSA

NAICS	Industry	Estab-lish-ments	Em-ploy-ment	Payroll		Sales, revenues ($ mil.)
				Total ($ mil.)	Per Empl. ($)	
221	Utilities	26	722	30.2	41,765	524.4

Sources: *Economic Census of the United States*, 1997. Only those industries are shown for which both employment and sales/revenue data were available. For the definition of MSAs, CMSAs, and PMSAs, please see the Introduction.

WASHINGTON, DC—MD—VA—WV PMSA

NAICS	Industry	Estab-lish-ments	Em-ploy-ment	Payroll		Sales, revenues ($ mil.)
				Total ($ mil.)	Per Empl. ($)	
221	Utilities	112	10,765	602.2	55,940	6,695.2
221210	Natural gas distribution	16	2,007	121.0	60,278	2,980.8

Sources: *Economic Census of the United States*, 1997. Only those industries are shown for which both employment and sales/revenue data were available. For the definition of MSAs, CMSAs, and PMSAs, please see the Introduction.

WHEELING, WV—OH MSA

NAICS	Industry	Estab-lish-ments	Em-ploy-ment	Payroll		Sales, revenues ($ mil.)
				Total ($ mil.)	Per Empl. ($)	
221	Utilities	12	791	39.6	50,096	439.9

Sources: *Economic Census of the United States*, 1997. Only those industries are shown for which both employment and sales/revenue data were available. For the definition of MSAs, CMSAs, and PMSAs, please see the Introduction.

WICHITA, KS MSA

NAICS	Industry	Estab-lish-ments	Em-ploy-ment	Payroll		Sales, revenues ($ mil.)
				Total ($ mil.)	Per Empl. ($)	
221	Utilities	18	948	46.8	49,402	470.0

Sources: *Economic Census of the United States*, 1997. Only those industries are shown for which both employment and sales/revenue data were available. For the definition of MSAs, CMSAs, and PMSAs, please see the Introduction.

WILLIAMSPORT, PA MSA

NAICS	Industry	Estab-lish-ments	Em-ploy-ment	Payroll		Sales, revenues ($ mil.)
				Total ($ mil.)	Per Empl. ($)	
221	Utilities	8	355	17.2	48,454	221.5

Sources: *Economic Census of the United States*, 1997. Only those industries are shown for which both employment and sales/revenue data were available. For the definition of MSAs, CMSAs, and PMSAs, please see the Introduction.

WILMINGTON, NC MSA

NAICS	Industry	Estab-lish-ments	Em-ploy-ment	Payroll		Sales, revenues ($ mil.)
				Total ($ mil.)	Per Empl. ($)	
221	Utilities	14	1,489	80.2	53,850	570.3

Sources: *Economic Census of the United States*, 1997. Only those industries are shown for which both employment and sales/revenue data were available. For the definition of MSAs, CMSAs, and PMSAs, please see the Introduction.

WORCESTER, MA—CT PMSA

NAICS	Industry	Estab-lish-ments	Em-ploy-ment	Payroll		Sales, revenues ($ mil.)
				Total ($ mil.)	Per Empl. ($)	
221	Utilities	27	2,597	147.9	56,946	630.9

Sources: *Economic Census of the United States*, 1997. Only those industries are shown for which both employment and sales/revenue data were available. For the definition of MSAs, CMSAs, and PMSAs, please see the Introduction.

YAKIMA, WA MSA

NAICS	Industry	Estab-lish-ments	Em-ploy-ment	Payroll		Sales, revenues ($ mil.)
				Total ($ mil.)	Per Empl. ($)	
221	Utilities	19	297	12.8	43,125	93.3

Sources: *Economic Census of the United States*, 1997. Only those industries are shown for which both employment and sales/revenue data were available. For the definition of MSAs, CMSAs, and PMSAs, please see the Introduction.

YORK, PA MSA

NAICS	Industry	Estab-lish-ments	Em-ploy-ment	Payroll		Sales, revenues ($ mil.)
				Total ($ mil.)	Per Empl. ($)	
221	Utilities	16	1,480	92.4	62,428	963.8

Sources: *Economic Census of the United States*, 1997. Only those industries are shown for which both employment and sales/revenue data were available. For the definition of MSAs, CMSAs, and PMSAs, please see the Introduction.

YOUNGSTOWN—WARREN, OH MSA

| NAICS | Industry | Estab-lish-ments | Em-ploy-ment | Payroll | | Sales, revenues ($ mil.) |
				Total ($ mil.)	Per Empl. ($)	
221	Utilities	16	951	47.2	49,678	616.2

Sources: *Economic Census of the United States*, 1997. Only those industries are shown for which both employment and sales/revenue data were available. For the definition of MSAs, CMSAs, and PMSAs, please see the Introduction.

YUBA CITY, CA MSA

| NAICS | Industry | Estab-lish-ments | Em-ploy-ment | Payroll | | Sales, revenues ($ mil.) |
				Total ($ mil.)	Per Empl. ($)	
221	Utilities	9	264	16.5	62,451	122.1

Sources: *Economic Census of the United States*, 1997. Only those industries are shown for which both employment and sales/revenue data were available. For the definition of MSAs, CMSAs, and PMSAs, please see the Introduction.

YUMA, AZ MSA

| NAICS | Industry | Estab-lish-ments | Em-ploy-ment | Payroll | | Sales, revenues ($ mil.) |
				Total ($ mil.)	Per Empl. ($)	
221	Utilities	8	227	10.7	47,137	52.8

Sources: *Economic Census of the United States*, 1997. Only those industries are shown for which both employment and sales/revenue data were available. For the definition of MSAs, CMSAs, and PMSAs, please see the Introduction.

Appendix III

METRO DATA - TRANSPORTATION

ABILENE, TX MSA

NAICS	Industry	Estab-lish-ments	Em-ploy-ment	Payroll		Sales, reven. ($ mil.)
				Total ($ mil.)	Per Empl. ($)	
48-49	Transportation and warehousing	83	1,057	23.0	21,763	55.7
484	Truck transportation	59	590	13.1	22,214	31.8
4841	General freight trucking	27	337	8.6	25,401	18.3
48412	General freight trucking, long-distance	22	293	7.7	26,416	16.3
484121	General freight trucking, long-distance, truckload (tl)	11	142	4.0	27,951	5.8
484122	General freight trucking, long-distance, less than truckload (ltl)	11	151	3.8	24,974	10.4
4842	Specialized freight trucking	32	253	4.5	17,968	13.6
484210	Used household and office goods moving	11	147	1.8	11,905	4.6
484220	Specialized freight (except used goods) trucking, local	14	44	1.5	33,500	5.2
488	Support activities for transportation	10	306	6.9	22,516	15.8
492	Couriers and messengers	8	76	1.7	21,934	4.6

Sources: *Economic Census of the United States*, 1997. Only those industries are shown for which both employment and sales/revenue data were available. For the definition of MSAs, CMSAs, and PMSAs, please see the Introduction.

AKRON, OH PMSA

NAICS	Industry	Estab-lish-ments	Em-ploy-ment	Payroll		Sales, reven. ($ mil.)
				Total ($ mil.)	Per Empl. ($)	
48-49	Transportation and warehousing	402	7,080	260.5	36,792	803.9
481	Air transportation	4	29	0.8	27,207	4.0
484	Truck transportation	268	5,514	221.1	40,100	661.6
4841	General freight trucking	129	4,314	178.3	41,323	327.4
484110	General freight trucking, local	49	341	9.4	27,660	27.3
4841101	General freight trucking without storage, local, truckload (tl)	33	227	6.4	28,242	21.5
48412	General freight trucking, long-distance	80	3,973	168.8	42,496	300.1
484121	General freight trucking, long-distance, truckload (tl)	54	472	15.4	32,646	69.3
484122	General freight trucking, long-distance, less than truckload (ltl)	26	3,501	153.4	43,824	230.8
4842	Specialized freight trucking	139	1,200	42.8	35,703	334.2
484210	Used household and office goods moving	17	178	4.5	25,309	9.7
484220	Specialized freight (except used goods) trucking, local	99	415	13.2	31,723	54.1
4842203	Dump trucking	67	273	8.5	31,245	38.5
4842204	Specialized trucking without storage, local	21	97	3.2	33,392	9.4
484230	Specialized freight (except used goods) trucking, long-distance	23	607	25.2	41,473	270.3
4842303	Other specialized trucking, long-distance	19	573	24.5	42,729	267.9
485	Transit and ground passenger transportation	16	249	3.0	12,197	7.9
488	Support activities for transportation	74	454	15.3	33,804	55.0
488410	Motor vehicle towing	18	139	2.7	19,165	7.4
488510	Freight transportation arrangement	51	285	11.9	41,919	43.7
4885102	Arrangement of transportation of freight and cargo	45	249	10.3	41,418	35.0
492	Couriers and messengers	19	428	8.9	20,783	45.1
492210	Local messengers and local delivery	11	27	0.7	24,407	2.5
4931	Warehousing and storage	18	379	10.4	27,517	24.9

Sources: *Economic Census of the United States*, 1997. Only those industries are shown for which both employment and sales/revenue data were available. For the definition of MSAs, CMSAs, and PMSAs, please see the Introduction.

ALBANY, GA MSA

NAICS	Industry	Estab-lish-ments	Em-ploy-ment	Payroll		Sales, reven. ($ mil.)
				Total ($ mil.)	Per Empl. ($)	
48-49	Transportation and warehousing	70	1,271	36.6	28,790	134.5
484	Truck transportation	43	928	28.5	30,685	100.9
4841	General freight trucking	30	825	26.2	31,752	93.8
48412	General freight trucking, long-distance	24	788	25.5	32,420	89.0
484121	General freight trucking, long-distance, truckload (tl)	14	470	15.1	32,200	60.4
4842	Specialized freight trucking	13	103	2.3	22,146	7.1
488	Support activities for transportation	8	82	2.0	24,866	7.4
492	Couriers and messengers	3	51	1.5	29,471	3.7
493	Warehousing and storage	8	179	3.9	21,894	15.6

Sources: *Economic Census of the United States*, 1997. Only those industries are shown for which both employment and sales/revenue data were available. For the definition of MSAs, CMSAs, and PMSAs, please see the Introduction.

ALBANY—SCHENECTADY—TROY, NY MSA

NAICS	Industry	Estab-lish-ments	Em-ploy-ment	Payroll Total ($ mil.)	Payroll Per Empl. ($)	Sales, reven. ($ mil.)
48-49	Transportation and warehousing	367	6,239	156.0	24,999	439.4
484	Truck transportation	210	2,563	77.7	30,312	249.6
4841	General freight trucking	78	1,502	46.5	30,927	139.0
484110	General freight trucking, local	24	258	6.0	23,279	14.3
4841101	General freight trucking without storage, local, truckload (tl)	14	140	3.6	25,457	8.1
48412	General freight trucking, long-distance	54	1,244	40.4	32,514	124.6
484121	General freight trucking, long-distance, truckload (tl)	35	628	15.2	24,205	51.3
484122	General freight trucking, long-distance, less than truckload (ltl)	19	616	25.2	40,984	73.3
4842	Specialized freight trucking	132	1,061	31.2	29,441	110.7
484210	Used household and office goods moving	27	274	6.5	23,708	19.7
4842101	Used household and office goods moving, local, without storage	11	57	1.1	19,719	4.5
484220	Specialized freight (except used goods) trucking, local	71	270	7.3	26,985	31.1
4842201	Hazardous materials trucking (except waste), local	12	51	1.7	33,039	8.1
4842203	Dump trucking	33	106	3.4	31,877	15.3
4842204	Specialized trucking without storage, local	14	63	1.0	15,857	3.6
484230	Specialized freight (except used goods) trucking, long-distance	34	517	17.5	33,762	59.9
4842303	Other specialized trucking, long-distance	21	358	13.0	36,176	43.3
485	Transit and ground passenger transportation	52	2,120	40.4	19,063	61.0
4853	Taxi and limousine service	17	484	4.6	9,473	7.4
4854101	School bus service	13	672	8.6	12,830	16.8
487	Scenic and sightseeing transportation	6	16	0.3	15,625	1.2
488	Support activities for transportation	42	333	9.5	28,595	24.0
488510	Freight transportation arrangement	23	111	3.5	31,351	12.0
4885102	Arrangement of transportation of freight and cargo	17	85	2.8	32,894	10.1
492110	Couriers	17	578	13.4	23,253	60.6
4931	Warehousing and storage	22	320	7.8	24,372	24.3
4931101	General warehousing and storage (except in foreign trade zones)	14	284	6.8	24,039	21.7

Sources: *Economic Census of the United States*, 1997. Only those industries are shown for which both employment and sales/revenue data were available. For the definition of MSAs, CMSAs, and PMSAs, please see the Introduction.

ALBUQUERQUE, NM MSA

NAICS	Industry	Estab-lish-ments	Em-ploy-ment	Payroll Total ($ mil.)	Payroll Per Empl. ($)	Sales, reven. ($ mil.)
48-49	Transportation and warehousing	340	5,755	154.5	26,845	471.6
484	Truck transportation	184	3,189	110.1	34,538	277.6
4841	General freight trucking	86	2,395	88.7	37,037	208.2
484110	General freight trucking, local	21	233	6.9	29,691	23.9
4841101	General freight trucking without storage, local, truckload (tl)	14	124	3.2	26,105	15.2
48412	General freight trucking, long-distance	65	2,162	81.8	37,829	184.3
484121	General freight trucking, long-distance, truckload (tl)	48	1,492	52.7	35,334	142.5
484122	General freight trucking, long-distance, less than truckload (ltl)	17	670	29.1	43,385	41.8
4842	Specialized freight trucking	98	794	21.4	27,001	69.4
484210	Used household and office goods moving	18	204	4.9	24,083	15.8
484220	Specialized freight (except used goods) trucking, local	51	194	4.5	23,335	20.1
4842203	Dump trucking	22	73	1.4	18,685	5.6
4842204	Specialized trucking without storage, local	19	76	2.0	26,921	9.3
484230	Specialized freight (except used goods) trucking, long-distance	29	396	12.0	30,301	33.4
4842303	Other specialized trucking, long-distance	24	339	10.6	31,133	28.1
485	Transit and ground passenger transportation	35	1,023	11.1	10,844	29.8
4854101	School bus service	19	707	6.2	8,827	15.7
486	Pipeline transportation	8	48	3.2	67,271	62.8
488	Support activities for transportation	55	556	9.0	16,243	27.0
4881	Support activities for air transportation	14	340	5.4	15,847	16.4
488410	Motor vehicle towing	18	127	2.1	16,622	5.9
488510	Freight transportation arrangement	17	63	0.9	14,571	3.1
4885102	Arrangement of transportation of freight and cargo	12	39	0.6	15,872	1.7
492	Couriers and messengers	27	622	13.0	20,957	42.5
4931	Warehousing and storage	15	64	1.4	21,828	6.0
4931101	General warehousing and storage (except in foreign trade zones)	11	51	1.1	22,078	4.8

Sources: *Economic Census of the United States*, 1997. Only those industries are shown for which both employment and sales/revenue data were available. For the definition of MSAs, CMSAs, and PMSAs, please see the Introduction.

ALEXANDRIA, LA MSA

NAICS	Industry	Estab-lish-ments	Em-ploy-ment	Payroll		Sales, reven. ($ mil.)
				Total ($ mil.)	Per Empl. ($)	
48-49	Transportation and warehousing	90	986	27.0	27,372	129.2
484	Truck transportation	63	663	16.7	25,149	63.6
4841	General freight trucking	28	476	13.0	27,345	49.5
48412	General freight trucking, long-distance	23	438	12.2	27,950	47.7
484121	General freight trucking, long-distance, truckload (tl)	16	302	8.9	29,421	39.4
4842	Specialized freight trucking	35	187	3.7	19,561	14.1
484220	Specialized freight (except used goods) trucking, local	26	87	1.9	22,241	9.1
4842203	Dump trucking	13	46	1.0	21,283	6.0
486	Pipeline transportation	5	89	5.0	55,910	42.5
488	Support activities for transportation	6	110	2.7	24,745	12.9
492	Couriers and messengers	5	63	1.4	21,857	4.3

Sources: Economic Census of the United States, 1997. Only those industries are shown for which both employment and sales/revenue data were available. For the definition of MSAs, CMSAs, and PMSAs, please see the Introduction.

ALLENTOWN—BETHLEHEM—EASTON, PA MSA

NAICS	Industry	Estab-lish-ments	Em-ploy-ment	Payroll		Sales, reven. ($ mil.)
				Total ($ mil.)	Per Empl. ($)	
48-49	Transportation and warehousing	278	5,301	138.9	26,207	536.4
484	Truck transportation	167	2,445	72.7	29,739	255.0
4841	General freight trucking	78	1,474	44.8	30,381	162.7
484110	General freight trucking, local	22	230	5.6	24,470	17.3
4841101	General freight trucking without storage, local, truckload (tl)	14	114	2.9	25,728	11.2
48412	General freight trucking, long-distance	56	1,244	39.2	31,473	145.3
484121	General freight trucking, long-distance, truckload (tl)	37	563	15.9	28,236	67.0
484122	General freight trucking, long-distance, less than truckload (ltl)	19	681	23.3	34,150	78.4
4842	Specialized freight trucking	89	971	27.9	28,765	92.4
484210	Used household and office goods moving	11	153	4.0	26,275	11.4
484220	Specialized freight (except used goods) trucking, local	55	379	10.3	27,074	41.1
4842203	Dump trucking	26	198	5.7	28,606	24.7
4842204	Specialized trucking without storage, local	17	97	2.7	28,000	11.3
484230	Specialized freight (except used goods) trucking, long-distance	23	439	13.6	31,093	39.9
4842303	Other specialized trucking, long-distance	17	363	10.6	29,102	31.0
485	Transit and ground passenger transportation	38	1,125	16.4	14,556	40.2
4854101	School bus service	15	499	5.1	10,253	12.9
488510	Freight transportation arrangement	12	48	1.4	28,333	4.8
492	Couriers and messengers	15	526	8.3	15,825	45.2
492110	Couriers	12	478	7.5	15,676	42.0
4931	Warehousing and storage	16	622	19.6	31,571	66.8
4931101	General warehousing and storage (except in foreign trade zones)	11	232	8.4	36,216	31.2

Sources: Economic Census of the United States, 1997. Only those industries are shown for which both employment and sales/revenue data were available. For the definition of MSAs, CMSAs, and PMSAs, please see the Introduction.

ALTOONA, PA MSA

NAICS	Industry	Estab-lish-ments	Em-ploy-ment	Payroll		Sales, reven. ($ mil.)
				Total ($ mil.)	Per Empl. ($)	
48-49	Transportation and warehousing	86	1,315	33.0	25,091	106.2
484	Truck transportation	56	811	24.0	29,551	71.5
4841	General freight trucking	27	532	16.0	30,000	46.5
48412	General freight trucking, long-distance	18	420	14.2	33,862	39.8
484122	General freight trucking, long-distance, less than truckload (ltl)	11	239	8.8	36,649	22.8
4842	Specialized freight trucking	29	279	8.0	28,695	25.0
484220	Specialized freight (except used goods) trucking, local	17	127	4.4	34,488	12.6
488	Support activities for transportation	9	121	3.5	28,950	12.9
492	Couriers and messengers	7	102	2.3	22,127	7.6

Sources: Economic Census of the United States, 1997. Only those industries are shown for which both employment and sales/revenue data were available. For the definition of MSAs, CMSAs, and PMSAs, please see the Introduction.

AMARILLO, TX MSA

NAICS	Industry	Estab-lish-ments	Em-ploy-ment	Payroll		Sales, reven. ($ mil.)
				Total ($ mil.)	Per Empl. ($)	
48-49	Transportation and warehousing	154	1,900	53.3	28,027	214.3
484	Truck transportation	111	1,308	36.7	28,089	137.3
4841	General freight trucking	55	840	23.8	28,323	84.8
48412	General freight trucking, long-distance	46	741	21.6	29,134	76.2
484121	General freight trucking, long-distance, truckload (tl)	34	583	17.8	30,535	63.3
484122	General freight trucking, long-distance, less than truckload (ltl)	12	158	3.8	23,962	13.0
4842	Specialized freight trucking	56	468	12.9	27,669	52.5
484220	Specialized freight (except used goods) trucking, local	22	125	3.7	29,480	21.2
484230	Specialized freight (except used goods) trucking, long-distance	25	262	7.6	29,130	26.3
488	Support activities for transportation	18	278	7.9	28,324	23.9
492	Couriers and messengers	10	128	2.9	23,023	8.0
493	Warehousing and storage	5	68	2.4	35,382	10.5

Sources: Economic Census of the United States, 1997. Only those industries are shown for which both employment and sales/revenue data were available. For the definition of MSAs, CMSAs, and PMSAs, please see the Introduction.

ANCHORAGE, AK MSA

NAICS	Industry	Estab-lish-ments	Em-ploy-ment	Payroll		Sales, reven. ($ mil.)
				Total ($ mil.)	Per Empl. ($)	
48-49	Transportation and warehousing	283	7,726	394.1	51,012	2,612.8
481	Air transportation	49	1,564	54.4	34,779	219.5
48111	Scheduled air transportation	22	1,372	46.6	33,980	177.5
481111	Scheduled passenger air transportation	14	985	29.7	30,202	102.7
48121	Nonscheduled air transportation	27	192	7.8	40,495	41.9
481211	Nonscheduled chartered passenger air transportation	19	83	3.4	41,373	14.5
483	Water transportation	6	172	13.9	80,529	53.6
484	Truck transportation	83	2,067	100.3	48,512	432.8
4841	General freight trucking	34	1,010	46.5	46,003	262.8
484110	General freight trucking, local	13	178	8.9	50,051	30.2
48412	General freight trucking, long-distance	21	832	37.6	45,137	232.6
484121	General freight trucking, long-distance, truckload (tl)	14	455	25.2	55,457	182.3
4842	Specialized freight trucking	49	1,057	53.8	50,910	170.0
484210	Used household and office goods moving	18	347	8.7	25,020	25.8
484220	Specialized freight (except used goods) trucking, local	24	654	43.1	65,943	134.0
487210	Scenic and sightseeing transportation, water	11	66	2.4	35,894	11.0
488	Support activities for transportation	73	1,499	47.7	31,822	153.4
4881	Support activities for air transportation	34	822	20.9	25,376	88.7
4881191	Airport operation and terminal services	11	516	11.3	21,911	23.3
488190	Other support activities for air transportation	23	306	9.6	31,219	65.4
4883	Support activities for water transportation	11	316	15.9	50,282	29.8
488510	Freight transportation arrangement	21	343	10.5	30,755	33.6
4885101	Freight forwarding	16	315	9.5	30,083	27.3
493	Warehousing and storage	6	39	0.9	23,077	2.4

Sources: Economic Census of the United States, 1997. Only those industries are shown for which both employment and sales/revenue data were available. For the definition of MSAs, CMSAs, and PMSAs, please see the Introduction.

ANN ARBOR, MI PMSA

NAICS	Industry	Estab-lish-ments	Em-ploy-ment	Payroll Total ($ mil.)	Payroll Per Empl. ($)	Sales, reven. ($ mil.)
48-49	Transportation and warehousing	210	4,699	166.8	35,496	553.4
481	Air transportation	10	870	27.4	31,487	100.6
484	Truck transportation	131	1,261	48.3	38,294	132.4
4841	General freight trucking	50	671	24.3	36,225	55.2
484110	General freight trucking, local	19	164	4.2	25,372	9.8
48412	General freight trucking, long-distance	31	507	20.1	39,736	45.4
484121	General freight trucking, long-distance, truckload (tl)	25	100	3.5	34,930	21.6
4842	Specialized freight trucking	81	590	24.0	40,647	77.2
484210	Used household and office goods moving	11	172	3.2	18,837	9.9
484220	Specialized freight (except used goods) trucking, local	56	299	12.9	43,211	43.2
4842203	Dump trucking	24	140	7.3	52,493	28.7
4842204	Specialized trucking without storage, local	20	128	4.9	38,461	11.5
484230	Specialized freight (except used goods) trucking, long-distance	14	119	7.8	65,731	24.1
486	Pipeline transportation	3	42	2.0	47,143	22.7
488	Support activities for transportation	33	456	7.9	17,342	34.8
488410	Motor vehicle towing	12	112	2.2	19,643	5.2
492	Couriers and messengers	14	1,710	74.2	43,404	246.9

Sources: Economic Census of the United States, 1997. Only those industries are shown for which both employment and sales/revenue data were available. For the definition of MSAs, CMSAs, and PMSAs, please see the Introduction.

ANNISTON, AL MSA

NAICS	Industry	Estab-lish-ments	Em-ploy-ment	Payroll Total ($ mil.)	Payroll Per Empl. ($)	Sales, reven. ($ mil.)
48-49	Transportation and warehousing	57	779	17.9	22,953	59.2
484	Truck transportation	40	545	14.1	25,853	45.3
4841	General freight trucking	24	461	12.8	27,866	41.0
48412	General freight trucking, long-distance	19	457	12.7	27,882	40.3
4842	Specialized freight trucking	16	84	1.2	14,810	4.2
484220	Specialized freight (except used goods) trucking, local	11	39	0.5	13,333	2.6
488	Support activities for transportation	4	81	1.8	22,148	3.5
493	Warehousing and storage	3	46	0.6	13,696	3.1

Sources: Economic Census of the United States, 1997. Only those industries are shown for which both employment and sales/revenue data were available. For the definition of MSAs, CMSAs, and PMSAs, please see the Introduction.

APPLETON—OSHKOSH—NEENAH, WI MSA

NAICS	Industry	Estab-lish-ments	Em-ploy-ment	Payroll Total ($ mil.)	Payroll Per Empl. ($)	Sales, reven. ($ mil.)
48-49	Transportation and warehousing	301	4,636	139.1	30,013	499.8
484	Truck transportation	207	2,935	98.3	33,479	350.7
4841	General freight trucking	111	2,504	85.1	33,974	287.4
484110	General freight trucking, local	26	326	10.7	32,902	30.4
4841101	General freight trucking without storage, local, truckload (tl)	19	200	7.5	37,560	21.9
48412	General freight trucking, long-distance	85	2,178	74.3	34,135	257.0
484121	General freight trucking, long-distance, truckload (tl)	64	1,809	59.5	32,892	202.1
484122	General freight trucking, long-distance, less than truckload (ltl)	21	369	14.8	40,228	54.9
4842	Specialized freight trucking	96	431	13.2	30,599	63.3
484210	Used household and office goods moving	14	138	4.0	29,217	13.9
484220	Specialized freight (except used goods) trucking, local	62	214	6.9	32,117	27.5
4842202	Agricultural products trucking without storage, local	34	104	2.4	22,923	9.6
4842203	Dump trucking	15	77	3.7	47,429	14.4
484230	Specialized freight (except used goods) trucking, long-distance	20	79	2.3	28,899	21.8
485	Transit and ground passenger transportation	27	757	7.9	10,425	20.0
4854101	School bus service	16	574	5.5	9,566	14.0
488	Support activities for transportation	20	346	17.4	50,153	62.7
492	Couriers and messengers	16	219	5.0	23,055	23.7
4931101	General warehousing and storage (except in foreign trade zones)	24	252	7.3	28,996	27.1

Sources: Economic Census of the United States, 1997. Only those industries are shown for which both employment and sales/revenue data were available. For the definition of MSAs, CMSAs, and PMSAs, please see the Introduction.

ASHEVILLE, NC MSA

NAICS	Industry	Estab-lish-ments	Em-ploy-ment	Payroll		Sales, reven. ($ mil.)
				Total ($ mil.)	Per Empl. ($)	
48-49	Transportation and warehousing	143	1,644	42.0	25,526	127.3
484	Truck transportation	106	1,251	33.5	26,767	99.5
4841	General freight trucking	48	838	24.3	28,956	67.3
484110	General freight trucking, local	14	77	1.7	22,597	8.8
48412	General freight trucking, long-distance	34	761	22.5	29,599	58.6
484121	General freight trucking, long-distance, truckload (tl)	17	435	12.2	27,952	28.8
484122	General freight trucking, long-distance, less than truckload (ltl)	17	326	10.4	31,798	29.8
4842	Specialized freight trucking	58	413	9.2	22,327	32.2
484220	Specialized freight (except used goods) trucking, local	36	241	5.8	24,075	20.8
4842203	Dump trucking	23	186	4.8	25,586	16.7
484230	Specialized freight (except used goods) trucking, long-distance	15	65	1.5	23,492	5.9
4842303	Other specialized trucking, long-distance	12	60	1.5	24,283	5.5
485	Transit and ground passenger transportation	7	98	1.9	18,980	4.9
488	Support activities for transportation	12	61	1.2	19,213	2.6
492	Couriers and messengers	11	188	4.1	21,798	16.1

Sources: *Economic Census of the United States*, 1997. Only those industries are shown for which both employment and sales/revenue data were available. For the definition of MSAs, CMSAs, and PMSAs, please see the Introduction.

ATHENS, GA MSA

NAICS	Industry	Estab-lish-ments	Em-ploy-ment	Payroll		Sales, reven. ($ mil.)
				Total ($ mil.)	Per Empl. ($)	
48-49	Transportation and warehousing	54	585	16.5	28,289	80.7
484	Truck transportation	35	356	10.5	29,452	42.0
4841	General freight trucking	21	232	7.2	31,069	22.4
48412	General freight trucking, long-distance	16	223	7.1	31,628	21.7
4842	Specialized freight trucking	14	124	3.3	26,427	19.5

Sources: *Economic Census of the United States*, 1997. Only those industries are shown for which both employment and sales/revenue data were available. For the definition of MSAs, CMSAs, and PMSAs, please see the Introduction.

ATLANTA, GA MSA

NAICS	Industry	Estab-lish-ments	Em-ploy-ment	Payroll Total ($ mil.)	Payroll Per Empl. ($)	Sales, reven. ($ mil.)
48-49	Transportation and warehousing	2,303	56,336	1,632.6	28,980	5,685.0
481	Air transportation	54	1,041	36.3	34,908	241.1
483111	Deep sea freight transportation	13	315	14.1	44,829	181.0
484	Truck transportation	1,178	29,506	932.9	31,617	2,740.7
4841	General freight trucking	560	19,222	639.3	33,257	1,770.2
484110	General freight trucking, local	179	1,963	49.1	25,024	157.4
4841101	General freight trucking without storage, local, truckload (tl)	107	772	22.3	28,940	87.1
4841102	General freight trucking without storage, local, less than truckload (ltl)	47	738	15.2	20,641	33.0
4841103	General freight trucking with storage, local, truckload (tl)	11	115	3.2	27,730	11.3
4841104	General freight trucking with storage, local, less than truckload (ltl)	14	338	8.4	24,731	26.1
48412	General freight trucking, long-distance	381	17,259	590.1	34,193	1,612.9
484121	General freight trucking, long-distance, truckload (tl)	299	6,968	216.0	30,997	797.3
484122	General freight trucking, long-distance, less than truckload (ltl)	82	10,291	374.1	36,357	815.5
4842	Specialized freight trucking	618	10,284	293.6	28,553	970.5
484210	Used household and office goods moving	112	2,118	59.0	27,867	183.8
4842101	Used household and office goods moving, local, without storage	43	564	10.4	18,420	28.9
4842102	Used household and office goods moving, long-distance	52	1,396	45.1	32,309	146.0
4842103	Used household and office goods moving, local, with storage	17	158	3.5	22,348	9.0
484220	Specialized freight (except used goods) trucking, local	374	2,116	54.3	25,679	207.8
4842201	Hazardous materials trucking (except waste), local	21	277	9.6	34,819	27.5
4842202	Agricultural products trucking without storage, local	20	51	1.1	21,882	3.8
4842203	Dump trucking	247	1,089	24.8	22,810	115.2
4842204	Specialized trucking without storage, local	81	511	14.1	27,556	51.0
484230	Specialized freight (except used goods) trucking, long-distance	132	6,050	180.3	29,798	578.9
4842301	Hazardous materials trucking (except waste), long-distance	21	896	28.6	31,890	78.2
4842302	Agricultural products trucking, long-distance	22	157	5.5	34,834	18.1
4842303	Other specialized trucking, long-distance	89	4,997	146.2	29,265	482.6
4853	Taxi and limousine service	68	339	5.3	15,493	29.7
485310	Taxi service	28	156	2.3	14,705	8.3
485320	Limousine service	40	183	3.0	16,164	21.4
485510	Charter bus industry	21	370	6.5	17,489	23.3
4855102	Charter bus service, interstate/interurban	13	289	5.1	17,727	16.6
48599	Other transit and ground passenger transportation	33	609	8.1	13,232	19.8
485991	Special needs transportation	18	342	4.6	13,477	13.5
485999	All other transit and ground passenger transportation	15	267	3.4	12,918	6.3
486	Pipeline transportation	20	577	31.5	54,591	545.5
488	Support activities for transportation	567	6,424	176.1	27,418	571.2
4881	Support activities for air transportation	63	2,175	37.0	17,001	101.4
48811	Airport operations	26	1,707	25.8	15,107	67.5
488190	Other support activities for air transportation	37	468	11.2	23,910	33.9
488410	Motor vehicle towing	104	670	13.4	19,969	39.3
488510	Freight transportation arrangement	358	3,012	111.8	37,118	362.6
4885101	Freight forwarding	146	1,520	52.9	34,816	184.6
4885102	Arrangement of transportation of freight and cargo	212	1,492	58.9	39,464	178.0
492	Couriers and messengers	182	13,762	330.0	23,978	1,006.5
492110	Couriers	101	11,963	293.7	24,548	901.9
4921101	Courier services (except by air)	36	8,092	190.5	23,547	466.3
4921102	Air courier services	65	3,871	103.1	26,641	435.5
492210	Local messengers and local delivery	81	1,799	36.3	20,187	104.6
4931	Warehousing and storage	145	3,003	86.0	28,631	296.2
4931101	General warehousing and storage (except in foreign trade zones)	99	1,751	45.1	25,770	159.5
4931201	Refrigerated products warehousing	13	472	20.5	43,362	61.2

Sources: Economic Census of the United States, 1997. Only those industries are shown for which both employment and sales/revenue data were available. For the definition of MSAs, CMSAs, and PMSAs, please see the Introduction.

ATLANTIC CAPE MAY, NJ PMSA

NAICS	Industry	Estab-lish-ments	Em-ploy-ment	Payroll Total ($ mil.)	Payroll Per Empl. ($)	Sales, reven. ($ mil.)
48-49	Transportation and warehousing	176	2,186	45.2	20,677	161.5
484	Truck transportation	71	358	10.0	28,036	38.3
4841	General freight trucking	18	125	4.1	32,984	12.5
484110	General freight trucking, local	11	77	2.4	31,558	5.8
4842	Specialized freight trucking	53	233	5.9	25,382	25.8
484220	Specialized freight (except used goods) trucking, local	30	111	2.8	24,811	10.4
4842203	Dump trucking	21	94	2.3	24,500	8.3
485	Transit and ground passenger transportation	40	1,483	22.1	14,870	54.4

Sources: Economic Census of the United States, 1997. Only those industries are shown for which both employment and sales/revenue data were available. For the definition of MSAs, CMSAs, and PMSAs, please see the Introduction.

AUGUSTA—AIKEN, GA—SC MSA

NAICS	Industry	Estab-lish-ments	Em-ploy-ment	Payroll Total ($ mil.)	Payroll Per Empl. ($)	Sales, reven. ($ mil.)
48-49	Transportation and warehousing	193	2,105	56.8	27,004	261.5
484	Truck transportation	128	1,427	37.8	26,474	129.6
4841	General freight trucking	56	796	23.6	29,678	79.5
484110	General freight trucking, local	14	121	3.2	26,694	11.9
48412	General freight trucking, long-distance	42	675	20.4	30,213	67.6
484121	General freight trucking, long-distance, truckload (tl)	28	371	10.5	28,296	37.1
484122	General freight trucking, long-distance, less than truckload (ltl)	14	304	9.9	32,553	30.5
4842	Specialized freight trucking	72	631	14.2	22,431	50.1
484210	Used household and office goods moving	15	156	3.2	20,513	9.4
484220	Specialized freight (except used goods) trucking, local	38	357	7.6	21,235	26.9
4842203	Dump trucking	16	190	3.5	18,463	14.1
484230	Specialized freight (except used goods) trucking, long-distance	19	118	3.4	28,585	13.8
488510	Freight transportation arrangement	11	28	0.8	28,464	2.1
4931	Warehousing and storage	12	93	1.8	19,548	9.4

Sources: Economic Census of the United States, 1997. Only those industries are shown for which both employment and sales/revenue data were available. For the definition of MSAs, CMSAs, and PMSAs, please see the Introduction.

AUSTIN—SAN MARCOS, TX MSA

NAICS	Industry	Estab-lish-ments	Em-ploy-ment	Payroll Total ($ mil.)	Payroll Per Empl. ($)	Sales, reven. ($ mil.)
48-49	Transportation and warehousing	479	5,537	123.4	22,283	515.7
481	Air transportation	12	215	3.8	17,842	21.2
484	Truck transportation	279	2,586	61.5	23,794	223.1
4841	General freight trucking	88	1,320	33.1	25,040	115.7
484110	General freight trucking, local	27	244	4.3	17,500	14.2
4841101	General freight trucking without storage, local, truckload (tl)	14	77	1.3	17,052	6.3
48412	General freight trucking, long-distance	61	1,076	28.8	26,750	101.5
484121	General freight trucking, long-distance, truckload (tl)	43	669	16.1	24,069	55.9
484122	General freight trucking, long-distance, less than truckload (ltl)	18	407	12.7	31,157	45.6
4842	Specialized freight trucking	191	1,266	28.5	22,495	107.4
484210	Used household and office goods moving	43	495	9.9	19,909	33.2
4842101	Used household and office goods moving, local, without storage	23	134	1.9	13,918	6.3
4842102	Used household and office goods moving, long-distance	12	249	5.8	23,177	19.0
484220	Specialized freight (except used goods) trucking, local	118	589	13.7	23,329	52.4
4842203	Dump trucking	85	375	7.9	20,965	36.7
4842204	Specialized trucking without storage, local	23	172	4.9	28,715	12.2
484230	Specialized freight (except used goods) trucking, long-distance	30	182	4.9	26,830	21.9
4842303	Other specialized trucking, long-distance	21	131	3.5	26,786	17.9
485	Transit and ground passenger transportation	22	733	8.9	12,085	33.1
486	Pipeline transportation	10	47	2.1	45,362	16.7
487	Scenic and sightseeing transportation	8	20	0.4	21,550	2.3
488	Support activities for transportation	88	991	26.3	26,493	91.8
4881	Support activities for air transportation	24	441	10.4	23,651	34.9
4881191	Airport operation and terminal services	11	225	2.8	12,404	9.5
488190	Other support activities for air transportation	13	216	7.6	35,366	25.4
488410	Motor vehicle towing	28	163	4.0	24,282	11.0
488510	Freight transportation arrangement	28	332	11.2	33,660	42.7
4885101	Freight forwarding	14	93	2.7	29,118	12.2
4885102	Arrangement of transportation of freight and cargo	14	239	8.5	35,427	30.5
492	Couriers and messengers	44	851	17.9	21,002	120.8
492110	Couriers	21	590	13.0	22,085	104.0
4921102	Air courier services	16	488	11.7	23,963	96.2
492210	Local messengers and local delivery	23	261	4.8	18,556	16.9
4931	Warehousing and storage	16	94	2.5	26,234	6.6

Sources: Economic Census of the United States, 1997. Only those industries are shown for which both employment and sales/revenue data were available. For the definition of MSAs, CMSAs, and PMSAs, please see the Introduction.

BAKERSFIELD, CA MSA

NAICS	Industry	Estab-lish-ments	Em-ploy-ment	Payroll		Sales, reven. ($ mil.)
				Total ($ mil.)	Per Empl. ($)	
48-49	Transportation and warehousing	319	4,588	128.6	28,029	485.8
484	Truck transportation	215	2,540	74.4	29,303	248.4
4841	General freight trucking	60	519	16.3	31,418	53.8
484110	General freight trucking, local	25	191	5.2	27,058	17.1
4841101	General freight trucking without storage, local, truckload (tl)	18	114	2.7	23,737	10.0
48412	General freight trucking, long-distance	35	328	11.1	33,957	36.7
484121	General freight trucking, long-distance, truckload (tl)	24	202	6.5	32,233	19.9
484122	General freight trucking, long-distance, less than truckload (ltl)	11	126	4.6	36,722	16.9
4842	Specialized freight trucking	155	2,021	58.1	28,760	194.6
484210	Used household and office goods moving	15	192	5.8	30,115	14.8
484220	Specialized freight (except used goods) trucking, local	97	989	25.1	25,346	104.3
4842203	Dump trucking	23	441	8.0	18,175	42.2
4842204	Specialized trucking without storage, local	28	333	10.6	31,931	31.6
484230	Specialized freight (except used goods) trucking, long-distance	43	840	27.3	32,469	75.4
4842302	Agricultural products trucking, long-distance	13	71	2.4	33,535	8.8
4842303	Other specialized trucking, long-distance	23	464	13.7	29,593	41.8
488	Support activities for transportation	43	996	22.3	22,386	69.9
488190	Other support activities for air transportation	13	788	17.6	22,278	54.0
488410	Motor vehicle towing	16	120	2.2	17,925	8.0
492	Couriers and messengers	20	199	3.9	19,628	12.8
492110	Couriers	12	153	3.4	22,255	11.0
4931	Warehousing and storage	13	213	4.8	22,465	23.4

Sources: Economic Census of the United States, 1997. Only those industries are shown for which both employment and sales/revenue data were available. For the definition of MSAs, CMSAs, and PMSAs, please see the Introduction.

BALTIMORE, MD PMSA

NAICS	Industry	Estab-lish-ments	Em-ploy-ment	Payroll		Sales, reven. ($ mil.)
				Total ($ mil.)	Per Empl. ($)	
48-49	Transportation and warehousing	1,707	27,009	720.7	26,683	2,495.5
481	Air transportation	22	412	9.1	22,019	147.4
484	Truck transportation	776	9,896	287.2	29,018	1,085.8
4841	General freight trucking	288	5,003	166.4	33,264	660.3
484110	General freight trucking, local	120	1,120	27.8	24,844	92.1
4841101	General freight trucking without storage, local, truckload (tl)	78	510	12.9	25,275	50.2
4841102	General freight trucking without storage, local, less than truckload (ltl)	27	435	11.3	25,917	27.0
48412	General freight trucking, long-distance	168	3,883	138.6	35,693	568.1
484121	General freight trucking, long-distance, truckload (tl)	128	2,025	65.5	32,356	349.4
484122	General freight trucking, long-distance, less than truckload (ltl)	40	1,858	73.1	39,330	218.7
4842	Specialized freight trucking	488	4,893	120.7	24,676	425.5
484210	Used household and office goods moving	103	1,776	30.2	17,015	104.7
4842102	Used household and office goods moving, long-distance	30	386	9.8	25,337	43.9
484220	Specialized freight (except used goods) trucking, local	305	1,816	42.5	23,406	161.0
4842202	Agricultural products trucking without storage, local	20	133	4.0	30,015	11.0
4842203	Dump trucking	166	901	19.4	21,584	83.8
4842204	Specialized trucking without storage, local	96	498	11.5	23,151	37.5
484230	Specialized freight (except used goods) trucking, long-distance	80	1,301	48.0	36,909	159.8
4842303	Other specialized trucking, long-distance	62	1,041	39.9	38,340	131.3
485	Transit and ground passenger transportation	328	4,583	63.1	13,759	164.0
485410	School and employee bus transportation	184	2,467	28.0	11,360	67.3
485510	Charter bus industry	30	627	10.6	16,850	34.7
488	Support activities for transportation	367	6,379	180.4	28,280	498.2
4881	Support activities for air transportation	23	826	13.6	16,420	34.5
4881191	Airport operation and terminal services	12	740	11.3	15,327	30.1
488190	Other support activities for air transportation	11	86	2.2	25,826	4.4
4883	Support activities for water transportation	41	2,496	74.4	29,821	182.4
4884	Support activities for road transportation	78	486	10.3	21,237	26.5
488410	Motor vehicle towing	68	397	8.5	21,494	23.1
488510	Freight transportation arrangement	204	2,006	69.6	34,717	197.0
48899	Other support activities for transportation	12	102	2.6	25,049	7.6
492110	Couriers	44	3,522	123.6	35,099	288.8
4931	Warehousing and storage	58	1,063	29.6	27,863	127.4

Sources: Economic Census of the United States, 1997. Only those industries are shown for which both employment and sales/revenue data were available. For the definition of MSAs, CMSAs, and PMSAs, please see the Introduction.

BANGOR, ME MSA

NAICS	Industry	Estab-lish-ments	Em-ploy-ment	Payroll		Sales, reven. ($ mil.)
				Total ($ mil.)	Per Empl. ($)	
48-49	Transportation and warehousing	83	1,448	35.6	24,557	125.9
484	Truck transportation	55	970	27.6	28,502	96.1
4841	General freight trucking	26	571	19.7	34,557	65.9
48412	General freight trucking, long-distance	18	427	15.0	35,239	48.5
484121	General freight trucking, long-distance, truckload (tl)	12	356	12.1	33,924	39.7
4842	Specialized freight trucking	29	399	7.9	19,837	30.2
484220	Specialized freight (except used goods) trucking, local	15	125	2.5	19,632	12.0
485	Transit and ground passenger transportation	6	222	2.5	11,473	7.7
492	Couriers and messengers	7	123	2.8	22,984	7.5
493	Warehousing and storage	4	48	1.2	24,688	6.1

Sources: *Economic Census of the United States*, 1997. Only those industries are shown for which both employment and sales/revenue data were available. For the definition of MSAs, CMSAs, and PMSAs, please see the Introduction.

BARNSTABLE—YARMOUTH, MA MSA

NAICS	Industry	Estab-lish-ments	Em-ploy-ment	Payroll		Sales, reven. ($ mil.)
				Total ($ mil.)	Per Empl. ($)	
48-49	Transportation and warehousing	77	822	20.1	24,504	66.1
481	Air transportation	6	135	3.4	24,985	12.1
4842	Specialized freight trucking	17	75	1.7	22,613	7.1
484220	Specialized freight (except used goods) trucking, local	12	22	0.6	26,818	3.5
485	Transit and ground passenger transportation	17	334	4.9	14,796	13.5
487	Scenic and sightseeing transportation	13	73	3.8	51,452	14.0

Sources: *Economic Census of the United States*, 1997. Only those industries are shown for which both employment and sales/revenue data were available. For the definition of MSAs, CMSAs, and PMSAs, please see the Introduction.

BATON ROUGE, LA MSA

NAICS	Industry	Estab-lish-ments	Em-ploy-ment	Payroll		Sales, reven. ($ mil.)
				Total ($ mil.)	Per Empl. ($)	
48-49	Transportation and warehousing	433	6,307	178.0	28,229	733.1
483211	Inland water freight transportation	11	545	16.4	30,026	126.2
484	Truck transportation	254	2,705	74.4	27,507	296.9
4841	General freight trucking	90	1,310	37.2	28,433	150.3
484110	General freight trucking, local	27	209	4.0	19,124	14.5
4841101	General freight trucking without storage, local, truckload (tl)	21	188	3.6	19,202	13.6
48412	General freight trucking, long-distance	63	1,101	33.3	30,200	135.8
484121	General freight trucking, long-distance, truckload (tl)	47	688	21.4	31,102	101.4
484122	General freight trucking, long-distance, less than truckload (ltl)	16	413	11.9	28,697	34.4
4842	Specialized freight trucking	164	1,395	37.2	26,638	146.6
484210	Used household and office goods moving	13	149	2.7	18,148	7.3
484220	Specialized freight (except used goods) trucking, local	96	503	10.8	21,425	40.1
4842203	Dump trucking	52	139	3.1	22,597	15.4
4842204	Specialized trucking without storage, local	25	274	6.1	22,259	19.2
484230	Specialized freight (except used goods) trucking, long-distance	55	743	23.7	31,869	99.2
4842301	Hazardous materials trucking (except waste), long-distance	29	563	18.7	33,178	75.6
4842303	Other specialized trucking, long-distance	20	146	4.5	30,986	21.7
485	Transit and ground passenger transportation	17	183	2.3	12,770	8.7
486	Pipeline transportation	9	121	6.4	53,107	88.8
488	Support activities for transportation	89	1,894	58.7	31,001	144.6
4883	Support activities for water transportation	37	1,580	50.7	32,099	120.9
488320	Marine cargo handling	13	1,116	38.0	34,052	80.3
488330	Navigational services to shipping	11	301	7.2	24,003	23.6
488410	Motor vehicle towing	19	119	2.3	19,647	8.2
488510	Freight transportation arrangement	23	120	3.8	31,292	9.1
4885102	Arrangement of transportation of freight and cargo	19	110	3.6	32,473	8.3
492	Couriers and messengers	23	370	6.7	18,178	23.1
492110	Couriers	14	269	5.4	20,257	19.6
4931	Warehousing and storage	21	335	9.6	28,761	32.3
4931101	General warehousing and storage (except in foreign trade zones)	14	209	6.3	30,191	17.2

Sources: *Economic Census of the United States*, 1997. Only those industries are shown for which both employment and sales/revenue data were available. For the definition of MSAs, CMSAs, and PMSAs, please see the Introduction.

BEAUMONT—PORT ARTHUR, TX MSA

NAICS	Industry	Estab-lish-ments	Em-ploy-ment	Payroll Total ($ mil.)	Payroll Per Empl. ($)	Sales, reven. ($ mil.)
48-49	Transportation and warehousing	266	3,840	127.9	33,297	588.5
484	Truck transportation	123	1,296	32.9	25,413	110.3
4841	General freight trucking	48	710	17.6	24,775	46.1
484110	General freight trucking, local	16	335	7.7	22,872	19.6
4841101	General freight trucking without storage, local, truckload (tl)	12	237	6.1	25,692	14.3
48412	General freight trucking, long-distance	32	375	9.9	26,475	26.6
484121	General freight trucking, long-distance, truckload (tl)	21	210	6.0	28,724	13.6
484122	General freight trucking, long-distance, less than truckload (ltl)	11	165	3.9	23,612	13.0
4842	Specialized freight trucking	75	586	15.3	26,186	64.2
484220	Specialized freight (except used goods) trucking, local	41	243	4.4	18,156	20.6
4842203	Dump trucking	25	128	2.6	20,195	12.7
484230	Specialized freight (except used goods) trucking, long-distance	29	308	10.3	33,510	41.2
4842301	Hazardous materials trucking (except waste), long-distance	15	232	8.6	36,966	31.6
486	Pipeline transportation	25	420	21.2	50,424	217.9
488	Support activities for transportation	72	767	25.1	32,737	81.1
4883	Support activities for water transportation	35	395	15.5	39,246	51.4
488330	Navigational services to shipping	19	189	9.2	48,598	26.3
488410	Motor vehicle towing	13	62	1.2	19,129	3.4
488510	Freight transportation arrangement	19	106	3.2	29,991	8.8
492	Couriers and messengers	6	89	3.5	39,371	11.4
4931	Warehousing and storage	18	298	7.7	25,685	26.0

Sources: Economic Census of the United States, 1997. Only those industries are shown for which both employment and sales/revenue data were available. For the definition of MSAs, CMSAs, and PMSAs, please see the Introduction.

BELLINGHAM, WA MSA

NAICS	Industry	Estab-lish-ments	Em-ploy-ment	Payroll Total ($ mil.)	Payroll Per Empl. ($)	Sales, reven. ($ mil.)
48-49	Transportation and warehousing	151	1,496	41.6	27,775	149.3
484	Truck transportation	85	663	19.0	28,722	72.0
4841	General freight trucking	27	286	9.0	31,629	31.6
48412	General freight trucking, long-distance	20	261	8.2	31,544	29.9
484121	General freight trucking, long-distance, truckload (tl)	15	226	6.8	30,283	23.0
4842	Specialized freight trucking	58	377	10.0	26,517	40.4
484220	Specialized freight (except used goods) trucking, local	36	151	4.1	26,894	16.0
4842202	Agricultural products trucking without storage, local	16	56	1.6	29,161	7.6
484230	Specialized freight (except used goods) trucking, long-distance	18	175	4.9	28,194	20.7
488	Support activities for transportation	36	360	10.3	28,694	25.8
488510	Freight transportation arrangement	22	273	7.2	26,216	17.0
4885102	Arrangement of transportation of freight and cargo	15	224	6.0	26,768	12.9
492	Couriers and messengers	10	57	1.3	23,175	3.4
493	Warehousing and storage	8	208	5.5	26,433	19.5

Sources: Economic Census of the United States, 1997. Only those industries are shown for which both employment and sales/revenue data were available. For the definition of MSAs, CMSAs, and PMSAs, please see the Introduction.

BENTON HARBOR, MI MSA

NAICS	Industry	Estab-lish-ments	Em-ploy-ment	Payroll Total ($ mil.)	Payroll Per Empl. ($)	Sales, reven. ($ mil.)
48-49	Transportation and warehousing	72	617	15.5	25,125	58.2
484	Truck transportation	46	304	8.5	28,046	28.4
4841	General freight trucking	28	172	4.0	22,988	11.9
48412	General freight trucking, long-distance	20	127	3.2	25,031	9.1
4842	Specialized freight trucking	18	132	4.6	34,636	16.6
486	Pipeline transportation	4	31	1.5	48,290	16.9
488	Support activities for transportation	6	89	1.1	12,101	2.4

Sources: Economic Census of the United States, 1997. Only those industries are shown for which both employment and sales/revenue data were available. For the definition of MSAs, CMSAs, and PMSAs, please see the Introduction.

BERGEN—PASSAIC, NJ PMSA

NAICS	Industry	Estab-lish-ments	Em-ploy-ment	Payroll Total ($ mil.)	Payroll Per Empl. ($)	Sales, reven. ($ mil.)
48-49	Transportation and warehousing	1,187	14,942	450.2	30,129	1,561.0
481	Air transportation	27	490	27.1	55,259	99.9
48121	Nonscheduled air transportation	20	274	19.5	71,168	91.5
484	Truck transportation	492	4,685	156.0	33,294	523.9
4841	General freight trucking	228	2,603	93.7	36,009	313.8
484110	General freight trucking, local	148	1,072	31.0	28,878	92.4
4841101	General freight trucking without storage, local, truckload (tl)	81	614	18.6	30,363	58.0
4841102	General freight trucking without storage, local, less than truckload (ltl)	56	305	7.7	25,154	23.1
48412	General freight trucking, long-distance	80	1,531	62.8	41,002	221.4
484121	General freight trucking, long-distance, truckload (tl)	59	744	27.7	37,280	116.7
484122	General freight trucking, long-distance, less than truckload (ltl)	21	787	35.0	44,521	104.7
4842	Specialized freight trucking	264	2,082	62.3	29,900	210.1
484210	Used household and office goods moving	86	769	19.9	25,932	57.7
4842101	Used household and office goods moving, local, without storage	36	176	3.5	19,915	10.9
4842102	Used household and office goods moving, long-distance	29	448	13.7	30,542	37.8
4842103	Used household and office goods moving, local, with storage	21	145	2.8	18,993	9.0
484220	Specialized freight (except used goods) trucking, local	130	782	24.0	30,751	82.3
4842203	Dump trucking	47	259	6.9	26,788	22.2
4842204	Specialized trucking without storage, local	55	286	8.1	28,276	34.9
484230	Specialized freight (except used goods) trucking, long-distance	48	531	18.3	34,394	70.1
4842303	Other specialized trucking, long-distance	39	504	17.0	33,806	65.3
485	Transit and ground passenger transportation	244	4,633	93.7	20,222	243.7
48511	Urban transit systems	13	690	23.1	33,500	48.8
4853	Taxi and limousine service	139	1,358	23.8	17,539	86.9
485310	Taxi service	33	519	5.7	10,969	14.4
485320	Limousine service	106	839	18.1	21,603	72.5
485410	School and employee bus transportation	45	2,001	27.8	13,915	60.0
485510	Charter bus industry	15	94	2.0	21,585	6.4
4855102	Charter bus service, interstate/interurban	11	72	1.5	20,292	4.8
48599	Other transit and ground passenger transportation	23	139	2.5	17,871	7.5
485991	Special needs transportation	13	116	2.0	17,284	4.8
488	Support activities for transportation	266	2,019	83.2	41,189	311.9
4881	Support activities for air transportation	18	311	13.3	42,704	76.7
488190	Other support activities for air transportation	11	106	4.8	45,236	17.6
488410	Motor vehicle towing	44	180	4.6	25,461	13.8
488510	Freight transportation arrangement	184	1,364	56.6	41,512	196.9
4885101	Freight forwarding	76	605	17.7	29,190	109.6
4885102	Arrangement of transportation of freight and cargo	108	759	39.0	51,335	87.4
492	Couriers and messengers	83	1,847	52.8	28,602	181.5
492110	Couriers	36	1,421	41.0	28,863	135.8
4921101	Courier services (except by air)	23	537	12.9	24,006	41.2
4921102	Air courier services	13	884	28.1	31,813	94.6
492210	Local messengers and local delivery	47	426	11.8	27,732	45.7
4931	Warehousing and storage	56	749	17.3	23,130	58.8
4931101	General warehousing and storage (except in foreign trade zones)	41	612	13.8	22,564	49.4

Sources: Economic Census of the United States, 1997. Only those industries are shown for which both employment and sales/revenue data were available. For the definition of MSAs, CMSAs, and PMSAs, please see the Introduction.

BILLINGS, MT MSA

NAICS	Industry	Estab-lish-ments	Em-ploy-ment	Payroll Total ($ mil.)	Payroll Per Empl. ($)	Sales, reven. ($ mil.)
48-49	Transportation and warehousing	161	2,376	55.8	23,485	268.6
484	Truck transportation	117	1,353	33.4	24,687	161.5
4841	General freight trucking	55	782	18.1	23,120	88.5
48412	General freight trucking, long-distance	46	738	17.6	23,817	84.4
484121	General freight trucking, long-distance, truckload (tl)	36	531	12.1	22,780	67.0
4842	Specialized freight trucking	62	571	15.3	26,832	73.1
484220	Specialized freight (except used goods) trucking, local	23	163	4.1	25,258	15.1
4842204	Specialized trucking without storage, local	13	50	1.3	25,500	4.7
484230	Specialized freight (except used goods) trucking, long-distance	35	329	9.8	29,790	53.5
4842302	Agricultural products trucking, long-distance	11	87	1.9	21,425	8.7
4842303	Other specialized trucking, long-distance	15	211	6.9	32,692	39.1

Sources: Economic Census of the United States, 1997. Only those industries are shown for which both employment and sales/revenue data were available. For the definition of MSAs, CMSAs, and PMSAs, please see the Introduction.

BILOXI—GULFPORT—PASCAGOULA, MS MSA

NAICS	Industry	Estab-lish-ments	Em-ploy-ment	Payroll		Sales, reven. ($ mil.)
				Total ($ mil.)	Per Empl. ($)	
48-49	Transportation and warehousing	201	2,370	57.6	24,306	213.5
483	Water transportation	9	201	6.7	33,577	21.4
484	Truck transportation	100	1,066	26.9	25,279	122.5
4841	General freight trucking	51	697	19.7	28,255	97.3
484110	General freight trucking, local	13	101	2.4	23,436	8.7
48412	General freight trucking, long-distance	38	596	17.3	29,072	88.6
484121	General freight trucking, long-distance, truckload (tl)	32	519	15.4	29,697	82.9
4842	Specialized freight trucking	49	369	7.3	19,656	25.1
484210	Used household and office goods moving	13	170	3.3	19,647	9.6
484220	Specialized freight (except used goods) trucking, local	29	162	3.3	20,414	13.9
4842203	Dump trucking	15	111	2.5	22,396	10.6
485	Transit and ground passenger transportation	11	177	1.8	10,446	4.6
488	Support activities for transportation	48	708	16.0	22,552	45.1
4883	Support activities for water transportation	19	569	13.2	23,160	35.4
488510	Freight transportation arrangement	12	48	1.2	24,688	3.5
492	Couriers and messengers	8	74	1.8	24,581	6.0
493	Warehousing and storage	9	111	3.0	27,090	8.8

Sources: *Economic Census of the United States*, 1997. Only those industries are shown for which both employment and sales/revenue data were available. For the definition of MSAs, CMSAs, and PMSAs, please see the Introduction.

BINGHAMTON, NY MSA

NAICS	Industry	Estab-lish-ments	Em-ploy-ment	Payroll		Sales, reven. ($ mil.)
				Total ($ mil.)	Per Empl. ($)	
48-49	Transportation and warehousing	96	1,571	37.5	23,898	130.5
481	Air transportation	3	134	4.0	30,209	19.2
484	Truck transportation	65	860	24.7	28,714	77.4
4841	General freight trucking	28	506	17.5	34,597	57.5
484110	General freight trucking, local	11	212	7.6	35,698	21.1
48412	General freight trucking, long-distance	17	294	9.9	33,803	36.4
4842	Specialized freight trucking	37	354	7.2	20,305	19.9
484220	Specialized freight (except used goods) trucking, local	21	57	1.3	22,070	4.3
4842203	Dump trucking	11	24	0.5	19,208	2.1
485	Transit and ground passenger transportation	14	420	4.2	9,986	11.3
492	Couriers and messengers	5	129	3.0	22,977	15.0

Sources: *Economic Census of the United States*, 1997. Only those industries are shown for which both employment and sales/revenue data were available. For the definition of MSAs, CMSAs, and PMSAs, please see the Introduction.

BIRMINGHAM, AL MSA

NAICS	Industry	Estab-lish-ments	Em-ploy-ment	Payroll		Sales, reven. ($ mil.)
				Total ($ mil.)	Per Empl. ($)	
48-49	Transportation and warehousing	514	10,651	310.9	29,194	1,145.7
484	Truck transportation	343	5,177	149.0	28,775	679.6
4841	General freight trucking	166	3,707	111.2	29,987	522.3
484110	General freight trucking, local	46	372	9.7	26,027	41.5
4841101	General freight trucking without storage, local, truckload (tl)	33	235	6.5	27,638	31.6
48412	General freight trucking, long-distance	120	3,335	101.5	30,429	480.7
484121	General freight trucking, long-distance, truckload (tl)	92	1,651	46.3	28,054	311.5
484122	General freight trucking, long-distance, less than truckload (ltl)	28	1,684	55.2	32,758	169.2
4842	Specialized freight trucking	177	1,470	37.8	25,716	157.3
484210	Used household and office goods moving	28	294	6.0	20,299	17.2
4842101	Used household and office goods moving, local, without storage	12	76	1.2	15,711	3.4
4842102	Used household and office goods moving, long-distance	11	171	3.6	20,825	10.5
484220	Specialized freight (except used goods) trucking, local	108	648	13.9	21,421	63.2
4842203	Dump trucking	72	451	9.6	21,392	41.9
4842204	Specialized trucking without storage, local	19	49	0.8	16,735	3.8
484230	Specialized freight (except used goods) trucking, long-distance	41	528	18.0	34,004	76.9
4842303	Other specialized trucking, long-distance	26	357	13.1	36,765	46.4
485	Transit and ground passenger transportation	22	394	6.2	15,822	12.8
4853	Taxi and limousine service	11	56	0.7	11,607	2.7
486	Pipeline transportation	9	132	10.9	82,462	120.9
488	Support activities for transportation	68	653	15.4	23,562	59.5
488410	Motor vehicle towing	17	141	3.3	23,468	14.2
488510	Freight transportation arrangement	31	129	3.9	29,876	14.3
4885101	Freight forwarding	11	38	0.9	22,553	4.2
4885102	Arrangement of transportation of freight and cargo	20	91	3.0	32,934	10.2
492	Couriers and messengers	35	4,033	124.3	30,828	252.9
492110	Couriers	23	3,824	121.2	31,689	246.1
492210	Local messengers and local delivery	12	209	3.2	15,077	6.7
4931	Warehousing and storage	26	216	4.3	20,014	16.0
4931101	General warehousing and storage (except in foreign trade zones)	18	136	2.7	19,713	10.9

Sources: Economic Census of the United States, 1997. Only those industries are shown for which both employment and sales/revenue data were available. For the definition of MSAs, CMSAs, and PMSAs, please see the Introduction.

BISMARCK, ND MSA

NAICS	Industry	Estab-lish-ments	Em-ploy-ment	Payroll		Sales, reven. ($ mil.)
				Total ($ mil.)	Per Empl. ($)	
48-49	Transportation and warehousing	107	1,488	39.0	26,193	139.1
4841	General freight trucking	52	900	26.5	29,478	67.8
484110	General freight trucking, local	12	151	2.4	16,219	6.9
48412	General freight trucking, long-distance	40	749	24.1	32,151	61.0
484121	General freight trucking, long-distance, truckload (tl)	29	444	17.0	38,189	47.2
484122	General freight trucking, long-distance, less than truckload (ltl)	11	305	7.1	23,361	13.8
484220	Specialized freight (except used goods) trucking, local	15	57	0.7	12,246	4.8

Sources: Economic Census of the United States, 1997. Only those industries are shown for which both employment and sales/revenue data were available. For the definition of MSAs, CMSAs, and PMSAs, please see the Introduction.

BLOOMINGTON, IN MSA

NAICS	Industry	Estab-lish-ments	Em-ploy-ment	Payroll		Sales, reven. ($ mil.)
				Total ($ mil.)	Per Empl. ($)	
48-49	Transportation and warehousing	59	663	16.0	24,119	50.2
484	Truck transportation	41	382	10.4	27,196	36.6
4841	General freight trucking	17	253	7.3	28,696	25.4
4842	Specialized freight trucking	24	129	3.1	24,256	11.2
484220	Specialized freight (except used goods) trucking, local	12	46	1.1	23,087	5.1
485	Transit and ground passenger transportation	9	190	3.3	17,179	5.9

Sources: Economic Census of the United States, 1997. Only those industries are shown for which both employment and sales/revenue data were available. For the definition of MSAs, CMSAs, and PMSAs, please see the Introduction.

BLOOMINGTON—NORMAL, IL MSA

| NAICS | Industry | Estab-lish-ments | Em-ploy-ment | Payroll | | Sales, reven. ($ mil.) |
				Total ($ mil.)	Per Empl. ($)	
48-49	Transportation and warehousing	99	1,828	53.9	29,481	162.4
484	Truck transportation	71	1,136	39.5	34,783	117.7
4841	General freight trucking	28	815	29.4	36,048	80.0
48412	General freight trucking, long-distance	22	800	29.1	36,369	78.5
484121	General freight trucking, long-distance, truckload (tl)	16	146	3.1	21,363	12.7
4842	Specialized freight trucking	43	321	10.1	31,570	37.7
484220	Specialized freight (except used goods) trucking, local	21	56	1.4	24,786	7.7
484230	Specialized freight (except used goods) trucking, long-distance	16	138	5.6	40,399	20.1
4842302	Agricultural products trucking, long-distance	11	50	1.0	19,900	5.7
485	Transit and ground passenger transportation	8	117	1.0	8,231	2.5
488	Support activities for transportation	7	42	1.3	30,500	3.3

Sources: Economic Census of the United States, 1997. Only those industries are shown for which both employment and sales/revenue data were available. For the definition of MSAs, CMSAs, and PMSAs, please see the Introduction.

BOISE CITY, ID MSA

| NAICS | Industry | Estab-lish-ments | Em-ploy-ment | Payroll | | Sales, reven. ($ mil.) |
				Total ($ mil.)	Per Empl. ($)	
48-49	Transportation and warehousing	366	3,767	88.5	23,487	332.8
48121	Nonscheduled air transportation	11	106	4.3	40,340	13.9
484	Truck transportation	234	2,043	54.8	26,817	200.5
4841	General freight trucking	126	1,159	33.9	29,232	118.9
484110	General freight trucking, local	25	182	4.8	26,505	12.7
4841101	General freight trucking without storage, local, truckload (tl)	19	91	2.2	23,714	7.2
48412	General freight trucking, long-distance	101	977	29.1	29,740	106.2
484121	General freight trucking, long-distance, truckload (tl)	84	525	17.0	32,425	67.5
484122	General freight trucking, long-distance, less than truckload (ltl)	17	452	12.0	26,622	38.6
4842	Specialized freight trucking	108	884	20.9	23,650	81.6
484210	Used household and office goods moving	16	245	5.4	22,061	16.7
484220	Specialized freight (except used goods) trucking, local	51	145	3.1	21,710	13.9
4842202	Agricultural products trucking without storage, local	19	54	1.0	18,333	5.0
4842203	Dump trucking	13	43	1.1	24,744	5.4
484230	Specialized freight (except used goods) trucking, long-distance	41	494	12.4	25,008	51.1
4842302	Agricultural products trucking, long-distance	18	143	2.9	20,601	15.0
4842303	Other specialized trucking, long-distance	17	316	8.6	27,291	34.5
485	Transit and ground passenger transportation	24	668	8.1	12,067	18.6
488	Support activities for transportation	51	363	7.3	20,094	29.2
4881	Support activities for air transportation	17	213	2.7	12,822	10.5
488410	Motor vehicle towing	14	47	1.0	20,574	3.7
488510	Freight transportation arrangement	17	98	3.5	36,041	14.5
4885102	Arrangement of transportation of freight and cargo	12	63	2.6	41,508	11.6
492	Couriers and messengers	27	374	7.5	19,984	26.8
492110	Couriers	13	250	6.1	24,328	23.6
492210	Local messengers and local delivery	14	124	1.4	11,226	3.2

Sources: Economic Census of the United States, 1997. Only those industries are shown for which both employment and sales/revenue data were available. For the definition of MSAs, CMSAs, and PMSAs, please see the Introduction.

BOSTON, MA—NH PMSA

NAICS	Industry	Estab-lish-ments	Em-ploy-ment	Payroll		Sales, reven. ($ mil.)
				Total ($ mil.)	Per Empl. ($)	
48-49	Transportation and warehousing	1,799	32,381	885.5	27,347	3,066.2
481	Air transportation	53	615	21.9	35,543	321.9
48111	Scheduled air transportation	41	462	16.2	35,050	286.2
48121	Nonscheduled air transportation	12	153	5.7	37,033	35.7
484	Truck transportation	707	8,080	244.2	30,225	797.7
4841	General freight trucking	238	3,163	113.8	35,968	336.1
484110	General freight trucking, local	132	984	29.7	30,172	89.3
4841101	General freight trucking without storage, local, truckload (tl)	71	437	15.0	34,272	45.2
4841102	General freight trucking without storage, local, less than truckload (ltl)	54	345	11.3	32,617	33.5
48412	General freight trucking, long-distance	106	2,179	84.1	38,586	246.8
484121	General freight trucking, long-distance, truckload (tl)	75	1,051	37.0	35,168	114.3
484122	General freight trucking, long-distance, less than truckload (ltl)	31	1,128	47.1	41,770	132.5
4842	Specialized freight trucking	469	4,917	130.5	26,531	461.6
484210	Used household and office goods moving	148	1,988	52.2	26,238	142.2
4842101	Used household and office goods moving, local, without storage	67	568	9.6	16,903	32.7
4842102	Used household and office goods moving, long-distance	38	711	19.3	27,155	59.6
4842103	Used household and office goods moving, local, with storage	43	709	23.3	32,797	49.8
484220	Specialized freight (except used goods) trucking, local	253	1,508	36.5	24,229	198.9
4842201	Hazardous materials trucking (except waste), local	21	99	3.4	34,253	13.1
4842202	Agricultural products trucking without storage, local	11	23	0.6	27,826	3.3
4842203	Dump trucking	131	409	16.1	39,262	79.1
4842204	Specialized trucking without storage, local	86	963	15.9	16,549	101.6
484230	Specialized freight (except used goods) trucking, long-distance	68	1,421	41.8	29,385	120.5
4842303	Other specialized trucking, long-distance	58	1,362	39.7	29,145	114.2
485	Transit and ground passenger transportation	331	7,574	129.9	17,151	311.9
485113	Bus and motor vehicle transit systems	14	269	4.1	15,260	10.3
4853	Taxi and limousine service	169	2,292	43.9	19,137	98.8
485310	Taxi service	102	993	16.6	16,756	43.7
485320	Limousine service	67	1,299	27.2	20,957	55.1
485410	School and employee bus transportation	60	2,599	34.6	13,306	80.1
485510	Charter bus industry	15	780	17.3	22,144	49.4
48599	Other transit and ground passenger transportation	65	1,316	22.4	17,040	55.9
485991	Special needs transportation	46	1,115	17.1	15,375	37.0
485999	All other transit and ground passenger transportation	19	201	5.3	26,274	18.9
487210	Scenic and sightseeing transportation, water	26	198	5.5	27,611	22.3
488	Support activities for transportation	377	3,816	118.7	31,099	373.2
4881	Support activities for air transportation	24	782	18.0	23,073	52.7
488410	Motor vehicle towing	80	414	8.1	19,606	29.0
488510	Freight transportation arrangement	242	2,144	82.9	38,661	266.2
4885101	Freight forwarding	126	1,412	56.1	39,712	181.7
4885102	Arrangement of transportation of freight and cargo	116	732	26.8	36,633	84.5
492110	Couriers	106	8,928	261.4	29,278	691.3
4921101	Courier services (except by air)	51	5,660	157.3	27,796	342.9
4921102	Air courier services	55	3,268	104.1	31,844	348.4
4931	Warehousing and storage	90	1,363	42.5	31,216	152.2
4931101	General warehousing and storage (except in foreign trade zones)	62	910	27.6	30,297	97.3
4931201	Refrigerated products warehousing	14	207	7.7	37,184	28.8

Sources: *Economic Census of the United States*, 1997. Only those industries are shown for which both employment and sales/revenue data were available. For the definition of MSAs, CMSAs, and PMSAs, please see the Introduction.

BOSTON—WORCESTER—LAWRENCE, MA—NH—ME—CT CMSA

NAICS	Industry	Estab-lish-ments	Em-ploy-ment	Payroll		Sales, reven. ($ mil.)
				Total ($ mil.)	Per Empl. ($)	
48-49	Transportation and warehousing	3,060	55,077	1,448.7	26,303	4,722.6
48111	Scheduled air transportation	46	486	17.2	35,432	290.0
484	Truck transportation	1,406	14,945	472.0	31,583	1,596.9
4841	General freight trucking	531	7,134	253.0	35,466	810.0
484122	General freight trucking, long-distance, less than truckload (ltl)	95	3,166	127.4	40,236	412.4
4842	Specialized freight trucking	875	7,811	219.0	28,038	786.9
4842101	Used household and office goods moving, local, without storage	110	776	15.0	19,302	49.1
484220	Specialized freight (except used goods) trucking, local	486	2,572	66.5	25,860	338.3
48599	Other transit and ground passenger transportation	111	2,429	39.6	16,304	92.2
488	Support activities for transportation	526	4,856	148.7	30,622	469.5
4921101	Courier services (except by air)	76	10,595	300.5	28,363	644.6

Sources: *Economic Census of the United States*, 1997. Only those industries are shown for which both employment and sales/revenue data were available. For the definition of MSAs, CMSAs, and PMSAs, please see the Introduction.

BOULDER—LONGMONT, CO PMSA

| NAICS | Industry | Estab-lish-ments | Em-ploy-ment | Payroll | | Sales, reven. ($ mil.) |
				Total ($ mil.)	Per Empl. ($)	
48-49	Transportation and warehousing	100	1,387	27.5	19,795	118.1
481	Air transportation	5	22	0.9	42,500	3.3
484	Truck transportation	41	291	8.5	29,096	35.1
4841	General freight trucking	12	73	2.4	32,205	11.6
4842	Specialized freight trucking	29	218	6.1	28,055	23.6
484210	Used household and office goods moving	16	164	4.4	26,659	15.3
485	Transit and ground passenger transportation	7	361	5.1	14,205	14.1
488	Support activities for transportation	29	469	7.5	15,972	42.6
492	Couriers and messengers	13	237	5.3	22,435	22.3

Sources: Economic Census of the United States, 1997. Only those industries are shown for which both employment and sales/revenue data were available. For the definition of MSAs, CMSAs, and PMSAs, please see the Introduction.

BRAZORIA, TX PMSA

| NAICS | Industry | Estab-lish-ments | Em-ploy-ment | Payroll | | Sales, reven. ($ mil.) |
				Total ($ mil.)	Per Empl. ($)	
48-49	Transportation and warehousing	132	1,613	45.8	28,383	223.6
481	Air transportation	7	82	2.2	27,220	11.6
483	Water transportation	5	144	3.4	23,646	9.1
484	Truck transportation	75	1,065	30.6	28,709	105.9
4841	General freight trucking	28	387	10.8	27,840	27.9
484110	General freight trucking, local	14	89	1.9	21,854	7.9
48412	General freight trucking, long-distance	14	298	8.8	29,628	20.0
4842	Specialized freight trucking	47	678	19.8	29,205	78.1
484220	Specialized freight (except used goods) trucking, local	18	139	4.7	34,115	17.5
4842203	Dump trucking	12	96	3.5	36,302	13.3
484230	Specialized freight (except used goods) trucking, long-distance	21	458	13.8	30,068	57.7
488	Support activities for transportation	24	228	6.3	27,654	18.4

Sources: Economic Census of the United States, 1997. Only those industries are shown for which both employment and sales/revenue data were available. For the definition of MSAs, CMSAs, and PMSAs, please see the Introduction.

BREMERTON, WA PMSA

| NAICS | Industry | Estab-lish-ments | Em-ploy-ment | Payroll | | Sales, reven. ($ mil.) |
				Total ($ mil.)	Per Empl. ($)	
48-49	Transportation and warehousing	95	909	19.3	21,260	58.6
484	Truck transportation	48	321	7.4	23,056	23.2
4841	General freight trucking	12	35	1.5	42,114	3.9
4842	Specialized freight trucking	36	286	5.9	20,724	19.3
484210	Used household and office goods moving	19	230	4.2	18,391	13.0
484220	Specialized freight (except used goods) trucking, local	13	53	1.6	30,094	5.9
488	Support activities for transportation	21	111	2.6	23,072	7.3

Sources: Economic Census of the United States, 1997. Only those industries are shown for which both employment and sales/revenue data were available. For the definition of MSAs, CMSAs, and PMSAs, please see the Introduction.

BRIDGEPORT, CT PMSA

| NAICS | Industry | Estab-lish-ments | Em-ploy-ment | Payroll | | Sales, reven. ($ mil.) |
				Total ($ mil.)	Per Empl. ($)	
48-49	Transportation and warehousing	161	2,866	84.8	29,572	401.2
484	Truck transportation	72	1,115	36.7	32,946	104.9
4841	General freight trucking	29	600	21.5	35,750	41.6
48412	General freight trucking, long-distance	20	526	20.1	38,156	38.0
4842	Specialized freight trucking	43	515	15.3	29,680	63.3
484210	Used household and office goods moving	20	438	12.9	29,557	54.1
484220	Specialized freight (except used goods) trucking, local	20	56	1.6	29,232	7.0
4842203	Dump trucking	12	41	1.2	30,366	4.3
485	Transit and ground passenger transportation	36	1,068	16.3	15,219	41.7
4853	Taxi and limousine service	19	218	3.8	17,638	10.2
485320	Limousine service	13	169	3.1	18,130	8.0
4854101	School bus service	11	723	10.0	13,780	25.3
488510	Freight transportation arrangement	17	58	2.8	48,155	10.7
4885102	Arrangement of transportation of freight and cargo	13	45	2.4	52,311	9.2

Sources: *Economic Census of the United States*, 1997. Only those industries are shown for which both employment and sales/revenue data were available. For the definition of MSAs, CMSAs, and PMSAs, please see the Introduction.

BROCKTON, MA PMSA

| NAICS | Industry | Estab-lish-ments | Em-ploy-ment | Payroll | | Sales, reven. ($ mil.) |
				Total ($ mil.)	Per Empl. ($)	
48-49	Transportation and warehousing	172	2,396	60.5	25,267	238.6
484	Truck transportation	110	1,238	40.8	32,969	167.0
4841	General freight trucking	46	854	28.4	33,200	108.0
484110	General freight trucking, local	17	200	6.3	31,575	18.7
48412	General freight trucking, long-distance	29	654	22.0	33,697	89.3
484121	General freight trucking, long-distance, truckload (tl)	14	217	6.4	29,424	33.1
484122	General freight trucking, long-distance, less than truckload (ltl)	15	437	15.7	35,819	56.2
4842	Specialized freight trucking	64	384	12.5	32,456	59.0
484210	Used household and office goods moving	16	70	2.1	29,386	5.8
484220	Specialized freight (except used goods) trucking, local	38	193	6.0	31,083	33.9
4842203	Dump trucking	25	76	2.0	26,105	7.8
485	Transit and ground passenger transportation	28	791	9.3	11,736	22.8
4854101	School bus service	14	494	5.8	11,836	13.9

Sources: *Economic Census of the United States*, 1997. Only those industries are shown for which both employment and sales/revenue data were available. For the definition of MSAs, CMSAs, and PMSAs, please see the Introduction.

BROWNSVILLE—HARLINGEN—SAN BENITO, TX MSA

| NAICS | Industry | Estab-lish-ments | Em-ploy-ment | Payroll | | Sales, reven. ($ mil.) |
				Total ($ mil.)	Per Empl. ($)	
48-49	Transportation and warehousing	284	2,784	58.5	21,028	250.2
481	Air transportation	5	12	0.4	33,083	8.5
484	Truck transportation	142	948	21.9	23,062	115.4
4841	General freight trucking	94	748	18.3	24,516	93.5
484110	General freight trucking, local	18	79	1.5	19,468	6.2
4841101	General freight trucking without storage, local, truckload (tl)	13	34	0.6	17,029	3.7
48412	General freight trucking, long-distance	76	669	16.8	25,112	87.2
484121	General freight trucking, long-distance, truckload (tl)	62	475	12.1	25,396	64.6
484122	General freight trucking, long-distance, less than truckload (ltl)	14	194	4.7	24,418	22.7
4842	Specialized freight trucking	48	200	3.5	17,625	22.0
484220	Specialized freight (except used goods) trucking, local	24	72	1.1	15,847	6.6
484230	Specialized freight (except used goods) trucking, long-distance	15	66	1.8	26,985	13.0
485	Transit and ground passenger transportation	8	163	3.0	18,699	12.2
488	Support activities for transportation	93	1,217	23.3	19,118	67.4
4883	Support activities for water transportation	12	298	6.2	20,681	16.7
488510	Freight transportation arrangement	63	694	13.4	19,350	38.3
4885101	Freight forwarding	26	189	2.7	14,397	10.0
4885102	Arrangement of transportation of freight and cargo	37	505	10.7	21,204	28.3
492	Couriers and messengers	10	182	4.8	26,478	27.6
4931	Warehousing and storage	17	216	4.0	18,440	14.8

Sources: *Economic Census of the United States*, 1997. Only those industries are shown for which both employment and sales/revenue data were available. For the definition of MSAs, CMSAs, and PMSAs, please see the Introduction.

BRYAN—COLLEGE STATION, TX MSA

NAICS	Industry	Estab-lish-ments	Em-ploy-ment	Payroll		Sales, reven. ($ mil.)
				Total ($ mil.)	Per Empl. ($)	
48-49	Transportation and warehousing	59	418	7.3	17,373	26.1
484	Truck transportation	36	309	4.5	14,450	16.5
4841	General freight trucking	15	216	2.9	13,509	10.8
4842	Specialized freight trucking	21	93	1.5	16,634	5.7
484220	Specialized freight (except used goods) trucking, local	13	54	0.9	15,852	3.3
492	Couriers and messengers	4	41	1.3	31,951	3.9

Sources: Economic Census of the United States, 1997. Only those industries are shown for which both employment and sales/revenue data were available. For the definition of MSAs, CMSAs, and PMSAs, please see the Introduction.

BUFFALO—NIAGARA FALLS, NY MSA

NAICS	Industry	Estab-lish-ments	Em-ploy-ment	Payroll		Sales, reven. ($ mil.)
				Total ($ mil.)	Per Empl. ($)	
48-49	Transportation and warehousing	653	13,926	369.8	26,552	1,130.7
484	Truck transportation	325	4,511	148.2	32,843	461.5
4841	General freight trucking	142	2,747	96.4	35,110	277.4
484110	General freight trucking, local	51	406	9.6	23,613	34.8
4841101	General freight trucking without storage, local, truckload (tl)	29	245	6.4	26,102	24.4
4841102	General freight trucking without storage, local, less than truckload (ltl)	19	130	2.5	18,938	7.2
48412	General freight trucking, long-distance	91	2,341	86.9	37,104	242.6
484121	General freight trucking, long-distance, truckload (tl)	64	756	19.3	25,581	81.4
484122	General freight trucking, long-distance, less than truckload (ltl)	27	1,585	67.5	42,600	161.1
4842	Specialized freight trucking	183	1,764	51.7	29,312	184.1
484210	Used household and office goods moving	33	376	8.5	22,585	23.6
4842101	Used household and office goods moving, local, without storage	16	107	2.6	24,140	6.5
4842102	Used household and office goods moving, long-distance	13	218	4.8	22,170	14.2
484220	Specialized freight (except used goods) trucking, local	110	692	19.2	27,736	73.1
4842203	Dump trucking	64	422	13.0	30,742	49.0
4842204	Specialized trucking without storage, local	32	129	2.6	20,217	13.3
484230	Specialized freight (except used goods) trucking, long-distance	40	696	24.0	34,514	87.4
4842303	Other specialized trucking, long-distance	24	548	19.2	35,078	71.8
485	Transit and ground passenger transportation	92	3,336	38.3	11,477	100.3
4853	Taxi and limousine service	38	253	2.1	8,146	6.1
485310	Taxi service	15	165	1.6	9,703	3.9
485320	Limousine service	23	88	0.5	5,227	2.2
48599	Other transit and ground passenger transportation	16	440	6.1	13,770	12.5
488	Support activities for transportation	129	1,861	53.7	28,844	153.2
488410	Motor vehicle towing	15	99	2.0	19,848	4.9
488510	Freight transportation arrangement	93	1,290	40.2	31,130	111.4
4885101	Freight forwarding	27	328	10.9	33,299	33.4
4885102	Arrangement of transportation of freight and cargo	66	962	29.2	30,391	77.9
492	Couriers and messengers	41	3,092	83.1	26,863	216.5
492110	Couriers	13	2,855	79.2	27,746	204.4
492210	Local messengers and local delivery	28	237	3.8	16,224	12.0
4931	Warehousing and storage	40	572	12.8	22,404	44.9
493110	General warehousing and storage	25	372	7.5	20,153	25.4

Sources: Economic Census of the United States, 1997. Only those industries are shown for which both employment and sales/revenue data were available. For the definition of MSAs, CMSAs, and PMSAs, please see the Introduction.

BURLINGTON, VT MSA

NAICS	Industry	Estab-lish-ments	Em-ploy-ment	Payroll		Sales, reven. ($ mil.)
				Total ($ mil.)	Per Empl. ($)	
48-49	Transportation and warehousing	110	1,850	40.2	21,742	133.2
484	Truck transportation	57	743	21.2	28,520	66.9
4841	General freight trucking	25	514	14.9	28,934	46.2
484122	General freight trucking, long-distance, less than truckload (ltl)	13	363	10.4	28,565	30.9
4842	Specialized freight trucking	32	229	6.3	27,590	20.6
484220	Specialized freight (except used goods) trucking, local	20	79	2.3	29,405	9.6
485	Transit and ground passenger transportation	15	360	6.5	17,936	15.4
488	Support activities for transportation	10	44	1.0	21,795	3.2
492	Couriers and messengers	17	564	8.0	14,234	37.1
492110	Couriers	12	551	7.8	14,232	36.5

Sources: Economic Census of the United States, 1997. Only those industries are shown for which both employment and sales/revenue data were available. For the definition of MSAs, CMSAs, and PMSAs, please see the Introduction.

CANTON—MASSILLON, OH MSA

NAICS	Industry	Estab-lish-ments	Em-ploy-ment	Payroll Total ($ mil.)	Payroll Per Empl. ($)	Sales, reven. ($ mil.)
48-49	Transportation and warehousing	218	2,690	58.0	21,558	224.3
484	Truck transportation	175	2,240	48.5	21,658	200.0
4841	General freight trucking	72	774	21.9	28,345	107.3
484110	General freight trucking, local	22	125	2.6	20,992	9.8
4841101	General freight trucking without storage, local, truckload (tl)	18	102	2.2	21,686	8.7
48412	General freight trucking, long-distance	50	649	19.3	29,761	97.5
484121	General freight trucking, long-distance, truckload (tl)	39	527	14.5	27,596	77.0
484122	General freight trucking, long-distance, less than truckload (ltl)	11	122	4.8	39,115	20.5
4842	Specialized freight trucking	103	1,466	26.6	18,128	92.8
484210	Used household and office goods moving	14	99	2.4	23,879	7.1
484220	Specialized freight (except used goods) trucking, local	71	310	6.2	19,900	27.5
4842203	Dump trucking	41	153	3.1	20,144	17.7
4842204	Specialized trucking without storage, local	14	96	1.7	17,437	4.8
484230	Specialized freight (except used goods) trucking, long-distance	18	1,057	18.0	17,069	58.2
4842303	Other specialized trucking, long-distance	14	471	6.3	13,278	26.9
485	Transit and ground passenger transportation	7	63	0.5	7,698	1.4
488	Support activities for transportation	22	87	1.6	17,931	4.8
492	Couriers and messengers	4	108	2.7	24,741	6.8

Sources: *Economic Census of the United States,* 1997. Only those industries are shown for which both employment and sales/revenue data were available. For the definition of MSAs, CMSAs, and PMSAs, please see the Introduction.

CASPER, WY MSA

NAICS	Industry	Estab-lish-ments	Em-ploy-ment	Payroll Total ($ mil.)	Payroll Per Empl. ($)	Sales, reven. ($ mil.)
48-49	Transportation and warehousing	82	824	23.0	27,900	120.4
481	Air transportation	3	50	1.1	21,260	5.8
484	Truck transportation	55	466	11.9	25,532	50.0
4841	General freight trucking	23	198	4.7	23,778	23.7
484121	General freight trucking, long-distance, truckload (tl)	18	166	4.2	25,452	20.1
4842	Specialized freight trucking	32	268	7.2	26,828	26.3
484220	Specialized freight (except used goods) trucking, local	12	55	1.3	22,800	5.8
484230	Specialized freight (except used goods) trucking, long-distance	14	172	4.9	28,477	17.4
486	Pipeline transportation	7	184	8.0	43,429	59.1
488	Support activities for transportation	4	17	0.2	13,706	0.7
492	Couriers and messengers	7	70	1.4	20,571	3.8

Sources: *Economic Census of the United States,* 1997. Only those industries are shown for which both employment and sales/revenue data were available. For the definition of MSAs, CMSAs, and PMSAs, please see the Introduction.

CEDAR RAPIDS, IA MSA

NAICS	Industry	Estab-lish-ments	Em-ploy-ment	Payroll Total ($ mil.)	Payroll Per Empl. ($)	Sales, reven. ($ mil.)
48-49	Transportation and warehousing	169	2,597	72.7	28,010	407.4
484	Truck transportation	109	1,938	55.8	28,807	324.8
4841	General freight trucking	66	1,161	34.0	29,252	245.1
484110	General freight trucking, local	13	173	4.1	23,428	9.8
48412	General freight trucking, long-distance	53	988	29.9	30,272	235.3
484121	General freight trucking, long-distance, truckload (tl)	40	716	20.2	28,230	203.8
484122	General freight trucking, long-distance, less than truckload (ltl)	13	272	9.7	35,647	31.5
4842	Specialized freight trucking	43	777	21.9	28,142	79.7
484220	Specialized freight (except used goods) trucking, local	22	85	2.3	27,424	7.6
484230	Specialized freight (except used goods) trucking, long-distance	12	86	2.5	29,593	11.4
488	Support activities for transportation	22	162	4.9	30,130	34.3
488510	Freight transportation arrangement	13	54	2.0	36,130	20.3
492110	Couriers	11	178	4.5	25,084	23.8
493	Warehousing and storage	6	147	3.8	25,762	11.0

Sources: *Economic Census of the United States,* 1997. Only those industries are shown for which both employment and sales/revenue data were available. For the definition of MSAs, CMSAs, and PMSAs, please see the Introduction.

CHAMPAIGN—URBANA, IL MSA

NAICS	Industry	Estab-lish-ments	Em-ploy-ment	Payroll		Sales, reven. ($ mil.)
				Total ($ mil.)	Per Empl. ($)	
48-49	Transportation and warehousing	94	1,723	46.3	26,876	220.1
484	Truck transportation	64	1,290	38.3	29,664	192.4
4841	General freight trucking	37	1,135	33.5	29,528	174.9
484110	General freight trucking, local	12	70	1.9	26,757	4.9
48412	General freight trucking, long-distance	25	1,065	31.6	29,710	170.0
484121	General freight trucking, long-distance, truckload (tl)	21	1,038	31.0	29,819	167.7
4842	Specialized freight trucking	27	155	4.8	30,665	17.5
484220	Specialized freight (except used goods) trucking, local	14	25	0.6	23,720	3.9
485	Transit and ground passenger transportation	9	178	2.3	12,787	4.7
488	Support activities for transportation	10	142	3.2	22,268	8.9
492	Couriers and messengers	6	77	2.0	25,883	8.3

Sources: Economic Census of the United States, 1997. Only those industries are shown for which both employment and sales/revenue data were available. For the definition of MSAs, CMSAs, and PMSAs, please see the Introduction.

CHARLESTON, WV MSA

NAICS	Industry	Estab-lish-ments	Em-ploy-ment	Payroll		Sales, reven. ($ mil.)
				Total ($ mil.)	Per Empl. ($)	
48-49	Transportation and warehousing	190	3,438	121.5	35,351	637.4
484	Truck transportation	116	1,423	41.6	29,220	157.5
4841	General freight trucking	42	662	21.6	32,687	49.7
484110	General freight trucking, local	19	209	7.1	33,761	14.1
48412	General freight trucking, long-distance	23	453	14.6	32,192	35.6
484121	General freight trucking, long-distance, truckload (tl)	14	142	4.9	34,204	11.0
4842	Specialized freight trucking	74	761	19.9	26,204	107.8
484220	Specialized freight (except used goods) trucking, local	40	344	7.9	22,933	35.2
4842203	Dump trucking	24	201	4.4	22,070	22.4
484230	Specialized freight (except used goods) trucking, long-distance	26	340	10.2	30,018	67.9
4842301	Hazardous materials trucking (except waste), long-distance	16	187	5.4	28,995	35.0
486210	Pipeline transportation of natural gas	19	1,197	60.8	50,809	401.4
488	Support activities for transportation	23	183	4.0	21,623	21.3
492	Couriers and messengers	16	379	6.5	17,053	26.0
493	Warehousing and storage	4	26	0.8	29,192	3.5

Sources: Economic Census of the United States, 1997. Only those industries are shown for which both employment and sales/revenue data were available. For the definition of MSAs, CMSAs, and PMSAs, please see the Introduction.

CHARLESTON—NORTH CHARLESTON, SC MSA

NAICS	Industry	Estab-lish-ments	Em-ploy-ment	Payroll		Sales, reven. ($ mil.)
				Total ($ mil.)	Per Empl. ($)	
48-49	Transportation and warehousing	478	8,412	191.6	22,773	725.9
484	Truck transportation	216	2,325	64.1	27,588	236.7
4841	General freight trucking	122	1,564	45.1	28,865	155.9
484110	General freight trucking, local	30	132	2.8	21,311	20.2
4841101	General freight trucking without storage, local, truckload (tl)	25	95	2.3	24,021	19.0
48412	General freight trucking, long-distance	92	1,432	42.3	29,561	135.6
484121	General freight trucking, long-distance, truckload (tl)	70	951	27.0	28,331	90.3
484122	General freight trucking, long-distance, less than truckload (ltl)	22	481	15.4	31,954	45.4
4842	Specialized freight trucking	94	761	19.0	24,965	80.8
484210	Used household and office goods moving	20	255	4.1	16,271	11.3
484220	Specialized freight (except used goods) trucking, local	44	325	9.5	29,274	46.6
4842203	Dump trucking	25	244	7.1	29,164	34.8
4842204	Specialized trucking without storage, local	13	56	1.3	23,607	6.5
484230	Specialized freight (except used goods) trucking, long-distance	30	181	5.3	29,475	22.8
4842303	Other specialized trucking, long-distance	17	58	1.5	25,448	6.8
488	Support activities for transportation	152	4,233	91.3	21,573	252.4
4883	Support activities for water transportation	28	2,815	50.0	17,766	114.7
488320	Marine cargo handling	11	2,622	45.6	17,373	99.3
488410	Motor vehicle towing	22	101	1.3	13,347	6.0
488510	Freight transportation arrangement	82	839	28.1	33,510	75.7
4885101	Freight forwarding	31	192	6.1	31,719	17.7
4885102	Arrangement of transportation of freight and cargo	51	647	22.0	34,042	58.0
4931	Warehousing and storage	27	533	13.2	24,690	45.5
4931101	General warehousing and storage (except in foreign trade zones)	21	457	10.9	23,897	34.8

Sources: Economic Census of the United States, 1997. Only those industries are shown for which both employment and sales/revenue data were available. For the definition of MSAs, CMSAs, and PMSAs, please see the Introduction.

CHARLOTTE—GASTONIA—ROCK HILL, NC—SC MSA

NAICS	Industry	Estab-lish-ments	Em-ploy-ment	Payroll		Sales, reven. ($ mil.)
				Total ($ mil.)	Per Empl. ($)	
48-49	Transportation and warehousing	970	24,744	714.0	28,855	2,117.4
481	Air transportation	25	930	31.1	33,468	179.4
48111	Scheduled air transportation	12	830	27.6	33,216	160.5
48121	Nonscheduled air transportation	13	100	3.6	35,560	18.9
484	Truck transportation	559	13,464	417.2	30,988	1,149.7
4841	General freight trucking	296	10,987	345.5	31,443	892.3
484110	General freight trucking, local	86	723	14.3	19,740	58.5
4841101	General freight trucking without storage, local, truckload (tl)	60	243	6.5	26,741	43.0
4841102	General freight trucking without storage, local, less than truckload (ltl)	20	287	3.9	13,498	6.0
48412	General freight trucking, long-distance	210	10,264	331.2	32,267	833.8
484121	General freight trucking, long-distance, truckload (tl)	167	4,322	124.0	28,698	437.1
484122	General freight trucking, long-distance, less than truckload (ltl)	43	5,942	207.2	34,864	396.7
4842	Specialized freight trucking	263	2,477	71.8	28,972	257.4
484210	Used household and office goods moving	53	729	18.9	25,883	57.9
4842101	Used household and office goods moving, local, without storage	20	100	1.8	18,370	4.6
4842102	Used household and office goods moving, long-distance	22	514	14.4	27,918	45.5
4842103	Used household and office goods moving, local, with storage	11	115	2.7	23,322	7.8
484220	Specialized freight (except used goods) trucking, local	148	1,049	29.2	27,794	94.5
4842203	Dump trucking	93	836	23.1	27,609	72.0
4842204	Specialized trucking without storage, local	30	96	2.5	26,302	9.6
484230	Specialized freight (except used goods) trucking, long-distance	62	699	23.7	33,960	105.1
4842301	Hazardous materials trucking (except waste), long-distance	15	172	6.1	35,174	17.5
4842303	Other specialized trucking, long-distance	37	484	16.6	34,395	83.0
4853	Taxi and limousine service	19	217	2.1	9,567	5.3
485510	Charter bus industry	13	137	2.1	15,672	7.6
486	Pipeline transportation	6	25	1.1	43,120	18.1
488	Support activities for transportation	195	1,794	50.2	28,004	168.2
4881	Support activities for air transportation	18	410	7.3	17,893	29.5
488410	Motor vehicle towing	37	248	5.6	22,710	17.2
488510	Freight transportation arrangement	127	982	33.8	34,398	109.6
4885101	Freight forwarding	61	590	22.3	37,829	68.4
4885102	Arrangement of transportation of freight and cargo	66	392	11.5	29,235	41.2
492	Couriers and messengers	74	7,156	182.9	25,558	452.7
492110	Couriers	44	6,816	178.0	26,114	438.7
4921101	Courier services (except by air)	23	5,992	154.0	25,694	335.1
4921102	Air courier services	21	824	24.0	29,169	103.6
492210	Local messengers and local delivery	30	340	4.9	14,412	14.1
4931	Warehousing and storage	57	929	24.1	25,934	74.0
4931101	General warehousing and storage (except in foreign trade zones)	42	792	19.7	24,814	59.3

Sources: *Economic Census of the United States*, 1997. Only those industries are shown for which both employment and sales/revenue data were available. For the definition of MSAs, CMSAs, and PMSAs, please see the Introduction.

CHARLOTTESVILLE, VA MSA

NAICS	Industry	Estab-lish-ments	Em-ploy-ment	Payroll		Sales, reven. ($ mil.)
				Total ($ mil.)	Per Empl. ($)	
48-49	Transportation and warehousing	79	609	17.3	28,391	69.3
484	Truck transportation	53	276	7.0	25,297	23.9
4841	General freight trucking	15	93	3.0	31,839	11.4
4842	Specialized freight trucking	38	183	4.0	21,973	12.5
484220	Specialized freight (except used goods) trucking, local	28	68	1.3	18,676	6.4
4842203	Dump trucking	22	49	1.0	19,776	4.3
492	Couriers and messengers	6	135	3.4	25,119	5.8

Sources: *Economic Census of the United States*, 1997. Only those industries are shown for which both employment and sales/revenue data were available. For the definition of MSAs, CMSAs, and PMSAs, please see the Introduction.

CHATTANOOGA, TN—GA MSA

NAICS	Industry	Estab-lish-ments	Em-ploy-ment	Payroll		Sales, reven. ($ mil.)
				Total ($ mil.)	Per Empl. ($)	
48-49	Transportation and warehousing	288	7,215	203.2	28,157	578.5
484	Truck transportation	177	5,755	174.0	30,228	476.7
4841	General freight trucking	110	4,988	154.1	30,904	402.0
484110	General freight trucking, local	28	192	4.7	24,604	17.0
4841101	General freight trucking without storage, local, truckload (tl)	18	91	2.5	27,033	11.9
48412	General freight trucking, long-distance	82	4,796	149.4	31,156	385.0
484121	General freight trucking, long-distance, truckload (tl)	58	3,965	119.1	30,047	297.5
484122	General freight trucking, long-distance, less than truckload (ltl)	24	831	30.3	36,450	87.5
4842	Specialized freight trucking	67	767	19.8	25,832	74.6
484220	Specialized freight (except used goods) trucking, local	36	218	5.5	25,211	26.7
4842203	Dump trucking	30	160	4.3	26,906	22.1
484230	Specialized freight (except used goods) trucking, long-distance	23	401	10.8	26,970	36.5
4842303	Other specialized trucking, long-distance	12	175	5.0	28,811	16.4
485	Transit and ground passenger transportation	16	125	1.8	14,112	4.8
487	Scenic and sightseeing transportation	3	58	0.7	11,724	3.7
488	Support activities for transportation	46	263	6.0	22,787	16.1
488410	Motor vehicle towing	14	103	3.0	28,913	8.6
488510	Freight transportation arrangement	19	65	1.5	22,692	3.8
4885102	Arrangement of transportation of freight and cargo	11	39	0.8	21,051	2.4
492	Couriers and messengers	28	549	8.1	14,843	32.3
492110	Couriers	11	384	5.7	14,956	25.3
492210	Local messengers and local delivery	17	165	2.4	14,582	7.0
493	Warehousing and storage	9	361	9.1	25,141	25.8

Sources: *Economic Census of the United States*, 1997. Only those industries are shown for which both employment and sales/revenue data were available. For the definition of MSAs, CMSAs, and PMSAs, please see the Introduction.

CHEYENNE, WY MSA

NAICS	Industry	Estab-lish-ments	Em-ploy-ment	Payroll		Sales, reven. ($ mil.)
				Total ($ mil.)	Per Empl. ($)	
48-49	Transportation and warehousing	72	697	17.8	25,577	68.7
484	Truck transportation	50	542	13.2	24,277	44.8
4841	General freight trucking	24	282	7.3	25,936	20.9
48412	General freight trucking, long-distance	18	241	7.1	29,286	19.9
484121	General freight trucking, long-distance, truckload (tl)	13	225	6.7	29,689	17.7
4842	Specialized freight trucking	26	260	5.8	22,477	23.8
484230	Specialized freight (except used goods) trucking, long-distance	13	120	3.4	28,175	15.6
488	Support activities for transportation	10	48	0.9	18,417	2.9
492	Couriers and messengers	4	30	0.7	22,200	1.4

Sources: *Economic Census of the United States*, 1997. Only those industries are shown for which both employment and sales/revenue data were available. For the definition of MSAs, CMSAs, and PMSAs, please see the Introduction.

CHICAGO, IL PMSA

NAICS	Industry	Estab-lish-ments	Em-ploy-ment	Payroll Total ($ mil.)	Payroll Per Empl. ($)	Sales, reven. ($ mil.)
48-49	Transportation and warehousing	5,187	108,148	3,134.0	28,979	11,401.5
481	Air transportation	100	1,676	60.8	36,293	865.9
48111	Scheduled air transportation	74	1,362	50.1	36,797	795.9
48121	Nonscheduled air transportation	26	314	10.7	34,108	70.1
481211	Nonscheduled chartered passenger air transportation	19	263	9.3	35,209	61.7
483	Water transportation	32	785	29.9	38,082	271.9
483111	Deep sea freight transportation	18	406	17.9	44,200	229.1
484	Truck transportation	2,727	38,083	1,375.0	36,106	4,877.0
4841	General freight trucking	1,356	26,258	968.8	36,897	2,747.1
484110	General freight trucking, local	755	7,692	242.2	31,491	742.4
4841101	General freight trucking without storage, local, truckload (tl)	451	4,124	136.0	32,976	468.5
4841102	General freight trucking without storage, local, less than truckload (ltl)	263	2,917	85.3	29,241	204.0
4841103	General freight trucking with storage, local, truckload (tl)	27	321	10.7	33,371	44.4
4841104	General freight trucking with storage, local, less than truckload (ltl)	14	330	10.2	30,997	25.5
48412	General freight trucking, long-distance	601	18,566	726.6	39,137	2,004.7
484121	General freight trucking, long-distance, truckload (tl)	426	6,773	247.3	36,513	868.3
484122	General freight trucking, long-distance, less than truckload (ltl)	175	11,793	479.3	40,644	1,136.4
4842	Specialized freight trucking	1,371	11,825	406.2	34,350	2,129.9
484210	Used household and office goods moving	296	4,423	135.3	30,582	1,081.0
4842102	Used household and office goods moving, long-distance	93	2,438	82.9	34,019	920.9
484220	Specialized freight (except used goods) trucking, local	872	4,760	165.4	34,744	652.2
4842201	Hazardous materials trucking (except waste), local	38	208	9.5	45,476	25.1
4842203	Dump trucking	505	2,013	76.2	37,858	346.1
4842205	Specialized trucking with storage, local	27	428	15.3	35,801	38.8
484230	Specialized freight (except used goods) trucking, long-distance	203	2,642	105.5	39,948	396.7
4842301	Hazardous materials trucking (except waste), long-distance	38	547	21.8	39,896	72.8
4842302	Agricultural products trucking, long-distance	29	145	3.9	26,600	15.3
4842303	Other specialized trucking, long-distance	136	1,950	79.9	40,955	308.6
485	Transit and ground passenger transportation	567	13,957	222.6	15,946	635.3
4853	Taxi and limousine service	324	2,194	48.9	22,294	185.1
485310	Taxi service	106	447	9.5	21,159	57.7
485320	Limousine service	218	1,747	39.5	22,584	127.3
485510	Charter bus industry	36	595	12.1	20,321	37.8
4855101	Charter bus service, local	15	281	5.1	18,128	16.4
4855102	Charter bus service, interstate/interurban	21	314	7.0	22,283	21.4
48599	Other transit and ground passenger transportation	68	1,617	30.4	18,808	75.2
485991	Special needs transportation	45	953	18.9	19,851	35.9
485999	All other transit and ground passenger transportation	23	664	11.5	17,312	39.3
486	Pipeline transportation	26	954	60.0	62,941	364.7
488	Support activities for transportation	1,166	15,431	539.1	34,938	1,780.8
4881	Support activities for air transportation	63	1,655	37.2	22,458	109.2
4881191	Airport operation and terminal services	28	1,133	21.0	18,503	64.0
488190	Other support activities for air transportation	35	522	16.2	31,042	45.2
4882101	Support activities incidental to rail transportation	54	2,084	64.2	30,811	325.1
488320	Marine cargo handling	13	392	17.2	43,878	55.7
488390	Other support activities for water transportation	16	90	2.8	31,344	13.4
4884	Support activities for road transportation	190	1,201	30.2	25,115	88.3
488410	Motor vehicle towing	179	1,139	27.1	23,773	77.5
488490	Other support activities for road transportation	11	62	3.1	49,758	10.9
488510	Freight transportation arrangement	782	9,518	372.7	39,159	1,145.1
4885101	Freight forwarding	365	5,502	211.2	38,379	688.8
4885102	Arrangement of transportation of freight and cargo	417	4,016	161.5	40,226	456.3
4931	Warehousing and storage	218	4,576	143.9	31,439	436.4
4931201	Refrigerated products warehousing	14	776	21.8	28,080	69.3

Sources: Economic Census of the United States, 1997. Only those industries are shown for which both employment and sales/revenue data were available. For the definition of MSAs, CMSAs, and PMSAs, please see the Introduction.

CHICAGO—GARY—KENOSHA, IL—IN—WI CMSA

NAICS	Industry	Estab-lish-ments	Em-ploy-ment	Payroll Total ($ mil.)	Per Empl. ($)	Sales, reven. ($ mil.)
48-49	Transportation and warehousing	5,791	118,565	3,412.9	28,785	12,593.7
483111	Deep sea freight transportation	18	406	17.9	44,200	229.1
484	Truck transportation	3,137	45,050	1,578.9	35,049	5,705.9
4841	General freight trucking	1,535	30,662	1,090.9	35,577	3,249.5
484110	General freight trucking, local	808	8,116	254.3	31,327	801.3
4841103	General freight trucking with storage, local, truckload (tl)	27	321	10.7	33,371	44.4
4841104	General freight trucking with storage, local, less than truckload (ltl)	14	330	10.2	30,997	25.5
48412	General freight trucking, long-distance	727	22,546	836.6	37,107	2,448.2
484121	General freight trucking, long-distance, truckload (tl)	535	10,202	336.4	32,976	1,247.9
484122	General freight trucking, long-distance, less than truckload (ltl)	192	12,344	500.2	40,521	1,200.2
4842	Specialized freight trucking	1,602	14,388	488.1	33,922	2,456.4
484210	Used household and office goods moving	324	4,842	149.6	30,899	1,110.2
4842102	Used household and office goods moving, long-distance	101	2,701	94.6	35,029	943.3
484220	Specialized freight (except used goods) trucking, local	1,004	5,788	196.6	33,970	757.0
4842203	Dump trucking	583	2,676	96.2	35,957	409.8
484230	Specialized freight (except used goods) trucking, long-distance	274	3,758	141.8	37,745	589.3
4859992	All other passenger transportation	11	40	1.1	26,650	2.4
486	Pipeline transportation	38	1,147	69.6	60,662	461.8
4882101	Support activities incidental to rail transportation	61	2,269	71.6	31,561	357.8
492	Couriers and messengers	348	32,357	691.9	21,382	2,150.7
492110	Couriers	151	29,882	633.6	21,204	1,997.1
492210	Local messengers and local delivery	197	2,475	58.2	23,533	153.6
493190	Other warehousing and storage	56	903	28.9	32,035	101.6

Sources: Economic Census of the United States, 1997. Only those industries are shown for which both employment and sales/revenue data were available. For the definition of MSAs, CMSAs, and PMSAs, please see the Introduction.

CHICO—PARADISE, CA MSA

NAICS	Industry	Estab-lish-ments	Em-ploy-ment	Payroll Total ($ mil.)	Per Empl. ($)	Sales, reven. ($ mil.)
48-49	Transportation and warehousing	80	975	17.7	18,199	73.0
484	Truck transportation	52	470	8.9	18,921	34.1
4841	General freight trucking	16	186	5.6	30,317	20.6
48412	General freight trucking, long-distance	11	130	3.9	30,169	15.4
4842	Specialized freight trucking	36	284	3.3	11,458	13.5
484220	Specialized freight (except used goods) trucking, local	19	38	1.0	27,474	5.4
484230	Specialized freight (except used goods) trucking, long-distance	13	212	1.7	8,080	6.4
485	Transit and ground passenger transportation	6	267	3.1	11,670	6.3
488	Support activities for transportation	14	114	2.2	19,193	6.6
492	Couriers and messengers	4	59	1.5	24,881	4.3

Sources: Economic Census of the United States, 1997. Only those industries are shown for which both employment and sales/revenue data were available. For the definition of MSAs, CMSAs, and PMSAs, please see the Introduction.

CINCINNATI, OH—KY—IN PMSA

NAICS	Industry	Estab-lish-ments	Em-ploy-ment	Payroll Total ($ mil.)	Payroll Per Empl. ($)	Sales, reven. ($ mil.)
48-49	Transportation and warehousing	940	23,486	694.1	29,554	2,589.0
484	Truck transportation	506	6,255	204.5	32,696	726.7
4841	General freight trucking	239	4,315	151.1	35,027	499.9
484110	General freight trucking, local	91	871	25.1	28,850	85.6
4841101	General freight trucking without storage, local, truckload (tl)	52	408	13.1	32,132	56.2
4841102	General freight trucking without storage, local, less than truckload (ltl)	34	431	11.2	25,972	25.3
48412	General freight trucking, long-distance	148	3,444	126.0	36,589	414.2
484121	General freight trucking, long-distance, truckload (tl)	106	991	30.5	30,755	180.7
484122	General freight trucking, long-distance, less than truckload (ltl)	42	2,453	95.5	38,946	233.5
4842	Specialized freight trucking	267	1,940	53.4	27,510	226.8
484210	Used household and office goods moving	32	385	9.6	24,818	34.1
484220	Specialized freight (except used goods) trucking, local	182	995	27.2	27,353	106.9
4842203	Dump trucking	116	550	14.5	26,311	65.8
4842204	Specialized trucking without storage, local	45	278	7.9	28,317	24.1
484230	Specialized freight (except used goods) trucking, long-distance	53	560	16.6	29,641	85.8
4842303	Other specialized trucking, long-distance	36	391	10.6	27,130	58.6
4854101	School bus service	21	1,116	13.4	12,047	32.7
485510	Charter bus industry	12	316	4.8	15,057	13.2
488	Support activities for transportation	193	2,096	54.6	26,054	211.6
4882101	Support activities incidental to rail transportation	11	235	4.7	19,791	43.1
4884	Support activities for road transportation	39	234	4.5	19,197	12.0
488410	Motor vehicle towing	36	201	3.8	18,910	10.6
488510	Freight transportation arrangement	98	861	29.6	34,403	98.3
4885101	Freight forwarding	40	439	14.5	33,114	46.3
4885102	Arrangement of transportation of freight and cargo	58	422	15.1	35,744	52.0
492	Couriers and messengers	77	7,639	253.4	33,174	458.1
492110	Couriers	33	7,091	239.9	33,830	416.4
492210	Local messengers and local delivery	44	548	13.5	24,688	41.7
4931	Warehousing and storage	40	758	20.6	27,218	77.9
4931101	General warehousing and storage (except in foreign trade zones)	30	497	12.8	25,821	56.2

Sources: Economic Census of the United States, 1997. Only those industries are shown for which both employment and sales/revenue data were available. For the definition of MSAs, CMSAs, and PMSAs, please see the Introduction.

CINCINNATI—HAMILTON, OH—KY—IN CMSA

NAICS	Industry	Estab-lish-ments	Em-ploy-ment	Payroll Total ($ mil.)	Payroll Per Empl. ($)	Sales, reven. ($ mil.)
48-49	Transportation and warehousing	1,123	27,872	801.7	28,764	2,936.0
484	Truck transportation	631	9,618	295.5	30,729	1,015.5
4841	General freight trucking	296	6,199	201.1	32,443	619.1
484110	General freight trucking, local	106	1,240	31.2	25,191	113.2
4841101	General freight trucking without storage, local, truckload (tl)	63	596	17.2	28,881	81.0
48412	General freight trucking, long-distance	190	4,959	169.9	34,257	505.9
484121	General freight trucking, long-distance, truckload (tl)	141	1,648	48.1	29,211	246.2
484122	General freight trucking, long-distance, less than truckload (ltl)	49	3,311	121.7	36,768	259.8
4842	Specialized freight trucking	335	3,419	94.4	27,620	396.3
484210	Used household and office goods moving	43	1,021	24.5	24,003	100.0
484220	Specialized freight (except used goods) trucking, local	222	1,240	33.7	27,181	133.5
4842203	Dump trucking	144	664	17.3	26,056	81.4
484230	Specialized freight (except used goods) trucking, long-distance	70	1,158	36.2	31,278	162.8
4842301	Hazardous materials trucking (except waste), long-distance	11	230	7.4	32,065	24.3
4842303	Other specialized trucking, long-distance	49	822	24.8	30,225	119.7
488	Support activities for transportation	220	2,274	59.7	26,249	228.5
4882101	Support activities incidental to rail transportation	11	235	4.7	19,791	43.1
488510	Freight transportation arrangement	112	937	32.1	34,222	108.1
4931	Warehousing and storage	49	915	24.2	26,475	97.1

Sources: Economic Census of the United States, 1997. Only those industries are shown for which both employment and sales/revenue data were available. For the definition of MSAs, CMSAs, and PMSAs, please see the Introduction.

CLARKSVILLE—HOPKINSVILLE, TN—KY MSA

NAICS	Industry	Estab-lish-ments	Em-ploy-ment	Payroll		Sales, reven. ($ mil.)
				Total ($ mil.)	Per Empl. ($)	
48-49	Transportation and warehousing	89	666	15.8	23,721	47.3
484	Truck transportation	66	451	11.4	25,310	37.1
4841	General freight trucking	24	109	3.7	33,798	12.7
48412	General freight trucking, long-distance	18	87	3.0	34,690	10.5
4842	Specialized freight trucking	42	342	7.7	22,605	24.4
484210	Used household and office goods moving	12	222	4.7	21,369	11.7
484220	Specialized freight (except used goods) trucking, local	22	72	1.7	23,819	8.1
485	Transit and ground passenger transportation	8	84	0.9	10,238	2.2
488	Support activities for transportation	9	97	2.5	25,701	5.0

Sources: Economic Census of the United States, 1997. Only those industries are shown for which both employment and sales/revenue data were available. For the definition of MSAs, CMSAs, and PMSAs, please see the Introduction.

CLEVELAND—AKRON, OH CMSA

NAICS	Industry	Estab-lish-ments	Em-ploy-ment	Payroll		Sales, reven. ($ mil.)
				Total ($ mil.)	Per Empl. ($)	
48-49	Transportation and warehousing	1,679	27,580	894.3	32,425	3,068.9
481	Air transportation	16	141	3.9	27,695	31.8
48121	Nonscheduled air transportation	11	131	3.6	27,489	29.2
484	Truck transportation	1,022	14,023	500.2	35,671	1,863.3
4841	General freight trucking	459	9,228	339.0	36,732	1,011.2
484110	General freight trucking, local	188	1,572	44.5	28,331	150.1
4841101	General freight trucking without storage, local, truckload (tl)	114	655	18.0	27,463	80.5
48412	General freight trucking, long-distance	271	7,656	294.4	38,457	861.1
484121	General freight trucking, long-distance, truckload (tl)	211	2,959	92.9	31,393	492.6
484122	General freight trucking, long-distance, less than truckload (ltl)	60	4,697	201.5	42,907	368.6
4842	Specialized freight trucking	563	4,795	161.2	33,628	852.0
484210	Used household and office goods moving	91	1,125	31.4	27,906	92.2
4842102	Used household and office goods moving, long-distance	40	744	23.9	32,085	73.0
484220	Specialized freight (except used goods) trucking, local	368	1,861	57.0	30,637	305.9
4842202	Agricultural products trucking without storage, local	25	77	2.0	26,494	10.8
4842203	Dump trucking	229	1,029	33.5	32,550	145.7
4842204	Specialized trucking without storage, local	92	562	15.4	27,365	48.0
484230	Specialized freight (except used goods) trucking, long-distance	104	1,809	72.8	40,264	453.9
4842301	Hazardous materials trucking (except waste), long-distance	12	88	2.7	30,636	8.3
4842302	Agricultural products trucking, long-distance	13	64	2.2	34,969	7.4
4842303	Other specialized trucking, long-distance	79	1,657	67.9	40,980	438.2
485	Transit and ground passenger transportation	96	2,310	35.6	15,423	98.9
4853	Taxi and limousine service	45	438	6.6	14,982	27.9
485310	Taxi service	19	266	4.5	16,797	19.0
485320	Limousine service	26	172	2.1	12,174	8.9
488	Support activities for transportation	333	3,120	90.8	29,102	283.0
4883	Support activities for water transportation	15	391	11.0	28,202	31.9
488410	Motor vehicle towing	76	496	9.3	18,683	26.4
488510	Freight transportation arrangement	199	1,369	54.9	40,083	178.9
4885101	Freight forwarding	49	464	20.3	43,808	57.8
4885102	Arrangement of transportation of freight and cargo	150	905	34.5	38,173	121.0
492	Couriers and messengers	97	5,848	183.8	31,438	448.5
492110	Couriers	44	5,435	173.7	31,961	397.2
4921101	Courier services (except by air)	19	4,198	134.8	32,116	248.3
4921102	Air courier services	25	1,237	38.9	31,434	148.9
492210	Local messengers and local delivery	53	413	10.1	24,554	51.3
4931	Warehousing and storage	82	1,390	32.7	23,519	94.1

Sources: Economic Census of the United States, 1997. Only those industries are shown for which both employment and sales/revenue data were available. For the definition of MSAs, CMSAs, and PMSAs, please see the Introduction.

CLEVELAND—LORAIN—ELYRIA, OH PMSA

NAICS	Industry	Estab-lish-ments	Em-ploy-ment	Payroll		Sales, reven. ($ mil.)
				Total ($ mil.)	Per Empl. ($)	
48-49	Transportation and warehousing	1,277	20,500	633.8	30,917	2,265.0
481	Air transportation	12	112	3.1	27,821	27.7
48311	Deep sea, coastal, and Great Lakes water transportation	13	627	40.7	64,931	214.0
484	Truck transportation	754	8,509	279.1	32,800	1,201.7
4841	General freight trucking	330	4,914	160.7	32,702	683.8
484110	General freight trucking, local	139	1,231	35.1	28,517	122.8
4841101	General freight trucking without storage, local, truckload (tl)	81	428	11.6	27,049	59.0
4841102	General freight trucking without storage, local, less than truckload (ltl)	49	713	21.8	30,642	57.2
48412	General freight trucking, long-distance	191	3,683	125.6	34,100	561.0
484121	General freight trucking, long-distance, truckload (tl)	157	2,487	77.5	31,155	423.3
484122	General freight trucking, long-distance, less than truckload (ltl)	34	1,196	48.1	40,224	137.8
4842	Specialized freight trucking	424	3,595	118.4	32,935	517.9
484210	Used household and office goods moving	74	947	26.9	28,394	82.5
4842101	Used household and office goods moving, local, without storage	31	166	2.7	16,277	7.8
4842102	Used household and office goods moving, long-distance	32	660	20.9	31,594	66.3
4842103	Used household and office goods moving, local, with storage	11	121	3.3	27,562	8.4
484220	Specialized freight (except used goods) trucking, local	269	1,446	43.8	30,325	251.7
4842202	Agricultural products trucking without storage, local	19	66	1.8	27,394	9.8
4842203	Dump trucking	162	756	25.0	33,021	107.1
4842204	Specialized trucking without storage, local	71	465	12.1	26,108	38.6
484230	Specialized freight (except used goods) trucking, long-distance	81	1,202	47.7	39,654	183.6
4842302	Agricultural products trucking, long-distance	13	64	2.2	34,969	7.4
4842303	Other specialized trucking, long-distance	60	1,084	43.4	40,055	170.3
485	Transit and ground passenger transportation	80	2,061	32.6	15,813	91.0
4853	Taxi and limousine service	37	365	5.3	14,625	24.3
485310	Taxi service	16	209	3.5	16,967	16.4
485320	Limousine service	21	156	1.8	11,487	8.0
485991	Special needs transportation	17	148	2.5	16,905	6.4
486	Pipeline transportation	6	76	4.2	55,658	26.1
488	Support activities for transportation	259	2,666	75.4	28,301	228.0
4881	Support activities for air transportation	19	640	9.7	15,134	28.5
488190	Other support activities for air transportation	11	65	2.4	37,354	9.5
4883	Support activities for water transportation	15	391	11.0	28,202	31.9
488410	Motor vehicle towing	58	357	6.6	18,496	19.0
488510	Freight transportation arrangement	148	1,084	42.9	39,601	135.2
4885101	Freight forwarding	43	428	18.7	43,675	49.2
4885102	Arrangement of transportation of freight and cargo	105	656	24.2	36,942	86.0
492	Couriers and messengers	78	5,420	175.0	32,279	403.4
492110	Couriers	36	5,034	165.5	32,871	354.6
4921101	Courier services (except by air)	15	3,948	131.5	33,306	235.1
4921102	Air courier services	21	1,086	34.0	31,288	119.4
492210	Local messengers and local delivery	42	386	9.5	24,565	48.8
4931	Warehousing and storage	64	1,011	22.3	22,021	69.2
4931101	General warehousing and storage (except in foreign trade zones)	51	630	14.0	22,271	46.8

Sources: Economic Census of the United States, 1997. Only those industries are shown for which both employment and sales/revenue data were available. For the definition of MSAs, CMSAs, and PMSAs, please see the Introduction.

COLORADO SPRINGS, CO MSA

NAICS	Industry	Estab-lish-ments	Em-ploy-ment	Payroll		Sales, reven. ($ mil.)
				Total ($ mil.)	Per Empl. ($)	
48-49	Transportation and warehousing	213	2,870	84.8	29,556	265.5
481	Air transportation	4	62	0.7	11,016	6.8
484	Truck transportation	118	897	23.1	25,792	89.7
4841	General freight trucking	44	383	11.4	29,726	45.3
48412	General freight trucking, long-distance	39	317	9.9	31,158	38.8
484121	General freight trucking, long-distance, truckload (tl)	27	165	4.4	26,927	20.0
484122	General freight trucking, long-distance, less than truckload (ltl)	12	152	5.4	35,750	18.8
4842	Specialized freight trucking	74	514	11.7	22,860	44.3
484210	Used household and office goods moving	31	333	6.6	19,838	21.0
4842102	Used household and office goods moving, long-distance	14	178	3.9	21,848	12.5
4842103	Used household and office goods moving, local, with storage	11	120	2.3	19,258	7.3
484220	Specialized freight (except used goods) trucking, local	37	131	4.1	31,511	20.4
4842203	Dump trucking	20	35	0.7	20,257	7.5
4842204	Specialized trucking without storage, local	11	63	2.7	42,508	9.4
485	Transit and ground passenger transportation	10	307	8.0	25,909	17.1
488	Support activities for transportation	43	701	13.5	19,285	32.3
4881	Support activities for air transportation	16	553	10.7	19,365	24.0
488410	Motor vehicle towing	18	97	1.4	14,577	4.4
492	Couriers and messengers	23	682	29.4	43,104	86.4
492110	Couriers	13	589	27.7	47,098	83.2
4931	Warehousing and storage	11	196	8.5	43,520	23.4

Sources: Economic Census of the United States, 1997. Only those industries are shown for which both employment and sales/revenue data were available. For the definition of MSAs, CMSAs, and PMSAs, please see the Introduction.

COLUMBIA, MO MSA

NAICS	Industry	Estab-lish-ments	Em-ploy-ment	Payroll		Sales, reven. ($ mil.)
				Total ($ mil.)	Per Empl. ($)	
48-49	Transportation and warehousing	86	1,095	25.5	23,314	104.9
484	Truck transportation	54	537	15.1	28,153	51.8
4841	General freight trucking	29	291	10.6	36,354	38.7
48412	General freight trucking, long-distance	20	253	10.0	39,407	36.8
484122	General freight trucking, long-distance, less than truckload (ltl)	11	206	8.3	40,466	30.1
4842	Specialized freight trucking	25	246	4.5	18,451	13.1
484220	Specialized freight (except used goods) trucking, local	12	76	1.7	22,882	5.2
485	Transit and ground passenger transportation	7	302	4.0	13,109	9.2
492	Couriers and messengers	16	167	3.3	19,593	21.3
492110	Couriers	11	147	3.1	20,782	20.5

Sources: Economic Census of the United States, 1997. Only those industries are shown for which both employment and sales/revenue data were available. For the definition of MSAs, CMSAs, and PMSAs, please see the Introduction.

COLUMBIA, SC MSA

NAICS	Industry	Estab-lish-ments	Em-ploy-ment	Payroll		Sales, reven. ($ mil.)
				Total ($ mil.)	Per Empl. ($)	
48-49	Transportation and warehousing	232	7,112	183.5	25,802	863.1
484	Truck transportation	131	2,270	67.7	29,845	215.3
4841	General freight trucking	69	1,437	43.5	30,285	137.5
484110	General freight trucking, local	18	112	2.4	21,312	12.8
4841101	General freight trucking without storage, local, truckload (tl)	12	83	2.0	24,398	12.1
48412	General freight trucking, long-distance	51	1,325	41.1	31,044	124.7
484121	General freight trucking, long-distance, truckload (tl)	32	442	11.7	26,369	58.0
484122	General freight trucking, long-distance, less than truckload (ltl)	19	883	29.5	33,384	66.7
4842	Specialized freight trucking	62	833	24.2	29,086	77.7
484210	Used household and office goods moving	13	249	6.0	23,920	15.6
484220	Specialized freight (except used goods) trucking, local	32	360	9.1	25,314	37.1
4842203	Dump trucking	15	180	5.4	30,006	22.3
484230	Specialized freight (except used goods) trucking, long-distance	17	224	9.2	40,893	25.0
4842303	Other specialized trucking, long-distance	11	146	6.8	46,562	17.7
488510	Freight transportation arrangement	20	106	2.7	25,208	12.6
4885102	Arrangement of transportation of freight and cargo	14	48	1.6	33,667	9.3
492	Couriers and messengers	22	4,081	99.0	24,262	249.1
492110	Couriers	13	3,990	98.0	24,554	246.5
4931101	General warehousing and storage (except in foreign trade zones)	14	127	2.4	19,094	12.8

Sources: Economic Census of the United States, 1997. Only those industries are shown for which both employment and sales/revenue data were available. For the definition of MSAs, CMSAs, and PMSAs, please see the Introduction.

COLUMBUS, GA—AL MSA

NAICS	Industry	Estab-lish-ments	Em-ploy-ment	Payroll		Sales, reven. ($ mil.)
				Total ($ mil.)	Per Empl. ($)	
48-49	Transportation and warehousing	141	1,993	39.9	20,045	141.1
484	Truck transportation	98	1,143	26.0	22,712	92.8
4841	General freight trucking	48	599	17.1	28,621	63.4
484110	General freight trucking, local	15	107	2.0	18,794	8.1
48412	General freight trucking, long-distance	33	492	15.1	30,758	55.2
484121	General freight trucking, long-distance, truckload (tl)	23	269	6.6	24,446	21.8
4842	Specialized freight trucking	50	544	8.8	16,206	29.4
484210	Used household and office goods moving	21	224	3.6	15,884	10.1
4842103	Used household and office goods moving, local, with storage	12	181	2.9	15,967	7.9
484220	Specialized freight (except used goods) trucking, local	24	301	4.7	15,635	16.4
4842203	Dump trucking	17	250	3.5	13,980	12.7
485	Transit and ground passenger transportation	15	170	2.3	13,735	4.4
488	Support activities for transportation	8	480	6.7	13,996	23.6
492	Couriers and messengers	5	91	2.1	23,484	8.2
493	Warehousing and storage	10	95	2.4	25,463	9.3

Sources: Economic Census of the United States, 1997. Only those industries are shown for which both employment and sales/revenue data were available. For the definition of MSAs, CMSAs, and PMSAs, please see the Introduction.

COLUMBUS, OH MSA

NAICS	Industry	Estab-lish-ments	Em-ploy-ment	Payroll		Sales, reven. ($ mil.)
				Total ($ mil.)	Per Empl. ($)	
48-49	Transportation and warehousing	860	20,166	615.9	30,544	1,989.8
481	Air transportation	21	1,027	29.6	28,795	238.9
484	Truck transportation	526	9,097	309.8	34,051	958.3
4841	General freight trucking	276	7,047	253.6	35,989	729.6
484110	General freight trucking, local	107	1,007	26.1	25,918	91.7
4841101	General freight trucking without storage, local, truckload (tl)	69	611	16.9	27,717	59.0
4841102	General freight trucking without storage, local, less than truckload (ltl)	32	282	7.0	24,936	26.0
48412	General freight trucking, long-distance	169	6,040	227.5	37,668	637.8
484121	General freight trucking, long-distance, truckload (tl)	134	2,985	96.9	32,468	410.5
484122	General freight trucking, long-distance, less than truckload (ltl)	35	3,055	130.6	42,750	227.3
4842	Specialized freight trucking	250	2,050	56.1	27,386	228.7
484210	Used household and office goods moving	34	702	18.6	26,486	51.6
4842101	Used household and office goods moving, local, without storage	16	124	1.7	14,105	5.2
484220	Specialized freight (except used goods) trucking, local	168	687	19.2	27,932	99.4
4842203	Dump trucking	115	406	12.0	29,618	71.4
4842204	Specialized trucking without storage, local	30	147	3.2	21,844	12.7
484230	Specialized freight (except used goods) trucking, long-distance	48	661	18.4	27,776	77.7
4842303	Other specialized trucking, long-distance	29	434	11.2	25,899	53.4
4853	Taxi and limousine service	16	200	3.0	15,155	10.1
485410	School and employee bus transportation	14	283	3.5	12,505	6.9
488	Support activities for transportation	141	1,707	49.0	28,684	154.2
4881	Support activities for air transportation	18	218	3.9	18,101	7.7
488410	Motor vehicle towing	29	227	4.0	17,511	11.5
488510	Freight transportation arrangement	84	1,139	38.2	33,572	122.0
4885101	Freight forwarding	35	304	10.4	34,184	41.5
4885102	Arrangement of transportation of freight and cargo	49	835	27.8	33,349	80.6
492	Couriers and messengers	58	5,595	155.5	27,800	373.0
492110	Couriers	28	5,369	150.4	28,006	349.0
492210	Local messengers and local delivery	30	226	5.2	22,916	24.0
4931	Warehousing and storage	52	1,452	37.8	26,010	112.4
4931101	General warehousing and storage (except in foreign trade zones)	34	1,042	27.5	26,428	79.2
493190	Other warehousing and storage	12	253	6.2	24,597	18.5

Sources: Economic Census of the United States, 1997. Only those industries are shown for which both employment and sales/revenue data were available. For the definition of MSAs, CMSAs, and PMSAs, please see the Introduction.

CORPUS CHRISTI, TX MSA

NAICS	Industry	Estab-lish-ments	Em-ploy-ment	Payroll		Sales, reven. ($ mil.)
				Total ($ mil.)	Per Empl. ($)	
48-49	Transportation and warehousing	240	2,738	80.0	29,201	337.3
484	Truck transportation	117	1,358	34.9	25,688	112.2
4841	General freight trucking	49	603	14.1	23,448	40.6
484110	General freight trucking, local	18	181	4.3	23,740	13.7
4841101	General freight trucking without storage, local, truckload (tl)	14	121	3.2	26,058	11.0
48412	General freight trucking, long-distance	31	422	9.8	23,322	26.9
484121	General freight trucking, long-distance, truckload (tl)	20	298	6.4	21,631	14.9
484122	General freight trucking, long-distance, less than truckload (ltl)	11	124	3.4	27,387	12.0
4842	Specialized freight trucking	68	755	20.7	27,477	71.6
484220	Specialized freight (except used goods) trucking, local	28	161	4.4	27,248	27.7
484230	Specialized freight (except used goods) trucking, long-distance	32	426	13.0	30,408	37.0
4842303	Other specialized trucking, long-distance	16	188	5.5	29,319	17.8
4862101	Natural gas transmission	13	99	4.7	47,141	70.9
487	Scenic and sightseeing transportation	10	83	1.2	13,904	4.5
488	Support activities for transportation	63	726	26.2	36,073	63.9
4883	Support activities for water transportation	28	198	8.1	41,051	20.9
488330	Navigational services to shipping	12	45	3.4	76,022	8.4
488390	Other support activities for water transportation	11	116	3.8	32,379	9.1
492	Couriers and messengers	12	182	4.5	24,478	15.8
493	Warehousing and storage	8	83	2.8	34,096	22.8

Sources: *Economic Census of the United States*, 1997. Only those industries are shown for which both employment and sales/revenue data were available. For the definition of MSAs, CMSAs, and PMSAs, please see the Introduction.

CUMBERLAND, MD—WV MSA

NAICS	Industry	Estab-lish-ments	Em-ploy-ment	Payroll		Sales, reven. ($ mil.)
				Total ($ mil.)	Per Empl. ($)	
48-49	Transportation and warehousing	69	644	12.0	18,686	42.6
484	Truck transportation	36	425	9.0	21,193	28.3
4841	General freight trucking	12	231	5.2	22,299	16.9
4842	Specialized freight trucking	24	194	3.9	19,876	11.4
484220	Specialized freight (except used goods) trucking, local	17	118	2.0	16,983	7.0
4842203	Dump trucking	12	99	1.7	16,848	5.9
485	Transit and ground passenger transportation	24	114	0.8	6,675	3.3
4854101	School bus service	18	94	0.6	6,223	1.6

Sources: *Economic Census of the United States*, 1997. Only those industries are shown for which both employment and sales/revenue data were available. For the definition of MSAs, CMSAs, and PMSAs, please see the Introduction.

DALLAS, TX PMSA

NAICS	Industry	Estab-lish-ments	Em-ploy-ment	Payroll		Sales, reven. ($ mil.)
				Total ($ mil.)	Per Empl. ($)	
48-49	Transportation and warehousing	1,777	49,911	1,482.8	29,708	5,975.6
481	Air transportation	62	1,828	69.2	37,839	434.6
48111	Scheduled air transportation	28	666	22.2	33,366	170.8
481111	Scheduled passenger air transportation	22	547	17.8	32,484	137.2
48121	Nonscheduled air transportation	34	1,162	46.9	40,403	263.8
48311	Deep sea, coastal, and Great Lakes water transportation	12	982	38.6	39,295	615.2
484	Truck transportation	959	22,665	705.4	31,123	2,206.9
4841	General freight trucking	485	15,226	509.5	33,464	1,410.6
484110	General freight trucking, local	186	1,759	47.3	26,869	147.3
4841101	General freight trucking without storage, local, truckload (tl)	110	768	21.4	27,911	73.0
4841102	General freight trucking without storage, local, less than truckload (ltl)	56	669	17.5	26,143	48.2
4841103	General freight trucking with storage, local, truckload (tl)	13	237	6.6	27,768	19.6
48412	General freight trucking, long-distance	299	13,467	462.3	34,325	1,263.3
484121	General freight trucking, long-distance, truckload (tl)	239	4,871	139.7	28,682	635.1
484122	General freight trucking, long-distance, less than truckload (ltl)	60	8,596	322.5	37,523	628.2
4842	Specialized freight trucking	474	7,439	195.9	26,333	796.3
484210	Used household and office goods moving	106	2,163	52.5	24,272	191.3
4842101	Used household and office goods moving, local, without storage	41	620	11.0	17,794	26.9
4842102	Used household and office goods moving, long-distance	40	896	28.0	31,209	121.5
4842103	Used household and office goods moving, local, with storage	25	647	13.5	20,875	42.9
484220	Specialized freight (except used goods) trucking, local	238	1,570	34.6	22,017	172.3
4842202	Agricultural products trucking without storage, local	16	49	0.7	14,959	3.5
4842203	Dump trucking	131	686	14.3	20,835	90.5
4842204	Specialized trucking without storage, local	79	455	11.5	25,323	50.1
484230	Specialized freight (except used goods) trucking, long-distance	130	3,706	108.8	29,365	432.7
4842301	Hazardous materials trucking (except waste), long-distance	12	76	3.2	42,276	10.3
4842302	Agricultural products trucking, long-distance	24	209	4.4	21,139	26.7
4842303	Other specialized trucking, long-distance	94	3,421	101.2	29,580	395.8
485	Transit and ground passenger transportation	90	2,450	34.6	14,115	93.3
4853	Taxi and limousine service	49	558	8.2	14,754	24.7
485320	Limousine service	40	428	7.0	16,444	18.8
485510	Charter bus industry	12	196	3.2	16,536	11.9
486	Pipeline transportation	17	494	22.9	46,368	420.5
487	Scenic and sightseeing transportation	7	13	0.4	32,308	1.2
488	Support activities for transportation	340	6,692	245.9	36,748	1,029.5
4881	Support activities for air transportation	89	3,427	139.3	40,636	714.9
48811	Airport operations	23	359	6.4	17,811	23.1
488190	Other support activities for air transportation	66	3,068	132.9	43,307	691.8
4884	Support activities for road transportation	84	810	17.9	22,133	56.2
488410	Motor vehicle towing	78	670	16.3	24,276	49.6
488510	Freight transportation arrangement	152	1,834	63.9	34,824	189.3
4885101	Freight forwarding	51	850	29.1	34,222	90.3
4885102	Arrangement of transportation of freight and cargo	101	984	34.8	35,343	99.0
492	Couriers and messengers	197	13,101	325.3	24,833	1,029.0
492110	Couriers	98	11,928	296.5	24,858	950.9
4921101	Courier services (except by air)	33	9,082	215.8	23,757	540.2
4921102	Air courier services	65	2,846	80.7	28,373	410.7
492210	Local messengers and local delivery	99	1,173	28.8	24,572	78.1
4931	Warehousing and storage	93	1,686	40.5	23,993	145.4
4931101	General warehousing and storage (except in foreign trade zones)	63	1,081	25.8	23,872	98.6
493190	Other warehousing and storage	18	296	5.7	19,270	20.2

Sources: *Economic Census of the United States*, 1997. Only those industries are shown for which both employment and sales/revenue data were available. For the definition of MSAs, CMSAs, and PMSAs, please see the Introduction.

DALLAS—FORT WORTH, TX CMSA

NAICS	Industry	Estab-lish-ments	Em-ploy-ment	Payroll		Sales, reven. ($ mil.)
				Total ($ mil.)	Per Empl. ($)	
48-49	Transportation and warehousing	2,633	65,028	1,892.8	29,108	7,613.8
481	Air transportation	76	2,333	90.8	38,941	612.2
48311	Deep sea, coastal, and Great Lakes water transportation	12	982	38.6	39,295	615.2
484	Truck transportation	1,420	28,941	876.1	30,273	2,908.3
4841	General freight trucking	711	18,450	594.5	32,222	1,738.3
484110	General freight trucking, local	273	2,696	65.7	24,380	205.4
4841101	General freight trucking without storage, local, truckload (tl)	165	1,116	29.2	26,201	102.4
4841102	General freight trucking without storage, local, less than truckload (ltl)	78	1,183	26.2	22,181	71.5
4841103	General freight trucking with storage, local, truckload (tl)	19	268	7.7	28,593	22.3
4841104	General freight trucking with storage, local, less than truckload (ltl)	11	129	2.6	20,047	9.2
48412	General freight trucking, long-distance	438	15,754	528.8	33,564	1,532.9
484121	General freight trucking, long-distance, truckload (tl)	348	6,355	179.6	28,255	801.6
484122	General freight trucking, long-distance, less than truckload (ltl)	90	9,399	349.2	37,154	731.3
4842	Specialized freight trucking	709	10,491	281.6	26,846	1,170.0
484210	Used household and office goods moving	146	2,699	65.2	24,147	241.2
4842101	Used household and office goods moving, local, without storage	55	675	12.0	17,763	30.8
4842102	Used household and office goods moving, long-distance	57	1,137	33.5	29,491	153.3
4842103	Used household and office goods moving, local, with storage	34	887	19.7	22,156	57.0
484220	Specialized freight (except used goods) trucking, local	372	2,343	54.6	23,283	268.9
4842203	Dump trucking	213	979	20.8	21,270	124.5
4842204	Specialized trucking without storage, local	119	753	20.7	27,533	100.5
4842205	Specialized trucking with storage, local	13	524	11.5	21,922	36.5
484230	Specialized freight (except used goods) trucking, long-distance	191	5,449	161.9	29,714	659.9
4842301	Hazardous materials trucking (except waste), long-distance	22	659	18.2	27,616	62.6
4842302	Agricultural products trucking, long-distance	34	346	8.2	23,806	38.6
4842303	Other specialized trucking, long-distance	135	4,444	135.5	30,485	558.7
485	Transit and ground passenger transportation	123	3,980	59.0	14,820	140.5
4853	Taxi and limousine service	61	661	9.7	14,694	29.8
485310	Taxi service	12	187	1.8	9,529	8.4
485320	Limousine service	49	474	7.9	16,732	21.3
485510	Charter bus industry	23	469	6.7	14,277	24.3
4855102	Charter bus service, interstate/interurban	14	234	3.6	15,573	14.1
487	Scenic and sightseeing transportation	7	13	0.4	32,308	1.2
488	Support activities for transportation	575	11,392	383.4	33,656	1,492.5
4881	Support activities for air transportation	147	5,457	190.6	34,920	916.6
48811	Airport operations	42	1,439	22.3	15,516	75.2
488190	Other support activities for air transportation	105	4,018	168.2	41,869	841.4
4882101	Support activities incidental to rail transportation	14	888	31.9	35,976	94.0
4884	Support activities for road transportation	121	1,248	26.3	21,095	76.4
488410	Motor vehicle towing	111	890	21.2	23,848	63.6
488510	Freight transportation arrangement	282	3,737	133.4	35,694	402.6
4885101	Freight forwarding	125	1,939	70.0	36,125	244.5
4885102	Arrangement of transportation of freight and cargo	157	1,798	63.3	35,229	158.2
492	Couriers and messengers	262	14,397	357.6	24,841	1,181.3
492110	Couriers	124	12,891	318.0	24,666	1,069.6
4921101	Courier services (except by air)	47	9,623	223.8	23,255	608.4
4921102	Air courier services	77	3,268	94.2	28,823	461.3
492210	Local messengers and local delivery	138	1,506	39.7	26,332	111.7
4931	Warehousing and storage	133	2,425	61.4	25,318	219.8
4931101	General warehousing and storage (except in foreign trade zones)	88	1,506	36.2	24,031	136.3

Sources: Economic Census of the United States, 1997. Only those industries are shown for which both employment and sales/revenue data were available. For the definition of MSAs, CMSAs, and PMSAs, please see the Introduction.

DANBURY, CT PMSA

NAICS	Industry	Estab-lish-ments	Em-ploy-ment	Payroll		Sales, reven. ($ mil.)
				Total ($ mil.)	Per Empl. ($)	
48-49	Transportation and warehousing	93	1,307	31.0	23,712	92.0
484	Truck transportation	35	277	7.9	28,635	30.4
4842	Specialized freight trucking	29	203	5.4	26,764	19.9
484210	Used household and office goods moving	13	143	4.1	28,566	13.1
484220	Specialized freight (except used goods) trucking, local	16	60	1.3	22,467	6.8
4842203	Dump trucking	11	36	0.8	21,833	4.0
485	Transit and ground passenger transportation	22	601	7.6	12,614	20.7
488	Support activities for transportation	23	129	5.5	42,372	14.1
492	Couriers and messengers	8	212	7.1	33,627	15.7

Sources: Economic Census of the United States, 1997. Only those industries are shown for which both employment and sales/revenue data were available. For the definition of MSAs, CMSAs, and PMSAs, please see the Introduction.

DANVILLE, VA MSA

NAICS	Industry	Estab-lish-ments	Em-ploy-ment	Payroll		Sales, reven. ($ mil.)
				Total ($ mil.)	Per Empl. ($)	
48-49	Transportation and warehousing	61	405	10.0	24,802	44.3
484	Truck transportation	43	311	7.5	24,090	28.9
4841	General freight trucking	20	183	4.8	26,279	19.3
4842	Specialized freight trucking	23	128	2.7	20,961	9.7
488	Support activities for transportation	4	11	0.4	35,182	0.9

Sources: *Economic Census of the United States*, 1997. Only those industries are shown for which both employment and sales/revenue data were available. For the definition of MSAs, CMSAs, and PMSAs, please see the Introduction.

DAVENPORT—MOLINE—ROCK ISLAND, IA—IL MSA

NAICS	Industry	Estab-lish-ments	Em-ploy-ment	Payroll		Sales, reven. ($ mil.)
				Total ($ mil.)	Per Empl. ($)	
48-49	Transportation and warehousing	291	4,472	131.0	29,294	440.8
484	Truck transportation	196	3,081	98.1	31,824	273.4
4841	General freight trucking	92	2,306	78.7	34,124	205.8
484110	General freight trucking, local	28	203	5.3	25,956	16.1
4841101	General freight trucking without storage, local, truckload (tl)	20	104	2.7	25,798	9.7
48412	General freight trucking, long-distance	64	2,103	73.4	34,913	189.7
484121	General freight trucking, long-distance, truckload (tl)	41	864	22.6	26,132	93.7
484122	General freight trucking, long-distance, less than truckload (ltl)	23	1,239	50.8	41,036	95.9
4842	Specialized freight trucking	104	775	19.4	24,979	67.6
484210	Used household and office goods moving	19	249	3.7	14,823	11.1
4842102	Used household and office goods moving, long-distance	11	194	2.6	13,196	7.8
484220	Specialized freight (except used goods) trucking, local	65	209	4.9	23,646	25.8
4842202	Agricultural products trucking without storage, local	14	73	1.6	22,014	5.7
4842203	Dump trucking	41	113	2.9	25,372	18.2
484230	Specialized freight (except used goods) trucking, long-distance	20	317	10.7	33,836	30.7
488	Support activities for transportation	40	602	16.0	26,646	75.3
4884	Support activities for road transportation	12	85	1.4	16,235	3.8
488510	Freight transportation arrangement	13	47	1.9	39,511	7.8
4931	Warehousing and storage	12	112	3.3	29,196	14.0

Sources: *Economic Census of the United States*, 1997. Only those industries are shown for which both employment and sales/revenue data were available. For the definition of MSAs, CMSAs, and PMSAs, please see the Introduction.

DAYTON—SPRINGFIELD, OH MSA

NAICS	Industry	Estab-lish-ments	Em-ploy-ment	Payroll Total ($ mil.)	Payroll Per Empl. ($)	Sales, reven. ($ mil.)
48-49	Transportation and warehousing	419	10,704	357.1	33,359	938.1
481	Air transportation	15	872	36.5	41,838	97.9
484	Truck transportation	246	4,774	177.4	37,163	531.0
4841	General freight trucking	123	3,421	132.0	38,584	397.4
484110	General freight trucking, local	48	338	9.4	27,953	32.5
4841101	General freight trucking without storage, local, truckload (tl)	30	210	6.3	29,890	24.3
48412	General freight trucking, long-distance	75	3,083	122.5	39,749	364.9
484121	General freight trucking, long-distance, truckload (tl)	56	2,337	75.1	32,134	200.5
484122	General freight trucking, long-distance, less than truckload (ltl)	19	746	47.4	63,605	164.4
4842	Specialized freight trucking	123	1,353	45.4	33,572	133.6
484210	Used household and office goods moving	23	364	6.3	17,363	19.9
4842102	Used household and office goods moving, long-distance	12	257	4.3	16,580	13.6
484220	Specialized freight (except used goods) trucking, local	73	466	13.2	28,335	51.0
4842203	Dump trucking	49	226	5.8	25,575	31.5
4842204	Specialized trucking without storage, local	14	213	6.8	32,014	17.6
484230	Specialized freight (except used goods) trucking, long-distance	27	523	25.9	49,520	62.8
4842303	Other specialized trucking, long-distance	21	498	25.6	51,341	61.4
488	Support activities for transportation	77	1,117	23.8	21,347	75.2
4881	Support activities for air transportation	16	394	6.6	16,629	26.4
4884	Support activities for road transportation	21	275	4.7	17,175	11.1
488410	Motor vehicle towing	17	252	4.4	17,548	10.3
488510	Freight transportation arrangement	35	345	8.7	25,151	33.2
4885101	Freight forwarding	15	106	2.8	26,500	-11.9
4885102	Arrangement of transportation of freight and cargo	20	239	5.9	24,552	21.3
492	Couriers and messengers	36	3,495	110.4	31,582	196.1
492110	Couriers	17	3,079	101.8	33,070	174.9
492210	Local messengers and local delivery	19	416	8.6	20,572	21.2
4931	Warehousing and storage	20	135	3.3	24,637	18.1
4931101	General warehousing and storage (except in foreign trade zones)	15	95	2.5	26,547	12.8

Sources: *Economic Census of the United States*, 1997. Only those industries are shown for which both employment and sales/revenue data were available. For the definition of MSAs, CMSAs, and PMSAs, please see the Introduction.

DAYTONA BEACH, FL MSA

NAICS	Industry	Estab-lish-ments	Em-ploy-ment	Payroll Total ($ mil.)	Payroll Per Empl. ($)	Sales, reven. ($ mil.)
48-49	Transportation and warehousing	176	1,260	24.5	19,449	81.2
484	Truck transportation	93	395	9.5	24,157	39.2
4841	General freight trucking	39	166	4.2	25,428	19.0
484110	General freight trucking, local	11	47	1.1	24,064	4.5
48412	General freight trucking, long-distance	28	119	3.1	25,966	14.5
484121	General freight trucking, long-distance, truckload (tl)	24	71	1.7	23,549	8.9
4842	Specialized freight trucking	54	229	5.3	23,236	20.2
484210	Used household and office goods moving	18	76	1.8	23,145	7.6
484220	Specialized freight (except used goods) trucking, local	26	87	1.5	16,977	5.7
485	Transit and ground passenger transportation	14	429	7.9	18,357	13.8
487210	Scenic and sightseeing transportation, water	11	40	0.6	14,175	2.0
488	Support activities for transportation	38	241	2.9	11,954	13.8
4881	Support activities for air transportation	13	151	1.7	10,934	10.2
488510	Freight transportation arrangement	13	22	0.5	22,182	1.1
492	Couriers and messengers	10	87	2.4	27,828	8.7
493	Warehousing and storage	3	27	0.7	24,333	1.4

Sources: *Economic Census of the United States*, 1997. Only those industries are shown for which both employment and sales/revenue data were available. For the definition of MSAs, CMSAs, and PMSAs, please see the Introduction.

DECATUR, AL MSA

NAICS	Industry	Estab-lish-ments	Em-ploy-ment	Payroll		Sales, reven. ($ mil.)
				Total ($ mil.)	Per Empl. ($)	
48-49	Transportation and warehousing	90	845	18.4	21,798	74.9
484	Truck transportation	70	682	15.5	22,790	65.2
4841	General freight trucking	47	529	11.8	22,259	52.8
48412	General freight trucking, long-distance	38	472	10.9	23,102	49.4
484121	General freight trucking, long-distance, truckload (tl)	30	233	4.9	21,099	33.0
4842	Specialized freight trucking	23	153	3.8	24,627	12.4
488	Support activities for transportation	10	77	1.5	19,870	4.2
493	Warehousing and storage	4	38	0.8	20,526	3.9

Sources: *Economic Census of the United States*, 1997. Only those industries are shown for which both employment and sales/revenue data were available. For the definition of MSAs, CMSAs, and PMSAs, please see the Introduction.

DECATUR, IL MSA

NAICS	Industry	Estab-lish-ments	Em-ploy-ment	Payroll		Sales, reven. ($ mil.)
				Total ($ mil.)	Per Empl. ($)	
48-49	Transportation and warehousing	102	4,152	127.1	30,606	612.3
484	Truck transportation	71	803	22.2	27,675	77.1
4841	General freight trucking	30	456	13.6	29,814	43.0
484110	General freight trucking, local	12	51	0.8	14,863	2.7
48412	General freight trucking, long-distance	18	405	12.8	31,696	40.3
484121	General freight trucking, long-distance, truckload (tl)	14	352	10.7	30,506	31.4
4842	Specialized freight trucking	41	347	8.6	24,865	34.1
484220	Specialized freight (except used goods) trucking, local	22	88	1.6	17,818	7.5
4842203	Dump trucking	12	59	1.1	17,949	5.2
484230	Specialized freight (except used goods) trucking, long-distance	12	126	4.6	36,444	17.0
488	Support activities for transportation	9	116	2.7	23,543	9.4
493	Warehousing and storage	6	56	1.5	26,786	5.2

Sources: *Economic Census of the United States*, 1997. Only those industries are shown for which both employment and sales/revenue data were available. For the definition of MSAs, CMSAs, and PMSAs, please see the Introduction.

DENVER, CO PMSA

NAICS	Industry	Estab-lish-ments	Em-ploy-ment	Payroll		Sales, reven. ($ mil.)
				Total ($ mil.)	Per Empl. ($)	
48-49	Transportation and warehousing	1,115	26,420	733.9	27,778	2,533.2
481	Air transportation	31	1,518	52.0	34,265	402.1
48111	Scheduled air transportation	15	1,266	46.0	36,342	376.1
48121	Nonscheduled air transportation	16	252	6.0	23,833	26.0
481211	Nonscheduled chartered passenger air transportation	13	244	5.9	24,012	25.3
484	Truck transportation	605	10,564	330.9	31,327	1,085.0
4841	General freight trucking	278	7,213	233.8	32,416	694.9
484110	General freight trucking, local	96	1,147	27.6	24,036	86.0
4841101	General freight trucking without storage, local, truckload (tl)	51	254	6.3	24,811	27.2
4841102	General freight trucking without storage, local, less than truckload (ltl)	35	556	13.3	23,844	31.4
48412	General freight trucking, long-distance	182	6,066	206.2	34,000	608.8
484121	General freight trucking, long-distance, truckload (tl)	135	2,783	80.3	28,851	350.8
484122	General freight trucking, long-distance, less than truckload (ltl)	47	3,283	126.0	38,365	258.0
4842	Specialized freight trucking	327	3,351	97.1	28,985	390.1
484210	Used household and office goods moving	69	1,591	46.3	29,075	108.1
4842101	Used household and office goods moving, local, without storage	27	261	5.6	21,506	14.7
4842102	Used household and office goods moving, long-distance	19	671	25.1	37,461	54.9
4842103	Used household and office goods moving, local, with storage	23	659	15.5	23,536	38.6
484220	Specialized freight (except used goods) trucking, local	177	1,129	29.6	26,183	106.0
4842203	Dump trucking	101	373	9.5	25,359	44.8
4842204	Specialized trucking without storage, local	52	367	9.6	26,128	29.8
484230	Specialized freight (except used goods) trucking, long-distance	81	631	21.3	33,769	176.0
4842301	Hazardous materials trucking (except waste), long-distance	11	196	6.7	34,398	106.9
4842303	Other specialized trucking, long-distance	63	412	14.1	34,308	66.0
485	Transit and ground passenger transportation	64	2,050	33.6	16,393	90.4
4853	Taxi and limousine service	26	391	5.3	13,652	19.1
485320	Limousine service	21	223	2.4	10,848	8.6
48599	Other transit and ground passenger transportation	14	384	6.3	16,375	15.0
488	Support activities for transportation	239	2,555	60.5	23,669	228.7
4881	Support activities for air transportation	37	1,002	16.9	16,874	56.6
4881191	Airport operation and terminal services	13	715	10.7	14,937	20.0
488190	Other support activities for air transportation	24	287	6.2	21,700	36.6
4884	Support activities for road transportation	55	544	12.5	22,934	41.6
488410	Motor vehicle towing	49	430	9.0	21,009	25.4
488510	Freight transportation arrangement	125	778	25.8	33,130	118.0
4885101	Freight forwarding	51	442	14.9	33,649	68.5
4885102	Arrangement of transportation of freight and cargo	74	336	10.9	32,446	49.5
492	Couriers and messengers	106	8,976	223.7	24,926	591.0
492110	Couriers	53	7,873	203.7	25,870	547.9
492210	Local messengers and local delivery	53	1,103	20.1	18,191	43.1
4931	Warehousing and storage	49	354	12.1	34,251	43.6
4931101	General warehousing and storage (except in foreign trade zones)	30	197	7.8	39,447	26.2
493190	Other warehousing and storage	13	63	1.4	22,127	3.2

Sources: Economic Census of the United States, 1997. Only those industries are shown for which both employment and sales/revenue data were available. For the definition of MSAs, CMSAs, and PMSAs, please see the Introduction.

DENVER—BOULDER—GREELEY, CO CMSA

NAICS	Industry	Estab-lish-ments	Em-ploy-ment	Payroll		Sales, reven. ($ mil.)
				Total ($ mil.)	Per Empl. ($)	
48-49	Transportation and warehousing	1,387	29,043	792.8	27,299	2,823.2
481	Air transportation	36	1,540	52.9	34,383	405.4
484	Truck transportation	785	11,772	364.4	30,955	1,269.7
4841	General freight trucking	353	7,830	251.5	32,118	817.9
4841102	General freight trucking without storage, local, less than truckload (ltl)	40	614	15.1	24,643	36.4
484121	General freight trucking, long-distance, truckload (tl)	180	3,198	91.5	28,607	440.5
4842	Specialized freight trucking	432	3,942	112.9	28,646	451.8
484210	Used household and office goods moving	91	1,811	51.9	28,680	129.2
484220	Specialized freight (except used goods) trucking, local	228	1,342	35.7	26,593	127.4
4842201	Hazardous materials trucking (except waste), local	11	68	2.3	34,191	6.5
484230	Specialized freight (except used goods) trucking, long-distance	113	789	25.3	32,058	195.2
4842302	Agricultural products trucking, long-distance	25	109	2.7	24,606	15.5
485	Transit and ground passenger transportation	75	2,471	39.6	16,008	107.0
488	Support activities for transportation	285	3,131	70.8	22,608	280.6
4881	Support activities for air transportation	53	1,423	23.2	16,334	94.8
488510	Freight transportation arrangement	139	826	27.3	33,011	123.7
492	Couriers and messengers	125	9,311	230.7	24,772	619.0
492110	Couriers	64	8,109	209.7	25,856	573.4
492210	Local messengers and local delivery	61	1,202	21.0	17,458	45.5
4931902	Specialized goods warehousing and storage	13	62	1.4	21,774	3.3

Sources: Economic Census of the United States, 1997. Only those industries are shown for which both employment and sales/revenue data were available. For the definition of MSAs, CMSAs, and PMSAs, please see the Introduction.

DES MOINES, IA MSA

NAICS	Industry	Estab-lish-ments	Em-ploy-ment	Payroll		Sales, reven. ($ mil.)
				Total ($ mil.)	Per Empl. ($)	
48-49	Transportation and warehousing	382	11,250	313.7	27,885	1,017.1
481	Air transportation	7	75	1.6	20,693	8.1
484	Truck transportation	246	5,750	178.6	31,069	634.5
4841	General freight trucking	138	4,762	152.0	31,928	539.5
484110	General freight trucking, local	36	285	7.7	26,891	40.7
4841101	General freight trucking without storage, local, truckload (tl)	22	194	5.6	28,856	35.4
4841102	General freight trucking without storage, local, less than truckload (ltl)	14	91	2.1	22,703	5.3
48412	General freight trucking, long-distance	102	4,477	144.4	32,249	498.8
484121	General freight trucking, long-distance, truckload (tl)	73	3,514	109.9	31,271	414.4
484122	General freight trucking, long-distance, less than truckload (ltl)	29	963	34.5	35,817	84.3
4842	Specialized freight trucking	108	988	26.6	26,927	95.0
484210	Used household and office goods moving	16	203	4.5	22,187	13.6
484220	Specialized freight (except used goods) trucking, local	62	280	7.8	27,929	33.1
4842203	Dump trucking	34	224	6.6	29,464	29.0
4842204	Specialized trucking without storage, local	14	35	0.7	20,543	2.0
484230	Specialized freight (except used goods) trucking, long-distance	30	505	14.3	28,277	48.3
4842303	Other specialized trucking, long-distance	16	314	9.5	30,379	32.6
486	Pipeline transportation	6	115	6.2	53,583	62.8
488	Support activities for transportation	49	373	7.3	19,542	25.0
488410	Motor vehicle towing	14	85	1.2	14,553	4.3
488510	Freight transportation arrangement	20	115	3.9	33,748	12.3
4885102	Arrangement of transportation of freight and cargo	17	99	3.4	34,535	10.3
492	Couriers and messengers	43	4,196	105.7	25,194	245.9
492110	Couriers	23	3,851	100.9	26,205	233.9
492210	Local messengers and local delivery	20	345	4.8	13,913	12.0
4931	Warehousing and storage	15	540	12.6	23,370	34.6

Sources: *Economic Census of the United States*, 1997. Only those industries are shown for which both employment and sales/revenue data were available. For the definition of MSAs, CMSAs, and PMSAs, please see the Introduction.

DETROIT, MI PMSA

NAICS	Industry	Estab-lish-ments	Em-ploy-ment	Payroll		Sales, reven. ($ mil.)
				Total ($ mil.)	Per Empl. ($)	
48-49	Transportation and warehousing	1,991	43,291	1,383.5	31,959	5,516.3
481	Air transportation	47	1,894	65.8	34,754	371.3
48111	Scheduled air transportation	26	1,339	39.3	29,341	224.5
48121	Nonscheduled air transportation	21	555	26.5	47,814	146.7
484	Truck transportation	1,135	21,606	740.9	34,292	3,273.2
4841	General freight trucking	518	14,849	467.8	31,501	2,333.7
484110	General freight trucking, local	248	3,509	126.8	36,144	502.0
4841101	General freight trucking without storage, local, truckload (tl)	177	1,875	56.6	30,201	339.7
4841102	General freight trucking without storage, local, less than truckload (ltl)	60	1,398	63.8	45,649	147.0
48412	General freight trucking, long-distance	270	11,340	340.9	30,065	1,831.7
484121	General freight trucking, long-distance, truckload (tl)	201	7,668	199.8	26,052	1,363.9
484122	General freight trucking, long-distance, less than truckload (ltl)	69	3,672	141.2	38,444	467.8
4842	Specialized freight trucking	617	6,757	273.1	40,424	939.5
484210	Used household and office goods moving	104	1,502	44.8	29,857	138.2
4842101	Used household and office goods moving, local, without storage	51	414	8.0	19,382	22.8
4842102	Used household and office goods moving, local, long-distance	34	752	25.1	33,338	86.9
4842103	Used household and office goods moving, local, with storage	19	336	11.8	34,973	28.4
484220	Specialized freight (except used goods) trucking, local	367	2,712	112.7	41,562	386.1
4842202	Agricultural products trucking without storage, local	28	132	3.8	28,742	12.2
4842203	Dump trucking	194	1,250	59.0	47,189	213.4
4842204	Specialized trucking without storage, local	127	1,144	42.1	36,778	139.1
484230	Specialized freight (except used goods) trucking, long-distance	146	2,543	115.6	45,453	415.3
4842301	Hazardous materials trucking (except waste), long-distance	12	149	4.6	31,154	13.9
4842302	Agricultural products trucking, long-distance	15	51	1.2	24,137	4.5
4842303	Other specialized trucking, long-distance	119	2,343	109.7	46,826	396.8
485	Transit and ground passenger transportation	134	2,173	34.7	15,970	88.7
4853	Taxi and limousine service	64	437	5.2	11,817	18.3
485410	School and employee bus transportation	17	710	10.1	14,228	22.3
4854101	School bus service	14	700	10.1	14,360	22.2
485510	Charter bus industry	12	240	3.9	16,408	13.1
48599	Other transit and ground passenger transportation	35	525	7.9	15,038	22.9
485991	Special needs transportation	24	226	3.0	13,398	8.6
485999	All other transit and ground passenger transportation	11	299	4.9	16,278	14.4
488	Support activities for transportation	429	6,463	186.4	28,843	594.7
4881	Support activities for air transportation	41	1,162	23.6	20,347	65.2
4881191	Airport operation and terminal services	18	750	12.5	16,664	28.4
488190	Other support activities for air transportation	23	412	11.1	27,051	36.8
4882101	Support activities incidental to rail transportation	22	433	13.1	30,143	28.3
4883	Support activities for water transportation	26	165	8.5	51,352	21.4
488390	Other support activities for water transportation	14	30	0.8	25,267	1.9
4883901	Other services incidental to water transportation	11	21	0.5	22,333	1.2
4884	Support activities for road transportation	117	923	20.9	22,612	60.6
488410	Motor vehicle towing	110	742	15.2	20,453	44.9
488510	Freight transportation arrangement	205	3,175	98.6	31,058	333.2
4885101	Freight forwarding	80	1,589	46.1	29,037	178.5
4885102	Arrangement of transportation of freight and cargo	125	1,586	52.5	33,084	154.7
48899	Other support activities for transportation	18	605	21.8	35,970	86.0
492	Couriers and messengers	127	8,503	251.9	29,629	598.4
492110	Couriers	56	7,795	233.6	29,974	565.9
4921101	Courier services (except by air)	16	5,938	176.3	29,690	331.6
4921102	Air courier services	40	1,857	57.4	30,883	234.3
492210	Local messengers and local delivery	71	708	18.3	25,829	32.5
4931	Warehousing and storage	83	1,434	38.2	26,669	159.4
4931101	General warehousing and storage (except in foreign trade zones)	48	923	23.3	25,270	107.7
4931902	Specialized goods warehousing and storage	23	379	11.1	29,377	32.7

Sources: *Economic Census of the United States,* 1997. Only those industries are shown for which both employment and sales/revenue data were available. For the definition of MSAs, CMSAs, and PMSAs, please see the Introduction.

DETROIT—ANN ARBOR—FLINT, MI CMSA

NAICS	Industry	Estab-lish-ments	Em-ploy-ment	Payroll		Sales, reven. ($ mil.)
				Total ($ mil.)	Per Empl. ($)	
48-49	Transportation and warehousing	2,362	49,838	1,616.9	32,444	6,260.6
48111	Scheduled air transportation	33	1,831	53.7	29,347	282.1
484	Truck transportation	1,374	24,010	839.7	34,975	3,529.5
4841	General freight trucking	623	16,115	510.3	31,666	2,441.8
484110	General freight trucking, local	284	3,724	132.5	35,590	516.8
4841101	General freight trucking without storage, local, truckload (tl)	198	2,007	60.2	29,971	349.4
48412	General freight trucking, long-distance	339	12,391	377.8	30,487	1,925.0
484121	General freight trucking, long-distance, truckload (tl)	253	8,156	213.4	26,160	1,415.7
484122	General freight trucking, long-distance, less than truckload (ltl)	86	4,235	164.4	38,818	509.3
4842	Specialized freight trucking	751	7,895	329.5	41,729	1,087.7
484210	Used household and office goods moving	126	1,810	53.2	29,385	161.2
4842102	Used household and office goods moving, long-distance	38	972	32.2	33,085	105.9
484220	Specialized freight (except used goods) trucking, local	451	3,066	127.6	41,627	439.5
4842201	Hazardous materials trucking (except waste), local	13	81	2.6	31,963	8.9
4842202	Agricultural products trucking without storage, local	40	163	4.5	27,460	15.6
4842203	Dump trucking	236	1,425	67.7	47,519	249.5
4842204	Specialized trucking without storage, local	154	1,280	47.3	36,915	151.5
484230	Specialized freight (except used goods) trucking, long-distance	174	3,019	148.6	49,234	486.9
4842303	Other specialized trucking, long-distance	143	2,810	142.5	50,723	467.3
48599	Other transit and ground passenger transportation	35	525	7.9	15,038	22.9
485991	Special needs transportation	24	226	3.0	13,398	8.6
485999	All other transit and ground passenger transportation	11	299	4.9	16,278	14.4
488	Support activities for transportation	484	7,051	197.1	27,951	638.2
4883	Support activities for water transportation	26	165	8.5	51,352	21.4
488390	Other support activities for water transportation	14	30	0.8	25,267	1.9
4883901	Other services incidental to water transportation	11	21	0.5	22,333	1.2
488410	Motor vehicle towing	134	900	18.2	20,239	53.7
488510	Freight transportation arrangement	220	3,269	101.0	30,882	338.9
488991	Packing and crating	17	657	23.2	35,254	91.3
492	Couriers and messengers	151	10,464	332.7	31,796	876.4
492110	Couriers	69	9,656	312.2	32,330	839.9
492210	Local messengers and local delivery	82	808	20.5	25,423	36.4
493190	Other warehousing and storage	27	444	12.8	28,881	36.9

Sources: Economic Census of the United States, 1997. Only those industries are shown for which both employment and sales/revenue data were available. For the definition of MSAs, CMSAs, and PMSAs, please see the Introduction.

DOTHAN, AL MSA

NAICS	Industry	Estab-lish-ments	Em-ploy-ment	Payroll		Sales, reven. ($ mil.)
				Total ($ mil.)	Per Empl. ($)	
48-49	Transportation and warehousing	123	3,598	110.9	30,831	246.4
484	Truck transportation	90	1,415	37.2	26,310	111.8
4841	General freight trucking	43	1,079	30.2	28,020	89.9
484110	General freight trucking, local	12	46	0.7	15,413	3.0
48412	General freight trucking, long-distance	31	1,033	29.5	28,582	87.0
484121	General freight trucking, long-distance, truckload (tl)	19	824	23.0	27,931	68.9
484122	General freight trucking, long-distance, less than truckload (ltl)	12	209	6.5	31,148	18.1
4842	Specialized freight trucking	47	336	7.0	20,818	21.9
484220	Specialized freight (except used goods) trucking, local	19	65	1.1	17,569	4.2
484230	Specialized freight (except used goods) trucking, long-distance	20	88	1.6	17,841	6.9
4842303	Other specialized trucking, long-distance	14	56	1.0	17,982	4.4
488	Support activities for transportation	19	2,005	70.3	35,046	121.6
492	Couriers and messengers	5	75	1.5	19,693	4.7
493	Warehousing and storage	4	65	1.4	20,985	6.3

Sources: Economic Census of the United States, 1997. Only those industries are shown for which both employment and sales/revenue data were available. For the definition of MSAs, CMSAs, and PMSAs, please see the Introduction.

DOVER, DE MSA

NAICS	Industry	Estab-lish-ments	Em-ploy-ment	Payroll		Sales, reven. ($ mil.)
				Total ($ mil.)	Per Empl. ($)	
48-49	Transportation and warehousing	124	1,284	26.8	20,873	92.2
484	Truck transportation	62	449	10.5	23,290	47.8
4841	General freight trucking	26	235	5.4	22,843	27.4
48412	General freight trucking, long-distance	18	141	3.7	26,262	21.8
4842	Specialized freight trucking	36	214	5.1	23,780	20.3
484220	Specialized freight (except used goods) trucking, local	16	70	1.8	25,043	4.4
4842203	Dump trucking	11	12	0.3	25,667	1.4
485	Transit and ground passenger transportation	42	675	12.3	18,237	28.9
4854101	School bus service	31	329	2.6	8,052	8.1

Sources: *Economic Census of the United States*, 1997. Only those industries are shown for which both employment and sales/revenue data were available. For the definition of MSAs, CMSAs, and PMSAs, please see the Introduction.

DUBUQUE, IA MSA

NAICS	Industry	Estab-lish-ments	Em-ploy-ment	Payroll		Sales, reven. ($ mil.)
				Total ($ mil.)	Per Empl. ($)	
48-49	Transportation and warehousing	95	868	23.4	26,977	90.4
481	Air transportation	3	6	0.2	34,167	2.0
484	Truck transportation	72	706	19.7	27,941	78.9
4841	General freight trucking	43	538	16.5	30,704	67.7
48412	General freight trucking, long-distance	37	499	15.7	31,443	64.4
484121	General freight trucking, long-distance, truckload (tl)	31	394	12.2	31,013	51.5
4842	Specialized freight trucking	29	168	3.2	19,089	11.2
484220	Specialized freight (except used goods) trucking, local	19	107	2.1	19,981	6.1
485	Transit and ground passenger transportation	3	29	0.5	18,241	1.8
488	Support activities for transportation	9	49	1.3	27,408	3.4
492	Couriers and messengers	4	62	1.2	19,000	2.7

Sources: *Economic Census of the United States*, 1997. Only those industries are shown for which both employment and sales/revenue data were available. For the definition of MSAs, CMSAs, and PMSAs, please see the Introduction.

DULUTH—SUPERIOR, MN—WI MSA

NAICS	Industry	Estab-lish-ments	Em-ploy-ment	Payroll		Sales, reven. ($ mil.)
				Total ($ mil.)	Per Empl. ($)	
48-49	Transportation and warehousing	218	2,002	70.6	35,240	420.7
484	Truck transportation	130	914	25.9	28,382	92.4
4841	General freight trucking	43	560	18.2	32,513	60.4
484110	General freight trucking, local	13	28	0.6	22,000	3.3
48412	General freight trucking, long-distance	30	532	17.6	33,066	57.1
484121	General freight trucking, long-distance, truckload (tl)	17	403	13.4	33,340	43.8
484122	General freight trucking, long-distance, less than truckload (ltl)	13	129	4.2	32,209	13.3
4842	Specialized freight trucking	87	354	7.7	21,847	32.0
484210	Used household and office goods moving	12	73	1.6	21,274	4.7
484220	Specialized freight (except used goods) trucking, local	66	240	5.3	22,279	23.5
4842203	Dump trucking	31	110	3.2	29,164	13.7
4842204	Specialized trucking without storage, local	15	76	1.4	18,342	5.2
485	Transit and ground passenger transportation	22	303	3.2	10,488	12.1
488	Support activities for transportation	35	208	8.8	42,361	31.2
4883	Support activities for water transportation	13	106	6.4	60,255	23.7
492	Couriers and messengers	14	146	3.8	26,253	10.8

Sources: *Economic Census of the United States*, 1997. Only those industries are shown for which both employment and sales/revenue data were available. For the definition of MSAs, CMSAs, and PMSAs, please see the Introduction.

DUTCHESS COUNTY, NY PMSA

NAICS	Industry	Estab-lish-ments	Em-ploy-ment	Payroll		Sales, reven. ($ mil.)
				Total ($ mil.)	Per Empl. ($)	
48-49	Transportation and warehousing	96	1,004	19.4	19,312	58.5
484	Truck transportation	55	384	10.1	26,398	35.9
4841	General freight trucking	12	21	0.7	34,000	4.5
4842	Specialized freight trucking	43	363	9.4	25,959	31.3
484220	Specialized freight (except used goods) trucking, local	31	118	3.5	29,839	13.2
4842203	Dump trucking	18	88	2.9	32,841	10.9

Sources: Economic Census of the United States, 1997. Only those industries are shown for which both employment and sales/revenue data were available. For the definition of MSAs, CMSAs, and PMSAs, please see the Introduction.

EAU CLAIRE, WI MSA

NAICS	Industry	Estab-lish-ments	Em-ploy-ment	Payroll		Sales, reven. ($ mil.)
				Total ($ mil.)	Per Empl. ($)	
48-49	Transportation and warehousing	145	1,376	28.0	20,358	99.9
484	Truck transportation	113	740	18.6	25,157	63.6
4841	General freight trucking	52	430	11.5	26,756	34.7
484110	General freight trucking, local	11	41	0.9	21,707	3.8
48412	General freight trucking, long-distance	41	389	10.6	27,288	31.0
484121	General freight trucking, long-distance, truckload (tl)	35	316	8.6	27,370	20.9
4842	Specialized freight trucking	61	310	7.1	22,939	28.9
484220	Specialized freight (except used goods) trucking, local	37	144	3.5	24,576	16.3
4842202	Agricultural products trucking without storage, local	18	45	0.5	11,711	3.4
4842203	Dump trucking	13	53	1.5	29,075	8.5
485	Transit and ground passenger transportation	15	411	4.3	10,389	12.4
492	Couriers and messengers	5	111	2.2	19,847	5.6
493	Warehousing and storage	5	55	1.1	20,418	4.1

Sources: Economic Census of the United States, 1997. Only those industries are shown for which both employment and sales/revenue data were available. For the definition of MSAs, CMSAs, and PMSAs, please see the Introduction.

EL PASO, TX MSA

NAICS	Industry	Estab-lish-ments	Em-ploy-ment	Payroll		Sales, reven. ($ mil.)
				Total ($ mil.)	Per Empl. ($)	
48-49	Transportation and warehousing	547	6,611	199.3	30,142	1,643.5
484	Truck transportation	322	3,508	87.3	24,877	374.3
4841	General freight trucking	197	2,403	65.0	27,040	260.4
484110	General freight trucking, local	54	377	9.4	24,984	33.7
4841101	General freight trucking without storage, local, truckload (tl)	38	276	7.8	28,127	27.8
48412	General freight trucking, long-distance	143	2,026	55.6	27,423	226.7
484121	General freight trucking, long-distance, truckload (tl)	112	1,119	27.4	24,505	109.9
484122	General freight trucking, long-distance, less than truckload (ltl)	31	907	28.1	31,022	116.7
4842	Specialized freight trucking	125	1,105	22.3	20,172	113.9
484210	Used household and office goods moving	40	363	6.8	18,623	22.4
4842101	Used household and office goods moving, local, without storage	11	50	0.9	18,900	2.9
4842102	Used household and office goods moving, long-distance	13	130	2.5	19,569	10.6
4842103	Used household and office goods moving, local, with storage	16	183	3.3	17,874	8.9
484220	Specialized freight (except used goods) trucking, local	51	311	5.0	15,929	28.2
4842203	Dump trucking	26	132	2.1	16,159	10.6
4842204	Specialized trucking without storage, local	13	118	1.9	15,822	11.8
484230	Specialized freight (except used goods) trucking, long-distance	34	431	10.6	24,538	63.3
4842303	Other specialized trucking, long-distance	18	209	5.4	26,010	20.5
488	Support activities for transportation	119	1,257	29.8	23,672	90.0
4881	Support activities for air transportation	13	107	2.3	21,710	7.5
488410	Motor vehicle towing	13	122	2.1	17,082	5.8
488510	Freight transportation arrangement	88	999	24.6	24,624	75.0
4885101	Freight forwarding	35	357	8.9	24,913	32.1
4885102	Arrangement of transportation of freight and cargo	53	642	15.7	24,463	43.0
492110	Couriers	11	239	6.6	27,556	40.8
4931	Warehousing and storage	38	567	11.9	20,974	63.4
4931101	General warehousing and storage (except in foreign trade zones)	30	387	9.4	24,346	40.9

Sources: Economic Census of the United States, 1997. Only those industries are shown for which both employment and sales/revenue data were available. For the definition of MSAs, CMSAs, and PMSAs, please see the Introduction.

ELKHART—GOSHEN, IN MSA

NAICS	Industry	Estab-lish-ments	Em-ploy-ment	Payroll Total ($ mil.)	Payroll Per Empl. ($)	Sales, reven. ($ mil.)
48-49	Transportation and warehousing	118	1,805	49.5	27,420	299.3
481	Air transportation	3	16	0.4	24,250	2.1
484	Truck transportation	85	1,510	43.3	28,665	265.3
4841	General freight trucking	37	700	21.1	30,150	75.4
48412	General freight trucking, long-distance	33	685	20.8	30,350	73.8
484121	General freight trucking, long-distance, truckload (tl)	26	565	16.7	29,607	60.1
4842	Specialized freight trucking	48	810	22.2	27,381	189.8
484230	Specialized freight (except used goods) trucking, long-distance	18	606	17.5	28,931	173.0
4842303	Other specialized trucking, long-distance	12	560	16.1	28,745	163.6
488	Support activities for transportation	20	153	3.0	19,797	12.3
492	Couriers and messengers	3	29	0.3	8,966	0.6

Sources: Economic Census of the United States, 1997. Only those industries are shown for which both employment and sales/revenue data were available. For the definition of MSAs, CMSAs, and PMSAs, please see the Introduction.

ELMIRA, NY MSA

NAICS	Industry	Estab-lish-ments	Em-ploy-ment	Payroll Total ($ mil.)	Payroll Per Empl. ($)	Sales, reven. ($ mil.)
48-49	Transportation and warehousing	43	802	18.9	23,602	67.6
481	Air transportation	3	39	0.7	18,154	8.7
484	Truck transportation	23	283	8.6	30,505	25.2
4841	General freight trucking	13	179	4.8	26,810	17.4
488	Support activities for transportation	7	37	0.9	24,378	4.2
492	Couriers and messengers	5	74	2.0	27,622	8.1

Sources: Economic Census of the United States, 1997. Only those industries are shown for which both employment and sales/revenue data were available. For the definition of MSAs, CMSAs, and PMSAs, please see the Introduction.

ENID, OK MSA

NAICS	Industry	Estab-lish-ments	Em-ploy-ment	Payroll Total ($ mil.)	Payroll Per Empl. ($)	Sales, reven. ($ mil.)
48-49	Transportation and warehousing	50	605	16.6	27,438	94.9
484	Truck transportation	31	419	10.9	25,955	41.6
4842	Specialized freight trucking	21	207	5.6	27,184	22.0

Sources: Economic Census of the United States, 1997. Only those industries are shown for which both employment and sales/revenue data were available. For the definition of MSAs, CMSAs, and PMSAs, please see the Introduction.

ERIE, PA MSA

NAICS	Industry	Estab-lish-ments	Em-ploy-ment	Payroll Total ($ mil.)	Payroll Per Empl. ($)	Sales, reven. ($ mil.)
48-49	Transportation and warehousing	133	1,551	43.1	27,775	152.4
484	Truck transportation	84	944	30.5	32,302	102.6
4841	General freight trucking	30	673	23.2	34,483	78.0
48412	General freight trucking, long-distance	23	618	22.0	35,626	72.0
484121	General freight trucking, long-distance, truckload (tl)	14	385	12.4	32,234	44.2
4842	Specialized freight trucking	54	271	7.3	26,886	24.6
484220	Specialized freight (except used goods) trucking, local	39	161	4.4	27,466	15.6
4842203	Dump trucking	25	88	2.8	32,375	11.1
485	Transit and ground passenger transportation	12	355	4.0	11,206	10.1
488	Support activities for transportation	19	86	2.1	24,651	9.1
492	Couriers and messengers	7	93	2.2	24,129	7.7
493	Warehousing and storage	3	22	0.5	20,682	2.4

Sources: Economic Census of the United States, 1997. Only those industries are shown for which both employment and sales/revenue data were available. For the definition of MSAs, CMSAs, and PMSAs, please see the Introduction.

EUGENE—SPRINGFIELD, OR MSA

NAICS	Industry	Estab-lish-ments	Em-ploy-ment	Payroll		Sales, reven. ($ mil.)
				Total ($ mil.)	Per Empl. ($)	
48-49	Transportation and warehousing	230	2,580	64.9	25,173	259.0
484	Truck transportation	156	1,840	49.5	26,896	182.8
4841	General freight trucking	60	1,254	36.0	28,685	135.8
484110	General freight trucking, local	17	314	10.2	32,449	23.1
4841101	General freight trucking without storage, local, truckload (tl)	12	277	8.9	32,162	19.1
48412	General freight trucking, long-distance	43	940	25.8	27,428	112.8
484121	General freight trucking, long-distance, truckload (tl)	34	833	21.0	25,209	95.1
4842	Specialized freight trucking	96	586	13.5	23,067	47.0
484220	Specialized freight (except used goods) trucking, local	63	245	5.4	22,086	21.8
4842202	Agricultural products trucking without storage, local	25	111	2.5	22,288	9.7
4842203	Dump trucking	23	72	1.5	20,958	6.5
484230	Specialized freight (except used goods) trucking, long-distance	23	221	5.1	23,208	16.1
485	Transit and ground passenger transportation	18	225	2.6	11,436	7.8
488	Support activities for transportation	27	272	5.7	20,963	23.0
488510	Freight transportation arrangement	11	60	1.4	22,550	8.2
492	Couriers and messengers	18	170	3.3	19,635	12.3

Sources: *Economic Census of the United States*, 1997. Only those industries are shown for which both employment and sales/revenue data were available. For the definition of MSAs, CMSAs, and PMSAs, please see the Introduction.

EVANSVILLE—HENDERSON, IN—KY MSA

NAICS	Industry	Estab-lish-ments	Em-ploy-ment	Payroll		Sales, reven. ($ mil.)
				Total ($ mil.)	Per Empl. ($)	
48-49	Transportation and warehousing	234	4,032	103.4	25,635	695.9
484	Truck transportation	138	2,513	69.7	27,723	573.7
4841	General freight trucking	83	1,412	39.3	27,821	138.8
484110	General freight trucking, local	27	424	9.2	21,724	22.8
4841101	General freight trucking without storage, local, truckload (tl)	14	158	3.9	24,911	10.9
4841102	General freight trucking without storage, local, less than truckload (ltl)	13	266	5.3	19,831	11.8
48412	General freight trucking, long-distance	56	988	30.1	30,437	116.0
484121	General freight trucking, long-distance, truckload (tl)	39	539	15.3	28,429	69.1
484122	General freight trucking, long-distance, less than truckload (ltl)	17	449	14.7	32,849	47.0
4842	Specialized freight trucking	55	1,101	30.4	27,598	434.9
4842203	Dump trucking	23	359	9.3	25,822	61.5
485	Transit and ground passenger transportation	26	182	1.4	7,445	4.5
4854101	School bus service	17	64	0.3	5,172	1.3
488	Support activities for transportation	34	422	10.0	23,671	45.2
4931101	General warehousing and storage (except in foreign trade zones)	16	639	15.5	24,297	41.1

Sources: *Economic Census of the United States*, 1997. Only those industries are shown for which both employment and sales/revenue data were available. For the definition of MSAs, CMSAs, and PMSAs, please see the Introduction.

FARGO—MOORHEAD, ND—MN MSA

NAICS	Industry	Estab-lish-ments	Em-ploy-ment	Payroll		Sales, reven. ($ mil.)
				Total ($ mil.)	Per Empl. ($)	
48-49	Transportation and warehousing	240	3,320	78.6	23,667	350.3
484	Truck transportation	185	2,406	62.3	25,900	291.3
4841	General freight trucking	110	1,926	50.6	26,256	214.3
484110	General freight trucking, local	14	160	5.5	34,250	16.5
48412	General freight trucking, long-distance	96	1,766	45.1	25,532	197.8
484121	General freight trucking, long-distance, truckload (tl)	79	1,436	36.0	25,095	165.5
484122	General freight trucking, long-distance, less than truckload (ltl)	17	330	9.1	27,430	32.3
4842	Specialized freight trucking	75	480	11.7	24,471	77.0
484220	Specialized freight (except used goods) trucking, local	27	155	2.8	18,213	14.9
4842203	Dump trucking	12	21	0.9	41,714	3.6
484230	Specialized freight (except used goods) trucking, long-distance	41	286	8.1	28,339	59.9
4842302	Agricultural products trucking, long-distance	18	31	0.8	25,452	5.8
4842303	Other specialized trucking, long-distance	19	227	6.6	29,225	51.4
485	Transit and ground passenger transportation	17	326	3.1	9,417	7.0
492	Couriers and messengers	8	221	4.7	21,262	12.3

Sources: *Economic Census of the United States*, 1997. Only those industries are shown for which both employment and sales/revenue data were available. For the definition of MSAs, CMSAs, and PMSAs, please see the Introduction.

FAYETTEVILLE, NC MSA

NAICS	Industry	Estab-lish-ments	Em-ploy-ment	Payroll Total ($ mil.)	Payroll Per Empl. ($)	Sales, reven. ($ mil.)
48-49	Transportation and warehousing	144	1,834	46.7	25,480	128.8
484	Truck transportation	110	1,409	38.8	27,547	94.9
4841	General freight trucking	44	744	25.5	34,324	59.9
484110	General freight trucking, local	12	58	0.9	15,517	2.7
48412	General freight trucking, long-distance	32	686	24.6	35,914	57.3
484121	General freight trucking, long-distance, truckload (tl)	18	273	12.3	44,993	24.5
484122	General freight trucking, long-distance, less than truckload (ltl)	14	413	12.4	29,913	32.8
4842	Specialized freight trucking	66	665	13.3	19,965	35.0
484210	Used household and office goods moving	28	421	8.1	19,221	19.4
4842102	Used household and office goods moving, long-distance	14	234	4.6	19,594	10.1
484220	Specialized freight (except used goods) trucking, local	28	200	4.1	20,540	12.0
4842203	Dump trucking	15	105	2.4	22,590	6.9
485	Transit and ground passenger transportation	8	111	1.3	11,640	4.9
488	Support activities for transportation	15	139	3.3	23,871	13.7
492	Couriers and messengers	6	158	2.9	18,576	11.5

Sources: *Economic Census of the United States*, 1997. Only those industries are shown for which both employment and sales/revenue data were available. For the definition of MSAs, CMSAs, and PMSAs, please see the Introduction.

FAYETTEVILLE—SPRINGDALE—ROGERS, AR MSA

NAICS	Industry	Estab-lish-ments	Em-ploy-ment	Payroll Total ($ mil.)	Payroll Per Empl. ($)	Sales, reven. ($ mil.)
48-49	Transportation and warehousing	249	6,972	217.8	31,246	664.7
484	Truck transportation	183	6,225	199.2	32,003	589.6
4841	General freight trucking	87	5,272	176.5	33,472	496.5
484110	General freight trucking, local	15	37	0.7	20,108	3.2
4841101	General freight trucking without storage, local, truckload (tl)	12	20	0.4	21,300	2.4
48412	General freight trucking, long-distance	72	5,235	175.7	33,567	493.3
484121	General freight trucking, long-distance, truckload (tl)	59	2,783	87.4	31,395	284.2
484122	General freight trucking, long-distance, less than truckload (ltl)	13	2,452	88.3	36,031	209.2
4842	Specialized freight trucking	96	953	22.8	23,875	93.1
484210	Used household and office goods moving	11	97	1.7	17,216	5.0
484220	Specialized freight (except used goods) trucking, local	61	132	2.4	17,902	15.8
4842202	Agricultural products trucking without storage, local	16	28	0.4	15,786	2.2
4842203	Dump trucking	36	81	1.5	18,815	11.6
484230	Specialized freight (except used goods) trucking, long-distance	24	724	18.7	25,856	72.3
4842303	Other specialized trucking, long-distance	12	571	15.7	27,434	56.9
485	Transit and ground passenger transportation	3	29	0.5	17,621	1.9
488	Support activities for transportation	35	236	7.7	32,826	25.2
488510	Freight transportation arrangement	18	169	6.3	37,574	20.8
492	Couriers and messengers	7	217	3.6	16,369	16.0
4931	Warehousing and storage	15	219	5.6	25,772	23.1

Sources: *Economic Census of the United States*, 1997. Only those industries are shown for which both employment and sales/revenue data were available. For the definition of MSAs, CMSAs, and PMSAs, please see the Introduction.

FITCHBURG—LEOMINSTER, MA PMSA

NAICS	Industry	Estab-lish-ments	Em-ploy-ment	Payroll Total ($ mil.)	Payroll Per Empl. ($)	Sales, reven. ($ mil.)
48-49	Transportation and warehousing	81	1,109	21.3	19,164	51.8
484	Truck transportation	43	211	6.0	28,204	18.5
4841	General freight trucking	18	128	3.4	26,750	9.8
4842	Specialized freight trucking	25	83	2.5	30,446	8.7
484220	Specialized freight (except used goods) trucking, local	17	40	0.8	20,675	3.8
485	Transit and ground passenger transportation	25	723	10.0	13,806	19.4
4853	Taxi and limousine service	11	79	0.9	11,291	2.1
493	Warehousing and storage	4	104	3.0	29,308	8.7

Sources: *Economic Census of the United States*, 1997. Only those industries are shown for which both employment and sales/revenue data were available. For the definition of MSAs, CMSAs, and PMSAs, please see the Introduction.

FLAGSTAFF, AZ—UT MSA

NAICS	Industry	Estab-lish-ments	Em-ploy-ment	Payroll Total ($ mil.)	Payroll Per Empl. ($)	Sales, reven. ($ mil.)
48-49	Transportation and warehousing	112	1,347	29.4	21,815	190.6
484	Truck transportation	60	394	9.6	24,363	26.8
4841	General freight trucking	20	202	4.7	23,495	10.4
4842	Specialized freight trucking	40	192	4.9	25,276	16.3
484220	Specialized freight (except used goods) trucking, local	26	93	2.1	22,333	7.7
4842203	Dump trucking	14	51	1.2	22,784	4.7
486	Pipeline transportation	6	62	3.7	60,161	104.1
487	Scenic and sightseeing transportation	8	324	6.2	19,167	27.3
488410	Motor vehicle towing	11	53	0.9	17,906	3.7

Sources: *Economic Census of the United States*, 1997. Only those industries are shown for which both employment and sales/revenue data were available. For the definition of MSAs, CMSAs, and PMSAs, please see the Introduction.

FLINT, MI PMSA

NAICS	Industry	Estab-lish-ments	Em-ploy-ment	Payroll Total ($ mil.)	Payroll Per Empl. ($)	Sales, reven. ($ mil.)
48-49	Transportation and warehousing	161	1,848	66.6	36,041	190.9
484	Truck transportation	108	1,143	50.6	44,226	123.9
4841	General freight trucking	55	595	18.2	30,637	52.9
484110	General freight trucking, local	17	51	1.5	30,333	5.1
4841101	General freight trucking without storage, local, truckload (tl)	11	21	0.5	25,143	2.4
48412	General freight trucking, long-distance	38	544	16.7	30,665	47.9
484121	General freight trucking, long-distance, truckload (tl)	27	388	10.1	26,044	30.2
484122	General freight trucking, long-distance, less than truckload (ltl)	11	156	6.6	42,160	17.7
4842	Specialized freight trucking	53	548	32.3	58,980	71.0
484210	Used household and office goods moving	11	136	5.1	37,515	13.2
484220	Specialized freight (except used goods) trucking, local	28	55	2.0	36,218	10.2
4842203	Dump trucking	18	35	1.4	39,400	7.4
4842303	Other specialized trucking, long-distance	14	357	25.2	70,664	47.5
485	Transit and ground passenger transportation	8	166	2.6	15,855	8.2
488	Support activities for transportation	22	132	2.8	20,932	8.7
488410	Motor vehicle towing	12	46	0.8	18,239	3.6
492	Couriers and messengers	10	251	6.6	26,139	31.1

Sources: *Economic Census of the United States*, 1997. Only those industries are shown for which both employment and sales/revenue data were available. For the definition of MSAs, CMSAs, and PMSAs, please see the Introduction.

FLORENCE, AL MSA

NAICS	Industry	Estab-lish-ments	Em-ploy-ment	Payroll Total ($ mil.)	Payroll Per Empl. ($)	Sales, reven. ($ mil.)
48-49	Transportation and warehousing	69	909	17.5	19,296	127.4
484	Truck transportation	42	732	13.3	18,165	102.2
4841	General freight trucking	23	583	9.9	16,979	93.9
48412	General freight trucking, long-distance	20	575	9.7	16,809	92.7
4842	Specialized freight trucking	19	149	3.4	22,805	8.3
484220	Specialized freight (except used goods) trucking, local	11	65	1.1	16,277	2.9
485	Transit and ground passenger transportation	6	72	1.1	14,875	4.2
487	Scenic and sightseeing transportation	3	3	0.0	14,000	0.3
488	Support activities for transportation	11	35	0.8	22,829	3.0

Sources: *Economic Census of the United States*, 1997. Only those industries are shown for which both employment and sales/revenue data were available. For the definition of MSAs, CMSAs, and PMSAs, please see the Introduction.

FLORENCE, SC MSA

NAICS	Industry	Estab-lish-ments	Em-ploy-ment	Payroll Total ($ mil.)	Payroll Per Empl. ($)	Sales, reven. ($ mil.)
48-49	Transportation and warehousing	80	992	26.2	26,365	76.2
484	Truck transportation	51	642	19.0	29,544	55.2
4841	General freight trucking	26	452	14.1	31,128	38.8
48412	General freight trucking, long-distance	21	396	13.3	33,662	36.7
484121	General freight trucking, long-distance, truckload (tl)	11	53	1.7	31,736	5.9
4842	Specialized freight trucking	25	190	4.9	25,774	16.4
484220	Specialized freight (except used goods) trucking, local	11	81	1.8	21,741	6.3
492	Couriers and messengers	5	114	2.4	21,263	8.8
493	Warehousing and storage	6	143	3.1	21,734	5.8

Sources: *Economic Census of the United States*, 1997. Only those industries are shown for which both employment and sales/revenue data were available. For the definition of MSAs, CMSAs, and PMSAs, please see the Introduction.

FORT COLLINS—LOVELAND, CO MSA

NAICS	Industry	Estab-lish-ments	Em-ploy-ment	Payroll Total ($ mil.)	Payroll Per Empl. ($)	Sales, reven. ($ mil.)
48-49	Transportation and warehousing	136	1,156	33.9	29,323	97.1
481	Air transportation	4	45	1.7	38,533	9.8
484	Truck transportation	91	668	22.5	33,632	60.0
4841	General freight trucking	46	414	16.9	40,836	40.9
484110	General freight trucking, local	14	58	1.3	22,397	6.1
4841101	General freight trucking without storage, local, truckload (tl)	11	40	1.0	25,775	5.4
48412	General freight trucking, long-distance	32	356	15.6	43,840	34.8
484121	General freight trucking, long-distance, truckload (tl)	26	307	13.8	44,847	25.9
4842	Specialized freight trucking	45	254	5.6	21,890	19.2
484210	Used household and office goods moving	12	125	2.1	16,936	6.6
484220	Specialized freight (except used goods) trucking, local	28	107	2.9	26,963	10.3
4842203	Dump trucking	12	51	1.3	25,804	4.7
4842204	Specialized trucking without storage, local	12	50	1.4	28,300	4.9
485	Transit and ground passenger transportation	9	101	1.8	17,366	2.8
488	Support activities for transportation	18	164	4.4	26,707	12.1
492	Couriers and messengers	8	126	3.0	23,516	9.2
493	Warehousing and storage	6	52	0.6	11,538	3.2

Sources: *Economic Census of the United States*, 1997. Only those industries are shown for which both employment and sales/revenue data were available. For the definition of MSAs, CMSAs, and PMSAs, please see the Introduction.

FORT LAUDERDALE, FL PMSA

NAICS	Industry	Estab-lish-ments	Em-ploy-ment	Payroll		Sales, reven. ($ mil.)
				Total ($ mil.)	Per Empl. ($)	
48-49	Transportation and warehousing	995	13,722	310.7	22,640	1,590.3
481	Air transportation	52	845	26.0	30,770	157.6
48111	Scheduled air transportation	28	587	18.4	31,290	105.4
481111	Scheduled passenger air transportation	23	432	13.8	31,981	86.2
48121	Nonscheduled air transportation	24	258	7.6	29,589	52.2
483	Water transportation	30	1,591	48.1	30,258	461.2
48311	Deep sea, coastal, and Great Lakes water transportation	24	1,466	44.6	30,419	449.7
484	Truck transportation	317	2,424	69.7	28,749	299.2
4841	General freight trucking	106	1,115	37.3	33,430	144.3
484110	General freight trucking, local	49	336	8.9	26,423	28.7
4841102	General freight trucking without storage, local, less than truckload (ltl)	19	244	6.5	26,643	15.0
48412	General freight trucking, long-distance	57	779	28.4	36,453	115.6
484121	General freight trucking, long-distance, truckload (tl)	43	253	9.8	38,632	56.6
484122	General freight trucking, long-distance, less than truckload (ltl)	14	526	18.6	35,405	59.0
4842	Specialized freight trucking	211	1,309	32.4	24,761	155.0
484210	Used household and office goods moving	76	578	12.1	20,976	49.0
4842101	Used household and office goods moving, local, without storage	30	66	1.1	16,621	5.0
4842102	Used household and office goods moving, long-distance	29	321	7.2	22,445	30.1
4842103	Used household and office goods moving, local, with storage	17	191	3.8	20,010	14.0
484220	Specialized freight (except used goods) trucking, local	100	421	11.4	26,971	69.4
4842202	Agricultural products trucking without storage, local	13	33	0.7	22,455	3.0
4842203	Dump trucking	43	172	5.2	30,314	45.1
4842204	Specialized trucking without storage, local	31	119	2.4	20,345	11.8
484230	Specialized freight (except used goods) trucking, long-distance	35	310	8.9	28,816	36.5
4842303	Other specialized trucking, long-distance	18	98	1.7	17,306	9.0
4853	Taxi and limousine service	55	141	2.4	16,879	11.2
485310	Taxi service	14	53	0.9	16,208	3.4
485320	Limousine service	41	88	1.5	17,284	7.8
48599	Other transit and ground passenger transportation	21	261	4.3	16,287	8.6
485991	Special needs transportation	13	248	4.1	16,520	8.1
487210	Scenic and sightseeing transportation, water	47	964	11.5	11,882	75.2
4872101	Excursion and sightseeing boats (including dinner cruises)	17	901	10.1	11,210	70.1
4872102	Charter fishing and party fishing boats	30	63	1.4	21,492	5.1
488	Support activities for transportation	330	4,864	81.2	16,694	297.1
4881	Support activities for air transportation	76	1,524	32.7	21,426	125.1
48811	Airport operations	22	1,019	18.9	18,502	60.0
488190	Other support activities for air transportation	54	505	13.8	27,325	65.0
4883	Support activities for water transportation	63	2,505	27.2	10,844	104.8
488320	Marine cargo handling	11	1,359	17.4	12,773	58.4
488330	Navigational services to shipping	13	102	2.6	25,667	23.0
4884	Support activities for road transportation	67	403	8.3	20,519	26.7
488410	Motor vehicle towing	61	325	5.9	18,003	20.0
488510	Freight transportation arrangement	116	393	12.4	31,491	38.6
4885101	Freight forwarding	40	110	2.7	24,964	11.2
4885102	Arrangement of transportation of freight and cargo	76	283	9.6	34,028	27.4
492	Couriers and messengers	93	1,718	49.4	28,770	195.8
492110	Couriers	47	1,494	44.7	29,940	176.9
4921101	Courier services (except by air)	23	158	2.7	17,101	14.7
4921102	Air courier services	24	1,336	42.0	31,459	162.2
492210	Local messengers and local delivery	46	224	4.7	20,964	18.9
4931	Warehousing and storage	29	264	7.1	26,894	27.0
4931101	General warehousing and storage (except in foreign trade zones)	17	168	4.8	28,673	15.0

Sources: *Economic Census of the United States*, 1997. Only those industries are shown for which both employment and sales/revenue data were available. For the definition of MSAs, CMSAs, and PMSAs, please see the Introduction.

FORT MYERS—CAPE CORAL, FL MSA

NAICS	Industry	Establishments	Employment	Payroll Total ($ mil.)	Payroll Per Empl. ($)	Sales, reven. ($ mil.)
48-49	Transportation and warehousing	219	1,502	32.9	21,936	151.0
483	Water transportation	10	78	1.2	15,846	4.8
484	Truck transportation	105	691	17.9	25,863	82.0
4841	General freight trucking	33	255	8.2	32,063	30.1
48412	General freight trucking, long-distance	25	212	7.0	33,009	27.1
484121	General freight trucking, long-distance, truckload (tl)	12	38	1.3	33,947	8.7
484122	General freight trucking, long-distance, less than truckload (ltl)	13	174	5.7	32,805	18.4
4842	Specialized freight trucking	72	436	9.7	22,236	51.9
484210	Used household and office goods moving	17	118	2.2	18,847	8.2
484220	Specialized freight (except used goods) trucking, local	43	255	5.7	22,525	36.3
4842203	Dump trucking	32	177	3.8	21,345	30.9
484230	Specialized freight (except used goods) trucking, long-distance	12	63	1.7	27,413	7.3
485	Transit and ground passenger transportation	22	212	2.7	12,802	9.9
487	Scenic and sightseeing transportation	8	38	0.7	17,737	1.9
488	Support activities for transportation	47	252	4.3	17,139	25.3
488510	Freight transportation arrangement	20	71	1.5	20,606	16.4
4885102	Arrangement of transportation of freight and cargo	14	57	1.3	22,509	15.4
492	Couriers and messengers	17	183	5.2	28,279	20.3
493	Warehousing and storage	7	18	0.4	20,444	2.0

Sources: Economic Census of the United States, 1997. Only those industries are shown for which both employment and sales/revenue data were available. For the definition of MSAs, CMSAs, and PMSAs, please see the Introduction.

FORT PIERCE—PORT ST. LUCIE, FL MSA

NAICS	Industry	Establishments	Employment	Payroll Total ($ mil.)	Payroll Per Empl. ($)	Sales, reven. ($ mil.)
48-49	Transportation and warehousing	156	1,599	45.9	28,734	127.2
481	Air transportation	5	7	0.3	42,143	1.5
484	Truck transportation	70	1,146	36.3	31,654	84.9
4841	General freight trucking	24	148	8.8	59,547	17.7
484110	General freight trucking, local	11	106	2.9	27,557	4.8
48412	General freight trucking, long-distance	13	42	5.9	140,286	13.0
4842	Specialized freight trucking	46	998	27.5	27,518	67.2
484210	Used household and office goods moving	15	86	1.6	18,326	5.7
484220	Specialized freight (except used goods) trucking, local	16	67	1.2	18,164	3.9
484230	Specialized freight (except used goods) trucking, long-distance	15	845	24.7	29,195	57.7
485	Transit and ground passenger transportation	12	76	0.6	8,066	3.3
488	Support activities for transportation	46	205	4.6	22,576	16.1
488510	Freight transportation arrangement	12	40	1.4	35,650	2.4
493	Warehousing and storage	5	33	0.7	21,788	2.0

Sources: Economic Census of the United States, 1997. Only those industries are shown for which both employment and sales/revenue data were available. For the definition of MSAs, CMSAs, and PMSAs, please see the Introduction.

FORT SMITH, AR—OK MSA

NAICS	Industry	Establishments	Employment	Payroll Total ($ mil.)	Payroll Per Empl. ($)	Sales, reven. ($ mil.)
48-49	Transportation and warehousing	206	4,636	134.8	29,066	519.8
484	Truck transportation	160	4,220	124.4	29,490	463.9
4841	General freight trucking	109	4,026	119.9	29,774	441.7
484110	General freight trucking, local	11	81	1.3	16,469	6.1
48412	General freight trucking, long-distance	98	3,945	118.5	30,047	435.6
484121	General freight trucking, long-distance, truckload (tl)	78	3,661	110.8	30,275	415.1
484122	General freight trucking, long-distance, less than truckload (ltl)	20	284	7.7	27,109	20.5
4842	Specialized freight trucking	51	194	4.6	23,582	22.2
4842203	Dump trucking	16	37	0.8	22,324	3.3
484230	Specialized freight (except used goods) trucking, long-distance	19	100	2.4	24,490	14.6
488	Support activities for transportation	21	159	3.8	23,654	18.5
488510	Freight transportation arrangement	13	130	3.2	24,646	16.4
492	Couriers and messengers	10	80	1.9	23,200	8.0
493	Warehousing and storage	7	130	3.3	25,346	10.1

Sources: Economic Census of the United States, 1997. Only those industries are shown for which both employment and sales/revenue data were available. For the definition of MSAs, CMSAs, and PMSAs, please see the Introduction.

FORT WALTON BEACH, FL MSA

NAICS	Industry	Estab-lish-ments	Em-ploy-ment	Payroll		Sales, reven. ($ mil.)
				Total ($ mil.)	Per Empl. ($)	
48-49	Transportation and warehousing	89	536	11.5	21,491	37.0
484	Truck transportation	23	177	4.3	24,316	14.1
4842	Specialized freight trucking	16	157	3.9	24,885	12.6
485	Transit and ground passenger transportation	6	64	0.6	9,203	1.5
487210	Scenic and sightseeing transportation, water	35	60	1.2	19,417	5.4
4872102	Charter fishing and party fishing boats	30	56	1.0	18,286	4.9

Sources: *Economic Census of the United States*, 1997. Only those industries are shown for which both employment and sales/revenue data were available. For the definition of MSAs, CMSAs, and PMSAs, please see the Introduction.

FORT WAYNE, IN MSA

NAICS	Industry	Estab-lish-ments	Em-ploy-ment	Payroll		Sales, reven. ($ mil.)
				Total ($ mil.)	Per Empl. ($)	
48-49	Transportation and warehousing	319	6,674	217.3	32,557	1,407.1
481	Air transportation	7	71	1.5	21,634	12.8
484	Truck transportation	231	5,652	193.5	34,241	1,300.4
4841	General freight trucking	136	2,434	80.7	33,150	395.3
484110	General freight trucking, local	39	398	9.3	23,329	32.3
4841101	General freight trucking without storage, local, truckload (tl)	28	222	4.5	20,387	14.7
48412	General freight trucking, long-distance	97	2,036	71.4	35,069	363.0
484121	General freight trucking, long-distance, truckload (tl)	74	1,103	35.1	31,831	103.3
484122	General freight trucking, long-distance, less than truckload (ltl)	23	933	36.3	38,897	259.7
4842	Specialized freight trucking	95	3,218	112.8	35,066	905.1
4842302	Agricultural products trucking, long-distance	11	50	0.9	18,360	2.8
488	Support activities for transportation	28	242	6.3	25,835	24.1
488410	Motor vehicle towing	11	59	0.8	13,017	2.4
492	Couriers and messengers	24	325	6.9	21,317	35.0
492210	Local messengers and local delivery	14	83	1.8	22,169	4.8
4931	Warehousing and storage	18	231	5.5	23,840	18.0
4931101	General warehousing and storage (except in foreign trade zones)	14	202	4.7	23,079	12.6

Sources: *Economic Census of the United States*, 1997. Only those industries are shown for which both employment and sales/revenue data were available. For the definition of MSAs, CMSAs, and PMSAs, please see the Introduction.

FORT WORTH—ARLINGTON, TX PMSA

NAICS	Industry	Estab-lish-ments	Em-ploy-ment	Payroll		Sales, reven. ($ mil.)
				Total ($ mil.)	Per Empl. ($)	
48-49	Transportation and warehousing	856	15,117	410.1	27,126	1,638.1
481	Air transportation	14	505	21.7	42,929	177.5
484	Truck transportation	461	6,276	170.7	27,203	701.3
4841	General freight trucking	226	3,224	85.0	26,359	327.7
484110	General freight trucking, local	87	937	18.5	19,709	58.0
4841101	General freight trucking without storage, local, truckload (tl)	55	348	7.8	22,425	29.4
4841102	General freight trucking without storage, local, less than truckload (ltl)	22	514	8.8	17,023	23.3
48412	General freight trucking, long-distance	139	2,287	66.5	29,084	269.6
484121	General freight trucking, long-distance, truckload (tl)	109	1,484	39.8	26,853	166.5
484122	General freight trucking, long-distance, less than truckload (ltl)	30	803	26.7	33,207	103.1
4842	Specialized freight trucking	235	3,052	85.7	28,095	373.7
484210	Used household and office goods moving	40	536	12.7	23,642	49.9
4842101	Used household and office goods moving, local, without storage	14	55	1.0	17,418	4.0
4842102	Used household and office goods moving, long-distance	17	241	5.6	23,104	31.8
484220	Specialized freight (except used goods) trucking, local	134	773	20.0	25,854	96.6
4842203	Dump trucking	82	293	6.5	22,287	34.0
4842204	Specialized trucking without storage, local	40	298	9.2	30,906	50.4
484230	Specialized freight (except used goods) trucking, long-distance	61	1,743	53.1	30,458	227.2
4842303	Other specialized trucking, long-distance	41	1,023	34.3	33,512	163.0
485	Transit and ground passenger transportation	33	1,530	24.4	15,948	47.2
4853	Taxi and limousine service	12	103	1.5	14,369	5.1
485510	Charter bus industry	11	273	3.5	12,656	12.3
488	Support activities for transportation	235	4,700	137.5	29,254	463.0
4881	Support activities for air transportation	58	2,030	51.3	25,269	201.7
4881191	Airport operation and terminal services	19	1,080	15.9	14,754	52.1
488190	Other support activities for air transportation	39	950	35.4	37,224	149.5
4884	Support activities for road transportation	37	438	8.4	19,176	20.2
488410	Motor vehicle towing	33	220	5.0	22,545	14.0
488510	Freight transportation arrangement	130	1,903	69.5	36,532	213.3
4885101	Freight forwarding	74	1,089	41.0	37,611	154.2
4885102	Arrangement of transportation of freight and cargo	56	814	28.6	35,090	59.1
492	Couriers and messengers	65	1,296	32.3	24,921	152.3
492110	Couriers	26	963	21.5	22,289	118.8
4921101	Courier services (except by air)	14	541	8.0	14,823	68.2
4921102	Air courier services	12	422	13.4	31,860	50.6
492210	Local messengers and local delivery	39	333	10.8	32,532	33.6
4931	Warehousing and storage	40	739	20.9	28,341	74.4
4931101	General warehousing and storage (except in foreign trade zones)	25	425	10.4	24,433	37.6

Sources: *Economic Census of the United States*, 1997. Only those industries are shown for which both employment and sales/revenue data were available. For the definition of MSAs, CMSAs, and PMSAs, please see the Introduction.

FRESNO, CA MSA

NAICS	Industry	Estab-lish-ments	Em-ploy-ment	Payroll		Sales, reven. ($ mil.)
				Total ($ mil.)	Per Empl. ($)	
48-49	Transportation and warehousing	533	5,709	148.9	26,073	618.0
484	Truck transportation	377	3,807	108.4	28,479	455.0
4841	General freight trucking	171	2,655	75.2	28,322	307.8
484110	General freight trucking, local	58	565	15.2	26,851	72.7
4841101	General freight trucking without storage, local, truckload (tl)	41	329	8.3	25,219	50.6
48412	General freight trucking, long-distance	113	2,090	60.0	28,720	235.1
484121	General freight trucking, long-distance, truckload (tl)	85	1,548	41.7	26,949	145.0
484122	General freight trucking, long-distance, less than truckload (ltl)	28	542	18.3	33,779	90.1
4842	Specialized freight trucking	206	1,152	33.2	28,841	147.3
484210	Used household and office goods moving	19	144	3.1	21,569	8.0
484220	Specialized freight (except used goods) trucking, local	136	523	15.8	30,262	78.1
4842202	Agricultural products trucking without storage, local	67	168	6.6	39,048	28.9
4842203	Dump trucking	35	270	7.0	26,085	37.9
4842204	Specialized trucking without storage, local	29	62	1.9	29,887	9.9
484230	Specialized freight (except used goods) trucking, long-distance	51	485	14.3	29,468	61.2
4842302	Agricultural products trucking, long-distance	32	232	5.6	24,216	23.6
485	Transit and ground passenger transportation	21	536	9.4	17,468	20.7
488	Support activities for transportation	73	450	12.4	27,489	50.7
488410	Motor vehicle towing	26	127	2.7	21,591	7.8
488510	Freight transportation arrangement	33	162	5.9	36,432	25.9
4885102	Arrangement of transportation of freight and cargo	25	135	5.2	38,622	23.5
492	Couriers and messengers	24	427	7.4	17,433	28.3
492210	Local messengers and local delivery	14	152	2.2	14,513	7.4
4931	Warehousing and storage	24	314	6.2	19,723	26.4
4931101	General warehousing and storage (except in foreign trade zones)	13	118	2.1	18,042	7.7

Sources: *Economic Census of the United States*, 1997. Only those industries are shown for which both employment and sales/revenue data were available. For the definition of MSAs, CMSAs, and PMSAs, please see the Introduction.

GADSDEN, AL MSA

NAICS	Industry	Estab-lish-ments	Em-ploy-ment	Payroll		Sales, reven. ($ mil.)
				Total ($ mil.)	Per Empl. ($)	
48-49	Transportation and warehousing	59	950	23.2	24,437	76.9
484	Truck transportation	45	633	16.7	26,408	55.7
4841	General freight trucking	26	547	15.0	27,450	49.5
48412	General freight trucking, long-distance	19	535	14.8	27,755	48.6
484121	General freight trucking, long-distance, truckload (tl)	15	451	11.0	24,457	38.1
4842	Specialized freight trucking	19	86	1.7	19,779	6.2
488	Support activities for transportation	6	45	0.8	17,711	3.4
493	Warehousing and storage	4	167	3.8	22,725	13.0

Sources: *Economic Census of the United States*, 1997. Only those industries are shown for which both employment and sales/revenue data were available. For the definition of MSAs, CMSAs, and PMSAs, please see the Introduction.

GAINESVILLE, FL MSA

NAICS	Industry	Estab-lish-ments	Em-ploy-ment	Payroll		Sales, reven. ($ mil.)
				Total ($ mil.)	Per Empl. ($)	
48-49	Transportation and warehousing	55	426	8.4	19,746	36.4
481	Air transportation	3	38	0.7	18,342	6.4
484	Truck transportation	26	182	3.5	19,258	15.5
4842	Specialized freight trucking	20	160	2.8	17,600	12.9
485	Transit and ground passenger transportation	5	40	0.5	11,825	2.5
488	Support activities for transportation	10	81	1.5	19,099	5.9
492	Couriers and messengers	8	81	2.1	25,346	5.6

Sources: *Economic Census of the United States*, 1997. Only those industries are shown for which both employment and sales/revenue data were available. For the definition of MSAs, CMSAs, and PMSAs, please see the Introduction.

GALVESTON—TEXAS CITY, TX PMSA

NAICS	Industry	Estab-lish-ments	Em-ploy-ment	Payroll		Sales, reven. ($ mil.)
				Total ($ mil.)	Per Empl. ($)	
48-49	Transportation and warehousing	137	1,841	54.1	29,372	233.8
481	Air transportation	4	59	2.3	38,983	10.4
483	Water transportation	9	320	9.1	28,306	45.1
484	Truck transportation	38	349	11.3	32,347	37.5
4841	General freight trucking	12	88	2.2	24,580	6.9
4842	Specialized freight trucking	26	261	9.1	34,966	30.5
484220	Specialized freight (except used goods) trucking, local	14	110	3.3	30,182	11.2
486	Pipeline transportation	6	97	4.6	47,928	43.7
488	Support activities for transportation	56	599	17.7	29,606	62.7
4883	Support activities for water transportation	36	514	15.9	31,025	57.8
488330	Navigational services to shipping	15	122	6.0	48,795	14.6
4883302	Navigational services	11	26	2.7	105,346	7.1
493	Warehousing and storage	5	195	5.7	29,308	23.8

Sources: *Economic Census of the United States*, 1997. Only those industries are shown for which both employment and sales/revenue data were available. For the definition of MSAs, CMSAs, and PMSAs, please see the Introduction.

GARY, IN PMSA

NAICS	Industry	Estab-lish-ments	Em-ploy-ment	Payroll		Sales, reven. ($ mil.)
				Total ($ mil.)	Per Empl. ($)	
48-49	Transportation and warehousing	442	8,123	214.0	26,341	926.1
484	Truck transportation	297	5,686	156.2	27,467	683.3
4841	General freight trucking	129	3,588	93.9	26,170	412.7
484110	General freight trucking, local	41	361	10.5	29,017	54.7
4841101	General freight trucking without storage, local, truckload (tl)	36	311	9.6	30,714	52.8
48412	General freight trucking, long-distance	88	3,227	83.4	25,852	358.0
484121	General freight trucking, long-distance, truckload (tl)	76	2,963	72.9	24,597	324.4
484122	General freight trucking, long-distance, less than truckload (ltl)	12	264	10.5	39,936	33.6
4842	Specialized freight trucking	168	2,098	62.3	29,685	270.7
484210	Used household and office goods moving	21	185	3.0	16,411	7.6
4842101	Used household and office goods moving, local, without storage	13	88	1.5	16,830	3.5
484220	Specialized freight (except used goods) trucking, local	99	936	28.5	30,453	96.1
4842201	Hazardous materials trucking (except waste), local	11	109	3.4	31,413	9.3
4842203	Dump trucking	55	611	18.7	30,571	58.7
4842204	Specialized trucking without storage, local	25	166	4.8	28,633	24.8
484230	Specialized freight (except used goods) trucking, long-distance	48	977	30.7	31,464	167.0
4842303	Other specialized trucking, long-distance	34	834	24.7	29,633	148.6
486	Pipeline transportation	9	137	6.9	50,226	71.5
488	Support activities for transportation	56	482	16.5	34,207	57.0
488410	Motor vehicle towing	18	127	3.5	27,559	10.1
488510	Freight transportation arrangement	27	142	4.4	30,859	15.2
4885102	Arrangement of transportation of freight and cargo	20	108	3.9	35,954	13.7
4931	Warehousing and storage	23	352	11.0	31,216	40.0
4931101	General warehousing and storage (except in foreign trade zones)	13	190	6.3	33,274	21.6

Sources: Economic Census of the United States, 1997. Only those industries are shown for which both employment and sales/revenue data were available. For the definition of MSAs, CMSAs, and PMSAs, please see the Introduction.

GLENS FALLS, NY MSA

NAICS	Industry	Estab-lish-ments	Em-ploy-ment	Payroll		Sales, reven. ($ mil.)
				Total ($ mil.)	Per Empl. ($)	
48-49	Transportation and warehousing	49	363	9.0	24,868	32.6
484	Truck transportation	34	269	6.4	23,978	23.6
4841	General freight trucking	13	77	2.1	27,779	7.6
4842	Specialized freight trucking	21	192	4.3	22,453	16.0
488	Support activities for transportation	3	28	0.8	27,321	2.8

Sources: Economic Census of the United States, 1997. Only those industries are shown for which both employment and sales/revenue data were available. For the definition of MSAs, CMSAs, and PMSAs, please see the Introduction.

GOLDSBORO, NC MSA

NAICS	Industry	Estab-lish-ments	Em-ploy-ment	Payroll		Sales, reven. ($ mil.)
				Total ($ mil.)	Per Empl. ($)	
48-49	Transportation and warehousing	61	471	11.4	24,308	51.3
484	Truck transportation	43	374	9.8	26,329	46.3
4842	Specialized freight trucking	33	294	8.2	27,799	29.8
485	Transit and ground passenger transportation	5	37	0.3	9,081	0.6
493	Warehousing and storage	6	42	0.8	20,143	2.9

Sources: Economic Census of the United States, 1997. Only those industries are shown for which both employment and sales/revenue data were available. For the definition of MSAs, CMSAs, and PMSAs, please see the Introduction.

GRAND FORKS, ND—MN MSA

| NAICS | Industry | Estab-lish-ments | Em-ploy-ment | Payroll | | Sales, reven. ($ mil.) |
				Total ($ mil.)	Per Empl. ($)	
48-49	Transportation and warehousing	100	884	18.3	20,698	97.2
484	Truck transportation	75	647	13.4	20,743	78.3
4841	General freight trucking	27	226	5.7	25,159	46.7
484121	General freight trucking, long-distance, truckload (tl)	16	175	4.1	23,314	40.7
4842	Specialized freight trucking	48	421	7.7	18,373	31.7
484220	Specialized freight (except used goods) trucking, local	26	274	4.2	15,226	17.3
4842202	Agricultural products trucking without storage, local	11	201	2.3	11,308	7.7
484230	Specialized freight (except used goods) trucking, long-distance	15	71	1.6	22,930	9.2
4842302	Agricultural products trucking, long-distance	11	61	1.4	22,213	7.3
488	Support activities for transportation	9	68	1.5	21,338	6.6
493	Warehousing and storage	3	13	0.2	12,846	0.4

Sources: *Economic Census of the United States*, 1997. Only those industries are shown for which both employment and sales/revenue data were available. For the definition of MSAs, CMSAs, and PMSAs, please see the Introduction.

GRAND JUNCTION, CO MSA

| NAICS | Industry | Estab-lish-ments | Em-ploy-ment | Payroll | | Sales, reven. ($ mil.) |
				Total ($ mil.)	Per Empl. ($)	
48-49	Transportation and warehousing	89	1,206	28.1	23,272	113.6
484	Truck transportation	63	520	13.9	26,729	54.1
4841	General freight trucking	27	283	7.7	27,219	26.7
48412	General freight trucking, long-distance	21	265	7.5	28,136	25.8
484121	General freight trucking, long-distance, truckload (tl)	12	169	4.6	27,467	15.4
4842	Specialized freight trucking	36	237	6.2	26,143	27.4
484220	Specialized freight (except used goods) trucking, local	15	88	3.1	34,875	12.1
484230	Specialized freight (except used goods) trucking, long-distance	14	107	2.1	19,486	7.9
488	Support activities for transportation	10	239	7.3	30,611	31.4
492	Couriers and messengers	5	121	1.9	15,843	5.3

Sources: *Economic Census of the United States*, 1997. Only those industries are shown for which both employment and sales/revenue data were available. For the definition of MSAs, CMSAs, and PMSAs, please see the Introduction.

GRAND RAPIDS—MUSKEGON—HOLLAND, MI MSA

NAICS	Industry	Estab-lish-ments	Em-ploy-ment	Payroll		Sales, reven. ($ mil.)
				Total ($ mil.)	Per Empl. ($)	
48-49	Transportation and warehousing	534	11,757	394.7	33,570	1,099.9
481	Air transportation	13	120	2.8	23,583	21.3
484	Truck transportation	337	6,124	216.8	35,406	692.9
4841	General freight trucking	197	4,943	179.7	36,352	563.9
484110	General freight trucking, local	47	438	10.6	24,242	36.1
4841101	General freight trucking without storage, local, truckload (tl)	31	216	4.6	21,426	19.5
48412	General freight trucking, long-distance	150	4,505	169.1	37,529	527.8
484121	General freight trucking, long-distance, truckload (tl)	111	3,000	109.2	36,412	348.0
484122	General freight trucking, long-distance, less than truckload (ltl)	39	1,505	59.8	39,755	179.8
4842	Specialized freight trucking	140	1,181	37.1	31,447	129.0
484210	Used household and office goods moving	20	358	10.9	30,330	28.0
484220	Specialized freight (except used goods) trucking, local	86	437	13.2	30,137	59.4
4842202	Agricultural products trucking without storage, local	22	76	1.6	21,013	14.8
4842203	Dump trucking	45	224	8.1	36,022	34.1
484230	Specialized freight (except used goods) trucking, long-distance	34	386	13.1	33,966	41.6
4842303	Other specialized trucking, long-distance	21	236	8.3	35,076	23.7
485	Transit and ground passenger transportation	18	285	5.5	19,207	17.3
487	Scenic and sightseeing transportation	8	2	0.2	92,500	0.7
488	Support activities for transportation	87	616	14.6	23,744	41.9
4884	Support activities for road transportation	33	315	6.7	21,133	14.4
488410	Motor vehicle towing	29	174	3.1	17,701	8.4
488510	Freight transportation arrangement	41	176	6.2	35,347	20.3
4885101	Freight forwarding	12	44	1.3	28,977	4.9
4885102	Arrangement of transportation of freight and cargo	29	132	4.9	37,470	15.4
492	Couriers and messengers	39	4,360	142.6	32,717	278.2
492110	Couriers	21	4,087	137.7	33,704	268.4
4921102	Air courier services	12	587	15.1	25,719	61.1
492210	Local messengers and local delivery	18	273	4.9	17,938	9.8
4931	Warehousing and storage	26	182	5.2	28,813	21.2
4931101	General warehousing and storage (except in foreign trade zones)	19	111	3.4	30,297	12.3

Sources: *Economic Census of the United States*, 1997. Only those industries are shown for which both employment and sales/revenue data were available. For the definition of MSAs, CMSAs, and PMSAs, please see the Introduction.

GREAT FALLS, MT MSA

NAICS	Industry	Estab-lish-ments	Em-ploy-ment	Payroll		Sales, reven. ($ mil.)
				Total ($ mil.)	Per Empl. ($)	
48-49	Transportation and warehousing	83	601	11.3	18,765	53.4
484	Truck transportation	66	366	7.9	21,702	45.1
4841	General freight trucking	31	161	3.6	22,292	16.8
484110	General freight trucking, local	11	27	0.5	16,963	2.4
48412	General freight trucking, long-distance	20	134	3.1	23,366	14.4
484121	General freight trucking, long-distance, truckload (tl)	16	114	2.3	20,588	10.9
4842	Specialized freight trucking	35	205	4.4	21,239	28.3
484210	Used household and office goods moving	12	112	2.4	21,759	19.7
484220	Specialized freight (except used goods) trucking, local	13	56	1.3	23,107	6.0
485	Transit and ground passenger transportation	5	137	1.1	8,197	2.5
492	Couriers and messengers	6	74	1.8	24,581	4.6

Sources: *Economic Census of the United States*, 1997. Only those industries are shown for which both employment and sales/revenue data were available. For the definition of MSAs, CMSAs, and PMSAs, please see the Introduction.

GREELEY, CO PMSA

NAICS	Industry	Establish-ments	Em-ploy-ment	Payroll Total ($ mil.)	Payroll Per Empl. ($)	Sales, reven. ($ mil.)
48-49	Transportation and warehousing	172	1,236	31.5	25,471	171.9
484	Truck transportation	139	917	25.0	27,262	149.6
4841	General freight trucking	63	544	15.3	28,165	111.4
484110	General freight trucking, local	21	130	3.8	29,315	18.9
4841101	General freight trucking without storage, local, truckload (tl)	16	72	1.9	26,903	13.9
48412	General freight trucking, long-distance	42	414	11.5	27,804	92.5
4842	Specialized freight trucking	76	373	9.7	25,944	38.2
484220	Specialized freight (except used goods) trucking, local	42	173	4.7	27,162	15.5
4842203	Dump trucking	19	64	1.9	28,937	7.4
484230	Specialized freight (except used goods) trucking, long-distance	28	144	3.7	25,486	17.0
4842302	Agricultural products trucking, long-distance	18	86	2.3	26,174	12.4
485	Transit and ground passenger transportation	4	60	0.8	13,683	2.5
488	Support activities for transportation	17	107	2.8	26,355	9.3
492	Couriers and messengers	6	98	1.6	16,337	5.7
493	Warehousing and storage	6	54	1.2	22,981	4.8

Sources: Economic Census of the United States, 1997. Only those industries are shown for which both employment and sales/revenue data were available. For the definition of MSAs, CMSAs, and PMSAs, please see the Introduction.

GREEN BAY, WI MSA

NAICS	Industry	Establish-ments	Em-ploy-ment	Payroll Total ($ mil.)	Payroll Per Empl. ($)	Sales, reven. ($ mil.)
48-49	Transportation and warehousing	244	6,451	226.2	35,061	934.1
484	Truck transportation	184	5,230	200.0	38,232	820.0
4841	General freight trucking	89	4,630	184.1	39,756	758.8
484110	General freight trucking, local	21	195	4.4	22,467	18.5
4841101	General freight trucking without storage, local, truckload (tl)	12	81	1.9	23,926	9.2
48412	General freight trucking, long-distance	68	4,435	179.7	40,516	740.3
484121	General freight trucking, long-distance, truckload (tl)	60	4,272	172.5	40,389	710.1
4842	Specialized freight trucking	95	600	15.9	26,468	61.2
484220	Specialized freight (except used goods) trucking, local	72	264	7.3	27,633	24.1
4842203	Dump trucking	51	175	4.9	28,183	17.3
484230	Specialized freight (except used goods) trucking, long-distance	14	247	6.9	28,020	32.0
485	Transit and ground passenger transportation	16	492	5.9	12,073	17.0
488	Support activities for transportation	20	351	11.4	32,578	67.8
492	Couriers and messengers	9	157	3.4	21,567	9.8
4931	Warehousing and storage	11	203	5.0	24,419	17.1

Sources: Economic Census of the United States, 1997. Only those industries are shown for which both employment and sales/revenue data were available. For the definition of MSAs, CMSAs, and PMSAs, please see the Introduction.

GREENSBORO—WINSTON-SALEM—HIGH POINT, NC MSA

NAICS	Industry	Estab- lish- ments	Em- ploy- ment	Payroll		Sales, reven. ($ mil.)
				Total ($ mil.)	Per Empl. ($)	
48-49	Transportation and warehousing	814	16,074	484.7	30,156	1,376.9
481	Air transportation	14	138	4.9	35,732	27.8
484	Truck transportation	517	10,901	342.9	31,457	861.2
4841	General freight trucking	247	7,016	234.7	33,458	553.0
484110	General freight trucking, local	75	725	17.8	24,506	56.0
4841101	General freight trucking without storage, local, truckload (tl)	48	246	5.6	22,606	26.8
4841102	General freight trucking without storage, local, less than truckload (ltl)	22	450	11.2	24,931	26.6
48412	General freight trucking, long-distance	172	6,291	217.0	34,489	497.0
484121	General freight trucking, long-distance, truckload (tl)	133	2,733	91.8	33,572	287.4
484122	General freight trucking, long-distance, less than truckload (ltl)	39	3,558	125.2	35,193	209.6
4842	Specialized freight trucking	270	3,885	108.2	27,846	308.2
484210	Used household and office goods moving	53	1,301	31.7	24,333	81.8
4842102	Used household and office goods moving, long-distance	30	1,150	28.6	24,871	74.4
484220	Specialized freight (except used goods) trucking, local	161	935	24.7	26,371	85.3
4842202	Agricultural products trucking without storage, local	18	72	1.6	22,056	6.1
4842203	Dump trucking	102	492	12.7	25,756	49.6
4842204	Specialized trucking without storage, local	35	333	9.3	27,952	26.1
484230	Specialized freight (except used goods) trucking, long-distance	56	1,649	51.9	31,453	141.0
4842303	Other specialized trucking, long-distance	36	1,476	46.5	31,532	119.4
485	Transit and ground passenger transportation	50	565	8.5	14,989	20.5
4853	Taxi and limousine service	28	104	0.8	7,346	3.0
485310	Taxi service	21	85	0.7	8,118	2.5
485510	Charter bus industry	12	169	2.6	15,550	10.1
487	Scenic and sightseeing transportation	3	7	0.0	3,857	0.2
488	Support activities for transportation	122	2,701	89.5	33,128	292.8
488190	Other support activities for air transportation	12	1,428	53.4	37,361	130.7
488410	Motor vehicle towing	26	141	2.9	20,766	9.0
488510	Freight transportation arrangement	67	456	14.3	31,458	47.2
4885101	Freight forwarding	25	272	8.2	30,169	19.6
4885102	Arrangement of transportation of freight and cargo	42	184	6.1	33,364	27.6
492	Couriers and messengers	51	979	20.0	20,443	79.9
492110	Couriers	28	874	18.1	20,672	75.0
4921101	Courier services (except by air)	12	315	3.7	11,632	13.4
4921102	Air courier services	16	559	14.4	25,766	61.6
492210	Local messengers and local delivery	23	105	1.9	18,543	4.9
4931	Warehousing and storage	50	711	15.0	21,058	40.0
4931101	General warehousing and storage (except in foreign trade zones)	34	615	13.6	22,161	33.7

Sources: Economic Census of the United States, 1997. Only those industries are shown for which both employment and sales/revenue data were available. For the definition of MSAs, CMSAs, and PMSAs, please see the Introduction.

GREENVILLE, NC MSA

NAICS	Industry	Estab- lish- ments	Em- ploy- ment	Payroll		Sales, reven. ($ mil.)
				Total ($ mil.)	Per Empl. ($)	
48-49	Transportation and warehousing	75	585	12.1	20,612	46.7
484	Truck transportation	44	317	6.7	20,981	26.0
4841	General freight trucking	16	229	4.7	20,472	16.9
4842	Specialized freight trucking	28	88	2.0	22,307	9.1
484220	Specialized freight (except used goods) trucking, local	17	44	1.1	23,977	4.4
488	Support activities for transportation	7	55	1.7	31,073	5.9
492	Couriers and messengers	7	128	1.7	13,203	6.9
493	Warehousing and storage	7	39	1.3	33,308	5.2

Sources: Economic Census of the United States, 1997. Only those industries are shown for which both employment and sales/revenue data were available. For the definition of MSAs, CMSAs, and PMSAs, please see the Introduction.

GREENVILLE—SPARTANBURG—ANDERSON, SC MSA

NAICS	Industry	Estab-lish-ments	Em-ploy-ment	Payroll		Sales, reven. ($ mil.)
				Total ($ mil.)	Per Empl. ($)	
48-49	Transportation and warehousing	520	10,844	341.8	31,521	1,031.6
484	Truck transportation	316	6,464	200.0	30,937	562.4
4841	General freight trucking	174	4,626	146.2	31,604	371.6
484110	General freight trucking, local	47	418	8.9	21,270	28.3
4841101	General freight trucking without storage, local, truckload (tl)	33	185	5.0	27,108	20.6
48412	General freight trucking, long-distance	127	4,208	137.3	32,631	343.3
484121	General freight trucking, long-distance, truckload (tl)	86	1,383	37.3	26,942	144.0
484122	General freight trucking, long-distance, less than truckload (ltl)	41	2,825	100.0	35,416	199.3
4842	Specialized freight trucking	142	1,838	53.8	29,257	190.8
484210	Used household and office goods moving	22	459	12.0	26,174	26.9
484220	Specialized freight (except used goods) trucking, local	65	484	12.2	25,157	38.2
4842203	Dump trucking	25	253	5.7	22,632	18.7
4842204	Specialized trucking without storage, local	23	156	4.3	27,417	13.6
484230	Specialized freight (except used goods) trucking, long-distance	55	895	29.6	33,056	125.7
4842301	Hazardous materials trucking (except waste), long-distance	21	222	6.9	30,977	45.2
4842303	Other specialized trucking, long-distance	25	640	21.8	34,117	75.9
488	Support activities for transportation	84	2,930	109.5	37,364	302.9
488410	Motor vehicle towing	21	58	0.8	14,155	3.6
488510	Freight transportation arrangement	38	255	8.2	32,102	44.9
4885101	Freight forwarding	16	126	4.4	35,294	20.6
4885102	Arrangement of transportation of freight and cargo	22	129	3.7	28,984	24.3
492	Couriers and messengers	32	584	11.7	20,005	57.8
492110	Couriers	17	403	9.2	22,861	51.5
492210	Local messengers and local delivery	15	181	2.5	13,646	6.3
4931	Warehousing and storage	48	624	14.8	23,702	50.8
4931101	General warehousing and storage (except in foreign trade zones)	35	477	10.3	21,667	34.4

Sources: Economic Census of the United States, 1997. Only those industries are shown for which both employment and sales/revenue data were available. For the definition of MSAs, CMSAs, and PMSAs, please see the Introduction.

HAGERSTOWN, MD PMSA

NAICS	Industry	Estab-lish-ments	Em-ploy-ment	Payroll		Sales, reven. ($ mil.)
				Total ($ mil.)	Per Empl. ($)	
48-49	Transportation and warehousing	118	2,037	64.0	31,427	143.1
484	Truck transportation	60	1,561	53.6	34,316	106.2
4841	General freight trucking	34	1,410	50.0	35,496	90.7
484110	General freight trucking, local	11	57	1.7	30,509	4.7
48412	General freight trucking, long-distance	23	1,353	48.3	35,707	86.0
484121	General freight trucking, long-distance, truckload (tl)	18	961	31.4	32,639	54.5
4842	Specialized freight trucking	26	151	3.5	23,298	15.5
488	Support activities for transportation	19	156	3.9	24,910	12.5

Sources: Economic Census of the United States, 1997. Only those industries are shown for which both employment and sales/revenue data were available. For the definition of MSAs, CMSAs, and PMSAs, please see the Introduction.

HAMILTON—MIDDLETOWN, OH PMSA

NAICS	Industry	Estab-lish-ments	Em-ploy-ment	Payroll Total ($ mil.)	Payroll Per Empl. ($)	Sales, reven. ($ mil.)
48-49	Transportation and warehousing	183	4,386	107.6	24,538	346.9
484	Truck transportation	125	3,363	91.0	27,070	288.8
4841	General freight trucking	57	1,884	50.0	26,526	119.3
484110	General freight trucking, local	15	369	6.1	16,556	27.6
4841101	General freight trucking without storage, local, truckload (tl)	11	188	4.1	21,824	24.8
48412	General freight trucking, long-distance	42	1,515	43.9	28,954	91.7
484121	General freight trucking, long-distance, truckload (tl)	35	657	17.7	26,883	65.5
4842	Specialized freight trucking	68	1,479	41.1	27,763	169.5
484210	Used household and office goods moving	11	636	15.0	23,509	65.9
484220	Specialized freight (except used goods) trucking, local	40	245	6.5	26,486	26.6
4842203	Dump trucking	28	114	2.8	24,825	15.6
484230	Specialized freight (except used goods) trucking, long-distance	17	598	19.6	32,811	76.9
4842303	Other specialized trucking, long-distance	13	431	14.2	33,032	61.1
485	Transit and ground passenger transportation	15	633	6.1	9,651	11.1
488	Support activities for transportation	27	178	5.1	28,545	16.8
488510	Freight transportation arrangement	14	76	2.4	32,171	9.8
493	Warehousing and storage	9	157	3.6	22,892	19.1

Sources: *Economic Census of the United States*, 1997. Only those industries are shown for which both employment and sales/revenue data were available. For the definition of MSAs, CMSAs, and PMSAs, please see the Introduction.

HARRISBURG—LEBANON—CARLISLE, PA MSA

NAICS	Industry	Estab-lish-ments	Em-ploy-ment	Payroll Total ($ mil.)	Payroll Per Empl. ($)	Sales, reven. ($ mil.)
48-49	Transportation and warehousing	327	18,954	547.0	28,859	1,359.1
484	Truck transportation	167	9,742	323.1	33,165	690.4
4841	General freight trucking	89	8,541	288.1	33,732	552.2
484110	General freight trucking, local	25	460	9.5	20,746	23.3
4841101	General freight trucking without storage, local, truckload (tl)	13	111	2.6	23,595	8.0
48412	General freight trucking, long-distance	64	8,081	278.6	34,472	528.9
484121	General freight trucking, long-distance, truckload (tl)	44	4,180	130.0	31,111	356.6
484122	General freight trucking, long-distance, less than truckload (ltl)	20	3,901	148.5	38,073	172.3
4842	Specialized freight trucking	78	1,201	35.0	29,129	138.2
484210	Used household and office goods moving	11	352	10.3	29,332	22.1
484220	Specialized freight (except used goods) trucking, local	43	365	9.1	24,890	29.6
4842203	Dump trucking	13	44	1.1	25,273	4.2
4842204	Specialized trucking without storage, local	14	86	2.4	28,151	12.1
484230	Specialized freight (except used goods) trucking, long-distance	24	484	15.6	32,178	86.4
4842303	Other specialized trucking, long-distance	17	445	14.3	32,207	82.7
485	Transit and ground passenger transportation	52	1,581	17.0	10,760	47.2
4854101	School bus service	39	1,320	13.1	9,886	36.8
486	Pipeline transportation	10	109	5.7	51,908	80.3
488510	Freight transportation arrangement	21	215	4.7	21,735	15.2
4885102	Arrangement of transportation of freight and cargo	12	66	2.1	32,288	7.1
492	Couriers and messengers	18	4,708	133.2	28,298	331.9
492110	Couriers	11	4,621	131.4	28,446	323.1
4931	Warehousing and storage	34	1,869	42.2	22,553	128.2

Sources: *Economic Census of the United States*, 1997. Only those industries are shown for which both employment and sales/revenue data were available. For the definition of MSAs, CMSAs, and PMSAs, please see the Introduction.

HARTFORD, CT MSA

NAICS	Industry	Estab-lish-ments	Em-ploy-ment	Payroll		Sales, reven. ($ mil.)
				Total ($ mil.)	Per Empl. ($)	
48-49	Transportation and warehousing	528	12,701	361.0	28,419	1,076.5
484	Truck transportation	240	2,531	92.0	36,339	335.8
4841	General freight trucking	100	1,465	52.1	35,534	195.5
484110	General freight trucking, local	47	425	12.7	29,805	53.8
4841101	General freight trucking without storage, local, truckload (tl)	21	244	8.8	36,090	39.5
4841102	General freight trucking without storage, local, less than truckload (ltl)	21	118	2.9	24,610	11.3
48412	General freight trucking, long-distance	53	1,040	39.4	37,876	141.7
484121	General freight trucking, long-distance, truckload (tl)	38	499	16.1	32,190	74.7
484122	General freight trucking, long-distance, less than truckload (ltl)	15	541	23.3	43,120	67.0
4842	Specialized freight trucking	140	1,066	39.9	37,446	140.3
484210	Used household and office goods moving	42	634	22.6	35,692	79.4
484220	Specialized freight (except used goods) trucking, local	76	271	10.7	39,605	39.2
4842203	Dump trucking	39	92	3.5	37,859	17.6
4842204	Specialized trucking without storage, local	23	154	6.0	39,065	15.3
484230	Specialized freight (except used goods) trucking, long-distance	22	161	6.6	40,714	21.7
485	Transit and ground passenger transportation	98	2,700	50.6	18,751	125.8
4853	Taxi and limousine service	30	302	4.7	15,626	13.2
4854101	School bus service	44	1,628	25.6	15,719	60.7
488	Support activities for transportation	102	1,380	39.5	28,646	150.8
4881	Support activities for air transportation	25	855	18.1	21,187	60.4
48811	Airport operations	12	536	5.9	11,093	20.1
488190	Other support activities for air transportation	13	319	12.2	38,147	40.2
488510	Freight transportation arrangement	62	446	19.2	43,058	67.6
492110	Couriers	27	5,390	161.7	29,991	371.7

Sources: *Economic Census of the United States*, 1997. Only those industries are shown for which both employment and sales/revenue data were available. For the definition of MSAs, CMSAs, and PMSAs, please see the Introduction.

HATTIESBURG, MS MSA

NAICS	Industry	Estab-lish-ments	Em-ploy-ment	Payroll		Sales, reven. ($ mil.)
				Total ($ mil.)	Per Empl. ($)	
48-49	Transportation and warehousing	111	848	22.4	26,364	94.3
484	Truck transportation	83	669	17.6	26,293	65.4
4841	General freight trucking	37	361	9.3	25,687	35.9
484110	General freight trucking, local	13	42	0.9	21,619	5.0
48412	General freight trucking, long-distance	24	319	8.4	26,223	30.9
484121	General freight trucking, long-distance, truckload (tl)	18	205	5.4	26,366	22.5
4842	Specialized freight trucking	46	308	8.3	27,003	29.5
484220	Specialized freight (except used goods) trucking, local	30	141	3.2	22,539	11.5
484230	Specialized freight (except used goods) trucking, long-distance	13	132	4.3	32,379	13.7
486	Pipeline transportation	4	37	1.6	42,027	18.3
488	Support activities for transportation	12	39	0.7	18,744	2.9

Sources: *Economic Census of the United States*, 1997. Only those industries are shown for which both employment and sales/revenue data were available. For the definition of MSAs, CMSAs, and PMSAs, please see the Introduction.

HICKORY—MORGANTON—LENOIR, NC MSA

NAICS	Industry	Estab-lish-ments	Em-ploy-ment	Payroll		Sales, reven. ($ mil.)
				Total ($ mil.)	Per Empl. ($)	
48-49	Transportation and warehousing	218	4,149	112.5	27,121	372.2
484	Truck transportation	171	3,612	101.5	28,089	326.6
4841	General freight trucking	103	3,005	88.8	29,556	280.0
484110	General freight trucking, local	25	304	7.0	23,039	17.8
4841101	General freight trucking without storage, local, truckload (tl)	17	60	1.2	20,467	6.7
48412	General freight trucking, long-distance	78	2,701	81.8	30,290	262.2
484121	General freight trucking, long-distance, truckload (tl)	44	810	25.7	31,725	89.2
484122	General freight trucking, long-distance, less than truckload (ltl)	34	1,891	56.1	29,675	173.0
4842	Specialized freight trucking	68	607	12.6	20,829	46.7
484210	Used household and office goods moving	16	290	5.7	19,576	15.7
484220	Specialized freight (except used goods) trucking, local	39	151	2.8	18,583	10.3
4842203	Dump trucking	21	61	1.1	18,098	6.3
484230	Specialized freight (except used goods) trucking, long-distance	13	166	4.2	25,060	20.7
488	Support activities for transportation	19	93	2.3	24,376	10.8
488510	Freight transportation arrangement	13	52	1.3	24,269	7.1
492	Couriers and messengers	9	229	4.5	19,721	15.3

Sources: Economic Census of the United States, 1997. Only those industries are shown for which both employment and sales/revenue data were available. For the definition of MSAs, CMSAs, and PMSAs, please see the Introduction.

HONOLULU, HI MSA

NAICS	Industry	Estab-lish-ments	Em-ploy-ment	Payroll		Sales, reven. ($ mil.)
				Total ($ mil.)	Per Empl. ($)	
48-49	Transportation and warehousing	395	12,496	339.6	27,176	965.3
481	Air transportation	23	738	19.3	26,108	111.5
481111	Scheduled passenger air transportation	12	578	16.0	27,666	100.1
483	Water transportation	10	948	31.5	33,237	158.1
484	Truck transportation	114	2,131	61.9	29,043	187.3
4841	General freight trucking	46	777	22.4	28,879	77.5
484110	General freight trucking, local	30	611	16.9	27,735	44.8
48412	General freight trucking, long-distance	16	166	5.5	33,090	32.7
4842	Specialized freight trucking	68	1,354	39.5	29,137	109.8
484210	Used household and office goods moving	16	790	25.5	32,223	59.9
4842203	Dump trucking	30	165	4.2	25,624	14.2
4842204	Specialized trucking without storage, local	15	229	3.8	16,751	10.8
4853	Taxi and limousine service	31	290	5.0	17,355	14.4
485310	Taxi service	12	107	1.7	15,439	5.3
485320	Limousine service	19	183	3.4	18,475	9.1
487	Scenic and sightseeing transportation	44	2,146	38.5	17,945	125.1
4871101	Sightseeing buses	12	1,230	24.7	20,108	63.2
487210	Scenic and sightseeing transportation, water	27	858	12.4	14,399	55.2
4872101	Excursion and sightseeing boats (including dinner cruises)	17	838	12.0	14,279	53.9
488	Support activities for transportation	97	2,257	70.6	31,259	166.9
4881	Support activities for air transportation	16	1,100	21.1	19,204	42.9
4883	Support activities for water transportation	17	749	37.9	50,618	77.6
488510	Freight transportation arrangement	51	289	10.1	34,799	41.7
4885101	Freight forwarding	29	153	4.8	31,359	22.5
4885102	Arrangement of transportation of freight and cargo	22	136	5.3	38,669	19.3
492	Couriers and messengers	36	1,097	28.6	26,077	75.3
492110	Couriers	17	905	25.2	27,875	66.1
492210	Local messengers and local delivery	19	192	3.4	17,599	9.2

Sources: Economic Census of the United States, 1997. Only those industries are shown for which both employment and sales/revenue data were available. For the definition of MSAs, CMSAs, and PMSAs, please see the Introduction.

HOUMA, LA MSA

NAICS	Industry	Estab-lish-ments	Em-ploy-ment	Payroll		Sales, reven. ($ mil.)
				Total ($ mil.)	Per Empl. ($)	
48-49	Transportation and warehousing	317	5,315	151.5	28,503	688.6
483	Water transportation	125	2,751	83.5	30,340	304.0
48311	Deep sea, coastal, and Great Lakes water transportation	76	1,914	59.7	31,167	231.0
483113	Coastal and Great Lakes freight transportation	65	1,678	54.5	32,496	198.3
4831131	Coastal and intercoastal freight transportation	26	745	19.3	25,843	80.5
4831133	Coastal and intercoastal towing service	39	933	35.3	37,808	117.8
48321	Inland water transportation	49	837	23.8	28,449	73.0
483211	Inland water freight transportation	34	739	22.5	30,502	69.3
4832111	Inland waterways freight transportation (except towing)	13	120	2.5	20,858	5.6
4832112	Inland waterways towing transportation	21	619	20.0	32,372	63.6
483212	Inland water passenger transportation	15	98	1.3	12,969	3.7
484	Truck transportation	64	857	19.0	22,121	49.1
4841	General freight trucking	29	713	16.0	22,505	35.2
48412	General freight trucking, long-distance	23	704	15.9	22,554	34.1
484121	General freight trucking, long-distance, truckload (tl)	16	475	11.9	25,044	20.1
4842	Specialized freight trucking	35	144	2.9	20,222	13.9
484220	Specialized freight (except used goods) trucking, local	25	120	2.4	20,017	12.1
4842203	Dump trucking	15	51	1.0	20,039	6.1
486	Pipeline transportation	14	288	15.7	54,354	207.1
487	Scenic and sightseeing transportation	9	55	0.9	15,836	8.1
488	Support activities for transportation	87	1,155	26.3	22,758	83.7
4883	Support activities for water transportation	63	1,059	23.5	22,153	67.0
488330	Navigational services to shipping	41	557	16.3	29,241	47.7
4883301	Tugboat service (including fleeting and harbor service)	36	527	15.8	29,981	46.6
4883901	Other services incidental to water transportation	15	462	6.1	13,156	15.2

Sources: Economic Census of the United States, 1997. Only those industries are shown for which both employment and sales/revenue data were available. For the definition of MSAs, CMSAs, and PMSAs, please see the Introduction.

HOUSTON, TX PMSA

NAICS	Industry	Estab-lish-ments	Em-ploy-ment	Payroll Total ($ mil.)	Payroll Per Empl. ($)	Sales, reven. ($ mil.)
48-49	Transportation and warehousing	2,442	56,743	1,978.1	34,861	10,164.8
481	Air transportation	68	948	38.0	40,077	419.6
48111	Scheduled air transportation	38	766	30.8	40,255	377.9
481111	Scheduled passenger air transportation	31	706	28.7	40,627	362.0
48121	Nonscheduled air transportation	30	182	7.2	39,330	41.7
481211	Nonscheduled chartered passenger air transportation	25	128	5.0	39,055	34.7
483	Water transportation	79	3,828	146.8	38,361	971.0
48311	Deep sea, coastal, and Great Lakes water transportation	54	2,133	93.0	43,578	691.4
483111	Deep sea freight transportation	39	1,219	51.0	41,821	442.2
483113	Coastal and Great Lakes freight transportation	15	914	42.0	45,920	249.2
48321	Inland water transportation	25	1,695	53.9	31,795	279.7
484	Truck transportation	961	17,640	523.2	29,658	1,933.2
4841	General freight trucking	439	9,739	291.8	29,965	1,047.1
484110	General freight trucking, local	182	1,912	51.7	27,030	212.3
4841101	General freight trucking without storage, local, truckload (tl)	119	1,379	38.4	27,833	162.1
4841102	General freight trucking without storage, local, less than truckload (ltl)	44	354	8.5	23,932	30.8
4841103	General freight trucking with storage, local, truckload (tl)	12	95	2.6	27,000	12.0
48412	General freight trucking, long-distance	257	7,827	240.2	30,683	834.8
484121	General freight trucking, long-distance, truckload (tl)	205	3,912	112.7	28,805	457.7
484122	General freight trucking, long-distance, less than truckload (ltl)	52	3,915	127.5	32,558	377.2
4842	Specialized freight trucking	522	7,901	231.3	29,279	886.1
484210	Used household and office goods moving	101	1,798	45.3	25,181	165.5
4842101	Used household and office goods moving, local, without storage	32	277	4.9	17,700	15.5
4842102	Used household and office goods moving, long-distance	42	961	26.3	27,363	106.5
4842103	Used household and office goods moving, local, with storage	27	560	14.1	25,136	43.6
484220	Specialized freight (except used goods) trucking, local	272	2,323	64.6	27,827	250.3
4842201	Hazardous materials trucking (except waste), local	21	411	15.2	37,000	43.1
4842202	Agricultural products trucking without storage, local	14	57	1.8	31,526	7.1
4842203	Dump trucking	143	544	11.8	21,778	76.3
4842204	Specialized trucking without storage, local	82	1,023	27.9	27,291	96.0
4842205	Specialized trucking with storage, local	12	288	7.9	27,330	27.8
484230	Specialized freight (except used goods) trucking, long-distance	149	3,780	121.4	32,120	470.3
4842301	Hazardous materials trucking (except waste), long-distance	48	1,589	51.8	32,580	193.9
4842302	Agricultural products trucking, long-distance	15	86	4.1	47,767	23.5
4842303	Other specialized trucking, long-distance	86	2,105	65.5	31,134	252.9
485	Transit and ground passenger transportation	78	1,541	26.9	17,475	84.5
4853	Taxi and limousine service	41	650	12.5	19,302	39.7
485510	Charter bus industry	12	293	4.4	15,143	15.3
48599	Other transit and ground passenger transportation	14	86	1.4	15,791	5.4
486	Pipeline transportation	132	5,461	360.4	65,990	3,736.0
486110	Pipeline transportation of crude oil	22	1,192	75.1	63,010	452.0
486210	Pipeline transportation of natural gas	86	3,698	250.5	67,749	2,919.6
4869	Other pipeline transportation	24	571	34.7	60,820	364.4
488	Support activities for transportation	782	16,816	572.4	34,039	1,875.2
4881	Support activities for air transportation	61	1,442	30.9	21,431	154.2
4881191	Airport operation and terminal services	28	930	13.1	14,117	41.5
488190	Other support activities for air transportation	33	512	17.8	34,717	112.8
4882101	Support activities incidental to rail transportation	14	222	6.4	28,950	27.2
4883	Support activities for water transportation	127	4,543	107.5	23,663	314.7
488320	Marine cargo handling	31	3,576	68.7	19,204	164.8
488330	Navigational services to shipping	40	370	16.1	43,416	83.5
4883301	Tugboat service (including fleeting and harbor service)	12	309	10.2	33,113	66.5
4883902	Marine cargo inspectors and surveyors	21	309	11.9	38,388	34.1
4884	Support activities for road transportation	75	709	13.2	18,581	43.9
488410	Motor vehicle towing	62	466	9.4	20,197	36.4
488490	Other support activities for road transportation	13	243	3.8	15,481	7.5
488510	Freight transportation arrangement	466	4,904	187.0	38,122	519.0
4885101	Freight forwarding	183	2,591	96.8	37,342	283.9
4885102	Arrangement of transportation of freight and cargo	283	2,313	90.2	38,997	235.1
48899	Other support activities for transportation	39	4,996	227.4	45,526	816.1
492110	Couriers	86	6,162	173.1	28,086	529.8
4921101	Courier services (except by air)	25	3,844	106.5	27,717	228.6
4921102	Air courier services	61	2,318	66.5	28,698	301.3
4931	Warehousing and storage	119	2,703	97.0	35,899	477.6
4931101	General warehousing and storage (except in foreign trade zones)	73	860	22.1	25,743	78.3
493190	Other warehousing and storage	36	1,584	69.4	43,838	376.4

Sources: Economic Census of the United States, 1997. Only those industries are shown for which both employment and sales/revenue data were available. For the definition of MSAs, CMSAs, and PMSAs, please see the Introduction.

HOUSTON—GALVESTON—BRAZORIA, TX CMSA

NAICS	Industry	Estab-lish-ments	Em-ploy-ment	Payroll Total ($ mil.)	Payroll Per Empl. ($)	Sales, reven. ($ mil.)
48-49	Transportation and warehousing	2,711	60,197	2,077.9	34,519	10,622.2
481	Air transportation	79	1,089	42.5	39,050	441.6
48111	Scheduled air transportation	38	766	30.8	40,255	377.9
481111	Scheduled passenger air transportation	31	706	28.7	40,627	362.0
48121	Nonscheduled air transportation	41	323	11.7	36,192	63.7
481211	Nonscheduled chartered passenger air transportation	32	202	7.4	36,535	47.6
483	Water transportation	93	4,292	159.3	37,117	1,025.3
48311	Deep sea, coastal, and Great Lakes water transportation	62	2,443	102.2	41,829	732.2
48321	Inland water transportation	31	1,849	57.1	30,891	293.1
484	Truck transportation	1,074	19,054	565.0	29,654	2,076.6
4841	General freight trucking	479	10,214	304.8	29,839	1,081.9
484110	General freight trucking, local	199	2,006	53.8	26,797	220.6
4841103	General freight trucking with storage, local, truckload (tl)	12	95	2.6	27,000	12.0
48412	General freight trucking, long-distance	280	8,208	251.0	30,582	861.4
4842	Specialized freight trucking	595	8,840	260.3	29,441	994.7
484210	Used household and office goods moving	113	1,888	46.7	24,733	168.7
4842102	Used household and office goods moving, long-distance	47	1,014	27.2	26,803	108.4
484220	Specialized freight (except used goods) trucking, local	304	2,572	72.7	28,267	278.9
4842203	Dump trucking	163	671	15.9	23,757	92.7
4842204	Specialized trucking without storage, local	90	1,058	28.7	27,104	99.0
4842205	Specialized trucking with storage, local	12	288	7.9	27,330	27.8
484230	Specialized freight (except used goods) trucking, long-distance	178	4,380	140.9	32,160	547.0
4842301	Hazardous materials trucking (except waste), long-distance	62	1,900	63.0	33,137	235.1
488	Support activities for transportation	862	17,643	596.4	33,806	1,956.3
4881	Support activities for air transportation	68	1,469	31.3	21,324	155.8
4881191	Airport operation and terminal services	32	944	13.3	14,121	42.3
488190	Other support activities for air transportation	36	525	18.0	34,276	113.5
4882101	Support activities incidental to rail transportation	17	282	7.8	27,730	31.4
4883	Support activities for water transportation	172	5,175	126.7	24,479	381.0
488320	Marine cargo handling	44	3,859	73.1	18,953	180.5
488510	Freight transportation arrangement	479	4,957	188.7	38,061	523.3
4921101	Courier services (except by air)	25	3,844	106.5	27,717	228.6
4931902	Specialized goods warehousing and storage	38	1,523	68.4	44,906	381.0

Sources: *Economic Census of the United States*, 1997. Only those industries are shown for which both employment and sales/revenue data were available. For the definition of MSAs, CMSAs, and PMSAs, please see the Introduction.

HUNTINGTON—ASHLAND, WV—KY—OH MSA

NAICS	Industry	Estab-lish-ments	Em-ploy-ment	Payroll Total ($ mil.)	Payroll Per Empl. ($)	Sales, reven. ($ mil.)
48-49	Transportation and warehousing	202	2,309	64.3	27,854	231.5
484	Truck transportation	133	1,091	31.7	29,044	135.7
4841	General freight trucking	37	326	9.1	27,942	39.1
484110	General freight trucking, local	11	43	0.9	19,814	2.5
48412	General freight trucking, long-distance	26	283	8.3	29,177	36.5
484121	General freight trucking, long-distance, truckload (tl)	22	211	5.7	26,981	27.8
4842	Specialized freight trucking	96	765	22.6	29,514	96.6
484220	Specialized freight (except used goods) trucking, local	69	434	11.6	26,684	52.9
4842203	Dump trucking	40	273	7.5	27,374	36.0
4842204	Specialized trucking without storage, local	16	76	1.4	18,250	7.3
484230	Specialized freight (except used goods) trucking, long-distance	24	299	9.9	33,187	40.9
488	Support activities for transportation	33	650	16.6	25,591	47.3
4883	Support activities for water transportation	17	485	14.1	29,089	40.4
492	Couriers and messengers	8	140	2.6	18,493	6.8
493	Warehousing and storage	5	80	1.6	20,037	5.0

Sources: *Economic Census of the United States*, 1997. Only those industries are shown for which both employment and sales/revenue data were available. For the definition of MSAs, CMSAs, and PMSAs, please see the Introduction.

HUNTSVILLE, AL MSA

NAICS	Industry	Estab-lish-ments	Em-ploy-ment	Payroll		Sales, reven. ($ mil.)
				Total ($ mil.)	Per Empl. ($)	
48-49	Transportation and warehousing	151	1,797	40.7	22,648	156.7
484	Truck transportation	82	828	22.2	26,809	83.0
4841	General freight trucking	40	581	17.4	29,988	66.9
484110	General freight trucking, local	12	71	1.6	22,366	6.3
48412	General freight trucking, long-distance	28	510	15.8	31,049	60.6
484121	General freight trucking, long-distance, truckload (tl)	21	214	4.4	20,734	23.3
4842	Specialized freight trucking	42	247	4.8	19,332	16.1
484210	Used household and office goods moving	15	158	3.3	20,766	8.2
484220	Specialized freight (except used goods) trucking, local	19	76	1.1	14,579	5.2
4842203	Dump trucking	11	44	0.7	16,682	3.7
488	Support activities for transportation	33	299	5.6	18,686	16.8
488510	Freight transportation arrangement	13	82	2.1	25,866	6.0
4931	Warehousing and storage	11	207	4.1	19,923	11.4

Sources: Economic Census of the United States, 1997. Only those industries are shown for which both employment and sales/revenue data were available. For the definition of MSAs, CMSAs, and PMSAs, please see the Introduction.

INDIANAPOLIS, IN MSA

NAICS	Industry	Estab-lish-ments	Em-ploy-ment	Payroll		Sales, reven. ($ mil.)
				Total ($ mil.)	Per Empl. ($)	
48-49	Transportation and warehousing	1,027	29,611	836.4	28,245	2,572.8
481	Air transportation	16	411	17.3	41,983	69.5
484	Truck transportation	669	13,699	443.9	32,400	1,513.6
4841	General freight trucking	327	8,929	305.7	34,242	985.6
484110	General freight trucking, local	84	930	23.1	24,839	64.1
4841101	General freight trucking without storage, local, truckload (tl)	59	548	14.8	27,077	45.4
4841102	General freight trucking without storage, local, less than truckload (ltl)	22	363	7.6	20,953	16.7
48412	General freight trucking, long-distance	243	7,999	282.6	35,336	921.4
484121	General freight trucking, long-distance, truckload (tl)	196	4,122	130.5	31,664	547.3
484122	General freight trucking, long-distance, less than truckload (ltl)	47	3,877	152.1	39,240	374.2
4842	Specialized freight trucking	342	4,770	138.1	28,953	528.0
484210	Used household and office goods moving	56	2,398	67.8	28,286	267.5
4842101	Used household and office goods moving, local, without storage	25	330	5.0	15,048	13.5
4842102	Used household and office goods moving, long-distance	24	1,921	59.6	31,011	245.8
484220	Specialized freight (except used goods) trucking, local	207	1,452	42.8	29,501	147.8
4842202	Agricultural products trucking without storage, local	27	98	2.7	27,112	12.1
4842203	Dump trucking	116	762	21.5	28,257	85.6
4842204	Specialized trucking without storage, local	57	253	7.9	31,399	25.1
484230	Specialized freight (except used goods) trucking, long-distance	79	920	27.4	29,826	112.7
4842301	Hazardous materials trucking (except waste), long-distance	13	218	7.2	33,115	24.4
4842302	Agricultural products trucking, long-distance	20	154	4.4	28,338	10.3
4842303	Other specialized trucking, long-distance	46	548	15.9	28,936	78.0
485	Transit and ground passenger transportation	49	1,218	17.3	14,183	53.1
4853	Taxi and limousine service	20	191	2.6	13,707	11.4
485310	Taxi service	11	149	2.1	14,168	9.8
488	Support activities for transportation	172	2,543	61.0	23,993	173.8
4881	Support activities for air transportation	20	1,327	28.5	21,489	67.3
4884	Support activities for road transportation	43	283	4.9	17,477	12.0
488410	Motor vehicle towing	40	275	4.9	17,851	11.9
488510	Freight transportation arrangement	87	754	23.6	31,340	79.1
4885101	Freight forwarding	39	496	15.6	31,524	52.4
4885102	Arrangement of transportation of freight and cargo	48	258	8.0	30,984	26.8
48899	Other support activities for transportation	15	113	2.5	21,708	11.8
492	Couriers and messengers	72	10,379	258.9	24,946	637.2
492110	Couriers	32	10,178	254.8	25,030	619.8
492210	Local messengers and local delivery	40	201	4.2	20,701	17.4
4931	Warehousing and storage	37	1,237	32.1	25,956	80.5
4931101	General warehousing and storage (except in foreign trade zones)	27	869	22.2	25,542	50.8

Sources: Economic Census of the United States, 1997. Only those industries are shown for which both employment and sales/revenue data were available. For the definition of MSAs, CMSAs, and PMSAs, please see the Introduction.

IOWA CITY, IA MSA

NAICS	Industry	Establishments	Employment	Payroll		Sales, reven. ($ mil.)
				Total ($ mil.)	Per Empl. ($)	
48-49	Transportation and warehousing	55	1,669	47.3	28,365	307.9
484	Truck transportation	33	1,292	37.8	29,238	263.0
4841	General freight trucking	20	1,186	35.3	29,723	252.4
4842	Specialized freight trucking	13	106	2.5	23,811	10.6
485	Transit and ground passenger transportation	8	189	1.8	9,497	3.7
486	Pipeline transportation	4	56	5.3	93,982	32.8

Sources: Economic Census of the United States, 1997. Only those industries are shown for which both employment and sales/revenue data were available. For the definition of MSAs, CMSAs, and PMSAs, please see the Introduction.

JACKSON, MI MSA

NAICS	Industry	Establishments	Employment	Payroll		Sales, reven. ($ mil.)
				Total ($ mil.)	Per Empl. ($)	
48-49	Transportation and warehousing	72	844	29.9	35,402	99.4
484	Truck transportation	47	696	26.0	37,292	85.1
4841	General freight trucking	25	373	15.1	40,606	55.2
48412	General freight trucking, long-distance	18	339	14.1	41,634	50.4
484121	General freight trucking, long-distance, truckload (tl)	11	92	2.4	26,261	15.2
4842	Specialized freight trucking	22	323	10.8	33,464	29.9
485	Transit and ground passenger transportation	6	40	0.4	10,150	1.4
488	Support activities for transportation	8	37	1.3	34,568	3.4

Sources: Economic Census of the United States, 1997. Only those industries are shown for which both employment and sales/revenue data were available. For the definition of MSAs, CMSAs, and PMSAs, please see the Introduction.

JACKSON, MS MSA

NAICS	Industry	Establishments	Employment	Payroll		Sales, reven. ($ mil.)
				Total ($ mil.)	Per Empl. ($)	
48-49	Transportation and warehousing	281	6,986	210.2	30,091	712.2
484	Truck transportation	187	4,430	140.0	31,592	439.6
4841	General freight trucking	102	2,819	91.2	32,355	245.7
484110	General freight trucking, local	31	125	2.6	20,408	8.1
4841101	General freight trucking without storage, local, truckload (tl)	18	55	1.4	24,764	4.4
48412	General freight trucking, long-distance	71	2,694	88.7	32,910	237.6
484121	General freight trucking, long-distance, truckload (tl)	52	1,391	38.3	27,507	157.0
484122	General freight trucking, long-distance, less than truckload (ltl)	19	1,303	50.4	38,678	80.5
4842	Specialized freight trucking	85	1,611	48.7	30,256	193.9
484210	Used household and office goods moving	16	177	3.8	21,384	12.4
484220	Specialized freight (except used goods) trucking, local	38	112	2.1	18,420	11.6
4842203	Dump trucking	30	84	1.5	17,821	9.8
484230	Specialized freight (except used goods) trucking, long-distance	31	1,322	42.9	32,447	169.9
4842301	Hazardous materials trucking (except waste), long-distance	13	162	5.8	35,525	24.0
486	Pipeline transportation	5	124	7.6	61,532	64.3
488	Support activities for transportation	46	1,373	43.4	31,631	145.9
488510	Freight transportation arrangement	18	83	3.1	37,096	19.0
492110	Couriers	12	388	7.2	18,665	28.2
493	Warehousing and storage	9	90	1.9	21,600	9.5

Sources: Economic Census of the United States, 1997. Only those industries are shown for which both employment and sales/revenue data were available. For the definition of MSAs, CMSAs, and PMSAs, please see the Introduction.

JACKSON, TN MSA

NAICS	Industry	Estab-lish-ments	Em-ploy-ment	Payroll Total ($ mil.)	Payroll Per Empl. ($)	Sales, reven. ($ mil.)
48-49	Transportation and warehousing	102	1,416	38.3	27,048	158.7
484	Truck transportation	78	1,165	34.3	29,412	146.0
4841	General freight trucking	55	1,026	30.8	30,030	134.4
48412	General freight trucking, long-distance	47	1,016	30.6	30,078	132.6
484121	General freight trucking, long-distance, truckload (tl)	36	593	18.3	30,776	92.8
484122	General freight trucking, long-distance, less than truckload (ltl)	11	423	12.3	29,099	39.7
4842	Specialized freight trucking	23	139	3.5	24,849	11.7
484220	Specialized freight (except used goods) trucking, local	15	50	1.1	21,660	5.2
4842203	Dump trucking	12	43	0.9	21,884	4.8
488	Support activities for transportation	8	114	1.8	15,588	5.5
492	Couriers and messengers	6	58	0.7	11,500	2.0
493	Warehousing and storage	3	37	0.8	22,405	2.4

Sources: Economic Census of the United States, 1997. Only those industries are shown for which both employment and sales/revenue data were available. For the definition of MSAs, CMSAs, and PMSAs, please see the Introduction.

JACKSONVILLE, FL MSA

NAICS	Industry	Estab-lish-ments	Em-ploy-ment	Payroll Total ($ mil.)	Payroll Per Empl. ($)	Sales, reven. ($ mil.)
48-49	Transportation and warehousing	861	21,596	628.0	29,081	2,894.8
481	Air transportation	10	474	11.4	23,983	48.0
483	Water transportation	26	1,345	63.7	47,349	751.6
48311	Deep sea, coastal, and Great Lakes water transportation	19	1,174	58.3	49,641	734.9
484	Truck transportation	381	7,420	221.8	29,893	1,196.6
4841	General freight trucking	184	5,259	154.8	29,435	981.5
484110	General freight trucking, local	65	690	21.3	30,868	85.7
4841101	General freight trucking without storage, local, truckload (tl)	51	395	11.8	29,876	64.2
48412	General freight trucking, long-distance	119	4,569	133.5	29,219	895.9
484121	General freight trucking, long-distance, truckload (tl)	96	3,136	91.0	29,022	791.1
484122	General freight trucking, long-distance, less than truckload (ltl)	23	1,433	42.5	29,648	104.8
4842	Specialized freight trucking	197	2,161	67.0	31,007	215.1
484210	Used household and office goods moving	46	470	8.9	18,843	29.9
4842101	Used household and office goods moving, local, without storage	16	145	3.4	23,152	12.2
4842102	Used household and office goods moving, long-distance	16	218	4.1	18,803	11.6
4842103	Used household and office goods moving, local, with storage	14	107	1.4	13,084	6.1
484220	Specialized freight (except used goods) trucking, local	89	464	12.0	25,869	43.7
4842203	Dump trucking	48	173	3.6	20,919	18.9
4842204	Specialized trucking without storage, local	24	97	2.4	24,330	8.8
484230	Specialized freight (except used goods) trucking, long-distance	62	1,227	46.1	37,610	141.4
4842303	Other specialized trucking, long-distance	44	1,092	42.6	39,023	129.7
485	Transit and ground passenger transportation	118	1,395	15.1	10,806	48.0
4853	Taxi and limousine service	15	62	0.7	11,565	4.9
485410	School and employee bus transportation	92	1,114	9.9	8,921	29.9
487	Scenic and sightseeing transportation	17	335	3.5	10,522	11.7
487210	Scenic and sightseeing transportation, water	12	241	2.5	10,440	8.7
488	Support activities for transportation	209	4,561	133.3	29,226	398.0
4881	Support activities for air transportation	19	1,118	55.6	49,710	117.7
488320	Marine cargo handling	12	1,609	23.7	14,710	47.0
488330	Navigational services to shipping	26	36	2.1	58,167	7.4
4883302	Navigational services	23	26	2.0	77,192	7.1
488390	Other support activities for water transportation	16	50	2.3	45,340	4.7
488510	Freight transportation arrangement	87	521	17.7	33,994	74.4
4885101	Freight forwarding	27	197	7.0	35,609	36.5
4885102	Arrangement of transportation of freight and cargo	60	324	10.7	33,012	37.9
492	Couriers and messengers	53	4,771	148.0	31,015	317.6
492110	Couriers	24	4,593	144.4	31,445	303.5
492210	Local messengers and local delivery	29	178	3.5	19,921	14.1
4931	Warehousing and storage	47	1,295	31.3	24,175	123.3
4931101	General warehousing and storage (except in foreign trade zones)	31	873	20.8	23,790	52.1

Sources: Economic Census of the United States, 1997. Only those industries are shown for which both employment and sales/revenue data were available. For the definition of MSAs, CMSAs, and PMSAs, please see the Introduction.

JACKSONVILLE, NC MSA

NAICS	Industry	Estab-lish-ments	Em-ploy-ment	Payroll		Sales, reven. ($ mil.)
				Total ($ mil.)	Per Empl. ($)	
48-49	Transportation and warehousing	94	704	13.6	19,267	64.0
481	Air transportation	3	59	0.8	12,797	5.5
484	Truck transportation	56	524	11.7	22,345	54.8
4842	Specialized freight trucking	48	310	5.8	18,655	22.8
484210	Used household and office goods moving	16	150	2.4	15,880	7.9
484220	Specialized freight (except used goods) trucking, local	29	157	3.3	21,325	14.2
4842203	Dump trucking	23	128	2.9	22,313	12.9
485	Transit and ground passenger transportation	26	85	0.8	9,682	2.9
4853	Taxi and limousine service	20	34	0.2	6,912	0.6
492	Couriers and messengers	3	15	0.1	8,733	0.5

Sources: *Economic Census of the United States*, 1997. Only those industries are shown for which both employment and sales/revenue data were available. For the definition of MSAs, CMSAs, and PMSAs, please see the Introduction.

JAMESTOWN, NY MSA

NAICS	Industry	Estab-lish-ments	Em-ploy-ment	Payroll		Sales, reven. ($ mil.)
				Total ($ mil.)	Per Empl. ($)	
48-49	Transportation and warehousing	85	878	19.8	22,579	78.1
484	Truck transportation	54	399	10.7	26,917	47.5
4841	General freight trucking	26	213	5.9	27,540	30.7
48412	General freight trucking, long-distance	19	161	4.4	27,031	18.1
484121	General freight trucking, long-distance, truckload (tl)	14	119	2.9	24,513	10.9
4842	Specialized freight trucking	28	186	4.9	26,204	16.8
484220	Specialized freight (except used goods) trucking, local	14	74	1.9	25,946	7.2
485	Transit and ground passenger transportation	16	235	2.1	9,085	6.0
488	Support activities for transportation	8	164	4.6	27,939	16.0

Sources: *Economic Census of the United States*, 1997. Only those industries are shown for which both employment and sales/revenue data were available. For the definition of MSAs, CMSAs, and PMSAs, please see the Introduction.

JANESVILLE—BELOIT, WI MSA

NAICS	Industry	Estab-lish-ments	Em-ploy-ment	Payroll		Sales, reven. ($ mil.)
				Total ($ mil.)	Per Empl. ($)	
48-49	Transportation and warehousing	103	1,444	50.3	34,818	170.1
484	Truck transportation	79	984	41.4	42,042	137.3
4841	General freight trucking	36	339	10.7	31,519	49.8
48412	General freight trucking, long-distance	31	329	10.5	31,878	48.7
484121	General freight trucking, long-distance, truckload (tl)	28	259	7.6	29,529	38.9
4842	Specialized freight trucking	43	645	30.7	47,572	87.5
484220	Specialized freight (except used goods) trucking, local	19	54	1.4	25,019	4.6
4842203	Dump trucking	12	33	1.0	28,879	3.0
484230	Specialized freight (except used goods) trucking, long-distance	18	528	26.9	50,875	77.2
485	Transit and ground passenger transportation	11	332	4.4	13,181	16.0
488	Support activities for transportation	6	42	0.9	21,500	3.9

Sources: *Economic Census of the United States*, 1997. Only those industries are shown for which both employment and sales/revenue data were available. For the definition of MSAs, CMSAs, and PMSAs, please see the Introduction.

JERSEY CITY, NJ PMSA

NAICS	Industry	Estab-lish-ments	Em-ploy-ment	Payroll		Sales, reven. ($ mil.)
				Total ($ mil.)	Per Empl. ($)	
48-49	Transportation and warehousing	854	22,881	726.4	31,747	2,262.9
48311	Deep sea, coastal, and Great Lakes water transportation	12	660	19.5	29,602	221.8
484	Truck transportation	419	7,798	276.1	35,412	824.1
4841	General freight trucking	267	6,155	221.4	35,967	664.3
484110	General freight trucking, local	192	2,513	78.3	31,166	259.1
4841101	General freight trucking without storage, local, truckload (tl)	119	952	28.3	29,737	101.6
4841102	General freight trucking without storage, local, less than truckload (ltl)	55	1,100	34.9	31,736	106.3
48412	General freight trucking, long-distance	75	3,642	143.1	39,280	405.2
484121	General freight trucking, long-distance, truckload (tl)	50	1,272	51.4	40,429	230.9
484122	General freight trucking, long-distance, less than truckload (ltl)	25	2,370	91.6	38,664	174.2
4842	Specialized freight trucking	152	1,643	54.8	33,332	159.8
484210	Used household and office goods moving	41	364	10.9	29,942	30.2
4842101	Used household and office goods moving, local, without storage	22	185	4.7	25,654	11.5
4842103	Used household and office goods moving, local, with storage	11	61	1.6	26,721	4.0
484220	Specialized freight (except used goods) trucking, local	90	1,052	36.7	34,905	103.0
4842204	Specialized trucking without storage, local	35	504	19.8	39,347	48.7
4842205	Specialized trucking with storage, local	15	445	13.9	31,261	41.4
484230	Specialized freight (except used goods) trucking, long-distance	21	227	7.1	31,476	26.6
4842303	Other specialized trucking, long-distance	16	213	6.6	30,751	20.9
485	Transit and ground passenger transportation	117	1,840	28.1	15,279	72.5
485113	Bus and motor vehicle transit systems	34	359	7.8	21,696	18.0
485510	Charter bus industry	12	246	8.2	33,435	25.6
488	Support activities for transportation	181	4,104	180.0	43,863	468.8
4883	Support activities for water transportation	16	637	32.0	50,160	82.6
488510	Freight transportation arrangement	147	3,244	141.8	43,724	348.9
4885101	Freight forwarding	60	1,122	40.8	36,373	120.5
4885102	Arrangement of transportation of freight and cargo	87	2,122	101.0	47,611	228.4
4931	Warehousing and storage	76	2,767	84.0	30,342	278.7
4931101	General warehousing and storage (except in foreign trade zones)	58	1,831	47.8	26,108	152.1
4931902	Specialized goods warehousing and storage	11	510	21.1	41,412	91.2

Sources: *Economic Census of the United States*, 1997. Only those industries are shown for which both employment and sales/revenue data were available. For the definition of MSAs, CMSAs, and PMSAs, please see the Introduction.

JOHNSON CITY—KINGSPORT—BRISTOL, TN—VA MSA

NAICS	Industry	Estab-lish-ments	Em-ploy-ment	Payroll		Sales, reven. ($ mil.)
				Total ($ mil.)	Per Empl. ($)	
48-49	Transportation and warehousing	282	3,644	75.4	20,689	269.5
481	Air transportation	3	11	0.4	35,636	1.5
484	Truck transportation	213	2,512	59.3	23,598	211.8
4841	General freight trucking	105	1,851	44.3	23,931	145.1
484110	General freight trucking, local	22	217	5.1	23,295	21.1
4841101	General freight trucking without storage, local, truckload (tl)	15	152	4.0	26,007	18.3
48412	General freight trucking, long-distance	83	1,634	39.2	24,015	124.0
484121	General freight trucking, long-distance, truckload (tl)	67	1,139	23.5	20,630	83.4
484122	General freight trucking, long-distance, less than truckload (ltl)	16	495	15.7	31,804	40.5
4842	Specialized freight trucking	108	661	15.0	22,667	66.7
484210	Used household and office goods moving	19	127	2.5	19,976	9.5
484220	Specialized freight (except used goods) trucking, local	58	252	4.5	17,988	20.4
4842202	Agricultural products trucking without storage, local	15	55	1.0	18,727	4.1
4842203	Dump trucking	31	130	2.3	17,654	12.2
484230	Specialized freight (except used goods) trucking, long distance	31	282	7.9	28,060	36.9
4842303	Other specialized trucking, long-distance	11	134	3.7	27,545	14.2
485	Transit and ground passenger transportation	24	772	7.7	9,988	20.6
488	Support activities for transportation	19	89	1.6	18,236	6.8
492	Couriers and messengers	15	220	4.7	21,223	19.8

Sources: *Economic Census of the United States*, 1997. Only those industries are shown for which both employment and sales/revenue data were available. For the definition of MSAs, CMSAs, and PMSAs, please see the Introduction.

JOHNSTOWN, PA MSA

NAICS	Industry	Estab-lish-ments	Em-ploy-ment	Payroll		Sales, reven. ($ mil.)
				Total ($ mil.)	Per Empl. ($)	
48-49	Transportation and warehousing	199	2,072	39.7	19,150	160.9
484	Truck transportation	145	1,254	29.8	23,729	119.1
4841	General freight trucking	39	665	16.9	25,367	61.7
48412	General freight trucking, long-distance	29	622	15.8	25,424	57.3
484121	General freight trucking, long-distance, truckload (tl)	24	334	8.5	25,518	31.1
4842	Specialized freight trucking	106	589	12.9	21,879	57.4
484220	Specialized freight (except used goods) trucking, local	93	511	11.0	21,509	51.2
4842203	Dump trucking	68	375	8.3	22,093	35.8
4842204	Specialized trucking without storage, local	14	83	1.7	20,590	12.6
485	Transit and ground passenger transportation	38	662	5.5	8,370	18.3
485410	School and employee bus transportation	32	570	4.4	7,789	13.5
488	Support activities for transportation	6	57	1.5	25,596	6.8

Sources: Economic Census of the United States, 1997. Only those industries are shown for which both employment and sales/revenue data were available. For the definition of MSAs, CMSAs, and PMSAs, please see the Introduction.

JONESBORO, AR MSA

NAICS	Industry	Estab-lish-ments	Em-ploy-ment	Payroll		Sales, reven. ($ mil.)
				Total ($ mil.)	Per Empl. ($)	
48-49	Transportation and warehousing	107	1,066	24.1	22,623	97.8
484	Truck transportation	85	869	20.7	23,838	86.7
4841	General freight trucking	54	759	18.6	24,469	77.5
48412	General freight trucking, long-distance	44	682	16.5	24,147	70.7
484121	General freight trucking, long-distance, truckload (tl)	34	500	10.6	21,154	46.9
4842	Specialized freight trucking	31	110	2.1	19,482	9.2
484220	Specialized freight (except used goods) trucking, local	20	87	1.5	17,437	6.3
4842203	Dump trucking	12	42	0.7	17,262	3.6
492	Couriers and messengers	7	111	2.1	19,144	6.5
493	Warehousing and storage	3	5	0.1	14,600	1.3

Sources: Economic Census of the United States, 1997. Only those industries are shown for which both employment and sales/revenue data were available. For the definition of MSAs, CMSAs, and PMSAs, please see the Introduction.

JOPLIN, MO MSA

NAICS	Industry	Estab-lish-ments	Em-ploy-ment	Payroll		Sales, reven. ($ mil.)
				Total ($ mil.)	Per Empl. ($)	
48-49	Transportation and warehousing	203	6,046	167.9	27,770	579.5
484	Truck transportation	155	5,278	153.2	29,017	506.1
4841	General freight trucking	97	4,542	136.1	29,970	442.2
484110	General freight trucking, local	17	90	1.7	19,300	6.9
48412	General freight trucking, long-distance	80	4,452	134.4	30,186	435.4
484121	General freight trucking, long-distance, truckload (tl)	74	4,244	127.3	30,003	414.6
4842	Specialized freight trucking	58	736	17.0	23,136	63.8
484220	Specialized freight (except used goods) trucking, local	31	235	4.8	20,362	21.3
4842203	Dump trucking	13	177	3.6	20,085	16.5
484230	Specialized freight (except used goods) trucking, long-distance	22	473	11.9	25,186	41.8
4842302	Agricultural products trucking, long-distance	11	89	0.7	8,079	4.1
488	Support activities for transportation	16	425	7.1	16,645	38.3
492	Couriers and messengers	14	111	2.4	21,865	9.3
493	Warehousing and storage	5	138	3.0	22,043	12.5

Sources: Economic Census of the United States, 1997. Only those industries are shown for which both employment and sales/revenue data were available. For the definition of MSAs, CMSAs, and PMSAs, please see the Introduction.

KALAMAZOO—BATTLE CREEK, MI MSA

NAICS	Industry	Estab-lish-ments	Em-ploy-ment	Payroll		Sales, reven. ($ mil.)
				Total ($ mil.)	Per Empl. ($)	
48-49	Transportation and warehousing	196	2,659	76.2	28,650	264.6
481	Air transportation	3	43	1.0	22,465	5.6
484	Truck transportation	126	1,523	47.6	31,253	158.5
4841	General freight trucking	60	1,034	33.1	32,002	114.3
484110	General freight trucking, local	17	297	8.1	27,441	30.4
48412	General freight trucking, long-distance	43	737	24.9	33,840	83.9
484121	General freight trucking, long-distance, truckload (tl)	31	447	12.1	27,083	42.0
484122	General freight trucking, long-distance, less than truckload (ltl)	12	290	12.8	44,255	41.8
4842	Specialized freight trucking	66	489	14.5	29,671	44.2
484210	Used household and office goods moving	13	151	3.7	24,795	9.4
484220	Specialized freight (except used goods) trucking, local	35	140	3.8	27,400	15.4
4842204	Specialized trucking without storage, local	15	45	1.1	24,667	4.5
484230	Specialized freight (except used goods) trucking, long-distance	18	198	6.9	34,995	19.4
4842303	Other specialized trucking, long-distance	13	153	5.7	36,961	13.7
488	Support activities for transportation	28	566	16.0	28,330	53.5
492	Couriers and messengers	14	301	6.4	21,146	25.5
4931	Warehousing and storage	14	154	3.7	23,760	13.2

Sources: Economic Census of the United States, 1997. Only those industries are shown for which both employment and sales/revenue data were available. For the definition of MSAs, CMSAs, and PMSAs, please see the Introduction.

KANKAKEE, IL PMSA

NAICS	Industry	Estab-lish-ments	Em-ploy-ment	Payroll		Sales, reven. ($ mil.)
				Total ($ mil.)	Per Empl. ($)	
48-49	Transportation and warehousing	79	849	25.3	29,744	106.0
484	Truck transportation	60	573	19.2	33,531	69.2
4841	General freight trucking	28	472	16.1	34,191	53.5
48412	General freight trucking, long-distance	21	437	15.3	35,080	51.3
4842	Specialized freight trucking	32	101	3.1	30,446	15.8
484230	Specialized freight (except used goods) trucking, long-distance	16	47	1.6	33,149	11.2
486	Pipeline transportation	3	56	2.7	47,357	25.7

Sources: Economic Census of the United States, 1997. Only those industries are shown for which both employment and sales/revenue data were available. For the definition of MSAs, CMSAs, and PMSAs, please see the Introduction.

KANSAS CITY, MO—KS MSA

NAICS	Industry	Estab-lish-ments	Em-ploy-ment	Payroll Total ($ mil.)	Payroll Per Empl. ($)	Sales, reven. ($ mil.)
48-49	Transportation and warehousing	1,320	28,558	784.7	27,477	2,396.6
484	Truck transportation	723	13,103	419.4	32,006	1,293.5
4841	General freight trucking	365	9,996	325.5	32,567	943.5
484110	General freight trucking, local	130	1,218	33.2	27,266	121.5
4841101	General freight trucking without storage, local, truckload (tl)	82	729	20.7	28,431	80.4
4841102	General freight trucking without storage, local, less than truckload (ltl)	38	433	10.9	25,111	30.7
48412	General freight trucking, long-distance	235	8,778	292.3	33,302	822.0
484121	General freight trucking, long-distance, truckload (tl)	181	4,906	148.4	30,245	514.0
484122	General freight trucking, long-distance, less than truckload (ltl)	54	3,872	143.9	37,175	307.9
4842	Specialized freight trucking	358	3,107	93.8	30,201	350.0
484210	Used household and office goods moving	70	1,014	22.9	22,546	73.7
4842101	Used household and office goods moving, local, without storage	30	164	2.1	12,793	6.2
4842102	Used household and office goods moving, long-distance	26	711	18.0	25,301	60.8
4842103	Used household and office goods moving, local, with storage	14	139	2.8	19,964	6.7
484220	Specialized freight (except used goods) trucking, local	210	1,062	28.7	27,045	139.4
4842201	Hazardous materials trucking (except waste), local	11	121	3.6	29,769	20.9
4842203	Dump trucking	128	627	16.0	25,464	73.9
4842204	Specialized trucking without storage, local	59	248	6.6	26,681	32.3
484230	Specialized freight (except used goods) trucking, long-distance	78	1,031	42.3	40,982	136.9
4842301	Hazardous materials trucking (except waste), long-distance	13	142	3.2	22,521	10.9
4842302	Agricultural products trucking, long-distance	22	93	2.2	23,183	22.5
4842303	Other specialized trucking, long-distance	43	796	36.9	46,354	103.4
485	Transit and ground passenger transportation	132	4,223	62.2	14,721	145.7
4853	Taxi and limousine service	30	138	1.7	12,181	6.9
485320	Limousine service	20	103	1.2	11,194	4.6
485410	School and employee bus transportation	73	3,575	50.1	14,007	117.0
48599	Other transit and ground passenger transportation	17	244	2.8	11,545	6.6
485999	All other transit and ground passenger transportation	11	167	1.6	9,802	4.3
486	Pipeline transportation	21	227	11.5	50,859	88.2
486210	Pipeline transportation of natural gas	11	103	5.7	55,320	38.3
488	Support activities for transportation	233	2,706	74.7	27,620	225.8
4881	Support activities for air transportation	24	716	19.5	27,193	41.9
4881191	Airport operation and terminal services	12	598	16.5	27,579	32.0
488190	Other support activities for air transportation	12	118	3.0	25,237	10.0
4882101	Support activities incidental to rail transportation	15	384	9.8	25,451	32.4
4884	Support activities for road transportation	52	434	9.4	21,583	27.7
488410	Motor vehicle towing	45	336	7.1	21,089	21.7
488510	Freight transportation arrangement	136	1,002	33.7	33,599	118.3
4885101	Freight forwarding	47	387	12.4	32,119	41.8
4885102	Arrangement of transportation of freight and cargo	89	615	21.2	34,530	76.5
492	Couriers and messengers	114	6,559	173.6	26,464	446.5
492110	Couriers	40	5,697	157.7	27,687	393.1
4921101	Courier services (except by air)	18	4,794	130.4	27,202	288.8
4921102	Air courier services	22	903	27.3	30,261	104.3
492210	Local messengers and local delivery	74	862	15.8	18,381	53.4
4931	Warehousing and storage	70	1,530	39.4	25,722	148.0
4931101	General warehousing and storage (except in foreign trade zones)	51	1,010	22.1	21,913	72.4

Sources: *Economic Census of the United States*, 1997. Only those industries are shown for which both employment and sales/revenue data were available. For the definition of MSAs, CMSAs, and PMSAs, please see the Introduction.

KENOSHA, WI PMSA

NAICS	Industry	Estab-lish-ments	Em-ploy-ment	Payroll Total ($ mil.)	Payroll Per Empl. ($)	Sales, reven. ($ mil.)
48-49	Transportation and warehousing	83	1,445	39.7	27,440	160.0
484	Truck transportation	53	708	28.5	40,270	76.3
4841	General freight trucking	22	344	12.0	34,831	36.2
48412	General freight trucking, long-distance	17	316	11.2	35,573	34.1
4842	Specialized freight trucking	31	364	16.5	45,409	40.1
4842203	Dump trucking	15	38	1.0	25,658	3.7
485	Transit and ground passenger transportation	9	296	3.1	10,628	6.8
488	Support activities for transportation	15	338	6.6	19,536	69.2

Sources: *Economic Census of the United States*, 1997. Only those industries are shown for which both employment and sales/revenue data were available. For the definition of MSAs, CMSAs, and PMSAs, please see the Introduction.

KILLEEN—TEMPLE, TX MSA

NAICS	Industry	Estab-lish-ments	Em-ploy-ment	Payroll		Sales, reven. ($ mil.)
				Total ($ mil.)	Per Empl. ($)	
48-49	Transportation and warehousing	104	1,844	48.9	26,497	120.3
484	Truck transportation	82	979	24.0	24,470	78.7
4841	General freight trucking	37	665	17.8	26,808	60.4
48412	General freight trucking, long-distance	27	435	13.0	29,830	46.1
484121	General freight trucking, long-distance, truckload (tl)	24	375	11.9	31,725	41.2
4842	Specialized freight trucking	45	314	6.1	19,519	18.3
484210	Used household and office goods moving	25	241	4.7	19,643	13.6
4842103	Used household and office goods moving, local, with storage	17	155	2.6	16,800	7.8
484220	Specialized freight (except used goods) trucking, local	16	54	1.1	20,093	3.5
485	Transit and ground passenger transportation	5	200	2.2	11,040	5.4

Sources: Economic Census of the United States, 1997. Only those industries are shown for which both employment and sales/revenue data were available. For the definition of MSAs, CMSAs, and PMSAs, please see the Introduction.

KNOXVILLE, TN MSA

NAICS	Industry	Estab-lish-ments	Em-ploy-ment	Payroll		Sales, reven. ($ mil.)
				Total ($ mil.)	Per Empl. ($)	
48-49	Transportation and warehousing	484	6,539	176.3	26,966	587.3
484	Truck transportation	267	4,956	146.0	29,464	472.4
4841	General freight trucking	147	3,840	114.2	29,748	365.1
484110	General freight trucking, local	31	220	5.3	23,909	26.5
4841101	General freight trucking without storage, local, truckload (tl)	22	165	4.7	28,194	25.2
48412	General freight trucking, long-distance	116	3,620	109.0	30,103	338.5
484121	General freight trucking, long-distance, truckload (tl)	90	2,143	58.5	27,295	223.2
484122	General freight trucking, long-distance, less than truckload (ltl)	26	1,477	50.5	34,177	115.3
4842	Specialized freight trucking	120	1,116	31.8	28,487	107.3
484210	Used household and office goods moving	23	275	5.5	20,040	16.9
484220	Specialized freight (except used goods) trucking, local	65	404	8.6	21,329	34.1
4842203	Dump trucking	39	285	5.8	20,267	22.1
4842204	Specialized trucking without storage, local	17	65	1.6	25,246	7.6
484230	Specialized freight (except used goods) trucking, long-distance	32	437	17.7	40,419	56.4
4842303	Other specialized trucking, long-distance	20	344	11.6	33,619	34.2
485	Transit and ground passenger transportation	113	551	5.7	10,341	24.8
4854101	School bus service	95	416	3.3	7,853	12.0
488	Support activities for transportation	56	399	10.6	26,624	33.3
488410	Motor vehicle towing	20	135	3.7	27,474	7.6
488510	Freight transportation arrangement	21	61	1.7	27,066	6.5
4885102	Arrangement of transportation of freight and cargo	18	51	1.4	27,510	4.7
492	Couriers and messengers	22	404	8.1	20,111	34.3
492110	Couriers	13	342	7.5	21,924	30.3
4931101	General warehousing and storage (except in foreign trade zones)	13	172	4.0	23,360	7.8

Sources: Economic Census of the United States, 1997. Only those industries are shown for which both employment and sales/revenue data were available. For the definition of MSAs, CMSAs, and PMSAs, please see the Introduction.

KOKOMO, IN MSA

NAICS	Industry	Estab-lish-ments	Em-ploy-ment	Payroll		Sales, reven. ($ mil.)
				Total ($ mil.)	Per Empl. ($)	
48-49	Transportation and warehousing	48	531	14.9	28,134	57.8
484	Truck transportation	35	392	12.4	31,597	49.1
4841	General freight trucking	18	306	9.8	31,958	39.9
48412	General freight trucking, long-distance	14	282	9.1	32,372	38.3
484121	General freight trucking, long-distance, truckload (tl)	11	196	5.2	26,633	24.2
4842	Specialized freight trucking	17	86	2.6	30,314	9.3
484220	Specialized freight (except used goods) trucking, local	12	27	0.5	19,407	3.2

Sources: Economic Census of the United States, 1997. Only those industries are shown for which both employment and sales/revenue data were available. For the definition of MSAs, CMSAs, and PMSAs, please see the Introduction.

LA CROSSE, WI—MN MSA

NAICS	Industry	Establishments	Employment	Payroll Total ($ mil.)	Payroll Per Empl. ($)	Sales, reven. ($ mil.)
48-49	Transportation and warehousing	103	1,181	32.6	27,607	94.4
484	Truck transportation	66	724	25.8	35,688	72.7
4841	General freight trucking	31	505	17.5	34,679	51.5
484110	General freight trucking, local	11	238	8.0	33,735	22.6
48412	General freight trucking, long-distance	20	267	9.5	35,521	28.9
4842	Specialized freight trucking	35	219	8.3	38,014	21.2
484220	Specialized freight (except used goods) trucking, local	25	141	6.4	45,121	15.5
485	Transit and ground passenger transportation	14	291	2.8	9,474	7.0
488	Support activities for transportation	6	32	0.9	29,437	4.0
492	Couriers and messengers	10	93	1.8	19,785	7.8
493	Warehousing and storage	3	18	0.4	24,611	1.1

Sources: Economic Census of the United States, 1997. Only those industries are shown for which both employment and sales/revenue data were available. For the definition of MSAs, CMSAs, and PMSAs, please see the Introduction.

LAFAYETTE, IN MSA

NAICS	Industry	Establishments	Employment	Payroll Total ($ mil.)	Payroll Per Empl. ($)	Sales, reven. ($ mil.)
48-49	Transportation and warehousing	108	1,199	38.6	32,163	116.4
484	Truck transportation	82	865	31.2	36,072	91.4
4841	General freight trucking	35	468	17.7	37,859	51.1
484110	General freight trucking, local	12	120	8.4	69,908	13.9
48412	General freight trucking, long-distance	23	348	9.3	26,807	37.2
484121	General freight trucking, long-distance, truckload (tl)	18	231	6.6	28,459	28.0
4842	Specialized freight trucking	47	397	13.5	33,965	40.3
484220	Specialized freight (except used goods) trucking, local	24	114	3.1	27,289	10.5
4842203	Dump trucking	15	88	2.6	29,170	8.3
484230	Specialized freight (except used goods) trucking, long-distance	20	250	9.3	37,096	27.2
4842303	Other specialized trucking, long-distance	12	190	7.5	39,537	20.4
488	Support activities for transportation	7	76	1.6	21,711	6.1
493	Warehousing and storage	7	142	3.9	27,338	10.1

Sources: Economic Census of the United States, 1997. Only those industries are shown for which both employment and sales/revenue data were available. For the definition of MSAs, CMSAs, and PMSAs, please see the Introduction.

LAFAYETTE, LA MSA

NAICS	Industry	Establishments	Employment	Payroll Total ($ mil.)	Payroll Per Empl. ($)	Sales, reven. ($ mil.)
48-49	Transportation and warehousing	267	5,510	150.8	27,361	516.4
483	Water transportation	14	703	19.6	27,828	103.6
484	Truck transportation	159	2,699	63.5	23,532	166.8
4841	General freight trucking	63	1,970	47.0	23,849	101.4
484110	General freight trucking, local	14	176	3.3	18,830	10.6
48412	General freight trucking, long-distance	49	1,794	43.7	24,342	90.8
484121	General freight trucking, long-distance, truckload (tl)	38	1,428	34.8	24,400	63.1
484122	General freight trucking, long-distance, less than truckload (ltl)	11	366	8.8	24,115	27.7
4842	Specialized freight trucking	96	729	16.5	22,676	65.3
484220	Specialized freight (except used goods) trucking, local	60	282	4.9	17,496	23.9
4842203	Dump trucking	23	79	1.3	16,873	6.9
4842204	Specialized trucking without storage, local	24	150	2.7	17,787	11.1
484230	Specialized freight (except used goods) trucking, long-distance	29	396	10.6	26,864	39.1
4842303	Other specialized trucking, long-distance	19	257	6.2	24,101	27.3
485	Transit and ground passenger transportation	19	228	3.3	14,329	9.9
486	Pipeline transportation	24	281	13.8	49,249	139.6
486210	Pipeline transportation of natural gas	17	235	11.8	50,123	115.7
488	Support activities for transportation	26	424	5.1	11,991	15.3
492	Couriers and messengers	9	144	3.3	22,799	13.6
493	Warehousing and storage	6	29	0.9	32,207	5.1

Sources: Economic Census of the United States, 1997. Only those industries are shown for which both employment and sales/revenue data were available. For the definition of MSAs, CMSAs, and PMSAs, please see the Introduction.

LAKE CHARLES, LA MSA

NAICS	Industry	Estab-lish-ments	Em-ploy-ment	Payroll		Sales, reven. ($ mil.)
				Total ($ mil.)	Per Empl. ($)	
48-49	Transportation and warehousing	160	1,783	58.8	32,965	254.1
484	Truck transportation	96	863	20.0	23,203	68.0
4841	General freight trucking	38	555	12.2	22,054	41.1
484110	General freight trucking, local	11	49	0.9	19,204	5.0
48412	General freight trucking, long-distance	27	506	11.3	22,330	36.1
484121	General freight trucking, long-distance, truckload (tl)	23	384	8.7	22,760	28.8
4842	Specialized freight trucking	58	308	7.8	25,273	27.0
4842203	Dump trucking	17	33	0.6	17,939	3.1
484230	Specialized freight (except used goods) trucking, long-distance	28	209	6.0	28,732	19.9
4842301	Hazardous materials trucking (except waste), long-distance	16	153	4.3	27,837	14.5
4842303	Other specialized trucking, long-distance	12	56	1.7	31,179	5.3
486	Pipeline transportation	12	113	5.7	50,805	57.1
488	Support activities for transportation	28	308	16.1	52,386	28.3
4883	Support activities for water transportation	11	251	15.0	59,657	24.8
492	Couriers and messengers	7	79	1.7	21,038	4.9

Sources: Economic Census of the United States, 1997. Only those industries are shown for which both employment and sales/revenue data were available. For the definition of MSAs, CMSAs, and PMSAs, please see the Introduction.

LAKELAND—WINTER HAVEN, FL MSA

NAICS	Industry	Estab-lish-ments	Em-ploy-ment	Payroll		Sales, reven. ($ mil.)
				Total ($ mil.)	Per Empl. ($)	
48-49	Transportation and warehousing	355	5,254	150.6	28,661	586.6
484	Truck transportation	254	4,419	128.6	29,105	483.8
4841	General freight trucking	128	1,831	55.8	30,448	215.6
484110	General freight trucking, local	48	260	5.2	19,931	25.1
4841101	General freight trucking without storage, local, truckload (tl)	41	241	4.8	19,938	23.7
48412	General freight trucking, long-distance	80	1,571	50.6	32,189	190.6
484121	General freight trucking, long-distance, truckload (tl)	72	1,313	43.4	33,023	176.0
4842	Specialized freight trucking	126	2,588	72.9	28,154	268.2
484210	Used household and office goods moving	12	90	1.6	17,800	8.4
484220	Specialized freight (except used goods) trucking, local	60	366	8.9	24,189	49.4
4842202	Agricultural products trucking without storage, local	17	51	0.8	15,804	3.5
4842203	Dump trucking	24	272	6.7	24,621	40.1
484230	Specialized freight (except used goods) trucking, long-distance	54	2,132	62.4	29,272	210.4
4842303	Other specialized trucking, long-distance	22	1,620	48.2	29,763	165.6
485	Transit and ground passenger transportation	8	106	1.4	13,387	3.4
488	Support activities for transportation	65	421	12.5	29,770	57.2
488190	Other support activities for air transportation	11	103	3.2	31,155	14.5
4884	Support activities for road transportation	19	75	1.4	18,427	4.6
488510	Freight transportation arrangement	31	188	6.4	34,080	32.8
4885102	Arrangement of transportation of freight and cargo	25	161	5.8	36,267	31.2
492	Couriers and messengers	10	117	3.1	26,675	7.5
4931	Warehousing and storage	13	165	4.2	25,152	23.5

Sources: Economic Census of the United States, 1997. Only those industries are shown for which both employment and sales/revenue data were available. For the definition of MSAs, CMSAs, and PMSAs, please see the Introduction.

LANCASTER, PA MSA

NAICS	Industry	Estab-lish-ments	Em-ploy-ment	Payroll Total ($ mil.)	Payroll Per Empl. ($)	Sales, reven. ($ mil.)
48-49	Transportation and warehousing	258	4,414	130.8	29,638	329.9
481	Air transportation	5	24	0.6	23,333	5.1
484	Truck transportation	185	2,806	100.4	35,785	231.3
4841	General freight trucking	92	1,861	72.6	39,025	140.5
484110	General freight trucking, local	19	101	2.9	28,683	11.3
4841101	General freight trucking without storage, local, truckload (tl)	13	76	2.2	28,961	7.8
48412	General freight trucking, long-distance	73	1,760	69.7	39,619	129.2
484121	General freight trucking, long-distance, truckload (tl)	58	560	17.0	30,387	72.2
484122	General freight trucking, long-distance, less than truckload (ltl)	15	1,200	52.7	43,927	57.1
4842	Specialized freight trucking	93	945	27.8	29,404	90.7
484220	Specialized freight (except used goods) trucking, local	50	308	8.2	26,497	30.1
4842202	Agricultural products trucking without storage, local	12	95	2.5	26,358	8.7
4842203	Dump trucking	22	123	3.5	28,366	15.0
484230	Specialized freight (except used goods) trucking, long-distance	39	501	15.8	31,617	49.5
4842302	Agricultural products trucking, long-distance	20	226	5.9	26,296	19.0
4842303	Other specialized trucking, long-distance	16	264	9.6	36,538	29.4
485	Transit and ground passenger transportation	22	934	13.6	14,593	28.4
4854101	School bus service	13	649	7.2	11,037	15.9
488	Support activities for transportation	17	117	3.2	27,581	11.4
492	Couriers and messengers	12	295	6.5	22,014	16.4
493	Warehousing and storage	8	165	4.7	28,709	17.4

Sources: *Economic Census of the United States*, 1997. Only those industries are shown for which both employment and sales/revenue data were available. For the definition of MSAs, CMSAs, and PMSAs, please see the Introduction.

LANSING—EAST LANSING, MI MSA

NAICS	Industry	Estab-lish-ments	Em-ploy-ment	Payroll Total ($ mil.)	Payroll Per Empl. ($)	Sales, reven. ($ mil.)
48-49	Transportation and warehousing	195	1,859	63.9	34,391	218.8
481	Air transportation	4	26	0.4	16,192	5.7
484	Truck transportation	134	1,034	46.9	45,362	163.5
4841	General freight trucking	49	345	11.2	32,603	71.8
484110	General freight trucking, local	20	106	3.0	27,849	8.1
4841101	General freight trucking without storage, local, truckload (tl)	17	86	2.6	29,907	7.1
48412	General freight trucking, long-distance	29	239	8.3	34,711	63.8
484121	General freight trucking, long-distance, truckload (tl)	25	144	4.0	27,951	48.5
4842	Specialized freight trucking	85	689	35.7	51,750	91.7
484210	Used household and office goods moving	17	129	3.3	25,527	11.1
484220	Specialized freight (except used goods) trucking, local	42	155	5.1	32,697	18.7
4842203	Dump trucking	22	70	2.3	32,257	8.3
484230	Specialized freight (except used goods) trucking, long-distance	26	405	27.3	67,395	61.9
4842303	Other specialized trucking, long-distance	16	363	24.8	68,278	55.8
485	Transit and ground passenger transportation	9	376	6.0	16,072	13.8
488	Support activities for transportation	27	199	5.1	25,693	16.1
492	Couriers and messengers	16	206	5.0	24,068	16.3

Sources: *Economic Census of the United States*, 1997. Only those industries are shown for which both employment and sales/revenue data were available. For the definition of MSAs, CMSAs, and PMSAs, please see the Introduction.

LAREDO, TX MSA

NAICS	Industry	Estab-lish-ments	Em-ploy-ment	Payroll		Sales, reven. ($ mil.)
				Total ($ mil.)	Per Empl. ($)	
48-49	Transportation and warehousing	753	8,707	189.4	21,749	711.3
484	Truck transportation	252	3,269	79.6	24,351	347.3
4841	General freight trucking	195	2,534	64.6	25,509	295.7
484110	General freight trucking, local	86	538	11.0	20,422	36.5
4841101	General freight trucking without storage, local, truckload (tl)	68	265	4.0	15,121	15.4
48412	General freight trucking, long-distance	109	1,996	53.7	26,881	259.2
484121	General freight trucking, long-distance, truckload (tl)	93	1,630	41.3	25,345	194.7
484122	General freight trucking, long-distance, less than truckload (ltl)	16	366	12.3	33,721	64.5
4842	Specialized freight trucking	57	735	15.0	20,355	51.6
484220	Specialized freight (except used goods) trucking, local	35	174	3.1	17,851	12.8
4842203	Dump trucking	19	75	1.4	18,867	5.4
4842204	Specialized trucking without storage, local	13	85	1.5	17,600	6.6
484230	Specialized freight (except used goods) trucking, long-distance	14	66	1.0	15,242	6.7
488	Support activities for transportation	460	5,065	101.7	20,075	293.5
488510	Freight transportation arrangement	443	4,843	97.2	20,074	282.8
4885101	Freight forwarding	242	2,634	47.6	18,088	159.7
4885102	Arrangement of transportation of freight and cargo	201	2,209	49.6	22,442	123.1
492	Couriers and messengers	13	79	2.3	29,203	27.5
4931	Warehousing and storage	15	187	3.3	17,829	14.1

Sources: Economic Census of the United States, 1997. Only those industries are shown for which both employment and sales/revenue data were available. For the definition of MSAs, CMSAs, and PMSAs, please see the Introduction.

LAS CRUCES, NM MSA

NAICS	Industry	Estab-lish-ments	Em-ploy-ment	Payroll		Sales, reven. ($ mil.)
				Total ($ mil.)	Per Empl. ($)	
48-49	Transportation and warehousing	84	921	16.6	18,074	90.9
484	Truck transportation	54	417	9.4	22,482	66.0
4841	General freight trucking	20	252	6.9	27,492	51.0
48412	General freight trucking, long-distance	15	249	6.8	27,486	50.6
4842	Specialized freight trucking	34	165	2.4	14,830	15.0
484220	Specialized freight (except used goods) trucking, local	24	79	1.1	14,253	9.7
4842203	Dump trucking	13	30	0.4	12,967	2.9
485	Transit and ground passenger transportation	6	343	4.1	11,907	9.7
488	Support activities for transportation	15	41	0.9	22,756	3.1
493	Warehousing and storage	3	17	0.4	24,412	1.3

Sources: Economic Census of the United States, 1997. Only those industries are shown for which both employment and sales/revenue data were available. For the definition of MSAs, CMSAs, and PMSAs, please see the Introduction.

LAS VEGAS, NV—AZ MSA

NAICS	Industry	Estab-lish-ments	Em-ploy-ment	Payroll		Sales, reven. ($ mil.)
				Total ($ mil.)	Per Empl. ($)	
48-49	Transportation and warehousing	544	13,336	288.3	21,620	998.8
481	Air transportation	30	783	21.2	27,063	86.8
48111	Scheduled air transportation	13	432	10.1	23,338	53.5
48121	Nonscheduled air transportation	17	351	11.1	31,647	33.3
484	Truck transportation	249	2,950	86.8	29,430	274.2
4841	General freight trucking	114	1,498	47.8	31,902	144.6
484110	General freight trucking, local	36	342	8.5	24,904	23.9
4841102	General freight trucking without storage, local, less than truckload (ltl)	16	237	5.4	22,595	12.8
48412	General freight trucking, long-distance	78	1,156	39.3	33,972	120.7
484121	General freight trucking, long-distance, truckload (tl)	51	616	21.0	34,151	61.2
484122	General freight trucking, long-distance, less than truckload (ltl)	27	540	18.2	33,769	59.5
4842	Specialized freight trucking	135	1,452	39.0	26,879	129.6
484210	Used household and office goods moving	28	437	11.2	25,616	35.6
4842103	Used household and office goods moving, local, with storage	13	219	6.0	27,557	14.7
484220	Specialized freight (except used goods) trucking, local	76	772	19.8	25,642	70.3
4842203	Dump trucking	44	474	14.1	29,844	54.4
4842204	Specialized trucking without storage, local	29	284	5.5	19,197	14.9
484230	Specialized freight (except used goods) trucking, long-distance	31	243	8.0	33,082	23.7
4842303	Other specialized trucking, long-distance	21	179	6.6	37,101	17.8
485	Transit and ground passenger transportation	50	6,274	106.9	17,044	252.3
485310	Taxi service	14	3,907	64.1	16,415	141.8
48599	Other transit and ground passenger transportation	17	583	9.3	16,007	19.8
4881	Support activities for air transportation	27	931	16.2	17,353	58.0
4881191	Airport operation and terminal services	12	668	11.2	16,817	32.6
488190	Other support activities for air transportation	15	263	4.9	18,715	25.4
488510	Freight transportation arrangement	42	187	4.6	24,439	37.9
4885101	Freight forwarding	12	72	2.4	33,597	28.1
4885102	Arrangement of transportation of freight and cargo	30	115	2.2	18,704	9.8
492110	Couriers	29	612	15.9	25,959	55.4
4921101	Courier services (except by air)	16	247	4.9	20,000	17.9
4921102	Air courier services	13	365	10.9	29,992	37.5
4931101	General warehousing and storage (except in foreign trade zones)	16	237	4.7	19,806	12.5

Sources: *Economic Census of the United States*, 1997. Only those industries are shown for which both employment and sales/revenue data were available. For the definition of MSAs, CMSAs, and PMSAs, please see the Introduction.

LAWRENCE, KS MSA

NAICS	Industry	Estab-lish-ments	Em-ploy-ment	Payroll		Sales, reven. ($ mil.)
				Total ($ mil.)	Per Empl. ($)	
48-49	Transportation and warehousing	40	446	7.0	15,762	20.8
484	Truck transportation	25	135	3.4	25,289	11.6
4842	Specialized freight trucking	17	43	0.6	14,186	2.4
485	Transit and ground passenger transportation	7	243	2.2	8,988	5.1
488	Support activities for transportation	5	46	0.6	12,870	2.0

Sources: *Economic Census of the United States*, 1997. Only those industries are shown for which both employment and sales/revenue data were available. For the definition of MSAs, CMSAs, and PMSAs, please see the Introduction.

LAWRENCE, MA—NH PMSA

NAICS	Industry	Estab-lish-ments	Em-ploy-ment	Payroll Total ($ mil.)	Payroll Per Empl. ($)	Sales, reven. ($ mil.)
48-49	Transportation and warehousing	174	2,179	51.7	23,717	115.3
481	Air transportation	5	150	11.9	79,320	17.4
484	Truck transportation	90	572	17.3	30,227	41.8
4841	General freight trucking	34	344	12.3	35,831	20.2
484110	General freight trucking, local	20	156	3.7	23,442	8.6
4841101	General freight trucking without storage, local, truckload (tl)	12	94	1.8	18,787	3.7
48412	General freight trucking, long-distance	14	188	8.7	46,112	11.6
4842	Specialized freight trucking	56	228	5.0	21,772	21.6
484210	Used household and office goods moving	13	75	1.2	16,533	4.9
484220	Specialized freight (except used goods) trucking, local	37	111	2.5	22,225	13.4
4842203	Dump trucking	22	30	1.1	35,900	4.5
485	Transit and ground passenger transportation	42	1,207	16.1	13,316	36.8
4853	Taxi and limousine service	16	110	1.2	10,627	3.9
4854101	School bus service	15	852	9.8	11,520	23.0
493	Warehousing and storage	8	131	3.8	29,252	9.6

Sources: Economic Census of the United States, 1997. Only those industries are shown for which both employment and sales/revenue data were available. For the definition of MSAs, CMSAs, and PMSAs, please see the Introduction.

LAWTON, OK MSA

NAICS	Industry	Estab-lish-ments	Em-ploy-ment	Payroll Total ($ mil.)	Payroll Per Empl. ($)	Sales, reven. ($ mil.)
48-49	Transportation and warehousing	48	456	8.7	19,018	28.1
484	Truck transportation	33	347	6.9	19,775	22.4
4841	General freight trucking	11	98	2.0	19,918	7.4
4842	Specialized freight trucking	22	249	4.9	19,719	15.0
488	Support activities for transportation	4	28	0.2	7,750	1.0

Sources: Economic Census of the United States, 1997. Only those industries are shown for which both employment and sales/revenue data were available. For the definition of MSAs, CMSAs, and PMSAs, please see the Introduction.

LEWISTON—AUBURN, ME MSA

NAICS	Industry	Estab-lish-ments	Em-ploy-ment	Payroll Total ($ mil.)	Payroll Per Empl. ($)	Sales, reven. ($ mil.)
48-49	Transportation and warehousing	72	677	15.5	22,874	59.5
484	Truck transportation	46	326	9.7	29,856	41.4
4841	General freight trucking	20	235	7.8	33,191	30.1
48412	General freight trucking, long-distance	15	218	6.9	31,587	26.7
4842	Specialized freight trucking	26	91	1.9	21,242	11.3
485	Transit and ground passenger transportation	9	126	1.5	11,730	3.9
488	Support activities for transportation	10	119	2.5	20,849	6.6
493	Warehousing and storage	3	70	1.3	18,343	4.4

Sources: Economic Census of the United States, 1997. Only those industries are shown for which both employment and sales/revenue data were available. For the definition of MSAs, CMSAs, and PMSAs, please see the Introduction.

LEXINGTON, KY MSA

NAICS	Industry	Estab-lish-ments	Em-ploy-ment	Payroll Total ($ mil.)	Payroll Per Empl. ($)	Sales, reven. ($ mil.)
48-49	Transportation and warehousing	246	3,779	103.3	27,327	326.2
484	Truck transportation	158	2,587	77.7	30,041	217.9
4841	General freight trucking	83	1,610	50.8	31,540	139.0
484110	General freight trucking, local	26	297	6.8	22,842	16.9
48412	General freight trucking, long-distance	57	1,313	44.0	33,507	122.1
484121	General freight trucking, long-distance, truckload (tl)	40	511	14.4	28,082	50.7
484122	General freight trucking, long-distance, less than truckload (ltl)	17	802	29.6	36,964	71.5
4842	Specialized freight trucking	75	977	26.9	27,571	78.9
484210	Used household and office goods moving	15	253	4.1	16,174	13.2
484220	Specialized freight (except used goods) trucking, local	44	506	14.3	28,219	40.5
4842203	Dump trucking	22	310	8.5	27,323	25.1
484230	Specialized freight (except used goods) trucking, long-distance	16	218	8.6	39,294	25.1
488510	Freight transportation arrangement	14	66	1.2	18,742	4.7
4931101	General warehousing and storage (except in foreign trade zones)	11	234	6.8	28,932	19.2

Sources: Economic Census of the United States, 1997. Only those industries are shown for which both employment and sales/revenue data were available. For the definition of MSAs, CMSAs, and PMSAs, please see the Introduction.

LIMA, OH MSA

NAICS	Industry	Estab-lish-ments	Em-ploy-ment	Payroll Total ($ mil.)	Payroll Per Empl. ($)	Sales, reven. ($ mil.)
48-49	Transportation and warehousing	127	1,620	47.2	29,136	184.6
484	Truck transportation	101	1,329	39.1	29,427	157.3
4841	General freight trucking	48	914	27.3	29,885	105.0
484110	General freight trucking, local	16	256	5.9	22,910	17.2
4841101	General freight trucking without storage, local, truckload (tl)	12	172	5.2	30,163	14.9
48412	General freight trucking, long-distance	32	658	21.5	32,599	87.8
484121	General freight trucking, long-distance, truckload (tl)	21	407	12.2	30,047	52.8
484122	General freight trucking, long-distance, less than truckload (ltl)	11	251	9.2	36,737	34.9
4842	Specialized freight trucking	53	415	11.8	28,419	52.3
484220	Specialized freight (except used goods) trucking, local	30	205	6.5	31,902	17.0
4842203	Dump trucking	13	34	0.8	24,441	4.7
486	Pipeline transportation	4	58	2.7	46,776	13.0
488	Support activities for transportation	10	101	2.4	24,168	6.8

Sources: Economic Census of the United States, 1997. Only those industries are shown for which both employment and sales/revenue data were available. For the definition of MSAs, CMSAs, and PMSAs, please see the Introduction.

LINCOLN, NE MSA

NAICS	Industry	Estab-lish-ments	Em-ploy-ment	Payroll Total ($ mil.)	Payroll Per Empl. ($)	Sales, reven. ($ mil.)
48-49	Transportation and warehousing	159	4,215	138.8	32,940	525.1
481	Air transportation	4	45	1.0	23,178	7.2
484	Truck transportation	104	2,890	100.2	34,679	359.7
4841	General freight trucking	51	2,585	93.1	36,018	333.3
484110	General freight trucking, local	15	135	3.4	25,370	10.0
48412	General freight trucking, long-distance	36	2,450	89.7	36,605	323.4
484121	General freight trucking, long-distance, truckload (tl)	29	2,359	86.2	36,540	310.9
4842	Specialized freight trucking	53	305	7.1	23,331	26.3
484210	Used household and office goods moving	13	73	1.4	19,164	4.6
484220	Specialized freight (except used goods) trucking, local	30	146	3.4	23,247	13.1
4842203	Dump trucking	14	55	1.2	21,800	6.4
488	Support activities for transportation	18	828	30.6	37,005	129.2
493	Warehousing and storage	7	70	1.6	22,286	5.8

Sources: Economic Census of the United States, 1997. Only those industries are shown for which both employment and sales/revenue data were available. For the definition of MSAs, CMSAs, and PMSAs, please see the Introduction.

LITTLE ROCK—NORTH LITTLE ROCK, AR MSA

NAICS	Industry	Estab-lish-ments	Em-ploy-ment	Payroll Total ($ mil.)	Payroll Per Empl. ($)	Sales, reven. ($ mil.)
48-49	Transportation and warehousing	344	12,549	354.2	28,227	1,065.6
484	Truck transportation	227	5,583	167.2	29,951	470.9
4841	General freight trucking	104	4,471	139.4	31,183	373.1
484110	General freight trucking, local	18	138	3.8	27,362	11.8
48412	General freight trucking, long-distance	86	4,333	135.6	31,304	361.3
484121	General freight trucking, long-distance, truckload (tl)	65	2,687	81.6	30,374	216.4
484122	General freight trucking, long-distance, less than truckload (ltl)	21	1,646	54.0	32,823	144.9
4842	Specialized freight trucking	123	1,112	27.8	25,001	97.8
484210	Used household and office goods moving	22	241	3.6	14,739	12.5
4842101	Used household and office goods moving, local, without storage	12	31	0.4	11,419	1.2
484220	Specialized freight (except used goods) trucking, local	68	315	6.1	19,333	28.4
4842203	Dump trucking	35	174	2.7	15,333	17.2
4842204	Specialized trucking without storage, local	22	99	2.6	25,818	8.9
484230	Specialized freight (except used goods) trucking, long-distance	33	556	18.2	32,660	57.0
4842302	Agricultural products trucking, long-distance	11	50	1.1	22,320	8.0
4842303	Other specialized trucking, long-distance	15	418	14.1	33,617	40.1
485	Transit and ground passenger transportation	17	266	6.6	24,771	17.5
488	Support activities for transportation	53	697	19.1	27,466	72.0
4881	Support activities for air transportation	14	407	10.9	26,789	47.3
488410	Motor vehicle towing	11	116	2.0	17,509	6.3
488510	Freight transportation arrangement	24	126	5.0	39,413	13.1
4885102	Arrangement of transportation of freight and cargo	20	119	4.7	39,723	12.4
492	Couriers and messengers	26	5,196	137.5	26,461	331.3
492110	Couriers	15	4,902	131.9	26,916	318.5
492210	Local messengers and local delivery	11	294	5.5	18,867	12.7
493	Warehousing and storage	10	177	5.2	29,164	19.5

Sources: Economic Census of the United States, 1997. Only those industries are shown for which both employment and sales/revenue data were available. For the definition of MSAs, CMSAs, and PMSAs, please see the Introduction.

LONGVIEW—MARSHALL, TX MSA

NAICS	Industry	Estab-lish-ments	Em-ploy-ment	Payroll Total ($ mil.)	Payroll Per Empl. ($)	Sales, reven. ($ mil.)
48-49	Transportation and warehousing	140	1,878	49.2	26,202	220.0
484	Truck transportation	90	1,104	27.5	24,948	98.6
4841	General freight trucking	48	615	15.0	24,426	55.6
48412	General freight trucking, long-distance	38	535	13.4	25,135	51.0
484121	General freight trucking, long-distance, truckload (tl)	32	461	11.6	25,167	42.0
4842	Specialized freight trucking	42	489	12.5	25,605	43.1
484220	Specialized freight (except used goods) trucking, local	23	202	5.2	25,540	19.1
484230	Specialized freight (except used goods) trucking, long-distance	16	270	7.2	26,530	22.9
485	Transit and ground passenger transportation	3	50	0.4	7,560	0.9
486	Pipeline transportation	15	189	8.2	43,153	84.9
488	Support activities for transportation	26	465	11.2	23,996	29.7
493	Warehousing and storage	3	30	0.7	23,867	2.8

Sources: Economic Census of the United States, 1997. Only those industries are shown for which both employment and sales/revenue data were available. For the definition of MSAs, CMSAs, and PMSAs, please see the Introduction.

LOS ANGELES—LONG BEACH, CA PMSA

NAICS	Industry	Establishments	Employment	Payroll Total ($ mil.)	Payroll Per Empl. ($)	Sales, reven. ($ mil.)
48-49	Transportation and warehousing	4,722	109,979	3,519.9	32,005	14,953.1
481	Air transportation	177	4,691	184.4	39,308	2,427.0
48111	Scheduled air transportation	113	3,804	140.5	36,926	2,200.2
481111	Scheduled passenger air transportation	82	3,151	114.7	36,408	1,932.4
481112	Scheduled freight air transportation	31	653	25.7	39,429	267.8
48121	Nonscheduled air transportation	64	887	43.9	49,521	226.8
481211	Nonscheduled chartered passenger air transportation	53	681	30.6	44,962	204.4
483	Water transportation	37	3,343	120.1	35,928	1,267.7
48311	Deep sea, coastal, and Great Lakes water transportation	34	3,311	119.2	35,999	1,266.0
483111	Deep sea freight transportation	17	693	42.2	60,876	760.9
484	Truck transportation	1,750	27,561	796.1	28,885	3,113.8
4841	General freight trucking	851	17,821	543.3	30,484	2,126.3
484110	General freight trucking, local	558	7,564	206.6	27,313	795.8
4841101	General freight trucking without storage, local, truckload (tl)	309	2,849	81.9	28,752	380.9
4841102	General freight trucking without storage, local, less than truckload (ltl)	175	3,238	86.0	26,565	244.0
4841103	General freight trucking with storage, local, truckload (tl)	43	1,016	25.6	25,213	101.0
4841104	General freight trucking with storage, local, less than truckload (ltl)	31	461	13.0	28,295	69.8
48412	General freight trucking, long-distance	293	10,257	336.7	32,824	1,330.5
484121	General freight trucking, long-distance, truckload (tl)	194	3,914	116.3	29,710	518.6
484122	General freight trucking, long-distance, less than truckload (ltl)	99	6,343	220.4	34,745	811.9
4842	Specialized freight trucking	899	9,740	252.8	25,959	987.5
484210	Used household and office goods moving	278	3,257	79.6	24,427	260.0
4842101	Used household and office goods moving, local, without storage	106	609	9.0	14,834	36.0
4842102	Used household and office goods moving, long-distance	63	920	30.7	33,404	90.9
4842103	Used household and office goods moving, local, with storage	109	1,728	39.8	23,029	133.0
484220	Specialized freight (except used goods) trucking, local	491	4,620	108.9	23,565	410.2
4842201	Hazardous materials trucking (except waste), local	25	807	31.8	39,436	82.2
4842202	Agricultural products trucking without storage, local	39	281	7.9	28,032	31.2
4842203	Dump trucking	206	818	19.6	24,009	101.2
4842204	Specialized trucking without storage, local	197	2,252	36.2	16,089	141.1
4842205	Specialized trucking with storage, local	24	462	13.3	28,786	54.5
484230	Specialized freight (except used goods) trucking, long-distance	130	1,863	64.4	34,575	317.4
4842301	Hazardous materials trucking (except waste), long-distance	18	548	19.7	36,005	94.3
4842302	Agricultural products trucking, long-distance	36	296	9.5	32,182	42.7
4842303	Other specialized trucking, long-distance	76	1,019	35.2	34,500	180.4
48511	Urban transit systems	23	1,234	34.9	28,262	88.9
4853	Taxi and limousine service	123	1,814	34.1	18,790	129.2
485310	Taxi service	19	317	8.4	26,587	33.9
485320	Limousine service	104	1,497	25.7	17,139	95.3
485410	School and employee bus transportation	35	3,414	54.1	15,856	133.1
4854101	School bus service	32	3,244	51.9	15,997	129.2
485510	Charter bus industry	52	1,139	23.5	20,594	81.3
4855101	Charter bus service, local	21	546	10.2	18,771	36.6
4855102	Charter bus service, interstate/interurban	31	593	13.2	22,272	44.7
48599	Other transit and ground passenger transportation	89	2,686	40.4	15,024	135.8
485991	Special needs transportation	58	1,752	27.0	15,410	98.5
485999	All other transit and ground passenger transportation	31	934	13.4	14,300	37.3
4859991	Scheduled airport shuttle service	24	829	12.0	14,476	33.5
488	Support activities for transportation	1,607	30,279	1,276.3	42,150	3,560.7
4881	Support activities for air transportation	132	5,856	131.0	22,365	436.0
48811	Airport operations	56	3,585	67.4	18,796	205.6
488190	Other support activities for air transportation	76	2,271	63.6	27,998	230.5
4882101	Support activities incidental to rail transportation	17	835	22.8	27,363	92.4
4883	Support activities for water transportation	64	8,133	587.7	72,262	1,307.4
488320	Marine cargo handling	27	7,603	559.8	73,633	1,159.2
488330	Navigational services to shipping	11	295	16.6	56,237	51.7
4884	Support activities for road transportation	242	2,719	67.9	24,989	179.2
488410	Motor vehicle towing	217	2,412	60.2	24,943	160.8
488490	Other support activities for road transportation	25	307	7.8	25,349	18.4
4884903	Fixed facilities and inspection and weighing services for motor transportation vehicles	11	99	4.8	48,859	10.6
4884904	Support activities incidental to road transportation	14	208	2.9	14,159	7.8
488510	Freight transportation arrangement	1,128	12,573	462.4	36,776	1,532.5
4885101	Freight forwarding	650	7,671	278.9	36,355	977.6
4885102	Arrangement of transportation of freight and cargo	478	4,902	183.5	37,434	554.9
488991	Packing and crating	24	163	4.4	27,092	13.1
492	Couriers and messengers	455	21,176	517.6	24,442	1,525.1
492110	Couriers	231	16,124	441.8	27,399	1,337.6
4921101	Courier services (except by air)	75	8,410	216.2	25,706	485.7
4921102	Air courier services	156	7,714	225.6	29,245	851.9
492210	Local messengers and local delivery	224	5,052	75.8	15,004	187.4
4931	Warehousing and storage	234	5,268	137.5	26,100	488.5
4931101	General warehousing and storage (except in foreign trade zones)	161	3,472	85.5	24,634	286.4
493120	Refrigerated warehousing and storage	33	1,128	30.5	27,001	108.4
4931902	Specialized goods warehousing and storage	27	363	16.5	45,515	74.1

Sources: *Economic Census of the United States*, 1997. Only those industries are shown for which both employment and sales/revenue data were available. For the definition of MSAs, CMSAs, and PMSAs, please see the Introduction.

LOS ANGELES—RIVERSIDE—ORANGE COUNTY, CA CMSA

NAICS	Industry	Estab-lish-ments	Em-ploy-ment	Payroll		Sales, reven. ($ mil.)
				Total ($ mil.)	Per Empl. ($)	
48-49	Transportation and warehousing	7,345	172,463	5,166.2	29,956	21,613.2
484	Truck transportation	3,235	48,249	1,428.1	29,600	5,355.4
4841	General freight trucking	1,439	29,782	939.7	31,551	3,445.3
484110	General freight trucking, local	843	11,367	308.6	27,152	1,169.0
4841101	General freight trucking without storage, local, truckload (tl)	475	4,159	119.5	28,743	551.5
4841104	General freight trucking with storage, local, less than truckload (ltl)	42	813	22.9	28,199	93.4
48412	General freight trucking, long-distance	596	18,415	631.0	34,267	2,276.3
484121	General freight trucking, long-distance, truckload (tl)	410	7,189	217.9	30,304	926.1
484122	General freight trucking, long-distance, less than truckload (ltl)	186	11,226	413.2	36,805	1,350.3
4842	Specialized freight trucking	1,796	18,467	488.5	26,452	1,910.1
484210	Used household and office goods moving	518	6,168	150.7	24,437	562.6
4842101	Used household and office goods moving, local, without storage	205	1,281	21.3	16,615	76.8
4842102	Used household and office goods moving, long-distance	144	2,114	61.6	29,145	282.9
4842103	Used household and office goods moving, local, with storage	169	2,773	67.8	24,462	202.8
484220	Specialized freight (except used goods) trucking, local	1,005	8,823	226.4	25,656	861.6
4842201	Hazardous materials trucking (except waste), local	44	1,087	40.1	36,932	104.0
4842202	Agricultural products trucking without storage, local	113	727	17.2	23,711	66.0
4842203	Dump trucking	454	2,263	59.8	26,443	322.1
4842204	Specialized trucking without storage, local	361	4,092	89.9	21,970	289.5
4842205	Specialized trucking with storage, local	33	654	19.2	29,422	80.0
484230	Specialized freight (except used goods) trucking, long-distance	273	3,476	111.4	32,047	485.9
4842303	Other specialized trucking, long-distance	158	2,306	73.8	32,011	311.3
485113	Bus and motor vehicle transit systems	31	1,479	39.4	26,659	100.0
4853	Taxi and limousine service	198	2,567	45.9	17,863	162.4
485310	Taxi service	37	609	13.2	21,612	46.6
485320	Limousine service	161	1,958	32.7	16,697	115.8
4854101	School bus service	58	5,443	84.2	15,463	202.9
4855101	Charter bus service, local	41	726	13.0	17,959	46.0
48599	Other transit and ground passenger transportation	143	4,018	62.4	15,526	189.5
485991	Special needs transportation	94	2,647	40.6	15,332	124.9
485999	All other transit and ground passenger transportation	49	1,371	21.8	15,902	64.7
4872102	Charter fishing and party fishing boats	54	276	3.7	13,475	20.1
488	Support activities for transportation	2,082	34,635	1,399.3	40,403	3,999.5
4881	Support activities for air transportation	211	6,826	153.1	22,433	512.6
48811	Airport operations	85	4,130	78.4	18,994	246.1
488190	Other support activities for air transportation	126	2,696	74.7	27,701	266.5
4883	Support activities for water transportation	79	8,248	590.7	71,613	1,315.9
4884	Support activities for road transportation	436	4,363	104.4	23,925	294.6
488410	Motor vehicle towing	402	3,884	93.0	23,932	256.9
488490	Other support activities for road transportation	34	479	11.4	23,873	37.7
488510	Freight transportation arrangement	1,290	13,916	517.1	37,155	1,743.3
4885101	Freight forwarding	709	8,271	301.4	36,444	1,079.3
4885102	Arrangement of transportation of freight and cargo	581	5,645	215.6	38,196	664.0
492	Couriers and messengers	657	43,203	996.5	23,065	2,830.5
492110	Couriers	332	35,190	877.5	24,935	2,533.8
492210	Local messengers and local delivery	325	8,013	119.0	14,854	296.7
4931	Warehousing and storage	334	7,306	194.3	26,597	696.7
4931101	General warehousing and storage (except in foreign trade zones)	219	4,710	118.2	25,086	389.7
4931902	Specialized goods warehousing and storage	46	557	21.9	39,250	94.8

Sources: Economic Census of the United States, 1997. Only those industries are shown for which both employment and sales/revenue data were available. For the definition of MSAs, CMSAs, and PMSAs, please see the Introduction.

LOUISVILLE, KY—IN MSA

NAICS	Industry	Estab-lish-ments	Em-ploy-ment	Payroll		Sales, reven. ($ mil.)
				Total ($ mil.)	Per Empl. ($)	
48-49	Transportation and warehousing	667	24,717	797.6	32,269	3,604.0
484	Truck transportation	410	6,986	215.2	30,810	879.4
4841	General freight trucking	200	4,680	146.1	31,224	617.7
484110	General freight trucking, local	56	585	14.0	24,000	45.6
4841101	General freight trucking without storage, local, truckload (tl)	38	314	7.2	22,825	28.5
48412	General freight trucking, long-distance	144	4,095	132.1	32,256	572.1
484121	General freight trucking, long-distance, truckload (tl)	118	2,475	70.3	28,395	367.4
484122	General freight trucking, long-distance, less than truckload (ltl)	26	1,620	61.8	38,154	204.7
4842	Specialized freight trucking	210	2,306	69.1	29,972	261.7
484210	Used household and office goods moving	36	552	12.2	22,060	50.1
4842101	Used household and office goods moving, local, without storage	11	110	1.6	14,500	4.8
4842102	Used household and office goods moving, long-distance	15	322	8.3	25,891	38.3
484220	Specialized freight (except used goods) trucking, local	116	831	22.3	26,785	83.6
4842203	Dump trucking	59	438	12.6	28,728	47.9
4842204	Specialized trucking without storage, local	32	277	7.2	25,892	22.2
484230	Specialized freight (except used goods) trucking, long-distance	58	923	34.7	37,573	128.0
4842301	Hazardous materials trucking (except waste), long-distance	15	133	4.6	34,414	14.4
4842303	Other specialized trucking, long-distance	37	776	29.7	38,290	112.2
4853	Taxi and limousine service	13	412	5.9	14,405	10.5
4854101	School bus service	12	177	2.6	14,644	9.3
488	Support activities for transportation	98	1,729	38.5	22,289	113.5
4882101	Support activities incidental to rail transportation	11	401	10.3	25,661	21.2
488410	Motor vehicle towing	21	159	2.6	16,396	7.3
488510	Freight transportation arrangement	41	670	17.1	25,561	46.2
4885102	Arrangement of transportation of freight and cargo	33	637	15.6	24,474	40.9
4931	Warehousing and storage	44	919	26.6	28,984	92.9
4931101	General warehousing and storage (except in foreign trade zones)	30	599	18.4	30,775	69.9

Sources: *Economic Census of the United States*, 1997. Only those industries are shown for which both employment and sales/revenue data were available. For the definition of MSAs, CMSAs, and PMSAs, please see the Introduction.

LOWELL, MA—NH PMSA

NAICS	Industry	Estab-lish-ments	Em-ploy-ment	Payroll		Sales, reven. ($ mil.)
				Total ($ mil.)	Per Empl. ($)	
48-49	Transportation and warehousing	134	2,458	73.1	29,742	202.5
484	Truck transportation	89	1,576	61.6	39,092	171.5
4841	General freight trucking	41	937	35.8	38,215	99.1
484110	General freight trucking, local	17	162	3.0	18,241	7.4
48412	General freight trucking, long-distance	24	775	32.9	42,390	91.8
484121	General freight trucking, long-distance, truckload (tl)	12	151	5.9	38,808	17.2
484122	General freight trucking, long-distance, less than truckload (ltl)	12	624	27.0	43,256	74.6
4842	Specialized freight trucking	48	639	25.8	40,379	72.3
484210	Used household and office goods moving	18	341	13.4	39,217	31.6
4842101	Used household and office goods moving, local, without storage	11	75	2.1	27,440	4.8
484220	Specialized freight (except used goods) trucking, local	24	132	4.6	34,727	17.3
4842203	Dump trucking	17	52	1.4	27,635	6.0
485	Transit and ground passenger transportation	27	717	7.1	9,852	19.4
4854101	School bus service	11	499	4.4	8,780	12.0
488	Support activities for transportation	11	133	3.9	29,113	9.7

Sources: *Economic Census of the United States*, 1997. Only those industries are shown for which both employment and sales/revenue data were available. For the definition of MSAs, CMSAs, and PMSAs, please see the Introduction.

LUBBOCK, TX MSA

NAICS	Industry	Estab-lish-ments	Em-ploy-ment	Payroll		Sales, reven. ($ mil.)
				Total ($ mil.)	Per Empl. ($)	
48-49	Transportation and warehousing	165	2,640	59.6	22,580	236.8
481	Air transportation	3	32	0.6	17,594	2.3
484	Truck transportation	102	1,362	36.8	27,047	145.5
4841	General freight trucking	46	721	19.2	26,599	67.7
48412	General freight trucking, long-distance	36	578	16.4	28,330	56.1
484121	General freight trucking, long-distance, truckload (tl)	28	442	12.9	29,215	44.1
4842	Specialized freight trucking	56	641	17.7	27,551	77.8
484210	Used household and office goods moving	13	132	2.1	15,803	6.8
484220	Specialized freight (except used goods) trucking, local	25	189	4.2	22,444	14.9
484230	Specialized freight (except used goods) trucking, long-distance	18	320	11.3	35,412	56.1
488	Support activities for transportation	24	144	2.3	16,257	6.6
492	Couriers and messengers	17	299	5.8	19,475	22.3
493	Warehousing and storage	10	245	6.4	26,020	39.4

Sources: Economic Census of the United States, 1997. Only those industries are shown for which both employment and sales/revenue data were available. For the definition of MSAs, CMSAs, and PMSAs, please see the Introduction.

LYNCHBURG, VA MSA

NAICS	Industry	Estab-lish-ments	Em-ploy-ment	Payroll		Sales, reven. ($ mil.)
				Total ($ mil.)	Per Empl. ($)	
48-49	Transportation and warehousing	161	1,779	44.2	24,864	182.9
484	Truck transportation	115	1,292	31.7	24,502	132.0
4841	General freight trucking	66	865	22.0	25,486	100.3
484110	General freight trucking, local	18	111	2.5	22,613	6.4
4841101	General freight trucking without storage, local, truckload (tl)	14	70	1.2	17,157	4.1
48412	General freight trucking, long-distance	48	754	19.5	25,908	93.9
484121	General freight trucking, long-distance, truckload (tl)	43	645	15.6	24,212	69.9
4842	Specialized freight trucking	49	427	9.6	22,508	31.7
484220	Specialized freight (except used goods) trucking, local	27	196	4.5	22,990	17.4
4842203	Dump trucking	18	164	4.0	24,482	16.1
484230	Specialized freight (except used goods) trucking, long-distance	12	152	3.5	22,875	9.0
488	Support activities for transportation	16	187	5.7	30,626	19.1
493	Warehousing and storage	7	35	1.1	32,371	4.0

Sources: Economic Census of the United States, 1997. Only those industries are shown for which both employment and sales/revenue data were available. For the definition of MSAs, CMSAs, and PMSAs, please see the Introduction.

MACON, GA MSA

NAICS	Industry	Estab-lish-ments	Em-ploy-ment	Payroll		Sales, reven. ($ mil.)
				Total ($ mil.)	Per Empl. ($)	
48-49	Transportation and warehousing	167	1,970	44.1	22,372	149.5
484	Truck transportation	103	922	24.1	26,163	75.4
4841	General freight trucking	49	554	16.1	29,096	48.1
484110	General freight trucking, local	17	70	1.5	20,843	6.2
4841101	General freight trucking without storage, local, truckload (tl)	12	40	0.8	19,525	4.7
48412	General freight trucking, long-distance	32	484	14.7	30,289	41.9
484121	General freight trucking, long-distance, truckload (tl)	18	180	4.7	26,283	15.0
484122	General freight trucking, long-distance, less than truckload (ltl)	14	304	9.9	32,661	26.9
4842	Specialized freight trucking	54	368	8.0	21,747	27.3
484220	Specialized freight (except used goods) trucking, local	33	152	4.5	29,362	18.1
4842203	Dump trucking	21	92	2.9	31,674	13.8
484230	Specialized freight (except used goods) trucking, long-distance	11	72	2.1	29,097	4.4
488	Support activities for transportation	27	574	11.3	19,767	48.1
488410	Motor vehicle towing	14	69	1.2	17,855	4.1
4931	Warehousing and storage	14	147	2.6	17,687	7.9

Sources: Economic Census of the United States, 1997. Only those industries are shown for which both employment and sales/revenue data were available. For the definition of MSAs, CMSAs, and PMSAs, please see the Introduction.

MADISON, WI MSA

NAICS	Industry	Estab-lish-ments	Em-ploy-ment	Payroll Total ($ mil.)	Payroll Per Empl. ($)	Sales, reven. ($ mil.)
48-49	Transportation and warehousing	287	3,689	79.6	21,581	270.1
481	Air transportation	6	84	2.0	23,405	8.2
484	Truck transportation	191	1,721	45.6	26,493	165.8
4841	General freight trucking	80	1,000	30.2	30,174	109.6
484110	General freight trucking, local	28	264	6.8	25,693	23.8
4841101	General freight trucking without storage, local, truckload (tl)	18	148	3.7	24,804	15.2
484121	General freight trucking, long-distance	52	736	23.4	31,781	85.9
484121	General freight trucking, long-distance, truckload (tl)	41	389	12.8	32,972	42.8
484122	General freight trucking, long-distance, less than truckload (ltl)	11	347	10.6	30,447	43.0
4842	Specialized freight trucking	111	721	15.4	21,388	56.2
484210	Used household and office goods moving	17	174	2.9	16,707	8.2
484220	Specialized freight (except used goods) trucking, local	73	418	9.4	22,538	32.6
4842202	Agricultural products trucking without storage, local	13	58	2.6	45,534	10.2
4842203	Dump trucking	51	74	2.7	37,014	12.9
484230	Specialized freight (except used goods) trucking, long-distance	21	129	3.1	23,977	15.4
485	Transit and ground passenger transportation	33	1,013	12.4	12,194	28.1
4854101	School bus service	17	444	4.2	9,367	10.4
487	Scenic and sightseeing transportation	4	21	0.4	17,857	1.4
488	Support activities for transportation	19	97	2.3	23,351	6.8
492	Couriers and messengers	25	682	15.5	22,667	52.5
492110	Couriers	13	588	14.3	24,291	49.0
492210	Local messengers and local delivery	12	94	1.2	12,511	3.5
493	Warehousing and storage	9	71	1.6	22,549	7.3

Sources: Economic Census of the United States, 1997. Only those industries are shown for which both employment and sales/revenue data were available. For the definition of MSAs, CMSAs, and PMSAs, please see the Introduction.

MANCHESTER, NH PMSA

NAICS	Industry	Estab-lish-ments	Em-ploy-ment	Payroll Total ($ mil.)	Payroll Per Empl. ($)	Sales, reven. ($ mil.)
48-49	Transportation and warehousing	102	1,316	37.4	28,449	130.6
484	Truck transportation	49	516	17.5	33,942	56.8
4841	General freight trucking	21	346	12.3	35,587	37.6
48412	General freight trucking, long-distance	13	283	11.2	39,484	34.8
4842	Specialized freight trucking	28	170	5.2	30,594	19.2
484220	Specialized freight (except used goods) trucking, local	17	110	3.1	28,464	10.8
488	Support activities for transportation	18	100	3.2	31,690	7.2
488410	Motor vehicle towing	11	49	0.8	16,429	2.7
492110	Couriers	18	472	13.5	28,564	57.6
4921102	Air courier services	12	391	12.0	30,670	49.4

Sources: Economic Census of the United States, 1997. Only those industries are shown for which both employment and sales/revenue data were available. For the definition of MSAs, CMSAs, and PMSAs, please see the Introduction.

MANSFIELD, OH MSA

NAICS	Industry	Estab-lish-ments	Em-ploy-ment	Payroll Total ($ mil.)	Payroll Per Empl. ($)	Sales, reven. ($ mil.)
48-49	Transportation and warehousing	107	1,030	25.9	25,162	96.5
484	Truck transportation	73	641	17.5	27,324	62.1
4841	General freight trucking	41	405	11.5	28,323	41.1
48412	General freight trucking, long-distance	35	380	11.1	29,195	39.9
484121	General freight trucking, long-distance, truckload (tl)	25	179	4.7	26,413	17.2
4842	Specialized freight trucking	32	236	6.0	25,610	21.0
484220	Specialized freight (except used goods) trucking, local	21	95	2.3	23,989	10.7
485	Transit and ground passenger transportation	9	91	0.9	9,352	2.0
488	Support activities for transportation	17	99	2.1	21,333	5.7

Sources: Economic Census of the United States, 1997. Only those industries are shown for which both employment and sales/revenue data were available. For the definition of MSAs, CMSAs, and PMSAs, please see the Introduction.

MCALLEN—EDINBURG—MISSION, TX MSA

| NAICS | Industry | Estab-lish-ments | Em-ploy-ment | Payroll | | Sales, reven. ($ mil.) |
				Total ($ mil.)	Per Empl. ($)	
48-49	Transportation and warehousing	338	2,618	55.2	21,087	233.7
484	Truck transportation	199	1,644	37.3	22,698	159.8
4841	General freight trucking	101	1,132	24.4	21,523	111.6
484110	General freight trucking, local	29	162	2.4	14,562	9.9
4841101	General freight trucking without storage, local, truckload (tl)	19	84	1.1	13,000	6.3
48412	General freight trucking, long-distance	72	970	22.0	22,686	101.7
484121	General freight trucking, long-distance, truckload (tl)	64	908	19.6	21,553	88.5
4842	Specialized freight trucking	98	512	13.0	25,295	48.2
484210	Used household and office goods moving	11	35	0.6	17,257	2.4
484220	Specialized freight (except used goods) trucking, local	57	317	10.1	31,760	33.1
4842202	Agricultural products trucking without storage, local	15	45	0.7	15,467	3.1
4842203	Dump trucking	27	119	1.7	13,874	11.8
4842204	Specialized trucking without storage, local	15	153	7.7	50,464	18.2
484230	Specialized freight (except used goods) trucking, long-distance	30	160	2.3	14,244	12.7
4842302	Agricultural products trucking, long-distance	17	121	1.6	13,521	9.1
488	Support activities for transportation	95	601	11.7	19,502	39.8
488410	Motor vehicle towing	12	35	0.4	11,457	1.6
488510	Freight transportation arrangement	71	446	9.4	21,034	30.8
4885101	Freight forwarding	15	103	1.7	16,097	7.9
4885102	Arrangement of transportation of freight and cargo	56	343	7.7	22,516	22.9
492	Couriers and messengers	6	53	1.5	28,264	4.3
4931	Warehousing and storage	13	187	2.6	13,856	15.2

Sources: *Economic Census of the United States*, 1997. Only those industries are shown for which both employment and sales/revenue data were available. For the definition of MSAs, CMSAs, and PMSAs, please see the Introduction.

MEDFORD—ASHLAND, OR MSA

| NAICS | Industry | Estab-lish-ments | Em-ploy-ment | Payroll | | Sales, reven. ($ mil.) |
				Total ($ mil.)	Per Empl. ($)	
48-49	Transportation and warehousing	154	2,357	72.5	30,748	243.7
484	Truck transportation	104	1,186	36.0	30,312	158.4
4841	General freight trucking	58	688	21.8	31,625	105.4
484110	General freight trucking, local	14	103	2.7	26,534	4.7
48412	General freight trucking, long-distance	44	585	19.0	32,521	100.6
484121	General freight trucking, long-distance, truckload (tl)	32	405	13.7	33,842	88.2
484122	General freight trucking, long-distance, less than truckload (ltl)	12	180	5.3	29,550	12.5
4842	Specialized freight trucking	46	498	14.2	28,498	53.0
484220	Specialized freight (except used goods) trucking, local	25	104	2.3	22,125	9.4
484230	Specialized freight (except used goods) trucking, long-distance	18	369	11.3	30,729	42.3
485	Transit and ground passenger transportation	10	205	1.9	9,224	5.3
488	Support activities for transportation	21	265	9.2	34,608	26.1
4885102	Arrangement of transportation of freight and cargo	17	206	7.9	38,539	21.6
492	Couriers and messengers	6	86	2.1	24,407	6.2

Sources: *Economic Census of the United States*, 1997. Only those industries are shown for which both employment and sales/revenue data were available. For the definition of MSAs, CMSAs, and PMSAs, please see the Introduction.

MELBOURNE—TITUSVILLE—PALM BAY, FL MSA

NAICS	Industry	Estab-lish-ments	Em-ploy-ment	Payroll Total ($ mil.)	Payroll Per Empl. ($)	Sales, reven. ($ mil.)
48-49	Transportation and warehousing	200	7,393	212.6	28,763	943.0
484	Truck transportation	86	486	11.4	23,368	43.3
4841	General freight trucking	24	86	2.3	27,163	11.8
48412	General freight trucking, long-distance	16	72	1.9	26,278	9.5
4842	Specialized freight trucking	62	400	9.0	22,552	31.5
484210	Used household and office goods moving	19	216	4.4	20,583	12.9
4842102	Used household and office goods moving, long-distance	11	162	3.6	22,377	10.5
484220	Specialized freight (except used goods) trucking, local	27	109	2.3	21,037	8.5
4842203	Dump trucking	15	67	1.2	18,090	5.7
484230	Specialized freight (except used goods) trucking, long-distance	16	75	2.3	30,427	10.1
4842303	Other specialized trucking, long-distance	12	38	1.0	26,447	6.7
487	Scenic and sightseeing transportation	6	28	0.5	16,071	1.6
4881	Support activities for air transportation	17	343	11.9	34,781	47.8
488510	Freight transportation arrangement	13	47	1.7	35,532	6.2
492	Couriers and messengers	16	179	4.3	23,872	20.3
493	Warehousing and storage	7	51	1.6	31,431	12.3

Sources: Economic Census of the United States, 1997. Only those industries are shown for which both employment and sales/revenue data were available. For the definition of MSAs, CMSAs, and PMSAs, please see the Introduction.

MEMPHIS, TN—AR—MS MSA

NAICS	Industry	Estab-lish-ments	Em-ploy-ment	Payroll Total ($ mil.)	Payroll Per Empl. ($)	Sales, reven. ($ mil.)
48-49	Transportation and warehousing	924	24,268	841.2	34,664	2,522.5
483	Water transportation	8	295	9.8	33,088	57.3
484	Truck transportation	423	13,832	477.7	34,539	1,393.1
4841	General freight trucking	240	11,744	406.9	34,644	1,112.1
484110	General freight trucking, local	69	620	15.6	25,229	52.5
4841101	General freight trucking without storage, local, truckload (tl)	43	294	8.4	28,626	35.0
4841102	General freight trucking without storage, local, less than truckload (ltl)	16	253	5.3	20,881	11.5
48412	General freight trucking, long-distance	171	11,124	391.2	35,169	1,059.6
484121	General freight trucking, long-distance, truckload (tl)	131	6,077	192.3	31,636	690.8
484122	General freight trucking, long-distance, less than truckload (ltl)	40	5,047	199.0	39,424	368.8
4842	Specialized freight trucking	183	2,088	70.9	33,948	281.0
484210	Used household and office goods moving	34	504	13.8	27,442	52.7
484220	Specialized freight (except used goods) trucking, local	89	528	13.5	25,576	58.3
4842203	Dump trucking	49	150	3.6	24,307	16.5
4842204	Specialized trucking without storage, local	24	218	5.3	24,440	20.4
484230	Specialized freight (except used goods) trucking, long-distance	60	1,056	43.5	41,239	170.0
4842301	Hazardous materials trucking (except waste), long-distance	14	204	6.7	32,887	26.8
4842303	Other specialized trucking, long-distance	36	838	36.5	43,518	139.9
485	Transit and ground passenger transportation	27	1,175	15.9	13,559	43.8
488	Support activities for transportation	200	3,008	90.4	30,069	279.9
4881	Support activities for air transportation	23	529	11.7	22,200	52.7
488190	Other support activities for air transportation	16	347	9.7	27,821	48.1
4882101	Support activities incidental to rail transportation	12	173	3.4	19,827	31.1
4883	Support activities for water transportation	17	263	7.0	26,745	34.5
488410	Motor vehicle towing	33	152	3.3	22,013	10.7
488510	Freight transportation arrangement	108	1,744	62.1	35,580	146.9
4885101	Freight forwarding	40	857	25.8	30,063	57.2
4885102	Arrangement of transportation of freight and cargo	68	887	36.3	40,911	89.6
492	Couriers and messengers	160	4,437	204.7	46,131	582.0
492110	Couriers	135	4,088	195.1	47,713	558.0
4921101	Courier services (except by air)	16	613	8.2	13,400	29.1
4921102	Air courier services	119	3,475	186.8	53,766	528.9
492210	Local messengers and local delivery	25	349	9.6	27,599	24.0
4931	Warehousing and storage	91	1,406	37.5	26,654	136.3
4931101	General warehousing and storage (except in foreign trade zones)	57	774	21.2	27,358	68.9
493190	Other warehousing and storage	17	356	9.2	25,770	35.9

Sources: Economic Census of the United States, 1997. Only those industries are shown for which both employment and sales/revenue data were available. For the definition of MSAs, CMSAs, and PMSAs, please see the Introduction.

MERCED, CA MSA

NAICS	Industry	Estab-lish-ments	Em-ploy-ment	Payroll		Sales, reven. ($ mil.)
				Total ($ mil.)	Per Empl. ($)	
48-49	Transportation and warehousing	116	1,208	31.7	26,233	118.0
484	Truck transportation	95	884	26.5	30,019	103.9
4841	General freight trucking	26	308	7.8	25,231	27.3
48412	General freight trucking, long-distance	16	250	6.5	26,148	17.1
484121	General freight trucking, long-distance, truckload (tl)	13	204	4.6	22,397	11.9
4842	Specialized freight trucking	69	576	18.8	32,580	76.6
484220	Specialized freight (except used goods) trucking, local	45	201	5.2	25,896	28.8
4842202	Agricultural products trucking without storage, local	31	143	4.1	28,615	24.3
484230	Specialized freight (except used goods) trucking, long-distance	19	334	13.0	38,979	46.1
485	Transit and ground passenger transportation	4	181	2.8	15,713	6.9
488	Support activities for transportation	12	121	1.7	14,289	5.5

Sources: *Economic Census of the United States*, 1997. Only those industries are shown for which both employment and sales/revenue data were available. For the definition of MSAs, CMSAs, and PMSAs, please see the Introduction.

MIAMI, FL PMSA

NAICS	Industry	Estab-lish-ments	Em-ploy-ment	Payroll Total ($ mil.)	Payroll Per Empl. ($)	Sales, reven. ($ mil.)
48-49	Transportation and warehousing	2,510	55,863	1,782.5	31,908	8,456.9
481	Air transportation	131	5,774	167.5	29,015	1,271.7
48111	Scheduled air transportation	98	5,433	157.1	28,922	1,167.7
481111	Scheduled passenger air transportation	72	2,728	80.0	29,319	669.4
481112	Scheduled freight air transportation	26	2,705	77.1	28,521	498.3
48121	Nonscheduled air transportation	33	341	10.4	30,507	104.1
481211	Nonscheduled chartered passenger air transportation	20	151	3.8	25,490	30.5
483	Water transportation	47	6,901	259.1	37,549	3,032.5
48311	Deep sea, coastal, and Great Lakes water transportation	43	6,878	258.7	37,612	3,031.0
483112	Deep sea passenger transportation	12	5,870	222.3	37,869	2,425.1
484	Truck transportation	500	14,613	600.6	41,101	1,783.6
4841	General freight trucking	263	12,871	562.7	43,719	1,626.7
484110	General freight trucking, local	155	874	21.3	24,314	71.3
4841101	General freight trucking without storage, local, truckload (tl)	85	424	9.8	23,116	40.8
4841102	General freight trucking without storage, local, less than truckload (ltl)	49	270	5.8	21,530	17.8
4841103	General freight trucking with storage, local, truckload (tl)	12	148	5.0	33,838	10.0
48412	General freight trucking, long-distance	108	11,997	541.5	45,133	1,555.5
484121	General freight trucking, long-distance, truckload (tl)	73	10,371	486.2	46,878	1,367.2
484122	General freight trucking, long-distance, less than truckload (ltl)	35	1,626	55.3	34,002	188.2
4842	Specialized freight trucking	237	1,742	37.9	21,757	156.8
484210	Used household and office goods moving	79	493	10.6	21,469	38.8
4842101	Used household and office goods moving, local, without storage	39	158	3.3	20,759	10.8
4842102	Used household and office goods moving, long-distance	13	104	2.8	26,952	9.4
4842103	Used household and office goods moving, local, with storage	27	231	4.5	19,485	18.6
484220	Specialized freight (except used goods) trucking, local	114	657	14.8	22,600	71.2
4842202	Agricultural products trucking without storage, local	19	121	1.3	10,471	5.3
4842203	Dump trucking	40	175	3.9	22,440	33.8
4842204	Specialized trucking without storage, local	40	237	7.1	29,772	24.5
4842205	Specialized trucking with storage, local	12	106	2.4	22,689	7.2
484230	Specialized freight (except used goods) trucking, long-distance	44	592	12.5	21,061	46.8
4842302	Agricultural products trucking, long-distance	14	200	4.1	20,590	12.3
4842303	Other specialized trucking, long-distance	30	392	8.4	21,301	34.5
485	Transit and ground passenger transportation	130	1,402	30.8	21,989	90.2
4853	Taxi and limousine service	52	175	3.2	18,091	18.8
485310	Taxi service	27	69	1.0	13,812	4.1
485320	Limousine service	25	106	2.2	20,877	14.7
4854101	School bus service	18	157	2.1	13,178	5.5
48599	Other transit and ground passenger transportation	37	376	6.6	17,644	19.3
485991	Special needs transportation	28	312	5.1	16,500	16.9
487210	Scenic and sightseeing transportation, water	36	243	4.4	17,909	27.1
4872101	Excursion and sightseeing boats (including dinner cruises)	11	107	3.1	28,785	13.8
4872102	Charter fishing and party fishing boats	25	136	1.3	9,353	13.4
488	Support activities for transportation	1,308	18,224	479.5	26,312	1,432.9
4881	Support activities for air transportation	141	7,590	182.1	23,996	526.3
4881191	Airport operation and terminal services	49	4,361	67.4	15,467	158.3
488190	Other support activities for air transportation	92	3,229	114.7	35,517	368.0
4883	Support activities for water transportation	85	2,961	80.4	27,138	167.8
488320	Marine cargo handling	15	2,305	53.7	23,288	100.8
488330	Navigational services to shipping	25	201	8.0	39,592	18.9
4883302	Navigational services	19	34	3.3	96,559	7.2
488390	Other support activities for water transportation	36	226	8.5	37,407	21.4
4883901	Other services incidental to water transportation	25	106	4.3	40,368	11.4
488410	Motor vehicle towing	59	481	8.2	17,069	26.5
488510	Freight transportation arrangement	990	6,821	201.3	29,509	688.7
4885101	Freight forwarding	617	4,433	128.3	28,942	449.1
4885102	Arrangement of transportation of freight and cargo	373	2,388	73.0	30,563	239.6
492	Couriers and messengers	283	7,525	214.5	28,502	746.3
492110	Couriers	159	6,804	199.5	29,314	686.0
4921101	Courier services (except by air)	61	4,917	132.9	27,028	437.8
4921102	Air courier services	98	1,887	66.6	35,269	248.1
492210	Local messengers and local delivery	124	721	15.0	20,839	60.4
4931	Warehousing and storage	68	1,164	25.5	21,935	66.2
4931101	General warehousing and storage (except in foreign trade zones)	48	762	17.0	22,306	40.8

Sources: *Economic Census of the United States*, 1997. Only those industries are shown for which both employment and sales/revenue data were available. For the definition of MSAs, CMSAs, and PMSAs, please see the Introduction.

MIAMI—FORT LAUDERDALE, FL CMSA

NAICS	Industry	Estab-lish-ments	Em-ploy-ment	Payroll Total ($ mil.)	Payroll Per Empl. ($)	Sales, reven. ($ mil.)
48-49	Transportation and warehousing	3,505	69,585	2,093.1	30,080	10,047.2
481	Air transportation	183	6,619	193.5	29,239	1,429.3
48111	Scheduled air transportation	126	6,020	175.5	29,153	1,273.0
481111	Scheduled passenger air transportation	95	3,160	93.8	29,683	755.6
481112	Scheduled freight air transportation	31	2,860	81.7	28,566	517.5
48121	Nonscheduled air transportation	57	599	18.0	30,112	156.3
483	Water transportation	77	8,492	307.3	36,183	3,493.7
48311	Deep sea, coastal, and Great Lakes water transportation	67	8,344	303.3	36,348	3,480.8
484	Truck transportation	817	17,037	670.3	39,344	2,082.8
4841	General freight trucking	369	13,986	600.0	42,899	1,771.0
484110	General freight trucking, local	204	1,210	30.1	24,899	100.0
4841102	General freight trucking without storage, local, less than truckload (ltl)	68	514	12.3	23,957	32.9
48412	General freight trucking, long-distance	165	12,776	569.9	44,604	1,671.1
484121	General freight trucking, long-distance, truckload (tl)	116	10,624	495.9	46,682	1,423.8
484122	General freight trucking, long-distance, less than truckload (ltl)	49	2,152	73.9	34,345	247.3
4842	Specialized freight trucking	448	3,051	70.3	23,046	311.8
484210	Used household and office goods moving	155	1,071	22.7	21,203	87.8
4842101	Used household and office goods moving, local, without storage	69	224	4.4	19,540	15.8
4842102	Used household and office goods moving, long-distance	42	425	10.0	23,548	39.5
4842103	Used household and office goods moving, local, with storage	44	422	8.3	19,723	32.5
484220	Specialized freight (except used goods) trucking, local	214	1,078	26.2	24,307	140.6
4842202	Agricultural products trucking without storage, local	32	154	2.0	13,039	8.3
4842203	Dump trucking	83	347	9.1	26,343	79.0
4842204	Specialized trucking without storage, local	71	356	9.5	26,621	36.3
4842205	Specialized trucking with storage, local	18	159	3.5	21,799	10.7
484230	Specialized freight (except used goods) trucking, long-distance	79	902	21.4	23,726	83.4
4842302	Agricultural products trucking, long-distance	23	242	4.8	19,888	14.6
4842303	Other specialized trucking, long-distance	48	490	10.0	20,502	43.5
4853	Taxi and limousine service	107	316	5.5	17,551	30.0
485310	Taxi service	41	122	1.8	14,852	7.5
485320	Limousine service	66	194	3.7	19,247	22.5
485410	School and employee bus transportation	22	181	2.5	13,890	6.4
485510	Charter bus industry	16	830	13.9	16,693	39.1
4855101	Charter bus service, local	11	581	5.9	10,189	19.2
48599	Other transit and ground passenger transportation	58	637	10.9	17,088	27.9
485991	Special needs transportation	41	560	9.2	16,509	25.1
485999	All other transit and ground passenger transportation	17	77	1.6	21,299	2.9
4859991	Scheduled airport shuttle service	11	67	1.5	22,134	2.3
487	Scenic and sightseeing transportation	92	1,237	17.6	14,248	114.7
487210	Scenic and sightseeing transportation, water	83	1,207	15.8	13,095	102.4
4872101	Excursion and sightseeing boats (including dinner cruises)	28	1,008	13.2	13,075	83.9
4872102	Charter fishing and party fishing boats	55	199	2.6	13,196	18.5
488	Support activities for transportation	1,638	23,088	560.7	24,286	1,730.0
4881	Support activities for air transportation	217	9,114	214.8	23,567	651.3
48811	Airport operations	71	5,380	86.3	16,042	218.4
488190	Other support activities for air transportation	146	3,734	128.5	34,409	433.0
4883	Support activities for water transportation	148	5,466	107.5	19,671	272.6
488320	Marine cargo handling	26	3,664	71.0	19,388	159.1
488330	Navigational services to shipping	38	303	10.6	34,904	42.0
488410	Motor vehicle towing	120	806	14.1	17,445	46.4
488510	Freight transportation arrangement	1,106	7,214	213.7	29,617	727.3
4885101	Freight forwarding	657	4,543	131.0	28,845	460.3
4885102	Arrangement of transportation of freight and cargo	449	2,671	82.6	30,930	267.0
492	Couriers and messengers	376	9,243	263.9	28,552	942.1
492110	Couriers	206	8,298	244.2	29,427	862.8
4921101	Courier services (except by air)	84	5,075	135.6	26,719	452.5
4921102	Air courier services	122	3,223	108.6	33,690	410.3
492210	Local messengers and local delivery	170	945	19.7	20,869	79.3
4931	Warehousing and storage	97	1,428	32.6	22,852	93.2
4931101	General warehousing and storage (except in foreign trade zones)	65	930	21.8	23,456	55.9
4931201	Refrigerated products warehousing	15	305	6.6	21,797	21.5
4931902	Specialized goods warehousing and storage	17	193	4.2	21,606	15.8

Sources: Economic Census of the United States, 1997. Only those industries are shown for which both employment and sales/revenue data were available. For the definition of MSAs, CMSAs, and PMSAs, please see the Introduction.

MIDDLESEX—SOMERSET—HUNTERDON, NJ PMSA

NAICS	Industry	Establishments	Employment	Payroll		Sales, reven. ($ mil.)
				Total ($ mil.)	Per Empl. ($)	
48-49	Transportation and warehousing	1,066	21,027	634.8	30,191	2,441.1
484	Truck transportation	549	7,441	275.5	37,021	1,031.8
4841	General freight trucking	264	4,632	182.5	39,394	687.2
484110	General freight trucking, local	134	895	33.6	37,523	116.9
4841101	General freight trucking without storage, local, truckload (tl)	77	552	22.1	40,007	74.7
4841102	General freight trucking without storage, local, less than truckload (ltl)	49	219	7.9	36,283	26.2
484112	General freight trucking, long-distance	130	3,737	148.9	39,842	570.3
484121	General freight trucking, long-distance, truckload (tl)	85	1,604	68.3	42,590	231.1
484122	General freight trucking, long-distance, less than truckload (ltl)	45	2,133	80.6	37,775	339.2
4842	Specialized freight trucking	285	2,809	93.0	33,107	344.7
484210	Used household and office goods moving	56	864	26.5	30,655	98.6
4842101	Used household and office goods moving, local, without storage	20	90	1.3	14,389	4.2
4842102	Used household and office goods moving, long-distance	22	544	18.0	33,022	70.5
4842103	Used household and office goods moving, local, with storage	14	230	7.2	31,422	23.9
484220	Specialized freight (except used goods) trucking, local	178	996	28.4	28,466	107.7
4842201	Hazardous materials trucking (except waste), local	14	49	1.7	34,286	3.8
4842203	Dump trucking	84	322	11.5	35,590	43.2
4842204	Specialized trucking without storage, local	66	486	10.2	21,023	42.4
484230	Specialized freight (except used goods) trucking, long-distance	51	949	38.2	40,211	138.3
4842301	Hazardous materials trucking (except waste), long-distance	18	348	13.4	38,408	48.2
4842303	Other specialized trucking, long-distance	30	589	24.7	41,935	88.7
485	Transit and ground passenger transportation	155	3,399	48.4	14,244	119.6
4853	Taxi and limousine service	84	586	8.1	13,833	23.8
485310	Taxi service	27	96	0.9	9,604	3.1
485320	Limousine service	57	490	7.2	14,661	20.8
485410	School and employee bus transportation	33	2,074	26.3	12,665	60.0
485510	Charter bus industry	13	241	4.7	19,485	9.3
486	Pipeline transportation	4	76	4.2	54,829	59.6
488	Support activities for transportation	172	2,196	85.1	38,731	269.0
488410	Motor vehicle towing	31	184	4.1	22,446	13.7
488510	Freight transportation arrangement	113	1,670	71.0	42,490	219.0
4885101	Freight forwarding	43	785	27.3	34,832	91.2
4885102	Arrangement of transportation of freight and cargo	70	885	43.6	49,284	127.8
492	Couriers and messengers	77	4,651	127.8	27,468	438.4
492110	Couriers	34	4,129	117.9	28,549	402.8
492210	Local messengers and local delivery	43	522	9.9	18,916	35.5
4931	Warehousing and storage	93	3,103	84.2	27,137	260.1
4931101	General warehousing and storage (except in foreign trade zones)	73	2,502	62.1	24,827	179.1
493190	Other warehousing and storage	15	395	16.4	41,559	64.4
4931902	Specialized goods warehousing and storage	12	357	15.5	43,443	61.1

Sources: *Economic Census of the United States*, 1997. Only those industries are shown for which both employment and sales/revenue data were available. For the definition of MSAs, CMSAs, and PMSAs, please see the Introduction.

MILWAUKEE—RACINE, WI CMSA

NAICS	Industry	Establishments	Employment	Payroll		Sales, reven. ($ mil.)
				Total ($ mil.)	Per Empl. ($)	
48-49	Transportation and warehousing	1,159	23,898	631.8	26,438	2,038.8
481	Air transportation	18	345	8.5	24,614	54.4
48111	Scheduled air transportation	11	224	5.5	24,746	37.5
484	Truck transportation	690	9,742	311.7	32,000	1,183.6
4841	General freight trucking	313	6,965	227.4	32,647	883.4
484110	General freight trucking, local	123	1,501	43.8	29,153	111.3
484112	General freight trucking, long-distance	190	5,464	183.6	33,606	772.1
484121	General freight trucking, long-distance, truckload (tl)	130	2,929	93.1	31,784	443.7
484122	General freight trucking, long-distance, less than truckload (ltl)	60	2,535	90.5	35,712	328.4
4842	Specialized freight trucking	377	2,777	84.4	30,378	300.2
484220	Specialized freight (except used goods) trucking, local	271	1,310	42.9	32,733	166.9
4842202	Agricultural products trucking without storage, local	23	84	1.5	17,679	4.8
4842203	Dump trucking	188	670	22.2	33,072	108.0
4842204	Specialized trucking without storage, local	42	441	15.9	35,973	46.0
485	Transit and ground passenger transportation	168	4,811	61.6	12,797	150.8
485310	Taxi service	16	121	1.1	9,066	3.7
485410	School and employee bus transportation	53	3,679	43.7	11,873	103.8
48599	Other transit and ground passenger transportation	60	543	8.2	15,192	20.8
485991	Special needs transportation	56	534	8.1	15,230	20.4
488	Support activities for transportation	152	1,463	41.9	28,643	136.6
488510	Freight transportation arrangement	87	636	22.3	35,079	74.6

Sources: *Economic Census of the United States*, 1997. Only those industries are shown for which both employment and sales/revenue data were available. For the definition of MSAs, CMSAs, and PMSAs, please see the Introduction.

MILWAUKEE—WAUKESHA, WI PMSA

NAICS	Industry	Estab-lish-ments	Em-ploy-ment	Payroll		Sales, reven. ($ mil.)
				Total ($ mil.)	Per Empl. ($)	
48-49	Transportation and warehousing	1,023	22,152	584.7	26,396	1,861.7
481	Air transportation	18	345	8.5	24,614	54.4
48111	Scheduled air transportation	11	224	5.5	24,746	37.5
484	Truck transportation	595	8,679	277.0	31,914	1,044.1
4841	General freight trucking	286	6,290	203.9	32,416	793.1
484110	General freight trucking, local	115	1,414	40.9	28,938	102.9
4841101	General freight trucking without storage, local, truckload (tl)	66	663	18.9	28,469	52.0
4841102	General freight trucking without storage, local, less than truckload (ltl)	46	729	21.4	29,306	49.2
48412	General freight trucking, long-distance	171	4,876	163.0	33,425	690.2
484121	General freight trucking, long-distance, truckload (tl)	115	2,349	72.7	30,964	362.6
484122	General freight trucking, long-distance, less than truckload (ltl)	56	2,527	90.2	35,712	327.6
4842	Specialized freight trucking	309	2,389	73.1	30,590	251.0
484210	Used household and office goods moving	50	807	21.1	26,088	62.3
484220	Specialized freight (except used goods) trucking, local	218	1,130	37.7	33,388	139.9
4842201	Hazardous materials trucking (except waste), local	14	91	2.6	28,242	5.4
4842203	Dump trucking	152	546	18.4	33,749	85.1
4842204	Specialized trucking without storage, local	32	405	15.1	37,343	43.8
484230	Specialized freight (except used goods) trucking, long-distance	41	452	14.3	31,633	48.8
4842303	Other specialized trucking, long-distance	30	406	12.9	31,778	41.7
485	Transit and ground passenger transportation	153	4,352	55.2	12,687	136.3
4853	Taxi and limousine service	40	281	3.4	11,964	10.6
485310	Taxi service	16	121	1.1	9,066	3.7
485320	Limousine service	24	160	2.3	14,156	6.9
485410	School and employee bus transportation	47	3,322	39.8	11,983	92.8
48599	Other transit and ground passenger transportation	56	532	8.1	15,235	20.4
485991	Special needs transportation	52	523	8.0	15,275	19.9
488	Support activities for transportation	137	1,365	39.4	28,885	127.3
4884	Support activities for road transportation	31	201	4.0	19,891	11.3
488410	Motor vehicle towing	28	184	3.7	20,370	10.9
488510	Freight transportation arrangement	80	586	20.8	35,495	68.1
4885101	Freight forwarding	39	325	11.3	34,815	35.2
4885102	Arrangement of transportation of freight and cargo	41	261	9.5	36,341	33.0
492	Couriers and messengers	78	6,903	190.0	27,519	444.7
492110	Couriers	32	6,334	177.6	28,046	421.0
492210	Local messengers and local delivery	46	569	12.3	21,654	23.7
4931	Warehousing and storage	33	474	13.5	28,527	48.0
4931101	General warehousing and storage (except in foreign trade zones)	21	326	9.7	29,620	35.1

Sources: *Economic Census of the United States*, 1997. Only those industries are shown for which both employment and sales/revenue data were available. For the definition of MSAs, CMSAs, and PMSAs, please see the Introduction.

MINNEAPOLIS—ST. PAUL, MN—WI MSA

NAICS	Industry	Estab-lish-ments	Em-ploy-ment	Payroll		Sales, reven. ($ mil.)
				Total ($ mil.)	Per Empl. ($)	
48-49	Transportation and warehousing	1,770	36,283	972.5	26,804	3,809.4
481	Air transportation	35	1,066	39.3	36,858	178.2
484	Truck transportation	958	13,335	444.9	33,362	1,966.8
4841	General freight trucking	465	9,659	334.5	34,633	1,474.5
484110	General freight trucking, local	201	1,694	49.1	29,012	158.9
4841101	General freight trucking without storage, local, truckload (tl)	118	799	24.5	30,671	95.9
4841102	General freight trucking without storage, local, less than truckload (ltl)	73	850	23.4	27,540	59.6
48412	General freight trucking, long-distance	264	7,965	285.4	35,829	1,315.5
484121	General freight trucking, long-distance, truckload (tl)	205	4,864	163.7	33,663	923.6
484122	General freight trucking, long-distance, less than truckload (ltl)	59	3,101	121.6	39,226	391.9
4842	Specialized freight trucking	493	3,676	110.4	30,020	492.4
484210	Used household and office goods moving	91	1,356	37.4	27,568	148.0
4842101	Used household and office goods moving, local, without storage	31	210	3.9	18,552	9.9
4842102	Used household and office goods moving, long-distance	44	785	23.7	30,215	113.6
4842103	Used household and office goods moving, local, with storage	16	361	9.8	27,055	24.6
484220	Specialized freight (except used goods) trucking, local	291	1,355	37.5	27,708	185.8
4842203	Dump trucking	154	456	14.3	31,456	86.1
4842204	Specialized trucking without storage, local	77	460	12.2	26,537	47.0
484230	Specialized freight (except used goods) trucking, long-distance	111	965	35.4	36,712	158.6
4842301	Hazardous materials trucking (except waste), long-distance	13	137	4.6	33,380	37.7
4842302	Agricultural products trucking, long-distance	25	118	3.0	25,305	22.6
4842303	Other specialized trucking, long-distance	73	710	27.9	39,251	98.3
485	Transit and ground passenger transportation	205	7,079	98.1	13,853	233.7
4853	Taxi and limousine service	55	519	8.3	15,979	25.5
485310	Taxi service	26	165	3.4	20,491	8.9
485320	Limousine service	29	354	4.9	13,876	16.7
485410	School and employee bus transportation	76	4,626	57.9	12,520	128.7
485510	Charter bus industry	14	247	3.6	14,721	10.3
48599	Other transit and ground passenger transportation	50	1,225	20.6	16,855	44.1
485991	Special needs transportation	40	1,088	18.7	17,206	38.3
488	Support activities for transportation	334	3,581	112.2	31,329	430.9
4881191	Airport operation and terminal services	13	649	13.5	20,761	96.8
488410	Motor vehicle towing	72	615	11.4	18,593	33.5
488510	Freight transportation arrangement	193	1,861	71.1	38,213	243.0
4885101	Freight forwarding	84	1,083	42.0	38,784	128.7
4885102	Arrangement of transportation of freight and cargo	109	778	29.1	37,418	114.3
492	Couriers and messengers	153	10,110	242.3	23,964	685.3
492110	Couriers	49	7,697	195.8	25,438	550.4
492210	Local messengers and local delivery	104	2,413	46.5	19,260	134.9
4931	Warehousing and storage	51	787	22.5	28,602	135.0
4931101	General warehousing and storage (except in foreign trade zones)	32	414	11.1	26,768	96.7

Sources: *Economic Census of the United States*, 1997. Only those industries are shown for which both employment and sales/revenue data were available. For the definition of MSAs, CMSAs, and PMSAs, please see the Introduction.

MOBILE, AL MSA

NAICS	Industry	Estab-lish-ments	Em-ploy-ment	Payroll		Sales, reven. ($ mil.)
				Total ($ mil.)	Per Empl. ($)	
48-49	Transportation and warehousing	452	6,772	171.6	25,339	647.6
484	Truck transportation	228	2,939	73.2	24,907	257.4
4841	General freight trucking	108	1,968	49.8	25,318	171.3
484110	General freight trucking, local	24	244	4.8	19,713	19.1
4841101	General freight trucking without storage, local, truckload (tl)	20	229	4.6	20,026	18.5
48412	General freight trucking, long-distance	84	1,724	45.0	26,111	152.2
484121	General freight trucking, long-distance, truckload (tl)	64	1,149	27.3	23,736	104.4
484122	General freight trucking, long-distance, less than truckload (ltl)	20	575	17.7	30,857	47.8
4842	Specialized freight trucking	120	971	23.4	24,074	86.1
484210	Used household and office goods moving	20	208	3.2	15,187	9.4
484220	Specialized freight (except used goods) trucking, local	57	269	6.0	22,487	26.7
4842202	Agricultural products trucking without storage, local	12	54	1.0	18,667	6.2
4842203	Dump trucking	26	119	2.3	19,580	10.9
4842204	Specialized trucking without storage, local	14	78	2.3	28,897	8.1
484230	Specialized freight (except used goods) trucking, long-distance	43	494	14.2	28,680	50.0
4842301	Hazardous materials trucking (except waste), long-distance	18	245	7.6	30,898	24.5
4842303	Other specialized trucking, long-distance	18	221	5.9	26,647	21.2
486	Pipeline transportation	6	61	2.7	44,525	25.3
487210	Scenic and sightseeing transportation, water	19	40	0.5	13,075	1.9
488	Support activities for transportation	121	2,027	54.4	26,862	181.1
4883	Support activities for water transportation	50	1,279	33.5	26,215	91.6
488320	Marine cargo handling	19	933	24.2	25,895	39.9
488510	Freight transportation arrangement	51	538	17.3	32,113	44.7
4885102	Arrangement of transportation of freight and cargo	42	445	14.1	31,598	33.9
492	Couriers and messengers	21	354	8.1	22,828	27.6
492110	Couriers	11	313	7.1	22,591	25.5
4931	Warehousing and storage	20	283	8.2	29,145	24.9
4931101	General warehousing and storage (except in foreign trade zones)	11	224	6.6	29,286	17.0

Sources: Economic Census of the United States, 1997. Only those industries are shown for which both employment and sales/revenue data were available. For the definition of MSAs, CMSAs, and PMSAs, please see the Introduction.

MODESTO, CA MSA

NAICS	Industry	Estab-lish-ments	Em-ploy-ment	Payroll		Sales, reven. ($ mil.)
				Total ($ mil.)	Per Empl. ($)	
48-49	Transportation and warehousing	263	3,136	81.5	25,983	301.8
484	Truck transportation	196	1,939	55.4	28,568	210.9
4841	General freight trucking	77	914	26.0	28,406	87.0
484110	General freight trucking, local	35	261	7.1	27,372	31.3
4841101	General freight trucking without storage, local, truckload (tl)	29	194	5.1	26,232	21.3
48412	General freight trucking, long-distance	42	653	18.8	28,819	55.7
484121	General freight trucking, long-distance, truckload (tl)	38	602	17.2	28,508	48.7
4842	Specialized freight trucking	119	1,025	29.4	28,713	123.9
484210	Used household and office goods moving	16	101	1.8	17,653	5.8
484220	Specialized freight (except used goods) trucking, local	69	427	12.0	28,091	60.6
4842202	Agricultural products trucking without storage, local	35	174	6.0	34,707	25.2
4842203	Dump trucking	16	103	2.4	23,369	21.4
4842204	Specialized trucking without storage, local	12	117	2.5	21,308	10.1
484230	Specialized freight (except used goods) trucking, long-distance	34	497	15.7	31,495	57.6
4842302	Agricultural products trucking, long-distance	21	307	10.6	34,443	38.8
485	Transit and ground passenger transportation	9	452	6.9	15,195	19.7
488	Support activities for transportation	35	219	4.7	21,594	15.4
488410	Motor vehicle towing	16	62	1.1	17,516	4.8
492	Couriers and messengers	10	134	3.2	23,582	8.5
493	Warehousing and storage	9	321	9.0	28,184	37.5

Sources: Economic Census of the United States, 1997. Only those industries are shown for which both employment and sales/revenue data were available. For the definition of MSAs, CMSAs, and PMSAs, please see the Introduction.

MONMOUTH—OCEAN, NJ PMSA

NAICS	Industry	Estab-lish-ments	Em-ploy-ment	Payroll Total ($ mil.)	Payroll Per Empl. ($)	Sales, reven. ($ mil.)
48-49	Transportation and warehousing	584	5,581	114.8	20,561	407.4
484	Truck transportation	267	1,409	39.9	28,285	163.2
4841	General freight trucking	112	527	17.8	33,702	79.4
484110	General freight trucking, local	61	224	7.9	35,210	28.5
4841101	General freight trucking without storage, local, truckload (tl)	37	158	5.7	35,930	19.4
48412	General freight trucking, long-distance	51	303	9.9	32,587	50.8
484121	General freight trucking, long-distance, truckload (tl)	35	158	4.2	26,519	27.0
484122	General freight trucking, long-distance, less than truckload (ltl)	16	145	5.7	39,200	23.8
4842	Specialized freight trucking	155	882	22.1	25,048	83.8
484210	Used household and office goods moving	32	207	4.4	21,319	12.6
484220	Specialized freight (except used goods) trucking, local	98	501	12.5	24,888	55.0
4842203	Dump trucking	53	153	5.3	34,575	29.8
484230	Specialized freight (except used goods) trucking, long-distance	25	174	5.2	29,943	16.2
4842303	Other specialized trucking, long-distance	15	101	2.4	23,752	8.2
485	Transit and ground passenger transportation	127	2,994	41.1	13,733	109.4
4853	Taxi and limousine service	70	480	6.2	12,852	17.8
485310	Taxi service	24	88	0.9	9,898	2.4
485320	Limousine service	46	392	5.3	13,515	15.4
4854101	School bus service	27	1,563	19.9	12,717	42.3
487210	Scenic and sightseeing transportation, water	45	123	2.1	17,301	8.6
488	Support activities for transportation	97	426	13.0	30,613	59.1
488410	Motor vehicle towing	25	63	1.4	21,571	5.9
488510	Freight transportation arrangement	49	191	6.9	36,199	35.4
4885101	Freight forwarding	18	63	3.0	46,905	13.1
4885102	Arrangement of transportation of freight and cargo	31	128	4.0	30,930	22.3

Sources: Economic Census of the United States, 1997. Only those industries are shown for which both employment and sales/revenue data were available. For the definition of MSAs, CMSAs, and PMSAs, please see the Introduction.

MONROE, LA MSA

NAICS	Industry	Estab-lish-ments	Em-ploy-ment	Payroll Total ($ mil.)	Payroll Per Empl. ($)	Sales, reven. ($ mil.)
48-49	Transportation and warehousing	122	1,438	38.6	26,835	140.5
484	Truck transportation	82	968	29.2	30,156	99.5
4841	General freight trucking	57	845	26.7	31,593	88.9
484110	General freight trucking, local	14	80	1.7	20,825	7.1
4841101	General freight trucking without storage, local, truckload (tl)	11	62	1.4	22,032	6.4
48412	General freight trucking, long-distance	43	765	25.0	32,719	81.8
484121	General freight trucking, long-distance, truckload (tl)	33	608	20.4	33,602	67.2
4842	Specialized freight trucking	25	123	2.5	20,285	10.6
484220	Specialized freight (except used goods) trucking, local	11	36	0.9	25,000	4.3
488	Support activities for transportation	12	147	2.6	17,741	9.4
492	Couriers and messengers	7	80	1.8	22,175	3.6
493	Warehousing and storage	6	132	2.8	20,841	10.0

Sources: Economic Census of the United States, 1997. Only those industries are shown for which both employment and sales/revenue data were available. For the definition of MSAs, CMSAs, and PMSAs, please see the Introduction.

MONTGOMERY, AL MSA

NAICS	Industry	Estab-lish-ments	Em-ploy-ment	Payroll		Sales, reven. ($ mil.)
				Total ($ mil.)	Per Empl. ($)	
48-49	Transportation and warehousing	186	2,512	55.5	22,097	203.7
484	Truck transportation	127	1,541	37.6	24,416	144.9
4841	General freight trucking	58	847	22.9	26,985	85.5
48412	General freight trucking, long-distance	52	825	22.5	27,310	84.2
484121	General freight trucking, long-distance, truckload (tl)	39	480	12.1	25,179	56.6
484122	General freight trucking, long-distance, less than truckload (ltl)	13	345	10.4	30,275	27.6
4842	Specialized freight trucking	69	694	14.8	21,281	59.3
484210	Used household and office goods moving	13	200	3.9	19,480	9.4
484220	Specialized freight (except used goods) trucking, local	43	302	5.2	17,083	30.5
4842203	Dump trucking	27	207	3.6	17,251	25.0
484230	Specialized freight (except used goods) trucking, long-distance	13	192	5.7	29,760	19.4
488	Support activities for transportation	14	242	6.0	24,632	18.5
492	Couriers and messengers	9	168	3.7	22,280	14.1
4931	Warehousing and storage	17	201	4.0	19,672	12.2

Sources: Economic Census of the United States, 1997. Only those industries are shown for which both employment and sales/revenue data were available. For the definition of MSAs, CMSAs, and PMSAs, please see the Introduction.

MUNCIE, IN MSA

NAICS	Industry	Estab-lish-ments	Em-ploy-ment	Payroll		Sales, reven. ($ mil.)
				Total ($ mil.)	Per Empl. ($)	
48-49	Transportation and warehousing	61	2,173	64.3	29,591	211.3
484	Truck transportation	40	1,866	59.5	31,900	192.3
4841	General freight trucking	27	1,774	56.1	31,607	183.5
48412	General freight trucking, long-distance	19	1,691	51.6	30,492	176.1
4842	Specialized freight trucking	13	92	3.5	37,554	8.8
485	Transit and ground passenger transportation	6	181	1.7	9,326	4.7
486	Pipeline transportation	3	19	0.9	47,421	6.7
493	Warehousing and storage	5	34	0.5	14,147	3.1

Sources: Economic Census of the United States, 1997. Only those industries are shown for which both employment and sales/revenue data were available. For the definition of MSAs, CMSAs, and PMSAs, please see the Introduction.

MYRTLE BEACH, SC MSA

NAICS	Industry	Estab-lish-ments	Em-ploy-ment	Payroll		Sales, reven. ($ mil.)
				Total ($ mil.)	Per Empl. ($)	
48-49	Transportation and warehousing	109	756	13.7	18,175	57.6
484	Truck transportation	52	328	6.4	19,598	29.5
4841	General freight trucking	17	142	3.9	27,521	17.0
4842	Specialized freight trucking	35	186	2.5	13,548	12.5
484220	Specialized freight (except used goods) trucking, local	20	97	0.9	9,639	6.4
488	Support activities for transportation	16	132	2.3	17,250	6.4
492	Couriers and messengers	9	113	2.4	21,062	11.6

Sources: Economic Census of the United States, 1997. Only those industries are shown for which both employment and sales/revenue data were available. For the definition of MSAs, CMSAs, and PMSAs, please see the Introduction.

NAPLES, FL MSA

| NAICS | Industry | Estab-lish-ments | Em-ploy-ment | Payroll | | Sales, reven. ($ mil.) |
				Total ($ mil.)	Per Empl. ($)	
48-49	Transportation and warehousing	133	699	16.6	23,747	78.0
481	Air transportation	9	65	2.3	35,846	15.1
484	Truck transportation	54	193	4.7	24,580	17.1
4842	Specialized freight trucking	48	182	4.5	24,522	15.0
484210	Used household and office goods moving	14	116	3.1	26,914	7.2
484220	Specialized freight (except used goods) trucking, local	30	44	0.9	20,568	5.7
485	Transit and ground passenger transportation	13	74	0.7	9,054	2.7
487	Scenic and sightseeing transportation	19	148	2.2	14,858	7.3
487210	Scenic and sightseeing transportation, water	16	99	1.6	16,263	5.1
488	Support activities for transportation	28	122	4.2	34,057	28.1

Sources: Economic Census of the United States, 1997. Only those industries are shown for which both employment and sales/revenue data were available. For the definition of MSAs, CMSAs, and PMSAs, please see the Introduction.

NASHUA, NH PMSA

| NAICS | Industry | Estab-lish-ments | Em-ploy-ment | Payroll | | Sales, reven. ($ mil.) |
				Total ($ mil.)	Per Empl. ($)	
48-49	Transportation and warehousing	96	5,782	160.5	27,757	346.6
484	Truck transportation	48	417	10.8	25,894	40.3
4841	General freight trucking	19	147	4.5	30,633	15.0
48412	General freight trucking, long-distance	13	129	3.7	28,977	13.0
4842	Specialized freight trucking	29	270	6.3	23,315	25.3
484220	Specialized freight (except used goods) trucking, local	11	34	0.5	14,853	3.4
485	Transit and ground passenger transportation	15	435	4.5	10,448	11.3

Sources: Economic Census of the United States, 1997. Only those industries are shown for which both employment and sales/revenue data were available. For the definition of MSAs, CMSAs, and PMSAs, please see the Introduction.

NASHVILLE, TN MSA

| NAICS | Industry | Estab-lish-ments | Em-ploy-ment | Payroll | | Sales, reven. ($ mil.) |
				Total ($ mil.)	Per Empl. ($)	
48-49	Transportation and warehousing	757	22,048	677.6	30,733	1,934.7
481	Air transportation	20	319	7.9	24,771	40.0
48121	Nonscheduled air transportation	12	143	3.8	26,322	19.6
484	Truck transportation	427	11,371	388.1	34,132	1,074.2
4841	General freight trucking	241	8,870	306.3	34,533	790.3
484110	General freight trucking, local	57	552	15.6	28,263	48.4
4841101	General freight trucking without storage, local, truckload (tl)	34	277	8.5	30,726	33.0
4841102	General freight trucking without storage, local, less than truckload (ltl)	17	247	6.7	26,988	14.1
48412	General freight trucking, long-distance	184	8,318	290.7	34,949	741.8
484121	General freight trucking, long-distance, truckload (tl)	147	4,376	129.2	29,522	470.4
484122	General freight trucking, long-distance, less than truckload (ltl)	37	3,942	161.5	40,974	271.4
4842	Specialized freight trucking	186	2,501	81.8	32,711	284.0
484210	Used household and office goods moving	39	489	11.4	23,268	31.6
4842101	Used household and office goods moving, local, without storage	15	70	1.1	15,914	4.3
4842102	Used household and office goods moving, long-distance	17	304	7.9	25,941	19.4
484220	Specialized freight (except used goods) trucking, local	89	521	12.6	24,106	44.3
4842203	Dump trucking	53	323	7.8	24,229	30.3
4842204	Specialized trucking without storage, local	22	98	2.5	25,551	7.4
484230	Specialized freight (except used goods) trucking, long-distance	58	1,491	57.9	38,814	208.0
4842303	Other specialized trucking, long-distance	44	1,162	49.5	42,571	140.4
485	Transit and ground passenger transportation	64	1,096	24.6	22,456	55.3
4853	Taxi and limousine service	15	128	1.8	14,109	4.5
4854101	School bus service	26	51	0.6	10,980	2.2
486	Pipeline transportation	10	77	4.9	63,597	52.6
488	Support activities for transportation	129	1,668	45.7	27,373	166.8
4881	Support activities for air transportation	21	496	13.9	28,067	47.7
48811	Airport operations	11	133	2.3	17,353	10.3
488410	Motor vehicle towing	33	366	8.3	22,765	35.1
488510	Freight transportation arrangement	63	603	18.8	31,144	69.1
4885101	Freight forwarding	25	357	10.4	29,165	46.3
4885102	Arrangement of transportation of freight and cargo	38	246	8.4	34,016	22.8
492	Couriers and messengers	51	6,405	167.6	26,162	409.2
492110	Couriers	25	6,143	163.2	26,563	394.8
492210	Local messengers and local delivery	26	262	4.4	16,771	14.4
4931	Warehousing and storage	43	727	26.1	35,880	69.7
4931101	General warehousing and storage (except in foreign trade zones)	29	443	17.4	39,305	46.0

Sources: Economic Census of the United States, 1997. Only those industries are shown for which both employment and sales/revenue data were available. For the definition of MSAs, CMSAs, and PMSAs, please see the Introduction.

NASSAU—SUFFOLK, NY PMSA

NAICS	Industry	Estab-lish-ments	Em-ploy-ment	Payroll		Sales, reven. ($ mil.)
				Total ($ mil.)	Per Empl. ($)	
48-49	Transportation and warehousing	1,888	27,155	745.6	27,456	2,648.5
484	Truck transportation	728	5,641	170.7	30,254	621.3
4841	General freight trucking	268	2,240	81.4	36,328	285.4
484110	General freight trucking, local	178	951	29.6	31,131	89.3
4841101	General freight trucking without storage, local, truckload (tl)	90	388	13.4	34,497	44.0
4841102	General freight trucking without storage, local, less than truckload (ltl)	78	463	13.1	28,194	36.6
48412	General freight trucking, long-distance	90	1,289	51.8	40,161	196.0
484121	General freight trucking, long-distance, truckload (tl)	63	559	21.6	38,637	87.6
484122	General freight trucking, long-distance, less than truckload (ltl)	27	730	30.2	41,329	108.4
4842	Specialized freight trucking	460	3,401	89.3	26,253	335.9
484210	Used household and office goods moving	127	1,127	24.9	22,138	85.4
4842101	Used household and office goods moving, local, without storage	54	312	5.3	16,856	18.1
4842102	Used household and office goods moving, long-distance	35	530	12.4	23,315	43.3
4842103	Used household and office goods moving, local, with storage	38	285	7.3	25,730	24.0
484220	Specialized freight (except used goods) trucking, local	290	1,979	53.2	26,867	215.0
4842201	Hazardous materials trucking (except waste), local	19	50	1.1	22,520	7.5
4842203	Dump trucking	112	339	12.5	36,900	48.4
4842204	Specialized trucking without storage, local	129	1,483	37.3	25,147	150.2
484230	Specialized freight (except used goods) trucking, long-distance	43	295	11.2	37,864	35.5
4842303	Other specialized trucking, long-distance	35	271	10.4	38,288	33.8
485	Transit and ground passenger transportation	378	9,835	167.2	17,000	397.2
4853	Taxi and limousine service	255	1,411	20.2	14,325	78.9
485310	Taxi service	80	360	6.0	16,556	18.7
485320	Limousine service	175	1,051	14.3	13,561	60.2
485410	School and employee bus transportation	61	7,066	114.6	16,219	244.9
48599	Other transit and ground passenger transportation	42	651	14.5	22,200	28.7
485991	Special needs transportation	33	540	10.4	19,317	19.3
4872102	Charter fishing and party fishing boats	35	92	1.2	13,304	4.8
488	Support activities for transportation	454	4,187	173.0	41,325	577.5
4881	Support activities for air transportation	40	814	32.4	39,785	154.2
488190	Other support activities for air transportation	31	784	31.5	40,149	150.8
4883	Support activities for water transportation	17	275	8.4	30,444	24.5
4884	Support activities for road transportation	67	444	12.1	27,158	33.5
4885101	Freight forwarding	162	1,510	74.4	49,284	225.5
492110	Couriers	52	4,613	139.2	30,176	453.5
4931	Warehousing and storage	32	434	10.7	24,597	37.0
4931101	General warehousing and storage (except in foreign trade zones)	21	285	6.2	21,660	18.8

Sources: *Economic Census of the United States*, 1997. Only those industries are shown for which both employment and sales/revenue data were available. For the definition of MSAs, CMSAs, and PMSAs, please see the Introduction.

NEW BEDFORD, MA PMSA

NAICS	Industry	Estab-lish-ments	Em-ploy-ment	Payroll		Sales, reven. ($ mil.)
				Total ($ mil.)	Per Empl. ($)	
48-49	Transportation and warehousing	93	1,180	23.5	19,908	68.5
484	Truck transportation	37	314	8.0	25,439	31.3
4841	General freight trucking	14	130	4.1	31,177	15.5
4842	Specialized freight trucking	23	184	3.9	21,386	15.8
484220	Specialized freight (except used goods) trucking, local	15	74	2.7	36,554	9.2
485	Transit and ground passenger transportation	25	666	9.2	13,875	19.9
488	Support activities for transportation	17	113	3.3	29,124	7.7

Sources: *Economic Census of the United States*, 1997. Only those industries are shown for which both employment and sales/revenue data were available. For the definition of MSAs, CMSAs, and PMSAs, please see the Introduction.

NEW HAVEN—MERIDEN, CT PMSA

| NAICS | Industry | Estab-lish-ments | Em-ploy-ment | Payroll | | Sales, reven. ($ mil.) |
				Total ($ mil.)	Per Empl. ($)	
48-49	Transportation and warehousing	266	3,911	108.1	27,651	425.6
484	Truck transportation	151	1,491	54.0	36,206	168.7
4841	General freight trucking	57	783	30.1	38,499	92.8
484110	General freight trucking, local	26	132	3.8	28,841	18.1
4841101	General freight trucking without storage, local, truckload (tl)	11	48	1.6	32,750	9.4
48412	General freight trucking, long-distance	31	651	26.3	40,458	74.7
484121	General freight trucking, long-distance, truckload (tl)	21	246	8.7	35,411	23.5
4842	Specialized freight trucking	94	708	23.8	33,669	76.0
484210	Used household and office goods moving	26	221	6.1	27,511	23.0
484220	Specialized freight (except used goods) trucking, local	53	281	11.2	39,989	33.2
4842203	Dump trucking	19	34	1.0	29,235	4.9
4842204	Specialized trucking without storage, local	25	227	9.2	40,608	23.2
484230	Specialized freight (except used goods) trucking, long-distance	15	206	6.5	31,655	19.7
485	Transit and ground passenger transportation	45	1,231	18.7	15,171	44.3
485320	Limousine service	11	196	2.4	12,301	6.7
4854101	School bus service	19	839	11.8	14,060	28.1
488	Support activities for transportation	38	465	13.7	29,518	116.1
488510	Freight transportation arrangement	17	184	5.5	29,995	71.4
492	Couriers and messengers	11	369	10.8	29,168	43.0
493	Warehousing and storage	8	150	3.8	25,367	15.6

Sources: *Economic Census of the United States*, 1997. Only those industries are shown for which both employment and sales/revenue data were available. For the definition of MSAs, CMSAs, and PMSAs, please see the Introduction.

NEW LONDON—NORWICH, CT—RI MSA

| NAICS | Industry | Estab-lish-ments | Em-ploy-ment | Payroll | | Sales, reven. ($ mil.) |
				Total ($ mil.)	Per Empl. ($)	
48-49	Transportation and warehousing	111	1,245	37.9	30,449	112.8
484	Truck transportation	56	467	15.4	32,908	47.7
4841	General freight trucking	16	142	5.5	38,486	22.3
48412	General freight trucking, long-distance	11	99	3.9	39,889	14.2
4842	Specialized freight trucking	40	325	9.9	30,471	25.5
484210	Used household and office goods moving	11	141	3.5	24,496	7.7
484220	Specialized freight (except used goods) trucking, local	20	73	2.1	28,932	6.3
4842203	Dump trucking	15	47	1.2	25,064	4.0
485	Transit and ground passenger transportation	19	359	6.3	17,429	17.2

Sources: *Economic Census of the United States*, 1997. Only those industries are shown for which both employment and sales/revenue data were available. For the definition of MSAs, CMSAs, and PMSAs, please see the Introduction.

NEW ORLEANS, LA MSA

NAICS	Industry	Estab-lish-ments	Em-ploy-ment	Payroll		Sales, reven. ($ mil.)
				Total ($ mil.)	Per Empl. ($)	
48-49	Transportation and warehousing	1,128	29,589	863.8	29,193	3,492.5
481211	Nonscheduled chartered passenger air transportation	11	241	7.4	30,515	35.5
483	Water transportation	139	6,125	179.3	29,271	1,051.6
48311	Deep sea, coastal, and Great Lakes water transportation	77	4,567	127.6	27,931	724.5
483113	Coastal and Great Lakes freight transportation	56	3,318	105.7	31,847	488.2
4831131	Coastal and intercoastal freight transportation	27	2,877	94.8	32,965	422.3
4831133	Coastal and intercoastal towing service	29	441	10.8	24,558	65.9
48321	Inland water transportation	62	1,558	51.7	33,197	327.1
4832111	Inland waterways freight transportation (except towing)	23	885	32.6	36,885	264.1
484	Truck transportation	321	4,402	116.4	26,443	436.5
4841	General freight trucking	157	2,918	85.7	29,368	310.7
484110	General freight trucking, local	67	501	9.9	19,778	39.6
4841101	General freight trucking without storage, local, truckload (tl)	54	352	6.7	19,040	30.2
48412	General freight trucking, long-distance	90	2,417	75.8	31,356	271.0
484121	General freight trucking, long-distance, truckload (tl)	66	1,329	39.2	29,476	176.7
484122	General freight trucking, long-distance, less than truckload (ltl)	24	1,088	36.6	33,653	94.3
4842	Specialized freight trucking	164	1,484	30.7	20,691	125.8
484210	Used household and office goods moving	29	551	10.0	18,064	33.4
4842102	Used household and office goods moving, long-distance	13	232	4.6	19,845	19.5
484220	Specialized freight (except used goods) trucking, local	97	620	11.6	18,637	57.3
4842203	Dump trucking	54	265	4.9	18,626	25.9
4842204	Specialized trucking without storage, local	28	120	2.5	20,658	9.3
484230	Specialized freight (except used goods) trucking, long-distance	38	313	9.2	29,383	35.1
4842301	Hazardous materials trucking (except waste), long-distance	13	91	3.7	40,813	15.7
4842303	Other specialized trucking, long-distance	25	222	5.5	24,698	19.5
485	Transit and ground passenger transportation	73	2,456	79.4	32,341	147.6
4853	Taxi and limousine service	32	310	3.8	12,316	11.8
485310	Taxi service	15	77	1.1	14,494	3.0
485320	Limousine service	17	233	2.7	11,597	8.7
48599	Other transit and ground passenger transportation	15	239	4.2	17,393	10.7
486	Pipeline transportation	22	447	24.5	54,765	176.9
486110	Pipeline transportation of crude oil	15	213	12.0	56,512	92.8
487210	Scenic and sightseeing transportation, water	16	1,157	34.3	29,621	162.6
4872101	Excursion and sightseeing boats (including dinner cruises)	11	1,145	34.1	29,744	161.9
488	Support activities for transportation	431	7,709	233.5	30,286	966.8
4883	Support activities for water transportation	184	5,262	161.6	30,703	735.8
488320	Marine cargo handling	40	1,734	51.5	29,686	185.5
488330	Navigational services to shipping	80	1,838	55.4	30,168	286.2
4883301	Tugboat service (including fleeting and harbor service)	44	1,503	44.3	29,488	209.4
488390	Other support activities for water transportation	54	816	25.8	31,571	86.1
4883901	Other services incidental to water transportation	38	602	17.7	29,387	58.4
4883902	Marine cargo inspectors and surveyors	16	214	8.1	37,715	27.7
4884	Support activities for road transportation	30	225	4.9	21,991	15.0
488410	Motor vehicle towing	23	157	3.0	19,318	10.8
488510	Freight transportation arrangement	191	1,561	58.3	37,379	154.9
4885101	Freight forwarding	47	498	17.4	34,843	48.8
4885102	Arrangement of transportation of freight and cargo	144	1,063	41.0	38,567	106.1
492	Couriers and messengers	58	5,607	147.1	26,236	346.9
492110	Couriers	38	5,483	144.8	26,413	338.4
492210	Local messengers and local delivery	20	124	2.3	18,427	8.5
4931	Warehousing and storage	44	1,161	36.8	31,655	140.0
4931101	General warehousing and storage (except in foreign trade zones)	16	257	5.1	19,770	17.2
493190	Other warehousing and storage	18	596	23.2	38,930	95.3

Sources: Economic Census of the United States, 1997. Only those industries are shown for which both employment and sales/revenue data were available. For the definition of MSAs, CMSAs, and PMSAs, please see the Introduction.

NEW YORK, NY PMSA

NAICS	Industry	Estab-lish-ments	Em-ploy-ment	Payroll		Sales, reven. ($ mil.)
				Total ($ mil.)	Per Empl. ($)	
48-49	Transportation and warehousing	5,232	94,840	2,695.5	28,421	10,693.8
481	Air transportation	167	7,809	318.1	40,730	3,027.7
48111	Scheduled air transportation	146	7,363	300.6	40,821	2,936.1
481111	Scheduled passenger air transportation	121	6,493	263.7	40,618	2,558.5
481112	Scheduled freight air transportation	25	870	36.8	42,334	377.5
48121	Nonscheduled air transportation	21	446	17.5	39,226	91.6
483	Water transportation	84	3,521	140.4	39,885	979.1
48311	Deep sea, coastal, and Great Lakes water transportation	74	3,330	132.2	39,704	949.3
483111	Deep sea freight transportation	49	1,532	79.5	51,892	615.5
484	Truck transportation	1,227	12,694	341.7	26,916	1,072.9
4841	General freight trucking	493	4,322	140.2	32,428	427.2
484110	General freight trucking, local	366	2,396	68.2	28,477	197.2
4841101	General freight trucking without storage, local, truckload (tl)	178	1,266	33.6	26,555	96.9
4841102	General freight trucking without storage, local, less than truckload (ltl)	153	879	25.1	28,579	70.7
4841103	General freight trucking with storage, local, truckload (tl)	18	144	6.0	41,896	17.0
4841104	General freight trucking with storage, local, less than truckload (ltl)	17	107	3.5	32,336	12.5
48412	General freight trucking, long-distance	127	1,926	71.9	37,343	230.0
484121	General freight trucking, long-distance, truckload (tl)	84	804	27.5	34,216	93.0
484122	General freight trucking, long-distance, less than truckload (ltl)	43	1,122	44.4	39,583	137.0
4842	Specialized freight trucking	734	8,372	201.5	24,071	645.8
484210	Used household and office goods moving	317	4,425	92.0	20,795	287.6
4842101	Used household and office goods moving, local, without storage	159	1,284	32.6	25,390	93.9
4842102	Used household and office goods moving, long-distance	76	1,013	25.2	24,828	99.9
4842103	Used household and office goods moving, local, with storage	82	2,128	34.3	16,103	93.8
484220	Specialized freight (except used goods) trucking, local	344	3,375	93.9	27,824	303.5
4842201	Hazardous materials trucking (except waste), local	27	252	7.5	29,940	26.3
4842202	Agricultural products trucking without storage, local	41	117	2.9	24,598	11.1
4842203	Dump trucking	104	291	8.7	29,746	37.1
4842204	Specialized trucking without storage, local	148	2,093	57.5	27,473	184.8
4842205	Specialized trucking with storage, local	24	622	17.3	27,855	44.3
484230	Specialized freight (except used goods) trucking, long-distance	73	572	15.6	27,264	54.6
4842301	Hazardous materials trucking (except waste), long-distance	11	74	3.0	40,041	6.4
4842303	Other specialized trucking, long-distance	52	427	10.7	24,974	40.6
485	Transit and ground passenger transportation	1,672	25,835	608.7	23,560	1,753.5
48511	Urban transit systems	37	2,570	119.4	46,463	203.9
4853	Taxi and limousine service	1,170	5,977	123.5	20,661	795.9
485310	Taxi service	744	1,915	33.3	17,369	220.9
485320	Limousine service	426	4,062	90.2	22,212	575.0
485410	School and employee bus transportation	200	11,834	243.9	20,612	481.4
4854101	School bus service	196	11,573	241.7	20,887	476.3
485510	Charter bus industry	65	1,434	26.9	18,785	75.4
4855101	Charter bus service, local	33	900	16.0	17,730	36.2
4855102	Charter bus service, interstate/interurban	32	534	11.0	20,562	39.2
48599	Other transit and ground passenger transportation	190	3,416	65.0	19,032	153.8
485991	Special needs transportation	148	2,830	51.5	18,182	116.9
485999	All other transit and ground passenger transportation	42	586	13.6	23,135	37.0
4859991	Scheduled airport shuttle service	31	555	12.8	23,025	35.4
4859992	All other passenger transportation	11	31	0.8	25,097	1.6
487210	Scenic and sightseeing transportation, water	32	387	10.3	26,612	44.0
4872102	Charter fishing and party fishing boats	24	124	3.2	25,766	14.7
488	Support activities for transportation	1,313	17,152	570.8	33,277	1,693.6
4881	Support activities for air transportation	48	6,051	123.1	20,338	266.4
4881191	Airport operation and terminal services	29	5,256	97.6	18,575	188.9
488190	Other support activities for air transportation	19	795	25.4	31,995	77.5
4883	Support activities for water transportation	59	1,262	48.0	38,071	132.4
488320	Marine cargo handling	12	671	23.9	35,611	65.6
488330	Navigational services to shipping	24	417	16.1	38,707	49.7
488390	Other support activities for water transportation	23	174	8.0	46,029	17.1
488410	Motor vehicle towing	132	662	13.5	20,414	52.9
488510	Freight transportation arrangement	1,025	8,591	373.3	43,455	1,202.0
4885101	Freight forwarding	507	4,419	180.3	40,802	654.1
4885102	Arrangement of transportation of freight and cargo	518	4,172	193.0	46,265	547.9
48899	Other support activities for transportation	38	481	10.5	21,923	33.9
488991	Packing and crating	31	427	9.3	21,726	28.6
492	Couriers and messengers	583	25,484	650.7	25,532	1,906.0
492110	Couriers	258	17,076	507.4	29,712	1,525.9
4921101	Courier services (except by air)	87	9,800	286.0	29,188	621.0
4921102	Air courier services	171	7,276	221.3	30,419	904.8
492210	Local messengers and local delivery	325	8,408	143.3	17,042	380.1
4931	Warehousing and storage	136	1,729	48.2	27,864	179.4
4931101	General warehousing and storage (except in foreign trade zones)	82	1,177	31.1	26,408	82.8
493190	Other warehousing and storage	47	406	11.4	28,037	79.3
4931901	Household goods warehousing and storage	23	114	3.1	26,789	13.5
4931902	Specialized goods warehousing and storage	24	292	8.3	28,524	65.8

Sources: Economic Census of the United States, 1997. Only those industries are shown for which both employment and sales/revenue data were available. For the definition of MSAs, CMSAs, and PMSAs, please see the Introduction.

NEW YORK—NORTHERN NEW JERSEY—LONG ISLAND, NY—NJ—CT—PA CMSA

NAICS	Industry	Estab-lish-ments	Em-ploy-ment	Payroll		Sales, reven. ($ mil.)
				Total ($ mil.)	Per Empl. ($)	
48-49	Transportation and warehousing	13,867	254,790	7,594.8	29,808	28,432.2
481	Air transportation	293	10,086	411.0	40,747	3,749.1
48111	Scheduled air transportation	200	8,714	346.9	39,814	3,393.8
481111	Scheduled passenger air transportation	157	7,605	302.9	39,823	2,950.9
481112	Scheduled freight air transportation	43	1,109	44.1	39,749	442.8
48121	Nonscheduled air transportation	93	1,372	64.0	46,672	355.3
481211	Nonscheduled chartered passenger air transportation	81	1,164	57.6	49,450	335.6
48311	Deep sea, coastal, and Great Lakes water transportation	207	7,796	327.7	42,032	4,016.6
483113	Coastal and Great Lakes freight transportation	84	2,105	94.1	44,705	682.6
4831131	Coastal and intercoastal freight transportation	58	1,497	69.4	46,357	537.7
4832111	Inland waterways freight transportation (except towing)	18	205	9.7	47,146	33.3
484	Truck transportation	5,020	57,650	1,870.1	32,439	6,111.1
4841	General freight trucking	2,180	31,700	1,131.7	35,701	3,602.5
484110	General freight trucking, local	1,358	10,092	301.7	29,896	986.4
4841102	General freight trucking without storage, local, less than truckload (ltl)	513	3,769	107.4	28,489	322.0
4841103	General freight trucking with storage, local, truckload (tl)	62	889	28.4	31,955	100.1
48412	General freight trucking, long-distance	822	21,608	830.0	38,412	2,616.1
4842	Specialized freight trucking	2,840	25,950	738.4	28,453	2,508.6
484210	Used household and office goods moving	864	10,302	250.9	24,352	807.9
4842103	Used household and office goods moving, local, with storage	220	3,559	73.8	20,737	217.4
484220	Specialized freight (except used goods) trucking, local	1,576	10,902	321.5	29,493	1,139.0
4842201	Hazardous materials trucking (except waste), local	121	533	17.2	32,349	56.0
4842205	Specialized trucking with storage, local	83	1,612	48.8	30,245	142.7
484230	Specialized freight (except used goods) trucking, long-distance	400	4,746	165.9	34,966	561.6
4842301	Hazardous materials trucking (except waste), long-distance	82	929	35.2	37,868	127.0
48511	Urban transit systems	123	8,799	352.3	40,036	610.9
485210	Interurban and rural bus transportation	50	7,531	282.4	37,499	363.8
4853	Taxi and limousine service	2,073	13,436	256.4	19,082	1,193.3
485410	School and employee bus transportation	531	33,329	542.2	16,267	1,141.0
4854101	School bus service	518	33,000	538.8	16,327	1,132.2
4854102	Employee bus service	13	329	3.4	10,267	8.8
48599	Other transit and ground passenger transportation	387	5,820	115.2	19,796	273.9
485991	Special needs transportation	289	4,588	84.7	18,462	183.3
485999	All other transit and ground passenger transportation	98	1,232	30.5	24,765	90.7
486	Pipeline transportation	24	385	23.1	60,083	326.6
486210	Pipeline transportation of natural gas	17	285	18.5	64,877	284.5
487210	Scenic and sightseeing transportation, water	138	642	15.6	24,310	65.3
488	Support activities for transportation	3,102	40,751	1,555.5	38,172	4,656.7
4881	Support activities for air transportation	180	9,436	218.6	23,163	666.3
4881191	Airport operation and terminal services	74	7,151	135.2	18,902	343.2
4883	Support activities for water transportation	166	5,788	258.7	44,702	696.6
488320	Marine cargo handling	30	3,944	178.3	45,206	464.7
488330	Navigational services to shipping	42	668	28.3	42,419	93.0
4884	Support activities for road transportation	413	2,245	54.5	24,265	172.6
488991	Packing and crating	87	1,110	26.1	23,485	79.5
492	Couriers and messengers	1,165	53,558	1,426.8	26,641	4,491.8
492110	Couriers	511	42,365	1,217.8	28,745	3,876.1
4921101	Courier services (except by air)	213	25,119	693.6	27,613	1,938.9
4921102	Air courier services	298	17,246	524.2	30,395	1,937.2
492210	Local messengers and local delivery	654	11,193	209.0	18,676	615.6
4931	Warehousing and storage	524	10,616	303.6	28,596	1,072.5
493110	General warehousing and storage	364	7,710	200.8	26,042	609.1
493190	Other warehousing and storage	128	1,919	69.1	36,001	345.2

Sources: *Economic Census of the United States*, 1997. Only those industries are shown for which both employment and sales/revenue data were available. For the definition of MSAs, CMSAs, and PMSAs, please see the Introduction.

NEWARK, NJ PMSA

NAICS	Industry	Estab-lish-ments	Em-ploy-ment	Payroll		Sales, reven. ($ mil.)
				Total ($ mil.)	Per Empl. ($)	
48-49	Transportation and warehousing	1,731	45,780	1,551.9	33,898	5,752.7
481	Air transportation	30	446	18.8	42,047	370.0
48111	Scheduled air transportation	23	356	13.3	37,483	332.0
481111	Scheduled passenger air transportation	15	246	9.8	39,858	275.9
48311	Deep sea, coastal, and Great Lakes water transportation	16	1,754	73.2	41,729	1,490.2
484	Truck transportation	783	11,034	376.2	34,094	1,234.1
4841	General freight trucking	344	7,120	243.0	34,123	797.7
484110	General freight trucking, local	192	1,454	40.2	27,654	145.5
4841101	General freight trucking without storage, local, truckload (tl)	110	702	21.2	30,219	80.4
4841102	General freight trucking without storage, local, less than truckload (ltl)	68	570	13.6	23,893	42.8
48412	General freight trucking, long-distance	152	5,666	202.7	35,783	652.2
484121	General freight trucking, long-distance, truckload (tl)	112	1,953	64.4	32,998	303.5
484122	General freight trucking, long-distance, less than truckload (ltl)	40	3,713	138.3	37,248	348.8
4842	Specialized freight trucking	439	3,914	133.2	34,040	436.4
484210	Used household and office goods moving	99	1,292	36.8	28,483	103.4
4842101	Used household and office goods moving, local, without storage	44	184	3.7	19,842	11.6
4842102	Used household and office goods moving, long-distance	39	795	22.5	28,313	65.3
4842103	Used household and office goods moving, local, with storage	16	313	10.6	33,994	26.5
484220	Specialized freight (except used goods) trucking, local	242	1,182	42.8	36,245	168.0
4842201	Hazardous materials trucking (except waste), local	18	45	2.2	48,511	5.5
4842202	Agricultural products trucking without storage, local	21	50	2.0	39,820	5.9
4842203	Dump trucking	125	426	15.2	35,596	89.4
4842204	Specialized trucking without storage, local	66	450	17.5	38,971	50.9
4842205	Specialized trucking with storage, local	12	211	6.0	28,275	16.3
484230	Specialized freight (except used goods) trucking, long-distance	98	1,440	53.6	37,217	165.1
4842301	Hazardous materials trucking (except waste), long-distance	27	271	9.3	34,133	35.1
4842303	Other specialized trucking, long-distance	64	1,137	43.1	37,928	124.6
485	Transit and ground passenger transportation	314	14,705	473.8	32,222	721.2
4853	Taxi and limousine service	166	1,323	26.6	20,125	71.4
485310	Taxi service	35	119	1.8	15,269	6.0
485320	Limousine service	131	1,204	24.8	20,605	65.4
485410	School and employee bus transportation	64	3,018	36.6	12,134	83.7
48599	Other transit and ground passenger transportation	51	734	16.3	22,181	45.6
485991	Special needs transportation	34	454	9.2	20,181	18.5
485999	All other transit and ground passenger transportation	17	280	7.1	25,425	27.1
488	Support activities for transportation	365	8,149	332.3	40,783	908.4
4881	Support activities for air transportation	20	1,401	26.1	18,626	80.6
488119	Other airport operations	12	1,305	23.1	17,713	71.4
4883	Support activities for water transportation	20	3,075	146.8	47,738	381.8
488320	Marine cargo handling	11	2,773	128.0	46,159	336.2
4884	Support activities for road transportation	54	299	9.2	30,890	25.1
488510	Freight transportation arrangement	248	3,135	141.4	45,105	392.3
4885101	Freight forwarding	120	1,630	67.8	41,589	221.7
4885102	Arrangement of transportation of freight and cargo	128	1,505	73.6	48,912	170.7
48899	Other support activities for transportation	16	174	5.1	29,138	18.5
492	Couriers and messengers	124	8,430	233.9	27,747	853.1
492110	Couriers	58	7,914	220.5	27,858	802.5
4921101	Courier services (except by air)	25	3,511	100.8	28,717	348.6
4921102	Air courier services	33	4,403	119.6	27,173	453.9
492210	Local messengers and local delivery	66	516	13.4	26,035	50.6
4931	Warehousing and storage	81	1,113	37.2	33,447	116.1
4931101	General warehousing and storage (except in foreign trade zones)	56	784	25.5	32,570	80.6
493190	Other warehousing and storage	21	229	8.4	36,786	24.2
4931902	Specialized goods warehousing and storage	17	152	5.3	34,730	17.3

Sources: *Economic Census of the United States*, 1997. Only those industries are shown for which both employment and sales/revenue data were available. For the definition of MSAs, CMSAs, and PMSAs, please see the Introduction.

NEWBURGH, NY—PA PMSA

NAICS	Industry	Estab-lish-ments	Em-ploy-ment	Payroll		Sales, reven. ($ mil.)
				Total ($ mil.)	Per Empl. ($)	
48-49	Transportation and warehousing	196	4,269	122.6	28,712	272.9
484	Truck transportation	92	2,149	77.2	35,919	135.1
4841	General freight trucking	46	1,773	67.3	37,973	103.2
484110	General freight trucking, local	21	246	3.8	15,280	20.4
4841101	General freight trucking without storage, local, truckload (tl)	15	210	3.2	15,238	19.5
48412	General freight trucking, long-distance	25	1,527	63.6	41,629	82.8
484121	General freight trucking, long-distance, truckload (tl)	14	290	10.1	34,852	39.9
484122	General freight trucking, long-distance, less than truckload (ltl)	11	1,237	53.5	43,217	42.9
4842	Specialized freight trucking	46	376	9.9	26,231	31.9
484220	Specialized freight (except used goods) trucking, local	34	242	5.5	22,554	14.8
4842203	Dump trucking	15	35	1.3	37,829	6.2
485	Transit and ground passenger transportation	58	1,146	17.9	15,589	39.3
485410	School and employee bus transportation	19	808	12.0	14,832	24.8

Sources: *Economic Census of the United States*, 1997. Only those industries are shown for which both employment and sales/revenue data were available. For the definition of MSAs, CMSAs, and PMSAs, please see the Introduction.

NORFOLK—VIRGINIA BEACH—NEWPORT NEWS, VA—NC MSA

NAICS	Industry	Estab-lish-ments	Em-ploy-ment	Payroll		Sales, reven. ($ mil.)
				Total ($ mil.)	Per Empl. ($)	
48-49	Transportation and warehousing	870	14,186	423.2	29,836	1,335.3
484	Truck transportation	418	4,572	132.2	28,911	394.3
4841	General freight trucking	184	2,163	63.5	29,376	212.8
484110	General freight trucking, local	70	480	12.0	24,990	37.3
4841101	General freight trucking without storage, local, truckload (tl)	51	295	7.3	24,708	26.8
48412	General freight trucking, long-distance	114	1,683	51.5	30,627	175.5
484121	General freight trucking, long-distance, truckload (tl)	90	1,005	29.0	28,821	110.5
484122	General freight trucking, long-distance, less than truckload (ltl)	24	678	22.6	33,304	64.9
4842	Specialized freight trucking	234	2,409	68.6	28,494	181.5
484210	Used household and office goods moving	57	970	19.2	19,756	62.2
4842101	Used household and office goods moving, local, without storage	16	83	1.6	18,723	3.7
4842102	Used household and office goods moving, long-distance	25	587	11.7	19,981	44.7
4842103	Used household and office goods moving, local, with storage	16	300	5.9	19,600	13.7
484220	Specialized freight (except used goods) trucking, local	134	668	15.5	23,254	62.3
4842203	Dump trucking	95	401	8.0	19,845	37.9
4842204	Specialized trucking without storage, local	27	215	6.4	29,753	20.7
484230	Specialized freight (except used goods) trucking, long-distance	43	771	33.9	44,029	57.0
4842303	Other specialized trucking, long-distance	27	712	32.1	45,107	50.3
485	Transit and ground passenger transportation	54	860	10.0	11,657	30.3
485310	Taxi service	12	186	2.6	14,226	6.2
487	Scenic and sightseeing transportation	10	133	1.8	13,414	7.4
488	Support activities for transportation	240	5,521	173.7	31,463	464.3
4881	Support activities for air transportation	21	633	13.0	20,559	46.1
4881191	Airport operation and terminal services	13	473	7.7	16,239	31.3
4883	Support activities for water transportation	48	3,482	121.0	34,746	297.1
488320	Marine cargo handling	11	1,595	45.2	28,361	95.2
488330	Navigational services to shipping	15	376	8.9	23,782	49.9
488390	Other support activities for water transportation	15	123	2.3	18,959	6.3
4883901	Other services incidental to water transportation	12	109	1.7	15,523	4.9
488410	Motor vehicle towing	56	357	5.7	15,885	14.7
488510	Freight transportation arrangement	101	983	32.3	32,840	96.4
4885101	Freight forwarding	40	283	8.9	31,389	29.7
4885102	Arrangement of transportation of freight and cargo	61	700	23.4	33,427	66.7
492	Couriers and messengers	43	721	15.3	21,251	56.0
492110	Couriers	17	434	12.2	28,207	46.6
492210	Local messengers and local delivery	26	287	3.1	10,732	9.4
4931	Warehousing and storage	51	607	14.0	23,115	52.5
4931101	General warehousing and storage (except in foreign trade zones)	25	256	6.4	25,051	24.8
4931902	Specialized goods warehousing and storage	11	119	3.7	31,437	11.4

Sources: *Economic Census of the United States*, 1997. Only those industries are shown for which both employment and sales/revenue data were available. For the definition of MSAs, CMSAs, and PMSAs, please see the Introduction.

OAKLAND, CA PMSA

NAICS	Industry	Estab-lish-ments	Em-ploy-ment	Payroll		Sales, reven. ($ mil.)
				Total ($ mil.)	Per Empl. ($)	
48-49	Transportation and warehousing	1,188	30,207	935.8	30,979	3,006.3
48311	Deep sea, coastal, and Great Lakes water transportation	14	1,200	69.8	58,187	444.3
483111	Deep sea freight transportation	11	1,165	68.1	58,451	438.9
484	Truck transportation	646	8,998	286.7	31,864	1,056.8
4841	General freight trucking	259	4,751	159.0	33,474	542.7
484110	General freight trucking, local	152	2,034	57.0	28,019	196.2
4841101	General freight trucking without storage, local, truckload (tl)	100	1,068	28.6	26,780	112.1
4841102	General freight trucking without storage, local, less than truckload (ltl)	34	737	21.6	29,300	60.1
48412	General freight trucking, long-distance	107	2,717	102.0	37,558	346.5
484121	General freight trucking, long-distance, truckload (tl)	60	557	26.0	46,625	109.0
484122	General freight trucking, long-distance, less than truckload (ltl)	47	2,160	76.1	35,220	237.5
4842	Specialized freight trucking	387	4,247	127.7	30,062	514.1
484210	Used household and office goods moving	114	1,888	57.3	30,327	204.5
4842101	Used household and office goods moving, local, without storage	51	350	7.4	21,094	20.7
4842102	Used household and office goods moving, long-distance	27	467	10.8	23,036	42.7
4842103	Used household and office goods moving, local, with storage	36	1,071	39.1	36,524	141.0
484220	Specialized freight (except used goods) trucking, local	220	1,757	48.9	27,815	237.5
4842203	Dump trucking	111	798	23.5	29,420	131.4
4842204	Specialized trucking without storage, local	90	722	22.5	31,100	94.9
484230	Specialized freight (except used goods) trucking, long-distance	53	602	21.5	35,786	72.1
4842301	Hazardous materials trucking (except waste), long-distance	14	113	4.0	35,150	12.4
4842303	Other specialized trucking, long-distance	29	435	13.6	31,349	47.2
485	Transit and ground passenger transportation	77	2,288	36.8	16,069	92.9
485320	Limousine service	16	124	2.5	19,911	5.3
485510	Charter bus industry	15	117	2.1	18,265	8.9
48599	Other transit and ground passenger transportation	22	448	6.9	15,386	15.8
485991	Special needs transportation	11	366	5.6	15,238	9.8
485999	All other transit and ground passenger transportation	11	82	1.3	16,049	6.1
488	Support activities for transportation	258	5,059	230.7	45,599	538.5
4881	Support activities for air transportation	29	648	14.0	21,540	38.4
4881191	Airport operation and terminal services	12	295	4.8	16,363	9.9
488190	Other support activities for air transportation	17	353	9.1	25,867	28.4
4883	Support activities for water transportation	39	2,081	133.9	64,342	282.3
488320	Marine cargo handling	16	1,911	126.7	66,294	260.7
4884	Support activities for road transportation	68	624	14.8	23,700	42.9
488410	Motor vehicle towing	63	544	12.7	23,379	38.4
488510	Freight transportation arrangement	99	1,395	60.4	43,295	158.5
4885101	Freight forwarding	53	400	12.2	30,415	52.3
4885102	Arrangement of transportation of freight and cargo	46	995	48.2	48,473	106.1
48899	Other support activities for transportation	14	70	1.0	14,657	3.2
492	Couriers and messengers	100	11,024	262.6	23,823	668.4
492110	Couriers	50	9,511	235.5	24,758	606.4
4921101	Courier services (except by air)	22	6,035	149.2	24,730	348.2
4921102	Air courier services	28	3,476	86.2	24,807	258.2
492210	Local messengers and local delivery	50	1,513	27.2	17,946	62.0
4931	Warehousing and storage	62	1,177	31.0	26,336	114.9
4931101	General warehousing and storage (except in foreign trade zones)	35	715	16.6	23,171	52.8
4931902	Specialized goods warehousing and storage	14	183	6.2	33,951	35.7

Sources: *Economic Census of the United States*, 1997. Only those industries are shown for which both employment and sales/revenue data were available. For the definition of MSAs, CMSAs, and PMSAs, please see the Introduction.

OCALA, FL MSA

NAICS	Industry	Estab-lish-ments	Em-ploy-ment	Payroll		Sales, reven. ($ mil.)
				Total ($ mil.)	Per Empl. ($)	
48-49	Transportation and warehousing	112	990	25.8	26,086	111.1
484	Truck transportation	85	789	21.7	27,545	90.8
4841	General freight trucking	39	569	17.0	29,875	70.7
48412	General freight trucking, long-distance	31	537	16.3	30,296	65.6
484121	General freight trucking, long-distance, truckload (tl)	19	169	4.9	28,858	14.7
484122	General freight trucking, long-distance, less than truckload (ltl)	12	368	11.4	30,957	51.0
4842	Specialized freight trucking	46	220	4.7	21,518	20.0
484220	Specialized freight (except used goods) trucking, local	20	101	1.9	19,040	8.8
484230	Specialized freight (except used goods) trucking, long-distance	19	101	2.6	25,584	10.4
4842303	Other specialized trucking, long-distance	14	79	2.1	26,228	8.5
485	Transit and ground passenger transportation	9	72	0.9	12,292	2.8
492	Couriers and messengers	6	72	1.6	22,097	6.8

Sources: *Economic Census of the United States*, 1997. Only those industries are shown for which both employment and sales/revenue data were available. For the definition of MSAs, CMSAs, and PMSAs, please see the Introduction.

ODESSA—MIDLAND, TX MSA

| NAICS | Industry | Estab-lish-ments | Em-ploy-ment | Payroll | | Sales, reven. ($ mil.) |
				Total ($ mil.)	Per Empl. ($)	
48-49	Transportation and warehousing	185	2,182	64.7	29,667	354.6
48121	Nonscheduled air transportation	11	33	0.7	21,030	3.8
484	Truck transportation	125	1,599	45.5	28,468	159.1
4841	General freight trucking	42	513	12.9	25,133	38.3
48412	General freight trucking, long-distance	35	428	11.1	25,979	32.2
484121	General freight trucking, long-distance, truckload (tl)	25	344	8.7	25,419	22.2
4842	Specialized freight trucking	83	1,086	32.6	30,043	120.7
484210	Used household and office goods moving	11	117	2.0	16,838	6.3
484220	Specialized freight (except used goods) trucking, local	45	575	20.0	34,736	75.0
4842203	Dump trucking	19	66	1.5	22,591	7.6
4842204	Specialized trucking without storage, local	23	502	18.3	36,482	66.8
484230	Specialized freight (except used goods) trucking, long-distance	27	394	10.7	27,117	39.4
4842303	Other specialized trucking, long-distance	18	310	8.2	26,510	32.6
486	Pipeline transportation	17	255	11.7	45,851	167.6
488	Support activities for transportation	14	98	2.9	29,459	11.7
492	Couriers and messengers	7	113	2.6	22,637	7.0

Sources: Economic Census of the United States, 1997. Only those industries are shown for which both employment and sales/revenue data were available. For the definition of MSAs, CMSAs, and PMSAs, please see the Introduction.

OKLAHOMA CITY, OK MSA

| NAICS | Industry | Estab-lish-ments | Em-ploy-ment | Payroll | | Sales, reven. ($ mil.) |
				Total ($ mil.)	Per Empl. ($)	
48-49	Transportation and warehousing	604	12,202	345.2	28,291	1,566.2
484	Truck transportation	377	6,172	180.2	29,194	600.6
4841	General freight trucking	183	3,832	119.1	31,075	377.3
484110	General freight trucking, local	54	441	8.9	20,150	32.7
4841101	General freight trucking without storage, local, truckload (tl)	35	186	3.6	19,210	16.8
48412	General freight trucking, long-distance	129	3,391	110.2	32,496	344.5
484121	General freight trucking, long-distance, truckload (tl)	100	1,928	59.8	31,016	210.8
484122	General freight trucking, long-distance, less than truckload (ltl)	29	1,463	50.4	34,448	133.7
4842	Specialized freight trucking	194	2,340	61.1	26,113	223.4
484210	Used household and office goods moving	28	304	7.3	24,079	21.2
4842101	Used household and office goods moving, local, without storage	12	75	0.9	12,467	2.1
484220	Specialized freight (except used goods) trucking, local	94	762	18.2	23,916	71.3
4842203	Dump trucking	49	342	7.9	23,173	33.2
4842204	Specialized trucking without storage, local	30	387	9.5	24,424	29.5
484230	Specialized freight (except used goods) trucking, long-distance	72	1,274	35.6	27,912	130.8
4842302	Agricultural products trucking, long-distance	14	120	2.1	17,225	10.7
4842303	Other specialized trucking, long-distance	48	960	27.4	28,552	101.8
486	Pipeline transportation	24	926	36.7	39,646	620.1
488	Support activities for transportation	107	1,592	37.3	23,442	97.7
4881	Support activities for air transportation	49	1,217	30.7	25,192	77.2
48811	Airport operations	16	406	6.0	14,660	27.2
488190	Other support activities for air transportation	33	811	24.7	30,465	50.0
488410	Motor vehicle towing	29	169	2.9	17,089	8.7
488510	Freight transportation arrangement	21	93	2.1	22,978	8.2
4885102	Arrangement of transportation of freight and cargo	17	58	1.4	24,879	5.7
492	Couriers and messengers	52	3,186	85.7	26,907	225.2
492110	Couriers	24	2,993	81.6	27,259	210.0
4921102	Air courier services	15	355	10.0	28,082	52.9
492210	Local messengers and local delivery	28	193	4.1	21,451	15.1
4931	Warehousing and storage	15	99	2.2	22,172	7.7

Sources: Economic Census of the United States, 1997. Only those industries are shown for which both employment and sales/revenue data were available. For the definition of MSAs, CMSAs, and PMSAs, please see the Introduction.

OLYMPIA, WA PMSA

NAICS	Industry	Estab-lish-ments	Em-ploy-ment	Payroll		Sales, reven. ($ mil.)
				Total ($ mil.)	Per Empl. ($)	
48-49	Transportation and warehousing	113	663	16.2	24,436	65.4
484	Truck transportation	79	341	10.1	29,686	44.1
4841	General freight trucking	31	156	5.1	32,577	21.3
48412	General freight trucking, long-distance	21	88	2.9	33,477	13.2
4842	Specialized freight trucking	48	185	5.0	27,249	22.8
484220	Specialized freight (except used goods) trucking, local	25	94	2.6	27,851	14.0
484230	Specialized freight (except used goods) trucking, long-distance	16	31	1.2	39,516	4.5
488	Support activities for transportation	17	60	1.7	28,400	5.9
492	Couriers and messengers	6	109	2.5	22,853	10.5

Sources: Economic Census of the United States, 1997. Only those industries are shown for which both employment and sales/revenue data were available. For the definition of MSAs, CMSAs, and PMSAs, please see the Introduction.

OMAHA, NE—IA MSA

NAICS	Industry	Estab-lish-ments	Em-ploy-ment	Payroll		Sales, reven. ($ mil.)
				Total ($ mil.)	Per Empl. ($)	
48-49	Transportation and warehousing	658	12,558	363.7	28,965	1,973.2
481	Air transportation	14	123	4.5	36,878	30.9
484	Truck transportation	436	5,837	184.1	31,543	1,347.7
4841	General freight trucking	259	4,481	148.0	33,028	1,194.4
484110	General freight trucking, local	78	480	11.8	24,540	34.9
4841101	General freight trucking without storage, local, truckload (tl)	49	271	7.1	26,269	24.6
48412	General freight trucking, long-distance	181	4,001	136.2	34,047	1,159.5
484121	General freight trucking, long-distance, truckload (tl)	152	3,115	104.2	33,451	1,067.9
484122	General freight trucking, long-distance, less than truckload (ltl)	29	886	32.0	36,142	91.6
4842	Specialized freight trucking	177	1,356	36.1	26,633	153.3
484210	Used household and office goods moving	43	508	11.7	23,124	41.8
4842102	Used household and office goods moving, long-distance	18	353	8.7	24,629	33.3
484220	Specialized freight (except used goods) trucking, local	82	337	7.7	22,736	37.6
4842202	Agricultural products trucking without storage, local	23	38	0.8	21,447	4.1
4842203	Dump trucking	38	154	4.5	28,955	23.2
4842204	Specialized trucking without storage, local	18	129	2.3	17,953	9.9
484230	Specialized freight (except used goods) trucking, long-distance	52	511	16.7	32,693	73.9
4842302	Agricultural products trucking, long-distance	20	84	1.9	23,190	12.4
4842303	Other specialized trucking, long-distance	28	307	11.2	36,463	50.8
488	Support activities for transportation	92	826	21.8	26,341	67.5
4881	Support activities for air transportation	17	206	4.3	20,922	22.9
488410	Motor vehicle towing	15	66	1.4	20,894	4.3
488510	Freight transportation arrangement	44	317	10.2	32,095	25.0
492	Couriers and messengers	48	4,182	112.7	26,942	259.0
492110	Couriers	20	3,910	106.2	27,151	243.5
492210	Local messengers and local delivery	28	272	6.5	23,945	15.5
4931	Warehousing and storage	25	406	12.3	30,244	36.3
4931201	Refrigerated products warehousing	11	302	9.5	31,603	30.1

Sources: Economic Census of the United States, 1997. Only those industries are shown for which both employment and sales/revenue data were available. For the definition of MSAs, CMSAs, and PMSAs, please see the Introduction.

ORANGE COUNTY, CA PMSA

| NAICS | Industry | Estab-lish-ments | Em-ploy-ment | Payroll | | Sales, reven. ($ mil.) |
				Total ($ mil.)	Per Empl. ($)	
48-49	Transportation and warehousing	952	28,630	738.0	25,776	3,434.6
484	Truck transportation	425	5,696	161.4	28,341	656.8
4841	General freight trucking	164	3,075	94.6	30,776	349.8
484110	General freight trucking, local	98	1,410	36.6	25,962	124.7
4841101	General freight trucking without storage, local, truckload (tl)	45	305	8.9	29,252	32.7
4841102	General freight trucking without storage, local, less than truckload (ltl)	43	844	20.4	24,148	75.5
48412	General freight trucking, long-distance	66	1,665	58.0	34,852	225.1
484121	General freight trucking, long-distance, truckload (tl)	41	509	15.3	30,037	61.4
484122	General freight trucking, long-distance, less than truckload (ltl)	25	1,156	42.7	36,972	163.8
4842	Specialized freight trucking	261	2,621	66.8	25,483	307.0
484210	Used household and office goods moving	114	1,404	36.6	26,103	189.0
4842101	Used household and office goods moving, local, without storage	53	400	7.1	17,758	19.7
4842102	Used household and office goods moving, long-distance	34	605	17.4	28,790	135.9
4842103	Used household and office goods moving, local, with storage	27	399	12.1	30,393	33.4
484220	Specialized freight (except used goods) trucking, local	121	947	19.1	20,178	88.0
4842203	Dump trucking	50	234	5.8	24,996	33.6
4842204	Specialized trucking without storage, local	54	490	6.0	12,186	23.5
484230	Specialized freight (except used goods) trucking, long-distance	26	270	11.0	40,870	30.0
4842303	Other specialized trucking, long-distance	17	200	9.1	45,500	23.9
485	Transit and ground passenger transportation	80	2,196	40.4	18,377	101.1
4853	Taxi and limousine service	33	419	7.2	17,239	18.3
485320	Limousine service	26	238	3.9	16,412	9.8
485510	Charter bus industry	15	256	4.6	17,914	15.8
48599	Other transit and ground passenger transportation	18	786	14.8	18,790	36.8
485991	Special needs transportation	11	469	8.4	17,898	14.5
487210	Scenic and sightseeing transportation, water	22	222	4.9	22,257	18.1
488	Support activities for transportation	219	2,142	69.7	32,546	247.1
4881	Support activities for air transportation	24	519	11.0	21,200	30.8
488190	Other support activities for air transportation	15	201	5.4	26,692	13.5
488410	Motor vehicle towing	65	598	15.0	25,127	43.6
488510	Freight transportation arrangement	109	927	41.5	44,751	155.4
4885101	Freight forwarding	45	501	20.1	40,050	93.2
4885102	Arrangement of transportation of freight and cargo	64	426	21.4	50,279	62.2
492	Couriers and messengers	121	12,065	263.8	21,867	697.7
492110	Couriers	60	9,572	228.3	23,846	609.4
4921101	Courier services (except by air)	30	7,763	178.0	22,935	433.9
4921102	Air courier services	30	1,809	50.2	27,755	175.5
492210	Local messengers and local delivery	61	2,493	35.6	14,268	88.3
4931	Warehousing and storage	45	608	16.6	27,342	74.4
4931101	General warehousing and storage (except in foreign trade zones)	27	284	7.6	26,930	29.9

Sources: *Economic Census of the United States*, 1997. Only those industries are shown for which both employment and sales/revenue data were available. For the definition of MSAs, CMSAs, and PMSAs, please see the Introduction.

ORLANDO, FL MSA

NAICS	Industry	Estab-lish-ments	Em-ploy-ment	Payroll Total ($ mil.)	Payroll Per Empl. ($)	Sales, reven. ($ mil.)
48-49	Transportation and warehousing	866	16,150	404.4	25,042	1,459.7
481	Air transportation	37	388	11.3	29,240	108.6
48111	Scheduled air transportation	15	198	5.4	27,247	74.9
48121	Nonscheduled air transportation	22	190	5.9	31,316	33.7
481211	Nonscheduled chartered passenger air transportation	15	35	0.8	23,657	4.0
484	Truck transportation	398	5,139	142.9	27,812	584.0
4841	General freight trucking	171	3,016	93.2	30,914	383.9
484110	General freight trucking, local	54	378	9.2	24,399	49.5
4841101	General freight trucking without storage, local, truckload (tl)	30	211	5.2	24,536	26.4
4841102	General freight trucking without storage, local, less than truckload (ltl)	21	151	3.7	24,762	21.9
48412	General freight trucking, long-distance	117	2,638	84.0	31,848	334.4
484121	General freight trucking, long-distance, truckload (tl)	91	1,056	28.7	27,163	169.3
484122	General freight trucking, long-distance, less than truckload (ltl)	26	1,582	55.3	34,975	165.1
4842	Specialized freight trucking	227	2,123	49.7	23,406	200.1
484210	Used household and office goods moving	51	560	12.2	21,800	44.4
4842101	Used household and office goods moving, local, without storage	16	55	0.8	14,709	3.1
4842102	Used household and office goods moving, long-distance	22	358	8.4	23,480	32.6
4842103	Used household and office goods moving, local, with storage	13	147	3.0	20,361	8.7
484220	Specialized freight (except used goods) trucking, local	116	560	13.1	23,304	55.6
4842202	Agricultural products trucking without storage, local	16	31	0.7	20,968	2.8
4842203	Dump trucking	50	303	6.3	20,700	31.7
4842204	Specialized trucking without storage, local	43	180	4.9	27,256	17.5
484230	Specialized freight (except used goods) trucking, long-distance	60	1,003	24.4	24,359	100.0
4842302	Agricultural products trucking, long-distance	16	85	1.8	21,106	15.2
4842303	Other specialized trucking, long-distance	40	867	21.1	24,303	82.0
485	Transit and ground passenger transportation	98	1,879	36.3	19,315	132.9
4853	Taxi and limousine service	33	295	6.9	23,312	25.6
485310	Taxi service	15	236	5.9	25,042	21.0
485320	Limousine service	18	59	1.0	16,390	4.6
485510	Charter bus industry	24	373	6.4	17,241	20.4
4855101	Charter bus service, local	12	190	4.1	21,395	12.9
4855102	Charter bus service, interstate/interurban	12	183	2.4	12,929	7.5
48599	Other transit and ground passenger transportation	30	1,079	20.8	19,312	76.1
485991	Special needs transportation	14	101	1.6	15,436	4.2
485999	All other transit and ground passenger transportation	16	978	19.3	19,713	71.9
4859991	Scheduled airport shuttle service	11	970	19.1	19,690	70.5
487110	Scenic and sightseeing transportation, land	11	27	0.5	19,000	1.8
488	Support activities for transportation	198	2,556	52.1	20,394	171.6
4881	Support activities for air transportation	40	1,516	27.6	18,206	77.5
48811	Airport operations	17	928	17.1	18,376	46.3
488190	Other support activities for air transportation	23	588	10.5	17,939	31.1
4884	Support activities for road transportation	54	589	11.0	18,703	32.8
488410	Motor vehicle towing	51	567	10.4	18,423	31.7
488510	Freight transportation arrangement	86	371	11.8	31,709	50.4
4885101	Freight forwarding	36	160	5.7	35,650	23.0
4885102	Arrangement of transportation of freight and cargo	50	211	6.1	28,720	27.5
492	Couriers and messengers	77	5,685	149.3	26,257	365.4
492110	Couriers	39	5,345	143.0	26,752	341.5
492210	Local messengers and local delivery	38	340	6.3	18,468	24.0
4931	Warehousing and storage	30	303	6.0	19,710	27.8
4931101	General warehousing and storage (except in foreign trade zones)	19	187	3.5	18,963	15.0

Sources: *Economic Census of the United States*, 1997. Only those industries are shown for which both employment and sales/revenue data were available. For the definition of MSAs, CMSAs, and PMSAs, please see the Introduction.

OWENSBORO, KY MSA

NAICS	Industry	Estab-lish-ments	Em-ploy-ment	Payroll Total ($ mil.)	Payroll Per Empl. ($)	Sales, reven. ($ mil.)
48-49	Transportation and warehousing	64	1,069	39.5	36,961	190.2
484	Truck transportation	40	388	10.1	26,116	41.7
4841	General freight trucking	19	259	7.2	27,931	28.4
48412	General freight trucking, long-distance	13	242	6.8	28,198	26.9
4842	Specialized freight trucking	21	129	2.9	22,473	13.3
484230	Specialized freight (except used goods) trucking, long-distance	11	66	1.7	25,621	9.5

Sources: *Economic Census of the United States*, 1997. Only those industries are shown for which both employment and sales/revenue data were available. For the definition of MSAs, CMSAs, and PMSAs, please see the Introduction.

PANAMA CITY, FL MSA

NAICS	Industry	Estab-lish-ments	Em-ploy-ment	Payroll		Sales, reven. ($ mil.)
				Total ($ mil.)	Per Empl. ($)	
48-49	Transportation and warehousing	106	833	20.5	24,599	69.4
483	Water transportation	7	108	3.8	35,102	14.1
484	Truck transportation	44	387	10.3	26,527	28.8
4841	General freight trucking	13	58	1.6	26,828	4.9
4842	Specialized freight trucking	31	329	8.7	26,474	23.9
484210	Used household and office goods moving	13	128	2.6	20,547	6.9
484220	Specialized freight (except used goods) trucking, local	14	91	2.3	25,549	7.5
485	Transit and ground passenger transportation	3	25	0.3	11,840	2.1
487210	Scenic and sightseeing transportation, water	18	102	0.9	9,078	3.1
4872102	Charter fishing and party fishing boats	14	83	0.6	7,759	2.0
488	Support activities for transportation	26	155	3.7	24,000	15.7
493	Warehousing and storage	3	3	0.1	26,333	0.6

Sources: Economic Census of the United States, 1997. Only those industries are shown for which both employment and sales/revenue data were available. For the definition of MSAs, CMSAs, and PMSAs, please see the Introduction.

PARKERSBURG—MARIETTA, WV—OH MSA

NAICS	Industry	Estab-lish-ments	Em-ploy-ment	Payroll		Sales, reven. ($ mil.)
				Total ($ mil.)	Per Empl. ($)	
48-49	Transportation and warehousing	120	1,444	34.2	23,677	137.0
484	Truck transportation	82	808	19.6	24,243	87.7
4841	General freight trucking	36	408	9.8	24,088	38.1
48412	General freight trucking, long-distance	26	312	8.1	26,106	33.0
484121	General freight trucking, long-distance, truckload (tl)	19	194	3.6	18,722	18.7
4842	Specialized freight trucking	46	400	9.8	24,400	49.6
484220	Specialized freight (except used goods) trucking, local	36	162	4.5	28,056	31.6
4842203	Dump trucking	22	85	2.6	30,294	16.7
485	Transit and ground passenger transportation	7	108	1.4	12,824	2.0
487	Scenic and sightseeing transportation	4	9	0.2	19,889	0.6
492	Couriers and messengers	3	45	1.2	26,622	1.6
493	Warehousing and storage	5	154	3.9	25,409	13.6

Sources: Economic Census of the United States, 1997. Only those industries are shown for which both employment and sales/revenue data were available. For the definition of MSAs, CMSAs, and PMSAs, please see the Introduction.

PENSACOLA, FL MSA

NAICS	Industry	Estab-lish-ments	Em-ploy-ment	Payroll		Sales, reven. ($ mil.)
				Total ($ mil.)	Per Empl. ($)	
48-49	Transportation and warehousing	236	2,729	67.8	24,853	224.1
484	Truck transportation	153	1,097	26.7	24,300	95.4
4841	General freight trucking	52	353	10.7	30,235	38.0
484110	General freight trucking, local	15	66	1.7	25,348	7.4
48412	General freight trucking, long-distance	37	287	9.0	31,359	30.6
484121	General freight trucking, long-distance, truckload (tl)	30	166	4.6	27,843	20.8
4842	Specialized freight trucking	101	744	16.0	21,484	57.4
484210	Used household and office goods moving	27	247	4.8	19,543	14.7
4842102	Used household and office goods moving, long-distance	13	133	2.9	21,902	9.2
484220	Specialized freight (except used goods) trucking, local	32	168	3.7	22,214	19.4
4842203	Dump trucking	14	88	1.4	16,273	6.3
484230	Specialized freight (except used goods) trucking, long-distance	42	329	7.4	22,568	23.3
485	Transit and ground passenger transportation	15	250	3.8	15,316	10.4
487	Scenic and sightseeing transportation	5	6	0.1	9,000	0.2
488	Support activities for transportation	37	1,104	31.1	28,126	81.6
492	Couriers and messengers	14	229	4.9	21,585	19.7
493	Warehousing and storage	7	12	0.3	21,250	2.4

Sources: Economic Census of the United States, 1997. Only those industries are shown for which both employment and sales/revenue data were available. For the definition of MSAs, CMSAs, and PMSAs, please see the Introduction.

PEORIA—PEKIN, IL MSA

NAICS	Industry	Estab- lish- ments	Em- ploy- ment	Payroll		Sales, reven. ($ mil.)
				Total ($ mil.)	Per Empl. ($)	
48-49	Transportation and warehousing	237	4,741	124.5	26,263	442.1
483	Water transportation	4	54	1.1	19,519	4.4
484	Truck transportation	152	3,189	91.9	28,833	289.1
4841	General freight trucking	72	2,574	75.5	29,342	237.0
484110	General freight trucking, local	18	106	2.5	23,519	7.7
4841101	General freight trucking without storage, local, truckload (tl)	15	104	2.4	22,981	7.3
48412	General freight trucking, long-distance	54	2,468	73.0	29,592	229.4
484121	General freight trucking, long-distance, truckload (tl)	45	2,173	63.9	29,423	199.9
4842	Specialized freight trucking	80	615	16.4	26,701	52.0
484220	Specialized freight (except used goods) trucking, local	61	194	5.1	26,490	19.8
4842202	Agricultural products trucking without storage, local	11	55	1.0	17,382	3.4
4842203	Dump trucking	42	114	3.3	28,868	13.7
484230	Specialized freight (except used goods) trucking, long-distance	15	221	6.0	26,941	20.2
485	Transit and ground passenger transportation	14	339	4.2	12,307	11.9
488	Support activities for transportation	30	649	15.2	23,407	55.4
492	Couriers and messengers	18	293	5.9	20,253	35.5
4931	Warehousing and storage	12	198	5.7	28,944	42.3

Sources: Economic Census of the United States, 1997. Only those industries are shown for which both employment and sales/revenue data were available. For the definition of MSAs, CMSAs, and PMSAs, please see the Introduction.

PHILADELPHIA, PA—NJ PMSA

NAICS	Industry	Estab-lish-ments	Em-ploy-ment	Payroll		Sales, reven. ($ mil.)
				Total ($ mil.)	Per Empl. ($)	
48-49	Transportation and warehousing	2,245	46,981	1,367.6	29,109	4,578.3
481	Air transportation	35	562	16.7	29,721	179.9
48111	Scheduled air transportation	20	365	8.7	23,852	155.7
48121	Nonscheduled air transportation	15	197	8.0	40,594	24.1
48311	Deep sea, coastal, and Great Lakes water transportation	33	1,132	60.4	53,387	330.3
483113	Coastal and Great Lakes freight transportation	16	890	49.9	56,012	185.6
484	Truck transportation	1,075	15,154	520.2	34,327	1,719.1
4841	General freight trucking	476	9,164	338.5	36,938	1,074.7
484110	General freight trucking, local	214	1,675	48.1	28,713	165.3
4841101	General freight trucking without storage, local, truckload (tl)	132	937	26.5	28,290	107.0
4841102	General freight trucking without storage, local, less than truckload (ltl)	71	616	18.8	30,531	51.8
48412	General freight trucking, long-distance	262	7,489	290.4	38,777	909.4
484121	General freight trucking, long-distance, truckload (tl)	195	2,902	93.8	32,327	439.4
484122	General freight trucking, long-distance, less than truckload (ltl)	67	4,587	196.6	42,858	470.0
4842	Specialized freight trucking	599	5,990	181.7	30,334	644.4
484210	Used household and office goods moving	152	2,167	58.6	27,021	171.2
4842101	Used household and office goods moving, local, without storage	61	369	9.0	24,287	23.1
4842102	Used household and office goods moving, long-distance	45	1,319	38.1	28,882	114.9
4842103	Used household and office goods moving, local, with storage	46	479	11.5	24,000	33.3
484220	Specialized freight (except used goods) trucking, local	307	1,792	48.5	27,080	171.4
4842201	Hazardous materials trucking (except waste), local	16	78	2.3	29,154	11.0
4842202	Agricultural products trucking without storage, local	22	151	4.3	28,781	11.0
4842203	Dump trucking	176	819	24.2	29,570	89.9
4842204	Specialized trucking without storage, local	83	625	15.0	24,021	52.1
484230	Specialized freight (except used goods) trucking, long-distance	140	2,031	74.6	36,741	301.7
4842301	Hazardous materials trucking (except waste), long-distance	29	463	17.5	37,827	74.1
4842302	Agricultural products trucking, long-distance	29	181	7.7	42,547	30.9
4842303	Other specialized trucking, long-distance	82	1,387	49.4	35,621	196.8
485	Transit and ground passenger transportation	307	8,793	138.6	15,767	339.5
4853	Taxi and limousine service	163	1,084	16.7	15,400	50.9
485310	Taxi service	93	232	3.1	13,405	10.3
485320	Limousine service	70	852	13.6	15,944	40.5
485410	School and employee bus transportation	63	4,583	63.4	13,825	131.4
4854101	School bus service	59	4,538	62.9	13,854	130.3
485510	Charter bus industry	21	576	11.6	20,123	27.8
48599	Other transit and ground passenger transportation	48	2,131	33.6	15,788	99.9
485991	Special needs transportation	37	1,857	29.8	16,050	89.7
485999	All other transit and ground passenger transportation	11	274	3.8	14,011	10.3
488	Support activities for transportation	473	7,106	227.2	31,970	671.0
4881	Support activities for air transportation	35	1,313	24.5	18,632	71.8
4881191	Airport operation and terminal services	17	957	13.5	14,153	38.9
488190	Other support activities for air transportation	18	356	10.9	30,674	33.0
4882101	Support activities incidental to rail transportation	12	181	4.8	26,735	40.3
4883	Support activities for water transportation	45	2,181	83.6	38,322	169.5
488320	Marine cargo handling	18	1,107	36.0	32,560	90.0
488390	Other support activities for water transportation	14	148	5.0	33,791	11.3
4884	Support activities for road transportation	99	421	7.4	17,570	22.8
488410	Motor vehicle towing	94	345	6.2	17,875	20.1
488510	Freight transportation arrangement	257	2,722	100.0	36,745	341.3
4885101	Freight forwarding	89	1,462	51.5	35,250	162.8
4885102	Arrangement of transportation of freight and cargo	168	1,260	48.5	38,480	178.5
48899	Other support activities for transportation	25	288	6.9	23,872	25.3
492	Couriers and messengers	167	11,067	306.8	27,718	917.7
492110	Couriers	84	10,440	292.5	28,018	869.5
4921101	Courier services (except by air)	43	7,492	194.9	26,018	436.0
4921102	Air courier services	41	2,948	97.6	33,101	433.5
492210	Local messengers and local delivery	83	627	14.2	22,711	48.1
4931	Warehousing and storage	115	2,620	73.1	27,903	243.5
4931101	General warehousing and storage (except in foreign trade zones)	75	1,269	34.7	27,321	99.7
4931201	Refrigerated products warehousing	18	866	27.2	31,364	89.1
4931902	Specialized goods warehousing and storage	14	110	3.8	34,909	32.9

Sources: Economic Census of the United States, 1997. Only those industries are shown for which both employment and sales/revenue data were available. For the definition of MSAs, CMSAs, and PMSAs, please see the Introduction.

PHILADELPHIA—WILMINGTON—ATLANTIC CITY, PA—NJ—DE—MD CMSA

NAICS	Industry	Estab-lish-ments	Em-ploy-ment	Payroll Total ($ mil.)	Payroll Per Empl. ($)	Sales, reven. ($ mil.)
48-49	Transportation and warehousing	2,902	58,037	1,647.2	28,381	5,557.0
481211	Nonscheduled chartered passenger air transportation	18	158	7.6	47,956	57.0
484	Truck transportation	1,428	20,053	661.4	32,983	2,199.5
4841	General freight trucking	607	11,979	421.2	35,163	1,363.5
484110	General freight trucking, local	262	1,917	54.8	28,574	192.0
48412	General freight trucking, long-distance	345	10,062	366.4	36,419	1,171.5
4842	Specialized freight trucking	821	8,074	240.2	29,749	835.9
484210	Used household and office goods moving	190	2,835	73.6	25,952	216.3
484220	Specialized freight (except used goods) trucking, local	429	2,427	67.3	27,733	239.3
484230	Specialized freight (except used goods) trucking, long-distance	202	2,812	99.3	35,317	380.3
4842303	Other specialized trucking, long-distance	106	1,868	62.3	33,362	234.5
485	Transit and ground passenger transportation	404	11,829	185.0	15,638	454.5
485410	School and employee bus transportation	96	5,967	78.3	13,122	168.9
485510	Charter bus industry	29	737	14.2	19,313	34.7
48599	Other transit and ground passenger transportation	57	2,490	40.1	16,097	114.6
4882101	Support activities incidental to rail transportation	18	348	7.8	22,546	49.3
488510	Freight transportation arrangement	284	2,815	103.9	36,921	355.5
4931201	Refrigerated products warehousing	26	989	31.4	31,765	101.4
493190	Other warehousing and storage	26	572	14.4	25,150	68.8

Sources: *Economic Census of the United States*, 1997. Only those industries are shown for which both employment and sales/revenue data were available. For the definition of MSAs, CMSAs, and PMSAs, please see the Introduction.

PHOENIX—MESA, AZ MSA

NAICS	Industry	Estab-lish-ments	Em-ploy-ment	Payroll Total ($ mil.)	Payroll Per Empl. ($)	Sales, reven. ($ mil.)
48-49	Transportation and warehousing	1,337	36,189	901.0	24,898	3,007.8
481	Air transportation	32	380	10.1	26,516	136.7
48111	Scheduled air transportation	15	299	6.8	22,652	123.4
48121	Nonscheduled air transportation	17	81	3.3	40,778	13.2
484	Truck transportation	790	19,909	501.0	25,167	1,719.3
4841	General freight trucking	382	15,584	394.0	25,284	1,332.1
484110	General freight trucking, local	150	1,766	40.6	22,969	120.8
4841101	General freight trucking without storage, local, truckload (tl)	96	654	14.8	22,615	55.4
48412	General freight trucking, long-distance	232	13,818	353.5	25,580	1,211.3
484121	General freight trucking, long-distance, truckload (tl)	192	11,749	281.6	23,972	1,018.6
484122	General freight trucking, long-distance, less than truckload (ltl)	40	2,069	71.8	34,708	192.7
4842	Specialized freight trucking	408	4,325	107.0	24,746	387.2
484210	Used household and office goods moving	82	1,523	32.2	21,164	89.9
4842101	Used household and office goods moving, local, without storage	38	384	8.7	22,651	19.4
4842102	Used household and office goods moving, long-distance	32	894	19.2	21,474	58.4
4842103	Used household and office goods moving, local, with storage	12	245	4.3	17,702	12.0
484220	Specialized freight (except used goods) trucking, local	241	1,733	42.7	24,643	158.1
4842202	Agricultural products trucking without storage, local	48	271	7.5	27,579	29.0
4842203	Dump trucking	112	806	16.1	20,025	63.4
4842204	Specialized trucking without storage, local	69	499	15.0	30,026	53.6
484230	Specialized freight (except used goods) trucking, long-distance	85	1,069	32.1	30,017	139.2
4842302	Agricultural products trucking, long-distance	26	197	4.5	23,091	29.5
4842303	Other specialized trucking, long-distance	52	835	26.3	31,471	105.6
485	Transit and ground passenger transportation	65	2,289	50.3	21,956	89.9
4853	Taxi and limousine service	27	203	3.1	15,113	11.3
485320	Limousine service	20	176	2.9	16,352	10.6
485510	Charter bus industry	15	255	3.9	15,114	14.5
488	Support activities for transportation	283	2,833	87.6	30,925	315.3
4881	Support activities for air transportation	59	1,316	47.7	36,246	127.3
48811	Airport operations	19	853	32.6	38,197	64.9
488190	Other support activities for air transportation	40	463	15.1	32,652	62.4
4884	Support activities for road transportation	74	594	13.0	21,928	30.0
488410	Motor vehicle towing	70	455	10.7	23,604	26.3
488510	Freight transportation arrangement	132	791	24.6	31,053	150.8
4885101	Freight forwarding	57	491	12.5	25,397	76.2
4885102	Arrangement of transportation of freight and cargo	75	300	12.1	40,310	74.6
492	Couriers and messengers	105	10,058	233.1	23,174	646.5
492110	Couriers	53	9,086	211.7	23,304	599.9
4921101	Courier services (except by air)	23	7,511	164.7	21,928	416.9
4921102	Air courier services	30	1,575	47.0	29,864	183.0
492210	Local messengers and local delivery	52	972	21.3	21,963	46.6
4931	Warehousing and storage	46	578	14.7	25,415	43.1
4931101	General warehousing and storage (except in foreign trade zones)	31	298	7.3	24,473	17.8

Sources: *Economic Census of the United States*, 1997. Only those industries are shown for which both employment and sales/revenue data were available. For the definition of MSAs, CMSAs, and PMSAs, please see the Introduction.

PINE BLUFF, AR MSA

NAICS	Industry	Estab-lish-ments	Em-ploy-ment	Payroll		Sales, reven. ($ mil.)
				Total ($ mil.)	Per Empl. ($)	
48-49	Transportation and warehousing	43	333	6.1	18,429	30.9
484220	Specialized freight (except used goods) trucking, local	11	33	0.6	16,909	4.1
488	Support activities for transportation	7	49	1.0	20,388	7.8
493	Warehousing and storage	5	95	1.6	16,516	9.2

Sources: *Economic Census of the United States*, 1997. Only those industries are shown for which both employment and sales/revenue data were available. For the definition of MSAs, CMSAs, and PMSAs, please see the Introduction.

PITTSBURGH, PA MSA

NAICS	Industry	Estab-lish-ments	Em-ploy-ment	Payroll		Sales, reven. ($ mil.)
				Total ($ mil.)	Per Empl. ($)	
48-49	Transportation and warehousing	1,157	25,695	655.6	25,516	2,512.6
481	Air transportation	29	760	16.4	21,607	131.2
48111	Scheduled air transportation	15	620	12.7	20,521	107.8
48121	Nonscheduled air transportation	14	140	3.7	26,414	23.5
484	Truck transportation	650	9,304	270.6	29,085	1,138.1
4841	General freight trucking	255	5,868	183.8	31,331	707.3
484110	General freight trucking, local	70	953	15.8	16,604	60.6
4841101	General freight trucking without storage, local, truckload (tl)	41	260	5.5	21,046	25.8
4841102	General freight trucking without storage, local, less than truckload (ltl)	18	201	4.2	20,662	10.8
48412	General freight trucking, long-distance	185	4,915	168.0	34,186	646.7
484121	General freight trucking, long-distance, truckload (tl)	148	2,397	70.4	29,377	404.3
484122	General freight trucking, long-distance, less than truckload (ltl)	37	2,518	97.6	38,764	242.4
4842	Specialized freight trucking	395	3,436	86.8	25,251	430.8
484210	Used household and office goods moving	73	1,124	27.8	24,705	86.9
4842101	Used household and office goods moving, local, without storage	26	155	2.4	15,471	9.0
4842102	Used household and office goods moving, long-distance	29	823	22.8	27,711	69.1
4842103	Used household and office goods moving, local, with storage	18	146	2.6	17,562	8.8
484220	Specialized freight (except used goods) trucking, local	244	1,583	39.2	24,766	166.1
4842201	Hazardous materials trucking (except waste), local	13	55	1.8	31,818	4.4
4842203	Dump trucking	155	952	22.1	23,233	107.6
4842204	Specialized trucking without storage, local	66	547	14.8	27,066	51.9
484230	Specialized freight (except used goods) trucking, long-distance	78	729	19.8	27,145	177.9
4842301	Hazardous materials trucking (except waste), long-distance	13	131	4.3	33,084	20.8
4842303	Other specialized trucking, long-distance	58	548	14.3	26,097	150.1
485	Transit and ground passenger transportation	139	5,247	62.7	11,942	181.8
4853	Taxi and limousine service	29	227	2.0	8,811	13.0
485320	Limousine service	21	166	1.1	6,819	5.6
485410	School and employee bus transportation	74	3,823	40.1	10,494	111.0
486210	Pipeline transportation of natural gas	21	470	23.2	49,457	220.2
488	Support activities for transportation	172	1,909	46.6	24,419	146.0
4881	Support activities for air transportation	14	574	7.8	13,512	17.5
4883	Support activities for water transportation	17	183	5.2	28,645	16.4
488410	Motor vehicle towing	35	164	2.6	15,909	8.8
488510	Freight transportation arrangement	85	718	26.4	36,777	91.6
4885101	Freight forwarding	37	305	12.6	41,170	34.0
4885102	Arrangement of transportation of freight and cargo	48	413	13.8	33,533	57.6
492	Couriers and messengers	76	6,456	191.1	29,603	419.6
492110	Couriers	35	6,014	183.1	30,449	394.8
492210	Local messengers and local delivery	41	442	8.0	18,095	24.8
4931	Warehousing and storage	43	663	20.0	30,186	59.9
4931101	General warehousing and storage (except in foreign trade zones)	34	454	14.3	31,405	39.8

Sources: *Economic Census of the United States*, 1997. Only those industries are shown for which both employment and sales/revenue data were available. For the definition of MSAs, CMSAs, and PMSAs, please see the Introduction.

PITTSFIELD, MA MSA

NAICS	Industry	Estab-lish-ments	Em-ploy-ment	Payroll		Sales, reven. ($ mil.)
				Total ($ mil.)	Per Empl. ($)	
48-49	Transportation and warehousing	40	573	9.3	16,209	25.1
484	Truck transportation	19	130	3.0	23,185	9.6
4842	Specialized freight trucking	13	96	1.9	19,760	6.2
485	Transit and ground passenger transportation	13	368	4.3	11,674	9.3

Sources: *Economic Census of the United States*, 1997. Only those industries are shown for which both employment and sales/revenue data were available. For the definition of MSAs, CMSAs, and PMSAs, please see the Introduction.

POCATELLO, ID MSA

| NAICS | Industry | Estab-lish-ments | Em-ploy-ment | Payroll | | Sales, reven. ($ mil.) |
				Total ($ mil.)	Per Empl. ($)	
48-49	Transportation and warehousing	43	519	10.5	20,247	39.3
484	Truck transportation	29	237	6.2	26,093	24.9
4841	General freight trucking	14	120	3.5	28,883	14.1
4842	Specialized freight trucking	15	117	2.7	23,231	10.8
488	Support activities for transportation	4	14	0.4	27,500	1.2
492	Couriers and messengers	3	60	0.9	15,083	2.9

Sources: Economic Census of the United States, 1997. Only those industries are shown for which both employment and sales/revenue data were available. For the definition of MSAs, CMSAs, and PMSAs, please see the Introduction.

PORTLAND, ME MSA

| NAICS | Industry | Estab-lish-ments | Em-ploy-ment | Payroll | | Sales, reven. ($ mil.) |
				Total ($ mil.)	Per Empl. ($)	
48-49	Transportation and warehousing	181	2,537	74.0	29,181	302.8
484	Truck transportation	78	1,413	45.3	32,054	162.6
4841	General freight trucking	42	834	26.5	31,784	84.2
48412	General freight trucking, long-distance	35	741	25.2	34,053	81.8
484121	General freight trucking, long-distance, truckload (tl)	21	480	14.9	30,948	49.1
484122	General freight trucking, long-distance, less than truckload (ltl)	14	261	10.4	39,762	32.7
4842	Specialized freight trucking	36	579	18.8	32,442	78.5
484220	Specialized freight (except used goods) trucking, local	17	59	1.3	22,610	6.3
4842204	Specialized trucking without storage, local	11	48	1.1	21,917	2.7
485	Transit and ground passenger transportation	16	165	2.9	17,430	7.8
487	Scenic and sightseeing transportation	7	67	1.6	24,284	5.4
488	Support activities for transportation	43	246	5.8	23,711	23.6
4883	Support activities for water transportation	15	98	2.9	29,469	9.1
488510	Freight transportation arrangement	16	87	2.4	27,736	12.7
4885102	Arrangement of transportation of freight and cargo	13	72	2.0	27,958	12.0
492	Couriers and messengers	18	444	11.5	25,795	42.3
492110	Couriers	12	375	10.3	27,419	39.5
493	Warehousing and storage	5	87	2.7	30,460	11.0

Sources: Economic Census of the United States, 1997. Only those industries are shown for which both employment and sales/revenue data were available. For the definition of MSAs, CMSAs, and PMSAs, please see the Introduction.

PORTLAND—SALEM, OR—WA CMSA

| NAICS | Industry | Estab-lish-ments | Em-ploy-ment | Payroll | | Sales, reven. ($ mil.) |
				Total ($ mil.)	Per Empl. ($)	
48-49	Transportation and warehousing	1,525	28,808	917.3	31,843	2,850.7
484	Truck transportation	879	13,201	423.0	32,041	1,222.1
4841	General freight trucking	338	8,425	281.0	33,354	792.1
484110	General freight trucking, local	107	1,642	44.5	27,091	135.6
48412	General freight trucking, long-distance	231	6,783	236.5	34,870	656.4
484121	General freight trucking, long-distance, truckload (tl)	183	2,648	82.8	31,268	337.1
484122	General freight trucking, long-distance, less than truckload (ltl)	48	4,135	153.7	37,177	319.4
4842	Specialized freight trucking	541	4,776	142.0	29,726	430.1
484210	Used household and office goods moving	52	923	26.6	28,784	68.3
484220	Specialized freight (except used goods) trucking, local	382	1,688	42.7	25,311	168.0
4842202	Agricultural products trucking without storage, local	66	222	6.0	26,955	20.5
4842203	Dump trucking	221	760	18.2	23,984	75.8
484230	Specialized freight (except used goods) trucking, long-distance	107	2,165	72.7	33,570	193.8
4854101	School bus service	27	1,286	14.3	11,115	34.8
488	Support activities for transportation	352	4,461	186.0	41,685	460.8
4883	Support activities for water transportation	39	1,397	102.4	73,271	186.0
488320	Marine cargo handling	12	1,186	92.7	78,148	148.9
488510	Freight transportation arrangement	192	1,377	49.8	36,179	175.2
4931	Warehousing and storage	55	656	21.5	32,791	88.4

Sources: Economic Census of the United States, 1997. Only those industries are shown for which both employment and sales/revenue data were available. For the definition of MSAs, CMSAs, and PMSAs, please see the Introduction.

PORTLAND—VANCOUVER, OR—WA PMSA

NAICS	Industry	Estab-lish-ments	Em-ploy-ment	Payroll		Sales, reven. ($ mil.)
				Total ($ mil.)	Per Empl. ($)	
48-49	Transportation and warehousing	1,334	26,268	839.1	31,944	2,588.4
481	Air transportation	21	443	13.7	30,993	170.9
48121	Nonscheduled air transportation	12	226	7.0	31,146	41.4
484	Truck transportation	757	12,280	395.4	32,195	1,126.5
4841	General freight trucking	292	8,099	271.6	33,535	753.2
484110	General freight trucking, local	95	1,556	41.9	26,956	125.3
4841101	General freight trucking without storage, local, truckload (tl)	67	709	18.0	25,450	61.6
48412	General freight trucking, long-distance	197	6,543	229.7	35,099	627.9
484121	General freight trucking, long-distance, truckload (tl)	156	2,468	78.8	31,912	321.9
484122	General freight trucking, long-distance, less than truckload (ltl)	41	4,075	150.9	37,029	306.1
4842	Specialized freight trucking	465	4,181	123.8	29,600	373.3
484210	Used household and office goods moving	46	863	25.2	29,175	65.0
4842101	Used household and office goods moving, local, without storage	11	49	0.8	16,388	2.0
4842102	Used household and office goods moving, long-distance	23	423	12.3	29,005	37.4
4842103	Used household and office goods moving, local, with storage	12	391	12.1	30,962	25.6
484220	Specialized freight (except used goods) trucking, local	328	1,490	36.9	24,734	149.3
4842202	Agricultural products trucking without storage, local	49	136	3.6	26,324	13.5
4842203	Dump trucking	192	674	15.4	22,921	66.6
4842204	Specialized trucking without storage, local	78	553	13.4	24,152	44.9
484230	Specialized freight (except used goods) trucking, long-distance	91	1,828	61.7	33,768	159.0
4842302	Agricultural products trucking, long-distance	26	223	5.3	23,964	19.3
4842303	Other specialized trucking, long-distance	57	1,469	51.3	34,956	128.3
485	Transit and ground passenger transportation	78	2,168	29.8	13,768	73.6
4853	Taxi and limousine service	33	467	6.4	13,670	18.6
485310	Taxi service	11	231	3.6	15,407	11.1
485320	Limousine service	22	236	2.8	11,970	7.6
4854101	School bus service	20	1,108	12.7	11,434	30.6
488	Support activities for transportation	326	4,344	183.2	42,170	446.3
488190	Other support activities for air transportation	18	302	7.1	23,576	21.5
4883	Support activities for water transportation	39	1,397	102.4	73,271	186.0
488320	Marine cargo handling	12	1,186	92.7	78,148	148.9
488410	Motor vehicle towing	60	576	11.5	20,030	37.9
488510	Freight transportation arrangement	184	1,348	49.1	36,444	171.2
4885101	Freight forwarding	64	644	23.0	35,694	77.0
4885102	Arrangement of transportation of freight and cargo	120	704	26.1	37,129	94.2
492	Couriers and messengers	74	5,698	159.1	27,923	405.1
492110	Couriers	37	5,344	152.7	28,577	391.1
492210	Local messengers and local delivery	37	354	6.4	18,048	14.1
4931	Warehousing and storage	47	524	17.3	32,994	67.5
4931101	General warehousing and storage (except in foreign trade zones)	30	216	7.2	33,310	23.5

Sources: *Economic Census of the United States*, 1997. Only those industries are shown for which both employment and sales/revenue data were available. For the definition of MSAs, CMSAs, and PMSAs, please see the Introduction.

PORTSMOUTH—ROCHESTER, NH—ME PMSA

NAICS	Industry	Estab-lish-ments	Em-ploy-ment	Payroll		Sales, reven. ($ mil.)
				Total ($ mil.)	Per Empl. ($)	
48-49	Transportation and warehousing	161	2,913	47.0	16,133	195.1
484	Truck transportation	86	571	15.0	26,335	71.4
4841	General freight trucking	32	188	5.7	30,362	32.8
484110	General freight trucking, local	12	31	0.9	29,000	4.5
48412	General freight trucking, long-distance	20	157	4.8	30,631	28.3
4842	Specialized freight trucking	54	383	9.3	24,358	38.6
484210	Used household and office goods moving	17	169	3.6	21,219	9.9
484220	Specialized freight (except used goods) trucking, local	30	171	4.6	26,813	24.9
4842203	Dump trucking	15	105	3.3	31,048	18.7
485	Transit and ground passenger transportation	30	587	7.3	12,518	18.9
4853	Taxi and limousine service	14	147	1.8	12,061	4.2

Sources: *Economic Census of the United States*, 1997. Only those industries are shown for which both employment and sales/revenue data were available. For the definition of MSAs, CMSAs, and PMSAs, please see the Introduction.

PROVIDENCE—FALL RIVER—WARWICK, RI—MA MSA

NAICS	Industry	Estab-lish-ments	Em-ploy-ment	Payroll		Sales, reven. ($ mil.)
				Total ($ mil.)	Per Empl. ($)	
48-49	Transportation and warehousing	627	7,129	177.6	24,914	714.0
484	Truck transportation	329	2,974	93.8	31,548	414.8
4841	General freight trucking	123	1,786	60.2	33,706	212.4
484110	General freight trucking, local	42	224	7.7	34,585	31.8
4841101	General freight trucking without storage, local, truckload (tl)	27	170	6.2	36,706	27.3
4841102	General freight trucking without storage, local, less than truckload (ltl)	12	33	1.0	29,545	2.8
48412	General freight trucking, long-distance	81	1,562	52.5	33,580	180.6
484121	General freight trucking, long-distance, truckload (tl)	53	714	24.7	34,646	86.6
484122	General freight trucking, long-distance, less than truckload (ltl)	28	848	27.7	32,683	94.1
4842	Specialized freight trucking	206	1,188	33.6	28,305	202.4
484210	Used household and office goods moving	58	672	19.5	29,009	137.1
4842101	Used household and office goods moving, local, without storage	33	156	4.8	30,526	11.3
484220	Specialized freight (except used goods) trucking, local	117	329	9.4	28,571	33.4
4842203	Dump trucking	77	120	3.0	25,300	14.0
484230	Specialized freight (except used goods) trucking, long-distance	31	187	4.7	25,305	31.8
4842303	Other specialized trucking, long-distance	24	157	4.1	26,038	29.4
485	Transit and ground passenger transportation	102	2,269	32.5	14,339	83.4
4853	Taxi and limousine service	43	226	2.5	11,093	9.6
485310	Taxi service	29	91	1.3	14,066	5.4
485320	Limousine service	14	135	1.2	9,089	4.1
4854101	School bus service	39	1,597	16.6	10,405	39.1
488	Support activities for transportation	100	1,008	27.1	26,892	96.3
4881	Support activities for air transportation	13	347	8.0	23,196	35.5
4883	Support activities for water transportation	16	164	4.2	25,506	16.2
488410	Motor vehicle towing	28	71	1.2	17,141	5.1
492210	Local messengers and local delivery	39	253	5.5	21,747	13.6
4931101	General warehousing and storage (except in foreign trade zones)	15	105	2.9	27,533	9.7

Sources: Economic Census of the United States, 1997. Only those industries are shown for which both employment and sales/revenue data were available. For the definition of MSAs, CMSAs, and PMSAs, please see the Introduction.

PROVO—OREM, UT MSA

NAICS	Industry	Estab-lish-ments	Em-ploy-ment	Payroll		Sales, reven. ($ mil.)
				Total ($ mil.)	Per Empl. ($)	
48-49	Transportation and warehousing	110	1,305	36.5	27,959	147.6
484	Truck transportation	80	629	15.1	23,957	66.7
4841	General freight trucking	38	435	9.9	22,729	47.7
4841101	General freight trucking without storage, local, truckload (tl)	14	122	3.0	24,246	18.7
48412	General freight trucking, long-distance	24	313	6.9	22,137	29.0
484121	General freight trucking, long-distance, truckload (tl)	21	269	5.5	20,595	23.0
4842	Specialized freight trucking	42	194	5.2	26,711	19.0
484220	Specialized freight (except used goods) trucking, local	31	123	3.6	29,285	13.4
4842203	Dump trucking	23	63	2.3	36,841	9.6
488	Support activities for transportation	16	37	1.0	26,405	15.5
492	Couriers and messengers	3	80	1.8	22,687	5.1

Sources: Economic Census of the United States, 1997. Only those industries are shown for which both employment and sales/revenue data were available. For the definition of MSAs, CMSAs, and PMSAs, please see the Introduction.

PUEBLO, CO MSA

NAICS	Industry	Estab-lish-ments	Em-ploy-ment	Payroll		Sales, reven. ($ mil.)
				Total ($ mil.)	Per Empl. ($)	
48-49	Transportation and warehousing	67	445	11.1	24,867	34.1
484	Truck transportation	43	263	7.3	27,814	22.5
4841	General freight trucking	17	80	2.3	28,763	10.8
48412	General freight trucking, long-distance	12	66	1.9	29,000	8.0
4842	Specialized freight trucking	26	183	5.0	27,399	11.7
484220	Specialized freight (except used goods) trucking, local	14	98	3.6	36,969	6.9
488	Support activities for transportation	8	55	1.2	21,964	4.9
492	Couriers and messengers	7	68	1.6	23,912	4.3

Sources: Economic Census of the United States, 1997. Only those industries are shown for which both employment and sales/revenue data were available. For the definition of MSAs, CMSAs, and PMSAs, please see the Introduction.

PUNTA GORDA, FL MSA

NAICS	Industry	Estab-lish-ments	Em-ploy-ment	Payroll		Sales, reven. ($ mil.)
				Total ($ mil.)	Per Empl. ($)	
48-49	Transportation and warehousing	38	237	5.8	24,291	25.8
484	Truck transportation	17	125	3.0	23,856	17.0
4842	Specialized freight trucking	11	121	2.8	23,223	16.0
485	Transit and ground passenger transportation	5	11	0.1	12,636	0.6

Sources: Economic Census of the United States, 1997. Only those industries are shown for which both employment and sales/revenue data were available. For the definition of MSAs, CMSAs, and PMSAs, please see the Introduction.

RACINE, WI PMSA

NAICS	Industry	Estab-lish-ments	Em-ploy-ment	Payroll		Sales, reven. ($ mil.)
				Total ($ mil.)	Per Empl. ($)	
48-49	Transportation and warehousing	136	1,746	47.1	26,977	177.2
484	Truck transportation	95	1,063	34.8	32,705	139.5
4841	General freight trucking	27	675	23.5	34,793	90.3
48412	General freight trucking, long-distance	19	588	20.6	35,109	81.9
484121	General freight trucking, long-distance, truckload (tl)	15	580	20.4	35,102	81.1
4842	Specialized freight trucking	68	388	11.3	29,072	49.2
484220	Specialized freight (except used goods) trucking, local	53	180	5.2	28,617	27.0
4842203	Dump trucking	36	124	3.7	30,089	22.9
485	Transit and ground passenger transportation	15	459	6.4	13,837	14.5
488	Support activities for transportation	15	98	2.5	25,265	9.3

Sources: Economic Census of the United States, 1997. Only those industries are shown for which both employment and sales/revenue data were available. For the definition of MSAs, CMSAs, and PMSAs, please see the Introduction.

RALEIGH—DURHAM—CHAPEL HILL, NC MSA

NAICS	Industry	Estab-lish-ments	Em-ploy-ment	Payroll		Sales, reven. ($ mil.)
				Total ($ mil.)	Per Empl. ($)	
48-49	Transportation and warehousing	574	10,116	267.7	26,459	807.5
484	Truck transportation	336	3,857	112.5	29,159	360.2
4841	General freight trucking	125	1,773	56.5	31,881	191.4
484110	General freight trucking, local	31	253	5.5	21,561	15.1
4841101	General freight trucking without storage, local, truckload (tl)	20	109	2.6	24,000	7.0
48412	General freight trucking, long-distance	94	1,520	51.1	33,599	176.3
484121	General freight trucking, long-distance, truckload (tl)	58	327	9.6	29,248	37.6
484122	General freight trucking, long-distance, less than truckload (ltl)	36	1,193	41.5	34,791	138.7
4842	Specialized freight trucking	211	2,084	55.9	26,844	168.8
484210	Used household and office goods moving	35	437	11.0	25,261	29.7
4842101	Used household and office goods moving, local, without storage	15	95	2.1	21,642	5.6
4842102	Used household and office goods moving, long-distance	11	215	6.0	27,716	15.9
484220	Specialized freight (except used goods) trucking, local	143	1,320	35.1	26,621	109.9
4842203	Dump trucking	93	447	10.0	22,461	41.1
4842204	Specialized trucking without storage, local	21	121	3.2	26,521	10.2
484230	Specialized freight (except used goods) trucking, long-distance	33	327	9.8	29,859	29.2
4842303	Other specialized trucking, long-distance	18	173	4.5	26,243	12.7
485	Transit and ground passenger transportation	45	868	13.7	15,798	38.0
4853	Taxi and limousine service	18	194	2.1	10,773	7.8
485310	Taxi service	13	53	0.6	10,849	2.5
48599	Other transit and ground passenger transportation	13	117	1.1	9,453	3.0
488	Support activities for transportation	95	634	16.1	25,356	52.0
4881	Support activities for air transportation	15	285	5.0	17,372	11.1
488410	Motor vehicle towing	32	147	2.9	19,769	9.6
488510	Freight transportation arrangement	43	183	7.7	42,273	29.7
4885101	Freight forwarding	28	120	4.3	36,000	21.3
4885102	Arrangement of transportation of freight and cargo	15	63	3.4	54,222	8.4
492	Couriers and messengers	56	4,167	107.3	25,758	272.9
492110	Couriers	30	3,851	102.3	26,561	261.3
4921101	Courier services (except by air)	14	3,180	82.8	26,034	173.0
4921102	Air courier services	16	671	19.5	29,060	88.3
492210	Local messengers and local delivery	26	316	5.0	15,972	11.6
4931	Warehousing and storage	26	455	13.5	29,730	44.0
4931101	General warehousing and storage (except in foreign trade zones)	13	271	8.5	31,502	24.7

Sources: Economic Census of the United States, 1997. Only those industries are shown for which both employment and sales/revenue data were available. For the definition of MSAs, CMSAs, and PMSAs, please see the Introduction.

RAPID CITY, SD MSA

NAICS	Industry	Estab-lish-ments	Em-ploy-ment	Payroll		Sales, reven. ($ mil.)
				Total ($ mil.)	Per Empl. ($)	
48-49	Transportation and warehousing	104	798	17.4	21,744	75.3
481	Air transportation	7	102	1.4	13,431	8.8
484	Truck transportation	63	440	11.6	26,423	52.0
4841	General freight trucking	36	243	7.0	28,765	32.9
484110	General freight trucking, local	12	57	2.0	34,246	7.3
48412	General freight trucking, long-distance	24	186	5.0	27,086	25.5
484121	General freight trucking, long-distance, truckload (tl)	15	139	3.6	26,129	19.6
4842	Specialized freight trucking	27	197	4.6	23,533	19.1
484220	Specialized freight (except used goods) trucking, local	12	59	1.6	27,017	8.2
488	Support activities for transportation	6	13	0.3	20,615	0.8
492	Couriers and messengers	13	84	1.7	20,631	4.2

Sources: Economic Census of the United States, 1997. Only those industries are shown for which both employment and sales/revenue data were available. For the definition of MSAs, CMSAs, and PMSAs, please see the Introduction.

READING, PA MSA

NAICS	Industry	Estab-lish-ments	Em-ploy-ment	Payroll		Sales, reven. ($ mil.)
				Total ($ mil.)	Per Empl. ($)	
48-49	Transportation and warehousing	176	2,845	74.9	26,325	272.0
484	Truck transportation	121	1,423	47.0	33,056	168.9
4841	General freight trucking	46	760	28.6	37,678	89.2
484110	General freight trucking, local	19	94	2.7	28,489	9.6
4841101	General freight trucking without storage, local, truckload (tl)	11	39	1.2	31,872	5.9
48412	General freight trucking, long-distance	27	666	26.0	38,974	79.6
484121	General freight trucking, long-distance, truckload (tl)	18	288	10.2	35,309	34.0
4842	Specialized freight trucking	75	663	18.4	27,757	79.7
484220	Specialized freight (except used goods) trucking, local	45	262	6.7	25,439	29.9
4842203	Dump trucking	28	181	4.0	22,227	20.4
484230	Specialized freight (except used goods) trucking, long-distance	20	344	10.3	30,006	43.0
485	Transit and ground passenger transportation	15	673	9.2	13,632	25.7
488	Support activities for transportation	20	120	3.0	25,108	10.8
492	Couriers and messengers	6	216	4.7	21,537	9.8
493	Warehousing and storage	7	211	5.3	25,118	14.4

Sources: Economic Census of the United States, 1997. Only those industries are shown for which both employment and sales/revenue data were available. For the definition of MSAs, CMSAs, and PMSAs, please see the Introduction.

REDDING, CA MSA

NAICS	Industry	Estab-lish-ments	Em-ploy-ment	Payroll		Sales, reven. ($ mil.)
				Total ($ mil.)	Per Empl. ($)	
48-49	Transportation and warehousing	137	1,287	30.2	23,482	105.9
484	Truck transportation	107	822	22.2	27,060	80.3
4841	General freight trucking	36	385	10.9	28,314	38.4
484110	General freight trucking, local	13	144	4.6	31,951	15.6
48412	General freight trucking, long-distance	23	241	6.3	26,141	22.8
484121	General freight trucking, long-distance, truckload (tl)	18	144	4.2	29,083	17.4
4842	Specialized freight trucking	71	437	11.3	25,954	41.9
484210	Used household and office goods moving	12	54	0.9	15,870	3.3
484220	Specialized freight (except used goods) trucking, local	43	156	4.5	28,782	18.4
4842203	Dump trucking	18	39	0.9	23,667	7.3
4842204	Specialized trucking without storage, local	15	61	1.7	28,197	5.0
484230	Specialized freight (except used goods) trucking, long-distance	16	227	6.0	26,410	20.2
488	Support activities for transportation	10	98	2.1	21,561	6.2
492	Couriers and messengers	10	167	2.9	17,222	11.0

Sources: Economic Census of the United States, 1997. Only those industries are shown for which both employment and sales/revenue data were available. For the definition of MSAs, CMSAs, and PMSAs, please see the Introduction.

RENO, NV MSA

| NAICS | Industry | Estab-lish-ments | Em-ploy-ment | Payroll | | Sales, reven. ($ mil.) |
				Total ($ mil.)	Per Empl. ($)	
48-49	Transportation and warehousing	215	4,117	106.2	25,797	384.6
484	Truck transportation	101	1,905	62.4	32,738	221.1
4841	General freight trucking	57	1,375	44.9	32,663	165.3
484110	General freight trucking, local	14	292	8.5	29,058	20.3
48412	General freight trucking, long-distance	43	1,083	36.4	33,634	145.1
484121	General freight trucking, long-distance, truckload (tl)	22	197	6.8	34,716	21.0
484122	General freight trucking, long-distance, less than truckload (ltl)	21	886	29.6	33,394	124.1
4842	Specialized freight trucking	44	530	17.5	32,932	55.8
484220	Specialized freight (except used goods) trucking, local	23	114	3.6	31,798	15.0
4842203	Dump trucking	12	79	2.8	35,076	11.4
4842204	Specialized trucking without storage, local	11	35	0.9	24,400	3.6
484230	Specialized freight (except used goods) trucking, long-distance	11	261	9.7	37,303	31.1
488	Support activities for transportation	43	604	13.0	21,584	40.2
488510	Freight transportation arrangement	18	152	3.7	24,158	10.7
492	Couriers and messengers	26	414	9.1	21,915	43.9
492110	Couriers	14	336	7.5	22,196	39.5
492210	Local messengers and local delivery	12	78	1.6	20,705	4.4
4931	Warehousing and storage	16	287	7.8	27,279	23.1
4931101	General warehousing and storage (except in foreign trade zones)	11	258	7.0	27,136	21.1

Sources: *Economic Census of the United States*, 1997. Only those industries are shown for which both employment and sales/revenue data were available. For the definition of MSAs, CMSAs, and PMSAs, please see the Introduction.

RICHLAND—KENNEWICK—PASCO, WA MSA

| NAICS | Industry | Estab-lish-ments | Em-ploy-ment | Payroll | | Sales, reven. ($ mil.) |
				Total ($ mil.)	Per Empl. ($)	
48-49	Transportation and warehousing	111	1,229	28.9	23,554	136.4
481	Air transportation	3	25	0.5	18,560	3.8
484	Truck transportation	64	468	12.1	25,853	42.2
4841	General freight trucking	22	164	5.4	32,884	18.2
48412	General freight trucking, long-distance	14	91	3.0	33,407	11.3
4842	Specialized freight trucking	42	304	6.7	22,059	24.0
484220	Specialized freight (except used goods) trucking, local	18	79	2.3	28,924	9.3
484230	Specialized freight (except used goods) trucking, long-distance	15	97	2.5	25,619	9.8
488	Support activities for transportation	14	189	3.0	16,127	26.4
492	Couriers and messengers	10	152	2.8	18,316	10.2
4931	Warehousing and storage	13	284	9.0	31,634	47.4

Sources: *Economic Census of the United States*, 1997. Only those industries are shown for which both employment and sales/revenue data were available. For the definition of MSAs, CMSAs, and PMSAs, please see the Introduction.

RICHMOND—PETERSBURG, VA MSA

| NAICS | Industry | Estab-lish-ments | Em-ploy-ment | Payroll | | Sales, reven. ($ mil.) |
				Total ($ mil.)	Per Empl. ($)	
48-49	Transportation and warehousing	585	14,801	403.1	27,234	1,143.8
484	Truck transportation	323	5,340	162.9	30,501	461.9
4841	General freight trucking	140	4,038	130.6	32,336	350.4
484110	General freight trucking, local	38	415	11.3	27,313	30.4
4841101	General freight trucking without storage, local, truckload (tl)	26	258	7.5	28,950	21.8
48412	General freight trucking, long-distance	102	3,623	119.2	32,912	320.0
484121	General freight trucking, long-distance, truckload (tl)	75	2,174	68.1	31,334	199.7
484122	General freight trucking, long-distance, less than truckload (ltl)	27	1,449	51.1	35,279	120.2
4842	Specialized freight trucking	183	1,302	32.3	24,810	111.5
484210	Used household and office goods moving	31	498	9.9	19,906	26.8
4842101	Used household and office goods moving, local, without storage	12	54	0.7	12,667	2.5
4842102	Used household and office goods moving, long-distance	14	399	8.4	21,170	22.0
484220	Specialized freight (except used goods) trucking, local	131	467	11.2	23,880	43.2
4842202	Agricultural products trucking without storage, local	11	26	0.4	17,077	1.5
4842203	Dump trucking	93	245	4.5	18,331	25.1
4842204	Specialized trucking without storage, local	23	120	3.7	30,783	11.2
484230	Specialized freight (except used goods) trucking, long-distance	21	337	11.2	33,347	41.5
485	Transit and ground passenger transportation	45	1,150	24.8	21,596	38.9
485310	Taxi service	11	76	0.6	8,053	2.3
488	Support activities for transportation	92	892	18.5	20,786	56.1
488410	Motor vehicle towing	39	234	3.8	16,380	12.5
488510	Freight transportation arrangement	40	292	10.2	35,010	30.1
4885102	Arrangement of transportation of freight and cargo	30	242	9.0	36,996	25.6
492	Couriers and messengers	54	6,057	161.5	26,665	367.4
492110	Couriers	25	5,491	152.7	27,811	347.1
492210	Local messengers and local delivery	29	566	8.8	15,542	20.3
4931	Warehousing and storage	38	1,064	23.4	21,991	62.6
4931101	General warehousing and storage (except in foreign trade zones)	26	530	11.9	22,411	34.4

Sources: Economic Census of the United States, 1997. Only those industries are shown for which both employment and sales/revenue data were available. For the definition of MSAs, CMSAs, and PMSAs, please see the Introduction.

RIVERSIDE—SAN BERNARDINO, CA PMSA

NAICS	Industry	Estab-lish-ments	Em-ploy-ment	Payroll		Sales, reven. ($ mil.)
				Total ($ mil.)	Per Empl. ($)	
48-49	Transportation and warehousing	1,374	30,745	829.8	26,989	2,907.3
481	Air transportation	21	519	15.9	30,719	70.6
48121	Nonscheduled air transportation	15	185	6.9	37,038	29.2
484	Truck transportation	889	13,632	434.9	31,905	1,452.1
4841	General freight trucking	379	8,395	285.4	33,997	906.7
484110	General freight trucking, local	166	2,235	61.0	27,313	234.3
4841101	General freight trucking without storage, local, truckload (tl)	106	951	27.2	28,636	131.5
4841102	General freight trucking without storage, local, less than truckload (ltl)	45	901	23.8	26,446	65.0
48412	General freight trucking, long-distance	213	6,160	224.4	36,422	672.3
484121	General freight trucking, long-distance, truckload (tl)	161	2,681	83.2	31,020	330.6
484122	General freight trucking, long-distance, less than truckload (ltl)	52	3,479	141.2	40,585	341.7
4842	Specialized freight trucking	510	5,237	149.5	28,552	545.4
484210	Used household and office goods moving	104	1,262	29.9	23,666	99.0
4842101	Used household and office goods moving, local, without storage	38	232	4.6	19,914	19.3
4842102	Used household and office goods moving, long-distance	41	509	11.5	22,664	49.7
4842103	Used household and office goods moving, local, with storage	25	521	13.7	26,317	30.0
484220	Specialized freight (except used goods) trucking, local	310	2,784	89.7	32,214	330.4
4842202	Agricultural products trucking without storage, local	51	312	6.8	21,676	24.1
4842203	Dump trucking	160	1,078	31.3	29,034	173.9
4842204	Specialized trucking without storage, local	84	1,170	45.4	38,773	116.0
484230	Specialized freight (except used goods) trucking, long-distance	96	1,191	30.0	25,170	115.9
4842302	Agricultural products trucking, long-distance	35	214	5.2	24,322	21.9
4842303	Other specialized trucking, long-distance	54	955	24.3	25,436	88.0
4853	Taxi and limousine service	29	214	3.0	13,879	9.8
485320	Limousine service	23	155	2.3	14,961	7.8
4854101	School bus service	15	1,368	18.8	13,760	44.1
485510	Charter bus industry	26	342	6.4	18,582	19.3
4855101	Charter bus service, local	13	97	1.5	15,629	5.9
4855102	Charter bus service, interstate/interurban	13	245	4.8	19,751	13.5
48599	Other transit and ground passenger transportation	25	409	5.0	12,210	11.1
485991	Special needs transportation	19	399	4.8	12,103	10.5
488	Support activities for transportation	205	1,851	41.3	22,293	146.7
4881	Support activities for air transportation	44	386	8.8	22,697	34.2
48811	Airport operations	16	209	5.0	23,842	22.0
488190	Other support activities for air transportation	28	177	3.8	21,345	12.3
488410	Motor vehicle towing	100	715	13.6	19,015	41.3
488510	Freight transportation arrangement	41	375	10.3	27,557	40.5
4885102	Arrangement of transportation of freight and cargo	31	283	8.1	28,608	32.9
492	Couriers and messengers	70	9,703	209.7	21,616	589.5
492110	Couriers	35	9,326	203.4	21,814	573.4
492210	Local messengers and local delivery	35	377	6.3	16,732	16.1
4931	Warehousing and storage	46	1,317	37.5	28,484	118.4
4931101	General warehousing and storage (except in foreign trade zones)	26	917	24.2	26,346	70.8
493190	Other warehousing and storage	11	168	3.5	20,857	17.3

Sources: Economic Census of the United States, 1997. Only those industries are shown for which both employment and sales/revenue data were available. For the definition of MSAs, CMSAs, and PMSAs, please see the Introduction.

ROANOKE, VA MSA

NAICS	Industry	Estab-lish-ments	Em-ploy-ment	Payroll		Sales, reven. ($ mil.)
				Total ($ mil.)	Per Empl. ($)	
48-49	Transportation and warehousing	159	2,616	69.0	26,388	211.3
484	Truck transportation	100	1,837	53.7	29,236	149.1
4841	General freight trucking	54	1,287	38.3	29,757	104.5
484110	General freight trucking, local	16	202	5.8	28,550	17.1
48412	General freight trucking, long-distance	38	1,085	32.5	29,982	87.4
484121	General freight trucking, long-distance, truckload (tl)	22	414	8.7	21,027	28.3
484122	General freight trucking, long-distance, less than truckload (ltl)	16	671	23.8	35,507	59.1
4842	Specialized freight trucking	46	550	15.4	28,018	44.6
484210	Used household and office goods moving	16	265	6.2	23,464	18.9
484220	Specialized freight (except used goods) trucking, local	23	176	5.8	33,063	16.6
4842203	Dump trucking	12	52	1.2	23,423	3.0
488	Support activities for transportation	19	194	4.0	20,541	13.9
492	Couriers and messengers	22	356	7.8	21,935	32.2
492110	Couriers	15	247	6.0	24,344	28.2

Sources: Economic Census of the United States, 1997. Only those industries are shown for which both employment and sales/revenue data were available. For the definition of MSAs, CMSAs, and PMSAs, please see the Introduction.

ROCHESTER, MN MSA

NAICS	Industry	Estab-lish-ments	Em-ploy-ment	Payroll Total ($ mil.)	Payroll Per Empl. ($)	Sales, reven. ($ mil.)
48-49	Transportation and warehousing	91	1,600	36.6	22,863	129.5
484	Truck transportation	52	701	22.9	32,686	93.5
4841	General freight trucking	24	421	14.2	33,741	53.7
48412	General freight trucking, long-distance	17	293	11.0	37,631	47.6
484121	General freight trucking, long-distance, truckload (tl)	13	247	9.2	37,352	40.6
4842	Specialized freight trucking	28	280	8.7	31,100	39.8
484220	Specialized freight (except used goods) trucking, local	14	35	1.0	27,914	4.4
485	Transit and ground passenger transportation	18	599	7.0	11,715	16.5
488	Support activities for transportation	10	114	2.2	19,614	9.1
492	Couriers and messengers	6	117	2.8	23,521	6.3

Sources: *Economic Census of the United States*, 1997. Only those industries are shown for which both employment and sales/revenue data were available. For the definition of MSAs, CMSAs, and PMSAs, please see the Introduction.

ROCHESTER, NY MSA

NAICS	Industry	Estab-lish-ments	Em-ploy-ment	Payroll Total ($ mil.)	Payroll Per Empl. ($)	Sales, reven. ($ mil.)
48-49	Transportation and warehousing	434	6,473	158.0	24,409	488.6
481	Air transportation	5	18	0.5	29,778	3.9
484	Truck transportation	258	2,359	71.4	30,269	261.8
4841	General freight trucking	94	1,429	46.7	32,684	160.1
484110	General freight trucking, local	41	337	8.0	23,760	22.1
4841101	General freight trucking without storage, local, truckload (tl)	21	189	4.3	22,556	13.7
48412	General freight trucking, long-distance	53	1,092	38.7	35,439	138.0
484121	General freight trucking, long-distance, truckload (tl)	35	645	20.1	31,124	79.8
484122	General freight trucking, long-distance, less than truckload (ltl)	18	447	18.6	41,664	58.2
4842	Specialized freight trucking	164	930	24.7	26,558	101.7
484210	Used household and office goods moving	23	329	8.4	25,502	26.4
4842102	Used household and office goods moving, long-distance	12	272	7.2	26,471	23.2
484220	Specialized freight (except used goods) trucking, local	104	359	9.2	25,638	35.1
4842202	Agricultural products trucking without storage, local	11	40	1.1	26,575	4.4
4842203	Dump trucking	62	188	5.1	27,048	22.0
4842204	Specialized trucking without storage, local	19	79	1.8	23,266	5.1
484230	Specialized freight (except used goods) trucking, long-distance	37	242	7.1	29,360	40.2
4842302	Agricultural products trucking, long-distance	12	80	1.8	22,788	9.1
4842303	Other specialized trucking, long-distance	20	144	4.6	32,062	28.4
485	Transit and ground passenger transportation	47	2,413	42.5	17,623	67.6
4854101	School bus service	16	1,303	12.7	9,723	29.0
48599	Other transit and ground passenger transportation	15	398	7.0	17,678	10.5
486	Pipeline transportation	5	28	1.4	49,750	8.6
487	Scenic and sightseeing transportation	6	4	0.2	50,500	0.9
488	Support activities for transportation	51	695	17.0	24,388	43.2
4881	Support activities for air transportation	14	190	2.2	11,521	5.5
488510	Freight transportation arrangement	22	233	9.6	41,219	27.5
4885101	Freight forwarding	12	120	5.3	43,900	18.1
492	Couriers and messengers	30	735	18.8	25,544	78.0
492110	Couriers	14	462	13.8	29,786	66.3
492210	Local messengers and local delivery	16	273	5.0	18,366	11.7
4931	Warehousing and storage	32	221	6.2	28,127	24.6
4931101	General warehousing and storage (except in foreign trade zones)	13	60	1.6	25,933	6.2
4931201	Refrigerated products warehousing	14	119	3.3	27,378	14.3

Sources: *Economic Census of the United States*, 1997. Only those industries are shown for which both employment and sales/revenue data were available. For the definition of MSAs, CMSAs, and PMSAs, please see the Introduction.

ROCKFORD, IL MSA

NAICS	Industry	Estab-lish-ments	Em-ploy-ment	Payroll		Sales, reven. ($ mil.)
				Total ($ mil.)	Per Empl. ($)	
48-49	Transportation and warehousing	232	3,384	109.6	32,390	633.3
481	Air transportation	4	47	1.3	28,255	5.7
484	Truck transportation	162	1,926	69.8	36,229	455.8
4841	General freight trucking	93	1,545	55.6	35,959	393.6
484110	General freight trucking, local	36	199	4.6	23,251	15.1
4841101	General freight trucking without storage, local, truckload (tl)	22	122	3.2	26,172	11.0
48412	General freight trucking, long-distance	57	1,346	50.9	37,837	378.5
484121	General freight trucking, long-distance, truckload (tl)	40	760	25.3	33,224	296.7
484122	General freight trucking, long-distance, less than truckload (ltl)	17	586	25.7	43,821	81.7
4842	Specialized freight trucking	69	381	14.2	37,328	62.3
484220	Specialized freight (except used goods) trucking, local	43	95	2.2	22,695	17.7
4842203	Dump trucking	22	47	1.2	24,745	12.9
484230	Specialized freight (except used goods) trucking, long-distance	21	237	11.2	47,190	42.1
485	Transit and ground passenger transportation	18	348	3.7	10,724	10.2
4853	Taxi and limousine service	11	53	0.3	5,811	0.9
486	Pipeline transportation	4	10	0.3	34,600	11.3
488	Support activities for transportation	26	534	20.5	38,358	92.1
492	Couriers and messengers	11	193	4.4	22,984	22.4
493	Warehousing and storage	7	326	9.5	29,153	35.8

Sources: *Economic Census of the United States*, 1997. Only those industries are shown for which both employment and sales/revenue data were available. For the definition of MSAs, CMSAs, and PMSAs, please see the Introduction.

ROCKY MOUNT, NC MSA

NAICS	Industry	Estab-lish-ments	Em-ploy-ment	Payroll		Sales, reven. ($ mil.)
				Total ($ mil.)	Per Empl. ($)	
48-49	Transportation and warehousing	86	947	22.0	23,195	76.8
484	Truck transportation	59	549	15.9	28,967	54.5
4841	General freight trucking	24	419	13.3	31,711	39.6
48412	General freight trucking, long-distance	18	397	12.6	31,804	38.0
484121	General freight trucking, long-distance, truckload (tl)	14	297	8.9	29,798	23.5
4842	Specialized freight trucking	35	130	2.6	20,123	15.0
484220	Specialized freight (except used goods) trucking, local	19	60	1.2	19,750	5.4
4842203	Dump trucking	12	44	0.8	17,114	3.3
484230	Specialized freight (except used goods) trucking, long-distance	11	58	1.2	20,103	8.9
485	Transit and ground passenger transportation	7	53	0.4	7,226	1.4
488	Support activities for transportation	11	91	2.4	26,187	9.4
493	Warehousing and storage	5	96	2.1	22,094	7.8

Sources: *Economic Census of the United States*, 1997. Only those industries are shown for which both employment and sales/revenue data were available. For the definition of MSAs, CMSAs, and PMSAs, please see the Introduction.

SACRAMENTO, CA PMSA

NAICS	Industry	Estab-lish-ments	Em-ploy-ment	Payroll		Sales, reven. ($ mil.)
				Total ($ mil.)	Per Empl. ($)	
48-49	Transportation and warehousing	551	12,723	331.4	26,051	949.8
484	Truck transportation	292	4,106	119.3	29,048	396.2
4841	General freight trucking	115	2,865	91.9	32,077	263.5
484110	General freight trucking, local	50	366	9.3	25,273	27.3
4841101	General freight trucking without storage, local, truckload (tl)	35	272	7.4	27,338	20.7
4841102	General freight trucking without storage, local, less than truckload (ltl)	11	77	1.1	14,247	4.5
48412	General freight trucking, long-distance	65	2,499	82.6	33,073	236.2
484121	General freight trucking, long-distance, truckload (tl)	39	1,137	34.3	30,168	109.5
484122	General freight trucking, long-distance, less than truckload (ltl)	26	1,362	48.3	35,499	126.7
4842	Specialized freight trucking	177	1,241	27.4	22,055	132.7
484210	Used household and office goods moving	53	580	10.8	18,700	40.1
4842101	Used household and office goods moving, local, without storage	23	129	2.3	17,922	9.6
4842102	Used household and office goods moving, long-distance	12	253	4.4	17,530	15.7
4842103	Used household and office goods moving, local, with storage	18	198	4.1	20,702	14.9
484220	Specialized freight (except used goods) trucking, local	101	558	14.2	25,536	82.0
4842202	Agricultural products trucking without storage, local	12	18	0.9	48,167	6.1
4842203	Dump trucking	61	370	8.6	23,332	60.4
4842204	Specialized trucking without storage, local	24	108	2.8	25,796	9.3
484230	Specialized freight (except used goods) trucking, long-distance	23	103	2.3	22,087	10.5
4842303	Other specialized trucking, long-distance	13	89	1.9	21,270	6.7
4853	Taxi and limousine service	18	141	1.9	13,135	5.6
485320	Limousine service	11	76	1.0	12,763	3.1
485510	Charter bus industry	11	260	5.4	20,808	15.5
48599	Other transit and ground passenger transportation	14	291	4.3	14,670	10.3
488	Support activities for transportation	103	888	19.1	21,514	61.9
4881	Support activities for air transportation	24	299	5.6	18,813	20.3
488190	Other support activities for air transportation	15	163	3.7	22,804	15.9
488410	Motor vehicle towing	48	431	10.1	23,427	27.6
488510	Freight transportation arrangement	22	94	2.2	23,883	10.3
4885102	Arrangement of transportation of freight and cargo	15	63	1.7	26,381	8.4
492	Couriers and messengers	65	6,124	160.1	26,144	385.8
492110	Couriers	38	5,620	151.7	26,998	366.0
4921101	Courier services (except by air)	14	4,550	123.5	27,140	251.1
4921102	Air courier services	24	1,070	28.2	26,396	114.9
492210	Local messengers and local delivery	27	504	8.4	16,615	19.7
4931	Warehousing and storage	20	411	9.6	23,389	33.6
4931101	General warehousing and storage (except in foreign trade zones)	13	62	1.3	20,516	3.4

Sources: Economic Census of the United States, 1997. Only those industries are shown for which both employment and sales/revenue data were available. For the definition of MSAs, CMSAs, and PMSAs, please see the Introduction.

SACRAMENTO—YOLO, CA CMSA

NAICS	Industry	Estab-lish-ments	Em-ploy-ment	Payroll		Sales, reven. ($ mil.)
				Total ($ mil.)	Per Empl. ($)	
48-49	Transportation and warehousing	707	15,612	422.3	27,050	1,227.7
484	Truck transportation	396	6,254	190.5	30,457	600.5
4841	General freight trucking	159	4,484	144.3	32,178	398.2
484110	General freight trucking, local	69	991	24.8	24,994	57.0
4841102	General freight trucking without storage, local, less than truckload (ltl)	17	609	14.4	23,583	24.0
48412	General freight trucking, long-distance	90	3,493	119.5	34,216	341.2
484121	General freight trucking, long-distance, truckload (tl)	53	1,569	47.9	30,515	160.8
484122	General freight trucking, long-distance, less than truckload (ltl)	37	1,924	71.6	37,233	180.3
4842	Specialized freight trucking	237	1,770	46.2	26,098	202.3
4842102	Used household and office goods moving, long-distance	12	253	4.4	17,530	15.7
484220	Specialized freight (except used goods) trucking, local	135	815	23.7	29,103	114.6
4842202	Agricultural products trucking without storage, local	30	60	2.8	46,983	11.4
4842203	Dump trucking	70	442	10.7	24,183	72.9
485320	Limousine service	11	76	1.0	12,763	3.1
485510	Charter bus industry	11	260	5.4	20,808	15.5
488	Support activities for transportation	130	1,239	30.4	24,565	108.6
488410	Motor vehicle towing	59	522	12.3	23,563	34.3
488510	Freight transportation arrangement	30	256	8.6	33,590	31.7
4885101	Freight forwarding	11	166	6.2	37,199	18.9
4885102	Arrangement of transportation of freight and cargo	19	90	2.4	26,933	12.8
492	Couriers and messengers	74	6,263	162.6	25,961	393.4
492110	Couriers	41	5,669	152.8	26,945	369.9
4921101	Courier services (except by air)	17	4,599	124.5	27,073	255.0
4921102	Air courier services	24	1,070	28.2	26,396	114.9
492210	Local messengers and local delivery	33	594	9.8	16,567	23.5
4931	Warehousing and storage	30	600	14.7	24,548	50.5

Sources: Economic Census of the United States, 1997. Only those industries are shown for which both employment and sales/revenue data were available. For the definition of MSAs, CMSAs, and PMSAs, please see the Introduction.

SAGINAW—BAY CITY—MIDLAND, MI MSA

NAICS	Industry	Estab-lish-ments	Em-ploy-ment	Payroll		Sales, reven. ($ mil.)
				Total ($ mil.)	Per Empl. ($)	
48-49	Transportation and warehousing	199	2,310	71.1	30,781	290.1
484	Truck transportation	131	1,636	55.5	33,950	200.0
4841	General freight trucking	61	710	22.9	32,313	96.1
484110	General freight trucking, local	17	65	1.1	17,308	5.1
4841101	General freight trucking without storage, local, truckload (tl)	14	52	1.0	18,404	4.8
48412	General freight trucking, long-distance	44	645	21.8	33,825	91.0
484121	General freight trucking, long-distance, truckload (tl)	33	429	11.8	27,552	60.2
484122	General freight trucking, long-distance, less than truckload (ltl)	11	216	10.0	46,282	30.8
4842	Specialized freight trucking	70	926	32.6	35,205	103.9
484220	Specialized freight (except used goods) trucking, local	45	550	14.2	25,749	52.8
4842203	Dump trucking	26	428	12.4	29,000	43.1
4842204	Specialized trucking without storage, local	14	56	0.9	15,750	3.5
484230	Specialized freight (except used goods) trucking, long-distance	15	222	12.7	57,090	37.5
488	Support activities for transportation	24	138	3.3	24,109	14.2
488410	Motor vehicle towing	13	87	1.7	20,011	4.8
492	Couriers and messengers	17	337	6.6	19,620	23.2
492110	Couriers	11	277	5.2	18,939	21.2

Sources: *Economic Census of the United States*, 1997. Only those industries are shown for which both employment and sales/revenue data were available. For the definition of MSAs, CMSAs, and PMSAs, please see the Introduction.

SALEM, OR PMSA

NAICS	Industry	Estab-lish-ments	Em-ploy-ment	Payroll		Sales, reven. ($ mil.)
				Total ($ mil.)	Per Empl. ($)	
48-49	Transportation and warehousing	191	2,540	78.2	30,798	262.3
484	Truck transportation	122	921	27.6	29,990	95.7
4841	General freight trucking	46	326	9.4	28,859	38.8
484110	General freight trucking, local	12	86	2.5	29,535	10.3
48412	General freight trucking, long-distance	34	240	6.9	28,617	28.5
484121	General freight trucking, long-distance, truckload (tl)	27	180	4.0	22,433	15.2
4842	Specialized freight trucking	76	595	18.2	30,610	56.8
484220	Specialized freight (except used goods) trucking, local	54	198	5.9	29,657	18.7
4842202	Agricultural products trucking without storage, local	17	86	2.4	27,953	7.0
4842203	Dump trucking	29	86	2.8	32,314	9.2
484230	Specialized freight (except used goods) trucking, long-distance	16	337	11.0	32,496	34.8
488	Support activities for transportation	26	117	2.8	23,684	14.4
493	Warehousing and storage	8	132	4.2	31,985	20.9

Sources: *Economic Census of the United States*, 1997. Only those industries are shown for which both employment and sales/revenue data were available. For the definition of MSAs, CMSAs, and PMSAs, please see the Introduction.

SALINAS, CA MSA

NAICS	Industry	Estab-lish-ments	Em-ploy-ment	Payroll		Sales, reven. ($ mil.)
				Total ($ mil.)	Per Empl. ($)	
48-49	Transportation and warehousing	205	2,062	59.6	28,882	220.1
484	Truck transportation	114	1,071	30.0	28,042	127.8
4841	General freight trucking	28	268	10.1	37,675	45.5
484110	General freight trucking, local	19	162	5.6	34,352	23.0
4841101	General freight trucking without storage, local, truckload (tl)	14	120	3.8	32,058	16.1
4842	Specialized freight trucking	86	803	19.9	24,827	82.3
484210	Used household and office goods moving	20	323	6.7	20,796	17.3
484220	Specialized freight (except used goods) trucking, local	49	272	7.7	28,294	40.2
4842202	Agricultural products trucking without storage, local	21	108	2.7	25,370	12.0
4842203	Dump trucking	18	112	3.5	31,491	24.2
484230	Specialized freight (except used goods) trucking, long-distance	17	208	5.5	26,553	24.9
4842302	Agricultural products trucking, long-distance	13	140	4.3	30,764	18.3
485	Transit and ground passenger transportation	14	231	4.7	20,277	11.2
488	Support activities for transportation	43	340	11.7	34,524	34.3
488410	Motor vehicle towing	11	67	1.9	27,791	5.8
488510	Freight transportation arrangement	18	203	6.8	33,714	18.9
4931	Warehousing and storage	16	236	8.5	35,975	31.1

Sources: *Economic Census of the United States*, 1997. Only those industries are shown for which both employment and sales/revenue data were available. For the definition of MSAs, CMSAs, and PMSAs, please see the Introduction.

SALT LAKE CITY—OGDEN, UT MSA

NAICS	Industry	Estab-lish-ments	Em-ploy-ment	Payroll Total ($ mil.)	Payroll Per Empl. ($)	Sales, reven. ($ mil.)
48-49	Transportation and warehousing	696	23,819	661.0	27,750	2,304.8
484	Truck transportation	433	14,882	430.1	28,898	1,393.0
4841	General freight trucking	239	12,548	365.6	29,136	1,142.4
484110	General freight trucking, local	61	780	19.9	25,453	61.4
4841101	General freight trucking without storage, local, truckload (tl)	44	392	9.6	24,571	38.6
48412	General freight trucking, long-distance	178	11,768	345.8	29,381	1,081.0
484121	General freight trucking, long-distance, truckload (tl)	142	9,059	253.9	28,031	861.7
484122	General freight trucking, long-distance, less than truckload (ltl)	36	2,709	91.8	33,893	219.3
4842	Specialized freight trucking	194	2,334	64.5	27,617	250.6
484210	Used household and office goods moving	28	629	13.5	21,437	39.3
4842102	Used household and office goods moving, long-distance	14	398	8.2	20,593	26.1
484220	Specialized freight (except used goods) trucking, local	114	622	18.6	29,947	73.5
4842203	Dump trucking	75	389	13.9	35,645	55.5
4842204	Specialized trucking without storage, local	22	114	2.8	24,912	11.4
484230	Specialized freight (except used goods) trucking, long-distance	52	1,083	32.3	29,869	137.8
4842301	Hazardous materials trucking (except waste), long-distance	18	207	6.0	29,193	26.8
4842303	Other specialized trucking, long-distance	28	798	23.8	29,767	97.7
485	Transit and ground passenger transportation	26	533	8.2	15,370	23.7
488	Support activities for transportation	134	1,725	32.0	18,546	94.9
4881	Support activities for air transportation	23	923	13.3	14,377	37.0
4881191	Airport operation and terminal services	13	865	11.8	13,681	31.1
488410	Motor vehicle towing	24	142	2.7	19,176	8.8
488510	Freight transportation arrangement	70	408	12.8	31,299	41.0
492	Couriers and messengers	47	5,047	135.6	26,870	334.3
4931	Warehousing and storage	30	228	6.4	28,263	28.8

Sources: *Economic Census of the United States*, 1997. Only those industries are shown for which both employment and sales/revenue data were available. For the definition of MSAs, CMSAs, and PMSAs, please see the Introduction.

SAN ANGELO, TX MSA

NAICS	Industry	Estab-lish-ments	Em-ploy-ment	Payroll Total ($ mil.)	Payroll Per Empl. ($)	Sales, reven. ($ mil.)
48-49	Transportation and warehousing	53	386	7.6	19,707	31.8
484	Truck transportation	29	195	3.1	15,985	11.9
4841	General freight trucking	11	66	1.0	15,197	3.7
4842	Specialized freight trucking	18	129	2.1	16,388	8.2
488	Support activities for transportation	8	64	1.6	24,328	4.3

Sources: *Economic Census of the United States*, 1997. Only those industries are shown for which both employment and sales/revenue data were available. For the definition of MSAs, CMSAs, and PMSAs, please see the Introduction.

SAN ANTONIO, TX MSA

NAICS	Industry	Estab-lish-ments	Em-ploy-ment	Payroll Total ($ mil.)	Payroll Per Empl. ($)	Sales, reven. ($ mil.)
48-49	Transportation and warehousing	774	15,123	394.4	26,083	1,132.2
484	Truck transportation	486	5,568	144.1	25,888	507.1
4841	General freight trucking	258	3,168	88.0	27,764	299.9
484110	General freight trucking, local	73	806	16.5	20,413	56.8
4841101	General freight trucking without storage, local, truckload (tl)	54	345	7.3	21,278	34.3
4841102	General freight trucking without storage, local, less than truckload (ltl)	15	399	7.7	19,223	18.0
48412	General freight trucking, long-distance	185	2,362	71.5	30,272	243.1
484121	General freight trucking, long-distance, truckload (tl)	156	1,727	48.8	28,277	171.0
484122	General freight trucking, long-distance, less than truckload (ltl)	29	635	22.7	35,698	72.1
4842	Specialized freight trucking	228	2,400	56.2	23,413	207.2
484210	Used household and office goods moving	59	778	14.3	18,395	47.6
4842101	Used household and office goods moving, local, without storage	22	184	1.9	10,386	4.3
4842102	Used household and office goods moving, long-distance	22	387	8.2	21,297	31.5
4842103	Used household and office goods moving, local, with storage	15	207	4.2	20,087	11.8
484220	Specialized freight (except used goods) trucking, local	129	680	15.1	22,218	82.4
4842203	Dump trucking	94	466	11.3	24,313	68.3
4842204	Specialized trucking without storage, local	22	173	3.0	17,272	10.7
484230	Specialized freight (except used goods) trucking, long-distance	40	942	26.8	28,420	77.3
4842303	Other specialized trucking, long-distance	20	343	7.7	22,475	28.5
485	Transit and ground passenger transportation	44	2,478	57.9	23,352	63.3
4853	Taxi and limousine service	18	242	2.6	10,661	9.3
488	Support activities for transportation	135	1,779	49.6	27,902	156.5
4881	Support activities for air transportation	42	1,203	32.9	27,326	102.4
48811	Airport operations	11	658	16.0	24,356	44.6
488190	Other support activities for air transportation	31	545	16.8	30,912	57.9
488410	Motor vehicle towing	32	121	2.5	20,620	7.9
488510	Freight transportation arrangement	48	318	11.9	37,513	41.3
4885101	Freight forwarding	15	104	2.7	26,298	15.6
4885102	Arrangement of transportation of freight and cargo	33	214	9.2	42,963	25.7
492	Couriers and messengers	69	4,660	128.4	27,543	301.7
492110	Couriers	28	4,363	121.2	27,778	281.6
492210	Local messengers and local delivery	41	297	7.2	24,091	20.1
4931	Warehousing and storage	25	211	3.3	15,706	11.0
4931101	General warehousing and storage (except in foreign trade zones)	17	52	0.7	12,827	3.2

Sources: Economic Census of the United States, 1997. Only those industries are shown for which both employment and sales/revenue data were available. For the definition of MSAs, CMSAs, and PMSAs, please see the Introduction.

SAN DIEGO, CA MSA

NAICS	Industry	Estab-lish-ments	Em-ploy-ment	Payroll		Sales, reven. ($ mil.)
				Total ($ mil.)	Per Empl. ($)	
48-49	Transportation and warehousing	1,060	14,863	355.2	23,901	1,323.4
481	Air transportation	37	386	9.2	23,839	62.0
48111	Scheduled air transportation	15	280	6.3	22,600	47.8
48121	Nonscheduled air transportation	22	106	2.9	27,113	14.2
481211	Nonscheduled chartered passenger air transportation	16	89	2.6	29,416	11.4
484	Truck transportation	457	4,520	120.2	26,593	530.6
4841	General freight trucking	164	1,751	47.7	27,268	205.2
484110	General freight trucking, local	88	793	16.2	20,446	57.7
4841101	General freight trucking without storage, local, truckload (tl)	60	466	8.4	18,112	34.9
48412	General freight trucking, long-distance	76	958	31.5	32,915	147.5
484121	General freight trucking, long-distance, truckload (tl)	42	343	9.2	26,758	43.1
484122	General freight trucking, long-distance, less than truckload (ltl)	34	615	22.4	36,350	104.4
4842	Specialized freight trucking	293	2,769	72.5	26,166	325.3
484210	Used household and office goods moving	132	1,466	36.5	24,909	139.7
4842101	Used household and office goods moving, local, without storage	55	320	5.3	16,416	14.6
4842102	Used household and office goods moving, long-distance	42	666	17.6	26,381	75.0
4842103	Used household and office goods moving, local, with storage	35	480	13.7	28,527	50.0
484220	Specialized freight (except used goods) trucking, local	126	1,000	25.2	25,248	129.5
4842203	Dump trucking	68	520	15.0	28,769	93.2
4842204	Specialized trucking without storage, local	40	385	7.5	19,540	23.1
484230	Specialized freight (except used goods) trucking, long-distance	35	303	10.7	35,284	56.2
4842303	Other specialized trucking, long-distance	22	190	5.9	31,295	35.2
485	Transit and ground passenger transportation	85	3,800	84.1	22,122	128.8
4853	Taxi and limousine service	33	736	8.7	11,842	22.8
485310	Taxi service	11	262	4.3	16,473	8.8
485320	Limousine service	22	474	4.4	9,283	13.9
485510	Charter bus industry	12	289	4.8	16,626	14.8
48599	Other transit and ground passenger transportation	22	319	4.2	13,016	9.6
485999	All other transit and ground passenger transportation	14	123	1.0	8,293	3.1
487210	Scenic and sightseeing transportation, water	51	431	6.6	15,329	36.9
4872102	Charter fishing and party fishing boats	44	329	5.3	15,979	30.8
488	Support activities for transportation	296	3,338	82.8	24,809	245.3
4881	Support activities for air transportation	46	1,021	21.6	21,164	53.4
4881191	Airport operation and terminal services	20	837	14.7	17,597	30.2
488190	Other support activities for air transportation	26	184	6.9	37,386	23.2
4883	Support activities for water transportation	18	240	5.8	24,375	16.4
488410	Motor vehicle towing	77	828	19.1	23,079	48.7
488510	Freight transportation arrangement	147	1,191	34.9	29,321	122.0
4885101	Freight forwarding	77	552	19.7	35,605	72.7
4885102	Arrangement of transportation of freight and cargo	70	639	15.3	23,892	49.3
492	Couriers and messengers	87	2,043	44.0	21,527	217.3
492110	Couriers	43	1,289	31.8	24,652	185.7
4921101	Courier services (except by air)	19	377	6.1	16,117	25.1
4921102	Air courier services	24	912	25.7	28,181	160.6
492210	Local messengers and local delivery	44	754	12.2	16,183	31.6
4931	Warehousing and storage	32	206	5.0	24,155	18.1
493110	General warehousing and storage	22	134	3.7	27,978	12.0

Sources: *Economic Census of the United States*, 1997. Only those industries are shown for which both employment and sales/revenue data were available. For the definition of MSAs, CMSAs, and PMSAs, please see the Introduction.

SAN FRANCISCO, CA PMSA

NAICS	Industry	Estab-lish-ments	Em-ploy-ment	Payroll		Sales, reven. ($ mil.)
				Total ($ mil.)	Per Empl. ($)	
48-49	Transportation and warehousing	1,222	28,227	910.6	32,260	3,634.5
481	Air transportation	58	814	32.1	39,378	480.6
48111	Scheduled air transportation	48	775	30.1	38,775	473.0
48311	Deep sea, coastal, and Great Lakes water transportation	13	1,497	89.3	59,664	848.2
484	Truck transportation	321	4,243	110.3	26,001	349.0
4841	General freight trucking	108	2,026	56.0	27,658	169.1
484110	General freight trucking, local	82	844	22.2	26,344	60.8
4841101	General freight trucking without storage, local, truckload (tl)	35	497	10.4	20,988	33.0
4841102	General freight trucking without storage, local, less than truckload (ltl)	41	271	8.7	32,207	20.4
48412	General freight trucking, long-distance	26	1,182	33.8	28,596	108.3
484121	General freight trucking, long-distance, truckload (tl)	17	921	24.5	26,578	72.3
4842	Specialized freight trucking	213	2,217	54.3	24,487	179.9
484210	Used household and office goods moving	89	1,207	27.2	22,546	77.5
4842101	Used household and office goods moving, local, without storage	41	390	8.3	21,372	23.0
4842103	Used household and office goods moving, local, with storage	39	565	13.7	24,161	39.7
484220	Specialized freight (except used goods) trucking, local	100	757	18.4	24,255	77.0
4842203	Dump trucking	47	250	7.2	28,932	44.0
4842204	Specialized trucking without storage, local	38	271	6.6	24,376	19.7
484230	Specialized freight (except used goods) trucking, long-distance	24	253	8.7	34,439	25.4
4842303	Other specialized trucking, long-distance	15	175	5.7	32,537	19.4
485	Transit and ground passenger transportation	130	2,999	57.3	19,096	175.1
4853	Taxi and limousine service	77	975	16.6	16,978	76.2
485310	Taxi service	26	375	6.6	17,640	36.7
485320	Limousine service	51	600	9.9	16,565	39.5
485510	Charter bus industry	20	419	8.2	19,604	23.9
4855101	Charter bus service, local	15	377	7.4	19,660	20.8
48599	Other transit and ground passenger transportation	26	1,021	18.4	17,996	43.3
485999	All other transit and ground passenger transportation	16	836	15.2	18,200	35.9
488	Support activities for transportation	474	7,647	289.8	37,892	933.4
4881	Support activities for air transportation	23	1,288	26.7	20,740	55.7
4883	Support activities for water transportation	21	1,035	64.4	62,265	286.6
488410	Motor vehicle towing	48	568	10.6	18,676	33.6
488510	Freight transportation arrangement	371	4,643	185.1	39,865	545.8
4885101	Freight forwarding	234	3,068	121.1	39,458	373.0
4885102	Arrangement of transportation of freight and cargo	137	1,575	64.0	40,658	172.8
492	Couriers and messengers	140	9,411	283.4	30,112	708.4
492110	Couriers	82	7,716	250.3	32,439	647.4
4921101	Courier services (except by air)	25	5,142	158.6	30,843	304.8
4921102	Air courier services	57	2,574	91.7	35,627	342.7
492210	Local messengers and local delivery	58	1,695	33.1	19,515	60.9
4931	Warehousing and storage	30	313	9.3	29,767	28.4
4931101	General warehousing and storage (except in foreign trade zones)	19	160	3.9	24,425	12.8

Sources: *Economic Census of the United States*, 1997. Only those industries are shown for which both employment and sales/revenue data were available. For the definition of MSAs, CMSAs, and PMSAs, please see the Introduction.

SAN FRANCISCO—OAKLAND—SAN JOSE, CA CMSA

NAICS	Industry	Estab-lish-ments	Em-ploy-ment	Payroll		Sales, reven. ($ mil.)
				Total ($ mil.)	Per Empl. ($)	
48-49	Transportation and warehousing	3,546	76,078	2,341.6	30,778	8,552.7
48111	Scheduled air transportation	58	1,014	35.2	34,699	499.5
484	Truck transportation	1,611	21,735	656.8	30,217	2,401.3
4841	General freight trucking	572	11,107	350.5	31,555	1,189.6
484110	General freight trucking, local	338	4,374	126.9	29,012	401.9
48412	General freight trucking, long-distance	234	6,733	223.6	33,207	787.7
4842	Specialized freight trucking	1,039	10,628	306.3	28,819	1,211.6
484210	Used household and office goods moving	321	4,579	120.0	26,210	397.1
4842101	Used household and office goods moving, local, without storage	148	1,119	23.1	20,640	62.9
4842102	Used household and office goods moving, long-distance	67	1,318	32.2	24,450	120.4
4842103	Used household and office goods moving, local, with storage	106	2,142	64.7	30,204	213.8
484220	Specialized freight (except used goods) trucking, local	574	4,237	117.6	27,759	569.8
4842202	Agricultural products trucking without storage, local	42	234	6.8	29,103	32.2
4842203	Dump trucking	313	2,019	57.7	28,573	347.5
4842205	Specialized trucking with storage, local	18	545	10.2	18,657	27.5
484230	Specialized freight (except used goods) trucking, long-distance	144	1,812	68.7	37,892	244.7
4842303	Other specialized trucking, long-distance	74	947	33.5	35,348	103.9
485113	Bus and motor vehicle transit systems	11	630	11.7	18,556	22.0
4853	Taxi and limousine service	158	1,863	29.3	15,732	112.4
485410	School and employee bus transportation	21	1,683	32.0	19,020	70.4
485510	Charter bus industry	45	787	16.2	20,604	48.4
485999	All other transit and ground passenger transportation	38	1,230	20.9	17,007	54.1
4859991	Scheduled airport shuttle service	29	1,195	20.6	17,230	50.4
488	Support activities for transportation	924	14,835	575.1	38,765	1,639.0
4881	Support activities for air transportation	82	2,403	50.3	20,918	121.9
48811	Airport operations	33	1,403	25.8	18,363	59.2
488190	Other support activities for air transportation	49	1,000	24.5	24,504	62.6
488390	Other support activities for water transportation	26	174	7.1	41,057	27.5
488410	Motor vehicle towing	203	1,885	43.4	23,032	124.6
488510	Freight transportation arrangement	511	6,458	258.3	40,004	752.9
4885101	Freight forwarding	309	3,670	140.1	38,166	453.9
4885102	Arrangement of transportation of freight and cargo	202	2,788	118.3	42,424	299.0
48899	Other support activities for transportation	33	395	10.1	25,613	34.4
492	Couriers and messengers	331	23,372	620.8	26,562	1,696.7
492110	Couriers	181	19,234	541.9	28,173	1,531.5
492210	Local messengers and local delivery	150	4,138	78.9	19,071	165.3
4931201	Refrigerated products warehousing	22	495	14.6	29,509	52.9
493190	Other warehousing and storage	41	465	15.9	34,088	64.6
4931902	Specialized goods warehousing and storage	36	434	15.3	35,343	61.8

Sources: *Economic Census of the United States*, 1997. Only those industries are shown for which both employment and sales/revenue data were available. For the definition of MSAs, CMSAs, and PMSAs, please see the Introduction.

SAN JOSE, CA PMSA

NAICS	Industry	Estab-lish-ments	Em-ploy-ment	Payroll Total ($ mil.)	Payroll Per Empl. ($)	Sales, reven. ($ mil.)
48-49	Transportation and warehousing	541	10,395	291.0	27,990	1,096.9
484	Truck transportation	270	4,769	154.1	32,320	572.9
4841	General freight trucking	93	2,711	88.0	32,467	306.8
484110	General freight trucking, local	49	1,136	38.0	33,429	106.7
4841101	General freight trucking without storage, local, truckload (tl)	24	253	8.1	32,091	25.1
4841102	General freight trucking without storage, local, less than truckload (ltl)	18	473	14.3	30,326	37.4
48412	General freight trucking, long-distance	44	1,575	50.0	31,774	200.1
484121	General freight trucking, long-distance, truckload (tl)	26	809	19.1	23,627	73.0
484122	General freight trucking, long-distance, less than truckload (ltl)	18	766	30.9	40,379	127.1
4842	Specialized freight trucking	177	2,058	66.1	32,126	266.0
484210	Used household and office goods moving	51	897	25.4	28,276	76.9
4842101	Used household and office goods moving, local, without storage	21	211	5.0	23,763	11.8
4842102	Used household and office goods moving, long-distance	17	412	13.3	32,369	46.4
4842103	Used household and office goods moving, local, with storage	13	274	7.0	25,599	18.7
484220	Specialized freight (except used goods) trucking, local	105	791	22.6	28,623	118.9
4842203	Dump trucking	71	476	14.3	30,021	98.2
4842204	Specialized trucking without storage, local	24	96	2.6	27,271	7.7
484230	Specialized freight (except used goods) trucking, long-distance	21	370	18.1	48,946	70.2
485	Transit and ground passenger transportation	61	1,232	21.3	17,263	54.2
4853	Taxi and limousine service	36	449	6.9	15,303	20.9
485320	Limousine service	27	353	5.1	14,436	13.7
48599	Other transit and ground passenger transportation	14	304	5.0	16,352	10.6
488	Support activities for transportation	105	1,417	37.5	26,441	111.6
4881	Support activities for air transportation	18	383	8.1	21,031	23.5
488190	Other support activities for air transportation	11	182	5.5	30,385	18.0
488410	Motor vehicle towing	49	460	13.3	28,974	33.2
488510	Freight transportation arrangement	26	230	7.1	30,774	30.7
4885101	Freight forwarding	17	183	6.2	33,607	26.7
492	Couriers and messengers	66	2,429	62.0	25,534	284.1
492110	Couriers	36	1,662	46.3	27,862	249.0
4921101	Courier services (except by air)	13	357	6.1	17,014	16.7
4921102	Air courier services	23	1,305	40.2	30,829	232.2
492210	Local messengers and local delivery	30	767	15.7	20,490	35.2
4931101	General warehousing and storage (except in foreign trade zones)	16	218	5.6	25,757	16.4

Sources: Economic Census of the United States, 1997. Only those industries are shown for which both employment and sales/revenue data were available. For the definition of MSAs, CMSAs, and PMSAs, please see the Introduction.

SAN LUIS OBISPO—ATASCADERO—PASO ROBLES, CA MSA

NAICS	Industry	Estab-lish-ments	Em-ploy-ment	Payroll Total ($ mil.)	Payroll Per Empl. ($)	Sales, reven. ($ mil.)
48-49	Transportation and warehousing	97	973	25.9	26,594	117.0
484	Truck transportation	51	311	9.1	29,395	46.7
4841	General freight trucking	20	142	4.5	31,866	14.8
48412	General freight trucking, long-distance	12	92	3.0	32,185	10.1
4842	Specialized freight trucking	31	169	4.6	27,320	31.9
484220	Specialized freight (except used goods) trucking, local	20	74	1.9	25,486	9.6
4842203	Dump trucking	13	51	1.3	25,098	6.9
486	Pipeline transportation	7	103	4.9	47,689	39.7
488	Support activities for transportation	14	93	1.7	18,538	6.3

Sources: Economic Census of the United States, 1997. Only those industries are shown for which both employment and sales/revenue data were available. For the definition of MSAs, CMSAs, and PMSAs, please see the Introduction.

SANTA BARBARA—SANTA MARIA—LOMPOC, CA MSA

NAICS	Industry	Estab-lish-ments	Em-ploy-ment	Payroll		Sales, reven. ($ mil.)
				Total ($ mil.)	Per Empl. ($)	
48-49	Transportation and warehousing	189	2,594	69.3	26,726	232.3
484	Truck transportation	91	730	15.9	21,810	52.3
4841	General freight trucking	26	151	4.0	26,603	14.6
484110	General freight trucking, local	11	47	0.9	18,404	3.5
48412	General freight trucking, long-distance	15	104	3.2	30,308	11.1
484121	General freight trucking, long-distance, truckload (tl)	11	82	2.3	28,354	8.2
4842	Specialized freight trucking	65	579	11.9	20,560	37.7
484210	Used household and office goods moving	22	213	3.3	15,310	9.5
484220	Specialized freight (except used goods) trucking, local	35	301	6.9	22,887	22.6
4842203	Dump trucking	24	209	5.7	27,129	17.1
485	Transit and ground passenger transportation	17	387	5.7	14,610	10.4
488	Support activities for transportation	26	569	20.2	35,434	36.7
488410	Motor vehicle towing	11	73	1.7	22,863	5.2
492	Couriers and messengers	16	328	7.9	24,131	25.7
492110	Couriers	11	172	5.2	30,203	18.3

Sources: Economic Census of the United States, 1997. Only those industries are shown for which both employment and sales/revenue data were available. For the definition of MSAs, CMSAs, and PMSAs, please see the Introduction.

SANTA CRUZ—WATSONVILLE, CA PMSA

NAICS	Industry	Estab-lish-ments	Em-ploy-ment	Payroll		Sales, reven. ($ mil.)
				Total ($ mil.)	Per Empl. ($)	
48-49	Transportation and warehousing	123	1,507	37.0	24,525	149.1
484	Truck transportation	73	791	20.8	26,281	94.9
4841	General freight trucking	16	296	8.3	28,101	32.4
4842	Specialized freight trucking	57	495	12.5	25,192	62.5
484210	Used household and office goods moving	14	95	1.4	14,726	11.6
484220	Specialized freight (except used goods) trucking, local	30	159	3.8	23,943	21.2
4842203	Dump trucking	12	81	2.2	26,741	15.0
4842204	Specialized trucking without storage, local	13	49	0.6	13,204	3.8
484230	Specialized freight (except used goods) trucking, long-distance	13	241	7.3	30,141	29.7
488410	Motor vehicle towing	13	99	1.9	18,788	5.2
4931201	Refrigerated products warehousing	11	229	5.7	24,690	24.3

Sources: Economic Census of the United States, 1997. Only those industries are shown for which both employment and sales/revenue data were available. For the definition of MSAs, CMSAs, and PMSAs, please see the Introduction.

SANTA FE, NM MSA

NAICS	Industry	Estab-lish-ments	Em-ploy-ment	Payroll		Sales, reven. ($ mil.)
				Total ($ mil.)	Per Empl. ($)	
48-49	Transportation and warehousing	53	364	7.8	21,426	29.5
481	Air transportation	5	16	0.6	38,125	2.9
484	Truck transportation	15	97	1.7	17,938	6.2
4842	Specialized freight trucking	11	83	1.4	17,133	4.7
485	Transit and ground passenger transportation	9	93	1.4	15,108	2.7
488	Support activities for transportation	16	68	1.7	24,574	7.4

Sources: Economic Census of the United States, 1997. Only those industries are shown for which both employment and sales/revenue data were available. For the definition of MSAs, CMSAs, and PMSAs, please see the Introduction.

SANTA ROSA, CA PMSA

NAICS	Industry	Estab-lish-ments	Em-ploy-ment	Payroll		Sales, reven. ($ mil.)
				Total ($ mil.)	Per Empl. ($)	
48-49	Transportation and warehousing	252	2,454	61.2	24,947	222.0
484	Truck transportation	163	1,218	35.1	28,818	155.4
4841	General freight trucking	54	605	19.3	31,853	72.7
484110	General freight trucking, local	29	234	6.5	27,842	23.7
4841101	General freight trucking without storage, local, truckload (tl)	18	90	2.9	32,611	13.3
48412	General freight trucking, long-distance	25	371	12.8	34,383	49.0
484121	General freight trucking, long-distance, truckload (tl)	17	268	8.5	31,578	29.9
4842	Specialized freight trucking	109	613	15.8	25,822	82.6
484210	Used household and office goods moving	19	117	2.7	23,385	8.3
484220	Specialized freight (except used goods) trucking, local	78	453	11.9	26,223	67.0
4842202	Agricultural products trucking without storage, local	11	58	1.6	26,793	5.9
4842203	Dump trucking	51	313	7.6	24,387	47.7
484230	Specialized freight (except used goods) trucking, long-distance	12	43	1.2	28,233	7.4
485	Transit and ground passenger transportation	27	609	11.4	18,755	28.3
48599	Other transit and ground passenger transportation	11	167	2.8	16,778	7.9
488410	Motor vehicle towing	15	98	1.9	19,388	6.0
492	Couriers and messengers	14	227	5.4	23,634	12.6
4931	Warehousing and storage	13	55	1.2	22,091	4.3

Sources: Economic Census of the United States, 1997. Only those industries are shown for which both employment and sales/revenue data were available. For the definition of MSAs, CMSAs, and PMSAs, please see the Introduction.

SARASOTA—BRADENTON, FL MSA

NAICS	Industry	Estab-lish-ments	Em-ploy-ment	Payroll		Sales, reven. ($ mil.)
				Total ($ mil.)	Per Empl. ($)	
48-49	Transportation and warehousing	201	1,408	34.1	24,241	149.3
484	Truck transportation	101	746	18.0	24,111	66.4
4841	General freight trucking	36	271	6.9	25,494	27.3
484110	General freight trucking, local	13	25	0.5	21,880	4.0
48412	General freight trucking, long-distance	23	246	6.4	25,862	23.2
4842	Specialized freight trucking	65	475	11.1	23,322	39.1
484210	Used household and office goods moving	22	213	5.1	24,000	14.4
484220	Specialized freight (except used goods) trucking, local	26	163	3.3	20,135	13.5
4842203	Dump trucking	16	112	2.5	21,893	11.4
484230	Specialized freight (except used goods) trucking, long-distance	17	99	2.7	27,111	11.1
485	Transit and ground passenger transportation	22	54	0.8	14,426	3.0
4853	Taxi and limousine service	11	22	0.4	17,273	1.8
488	Support activities for transportation	41	268	5.4	19,993	20.4
488410	Motor vehicle towing	16	67	1.4	20,224	4.1
492	Couriers and messengers	12	163	4.3	26,663	13.8

Sources: Economic Census of the United States, 1997. Only those industries are shown for which both employment and sales/revenue data were available. For the definition of MSAs, CMSAs, and PMSAs, please see the Introduction.

SAVANNAH, GA MSA

NAICS	Industry	Estab-lish-ments	Em-ploy-ment	Payroll		Sales, reven. ($ mil.)
				Total ($ mil.)	Per Empl. ($)	
48-49	Transportation and warehousing	345	6,404	153.3	23,934	511.5
484	Truck transportation	171	1,881	52.2	27,744	193.6
4841	General freight trucking	95	1,204	34.6	28,748	131.1
484110	General freight trucking, local	26	218	4.5	20,550	20.8
4841101	General freight trucking without storage, local, truckload (tl)	21	180	3.5	19,306	17.5
48412	General freight trucking, long-distance	69	986	30.1	30,561	110.3
484121	General freight trucking, long-distance, truckload (tl)	53	630	18.2	28,830	77.0
484122	General freight trucking, long-distance, less than truckload (ltl)	16	356	12.0	33,624	33.3
4842	Specialized freight trucking	76	677	17.6	25,959	62.5
484210	Used household and office goods moving	15	190	3.9	20,468	11.4
484220	Specialized freight (except used goods) trucking, local	31	135	3.0	22,474	12.7
4842203	Dump trucking	18	86	2.0	23,663	9.7
484230	Specialized freight (except used goods) trucking, long-distance	30	352	10.7	30,259	38.4
4842301	Hazardous materials trucking (except waste), long-distance	14	200	6.3	31,540	20.2
488	Support activities for transportation	113	3,771	82.3	21,826	231.1
4883	Support activities for water transportation	30	2,950	59.8	20,282	159.8
488510	Freight transportation arrangement	63	616	19.2	31,114	50.2
4885101	Freight forwarding	18	168	5.6	33,113	14.1
4885102	Arrangement of transportation of freight and cargo	45	448	13.6	30,364	36.1
4931	Warehousing and storage	18	226	8.2	36,265	36.2

Sources: Economic Census of the United States, 1997. Only those industries are shown for which both employment and sales/revenue data were available. For the definition of MSAs, CMSAs, and PMSAs, please see the Introduction.

SCRANTON—WILKES-BARRE—HAZLETON, PA MSA

NAICS	Industry	Estab-lish-ments	Em-ploy-ment	Payroll		Sales, reven. ($ mil.)
				Total ($ mil.)	Per Empl. ($)	
48-49	Transportation and warehousing	416	6,887	193.9	28,158	705.0
484	Truck transportation	259	4,402	151.5	34,409	536.1
4841	General freight trucking	135	3,026	95.4	31,522	350.2
484110	General freight trucking, local	40	378	9.0	23,910	28.8
4841101	General freight trucking without storage, local, truckload (tl)	29	181	5.3	29,343	19.6
48412	General freight trucking, long-distance	95	2,648	86.3	32,609	321.4
484121	General freight trucking, long-distance, truckload (tl)	73	2,072	64.6	31,184	251.2
484122	General freight trucking, long-distance, less than truckload (ltl)	22	576	21.7	37,734	70.2
4842	Specialized freight trucking	124	1,376	56.1	40,759	185.9
484210	Used household and office goods moving	21	192	4.7	24,464	12.9
484220	Specialized freight (except used goods) trucking, local	79	385	11.1	28,881	39.6
4842203	Dump trucking	56	244	7.1	29,152	26.3
4842204	Specialized trucking without storage, local	11	86	2.2	25,279	6.6
484230	Specialized freight (except used goods) trucking, long-distance	24	799	40.3	50,398	133.4
4842303	Other specialized trucking, long-distance	17	769	39.3	51,099	127.3
485	Transit and ground passenger transportation	95	1,456	16.6	11,393	54.6
4853	Taxi and limousine service	12	192	1.8	9,255	4.5
485410	School and employee bus transportation	64	899	8.7	9,638	24.8
485510	Charter bus industry	13	289	5.5	18,862	21.2
488	Support activities for transportation	29	305	5.8	19,013	50.0
4931101	General warehousing and storage (except in foreign trade zones)	15	316	9.4	29,706	20.9

Sources: Economic Census of the United States, 1997. Only those industries are shown for which both employment and sales/revenue data were available. For the definition of MSAs, CMSAs, and PMSAs, please see the Introduction.

SEATTLE—BELLEVUE—EVERETT, WA PMSA

NAICS	Industry	Estab-lish-ments	Em-ploy-ment	Payroll Total ($ mil.)	Payroll Per Empl. ($)	Sales, reven. ($ mil.)
48-49	Transportation and warehousing	1,522	35,626	1,212.6	34,037	4,201.0
48111	Scheduled air transportation	27	355	12.3	34,761	272.2
483	Water transportation	55	3,350	156.0	46,557	1,053.6
484	Truck transportation	590	8,551	277.3	32,434	963.9
4841	General freight trucking	251	4,720	160.2	33,942	569.7
484110	General freight trucking, local	117	1,534	46.7	30,467	141.6
4841101	General freight trucking without storage, local, truckload (tl)	69	811	24.6	30,296	78.8
4841102	General freight trucking without storage, local, less than truckload (ltl)	41	652	20.1	30,891	57.8
48412	General freight trucking, long-distance	134	3,186	113.5	35,615	428.1
484121	General freight trucking, long-distance, truckload (tl)	93	1,160	37.5	32,347	150.9
484122	General freight trucking, long-distance, less than truckload (ltl)	41	2,026	75.9	37,486	277.2
4842	Specialized freight trucking	339	3,831	117.1	30,576	394.3
484210	Used household and office goods moving	89	1,536	44.0	28,629	145.1
4842101	Used household and office goods moving, local, without storage	28	191	4.0	20,775	14.0
4842102	Used household and office goods moving, long-distance	32	771	22.3	28,938	92.6
4842103	Used household and office goods moving, local, with storage	29	574	17.7	30,828	38.5
484220	Specialized freight (except used goods) trucking, local	174	1,071	32.9	30,705	127.2
4842202	Agricultural products trucking without storage, local	29	77	2.1	27,442	8.2
4842203	Dump trucking	73	292	10.0	34,199	35.9
4842204	Specialized trucking without storage, local	63	634	18.7	29,467	77.9
484230	Specialized freight (except used goods) trucking, long-distance	76	1,224	40.3	32,905	122.0
4842302	Agricultural products trucking, long-distance	20	42	1.1	25,667	6.1
4842303	Other specialized trucking, long-distance	48	1,063	35.7	33,593	107.5
485	Transit and ground passenger transportation	63	2,064	37.3	18,051	89.8
48599	Other transit and ground passenger transportation	17	743	11.9	16,003	26.3
488	Support activities for transportation	555	10,224	427.9	41,851	961.9
4881	Support activities for air transportation	50	3,609	108.6	30,101	261.5
4881191	Airport operation and terminal services	19	895	13.8	15,375	45.7
488190	Other support activities for air transportation	31	2,714	94.9	34,957	215.7
4883	Support activities for water transportation	84	2,260	176.1	77,923	276.7
488320	Marine cargo handling	17	1,931	160.1	82,935	225.5
488330	Navigational services to shipping	33	203	10.8	53,005	34.0
4883901	Other services incidental to water transportation	23	60	2.3	37,850	5.8
4884	Support activities for road transportation	93	690	15.0	21,717	39.4
488410	Motor vehicle towing	80	569	12.7	22,308	34.8
488490	Other support activities for road transportation	13	121	2.3	18,942	4.6
488510	Freight transportation arrangement	315	3,446	124.4	36,104	374.1
4885101	Freight forwarding	171	2,267	78.5	34,639	244.0
4885102	Arrangement of transportation of freight and cargo	144	1,179	45.9	38,919	130.1
492	Couriers and messengers	111	8,598	227.6	26,466	569.9
492110	Couriers	63	7,738	211.0	27,269	533.6
4921101	Courier services (except by air)	26	6,337	165.8	26,160	356.7
4921102	Air courier services	37	1,401	45.2	32,285	176.9
492210	Local messengers and local delivery	48	860	16.5	19,244	36.3
4931	Warehousing and storage	72	1,546	46.0	29,729	149.6
4931101	General warehousing and storage (except in foreign trade zones)	41	801	23.7	29,556	81.3
493120	Refrigerated warehousing and storage	15	498	13.8	27,801	34.1
4931902	Specialized goods warehousing and storage	12	109	3.4	30,798	18.5

Sources: *Economic Census of the United States*, 1997. Only those industries are shown for which both employment and sales/revenue data were available. For the definition of MSAs, CMSAs, and PMSAs, please see the Introduction.

SEATTLE—TACOMA—BREMERTON, WA CMSA

NAICS	Industry	Estab-lish-ments	Em-ploy-ment	Payroll Total ($ mil.)	Payroll Per Empl. ($)	Sales, reven. ($ mil.)
48-49	Transportation and warehousing	2,145	44,753	1,497.9	33,470	5,587.5
484	Truck transportation	968	14,295	466.4	32,624	1,619.6
4841	General freight trucking	400	8,504	296.1	34,816	1,027.9
484121	General freight trucking, long-distance, truckload (tl)	177	4,246	150.7	35,489	538.2
4842	Specialized freight trucking	568	5,791	170.3	29,405	591.6
484210	Used household and office goods moving	162	2,408	62.7	26,039	205.0
484220	Specialized freight (except used goods) trucking, local	276	1,592	49.1	30,827	192.5
4842202	Agricultural products trucking without storage, local	50	136	3.2	23,684	12.6
4842203	Dump trucking	119	632	21.5	34,000	81.2
484230	Specialized freight (except used goods) trucking, long-distance	130	1,791	58.5	32,667	194.2
4842303	Other specialized trucking, long-distance	72	1,509	49.4	32,716	162.6
488	Support activities for transportation	683	11,271	457.8	40,618	1,087.3
4881	Support activities for air transportation	71	3,760	112.9	30,031	277.9
48811	Airport operations	25	932	14.7	15,795	49.2
488190	Other support activities for air transportation	46	2,828	98.2	34,723	228.7
4883	Support activities for water transportation	108	2,478	185.4	74,822	336.3
488330	Navigational services to shipping	44	219	11.9	54,283	36.7
488490	Other support activities for road transportation	17	218	3.6	16,716	6.9
4885101	Freight forwarding	195	2,449	85.2	34,798	265.6
493120	Refrigerated warehousing and storage	20	556	15.9	28,534	39.0

Sources: Economic Census of the United States, 1997. Only those industries are shown for which both employment and sales/revenue data were available. For the definition of MSAs, CMSAs, and PMSAs, please see the Introduction.

SHARON, PA MSA

NAICS	Industry	Estab-lish-ments	Em-ploy-ment	Payroll Total ($ mil.)	Payroll Per Empl. ($)	Sales, reven. ($ mil.)
48-49	Transportation and warehousing	84	1,141	25.0	21,935	93.5
484	Truck transportation	54	718	19.3	26,903	70.3
4841	General freight trucking	20	479	13.9	29,050	43.2
484121	General freight trucking, long-distance, truckload (tl)	13	248	5.2	21,081	24.5
4842	Specialized freight trucking	34	239	5.4	22,598	27.1
484220	Specialized freight (except used goods) trucking, local	24	107	2.0	18,318	12.6
4842203	Dump trucking	16	70	1.5	21,257	7.8
485	Transit and ground passenger transportation	21	397	5.3	13,287	20.6
4854101	School bus service	16	149	1.3	8,510	3.7
493	Warehousing and storage	5	11	0.3	23,727	2.0

Sources: Economic Census of the United States, 1997. Only those industries are shown for which both employment and sales/revenue data were available. For the definition of MSAs, CMSAs, and PMSAs, please see the Introduction.

SHEBOYGAN, WI MSA

NAICS	Industry	Estab-lish-ments	Em-ploy-ment	Payroll Total ($ mil.)	Payroll Per Empl. ($)	Sales, reven. ($ mil.)
48-49	Transportation and warehousing	89	793	17.8	22,414	60.2
484	Truck transportation	65	477	12.4	25,962	45.6
4841	General freight trucking	37	314	8.1	25,697	32.8
48412	General freight trucking, long-distance	28	231	6.1	26,255	26.1
4842	Specialized freight trucking	28	163	4.3	26,472	12.9
484220	Specialized freight (except used goods) trucking, local	21	152	4.0	26,283	11.9
4842202	Agricultural products trucking without storage, local	11	52	0.9	17,442	4.2
485	Transit and ground passenger transportation	13	235	3.4	14,536	8.0

Sources: Economic Census of the United States, 1997. Only those industries are shown for which both employment and sales/revenue data were available. For the definition of MSAs, CMSAs, and PMSAs, please see the Introduction.

SHERMAN—DENISON, TX MSA

NAICS	Industry	Estab-lish-ments	Em-ploy-ment	Payroll		Sales, reven. ($ mil.)
				Total ($ mil.)	Per Empl. ($)	
48-49	Transportation and warehousing	63	507	12.4	24,438	49.1
484	Truck transportation	50	397	10.2	25,746	41.7
4841	General freight trucking	24	218	5.4	24,936	24.4
48412	General freight trucking, long-distance	20	188	4.9	26,266	23.1
484121	General freight trucking, long-distance, truckload (tl)	15	96	2.0	20,771	11.2
4842	Specialized freight trucking	26	179	4.8	26,732	17.3
484220	Specialized freight (except used goods) trucking, local	19	76	1.8	23,395	7.2
488	Support activities for transportation	4	16	0.3	20,625	1.2
492	Couriers and messengers	5	38	1.0	25,474	3.7

Sources: *Economic Census of the United States*, 1997. Only those industries are shown for which both employment and sales/revenue data were available. For the definition of MSAs, CMSAs, and PMSAs, please see the Introduction.

SHREVEPORT—BOSSIER CITY, LA MSA

NAICS	Industry	Estab-lish-ments	Em-ploy-ment	Payroll		Sales, reven. ($ mil.)
				Total ($ mil.)	Per Empl. ($)	
48-49	Transportation and warehousing	223	3,769	120.9	32,074	621.7
484	Truck transportation	142	1,806	54.6	30,216	176.8
4841	General freight trucking	71	914	24.6	26,967	71.3
48412	General freight trucking, long-distance	61	841	23.3	27,665	65.0
484121	General freight trucking, long-distance, truckload (tl)	45	378	8.7	22,971	33.6
484122	General freight trucking, long-distance, less than truckload (ltl)	16	463	14.6	31,497	31.4
4842	Specialized freight trucking	71	892	29.9	33,545	105.5
484210	Used household and office goods moving	12	125	2.6	20,464	8.2
484220	Specialized freight (except used goods) trucking, local	46	292	6.6	22,596	26.2
4842203	Dump trucking	17	113	2.6	22,973	10.7
4842204	Specialized trucking without storage, local	16	111	3.1	27,865	11.2
484230	Specialized freight (except used goods) trucking, long-distance	13	475	20.8	43,718	71.1
493	Warehousing and storage	9	117	2.7	23,470	11.5

Sources: *Economic Census of the United States*, 1997. Only those industries are shown for which both employment and sales/revenue data were available. For the definition of MSAs, CMSAs, and PMSAs, please see the Introduction.

SIOUX CITY, IA—NE MSA

NAICS	Industry	Estab-lish-ments	Em-ploy-ment	Payroll		Sales, reven. ($ mil.)
				Total ($ mil.)	Per Empl. ($)	
48-49	Transportation and warehousing	139	2,432	59.9	24,639	299.2
484	Truck transportation	105	1,609	41.0	25,503	240.4
4841	General freight trucking	53	1,063	28.5	26,798	122.0
48412	General freight trucking, long-distance	43	1,043	28.2	27,084	120.1
484121	General freight trucking, long-distance, truckload (tl)	32	909	23.5	25,894	102.7
484122	General freight trucking, long-distance, less than truckload (ltl)	11	134	4.7	35,157	17.4
4842	Specialized freight trucking	52	546	12.5	22,982	118.4
484220	Specialized freight (except used goods) trucking, local	20	139	3.0	21,633	12.7
484230	Specialized freight (except used goods) trucking, long-distance	25	363	8.6	23,614	103.0
488	Support activities for transportation	9	101	2.8	27,515	9.0
492	Couriers and messengers	5	79	1.6	20,127	4.2
493	Warehousing and storage	9	455	12.1	26,618	35.5

Sources: *Economic Census of the United States*, 1997. Only those industries are shown for which both employment and sales/revenue data were available. For the definition of MSAs, CMSAs, and PMSAs, please see the Introduction.

SIOUX FALLS, SD MSA

NAICS	Industry	Estab-lish-ments	Em-ploy-ment	Payroll Total ($ mil.)	Payroll Per Empl. ($)	Sales, reven. ($ mil.)
48-49	Transportation and warehousing	273	3,210	75.0	23,372	421.6
484	Truck transportation	211	2,102	57.9	27,523	350.6
4841	General freight trucking	138	1,713	47.0	27,417	291.7
484110	General freight trucking, local	25	192	4.2	21,917	18.0
4841101	General freight trucking without storage, local, truckload (tl)	19	111	2.7	24,081	13.3
48412	General freight trucking, long-distance	113	1,521	42.8	28,111	273.8
484121	General freight trucking, long-distance, truckload (tl)	100	1,200	31.0	25,854	249.6
484122	General freight trucking, long-distance, less than truckload (ltl)	13	321	11.7	36,548	24.1
4842	Specialized freight trucking	73	389	10.9	27,990	58.9
484220	Specialized freight (except used goods) trucking, local	26	175	5.2	29,754	15.3
484230	Specialized freight (except used goods) trucking, long-distance	38	142	3.7	25,993	38.7
4842302	Agricultural products trucking, long-distance	24	104	2.7	25,760	29.4
485	Transit and ground passenger transportation	16	509	4.6	8,998	13.1
486	Pipeline transportation	3	21	1.0	48,095	9.6
492	Couriers and messengers	17	338	6.5	19,249	26.1
493	Warehousing and storage	6	97	2.1	21,423	8.5

Sources: Economic Census of the United States, 1997. Only those industries are shown for which both employment and sales/revenue data were available. For the definition of MSAs, CMSAs, and PMSAs, please see the Introduction.

SOUTH BEND, IN MSA

NAICS	Industry	Estab-lish-ments	Em-ploy-ment	Payroll Total ($ mil.)	Payroll Per Empl. ($)	Sales, reven. ($ mil.)
48-49	Transportation and warehousing	140	3,316	95.7	28,857	292.8
484	Truck transportation	92	2,451	78.2	31,919	237.7
4841	General freight trucking	48	1,924	63.9	33,227	185.7
484110	General freight trucking, local	11	133	3.2	24,195	7.1
48412	General freight trucking, long-distance	37	1,791	60.7	33,897	178.6
484121	General freight trucking, long-distance, truckload (tl)	16	678	20.0	29,560	68.5
484122	General freight trucking, long-distance, less than truckload (ltl)	21	1,113	40.7	36,539	110.1
4842	Specialized freight trucking	44	527	14.3	27,146	52.0
484220	Specialized freight (except used goods) trucking, local	20	113	3.0	26,593	9.7
484230	Specialized freight (except used goods) trucking, long-distance	14	304	8.4	27,668	35.2
4842303	Other specialized trucking, long-distance	11	275	7.9	28,753	33.9
485	Transit and ground passenger transportation	9	361	5.7	15,778	11.8
488	Support activities for transportation	17	81	2.2	26,556	9.0
492	Couriers and messengers	15	400	9.0	22,588	31.5
493	Warehousing and storage	4	14	0.4	29,000	1.8

Sources: Economic Census of the United States, 1997. Only those industries are shown for which both employment and sales/revenue data were available. For the definition of MSAs, CMSAs, and PMSAs, please see the Introduction.

SPOKANE, WA MSA

NAICS	Industry	Estab-lish-ments	Em-ploy-ment	Payroll Total ($ mil.)	Payroll Per Empl. ($)	Sales, reven. ($ mil.)
48-49	Transportation and warehousing	206	3,761	89.2	23,707	329.5
484	Truck transportation	129	2,383	64.8	27,194	231.9
4841	General freight trucking	72	1,953	53.3	27,305	199.5
484110	General freight trucking, local	18	263	7.1	26,932	17.2
48412	General freight trucking, long-distance	54	1,690	46.2	27,363	182.3
484121	General freight trucking, long-distance, truckload (tl)	40	1,300	35.4	27,260	142.4
484122	General freight trucking, long-distance, less than truckload (ltl)	14	390	10.8	27,708	39.9
4842	Specialized freight trucking	57	430	11.5	26,688	32.5
484210	Used household and office goods moving	11	178	4.8	27,169	12.2
484220	Specialized freight (except used goods) trucking, local	26	88	2.3	25,648	7.8
4842203	Dump trucking	12	46	1.2	26,109	3.7
4842204	Specialized trucking without storage, local	11	39	1.0	25,487	3.8
484230	Specialized freight (except used goods) trucking, long-distance	20	164	4.4	26,726	12.5
4842303	Other specialized trucking, long-distance	11	114	2.9	25,570	7.5
485	Transit and ground passenger transportation	19	555	5.6	10,058	15.2
488	Support activities for transportation	27	304	6.1	19,954	19.3
488510	Freight transportation arrangement	12	86	2.4	28,244	7.0
492	Couriers and messengers	19	402	7.4	18,371	27.2

Sources: Economic Census of the United States, 1997. Only those industries are shown for which both employment and sales/revenue data were available. For the definition of MSAs, CMSAs, and PMSAs, please see the Introduction.

SPRINGFIELD, IL MSA

NAICS	Industry	Establishments	Employment	Payroll		Sales, reven. ($ mil.)
				Total ($ mil.)	Per Empl. ($)	
48-49	Transportation and warehousing	113	1,791	44.7	24,958	156.4
484	Truck transportation	80	975	22.8	23,398	75.4
4841	General freight trucking	36	804	19.3	23,960	57.1
484110	General freight trucking, local	11	66	2.1	31,394	5.0
48412	General freight trucking, long-distance	25	738	17.2	23,295	52.1
484121	General freight trucking, long-distance, truckload (tl)	16	563	7.4	13,153	23.5
4842	Specialized freight trucking	44	171	3.5	20,754	18.3
484220	Specialized freight (except used goods) trucking, local	30	60	1.2	20,433	10.2
4842203	Dump trucking	16	39	0.8	21,282	7.8
485	Transit and ground passenger transportation	6	352	3.2	8,960	5.6
492	Couriers and messengers	8	84	2.0	23,548	8.1

Sources: *Economic Census of the United States*, 1997. Only those industries are shown for which both employment and sales/revenue data were available. For the definition of MSAs, CMSAs, and PMSAs, please see the Introduction.

SPRINGFIELD, MA MSA

NAICS	Industry	Establishments	Employment	Payroll		Sales, reven. ($ mil.)
				Total ($ mil.)	Per Empl. ($)	
48-49	Transportation and warehousing	252	5,073	118.6	23,379	355.1
484	Truck transportation	134	1,861	57.3	30,775	193.6
4841	General freight trucking	70	1,356	43.1	31,809	153.2
484110	General freight trucking, local	26	245	6.6	26,988	16.3
4841101	General freight trucking without storage, local, truckload (tl)	13	127	4.3	34,142	11.3
48412	General freight trucking, long-distance	44	1,111	36.5	32,872	136.9
484121	General freight trucking, long-distance, truckload (tl)	31	517	16.7	32,381	69.8
484122	General freight trucking, long-distance, less than truckload (ltl)	13	594	19.8	33,300	67.0
4842	Specialized freight trucking	64	505	14.1	27,998	40.4
484210	Used household and office goods moving	18	210	4.2	19,952	11.7
484220	Specialized freight (except used goods) trucking, local	35	105	3.5	33,048	13.2
4842203	Dump trucking	21	28	1.0	37,357	5.3
484230	Specialized freight (except used goods) trucking, long-distance	11	190	6.5	34,100	15.5
485	Transit and ground passenger transportation	49	2,362	40.0	16,926	94.0
4854101	School bus service	14	962	11.2	11,594	20.0
488510	Freight transportation arrangement	19	152	3.9	25,658	12.7

Sources: *Economic Census of the United States*, 1997. Only those industries are shown for which both employment and sales/revenue data were available. For the definition of MSAs, CMSAs, and PMSAs, please see the Introduction.

SPRINGFIELD, MO MSA

NAICS	Industry	Establishments	Employment	Payroll		Sales, reven. ($ mil.)
				Total ($ mil.)	Per Empl. ($)	
48-49	Transportation and warehousing	386	5,682	154.3	27,163	822.5
484	Truck transportation	282	4,537	132.6	29,218	751.1
4841	General freight trucking	189	2,694	80.9	30,023	311.4
484110	General freight trucking, local	42	369	8.0	21,678	43.1
4841101	General freight trucking without storage, local, truckload (tl)	20	220	4.7	21,364	34.5
48412	General freight trucking, long-distance	147	2,325	72.9	31,348	268.3
484121	General freight trucking, long-distance, truckload (tl)	117	1,596	41.9	26,249	219.1
484122	General freight trucking, long-distance, less than truckload (ltl)	30	729	31.0	42,512	49.2
4842	Specialized freight trucking	93	1,843	51.7	28,041	439.7
484210	Used household and office goods moving	17	165	2.8	16,739	6.6
484220	Specialized freight (except used goods) trucking, local	42	169	2.8	16,355	10.6
4842203	Dump trucking	15	62	1.2	18,565	4.1
4842204	Specialized trucking without storage, local	12	89	1.3	15,124	4.9
484230	Specialized freight (except used goods) trucking, long-distance	34	1,509	46.2	30,585	422.5
485	Transit and ground passenger transportation	18	415	4.8	11,643	12.5
488	Support activities for transportation	46	405	10.0	24,795	29.9
488510	Freight transportation arrangement	25	118	2.9	24,847	8.0
4885102	Arrangement of transportation of freight and cargo	20	75	1.8	23,400	5.0
492	Couriers and messengers	24	243	4.8	19,646	19.2
492110	Couriers	11	167	3.8	22,766	17.0
492210	Local messengers and local delivery	13	76	1.0	12,789	2.2

Sources: *Economic Census of the United States*, 1997. Only those industries are shown for which both employment and sales/revenue data were available. For the definition of MSAs, CMSAs, and PMSAs, please see the Introduction.

ST. CLOUD, MN MSA

NAICS	Industry	Estab-lish-ments	Em-ploy-ment	Payroll		Sales, reven. ($ mil.)
				Total ($ mil.)	Per Empl. ($)	
48-49	Transportation and warehousing	175	2,802	69.7	24,876	308.3
484	Truck transportation	132	1,794	49.6	27,640	252.2
4841	General freight trucking	63	1,603	45.1	28,160	220.2
484110	General freight trucking, local	17	213	4.9	23,066	20.4
48412	General freight trucking, long-distance	46	1,390	40.2	28,940	199.9
484121	General freight trucking, long-distance, truckload (tl)	36	1,299	36.8	28,323	185.8
4842	Specialized freight trucking	69	191	4.4	23,283	32.0
484220	Specialized freight (except used goods) trucking, local	40	97	2.0	20,722	9.4
4842202	Agricultural products trucking without storage, local	23	77	0.9	12,156	5.1
484230	Specialized freight (except used goods) trucking, long-distance	24	71	1.9	26,958	20.7
4842303	Other specialized trucking, long-distance	13	45	1.4	31,333	9.3
485	Transit and ground passenger transportation	17	473	5.7	12,089	14.8
4854101	School bus service	11	344	3.7	10,852	9.6
492	Couriers and messengers	8	398	11.3	28,410	25.1

Sources: Economic Census of the United States, 1997. Only those industries are shown for which both employment and sales/revenue data were available. For the definition of MSAs, CMSAs, and PMSAs, please see the Introduction.

ST. JOSEPH, MO MSA

NAICS	Industry	Estab-lish-ments	Em-ploy-ment	Payroll		Sales, reven. ($ mil.)
				Total ($ mil.)	Per Empl. ($)	
48-49	Transportation and warehousing	121	1,140	25.4	22,249	103.7
484	Truck transportation	91	698	18.8	26,920	85.8
4841	General freight trucking	66	577	16.5	28,603	74.5
484110	General freight trucking, local	13	78	2.2	28,244	6.3
48412	General freight trucking, long-distance	53	499	14.3	28,659	68.2
484121	General freight trucking, long-distance, truckload (tl)	46	440	12.0	27,232	57.7
4842	Specialized freight trucking	25	121	2.3	18,893	11.3
484220	Specialized freight (except used goods) trucking, local	14	40	0.8	20,575	3.1
485	Transit and ground passenger transportation	9	304	3.1	10,329	7.0
488	Support activities for transportation	7	22	0.6	25,727	1.5
492	Couriers and messengers	10	70	1.5	22,043	4.5
493	Warehousing and storage	4	46	1.3	28,804	4.9

Sources: Economic Census of the United States, 1997. Only those industries are shown for which both employment and sales/revenue data were available. For the definition of MSAs, CMSAs, and PMSAs, please see the Introduction.

ST. LOUIS, MO—IL MSA

NAICS	Industry	Estab-lish-ments	Em-ploy-ment	Payroll		Sales, reven. ($ mil.)
				Total ($ mil.)	Per Empl. ($)	
48-49	Transportation and warehousing	1,848	36,716	925.6	25,209	4,500.6
48121	Nonscheduled air transportation	16	250	10.7	42,952	33.0
481211	Nonscheduled chartered passenger air transportation	13	235	10.4	44,383	32.0
483	Water transportation	22	412	13.5	32,675	300.9
483211	Inland water freight transportation	14	231	10.0	43,442	245.7
4832111	Inland waterways freight transportation (except towing)	11	189	7.9	41,603	210.1
484	Truck transportation	1,117	15,138	467.0	30,846	2,927.8
4841	General freight trucking	537	8,739	292.6	33,483	939.0
484110	General freight trucking, local	243	1,931	55.2	28,608	205.5
4841101	General freight trucking without storage, local, truckload (tl)	138	1,199	35.8	29,837	141.5
4841102	General freight trucking without storage, local, less than truckload (ltl)	89	622	16.8	26,961	52.6
48412	General freight trucking, long-distance	294	6,808	237.4	34,865	733.5
484121	General freight trucking, long-distance, truckload (tl)	242	3,637	115.6	31,787	482.5
484122	General freight trucking, long-distance, less than truckload (ltl)	52	3,171	121.8	38,396	251.1
4842	Specialized freight trucking	580	6,399	174.3	27,246	1,988.7
484210	Used household and office goods moving	120	3,194	75.6	23,673	1,646.6
4842101	Used household and office goods moving, local, without storage	48	328	5.4	16,448	14.1
4842102	Used household and office goods moving, long-distance	41	2,323	56.9	24,495	1,603.4
4842103	Used household and office goods moving, local, with storage	31	543	13.3	24,523	29.2
484220	Specialized freight (except used goods) trucking, local	362	1,881	43.9	23,314	175.1
4842202	Agricultural products trucking without storage, local	33	214	4.4	20,575	22.5
4842203	Dump trucking	227	1,000	25.0	24,974	110.3
4842204	Specialized trucking without storage, local	82	531	10.9	20,599	30.1
484230	Specialized freight (except used goods) trucking, long-distance	98	1,324	54.9	41,449	166.9
4842301	Hazardous materials trucking (except waste), long-distance	28	262	8.5	32,531	28.0
4842302	Agricultural products trucking, long-distance	20	67	1.2	17,701	5.3
4842303	Other specialized trucking, long-distance	50	995	45.2	45,396	133.7
485	Transit and ground passenger transportation	135	5,022	59.5	11,853	155.6
4853	Taxi and limousine service	47	368	6.2	16,940	19.3
485310	Taxi service	27	212	4.1	19,203	13.7
485320	Limousine service	20	156	2.2	13,865	5.6
485410	School and employee bus transportation	56	3,956	42.8	10,810	104.4
4854101	School bus service	53	3,806	40.3	10,587	97.7
485510	Charter bus industry	12	266	3.1	11,820	11.0
48599	Other transit and ground passenger transportation	14	289	4.1	14,232	10.0
486	Pipeline transportation	13	146	7.0	47,979	65.3
488	Support activities for transportation	350	7,285	142.4	19,541	420.9
4881	Support activities for air transportation	37	4,304	54.0	12,551	134.1
4881191	Airport operation and terminal services	17	3,423	31.7	9,274	42.0
488190	Other support activities for air transportation	20	881	22.3	25,284	92.1
4882101	Support activities incidental to rail transportation	18	887	28.3	31,888	77.9
4883	Support activities for water transportation	29	536	17.0	31,627	75.1
488330	Navigational services to shipping	13	417	11.5	27,516	50.3
4884	Support activities for road transportation	63	472	8.4	17,900	22.5
488410	Motor vehicle towing	58	405	7.6	18,644	20.9
488510	Freight transportation arrangement	187	989	32.7	33,087	103.6
4885101	Freight forwarding	77	480	15.7	32,702	62.1
4885102	Arrangement of transportation of freight and cargo	110	509	17.0	33,450	41.5
48899	Other support activities for transportation	16	97	1.9	19,845	7.6
492	Couriers and messengers	116	7,804	208.8	26,758	519.2
492110	Couriers	39	6,066	176.6	29,108	429.2
492210	Local messengers and local delivery	77	1,738	32.3	18,558	89.9
4931	Warehousing and storage	68	629	16.1	25,542	74.2
4931101	General warehousing and storage (except in foreign trade zones)	52	475	11.2	23,680	49.8
493190	Other warehousing and storage	12	90	2.8	31,033	7.5

Sources: Economic Census of the United States, 1997. Only those industries are shown for which both employment and sales/revenue data were available. For the definition of MSAs, CMSAs, and PMSAs, please see the Introduction.

STAMFORD—NORWALK, CT PMSA

NAICS	Industry	Estab-lish-ments	Em-ploy-ment	Payroll		Sales, reven. ($ mil.)
				Total ($ mil.)	Per Empl. ($)	
48-49	Transportation and warehousing	274	4,827	203.9	42,249	1,049.4
48311	Deep sea, coastal, and Great Lakes water transportation	28	916	47.9	52,330	665.2
484	Truck transportation	45	570	17.5	30,726	58.1
4842	Specialized freight trucking	35	220	6.4	28,900	22.7
484210	Used household and office goods moving	19	149	4.5	29,899	13.2
484220	Specialized freight (except used goods) trucking, local	13	51	1.5	29,275	8.3
485	Transit and ground passenger transportation	68	1,404	33.1	23,573	77.5
4853	Taxi and limousine service	51	787	24.3	30,915	56.4
485320	Limousine service	46	765	23.9	31,297	55.0
488	Support activities for transportation	90	899	70.9	78,859	154.1
488510	Freight transportation arrangement	67	636	60.9	95,819	131.5
4885101	Freight forwarding	11	201	10.4	51,836	41.4
4885102	Arrangement of transportation of freight and cargo	56	435	50.5	116,143	90.1
492	Couriers and messengers	25	515	18.5	36,004	59.9
492110	Couriers	15	463	17.0	36,700	54.3
493	Warehousing and storage	8	182	5.3	29,396	24.4

Sources: Economic Census of the United States, 1997. Only those industries are shown for which both employment and sales/revenue data were available. For the definition of MSAs, CMSAs, and PMSAs, please see the Introduction.

STATE COLLEGE, PA MSA

NAICS	Industry	Estab-lish-ments	Em-ploy-ment	Payroll		Sales, reven. ($ mil.)
				Total ($ mil.)	Per Empl. ($)	
48-49	Transportation and warehousing	90	1,271	22.7	17,869	88.3
481	Air transportation	4	97	2.7	27,660	14.1
484	Truck transportation	53	490	13.1	26,743	54.9
4841	General freight trucking	15	271	8.4	30,956	35.7
4842	Specialized freight trucking	38	219	4.7	21,530	19.2
484220	Specialized freight (except used goods) trucking, local	33	129	2.5	19,039	11.9
4842203	Dump trucking	25	117	2.1	18,274	10.3
485	Transit and ground passenger transportation	22	527	3.8	7,194	10.7
4854101	School bus service	19	401	2.1	5,130	6.7
488	Support activities for transportation	7	67	1.1	16,582	3.7
492	Couriers and messengers	4	90	2.0	22,467	5.0

Sources: Economic Census of the United States, 1997. Only those industries are shown for which both employment and sales/revenue data were available. For the definition of MSAs, CMSAs, and PMSAs, please see the Introduction.

STEUBENVILLE—WEIRTON, OH—WV MSA

NAICS	Industry	Estab-lish-ments	Em-ploy-ment	Payroll		Sales, reven. ($ mil.)
				Total ($ mil.)	Per Empl. ($)	
48-49	Transportation and warehousing	90	812	17.0	20,989	80.7
484	Truck transportation	68	565	13.1	23,129	69.6
4841	General freight trucking	22	299	6.5	21,769	32.8
4842	Specialized freight trucking	46	266	6.6	24,658	36.8
484220	Specialized freight (except used goods) trucking, local	34	231	4.9	21,251	20.1
4842203	Dump trucking	24	181	3.8	21,017	16.3
485	Transit and ground passenger transportation	4	40	0.6	14,500	1.0
488	Support activities for transportation	12	134	2.7	20,194	6.9

Sources: Economic Census of the United States, 1997. Only those industries are shown for which both employment and sales/revenue data were available. For the definition of MSAs, CMSAs, and PMSAs, please see the Introduction.

STOCKTON—LODI, CA MSA

NAICS	Industry	Estab-lish-ments	Em-ploy-ment	Payroll		Sales, reven. ($ mil.)
				Total ($ mil.)	Per Empl. ($)	
48-49	Transportation and warehousing	414	7,876	241.0	30,600	811.3
484	Truck transportation	299	4,551	145.6	31,996	557.9
4841	General freight trucking	146	2,954	98.7	33,398	358.0
484110	General freight trucking, local	55	861	25.3	29,359	97.0
4841101	General freight trucking without storage, local, truckload (tl)	42	509	16.7	32,713	59.1
48412	General freight trucking, long-distance	91	2,093	73.4	35,060	261.0
484121	General freight trucking, long-distance, truckload (tl)	71	1,281	43.3	33,800	184.5
484122	General freight trucking, long-distance, less than truckload (ltl)	20	812	30.1	37,047	76.4
4842	Specialized freight trucking	153	1,597	47.0	29,404	199.9
484210	Used household and office goods moving	17	95	1.7	18,126	6.8
484220	Specialized freight (except used goods) trucking, local	96	904	26.5	29,284	115.9
4842202	Agricultural products trucking without storage, local	37	319	11.0	34,602	39.8
4842203	Dump trucking	37	478	12.3	25,684	61.7
4842204	Specialized trucking without storage, local	17	49	1.0	20,388	4.6
484230	Specialized freight (except used goods) trucking, long-distance	40	598	18.8	31,376	77.2
4842302	Agricultural products trucking, long-distance	27	209	5.7	27,249	19.6
485	Transit and ground passenger transportation	18	357	5.0	14,048	12.5
488	Support activities for transportation	52	425	10.4	24,546	32.2
488410	Motor vehicle towing	20	126	2.8	22,373	8.3
488510	Freight transportation arrangement	16	71	2.4	34,296	7.3
492110	Couriers	11	185	4.1	22,368	19.8
4931	Warehousing and storage	26	2,274	74.1	32,566	180.6
4931101	General warehousing and storage (except in foreign trade zones)	18	2,134	66.7	31,271	150.1

Sources: *Economic Census of the United States*, 1997. Only those industries are shown for which both employment and sales/revenue data were available. For the definition of MSAs, CMSAs, and PMSAs, please see the Introduction.

SUMTER, SC MSA

NAICS	Industry	Estab-lish-ments	Em-ploy-ment	Payroll		Sales, reven. ($ mil.)
				Total ($ mil.)	Per Empl. ($)	
48-49	Transportation and warehousing	43	464	9.3	20,011	33.9
484	Truck transportation	27	318	7.1	22,302	26.1
4841	General freight trucking	14	164	4.4	27,128	17.4
484121	General freight trucking, long-distance, truckload (tl)	11	155	4.3	28,058	16.5
4842	Specialized freight trucking	13	154	2.6	17,162	8.8
488	Support activities for transportation	7	55	0.8	13,818	2.7

Sources: *Economic Census of the United States*, 1997. Only those industries are shown for which both employment and sales/revenue data were available. For the definition of MSAs, CMSAs, and PMSAs, please see the Introduction.

SYRACUSE, NY MSA

NAICS	Industry	Estab-lish-ments	Em-ploy-ment	Payroll Total ($ mil.)	Payroll Per Empl. ($)	Sales, reven. ($ mil.)
48-49	Transportation and warehousing	353	10,954	270.9	24,729	779.2
481	Air transportation	6	26	0.8	29,923	6.8
484	Truck transportation	200	3,967	111.8	28,193	374.2
4841	General freight trucking	101	3,312	94.4	28,508	305.8
484110	General freight trucking, local	33	1,276	27.2	21,301	73.2
4841101	General freight trucking without storage, local, truckload (tl)	16	1,076	21.8	20,265	58.3
4841102	General freight trucking without storage, local, less than truckload (ltl)	17	200	5.4	26,875	14.9
484122	General freight trucking, long-distance	68	2,036	67.2	33,026	232.6
484121	General freight trucking, long-distance, truckload (tl)	48	902	25.7	28,540	90.5
484122	General freight trucking, long-distance, less than truckload (ltl)	20	1,134	41.5	36,593	142.1
4842	Specialized freight trucking	99	655	17.4	26,600	68.3
484210	Used household and office goods moving	16	192	4.1	21,411	11.2
484220	Specialized freight (except used goods) trucking, local	55	182	5.9	32,451	28.0
4842203	Dump trucking	31	131	4.9	37,053	24.5
4842204	Specialized trucking without storage, local	11	23	0.5	22,478	1.8
484230	Specialized freight (except used goods) trucking, long-distance	28	281	7.4	26,356	29.1
4842303	Other specialized trucking, long-distance	15	108	2.7	24,620	13.1
485	Transit and ground passenger transportation	55	1,611	26.5	16,473	42.2
4853	Taxi and limousine service	21	251	2.9	11,386	6.0
485310	Taxi service	13	207	2.6	12,440	4.7
4854101	School bus service	15	612	7.0	11,467	15.9
485991	Special needs transportation	11	179	2.7	14,849	5.7
488	Support activities for transportation	37	455	9.9	21,681	29.2
488510	Freight transportation arrangement	21	110	3.9	35,073	13.6
4885102	Arrangement of transportation of freight and cargo	15	79	2.5	31,127	10.1
492	Couriers and messengers	27	4,455	109.4	24,561	271.4
492110	Couriers	15	4,210	105.9	25,154	262.4
492210	Local messengers and local delivery	12	245	3.5	14,371	9.0
4931	Warehousing and storage	22	394	10.4	26,472	43.7
4931101	General warehousing and storage (except in foreign trade zones)	16	218	5.6	25,463	16.9

Sources: Economic Census of the United States, 1997. Only those industries are shown for which both employment and sales/revenue data were available. For the definition of MSAs, CMSAs, and PMSAs, please see the Introduction.

TACOMA, WA PMSA

NAICS	Industry	Estab-lish-ments	Em-ploy-ment	Payroll Total ($ mil.)	Payroll Per Empl. ($)	Sales, reven. ($ mil.)
48-49	Transportation and warehousing	415	7,555	249.8	33,058	1,262.4
484	Truck transportation	251	5,082	171.5	33,746	588.4
4841	General freight trucking	106	3,593	129.3	35,990	433.1
484110	General freight trucking, local	34	389	10.3	26,452	27.8
4841101	General freight trucking without storage, local, truckload (tl)	24	179	5.3	29,536	15.6
484122	General freight trucking, long-distance	72	3,204	119.0	37,148	405.3
484121	General freight trucking, long-distance, truckload (tl)	62	3,017	111.2	36,869	379.3
4842	Specialized freight trucking	145	1,489	42.2	28,330	155.3
484210	Used household and office goods moving	47	582	13.3	22,854	42.6
4842102	Used household and office goods moving, long-distance	22	363	7.7	21,275	27.7
4842103	Used household and office goods moving, local, with storage	17	189	4.8	25,344	12.4
484220	Specialized freight (except used goods) trucking, local	64	374	12.0	32,029	45.4
4842202	Agricultural products trucking without storage, local	14	39	0.6	16,487	2.5
4842203	Dump trucking	27	277	9.6	34,513	37.5
4842204	Specialized trucking without storage, local	18	36	0.9	24,528	3.4
484230	Specialized freight (except used goods) trucking, long-distance	34	533	16.9	31,715	67.3
4842303	Other specialized trucking, long-distance	17	438	13.4	30,591	54.2
488	Support activities for transportation	90	876	25.7	29,292	112.2
4883	Support activities for water transportation	16	190	8.2	43,368	56.9
4884	Support activities for road transportation	26	281	4.4	15,502	11.6
488410	Motor vehicle towing	22	184	3.0	16,326	9.3
488510	Freight transportation arrangement	31	212	7.3	34,264	24.1
4885101	Freight forwarding	18	171	5.9	34,743	18.6
4885102	Arrangement of transportation of freight and cargo	13	41	1.3	32,268	5.6
4931	Warehousing and storage	19	316	11.1	35,082	25.4

Sources: Economic Census of the United States, 1997. Only those industries are shown for which both employment and sales/revenue data were available. For the definition of MSAs, CMSAs, and PMSAs, please see the Introduction.

TALLAHASSEE, FL MSA

| NAICS | Industry | Estab-lish-ments | Em-ploy-ment | Payroll | | Sales, reven. ($ mil.) |
				Total ($ mil.)	Per Empl. ($)	
48-49	Transportation and warehousing	90	1,260	25.4	20,156	108.4
481	Air transportation	4	78	1.3	16,449	14.3
484	Truck transportation	47	594	13.2	22,261	39.4
4841	General freight trucking	17	160	4.7	29,525	11.2
48412	General freight trucking, long-distance	12	124	3.7	29,718	8.5
4842	Specialized freight trucking	30	434	8.5	19,583	28.2
484220	Specialized freight (except used goods) trucking, local	17	245	4.3	17,641	14.7
485	Transit and ground passenger transportation	11	246	4.1	16,561	7.7
492	Couriers and messengers	11	215	3.8	17,442	16.5

Sources: Economic Census of the United States, 1997. Only those industries are shown for which both employment and sales/revenue data were available. For the definition of MSAs, CMSAs, and PMSAs, please see the Introduction.

TAMPA—ST. PETERSBURG—CLEARWATER, FL MSA

| NAICS | Industry | Estab-lish-ments | Em-ploy-ment | Payroll | | Sales, reven. ($ mil.) |
				Total ($ mil.)	Per Empl. ($)	
48-49	Transportation and warehousing	1,121	15,114	405.7	26,845	1,752.0
481	Air transportation	20	111	2.8	25,162	33.4
48121	Nonscheduled air transportation	11	34	1.0	29,235	5.6
48311	Deep sea, coastal, and Great Lakes water transportation	19	530	32.7	61,649	363.1
484	Truck transportation	536	7,100	204.9	28,861	709.9
4841	General freight trucking	213	3,892	126.6	32,537	374.8
484110	General freight trucking, local	81	348	6.7	19,224	30.9
4841101	General freight trucking without storage, local, truckload (tl)	51	188	4.1	21,734	18.3
4841102	General freight trucking without storage, local, less than truckload (ltl)	25	92	1.6	17,511	9.5
48412	General freight trucking, long-distance	132	3,544	119.9	33,845	344.0
484121	General freight trucking, long-distance, truckload (tl)	98	1,763	62.0	35,181	161.9
484122	General freight trucking, long-distance, less than truckload (ltl)	34	1,781	57.9	32,522	182.1
4842	Specialized freight trucking	323	3,208	78.3	24,400	335.0
484210	Used household and office goods moving	80	774	15.8	20,372	80.7
4842101	Used household and office goods moving, local, without storage	36	196	3.6	18,577	11.1
4842102	Used household and office goods moving, long-distance	26	395	8.4	21,248	60.9
4842103	Used household and office goods moving, local, with storage	18	183	3.7	20,404	8.7
484220	Specialized freight (except used goods) trucking, local	169	1,072	21.9	20,407	117.1
4842201	Hazardous materials trucking (except waste), local	12	120	3.9	32,233	9.8
4842203	Dump trucking	96	559	10.1	17,989	78.4
4842204	Specialized trucking without storage, local	43	289	5.8	20,090	21.9
484230	Specialized freight (except used goods) trucking, long-distance	74	1,362	40.6	29,832	137.2
4842301	Hazardous materials trucking (except waste), long-distance	11	366	11.2	30,478	30.9
4842302	Agricultural products trucking, long-distance	15	37	0.8	22,649	6.7
4842303	Other specialized trucking, long-distance	48	959	28.6	29,862	99.7
485	Transit and ground passenger transportation	75	1,367	17.9	13,108	58.5
4853	Taxi and limousine service	38	466	5.0	10,815	23.0
485310	Taxi service	16	252	3.0	11,929	9.3
485320	Limousine service	22	214	2.0	9,505	13.7
48599	Other transit and ground passenger transportation	21	541	7.8	14,412	17.5
487210	Scenic and sightseeing transportation, water	32	593	11.6	19,592	28.9
4872101	Excursion and sightseeing boats (including dinner cruises)	12	252	5.4	21,250	10.7
4872102	Charter fishing and party fishing boats	20	341	6.3	18,367	18.2
488	Support activities for transportation	274	2,750	69.7	25,337	262.9
4881	Support activities for air transportation	34	869	15.8	18,150	62.6
48811	Airport operations	13	333	4.7	14,051	23.5
488190	Other support activities for air transportation	21	536	11.1	20,696	39.1
4883	Support activities for water transportation	56	532	22.7	42,605	98.8
488330	Navigational services to shipping	22	203	9.8	48,320	27.4
488390	Other support activities for water transportation	21	70	5.1	73,400	45.4
4884	Support activities for road transportation	46	644	9.3	14,382	19.8
488410	Motor vehicle towing	40	244	4.9	20,102	13.5
488510	Freight transportation arrangement	118	588	19.6	33,369	64.2
4885101	Freight forwarding	42	188	5.5	29,372	19.9
4885102	Arrangement of transportation of freight and cargo	76	400	14.1	35,248	44.4
48899	Other support activities for transportation	14	73	1.0	13,959	4.8
492	Couriers and messengers	103	1,690	41.2	24,383	180.1
492110	Couriers	55	1,342	34.5	25,682	151.9
4921101	Courier services (except by air)	31	409	8.3	20,284	35.0
4921102	Air courier services	24	933	26.2	28,048	116.9
492210	Local messengers and local delivery	48	348	6.7	19,376	28.2
4931	Warehousing and storage	46	706	18.5	26,214	68.4
4931101	General warehousing and storage (except in foreign trade zones)	22	403	9.1	22,648	26.8
4931201	Refrigerated products warehousing	11	207	6.2	29,773	19.7

Sources: Economic Census of the United States, 1997. Only those industries are shown for which both employment and sales/revenue data were available. For the definition of MSAs, CMSAs, and PMSAs, please see the Introduction.

TERRE HAUTE, IN MSA

NAICS	Industry	Estab-lish-ments	Em-ploy-ment	Payroll		Sales, reven. ($ mil.)
				Total ($ mil.)	Per Empl. ($)	
48-49	Transportation and warehousing	113	1,435	29.2	20,371	188.0
484	Truck transportation	83	749	19.1	25,522	68.3
4841	General freight trucking	43	467	12.4	26,559	42.9
48412	General freight trucking, long-distance	36	448	12.0	26,824	41.0
484121	General freight trucking, long-distance, truckload (tl)	31	349	9.3	26,513	31.8
4842	Specialized freight trucking	40	282	6.7	23,805	25.4
484220	Specialized freight (except used goods) trucking, local	23	174	3.9	22,420	15.9
4842203	Dump trucking	15	83	1.9	23,373	10.2
484230	Specialized freight (except used goods) trucking, long-distance	12	78	2.3	29,218	7.9
488	Support activities for transportation	11	87	2.5	28,253	11.6

Sources: Economic Census of the United States, 1997. Only those industries are shown for which both employment and sales/revenue data were available. For the definition of MSAs, CMSAs, and PMSAs, please see the Introduction.

TEXARKANA, TX—TEXARKANA, AR MSA

NAICS	Industry	Estab-lish-ments	Em-ploy-ment	Payroll		Sales, reven. ($ mil.)
				Total ($ mil.)	Per Empl. ($)	
48-49	Transportation and warehousing	78	1,010	24.4	24,171	95.8
484	Truck transportation	56	464	10.2	22,032	48.6
4841	General freight trucking	24	325	7.3	22,440	38.4
48412	General freight trucking, long-distance	19	265	6.2	23,351	33.7
484121	General freight trucking, long-distance, truckload (tl)	16	163	3.9	23,730	25.8
4842	Specialized freight trucking	32	139	2.9	21,079	10.2
484220	Specialized freight (except used goods) trucking, local	16	66	1.5	22,667	5.3
484230	Specialized freight (except used goods) trucking, long-distance	11	46	1.0	22,630	3.6
488	Support activities for transportation	10	282	9.0	31,816	23.2
492	Couriers and messengers	6	79	1.6	20,519	5.0

Sources: Economic Census of the United States, 1997. Only those industries are shown for which both employment and sales/revenue data were available. For the definition of MSAs, CMSAs, and PMSAs, please see the Introduction.

TOLEDO, OH MSA

NAICS	Industry	Estab-lish-ments	Em-ploy-ment	Payroll		Sales, reven. ($ mil.)
				Total ($ mil.)	Per Empl. ($)	
48-49	Transportation and warehousing	383	6,418	199.2	31,034	687.0
481	Air transportation	6	75	1.9	25,267	12.5
484	Truck transportation	245	4,342	142.8	32,880	461.5
4841	General freight trucking	140	3,253	111.2	34,186	348.5
484110	General freight trucking, local	52	616	18.3	29,735	58.0
4841101	General freight trucking without storage, local, truckload (tl)	37	487	15.5	31,924	50.2
48412	General freight trucking, long-distance	88	2,637	92.9	35,226	290.5
484121	General freight trucking, long-distance, truckload (tl)	71	1,216	37.2	30,592	157.1
484122	General freight trucking, long-distance, less than truckload (ltl)	17	1,421	55.7	39,191	133.4
4842	Specialized freight trucking	105	1,089	31.6	28,976	113.0
484210	Used household and office goods moving	16	251	4.7	18,861	14.7
484220	Specialized freight (except used goods) trucking, local	60	427	11.8	27,749	52.0
4842203	Dump trucking	29	217	5.2	24,051	29.7
4842204	Specialized trucking without storage, local	20	165	5.4	32,770	16.9
484230	Specialized freight (except used goods) trucking, long-distance	29	411	15.0	36,428	46.3
4842303	Other specialized trucking, long-distance	17	318	11.7	36,682	35.4
485	Transit and ground passenger transportation	17	299	4.6	15,485	14.5
486	Pipeline transportation	6	139	6.7	47,935	33.9
488	Support activities for transportation	61	804	26.3	32,670	102.2
488410	Motor vehicle towing	11	42	0.7	16,357	2.4
488510	Freight transportation arrangement	32	427	12.8	30,087	37.9
4885102	Arrangement of transportation of freight and cargo	26	299	8.2	27,375	23.3
492110	Couriers	13	512	10.8	21,162	40.1
4931	Warehousing and storage	13	146	4.3	29,137	16.5

Sources: Economic Census of the United States, 1997. Only those industries are shown for which both employment and sales/revenue data were available. For the definition of MSAs, CMSAs, and PMSAs, please see the Introduction.

TOPEKA, KS MSA

NAICS	Industry	Estab-lish-ments	Em-ploy-ment	Payroll		Sales, reven. ($ mil.)
				Total ($ mil.)	Per Empl. ($)	
48-49	Transportation and warehousing	100	1,030	21.3	20,668	67.4
484	Truck transportation	53	449	12.9	28,693	36.0
4841	General freight trucking	20	291	9.3	31,863	23.9
48412	General freight trucking, long-distance	17	287	9.2	32,028	23.6
4842	Specialized freight trucking	33	158	3.6	22,854	12.1
4842203	Dump trucking	12	14	0.6	41,214	3.3
485	Transit and ground passenger transportation	12	310	2.7	8,842	6.9
488	Support activities for transportation	13	85	1.7	19,541	7.7
492	Couriers and messengers	11	122	2.6	21,328	10.1
493	Warehousing and storage	6	38	0.9	23,289	2.6

Sources: *Economic Census of the United States*, 1997. Only those industries are shown for which both employment and sales/revenue data were available. For the definition of MSAs, CMSAs, and PMSAs, please see the Introduction.

TRENTON, NJ PMSA

NAICS	Industry	Estab-lish-ments	Em-ploy-ment	Payroll		Sales, reven. ($ mil.)
				Total ($ mil.)	Per Empl. ($)	
48-49	Transportation and warehousing	154	3,267	84.7	25,926	294.8
484	Truck transportation	56	612	20.9	34,193	71.4
4841	General freight trucking	25	354	13.3	37,678	41.0
484110	General freight trucking, local	12	47	1.4	29,574	3.6
48412	General freight trucking, long-distance	13	307	11.9	38,919	37.4
4842	Specialized freight trucking	31	258	7.6	29,411	30.4
484220	Specialized freight (except used goods) trucking, local	17	74	2.0	27,095	7.8
485	Transit and ground passenger transportation	40	1,890	38.3	20,287	75.3
4853	Taxi and limousine service	15	477	10.1	21,111	21.9
4854101	School bus service	11	591	8.6	14,560	15.9
488	Support activities for transportation	29	167	5.5	32,683	22.1
488510	Freight transportation arrangement	14	47	1.8	38,702	9.1
492	Couriers and messengers	12	401	12.1	30,187	40.3
493	Warehousing and storage	10	118	4.7	39,958	52.7

Sources: *Economic Census of the United States*, 1997. Only those industries are shown for which both employment and sales/revenue data were available. For the definition of MSAs, CMSAs, and PMSAs, please see the Introduction.

TUCSON, AZ MSA

NAICS	Industry	Estab-lish-ments	Em-ploy-ment	Payroll		Sales, reven. ($ mil.)
				Total ($ mil.)	Per Empl. ($)	
48-49	Transportation and warehousing	308	3,768	87.8	23,312	394.1
481	Air transportation	8	199	5.9	29,663	34.8
484	Truck transportation	138	1,207	28.6	23,669	98.2
4841	General freight trucking	54	439	11.6	26,310	46.0
484110	General freight trucking, local	14	139	3.0	21,504	9.3
48412	General freight trucking, long-distance	40	300	8.6	28,537	36.7
484121	General freight trucking, long-distance, truckload (tl)	28	105	2.4	23,267	9.5
484122	General freight trucking, long-distance, less than truckload (ltl)	12	195	6.1	31,374	27.2
4842	Specialized freight trucking	84	768	17.0	22,160	52.2
484210	Used household and office goods moving	27	316	5.4	17,085	13.8
484220	Specialized freight (except used goods) trucking, local	39	276	5.7	20,630	21.7
4842203	Dump trucking	25	168	3.0	17,762	13.2
484230	Specialized freight (except used goods) trucking, long-distance	18	176	5.9	33,670	16.8
4842303	Other specialized trucking, long-distance	11	151	5.4	36,040	14.4
48599	Other transit and ground passenger transportation	16	412	5.9	14,303	14.3
488	Support activities for transportation	69	979	27.2	27,800	83.9
4881	Support activities for air transportation	23	613	19.5	31,809	58.3
48811	Airport operations	11	142	2.5	17,387	7.6
488190	Other support activities for air transportation	12	471	17.0	36,157	50.7
488410	Motor vehicle towing	19	153	2.6	17,222	7.1
488510	Freight transportation arrangement	22	103	3.0	28,777	11.7
4885102	Arrangement of transportation of freight and cargo	16	55	1.6	28,582	6.2
492	Couriers and messengers	38	544	11.5	21,112	51.2

Sources: *Economic Census of the United States*, 1997. Only those industries are shown for which both employment and sales/revenue data were available. For the definition of MSAs, CMSAs, and PMSAs, please see the Introduction.

TULSA, OK MSA

NAICS	Industry	Estab-lish-ments	Em-ploy-ment	Payroll		Sales, reven. ($ mil.)
				Total ($ mil.)	Per Empl. ($)	
48-49	Transportation and warehousing	479	8,891	300.4	33,790	1,659.5
484	Truck transportation	258	4,778	142.0	29,714	522.9
4841	General freight trucking	125	3,588	111.5	31,081	404.2
484110	General freight trucking, local	32	131	3.1	23,336	9.2
4841101	General freight trucking without storage, local, truckload (tl)	19	57	0.8	13,895	3.3
4841102	General freight trucking without storage, local, less than truckload (ltl)	13	74	2.3	30,608	5.9
48412	General freight trucking, long-distance	93	3,457	108.5	31,375	395.0
484121	General freight trucking, long-distance, truckload (tl)	68	2,716	85.2	31,371	321.9
484122	General freight trucking, long-distance, less than truckload (ltl)	25	741	23.3	31,387	73.1
4842	Specialized freight trucking	133	1,190	30.5	25,591	118.8
484210	Used household and office goods moving	26	358	7.7	21,383	26.6
4842101	Used household and office goods moving, local, without storage	11	74	0.6	8,757	2.0
4842102	Used household and office goods moving, long-distance	12	230	6.3	27,200	22.1
484220	Specialized freight (except used goods) trucking, local	60	384	9.7	25,367	38.4
4842203	Dump trucking	24	197	5.8	29,574	26.2
4842204	Specialized trucking without storage, local	23	126	2.9	22,889	8.5
484230	Specialized freight (except used goods) trucking, long-distance	47	448	13.1	29,145	53.8
4842301	Hazardous materials trucking (except waste), long-distance	13	140	4.0	28,900	18.0
4842303	Other specialized trucking, long-distance	25	281	8.5	30,238	32.5
486	Pipeline transportation	34	1,883	104.0	55,218	902.9
486210	Pipeline transportation of natural gas	23	1,363	70.0	51,334	661.8
488	Support activities for transportation	105	1,197	32.5	27,140	128.8
4881	Support activities for air transportation	31	689	18.1	26,226	85.8
488190	Other support activities for air transportation	24	445	12.4	27,861	59.8
488410	Motor vehicle towing	16	100	2.4	23,730	6.5
488510	Freight transportation arrangement	47	256	8.0	31,375	23.9
4885101	Freight forwarding	20	143	4.5	31,294	14.1
4885102	Arrangement of transportation of freight and cargo	27	113	3.6	31,478	9.7
492	Couriers and messengers	41	574	14.2	24,749	60.7
492110	Couriers	18	343	11.1	32,309	50.7
492210	Local messengers and local delivery	23	231	3.1	13,524	10.0
4931	Warehousing and storage	17	47	1.0	21,723	4.2

Sources: Economic Census of the United States, 1997. Only those industries are shown for which both employment and sales/revenue data were available. For the definition of MSAs, CMSAs, and PMSAs, please see the Introduction.

TUSCALOOSA, AL MSA

NAICS	Industry	Estab-lish-ments	Em-ploy-ment	Payroll		Sales, reven. ($ mil.)
				Total ($ mil.)	Per Empl. ($)	
48-49	Transportation and warehousing	116	1,348	32.4	24,016	154.9
484	Truck transportation	94	853	19.1	22,406	96.7
4841	General freight trucking	40	480	11.3	23,462	67.4
48412	General freight trucking, long-distance	31	415	10.2	24,675	61.9
4842	Specialized freight trucking	54	373	7.8	21,046	29.3
484220	Specialized freight (except used goods) trucking, local	37	238	4.4	18,471	15.7
4842203	Dump trucking	21	146	3.0	20,342	10.6
484230	Specialized freight (except used goods) trucking, long-distance	12	86	2.6	30,093	11.7
488	Support activities for transportation	4	52	1.1	21,135	1.8
492	Couriers and messengers	5	34	0.9	25,912	2.7
493	Warehousing and storage	4	77	2.5	33,052	10.1

Sources: Economic Census of the United States, 1997. Only those industries are shown for which both employment and sales/revenue data were available. For the definition of MSAs, CMSAs, and PMSAs, please see the Introduction.

TYLER, TX MSA

NAICS	Industry	Estab-lish-ments	Em-ploy-ment	Payroll		Sales, reven. ($ mil.)
				Total ($ mil.)	Per Empl. ($)	
48-49	Transportation and warehousing	104	1,392	27.5	19,753	99.4
484	Truck transportation	76	1,014	19.3	19,081	70.6
4841	General freight trucking	40	705	15.4	21,884	58.9
48412	General freight trucking, long-distance	33	598	13.3	22,239	52.1
484121	General freight trucking, long-distance, truckload (tl)	23	361	7.6	21,047	31.9
4842	Specialized freight trucking	36	309	3.9	12,686	11.7
484220	Specialized freight (except used goods) trucking, local	18	47	1.0	21,362	4.5
4842203	Dump trucking	12	25	0.6	25,640	3.0
488	Support activities for transportation	12	181	4.3	23,983	13.1
492	Couriers and messengers	6	99	2.5	25,556	9.2

Sources: Economic Census of the United States, 1997. Only those industries are shown for which both employment and sales/revenue data were available. For the definition of MSAs, CMSAs, and PMSAs, please see the Introduction.

UTICA—ROME, NY MSA

NAICS	Industry	Estab-lish-ments	Em-ploy-ment	Payroll		Sales, reven. ($ mil.)
				Total ($ mil.)	Per Empl. ($)	
48-49	Transportation and warehousing	135	1,794	42.5	23,683	111.7
481	Air transportation	4	33	0.8	25,152	10.4
484	Truck transportation	85	845	28.0	33,157	59.8
4841	General freight trucking	31	402	15.9	39,488	24.7
484110	General freight trucking, local	13	52	1.1	21,269	3.6
48412	General freight trucking, long-distance	18	350	14.8	42,194	21.1
484121	General freight trucking, long-distance, truckload (tl)	14	325	13.8	42,542	17.6
4842	Specialized freight trucking	54	443	12.1	27,413	35.2
484220	Specialized freight (except used goods) trucking, local	29	106	2.9	27,038	11.3
4842203	Dump trucking	15	51	1.6	31,824	7.1
484230	Specialized freight (except used goods) trucking, long-distance	18	243	6.9	28,572	18.0
485	Transit and ground passenger transportation	23	714	9.1	12,709	22.7
488	Support activities for transportation	8	38	1.0	27,079	3.2
492	Couriers and messengers	6	134	2.3	17,425	7.1

Sources: Economic Census of the United States, 1997. Only those industries are shown for which both employment and sales/revenue data were available. For the definition of MSAs, CMSAs, and PMSAs, please see the Introduction.

VALLEJO—FAIRFIELD—NAPA, CA PMSA

NAICS	Industry	Estab-lish-ments	Em-ploy-ment	Payroll		Sales, reven. ($ mil.)
				Total ($ mil.)	Per Empl. ($)	
48-49	Transportation and warehousing	220	3,288	106.0	32,249	443.8
484	Truck transportation	138	1,716	49.7	28,974	172.4
4841	General freight trucking	42	718	19.8	27,581	65.9
484110	General freight trucking, local	17	101	2.4	23,426	10.7
4841101	General freight trucking without storage, local, truckload (tl)	11	69	1.5	21,913	7.6
48412	General freight trucking, long-distance	25	617	17.4	28,261	55.2
484121	General freight trucking, long-distance, truckload (tl)	21	582	15.7	27,019	48.2
4842	Specialized freight trucking	96	998	29.9	29,977	106.5
484210	Used household and office goods moving	34	375	6.0	16,125	18.4
4842101	Used household and office goods moving, local, without storage	17	88	1.3	14,216	3.1
484220	Specialized freight (except used goods) trucking, local	41	320	12.1	37,669	48.2
4842203	Dump trucking	21	101	2.9	28,614	11.2
4842204	Specialized trucking without storage, local	12	150	6.4	42,493	18.6
484230	Specialized freight (except used goods) trucking, long-distance	21	303	11.8	38,997	39.9
488	Support activities for transportation	42	339	8.6	25,484	33.1
4884	Support activities for road transportation	19	125	3.1	24,896	8.6
488410	Motor vehicle towing	15	116	3.0	25,879	8.2
4931	Warehousing and storage	11	78	2.8	35,590	10.9

Sources: Economic Census of the United States, 1997. Only those industries are shown for which both employment and sales/revenue data were available. For the definition of MSAs, CMSAs, and PMSAs, please see the Introduction.

VENTURA, CA PMSA

| NAICS | Industry | Estab-lish-ments | Em-ploy-ment | Payroll | | Sales, reven. ($ mil.) |
				Total ($ mil.)	Per Empl. ($)	
48-49	Transportation and warehousing	297	3,109	78.6	25,272	318.2
484	Truck transportation	171	1,360	35.7	26,237	132.8
4841	General freight trucking	45	491	16.4	33,316	62.6
484110	General freight trucking, local	21	158	4.4	27,772	14.3
4841101	General freight trucking without storage, local, truckload (tl)	15	54	1.5	27,278	6.4
48412	General freight trucking, long-distance	24	333	12.0	35,946	48.3
484121	General freight trucking, long-distance, truckload (tl)	14	85	3.1	36,659	15.5
4842	Specialized freight trucking	126	869	19.3	22,238	70.2
484210	Used household and office goods moving	22	245	4.7	18,996	14.6
484220	Specialized freight (except used goods) trucking, local	83	472	8.7	18,439	33.0
4842202	Agricultural products trucking without storage, local	15	106	2.2	20,396	8.3
4842203	Dump trucking	38	133	3.1	22,955	13.4
4842204	Specialized trucking without storage, local	26	180	2.3	12,972	9.0
484230	Specialized freight (except used goods) trucking, long-distance	21	152	6.0	39,263	22.5
4842303	Other specialized trucking, long-distance	11	132	5.3	39,932	19.0
485	Transit and ground passenger transportation	31	608	9.2	15,158	24.6
4853	Taxi and limousine service	13	120	1.6	13,142	5.1
48599	Other transit and ground passenger transportation	11	137	2.3	16,547	5.8
488	Support activities for transportation	51	363	12.1	33,336	44.9
4881	Support activities for air transportation	11	65	2.4	36,877	11.6
488410	Motor vehicle towing	20	159	4.2	26,208	11.2
488510	Freight transportation arrangement	12	41	2.9	69,585	14.9
492	Couriers and messengers	11	259	5.3	20,622	18.3
493	Warehousing and storage	9	113	2.7	23,735	15.3

Sources: *Economic Census of the United States*, 1997. Only those industries are shown for which both employment and sales/revenue data were available. For the definition of MSAs, CMSAs, and PMSAs, please see the Introduction.

VICTORIA, TX MSA

| NAICS | Industry | Estab-lish-ments | Em-ploy-ment | Payroll | | Sales, reven. ($ mil.) |
				Total ($ mil.)	Per Empl. ($)	
48-49	Transportation and warehousing	59	702	20.9	29,724	106.0
484	Truck transportation	36	384	9.7	25,310	26.9
4841	General freight trucking	19	219	5.5	25,027	12.7
48412	General freight trucking, long-distance	13	131	3.3	24,931	8.2
4842	Specialized freight trucking	17	165	4.2	25,685	14.2
486	Pipeline transportation	8	103	6.0	58,146	65.6
488	Support activities for transportation	6	150	3.5	23,133	7.9
492	Couriers and messengers	5	38	0.8	21,526	2.8

Sources: *Economic Census of the United States*, 1997. Only those industries are shown for which both employment and sales/revenue data were available. For the definition of MSAs, CMSAs, and PMSAs, please see the Introduction.

VINELAND—MILLVILLE—BRIDGETON, NJ PMSA

| NAICS | Industry | Estab-lish-ments | Em-ploy-ment | Payroll | | Sales, reven. ($ mil.) |
				Total ($ mil.)	Per Empl. ($)	
48-49	Transportation and warehousing	103	3,166	85.2	26,924	338.5
484	Truck transportation	58	2,172	61.6	28,363	213.1
4841	General freight trucking	24	1,701	46.7	27,435	166.7
484110	General freight trucking, local	11	48	1.3	26,479	6.0
48412	General freight trucking, long-distance	13	1,653	45.4	27,463	160.7
4842	Specialized freight trucking	34	471	14.9	31,715	46.4
484220	Specialized freight (except used goods) trucking, local	19	144	4.5	31,049	13.7
485	Transit and ground passenger transportation	12	330	3.9	11,782	11.2

Sources: *Economic Census of the United States*, 1997. Only those industries are shown for which both employment and sales/revenue data were available. For the definition of MSAs, CMSAs, and PMSAs, please see the Introduction.

VISALIA—TULARE—PORTERVILLE, CA MSA

| NAICS | Industry | Estab-lish-ments | Em-ploy-ment | Payroll | | Sales, reven. ($ mil.) |
				Total ($ mil.)	Per Empl. ($)	
48-49	Transportation and warehousing	204	2,514	71.7	28,529	254.3
484	Truck transportation	149	1,712	52.8	30,844	155.0
4841	General freight trucking	40	799	29.3	36,622	61.6
484110	General freight trucking, local	15	62	1.8	29,613	10.5
4841101	General freight trucking without storage, local, truckload (tl)	12	56	1.6	28,804	9.6
48412	General freight trucking, long-distance	25	737	27.4	37,212	51.1
484121	General freight trucking, long-distance, truckload (tl)	21	669	24.8	37,133	44.6
4842	Specialized freight trucking	109	913	23.5	25,788	93.4
484220	Specialized freight (except used goods) trucking, local	68	338	8.4	24,976	36.0
4842202	Agricultural products trucking without storage, local	45	241	5.7	23,515	23.8
484230	Specialized freight (except used goods) trucking, long-distance	38	560	14.6	26,150	56.3
4842302	Agricultural products trucking, long-distance	26	419	11.0	26,353	42.4
485	Transit and ground passenger transportation	9	202	2.4	11,950	7.3
488	Support activities for transportation	21	188	3.8	19,952	21.4
4931	Warehousing and storage	13	202	4.5	22,208	18.8

Sources: Economic Census of the United States, 1997. Only those industries are shown for which both employment and sales/revenue data were available. For the definition of MSAs, CMSAs, and PMSAs, please see the Introduction.

WACO, TX MSA

| NAICS | Industry | Estab-lish-ments | Em-ploy-ment | Payroll | | Sales, reven. ($ mil.) |
				Total ($ mil.)	Per Empl. ($)	
48-49	Transportation and warehousing	102	1,653	34.4	20,832	114.8
484	Truck transportation	69	1,008	24.6	24,438	83.2
4841	General freight trucking	32	505	11.8	23,416	42.2
48412	General freight trucking, long-distance	22	334	8.6	25,632	33.5
484121	General freight trucking, long-distance, truckload (tl)	13	118	2.4	20,034	10.3
4842	Specialized freight trucking	37	503	12.8	25,465	41.0
484220	Specialized freight (except used goods) trucking, local	15	114	2.0	17,316	6.9
484230	Specialized freight (except used goods) trucking, long-distance	16	352	10.1	28,585	32.2
4842303	Other specialized trucking, long-distance	11	324	9.7	29,923	30.2
485	Transit and ground passenger transportation	10	300	3.2	10,597	6.6
488	Support activities for transportation	11	87	1.6	18,885	6.3
492	Couriers and messengers	8	182	2.8	15,313	10.2

Sources: Economic Census of the United States, 1997. Only those industries are shown for which both employment and sales/revenue data were available. For the definition of MSAs, CMSAs, and PMSAs, please see the Introduction.

WASHINGTON, DC—MD—VA—WV PMSA

NAICS	Industry	Estab-lish-ments	Em-ploy-ment	Payroll Total ($ mil.)	Payroll Per Empl. ($)	Sales, reven. ($ mil.)
48-49	Transportation and warehousing	2,006	31,665	884.4	27,931	3,902.3
481	Air transportation	71	1,762	56.9	32,275	577.8
481111	Scheduled passenger air transportation	45	1,566	47.2	30,158	534.7
484	Truck transportation	874	10,277	276.5	26,901	856.2
4841	General freight trucking	220	2,892	93.2	32,232	306.9
484110	General freight trucking, local	98	915	26.4	28,834	70.7
4841101	General freight trucking without storage, local, truckload (tl)	65	348	9.0	25,885	30.8
4841102	General freight trucking without storage, local, less than truckload (ltl)	23	287	8.9	30,861	20.0
48412	General freight trucking, long-distance	122	1,977	66.8	33,805	236.2
484121	General freight trucking, long-distance, truckload (tl)	96	1,292	40.3	31,192	160.0
484122	General freight trucking, long-distance, less than truckload (ltl)	26	685	26.5	38,733	76.3
4842	Specialized freight trucking	654	7,385	183.2	24,813	549.3
484210	Used household and office goods moving	200	4,425	112.3	25,367	290.1
4842101	Used household and office goods moving, local, without storage	73	582	12.7	21,823	34.8
4842102	Used household and office goods moving, long-distance	61	1,590	46.5	29,234	135.4
4842103	Used household and office goods moving, local, with storage	66	2,253	53.1	23,554	119.8
484220	Specialized freight (except used goods) trucking, local	398	2,338	51.2	21,883	199.3
4842202	Agricultural products trucking without storage, local	28	342	5.2	15,196	16.7
4842203	Dump trucking	246	1,188	28.6	24,078	120.6
4842204	Specialized trucking without storage, local	111	736	15.8	21,486	58.3
484230	Specialized freight (except used goods) trucking, long-distance	56	622	19.8	31,883	60.0
4842303	Other specialized trucking, long-distance	37	449	15.2	33,882	45.7
485	Transit and ground passenger transportation	307	4,098	71.4	17,428	256.7
4853	Taxi and limousine service	116	1,292	26.7	20,703	134.7
485310	Taxi service	40	569	9.9	17,381	43.5
485320	Limousine service	76	723	16.9	23,317	91.2
485410	School and employee bus transportation	101	879	11.3	12,811	33.1
485510	Charter bus industry	30	549	11.9	21,658	37.2
4855101	Charter bus service, local	11	85	2.1	24,212	7.5
4855102	Charter bus service, interstate/interurban	19	464	9.8	21,190	29.7
485999	All other transit and ground passenger transportation	16	144	3.4	23,583	14.1
486210	Pipeline transportation of natural gas	17	329	28.6	87,052	83.5
488	Support activities for transportation	379	4,869	144.2	29,610	439.4
4881	Support activities for air transportation	57	2,351	52.7	22,414	137.9
48811	Airport operations	28	1,536	27.8	18,118	79.6
488190	Other support activities for air transportation	29	815	24.9	30,509	58.2
4884	Support activities for road transportation	129	843	20.2	23,948	68.7
488410	Motor vehicle towing	123	755	17.8	23,607	55.4
488510	Freight transportation arrangement	158	1,174	49.4	42,055	166.9
4885101	Freight forwarding	80	768	32.2	41,964	118.9
4885102	Arrangement of transportation of freight and cargo	78	406	17.1	42,229	48.0
492	Couriers and messengers	273	9,131	270.5	29,619	829.0
492110	Couriers	120	7,408	235.2	31,749	684.7
4921101	Courier services (except by air)	41	4,314	141.4	32,766	276.5
4921102	Air courier services	79	3,094	93.8	30,331	408.2
492210	Local messengers and local delivery	153	1,723	35.3	20,461	144.3
4931	Warehousing and storage	51	554	14.3	25,859	45.2
4931101	General warehousing and storage (except in foreign trade zones)	36	425	11.7	27,478	33.2

Sources: Economic Census of the United States, 1997. Only those industries are shown for which both employment and sales/revenue data were available. For the definition of MSAs, CMSAs, and PMSAs, please see the Introduction.

WASHINGTON—BALTIMORE, DC—MD—VA—WV CMSA

NAICS	Industry	Estab-lish-ments	Em-ploy-ment	Payroll Total ($ mil.)	Payroll Per Empl. ($)	Sales, reven. ($ mil.)
48-49	Transportation and warehousing	3,831	60,711	1,669.1	27,493	6,540.9
484	Truck transportation	1,710	21,734	617.2	28,397	2,048.2
4841	General freight trucking	542	9,305	309.7	33,282	1,057.8
484110	General freight trucking, local	229	2,092	55.9	26,743	167.5
48412	General freight trucking, long-distance	313	7,213	253.7	35,178	890.3
484121	General freight trucking, long-distance, truckload (tl)	242	4,278	137.2	32,068	563.8
484122	General freight trucking, long-distance, less than truckload (ltl)	71	2,935	116.6	39,711	326.5
4842	Specialized freight trucking	1,168	12,429	307.5	24,741	990.3
4842204	Specialized trucking without storage, local	213	1,262	28.3	22,414	98.3
4842301	Hazardous materials trucking (except waste), long-distance	14	233	7.5	32,326	27.1
488	Support activities for transportation	765	11,404	328.5	28,802	950.1
488490	Other support activities for road transportation	16	177	4.2	23,463	16.7
488510	Freight transportation arrangement	368	3,212	120.1	37,389	367.7
4921102	Air courier services	108	4,234	131.5	31,062	552.3

Sources: Economic Census of the United States, 1997. Only those industries are shown for which both employment and sales/revenue data were available. For the definition of MSAs, CMSAs, and PMSAs, please see the Introduction.

WATERBURY, CT PMSA

NAICS	Industry	Estab-lish-ments	Em-ploy-ment	Payroll		Sales, reven. ($ mil.)
				Total ($ mil.)	Per Empl. ($)	
48-49	Transportation and warehousing	85	1,133	21.2	18,726	70.5
484	Truck transportation	49	350	9.7	27,697	35.4
4841	General freight trucking	19	146	5.3	36,082	18.7
48412	General freight trucking, long-distance	14	113	4.2	36,779	14.8
484121	General freight trucking, long-distance, truckload (tl)	11	42	0.9	21,857	4.2
4842	Specialized freight trucking	30	204	4.4	21,696	16.7
484220	Specialized freight (except used goods) trucking, local	20	153	3.3	21,791	13.4
4842203	Dump trucking	11	62	1.9	30,774	9.6
485	Transit and ground passenger transportation	19	689	9.0	13,032	23.2

Sources: *Economic Census of the United States*, 1997. Only those industries are shown for which both employment and sales/revenue data were available. For the definition of MSAs, CMSAs, and PMSAs, please see the Introduction.

WATERLOO—CEDAR FALLS, IA MSA

NAICS	Industry	Estab-lish-ments	Em-ploy-ment	Payroll		Sales, reven. ($ mil.)
				Total ($ mil.)	Per Empl. ($)	
48-49	Transportation and warehousing	95	1,178	32.4	27,511	185.1
481	Air transportation	3	29	0.5	16,690	5.6
484	Truck transportation	60	649	20.1	30,932	140.5
4841	General freight trucking	38	554	17.7	31,939	131.1
48412	General freight trucking, long-distance	29	528	17.2	32,513	129.6
484121	General freight trucking, long-distance, truckload (tl)	22	377	11.4	30,284	112.3
4842	Specialized freight trucking	22	95	2.4	25,063	9.4
484220	Specialized freight (except used goods) trucking, local	13	51	1.3	24,569	4.9
488	Support activities for transportation	13	122	3.5	28,852	8.9
492	Couriers and messengers	7	105	1.9	18,314	5.1
493	Warehousing and storage	5	126	3.4	27,349	9.7

Sources: *Economic Census of the United States*, 1997. Only those industries are shown for which both employment and sales/revenue data were available. For the definition of MSAs, CMSAs, and PMSAs, please see the Introduction.

WAUSAU, WI MSA

NAICS	Industry	Estab-lish-ments	Em-ploy-ment	Payroll		Sales, reven. ($ mil.)
				Total ($ mil.)	Per Empl. ($)	
48-49	Transportation and warehousing	178	1,992	53.8	27,011	450.6
484	Truck transportation	125	1,258	43.6	34,679	347.3
4841	General freight trucking	74	942	35.3	37,451	130.6
484110	General freight trucking, local	18	86	4.0	46,698	12.5
4841101	General freight trucking without storage, local, truckload (tl)	13	67	3.4	51,090	10.8
48412	General freight trucking, long-distance	56	856	31.3	36,522	118.0
484121	General freight trucking, long-distance, truckload (tl)	43	711	26.0	36,636	93.5
484122	General freight trucking, long-distance, less than truckload (ltl)	13	145	5.2	35,966	24.5
4842	Specialized freight trucking	51	316	8.3	26,415	216.7
4842203	Dump trucking	16	47	1.5	31,830	6.6
485	Transit and ground passenger transportation	20	495	4.6	9,220	11.5
488	Support activities for transportation	13	76	1.8	24,184	13.1
493	Warehousing and storage	7	53	1.2	21,925	5.0

Sources: *Economic Census of the United States*, 1997. Only those industries are shown for which both employment and sales/revenue data were available. For the definition of MSAs, CMSAs, and PMSAs, please see the Introduction.

WEST PALM BEACH—BOCA RATON, FL MSA

| NAICS | Industry | Estab-lish-ments | Em-ploy-ment | Payroll | | Sales, reven. ($ mil.) |
				Total ($ mil.)	Per Empl. ($)	
48-49	Transportation and warehousing	555	4,631	127.2	27,473	534.5
481	Air transportation	28	141	5.0	35,567	71.5
481211	Nonscheduled chartered passenger air transportation	15	38	1.6	42,289	9.5
483	Water transportation	15	218	3.9	17,734	19.4
484	Truck transportation	191	1,496	46.7	31,246	176.7
4841	General freight trucking	63	763	25.8	33,814	90.4
484110	General freight trucking, local	22	93	2.6	28,054	9.8
4841101	General freight trucking without storage, local, truckload (tl)	16	65	2.0	30,431	6.9
48412	General freight trucking, long-distance	41	670	23.2	34,613	80.6
484121	General freight trucking, long-distance, truckload (tl)	26	314	11.1	35,439	37.6
484122	General freight trucking, long-distance, less than truckload (ltl)	15	356	12.1	33,885	42.9
4842	Specialized freight trucking	128	733	20.9	28,573	86.3
484210	Used household and office goods moving	44	327	7.1	21,765	21.5
4842101	Used household and office goods moving, local, without storage	18	66	0.8	12,000	2.8
4842103	Used household and office goods moving, local, with storage	18	196	4.3	22,153	13.4
484220	Specialized freight (except used goods) trucking, local	53	219	6.4	29,256	31.7
4842203	Dump trucking	28	108	2.4	22,454	20.7
4842204	Specialized trucking without storage, local	14	68	1.5	21,632	7.1
484230	Specialized freight (except used goods) trucking, long-distance	31	187	7.4	39,679	33.1
4842303	Other specialized trucking, long-distance	24	159	6.7	42,119	30.9
485	Transit and ground passenger transportation	65	585	9.5	16,197	31.2
4853	Taxi and limousine service	34	377	6.3	16,719	16.6
485320	Limousine service	26	266	4.4	16,549	10.4
48599	Other transit and ground passenger transportation	26	107	1.4	13,243	6.3
485991	Special needs transportation	17	86	1.2	14,093	4.7
487210	Scenic and sightseeing transportation, water	41	103	2.3	22,107	9.3
4872102	Charter fishing and party fishing boats	32	62	1.6	26,242	6.2
488	Support activities for transportation	145	1,393	42.2	30,303	152.6
4881	Support activities for air transportation	35	578	14.0	24,171	66.1
4881191	Airport operation and terminal services	16	474	11.4	24,019	58.6
488190	Other support activities for air transportation	19	104	2.6	24,865	7.6
488390	Other support activities for water transportation	13	16	0.4	25,812	1.4
488410	Motor vehicle towing	28	157	2.9	18,580	7.1
488510	Freight transportation arrangement	42	561	22.9	40,824	72.1
4885102	Arrangement of transportation of freight and cargo	32	519	21.5	41,489	63.7
492	Couriers and messengers	46	625	15.5	24,795	59.1
492110	Couriers	19	503	13.5	26,797	48.7
492210	Local messengers and local delivery	27	122	2.0	16,541	10.4
4931	Warehousing and storage	19	58	1.4	23,397	12.1
4931101	General warehousing and storage (except in foreign trade zones)	13	45	1.1	24,267	5.2

Sources: *Economic Census of the United States*, 1997. Only those industries are shown for which both employment and sales/revenue data were available. For the definition of MSAs, CMSAs, and PMSAs, please see the Introduction.

WHEELING, WV—OH MSA

| NAICS | Industry | Estab-lish-ments | Em-ploy-ment | Payroll | | Sales, reven. ($ mil.) |
				Total ($ mil.)	Per Empl. ($)	
48-49	Transportation and warehousing	103	756	18.9	25,013	83.6
484	Truck transportation	78	527	13.2	25,017	53.3
4841	General freight trucking	22	148	5.1	34,453	14.2
48412	General freight trucking, long-distance	15	122	4.6	37,557	12.3
4842	Specialized freight trucking	56	379	8.1	21,332	39.2
484220	Specialized freight (except used goods) trucking, local	44	298	6.0	20,054	32.2
488	Support activities for transportation	11	51	1.4	27,549	14.2
492	Couriers and messengers	4	70	1.5	22,029	3.4

Sources: *Economic Census of the United States*, 1997. Only those industries are shown for which both employment and sales/revenue data were available. For the definition of MSAs, CMSAs, and PMSAs, please see the Introduction.

WICHITA FALLS, TX MSA

NAICS	Industry	Estab-lish-ments	Em-ploy-ment	Payroll		Sales, reven. ($ mil.)
				Total ($ mil.)	Per Empl. ($)	
48-49	Transportation and warehousing	84	936	21.6	23,028	91.0
484	Truck transportation	58	578	12.2	21,029	44.4
4841	General freight trucking	29	401	8.9	22,177	29.4
48412	General freight trucking, long-distance	21	287	7.7	26,843	22.3
484121	General freight trucking, long-distance, truckload (tl)	13	177	4.9	27,876	13.3
4842	Specialized freight trucking	29	177	3.3	18,429	15.0
484220	Specialized freight (except used goods) trucking, local	13	47	0.9	18,979	4.0
488	Support activities for transportation	10	109	5.7	52,257	22.0
492	Couriers and messengers	4	36	1.0	27,556	3.5

Sources: Economic Census of the United States, 1997. Only those industries are shown for which both employment and sales/revenue data were available. For the definition of MSAs, CMSAs, and PMSAs, please see the Introduction.

WICHITA, KS MSA

NAICS	Industry	Estab-lish-ments	Em-ploy-ment	Payroll		Sales, reven. ($ mil.)
				Total ($ mil.)	Per Empl. ($)	
48-49	Transportation and warehousing	340	5,031	133.5	26,542	503.2
484	Truck transportation	205	2,608	74.1	28,396	263.4
4841	General freight trucking	93	1,675	52.8	31,529	185.7
484110	General freight trucking, local	27	423	11.0	26,106	30.5
4841102	General freight trucking without storage, local, less than truckload (ltl)	13	327	8.9	27,263	22.3
48412	General freight trucking, long-distance	66	1,252	41.8	33,361	155.3
484121	General freight trucking, long-distance, truckload (tl)	44	548	15.1	27,564	76.8
484122	General freight trucking, long-distance, less than truckload (ltl)	22	704	26.7	37,874	78.5
4842	Specialized freight trucking	112	933	21.2	22,773	77.7
484210	Used household and office goods moving	16	310	6.4	20,581	17.9
484220	Specialized freight (except used goods) trucking, local	68	400	9.3	23,353	36.4
4842202	Agricultural products trucking without storage, local	16	83	1.4	16,892	6.4
4842203	Dump trucking	33	183	3.9	21,536	16.6
4842204	Specialized trucking without storage, local	19	134	4.0	29,836	13.3
484230	Specialized freight (except used goods) trucking, long-distance	28	223	5.5	24,780	23.4
4842302	Agricultural products trucking, long-distance	16	71	2.0	27,535	10.3
485	Transit and ground passenger transportation	16	717	7.3	10,240	15.9
486	Pipeline transportation	18	268	13.0	48,623	61.9
488	Support activities for transportation	57	799	24.5	30,677	104.4
488190	Other support activities for air transportation	16	487	17.9	36,782	78.3
488510	Freight transportation arrangement	25	109	3.3	30,229	13.7
4885102	Arrangement of transportation of freight and cargo	20	93	2.9	30,914	11.9
492	Couriers and messengers	28	465	10.3	22,123	40.4
492110	Couriers	17	384	8.9	23,305	37.5
492210	Local messengers and local delivery	11	81	1.3	16,519	3.0
493	Warehousing and storage	10	97	2.5	25,948	9.6

Sources: Economic Census of the United States, 1997. Only those industries are shown for which both employment and sales/revenue data were available. For the definition of MSAs, CMSAs, and PMSAs, please see the Introduction.

WILLIAMSPORT, PA MSA

NAICS	Industry	Estab-lish-ments	Em-ploy-ment	Payroll		Sales, reven. ($ mil.)
				Total ($ mil.)	Per Empl. ($)	
48-49	Transportation and warehousing	76	842	20.7	24,546	86.1
481	Air transportation	3	31	0.4	13,258	4.1
484	Truck transportation	44	481	14.6	30,393	53.0
4841	General freight trucking	19	145	3.9	26,793	16.1
48412	General freight trucking, long-distance	15	134	3.8	28,261	15.5
4842	Specialized freight trucking	25	336	10.7	31,946	36.9
484220	Specialized freight (except used goods) trucking, local	17	67	1.5	21,746	11.1
485	Transit and ground passenger transportation	15	125	0.9	7,104	3.3
4854101	School bus service	12	97	0.6	6,515	2.6
492	Couriers and messengers	6	100	2.4	24,120	8.5

Sources: Economic Census of the United States, 1997. Only those industries are shown for which both employment and sales/revenue data were available. For the definition of MSAs, CMSAs, and PMSAs, please see the Introduction.

WILMINGTON, NC MSA

NAICS	Industry	Estab-lish-ments	Em-ploy-ment	Payroll		Sales, reven. ($ mil.)
				Total ($ mil.)	Per Empl. ($)	
48-49	Transportation and warehousing	223	2,851	66.1	23,179	219.4
483	Water transportation	5	95	2.3	23,884	11.8
484	Truck transportation	125	1,182	34.2	28,895	121.4
4841	General freight trucking	58	621	18.4	29,705	61.6
484110	General freight trucking, local	16	89	1.4	15,461	8.4
4841101	General freight trucking without storage, local, truckload (tl)	11	71	1.0	14,634	5.0
48412	General freight trucking, long-distance	42	532	17.1	32,088	53.2
484121	General freight trucking, long-distance, truckload (tl)	28	322	9.0	27,854	28.9
484122	General freight trucking, long-distance, less than truckload (ltl)	14	210	8.1	38,581	24.3
4842	Specialized freight trucking	67	561	15.7	27,998	59.8
484210	Used household and office goods moving	11	62	1.6	26,194	4.6
484220	Specialized freight (except used goods) trucking, local	35	216	5.8	26,819	18.8
4842203	Dump trucking	21	132	3.2	24,356	11.2
484230	Specialized freight (except used goods) trucking, long-distance	21	283	8.3	29,293	36.4
485	Transit and ground passenger transportation	7	78	1.4	18,128	3.3
488	Support activities for transportation	60	1,207	21.3	17,626	59.2
4883	Support activities for water transportation	19	906	12.7	14,025	31.3
488510	Freight transportation arrangement	31	224	7.2	32,161	22.4
4885102	Arrangement of transportation of freight and cargo	24	177	5.6	31,390	14.7
493	Warehousing and storage	8	89	2.8	31,944	10.0

Sources: *Economic Census of the United States*, 1997. Only those industries are shown for which both employment and sales/revenue data were available. For the definition of MSAs, CMSAs, and PMSAs, please see the Introduction.

WILMINGTON—NEWARK, DE—MD PMSA

NAICS	Industry	Estab-lish-ments	Em-ploy-ment	Payroll		Sales, reven. ($ mil.)
				Total ($ mil.)	Per Empl. ($)	
48-49	Transportation and warehousing	378	5,704	149.2	26,150	478.6
484	Truck transportation	224	2,369	69.6	29,370	228.9
4841	General freight trucking	89	989	31.9	32,292	109.6
484110	General freight trucking, local	26	117	3.0	25,470	14.9
48412	General freight trucking, long-distance	63	872	29.0	33,208	94.8
484121	General freight trucking, long-distance, truckload (tl)	52	595	18.2	30,523	56.9
484122	General freight trucking, long-distance, less than truckload (ltl)	11	277	10.8	38,975	37.8
4842	Specialized freight trucking	135	1,380	37.6	27,275	119.3
484210	Used household and office goods moving	21	485	10.6	21,885	28.6
484220	Specialized freight (except used goods) trucking, local	73	380	11.6	30,411	43.9
4842203	Dump trucking	52	190	4.2	22,011	19.5
484230	Specialized freight (except used goods) trucking, long-distance	41	515	15.5	30,039	46.9
4842301	Hazardous materials trucking (except waste), long-distance	21	124	4.8	39,024	17.1
4842303	Other specialized trucking, long-distance	16	342	9.8	28,529	25.7
485	Transit and ground passenger transportation	45	1,223	20.4	16,683	49.3
485410	School and employee bus transportation	22	668	7.5	11,193	19.2
488	Support activities for transportation	60	1,128	30.3	26,820	98.1
4881	Support activities for air transportation	15	349	12.5	35,891	50.5
488190	Other support activities for air transportation	11	301	10.3	34,070	43.0
4883	Support activities for water transportation	12	454	10.7	23,463	28.1
488510	Freight transportation arrangement	16	38	1.8	46,579	3.9
492	Couriers and messengers	12	436	12.7	29,213	45.0

Sources: *Economic Census of the United States*, 1997. Only those industries are shown for which both employment and sales/revenue data were available. For the definition of MSAs, CMSAs, and PMSAs, please see the Introduction.

WORCESTER, MA—CT PMSA

NAICS	Industry	Estab-lish-ments	Em-ploy-ment	Payroll		Sales, reven. ($ mil.)
				Total ($ mil.)	Per Empl. ($)	
48-49	Transportation and warehousing	248	3,363	88.2	26,223	307.3
484	Truck transportation	147	1,450	50.8	35,026	200.7
4841	General freight trucking	68	897	32.8	36,517	135.9
484110	General freight trucking, local	30	234	7.3	31,321	22.4
4841101	General freight trucking without storage, local, truckload (tl)	16	164	5.3	32,012	16.1
48412	General freight trucking, long-distance	38	663	25.4	38,351	113.5
484121	General freight trucking, long-distance, truckload (tl)	22	168	5.9	34,982	22.0
484122	General freight trucking, long-distance, less than truckload (ltl)	16	495	19.5	39,495	91.5
4842	Specialized freight trucking	79	553	18.0	32,606	64.8
484210	Used household and office goods moving	14	118	2.6	21,703	10.8
484220	Specialized freight (except used goods) trucking, local	44	199	5.2	25,995	22.8
4842203	Dump trucking	28	79	2.0	25,076	8.7
4842204	Specialized trucking without storage, local	11	64	1.6	25,484	6.4
484230	Specialized freight (except used goods) trucking, long-distance	21	236	10.3	43,631	31.2
485	Transit and ground passenger transportation	45	1,306	20.2	15,433	48.4
4853	Taxi and limousine service	20	118	1.2	10,449	3.6
485310	Taxi service	12	51	0.8	15,686	1.7
48599	Other transit and ground passenger transportation	12	215	3.3	15,353	8.3
488510	Freight transportation arrangement	11	87	2.2	25,264	8.5

Sources: *Economic Census of the United States*, 1997. Only those industries are shown for which both employment and sales/revenue data were available. For the definition of MSAs, CMSAs, and PMSAs, please see the Introduction.

YAKIMA, WA MSA

NAICS	Industry	Estab-lish-ments	Em-ploy-ment	Payroll		Sales, reven. ($ mil.)
				Total ($ mil.)	Per Empl. ($)	
48-49	Transportation and warehousing	162	1,610	40.2	24,973	148.5
484	Truck transportation	108	1,134	29.7	26,202	105.9
4841	General freight trucking	55	857	22.4	26,095	79.8
484110	General freight trucking, local	11	146	3.6	24,356	11.4
48412	General freight trucking, long-distance	44	711	18.8	26,451	68.4
484121	General freight trucking, long-distance, truckload (tl)	35	633	16.2	25,558	59.9
4842	Specialized freight trucking	53	277	7.3	26,534	26.1
484220	Specialized freight (except used goods) trucking, local	26	68	1.7	24,294	7.0
4842202	Agricultural products trucking without storage, local	14	54	1.5	27,574	6.2
484230	Specialized freight (except used goods) trucking, long-distance	21	169	5.1	30,213	17.3
4842302	Agricultural products trucking, long-distance	16	103	3.2	30,650	11.1
488	Support activities for transportation	28	127	4.1	31,913	11.9
488510	Freight transportation arrangement	20	93	2.7	29,086	8.2
4931	Warehousing and storage	12	98	2.2	22,235	12.0

Sources: *Economic Census of the United States*, 1997. Only those industries are shown for which both employment and sales/revenue data were available. For the definition of MSAs, CMSAs, and PMSAs, please see the Introduction.

YOLO, CA PMSA

NAICS	Industry	Estab-lish-ments	Em-ploy-ment	Payroll		Sales, reven. ($ mil.)
				Total ($ mil.)	Per Empl. ($)	
48-49	Transportation and warehousing	156	2,889	90.9	31,452	277.9
484	Truck transportation	104	2,148	71.2	33,150	204.3
4841	General freight trucking	44	1,619	52.4	32,356	134.7
484110	General freight trucking, local	19	625	15.5	24,830	29.7
48412	General freight trucking, long-distance	25	994	36.9	37,088	105.0
484121	General freight trucking, long-distance, truckload (tl)	14	432	13.6	31,428	51.4
484122	General freight trucking, long-distance, less than truckload (ltl)	11	562	23.3	41,438	53.6
4842	Specialized freight trucking	60	529	18.8	35,582	69.6
484220	Specialized freight (except used goods) trucking, local	34	257	9.5	36,848	32.6
4842202	Agricultural products trucking without storage, local	18	42	2.0	46,476	5.3
4842302	Agricultural products trucking, long-distance	17	106	4.4	41,717	21.8
488	Support activities for transportation	27	351	11.3	32,285	46.8
488410	Motor vehicle towing	11	91	2.2	24,209	6.7
492	Couriers and messengers	9	139	2.5	17,914	7.7
493	Warehousing and storage	10	189	5.1	27,069	16.9

Sources: *Economic Census of the United States*, 1997. Only those industries are shown for which both employment and sales/revenue data were available. For the definition of MSAs, CMSAs, and PMSAs, please see the Introduction.

YORK, PA MSA

| NAICS | Industry | Estab-lish-ments | Em-ploy-ment | Payroll | | Sales, reven. ($ mil.) |
				Total ($ mil.)	Per Empl. ($)	
48-49	Transportation and warehousing	170	3,709	102.7	27,697	399.3
484	Truck transportation	106	2,143	73.9	34,478	250.7
4841	General freight trucking	56	1,882	66.9	35,531	224.8
484110	General freight trucking, local	19	114	3.2	28,395	11.9
4841101	General freight trucking without storage, local, truckload (tl)	16	97	2.7	28,330	10.6
48412	General freight trucking, long-distance	37	1,768	63.6	35,991	212.9
484121	General freight trucking, long-distance, truckload (tl)	27	832	27.1	32,560	99.5
4842	Specialized freight trucking	50	261	7.0	26,885	25.9
484220	Specialized freight (except used goods) trucking, local	30	85	1.6	19,259	6.9
4842203	Dump trucking	11	30	0.5	17,167	3.1
484230	Specialized freight (except used goods) trucking, long-distance	15	101	3.2	32,168	10.7
4842303	Other specialized trucking, long-distance	12	95	3.1	32,368	10.0
485	Transit and ground passenger transportation	18	640	7.5	11,775	21.3
4854101	School bus service	12	500	5.6	11,124	12.7
488	Support activities for transportation	22	344	6.4	18,541	76.0
488510	Freight transportation arrangement	13	266	5.3	19,786	70.8
493	Warehousing and storage	10	365	8.8	24,195	27.6

Sources: *Economic Census of the United States*, 1997. Only those industries are shown for which both employment and sales/revenue data were available. For the definition of MSAs, CMSAs, and PMSAs, please see the Introduction.

YOUNGSTOWN—WARREN, OH MSA

| NAICS | Industry | Estab-lish-ments | Em-ploy-ment | Payroll | | Sales, reven. ($ mil.) |
				Total ($ mil.)	Per Empl. ($)	
48-49	Transportation and warehousing	370	4,862	139.2	28,633	705.4
484	Truck transportation	250	3,395	109.9	32,366	587.0
4841	General freight trucking	129	2,025	63.3	31,268	346.3
484110	General freight trucking, local	41	427	11.4	26,621	40.0
4841101	General freight trucking without storage, local, truckload (tl)	32	221	5.5	24,674	20.6
48412	General freight trucking, long-distance	88	1,598	51.9	32,509	306.3
484121	General freight trucking, long-distance, truckload (tl)	75	1,284	40.5	31,532	247.9
484122	General freight trucking, long-distance, less than truckload (ltl)	13	314	11.5	36,506	58.3
4842	Specialized freight trucking	121	1,370	46.6	33,990	240.8
484210	Used household and office goods moving	17	155	2.6	16,935	7.5
484220	Specialized freight (except used goods) trucking, local	72	399	11.9	29,930	83.1
4842203	Dump trucking	50	314	9.9	31,490	73.8
4842204	Specialized trucking without storage, local	14	58	1.6	28,259	5.8
484230	Specialized freight (except used goods) trucking, long-distance	32	816	32.0	39,214	150.1
4842303	Other specialized trucking, long-distance	19	563	23.3	41,467	103.5
485	Transit and ground passenger transportation	15	274	2.8	10,376	7.4
488	Support activities for transportation	72	622	14.2	22,757	49.7
488410	Motor vehicle towing	22	111	1.6	14,126	4.6
488510	Freight transportation arrangement	30	132	3.7	27,689	20.8
4885102	Arrangement of transportation of freight and cargo	25	116	3.3	28,336	18.4
492	Couriers and messengers	12	169	4.0	23,456	15.6
4931	Warehousing and storage	11	352	7.0	19,781	32.4

Sources: *Economic Census of the United States*, 1997. Only those industries are shown for which both employment and sales/revenue data were available. For the definition of MSAs, CMSAs, and PMSAs, please see the Introduction.

YUBA CITY, CA MSA

| NAICS | Industry | Estab-lish-ments | Em-ploy-ment | Payroll | | Sales, reven. ($ mil.) |
				Total ($ mil.)	Per Empl. ($)	
48-49	Transportation and warehousing	90	628	15.4	24,446	59.6
484	Truck transportation	64	421	9.7	23,000	40.7
4841	General freight trucking	17	80	1.7	21,025	10.0
4842	Specialized freight trucking	47	341	8.0	23,463	30.7
484210	Used household and office goods moving	11	120	1.6	12,950	4.6
484220	Specialized freight (except used goods) trucking, local	30	189	5.6	29,651	20.7
4842203	Dump trucking	19	138	4.4	31,899	15.7
485	Transit and ground passenger transportation	6	74	1.0	13,892	3.6
493	Warehousing and storage	5	44	1.4	32,727	5.5

Sources: *Economic Census of the United States*, 1997. Only those industries are shown for which both employment and sales/revenue data were available. For the definition of MSAs, CMSAs, and PMSAs, please see the Introduction.

YUMA, AZ MSA

NAICS	Industry	Estab-lish-ments	Em-ploy-ment	Payroll		Sales, reven. ($ mil.)
				Total ($ mil.)	Per Empl. ($)	
48-49	Transportation and warehousing	75	646	15.4	23,816	56.2
484	Truck transportation	47	406	11.1	27,397	36.9
4841	General freight trucking	15	264	8.0	30,186	21.8
4842	Specialized freight trucking	32	142	3.2	22,211	15.1
484220	Specialized freight (except used goods) trucking, local	16	54	1.2	23,111	5.3
4842202	Agricultural products trucking without storage, local	11	29	0.8	28,931	3.7
484230	Specialized freight (except used goods) trucking, long-distance	12	39	1.0	24,692	4.0
485	Transit and ground passenger transportation	5	49	0.3	5,510	1.3
488	Support activities for transportation	9	43	0.8	18,488	2.5
492	Couriers and messengers	3	25	0.6	22,600	2.3
493	Warehousing and storage	4	45	0.7	16,311	1.8

Sources: *Economic Census of the United States*, 1997. Only those industries are shown for which both employment and sales/revenue data were available. For the definition of MSAs, CMSAs, and PMSAs, please see the Introduction.

INDEXES

SIC INDEX

NAICS INDEX

SUBJECT INDEX

COMPANY INDEX

SIC INDEX

This index holds references to all SIC-denominated industries. Items shown in bold are Standard Industrial Classification codes (SICs). Page references (dashed items) are to the NAICS industry which is either identical to the SIC industry or incorporates all or a part of it. NAICS stands for North American Industry Classification System. The index is in two parts. The first part is sorted by SIC number. The second is arranged alphabetically by the industry name. The SIC code is shown in parentheses after the name. To find industries by NAICS code, please see the NAICS Index. This index provides an interesting view of the way in which SICs have been distributed among the new NAICS codes.

Bold items are SICs. Dashed items are NAICS codes. Numbers following p. are page references.

Bold items are SICs. Dashed items are NAICS codes. Numbers following p. are page references.

Bold items are SICs. Dashed items are NAICS codes. Numbers following p. are page references.

NAICS INDEX

This index holds references to all NAICS-denominated industries. NAICS stands for North American Industry Classification System. Page references are to the starting page of the industry. The index is in two parts. The first part is sorted by NAICS number. The second is arranged alphabetically by industry name. The NAICS code is shown in parentheses after the name. To find industries by Standard Industrial Classification (SIC) code, please see the SIC Index. NAICS 111930 also includes NAICS 111940, Hay Farming, and 111999, All Other Crop Farming. NAICS 112500 also includes 112990, All Other Animal Production.

Numbers following p. are page references.

NAICS INDEX

SUBJECT INDEX

This index holds references to more than 1,500 products, services, industrial activities, and names of metropolitan areas. All references are to page numbers. Pages refer to the starting page of the industry in which a product is made or a service is performed. For an explanation of the designations MSA, CMSA, and PMSA—which follow metro areas—please see the Introduction.

Subject Index

Numbers following p. or pp. are page references.

Numbers following p. or pp. are page references.

Numbers following p. or pp. are page references.

Numbers following p. or pp. are page references.

Numbers following p. or pp. are page references.

Subject Index

COMPANY INDEX

This index shows, in alphabetical order, more than 2,400 companies in *Infrastructure Industries USA*. Organizations may be public or private companies, subsidiaries or divisions of companies, joint ventures or affiliates, or corporate groups. Each company entry is followed by one or more page numbers. One or more NAICS codes are shown for each organization, indicating the industry or industries in which it participates.

Allen's Hatchery Inc., p. 106 [NAICS 11230]

Alliance Shippers Inc., p. 448 [NAICS 488510]

Alliant Energy, p. 215 [NAICS 221210]

Allied Construction Services Inc., p. 285 [NAICS 235420]

Allied Holdings Inc., pp. 361, 364, 367 [NAICS 484110, 484121, 484122]

Allied Marine Industries Inc., p. 438 [NAICS 488330]

Allied Realty Co., pp. 453, 461 [NAICS 488999, 493110]

Aloha Airgroup Inc., pp. 334, 337 [NAICS 481111, 481112]

Aloha Airlines Inc., pp. 334, 337 [NAICS 481111, 481112]

Alta Gold Co., pp. 144, 147, 151, 155 [NAICS 212221, 212222, 212234, 212299]

Altair International, p. 316 [NAICS 235930]

Alter Barge Co., p. 357 [NAICS 483211]

Alter Barge Line Inc., p. 357 [NAICS 483211]

Alvan Motor Freight Inc., p. 361 [NAICS 484110]

AMBAR Inc., p. 189 [NAICS 213112]

AMCOL International Corp., pp. 175, 364, 367 [NAICS 212325, 484121, 484122]

Amerada Hess Corp., p. 128 [NAICS 211111]

Ameren Corp., p. 212 [NAICS 221122]

America West Airlines Inc., pp. 334, 337 [NAICS 481111, 481112]

America West Holdings Corp., pp. 334, 337 [NAICS 481111, 481112]

American Absorbents Natural, p. 183 [NAICS 212399]

American Airlines Inc., pp. 334, 337 [NAICS 481111, 481112]

American Classic Voyages Co., p. 417 [NAICS 487210]

American Commercial Lines Inc., p. 357 [NAICS 483211]

American Eco Corp., pp. 266, 327 [NAICS 234990, 235990]

American Electric Power Inc., p. 212 [NAICS 221122]

American Freightways Corp., pp. 361, 364, 367 [NAICS 484110, 484121, 484122]

American Medical Response Inc., p. 402 [NAICS 485999]

American Mine Services Inc., p. 195 [NAICS 213114]

American Nursery Products Inc., p. 34 [NAICS 111400]

American Pop Corn Co., p. 10 [NAICS 111100]

American President Lines Ltd., p. 347 [NAICS 483111]

American Residential Services, p. 270 [NAICS 235110]

American River Transportation, p. 357 [NAICS 483211]

American Steamship Co., p. 352 [NAICS 483113]

American Trading & Production, p. 128 [NAICS 211111]

American Trans Air Inc., pp. 334, 337, 340 [NAICS 481111, 481112, 481211]

American Water Works Inc., p. 218 [NAICS 221310]

Americold Logistics, p. 464 [NAICS 493120]

Americomm Resources Corp., p. 144 [NAICS 212221]

Ameriflight Inc., pp. 334, 337 [NAICS 481111, 481112]

AmeriGas Inc., p. 215 [NAICS 221210]

Amerihost Properties Inc., p. 236 [NAICS 233220]

Amerijet International Inc., p. 455 [NAICS 492110]

AmeriLink Corp., p. 259 [NAICS 234920]

Amfac/JMB Hawaii Inc., pp. 26, 228 [NAICS 111300, 233110]

Amis Materials Co., p. 165 [NAICS 212319]

Amoco Co., p. 128 [NAICS 211111]

Amoco Tulsa Technology Center, p. 189 [NAICS 213112]

AMR Corp., pp. 334, 337, 455 [NAICS 481111, 481112, 492110]

AMREP Corp., pp. 228, 232 [NAICS 233110, 233210]

Amtran Inc., pp. 334, 337, 340 [NAICS 481111, 481112, 481211]

Amvest Corp., p. 134 [NAICS 212111]

A.N. Deringer Inc., pp. 448, 461 [NAICS 488510, 493110]

Anadarko Petroleum Corp., p. 128 [NAICS 211111]

Anadrill Schlumberger, p. 186 [NAICS 213111]

Anderson Transfer, p. 461 [NAICS 493110]

Andrew Roby General Contractor, p. 236 [NAICS 233220]

Anglogold Colorado Corp., p. 144 [NAICS 212221]

AngloGold North America Inc., p. 144 [NAICS 212221]

Anjou Intern. Management, p. 270 [NAICS 235110]

Anning-Johnson Co., p. 285 [NAICS 235420]

ANR Coal Company L.L.C., pp. 134, 137 [NAICS 212111, 212112]

ANR Pipeline Co., p. 407 [NAICS 486210]

Anschutz Corp., p. 189 [NAICS 213112]

Anthony Farms Inc., p. 18 [NAICS 111200]

Anthony Pools, p. 327 [NAICS 235990]

A.P. Orleans Co., p. 232 [NAICS 233210]

APAC Construction Group, p. 252 [NAICS 234120]

APAC Inc., p. 248 [NAICS 234110]

Apache Corp., pp. 128, 189 [NAICS 211111, 213112]

APC Warehouse Co., pp. 435, 461 [NAICS 488320, 493110]

Apex Industries Inc., p. 270 [NAICS 235110]

APi Group Inc., p. 285 [NAICS 235420]

Appalachian Power Co., p. 212 [NAICS 221122]

Aquila Gas Pipeline Corp., p. 215 [NAICS 221210]

Arabian Shield Development Co., pp. 144, 149 [NAICS 212221, 212231]

Arbor Acres Farm Inc., p. 106 [NAICS 11230]

Arch Coal Inc., p. 134 [NAICS 212111]

Arctic Slope Regional Corp., p. 128 [NAICS 211111]

Arctic Slope World Services Inc., pp. 266, 327, 453 [NAICS 234990, 235990, 488999]

Arends Brothers Inc., pp. 42, 66 [NAICS 11193-94-99, 111900]

Argenbright Inc., pp. 381, 383, 385 [NAICS 485112, 485113, 485119]

Argonaut Constructors Inc., p. 259 [NAICS 234920]

Arguss Communications Group, p. 278 [NAICS 235310]

Arguss Holdings Inc., p. 278 [NAICS 235310]

Arizona Public Service Co., p. 212 [NAICS 221122]

Arkansas Best Corp., pp. 364, 367 [NAICS 484121, 484122]

Arkansas Best Holdings Corp., pp. 364, 367 [NAICS 484121, 484122]

Armor Deck Inc., p. 285 [NAICS 235420]

Arnold Industries Inc., pp. 364, 367, 461 [NAICS 484121, 484122, 493110]

Arnold Transportation Service, p. 361 [NAICS 484110]

Arrow Air Inc., pp. 334, 337 [NAICS 481111, 481112]

Artesian Resources Corp., p. 218 [NAICS 221310]

Artic Express Inc., p. 361 [NAICS 484110]

Arvida/JMB Partners, pp. 232, 236 [NAICS 233210, 233220]

Asarco Inc., pp. 144, 149, 151 [NAICS 212221, 212231, 212234]

Aspen Exploration Corp., p. 144 [NAICS 212221]

Asplundh Construction Corp., p. 259 [NAICS 234920]

Associated Freezers Inc., p. 464 [NAICS 493120]

Associated Pipe Line Contractors, p. 259 [NAICS 234920]

Associated Potato Growers Inc., p. 467 [NAICS 493130]

Astral Airlines Inc., pp. 334, 337 [NAICS 481111, 481112]

A.T. Massey Coal Company Inc., p. 134 [NAICS 212111]

ATC Leasing Co., pp. 347, 352 [NAICS 483111, 483113]

Atlanta Gas Light Co., p. 215 [NAICS 221210]

Atlantic Coast Airlines Holdings, pp. 334, 337 [NAICS 481111, 481112]

Atlantic Coast Airlines Inc., pp. 334, 337 [NAICS 481111, 481112]

Atlantic Container Line, p. 347 [NAICS 483111]

Atlantic Express Transportation, p. 394 [NAICS 485410]

Atlantic Richfield Co., pp. 128, 189 [NAICS 211111, 213112]

Atlas Air Inc., pp. 334, 337 [NAICS 481111, 481112]

Atlas Corp., pp. 144, 183 [NAICS 212221, 212399]

Atlas Van Lines Inc., pp. 361, 364, 367, 448 [NAICS 484110, 484121, 484122, 488510]

Atlas World Group Inc., pp. 361, 364, 367, 448 [NAICS 484110, 484121, 484122, 488510]

ATMOS Energy Corp., p. 215 [NAICS 221210]

Atrex Inc., p. 259 [NAICS 234920]

Attebury Grain Inc., p. 467 [NAICS 493130]

Atwood Oceanics Inc., pp. 186, 189 [NAICS 213111, 213112]

Auchter Co., p. 266 [NAICS 234990]

Austin Co., pp. 240, 244 [NAICS 233310, 233320]

Austin Commercial Inc., p. 240 [NAICS 233310]

Austin Industries Inc., pp. 240, 244, 248, 252 [NAICS 233310, 233320, 234110, 234120]

AutoNation Inc., p. 278 [NAICS 235310]

Avatar Holdings Inc., p. 228 [NAICS 233110]

Numbers following p. or pp. are page references. Bracketed items indicate industries. Page references are to the starting pages of company tables.

Cal-Maine Foods Inc., p. 106 [NAICS 11230]

Calavo Growers of California, p. 26 [NAICS 111300]

Caldwell Milling Company Inc., p. 106 [NAICS 11230]

Calhoun Builders Inc., p. 236 [NAICS 233220]

California Cartage Co., p. 461 [NAICS 493110]

California Water Service Group, p. 218 [NAICS 221310]

Calnev Pipe Line Co., p. 410 [NAICS 486910]

Calpine Natural Gas Co., p. 186 [NAICS 213111]

Calumet Farm Inc., p. 122 [NAICS 112500-112900]

Canandaigua Brands Inc., p. 26 [NAICS 111300]

Cannon and Wendt Electric Inc., p. 278 [NAICS 235310]

Cannon Sline Inc., p. 274 [NAICS 235210]

Canyon Resources Corp., pp. 144, 147, 183 [NAICS 212221, 212222, 212399]

Capital Cargo Airlines, pp. 334, 337 [NAICS 481111, 481112]

Capital City Companies Inc., p. 461 [NAICS 493110]

Capital Development Co., p. 228 [NAICS 233110]

Capital Pacific Holdings Inc., pp. 232, 236 [NAICS 233210, 233220]

Capitol Aggregates Ltd., p. 160 [NAICS 212312]

Caprock Industries Inc., p. 82 [NAICS 112112]

Cardinal Fence and Security Inc., p. 327 [NAICS 235990]

Carey International Inc., p. 402 [NAICS 485999]

Carey Limousine of San Fancisco, p. 402 [NAICS 485999]

Carl Bolander and Sons Co., pp. 316, 320 [NAICS 235930, 235940]

Carlson Group Inc., p. 244 [NAICS 233320]

Carnival Corp., pp. 350, 355 [NAICS 483112, 483114]

Carolina Coach Company Inc., p. 387 [NAICS 485210]

Carolina Power and Light Co., p. 212 [NAICS 221122]

Carrier Aircraft Interiors, p. 424 [NAICS 488119]

Carson Concrete Corp., p. 302 [NAICS 235710]

Carson Oil Company Inc., p. 270 [NAICS 235110]

Carwell Elevator Company Inc., p. 467 [NAICS 493130]

Carylon Corp., p. 221 [NAICS 221320]

CASAS Intern. Brokerage Inc., p. 448 [NAICS 488510]

Casden Co., p. 228 [NAICS 233110]

Case Foundation Co., pp. 302, 316 [NAICS 235710, 235930]

Casmyn Corp., pp. 144, 183 [NAICS 212221, 212399]

Cassens Corp., pp. 364, 367 [NAICS 484121, 484122]

Castle Energy Corp., p. 407 [NAICS 486210]

Catalina Channel Express Inc., p. 359 [NAICS 483212]

Cayuga Crushed Stone Inc., p. 165 [NAICS 212319]

C.C. Myers Inc., pp. 248, 252 [NAICS 234110, 234120]

CCAIR Inc., pp. 334, 337 [NAICS 481111, 481112]

CCC Group Inc., p. 266 [NAICS 234990]

C.C.W. Group, p. 461 [NAICS 493110]

Ceanic Corp., p. 189 [NAICS 213112]

Cedar Falls Municipal Gas, p. 407 [NAICS 486210]

Cedar Falls Utilities, p. 218 [NAICS 221310]

CEI West Roofing Co., p. 298 [NAICS 235610]

Celadon Group Inc., pp. 364, 367 [NAICS 484121, 484122]

Celadon Trucking Services Inc., pp. 364, 367 [NAICS 484121, 484122]

Celite Corp., p. 183 [NAICS 212399]

Center Brothers Inc., pp. 292, 295 [NAICS 235510, 235520]

Centex Construction Group Inc., p. 244 [NAICS 233320]

Centex Construction Inc., pp. 244, 266 [NAICS 233320, 234990]

Centex Corp., pp. 228, 232 [NAICS 233110, 233210]

Centex-Rodgers Inc., p. 240 [NAICS 233310]

Centex-Rooney Construction Inc., p. 236 [NAICS 233220]

Centra Inc., pp. 364, 367 [NAICS 484121, 484122]

Central Allied Enterprises Inc., p. 302 [NAICS 235710]

Central and South West Corp., p. 212 [NAICS 221122]

Central Cold Storage Inc., p. 464 [NAICS 493120]

Central Gulf Lines Inc., pp. 347, 352 [NAICS 483111, 483113]

Central Industries Inc., p. 186 [NAICS 213111]

Central New York Regional, pp. 381, 383, 385 [NAICS 485112, 485113, 485119]

Central Power and Light Co., p. 212 [NAICS 221122]

Central Transport Intern. Inc., p. 448 [NAICS 488510]

Central Washington Grain, pp. 10, 467 [NAICS 111100, 493130]

Century Geophysical Corp., p. 195 [NAICS 213114]

C.F. Bean Corp., p. 266 [NAICS 234990]

CGB Enterprises Inc., pp. 364, 367, 446 [NAICS 484121, 484122, 488490]

CH Energy Group Inc., p. 215 [NAICS 221210]

C.H. Heist Corp., p. 285 [NAICS 235420]

C.H. Robinson Company Inc., p. 448 [NAICS 488510]

Challenge Air Cargo Inc., pp. 334, 337 [NAICS 481111, 481112]

Chalone Wine Group Ltd., p. 26 [NAICS 111300]

Chandler and Associates Inc., p. 186 [NAICS 213111]

Chapman Corp., pp. 270, 278 [NAICS 235110, 235310]

Charles C. Hart Seed Co., p. 34 [NAICS 111400]

Charles F. Evans Company Inc., p. 298 [NAICS 235610]

Charles River Laboratories, p. 122 [NAICS 112500-112900]

Chateau Montelena, p. 26 [NAICS 111300]

Chateau Potelle Winery, p. 26 [NAICS 111300]

Chemetall Foote Corp., p. 181 [NAICS 212393]

ChemFirst Inc., p. 144 [NAICS 212221]

Chesapeake Energy Corp., p. 186 [NAICS 213111]

Chesapeake Operating Inc., p. 186 [NAICS 213111]

Chevron Corp., p. 128 [NAICS 211111]

Chevron Industries, p. 189 [NAICS 213112]

Chevron Overseas Petroleum Inc., p. 189 [NAICS 213112]

Chevron Shipping Co., p. 347 [NAICS 483111]

CHI Construction Co., p. 232 [NAICS 233210]

Chicago Bridge and Iron Co., pp. 252, 266 [NAICS 234120, 234990]

Chief Consolidated Mining Co., pp. 144, 147 [NAICS 212221, 212222]

Chief Wenatchee, p. 464 [NAICS 493120]

Chiquita Brands International Inc., p. 26 [NAICS 111300]

Choice Parcel Service Inc., p. 455 [NAICS 492110]

Cianbro Corp., pp. 248, 252, 266 [NAICS 234110, 234120, 234990]

CILCORP Inc., p. 215 [NAICS 221210]

CINergy Corp., p. 212 [NAICS 221122]

Circle International Group Inc., p. 448 [NAICS 488510]

CITGO Petroleum Corp., p. 410 [NAICS 486910]

Citizens Utilities Co., pp. 215, 218 [NAICS 221210, 221310]

Citrus Corp., p. 407 [NAICS 486210]

City Sprint, p. 455 [NAICS 492110]

C.J. Hughes Construction Co., p. 259 [NAICS 234920]

Clark Construction Group Inc., pp. 240, 244 [NAICS 233310, 233320]

Clark Enterprises Inc., p. 244 [NAICS 233320]

Clark Grave Vault Co., p. 327 [NAICS 235990]

Classic Transportation Group, pp. 397, 402 [NAICS 485510, 485999]

Classical Cruises, pp. 350, 355 [NAICS 483112, 483114]

Cleveland-Cliffs Inc., p. 142 [NAICS 212210]

Cleveland Consolidated, pp. 270, 278 [NAICS 235110, 235310]

Cleveland Electric Illuminating, p. 212 [NAICS 221122]

Cliffs Drilling Co., pp. 186, 189 [NAICS 213111, 213112]

Clipper Exxpress Co., p. 448 [NAICS 488510]

Clipper Navigation Inc., p. 417 [NAICS 487210]

Clos du Bois Wines, p. 26 [NAICS 111300]

Cloverland Electric Coop., p. 212 [NAICS 221122]

C.M. Holtzinger Fruit Inc., p. 26 [NAICS 111300]

CMS Energy Corp., pp. 128, 212 [NAICS 211111, 221122]

CNF Transportation Inc., pp. 364, 367, 448, 455 [NAICS 484121, 484122, 488510, 492110]

CNG Transmission Corp., p. 407 [NAICS 486210]

Coach Farm Inc., p. 90 [NAICS 112120]

Coach USA Inc., p. 379 [NAICS 485111]

Coal Properties Corp., p. 134 [NAICS 212111]

Coast Machinery Movers, p. 323 [NAICS 235950]

Coastal Corp., pp. 128, 134, 364, 367 [NAICS 211111, 212111, 484121, 484122]

Coastal Oil and Gas Corp., p. 189 [NAICS 213112]

Coastal Towing Inc., p. 438 [NAICS 488330]

Coastal Transportation Inc., p. 352 [NAICS 483113]

Coca-Cola Swire Pacific Holdings, pp. 334, 337 [NAICS 481111, 481112]

Cochran Inc., p. 278 [NAICS 235310]

Numbers following p. or pp. are page references. Bracketed items indicate industries. Page references are to the starting pages of company tables.

852

Numbers following p. or pp. are page references. Bracketed items indicate industries. Page references are to the starting pages of company tables.

853

Company Index

Numbers following p. or pp. are page references. Bracketed items indicate industries. Page references are to the starting pages of company tables.

Electric Machinery Enterprises, p. 278 [NAICS 235310]

Electrical Construction Co., p. 278 [NAICS 235310]

Electro-Coal Transfer, pp. 352, 435 [NAICS 483113, 488320]

Electro Management Inc., p. 278 [NAICS 235310]

Electronic Data Carriers Inc., p. 361 [NAICS 484110]

Elenburg Exploration Inc., p. 186 [NAICS 213111]

Elf Exploration Inc., p. 189 [NAICS 213112]

Elkhart Cooperative Equity, p. 467 [NAICS 493130]

Elkin Co., p. 106 [NAICS 11230]

Elliott Homes Inc., p. 228 [NAICS 233110]

Elliott-Lewis Corp., p. 270 [NAICS 235110]

Elmhurst-Chicago Stone, p. 160 [NAICS 212312]

Elmira Water Board, p. 218 [NAICS 221310]

Elston-Richards Inc., p. 361 [NAICS 484110]

EMCOR Group Inc., pp. 259, 270, 278 [NAICS 234920, 235110, 235310]

Emergency Medical Service, p. 402 [NAICS 485999]

Emery Air Charter Inc., p. 340 [NAICS 481211]

Emery Worldwide, p. 455 [NAICS 492110]

Emma Cooperative Elevator Co., p. 467 [NAICS 493130]

Emons Transportation Group Inc., p. 430 [NAICS 488210]

Empire Airlines Inc., pp. 334, 337, 455 [NAICS 481111, 481112, 492110]

Empire District Electric Co., p. 218 [NAICS 221310]

Empire State Coca-Cola Co., p. 461 [NAICS 493110]

Enbrery Inc, p. 405 [NAICS 486110]

Encina Gas Marketing Inc., p. 407 [NAICS 486210]

Energen Corp., p. 215 [NAICS 221210]

Energy Corporation of America, p. 131 [NAICS 211112]

Energy East Corp., p. 215 [NAICS 221210]

Engelberth Construction Inc., p. 236 [NAICS 233220]

Engle Homes Inc., p. 232 [NAICS 233210]

Enogex Inc., pp. 215, 407 [NAICS 221210, 486210]

Enron Corp., pp. 128, 215 [NAICS 211111, 221210]

Enron Power Corp., p. 266 [NAICS 234990]

ENSCO International Inc., pp. 186, 435 [NAICS 213111, 488320]

ENSERCH Corp., pp. 128, 215 [NAICS 211111, 221210]

Entergy Corp., p. 212 [NAICS 221122]

Entergy Gulf States Inc., p. 212 [NAICS 221122]

Entergy Louisiana Inc., p. 212 [NAICS 221122]

Enterprise Products Partners L.P., p. 131 [NAICS 211112]

Environmental & Foundation, p. 195 [NAICS 213114]

EOG Resources Inc., pp. 128, 189 [NAICS 211111, 213112]

EOTT Energy Corp., pp. 364, 367 [NAICS 484121, 484122]

EOTT Energy Operating L.P., p. 448 [NAICS 488510]

Epps Aviation Inc., p. 340 [NAICS 481211]

Equitable Resources Inc., pp. 128, 215 [NAICS 211111, 221210]

Equitrans L.P., p. 407 [NAICS 486210]

Era Aviation Inc., pp. 334, 337 [NAICS 481111, 481112]

ERC Properties Inc., p. 228 [NAICS 233110]

Ermco Inc., p. 278 [NAICS 235310]

Estes Express Lines Inc., pp. 364, 367 [NAICS 484121, 484122]

Estridge Group, p. 232 [NAICS 233210]

Etranco Inc., p. 361 [NAICS 484110]

ETS Pacific Inc., p. 263 [NAICS 234930]

Europa Cruise Line Ltd., pp. 350, 355 [NAICS 483112, 483114]

Europa Cruises Corp., pp. 350, 355 [NAICS 483112, 483114]

European Cruises Inc., pp. 350, 355 [NAICS 483112, 483114]

Evergreen Intern. Airlines Inc., p. 340 [NAICS 481211]

Evergreen Intern. Aviation Inc., pp. 334, 337 [NAICS 481111, 481112]

E.W. Corrigan Construction Co., p. 236 [NAICS 233220]

Executive Jet Inc., p. 340 [NAICS 481211]

Exel Logistics Inc., pp. 361, 448, 461 [NAICS 484110, 488510, 493110]

Exhibit Systems Inc., p. 461 [NAICS 493110]

Expeditors Intern. of Washington, p. 448 [NAICS 488510]

Express Marine Inc., p. 352 [NAICS 483113]

Express One International Inc., pp. 334, 337 [NAICS 481111, 481112]

Exxon Coal and Minerals Co., pp. 134, 151, 193 [NAICS 212111, 212234, 213113]

Exxon Mobil Corp., pp. 128, 153, 407 [NAICS 211111, 212291, 486210]

Exxon Mobil U.S.A., pp. 128, 189 [NAICS 211111, 213112]

F. Richard Wilton Jr. Inc., p. 285 [NAICS 235420]

Facilities Management Inc., p. 221 [NAICS 221320]

Fairfield Maxwell Corp., pp. 189, 347 [NAICS 213112, 483111]

Fairman Drilling Co., p. 186 [NAICS 213111]

Falcon Seaboard Resources Inc., p. 407 [NAICS 486210]

Falkirk Mining Co., p. 134 [NAICS 212111]

Fall River Feedyard L.L.C., p. 82 [NAICS 112112]

Farm Fish Inc., p. 122 [NAICS 112500-112900]

Farm Fresh Catfish Co., p. 122 [NAICS 112500-112900]

Farmers Association Talmage, p. 467 [NAICS 493130]

Farmers Co-op Elevator, p. 467 [NAICS 493130]

Farmers Cooperative Association, p. 467 [NAICS 493130]

Farmers Cooperative Compress, p. 467 [NAICS 493130]

Farmers Cooperative Mill Elevator, p. 467 [NAICS 493130]

Farmland Grain, p. 467 [NAICS 493130]

Farrar Oil Co., p. 122 [NAICS 112500-112900]

Farrell Lines Inc., p. 347 [NAICS 483111]

Fasco Mills Co., p. 467 [NAICS 493130]

Feather Crest Farms Inc., p. 106 [NAICS 11230]

Federal Compress & Warehouse, p. 467 [NAICS 493130]

Federal Express Corp., pp. 347, 361, 455 [NAICS 483111, 484110, 492110]

Federal Warehouse Co., pp. 361, 453, 461 [NAICS 484110, 488999, 493110]

FedEx Corp., pp. 347, 361, 364, 367, 455 [NAICS 483111, 484110, 484121, 484122, 492110]

Fess Parker Winery and Vineyard, p. 26 [NAICS 111300]

Field and Associates Inc., pp. 285, 298 [NAICS 235420, 235610]

FINA Inc., pp. 128, 189 [NAICS 211111, 213112]

Fina Oil and Chemical Co., p. 189 [NAICS 213112]

FirstEnergy Corp., p. 212 [NAICS 221122]

Fisher Sand and Gravel Co., p. 168 [NAICS 212321]

Fisher Tank Co., p. 309 [NAICS 235910]

Fisher Vineyard, p. 26 [NAICS 111300]

Fitchburg Gas & Electric Light, p. 407 [NAICS 486210]

Flatiron Structures L.L.C., pp. 248, 252 [NAICS 234110, 234120]

Fleet Yacht Charters, p. 441 [NAICS 488390]

Fletcher Granite Company Inc., p. 158 [NAICS 212311]

Fletcher Pacific Construction Ltd., pp. 236, 248 [NAICS 233220, 234110]

Flight International Group Inc., p. 424 [NAICS 488119]

Flight International Inc., p. 340 [NAICS 481211]

Flight Services Group Inc., p. 340 [NAICS 481211]

Flint Engineering & Construction, p. 259 [NAICS 234920]

Flint Industries Inc., pp. 240, 244, 266 [NAICS 233310, 233320, 234990]

Flippo Construction Company Inc., pp. 252, 259 [NAICS 234120, 234920]

Florida Crushed Stone Co., p. 160 [NAICS 212312]

Florida East Coast Industries Inc., p. 228 [NAICS 233110]

Florida Power and Light Co., p. 212 [NAICS 221122]

Florida Power Corp., p. 212 [NAICS 221122]

Florida Progress Corp., p. 212 [NAICS 221122]

Florida Public Utilities Co., pp. 212, 218 [NAICS 221122, 221310]

Florida Rock and Sand Inc., p. 168 [NAICS 212321]

Florida Rock Industries Inc., p. 168 [NAICS 212321]

Floyd and Beasley Transfer, p. 461 [NAICS 493110]

Fluidics Inc., p. 270 [NAICS 235110]

Fluor Corp., pp. 134, 240, 266 [NAICS 212111, 233310, 234990]

FMC Corp. Lithium Div., p. 158 [NAICS 212311]

Focus Group Inc., p. 228 [NAICS 233110]

Forbes Homes Inc., p. 228 [NAICS 233110]

Forcenergy Inc., p. 189 [NAICS 213112]

Forest Lines Inc., pp. 347, 352 [NAICS 483111, 483113]

Fortress Group Inc., p. 236 [NAICS 233220]

Forward Air Corp., p. 361 [NAICS 484110]

Foss Maritime Co., p. 438 [NAICS 488330]

Foster Brothers Inc., p. 228 [NAICS 233110]

Foster Poultry Farms Inc., p. 106 [NAICS 11230]

Numbers following p. or pp. are page references. Bracketed items indicate industries. Page references are to the starting pages of company tables.

Company Index

855

Numbers following p. or pp. are page references. Bracketed items indicate industries. Page references are to the starting pages of company tables.

856

Hardaway Group Inc., p. 236 [NAICS 233220]
Harder Mechanical Contractors, p. 270 [NAICS 235110]
Hardin Construction Group Inc., p. 244 [NAICS 233320]
Hardrives of Delray Inc., p. 248 [NAICS 234110]
Harken Energy Corp., p. 186 [NAICS 213111]
Harkins Builders Inc., p. 236 [NAICS 233220]
Harmon Contract, pp. 309, 313 [NAICS 235910, 235920]
Harper Bros. Inc., pp. 160, 248 [NAICS 212312, 234110]
Harper Contracting, p. 316 [NAICS 235930]
Harper Industries Inc., p. 248 [NAICS 234110]
Harper Investments Inc., pp. 168, 316 [NAICS 212321, 235930]
Harris Farms Inc., pp. 18, 42, 58 [NAICS 111200, 111900, 111920]
Harry F. Ortlip Co., p. 278 [NAICS 235310]
Harry Grodsky and Company Inc., p. 270 [NAICS 235110]
Harry Singh and Sons, p. 18 [NAICS 111200]
Hartco Inc., p. 455 [NAICS 492110]
Hartman-Walsh Painting Co., pp. 274, 327 [NAICS 235210, 235990]
Hartsfield Atlanta Intern. Airport, p. 424 [NAICS 488119]
Haskell Co., pp. 240, 244 [NAICS 233310, 233320]
Hathaway Dinwiddie Construction, pp. 240, 244 [NAICS 233310, 233320]
Havens Steel Co., p. 309 [NAICS 235910]
Haverhill Coop., p. 467 [NAICS 493130]
Hawaiian Airlines Inc., pp. 334, 337, 455 [NAICS 481111, 481112, 492110]
Hawaiian Bitumuls & Paving, p. 248 [NAICS 234110]
Hawaiian Electric Company Inc., p. 212 [NAICS 221122]
Hawaiian Electric Industries Inc., pp. 228, 448 [NAICS 233110, 488510]
Hawthorne Corp., p. 424 [NAICS 488119]
Hayward Baker Inc., p. 327 [NAICS 235990]
H.B. Zachry Co., p. 259 [NAICS 234920]
HBE Corp., pp. 240, 244 [NAICS 233310, 233320]
H.C. Spinks Clay Company Inc., pp. 74, 173 [NAICS 112111, 212324]
HCB Contractors, p. 244 [NAICS 233320]
H.E. Sargent Inc., p. 248 [NAICS 234110]
Heartland Express Inc., pp. 364, 367 [NAICS 484121, 484122]
Hechinger Investment Co., p. 232 [NAICS 233210]
Hecla Mining Co., pp. 144, 147, 149, 173 [NAICS 212221, 212222, 212231, 212324]
Helicopters Services Inc., p. 340 [NAICS 481211]
Helix Electric Inc., p. 278 [NAICS 235310]
Helmerich and Payne Inc., pp. 186, 189, 228 [NAICS 213111, 213112, 233110]
Helmerich & Payne Intern., p. 186 [NAICS 213111]
Henderson Electric Company Inc., p. 278 [NAICS 235310]
Henderson Excavating Co., p. 316 [NAICS 235930]
Henkels & McCoy Inc. Northeast, pp. 259, 270, 278, 323, 327 [NAICS 234920, 235110, 235310, 235950, 235990]

Henry Fischer Builder Inc., pp. 232, 236 [NAICS 233210, 233220]
Hensel Phelps Construction Co., pp. 244, 248 [NAICS 233320, 234110]
Herman Goldner Company Inc., p. 270 [NAICS 235110]
Hermann Engelmann Greenhouses, p. 34 [NAICS 111400]
Herzog Contracting Corp., pp. 248, 252, 266 [NAICS 234110, 234120, 234990]
Hess Collection Winery, p. 26 [NAICS 111300]
Hickman Drilling Co., p. 186 [NAICS 213111]
Hickory Construction Co., p. 252 [NAICS 234120]
Higgins Erectors and Haulers Inc., p. 309 [NAICS 235910]
High Island Offshore System, p. 407 [NAICS 486210]
Highlines Construction Inc., p. 259 [NAICS 234920]
Hilltop Basic Resources Inc., p. 168 [NAICS 212321]
Hinkle Corp., p. 248 [NAICS 234110]
H.J. Russell and Co., p. 232 [NAICS 233210]
H.J. Stabile and Son Inc., pp. 232, 236 [NAICS 233210, 233220]
H.N. Donahoo Contracting Inc., p. 259 [NAICS 234920]
Hodges Truck Company Inc., pp. 327, 361 [NAICS 235990, 484110]
Hoffman Corp., pp. 240, 244 [NAICS 233310, 233320]
Holland America Line Westours, pp. 350, 355 [NAICS 483112, 483114]
Holman United, p. 461 [NAICS 493110]
Homestake Mining Co., pp. 144, 147 [NAICS 212221, 212222]
Honolulu Painting Company Ltd., p. 274 [NAICS 235210]
Honolulu Shipyard Inc., p. 298 [NAICS 235610]
Hood Corp., pp. 259, 278 [NAICS 234920, 235310]
Hooper Construction Corp., pp. 270, 278 [NAICS 235110, 235310]
Hope Communities Inc., p. 228 [NAICS 233110]
Horizon Air Industries Inc., pp. 334, 337 [NAICS 481111, 481112]
Horizon Offshore, p. 263 [NAICS 234930]
Horst Construction Company Inc., p. 236 [NAICS 233220]
Houston Lighting and Power Co., p. 212 [NAICS 221122]
Hovnanian Enterprises Inc., pp. 232, 236 [NAICS 233210, 233220]
Howard's Express Inc., p. 361 [NAICS 484110]
Howell Asphalt Company Inc., p. 252 [NAICS 234120]
Howell Corp. (Houston, Texas), p. 189 [NAICS 213112]
HPC Inc., p. 274 [NAICS 235210]
HSI GeoTrans Inc., p. 327 [NAICS 235990]
Hub Group Inc., pp. 435, 448 [NAICS 488320, 488510]
Hub Group Distribution Services, p. 461 [NAICS 493110]
Hubbard Construction Co., pp. 248, 266 [NAICS 234110, 234990]

Huber, Hunt and Nichols Inc., pp. 240, 244, 248 [NAICS 233310, 233320, 234110]
Hudson General Corp., p. 424 [NAICS 488119]
Hudson General L.L.C., p. 424 [NAICS 488119]
Huffco Group Inc., p. 131 [NAICS 211112]
Hulcher Services Inc., p. 453 [NAICS 488999]
Hunt Building Corp., p. 236 [NAICS 233220]
Hunt Consolidated Inc., p. 128 [NAICS 211111]
Hunt Corp. (Indianapolis, Indiana), p. 240 [NAICS 233310]
Hunter Ambulette-Ambulance Inc., p. 402 [NAICS 485999]
Hvide Marine Inc., pp. 347, 352, 438 [NAICS 483111, 483113, 488330]
Hy-Tek Material Handling Inc., p. 323 [NAICS 235950]
Hylive, p. 106 [NAICS 11230]
I and OA Slutzky Inc., p. 252 [NAICS 234120]
ICO Inc., p. 189 [NAICS 213112]
ICOS Corporation of America, p. 282 [NAICS 235410]
Illinois Central Corp., p. 430 [NAICS 488210]
Illinois Power Co., p. 212 [NAICS 221122]
Illinova Corp., p. 212 [NAICS 221122]
Illinova Generating Co., p. 212 [NAICS 221122]
IMC-Agrico Co., p. 179 [NAICS 212392]
IMC Chemicals Inc., p. 177 [NAICS 212391]
IMC Kalium, p. 177 [NAICS 212391]
Imperial Petroleum Inc., p. 131 [NAICS 211112]
Imperial Power Services Inc., p. 224 [NAICS 221330]
Independence Excavating Inc., p. 316 [NAICS 235930]
Indiana Energy Inc., p. 215 [NAICS 221210]
Indiana Freight Traffic Analysts, p. 453 [NAICS 488999]
Indiana Harbor Belt Railroad Co., p. 430 [NAICS 488210]
Indianapolis Water Co., p. 218 [NAICS 221310]
Industrial Roofing Co., p. 298 [NAICS 235610]
Ingalls Feed Yard, p. 82 [NAICS 112112]
Ingram Industries Inc., p. 357 [NAICS 483211]
Inland-Joseph Fruit Co., p. 467 [NAICS 493130]
Insituform East Inc., p. 259 [NAICS 234920]
Insituform Plains Inc., p. 259 [NAICS 234920]
Insituform Technologies USA Inc., p. 259 [NAICS 234920]
Inter-Maritime Forwarding Inc., p. 448 [NAICS 488510]
Intermountain Electric Inc., p. 278 [NAICS 235310]
Intern. Terminal Operating Inc., p. 435 [NAICS 488320]
International Cargo Group Inc., p. 448 [NAICS 488510]
International Chimney Corp., p. 282 [NAICS 235410]
International Shipholding Corp., pp. 347, 435 [NAICS 483111, 488320]
International Total Services Inc., p. 424 [NAICS 488119]
Interstate General Company L.P., p. 228 [NAICS 233110]
Interstate Highway Construction, p. 248 [NAICS 234110]

Numbers following p. or pp. are page references. Bracketed items indicate industries. Page references are to the starting pages of company tables.

857

Numbers following p. or pp. are page references. Bracketed items indicate industries. Page references are to the starting pages of company tables.

859

Numbers following p. or pp. are page references. Bracketed items indicate industries. Page references are to the starting pages of company tables.

Numbers following p. or pp. are page references. Bracketed items indicate industries. Page references are to the starting pages of company tables.

Proven Alternatives Inc., pp. 323, 327 [NAICS 235950, 235990]
PS Marcato Elevator Inc., p. 323 [NAICS 235950]
PSA Airlines Inc., pp. 334, 337 [NAICS 481111, 481112]
PSF Industries Inc., pp. 309, 323 [NAICS 235910, 235950]
P.T. Ferro Construction Co., p. 316 [NAICS 235930]
Public Service Electric & Gas Co., p. 212 [NAICS 221122]
Public Service Enterprise Group, p. 212 [NAICS 221122]
Public Service of Colorado, p. 212 [NAICS 221122]
Public Service of New Mexico, p. 218 [NAICS 221310]
Public Service of North Carolina, p. 189 [NAICS 213112]
Pulte Corp., p. 232 [NAICS 233210]
Pulte Diversified Companies Inc., p. 232 [NAICS 233210]
P.W. Stephens Residential Inc., p. 327 [NAICS 235990]
Quality Distribution Inc., pp. 364, 367 [NAICS 484121, 484122]
Questar Corp., pp. 128, 215 [NAICS 211111, 221210]
Questar Pipeline Co., p. 407 [NAICS 486210]
Quintana Petroleum Corp., p. 189 [NAICS 213112]
R and B Falcon Corp., p. 186 [NAICS 213111]
R. Roese Contracting Inc., p. 259 [NAICS 234920]
R.A. Bright Construction Inc., p. 316 [NAICS 235930]
Raba-Kistner Consultants Inc., pp. 306, 327 [NAICS 235810, 235990]
Rail Van Inc., p. 361 [NAICS 484110]
Rainier Cold Storage Inc., p. 464 [NAICS 493120]
Ralph M. Parsons Co., p. 240 [NAICS 233310]
Ramcon Engineering, p. 327 [NAICS 235990]
Ramos Oil Company Inc., p. 186 [NAICS 213111]
Randall and Blake Inc., p. 181 [NAICS 212393]
Ranger Construction, p. 252 [NAICS 234120]
Ray-Carroll County Grain, p. 467 [NAICS 493130]
Ray Wilson Co., pp. 302, 327 [NAICS 235710, 235990]
Raygal Inc., p. 323 [NAICS 235950]
Raytheon Aerospace Co., p. 424 [NAICS 488119]
Raytheon Engineers, p. 240 [NAICS 233310]
R.D. Offutt Co., p. 18 [NAICS 111200]
R.E. Purcell Construction Co., p. 236 [NAICS 233220]
Reading Anthracite Co., p. 140 [NAICS 212113]
Red River Mining, p. 134 [NAICS 212111]
Redgwick Construction Co., p. 316 [NAICS 235930]
Redland Stone Products Co., p. 160 [NAICS 212312]
Reedy Industries Inc., p. 270 [NAICS 235110]
Reeve Aleutian Airways Inc., pp. 334, 337 [NAICS 481111, 481112]
Reeve Cattle Co., p. 82 [NAICS 112112]
Ref-Chem Corp., p. 266 [NAICS 234990]
Reitz Coal Co., p. 134 [NAICS 212111]
Reliable Contracting Inc., p. 228 [NAICS 233110]
Reliance Elevator Co., p. 323 [NAICS 235950]
Reliant Energy Inc., p. 212 [NAICS 221122]

Renaissance Cruises Inc., pp. 350, 355 [NAICS 483112, 483114]
Rescar Inc., p. 453 [NAICS 488999]
Reserve Industries Corp., pp. 153, 171 [NAICS 212291, 212322]
Resurrection Mining Co., p. 149 [NAICS 212231]
Reunion Energy Co., p. 186 [NAICS 213111]
Rex Moore Electrical Contractors, p. 278 [NAICS 235310]
Reynolds Inc., pp. 259, 266 [NAICS 234920, 234990]
RFI Communications & Security, p. 278 [NAICS 235310]
RGC (USA) Mineral Sands Inc., p. 155 [NAICS 212299]
R.H. White Construction Inc., p. 259 [NAICS 234920]
Rhode Construction Co., p. 259 [NAICS 234920]
Rice Fruit Co., p. 26 [NAICS 111300]
Richard A. Heaps Electrical, p. 259 [NAICS 234920]
Richmond American Homes Inc., pp. 228, 232 [NAICS 233110, 233210]
Richmor Aviation Inc., p. 340 [NAICS 481211]
Riechmann Distribution Inc., p. 464 [NAICS 493120]
Rieth-Riley Company Inc., pp. 252, 266 [NAICS 234120, 234990]
Rio Tinto Services Inc., p. 183 [NAICS 212399]
Ritchie Corp., p. 248 [NAICS 234110]
Rite Stuff Foods Inc., p. 461 [NAICS 493110]
R.L. Coolsaet Construction Co., p. 259 [NAICS 234920]
Roadway Express Inc., pp. 364, 367 [NAICS 484121, 484122]
Robert Mondavi Corp., p. 26 [NAICS 111300]
Rock-it Cargo USA Inc., p. 448 [NAICS 488510]
Rock of Ages Corp., p. 158 [NAICS 212311]
Rock-Tred Corp., p. 327 [NAICS 235990]
Rocky Flats Environmental, p. 266 [NAICS 234990]
Rodney Strong Vineyards, p. 26 [NAICS 111300]
Rogers Group Inc., pp. 168, 248, 252 [NAICS 212321, 234110, 234120]
Romar Transportation Systems, pp. 361, 453, 461 [NAICS 484110, 488999, 493110]
Roode Packing Company Inc., p. 82 [NAICS 112112]
Rooney Brothers Co., pp. 240, 244 [NAICS 233310, 233320]
Rose Construction Co., p. 316 [NAICS 235930]
Ross Aviation Inc., pp. 334, 337 [NAICS 481111, 481112]
Roth Bros. Inc., pp. 270, 298 [NAICS 235110, 235610]
Rouse Co., p. 232 [NAICS 233210]
Rowan Companies Inc., p. 186 [NAICS 213111]
Rowe Corp., p. 259 [NAICS 234920]
Royal Caribbean Cruises Ltd., pp. 350, 355 [NAICS 483112, 483114]
Royal Citrus Co., p. 26 [NAICS 111300]
Royal Crescent Valley Inc., p. 144 [NAICS 212221]
Royal Gold Inc., p. 195 [NAICS 213114]
Royal Packing Co., p. 18 [NAICS 111200]
Royce Homes Inc., p. 232 [NAICS 233210]

RPC Inc., pp. 189, 361 [NAICS 213112, 484110]
RTK Corp., p. 278 [NAICS 235310]
Rudolph and Sletten Inc., pp. 240, 244 [NAICS 233310, 233320]
Rudolph/Libbe Companies Inc., pp. 270, 278 [NAICS 235110, 235310]
Rugby Farmers Union Elevator, p. 467 [NAICS 493130]
Ruhlin Co., p. 248 [NAICS 234110]
Rural/Metro Corp., p. 402 [NAICS 485999]
Rural Metro Inc., p. 402 [NAICS 485999]
Russell Lands Inc., p. 228 [NAICS 233110]
Russo Farms Inc., p. 18 [NAICS 111200]
Ryan Companies US Inc., p. 228 [NAICS 233110]
Ryan Homes, p. 232 [NAICS 233210]
Ryan Incorporated Central, p. 316 [NAICS 235930]
Ryder Student Transportation, p. 394 [NAICS 485410]
Ryland Group Inc., p. 232 [NAICS 233210]
S & B Engineers & Constructors, p. 266 [NAICS 234990]
Sabine Pipe Line Co., p. 413 [NAICS 486990]
Sachs Electric Co., p. 278 [NAICS 235310]
Saddle Creek Corp., p. 461 [NAICS 493110]
Safety-Kleen Corp. Oklahoma, p. 361 [NAICS 484110]
Saga Transport (U.S.A.) Inc., p. 448 [NAICS 488510]
Saia Motor Freight Line Inc., pp. 361, 364, 367 [NAICS 484110, 484121, 484122]
St. Joe Paper Co., p. 228 [NAICS 233110]
St. Louis Helicopter Airways Inc., p. 340 [NAICS 481211]
St. Supery Vineyards and Winery, p. 26 [NAICS 111300]
Salem National Corp., p. 361 [NAICS 484110]
Salient 3 Communications Inc., p. 228 [NAICS 233110]
Salt Chuk Resources, p. 352 [NAICS 483113]
Salt River Project Agricultural, pp. 212, 218 [NAICS 221122, 221310]
Salyer American Corp., pp. 18, 42, 58 [NAICS 111200, 111900, 111920]
Samedan Oil Corp., p. 128 [NAICS 211111]
San Diego Gas and Electric Co., pp. 212, 215 [NAICS 221122, 221210]
San Diego Transit Corp., p. 387 [NAICS 485210]
San Gabriel Valley Water Co., p. 218 [NAICS 221310]
San Jose Water Co., p. 218 [NAICS 221310]
San Rafael Rock Quarry Inc., p. 165 [NAICS 212319]
Santa Fe International Corp., pp. 160, 186 [NAICS 212312, 213111]
Sargent Electric Co., p. 278 [NAICS 235310]
Sauer Industries Inc., p. 327 [NAICS 235990]
Savage Industries Inc., p. 361 [NAICS 484110]
Savage Zinc Inc., p. 149 [NAICS 212231]
Saxton Inc., pp. 228, 282, 285, 302 [NAICS 233110, 235410, 235420, 235710]
SCANA Corp., p. 212 [NAICS 221122]
Scenic Airlines Inc., p. 340 [NAICS 481211]
Schaake Packing Co., p. 82 [NAICS 112112]
Scheid Vineyards Inc., p. 26 [NAICS 111300]

Numbers following p. or pp. are page references. Bracketed items indicate industries. Page references are to the starting pages of company tables.

864

Company Index

Numbers following p. or pp. are page references. Bracketed items indicate industries. Page references are to the starting pages of company tables.

Wesseln Construction Inc., p. 236 [NAICS 233220]

Western Aircraft Inc., p. 424 [NAICS 488119]

Western Atlas International Inc., pp. 128, 189 [NAICS 211111, 213112]

Western Atlas Logging Services, p. 189 [NAICS 213112]

Western Gas Resources Inc., p. 128 [NAICS 211111]

Western Mobile Denver Paving, pp. 248, 252 [NAICS 234110, 234120]

Western Pioneer Inc., pp. 352, 357 [NAICS 483113, 483211]

Western States Minerals Corp., p. 144 [NAICS 212221]

Western Waterproofing Inc., p. 327 [NAICS 235990]

WestEx Inc., p. 448 [NAICS 488510]

Westmoreland Coal Co., p. 137 [NAICS 212112]

WesTower Corp., p. 274 [NAICS 235210]

Westwood Shipping Lines, p. 347 [NAICS 483111]

Westwood Swinerton, p. 228 [NAICS 233110]

W.G. Lockhart Construction Co., p. 259 [NAICS 234920]

W.G. Thompson Inc., p. 274 [NAICS 235210]

White Cap Industries Inc., p. 274 [NAICS 235210]

Whiting-Turner Contracting Co., pp. 240, 244 [NAICS 233310, 233320]

Wice Freight Service Inc., p. 448 [NAICS 488510]

Wicor Inc., p. 215 [NAICS 221210]

Wight Nurseries Inc., p. 34 [NAICS 111400]

Wilcox Farms Inc., p. 90 [NAICS 112120]

Willamette Valley Vineyards Inc., p. 26 [NAICS 111300]

William Bolthouse Farms Inc., p. 18 [NAICS 111200]

William E. Buchan Inc., pp. 228, 232 [NAICS 233110, 233210]

William Lyon Homes Inc., p. 236 [NAICS 233220]

William Penn Aviation Inc., p. 424 [NAICS 488119]

Williams Companies Inc., pp. 407, 410 [NAICS 486210, 486910]

Williams Group International, p. 274 [NAICS 235210]

Williams Industries Inc., p. 309 [NAICS 235910]

Williamsburg Winery Ltd., p. 26 [NAICS 111300]

Williard Inc., pp. 266, 270, 278 [NAICS 234990, 235110, 235310]

Williston Basin Interstate Pipeline, p. 407 [NAICS 486210]

Wilson Farms Inc., pp. 18, 106 [NAICS 11230, 111200]

Windsor Inc., p. 417 [NAICS 487210]

Wingra Stone Company Inc., pp. 165, 302 [NAICS 212319, 235710]

Wings West Airlines Inc., pp. 334, 337 [NAICS 481111, 481112]

Wisconsin Electric Power Co., p. 215 [NAICS 221210]

Wisconsin Energy Corp., pp. 212, 215 [NAICS 221122, 221210]

W.L. Hailey and Company Inc., pp. 252, 259 [NAICS 234120, 234920]

WLR Foods Inc., p. 464 [NAICS 493120]

W.M. Lyles Co., p. 221 [NAICS 221320]

WMOG Inc., p. 252 [NAICS 234120]

W.O. Operating Co., p. 186 [NAICS 213111]

Wohlsen Construction Co., p. 232 [NAICS 233210]

Wolcott and Lincoln Inc., p. 467 [NAICS 493130]

Wolfsen Inc., pp. 42, 66 [NAICS 11193-94-99, 111900]

Wolverine Gas and Oil Co., p. 407 [NAICS 486210]

Woodruff and Sons Inc., p. 259 [NAICS 234920]

World Airways Inc., pp. 334, 337 [NAICS 481111, 481112]

World Minerals Inc., p. 183 [NAICS 212399]

World Yacht Inc., p. 417 [NAICS 487210]

W.W. Boxley Co., pp. 160, 163 [NAICS 212312, 212313]

W.W. Gay Mechanical, p. 270 [NAICS 235110]

Wyodak Resources Development, p. 134 [NAICS 212111]

Wyoming Sand and Stone Co., p. 168 [NAICS 212321]

Yankee Energy System Inc., p. 215 [NAICS 221210]

Yankee Gas Services Co., p. 215 [NAICS 221210]

Yantis Corp., p. 259 [NAICS 234920]

Yellow Cab Company Inc., p. 389 [NAICS 485310]

Yellow Cab-Delaware Inc., p. 389 [NAICS 485310]

Yellow Corp., pp. 364, 367, 448 [NAICS 484121, 484122, 488510]

Yellow Freight System Inc., pp. 364, 367 [NAICS 484121, 484122]

Yoder Brothers Inc., p. 34 [NAICS 111400]

York Hill Trap Rock Quarry, p. 165 [NAICS 212319]

York Water Co., p. 218 [NAICS 221310]

Young Sales Corp., pp. 285, 298 [NAICS 235420, 235610]

Youngstown Thermal L.P., p. 224 [NAICS 221330]

Yukon-Pacific Corp., p. 131 [NAICS 211112]

Zantop International Airlines Inc., pp. 340, 455 [NAICS 481211, 492110]

Zaring National Corp., p. 232 [NAICS 233210]

Zeigler Coal Holding Co., p. 137 [NAICS 212112]

Zelenka Nursery Inc., p. 34 [NAICS 111400]

Zemex Industrial Minerals Inc., pp. 171, 173, 175, 183 [NAICS 212322, 212324, 212325, 212399]

Zenith Drilling Corp., p. 186 [NAICS 213111]

Zenith Tech Inc., p. 252 [NAICS 234120]

Numbers following p. or pp. are page references. Bracketed items indicate industries. Page references are to the starting pages of company tables.